EMPLOYMENT, HOURS, AND EARNINGS

STATES AND AREAS

Ninth Edition
2014

EMPLOYMENT, HOURS, AND EARNINGS

STATES AND AREAS

Ninth Edition
2014

Edited by Gwenavere W. Dunn

Lanham, MD

Published in the United States of America
by Bernan Press, a wholly owned subsidiary of
The Rowman & Littlefield Publishing Group, Inc.
4501 Forbes Boulevard, Suite 200
Lanham, Maryland 20706

Bernan Press
800-865-3457
info@bernan.com
www.bernan.com

ISBN-13: 978-1-59888-727-3
e-ISBN-13: 978-1-59888-728-0

♾ ™ The paper used in this publication meets the minimum requirements of American National Standard
for Information Sciences—Permanence of Paper for Printed Library Materials, ANSI/NISO Z39.48-1992.
Manufactured in the United States of America.

CONTENTS

PART A: STATE DATA—*Continued*

PART B: METROPOLITAN STATISTICAL AREA (MSA) DATA

PART B: METROPOLITAN STATISTICAL AREA (MSA) DATA—*Continued*

APPENDIX

PREFACE

Bernan Press proudly presents the ninth edition of *Employment, Hours, and Earnings: States and Areas, 2014*. A special addition to Bernan Press's *Handbook of U.S. Labor Statistics: Employment, Earnings, Prices, Productivity, and Other Labor Data*, this reference is a consolidated wealth of employment information, providing monthly and annual data on hours worked and earnings made by industry across America for the years 2002 through 2013, including figures and summary information spanning years 2000 through 2013. These data, compiled by the Bureau of Labor Statistics (BLS), are presented for states and metropolitan statistical areas.

This edition features:

- Nearly 300 tables with data on employment for each state, the District of Columbia, and the nation's 75 largest metropolitan statistical areas (MSAs)

- Detailed, non-seasonally adjusted industry data organized by month and year

- Hours and earnings data for each state, by industry

- An introduction for each state and the District of Columbia that denotes salient data and noteworthy trends, including changes in population and the civilian labor force, industry increases and declines, employment and unemployment statistics, and a chart detailing employment percentages, by industry

- Ranking of the 75 largest MSAs, including Census population estimates for 2013, unemployment rates for 2011 through 2013, and the percent change in total nonfarm employment from 2002 through 2013

- Concise technical notes that explain pertinent facts about the data, including sources, definitions, and significant changes; and provides references for further guidance

- A comprehensive appendix that details the geographical components of the 75 largest MSAs

The employment, hours, and earnings data in this publication provide a detailed and timely picture of the 50 states, the District of Columbia, and the nation's 75 largest MSAs. These data can be used to analyze key factors affecting state and local economies and to compare national cyclical trends to local-level economic activity.

This reference is an excellent source of information for analysts in both the public and private sectors. Readers who are involved in public policy can use these data to determine the health of the economy, to clearly identify which sectors are growing and which are declining, and to determine the need for federal assistance. State and local jurisdictions can use the data to determine the need for services, including training and unemployment assistance, and for planning and budgetary purposes. In addition, the data can be used to forecast tax revenue. In private industry, the data can be used by business owners to compare their business to the economy as a whole, and to identify suitable areas when making decisions about plant locations, wholesale and retail trade outlets, and for locating a particular sector base.

Gwenavere W. Dunn is a consulting writer and editor and holds a Master of Science degree in Human Resource Management from Trinity Washington University. She is a former senior editor with the Board of Governors of the Federal Reserve System and former managing editor of the *Federal Reserve Bulletin*. More recently she was assistant editor of *The State and Metropolitan Area Data Book, 2013*; *Race and Employment in America, 2013*; *The Almanac of American Education, 2013*; and *The Who, What, and Where of America, 2014*, as well as editor of *Crime in the United States, 2014*, published by Bernan Press.

In this ninth edition, *Employment, Hours, and Earnings: States and Areas* presents monthly and annual average data on employment for each state, the District of Columbia, and the nation's 75 largest metropolitan statistical areas (MSAs). In addition, hours and earnings data are provided, where available, for each state. The industry data are based on the North American Industry Classification System (NAICS), which is discussed in greater detail later in these notes. The employment data are presented on a monthly and annual basis for 2002 through 2013. The hours and earnings data are available from 2009 through 2013.

The Bureau of Labor Statistics (BLS), the statistical agency within the U.S. Department of Labor, conducts the Current Employment Statistics (CES) survey to provide industry data on the employment, hours, and earnings of workers on nonfarm payrolls. The unemployment data and the civilian labor force estimates in this publication were obtained from the Local Area Unemployment Statistics (LAUS) program, which provides monthly employment and unemployment data for approximately 7,300 geographic areas including Census regions and divisions, states, counties, metropolitan areas, and many cities and towns.

The data from both the CES and LAUS are derived from federal and state cooperative collection efforts in which state employment security agencies prepare data using concepts, definitions, and technical procedures prescribed by the BLS. Although the estimation of the two data sets are based on differing methodologies (described in more detail later in this section), their inclusion together in this reference is intended to provide a broad overview of state and local labor market conditions.

THE CURRENT EMPLOYMENT STATISTICS (CES) SURVEY—EMPLOYMENT, HOURS, AND EARNINGS DATA

The CES survey is a monthly survey commonly referred to as the establishment or payroll survey that provides estimates of employment, hours, and earnings data by industry. Its estimates are derived from a sample of about 145,000 private nonfarm businesses and federal, state, and local government entities, which cover approximately 557,000 individual worksites in all 50 states, the District of Columbia, Puerto Rico, the U.S. Virgin Islands, and more than 350 metropolitan areas and divisions. These establishments are classified on the basis of their primary activity by major industry groupings in accordance with NAICS. For an establishment engaging in more than one activity, the entire establishment is included under the industry indicated as the principal activity.

All establishments with 1,000 employees or more are asked to participate in the survey, along with a representative sample of smaller businesses. The BLS Regional Data Collection Centers gather the data every month. Each firm is initially enrolled by telephone and the data is then collected for several months by a process called Computer Assisted Telephone Interviewing (CATI). Whenever possible, respondents are transferred to a self-reporting mode such as Touchtone Data Entry (TDE), fax, or Internet collection. Gathering data via the Internet is one of the fastest growing forms of data collection, but still remains a relatively small percentage of the total data collected each month. Electronic Data Interchange (EDI), in which each firm provides the BLS with an electronic file in a prescribed format, remains the most popular method for collecting data.

State estimation procedures are designed to produce accurate data for each individual state. The BLS independently develops the national series and does not force state estimates to sum to the national total. Because each state series is subject to larger sampling and nonsampling errors than the national series, summing them cumulates individual state level errors and can cause significant distortions at an aggregate level. As a result of these statistical limitations, the BLS does not compile a "sum of states" employment series, and cautions users that doing so may result in a series with a relatively large and volatile error structure.

More information on the exact methodology used to obtain data for employment, hours, and earnings was originally detailed in the *BLS Handbook of Methods*. The *Handbook* is updated online and can be found at www.bls.gov/opub/hom. Information on the CES survey can also be found on the BLS website at www.bls.gov/ces/cesprog.htm.

CONCEPTS

Employment is the total number of persons employed either full- or part-time in nonfarm business establishments during a specific payroll period. Temporary employees are included as well as civilian government employees. Unpaid family members working in a family-owned business, domestic workers in private homes, farm employees, and self-employed persons are excluded from the CES, as well as military personnel and employees of the Central Intelligence Agency, the National Security Agency, the National Imagery and Mapping Agency, and the Defense Intelligence Agency. In addition, employees on layoff, on leave without pay, on strike for the entire pay period, or who had been hired but did not start work during the pay period are also excluded.

The reference period includes all persons who worked during or received pay for any part of the pay period that includes the 12th of the month, a standard for all federal agencies collecting employment data from business establishments. Workers who are on paid sick leave (when pay is received directly from the employer) or paid holiday or vacation, or who worked during only part of the specified pay period (because of unemployment or strike during the rest of the pay period) are counted as employed. Employees on the payroll of more than one establishment during the pay period are counted in each establishment that reports them, whether the duplication is due to turnover or dual jobholding.

Nonfarm employment includes employment in all goods-producing and service-providing industries. The goods-producing sector includes mining and logging, construction, and manufacturing, the last of which is made up of durable and nondurable goods (these breakdowns are not provided in this publication). The service-providing sector includes both private service-providing and government employment. Private service sector employment includes trade, transportation, and utilities (which comprises wholesale trade, retail trade, and transportation and utilities); information; financial activities; professional and business services; educational and health services; leisure and hospitality; and other services. Government employment encompasses federal-, state-, and local-level civilian employees. Subcategories of these industries are available on the BLS website at www.bls.gov/sae.

Unemployment consists of those who were not employed during the reference week but were available for work, except for temporary illness, and had made specific efforts to find employment some time during the 4-week period ending with the reference week. Persons who were waiting to be recalled to a job from which they had been laid off are classified as unemployed whether or not they have been looking for another job.

The *unemployment rate* is the number of unemployed persons as a percent of the civilian labor force.

The *civilian labor force* consists of all persons classified as employed or unemployed as described above.

Hours and earnings data for each state are based on reports from industry payrolls and the corresponding hours paid for construction workers, production workers, and nonsupervisory workers. The data include workers who received pay for any part of the pay period that includes the 12th day of the month. Because not all sample respondents report production worker hours and earnings data, insufficient sample sizes preclude hours and earnings data from many sectors in many states. Therefore, the data available, and thus published, vary from state to state.

The payroll for these workers is reported before deductions of any kind, including Social Security, unemployment insurance, group health insurance, withholding taxes, retirement plans, or union dues.

Included in the payroll report of earnings is pay for all hours worked, including overtime, shift premiums, vacations, holiday, and sick-leave pay. Bonuses and commissions are excluded unless they are earned and paid regularly

each pay period. Benefits, such as health insurance and contribution to a retirement fund, are also excluded.

Hours include all hours worked (including overtime hours) and hours paid for holidays, vacations, and sick leave during the pay period that includes the 12th day of the month. Average weekly hours differ from the concept of scheduled hours worked because of factors such as unpaid absenteeism, labor turnover, part-time work, and strikes as well as fluctuations in work schedules. Average weekly hours are typically lower than scheduled hours of work.

Average hourly earnings are derived by dividing gross payrolls by total hours, reflecting the actual earnings of workers (including premium pay). They differ from wage rates, which are the amounts stipulated for a given unit of work or time. Average hourly earnings do not represent total labor costs per hour because they exclude retroactive payments and irregular bonuses, employee benefits, and the employer's share of payroll taxes. Earnings for employees not included in the production worker or nonsupervisory categories are not reflected in the estimates in this publication.

Average weekly earnings are derived by multiplying average weekly hours by average hourly earnings.

Users should note that in the context of historical data, long-term trends in hours and earnings data also reflect structural changes, such as the changing mixes of full-time and part-time employees and highly paid and lower-wage workers within businesses and across industries.

METROPOLITAN STATISTICAL AREAS (MSAs) AND NEW ENGLAND CITY AND TOWN AREAS (NECTAs)

A metropolitan statistical area (MSA) is a core area with a large population nucleus, combined with adjacent communities that have high degrees of economic and social integration with the core area. The standard definition of a MSA is determined by the Office of Management and Budget (OMB), which updates the definition based on the decennial census and updated information provided by the Census Bureau between the censuses. Each MSA must have at least one urbanized area of 50,000 inhabitants or more.

New England city and town areas (NECTAs) are similar to MSAs, but are defined using cities and towns instead of counties in the six New England states. BLS only provides employment data on NECTAs in the New England region. Employment and Unemployment data are provided for the following NECTAs in this publication: Boston–Cambridge–Quincy, MA–NH; Bridgeport–Stamford–Norwalk, CT; Hartford–West Hartford–East Hartford, CT; New Haven, CT; and Providence–Fall River–Warwick, RI–MA. All other areas are MSAs.

The appendix details the geographic components for each MSA and NECTA.

REVISIONS TO THE DATA

North American Industry Classification System (NAICS)

The most far-reaching revision of the CES data occurred when the industrial classification system was changed from the 60-year-old Standard Industrial Classification (SIC) system to the North American Industry Classification System (NAICS) in January 2003. The revision changed the way establishments were classified into industries in order to more accurately reflect the current composition of U.S. businesses. In March 2008, the CES state and area nonfarm payroll series was converted to the 2007 NAICS series. This resulted in relatively minor changes. In February 2012, CES updated the national payroll series to NAICS 2012 from NAICS 2007. This resulted in minor content changes within the Manufacturing and Retail trade sectors as well as minor coding changes within the Utilities and Leisure and hospitality sectors. Several industry titles and descriptions were updated as well. More information on the NAICS conversion can be found at www.bls.gov/ces/cesnaics12.htm.

NAICS was adopted as the standard measure of industry classification by statistical agencies in the United States, Canada, and Mexico to enhance the comparability of economic data across the North American Free Trade Association (NAFTA) trade area. Comparison between the NAICS and the old SIC are limited, however, the historical industry series from April 1995 through 2001 are available on both SIC and NAICS bases. The BLS has not updated the SIC data nor (for the most part) linked the historical SIC data with the current NAICS data.

Benchmark Revisions

Employment estimates are adjusted annually to a complete count of jobs—called benchmarks—which are primarily derived from tax reports submitted by employers covered by state unemployment laws (which cover most establishments). In this re-anchoring of sample-based employment estimates to full population counts, the original sample-based estimates are replaced with the benchmark data from the previous year. The benchmark information is used to adjust monthly estimates between the new benchmark and the preceding benchmark, thereby preserving the continuity of the series and establishing the level of employment for the new benchmark month.

Seasonal Adjustment

Over the course of a year, the size of a state's employment level undergoes sharp fluctuations because of changes in the weather, reduced or expanded production, harvests, major holidays, and the like. Because these seasonal events follow a more or less regular pattern each year, adjusting the data on a month-to-month basis may eliminate their influence on data trends. These adjustments make it easier for users to observe the cyclical and other nonseasonal movements in the data series, but it must be noted that the seasonally adjusted series are only an approximation based on past experience. The seasonally adjusted data have a broader margin of error than the unadjusted data because they are subject to both sampling and other errors in the seasonal adjustment process. The data presented in this publication are not seasonally adjusted; therefore, the month-to-month variations in the data contain seasonal variations that may distort month-to-month comparisons. Data for the MSAs are also not seasonally adjusted, as the sample sizes do not allow for reliable estimates for seasonal adjustment factors.

THE LOCAL AREA UNEMPLOYMENT STATISTICS (LAUS) PROGRAM

The Local Area Unemployment Statistics (LAUS) program provides monthly and annual estimates on several labor force concepts, including employment, unemployment, labor force totals, and the employment-population ratio. The unemployment data as well as the civilian labor force estimates presented in this publication are from the LAUS program. The unemployment rate is shown for each state in 2000, 2010, and 2013 along with the rank for each state. The rankings are from lowest to highest. In 2013, unemployment ranged from a low of 2.9 percent in North Dakota to 9.8 percent in Nevada. Therefore, North Dakota is ranked first and Nevada is ranked 51st. Unemployment data are not available by industry.

The concepts and definitions underlying the LAUS program come from the Current Population Survey (CPS), the household survey conducted by the Census Bureau for the BLS. The LAUS models combine current and historical data from the CPS, Current Employment Statistics (CES), and the State Unemployment Insurance (UI) Systems. Numerous conceptual and technical differences exist between the household and establishment surveys, and estimates of monthly employment changes from these two surveys usually do not match in size or even direction. As a result, the unemployment data and the civilian labor force estimates on each state header page presented in this edition are not directly comparable to the employment data. However, this publication includes this information to provide complementary information on labor market conditions in each state and the District of Columbia. Monthly and annual data are available from the BLS on their website at www.bls.gov/lau. More information on the differences between the surveys, as well as guidance on the complex methods used to obtain the LAUS data, is provided on the BLS website at www.bls.gov/lau/laufaq.htm.

PART A

STATE DATA

ALABAMA
At a Glance

Population:
  2000 census: 4,447,207
  2010 census: 4,779,736
  2013 estimate: 4,833,722

Percent change in population:
2000–2010: 7.5%
2010–2013: 1.1%

Percent change in total nonfarm employment:
  2000–2010: -3.1%
  2010–2013: 1.7%

Industry with the largest growth in employment, 2000–2013 (thousands):
  Education and Health Services, 46.2

Industry with the largest decline or smallest growth in employment, 2000–2013 (thousands):
  Manufacturing, -102.3

Civilian labor force:
  2000: 2,154,545
  2010: 2,179,163
  2013: 2,138,048

Unemployment rate and rank among states (lowest to highest):
  2000: 4.1%, 32nd
  2010: 9.5%, 32nd
  2013: 6.5%, 18th

Over-the-year change in unemployment rates:
  2010–2011: -0.5%
  2011–2012: -1.4%
  2012–2013: -0.6%

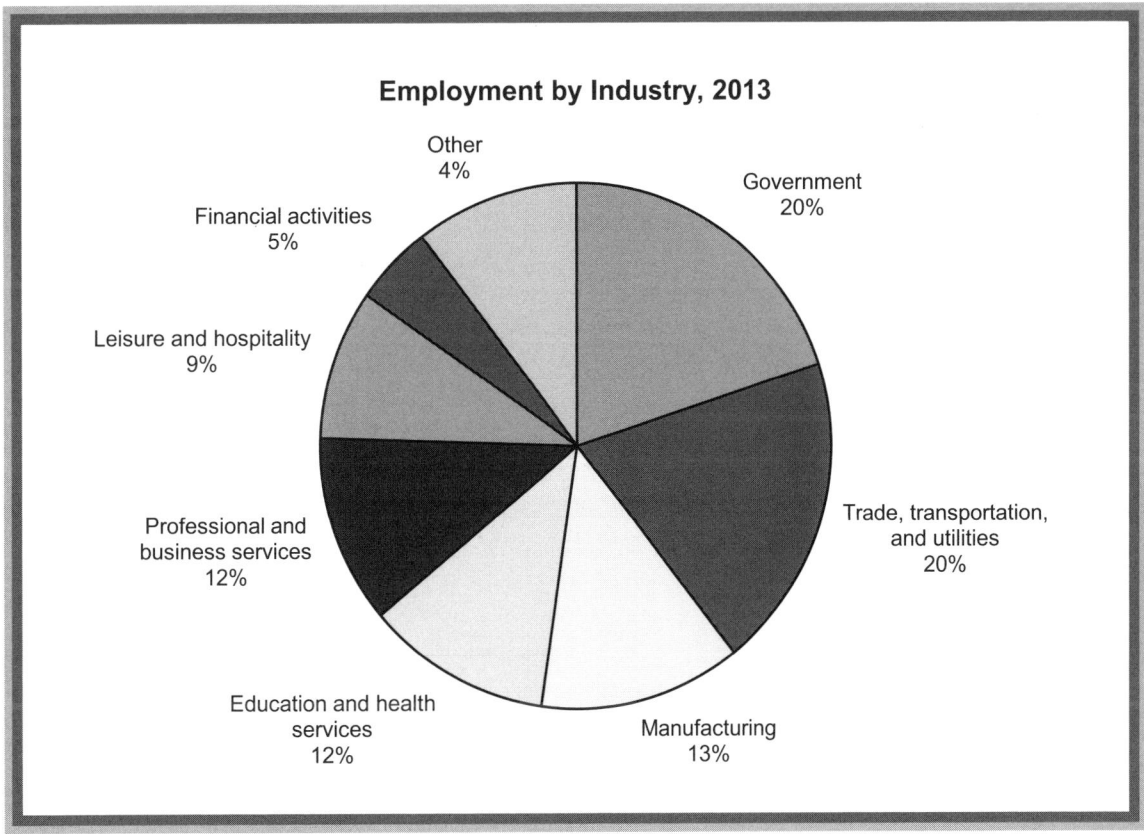

Employment by Industry, 2013

Other
4%

Government
20%

Financial activities
5%

Leisure and hospitality
9%

Trade, transportation,
and utilities
20%

Professional and
business services
12%

Education and health
services
12%

Manufacturing
13%

1. Employment by Industry: Alabama, Selected Years, 2002–2013

(Numbers in thousands, not seasonally adjusted)

Industry and year	January	February	March	April	May	June	July	August	September	October	November	December	Annual average
Total Nonfarm													
2002	1,859.7	1,868.4	1,882.6	1,888.3	1,891.6	1,886.1	1,872.4	1,879.8	1,888.3	1,889.9	1,897.0	1,894.8	1,883.2
2003	1,857.0	1,864.0	1,875.0	1,879.1	1,882.2	1,875.8	1,862.1	1,869.3	1,877.1	1,883.7	1,889.6	1,891.8	1,875.6
2004	1,862.6	1,872.4	1,886.5	1,899.3	1,903.8	1,908.8	1,900.9	1,903.9	1,908.4	1,915.6	1,926.2	1,932.4	1,901.7
2005	1,899.8	1,910.5	1,925.1	1,943.1	1,948.2	1,951.4	1,939.6	1,947.9	1,958.2	1,961.9	1,974.2	1,979.2	1,944.9
2006	1,944.9	1,956.1	1,974.5	1,978.5	1,984.2	1,994.6	1,972.0	1,981.0	1,990.4	1,984.2	1,994.6	2,000.1	1,979.6
2007	1,974.9	1,987.3	2,004.4	2,000.9	2,009.4	2,018.4	1,994.0	2,004.4	2,013.3	2,012.4	2,022.0	2,026.7	2,005.7
2008	1,986.0	1,994.5	2,002.7	2,008.7	2,012.5	2,012.1	1,989.0	1,991.1	1,992.2	1,981.3	1,970.9	1,964.4	1,992.1
2009	1,905.6	1,899.9	1,900.1	1,900.1	1,899.7	1,895.5	1,873.5	1,870.8	1,872.6	1,868.4	1,875.8	1,876.0	1,886.5
2010	1,840.1	1,844.6	1,860.7	1,872.1	1,888.2	1,889.3	1,870.4	1,868.7	1,872.3	1,877.1	1,883.4	1,882.4	1,870.8
2011	1,839.4	1,853.3	1,865.6	1,875.0	1,877.8	1,878.2	1,863.2	1,868.3	1,879.6	1,873.5	1,883.6	1,882.7	1,870.0
2012	1,850.5	1,862.1	1,880.5	1,889.2	1,893.0	1,897.2	1,874.0	1,884.3	1,890.7	1,892.6	1,904.8	1,903.2	1,885.2
2013	1,865.9	1,881.4	1,896.5	1,905.4	1,912.8	1,915.2	1,896.6	1,904.3	1,906.2	1,915.5	1,920.7	1,919.9	1,903.4
Total Private													
2002	1,507.2	1,512.5	1,526.0	1,530.0	1,534.1	1,534.8	1,531.1	1,537.2	1,532.0	1,529.7	1,535.4	1,533.4	1,528.6
2003	1,498.7	1,502.0	1,512.1	1,515.7	1,518.9	1,521.4	1,517.7	1,522.9	1,517.7	1,521.1	1,526.5	1,530.3	1,517.1
2004	1,503.9	1,510.7	1,524.6	1,536.5	1,541.9	1,550.0	1,552.1	1,553.3	1,548.4	1,553.9	1,563.1	1,569.2	1,542.3
2005	1,539.7	1,547.5	1,561.6	1,578.3	1,582.7	1,587.2	1,587.2	1,592.8	1,595.3	1,594.5	1,606.1	1,611.4	1,582.0
2006	1,578.2	1,587.1	1,603.9	1,606.4	1,611.2	1,622.4	1,612.0	1,618.4	1,618.8	1,610.3	1,619.8	1,624.8	1,609.4
2007	1,600.7	1,610.7	1,626.5	1,622.5	1,630.1	1,639.3	1,629.4	1,635.8	1,635.5	1,632.0	1,640.1	1,644.9	1,629.0
2008	1,605.7	1,610.4	1,617.4	1,622.1	1,624.4	1,624.2	1,616.8	1,616.1	1,609.1	1,593.7	1,583.7	1,576.6	1,608.4
2009	1,522.5	1,514.7	1,514.0	1,511.6	1,510.9	1,507.9	1,502.3	1,497.6	1,490.6	1,481.6	1,488.5	1,488.0	1,502.5
2010	1,456.0	1,458.0	1,471.1	1,480.9	1,487.9	1,494.7	1,494.2	1,492.6	1,488.4	1,490.1	1,495.2	1,494.3	1,483.6
2011	1,455.2	1,466.6	1,477.8	1,487.2	1,490.4	1,494.0	1,491.6	1,497.0	1,499.4	1,491.7	1,500.3	1,501.8	1,487.8
2012	1,472.4	1,480.7	1,496.9	1,506.4	1,510.9	1,517.8	1,508.2	1,517.8	1,516.0	1,512.8	1,523.7	1,522.8	1,507.2
2013	1,489.3	1,501.0	1,513.9	1,522.8	1,530.9	1,536.7	1,527.0	1,534.5	1,531.0	1,536.5	1,541.0	1,542.0	1,525.6
Goods Producing													
2002	420.1	419.9	422.5	422.3	423.5	422.2	418.9	421.9	421.4	420.1	418.3	415.7	420.6
2003	408.4	408.2	409.7	407.8	407.6	406.4	402.6	404.7	404.1	405.6	403.9	404.3	406.1
2004	398.3	400.1	402.7	404.5	405.9	407.0	409.0	408.3	409.2	412.1	412.1	412.4	406.8
2005	405.6	406.8	411.0	416.8	417.5	417.5	418.0	419.6	421.3	422.2	424.6	425.4	417.2
2006	421.6	423.7	427.6	427.9	428.0	430.5	427.7	427.2	426.6	423.3	422.3	422.6	425.8
2007	420.1	421.6	423.9	420.9	421.3	423.9	421.0	421.8	423.2	423.0	421.0	420.6	421.9
2008	413.2	412.5	412.1	411.1	411.2	411.1	409.0	406.0	404.6	397.1	389.8	386.1	405.3
2009	369.7	363.7	360.9	356.0	352.9	348.9	347.3	344.3	342.3	339.5	339.2	339.1	350.3
2010	332.1	331.5	334.3	336.6	338.3	339.4	338.6	337.4	336.8	335.3	333.9	331.9	335.5
2011	322.5	326.3	329.0	330.0	331.5	332.5	331.2	332.6	332.7	331.4	332.4	333.8	330.5
2012	328.5	329.9	333.3	335.1	335.5	336.9	336.7	338.2	337.9	339.0	339.0	339.6	335.8
2013	334.7	336.1	340.5	341.1	341.3	342.8	341.0	342.5	342.0	341.7	340.3	339.6	340.3
Service-Providing													
2002	1,439.6	1,448.5	1,460.1	1,466.0	1,468.1	1,463.9	1,453.5	1,457.9	1,466.9	1,469.8	1,478.7	1,479.1	1,462.7
2003	1,448.6	1,455.8	1,465.3	1,471.3	1,474.6	1,469.4	1,459.5	1,464.6	1,473.0	1,478.1	1,485.7	1,487.5	1,469.5
2004	1,464.3	1,472.3	1,483.8	1,494.8	1,497.9	1,501.8	1,491.9	1,495.6	1,499.2	1,503.5	1,514.1	1,520.0	1,494.9
2005	1,494.2	1,503.7	1,514.1	1,526.3	1,530.7	1,533.9	1,521.6	1,528.3	1,536.9	1,539.7	1,549.6	1,553.8	1,527.7
2006	1,523.3	1,532.4	1,546.9	1,550.6	1,556.2	1,564.1	1,544.3	1,553.8	1,563.8	1,560.9	1,572.3	1,577.5	1,553.8
2007	1,554.8	1,565.7	1,580.5	1,580.0	1,588.1	1,594.5	1,573.0	1,582.6	1,590.1	1,589.4	1,601.0	1,606.1	1,583.8
2008	1,572.8	1,582.0	1,590.6	1,597.6	1,601.3	1,601.0	1,580.0	1,585.1	1,587.6	1,584.2	1,581.1	1,578.3	1,586.8
2009	1,535.9	1,536.2	1,539.2	1,544.1	1,546.8	1,546.6	1,526.2	1,526.5	1,530.3	1,528.9	1,536.6	1,536.9	1,536.2
2010	1,508.0	1,513.1	1,526.4	1,535.5	1,549.9	1,549.9	1,531.8	1,531.3	1,535.5	1,541.8	1,549.5	1,550.5	1,535.3
2011	1,516.9	1,527.0	1,536.6	1,545.0	1,546.3	1,545.7	1,532.0	1,535.7	1,546.9	1,542.1	1,551.2	1,548.9	1,539.5
2012	1,522.0	1,532.2	1,547.2	1,554.1	1,557.5	1,560.3	1,537.3	1,546.1	1,552.8	1,553.6	1,565.8	1,563.6	1,549.4
2013	1,531.2	1,545.3	1,556.0	1,564.3	1,571.5	1,572.4	1,555.6	1,561.8	1,564.2	1,573.8	1,580.4	1,580.3	1,563.1
Mining and Logging													
2002	13.2	13.1	13.2	13.0	13.0	13.0	12.9	13.0	12.9	12.6	12.5	12.5	12.9
2003	12.5	12.4	12.5	12.5	12.5	12.5	12.4	12.5	12.6	12.5	12.5	12.5	12.5
2004	12.2	12.2	12.2	12.2	12.3	12.4	12.4	12.5	12.6	12.7	12.6	12.7	12.4
2005	12.7	12.7	12.7	12.8	13.0	13.0	13.1	13.0	13.2	13.0	13.1	13.1	13.0
2006	13.0	13.1	13.1	13.0	13.0	13.2	13.1	13.1	13.2	12.9	13.0	13.1	13.1
2007	12.9	13.0	13.1	12.8	12.9	12.9	12.8	12.9	12.8	12.8	12.7	12.8	12.9
2008	12.5	12.6	12.6	12.6	12.4	12.5	12.6	12.6	12.7	12.6	12.5	12.5	12.6
2009	12.2	12.2	11.9	11.8	11.7	11.8	11.8	11.6	11.7	11.7	11.7	11.6	11.8
2010	11.7	11.7	11.7	11.9	12.0	12.0	12.1	12.2	12.1	12.3	12.2	12.2	12.0
2011	12.1	12.1	12.1	12.3	12.4	12.5	12.3	12.5	12.6	12.5	12.5	12.6	12.4
2012	12.7	12.6	12.5	12.5	12.5	12.6	12.8	12.8	12.7	12.6	12.6	12.6	12.6
2013	12.3	12.3	12.4	12.1	12.2	12.2	11.9	12.0	12.0	11.9	12.1	12.0	12.1
Construction													
2002	96.8	98.3	100.5	99.7	100.9	100.0	100.3	101.4	102.1	102.7	101.1	99.2	100.3
2003	97.3	97.6	99.3	98.4	98.8	98.9	99.0	100.1	100.7	103.2	102.4	101.7	99.8
2004	99.6	101.2	103.0	102.4	102.6	102.6	104.1	103.1	103.2	104.9	104.0	103.3	102.8
2005	100.6	101.6	104.2	106.2	105.4	105.2	105.2	106.2	107.0	108.6	108.6	107.5	105.5
2006	105.1	106.2	109.5	110.2	110.2	111.1	110.4	111.0	111.7	111.1	111.0	110.2	109.8
2007	109.4	110.7	113.2	112.0	112.3	113.1	112.0	113.2	114.7	114.9	113.6	113.1	112.7
2008	109.5	110.0	110.4	110.3	110.9	110.7	110.1	109.0	108.8	105.9	103.8	102.3	108.5
2009	94.8	93.6	94.3	92.9	93.3	92.9	92.0	90.5	89.7	88.5	89.0	89.3	91.7
2010	85.4	85.4	87.4	88.2	89.1	90.2	89.3	88.2	87.8	86.8	85.1	83.5	87.2
2011	77.2	79.2	81.1	80.8	82.0	81.8	81.2	81.1	81.9	81.0	80.7	80.6	80.7
2012	76.7	77.7	79.9	80.3	79.9	80.0	79.7	80.2	80.2	80.7	80.0	79.3	79.6
2013	76.5	76.9	79.9	80.5	80.3	80.5	79.9	80.5	80.0	80.0	77.6	76.9	79.1

1. Employment by Industry: Alabama, Selected Years, 2002–2013—*Continued*

(Numbers in thousands, not seasonally adjusted)

Industry and year	January	February	March	April	May	June	July	August	September	October	November	December	Annual average
Manufacturing													
2002	310.1	308.5	308.8	309.6	309.6	309.2	305.7	307.5	306.4	304.8	304.7	304.0	307.4
2003	298.6	298.2	297.9	296.9	296.3	295.0	291.2	292.1	290.8	289.9	289.0	290.1	293.8
2004	286.5	286.7	287.5	289.9	291.0	292.0	292.5	292.7	293.4	294.5	295.5	296.4	291.6
2005	292.3	292.5	294.1	297.8	299.1	299.3	299.7	300.4	301.1	300.6	302.9	304.8	298.7
2006	303.5	304.4	305.0	304.7	304.8	306.2	304.2	303.1	301.7	299.3	298.3	299.3	302.9
2007	297.8	297.9	297.6	296.1	296.1	297.9	296.2	295.7	295.7	295.3	294.7	294.7	296.3
2008	291.2	289.9	289.1	288.2	287.9	287.9	286.3	284.4	283.1	278.6	273.5	271.3	284.3
2009	262.7	257.9	254.7	251.3	247.9	244.2	243.5	242.2	240.9	239.3	238.5	238.2	246.8
2010	235.0	234.4	235.2	236.5	237.2	237.2	237.2	237.0	236.9	236.2	236.6	236.2	236.3
2011	233.2	235.0	235.8	236.9	237.1	238.2	237.7	239.0	238.2	237.9	239.2	240.6	237.4
2012	239.1	239.6	240.9	242.3	243.1	244.3	244.2	245.2	245.0	245.7	246.4	247.7	243.6
2013	245.9	246.9	248.2	248.5	248.8	250.1	249.2	250.0	250.0	249.8	250.6	250.7	249.1
Trade, Transportation, and Utilities													
2002	371.1	369.3	372.0	370.1	371.0	370.5	371.0	370.0	368.6	370.2	377.0	380.9	371.8
2003	366.0	364.2	367.1	368.1	369.2	370.7	372.2	372.9	371.9	374.4	379.5	383.5	371.6
2004	371.3	370.8	374.5	375.0	375.9	377.0	376.4	376.0	374.4	377.3	384.1	389.6	376.9
2005	376.6	376.0	378.3	380.5	381.6	382.9	382.4	382.8	382.5	383.3	391.2	396.3	382.9
2006	382.6	381.5	385.4	384.1	385.2	387.4	386.3	387.3	388.1	388.9	396.8	401.7	387.9
2007	387.8	387.5	391.8	390.8	394.4	396.2	395.2	394.8	395.1	394.9	402.6	406.0	394.8
2008	390.7	388.8	391.1	389.6	390.2	390.4	389.6	389.8	388.4	385.9	389.0	390.2	389.5
2009	371.3	367.5	366.8	364.9	366.0	366.0	364.4	363.2	363.0	361.1	366.8	368.7	365.8
2010	356.7	355.7	358.6	359.1	360.7	361.2	360.7	360.8	359.9	363.1	368.8	372.0	361.4
2011	358.8	358.8	360.7	362.0	362.5	364.0	364.2	364.9	364.1	365.1	371.5	374.3	364.2
2012	361.9	360.3	363.5	363.8	365.5	366.4	364.3	364.7	364.4	366.2	374.9	376.7	366.1
2013	361.7	362.1	364.2	365.1	367.1	369.1	368.3	369.2	367.9	371.8	378.3	382.1	368.9
Wholesale Trade													
2002	79.9	79.5	79.5	78.7	78.6	78.6	78.5	78.5	78.4	78.0	78.2	78.4	78.7
2003	76.8	76.8	77.0	76.6	77.1	77.2	77.3	77.3	77.4	77.9	77.9	78.1	77.3
2004	76.9	77.0	77.6	78.1	78.3	78.6	78.7	78.7	78.5	79.0	78.8	79.1	78.3
2005	78.1	78.4	78.8	79.3	79.3	79.5	79.8	79.7	80.0	79.9	80.0	80.5	79.4
2006	79.9	80.3	81.0	81.0	81.5	81.9	81.9	82.0	82.1	81.9	82.1	82.5	81.5
2007	81.3	81.6	82.1	81.9	82.3	82.8	82.2	82.2	82.4	82.5	82.3	82.4	82.2
2008	80.8	80.8	81.0	81.0	81.3	81.3	80.9	80.8	80.7	80.4	79.5	79.1	80.6
2009	77.0	76.3	75.9	75.0	74.8	74.4	73.6	73.6	73.3	73.3	73.2	72.9	74.4
2010	71.7	71.5	71.5	71.8	72.1	71.9	72.0	71.9	71.6	72.1	71.9	71.8	71.8
2011	70.9	71.3	71.5	71.8	71.9	71.9	72.3	72.5	72.4	72.9	72.7	72.9	72.1
2012	71.9	72.0	72.5	72.6	72.9	73.0	72.6	72.6	72.6	73.0	72.9	73.0	72.6
2013	72.0	72.4	72.5	72.8	73.1	73.1	73.2	73.4	73.5	75.2	74.6	74.1	73.3
Retail Trade													
2002	226.4	225.0	227.3	225.5	225.8	225.2	225.3	224.1	223.0	225.3	231.9	235.7	226.7
2003	223.5	222.2	224.8	226.6	226.6	227.7	228.7	229.6	228.7	230.7	236.0	239.7	228.7
2004	229.5	228.8	231.0	231.2	231.5	231.8	231.1	230.7	229.6	231.9	238.7	243.4	232.4
2005	232.7	231.5	233.1	234.3	234.9	235.4	234.6	235.2	234.3	234.7	242.4	246.3	235.8
2006	234.2	232.7	235.2	233.6	233.9	234.9	234.0	234.6	234.9	236.2	243.5	247.1	236.2
2007	236.4	235.7	238.9	238.5	240.8	241.7	241.5	241.0	240.7	240.7	248.0	250.5	241.2
2008	239.1	237.5	239.7	237.7	237.8	238.2	237.2	237.2	236.0	234.6	239.0	240.6	237.9
2009	227.5	224.7	224.7	224.0	224.8	225.1	224.4	223.0	223.2	221.8	227.5	229.0	225.0
2010	220.0	219.2	221.9	221.5	222.4	222.9	222.0	222.1	221.2	224.1	229.8	232.3	223.3
2011	221.5	220.7	222.1	223.3	223.3	224.5	224.4	224.5	223.7	224.6	231.1	232.9	224.7
2012	222.5	220.2	222.2	222.3	223.6	224.0	222.6	222.5	222.0	223.5	232.0	232.9	224.2
2013	219.6	219.4	221.1	222.0	223.4	225.1	224.5	225.0	223.7	225.0	232.6	235.2	224.7
Transportation and Utilities													
2002	64.8	64.8	65.2	65.9	66.6	66.7	67.2	67.4	67.2	66.9	66.9	66.8	66.4
2003	65.7	65.2	65.3	64.9	65.5	65.8	66.2	66.0	65.8	65.8	65.6	65.7	65.6
2004	64.9	65.0	65.9	65.7	66.1	66.6	66.6	66.6	66.3	66.4	66.6	67.1	66.2
2005	65.8	66.1	66.4	66.9	67.4	68.0	68.0	67.9	68.2	68.7	68.8	69.5	67.6
2006	68.5	68.5	69.2	69.5	69.8	70.6	70.4	70.7	71.1	70.8	71.2	72.1	70.2
2007	70.1	70.2	70.8	70.4	71.3	71.7	71.5	71.6	72.0	71.7	72.3	73.1	71.4
2008	70.8	70.5	70.4	70.9	71.1	70.9	71.5	71.8	71.7	70.9	70.5	70.5	71.0
2009	66.8	66.5	66.2	65.9	66.4	66.5	66.4	66.6	66.5	66.0	66.1	66.8	66.4
2010	65.0	65.0	65.2	65.8	66.2	66.4	66.7	66.8	67.1	66.9	67.1	67.9	66.3
2011	66.4	66.8	67.1	66.9	67.3	67.6	67.5	67.9	68.0	67.6	67.7	68.5	67.4
2012	67.5	68.1	68.8	68.9	69.0	69.4	69.1	69.6	69.8	69.7	70.0	70.8	69.2
2013	70.1	70.3	70.6	70.3	70.6	70.9	70.6	70.8	70.7	71.6	71.1	72.8	70.9
Information													
2002	32.9	32.6	32.8	32.5	32.4	32.4	32.3	31.9	31.4	31.4	31.4	31.3	32.1
2003	30.7	30.8	30.8	29.8	29.9	30.0	30.0	29.7	29.3	29.5	29.8	29.9	30.0
2004	29.5	29.4	29.5	29.6	29.6	29.7	29.7	29.5	29.3	29.3	29.5	29.6	29.5
2005	29.3	29.3	29.3	29.4	29.3	29.3	29.3	29.3	29.0	28.9	29.0	29.1	29.2
2006	28.7	28.7	28.8	28.7	28.8	28.8	28.5	28.4	28.2	28.1	28.2	28.3	28.5
2007	27.9	28.1	28.2	28.2	28.4	28.4	28.0	27.9	27.7	27.7	27.9	27.9	28.0
2008	27.4	27.3	27.3	27.3	27.3	27.1	26.9	26.8	26.4	26.2	26.2	26.3	26.9
2009	25.8	25.6	25.5	25.3	25.3	25.4	24.9	24.8	24.7	24.6	24.7	24.8	25.1
2010	24.5	24.4	24.3	24.1	24.2	24.2	24.0	23.9	23.7	23.7	23.7	23.6	24.0
2011	23.5	23.4	23.2	23.1	23.3	23.3	23.2	23.1	23.1	22.7	22.8	22.8	23.1
2012	22.9	22.9	22.9	22.8	22.8	22.8	22.7	22.6	22.5	22.2	22.4	22.4	22.7
2013	22.4	22.3	22.3	22.3	22.8	22.8	22.8	22.7	22.4	22.3	22.4	22.4	22.5

1. Employment by Industry: Alabama, Selected Years, 2002–2013—*Continued*

(Numbers in thousands, not seasonally adjusted)

Industry and year	January	February	March	April	May	June	July	August	September	October	November	December	Annual average
Financial Activities													
2002	96.8	96.4	96.7	97.3	97.6	97.8	97.9	97.8	97.0	97.0	96.8	97.2	97.2
2003	95.9	95.5	95.7	96.0	96.2	96.8	97.3	97.2	96.4	96.3	96.4	96.7	96.4
2004	95.6	95.9	96.2	96.5	96.8	97.7	97.7	97.8	97.2	97.7	97.7	97.9	97.1
2005	96.2	96.8	97.3	97.6	97.6	98.2	98.4	98.1	98.5	101.2	99.9	100.1	98.3
2006	97.1	98.3	98.5	98.4	98.8	99.4	99.1	99.1	98.9	98.8	99.1	99.7	98.8
2007	99.0	99.1	99.7	99.2	99.7	100.6	100.3	100.2	100.1	99.8	100.0	100.2	99.8
2008	98.8	99.2	99.2	99.2	99.2	99.6	99.8	99.7	99.2	99.0	98.4	98.2	99.1
2009	96.9	96.6	96.6	96.6	96.9	96.9	96.4	95.8	95.0	94.3	93.7	93.6	95.8
2010	92.1	92.0	92.4	92.3	92.5	92.7	92.2	91.8	91.2	91.7	91.7	91.9	92.0
2011	91.1	91.5	91.6	92.4	93.8	93.0	93.2	92.5	93.3	92.1	92.0	91.8	92.4
2012	90.6	91.1	91.5	91.7	92.2	92.7	93.5	93.4	93.6	93.5	94.0	93.9	92.6
2013	93.2	93.3	93.8	93.7	93.9	94.3	94.5	94.6	93.9	94.7	95.0	95.4	94.2
Professional and Business Services													
2002	178.9	180.6	184.6	185.9	185.6	187.2	187.5	190.6	189.8	190.1	189.1	187.7	186.5
2003	184.1	185.8	187.4	188.2	188.2	188.7	187.9	189.5	189.3	189.5	190.3	190.3	188.3
2004	188.9	190.2	192.7	196.5	197.6	200.0	201.0	202.5	201.3	202.1	201.4	202.4	198.1
2005	200.1	202.9	204.2	206.8	206.3	207.8	209.7	212.0	213.5	214.7	215.4	214.9	209.0
2006	208.8	211.4	213.5	213.7	213.7	216.7	214.2	217.1	217.8	216.7	217.0	217.1	214.8
2007	215.4	218.1	221.1	219.8	219.9	221.7	218.8	221.8	222.4	222.2	223.7	224.8	220.8
2008	220.1	221.5	222.2	223.8	222.1	222.1	220.0	220.5	220.1	219.7	216.8	214.1	220.3
2009	205.6	205.3	204.7	205.5	203.4	205.0	205.0	205.0	202.9	202.6	203.8	203.3	204.3
2010	200.3	201.5	203.4	206.1	207.0	210.9	212.9	212.0	212.2	212.8	213.8	213.9	208.9
2011	208.2	211.1	211.9	212.8	212.2	213.1	212.4	214.6	216.8	215.4	215.3	215.6	213.3
2012	210.3	213.7	215.9	217.3	218.2	219.5	217.3	221.6	220.9	219.5	219.8	218.2	217.7
2013	212.7	216.2	218.2	219.3	219.6	220.9	218.7	220.5	219.2	220.2	219.3	219.7	218.7
Education and Health Services													
2002	177.1	180.9	181.2	183.2	182.5	182.2	181.0	182.7	185.0	185.9	188.3	187.1	183.1
2003	184.4	186.2	186.5	187.7	187.4	185.7	185.6	185.8	186.6	188.1	190.0	189.3	186.9
2004	188.0	189.4	190.0	192.3	191.7	191.7	191.9	192.9	194.3	195.1	197.7	197.7	192.7
2005	196.0	197.3	198.2	199.4	200.1	199.1	199.2	200.3	202.6	200.7	202.2	201.8	199.7
2006	199.6	200.4	202.1	203.2	203.8	203.1	202.0	203.9	205.3	205.5	207.5	206.5	203.6
2007	204.8	206.6	207.5	207.8	208.3	207.8	207.3	209.8	210.1	210.5	211.4	212.1	208.7
2008	208.2	210.1	210.7	211.1	211.8	210.4	210.0	211.6	212.3	212.8	212.3	211.8	211.1
2009	209.2	209.8	209.9	210.7	211.3	209.3	209.7	211.0	211.7	212.3	214.1	212.7	211.0
2010	210.9	212.4	212.4	213.4	213.7	212.5	214.0	215.4	216.1	216.7	217.3	216.2	214.3
2011	213.2	214.3	215.7	215.8	215.7	213.9	214.0	215.3	217.8	217.3	218.7	217.6	215.8
2012	216.0	216.7	218.1	218.9	217.8	217.3	214.9	218.0	220.2	219.6	221.6	221.8	218.4
2013	218.0	221.6	220.3	221.2	223.0	220.6	217.7	220.6	223.2	224.5	225.6	225.1	221.8
Leisure and Hospitality													
2002	144.3	146.2	149.2	151.9	154.6	155.9	156.3	156.2	153.5	150.3	150.1	149.6	151.5
2003	146.1	148.0	151.5	154.5	156.4	158.6	158.3	159.3	157.1	154.9	154.4	154.3	154.5
2004	151.2	153.5	157.2	160.2	162.2	164.1	164.1	164.2	161.3	159.1	159.4	158.4	159.6
2005	155.1	157.5	162.0	166.4	168.5	170.4	168.7	169.6	167.2	163.6	163.9	163.6	164.7
2006	160.3	163.3	167.6	170.1	172.6	174.9	173.5	174.8	173.4	169.0	168.8	168.7	169.8
2007	165.8	169.2	172.9	174.6	176.7	178.9	177.6	178.5	176.1	172.9	172.3	171.9	174.0
2008	166.3	169.2	172.7	177.8	180.3	181.2	179.3	179.9	176.6	171.8	170.3	169.3	174.6
2009	163.8	166.0	169.2	172.3	174.6	175.7	174.0	173.4	171.5	167.5	166.9	166.4	170.1
2010	160.3	161.0	165.9	169.5	171.4	173.0	170.9	171.0	168.8	166.5	166.5	165.5	167.5
2011	159.5	162.3	166.5	171.5	171.8	174.1	173.7	174.7	172.4	168.5	168.0	166.7	169.1
2012	163.1	166.3	170.9	176.1	178.2	180.6	177.7	178.8	176.6	172.7	172.7	171.0	173.7
2013	167.9	170.4	174.8	180.2	183.2	185.4	183.7	184.1	182.4	181.3	181.0	178.9	179.4
Other Services													
2002	86.0	86.6	87.0	86.8	86.9	86.6	86.2	86.1	85.3	84.7	84.4	83.9	85.9
2003	83.1	83.3	83.4	83.6	84.0	84.5	83.8	83.8	83.0	82.8	82.2	82.0	83.3
2004	81.1	81.4	81.8	81.9	82.2	82.8	82.3	82.1	81.4	81.2	81.2	81.2	81.7
2005	80.8	80.9	81.3	81.4	81.8	82.0	81.5	81.1	80.7	79.9	79.9	80.2	81.0
2006	79.5	79.8	80.4	80.3	80.3	81.6	80.7	80.6	80.5	80.0	80.1	80.2	80.3
2007	79.9	80.5	81.4	81.2	81.4	81.8	81.2	81.0	80.8	81.0	81.2	81.4	81.1
2008	81.0	81.8	82.1	82.2	82.3	82.3	82.2	81.8	81.5	81.2	80.9	80.6	81.7
2009	80.2	80.2	80.4	80.3	80.5	80.7	80.6	80.1	79.5	79.7	79.3	79.4	80.1
2010	79.1	79.5	79.8	79.8	80.1	80.8	80.9	80.3	79.7	80.3	79.5	79.3	79.9
2011	78.4	78.9	79.2	79.6	79.6	80.1	79.7	79.3	79.2	79.2	79.6	79.2	79.3
2012	79.1	79.8	80.8	80.7	80.7	81.6	81.1	80.5	79.9	80.1	79.3	79.2	80.2
2013	78.7	79.0	79.8	79.9	80.0	80.8	80.3	80.3	80.0	80.0	79.1	78.8	79.7
Government													
2002	352.5	355.9	356.6	358.3	357.5	351.3	341.3	342.6	356.3	360.2	361.6	361.4	354.6
2003	358.3	362.0	362.9	363.4	363.3	354.4	344.4	346.4	359.4	362.6	363.1	361.5	358.5
2004	358.7	361.7	361.9	362.8	361.9	358.8	348.8	350.6	360.0	361.7	363.1	363.2	359.4
2005	360.1	363.0	363.5	364.8	365.5	364.2	352.4	355.1	362.9	367.4	368.1	367.8	362.9
2006	366.7	369.0	370.6	372.1	373.0	372.2	360.0	362.6	371.6	373.9	374.8	375.3	370.2
2007	374.2	376.6	377.9	378.4	379.3	379.1	364.6	368.6	377.8	380.4	381.9	381.8	376.7
2008	380.3	384.1	385.3	386.6	388.1	387.9	372.2	375.0	383.1	387.6	387.2	387.8	383.8
2009	383.1	385.2	386.1	388.5	388.8	387.6	371.2	373.2	382.0	386.8	387.3	388.0	384.0
2010	384.1	386.6	389.6	391.2	400.3	394.6	376.2	376.1	383.9	387.0	388.2	388.1	387.2
2011	384.2	386.7	387.8	387.8	387.4	384.2	371.6	371.3	380.2	381.8	383.3	380.9	382.3
2012	378.1	381.4	383.6	382.8	382.1	379.4	365.8	366.5	374.7	379.8	381.1	380.4	378.0
2013	376.6	380.4	382.6	382.6	381.9	378.5	369.6	369.8	375.2	379.0	379.7	377.9	377.8

2. Average Weekly Hours by Selected Industry: Alabama, 2009–2013

(Not seasonally adjusted)

Industry and year	January	February	March	April	May	June	July	August	September	October	November	December	Annual average
Total Private													
2009	34.8	35.2	35.1	34.8	34.7	35.0	34.6	35.1	34.6	34.6	34.9	34.7	34.8
2010	34.6	34.8	34.8	35.0	35.5	35.2	35.4	35.5	35.0	35.2	35.3	35.1	35.1
2011	34.8	35.0	35.0	34.9	35.2	35.0	35.2	35.6	35.7	35.7	35.3	35.7	35.3
2012	35.5	35.9	35.7	36.2	35.6	35.8	35.9	36.0	36.4	36.1	36.1	36.6	36.0
2013	35.5	35.8	36.0	36.0	35.8	36.6	36.0	36.1	36.6	36.1	36.2	36.3	36.1
Goods-Producing													
2009	38.4	39.0	39.1	38.9	38.8	39.2	38.7	39.3	38.6	38.9	39.2	39.3	38.9
2010	39.4	39.5	39.4	39.6	40.4	40.1	40.4	40.4	40.2	40.6	40.7	40.5	40.1
2011	39.9	40.1	40.2	39.7	40.5	40.4	39.8	41.2	41.8	41.0	41.0	41.5	40.6
2012	41.2	41.8	41.8	42.3	42.0	42.1	41.5	42.7	42.9	42.8	43.2	43.2	42.3
2013	42.3	42.9	42.9	42.8	42.7	43.0	42.4	43.1	43.2	43.4	43.4	43.0	42.9
Construction													
2009	41.2	41.4	41.2	41.1	41.0	41.1	41.0	41.1	41.0	41.0	40.9	40.8	41.1
2010	41.2	41.6	41.9	42.3	42.4	42.3	42.2	42.4	42.3	42.5	42.4	42.5	42.2
2011	42.3	42.4	42.2	41.6	42.7	42.5	42.8	43.3	43.4	42.3	41.4	42.0	42.4
2012	39.0	40.7	41.1	42.1	41.3	40.8	40.1	40.9	40.2	40.2	39.7	39.3	40.4
2013	37.5	38.7	40.4	41.7	41.9	40.9	40.9	41.8	42.9	41.9	41.1	41.0	40.9
Manufacturing													
2009	41.3	41.4	41.3	41.3	41.2	41.1	41.1	41.2	41.0	41.1	41.2	41.3	41.2
2010	41.3	41.2	41.3	41.2	41.3	41.1	41.3	41.2	41.1	41.2	41.3	41.2	41.2
2011	41.0	41.2	41.2	40.4	40.8	40.6	40.3	41.2	41.5	40.6	40.7	41.2	40.9
2012	41.7	42.0	42.1	42.2	42.1	42.3	41.8	42.4	42.9	42.8	42.4	42.6	42.3
2013	41.8	42.5	42.3	41.9	41.7	42.3	41.7	42.4	42.3	42.9	43.1	42.7	42.3
Trade, Transportation, and Utilities													
2009	36.1	36.3	36.4	36.2	36.3	36.5	36.3	36.5	36.3	36.2	36.2	36.4	36.3
2010	36.3	36.4	36.3	36.6	36.9	36.7	36.5	36.6	36.5	36.6	36.5	36.7	36.5
2011	36.5	36.6	36.5	36.5	36.1	35.5	36.2	35.9	35.7	35.6	35.3	35.8	36.0
2012	35.7	36.1	35.3	36.1	35.3	35.9	35.6	35.1	36.2	35.8	36.2	36.0	35.8
2013	35.7	36.0	36.1	36.3	35.8	36.6	35.9	36.2	36.7	35.9	36.0	36.2	36.1
Financial Activities													
2009	36.8	36.6	36.6	36.4	37.4	36.9	36.1	36.8	36.7	36.5	37.1	36.6	36.7
2010	36.6	36.6	36.9	36.8	37.0	36.6	36.4	36.7	36.4	36.4	36.0	36.2	36.6
2011	36.4	36.6	36.3	35.9	36.0	37.2	36.2	36.4	36.8	36.4	37.8	37.1	36.6
2012	38.1	37.0	36.9	37.9	37.2	37.3	38.6	37.8	37.9	36.8	37.0	38.1	37.6
2013	37.3	37.3	36.9	37.1	37.3	38.6	37.1	36.9	38.1	36.8	37.0	37.5	37.3
Professional and Business Services													
2009	35.8	35.9	36.0	36.2	36.1	36.3	36.1	36.2	36.0	36.0	36.1	36.0	36.1
2010	35.9	36.0	36.1	36.3	36.5	36.4	36.6	36.8	36.7	36.8	36.8	36.8	36.5
2011	36.6	36.7	36.9	37.3	37.5	36.8	36.8	37.1	37.1	37.5	36.3	36.8	37.0
2012	36.1	36.6	36.2	36.9	36.7	36.6	36.7	36.8	37.0	36.5	36.1	36.4	36.5
2013	35.6	36.0	36.7	36.9	36.4	37.5	36.8	36.9	38.0	37.3	37.4	37.3	36.9
Education and Health Services													
2009	35.3	35.5	35.0	34.7	34.4	34.3	34.4	34.8	34.4	34.5	34.8	34.5	34.7
2010	34.6	34.5	34.7	34.5	35.0	34.6	34.8	35.0	35.0	34.8	35.0	34.8	34.8
2011	35.1	35.3	34.9	34.4	35.1	34.7	35.1	35.0	35.3	35.1	34.5	34.7	34.9
2012	34.6	34.4	34.6	34.8	34.1	34.0	34.5	34.1	34.7	34.0	34.0	34.4	34.3
2013	33.9	33.9	33.8	33.4	33.4	34.2	33.5	33.6	33.9	33.1	33.5	33.9	33.7
Leisure and Hospitality													
2009	25.3	25.5	25.5	25.6	25.8	26.7	26.2	26.4	26.0	26.3	26.5	26.3	26.0
2010	26.5	27.0	27.0	27.2	27.3	27.1	27.3	26.8	26.5	26.7	26.5	26.6	26.9
2011	26.4	26.5	26.5	26.5	26.4	27.1	27.1	27.1	26.7	27.4	27.0	27.5	26.9
2012	26.5	27.3	27.3	27.1	26.5	26.7	27.2	27.1	26.0	26.3	25.8	26.4	26.7
2013	25.5	26.2	26.6	26.3	26.3	27.0	26.8	26.9	26.4	26.5	26.3	26.5	26.4
Other Services													
2009	30.0	30.3	30.7	30.9	31.7	30.9	31.0	31.3	30.2	30.4	30.3	29.9	30.6
2010	30.0	30.0	29.7	29.8	30.1	30.2	30.3	30.5	30.2	30.1	30.2	30.4	30.1
2011	30.4	30.4	30.5	30.9	31.7	31.6	31.9	32.5	32.1	32.6	31.4	31.2	31.4
2012	29.8	31.6	31.9	32.1	30.7	32.0	32.2	32.4	33.5	34.2	33.0	33.4	32.2
2013	31.8	30.9	32.2	32.8	32.5	35.2	33.0	32.7	34.9	33.7	33.4	33.9	33.1

3. Average Hourly Earnings by Selected Industry: Alabama, 2009–2013

(Dollars, not seasonally adjusted)

Industry and year	January	February	March	April	May	June	July	August	September	October	November	December	Annual average
Total Private													
2009	19.82	19.87	19.57	19.69	19.64	19.41	19.44	19.58	19.66	19.70	19.86	19.87	19.68
2010	19.95	19.94	19.95	19.94	19.90	19.79	19.70	19.68	19.83	19.81	19.87	19.95	19.86
2011	19.97	19.95	19.85	20.04	20.24	20.20	20.19	20.20	20.34	20.43	20.20	20.08	20.14
2012	20.41	20.30	20.31	20.38	20.09	20.21	20.14	19.94	20.18	20.04	20.16	20.40	20.21
2013	20.26	20.27	20.24	20.11	19.97	20.09	20.03	20.12	20.35	20.18	20.09	20.46	20.18
Goods-Producing													
2009	20.84	21.01	20.94	21.07	20.87	20.91	21.09	20.92	21.20	21.20	21.32	21.22	21.05
2010	21.25	21.36	21.32	21.24	21.18	21.26	21.40	21.33	21.51	21.45	21.47	21.70	21.37
2011	21.77	21.54	21.53	21.36	21.56	21.66	22.18	21.93	22.13	22.08	21.87	21.57	21.77
2012	21.83	21.64	21.72	21.99	21.47	21.72	21.74	21.60	21.44	21.39	21.68	22.09	21.69
2013	21.93	22.05	22.25	22.01	21.75	21.92	22.00	21.84	21.96	21.98	21.96	22.37	22.00
Construction													
2009	17.97	18.20	18.13	18.04	17.94	18.04	18.04	18.07	18.03	18.08	18.05	18.00	18.05
2010	17.96	18.16	18.19	18.16	18.22	18.38	18.36	18.49	18.46	18.55	18.50	18.53	18.33
2011	18.41	18.50	18.69	18.38	19.46	19.59	19.68	19.46	19.60	19.68	19.85	19.07	19.21
2012	19.61	19.49	19.80	19.49	19.81	20.34	20.29	20.51	20.36	20.60	20.95	20.38	20.14
2013	20.16	20.60	21.27	20.63	20.45	21.08	20.99	20.79	21.23	21.57	21.33	23.05	21.10
Manufacturing													
2009	20.35	20.40	20.38	20.44	20.37	20.32	20.37	20.43	20.34	20.38	20.41	20.45	20.39
2010	20.47	20.43	20.46	20.52	20.53	20.51	20.61	20.58	20.56	20.63	20.66	20.62	20.55
2011	20.51	20.62	20.52	20.67	20.56	20.83	21.06	20.97	21.00	21.28	20.97	20.96	20.83
2012	21.21	21.13	21.00	21.70	20.99	21.22	21.33	21.11	21.07	20.99	20.83	20.93	21.12
2013	20.92	21.13	21.36	21.33	21.18	21.35	21.58	21.49	21.62	21.60	21.68	21.97	21.44
Trade, Transportation, and Utilities													
2009	16.80	16.93	16.97	16.86	16.96	17.12	17.03	17.14	17.05	17.00	17.06	17.12	17.00
2010	17.11	17.12	17.10	17.12	17.27	17.33	17.27	17.31	17.29	17.31	17.25	17.34	17.24
2011	17.25	17.31	17.34	17.66	18.71	18.48	18.54	18.62	18.87	18.93	18.41	18.44	18.21
2012	18.68	18.60	18.38	18.47	18.23	18.65	18.28	18.01	18.28	18.32	17.99	18.20	18.34
2013	18.16	18.27	18.23	17.80	17.92	18.03	17.81	17.83	18.11	18.04	17.80	18.18	18.01
Financial Activities													
2009	20.33	20.47	20.48	20.54	20.22	20.49	20.70	20.68	20.76	20.79	20.72	20.76	20.58
2010	20.83	20.97	20.90	20.84	20.75	20.75	20.75	20.68	20.63	20.64	20.89	20.73	20.77
2011	20.57	20.54	20.76	21.23	21.53	21.19	20.98	20.95	21.12	21.54	20.59	20.58	20.97
2012	21.20	21.03	21.12	21.36	21.51	21.21	21.21	20.62	20.95	20.93	20.94	21.41	21.12
2013	21.03	21.32	21.57	21.49	21.66	21.47	21.47	21.51	21.78	21.04	20.85	21.33	21.38
Professional and Business Services													
2009	24.48	24.52	24.55	24.67	24.56	24.65	24.54	24.59	24.50	24.51	24.59	24.53	24.56
2010	24.50	24.56	24.60	24.43	24.32	24.27	24.31	24.39	24.34	24.34	24.36	24.41	24.40
2011	24.34	24.40	24.38	24.39	24.25	23.89	23.75	23.45	23.43	23.31	23.04	22.65	23.77
2012	23.51	23.23	23.29	23.28	22.95	22.65	22.90	22.90	22.99	22.66	22.73	22.75	22.98
2013	23.01	23.28	23.06	23.31	23.02	23.00	23.03	23.17	23.37	22.82	22.82	23.62	23.13
Education and Health Services													
2009	19.40	19.42	19.26	19.39	19.60	19.52	19.51	19.79	19.80	19.82	19.81	19.85	19.60
2010	19.74	19.74	19.74	20.04	19.78	19.94	19.83	19.75	19.70	19.88	19.84	19.91	19.82
2011	19.70	19.71	19.52	20.11	19.69	20.26	20.22	20.40	20.38	20.73	20.65	20.70	20.17
2012	20.64	20.69	20.53	20.64	20.44	20.80	20.78	20.88	21.14	20.78	21.23	21.39	20.83
2013	20.87	20.95	20.97	20.91	20.65	20.94	20.81	20.99	21.07	21.00	20.93	20.96	20.92
Leisure and Hospitality													
2009	9.95	10.06	10.05	10.08	10.17	10.17	10.15	10.23	10.28	10.30	10.25	10.24	10.16
2010	10.29	10.32	10.30	10.34	10.34	10.30	10.37	10.41	10.41	10.44	10.59	10.64	10.40
2011	10.74	10.70	10.62	10.67	10.71	10.57	10.53	10.62	10.53	10.58	10.65	10.90	10.65
2012	10.85	10.93	10.87	10.92	10.94	10.90	10.89	10.80	11.02	11.02	11.09	11.23	10.95
2013	11.19	11.15	11.10	11.00	10.98	10.88	10.88	10.84	10.84	10.87	10.82	11.05	10.96
Other Services													
2009	16.20	16.28	16.09	16.09	15.58	15.40	15.65	15.58	15.77	15.77	15.89	15.84	15.84
2010	15.92	15.96	16.10	16.19	16.14	15.88	16.11	16.22	16.34	16.34	16.22	16.03	16.12
2011	16.10	16.19	16.32	16.78	17.41	17.75	17.45	17.51	17.17	17.34	18.19	18.87	17.27
2012	19.21	18.38	18.73	19.10	18.63	19.59	18.79	19.03	19.61	19.81	19.69	20.08	19.23
2013	19.95	19.92	19.79	19.83	19.99	20.55	19.89	20.60	20.27	20.13	20.15	20.18	20.11

4. Average Weekly Earnings by Selected Industry: Alabama, 2009–2013

(Dollars, not seasonally adjusted)

Industry and year	January	February	March	April	May	June	July	August	September	October	November	December	Annual average
Total Private													
2009	689.7	699.4	686.9	685.2	681.5	679.4	672.6	687.3	680.2	681.6	693.1	689.5	684.9
2010	690.3	693.9	694.3	697.9	706.5	696.6	697.4	698.6	694.1	697.3	701.4	700.3	697.1
2011	695.0	698.3	694.8	699.4	712.5	707.0	710.7	719.1	726.1	729.4	713.1	716.9	710.9
2012	724.6	728.8	725.1	737.8	715.2	723.5	723.0	717.8	734.6	723.4	727.8	746.6	727.6
2013	719.2	725.7	728.6	724.0	714.9	735.3	721.1	726.3	744.8	728.5	727.3	742.7	728.5
Goods-Producing													
2009	800.3	819.4	818.8	819.6	809.8	819.7	816.2	822.2	818.3	824.7	835.7	834.0	818.9
2010	837.3	843.7	840.0	841.1	855.7	852.5	864.6	861.7	864.7	870.9	873.8	878.9	856.9
2011	868.6	863.8	865.5	848.0	873.2	875.1	882.8	903.5	925.0	905.3	896.7	895.2	883.9
2012	899.4	904.6	907.9	930.2	901.7	914.4	902.2	922.3	919.8	915.5	936.6	954.3	917.5
2013	927.6	946.0	954.5	942.0	928.7	942.6	932.8	941.3	948.7	953.9	953.1	961.9	943.8
Construction													
2009	740.4	753.5	747.0	741.4	735.5	741.4	739.6	742.7	739.2	741.3	738.3	734.4	741.9
2010	740.0	755.5	762.2	768.2	772.5	777.5	774.8	784.0	780.9	788.4	784.4	787.5	773.5
2011	778.7	784.4	788.7	764.6	830.9	832.6	842.3	842.6	850.6	832.5	821.8	800.9	814.5
2012	764.8	793.2	813.8	820.5	818.2	829.9	813.6	838.9	818.5	828.1	831.7	800.9	813.7
2013	756.0	797.2	859.3	860.3	856.9	862.2	858.5	869.0	910.8	903.8	876.7	945.1	863.0
Manufacturing													
2009	840.5	844.6	841.7	844.2	839.2	835.2	837.2	841.7	833.9	837.6	840.9	844.6	840.1
2010	845.4	841.7	845.0	845.4	847.9	843.0	851.2	847.9	845.0	850.0	853.3	849.5	846.7
2011	840.9	849.5	845.4	835.1	838.9	845.7	848.7	864.0	871.5	864.0	853.5	863.6	852.0
2012	884.5	887.5	884.1	915.7	883.7	897.6	891.6	895.1	903.9	898.4	883.2	891.6	893.4
2013	874.5	898.0	903.5	893.7	883.2	903.1	899.9	911.2	914.5	926.6	934.4	938.1	906.9
Trade, Transportation, and Utilities													
2009	606.5	614.6	617.7	610.3	615.7	624.9	618.2	625.6	618.9	615.4	617.6	623.2	617.1
2010	621.1	623.2	620.7	626.6	637.3	636.0	630.4	633.6	631.1	633.6	629.6	636.4	629.3
2011	629.6	633.6	632.9	644.6	675.4	656.0	671.2	668.5	673.7	673.9	649.9	660.2	655.6
2012	666.9	671.5	648.8	666.8	643.5	669.5	650.8	632.2	661.7	655.9	651.2	655.2	656.6
2013	648.3	657.7	658.1	646.1	641.5	659.9	639.4	645.5	664.6	647.6	640.8	658.1	650.2
Financial Activities													
2009	748.1	749.2	749.6	747.7	756.2	756.1	747.3	761.0	761.9	758.8	768.7	759.8	755.3
2010	762.4	767.5	771.2	766.9	767.8	755.1	755.3	759.0	750.9	751.3	752.0	750.4	760.2
2011	748.8	745.6	745.3	764.3	800.9	767.1	763.7	771.0	768.8	814.2	766.0	763.5	767.5
2012	807.7	778.1	779.3	809.5	800.2	791.1	818.7	779.4	794.0	770.2	774.8	815.7	794.1
2013	784.4	795.2	795.9	797.3	807.9	828.7	796.5	793.7	829.8	774.3	771.5	799.9	797.5
Professional and Business Services													
2009	876.4	880.3	883.8	893.1	886.6	894.8	885.9	890.2	882.0	882.4	887.7	883.1	886.6
2010	879.6	884.2	888.1	886.8	887.7	883.4	889.8	897.6	893.3	895.7	896.5	898.3	890.6
2011	890.8	895.5	899.6	909.8	909.4	879.2	874.0	870.0	869.3	874.1	836.4	833.5	879.5
2012	848.7	850.2	843.1	859.0	842.3	829.0	840.4	842.7	850.6	827.1	820.6	828.1	838.8
2013	819.2	838.1	846.3	860.1	837.9	862.5	847.5	855.0	888.1	851.2	853.5	881.0	853.5
Education and Health Services													
2009	684.8	689.4	674.1	672.8	674.2	669.5	671.1	688.7	681.1	683.8	689.4	684.8	680.1
2010	683.0	681.0	685.0	691.4	692.3	689.9	690.1	691.3	689.5	691.8	694.4	692.9	689.7
2011	691.5	695.8	681.3	691.8	691.1	703.0	709.7	714.0	719.4	727.6	712.4	718.3	703.9
2012	714.1	711.7	710.3	718.3	697.0	707.2	716.9	712.0	733.6	706.5	721.8	735.8	714.5
2013	707.5	710.2	708.8	698.4	689.7	716.2	697.1	705.3	714.3	695.1	701.2	710.5	705.0
Leisure and Hospitality													
2009	251.7	256.5	256.3	258.1	262.4	271.5	265.9	270.1	267.3	270.9	271.6	269.3	264.2
2010	272.7	278.6	278.1	281.3	282.3	279.1	283.1	279.0	275.9	278.8	280.6	283.0	279.8
2011	283.5	283.6	281.4	282.8	282.7	286.5	285.4	287.8	281.2	289.9	287.6	299.8	286.5
2012	287.5	298.4	296.8	295.9	289.9	291.0	296.2	292.7	286.5	289.8	286.1	296.5	292.4
2013	285.4	292.1	295.3	289.3	288.8	293.8	291.6	291.6	286.2	288.1	284.6	292.8	289.3
Other Services													
2009	486.0	493.3	494.0	497.2	493.9	475.9	485.2	487.7	476.3	479.4	481.5	473.6	484.7
2010	477.6	478.8	478.2	482.5	485.8	479.6	488.1	494.7	493.5	491.8	489.8	487.3	485.2
2011	489.4	492.2	497.8	518.5	551.9	560.9	556.7	569.1	551.2	565.3	571.2	588.7	542.3
2012	572.5	580.8	597.5	613.1	571.9	626.9	605.0	616.6	656.9	677.5	649.8	670.7	619.2
2013	634.4	615.5	637.2	650.4	649.7	723.4	656.4	673.6	707.4	678.4	673.0	684.1	665.6

ALASKA
At a Glance

Population:
  2000 census: 626,932
  2010 census: 710,231
  2013 estimate: 735,132

Percent change in population:
  2000–2010: 13.3%
  2010–2012: 3.5%

Percent change in total nonfarm employment:
  2000–2010: 14.2%
  2010–2013: 3.6%

Industry with the largest growth in employment, 2000–2013 (thousands):
  Education and Health Services, 21.0

Industry with the largest decline or smallest growth in employment, 2000–2013 (thousands):
  Financial Activities, -1.7

Civilian labor force:
  2000: 319,002
  2010: 361,714
  2013: 364,188

Unemployment rate and rank among states (lowest to highest):
  2000: 6.2%, 51st
  2010: 8.0%, 17th
  2013: 6.5%, 18th

Over-the-year change in unemployment rates:
  2010–2011: -0.4%
  2011–2012: -0.7%
  2012–2013: -0.4%

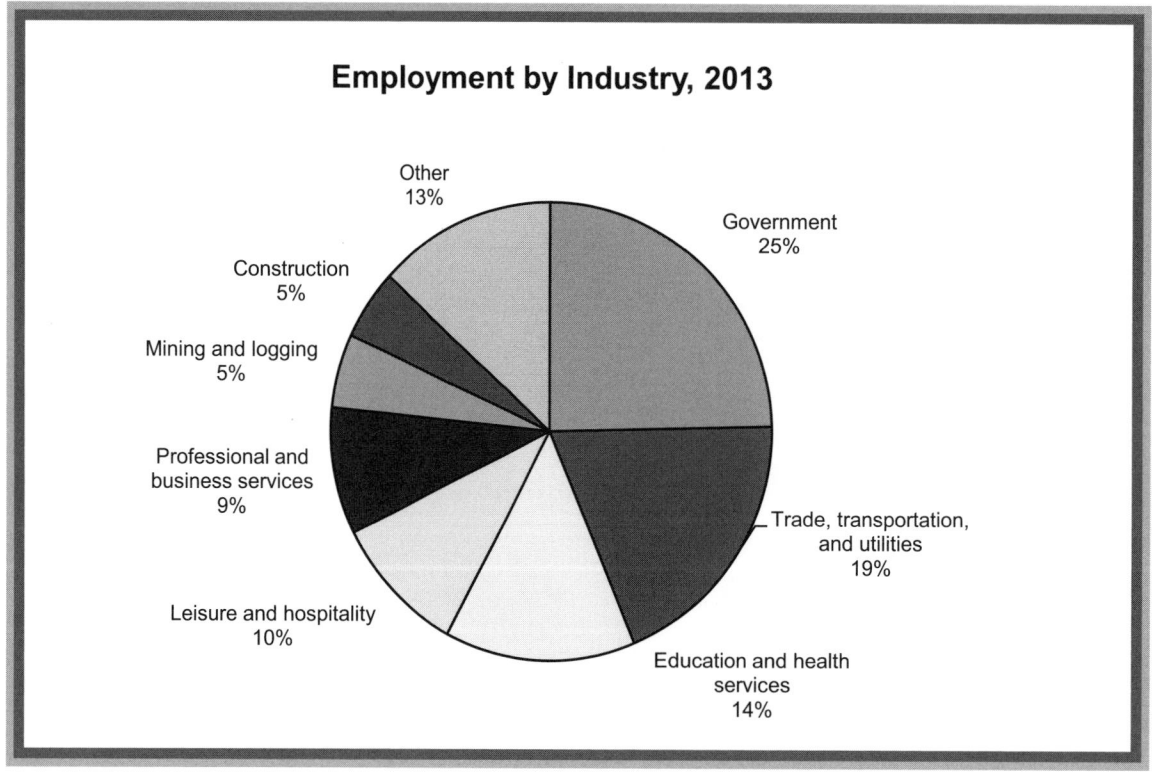

Employment by Industry, 2013

Other 13%
Construction 5%
Mining and logging 5%
Professional and business services 9%
Leisure and hospitality 10%
Government 25%
Trade, transportation, and utilities 19%
Education and health services 14%

1. Employment by Industry: Alaska, Selected Years, 2002–2013

(Numbers in thousands, not seasonally adjusted)

Industry and year	January	February	March	April	May	June	July	August	September	October	November	December	Annual average
Total Nonfarm													
2002	270.0	279.1	282.4	286.0	296.7	307.4	313.8	314.5	308.6	296.0	286.7	284.9	293.8
2003	277.2	283.5	286.5	289.2	302.7	313.6	318.7	319.1	313.3	298.2	289.2	287.2	298.2
2004	282.3	285.8	290.2	294.3	305.3	318.0	326.1	324.9	319.7	304.5	295.0	293.3	303.3
2005	287.7	292.0	295.3	300.3	312.5	324.5	332.4	332.1	324.6	307.7	300.2	296.1	308.8
2006	290.4	297.0	301.4	306.4	318.8	335.8	336.7	336.3	329.1	310.2	303.9	300.7	313.9
2007	295.3	302.0	304.9	308.9	321.1	335.6	338.8	339.5	331.2	314.3	307.1	303.7	316.9
2008	299.3	305.1	307.5	312.1	326.3	340.1	345.4	344.6	336.4	318.1	310.7	308.2	321.2
2009	301.6	306.8	308.0	312.8	322.2	337.3	343.0	341.7	333.1	316.7	309.6	306.3	319.9
2010	301.9	306.1	308.6	314.7	324.9	342.9	348.7	347.0	340.5	323.9	316.6	313.4	324.1
2011	307.8	313.5	315.8	320.4	329.8	348.1	353.3	351.9	346.5	328.4	320.5	317.5	329.5
2012	312.1	319.4	322.2	326.2	337.3	354.0	357.3	356.4	348.6	335.9	324.7	321.3	334.6
2013	314.3	321.8	324.2	328.5	339.3	354.3	359.3	359.4	350.8	332.9	324.5	320.8	335.8
Total Private													
2002	192.7	199.0	201.5	204.3	215.0	227.5	238.4	237.5	227.0	214.2	204.9	202.2	213.7
2003	197.6	201.8	203.9	206.3	219.3	232.3	242.2	241.7	231.0	215.9	207.3	205.2	217.0
2004	201.8	204.4	207.6	211.6	223.0	238.0	249.8	248.0	238.5	222.3	213.1	211.0	222.4
2005	207.8	210.4	213.2	217.4	229.6	244.6	256.6	255.3	243.3	225.5	218.1	214.4	228.0
2006	211.8	215.3	219.0	223.2	235.5	253.8	260.8	259.1	247.1	228.1	222.1	219.1	232.9
2007	216.4	220.1	222.3	225.8	238.0	255.1	263.1	262.6	249.2	231.1	224.4	221.2	235.8
2008	218.9	222.7	224.8	228.1	243.4	258.0	268.1	265.9	252.9	234.1	226.9	224.9	239.1
2009	220.0	223.2	224.4	227.1	238.8	253.0	263.6	261.4	248.2	230.7	224.1	220.8	236.3
2010	218.8	220.9	222.9	227.6	239.1	256.1	267.6	265.0	253.2	236.5	229.8	226.7	238.7
2011	223.6	227.7	230.3	233.8	244.9	262.4	273.4	271.8	260.3	241.8	234.6	231.6	244.7
2012	230.1	234.1	236.4	240.3	252.5	269.7	278.3	276.0	263.0	250.2	239.5	236.3	250.5
2013	233.1	237.7	239.9	243.6	255.1	270.8	281.4	280.6	267.4	249.4	241.3	237.5	253.2
Goods-Producing													
2002	30.8	34.8	35.2	34.5	36.2	40.8	48.6	47.6	43.4	38.9	33.6	30.9	37.9
2003	31.1	34.7	35.3	33.8	37.1	43.2	50.7	49.1	44.3	39.4	33.7	30.7	38.6
2004	33.7	35.0	35.6	35.7	38.3	44.9	53.2	50.8	46.1	40.5	35.2	32.3	40.1
2005	35.4	36.6	37.6	37.7	39.8	46.2	54.7	53.5	48.0	42.1	37.4	34.1	41.9
2006	36.3	38.2	39.3	40.1	41.7	50.5	56.5	54.6	49.1	43.4	39.1	35.7	43.7
2007	38.0	39.7	40.1	40.6	42.1	50.0	57.3	56.3	50.5	44.8	40.1	36.8	44.7
2008	38.5	40.7	41.2	41.2	43.8	51.3	58.6	57.2	51.4	45.1	40.1	37.8	45.6
2009	38.8	40.7	41.0	41.1	42.7	50.3	58.3	55.7	48.2	42.0	38.1	35.0	44.3
2010	37.3	38.5	39.4	39.9	41.9	49.9	58.7	56.2	50.1	43.6	39.3	36.2	44.3
2011	37.6	40.0	40.9	41.0	42.7	51.5	59.9	58.2	52.4	45.3	40.3	37.1	45.6
2012	39.6	42.1	43.3	43.5	45.6	54.0	61.2	59.1	52.2	47.2	41.9	38.6	47.4
2013	40.3	43.0	44.2	44.7	45.8	54.0	62.1	60.3	54.4	48.8	43.6	40.4	48.5
Service-Providing													
2002	239.2	244.3	247.2	251.5	260.5	266.6	265.2	266.9	265.2	257.1	253.1	254.0	255.9
2003	246.1	248.8	251.2	255.4	265.6	270.4	268.0	270.0	269.0	258.8	255.5	256.5	259.6
2004	248.6	250.8	254.6	258.6	267.0	273.1	272.9	274.1	273.6	264.0	259.8	261.0	263.2
2005	252.3	255.4	257.7	262.6	272.7	278.3	277.7	278.6	276.6	265.6	262.8	262.0	266.9
2006	254.1	258.8	262.1	266.3	277.1	285.3	280.2	281.7	280.0	266.8	264.8	265.0	270.2
2007	257.3	262.3	264.8	268.3	279.0	285.6	281.5	283.2	280.7	269.5	267.0	266.9	272.2
2008	260.8	264.4	266.3	270.9	282.5	288.8	286.8	287.4	285.0	273.0	270.6	270.4	275.6
2009	262.8	266.1	267.0	271.7	279.5	287.0	284.7	286.0	284.9	274.7	271.5	271.3	275.6
2010	264.6	267.6	269.2	274.8	283.0	293.0	290.0	290.8	290.4	280.3	277.3	277.2	279.9
2011	270.2	273.5	274.9	279.4	287.1	296.6	293.4	293.7	294.1	283.1	280.2	280.4	283.9
2012	272.5	277.3	278.9	282.7	291.7	300.0	296.1	297.3	296.4	288.7	282.8	282.7	287.3
2013	274.0	278.8	280.0	283.8	293.5	300.3	297.2	299.1	296.4	284.1	280.9	280.4	287.4
Mining and Logging													
2002	10.5	10.7	10.8	11.1	10.9	11.1	11.6	11.5	11.2	11.1	10.8	10.5	11.0
2003	10.0	10.2	10.3	10.2	10.4	10.3	10.4	10.4	10.3	10.0	9.8	9.7	10.2
2004	9.4	9.7	9.9	10.2	10.3	10.4	10.5	10.6	10.3	10.1	10.0	10.1	10.1
2005	9.9	10.3	10.5	10.4	10.5	10.8	11.1	11.2	11.2	11.3	11.3	11.3	10.8
2006	11.0	11.4	11.5	12.1	12.4	12.8	12.7	12.9	12.9	12.8	12.8	12.9	12.4
2007	12.9	13.2	13.3	13.5	13.6	14.1	14.3	14.5	14.5	14.5	14.2	14.3	13.9
2008	14.2	14.5	14.7	14.8	15.1	15.5	15.7	16.0	16.0	15.9	15.7	16.1	15.4
2009	15.4	15.6	15.5	15.4	15.5	15.8	15.3	15.4	15.1	14.5	14.4	14.3	15.2
2010	14.0	14.2	14.5	14.8	15.3	16.0	16.4	16.5	16.3	15.9	15.6	15.6	15.4
2011	14.8	15.2	15.3	15.5	15.8	16.4	16.8	16.9	16.7	16.5	16.1	16.4	16.0
2012	15.5	15.8	16.0	16.5	17.0	17.5	17.9	18.1	17.8	17.8	17.5	17.0	17.0
2013	16.4	16.9	17.3	17.2	17.4	18.0	18.0	18.2	17.9	17.7	17.4	17.4	17.5
Construction													
2002	12.2	12.4	12.8	13.4	15.8	18.1	19.0	19.6	18.9	17.7	15.5	14.3	15.8
2003	12.5	12.7	13.1	14.6	17.4	19.3	20.4	21.0	20.5	19.2	16.8	15.5	16.9
2004	13.7	13.8	14.1	15.3	17.7	20.1	21.4	21.7	21.0	19.6	17.5	16.2	17.7
2005	14.6	14.7	15.3	17.1	19.0	21.1	22.3	22.8	21.7	20.2	17.6	16.3	18.6
2006	14.5	14.7	15.3	16.6	18.8	21.0	21.4	21.5	21.0	19.8	17.4	16.1	18.2
2007	14.3	14.8	14.9	16.1	18.0	20.2	20.8	21.2	20.3	19.1	16.7	15.5	17.7
2008	13.7	14.1	14.5	15.7	17.8	19.9	20.7	21.2	20.1	18.7	15.7	14.7	17.2
2009	12.9	13.3	13.6	14.4	16.8	18.7	19.6	19.8	18.7	17.6	15.4	14.4	16.3
2010	12.8	12.7	12.9	14.1	16.3	18.6	19.6	19.8	19.0	17.9	15.2	14.1	16.1
2011	12.3	12.5	12.8	14.0	16.0	18.2	18.9	19.2	18.6	17.6	15.1	14.0	15.8
2012	13.1	13.2	13.6	14.5	16.6	18.9	19.8	20.2	19.1	18.2	15.3	14.3	16.4
2013	12.8	13.2	13.8	14.6	16.3	18.8	19.6	20.6	19.5	18.7	16.1	15.3	16.6

1. Employment by Industry: Alaska, Selected Years, 2002–2013—*Continued*

(Numbers in thousands, not seasonally adjusted)

Industry and year	January	February	March	April	May	June	July	August	September	October	November	December	Annual average
Manufacturing													
2002	8.1	11.7	11.6	10.0	9.5	11.6	18.0	16.5	13.3	10.1	7.3	6.1	11.2
2003	8.6	11.8	11.9	9.0	9.3	13.6	19.9	17.7	13.5	10.2	7.1	5.5	11.5
2004	10.6	11.5	11.6	10.2	10.3	14.4	21.3	18.5	14.8	10.8	7.7	6.0	12.3
2005	10.9	11.6	11.8	10.2	10.3	14.3	21.3	19.5	15.1	10.6	8.5	6.5	12.6
2006	10.8	12.1	12.5	11.4	10.5	16.7	22.4	20.2	15.2	10.8	8.9	6.7	13.2
2007	10.8	11.7	11.9	11.0	10.5	15.7	22.2	20.6	15.7	11.2	9.2	7.0	13.1
2008	10.6	12.1	12.0	10.7	10.9	15.9	22.2	20.0	15.3	10.5	8.7	7.0	13.0
2009	10.5	11.8	11.9	11.3	10.4	15.8	23.4	20.5	14.4	9.9	8.3	6.3	12.9
2010	10.5	11.6	12.0	11.0	10.3	15.3	22.7	19.9	14.8	9.8	8.5	6.5	12.7
2011	10.5	12.3	12.8	11.5	10.9	16.9	24.2	22.1	17.1	11.2	9.1	6.7	13.8
2012	11.0	13.1	13.7	12.5	12.0	17.6	23.5	20.8	15.3	11.5	9.4	7.3	14.0
2013	11.1	12.9	13.1	12.9	12.1	17.2	24.5	21.5	17.0	12.4	10.1	7.7	14.4
Trade, Transportation, and Utilities													
2002	56.6	57.0	57.9	58.8	62.4	64.9	66.3	66.4	64.1	61.2	59.4	59.3	61.2
2003	57.1	56.8	57.2	58.5	62.2	64.4	65.3	65.6	63.8	60.0	59.2	59.6	60.8
2004	57.0	57.0	58.0	59.5	63.6	65.8	67.5	67.4	65.7	62.0	60.7	60.7	62.1
2005	58.3	58.4	59.0	60.7	64.8	66.9	68.5	68.5	66.3	62.6	61.4	61.0	63.0
2006	59.4	58.9	60.0	61.6	65.8	68.6	69.0	69.0	66.5	62.2	61.8	61.9	63.7
2007	59.9	59.8	60.4	61.8	65.9	68.7	69.3	69.5	67.0	63.0	62.1	62.4	64.2
2008	60.8	60.6	61.3	62.5	66.9	69.0	69.8	69.5	67.2	63.0	62.3	62.5	64.6
2009	60.0	59.5	60.0	61.4	64.9	66.8	67.7	68.0	66.0	61.7	61.3	61.1	63.2
2010	58.9	58.6	59.0	60.6	64.2	66.9	67.7	67.8	65.2	61.7	61.0	61.3	62.7
2011	58.9	58.9	59.8	60.9	64.9	67.3	68.3	68.6	66.5	62.4	61.7	61.6	63.3
2012	59.8	59.6	59.8	61.5	65.3	67.7	68.5	68.6	66.9	64.1	62.0	62.2	63.8
2013	60.1	59.8	60.1	61.5	65.7	67.8	68.5	69.3	67.5	63.0	62.1	62.4	64.0
Wholesale Trade													
2002	5.7	5.7	5.8	6.1	6.2	6.5	7.0	6.9	6.4	6.0	5.9	5.9	6.2
2003	5.9	5.8	5.8	5.9	6.1	6.4	6.5	6.5	6.4	6.1	6.0	6.0	6.1
2004	5.9	6.0	6.1	6.1	6.2	6.4	6.6	6.6	6.4	6.2	6.0	6.1	6.2
2005	5.9	6.0	6.0	6.1	6.4	6.5	6.8	6.7	6.5	6.3	6.2	6.2	6.3
2006	6.2	6.2	6.3	6.3	6.6	6.8	7.0	7.0	6.8	6.5	6.3	6.4	6.5
2007	6.3	6.3	6.4	6.5	6.6	6.9	6.9	7.0	6.7	6.5	6.4	6.4	6.6
2008	6.3	6.3	6.3	6.4	6.6	6.8	7.0	6.9	6.6	6.3	6.2	6.2	6.5
2009	6.2	6.1	6.2	6.2	6.4	6.6	6.7	6.6	6.4	6.0	6.0	6.0	6.3
2010	5.9	5.9	6.0	6.1	6.3	6.5	6.8	6.8	6.4	6.2	6.1	6.2	6.3
2011	6.0	6.1	6.1	6.1	6.3	6.5	6.8	6.7	6.4	6.3	6.1	6.1	6.3
2012	6.0	6.0	6.0	6.2	6.3	6.5	6.6	6.6	6.6	6.4	6.4	6.5	6.3
2013	6.4	6.4	6.5	6.5	6.7	6.8	6.8	6.8	6.7	6.5	6.3	6.3	6.6
Retail Trade													
2002	32.0	31.9	32.2	32.6	34.2	35.4	35.8	35.6	34.9	34.3	34.0	34.2	33.9
2003	32.3	32.1	32.2	32.8	34.3	35.6	35.8	35.7	35.1	34.1	33.9	34.3	34.0
2004	32.4	32.2	32.8	33.7	35.4	36.9	37.3	37.2	36.3	35.3	35.4	35.5	35.0
2005	33.8	33.7	33.9	34.8	36.3	37.7	38.0	37.9	37.0	35.8	35.7	35.8	35.9
2006	34.3	33.6	34.0	34.9	36.5	37.9	37.8	37.5	36.5	35.4	35.5	35.7	35.8
2007	34.3	33.8	34.2	34.9	36.5	37.8	38.2	37.9	36.8	35.7	35.8	36.2	36.0
2008	35.0	34.3	34.6	35.3	36.7	37.9	38.1	37.6	36.8	36.0	35.9	36.0	36.2
2009	34.2	33.6	33.8	34.7	36.1	37.0	37.3	37.3	36.6	35.4	35.6	35.5	35.6
2010	34.0	33.7	33.7	34.7	35.9	37.2	37.4	37.1	36.0	35.2	35.4	35.5	35.5
2011	34.0	33.6	33.9	34.5	36.0	37.2	37.5	37.5	36.7	35.7	35.9	35.9	35.7
2012	34.5	34.0	34.0	34.7	36.2	37.3	37.4	37.3	36.5	35.8	35.7	35.7	35.8
2013	34.3	33.8	33.9	34.6	36.1	37.3	37.5	37.9	37.3	36.2	36.1	36.2	35.9
Transportation and Utilities													
2002	18.9	19.4	19.9	20.1	22.0	23.0	23.5	23.9	22.8	20.9	19.5	19.2	21.1
2003	18.9	18.9	19.2	19.8	21.8	22.4	23.0	23.4	22.3	19.8	19.3	19.3	20.7
2004	18.7	18.8	19.1	19.7	22.0	22.5	23.6	23.6	23.0	20.5	19.3	19.1	20.8
2005	18.6	18.7	19.1	19.8	22.1	22.7	23.7	23.9	22.8	20.5	19.5	19.0	20.9
2006	18.9	19.1	19.7	20.4	22.7	23.9	24.2	24.5	23.2	20.3	20.0	19.8	21.4
2007	19.3	19.7	19.8	20.4	22.8	24.0	24.2	24.6	23.5	20.8	19.9	19.8	21.6
2008	19.5	20.0	20.4	20.8	23.6	24.3	24.7	25.0	23.8	20.7	20.2	20.3	21.9
2009	19.6	19.8	20.0	20.5	22.4	23.2	23.7	24.1	23.0	20.3	19.7	19.6	21.3
2010	19.0	19.0	19.3	19.8	22.0	23.2	23.5	23.9	22.8	20.3	19.5	19.6	21.0
2011	18.9	19.2	19.8	20.3	22.6	23.6	24.0	24.4	23.4	20.4	19.7	19.6	21.3
2012	19.3	19.6	19.8	20.6	22.8	23.9	24.5	24.7	23.8	21.9	19.9	20.0	21.7
2013	19.4	19.6	19.7	20.4	22.9	23.7	24.2	24.6	23.5	20.3	19.7	19.9	21.5
Information													
2002	6.9	6.8	6.9	7.1	7.1	7.2	7.4	7.2	7.2	7.1	7.0	7.1	7.1
2003	6.8	6.8	6.8	6.9	7.0	7.1	7.1	7.0	7.0	6.9	6.9	6.9	6.9
2004	6.8	6.8	6.8	6.8	6.9	6.9	6.9	6.9	6.9	6.9	6.9	7.0	6.9
2005	6.8	6.9	6.9	6.9	7.0	7.0	7.0	7.0	7.0	6.9	7.0	7.0	7.0
2006	6.9	7.0	7.0	6.9	7.0	7.1	7.0	7.1	7.0	7.0	7.0	7.0	7.0
2007	6.9	6.9	6.9	6.8	6.9	7.0	7.0	7.0	7.0	6.9	6.9	6.9	6.9
2008	6.8	6.9	6.9	6.9	7.1	7.1	7.1	7.1	7.1	7.0	7.0	7.0	7.0
2009	6.7	6.8	6.7	6.6	6.5	6.6	6.6	6.5	6.5	6.5	6.4	6.4	6.6
2010	6.3	6.3	6.3	6.3	6.3	6.5	6.6	6.5	6.7	7.0	6.9	6.6	6.5
2011	6.3	6.3	6.4	6.4	6.3	6.4	6.4	6.3	6.2	6.3	6.3	6.3	6.3
2012	6.2	6.2	6.2	6.2	6.3	6.3	6.3	6.2	6.1	6.2	6.1	6.2	6.2
2013	6.0	6.0	6.0	6.1	6.2	6.2	6.2	6.2	6.3	6.2	6.3	6.2	6.2

1. Employment by Industry: Alaska, Selected Years, 2002–2013—*Continued*

(Numbers in thousands, not seasonally adjusted)

Industry and year	January	February	March	April	May	June	July	August	September	October	November	December	Annual average
Financial Activities													
2002	10.9	10.8	11.1	11.0	11.3	11.7	11.8	11.9	11.8	11.6	11.6	11.5	11.4
2003	11.3	11.4	11.6	11.7	12.0	12.3	12.5	12.6	12.4	12.1	12.0	12.0	12.0
2004	11.6	11.7	11.8	12.2	12.2	12.6	12.6	12.7	12.5	12.4	12.3	12.3	12.2
2005	12.1	12.0	12.0	12.2	12.4	12.8	13.0	12.9	12.9	12.8	12.7	12.5	12.5
2006	12.2	12.2	12.3	12.4	12.7	13.0	13.0	13.1	12.8	12.5	12.4	12.4	12.6
2007	12.0	12.2	12.3	12.3	12.6	13.0	12.9	13.1	12.7	12.5	12.3	12.3	12.5
2008	11.9	12.0	12.1	12.1	12.5	12.5	12.7	12.6	12.4	12.0	11.9	11.9	12.2
2009	11.8	11.8	11.8	11.9	12.1	12.4	12.6	12.6	12.2	12.3	12.2	12.1	12.2
2010	11.9	11.8	11.8	12.0	12.2	12.6	12.7	12.7	12.7	12.4	12.4	11.9	12.2
2011	11.9	12.0	12.0	12.0	12.1	12.5	12.7	12.7	12.3	12.1	12.0	11.9	12.2
2012	11.9	11.9	11.8	11.9	12.2	12.5	12.7	12.7	12.2	12.3	12.1	12.1	12.2
2013	11.8	11.9	11.8	12.0	12.1	12.7	12.9	12.8	12.2	12.1	11.9	11.9	12.2
Professional and Business Services													
2002	22.5	23.1	23.3	23.5	24.5	25.5	25.4	25.7	24.6	24.0	23.3	23.2	24.1
2003	23.0	22.9	23.2	23.8	25.3	26.2	26.0	26.4	25.2	24.2	23.5	23.7	24.5
2004	23.0	23.2	23.7	23.9	24.6	25.8	26.3	26.5	26.1	24.7	24.1	24.3	24.7
2005	23.1	23.6	23.5	24.2	25.5	26.9	27.0	27.3	26.3	24.7	24.3	24.3	25.1
2006	23.5	24.2	24.6	25.1	26.3	27.5	27.4	27.4	27.0	25.4	24.9	25.1	25.7
2007	24.6	25.1	25.3	25.9	27.3	28.3	28.1	28.2	27.7	26.3	26.1	25.9	26.6
2008	25.6	26.1	26.2	27.1	28.6	29.6	29.8	29.8	29.1	27.9	27.4	27.5	27.9
2009	26.6	27.0	27.1	27.1	28.3	29.1	29.1	29.1	28.6	27.4	26.7	26.7	27.7
2010	26.3	26.7	26.8	27.0	28.1	29.5	29.5	29.6	29.3	28.2	27.5	27.3	28.0
2011	26.9	27.5	27.4	28.1	29.0	30.3	30.1	29.8	29.9	28.9	28.6	28.6	28.8
2012	28.0	28.6	28.8	29.1	30.2	31.4	31.5	31.4	31.2	30.1	29.3	29.2	29.9
2013	28.6	29.4	29.3	29.6	30.6	31.5	31.5	32.0	30.8	29.4	29.2	28.6	30.0
Education and Health Services													
2002	29.4	29.8	30.1	30.5	30.9	31.2	31.2	31.4	31.2	31.6	31.9	32.3	31.0
2003	31.6	32.4	32.6	33.2	33.5	33.6	33.7	33.9	33.8	34.0	34.2	34.6	33.4
2004	34.2	34.6	34.9	35.2	35.4	35.3	35.0	34.8	35.1	35.3	35.5	35.9	35.1
2005	35.5	35.8	36.3	36.2	36.5	36.8	36.4	36.5	36.5	36.6	36.8	37.1	36.4
2006	36.8	37.3	37.4	37.6	37.9	38.0	37.7	37.7	37.6	37.2	37.4	37.5	37.5
2007	37.1	37.7	37.9	37.9	37.9	37.7	37.3	37.5	37.1	37.3	37.4	37.6	37.5
2008	37.4	37.9	38.1	38.1	38.3	38.1	38.3	38.3	38.1	38.4	38.6	38.9	38.2
2009	38.5	39.0	39.1	39.5	39.6	39.7	39.9	40.0	40.0	40.6	40.5	40.9	39.8
2010	40.8	41.2	41.3	41.9	42.1	42.2	42.4	42.3	42.6	43.1	43.2	43.5	42.2
2011	43.5	43.9	44.0	44.4	44.6	44.6	44.7	45.0	45.0	45.1	45.3	45.8	44.7
2012	45.4	46.0	46.0	46.2	46.4	46.5	45.6	45.7	45.5	46.6	46.8	46.9	46.1
2013	46.5	47.0	47.1	47.4	47.4	47.1	47.2	47.2	47.0	47.3	47.3	47.5	47.2
Leisure and Hospitality													
2002	24.0	24.9	25.0	26.9	30.5	34.3	35.7	35.4	33.0	28.3	26.7	26.6	29.3
2003	25.7	25.7	26.0	27.1	30.8	34.1	35.6	35.8	33.4	28.1	26.7	26.6	29.6
2004	24.9	25.3	25.9	27.1	30.5	35.0	37.1	37.5	34.8	29.2	27.2	27.4	30.2
2005	25.8	26.1	26.8	28.3	32.4	36.7	38.6	38.3	35.1	28.6	27.3	27.3	30.9
2006	25.8	26.5	27.2	28.5	32.9	37.9	38.8	38.9	35.7	29.0	28.1	28.2	31.5
2007	26.8	27.3	27.9	29.3	33.8	39.0	39.8	39.6	35.9	29.1	28.3	28.1	32.1
2008	27.0	27.4	27.8	29.0	34.8	38.9	40.3	39.9	36.2	29.2	28.3	28.1	32.2
2009	26.5	27.1	27.5	28.1	33.1	36.5	37.7	37.8	35.1	29.0	27.7	27.5	31.1
2010	26.4	26.9	27.2	28.6	32.9	36.9	38.4	38.4	35.5	29.2	28.5	28.8	31.5
2011	27.5	28.0	28.6	29.7	33.9	38.3	39.8	39.7	36.5	30.2	29.0	28.9	32.5
2012	27.9	28.4	29.1	30.4	34.7	39.4	40.7	40.5	37.2	32.1	29.7	29.6	33.3
2013	28.4	29.1	29.8	30.6	35.4	39.5	41.0	40.9	37.4	31.0	29.3	29.3	33.5
Other Services													
2002	11.6	11.8	12.0	12.0	12.1	11.9	12.0	11.9	11.7	11.5	11.4	11.3	11.8
2003	11.0	11.1	11.2	11.3	11.4	11.4	11.3	11.3	11.1	11.2	11.1	11.1	11.2
2004	10.6	10.8	10.9	11.2	11.5	11.7	11.2	11.4	11.3	11.3	11.2	11.1	11.2
2005	10.8	11.0	11.1	11.2	11.2	11.3	11.4	11.3	11.2	11.2	11.2	11.1	11.2
2006	10.9	11.0	11.2	11.0	11.2	11.2	11.4	11.3	11.4	11.4	11.4	11.3	11.2
2007	11.1	11.4	11.5	11.2	11.5	11.4	11.4	11.4	11.3	11.2	11.2	11.2	11.3
2008	10.9	11.1	11.2	11.2	11.4	11.5	11.5	11.5	11.4	11.5	11.3	11.2	11.3
2009	11.1	11.3	11.2	11.4	11.6	11.6	11.7	11.7	11.6	11.2	11.2	11.1	11.4
2010	10.9	10.9	11.1	11.3	11.4	11.6	11.6	11.5	11.4	11.3	11.2	11.1	11.3
2011	11.0	11.1	11.2	11.3	11.4	11.5	11.5	11.5	11.5	11.5	11.4	11.4	11.4
2012	11.3	11.3	11.4	11.5	11.8	11.9	11.8	11.8	11.7	11.6	11.6	11.5	11.6
2013	11.4	11.5	11.6	11.7	11.9	12.0	12.0	11.9	11.8	11.6	11.6	11.2	11.7
Government													
2002	77.3	80.1	80.9	81.7	81.7	79.9	75.4	77.0	81.6	81.8	81.8	82.7	80.2
2003	79.6	81.7	82.6	82.9	83.4	81.3	76.5	77.4	82.3	82.3	81.9	82.0	81.2
2004	80.5	81.4	82.6	82.7	82.3	80.0	76.3	76.9	81.2	82.2	81.9	82.3	80.9
2005	79.9	81.6	82.1	82.9	82.9	79.9	75.8	76.8	81.3	82.2	82.1	81.7	80.8
2006	78.6	81.7	82.4	83.2	83.3	82.0	75.9	77.2	82.0	82.1	81.8	81.6	81.0
2007	78.9	81.9	82.6	83.1	83.1	80.5	75.7	76.9	82.0	83.2	82.7	82.5	81.1
2008	80.4	82.4	82.7	84.0	82.9	82.1	77.3	78.7	83.5	84.0	83.8	83.3	82.1
2009	81.6	83.6	83.6	85.7	83.4	84.3	79.4	80.3	84.9	86.0	85.5	85.5	83.7
2010	83.1	85.2	85.7	87.1	85.8	86.8	81.1	82.0	87.3	87.4	86.8	86.7	85.4
2011	84.2	85.8	85.5	86.6	84.9	85.7	79.9	80.1	86.2	86.6	85.9	85.9	84.8
2012	82.0	85.3	85.8	85.9	84.8	84.3	79.0	80.4	85.6	85.7	85.2	85.0	84.1
2013	81.2	84.1	84.3	84.9	84.2	83.5	77.9	78.8	83.4	83.5	83.2	83.3	82.7

2. Average Weekly Hours by Selected Industry: Alaska, 2009–2013

(Not seasonally adjusted)

Industry and year	January	February	March	April	May	June	July	August	September	October	November	December	Annual average
Total Private													
2009	33.2	34.5	35.3	33.9	34.0	35.1	36.0	37.4	35.4	35.1	34.8	34.4	35.0
2010	34.1	34.7	34.7	34.3	37.1	36.1	36.8	36.8	34.2	34.4	34.5	35.5	35.3
2011	36.5	36.4	35.8	35.0	35.5	36.1	36.8	36.4	35.7	36.2	34.5	34.2	35.8
2012	34.6	34.7	34.5	34.6	34.5	35.7	37.2	36.9	36.4	35.3	34.6	34.7	35.4
2013	33.7	35.5	35.2	34.4	34.5	36.3	36.6	36.5	35.9	34.7	34.1	34.5	35.2
Goods-Producing													
2009	39.2	42.8	47.3	41.3	41.1	42.9	45.4	47.9	43.9	44.5	41.3	43.2	43.6
2010	42.2	42.9	42.6	39.9	40.4	38.7	39.2	39.5	30.9	31.0	31.5	31.3	37.5
2011	42.6	42.3	42.7	38.0	38.7	40.6	44.1	42.5	40.7	42.4	38.0	37.5	41.0
2012	36.4	38.1	37.7	35.5	37.5	39.4	43.4	43.9	42.3	40.5	38.3	39.3	39.7
2013	37.3	42.8	42.9	38.6	39.8	42.8	45.1	45.0	42.0	39.2	38.5	39.4	41.4
Construction													
2009	38.7	40.4	41.0	41.8	40.7	42.9	44.3	44.5	41.1	41.4	37.7	40.5	41.4
2010	39.8	40.7	39.7	41.4	38.3	39.0	38.6	38.3	37.2	35.2	33.2	34.1	37.9
2011	35.5	36.7	37.1	38.3	39.0	40.1	40.6	41.4	41.4	40.6	36.2	34.2	38.8
2012	34.5	35.2	34.3	34.7	37.4	39.5	40.6	40.6	40.8	39.4	36.6	38.5	38.0
2013	38.0	38.8	38.4	39.2	38.7	41.0	42.4	42.7	41.6	40.0	38.8	40.0	40.2
Manufacturing													
2009	35.5	40.5	52.1	31.5	31.5	36.6	41.3	49.5	42.6	44.1	41.4	42.1	41.2
2010	42.3	49.2	48.5	40.6	43.7	42.6	47.5	52.0	29.0	28.0	28.9	25.7	41.7
2011	40.0	47.3	47.7	41.0	40.4	44.7	52.2	47.0	40.3	45.6	38.7	40.7	44.8
2012	36.3	49.7	48.7	39.7	39.9	42.4	52.1	53.6	46.0	42.4	38.2	38.2	45.4
2013	36.0	53.0	52.7	37.6	40.8	44.6	50.3	49.7	40.7	33.8	33.1	32.7	43.6
Trade, Transportation, and Utilities													
2009	31.1	32.8	32.6	31.9	33.0	33.0	33.9	35.7	35.2	34.1	34.6	33.6	33.5
2010	33.3	33.8	33.5	33.6	34.6	34.1	34.5	35.0	33.5	33.6	34.6	37.4	34.3
2011	36.5	36.1	34.9	34.8	35.5	36.0	35.9	35.3	34.7	35.4	34.6	34.2	35.3
2012	34.4	34.5	34.2	34.6	34.3	35.6	36.1	35.2	34.8	33.5	33.8	33.3	34.6
2013	32.4	33.5	33.4	33.1	33.8	36.1	36.4	36.0	36.3	34.3	34.0	34.4	34.5
Professional and Business Services													
2009	34.8	35.0	35.2	35.7	35.2	37.0	36.2	38.4	36.0	36.8	37.0	36.1	36.1
2010	35.7	36.4	37.0	37.2	39.1	36.1	38.7	39.1	38.5	38.7	38.1	39.2	37.9
2011	40.2	39.3	38.6	38.1	38.3	38.8	38.3	38.6	38.3	38.6	37.0	37.0	38.4
2012	38.6	37.1	36.8	37.5	37.1	37.2	38.0	37.5	37.4	37.7	36.9	36.4	37.3
2013	35.4	36.6	35.9	35.9	35.5	36.8	36.6	36.9	36.5	36.5	35.7	36.1	36.2
Leisure and Hospitality													
2009	25.9	26.4	26.5	25.7	26.2	27.5	27.5	28.0	26.3	25.5	25.2	24.9	26.4
2010	24.1	25.2	26.0	25.4	25.0	25.1	27.1	24.3	21.5	22.6	23.6	23.6	24.5
2011	23.6	23.5	23.0	23.5	24.8	25.0	25.9	26.3	25.2	25.4	24.8	24.4	24.7
2012	25.2	25.7	26.2	26.8	26.1	28.2	30.0	29.1	29.3	28.2	27.0	27.8	27.6
2013	26.4	26.7	27.6	27.2	26.9	28.5	28.1	28.5	28.2	27.1	26.5	27.2	27.5

3. Average Hourly Earnings by Selected Industry: Alaska, 2009–2013

(Dollars, not seasonally adjusted)

Industry and year	January	February	March	April	May	June	July	August	September	October	November	December	Annual average
Total Private													
2009	24.80	24.65	24.39	25.22	25.02	24.42	24.26	24.37	24.98	25.41	25.03	25.30	24.80
2010	25.32	24.85	24.89	25.36	24.24	23.97	23.50	23.56	24.37	22.37	22.50	22.22	23.90
2011	23.61	23.55	23.82	24.68	24.46	24.24	24.20	24.32	25.39	25.27	25.23	25.36	24.51
2012	25.27	24.72	24.70	25.45	25.54	25.37	25.26	25.26	25.94	26.43	26.45	26.75	25.59
2013	26.43	26.05	26.07	26.57	26.43	26.30	26.50	26.79	27.40	27.57	27.50	27.55	26.76
Goods-Producing													
2009	29.60	27.63	25.70	30.21	31.00	29.19	27.63	27.04	30.73	31.37	30.64	32.13	29.20
2010	31.68	29.52	29.66	32.08	34.03	32.81	30.74	29.20	33.88	33.33	33.55	35.74	31.92
2011	32.83	31.94	31.59	35.93	35.36	34.10	30.82	31.33	34.91	33.94	35.24	35.63	33.42
2012	33.07	30.41	30.01	33.30	34.38	33.33	30.98	30.97	33.19	34.63	33.50	36.10	32.83
2013	33.35	31.55	30.62	33.80	34.18	32.94	32.27	33.24	35.41	36.15	36.75	36.45	33.77
Construction													
2009	31.54	32.21	32.40	33.74	33.58	35.38	35.11	35.30	36.12	35.24	33.80	33.83	34.25
2010	34.61	34.40	34.62	33.47	36.07	37.96	39.55	38.02	37.74	34.69	34.78	34.44	36.14
2011	35.38	36.10	35.73	36.49	35.51	36.98	36.94	36.47	37.25	35.61	34.46	35.79	36.16
2012	35.21	35.25	34.74	35.85	36.58	37.95	37.54	37.59	37.69	37.71	37.20	37.31	36.93
2013	35.89	37.18	36.07	36.63	36.27	36.91	37.74	38.22	37.91	37.58	37.53	36.76	37.17
Manufacturing													
2009	17.89	16.26	14.54	17.88	21.77	17.41	15.30	14.64	18.59	20.66	20.79	24.12	17.36
2010	21.10	18.06	19.15	22.48	23.30	19.81	17.30	16.15	19.70	21.67	22.75	25.98	19.44
2011	20.80	17.57	17.56	22.47	22.90	19.28	16.42	16.77	19.44	19.32	23.75	24.31	19.08
2012	19.98	16.80	17.08	21.13	22.95	18.89	16.81	16.71	18.52	21.08	23.65	24.98	18.91
2013	20.46	17.31	16.29	20.22	21.44	18.92	16.79	16.97	19.49	22.25	22.19	24.10	18.79
Trade, Transportation, and Utilities													
2009	20.16	20.42	20.84	20.38	20.02	19.64	20.03	21.12	20.64	21.29	20.99	20.83	20.53
2010	20.58	20.87	21.04	21.18	21.31	20.53	20.04	20.79	21.17	21.01	20.88	19.17	20.70
2011	20.71	20.68	20.49	20.75	20.55	19.78	19.78	19.97	20.34	20.66	20.64	20.60	20.42
2012	20.81	20.60	20.50	20.73	20.30	19.94	20.17	20.11	20.66	20.95	21.00	21.06	20.55
2013	21.16	20.91	21.59	21.45	20.75	20.50	20.77	21.00	21.58	21.93	21.86	22.32	21.30
Professional and Business Services													
2009	32.13	32.69	32.77	32.30	31.89	30.41	29.51	29.93	29.81	31.05	32.19	31.55	31.30
2010	31.84	31.55	31.21	31.36	31.63	31.24	30.70	30.97	31.25	31.88	32.79	33.01	31.61
2011	33.79	34.48	34.05	34.19	33.27	32.71	32.69	32.62	33.14	33.32	33.05	33.34	33.37
2012	32.91	31.75	32.38	33.00	32.47	32.62	32.62	33.09	32.95	33.06	33.17	34.34	32.93
2013	34.64	34.22	34.25	34.48	34.79	34.82	34.81	35.34	35.33	35.19	35.28	35.25	34.87
Leisure and Hospitality													
2009	13.06	13.20	13.37	13.37	12.83	12.96	12.95	13.16	13.12	13.40	13.45	13.75	13.19
2010	13.88	13.73	13.66	13.64	13.61	13.97	12.65	13.78	13.69	13.37	13.14	13.85	13.54
2011	13.84	14.03	14.29	14.21	13.96	13.97	13.60	13.90	13.69	14.18	14.02	14.17	13.98
2012	14.19	14.52	14.40	14.35	14.45	14.17	14.20	14.35	14.48	14.75	15.13	15.07	14.48
2013	14.93	15.14	15.05	15.12	15.31	15.05	15.31	15.45	15.71	15.73	16.02	16.00	15.40

4. Average Weekly Earnings by Selected Industry: Alaska, 2009–2013

(Dollars, not seasonally adjusted)

Industry and year	January	February	March	April	May	June	July	August	September	October	November	December	Annual average
Total Private													
2009	823.36	850.43	860.97	854.96	850.68	857.14	873.36	911.44	884.29	891.89	871.04	870.32	868.00
2010	863.41	862.30	863.68	869.85	899.30	865.32	864.80	867.01	833.45	769.53	776.25	788.81	843.67
2011	861.77	857.22	852.76	863.80	868.33	875.06	890.56	885.25	906.42	914.77	870.44	867.31	877.46
2012	874.34	857.78	852.15	880.57	881.13	905.71	939.67	932.09	944.22	932.98	915.17	928.23	905.89
2013	890.69	924.78	917.66	914.01	911.84	954.69	969.90	977.84	983.66	956.68	937.75	950.48	941.95
Goods-Producing													
2009	1,160.32	1,182.56	1,215.61	1,247.67	1,274.10	1,252.25	1,254.40	1,295.22	1,349.05	1,395.97	1,265.43	1,388.02	1,273.12
2010	1,336.90	1,266.41	1,263.52	1,279.99	1,374.81	1,269.75	1,205.01	1,153.40	1,046.89	1,033.23	1,056.83	1,118.66	1,197.00
2011	1,398.56	1,351.06	1,348.89	1,365.34	1,368.43	1,384.46	1,359.16	1,331.53	1,420.84	1,439.06	1,339.12	1,336.13	1,370.22
2012	1,203.75	1,158.62	1,131.38	1,182.15	1,289.25	1,313.20	1,344.53	1,359.58	1,403.94	1,402.52	1,359.65	1,418.73	1,303.35
2013	1,243.96	1,350.34	1,313.60	1,304.68	1,360.36	1,409.83	1,455.38	1,495.80	1,487.22	1,417.08	1,414.88	1,436.13	1,398.08
Construction													
2009	1,220.60	1,301.28	1,328.40	1,410.33	1,366.71	1,517.80	1,555.37	1,570.85	1,484.53	1,458.94	1,274.26	1,370.12	1,417.95
2010	1,377.48	1,400.08	1,374.41	1,385.66	1,381.48	1,480.44	1,526.63	1,456.17	1,403.93	1,221.09	1,154.70	1,174.40	1,369.71
2011	1,255.99	1,324.87	1,325.58	1,397.57	1,384.89	1,482.90	1,499.76	1,509.86	1,542.15	1,445.77	1,247.45	1,224.02	1,403.01
2012	1,214.75	1,240.80	1,191.58	1,244.00	1,368.09	1,499.03	1,524.12	1,526.15	1,537.75	1,485.77	1,361.52	1,436.44	1,403.34
2013	1,363.82	1,442.58	1,385.09	1,435.90	1,403.65	1,513.31	1,600.18	1,631.99	1,577.06	1,503.20	1,456.16	1,470.40	1,494.23
Manufacturing													
2009	635.10	658.53	757.53	563.22	685.76	637.21	631.89	724.68	791.93	911.11	860.71	1,015.45	715.23
2010	892.53	888.55	928.78	912.69	1,018.21	843.91	821.75	839.80	571.30	606.76	657.48	667.69	810.65
2011	832.00	831.06	837.61	921.27	925.16	861.82	857.12	788.19	783.43	880.99	919.13	989.42	854.78
2012	725.27	834.96	831.80	838.86	915.71	800.94	875.80	895.66	851.92	893.79	903.43	954.24	858.51
2013	736.56	917.43	858.48	760.27	874.75	843.83	844.54	843.41	793.24	752.05	734.49	788.07	819.24
Trade, Transportation, and Utilities													
2009	626.98	669.78	679.38	650.12	660.66	648.12	679.02	753.98	726.53	725.99	726.25	699.89	687.76
2010	685.31	705.41	704.84	711.65	737.33	700.07	691.38	727.65	709.20	705.94	722.45	716.96	710.01
2011	755.92	746.55	715.10	722.10	729.53	712.08	720.87	704.94	705.80	731.36	714.14	704.52	720.83
2012	715.86	710.70	701.10	717.26	696.29	709.86	728.14	707.87	718.97	701.83	709.80	701.30	711.03
2013	685.58	700.49	721.11	710.00	701.35	740.05	756.03	756.00	783.35	752.20	743.24	767.81	734.85
Professional and Business Services													
2009	1,118.12	1,144.15	1,153.50	1,153.11	1,122.53	1,125.17	1,068.26	1,149.31	1,073.16	1,142.64	1,191.03	1,138.96	1,129.93
2010	1,136.69	1,148.42	1,154.77	1,166.59	1,236.73	1,127.76	1,188.09	1,210.93	1,203.13	1,233.76	1,249.30	1,293.99	1,198.02
2011	1,358.36	1,355.06	1,314.33	1,302.64	1,274.24	1,269.15	1,252.03	1,259.13	1,269.26	1,286.15	1,222.85	1,233.58	1,281.41
2012	1,270.33	1,177.93	1,191.58	1,237.50	1,204.64	1,213.46	1,257.42	1,235.63	1,236.44	1,250.51	1,232.46	1,249.98	1,228.29
2013	1,226.26	1,252.45	1,229.58	1,237.83	1,235.05	1,281.38	1,274.05	1,304.05	1,289.55	1,284.44	1,259.50	1,272.53	1,262.29
Leisure and Hospitality													
2009	338.25	348.48	354.31	343.61	336.15	356.40	356.13	368.48	345.06	341.70	338.94	342.38	348.22
2010	334.51	346.00	355.16	346.46	340.25	350.65	342.82	334.85	287.46	304.87	310.10	326.86	331.73
2011	326.62	329.71	328.67	333.94	346.21	340.00	360.01	360.05	357.34	358.90	347.70	345.75	345.31
2012	357.59	373.16	377.28	384.58	377.15	399.59	426.00	417.59	424.26	415.95	408.51	418.95	399.65
2013	394.15	404.24	415.38	411.26	411.84	428.93	430.21	440.33	443.02	426.28	424.53	435.20	423.50

ARIZONA
At a Glance

Population:
  2000 census: 5,130,247
  2010 census: 6,392,017
  2013 estimate: 6,626,624

Percent change in population:
  2000–2010: 24.6%
  2010–2013: 3.7%

Percent change in total nonfarm employment:
  2000–2010: 6.4%
  2010–2013: 5.4%

Industry with the largest growth in employment, 2000–2013 (thousands):
  Education and Health Services, 161.5

Industry with the largest decline or smallest growth in employment, 2000–2013 (thousands):
  Manufacturing, -54.7

Civilian labor force:
  2000: 2,505,306
  2010: 3,105,648
  2013: 3,012,476

Unemployment rate and rank among states (lowest to highest):
  2000: 4.0%, 28th
  2010: 10.4%, 41st
  2013: 8.0%, 39th

Over-the-year change in unemployment rates:
  2010–2011: -1.0%
  2011–2012: -1.1%
  2012–2013: -0.3%

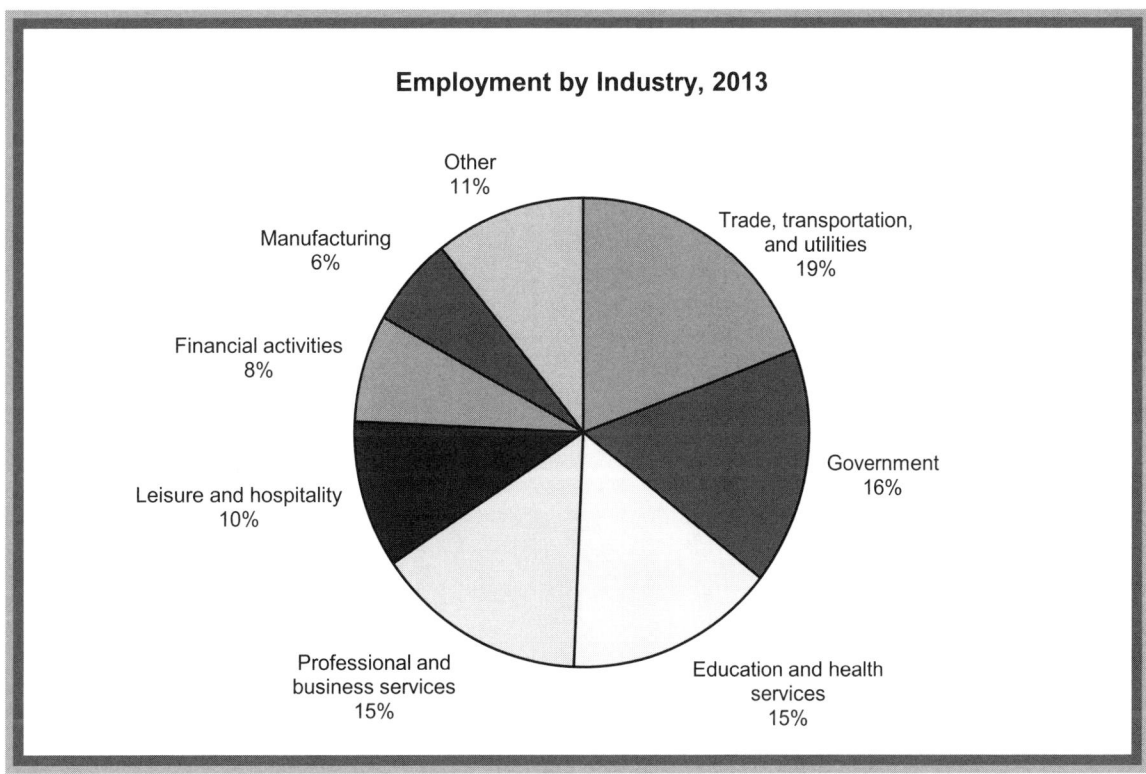

Employment by Industry, 2013

Other
11%

Trade, transportation, and utilities
19%

Manufacturing
6%

Financial activities
8%

Government
16%

Leisure and hospitality
10%

Professional and business services
15%

Education and health services
15%

1. Employment by Industry: Arizona, Selected Years, 2002–2013

(Numbers in thousands, not seasonally adjusted)

Industry and year	January	February	March	April	May	June	July	August	September	October	November	December	Annual average
Total Nonfarm													
2002	2,230.1	2,253.8	2,270.3	2,282.0	2,278.3	2,253.2	2,212.1	2,248.1	2,268.7	2,284.8	2,313.5	2,314.6	2,267.5
2003	2,255.5	2,281.9	2,294.9	2,300.3	2,302.6	2,274.0	2,242.3	2,282.5	2,305.9	2,333.9	2,350.3	2,366.4	2,299.2
2004	2,311.5	2,342.3	2,361.0	2,379.0	2,380.6	2,356.2	2,335.1	2,371.8	2,400.3	2,439.4	2,459.2	2,479.3	2,384.6
2005	2,416.7	2,458.2	2,477.4	2,509.8	2,511.6	2,485.0	2,472.0	2,511.3	2,549.7	2,562.1	2,589.5	2,608.6	2,512.7
2006	2,566.2	2,610.6	2,633.4	2,639.0	2,648.1	2,620.7	2,592.4	2,629.7	2,661.3	2,674.1	2,692.4	2,703.7	2,639.3
2007	2,636.3	2,674.2	2,692.1	2,682.1	2,687.1	2,655.7	2,629.4	2,668.1	2,688.7	2,701.3	2,718.4	2,719.7	2,679.4
2008	2,650.5	2,673.2	2,672.3	2,661.9	2,655.0	2,605.5	2,563.4	2,601.6	2,607.4	2,600.4	2,597.0	2,581.8	2,622.5
2009	2,498.7	2,493.7	2,485.1	2,467.5	2,451.8	2,391.6	2,363.5	2,387.6	2,400.6	2,407.4	2,421.8	2,422.1	2,432.6
2010	2,366.3	2,385.2	2,396.9	2,407.0	2,414.1	2,351.8	2,326.5	2,357.3	2,373.8	2,402.1	2,423.0	2,429.7	2,386.1
2011	2,380.6	2,403.0	2,415.9	2,427.2	2,426.7	2,362.4	2,338.4	2,393.4	2,423.0	2,441.1	2,465.0	2,468.3	2,412.1
2012	2,426.1	2,448.9	2,466.9	2,468.6	2,464.4	2,423.0	2,390.2	2,448.4	2,475.6	2,494.6	2,523.4	2,531.6	2,463.5
2013	2,479.0	2,505.5	2,518.3	2,525.5	2,523.1	2,470.9	2,448.4	2,498.4	2,526.7	2,542.6	2,567.5	2,576.6	2,515.2
Total Private													
2002	1,847.8	1,858.5	1,873.6	1,881.5	1,883.6	1,882.0	1,861.6	1,874.1	1,872.0	1,879.8	1,901.1	1,908.9	1,877.0
2003	1,866.7	1,877.9	1,891.1	1,897.0	1,900.7	1,899.3	1,889.7	1,904.4	1,909.0	1,928.0	1,944.6	1,960.1	1,905.7
2004	1,921.1	1,936.2	1,954.3	1,970.9	1,974.8	1,979.2	1,978.1	1,987.4	1,991.5	2,023.6	2,043.5	2,062.6	1,985.3
2005	2,021.1	2,043.6	2,065.5	2,097.3	2,101.8	2,106.4	2,106.6	2,122.3	2,138.6	2,147.2	2,173.1	2,193.3	2,109.7
2006	2,165.8	2,194.3	2,217.1	2,222.8	2,230.4	2,238.2	2,221.9	2,235.6	2,244.6	2,249.2	2,266.9	2,282.6	2,230.8
2007	2,226.5	2,248.6	2,265.2	2,255.6	2,261.2	2,264.1	2,244.3	2,256.1	2,255.6	2,264.5	2,278.5	2,280.5	2,258.4
2008	2,220.6	2,230.6	2,230.7	2,219.1	2,213.1	2,199.1	2,172.3	2,179.4	2,168.6	2,157.7	2,151.8	2,139.2	2,190.2
2009	2,068.6	2,054.1	2,047.2	2,027.3	2,018.1	1,999.8	1,981.6	1,982.6	1,973.6	1,976.8	1,990.5	1,994.9	2,009.6
2010	1,947.9	1,955.6	1,968.8	1,975.5	1,973.6	1,964.4	1,950.5	1,958.5	1,954.6	1,980.4	1,998.5	2,009.9	1,969.9
2011	1,968.8	1,980.3	1,993.9	2,003.7	2,004.9	1,993.1	1,984.1	1,998.1	2,005.6	2,020.2	2,042.6	2,052.6	2,004.0
2012	2,017.1	2,027.6	2,045.1	2,046.0	2,048.6	2,044.0	2,029.6	2,048.5	2,054.8	2,072.3	2,099.2	2,109.7	2,053.5
2013	2,066.4	2,082.4	2,096.2	2,102.1	2,104.4	2,097.1	2,087.7	2,104.9	2,107.5	2,119.9	2,144.3	2,157.2	2,105.8
Goods-Producing													
2002	363.5	363.5	365.1	364.8	365.6	367.4	367.0	368.4	365.1	362.7	361.2	359.4	364.5
2003	353.9	353.2	354.5	356.0	358.1	360.8	360.7	362.9	362.5	363.6	363.8	365.1	359.6
2004	360.6	363.7	366.6	368.9	371.6	377.1	380.5	381.7	383.2	388.4	389.9	393.1	377.1
2005	386.4	391.6	396.7	403.2	406.3	413.0	415.5	418.0	419.7	420.5	423.9	428.2	410.3
2006	423.7	430.4	435.0	437.9	440.4	445.0	443.5	442.6	439.8	434.6	430.1	428.5	436.0
2007	418.8	421.9	422.7	419.1	420.3	425.2	423.1	423.7	418.8	414.0	408.1	402.2	418.2
2008	391.5	388.9	386.8	383.1	381.6	380.2	376.2	373.5	367.1	357.8	347.3	338.6	372.7
2009	322.2	312.0	306.6	298.8	295.6	294.5	291.1	287.7	283.3	280.2	277.2	274.5	293.6
2010	267.7	267.8	268.7	271.0	271.2	272.7	273.0	272.3	270.6	272.5	271.9	271.3	270.9
2011	266.3	266.2	268.1	269.7	271.7	274.6	276.0	276.6	276.5	276.6	276.1	276.5	272.9
2012	273.7	274.9	278.5	279.5	281.7	285.7	287.0	288.9	288.7	289.1	289.0	288.7	283.8
2013	283.9	285.8	288.2	288.5	291.1	295.0	295.9	296.3	294.4	292.0	292.5	292.6	291.4
Service-Providing													
2002	1,866.6	1,890.3	1,905.2	1,917.2	1,912.7	1,885.8	1,845.1	1,879.7	1,903.6	1,922.1	1,952.3	1,955.2	1,903.0
2003	1,901.6	1,928.7	1,940.4	1,944.3	1,944.5	1,913.2	1,881.6	1,919.6	1,943.4	1,970.3	1,986.5	2,001.3	1,939.6
2004	1,950.9	1,978.6	1,994.4	2,010.1	2,009.0	1,979.1	1,954.6	1,990.1	2,017.1	2,051.0	2,069.3	2,086.2	2,007.5
2005	2,030.3	2,066.6	2,080.7	2,106.6	2,105.3	2,072.0	2,056.5	2,093.3	2,130.0	2,141.6	2,165.6	2,180.4	2,102.4
2006	2,142.5	2,180.2	2,198.4	2,201.1	2,207.7	2,175.7	2,148.9	2,187.1	2,221.5	2,239.5	2,262.3	2,275.2	2,203.3
2007	2,217.5	2,252.3	2,269.4	2,263.0	2,266.8	2,230.5	2,206.3	2,244.4	2,269.9	2,287.3	2,310.3	2,317.5	2,261.3
2008	2,259.0	2,284.3	2,285.5	2,278.8	2,273.4	2,225.3	2,187.2	2,228.1	2,240.3	2,242.6	2,249.7	2,243.2	2,249.8
2009	2,176.5	2,181.7	2,178.5	2,168.7	2,156.2	2,097.1	2,072.4	2,099.9	2,117.3	2,127.2	2,144.6	2,147.6	2,139.0
2010	2,098.6	2,117.4	2,128.2	2,136.0	2,142.9	2,079.1	2,053.5	2,085.0	2,103.2	2,129.6	2,151.1	2,158.4	2,115.3
2011	2,114.3	2,136.8	2,147.8	2,157.5	2,155.0	2,087.8	2,062.4	2,116.8	2,146.5	2,164.5	2,188.9	2,191.8	2,139.2
2012	2,152.4	2,174.0	2,188.4	2,189.1	2,182.7	2,137.3	2,103.2	2,159.5	2,186.9	2,205.5	2,234.4	2,242.9	2,179.7
2013	2,195.1	2,219.7	2,230.1	2,237.0	2,232.0	2,175.9	2,152.5	2,202.1	2,232.3	2,250.6	2,275.0	2,284.0	2,223.9
Mining and Logging													
2002	8.9	8.9	8.9	9.0	8.8	8.9	8.7	8.7	8.7	8.6	8.4	8.4	8.7
2003	8.2	8.0	7.9	8.0	8.0	8.1	8.1	8.1	8.0	8.0	8.0	8.0	8.0
2004	7.8	7.9	7.9	8.1	8.3	8.4	8.4	8.5	8.5	8.7	8.7	8.7	8.3
2005	8.6	8.7	8.8	9.0	9.1	9.3	8.1	8.0	8.0	8.0	8.4	9.0	8.6
2006	9.0	9.1	9.2	9.5	9.7	10.1	10.2	10.3	10.4	10.4	10.5	10.5	9.9
2007	10.5	10.5	10.7	10.7	10.9	11.2	11.8	12.1	12.1	12.3	12.4	12.5	11.5
2008	12.7	12.7	12.9	13.0	13.3	13.7	14.0	14.2	14.4	14.0	13.8	13.8	13.5
2009	12.6	12.1	12.1	10.9	10.6	10.7	10.7	10.8	10.7	10.8	10.8	10.8	11.1
2010	10.8	10.9	10.8	10.9	11.0	11.0	11.0	10.8	10.8	10.7	11.0	11.2	10.9
2011	11.3	11.4	11.5	11.2	11.4	11.6	11.2	11.3	11.4	12.1	12.1	12.2	11.6
2012	12.2	12.3	12.4	12.5	12.6	12.7	12.9	12.9	12.9	12.8	12.9	13.0	12.7
2013	13.0	13.1	13.1	13.2	13.3	13.6	13.7	13.7	13.4	13.4	13.2	13.3	13.3
Construction													
2002	167.0	167.4	169.7	170.1	172.0	174.0	174.1	176.6	174.8	174.3	173.9	172.4	172.2
2003	168.7	169.0	170.5	172.0	174.7	177.1	177.7	179.8	180.1	181.6	181.5	181.7	176.2
2004	178.3	180.6	183.0	185.8	187.9	191.4	194.3	195.7	197.1	201.0	201.8	203.8	191.7
2005	199.2	203.3	207.9	213.7	215.9	220.8	224.1	226.0	228.2	228.8	231.6	233.3	219.4
2006	229.7	234.4	238.7	241.1	244.0	247.5	246.1	245.6	243.8	240.0	237.8	235.4	240.3
2007	226.7	227.6	228.5	226.4	227.6	231.7	228.7	229.1	225.9	221.4	215.7	210.0	224.9
2008	200.7	198.8	198.2	195.1	193.6	192.0	188.6	186.3	181.1	173.9	165.8	158.8	186.1
2009	147.3	140.4	137.4	132.7	131.0	130.8	128.2	125.3	122.0	119.3	116.5	114.0	128.7
2010	109.0	109.0	109.9	111.8	111.6	113.0	113.3	113.0	111.8	113.1	112.0	110.7	111.5
2011	106.6	106.4	107.9	109.4	110.1	112.4	113.7	113.9	113.9	113.1	112.1	111.2	110.9
2012	108.8	109.3	112.0	112.6	114.1	117.0	118.1	119.8	120.1	120.7	120.5	119.5	116.0
2013	116.2	117.6	120.0	120.6	122.6	125.5	126.2	127.0	125.9	123.9	124.6	124.2	122.9

1. Employment by Industry: Arizona, Selected Years, 2002–2013—*Continued*

(Numbers in thousands, not seasonally adjusted)

Industry and year	January	February	March	April	May	June	July	August	September	October	November	December	Annual average
Manufacturing													
2002	187.6	187.2	186.5	185.7	184.8	184.5	184.2	183.1	181.6	179.8	178.9	178.6	183.5
2003	177.0	176.2	176.1	176.0	175.4	175.6	174.9	175.0	174.4	174.0	174.3	175.4	175.4
2004	174.5	175.2	175.7	175.0	175.4	177.3	177.8	177.5	177.6	178.7	179.4	180.6	177.1
2005	178.6	179.6	180.0	180.5	181.3	182.9	183.3	184.0	183.5	183.7	183.9	185.9	182.3
2006	185.0	186.9	187.1	187.3	186.7	187.4	187.2	186.7	185.6	184.2	181.8	182.6	185.7
2007	181.6	183.8	183.5	182.0	181.8	182.3	182.6	182.5	180.8	180.3	180.0	179.7	181.7
2008	178.1	177.4	175.7	175.0	174.7	174.5	173.6	173.0	171.6	169.9	167.7	166.0	173.1
2009	162.3	159.5	157.1	155.2	154.0	153.0	152.2	151.6	150.6	150.1	149.9	149.7	153.8
2010	147.9	147.9	148.0	148.3	148.6	148.7	148.9	148.5	148.1	148.4	148.8	149.4	148.5
2011	148.4	148.4	148.7	149.1	150.2	150.6	151.1	151.4	151.2	151.4	151.9	153.1	150.5
2012	152.7	153.3	154.1	154.4	155.0	156.0	156.0	156.2	155.7	155.6	155.6	156.2	155.1
2013	154.7	155.1	155.1	154.7	155.2	155.9	156.0	155.6	155.1	154.7	154.7	155.1	155.2
Trade, Transportation, and Utilities													
2002	437.2	434.0	436.7	437.4	439.1	439.9	435.3	436.8	438.1	442.1	452.9	460.9	440.9
2003	442.6	441.7	442.7	440.7	441.1	440.5	439.5	441.4	441.9	450.3	461.3	469.0	446.1
2004	453.6	453.1	455.0	456.8	458.4	458.8	459.1	460.5	459.0	468.4	481.0	488.8	462.7
2005	476.8	477.8	479.9	481.8	482.3	482.3	485.8	487.2	490.1	494.4	507.7	516.8	488.6
2006	502.1	501.6	505.9	505.7	506.4	506.4	507.8	509.8	510.9	517.9	531.3	540.4	512.2
2007	522.0	520.8	523.2	522.7	524.0	523.8	524.2	525.2	526.0	528.8	542.4	549.2	527.7
2008	527.9	525.2	524.2	518.7	519.2	517.8	510.4	511.4	507.5	508.6	514.8	515.3	516.8
2009	495.5	487.2	484.8	479.3	478.0	474.4	471.7	471.1	469.1	468.8	478.2	483.0	478.4
2010	467.9	466.7	467.2	467.6	467.7	465.6	463.1	463.0	459.9	465.6	476.6	482.8	467.8
2011	468.0	467.5	468.9	470.7	470.7	469.7	468.3	469.4	468.2	474.6	487.9	491.3	472.9
2012	475.9	472.5	474.3	473.2	473.5	472.3	470.2	470.6	471.2	476.4	491.5	495.7	476.4
2013	475.2	473.5	473.6	475.0	476.6	476.4	476.6	478.6	479.6	483.6	498.3	503.7	480.9
Wholesale Trade													
2002	94.2	94.4	95.0	93.5	94.3	94.0	93.4	93.4	93.3	94.0	94.6	95.4	94.1
2003	94.3	94.6	94.4	93.2	93.3	92.9	91.8	91.7	91.6	91.9	92.7	94.1	93.0
2004	94.3	94.5	94.8	94.5	94.9	95.3	95.8	95.8	94.5	96.4	97.0	98.5	95.5
2005	97.6	98.6	99.2	99.3	99.3	99.6	100.0	99.9	100.2	100.9	102.2	104.1	100.1
2006	103.5	104.3	104.8	104.6	104.7	105.3	105.6	105.8	106.2	106.8	107.9	109.4	105.7
2007	107.7	108.3	108.9	108.1	108.2	108.9	108.9	108.7	108.5	108.9	110.0	110.9	108.8
2008	109.3	109.7	109.6	108.3	108.4	107.9	107.0	107.1	106.9	107.2	107.1	106.8	107.9
2009	104.5	103.4	102.2	100.5	99.5	98.5	98.0	97.6	96.7	97.0	97.0	97.3	99.4
2010	95.8	96.1	96.3	96.2	96.1	95.8	95.3	94.7	93.9	94.8	95.6	95.9	95.5
2011	95.0	95.7	95.7	96.0	95.9	96.0	95.5	95.2	95.3	95.8	96.3	96.4	95.7
2012	95.4	95.8	96.5	96.3	96.4	96.8	96.4	96.3	96.4	96.9	97.5	97.7	96.5
2013	96.3	96.9	96.9	97.1	97.1	97.4	96.8	97.1	97.4	98.3	99.1	99.4	97.5
Retail Trade													
2002	268.9	265.6	267.0	268.6	269.2	269.4	265.8	266.8	268.4	270.6	280.7	287.8	270.7
2003	271.5	270.3	271.4	270.9	271.2	271.3	271.7	273.5	273.9	281.1	291.2	297.0	276.3
2004	282.4	281.8	282.7	284.5	285.5	285.5	285.1	286.4	286.6	292.0	303.9	309.9	288.9
2005	299.5	299.1	300.6	302.7	302.3	302.0	305.0	305.8	307.8	311.5	322.4	328.1	307.2
2006	316.0	314.8	318.2	317.8	318.2	317.6	318.2	319.2	319.1	325.7	337.4	343.1	322.1
2007	328.5	326.6	328.5	328.4	329.0	327.7	328.6	329.3	330.0	332.8	344.7	348.4	331.9
2008	331.9	328.4	327.7	323.7	324.0	323.3	317.5	318.0	314.8	315.9	321.4	321.3	322.3
2009	306.3	299.8	298.8	296.8	296.5	294.3	292.6	292.2	291.6	291.6	301.0	304.0	297.1
2010	292.5	291.0	291.4	291.7	291.7	289.7	288.0	287.9	285.5	289.6	299.2	302.5	291.7
2011	291.2	289.7	290.8	292.1	291.8	290.3	290.0	291.2	289.9	295.0	307.1	308.6	294.0
2012	296.6	292.8	293.6	293.1	293.6	291.9	290.2	290.5	291.2	295.7	309.7	311.8	295.9
2013	294.4	292.0	292.8	294.7	295.4	295.2	296.3	297.9	298.5	302.6	314.6	318.4	299.4
Transportation and Utilities													
2002	74.1	74.0	74.7	75.3	75.6	76.5	76.1	76.6	76.4	77.5	77.6	77.7	76.0
2003	76.8	76.8	76.9	76.6	76.6	76.3	76.0	76.2	76.4	77.3	77.4	77.9	76.8
2004	76.9	76.8	77.5	77.8	78.0	78.0	78.2	78.3	77.9	80.0	80.1	80.4	78.3
2005	79.7	80.1	80.1	79.8	80.7	80.7	80.8	81.5	82.1	82.0	83.1	84.6	81.3
2006	82.6	82.5	82.9	83.3	83.5	83.5	84.0	84.8	85.6	85.4	86.0	87.9	84.3
2007	85.8	85.9	85.8	86.2	86.8	87.2	86.7	87.2	87.5	87.1	87.7	89.9	87.0
2008	86.7	87.1	86.9	86.7	86.8	86.6	85.9	86.3	85.8	85.5	86.3	87.2	86.5
2009	84.7	84.0	83.8	82.0	82.0	81.6	81.1	81.3	80.8	80.2	80.2	81.7	82.0
2010	79.6	79.6	79.5	79.7	79.9	80.1	79.8	80.4	80.5	81.2	81.8	84.4	80.5
2011	81.8	82.1	82.4	82.6	83.0	83.4	82.8	83.0	83.0	83.8	84.5	86.3	83.2
2012	83.9	83.9	84.2	83.8	83.5	83.6	83.6	83.8	83.6	83.8	84.3	86.2	84.0
2013	84.5	84.6	83.9	83.2	84.1	83.8	83.5	83.6	83.7	82.7	84.6	85.9	84.0
Information													
2002	52.8	52.7	52.2	52.2	51.8	51.2	51.1	50.9	50.1	49.4	50.2	50.3	51.2
2003	49.0	49.3	49.5	49.5	49.4	49.5	48.9	48.7	48.0	48.1	49.1	48.9	49.0
2004	47.9	47.9	48.2	48.1	47.4	47.1	46.2	45.3	44.0	44.2	44.7	44.3	46.3
2005	43.6	44.2	44.5	45.3	45.5	45.1	44.7	44.5	44.0	44.3	44.9	45.5	44.7
2006	44.8	44.9	44.9	43.9	44.0	43.9	43.1	43.0	42.1	41.7	42.3	42.4	43.4
2007	40.6	41.5	41.4	41.7	42.3	42.1	41.8	41.5	41.1	40.8	41.7	41.3	41.5
2008	40.6	41.5	41.9	41.0	42.1	41.7	40.5	40.2	40.6	39.7	40.2	40.4	40.9
2009	39.1	39.4	38.8	38.8	39.1	38.3	37.9	37.6	37.0	36.4	36.9	36.8	38.0
2010	36.4	36.6	36.8	36.8	36.8	37.1	36.2	36.1	35.8	35.6	36.1	36.6	36.4
2011	36.2	36.3	36.4	36.6	36.8	37.0	37.3	37.3	37.1	37.5	38.4	38.4	37.1
2012	38.3	38.7	38.9	39.2	39.8	39.7	39.8	40.1	39.5	39.6	40.7	40.9	39.6
2013	40.6	41.2	41.4	41.4	42.1	41.7	41.9	42.1	41.3	40.5	41.2	42.1	41.5

1. Employment by Industry: Arizona, Selected Years, 2002–2013—*Continued*

(Numbers in thousands, not seasonally adjusted)

Industry and year	January	February	March	April	May	June	July	August	September	October	November	December	Annual average
Financial Activities													
2002	153.9	155.5	155.0	156.0	155.5	155.4	155.1	155.3	155.5	156.7	158.7	159.7	156.0
2003	157.6	158.5	160.1	159.9	160.7	161.2	162.1	163.3	162.6	162.6	162.9	163.8	161.3
2004	161.7	162.7	163.7	165.8	165.6	165.8	166.7	167.2	166.9	169.1	169.7	171.0	166.3
2005	169.1	170.6	171.3	174.0	174.4	175.4	176.9	178.6	179.6	181.1	181.9	183.3	176.4
2006	180.7	182.1	183.1	183.6	184.5	185.0	185.1	185.9	186.4	187.5	187.8	189.7	185.1
2007	186.8	188.4	189.1	189.1	188.9	188.6	187.9	185.6	184.5	183.3	183.1	183.8	186.6
2008	179.3	180.6	180.5	180.1	180.0	179.5	178.1	177.9	177.1	176.4	175.4	175.3	178.4
2009	171.6	171.5	171.3	170.9	171.0	170.4	170.0	170.0	168.7	168.5	168.3	169.2	170.1
2010	166.6	167.1	167.7	166.2	166.5	166.6	167.0	167.4	166.6	169.0	169.5	170.9	167.6
2011	168.3	169.2	169.8	170.5	170.4	171.0	171.5	172.0	172.0	172.7	173.3	175.3	171.3
2012	173.5	175.3	175.6	175.3	175.4	175.5	175.7	176.4	176.8	178.9	180.1	181.3	176.7
2013	179.5	182.2	182.2	183.1	183.9	184.4	184.4	184.7	184.9	187.4	190.4	193.1	185.0
Professional and Business Services													
2002	304.0	308.2	313.6	317.4	316.4	317.2	314.2	317.7	316.0	315.3	317.7	317.7	314.6
2003	309.4	313.8	317.9	320.3	321.2	322.2	318.8	321.7	323.3	326.6	326.9	329.9	321.0
2004	319.6	323.3	328.1	335.8	335.7	338.9	341.0	342.3	344.5	351.9	353.2	356.7	339.3
2005	346.6	352.1	356.7	364.2	363.8	367.1	368.3	372.0	375.4	374.8	377.8	380.3	366.6
2006	374.6	383.3	387.2	390.2	392.5	397.2	395.4	399.6	403.1	404.3	405.7	408.1	395.1
2007	395.4	400.2	404.8	402.7	402.9	405.5	402.8	406.4	405.1	408.5	409.8	407.6	404.3
2008	395.1	398.1	396.1	393.9	390.5	387.3	383.7	385.8	382.5	380.8	376.9	374.0	387.1
2009	359.2	356.2	353.4	349.5	345.3	342.7	341.0	338.8	337.6	342.1	345.0	345.4	346.4
2010	335.0	336.4	340.1	342.5	340.5	339.3	337.1	337.9	336.8	344.3	345.7	350.4	340.5
2011	341.1	344.4	346.4	347.8	344.2	343.1	343.2	344.9	346.6	351.0	353.8	358.6	347.1
2012	348.6	350.5	353.5	354.0	353.4	355.5	354.4	358.0	358.3	363.6	369.8	373.1	357.7
2013	367.1	367.2	370.3	372.2	371.7	372.8	370.1	371.5	371.1	375.1	376.2	377.1	371.9
Education and Health Services													
2002	228.5	230.6	231.9	231.3	233.0	232.4	228.6	233.8	235.7	239.1	241.5	242.3	234.1
2003	241.2	243.9	244.5	247.1	247.6	246.6	244.8	249.6	252.0	253.1	254.6	256.0	248.4
2004	255.2	256.9	258.2	260.5	261.2	260.5	257.9	262.7	265.1	269.0	270.3	272.1	262.5
2005	268.0	270.2	273.2	277.5	278.6	275.7	273.4	278.9	281.6	282.9	284.8	286.2	277.6
2006	284.5	288.2	290.9	291.4	292.6	291.5	289.8	295.6	298.2	299.8	301.9	305.0	294.1
2007	299.7	304.3	306.0	304.2	305.7	305.2	302.5	308.0	310.7	315.5	316.4	318.2	308.0
2008	314.0	318.6	320.1	322.1	323.5	320.9	319.5	325.1	327.8	329.8	331.9	333.6	323.9
2009	328.0	330.4	331.1	331.1	332.1	329.3	327.7	333.8	335.6	339.4	342.0	343.7	333.7
2010	339.2	340.7	342.2	342.0	343.1	339.8	337.8	344.6	346.3	351.8	353.3	353.2	344.5
2011	348.9	351.2	352.1	353.9	357.2	349.5	347.2	355.2	359.2	361.4	363.8	365.0	355.4
2012	362.0	365.1	365.9	366.1	366.3	361.6	357.1	365.4	368.5	370.7	372.9	374.4	366.3
2013	367.8	371.2	373.7	373.7	372.6	366.4	364.3	372.9	375.5	379.8	382.1	384.1	373.7
Leisure and Hospitality													
2002	223.0	228.4	232.5	235.7	235.2	230.8	224.3	225.1	225.3	228.3	232.6	232.2	229.5
2003	228.0	232.2	235.8	238.0	236.8	232.4	227.5	228.5	230.2	234.6	236.4	237.7	233.2
2004	234.7	239.5	244.9	246.2	246.0	241.8	237.2	238.1	239.4	242.4	244.5	246.0	241.7
2005	242.5	248.1	252.9	259.9	259.0	255.7	250.6	251.8	256.1	256.6	258.8	259.4	254.3
2006	258.1	264.2	268.9	271.6	270.1	267.6	261.3	262.6	266.6	267.5	271.0	271.1	266.7
2007	266.8	272.9	278.4	278.1	277.9	273.0	264.0	267.7	269.9	273.9	276.2	276.9	273.0
2008	272.0	276.3	279.1	279.2	275.1	270.3	263.2	265.3	266.0	265.6	266.2	263.8	270.2
2009	257.5	261.2	264.9	264.6	262.7	255.9	249.1	250.9	250.2	250.6	252.2	251.8	256.0
2010	247.3	251.7	257.1	261.2	259.1	254.2	248.3	249.8	251.4	253.8	257.1	256.2	253.9
2011	252.1	256.5	263.0	265.3	264.6	259.0	252.7	255.5	259.2	259.8	262.7	261.5	259.3
2012	259.9	265.0	272.2	272.6	271.8	266.5	259.4	263.5	266.0	267.8	268.4	268.8	266.8
2013	266.7	273.6	279.4	280.8	278.8	272.8	267.7	272.4	274.3	275.0	276.2	276.4	274.5
Other Services													
2002	84.9	85.6	86.6	86.7	87.0	87.7	86.0	86.1	86.2	86.2	86.3	86.4	86.3
2003	85.0	85.3	86.1	85.5	85.8	86.1	87.4	88.3	88.5	89.1	89.6	89.7	87.2
2004	87.8	89.1	89.6	88.8	88.9	89.2	89.5	89.6	89.4	90.2	90.2	90.6	89.4
2005	88.1	89.0	90.3	91.4	91.9	92.1	91.4	91.3	92.1	92.6	93.3	93.6	91.4
2006	97.3	99.6	101.2	98.5	99.9	101.6	95.9	96.5	97.5	95.9	96.8	97.4	98.2
2007	96.4	98.6	99.6	98.0	99.2	100.7	98.0	98.0	99.5	99.7	100.8	101.3	99.2
2008	100.2	101.4	102.0	101.0	101.1	101.4	100.7	100.2	100.0	99.0	99.1	98.2	100.4
2009	95.5	96.2	96.3	94.3	94.3	94.3	93.1	92.7	92.1	90.8	90.7	90.5	93.4
2010	87.8	88.6	89.0	88.2	88.7	89.1	88.0	87.4	87.2	87.8	88.3	88.5	88.2
2011	87.9	89.0	89.2	89.2	89.3	89.2	87.9	87.2	86.8	86.6	86.6	86.0	87.9
2012	85.2	85.6	86.2	86.1	86.7	87.2	86.0	85.6	85.8	86.2	86.8	86.8	86.2
2013	85.6	87.7	87.4	87.4	87.6	87.6	86.8	86.4	86.4	86.5	87.4	88.1	87.1
Government													
2002	382.3	395.3	396.7	400.5	394.7	371.2	350.5	374.0	396.7	405.0	412.4	405.7	390.4
2003	388.8	404.0	403.8	403.3	401.9	374.7	352.6	378.1	396.9	405.9	405.7	406.3	393.5
2004	390.4	406.1	406.7	408.1	405.8	377.0	357.0	384.4	408.8	415.8	415.7	416.7	399.4
2005	395.6	414.6	411.9	412.5	409.8	378.6	365.4	389.0	411.1	414.9	416.4	415.3	402.9
2006	400.4	416.3	416.3	416.2	417.7	382.5	370.5	394.1	416.7	424.9	425.5	421.1	408.5
2007	409.8	425.6	426.9	426.5	425.9	391.6	385.1	412.0	433.1	436.8	439.9	439.2	421.0
2008	429.9	442.6	441.6	442.8	441.9	406.4	391.1	422.2	438.8	442.7	445.2	442.6	432.3
2009	430.1	439.6	437.9	440.2	433.7	391.8	381.9	405.0	427.0	430.6	431.3	427.2	423.0
2010	418.4	429.6	428.1	431.5	440.5	387.4	376.0	398.8	419.2	421.7	424.5	419.8	416.3
2011	411.8	422.7	422.0	423.5	421.8	369.3	354.3	395.3	417.4	420.9	422.4	415.7	408.1
2012	409.0	421.3	421.8	422.6	415.8	379.0	360.6	399.9	420.8	422.3	424.2	421.9	409.9
2013	412.6	423.1	422.1	423.4	418.7	373.8	360.7	393.5	419.2	422.7	423.2	419.4	409.4

2. Average Weekly Hours by Selected Industry: Arizona, 2009–2013

(Not seasonally adjusted)

Industry and year	January	February	March	April	May	June	July	August	September	October	November	December	Annual average
Total Private													
2009	34.8	35.0	35.1	34.5	34.5	34.5	34.6	35.1	34.6	34.8	35.3	34.7	34.8
2010	34.5	35.3	35.0	34.9	35.5	35.4	35.4	35.8	35.1	35.2	35.4	35.0	35.2
2011	35.2	35.0	35.1	35.1	35.1	35.0	34.9	35.0	34.9	35.4	34.8	34.7	35.0
2012	35.0	34.6	34.8	35.1	34.8	35.0	35.3	34.8	35.3	34.9	35.0	35.2	35.0
2013	34.6	34.8	34.9	34.8	34.7	35.4	34.5	34.7	34.9	34.6	34.5	35.2	34.8
Goods-Producing													
2009	37.6	36.5	37.1	36.4	36.5	37.4	37.2	37.8	37.1	37.6	37.8	37.3	37.2
2010	37.3	37.3	36.9	37.7	38.0	37.9	38.3	38.4	37.9	38.6	38.4	38.3	37.9
2011	38.1	38.1	38.0	38.3	37.8	38.9	37.4	38.5	38.3	38.1	38.2	37.4	38.1
2012	37.7	37.2	37.7	38.1	38.7	39.3	38.4	38.8	38.8	38.8	38.5	38.7	38.4
2013	38.5	38.7	38.8	39.1	39.2	39.9	39.3	39.7	38.5	39.1	39.0	39.5	39.1
Construction													
2009	36.5	35.5	36.2	35.7	36.0	37.0	36.8	37.1	36.4	37.0	36.9	35.9	36.4
2010	36.1	36.3	35.4	36.4	36.5	37.3	37.0	37.3	36.5	37.8	36.7	36.4	36.6
2011	36.7	36.8	36.3	36.5	35.7	37.4	35.8	37.1	36.8	36.6	36.2	34.6	36.4
2012	36.1	35.3	36.4	36.5	37.0	37.7	36.6	37.2	37.5	37.6	36.7	36.8	36.8
2013	37.4	37.5	37.6	37.7	38.2	39.5	38.5	38.7	37.4	38.4	38.3	38.3	38.1
Manufacturing													
2009	38.4	37.4	38.0	37.0	36.9	37.7	37.7	38.5	37.7	38.1	38.6	38.5	37.9
2010	38.3	38.1	38.5	38.6	39.3	38.3	38.6	38.6	38.5	38.7	39.6	39.8	38.7
2011	39.2	39.2	39.5	39.9	39.8	40.4	39.1	39.9	40.0	39.7	40.4	40.9	39.8
2012	39.7	39.5	39.5	39.8	40.3	40.8	40.2	40.4	40.1	39.9	40.2	40.4	40.1
2013	39.5	39.6	39.7	40.3	40.1	40.2	40.0	40.6	39.4	39.6	39.5	40.4	39.9
Trade, Transportation, and Utilities													
2009	36.1	36.3	36.0	35.5	35.6	35.6	35.2	35.6	35.5	35.1	35.9	35.2	35.6
2010	34.7	35.2	34.9	35.0	35.9	35.4	35.5	36.1	35.4	35.6	35.9	36.1	35.5
2011	36.3	35.9	35.9	36.1	36.1	36.0	36.2	36.1	35.8	36.4	35.5	35.8	36.0
2012	35.7	35.7	35.8	36.1	35.8	36.3	36.5	35.7	36.2	36.0	36.0	36.3	36.0
2013	35.6	35.6	35.8	35.4	35.3	36.3	35.2	35.3	35.8	35.2	34.8	35.7	35.5
Financial Activities													
2009	37.2	37.3	37.4	37.0	35.9	36.2	37.1	37.6	37.2	37.5	38.4	37.7	37.2
2010	37.5	38.3	38.3	38.3	39.2	38.7	38.8	38.8	38.2	38.2	38.7	38.6	38.5
2011	39.5	38.9	38.7	38.8	39.5	39.2	39.7	39.0	39.5	39.9	39.2	38.6	39.2
2012	39.4	38.8	38.7	38.9	38.6	38.5	39.3	38.7	39.3	38.7	38.9	39.2	38.9
2013	38.6	38.4	38.2	38.5	38.3	38.6	37.6	38.5	38.4	38.2	38.2	39.0	38.4
Professional and Business Services													
2009	35.7	35.5	35.7	35.4	35.5	34.7	34.3	35.3	34.5	35.1	35.4	34.6	35.1
2010	34.8	35.0	34.4	34.7	35.6	34.8	35.0	36.0	35.2	35.5	35.7	34.8	35.1
2011	34.6	34.6	34.7	34.8	35.3	34.9	35.1	35.3	34.8	35.8	35.3	36.0	35.1
2012	35.9	35.6	35.3	36.2	36.0	36.4	36.9	36.7	36.9	36.1	36.3	36.8	36.3
2013	35.9	36.3	36.4	36.3	36.1	36.5	35.9	36.1	36.6	36.3	36.2	36.8	36.3
Education and Health Services													
2009	35.0	35.5	35.5	35.0	35.1	35.0	35.6	35.6	35.2	35.1	35.5	35.6	35.3
2010	35.1	35.4	35.2	34.8	34.8	34.7	34.3	34.4	33.8	34.2	34.1	34.3	34.6
2011	34.7	33.7	34.1	33.9	34.0	33.6	33.4	33.4	33.4	33.9	33.3	33.2	33.7
2012	33.5	33.0	33.3	33.5	33.2	33.0	33.6	33.5	33.9	33.6	33.5	33.9	33.5
2013	33.3	33.6	33.8	33.7	33.6	34.0	32.9	32.8	33.7	33.1	33.0	33.6	33.4
Leisure and Hospitality													
2009	26.7	27.5	27.7	27.1	26.9	26.5	26.5	26.7	26.8	26.4	27.1	26.4	26.9
2010	26.7	27.1	27.0	27.0	27.4	27.6	27.0	27.6	27.0	26.9	27.2	26.6	27.1
2011	27.1	27.5	27.1	27.1	26.6	26.0	25.9	26.0	26.6	27.0	26.6	26.2	26.6
2012	27.2	27.0	27.8	27.5	26.8	26.5	26.9	25.6	26.3	26.1	26.6	26.7	26.8
2013	25.9	26.3	26.8	26.3	26.2	26.9	26.0	25.7	26.1	26.0	26.2	26.6	26.3
Other Services													
2009	31.7	31.7	32.6	31.9	32.1	32.5	32.8	33.1	32.2	32.8	33.2	34.0	32.5
2010	34.3	34.1	34.6	34.2	34.4	34.3	33.6	33.7	33.3	33.1	33.1	33.0	33.8
2011	33.4	34.2	34.2	33.6	34.1	32.8	32.7	32.6	32.6	32.4	31.4	31.6	33.0
2012	32.9	32.5	32.8	32.1	31.6	31.7	31.8	31.4	32.0	31.2	31.5	31.4	31.9
2013	30.8	31.1	31.5	31.1	30.7	32.1	30.8	31.2	31.7	31.5	31.6	32.4	31.4

3. Average Hourly Earnings by Selected Industry: Arizona, 2009–2013

(Dollars, not seasonally adjusted)

Industry and year	January	February	March	April	May	June	July	August	September	October	November	December	Annual average
Total Private													
2009	21.71	21.93	21.78	21.85	21.90	21.87	22.13	22.08	22.17	22.27	22.20	22.55	22.03
2010	22.57	22.22	22.53	22.39	22.11	21.91	22.05	22.00	22.05	21.95	21.81	22.40	22.16
2011	22.57	22.59	22.59	22.75	22.73	22.40	22.61	22.40	22.53	22.61	22.41	22.54	22.56
2012	22.77	22.53	22.43	22.66	22.45	22.51	22.69	22.49	22.70	22.63	22.52	22.83	22.60
2013	22.74	22.73	22.57	22.85	22.79	23.05	23.01	23.17	23.45	23.08	23.21	23.29	23.00
Goods-Producing													
2009	22.61	22.92	23.01	23.13	23.11	23.16	23.21	22.92	23.27	23.24	23.29	23.69	23.12
2010	23.23	23.23	23.13	23.01	22.89	22.66	22.44	22.25	22.11	22.09	21.96	22.56	22.62
2011	22.43	22.84	23.20	23.24	23.24	22.88	23.06	23.03	23.12	23.29	23.42	24.08	23.15
2012	24.04	23.85	23.60	23.89	23.80	23.70	23.74	23.68	24.07	23.91	23.82	24.01	23.84
2013	23.90	23.81	23.78	23.71	23.63	23.72	23.82	23.85	24.08	24.02	24.23	24.38	23.91
Construction													
2009	22.23	22.46	22.20	22.38	22.41	22.63	22.53	22.40	23.00	22.86	22.91	23.25	22.59
2010	22.74	22.87	23.13	23.03	22.79	22.47	22.47	22.07	21.91	21.66	21.79	22.41	22.44
2011	22.25	22.57	22.89	22.52	22.08	21.66	21.53	21.91	21.87	21.85	21.79	22.39	22.10
2012	22.39	22.30	21.99	22.59	22.75	22.57	22.19	22.50	23.00	22.93	22.78	22.83	22.58
2013	22.69	22.52	22.62	22.40	22.54	22.70	22.96	23.45	23.42	23.47	23.53	23.61	23.00
Manufacturing													
2009	23.10	23.41	23.78	23.84	23.69	23.64	23.85	23.41	23.54	23.60	23.65	24.13	23.63
2010	23.71	23.55	23.09	22.91	22.95	22.80	22.31	22.38	22.28	22.45	22.06	22.58	22.75
2011	22.56	23.09	23.41	23.89	24.37	24.17	24.78	24.28	24.56	24.85	24.83	25.56	24.21
2012	25.45	25.13	25.00	25.02	24.71	24.69	25.12	24.70	24.98	24.70	24.63	24.96	24.92
2013	24.96	24.92	24.82	24.88	24.63	24.67	24.54	24.10	24.57	24.39	24.83	25.03	24.69
Trade, Transportation, and Utilities													
2009	20.64	20.86	20.33	20.32	20.28	20.60	21.06	20.55	20.61	20.88	20.69	20.64	20.62
2010	21.03	19.86	20.29	20.50	20.04	20.42	20.21	20.26	20.25	20.32	19.99	19.91	20.25
2011	20.14	20.15	20.15	20.25	20.25	19.96	20.29	19.90	20.37	20.80	20.56	20.51	20.28
2012	21.20	20.60	20.58	21.19	20.68	21.14	21.46	20.92	21.22	21.00	20.68	21.18	20.99
2013	21.30	21.20	21.05	21.27	21.06	21.06	20.97	20.83	21.11	20.68	20.63	20.38	20.96
Financial Activities													
2009	22.65	23.02	23.02	23.08	23.46	23.16	23.85	24.52	24.46	24.35	24.19	24.11	23.66
2010	24.02	24.49	23.89	24.00	23.82	23.28	23.50	23.57	23.21	23.01	22.76	23.03	23.54
2011	23.23	23.04	23.13	23.62	23.24	23.15	23.61	23.73	23.78	23.66	23.71	23.79	23.48
2012	23.97	23.65	24.32	24.70	24.28	24.34	24.28	24.02	24.31	24.30	24.43	24.84	24.29
2013	24.14	24.64	24.81	25.19	25.79	26.64	26.52	27.51	27.94	26.39	26.84	27.38	26.17
Professional and Business Services													
2009	25.59	26.04	26.49	26.52	26.50	26.47	26.94	26.71	26.42	26.26	26.70	26.43	26.42
2010	26.46	26.48	27.17	27.48	27.02	26.88	27.36	26.69	27.21	26.60	26.83	27.52	26.98
2011	28.02	28.16	27.93	28.11	27.82	27.31	27.26	26.99	27.15	26.90	26.40	25.94	27.32
2012	26.57	26.58	26.66	26.46	26.02	25.91	26.18	25.87	26.04	26.05	25.77	26.14	26.18
2013	26.05	26.03	25.73	25.61	25.64	25.84	25.48	25.30	25.58	25.50	25.74	25.50	25.67
Education and Health Services													
2009	23.53	23.50	23.56	23.60	23.63	23.37	23.31	23.45	23.60	23.77	23.51	23.43	23.52
2010	23.65	23.53	23.56	23.68	23.35	23.31	23.61	23.43	23.86	23.90	23.49	23.60	23.58
2011	23.53	23.88	23.89	23.85	23.92	23.46	23.65	23.53	23.56	23.17	23.29	23.56	23.61
2012	23.51	23.74	23.45	23.53	23.66	23.62	23.84	23.72	23.75	23.77	23.99	24.07	23.72
2013	24.26	24.09	24.03	24.42	23.97	24.31	24.48	24.26	24.53	24.62	24.77	25.20	24.41
Leisure and Hospitality													
2009	13.10	13.07	13.17	13.23	12.98	13.08	12.83	12.93	13.19	13.25	13.29	13.28	13.12
2010	13.22	13.31	13.28	13.44	13.49	13.22	12.97	13.02	12.93	13.06	13.21	13.41	13.22
2011	13.26	13.24	13.16	13.54	13.99	13.67	13.73	13.46	13.53	13.71	13.89	13.83	13.58
2012	13.91	13.81	13.73	13.56	13.54	13.40	13.31	13.33	13.40	13.60	13.58	13.56	13.56
2013	13.54	13.51	13.46	13.43	13.50	13.33	13.36	13.38	13.65	13.52	13.52	13.64	13.49
Other Services													
2009	16.42	16.61	16.19	16.54	16.20	16.13	16.05	16.24	16.49	16.13	16.16	15.85	16.25
2010	15.44	15.78	15.88	15.79	15.96	15.56	15.85	16.23	16.03	15.65	15.98	16.40	15.88
2011	16.12	16.29	16.49	16.89	16.83	16.71	17.15	16.88	16.92	16.89	17.30	17.40	16.81
2012	17.72	17.59	17.90	17.89	18.02	18.11	18.71	18.91	19.17	18.99	19.26	19.74	18.49
2013	19.35	19.35	19.24	20.07	19.79	19.84	19.83	19.98	20.54	20.25	20.46	20.45	19.93

4. Average Weekly Earnings by Selected Industry: Arizona, 2009–2013

(Dollars, not seasonally adjusted)

Industry and year	January	February	March	April	May	June	July	August	September	October	November	December	Annual average
Total Private													
2009	755.51	767.55	764.48	753.83	755.55	754.52	765.70	775.01	767.08	775.00	783.66	782.49	766.64
2010	778.67	784.37	788.55	781.41	784.91	775.61	780.57	787.60	773.96	772.64	772.07	784.00	780.03
2011	794.46	790.65	792.91	798.53	797.82	784.00	789.09	784.00	786.30	800.39	779.87	782.14	789.60
2012	796.95	779.54	780.56	795.37	781.26	787.85	800.96	782.65	801.31	789.79	788.20	803.62	791.00
2013	786.80	791.00	787.69	795.18	790.81	815.97	793.85	804.00	818.41	798.57	800.75	819.81	800.40
Goods-Producing													
2009	850.14	836.58	853.67	841.93	843.52	866.18	863.41	866.38	863.32	873.82	880.36	883.64	860.06
2010	866.48	866.48	853.50	867.48	869.82	858.81	859.45	854.40	837.97	852.67	843.26	864.05	857.30
2011	854.58	870.20	881.60	890.09	878.47	890.03	862.44	886.66	885.50	887.35	894.64	900.59	882.02
2012	906.31	887.22	889.72	910.21	921.06	931.41	911.62	918.78	933.92	927.71	917.07	929.19	915.46
2013	920.15	921.45	922.66	927.06	926.30	946.43	936.13	946.85	927.08	939.18	944.97	963.01	934.88
Construction													
2009	811.40	797.33	803.64	798.97	806.76	837.31	829.10	831.04	837.20	845.82	845.38	834.68	822.28
2010	820.91	830.18	818.80	838.29	831.84	838.13	831.39	823.21	799.72	818.75	799.69	815.72	821.30
2011	816.58	830.58	830.91	821.98	788.26	810.08	770.77	812.86	804.82	799.71	788.80	774.69	804.44
2012	808.28	787.19	800.44	824.54	841.75	850.89	812.15	837.00	862.50	862.17	836.03	840.14	830.94
2013	848.61	844.50	850.51	844.48	861.03	896.65	883.96	907.52	875.91	901.25	901.20	904.26	876.30
Manufacturing													
2009	887.04	875.53	903.64	882.08	874.16	891.23	899.15	901.29	887.46	899.16	912.89	929.01	895.58
2010	908.09	897.26	888.97	884.33	901.94	873.24	861.17	863.87	857.78	868.82	873.58	898.68	880.43
2011	884.35	905.13	924.70	953.21	969.93	976.47	968.90	968.77	982.40	986.55	1,003.13	1,045.40	963.56
2012	1,010.37	992.64	987.50	995.80	995.81	1,007.35	1,009.82	997.88	1,001.70	985.53	990.13	1,008.38	999.29
2013	985.92	986.83	985.35	1,002.66	987.66	991.73	981.60	978.46	968.06	965.84	980.79	1,011.21	985.13
Trade, Transportation, and Utilities													
2009	745.10	757.22	731.88	721.36	721.97	733.36	741.31	731.58	731.66	732.89	742.77	726.53	734.07
2010	729.74	699.07	708.12	717.50	719.44	722.87	717.46	731.39	716.85	723.39	717.64	718.75	718.88
2011	731.08	723.39	723.39	731.03	731.03	718.56	734.50	718.39	729.25	757.12	729.88	734.26	730.08
2012	756.84	735.42	736.76	764.96	740.34	767.38	783.29	746.84	768.16	756.00	744.48	768.83	755.64
2013	758.28	754.72	753.59	752.96	743.42	764.48	738.14	735.30	755.74	727.94	717.92	727.57	744.08
Financial Activities													
2009	842.58	858.65	860.95	853.96	842.21	838.39	884.84	921.95	909.91	913.13	928.90	908.95	880.15
2010	900.75	937.97	914.99	919.20	933.74	900.94	911.80	914.52	886.62	878.98	880.81	888.96	906.29
2011	917.59	896.26	895.13	916.46	917.98	907.48	937.32	925.47	939.31	944.03	929.43	918.29	920.42
2012	944.42	917.62	941.18	960.83	937.21	937.09	954.20	929.57	955.38	940.41	950.33	973.73	944.88
2013	931.80	946.18	947.74	969.82	987.76	1,028.30	997.15	1,059.14	1,072.90	1,008.10	1,025.29	1,067.82	1,004.93
Professional and Business Services													
2009	913.56	924.42	945.69	938.81	940.75	918.51	924.04	942.86	911.49	921.73	945.18	914.48	927.34
2010	920.81	926.80	934.65	953.56	961.91	935.42	957.60	960.84	957.79	944.30	957.83	957.70	947.00
2011	969.49	974.34	969.17	978.23	982.05	953.12	956.83	952.75	944.82	963.02	931.92	933.84	958.93
2012	953.86	946.25	941.10	957.85	936.72	943.12	966.04	949.43	960.88	940.41	935.45	961.95	950.33
2013	935.20	944.89	936.57	929.64	925.60	943.16	914.73	913.33	936.23	925.65	931.79	938.40	931.82
Education and Health Services													
2009	823.55	834.25	836.38	826.00	829.41	817.95	829.84	834.82	830.72	834.33	834.61	834.11	830.26
2010	830.12	832.96	829.31	824.06	812.58	808.86	809.82	805.99	806.47	817.38	801.01	809.48	815.87
2011	816.49	804.76	814.65	808.52	813.28	788.26	789.91	785.90	786.90	785.46	775.56	782.19	795.66
2012	787.59	783.42	780.89	788.26	785.51	779.46	801.02	794.62	805.13	798.67	803.67	815.97	794.62
2013	807.86	809.42	812.21	822.95	805.39	826.54	805.39	795.73	826.66	814.92	817.41	846.72	815.29
Leisure and Hospitality													
2009	349.77	359.43	364.81	358.53	349.16	346.62	340.00	345.23	353.49	349.80	360.16	350.59	352.93
2010	352.97	360.70	358.56	362.88	369.63	364.87	350.19	359.35	349.11	351.31	359.31	356.71	358.26
2011	359.35	364.10	356.64	366.93	372.13	355.42	355.61	349.96	359.90	370.17	369.47	362.35	361.23
2012	378.35	372.87	381.69	372.90	362.87	355.10	358.04	341.25	352.42	354.96	361.23	362.05	363.41
2013	350.69	355.31	360.73	353.21	353.70	358.58	347.36	343.87	356.27	351.52	354.22	362.82	354.79
Other Services													
2009	520.51	526.54	527.79	527.63	520.02	524.23	526.44	537.54	530.98	529.06	536.51	538.90	528.13
2010	529.59	538.10	549.45	540.02	549.02	533.71	532.56	546.95	533.80	518.02	528.94	541.20	536.74
2011	538.41	557.12	563.96	567.50	573.90	548.09	560.81	550.29	551.59	547.24	543.22	549.84	554.73
2012	582.99	571.68	587.12	574.27	569.43	574.09	594.98	593.77	613.44	592.49	606.69	619.84	589.83
2013	595.98	601.79	606.06	624.18	607.55	636.86	610.76	623.38	651.12	637.88	646.54	662.58	625.80

ARKANSAS
At a Glance

Population:
    2000 census: 2,673,293
    2010 census: 2,915,918
    2013 estimate: 2,959,918

Percent change in population:
    2000–2010: 9.1%
    2010–2013: 1.5%

Percent change in total nonfarm employment:
    2000–2010: 0.4%
    2010–2013: 1.2%

Industry with the largest growth in employment, 2000–2013 (thousands):
    Education and Health Services, 44.6

Industry with the largest decline or smallest growth in employment, 2000–2013 (thousands):
    Manufacturing, -87.9

Civilian labor force:
    2000: 1,260,256
    2010: 1,344,717
    2013: 1,326,528

Unemployment rate and rank among states (lowest to highest):
    2000: 4.2%, 33rd
    2010: 7.9%, 15th
    2013: 7.5%, 33rd

Over-the-year change in unemployment rates:
    2010–2011: 0.1%
    2011–2012: -0.5%
    2012–2013: 0.0%

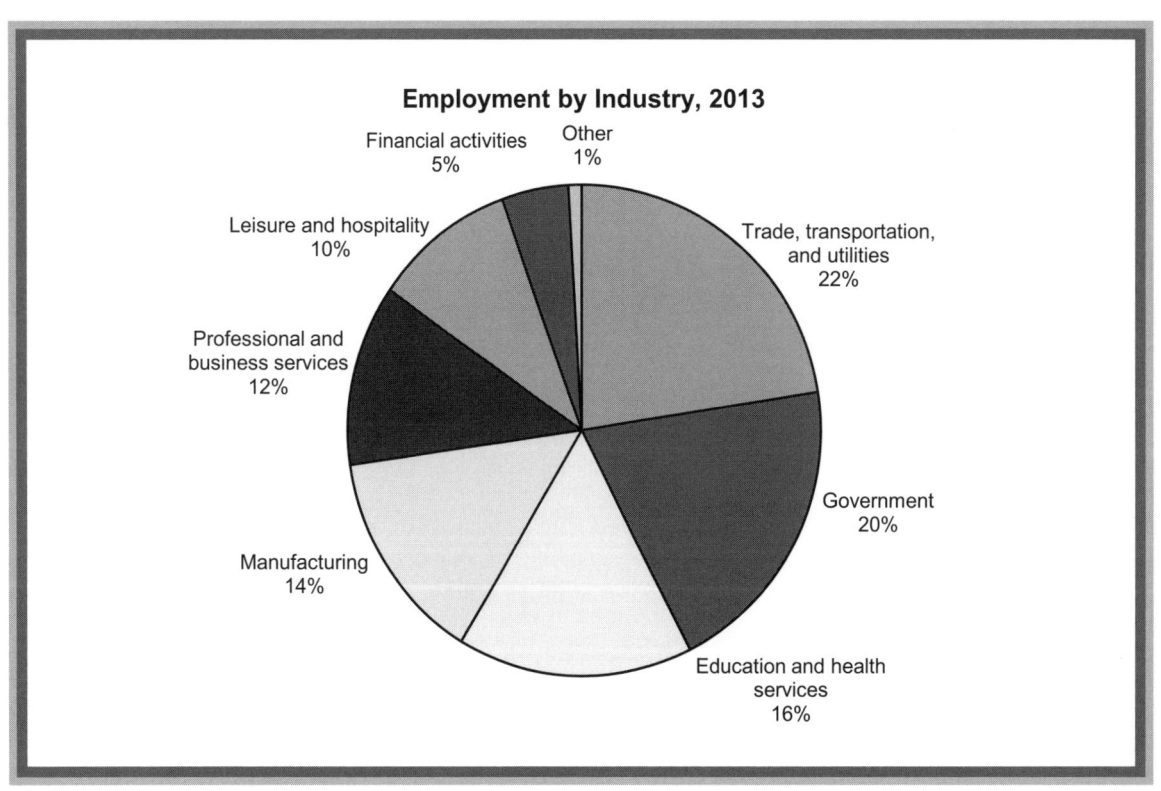

Employment by Industry, 2013

- Financial activities 5%
- Other 1%
- Leisure and hospitality 10%
- Trade, transportation, and utilities 22%
- Professional and business services 12%
- Manufacturing 14%
- Government 20%
- Education and health services 16%

1. Employment by Industry: Arkansas, Selected Years, 2002–2013

(Numbers in thousands, not seasonally adjusted)

Industry and year	January	February	March	April	May	June	July	August	September	October	November	December	Annual average
Total Nonfarm													
2002	1,125.3	1,132.8	1,144.1	1,148.4	1,155.3	1,155.0	1,138.2	1,143.2	1,157.2	1,151.7	1,151.8	1,152.4	1,146.3
2003	1,128.7	1,133.1	1,140.4	1,142.6	1,149.2	1,146.0	1,131.1	1,141.2	1,155.5	1,159.1	1,156.3	1,158.4	1,145.1
2004	1,135.2	1,142.5	1,152.9	1,157.7	1,162.2	1,161.1	1,146.8	1,155.4	1,169.0	1,168.7	1,172.0	1,173.6	1,158.1
2005	1,151.0	1,162.1	1,173.0	1,178.4	1,182.2	1,180.9	1,165.3	1,172.0	1,192.7	1,189.1	1,193.1	1,194.7	1,177.9
2006	1,178.2	1,186.6	1,198.5	1,203.8	1,206.7	1,205.3	1,184.1	1,193.2	1,208.6	1,205.5	1,205.7	1,207.3	1,198.6
2007	1,184.9	1,193.3	1,207.8	1,207.4	1,211.2	1,209.7	1,188.1	1,200.1	1,213.2	1,211.2	1,213.0	1,214.2	1,204.5
2008	1,190.8	1,200.0	1,207.9	1,207.9	1,212.6	1,208.4	1,189.8	1,198.4	1,211.8	1,205.4	1,200.8	1,195.9	1,202.5
2009	1,166.4	1,169.2	1,174.2	1,175.0	1,171.0	1,164.0	1,150.7	1,153.3	1,165.4	1,162.5	1,164.3	1,163.2	1,164.9
2010	1,134.9	1,138.6	1,155.1	1,164.0	1,175.0	1,177.3	1,158.2	1,162.8	1,172.6	1,171.7	1,172.4	1,173.5	1,163.0
2011	1,146.7	1,149.0	1,163.2	1,179.5	1,174.6	1,167.9	1,160.3	1,166.2	1,179.2	1,184.7	1,185.6	1,184.2	1,170.1
2012	1,158.5	1,166.8	1,178.7	1,183.2	1,186.5	1,181.8	1,160.9	1,168.6	1,181.1	1,182.0	1,183.9	1,185.6	1,176.5
2013	1,159.1	1,169.3	1,176.6	1,182.7	1,184.5	1,175.4	1,161.7	1,167.3	1,183.3	1,189.4	1,191.7	1,187.5	1,177.4
Total Private													
2002	930.4	933.8	944.1	949.6	956.8	962.1	957.7	959.7	961.0	952.6	951.3	952.1	950.9
2003	932.0	932.8	939.0	941.7	948.7	950.3	945.8	952.7	954.7	955.4	951.8	954.6	946.6
2004	935.7	939.3	948.9	954.8	959.7	964.4	962.5	964.6	966.1	963.4	965.2	968.0	957.7
2005	950.1	956.1	966.6	970.5	975.6	979.5	976.9	979.4	985.2	980.2	983.7	986.3	974.2
2006	972.6	976.6	987.3	992.0	996.1	1,001.2	992.3	996.2	997.8	993.2	992.1	995.0	991.0
2007	976.8	979.7	993.2	992.9	998.0	1,001.1	994.4	1,000.0	999.3	995.3	996.0	998.1	993.7
2008	979.8	983.6	990.6	990.5	995.0	996.6	992.3	996.0	995.3	986.8	981.4	977.3	988.8
2009	952.2	949.8	953.7	953.5	950.6	949.2	948.1	947.0	948.3	940.7	941.7	940.9	948.0
2010	920.6	920.5	934.1	941.9	947.5	956.4	951.9	954.9	954.4	951.1	951.1	952.8	944.8
2011	931.6	929.5	942.0	956.8	953.0	952.5	960.7	960.5	961.6	963.1	963.1	963.6	953.2
2012	944.5	946.9	957.6	962.5	966.4	967.1	960.0	964.9	964.2	961.8	962.3	965.0	960.3
2013	945.0	950.0	956.5	962.1	965.4	962.2	961.3	964.0	966.8	969.8	970.9	967.9	961.8
Goods-Producing													
2002	273.3	273.4	274.6	274.9	276.7	278.9	277.8	277.3	276.7	273.1	270.9	270.1	274.8
2003	265.2	263.5	263.9	263.1	264.0	264.5	263.4	264.6	264.8	264.3	261.3	262.0	263.7
2004	257.8	257.7	259.8	262.3	263.8	265.3	264.7	265.0	264.8	262.5	261.5	260.8	262.2
2005	258.7	259.2	261.3	261.9	264.0	265.2	264.4	265.4	266.7	265.2	265.5	265.6	263.6
2006	262.8	263.7	263.6	265.4	266.3	268.7	266.1	266.9	265.9	262.5	259.2	259.9	264.3
2007	256.2	255.1	258.1	257.5	258.2	258.5	257.1	257.1	256.4	254.6	253.1	253.5	256.3
2008	249.7	249.5	251.2	251.0	252.2	253.2	253.1	253.4	253.1	250.5	246.4	243.8	250.6
2009	235.9	232.5	230.3	227.0	224.9	224.0	224.5	225.2	224.6	220.1	219.1	218.3	225.5
2010	213.5	212.4	216.6	219.0	220.8	224.8	223.5	223.4	222.1	220.2	219.3	219.3	219.6
2011	214.0	213.9	216.5	218.5	218.1	217.9	220.3	219.1	219.3	217.6	216.7	216.1	217.3
2012	212.7	212.7	214.9	214.7	216.1	216.6	214.9	214.8	213.9	211.2	209.7	210.0	213.5
2013	206.7	206.9	207.9	207.3	208.4	208.5	208.7	208.6	208.3	208.2	207.6	206.8	207.8
Service-Providing													
2002	852.0	859.4	869.5	873.5	878.6	876.1	860.4	865.9	880.5	878.6	880.9	882.3	871.5
2003	863.5	869.6	876.5	879.5	885.2	881.5	867.7	876.6	890.7	894.8	895.0	896.4	881.4
2004	877.4	884.8	893.1	895.4	898.4	895.8	882.1	890.4	904.2	906.2	910.5	912.8	895.9
2005	892.3	902.9	911.7	916.5	918.2	915.7	900.9	906.6	926.0	923.9	927.6	929.1	914.3
2006	915.4	922.9	934.9	938.4	940.4	936.6	918.0	926.3	942.7	943.0	946.5	947.4	934.4
2007	928.7	938.2	949.7	949.9	953.0	951.2	931.0	943.0	956.8	956.6	959.9	960.7	948.2
2008	941.1	950.5	956.7	956.9	960.4	955.2	936.7	945.0	958.7	954.9	954.4	952.1	951.9
2009	930.5	936.7	943.9	948.0	946.1	940.0	926.2	928.1	940.8	942.4	945.2	944.9	939.4
2010	921.4	926.2	938.5	945.0	954.2	952.5	934.7	939.4	950.5	951.5	953.1	954.2	943.4
2011	932.7	935.1	946.7	961.0	956.5	950.0	940.0	947.1	959.9	967.1	968.9	968.1	952.8
2012	945.8	954.1	963.8	968.5	970.4	965.2	946.0	953.8	967.2	970.8	974.2	975.6	963.0
2013	952.4	962.4	968.7	975.4	976.1	966.9	953.0	958.7	975.0	981.2	984.1	980.7	969.6
Mining and Logging													
2002	6.5	6.5	6.6	6.6	6.8	6.9	6.9	7.0	7.0	6.9	6.9	6.8	6.8
2003	6.5	6.6	6.6	6.8	7.0	7.1	7.0	7.2	7.2	7.2	7.2	7.2	7.0
2004	7.0	6.9	6.9	6.9	7.0	7.0	7.0	7.2	7.2	7.0	6.8	6.8	7.0
2005	6.5	6.6	6.7	6.9	7.0	7.2	7.2	7.3	7.3	7.2	7.2	7.3	7.0
2006	6.8	6.8	6.9	7.4	7.6	7.8	7.7	7.8	8.1	8.0	8.1	8.2	7.6
2007	8.4	8.7	9.0	9.0	9.3	9.6	9.6	9.9	10.0	9.8	9.8	9.9	9.4
2008	9.9	9.8	10.0	10.2	10.6	10.8	11.0	11.0	11.1	11.3	11.4	11.2	10.7
2009	10.6	10.5	10.5	10.3	10.1	10.2	10.4	10.4	10.3	9.9	10.0	10.0	10.3
2010	9.9	9.8	10.2	10.6	10.8	11.0	10.8	10.9	10.9	10.9	10.9	11.0	10.6
2011	10.6	10.6	10.7	10.9	10.8	11.0	11.5	11.4	11.5	11.6	11.6	11.5	11.1
2012	11.3	11.2	11.3	11.1	11.1	11.0	10.7	10.5	10.3	10.1	10.1	10.0	10.7
2013	9.6	9.6	9.6	9.6	9.7	9.7	9.8	9.8	9.8	9.7	9.6	9.6	9.7
Construction													
2002	51.3	51.7	53.2	54.0	55.2	56.6	57.1	57.1	56.0	54.2	53.0	52.2	54.3
2003	49.3	48.7	49.5	50.1	51.3	51.7	51.9	52.4	52.2	51.9	50.5	50.2	50.8
2004	47.8	47.8	49.7	51.3	52.4	53.3	53.3	53.4	53.3	52.1	51.6	51.2	51.4
2005	50.3	50.9	52.5	53.8	55.3	55.7	56.0	56.5	56.8	55.9	55.9	56.2	54.7
2006	54.0	55.0	54.8	56.6	57.9	58.9	57.8	58.4	59.0	57.3	56.1	56.4	56.9
2007	53.9	53.6	56.4	56.7	57.4	58.0	57.1	57.5	57.2	56.3	56.0	55.5	56.3
2008	53.4	53.8	55.1	55.7	56.6	57.3	57.8	58.5	58.2	57.4	56.0	55.0	56.2
2009	52.1	51.9	51.6	51.0	50.7	51.7	53.2	53.6	53.3	50.5	49.9	49.2	51.6
2010	46.0	45.0	47.3	48.8	49.7	51.3	51.1	50.8	50.0	48.9	47.8	47.5	48.7
2011	43.6	43.6	45.5	47.3	47.2	48.3	49.3	48.8	49.2	48.6	48.1	47.8	47.3
2012	45.6	46.1	47.5	47.6	48.6	49.4	47.7	48.3	48.5	47.3	46.1	46.0	47.4
2013	43.9	44.4	45.3	45.4	46.3	46.2	46.3	46.3	46.0	46.5	46.1	45.2	45.7

1. Employment by Industry: Arkansas, Selected Years, 2002–2013—*Continued*

(Numbers in thousands, not seasonally adjusted)

Industry and year	January	February	March	April	May	June	July	August	September	October	November	December	Annual average
Manufacturing													
2002	215.5	215.2	214.8	214.3	214.7	215.4	213.8	213.2	213.7	212.0	211.0	211.1	213.7
2003	209.4	208.2	207.8	206.2	205.7	205.7	204.5	205.0	205.4	205.2	203.6	204.6	205.9
2004	203.0	203.0	203.2	204.1	204.4	205.0	204.4	204.4	204.3	203.4	203.1	202.8	203.8
2005	201.9	201.7	202.1	201.2	201.7	202.3	201.2	201.6	202.6	202.1	202.4	202.1	201.9
2006	202.0	201.9	201.9	201.4	200.8	202.0	200.6	200.7	198.8	197.2	195.0	195.3	199.8
2007	193.9	192.8	192.7	191.8	191.5	190.9	190.4	189.7	189.2	188.5	187.3	188.1	190.6
2008	186.4	185.9	186.1	185.1	185.0	185.1	184.3	183.9	183.8	181.8	179.0	177.6	183.7
2009	173.2	170.1	168.2	165.7	164.1	162.1	160.9	161.2	161.0	159.7	159.2	159.1	163.7
2010	157.6	157.6	159.1	159.6	160.3	162.5	161.6	161.7	161.2	160.4	160.6	160.8	160.3
2011	159.8	159.7	160.3	160.3	160.1	158.6	159.5	158.9	158.6	157.4	157.0	156.8	158.9
2012	155.8	155.4	156.1	156.0	156.4	156.2	156.5	156.0	155.1	153.8	153.5	154.0	155.4
2013	153.2	152.9	153.0	152.3	152.4	152.6	152.6	152.5	152.6	152.1	151.9	152.0	152.5
Trade, Transportation, and Utilities													
2002	236.9	236.9	239.8	240.4	242.0	242.5	241.6	241.4	241.8	240.4	243.0	244.4	240.9
2003	236.2	235.3	236.7	237.3	238.2	238.7	238.5	239.7	240.9	242.4	244.1	246.3	239.5
2004	237.6	237.6	239.3	240.1	241.4	242.2	242.1	242.4	243.2	243.2	245.8	248.7	242.0
2005	241.1	240.6	242.7	244.2	244.9	246.0	245.7	245.4	247.2	246.4	249.7	252.0	245.5
2006	244.8	244.4	247.8	247.3	248.8	248.8	247.7	248.3	249.2	249.6	252.5	254.6	248.7
2007	246.2	245.9	250.3	248.2	250.2	250.8	249.7	250.4	250.4	249.8	253.5	255.2	250.1
2008	247.2	246.4	248.2	247.2	248.3	248.7	247.1	247.2	246.4	244.2	245.9	246.3	246.9
2009	237.3	235.2	236.8	236.3	235.9	235.3	235.4	234.0	234.2	233.3	235.9	237.0	235.6
2010	229.7	228.7	231.6	231.9	233.6	235.7	235.6	236.1	234.8	236.6	239.6	241.4	234.6
2011	233.7	231.3	233.9	238.0	237.0	237.8	239.6	239.0	238.7	240.3	243.1	245.3	238.1
2012	238.2	237.0	239.5	240.7	241.7	242.4	241.4	241.7	241.5	241.4	245.0	246.5	241.4
2013	238.1	238.0	239.7	240.0	240.0	240.4	241.5	242.1	241.6	244.3	245.9	247.7	241.6
Wholesale Trade													
2002	44.2	44.2	44.8	44.9	45.1	45.6	45.3	45.2	45.3	44.9	44.6	44.6	44.9
2003	43.9	44.1	44.4	44.4	44.9	44.9	45.1	45.2	45.4	45.3	45.1	45.2	44.9
2004	44.6	44.8	45.4	46.0	46.5	46.8	46.9	46.5	46.6	46.5	46.6	47.1	46.2
2005	46.5	46.8	47.3	47.5	47.8	48.0	47.8	47.6	47.6	47.2	47.1	47.5	47.4
2006	46.9	47.1	47.5	47.9	48.2	48.5	48.1	48.1	48.2	47.9	47.9	48.2	47.9
2007	47.2	47.4	48.0	48.1	48.3	48.6	48.2	48.1	47.9	48.0	48.0	48.3	48.0
2008	47.8	48.1	48.4	48.6	48.9	49.0	48.9	48.8	48.8	48.4	48.2	48.1	48.5
2009	47.0	47.0	47.2	47.2	47.3	47.2	47.0	46.7	46.3	46.2	46.1	46.1	46.8
2010	45.3	45.4	46.0	46.4	46.6	47.0	46.6	46.4	46.0	46.5	46.3	46.3	46.2
2011	45.5	45.4	45.8	46.8	46.5	46.6	47.3	47.0	46.9	47.1	46.9	47.1	46.6
2012	46.5	46.6	47.1	47.9	48.0	48.2	47.4	47.4	47.1	46.9	46.7	46.9	47.2
2013	46.5	46.7	47.1	47.2	47.3	47.3	47.2	47.1	46.9	46.9	47.0	47.5	47.1
Retail Trade													
2002	128.6	127.5	129.1	129.7	130.8	130.7	130.1	129.5	129.4	128.8	131.8	133.5	130.0
2003	127.1	126.0	126.8	127.3	127.8	127.9	127.9	128.7	129.3	130.2	132.4	134.6	128.8
2004	128.5	128.1	129.4	129.8	130.5	130.7	130.3	130.6	130.6	131.1	134.0	135.6	130.8
2005	129.9	128.8	130.2	131.3	131.5	132.1	131.6	131.4	131.9	132.2	135.5	136.9	131.9
2006	131.8	130.9	133.5	132.6	133.6	132.9	132.2	132.7	132.6	133.2	136.0	137.5	133.3
2007	132.3	131.4	134.6	132.9	134.2	134.3	134.0	134.1	134.3	133.9	137.7	139.4	134.4
2008	133.7	132.6	133.9	132.8	133.6	134.2	133.4	133.7	132.9	131.6	133.9	135.1	133.5
2009	129.2	128.0	129.6	129.6	130.0	129.7	129.2	129.2	129.3	129.0	131.6	132.7	129.8
2010	126.7	125.6	127.5	127.7	128.9	130.1	129.8	130.1	128.9	130.4	133.5	134.8	129.5
2011	129.4	127.4	129.1	131.3	130.5	130.8	131.6	131.2	130.2	131.9	134.9	136.0	131.2
2012	130.9	129.8	131.2	131.9	132.5	132.6	132.5	132.3	132.3	132.3	136.0	136.6	132.6
2013	130.5	130.2	131.4	131.8	131.7	131.8	133.3	133.6	133.2	135.5	137.0	137.9	133.2
Transportation and Utilities													
2002	64.1	65.2	65.9	65.8	66.1	66.2	66.2	66.7	67.1	66.7	66.6	66.3	66.1
2003	65.2	65.2	65.5	65.6	65.5	65.4	65.5	65.8	66.2	66.9	66.6	66.5	65.8
2004	64.5	64.7	64.5	64.3	64.4	64.7	64.9	65.3	66.0	65.6	65.2	66.0	65.0
2005	64.7	65.0	65.2	65.4	65.6	65.9	66.3	66.4	67.7	67.0	67.1	67.6	66.2
2006	66.1	66.4	66.8	66.8	67.0	67.4	67.4	67.5	68.4	68.5	68.6	68.9	67.5
2007	66.7	67.1	67.7	67.2	67.7	67.9	67.5	68.2	68.2	67.9	67.8	67.5	67.6
2008	65.7	65.7	65.9	65.8	65.8	65.5	64.8	64.7	64.7	64.2	63.8	63.1	65.0
2009	61.1	60.2	60.0	59.5	58.6	58.4	59.2	58.1	58.6	58.1	58.2	58.2	59.0
2010	57.7	57.7	58.1	57.8	58.1	58.6	59.2	59.6	59.9	59.7	59.8	60.3	58.9
2011	58.8	58.5	59.0	59.9	60.0	60.4	60.7	60.8	61.6	61.3	61.3	62.2	60.4
2012	60.8	60.6	61.2	60.9	61.2	61.6	61.5	62.0	62.1	62.2	62.3	63.0	61.6
2013	61.1	61.1	61.2	61.0	61.0	61.3	61.0	61.4	61.5	61.9	61.9	62.3	61.4
Information													
2002	20.8	20.5	20.2	20.2	20.2	20.5	20.4	20.3	20.2	20.2	20.4	20.3	20.4
2003	20.1	20.1	20.1	19.9	20.0	20.2	20.4	20.3	20.1	20.2	20.3	20.3	20.2
2004	20.1	20.0	20.0	19.8	19.8	19.9	19.7	19.7	19.6	19.5	19.7	19.7	19.8
2005	19.6	19.8	19.7	19.4	19.4	19.3	19.2	19.3	19.0	19.0	19.0	19.0	19.3
2006	18.8	18.8	18.8	18.8	18.7	18.6	18.6	18.7	18.6	18.3	18.3	18.3	18.6
2007	18.4	18.4	18.4	18.4	18.4	18.2	18.1	18.1	18.0	17.8	17.8	17.8	18.2
2008	17.6	17.7	17.6	17.8	17.5	17.6	17.5	17.5	17.2	17.0	16.9	16.9	17.4
2009	16.5	16.4	16.4	16.4	16.5	16.5	16.4	16.2	16.0	15.8	15.7	15.7	16.2
2010	15.3	15.4	15.5	15.4	15.5	15.8	15.3	15.2	15.2	15.1	15.1	15.1	15.3
2011	15.0	15.0	14.9	14.9	14.9	14.9	14.9	14.9	14.7	14.7	14.7	14.7	14.9
2012	14.6	14.6	14.5	14.5	14.6	14.5	14.4	14.4	14.4	14.4	14.4	14.5	14.5
2013	14.2	14.2	14.2	14.1	14.2	14.3	14.3	14.2	14.1	14.0	14.1	14.1	14.2

1. Employment by Industry: Arkansas, Selected Years, 2002–2013—*Continued*

(Numbers in thousands, not seasonally adjusted)

Industry and year	January	February	March	April	May	June	July	August	September	October	November	December	Annual average
Financial Activities													
2002	49.4	49.2	49.5	49.5	49.7	50.0	50.0	49.9	49.8	49.3	49.4	49.8	49.6
2003	49.4	49.4	49.6	49.9	50.2	50.7	50.9	50.9	50.7	50.6	50.8	51.3	50.4
2004	50.2	50.3	50.5	50.7	50.9	51.3	51.2	51.1	51.1	50.8	50.9	51.4	50.9
2005	50.8	50.7	50.9	50.7	51.0	51.6	51.8	51.8	51.8	51.7	51.8	52.5	51.4
2006	51.8	51.8	52.0	52.2	52.5	52.9	52.9	53.1	53.0	52.7	52.9	53.2	52.6
2007	52.4	52.4	52.6	53.1	53.3	53.7	53.7	53.6	53.4	53.2	53.1	53.3	53.2
2008	52.6	52.6	52.7	52.5	52.7	52.7	52.5	52.5	52.3	51.6	51.5	52.0	52.4
2009	51.0	50.7	50.8	50.8	50.9	51.0	50.5	50.3	50.1	49.7	49.6	49.8	50.4
2010	48.7	48.6	48.5	48.8	48.7	49.1	48.9	48.9	48.7	48.8	48.8	49.1	48.8
2011	48.2	48.0	48.2	48.7	48.4	48.6	49.0	48.7	48.3	48.7	48.7	49.0	48.5
2012	48.5	48.6	48.7	48.8	49.1	49.4	49.2	49.4	49.1	49.1	49.2	49.4	49.0
2013	48.9	49.0	49.1	49.4	49.6	49.5	49.6	49.8	49.5	49.8	49.7	50.5	49.5
Professional and Business Services													
2002	96.4	96.9	99.1	100.4	101.2	102.4	102.3	103.3	104.5	103.7	102.6	102.9	101.3
2003	101.0	101.5	102.0	103.0	104.2	104.4	102.6	105.5	105.7	107.2	105.8	105.3	104.0
2004	105.2	105.2	106.5	107.1	107.1	107.9	109.0	109.7	109.3	110.4	110.7	110.7	108.2
2005	107.1	108.8	110.5	110.6	110.7	111.5	111.8	112.8	113.2	113.1	113.1	113.3	111.4
2006	111.5	112.9	115.1	114.5	114.9	115.6	114.0	114.6	115.6	115.1	114.7	114.6	114.4
2007	114.0	115.1	116.6	116.5	116.8	117.4	116.2	118.8	119.2	118.5	117.8	117.7	117.1
2008	115.0	117.2	117.3	117.0	117.8	117.2	116.4	117.9	118.1	117.9	116.3	115.5	117.0
2009	112.7	113.3	113.5	113.5	112.2	111.7	112.1	113.0	113.5	114.1	115.2	115.8	113.4
2010	114.1	115.0	117.3	118.6	118.5	119.4	119.5	120.2	120.5	120.1	119.5	120.1	118.6
2011	118.7	119.5	121.5	123.6	122.1	122.7	124.7	125.3	124.8	125.7	124.6	124.5	123.1
2012	121.6	122.7	124.2	125.9	125.7	125.2	125.4	125.7	125.6	126.7	126.0	126.6	125.1
2013	124.9	127.2	128.2	129.5	129.7	127.2	127.0	127.2	130.1	129.1	130.1	128.7	128.2
Education and Health Services													
2002	133.0	133.8	135.0	135.4	135.3	134.1	133.2	134.9	137.4	137.9	138.6	138.7	135.6
2003	137.3	138.6	139.6	139.8	140.0	137.9	136.7	138.4	141.4	142.2	142.0	142.4	139.7
2004	140.1	141.4	142.3	142.7	142.3	141.2	140.2	141.1	143.9	144.9	145.3	145.2	142.6
2005	144.1	145.4	145.8	146.0	146.0	144.1	143.6	144.9	148.1	149.1	148.9	148.6	146.2
2006	148.4	149.7	150.7	151.2	150.9	150.0	148.2	149.8	152.5	152.7	152.8	153.0	150.8
2007	150.8	153.0	153.9	154.2	154.4	153.6	152.2	154.3	156.0	156.3	156.7	157.0	154.4
2008	156.8	157.7	158.5	157.5	157.6	156.3	155.3	156.9	159.3	160.0	160.0	159.7	158.0
2009	158.2	160.2	161.6	163.5	162.6	161.2	161.0	161.6	165.0	165.8	165.9	166.0	162.7
2010	163.7	164.5	165.2	165.4	165.7	164.6	163.6	165.4	168.2	168.2	168.4	168.5	166.0
2011	165.4	165.2	166.5	168.0	167.0	163.5	164.2	166.2	170.0	171.1	171.7	171.3	167.5
2012	169.5	170.0	170.8	170.3	170.1	167.4	165.6	169.5	172.0	173.5	173.5	173.4	170.5
2013	170.4	171.6	171.5	172.5	172.6	169.3	168.1	170.4	173.0	174.3	175.0	174.1	171.9
Leisure and Hospitality													
2002	80.5	82.8	85.2	88.0	90.6	92.0	91.0	91.3	89.6	87.5	85.9	85.3	87.5
2003	82.6	84.3	86.6	88.0	91.0	92.2	92.0	92.1	90.2	87.7	86.7	86.1	88.3
2004	84.2	86.4	89.5	90.8	92.9	94.4	93.8	94.1	92.9	91.1	90.1	90.0	90.9
2005	87.5	90.1	93.5	94.9	96.6	98.3	97.1	96.8	96.2	93.4	93.3	92.7	94.2
2006	92.0	92.7	96.2	99.0	99.8	101.7	99.8	99.7	98.0	97.5	96.7	96.1	97.4
2007	94.0	94.9	97.8	99.7	101.3	102.8	101.8	102.1	100.6	99.9	98.8	98.2	99.3
2008	95.9	97.3	99.5	101.7	102.9	104.4	104.0	104.3	102.7	99.9	99.0	97.5	100.8
2009	95.6	96.5	99.1	100.9	102.6	104.1	103.1	102.1	100.7	98.3	97.0	95.2	99.6
2010	93.0	93.5	96.6	99.7	101.4	103.0	101.9	102.3	101.6	99.0	97.4	96.5	98.8
2011	93.8	94.0	97.3	101.3	102.1	103.3	103.7	103.7	102.4	101.4	100.1	99.1	100.2
2012	96.6	98.3	101.6	104.0	105.3	107.1	105.4	105.9	104.3	102.2	101.3	101.4	102.8
2013	99.1	100.3	102.9	106.0	107.5	109.2	108.6	108.5	107.1	106.9	105.6	103.2	105.4
Other Services													
2002	40.1	40.3	40.7	40.8	41.1	41.7	41.4	41.3	41.0	40.5	40.5	40.6	40.8
2003	40.2	40.1	40.5	40.7	41.1	41.7	41.3	41.2	40.9	40.8	40.8	40.9	40.9
2004	40.5	40.7	41.0	41.3	41.5	42.2	41.8	41.5	41.3	41.0	41.2	41.5	41.3
2005	41.2	41.5	42.2	42.8	43.0	43.5	43.3	43.0	43.0	42.3	42.4	42.6	42.6
2006	42.5	42.6	43.1	43.6	44.2	44.9	45.0	45.1	45.0	44.8	45.0	45.3	44.3
2007	44.8	44.9	45.5	45.3	45.4	46.1	45.6	45.6	45.3	45.2	45.2	45.4	45.4
2008	45.0	45.2	45.6	45.8	46.0	46.5	46.4	46.3	46.2	45.7	45.4	45.6	45.8
2009	45.0	45.0	45.2	45.1	45.0	45.4	45.1	44.6	44.2	43.6	43.3	43.1	44.6
2010	42.6	42.4	42.8	43.1	43.3	44.0	43.6	43.4	43.3	43.1	43.0	42.8	43.1
2011	42.8	42.6	43.2	43.8	43.4	43.8	44.3	43.6	43.4	43.6	43.5	43.6	43.5
2012	42.8	43.0	43.4	43.6	43.8	44.5	43.7	43.5	43.4	43.3	43.2	43.2	43.5
2013	42.7	42.8	43.0	43.3	43.4	43.8	43.5	43.2	43.1	43.2	42.9	42.8	43.1
Government													
2002	194.9	199.0	200.0	198.8	198.5	192.9	180.5	183.5	196.2	199.1	200.5	200.3	195.4
2003	196.7	200.3	201.4	200.9	200.5	195.7	185.3	188.5	200.8	203.7	204.5	203.8	198.5
2004	199.5	203.2	204.0	202.9	202.5	196.7	184.3	190.8	202.9	205.3	206.8	205.6	200.4
2005	200.9	206.0	206.4	207.9	206.6	201.4	188.4	192.6	207.5	208.9	209.4	208.4	203.7
2006	205.6	210.0	211.2	211.8	210.6	204.1	191.8	197.0	210.8	212.3	213.6	212.3	207.6
2007	208.1	213.6	214.6	214.5	213.2	208.6	193.7	200.1	213.9	215.9	217.0	216.1	210.8
2008	211.0	216.4	217.3	217.4	217.6	211.8	197.5	202.4	216.5	218.6	219.4	218.6	213.7
2009	214.2	219.4	220.5	221.5	220.4	214.8	202.6	206.3	217.1	221.8	222.6	222.3	217.0
2010	214.3	218.1	221.0	222.1	227.5	220.9	206.3	207.9	218.2	220.6	221.3	220.7	218.2
2011	215.1	219.5	221.2	222.7	221.6	215.4	199.6	205.7	217.6	221.6	222.5	220.6	216.9
2012	214.0	219.9	221.1	220.7	220.1	214.7	200.9	203.7	216.9	220.2	221.6	220.6	216.2
2013	214.1	219.3	220.1	220.6	219.1	213.2	200.4	203.3	216.5	219.6	220.8	219.6	215.6

2. Average Weekly Hours by Selected Industry: Arkansas, 2009–2013

(Not seasonally adjusted)

Industry and year	January	February	March	April	May	June	July	August	September	October	November	December	Annual average
Total Private													
2009	34.6	35.3	34.0	33.8	34.3	34.7	34.4	35.3	34.3	34.6	35.1	34.8	34.6
2010	34.3	33.6	34.7	34.9	35.2	35.4	35.0	35.5	34.8	35.0	34.7	35.1	34.9
2011	34.1	33.1	35.0	35.0	35.5	35.4	35.3	35.1	35.3	36.0	35.1	35.3	35.0
2012	35.2	34.5	34.8	35.1	34.7	34.9	35.2	35.0	35.2	34.6	34.7	35.2	34.9
2013	34.0	34.4	34.6	34.5	34.7	35.7	35.0	35.2	35.7	34.8	34.9	34.9	34.9
Goods-Producing													
2009	37.6	37.9	36.4	36.1	37.7	38.2	37.3	39.2	37.3	38.4	39.6	39.2	37.9
2010	39.4	37.0	39.6	39.7	39.6	39.9	39.3	39.3	38.8	39.5	39.2	39.4	39.2
2011	36.2	35.3	39.2	38.4	39.0	39.3	39.7	39.4	40.5	40.9	39.8	41.1	39.1
2012	40.2	40.0	40.4	41.1	40.6	41.1	40.9	41.1	41.8	41.2	41.2	41.8	40.9
2013	39.7	40.7	40.5	40.5	40.5	41.9	41.3	41.6	41.5	40.7	41.2	41.2	40.9
Construction													
2009	37.9	36.6	34.7	36.5	36.7	38.5	37.0	38.7	36.9	36.5	38.4	36.5	37.1
2010	38.3	36.3	38.3	39.2	37.2	38.8	37.7	38.0	36.2	37.0	36.2	36.7	37.5
2011	31.0	32.0	37.6	36.0	36.9	38.1	38.0	37.6	38.7	38.4	37.6	38.0	36.7
2012	36.7	36.2	38.2	38.4	38.8	39.0	39.1	38.7	38.8	38.3	38.2	39.4	38.3
2013	38.3	39.5	40.3	38.9	39.8	41.1	40.8	41.2	41.1	39.7	41.2	41.3	40.3
Manufacturing													
2009	37.4	37.8	37.3	35.9	37.5	37.0	36.4	38.3	37.6	39.4	39.2	39.9	37.8
2010	39.3	37.9	39.1	39.0	39.7	39.3	38.8	38.7	38.9	39.1	39.1	39.3	39.0
2011	38.3	36.9	39.4	39.3	39.7	39.7	40.3	40.3	41.1	41.8	40.7	41.9	39.9
2012	41.2	41.2	41.0	41.8	41.1	41.8	41.4	41.8	42.7	42.1	42.1	42.5	41.7
2013	39.9	40.9	40.5	41.0	40.6	42.0	41.4	41.7	41.5	41.1	41.2	41.0	41.1
Trade, Transportation, and Utilities													
2009	35.0	36.4	35.0	35.7	35.5	36.5	36.1	36.6	36.6	36.1	36.1	35.6	35.9
2010	35.7	35.5	36.1	36.5	36.8	37.0	37.2	37.5	36.9	36.8	36.3	37.3	36.6
2011	36.3	35.3	36.6	37.0	37.3	37.5	37.2	36.7	36.3	37.1	35.6	35.1	36.5
2012	34.6	34.6	35.1	36.0	35.5	35.5	35.4	35.3	35.6	35.4	34.3	34.9	35.2
2013	34.0	34.6	35.3	35.2	34.8	36.0	36.2	36.1	36.6	36.0	35.9	35.9	35.6
Financial Activities													
2009	37.9	37.4	37.2	36.8	37.1	37.1	37.0	38.0	37.4	37.8	38.2	37.1	37.4
2010	37.2	37.1	37.4	37.2	38.4	38.2	37.6	37.6	37.3	37.5	37.3	37.2	37.5
2011	38.0	36.4	38.0	37.2	38.0	37.5	37.6	37.8	37.2	38.7	37.4	37.5	37.6
2012	39.0	36.8	36.6	37.5	37.3	36.5	37.6	36.7	35.5	35.2	35.4	36.8	36.7
2013	34.7	35.4	35.0	35.1	35.3	36.6	34.4	35.5	36.2	34.8	35.5	36.5	35.4
Professional and Business Services													
2009	34.9	35.9	34.5	33.7	33.0	33.5	33.0	34.4	32.6	32.0	33.7	34.5	33.8
2010	33.3	33.2	34.2	34.5	34.9	34.1	33.4	35.1	33.2	32.8	33.1	32.7	33.7
2011	32.2	32.3	33.8	34.6	35.9	34.6	34.8	34.9	35.3	35.9	35.6	35.3	34.6
2012	35.6	34.7	35.4	36.4	35.7	35.5	36.2	36.4	35.9	35.2	36.1	35.7	35.7
2013	34.5	35.5	35.4	35.4	36.7	37.4	35.7	36.4	37.8	36.7	36.4	36.7	36.2
Education and Health Services													
2009	32.1	32.7	32.2	32.0	32.3	32.6	32.8	33.0	32.8	32.7	33.0	32.8	32.6
2010	32.2	31.5	32.3	32.5	33.1	33.3	32.5	33.1	32.7	32.4	32.3	32.1	32.5
2011	32.2	31.2	32.4	32.6	32.7	32.6	32.5	32.4	32.2	32.9	32.5	32.6	32.4
2012	32.9	32.0	32.7	33.6	33.0	33.1	33.4	33.0	33.7	33.2	33.3	33.9	33.2
2013	33.5	33.2	33.1	33.2	33.7	34.4	33.5	33.2	33.8	33.0	33.3	33.4	33.4
Leisure and Hospitality													
2009	26.3	27.1	26.5	26.5	27.1	27.3	27.8	27.7	26.2	27.1	25.7	25.7	26.8
2010	24.9	25.9	26.2	26.0	26.7	27.2	27.7	27.3	26.5	26.7	26.3	26.6	26.5
2011	25.7	25.0	26.1	25.6	25.9	26.2	25.9	25.9	25.9	26.3	25.6	25.5	25.8
2012	25.6	25.5	25.5	26.7	26.6	27.1	27.1	26.7	26.3	25.7	25.9	26.2	26.3
2013	25.1	25.7	26.4	26.3	25.6	26.9	26.4	26.3	26.3	25.7	25.3	24.1	25.8

3. Average Hourly Earnings by Selected Industry: Arkansas, 2009–2013

(Dollars, not seasonally adjusted)

Industry and year	January	February	March	April	May	June	July	August	September	October	November	December	Annual average
Total Private													
2009	17.73	17.85	17.91	18.01	18.05	17.82	17.79	17.90	17.99	18.10	18.27	18.28	17.97
2010	18.31	18.43	17.95	18.00	17.93	17.89	18.19	18.02	17.99	17.93	18.16	18.15	18.08
2011	18.58	18.62	18.26	18.21	18.38	18.12	18.16	18.13	18.42	18.54	18.40	18.52	18.36
2012	18.84	18.83	18.61	18.05	17.89	17.92	18.45	18.29	18.78	18.92	19.05	19.21	18.57
2013	19.11	19.03	19.01	19.07	19.02	19.13	19.23	19.22	19.61	19.41	19.54	19.92	19.28
Goods-Producing													
2009	17.47	17.74	17.69	17.54	17.38	17.16	17.10	17.08	17.15	17.15	17.15	17.39	17.33
2010	17.32	17.90	17.30	17.33	17.11	17.21	17.73	17.12	17.26	17.15	17.32	17.59	17.36
2011	18.26	18.39	18.02	18.03	18.28	17.93	17.91	18.09	18.21	18.25	18.29	18.62	18.19
2012	18.59	18.82	18.45	18.49	18.35	18.52	18.59	18.39	18.58	18.71	18.58	18.49	18.55
2013	18.92	18.41	18.63	18.58	18.81	18.94	18.95	18.89	19.34	19.40	19.61	19.73	19.02
Construction													
2009	18.90	19.08	19.20	19.18	19.06	18.32	18.15	18.00	18.11	18.40	18.03	19.01	18.61
2010	18.67	19.17	18.69	18.65	18.34	18.52	20.52	18.31	18.45	18.51	18.81	18.45	18.76
2011	19.30	19.01	18.23	18.08	18.15	17.58	17.69	17.87	18.08	18.56	18.33	18.33	18.23
2012	18.19	18.86	17.93	17.89	17.79	17.67	17.87	17.56	17.80	17.97	18.26	18.00	17.97
2013	17.18	17.41	17.64	17.69	18.13	18.21	18.51	18.42	19.09	19.78	20.24	21.29	18.66
Manufacturing													
2009	16.69	16.71	15.87	15.70	15.77	15.81	15.87	15.99	16.12	16.05	16.39	16.44	16.13
2010	16.45	16.64	16.38	16.43	16.37	16.52	16.67	16.70	16.85	16.65	16.82	16.94	16.62
2011	17.06	17.26	17.14	17.30	17.70	17.55	17.50	17.68	17.78	17.78	17.96	18.44	17.60
2012	18.46	18.56	18.38	18.42	18.28	18.56	18.63	18.48	18.63	18.76	18.52	18.50	18.52
2013	19.33	18.60	18.80	18.71	18.87	18.99	18.88	18.83	19.28	19.19	19.31	19.13	18.99
Trade, Transportation, and Utilities													
2009	16.99	16.98	17.10	17.15	17.20	17.03	17.17	17.44	17.29	17.32	17.59	17.65	17.24
2010	17.81	17.92	17.88	18.19	18.23	18.24	18.56	18.38	18.76	18.79	19.00	18.97	18.40
2011	18.87	18.94	18.79	19.08	19.15	18.83	19.05	18.43	18.83	18.70	18.31	18.66	18.80
2012	18.79	18.76	18.61	18.54	18.18	18.58	18.64	18.48	18.98	18.68	18.73	19.06	18.67
2013	18.76	18.82	18.84	18.92	18.66	18.70	19.53	19.66	19.99	19.58	19.69	20.13	19.29
Financial Activities													
2009	21.67	23.26	22.42	22.73	23.62	23.11	23.06	23.68	23.61	24.32	24.43	23.94	23.32
2010	23.75	23.99	23.68	23.33	23.72	23.66	23.37	23.80	23.40	23.31	23.34	23.45	23.57
2011	23.53	23.26	22.71	22.48	22.19	21.65	21.45	21.59	21.59	22.37	22.60	22.54	22.41
2012	24.12	24.35	24.04	24.86	24.63	23.65	25.77	24.63	25.06	26.28	26.31	25.45	24.92
2013	23.04	23.84	23.09	23.29	23.15	23.94	23.20	22.47	22.57	21.91	23.05	24.39	23.17
Professional and Business Services													
2009	20.23	20.16	20.23	20.28	20.32	20.75	20.65	20.49	20.46	20.27	20.65	20.41	20.41
2010	20.63	20.39	19.92	20.16	20.09	19.98	20.22	19.80	20.03	20.14	19.99	20.32	20.13
2011	20.65	20.78	20.04	19.96	20.72	20.49	20.83	20.80	21.22	21.45	21.95	21.61	20.89
2012	22.60	22.26	22.54	22.62	22.13	22.28	22.56	21.95	21.91	22.49	22.79	23.55	22.47
2013	24.59	23.75	23.46	23.99	23.13	23.04	23.09	22.20	22.73	22.61	22.41	22.82	23.14
Education and Health Services													
2009	16.31	16.16	16.40	16.32	16.44	16.39	16.51	16.66	16.83	17.10	16.91	16.95	16.59
2010	16.92	16.98	16.81	16.68	16.55	16.70	16.64	16.76	16.60	16.61	16.64	16.63	16.71
2011	16.52	16.87	16.88	16.69	16.80	16.99	17.22	17.30	17.40	17.58	17.45	17.51	17.11
2012	17.91	18.00	17.91	18.06	17.93	17.97	18.81	18.90	19.24	19.00	19.52	19.74	18.59
2013	19.35	19.70	19.78	19.79	19.99	20.38	19.95	20.71	20.92	20.78	20.60	20.67	20.22
Leisure and Hospitality													
2009	9.72	9.86	9.87	9.98	10.17	9.86	9.88	10.05	10.05	10.42	10.28	10.37	10.04
2010	10.48	10.51	10.33	10.28	10.19	10.08	10.06	10.21	10.10	10.30	10.21	10.18	10.24
2011	10.33	10.49	10.41	10.32	10.44	10.31	10.28	10.34	10.34	10.65	10.74	10.77	10.45
2012	10.81	10.66	10.48	9.68	9.71	9.64	9.73	9.86	9.92	9.98	9.98	10.03	10.02
2013	10.24	10.26	10.29	10.27	10.33	10.20	10.34	10.40	10.49	10.42	10.60	10.90	10.39

4. Average Weekly Earnings by Selected Industry: Arkansas, 2009–2013

(Dollars, not seasonally adjusted)

Industry and year	January	February	March	April	May	June	July	August	September	October	November	December	Annual average
Total Private													
2009	613.46	630.11	608.94	608.74	619.12	618.35	611.98	631.87	617.06	626.26	641.28	636.14	621.76
2010	628.03	619.25	622.87	628.20	631.14	633.31	636.65	639.71	626.05	627.55	630.15	637.07	630.99
2011	633.58	616.32	639.10	637.35	652.49	641.45	641.05	636.36	650.23	667.44	645.84	653.76	642.60
2012	663.17	649.64	647.63	633.56	620.78	625.41	649.44	640.15	661.06	654.63	661.04	676.19	648.09
2013	649.74	654.63	657.75	657.92	659.99	682.94	673.05	676.54	700.08	675.47	681.95	695.21	672.87
Goods-Producing													
2009	656.87	672.35	643.92	633.19	655.23	655.51	637.83	669.54	639.70	658.56	679.14	681.69	656.81
2010	682.41	662.30	685.08	688.00	677.56	686.68	696.79	672.82	669.69	677.43	678.94	693.05	680.51
2011	661.01	649.17	706.38	692.35	712.92	704.65	711.03	712.75	737.51	746.43	727.94	765.28	711.23
2012	747.32	752.80	745.38	759.94	745.01	761.17	760.33	755.83	776.64	770.85	765.50	772.88	758.70
2013	751.12	749.29	754.52	752.49	761.81	793.59	782.64	785.82	802.61	789.58	807.93	812.88	777.92
Construction													
2009	716.31	698.33	666.24	700.07	699.50	705.32	671.55	696.60	668.26	671.60	692.35	693.87	690.43
2010	715.06	695.87	715.83	731.08	682.25	718.58	773.60	695.78	667.89	684.87	680.92	677.12	703.50
2011	598.30	608.32	685.45	650.88	669.74	669.80	672.22	671.91	699.70	712.70	689.21	696.54	669.04
2012	667.57	682.73	684.93	686.98	690.25	689.13	698.72	679.57	690.64	688.25	697.53	709.20	688.25
2013	657.99	687.70	710.89	688.14	721.57	748.43	755.21	758.90	784.60	785.27	833.89	879.28	752.00
Manufacturing													
2009	624.21	631.64	591.95	563.63	591.38	584.97	577.67	612.42	606.11	632.37	642.49	655.96	609.71
2010	646.49	630.66	640.46	640.77	649.89	649.24	646.80	646.29	655.47	651.02	657.66	665.74	648.18
2011	653.40	636.89	675.32	679.89	702.69	696.74	705.25	712.50	730.76	743.20	730.97	772.64	702.24
2012	760.55	764.67	753.58	769.96	751.31	775.81	771.28	772.46	795.50	789.80	779.69	786.25	772.28
2013	771.27	760.74	761.40	767.11	766.12	797.58	781.63	785.21	800.12	788.71	795.57	784.33	780.49
Trade, Transportation, and Utilities													
2009	594.65	618.07	598.50	612.26	610.60	621.60	619.84	638.30	632.81	625.25	635.00	628.34	618.92
2010	635.82	636.16	645.47	663.94	670.86	674.88	690.43	689.25	692.24	691.47	689.70	707.58	673.44
2011	684.98	668.58	687.71	705.96	714.30	706.13	708.66	676.38	683.53	693.77	651.84	654.97	686.20
2012	650.13	649.10	653.21	667.44	645.39	659.59	659.86	652.34	675.69	661.27	642.44	665.19	657.18
2013	637.84	651.17	665.05	665.98	649.37	673.20	706.99	709.73	731.63	704.88	706.87	722.67	686.72
Financial Activities													
2009	821.29	869.92	834.02	836.46	876.30	857.38	853.22	899.84	883.01	919.30	933.23	888.17	872.17
2010	883.50	890.03	885.63	867.88	910.85	903.81	878.71	894.88	872.82	874.13	870.58	872.34	883.88
2011	894.14	846.66	862.98	836.26	843.22	811.88	806.52	816.10	803.15	904.42	845.24	845.25	842.62
2012	940.68	896.08	879.86	932.25	918.70	863.23	968.95	903.92	889.63	925.06	931.37	936.56	914.56
2013	799.49	843.94	808.15	817.48	817.20	876.20	798.08	797.69	817.03	762.47	818.28	890.24	820.22
Professional and Business Services													
2009	706.03	723.74	697.94	683.44	670.56	695.13	681.45	704.86	667.00	648.64	695.91	704.15	689.86
2010	686.98	676.95	681.26	695.52	701.14	681.32	675.35	694.98	665.00	660.59	661.67	664.46	678.38
2011	664.93	671.19	677.35	690.62	743.85	708.95	724.88	725.92	749.07	770.06	781.42	762.83	722.79
2012	804.56	772.42	797.92	823.37	790.04	790.94	816.67	798.98	786.57	791.65	822.72	840.74	802.18
2013	848.36	843.13	830.48	849.25	848.87	861.70	824.31	808.08	859.19	829.79	815.72	837.49	837.67
Education and Health Services													
2009	523.55	528.43	528.08	522.24	531.01	534.31	541.53	549.78	552.02	559.17	558.03	555.96	540.83
2010	544.82	534.87	542.96	542.10	547.81	556.11	540.80	554.76	542.82	538.16	537.47	533.82	543.08
2011	531.94	526.34	546.91	544.09	549.36	553.87	559.65	560.52	560.28	578.38	567.13	570.83	554.36
2012	589.24	576.00	585.66	606.82	591.69	594.81	628.25	623.70	648.39	630.80	650.02	669.19	617.19
2013	648.23	654.04	654.72	657.03	673.66	701.07	668.33	687.57	707.10	685.74	685.98	690.38	675.35
Leisure and Hospitality													
2009	255.64	267.21	261.56	264.47	275.61	269.18	274.66	278.39	263.31	282.38	264.20	266.51	269.07
2010	260.95	272.21	270.65	267.28	272.07	274.18	278.66	278.73	267.65	275.01	268.52	270.79	271.36
2011	265.48	262.25	271.70	264.19	270.40	270.12	266.25	267.81	267.81	280.10	274.94	274.64	269.61
2012	276.74	271.83	267.24	258.46	258.29	261.24	263.68	263.26	260.90	256.49	258.48	262.79	263.53
2013	257.02	263.68	271.66	270.10	264.45	274.38	272.98	273.52	275.89	267.79	268.18	262.69	268.06

CALIFORNIA
At a Glance

Population:
   2000 census: 33,871,653
   2010 census: 37,253,956
   2013 estimate: 38,332,521

Percent change in population:
   2000–2010: 10.0%
   2010–2013: 2.9%

Percent change in total nonfarm employment:
   2000–2010: -2.7%
   2010–2013: 6.6%

Industry with the largest growth in employment, 2000–2013 (thousands):
   Education and Health Services, 853.3

Industry with the largest decline or smallest growth in employment, 2000–2013 (thousands):
   Manufacturing, -529.9

Civilian labor force:
   2000: 16,857,578
   2010: 18,336,328
   2013: 18,596,818

Unemployment rate and rank among states (lowest to highest):
   2000: 4.9%, 43rd
   2010: 12.4%, 49th
   2013: 8.9%, 48th

Over-the-year change in unemployment rates:
   2010–2011: -0.6%
   2011–2012: -1.4%
   2012–2013: -1.5%

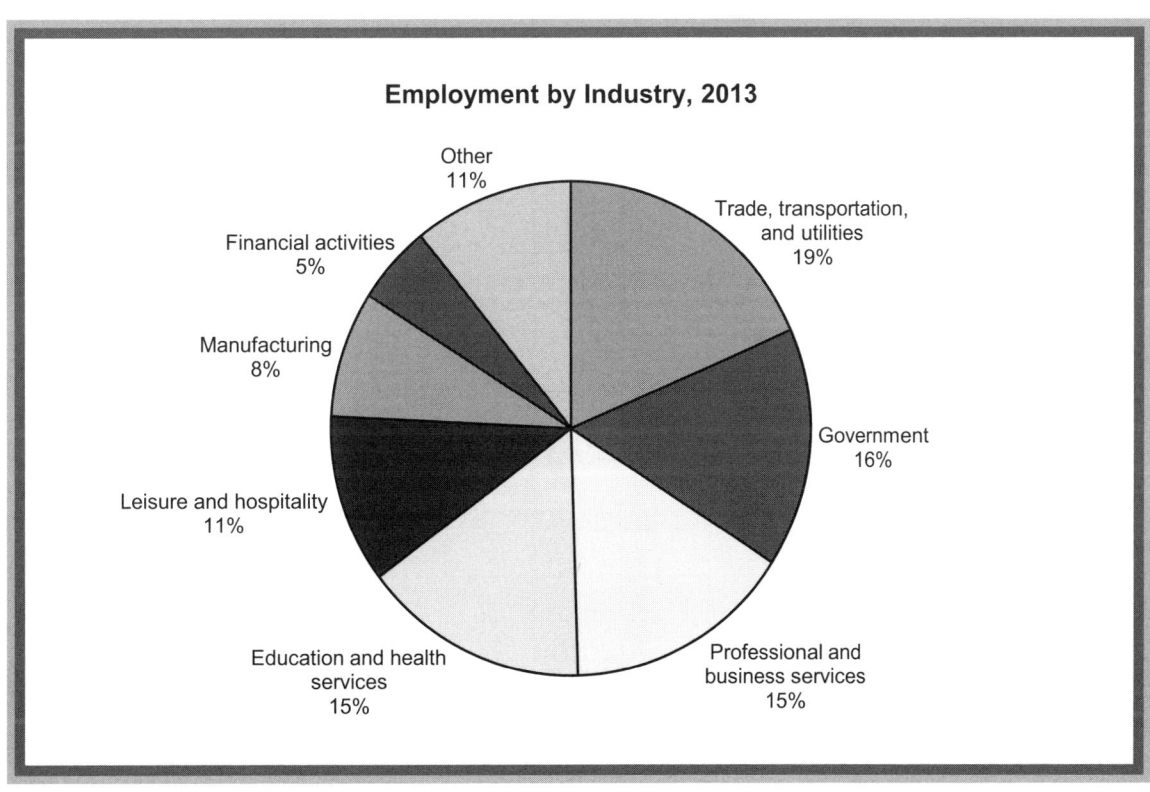

Employment by Industry, 2013

Other 11%
Trade, transportation, and utilities 19%
Financial activities 5%
Manufacturing 8%
Government 16%
Leisure and hospitality 11%
Education and health services 15%
Professional and business services 15%

1. Employment by Industry: California, Selected Years, 2002–2013

(Numbers in thousands, not seasonally adjusted)

Industry and year	January	February	March	April	May	June	July	August	September	October	November	December	Annual average
Total Nonfarm													
2002	14,360.9	14,453.8	14,587.5	14,579.5	14,663.9	14,715.9	14,487.7	14,539.8	14,601.7	14,641.9	14,712.5	14,743.5	14,590.7
2003	14,383.0	14,449.6	14,533.1	14,537.9	14,602.7	14,661.7	14,453.1	14,500.3	14,559.3	14,627.0	14,665.5	14,719.8	14,557.8
2004	14,415.3	14,512.9	14,626.9	14,647.5	14,730.5	14,792.7	14,687.8	14,697.8	14,771.8	14,869.0	14,944.5	14,983.8	14,723.4
2005	14,655.6	14,772.2	14,876.0	14,933.4	14,990.3	15,061.3	14,950.3	15,009.8	15,123.8	15,171.5	15,263.1	15,335.2	15,011.9
2006	14,980.4	15,106.2	15,190.3	15,193.3	15,305.0	15,393.6	15,223.7	15,276.8	15,364.5	15,399.9	15,465.0	15,509.7	15,284.0
2007	15,168.7	15,279.7	15,385.7	15,337.4	15,428.4	15,501.4	15,372.6	15,383.0	15,443.9	15,483.4	15,551.3	15,594.0	15,410.8
2008	15,188.0	15,279.9	15,332.1	15,342.8	15,378.3	15,404.2	15,193.7	15,180.4	15,207.8	15,179.6	15,119.9	15,080.4	15,240.6
2009	14,624.4	14,559.2	14,536.9	14,470.5	14,478.6	14,446.9	14,155.7	14,134.5	14,151.8	14,283.1	14,303.9	14,312.3	14,371.5
2010	13,976.9	14,017.1	14,085.5	14,216.8	14,308.3	14,320.8	14,111.6	14,135.9	14,194.1	14,342.3	14,392.9	14,422.5	14,210.4
2011	14,124.8	14,207.0	14,265.7	14,330.2	14,376.4	14,394.9	14,246.8	14,293.0	14,388.9	14,496.3	14,575.9	14,598.1	14,358.2
2012	14,369.8	14,466.7	14,551.0	14,593.5	14,692.2	14,758.9	14,581.4	14,659.5	14,725.0	14,942.0	15,055.6	15,080.2	14,706.3
2013	14,802.5	14,928.4	15,005.8	15,078.0	15,155.3	15,191.1	15,045.9	15,155.8	15,205.3	15,327.4	15,426.8	15,446.4	15,147.4
Total Private													
2002	11,938.3	12,004.0	12,108.3	12,089.0	12,166.9	12,223.8	12,128.7	12,197.7	12,193.7	12,175.0	12,229.3	12,268.8	12,143.6
2003	11,932.1	11,986.7	12,053.0	12,063.2	12,129.0	12,191.4	12,107.6	12,184.2	12,188.4	12,208.1	12,232.5	12,304.0	12,131.7
2004	12,018.0	12,100.6	12,196.7	12,212.0	12,292.4	12,354.2	12,374.7	12,408.9	12,415.9	12,457.1	12,513.2	12,564.3	12,325.7
2005	12,251.9	12,342.4	12,429.9	12,481.5	12,531.0	12,607.6	12,618.4	12,683.0	12,733.3	12,731.7	12,804.0	12,885.8	12,591.7
2006	12,549.2	12,649.3	12,716.9	12,716.4	12,819.4	12,909.5	12,856.2	12,923.1	12,942.7	12,918.6	12,962.8	13,017.3	12,831.8
2007	12,693.6	12,780.9	12,864.5	12,812.5	12,893.0	12,966.9	12,965.3	12,989.9	12,982.0	12,969.0	13,014.6	13,062.5	12,916.2
2008	12,676.8	12,742.7	12,777.8	12,780.6	12,806.5	12,830.8	12,769.1	12,766.6	12,732.9	12,650.2	12,576.9	12,549.3	12,721.7
2009	12,110.4	12,026.2	11,985.7	11,907.2	11,920.8	11,903.9	11,798.3	11,795.6	11,771.2	11,810.1	11,823.5	11,849.7	11,891.9
2010	11,532.7	11,557.1	11,605.3	11,690.5	11,736.2	11,789.4	11,781.4	11,825.3	11,823.6	11,894.7	11,927.7	11,979.8	11,762.0
2011	11,700.5	11,761.4	11,796.5	11,860.6	11,906.6	11,937.4	11,968.5	12,020.4	12,052.5	12,088.4	12,149.9	12,196.5	11,953.3
2012	11,987.4	12,058.4	12,122.9	12,167.8	12,258.6	12,333.1	12,329.7	12,402.1	12,407.5	12,556.2	12,648.9	12,688.1	12,330.1
2013	12,439.2	12,537.0	12,593.1	12,670.5	12,737.7	12,783.0	12,809.5	12,887.8	12,873.4	12,939.0	13,010.4	13,046.7	12,777.3
Goods-Producing													
2002	2,402.2	2,412.0	2,429.4	2,422.8	2,441.3	2,459.4	2,443.3	2,469.1	2,459.7	2,432.7	2,410.8	2,393.7	2,431.4
2003	2,334.6	2,332.0	2,345.2	2,340.0	2,357.6	2,379.7	2,370.9	2,400.8	2,399.8	2,378.1	2,362.0	2,361.3	2,363.5
2004	2,318.4	2,331.3	2,353.2	2,371.9	2,392.2	2,418.2	2,442.0	2,453.0	2,449.8	2,427.5	2,405.0	2,397.1	2,396.6
2005	2,336.3	2,363.4	2,384.6	2,403.5	2,419.6	2,448.9	2,472.7	2,490.6	2,493.5	2,473.2	2,460.3	2,456.6	2,433.6
2006	2,404.9	2,427.4	2,430.7	2,417.3	2,456.7	2,483.9	2,479.6	2,496.2	2,494.2	2,457.4	2,428.8	2,409.8	2,448.9
2007	2,356.3	2,368.2	2,385.2	2,371.9	2,390.0	2,418.0	2,424.7	2,428.9	2,410.2	2,376.6	2,347.5	2,325.7	2,383.6
2008	2,261.2	2,265.7	2,264.8	2,256.8	2,265.7	2,274.1	2,274.2	2,276.4	2,257.7	2,213.9	2,163.5	2,127.4	2,241.8
2009	2,042.2	1,993.7	1,977.7	1,945.8	1,944.8	1,940.9	1,921.4	1,919.8	1,902.4	1,882.0	1,862.9	1,839.7	1,931.1
2010	1,802.9	1,795.1	1,806.8	1,811.0	1,827.5	1,842.7	1,851.9	1,863.2	1,852.1	1,846.3	1,829.5	1,814.7	1,828.6
2011	1,787.4	1,794.3	1,797.0	1,813.2	1,829.2	1,845.4	1,867.3	1,881.7	1,879.9	1,867.5	1,851.4	1,840.6	1,837.9
2012	1,819.2	1,822.6	1,830.9	1,831.7	1,859.2	1,885.8	1,902.5	1,917.7	1,914.7	1,906.2	1,894.5	1,884.9	1,872.5
2013	1,860.1	1,874.5	1,882.3	1,890.9	1,905.9	1,927.3	1,945.5	1,964.6	1,958.3	1,940.5	1,936.6	1,924.9	1,917.6
Service-Providing													
2002	11,958.7	12,041.8	12,158.1	12,156.7	12,222.6	12,256.5	12,044.4	12,070.7	12,142.0	12,209.2	12,301.7	12,349.8	12,159.4
2003	12,048.4	12,117.6	12,187.9	12,197.9	12,245.1	12,282.0	12,082.2	12,099.5	12,159.5	12,248.9	12,303.5	12,358.5	12,194.3
2004	12,096.9	12,181.6	12,273.7	12,275.6	12,338.3	12,374.5	12,245.8	12,244.8	12,322.0	12,441.5	12,539.5	12,586.7	12,326.7
2005	12,319.3	12,408.8	12,491.4	12,529.9	12,570.7	12,612.4	12,477.6	12,519.2	12,630.3	12,698.3	12,802.8	12,878.6	12,578.3
2006	12,575.5	12,678.8	12,759.6	12,776.0	12,848.3	12,909.7	12,744.1	12,780.6	12,870.3	12,942.5	13,036.2	13,099.9	12,835.1
2007	12,812.4	12,911.5	13,000.5	12,965.5	13,038.4	13,083.4	12,947.9	12,954.1	13,033.7	13,106.8	13,203.8	13,268.3	13,027.2
2008	12,926.8	13,014.2	13,067.3	13,086.0	13,112.6	13,130.1	12,919.5	12,904.0	12,950.1	12,965.7	12,956.4	12,953.0	12,998.8
2009	12,582.2	12,565.5	12,559.2	12,524.7	12,533.8	12,506.0	12,234.3	12,214.7	12,249.4	12,401.1	12,441.0	12,472.6	12,440.4
2010	12,174.0	12,222.0	12,278.7	12,405.8	12,480.8	12,478.1	12,259.7	12,272.7	12,342.0	12,496.0	12,563.4	12,607.8	12,381.8
2011	12,337.4	12,412.7	12,468.7	12,517.0	12,547.2	12,549.5	12,379.5	12,411.3	12,509.0	12,628.8	12,724.5	12,757.5	12,520.3
2012	12,550.6	12,644.1	12,720.1	12,761.8	12,833.0	12,873.1	12,678.9	12,741.8	12,810.3	13,035.8	13,161.1	13,195.3	12,833.8
2013	12,942.4	13,053.9	13,123.5	13,187.1	13,249.4	13,263.8	13,100.4	13,191.2	13,247.0	13,386.9	13,490.2	13,521.5	13,229.8
Mining and Logging													
2002	22.5	22.4	22.1	22.1	23.0	23.6	23.6	23.9	23.9	23.8	23.6	22.7	23.1
2003	20.8	21.0	21.0	21.0	21.8	22.7	23.2	23.2	22.9	23.5	23.0	22.7	22.2
2004	21.5	21.6	21.7	22.2	23.0	23.4	23.4	23.5	23.5	23.8	23.3	22.9	22.8
2005	21.7	21.9	22.0	22.4	23.0	23.8	24.5	24.7	24.8	24.9	24.6	24.3	23.6
2006	23.0	23.4	23.3	23.4	24.8	25.7	26.2	26.6	26.7	26.4	25.9	25.2	25.1
2007	24.6	24.8	24.6	25.3	26.3	27.0	27.7	28.0	28.0	28.2	28.0	27.5	26.7
2008	26.6	27.0	27.0	27.9	28.6	29.2	29.9	30.0	29.9	30.2	29.5	28.7	28.7
2009	27.1	26.5	26.0	25.4	25.5	26.1	26.4	26.3	26.2	26.3	25.8	25.2	26.1
2010	25.0	24.6	25.1	25.4	27.0	27.5	28.1	28.2	28.2	28.1	27.7	27.0	26.8
2011	26.7	27.0	26.9	27.7	28.3	28.9	29.9	30.2	30.2	30.3	30.1	29.7	28.8
2012	29.3	29.0	29.0	29.2	30.3	31.0	31.8	32.0	31.6	31.4	31.1	30.4	30.5
2013	29.6	29.7	29.6	30.1	30.9	31.3	31.3	31.2	31.2	31.0	30.7	30.3	30.6
Construction													
2002	736.1	742.5	753.0	756.6	770.8	783.3	783.4	801.8	798.1	795.9	790.3	780.9	774.4
2003	755.0	752.3	764.9	770.1	788.6	805.9	810.9	827.0	826.6	825.4	819.3	815.7	796.8
2004	792.8	798.3	811.6	830.0	842.5	861.3	875.2	884.1	886.9	884.1	871.5	866.4	850.4
2005	823.8	844.8	862.3	880.4	895.0	915.7	931.5	942.8	947.4	944.2	940.1	935.6	905.3
2006	903.9	916.0	914.6	908.8	940.9	959.0	957.9	966.3	962.7	941.3	923.8	908.8	933.7
2007	874.6	879.9	894.0	890.6	903.5	917.8	918.7	919.8	905.3	886.9	868.9	850.8	892.6
2008	803.3	804.8	803.7	800.3	803.6	805.9	803.2	802.4	788.4	769.6	744.2	723.5	787.7
2009	674.4	644.7	644.1	630.4	632.2	632.3	621.7	619.6	607.6	600.2	594.2	576.2	623.1
2010	550.6	542.7	549.3	553.9	562.2	568.8	572.4	574.8	566.9	566.5	560.4	549.6	559.8
2011	532.7	535.1	534.3	545.8	554.4	562.8	578.6	584.6	584.0	580.6	575.5	567.3	561.3
2012	556.2	556.0	559.1	560.9	579.0	595.2	605.8	612.1	613.1	616.7	615.2	609.7	589.9
2013	597.6	606.5	612.6	618.6	628.3	640.4	651.5	660.6	656.7	654.5	656.2	650.7	636.2

1. Employment by Industry: California, Selected Years, 2002–2013—*Continued*

(Numbers in thousands, not seasonally adjusted)

Industry and year	January	February	March	April	May	June	July	August	September	October	November	December	Annual average
Manufacturing													
2002	1,643.6	1,647.1	1,654.3	1,644.1	1,647.5	1,652.5	1,636.3	1,643.4	1,637.7	1,613.0	1,596.9	1,590.1	1,633.9
2003	1,558.8	1,558.7	1,559.3	1,548.9	1,547.2	1,551.1	1,536.8	1,550.6	1,550.3	1,529.2	1,519.7	1,522.9	1,544.5
2004	1,504.1	1,511.4	1,519.9	1,519.7	1,526.7	1,533.5	1,543.4	1,545.4	1,539.4	1,519.6	1,510.2	1,507.8	1,523.4
2005	1,490.8	1,496.7	1,500.3	1,500.7	1,501.6	1,509.4	1,516.7	1,523.1	1,521.3	1,504.1	1,495.6	1,496.7	1,504.8
2006	1,478.0	1,488.0	1,492.8	1,485.1	1,491.0	1,499.2	1,495.5	1,503.3	1,504.8	1,489.7	1,479.1	1,475.8	1,490.2
2007	1,457.1	1,463.5	1,466.6	1,456.0	1,460.2	1,473.2	1,478.3	1,481.1	1,476.9	1,461.5	1,450.6	1,447.4	1,464.4
2008	1,431.3	1,433.9	1,434.1	1,428.6	1,433.5	1,439.0	1,441.1	1,444.0	1,439.4	1,414.1	1,389.8	1,375.2	1,425.3
2009	1,340.7	1,322.5	1,307.6	1,290.0	1,287.1	1,282.5	1,273.3	1,273.9	1,268.6	1,255.5	1,242.9	1,238.3	1,281.9
2010	1,227.3	1,227.8	1,232.4	1,231.7	1,238.3	1,246.4	1,251.4	1,260.2	1,257.0	1,251.7	1,241.4	1,238.1	1,242.0
2011	1,228.0	1,232.2	1,235.8	1,239.7	1,246.5	1,253.7	1,258.8	1,266.9	1,265.7	1,256.6	1,245.8	1,243.6	1,247.8
2012	1,233.7	1,237.6	1,242.8	1,241.6	1,249.9	1,259.6	1,264.9	1,273.6	1,270.0	1,258.1	1,248.2	1,244.8	1,252.1
2013	1,232.9	1,238.3	1,240.1	1,242.2	1,246.7	1,255.6	1,262.7	1,272.8	1,270.4	1,255.0	1,249.7	1,243.9	1,250.9
Trade, Transportation, and Utilities													
2002	2,695.9	2,678.4	2,692.8	2,689.4	2,705.2	2,724.7	2,710.5	2,717.9	2,726.0	2,728.7	2,780.2	2,828.4	2,723.2
2003	2,698.1	2,681.1	2,684.9	2,679.1	2,692.1	2,708.4	2,693.5	2,702.1	2,712.0	2,746.7	2,776.0	2,821.8	2,716.3
2004	2,700.5	2,690.4	2,705.2	2,707.9	2,727.1	2,746.7	2,744.8	2,749.6	2,755.9	2,786.6	2,846.1	2,881.4	2,753.5
2005	2,776.8	2,759.9	2,766.9	2,768.0	2,782.9	2,796.9	2,807.9	2,820.8	2,835.4	2,849.9	2,909.7	2,964.3	2,820.0
2006	2,829.8	2,814.2	2,827.2	2,826.7	2,846.4	2,866.4	2,866.2	2,879.9	2,888.5	2,899.7	2,964.8	3,006.9	2,876.4
2007	2,895.8	2,871.4	2,878.2	2,864.2	2,881.3	2,892.0	2,907.1	2,911.1	2,912.5	2,923.2	2,987.1	3,031.3	2,912.9
2008	2,894.3	2,867.6	2,863.2	2,848.2	2,852.0	2,853.7	2,843.1	2,836.3	2,827.8	2,818.4	2,837.5	2,850.1	2,849.4
2009	2,713.1	2,669.3	2,647.7	2,621.6	2,629.2	2,625.5	2,604.0	2,603.4	2,610.1	2,621.6	2,665.6	2,696.8	2,642.3
2010	2,598.0	2,578.3	2,578.0	2,590.2	2,604.7	2,613.5	2,616.5	2,628.1	2,627.8	2,650.8	2,706.5	2,742.3	2,627.9
2011	2,641.4	2,625.2	2,624.4	2,641.4	2,653.3	2,660.5	2,669.3	2,682.4	2,683.1	2,702.3	2,766.8	2,794.6	2,678.7
2012	2,704.3	2,673.7	2,677.6	2,685.3	2,704.4	2,717.5	2,724.0	2,734.7	2,737.7	2,757.5	2,843.1	2,863.9	2,735.3
2013	2,758.5	2,744.0	2,742.8	2,754.3	2,771.8	2,784.9	2,796.3	2,810.1	2,805.9	2,824.5	2,905.1	2,931.3	2,802.5
Wholesale Trade													
2002	641.9	645.3	649.4	649.3	651.7	654.3	650.6	652.7	652.9	649.8	650.3	651.8	650.0
2003	642.4	644.5	647.7	648.7	650.6	653.1	647.1	648.9	648.7	645.8	644.3	646.9	647.4
2004	639.5	643.0	646.3	648.4	651.9	657.2	655.9	656.0	655.9	659.7	660.8	661.6	653.0
2005	658.0	660.6	664.3	669.7	673.0	675.7	676.5	677.8	679.5	681.5	682.2	684.7	673.6
2006	681.4	688.0	692.2	695.0	699.1	704.9	704.2	705.7	708.3	706.6	707.4	710.2	700.3
2007	702.5	706.9	711.5	710.5	714.1	716.9	719.7	718.8	719.0	720.8	720.2	722.4	715.3
2008	710.6	711.8	713.7	710.4	710.0	709.1	705.4	703.1	699.5	696.0	688.9	684.0	703.5
2009	665.6	660.5	654.6	649.3	648.1	646.9	640.7	637.3	634.8	637.1	634.9	634.2	645.3
2010	629.8	631.1	632.8	641.8	645.3	647.2	648.4	649.1	648.6	650.8	651.1	651.9	644.0
2011	645.7	648.7	649.2	656.0	657.8	659.0	661.1	663.1	663.0	663.2	663.6	664.7	657.9
2012	659.5	662.9	665.6	669.1	674.3	677.2	678.7	681.8	681.2	684.0	686.2	687.6	675.7
2013	681.4	685.4	688.3	693.1	697.8	700.9	702.4	704.3	704.2	701.2	702.4	707.3	697.4
Retail Trade													
2002	1,568.2	1,545.6	1,558.0	1,551.9	1,561.8	1,575.8	1,567.1	1,570.8	1,579.3	1,585.7	1,637.9	1,684.2	1,582.2
2003	1,577.0	1,558.5	1,558.7	1,553.4	1,561.7	1,572.3	1,566.8	1,573.7	1,579.7	1,615.9	1,648.8	1,693.7	1,588.4
2004	1,589.5	1,575.6	1,584.0	1,584.3	1,597.1	1,607.9	1,604.7	1,609.3	1,611.3	1,631.1	1,689.9	1,728.3	1,617.8
2005	1,638.6	1,618.0	1,622.0	1,615.6	1,624.5	1,634.8	1,643.5	1,654.7	1,664.1	1,676.5	1,735.0	1,783.8	1,659.3
2006	1,663.6	1,640.6	1,646.5	1,644.3	1,654.1	1,663.5	1,666.2	1,676.0	1,677.0	1,690.6	1,752.6	1,785.9	1,680.1
2007	1,695.5	1,666.1	1,669.7	1,653.8	1,663.1	1,668.0	1,676.5	1,682.2	1,678.1	1,687.9	1,751.3	1,787.1	1,689.9
2008	1,682.1	1,649.1	1,646.8	1,635.1	1,633.1	1,635.7	1,633.0	1,627.6	1,619.9	1,618.7	1,647.5	1,662.5	1,640.9
2009	1,562.3	1,528.5	1,514.8	1,498.9	1,505.9	1,504.0	1,494.2	1,496.9	1,502.5	1,512.5	1,560.6	1,589.0	1,522.5
2010	1,507.7	1,487.3	1,486.1	1,489.3	1,496.3	1,500.7	1,502.4	1,510.8	1,509.0	1,528.0	1,582.6	1,611.6	1,517.7
2011	1,531.8	1,512.5	1,510.1	1,515.4	1,521.9	1,527.1	1,533.7	1,541.0	1,540.8	1,558.2	1,621.8	1,644.3	1,546.6
2012	1,570.7	1,538.0	1,536.8	1,537.9	1,547.4	1,551.4	1,555.1	1,560.5	1,560.9	1,578.1	1,659.5	1,671.7	1,572.3
2013	1,585.2	1,564.8	1,561.5	1,566.2	1,576.9	1,585.1	1,589.4	1,597.5	1,592.6	1,612.4	1,684.2	1,700.7	1,601.4
Transportation and Utilities													
2002	485.8	487.5	485.4	488.2	491.7	494.6	492.8	494.4	493.8	493.2	492.0	492.4	491.0
2003	478.7	478.1	478.5	477.0	479.8	483.0	479.6	479.5	483.6	485.0	482.9	481.2	480.6
2004	471.5	471.8	474.9	475.2	478.1	481.6	484.2	484.3	488.7	495.8	495.4	491.5	482.8
2005	480.2	481.3	480.6	482.7	485.4	486.4	487.9	488.3	491.8	491.9	492.5	495.8	487.1
2006	484.8	485.6	488.5	487.4	493.2	498.0	495.8	498.2	503.2	502.5	504.8	510.8	496.1
2007	497.8	498.4	497.0	499.9	504.1	507.1	510.9	510.1	515.4	514.5	515.6	521.8	507.7
2008	501.6	506.7	502.7	502.7	508.9	508.9	504.7	505.6	508.4	503.7	501.1	503.6	504.9
2009	485.2	480.3	478.3	473.4	475.2	474.6	469.1	469.2	472.8	472.0	470.1	473.6	474.5
2010	460.5	459.9	459.1	459.1	463.1	465.6	465.7	468.2	470.2	472.0	472.8	478.8	466.3
2011	463.9	464.0	465.1	470.0	473.6	474.4	474.5	478.3	479.3	480.9	481.4	485.6	474.3
2012	474.1	472.8	475.2	478.3	482.7	488.9	490.2	492.4	495.6	495.4	497.4	504.6	487.3
2013	491.9	493.8	493.0	495.0	497.1	498.9	504.5	508.3	509.1	510.9	518.5	523.3	503.7
Information													
2002	510.2	511.4	519.9	502.6	502.3	501.6	484.6	490.5	481.4	487.8	495.8	479.4	497.3
2003	480.3	487.1	481.7	470.7	475.2	467.9	467.1	478.4	466.3	476.9	483.7	477.8	476.1
2004	485.6	490.7	487.8	477.6	483.5	474.0	478.8	479.4	470.6	483.4	492.5	484.3	482.4
2005	473.1	477.0	480.7	470.3	469.9	470.3	466.9	473.2	472.5	471.4	480.2	478.0	473.6
2006	468.3	476.4	475.6	467.8	468.7	470.8	464.9	465.0	459.5	456.2	456.7	463.6	466.1
2007	463.5	471.4	473.7	464.8	470.3	473.8	471.7	476.0	474.7	464.5	470.7	478.3	471.1
2008	459.6	469.9	478.2	477.6	482.7	486.3	478.9	479.8	481.6	474.6	471.5	472.2	476.1
2009	450.9	452.0	454.3	442.8	440.8	442.8	438.0	437.5	438.0	428.9	431.3	438.3	441.3
2010	425.5	425.6	428.7	420.7	422.4	429.2	429.7	434.1	433.6	427.9	432.0	439.1	429.0
2011	430.9	431.3	432.8	428.1	427.7	429.7	431.2	433.0	429.2	431.1	429.2	433.2	430.6
2012	426.4	427.4	430.3	431.8	430.7	431.1	436.3	438.5	434.1	439.1	445.6	449.7	435.1
2013	438.7	442.1	443.9	444.3	443.8	448.0	450.6	454.2	453.7	457.1	465.2	463.6	450.4

1. Employment by Industry: California, Selected Years, 2002–2013—*Continued*

(Numbers in thousands, not seasonally adjusted)

Industry and year	January	February	March	April	May	June	July	August	September	October	November	December	Annual average
Financial Activities													
2002	828.8	834.4	837.7	838.7	842.4	847.4	846.2	851.5	851.8	853.9	860.2	867.6	846.7
2003	859.1	864.3	869.3	874.6	880.5	884.9	883.3	887.5	886.0	883.8	883.9	888.3	878.8
2004	879.9	883.5	887.9	889.4	892.0	895.1	900.3	901.7	900.2	900.7	903.2	908.2	895.2
2005	901.7	905.8	910.7	911.8	915.2	919.1	923.6	927.0	927.9	930.6	931.4	938.3	920.3
2006	926.9	929.7	932.8	931.9	935.7	934.9	928.3	927.9	925.2	920.4	918.7	921.1	927.8
2007	906.4	912.6	914.3	905.5	904.6	904.0	899.5	895.9	886.6	879.7	875.5	874.7	896.6
2008	856.5	857.5	855.9	849.2	847.6	845.8	843.4	840.0	832.8	828.1	822.9	822.2	841.8
2009	805.8	802.1	798.9	791.3	786.7	784.9	778.5	774.3	766.8	770.4	767.6	768.6	783.0
2010	756.6	757.7	759.3	758.8	758.7	761.1	760.9	760.8	758.9	762.7	761.1	765.3	760.2
2011	758.2	760.1	761.0	758.8	759.7	762.6	762.8	763.2	761.8	763.3	763.4	767.6	761.9
2012	761.3	765.1	768.8	767.3	770.5	774.3	777.3	778.0	775.4	779.4	780.2	784.2	773.5
2013	775.0	778.4	779.1	782.3	785.1	787.0	788.6	788.3	782.7	782.3	778.1	780.5	782.3
Professional and Business Services													
2002	2,096.2	2,109.4	2,132.3	2,115.0	2,117.8	2,125.6	2,112.3	2,127.6	2,123.7	2,120.8	2,127.8	2,130.8	2,119.9
2003	2,065.3	2,078.8	2,096.6	2,091.5	2,089.7	2,097.0	2,075.4	2,090.0	2,085.9	2,080.6	2,082.4	2,090.8	2,085.3
2004	2,033.8	2,055.6	2,079.0	2,079.0	2,086.7	2,102.6	2,102.8	2,116.0	2,112.9	2,126.4	2,133.8	2,145.8	2,097.9
2005	2,095.9	2,122.6	2,138.1	2,144.7	2,141.4	2,158.4	2,163.9	2,180.5	2,190.8	2,189.0	2,199.0	2,211.8	2,161.3
2006	2,166.4	2,194.2	2,211.0	2,217.2	2,227.2	2,252.8	2,249.8	2,269.0	2,274.7	2,281.9	2,285.6	2,291.4	2,243.4
2007	2,214.5	2,242.2	2,257.9	2,245.6	2,252.9	2,271.0	2,268.2	2,278.3	2,277.8	2,293.0	2,294.5	2,298.3	2,266.2
2008	2,227.0	2,248.7	2,254.3	2,256.9	2,248.4	2,255.0	2,246.6	2,252.0	2,243.5	2,231.0	2,208.1	2,193.8	2,238.8
2009	2,111.5	2,095.4	2,079.2	2,058.5	2,048.4	2,045.7	2,032.8	2,038.9	2,029.0	2,060.9	2,065.9	2,066.9	2,061.1
2010	2,005.6	2,027.2	2,037.0	2,057.3	2,057.5	2,076.1	2,079.7	2,092.4	2,087.5	2,122.4	2,120.7	2,121.7	2,073.8
2011	2,066.5	2,089.5	2,096.3	2,104.1	2,106.3	2,115.9	2,135.7	2,149.6	2,160.8	2,175.6	2,181.9	2,188.0	2,130.9
2012	2,153.8	2,186.1	2,201.4	2,206.4	2,216.2	2,237.8	2,239.5	2,258.6	2,261.2	2,290.9	2,302.5	2,304.2	2,238.2
2013	2,255.1	2,285.3	2,297.1	2,311.3	2,316.8	2,327.4	2,332.1	2,356.7	2,354.5	2,377.1	2,373.4	2,383.6	2,330.9
Education and Health Services													
2002	1,594.2	1,622.9	1,636.8	1,632.3	1,642.5	1,630.7	1,614.4	1,617.7	1,641.4	1,660.5	1,673.8	1,677.6	1,637.1
2003	1,651.2	1,677.5	1,693.3	1,712.1	1,720.3	1,714.2	1,690.1	1,690.4	1,715.3	1,731.0	1,740.9	1,750.5	1,707.2
2004	1,724.5	1,748.7	1,760.9	1,756.5	1,756.7	1,748.0	1,728.6	1,731.1	1,758.7	1,784.1	1,791.4	1,793.2	1,756.9
2005	1,763.8	1,786.8	1,795.6	1,805.3	1,808.6	1,798.1	1,773.6	1,777.3	1,809.3	1,830.0	1,839.9	1,839.9	1,802.3
2006	1,808.9	1,835.3	1,845.3	1,845.1	1,847.9	1,837.9	1,812.0	1,817.1	1,848.0	1,865.9	1,874.6	1,878.5	1,843.0
2007	1,861.8	1,895.2	1,911.2	1,905.2	1,913.3	1,900.8	1,886.2	1,889.4	1,922.9	1,947.4	1,960.1	1,965.7	1,913.3
2008	1,942.8	1,976.4	1,983.3	1,997.0	1,998.5	1,985.6	1,955.9	1,963.2	1,993.7	2,016.5	2,026.8	2,039.7	1,990.0
2009	2,009.5	2,034.1	2,044.8	2,052.2	2,055.7	2,042.0	2,013.3	2,016.5	2,039.8	2,070.0	2,071.6	2,077.7	2,043.9
2010	2,028.1	2,045.1	2,051.2	2,070.9	2,067.7	2,049.7	2,020.7	2,025.3	2,054.7	2,078.7	2,085.4	2,094.2	2,056.0
2011	2,059.3	2,084.6	2,091.9	2,096.5	2,093.7	2,072.8	2,039.7	2,044.5	2,078.3	2,102.3	2,114.7	2,128.0	2,083.9
2012	2,112.3	2,149.2	2,156.9	2,159.1	2,163.2	2,147.5	2,109.1	2,124.4	2,148.8	2,255.6	2,262.6	2,276.7	2,172.1
2013	2,260.8	2,292.2	2,302.7	2,309.7	2,308.3	2,282.1	2,270.3	2,286.7	2,307.4	2,350.7	2,352.6	2,361.8	2,307.1
Leisure and Hospitality													
2002	1,318.3	1,335.5	1,355.6	1,382.3	1,403.3	1,419.2	1,410.0	1,417.2	1,402.9	1,384.1	1,375.0	1,385.6	1,382.4
2003	1,345.9	1,362.7	1,376.5	1,388.7	1,404.4	1,425.8	1,425.3	1,432.5	1,418.7	1,406.9	1,401.8	1,411.7	1,400.1
2004	1,380.9	1,400.7	1,418.0	1,425.4	1,447.2	1,460.7	1,471.1	1,474.1	1,461.4	1,444.3	1,438.5	1,450.5	1,439.4
2005	1,408.5	1,424.5	1,446.1	1,468.6	1,483.0	1,502.3	1,504.9	1,509.6	1,497.4	1,483.1	1,480.9	1,492.9	1,475.2
2006	1,451.1	1,472.8	1,491.8	1,506.5	1,526.6	1,548.3	1,548.4	1,556.2	1,540.4	1,526.8	1,523.6	1,535.9	1,519.0
2007	1,496.8	1,514.2	1,534.7	1,548.1	1,569.4	1,590.5	1,593.5	1,595.5	1,580.0	1,567.2	1,562.8	1,571.7	1,560.4
2008	1,529.7	1,545.4	1,563.1	1,578.5	1,593.0	1,609.9	1,611.7	1,607.5	1,585.8	1,559.2	1,543.7	1,544.1	1,572.6
2009	1,489.9	1,491.6	1,494.3	1,504.2	1,522.4	1,529.3	1,526.5	1,522.7	1,504.9	1,491.8	1,477.0	1,482.3	1,503.1
2010	1,440.8	1,450.0	1,463.0	1,497.2	1,510.0	1,526.8	1,533.9	1,536.0	1,523.1	1,515.9	1,505.0	1,517.3	1,501.6
2011	1,476.8	1,491.1	1,506.6	1,524.8	1,541.0	1,554.4	1,565.1	1,569.6	1,561.3	1,547.0	1,544.7	1,546.7	1,535.8
2012	1,520.0	1,538.3	1,558.0	1,583.6	1,606.1	1,627.1	1,633.8	1,643.2	1,627.5	1,616.9	1,612.1	1,617.3	1,598.7
2013	1,590.1	1,612.5	1,634.8	1,662.5	1,688.1	1,706.0	1,708.3	1,709.2	1,694.4	1,686.5	1,678.3	1,685.0	1,671.3
Other Services													
2002	492.5	500.0	503.8	505.9	512.1	515.2	507.4	506.2	506.8	506.5	505.7	505.7	505.7
2003	497.6	503.2	505.5	506.5	509.2	513.5	502.0	502.5	504.4	504.1	501.8	501.8	504.3
2004	494.4	499.7	504.7	504.3	507.0	508.9	506.3	504.0	506.4	504.1	502.7	503.8	503.9
2005	495.8	502.4	507.2	509.3	510.4	513.6	504.9	504.0	506.5	504.5	502.8	504.0	505.5
2006	492.9	499.3	502.5	503.9	510.2	514.5	507.0	511.8	512.2	510.3	510.0	510.1	507.1
2007	498.5	505.7	509.3	507.2	511.2	516.8	514.4	514.8	517.3	517.4	516.4	516.8	512.2
2008	505.7	511.5	515.0	516.4	518.6	520.4	515.3	511.4	510.0	508.5	502.9	499.8	511.3
2009	487.5	488.0	488.8	491.8	492.8	492.8	483.8	482.5	480.2	484.5	481.6	479.4	486.1
2010	475.2	478.1	481.3	484.4	487.7	490.3	488.1	485.4	485.9	490.0	487.5	485.2	484.9
2011	480.0	485.3	486.5	493.7	495.7	496.1	497.4	496.4	498.1	499.3	497.8	497.8	493.7
2012	490.1	496.0	499.0	502.6	508.3	512.0	507.2	507.0	508.1	510.6	508.3	507.2	504.7
2013	500.9	508.0	510.4	515.2	517.9	520.3	517.8	518.0	516.5	520.3	521.1	516.0	515.2
Government													
2002	2,422.6	2,449.8	2,479.2	2,490.5	2,497.0	2,492.1	2,359.0	2,342.1	2,408.0	2,466.9	2,483.2	2,474.7	2,447.1
2003	2,450.9	2,462.9	2,480.1	2,474.7	2,473.7	2,470.3	2,345.5	2,316.1	2,370.9	2,418.9	2,433.0	2,415.8	2,426.1
2004	2,397.3	2,412.3	2,430.2	2,435.5	2,438.1	2,438.5	2,313.1	2,288.9	2,355.9	2,411.9	2,431.3	2,419.5	2,397.7
2005	2,403.7	2,429.8	2,446.1	2,451.9	2,459.3	2,453.7	2,331.9	2,326.8	2,390.5	2,439.8	2,459.1	2,449.4	2,420.2
2006	2,431.2	2,456.9	2,473.4	2,476.9	2,485.6	2,484.1	2,367.5	2,353.7	2,421.8	2,481.3	2,502.2	2,492.4	2,452.3
2007	2,475.1	2,498.8	2,521.2	2,524.9	2,535.4	2,534.5	2,407.3	2,393.1	2,461.9	2,514.4	2,536.7	2,531.5	2,494.6
2008	2,511.2	2,537.2	2,554.3	2,562.2	2,571.8	2,573.4	2,424.6	2,413.8	2,474.9	2,529.4	2,543.0	2,531.1	2,518.9
2009	2,514.0	2,533.0	2,551.2	2,563.3	2,557.8	2,543.0	2,357.4	2,338.9	2,380.6	2,473.0	2,480.4	2,462.6	2,479.6
2010	2,444.2	2,460.0	2,480.2	2,526.3	2,572.1	2,531.4	2,330.2	2,310.6	2,370.5	2,447.6	2,465.2	2,442.7	2,448.4
2011	2,424.3	2,445.6	2,469.2	2,469.6	2,469.8	2,457.5	2,278.3	2,272.6	2,336.4	2,407.9	2,426.0	2,401.6	2,404.9
2012	2,382.4	2,408.3	2,428.1	2,425.7	2,433.6	2,425.8	2,251.7	2,257.4	2,317.5	2,385.8	2,406.7	2,392.1	2,376.3
2013	2,363.3	2,391.4	2,412.7	2,407.5	2,417.6	2,408.1	2,236.4	2,268.0	2,331.9	2,388.4	2,416.4	2,399.7	2,370.1

2. Average Weekly Hours by Selected Industry: California, 2009–2013

(Not seasonally adjusted)

Industry and year	January	February	March	April	May	June	July	August	September	October	November	December	Annual average
Total Private													
2009	33.8	34.2	34.2	33.7	33.7	33.5	33.6	34.1	33.3	33.8	34.3	33.7	33.8
2010	33.5	33.6	33.6	33.7	34.6	33.9	33.9	34.8	33.8	34.1	33.9	34.2	34.0
2011	34.6	34.1	34.1	34.1	34.8	34.1	34.3	34.4	34.3	35.1	34.1	34.3	34.4
2012	34.7	34.0	34.0	34.5	34.1	34.3	35.0	34.4	35.0	34.1	34.0	34.8	34.4
2013	33.8	34.0	34.1	34.2	34.2	35.1	34.2	34.4	35.0	34.2	34.2	35.2	34.4
Goods-Producing													
2009	37.2	36.2	36.9	36.5	37.1	37.4	37.5	37.4	36.4	36.8	37.5	37.6	37.0
2010	37.1	37.2	37.7	37.7	38.2	37.9	37.9	38.7	37.5	38.5	38.8	39.0	38.0
2011	39.0	38.6	38.5	38.5	39.1	38.9	38.7	39.0	38.8	39.1	38.4	38.4	38.7
2012	38.5	38.1	38.1	37.6	38.3	38.6	38.7	38.7	39.0	38.9	38.4	39.0	38.5
2013	38.2	38.5	38.9	38.7	38.6	39.1	38.6	38.9	39.0	39.0	38.7	39.5	38.8
Construction													
2009	35.5	33.3	35.5	34.2	35.2	35.6	36.1	36.1	34.6	35.0	35.6	35.2	35.2
2010	35.3	34.1	35.4	33.9	34.9	35.3	35.8	36.4	34.6	35.4	34.7	35.0	35.1
2011	34.7	34.6	34.5	35.1	35.7	35.6	35.5	35.9	35.4	35.8	34.6	35.1	35.2
2012	35.8	35.1	35.2	34.0	36.4	36.7	36.3	36.5	36.7	36.8	35.9	36.5	36.0
2013	35.9	36.0	36.4	37.0	36.6	37.1	36.7	37.1	36.8	36.8	36.3	37.1	36.7
Manufacturing													
2009	38.0	37.6	37.5	37.5	37.9	38.2	37.0	37.8	37.4	37.8	38.5	39.0	37.8
2010	38.2	38.2	38.4	38.5	38.9	38.6	38.4	39.4	38.5	39.4	39.4	39.7	38.8
2011	39.7	39.2	39.2	39.1	39.7	39.5	38.8	39.1	39.1	39.5	39.2	39.1	39.3
2012	39.0	38.9	38.9	38.8	38.8	39.1	39.5	39.3	39.7	39.6	39.4	40.0	39.3
2013	39.1	39.5	39.9	39.6	39.7	40.2	39.6	39.9	40.2	40.3	40.1	40.9	39.9
Trade, Transportation, and Utilities													
2009	34.6	34.9	34.9	34.7	34.8	34.1	34.3	33.4	33.4	35.1	33.8	33.7	34.3
2010	33.3	33.3	33.4	33.6	34.4	34.0	34.1	34.9	34.3	34.3	34.0	34.7	34.0
2011	34.5	34.0	34.5	34.8	35.3	34.8	34.9	35.1	35.0	35.6	34.6	35.1	34.9
2012	34.8	34.4	34.5	35.0	34.6	34.8	35.4	34.9	35.3	34.3	34.4	35.1	34.8
2013	33.6	34.1	34.4	34.6	34.9	35.7	35.0	35.2	35.6	34.7	34.5	36.3	34.9
Financial Activities													
2009	36.1	37.4	37.2	36.2	36.1	36.3	36.7	37.9	36.6	36.7	38.0	36.5	36.8
2010	36.6	36.9	36.2	36.4	38.1	36.6	36.2	37.9	36.1	36.4	36.2	36.3	36.7
2011	37.2	36.0	35.7	36.0	37.1	36.5	36.7	36.3	36.8	38.1	36.7	36.5	36.6
2012	37.6	36.1	36.2	36.8	36.1	36.3	37.5	36.6	37.6	36.6	36.4	37.7	36.8
2013	36.0	36.1	36.3	36.2	36.3	37.6	36.3	36.4	37.3	36.4	36.5	38.0	36.6
Professional and Business Services													
2009	35.4	36.2	36.0	35.5	35.2	34.3	33.8	35.2	34.6	34.7	36.1	34.9	35.2
2010	35.1	35.2	35.4	35.5	36.5	35.5	35.5	36.6	35.2	35.7	35.3	35.6	35.6
2011	36.4	35.7	35.6	36.0	36.9	36.1	35.9	36.2	36.1	37.0	36.0	35.8	36.1
2012	36.3	35.6	35.6	36.4	35.7	35.7	36.4	35.8	36.6	35.5	35.4	36.5	36.0
2013	35.4	35.6	35.6	35.8	35.6	36.6	35.5	35.8	36.6	35.8	35.8	36.5	35.9
Education and Health Services													
2009	33.2	34.0	34.0	33.3	33.4	33.3	33.4	34.1	33.1	33.2	34.2	33.9	33.6
2010	33.8	33.6	33.4	33.5	34.3	33.4	33.3	34.1	33.6	33.4	33.3	33.5	33.6
2011	34.0	33.6	33.5	32.4	33.3	31.5	32.9	32.7	32.9	33.5	33.0	33.2	33.0
2012	34.2	33.2	33.2	33.9	33.1	33.4	34.1	33.2	34.1	33.3	33.4	34.1	33.6
2013	33.5	33.6	33.4	33.4	33.5	34.3	33.5	33.4	34.4	33.4	33.5	34.2	33.7
Leisure and Hospitality													
2009	25.5	26.3	26.1	25.6	25.5	25.8	26.0	27.5	26.2	26.1	27.0	25.9	26.1
2010	25.6	26.2	26.0	26.1	27.0	26.2	26.5	27.4	26.1	26.1	25.9	25.9	26.3
2011	26.6	26.6	26.4	26.5	27.2	26.5	26.6	26.7	26.0	26.9	26.0	26.1	26.5
2012	27.0	26.2	26.1	27.2	26.4	26.7	27.8	27.0	27.2	26.3	26.1	26.8	26.7
2013	25.9	26.2	26.2	26.2	26.3	27.2	26.4	26.6	26.9	26.1	26.0	26.9	26.4
Other Services													
2009	30.6	30.6	31.0	30.9	30.6	30.7	31.2	31.7	30.3	29.7	30.5	29.3	30.6
2010	30.7	30.6	30.5	30.5	31.9	31.1	31.4	32.2	31.2	31.0	30.3	30.3	31.0
2011	32.5	31.5	31.4	31.7	32.2	32.3	32.3	32.5	31.7	32.6	31.1	31.3	31.9
2012	32.3	31.3	31.3	31.6	31.2	31.3	32.5	31.9	32.1	30.6	30.2	31.4	31.5
2013	30.8	30.8	31.1	31.2	30.9	32.3	31.7	31.3	31.7	30.7	31.0	31.7	31.3

3. Average Hourly Earnings by Selected Industry: California, 2009–2013

(Dollars, not seasonally adjusted)

Industry and year	January	February	March	April	May	June	July	August	September	October	November	December	Annual average
Total Private													
2009	25.41	25.41	25.59	25.43	25.19	25.28	25.20	25.47	25.52	25.68	25.75	25.68	25.47
2010	26.40	26.25	26.22	26.38	26.39	26.19	26.28	26.33	26.29	26.35	26.52	26.67	26.36
2011	26.86	27.06	27.14	26.99	27.15	26.65	26.87	26.62	26.78	26.99	26.86	26.81	26.90
2012	27.23	26.96	26.89	27.09	26.81	26.76	26.79	26.48	26.88	26.71	26.75	27.15	26.87
2013	27.02	26.98	26.85	27.30	27.23	27.45	27.22	27.13	27.51	27.26	27.27	27.42	27.22
Goods-Producing													
2009	27.87	27.70	28.32	28.03	27.88	28.04	27.56	28.03	27.77	27.83	28.03	28.25	27.94
2010	27.90	27.03	27.41	28.19	28.58	28.35	28.47	28.60	28.69	28.65	28.71	28.91	28.30
2011	28.52	28.16	28.30	28.44	28.25	28.03	28.41	28.39	28.45	28.54	28.59	28.92	28.42
2012	28.72	28.50	28.64	28.94	28.61	28.49	28.35	28.18	28.55	28.46	28.64	28.98	28.59
2013	29.08	29.10	28.83	29.05	29.17	29.16	29.24	28.98	29.18	29.09	29.14	29.50	29.13
Construction													
2009	26.95	25.28	26.67	26.42	26.62	27.15	27.52	28.03	28.68	28.82	28.70	29.12	27.47
2010	28.77	26.61	26.94	26.82	26.90	27.42	27.92	28.27	28.46	28.61	29.00	29.40	27.94
2011	27.59	26.21	26.69	26.80	26.90	27.33	27.68	28.30	28.63	28.67	28.88	29.73	27.81
2012	28.98	29.26	29.38	29.63	29.59	29.52	29.77	29.83	30.06	30.15	30.38	30.89	29.81
2013	30.91	30.70	30.57	30.50	30.56	30.75	31.14	31.03	31.28	31.26	31.21	31.63	30.97
Manufacturing													
2009	26.97	26.70	27.08	26.71	26.72	26.55	26.68	26.64	26.68	26.76	27.16	27.37	26.84
2010	27.03	26.49	26.60	26.62	27.10	26.88	26.90	27.03	27.28	27.26	27.31	27.47	27.00
2011	27.07	26.72	26.96	27.28	27.14	26.80	27.02	26.92	27.03	27.27	27.40	27.56	27.10
2012	27.72	27.32	27.56	27.99	27.52	27.40	27.15	26.89	27.40	27.27	27.47	27.77	27.45
2013	27.92	28.05	27.85	28.16	28.33	28.20	28.13	27.77	27.96	27.84	27.94	28.28	28.04
Trade, Transportation, and Utilities													
2009	20.84	21.15	20.90	20.91	20.77	20.72	20.79	21.04	21.21	22.08	21.97	21.48	21.16
2010	24.27	24.39	24.08	23.97	24.07	23.66	23.55	23.32	23.19	23.23	23.15	22.99	23.64
2011	23.10	23.20	24.23	23.97	23.65	23.22	23.09	22.65	22.63	22.69	22.46	22.02	23.06
2012	22.54	22.33	22.06	22.28	21.82	21.78	21.75	21.35	21.80	21.57	21.50	21.96	21.89
2013	21.82	21.85	21.87	21.79	21.74	22.15	21.73	21.57	21.98	21.55	21.44	21.20	21.72
Financial Activities													
2009	31.02	30.84	30.44	30.14	30.21	29.80	30.53	30.94	31.13	30.75	30.93	30.94	30.64
2010	31.13	29.89	30.08	30.09	30.82	30.26	30.86	30.46	30.15	30.14	30.22	30.58	30.39
2011	31.14	31.17	30.59	30.25	30.66	29.78	29.71	30.04	30.16	30.37	30.12	29.89	30.32
2012	30.35	29.94	30.37	30.63	30.70	30.53	30.62	30.10	30.64	30.54	30.55	30.70	30.47
2013	30.77	30.82	30.79	31.47	31.31	31.54	31.51	31.72	31.95	31.61	31.76	32.22	31.46
Professional and Business Services													
2009	30.95	31.00	32.19	31.67	30.79	31.46	31.78	32.00	31.91	31.66	31.83	31.62	31.57
2010	32.18	32.34	32.14	32.47	32.22	32.10	32.39	32.69	32.41	32.47	32.89	33.16	32.46
2011	33.86	34.81	34.35	34.23	34.86	34.07	34.36	33.80	33.93	34.42	33.80	33.90	34.20
2012	34.55	33.87	33.76	34.19	33.71	33.79	34.18	33.49	34.10	33.51	33.79	34.59	33.96
2013	34.12	33.76	33.53	35.37	35.31	35.90	35.13	34.74	35.28	34.70	34.78	35.21	34.83
Education and Health Services													
2009	25.60	25.65	25.35	25.46	25.28	25.35	25.08	25.30	25.49	25.53	25.47	25.39	25.41
2010	25.19	25.38	25.26	25.51	25.12	25.15	25.29	25.37	25.60	25.62	25.93	26.25	25.47
2011	26.03	26.22	26.14	25.85	26.32	25.82	26.56	26.05	26.41	26.71	26.87	27.26	26.36
2012	27.55	27.45	27.35	27.50	27.47	27.59	27.59	27.61	27.75	27.59	27.61	27.86	27.58
2013	27.65	27.72	27.53	27.63	27.51	27.66	27.86	27.92	28.12	28.01	28.07	28.36	27.84
Leisure and Hospitality													
2009	14.48	14.35	14.27	14.22	14.30	14.28	14.24	14.19	14.23	14.29	14.47	14.74	14.34
2010	14.83	14.81	14.75	14.64	14.68	14.51	14.42	14.46	14.63	14.60	14.81	14.97	14.67
2011	14.90	15.00	14.91	14.76	14.89	14.72	14.71	14.71	14.79	14.76	14.61	14.65	14.78
2012	14.73	14.75	14.71	14.76	14.73	14.71	14.54	14.54	14.57	14.61	14.64	14.72	14.67
2013	14.66	14.86	14.73	14.79	14.87	14.85	14.83	14.88	15.05	14.97	15.14	15.20	14.90
Other Services													
2009	20.36	20.64	20.89	20.94	20.90	20.87	20.50	20.84	20.86	21.16	21.41	22.07	20.95
2010	21.42	21.32	20.98	20.79	19.99	19.76	19.81	20.21	19.90	20.19	20.44	20.66	20.45
2011	21.20	21.04	20.95	21.10	21.44	20.85	20.79	20.83	21.11	21.23	20.96	20.84	21.03
2012	21.23	21.34	21.20	21.37	20.78	20.78	21.01	20.70	21.36	21.29	21.45	21.88	21.20
2013	21.82	21.51	21.73	21.74	21.71	21.70	21.48	21.84	22.23	21.83	21.95	22.50	21.84

4. Average Weekly Earnings by Selected Industry: California, 2009–2013

(Dollars, not seasonally adjusted)

Industry and year	January	February	March	April	May	June	July	August	September	October	November	December	Annual average
Total Private													
2009	858.86	869.02	875.18	856.99	848.90	846.88	846.72	868.53	849.82	867.98	883.23	865.42	860.89
2010	884.40	882.00	880.99	889.01	913.09	887.84	890.89	916.28	888.60	898.54	899.03	912.11	896.24
2011	929.36	922.75	925.47	920.36	944.82	908.77	921.64	915.73	918.55	947.35	915.93	919.58	925.36
2012	944.88	916.64	914.26	934.61	914.22	917.87	937.65	910.91	940.80	910.81	909.50	944.82	924.33
2013	913.28	917.32	915.59	933.66	931.27	963.50	930.92	933.27	962.85	932.29	932.63	965.18	936.37
Goods-Producing													
2009	1,036.76	1,002.74	1,045.01	1,023.10	1,034.35	1,048.70	1,033.50	1,048.32	1,010.83	1,024.14	1,051.13	1,062.20	1,033.78
2010	1,035.09	1,005.52	1,033.36	1,062.76	1,091.76	1,074.47	1,079.01	1,106.82	1,075.88	1,103.03	1,113.95	1,127.49	1,075.40
2011	1,112.28	1,086.98	1,089.55	1,094.94	1,104.58	1,090.37	1,099.47	1,107.21	1,103.86	1,115.91	1,097.86	1,110.53	1,099.85
2012	1,105.72	1,085.85	1,091.18	1,088.14	1,095.76	1,099.71	1,097.15	1,090.57	1,113.45	1,107.09	1,099.78	1,130.22	1,100.72
2013	1,110.86	1,120.35	1,121.49	1,124.24	1,125.96	1,140.16	1,128.66	1,127.32	1,138.02	1,134.51	1,127.72	1,165.25	1,130.24
Construction													
2009	956.73	841.82	946.79	903.56	937.02	966.54	993.47	1,011.88	992.33	1,008.70	1,021.72	1,025.02	966.94
2010	1,015.58	907.40	953.68	909.20	938.81	967.93	999.54	1,029.03	984.72	1,012.79	1,006.30	1,029.00	980.69
2011	957.37	906.87	920.81	940.68	960.33	972.95	982.64	1,015.97	1,013.50	1,026.39	999.25	1,043.52	978.91
2012	1,037.48	1,027.03	1,034.18	1,007.42	1,077.08	1,083.38	1,080.65	1,088.80	1,103.20	1,109.52	1,090.64	1,127.49	1,073.16
2013	1,109.67	1,105.20	1,112.75	1,128.50	1,118.50	1,140.83	1,142.84	1,151.21	1,151.10	1,150.37	1,132.92	1,173.47	1,136.60
Manufacturing													
2009	1,024.86	1,003.92	1,015.50	1,001.63	1,012.69	1,014.21	987.16	1,006.99	997.83	1,011.53	1,045.66	1,067.43	1,014.55
2010	1,032.55	1,011.92	1,021.44	1,024.87	1,054.19	1,037.57	1,032.96	1,064.98	1,050.28	1,074.04	1,076.01	1,090.56	1,047.60
2011	1,074.68	1,047.42	1,056.83	1,066.65	1,077.46	1,058.60	1,048.38	1,052.57	1,056.87	1,077.17	1,074.08	1,077.60	1,065.03
2012	1,081.08	1,062.75	1,072.08	1,086.01	1,067.78	1,071.34	1,072.43	1,056.78	1,087.78	1,079.89	1,082.32	1,110.80	1,078.79
2013	1,091.67	1,107.98	1,111.22	1,115.14	1,124.70	1,133.64	1,113.95	1,108.02	1,123.99	1,121.95	1,120.39	1,156.65	1,118.80
Trade, Transportation, and Utilities													
2009	721.06	738.14	729.41	725.58	722.80	706.55	713.10	702.74	708.41	775.01	742.59	723.88	725.79
2010	808.19	812.19	804.27	805.39	828.01	804.44	803.06	813.87	795.42	796.79	787.10	797.75	803.76
2011	796.95	788.80	835.94	834.16	834.85	808.06	805.84	795.02	792.05	807.76	777.12	772.90	804.79
2012	784.39	768.15	761.07	779.80	754.97	757.94	769.95	745.12	769.54	739.85	739.60	770.80	761.77
2013	733.15	745.09	752.33	753.93	758.73	790.76	760.55	759.26	782.49	747.79	739.68	769.56	758.03
Financial Activities													
2009	1,119.82	1,153.42	1,132.37	1,091.07	1,090.58	1,081.74	1,120.45	1,172.63	1,139.36	1,128.53	1,175.34	1,129.31	1,127.55
2010	1,139.36	1,102.94	1,088.90	1,095.28	1,174.24	1,107.52	1,117.13	1,154.43	1,088.42	1,097.10	1,093.96	1,110.05	1,115.31
2011	1,158.41	1,122.12	1,092.06	1,089.00	1,137.49	1,086.97	1,090.36	1,090.45	1,109.89	1,157.10	1,105.40	1,090.99	1,109.71
2012	1,141.16	1,080.83	1,099.39	1,127.18	1,108.27	1,108.24	1,148.25	1,101.66	1,152.06	1,117.76	1,112.02	1,157.39	1,121.30
2013	1,107.72	1,112.60	1,117.68	1,139.21	1,136.55	1,185.90	1,143.81	1,154.61	1,191.74	1,150.60	1,159.24	1,224.36	1,151.44
Professional and Business Services													
2009	1,095.63	1,122.20	1,158.84	1,124.29	1,083.81	1,079.08	1,074.16	1,126.40	1,104.09	1,098.60	1,149.06	1,103.54	1,111.26
2010	1,129.52	1,138.37	1,137.76	1,152.69	1,176.03	1,139.55	1,149.85	1,196.45	1,140.83	1,159.18	1,161.02	1,180.50	1,155.58
2011	1,232.50	1,242.72	1,222.86	1,232.28	1,286.33	1,229.93	1,233.52	1,223.56	1,224.87	1,273.54	1,216.80	1,213.62	1,234.62
2012	1,254.17	1,205.77	1,201.86	1,244.52	1,203.45	1,206.30	1,244.15	1,198.94	1,248.06	1,189.61	1,196.17	1,262.54	1,222.56
2013	1,207.85	1,201.86	1,193.67	1,266.25	1,257.04	1,313.94	1,247.12	1,243.69	1,291.25	1,242.26	1,245.12	1,285.17	1,250.40
Education and Health Services													
2009	849.92	872.10	861.90	847.82	844.35	844.16	837.67	862.73	843.72	847.60	871.07	860.72	853.78
2010	851.42	852.77	843.68	854.59	861.62	840.01	842.16	865.12	860.16	855.71	863.47	879.38	855.79
2011	885.02	880.99	875.69	837.54	876.46	813.33	873.82	851.84	868.89	894.79	886.71	905.03	869.88
2012	942.21	911.34	908.02	932.25	909.26	921.51	940.82	916.65	946.28	918.75	922.17	950.03	926.69
2013	926.28	931.39	919.50	922.84	921.59	948.74	933.31	932.53	967.33	935.53	940.35	969.91	938.21
Leisure and Hospitality													
2009	369.24	377.41	372.45	364.03	364.65	368.42	370.24	390.23	372.83	372.97	390.69	381.77	374.27
2010	379.65	388.02	383.50	382.10	396.36	380.16	382.13	396.20	381.84	381.06	383.58	387.72	385.82
2011	396.34	399.00	393.62	391.14	405.01	390.08	391.29	392.76	384.54	397.04	379.86	382.37	391.67
2012	397.71	386.45	383.93	401.47	388.87	392.76	404.21	392.58	396.30	384.24	382.10	394.50	391.69
2013	379.69	389.33	385.93	387.50	391.08	403.92	391.51	395.81	404.85	390.72	393.64	408.88	393.36
Other Services													
2009	623.02	631.58	647.59	647.05	639.54	640.71	639.60	660.63	632.06	628.45	653.01	646.65	641.07
2010	657.59	652.39	639.89	634.10	637.68	614.54	622.03	650.76	620.88	625.89	629.55	626.00	633.95
2011	689.00	662.76	657.83	668.87	690.37	673.46	671.52	676.98	669.19	692.10	651.86	652.29	670.86
2012	685.73	667.94	663.56	675.29	648.34	650.41	682.83	660.33	685.66	651.47	647.79	687.03	667.80
2013	672.06	662.51	675.80	678.29	670.84	700.91	680.92	683.59	704.69	670.18	680.45	713.25	683.59

COLORADO
At a Glance

Population:
    2000 census: 4,302,086
    2010 census: 5,029,196
    2013 estimate: 5,268,367

Percent change in population:
    2000–2010: 16.9%
    2010–2013: 4.8%

Percent change in total nonfarm employment:
    2000–2010: 0.4%
    2010–2013: 4.8%

Industry with the largest growth in employment, 2000–2013 (thousands):
    Education and Health Services, 94.0

Industry with the largest decline or smallest growth in employment, 2000–2013 (thousands):
    Manufacturing, -56.1

Civilian labor force:
    2000: 2,364,990
    2010: 2,722,913
    2013: 2,754,870

Unemployment rate and rank among states (lowest to highest):
    2000: 2.78%, 3rd
    2010: 9.0%, 29th
    2013: 6.8%, 26th

Over-the-year change in unemployment rates:
    2010–2011: -0.5 %
    2011–2012: -0.7%
    2012–2013: -1.0%

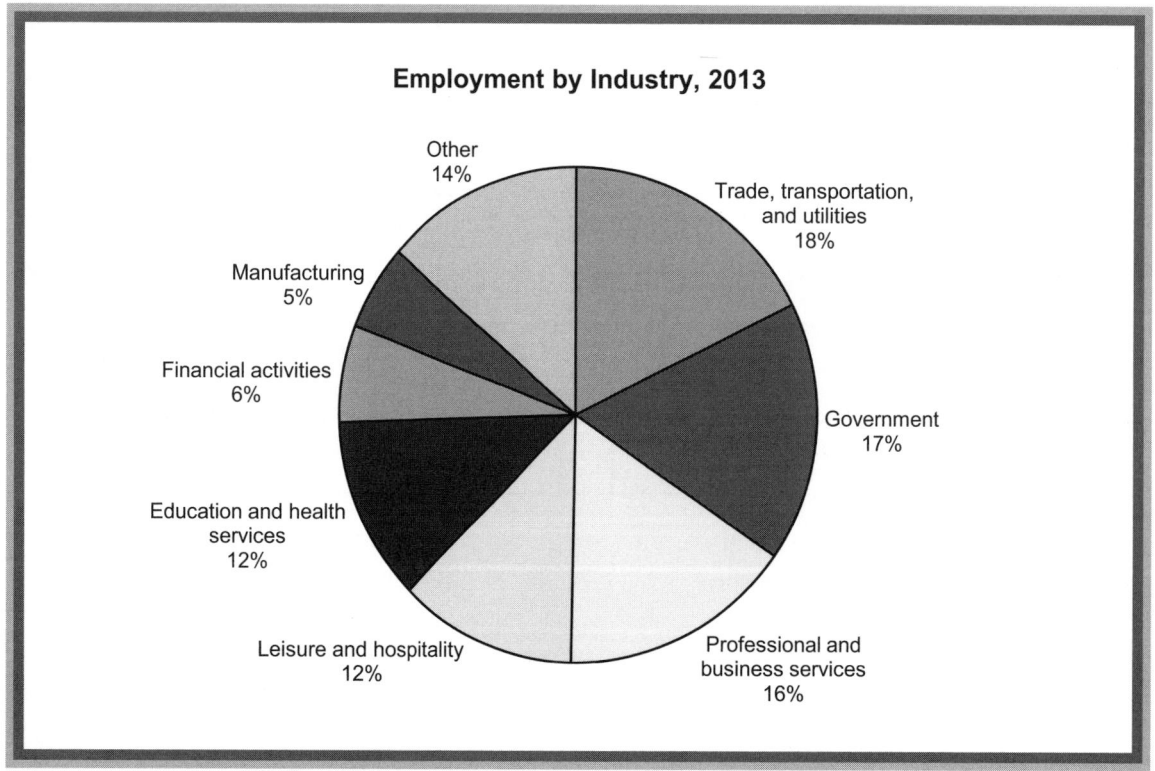

Employment by Industry, 2013

1. Employment by Industry: Colorado, Selected Years, 2002–2013

(Numbers in thousands, not seasonally adjusted)

Industry and year	January	February	March	April	May	June	July	August	September	October	November	December	Annual average
Total Nonfarm													
2002	2,148.8	2,159.6	2,172.9	2,181.8	2,191.1	2,214.2	2,193.6	2,199.7	2,189.0	2,178.8	2,183.0	2,197.7	2,184.2
2003	2,131.3	2,135.4	2,139.3	2,138.4	2,147.2	2,169.2	2,156.1	2,163.7	2,158.0	2,159.4	2,158.0	2,177.4	2,152.8
2004	2,123.5	2,132.9	2,151.8	2,168.0	2,174.1	2,201.8	2,190.0	2,196.3	2,197.2	2,196.0	2,199.6	2,224.4	2,179.6
2005	2,163.5	2,181.9	2,199.1	2,207.3	2,215.8	2,244.6	2,238.4	2,241.4	2,247.7	2,244.0	2,251.3	2,276.6	2,226.0
2006	2,220.1	2,235.2	2,255.0	2,259.9	2,274.3	2,307.4	2,286.4	2,294.1	2,295.1	2,293.3	2,303.0	2,325.8	2,279.1
2007	2,262.6	2,280.5	2,306.4	2,313.1	2,327.7	2,358.3	2,342.1	2,350.4	2,352.3	2,350.5	2,359.1	2,372.9	2,331.3
2008	2,314.5	2,330.9	2,343.6	2,349.0	2,359.8	2,379.0	2,363.3	2,369.4	2,361.0	2,351.9	2,341.0	2,340.5	2,350.3
2009	2,271.2	2,261.9	2,257.9	2,248.2	2,250.9	2,258.8	2,238.1	2,235.5	2,231.9	2,231.3	2,227.0	2,234.7	2,245.6
2010	2,174.8	2,188.5	2,201.2	2,211.8	2,225.6	2,241.0	2,231.5	2,234.2	2,228.7	2,236.5	2,238.5	2,254.8	2,222.3
2011	2,202.9	2,213.5	2,229.0	2,248.1	2,252.7	2,274.7	2,263.5	2,274.3	2,280.2	2,277.6	2,285.0	2,301.7	2,258.6
2012	2,249.6	2,263.2	2,282.6	2,292.6	2,303.1	2,330.8	2,319.3	2,329.0	2,330.4	2,341.1	2,351.1	2,363.6	2,313.0
2013	2,311.0	2,332.3	2,349.9	2,359.1	2,371.8	2,397.6	2,390.2	2,404.2	2,404.3	2,408.5	2,417.4	2,426.5	2,381.1
Total Private													
2002	1,804.7	1,804.7	1,814.7	1,823.6	1,828.8	1,858.5	1,854.9	1,859.2	1,832.5	1,814.0	1,817.1	1,833.0	1,828.8
2003	1,780.8	1,774.9	1,776.8	1,778.0	1,781.0	1,813.4	1,818.1	1,825.0	1,801.8	1,797.0	1,795.7	1,816.8	1,796.6
2004	1,773.9	1,773.5	1,789.6	1,804.4	1,807.8	1,842.7	1,851.4	1,855.0	1,836.8	1,829.0	1,831.8	1,857.9	1,821.2
2005	1,810.7	1,817.2	1,833.2	1,839.8	1,845.1	1,881.6	1,893.2	1,896.3	1,882.7	1,873.1	1,880.6	1,906.9	1,863.4
2006	1,863.3	1,866.8	1,883.4	1,889.1	1,899.8	1,939.3	1,937.6	1,942.7	1,925.3	1,918.1	1,927.0	1,950.5	1,911.9
2007	1,902.3	1,905.8	1,928.4	1,934.6	1,945.7	1,983.7	1,986.6	1,991.1	1,972.8	1,966.4	1,973.5	1,988.9	1,956.7
2008	1,943.8	1,947.6	1,957.3	1,962.1	1,967.2	1,997.0	1,998.7	1,999.5	1,972.5	1,956.4	1,945.0	1,947.2	1,966.2
2009	1,888.7	1,869.8	1,863.2	1,851.6	1,849.4	1,868.9	1,869.0	1,864.5	1,839.4	1,831.2	1,827.8	1,837.8	1,855.1
2010	1,792.4	1,792.5	1,801.4	1,811.7	1,814.0	1,846.5	1,857.0	1,860.2	1,835.8	1,836.2	1,837.1	1,856.3	1,828.4
2011	1,819.5	1,817.6	1,830.6	1,847.7	1,849.4	1,882.4	1,891.9	1,902.0	1,884.8	1,876.4	1,883.1	1,903.0	1,865.7
2012	1,865.8	1,866.8	1,883.0	1,891.8	1,898.7	1,936.8	1,946.2	1,951.4	1,932.2	1,937.8	1,945.9	1,961.9	1,918.2
2013	1,919.2	1,926.8	1,942.1	1,950.4	1,958.6	1,996.5	2,009.1	2,018.0	1,995.4	1,992.6	2,000.3	2,013.9	1,976.9
Goods-Producing													
2002	328.1	327.2	330.7	334.4	340.2	344.6	343.9	343.7	337.8	334.6	329.7	324.7	335.0
2003	312.2	309.4	308.8	310.9	315.6	321.0	320.9	320.7	316.9	317.2	313.2	310.4	314.8
2004	301.1	300.0	304.7	310.7	314.7	321.8	324.2	324.4	322.4	322.8	319.9	317.6	315.4
2005	307.4	310.0	314.3	317.3	322.1	330.5	335.3	336.6	334.9	333.8	333.0	331.3	325.5
2006	323.1	324.3	328.8	331.5	337.4	345.1	344.3	344.5	342.0	340.3	336.9	334.7	336.1
2007	321.2	321.8	328.7	332.4	339.7	347.4	348.5	348.5	344.6	345.3	342.6	337.0	338.1
2008	326.2	326.0	328.4	330.7	336.6	342.3	341.7	341.4	336.6	334.2	328.0	318.7	332.6
2009	300.9	293.9	289.9	284.9	285.1	287.0	285.5	282.9	278.6	276.1	272.1	265.7	283.6
2010	255.0	253.5	254.9	259.2	262.8	268.6	270.7	270.1	268.2	269.2	266.9	265.0	263.7
2011	254.8	253.6	257.4	263.8	266.3	272.6	275.5	277.4	276.0	276.8	275.2	273.1	268.5
2012	265.0	264.4	266.9	270.9	275.8	281.4	283.3	284.2	282.4	284.8	283.3	281.4	277.0
2013	273.5	275.1	278.8	281.7	288.1	295.0	297.6	300.3	298.3	298.9	297.2	293.2	289.8
Service-Providing													
2002	1,820.7	1,832.4	1,842.2	1,847.4	1,850.9	1,869.6	1,849.7	1,856.0	1,851.2	1,844.2	1,853.3	1,873.0	1,849.2
2003	1,819.1	1,826.0	1,830.5	1,827.5	1,831.6	1,848.2	1,835.2	1,843.0	1,841.1	1,842.2	1,844.8	1,867.0	1,838.0
2004	1,822.4	1,832.9	1,847.1	1,857.3	1,859.4	1,880.0	1,865.8	1,871.9	1,874.8	1,873.2	1,879.7	1,906.8	1,864.3
2005	1,856.1	1,871.9	1,884.8	1,890.0	1,893.7	1,914.1	1,903.1	1,904.8	1,912.8	1,910.2	1,918.3	1,945.3	1,900.4
2006	1,897.0	1,910.9	1,926.2	1,928.4	1,936.9	1,962.3	1,942.1	1,949.6	1,953.1	1,953.0	1,966.1	1,991.1	1,943.1
2007	1,941.4	1,958.7	1,977.7	1,980.7	1,988.0	2,010.9	1,993.6	2,001.9	2,007.7	2,005.2	2,016.5	2,035.9	1,993.2
2008	1,988.3	2,004.9	2,015.2	2,018.3	2,023.2	2,036.7	2,021.6	2,028.0	2,024.4	2,017.7	2,013.0	2,021.8	2,017.8
2009	1,970.3	1,968.0	1,968.0	1,963.3	1,965.8	1,971.8	1,952.6	1,952.6	1,953.3	1,955.2	1,954.9	1,969.0	1,962.1
2010	1,919.8	1,935.0	1,946.3	1,952.6	1,962.8	1,972.4	1,960.8	1,964.1	1,960.5	1,967.3	1,971.6	1,989.8	1,958.6
2011	1,948.1	1,959.9	1,971.6	1,984.3	1,986.4	2,002.1	1,988.0	1,996.9	2,004.2	2,000.8	2,009.8	2,028.6	1,990.1
2012	1,984.6	1,998.8	2,015.7	2,021.7	2,027.3	2,049.4	2,036.0	2,044.8	2,048.0	2,056.3	2,067.8	2,082.2	2,036.1
2013	2,037.5	2,057.2	2,071.1	2,077.4	2,083.7	2,102.6	2,092.6	2,103.9	2,106.0	2,109.6	2,120.2	2,133.3	2,091.3
Mining and Logging													
2002	12.9	12.8	12.9	12.8	12.9	13.1	13.2	13.1	13.1	13.0	12.8	12.7	12.9
2003	12.5	12.6	12.7	12.8	13.1	13.3	13.4	13.5	13.4	13.6	13.6	13.5	13.2
2004	13.2	13.4	13.6	13.9	14.2	14.5	14.9	15.1	15.0	15.0	15.2	15.3	14.4
2005	15.4	15.8	16.1	16.2	16.5	17.2	17.7	18.1	18.1	18.2	18.5	18.7	17.2
2006	18.7	19.1	19.6	19.7	20.3	21.1	21.6	22.2	22.2	22.7	22.8	23.3	21.1
2007	23.1	23.6	23.9	24.5	25.2	25.9	25.9	26.2	25.8	25.9	26.2	26.2	25.2
2008	26.4	26.7	26.8	27.5	28.0	28.6	28.9	29.2	29.2	30.0	30.2	29.9	28.5
2009	28.4	27.0	26.0	24.2	23.9	23.6	23.1	23.0	22.9	22.8	22.7	22.8	24.2
2010	22.5	22.8	23.0	23.5	23.9	24.4	25.0	25.2	25.1	25.4	25.5	26.0	24.4
2011	25.7	25.9	26.3	26.8	27.2	27.9	28.5	28.9	28.7	29.5	29.8	30.1	27.9
2012	30.0	30.2	30.3	30.2	30.4	30.7	30.7	30.6	30.1	30.1	29.9	29.9	30.3
2013	29.5	29.6	29.6	29.6	30.0	30.5	30.8	31.2	31.2	31.5	31.3	31.3	30.5
Construction													
2002	150.5	151.3	154.5	158.8	164.3	168.4	168.5	168.8	164.5	162.2	158.5	154.3	160.4
2003	145.2	143.1	143.4	145.6	150.3	155.3	156.1	155.9	153.4	153.7	149.8	147.2	149.9
2004	140.1	138.7	142.7	147.7	151.1	156.3	158.3	158.2	157.0	157.4	154.8	152.7	151.3
2005	144.7	146.3	150.1	153.3	157.7	164.6	168.1	169.3	168.3	167.2	166.0	164.2	160.0
2006	157.7	158.3	161.9	164.7	169.7	175.7	174.6	174.4	172.6	170.7	167.6	165.3	167.8
2007	154.0	154.4	160.5	164.1	169.8	175.7	176.9	176.7	173.1	173.1	170.1	164.7	167.8
2008	155.4	155.6	157.9	160.0	165.0	169.6	169.5	169.2	166.0	163.4	158.5	151.3	161.8
2009	138.4	134.8	133.3	131.4	132.7	135.5	135.0	133.2	130.0	127.9	124.6	118.9	131.3
2010	110.3	108.6	109.6	112.9	115.3	119.3	120.6	119.6	118.2	118.3	115.8	113.1	115.1
2011	104.3	102.7	105.3	110.1	111.6	116.0	117.5	118.6	117.5	117.5	115.7	113.0	112.5
2012	106.5	105.4	107.4	111.0	115.1	119.2	120.5	121.4	120.5	122.4	121.1	119.4	115.8
2013	113.4	114.4	117.5	120.3	125.9	131.3	133.2	135.3	133.8	133.6	131.3	127.8	126.5

1. Employment by Industry: Colorado, Selected Years, 2002–2013—*Continued*

(Numbers in thousands, not seasonally adjusted)

Industry and year	January	February	March	April	May	June	July	August	September	October	November	December	Annual average
Manufacturing													
2002	164.7	163.1	163.3	162.8	163.0	163.1	162.2	161.8	160.2	159.4	158.4	157.7	161.6
2003	154.5	153.7	152.7	152.5	152.2	152.4	151.4	151.3	150.1	150.1	149.9	149.7	151.7
2004	147.8	147.9	148.4	149.1	149.4	151.0	151.0	151.1	150.4	150.4	149.9	149.6	149.7
2005	147.3	147.9	148.1	147.8	147.9	148.7	149.5	149.2	148.5	148.4	148.5	148.4	148.4
2006	146.7	146.9	147.3	147.1	147.4	148.3	148.1	147.9	147.2	146.9	146.5	146.1	147.2
2007	144.1	143.8	144.3	143.8	144.7	145.8	145.7	145.6	145.7	146.3	146.3	146.1	145.2
2008	144.4	143.7	143.7	143.2	143.6	144.1	143.3	143.0	141.4	140.8	139.3	137.5	142.3
2009	134.1	132.1	130.6	129.3	128.5	127.9	127.4	126.7	125.7	125.4	124.8	124.0	128.0
2010	122.2	122.1	122.3	122.8	123.6	124.9	125.1	125.3	124.9	125.5	125.6	125.9	124.2
2011	124.8	125.0	125.8	126.9	127.5	128.7	129.5	129.9	129.8	129.8	129.7	130.0	128.1
2012	128.5	128.8	129.2	129.7	130.3	131.5	132.1	132.2	131.8	132.3	132.3	132.1	130.9
2013	130.6	131.1	131.7	131.8	132.2	133.2	133.6	133.8	133.3	133.8	134.6	134.1	132.8
Trade, Transportation, and Utilities													
2002	409.0	405.3	406.4	408.1	410.3	415.0	413.7	413.6	410.6	409.8	418.3	424.6	412.1
2003	405.6	401.6	400.8	399.2	399.3	402.0	402.5	404.1	402.6	405.4	412.2	418.3	404.5
2004	401.7	397.7	399.3	401.5	403.2	406.9	407.9	408.6	406.3	408.2	415.6	422.8	406.6
2005	405.8	403.7	406.1	405.9	407.4	411.7	413.7	413.3	414.3	416.7	425.1	431.8	413.0
2006	414.2	409.5	411.9	413.3	414.8	419.6	418.9	419.6	418.7	421.9	431.2	438.3	419.3
2007	424.2	419.7	422.3	422.7	424.4	428.9	430.5	430.8	429.7	431.6	440.1	445.3	429.2
2008	430.9	426.6	428.2	427.7	427.8	431.5	431.8	431.7	427.8	426.1	428.8	432.1	429.3
2009	413.4	406.4	403.2	400.7	401.5	404.0	402.7	402.1	399.4	399.9	404.2	408.4	403.8
2010	393.0	391.0	391.6	392.7	394.6	398.6	400.0	400.4	396.5	398.8	404.5	409.6	397.6
2011	395.1	392.6	393.8	397.2	398.9	402.6	403.9	404.8	401.8	403.6	410.9	415.6	401.7
2012	402.5	399.2	401.1	402.6	405.3	409.9	411.3	411.4	409.8	413.5	422.5	427.1	409.7
2013	412.6	410.7	412.0	413.2	415.7	420.3	421.8	423.7	421.3	421.7	427.8	432.7	419.5
Wholesale Trade													
2002	95.7	95.7	95.7	95.6	95.7	95.8	95.6	95.1	94.5	93.9	93.7	94.0	95.1
2003	92.8	92.3	92.4	92.2	92.2	92.5	92.2	91.9	91.5	91.9	91.5	91.8	92.1
2004	90.6	90.7	91.2	91.6	91.8	92.5	92.3	92.4	92.3	92.4	92.6	92.8	91.9
2005	91.7	92.1	92.6	92.9	93.2	93.7	94.2	94.4	94.4	94.2	94.3	94.7	93.5
2006	93.9	94.3	94.9	95.4	96.1	97.2	97.0	97.4	97.2	97.5	97.9	98.5	96.4
2007	97.2	97.7	98.4	98.7	99.2	100.0	99.9	100.0	99.6	100.2	100.3	100.5	99.3
2008	99.5	99.8	100.1	100.4	100.7	101.0	101.0	100.7	100.2	99.7	99.0	98.8	100.1
2009	96.7	95.7	94.7	93.8	93.6	93.4	92.8	92.4	91.7	91.7	91.3	91.4	93.3
2010	90.1	89.9	90.0	90.4	90.6	91.1	91.3	91.3	90.9	91.3	91.2	91.4	90.8
2011	90.5	90.6	91.0	91.6	91.9	92.3	92.6	92.8	92.5	92.4	92.5	92.6	91.9
2012	91.7	92.1	92.7	93.3	93.8	94.5	94.9	95.0	94.8	95.3	95.3	95.8	94.1
2013	94.6	95.1	95.5	96.0	96.4	97.2	97.3	97.5	97.2	96.8	96.9	96.8	96.4
Retail Trade													
2002	240.2	236.4	237.6	239.1	240.8	244.9	243.5	243.5	241.3	241.3	249.1	254.5	242.7
2003	238.7	235.4	234.6	234.5	235.5	238.0	238.3	239.9	239.0	240.9	247.2	252.2	239.5
2004	238.8	234.7	235.6	236.9	238.3	240.7	241.4	242.2	240.4	242.4	249.5	254.7	241.3
2005	240.9	238.3	240.3	240.1	241.9	244.8	245.7	245.1	246.2	248.4	256.4	261.0	245.8
2006	246.3	241.4	243.0	244.2	245.0	247.4	247.3	247.5	246.8	250.0	258.4	262.5	248.3
2007	251.1	246.7	248.4	248.3	249.6	252.6	254.3	254.4	253.8	254.7	262.2	265.4	253.5
2008	254.0	250.3	251.4	250.7	250.6	253.5	253.7	254.1	251.7	251.3	254.3	256.1	252.6
2009	242.9	237.9	236.3	234.3	236.0	238.2	237.8	237.6	236.2	236.7	241.6	244.0	238.3
2010	232.9	230.8	231.5	233.1	234.8	237.9	239.3	239.4	236.2	237.6	243.0	245.9	236.9
2011	235.0	233.0	233.7	236.5	237.9	240.5	241.1	242.0	239.6	241.1	247.6	250.4	239.9
2012	240.1	236.4	237.8	238.8	240.8	243.9	244.6	244.5	243.3	245.1	253.2	255.8	243.7
2013	244.2	241.8	242.9	244.0	245.9	249.4	250.7	252.0	250.0	251.4	256.9	259.5	249.1
Transportation and Utilities													
2002	73.1	73.2	73.1	73.4	73.8	74.3	74.6	75.0	74.8	74.6	75.5	76.1	74.3
2003	74.1	73.9	73.8	72.5	71.6	71.5	72.0	72.3	72.1	72.6	73.5	74.3	72.9
2004	72.3	72.3	72.5	73.0	73.1	73.7	74.2	74.0	73.6	73.4	73.5	75.3	73.4
2005	73.2	73.3	73.2	72.9	72.3	73.2	73.8	73.8	73.7	74.1	74.4	76.1	73.7
2006	74.0	73.8	74.0	73.7	73.7	75.0	74.6	74.7	74.7	74.4	74.9	77.3	74.6
2007	75.9	75.3	75.5	75.7	75.6	76.3	76.3	76.4	76.3	76.7	77.6	79.4	76.4
2008	77.4	76.5	76.7	76.6	76.5	77.0	77.1	76.9	75.9	75.1	75.5	77.2	76.5
2009	73.8	72.8	72.2	72.6	71.9	72.4	72.1	72.1	71.5	71.5	71.3	73.0	72.3
2010	70.0	70.3	70.1	69.2	69.2	69.6	69.4	69.7	69.4	69.9	70.3	72.3	70.0
2011	69.6	69.0	69.1	69.1	69.1	69.8	70.2	70.0	69.7	70.1	70.8	72.6	69.9
2012	70.7	70.7	70.6	70.5	70.7	71.5	71.8	71.9	71.7	73.1	74.0	75.5	71.9
2013	73.8	73.8	73.6	73.2	73.4	73.7	73.8	74.2	74.1	73.5	74.0	76.4	74.0
Information													
2002	98.1	97.0	96.2	95.2	94.1	93.7	91.7	91.0	89.9	89.3	89.4	88.6	92.9
2003	86.5	86.1	85.7	84.9	84.8	84.8	84.5	84.2	83.3	83.1	83.6	83.7	84.6
2004	82.7	82.8	82.6	81.9	81.9	81.9	81.2	80.9	79.5	79.3	79.6	79.6	81.2
2005	78.3	77.9	77.8	77.1	77.1	77.1	76.8	76.4	76.0	75.8	76.0	76.2	76.9
2006	75.8	75.6	75.8	75.4	75.7	75.7	75.3	75.2	74.7	75.0	75.4	75.5	75.4
2007	74.9	75.0	75.0	75.8	76.2	77.0	76.7	76.8	76.3	77.3	77.6	77.9	76.4
2008	77.4	77.6	77.4	77.2	77.0	77.2	77.0	76.8	76.3	76.1	76.0	76.1	76.8
2009	76.7	76.2	76.0	75.4	75.0	74.8	74.5	73.9	73.5	73.5	73.6	72.9	74.7
2010	72.2	71.9	72.0	71.7	71.8	72.3	71.8	72.0	71.5	71.9	72.5	72.5	72.0
2011	72.3	72.2	71.8	71.8	71.6	71.5	71.2	71.1	70.9	70.7	70.8	70.5	71.4
2012	70.2	70.2	70.3	69.7	69.8	70.0	69.6	69.5	69.2	69.4	69.7	69.9	69.8
2013	69.5	69.7	69.7	69.4	69.6	70.3	70.4	70.4	69.7	69.7	68.7	69.9	70.1	69.8

1. Employment by Industry: Colorado, Selected Years, 2002–2013—*Continued*

(Numbers in thousands, not seasonally adjusted)

Industry and year	January	February	March	April	May	June	July	August	September	October	November	December	Annual average
Financial Activities													
2002	147.7	148.3	148.7	147.8	147.6	149.0	149.3	150.2	149.6	150.3	151.8	154.1	149.5
2003	152.4	152.8	153.2	153.3	153.2	154.6	155.5	156.0	154.6	154.2	153.8	155.9	154.1
2004	153.5	153.8	154.2	154.0	153.3	154.7	155.2	155.2	154.6	154.6	154.8	157.1	154.6
2005	155.2	156.0	157.0	157.2	157.1	158.7	159.6	160.0	159.9	159.3	159.9	162.4	158.5
2006	159.3	159.8	160.2	160.0	160.0	161.3	161.0	161.1	160.3	159.8	160.1	162.3	160.4
2007	159.6	160.1	160.4	159.9	159.2	160.5	160.3	160.0	158.7	157.8	157.9	159.2	159.5
2008	157.0	157.4	157.7	156.9	156.0	156.6	156.6	155.7	154.0	153.2	152.5	153.7	155.6
2009	150.5	149.8	149.1	148.7	147.9	148.3	147.9	147.7	146.1	146.1	145.9	147.4	148.0
2010	144.9	144.6	144.7	144.2	143.2	144.2	144.7	144.7	143.6	143.7	143.6	145.7	144.3
2011	143.6	143.4	143.5	143.3	142.8	144.0	144.1	144.4	143.7	143.3	144.3	146.2	143.9
2012	144.3	144.7	145.4	145.3	145.2	146.8	147.3	147.7	146.8	147.8	148.3	150.3	146.7
2013	148.6	149.4	150.3	150.2	149.8	151.3	152.0	152.1	151.2	151.2	150.7	151.9	150.7
Professional and Business Services													
2002	290.7	293.1	294.9	299.5	302.1	303.8	301.7	304.8	300.9	298.0	295.6	295.4	298.4
2003	284.8	285.9	286.6	290.6	292.9	298.0	298.5	301.2	298.0	299.2	296.2	298.4	294.2
2004	289.4	292.0	295.9	304.0	305.9	311.3	313.8	314.6	312.5	312.2	310.3	313.0	306.2
2005	304.7	305.8	308.5	316.2	318.0	322.7	325.0	326.1	324.9	324.6	323.6	326.6	318.9
2006	316.7	320.4	323.6	329.3	333.7	340.4	339.7	341.9	340.0	339.4	338.9	341.0	333.8
2007	333.9	335.8	340.7	346.0	350.7	356.9	356.5	358.3	357.1	355.1	352.7	353.2	349.7
2008	344.2	347.0	348.4	354.7	356.2	360.4	359.9	361.3	357.6	355.7	350.5	348.2	353.7
2009	335.8	331.9	330.9	331.8	332.6	334.3	333.5	332.4	329.4	330.2	329.5	328.9	331.8
2010	319.4	321.1	323.8	329.4	331.4	335.6	337.1	337.4	332.8	334.8	333.6	332.6	330.8
2011	328.5	330.0	330.8	338.7	341.4	344.8	346.4	348.8	346.6	346.6	347.1	347.8	341.5
2012	340.3	342.2	345.0	351.7	355.7	360.8	362.9	365.1	362.7	367.5	365.0	363.6	356.9
2013	356.3	359.5	362.8	368.0	371.7	376.7	378.7	381.2	378.0	380.6	381.8	380.0	372.9
Education and Health Services													
2002	204.2	205.7	206.4	208.0	208.7	208.4	207.7	209.1	209.7	210.2	211.4	212.0	208.5
2003	209.8	211.1	211.7	212.4	212.9	213.1	212.3	213.1	213.5	214.5	215.2	216.1	213.0
2004	214.7	216.0	217.1	217.6	218.2	218.3	217.0	218.1	219.5	220.5	221.6	223.1	218.5
2005	220.3	223.0	223.5	224.0	225.0	225.3	223.6	224.6	225.2	225.5	226.9	228.0	224.6
2006	225.9	228.5	229.3	230.0	231.1	231.2	229.4	230.8	232.1	233.9	235.3	236.5	231.2
2007	233.7	236.8	238.4	238.8	239.9	240.1	238.7	240.5	241.7	243.8	245.7	247.1	240.4
2008	244.5	247.6	248.0	248.8	250.2	249.3	248.9	250.6	251.6	254.2	256.1	256.1	250.5
2009	254.1	255.8	256.0	256.5	257.2	256.4	256.1	256.8	256.9	259.5	260.4	261.2	257.2
2010	258.9	261.3	262.1	263.5	264.4	263.8	263.6	265.0	265.3	268.6	269.3	270.3	264.7
2011	268.0	270.0	271.4	272.5	273.1	272.3	271.9	274.2	275.6	277.1	277.8	280.2	273.7
2012	277.4	280.1	281.0	281.2	281.5	281.4	280.7	282.3	283.4	285.9	287.1	288.9	282.6
2013	281.2	283.5	284.3	285.7	285.8	284.5	284.6	286.9	287.6	290.3	293.8	292.8	286.8
Leisure and Hospitality													
2002	242.2	243.4	246.1	245.2	240.3	256.9	259.6	260.0	248.7	237.2	236.0	248.5	247.0
2003	243.8	242.8	244.8	241.2	236.6	252.5	256.6	258.8	247.6	238.2	236.1	247.9	245.6
2004	244.8	245.5	249.7	248.2	244.0	259.6	263.5	264.5	253.9	243.3	242.2	256.1	251.3
2005	250.8	252.7	257.5	253.7	250.0	266.0	269.7	270.0	259.1	249.5	248.6	262.5	257.5
2006	258.5	259.0	263.3	259.2	256.5	273.7	277.2	277.9	266.7	257.4	258.7	271.0	264.9
2007	263.4	264.7	270.0	266.5	263.0	278.6	281.9	282.6	271.7	262.5	264.1	275.7	270.4
2008	269.7	271.1	274.5	271.7	268.7	283.7	286.4	285.9	273.3	262.3	259.1	268.7	272.9
2009	262.2	261.3	263.5	260.2	256.6	269.4	274.5	274.7	262.6	253.3	250.0	260.7	262.4
2010	256.7	257.0	259.9	259.3	253.7	270.1	275.7	277.2	265.6	257.4	255.0	268.6	263.0
2011	265.4	264.1	269.4	267.0	261.6	279.5	284.1	286.0	275.8	264.6	263.4	275.4	271.4
2012	272.0	271.5	278.1	275.0	269.8	289.3	293.7	294.0	281.6	272.5	274.0	284.3	279.7
2013	281.2	282.6	287.4	285.3	280.3	299.6	305.1	304.5	291.6	283.5	281.1	295.0	289.8
Other Services													
2002	84.7	84.7	85.3	85.4	85.5	87.1	87.3	86.8	85.3	84.6	84.9	85.1	85.6
2003	85.7	85.2	85.2	85.5	85.7	87.4	87.3	86.9	85.3	85.2	85.4	86.1	85.9
2004	86.0	85.7	85.7	86.1	86.5	86.6	88.2	88.6	88.7	88.1	88.1	87.8	87.4
2005	88.2	88.1	88.5	88.4	88.4	89.6	89.5	89.3	88.4	87.9	87.5	88.1	88.5
2006	89.8	89.7	90.5	90.4	90.6	92.3	91.8	91.7	90.8	90.4	90.5	91.2	90.8
2007	91.4	91.9	92.9	92.5	92.6	94.3	93.5	93.6	93.0	93.0	92.8	93.5	92.9
2008	93.9	94.3	94.7	94.4	94.7	96.0	96.4	96.1	95.3	94.6	94.0	93.6	94.8
2009	95.1	94.5	94.6	93.4	93.5	94.7	94.3	94.0	92.9	92.6	92.1	92.6	93.7
2010	92.3	92.1	92.4	91.7	92.1	93.3	93.4	93.4	93.4	92.3	91.8	91.7	92.4
2011	91.8	91.7	92.5	93.4	93.7	95.1	94.8	95.3	94.4	93.7	93.6	94.2	93.7
2012	94.1	94.5	95.2	95.4	95.6	97.2	97.4	97.2	96.3	96.4	96.0	96.4	96.0
2013	96.3	96.3	96.8	96.9	97.6	98.8	98.9	98.9	97.7	97.7	98.0	98.2	97.7
Government													
2002	344.1	354.9	358.2	358.2	362.3	355.7	338.7	340.5	356.5	364.8	365.9	364.7	355.4
2003	350.5	360.5	362.5	360.4	366.2	355.8	338.0	338.7	356.2	362.4	362.3	360.6	356.2
2004	349.6	359.4	362.2	363.6	366.3	359.1	338.6	341.3	360.4	367.0	367.8	366.5	358.5
2005	352.8	364.7	365.9	367.5	370.7	363.0	345.2	345.1	365.0	370.9	370.7	369.7	362.6
2006	356.8	368.4	371.6	370.8	374.5	368.1	348.8	351.4	368.8	375.2	376.0	375.3	367.2
2007	360.3	374.7	378.0	378.5	382.0	374.6	355.5	359.3	379.5	384.1	385.6	384.0	374.7
2008	370.7	383.3	386.3	386.9	392.6	382.0	364.6	369.9	388.5	395.5	396.0	393.3	384.1
2009	382.5	392.1	394.7	396.6	401.5	389.9	369.1	371.0	392.5	400.1	399.2	396.9	390.5
2010	382.4	396.0	399.8	400.1	411.6	394.5	374.5	374.0	392.9	400.3	401.4	398.5	393.8
2011	383.4	395.9	398.4	400.4	403.3	392.3	371.6	372.3	395.4	401.2	401.9	398.7	392.9
2012	383.8	396.4	399.6	400.8	404.4	394.0	373.1	377.6	398.2	403.3	405.2	401.7	394.8
2013	391.8	405.5	407.8	408.7	413.2	401.1	381.1	386.2	408.9	415.9	417.1	412.6	404.2

2. Average Weekly Hours by Selected Industry: Colorado, 2009–2013

(Not seasonally adjusted)

Industry and year	January	February	March	April	May	June	July	August	September	October	November	December	Annual average
Total Private													
2009	33.9	34.6	34.8	34.2	34.4	34.5	34.6	34.8	34.2	34.1	34.5	33.4	34.3
2010	33.6	33.6	33.5	33.8	34.8	34.6	34.7	35.0	34.4	34.4	34.5	34.2	34.3
2011	34.3	33.9	33.9	34.2	35.1	34.5	34.7	34.5	34.6	35.4	34.7	34.6	34.5
2012	35.0	34.4	34.3	35.1	34.6	34.9	35.6	35.0	35.5	35.0	34.7	35.4	35.0
2013	34.3	34.5	34.7	34.4	34.6	35.6	34.8	34.9	35.2	34.6	34.8	35.1	34.8
Goods-Producing													
2009	37.6	37.6	38.2	36.7	37.8	38.1	38.0	38.2	37.4	37.9	38.2	36.6	37.7
2010	37.5	37.3	37.2	37.5	38.1	38.4	38.5	38.8	37.9	38.4	38.3	38.1	38.0
2011	36.5	37.0	37.5	38.5	39.1	38.9	39.2	38.9	39.4	39.5	39.2	38.7	38.6
2012	37.4	37.1	37.9	38.1	38.5	39.0	39.4	39.1	39.2	39.8	39.1	38.5	38.6
2013	37.5	37.6	38.0	37.7	38.6	39.6	39.1	40.0	39.2	39.4	39.1	39.6	38.8
Construction													
2009	36.4	36.5	37.5	37.4	38.5	38.9	39.4	39.4	37.3	38.1	38.5	36.3	37.8
2010	38.0	37.2	36.8	37.5	37.8	39.3	39.6	39.7	38.3	39.0	38.8	38.5	38.4
2011	35.3	35.8	36.6	37.6	38.2	38.0	38.7	38.4	38.2	38.4	37.4	36.8	37.5
2012	36.3	35.6	36.7	36.6	36.7	37.9	38.8	37.9	37.4	39.3	38.3	37.8	37.5
2013	36.8	37.0	37.6	36.7	37.7	38.9	38.7	39.6	39.0	39.3	38.9	38.4	38.3
Manufacturing													
2009	38.7	38.4	38.5	37.8	38.1	38.2	38.0	38.3	37.6	37.8	38.4	36.7	38.0
2010	36.6	37.1	37.5	37.5	38.5	38.1	38.1	38.5	37.8	38.0	38.2	38.6	37.9
2011	37.9	38.2	38.5	39.2	39.6	39.5	39.5	39.1	39.8	40.0	39.9	40.2	39.3
2012	37.8	37.9	38.5	39.1	39.6	39.8	39.4	40.1	40.5	40.0	39.7	38.9	39.3
2013	38.1	38.6	38.3	38.7	39.1	40.0	39.1	40.2	39.6	39.6	39.2	39.8	39.2
Trade, Transportation, and Utilities													
2009	34.2	35.0	35.0	34.8	34.9	35.1	35.3	35.5	35.1	34.8	34.8	34.0	34.9
2010	34.1	34.3	34.4	34.4	35.0	35.0	34.8	35.4	34.9	34.9	35.8	35.9	34.9
2011	35.7	35.0	35.0	35.2	36.0	35.8	36.2	36.0	36.3	36.8	36.2	36.3	35.9
2012	36.9	36.2	35.8	36.5	35.4	35.7	36.4	35.6	36.2	35.4	35.2	36.2	36.0
2013	34.8	35.2	35.4	35.0	35.2	36.3	35.8	35.7	35.9	35.0	35.1	35.8	35.4
Financial Activities													
2009	34.9	35.4	35.7	35.4	35.3	35.3	35.2	35.2	34.6	34.8	36.1	35.3	35.3
2010	35.7	35.6	35.7	34.6	35.9	35.7	36.1	36.4	35.9	35.5	36.2	36.2	35.8
2011	37.1	36.6	36.7	36.9	38.4	36.4	36.9	36.8	37.0	37.8	36.8	36.3	37.0
2012	38.6	36.9	36.4	37.5	36.7	36.9	38.6	37.3	38.2	37.2	37.4	38.5	37.5
2013	37.7	37.2	37.3	37.5	36.9	38.4	37.3	37.0	37.8	36.7	36.6	37.5	37.3
Professional and Business Services													
2009	35.9	36.6	36.4	36.4	36.2	36.7	36.6	36.9	36.3	36.5	37.3	35.6	36.4
2010	35.9	35.7	36.0	36.5	36.8	36.9	37.1	37.5	37.0	36.8	37.1	36.8	36.7
2011	36.9	36.7	36.2	36.6	37.2	36.6	36.5	36.3	36.2	37.3	36.5	36.7	36.6
2012	37.3	37.0	36.7	38.0	37.2	37.4	37.7	37.4	38.2	37.5	37.0	38.6	37.5
2013	36.9	37.2	37.1	36.8	37.2	38.3	36.9	37.3	37.6	37.2	37.4	37.6	37.3
Education and Health Services													
2009	34.7	35.1	35.0	34.5	34.4	34.1	34.1	34.4	34.1	34.0	34.0	33.6	34.3
2010	33.8	33.7	32.9	33.2	33.4	33.0	33.0	33.5	33.1	32.9	33.1	32.8	33.2
2011	33.5	33.5	33.0	33.3	33.4	33.0	33.0	32.7	33.0	34.1	33.2	33.4	33.3
2012	33.3	32.7	31.9	32.8	32.5	32.8	33.1	32.8	33.2	32.6	32.8	33.4	32.8
2013	32.4	32.5	32.2	32.3	32.0	32.6	31.8	31.8	32.3	31.8	32.1	32.1	32.2
Leisure and Hospitality													
2009	23.9	24.3	24.7	24.3	24.6	25.2	25.5	26.3	25.1	24.3	24.1	24.0	24.7
2010	24.7	25.4	25.1	24.9	26.0	26.2	26.5	27.4	26.1	25.9	25.3	24.8	25.7
2011	25.4	25.4	26.3	25.7	26.8	26.9	27.1	26.8	26.3	27.1	26.2	26.2	26.4
2012	27.0	26.7	27.3	27.2	26.9	27.6	28.2	27.8	28.1	27.3	26.8	27.5	27.4
2013	27.1	27.7	28.0	27.0	27.5	28.6	28.1	28.1	27.7	26.8	27.0	26.7	27.5
Other Services													
2009	33.0	33.1	33.0	32.7	33.4	33.4	32.8	33.8	33.4	33.2	34.2	32.6	33.2
2010	32.7	30.9	31.3	31.2	31.8	32.0	32.9	33.3	32.8	32.2	32.6	33.1	32.2
2011	33.3	31.6	31.1	31.0	33.2	32.6	32.1	32.4	32.6	34.0	32.6	33.3	32.5
2012	35.1	33.9	33.4	35.0	33.9	34.1	35.6	35.6	34.6	34.1	34.8	35.3	34.6
2013	34.5	34.3	34.4	33.9	33.9	34.9	33.3	33.5	34.1	33.4	33.9	34.6	34.1

3. Average Hourly Earnings by Selected Industry: Colorado, 2009–2013

(Dollars, not seasonally adjusted)

Industry and year	January	February	March	April	May	June	July	August	September	October	November	December	Annual average
Total Private													
2009	27.96	28.17	28.33	27.98	27.57	27.43	27.64	27.82	27.43	27.56	27.93	27.95	27.81
2010	27.75	28.22	28.04	28.43	28.43	27.83	27.78	28.12	28.12	28.01	28.09	28.15	28.08
2011	28.39	28.35	28.29	28.21	28.24	27.88	28.15	28.07	28.14	28.47	28.37	28.32	28.24
2012	28.72	28.33	28.24	28.50	27.96	27.77	27.91	27.73	28.10	27.93	28.22	28.31	28.14
2013	28.33	28.32	28.01	28.08	27.89	28.08	27.82	27.79	27.93	27.72	27.60	28.03	27.96
Goods-Producing													
2009	29.89	29.53	29.64	29.93	29.72	29.68	29.33	29.52	29.15	29.36	29.11	29.85	29.56
2010	29.72	29.92	29.76	29.55	29.83	29.74	29.72	29.79	30.06	29.87	29.78	30.17	29.83
2011	30.44	30.32	30.43	30.26	29.85	30.27	30.13	30.22	30.26	30.41	30.15	30.75	30.29
2012	30.87	30.31	30.53	30.73	30.33	29.93	30.16	30.03	30.15	30.06	30.06	30.20	30.28
2013	30.50	30.22	29.95	29.68	29.93	29.97	30.09	29.91	30.18	29.96	30.18	30.31	30.07
Construction													
2009	29.20	29.16	28.86	28.75	28.53	28.29	28.29	28.61	28.70	29.27	29.23	29.63	28.86
2010	29.65	30.22	30.42	29.11	29.05	28.63	29.01	28.98	29.35	28.87	28.79	29.14	29.22
2011	29.64	29.54	29.69	28.92	28.35	28.50	29.14	28.79	29.08	29.12	29.33	29.15	29.08
2012	28.31	28.42	28.77	28.64	28.60	28.46	28.70	28.55	28.75	29.14	29.71	29.58	28.82
2013	29.63	29.72	29.34	28.88	29.47	29.25	29.29	29.61	30.08	29.71	29.65	30.39	29.58
Manufacturing													
2009	29.93	29.31	29.55	30.02	29.85	29.90	29.57	29.76	29.19	29.20	28.90	29.77	29.58
2010	29.75	29.87	29.58	29.60	30.02	29.93	29.82	29.91	30.15	30.22	30.12	30.42	29.95
2011	30.60	30.47	30.58	30.61	30.29	30.80	30.42	30.47	30.41	30.64	30.26	31.02	30.55
2012	31.39	30.66	30.86	31.14	30.68	30.22	30.47	30.36	30.47	30.24	30.05	30.32	30.57
2013	30.70	30.32	30.07	29.87	30.01	30.10	30.26	29.93	30.15	29.99	30.32	30.25	30.16
Trade, Transportation, and Utilities													
2009	22.55	22.62	22.59	23.16	22.39	22.37	21.46	21.47	21.61	21.16	21.10	21.00	21.95
2010	21.47	22.11	21.50	22.39	22.84	22.54	22.99	22.80	23.17	23.25	23.61	23.83	22.73
2011	24.25	24.73	24.46	24.89	25.38	25.06	25.49	25.18	25.74	25.69	26.06	25.11	25.18
2012	25.40	25.30	25.14	25.65	25.00	24.88	25.32	25.33	25.59	24.97	25.35	24.97	25.24
2013	25.31	25.06	24.32	24.59	24.22	24.41	24.25	24.11	24.21	24.02	23.39	23.67	24.29
Financial Activities													
2009	40.42	42.19	43.26	41.48	41.41	40.49	40.92	41.82	39.72	41.15	41.98	41.57	41.37
2010	40.01	40.11	40.68	41.69	42.21	40.86	41.23	42.14	41.10	41.69	42.03	42.46	41.36
2011	43.10	42.87	42.82	42.75	43.56	42.39	42.18	42.58	40.61	42.77	41.54	41.60	42.40
2012	41.80	40.80	41.01	42.25	40.99	41.46	42.28	41.26	41.70	40.79	41.65	41.70	41.48
2013	40.95	40.74	41.71	43.33	42.66	44.08	43.50	43.44	44.62	43.44	43.17	43.93	42.97
Professional and Business Services													
2009	32.18	32.06	32.07	30.70	30.37	29.92	29.67	29.99	30.07	29.38	29.64	30.21	30.52
2010	30.48	30.40	30.26	29.51	29.81	29.39	29.70	30.08	29.97	30.39	30.18	30.30	30.03
2011	31.44	30.97	30.68	30.55	30.12	29.45	29.99	29.99	30.11	30.39	30.35	30.48	30.36
2012	31.19	30.92	30.58	30.54	30.28	29.77	29.77	29.88	29.73	30.51	29.84	30.40	30.29
2013	30.82	31.00	30.82	30.45	30.47	30.33	30.10	30.40	30.48	30.39	30.56	30.98	30.56
Education and Health Services													
2009	25.92	25.74	26.03	26.09	26.15	26.09	26.14	25.98	25.79	25.83	25.89	25.70	25.94
2010	25.76	25.98	26.01	25.91	26.09	26.10	26.09	26.06	26.04	26.40	26.42	26.54	26.12
2011	26.95	26.27	26.17	26.19	26.18	26.27	26.78	26.34	26.41	26.47	26.56	26.59	26.43
2012	26.87	26.44	26.41	26.27	26.10	26.00	26.06	26.04	26.14	25.93	26.09	26.17	26.21
2013	25.89	25.74	25.24	25.31	25.15	25.01	24.98	25.03	25.03	25.02	24.91	25.38	25.22
Leisure and Hospitality													
2009	15.55	15.40	15.17	15.16	15.02	15.40	15.26	15.53	15.71	15.34	15.22	15.45	15.35
2010	15.37	15.29	15.01	15.16	15.25	15.26	14.91	15.23	15.54	15.45	15.35	15.65	15.29
2011	15.55	15.46	15.49	15.42	15.38	14.96	15.02	14.90	15.21	15.03	15.11	15.17	15.21
2012	14.98	15.18	15.00	15.26	15.18	15.06	14.93	14.85	15.16	15.20	15.29	15.52	15.13
2013	15.59	15.70	15.59	15.41	15.37	14.99	14.89	14.74	15.13	15.15	15.15	15.32	15.23
Other Services													
2009	22.67	22.38	22.19	22.71	21.95	21.82	21.67	21.71	21.95	21.93	22.08	22.35	22.11
2010	22.36	22.05	22.14	22.10	21.86	21.83	21.76	21.81	21.95	21.80	21.77	22.35	21.98
2011	22.60	21.56	21.22	21.03	20.83	20.57	19.61	19.25	19.88	19.30	19.38	19.12	20.33
2012	19.89	20.14	19.87	19.56	20.08	20.00	19.78	19.93	20.17	20.48	20.10	21.00	20.08
2013	21.42	21.93	21.28	21.48	21.72	21.29	20.81	21.03	21.42	21.64	21.66	21.97	21.46

4. Average Weekly Earnings by Selected Industry: Colorado, 2009–2013

(Dollars, not seasonally adjusted)

Industry and year	January	February	March	April	May	June	July	August	September	October	November	December	Annual average
Total Private													
2009	818.01	835.94	841.12	812.25	813.90	807.65	816.21	823.37	804.38	805.78	819.72	798.26	815.65
2010	796.66	795.98	795.96	806.81	834.16	817.60	822.39	832.30	812.18	819.75	823.17	823.88	816.00
2011	826.97	816.65	809.19	821.48	838.89	811.79	824.13	815.93	825.56	860.57	836.62	837.32	826.28
2012	858.90	825.60	830.75	872.94	847.01	854.70	880.03	855.05	883.60	861.35	859.52	891.37	861.35
2013	861.27	873.20	876.52	876.86	881.26	917.41	888.79	890.30	921.18	892.68	904.10	920.32	892.27
Goods-Producing													
2009	994.52	1,004.30	1,022.23	996.04	996.03	976.88	974.70	980.59	956.69	968.35	975.63	947.94	983.22
2010	974.25	961.22	957.53	980.63	989.84	984.58	994.07	998.71	972.89	983.42	993.89	997.46	982.30
2011	963.24	969.03	973.88	1,004.08	1,002.13	999.73	991.76	980.28	1,005.88	1,003.30	990.58	994.59	991.25
2012	969.03	952.73	963.80	974.98	978.29	1,002.30	1,004.70	999.79	1,013.71	1,022.86	1,013.86	1,027.95	993.95
2013	1,004.63	1,018.21	1,030.18	1,021.67	1,043.74	1,079.89	1,062.74	1,080.00	1,083.88	1,085.86	1,083.46	1,109.99	1,059.24
Construction													
2009	903.45	894.62	920.63	921.16	935.94	924.26	927.08	927.48	873.19	915.92	924.77	876.28	910.98
2010	913.52	884.62	868.48	891.75	909.09	922.76	928.22	930.97	900.82	917.67	930.42	921.69	910.46
2011	843.32	859.92	880.96	924.21	919.86	910.86	912.55	904.32	898.46	905.09	889.00	881.36	895.13
2012	854.87	836.24	866.85	854.24	862.45	853.89	888.52	888.38	878.90	918.05	903.50	918.16	878.25
2013	905.28	925.74	938.87	909.06	955.32	979.50	970.21	990.79	1,000.35	1,032.80	1,018.40	1,023.74	973.59
Manufacturing													
2009	1,071.60	1,065.60	1,069.15	1,047.82	1,051.18	1,046.30	1,033.60	1,037.55	1,017.46	1,031.56	1,045.63	1,003.01	1,042.34
2010	998.08	1,003.93	1,025.25	1,034.63	1,054.13	1,036.70	1,047.37	1,045.66	1,021.36	1,028.66	1,046.30	1,058.80	1,033.91
2011	1,042.63	1,041.33	1,039.89	1,053.30	1,052.17	1,053.47	1,034.90	1,023.64	1,071.02	1,062.80	1,041.39	1,056.86	1,048.13
2012	1,020.22	1,016.86	1,011.78	1,041.23	1,044.25	1,085.74	1,046.46	1,048.62	1,075.68	1,056.40	1,055.62	1,060.41	1,047.74
2013	1,040.13	1,060.34	1,049.42	1,065.41	1,043.58	1,075.60	1,052.57	1,069.72	1,090.58	1,057.32	1,070.55	1,086.14	1,063.50
Trade, Transportation, and Utilities													
2009	667.58	681.45	686.00	681.73	680.55	683.40	690.47	694.74	677.78	672.68	677.56	659.94	679.85
2010	651.99	657.19	662.54	666.33	681.80	674.45	675.47	687.47	677.06	686.83	698.46	704.36	677.06
2011	705.79	689.15	678.65	684.99	718.56	704.19	725.45	724.32	747.05	774.64	768.16	766.29	724.82
2012	808.85	769.25	774.00	821.98	778.80	788.61	816.09	795.30	833.69	786.59	782.14	833.32	800.28
2013	793.79	794.46	795.08	794.85	805.02	843.25	816.24	810.75	842.93	795.20	805.90	820.89	809.24
Financial Activities													
2009	763.61	775.61	783.97	770.30	784.01	786.13	781.44	775.81	752.55	759.34	796.73	773.07	775.89
2010	787.90	796.73	766.12	733.17	781.54	762.91	775.07	784.78	781.18	782.42	807.26	817.40	781.51
2011	837.35	824.23	830.89	854.97	919.30	859.40	887.81	881.36	883.56	943.87	894.98	883.91	875.79
2012	946.47	939.11	930.02	978.00	937.69	961.98	1,050.69	981.74	1,037.51	1,008.12	1,005.69	1,041.43	984.75
2013	1,020.54	1,030.44	1,036.57	1,054.88	1,058.29	1,110.14	1,083.57	1,098.90	1,148.36	1,086.69	1,106.05	1,144.88	1,080.95
Professional and Business Services													
2009	1,078.44	1,093.97	1,096.37	1,071.25	1,061.75	1,068.34	1,063.96	1,077.11	1,056.33	1,067.99	1,101.84	1,071.56	1,074.16
2010	1,080.95	1,064.93	1,069.56	1,073.47	1,084.13	1,074.53	1,075.90	1,090.88	1,071.89	1,073.09	1,097.05	1,094.43	1,079.71
2011	1,114.75	1,098.06	1,075.50	1,092.14	1,102.24	1,063.60	1,077.48	1,062.14	1,059.57	1,134.67	1,081.86	1,098.80	1,087.02
2012	1,134.67	1,085.21	1,092.56	1,162.80	1,111.54	1,112.65	1,129.87	1,102.55	1,133.01	1,095.75	1,092.98	1,169.19	1,118.25
2013	1,129.14	1,152.83	1,147.87	1,145.95	1,154.69	1,225.98	1,174.16	1,174.95	1,205.83	1,174.40	1,182.21	1,218.24	1,174.58
Education and Health Services													
2009	790.81	804.14	806.75	771.08	779.50	769.64	771.34	783.63	779.53	780.98	788.80	782.54	783.41
2010	774.02	783.86	789.93	801.12	807.28	797.28	797.61	807.02	789.44	787.96	789.77	783.92	792.48
2011	799.31	810.70	799.59	810.19	814.96	804.21	801.90	801.48	804.87	832.72	818.38	817.97	810.86
2012	819.85	797.55	793.67	817.05	802.43	813.77	823.53	799.01	822.36	796.74	809.50	813.96	808.52
2013	781.49	784.55	770.87	775.20	759.36	774.25	754.61	753.66	765.51	750.48	757.56	758.52	766.36
Leisure and Hospitality													
2009	342.01	350.89	357.90	347.98	346.61	352.55	359.81	373.46	354.66	343.36	339.09	342.24	350.99
2010	351.23	358.39	361.19	353.83	360.62	362.61	374.18	385.79	365.14	361.56	353.44	351.66	361.86
2011	362.46	368.55	381.61	370.85	381.63	374.99	383.19	377.34	377.14	388.61	378.59	376.23	377.52
2012	393.93	386.62	401.04	412.35	399.47	406.27	412.28	402.82	415.32	408.14	404.95	418.55	405.52
2013	415.44	424.64	429.80	416.61	420.48	426.14	420.94	424.87	424.36	412.45	413.64	407.18	419.10
Other Services													
2009	678.81	689.47	686.40	677.87	691.71	694.72	682.57	699.32	685.37	684.58	703.84	659.82	685.91
2010	659.56	630.98	642.59	646.78	674.16	674.56	681.69	693.64	678.30	672.34	691.77	696.42	669.44
2011	697.64	663.92	655.28	654.10	707.16	682.64	702.35	684.61	704.16	722.16	696.01	719.28	691.28
2012	738.50	718.34	721.77	754.95	727.16	736.56	787.12	763.26	760.51	740.99	746.11	775.54	747.36
2013	731.75	747.74	760.24	752.24	738.68	768.50	716.62	717.57	756.34	753.17	778.34	788.19	751.56

CONNECTICUT
At a Glance

Population:
   2000 census: 3,405,650
   2010 census: 3,574,097
   2013 estimate: 3,596,080

Percent change in population:
   2000–2010: 4.9%
   2010–2013: 0.6%

Percent change in total nonfarm employment:
   2000–2010: -5.0%
   2010–2013: 2.9%

Industry with the largest growth in employment, 2000–2013 (thousands):
   Education and Health Services, 76.6

Industry with the largest decline or smallest growth in employment, 2000–2013 (thousands):
   Manufacturing, -71.9

Civilian labor force:
   2000: 1,736,831
   2010: 1,915,220
   2013: 1,859,926

Unemployment rate and rank among states (lowest to highest):
   2000: 2.3%, 1st
   2010: 9.3%, 31st
   2013: 7.8%, 38th

Over-the-year change in unemployment rates:
   2010–2011: -0.4%
   2011–2012: -0.6%
   2012–2013: -0.5%

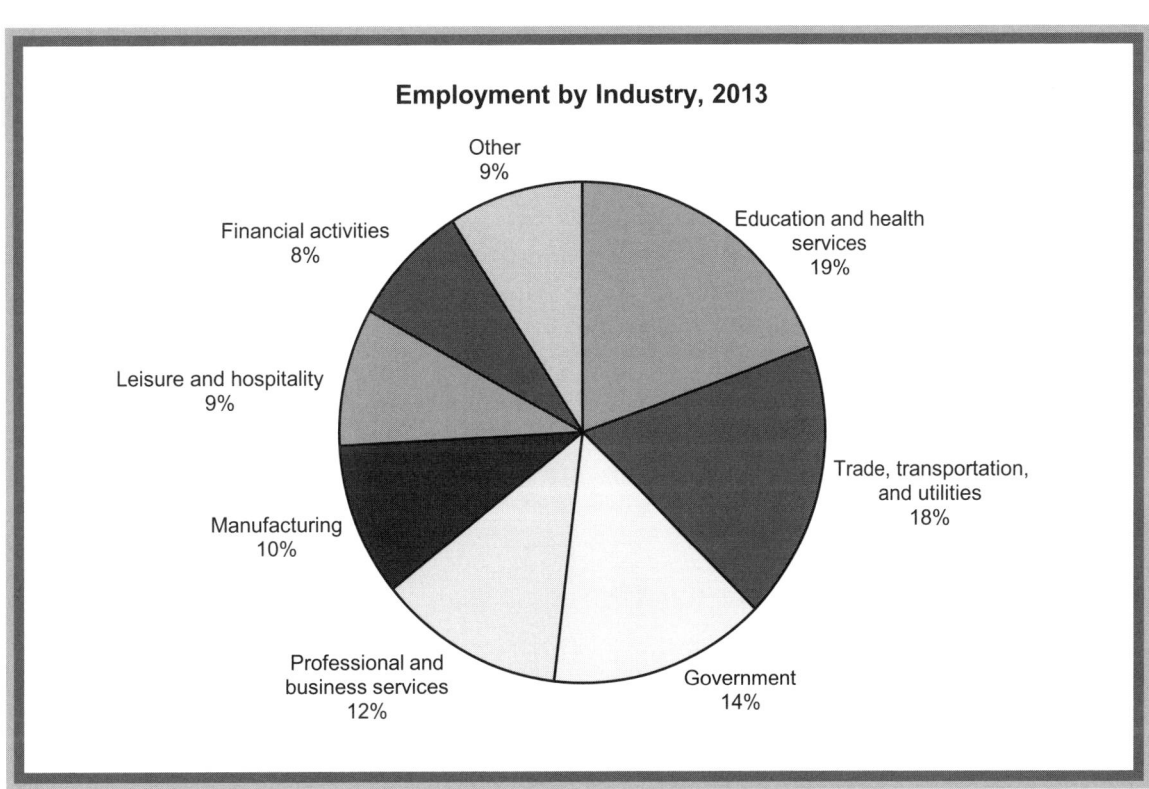

Employment by Industry, 2013

Other
9%

Education and health services
19%

Financial activities
8%

Trade, transportation, and utilities
18%

Leisure and hospitality
9%

Manufacturing
10%

Government
14%

Professional and business services
12%

1. Employment by Industry: Connecticut, Selected Years, 2002–2013

(Numbers in thousands, not seasonally adjusted)

Industry and year	January	February	March	April	May	June	July	August	September	October	November	December	Annual average
Total Nonfarm													
2002	1,648.1	1,648.7	1,657.5	1,670.2	1,679.9	1,687.0	1,655.0	1,652.0	1,663.3	1,665.2	1,673.1	1,678.2	1,664.9
2003	1,630.9	1,626.0	1,630.8	1,641.6	1,653.8	1,659.7	1,633.2	1,630.5	1,642.6	1,655.7	1,663.3	1,665.7	1,644.5
2004	1,616.6	1,618.6	1,627.7	1,646.3	1,658.3	1,667.0	1,644.2	1,642.0	1,655.7	1,664.6	1,675.4	1,681.3	1,649.8
2005	1,630.3	1,636.0	1,639.6	1,663.5	1,670.4	1,681.7	1,653.9	1,651.0	1,668.0	1,673.3	1,683.9	1,692.8	1,662.0
2006	1,648.5	1,650.7	1,656.0	1,678.4	1,687.3	1,698.5	1,672.5	1,673.7	1,685.3	1,694.5	1,704.9	1,716.6	1,680.6
2007	1,666.5	1,668.4	1,671.9	1,689.8	1,705.6	1,720.4	1,691.4	1,690.4	1,704.3	1,714.2	1,724.2	1,730.9	1,698.2
2008	1,685.3	1,687.8	1,692.5	1,705.6	1,717.7	1,724.5	1,690.4	1,686.7	1,697.2	1,700.9	1,701.4	1,698.0	1,699.0
2009	1,639.1	1,634.7	1,626.9	1,627.0	1,639.7	1,640.7	1,608.5	1,602.5	1,617.4	1,623.1	1,628.3	1,631.3	1,626.6
2010	1,569.1	1,571.8	1,575.2	1,600.3	1,622.4	1,625.1	1,607.3	1,604.2	1,616.8	1,629.1	1,635.5	1,639.2	1,608.0
2011	1,591.4	1,598.0	1,600.3	1,627.8	1,634.9	1,638.2	1,622.6	1,616.9	1,632.6	1,639.0	1,647.0	1,653.0	1,625.1
2012	1,609.4	1,615.5	1,623.1	1,635.1	1,648.1	1,655.6	1,634.2	1,630.4	1,645.2	1,655.2	1,664.3	1,669.2	1,640.4
2013	1,621.3	1,618.8	1,629.6	1,652.0	1,664.7	1,678.1	1,656.4	1,648.7	1,656.2	1,669.8	1,680.0	1,681.2	1,654.7
Total Private													
2002	1,399.4	1,393.8	1,401.7	1,415.6	1,425.7	1,436.9	1,423.9	1,418.1	1,416.5	1,413.6	1,417.8	1,423.7	1,415.6
2003	1,380.6	1,373.4	1,377.6	1,390.1	1,402.6	1,413.6	1,405.0	1,400.4	1,400.4	1,408.2	1,413.0	1,417.0	1,398.5
2004	1,374.3	1,371.2	1,378.9	1,398.2	1,411.4	1,425.0	1,419.2	1,413.7	1,416.3	1,417.5	1,425.3	1,432.6	1,407.0
2005	1,388.8	1,389.1	1,393.2	1,414.9	1,422.6	1,437.1	1,428.8	1,422.6	1,424.8	1,424.1	1,432.1	1,440.9	1,418.3
2006	1,402.9	1,401.3	1,406.8	1,428.2	1,437.5	1,453.7	1,444.4	1,440.9	1,441.4	1,444.3	1,451.8	1,463.1	1,434.7
2007	1,419.0	1,416.0	1,420.1	1,437.5	1,453.6	1,471.9	1,460.5	1,456.2	1,456.1	1,458.2	1,465.5	1,472.9	1,449.0
2008	1,432.7	1,430.1	1,435.8	1,448.6	1,460.1	1,472.2	1,456.6	1,450.4	1,447.1	1,443.4	1,441.6	1,439.9	1,446.5
2009	1,387.4	1,379.0	1,371.9	1,372.2	1,384.7	1,392.4	1,379.4	1,372.3	1,373.3	1,372.9	1,375.2	1,379.6	1,378.4
2010	1,323.3	1,322.0	1,327.3	1,352.9	1,368.4	1,381.2	1,379.4	1,375.1	1,376.4	1,381.7	1,386.6	1,391.3	1,363.8
2011	1,350.4	1,352.9	1,355.2	1,380.4	1,390.0	1,401.4	1,398.0	1,393.5	1,394.0	1,394.6	1,401.1	1,407.1	1,384.9
2012	1,371.0	1,371.2	1,379.1	1,392.3	1,406.8	1,419.9	1,411.1	1,407.2	1,407.8	1,413.2	1,419.4	1,423.9	1,401.9
2013	1,381.1	1,377.5	1,387.6	1,409.1	1,421.6	1,435.5	1,428.2	1,424.8	1,421.9	1,430.6	1,438.1	1,439.1	1,416.3
Goods-Producing													
2002	277.2	274.5	275.5	277.7	278.8	280.2	276.3	276.6	275.2	272.7	270.9	268.5	275.3
2003	261.0	257.3	257.9	261.5	264.1	266.2	264.3	265.1	264.4	264.2	264.0	262.4	262.7
2004	255.1	253.4	256.5	262.2	264.8	268.1	267.6	268.2	267.8	267.2	266.8	265.5	263.6
2005	258.0	255.9	257.1	261.7	263.8	267.0	265.6	265.2	263.6	262.4	261.9	260.2	261.9
2006	255.4	254.8	253.5	261.0	262.8	266.5	265.8	265.7	263.9	262.9	262.3	261.7	261.4
2007	255.1	253.0	254.8	258.4	261.0	265.1	264.2	264.5	262.7	261.8	261.4	259.3	260.1
2008	252.5	250.4	251.4	254.9	256.9	259.0	257.2	256.9	254.8	252.4	249.0	244.7	253.3
2009	233.9	229.3	227.5	227.4	228.4	229.8	226.8	225.7	225.0	222.7	221.2	219.3	226.4
2010	209.2	207.1	208.2	214.0	216.8	220.0	220.5	220.5	220.3	219.7	219.4	218.0	216.1
2011	211.4	211.2	212.3	216.4	219.0	222.2	222.8	223.0	221.8	221.0	221.0	219.1	218.4
2012	213.1	212.4	212.9	215.6	217.5	220.4	220.5	220.5	218.8	219.1	218.2	217.6	217.2
2013	212.3	211.4	212.5	216.5	219.4	221.9	222.6	222.1	220.6	220.7	219.4	217.9	218.1
Service-Providing													
2002	1,370.9	1,374.2	1,382.0	1,392.5	1,401.1	1,406.8	1,378.7	1,375.4	1,388.1	1,392.5	1,402.2	1,409.7	1,389.5
2003	1,369.9	1,368.7	1,372.9	1,380.1	1,389.7	1,393.5	1,368.9	1,365.4	1,378.2	1,391.5	1,399.3	1,403.3	1,381.8
2004	1,361.5	1,365.2	1,371.2	1,384.1	1,393.5	1,398.9	1,376.6	1,373.8	1,387.9	1,397.4	1,408.6	1,415.8	1,386.2
2005	1,372.3	1,380.1	1,382.5	1,401.8	1,406.6	1,414.7	1,388.3	1,385.8	1,404.4	1,410.9	1,422.0	1,432.6	1,400.2
2006	1,393.1	1,395.9	1,402.5	1,417.4	1,424.5	1,432.0	1,406.7	1,408.0	1,421.4	1,431.6	1,442.6	1,454.9	1,419.2
2007	1,411.4	1,415.4	1,417.1	1,431.4	1,444.6	1,455.3	1,427.2	1,425.9	1,441.6	1,452.4	1,462.8	1,471.6	1,438.1
2008	1,432.8	1,437.4	1,441.1	1,450.7	1,460.8	1,465.5	1,433.2	1,429.8	1,442.4	1,448.5	1,452.4	1,453.3	1,445.7
2009	1,405.2	1,405.4	1,399.4	1,399.6	1,411.3	1,410.9	1,381.7	1,376.8	1,392.4	1,400.4	1,407.1	1,412.0	1,400.2
2010	1,359.9	1,364.7	1,367.0	1,386.3	1,405.6	1,405.1	1,386.8	1,383.7	1,396.5	1,409.4	1,416.1	1,421.2	1,391.9
2011	1,380.0	1,386.8	1,388.0	1,411.4	1,415.9	1,416.0	1,399.8	1,393.9	1,410.8	1,418.0	1,426.0	1,433.9	1,406.7
2012	1,396.3	1,403.1	1,410.2	1,419.5	1,430.6	1,435.2	1,413.7	1,409.9	1,426.4	1,436.1	1,446.1	1,451.6	1,423.2
2013	1,409.0	1,407.4	1,417.1	1,435.5	1,445.3	1,456.2	1,433.8	1,426.6	1,435.6	1,449.1	1,460.6	1,463.3	1,436.6
Mining and Logging													
2002	0.7	0.6	0.7	0.7	0.8	0.8	0.8	0.8	0.8	0.8	0.8	0.8	0.8
2003	0.7	0.6	0.6	0.7	0.8	0.8	0.8	0.8	0.8	0.8	0.8	0.7	0.7
2004	0.6	0.6	0.7	0.7	0.8	0.8	0.8	0.8	0.8	0.8	0.8	0.7	0.7
2005	0.7	0.6	0.6	0.7	0.8	0.8	0.8	0.8	0.8	0.8	0.8	0.7	0.7
2006	0.7	0.7	0.7	0.8	0.8	0.8	0.8	0.8	0.8	0.8	0.8	0.7	0.8
2007	0.7	0.6	0.6	0.7	0.7	0.8	0.8	0.8	0.8	0.8	0.8	0.7	0.7
2008	0.7	0.6	0.7	0.7	0.8	0.8	0.8	0.8	0.8	0.8	0.8	0.7	0.8
2009	0.6	0.6	0.6	0.6	0.7	0.7	0.7	0.7	0.7	0.6	0.6	0.6	0.6
2010	0.5	0.5	0.5	0.6	0.6	0.6	0.6	0.6	0.6	0.6	0.6	0.6	0.6
2011	0.5	0.5	0.5	0.5	0.6	0.6	0.6	0.6	0.6	0.6	0.6	0.6	0.6
2012	0.5	0.5	0.5	0.6	0.6	0.6	0.6	0.6	0.6	0.6	0.6	0.5	0.6
2013	0.5	0.5	0.5	0.5	0.6	0.6	0.6	0.6	0.6	0.6	0.6	0.6	0.6
Construction													
2002	59.4	58.5	59.9	63.3	65.0	66.4	66.8	66.7	65.5	64.5	63.7	61.3	63.4
2003	56.2	54.3	55.2	59.1	62.4	64.0	65.9	66.4	65.6	65.5	65.3	63.3	61.9
2004	57.5	56.4	58.6	64.3	66.9	68.7	69.9	70.5	69.9	69.5	68.8	67.1	65.7
2005	60.9	59.6	60.5	65.2	67.1	69.0	70.0	70.1	68.9	67.7	67.2	65.1	65.9
2006	60.9	60.4	61.9	66.0	67.8	69.8	70.9	71.3	70.2	69.8	68.9	67.6	67.1
2007	62.6	60.7	62.4	67.1	69.7	71.9	72.7	72.9	71.9	71.7	71.0	68.8	68.6
2008	63.0	61.9	62.9	66.2	67.5	68.4	68.6	68.4	67.1	65.8	63.5	60.5	65.3
2009	53.8	52.0	51.8	53.7	55.5	56.7	56.8	56.6	56.1	55.2	54.2	52.2	54.6
2010	44.3	42.9	43.6	49.1	50.9	52.3	53.3	53.7	53.1	52.9	52.6	50.9	50.0
2011	45.6	45.3	46.0	50.1	52.1	53.8	54.8	55.1	54.7	54.3	54.4	52.2	51.5
2012	47.3	46.4	47.3	50.2	51.6	53.1	54.1	54.4	54.0	54.4	53.6	52.5	51.6
2013	47.9	47.1	48.2	52.3	54.7	55.8	56.9	57.2	56.7	56.8	56.7	55.0	53.8

1. Employment by Industry: Connecticut, Selected Years, 2002–2013—*Continued*

(Numbers in thousands, not seasonally adjusted)

Industry and year	January	February	March	April	May	June	July	August	September	October	November	December	Annual average
Manufacturing													
2002	217.1	215.4	214.9	213.7	213.0	213.0	208.7	209.1	208.9	207.4	206.4	206.4	211.2
2003	204.1	202.4	202.1	201.7	200.9	201.4	197.6	197.9	198.0	197.9	197.9	198.4	200.0
2004	197.0	196.4	197.2	197.2	197.1	198.6	196.9	196.9	197.1	196.9	197.2	197.7	197.2
2005	196.4	195.7	196.0	195.8	195.9	197.2	194.8	194.3	193.9	193.9	193.9	194.4	195.2
2006	193.8	193.7	190.9	194.2	194.2	195.9	194.1	193.6	192.9	192.3	192.6	193.4	193.5
2007	191.8	191.7	191.8	190.6	190.6	192.4	190.7	190.8	190.0	189.3	189.6	189.8	190.8
2008	188.8	187.9	187.8	188.0	188.6	189.8	187.8	187.7	186.9	185.8	184.7	183.5	187.3
2009	179.5	176.7	175.1	173.1	172.2	172.4	169.3	168.4	168.2	166.9	166.4	166.5	171.2
2010	164.4	163.7	164.1	164.3	165.3	167.1	166.6	166.2	166.6	166.2	166.2	166.5	165.6
2011	165.3	165.4	165.8	165.8	166.3	167.8	167.4	167.3	166.5	166.1	166.0	166.3	166.3
2012	165.3	165.5	165.1	164.8	165.3	166.7	165.8	165.5	164.2	164.1	164.0	164.6	165.1
2013	163.9	163.8	163.8	163.7	164.1	165.5	165.1	164.3	163.3	163.3	162.1	162.3	163.8
Trade, Transportation, and Utilities													
2002	309.4	303.8	305.4	307.7	309.7	312.7	305.9	304.3	308.6	308.2	314.3	320.4	309.2
2003	306.3	300.9	302.5	301.4	304.0	306.9	300.5	299.4	303.9	308.5	313.6	318.1	305.5
2004	304.9	301.0	302.3	303.7	306.4	309.3	304.4	302.6	307.2	310.5	318.3	324.2	307.9
2005	310.2	306.3	306.6	308.4	310.0	312.4	306.2	304.9	309.2	310.2	317.5	324.5	310.5
2006	311.7	305.4	307.3	308.6	310.3	313.2	306.2	305.0	308.4	311.2	318.8	325.1	310.9
2007	311.2	305.3	306.6	306.3	311.4	314.9	308.2	306.7	310.4	312.7	320.3	327.0	311.8
2008	314.7	308.1	308.9	308.2	310.9	313.1	306.2	304.7	307.6	307.9	312.4	316.4	309.9
2009	300.4	294.3	292.3	287.8	293.1	295.5	288.0	286.9	290.2	291.9	297.3	301.8	293.3
2010	287.2	282.2	283.0	283.1	289.2	293.0	288.0	287.2	288.9	292.4	298.6	304.3	289.8
2011	290.4	287.0	287.2	291.2	293.0	295.7	290.0	289.6	291.7	293.6	299.8	305.8	292.9
2012	294.9	289.6	291.6	291.1	295.9	298.3	291.7	291.3	294.3	297.6	305.1	308.6	295.8
2013	296.0	289.9	292.6	295.2	297.9	301.3	295.4	295.4	297.6	300.7	309.3	312.9	298.7
Wholesale Trade													
2002	65.9	65.5	65.7	66.1	66.3	66.4	66.3	66.2	66.0	65.8	65.8	66.2	66.0
2003	65.3	65.0	65.4	65.4	65.5	66.0	65.5	65.4	65.2	65.5	65.6	65.7	65.5
2004	64.8	64.9	65.4	65.9	66.2	66.7	66.0	66.0	65.8	65.4	65.8	66.2	65.8
2005	65.7	65.4	65.6	65.9	66.3	66.7	66.8	66.8	66.9	66.9	67.1	67.5	66.5
2006	66.9	66.8	67.1	67.5	67.7	68.1	67.7	67.6	67.3	67.7	67.7	67.9	67.5
2007	67.5	67.5	67.5	67.7	67.9	68.6	68.5	68.6	68.7	68.7	68.7	69.5	68.3
2008	69.2	69.1	69.5	69.4	69.8	70.0	69.4	69.1	68.9	68.7	68.6	68.4	69.2
2009	67.2	66.5	65.9	65.2	65.1	65.1	64.6	64.4	64.2	63.7	63.4	63.6	64.9
2010	61.9	61.6	61.9	62.3	62.7	63.3	63.1	63.2	62.8	62.7	63.1	63.4	62.7
2011	62.2	62.3	62.4	63.1	63.2	63.7	63.5	63.5	63.1	63.1	63.0	63.1	63.0
2012	62.6	62.6	62.8	63.2	63.5	63.8	63.4	63.3	62.9	63.4	63.2	63.3	63.2
2013	62.5	62.2	62.7	63.2	63.3	63.8	63.6	63.4	63.1	63.7	63.7	63.8	63.3
Retail Trade													
2002	194.9	189.5	191.1	192.0	193.7	196.5	193.2	192.9	192.8	192.0	198.2	204.0	194.2
2003	192.1	187.3	188.2	187.5	189.6	191.6	189.3	189.3	189.3	192.2	197.3	201.7	191.3
2004	191.1	187.2	188.0	188.0	189.9	191.9	191.4	190.4	190.3	192.2	199.2	204.6	192.0
2005	193.0	189.3	189.1	190.1	191.0	192.4	190.2	189.8	189.2	190.4	196.7	202.2	192.0
2006	192.3	186.4	187.8	188.7	189.8	191.9	189.6	189.4	188.4	190.5	197.8	202.4	191.3
2007	191.1	185.5	186.7	186.4	190.6	192.9	190.4	190.0	188.7	190.7	198.0	202.7	191.1
2008	192.9	186.5	186.8	185.8	187.9	189.5	186.7	186.8	185.1	185.6	190.1	193.3	188.1
2009	181.2	176.3	175.2	173.9	177.1	179.5	176.5	176.8	175.9	178.0	183.7	186.9	178.4
2010	176.6	172.0	172.5	173.6	177.0	179.8	178.7	178.3	176.2	179.6	184.9	188.9	178.2
2011	179.1	175.4	175.3	178.1	179.4	181.1	179.3	179.7	178.1	180.1	186.0	190.6	180.2
2012	182.2	177.0	178.4	178.4	181.5	183.3	181.0	181.0	179.6	182.2	189.5	191.8	182.2
2013	182.3	177.6	178.4	180.3	182.4	184.7	183.1	183.8	181.6	183.6	190.7	193.1	183.5
Transportation and Utilities													
2002	48.6	48.8	48.6	49.6	49.7	49.8	46.4	45.2	49.8	50.4	50.3	50.2	49.0
2003	48.9	48.6	48.9	48.5	48.9	49.3	45.7	44.7	49.4	50.8	50.7	50.7	48.8
2004	49.0	48.9	48.9	49.8	50.3	50.7	47.0	46.2	51.1	52.9	53.3	53.4	50.1
2005	51.5	51.6	51.9	52.4	52.7	53.3	49.2	48.3	53.1	52.9	53.7	54.8	52.1
2006	52.5	52.2	52.4	52.4	52.8	53.2	48.9	48.0	52.7	53.0	53.3	54.8	52.2
2007	52.6	52.3	52.4	52.2	52.9	53.4	49.3	48.1	53.0	53.3	53.6	54.8	52.3
2008	52.6	52.5	52.6	53.0	53.2	53.6	50.1	48.8	53.6	53.6	53.7	54.7	52.7
2009	52.0	51.5	51.2	48.7	50.9	50.9	46.9	45.7	50.1	50.2	50.2	51.3	50.0
2010	48.7	48.6	48.6	47.2	49.5	49.9	46.2	45.7	49.9	50.1	50.6	52.0	48.9
2011	49.1	49.3	49.5	50.0	50.4	50.9	47.2	46.4	50.5	50.4	50.8	52.1	49.7
2012	50.1	50.0	50.4	49.5	50.9	51.2	47.3	47.0	51.8	52.0	52.4	53.5	50.5
2013	51.2	50.1	51.5	51.7	52.2	52.8	48.7	48.2	52.9	53.4	54.9	56.0	52.0
Information													
2002	42.2	41.9	41.8	41.5	41.4	41.5	41.0	40.7	40.2	40.0	39.9	40.0	41.0
2003	40.1	39.9	39.8	39.6	39.5	39.8	39.6	39.5	39.1	39.2	39.4	39.5	39.6
2004	39.2	38.8	38.9	38.9	39.0	39.4	39.3	39.3	38.8	38.6	38.9	38.8	39.0
2005	38.5	38.6	38.3	38.2	38.2	38.5	38.2	38.0	37.6	37.5	37.7	37.8	38.1
2006	37.9	37.9	37.9	37.7	37.8	37.9	38.0	38.0	37.7	37.8	38.1	38.3	37.9
2007	37.5	37.9	37.7	38.0	39.0	38.6	38.8	38.9	39.2	39.0	38.1	38.2	38.4
2008	37.9	38.2	37.9	38.5	38.6	38.6	37.9	38.1	37.1	36.9	36.9	37.0	37.8
2009	36.4	36.3	35.5	35.1	34.6	34.5	34.3	34.0	33.3	32.7	32.8	32.3	34.3
2010	31.8	31.7	31.6	31.5	31.7	31.6	31.6	32.0	31.8	31.6	31.7	31.8	31.7
2011	31.5	31.5	31.5	31.4	31.3	31.3	31.5	31.5	31.1	31.0	31.3	31.2	31.3
2012	31.3	31.5	31.0	31.0	31.2	31.0	31.2	31.6	31.4	31.4	31.9	31.5	31.3
2013	31.5	32.3	32.0	31.6	32.1	32.2	32.4	32.4	31.7	31.6	31.6	31.4	31.9

1. Employment by Industry: Connecticut, Selected Years, 2002–2013—*Continued*

(Numbers in thousands, not seasonally adjusted)

Industry and year	January	February	March	April	May	June	July	August	September	October	November	December	Annual average
Financial Activities													
2002	142.8	142.1	142.1	141.4	142.1	143.4	143.9	143.8	142.5	141.8	142.5	143.1	142.6
2003	142.4	141.7	141.7	142.6	143.3	144.7	144.3	144.0	142.4	141.5	141.4	142.0	142.7
2004	140.1	139.6	139.8	139.7	140.1	141.6	142.0	142.1	140.7	140.3	140.7	141.1	140.7
2005	140.5	140.5	140.5	141.6	141.5	143.4	144.2	144.0	142.7	142.4	142.6	143.5	142.3
2006	143.0	142.7	142.9	142.9	143.4	145.1	145.6	145.8	144.5	144.6	145.1	145.6	144.3
2007	144.9	144.4	144.1	144.1	144.4	146.3	146.2	145.7	144.0	143.6	143.5	144.1	144.6
2008	143.0	143.3	144.0	143.2	143.5	145.3	144.8	144.9	142.8	142.0	142.1	142.0	143.4
2009	139.7	139.3	139.4	137.7	137.5	138.5	138.2	137.6	135.8	135.9	135.9	136.0	137.6
2010	134.1	134.1	134.4	133.9	134.3	136.2	136.7	137.0	135.2	135.1	135.6	135.8	135.2
2011	135.3	135.2	135.2	134.9	134.9	135.6	136.6	136.4	134.4	134.0	133.9	134.1	135.0
2012	133.1	132.9	133.1	132.9	133.1	134.7	134.9	134.4	132.7	132.7	132.3	132.2	133.3
2013	131.8	131.2	130.9	130.7	130.9	132.8	133.1	132.4	130.8	131.4	132.3	132.6	131.7
Professional and Business Services													
2002	197.7	197.7	200.7	203.2	203.9	206.2	203.3	204.1	203.4	201.6	201.2	201.0	202.0
2003	193.5	193.4	194.4	196.9	197.1	198.5	196.6	197.7	197.8	198.1	198.7	198.3	196.8
2004	191.2	191.3	193.4	196.7	197.7	200.7	199.3	199.6	199.4	197.2	198.5	199.6	197.1
2005	191.9	193.2	195.3	199.1	199.2	203.1	202.4	202.3	203.3	202.2	203.1	204.0	199.9
2006	196.0	198.5	200.8	204.6	204.7	208.8	205.0	206.2	206.8	205.7	206.3	208.3	204.3
2007	199.4	200.4	201.6	206.1	207.7	211.4	207.4	208.2	207.8	208.2	208.7	210.4	206.4
2008	203.6	203.3	205.0	207.9	207.5	210.2	206.9	206.2	204.8	202.6	200.9	199.8	204.9
2009	192.3	189.7	188.6	190.5	189.8	190.7	187.8	188.3	187.8	188.6	188.8	189.9	189.4
2010	179.5	181.6	182.8	190.9	191.2	193.7	193.1	192.8	192.5	193.7	193.3	193.7	189.9
2011	188.1	189.9	189.6	196.7	196.4	198.7	198.1	197.8	198.2	199.1	200.9	201.2	196.2
2012	194.7	195.2	198.7	203.2	203.3	205.4	204.6	204.5	204.5	204.4	204.9	204.4	202.3
2013	196.9	198.9	199.6	204.8	205.5	207.7	206.9	208.1	206.6	207.0	207.2	206.2	204.6
Education and Health Services													
2002	255.1	258.9	258.9	260.3	259.6	257.1	255.9	253.7	259.4	264.4	266.5	266.9	259.7
2003	261.1	264.3	263.0	265.1	264.6	261.4	260.0	257.0	262.4	268.5	270.0	270.3	264.0
2004	264.4	268.2	267.0	270.3	270.3	266.6	264.3	261.3	268.3	274.0	275.0	274.8	268.7
2005	269.0	273.4	271.8	275.6	274.0	270.1	268.6	265.9	273.1	278.3	279.7	279.8	273.3
2006	274.7	278.4	277.2	280.9	279.5	276.1	275.8	273.7	280.6	284.8	286.4	287.2	279.6
2007	282.1	286.6	285.2	289.3	287.5	285.9	283.8	281.3	288.5	293.0	294.7	295.4	287.8
2008	290.7	295.8	295.3	297.9	296.2	294.4	292.2	289.8	296.8	302.2	304.6	304.7	296.7
2009	299.1	304.3	301.6	302.8	301.9	299.0	298.4	296.3	302.3	306.7	307.5	308.4	302.4
2010	301.8	304.9	304.4	308.8	307.3	304.1	302.9	300.6	308.0	312.8	313.9	313.8	306.9
2011	310.1	313.0	312.7	315.9	315.0	311.2	309.1	307.0	314.2	316.1	317.3	317.8	313.3
2012	313.0	317.9	317.2	318.4	318.5	315.4	312.5	310.6	318.4	321.9	322.7	324.7	317.6
2013	316.8	319.7	320.7	323.4	321.7	319.3	316.1	315.0	322.3	328.4	330.2	329.2	321.9
Leisure and Hospitality													
2002	112.9	113.0	115.0	120.8	126.4	131.4	133.5	131.6	125.2	122.9	120.2	121.0	122.8
2003	114.7	114.6	116.4	121.3	127.8	132.9	136.1	134.7	128.7	126.2	123.9	124.1	125.1
2004	117.9	117.5	119.2	124.4	130.5	136.0	138.3	137.0	131.8	127.5	124.8	126.0	127.6
2005	119.1	119.5	121.5	127.6	133.0	138.5	139.5	138.8	132.8	128.6	126.9	127.7	129.5
2006	122.1	121.8	124.8	129.3	135.2	141.6	142.8	141.7	135.7	133.1	130.6	132.3	132.6
2007	125.4	125.2	126.5	131.4	138.5	144.4	146.4	146.0	139.5	136.1	135.0	134.5	135.7
2008	127.5	128.3	130.3	134.8	142.7	147.1	147.4	146.1	140.7	136.8	133.3	133.0	137.3
2009	124.2	124.9	125.9	129.9	138.1	142.2	143.8	141.9	137.8	133.7	131.0	130.9	133.7
2010	120.3	121.3	123.3	130.8	137.4	141.0	144.4	143.1	139.1	135.8	133.6	133.3	133.6
2011	124.3	125.7	127.2	133.7	139.8	145.0	148.1	146.6	142.5	140.0	137.0	137.6	137.3
2012	130.8	131.5	134.3	139.2	145.9	152.1	152.6	151.3	145.8	143.7	141.7	142.7	142.6
2013	134.7	133.0	137.7	145.0	151.7	157.0	158.2	156.3	150.4	149.4	146.8	146.8	147.3
Other Services													
2002	62.1	61.9	62.3	63.0	63.8	64.4	64.1	63.3	62.0	62.0	62.3	62.8	62.8
2003	61.5	61.3	61.9	61.7	62.2	63.2	63.6	63.0	61.7	62.0	62.0	62.3	62.2
2004	61.5	61.4	61.8	62.3	62.6	63.3	64.0	63.6	62.3	62.2	62.3	62.6	62.5
2005	61.6	61.7	62.1	62.7	62.9	64.1	64.1	63.5	62.5	62.5	62.7	63.4	62.8
2006	62.1	61.8	62.4	63.2	63.8	64.5	65.2	64.8	63.8	64.2	64.2	64.6	63.7
2007	63.4	63.2	63.6	63.9	64.1	65.3	65.5	64.9	64.0	63.8	63.8	64.0	64.1
2008	62.8	62.7	63.0	63.2	63.7	64.5	64.0	63.7	62.5	62.6	62.4	62.3	63.1
2009	61.4	60.9	61.1	61.0	61.3	62.2	62.1	61.6	61.1	60.7	60.7	61.0	61.3
2010	59.4	59.1	59.6	59.9	60.5	61.6	62.2	61.9	60.6	60.6	60.5	60.6	60.5
2011	59.3	59.4	59.5	60.2	60.6	61.7	61.8	61.6	60.1	59.8	59.9	60.3	60.4
2012	60.1	60.2	60.3	60.9	61.4	62.6	63.1	63.0	61.9	62.4	62.6	62.2	61.7
2013	61.1	61.1	61.6	61.9	62.4	63.3	63.5	63.1	61.9	61.4	61.3	62.1	62.1
Government													
2002	248.7	254.9	255.8	254.6	254.2	250.1	231.1	233.9	246.8	251.6	255.3	254.5	249.3
2003	250.3	252.6	253.2	251.5	251.2	246.1	228.2	230.1	242.2	247.5	250.3	248.7	246.0
2004	242.3	247.4	248.8	248.1	246.9	242.0	225.0	228.3	239.4	247.1	250.1	248.7	242.8
2005	241.5	246.9	246.4	248.6	247.8	244.6	225.1	228.4	243.2	249.2	251.8	251.9	243.8
2006	245.6	249.4	249.2	250.2	249.8	244.8	228.1	232.8	243.9	250.2	253.1	253.5	245.9
2007	247.5	252.4	251.8	252.3	252.0	248.5	230.9	234.2	248.2	256.0	258.7	258.0	249.2
2008	252.6	257.7	256.7	257.0	257.6	252.3	233.8	236.3	250.1	257.5	259.8	258.1	252.5
2009	251.7	255.7	255.0	254.8	255.0	248.3	229.1	230.2	244.1	250.2	253.1	251.7	248.2
2010	245.8	249.8	247.9	247.4	254.0	243.9	227.9	229.1	240.4	247.4	248.9	247.9	244.2
2011	241.0	245.1	245.1	247.4	244.9	236.8	224.6	223.4	238.6	244.4	245.9	245.9	240.3
2012	238.4	244.3	244.0	242.8	241.3	235.7	223.1	223.2	237.4	242.0	244.9	245.3	238.5
2013	240.2	241.3	242.0	242.9	243.1	242.6	228.2	223.9	234.3	239.2	241.9	242.1	238.5

2. Average Weekly Hours by Selected Industry: Connecticut, 2009–2013

(Not seasonally adjusted)

Industry and year	January	February	March	April	May	June	July	August	September	October	November	December	Annual average
Total Private													
2009	33.3	33.4	33.1	32.7	33.1	32.9	33.0	33.1	33.0	32.4	33.0	32.7	33.0
2010	33.0	32.5	33.1	33.3	33.5	33.3	33.3	33.6	33.4	33.6	33.5	33.8	33.3
2011	33.2	33.6	33.7	33.7	34.1	33.8	33.9	34.1	34.1	34.4	34.1	34.2	33.9
2012	34.2	33.8	33.9	34.3	33.7	33.8	34.0	33.9	34.3	34.0	34.0	34.2	34.0
2013	33.2	33.0	33.2	33.6	33.6	34.0	33.6	33.6	34.2	33.7	33.6	33.6	33.6
Goods-Producing													
2009	38.0	37.7	37.8	37.0	37.9	38.0	38.6	38.3	38.4	38.3	38.8	38.5	38.1
2010	38.5	37.6	38.7	38.9	38.9	39.0	39.1	38.9	39.0	38.6	38.9	38.9	38.8
2011	36.8	38.1	38.5	38.5	38.6	38.7	38.8	39.1	39.0	39.0	39.2	39.4	38.6
2012	39.0	39.2	39.2	39.6	38.8	39.3	38.8	39.0	39.5	39.3	39.4	40.0	39.3
2013	39.5	38.6	39.6	39.7	39.6	40.0	39.4	40.3	40.4	39.8	39.7	39.6	39.7
Construction													
2009	34.3	35.0	35.5	35.4	36.6	36.5	37.2	37.4	36.4	36.8	36.5	35.5	36.1
2010	35.4	34.6	35.7	36.5	36.8	37.4	37.4	37.8	37.5	37.3	37.1	36.8	36.8
2011	34.0	35.4	35.9	35.9	36.5	36.8	36.9	37.8	37.2	36.6	36.3	37.1	36.4
2012	35.9	36.5	36.7	37.6	37.4	37.5	37.4	37.6	38.7	38.2	38.5	38.7	37.6
2013	38.7	37.6	38.7	38.8	39.1	37.9	38.6	39.8	39.4	37.7	37.7	35.9	38.3
Manufacturing													
2009	40.0	39.2	39.1	38.2	38.7	38.8	39.3	38.9	39.3	39.2	39.9	39.9	39.2
2010	39.9	39.1	39.9	39.8	39.8	39.6	39.7	39.4	39.7	39.3	39.7	40.1	39.7
2011	38.2	39.3	39.5	39.5	39.5	39.6	39.7	39.8	39.9	40.1	40.4	40.4	39.7
2012	40.1	40.1	40.0	40.3	39.4	40.0	39.4	39.6	39.9	39.8	39.9	40.6	39.9
2013	39.8	38.9	39.9	40.0	39.8	40.6	39.6	40.4	40.7	40.4	40.4	40.9	40.1
Trade, Transportation, and Utilities													
2009	33.7	33.4	33.4	33.0	33.5	33.3	33.2	33.3	33.6	33.0	33.3	33.8	33.4
2010	33.2	32.7	33.0	33.1	33.7	33.7	33.3	33.5	33.6	33.8	33.7	34.2	33.5
2011	33.9	34.5	34.4	34.5	34.7	34.3	34.2	34.4	34.8	35.1	35.0	35.3	34.6
2012	34.8	34.6	34.7	34.9	34.8	34.4	34.8	34.2	34.9	34.6	34.8	34.7	34.7
2013	33.7	33.5	33.8	34.0	34.0	34.0	33.7	33.6	33.8	33.4	33.4	33.9	33.7
Financial Activities													
2009	35.8	35.8	35.9	35.4	35.5	35.7	35.2	36.0	35.5	35.7	37.1	36.0	35.8
2010	36.0	36.1	36.5	36.2	37.2	36.7	36.9	37.2	36.6	36.8	37.1	37.3	36.7
2011	37.3	37.0	37.1	36.8	37.4	36.8	36.8	36.8	37.0	37.7	37.0	37.0	37.1
2012	37.9	36.6	36.7	37.4	36.6	36.9	38.1	37.1	37.7	36.9	37.1	37.9	37.2
2013	36.6	37.3	37.2	37.1	36.9	37.7	36.5	36.7	37.9	37.1	37.2	37.9	37.2
Professional and Business Services													
2009	33.0	33.6	33.2	33.2	33.5	33.1	33.1	33.5	32.7	33.2	34.1	33.0	33.3
2010	33.4	32.8	33.6	34.0	34.4	33.8	33.3	34.0	33.3	33.4	33.5	33.7	33.6
2011	33.7	33.8	34.0	34.0	35.2	35.1	35.0	34.8	35.0	34.9	34.4	34.4	34.5
2012	34.7	33.8	34.3	35.0	34.8	35.2	35.4	35.0	35.7	34.7	34.9	35.3	34.9
2013	33.7	33.7	34.1	35.0	35.0	35.8	34.7	34.2	35.7	35.0	34.5	34.7	34.7
Education and Health Services													
2009	30.7	31.0	30.5	30.0	30.1	30.1	30.3	30.3	30.8	30.7	30.7	30.5	30.5
2010	30.7	30.0	30.3	30.4	30.6	30.6	30.9	31.1	30.6	30.5	30.3	30.6	30.5
2011	30.2	30.6	30.7	30.9	30.9	30.8	31.0	31.2	31.0	31.1	30.9	31.3	30.9
2012	31.4	31.0	31.0	31.3	31.0	30.9	31.0	31.2	30.9	31.2	31.0	31.4	31.1
2013	31.2	31.2	31.2	31.3	31.1	31.4	31.3	31.2	31.4	31.2	31.2	31.0	31.2
Leisure and Hospitality													
2009	25.6	27.0	26.0	26.5	26.5	25.9	26.5	26.5	26.2	26.8	26.7	25.9	26.3
2010	25.0	25.1	25.1	26.5	26.3	25.9	26.7	26.8	26.5	26.8	26.7	26.3	26.2
2011	25.0	26.4	26.2	26.4	26.6	26.7	27.0	26.8	26.7	27.0	27.1	26.9	26.6
2012	26.0	26.1	26.1	26.3	25.8	26.0	26.5	26.8	26.4	26.0	25.5	26.1	26.1
2013	24.5	24.4	24.9	26.0	26.2	26.3	26.8	26.8	26.7	26.1	25.7	24.8	25.8
Other Services													
2009	29.2	28.8	28.8	28.7	29.5	29.7	29.6	29.7	29.5	29.8	29.7	29.2	29.3
2010	29.0	28.8	29.0	28.7	29.1	28.9	30.2	30.2	29.7	30.3	30.1	30.1	29.5
2011	29.4	29.9	29.2	29.9	30.8	30.5	31.8	32.0	31.0	32.1	31.1	31.2	30.8
2012	31.9	31.7	31.8	32.0	30.8	31.2	31.3	32.1	31.6	31.2	31.0	30.7	31.4
2013	30.5	30.2	30.0	29.8	30.5	31.1	31.7	31.7	31.6	31.3	31.7	30.7	30.9

3. Average Hourly Earnings by Selected Industry: Connecticut, 2009–2013

(Dollars, not seasonally adjusted)

Industry and year	January	February	March	April	May	June	July	August	September	October	November	December	Annual average
Total Private													
2009	27.96	28.17	28.33	27.98	27.57	27.43	27.64	27.82	27.43	27.56	27.93	27.95	27.81
2010	27.75	28.22	28.04	28.43	28.43	27.83	27.78	28.12	28.12	28.01	28.09	28.15	28.08
2011	28.39	28.35	28.29	28.21	28.24	27.88	28.15	28.07	28.14	28.47	28.37	28.32	28.24
2012	28.72	28.33	28.24	28.50	27.96	27.77	27.91	27.73	28.10	27.93	28.22	28.31	28.14
2013	28.33	28.32	28.01	28.08	27.89	28.08	27.82	27.79	27.93	27.72	27.60	28.03	27.96
Goods-Producing													
2009	29.89	29.53	29.64	29.93	29.72	29.68	29.33	29.52	29.15	29.36	29.11	29.85	29.56
2010	29.72	29.92	29.76	29.55	29.83	29.74	29.72	29.79	30.06	29.87	29.78	30.17	29.83
2011	30.44	30.32	30.43	30.26	29.85	30.27	30.13	30.22	30.26	30.41	30.15	30.75	30.29
2012	30.87	30.31	30.53	30.73	30.33	29.93	30.16	30.03	30.15	30.06	30.06	30.20	30.28
2013	30.50	30.22	29.95	29.68	29.93	29.97	30.09	29.91	30.18	29.96	30.18	30.31	30.07
Construction													
2009	29.20	29.16	28.86	28.75	28.53	28.29	28.29	28.61	28.70	29.27	29.23	29.63	28.86
2010	29.65	30.22	30.42	29.11	29.05	28.63	29.01	28.98	29.35	28.87	28.79	29.14	29.22
2011	29.64	29.54	29.69	28.92	28.35	28.50	29.14	28.79	29.08	29.12	29.33	29.15	29.08
2012	28.31	28.42	28.77	28.64	28.60	28.46	28.70	28.55	28.75	29.14	29.71	29.58	28.82
2013	29.63	29.72	29.34	28.88	29.47	29.25	29.29	29.61	30.08	29.71	29.65	30.39	29.58
Manufacturing													
2009	29.93	29.31	29.55	30.02	29.85	29.90	29.57	29.76	29.19	29.20	28.90	29.77	29.58
2010	29.75	29.87	29.58	29.60	30.02	29.93	29.82	29.91	30.15	30.22	30.12	30.42	29.95
2011	30.60	30.47	30.58	30.61	30.29	30.80	30.42	30.47	30.41	30.64	30.26	31.02	30.55
2012	31.39	30.66	30.86	31.14	30.68	30.22	30.47	30.36	30.47	30.24	30.05	30.32	30.57
2013	30.70	30.32	30.07	29.87	30.01	30.10	30.26	29.93	30.15	29.99	30.32	30.25	30.16
Trade, Transportation, and Utilities													
2009	22.55	22.62	22.59	23.16	22.39	22.37	21.46	21.47	21.61	21.16	21.10	21.00	21.95
2010	21.47	22.11	21.50	22.39	22.84	22.54	22.99	22.80	23.17	23.25	23.61	23.83	22.73
2011	24.25	24.73	24.46	24.89	25.38	25.06	25.49	25.18	25.74	25.69	26.06	25.11	25.18
2012	25.40	25.30	25.14	25.65	25.00	24.88	25.32	25.33	25.59	24.97	25.35	24.97	25.24
2013	25.31	25.06	24.32	24.59	24.22	24.41	24.25	24.11	24.21	24.02	23.39	23.67	24.29
Financial Activities													
2009	40.42	42.19	43.26	41.48	41.41	40.49	40.92	41.82	39.72	41.15	41.98	41.57	41.37
2010	40.01	40.11	40.68	41.69	42.21	40.86	41.23	42.14	41.10	41.69	42.03	42.46	41.36
2011	43.10	42.87	42.82	42.75	43.56	42.39	42.18	42.58	40.61	42.77	41.54	41.60	42.40
2012	41.80	40.80	41.01	42.25	40.99	41.46	42.28	41.26	41.70	40.79	41.65	41.70	41.48
2013	40.95	40.74	41.71	43.33	42.66	44.08	43.50	43.44	44.62	43.44	43.17	43.93	42.97
Professional and Business Services													
2009	32.18	32.06	32.07	30.70	30.37	29.92	29.67	29.99	30.07	29.38	29.64	30.21	30.52
2010	30.48	30.40	30.26	29.51	29.81	29.39	29.70	30.08	29.97	30.39	30.18	30.30	30.03
2011	31.44	30.97	30.68	30.55	30.12	29.45	29.99	29.99	30.11	30.39	30.35	30.48	30.36
2012	31.19	30.92	30.58	30.54	30.28	29.77	29.88	29.73	30.51	29.84	30.00	30.40	30.29
2013	30.82	31.00	30.82	30.45	30.47	30.33	30.10	30.40	30.48	30.39	30.56	30.98	30.56
Education and Health Services													
2009	25.92	25.74	26.03	26.09	26.15	26.09	26.14	25.98	25.79	25.83	25.89	25.70	25.94
2010	25.76	25.98	26.01	25.91	26.09	26.10	26.09	26.06	26.04	26.40	26.42	26.54	26.12
2011	26.95	26.27	26.17	26.19	26.18	26.27	26.78	26.34	26.41	26.47	26.56	26.59	26.43
2012	26.87	26.44	26.41	26.27	26.10	26.00	26.06	26.04	26.14	25.93	26.09	26.17	26.21
2013	25.89	25.74	25.24	25.31	25.15	25.01	24.98	25.03	25.03	25.02	24.91	25.38	25.22
Leisure and Hospitality													
2009	15.55	15.40	15.17	15.16	15.02	15.40	15.26	15.53	15.71	15.34	15.22	15.45	15.35
2010	15.37	15.29	15.01	15.16	15.25	15.26	14.91	15.23	15.54	15.45	15.35	15.65	15.29
2011	15.55	15.46	15.49	15.42	15.38	14.96	15.02	14.90	15.21	15.03	15.11	15.17	15.21
2012	14.98	15.18	15.00	15.26	15.18	15.06	14.93	14.85	15.16	15.20	15.29	15.52	15.13
2013	15.59	15.70	15.59	15.41	15.37	14.99	14.89	14.74	15.13	15.15	15.15	15.32	15.23
Other Services													
2009	22.67	22.38	22.19	22.71	21.95	21.82	21.67	21.71	21.95	21.93	22.08	22.35	22.11
2010	22.36	22.05	22.14	22.10	21.86	21.83	21.76	21.81	21.95	21.80	21.77	22.35	21.98
2011	22.60	21.56	21.22	21.03	20.83	20.57	19.61	19.25	19.88	19.30	19.38	19.12	20.33
2012	19.89	20.14	19.87	19.56	20.08	20.00	19.78	19.93	20.17	20.48	20.10	21.00	20.08
2013	21.42	21.93	21.28	21.48	21.72	21.29	20.81	21.03	21.42	21.64	21.66	21.97	21.46

4. Average Weekly Earnings by Selected Industry: Connecticut, 2009–2013

(Dollars, not seasonally adjusted)

Industry and year	January	February	March	April	May	June	July	August	September	October	November	December	Annual average
Total Private													
2009	931.07	940.88	937.72	914.95	912.57	902.45	912.12	920.84	905.19	892.94	921.69	913.97	917.73
2010	915.75	917.15	928.12	946.72	952.41	926.74	925.07	944.83	939.21	941.14	941.02	951.47	935.06
2011	942.55	952.56	953.37	950.68	962.98	942.34	954.29	957.19	959.57	979.37	967.42	968.54	957.34
2012	982.22	957.55	957.34	977.55	942.25	938.63	948.94	940.05	963.83	949.62	959.48	968.20	956.76
2013	940.56	934.56	929.93	943.49	937.10	954.72	934.75	933.74	955.21	934.16	927.36	941.81	939.46
Goods-Producing													
2009	1,135.82	1,113.28	1,120.39	1,107.41	1,126.39	1,127.84	1,132.14	1,130.62	1,119.36	1,124.49	1,129.47	1,149.23	1,126.24
2010	1,144.22	1,124.99	1,151.71	1,149.50	1,160.39	1,159.86	1,162.05	1,158.83	1,172.34	1,152.98	1,158.44	1,173.61	1,157.40
2011	1,120.19	1,155.19	1,171.56	1,165.01	1,152.21	1,171.45	1,169.04	1,181.60	1,180.14	1,185.99	1,181.88	1,211.55	1,169.19
2012	1,203.93	1,188.15	1,196.78	1,216.91	1,176.80	1,176.25	1,170.21	1,171.17	1,190.93	1,181.36	1,184.36	1,208.00	1,190.00
2013	1,204.75	1,166.49	1,186.02	1,178.30	1,185.23	1,198.80	1,185.55	1,205.37	1,219.27	1,192.41	1,198.15	1,200.28	1,193.78
Construction													
2009	1,001.56	1,020.60	1,024.53	1,017.75	1,044.20	1,032.59	1,052.39	1,070.01	1,044.68	1,077.14	1,066.90	1,051.87	1,041.85
2010	1,049.61	1,045.61	1,085.99	1,062.52	1,069.04	1,070.76	1,084.97	1,095.44	1,100.63	1,076.85	1,068.11	1,072.35	1,075.30
2011	1,007.76	1,045.72	1,065.87	1,038.23	1,034.78	1,048.80	1,075.27	1,088.26	1,081.78	1,065.79	1,064.68	1,081.47	1,058.51
2012	1,016.33	1,037.33	1,055.86	1,076.86	1,069.64	1,067.25	1,073.38	1,073.48	1,112.63	1,113.15	1,143.84	1,144.75	1,083.63
2013	1,146.68	1,117.47	1,135.46	1,120.54	1,152.28	1,108.58	1,130.59	1,178.48	1,185.15	1,120.07	1,117.81	1,091.00	1,132.91
Manufacturing													
2009	1,197.20	1,148.95	1,155.41	1,146.76	1,155.20	1,160.12	1,162.10	1,157.66	1,147.17	1,144.64	1,153.11	1,187.82	1,159.54
2010	1,187.03	1,167.92	1,180.24	1,178.08	1,194.80	1,185.23	1,183.85	1,178.45	1,196.96	1,187.65	1,195.76	1,219.84	1,189.02
2011	1,168.92	1,197.47	1,207.91	1,209.10	1,196.46	1,219.68	1,207.67	1,212.71	1,213.36	1,228.66	1,222.50	1,253.21	1,212.84
2012	1,258.74	1,229.47	1,234.40	1,254.94	1,208.79	1,208.80	1,200.52	1,202.26	1,215.75	1,203.55	1,199.00	1,230.99	1,219.74
2013	1,221.86	1,179.45	1,199.79	1,194.80	1,194.40	1,222.06	1,198.30	1,209.17	1,227.11	1,211.60	1,224.93	1,237.23	1,209.42
Trade, Transportation, and Utilities													
2009	759.94	755.51	754.51	764.28	750.07	744.92	712.47	714.95	726.10	698.28	702.63	709.80	733.13
2010	712.80	723.00	709.50	741.11	769.71	759.60	765.57	763.80	778.51	785.85	795.66	814.99	761.46
2011	822.08	853.19	841.42	858.71	880.69	859.56	871.76	866.19	895.75	901.72	912.10	886.38	871.23
2012	883.92	875.38	872.36	895.19	870.00	855.87	881.14	866.29	893.09	863.96	882.18	866.46	875.83
2013	852.95	839.51	822.02	836.06	823.48	829.94	817.23	810.10	818.30	802.27	781.23	802.41	818.57
Financial Activities													
2009	1,447.04	1,510.40	1,553.03	1,468.39	1,470.06	1,445.49	1,440.38	1,505.52	1,410.06	1,469.06	1,557.46	1,496.52	1,481.05
2010	1,440.36	1,447.97	1,484.82	1,509.18	1,570.21	1,499.56	1,521.39	1,567.61	1,504.26	1,534.19	1,559.31	1,583.76	1,517.91
2011	1,607.63	1,586.19	1,588.62	1,573.20	1,629.14	1,559.95	1,552.22	1,566.94	1,502.57	1,612.43	1,536.98	1,539.20	1,573.04
2012	1,584.22	1,493.28	1,505.07	1,580.15	1,500.23	1,529.87	1,610.87	1,530.75	1,572.09	1,505.15	1,545.22	1,580.43	1,543.06
2013	1,498.77	1,519.60	1,551.61	1,607.54	1,574.15	1,661.82	1,587.75	1,594.25	1,691.10	1,611.62	1,605.92	1,664.95	1,598.48
Professional and Business Services													
2009	1,061.94	1,077.22	1,064.72	1,019.24	1,017.40	990.35	982.08	1,004.67	983.29	975.42	1,010.72	996.93	1,016.32
2010	1,018.03	997.12	1,016.74	1,003.34	1,025.46	993.38	989.01	1,022.72	998.00	1,015.03	1,011.03	1,021.11	1,009.01
2011	1,059.53	1,046.79	1,043.12	1,038.70	1,060.22	1,033.70	1,049.65	1,043.65	1,053.85	1,060.61	1,044.04	1,048.51	1,047.42
2012	1,082.29	1,045.10	1,048.89	1,068.90	1,053.74	1,047.90	1,057.75	1,040.55	1,089.21	1,035.45	1,047.00	1,073.12	1,057.12
2013	1,038.63	1,044.70	1,050.96	1,065.75	1,066.45	1,085.81	1,044.47	1,039.68	1,088.14	1,063.65	1,054.32	1,075.01	1,060.43
Education and Health Services													
2009	795.74	797.94	793.92	782.70	787.12	785.31	792.04	787.19	794.33	792.98	794.82	783.85	791.17
2010	790.83	779.40	788.10	787.66	798.35	798.66	806.18	810.47	796.82	805.20	800.53	812.12	796.66
2011	813.89	803.86	803.42	809.27	808.96	809.12	830.18	821.81	818.71	823.22	820.70	832.27	816.69
2012	843.72	819.64	818.71	822.25	809.10	803.40	807.86	812.45	807.73	809.02	808.79	821.74	815.13
2013	807.77	803.09	787.49	792.20	782.17	785.31	781.87	780.94	785.94	780.62	777.19	786.78	786.86
Leisure and Hospitality													
2009	398.08	415.80	394.42	401.74	398.03	398.86	404.39	411.55	411.60	411.11	406.37	400.16	403.71
2010	384.25	383.78	376.75	401.74	401.08	395.23	398.10	408.16	411.81	414.06	409.85	411.60	400.60
2011	388.75	408.14	405.84	407.09	409.11	399.43	405.54	399.32	406.11	405.81	409.48	408.07	404.59
2012	389.48	396.20	391.50	401.34	391.64	391.56	395.65	397.98	400.22	395.20	389.90	405.07	394.89
2013	381.96	383.08	388.19	400.66	402.69	394.24	399.05	395.03	403.97	395.42	389.36	379.94	392.93
Other Services													
2009	661.96	644.54	639.07	651.78	647.53	648.05	641.43	644.79	647.53	653.51	655.78	652.62	647.82
2010	648.44	635.04	642.06	634.27	636.13	630.89	657.15	658.66	651.92	660.54	655.28	672.74	648.41
2011	664.44	644.64	619.62	628.80	641.56	627.39	623.60	616.00	616.28	619.53	602.72	596.54	626.16
2012	634.49	638.44	631.87	625.92	618.46	624.00	619.11	639.75	637.37	638.98	623.10	644.70	630.51
2013	653.31	662.29	638.40	640.10	662.46	662.12	659.68	666.65	676.87	677.33	686.62	674.48	663.42

DELAWARE
At a Glance

Population:
    2000 census: 783,559
    2010 census: 897,934
    2013 estimate: 925,749

Percent change in population:
    2000–2010: 14.6%
    2010–2013: 3.1%

Percent change in total nonfarm employment:
    2000–2010: -1.6%
    2010–2013: 3.3%

Industry with the largest growth in employment, 2000–2013 (thousands):
    Education and Health Services, 23.7

Industry with the largest decline or smallest growth in employment, 2000–2013 (thousands):
    Manufacturing, -16.2

Civilian labor force:
    2000: 416,503
    2010: 436,052
    2013: 443,020

Unemployment rate and rank among states (lowest to highest):
    2000: 3.3%, 14th
    2010: 8.0%, 17th
    2013: 6.7%, 23rd

Over-the-year change in unemployment rates:
    2010–2011: -0.6%
    2011–2012: -0.3
    2012–2013: -0.4

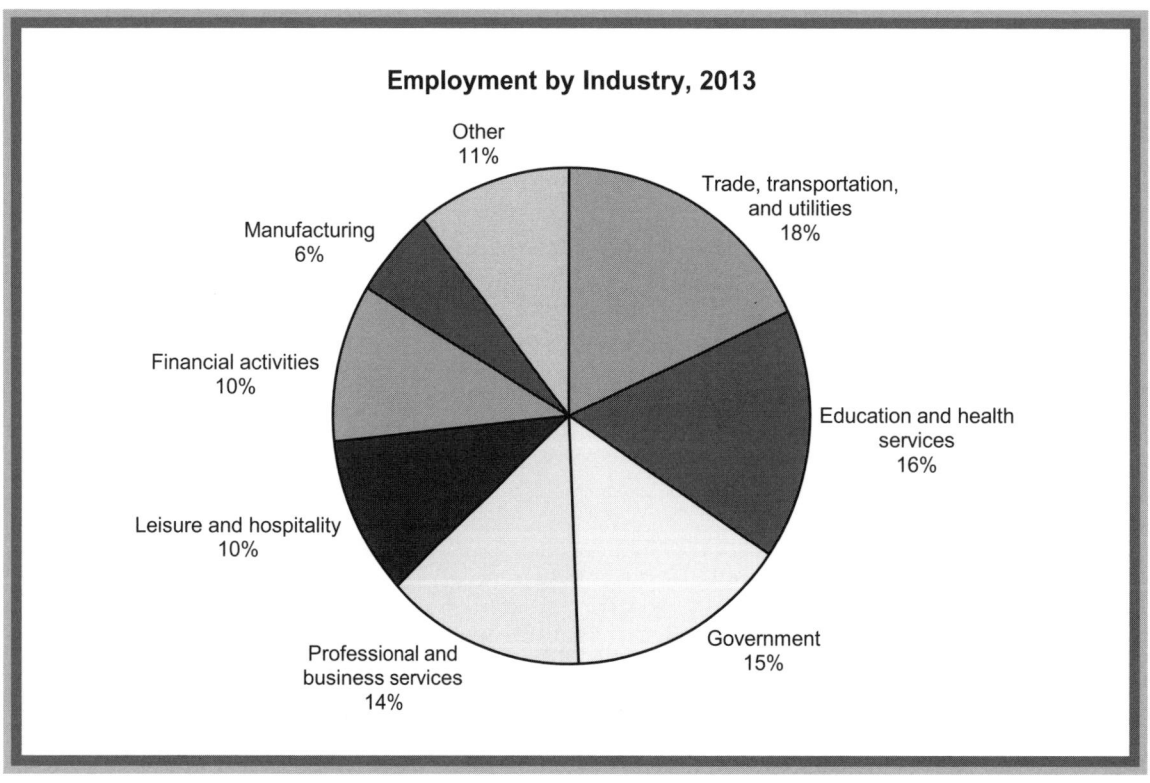

Employment by Industry, 2013

Other 11%
Trade, transportation, and utilities 18%
Manufacturing 6%
Financial activities 10%
Education and health services 16%
Leisure and hospitality 10%
Professional and business services 14%
Government 15%

1. Employment by Industry: Delaware, Selected Years, 2002–2013

(Numbers in thousands, not seasonally adjusted)

Industry and year	January	February	March	April	May	June	July	August	September	October	November	December	Annual average
Total Nonfarm													
2002	404.3	405.9	408.8	412.5	418.2	420.2	419.5	418.9	420.5	416.8	419.3	419.9	415.4
2003	404.1	401.5	405.7	411.0	417.2	422.5	419.2	419.2	420.2	420.9	422.4	424.1	415.7
2004	412.0	413.9	418.7	419.4	425.9	431.3	428.3	427.9	428.6	430.2	432.5	432.3	425.1
2005	418.6	419.5	424.4	430.6	434.9	436.3	436.0	436.2	437.4	437.6	442.5	441.3	432.9
2006	427.5	428.0	432.5	436.3	441.6	444.3	439.6	439.2	439.9	441.0	442.9	444.8	438.1
2007	428.7	427.6	432.8	436.7	442.3	445.8	441.6	441.1	440.2	440.5	444.3	445.7	438.9
2008	430.7	431.8	434.9	439.7	441.8	443.7	439.7	438.2	436.3	435.4	435.9	433.4	436.8
2009	415.7	414.2	415.0	416.9	422.0	421.5	416.7	415.6	415.0	416.1	415.7	414.8	416.6
2010	399.9	397.2	403.9	411.5	417.2	419.8	420.2	418.9	419.3	418.0	419.2	420.3	413.8
2011	406.7	407.7	411.6	419.6	420.0	421.5	420.5	418.4	419.6	418.3	420.1	420.8	417.1
2012	406.8	407.6	412.4	416.7	422.1	423.5	422.8	421.9	421.8	423.6	426.9	427.3	419.5
2013	412.8	414.9	419.4	424.0	429.0	431.1	431.3	431.2	430.4	432.3	436.5	435.9	427.4
Total Private													
2002	348.6	348.9	351.1	354.6	360.5	364.0	364.7	365.5	363.0	358.2	360.0	360.9	358.3
2003	347.4	344.2	348.0	352.8	358.6	365.3	364.3	365.4	363.0	362.5	364.1	365.6	358.4
2004	354.9	356.1	359.9	361.3	367.3	374.0	373.1	373.2	370.4	371.7	373.8	373.5	367.4
2005	360.6	360.6	364.3	370.0	374.1	378.2	378.5	379.8	377.5	375.9	380.6	379.7	373.3
2006	367.6	366.9	370.1	373.8	378.3	384.7	381.2	382.1	379.5	378.8	380.3	382.3	377.1
2007	368.1	365.9	369.9	373.5	378.8	385.1	382.1	382.5	378.7	376.9	380.4	382.0	377.0
2008	368.6	369.0	370.9	375.2	377.2	382.2	379.4	378.6	373.6	371.2	371.9	369.6	374.0
2009	353.6	350.6	349.9	351.7	356.9	359.6	357.2	356.3	352.4	350.8	350.4	350.1	353.3
2010	337.9	334.2	339.2	346.2	350.8	356.4	358.7	358.6	355.6	353.2	353.8	355.1	350.0
2011	344.0	344.0	346.7	353.3	355.0	359.2	359.8	358.3	356.0	353.2	354.9	355.8	353.4
2012	344.6	343.7	347.3	351.7	356.7	361.0	362.0	362.1	358.4	358.7	361.8	362.2	355.9
2013	351.4	350.9	354.0	358.4	363.2	368.1	370.1	371.0	366.5	367.0	370.3	370.9	363.5
Goods-Producing													
2002	60.5	61.1	61.2	59.7	61.8	62.2	62.3	62.2	61.9	61.1	60.8	60.8	61.3
2003	57.5	57.1	57.9	58.7	60.2	61.8	60.5	61.2	61.4	62.0	61.8	60.5	60.1
2004	58.7	59.1	60.1	60.8	61.2	62.2	62.2	62.1	61.2	61.7	61.6	61.0	61.0
2005	58.1	59.0	60.0	61.2	61.9	61.1	61.1	62.4	62.3	61.9	64.2	61.2	61.2
2006	61.7	61.3	62.0	62.7	63.1	64.1	63.0	63.7	63.8	63.7	63.2	62.8	62.9
2007	60.3	59.0	60.1	60.6	61.5	61.9	60.9	61.4	60.5	59.9	61.0	60.4	60.6
2008	57.3	58.1	58.0	58.6	57.6	58.6	56.9	56.8	55.5	54.7	55.4	53.9	56.8
2009	50.5	48.9	48.3	48.2	48.5	48.5	47.8	47.7	46.9	47.2	46.8	46.1	48.0
2010	44.4	42.9	43.9	45.4	45.5	46.3	45.9	46.1	45.8	45.8	45.6	45.5	45.3
2011	44.0	43.9	44.7	45.8	46.0	45.8	45.7	45.0	45.0	45.2	44.7	44.5	45.0
2012	43.0	42.7	42.9	43.7	44.3	44.5	45.2	45.0	44.9	44.7	44.8	44.6	44.2
2013	43.9	43.5	43.7	44.2	44.7	45.1	45.3	45.8	45.6	45.9	46.4	45.9	45.0
Service-Providing													
2002	343.8	344.8	347.6	352.8	356.4	358.0	357.2	356.7	358.6	355.7	358.5	359.1	354.1
2003	346.6	344.4	347.8	352.3	357.0	360.7	358.7	358.0	358.8	358.9	360.6	363.6	355.6
2004	353.3	354.8	358.6	358.6	364.7	369.1	366.1	365.8	367.4	368.5	370.9	371.3	364.1
2005	360.5	360.5	364.4	369.4	373.0	375.2	374.9	373.8	375.1	375.7	378.3	380.1	371.7
2006	365.8	366.7	370.5	373.6	378.5	380.2	376.6	375.5	376.1	377.3	379.7	382.0	375.2
2007	368.4	368.6	372.7	376.1	380.8	383.9	380.7	379.7	379.7	380.6	383.3	385.3	378.3
2008	373.4	373.7	376.9	381.1	384.2	385.1	382.8	381.4	380.8	380.7	380.5	379.5	380.0
2009	365.2	365.3	366.7	368.7	373.5	373.0	368.9	367.9	368.1	368.9	368.9	368.7	368.7
2010	355.5	354.3	360.0	366.1	371.7	373.5	374.3	372.8	373.5	372.2	373.6	374.8	368.5
2011	362.7	363.8	366.9	373.8	374.0	375.7	374.8	373.4	374.6	373.1	375.4	376.3	372.0
2012	363.8	364.9	369.5	373.0	377.8	379.0	377.6	376.9	376.9	378.9	382.1	382.7	375.3
2013	368.9	371.4	375.7	379.8	384.3	386.0	386.0	385.4	384.8	386.4	390.1	390.0	382.4
Mining, Logging, and Construction													
2002	23.4	23.1	23.2	24.0	24.4	24.9	25.3	25.1	24.6	24.1	24.0	24.2	24.2
2003	23.0	21.6	22.2	23.4	24.3	24.9	25.5	25.5	25.2	25.7	25.8	25.6	24.4
2004	24.4	24.1	25.1	25.8	26.1	27.0	27.4	27.5	27.3	27.7	27.6	26.8	26.4
2005	25.9	25.5	26.3	27.5	27.9	28.5	28.7	28.5	28.4	29.6	30.4	28.9	28.0
2006	28.0	27.8	28.3	29.3	29.6	30.5	30.1	30.2	30.1	30.1	29.5	29.1	29.4
2007	27.2	26.0	26.8	27.4	28.0	28.2	28.1	28.0	28.0	27.3	27.5	26.9	27.5
2008	25.7	25.1	25.3	26.3	26.1	26.1	25.8	25.6	24.7	23.8	23.6	22.7	25.1
2009	20.7	19.9	20.1	20.0	20.4	20.6	20.4	20.3	19.6	19.8	19.5	19.1	20.0
2010	18.0	17.1	18.0	19.3	19.6	20.1	19.9	20.1	19.8	20.0	20.0	19.9	19.3
2011	18.7	18.6	19.3	20.2	20.1	19.9	19.6	19.1	19.2	19.3	18.9	18.8	19.3
2012	17.7	17.3	17.4	18.1	18.5	18.7	19.1	19.1	19.0	19.1	19.3	19.2	18.5
2013	18.5	18.3	18.6	19.1	19.5	19.7	20.0	20.3	20.1	20.4	21.0	20.6	19.7

1. Employment by Industry: Delaware, Selected Years, 2002–2013—*Continued*

(Numbers in thousands, not seasonally adjusted)

Industry and year	January	February	March	April	May	June	July	August	September	October	November	December	Annual average
Manufacturing													
2002	37.1	38.0	38.0	35.7	37.4	37.3	37.0	37.1	37.3	37.0	36.8	36.6	37.1
2003	34.5	35.5	35.7	35.3	35.9	36.9	35.0	35.7	36.2	36.3	36.0	34.9	35.7
2004	34.3	35.0	35.0	35.0	35.1	35.2	34.8	34.6	33.9	34.0	34.0	34.2	34.6
2005	32.2	33.5	33.7	33.7	34.0	32.6	32.4	33.9	33.9	32.3	33.8	32.3	33.2
2006	33.7	33.5	33.7	33.4	33.5	33.6	32.9	33.5	33.7	33.6	33.7	33.7	33.5
2007	33.1	33.0	33.3	33.2	33.5	33.7	32.8	33.4	32.5	32.6	33.5	33.5	33.2
2008	31.6	33.0	32.7	32.3	31.5	32.5	31.1	31.2	30.8	30.9	31.8	31.2	31.7
2009	29.8	29.0	28.2	28.2	28.1	27.9	27.4	27.4	27.3	27.4	27.3	27.0	27.9
2010	26.4	25.8	25.9	26.1	25.9	26.2	26.0	26.0	26.0	25.8	25.6	25.6	25.9
2011	25.3	25.3	25.4	25.6	25.9	25.9	26.1	25.9	25.8	25.9	25.8	25.7	25.7
2012	25.3	25.4	25.5	25.6	25.8	25.8	26.1	25.9	25.9	25.6	25.5	25.4	25.7
2013	25.4	25.2	25.1	25.1	25.2	25.4	25.3	25.5	25.5	25.5	25.4	25.3	25.3
Trade, Transportation, and Utilities													
2002	74.9	74.2	75.1	75.4	76.9	77.8	77.8	77.7	77.9	77.3	79.0	80.4	77.0
2003	76.1	75.1	76.2	77.0	78.3	79.4	78.9	79.4	79.1	79.8	81.3	83.3	78.7
2004	78.6	78.1	78.7	79.4	80.2	81.8	81.3	81.0	80.8	81.5	83.6	84.5	80.8
2005	79.9	78.9	79.8	80.3	81.1	81.8	82.1	82.1	81.7	82.5	84.5	86.1	81.7
2006	81.1	80.1	80.9	81.7	82.8	83.5	83.0	82.4	81.9	82.5	84.7	85.6	82.5
2007	81.9	80.6	81.1	81.3	82.9	83.9	83.8	83.7	83.2	82.8	85.2	86.1	83.0
2008	81.5	80.4	80.9	80.4	81.3	81.9	81.3	80.9	80.3	80.7	81.7	82.6	81.2
2009	76.3	74.9	74.7	74.3	75.1	75.5	75.0	74.9	74.9	74.8	76.3	76.8	75.3
2010	72.6	71.2	72.2	73.2	74.5	75.2	75.0	74.8	74.8	75.1	77.1	78.0	74.5
2011	74.0	73.4	73.7	75.1	75.3	76.1	75.6	75.5	75.4	75.3	77.7	78.5	75.5
2012	74.4	73.4	74.3	74.6	75.9	76.1	75.8	75.7	75.3	76.2	79.1	79.4	75.9
2013	75.0	74.4	75.2	76.0	76.8	77.3	77.6	78.0	78.1	78.3	79.7	81.1	77.3
Wholesale Trade													
2002	13.3	13.2	13.6	13.5	13.7	13.8	13.8	13.9	13.8	13.7	13.6	13.7	13.6
2003	13.6	13.6	13.9	14.0	14.3	14.2	14.4	14.5	14.4	14.3	14.3	14.4	14.2
2004	14.3	14.3	14.4	14.7	14.8	14.9	15.0	14.9	14.8	15.0	14.9	14.9	14.7
2005	14.8	14.8	14.9	14.9	14.9	14.8	14.8	14.9	14.8	15.0	15.1	15.3	14.9
2006	14.9	15.0	15.0	15.2	15.3	15.3	15.3	15.2	15.1	15.0	14.9	15.2	15.1
2007	14.8	14.7	14.7	14.9	15.0	15.1	15.2	15.2	15.0	14.8	14.9	14.9	14.9
2008	14.7	14.7	14.8	14.6	14.8	14.7	14.7	14.5	14.4	14.5	14.4	14.2	14.6
2009	13.7	13.6	13.5	13.5	13.4	13.2	13.2	13.1	12.9	12.9	12.8	12.7	13.2
2010	12.4	12.5	12.5	12.6	12.6	12.5	12.6	12.5	12.6	12.4	12.4	12.4	12.5
2011	12.5	12.6	12.5	12.6	12.5	12.6	12.6	12.6	12.5	12.5	12.5	12.5	12.5
2012	12.4	12.4	12.6	12.6	12.5	12.5	12.5	12.4	12.3	12.3	12.3	12.3	12.4
2013	12.0	12.1	12.2	12.2	12.3	12.3	12.3	12.3	12.3	12.2	12.2	12.2	12.2
Retail Trade													
2002	49.6	48.7	49.3	49.7	50.7	51.7	51.9	51.9	51.6	51.0	52.8	54.2	51.1
2003	50.0	49.0	49.8	50.5	51.3	52.4	52.4	52.8	51.8	52.4	53.8	55.1	51.8
2004	51.0	50.3	50.7	51.1	51.9	53.2	53.1	53.2	52.4	52.8	54.9	55.7	52.5
2005	52.0	51.1	51.6	52.3	53.1	53.8	54.4	54.4	53.4	53.7	55.6	57.0	53.5
2006	52.9	51.7	52.4	52.9	53.6	54.2	54.3	53.9	52.8	53.2	55.7	56.1	53.6
2007	53.1	52.1	52.7	52.8	53.9	54.9	55.1	54.9	54.2	54.1	56.5	57.2	54.3
2008	53.4	52.2	52.5	52.2	52.8	53.6	53.2	53.1	52.2	52.4	53.5	54.3	53.0
2009	49.9	48.6	48.6	48.4	49.2	49.9	50.2	50.1	49.5	49.4	51.0	51.6	49.7
2010	48.0	46.7	47.6	48.5	49.6	50.5	50.9	50.8	49.9	50.3	52.3	53.0	49.8
2011	49.2	48.5	48.9	50.1	50.3	51.1	51.3	51.4	50.4	50.2	52.5	53.1	50.6
2012	49.6	48.6	49.2	49.9	50.7	51.2	51.2	51.1	50.0	50.4	53.0	53.1	50.7
2013	49.4	48.9	49.5	50.2	50.9	51.6	52.0	52.4	51.4	51.5	52.7	53.9	51.2
Transportation and Utilities													
2002	12.0	12.3	12.2	12.2	12.5	12.3	12.1	11.9	12.5	12.6	12.6	12.5	12.3
2003	12.5	12.5	12.5	12.5	12.7	12.8	12.1	12.1	12.9	13.1	13.2	13.8	12.7
2004	13.3	13.5	13.6	13.6	13.5	13.7	13.2	12.9	13.6	13.7	13.8	13.9	13.5
2005	13.1	13.0	13.3	13.1	13.1	13.2	12.9	12.8	13.5	13.8	13.8	13.8	13.3
2006	13.3	13.4	13.5	13.6	13.9	14.0	13.4	13.3	14.0	14.3	14.1	14.3	13.8
2007	14.0	13.8	13.7	13.6	14.0	13.9	13.5	13.6	14.0	13.9	13.8	14.0	13.8
2008	13.4	13.5	13.6	13.6	13.7	13.6	13.4	13.3	13.7	13.8	13.8	14.1	13.6
2009	12.7	12.7	12.6	12.4	12.5	12.4	11.6	11.7	12.5	12.5	12.5	12.5	12.4
2010	12.2	12.0	12.1	12.1	12.3	12.2	11.5	11.5	12.3	12.4	12.4	12.6	12.1
2011	12.3	12.3	12.3	12.4	12.5	12.4	11.7	11.5	12.5	12.6	12.7	12.9	12.3
2012	12.4	12.4	12.5	12.1	12.7	12.4	12.1	12.2	13.0	13.5	13.8	14.0	12.8
2013	13.6	13.4	13.5	13.6	13.6	13.4	13.3	13.3	14.4	14.6	14.8	15.0	13.9
Information													
2002	7.8	7.8	7.8	7.7	7.7	7.8	7.8	7.9	7.7	7.6	7.7	7.6	7.7
2003	7.5	7.5	7.5	7.4	7.4	7.4	7.4	7.4	7.3	7.1	7.2	7.2	7.4
2004	7.3	7.2	7.3	7.0	7.0	7.0	7.0	7.0	6.9	7.0	7.0	7.0	7.1
2005	6.4	6.4	6.5	6.7	6.8	6.8	6.8	6.7	6.7	6.8	6.8	6.8	6.7
2006	6.7	6.7	6.6	6.6	6.6	6.7	6.7	6.8	6.7	6.7	6.8	6.8	6.7
2007	6.8	6.8	6.8	6.8	6.8	6.9	7.0	7.0	7.0	7.1	7.1	7.1	6.9
2008	7.0	7.1	7.1	7.1	7.1	7.2	7.0	7.1	7.0	7.0	6.9	6.8	7.0
2009	6.8	6.7	6.7	6.6	6.6	6.5	6.5	6.4	6.3	6.4	6.2	6.1	6.5
2010	5.9	5.9	6.0	6.1	6.0	6.0	6.0	6.0	5.9	6.0	5.9	5.8	6.0
2011	5.8	5.8	5.8	5.8	5.6	5.8	5.7	5.2	5.7	5.5	5.6	5.7	5.7
2012	5.6	5.6	5.6	5.5	5.5	5.5	5.4	5.5	5.3	5.3	5.3	5.3	5.5
2013	5.3	5.4	5.3	5.3	5.2	5.2	5.2	5.3	5.2	5.1	5.3	5.3	5.3

1. Employment by Industry: Delaware, Selected Years, 2002–2013—*Continued*

(Numbers in thousands, not seasonally adjusted)

Industry and year	January	February	March	April	May	June	July	August	September	October	November	December	Annual average
Financial Activities													
2002	46.7	46.6	46.6	46.3	46.5	46.7	47.1	46.9	46.2	45.8	45.8	45.8	46.4
2003	45.5	45.3	45.2	45.6	45.6	45.7	46.5	46.0	45.3	44.2	44.2	44.2	45.3
2004	44.1	44.1	44.3	44.3	44.6	45.0	45.6	45.7	45.0	44.4	44.6	44.5	44.7
2005	45.1	45.1	44.9	44.8	45.0	45.3	45.9	45.8	45.3	45.1	45.2	45.2	45.2
2006	44.5	44.4	44.2	44.5	44.4	44.6	44.7	45.3	45.0	44.9	45.0	45.2	44.7
2007	44.8	44.9	44.9	45.1	45.3	45.8	45.8	45.6	45.2	45.3	45.2	45.2	45.3
2008	45.0	45.0	45.2	45.5	45.7	46.3	46.5	46.2	45.5	45.3	45.0	44.6	45.5
2009	44.3	44.0	43.9	43.9	44.2	44.5	44.6	44.2	43.9	43.3	43.1	43.0	43.9
2010	42.4	42.4	42.6	42.5	42.5	43.1	43.4	43.4	43.0	42.3	42.2	42.8	42.7
2011	42.3	42.4	42.3	42.3	42.2	42.8	43.1	42.8	42.3	41.4	41.3	41.6	42.2
2012	41.3	41.3	41.5	41.5	42.0	42.7	43.3	43.4	42.7	42.8	42.9	43.3	42.4
2013	42.9	43.2	43.2	43.2	43.4	44.1	44.6	44.7	44.1	44.3	44.4	44.8	43.9
Professional and Business Services													
2002	61.0	60.6	60.3	61.2	61.0	60.1	60.5	60.9	60.9	60.5	60.8	61.3	60.8
2003	59.1	57.9	58.2	58.3	58.7	58.9	58.5	58.5	58.8	59.6	59.8	60.8	58.9
2004	59.8	61.2	61.8	60.1	61.5	62.2	61.4	61.7	61.5	62.4	63.0	63.5	61.7
2005	60.8	60.7	61.2	62.6	62.7	63.1	62.7	62.7	62.7	62.7	63.3	64.3	62.5
2006	60.8	61.0	61.5	61.3	61.4	61.2	60.7	61.0	60.7	60.7	60.9	62.6	61.2
2007	58.3	58.5	59.4	60.2	60.5	61.0	60.3	60.3	60.2	60.6	61.5	62.7	60.3
2008	59.6	59.4	59.4	60.3	59.9	60.0	59.6	59.4	59.0	59.0	59.5	59.5	59.6
2009	56.0	55.9	55.7	55.8	56.2	56.1	55.1	54.9	54.5	55.0	55.3	56.2	55.6
2010	53.2	53.3	53.5	54.1	54.7	55.0	55.7	55.5	55.2	55.7	55.5	56.7	54.8
2011	53.9	54.2	54.1	55.8	55.3	55.6	55.7	55.8	55.6	56.0	57.1	57.5	55.6
2012	54.8	54.5	55.1	56.0	55.8	55.8	55.9	56.0	55.9	56.9	58.3	58.5	56.1
2013	55.8	55.4	56.3	57.1	57.1	57.5	58.3	58.6	58.0	59.6	61.7	61.5	58.1
Education and Health Services													
2002	48.4	48.8	49.1	49.5	49.7	49.5	49.0	49.7	50.2	50.3	50.6	50.7	49.6
2003	50.7	50.7	51.1	51.3	51.4	51.4	50.8	51.1	51.9	52.3	52.6	52.9	51.5
2004	52.3	52.4	52.7	52.9	53.2	53.2	52.6	52.7	53.6	54.9	54.8	55.1	53.4
2005	54.7	54.9	55.3	55.6	55.8	55.9	55.0	55.1	55.9	56.1	56.4	56.6	55.6
2006	56.5	56.7	57.0	57.4	57.7	57.9	58.0	57.9	58.3	58.6	59.1	59.2	57.9
2007	58.9	59.0	59.3	59.6	59.9	59.8	59.5	59.6	60.5	60.8	61.0	61.4	59.9
2008	61.4	62.0	61.9	62.6	62.8	62.7	62.1	62.4	62.9	63.0	63.4	63.4	62.6
2009	63.3	63.4	63.4	63.6	63.8	63.5	63.3	63.4	63.5	64.1	64.3	64.2	63.7
2010	63.7	63.6	64.2	64.8	64.9	64.5	65.1	65.4	65.2	65.3	65.5	65.5	64.8
2011	65.4	65.6	66.2	66.7	66.5	66.2	66.3	66.4	66.8	67.3	67.4	68.0	66.6
2012	67.3	67.4	67.8	68.1	68.4	68.5	68.3	68.4	69.0	69.5	69.7	70.0	68.5
2013	69.3	69.6	69.8	69.6	69.8	69.5	69.5	69.7	69.7	70.0	70.4	70.5	69.8
Leisure and Hospitality													
2002	32.4	32.6	33.7	37.0	38.9	41.5	42.0	42.0	40.4	37.3	37.1	36.0	37.6
2003	33.3	33.0	34.2	36.6	38.9	42.1	43.1	43.1	40.8	38.9	38.4	37.9	38.4
2004	35.5	35.3	36.1	38.2	40.9	43.6	44.1	44.1	42.7	40.6	40.0	38.7	40.0
2005	36.3	36.3	37.2	39.2	41.2	44.4	45.0	45.0	43.1	40.7	40.0	39.2	40.6
2006	36.3	36.6	37.6	39.3	42.0	46.1	44.6	44.7	43.1	41.3	40.1	39.3	40.9
2007	36.8	37.0	38.0	39.7	41.7	45.3	44.6	44.9	42.2	40.3	39.3	38.9	40.7
2008	36.8	36.9	38.3	40.3	42.4	44.8	45.4	45.3	43.2	41.3	39.9	38.7	41.1
2009	36.6	37.0	37.5	39.6	42.5	44.7	44.9	44.9	42.8	40.6	39.0	38.3	40.7
2010	36.4	35.9	37.4	40.5	43.0	46.1	47.7	47.5	45.9	43.4	42.4	41.2	42.3
2011	39.1	39.2	40.4	42.3	44.5	46.9	47.8	47.8	45.6	43.0	41.7	40.6	43.2
2012	38.9	39.4	40.7	42.7	45.2	47.8	48.2	48.2	45.7	43.6	42.0	41.3	43.6
2013	39.7	39.8	40.9	43.2	46.5	49.2	49.5	48.8	46.1	44.1	42.5	41.9	44.4
Other Services													
2002	16.9	17.2	17.3	17.8	18.0	18.4	18.2	18.2	17.8	18.3	18.2	18.3	17.9
2003	17.7	17.6	17.7	17.9	18.1	18.6	18.6	18.7	18.4	18.6	18.8	18.8	18.3
2004	18.6	18.7	18.9	18.6	18.7	19.0	18.9	18.9	18.7	19.2	19.2	19.2	18.9
2005	19.3	19.3	19.4	19.6	19.6	19.8	19.9	20.0	19.8	20.1	20.2	20.3	19.8
2006	20.0	20.1	20.3	20.3	20.3	20.6	20.5	20.3	20.0	20.4	20.5	20.8	20.3
2007	20.3	20.1	20.3	20.2	20.2	20.5	20.2	20.0	19.9	20.1	20.1	20.2	20.2
2008	20.0	20.1	20.1	20.4	20.4	20.7	20.6	20.5	20.2	20.2	20.1	20.1	20.3
2009	19.8	19.8	19.7	19.7	20.0	20.3	20.0	19.9	19.6	19.4	19.4	19.4	19.8
2010	19.3	19.0	19.4	19.6	19.7	20.2	19.9	20.0	19.7	19.7	19.6	19.6	19.6
2011	19.5	19.5	19.5	19.5	19.6	20.0	19.9	19.8	19.6	19.5	19.4	19.4	19.6
2012	19.3	19.4	19.4	19.6	19.6	20.1	19.9	19.9	19.6	19.7	19.7	19.8	19.7
2013	19.5	19.6	19.6	19.8	19.7	20.2	20.1	20.1	19.7	19.7	19.9	19.9	19.8
Government													
2002	55.7	57.0	57.7	57.9	57.7	56.2	54.8	53.4	57.5	58.6	59.3	59.0	57.1
2003	56.7	57.3	57.7	58.2	58.6	57.2	54.9	53.8	57.2	58.4	58.3	58.5	57.2
2004	57.1	57.8	58.8	58.1	58.6	57.3	55.2	54.7	58.2	58.5	58.7	58.8	57.7
2005	58.0	58.9	60.1	60.6	60.8	58.1	57.5	56.4	59.9	61.7	61.9	61.6	59.6
2006	59.9	61.1	62.4	62.5	63.3	59.6	58.4	57.1	60.4	62.2	62.6	62.5	61.0
2007	60.6	61.7	62.9	63.2	63.5	60.7	59.5	58.6	61.5	63.6	63.9	63.7	62.0
2008	62.1	62.8	64.0	64.5	64.6	61.5	60.3	59.6	62.7	64.2	64.0	63.8	62.8
2009	62.1	63.6	65.1	65.2	65.1	61.9	59.5	59.3	62.6	65.3	65.3	64.7	63.3
2010	62.0	63.0	64.7	65.3	66.4	63.4	61.5	60.3	63.7	64.8	65.4	65.2	63.8
2011	62.7	63.7	64.9	66.3	65.0	62.3	60.7	60.1	63.6	65.1	65.2	65.0	63.7
2012	62.2	63.9	65.1	65.0	65.4	62.5	60.8	59.8	63.4	64.9	65.1	65.1	63.6
2013	61.4	64.0	65.4	65.6	65.8	63.0	61.2	60.2	63.9	65.3	66.2	65.0	63.9

2. Average Weekly Hours by Selected Industry: Delaware, 2009–2013

(Not seasonally adjusted)

Industry and year	January	February	March	April	May	June	July	August	September	October	November	December	Annual average
Total Private													
2009	32.6	32.7	32.8	32.6	32.8	32.8	32.8	33.3	32.7	32.4	32.4	32.4	32.7
2010	32.4	31.6	32.8	32.7	33.0	32.5	32.5	32.7	32.0	32.2	32.2	32.7	32.4
2011	32.8	32.8	32.6	32.8	32.8	33.2	33.4	33.3	33.3	33.6	33.1	33.3	33.1
2012	33.1	33.0	33.0	33.2	32.8	32.9	33.2	33.3	32.7	32.5	32.8	33.3	33.0
2013	32.0	32.4	32.7	32.4	32.4	32.9	32.5	32.9	33.0	32.2	32.4	32.8	32.6
Goods-Producing													
2009	36.0	36.0	36.2	36.4	37.1	37.3	37.6	37.5	36.9	37.5	36.9	37.9	36.9
2010	37.4	36.4	37.2	36.6	36.8	37.2	36.9	36.9	36.5	37.7	37.5	38.1	37.1
2011	36.9	37.3	37.1	37.3	38.7	38.3	38.9	38.8	39.7	38.7	38.5	39.4	38.3
2012	38.7	38.4	37.9	37.9	38.0	37.7	37.0	37.6	37.5	36.8	37.0	38.0	37.7
2013	37.1	37.5	37.7	37.4	37.8	37.9	37.2	38.1	38.5	38.3	38.6	38.5	37.9
Construction													
2009	35.7	36.2	36.1	34.9	36.0	35.5	36.3	36.2	35.4	35.8	35.8	36.6	35.9
2010	35.2	34.6	34.8	34.7	34.4	35.2	34.5	34.9	34.2	35.2	35.9	36.4	35.0
2011	35.2	35.7	35.4	36.1	36.6	37.1	37.7	37.6	39.1	36.9	38.0	38.0	36.9
2012	37.4	37.9	37.0	37.3	37.7	37.7	37.5	37.9	38.8	38.0	37.4	37.9	37.7
2013	37.6	37.6	37.8	36.8	38.1	36.5	35.7	37.2	37.9	37.2	38.5	37.5	37.4
Manufacturing													
2009	36.2	35.7	36.2	37.5	37.9	38.7	38.6	38.4	38.0	38.7	37.8	38.8	37.7
2010	38.8	37.6	38.8	38.1	38.6	38.8	38.8	38.5	38.3	39.5	38.7	39.4	38.6
2011	38.3	38.5	38.5	38.3	40.4	39.2	40.0	39.7	40.0	40.0	38.8	40.6	39.3
2012	39.6	38.7	38.5	38.3	38.3	37.7	36.7	37.2	36.7	36.0	36.7	38.0	37.7
2013	36.8	37.4	37.5	37.8	37.7	39.0	38.4	38.9	38.9	39.1	38.6	39.2	38.3
Trade, Transportation, and Utilities													
2009	32.8	33.0	33.0	32.9	33.5	33.1	33.1	33.1	33.5	32.7	32.5	33.0	33.0
2010	33.0	31.7	32.5	33.5	33.9	33.2	32.5	33.0	32.5	32.8	32.8	33.2	32.9
2011	33.3	33.0	33.2	33.0	33.8	33.4	33.7	33.4	33.5	33.4	33.4	33.1	33.4
2012	32.9	32.8	33.3	33.6	32.9	33.0	33.4	33.5	32.6	32.7	33.1	33.3	33.1
2013	31.6	32.2	32.8	32.6	32.4	32.6	32.9	32.8	32.5	32.1	32.4	33.6	32.5
Financial Activities													
2009	38.2	37.5	37.5	37.0	36.9	36.8	36.1	35.8	35.3	35.2	34.6	35.0	36.3
2010	35.4	36.0	36.7	36.1	36.7	36.1	36.2	36.5	36.2	36.3	36.5	36.9	36.3
2011	37.2	37.1	37.3	37.3	38.0	37.9	38.3	37.9	38.1	38.9	37.8	37.1	37.7
2012	37.8	36.7	37.2	36.8	36.9	36.0	36.4	36.2	36.8	35.8	35.9	36.4	36.6
2013	35.5	35.4	35.9	36.1	36.2	37.1	36.3	36.3	37.7	36.2	36.4	36.4	36.3
Professional and Business Services													
2009	33.1	33.9	33.7	33.6	32.9	32.7	32.6	33.3	32.9	33.2	33.6	32.7	33.2
2010	32.6	31.5	32.2	32.8	33.5	34.0	33.2	34.1	33.1	33.1	33.3	33.7	33.1
2011	33.9	33.7	33.1	33.8	34.5	33.8	33.3	34.4	34.3	35.6	34.0	34.7	34.1
2012	34.6	33.5	34.8	35.1	35.4	36.0	36.3	36.5	37.4	37.2	36.2	37.8	35.9
2013	34.2	35.0	35.7	35.3	35.4	36.0	33.8	35.3	36.2	34.5	34.2	35.5	35.1
Education and Health Services													
2009	32.0	32.6	33.2	33.2	33.6	33.8	34.3	34.5	34.6	33.9	34.1	33.6	33.6
2010	34.2	33.6	33.5	33.7	34.3	33.9	34.0	33.7	33.7	33.2	32.9	33.5	33.7
2011	33.7	33.3	33.4	33.5	33.8	33.5	33.7	33.2	33.4	33.3	33.1	33.5	33.5
2012	33.2	34.6	33.5	33.5	33.2	33.3	33.2	33.0	31.7	31.4	32.6	32.4	33.0
2013	32.3	32.1	32.1	32.0	31.8	32.5	31.8	32.1	32.6	31.9	31.9	31.5	32.1
Leisure and Hospitality													
2009	23.9	24.6	24.3	24.5	24.3	25.2	25.7	25.9	24.5	23.8	23.6	23.8	24.6
2010	23.1	22.6	23.1	23.8	23.4	23.9	24.6	24.7	23.7	23.7	23.6	23.3	23.7
2011	23.7	24.0	24.0	24.6	24.2	24.7	25.6	25.9	24.4	24.8	24.4	24.5	24.6
2012	23.9	24.4	24.7	24.8	24.9	25.7	26.9	26.8	25.0	25.5	24.9	25.6	25.3
2013	24.3	25.0	25.4	24.9	25.0	26.0	26.7	27.2	25.4	24.1	24.4	24.5	25.3

3. Average Hourly Earnings by Selected Industry: Delaware, 2009–2013

(Dollars, not seasonally adjusted)

Industry and year	January	February	March	April	May	June	July	August	September	October	November	December	Annual average
Total Private													
2009	22.49	22.53	22.43	22.04	21.69	21.46	22.04	22.63	22.64	22.57	22.71	22.41	22.30
2010	22.76	23.21	22.59	22.91	22.84	22.66	22.42	22.63	22.51	22.74	22.51	22.84	22.72
2011	22.85	22.58	22.40	22.45	22.25	21.87	21.81	22.00	22.39	22.42	22.26	22.54	22.32
2012	22.47	21.95	21.97	22.06	21.61	21.47	21.75	21.51	22.28	22.30	22.12	22.66	22.01
2013	22.72	22.77	22.67	22.52	22.23	21.97	21.59	21.51	22.05	21.96	21.81	21.84	22.13
Goods-Producing													
2009	22.60	22.87	22.96	22.68	22.53	22.36	22.56	22.86	23.12	22.59	23.03	22.91	22.75
2010	22.81	23.71	23.64	23.23	23.63	23.68	23.57	23.78	23.67	23.36	23.93	23.61	23.55
2011	24.12	24.13	23.98	23.98	23.44	23.66	23.44	23.37	23.75	23.50	23.61	23.60	23.71
2012	23.61	23.34	23.51	23.77	24.15	23.96	24.21	24.12	24.49	24.95	24.60	24.95	24.14
2013	24.71	25.07	25.17	24.89	25.14	25.06	25.05	24.91	25.08	25.10	24.88	24.16	24.93
Construction													
2009	26.46	26.64	26.21	25.85	25.13	25.54	25.03	25.50	26.09	25.24	25.62	26.19	25.79
2010	25.80	26.77	27.23	26.77	27.80	28.08	28.10	28.47	28.36	27.61	28.21	27.51	27.59
2011	28.35	28.20	27.79	27.51	27.24	27.37	27.15	27.24	27.86	27.59	27.63	27.40	27.60
2012	27.33	27.11	27.31	27.28	28.50	28.40	28.45	28.70	28.88	29.48	28.39	29.24	28.29
2013	29.13	29.89	29.89	29.13	29.34	29.44	29.69	28.86	29.09	29.00	28.24	26.68	29.00
Manufacturing													
2009	19.94	20.25	20.65	20.59	20.73	20.21	20.83	21.01	21.14	20.83	21.28	20.73	20.68
2010	20.97	21.85	21.40	20.84	20.81	20.62	20.48	20.49	20.47	20.43	20.83	20.82	20.83
2011	21.25	21.34	21.30	21.37	20.76	20.96	20.81	20.66	20.76	20.68	20.72	21.00	20.96
2012	21.14	20.82	21.00	21.35	21.07	20.75	21.02	20.67	21.08	21.39	21.68	21.73	21.14
2013	21.40	21.55	21.66	21.76	21.86	21.87	21.65	21.91	22.01	22.13	22.11	22.20	21.85
Trade, Transportation, and Utilities													
2009	18.48	18.41	18.45	18.34	18.16	18.06	18.15	18.19	17.94	18.02	18.02	17.85	18.17
2010	18.40	18.73	18.40	18.59	18.40	18.79	18.84	19.12	19.22	18.91	18.88	19.11	18.79
2011	19.41	19.09	19.23	19.68	19.57	19.29	19.32	19.40	19.35	19.47	19.25	19.66	19.39
2012	19.56	19.50	19.39	19.31	18.87	18.83	19.16	18.87	19.21	19.01	18.71	19.08	19.12
2013	19.18	19.23	18.94	19.25	18.88	19.00	18.74	18.58	19.00	18.88	18.45	18.49	18.88
Financial Activities													
2009	27.16	27.62	27.71	27.15	26.13	25.91	26.65	26.30	26.31	26.80	26.74	26.32	26.74
2010	27.00	27.21	27.14	27.15	26.81	26.94	26.88	27.26	27.09	27.55	26.92	27.35	27.11
2011	28.21	27.38	27.40	27.79	27.32	26.21	25.92	26.58	26.68	27.35	25.99	26.12	26.91
2012	26.99	26.67	26.06	27.36	26.25	26.19	28.04	26.32	27.23	26.46	26.31	27.60	26.79
2013	27.59	27.40	27.63	26.84	25.92	26.18	25.96	25.68	25.43	23.09	23.46	23.56	25.70
Professional and Business Services													
2009	29.23	29.45	29.32	28.28	28.05	27.64	27.81	27.80	27.62	27.44	28.04	27.31	28.17
2010	27.36	28.18	27.19	26.76	27.08	27.14	27.09	27.21	27.13	27.73	27.73	27.76	27.36
2011	27.82	27.28	26.96	26.68	26.88	26.10	26.01	26.51	26.48	26.50	26.81	26.90	26.74
2012	26.70	26.00	25.51	25.42	24.56	24.53	24.87	24.90	25.20	24.73	25.17	25.21	25.22
2013	26.49	26.84	27.07	27.31	27.26	27.12	26.52	26.81	27.64	27.51	27.75	28.13	27.22
Education and Health Services													
2009	21.65	21.60	21.40	21.26	21.07	21.21	20.87	20.25	20.63	20.96	21.31	21.23	21.11
2010	21.18	21.18	21.13	21.45	21.47	21.76	21.79	22.31	22.06	22.33	21.87	22.47	21.75
2011	21.69	21.84	21.70	22.02	21.83	22.13	22.43	22.06	22.67	22.61	22.53	23.09	22.22
2012	23.31	22.34	23.26	22.63	22.70	22.82	22.87	23.14	24.55	24.82	24.01	24.87	23.43
2013	24.03	23.94	23.82	23.48	23.11	22.88	22.95	22.78	22.94	23.28	23.14	23.22	23.30
Leisure and Hospitality													
2009	12.83	12.87	12.86	12.61	12.77	12.63	12.36	12.39	12.79	12.88	12.94	12.97	12.73
2010	13.26	13.51	13.20	12.75	13.01	12.84	13.14	13.39	13.33	13.44	13.03	13.31	13.18
2011	13.40	13.23	13.34	12.87	12.93	12.73	12.85	12.82	13.25	13.33	13.47	13.74	13.14
2012	13.94	13.67	13.68	13.60	13.44	12.99	12.93	12.70	12.69	12.81	13.39	13.72	13.26
2013	13.99	13.72	13.54	13.41	13.34	12.81	12.58	12.56	12.94	13.01	12.88	13.02	13.11

4. Average Weekly Earnings by Selected Industry: Delaware, 2009–2013

(Dollars, not seasonally adjusted)

Industry and year	January	February	March	April	May	June	July	August	September	October	November	December	Annual average
Total Private													
2009	733.17	736.73	735.70	718.50	711.43	703.89	722.91	753.58	740.33	731.27	735.80	726.08	729.21
2010	737.42	733.44	740.95	749.16	753.72	736.45	728.65	740.00	720.32	732.23	724.82	746.87	736.13
2011	749.48	740.62	730.24	736.36	738.70	721.71	728.45	732.60	745.59	753.31	736.81	750.58	738.79
2012	743.76	724.35	725.01	732.39	708.81	706.36	722.10	716.28	728.56	724.75	725.54	754.58	726.33
2013	727.04	737.75	741.31	729.65	720.25	722.81	701.68	707.68	727.65	707.11	706.64	716.35	721.11
Goods-Producing													
2009	813.60	823.32	831.15	825.55	835.86	834.03	848.26	857.25	853.13	847.13	849.81	868.29	839.48
2010	853.09	863.04	879.41	850.22	869.58	880.90	869.73	877.48	863.96	880.67	897.38	899.54	873.71
2011	890.03	900.05	889.66	894.45	907.13	906.18	911.82	906.76	942.88	909.45	908.99	929.84	908.09
2012	913.71	896.26	891.03	900.88	917.70	903.29	895.77	906.91	918.38	918.16	910.20	948.10	910.08
2013	916.74	940.13	948.91	930.89	950.29	949.77	931.86	949.07	965.58	961.33	960.37	930.16	944.85
Construction													
2009	944.62	964.37	946.18	902.17	904.68	906.67	908.59	923.10	923.59	903.59	917.20	958.55	925.86
2010	908.16	926.24	947.60	928.92	956.32	988.42	969.45	993.60	969.91	971.87	1,012.74	1,001.36	965.65
2011	997.92	1,006.74	983.77	993.11	996.98	1,015.43	1,023.56	1,024.22	1,089.33	1,018.07	1,049.94	1,041.20	1,018.44
2012	1,022.14	1,027.47	1,010.47	1,017.54	1,074.45	1,070.68	1,066.88	1,087.73	1,120.54	1,120.24	1,061.79	1,108.20	1,066.53
2013	1,095.29	1,123.86	1,129.84	1,071.98	1,117.85	1,074.56	1,059.93	1,073.59	1,102.51	1,078.80	1,087.24	1,000.50	1,084.60
Manufacturing													
2009	721.83	722.93	747.53	772.13	785.67	782.13	804.04	806.78	803.32	806.12	804.38	804.32	779.64
2010	813.64	821.56	830.32	794.00	803.27	800.06	794.62	788.87	784.00	806.99	806.12	820.31	804.04
2011	813.88	821.59	820.05	818.47	838.70	821.63	832.40	820.20	830.40	827.20	803.94	852.60	823.73
2012	837.14	805.73	808.50	817.71	806.98	782.28	771.43	768.92	773.64	770.04	795.66	825.74	796.98
2013	787.52	805.97	812.25	822.53	824.12	852.93	831.36	852.30	856.19	865.28	853.45	870.24	836.86
Trade, Transportation, and Utilities													
2009	606.14	607.53	608.85	603.39	608.36	597.79	600.77	602.09	600.99	589.25	585.65	589.05	599.61
2010	607.20	593.74	598.00	622.77	623.76	623.83	612.30	630.96	624.65	620.25	619.26	634.45	618.19
2011	646.35	629.97	638.44	649.44	661.47	644.29	651.08	647.96	648.23	650.30	642.95	650.75	647.63
2012	643.52	639.60	645.69	648.82	620.82	621.39	639.94	632.15	626.25	621.63	619.30	635.36	632.87
2013	606.09	619.21	621.23	627.55	611.71	619.40	616.55	609.42	617.50	606.05	597.78	621.26	613.60
Financial Activities													
2009	1,037.51	1,035.75	1,039.13	1,004.55	964.20	953.49	962.07	941.54	928.74	943.36	925.20	921.20	970.66
2010	955.80	979.56	996.04	980.12	983.93	972.53	973.06	994.99	980.66	1,000.07	982.58	1,009.22	984.09
2011	1,049.41	1,015.80	1,022.02	1,036.57	1,038.16	993.36	992.74	1,007.38	1,016.51	1,063.92	982.42	969.05	1,014.51
2012	1,020.22	978.79	969.43	1,006.85	968.63	942.84	1,020.66	952.78	1,002.06	947.27	944.53	1,004.64	980.51
2013	979.45	969.96	991.92	968.92	938.30	971.28	942.35	932.18	958.71	835.86	853.94	857.58	932.91
Professional and Business Services													
2009	967.51	998.36	988.08	950.21	922.85	903.83	906.61	925.74	908.70	911.01	942.14	893.04	935.24
2010	891.94	887.67	875.52	877.73	907.18	922.76	899.39	927.86	898.00	917.86	923.41	935.51	905.62
2011	943.10	919.34	892.38	901.78	927.36	882.18	866.13	911.94	908.26	943.40	911.54	933.43	911.83
2012	923.82	871.00	887.75	892.24	869.42	883.08	902.78	908.85	942.48	919.96	911.15	952.94	905.40
2013	905.96	939.40	966.40	964.04	965.00	976.32	896.38	946.39	1,000.57	949.10	949.05	998.62	955.42
Education and Health Services													
2009	692.80	704.16	710.48	705.83	707.95	716.90	715.84	698.63	713.80	710.54	726.67	713.33	709.30
2010	724.36	711.65	707.86	722.87	736.42	737.66	740.86	751.85	743.42	741.36	719.52	752.75	732.98
2011	730.95	727.27	724.78	737.67	737.85	741.36	755.89	732.39	757.18	752.91	745.74	773.52	744.37
2012	773.89	772.96	779.21	758.11	753.64	759.91	759.28	763.62	778.24	779.35	782.73	805.79	773.19
2013	776.17	768.47	764.62	751.36	734.90	743.60	729.81	731.24	747.84	742.63	738.17	731.43	747.93
Leisure and Hospitality													
2009	306.64	316.60	312.50	308.95	310.31	318.28	317.65	320.90	313.36	306.54	305.38	308.69	313.16
2010	306.31	305.33	304.92	303.45	304.43	306.88	323.24	330.73	315.92	318.53	307.51	310.12	312.37
2011	317.58	317.52	320.16	316.60	312.91	314.43	328.96	332.04	323.30	330.58	328.67	336.63	323.24
2012	333.17	333.55	337.90	337.28	334.66	333.84	347.82	340.36	317.25	326.66	333.41	351.23	335.48
2013	339.96	343.00	343.92	333.91	333.50	333.06	335.89	341.63	328.68	313.54	314.27	318.99	331.68

DISTRICT OF COLUMBIA
At a Glance

Population:
  2000 census: 572,086
  2010 census: 601,723
  2013 estimate: 646,449

Percent change in population:
  2000–2010: 5.2%
  2010–2013: 7.4%

Percent change in total nonfarm employment:
  2000–2010: 9.5%
  2010–2013: 4.6%

Industry with the largest growth in employment, 2000–2013 (thousands):
  Education and Health Services, 36.1

Industry with the largest decline or smallest growth in employment, 2000–2013 (thousands):
  Information, -8.4

Civilian labor force:
  2000: 309,421
  2010: 346,126
  2013: 370,482

Unemployment rate and rank among states (lowest to highest):
  2000: 5.7%, 49th
  2010: 10.1%, 38th
  2013: 8.3%, 44th

Over-the-year change in unemployment rates:
  2010–2011: 0.1%
  2011–2012: -1.1%
  2012–2013: -0.8%

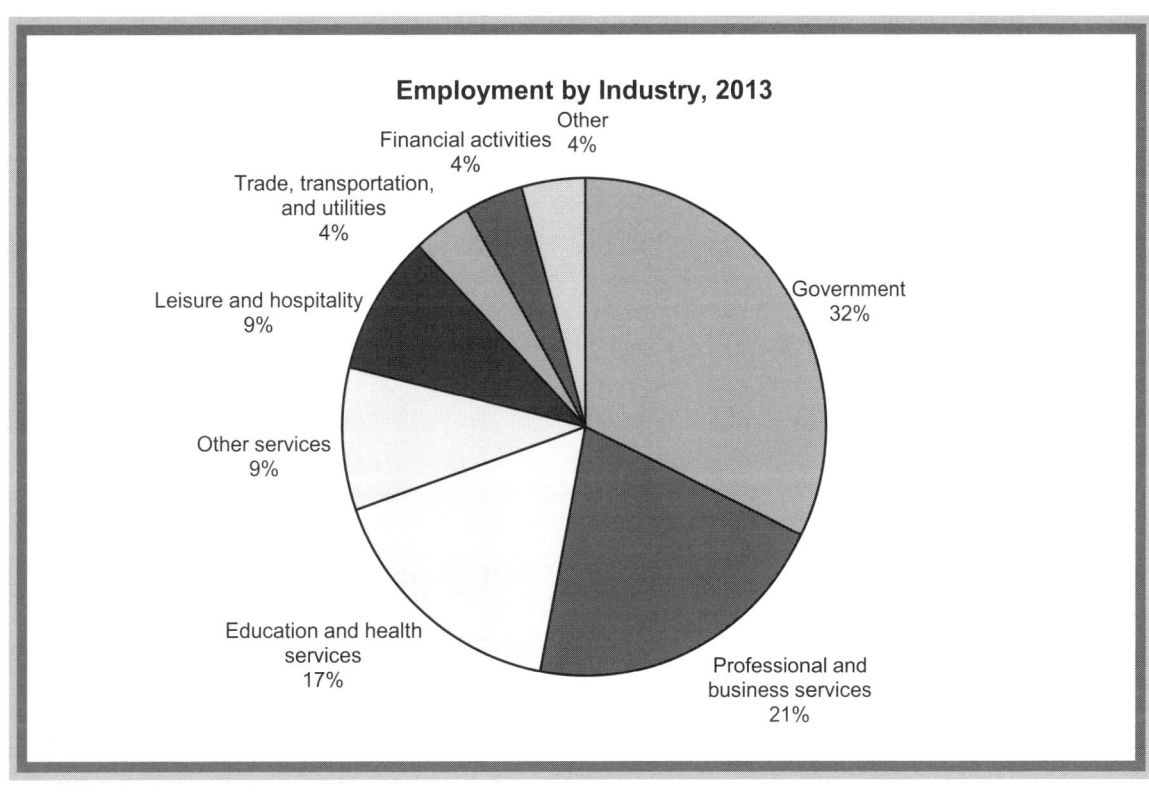

Employment by Industry, 2013

Other 4%
Financial activities 4%
Trade, transportation, and utilities 4%
Leisure and hospitality 9%
Other services 9%
Education and health services 17%
Professional and business services 21%
Government 32%

1. Employment by Industry: District of Columbia, Selected Years, 2002–2013

(Numbers in thousands, not seasonally adjusted)

Industry and year	January	February	March	April	May	June	July	August	September	October	November	December	Annual average
Total Nonfarm													
2002	648.3	653.3	660.3	662.6	660.9	664.8	674.4	669.9	666.9	667.4	670.9	671.1	664.2
2003	656.9	659.0	665.2	666.3	665.7	666.5	672.6	663.7	665.8	667.0	668.0	669.5	665.5
2004	657.9	665.1	670.7	673.8	673.9	676.6	680.0	679.0	675.0	678.8	680.8	678.6	674.2
2005	670.3	676.0	679.3	681.9	681.6	683.3	688.1	684.8	679.7	684.2	688.5	688.7	682.2
2006	675.4	681.8	686.2	685.3	684.6	689.4	695.5	689.8	685.3	691.4	693.6	693.4	687.6
2007	680.7	689.2	692.0	692.1	689.6	691.3	701.4	695.5	690.3	700.0	701.1	701.8	693.8
2008	689.0	693.6	698.2	701.2	702.7	704.1	720.0	715.9	705.1	705.9	706.0	704.5	703.9
2009	697.8	697.4	697.2	696.5	697.3	698.1	718.1	706.6	694.2	703.8	706.8	705.6	701.6
2010	698.2	695.5	703.4	713.6	715.5	715.6	732.1	707.7	711.1	717.2	718.4	717.3	712.1
2011	713.9	716.9	721.4	727.8	723.8	726.3	740.8	724.7	730.3	729.8	729.7	729.1	726.2
2012	721.9	725.1	729.9	730.9	733.9	732.9	743.1	729.0	736.1	744.0	745.8	744.8	734.8
2013	733.6	738.4	741.5	746.8	746.8	742.1	754.7	740.3	747.9	751.3	750.8	748.6	745.2
Total Private													
2002	418.0	424.2	430.5	433.8	431.4	432.3	434.3	432.3	435.0	438.2	440.5	439.9	432.5
2003	427.3	429.4	434.2	435.9	435.2	434.3	435.5	432.2	435.6	438.1	439.8	441.0	434.9
2004	429.0	436.5	441.3	444.5	445.4	445.7	443.8	441.4	445.0	447.8	448.6	446.0	442.9
2005	438.6	444.8	448.1	450.1	449.7	448.6	446.1	443.4	448.8	452.0	455.5	456.1	448.5
2006	443.6	450.4	454.8	455.3	453.9	455.9	452.7	449.4	454.6	460.2	462.4	462.0	454.6
2007	453.8	461.4	464.9	465.2	462.3	461.3	459.8	456.9	461.6	467.3	469.0	469.5	462.8
2008	458.1	463.0	467.1	471.4	471.8	470.1	471.5	469.5	472.6	471.7	471.7	469.6	469.0
2009	463.7	463.4	463.3	462.0	462.0	459.3	458.3	454.4	455.9	463.3	465.5	465.2	461.4
2010	456.9	454.8	462.5	471.5	470.7	468.1	464.2	461.4	465.1	468.4	469.4	469.5	465.2
2011	467.0	470.5	474.6	481.7	477.3	477.8	480.1	478.1	483.6	486.1	486.5	486.1	479.1
2012	479.5	483.8	488.0	490.1	492.6	489.3	488.3	486.9	494.5	501.3	503.2	502.8	491.7
2013	493.4	498.8	501.6	507.6	507.7	502.6	504.9	502.9	509.1	513.2	513.7	511.5	505.6
Goods-Producing													
2002	14.3	14.4	14.6	14.4	14.9	15.3	15.9	16.2	16.3	16.5	16.4	16.3	15.5
2003	15.6	15.4	15.8	15.4	15.2	15.4	15.7	15.7	15.7	15.4	15.2	14.9	15.5
2004	14.3	14.4	14.7	14.9	15.1	14.7	15.0	14.8	14.8	15.0	15.0	14.8	14.8
2005	14.5	14.8	14.8	15.1	15.2	15.2	14.8	14.9	14.5	14.3	14.4	14.4	14.7
2006	13.7	14.0	14.2	14.1	14.3	14.5	14.7	14.8	14.6	14.2	14.0	13.8	14.2
2007	13.9	13.7	13.8	13.9	14.3	14.5	14.6	15.0	14.9	14.8	14.7	14.2	14.4
2008	14.4	14.5	14.5	14.1	14.5	14.6	14.6	15.0	14.5	14.6	14.5	14.2	14.5
2009	14.0	14.0	13.5	13.4	13.4	13.3	12.8	12.7	12.4	11.9	11.7	11.6	12.9
2010	11.3	10.4	11.2	11.8	11.8	11.8	12.2	12.0	11.8	12.1	12.0	12.0	11.7
2011	12.1	12.1	12.3	12.8	13.0	13.2	14.1	14.1	13.8	13.6	13.5	13.6	13.2
2012	13.5	13.8	14.1	14.5	14.7	14.9	15.0	15.0	14.9	15.2	14.9	14.8	14.6
2013	14.5	14.6	14.7	14.5	14.9	15.1	15.6	15.7	15.1	14.7	14.5	14.1	14.8
Service-Providing													
2002	634.0	638.9	645.7	648.2	646.0	649.5	658.5	653.7	650.6	650.9	654.5	654.8	648.8
2003	641.3	643.6	649.4	650.9	650.5	651.1	656.9	648.0	650.1	651.6	652.8	654.6	650.1
2004	643.6	650.7	656.0	658.9	658.8	661.9	665.0	664.2	660.2	663.8	665.8	663.8	659.4
2005	655.8	661.2	664.5	666.8	666.4	668.1	673.3	669.9	665.2	669.9	674.1	674.3	667.5
2006	661.7	667.8	672.0	671.2	670.3	674.9	680.8	675.0	670.7	677.2	679.6	679.6	673.4
2007	666.8	675.5	678.2	678.2	675.3	676.8	686.8	680.5	675.4	685.2	686.4	687.6	679.4
2008	674.6	679.1	683.7	687.1	688.2	689.5	705.4	700.9	690.6	691.3	691.5	690.3	689.4
2009	683.8	683.4	683.7	683.1	683.9	684.8	705.3	693.9	681.8	691.9	695.1	694.0	688.7
2010	686.9	685.1	692.2	701.8	703.7	703.8	719.9	695.7	699.3	705.1	706.4	705.3	700.4
2011	701.8	704.8	709.1	715.0	710.8	713.1	726.7	710.6	716.5	716.2	716.2	715.5	713.0
2012	708.4	711.3	715.8	716.4	719.2	718.0	728.1	714.0	721.2	728.8	730.9	730.0	720.2
2013	719.1	723.8	726.8	732.3	731.9	727.0	739.1	724.6	732.8	736.6	736.3	734.5	730.4
Mining, Logging, and Construction													
2002	11.1	11.3	11.4	11.5	12.0	12.4	12.8	13.1	13.2	13.4	13.3	13.3	12.4
2003	13.0	12.8	13.2	12.8	12.7	12.9	13.2	13.2	13.2	12.9	12.7	12.4	12.9
2004	11.9	11.9	12.2	12.5	12.7	12.3	12.5	12.3	12.3	12.6	12.6	12.5	12.4
2005	12.3	12.6	12.6	12.9	13.0	13.0	12.7	12.8	12.5	12.4	12.5	12.4	12.6
2006	11.9	12.2	12.4	12.3	12.5	12.7	13.0	13.1	12.9	12.5	12.3	12.1	12.5
2007	12.2	12.0	12.1	12.2	12.6	12.8	12.9	13.4	13.2	13.1	13.0	12.5	12.7
2008	12.7	12.8	12.8	12.6	12.9	13.0	13.1	13.5	13.1	13.2	13.1	12.8	13.0
2009	12.6	12.6	12.2	12.1	12.1	12.0	11.5	11.4	11.2	10.7	10.5	10.4	11.6
2010	10.1	9.2	10.1	10.7	10.7	10.7	11.1	11.0	10.7	11.0	11.0	11.0	10.6
2011	11.0	11.1	11.2	11.7	11.9	12.1	13.0	13.1	12.8	12.6	12.5	12.6	12.1
2012	12.5	12.8	13.0	13.5	13.7	13.9	14.0	14.0	13.9	14.2	13.9	13.8	13.6
2013	13.5	13.6	13.7	13.5	13.9	14.1	14.6	14.7	14.1	13.8	13.6	13.3	13.9

1. Employment by Industry: District of Columbia, Selected Years, 2002–2013—*Continued*

(Numbers in thousands, not seasonally adjusted)

Industry and year	January	February	March	April	May	June	July	August	September	October	November	December	Annual average
Manufacturing													
2002	3.2	3.1	3.2	2.9	2.9	2.9	3.1	3.1	3.1	3.1	3.1	3.0	3.1
2003	2.6	2.6	2.6	2.6	2.5	2.5	2.5	2.5	2.5	2.5	2.5	2.5	2.5
2004	2.4	2.5	2.5	2.4	2.4	2.4	2.5	2.5	2.5	2.4	2.4	2.3	2.4
2005	2.2	2.2	2.2	2.2	2.2	2.2	2.1	2.1	2.0	1.9	1.9	2.0	2.1
2006	1.8	1.8	1.8	1.8	1.8	1.8	1.7	1.7	1.7	1.7	1.7	1.7	1.8
2007	1.7	1.7	1.7	1.7	1.7	1.7	1.7	1.6	1.7	1.7	1.7	1.7	1.7
2008	1.7	1.7	1.7	1.5	1.6	1.6	1.5	1.5	1.4	1.4	1.4	1.4	1.5
2009	1.4	1.4	1.3	1.3	1.3	1.3	1.3	1.3	1.2	1.2	1.2	1.2	1.3
2010	1.2	1.2	1.1	1.1	1.1	1.1	1.1	1.0	1.1	1.1	1.0	1.0	1.1
2011	1.1	1.0	1.1	1.1	1.1	1.1	1.1	1.0	1.0	1.0	1.0	1.0	1.1
2012	1.0	1.0	1.1	1.0	1.0	1.0	1.0	1.0	1.0	1.0	1.0	1.0	1.0
2013	1.0	1.0	1.0	1.0	1.0	1.0	1.0	1.0	1.0	0.9	0.9	0.8	1.0
Trade, Transportation, and Utilities													
2002	27.5	27.7	27.4	27.6	27.7	28.0	27.9	27.6	27.7	27.9	28.4	29.0	27.9
2003	27.5	27.3	27.7	27.5	27.6	28.1	27.9	27.9	27.9	28.3	28.7	29.2	28.0
2004	27.8	27.7	28.1	27.9	28.1	28.3	27.8	27.4	27.6	27.6	28.0	28.4	27.9
2005	27.3	27.1	27.6	27.4	27.5	27.6	27.8	27.5	27.6	28.2	28.4	29.3	27.8
2006	28.1	27.9	27.8	27.5	27.6	27.9	27.7	27.6	27.8	27.9	28.2	28.6	27.9
2007	27.5	27.2	27.4	27.8	27.9	27.9	27.7	27.5	27.6	27.6	28.1	28.4	27.7
2008	27.4	27.5	27.4	27.9	27.9	28.2	28.3	27.9	28.0	27.6	28.3	28.5	27.9
2009	27.3	26.8	26.7	26.8	26.6	26.5	26.5	26.4	26.5	27.0	27.5	27.5	26.8
2010	26.9	26.1	26.9	27.4	27.4	27.6	27.4	27.2	27.2	27.6	28.1	28.2	27.3
2011	27.3	27.1	27.1	27.5	27.3	27.2	27.1	27.1	27.3	27.9	28.1	28.3	27.4
2012	27.4	27.4	27.5	27.7	28.0	28.2	28.0	28.0	28.2	28.3	29.1	29.4	28.1
2013	28.5	28.6	28.6	28.7	28.7	28.8	28.6	28.8	29.0	29.2	29.8	30.9	29.0
Wholesale Trade													
2002	4.1	4.2	4.2	4.2	4.2	4.3	4.5	4.4	4.5	4.5	4.5	4.6	4.4
2003	4.5	4.5	4.5	4.4	4.5	4.5	4.6	4.5	4.5	4.6	4.6	4.6	4.5
2004	4.5	4.6	4.5	4.6	4.6	4.6	4.6	4.5	4.6	4.5	4.6	4.6	4.6
2005	4.6	4.6	4.6	4.6	4.6	4.7	4.6	4.6	4.6	4.5	4.6	4.6	4.6
2006	4.7	4.7	4.6	4.6	4.6	4.6	4.7	4.7	4.7	4.7	4.7	4.8	4.7
2007	4.8	4.8	4.8	4.8	4.8	4.8	4.8	4.8	4.8	4.8	4.8	4.8	4.8
2008	4.7	4.8	4.7	4.7	4.7	4.9	5.0	4.9	4.8	4.8	4.7	4.7	4.8
2009	4.7	4.6	4.6	4.6	4.6	4.6	4.6	4.5	4.5	4.6	4.6	4.6	4.6
2010	4.6	4.6	4.6	4.7	4.7	4.8	4.7	4.6	4.6	4.7	4.7	4.7	4.7
2011	4.6	4.6	4.6	4.6	4.6	4.5	4.5	4.7	4.6	4.8	4.8	4.8	4.6
2012	4.8	4.9	4.9	4.9	5.0	5.1	5.0	5.1	5.1	5.0	5.0	5.0	5.0
2013	4.9	5.0	4.9	4.8	4.9	4.9	4.9	4.9	4.9	4.9	5.0	4.9	4.9
Retail Trade													
2002	17.3	17.2	17.0	17.0	17.1	17.2	17.0	16.8	16.9	17.0	17.5	18.0	17.2
2003	16.7	16.6	16.7	16.8	16.8	17.3	17.0	17.1	17.2	17.5	17.9	18.5	17.2
2004	17.2	17.1	17.3	17.4	17.6	17.9	17.6	17.4	17.5	17.6	17.9	18.4	17.6
2005	17.4	17.1	17.5	17.3	17.4	17.4	17.6	17.4	17.5	17.9	18.2	18.9	17.6
2006	18.0	17.9	17.8	17.5	17.5	17.9	17.8	17.7	18.0	18.2	18.5	18.8	18.0
2007	18.0	17.8	17.8	18.2	18.2	18.3	18.1	17.9	18.0	18.2	18.6	18.9	18.2
2008	18.1	18.2	18.2	18.6	18.5	18.6	18.5	18.3	18.5	18.1	18.9	19.0	18.5
2009	18.0	17.6	17.5	17.5	17.3	17.3	17.3	17.4	17.6	18.1	18.7	18.8	17.8
2010	18.3	17.5	18.1	18.4	18.4	18.5	18.4	18.3	18.3	18.6	19.1	19.3	18.4
2011	18.6	18.4	18.3	18.6	18.5	18.4	18.3	18.1	18.5	18.9	19.2	19.5	18.6
2012	18.6	18.5	18.5	18.6	18.8	18.8	18.8	18.7	18.9	19.1	20.0	20.3	19.0
2013	19.5	19.5	19.5	19.6	19.6	19.6	19.5	19.7	20.0	20.2	20.8	22.0	20.0
Transportation and Utilities													
2002	6.1	6.3	6.2	6.4	6.4	6.5	6.4	6.4	6.3	6.4	6.4	6.4	6.4
2003	6.3	6.2	6.5	6.3	6.3	6.3	6.3	6.3	6.2	6.2	6.2	6.1	6.3
2004	6.1	6.0	6.3	5.9	5.9	5.8	5.6	5.5	5.5	5.5	5.5	5.4	5.8
2005	5.3	5.4	5.5	5.5	5.5	5.5	5.6	5.5	5.5	5.7	5.7	5.8	5.5
2006	5.4	5.3	5.4	5.4	5.5	5.4	5.2	5.2	5.1	5.0	5.0	5.0	5.2
2007	4.7	4.6	4.8	4.8	4.9	4.8	4.8	4.8	4.8	4.6	4.7	4.7	4.8
2008	4.6	4.5	4.5	4.6	4.7	4.7	4.8	4.7	4.7	4.7	4.7	4.8	4.7
2009	4.6	4.6	4.6	4.7	4.7	4.6	4.6	4.5	4.4	4.3	4.2	4.1	4.5
2010	4.0	4.0	4.2	4.3	4.3	4.3	4.3	4.3	4.3	4.3	4.3	4.2	4.2
2011	4.1	4.1	4.2	4.3	4.2	4.3	4.3	4.3	4.2	4.2	4.1	4.0	4.2
2012	4.0	4.0	4.1	4.2	4.2	4.3	4.2	4.2	4.2	4.2	4.1	4.1	4.2
2013	4.1	4.1	4.2	4.3	4.2	4.3	4.2	4.2	4.1	4.1	4.0	4.0	4.2
Information													
2002	25.7	25.6	26.0	25.7	25.7	25.8	25.3	25.3	25.1	24.6	24.7	24.7	25.4
2003	25.0	25.3	25.4	24.5	24.6	24.4	24.5	24.4	24.4	23.9	24.0	23.8	24.5
2004	24.3	24.1	24.2	24.0	24.1	24.1	24.4	24.4	24.0	22.9	22.8	22.7	23.8
2005	22.8	23.0	22.8	22.6	22.4	22.6	22.7	22.5	22.4	22.2	22.3	22.3	22.6
2006	22.0	21.9	22.2	22.1	22.1	22.4	22.4	22.2	22.3	22.0	22.1	22.1	22.2
2007	22.4	22.5	22.4	21.8	21.8	22.2	22.5	22.3	21.4	21.3	21.3	21.3	21.9
2008	21.1	21.2	21.3	20.9	21.0	20.9	21.0	21.0	20.8	20.6	20.6	20.4	20.9
2009	19.8	19.7	19.0	19.4	19.3	19.4	19.1	18.8	18.6	18.6	18.5	18.5	19.1
2010	18.5	18.4	18.5	18.7	18.6	18.9	19.0	18.7	18.8	18.7	18.5	18.7	18.7
2011	18.3	18.5	18.6	18.8	18.5	18.7	18.4	17.9	18.2	18.0	18.0	18.2	18.3
2012	17.5	17.7	17.6	17.3	17.4	17.7	17.4	17.7	17.7	17.3	17.6	17.4	17.5
2013	17.1	17.2	17.2	16.9	17.0	17.2	17.3	17.4	17.1	17.0	17.1	17.0	17.1

1. Employment by Industry: District of Columbia, Selected Years, 2002–2013—*Continued*

(Numbers in thousands, not seasonally adjusted)

Industry and year	January	February	March	April	May	June	July	August	September	October	November	December	Annual average
Financial Activities													
2002	30.4	30.6	30.9	30.3	30.3	30.6	31.0	31.2	31.0	31.2	31.3	31.3	30.8
2003	30.8	30.8	30.8	30.9	31.0	31.0	31.1	30.9	30.7	30.4	30.3	30.5	30.8
2004	30.0	30.1	30.2	30.8	31.0	31.2	30.6	30.5	30.5	30.6	30.7	30.7	30.6
2005	29.9	30.1	29.8	30.6	30.7	30.5	30.3	30.2	30.3	30.1	30.0	30.4	30.2
2006	29.5	29.7	29.9	29.2	29.3	29.4	29.6	29.6	29.5	29.3	29.1	29.2	29.4
2007	29.5	29.7	29.7	29.3	29.0	29.1	29.3	29.1	28.9	28.9	29.0	28.9	29.2
2008	28.3	28.4	28.3	28.4	28.3	28.4	28.2	28.2	28.2	27.8	27.8	27.6	28.2
2009	27.2	26.9	26.8	26.6	26.6	26.9	26.8	26.8	26.9	27.0	27.1	27.2	26.9
2010	26.8	26.7	27.0	27.1	27.1	27.3	26.6	26.5	26.1	27.0	27.2	27.2	26.9
2011	27.1	27.0	27.2	27.5	27.5	27.4	27.7	27.9	27.9	27.9	28.0	28.1	27.6
2012	28.1	28.1	28.2	28.2	28.1	28.4	28.2	28.1	28.0	28.3	28.4	28.3	28.2
2013	28.2	28.4	28.6	28.6	28.4	28.7	28.7	28.8	28.8	28.8	29.0	28.9	28.7
Professional and Business Services													
2002	135.2	136.2	137.5	139.3	139.1	141.1	141.2	140.2	139.5	139.6	140.0	140.5	139.1
2003	137.7	137.9	138.8	142.3	143.0	144.2	143.4	142.4	142.3	142.2	142.3	143.3	141.7
2004	137.7	139.5	140.9	142.9	144.0	146.8	146.2	145.5	145.1	146.0	145.5	146.1	143.9
2005	144.2	145.5	147.0	147.4	147.8	150.3	150.3	149.5	149.4	149.5	149.6	150.1	148.4
2006	147.4	149.2	150.5	151.4	152.1	155.8	153.7	152.5	152.3	153.4	153.5	153.5	152.1
2007	150.7	152.3	152.8	152.6	153.5	155.4	153.1	152.7	151.7	152.3	152.9	153.3	152.8
2008	150.5	152.0	153.3	153.6	153.6	155.0	153.6	152.9	151.9	151.8	150.6	150.1	152.4
2009	149.2	148.9	148.5	146.1	146.4	148.4	148.7	147.1	145.4	147.1	147.7	148.0	147.6
2010	145.8	145.8	147.3	148.7	148.6	150.0	149.1	148.2	146.8	147.2	147.2	147.4	147.7
2011	146.7	147.4	148.4	150.4	150.5	151.8	152.7	152.1	150.2	151.8	151.5	151.0	150.4
2012	150.7	151.5	152.7	152.6	152.9	154.4	155.6	154.9	153.7	156.2	156.9	156.5	154.1
2013	153.3	154.6	154.9	155.6	155.5	156.8	157.2	156.7	155.0	155.5	156.2	156.4	155.6
Education and Health Services													
2002	86.9	89.7	92.1	92.1	88.5	85.6	86.3	86.5	89.5	92.2	93.5	92.4	89.6
2003	88.3	89.7	90.7	89.1	86.8	84.1	86.4	85.5	88.8	90.8	91.8	91.4	88.6
2004	89.7	94.2	94.9	94.7	92.2	89.0	88.8	88.2	92.1	94.5	95.1	93.5	92.2
2005	91.6	94.7	94.6	93.8	91.5	87.4	86.5	86.0	91.3	94.6	97.4	96.4	92.2
2006	92.6	96.0	96.4	96.6	93.1	88.8	88.3	87.5	92.6	97.1	99.4	98.8	93.9
2007	97.3	101.6	102.4	101.3	96.9	92.1	92.3	91.5	97.5	102.9	103.0	103.2	98.5
2008	99.4	100.8	101.5	102.6	102.2	97.8	99.7	99.7	103.8	104.8	105.9	106.2	102.0
2009	104.9	106.0	106.6	106.8	105.3	100.3	100.9	100.2	103.4	107.9	109.1	108.9	105.0
2010	107.4	107.2	108.4	111.3	110.4	104.7	103.1	103.5	109.6	109.1	109.9	109.9	107.9
2011	112.7	113.6	114.1	114.3	110.3	108.5	109.4	108.6	115.6	115.5	115.9	116.0	112.9
2012	114.6	115.2	115.5	116.3	116.2	109.9	107.7	108.7	118.0	121.1	122.3	122.8	115.7
2013	120.5	122.3	122.7	125.2	124.4	116.6	118.8	118.2	126.2	129.4	129.6	128.0	123.5
Leisure and Hospitality													
2002	43.4	44.9	46.7	48.3	49.2	49.5	49.6	48.5	49.3	49.9	49.9	49.3	48.2
2003	47.4	47.7	49.2	50.3	50.8	50.5	49.6	48.9	49.4	50.5	50.6	50.4	49.6
2004	48.0	49.0	50.3	50.9	52.1	52.1	51.3	51.0	51.6	52.1	51.9	51.0	50.9
2005	50.5	51.5	52.8	54.2	55.4	55.1	54.1	53.4	54.4	54.4	54.3	53.8	53.7
2006	51.7	52.7	54.3	54.6	55.3	55.8	54.5	53.9	54.5	54.9	54.3	53.6	54.2
2007	51.5	52.8	54.5	56.3	56.3	56.4	56.4	55.7	56.5	56.4	56.6	56.3	55.5
2008	53.9	55.2	56.4	59.1	59.2	59.0	59.1	58.6	59.4	58.9	58.1	56.6	57.8
2009	56.0	56.0	57.4	58.4	59.8	59.1	58.5	57.8	58.6	59.2	59.1	58.4	58.2
2010	56.1	56.1	58.6	61.7	61.4	61.4	60.5	59.6	59.6	60.9	60.4	59.7	59.7
2011	57.2	58.5	60.1	63.9	63.5	63.5	62.6	63.0	63.8	64.3	64.2	63.2	62.3
2012	60.7	62.5	64.4	66.3	67.7	67.4	66.7	66.0	66.3	66.6	65.4	64.7	65.4
2013	63.1	64.6	66.3	69.2	69.6	69.4	68.8	68.1	68.7	69.1	68.5	67.3	67.7
Other Services													
2002	54.6	55.1	55.3	56.1	56.0	56.4	57.1	56.8	56.6	56.3	56.3	56.4	56.1
2003	55.0	55.3	55.8	55.9	56.2	56.6	56.9	56.5	56.4	56.6	56.9	57.5	56.3
2004	57.2	57.5	58.0	58.4	58.8	59.5	59.7	59.6	59.3	59.1	59.6	58.8	58.8
2005	57.8	58.1	58.7	59.0	59.2	59.9	59.6	59.4	58.9	58.7	59.1	59.4	59.0
2006	58.6	59.0	59.5	59.8	60.1	61.3	61.8	61.3	61.0	61.4	61.8	62.4	60.7
2007	61.0	61.6	61.9	62.2	62.6	63.7	63.9	63.1	63.1	63.1	63.4	63.9	62.8
2008	63.1	63.4	64.4	64.8	65.1	66.2	67.0	66.2	66.0	65.6	65.9	66.0	65.3
2009	65.3	65.1	64.8	64.5	64.6	65.4	65.0	64.6	64.1	64.6	64.8	65.1	64.8
2010	64.1	64.1	64.6	64.8	65.4	66.4	66.3	65.7	65.2	65.8	66.1	66.4	65.4
2011	65.6	66.3	66.8	66.5	66.7	67.5	68.1	67.4	66.8	67.1	67.3	67.7	67.0
2012	67.0	67.6	68.0	67.2	67.6	68.4	69.7	68.5	68.1	68.3	68.6	68.9	68.2
2013	68.2	68.5	68.6	68.9	69.2	70.0	69.9	69.2	69.2	69.5	69.0	68.9	69.1
Government													
2002	230.3	229.1	229.8	228.8	229.5	232.5	240.1	237.6	231.9	229.2	230.4	231.2	231.7
2003	229.6	229.6	231.0	230.4	230.5	232.2	237.1	231.5	230.2	228.9	228.2	228.5	230.6
2004	228.9	228.6	229.4	229.3	228.5	230.9	236.2	237.6	230.0	231.0	232.2	232.6	231.3
2005	231.7	231.2	231.2	231.8	231.9	234.7	242.0	241.4	230.9	232.2	233.0	232.6	233.7
2006	231.8	231.4	231.4	230.0	230.7	233.5	242.8	240.4	230.7	231.2	231.2	231.4	233.0
2007	226.9	227.8	227.1	226.9	227.3	230.0	241.6	238.6	228.7	232.7	232.1	232.3	231.0
2008	230.9	230.6	231.1	229.8	230.9	234.0	248.5	246.4	232.5	234.2	234.3	234.9	234.8
2009	234.1	234.0	233.9	234.5	235.3	238.8	259.8	252.2	238.3	240.5	241.3	240.4	240.3
2010	241.3	240.7	240.9	242.1	244.8	247.5	267.9	246.3	246.0	248.8	249.0	247.8	246.9
2011	246.9	246.4	246.8	246.1	246.5	248.5	260.7	246.6	246.7	243.7	243.2	243.0	247.1
2012	242.4	241.3	241.9	240.8	241.3	243.6	254.8	242.1	241.6	242.7	242.6	242.0	243.1
2013	240.2	239.6	239.9	239.2	239.1	239.5	249.8	237.4	238.8	238.1	237.1	237.1	239.7

2. Average Weekly Hours by Selected Industry: District of Columbia, 2009–2013

(Not seasonally adjusted)

Industry and year	January	February	March	April	May	June	July	August	September	October	November	December	Annual average
Total Private													
2009	36.7	36.8	36.5	36.2	35.9	36.1	36.0	36.6	36.2	36.0	36.4	35.6	36.2
2010	35.8	34.6	34.8	35.1	35.4	34.8	34.1	35.2	35.1	35.6	35.6	35.8	35.2
2011	36.3	35.7	35.0	35.3	35.9	35.3	35.3	35.3	35.2	36.2	35.1	35.0	35.5
2012	35.7	35.0	35.3	36.1	35.5	35.6	36.5	35.4	36.4	35.6	35.8	36.4	35.8
2013	35.6	36.0	35.7	35.6	35.7	36.7	35.5	35.7	36.5	35.7	35.9	36.6	35.9
Goods-Producing													
2009	32.1	32.4	32.6	32.4	32.7	32.8	33.0	33.0	32.7	33.0	32.5	32.6	32.6
2010	32.7	32.9	32.7	33.3	33.6	34.1	36.2	34.8	35.1	35.1	35.7	33.7	34.2
2011	34.5	35.7	36.7	36.3	37.0	38.2	36.7	37.6	38.7	38.1	36.4	36.3	36.9
2012	36.6	35.9	37.6	38.8	37.4	36.2	38.2	37.0	37.5	35.3	36.0	36.7	36.9
2013	37.3	37.3	38.1	36.2	38.0	37.4	37.7	38.9	40.7	37.2	37.2	38.4	37.9
Trade, Transportation, and Utilities													
2009	37.0	36.7	36.8	36.6	36.1	36.4	36.6	36.9	36.7	36.3	35.8	35.3	36.4
2010	35.6	33.3	34.0	34.5	35.6	35.5	35.9	36.4	35.2	35.5	35.2	35.3	35.2
2011	35.3	35.3	35.3	35.3	34.8	35.3	35.9	36.3	35.7	36.8	36.2	36.5	35.7
2012	37.9	37.0	38.3	39.2	38.6	38.8	40.3	39.1	38.7	38.6	38.7	37.6	38.5
2013	37.9	36.9	36.9	37.8	37.6	37.3	36.9	36.0	36.7	36.1	35.9	36.0	36.8
Professional and Business Services													
2009	37.1	37.3	37.0	36.7	36.4	36.8	36.8	37.7	37.1	36.6	37.5	36.2	36.9
2010	36.3	35.2	34.6	34.7	34.6	33.6	32.3	34.0	33.2	33.6	33.6	33.9	34.1
2011	34.5	33.7	32.9	33.8	34.6	33.9	33.6	34.2	34.3	35.6	34.7	34.6	34.2
2012	35.5	35.1	34.8	36.0	35.1	35.5	36.3	35.4	36.3	35.1	35.4	36.3	35.6
2013	35.3	36.2	35.5	35.4	35.7	37.7	35.9	36.4	37.5	36.0	36.8	37.5	36.3
Leisure and Hospitality													
2009	32.9	32.8	32.9	32.9	33.1	33.6	33.5	33.2	33.1	33.0	32.7	32.1	33.0
2010	32.7	31.2	33.6	34.1	34.2	33.6	33.2	33.9	32.6	32.7	32.4	31.6	33.0
2011	30.3	31.6	32.3	32.6	32.5	31.6	31.6	30.6	31.2	30.5	30.2	29.4	31.2
2012	29.6	29.6	29.3	29.6	29.9	30.2	30.4	29.3	30.7	30.6	30.2	30.7	30.0
2013	30.6	31.8	31.4	31.6	30.9	30.1	30.1	29.8	30.7	30.1	30.0	29.9	30.6
Other Services													
2009	35.1	35.3	35.8	35.7	35.8	35.7	36.0	36.3	35.9	36.1	36.3	35.9	35.8
2010	35.8	36.0	36.2	36.2	36.4	36.1	36.1	36.5	36.2	36.1	36.3	36.4	36.2
2011	36.7	35.8	35.3	35.1	35.9	35.3	35.6	35.2	34.7	35.5	34.7	34.9	35.4
2012	35.4	34.6	34.9	35.5	35.1	35.3	35.7	35.4	36.3	35.6	35.9	36.3	35.5
2013	35.2	35.9	35.9	35.7	35.9	36.9	35.2	35.9	36.3	36.0	35.7	36.4	35.9

3. Average Hourly Earnings by Selected Industry: District of Columbia, 2009–2013

(Dollars, not seasonally adjusted)

Industry and year	January	February	March	April	May	June	July	August	September	October	November	December	Annual average
Total Private													
2009	30.89	31.50	31.38	31.17	30.94	31.07	30.70	31.43	31.11	31.45	32.33	32.40	31.37
2010	32.74	33.68	33.85	34.29	34.61	33.52	34.22	34.54	34.25	34.49	34.64	35.24	34.18
2011	35.63	34.72	35.24	35.12	35.58	34.86	35.18	34.98	35.59	36.23	35.68	36.46	35.44
2012	37.11	36.38	36.36	37.06	36.03	36.24	37.30	36.65	37.32	36.95	36.87	37.72	36.84
2013	37.36	38.21	37.85	37.93	37.92	38.68	37.83	37.92	38.80	38.46	38.82	39.77	38.31
Goods-Producing													
2009	32.91	32.97	33.23	33.09	33.62	33.92	33.52	33.41	33.58	33.63	34.04	34.30	33.50
2010	34.38	35.29	33.32	32.42	32.23	32.32	30.63	29.79	29.17	29.39	29.15	30.93	31.46
2011	30.76	30.33	29.21	29.21	29.01	28.91	29.00	29.30	28.96	28.40	29.14	31.09	29.41
2012	34.12	32.30	32.22	31.08	31.45	31.55	32.10	32.28	32.46	32.76	33.18	34.18	32.45
2013	33.55	34.05	33.93	32.60	32.20	31.82	32.38	32.86	32.22	32.84	33.22	33.15	32.89
Trade, Transportation, and Utilities													
2009	23.39	23.55	23.61	23.89	23.68	23.71	23.60	23.84	23.24	23.72	24.55	24.18	23.75
2010	24.39	25.09	24.32	24.03	23.52	24.06	24.75	23.93	23.61	23.03	23.85	23.28	23.98
2011	23.55	23.19	22.82	22.98	23.12	22.53	22.66	23.37	24.20	25.26	24.43	23.47	23.48
2012	24.96	24.58	25.44	26.45	25.25	25.94	27.15	26.50	26.24	25.70	24.96	24.97	25.69
2013	24.39	25.46	25.25	25.12	24.81	24.61	23.57	24.11	24.07	25.00	24.47	24.87	24.65
Professional and Business Services													
2009	37.00	37.96	38.33	38.23	37.59	37.95	37.33	37.71	37.25	37.57	38.00	38.22	37.76
2010	38.69	39.79	39.25	39.47	40.14	38.10	38.52	39.64	38.60	38.33	38.85	39.48	39.08
2011	39.51	38.52	39.23	39.46	40.49	40.05	40.84	40.00	41.16	42.30	41.77	43.18	40.57
2012	44.61	43.60	43.42	44.15	43.51	43.79	44.90	43.64	45.36	44.55	44.40	46.01	44.34
2013	45.76	47.03	46.87	46.51	46.41	47.43	46.74	46.34	48.10	47.45	48.06	49.33	47.19
Leisure and Hospitality													
2009	16.82	16.70	16.63	16.66	16.53	16.41	16.28	16.39	16.50	16.77	17.35	17.57	16.71
2010	17.25	17.96	17.63	18.06	17.31	17.02	16.66	16.80	17.25	17.42	17.61	18.05	17.41
2011	17.82	17.83	18.17	18.18	18.46	17.95	17.57	17.24	17.86	18.10	17.76	18.09	17.92
2012	17.14	17.44	17.34	17.37	17.57	17.39	17.22	17.10	17.55	18.18	17.91	17.89	17.51
2013	17.87	18.63	17.83	18.03	17.92	17.70	17.16	17.34	17.44	17.90	16.90	17.67	17.70
Other Services													
2009	38.88	39.08	38.75	38.71	38.44	38.77	38.81	39.12	39.35	39.14	39.33	39.06	38.95
2010	39.54	39.23	38.49	39.13	39.23	38.15	39.11	39.97	39.98	40.22	40.59	40.81	39.54
2011	41.60	40.23	41.61	40.62	40.67	39.61	39.36	39.60	40.68	40.00	39.88	40.36	40.35
2012	41.29	39.52	38.93	40.26	39.44	39.21	40.21	39.98	40.70	40.36	40.12	41.10	40.10
2013	40.49	40.70	40.05	41.32	41.53	41.45	40.37	40.74	41.49	40.49	41.21	42.57	41.04

4. Average Weekly Earnings by Selected Industry: District of Columbia, 2009–2013

(Dollars, not seasonally adjusted)

Industry and year	January	February	March	April	May	June	July	August	September	October	November	December	Annual average
Total Private													
2009	1,133.66	1,159.20	1,145.37	1,128.35	1,110.75	1,121.63	1,105.20	1,150.34	1,126.18	1,132.20	1,176.81	1,153.44	1,135.59
2010	1,172.09	1,165.33	1,177.98	1,203.58	1,225.19	1,166.50	1,166.90	1,215.81	1,202.18	1,227.84	1,233.18	1,261.59	1,203.14
2011	1,293.37	1,239.50	1,233.40	1,239.74	1,277.32	1,230.56	1,241.85	1,234.79	1,252.77	1,311.53	1,252.37	1,276.10	1,258.12
2012	1,324.83	1,273.30	1,283.51	1,337.87	1,279.07	1,290.14	1,361.45	1,297.41	1,358.45	1,315.42	1,319.95	1,373.01	1,318.87
2013	1,330.02	1,375.56	1,351.25	1,350.31	1,353.74	1,419.56	1,342.97	1,353.74	1,416.20	1,373.02	1,393.64	1,455.58	1,375.33
Goods-Producing													
2009	1,056.41	1,068.23	1,083.30	1,072.12	1,099.37	1,112.58	1,106.16	1,102.53	1,098.07	1,109.79	1,106.30	1,118.18	1,092.10
2010	1,124.23	1,161.04	1,089.56	1,079.59	1,082.93	1,102.11	1,108.81	1,036.69	1,023.87	1,031.59	1,040.66	1,042.34	1,075.93
2011	1,061.22	1,082.78	1,072.01	1,060.32	1,073.37	1,104.36	1,064.30	1,101.68	1,120.75	1,082.04	1,060.70	1,128.57	1,085.23
2012	1,248.79	1,159.57	1,211.47	1,205.90	1,176.23	1,142.11	1,226.22	1,194.36	1,217.25	1,156.43	1,194.48	1,254.41	1,197.41
2013	1,251.42	1,270.07	1,292.73	1,180.12	1,223.60	1,190.07	1,220.73	1,278.25	1,311.35	1,221.65	1,235.78	1,272.96	1,246.53
Trade, Transportation, and Utilities													
2009	865.43	864.29	868.85	874.37	854.85	863.04	863.76	879.70	852.91	861.04	878.89	853.55	864.50
2010	868.28	835.50	826.88	829.04	837.31	854.13	888.53	871.05	831.07	817.57	839.52	821.78	844.10
2011	831.32	818.61	805.55	811.19	804.58	795.31	813.49	848.33	863.94	929.57	884.37	856.66	838.24
2012	945.98	909.46	974.35	1,036.84	974.65	1,006.47	1,094.15	1,036.15	1,015.49	992.02	965.95	938.87	989.07
2013	924.38	939.47	931.73	949.54	932.86	917.95	869.73	867.96	883.37	902.50	878.47	895.32	907.12
Professional and Business Services													
2009	1,372.70	1,415.91	1,418.21	1,403.04	1,368.28	1,396.56	1,373.74	1,421.67	1,381.98	1,375.06	1,425.00	1,383.56	1,393.34
2010	1,404.45	1,400.61	1,358.05	1,369.61	1,388.84	1,280.16	1,244.20	1,347.76	1,281.52	1,287.89	1,305.36	1,338.37	1,332.63
2011	1,363.10	1,298.12	1,290.67	1,333.75	1,400.95	1,357.70	1,372.22	1,368.00	1,411.79	1,505.88	1,449.42	1,494.03	1,387.49
2012	1,583.66	1,530.36	1,511.02	1,589.40	1,527.20	1,554.55	1,629.87	1,544.86	1,646.57	1,563.71	1,571.76	1,670.16	1,578.50
2013	1,615.33	1,702.49	1,663.89	1,646.45	1,656.84	1,788.11	1,677.97	1,686.78	1,803.75	1,708.20	1,768.61	1,849.88	1,713.00
Leisure and Hospitality													
2009	553.38	547.76	547.13	548.11	547.14	551.38	545.38	544.15	546.15	553.41	567.35	564.00	551.43
2010	564.08	560.35	592.37	615.85	592.00	571.87	553.11	569.52	562.35	569.63	570.56	570.38	574.53
2011	539.95	563.43	586.89	592.67	599.95	567.22	555.21	527.54	557.23	552.05	536.35	531.85	559.10
2012	507.34	516.22	508.06	514.15	525.34	525.18	523.49	501.03	538.79	556.31	540.88	549.22	525.30
2013	546.82	592.43	559.86	569.75	553.73	532.77	516.52	516.73	535.41	538.79	507.00	528.33	541.62
Other Services													
2009	1,364.69	1,379.52	1,387.25	1,381.95	1,376.15	1,384.09	1,397.16	1,420.06	1,412.67	1,412.95	1,427.68	1,402.25	1,394.41
2010	1,415.53	1,412.28	1,393.34	1,416.51	1,427.97	1,377.22	1,411.87	1,458.91	1,447.28	1,451.94	1,473.42	1,485.48	1,431.35
2011	1,526.72	1,440.23	1,468.83	1,425.76	1,460.05	1,398.23	1,401.22	1,393.92	1,411.60	1,420.00	1,383.84	1,408.56	1,428.39
2012	1,461.67	1,367.39	1,358.66	1,429.23	1,384.34	1,384.11	1,435.50	1,415.29	1,477.41	1,436.82	1,440.31	1,491.93	1,423.55
2013	1,425.25	1,461.13	1,437.80	1,475.12	1,490.93	1,529.51	1,421.02	1,462.57	1,506.09	1,457.64	1,471.20	1,549.55	1,473.34

FLORIDA
At a Glance

Population:
   2000 census: 15,982,571
   2010 census: 18,801,310
   2013 estimate: 19,552,860

Percent change in population:
   2000–2010: 17.6%
   2010–2013: 4.0%

Percent change in total nonfarm employment:
   2000–2010: 1.5%
   2010–2013: 5.7%

Industry with the largest growth in employment, 2000–2013 (thousands):
   Education and Health Services, 288.5

Industry with the largest decline or smallest growth in employment, 2000–2013 (thousands):
   Manufacturing, -155.4

Civilian labor force:
   2000: 7,869,690
   2010: 9,167,310
   2013: 9,432,291

Unemployment rate and rank among states (lowest to highest):
   2000: 3.8%, 25th
   2010: 11.3%, 47th
   2013: 7.2%, 30th

Over-the-year change in unemployment rates:
   2010–2011: -1.0%
   2011–2012: -1.5
   2012–2013: -1.6

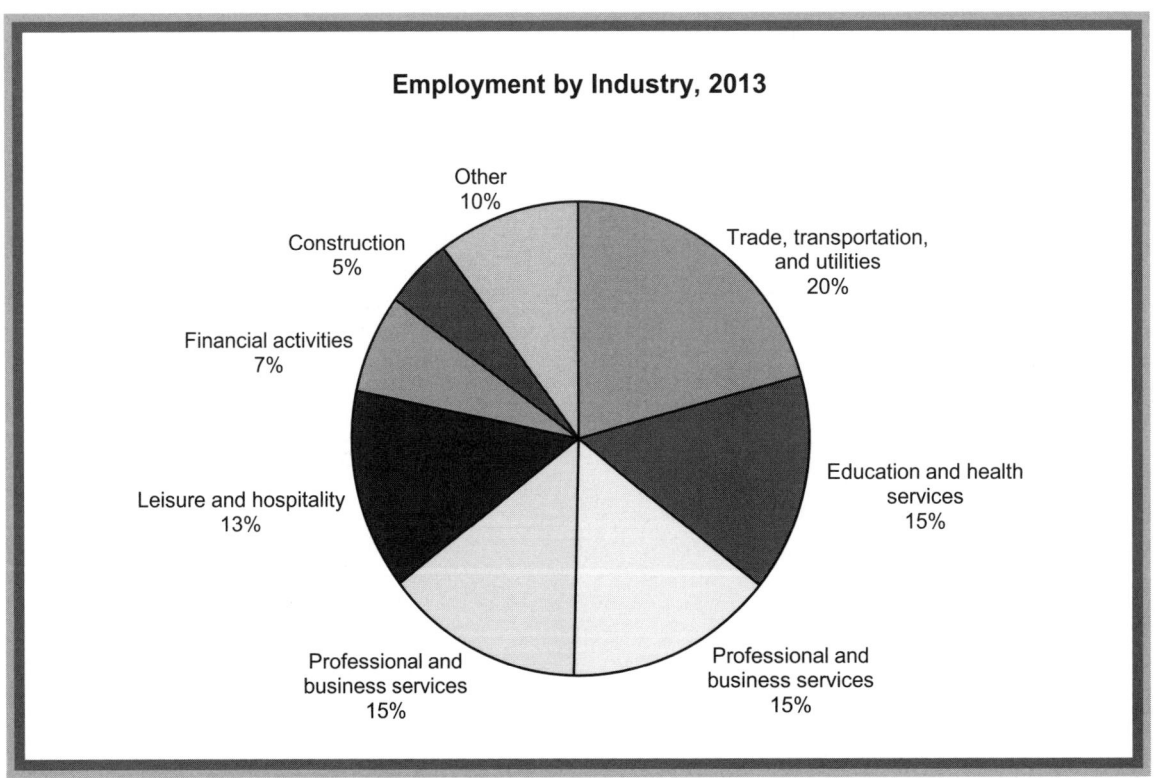

Employment by Industry, 2013

Other
10%

Construction
5%

Financial activities
7%

Trade, transportation,
and utilities
20%

Leisure and hospitality
13%

Education and health
services
15%

Professional and
business services
15%

Professional and
business services
15%

1. Employment by Industry: Florida, Selected Years, 2002–2013

(Numbers in thousands, not seasonally adjusted)

Industry and year	January	February	March	April	May	June	July	August	September	October	November	December	Annual average
Total Nonfarm													
2002	7,072.6	7,128.2	7,189.8	7,169.7	7,181.5	7,099.5	7,020.2	7,126.5	7,137.3	7,167.2	7,236.1	7,293.3	7,151.8
2003	7,159.6	7,215.0	7,270.3	7,245.0	7,249.3	7,167.1	7,099.4	7,200.1	7,220.4	7,265.6	7,313.4	7,385.5	7,232.6
2004	7,314.9	7,386.8	7,452.8	7,489.1	7,493.5	7,426.0	7,387.4	7,475.0	7,452.7	7,536.7	7,638.5	7,718.1	7,481.0
2005	7,603.4	7,686.3	7,732.9	7,775.6	7,793.6	7,699.6	7,679.2	7,796.1	7,841.0	7,847.8	7,922.1	7,995.5	7,781.1
2006	7,863.4	7,938.0	8,018.5	7,998.8	8,016.4	7,931.8	7,858.6	7,975.2	7,991.3	7,993.2	8,076.6	8,133.4	7,982.9
2007	7,992.0	8,058.7	8,122.9	8,074.9	8,069.5	7,960.9	7,851.9	7,951.3	7,937.8	7,927.0	7,999.8	8,032.7	7,998.3
2008	7,851.4	7,907.3	7,928.8	7,845.1	7,813.7	7,672.5	7,562.4	7,636.9	7,608.3	7,579.6	7,586.9	7,586.1	7,714.9
2009	7,377.7	7,377.1	7,372.3	7,324.4	7,284.4	7,152.3	7,063.8	7,131.1	7,125.5	7,150.8	7,204.6	7,224.0	7,232.3
2010	7,095.1	7,145.5	7,192.7	7,213.1	7,236.4	7,115.1	7,057.8	7,143.5	7,133.2	7,196.8	7,258.1	7,286.9	7,172.9
2011	7,173.5	7,224.0	7,270.9	7,307.9	7,277.6	7,163.9	7,126.6	7,212.5	7,238.8	7,280.9	7,356.7	7,389.6	7,251.9
2012	7,283.4	7,344.9	7,404.8	7,423.9	7,414.4	7,320.6	7,265.9	7,364.6	7,379.6	7,451.9	7,540.3	7,565.5	7,396.7
2013	7,443.9	7,519.6	7,573.4	7,581.1	7,582.2	7,490.2	7,456.4	7,565.3	7,577.2	7,657.9	7,736.9	7,766.7	7,579.2
Total Private													
2002	6,038.7	6,084.0	6,141.0	6,120.4	6,127.8	6,121.6	6,056.2	6,078.3	6,080.7	6,105.2	6,171.3	6,225.8	6,112.6
2003	6,106.9	6,151.5	6,203.2	6,179.4	6,177.3	6,173.2	6,118.4	6,143.1	6,157.5	6,194.6	6,239.6	6,309.8	6,179.5
2004	6,250.3	6,309.0	6,372.2	6,409.6	6,414.0	6,422.5	6,395.2	6,403.5	6,376.6	6,452.8	6,546.6	6,624.8	6,414.8
2005	6,522.3	6,592.8	6,637.1	6,680.1	6,694.9	6,700.4	6,678.5	6,713.0	6,743.1	6,739.7	6,811.2	6,885.9	6,699.9
2006	6,763.1	6,827.1	6,903.8	6,887.4	6,908.5	6,917.7	6,843.8	6,872.3	6,876.2	6,864.3	6,939.9	7,000.0	6,883.7
2007	6,868.2	6,923.6	6,982.3	6,935.7	6,933.9	6,919.9	6,810.8	6,821.2	6,799.6	6,781.4	6,848.5	6,883.3	6,875.7
2008	6,711.1	6,755.5	6,779.6	6,698.2	6,672.8	6,627.8	6,518.6	6,503.8	6,466.1	6,433.7	6,442.1	6,446.6	6,588.0
2009	6,244.6	6,237.9	6,235.4	6,181.8	6,153.9	6,116.9	6,029.6	6,017.4	6,001.6	6,022.2	6,072.8	6,098.7	6,117.7
2010	5,973.2	6,017.5	6,064.3	6,079.0	6,074.7	6,067.1	6,024.5	6,031.4	6,017.9	6,074.5	6,132.7	6,169.9	6,060.6
2011	6,058.9	6,099.7	6,148.2	6,185.1	6,167.0	6,145.5	6,114.7	6,128.9	6,146.9	6,173.7	6,249.3	6,287.8	6,158.8
2012	6,188.7	6,238.4	6,299.1	6,323.8	6,324.9	6,315.4	6,266.7	6,289.6	6,294.6	6,354.2	6,439.8	6,471.0	6,317.2
2013	6,353.7	6,419.5	6,472.0	6,481.8	6,493.0	6,487.3	6,462.4	6,493.5	6,494.8	6,563.1	6,637.0	6,673.8	6,502.7
Goods-Producing													
2002	937.5	938.5	941.6	936.9	939.5	941.0	932.3	939.3	938.7	942.5	945.6	946.4	940.0
2003	932.4	936.0	939.2	931.7	937.2	941.9	935.9	942.0	944.9	946.8	947.5	955.3	940.9
2004	953.1	962.7	974.2	980.2	984.7	992.7	995.6	998.6	997.9	1,007.5	1,015.6	1,024.4	990.6
2005	1,013.8	1,024.5	1,032.5	1,043.4	1,052.2	1,061.6	1,066.1	1,072.9	1,081.5	1,082.6	1,089.7	1,098.8	1,060.0
2006	1,085.7	1,099.2	1,111.6	1,110.2	1,117.3	1,123.6	1,110.2	1,112.0	1,109.5	1,098.3	1,093.7	1,091.4	1,105.2
2007	1,063.3	1,064.2	1,068.6	1,048.1	1,047.2	1,048.8	1,022.7	1,019.2	1,009.5	990.8	983.6	977.1	1,028.6
2008	945.2	944.0	938.8	915.5	911.9	908.8	886.6	880.1	872.7	852.8	838.1	823.5	893.2
2009	784.9	771.5	762.4	741.3	734.7	730.6	714.5	708.3	701.9	693.2	687.4	683.2	726.2
2010	660.6	662.1	664.5	668.6	669.1	672.4	673.1	670.7	666.2	661.3	658.4	657.0	665.3
2011	643.0	645.6	648.4	651.4	652.9	655.3	656.0	657.5	659.6	656.9	658.1	658.4	653.6
2012	649.1	651.9	657.8	657.1	661.9	667.1	665.3	670.5	672.0	673.8	677.5	677.1	665.1
2013	666.1	672.3	678.7	681.5	688.0	692.9	697.2	704.8	707.1	714.1	722.4	724.7	695.8
Service-Providing													
2002	6,135.1	6,189.7	6,248.2	6,232.8	6,242.0	6,158.5	6,087.9	6,187.2	6,198.6	6,224.7	6,290.5	6,346.9	6,211.8
2003	6,227.2	6,279.0	6,331.1	6,313.3	6,312.1	6,225.2	6,163.5	6,258.1	6,275.5	6,318.8	6,365.9	6,430.2	6,291.7
2004	6,361.8	6,424.1	6,478.6	6,508.9	6,508.8	6,433.3	6,391.8	6,476.4	6,454.8	6,529.2	6,622.9	6,693.7	6,490.4
2005	6,589.6	6,661.8	6,700.4	6,732.2	6,741.4	6,638.0	6,613.1	6,723.2	6,759.5	6,765.2	6,832.4	6,896.7	6,721.1
2006	6,777.7	6,838.8	6,906.9	6,888.6	6,899.1	6,808.2	6,748.4	6,863.2	6,881.8	6,894.9	6,982.9	7,042.0	6,877.7
2007	6,928.7	6,993.9	7,054.3	7,026.8	7,022.3	6,912.1	6,829.2	6,932.1	6,928.3	6,936.2	7,016.2	7,055.6	6,969.6
2008	6,906.2	6,963.3	6,990.0	6,929.6	6,901.8	6,763.7	6,675.8	6,756.8	6,735.6	6,726.8	6,748.8	6,762.6	6,821.8
2009	6,592.8	6,605.6	6,609.9	6,583.1	6,549.7	6,421.7	6,349.3	6,422.8	6,423.6	6,457.6	6,517.2	6,540.8	6,506.2
2010	6,434.5	6,483.4	6,528.2	6,544.5	6,567.3	6,442.7	6,384.7	6,472.8	6,467.0	6,535.5	6,599.7	6,629.9	6,507.5
2011	6,530.5	6,578.4	6,622.5	6,656.5	6,624.7	6,508.6	6,470.6	6,555.0	6,579.2	6,624.0	6,698.6	6,731.2	6,598.3
2012	6,634.3	6,693.0	6,747.0	6,766.8	6,752.5	6,653.5	6,600.6	6,694.1	6,707.6	6,778.1	6,862.8	6,888.4	6,731.6
2013	6,777.8	6,847.3	6,894.7	6,899.6	6,894.2	6,797.3	6,759.2	6,860.5	6,870.1	6,943.8	7,014.5	7,042.0	6,883.4
Mining and Logging													
2002	7.3	7.4	7.3	7.3	7.3	7.3	7.2	7.2	7.1	7.0	7.0	7.0	7.2
2003	7.1	7.0	7.0	6.9	7.1	7.1	7.1	7.2	7.2	7.2	7.2	7.2	7.1
2004	7.2	7.2	7.2	7.2	7.1	7.1	7.1	7.1	7.1	7.1	7.1	7.1	7.1
2005	7.1	7.1	7.1	7.2	7.2	7.2	7.2	7.2	7.0	6.8	6.8	6.9	7.1
2006	6.6	6.6	6.7	6.7	6.7	6.8	6.6	6.4	6.5	6.5	6.6	6.6	6.6
2007	6.7	6.8	6.7	6.8	6.8	6.9	6.6	6.7	6.6	6.6	6.7	6.7	6.7
2008	6.6	6.6	6.5	6.4	6.3	6.2	6.1	6.1	6.0	5.9	5.8	5.8	6.2
2009	5.7	5.6	5.5	5.5	5.5	5.5	5.4	5.4	5.4	5.4	5.4	5.4	5.5
2010	5.3	5.3	5.2	5.3	5.3	5.4	5.4	5.5	5.6	5.6	5.7	5.7	5.4
2011	5.7	5.7	5.7	5.7	5.7	5.7	5.6	5.6	5.6	5.6	5.6	5.6	5.7
2012	5.6	5.6	5.6	5.6	5.7	5.7	5.6	5.6	5.6	5.6	5.7	5.7	5.6
2013	5.7	5.7	5.7	5.7	5.6	5.6	5.6	5.7	5.6	5.6	5.6	5.7	5.7
Construction													
2002	495.9	497.0	499.8	498.5	502.0	503.7	500.3	506.9	507.6	513.5	516.1	516.8	504.8
2003	507.6	512.0	515.4	513.3	519.1	524.2	524.0	529.2	531.5	534.2	535.6	541.5	524.0
2004	540.7	548.2	557.1	561.9	565.2	572.4	576.9	579.6	580.4	590.5	597.1	603.7	572.8
2005	597.3	605.8	612.3	621.9	629.1	636.9	643.2	649.1	656.8	659.0	665.7	672.3	637.5
2006	661.7	673.4	684.3	685.1	690.9	696.1	687.9	690.0	688.1	680.4	676.3	672.6	682.2
2007	650.0	651.0	655.1	637.3	636.9	639.0	619.0	616.2	608.6	593.2	587.2	581.2	622.9
2008	554.4	553.6	550.6	531.1	528.8	527.1	511.1	506.0	501.0	486.4	475.4	465.3	515.9
2009	434.1	426.2	421.4	407.0	402.8	400.6	390.8	386.0	381.6	374.7	368.9	365.4	396.6
2010	347.5	349.2	351.5	355.1	353.8	356.1	357.8	355.7	351.6	347.3	343.3	340.4	350.8
2011	328.5	330.3	332.6	334.3	334.8	336.1	337.4	338.1	340.5	337.5	338.1	337.6	335.5
2012	328.8	330.9	335.1	334.9	338.4	343.1	342.6	347.0	349.2	350.4	352.8	352.1	342.1
2013	344.4	348.5	353.6	355.7	360.5	364.1	369.9	376.4	378.3	386.4	390.8	390.9	368.3

1. Employment by Industry: Florida, Selected Years, 2002–2013—*Continued*

(Numbers in thousands, not seasonally adjusted)

Industry and year	January	February	March	April	May	June	July	August	September	October	November	December	Annual average
Manufacturing													
2002	434.3	434.1	434.5	431.1	430.2	430.0	424.8	425.2	424.0	422.0	422.5	422.6	427.9
2003	417.7	417.0	416.8	411.5	411.0	410.6	404.8	405.6	406.2	405.4	404.7	406.6	409.8
2004	405.2	407.3	409.9	411.1	412.4	413.2	411.6	411.9	410.4	410.0	411.4	413.6	410.7
2005	409.4	411.6	413.1	414.3	415.9	417.5	415.7	416.6	417.7	416.8	417.2	419.6	415.5
2006	417.4	419.2	420.6	418.4	419.7	420.7	415.7	415.6	414.9	411.4	410.8	412.2	416.4
2007	406.6	407.0	406.8	404.0	403.5	402.9	397.1	396.3	394.3	391.0	389.7	389.2	399.0
2008	384.2	383.8	381.7	378.0	376.8	375.5	369.4	368.0	365.7	360.5	356.9	352.4	371.1
2009	345.1	339.7	335.5	328.8	326.4	324.5	318.3	316.9	314.9	313.1	313.1	312.4	324.1
2010	307.8	307.6	307.8	308.2	310.0	310.9	309.9	309.5	309.0	308.4	309.4	310.9	309.1
2011	308.8	309.6	310.1	311.4	312.4	313.5	313.0	313.8	313.5	313.8	314.4	315.2	312.5
2012	314.7	315.4	317.1	316.6	317.8	318.3	317.1	317.9	317.2	317.8	319.0	319.3	317.4
2013	316.0	318.1	319.4	320.1	321.9	323.2	321.7	322.7	323.2	322.1	326.0	328.1	321.9
Trade, Transportation, and Utilities													
2002	1,510.3	1,501.1	1,508.4	1,501.1	1,502.1	1,496.6	1,485.1	1,491.3	1,492.2	1,499.3	1,526.2	1,555.1	1,505.7
2003	1,495.9	1,488.3	1,490.8	1,486.2	1,486.6	1,482.4	1,478.0	1,483.5	1,487.9	1,501.6	1,528.5	1,558.8	1,497.4
2004	1,516.1	1,513.8	1,520.6	1,525.2	1,528.1	1,526.4	1,525.0	1,526.7	1,520.9	1,543.0	1,583.0	1,614.3	1,536.9
2005	1,566.1	1,569.2	1,576.0	1,586.7	1,591.8	1,590.4	1,591.0	1,596.7	1,600.6	1,608.1	1,636.8	1,668.3	1,598.5
2006	1,618.5	1,617.6	1,629.0	1,625.2	1,628.0	1,625.9	1,615.2	1,619.6	1,619.2	1,626.5	1,663.5	1,693.0	1,631.8
2007	1,639.8	1,636.6	1,645.5	1,639.6	1,644.3	1,639.1	1,623.2	1,624.9	1,624.8	1,628.1	1,668.1	1,688.8	1,641.9
2008	1,632.7	1,628.0	1,628.8	1,610.0	1,606.7	1,595.0	1,576.9	1,574.6	1,565.6	1,562.8	1,579.8	1,594.2	1,596.3
2009	1,527.6	1,514.4	1,505.7	1,489.6	1,486.5	1,477.9	1,461.3	1,459.8	1,456.9	1,462.6	1,492.5	1,510.8	1,487.1
2010	1,464.4	1,462.9	1,467.7	1,468.8	1,470.6	1,468.9	1,457.9	1,461.3	1,456.4	1,474.0	1,508.4	1,531.0	1,474.4
2011	1,484.4	1,482.4	1,487.3	1,495.5	1,494.0	1,491.4	1,489.5	1,493.9	1,495.1	1,506.9	1,546.7	1,566.0	1,502.8
2012	1,522.9	1,520.4	1,526.7	1,527.0	1,531.4	1,528.0	1,519.8	1,522.7	1,524.3	1,537.4	1,582.0	1,598.7	1,536.8
2013	1,550.5	1,550.2	1,554.3	1,556.2	1,561.0	1,563.3	1,558.5	1,563.8	1,563.7	1,580.9	1,616.3	1,645.4	1,572.0
Wholesale Trade													
2002	318.4	319.7	320.5	318.5	320.0	319.6	318.2	319.1	319.8	320.9	322.8	324.7	320.2
2003	319.9	320.8	321.3	320.8	320.9	320.6	320.3	321.1	322.1	322.6	324.1	327.2	321.8
2004	325.9	328.3	330.0	330.8	332.3	332.9	331.8	332.4	331.8	335.0	338.1	340.5	332.5
2005	338.2	340.5	341.3	344.4	346.4	346.4	346.1	346.9	348.1	348.4	350.0	353.6	345.9
2006	349.3	352.0	354.0	354.9	356.6	357.1	355.2	356.1	356.6	357.4	359.0	361.8	355.8
2007	360.2	362.7	363.8	362.4	363.3	363.1	359.2	359.1	358.9	359.4	360.4	362.0	361.2
2008	356.4	358.0	357.5	353.7	354.0	352.3	347.9	346.9	346.0	344.2	342.7	342.5	350.2
2009	333.5	332.3	329.3	325.7	324.8	322.2	317.9	317.0	315.5	316.2	316.9	318.3	322.5
2010	311.8	312.8	313.4	313.4	315.0	313.8	311.4	311.7	311.1	313.2	314.3	316.6	313.2
2011	309.8	311.2	312.1	313.0	312.5	311.8	310.7	310.8	311.2	312.3	313.7	316.7	312.1
2012	312.8	314.8	316.4	317.6	318.6	317.8	316.7	317.2	317.6	319.6	321.8	323.1	317.8
2013	318.3	320.1	321.2	321.2	322.4	321.8	319.6	320.6	321.2	321.2	322.0	324.5	321.2
Retail Trade													
2002	946.9	936.8	941.5	936.4	936.8	932.7	923.0	928.5	929.3	935.6	959.6	983.0	940.8
2003	936.3	928.9	930.8	926.5	928.3	926.5	923.2	927.3	930.7	943.6	968.4	991.4	938.5
2004	953.4	948.0	952.2	955.1	957.5	956.1	954.7	953.8	948.8	964.7	998.5	1,022.0	963.7
2005	982.5	982.2	987.0	993.1	995.2	995.7	996.7	1,001.2	1,002.5	1,009.9	1,033.6	1,056.0	1,003.0
2006	1,017.3	1,013.5	1,021.3	1,017.0	1,017.9	1,016.3	1,010.2	1,011.7	1,010.0	1,017.4	1,050.3	1,069.4	1,022.7
2007	1,027.6	1,022.3	1,028.8	1,023.0	1,027.5	1,023.0	1,013.2	1,014.5	1,013.9	1,016.2	1,051.6	1,065.5	1,027.3
2008	1,023.8	1,016.9	1,017.8	1,005.1	1,002.2	995.2	984.2	982.8	976.6	975.3	992.6	1,001.4	997.8
2009	953.5	943.8	939.5	929.9	929.0	924.8	915.4	915.6	915.0	919.9	947.7	959.2	932.8
2010	926.6	923.2	926.8	928.4	929.1	929.2	921.6	924.7	921.0	934.5	964.9	979.1	934.1
2011	943.8	939.5	942.2	947.8	947.0	945.1	944.0	948.3	948.6	958.5	993.9	1,004.6	955.3
2012	972.3	966.6	970.6	970.2	973.3	970.2	964.1	966.5	967.5	977.0	1,016.2	1,025.6	978.3
2013	988.9	985.6	987.5	988.8	992.2	995.1	994.5	997.9	996.6	1,011.8	1,041.6	1,060.6	1,003.4
Transportation and Utilities													
2002	245.0	244.6	246.4	246.2	245.3	244.3	243.9	243.7	243.1	242.8	243.8	247.4	244.7
2003	239.7	238.6	238.7	238.9	237.4	235.3	234.5	235.1	235.1	235.4	236.0	240.2	237.1
2004	236.8	237.5	238.4	239.3	238.3	237.4	238.5	240.5	240.3	243.3	246.4	251.8	240.7
2005	245.4	246.5	247.7	249.2	250.2	248.3	248.2	248.6	250.0	249.8	253.2	258.7	249.7
2006	251.9	252.1	253.7	253.3	253.5	252.5	249.8	251.8	252.6	251.7	254.2	261.8	253.2
2007	252.0	251.6	252.9	254.2	253.5	253.0	250.8	251.3	252.0	252.5	256.1	261.3	253.4
2008	252.5	253.1	253.5	251.2	250.5	247.5	244.8	244.9	243.0	243.3	244.5	250.3	248.3
2009	240.6	238.3	236.9	234.0	232.7	230.9	228.0	227.2	226.4	226.5	227.9	233.3	231.9
2010	226.0	226.9	227.5	227.0	226.5	225.9	224.9	224.9	224.3	226.3	229.2	235.3	227.1
2011	230.8	231.7	233.1	234.7	234.5	234.5	234.8	234.8	235.3	236.1	239.1	244.7	235.3
2012	237.8	239.0	239.7	239.2	239.5	240.0	239.0	239.0	239.2	240.8	244.0	250.0	240.6
2013	243.3	244.5	245.6	246.2	246.4	246.4	244.4	245.3	245.9	247.9	252.7	260.3	247.4
Information													
2002	177.5	177.0	177.2	175.0	175.3	174.8	173.3	172.7	171.8	171.2	171.8	172.4	174.2
2003	168.7	169.0	169.4	167.1	168.1	167.7	167.5	167.5	166.5	166.3	167.0	167.7	167.7
2004	164.5	163.9	165.0	163.8	164.5	164.9	163.8	163.9	162.7	163.7	165.0	165.6	164.3
2005	163.3	164.1	164.3	163.5	165.2	165.3	164.9	164.9	165.4	164.0	165.0	165.4	164.6
2006	161.9	162.7	162.9	162.6	163.7	164.4	164.1	163.4	162.4	162.2	163.2	164.0	163.1
2007	161.6	162.6	163.2	163.8	164.5	164.8	163.1	162.8	161.4	161.2	161.2	161.7	162.7
2008	160.1	160.6	160.4	159.1	159.3	158.8	157.9	156.6	154.3	153.8	153.4	152.4	157.2
2009	149.3	148.9	147.9	146.3	145.5	145.1	142.9	141.7	139.8	139.3	139.2	139.3	143.8
2010	137.7	137.4	138.2	137.2	137.0	137.1	136.8	136.9	136.0	136.6	137.1	136.7	137.1
2011	136.2	136.3	136.2	135.8	135.9	135.8	135.7	135.4	135.2	135.0	135.6	135.4	135.7
2012	134.1	134.0	133.9	133.8	133.6	133.4	133.4	133.0	132.0	133.9	133.9	134.0	133.6
2013	132.8	133.1	133.7	133.6	133.6	134.4	134.4	134.5	133.8	134.4	133.8	134.9	133.9

1. Employment by Industry: Florida, Selected Years, 2002–2013—*Continued*

(Numbers in thousands, not seasonally adjusted)

Industry and year	January	February	March	April	May	June	July	August	September	October	November	December	Annual average
Financial Activities													
2002	479.7	481.9	483.5	482.0	482.9	485.1	485.7	487.0	485.7	486.7	489.5	491.9	485.1
2003	486.1	487.9	489.9	491.9	493.8	496.5	497.8	500.1	499.6	500.5	500.5	505.1	495.8
2004	500.7	503.7	507.1	511.4	512.7	514.7	517.0	517.8	516.0	520.8	522.8	527.8	514.4
2005	522.3	526.2	528.1	533.6	536.3	540.2	542.6	544.3	545.5	548.5	552.0	558.2	539.8
2006	548.3	552.5	556.0	556.7	558.7	560.2	556.9	557.6	555.6	556.9	557.9	562.3	556.6
2007	550.7	554.3	556.3	554.0	554.5	555.7	552.2	550.5	547.3	545.1	546.0	547.7	551.2
2008	537.4	538.2	538.2	532.5	531.8	529.7	524.9	522.4	517.9	513.9	511.6	512.1	525.9
2009	497.7	495.7	493.9	491.3	490.6	490.0	485.7	483.7	479.3	479.6	480.0	481.2	487.4
2010	473.1	474.3	476.0	475.6	476.9	478.7	478.5	478.7	475.9	480.4	482.4	485.5	478.0
2011	478.9	480.7	483.3	484.3	484.4	484.9	487.0	488.2	489.3	490.4	491.4	495.0	486.5
2012	488.8	491.7	494.4	496.5	497.9	500.1	500.2	501.2	500.4	504.8	507.2	509.7	499.4
2013	503.2	506.0	508.7	510.1	511.4	514.0	514.4	515.6	514.7	517.4	517.0	518.7	512.6
Professional and Business Services													
2002	920.9	942.3	956.5	957.5	958.6	956.1	945.0	940.4	941.8	946.3	958.3	965.2	949.1
2003	947.0	965.3	982.1	979.5	970.2	966.7	947.9	950.8	950.9	968.9	969.6	975.4	964.5
2004	969.7	989.3	1,005.8	1,025.2	1,023.4	1,028.7	1,022.2	1,023.3	1,019.4	1,042.9	1,059.5	1,076.3	1,023.8
2005	1,059.2	1,080.6	1,087.4	1,097.0	1,096.9	1,098.4	1,096.1	1,106.0	1,115.3	1,107.7	1,121.6	1,132.1	1,099.9
2006	1,111.5	1,126.6	1,146.7	1,143.3	1,149.7	1,156.4	1,143.2	1,152.9	1,158.2	1,150.1	1,163.1	1,174.3	1,148.0
2007	1,155.5	1,170.9	1,182.0	1,170.3	1,166.3	1,164.1	1,143.5	1,147.1	1,140.4	1,139.7	1,145.1	1,148.9	1,156.2
2008	1,102.2	1,117.3	1,121.4	1,104.1	1,095.9	1,088.7	1,067.6	1,066.5	1,063.5	1,059.7	1,053.6	1,052.5	1,082.8
2009	1,009.1	1,009.9	1,007.2	998.6	993.4	991.5	977.1	977.6	978.3	987.5	996.2	999.1	993.8
2010	977.9	990.0	998.0	1,000.5	1,000.5	1,005.2	1,001.7	1,007.4	1,007.7	1,022.5	1,027.3	1,033.9	1,006.1
2011	1,014.9	1,028.6	1,035.9	1,043.8	1,036.6	1,034.7	1,027.7	1,030.2	1,033.7	1,039.9	1,049.8	1,056.9	1,036.1
2012	1,034.6	1,050.4	1,061.5	1,074.8	1,073.2	1,072.9	1,065.4	1,071.8	1,072.6	1,093.8	1,105.7	1,108.6	1,073.8
2013	1,082.1	1,099.9	1,108.4	1,108.4	1,113.3	1,112.7	1,111.8	1,119.5	1,120.6	1,134.7	1,145.6	1,144.0	1,116.8
Education and Health Services													
2002	860.0	867.8	875.4	872.3	875.6	874.3	864.4	873.8	882.1	888.4	894.5	898.8	877.3
2003	890.3	900.6	906.4	905.3	908.7	906.8	899.8	908.6	918.5	921.2	923.8	929.2	909.9
2004	922.7	930.8	935.0	937.9	940.6	936.6	928.6	934.0	935.4	942.8	948.7	951.7	937.1
2005	942.7	951.5	954.6	959.3	960.7	955.3	950.7	959.8	967.5	969.4	972.8	978.3	960.2
2006	967.0	975.4	982.0	982.2	986.1	983.5	974.5	985.3	992.7	994.6	1,001.2	1,007.0	986.0
2007	996.9	1,007.9	1,013.2	1,015.2	1,017.6	1,015.5	1,003.3	1,014.0	1,021.9	1,025.2	1,031.7	1,036.5	1,016.5
2008	1,026.7	1,036.3	1,040.8	1,038.5	1,041.2	1,034.3	1,022.7	1,030.5	1,036.8	1,042.9	1,049.9	1,054.4	1,037.9
2009	1,037.4	1,044.2	1,048.3	1,048.1	1,051.1	1,044.8	1,036.2	1,043.1	1,051.1	1,064.8	1,071.3	1,073.7	1,051.2
2010	1,059.3	1,066.7	1,071.5	1,072.8	1,074.2	1,066.5	1,057.2	1,061.3	1,066.9	1,081.0	1,086.6	1,086.2	1,070.9
2011	1,077.4	1,085.1	1,087.5	1,096.2	1,094.8	1,083.9	1,075.1	1,082.4	1,094.2	1,100.2	1,107.1	1,108.5	1,091.0
2012	1,093.8	1,101.9	1,106.3	1,112.0	1,113.0	1,104.3	1,091.8	1,103.6	1,113.0	1,119.9	1,125.0	1,126.7	1,109.3
2013	1,115.0	1,125.9	1,129.6	1,131.7	1,131.0	1,119.3	1,107.5	1,120.5	1,127.4	1,137.8	1,145.9	1,145.9	1,128.1
Leisure and Hospitality													
2002	850.6	870.7	890.0	890.4	887.1	885.4	864.1	866.5	860.8	860.4	872.6	882.1	873.4
2003	873.6	888.6	906.6	900.0	894.8	892.5	878.8	879.5	877.4	878.7	892.2	905.2	889.0
2004	907.9	926.7	945.3	945.2	938.1	933.5	920.9	917.8	903.6	912.4	929.2	941.7	926.9
2005	931.7	951.2	967.6	969.0	963.7	961.0	941.5	943.6	940.7	936.3	949.2	959.3	951.2
2006	949.1	968.4	987.6	980.4	976.1	971.9	952.9	954.3	949.7	946.4	965.5	974.2	964.7
2007	966.8	989.2	1,011.8	1,006.9	1,001.6	993.2	972.1	971.5	963.4	959.9	978.8	986.3	983.5
2008	973.9	995.7	1,013.7	1,005.5	993.9	982.5	959.0	951.8	938.8	934.5	945.1	949.0	970.3
2009	933.9	948.5	964.4	961.4	947.7	934.1	913.3	905.7	897.8	897.4	908.1	912.8	927.1
2010	904.2	926.1	948.7	955.0	946.8	939.1	923.0	920.1	914.9	922.2	935.4	942.6	931.5
2011	931.5	946.5	973.0	979.6	970.5	963.1	948.9	947.1	945.4	949.0	964.1	970.5	957.4
2012	967.9	988.7	1,016.9	1,019.0	1,010.8	1,006.2	990.7	987.0	980.0	988.4	1,005.0	1,011.6	997.7
2013	1,001.8	1,027.3	1,052.1	1,052.4	1,047.0	1,043.2	1,033.5	1,029.3	1,021.8	1,037.2	1,047.5	1,050.0	1,036.9
Other Services													
2002	302.2	304.7	308.4	305.2	306.7	308.3	306.3	307.3	307.6	310.4	312.8	313.9	307.8
2003	312.9	315.8	318.8	317.7	317.9	318.7	312.7	311.1	311.8	310.6	310.5	313.1	314.3
2004	315.6	318.1	319.2	320.7	321.9	325.0	322.1	321.4	320.7	319.7	322.8	323.0	320.9
2005	323.2	325.5	326.6	327.6	328.1	328.2	325.6	324.8	326.6	323.1	324.1	325.5	325.7
2006	321.1	324.7	328.0	326.8	328.9	331.8	326.8	327.2	328.9	329.3	331.8	333.8	328.3
2007	333.6	337.3	341.7	337.8	337.9	338.7	331.7	331.2	330.9	331.4	334.0	336.3	335.2
2008	332.9	335.4	337.5	333.0	332.1	330.0	323.0	321.3	316.5	313.3	310.6	308.5	324.5
2009	304.7	304.8	305.6	305.2	304.4	302.9	298.6	297.5	296.5	297.8	298.1	298.6	301.2
2010	296.0	298.0	299.7	300.5	299.6	299.2	296.3	295.0	293.9	296.5	297.1	297.0	297.4
2011	292.6	294.5	296.6	298.5	297.9	296.4	294.8	294.2	294.4	295.4	296.5	297.1	295.7
2012	297.5	299.4	301.6	303.6	303.1	303.4	300.1	299.8	300.3	302.2	303.5	304.6	301.6
2013	302.2	304.8	306.5	307.9	307.7	307.5	305.1	305.5	305.7	306.6	308.5	310.2	306.5
Government													
2002	1,033.9	1,044.2	1,048.8	1,049.3	1,053.7	977.9	964.0	1,048.2	1,056.6	1,062.0	1,064.8	1,067.5	1,039.2
2003	1,052.7	1,063.5	1,067.1	1,065.6	1,072.0	993.9	981.0	1,057.0	1,062.9	1,071.0	1,073.8	1,075.7	1,053.0
2004	1,064.6	1,077.8	1,080.6	1,079.5	1,079.5	1,003.5	992.2	1,071.5	1,076.1	1,083.9	1,091.9	1,093.3	1,066.2
2005	1,081.1	1,093.5	1,095.8	1,095.5	1,098.7	999.2	1,000.7	1,083.1	1,097.9	1,108.1	1,110.9	1,109.6	1,081.2
2006	1,100.3	1,110.9	1,114.7	1,111.4	1,107.9	1,014.1	1,014.8	1,102.9	1,115.1	1,128.9	1,136.7	1,133.4	1,099.3
2007	1,123.8	1,135.1	1,140.6	1,139.2	1,135.6	1,041.0	1,041.1	1,130.1	1,138.2	1,145.6	1,151.3	1,149.4	1,122.6
2008	1,140.3	1,151.8	1,149.2	1,146.9	1,140.9	1,044.7	1,043.8	1,133.1	1,142.2	1,145.9	1,144.8	1,139.5	1,126.9
2009	1,133.1	1,139.2	1,136.9	1,142.6	1,130.5	1,035.4	1,034.2	1,113.7	1,123.9	1,128.6	1,131.8	1,125.3	1,114.6
2010	1,121.9	1,128.0	1,128.4	1,134.1	1,161.7	1,048.0	1,033.3	1,112.1	1,115.3	1,122.3	1,125.4	1,117.0	1,112.3
2011	1,114.6	1,124.3	1,122.7	1,122.8	1,110.6	1,018.4	1,011.9	1,083.6	1,091.9	1,107.2	1,107.4	1,101.8	1,093.1
2012	1,094.7	1,106.5	1,105.7	1,100.1	1,089.5	1,005.2	999.2	1,075.0	1,085.0	1,097.7	1,100.5	1,094.5	1,079.5
2013	1,090.2	1,100.1	1,101.4	1,099.3	1,089.2	1,002.9	994.0	1,071.8	1,082.4	1,094.8	1,099.9	1,092.9	1,076.6

2. Average Weekly Hours by Selected Industry: Florida, 2009–2013

(Not seasonally adjusted)

Industry and year	January	February	March	April	May	June	July	August	September	October	November	December	Annual average
Total Private													
2009	34.7	35.0	34.9	34.8	34.7	34.8	35.0	35.2	35.1	34.9	35.4	35.4	35.0
2010	35.4	35.6	35.5	35.8	36.0	35.6	35.4	35.6	34.9	35.2	35.2	35.2	35.5
2011	35.4	35.2	35.1	35.2	35.0	34.7	34.7	34.5	34.4	34.7	34.5	34.6	34.8
2012	34.5	34.4	34.5	34.4	34.1	34.1	34.5	34.2	34.3	34.1	34.2	34.6	34.3
2013	34.1	34.5	34.5	34.3	34.2	34.5	34.2	34.4	34.5	34.2	34.3	34.6	34.4
Goods-Producing													
2009	37.8	38.7	38.5	38.0	38.1	38.4	38.9	39.1	40.2	41.0	41.7	41.8	39.3
2010	41.4	40.3	40.1	40.6	40.9	40.8	39.8	39.8	39.0	39.7	39.8	39.5	40.1
2011	39.4	39.2	39.5	40.1	40.0	40.2	39.8	39.6	40.2	40.1	40.2	40.4	39.9
2012	40.2	39.8	40.1	40.5	40.4	40.3	40.1	40.2	40.4	40.4	40.4	40.3	40.3
2013	39.6	40.1	40.3	40.1	40.1	40.2	39.6	39.9	40.2	39.9	40.1	40.7	40.1
Construction													
2009	38.3	39.4	39.1	38.3	38.4	38.8	38.4	38.4	38.9	41.0	41.0	40.9	39.2
2010	40.0	39.4	39.1	40.3	40.7	40.7	40.0	39.8	39.0	39.6	39.8	39.6	39.8
2011	39.5	39.1	39.5	40.4	40.3	40.7	40.2	40.0	40.4	40.7	40.6	40.4	40.2
2012	40.0	39.5	39.7	40.4	40.3	39.9	39.7	40.1	40.0	40.3	40.2	39.9	40.0
2013	39.1	39.0	39.6	39.5	39.3	39.3	38.9	39.3	39.4	39.2	39.2	39.6	39.3
Manufacturing													
2009	37.3	37.8	38.0	37.5	37.5	37.7	37.3	38.0	37.8	37.4	38.2	39.0	37.8
2010	40.1	38.8	38.9	38.9	39.1	39.1	38.3	38.6	38.0	38.5	39.6	39.6	39.0
2011	38.9	39.0	39.0	39.3	39.3	39.2	38.9	38.8	39.7	39.2	39.5	40.2	39.3
2012	40.2	39.9	40.3	40.3	40.2	40.3	40.2	39.9	40.5	40.1	40.2	40.4	40.2
2013	39.8	40.9	40.8	40.5	40.8	41.1	40.4	40.5	40.9	40.5	40.9	41.8	40.7
Trade, Transportation, and Utilities													
2009	34.6	35.1	35.0	34.8	34.9	34.7	34.8	35.0	34.7	34.6	35.0	35.1	34.9
2010	35.3	35.7	35.6	36.9	36.8	36.1	35.9	36.0	35.2	35.7	35.7	36.0	35.9
2011	35.3	35.7	35.5	35.4	35.0	34.6	34.6	34.1	33.9	33.8	33.7	34.1	34.6
2012	33.5	33.7	33.5	32.9	32.9	32.7	32.8	32.7	33.1	32.8	33.1	33.3	33.1
2013	32.8	33.2	33.2	32.8	33.0	33.1	32.9	32.8	32.9	32.6	32.7	33.1	32.9
Financial Activities													
2009	37.6	37.3	37.2	37.6	37.5	37.6	37.5	37.8	37.3	37.1	37.8	38.1	37.5
2010	37.7	38.1	38.3	37.8	38.9	38.1	37.9	38.8	38.1	37.8	37.7	37.4	38.0
2011	37.5	37.1	36.9	37.0	37.5	36.9	37.7	36.5	37.2	37.9	37.0	37.0	37.2
2012	37.7	37.0	36.8	37.3	36.4	36.8	37.6	36.8	37.6	37.0	37.5	39.1	37.3
2013	37.9	38.1	37.8	37.9	37.8	38.4	37.5	38.0	38.2	37.7	38.0	37.9	37.9
Professional and Business Services													
2009	35.7	36.3	36.1	36.3	36.2	36.9	36.9	37.1	37.2	36.8	37.2	36.6	36.6
2010	36.0	36.7	36.1	36.4	36.5	35.9	35.9	36.5	35.6	36.1	36.3	36.4	36.2
2011	36.7	36.8	36.6	36.9	37.1	36.7	36.3	36.5	36.3	37.0	36.6	36.7	36.7
2012	36.5	36.0	36.3	36.7	36.2	36.1	36.7	36.5	36.7	36.1	36.4	36.7	36.4
2013	35.8	36.0	36.0	36.2	35.9	36.7	36.6	36.8	37.2	36.6	36.4	36.8	36.4
Education and Health Services													
2009	35.4	35.7	35.7	35.7	35.7	35.3	35.6	35.2	35.2	35.1	35.3	35.3	35.4
2010	35.6	35.3	35.3	35.2	35.4	35.0	35.1	35.2	34.8	35.1	35.0	34.9	35.2
2011	35.3	35.0	34.8	34.8	34.5	34.1	34.2	34.1	34.1	34.5	34.0	34.1	34.5
2012	34.2	34.3	34.0	34.2	34.0	34.4	34.7	34.5	34.4	34.4	34.3	34.8	34.3
2013	34.7	34.9	34.8	34.7	34.7	34.8	34.6	34.6	34.9	34.8	35.0	34.8	34.8
Leisure and Hospitality													
2009	28.0	28.4	28.2	28.4	27.9	27.7	28.2	28.5	28.4	28.2	28.6	29.6	28.3
2010	29.8	30.4	30.5	29.7	29.7	30.1	29.5	29.4	28.3	27.7	27.8	27.9	29.2
2011	28.6	28.8	29.0	28.5	27.8	27.4	27.7	27.6	26.5	27.5	27.7	27.2	27.9
2012	27.8	28.2	28.7	28.1	27.4	27.1	27.9	27.1	26.8	27.0	27.4	27.3	27.6
2013	27.5	28.1	28.3	27.8	27.3	27.6	27.5	27.4	26.8	26.9	27.3	27.9	27.5
Other Services													
2009	34.0	33.8	34.2	33.8	33.9	33.8	33.6	34.0	34.3	34.4	34.9	34.7	34.1
2010	35.1	35.0	34.9	34.8	35.3	34.0	34.6	35.6	34.5	35.1	34.8	34.9	34.9
2011	35.4	34.9	34.7	34.7	35.2	33.9	34.2	34.5	34.1	34.4	33.7	33.4	34.4
2012	32.7	32.8	32.9	33.2	32.8	32.6	33.7	33.6	33.2	32.7	33.0	33.8	33.1
2013	33.4	33.4	33.7	33.9	33.3	33.9	33.3	33.4	33.1	32.8	32.7	33.0	33.3

3. Average Hourly Earnings by Selected Industry: Florida, 2009–2013

(Dollars, not seasonally adjusted)

Industry and year	January	February	March	April	May	June	July	August	September	October	November	December	Annual average
Total Private													
2009	21.52	21.68	21.60	21.37	21.60	21.38	21.64	21.80	21.62	21.66	21.80	21.65	21.61
2010	21.39	21.56	21.48	21.50	21.28	21.20	21.31	21.27	21.51	21.68	21.55	21.59	21.44
2011	21.66	21.62	21.43	21.46	21.50	21.36	21.34	21.26	21.46	21.59	21.42	21.41	21.46
2012	21.67	21.46	21.40	21.81	21.44	21.55	21.57	21.41	21.79	21.77	21.65	21.93	21.62
2013	21.89	21.81	21.75	21.91	21.89	22.06	21.93	21.85	22.11	22.01	22.01	22.22	21.95
Goods-Producing													
2009	22.94	22.72	23.24	22.69	22.89	22.52	22.99	23.12	22.56	22.72	22.61	23.47	22.87
2010	22.33	22.28	22.76	22.12	22.15	22.05	22.13	21.89	22.04	22.07	22.07	22.29	22.18
2011	22.48	22.67	22.53	22.54	22.54	22.39	22.33	22.54	22.42	22.54	22.31	22.37	22.47
2012	22.50	22.48	22.78	22.75	22.61	22.74	22.78	22.95	22.94	22.88	22.94	22.95	22.78
2013	23.27	22.93	22.95	23.02	22.95	22.94	23.11	23.05	23.01	22.90	22.65	22.94	22.97
Construction													
2009	21.99	21.58	21.82	21.85	21.76	21.73	22.34	22.44	22.42	22.21	21.48	21.98	21.96
2010	21.59	21.77	21.81	21.62	21.53	21.51	21.42	21.18	21.12	21.41	21.66	21.75	21.53
2011	22.16	22.19	22.20	22.21	21.92	21.74	21.46	21.62	21.31	21.27	21.09	21.10	21.68
2012	20.97	21.31	21.65	21.71	21.68	21.69	21.76	21.91	22.09	22.07	22.13	22.20	21.77
2013	22.68	22.48	22.37	22.41	22.41	22.26	22.52	22.45	22.13	22.15	21.75	22.09	22.30
Manufacturing													
2009	23.87	23.93	24.67	24.17	24.20	24.05	24.35	24.52	24.40	24.99	25.58	25.23	24.49
2010	24.69	24.24	24.98	24.65	24.15	24.15	24.24	23.85	24.11	23.83	23.39	23.55	24.19
2011	23.13	23.45	23.15	23.13	23.45	23.34	23.56	23.79	23.83	24.16	23.87	23.90	23.57
2012	24.25	23.83	24.07	24.00	23.74	23.96	23.95	24.13	23.87	23.77	23.82	23.74	23.93
2013	23.92	23.37	23.58	23.74	23.62	23.78	23.87	23.83	24.09	23.85	23.71	23.89	23.77
Trade, Transportation, and Utilities													
2009	19.02	19.08	19.18	18.73	18.87	18.67	18.99	19.22	19.31	19.16	19.55	19.23	19.08
2010	19.30	19.30	19.20	19.05	18.49	18.12	18.32	18.40	18.98	18.92	18.73	18.80	18.80
2011	18.74	18.86	18.41	18.46	18.30	18.06	17.78	17.65	18.06	18.10	18.03	18.18	18.22
2012	18.18	17.91	18.02	18.76	18.31	18.33	18.35	18.18	18.52	18.58	18.31	18.83	18.36
2013	18.83	18.75	18.81	18.93	18.78	18.88	18.87	18.74	19.16	19.09	19.18	19.17	18.93
Financial Activities													
2009	25.30	26.76	26.73	27.00	27.07	26.80	27.20	27.88	27.26	27.30	27.57	26.62	26.95
2010	26.23	26.98	26.25	26.42	26.24	26.07	26.10	25.97	25.36	25.76	25.60	26.03	26.08
2011	25.82	25.59	25.74	25.66	26.16	25.81	25.22	25.06	24.90	25.46	25.40	25.10	25.49
2012	25.46	25.16	25.66	25.94	25.32	25.60	25.45	25.26	25.77	25.47	25.28	25.16	25.46
2013	24.67	25.13	25.07	25.36	25.21	25.78	25.76	25.62	26.16	26.04	26.39	26.90	25.68
Professional and Business Services													
2009	23.20	23.44	23.52	23.50	23.55	23.54	23.85	23.93	23.57	23.61	23.54	23.64	23.57
2010	23.11	22.95	23.22	23.83	23.90	24.10	24.40	24.00	24.57	24.79	24.62	24.99	24.05
2011	25.26	24.75	24.61	24.73	24.88	24.78	25.08	25.01	25.16	25.45	25.16	25.46	25.03
2012	25.90	25.64	25.07	25.59	24.95	25.16	25.27	24.61	25.41	25.24	25.09	25.57	25.29
2013	25.32	25.48	25.43	25.56	25.48	25.85	25.18	24.92	25.33	25.07	25.13	25.60	25.36
Education and Health Services													
2009	22.79	22.75	22.97	22.88	22.93	23.51	23.42	23.54	23.39	23.28	23.23	23.23	23.16
2010	23.28	23.48	23.46	23.68	23.35	23.45	23.27	23.42	23.52	23.51	23.34	23.53	23.44
2011	23.56	23.14	23.20	23.25	23.26	23.39	23.57	23.45	23.74	23.77	23.79	23.79	23.49
2012	24.21	23.98	24.08	24.30	23.99	24.12	24.16	24.01	24.30	24.60	24.59	24.88	24.27
2013	24.85	24.63	24.57	24.83	24.90	24.99	24.90	25.01	24.89	24.82	24.68	24.88	24.83
Leisure and Hospitality													
2009	13.81	13.81	13.98	14.52	14.53	14.17	14.10	13.94	13.91	14.14	14.38	14.18	14.12
2010	14.19	14.42	14.51	14.22	14.13	14.09	14.01	13.93	13.86	13.86	13.76	13.71	14.07
2011	13.75	13.89	13.88	13.78	13.68	13.29	13.29	13.12	13.46	13.44	13.41	13.38	13.54
2012	13.61	13.81	13.87	13.89	13.70	13.49	13.37	13.49	13.50	13.49	13.64	13.51	13.62
2013	13.69	13.59	13.53	13.44	13.45	13.33	13.30	13.26	13.22	13.46	13.45	13.51	13.44
Other Services													
2009	20.62	20.61	20.85	20.80	20.74	20.68	20.68	20.36	20.51	20.78	20.92	20.98	20.71
2010	20.43	20.45	20.28	20.18	20.05	19.82	19.60	19.33	19.27	18.89	19.07	19.13	19.71
2011	19.35	19.13	19.07	18.69	18.99	19.06	18.85	18.80	18.48	18.40	18.70	18.49	18.84
2012	18.83	18.69	18.83	18.73	18.64	18.54	18.51	18.40	18.84	18.64	18.83	18.84	18.69
2013	18.67	18.73	18.53	18.80	18.80	18.99	18.94	18.83	19.03	18.86	19.18	19.33	18.89

4. Average Weekly Earnings by Selected Industry: Florida, 2009–2013

(Dollars, not seasonally adjusted)

Industry and year	January	February	March	April	May	June	July	August	September	October	November	December	Annual average
Total Private													
2009	746.74	758.80	753.84	743.68	749.52	744.02	757.40	767.36	758.86	755.93	771.72	766.41	756.35
2010	757.21	767.54	762.54	769.70	766.08	754.72	754.37	757.21	750.70	763.14	758.56	759.97	761.12
2011	766.76	761.02	752.19	755.39	752.50	741.19	740.50	733.47	738.22	749.17	738.99	740.79	746.81
2012	747.62	738.22	738.30	750.26	731.10	734.86	744.17	732.22	747.40	742.36	740.43	758.78	741.57
2013	746.45	752.45	750.38	751.51	748.64	761.07	750.01	751.64	762.80	752.74	754.94	768.81	755.08
Goods-Producing													
2009	867.13	879.26	894.74	862.22	872.11	864.77	894.31	903.99	906.91	931.52	942.84	981.05	898.79
2010	924.46	897.88	912.68	898.07	905.94	899.64	880.77	871.22	859.56	876.18	878.39	880.46	889.42
2011	885.71	888.66	889.94	903.85	901.60	900.08	888.73	892.58	901.28	903.85	896.86	903.75	896.55
2012	904.50	894.70	913.48	921.38	913.44	916.42	913.48	922.59	926.78	924.35	926.78	924.89	918.03
2013	921.49	919.49	924.89	923.10	920.30	922.19	915.16	919.70	925.00	913.71	908.27	933.66	921.10
Construction													
2009	842.22	850.25	853.16	836.86	835.58	843.12	857.86	861.70	872.14	910.61	880.68	898.98	860.83
2010	863.60	857.74	852.77	871.29	876.27	875.46	856.80	842.96	823.68	847.84	862.07	861.30	856.89
2011	875.32	867.63	876.90	897.28	883.38	884.82	862.69	864.80	860.92	865.69	856.25	852.44	871.54
2012	838.80	841.75	859.51	877.08	873.70	865.43	863.87	878.59	883.60	889.42	889.63	885.78	870.80
2013	886.79	876.72	885.85	885.20	880.71	874.82	876.03	882.29	871.92	868.28	852.60	874.76	876.39
Manufacturing													
2009	890.35	904.55	937.46	906.38	907.50	906.69	908.26	931.76	922.32	934.63	977.16	983.97	925.72
2010	990.07	940.51	971.72	958.89	960.30	944.27	928.39	920.61	916.18	917.46	926.24	932.58	943.41
2011	899.76	914.55	902.85	909.01	921.59	914.93	916.48	923.05	946.05	947.07	942.87	960.78	926.30
2012	974.85	950.82	970.02	967.20	954.35	965.59	962.79	962.79	966.74	953.18	957.56	959.10	961.99
2013	952.02	955.83	962.06	961.47	963.70	977.36	964.35	965.12	985.28	965.93	969.74	998.60	967.44
Trade, Transportation, and Utilities													
2009	658.09	669.71	671.30	651.80	658.56	647.85	660.85	672.70	670.06	662.94	684.25	674.97	665.89
2010	681.29	689.01	683.52	702.95	680.43	654.13	657.69	662.40	668.10	675.44	668.66	676.80	674.92
2011	661.52	673.30	653.56	653.48	640.50	624.88	615.19	601.87	612.23	611.78	607.61	619.94	630.41
2012	609.03	603.57	603.67	617.20	602.40	599.39	601.88	594.49	613.01	609.42	606.06	627.04	607.72
2013	617.62	622.50	624.49	620.90	619.74	624.93	620.82	614.67	630.36	622.33	627.19	634.53	622.80
Financial Activities													
2009	951.28	998.15	994.36	1,015.20	1,015.13	1,007.68	1,020.00	1,053.86	1,016.80	1,012.83	1,042.15	1,014.22	1,010.63
2010	988.87	1,027.94	1,005.38	998.68	1,020.74	993.27	989.19	1,007.64	966.22	973.73	965.12	973.52	991.04
2011	968.25	949.39	949.81	949.42	981.00	952.39	950.79	914.69	926.28	964.93	939.80	928.70	948.23
2012	959.84	930.92	944.29	967.56	921.65	942.08	956.92	929.57	968.95	942.39	948.00	983.76	949.66
2013	934.99	957.45	947.65	961.14	952.94	989.95	966.00	973.56	999.31	981.71	1,002.82	1,019.51	973.27
Professional and Business Services													
2009	828.24	850.87	849.07	853.05	852.51	868.63	880.07	887.80	876.80	868.85	875.69	865.22	862.66
2010	831.96	842.27	838.24	867.41	872.35	865.19	875.96	876.00	874.69	894.92	893.71	909.64	870.61
2011	927.04	910.80	900.73	912.54	923.05	909.43	910.40	912.87	913.31	941.65	920.86	934.38	918.60
2012	945.35	923.04	910.04	939.15	903.19	908.28	927.41	898.27	932.55	911.16	913.28	938.42	920.56
2013	906.46	917.28	915.48	925.27	914.73	948.70	921.59	917.06	942.28	917.56	914.73	942.08	923.10
Education and Health Services													
2009	806.77	812.18	820.03	816.82	818.60	829.90	833.75	828.61	823.33	817.13	820.02	820.02	819.86
2010	828.77	828.84	828.14	833.54	826.59	820.75	816.78	824.38	818.50	825.20	816.90	821.20	825.09
2011	831.67	809.90	807.36	809.10	802.47	797.60	806.09	799.65	809.53	820.07	808.86	811.24	810.41
2012	827.98	822.51	818.72	831.06	815.66	829.73	838.35	828.35	835.92	846.24	843.44	865.82	832.46
2013	862.30	859.59	855.04	861.60	864.03	869.65	861.54	865.35	868.66	863.74	863.80	865.82	864.08
Leisure and Hospitality													
2009	386.68	392.20	394.24	412.37	405.39	392.51	397.62	397.29	395.04	398.75	411.27	419.73	399.60
2010	422.86	438.37	442.56	422.33	419.66	424.11	413.30	409.54	392.24	383.92	382.53	382.51	410.84
2011	393.25	400.03	402.52	392.73	380.30	364.15	368.13	362.11	356.69	369.60	371.46	363.94	377.77
2012	378.36	389.44	398.07	390.31	375.38	365.58	373.02	365.58	361.80	364.23	373.74	368.82	375.91
2013	376.48	381.88	382.90	373.63	367.19	367.91	365.75	363.32	354.30	362.07	367.19	376.93	369.60
Other Services													
2009	701.08	696.62	713.07	703.04	703.09	698.98	694.85	692.24	703.49	714.83	730.11	728.01	706.21
2010	717.09	715.75	707.77	702.26	707.77	673.88	678.16	688.15	664.82	663.04	663.64	667.64	687.88
2011	684.99	667.64	661.73	648.54	668.45	646.13	644.67	648.60	630.17	632.96	630.19	617.57	648.10
2012	615.74	613.03	619.51	621.84	611.39	604.40	623.79	618.24	625.49	609.53	621.39	636.79	618.64
2013	623.58	625.58	624.46	637.32	626.04	643.76	630.70	628.92	629.89	618.61	627.19	637.89	629.04

GEORGIA
At a Glance

Population:
    2000 census: 8,186,653
    2010 census: 9,687,653
    2013 estimate: 9,992,167

Percent change in population:
    2000–2010: 18.3%
    2010–2013: 3.1%

Percent change in total nonfarm employment:
    2000–2010: -2.2%
    2010–2013: 4.5%

Industry with the largest growth in employment, 2000–2013 (thousands):
    Education and Health Services, 156.1

Industry with the largest decline or smallest growth in employment, 2000–2013 (thousands):
    Manufacturing, -181.0

Civilian labor force:
    2000: 4,242,889
    2010: 4,713,978
    2013: 4,767,323

Unemployment rate and rank among states (lowest to highest):
    2000: 3.5%, 19th
    2010: 10.2%, 39th
    2013: 8.2%, 41st

Over-the-year change in unemployment rates:
    2010–2011: -0.3%
    2011–2012: -0.9%
    2012–2013: -0.8%

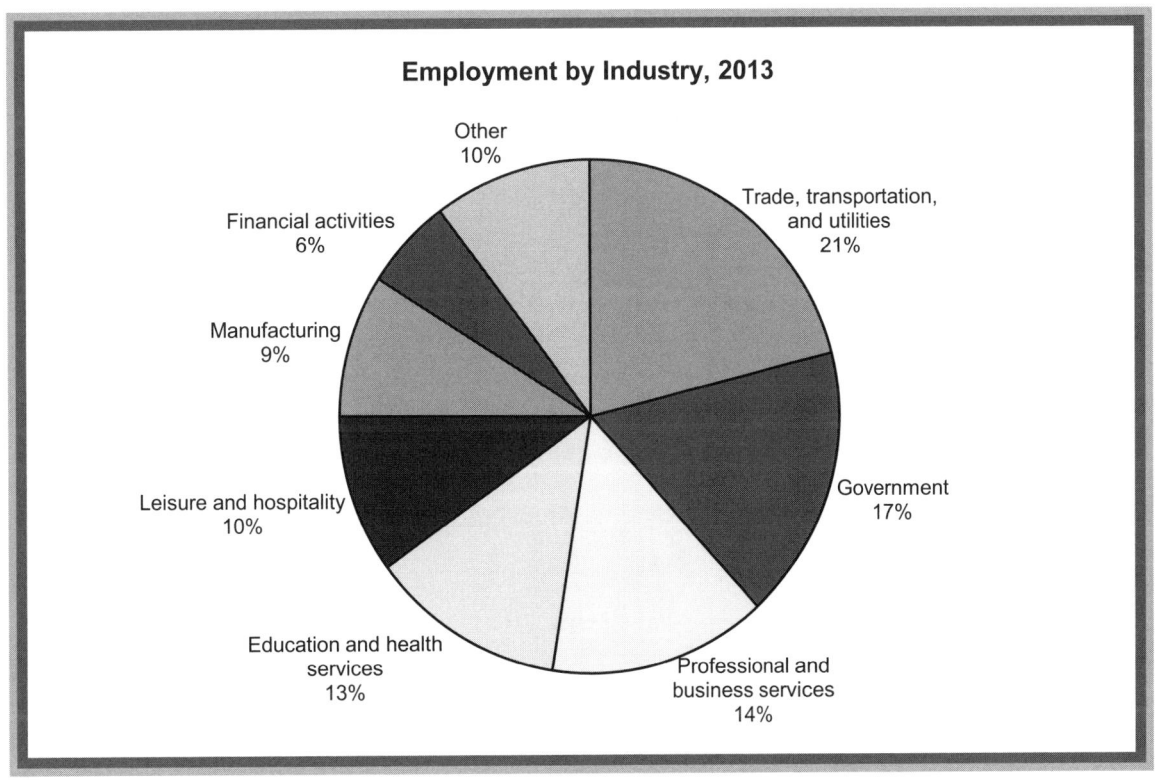

Employment by Industry, 2013

Other
10%

Financial activities
6%

Manufacturing
9%

Leisure and hospitality
10%

Education and health services
13%

Professional and business services
14%

Trade, transportation, and utilities
21%

Government
17%

1. Employment by Industry: Georgia, Selected Years, 2002–2013

(Numbers in thousands, not seasonally adjusted)

Industry and year	January	February	March	April	May	June	July	August	September	October	November	December	Annual average
Total Nonfarm													
2002	3,844.5	3,861.1	3,888.0	3,898.2	3,912.8	3,923.5	3,869.4	3,903.6	3,902.0	3,908.9	3,924.0	3,930.6	3,897.2
2003	3,824.0	3,835.8	3,857.3	3,861.2	3,872.0	3,867.3	3,845.6	3,883.7	3,890.6	3,885.9	3,902.8	3,916.9	3,870.3
2004	3,841.3	3,860.9	3,889.6	3,913.6	3,923.7	3,917.2	3,908.9	3,945.8	3,932.5	3,967.8	3,986.2	3,991.7	3,923.3
2005	3,933.0	3,953.3	3,960.8	4,017.0	4,034.9	4,020.4	4,007.3	4,056.6	4,055.1	4,068.0	4,095.1	4,099.5	4,025.1
2006	4,039.0	4,060.2	4,079.1	4,105.2	4,121.1	4,114.1	4,081.4	4,123.1	4,119.3	4,150.0	4,172.6	4,175.5	4,111.7
2007	4,116.5	4,136.8	4,152.6	4,161.7	4,180.4	4,169.4	4,138.3	4,182.1	4,175.6	4,184.8	4,205.6	4,202.1	4,167.2
2008	4,132.1	4,151.4	4,152.5	4,158.1	4,169.1	4,141.8	4,101.6	4,128.8	4,104.9	4,094.9	4,082.1	4,059.8	4,123.1
2009	3,954.9	3,944.2	3,930.1	3,932.6	3,931.4	3,899.4	3,860.0	3,871.6	3,860.8	3,869.7	3,882.6	3,873.1	3,900.9
2010	3,795.8	3,808.3	3,828.1	3,860.1	3,892.3	3,868.2	3,853.6	3,869.3	3,860.5	3,893.6	3,906.7	3,897.6	3,861.2
2011	3,805.6	3,856.9	3,877.8	3,917.8	3,927.3	3,905.5	3,886.5	3,911.5	3,910.8	3,930.4	3,949.7	3,936.4	3,901.4
2012	3,877.5	3,899.0	3,922.3	3,956.0	3,972.8	3,958.4	3,927.1	3,962.1	3,956.0	3,993.0	4,023.7	4,010.6	3,954.9
2013	3,951.2	3,979.7	3,995.2	4,032.1	4,044.9	4,027.0	4,015.1	4,053.6	4,049.2	4,070.4	4,093.8	4,088.2	4,033.4
Total Private													
2002	3,208.1	3,222.2	3,243.2	3,252.4	3,265.5	3,285.1	3,251.6	3,263.0	3,249.7	3,255.1	3,267.7	3,277.4	3,253.4
2003	3,172.3	3,179.2	3,199.2	3,203.9	3,217.1	3,225.4	3,222.5	3,242.3	3,238.4	3,228.6	3,244.1	3,259.6	3,219.4
2004	3,193.4	3,206.0	3,233.5	3,251.3	3,264.3	3,272.8	3,282.7	3,293.8	3,270.8	3,303.7	3,318.7	3,327.7	3,268.2
2005	3,272.9	3,285.8	3,291.9	3,348.0	3,366.3	3,364.7	3,370.6	3,389.1	3,381.1	3,390.7	3,415.6	3,420.9	3,358.1
2006	3,365.6	3,379.2	3,396.0	3,424.1	3,440.4	3,442.2	3,433.9	3,447.7	3,433.7	3,459.3	3,478.1	3,481.9	3,431.8
2007	3,429.4	3,440.8	3,455.0	3,466.1	3,484.9	3,485.4	3,478.8	3,496.2	3,479.5	3,481.3	3,498.6	3,496.1	3,474.3
2008	3,427.5	3,436.8	3,436.3	3,443.5	3,454.0	3,438.9	3,420.3	3,423.3	3,394.8	3,374.7	3,357.1	3,338.1	3,412.1
2009	3,239.0	3,222.4	3,207.7	3,210.4	3,213.3	3,196.6	3,182.1	3,177.7	3,153.2	3,162.4	3,174.3	3,167.5	3,192.2
2010	3,094.2	3,102.2	3,119.5	3,151.4	3,170.1	3,164.9	3,175.1	3,183.1	3,170.5	3,198.5	3,209.3	3,203.3	3,161.8
2011	3,117.1	3,161.7	3,180.6	3,224.6	3,232.3	3,222.9	3,224.1	3,236.9	3,225.2	3,239.9	3,256.2	3,245.9	3,214.0
2012	3,193.9	3,210.4	3,228.5	3,262.1	3,281.0	3,275.4	3,270.4	3,287.9	3,271.4	3,302.2	3,326.8	3,319.5	3,269.1
2013	3,265.7	3,288.1	3,302.1	3,339.0	3,356.2	3,352.6	3,361.5	3,383.6	3,368.4	3,386.8	3,409.1	3,406.4	3,351.6
Goods-Producing													
2002	678.4	684.1	686.8	685.7	686.3	687.6	684.3	684.0	680.5	675.5	672.7	670.2	681.3
2003	658.4	661.6	661.2	658.9	661.0	661.6	656.5	658.8	659.4	658.3	656.6	658.9	659.3
2004	648.2	651.5	655.3	656.1	656.7	661.5	664.8	666.3	662.7	667.2	666.5	666.7	660.3
2005	657.2	659.5	658.8	668.0	672.1	673.5	673.9	678.3	678.0	674.2	678.1	677.2	670.7
2006	672.0	674.8	676.1	679.0	681.9	685.0	681.7	684.7	682.0	678.8	674.4	671.7	678.5
2007	667.6	668.5	667.8	667.3	669.0	669.2	666.2	667.2	662.3	657.7	657.3	654.0	664.5
2008	643.8	642.3	638.7	634.4	633.7	631.0	626.0	623.5	617.0	608.9	596.9	586.9	623.6
2009	567.3	558.6	551.9	544.0	540.9	534.0	525.7	522.5	518.4	514.6	512.1	508.3	533.2
2010	500.0	499.1	500.1	501.9	505.4	505.1	507.6	507.9	506.6	506.3	505.5	502.2	504.0
2011	491.2	500.4	503.7	507.8	508.9	509.7	510.4	510.5	507.8	506.7	505.5	503.1	505.5
2012	498.2	499.7	501.0	503.1	504.6	505.3	506.2	507.4	506.7	508.2	509.2	506.6	504.7
2013	502.4	504.8	507.6	508.0	510.6	511.9	514.2	516.3	515.2	517.5	519.8	518.6	512.2
Service-Providing													
2002	3,166.1	3,177.0	3,201.2	3,212.5	3,226.5	3,235.9	3,185.1	3,219.6	3,221.5	3,233.4	3,251.3	3,260.4	3,215.9
2003	3,165.6	3,174.2	3,196.1	3,202.3	3,211.0	3,205.7	3,189.1	3,224.9	3,231.2	3,227.6	3,246.2	3,258.0	3,211.0
2004	3,193.1	3,209.4	3,234.3	3,257.5	3,267.0	3,255.7	3,244.1	3,279.5	3,269.8	3,300.6	3,319.7	3,325.0	3,263.0
2005	3,275.8	3,293.8	3,302.0	3,349.0	3,362.8	3,346.9	3,333.4	3,378.3	3,377.1	3,393.8	3,417.0	3,422.3	3,354.4
2006	3,367.0	3,385.4	3,403.0	3,426.2	3,439.2	3,429.1	3,399.7	3,438.4	3,437.3	3,471.2	3,498.2	3,503.8	3,433.2
2007	3,448.9	3,468.3	3,484.8	3,494.4	3,511.4	3,500.2	3,472.1	3,514.9	3,513.3	3,527.1	3,548.3	3,548.1	3,502.7
2008	3,488.3	3,509.1	3,513.8	3,523.7	3,535.4	3,510.8	3,475.6	3,505.3	3,487.9	3,486.0	3,485.2	3,472.9	3,499.5
2009	3,387.6	3,385.6	3,378.2	3,388.6	3,390.5	3,365.4	3,334.3	3,349.1	3,342.4	3,355.1	3,370.5	3,364.8	3,367.7
2010	3,295.8	3,309.2	3,328.0	3,358.2	3,386.9	3,363.1	3,346.0	3,361.4	3,353.9	3,387.3	3,401.2	3,395.4	3,357.2
2011	3,314.4	3,356.5	3,374.1	3,410.0	3,418.4	3,395.8	3,376.1	3,401.0	3,403.0	3,423.7	3,444.2	3,433.3	3,395.9
2012	3,379.3	3,399.3	3,421.3	3,452.9	3,468.2	3,453.1	3,420.9	3,454.7	3,449.3	3,484.8	3,514.5	3,504.0	3,450.2
2013	3,448.8	3,474.9	3,487.6	3,524.1	3,534.3	3,515.1	3,500.9	3,537.3	3,534.0	3,552.9	3,574.0	3,569.6	3,521.1
Mining and Logging													
2002	12.7	12.7	12.8	12.6	12.6	12.6	12.1	12.3	12.2	11.9	11.8	12.0	12.4
2003	12.1	12.1	12.1	12.2	12.4	12.4	12.3	12.4	12.4	12.3	12.4	12.4	12.3
2004	12.3	12.2	12.2	12.1	12.1	12.2	12.3	12.3	12.3	12.2	12.1	12.2	12.2
2005	11.8	11.9	11.9	12.1	12.2	12.2	12.3	12.3	12.2	12.1	12.1	12.1	12.1
2006	12.4	12.1	12.1	12.3	12.3	12.3	12.3	12.3	12.1	12.2	12.1	12.1	12.2
2007	12.1	12.1	12.1	12.0	12.0	11.9	11.9	11.9	11.9	11.8	11.7	11.6	11.9
2008	10.8	10.6	10.5	10.5	10.4	10.3	10.3	10.3	10.3	10.3	10.2	10.1	10.4
2009	9.7	9.5	9.3	9.4	9.4	9.4	9.3	9.4	9.2	9.3	9.3	9.2	9.4
2010	9.3	9.2	9.2	9.2	9.2	9.2	9.3	9.3	9.3	9.3	9.3	9.1	9.2
2011	9.0	9.1	9.0	9.0	9.0	9.0	9.1	9.1	9.0	8.9	8.8	8.7	9.0
2012	8.6	8.7	8.5	8.6	8.6	8.6	8.7	8.7	8.5	8.7	8.7	8.6	8.6
2013	8.7	8.7	8.7	8.9	8.9	8.8	8.9	8.9	8.8	8.9	9.0	9.0	8.9
Construction													
2002	195.2	197.8	199.1	198.3	199.0	200.0	199.3	199.5	198.2	196.5	195.8	194.3	197.8
2003	188.5	190.0	191.2	191.2	193.1	194.7	196.9	197.9	198.9	199.0	198.6	199.1	195.0
2004	193.7	193.3	196.0	196.8	197.2	200.4	203.7	203.6	200.9	204.4	204.0	203.7	199.8
2005	199.8	200.6	200.0	206.3	209.1	210.0	212.2	213.9	213.4	213.4	214.6	212.7	208.8
2006	209.2	211.0	212.5	215.4	217.9	220.6	223.0	224.5	223.7	223.6	222.9	221.4	218.8
2007	218.6	220.2	221.3	221.7	223.2	224.1	223.0	224.1	221.7	220.7	219.5	216.6	221.2
2008	211.1	211.4	209.9	208.7	209.5	208.1	206.9	204.5	201.2	197.4	193.0	187.7	204.1
2009	177.8	175.9	172.9	170.4	170.1	167.9	164.5	162.0	159.3	158.3	157.0	153.9	165.8
2010	148.1	148.4	148.9	150.1	151.0	150.6	152.0	151.6	150.7	150.3	149.5	145.6	149.7
2011	137.9	143.6	146.3	148.2	147.8	148.2	148.5	148.2	147.4	146.8	145.0	142.7	145.9
2012	138.3	139.3	139.9	140.9	140.9	141.2	142.7	143.5	142.7	143.6	143.5	141.3	141.5
2013	138.6	140.0	142.2	142.9	145.5	146.4	148.1	149.4	149.0	150.5	152.4	149.6	146.2

1. Employment by Industry: Georgia, Selected Years, 2002–2013—*Continued*

(Numbers in thousands, not seasonally adjusted)

Industry and year	January	February	March	April	May	June	July	August	September	October	November	December	Annual average
Manufacturing													
2002	470.5	473.6	474.9	474.8	474.7	475.0	472.9	472.2	470.1	467.1	465.1	463.9	471.2
2003	457.8	459.5	457.4	455.5	455.5	454.5	447.3	448.5	448.1	447.0	445.6	447.4	452.0
2004	442.2	446.0	447.1	447.2	447.4	448.9	448.8	450.4	449.6	450.7	450.4	450.8	448.3
2005	445.6	447.0	446.9	449.6	450.8	451.3	449.4	452.1	452.4	448.7	451.4	452.4	449.8
2006	450.4	451.7	451.5	451.3	451.7	452.1	446.4	447.9	446.2	443.0	439.4	438.2	447.5
2007	436.9	436.2	434.4	433.6	433.8	433.2	431.3	431.2	428.8	425.3	426.2	426.0	431.4
2008	421.9	420.3	418.3	415.2	413.8	412.6	408.8	408.7	405.5	401.2	393.7	389.1	409.1
2009	379.8	373.2	369.7	364.2	361.4	356.7	351.9	351.1	349.9	347.0	345.8	345.2	358.0
2010	342.6	341.5	342.0	342.6	345.2	345.3	346.3	347.0	346.6	346.7	346.7	347.5	345.0
2011	344.3	347.7	348.4	350.6	352.1	352.5	352.8	353.2	351.4	351.0	351.7	351.7	350.6
2012	351.3	351.7	352.6	353.6	355.1	355.5	354.8	355.2	355.5	355.9	357.0	356.7	354.6
2013	355.1	356.1	356.7	356.2	356.2	356.7	357.2	358.0	357.4	358.1	358.4	360.0	357.2
Trade, Transportation, and Utilities													
2002	835.2	830.5	834.0	833.7	837.1	840.6	832.8	834.0	833.4	844.4	858.4	871.0	840.4
2003	819.0	814.2	818.2	814.4	818.6	819.5	820.2	823.9	824.7	828.5	842.1	851.4	824.6
2004	817.4	813.9	820.0	820.9	825.7	826.3	829.5	830.8	826.6	837.8	852.4	860.6	830.2
2005	832.8	831.4	833.1	846.2	850.1	848.4	856.3	855.2	853.3	861.4	878.8	887.7	852.9
2006	856.2	853.2	857.4	865.0	870.4	869.0	865.2	867.3	866.9	880.1	898.6	906.2	871.3
2007	880.7	874.8	877.1	878.5	884.2	884.7	885.1	885.7	884.9	889.9	906.6	910.2	886.9
2008	883.5	879.3	880.2	876.6	877.7	874.0	873.1	872.3	867.6	864.4	868.6	869.6	873.9
2009	834.9	824.0	819.8	816.6	818.9	815.2	814.0	813.7	808.9	811.5	823.5	826.8	819.0
2010	799.6	797.2	798.9	802.6	807.5	806.7	809.2	810.3	806.1	819.0	830.4	835.1	810.2
2011	804.4	809.0	811.8	818.7	822.1	820.3	820.8	822.4	818.8	828.4	842.5	844.9	822.0
2012	823.4	820.4	822.6	828.3	833.5	830.3	830.4	831.5	828.1	838.4	857.1	858.2	833.5
2013	831.7	829.8	830.2	837.1	841.3	841.0	845.9	849.6	845.4	852.6	866.8	875.9	845.6
Wholesale Trade													
2002	206.1	206.1	207.4	207.2	207.2	207.8	206.3	205.8	205.0	207.5	206.7	206.7	206.7
2003	204.0	204.3	205.3	204.6	205.1	205.0	205.3	205.3	205.4	204.9	205.4	206.2	205.1
2004	202.8	202.9	204.2	205.7	206.8	207.2	207.7	208.3	207.2	209.1	209.2	209.6	206.7
2005	207.9	209.0	209.1	211.5	211.8	211.8	212.7	213.4	213.6	213.5	213.7	214.2	211.9
2006	211.8	212.6	213.0	214.2	215.8	215.4	216.2	216.3	216.5	219.2	218.2	218.4	215.6
2007	216.7	217.4	217.5	218.8	219.1	218.8	219.4	219.5	219.0	219.8	220.0	219.6	218.8
2008	218.0	218.8	218.2	219.0	219.0	218.0	217.7	217.9	217.0	216.2	213.8	211.6	217.1
2009	206.8	204.8	202.1	201.2	200.2	198.4	198.2	197.5	195.9	197.1	197.1	196.2	199.6
2010	194.2	194.5	194.4	195.7	196.4	195.8	196.4	196.4	195.0	197.1	197.0	195.8	195.7
2011	194.2	195.3	195.2	197.4	198.5	197.5	198.6	199.3	198.2	199.8	200.1	199.1	197.8
2012	198.1	199.3	199.3	200.9	202.3	201.5	202.6	203.1	202.0	204.4	204.8	204.3	201.9
2013	202.2	203.2	202.9	204.5	205.2	205.1	205.6	206.0	204.9	206.1	207.7	208.0	205.1
Retail Trade													
2002	453.9	449.3	452.2	449.9	452.4	453.9	449.9	451.3	452.6	453.4	467.3	479.0	455.4
2003	440.7	436.1	438.6	437.6	440.5	441.1	440.8	443.7	443.9	446.9	459.2	467.8	444.7
2004	439.8	436.3	440.1	439.1	441.8	442.3	443.4	443.6	441.2	449.2	462.7	470.9	445.9
2005	447.5	443.6	444.8	454.9	457.7	456.6	460.8	459.5	456.4	464.3	479.3	486.1	459.3
2006	464.3	460.3	462.9	468.0	470.6	468.6	464.0	465.4	463.6	474.1	492.9	497.5	471.0
2007	479.3	472.3	474.0	473.4	476.5	474.7	475.9	475.2	473.9	477.9	494.2	496.3	478.6
2008	474.5	469.2	470.3	466.7	467.0	464.0	464.0	463.5	459.9	459.0	466.0	467.5	466.0
2009	443.3	436.3	435.2	435.4	438.1	436.0	435.3	436.2	433.3	434.3	446.0	448.7	438.2
2010	428.6	425.9	427.3	430.0	432.7	432.0	433.2	433.8	430.3	439.0	450.1	453.4	434.7
2011	431.3	432.7	434.4	439.0	440.3	438.7	438.7	438.8	436.0	443.2	455.9	457.1	440.5
2012	440.5	436.4	438.1	441.1	444.0	441.7	441.7	442.0	439.7	447.1	464.1	463.4	445.0
2013	442.4	441.0	442.0	445.8	448.8	449.5	453.1	455.9	453.6	458.6	467.9	474.4	452.8
Transportation and Utilities													
2002	175.2	175.1	174.4	176.6	177.5	178.9	176.6	176.9	175.8	183.5	184.4	185.3	178.4
2003	174.3	173.8	174.3	172.2	173.0	173.4	174.1	174.9	175.4	176.7	177.5	177.4	174.8
2004	174.8	174.7	175.7	176.1	177.1	176.8	178.4	178.9	178.2	179.5	180.5	180.1	177.6
2005	177.4	178.8	179.2	179.8	180.6	180.0	182.8	182.3	183.3	183.6	185.8	187.4	181.8
2006	180.1	180.3	181.5	182.8	184.0	185.0	185.0	185.6	186.8	186.8	187.5	190.3	184.6
2007	184.7	185.1	185.6	186.3	188.6	191.2	189.8	191.0	192.0	192.2	192.4	194.3	189.4
2008	191.0	191.3	191.7	190.9	191.7	192.0	191.4	190.9	190.7	189.2	188.8	190.5	190.8
2009	184.8	182.9	182.5	180.0	180.6	180.8	180.5	180.0	179.7	180.1	180.4	181.9	181.2
2010	176.8	176.8	177.2	176.9	178.4	178.9	179.6	180.1	180.8	182.9	183.3	185.9	179.8
2011	178.9	181.0	182.2	182.3	183.3	184.1	183.5	184.3	184.6	185.4	186.5	188.7	183.7
2012	184.8	184.7	185.2	186.3	187.2	187.1	186.1	186.4	186.4	186.9	188.2	190.5	186.7
2013	187.1	185.6	185.3	186.8	187.3	186.4	187.2	187.7	186.9	187.9	191.2	193.5	187.7
Information													
2002	132.5	132.3	130.9	130.2	129.9	129.4	129.0	128.5	127.2	128.2	126.2	126.2	129.2
2003	126.4	125.4	123.3	121.3	120.2	119.7	118.0	117.4	115.0	114.7	115.6	115.4	119.4
2004	114.3	113.9	114.2	115.3	115.0	115.5	114.8	114.3	113.4	112.1	113.0	112.9	114.1
2005	111.9	112.2	112.6	112.5	111.7	113.1	112.5	111.1	111.2	111.7	112.6	113.1	112.2
2006	111.5	111.8	112.5	111.5	112.0	111.6	110.1	110.2	110.2	110.8	111.8	112.3	111.4
2007	112.8	112.5	112.5	111.0	111.6	111.7	111.3	111.4	111.3	110.4	111.0	111.0	111.5
2008	108.7	109.6	109.7	109.5	110.0	110.4	109.3	109.1	108.4	107.3	107.8	107.8	109.0
2009	106.9	106.7	106.1	105.7	105.5	105.3	104.1	103.8	103.3	102.2	102.3	103.0	104.6
2010	100.9	100.7	100.9	100.9	101.3	100.8	99.6	99.4	99.1	97.4	98.0	98.4	99.8
2011	97.4	98.1	98.0	98.6	98.4	97.9	98.9	99.1	98.7	98.8	100.3	98.5	98.6
2012	98.0	99.3	99.1	98.6	99.7	99.8	100.4	100.9	100.8	101.6	102.5	102.3	100.3
2013	100.7	101.8	101.8	102.3	102.9	102.3	102.2	102.6	102.0	101.7	102.5	102.7	102.1

1. Employment by Industry: Georgia, Selected Years, 2002–2013—*Continued*

(Numbers in thousands, not seasonally adjusted)

Industry and year	January	February	March	April	May	June	July	August	September	October	November	December	Annual average
Financial Activities													
2002	226.2	225.5	225.3	225.4	226.2	227.0	226.6	227.3	225.9	227.6	227.8	229.1	226.7
2003	224.9	224.8	226.4	226.6	228.1	229.5	230.6	231.4	231.1	228.1	228.2	229.0	228.2
2004	226.7	227.7	228.2	229.5	229.8	229.8	231.3	231.5	230.3	233.7	233.6	234.5	230.6
2005	234.1	235.1	234.8	235.7	236.9	237.1	236.5	237.5	237.1	239.8	240.0	241.4	237.2
2006	237.8	239.2	239.6	241.4	242.5	242.4	243.0	244.1	243.5	245.3	245.3	245.9	242.5
2007	242.3	243.9	243.8	243.4	243.5	243.4	243.9	243.8	242.0	242.3	242.2	241.8	243.0
2008	238.1	238.9	237.9	238.1	238.4	237.3	237.4	236.3	233.8	234.3	231.6	230.8	236.1
2009	228.0	226.9	225.4	224.9	225.0	224.4	223.9	222.7	220.6	220.5	220.0	219.9	223.5
2010	216.4	216.2	216.1	216.4	217.7	218.0	218.1	218.9	218.2	220.4	221.1	221.7	218.3
2011	219.0	219.6	219.7	222.5	223.1	223.4	223.8	224.8	224.7	225.9	226.1	226.3	223.2
2012	225.0	225.5	225.9	225.7	225.9	226.1	226.9	227.2	226.0	227.8	228.9	228.6	226.6
2013	226.4	227.3	227.6	229.0	229.7	230.0	231.5	232.2	230.5	231.7	233.6	233.9	230.3
Professional and Business Services													
2002	491.0	496.7	499.4	503.8	505.2	506.7	506.5	510.6	507.7	506.5	506.9	505.2	503.9
2003	482.5	487.2	490.0	491.3	489.4	492.2	495.7	501.1	500.6	499.5	500.2	502.6	494.4
2004	495.3	500.5	507.0	509.4	509.7	510.8	516.0	517.8	513.7	523.8	523.1	523.3	512.5
2005	519.1	524.2	524.5	531.0	532.4	533.7	536.4	544.5	545.7	547.5	548.3	546.4	536.1
2006	539.8	543.5	546.2	551.3	550.0	553.3	553.9	556.8	553.8	556.0	556.3	557.5	551.5
2007	549.9	555.1	560.6	558.9	561.8	563.6	562.4	569.7	567.7	569.2	569.7	574.7	563.6
2008	559.0	562.0	559.7	565.8	565.1	565.9	556.2	558.1	553.3	550.1	544.8	540.9	556.7
2009	516.2	514.3	509.6	508.3	505.7	508.2	508.0	507.0	504.9	515.9	518.9	519.4	511.4
2010	504.8	509.5	514.5	523.3	524.6	526.7	529.9	531.3	531.2	540.2	540.7	539.7	526.4
2011	519.6	532.7	536.5	547.3	545.4	545.9	545.6	550.1	550.8	552.2	554.3	553.1	544.5
2012	539.8	547.0	551.6	559.2	562.2	566.0	562.4	567.5	564.1	571.3	575.1	574.4	561.7
2013	563.9	573.9	577.4	583.1	585.3	587.8	589.7	595.4	595.5	595.5	597.8	593.3	586.6
Education and Health Services													
2002	362.7	366.2	370.3	370.5	371.6	371.3	369.4	374.4	375.9	377.8	379.9	380.0	372.5
2003	379.6	381.4	385.3	388.7	391.1	389.7	388.0	393.1	394.9	394.6	396.6	397.7	390.1
2004	396.0	399.0	400.3	401.9	403.2	399.7	401.5	406.2	405.0	412.3	413.7	413.3	404.3
2005	410.6	412.2	409.3	417.9	419.5	414.6	417.1	421.3	422.2	426.0	427.3	426.9	418.7
2006	427.2	429.7	429.0	431.3	432.5	427.2	429.0	432.8	432.6	442.7	443.7	442.8	433.4
2007	439.8	443.7	442.6	446.7	447.6	443.4	444.2	450.7	452.2	455.8	457.2	454.8	448.2
2008	451.6	456.6	455.9	457.4	459.2	452.0	453.4	459.7	458.9	463.5	464.8	463.9	458.1
2009	461.3	463.4	461.3	464.3	466.4	459.0	459.7	465.0	462.7	469.5	471.0	469.7	464.4
2010	466.4	469.9	470.8	473.4	475.8	469.4	471.8	477.9	477.7	484.8	485.0	482.9	475.5
2011	476.0	482.9	482.6	487.2	486.4	478.3	478.5	484.9	486.1	492.0	492.2	489.8	484.7
2012	486.2	490.9	491.2	495.5	496.3	488.8	487.6	497.1	497.8	503.7	505.2	503.4	495.3
2013	501.1	505.9	506.0	510.3	510.7	502.6	500.3	509.1	509.9	516.3	517.8	514.1	508.7
Leisure and Hospitality													
2002	321.3	325.5	334.4	343.0	348.4	361.0	346.8	347.7	343.0	338.5	338.3	339.1	340.6
2003	328.5	331.4	340.3	348.4	353.1	356.2	356.6	359.6	356.0	349.2	348.9	348.9	348.1
2004	340.6	344.6	352.0	361.2	366.9	370.7	366.9	369.5	363.6	361.8	361.2	361.6	360.1
2005	352.3	355.4	362.9	378.5	384.4	384.9	377.6	380.0	374.6	371.9	371.9	369.9	372.0
2006	364.2	369.6	377.7	385.3	390.6	392.6	389.7	391.3	385.6	386.3	388.5	387.0	384.0
2007	378.2	383.7	391.6	399.7	405.6	406.9	403.2	405.4	398.6	395.2	394.1	390.6	396.1
2008	383.3	387.2	393.4	400.2	407.2	405.1	402.4	402.3	395.4	386.6	383.3	379.9	393.9
2009	367.4	370.9	376.7	388.7	392.3	391.9	388.0	386.1	379.2	373.7	372.3	367.6	379.6
2010	355.2	358.1	366.4	379.2	382.9	383.6	383.0	382.8	377.9	375.9	374.1	370.7	374.2
2011	358.7	366.0	375.2	387.9	392.6	391.5	390.6	391.0	385.2	382.9	382.5	378.9	381.9
2012	372.8	376.1	385.7	398.6	404.9	404.4	401.4	402.3	395.3	397.2	395.1	393.8	394.0
2013	388.0	392.2	399.4	415.2	420.7	421.3	421.7	423.0	415.4	415.8	415.1	413.9	411.8
Other Services													
2002	160.8	161.4	162.1	160.1	160.8	161.5	156.2	156.5	156.1	156.6	157.5	156.6	158.9
2003	153.0	153.2	154.5	154.3	155.6	157.0	156.9	157.0	156.7	155.7	155.9	155.7	155.5
2004	154.9	154.9	156.5	157.0	157.3	158.5	157.9	157.4	155.5	155.0	155.2	154.8	156.2
2005	154.9	155.8	155.9	158.2	159.2	159.4	160.3	161.2	159.0	158.2	158.6	158.3	158.3
2006	156.9	157.4	157.5	159.3	160.5	161.1	161.3	160.5	159.1	159.3	159.5	158.5	159.2
2007	158.1	158.6	159.0	160.6	161.6	162.5	162.5	162.3	160.5	160.8	160.5	159.0	160.5
2008	159.5	160.9	160.8	161.5	162.7	163.2	162.5	162.0	160.4	159.6	159.3	158.3	160.9
2009	157.0	157.6	156.9	157.9	158.6	158.6	158.7	156.9	155.2	154.5	154.2	152.8	156.6
2010	150.9	151.5	151.8	153.7	154.9	154.6	155.9	154.6	153.7	154.5	154.5	152.6	153.6
2011	150.8	153.0	153.1	154.6	155.4	155.9	155.5	154.1	153.1	153.0	152.8	151.3	153.6
2012	150.5	151.5	151.4	153.1	153.9	154.7	155.1	154.0	152.6	154.0	153.7	152.2	153.1
2013	151.5	152.4	152.1	154.0	155.0	155.7	156.0	155.4	154.5	155.7	155.7	154.0	154.3
Government													
2002	636.4	638.9	644.8	645.8	647.3	638.4	617.8	640.6	652.3	653.8	656.3	653.2	643.8
2003	651.7	656.6	658.1	657.3	654.9	641.9	623.1	641.4	652.2	657.3	658.7	657.3	650.9
2004	647.9	654.9	656.1	662.3	659.4	644.4	626.2	652.0	661.7	664.1	667.5	664.0	655.0
2005	660.1	667.5	668.9	669.0	668.6	655.7	636.7	667.5	674.0	677.3	679.5	678.6	667.0
2006	673.4	681.0	683.1	681.1	680.7	671.9	647.5	675.4	685.6	690.7	694.5	693.6	679.9
2007	687.1	696.0	697.6	695.6	695.5	684.0	659.5	685.9	696.1	703.5	707.0	706.0	692.8
2008	704.6	714.6	716.2	714.6	715.1	702.9	681.3	705.5	710.1	720.2	725.0	721.7	711.0
2009	715.9	721.8	722.4	722.2	718.1	702.8	677.9	693.9	707.6	707.3	708.3	705.6	708.7
2010	701.6	706.1	708.6	708.7	722.2	703.3	678.5	686.2	690.0	695.1	697.4	694.3	699.3
2011	688.5	695.2	697.2	693.2	695.0	682.6	662.4	674.6	685.6	690.5	693.5	690.5	687.4
2012	683.6	688.6	693.8	693.9	691.8	683.0	656.7	674.2	684.6	690.8	696.9	691.1	685.8
2013	685.5	691.6	693.1	693.1	688.7	674.4	653.6	670.0	680.8	683.6	684.7	681.8	681.7

2. Average Weekly Hours by Selected Industry: Georgia, 2009–2013

(Not seasonally adjusted)

Industry and year	January	February	March	April	May	June	July	August	September	October	November	December	Annual average
Total Private													
2009	34.6	35.1	35.1	34.4	34.6	34.3	34.6	34.7	34.1	34.3	35.0	34.6	34.6
2010	34.3	34.2	34.4	34.9	35.2	34.9	34.7	35.1	34.7	34.9	34.8	34.8	34.7
2011	33.5	34.6	34.7	34.7	35.1	34.7	34.8	34.7	34.6	35.1	34.8	34.8	34.7
2012	35.0	34.8	34.8	35.2	34.8	34.9	35.2	35.0	35.6	34.9	34.9	35.5	35.0
2013	34.8	34.9	35.2	35.1	34.9	35.6	35.0	35.0	35.6	35.0	35.2	35.5	35.2
Goods-Producing													
2009	36.9	37.2	37.5	36.9	37.8	37.4	38.1	37.6	37.4	37.9	38.4	38.5	37.6
2010	38.4	37.5	38.2	39.0	39.3	39.0	39.0	38.7	38.2	38.9	38.7	39.1	38.7
2011	35.9	39.1	39.2	39.4	39.6	39.2	39.5	39.9	39.7	39.7	40.1	40.4	39.3
2012	39.1	39.4	39.6	39.9	39.7	40.1	39.4	39.7	40.2	40.1	40.3	40.8	39.9
2013	40.4	40.1	41.0	40.9	41.3	42.0	41.4	41.4	42.2	41.5	41.7	41.7	41.3
Construction													
2009	36.2	36.4	36.9	35.6	36.5	35.8	36.5	36.3	37.0	37.4	38.0	37.6	36.7
2010	36.9	35.9	36.0	36.6	37.0	37.3	37.5	38.0	37.7	38.8	38.7	38.3	37.4
2011	34.0	38.7	37.9	39.3	39.7	39.3	39.1	39.3	39.5	38.7	39.1	38.5	38.6
2012	37.3	38.5	38.5	39.8	39.0	39.1	40.1	39.6	40.1	39.9	40.5	39.7	39.3
2013	39.1	38.0	40.4	40.3	41.2	41.5	40.9	40.2	41.6	40.6	40.8	40.1	40.4
Manufacturing													
2009	37.3	37.0	37.3	37.3	37.9	37.8	38.7	38.5	37.7	38.4	39.0	39.4	38.0
2010	39.6	38.7	39.4	40.0	39.8	39.4	39.4	38.7	38.2	38.7	39.3	39.5	39.2
2011	36.8	39.3	39.9	39.4	39.5	39.3	39.9	40.4	40.0	40.2	40.6	41.5	39.7
2012	40.2	40.0	40.3	39.9	40.1	40.6	39.1	39.8	40.2	40.2	40.3	41.4	40.2
2013	41.2	41.2	41.2	41.2	41.3	42.2	41.6	42.1	42.4	41.9	42.2	42.5	41.8
Trade, Transportation, and Utilities													
2009	34.3	35.0	35.2	34.8	35.2	34.8	34.6	34.9	34.3	34.8	34.9	34.7	34.8
2010	34.2	34.2	34.0	34.6	35.1	34.9	34.8	35.5	34.9	34.9	34.9	35.0	34.8
2011	33.7	34.6	34.7	34.6	35.0	34.7	34.8	34.5	34.7	35.0	34.7	35.0	34.7
2012	34.9	34.9	34.7	34.7	34.6	34.5	34.8	34.4	34.6	34.3	34.6	35.0	34.7
2013	34.1	34.5	34.5	34.5	34.4	34.9	34.5	34.7	35.1	34.6	34.9	35.2	34.7
Financial Activities													
2009	36.2	36.6	36.2	35.1	34.8	34.6	35.1	36.2	36.0	36.2	36.1	34.6	35.6
2010	35.1	35.2	35.7	35.2	34.9	34.4	34.5	35.3	34.8	34.4	34.8	35.0	34.9
2011	36.3	35.0	35.5	35.1	36.5	35.6	35.9	35.4	35.6	37.2	35.9	35.8	35.8
2012	37.3	36.3	36.1	37.4	35.9	36.2	38.2	36.5	37.8	36.8	37.0	38.2	37.0
2013	36.8	36.9	36.7	36.9	36.9	38.1	37.0	37.1	38.2	36.6	36.7	38.0	37.2
Professional and Business Services													
2009	34.3	35.4	35.0	34.7	35.0	34.6	34.9	35.3	34.5	34.5	35.6	35.1	34.9
2010	34.1	34.8	35.0	35.4	35.2	34.9	35.1	35.4	35.0	35.0	34.9	35.1	35.0
2011	34.2	35.2	35.1	35.5	36.1	36.3	35.9	35.6	35.5	36.6	35.9	35.9	35.7
2012	36.4	36.2	36.4	37.6	36.9	36.8	37.4	38.3	38.9	37.5	37.0	38.3	37.3
2013	37.0	37.5	37.3	37.4	37.2	38.1	36.8	37.0	37.7	36.6	37.0	37.4	37.2
Education and Health Services													
2009	37.1	35.8	36.1	35.5	35.7	35.4	35.5	35.5	35.0	34.9	35.6	35.1	35.6
2010	34.8	34.7	34.9	35.0	35.5	35.2	35.1	35.3	35.3	35.1	35.3	35.1	35.1
2011	34.9	35.4	35.5	35.5	35.6	35.3	35.3	35.1	35.2	35.5	35.1	34.9	35.3
2012	35.6	34.6	34.6	34.7	34.6	34.4	34.8	34.5	35.1	34.5	34.2	34.9	34.7
2013	34.5	34.2	34.3	34.2	34.2	34.8	34.2	34.7	34.9	34.4	34.5	35.0	34.5
Leisure and Hospitality													
2009	28.1	29.0	29.0	28.4	28.5	27.7	28.1	27.8	27.2	27.6	27.5	27.7	28.1
2010	27.0	26.9	27.1	27.3	27.4	27.5	27.2	27.2	26.8	27.0	26.9	26.9	27.1
2011	25.3	26.9	27.0	27.0	27.2	26.7	26.9	26.8	26.2	26.5	26.3	26.3	26.6
2012	26.3	26.5	26.6	26.6	26.6	26.8	26.9	26.4	26.4	26.3	26.0	26.2	26.5
2013	25.6	26.2	26.6	26.6	26.4	26.9	26.3	26.0	26.1	26.1	26.2	26.4	26.3
Other Services													
2009	31.6	32.2	31.8	31.2	30.9	31.9	31.2	31.1	31.0	30.9	31.7	31.9	31.4
2010	31.7	32.2	32.3	32.9	33.3	32.9	33.2	33.5	33.7	33.3	33.5	33.6	33.0
2011	31.8	33.3	32.8	32.9	32.7	32.3	31.6	31.8	31.1	31.5	31.3	29.9	31.9
2012	30.4	30.3	30.8	30.7	29.4	30.2	30.4	30.7	31.4	30.2	30.2	31.1	30.5
2013	30.1	30.4	30.8	29.2	29.1	29.7	29.6	30.3	31.9	31.2	31.9	32.1	30.5

3. Average Hourly Earnings by Selected Industry: Georgia, 2009–2013

(Dollars, not seasonally adjusted)

Industry and year	January	February	March	April	May	June	July	August	September	October	November	December	Annual average
Total Private													
2009	21.10	21.49	21.32	21.07	20.53	20.70	20.82	21.05	21.00	20.99	21.46	21.37	21.08
2010	21.20	21.30	21.40	21.53	21.49	21.42	21.61	21.85	21.56	21.80	21.81	21.87	21.57
2011	22.40	21.77	21.61	21.83	21.77	21.72	21.78	21.75	21.80	21.98	21.83	21.78	21.83
2012	21.98	21.59	21.57	21.77	21.35	21.43	21.90	21.59	21.92	21.77	21.90	22.21	21.75
2013	22.21	22.40	22.15	22.26	22.18	22.44	22.34	22.45	22.77	22.61	22.71	23.06	22.47
Goods-Producing													
2009	20.31	20.06	20.10	20.30	20.05	20.69	20.54	20.80	21.03	21.05	21.53	21.36	20.64
2010	21.21	21.27	21.03	20.72	20.77	20.83	20.99	21.31	21.00	21.10	21.54	21.61	21.11
2011	21.84	21.21	20.99	21.31	21.47	21.94	21.82	21.63	21.87	22.10	21.88	22.14	21.68
2012	22.05	21.80	21.80	22.03	21.70	21.67	21.89	21.51	21.47	21.40	21.93	22.09	21.78
2013	21.86	22.16	22.00	22.08	22.22	22.53	22.47	22.42	22.51	22.39	22.50	22.85	22.34
Construction													
2009	20.90	20.58	20.71	20.53	20.39	21.08	21.28	21.62	21.94	21.98	21.75	21.61	21.18
2010	21.65	21.61	21.41	21.57	21.45	21.16	21.17	21.45	21.10	21.25	21.45	21.31	21.38
2011	22.29	21.18	21.02	21.39	21.39	21.66	21.48	21.53	21.78	22.17	21.93	22.34	21.67
2012	22.42	21.99	22.15	21.83	21.59	21.77	22.16	21.65	21.70	21.60	22.98	22.79	22.05
2013	22.47	22.91	22.39	22.21	22.49	22.54	22.48	22.59	22.91	22.51	22.46	22.88	22.57
Manufacturing													
2009	19.79	19.47	19.50	20.08	19.60	20.25	19.81	20.03	19.88	19.95	20.08	19.91	19.86
2010	19.86	20.12	19.98	19.73	19.93	19.26	20.48	20.76	20.44	20.56	20.39	20.80	20.28
2011	20.79	20.51	20.33	20.69	21.00	21.73	21.60	21.37	21.60	21.96	21.74	21.94	21.28
2012	21.80	21.62	21.58	22.07	21.71	21.58	21.69	21.49	21.35	21.32	21.45	21.78	21.62
2013	21.60	21.83	21.82	22.02	22.09	22.52	22.47	22.32	22.27	22.30	22.47	22.78	22.21
Trade, Transportation, and Utilities													
2009	19.94	20.25	20.26	20.11	19.70	19.73	19.75	19.96	19.69	19.16	19.63	19.44	19.80
2010	19.13	19.37	19.69	19.60	19.51	19.84	19.99	20.13	19.91	19.73	19.75	19.88	19.71
2011	20.19	20.04	20.11	20.16	20.20	20.08	20.22	20.21	20.16	20.26	19.92	20.07	20.13
2012	20.59	19.99	20.09	20.48	19.96	20.12	20.87	20.39	20.81	20.69	20.49	20.61	20.43
2013	20.47	20.64	20.13	20.12	20.24	20.54	20.39	20.37	20.59	20.48	20.46	20.76	20.43
Financial Activities													
2009	25.34	26.12	26.09	25.35	25.84	25.75	26.16	25.89	25.37	25.13	25.07	24.78	25.58
2010	24.69	25.08	24.81	25.55	25.65	25.20	25.50	25.66	25.24	24.80	24.46	24.59	25.10
2011	24.71	24.50	24.36	24.64	24.81	24.29	24.71	24.43	24.46	24.68	24.45	24.20	24.52
2012	24.81	25.18	25.50	26.39	26.59	27.09	27.10	27.29	28.55	27.92	27.04	28.78	26.87
2013	28.58	28.84	29.18	29.60	29.67	30.08	30.08	30.38	30.95	31.34	30.61	31.20	30.06
Professional and Business Services													
2009	27.20	27.32	27.16	26.35	26.11	26.15	25.74	26.15	26.31	26.39	27.00	27.00	26.58
2010	26.90	27.12	26.50	26.85	26.61	26.22	26.22	26.86	26.55	26.41	26.60	26.30	26.59
2011	27.57	26.41	26.35	26.56	26.60	26.70	26.81	26.81	26.84	27.02	27.20	27.23	26.84
2012	27.01	26.32	26.02	25.55	25.12	25.24	25.72	24.78	25.00	24.71	25.04	25.14	25.45
2013	25.47	25.63	25.16	25.52	25.28	25.66	25.53	25.69	26.09	25.55	26.18	26.64	25.70
Education and Health Services													
2009	21.28	21.88	21.74	22.10	21.65	21.89	22.02	21.97	21.85	22.40	22.49	22.16	21.95
2010	22.12	22.36	22.20	22.50	22.41	22.21	22.32	22.14	21.76	22.54	22.30	22.24	22.26
2011	22.60	22.11	21.87	22.19	21.83	21.86	22.25	21.94	21.91	22.22	22.24	22.01	22.08
2012	22.14	22.18	22.15	22.46	22.04	22.32	22.58	22.88	22.52	22.88	22.94	23.18	22.52
2013	23.34	23.88	23.89	23.73	23.50	23.57	23.79	24.00	24.10	24.09	24.10	23.94	23.83
Leisure and Hospitality													
2009	11.59	11.57	11.39	11.29	11.23	11.24	11.35	11.57	11.75	11.69	11.67	11.86	11.51
2010	11.70	11.80	11.83	11.87	11.90	11.72	11.77	12.00	12.02	12.02	12.12	12.07	11.90
2011	12.40	12.15	12.04	12.22	12.25	12.05	12.04	12.12	12.29	12.46	12.37	12.46	12.23
2012	12.29	12.36	12.22	12.25	12.21	12.08	12.26	12.07	12.15	12.11	12.10	12.17	12.19
2013	12.16	12.10	12.02	12.00	12.01	11.85	11.79	11.98	12.09	12.10	12.13	12.25	12.04
Other Services													
2009	16.67	16.91	17.01	16.93	16.74	16.89	16.91	17.19	17.40	17.69	17.63	17.90	17.15
2010	18.15	18.34	18.15	18.12	18.35	18.24	18.05	18.30	18.16	17.95	17.74	18.01	18.13
2011	18.74	18.12	17.77	18.12	17.81	17.72	17.74	17.39	17.66	17.89	17.55	18.02	17.88
2012	18.18	18.09	17.84	18.25	17.77	17.13	17.41	17.68	18.03	17.77	18.14	18.08	17.86
2013	18.07	18.55	18.66	19.22	19.20	18.93	18.46	18.74	18.93	19.71	19.38	19.64	18.97

4. Average Weekly Earnings by Selected Industry: Georgia, 2009–2013

(Dollars, not seasonally adjusted)

Industry and year	January	February	March	April	May	June	July	August	September	October	November	December	Annual average
Total Private													
2009	730.06	754.30	748.33	724.81	710.34	710.01	720.37	730.44	716.10	719.96	751.10	739.40	729.37
2010	727.16	728.46	736.16	751.40	756.45	747.56	749.87	766.94	748.13	760.82	758.99	761.08	748.48
2011	750.40	753.24	749.87	757.50	764.13	753.68	757.94	754.73	754.28	771.50	759.68	757.94	757.50
2012	769.30	751.33	750.64	766.30	742.98	747.91	770.88	755.65	780.35	759.77	764.31	788.46	761.25
2013	772.91	781.76	779.68	781.33	774.08	798.86	781.90	785.75	810.61	791.35	799.39	818.63	790.94
Goods-Producing													
2009	749.44	746.23	753.75	749.07	757.89	773.81	782.57	782.08	786.52	797.80	826.75	822.36	776.06
2010	814.46	797.63	803.35	808.08	816.26	812.37	818.61	824.70	802.20	820.79	833.60	844.95	816.96
2011	784.06	829.31	822.81	839.61	850.21	860.05	861.89	863.04	868.24	877.37	877.39	894.46	852.02
2012	862.16	858.92	863.28	879.00	861.49	868.97	862.47	853.95	863.09	858.14	883.78	901.27	869.02
2013	883.14	888.62	902.00	903.07	917.69	946.26	930.26	928.19	949.92	929.19	938.25	952.85	922.64
Construction													
2009	756.58	749.11	764.20	730.87	744.24	754.66	776.72	784.81	811.78	822.05	826.50	812.54	777.31
2010	798.89	775.80	770.76	789.46	793.65	789.27	793.88	815.10	795.47	824.50	830.12	816.17	799.61
2011	757.86	819.67	796.66	840.63	849.18	851.24	839.87	846.13	860.31	857.98	857.46	860.09	836.46
2012	836.27	846.62	852.78	868.83	842.01	851.21	888.62	857.34	870.17	861.84	930.69	904.76	866.57
2013	878.58	870.58	904.56	895.06	926.59	935.41	919.43	908.12	953.06	913.91	916.37	917.49	911.83
Manufacturing													
2009	738.17	720.39	727.35	748.98	742.84	765.45	766.65	771.16	749.48	766.08	783.12	784.45	754.68
2010	786.46	778.64	787.21	789.20	793.21	798.24	806.91	803.41	780.81	795.67	801.33	821.60	794.98
2011	765.07	806.04	811.17	815.19	829.50	853.99	861.84	863.35	864.00	882.79	882.64	910.51	844.82
2012	876.36	864.80	869.67	880.59	870.57	876.15	848.08	855.30	858.27	857.06	864.44	901.69	869.12
2013	889.92	899.40	898.98	907.22	912.32	950.34	934.75	939.67	944.25	934.37	948.23	968.15	928.38
Trade, Transportation, and Utilities													
2009	683.94	708.75	713.15	699.83	693.44	686.60	683.35	696.60	675.37	666.77	685.09	674.57	689.04
2010	654.25	662.45	669.46	678.16	684.80	692.42	695.65	714.62	694.86	688.58	689.28	695.80	685.91
2011	680.40	693.38	697.82	697.54	707.00	696.78	703.66	697.25	699.55	709.10	691.22	702.45	698.51
2012	718.59	697.65	697.12	710.66	690.62	694.14	726.28	701.42	720.03	709.67	708.95	721.35	708.92
2013	698.03	712.08	694.49	694.14	696.26	716.85	703.46	706.84	722.71	708.61	714.05	730.75	708.92
Financial Activities													
2009	917.31	955.99	944.46	889.79	899.23	890.95	918.22	937.22	913.32	909.71	905.03	857.39	910.65
2010	866.62	882.82	885.72	899.36	895.19	866.88	879.75	905.80	878.35	853.12	860.65	875.99	875.99
2011	896.97	857.50	864.78	864.86	905.57	864.72	887.09	864.82	870.78	918.10	877.76	866.36	877.82
2012	925.41	914.03	920.55	986.99	954.58	980.66	1,035.22	996.09	1,079.19	1,027.46	1,000.48	1,099.40	994.19
2013	1,051.74	1,064.20	1,070.91	1,092.24	1,094.82	1,146.05	1,112.96	1,127.10	1,182.29	1,147.04	1,123.39	1,185.60	1,118.23
Professional and Business Services													
2009	932.96	967.13	950.60	914.35	913.85	904.79	898.33	923.10	907.70	910.46	961.20	947.70	927.64
2010	917.29	943.78	927.50	950.49	936.67	915.08	920.32	950.84	929.25	924.35	928.34	923.13	930.65
2011	942.89	929.63	924.89	942.88	960.26	969.21	962.48	954.44	952.82	988.93	976.48	977.56	958.19
2012	983.16	952.78	947.13	960.68	926.93	928.83	961.93	949.07	972.50	926.63	926.48	962.86	949.29
2013	942.39	961.13	938.47	954.45	940.42	977.65	939.50	950.53	983.59	935.13	968.66	996.34	956.04
Education and Health Services													
2009	789.49	783.30	784.81	784.55	772.91	774.91	781.71	779.94	764.75	781.76	800.64	777.82	781.42
2010	769.78	775.89	774.78	787.50	795.56	781.79	783.43	781.54	768.13	791.15	787.19	780.62	781.33
2011	788.74	782.69	776.39	787.75	777.15	771.66	785.43	770.09	771.23	788.81	780.62	768.15	779.42
2012	788.18	767.43	766.39	779.36	762.58	767.81	785.78	789.36	790.45	789.36	784.55	808.98	781.44
2013	805.23	816.70	819.43	811.57	803.70	820.24	813.62	832.80	841.09	828.70	831.45	837.90	822.14
Leisure and Hospitality													
2009	325.68	335.53	330.31	320.64	320.06	311.35	318.94	321.65	319.60	322.64	320.93	328.52	323.43
2010	315.90	317.42	320.59	324.05	326.06	322.30	320.14	326.40	322.14	324.54	326.03	324.68	322.49
2011	313.72	326.84	325.08	329.94	333.20	321.74	323.88	324.82	322.00	330.19	325.33	327.70	325.32
2012	323.23	327.54	325.05	325.85	324.79	323.74	329.79	318.65	320.76	318.49	314.60	318.85	323.04
2013	311.30	317.02	319.73	319.20	317.06	318.77	310.08	311.48	315.55	315.81	317.81	323.40	316.65
Other Services													
2009	526.77	544.50	540.92	528.22	517.27	538.79	527.59	534.61	539.40	546.62	558.87	571.01	538.51
2010	575.36	590.55	586.25	596.15	611.06	600.10	599.26	613.05	611.99	597.74	594.29	605.14	598.29
2011	595.93	603.40	582.86	596.15	582.39	572.36	560.58	553.00	549.23	563.54	549.32	538.80	570.37
2012	552.67	548.13	549.47	560.28	522.44	517.33	529.26	542.78	566.14	536.65	547.83	562.29	544.73
2013	543.91	563.92	574.73	561.22	558.72	562.22	546.42	567.82	603.87	614.95	618.22	630.44	578.59

HAWAII
At a Glance

Population:
    2000 census: 1,211,497
    2010 census: 1,360,301
    2013 estimate: 1,404,054

Percent change in population:
    2000–2010: 12.3%
    2010–2013: 3.2%

Percent change in total nonfarm employment:
    2001–2010: 6.4%
    2010–2013: 5.2%

Industry with the largest growth in employment, 2000–2013 (thousands):
    Education and Health Services, 19.1

Industry with the largest decline or smallest growth in employment, 2000–2013 (thousands):
    Information, -3.8

Civilian labor force:
    2000: 609,018
    2010: 647,268
    2013: 648,825

Unemployment rate and rank among states (lowest to highest):
    2000: 4.0%, 28th
    2010: 6.7%, 7th
    2013: 4.8%, 8th

Over-the-year change in unemployment rates:
    2010–2011: -0.2%
    2011–2012: -0.8%
    2012–2013: -0.9%

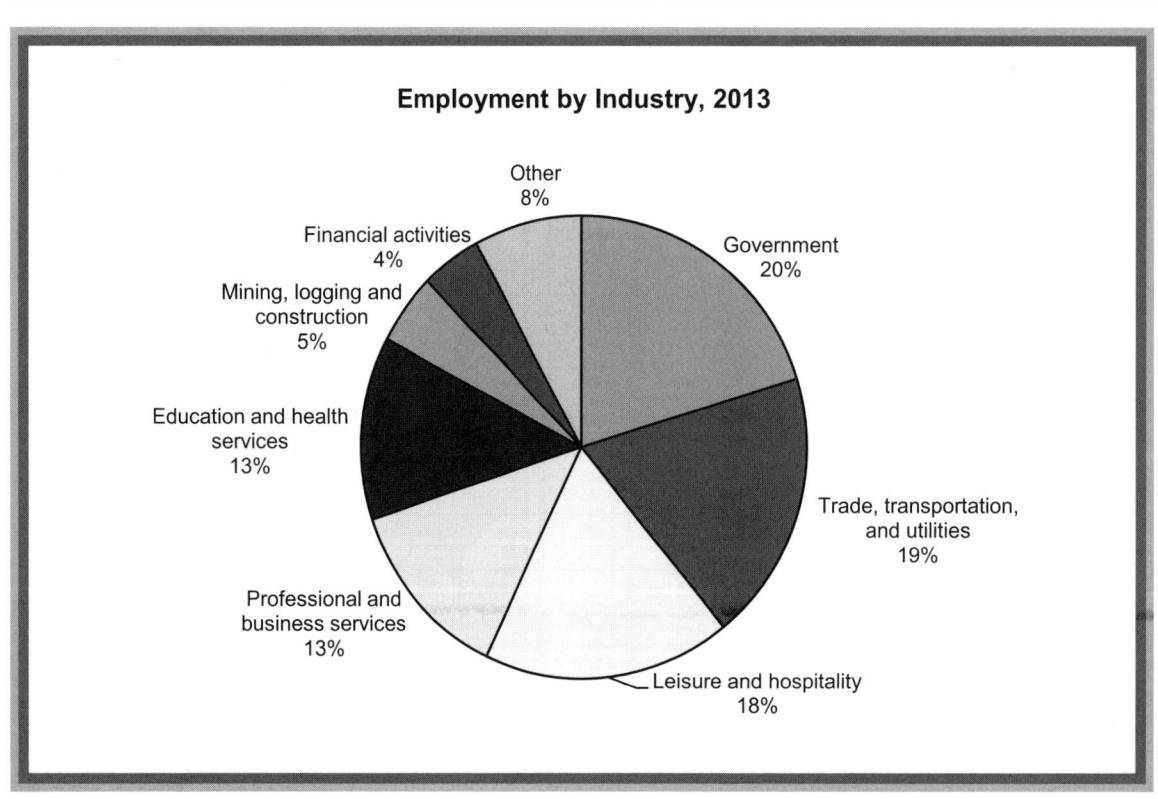

Employment by Industry, 2013

Other 8%
Financial activities 4%
Mining, logging and construction 5%
Education and health services 13%
Professional and business services 13%
Government 20%
Trade, transportation, and utilities 19%
Leisure and hospitality 18%

1. Employment by Industry: Hawaii, Selected Years, 2002–2013

(Numbers in thousands, not seasonally adjusted)

Industry and year	January	February	March	April	May	June	July	August	September	October	November	December	Annual average
Total Nonfarm													
2002	542.0	549.4	554.0	547.9	558.1	564.6	553.2	554.2	557.3	560.7	566.8	573.3	556.8
2003	559.6	564.5	567.8	562.7	568.2	568.9	562.3	563.4	566.1	570.0	576.2	581.9	567.6
2004	568.9	574.5	578.0	578.6	582.4	584.2	578.9	580.5	584.1	589.8	599.2	601.8	583.4
2005	585.0	593.1	597.4	598.5	602.0	604.4	597.3	601.3	604.2	605.8	611.8	618.9	601.6
2006	600.2	611.0	615.2	612.5	617.9	621.0	610.6	615.7	620.4	618.2	630.3	632.3	617.1
2007	615.0	622.9	626.5	618.5	627.1	630.5	618.0	619.7	624.6	626.4	632.3	637.0	624.9
2008	619.9	626.6	629.4	620.5	626.6	624.4	612.6	613.4	613.0	611.5	618.1	614.8	619.2
2009	597.6	599.3	600.6	594.8	595.0	594.3	583.0	580.8	584.3	587.1	588.6	592.5	591.5
2010	578.9	583.9	587.6	586.7	589.9	586.2	581.1	577.7	584.8	589.6	597.3	599.2	586.9
2011	580.7	592.1	595.8	592.7	593.4	591.2	587.5	584.8	593.9	597.1	603.1	608.4	593.4
2012	584.7	600.3	602.9	604.2	607.4	606.1	599.2	605.6	607.5	611.7	623.1	622.7	606.3
2013	600.1	615.8	618.7	615.1	619.6	616.5	612.2	609.9	617.7	621.7	632.2	632.0	617.6
Total Private													
2002	427.4	430.3	433.4	433.4	436.6	440.6	441.2	441.9	443.0	441.9	445.9	450.8	438.9
2003	440.7	442.9	445.4	443.7	445.8	447.8	448.4	450.3	451.8	450.3	454.9	460.0	448.5
2004	450.5	453.6	455.5	456.9	459.2	463.3	464.7	465.9	467.4	469.4	474.6	478.9	463.3
2005	468.8	472.1	475.2	477.1	479.3	482.9	483.3	485.6	487.7	485.7	490.0	496.3	482.0
2006	484.5	489.1	492.3	490.3	494.0	498.7	496.1	499.7	500.4	495.9	502.1	507.0	495.8
2007	495.1	498.7	501.6	498.6	501.8	507.0	502.6	504.3	503.7	502.7	506.8	510.4	502.8
2008	498.5	501.4	502.4	498.7	498.7	498.5	494.2	493.1	489.7	484.5	485.1	485.9	494.2
2009	472.5	472.2	471.6	465.8	464.8	466.3	462.8	462.0	461.9	461.7	462.4	465.5	465.8
2010	456.6	458.5	460.0	459.1	460.1	460.1	460.1	461.2	462.5	464.3	466.6	471.6	461.7
2011	460.5	465.2	468.1	465.5	465.2	465.8	467.9	469.3	471.4	471.2	475.7	480.3	468.8
2012	469.6	472.8	474.6	475.8	478.4	480.2	480.5	483.1	483.8	485.2	491.1	493.8	480.7
2013	484.5	487.8	490.3	489.7	490.4	491.6	493.4	494.0	493.9	495.2	500.3	502.8	492.8
Goods-Producing													
2002	40.0	39.9	40.6	40.2	40.6	41.6	41.8	42.1	41.7	41.8	42.1	42.2	41.2
2003	41.4	41.5	41.8	42.4	42.8	43.1	43.4	43.7	43.8	43.9	43.9	43.8	43.0
2004	42.9	43.3	42.7	43.8	44.3	45.1	45.4	45.5	45.8	45.9	46.3	46.7	44.8
2005	45.9	46.3	47.0	47.5	48.1	48.7	49.1	49.7	50.2	49.9	50.1	50.6	48.6
2006	49.5	49.8	50.1	50.1	50.9	51.7	52.0	52.8	53.5	53.1	53.9	54.6	51.8
2007	52.8	53.2	53.4	53.5	54.0	54.9	54.7	55.1	55.3	55.1	55.3	55.2	54.4
2008	53.9	54.1	54.0	53.7	53.2	53.3	53.0	52.9	52.4	51.4	50.8	50.1	52.7
2009	48.0	47.1	46.6	45.5	45.4	45.3	44.9	44.3	44.1	43.6	43.2	43.1	45.1
2010	42.2	41.9	42.0	41.7	41.7	41.5	41.7	41.6	41.7	42.1	42.2	42.4	41.9
2011	40.6	41.2	41.3	41.6	41.6	42.2	42.7	42.7	43.1	42.6	42.6	42.8	42.1
2012	41.7	41.8	41.8	41.7	41.9	42.6	42.7	43.1	43.6	43.8	44.1	44.1	42.7
2013	43.2	43.5	44.0	43.9	44.5	44.3	44.6	44.8	44.9	44.5	44.6	45.1	44.3
Service-Providing													
2002	502.0	509.5	513.4	507.7	517.5	523.0	511.4	512.1	515.6	518.9	524.7	531.1	515.6
2003	518.2	523.0	526.0	520.3	525.4	525.8	518.9	519.7	522.3	526.1	532.3	538.1	524.7
2004	526.0	531.2	535.3	534.8	538.1	539.1	533.5	535.0	538.3	543.9	552.9	555.1	538.6
2005	539.1	546.8	550.4	551.0	553.9	555.7	548.2	551.6	554.0	555.9	561.7	568.3	553.1
2006	550.7	561.2	565.1	562.4	567.0	569.3	558.6	562.9	566.9	565.1	576.4	577.7	565.3
2007	562.2	569.7	573.1	565.0	573.1	575.6	563.3	564.6	569.3	571.3	577.0	581.8	570.5
2008	566.0	572.5	575.4	566.8	573.4	571.1	559.6	560.5	560.6	560.1	567.3	564.7	566.5
2009	549.6	552.2	554.0	549.3	549.6	549.0	538.1	536.5	540.2	543.5	545.4	549.4	546.4
2010	536.7	542.0	545.6	545.0	548.2	544.7	539.4	536.1	543.1	547.5	555.1	556.8	545.0
2011	540.1	550.9	554.5	551.1	551.8	549.0	544.8	542.1	550.8	554.5	560.5	565.6	551.3
2012	543.0	558.5	561.1	562.5	565.5	563.5	556.5	562.5	563.9	567.9	579.0	578.6	563.5
2013	556.9	572.3	574.7	571.2	575.1	572.2	567.6	565.1	572.8	577.2	587.6	586.9	573.3
Mining, Logging, and Construction													
2002	24.4	24.3	24.9	25.1	25.4	26.2	26.6	27.0	26.8	26.9	27.1	27.2	26.0
2003	26.7	26.8	27.1	27.5	27.9	28.1	28.4	28.7	28.7	28.6	28.5	28.3	27.9
2004	27.6	27.9	27.4	28.4	28.9	29.5	30.0	30.1	30.4	30.6	30.9	31.3	29.4
2005	30.8	31.1	31.8	32.4	33.0	33.6	34.0	34.4	34.9	34.7	34.9	35.3	33.4
2006	34.5	34.7	34.9	35.0	35.7	36.4	36.7	37.3	37.9	37.8	38.4	39.0	36.5
2007	37.5	37.9	38.1	38.3	38.7	39.5	39.5	39.8	40.0	40.0	40.1	39.9	39.1
2008	38.9	39.0	38.9	38.6	38.1	38.2	38.1	37.9	37.7	37.0	36.3	35.6	37.9
2009	33.9	33.2	32.7	31.8	31.7	31.7	31.4	30.7	30.4	30.1	29.7	29.6	31.4
2010	29.0	28.8	28.9	28.8	28.8	28.7	28.9	28.7	28.8	29.1	29.1	29.2	28.9
2011	27.6	28.0	28.1	28.4	28.4	29.0	29.5	29.4	29.6	29.2	29.1	29.3	28.8
2012	28.4	28.4	28.5	28.5	28.8	29.4	29.5	29.8	30.2	30.4	30.5	30.5	29.4
2013	29.8	30.1	30.5	30.6	31.2	30.9	31.1	31.2	31.2	30.9	30.9	31.2	30.8

1. Employment by Industry: Hawaii, Selected Years, 2002–2013—*Continued*

(Numbers in thousands, not seasonally adjusted)

Industry and year	January	February	March	April	May	June	July	August	September	October	November	December	Annual average
Manufacturing													
2002	15.6	15.6	15.7	15.1	15.2	15.4	15.2	15.1	14.9	14.9	15.0	15.0	15.2
2003	14.7	14.7	14.7	14.9	14.9	15.0	15.0	15.0	15.1	15.3	15.4	15.5	15.0
2004	15.3	15.4	15.3	15.4	15.4	15.6	15.4	15.4	15.4	15.3	15.4	15.4	15.4
2005	15.1	15.2	15.2	15.1	15.1	15.1	15.1	15.3	15.3	15.2	15.2	15.3	15.2
2006	15.0	15.1	15.2	15.1	15.2	15.3	15.3	15.5	15.6	15.3	15.5	15.6	15.3
2007	15.3	15.3	15.3	15.2	15.3	15.4	15.2	15.3	15.3	15.1	15.2	15.3	15.3
2008	15.0	15.1	15.1	15.1	15.1	15.1	14.9	15.0	14.7	14.4	14.5	14.5	14.9
2009	14.1	13.9	13.9	13.7	13.7	13.6	13.5	13.6	13.7	13.5	13.5	13.5	13.7
2010	13.2	13.1	13.1	12.9	12.9	12.8	12.8	12.9	12.9	13.0	13.1	13.2	13.0
2011	13.0	13.2	13.2	13.2	13.2	13.2	13.2	13.3	13.5	13.4	13.5	13.5	13.3
2012	13.3	13.4	13.3	13.2	13.1	13.2	13.2	13.3	13.4	13.4	13.6	13.6	13.3
2013	13.4	13.4	13.5	13.3	13.3	13.4	13.5	13.6	13.7	13.6	13.7	13.9	13.5
Trade, Transportation, and Utilities													
2002	105.5	104.8	104.9	105.0	105.5	106.5	107.0	107.3	107.1	107.5	109.0	111.0	106.8
2003	107.4	107.0	106.8	106.2	106.4	106.9	107.6	107.9	108.0	108.2	110.1	112.2	107.9
2004	109.3	108.8	109.1	110.1	110.8	111.9	112.1	112.6	113.0	114.5	116.8	118.4	112.3
2005	114.9	114.9	115.2	115.5	116.4	117.3	118.2	118.7	119.1	118.9	120.7	122.9	117.7
2006	119.2	118.9	119.8	119.5	120.0	121.3	120.7	121.7	121.7	120.6	123.2	125.0	121.0
2007	121.6	120.3	121.4	120.3	120.8	121.6	121.3	121.4	121.2	121.5	124.5	126.4	121.9
2008	122.1	120.7	120.9	118.9	118.6	118.2	117.2	117.1	116.1	115.0	115.8	116.5	118.1
2009	113.4	112.3	111.7	110.3	110.0	110.5	110.2	109.8	110.1	110.0	111.4	112.8	111.0
2010	109.7	109.1	109.0	109.2	108.9	109.3	109.7	110.2	109.8	110.4	112.1	114.0	110.1
2011	110.8	110.3	110.5	110.1	110.0	110.3	111.0	111.2	111.2	112.3	114.4	116.1	111.5
2012	113.4	112.7	113.3	113.0	113.5	114.2	114.5	114.8	114.9	115.3	118.7	119.7	114.8
2013	115.9	115.6	116.0	115.5	115.6	116.2	116.3	116.6	116.6	118.0	120.4	121.3	117.0
Wholesale Trade													
2002	16.1	16.1	16.2	16.2	16.3	16.4	16.5	16.5	16.5	16.6	16.7	16.9	16.4
2003	16.5	16.5	16.6	16.6	16.7	16.7	16.8	16.8	16.8	16.8	16.8	16.9	16.7
2004	16.7	16.8	16.8	16.9	17.0	17.1	17.1	17.1	17.1	17.2	17.3	17.4	17.0
2005	17.1	17.3	17.4	17.4	17.5	17.6	17.7	17.8	17.9	17.9	17.9	18.1	17.6
2006	17.7	17.7	17.7	17.8	17.9	18.1	18.0	18.2	18.2	18.2	18.4	18.5	18.0
2007	18.2	18.2	18.4	18.3	18.4	18.6	18.6	18.7	18.8	18.8	19.0	19.1	18.6
2008	18.7	18.8	18.9	18.8	18.9	18.9	18.9	18.8	18.8	18.7	18.6	18.6	18.8
2009	18.2	18.1	18.0	17.9	17.8	17.8	17.8	17.7	17.8	17.7	17.7	17.8	17.9
2010	17.5	17.5	17.6	17.6	17.6	17.6	17.7	17.7	17.6	17.7	17.7	17.8	17.6
2011	17.4	17.3	17.3	17.4	17.4	17.4	17.5	17.5	17.5	17.6	17.6	17.8	17.5
2012	17.5	17.5	17.6	17.5	17.5	17.7	17.7	17.8	17.8	17.8	17.9	17.9	17.7
2013	17.7	17.7	17.8	17.7	17.7	17.7	17.7	17.7	17.7	17.8	18.0	17.9	17.8
Retail Trade													
2002	63.8	63.0	62.9	62.8	63.0	63.7	64.1	64.1	63.9	64.1	65.3	67.1	64.0
2003	64.0	63.4	63.1	62.8	63.0	63.7	64.3	64.4	64.3	64.6	66.4	68.4	64.4
2004	65.8	65.1	65.2	65.1	65.6	66.3	66.6	66.9	67.0	68.1	70.1	71.8	67.0
2005	68.5	68.1	68.2	67.8	68.0	68.3	69.1	69.3	69.3	69.7	71.3	73.3	69.2
2006	70.0	69.5	69.8	69.1	69.2	69.8	69.4	69.7	69.4	69.5	71.7	73.1	70.0
2007	70.4	69.4	70.1	69.3	69.6	70.1	69.9	69.8	69.6	69.8	72.4	73.8	70.4
2008	70.6	69.9	70.7	69.7	69.6	70.1	70.0	69.8	69.2	68.5	69.5	70.3	69.8
2009	67.9	67.0	66.6	65.6	65.3	65.8	65.7	65.5	65.9	66.0	67.5	68.6	66.5
2010	66.0	65.4	65.3	65.3	65.0	65.5	65.7	65.8	65.5	65.8	67.5	68.9	66.0
2011	66.6	66.0	66.2	65.9	65.8	66.1	66.5	66.6	66.7	67.3	69.3	70.5	67.0
2012	68.3	67.7	67.8	67.6	68.0	68.3	68.4	68.4	68.4	68.8	71.7	72.6	68.8
2013	69.4	68.8	69.1	68.7	68.7	69.1	69.2	69.2	69.2	70.1	72.6	73.3	69.8
Transportation and Utilities													
2002	25.6	25.7	25.8	26.0	26.2	26.4	26.4	26.7	26.7	26.8	27.0	27.0	26.4
2003	26.9	27.1	27.1	26.8	26.7	26.5	26.5	26.7	26.9	26.8	26.9	26.9	26.8
2004	26.8	26.9	27.1	28.1	28.2	28.5	28.4	28.6	28.9	29.2	29.4	29.2	28.3
2005	29.3	29.5	29.6	30.3	30.9	31.4	31.4	31.6	31.9	31.3	31.5	31.5	30.9
2006	31.5	31.7	32.3	32.6	32.9	33.4	33.3	33.8	34.1	32.9	33.1	33.4	32.9
2007	33.0	32.7	32.9	32.7	32.8	32.9	32.8	32.9	32.8	32.9	33.1	33.5	32.9
2008	32.8	32.0	31.3	30.4	30.1	29.2	28.3	28.5	28.1	27.8	27.7	27.6	29.5
2009	27.3	27.2	27.1	26.8	26.9	26.9	26.7	26.6	26.4	26.3	26.2	26.4	26.7
2010	26.2	26.2	26.1	26.3	26.3	26.2	26.3	26.7	26.7	26.9	26.9	27.3	26.5
2011	26.8	27.0	27.0	26.8	26.8	26.8	27.0	27.1	27.0	27.4	27.5	27.8	27.1
2012	27.6	27.5	27.9	27.9	28.0	28.2	28.4	28.6	28.7	28.7	29.1	29.2	28.3
2013	28.8	29.1	29.1	29.1	29.2	29.4	29.4	29.7	29.7	30.1	29.8	30.1	29.5
Information													
2002	11.7	11.7	11.6	11.5	11.5	11.3	11.2	11.3	12.0	11.1	11.1	11.7	11.5
2003	10.8	10.9	10.9	10.5	11.1	10.9	10.1	10.0	9.9	9.9	10.0	10.1	10.4
2004	10.2	10.1	10.4	10.2	10.5	10.6	11.1	11.0	11.1	11.1	11.6	11.5	10.8
2005	10.4	10.6	10.4	10.7	10.9	10.5	10.5	10.9	11.0	10.9	11.1	11.6	10.8
2006	10.8	11.1	10.9	10.2	11.0	10.8	10.3	10.5	11.0	10.3	10.8	10.9	10.7
2007	10.4	11.0	10.9	10.5	11.1	11.1	10.3	10.8	10.4	10.2	10.3	10.4	10.6
2008	9.6	10.1	10.4	10.4	10.7	11.1	9.9	9.6	9.6	9.4	9.8	10.0	10.1
2009	9.1	9.6	9.4	9.4	9.1	9.1	8.7	8.8	9.0	9.2	9.0	9.0	9.1
2010	8.9	9.7	9.9	9.5	10.7	10.0	8.8	9.4	11.1	9.8	9.4	10.3	9.8
2011	8.5	9.4	10.2	8.1	8.0	7.8	8.3	8.3	8.2	8.3	8.6	8.7	8.5
2012	8.3	8.4	8.5	8.4	8.4	7.8	8.1	8.3	8.4	8.6	9.2	8.9	8.4
2013	8.3	8.4	8.5	8.4	8.0	7.9	9.6	8.3	8.7	8.5	8.8	8.8	8.5

1. Employment by Industry: Hawaii, Selected Years, 2002–2013—*Continued*

(Numbers in thousands, not seasonally adjusted)

Industry and year	January	February	March	April	May	June	July	August	September	October	November	December	Annual average
Financial Activities													
2002	27.2	27.3	27.6	27.4	27.6	27.8	27.8	27.8	27.8	27.9	28.1	28.4	27.7
2003	27.7	27.9	28.1	28.0	28.2	28.5	28.6	28.8	28.6	28.6	28.5	28.8	28.4
2004	28.5	28.5	28.6	28.7	28.7	28.9	28.9	28.8	28.7	29.0	29.1	29.3	28.8
2005	28.7	29.0	29.0	28.9	29.1	29.2	29.4	29.5	29.5	29.5	29.7	29.9	29.3
2006	29.5	29.6	29.9	29.9	30.0	30.2	30.1	30.2	30.0	29.9	30.1	30.3	30.0
2007	29.9	30.0	30.2	29.9	30.0	30.2	30.2	30.1	29.9	30.0	29.9	30.1	30.0
2008	29.4	29.7	29.6	29.7	29.8	29.7	29.6	29.5	29.2	28.7	28.9	28.8	29.4
2009	27.9	27.9	27.8	27.8	27.8	27.8	27.6	27.6	27.5	27.5	27.4	27.5	27.7
2010	27.1	27.0	27.1	26.9	26.9	26.8	27.0	26.9	26.8	26.9	26.9	26.9	26.9
2011	26.5	26.5	26.6	26.6	26.5	26.5	26.7	26.7	26.6	26.5	26.8	26.8	26.6
2012	26.3	26.5	26.6	26.5	26.6	26.8	26.8	26.8	26.8	26.9	27.0	27.0	26.7
2013	26.7	26.8	27.0	27.0	27.1	27.1	27.2	27.1	27.0	27.3	27.4	27.4	27.1
Professional and Business Services													
2002	63.5	64.9	65.4	65.9	66.5	67.5	67.8	68.6	68.8	68.8	68.6	70.6	67.2
2003	69.0	68.6	69.2	68.9	68.8	69.6	69.4	70.3	70.8	69.6	70.6	71.1	69.7
2004	69.4	70.1	70.6	70.2	69.5	70.2	70.6	71.4	71.2	71.3	71.7	72.7	70.7
2005	71.9	72.5	73.1	73.6	73.0	74.0	74.2	74.9	74.8	75.1	76.1	77.3	74.2
2006	75.3	76.8	77.2	76.7	76.6	77.6	77.5	77.7	77.2	75.6	76.1	77.2	76.8
2007	75.1	75.7	76.0	75.0	75.3	77.1	76.4	76.6	76.8	77.1	77.2	78.1	76.4
2008	75.8	76.1	76.3	76.1	75.8	75.5	75.4	75.6	75.1	74.7	74.5	75.4	75.5
2009	73.1	72.9	72.9	71.5	71.0	71.1	70.5	70.4	70.0	71.2	70.8	71.6	71.4
2010	70.2	70.6	70.9	70.9	70.8	71.2	71.9	71.8	71.9	72.5	72.8	73.5	71.6
2011	73.2	74.3	75.0	75.2	74.7	75.0	74.7	75.5	75.8	75.8	76.5	77.6	75.3
2012	75.0	75.7	76.0	76.8	77.1	77.3	76.9	77.8	77.2	77.9	78.7	79.1	77.1
2013	78.0	78.9	79.4	79.3	78.9	79.0	79.3	79.8	79.6	80.3	80.2	80.3	79.4
Education and Health Services													
2002	61.6	62.6	62.9	63.0	63.5	63.4	63.5	62.5	63.7	63.8	64.9	64.3	63.3
2003	63.1	64.6	65.1	65.0	65.2	64.9	65.2	64.7	66.0	66.0	66.8	67.2	65.3
2004	65.5	66.6	67.1	66.9	67.7	67.7	67.4	67.0	68.3	68.5	69.4	69.9	67.7
2005	68.7	69.5	69.9	69.9	70.2	70.3	69.5	69.0	70.2	69.9	70.4	70.8	69.9
2006	68.9	70.1	70.7	70.7	71.4	71.8	70.6	71.2	71.7	71.8	72.6	73.0	71.2
2007	71.1	72.7	72.9	72.9	73.4	73.8	72.6	72.4	73.2	73.3	73.6	73.8	73.0
2008	72.5	73.7	73.9	73.8	74.2	74.7	74.0	73.8	74.4	74.7	75.2	75.5	74.2
2009	73.8	74.8	75.0	74.5	74.6	75.1	74.1	73.7	74.3	74.5	75.0	75.4	74.6
2010	74.5	75.2	75.6	75.2	75.6	75.3	74.9	74.6	74.6	75.9	75.9	76.3	75.3
2011	73.9	75.8	75.9	75.7	76.0	75.2	75.6	75.1	76.2	76.3	77.0	77.5	75.9
2012	75.0	76.4	76.1	76.7	77.4	76.8	76.7	77.2	77.9	78.1	78.3	79.1	77.1
2013	77.5	78.7	79.0	79.0	79.0	79.1	78.5	78.7	79.2	79.5	80.3	79.5	79.0
Leisure and Hospitality													
2002	94.7	95.8	96.8	96.8	97.7	98.7	98.3	98.5	98.0	97.2	98.2	98.6	97.4
2003	97.8	98.5	99.5	98.5	99.0	99.5	99.9	100.6	100.4	99.9	100.5	102.2	99.7
2004	100.9	102.1	102.6	102.7	103.1	104.2	104.7	105.1	104.9	104.4	105.0	105.5	103.8
2005	103.8	104.7	105.9	105.9	106.2	107.5	107.2	107.5	107.4	106.1	106.4	107.4	106.3
2006	105.9	107.1	107.8	107.3	107.9	109.1	108.9	109.3	109.0	108.2	108.9	109.5	108.2
2007	108.4	109.6	110.4	110.2	110.2	110.7	111.7	110.5	111.1	110.0	108.5	109.4	110.0
2008	108.5	109.7	109.8	108.6	108.7	108.7	108.1	107.5	105.8	103.6	103.1	102.7	107.1
2009	101.2	101.4	101.8	100.9	101.0	101.5	101.0	101.5	100.8	99.7	99.6	100.2	100.9
2010	98.8	99.4	99.8	99.7	99.4	100.0	100.2	100.8	100.7	100.7	101.4	102.3	100.3
2011	101.5	101.9	102.9	102.4	102.5	102.9	103.0	103.8	104.1	103.2	103.7	104.7	103.1
2012	104.3	105.4	106.3	106.5	107.1	108.3	108.6	108.7	108.4	108.1	108.5	109.5	107.5
2013	108.6	109.5	110.0	110.1	110.8	111.4	111.5	112.1	111.2	110.4	111.6	112.7	110.8
Other Services													
2002	23.2	23.3	23.6	23.6	23.7	23.8	23.8	23.8	23.9	23.8	23.9	24.0	23.7
2003	23.5	23.9	24.0	24.2	24.3	24.4	24.2	24.3	24.3	24.2	24.5	24.6	24.2
2004	23.8	24.1	24.4	24.3	24.6	24.7	24.5	24.5	24.4	24.7	24.7	24.9	24.5
2005	24.5	24.6	24.7	25.1	25.4	25.4	25.2	25.4	25.5	25.4	25.5	25.8	25.2
2006	25.4	25.7	25.9	25.9	26.2	26.2	26.0	26.3	26.3	26.4	26.5	26.5	26.1
2007	25.8	26.2	26.4	26.3	26.5	26.6	26.6	26.8	26.9	27.0	27.1	27.0	26.6
2008	26.7	27.3	27.5	27.5	27.7	27.3	27.0	27.1	27.1	27.0	27.0	26.9	27.2
2009	26.0	26.2	26.4	25.9	25.9	25.9	25.8	25.9	26.1	26.0	26.0	25.9	26.0
2010	25.2	25.6	25.7	26.0	26.1	26.0	25.9	25.9	25.9	26.0	25.9	25.9	25.8
2011	25.5	25.8	25.7	25.8	25.9	25.9	25.9	26.0	26.2	26.2	26.1	26.1	25.9
2012	25.6	25.9	26.0	26.2	26.4	26.4	26.2	26.4	26.6	26.5	26.6	26.4	26.3
2013	26.3	26.4	26.4	26.5	26.5	26.6	26.4	26.6	26.7	26.7	27.0	27.7	26.7
Government													
2002	114.6	119.1	120.6	114.5	121.5	124.0	112.0	112.3	114.3	118.8	120.9	122.5	117.9
2003	118.9	121.6	122.4	119.0	122.4	121.1	113.9	113.1	114.3	119.7	121.3	121.9	119.1
2004	118.4	120.9	122.5	121.7	123.2	120.9	114.2	114.6	116.7	120.4	124.6	122.9	120.1
2005	116.2	121.0	122.2	121.4	122.7	121.5	114.0	115.7	116.5	120.1	121.8	122.6	119.6
2006	115.7	121.9	122.9	122.2	123.9	122.3	114.5	116.0	120.0	122.3	128.2	125.3	121.3
2007	119.9	124.2	124.9	119.9	125.3	123.5	115.4	115.4	120.9	123.7	125.5	126.6	122.1
2008	121.4	125.2	127.0	121.8	127.9	125.9	118.4	120.3	123.3	127.0	133.0	128.9	125.0
2009	125.1	127.1	129.0	129.0	130.2	128.0	120.2	118.8	122.4	125.4	126.2	127.0	125.7
2010	122.3	125.4	127.6	127.6	129.8	126.1	121.0	116.5	122.3	125.3	130.7	127.6	125.2
2011	120.2	126.9	127.7	127.2	128.2	125.4	119.6	115.5	122.5	125.9	127.4	128.1	124.6
2012	115.1	127.5	128.3	128.4	129.0	125.9	118.7	122.5	123.7	126.5	132.0	128.9	125.5
2013	115.6	128.0	128.4	125.4	129.2	124.9	118.8	115.9	123.8	126.5	131.9	129.2	124.8

2. Average Weekly Hours by Selected Industry: Hawaii, 2009–2013

(Not seasonally adjusted)

Industry and year	January	February	March	April	May	June	July	August	September	October	November	December	Annual average
Total Private													
2009	32.3	33.4	33.0	32.5	32.3	32.5	32.3	32.6	32.0	32.2	32.7	32.2	32.5
2010	32.3	32.3	32.2	32.4	33.4	32.6	32.8	33.8	32.6	32.8	32.9	33.4	32.8
2011	34.1	33.3	33.0	33.4	34.1	33.4	33.2	33.1	33.1	34.0	32.7	32.6	33.4
2012	33.9	33.2	33.1	34.6	34.1	34.1	34.0	33.5	34.6	33.6	33.7	34.2	33.9
2013	33.0	33.1	33.1	33.2	33.0	34.1	33.2	33.0	33.8	32.9	32.6	33.6	33.2
Goods-Producing													
2009	36.1	36.6	37.0	36.5	36.4	35.4	36.2	35.5	34.3	34.3	34.7	36.1	35.8
2010	36.3	35.7	35.7	36.4	36.9	36.1	37.9	38.5	37.5	36.4	36.1	37.9	36.8
2011	36.3	37.7	36.6	37.9	37.2	36.8	36.8	36.4	36.6	35.1	33.7	35.7	36.4
2012	35.6	35.1	35.1	36.7	37.6	34.8	37.2	36.1	37.6	35.3	35.9	37.6	36.2
2013	35.3	35.2	35.7	36.3	36.4	34.8	37.4	36.5	37.1	37.3	34.6	37.2	36.2
Mining, Logging, and Construction													
2009	36.5	37.0	37.5	36.9	37.1	35.8	36.8	35.7	34.4	34.5	34.4	36.5	36.1
2010	37.1	36.0	35.8	36.8	37.4	36.2	38.5	38.9	37.9	36.2	36.2	37.8	37.0
2011	36.3	38.7	37.4	38.9	37.3	36.9	37.1	37.3	37.3	34.8	34.1	36.4	36.9
2012	36.5	36.2	35.5	37.7	38.3	35.1	37.8	35.9	37.9	35.1	36.4	37.8	36.7
2013	35.9	35.6	36.6	37.0	36.8	34.4	38.4	36.8	37.4	38.3	34.3	37.1	36.6
Manufacturing													
2009	35.2	35.7	35.7	35.4	35.1	34.4	34.7	35.1	34.2	34.1	35.2	35.3	35.0
2010	34.8	35.1	35.6	35.4	36.0	35.9	36.8	37.7	36.4	37.0	36.1	38.0	36.2
2011	36.3	35.8	34.9	35.5	36.8	36.6	35.9	34.2	35.0	35.5	32.9	34.1	35.4
2012	33.5	33.0	34.5	34.4	35.8	34.3	35.5	36.2	36.9	35.9	35.0	37.1	35.2
2013	34.1	34.4	33.8	34.6	35.6	35.6	35.2	35.9	36.5	35.0	35.4	37.4	35.3
Trade, Transportation, and Utilities													
2009	32.7	33.3	33.3	33.0	32.5	33.5	32.8	33.5	33.9	33.9	33.9	32.8	33.3
2010	32.7	33.5	32.9	33.4	34.5	34.5	34.0	34.1	33.6	33.8	34.2	35.0	33.9
2011	35.1	34.1	34.0	34.1	35.3	34.4	34.4	34.2	34.4	35.1	34.0	34.1	34.4
2012	35.0	33.8	33.4	34.2	33.5	33.9	34.3	33.2	34.2	32.9	33.0	34.5	33.8
2013	33.6	33.5	33.3	33.1	33.0	34.8	33.6	33.4	34.1	33.1	32.9	34.0	33.5
Professional and Business Services													
2009	31.8	33.0	33.0	32.6	32.4	32.7	32.3	32.6	32.1	32.6	33.3	33.0	32.6
2010	32.8	33.1	33.6	33.1	34.1	33.5	33.1	34.2	33.4	34.4	34.3	34.4	33.7
2011	35.1	35.6	35.2	35.9	34.8	34.6	33.8	33.2	33.0	34.6	33.9	34.5	34.5
2012	35.7	37.3	37.5	39.8	41.6	40.9	35.5	37.3	39.7	38.9	38.7	34.6	38.1
2013	33.8	34.5	34.1	34.7	34.4	35.5	34.1	34.0	35.5	35.1	34.5	35.5	34.7
Education and Health Services													
2009	30.8	32.5	31.7	30.9	30.8	30.2	30.9	31.2	30.8	30.2	31.0	30.7	31.0
2010	29.9	30.0	29.8	30.4	30.9	30.0	30.3	30.7	30.6	30.0	30.1	30.8	30.3
2011	32.4	31.7	31.2	31.3	32.8	31.5	31.2	31.6	31.8	33.2	32.0	31.8	31.9
2012	32.8	32.2	32.1	33.6	32.7	32.6	33.4	32.7	33.3	33.0	32.8	34.3	32.9
2013	33.4	33.1	33.3	33.5	33.3	34.4	33.8	33.3	34.2	33.3	32.9	33.0	33.5
Leisure and Hospitality													
2009	29.9	31.0	30.4	29.6	29.3	29.9	29.5	30.2	29.4	29.2	29.8	29.2	29.8
2010	29.6	29.2	29.4	28.9	29.9	29.0	29.4	30.9	28.8	29.3	29.6	29.4	29.4
2011	30.4	29.5	28.9	29.1	30.0	29.0	29.7	29.6	29.2	30.0	28.9	28.4	29.4
2012	30.1	29.0	28.8	30.1	29.1	30.0	30.9	29.9	30.4	29.5	30.0	30.8	29.9
2013	29.6	29.6	29.5	29.5	28.9	30.6	29.5	29.8	30.1	28.7	29.0	29.6	29.5

3. Average Hourly Earnings by Selected Industry: Hawaii, 2009–2013

(Dollars, not seasonally adjusted)

Industry and year	January	February	March	April	May	June	July	August	September	October	November	December	Annual average
Total Private													
2009	21.01	21.12	21.07	20.94	20.84	20.93	21.04	21.10	21.30	21.18	21.37	21.46	21.11
2010	21.39	21.38	21.38	21.33	21.36	21.35	21.65	21.90	22.02	21.97	21.82	22.20	21.65
2011	22.46	22.23	22.16	22.12	22.23	22.14	22.16	22.06	22.04	22.08	22.00	22.22	22.16
2012	22.39	22.35	22.54	22.49	22.40	22.45	23.01	22.77	23.08	22.84	22.99	23.23	22.72
2013	23.31	23.48	23.73	23.79	23.85	23.71	23.76	23.60	23.85	23.86	23.82	24.00	23.73
Goods-Producing													
2009	29.60	29.62	29.82	30.07	29.85	29.93	29.86	29.71	30.07	29.92	29.96	30.09	29.87
2010	30.15	29.76	29.84	30.25	30.22	30.26	30.42	30.17	30.63	30.20	30.15	30.66	30.23
2011	30.21	30.22	30.55	30.51	30.41	30.21	30.53	30.38	30.40	29.85	29.67	29.89	30.24
2012	30.21	30.89	30.17	30.73	30.80	30.16	30.78	30.31	30.64	30.34	31.61	30.91	30.64
2013	30.45	30.96	31.28	30.80	30.82	30.47	31.39	30.61	31.50	31.78	31.57	31.82	31.13
Mining, Logging, and Construction													
2009	32.76	32.77	33.10	33.40	33.03	33.22	33.27	33.40	33.82	33.73	33.97	33.81	33.33
2010	33.95	33.40	33.70	33.98	33.97	34.13	34.00	34.00	34.57	34.41	34.07	34.79	34.10
2011	34.50	34.32	34.80	34.69	34.81	34.67	34.98	34.54	34.81	34.56	33.93	34.07	34.56
2012	34.44	35.26	34.63	35.07	35.15	34.32	35.02	34.58	35.01	34.89	36.40	35.70	35.05
2013	35.13	35.64	35.83	35.22	35.32	35.36	35.73	35.02	35.92	36.20	36.87	36.92	35.77
Manufacturing													
2009	21.72	21.86	21.74	22.01	22.07	21.96	21.42	21.21	21.65	21.31	21.34	21.67	21.67
2010	21.24	21.50	21.25	21.61	21.55	21.54	21.40	21.34	21.53	21.00	21.46	21.59	21.42
2011	21.10	20.82	20.93	20.66	20.81	20.32	20.33	20.41	20.13	19.81	20.19	20.26	20.48
2012	20.41	20.67	20.28	20.44	20.57	20.66	20.70	20.88	20.53	20.28	20.41	19.97	20.48
2013	19.49	20.11	20.09	19.87	19.92	19.58	20.45	20.21	21.17	20.78	19.99	20.46	20.19
Trade, Transportation, and Utilities													
2009	18.20	18.40	18.35	18.57	18.56	18.54	18.70	18.83	18.96	18.67	19.00	18.94	18.64
2010	19.22	19.16	19.29	19.40	19.21	19.23	19.74	20.09	19.63	19.49	19.38	19.58	19.45
2011	20.24	19.66	19.48	19.53	19.61	19.29	20.12	19.49	19.54	19.73	19.98	20.28	19.75
2012	20.55	20.68	20.88	20.92	20.48	20.85	21.26	21.06	21.61	21.33	21.28	21.53	21.04
2013	21.68	21.87	22.25	22.43	22.60	22.36	22.31	22.50	22.92	22.70	22.71	22.86	22.44
Professional and Business Services													
2009	22.03	22.35	21.86	21.56	21.44	21.59	21.57	21.75	21.71	21.55	21.62	21.44	21.71
2010	21.74	21.80	22.16	22.16	22.85	22.72	23.07	23.38	23.55	23.41	23.51	23.14	22.81
2011	23.91	23.78	23.76	23.40	24.68	24.05	23.81	24.08	24.20	24.25	24.15	24.01	24.00
2012	24.30	23.69	23.72	23.41	22.78	23.08	23.72	23.32	23.30	22.98	23.22	24.22	23.45
2013	23.87	23.84	23.96	23.73	23.74	23.91	23.70	23.51	23.83	23.62	23.80	23.73	23.77
Education and Health Services													
2009	22.76	22.71	23.05	22.86	22.56	22.40	22.13	21.98	22.01	22.17	22.19	22.05	22.41
2010	22.09	21.87	21.74	21.60	21.37	21.54	21.33	21.66	21.89	22.11	22.13	22.42	21.81
2011	22.54	22.40	22.73	22.83	23.07	22.83	23.39	23.38	23.65	23.92	24.35	24.64	23.32
2012	24.93	24.77	25.68	24.99	25.33	25.81	26.46	26.41	26.60	26.62	26.55	26.61	25.91
2013	26.96	27.14	27.60	27.89	27.72	27.89	27.52	27.44	26.83	27.15	26.67	26.64	27.29
Leisure and Hospitality													
2009	17.16	17.11	16.93	17.04	16.71	17.17	17.04	16.86	17.20	16.76	17.08	17.32	17.03
2010	16.92	16.89	16.50	16.30	16.29	16.59	16.49	16.51	16.69	16.46	16.47	16.56	16.55
2011	16.49	16.56	16.76	16.81	16.62	16.72	16.82	16.89	16.85	16.72	16.01	16.03	16.61
2012	16.37	16.35	16.45	16.69	16.62	16.93	17.13	17.23	17.73	17.25	17.37	17.64	16.99
2013	18.04	18.15	18.15	18.19	18.20	18.05	18.08	17.76	17.96	17.87	18.05	18.54	18.09

4. Average Weekly Earnings by Selected Industry: Hawaii, 2009–2013

(Dollars, not seasonally adjusted)

Industry and year	January	February	March	April	May	June	July	August	September	October	November	December	Annual average
Total Private													
2009	678.62	705.41	695.31	680.55	673.13	680.23	679.59	687.86	681.60	682.00	698.80	691.01	686.08
2010	690.90	690.57	688.44	691.09	713.42	696.01	710.12	740.22	717.85	720.62	717.88	741.48	710.12
2011	765.89	740.26	731.28	738.81	758.04	739.48	735.71	730.19	729.52	750.72	719.40	724.37	740.14
2012	759.02	742.02	746.07	778.15	763.84	765.55	782.34	762.80	798.57	767.42	774.76	794.47	770.21
2013	769.23	777.19	785.46	789.83	787.05	808.51	788.83	778.80	806.13	784.99	776.53	806.40	787.84
Goods-Producing													
2009	1,068.56	1,084.09	1,103.34	1,097.56	1,086.54	1,059.52	1,080.93	1,054.71	1,031.40	1,026.26	1,039.61	1,086.25	1,069.35
2010	1,094.45	1,062.43	1,065.29	1,101.10	1,115.12	1,092.39	1,152.92	1,161.55	1,148.63	1,099.28	1,088.42	1,162.01	1,112.46
2011	1,096.62	1,139.29	1,118.13	1,156.33	1,131.25	1,111.73	1,123.50	1,105.83	1,112.64	1,047.74	999.88	1,067.07	1,100.74
2012	1,075.48	1,084.24	1,058.97	1,127.79	1,158.08	1,049.57	1,145.02	1,094.19	1,152.06	1,071.00	1,134.80	1,162.22	1,109.17
2013	1,074.89	1,089.79	1,116.70	1,118.04	1,121.85	1,060.36	1,173.99	1,117.27	1,168.65	1,185.39	1,092.32	1,183.70	1,126.91
Mining, Logging, and Construction													
2009	1,195.74	1,212.49	1,241.25	1,232.46	1,225.41	1,189.28	1,224.34	1,192.38	1,163.41	1,163.69	1,168.57	1,234.07	1,203.21
2010	1,259.55	1,202.40	1,206.46	1,250.46	1,270.48	1,235.51	1,317.47	1,322.60	1,310.20	1,245.64	1,233.33	1,315.06	1,261.70
2011	1,252.35	1,328.18	1,301.52	1,349.44	1,298.41	1,279.32	1,297.76	1,288.34	1,298.41	1,202.69	1,157.01	1,240.15	1,275.26
2012	1,257.06	1,276.41	1,229.37	1,322.14	1,346.25	1,204.63	1,323.76	1,241.42	1,326.88	1,224.64	1,324.96	1,349.46	1,286.34
2013	1,261.17	1,268.78	1,311.38	1,303.14	1,299.78	1,216.38	1,372.03	1,288.74	1,343.41	1,386.46	1,264.64	1,369.73	1,309.18
Manufacturing													
2009	764.54	780.40	776.12	779.15	774.66	755.42	743.27	744.47	740.43	726.67	751.17	764.95	758.45
2010	739.15	754.65	756.50	764.99	775.80	773.29	787.52	804.52	783.69	777.00	774.71	820.42	775.40
2011	765.93	745.36	730.46	733.43	765.81	743.71	729.85	698.02	704.55	703.26	664.25	690.87	724.99
2012	683.74	682.11	699.66	703.14	736.41	708.64	734.85	755.86	757.56	728.05	714.35	740.89	720.90
2013	664.61	691.78	679.04	687.50	709.15	697.05	719.84	725.54	772.71	727.30	707.65	765.20	712.71
Trade, Transportation, and Utilities													
2009	595.14	612.72	611.06	612.81	603.20	621.09	613.36	630.81	642.74	632.91	644.10	621.23	620.71
2010	628.49	641.86	634.64	647.96	662.75	663.44	685.19	685.07	659.57	658.76	662.80	685.30	659.36
2011	710.42	670.41	662.32	665.97	692.23	663.58	692.13	666.56	672.18	692.52	679.32	691.55	679.40
2012	719.25	698.98	697.39	715.46	686.08	706.82	729.22	699.19	739.06	701.76	702.24	742.79	711.15
2013	728.45	732.65	740.93	742.43	745.80	778.13	749.62	751.50	781.57	751.37	747.16	777.24	751.74
Professional and Business Services													
2009	700.55	737.55	721.38	702.86	694.66	705.99	696.71	709.05	696.89	702.53	719.95	707.52	707.75
2010	713.07	721.58	744.58	733.50	779.19	761.12	763.62	799.60	786.57	805.30	806.39	796.02	768.70
2011	839.24	846.57	836.35	840.06	858.86	832.13	804.78	799.46	798.60	839.05	818.69	828.35	828.00
2012	867.51	883.64	889.50	931.72	947.65	943.97	842.06	869.84	925.01	893.92	898.61	838.01	893.45
2013	806.81	822.48	817.04	823.43	816.66	848.81	808.17	799.34	845.97	829.06	821.10	842.42	824.82
Education and Health Services													
2009	701.01	738.08	730.69	706.37	694.85	676.48	683.82	685.78	677.91	669.53	687.89	676.94	694.71
2010	660.49	656.10	647.85	656.64	660.33	646.20	646.30	664.96	669.83	663.30	666.11	690.54	660.84
2011	730.30	710.08	709.18	714.58	756.70	719.15	729.77	738.81	752.07	794.14	779.20	783.55	743.91
2012	817.70	797.59	824.33	839.66	828.29	841.41	883.76	863.61	885.78	878.46	870.84	912.72	852.44
2013	900.46	898.33	919.08	934.32	923.08	959.42	930.18	913.75	917.59	904.10	877.44	879.12	914.22
Leisure and Hospitality													
2009	513.08	530.41	514.67	504.38	489.60	513.38	502.68	509.17	505.68	489.39	508.98	505.74	507.49
2010	500.83	493.19	485.10	471.07	487.07	481.11	484.81	510.16	480.67	482.28	487.51	486.86	486.57
2011	501.30	488.52	484.36	489.17	498.60	484.88	499.55	499.94	492.02	501.60	462.69	455.25	488.33
2012	492.74	474.15	473.76	502.37	483.64	507.90	529.32	515.18	538.99	508.88	521.10	543.31	508.00
2013	533.98	537.24	535.43	536.61	525.98	552.33	533.36	529.25	540.60	512.87	523.45	548.78	533.66

IDAHO
At a Glance

Population:
    2000 census: 1,293,953
    2010 census: 1,567,582
    2013 estimate: 1,612,136

Percent change in population:
    2000–2010: 21.1%
    2010–2013: 2.8%

Percent change in total nonfarm employment:
    2000–2010: 7.9%
    2010–2013: 5.7%

Industry with the largest growth in employment, 2000–2013 (thousands):
    Education and Health Services, 38.2

Industry with the largest decline or smallest growth in employment, 2000–2013 (thousands):
    Manufacturing, -10.5

Civilian labor force:
    2000: 662,958
    2010: 760,951
    2013: 775,407

Unemployment rate and rank among states (lowest to highest):
    2000: 4.6%, 41st
    2010: 8.7%, 28th
    2013: 6.2%, 15th

Over-the-year change in unemployment rates:
    2010–2011: -0.3%
    2011–2012: -1.1%
    2012–2013: -1.1%

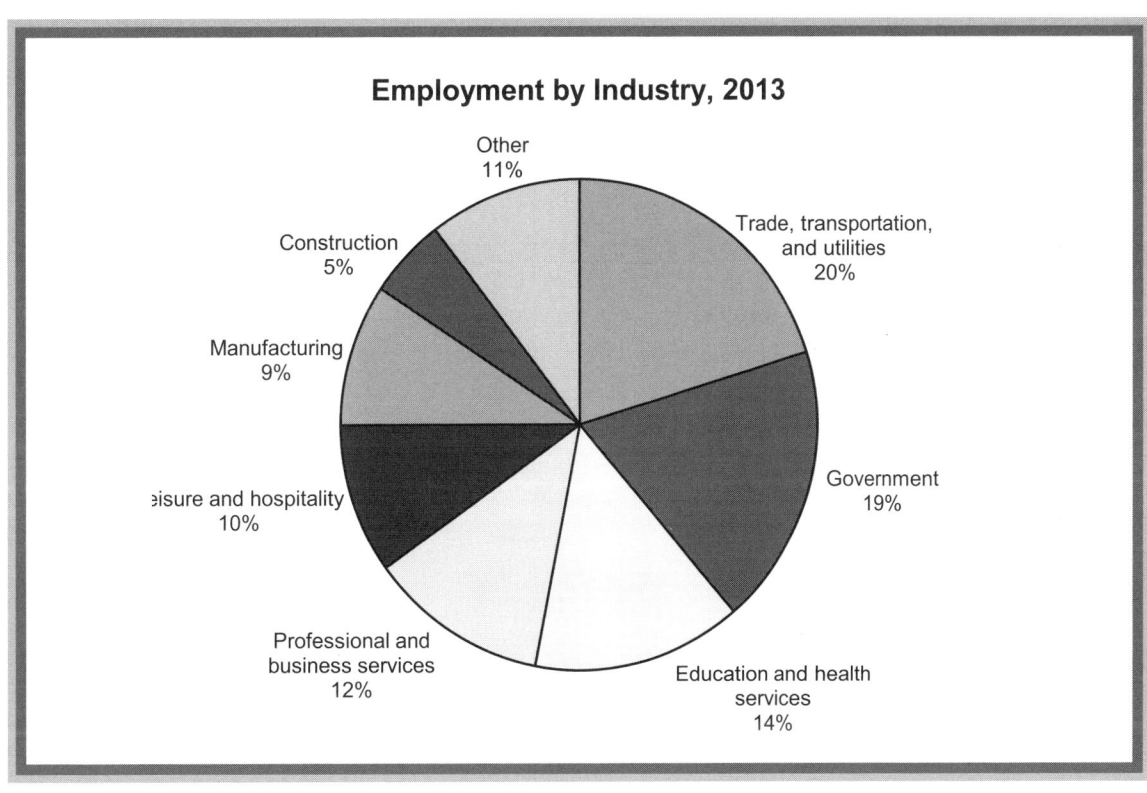

Employment by Industry, 2013

- Other 11%
- Trade, transportation, and utilities 20%
- Construction 5%
- Government 19%
- Manufacturing 9%
- Leisure and hospitality 10%
- Education and health services 14%
- Professional and business services 12%

1. Employment by Industry: Idaho, Selected Years, 2002–2013

(Numbers in thousands, not seasonally adjusted)

Industry and year	January	February	March	April	May	June	July	August	September	October	November	December	Annual average
Total Nonfarm													
2002	545.8	548.2	553.8	562.1	569.4	578.4	574.2	575.9	579.7	579.1	577.2	575.0	568.2
2003	555.3	556.5	561.2	564.8	571.5	580.4	574.9	578.2	583.1	581.0	578.6	578.2	572.0
2004	558.3	564.1	571.9	581.7	589.1	597.5	594.6	596.9	601.3	600.2	599.8	598.9	587.9
2005	581.5	588.5	594.4	603.2	609.5	617.9	617.5	621.1	628.4	624.0	624.6	625.0	611.3
2006	607.9	615.0	622.6	631.7	640.4	649.7	645.7	649.2	654.0	649.0	648.6	647.4	638.4
2007	628.2	635.5	642.3	649.8	659.6	668.7	661.6	665.3	666.9	661.6	661.3	658.3	654.9
2008	633.3	639.4	643.6	649.3	657.7	663.0	659.6	659.4	659.0	648.7	639.1	633.6	648.8
2009	606.7	605.5	604.1	607.8	612.8	618.1	610.9	611.0	614.2	612.9	608.7	605.5	609.9
2010	581.7	587.3	591.9	600.6	610.1	610.5	608.9	610.2	612.6	613.4	610.1	606.1	603.6
2011	585.9	592.6	595.2	605.8	612.6	616.1	616.8	618.3	624.0	621.9	621.1	618.9	610.8
2012	596.8	603.0	608.3	613.8	624.7	628.5	626.8	628.8	634.7	635.7	634.7	631.5	622.3
2013	612.5	620.1	626.1	634.6	644.0	648.3	645.5	646.3	649.9	650.0	643.6	638.7	638.3
Total Private													
2002	436.4	436.2	440.6	448.8	454.9	464.1	467.4	470.3	467.7	464.6	462.5	461.1	456.2
2003	444.7	443.9	447.1	451.5	456.0	465.3	467.1	471.4	469.2	465.1	463.2	463.6	459.0
2004	447.9	450.0	457.0	465.6	472.3	482.9	485.7	488.3	485.8	482.8	482.6	483.0	473.7
2005	469.4	472.6	477.8	486.4	492.1	501.8	508.4	512.3	511.7	505.9	506.8	508.5	496.1
2006	493.9	497.6	504.8	513.1	521.1	532.4	535.7	539.6	537.6	530.6	530.8	530.9	522.3
2007	515.1	518.7	525.1	531.6	540.4	550.8	551.0	553.5	547.8	542.1	542.3	539.6	538.2
2008	517.9	519.9	523.5	528.9	536.0	542.8	545.8	545.2	538.4	527.2	517.6	512.5	529.6
2009	489.0	485.9	483.0	484.3	489.9	496.2	498.4	498.1	495.6	491.5	487.7	487.5	490.4
2010	466.8	467.6	471.2	478.5	484.5	490.3	496.5	497.7	494.4	493.7	491.4	487.5	485.0
2011	472.8	473.9	476.0	485.8	491.4	498.9	505.7	507.1	506.4	502.7	502.3	500.1	493.6
2012	483.5	485.2	490.1	494.6	503.9	511.5	516.4	518.0	516.2	514.7	514.5	511.7	505.0
2013	496.9	500.3	506.0	514.1	522.2	529.4	534.7	535.7	531.5	527.5	521.9	518.1	519.9
Goods-Producing													
2002	100.0	98.8	99.6	101.8	105.5	108.8	110.5	111.0	110.0	109.2	107.8	105.7	105.7
2003	99.6	98.6	98.0	99.5	101.8	104.9	105.7	106.4	106.0	106.2	104.0	102.1	102.7
2004	97.9	97.9	99.8	103.1	105.5	108.8	110.4	111.4	110.4	110.6	109.1	107.7	106.1
2005	103.1	103.7	105.7	108.5	110.9	114.5	116.9	118.3	118.5	118.2	117.2	116.9	112.7
2006	112.4	113.5	115.9	118.8	122.4	127.1	128.1	128.4	127.8	126.0	124.5	122.6	123.3
2007	117.3	118.0	119.4	121.4	124.7	127.7	128.1	127.6	125.4	122.9	121.2	118.5	122.7
2008	111.6	110.2	110.7	112.0	114.6	116.7	117.2	116.5	114.8	111.8	106.5	102.9	112.1
2009	94.1	90.9	89.7	89.8	91.8	94.0	95.1	95.1	94.4	93.8	91.1	88.1	92.3
2010	83.3	82.6	83.4	85.4	87.6	89.9	91.3	92.2	91.6	91.6	89.7	86.2	87.9
2011	82.3	82.5	83.3	85.9	88.3	90.9	92.4	93.2	92.8	93.5	92.7	90.2	89.0
2012	86.4	86.2	86.9	88.6	91.8	94.6	96.0	96.6	95.8	96.4	95.4	93.9	92.4
2013	90.6	91.4	92.9	95.1	98.0	100.3	101.2	101.8	101.6	101.4	99.1	96.4	97.5
Service-Providing													
2002	445.8	449.4	454.2	460.3	463.9	469.6	463.7	464.9	469.7	469.9	469.4	469.3	462.5
2003	455.7	457.9	463.2	465.3	469.7	475.5	469.2	471.8	477.1	474.8	474.6	476.1	469.2
2004	460.4	466.2	472.1	478.6	483.6	488.7	484.2	485.5	490.9	489.6	490.7	491.2	481.8
2005	478.4	484.8	488.7	494.7	498.6	503.4	500.6	502.8	509.9	505.8	507.4	508.1	498.6
2006	495.5	501.5	506.7	512.9	518.0	522.6	517.6	520.8	526.2	523.0	524.1	524.8	516.1
2007	510.9	517.5	522.9	528.4	534.9	541.0	533.5	537.7	541.5	538.7	540.1	539.8	532.2
2008	521.7	529.2	532.9	537.3	543.1	546.3	542.4	542.9	544.2	536.9	532.6	530.7	536.7
2009	512.6	514.6	514.4	518.0	521.0	524.1	515.8	515.9	519.8	519.1	517.6	517.4	517.5
2010	498.4	504.7	508.5	515.2	522.5	520.6	517.6	518.0	521.0	521.8	520.4	519.9	515.7
2011	503.6	510.1	511.9	519.9	524.3	525.2	524.4	525.1	531.2	528.4	528.4	528.7	521.8
2012	510.4	516.8	521.4	525.2	532.9	533.9	530.8	532.2	538.9	539.3	539.3	537.6	529.9
2013	521.9	528.7	533.2	539.5	546.0	548.0	544.3	544.5	548.3	548.6	544.5	542.3	540.8
Mining and Logging													
2002	3.7	3.6	3.2	2.7	3.1	4.0	4.3	4.3	4.3	4.2	4.0	3.7	3.8
2003	3.5	3.2	2.9	2.7	3.1	3.7	4.1	4.2	4.2	4.1	3.9	3.6	3.6
2004	3.6	3.5	3.2	3.1	3.7	4.2	4.5	4.5	4.6	4.4	4.2	4.0	4.0
2005	3.8	3.6	3.5	3.4	3.8	4.3	4.5	4.7	4.7	4.6	4.3	4.2	4.1
2006	3.8	3.7	3.7	3.5	4.0	4.6	4.7	4.7	4.8	4.5	4.3	4.3	4.2
2007	4.0	4.0	3.8	3.6	4.3	4.8	4.9	5.0	4.9	4.7	4.6	4.4	4.4
2008	4.1	4.1	3.7	3.5	4.0	4.5	4.8	4.8	4.6	4.4	4.1	3.9	4.2
2009	3.4	3.2	2.7	2.5	2.7	3.2	3.6	3.7	3.7	3.6	3.4	3.2	3.2
2010	3.0	2.9	2.8	2.8	3.2	3.7	3.9	4.1	4.1	4.1	3.8	3.5	3.5
2011	3.4	3.4	3.3	3.1	3.3	3.9	4.3	4.4	4.4	4.4	4.3	4.1	3.9
2012	3.9	3.8	3.4	3.2	3.7	4.3	4.5	4.5	4.4	4.2	4.0	4.0	4.0
2013	3.8	3.7	3.6	3.5	3.9	4.2	4.4	4.4	4.3	4.3	4.1	4.0	4.0
Construction													
2002	31.5	31.0	31.9	34.4	37.3	38.6	40.0	40.1	39.4	39.0	38.0	36.8	36.5
2003	32.3	32.0	32.7	34.5	36.7	38.4	39.6	40.2	39.8	39.6	38.4	37.1	36.8
2004	33.6	33.5	35.4	38.3	40.1	41.8	43.0	43.7	43.0	42.8	42.1	41.1	39.9
2005	37.7	38.2	40.0	42.8	44.3	46.9	48.4	49.1	49.0	48.3	48.5	47.2	45.0
2006	44.4	45.4	47.4	50.1	52.8	55.9	56.2	56.5	55.6	54.3	53.5	51.4	52.0
2007	47.4	47.8	49.4	51.4	53.6	55.6	55.8	56.1	54.4	52.5	51.0	48.9	52.0
2008	43.3	42.1	43.2	44.8	46.9	48.2	48.5	48.2	47.1	45.0	42.2	39.8	44.9
2009	33.7	31.9	31.8	32.8	34.6	36.0	36.8	36.9	36.3	35.5	33.9	31.7	34.3
2010	28.1	27.6	28.6	30.2	31.8	32.9	33.9	34.2	33.7	32.9	31.8	29.4	31.3
2011	25.7	25.6	26.2	28.5	30.3	32.1	33.2	33.5	32.9	32.9	32.7	30.8	30.4
2012	27.5	27.3	28.0	29.4	31.3	32.8	33.9	34.2	33.8	33.8	32.9	31.8	31.4
2013	28.8	29.4	30.5	32.3	34.1	35.6	36.4	36.8	36.7	36.3	34.9	32.6	33.7

1. Employment by Industry: Idaho, Selected Years, 2002–2013—*Continued*

(Numbers in thousands, not seasonally adjusted)

Industry and year	January	February	March	April	May	June	July	August	September	October	November	December	Annual average
Manufacturing													
2002	64.8	64.2	64.5	64.7	65.1	66.2	66.2	66.6	66.3	66.0	65.8	65.2	65.5
2003	63.8	63.4	62.4	62.3	62.0	62.8	62.0	62.0	62.0	62.5	61.7	61.4	62.4
2004	60.7	60.9	61.2	61.7	61.7	62.8	62.9	63.2	62.8	63.4	62.8	62.6	62.2
2005	61.6	61.9	62.2	62.3	62.8	63.3	64.0	64.5	64.8	65.3	64.4	65.5	63.6
2006	64.2	64.4	64.8	65.2	65.6	66.6	67.2	67.2	67.4	67.2	66.7	66.9	66.1
2007	65.9	66.2	66.2	66.4	66.8	67.3	67.4	66.5	66.1	65.7	65.6	65.2	66.3
2008	64.2	64.0	63.8	63.7	63.7	64.0	63.9	63.5	63.1	62.4	60.2	59.2	63.0
2009	57.0	55.8	55.2	54.5	54.5	54.8	54.7	54.5	54.4	54.7	53.8	53.2	54.8
2010	52.2	52.1	52.0	52.4	52.6	53.3	53.5	53.9	53.8	54.6	54.1	53.3	53.2
2011	53.2	53.5	53.8	54.3	54.7	54.9	54.9	55.3	55.5	56.2	55.7	55.3	54.8
2012	55.0	55.1	55.5	56.0	56.8	57.5	57.6	57.9	57.6	58.4	58.5	58.1	57.0
2013	58.0	58.3	58.8	59.3	60.0	60.5	60.4	60.6	60.6	60.8	60.1	59.8	59.8
Trade, Transportation, and Utilities													
2002	113.7	112.8	113.5	114.8	116.0	116.8	116.6	117.1	117.2	116.9	118.6	119.1	116.1
2003	114.0	113.2	114.1	114.5	115.2	116.3	116.4	117.2	117.2	116.9	118.7	119.5	116.1
2004	114.1	113.7	114.9	116.6	118.1	119.1	119.5	119.5	119.3	119.9	121.8	122.9	118.3
2005	118.4	118.4	119.6	121.0	122.0	123.4	124.5	125.2	125.5	125.2	127.4	128.5	123.3
2006	123.6	123.3	124.4	126.0	127.3	129.0	128.8	129.8	130.2	130.3	132.6	133.6	128.2
2007	129.5	129.3	130.8	131.4	132.4	133.6	133.7	134.2	133.8	134.2	136.6	136.9	133.0
2008	131.4	130.6	131.1	131.6	132.6	133.3	133.9	133.7	132.3	131.6	132.0	131.8	132.2
2009	124.1	122.6	122.2	122.0	123.0	123.1	123.0	123.1	122.8	122.5	123.6	123.3	122.9
2010	119.1	118.0	118.6	120.0	121.2	121.8	122.5	123.5	122.2	122.9	124.2	124.3	121.5
2011	119.2	118.6	119.2	121.1	122.1	122.4	124.2	124.9	125.2	125.3	127.3	127.4	123.1
2012	123.1	122.3	123.4	123.8	125.6	126.5	127.6	127.9	128.0	128.6	130.4	130.2	126.5
2013	125.3	125.1	125.8	127.5	128.7	129.3	130.7	131.2	130.8	131.1	132.5	132.4	129.2
Wholesale Trade													
2002	23.9	24.1	24.3	24.5	24.7	24.8	24.6	24.4	24.7	24.5	24.7	24.4	24.5
2003	23.8	23.9	23.9	24.4	24.5	24.5	24.6	24.4	24.6	24.0	24.2	24.3	24.3
2004	23.8	24.0	24.4	24.7	24.9	25.1	25.4	25.4	25.5	25.4	25.5	25.4	25.0
2005	25.7	25.9	26.4	26.6	26.6	26.6	26.8	26.7	27.0	26.7	26.8	26.8	26.6
2006	26.1	26.4	26.7	27.0	27.1	27.3	27.1	27.1	27.3	27.1	27.4	27.4	27.0
2007	27.2	27.5	27.7	27.8	28.0	28.3	28.3	28.3	28.4	28.1	28.1	28.1	28.0
2008	27.6	27.7	27.9	27.8	28.0	28.1	28.3	28.0	28.1	27.8	27.5	27.3	27.8
2009	26.4	26.3	26.3	26.1	26.1	26.1	26.2	25.7	25.9	25.7	25.6	25.4	26.0
2010	25.2	25.2	25.5	25.9	26.1	26.2	26.5	26.5	26.2	26.4	26.2	26.1	26.0
2011	25.6	25.7	26.0	26.5	26.7	26.6	27.2	27.1	27.2	27.3	27.2	27.1	26.7
2012	26.7	26.9	27.4	27.6	27.9	27.9	28.5	28.1	28.2	28.4	28.1	28.1	27.8
2013	27.9	28.2	28.4	28.7	28.7	28.8	29.5	28.8	29.0	28.6	28.6	28.7	28.7
Retail Trade													
2002	70.9	69.7	70.3	71.3	72.2	72.7	72.9	73.1	72.8	72.5	74.2	75.0	72.3
2003	70.8	70.1	70.9	71.2	71.8	72.6	72.5	73.2	72.9	73.1	74.8	75.4	72.4
2004	71.0	70.5	71.1	72.5	73.7	74.2	74.4	74.4	74.0	74.6	76.4	77.4	73.7
2005	73.4	73.0	73.8	74.9	75.9	76.9	77.5	78.1	78.0	77.9	80.0	80.8	76.7
2006	77.3	76.6	77.5	78.5	79.7	80.7	80.9	81.6	81.7	82.0	83.9	84.5	80.4
2007	81.1	80.6	82.1	82.4	83.1	83.7	84.0	84.1	83.5	83.9	86.3	86.5	83.4
2008	82.4	81.5	82.0	82.4	83.1	83.4	83.8	83.6	82.2	81.7	82.6	82.4	82.6
2009	76.5	75.4	75.5	75.5	76.5	76.8	76.8	76.8	76.0	75.6	76.9	76.9	76.3
2010	73.4	72.4	73.1	74.0	74.9	75.2	75.5	76.0	74.9	75.3	76.7	76.6	74.8
2011	72.8	72.1	72.4	73.7	74.7	75.1	76.0	76.3	76.2	76.4	78.5	78.3	75.2
2012	75.0	74.2	74.8	75.3	76.7	77.5	78.0	78.0	77.7	78.1	80.3	79.9	77.1
2013	75.9	75.4	75.9	77.6	78.8	79.4	80.1	80.6	79.9	80.2	81.8	81.4	78.9
Transportation and Utilities													
2002	18.9	19.0	18.9	19.0	19.1	19.3	19.1	19.6	19.7	19.9	19.7	19.7	19.3
2003	19.4	19.2	19.3	18.9	18.9	19.2	19.3	19.6	19.7	19.8	19.7	19.8	19.4
2004	19.3	19.2	19.4	19.4	19.5	19.8	19.7	19.7	19.8	19.9	19.9	20.1	19.6
2005	19.3	19.5	19.4	19.5	19.5	19.9	20.2	20.4	20.5	20.6	20.6	20.9	20.0
2006	20.2	20.3	20.2	20.5	20.5	21.0	20.8	21.1	21.2	21.2	21.3	21.7	20.8
2007	21.2	21.2	21.0	21.2	21.3	21.6	21.4	21.8	21.9	22.2	22.2	22.3	21.6
2008	21.4	21.4	21.2	21.4	21.5	21.8	21.8	22.1	22.0	22.1	21.9	22.1	21.7
2009	21.2	20.9	20.4	20.4	20.4	20.2	20.0	20.6	20.9	21.2	21.1	21.0	20.7
2010	20.5	20.4	20.0	20.1	20.2	20.4	20.5	21.0	21.1	21.2	21.3	21.6	20.7
2011	20.8	20.8	20.8	20.9	20.7	20.7	21.0	21.5	21.8	21.6	21.6	22.0	21.2
2012	21.4	21.2	21.2	20.9	21.0	21.1	21.1	21.8	22.1	22.1	22.0	22.2	21.5
2013	21.5	21.5	21.5	21.2	21.2	21.1	21.1	21.8	21.9	22.3	22.1	22.3	21.6
Information													
2002	9.2	9.1	9.1	9.2	9.3	9.3	9.1	9.1	9.1	9.1	9.3	9.3	9.2
2003	9.1	9.1	9.1	9.2	9.2	9.2	9.1	9.1	9.1	9.1	9.3	9.3	9.2
2004	9.2	9.2	9.3	9.4	9.7	10.0	10.0	10.1	9.9	9.9	9.9	9.9	9.7
2005	10.0	10.1	10.1	10.3	10.4	10.4	10.5	10.3	10.3	10.5	10.4	10.6	10.3
2006	10.3	10.3	10.3	10.5	10.6	10.8	10.8	10.8	10.7	10.6	10.7	10.8	10.6
2007	10.6	10.6	10.7	10.8	10.9	11.0	10.9	11.0	10.8	10.9	11.0	11.0	10.9
2008	11.0	11.1	11.3	10.9	11.1	11.1	11.2	11.5	11.1	10.7	10.7	10.6	11.0
2009	10.4	10.5	10.3	10.0	10.0	10.1	10.0	9.8	9.7	9.7	9.8	9.8	10.0
2010	9.8	9.7	9.7	9.6	9.7	9.7	9.7	9.7	9.5	9.4	9.5	9.5	9.6
2011	9.4	9.3	9.3	9.5	9.6	9.6	9.6	9.6	9.4	9.4	9.4	9.5	9.5
2012	9.4	9.4	9.4	9.3	9.4	9.4	9.5	9.5	9.2	9.3	9.3	9.3	9.4
2013	9.1	9.1	9.3	9.4	9.5	9.5	9.5	9.5	9.3	9.2	9.2	9.3	9.3

1. Employment by Industry: Idaho, Selected Years, 2002–2013—*Continued*

(Numbers in thousands, not seasonally adjusted)

Industry and year	January	February	March	April	May	June	July	August	September	October	November	December	Annual average
Financial Activities													
2002	25.1	25.2	25.3	25.3	25.7	25.8	26.3	26.3	26.1	26.1	26.2	26.4	25.8
2003	26.1	26.1	26.3	26.5	26.8	27.2	27.5	27.6	27.4	27.4	27.3	27.6	27.0
2004	26.9	27.0	27.4	27.6	27.7	28.0	28.3	28.3	28.4	28.5	28.5	28.8	28.0
2005	28.3	28.5	28.4	28.8	29.1	29.6	30.2	30.4	30.5	30.5	30.7	30.8	29.7
2006	30.5	30.7	31.1	31.4	31.6	31.9	32.2	32.4	32.3	32.0	32.0	32.3	31.7
2007	31.8	31.9	32.0	32.3	32.7	32.7	33.0	32.8	32.4	32.3	32.5	32.4	32.4
2008	31.6	31.6	31.6	31.8	31.9	32.1	32.2	32.0	31.8	31.3	30.9	31.1	31.7
2009	30.1	30.0	29.8	29.8	29.7	29.7	29.7	29.5	29.2	29.3	29.2	29.4	29.6
2010	28.7	28.6	28.7	28.9	29.1	29.2	29.7	29.5	29.2	29.4	29.4	29.6	29.2
2011	29.2	29.2	29.2	29.5	29.7	29.9	30.4	30.3	30.3	30.2	30.2	30.3	29.9
2012	29.5	29.5	29.6	30.1	30.3	30.5	30.8	30.8	30.5	30.7	30.7	30.9	30.3
2013	30.4	30.6	30.7	31.0	31.3	31.4	31.7	31.9	31.5	31.2	30.5	30.2	31.0
Professional and Business Services													
2002	63.0	63.8	64.8	67.8	68.4	70.1	70.1	71.2	70.5	71.0	70.1	69.2	68.3
2003	65.5	66.3	67.5	68.6	69.2	70.8	70.0	71.4	71.2	70.2	69.8	69.6	69.2
2004	66.4	67.4	69.1	71.3	72.8	74.7	74.6	75.4	75.0	74.4	74.2	74.1	72.5
2005	70.8	72.6	73.8	76.3	77.3	78.4	79.1	80.0	79.9	78.2	78.6	78.1	76.9
2006	75.3	76.6	78.1	80.2	81.9	83.2	82.6	83.6	83.1	81.2	81.2	80.3	80.6
2007	76.8	78.1	79.5	82.2	83.5	85.3	84.5	85.7	85.1	83.9	83.2	82.4	82.5
2008	76.4	78.0	78.8	81.7	82.7	83.3	83.3	84.0	82.5	80.4	78.3	77.3	80.6
2009	73.8	73.5	72.8	73.7	74.5	75.3	75.4	75.9	76.0	75.5	74.9	74.6	74.7
2010	70.0	70.4	71.4	73.3	74.1	74.3	75.6	76.2	75.4	76.0	75.8	75.0	74.0
2011	72.2	72.3	72.6	74.2	74.8	75.9	76.9	77.8	77.5	76.5	76.0	75.1	75.2
2012	71.2	71.8	73.3	74.1	75.2	76.6	77.0	78.1	77.4	77.2	77.7	75.9	75.5
2013	72.6	73.3	74.9	76.0	77.6	79.2	79.3	80.3	79.4	78.0	77.0	76.0	77.0
Education and Health Services													
2002	58.6	58.9	59.4	59.8	58.9	59.1	59.0	59.1	60.4	60.8	61.3	61.6	59.7
2003	61.3	61.4	61.7	62.3	61.6	61.8	61.6	61.8	63.2	63.4	64.0	64.1	62.4
2004	63.2	64.0	64.6	65.2	64.4	65.0	64.4	64.6	66.3	67.0	67.6	67.3	65.3
2005	66.9	67.5	67.4	67.8	67.0	67.1	66.6	67.1	68.4	68.3	68.6	68.6	67.6
2006	67.8	68.5	69.2	69.2	68.8	68.8	69.9	70.4	71.8	72.1	72.7	72.7	70.2
2007	71.7	72.5	72.8	72.9	73.3	73.8	73.3	73.8	74.4	75.8	76.7	76.7	74.0
2008	75.9	77.0	77.5	77.5	77.3	77.5	77.6	76.3	78.0	79.2	79.3	79.6	77.7
2009	78.7	80.2	80.2	80.7	80.6	80.8	80.5	79.6	81.6	82.8	83.0	83.2	81.0
2010	80.9	83.0	83.5	83.8	84.0	83.6	83.6	81.9	84.3	85.7	85.9	85.7	83.8
2011	85.4	86.2	86.2	86.6	86.9	86.9	85.9	84.4	86.7	87.6	87.6	88.1	86.5
2012	86.8	87.7	88.1	88.1	88.7	88.4	87.5	86.3	88.8	89.8	89.9	90.1	88.4
2013	88.9	90.3	90.6	91.5	91.4	90.6	91.0	89.6	90.3	92.6	92.3	92.7	91.0
Leisure and Hospitality													
2002	49.5	50.0	50.8	52.1	53.1	56.0	57.2	57.8	56.3	53.4	51.2	51.9	53.3
2003	51.4	51.4	52.4	52.8	54.1	56.8	58.3	59.2	56.9	53.9	52.1	53.4	54.4
2004	52.5	53.0	53.8	54.0	55.7	58.7	59.6	60.1	58.2	54.4	53.4	54.2	55.6
2005	54.0	53.7	54.7	55.4	57.0	59.8	61.5	62.0	60.1	56.5	55.4	56.6	57.2
2006	55.7	56.2	57.2	58.2	59.6	62.3	63.6	64.5	62.5	59.4	58.2	59.6	59.8
2007	58.7	59.4	60.7	61.3	63.4	66.9	67.6	68.3	66.3	62.7	61.8	62.3	63.3
2008	60.5	61.3	61.9	62.1	64.3	66.8	68.2	68.9	66.1	61.2	59.1	58.4	63.2
2009	56.7	56.9	56.8	57.1	58.9	61.5	63.0	63.3	60.8	57.3	55.6	56.1	58.7
2010	54.2	54.3	54.9	56.6	57.8	60.6	62.3	63.2	61.2	57.8	56.1	56.5	58.0
2011	54.6	55.2	55.7	58.0	58.8	61.9	64.3	65.2	63.1	59.0	57.8	58.1	59.3
2012	56.1	57.2	58.2	59.4	61.4	63.7	65.8	66.7	64.8	61.0	59.7	60.0	61.2
2013	58.8	59.1	60.3	61.9	63.7	66.7	68.5	68.5	66.1	62.5	60.1	59.9	63.0
Other Services													
2002	17.3	17.6	18.1	18.0	18.0	18.2	18.6	18.7	18.1	18.1	18.0	17.9	18.1
2003	17.7	17.8	18.0	18.1	18.1	18.3	18.5	18.7	18.2	18.0	18.0	18.0	18.1
2004	17.7	17.8	18.1	18.4	18.4	18.6	18.9	18.9	18.3	18.1	18.1	18.1	18.3
2005	17.9	18.1	18.1	18.3	18.4	18.6	19.1	19.0	18.5	18.5	18.5	18.4	18.5
2006	18.3	18.5	18.6	18.8	18.9	19.3	19.7	19.7	19.2	19.0	18.9	19.0	19.0
2007	18.7	18.9	19.2	19.3	19.5	19.8	19.9	20.1	19.6	19.4	19.3	19.4	19.4
2008	19.5	20.1	20.6	21.3	21.5	22.0	22.2	22.3	21.8	21.0	20.8	20.8	21.2
2009	21.1	21.3	21.2	21.2	21.4	21.7	21.7	21.8	21.1	20.6	20.5	20.5	21.2
2010	20.8	21.0	21.0	20.9	21.0	21.2	21.8	21.5	21.0	20.9	20.8	20.7	21.1
2011	20.5	20.6	20.5	21.0	21.2	21.4	22.0	21.7	21.4	21.2	21.3	21.4	21.2
2012	21.0	21.1	21.2	21.2	21.5	21.8	22.2	22.1	21.7	21.7	21.4	21.4	21.5
2013	21.2	21.4	21.5	21.7	22.0	22.4	22.8	22.9	22.5	21.5	21.2	21.2	21.9
Government													
2002	109.4	112.0	113.2	113.3	114.5	114.3	106.8	105.6	112.0	114.5	114.7	113.9	112.0
2003	110.6	112.6	114.1	113.3	115.5	115.1	107.8	106.8	113.9	115.9	115.4	114.6	113.0
2004	110.4	114.1	114.9	116.1	116.8	114.6	108.9	108.6	115.5	117.4	117.2	115.9	114.2
2005	112.1	115.9	116.6	116.8	117.4	116.1	109.1	108.8	116.7	118.1	117.8	116.5	115.2
2006	114.0	117.4	117.8	118.6	119.3	117.3	110.0	109.6	116.4	118.4	117.8	116.5	116.1
2007	113.1	116.8	117.2	118.2	119.2	117.9	110.6	111.8	119.1	119.5	119.0	118.7	116.8
2008	115.4	119.5	120.1	120.4	121.7	120.2	113.8	114.2	120.6	121.5	121.5	121.1	119.2
2009	117.7	119.6	121.1	123.5	122.9	121.9	112.5	112.9	118.6	121.4	121.0	120.5	119.5
2010	114.9	119.7	120.7	122.1	125.6	120.2	112.4	112.5	118.2	119.7	118.7	118.6	118.6
2011	113.1	118.7	119.2	120.0	121.2	117.2	111.1	111.2	117.6	119.2	118.8	118.8	117.2
2012	113.3	117.8	118.2	119.2	120.8	117.0	110.4	110.8	118.5	121.0	120.2	119.8	117.3
2013	115.6	119.8	120.1	120.5	121.8	118.9	110.8	110.6	118.4	122.5	121.7	120.6	118.4

2. Average Weekly Hours by Selected Industry: Idaho, 2009–2013

(Not seasonally adjusted)

Industry and year	January	February	March	April	May	June	July	August	September	October	November	December	Annual average
Total Private													
2009	32.7	33.3	33.3	33.1	33.4	33.3	33.9	35.0	33.7	33.9	34.2	33.2	33.6
2010	33.2	33.1	33.0	33.3	33.4	33.2	33.6	34.4	33.6	33.6	33.5	33.6	33.5
2011	34.1	33.3	33.0	33.7	34.2	34.1	34.0	33.9	33.7	34.6	33.8	33.8	33.9
2012	33.9	33.3	33.0	34.0	33.1	33.6	34.0	33.7	34.2	33.4	32.9	33.8	33.6
2013	32.3	32.9	33.2	33.2	33.4	34.3	33.7	33.8	34.0	33.5	33.3	33.5	33.4
Goods-Producing													
2009	34.4	35.2	35.3	35.0	36.1	36.2	37.1	38.2	36.9	38.0	37.7	35.7	36.3
2010	35.3	36.1	36.7	36.0	36.3	36.7	37.0	38.5	38.3	38.2	38.4	39.8	37.3
2011	40.9	40.0	39.8	40.3	40.4	40.3	39.6	40.1	39.8	40.4	39.2	39.7	40.0
2012	39.7	38.9	38.2	39.3	38.8	39.3	39.1	39.2	39.6	38.7	37.6	38.5	38.9
2013	37.1	37.6	37.9	38.2	38.8	39.4	39.2	39.7	39.8	39.6	38.7	37.8	38.7
Construction													
2009	29.9	30.7	31.4	31.3	33.4	33.7	35.1	37.1	33.6	34.7	33.4	33.9	33.3
2010	31.9	33.0	35.4	34.5	33.2	34.8	35.7	36.8	36.4	36.5	36.9	35.0	35.0
2011	34.4	34.0	33.9	36.0	35.2	36.7	35.6	37.5	36.9	38.3	35.3	35.9	35.9
2012	34.3	33.9	31.2	33.7	35.2	37.6	37.5	37.2	37.0	36.5	33.4	33.8	35.2
2013	31.7	33.0	32.8	33.9	35.5	36.8	35.4	36.8	36.5	37.1	34.9	31.9	34.8
Manufacturing													
2009	36.3	37.3	37.0	36.7	37.0	37.2	37.6	38.1	38.0	39.1	39.7	38.2	37.7
2010	38.3	38.3	38.9	39.0	39.3	38.4	38.6	40.0	39.9	39.5	39.4	38.8	39.1
2011	40.6	39.5	39.6	39.9	40.6	40.0	39.4	39.3	39.4	40.0	39.4	40.0	39.8
2012	40.6	39.8	39.7	40.6	39.4	39.4	39.1	39.3	40.2	39.1	39.0	40.1	39.7
2013	38.9	39.4	40.0	40.0	40.1	40.4	40.6	40.8	41.1	40.9	40.7	40.3	40.3
Trade, Transportation, and Utilities													
2009	34.1	34.4	34.0	34.2	34.4	34.8	34.8	35.1	33.6	33.5	34.4	33.1	34.2
2010	32.9	32.7	31.7	32.7	33.6	33.5	33.9	34.8	34.0	33.9	33.9	34.0	33.5
2011	34.0	33.2	33.4	34.5	34.6	35.1	34.9	34.6	34.5	35.1	34.6	34.7	34.4
2012	33.6	33.8	33.7	34.2	33.6	34.3	34.4	34.3	34.0	34.2	34.0	34.6	34.1
2013	32.9	33.9	34.4	34.1	34.4	34.8	34.5	34.0	33.8	33.8	33.0	32.7	33.9
Financial Activities													
2009	37.2	37.4	37.2	36.5	36.1	35.9	36.7	38.1	37.0	37.0	38.0	36.5	36.9
2010	37.8	36.9	36.2	35.7	36.6	35.9	35.9	37.4	36.1	35.4	35.7	35.3	36.2
2011	36.5	36.3	35.7	36.2	37.1	36.3	36.4	36.5	36.5	37.6	36.1	35.9	36.4
2012	38.5	35.9	35.9	37.6	33.8	34.2	35.5	34.8	36.2	34.3	34.9	36.1	35.6
2013	34.3	35.1	34.9	35.1	34.8	36.6	34.8	35.4	37.1	35.0	36.2	38.0	35.6
Professional and Business Services													
2009	33.5	34.3	34.4	34.3	34.7	34.5	34.5	34.6	34.4	33.3	34.3	33.3	34.2
2010	33.8	33.3	34.0	34.6	33.3	33.1	33.7	34.4	33.9	33.8	34.0	33.7	33.8
2011	33.3	33.8	33.5	34.6	35.0	35.1	34.7	34.4	34.7	35.2	34.4	34.0	34.4
2012	33.5	33.8	33.3	34.7	35.0	35.3	36.2	35.5	37.1	35.4	34.0	35.2	34.9
2013	33.7	34.2	34.9	34.1	34.6	35.6	34.6	35.0	35.3	34.4	34.3	35.4	34.7
Education and Health Services													
2009	31.1	31.4	31.6	31.4	31.7	31.3	33.3	33.5	32.0	33.0	33.4	33.9	32.3
2010	34.3	33.4	33.0	33.2	33.3	32.9	32.4	32.5	31.9	32.6	32.2	32.0	32.8
2011	32.8	32.0	31.5	32.0	32.5	32.1	32.0	31.4	31.3	32.3	32.1	32.0	32.0
2012	32.4	31.9	31.5	32.3	31.5	31.3	31.7	31.6	32.6	31.6	31.6	32.2	31.8
2013	30.8	31.3	31.2	31.4	31.2	31.8	31.0	30.6	31.4	30.7	31.1	31.5	31.2
Leisure and Hospitality													
2009	23.8	25.7	25.6	24.2	25.2	23.9	24.5	25.4	23.2	22.8	21.5	21.5	24.0
2010	21.3	22.1	21.8	21.8	23.7	22.9	23.6	25.1	22.7	22.5	21.8	21.5	22.6
2011	22.1	21.6	21.0	21.2	22.4	21.8	23.1	23.0	22.0	23.6	22.3	21.9	22.2
2012	22.5	21.9	22.0	22.8	22.3	23.7	24.8	24.3	23.5	22.7	22.0	23.2	23.0
2013	21.8	22.9	23.5	23.6	23.3	25.8	25.8	26.1	26.2	24.7	24.4	25.6	24.5

3. Average Hourly Earnings by Selected Industry: Idaho, 2009–2013

(Dollars, not seasonally adjusted)

Industry and year	January	February	March	April	May	June	July	August	September	October	November	December	Annual average
Total Private													
2009	18.38	18.88	19.04	19.02	19.03	19.07	19.23	19.26	19.52	19.70	19.95	19.96	19.26
2010	20.38	20.68	20.99	20.92	20.98	20.76	22.05	21.09	20.97	21.07	21.17	21.26	21.03
2011	21.09	21.16	21.03	20.79	20.64	20.43	20.79	20.50	20.81	20.81	20.70	20.76	20.79
2012	20.81	21.10	20.96	21.18	21.01	20.94	20.94	20.85	21.17	21.09	21.10	21.27	21.04
2013	21.46	21.40	21.28	21.24	21.09	21.00	20.91	20.94	21.20	21.15	21.26	21.55	21.20
Goods-Producing													
2009	22.34	22.65	22.90	23.07	22.44	22.29	22.59	22.54	22.88	22.75	22.90	22.98	22.69
2010	23.47	24.14	24.28	24.12	24.10	23.87	24.20	24.05	24.14	24.38	24.30	23.82	24.08
2011	23.48	23.64	23.74	23.53	23.16	23.14	23.15	23.28	23.54	23.42	23.43	23.78	23.44
2012	23.81	23.75	23.79	23.93	24.17	23.95	24.20	23.87	24.19	23.78	24.03	23.97	23.96
2013	24.53	24.23	23.83	23.64	23.59	23.51	23.64	23.70	23.86	23.49	23.85	24.32	23.83
Construction													
2009	18.36	19.13	19.56	19.25	18.47	18.64	18.68	19.08	19.28	19.46	19.44	19.81	19.09
2010	19.12	20.20	20.61	20.87	21.17	21.08	21.18	21.50	21.97	21.53	21.47	22.05	21.12
2011	21.64	21.46	21.55	21.82	20.96	21.22	20.92	21.29	21.45	21.28	20.76	21.85	21.33
2012	21.68	21.13	21.12	21.02	21.41	20.65	20.88	20.46	20.53	19.77	20.26	20.13	20.71
2013	20.82	20.73	20.67	20.32	20.20	20.17	20.35	20.52	20.49	20.10	20.25	21.32	20.47
Manufacturing													
2009	23.20	23.58	23.62	24.10	24.07	23.85	24.31	24.17	24.43	23.99	24.24	24.20	23.98
2010	24.89	25.26	25.17	24.99	25.11	24.93	25.60	25.21	25.22	25.21	25.15	25.66	25.20
2011	25.16	25.13	25.19	24.91	24.50	24.42	24.64	24.65	24.89	24.71	24.79	24.79	24.81
2012	24.75	24.63	24.64	24.66	24.85	24.93	25.28	25.04	25.31	24.98	25.05	24.89	24.92
2013	25.30	24.99	24.64	24.56	24.52	24.56	24.68	24.73	24.99	24.62	24.99	25.09	24.80
Trade, Transportation, and Utilities													
2009	17.05	17.25	17.44	17.03	17.40	17.34	17.50	17.55	17.70	17.58	17.61	17.53	17.41
2010	17.76	18.20	17.81	17.69	17.75	17.70	17.71	17.81	17.61	17.70	17.52	17.45	17.72
2011	17.65	17.61	17.64	17.63	17.48	17.18	17.67	17.19	17.38	17.60	17.20	17.23	17.45
2012	17.79	17.42	17.48	17.65	17.38	17.36	17.45	17.69	18.00	17.37	17.36	17.38	17.53
2013	17.42	17.48	17.64	17.68	17.69	17.71	17.52	17.88	17.73	17.79	17.73	18.17	17.70
Financial Activities													
2009	20.41	20.28	20.30	20.85	20.56	20.81	21.56	21.97	21.06	21.41	21.01	21.01	20.94
2010	21.58	21.56	21.95	21.46	21.89	21.28	21.47	21.76	21.41	21.23	21.68	22.30	21.63
2011	20.78	20.31	20.60	20.41	20.84	20.39	20.73	20.26	20.77	20.87	20.78	20.62	20.62
2012	19.37	20.48	19.91	20.51	20.50	20.64	20.63	20.46	20.57	20.76	20.84	21.32	20.50
2013	21.02	21.32	21.14	20.97	21.04	21.04	20.95	20.83	20.48	20.34	20.70	21.22	20.92
Professional and Business Services													
2009	22.10	22.93	23.32	23.64	23.77	24.22	24.40	25.19	25.28	25.85	26.48	26.53	24.48
2010	27.09	27.21	28.15	28.23	28.31	27.80	32.07	27.93	27.21	27.23	27.32	27.58	28.02
2011	28.12	28.33	27.77	27.11	26.74	26.43	27.10	27.18	28.18	27.80	27.97	27.54	27.51
2012	27.65	28.43	28.06	28.00	27.87	27.71	27.49	26.95	26.94	27.31	27.09	26.98	27.52
2013	27.25	27.24	27.25	26.96	26.43	26.62	26.98	26.60	27.39	27.63	27.09	27.27	27.05
Education and Health Services													
2009	17.48	18.45	18.58	18.62	18.39	17.67	17.15	16.48	17.10	17.36	17.94	17.78	17.74
2010	18.44	18.22	18.44	18.57	19.55	19.37	19.45	20.31	20.47	20.28	20.61	20.73	19.53
2011	20.38	20.72	20.31	19.83	19.86	19.98	20.26	19.48	19.94	19.83	19.88	20.22	20.06
2012	19.92	20.27	20.31	20.91	20.31	20.68	20.69	20.51	20.71	21.02	21.04	20.93	20.61
2013	21.41	21.24	21.21	21.13	20.94	21.23	21.17	21.07	21.35	21.08	21.48	21.56	21.24
Leisure and Hospitality													
2009	10.11	10.38	10.36	10.39	10.65	10.42	10.23	10.33	10.18	10.53	10.69	10.66	10.40
2010	10.72	10.54	10.71	10.80	11.00	10.91	11.03	11.50	11.38	11.18	11.55	11.52	11.08
2011	11.37	11.41	11.47	11.38	11.46	11.07	11.48	11.43	11.44	11.53	11.61	11.77	11.45
2012	11.99	11.97	11.88	11.73	11.62	11.29	11.33	11.41	11.63	11.64	11.75	11.57	11.63
2013	11.44	11.46	11.51	11.51	11.74	11.34	11.31	11.26	11.72	11.76	12.03	12.28	11.61

4. Average Weekly Earnings by Selected Industry: Idaho, 2009–2013

(Dollars, not seasonally adjusted)

Industry and year	January	February	March	April	May	June	July	August	September	October	November	December	Annual average
Total Private													
2009	601.03	628.70	634.03	629.56	635.60	635.03	651.90	674.10	657.82	667.83	682.29	662.67	647.14
2010	676.62	684.51	692.67	696.64	700.73	689.23	740.88	725.50	704.59	707.95	709.20	714.34	704.51
2011	719.17	704.63	693.99	700.62	705.89	696.66	706.86	694.95	701.30	720.03	699.66	701.69	704.78
2012	705.46	702.63	691.68	720.12	695.43	703.58	711.96	702.65	724.01	704.41	694.19	718.93	706.94
2013	693.16	704.06	706.50	705.17	704.41	720.30	704.67	707.77	720.80	708.53	707.96	721.93	708.08
Goods-Producing													
2009	768.50	797.28	808.37	807.45	810.08	806.90	838.09	861.03	844.27	864.50	863.33	820.39	823.65
2010	828.49	871.45	891.08	868.32	874.83	876.03	895.40	925.93	924.56	931.32	933.12	948.04	898.18
2011	960.33	945.60	944.85	948.26	935.66	932.54	916.74	933.53	936.89	946.17	918.46	944.07	937.60
2012	945.26	923.88	908.78	940.45	937.80	941.24	946.22	935.70	957.92	920.29	903.53	922.85	932.04
2013	910.06	911.05	903.16	903.05	915.29	926.29	926.69	940.89	949.63	930.20	923.00	919.30	922.22
Construction													
2009	548.96	587.29	614.18	602.53	616.90	628.17	655.67	707.87	647.81	675.26	649.30	671.56	635.70
2010	609.93	666.60	729.59	720.02	702.84	733.58	756.13	791.20	799.71	785.85	792.24	771.75	739.20
2011	744.42	729.64	730.55	785.52	737.79	778.77	744.75	798.38	791.51	815.02	732.83	784.42	765.75
2012	743.62	716.31	658.94	708.37	753.63	776.44	783.00	761.11	759.61	721.61	676.68	680.39	728.99
2013	659.99	684.09	677.98	688.85	717.10	742.26	720.39	755.14	747.89	745.71	706.73	680.11	712.36
Manufacturing													
2009	842.16	879.53	873.94	884.47	890.59	887.22	914.06	920.88	928.34	938.01	962.33	924.44	904.05
2010	953.29	967.46	979.11	974.61	986.82	957.31	988.16	1,008.40	1,006.28	995.80	990.91	995.61	985.32
2011	1,021.50	992.64	997.52	993.91	994.70	976.80	970.82	968.75	980.67	988.40	976.73	991.60	987.44
2012	1,004.85	980.27	978.21	1,001.20	979.09	982.24	988.45	984.07	1,017.46	976.72	976.95	998.09	989.32
2013	984.17	984.61	985.60	982.40	983.25	992.22	1,002.01	1,008.98	1,027.09	1,006.96	1,017.09	1,011.13	999.44
Trade, Transportation, and Utilities													
2009	581.41	593.40	592.96	582.43	598.56	603.43	609.00	616.01	594.72	588.93	605.78	580.24	595.42
2010	584.30	595.14	564.58	578.46	596.40	592.95	600.37	619.79	598.74	600.03	593.93	593.30	593.62
2011	600.10	584.65	589.18	608.24	604.81	603.02	616.68	594.77	599.61	617.76	595.12	597.88	600.28
2012	597.74	588.80	589.08	603.63	583.97	595.45	600.28	606.77	612.00	594.05	590.24	601.35	597.77
2013	573.12	592.57	606.82	602.89	608.54	616.31	604.44	607.92	599.27	601.30	585.09	594.16	600.03
Financial Activities													
2009	759.25	758.47	755.16	761.03	742.22	747.08	791.25	837.06	779.22	792.17	798.38	766.87	772.69
2010	815.72	795.56	794.59	766.12	801.17	763.95	770.77	813.82	772.90	751.54	773.98	787.19	783.01
2011	758.47	737.25	735.42	738.84	773.16	740.16	754.57	739.49	758.11	784.71	750.16	740.26	750.57
2012	745.75	735.23	714.77	771.18	692.90	705.89	732.37	712.01	744.63	712.07	727.32	769.65	729.80
2013	720.99	748.33	737.79	736.05	732.19	770.06	729.06	737.38	759.81	711.90	749.34	806.36	744.75
Professional and Business Services													
2009	740.35	786.50	802.21	810.85	824.82	835.59	841.80	871.57	869.63	860.81	908.26	883.45	837.22
2010	915.64	906.09	957.10	976.76	942.72	920.18	1,080.76	960.79	922.42	920.37	928.88	929.45	947.08
2011	936.40	957.55	930.30	938.01	935.90	927.69	940.37	934.99	977.85	978.56	962.17	936.36	946.34
2012	926.28	960.93	934.40	971.60	975.45	978.16	995.14	956.73	999.47	966.77	921.06	949.70	960.45
2013	918.33	931.61	951.03	919.34	914.48	947.67	933.51	931.00	966.87	950.47	929.19	965.36	938.64
Education and Health Services													
2009	543.63	579.33	587.13	584.67	582.96	553.07	571.10	552.08	547.20	572.88	599.20	602.74	573.00
2010	632.49	608.55	608.52	616.52	651.02	637.27	630.18	660.08	652.99	661.13	663.64	663.36	640.58
2011	668.46	663.04	639.77	634.56	645.45	641.36	648.32	611.67	624.12	640.51	638.15	647.04	641.92
2012	645.41	646.61	639.77	675.39	639.77	647.28	655.87	648.12	675.15	664.23	664.86	673.95	655.40
2013	659.43	664.81	661.75	663.48	653.33	675.11	656.27	644.74	670.39	647.16	668.03	679.14	662.69
Leisure and Hospitality													
2009	240.62	266.77	265.22	251.44	268.38	249.04	250.64	262.38	236.18	240.08	229.84	229.19	249.60
2010	228.34	232.93	233.48	235.44	260.70	249.84	260.31	288.65	258.33	251.55	251.79	247.68	250.41
2011	251.28	246.46	240.87	241.26	256.70	241.33	265.19	262.89	251.68	272.11	258.90	257.76	254.19
2012	269.78	262.14	261.36	267.44	259.13	267.57	280.98	277.26	273.31	264.23	258.50	268.42	267.49
2013	249.39	262.43	270.49	271.64	273.54	292.57	291.80	293.89	307.06	290.47	293.53	314.37	284.45

ILLINOIS
At a Glance

Population:
  2000 census: 12,419,927
  2010 census: 12,830,632
  2013 estimate: 12,882,135

Percent change in population:
  2000–2010: 3.3%
  2010–2013: 0.4%

Percent change in total nonfarm employment:
  2000–2010: -7.1%
  2010–2013: 0.4%

Industry with the largest growth in employment, 2000–2013 (thousands):
  Education and Health Services, 195.6

Industry with the largest decline or smallest growth in employment, 2000–2013 (thousands):
  Manufacturing, -291.4

Civilian labor force:
  2000: 6,467,692
  2010: 6,616,840
  2013: 6,554,200

Unemployment rate and rank among states (lowest to highest):
  2000: 4.5%, 38th
  2010: 10.5%, 42nd
  2013: 9.2%, 49th

Over-the-year change in unemployment rates:
  2010–2011: -0.8%
  2011–2012: -0.8%
  2012–2013: 0.3%

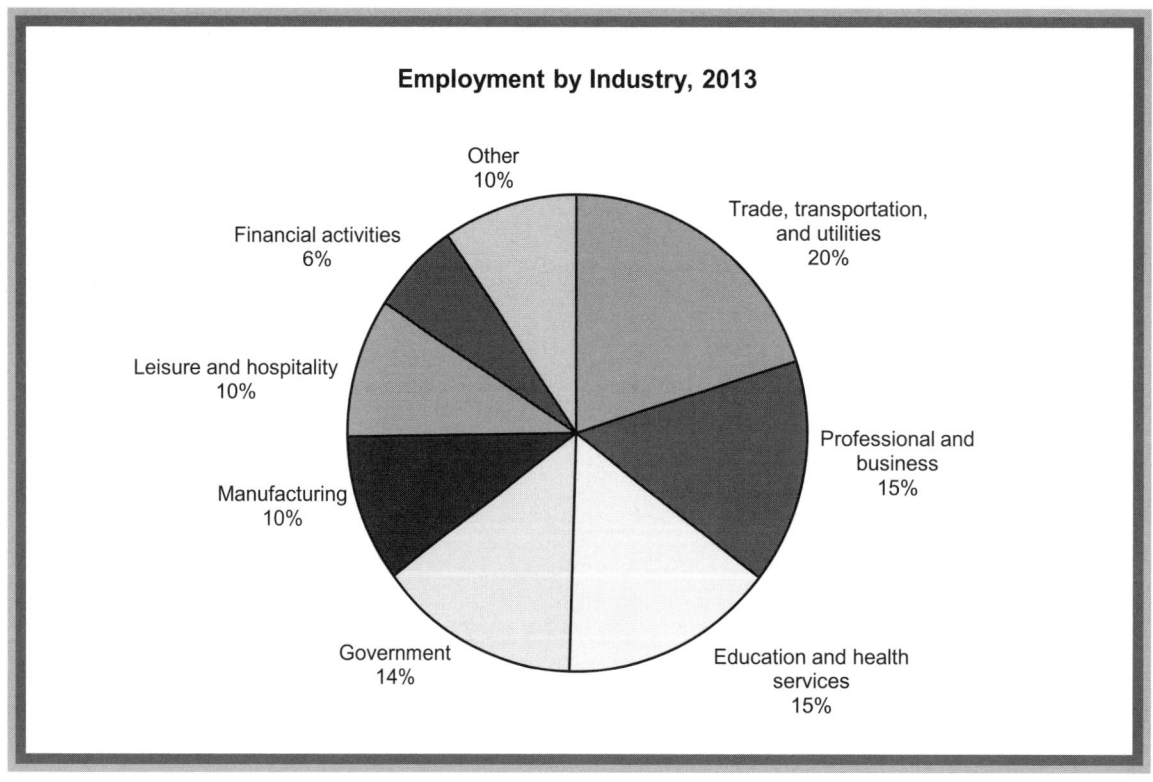

Employment by Industry, 2013

Other 10%
Trade, transportation, and utilities 20%
Financial activities 6%
Leisure and hospitality 10%
Manufacturing 10%
Government 14%
Professional and business 15%
Education and health services 15%

1. Employment by Industry: Illinois, Selected Years, 2002–2013

(Numbers in thousands, not seasonally adjusted)

Industry and year	January	February	March	April	May	June	July	August	September	October	November	December	Annual average
Total Nonfarm													
2002	5,778.6	5,781.4	5,819.3	5,875.3	5,921.8	5,948.7	5,897.0	5,910.8	5,914.5	5,914.1	5,926.8	5,918.3	5,883.9
2003	5,713.0	5,712.1	5,742.5	5,797.6	5,843.1	5,869.6	5,829.7	5,839.2	5,843.1	5,845.7	5,842.4	5,851.7	5,810.8
2004	5,666.8	5,673.3	5,723.9	5,789.2	5,842.7	5,877.9	5,855.2	5,855.0	5,854.9	5,872.1	5,882.2	5,897.6	5,815.9
2005	5,700.8	5,716.3	5,756.8	5,844.9	5,886.3	5,904.9	5,905.1	5,907.1	5,921.3	5,922.6	5,938.7	5,938.4	5,861.9
2006	5,774.8	5,798.4	5,845.0	5,904.9	5,953.7	6,003.7	5,966.3	5,972.5	5,982.5	5,987.1	6,002.3	6,001.7	5,932.7
2007	5,843.2	5,845.5	5,903.2	5,958.4	6,017.5	6,049.1	6,009.7	6,011.7	6,020.6	6,024.2	6,044.4	6,036.5	5,980.3
2008	5,869.4	5,874.8	5,903.8	5,962.1	6,011.8	6,023.1	5,984.9	5,982.4	5,972.9	5,967.4	5,940.3	5,899.7	5,949.4
2009	5,679.2	5,659.0	5,653.0	5,671.0	5,699.2	5,693.6	5,641.7	5,626.6	5,640.3	5,647.6	5,648.4	5,629.2	5,657.4
2010	5,462.4	5,482.7	5,515.5	5,595.9	5,655.8	5,663.2	5,612.7	5,636.0	5,654.2	5,687.1	5,698.0	5,688.3	5,612.7
2011	5,527.2	5,545.6	5,589.8	5,666.0	5,701.5	5,721.4	5,696.0	5,706.1	5,729.2	5,740.4	5,749.9	5,745.9	5,676.6
2012	5,595.1	5,617.1	5,670.0	5,729.4	5,773.9	5,798.1	5,761.0	5,777.7	5,807.8	5,813.1	5,833.1	5,821.6	5,749.8
2013	5,655.3	5,684.3	5,718.0	5,766.4	5,819.1	5,842.1	5,799.9	5,818.5	5,837.5	5,875.0	5,885.4	5,862.8	5,797.0
Total Private													
2002	4,932.8	4,915.3	4,946.8	4,999.5	5,040.3	5,083.5	5,069.0	5,088.1	5,064.3	5,042.3	5,049.9	5,043.0	5,022.9
2003	4,865.9	4,846.5	4,874.2	4,927.0	4,972.7	5,013.4	5,001.6	5,019.4	5,002.8	4,988.6	4,983.8	4,995.5	4,957.6
2004	4,829.6	4,821.1	4,867.3	4,934.3	4,988.1	5,036.6	5,034.4	5,039.2	5,021.2	5,016.1	5,022.6	5,044.8	4,971.3
2005	4,867.8	4,865.2	4,900.7	4,990.7	5,029.1	5,067.8	5,078.7	5,085.9	5,076.4	5,067.1	5,079.2	5,084.0	5,016.1
2006	4,942.5	4,945.0	4,988.3	5,050.2	5,095.7	5,158.7	5,146.2	5,157.4	5,136.8	5,133.3	5,144.4	5,148.9	5,087.3
2007	5,008.2	4,988.7	5,043.8	5,096.4	5,154.0	5,204.2	5,190.2	5,197.1	5,169.5	5,163.2	5,179.6	5,177.9	5,131.1
2008	5,027.8	5,010.5	5,038.8	5,094.4	5,140.6	5,172.4	5,158.7	5,163.8	5,117.8	5,097.4	5,070.0	5,033.2	5,093.8
2009	4,834.8	4,794.5	4,787.1	4,794.8	4,822.9	4,840.5	4,813.2	4,810.9	4,781.6	4,777.1	4,775.9	4,764.2	4,799.8
2010	4,618.2	4,616.3	4,649.4	4,724.1	4,769.8	4,809.0	4,794.4	4,818.6	4,804.6	4,828.6	4,838.2	4,835.6	4,758.9
2011	4,698.0	4,695.4	4,738.7	4,809.8	4,847.2	4,888.1	4,885.7	4,905.4	4,893.6	4,896.2	4,902.7	4,903.7	4,838.7
2012	4,775.9	4,777.2	4,827.0	4,882.6	4,927.3	4,972.0	4,962.3	4,983.5	4,970.7	4,967.3	4,984.9	4,978.4	4,917.4
2013	4,835.0	4,842.9	4,876.2	4,921.8	4,979.3	5,020.1	5,004.6	5,030.1	5,007.9	5,032.8	5,040.0	5,018.6	4,967.4
Goods-Producing													
2002	1,020.9	1,015.9	1,023.0	1,037.9	1,047.3	1,060.2	1,055.9	1,059.7	1,055.8	1,048.5	1,041.8	1,026.8	1,041.1
2003	982.6	975.7	982.6	999.2	1,009.1	1,018.3	1,013.7	1,016.3	1,010.5	999.8	990.7	981.5	998.3
2004	939.1	934.1	948.0	967.5	982.5	996.7	996.6	997.1	996.3	992.4	987.8	980.7	976.6
2005	931.9	931.2	940.0	963.7	974.0	984.9	984.1	985.2	984.0	980.1	976.5	963.5	966.6
2006	935.7	935.2	942.7	964.8	973.9	991.2	987.9	988.5	985.5	981.3	975.7	964.0	968.9
2007	931.2	918.6	936.6	953.0	967.3	980.6	975.6	975.8	970.8	963.8	961.1	947.5	956.8
2008	913.1	904.6	912.8	927.3	939.1	948.0	947.2	947.2	939.8	929.0	912.5	884.5	925.4
2009	831.9	818.0	813.3	807.3	805.8	808.8	804.7	804.6	800.9	793.8	783.3	766.9	803.3
2010	731.1	729.6	739.9	761.0	770.9	782.7	778.7	789.9	787.9	791.4	786.1	771.3	768.4
2011	743.6	742.6	755.1	773.2	784.1	796.7	799.5	802.2	796.1	793.4	787.9	776.7	779.3
2012	749.5	749.1	761.3	775.4	784.1	796.5	800.8	801.7	799.1	797.4	790.6	781.2	782.2
2013	752.8	753.2	759.2	767.7	782.6	794.4	795.8	798.3	794.7	792.9	787.9	770.1	779.1
Service-Providing													
2002	4,757.7	4,765.5	4,796.3	4,837.4	4,874.5	4,888.5	4,841.1	4,851.1	4,858.7	4,865.6	4,885.0	4,891.5	4,842.7
2003	4,730.4	4,736.4	4,759.9	4,798.4	4,834.0	4,851.3	4,816.0	4,822.9	4,832.6	4,845.9	4,851.7	4,870.2	4,812.5
2004	4,727.7	4,739.2	4,775.9	4,821.7	4,860.2	4,881.2	4,858.6	4,857.9	4,858.6	4,879.7	4,894.4	4,916.9	4,839.3
2005	4,768.9	4,785.1	4,816.8	4,881.2	4,912.3	4,920.0	4,921.0	4,921.9	4,937.3	4,942.5	4,962.2	4,974.9	4,895.3
2006	4,839.1	4,863.2	4,902.3	4,940.1	4,979.8	5,012.5	4,978.4	4,984.0	4,997.0	5,005.8	5,026.6	5,037.7	4,963.9
2007	4,912.0	4,926.9	4,966.6	5,005.4	5,050.2	5,068.5	5,034.1	5,035.9	5,049.8	5,060.4	5,083.3	5,089.0	5,023.5
2008	4,956.3	4,970.2	4,991.0	5,034.8	5,072.7	5,075.1	5,037.7	5,035.2	5,033.1	5,038.4	5,027.8	5,015.2	5,024.0
2009	4,847.3	4,841.0	4,839.7	4,863.7	4,893.4	4,884.8	4,837.0	4,822.0	4,839.4	4,853.8	4,865.1	4,862.3	4,854.1
2010	4,731.3	4,753.1	4,775.6	4,834.9	4,884.9	4,880.5	4,834.0	4,846.1	4,866.3	4,895.7	4,911.9	4,917.0	4,844.3
2011	4,783.6	4,803.0	4,834.7	4,892.8	4,917.4	4,924.7	4,896.5	4,903.9	4,933.1	4,947.0	4,962.0	4,969.2	4,897.3
2012	4,845.6	4,868.0	4,908.7	4,954.0	4,989.8	5,001.6	4,960.2	4,976.0	5,008.7	5,015.7	5,042.5	5,040.4	4,967.6
2013	4,902.5	4,931.1	4,958.8	4,998.7	5,036.5	5,047.7	5,004.1	5,020.2	5,042.8	5,082.1	5,097.5	5,092.7	5,017.9
Mining and Logging													
2002	9.6	9.5	9.7	9.6	9.6	9.8	9.7	9.7	9.7	9.8	9.7	9.7	9.7
2003	9.1	9.1	9.3	9.6	9.6	9.8	9.4	9.5	9.5	9.5	9.5	9.3	9.4
2004	8.6	8.6	9.0	9.3	9.5	9.7	9.7	9.7	9.8	9.5	9.6	9.5	9.4
2005	8.8	8.9	9.2	9.6	9.8	10.1	10.2	10.2	10.3	10.4	10.4	10.4	9.9
2006	10.0	9.9	10.0	10.1	10.4	10.6	10.5	10.3	10.3	10.4	10.3	10.2	10.3
2007	9.7	9.7	10.0	10.2	10.5	10.7	10.5	10.3	10.0	10.1	10.1	9.7	10.1
2008	9.3	9.3	9.6	9.5	9.9	9.9	9.9	10.1	10.0	10.0	9.9	9.8	9.8
2009	9.2	9.3	9.4	9.6	9.5	9.7	9.5	9.3	9.4	9.1	9.1	8.9	9.3
2010	8.4	8.4	8.5	9.0	9.1	9.3	9.5	9.4	9.6	9.6	9.5	9.4	9.1
2011	9.0	8.8	9.0	9.3	9.5	9.7	10.0	10.1	10.1	10.1	10.1	9.8	9.6
2012	9.6	9.6	9.9	10.3	10.3	10.4	10.6	10.6	10.4	10.2	10.2	10.0	10.2
2013	9.6	9.5	9.3	9.5	9.7	9.9	10.0	10.0	9.9	9.9	9.8	9.6	9.7
Construction													
2002	246.4	244.1	251.4	268.3	278.9	289.5	295.2	298.3	296.4	295.4	289.9	276.9	277.6
2003	246.8	240.8	248.2	268.1	280.1	289.4	295.1	297.7	294.0	287.4	280.1	270.1	274.8
2004	238.8	233.7	245.1	263.4	274.8	283.7	287.7	287.4	286.0	285.6	281.2	273.4	270.1
2005	236.7	235.7	243.1	263.5	273.8	281.6	285.0	285.8	285.6	284.8	280.5	266.4	268.5
2006	245.2	244.7	252.9	272.5	281.8	292.3	292.1	293.6	289.9	287.9	281.7	269.0	275.3
2007	244.5	233.6	249.8	266.5	279.8	288.9	289.4	290.1	287.2	284.3	278.9	263.8	271.4
2008	236.3	231.2	239.2	255.3	266.9	273.2	277.3	278.8	274.7	269.7	257.8	239.1	258.3
2009	205.8	201.9	206.1	214.1	221.8	227.7	231.2	231.0	227.8	224.2	215.3	199.7	217.2
2010	172.5	169.9	178.9	196.6	203.5	210.9	206.6	215.1	213.4	213.9	207.1	190.6	198.3
2011	168.9	167.7	177.2	192.3	201.7	209.5	212.4	214.0	210.2	206.3	200.0	188.7	195.7
2012	166.0	163.9	173.0	185.0	191.8	199.2	202.5	203.1	201.7	202.1	194.8	186.0	189.1
2013	164.4	164.6	170.1	180.2	193.6	201.1	206.8	207.9	207.0	205.1	200.2	181.3	190.2

1. Employment by Industry: Illinois, Selected Years, 2002–2013—*Continued*

(Numbers in thousands, not seasonally adjusted)

Industry and year	January	February	March	April	May	June	July	August	September	October	November	December	Annual average
Manufacturing													
2002	764.9	762.3	761.9	760.0	758.8	760.9	751.0	751.7	749.7	743.3	742.2	740.2	753.9
2003	726.7	725.8	725.1	721.5	719.4	719.1	709.2	709.1	707.0	702.9	701.1	702.1	714.1
2004	691.7	691.8	693.9	694.8	698.2	703.3	699.2	700.0	700.5	697.3	697.0	697.8	697.1
2005	686.4	686.6	687.7	690.6	690.4	693.2	688.9	689.2	688.1	684.9	685.6	686.7	688.2
2006	680.5	680.6	679.8	682.2	681.7	688.3	685.3	684.6	685.3	683.0	683.7	684.8	683.3
2007	677.0	675.3	676.8	676.3	677.0	681.0	675.7	675.4	673.6	669.4	672.1	674.0	675.3
2008	667.5	664.1	664.0	662.5	662.3	664.9	660.0	658.3	655.1	649.3	644.8	635.6	657.4
2009	616.9	606.8	597.8	583.6	574.5	571.4	564.0	564.3	563.7	560.5	558.9	558.3	576.7
2010	550.2	551.3	552.5	555.4	558.3	562.5	562.6	565.4	564.9	567.9	569.5	571.3	561.0
2011	565.7	566.1	568.9	571.6	572.9	577.5	577.1	578.1	575.8	577.0	577.8	578.2	573.9
2012	573.9	575.6	578.4	580.1	582.0	586.9	587.7	588.0	587.0	585.1	585.6	585.2	583.0
2013	578.8	579.1	579.8	578.0	579.3	583.4	579.0	580.4	577.8	577.9	577.9	579.2	579.2
Trade, Transportation, and Utilities													
2002	1,194.2	1,176.7	1,182.1	1,186.3	1,193.8	1,198.7	1,192.2	1,195.6	1,196.6	1,200.7	1,221.0	1,235.1	1,197.8
2003	1,180.2	1,168.0	1,171.1	1,173.2	1,181.7	1,186.2	1,173.0	1,177.0	1,178.7	1,185.8	1,201.8	1,217.3	1,182.8
2004	1,164.7	1,153.2	1,159.7	1,167.1	1,179.1	1,184.7	1,176.7	1,178.6	1,180.0	1,188.3	1,206.5	1,222.3	1,180.1
2005	1,170.9	1,159.2	1,166.4	1,176.0	1,184.5	1,188.6	1,184.2	1,187.0	1,188.4	1,193.0	1,213.1	1,230.2	1,186.8
2006	1,182.0	1,171.7	1,179.7	1,185.1	1,195.2	1,203.4	1,195.6	1,197.5	1,197.8	1,203.0	1,226.4	1,242.2	1,198.3
2007	1,201.3	1,185.7	1,196.3	1,195.8	1,209.8	1,217.5	1,210.4	1,210.1	1,211.1	1,214.5	1,240.7	1,254.6	1,212.3
2008	1,210.4	1,194.0	1,199.0	1,200.1	1,209.1	1,212.2	1,203.4	1,203.1	1,198.4	1,200.2	1,210.9	1,216.9	1,204.8
2009	1,161.9	1,143.9	1,138.2	1,134.0	1,140.7	1,141.7	1,128.8	1,129.4	1,127.1	1,129.9	1,145.2	1,153.2	1,139.5
2010	1,109.4	1,099.7	1,104.1	1,113.9	1,123.5	1,128.7	1,124.1	1,127.9	1,124.7	1,133.9	1,151.9	1,165.4	1,125.6
2011	1,126.0	1,116.8	1,122.2	1,133.2	1,140.1	1,145.4	1,141.7	1,145.9	1,145.4	1,152.3	1,171.4	1,185.3	1,143.8
2012	1,141.4	1,130.5	1,138.7	1,143.4	1,152.3	1,156.1	1,153.7	1,157.0	1,155.7	1,163.2	1,188.8	1,195.1	1,156.3
2013	1,148.0	1,138.9	1,143.1	1,148.1	1,158.2	1,165.4	1,161.4	1,166.4	1,163.1	1,172.5	1,199.0	1,211.5	1,164.6
Wholesale Trade													
2002	305.7	305.0	305.9	307.0	307.9	310.4	308.1	307.8	307.3	307.3	307.7	307.7	307.3
2003	303.6	303.2	304.2	304.2	305.0	305.6	303.9	302.4	301.2	300.8	300.8	301.0	303.0
2004	296.0	295.4	297.1	298.9	301.0	302.6	301.6	301.0	300.3	301.5	301.6	302.4	300.0
2005	296.7	296.9	299.5	302.0	303.1	305.2	305.2	304.7	304.7	304.7	305.4	306.6	302.9
2006	303.2	303.3	305.2	306.7	308.4	311.2	309.7	308.9	308.3	308.8	308.8	310.0	307.7
2007	305.9	305.5	307.6	308.8	310.7	313.8	312.8	312.1	311.7	312.9	312.9	313.8	310.7
2008	309.0	308.2	309.5	310.7	312.8	314.1	312.3	311.4	309.7	309.9	308.8	307.4	310.3
2009	299.2	296.7	295.6	293.8	293.2	293.2	290.4	289.1	287.1	287.9	287.6	287.5	291.8
2010	281.8	280.9	282.7	285.1	286.6	288.2	287.7	287.6	286.5	287.4	287.0	287.2	285.7
2011	284.3	284.3	285.9	288.6	289.7	292.0	292.2	291.8	290.8	291.5	291.2	292.1	289.5
2012	289.0	289.4	292.3	293.7	295.2	297.8	296.3	296.1	295.4	295.9	296.3	296.6	294.5
2013	293.9	294.0	295.7	296.6	298.7	301.6	301.1	300.2	299.6	298.2	299.3	298.3	298.1
Retail Trade													
2002	630.4	615.4	620.3	620.9	626.9	632.2	628.2	629.8	628.2	630.9	651.4	665.7	631.7
2003	621.0	611.1	613.4	614.7	621.0	626.4	620.3	623.5	622.1	627.5	643.7	658.8	625.3
2004	618.1	608.0	611.4	614.5	622.3	628.9	622.4	624.2	621.8	626.0	644.5	659.5	625.1
2005	619.9	608.1	611.4	617.0	623.2	626.6	625.8	627.4	624.1	627.3	645.4	659.3	626.3
2006	622.6	611.8	615.8	618.2	624.2	630.8	627.3	628.5	622.8	628.5	650.8	661.7	628.6
2007	632.8	618.0	624.5	623.3	632.6	638.2	635.6	634.1	630.3	632.4	657.1	667.1	635.5
2008	635.6	620.4	623.0	623.4	628.0	632.2	628.8	626.7	620.4	621.9	633.7	639.1	627.8
2009	604.1	590.7	587.6	588.6	594.8	597.9	593.2	592.9	588.5	590.4	605.6	611.4	595.5
2010	580.8	572.0	574.4	579.1	585.6	591.1	589.9	590.2	583.5	590.2	607.1	617.1	588.4
2011	587.0	577.5	580.2	586.8	591.2	595.7	594.6	597.1	592.3	598.1	616.3	625.8	595.2
2012	593.0	581.9	585.4	587.0	592.3	596.7	596.2	595.7	591.5	598.4	622.1	624.8	597.1
2013	592.0	582.8	584.6	587.3	594.3	601.8	599.7	600.8	596.6	603.6	627.3	636.9	600.6
Transportation and Utilities													
2002	258.1	256.3	255.9	258.4	259.0	256.1	255.9	258.0	261.1	262.5	261.9	261.7	258.7
2003	255.6	253.7	253.5	254.3	255.7	254.2	248.8	251.1	255.4	257.5	257.3	257.5	254.6
2004	250.6	249.8	251.2	253.7	255.8	253.2	252.7	253.4	257.9	260.8	260.4	260.4	255.0
2005	254.3	254.2	255.5	257.0	258.2	256.8	253.2	254.9	259.6	261.0	262.3	264.3	257.6
2006	256.2	256.6	258.7	260.2	262.6	261.4	258.6	260.1	266.7	265.7	266.8	270.5	262.0
2007	262.6	262.2	264.2	263.7	266.5	265.5	262.0	263.9	269.1	269.2	270.7	273.7	266.1
2008	265.8	265.4	266.5	266.0	268.3	265.9	262.3	265.0	268.3	268.4	268.4	270.4	266.7
2009	258.6	256.5	255.0	251.6	252.7	250.6	245.2	247.4	251.5	251.6	252.0	254.3	252.3
2010	246.8	246.8	247.0	249.7	251.3	249.4	246.5	250.1	254.7	256.3	257.8	261.1	251.5
2011	254.7	255.0	256.1	257.8	259.2	257.7	254.9	257.0	262.3	262.7	263.9	267.4	259.1
2012	259.4	259.2	261.0	262.7	264.8	261.6	261.2	265.2	268.8	268.9	270.4	273.7	264.7
2013	262.1	262.1	262.8	264.2	265.2	262.0	260.6	265.4	266.9	270.7	272.4	276.3	265.9
Information													
2002	141.3	140.6	140.4	140.3	140.0	139.6	136.7	136.2	133.5	133.0	132.5	132.0	137.2
2003	129.0	128.9	127.8	128.0	128.1	128.4	128.1	127.4	126.3	126.0	126.1	126.2	127.5
2004	122.2	122.1	121.8	121.6	121.7	121.8	121.1	120.4	118.9	119.2	119.3	120.0	120.8
2005	118.8	118.3	118.4	119.0	119.0	119.4	119.3	118.4	117.3	116.6	116.7	117.0	118.2
2006	116.4	116.0	116.2	116.9	117.1	117.4	117.1	116.3	115.1	115.3	115.3	115.9	116.3
2007	115.3	115.7	115.7	115.7	116.2	116.9	116.9	116.8	115.6	115.5	115.7	116.0	116.0
2008	115.4	115.4	115.9	115.6	115.9	115.8	115.5	115.0	113.0	112.1	111.7	111.6	114.4
2009	109.9	108.9	108.2	107.4	107.0	106.7	105.7	105.4	104.5	104.2	103.8	104.8	106.4
2010	103.3	102.3	102.3	102.1	102.1	102.4	101.8	101.9	100.6	100.9	100.9	101.1	101.8
2011	100.6	99.9	100.1	100.4	101.0	101.3	101.6	101.4	99.8	99.8	100.4	100.5	100.6
2012	100.2	99.8	100.1	100.4	101.1	100.5	100.5	100.2	99.1	99.9	99.8	100.0	100.1
2013	99.0	98.5	98.5	99.3	100.0	100.2	99.7	99.0	97.3	98.1	98.7	99.8	99.0

1. Employment by Industry: Illinois, Selected Years, 2002–2013—*Continued*

(Numbers in thousands, not seasonally adjusted)

Industry and year	January	February	March	April	May	June	July	August	September	October	November	December	Annual average
Financial Activities													
2002	398.7	398.3	399.1	398.2	399.4	403.3	402.7	402.9	400.1	400.2	401.3	403.7	400.7
2003	398.9	398.1	399.3	400.1	402.1	406.3	406.1	406.5	403.0	399.4	399.7	401.7	401.8
2004	396.7	396.2	398.0	397.0	398.6	402.5	403.0	403.0	399.1	398.7	398.8	401.7	399.4
2005	396.2	395.9	396.6	399.6	400.9	403.9	406.4	406.3	403.8	403.7	403.6	406.2	401.9
2006	401.0	401.1	402.4	403.2	404.5	408.1	408.6	408.7	405.6	406.0	405.7	407.3	405.2
2007	403.3	402.8	402.8	403.3	404.3	407.2	406.5	404.9	400.4	399.5	398.9	399.5	402.8
2008	393.6	393.5	393.7	393.4	394.1	396.0	394.3	393.7	388.6	387.6	385.7	385.7	391.7
2009	378.4	376.3	374.7	373.8	373.7	374.7	372.9	371.7	367.7	366.7	366.1	366.7	372.0
2010	361.3	360.7	360.8	362.3	363.2	365.9	365.6	365.9	362.8	364.7	364.7	366.0	363.7
2011	360.9	360.7	360.5	361.2	361.9	364.4	366.2	366.1	363.5	365.0	364.2	365.0	363.3
2012	361.1	361.5	362.1	363.6	365.2	368.6	369.6	370.0	367.3	366.7	366.3	367.8	365.8
2013	364.3	364.5	364.5	366.1	367.2	371.1	372.4	372.0	369.9	369.7	368.9	370.3	368.4
Professional and Business Services													
2002	771.2	769.7	773.2	789.7	792.8	799.3	802.8	810.9	806.4	799.3	795.5	786.8	791.5
2003	754.9	753.7	757.2	769.9	774.7	779.2	781.8	789.9	793.4	795.3	789.2	789.2	777.4
2004	758.5	762.3	771.0	791.9	798.3	810.7	813.5	817.1	815.8	815.5	811.8	817.8	798.7
2005	786.6	790.8	797.8	820.0	821.6	832.1	838.5	843.2	845.1	850.4	848.7	844.4	826.6
2006	815.2	819.1	830.0	847.3	852.4	866.4	866.5	873.1	870.6	874.9	870.2	865.2	854.2
2007	835.2	837.5	847.2	866.4	872.5	882.9	884.9	889.7	884.6	886.3	882.2	878.8	870.7
2008	846.7	848.9	850.5	866.0	869.7	874.0	872.5	875.0	865.0	860.9	850.6	838.8	859.9
2009	797.3	788.0	780.1	785.5	787.7	789.9	787.7	788.8	783.1	789.3	790.2	786.0	787.8
2010	762.0	766.1	768.9	795.3	799.8	809.6	813.0	818.6	815.6	825.1	825.1	823.2	801.9
2011	794.9	798.4	804.5	825.8	825.9	837.2	842.9	848.2	848.3	852.6	851.3	846.9	831.4
2012	824.5	827.3	837.1	856.4	862.7	875.8	875.0	882.6	882.8	882.3	886.0	880.1	864.4
2013	846.4	854.2	860.6	875.5	885.1	895.2	890.0	898.4	895.9	908.9	899.1	890.8	883.3
Education and Health Services													
2002	699.8	706.1	709.9	711.1	713.9	710.3	703.0	705.0	712.8	716.0	719.4	720.5	710.7
2003	709.0	712.2	716.0	715.6	717.9	716.7	712.7	715.1	720.5	724.8	727.2	728.7	718.0
2004	719.7	723.9	727.3	729.7	730.9	727.4	723.6	724.7	731.3	736.9	740.0	743.5	729.9
2005	734.6	738.3	740.1	745.5	746.9	741.7	740.8	740.8	748.8	752.4	755.1	757.2	745.2
2006	748.0	755.2	758.7	759.3	762.0	760.5	756.2	759.3	767.5	770.6	774.6	775.2	762.3
2007	765.9	773.8	777.4	777.6	779.2	777.3	772.7	774.1	782.4	788.6	793.0	795.2	779.8
2008	785.8	791.9	793.5	798.6	801.1	798.6	795.6	799.1	806.9	811.8	815.9	817.1	801.3
2009	806.5	812.4	816.1	815.3	817.6	814.7	810.3	809.7	816.2	823.0	826.4	828.0	816.4
2010	817.9	823.7	827.9	831.1	834.4	831.3	826.2	826.9	836.0	844.0	848.2	849.7	833.1
2011	838.4	844.0	848.9	847.1	848.7	845.6	838.9	840.6	852.0	855.9	858.6	863.1	848.5
2012	851.7	858.8	862.8	862.4	862.7	862.1	853.4	856.9	867.7	868.9	871.8	873.6	862.7
2013	865.6	873.7	878.3	876.1	877.1	871.5	863.4	870.5	878.7	886.6	892.3	887.1	876.7
Leisure and Hospitality													
2002	459.7	460.6	469.9	486.1	502.6	515.0	515.6	517.6	508.1	494.9	488.0	486.7	492.1
2003	464.7	463.5	471.5	492.3	509.2	522.0	520.8	521.7	513.7	501.0	493.6	494.0	497.3
2004	473.9	473.3	483.5	501.5	518.3	528.8	531.4	531.4	522.4	507.8	501.5	499.5	506.1
2005	476.4	478.5	487.0	511.0	525.4	534.8	537.8	537.7	530.9	514.3	508.4	506.4	512.4
2006	487.5	491.0	500.7	517.9	533.4	548.1	547.9	547.4	537.1	524.3	518.6	518.9	522.7
2007	500.7	499.2	509.4	526.6	544.6	555.9	553.7	556.0	544.6	534.9	527.6	524.7	531.5
2008	504.7	503.5	513.1	532.8	548.8	559.7	556.7	557.6	543.9	533.3	521.1	517.0	532.7
2009	493.4	491.4	499.5	515.1	532.4	541.3	538.0	537.1	527.9	514.9	506.0	502.7	516.6
2010	482.1	483.2	492.6	511.5	527.8	538.5	536.4	538.9	530.0	520.2	513.1	509.9	515.4
2011	488.4	487.5	500.0	519.5	534.1	543.8	542.2	549.0	538.2	527.6	520.5	516.0	522.2
2012	501.0	502.9	515.8	532.4	548.4	558.3	557.1	564.0	549.3	540.1	532.7	531.3	536.1
2013	513.2	513.3	524.0	540.7	559.1	570.1	569.0	572.2	557.8	551.9	543.0	537.6	546.0
Other Services													
2002	247.0	247.4	249.2	249.9	250.5	257.1	260.1	260.2	251.0	249.7	250.4	251.4	252.0
2003	246.6	246.4	248.7	248.7	249.9	256.3	265.4	265.5	256.7	256.5	255.5	256.9	254.4
2004	254.8	256.0	258.0	258.0	258.7	264.0	268.5	266.9	257.4	257.3	256.9	259.3	259.7
2005	252.4	253.0	254.4	255.9	256.8	262.4	267.6	267.3	258.1	256.6	257.1	259.1	258.4
2006	256.7	255.7	257.9	255.7	257.2	263.6	266.4	266.6	257.6	257.9	257.9	260.2	259.5
2007	255.3	255.4	258.4	258.0	260.1	265.9	269.5	269.7	260.0	260.1	260.4	261.6	261.2
2008	258.1	258.7	260.3	260.6	262.8	268.1	273.5	273.1	262.2	262.5	261.6	261.6	263.6
2009	255.5	255.6	257.0	256.4	258.0	262.7	265.1	264.2	254.2	255.3	254.9	255.9	257.9
2010	251.1	251.0	252.9	246.9	248.1	249.9	248.6	248.6	247.0	248.4	248.2	249.0	249.1
2011	245.2	245.5	247.4	249.4	251.4	253.7	252.7	252.0	250.3	249.6	248.4	250.2	249.7
2012	246.5	247.3	249.1	248.6	250.8	254.1	252.2	251.1	249.7	248.8	248.9	249.3	249.7
2013	245.7	246.6	248.0	248.3	250.0	252.2	252.9	253.3	250.5	252.2	251.1	251.4	250.2
Government													
2002	845.8	866.1	872.5	875.8	881.5	865.2	828.0	822.7	850.2	871.8	876.9	875.3	861.0
2003	847.1	865.6	868.3	870.6	870.4	856.2	828.1	819.8	840.3	857.1	858.6	856.2	853.2
2004	837.2	852.2	856.6	854.9	854.6	841.3	820.8	815.8	833.7	856.0	859.6	852.8	844.6
2005	833.0	851.1	856.1	854.2	857.2	837.1	826.4	821.2	844.9	855.5	859.5	854.4	845.9
2006	832.3	853.4	856.7	854.7	858.0	845.0	820.1	815.1	845.7	853.8	857.9	852.8	845.5
2007	835.0	856.8	859.4	862.0	863.5	844.9	819.5	814.6	851.1	861.0	864.8	858.6	849.3
2008	841.6	864.3	865.0	867.7	871.2	850.7	826.2	818.6	855.1	870.0	870.3	866.5	855.6
2009	844.4	864.5	865.9	876.2	876.3	853.1	828.5	815.7	858.7	870.5	872.5	865.0	857.6
2010	844.2	866.4	866.1	871.8	886.0	854.2	818.3	817.4	849.6	858.5	859.8	852.7	853.8
2011	829.2	850.2	851.1	856.2	854.3	833.3	810.3	800.7	835.6	844.2	847.2	842.2	837.9
2012	819.2	839.9	843.0	846.8	846.6	826.1	798.7	794.2	837.1	845.8	848.2	843.2	832.4
2013	820.3	841.4	841.8	844.6	839.8	822.0	795.3	788.4	829.6	842.2	845.4	844.2	829.6

2. Average Weekly Hours by Selected Industry: Illinois, 2009–2013

(Not seasonally adjusted)

Industry and year	January	February	March	April	May	June	July	August	September	October	November	December	Annual average
Total Private													
2009	34.1	34.5	34.5	34.4	34.4	34.4	34.4	34.5	34.5	34.4	34.5	34.5	34.4
2010	34.4	34.3	34.3	34.4	34.4	34.3	34.3	34.3	34.4	34.5	34.4	34.3	34.4
2011	34.3	34.3	34.4	34.5	34.7	34.5	34.5	34.5	34.6	35.0	34.6	34.7	34.6
2012	34.7	34.5	34.5	34.9	34.6	34.8	35.1	34.6	35.2	34.6	34.4	34.9	34.7
2013	33.9	34.2	34.3	34.3	34.3	34.8	34.3	34.5	34.9	34.6	34.6	35.0	34.5
Goods-Producing													
2009	38.8	38.8	39.2	39.1	39.3	39.4	39.3	39.5	39.4	39.6	39.7	39.6	39.3
2010	39.6	39.4	39.3	39.4	39.3	39.2	39.3	39.3	39.3	39.3	39.3	39.4	39.3
2011	39.3	39.2	39.5	39.5	40.1	39.6	39.2	39.9	39.8	40.0	39.5	39.9	39.6
2012	39.8	39.6	39.6	39.9	39.7	40.0	39.7	39.6	40.2	39.8	39.5	39.9	39.8
2013	38.9	38.9	39.4	39.3	39.3	39.9	39.6	40.3	40.4	40.2	39.9	40.5	39.7
Construction													
2009	36.3	37.5	37.6	37.6	37.7	37.9	37.8	38.0	37.9	38.1	38.1	38.2	37.7
2010	38.4	38.0	38.0	38.1	38.2	38.1	38.3	38.4	38.4	38.2	38.1	37.4	38.1
2011	37.4	37.3	37.6	37.9	38.6	38.3	39.4	39.6	39.2	39.0	37.5	37.8	38.4
2012	36.9	37.2	37.3	37.6	38.0	38.8	38.6	38.2	38.5	38.7	37.7	36.8	37.9
2013	36.0	35.7	35.9	35.4	37.6	37.8	37.2	37.9	38.0	37.9	36.8	36.8	37.0
Manufacturing													
2009	39.3	39.4	39.6	39.5	39.6	39.7	39.8	39.9	39.8	40.0	40.2	40.0	39.7
2010	40.2	40.1	40.3	40.4	40.5	40.3	40.2	40.2	40.2	40.4	40.5	40.9	40.4
2011	40.8	40.7	40.9	40.8	41.1	40.7	39.7	40.6	40.6	41.0	40.8	41.1	40.7
2012	41.0	40.6	40.5	40.7	40.7	40.7	40.4	40.4	41.0	40.4	40.4	41.2	40.7
2013	40.1	40.1	40.7	40.7	40.5	41.0	40.8	41.4	41.4	41.2	41.2	41.9	40.9
Trade, Transportation, and Utilities													
2009	33.6	33.9	33.9	33.9	33.9	33.7	33.8	33.9	33.9	33.8	34.0	34.2	33.9
2010	34.1	34.2	34.2	34.2	34.3	34.2	34.2	34.2	34.3	34.5	34.4	34.6	34.3
2011	34.6	34.5	34.5	34.7	35.0	35.0	35.1	35.0	35.2	35.5	35.2	35.2	35.0
2012	34.8	34.9	35.1	35.4	35.2	35.4	35.7	35.2	35.8	35.2	34.8	35.4	35.2
2013	34.3	34.7	35.0	34.8	35.2	35.2	35.0	35.0	35.4	35.3	34.9	35.6	35.0
Information													
2009	37.2	39.5	39.6	39.3	39.2	39.2	39.3	39.4	39.3	39.3	39.4	39.5	39.2
2010	39.3	39.1	39.0	39.1	39.2	39.1	39.2	39.2	39.1	39.0	38.9	38.5	39.1
2011	38.4	38.4	37.0	36.5	36.9	36.9	36.4	36.3	36.4	37.8	37.4	37.7	37.2
2012	37.8	37.1	37.0	37.4	36.7	36.5	37.1	36.7	37.9	36.5	36.9	37.3	37.1
2013	36.6	36.7	36.8	37.0	36.9	37.5	37.4	37.2	37.7	36.6	36.5	37.2	37.0
Financial Activities													
2009	36.4	37.0	37.0	36.9	36.8	36.8	37.0	37.1	37.0	36.8	36.8	36.7	36.9
2010	36.8	36.7	36.9	36.7	36.8	36.7	36.6	36.8	36.7	36.5	36.6	36.3	36.7
2011	36.4	36.6	36.6	36.6	36.7	36.3	36.6	36.3	36.6	37.8	37.7	37.3	36.8
2012	38.4	37.9	37.7	39.0	37.3	37.7	38.4	37.2	38.3	36.4	36.3	37.5	37.7
2013	35.9	36.5	36.5	36.6	36.2	37.1	35.6	35.7	37.3	36.1	36.1	37.1	36.4
Professional and Business Services													
2009	36.2	37.2	37.1	36.9	37.0	36.8	36.7	36.8	36.7	36.7	36.9	36.7	36.8
2010	36.5	36.4	36.4	36.5	36.6	36.5	36.4	36.5	36.4	36.5	36.4	35.9	36.4
2011	36.0	36.1	36.1	36.3	36.7	36.1	35.8	35.8	35.9	36.4	35.7	35.6	36.0
2012	35.9	35.6	35.7	36.4	36.3	36.5	36.4	36.1	37.0	36.3	36.1	36.7	36.3
2013	35.7	36.0	36.0	35.9	35.7	36.5	35.6	35.8	36.4	36.1	36.2	36.6	36.0
Education and Health Services													
2009	32.4	32.4	32.4	32.3	32.3	32.4	32.5	32.7	32.7	32.7	32.6	32.4	32.5
2010	32.4	32.3	32.1	32.2	32.3	32.2	32.1	32.4	32.6	32.8	32.7	32.8	32.4
2011	32.9	32.8	32.9	33.0	33.2	32.9	33.4	33.1	33.2	33.5	33.2	33.1	33.1
2012	33.7	33.1	32.8	33.1	32.8	32.9	33.4	32.9	33.3	32.6	33.0	33.0	33.0
2013	32.7	32.7	32.6	32.5	32.6	33.1	32.9	32.6	33.0	32.6	33.0	32.8	32.8
Leisure and Hospitality													
2009	25.0	26.1	26.1	26.0	26.1	26.2	26.0	25.8	25.7	25.5	25.7	25.6	25.8
2010	25.4	25.6	25.7	25.8	25.9	25.8	25.6	25.5	25.4	25.5	25.4	24.7	25.5
2011	24.6	24.5	25.2	25.2	25.0	25.3	25.2	25.2	25.1	25.4	25.2	25.5	25.1
2012	24.7	25.1	25.4	25.3	25.8	26.1	26.3	25.8	25.7	25.7	25.3	25.8	25.6
2013	24.5	24.9	25.4	25.4	25.8	26.3	25.7	26.0	25.9	26.0	25.8	25.9	25.6
Other Services													
2009	32.0	32.1	32.2	32.1	32.3	32.2	32.4	32.6	32.6	32.4	32.3	32.1	32.3
2010	32.1	32.3	32.2	32.4	32.3	32.3	32.2	32.2	32.1	32.3	32.2	32.2	32.2
2011	32.3	32.2	32.0	32.2	32.6	32.3	32.9	32.5	32.5	32.9	31.9	32.1	32.4
2012	32.7	31.6	31.5	32.0	31.6	31.5	32.2	31.3	31.8	31.4	31.2	32.2	31.7
2013	30.8	31.0	30.8	31.3	31.4	32.4	31.7	31.9	32.2	31.4	31.7	32.5	31.6

3. Average Hourly Earnings by Selected Industry: Illinois, 2009–2013

(Dollars, not seasonally adjusted)

Industry and year	January	February	March	April	May	June	July	August	September	October	November	December	Annual average
Total Private													
2009	22.81	23.04	23.11	23.07	22.97	22.99	23.07	23.12	23.12	23.10	23.13	23.12	23.05
2010	23.12	23.09	23.05	23.06	23.07	23.06	23.10	23.14	23.17	23.23	23.22	23.44	23.15
2011	23.45	23.37	23.15	23.36	23.55	23.38	23.60	23.54	23.70	23.98	23.83	23.95	23.58
2012	24.19	24.03	24.02	24.54	24.22	24.16	24.50	24.23	24.48	24.26	24.46	24.63	24.31
2013	24.68	24.73	24.67	24.77	24.71	24.85	24.81	24.72	25.04	24.78	24.89	25.04	24.81
Goods-Producing													
2009	24.62	24.74	24.99	25.04	24.89	24.81	24.97	25.04	25.06	25.00	25.14	25.00	24.94
2010	24.85	24.82	24.85	24.94	25.00	24.99	24.95	24.95	24.94	25.13	25.11	25.28	24.99
2011	25.31	25.24	25.23	25.50	25.67	25.62	26.04	25.94	25.91	26.29	26.13	26.17	25.76
2012	25.72	25.63	25.82	26.19	26.16	26.12	26.55	26.52	26.58	26.61	26.76	26.67	26.29
2013	26.34	26.44	26.32	26.23	26.55	26.72	26.82	26.74	26.87	26.87	27.06	26.79	26.65
Construction													
2009	31.52	32.18	32.29	32.23	32.16	32.03	32.15	32.20	32.22	32.20	32.29	32.48	32.16
2010	32.29	32.32	32.48	32.45	32.34	32.51	32.40	32.32	32.32	32.31	32.32	33.25	32.44
2011	33.22	33.24	32.91	33.15	33.18	33.23	33.20	33.32	32.98	33.50	33.66	33.89	33.29
2012	33.22	33.32	33.68	33.61	33.60	33.58	34.07	34.19	34.16	33.96	34.46	34.44	33.88
2013	33.81	34.46	34.02	33.82	33.49	33.73	34.45	34.11	34.23	34.32	34.63	34.15	34.11
Manufacturing													
2009	21.92	22.05	22.13	22.12	22.08	22.14	22.05	22.11	22.13	22.00	22.20	22.22	22.09
2010	22.12	22.19	22.15	22.32	22.47	22.38	23.33	23.38	23.39	23.48	23.67	23.94	22.91
2011	23.90	23.99	23.89	23.93	24.08	23.89	24.16	23.93	24.02	24.23	24.05	24.29	24.03
2012	24.13	23.94	23.91	24.21	24.01	23.81	24.12	24.02	24.15	24.14	24.36	24.71	24.13
2013	24.60	24.52	24.42	24.28	24.47	24.47	24.28	24.23	24.41	24.38	24.65	24.68	24.45
Trade, Transportation, and Utilities													
2009	19.51	19.69	19.85	19.74	19.67	19.83	19.75	19.80	19.80	19.70	19.72	20.00	19.76
2010	20.05	19.82	19.76	19.86	20.00	20.19	20.34	20.32	20.44	20.47	20.47	20.79	20.21
2011	20.69	20.55	20.21	20.70	20.95	20.73	21.19	20.88	21.26	21.59	21.40	21.50	20.98
2012	21.78	21.57	21.20	21.81	21.55	21.55	21.92	21.68	22.01	21.96	21.99	22.11	21.76
2013	22.39	22.29	22.38	22.88	22.56	22.73	22.74	22.48	22.54	22.67	22.46	22.63	22.56
Information													
2009	26.30	26.19	26.22	26.39	26.39	26.47	26.62	26.74	26.76	26.77	26.61	26.57	26.50
2010	26.57	26.45	26.62	26.76	26.62	26.56	26.53	26.56	26.53	26.53	26.68	26.86	26.61
2011	26.83	26.82	27.21	27.29	27.21	26.63	27.19	27.00	27.77	26.91	27.26	26.15	27.02
2012	26.68	26.78	27.04	27.91	27.80	27.64	27.74	27.49	28.11	28.09	28.12	28.85	27.69
2013	28.45	28.73	28.84	29.45	29.58	30.38	29.84	29.93	30.51	30.50	30.74	30.47	29.79
Financial Activities													
2009	27.97	29.04	29.04	28.95	29.05	28.93	28.94	29.05	29.03	29.13	29.05	29.00	28.93
2010	28.80	28.96	28.89	28.83	28.78	27.83	27.87	27.72	27.75	27.62	27.48	28.14	28.22
2011	28.22	28.29	28.10	28.53	29.00	28.28	28.22	28.61	28.65	29.28	29.13	29.36	28.64
2012	30.06	29.98	29.76	30.44	29.93	29.39	29.88	29.56	30.07	30.02	30.61	30.30	30.00
2013	29.97	30.67	30.15	30.46	30.49	30.22	30.47	30.70	31.08	30.64	31.38	31.55	30.65
Professional and Business Services													
2009	27.78	28.15	28.19	28.09	28.00	28.08	28.24	28.16	28.15	28.00	28.17	28.00	28.08
2010	28.07	28.04	28.04	28.02	28.02	28.00	28.12	28.22	28.26	28.37	28.38	28.15	28.14
2011	28.26	28.22	27.80	27.71	28.07	27.92	28.06	27.86	27.69	28.10	27.83	28.15	27.97
2012	28.83	28.26	28.44	28.75	28.20	28.15	28.69	27.83	28.21	27.67	27.94	28.65	28.30
2013	28.74	28.80	28.65	28.42	28.53	28.72	28.34	28.08	28.70	27.77	28.31	28.61	28.47
Education and Health Services													
2009	21.90	22.07	22.11	22.19	22.07	22.10	22.19	22.17	22.19	22.26	22.24	22.30	22.15
2010	22.35	22.51	22.46	22.33	22.33	22.43	22.29	22.42	22.38	22.21	22.15	22.52	22.36
2011	22.47	22.47	22.34	22.45	22.64	22.85	22.89	23.03	23.22	23.42	23.30	23.41	22.88
2012	23.33	23.57	23.72	23.89	24.03	24.14	24.17	24.09	24.09	24.13	24.39	24.27	23.99
2013	24.50	24.44	24.59	24.68	24.61	24.81	24.97	24.84	25.00	25.04	25.10	25.26	24.82
Leisure and Hospitality													
2009	12.41	12.62	12.58	12.57	12.57	12.55	12.60	12.80	12.80	12.67	12.48	12.40	12.59
2010	12.29	12.39	12.29	12.24	12.26	12.39	12.43	12.49	12.53	12.75	12.78	13.16	12.50
2011	13.16	13.23	13.12	13.29	12.65	12.47	12.48	12.65	12.96	12.40	12.59	12.80	12.81
2012	12.90	12.89	12.98	14.34	13.54	13.53	13.62	13.57	13.35	12.15	12.15	12.71	13.16
2013	12.60	12.51	12.63	12.72	12.79	12.61	12.53	13.02	13.14	12.43	11.97	12.55	12.63
Other Services													
2009	21.99	21.53	21.59	21.64	21.76	21.81	21.99	22.04	22.02	22.13	22.18	22.04	21.89
2010	22.21	22.00	22.16	22.08	22.10	22.07	22.08	22.07	22.00	22.01	22.03	22.39	22.10
2011	22.21	21.21	21.31	21.27	21.68	21.72	21.49	21.45	21.88	21.97	21.78	22.31	21.69
2012	22.59	22.35	22.64	22.98	22.78	22.53	23.10	22.93	23.10	23.17	23.37	23.83	22.95
2013	23.83	23.76	23.77	23.56	23.43	23.69	23.58	23.57	24.36	24.02	23.52	24.00	23.76

4. Average Weekly Earnings by Selected Industry: Illinois, 2009–2013

(Dollars, not seasonally adjusted)

Industry and year	January	February	March	April	May	June	July	August	September	October	November	December	Annual average
Total Private													
2009	777.82	794.88	797.30	793.61	790.17	790.86	793.61	797.64	797.64	794.64	797.99	797.64	792.92
2010	795.33	791.99	790.62	793.26	793.61	790.96	792.33	793.70	797.05	801.44	798.77	803.99	796.36
2011	804.34	801.59	796.36	805.92	817.19	806.61	814.20	812.13	820.02	839.30	824.52	831.07	815.87
2012	839.39	829.04	828.69	856.45	838.01	840.77	859.95	838.36	861.70	839.40	841.42	859.59	843.56
2013	836.65	845.77	846.18	849.61	847.55	864.78	850.98	852.84	873.90	857.39	861.19	876.40	855.95
Goods-Producing													
2009	955.26	959.91	979.61	979.06	978.18	977.51	981.32	989.08	987.36	990.00	998.06	990.00	980.14
2010	984.06	977.91	976.61	982.64	982.50	979.61	980.54	980.54	980.14	987.61	986.82	996.03	982.11
2011	994.68	989.41	996.59	1,007.25	1,029.37	1,014.55	1,020.77	1,035.01	1,031.22	1,051.60	1,032.14	1,044.18	1,020.10
2012	1,023.66	1,014.95	1,022.47	1,044.98	1,038.55	1,044.80	1,054.04	1,050.19	1,068.52	1,059.08	1,057.02	1,064.13	1,046.34
2013	1,024.63	1,028.52	1,037.01	1,030.84	1,043.42	1,066.13	1,062.07	1,077.62	1,085.55	1,080.17	1,079.69	1,085.00	1,058.01
Construction													
2009	1,144.18	1,206.75	1,214.10	1,211.85	1,212.43	1,213.94	1,215.27	1,223.60	1,221.14	1,226.82	1,230.25	1,240.74	1,212.43
2010	1,239.94	1,228.16	1,234.24	1,236.35	1,235.39	1,238.63	1,240.92	1,241.09	1,241.09	1,234.24	1,231.39	1,243.55	1,235.96
2011	1,242.43	1,239.85	1,237.42	1,256.39	1,280.75	1,272.71	1,308.08	1,319.47	1,292.82	1,306.50	1,262.25	1,281.04	1,278.34
2012	1,225.82	1,239.50	1,256.26	1,263.74	1,276.80	1,302.90	1,315.10	1,306.06	1,315.16	1,314.25	1,299.14	1,267.39	1,284.05
2013	1,217.16	1,230.22	1,221.32	1,197.23	1,259.22	1,274.99	1,281.54	1,292.77	1,300.74	1,300.73	1,274.38	1,256.72	1,262.07
Manufacturing													
2009	861.46	868.77	876.35	873.74	874.37	878.96	877.59	882.19	880.77	880.00	892.44	888.80	876.97
2010	889.22	889.82	892.65	901.73	910.04	901.91	937.87	939.88	940.28	948.59	958.64	979.15	925.56
2011	975.12	976.39	977.10	976.34	989.69	972.32	959.15	971.56	975.21	993.43	981.24	998.32	978.02
2012	989.33	971.96	968.36	985.35	977.21	969.07	974.45	970.41	990.15	975.26	984.14	1,018.05	982.09
2013	986.46	983.25	993.89	988.20	991.04	1,003.27	990.62	1,003.12	1,010.57	1,004.46	1,015.58	1,034.09	1,000.01
Trade, Transportation, and Utilities													
2009	655.54	667.49	672.92	669.19	666.81	668.27	667.55	671.22	671.22	665.86	670.48	684.00	669.86
2010	683.71	677.84	675.79	679.21	686.00	690.50	695.63	694.94	701.09	706.22	704.17	719.33	693.20
2011	715.87	708.98	697.25	718.29	733.25	725.55	743.77	730.80	748.35	766.45	753.28	756.80	734.30
2012	757.94	752.79	744.12	772.07	758.56	762.87	782.54	763.14	787.96	772.99	765.25	782.69	765.95
2013	767.98	773.46	783.30	796.22	794.11	800.10	795.90	786.80	797.92	800.25	783.85	805.63	789.60
Information													
2009	978.36	1,034.51	1,038.31	1,037.13	1,034.49	1,037.62	1,046.17	1,053.56	1,051.67	1,052.06	1,048.43	1,049.52	1,038.80
2010	1,044.20	1,034.20	1,038.18	1,046.32	1,043.50	1,038.50	1,039.98	1,041.15	1,037.32	1,034.67	1,037.85	1,034.11	1,040.45
2011	1,030.27	1,029.89	1,006.77	996.09	1,004.05	982.65	989.72	980.10	1,010.83	1,017.20	1,019.52	985.86	1,005.14
2012	1,008.50	993.54	1,000.48	1,043.83	1,020.26	1,008.86	1,029.15	1,008.88	1,065.37	1,025.29	1,037.63	1,076.11	1,027.30
2013	1,041.27	1,054.39	1,061.31	1,089.65	1,091.50	1,139.25	1,116.02	1,113.40	1,150.23	1,116.30	1,122.01	1,133.48	1,102.23
Financial Activities													
2009	1,018.11	1,074.48	1,074.48	1,068.26	1,069.04	1,064.62	1,070.78	1,077.76	1,074.11	1,071.98	1,069.04	1,064.30	1,067.52
2010	1,059.84	1,062.83	1,066.04	1,058.06	1,059.10	1,021.36	1,020.04	1,020.10	1,018.43	1,005.77	1,021.48	1,035.67	1,035.67
2011	1,027.21	1,035.41	1,028.46	1,044.20	1,064.30	1,026.56	1,032.85	1,038.54	1,048.59	1,106.78	1,098.20	1,095.13	1,053.95
2012	1,154.30	1,136.24	1,121.95	1,187.16	1,116.39	1,108.00	1,147.39	1,099.63	1,151.68	1,092.73	1,111.14	1,136.25	1,131.00
2013	1,075.92	1,119.46	1,100.48	1,114.84	1,103.74	1,121.16	1,084.73	1,095.99	1,159.28	1,106.10	1,132.82	1,170.51	1,115.66
Professional and Business Services													
2009	1,005.64	1,047.18	1,045.85	1,036.52	1,036.00	1,033.34	1,036.41	1,036.29	1,033.11	1,027.60	1,039.47	1,027.60	1,033.34
2010	1,024.56	1,020.66	1,020.66	1,022.73	1,025.53	1,022.00	1,023.57	1,030.03	1,028.66	1,035.51	1,033.03	1,010.59	1,024.30
2011	1,017.36	1,018.74	1,003.58	1,005.87	1,030.17	1,007.91	1,004.55	997.39	994.07	1,022.84	993.53	1,002.14	1,006.92
2012	1,035.00	1,006.06	1,015.31	1,046.50	1,023.66	1,027.48	1,044.32	1,004.66	1,043.77	1,004.42	1,008.63	1,051.46	1,027.29
2013	1,026.02	1,036.80	1,031.40	1,020.28	1,018.52	1,048.28	1,008.90	1,005.26	1,044.68	1,002.50	1,024.82	1,047.13	1,024.92
Education and Health Services													
2009	709.56	715.07	716.36	716.74	712.86	716.04	721.18	724.96	725.61	727.90	725.02	722.52	719.88
2010	724.14	727.07	720.97	719.03	721.26	722.25	715.51	726.41	729.59	728.49	724.31	738.66	724.46
2011	739.26	737.02	734.99	740.85	751.65	751.77	764.53	762.29	770.90	784.57	773.56	774.87	757.33
2012	786.22	780.17	778.02	790.76	788.18	794.21	807.28	792.56	802.20	786.64	804.87	800.91	791.67
2013	801.15	799.19	801.63	802.10	802.29	821.21	821.51	809.78	825.00	816.30	828.30	828.53	814.10
Leisure and Hospitality													
2009	310.25	329.38	328.34	326.82	328.08	328.81	327.60	330.24	328.96	323.09	320.74	317.44	324.82
2010	312.17	317.18	315.85	315.79	317.53	319.66	318.21	318.50	318.26	325.13	324.61	325.05	318.75
2011	323.74	324.14	330.62	334.91	316.25	315.49	314.50	318.78	325.30	314.96	317.27	326.40	321.53
2012	318.63	323.54	329.69	362.80	349.33	353.13	358.21	350.11	343.10	312.26	307.40	327.92	336.90
2013	308.70	311.50	320.80	323.09	329.98	331.64	322.02	338.52	340.33	323.18	308.83	325.05	323.33
Other Services													
2009	703.68	691.11	695.20	694.64	702.85	702.28	712.48	718.50	717.85	717.01	716.41	707.48	707.05
2010	712.94	710.60	713.55	715.39	713.83	712.86	710.98	710.65	706.20	710.92	709.37	720.96	711.62
2011	717.38	682.96	681.92	684.89	706.77	701.56	707.02	697.13	711.10	722.81	694.78	716.15	702.76
2012	738.69	706.26	713.16	735.36	719.85	709.70	743.82	717.71	734.58	727.54	729.14	767.33	727.52
2013	733.96	736.56	732.12	737.43	735.70	767.56	747.49	751.88	784.39	754.23	745.58	780.00	750.82

INDIANA
At a Glance

Population:
 2000 census: 6,080,827
 2010 census: 6,483,802
 2013 estimate: 6,570,902

Percent change in population:
 2000–2010: 6.6%
 2010–2013: 1.3%

Percent change in total nonfarm employment:
 2000–2010: -6.6%
 2010–2013: 4.7%

Industry with the largest growth in employment, 2000–2013 (thousands):
 Education and Health Services, 108.3

Industry with the largest decline or smallest growth in employment, 2000–2013 (thousands):
 Manufacturing, -172.5

Civilian labor force:
 2000: 3,144,379
 2010: 3,168,487
 2013: 3,179,935

Unemployment rate and rank among states (lowest to highest):
 2000: 2.9%, 10th
 2010: 10.0%, 36th
 2013: 7.5%, 33rd

Over-the-year change in unemployment rates:
 2010–2011: -1.1%
 2011–2012: -0.6%
 2012–2013: -0.6%

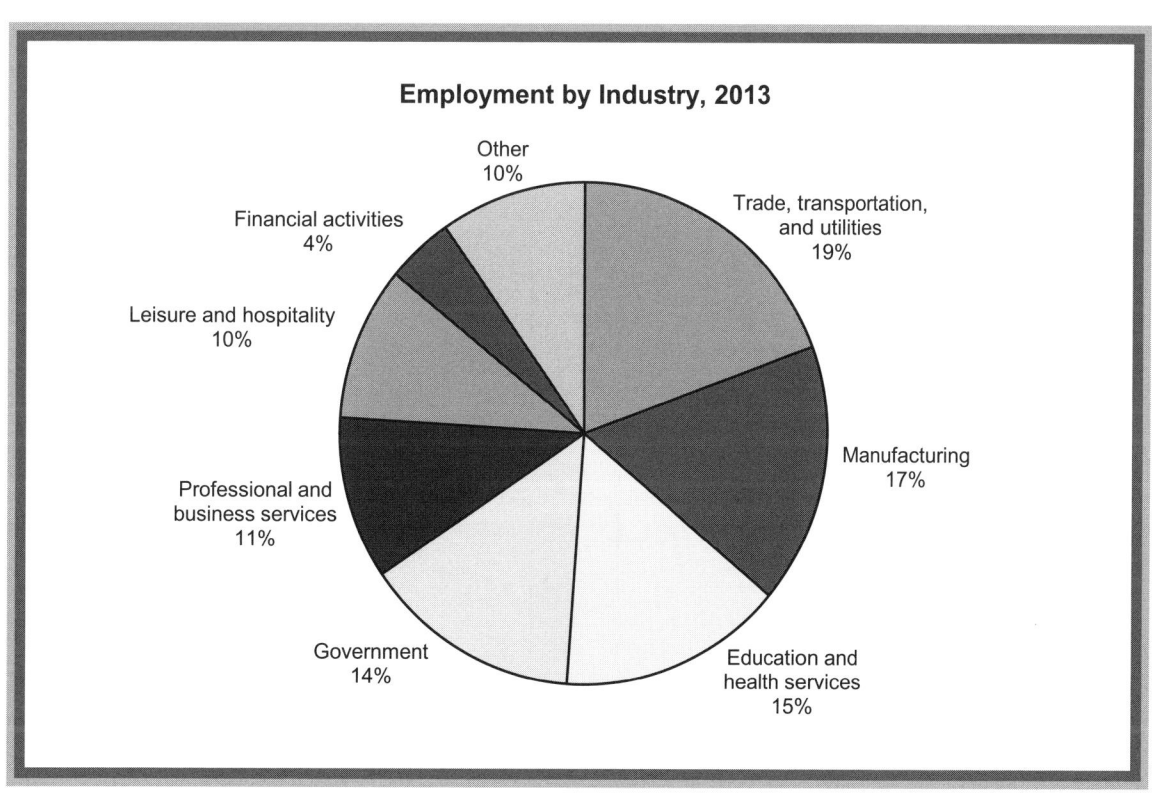

Employment by Industry, 2013

Other 10%

Financial activities 4%

Leisure and hospitality 10%

Professional and business services 11%

Government 14%

Trade, transportation, and utilities 19%

Manufacturing 17%

Education and health services 15%

1. Employment by Industry: Indiana, Selected Years, 2002–2013

(Numbers in thousands, not seasonally adjusted)

Industry and year	January	February	March	April	May	June	July	August	September	October	November	December	Annual average
Total Nonfarm													
2002	2,839.5	2,853.2	2,871.3	2,899.3	2,928.0	2,914.1	2,891.7	2,919.2	2,946.5	2,939.3	2,945.5	2,939.9	2,907.3
2003	2,853.0	2,856.3	2,875.7	2,901.1	2,926.2	2,903.0	2,861.0	2,894.1	2,929.4	2,943.5	2,942.8	2,940.3	2,902.2
2004	2,855.8	2,862.0	2,895.7	2,938.8	2,956.3	2,940.6	2,914.8	2,927.9	2,976.3	2,979.4	2,983.9	2,972.8	2,933.7
2005	2,887.2	2,905.6	2,928.1	2,968.8	2,979.6	2,961.3	2,930.4	2,945.8	3,003.1	3,005.2	3,008.9	2,999.3	2,960.3
2006	2,916.4	2,933.1	2,963.3	2,984.6	2,998.6	2,989.6	2,939.5	2,963.7	3,011.6	3,014.9	3,017.9	3,016.9	2,979.2
2007	2,927.2	2,930.3	2,971.1	2,995.0	3,016.3	3,006.5	2,955.5	2,990.5	3,024.2	3,027.8	3,032.5	3,021.6	2,991.5
2008	2,931.3	2,942.2	2,956.0	2,981.7	3,010.4	2,986.8	2,930.6	2,967.8	2,986.6	2,978.5	2,956.3	2,925.1	2,962.8
2009	2,796.2	2,794.7	2,799.5	2,808.0	2,816.8	2,781.0	2,719.6	2,756.4	2,804.7	2,815.1	2,816.2	2,808.2	2,793.0
2010	2,717.7	2,732.3	2,763.5	2,812.1	2,838.2	2,811.3	2,778.6	2,807.5	2,834.6	2,847.6	2,847.6	2,841.0	2,802.7
2011	2,765.1	2,781.5	2,815.2	2,856.6	2,880.0	2,845.8	2,795.6	2,834.1	2,895.7	2,899.7	2,901.9	2,904.3	2,848.0
2012	2,827.4	2,852.9	2,881.3	2,900.1	2,922.7	2,902.8	2,847.1	2,905.9	2,939.6	2,941.9	2,947.6	2,942.8	2,901.0
2013	2,849.6	2,882.6	2,901.9	2,931.3	2,944.0	2,930.2	2,876.5	2,946.5	2,969.1	2,988.6	2,999.1	2,980.6	2,933.3
Total Private													
2002	2,430.0	2,429.2	2,447.4	2,472.7	2,502.9	2,521.0	2,514.9	2,527.8	2,518.7	2,504.8	2,509.6	2,504.7	2,490.3
2003	2,434.4	2,425.3	2,441.9	2,469.6	2,493.2	2,499.9	2,482.3	2,502.1	2,497.7	2,504.5	2,503.9	2,500.8	2,479.6
2004	2,429.1	2,427.4	2,457.4	2,501.6	2,521.3	2,535.3	2,532.3	2,538.6	2,539.1	2,537.8	2,542.6	2,535.8	2,508.2
2005	2,458.4	2,466.4	2,489.1	2,529.8	2,543.6	2,558.4	2,550.4	2,559.0	2,564.0	2,562.3	2,568.1	2,561.6	2,534.3
2006	2,490.7	2,495.6	2,524.7	2,547.5	2,562.5	2,585.4	2,563.5	2,573.0	2,573.1	2,572.2	2,574.3	2,573.0	2,553.0
2007	2,499.2	2,489.7	2,527.1	2,553.8	2,578.6	2,596.5	2,575.6	2,582.1	2,581.0	2,581.1	2,585.3	2,575.0	2,560.4
2008	2,496.5	2,493.2	2,504.5	2,531.8	2,558.5	2,564.0	2,536.0	2,544.8	2,537.9	2,524.3	2,502.0	2,474.3	2,522.3
2009	2,356.6	2,346.9	2,348.0	2,357.5	2,362.4	2,362.8	2,341.1	2,348.9	2,357.6	2,357.4	2,363.5	2,356.4	2,354.9
2010	2,277.6	2,283.1	2,314.3	2,358.5	2,377.8	2,386.9	2,385.9	2,396.0	2,394.8	2,403.8	2,404.6	2,402.9	2,365.5
2011	2,335.7	2,344.3	2,376.3	2,414.2	2,433.6	2,437.3	2,431.8	2,446.4	2,455.9	2,457.9	2,458.5	2,460.8	2,421.1
2012	2,394.1	2,413.4	2,439.8	2,461.3	2,486.9	2,498.3	2,482.4	2,494.4	2,502.5	2,502.3	2,508.3	2,508.8	2,474.4
2013	2,427.3	2,447.2	2,465.9	2,496.1	2,521.1	2,531.0	2,514.7	2,535.0	2,537.4	2,550.8	2,561.9	2,545.9	2,511.2
Goods-Producing													
2002	725.8	726.2	731.2	737.9	746.4	756.5	755.5	760.1	755.2	747.9	745.0	737.0	743.7
2003	718.6	714.8	718.3	723.2	730.9	735.2	726.8	738.6	732.2	732.2	727.4	723.5	726.8
2004	703.2	701.6	710.5	723.6	732.6	740.0	735.2	741.7	738.8	734.2	730.4	726.6	726.5
2005	707.5	707.2	713.2	725.7	729.8	736.0	731.4	737.1	735.3	733.3	730.9	726.8	726.2
2006	710.2	707.8	715.8	723.6	728.1	738.2	729.9	734.1	727.9	724.3	718.9	716.1	722.9
2007	695.2	688.2	700.4	706.5	714.9	722.3	718.5	719.5	715.3	710.5	707.8	701.0	708.3
2008	679.2	676.7	675.7	681.2	689.2	692.9	676.7	682.0	673.0	663.1	649.0	628.8	672.3
2009	589.0	578.7	571.7	570.5	562.9	563.2	562.8	568.7	567.2	565.0	564.1	559.2	568.6
2010	540.7	538.7	548.8	564.7	572.1	579.1	585.0	586.2	582.4	583.3	578.1	574.9	569.5
2011	562.5	562.5	572.8	584.3	591.1	599.4	599.8	604.8	604.8	606.3	600.1	599.3	590.6
2012	588.4	590.1	598.6	608.2	616.1	626.3	626.5	627.7	624.0	623.4	618.7	617.3	613.8
2013	601.4	605.7	610.3	617.1	622.9	630.7	627.9	632.0	628.3	634.4	634.1	624.9	622.5
Service-Providing													
2002	2,113.7	2,127.0	2,140.1	2,161.4	2,181.6	2,157.6	2,136.2	2,159.1	2,191.3	2,191.4	2,200.5	2,202.9	2,163.6
2003	2,134.4	2,141.5	2,157.4	2,177.9	2,195.3	2,167.8	2,134.2	2,155.5	2,197.2	2,211.3	2,215.4	2,216.8	2,175.4
2004	2,152.6	2,160.4	2,185.2	2,215.2	2,223.7	2,200.6	2,179.6	2,186.2	2,237.5	2,245.2	2,253.5	2,246.2	2,207.2
2005	2,179.7	2,198.4	2,214.9	2,243.1	2,249.8	2,225.3	2,199.0	2,208.7	2,267.8	2,271.9	2,278.0	2,272.5	2,234.1
2006	2,206.2	2,225.3	2,247.5	2,261.0	2,270.5	2,251.4	2,209.6	2,229.6	2,283.7	2,290.6	2,299.0	2,300.8	2,256.3
2007	2,232.0	2,242.1	2,270.7	2,288.5	2,301.4	2,284.2	2,237.0	2,271.0	2,308.9	2,317.3	2,324.7	2,320.6	2,283.2
2008	2,252.1	2,265.5	2,280.3	2,300.5	2,321.2	2,293.9	2,253.9	2,285.8	2,313.6	2,315.4	2,307.3	2,296.3	2,290.5
2009	2,207.2	2,216.0	2,227.8	2,237.5	2,253.9	2,217.8	2,156.8	2,187.7	2,237.5	2,250.1	2,252.1	2,249.0	2,224.5
2010	2,177.0	2,193.6	2,214.7	2,247.4	2,266.1	2,232.2	2,193.6	2,221.3	2,252.2	2,264.3	2,269.5	2,266.1	2,233.2
2011	2,202.6	2,219.0	2,242.4	2,272.3	2,288.9	2,246.4	2,195.8	2,229.3	2,290.9	2,293.4	2,301.8	2,305.0	2,257.3
2012	2,239.0	2,262.8	2,282.7	2,291.9	2,306.6	2,276.5	2,220.6	2,278.2	2,315.6	2,318.5	2,328.9	2,325.5	2,287.2
2013	2,248.2	2,276.9	2,291.6	2,314.2	2,321.1	2,299.5	2,248.6	2,314.5	2,340.8	2,354.2	2,365.0	2,355.7	2,310.9
Mining and Logging													
2002	6.8	6.9	7.0	7.2	7.2	7.3	7.2	7.2	7.2	7.1	7.0	7.0	7.1
2003	6.6	6.7	6.7	7.0	7.0	7.1	7.1	7.1	7.2	7.1	7.1	7.0	7.0
2004	6.8	6.7	7.0	7.3	7.4	7.4	7.3	7.3	7.2	6.9	6.9	6.8	7.1
2005	6.7	6.7	6.8	7.0	7.0	7.1	7.0	7.0	6.9	6.9	6.9	6.8	6.9
2006	6.5	6.5	6.6	7.0	7.1	7.2	7.2	7.1	7.1	7.1	7.0	7.0	7.0
2007	6.8	6.7	6.9	7.0	7.1	7.1	7.1	7.1	7.1	7.0	6.9	6.8	7.0
2008	6.4	6.4	6.5	6.7	6.8	6.9	6.8	6.9	6.9	6.9	6.8	6.7	6.7
2009	6.3	6.3	6.5	6.6	6.7	6.8	6.8	6.8	6.8	6.7	6.7	6.5	6.6
2010	6.2	6.2	6.4	6.6	6.6	6.6	6.7	6.7	6.8	6.7	6.7	6.6	6.6
2011	6.3	6.4	6.6	6.7	6.8	6.9	6.9	7.0	6.9	7.0	7.0	6.9	6.8
2012	6.8	6.8	6.9	7.0	7.1	7.1	7.1	7.1	7.0	7.0	6.9	6.8	7.0
2013	6.7	6.7	6.7	6.9	6.9	7.0	7.1	7.1	7.1	7.1	7.1	7.0	7.0
Construction													
2002	134.4	133.5	137.0	142.9	147.9	152.3	155.2	155.1	152.6	149.5	148.1	143.6	146.0
2003	131.7	128.5	133.0	141.8	148.0	149.9	153.0	154.2	151.3	152.4	148.6	144.7	144.8
2004	131.4	129.6	136.5	146.7	152.6	155.6	158.9	156.8	155.0	153.5	151.1	146.5	147.9
2005	132.4	132.1	136.8	147.7	150.2	154.1	156.6	156.8	155.5	155.1	153.2	148.2	148.2
2006	136.9	136.1	140.9	148.0	153.4	157.1	157.3	157.8	156.2	156.4	154.3	152.0	150.5
2007	138.9	132.4	142.1	149.0	155.6	159.2	159.4	159.5	157.6	156.9	155.7	149.1	151.3
2008	135.5	133.2	137.6	143.6	148.7	151.8	153.2	152.0	150.0	149.2	143.3	133.7	144.3
2009	115.9	113.2	116.6	120.2	123.5	125.6	125.9	124.7	122.9	122.4	120.0	113.5	120.4
2010	100.3	98.3	104.5	115.0	118.3	121.1	126.1	124.7	121.9	123.0	120.9	114.0	115.7
2011	104.2	102.2	108.0	115.9	121.3	124.5	128.4	129.2	129.2	129.3	127.5	122.1	120.2
2012	112.4	111.2	116.9	123.8	127.4	130.9	131.9	132.0	131.5	130.8	127.4	123.7	125.0
2013	111.2	112.2	116.0	121.8	125.4	128.3	130.2	128.9	127.2	130.2	128.8	121.8	123.5

1. Employment by Industry: Indiana, Selected Years, 2002–2013—*Continued*

(Numbers in thousands, not seasonally adjusted)

Industry and year	January	February	March	April	May	June	July	August	September	October	November	December	Annual average
Manufacturing													
2002	584.6	585.8	587.2	587.8	591.3	596.9	593.1	597.8	595.4	591.3	589.9	586.4	590.6
2003	580.3	579.6	578.6	574.4	575.9	578.2	566.7	577.3	573.7	572.7	571.7	571.8	575.1
2004	565.0	565.3	567.0	569.6	572.6	577.0	569.0	577.6	576.6	573.8	572.4	573.3	571.6
2005	568.4	568.4	569.6	571.0	572.6	574.8	567.8	573.3	572.9	571.3	570.8	571.8	571.1
2006	566.8	565.2	568.3	568.6	567.6	573.9	565.4	569.2	564.6	560.8	557.6	557.1	565.4
2007	549.5	549.1	551.4	550.5	552.2	556.0	552.0	552.9	550.6	546.6	545.2	545.1	550.1
2008	537.3	537.1	531.6	530.9	533.7	534.2	516.7	523.1	516.1	507.0	498.9	488.4	521.3
2009	466.8	459.2	448.6	443.7	432.7	430.8	430.1	437.2	437.5	435.9	437.4	439.2	441.6
2010	434.2	434.2	437.9	443.1	447.2	451.4	452.2	454.8	453.7	453.6	450.5	454.3	447.3
2011	452.0	453.9	458.2	461.7	463.0	468.0	464.5	468.6	468.7	470.0	465.6	470.3	463.7
2012	469.2	472.1	474.8	477.4	481.6	488.3	487.5	488.6	485.5	485.6	484.4	486.8	481.8
2013	483.5	486.8	487.6	488.4	490.6	495.4	490.6	496.0	494.0	497.1	498.2	496.1	492.0
Trade, Transportation, and Utilities													
2002	579.0	572.6	574.5	575.9	581.1	584.0	582.7	583.2	580.7	579.3	590.8	595.6	581.6
2003	568.8	561.7	564.6	570.2	573.7	575.1	572.5	574.0	572.7	576.9	586.4	591.1	574.0
2004	566.6	561.1	565.9	572.2	576.9	579.4	579.9	580.5	576.5	581.4	591.2	596.1	577.3
2005	570.1	567.6	571.7	578.4	583.6	584.0	585.2	585.4	585.0	588.0	597.7	600.9	583.1
2006	576.9	572.6	577.4	579.2	584.4	587.0	584.8	585.7	584.5	587.8	598.6	602.8	585.1
2007	578.8	572.5	579.9	582.0	588.3	592.1	588.3	587.1	585.4	587.4	599.6	602.7	587.0
2008	576.4	571.9	574.4	577.2	583.9	584.9	582.0	583.0	578.9	578.6	582.0	582.4	579.6
2009	553.1	545.7	544.5	545.6	550.3	551.6	547.9	547.1	544.6	545.9	552.8	554.4	548.6
2010	532.3	527.1	532.3	537.6	542.5	544.9	545.5	545.3	542.1	547.9	555.9	558.4	542.7
2011	539.3	536.2	539.5	546.2	551.7	553.7	553.5	554.3	552.2	556.8	565.9	569.1	551.5
2012	549.8	546.1	550.4	554.6	561.1	564.2	562.1	561.5	561.0	564.7	577.4	579.0	561.0
2013	553.8	552.3	554.7	560.4	568.3	572.5	569.4	571.4	570.2	572.9	584.5	584.7	567.9
Wholesale Trade													
2002	119.7	119.3	119.3	120.0	120.6	121.1	120.5	119.9	119.2	118.5	118.3	118.3	119.6
2003	117.6	117.3	117.4	117.6	118.1	118.5	118.0	117.5	116.8	116.9	116.9	117.1	117.5
2004	116.1	116.3	117.5	118.9	119.8	120.6	121.2	120.8	119.8	120.5	120.5	120.6	119.4
2005	119.0	119.2	119.8	121.1	121.8	122.5	122.9	122.5	121.8	122.0	122.1	122.3	121.4
2006	121.1	121.2	122.0	122.8	123.8	125.0	124.4	123.8	123.4	123.6	123.5	123.9	123.2
2007	122.8	122.9	124.0	124.7	125.5	126.5	127.4	126.2	125.4	125.5	125.8	125.8	125.2
2008	124.0	124.1	124.6	125.3	126.2	126.4	125.9	125.2	124.2	123.7	122.6	121.7	124.5
2009	117.9	116.8	116.2	115.4	115.7	115.5	115.4	114.1	113.1	113.3	112.9	112.8	114.9
2010	111.3	111.1	112.1	113.1	113.5	113.8	114.5	113.6	113.0	113.2	112.7	112.4	112.9
2011	112.3	112.5	113.3	114.4	115.3	116.0	116.4	115.7	115.1	115.3	115.3	115.2	114.7
2012	114.2	114.3	115.2	115.9	116.9	117.8	117.8	116.8	116.4	116.3	116.0	116.1	116.1
2013	114.3	114.8	115.6	116.5	117.5	118.4	118.6	117.9	117.3	118.1	117.4	116.6	116.9
Retail Trade													
2002	338.8	333.7	335.8	336.3	340.5	342.8	340.7	340.6	339.1	337.7	348.4	353.8	340.7
2003	331.1	325.4	327.8	331.0	334.3	335.8	333.0	334.4	333.4	335.2	345.0	349.5	334.7
2004	329.7	323.8	326.1	328.3	332.0	333.8	332.0	332.3	329.3	332.3	341.9	346.3	332.3
2005	325.4	321.8	324.5	328.1	332.0	331.5	332.5	331.9	331.3	333.7	342.4	345.7	331.7
2006	326.9	322.0	325.0	325.9	329.0	329.8	328.5	329.3	327.6	330.5	340.3	343.4	329.9
2007	325.6	319.5	324.0	324.7	329.1	330.7	327.7	326.9	325.4	327.1	338.0	340.5	328.3
2008	321.3	316.8	317.9	319.0	323.7	324.3	323.4	323.5	321.2	321.6	326.4	327.8	322.2
2009	308.4	303.0	303.1	305.6	309.4	311.0	308.4	307.8	305.8	306.3	313.5	315.4	308.1
2010	299.7	294.9	297.8	300.9	304.4	305.9	305.6	305.3	302.0	306.8	314.5	316.9	304.6
2011	302.2	298.1	300.4	304.6	307.8	308.5	307.5	308.3	306.5	310.9	319.1	321.4	307.9
2012	306.9	302.6	305.0	307.8	312.0	313.1	311.8	311.2	310.9	314.6	326.2	326.0	312.3
2013	307.6	305.0	306.1	310.3	315.7	318.3	316.0	317.5	316.2	318.0	328.1	329.3	315.7
Transportation and Utilities													
2002	120.5	119.6	119.4	119.6	120.0	120.1	121.5	122.7	122.4	123.1	124.1	123.5	121.4
2003	120.1	119.0	119.4	121.6	121.3	120.8	121.5	122.1	122.5	124.8	124.5	124.5	121.8
2004	120.8	121.0	122.3	125.0	125.1	125.0	126.7	127.4	127.4	128.6	128.8	129.2	125.6
2005	125.7	126.6	127.4	129.2	129.8	130.0	129.8	131.0	131.9	132.3	133.2	132.9	130.0
2006	128.9	129.4	130.4	130.5	131.6	132.2	131.9	132.6	133.5	133.7	134.8	135.5	132.1
2007	130.4	130.1	131.9	132.6	133.7	134.9	133.2	134.0	134.6	134.8	135.8	136.4	133.5
2008	131.1	131.0	131.9	132.9	134.0	134.2	132.7	134.3	133.5	133.3	133.0	132.9	132.9
2009	126.8	125.9	125.2	124.6	125.2	125.1	124.1	125.2	125.7	126.3	126.4	126.2	125.6
2010	121.3	121.1	122.4	123.6	124.6	125.2	125.4	126.4	127.1	127.9	128.7	129.1	125.2
2011	124.8	125.6	125.8	127.2	128.6	129.2	129.6	130.3	130.6	130.6	131.5	132.5	128.9
2012	128.7	129.2	130.2	130.9	132.2	133.3	132.5	133.5	133.7	133.8	135.2	136.9	132.5
2013	131.9	132.5	133.0	133.6	135.1	135.8	134.8	136.0	136.7	136.8	139.0	138.8	135.3
Information													
2002	42.9	42.6	42.9	42.5	42.8	43.1	42.8	42.8	42.1	41.7	41.9	41.8	42.5
2003	41.0	40.7	41.1	40.8	41.4	42.0	41.9	42.1	41.4	41.0	41.2	41.3	41.3
2004	40.8	40.4	40.9	40.8	41.3	41.8	41.4	41.1	40.3	40.5	40.6	40.8	40.9
2005	40.0	40.1	40.1	40.2	40.7	41.0	40.8	40.7	40.0	39.7	40.0	40.4	40.3
2006	39.5	39.8	39.8	39.9	40.2	40.6	40.3	40.1	39.5	39.3	39.6	39.8	39.9
2007	39.5	39.6	39.5	39.6	40.1	40.6	40.6	40.5	39.9	39.6	39.9	40.0	40.0
2008	39.6	39.6	39.7	39.8	40.3	40.5	40.4	40.2	39.5	39.1	39.1	39.3	39.8
2009	38.6	38.4	38.1	37.8	38.1	38.4	37.8	37.6	36.8	36.4	36.5	36.7	37.6
2010	35.9	35.7	35.7	35.7	36.1	36.4	35.8	35.6	35.0	34.9	34.9	34.9	35.6
2011	34.4	34.2	34.4	34.3	34.8	35.1	35.0	35.1	35.0	35.0	35.2	35.4	34.8
2012	35.5	35.5	35.7	35.5	35.8	36.0	35.8	35.7	35.7	35.4	35.7	35.8	35.7
2013	35.7	35.6	35.8	35.8	35.7	36.0	36.3	35.9	35.4	35.3	35.4	35.6	35.7

1. Employment by Industry: Indiana, Selected Years, 2002–2013—*Continued*

(Numbers in thousands, not seasonally adjusted)

Industry and year	January	February	March	April	May	June	July	August	September	October	November	December	Annual average
Financial Activities													
2002	139.2	138.9	138.9	138.8	139.8	141.1	141.5	141.6	140.3	139.8	140.1	140.8	140.1
2003	139.5	139.5	140.2	140.5	141.9	143.1	143.2	143.3	141.8	141.0	140.4	140.9	141.3
2004	138.6	138.6	138.9	139.2	140.3	141.6	141.7	141.6	139.8	139.5	139.3	140.0	139.9
2005	137.2	137.2	137.2	138.0	138.7	139.9	140.4	140.7	139.6	139.0	138.8	139.4	138.8
2006	138.4	138.6	138.8	139.1	139.9	141.2	140.6	140.5	139.2	138.8	138.5	139.3	139.4
2007	137.5	137.8	138.1	138.4	139.1	140.3	140.1	139.6	138.5	138.2	137.7	138.0	138.6
2008	135.6	135.8	136.0	136.1	136.6	137.6	137.8	137.1	135.5	134.9	134.0	134.0	135.9
2009	132.3	131.7	131.6	131.5	132.0	132.4	132.3	131.8	130.4	130.0	129.5	129.9	131.3
2010	129.9	129.4	129.7	129.7	130.4	131.7	132.3	132.2	130.9	131.6	131.3	131.7	130.9
2011	130.9	130.9	131.3	131.0	131.9	132.5	132.6	132.0	130.9	130.7	130.3	130.5	131.3
2012	129.0	128.9	129.2	129.5	130.2	131.0	130.8	130.3	129.4	129.2	129.0	129.4	129.7
2013	127.6	127.3	127.3	127.8	129.2	130.4	130.6	130.5	129.7	129.0	129.4	130.2	129.1
Professional and Business Services													
2002	239.4	240.8	244.8	251.4	255.8	258.2	259.1	261.7	260.2	258.9	257.9	256.3	253.7
2003	246.5	246.5	248.2	251.2	254.4	255.4	254.4	257.8	257.8	259.7	260.1	257.4	254.1
2004	248.9	251.7	256.7	264.8	266.9	269.7	272.2	274.3	273.1	273.7	274.1	270.6	266.4
2005	260.5	264.1	266.8	273.1	274.2	276.2	276.2	279.8	280.4	281.2	280.5	278.2	274.3
2006	266.5	269.5	274.7	280.0	282.6	285.5	282.8	288.9	288.2	286.5	285.8	285.0	281.3
2007	275.8	276.8	283.5	289.6	292.3	294.0	290.1	295.7	295.5	295.1	293.7	292.0	289.5
2008	280.1	279.4	282.2	287.7	287.9	289.3	286.4	290.2	289.6	288.8	282.9	276.6	285.1
2009	259.4	257.7	258.3	259.1	257.9	259.1	255.8	260.8	263.1	267.7	271.1	269.2	261.6
2010	256.9	258.4	263.0	272.7	274.5	277.3	278.5	283.1	281.9	284.4	285.1	285.8	275.1
2011	275.3	276.2	282.2	288.7	287.2	287.0	287.4	292.4	295.5	295.9	295.9	295.0	288.2
2012	282.5	288.4	293.0	297.1	299.2	303.1	300.3	304.3	305.3	305.1	304.7	302.9	298.8
2013	290.4	291.8	296.7	302.8	303.8	307.2	309.1	314.3	315.0	317.4	318.7	316.1	306.9
Education and Health Services													
2002	345.2	347.3	348.4	349.4	348.6	344.1	342.7	344.5	353.5	355.7	357.2	357.8	349.5
2003	357.5	359.6	360.8	362.7	359.2	351.5	350.3	349.0	362.0	367.7	367.6	367.8	359.6
2004	365.3	367.3	369.5	372.7	365.0	359.0	360.3	356.3	373.7	378.1	379.7	376.8	368.6
2005	371.6	375.7	377.5	380.6	373.1	371.3	369.8	366.6	382.9	388.5	390.1	387.0	377.9
2006	381.7	386.7	389.5	389.8	382.4	380.8	377.6	374.0	390.5	396.7	397.2	394.5	386.8
2007	389.2	391.4	393.6	396.5	392.2	389.8	387.3	385.5	400.2	407.5	408.7	406.5	395.7
2008	401.1	404.2	405.4	407.2	405.7	400.7	397.6	394.4	410.2	416.3	417.6	419.0	406.6
2009	405.7	415.5	417.8	419.3	417.8	411.2	401.8	400.5	420.0	424.8	426.9	426.9	415.7
2010	413.0	423.6	427.4	430.1	426.4	416.5	409.4	412.1	427.5	431.6	433.6	433.0	423.7
2011	419.5	428.7	431.3	436.1	433.9	422.3	418.4	420.6	436.6	437.9	439.4	440.9	430.5
2012	427.1	438.7	438.5	434.1	432.3	420.7	413.2	418.8	438.3	439.7	442.5	443.8	432.3
2013	428.5	442.2	442.1	444.3	441.8	430.6	421.3	429.9	443.8	448.6	449.4	446.7	439.1
Leisure and Hospitality													
2002	250.5	252.1	257.1	266.2	276.3	280.9	278.7	282.1	276.1	271.2	266.5	265.0	268.6
2003	253.9	253.2	258.4	270.0	279.6	284.1	280.2	284.3	277.5	273.8	269.0	266.5	270.9
2004	255.0	255.3	262.5	274.4	283.6	287.7	285.6	287.2	281.8	275.1	272.4	269.9	274.2
2005	257.5	260.0	266.9	277.2	286.2	292.0	289.2	291.4	284.4	276.8	274.6	273.0	277.4
2006	263.2	266.0	272.6	279.2	287.2	293.3	289.8	292.2	286.4	282.5	279.9	279.1	281.0
2007	268.1	268.1	275.1	283.4	292.8	297.4	291.8	296.0	288.7	285.3	280.9	277.6	283.8
2008	267.9	268.8	273.8	284.0	294.9	297.8	295.5	298.8	293.2	285.3	280.1	277.2	284.8
2009	263.6	264.5	270.4	278.2	287.5	290.1	286.8	287.6	281.8	273.8	269.2	266.5	276.7
2010	256.3	257.7	263.5	273.4	280.9	284.8	283.1	285.9	279.8	274.8	270.5	269.1	273.3
2011	259.7	261.1	268.7	277.3	286.2	289.3	287.5	289.7	284.1	278.9	275.5	274.3	277.7
2012	266.2	269.6	277.1	284.7	293.6	297.5	294.8	297.3	291.2	286.1	282.5	282.5	285.3
2013	272.8	274.6	280.5	289.1	299.7	302.5	299.7	301.1	296.4	293.5	290.3	287.6	290.7
Other Services													
2002	108.0	108.7	109.6	110.6	112.1	113.1	111.9	111.8	110.6	110.3	110.2	110.4	110.6
2003	108.6	109.3	110.3	111.0	112.1	113.5	113.0	113.0	112.3	112.2	111.8	112.3	111.6
2004	110.7	111.4	112.5	113.9	114.7	116.1	116.0	115.9	115.1	115.3	114.9	115.0	114.3
2005	114.0	114.5	115.7	116.6	117.3	118.0	117.4	117.3	116.4	115.8	115.5	115.9	116.2
2006	114.3	114.6	116.1	116.7	117.7	118.8	117.7	117.5	116.9	116.3	115.8	116.4	116.6
2007	115.1	115.3	117.0	117.8	118.9	120.0	118.9	118.2	117.5	117.5	117.0	117.2	117.5
2008	116.6	116.8	117.3	118.6	120.0	120.3	119.6	119.1	118.0	118.2	117.3	117.0	118.2
2009	114.9	114.7	115.6	115.5	115.9	116.8	115.9	114.8	113.7	113.8	113.4	113.6	114.9
2010	112.6	112.5	113.9	114.6	114.9	116.2	116.3	115.6	115.2	115.3	115.2	115.1	114.8
2011	114.1	114.5	116.1	116.3	116.8	118.0	117.6	117.5	116.8	116.4	116.2	116.3	116.4
2012	115.6	116.1	117.3	117.6	118.6	119.5	118.9	118.8	117.9	118.4	117.7	118.1	117.9
2013	117.1	117.7	118.5	118.8	119.7	121.1	120.4	119.9	118.6	119.7	120.1	120.1	119.3
Government													
2002	409.5	424.0	423.9	426.6	425.1	393.1	376.8	391.4	427.8	434.5	435.9	435.2	417.0
2003	418.6	431.0	433.8	431.5	433.0	403.1	378.7	392.0	431.7	439.0	438.9	439.5	422.6
2004	426.7	434.6	438.3	437.2	435.0	405.3	382.5	389.3	437.2	441.6	441.3	437.0	425.5
2005	428.8	439.2	439.0	439.0	436.0	402.9	380.0	386.8	439.1	442.9	440.8	437.7	426.0
2006	425.7	437.5	438.6	437.1	436.1	404.2	376.0	390.7	438.5	442.7	443.6	443.9	426.2
2007	428.0	440.6	444.0	441.2	437.7	410.0	379.9	408.4	443.2	446.7	447.2	446.6	431.1
2008	434.8	449.0	451.5	449.9	451.9	422.8	394.6	423.0	448.7	454.2	454.3	450.8	440.5
2009	439.6	447.8	451.5	450.5	454.4	418.2	378.5	407.5	447.1	457.7	452.7	451.8	438.1
2010	440.1	449.2	449.2	453.6	460.4	424.4	392.7	411.5	439.8	443.8	443.0	438.1	437.2
2011	429.4	437.2	438.9	442.4	446.4	408.5	363.8	387.7	439.8	441.8	443.4	443.5	426.9
2012	433.3	439.5	441.5	438.8	435.8	404.5	364.7	411.5	437.1	439.6	439.3	434.0	426.6
2013	422.3	435.4	436.0	435.2	422.9	399.2	361.8	411.5	431.7	437.8	437.2	434.7	422.1

2. Average Weekly Hours by Selected Industry: Indiana, 2009–2013

(Not seasonally adjusted)

Industry and year	January	February	March	April	May	June	July	August	September	October	November	December	Annual average
Total Private													
2009	34.4	34.9	34.7	34.1	34.1	34.3	34.7	35.0	34.4	34.5	35.2	35.1	34.6
2010	34.8	34.5	35.0	35.0	35.1	35.1	35.1	35.4	35.2	35.0	35.3	34.8	35.0
2011	35.0	34.9	35.0	34.9	35.1	35.0	34.8	35.1	35.0	35.3	34.8	34.6	35.0
2012	34.5	34.6	34.6	35.0	34.5	34.8	35.0	34.7	34.8	34.6	34.5	34.8	34.7
2013	34.4	34.6	34.6	34.6	34.5	34.9	34.4	34.5	34.8	34.7	34.7	35.0	34.7
Goods-Producing													
2009	37.9	38.7	38.6	38.0	38.3	39.2	39.2	39.9	39.3	39.7	41.0	41.0	39.2
2010	40.5	39.8	40.6	40.6	40.7	41.0	40.8	41.1	41.0	41.5	41.6	41.5	40.9
2011	41.3	41.1	41.3	40.9	41.2	40.7	40.1	41.3	41.3	41.6	40.8	41.0	41.0
2012	40.7	40.8	40.6	41.5	40.8	41.1	41.4	41.1	41.0	40.8	40.8	41.0	41.0
2013	40.9	40.9	41.0	41.2	40.3	40.9	39.6	40.4	41.3	41.0	40.9	41.6	40.8
Construction													
2009	36.4	37.7	38.3	37.3	38.2	38.3	40.1	40.6	38.6	38.3	40.2	37.8	38.5
2010	38.5	36.6	38.7	39.6	38.1	39.4	40.7	40.6	38.4	40.2	39.3	38.1	39.1
2011	37.4	36.5	37.4	37.7	39.7	38.4	38.8	39.7	38.8	39.1	37.7	38.0	38.3
2012	36.5	37.4	38.2	39.1	38.8	39.8	39.4	39.9	39.9	39.6	40.6	38.1	39.0
2013	38.4	38.5	38.2	37.7	37.7	38.8	38.5	39.3	38.9	39.4	39.3	36.8	38.5
Manufacturing													
2009	37.2	37.7	37.7	37.3	37.6	38.7	38.2	39.0	38.8	39.4	40.7	41.4	38.6
2010	40.8	40.5	40.2	40.1	40.9	40.9	40.7	41.1	41.1	41.3	41.8	41.8	40.9
2011	41.8	41.8	42.0	41.6	41.4	41.1	40.3	41.5	41.5	41.9	41.3	41.5	41.5
2012	41.5	41.4	41.1	41.9	41.1	41.3	41.7	41.2	41.1	40.5	40.8	41.4	41.2
2013	41.2	41.2	41.4	41.8	40.6	41.2	39.6	40.4	41.5	41.1	41.0	42.3	41.1
Trade, Transportation, and Utilities													
2009	36.1	36.1	35.7	35.5	35.7	35.9	36.4	36.3	36.1	36.1	36.4	36.1	36.0
2010	35.8	36.0	36.1	36.5	36.7	36.5	36.6	36.8	36.6	36.6	36.5	36.3	36.4
2011	35.0	34.6	35.0	35.2	35.3	35.7	35.3	35.2	35.1	35.2	34.3	34.3	35.0
2012	33.9	34.0	34.4	34.8	34.6	35.0	34.8	34.6	34.6	34.4	34.0	34.1	34.4
2013	33.5	33.6	33.7	33.8	34.1	34.3	34.1	34.1	34.3	34.0	33.7	34.1	33.9
Financial Activities													
2009	36.3	36.6	36.1	35.3	36.2	35.6	35.5	36.6	36.3	36.8	37.8	38.0	36.4
2010	37.2	37.0	37.0	37.2	37.4	37.3	37.6	37.4	36.6	37.1	37.3	35.8	37.1
2011	36.8	36.4	36.3	36.8	37.5	36.9	37.1	36.3	36.5	36.9	36.4	36.6	36.7
2012	36.8	36.5	36.6	36.7	36.6	36.2	36.2	36.2	37.2	36.5	37.5	37.6	36.7
2013	37.3	37.3	37.3	36.9	37.0	37.5	37.0	36.7	36.9	37.0	37.2	37.0	37.1
Professional and Business Services													
2009	34.9	35.5	35.7	35.2	34.4	34.9	35.3	35.7	34.7	34.5	35.0	35.1	35.1
2010	35.6	35.3	35.2	35.2	35.6	35.3	35.2	37.1	35.5	35.8	36.6	36.1	35.7
2011	36.0	35.8	35.5	35.5	36.2	36.0	35.1	35.4	35.7	36.1	35.4	34.9	35.6
2012	35.2	35.1	34.6	35.9	35.0	35.1	35.1	34.6	35.2	34.8	35.1	35.5	35.1
2013	34.8	35.5	35.1	35.9	36.3	36.6	35.9	35.9	35.9	35.9	35.8	35.9	35.8
Education and Health Services													
2009	33.0	33.0	33.0	32.8	32.7	32.5	33.5	33.6	32.5	32.1	33.0	32.7	32.9
2010	32.4	32.1	32.2	32.3	32.6	32.4	32.2	32.4	32.3	31.9	32.4	32.4	32.3
2011	32.1	32.1	32.4	32.3	32.6	32.4	32.5	32.5	32.6	32.7	32.7	32.7	32.5
2012	32.7	32.8	32.7	32.8	32.3	32.7	32.9	32.7	33.0	33.0	32.9	33.1	32.8
2013	33.0	32.8	32.9	32.7	32.7	32.9	32.9	32.7	33.2	32.9	33.1	33.8	33.0
Leisure and Hospitality													
2009	24.4	25.7	25.5	24.8	25.3	25.6	25.9	26.3	25.4	25.3	25.5	25.2	25.4
2010	24.9	25.5	26.1	25.7	25.8	25.9	26.4	26.5	26.5	26.3	26.5	26.0	26.0
2011	25.8	26.3	26.4	26.3	26.4	26.3	26.3	26.2	25.8	26.0	26.0	25.6	26.1
2012	25.0	25.8	25.8	25.1	25.1	25.4	25.7	25.8	25.4	25.2	24.9	25.2	25.4
2013	24.2	24.5	24.6	24.6	24.8	25.3	25.3	25.2	25.0	24.8	25.0	24.7	24.8
Other Services													
2009	29.1	29.3	29.7	28.8	28.5	30.0	29.7	29.6	29.7	29.5	31.0	30.1	29.6
2010	29.7	29.4	29.9	28.7	29.3	29.9	30.1	29.8	30.2	30.1	30.0	28.9	29.7
2011	29.1	28.7	29.1	28.8	28.0	28.6	28.6	28.6	28.7	29.2	28.7	28.4	28.7
2012	28.8	28.8	29.1	28.8	28.8	29.2	30.1	29.0	28.2	28.6	28.5	29.1	28.9
2013	28.1	28.8	28.8	28.5	28.9	29.4	29.0	29.1	28.0	28.8	28.5	28.3	28.7

3. Average Hourly Earnings by Selected Industry: Indiana, 2009–2013

(Dollars, not seasonally adjusted)

Industry and year	January	February	March	April	May	June	July	August	September	October	November	December	Annual average
Total Private													
2009	20.50	20.99	20.74	20.67	20.54	20.51	20.41	20.36	20.50	20.34	20.52	20.59	20.56
2010	20.59	20.64	20.58	20.53	20.56	20.44	20.53	20.39	20.55	20.72	20.58	20.73	20.57
2011	20.79	20.55	20.43	20.29	20.43	20.32	20.61	20.63	20.70	20.99	20.87	21.12	20.64
2012	21.22	21.12	21.17	21.26	21.06	21.04	21.43	21.29	21.64	21.57	21.61	22.17	21.38
2013	22.07	22.05	22.03	22.05	21.77	21.95	21.91	21.99	22.26	22.08	22.24	22.54	22.08
Goods-Producing													
2009	23.54	24.18	23.87	24.00	23.86	23.71	23.83	23.45	23.66	23.51	23.92	23.30	23.73
2010	23.24	23.28	23.21	23.43	23.56	23.29	23.50	23.20	23.18	23.65	23.26	23.28	23.34
2011	23.32	22.91	23.12	23.00	23.27	23.18	23.51	23.57	23.64	24.11	23.99	24.43	23.51
2012	24.42	24.30	24.28	24.61	24.59	24.34	24.87	24.60	24.84	24.42	24.44	25.16	24.58
2013	24.92	24.91	24.65	24.66	24.37	24.75	24.68	24.23	24.81	24.54	24.90	25.22	24.72
Construction													
2009	23.83	24.04	24.30	24.59	24.31	24.49	24.56	24.47	24.60	24.38	24.40	24.56	24.39
2010	24.74	25.45	25.20	25.75	25.66	26.05	26.81	26.03	25.66	26.61	26.43	27.22	26.01
2011	26.65	26.33	26.45	26.09	26.62	26.14	26.07	26.21	26.33	26.05	26.68	26.94	26.37
2012	26.51	26.45	26.59	26.55	26.68	26.76	27.34	27.41	27.79	27.02	27.19	28.12	27.06
2013	28.28	28.04	28.24	28.42	27.77	27.02	26.86	26.29	26.49	26.79	26.14	25.98	27.16
Manufacturing													
2009	22.64	23.38	23.01	22.91	22.62	22.51	22.71	22.33	22.70	22.54	23.08	22.38	22.73
2010	22.27	22.30	22.22	22.32	22.60	22.19	22.26	22.27	22.43	22.73	22.31	22.26	22.35
2011	22.49	22.13	22.33	22.20	22.33	22.32	22.70	22.71	22.81	23.38	23.08	23.64	22.68
2012	23.81	23.71	23.52	23.96	23.92	23.61	24.16	23.78	23.99	23.66	23.70	24.44	23.86
2013	24.16	24.20	23.86	23.79	23.54	24.03	23.99	23.58	24.15	23.77	24.40	24.88	24.03
Trade, Transportation, and Utilities													
2009	18.31	18.34	18.53	18.24	18.20	18.60	18.30	18.66	18.78	18.65	18.80	19.07	18.54
2010	19.36	19.28	19.24	19.36	19.27	19.58	19.49	19.33	19.75	19.62	19.70	19.57	19.46
2011	20.04	19.59	19.31	19.23	19.35	19.12	19.30	19.27	19.36	19.54	19.49	19.30	19.41
2012	19.49	19.57	19.42	19.23	18.89	18.85	19.34	19.17	19.49	19.32	19.27	19.85	19.32
2013	19.63	19.80	19.99	19.67	19.50	19.77	19.84	20.08	20.15	20.13	20.27	20.48	19.95
Financial Activities													
2009	21.88	22.29	23.71	24.17	22.85	23.25	22.76	21.69	21.96	23.81	23.79	23.95	23.01
2010	24.45	24.17	24.40	23.36	23.81	23.94	23.57	23.99	24.09	23.43	22.87	24.17	23.85
2011	24.38	23.42	23.11	22.90	22.72	22.72	22.85	23.02	22.72	23.08	22.68	21.94	22.96
2012	23.16	22.24	22.41	22.72	22.06	22.11	22.67	22.15	22.90	22.92	22.94	23.32	22.64
2013	23.74	24.00	23.99	25.05	24.87	24.79	24.44	24.82	25.34	25.29	25.01	25.23	24.72
Professional and Business Services													
2009	21.21	21.64	21.05	20.83	21.31	21.22	21.19	21.05	20.83	19.22	19.48	19.65	20.71
2010	19.46	19.79	19.44	19.10	19.58	19.52	19.66	19.59	19.78	20.10	20.38	20.58	19.76
2011	20.86	20.67	20.67	20.49	20.94	20.78	21.37	21.28	21.18	21.27	21.63	21.83	21.08
2012	22.10	22.00	21.78	21.30	20.91	21.00	21.28	20.82	21.07	20.69	20.98	21.10	21.24
2013	21.10	21.29	21.17	21.13	21.05	21.29	21.65	21.97	22.23	21.86	22.21	22.48	21.63
Education and Health Services													
2009	21.64	21.56	21.50	21.50	21.62	21.58	21.56	21.40	21.54	21.48	21.42	21.85	21.55
2010	21.50	21.65	21.71	21.56	21.51	21.30	21.77	21.41	21.76	21.51	21.66	21.58	21.58
2011	21.54	21.72	21.59	21.43	21.59	21.84	22.23	22.13	22.07	22.27	21.95	22.42	21.90
2012	21.92	22.13	22.40	22.62	22.55	22.76	23.02	23.20	23.60	23.71	23.72	24.24	23.00
2013	23.89	23.74	24.11	24.25	23.92	24.11	24.08	24.47	24.24	24.06	24.01	24.30	24.10
Leisure and Hospitality													
2009	12.07	11.93	11.51	11.91	11.68	11.45	11.61	11.76	12.09	12.19	12.14	12.56	11.90
2010	12.80	12.88	12.72	12.29	12.25	12.31	12.29	12.15	12.34	12.27	12.25	12.85	12.44
2011	12.83	12.82	12.66	12.44	12.35	12.24	12.26	12.22	12.51	12.30	12.46	12.80	12.48
2012	12.91	12.67	12.49	12.36	12.22	12.03	12.11	11.95	12.05	12.24	12.33	12.59	12.32
2013	12.40	12.46	12.36	12.21	12.23	11.84	11.71	11.87	12.12	12.01	12.15	12.30	12.13
Other Services													
2009	17.95	18.32	18.14	17.89	18.14	17.11	17.44	18.23	18.41	18.75	19.00	19.23	18.22
2010	18.97	19.25	18.80	19.08	18.75	17.73	17.80	18.58	18.77	19.30	19.06	19.24	18.77
2011	18.96	18.85	18.62	18.31	18.13	17.59	16.99	16.73	16.60	16.49	16.94	17.56	
2012	17.00	16.70	17.09	17.05	16.99	17.06	17.00	17.04	17.64	17.23	17.19	17.84	17.15
2013	17.79	17.63	17.56	17.32	17.05	16.84	17.23	17.20	17.60	17.52	17.52	17.99	17.43

4. Average Weekly Earnings by Selected Industry: Indiana, 2009–2013

(Dollars, not seasonally adjusted)

Industry and year	January	February	March	April	May	June	July	August	September	October	November	December	Annual average
Total Private													
2009	705.20	732.55	719.68	704.85	700.41	703.49	708.23	712.60	705.20	701.73	722.30	722.71	711.38
2010	716.53	712.08	720.30	718.55	721.66	717.44	720.60	721.81	723.36	729.34	728.53	727.62	722.01
2011	727.65	717.20	715.05	708.12	717.09	711.20	717.23	724.11	724.50	740.95	726.28	730.75	722.40
2012	732.09	730.75	732.48	744.10	726.57	732.19	750.05	738.76	753.07	746.32	745.55	771.52	741.89
2013	759.21	762.93	762.24	762.93	751.07	766.06	753.70	758.66	774.65	766.18	771.73	788.90	766.18
Goods-Producing													
2009	892.17	935.77	921.38	912.00	913.84	929.43	934.14	935.66	929.84	933.35	980.72	955.30	930.22
2010	941.22	926.54	942.33	951.26	958.89	954.89	958.80	953.52	950.38	981.48	967.62	966.12	954.61
2011	963.12	941.60	954.86	940.70	958.72	943.43	942.75	973.44	976.33	1,002.98	978.79	1,001.63	963.91
2012	993.89	991.44	985.77	1,021.32	1,003.27	1,000.37	1,029.62	1,011.06	1,018.44	996.34	997.15	1,031.56	1,007.78
2013	1,019.23	1,018.82	1,010.65	1,015.99	982.11	1,012.28	977.33	978.89	1,024.65	1,006.14	1,018.41	1,049.15	1,008.58
Construction													
2009	867.41	906.31	930.69	917.21	928.64	937.97	984.86	993.48	949.56	933.75	980.88	928.37	939.02
2010	952.49	931.47	975.24	1,019.70	977.65	1,026.37	1,091.17	1,056.82	985.34	1,069.72	1,038.70	1,037.08	1,016.99
2011	996.71	961.05	989.23	983.59	1,056.81	1,003.78	1,011.52	1,040.54	1,021.60	1,018.56	1,005.84	1,023.72	1,009.97
2012	967.62	989.23	1,015.74	1,038.11	1,035.18	1,065.05	1,077.20	1,093.66	1,100.48	1,097.01	1,071.29	1,071.37	1,055.34
2013	1,085.95	1,079.54	1,078.77	1,071.43	1,046.93	1,048.38	1,034.11	1,033.20	1,030.46	1,055.53	1,027.30	956.06	1,045.66
Manufacturing													
2009	842.21	881.43	867.48	854.54	850.51	871.14	867.52	870.87	880.76	888.08	939.36	926.53	877.38
2010	908.62	903.15	893.24	895.03	924.34	907.57	905.98	915.30	921.87	938.75	932.56	930.47	914.12
2011	940.08	925.03	937.86	923.52	924.46	917.35	914.81	942.47	946.62	979.62	953.20	981.06	941.22
2012	988.12	981.59	966.67	1,003.92	983.11	975.09	1,007.47	979.74	985.99	958.23	966.96	1,011.82	983.03
2013	995.39	997.04	987.80	994.42	955.72	990.04	950.00	952.63	1,002.23	976.95	1,000.40	1,052.42	987.63
Trade, Transportation, and Utilities													
2009	660.99	662.07	661.52	647.52	649.74	667.74	666.12	677.36	677.96	673.27	684.32	688.43	667.44
2010	693.09	694.08	694.56	706.64	707.21	714.67	713.33	711.34	722.85	718.09	719.05	710.39	708.34
2011	701.40	677.81	675.85	676.90	683.06	682.58	681.29	678.30	679.54	687.81	668.51	661.99	679.35
2012	660.71	665.38	668.05	669.20	653.59	659.75	673.03	663.28	674.35	664.61	655.18	676.89	664.61
2013	657.61	665.28	673.66	664.85	664.95	678.11	676.54	684.73	691.15	684.42	683.10	698.37	676.31
Financial Activities													
2009	794.24	815.81	855.93	853.20	827.17	827.70	807.98	793.85	797.15	876.21	899.26	910.10	837.56
2010	909.54	894.29	902.80	868.99	890.49	892.96	886.23	897.23	881.69	869.25	853.05	865.29	884.84
2011	897.18	852.49	838.89	842.72	852.00	838.37	847.74	835.63	829.28	851.65	825.55	803.00	842.63
2012	852.29	811.76	820.21	833.82	807.40	800.38	820.65	801.83	851.88	836.58	860.25	876.83	830.89
2013	885.50	895.20	894.83	924.35	920.19	929.63	904.28	910.89	935.05	935.73	930.37	933.51	917.11
Professional and Business Services													
2009	740.23	768.22	751.49	733.22	733.06	740.58	748.01	751.49	722.80	663.09	681.80	689.72	726.92
2010	692.78	698.59	684.29	672.32	697.05	689.06	692.03	726.79	702.19	719.58	745.91	742.94	705.43
2011	750.96	739.99	733.79	727.40	758.03	748.08	750.09	753.31	756.13	767.85	765.70	761.87	750.45
2012	777.92	772.20	753.59	764.67	731.85	737.10	746.93	720.37	741.66	720.01	736.40	749.05	745.52
2013	734.28	755.80	743.07	758.57	764.12	779.21	777.24	788.72	798.06	784.77	795.12	807.03	774.35
Education and Health Services													
2009	714.12	711.48	709.50	705.20	706.97	701.35	722.26	719.04	700.05	689.51	706.86	714.50	709.00
2010	696.60	694.97	699.06	696.39	701.23	690.12	700.99	693.68	698.65	694.14	696.92	701.78	697.03
2011	691.43	697.21	699.52	692.19	703.83	707.62	722.48	719.23	719.48	728.23	717.77	733.13	711.75
2012	716.78	725.86	732.48	741.94	728.37	744.25	757.36	758.64	778.80	782.43	780.39	802.34	754.40
2013	788.37	778.67	793.22	792.98	782.18	793.22	792.23	800.17	804.77	791.57	794.73	821.34	795.30
Leisure and Hospitality													
2009	294.51	306.60	293.51	295.37	295.50	293.12	300.70	309.29	307.09	308.41	309.57	316.51	302.26
2010	318.72	328.44	331.99	315.85	316.05	318.83	324.46	321.98	327.01	322.70	324.63	334.10	323.44
2011	331.01	337.17	334.22	327.17	326.04	321.91	322.44	320.16	322.76	319.80	323.96	327.68	325.73
2012	322.75	326.89	322.24	310.24	306.72	305.56	311.23	308.31	306.07	308.45	307.02	317.27	312.93
2013	300.08	305.27	304.06	300.37	303.30	299.55	296.26	299.12	303.00	297.85	303.75	303.81	300.82
Other Services													
2009	522.35	536.78	538.76	515.23	516.99	513.30	517.97	539.61	546.78	553.13	589.00	578.82	539.31
2010	563.41	565.95	562.12	547.60	549.38	530.13	535.78	553.68	566.85	580.93	571.80	556.04	557.47
2011	551.74	541.00	541.84	527.33	507.64	503.07	485.91	478.48	475.56	484.72	473.26	481.10	503.97
2012	489.60	480.96	497.32	491.04	489.31	498.15	511.70	494.16	497.45	492.78	489.92	519.14	495.64
2013	499.90	507.74	505.73	493.62	492.75	495.10	499.67	500.52	492.80	504.58	499.32	509.12	500.24

IOWA
At a Glance

Population:
    2000 census: 2,926,538
    2010 census: 3,046,355
    2013 estimate: 3,062,309

Percent change in population:
    2000–2010: 4.1%
    2010–2013: 1.4%

Percent change in total nonfarm employment:
    2000–2010: -0.6%
    2010–2013: 4.1%

Industry with the largest growth in employment, 2000–2013 (thousands):
    Education and Health Services, 41.3

Industry with the largest decline or smallest growth in employment, 2000–2013 (thousands):
    Manufacturing, -37.1

Civilian labor force:
    2000: 1,601,920
    2010: 1,671,100
    2013: 1,671,320

Unemployment rate and rank among states (lowest to highest):
    2000: 2.8%, 8th
    2010: 6.3%, 5th
    2013: 4.6%, 6th

Over-the-year change in unemployment rates:
    2010–2011: -0.5%
    2011–2012: -0.6%
    2012–2013: -0.6%

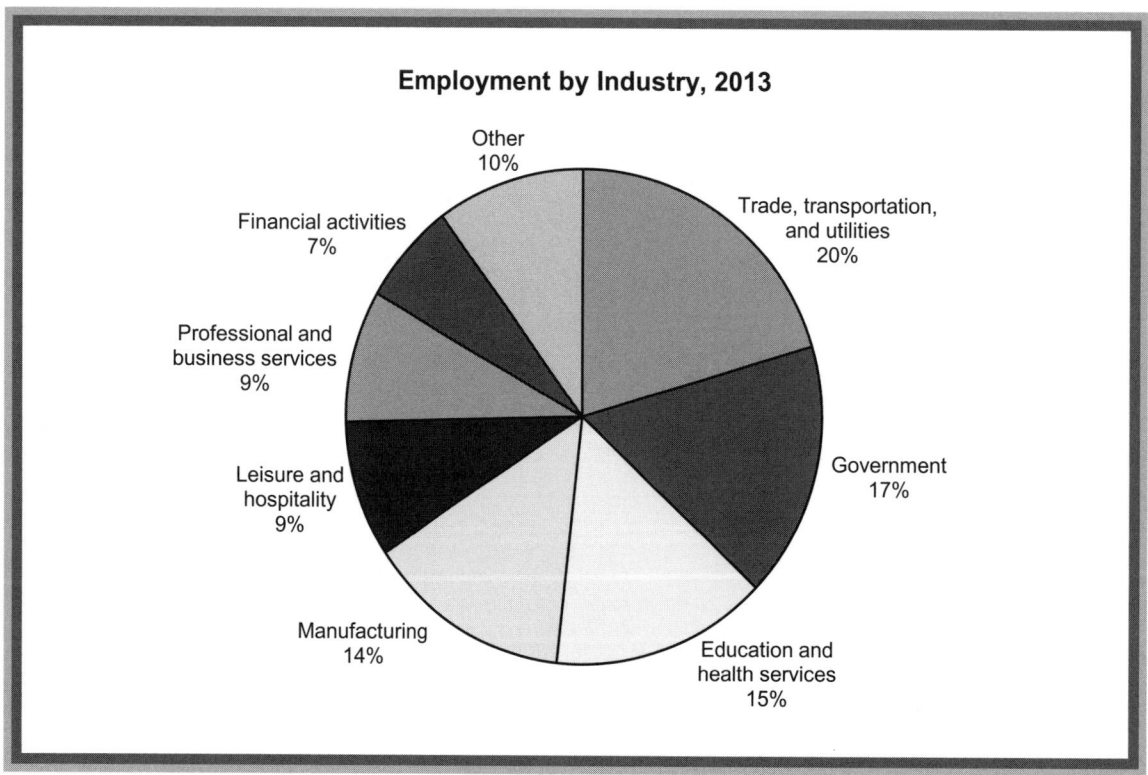

Employment by Industry, 2013

Other 10%
Financial activities 7%
Professional and business services 9%
Leisure and hospitality 9%
Manufacturing 14%
Education and health services 15%
Government 17%
Trade, transportation, and utilities 20%

1. Employment by Industry: Iowa, Selected Years, 2002–2013

(Numbers in thousands, not seasonally adjusted)

Industry and year	January	February	March	April	May	June	July	August	September	October	November	December	Annual average
Total Nonfarm													
2002	1,422.6	1,420.8	1,429.7	1,453.1	1,466.4	1,469.6	1,437.7	1,435.6	1,454.4	1,457.5	1,462.0	1,458.6	1,447.3
2003	1,411.9	1,411.4	1,420.5	1,440.2	1,453.7	1,455.2	1,427.0	1,430.3	1,450.8	1,460.6	1,462.4	1,461.3	1,440.4
2004	1,417.8	1,419.7	1,433.0	1,460.0	1,469.2	1,476.6	1,450.7	1,449.9	1,467.6	1,477.3	1,482.5	1,482.7	1,457.3
2005	1,434.2	1,442.3	1,459.1	1,483.4	1,494.3	1,499.3	1,473.1	1,472.6	1,496.0	1,501.7	1,505.7	1,504.3	1,480.5
2006	1,462.9	1,471.0	1,484.8	1,506.6	1,519.6	1,527.0	1,492.6	1,492.5	1,515.6	1,523.4	1,527.6	1,527.2	1,504.2
2007	1,482.6	1,485.7	1,496.4	1,517.8	1,534.1	1,542.2	1,508.5	1,508.8	1,529.3	1,538.6	1,545.9	1,538.9	1,519.1
2008	1,496.1	1,499.9	1,509.6	1,529.6	1,546.6	1,544.7	1,515.3	1,514.8	1,534.4	1,540.8	1,535.6	1,525.3	1,524.4
2009	1,471.7	1,472.0	1,473.0	1,488.5	1,497.8	1,493.6	1,460.6	1,461.3	1,479.2	1,487.2	1,486.8	1,476.8	1,479.0
2010	1,432.2	1,437.4	1,449.8	1,477.0	1,489.0	1,486.4	1,457.4	1,455.7	1,474.3	1,490.6	1,494.0	1,487.7	1,469.3
2011	1,443.8	1,449.9	1,460.9	1,489.1	1,500.4	1,499.8	1,477.7	1,479.8	1,501.5	1,509.7	1,513.5	1,507.8	1,486.2
2012	1,467.4	1,474.6	1,488.9	1,511.0	1,524.2	1,524.1	1,500.4	1,505.3	1,519.8	1,528.8	1,533.8	1,527.4	1,508.8
2013	1,484.2	1,493.3	1,501.6	1,521.2	1,540.1	1,543.8	1,526.0	1,530.4	1,543.0	1,560.8	1,561.8	1,549.3	1,529.6
Total Private													
2002	1,177.4	1,172.5	1,180.5	1,203.4	1,214.7	1,221.6	1,214.3	1,214.0	1,212.7	1,209.2	1,211.7	1,208.3	1,203.4
2003	1,168.9	1,162.7	1,170.7	1,190.1	1,201.7	1,207.5	1,203.1	1,207.5	1,206.7	1,209.8	1,210.1	1,208.4	1,195.6
2004	1,174.5	1,171.3	1,184.0	1,209.4	1,217.7	1,226.9	1,227.1	1,226.8	1,224.3	1,227.1	1,230.7	1,232.0	1,212.7
2005	1,191.8	1,194.3	1,209.7	1,233.2	1,241.8	1,250.8	1,248.9	1,248.2	1,250.5	1,249.9	1,252.6	1,251.9	1,235.3
2006	1,219.1	1,220.3	1,233.5	1,254.8	1,265.9	1,275.4	1,266.9	1,266.9	1,267.8	1,269.9	1,272.7	1,272.8	1,257.2
2007	1,235.0	1,232.0	1,242.8	1,263.8	1,277.6	1,288.7	1,279.9	1,280.3	1,279.0	1,281.7	1,287.8	1,281.8	1,269.2
2008	1,246.2	1,244.0	1,252.6	1,272.4	1,286.1	1,288.6	1,284.0	1,283.8	1,279.7	1,280.5	1,274.3	1,265.2	1,271.5
2009	1,218.6	1,213.3	1,213.3	1,227.4	1,234.7	1,235.8	1,226.3	1,227.1	1,224.8	1,226.5	1,225.4	1,217.6	1,224.2
2010	1,181.9	1,181.5	1,191.5	1,218.6	1,225.6	1,228.7	1,224.6	1,223.7	1,223.0	1,232.5	1,233.6	1,229.0	1,216.2
2011	1,194.2	1,194.4	1,204.4	1,231.2	1,241.1	1,244.5	1,241.8	1,243.6	1,247.5	1,251.8	1,254.7	1,249.5	1,233.2
2012	1,215.6	1,218.4	1,232.1	1,252.6	1,264.3	1,269.7	1,265.8	1,265.9	1,265.4	1,270.5	1,274.0	1,268.2	1,255.2
2013	1,234.0	1,236.8	1,244.6	1,263.6	1,279.5	1,287.5	1,287.2	1,288.9	1,285.8	1,297.3	1,296.8	1,286.2	1,274.0
Goods-Producing													
2002	284.3	281.7	284.2	293.4	298.8	303.3	302.3	300.8	297.3	295.2	293.9	289.1	293.7
2003	277.2	273.3	275.7	283.0	288.2	292.9	292.7	294.3	292.5	293.4	292.1	288.6	287.0
2004	277.9	275.7	280.8	291.4	295.3	302.0	303.8	301.4	300.5	300.4	300.1	297.9	293.9
2005	285.5	284.9	290.8	300.0	304.3	311.0	312.6	312.0	309.7	308.6	307.9	303.6	302.6
2006	295.7	295.0	298.8	306.2	310.4	316.3	316.1	315.6	313.0	310.8	309.0	305.5	307.7
2007	293.6	289.3	292.9	299.5	305.2	311.5	313.1	313.3	310.8	310.2	309.9	304.7	304.5
2008	293.9	290.9	293.0	301.0	307.7	311.0	312.8	312.5	308.7	305.5	300.8	292.3	302.5
2009	274.3	268.5	266.4	270.3	272.2	274.2	272.3	273.4	271.6	268.4	266.9	260.8	269.9
2010	250.0	248.5	252.1	263.7	266.4	270.5	272.3	272.1	270.7	270.7	269.6	263.8	264.2
2011	254.0	253.4	257.5	266.8	272.1	277.3	279.6	279.7	278.6	277.3	276.0	271.0	270.3
2012	261.5	260.9	266.3	275.0	280.4	285.2	286.4	286.0	283.6	283.6	281.6	278.2	277.4
2013	268.7	268.5	270.7	277.8	285.7	290.9	292.9	293.7	291.3	293.0	291.4	283.2	284.0
Service-Providing													
2002	1,138.3	1,139.1	1,145.5	1,159.7	1,167.6	1,166.3	1,135.4	1,134.8	1,157.1	1,162.3	1,168.1	1,169.5	1,153.6
2003	1,134.7	1,138.1	1,144.8	1,157.2	1,165.5	1,162.3	1,134.3	1,136.0	1,158.3	1,167.2	1,170.3	1,172.7	1,153.5
2004	1,139.9	1,144.0	1,152.2	1,168.6	1,173.9	1,174.6	1,146.9	1,148.5	1,167.1	1,176.9	1,182.4	1,184.8	1,163.3
2005	1,148.7	1,157.4	1,168.3	1,183.4	1,190.0	1,188.3	1,160.5	1,160.6	1,186.3	1,193.1	1,197.8	1,200.7	1,177.9
2006	1,167.2	1,176.0	1,186.0	1,200.4	1,209.2	1,210.7	1,176.5	1,176.9	1,202.6	1,212.6	1,218.6	1,221.7	1,196.5
2007	1,189.0	1,196.4	1,203.5	1,218.3	1,228.9	1,230.7	1,195.4	1,195.5	1,218.5	1,228.4	1,236.0	1,234.2	1,214.6
2008	1,202.2	1,209.0	1,216.6	1,228.6	1,238.9	1,233.7	1,202.5	1,202.3	1,225.7	1,235.3	1,234.8	1,233.0	1,221.9
2009	1,197.4	1,203.5	1,206.6	1,218.2	1,225.6	1,219.4	1,188.3	1,187.9	1,207.6	1,218.8	1,219.9	1,216.0	1,209.1
2010	1,182.2	1,188.9	1,197.7	1,213.3	1,222.6	1,215.9	1,185.1	1,183.6	1,203.6	1,219.9	1,224.4	1,223.9	1,205.1
2011	1,189.8	1,196.5	1,203.4	1,222.3	1,228.3	1,222.5	1,198.1	1,200.1	1,222.9	1,232.4	1,237.5	1,236.8	1,215.9
2012	1,205.9	1,213.7	1,222.6	1,236.0	1,243.8	1,238.9	1,214.0	1,219.3	1,236.2	1,245.2	1,252.2	1,249.2	1,231.4
2013	1,215.5	1,224.8	1,230.9	1,243.4	1,254.4	1,252.9	1,233.1	1,236.7	1,251.7	1,267.8	1,270.4	1,266.1	1,245.6
Mining and Logging													
2002	1.7	1.7	1.9	2.0	2.1	2.1	1.9	2.1	2.0	2.0	2.0	1.9	2.0
2003	1.5	1.5	1.6	1.9	2.0	2.1	2.0	2.2	2.2	2.1	2.1	2.0	1.9
2004	1.6	1.6	1.9	2.2	2.3	2.3	2.2	2.2	2.2	2.2	2.1	2.0	2.1
2005	1.7	1.7	2.0	2.1	2.2	2.3	2.3	2.3	2.2	2.2	2.2	2.0	2.1
2006	1.8	1.8	1.9	2.2	2.3	2.4	2.4	2.4	2.3	2.2	2.2	2.1	2.2
2007	1.8	1.7	2.0	2.1	2.2	2.3	2.3	2.3	2.3	2.3	2.3	2.1	2.1
2008	1.7	1.8	1.9	2.2	2.3	2.3	2.3	2.4	2.3	2.3	2.3	2.1	2.2
2009	1.6	1.8	2.0	2.3	2.4	2.4	2.4	2.5	2.4	2.3	2.3	2.1	2.2
2010	1.6	1.7	1.8	2.3	2.3	2.3	2.3	2.3	2.3	2.4	2.3	2.1	2.1
2011	1.7	1.8	1.8	2.2	2.3	2.4	2.4	2.4	2.4	2.4	2.3	2.2	2.2
2012	1.8	1.9	2.1	2.2	2.4	2.4	2.4	2.4	2.4	2.3	2.3	2.2	2.2
2013	1.8	1.8	2.0	2.1	2.4	2.4	2.4	2.4	2.4	2.4	2.4	2.2	2.2
Construction													
2002	54.8	53.1	55.4	62.9	67.1	70.2	71.2	70.9	68.6	68.2	67.1	63.4	64.4
2003	55.2	52.5	54.6	62.0	66.9	69.8	71.2	72.2	70.7	70.9	69.2	66.0	65.1
2004	57.5	55.6	59.7	67.9	70.8	74.3	75.4	75.2	73.5	72.3	71.7	69.2	68.6
2005	59.0	58.4	62.3	69.9	72.7	76.6	78.5	78.8	77.0	76.4	75.9	71.3	71.4
2006	64.9	64.6	67.1	72.8	76.3	79.7	80.8	80.7	79.7	77.8	76.2	72.4	74.4
2007	64.0	60.7	63.4	69.5	74.6	78.4	79.0	79.4	77.9	77.7	76.6	71.4	72.7
2008	63.1	60.5	62.4	70.0	75.9	78.4	81.6	81.5	79.4	78.0	75.0	69.8	73.0
2009	58.7	57.2	58.2	64.5	67.5	69.5	70.7	70.2	68.9	68.0	66.0	60.1	65.0
2010	51.6	50.3	52.3	62.2	64.7	67.2	68.1	67.2	66.1	66.0	64.5	58.8	61.6
2011	50.6	49.6	52.1	60.8	64.5	67.4	69.0	69.3	68.6	68.3	66.8	61.4	62.4
2012	54.1	52.9	56.5	63.8	67.4	69.9	70.5	70.6	69.2	69.2	67.0	63.9	64.6
2013	56.1	55.3	56.5	62.9	69.4	72.6	74.6	75.3	73.7	73.8	72.7	64.9	67.3

1. Employment by Industry: Iowa, Selected Years, 2002–2013—*Continued*

(Numbers in thousands, not seasonally adjusted)

Industry and year	January	February	March	April	May	June	July	August	September	October	November	December	Annual average
Manufacturing													
2002	227.8	226.9	226.9	228.5	229.6	231.0	229.2	227.8	226.7	225.0	224.8	223.8	227.3
2003	220.5	219.3	219.5	219.1	219.3	221.0	219.5	219.9	219.6	220.4	220.8	220.6	220.0
2004	218.8	218.5	219.2	221.3	222.2	225.4	226.2	224.0	224.8	225.9	226.3	226.7	223.3
2005	224.8	224.8	226.5	228.0	229.4	232.1	231.8	230.9	230.5	230.0	229.8	230.3	229.1
2006	229.0	228.6	229.8	231.2	231.8	234.2	232.9	232.5	231.0	230.8	230.6	231.0	231.1
2007	227.8	226.9	227.5	227.9	228.4	230.8	231.8	231.6	230.6	230.2	231.0	231.2	229.6
2008	229.1	228.6	228.7	228.8	229.5	230.3	228.9	228.6	227.0	225.2	223.5	220.4	227.4
2009	214.0	209.5	206.2	203.5	202.3	202.3	199.2	200.7	200.3	198.1	198.6	198.6	202.8
2010	196.8	196.5	198.0	199.2	199.4	201.0	201.9	202.6	202.3	202.3	202.8	202.9	200.5
2011	201.7	202.0	203.6	203.8	205.3	207.5	208.2	208.0	207.6	206.6	206.9	207.4	205.7
2012	205.6	206.1	207.7	209.0	210.6	212.9	213.5	213.0	212.0	212.1	212.3	212.1	210.6
2013	210.8	211.4	212.2	212.8	213.9	215.9	215.9	216.0	215.2	216.8	216.3	216.1	214.4
Trade, Transportation, and Utilities													
2002	303.6	299.1	300.3	304.2	305.6	307.9	307.2	307.4	306.0	306.4	310.9	312.3	305.9
2003	299.5	295.7	297.6	301.1	304.0	304.1	304.6	304.5	303.1	304.9	308.8	310.0	303.2
2004	299.5	296.8	298.6	302.7	304.0	305.4	307.1	307.1	304.8	306.0	310.7	313.0	304.6
2005	300.1	298.2	301.1	305.4	306.9	307.8	308.3	307.5	306.7	307.5	312.3	314.9	306.4
2006	303.8	301.5	303.6	308.0	309.9	311.1	309.3	308.6	307.6	309.5	314.3	316.5	308.6
2007	305.5	302.5	304.1	306.9	310.6	312.2	310.1	308.8	307.7	309.0	314.7	315.9	309.0
2008	306.6	304.1	306.0	307.5	310.6	311.2	310.6	310.5	308.7	310.4	313.2	314.3	309.5
2009	301.9	299.3	299.7	301.8	304.2	305.3	303.8	303.3	300.4	300.8	304.8	304.7	302.5
2010	294.7	291.9	293.8	298.5	300.5	302.1	301.0	300.6	297.9	301.2	305.0	306.8	299.5
2011	295.9	294.2	296.3	300.9	304.1	305.3	304.4	304.2	302.7	305.4	310.3	312.3	303.0
2012	301.4	299.3	300.7	304.2	307.3	309.0	308.5	308.1	307.3	309.1	315.1	316.1	307.2
2013	304.6	303.0	304.8	307.8	311.2	313.0	313.1	312.4	311.1	312.2	318.2	322.2	311.1
Wholesale Trade													
2002	65.8	65.4	65.5	66.9	66.8	67.3	68.8	68.0	67.3	67.0	66.5	66.0	66.8
2003	64.1	63.7	64.2	65.4	65.7	65.9	67.0	66.6	65.7	65.7	65.2	64.7	65.3
2004	63.9	63.7	64.4	66.2	66.1	66.6	67.8	67.4	66.6	67.0	67.0	66.8	66.1
2005	65.3	65.3	66.2	67.8	67.9	68.1	68.7	68.1	67.9	68.1	67.7	67.3	67.4
2006	66.6	66.3	66.8	68.0	68.1	68.3	68.4	67.9	67.7	67.5	67.7	67.1	67.5
2007	66.2	65.9	66.5	67.8	68.4	68.6	68.8	68.2	68.3	68.9	69.0	68.4	67.9
2008	67.3	67.2	67.8	68.7	69.8	69.6	69.8	69.2	68.5	69.4	68.7	68.2	68.7
2009	66.1	66.1	66.2	67.6	67.6	67.5'	67.6	66.7	66.0	66.9	66.8	66.4	66.8
2010	64.7	64.4	64.9	67.1	66.8	66.8	66.6	66.0	65.8	66.7	66.7	66.0	66.0
2011	65.0	64.8	65.5	67.0	67.5	67.6	67.6	67.1	67.2	68.4	68.7	68.1	67.0
2012	66.8	66.9	68.0	69.1	69.4	69.6	69.3	68.7	68.8	69.1	69.3	68.5	68.6
2013	67.3	67.4	67.8	69.2	70.5	70.4	70.1	69.7	69.0	69.5	69.7	70.2	69.2
Retail Trade													
2002	182.4	178.5	179.2	181.2	182.3	183.6	181.1	181.5	181.2	181.3	185.9	187.7	182.2
2003	179.0	175.8	176.6	178.7	180.8	181.0	180.1	180.0	179.7	180.9	185.3	186.9	180.4
2004	178.5	176.1	176.6	178.2	179.5	180.3	180.7	181.0	179.6	180.2	185.3	187.9	180.3
2005	177.6	175.6	176.8	179.0	180.2	180.8	180.4	180.1	179.1	179.5	184.3	186.7	180.0
2006	177.8	176.0	176.9	179.4	180.7	181.2	179.8	178.9	177.8	179.5	183.9	186.1	179.8
2007	178.0	175.3	175.7	177.1	179.6	180.6	179.4	178.3	177.0	177.6	182.7	184.3	178.8
2008	177.4	175.2	176.3	177.1	178.2	179.1	178.5	178.4	177.1	177.9	181.3	182.5	178.3
2009	174.7	172.5	172.8	173.8	175.9	177.3	176.3	176.3	174.0	173.8	177.6	177.6	175.2
2010	171.4	169.1	170.0	171.6	173.6	174.6	173.7	173.3	173.3	170.7	172.6	176.0	177.5	172.8
2011	170.8	169.1	170.1	172.6	174.7	175.5	175.1	175.0	173.3	174.8	179.0	180.9	174.2
2012	173.5	171.3	171.2	173.1	175.3	176.1	176.1	176.0	174.8	176.3	181.8	182.6	175.7
2013	174.6	172.8	173.8	175.4	177.0	178.5	179.0	178.7	178.0	178.7	182.6	184.6	177.8
Transportation and Utilities													
2002	55.4	55.2	55.6	56.1	56.5	57.0	57.3	57.9	57.5	58.1	58.5	58.6	57.0
2003	56.4	56.2	56.8	57.0	57.5	57.2	57.5	57.9	57.7	58.3	58.3	58.4	57.4
2004	57.1	57.0	57.6	58.3	58.4	58.5	58.6	58.7	58.6	58.8	58.4	58.3	58.2
2005	57.2	57.3	58.1	58.6	58.8	58.9	59.2	59.3	59.7	59.9	60.3	60.9	59.0
2006	59.4	59.2	59.9	60.6	61.1	61.6	61.1	61.8	62.1	62.5	62.7	63.3	61.3
2007	61.3	61.3	61.9	62.0	62.6	63.0	61.9	62.3	62.4	62.5	63.0	63.2	62.3
2008	61.9	61.7	61.9	61.7	62.6	62.5	62.3	62.9	63.1	63.1	63.2	63.6	62.5
2009	61.1	60.7	60.7	60.4	60.7	60.2	59.9	60.3	60.4	60.1	60.4	60.7	60.5
2010	58.6	58.4	58.9	59.8	60.1	60.7	60.7	61.3	61.4	61.9	62.3	63.3	60.6
2011	60.1	60.3	60.7	61.3	61.9	62.2	61.7	62.1	62.2	62.2	62.6	63.3	61.7
2012	61.1	61.1	61.5	62.0	62.6	63.3	63.1	63.4	63.7	63.7	64.0	65.0	62.9
2013	62.7	62.8	63.2	63.2	63.7	64.1	64.0	64.0	64.1	64.0	65.9	67.4	64.1
Information													
2002	35.6	35.6	35.4	35.5	35.6	35.6	34.8	34.7	34.4	34.4	34.7	34.5	35.1
2003	33.6	33.9	33.7	33.4	33.6	33.7	33.9	33.5	33.5	33.5	33.6	33.7	33.6
2004	33.3	33.3	33.4	33.6	33.6	33.7	34.0	34.0	33.7	33.7	33.9	34.0	33.7
2005	33.4	33.3	33.5	33.3	33.2	33.1	33.1	32.6	32.5	32.4	32.5	32.7	33.0
2006	32.2	32.4	32.6	32.9	33.0	33.2	33.1	33.0	33.0	33.1	33.4	33.7	33.0
2007	33.0	33.5	33.7	34.1	34.3	34.4	33.6	33.3	33.2	33.1	33.4	33.4	33.6
2008	33.2	33.5	33.5	33.8	33.9	33.6	32.6	32.3	32.3	31.9	31.7	32.9
2009	31.3	31.4	31.4	31.0	31.1	30.6	30.0	29.5	29.2	29.3	29.3	29.4	30.3
2010	29.0	29.2	29.0	29.1	29.2	28.8	28.6	28.3	27.7	28.2	28.4	28.7	28.7
2011	28.2	28.4	28.3	28.4	28.4	28.1	28.0	27.8	27.6	27.5	27.6	27.6	28.0
2012	27.2	27.4	27.6	27.3	27.2	27.1	26.8	26.6	26.3	26.5	26.8	26.5	26.9
2013	26.1	26.5	26.6	26.4	26.5	26.2	26.1	25.9	25.6	25.7	25.8	25.6	26.1

1. Employment by Industry: Iowa, Selected Years, 2002–2013—*Continued*

(Numbers in thousands, not seasonally adjusted)

Industry and year	January	February	March	April	May	June	July	August	September	October	November	December	Annual average
Financial Activities													
2002	93.0	93.0	93.3	93.7	93.7	94.7	95.0	94.7	93.8	93.8	93.7	94.2	93.9
2003	94.2	94.2	94.2	94.4	95.0	95.8	95.9	96.0	95.4	95.4	95.6	95.9	95.2
2004	95.3	95.4	95.4	96.3	96.7	97.6	98.1	98.3	97.3	97.3	97.3	98.1	96.9
2005	97.3	97.4	97.5	97.6	98.0	98.9	99.0	99.0	98.6	98.4	98.5	99.4	98.3
2006	98.8	99.0	99.7	99.8	100.4	101.6	101.5	101.3	101.2	101.1	100.9	101.8	100.6
2007	101.1	101.2	101.6	101.9	102.4	103.8	103.8	103.4	102.8	103.0	103.2	103.5	102.6
2008	102.6	102.7	102.8	102.6	102.8	103.6	103.6	103.2	102.0	101.8	101.9	102.4	102.7
2009	101.7	101.4	101.4	101.8	102.2	102.9	102.8	102.7	101.6	101.6	101.6	102.3	102.0
2010	101.2	100.9	101.2	100.8	101.2	101.9	101.7	101.6	100.8	101.1	101.1	101.7	101.3
2011	100.7	100.4	100.3	100.4	100.7	101.0	101.3	101.4	100.5	100.3	100.6	101.1	100.7
2012	100.2	100.1	100.5	101.2	101.6	102.5	102.5	102.3	101.8	102.1	102.3	103.0	101.7
2013	102.5	102.4	102.6	103.2	103.3	104.3	104.2	104.1	103.5	103.8	103.4	103.5	103.4
Professional and Business Services													
2002	102.4	102.6	103.7	105.5	105.5	107.5	107.4	107.0	107.0	106.1	106.9	106.1	105.6
2003	102.3	102.2	102.5	105.6	104.8	106.2	106.6	107.9	107.2	107.8	107.0	107.1	105.6
2004	104.1	104.3	105.3	108.8	108.3	109.2	110.0	110.2	108.7	110.9	110.8	110.7	108.4
2005	107.0	108.4	109.8	112.6	112.5	113.9	114.6	115.1	116.1	116.7	116.3	116.2	113.3
2006	111.7	112.6	114.3	116.8	117.2	118.7	118.5	118.8	118.7	120.0	120.4	119.4	117.3
2007	116.1	117.1	117.7	121.4	120.9	123.2	123.1	124.0	122.9	123.6	123.9	123.2	121.4
2008	119.6	119.9	120.4	123.5	123.6	124.8	126.2	125.7	124.5	125.2	122.4	121.3	123.1
2009	117.1	117.3	116.1	117.3	116.8	117.6	117.2	118.0	117.2	119.0	118.5	117.9	117.5
2010	115.6	116.7	117.6	121.6	121.1	122.0	123.6	124.1	123.1	125.3	125.1	124.5	121.7
2011	121.5	121.7	121.6	125.0	124.1	124.8	127.1	127.6	128.1	129.2	129.0	127.4	125.6
2012	124.8	125.8	127.4	129.8	129.4	131.3	132.5	132.3	132.0	132.3	131.4	129.7	129.9
2013	127.0	127.7	128.4	131.2	131.4	133.3	133.8	134.7	133.9	135.1	133.2	131.3	131.8
Education and Health Services													
2002	187.0	188.7	189.6	190.4	189.5	183.6	178.7	179.4	187.9	192.6	193.8	194.3	188.0
2003	189.9	191.9	193.1	191.9	190.4	185.3	180.3	180.6	188.7	193.7	194.6	194.5	189.6
2004	191.2	193.0	194.3	194.1	192.7	187.6	182.5	182.6	190.5	195.5	196.5	197.2	191.5
2005	193.1	195.5	196.7	197.2	196.0	191.1	186.7	186.8	195.5	199.9	200.9	201.5	195.1
2006	197.5	199.8	201.0	201.6	200.3	195.2	190.4	190.6	198.6	203.5	204.8	205.3	199.1
2007	201.2	204.1	205.5	205.7	204.1	199.2	193.7	194.7	203.1	208.2	210.1	209.8	203.3
2008	206.1	208.4	209.7	210.1	208.4	202.4	197.5	197.8	206.6	213.1	214.8	214.8	207.5
2009	210.5	212.9	213.9	214.6	212.5	206.4	201.6	202.1	211.1	218.4	219.2	219.3	211.9
2010	214.2	216.3	217.8	217.6	215.0	208.4	203.0	202.7	212.4	219.7	220.6	221.0	214.1
2011	215.6	218.0	219.1	221.5	218.6	211.3	205.6	206.0	216.6	224.0	225.0	225.2	217.2
2012	219.6	222.8	224.2	223.8	221.6	214.2	208.4	209.6	218.5	225.5	226.8	226.1	220.1
2013	221.5	223.6	224.2	224.7	223.0	217.3	213.4	214.0	221.8	232.1	232.0	230.7	223.2
Leisure and Hospitality													
2002	115.7	115.9	117.7	123.9	129.1	131.6	131.7	132.9	129.8	124.0	121.2	121.5	124.6
2003	116.6	116.0	118.0	124.4	129.4	132.8	132.6	134.2	130.1	124.8	122.3	122.2	125.3
2004	117.3	117.3	120.3	126.2	130.7	134.3	134.5	136.5	132.4	126.8	125.1	124.7	127.2
2005	120.1	121.1	124.3	130.7	134.6	137.7	137.6	138.6	135.2	130.3	128.1	127.3	130.5
2006	123.5	124.3	127.3	132.9	137.8	141.5	140.6	141.9	138.9	135.1	132.9	133.3	134.2
2007	127.9	127.9	130.2	136.7	142.1	145.3	144.2	144.9	140.9	136.8	134.8	133.4	137.1
2008	127.1	127.7	130.0	136.2	140.9	143.3	141.9	143.4	139.1	134.0	131.2	130.4	135.4
2009	124.6	125.2	127.0	132.9	137.8	140.6	140.3	140.7	136.6	131.9	128.2	126.2	132.7
2010	120.9	121.7	123.2	130.0	134.8	137.3	137.1	137.4	133.9	129.3	127.1	125.8	129.9
2011	122.1	122.2	124.9	131.7	136.4	139.6	138.7	139.8	136.5	131.1	129.4	127.9	131.7
2012	124.0	125.4	128.3	133.7	138.8	141.9	142.5	142.6	138.2	133.3	131.8	130.8	134.3
2013	126.4	127.9	130.0	134.9	140.2	143.9	144.9	145.1	140.4	138.0	134.6	132.2	136.5
Other Services													
2002	55.8	55.9	56.3	56.8	56.9	57.4	57.2	57.1	56.5	56.7	56.6	56.3	56.6
2003	55.6	55.5	55.9	56.3	56.3	56.7	56.5	56.5	56.2	56.3	56.1	56.4	56.2
2004	55.9	55.5	55.9	56.3	56.4	57.1	57.1	56.7	56.4	56.5	56.3	56.4	56.4
2005	55.3	55.5	56.0	56.4	56.3	57.3	57.0	56.6	56.2	56.1	56.1	56.3	56.3
2006	55.9	55.7	56.2	56.6	56.9	57.8	57.4	57.1	56.8	56.8	57.0	57.3	56.8
2007	56.6	56.4	57.1	57.6	58.0	59.1	58.3	57.9	57.6	57.8	57.8	57.9	57.7
2008	57.1	56.8	57.2	57.7	58.2	58.7	58.4	58.1	57.8	58.2	58.1	58.0	57.9
2009	57.2	57.3	57.4	57.7	57.9	58.5	58.3	57.4	57.1	57.1	56.9	57.0	57.5
2010	56.3	56.3	56.8	57.3	57.4	57.7	57.3	56.9	56.5	57.0	56.7	56.7	56.9
2011	56.2	56.1	56.4	56.5	56.7	57.1	57.1	57.1	56.9	57.0	56.8	57.0	56.7
2012	56.9	56.7	57.1	57.6	58.0	58.5	58.2	58.4	57.7	58.1	58.2	57.8	57.8
2013	57.2	57.2	57.3	57.6	58.2	58.6	58.8	59.0	58.2	57.4	58.2	57.5	57.9
Government													
2002	245.2	248.3	249.2	249.7	251.7	248.0	223.4	221.6	241.7	248.3	250.3	250.3	244.0
2003	243.0	248.7	249.8	250.1	252.0	247.7	223.9	222.8	244.1	250.8	252.3	252.9	244.8
2004	243.3	248.4	249.0	250.6	251.5	249.7	223.6	223.1	243.3	250.2	251.8	250.7	244.6
2005	242.4	248.0	249.4	250.2	252.5	248.5	224.2	224.4	245.5	251.8	253.1	252.4	245.2
2006	243.8	250.7	251.3	251.8	253.7	251.6	225.7	225.6	247.8	253.5	254.9	254.4	247.1
2007	247.6	253.7	253.6	254.0	256.5	253.5	228.6	228.5	250.3	256.9	258.1	257.1	249.9
2008	249.9	255.9	257.0	257.2	260.5	256.1	231.3	231.0	254.7	260.3	261.3	260.1	252.9
2009	253.1	258.7	259.7	261.1	263.1	257.8	234.3	234.2	254.4	260.7	261.4	259.2	254.8
2010	250.3	255.9	258.3	258.4	263.4	257.7	232.8	232.0	251.3	258.1	260.4	258.7	253.1
2011	249.6	255.5	256.5	257.9	259.3	255.3	235.9	236.2	254.0	257.9	258.8	258.3	252.9
2012	251.8	256.2	256.8	258.4	259.9	254.4	234.6	239.4	254.4	258.3	259.8	259.2	253.6
2013	250.2	256.5	257.0	257.6	260.6	256.3	238.8	241.5	257.2	263.5	265.0	263.1	255.6

2. Average Weekly Hours by Selected Industry: Iowa, 2009–2013

(Not seasonally adjusted)

Industry and year	January	February	March	April	May	June	July	August	September	October	November	December	Annual average
Total Private													
2009	32.8	33.3	32.8	32.8	32.8	33.1	33.4	34.0	33.8	33.9	34.1	33.3	33.3
2010	33.5	33.7	33.8	34.6	34.2	34.1	34.2	34.3	34.2	34.4	34.1	33.9	34.1
2011	33.8	33.2	33.5	33.8	34.1	34.0	33.9	34.0	34.1	34.6	34.2	34.2	34.0
2012	34.2	33.7	33.9	34.6	34.5	34.5	34.7	34.1	34.8	34.2	34.2	34.5	34.3
2013	33.7	33.9	33.8	34.0	34.4	35.1	34.5	34.7	35.1	34.7	34.7	34.9	34.5
Goods-Producing													
2009	36.8	37.3	36.7	36.5	37.2	38.2	38.1	39.0	39.7	40.2	40.0	38.0	38.1
2010	38.4	38.6	39.1	40.2	39.4	39.6	40.3	39.7	40.4	41.0	40.3	40.6	39.8
2011	39.8	38.6	39.3	39.5	40.3	40.1	40.0	40.7	40.4	41.0	40.4	40.5	40.1
2012	40.2	39.8	39.9	40.6	41.2	40.6	40.3	40.0	40.5	40.3	40.0	39.8	40.3
2013	38.9	38.8	39.4	39.7	40.7	41.1	41.0	41.2	41.4	41.6	41.2	41.1	40.5
Construction													
2009	37.1	38.0	37.4	38.5	38.1	41.8	42.4	42.2	42.0	41.6	41.5	38.5	40.1
2010	39.1	38.9	39.4	41.6	41.0	40.7	41.5	40.2	40.6	41.7	40.8	40.2	40.5
2011	39.0	37.9	38.8	39.5	41.2	41.7	40.7	41.9	41.3	41.3	39.5	38.8	40.3
2012	38.4	38.2	38.9	39.3	42.3	40.6	40.9	41.1	40.2	40.8	39.0	38.1	39.9
2013	36.5	36.9	38.0	38.2	42.0	41.2	42.7	42.6	42.9	43.6	42.0	40.6	40.9
Manufacturing													
2009	36.7	37.1	36.4	35.9	37.0	37.9	37.3	38.6	39.6	40.4	40.1	39.2	38.0
2010	39.2	39.4	39.8	40.5	40.3	40.5	40.6	40.3	41.0	41.7	41.7	41.0	40.5
2011	40.4	39.9	40.5	40.4	40.6	40.0	40.4	40.8	40.8	41.6	41.4	41.7	40.7
2012	41.4	41.0	40.8	41.6	41.2	41.1	40.5	40.0	41.1	40.4	40.6	40.6	40.9
2013	40.0	39.6	40.0	40.3	40.1	41.0	40.2	40.5	40.7	40.8	40.9	41.3	40.5
Trade, Transportation, and Utilities													
2009	31.3	31.6	31.8	32.1	31.6	31.7	32.1	32.4	32.3	32.3	33.1	31.5	32.0
2010	31.7	32.0	32.2	33.1	32.6	32.8	33.1	33.3	33.2	33.7	32.6	32.6	32.7
2011	32.3	31.9	31.8	32.6	32.9	32.7	32.7	33.0	32.9	33.0	33.0	32.7	32.6
2012	32.5	32.3	32.9	33.4	33.5	33.3	33.5	33.1	33.5	32.8	33.0	32.8	33.1
2013	32.3	32.7	32.4	32.5	33.1	33.4	32.9	33.2	33.7	33.5	33.2	33.2	33.0
Financial Activities													
2009	36.1	36.5	35.9	35.7	35.9	36.0	36.7	37.3	36.9	37.0	37.8	36.9	36.6
2010	37.5	38.1	37.6	37.7	38.3	37.9	37.8	38.8	37.9	37.9	38.5	37.8	38.0
2011	38.4	37.6	37.6	37.4	38.3	37.7	37.8	37.6	37.9	38.6	38.1	37.9	37.9
2012	38.7	38.2	38.1	39.0	38.4	38.1	38.5	37.7	38.8	38.0	38.0	38.8	38.4
2013	37.7	38.0	37.8	37.9	37.9	38.9	38.1	38.4	39.1	38.1	38.2	39.2	38.3
Professional and Business Services													
2009	32.6	33.8	32.5	32.3	32.2	32.9	33.5	33.4	32.6	33.4	33.8	33.2	33.0
2010	33.6	33.8	34.3	35.0	35.1	34.3	34.6	34.8	34.1	34.3	34.0	33.4	34.3
2011	33.3	32.8	33.7	34.3	34.7	34.7	34.2	33.8	34.3	34.9	34.5	34.0	34.1
2012	33.9	33.4	33.6	34.7	34.4	34.3	34.6	34.3	35.5	34.3	34.4	35.1	34.4
2013	33.3	33.7	33.3	33.9	34.1	35.7	33.9	34.5	34.9	34.5	34.6	35.5	34.3
Education and Health Services													
2009	32.6	32.7	31.4	31.7	31.3	31.2	31.7	32.1	31.4	31.2	31.5	31.0	31.6
2010	31.3	31.1	31.0	31.8	31.5	31.6	30.9	31.0	30.8	30.4	30.9	30.8	31.1
2011	31.2	30.8	30.9	31.2	31.3	31.3	31.1	31.1	31.1	31.4	31.2	31.4	31.2
2012	31.6	31.1	31.0	31.8	31.4	31.4	32.0	31.3	32.2	31.3	31.5	32.4	31.6
2013	32.0	31.8	31.7	31.7	31.5	32.4	31.5	31.4	32.1	31.3	31.7	31.7	31.7
Leisure and Hospitality													
2009	23.6	24.3	24.6	24.4	24.7	25.2	25.7	25.6	24.6	24.5	24.9	23.8	24.7
2010	23.5	23.8	23.9	24.4	23.8	24.6	24.3	24.4	24.3	24.1	24.3	24.0	24.1
2011	24.4	24.4	23.9	23.9	23.7	24.0	23.7	24.1	24.0	24.4	23.8	23.6	24.0
2012	23.7	23.6	23.8	23.8	23.6	24.6	24.8	24.6	24.8	24.2	24.3	24.2	24.2
2013	23.9	24.3	24.5	24.2	24.8	25.5	25.0	24.8	24.6	24.2	24.5	24.6	24.6
Other Services													
2009	27.2	27.9	27.9	27.8	27.8	28.4	27.8	29.1	28.2	28.1	27.7	27.1	27.9
2010	27.9	27.9	28.3	28.9	28.3	28.5	29.2	29.3	28.8	29.3	28.3	28.3	28.6
2011	28.5	28.3	29.1	29.1	29.4	30.1	29.6	29.0	29.0	29.7	28.3	28.3	29.0
2012	28.7	28.4	28.4	29.8	28.9	29.9	31.8	29.9	30.7	29.1	29.3	29.6	29.5
2013	29.6	29.1	28.3	28.7	28.6	29.4	29.8	29.9	29.7	28.9	27.6	29.2	29.1

3. Average Hourly Earnings by Selected Industry: Iowa, 2009–2013

(Dollars, not seasonally adjusted)

Industry and year	January	February	March	April	May	June	July	August	September	October	November	December	Annual average
Total Private													
2009	19.78	19.94	19.77	19.77	19.93	19.86	20.05	20.04	19.94	20.09	20.30	20.61	20.01
2010	20.27	20.80	20.44	20.46	20.33	20.18	20.10	20.23	20.46	20.51	20.26	20.49	20.38
2011	20.23	20.37	20.12	20.19	20.14	19.97	20.17	20.08	20.29	20.42	20.25	20.45	20.22
2012	20.64	20.60	20.54	20.83	20.69	20.54	20.87	20.70	21.11	21.10	21.22	21.52	20.87
2013	21.52	21.46	21.38	21.58	21.38	21.40	21.38	21.41	21.68	21.63	21.78	22.15	21.56
Goods-Producing													
2009	20.39	20.55	20.90	20.36	20.45	20.73	20.61	20.92	20.63	20.55	20.88	21.03	20.67
2010	21.07	20.97	21.02	20.77	20.88	20.71	20.68	20.79	20.73	21.04	20.83	20.85	20.86
2011	20.38	20.53	20.16	20.20	20.30	20.04	20.07	20.04	20.40	20.57	20.45	20.90	20.34
2012	21.02	20.85	20.94	21.39	21.58	21.22	21.58	21.62	22.03	21.73	21.84	22.51	21.54
2013	21.83	22.11	22.09	22.20	22.05	22.18	22.20	22.10	22.49	22.29	22.51	23.42	22.30
Construction													
2009	22.01	21.72	21.85	21.85	21.77	22.49	22.30	22.36	22.27	22.38	22.54	22.48	22.19
2010	22.82	22.72	23.11	22.43	22.51	22.52	22.20	22.26	22.54	22.76	22.35	22.89	22.57
2011	22.57	22.71	22.64	22.49	22.49	22.18	22.05	22.08	22.75	22.31	22.12	22.68	22.40
2012	22.94	22.95	23.03	22.96	24.10	22.54	22.23	22.86	23.31	23.13	22.91	23.80	23.06
2013	23.94	24.57	24.84	24.45	23.78	23.45	23.56	23.45	23.54	24.05	24.35	24.94	24.02
Manufacturing													
2009	19.77	20.04	20.46	19.68	19.83	19.92	20.22	20.61	20.23	20.07	20.44	20.75	20.17
2010	20.69	20.60	20.50	20.28	20.36	20.12	20.14	20.28	20.09	20.41	20.33	20.83	20.38
2011	20.28	20.40	19.87	19.83	19.83	19.51	19.59	19.50	19.70	20.11	20.00	20.43	19.92
2012	20.53	20.28	20.33	20.92	20.64	20.83	21.43	21.22	21.61	21.22	21.47	22.08	21.05
2013	21.06	21.22	21.08	21.33	21.29	21.62	21.48	21.39	21.93	21.42	21.63	22.78	21.53
Trade, Transportation, and Utilities													
2009	18.12	18.42	18.21	18.55	18.16	17.90	18.02	17.95	17.12	17.24	17.18	16.44	17.77
2010	16.45	16.73	16.49	16.74	16.90	17.14	16.89	17.29	17.54	16.85	16.88	16.95	16.91
2011	17.33	17.57	17.49	17.55	17.47	17.38	17.54	17.39	17.61	17.64	17.52	17.39	17.49
2012	17.72	17.99	17.75	18.07	17.85	17.90	17.99	17.74	17.98	17.97	17.86	17.75	17.88
2013	17.90	18.19	18.09	18.27	17.85	17.95	17.84	18.06	18.54	18.59	18.74	18.80	18.24
Financial Activities													
2009	25.31	25.66	25.90	25.42	25.95	25.84	26.01	25.89	25.55	25.66	25.73	25.69	25.72
2010	25.48	25.64	25.43	25.78	25.59	25.63	25.52	25.41	25.54	25.49	25.18	25.38	25.51
2011	25.52	25.96	25.61	25.87	26.03	25.96	25.90	25.95	25.90	26.05	25.99	26.05	25.90
2012	25.92	26.11	26.13	26.56	26.48	26.88	27.36	26.74	27.61	27.88	28.76	28.86	27.11
2013	29.30	28.57	28.18	28.34	29.46	29.22	29.09	28.79	28.91	28.81	28.97	28.80	28.87
Professional and Business Services													
2009	23.48	23.71	21.73	21.23	22.49	21.62	21.72	22.07	21.67	21.42	21.45	21.62	22.02
2010	21.32	21.13	20.47	21.20	21.52	21.12	21.06	21.35	21.64	22.13	21.83	22.22	21.42
2011	22.16	22.20	21.74	21.26	21.41	20.81	21.26	21.02	21.00	21.39	20.83	21.06	21.33
2012	21.60	20.98	20.89	20.70	20.51	19.97	20.18	20.11	20.29	20.42	20.48	20.90	20.58
2013	21.83	21.61	21.84	21.97	21.61	21.84	22.26	22.53	22.73	22.76	22.95	23.65	22.31
Education and Health Services													
2009	18.37	18.25	18.21	19.48	18.73	18.97	19.10	19.01	19.37	20.27	19.26	20.21	19.10
2010	19.46	19.39	19.39	19.84	19.26	19.17	19.51	19.53	19.92	20.40	19.70	20.65	19.69
2011	20.43	20.62	20.51	20.97	20.65	20.75	21.28	21.03	21.32	21.38	21.19	21.42	20.96
2012	21.64	21.61	21.58	21.92	21.50	21.64	22.24	22.17	22.53	22.51	22.43	22.50	22.03
2013	22.40	22.03	21.90	22.33	21.35	21.18	21.26	21.40	21.11	21.14	21.21	21.32	21.55
Leisure and Hospitality													
2009	11.83	11.82	11.78	11.84	11.73	11.58	11.57	11.73	11.94	11.93	11.95	12.25	11.82
2010	12.34	12.24	12.03	11.91	11.88	11.57	11.68	11.63	11.66	11.57	11.55	11.70	11.80
2011	11.69	11.76	11.74	11.79	11.77	11.55	11.80	11.59	11.69	11.64	11.78	11.93	11.73
2012	11.87	12.00	11.92	12.00	11.96	11.62	11.71	11.77	11.96	12.30	12.35	12.64	12.00
2013	12.44	12.36	12.30	12.30	12.19	11.95	11.99	12.15	12.23	12.38	12.42	12.70	12.28
Other Services													
2009	15.61	15.66	15.80	15.67	15.85	15.53	15.48	15.56	16.27	15.98	16.39	16.56	15.86
2010	16.45	16.31	16.82	16.29	16.75	16.66	16.35	16.77	16.90	17.34	17.59	17.27	16.79
2011	17.43	17.38	17.19	17.45	17.57	17.92	18.25	19.04	19.05	19.14	19.31	18.76	18.21
2012	18.50	18.79	18.60	18.66	18.63	18.37	19.24	19.55	19.85	19.60	19.98	20.06	19.16
2013	19.49	19.54	19.16	19.22	18.97	19.07	18.66	18.64	19.42	18.97	18.65	19.06	19.07

4. Average Weekly Earnings by Selected Industry: Iowa, 2009–2013

(Dollars, not seasonally adjusted)

Industry and year	January	February	March	April	May	June	July	August	September	October	November	December	Annual average
Total Private													
2009	648.78	664.00	648.46	648.46	653.70	657.37	669.67	681.36	673.97	681.05	692.23	686.31	666.33
2010	679.05	700.96	690.87	707.92	695.29	688.14	687.42	693.89	699.73	705.54	690.87	694.61	694.96
2011	683.77	676.28	674.02	682.42	686.77	678.98	683.76	682.72	691.89	706.53	692.55	699.39	687.48
2012	705.89	694.22	696.31	720.72	713.81	708.63	724.19	705.87	734.63	721.62	725.72	742.44	715.84
2013	725.22	727.49	722.64	733.72	735.47	751.14	737.61	742.93	760.97	750.56	755.77	773.04	743.82
Goods-Producing													
2009	750.35	766.52	767.03	743.14	760.74	791.89	785.24	815.88	819.01	826.11	835.20	799.14	787.53
2010	809.09	809.44	821.88	834.95	822.67	820.12	833.40	825.36	837.49	862.64	839.45	846.51	830.23
2011	811.12	792.46	792.29	797.90	818.09	803.60	802.80	815.63	824.16	843.37	826.18	846.45	815.63
2012	845.00	829.83	835.51	868.43	889.10	861.53	869.67	864.80	892.22	875.72	873.60	895.90	868.06
2013	849.19	857.87	870.35	881.34	897.44	911.60	910.20	910.52	931.09	927.26	927.41	962.56	903.15
Construction													
2009	816.57	825.36	817.19	841.23	829.44	940.08	945.52	943.59	935.34	931.01	935.41	865.48	889.82
2010	892.26	883.81	910.53	933.09	922.91	916.56	921.30	894.85	915.12	949.09	911.88	920.18	914.09
2011	880.23	860.71	878.43	888.36	926.59	924.91	897.44	925.15	939.58	921.40	873.74	879.98	902.72
2012	880.90	876.69	895.87	902.33	1,019.43	915.12	909.21	939.55	937.06	943.70	893.49	906.78	920.09
2013	873.81	906.63	943.92	933.99	998.76	966.14	1,006.01	998.97	1,009.87	1,048.58	1,022.70	1,012.56	982.42
Manufacturing													
2009	725.56	743.48	744.74	706.51	733.71	754.97	754.21	795.55	801.11	810.83	819.64	813.40	766.46
2010	811.05	811.64	815.90	821.34	820.51	814.86	817.68	817.28	823.69	851.10	847.76	854.03	825.39
2011	819.31	813.96	804.74	801.13	805.10	780.40	791.44	795.60	803.76	836.58	828.00	851.93	810.74
2012	849.94	831.48	829.46	870.27	850.37	856.11	867.92	848.80	888.17	857.29	871.68	896.45	860.95
2013	842.40	840.31	843.20	859.60	853.73	886.42	863.50	866.30	892.55	873.94	884.67	940.81	871.97
Trade, Transportation, and Utilities													
2009	567.16	582.07	579.08	595.46	573.86	567.43	578.44	581.58	552.98	556.85	568.66	517.86	568.64
2010	521.47	535.36	530.98	554.09	550.94	562.19	559.06	575.76	582.33	567.85	550.29	552.57	552.96
2011	559.76	560.48	556.18	572.13	574.76	566.33	573.56	573.87	579.37	582.12	578.16	568.65	570.17
2012	575.90	581.08	583.98	603.54	597.98	596.07	602.67	587.19	602.33	589.42	589.38	582.20	591.83
2013	578.17	594.81	586.12	593.78	590.84	599.53	586.94	599.59	624.80	622.77	622.17	624.16	601.92
Financial Activities													
2009	913.69	936.59	929.81	907.49	931.61	930.24	954.57	965.70	942.80	949.42	972.59	947.96	941.35
2010	955.50	976.88	956.17	971.91	980.10	971.38	964.66	985.91	967.97	966.07	969.43	959.36	969.38
2011	979.97	976.10	962.94	967.54	996.95	978.69	979.02	975.72	981.61	1,005.53	990.22	987.30	981.61
2012	1,003.10	997.40	995.55	1,035.84	1,016.83	1,024.13	1,053.36	1,008.10	1,071.27	1,059.44	1,092.88	1,119.77	1,041.02
2013	1,104.61	1,085.66	1,065.20	1,074.09	1,116.53	1,136.66	1,108.33	1,105.54	1,130.38	1,097.66	1,106.65	1,128.96	1,105.72
Professional and Business Services													
2009	765.45	801.40	706.23	685.73	724.18	711.30	727.62	737.14	706.44	715.43	725.01	717.78	726.66
2010	716.35	714.19	702.12	742.00	755.35	724.42	728.68	742.98	737.92	759.06	742.22	742.15	734.71
2011	737.93	728.16	732.64	729.22	742.93	722.11	727.09	710.48	720.30	746.51	718.64	716.04	727.35
2012	732.24	700.73	701.90	718.29	705.54	684.97	698.23	689.77	720.30	700.41	704.51	733.59	707.95
2013	726.94	728.26	727.27	744.78	736.90	779.69	754.61	777.29	793.28	785.22	794.07	839.58	765.23
Education and Health Services													
2009	598.86	596.78	571.79	617.52	586.25	591.86	605.47	610.22	608.22	632.42	606.69	626.51	603.56
2010	609.10	603.03	601.09	630.91	606.69	605.77	602.86	605.43	613.54	620.16	608.73	636.02	612.36
2011	637.42	635.10	633.76	654.26	646.35	649.48	661.81	654.03	663.05	671.33	661.13	672.59	653.95
2012	683.82	672.07	668.98	697.06	675.10	679.50	711.68	693.92	725.47	704.56	706.55	729.00	696.15
2013	716.80	700.55	694.23	707.86	672.53	686.23	669.69	671.96	677.63	661.68	672.36	675.84	683.14
Leisure and Hospitality													
2009	279.19	287.23	289.79	288.90	289.73	291.82	297.35	300.29	293.72	292.29	297.56	291.55	291.95
2010	289.99	291.31	287.52	290.60	282.74	284.62	283.82	283.77	283.34	278.84	280.67	280.80	284.38
2011	285.24	286.94	280.59	281.78	278.95	277.20	279.66	279.32	280.56	284.02	280.36	281.55	281.52
2012	281.32	283.20	283.70	285.60	282.26	285.85	290.41	289.54	296.61	297.66	300.11	305.89	290.40
2013	297.32	300.35	301.35	297.66	302.31	304.73	299.75	301.32	300.86	299.60	304.29	312.42	302.09
Other Services													
2009	424.59	436.91	440.82	435.63	440.63	441.05	430.34	452.80	458.81	449.04	454.00	448.78	442.49
2010	458.96	455.05	476.01	470.78	474.03	474.81	477.42	491.36	486.72	508.06	497.80	488.74	480.19
2011	496.76	491.85	500.23	507.80	516.56	539.39	540.20	552.16	552.45	568.46	546.47	530.91	528.09
2012	530.95	533.64	528.24	556.07	538.41	549.26	611.83	584.55	609.40	570.36	585.41	593.78	565.22
2013	576.90	568.61	542.23	551.61	542.54	560.66	556.07	557.34	576.77	548.23	514.74	556.55	554.94

KANSAS
At a Glance

Population:
    2000 census: 2,688,925
    2010 census: 2,853,118
    2013 estimate: 2,893,957

Percent change in population:
    2000–2010: 6.1%
    2010–2013: 1.4%

Percent change in total nonfarm employment:
    2000–2010: -1.3%
    2010–2013: 3.3%

Industry with the largest growth in employment, 2000–2013 (thousands):
    Education and Health Services, 39.8

Industry with the largest decline or smallest growth in employment, 2000–2013 (thousands):
    Manufacturing, -37.8

Civilian labor force:
    2000: 1,408,103
    2010: 1,503,659
    2013: 1,483,720

Unemployment rate and rank among states (lowest to highest):
    2000: 3.8%, 25th
    2010: 7.1%, 11th
    2013: 5.4%, 11th

Over-the-year change in unemployment rates:
    2010–2011: -0.6%
    2011–2012: -0.7%
    2012–2013: -0.4%

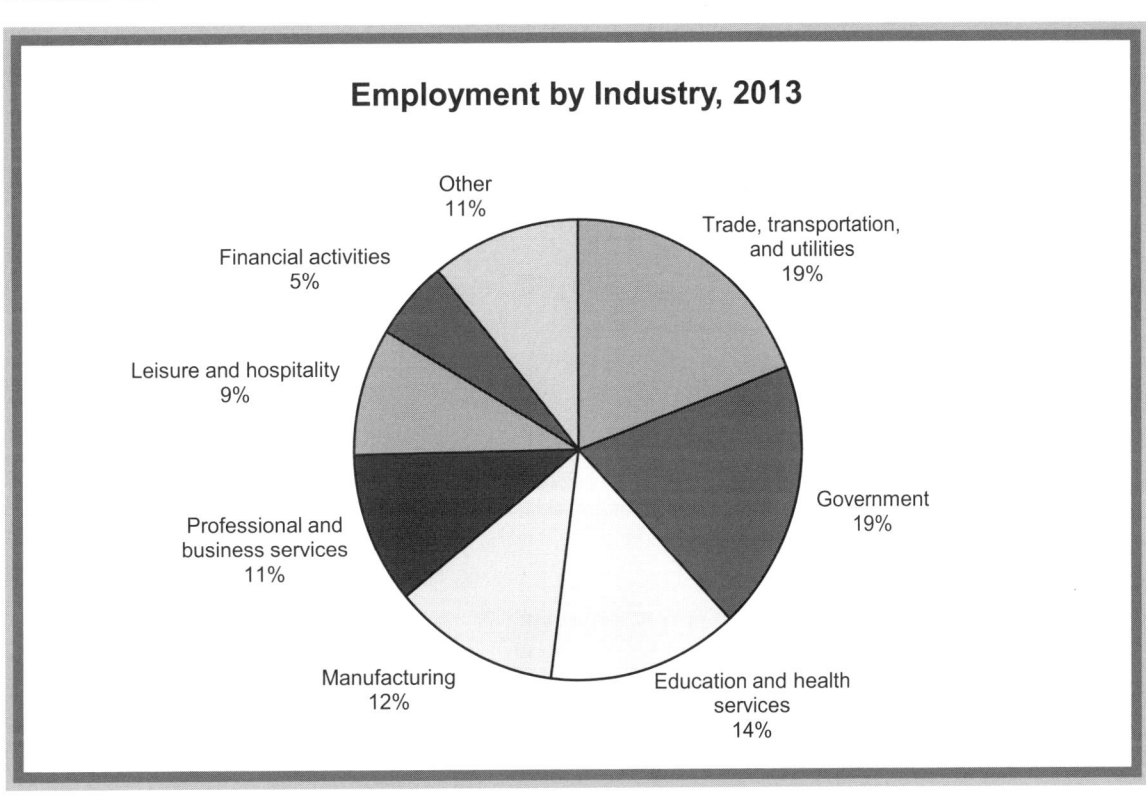

Employment by Industry, 2013

Other 11%
Trade, transportation, and utilities 19%
Financial activities 5%
Leisure and hospitality 9%
Professional and business services 11%
Manufacturing 12%
Education and health services 14%
Government 19%

1. Employment by Industry: Kansas, Selected Years, 2002–2013

(Numbers in thousands, not seasonally adjusted)

Industry and year	January	February	March	April	May	June	July	August	September	October	November	December	Annual average
Total Nonfarm													
2002	1,320.9	1,319.8	1,331.7	1,345.4	1,352.0	1,354.6	1,325.9	1,324.7	1,339.7	1,335.9	1,341.7	1,340.6	1,336.1
2003	1,301.0	1,302.0	1,307.9	1,316.3	1,325.4	1,324.7	1,297.5	1,295.8	1,315.6	1,320.7	1,325.0	1,326.3	1,313.2
2004	1,290.4	1,291.1	1,308.0	1,327.9	1,336.2	1,339.9	1,316.0	1,312.8	1,339.6	1,342.2	1,346.2	1,349.3	1,325.0
2005	1,302.6	1,315.3	1,329.3	1,338.2	1,344.3	1,349.4	1,311.8	1,312.1	1,341.3	1,344.7	1,352.3	1,355.9	1,333.1
2006	1,318.0	1,333.3	1,346.0	1,351.6	1,361.4	1,369.7	1,330.3	1,335.8	1,369.9	1,371.8	1,374.5	1,384.0	1,353.9
2007	1,341.2	1,351.9	1,372.9	1,377.7	1,387.1	1,397.5	1,369.5	1,368.2	1,391.3	1,396.9	1,404.7	1,402.2	1,380.1
2008	1,366.1	1,377.2	1,389.4	1,399.6	1,406.0	1,405.1	1,375.3	1,370.2	1,395.6	1,403.7	1,402.5	1,399.1	1,390.8
2009	1,358.2	1,355.6	1,356.0	1,356.4	1,359.6	1,349.7	1,318.4	1,313.4	1,333.5	1,339.0	1,341.9	1,337.9	1,343.3
2010	1,300.5	1,304.1	1,314.8	1,333.3	1,345.7	1,341.4	1,317.5	1,318.0	1,331.8	1,346.8	1,344.8	1,344.8	1,328.6
2011	1,314.8	1,316.4	1,326.2	1,346.9	1,353.5	1,340.7	1,324.8	1,328.2	1,348.1	1,357.6	1,359.6	1,354.6	1,339.3
2012	1,331.4	1,339.4	1,351.0	1,359.9	1,370.2	1,365.7	1,337.0	1,343.8	1,360.5	1,374.4	1,377.2	1,375.1	1,357.1
2013	1,341.7	1,352.9	1,358.9	1,376.3	1,381.9	1,375.6	1,355.5	1,361.3	1,384.2	1,394.5	1,400.4	1,392.0	1,372.9
Total Private													
2002	1,070.4	1,067.7	1,075.7	1,088.8	1,093.1	1,098.9	1,093.3	1,093.9	1,090.7	1,081.6	1,085.3	1,084.1	1,085.3
2003	1,050.4	1,049.4	1,052.2	1,060.6	1,066.9	1,069.6	1,066.0	1,067.7	1,068.1	1,066.1	1,068.2	1,068.6	1,062.8
2004	1,041.0	1,039.1	1,053.0	1,070.1	1,076.5	1,083.0	1,085.9	1,085.4	1,087.9	1,085.4	1,087.7	1,090.1	1,073.8
2005	1,057.2	1,061.1	1,071.3	1,079.5	1,084.7	1,092.5	1,089.7	1,089.6	1,089.7	1,086.2	1,091.9	1,094.7	1,082.3
2006	1,069.9	1,075.1	1,084.8	1,091.8	1,097.9	1,109.2	1,104.6	1,108.3	1,112.4	1,109.1	1,110.4	1,118.8	1,099.4
2007	1,090.0	1,091.8	1,109.5	1,115.0	1,121.9	1,131.4	1,132.9	1,133.2	1,131.5	1,131.9	1,137.8	1,135.4	1,121.9
2008	1,111.8	1,114.5	1,122.8	1,133.5	1,135.8	1,144.5	1,140.4	1,134.8	1,134.9	1,135.7	1,132.6	1,128.6	1,130.8
2009	1,096.0	1,089.4	1,088.1	1,087.3	1,085.9	1,087.7	1,083.0	1,079.5	1,073.4	1,071.5	1,072.9	1,069.0	1,082.0
2010	1,040.6	1,040.6	1,047.2	1,064.4	1,069.6	1,074.7	1,075.7	1,074.7	1,068.9	1,080.2	1,080.5	1,079.9	1,066.4
2011	1,053.2	1,053.0	1,061.0	1,078.9	1,084.5	1,084.4	1,086.7	1,088.2	1,085.7	1,091.8	1,093.8	1,091.9	1,079.4
2012	1,073.7	1,076.4	1,086.5	1,095.3	1,102.6	1,110.5	1,102.4	1,103.9	1,101.5	1,108.5	1,110.9	1,111.0	1,098.6
2013	1,085.7	1,089.5	1,095.3	1,110.4	1,117.9	1,124.7	1,123.5	1,125.7	1,123.5	1,129.1	1,134.4	1,128.2	1,115.7
Goods-Producing													
2002	251.6	250.1	251.8	254.0	255.6	258.4	257.0	258.0	255.9	251.3	249.9	248.1	253.5
2003	239.9	241.2	242.2	242.5	245.6	245.2	245.9	246.5	245.5	245.2	244.1	242.3	243.8
2004	237.0	235.0	240.5	245.4	246.9	249.4	253.2	252.2	251.7	251.8	250.5	250.2	247.0
2005	240.4	241.7	245.9	248.5	251.0	254.8	255.7	255.3	253.2	252.6	252.6	251.5	250.3
2006	247.0	248.8	251.1	252.7	254.7	259.9	260.5	260.6	259.2	257.8	256.4	257.1	255.5
2007	251.9	250.2	256.2	256.7	258.7	263.5	265.5	265.8	264.8	263.9	264.7	262.5	260.4
2008	257.1	256.7	260.1	262.2	261.5	267.3	267.9	261.7	264.5	262.4	259.5	256.4	261.4
2009	245.6	241.9	239.7	236.5	232.8	233.6	232.3	231.1	227.8	226.6	224.5	220.6	232.8
2010	214.1	213.6	215.7	221.4	222.8	225.9	227.9	227.7	226.4	226.9	224.9	222.9	222.5
2011	214.4	213.8	217.7	221.8	223.3	225.5	227.2	227.3	226.5	228.0	226.7	225.6	223.2
2012	222.0	221.6	225.8	225.9	228.5	230.8	231.4	231.0	230.5	230.4	229.0	226.8	227.8
2013	222.2	223.0	225.0	228.8	230.6	233.0	233.5	233.5	233.2	233.6	232.9	229.6	229.9
Service-Providing													
2002	1,069.3	1,069.7	1,079.9	1,091.4	1,096.4	1,096.2	1,068.9	1,066.7	1,083.8	1,084.6	1,091.8	1,092.5	1,082.6
2003	1,061.1	1,060.8	1,065.7	1,073.8	1,079.8	1,079.5	1,051.6	1,049.3	1,070.1	1,075.5	1,080.9	1,084.0	1,069.3
2004	1,053.4	1,056.1	1,067.5	1,082.5	1,089.3	1,090.5	1,062.8	1,060.6	1,087.9	1,090.4	1,095.7	1,099.1	1,078.0
2005	1,062.2	1,073.6	1,083.4	1,089.7	1,093.3	1,094.6	1,056.1	1,056.8	1,088.1	1,092.1	1,099.7	1,104.4	1,082.8
2006	1,071.0	1,084.5	1,094.9	1,098.9	1,106.7	1,109.8	1,069.8	1,075.2	1,110.7	1,114.0	1,118.1	1,126.9	1,098.4
2007	1,089.3	1,101.7	1,116.7	1,121.0	1,128.4	1,134.0	1,104.0	1,102.4	1,126.5	1,133.0	1,140.0	1,139.7	1,119.7
2008	1,109.0	1,120.5	1,129.3	1,137.4	1,144.5	1,137.8	1,107.4	1,108.5	1,131.1	1,141.3	1,143.0	1,142.7	1,129.4
2009	1,112.6	1,113.7	1,116.3	1,119.9	1,126.8	1,116.1	1,086.1	1,082.3	1,105.7	1,112.4	1,117.4	1,117.3	1,110.6
2010	1,086.4	1,090.5	1,099.1	1,111.9	1,122.9	1,115.5	1,089.6	1,090.3	1,105.4	1,119.9	1,119.9	1,121.9	1,106.1
2011	1,100.4	1,102.6	1,108.5	1,125.1	1,130.2	1,115.2	1,097.6	1,100.9	1,121.6	1,129.6	1,132.9	1,129.0	1,116.1
2012	1,109.4	1,117.8	1,125.2	1,134.0	1,141.7	1,134.9	1,105.6	1,112.8	1,130.0	1,144.0	1,148.2	1,148.3	1,129.3
2013	1,119.5	1,129.9	1,133.9	1,147.5	1,151.3	1,142.6	1,122.0	1,127.8	1,151.0	1,160.9	1,167.5	1,162.4	1,143.0
Mining and Logging													
2002	6.6	6.5	6.5	6.6	6.6	6.7	6.6	6.5	6.5	6.4	6.4	6.4	6.5
2003	6.2	6.2	6.3	6.4	6.5	6.6	6.6	6.7	6.7	6.7	6.8	6.8	6.5
2004	6.6	6.5	6.7	6.8	6.9	7.0	7.3	7.5	7.6	7.4	7.3	7.3	7.1
2005	7.2	7.3	7.3	7.4	7.5	7.6	7.6	7.7	7.7	7.9	7.9	8.0	7.6
2006	8.0	8.2	8.4	8.3	8.5	8.7	8.8	8.9	8.9	8.9	9.0	9.1	8.6
2007	8.9	8.9	9.0	9.2	9.1	9.1	9.3	9.3	9.2	9.3	9.3	9.4	9.2
2008	9.4	9.4	9.5	9.6	9.6	9.7	10.0	10.2	10.1	10.0	9.9	9.8	9.8
2009	8.7	8.3	8.1	7.8	7.7	7.8	8.0	8.0	8.0	8.1	8.0	8.1	8.1
2010	7.8	7.9	8.0	8.3	8.3	8.4	8.5	8.5	8.5	8.8	8.6	8.6	8.4
2011	8.4	8.3	8.5	8.8	8.8	9.0	9.5	9.5	9.4	9.5	9.5	9.6	9.1
2012	9.5	9.5	9.6	9.6	9.8	10.0	10.3	10.3	10.1	10.5	10.5	10.5	10.0
2013	10.1	10.1	10.1	10.4	10.5	10.4	10.7	10.6	10.5	10.6	10.6	10.6	10.4
Construction													
2002	58.2	57.7	59.5	62.3	64.1	66.3	67.1	66.7	65.2	64.3	63.5	62.3	63.1
2003	58.0	58.2	59.7	62.3	63.9	65.6	65.8	65.8	64.8	64.3	63.1	60.8	62.7
2004	57.4	54.7	59.0	63.3	64.1	66.5	67.6	66.8	65.8	65.4	64.1	63.0	63.1
2005	55.1	56.0	59.3	61.7	63.3	65.6	66.7	66.6	65.3	64.5	63.6	61.6	62.4
2006	59.2	59.8	61.7	63.2	64.4	67.2	67.7	67.4	66.3	64.6	63.9	64.4	64.1
2007	60.6	57.8	62.5	63.6	64.8	67.8	68.5	68.6	67.8	67.3	67.0	64.4	65.1
2008	59.9	59.0	61.8	64.5	66.3	68.2	68.5	67.9	66.3	65.1	63.8	62.2	64.5
2009	56.1	55.5	56.2	57.3	58.9	60.3	61.4	60.0	58.4	57.0	55.9	53.1	57.5
2010	47.2	46.7	49.2	53.8	54.7	56.9	58.6	58.4	57.4	57.6	55.5	53.2	54.1
2011	47.1	46.8	49.9	52.6	53.9	55.2	56.0	55.8	55.6	56.3	54.7	53.1	53.1
2012	50.5	50.4	53.9	54.8	56.2	57.8	57.6	57.2	56.7	56.2	54.9	53.5	55.0
2013	50.0	50.9	52.1	55.4	56.7	59.1	59.9	60.2	60.0	60.5	59.1	56.5	56.7

1. Employment by Industry: Kansas, Selected Years, 2002–2013—*Continued*

(Numbers in thousands, not seasonally adjusted)

Industry and year	January	February	March	April	May	June	July	August	September	October	November	December	Annual average
Manufacturing													
2002	186.8	185.9	185.8	185.1	184.9	185.4	183.3	184.8	184.2	180.6	180.0	179.4	183.9
2003	175.7	176.8	176.2	173.8	175.2	173.0	173.5	174.0	174.0	174.2	174.2	174.7	174.6
2004	173.0	173.8	174.8	175.3	175.9	175.9	178.3	177.9	178.3	179.0	179.1	179.9	176.8
2005	178.1	178.4	179.3	179.4	180.2	181.6	181.4	181.0	180.2	180.2	181.1	181.9	180.2
2006	179.8	180.8	181.0	181.2	181.8	184.0	184.0	184.3	184.0	184.3	183.5	184.4	182.8
2007	182.4	183.5	184.7	183.9	184.8	186.6	187.7	187.9	187.8	187.3	188.4	188.7	186.1
2008	187.8	188.3	188.8	188.1	185.6	189.4	189.4	183.6	188.1	187.3	185.8	184.4	187.2
2009	180.8	178.1	175.4	171.4	166.2	165.5	162.9	163.1	161.4	161.5	160.6	159.4	167.2
2010	159.1	159.0	158.5	159.3	159.8	160.6	160.8	160.8	160.5	160.5	160.8	161.1	160.1
2011	158.9	158.7	159.3	160.4	160.6	161.3	161.7	162.0	161.5	162.2	162.5	162.9	161.0
2012	162.0	161.7	162.3	161.5	162.5	163.0	163.5	163.5	163.7	163.7	163.6	162.8	162.8
2013	162.1	162.0	162.8	163.0	163.4	163.5	162.9	162.7	162.7	162.5	163.2	162.5	162.8
Trade, Transportation, and Utilities													
2002	266.2	262.4	262.7	266.0	267.1	268.4	265.7	265.7	265.2	265.4	268.9	270.5	266.2
2003	259.7	257.6	257.9	259.6	260.9	261.0	260.6	261.4	262.0	262.5	266.0	268.1	261.4
2004	258.2	256.1	257.1	259.8	262.1	263.3	261.4	261.3	263.2	262.8	266.8	268.3	261.7
2005	258.2	257.1	258.1	259.3	260.6	261.3	260.0	260.3	259.9	260.0	264.4	267.0	260.5
2006	256.9	255.7	257.3	257.6	258.7	259.9	258.3	259.7	260.4	260.1	263.7	267.4	259.6
2007	258.4	257.2	261.0	260.7	262.3	263.4	262.9	263.0	262.4	263.6	268.0	269.2	262.7
2008	260.9	259.5	260.4	260.9	261.9	263.0	263.6	262.5	261.1	262.6	265.3	266.2	262.3
2009	257.6	255.3	255.0	254.0	254.4	255.1	253.7	252.7	251.6	252.4	255.5	256.3	254.5
2010	247.8	246.4	247.5	250.4	252.0	253.2	252.9	252.5	251.1	254.4	257.8	259.2	252.1
2011	251.2	249.9	249.3	254.0	255.6	255.2	255.1	255.2	254.4	256.6	260.7	261.6	254.9
2012	254.5	252.8	253.9	255.6	257.2	259.3	256.2	256.5	256.0	258.7	262.7	263.7	257.3
2013	255.9	254.8	255.3	257.5	259.2	260.6	260.3	261.5	260.6	262.9	267.5	268.5	260.4
Wholesale Trade													
2002	60.2	60.1	60.3	60.8	60.8	61.6	61.6	61.0	60.4	59.8	59.6	59.6	60.5
2003	58.2	58.1	58.1	58.0	58.3	59.2	59.0	58.4	57.8	57.8	57.8	58.0	58.2
2004	56.6	56.6	57.0	57.4	58.0	59.3	59.4	58.9	58.5	58.5	58.4	58.2	58.1
2005	57.7	57.8	58.1	58.9	59.1	60.4	60.0	59.6	59.3	58.4	58.5	58.8	58.9
2006	58.1	58.3	58.5	57.5	57.9	59.3	59.2	58.9	58.8	58.4	58.3	58.9	58.5
2007	58.4	58.4	59.1	58.8	59.0	60.3	60.4	59.7	59.4	60.1	60.1	60.0	59.5
2008	60.2	60.0	59.9	60.2	60.5	61.3	61.9	60.9	60.4	60.6	60.5	60.2	60.6
2009	60.4	60.1	60.1	58.6	58.5	59.2	59.4	58.4	58.0	58.0	57.8	57.4	58.8
2010	56.6	56.6	56.8	58.3	58.4	59.2	59.2	58.4	57.9	58.2	57.8	57.7	57.9
2011	57.4	57.4	57.8	58.3	58.7	59.3	59.5	59.0	58.6	58.8	58.7	58.8	58.5
2012	58.2	58.2	58.5	58.5	58.9	60.2	59.2	59.0	58.4	58.7	58.5	58.7	58.8
2013	58.5	58.4	58.4	58.9	59.2	60.1	61.5	61.1	60.6	60.7	61.6	61.0	60.0
Retail Trade													
2002	153.9	150.7	150.9	152.6	153.5	154.1	152.1	152.2	152.2	152.6	156.3	158.0	153.3
2003	149.5	147.5	147.9	148.8	149.7	150.0	149.7	150.7	151.0	151.4	155.0	157.0	150.7
2004	150.3	148.2	149.0	150.1	151.5	151.5	149.6	149.2	151.3	150.4	154.5	156.3	151.0
2005	148.1	146.8	147.3	147.9	148.9	148.8	147.7	147.3	147.1	148.2	152.1	153.7	148.7
2006	146.3	145.0	146.3	147.0	147.8	147.7	146.8	147.2	147.6	147.7	151.2	153.3	147.8
2007	146.3	145.3	147.8	147.3	148.5	148.1	148.2	148.1	147.4	148.3	152.3	153.3	148.4
2008	146.7	145.3	146.5	146.5	147.2	147.5	147.5	147.0	146.0	145.9	148.6	149.4	147.0
2009	142.2	140.5	140.7	141.6	142.4	142.4	141.5	141.3	141.1	141.7	144.5	145.4	142.1
2010	139.4	138.0	138.7	139.9	141.1	141.2	140.7	140.4	139.2	141.2	144.5	145.5	140.8
2011	139.2	138.0	139.0	141.2	142.0	141.9	141.7	141.4	140.7	142.2	146.1	146.5	141.7
2012	141.3	139.7	140.6	141.5	142.5	143.0	142.5	142.1	141.9	143.5	147.4	147.9	142.8
2013	141.3	140.4	141.0	142.2	143.2	144.1	144.0	144.7	144.4	146.4	148.5	149.2	144.1
Transportation and Utilities													
2002	52.1	51.6	51.5	52.6	52.8	52.7	52.0	52.5	52.6	53.0	53.0	52.9	52.4
2003	52.0	52.0	51.9	52.8	52.9	51.8	51.9	52.3	53.2	53.3	53.2	53.1	52.5
2004	51.3	51.3	51.1	52.3	52.6	52.5	52.4	53.2	53.4	53.9	53.9	53.8	52.6
2005	52.4	52.5	52.7	52.5	52.6	52.1	52.3	53.4	53.5	53.4	53.8	54.5	53.0
2006	52.5	52.4	52.5	53.1	53.0	52.9	52.3	53.6	54.0	54.0	54.2	55.2	53.3
2007	53.7	53.5	54.1	54.6	54.8	55.0	54.3	55.2	55.6	55.2	55.6	55.9	54.8
2008	54.0	54.2	54.0	54.2	54.2	54.2	54.2	54.6	54.7	56.1	56.2	56.6	54.8
2009	55.0	54.7	54.2	53.8	53.5	53.5	52.8	53.0	52.5	52.7	53.2	53.5	53.5
2010	51.8	51.8	52.0	52.2	52.5	52.8	53.0	53.7	54.0	55.0	55.5	56.0	53.4
2011	54.6	54.5	52.5	54.5	54.9	54.0	53.9	54.8	55.1	55.6	55.9	56.3	54.7
2012	55.0	54.9	54.8	55.6	55.8	56.1	54.5	55.4	55.7	56.5	56.8	57.1	55.7
2013	56.1	56.0	55.9	56.4	56.8	56.4	54.8	55.7	55.6	55.8	57.4	58.3	56.3
Information													
2002	50.4	50.2	50.3	50.4	49.8	49.6	49.2	48.7	48.0	47.3	47.7	47.7	49.1
2003	47.2	46.4	46.1	45.5	45.0	45.2	44.6	44.0	43.8	43.4	43.5	43.5	44.9
2004	43.5	43.2	43.0	43.0	43.0	43.0	42.7	42.2	41.6	40.4	40.5	40.9	42.3
2005	40.6	40.7	40.4	40.7	40.6	40.5	40.4	39.8	39.6	38.6	39.0	39.3	40.0
2006	39.1	39.1	39.5	40.6	40.6	41.0	40.9	40.7	40.6	41.0	41.2	41.4	40.5
2007	41.7	41.7	41.8	41.8	41.8	41.8	41.9	41.5	40.9	40.6	40.6	40.6	41.4
2008	40.4	40.4	40.3	40.3	39.8	39.8	39.7	39.2	38.4	38.6	38.0	37.9	39.4
2009	37.2	36.9	36.8	37.1	36.7	36.2	35.8	35.2	34.4	32.5	32.3	32.4	35.3
2010	31.8	31.6	31.4	31.4	31.2	30.9	30.5	30.2	29.7	29.6	29.5	29.6	30.6
2011	29.3	29.3	29.2	28.9	28.2	28.1	27.9	27.7	27.4	27.4	27.4	27.5	28.2
2012	27.9	27.7	27.8	27.7	27.8	27.8	27.7	27.5	27.4	27.5	27.6	27.7	27.7
2013	27.3	27.2	27.2	27.3	27.4	27.5	27.8	27.9	27.6	27.6	27.7	27.7	27.5

1. Employment by Industry: Kansas, Selected Years, 2002–2013—*Continued*

(Numbers in thousands, not seasonally adjusted)

Industry and year	January	February	March	April	May	June	July	August	September	October	November	December	Annual average
Financial Activities													
2002	68.2	68.4	68.8	68.4	68.7	69.0	69.5	69.3	68.8	69.0	69.3	69.6	68.9
2003	68.5	68.5	69.0	69.5	69.6	70.0	70.1	70.5	69.7	69.6	69.4	69.7	69.5
2004	68.8	69.0	69.6	69.9	70.0	70.6	71.0	70.8	70.0	69.8	69.7	70.3	70.0
2005	69.3	69.4	69.6	70.0	70.1	70.7	71.1	71.0	70.8	71.0	71.1	71.8	70.5
2006	70.9	70.8	71.0	71.6	72.1	72.5	73.3	73.2	73.0	72.9	73.3	74.2	72.4
2007	73.2	73.3	73.9	73.7	74.1	74.7	75.1	74.9	74.5	74.1	74.1	74.5	74.2
2008	73.0	73.2	73.0	73.4	73.5	73.9	73.8	73.7	73.0	73.2	73.0	73.4	73.3
2009	72.0	72.0	71.9	71.4	71.5	72.0	72.7	72.8	71.9	72.3	72.5	72.7	72.1
2010	71.5	71.5	71.3	71.7	72.1	72.2	72.3	72.2	71.4	72.3	72.3	72.6	72.0
2011	71.5	71.3	71.5	72.2	73.3	73.5	74.0	74.1	73.6	74.1	74.0	74.3	73.1
2012	73.7	74.1	74.4	74.7	74.6	75.1	75.1	74.9	74.1	74.4	74.7	75.1	74.6
2013	74.2	74.4	74.2	75.1	75.6	76.6	76.6	76.4	75.8	75.8	76.5	76.8	75.7
Professional and Business Services													
2002	124.5	125.4	127.4	130.2	129.5	130.7	131.2	130.8	130.2	127.2	128.0	127.7	128.6
2003	123.5	123.1	122.9	126.0	125.5	127.7	124.9	125.3	124.6	124.6	124.7	126.2	124.9
2004	121.0	122.1	125.1	127.8	127.8	129.7	130.1	131.6	132.0	131.6	131.9	132.7	128.6
2005	127.8	128.7	130.5	131.8	131.3	133.0	133.9	135.2	135.3	135.8	136.8	137.7	133.2
2006	133.5	135.5	137.5	138.0	137.2	139.2	138.0	138.6	140.2	140.5	140.5	142.0	138.4
2007	138.1	139.5	141.3	143.5	144.0	145.0	146.6	147.7	148.0	147.8	149.2	148.4	144.9
2008	143.9	145.1	147.0	149.1	148.8	150.3	149.4	149.9	149.5	150.2	149.6	148.1	148.4
2009	142.8	141.2	140.8	141.6	140.9	140.9	140.5	139.8	138.8	140.0	141.1	141.2	140.8
2010	137.7	137.6	139.2	144.7	143.8	144.4	146.5	146.3	144.3	147.6	147.2	147.5	143.9
2011	143.7	144.5	146.0	149.3	148.3	147.3	148.8	149.6	149.9	151.1	151.3	149.7	148.3
2012	147.9	149.1	150.7	153.4	153.5	155.3	153.8	154.4	154.7	157.7	157.2	157.7	153.8
2013	154.0	155.5	157.1	160.9	160.5	162.4	163.5	164.6	164.7	166.1	167.8	166.1	161.9
Education and Health Services													
2002	154.2	155.1	155.9	157.8	158.4	157.1	155.8	156.3	158.7	159.0	159.5	159.6	157.3
2003	156.0	156.2	155.9	158.2	157.8	155.6	155.4	155.7	158.2	158.5	158.8	158.8	157.1
2004	157.4	158.2	159.3	160.4	160.6	159.6	160.4	160.5	162.9	164.2	164.6	164.2	161.0
2005	163.3	163.9	164.2	165.1	165.1	164.4	161.7	161.8	164.6	163.8	164.4	165.0	163.9
2006	163.1	164.3	165.1	165.6	166.3	166.3	164.3	164.9	168.5	169.0	169.1	169.9	166.4
2007	167.6	168.8	170.1	170.7	171.0	171.3	170.0	170.4	173.0	174.3	174.5	174.8	171.4
2008	173.4	174.9	175.6	177.0	177.2	176.6	174.2	175.5	177.6	178.6	179.2	179.2	176.6
2009	178.2	179.0	179.1	179.9	180.3	179.7	178.5	178.9	180.5	181.9	182.2	182.4	180.1
2010	179.1	180.1	180.1	179.5	180.1	179.3	178.2	178.5	179.8	182.5	183.2	183.5	180.3
2011	183.8	184.2	184.3	185.9	186.3	184.4	183.2	183.8	185.2	186.5	187.0	186.9	185.1
2012	184.4	185.2	185.5	186.2	186.9	186.2	184.3	185.2	186.7	188.2	188.9	189.5	186.4
2013	186.9	187.0	187.3	188.1	188.4	187.6	185.7	186.0	187.1	190.0	190.2	189.5	187.8
Leisure and Hospitality													
2002	103.0	103.7	106.0	108.9	110.9	111.8	111.8	112.3	110.6	109.5	109.2	108.0	108.8
2003	103.4	103.9	105.5	106.9	109.4	111.7	111.5	111.5	111.3	109.4	108.7	106.8	108.3
2004	103.0	103.2	105.7	110.2	112.8	113.9	114.0	113.9	113.1	111.6	110.6	110.3	110.2
2005	105.5	106.8	109.2	111.3	113.3	115.2	114.8	114.5	113.9	111.7	111.1	110.3	111.5
2006	107.6	108.7	110.7	114.1	116.4	118.4	117.9	118.9	118.2	116.2	114.7	114.9	114.7
2007	108.3	109.8	113.0	115.4	117.7	119.3	118.8	117.6	115.6	114.4	113.7	112.6	114.7
2008	110.7	111.5	113.0	116.9	119.2	120.3	118.3	118.9	117.5	116.5	114.6	114.4	116.0
2009	109.9	110.1	112.0	114.1	116.6	117.8	117.4	117.2	116.3	113.5	112.5	111.4	114.1
2010	107.1	108.2	110.3	113.4	115.8	117.4	116.3	116.2	114.9	114.2	113.4	112.5	113.3
2011	108.3	108.5	111.4	115.1	117.9	119.2	118.9	119.1	117.0	115.9	114.8	114.4	115.0
2012	112.3	114.3	116.9	120.2	122.5	124.5	122.8	123.3	120.4	119.7	119.1	118.9	119.6
2013	114.9	116.4	118.2	121.3	124.8	125.8	125.0	124.6	123.0	120.9	119.3	117.5	121.0
Other Services													
2002	52.3	52.4	52.8	53.1	53.1	53.9	53.1	52.8	53.3	52.9	52.8	52.9	53.0
2003	52.2	52.5	52.7	52.4	53.1	53.2	53.0	52.8	53.0	52.9	53.0	53.2	52.8
2004	52.1	52.3	52.7	53.6	53.3	53.5	53.1	52.9	53.4	53.2	53.1	53.2	53.0
2005	52.1	52.8	53.4	52.8	52.7	52.6	52.1	51.7	52.4	52.7	52.5	52.1	52.5
2006	51.8	52.2	52.6	51.6	51.9	52.0	51.4	51.7	52.3	51.6	51.5	51.9	51.9
2007	50.8	51.3	52.2	52.5	52.3	52.4	52.1	52.3	52.3	53.2	53.0	52.8	52.3
2008	52.4	53.2	53.4	53.7	53.9	53.3	53.5	53.4	53.3	53.6	53.4	53.0	53.3
2009	52.7	53.0	52.8	52.7	52.7	52.4	52.1	51.8	52.1	52.3	52.3	52.0	52.4
2010	51.5	51.6	51.7	51.9	51.8	51.4	51.1	51.1	51.3	52.7	52.2	52.1	51.7
2011	51.0	51.5	51.6	51.7	51.6	51.2	51.6	51.4	51.7	52.2	51.9	51.9	51.6
2012	51.0	51.6	51.5	51.6	51.6	51.5	51.1	51.1	51.7	51.9	51.7	51.7	51.5
2013	50.3	51.2	51.0	51.4	51.4	51.2	51.1	51.2	51.5	52.2	52.5	52.5	51.5
Government													
2002	250.5	252.1	256.0	256.6	258.9	255.7	232.6	230.8	249.0	254.3	256.4	256.5	250.8
2003	250.6	252.6	255.7	255.7	258.5	255.1	231.5	228.1	247.5	254.6	256.8	257.7	250.4
2004	249.4	252.0	255.0	257.8	259.7	256.9	230.1	227.4	251.7	256.8	258.5	259.2	251.2
2005	245.4	254.2	258.0	258.7	259.6	256.9	222.1	222.5	251.6	258.5	260.4	261.2	250.8
2006	248.1	258.2	261.2	259.8	263.5	260.5	225.7	227.5	257.5	262.7	264.1	265.2	254.5
2007	251.2	260.1	263.4	262.7	265.2	266.1	236.6	235.0	259.8	265.0	266.9	266.8	258.2
2008	254.3	262.7	266.6	266.1	270.2	260.6	234.9	235.4	260.7	268.0	269.9	270.5	260.0
2009	262.2	266.2	267.9	269.1	273.7	262.0	235.4	233.9	260.1	267.5	269.0	268.9	261.3
2010	259.9	263.5	267.6	268.9	276.1	266.7	241.8	243.3	262.9	266.6	264.3	264.9	262.2
2011	261.6	263.4	265.2	268.0	269.0	256.3	238.1	240.0	262.4	265.8	265.8	262.7	259.9
2012	257.7	263.0	264.5	264.6	267.6	255.2	234.6	239.9	259.0	265.9	266.3	264.1	258.5
2013	256.0	263.4	263.6	265.9	264.0	250.9	232.0	235.6	260.7	265.4	266.0	263.8	257.3

2. Average Weekly Hours by Selected Industry: Kansas, 2009–2013

(Not seasonally adjusted)

Industry and year	January	February	March	April	May	June	July	August	September	October	November	December	Annual average
Total Private													
2009	33.8	34.2	34.1	33.5	33.4	34.1	34.2	35.4	34.3	34.2	34.9	33.8	34.2
2010	33.6	33.6	33.5	34.0	34.4	34.5	34.3	34.7	33.9	34.2	34.1	34.4	34.1
2011	33.9	33.8	34.1	34.4	34.8	34.7	34.7	34.5	34.5	35.2	34.5	34.6	34.5
2012	34.7	34.3	34.6	34.9	34.6	35.1	35.2	35.1	35.5	34.8	34.8	35.2	34.9
2013	34.3	34.4	34.5	34.5	34.3	35.3	34.6	34.5	35.1	34.5	34.4	34.8	34.6
Goods-Producing													
2009	39.0	39.1	39.6	38.7	39.1	39.6	39.7	43.9	42.1	43.0	43.7	41.9	40.7
2010	42.1	41.2	41.6	42.6	42.7	42.8	41.8	41.9	40.5	41.5	41.1	41.9	41.8
2011	39.6	40.6	41.5	41.7	42.1	42.2	41.7	41.5	42.0	42.2	41.5	40.9	41.5
2012	41.0	40.3	40.9	41.4	41.6	41.8	41.8	41.8	41.3	41.6	41.5	41.6	41.4
2013	40.4	40.4	41.2	40.9	40.5	41.6	41.5	41.5	41.7	41.9	41.6	42.0	41.3
Construction													
2009	35.6	36.5	37.3	36.2	38.5	37.8	39.9	41.2	36.3	39.2	40.5	36.6	38.0
2010	39.0	36.8	37.7	41.1	40.0	41.9	43.2	43.4	39.8	41.7	39.0	40.7	40.5
2011	36.0	36.2	38.4	39.8	41.0	40.9	40.8	39.5	41.1	40.4	38.3	38.7	39.4
2012	37.9	36.9	38.6	38.6	39.8	39.6	39.6	40.2	38.9	40.0	38.9	38.8	39.0
2013	36.7	37.6	37.4	36.9	39.2	40.1	39.4	39.2	39.5	40.3	38.9	37.9	38.7
Manufacturing													
2009	39.8	39.5	40.0	39.1	38.8	39.9	39.3	44.6	43.7	44.2	44.6	43.7	41.4
2010	43.0	42.6	42.8	42.8	43.6	43.0	42.1	42.0	41.6	41.9	42.4	42.5	42.5
2011	41.4	41.4	42.0	41.8	41.9	42.1	41.5	41.9	41.8	42.4	42.4	41.6	41.8
2012	42.0	41.4	41.5	42.5	42.1	42.6	42.5	42.2	42.1	42.1	42.6	43.0	42.2
2013	41.9	41.5	42.7	42.4	42.2	43.4	43.1	43.2	43.3	43.3	43.2	43.9	42.8
Trade, Transportation, and Utilities													
2009	34.1	34.4	34.3	33.8	34.0	34.5	35.0	35.3	34.3	34.0	34.4	34.4	34.4
2010	33.9	33.5	32.5	34.0	33.7	34.1	34.0	34.2	33.4	33.4	32.6	32.7	33.5
2011	32.5	32.1	33.0	33.5	34.0	33.9	34.1	34.0	33.7	34.2	33.8	34.7	33.6
2012	35.1	34.4	34.7	35.3	35.4	35.7	36.0	35.6	36.1	35.5	35.8	35.8	35.5
2013	34.8	34.8	34.9	34.4	34.5	35.0	34.4	34.2	34.8	34.1	34.0	34.3	34.5
Financial Activities													
2009	36.5	37.7	37.1	36.4	36.2	36.4	36.6	37.9	36.7	36.8	38.1	36.3	36.9
2010	36.2	36.4	36.3	36.5	37.0	36.8	36.9	37.9	36.9	37.3	36.8	37.1	36.8
2011	38.1	37.4	37.2	37.1	37.6	37.1	37.2	37.0	37.0	38.4	37.5	37.5	37.4
2012	37.1	36.6	36.8	37.5	35.7	36.8	36.9	36.0	37.3	35.9	36.0	37.4	36.7
2013	35.8	36.8	36.5	36.3	36.0	38.0	36.2	36.2	37.2	35.8	36.5	36.7	36.5
Professional and Business Services													
2009	32.9	34.1	34.2	32.7	33.0	33.4	33.0	33.0	32.4	32.4	33.5	31.9	33.0
2010	31.0	32.1	32.4	32.5	32.7	33.0	33.2	34.4	33.8	34.5	34.4	34.1	33.2
2011	34.9	35.2	35.0	35.6	35.7	35.8	35.7	35.4	35.3	36.3	35.6	35.4	35.5
2012	35.2	34.8	35.0	35.5	34.8	35.1	35.4	35.5	36.3	35.0	34.8	35.2	35.2
2013	34.3	35.1	34.8	35.4	35.7	37.0	35.7	36.0	36.2	36.3	36.1	36.4	35.8
Education and Health Services													
2009	32.1	31.5	31.5	32.6	31.0	33.1	33.1	33.2	32.7	31.2	32.2	31.3	32.1
2010	31.4	31.2	31.3	31.2	32.2	31.4	31.7	32.2	31.7	31.8	31.6	31.7	31.6
2011	32.3	31.8	31.3	31.6	32.3	32.1	32.2	31.9	32.0	32.3	31.5	31.7	31.9
2012	32.5	31.9	31.7	31.9	31.3	31.8	32.0	31.2	32.0	31.2	31.2	32.4	31.8
2013	31.7	31.4	31.3	31.6	31.1	32.2	31.7	31.5	32.5	31.3	31.4	32.1	31.6
Leisure and Hospitality													
2009	23.0	24.0	23.6	23.4	23.9	24.4	24.2	24.5	23.6	23.5	24.0	22.9	23.8
2010	22.6	23.1	23.3	23.4	23.8	24.3	24.2	24.7	24.0	24.2	23.7	24.3	23.8
2011	24.1	24.1	24.6	24.7	24.6	24.8	24.6	25.3	24.9	25.9	25.2	25.0	24.8
2012	25.0	25.4	25.2	25.1	25.3	26.0	25.8	25.9	25.6	25.0	24.2	24.5	25.3
2013	23.8	24.0	24.1	24.0	24.0	24.7	23.7	23.7	23.7	23.6	23.5	23.5	23.9
Other Services													
2009	31.4	32.8	32.0	31.3	30.0	29.6	31.5	32.8	30.0	30.4	31.2	30.1	31.1
2010	30.1	31.1	30.7	30.5	30.2	31.7	32.0	32.1	30.7	30.4	30.0	30.4	30.8
2011	30.9	30.1	30.6	30.8	30.7	32.3	31.9	31.1	30.0	31.1	30.6	30.8	30.9
2012	29.4	30.1	29.8	29.9	30.2	31.6	31.2	30.9	30.5	29.7	30.5	30.8	30.4
2013	31.5	29.8	29.7	29.7	29.4	31.7	31.6	31.2	31.0	29.5	29.7	30.3	30.4

3. Average Hourly Earnings by Selected Industry: Kansas, 2009–2013

(Dollars, not seasonally adjusted)

Industry and year	January	February	March	April	May	June	July	August	September	October	November	December	Annual average
Total Private													
2009	20.40	20.54	20.40	20.27	20.46	20.07	20.22	19.57	19.82	20.12	20.13	20.16	20.18
2010	20.07	20.19	19.97	20.04	20.22	19.79	20.03	20.12	20.40	20.18	19.86	20.06	20.08
2011	20.58	20.65	20.34	20.45	20.47	20.36	20.47	20.44	20.42	20.63	20.67	20.63	20.51
2012	21.09	20.98	20.91	21.13	21.01	20.83	21.11	20.84	21.07	21.09	21.00	21.26	21.03
2013	21.42	21.47	21.36	21.50	21.38	21.44	21.32	21.32	21.49	21.48	21.52	21.70	21.45
Goods-Producing													
2009	22.56	22.28	22.38	22.64	22.80	22.34	22.34	20.03	20.60	21.26	21.31	22.68	21.91
2010	21.55	21.84	21.42	21.46	21.61	20.81	21.04	21.10	21.61	21.63	20.92	21.17	21.34
2011	21.58	21.87	21.88	21.82	21.75	21.73	21.70	21.86	21.91	22.06	22.07	22.24	21.87
2012	22.10	22.28	22.18	21.79	21.80	21.63	21.80	21.94	21.92	21.89	21.87	22.10	21.94
2013	21.61	21.84	21.43	21.43	21.12	21.64	21.59	21.66	22.12	22.16	22.50	22.88	21.84
Construction													
2009	21.82	21.46	21.99	22.43	22.65	22.04	21.89	21.70	22.38	22.59	23.09	23.66	22.30
2010	23.05	23.55	22.72	22.41	22.43	22.07	21.21	20.90	21.22	21.45	21.39	21.71	21.93
2011	21.76	21.63	21.12	21.18	21.68	21.58	21.36	21.82	22.09	22.17	22.66	22.49	21.80
2012	22.35	23.43	23.21	22.61	22.60	22.06	22.49	22.80	22.96	23.17	23.30	23.66	22.88
2013	23.08	23.27	21.49	21.94	22.01	22.38	22.34	22.28	22.65	23.08	23.65	23.80	22.67
Manufacturing													
2009	22.76	22.39	22.26	22.52	22.70	22.41	22.52	19.47	20.09	20.81	20.69	22.59	21.74
2010	21.12	21.35	21.05	21.24	21.48	21.09	20.99	21.20	21.80	21.78	20.79	21.06	21.24
2011	21.66	22.09	22.25	22.12	21.92	21.76	21.81	21.87	21.80	22.00	21.78	22.17	21.94
2012	22.00	21.91	21.76	21.55	21.58	21.52	21.51	21.60	21.51	21.34	21.31	21.56	21.59
2013	21.17	21.40	21.37	21.23	21.01	21.69	21.58	21.64	21.85	21.70	22.03	22.13	21.57
Trade, Transportation, and Utilities													
2009	17.99	18.10	18.31	18.02	18.08	17.77	17.95	18.28	18.34	18.70	18.66	17.95	18.18
2010	17.88	17.97	18.17	18.28	18.26	18.10	18.07	18.23	18.38	18.11	18.09	18.18	18.14
2011	18.37	18.44	18.27	18.67	18.69	18.68	18.71	18.64	18.82	19.34	19.25	18.96	18.74
2012	19.88	19.13	19.22	19.85	19.33	19.52	19.90	19.82	20.37	20.90	20.25	20.64	19.91
2013	21.11	20.94	21.00	21.03	20.62	20.82	20.55	20.51	20.44	20.47	19.98	20.09	20.63
Financial Activities													
2009	21.43	22.48	23.14	21.68	22.51	21.94	22.22	22.76	22.32	22.56	23.56	22.86	22.46
2010	23.27	23.23	22.69	23.10	23.46	23.17	23.88	23.91	23.81	23.89	23.91	22.88	23.52
2011	23.86	23.40	23.10	23.48	23.85	23.46	23.65	23.33	23.40	23.45	23.16	22.73	23.41
2012	24.27	24.32	23.09	23.49	24.45	24.15	23.88	23.71	24.28	23.87	23.76	23.88	23.93
2013	24.54	24.80	24.52	24.47	25.41	24.91	24.92	25.56	25.38	25.65	26.06	25.70	25.16
Professional and Business Services													
2009	26.23	26.27	25.52	25.53	25.86	25.46	25.92	24.93	25.59	25.24	25.35	24.60	25.55
2010	25.03	24.44	24.21	23.99	24.23	23.77	23.71	23.94	25.01	24.59	24.86	25.65	24.46
2011	26.07	25.45	25.16	24.99	25.29	25.00	25.40	25.12	24.52	24.75	24.56	24.91	25.09
2012	25.16	24.94	24.89	25.02	24.79	24.43	24.67	23.95	23.96	23.97	23.79	24.35	24.48
2013	24.29	24.13	23.83	24.16	23.81	23.72	23.57	23.46	24.05	23.72	23.66	23.60	23.83
Education and Health Services													
2009	17.90	18.35	17.76	18.08	18.40	18.14	18.40	17.77	17.90	18.34	17.43	17.90	18.03
2010	18.26	18.90	18.40	18.42	18.98	18.93	19.23	18.72	18.89	18.83	19.08	19.65	18.86
2011	20.02	20.39	19.55	19.48	19.21	19.34	19.36	19.34	19.41	19.47	19.57	19.41	19.54
2012	19.55	19.59	19.65	19.89	19.76	19.73	19.92	20.00	19.91	19.89	19.81	19.81	19.79
2013	19.76	19.95	20.05	20.60	20.85	20.90	20.88	20.91	21.04	21.15	21.33	21.52	20.75
Leisure and Hospitality													
2009	11.04	10.88	10.66	10.74	10.81	10.71	10.71	10.70	10.83	10.97	10.97	11.04	10.83
2010	11.04	11.04	10.90	11.17	10.96	10.73	10.67	10.70	10.74	10.90	10.97	10.75	10.88
2011	10.89	11.20	11.10	11.07	11.00	10.98	11.12	11.53	11.52	11.46	11.43	11.42	11.23
2012	11.56	11.39	11.27	11.29	11.31	11.25	11.21	10.89	11.11	11.18	11.13	11.31	11.24
2013	11.30	11.29	11.30	11.38	11.35	11.01	11.18	11.24	11.37	11.25	11.26	11.40	11.28
Other Services													
2009	20.32	20.45	20.68	20.85	21.05	21.31	21.56	21.34	21.09	21.02	21.27	20.87	20.98
2010	20.82	20.55	20.52	20.63	20.31	19.80	19.99	19.95	19.51	19.21	18.89	18.84	19.92
2011	19.42	19.71	19.39	19.69	19.65	19.29	19.17	19.36	19.11	19.34	19.29	19.32	19.39
2012	20.30	19.48	19.73	19.91	19.78	19.61	20.03	20.02	20.05	19.81	19.88	19.89	19.87
2013	20.76	20.50	20.84	20.69	21.22	21.31	21.46	21.35	21.07	21.08	21.12	22.11	21.13

4. Average Weekly Earnings by Selected Industry: Kansas, 2009–2013

(Dollars, not seasonally adjusted)

Industry and year	January	February	March	April	May	June	July	August	September	October	November	December	Annual average
Total Private													
2009	689.52	702.47	695.64	679.05	683.36	684.39	691.52	692.78	679.83	688.10	702.54	681.41	690.16
2010	674.35	678.38	669.00	681.36	695.57	682.76	687.03	698.16	691.56	690.16	677.23	690.06	684.73
2011	697.66	697.97	693.59	703.48	712.36	706.49	710.31	705.18	704.49	726.18	713.12	713.80	707.60
2012	731.82	719.61	723.49	737.44	726.95	731.13	743.07	731.48	747.99	733.93	730.80	748.35	733.95
2013	734.71	738.57	736.92	741.75	733.33	756.83	737.67	735.54	754.30	741.06	740.29	755.16	742.17
Goods-Producing													
2009	879.84	871.15	886.25	876.17	891.48	884.66	886.90	879.32	867.26	914.18	931.25	950.29	891.74
2010	907.26	899.81	891.07	914.20	922.75	890.67	879.47	884.09	875.21	897.65	859.81	887.02	892.01
2011	854.57	887.92	908.02	909.89	915.68	917.01	904.89	907.19	920.22	930.93	915.91	909.62	907.61
2012	906.10	897.88	907.16	902.11	906.88	904.13	911.24	917.09	905.30	910.62	907.61	919.36	908.32
2013	873.04	882.34	882.92	876.49	855.36	900.22	895.99	898.89	922.40	928.50	936.00	960.96	901.99
Construction													
2009	776.79	783.29	820.23	811.97	872.03	833.11	873.41	894.04	812.39	885.53	935.15	865.96	847.40
2010	898.95	866.64	856.54	921.05	897.20	924.73	916.27	907.06	844.56	894.47	834.21	883.60	888.17
2011	783.36	783.01	811.01	842.96	888.88	882.62	871.49	861.89	907.90	895.67	867.88	870.36	858.92
2012	847.07	864.57	895.91	872.75	899.48	873.58	890.60	916.56	893.14	926.80	906.37	918.01	892.32
2013	847.04	874.95	803.73	809.59	862.79	897.44	880.20	873.38	894.68	930.12	919.99	902.02	877.33
Manufacturing													
2009	905.85	884.41	890.40	880.53	880.76	894.16	885.04	868.36	877.93	919.80	922.77	987.18	900.04
2010	908.16	909.51	900.94	909.07	936.53	906.87	883.68	890.40	906.88	912.58	881.50	895.05	902.70
2011	896.72	914.53	934.50	924.62	918.45	916.10	905.12	916.35	911.24	932.80	923.47	922.27	917.09
2012	924.00	907.07	903.04	915.88	908.52	916.75	914.18	911.52	905.57	898.41	907.81	927.08	911.10
2013	887.02	888.10	912.50	900.15	886.62	941.35	930.10	934.85	946.11	939.61	951.70	971.51	923.20
Trade, Transportation, and Utilities													
2009	613.46	622.64	628.03	609.08	614.72	613.07	628.25	645.28	629.06	635.80	641.90	617.48	625.39
2010	606.13	602.00	590.53	621.52	615.36	617.21	614.38	623.47	613.89	604.87	589.73	594.49	607.69
2011	597.03	591.92	602.91	625.45	635.46	633.25	638.01	633.76	634.23	661.43	650.65	657.91	629.66
2012	697.79	658.07	666.93	700.71	684.28	696.86	716.40	705.59	735.36	741.95	724.95	738.91	706.81
2013	734.63	728.71	732.90	723.43	711.39	728.70	706.92	701.44	711.31	698.03	679.32	689.09	711.74
Financial Activities													
2009	782.20	847.50	858.49	789.15	814.86	798.62	813.25	862.60	819.14	830.21	897.64	829.82	828.77
2010	842.37	845.57	823.65	843.15	868.02	852.66	881.17	906.19	878.59	891.10	879.89	885.95	865.54
2011	909.07	875.16	859.32	871.11	896.76	870.37	879.78	863.21	865.80	900.48	868.50	852.38	875.53
2012	900.42	890.11	849.71	880.88	872.87	888.72	881.17	853.56	905.64	856.93	855.36	893.11	878.23
2013	878.53	912.64	894.98	888.26	914.76	946.58	902.10	925.27	944.14	918.27	951.19	943.19	918.34
Professional and Business Services													
2009	862.97	895.81	872.78	834.83	853.38	850.36	855.36	822.69	829.12	817.78	849.23	784.74	843.15
2010	775.93	784.52	784.40	779.68	792.32	784.41	787.17	823.54	845.34	848.36	855.18	874.67	812.07
2011	909.84	895.84	880.60	889.64	902.85	895.00	906.78	889.25	865.56	898.43	874.34	881.81	890.70
2012	885.63	867.91	871.15	888.21	862.69	857.49	873.32	850.23	869.75	838.95	827.89	857.12	861.70
2013	833.15	846.96	829.28	855.26	850.02	877.64	841.45	844.56	870.61	861.04	854.13	859.04	853.11
Education and Health Services													
2009	574.59	578.03	559.44	589.41	570.40	600.43	609.04	589.96	585.33	572.21	561.25	560.27	578.76
2010	573.36	589.68	575.92	574.70	611.16	594.40	609.59	602.78	598.81	598.79	602.93	622.91	595.98
2011	646.65	648.40	611.92	615.57	620.48	620.81	623.39	616.95	621.12	628.88	616.46	615.30	623.33
2012	635.38	624.92	622.91	634.49	618.49	627.41	637.44	624.00	637.12	620.57	618.07	641.84	629.32
2013	626.39	626.43	627.57	650.96	648.44	672.98	661.90	658.67	683.80	662.00	669.76	690.79	655.70
Leisure and Hospitality													
2009	253.92	261.12	251.58	251.32	258.36	261.32	259.18	262.15	255.59	257.80	263.28	252.82	257.75
2010	249.50	255.02	253.97	261.38	260.85	260.74	258.21	264.29	257.76	263.78	259.99	261.23	258.94
2011	262.45	269.92	273.06	273.43	270.60	272.30	273.55	291.71	286.85	296.81	288.04	285.50	278.50
2012	289.00	289.31	284.00	283.38	286.14	292.50	289.22	282.05	284.42	279.50	269.35	277.10	284.37
2013	268.94	270.96	272.33	273.12	272.40	271.95	264.97	266.39	269.47	265.50	264.61	267.90	269.59
Other Services													
2009	638.05	670.76	661.76	652.61	631.50	630.78	679.14	699.95	632.70	639.01	663.62	628.19	652.48
2010	626.68	639.11	629.96	629.22	613.36	627.66	639.68	640.40	598.96	583.98	566.70	572.74	613.54
2011	600.08	593.27	593.33	606.45	603.26	623.07	611.52	602.10	573.30	601.47	590.27	595.06	599.15
2012	596.82	586.35	587.95	595.31	597.36	619.68	624.94	618.62	611.53	588.36	606.34	612.61	604.05
2013	653.94	610.90	618.95	614.49	623.87	675.53	678.14	666.12	653.17	621.86	627.26	669.93	642.35

KENTUCKY
At a Glance

Population:
    2000 census: 4,042,193
    2010 census: 4,339,367
    2013 estimate: 4,395,295

Percent change in population:
    2000–2010: 7.4%
    2010–2013: 1.3%

Percent change in total nonfarm employment:
    2000–2010: -4.3%
    2010–2013: 3.7%

Industry with the largest growth in employment, 2000–2013 (thousands):
    Professional and Business Services, 39.4

Industry with the largest decline or smallest growth in employment, 2000–2013 (thousands):
    Manufacturing, -82.4

Civilian labor force:
    2000: 1,949,013
    2010: 2,068,269
    2013: 2,065,873

Unemployment rate and rank among states (lowest to highest):
    2000: 4.2%, 33rd
    2010: 10.2%, 39th
    2013: 8.3%, 44th

Over-the-year change in unemployment rates:
    2010–2011: -0.7%
    2010–2012: -1.2%
    2012–2013: 0.0%

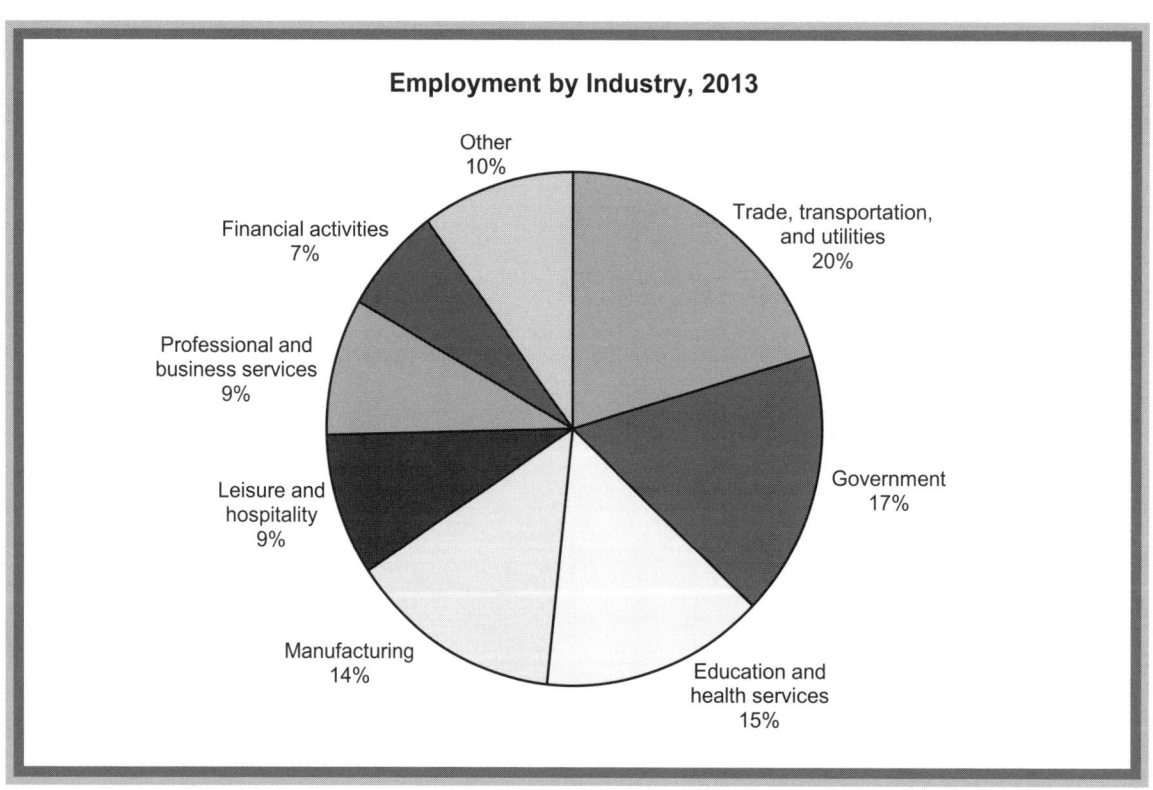

Employment by Industry, 2013

Other 10%
Trade, transportation, and utilities 20%
Financial activities 7%
Professional and business services 9%
Government 17%
Leisure and hospitality 9%
Manufacturing 14%
Education and health services 15%

1. Employment by Industry: Kentucky, Selected Years, 2002–2013

(Numbers in thousands, not seasonally adjusted)

Industry and year	January	February	March	April	May	June	July	August	September	October	November	December	Annual average
Total Nonfarm													
2002	1,759.3	1,761.9	1,774.7	1,788.2	1,801.0	1,801.2	1,782.4	1,790.2	1,796.5	1,800.0	1,807.2	1,803.2	1,788.8
2003	1,754.6	1,752.4	1,767.8	1,781.0	1,794.2	1,792.4	1,769.3	1,784.4	1,795.2	1,798.9	1,803.1	1,806.8	1,783.3
2004	1,760.6	1,763.0	1,779.0	1,797.5	1,804.1	1,808.2	1,788.0	1,802.7	1,812.3	1,817.5	1,824.7	1,825.6	1,798.6
2005	1,778.7	1,787.1	1,801.4	1,823.5	1,833.6	1,837.7	1,817.1	1,834.2	1,841.9	1,840.5	1,850.1	1,848.4	1,824.5
2006	1,810.0	1,814.0	1,836.0	1,846.2	1,857.5	1,858.9	1,832.8	1,850.1	1,856.8	1,855.8	1,866.4	1,876.9	1,846.8
2007	1,830.6	1,830.8	1,849.8	1,865.6	1,882.3	1,886.0	1,859.4	1,869.1	1,875.1	1,875.6	1,888.2	1,887.6	1,866.7
2008	1,838.9	1,839.7	1,848.2	1,862.5	1,878.8	1,871.6	1,848.5	1,858.9	1,848.2	1,845.0	1,844.9	1,835.7	1,851.7
2009	1,764.9	1,756.3	1,762.1	1,774.3	1,779.2	1,775.1	1,758.5	1,763.6	1,768.1	1,772.3	1,779.9	1,777.8	1,769.3
2010	1,725.4	1,718.9	1,743.1	1,769.7	1,785.1	1,786.2	1,765.0	1,770.6	1,781.5	1,790.7	1,797.3	1,802.2	1,769.6
2011	1,748.4	1,753.7	1,771.8	1,792.9	1,796.8	1,801.7	1,783.8	1,801.8	1,810.3	1,810.6	1,824.1	1,824.5	1,793.4
2012	1,782.2	1,786.6	1,804.3	1,819.5	1,831.9	1,835.4	1,811.8	1,823.5	1,829.5	1,833.9	1,848.0	1,849.5	1,821.3
2013	1,801.3	1,804.9	1,819.6	1,835.2	1,847.5	1,844.2	1,825.0	1,844.5	1,848.7	1,841.9	1,850.8	1,856.1	1,835.0
Total Private													
2002	1,447.0	1,445.5	1,456.5	1,468.8	1,481.3	1,486.3	1,479.7	1,488.7	1,480.7	1,481.6	1,487.5	1,485.2	1,474.1
2003	1,441.9	1,435.3	1,450.0	1,462.5	1,473.9	1,479.1	1,470.1	1,483.5	1,483.1	1,485.9	1,489.6	1,495.2	1,470.8
2004	1,451.3	1,450.3	1,464.7	1,481.9	1,490.3	1,499.1	1,489.6	1,503.5	1,501.8	1,505.2	1,511.4	1,514.0	1,488.6
2005	1,469.1	1,473.2	1,486.2	1,506.2	1,515.3	1,524.4	1,514.2	1,526.2	1,526.3	1,522.9	1,531.3	1,530.7	1,510.5
2006	1,496.1	1,495.9	1,516.4	1,524.7	1,534.9	1,543.7	1,526.1	1,537.4	1,536.3	1,533.5	1,543.1	1,554.1	1,528.5
2007	1,512.8	1,508.8	1,526.2	1,539.1	1,554.1	1,562.7	1,545.5	1,550.9	1,550.0	1,550.1	1,561.0	1,559.9	1,543.4
2008	1,516.3	1,513.6	1,521.0	1,535.8	1,550.9	1,549.7	1,537.7	1,543.5	1,528.4	1,519.7	1,518.9	1,510.4	1,528.8
2009	1,447.1	1,436.5	1,439.4	1,446.2	1,450.0	1,450.5	1,444.1	1,444.7	1,442.0	1,441.5	1,448.7	1,447.7	1,444.9
2010	1,400.7	1,390.9	1,412.1	1,435.4	1,443.5	1,450.9	1,446.0	1,451.0	1,450.4	1,456.6	1,462.2	1,468.2	1,439.0
2011	1,419.3	1,419.6	1,435.5	1,454.8	1,458.7	1,467.6	1,462.0	1,474.0	1,474.0	1,472.4	1,484.1	1,484.1	1,458.8
2012	1,446.2	1,446.1	1,461.7	1,475.1	1,488.5	1,497.8	1,489.0	1,495.6	1,492.5	1,494.4	1,507.3	1,509.0	1,483.6
2013	1,466.5	1,465.1	1,478.3	1,494.0	1,506.0	1,508.5	1,501.9	1,515.0	1,511.5	1,502.6	1,509.5	1,514.8	1,497.8
Goods-Producing													
2002	378.6	377.0	378.2	379.3	380.2	382.0	378.1	381.3	379.0	378.9	377.2	375.0	378.7
2003	364.4	360.6	363.4	365.1	367.5	369.1	367.7	370.3	370.7	371.1	369.4	370.4	367.5
2004	361.0	358.9	361.4	365.0	368.0	370.2	363.4	371.5	371.3	370.1	370.1	369.3	366.7
2005	358.9	359.1	362.2	366.8	369.4	372.3	365.4	372.0	372.3	371.8	372.5	370.6	367.8
2006	364.3	362.6	365.6	366.7	368.6	371.3	364.4	371.1	369.8	364.1	363.8	367.7	366.7
2007	358.7	356.1	358.5	363.5	366.1	369.8	362.7	364.6	367.2	362.6	365.9	361.8	363.1
2008	353.9	352.5	353.6	355.6	362.1	360.1	354.4	357.6	353.6	349.5	348.4	340.0	353.4
2009	321.4	317.5	314.6	313.5	311.4	310.3	307.4	308.0	307.7	306.0	305.1	303.0	310.5
2010	292.1	286.1	293.2	297.9	299.3	300.8	299.7	303.6	304.6	305.0	303.4	301.8	299.0
2011	292.5	293.1	296.7	301.7	302.9	307.2	302.8	308.7	309.0	308.0	309.1	307.3	303.3
2012	302.3	300.7	305.4	308.1	311.1	315.2	314.8	315.9	315.7	315.3	315.3	313.9	311.1
2013	306.5	306.1	308.7	311.1	314.4	317.1	313.6	318.1	319.0	317.4	313.8	310.0	313.0
Service-Providing													
2002	1,380.7	1,384.9	1,396.5	1,408.9	1,420.8	1,419.2	1,404.3	1,408.9	1,417.5	1,421.1	1,430.0	1,428.2	1,410.1
2003	1,390.2	1,391.8	1,404.4	1,415.9	1,426.7	1,423.3	1,401.6	1,414.1	1,424.5	1,427.8	1,433.7	1,436.4	1,415.9
2004	1,399.6	1,404.1	1,417.6	1,432.5	1,436.1	1,438.0	1,424.6	1,431.2	1,441.0	1,447.4	1,454.6	1,456.3	1,431.9
2005	1,419.8	1,428.0	1,439.2	1,456.7	1,464.2	1,465.4	1,451.7	1,462.2	1,469.6	1,468.7	1,477.6	1,477.8	1,456.7
2006	1,445.7	1,451.4	1,470.4	1,479.5	1,488.9	1,487.6	1,468.4	1,479.0	1,487.0	1,491.7	1,502.6	1,509.2	1,480.1
2007	1,471.9	1,474.7	1,491.3	1,502.1	1,516.2	1,516.2	1,496.7	1,504.5	1,507.9	1,513.0	1,522.3	1,525.8	1,503.6
2008	1,485.0	1,487.2	1,494.6	1,506.9	1,516.7	1,511.5	1,494.1	1,501.3	1,494.6	1,495.5	1,496.5	1,495.7	1,498.3
2009	1,443.5	1,438.8	1,447.5	1,460.8	1,467.8	1,464.8	1,451.1	1,455.6	1,460.4	1,466.3	1,474.8	1,474.8	1,458.9
2010	1,433.3	1,432.8	1,449.9	1,471.8	1,485.8	1,485.4	1,465.3	1,467.0	1,476.9	1,485.7	1,493.9	1,500.4	1,470.7
2011	1,455.9	1,460.6	1,475.1	1,491.2	1,493.9	1,494.5	1,481.0	1,493.1	1,501.3	1,502.6	1,515.0	1,517.2	1,490.1
2012	1,479.9	1,485.9	1,498.9	1,511.4	1,520.8	1,520.2	1,497.0	1,507.6	1,513.8	1,518.6	1,532.7	1,535.6	1,510.2
2013	1,494.8	1,498.8	1,510.9	1,524.1	1,533.1	1,527.1	1,511.4	1,526.4	1,529.7	1,524.5	1,537.0	1,546.1	1,522.0
Mining and Logging													
2002	21.2	21.0	20.8	20.4	20.4	20.5	20.2	20.2	20.2	19.8	19.8	19.7	20.4
2003	19.4	19.3	19.3	18.7	18.6	18.8	18.7	18.9	19.1	19.0	19.0	19.5	19.0
2004	19.1	18.9	19.2	19.6	19.6	19.8	19.7	19.8	19.7	20.1	20.1	20.3	19.7
2005	20.1	20.1	20.5	20.9	21.2	21.5	21.6	21.8	22.2	22.3	22.6	22.7	21.5
2006	22.3	22.3	22.7	22.9	23.0	23.2	23.2	23.1	23.1	22.9	22.9	22.9	22.9
2007	22.2	22.2	22.4	22.1	22.0	22.2	22.0	22.1	22.1	22.1	22.1	22.2	22.1
2008	22.2	22.1	22.3	22.8	23.4	23.7	24.0	24.6	24.8	25.4	25.5	25.6	23.9
2009	25.1	25.0	25.2	24.9	24.3	24.0	23.0	22.7	22.8	22.1	22.1	22.0	23.6
2010	21.3	21.3	21.5	21.8	21.9	22.3	22.2	22.4	22.5	22.4	22.5	22.7	22.1
2011	22.0	22.1	22.3	22.7	22.9	23.2	23.4	23.5	23.4	23.2	23.2	23.3	22.9
2012	23.0	22.5	22.1	21.6	21.1	21.0	20.4	19.9	19.5	18.7	18.6	18.1	20.5
2013	17.6	17.2	17.6	17.5	17.7	17.8	17.7	17.7	17.6	17.4	17.5	17.6	17.6
Construction													
2002	77.9	78.2	79.7	82.0	83.4	85.1	85.7	86.7	86.2	86.1	85.3	83.3	83.3
2003	76.6	74.2	78.4	82.4	84.4	85.5	86.5	86.3	86.0	87.1	85.4	83.8	83.1
2004	77.5	76.5	78.8	82.6	84.5	86.0	87.5	86.9	86.7	85.8	85.2	83.7	83.5
2005	76.2	77.4	79.5	83.2	85.6	87.6	89.1	88.0	87.2	87.0	86.0	84.0	84.2
2006	78.8	78.2	80.2	82.1	84.3	85.5	85.8	86.0	85.2	84.4	84.0	83.1	83.1
2007	77.4	75.5	80.9	84.3	86.5	88.3	88.7	89.1	88.9	89.3	88.4	85.8	85.3
2008	79.1	77.8	79.6	84.0	87.8	88.4	88.8	88.7	87.7	86.4	83.9	81.0	84.4
2009	72.7	71.1	71.9	73.3	74.4	75.4	76.1	75.5	75.1	75.3	74.1	71.9	73.9
2010	63.6	61.5	64.7	68.2	68.7	69.2	71.1	70.6	70.1	70.6	69.3	66.7	67.9
2011	60.4	60.7	63.7	67.5	69.0	71.3	70.9	71.3	70.6	69.5	69.4	67.3	67.6
2012	62.2	62.3	64.3	66.9	68.4	69.9	70.1	70.0	69.7	69.0	68.5	66.5	67.3
2013	61.4	61.5	63.5	65.8	68.3	70.0	70.8	71.2	71.6	71.6	68.4	64.7	67.4

1. Employment by Industry: Kentucky, Selected Years, 2002–2013—*Continued*

(Numbers in thousands, not seasonally adjusted)

Industry and year	January	February	March	April	May	June	July	August	September	October	November	December	Annual average
Manufacturing													
2002	279.5	277.8	277.7	276.9	276.4	276.4	272.2	274.4	272.6	273.0	272.1	272.0	275.1
2003	268.4	267.1	265.7	264.0	264.5	264.8	262.5	265.1	265.6	265.0	265.0	267.1	265.4
2004	264.4	263.5	263.4	262.8	263.9	264.4	256.2	264.8	264.9	264.2	264.8	265.3	263.6
2005	262.6	261.6	262.2	262.7	262.6	263.2	254.7	262.2	262.9	262.5	263.9	263.9	262.1
2006	263.2	262.1	262.7	261.7	261.3	262.6	255.4	262.0	261.5	256.8	256.9	261.7	260.7
2007	259.1	258.4	255.2	257.1	257.6	259.3	252.0	253.4	256.2	251.2	255.4	253.8	255.7
2008	252.6	252.6	251.7	248.8	250.9	248.0	241.6	244.3	241.1	237.7	239.0	233.4	245.1
2009	223.6	221.4	217.5	215.3	212.7	210.9	208.3	209.8	209.8	208.6	208.9	209.1	213.0
2010	207.2	203.3	207.0	207.9	208.7	209.3	206.4	210.6	212.0	212.0	211.6	212.4	209.0
2011	210.1	210.3	210.7	211.5	211.0	212.7	208.5	213.9	215.0	215.3	216.5	216.7	212.7
2012	217.1	215.9	219.0	219.6	221.6	224.3	224.3	226.0	226.5	227.6	228.2	229.3	223.3
2013	227.5	227.4	227.6	227.8	228.4	229.3	225.1	229.2	229.8	228.4	227.9	227.7	228.0
Trade, Transportation, and Utilities													
2002	370.1	367.1	369.5	369.1	371.7	372.1	371.7	372.3	370.6	372.1	378.9	382.8	372.3
2003	366.0	362.9	365.9	366.8	369.7	370.2	369.0	372.2	371.5	373.9	379.2	383.5	370.9
2004	367.9	365.3	368.1	370.0	372.2	373.6	371.7	373.5	373.5	377.0	383.1	386.5	373.5
2005	372.4	370.1	372.7	375.1	377.5	378.5	378.3	379.0	377.8	377.9	385.5	388.7	377.8
2006	374.7	371.6	376.5	377.1	380.2	381.9	378.5	379.4	379.1	381.9	389.2	394.2	380.4
2007	381.1	378.2	383.2	382.9	386.4	388.3	384.9	384.9	385.2	387.6	394.4	396.6	386.1
2008	381.1	377.7	378.8	380.4	383.1	383.4	381.2	382.1	378.0	377.5	383.0	386.2	381.0
2009	366.0	360.0	360.2	360.6	362.8	363.4	361.2	360.9	360.4	360.9	367.3	370.5	362.9
2010	354.7	352.0	355.1	357.4	359.9	361.2	360.4	361.2	359.8	363.9	370.2	375.2	360.9
2011	358.7	356.9	360.0	362.0	363.2	365.4	365.0	366.2	365.2	367.2	376.4	379.6	365.5
2012	363.9	362.0	364.9	366.4	369.2	370.5	368.6	369.3	369.1	369.1	377.0	379.7	369.1
2013	364.3	362.3	364.8	366.1	369.1	370.7	369.1	371.1	370.6	366.4	372.7	379.6	368.9
Wholesale Trade													
2002	72.2	72.1	71.5	71.8	72.3	72.2	71.9	72.1	71.8	72.3	72.8	73.2	72.2
2003	72.8	72.6	72.4	72.7	73.2	73.4	73.0	73.5	73.3	73.2	73.7	74.3	73.2
2004	73.7	73.5	73.6	73.9	73.9	74.1	74.3	74.2	73.9	74.2	74.8	75.2	74.1
2005	74.3	74.0	74.1	74.4	74.6	74.6	74.5	74.6	74.5	74.5	74.8	75.2	74.5
2006	74.7	74.7	75.4	75.8	76.2	76.5	75.9	76.0	75.9	76.5	76.7	77.3	76.0
2007	76.6	76.6	77.2	77.2	77.2	77.6	77.0	76.9	77.0	76.8	76.9	77.2	77.0
2008	76.5	76.6	76.6	76.4	76.6	76.9	76.5	76.4	75.8	75.9	75.9	75.7	76.3
2009	73.9	72.9	72.6	72.4	72.5	72.3	72.1	71.8	71.7	71.7	72.2	72.6	72.4
2010	71.4	71.1	71.4	71.2	71.6	71.9	72.0	71.8	71.7	72.0	72.1	72.2	71.7
2011	71.0	71.4	71.7	71.4	71.6	72.0	72.5	72.6	72.5	72.4	72.5	72.8	72.0
2012	71.9	72.0	72.2	72.4	72.7	72.9	72.8	73.2	73.2	73.1	73.3	73.5	72.8
2013	73.2	73.2	73.6	73.6	73.9	74.5	74.4	74.5	74.4	74.0	73.4	74.6	73.9
Retail Trade													
2002	209.6	207.5	210.6	211.4	213.3	213.8	211.2	211.4	210.8	210.9	217.3	220.6	212.4
2003	207.3	204.3	206.4	207.5	209.8	210.2	209.7	211.3	211.2	212.3	217.6	221.0	210.7
2004	208.4	206.1	208.1	209.2	210.8	211.6	209.4	210.6	211.0	212.4	218.0	220.8	211.4
2005	210.0	207.7	209.5	210.6	212.5	212.7	212.2	212.0	210.9	211.1	217.5	220.3	212.3
2006	209.8	207.4	210.5	210.5	212.3	212.2	210.2	210.5	209.2	211.2	217.4	220.0	211.8
2007	211.0	208.5	212.3	212.0	214.8	214.8	213.6	212.8	212.2	212.7	219.0	220.4	213.7
2008	210.4	208.1	209.8	210.1	211.5	211.8	210.9	211.2	208.7	208.3	212.6	214.0	210.6
2009	202.2	198.4	199.0	200.8	202.5	203.0	201.7	200.8	200.3	200.7	205.5	206.8	201.8
2010	197.0	195.2	197.6	199.5	201.1	200.7	200.5	200.7	198.8	201.7	205.9	207.6	200.5
2011	198.3	196.2	198.3	200.7	201.3	201.5	200.6	201.1	199.2	201.2	207.0	208.7	201.2
2012	199.8	197.3	199.7	201.3	203.5	204.1	202.8	202.4	201.8	202.8	209.0	209.6	202.8
2013	199.7	198.1	199.6	201.1	203.2	204.0	203.0	203.6	202.4	199.6	204.9	207.2	202.2
Transportation and Utilities													
2002	88.3	87.5	87.4	85.9	86.1	86.1	88.6	88.8	88.0	88.9	88.8	89.0	87.8
2003	85.9	86.0	87.1	86.6	86.7	86.6	86.3	87.4	87.0	88.4	87.9	88.2	87.0
2004	85.8	85.7	86.4	86.9	87.5	87.9	88.0	88.7	88.6	90.4	90.3	90.5	88.1
2005	88.1	88.4	89.1	90.1	90.4	91.2	91.6	92.4	92.4	92.3	93.2	93.2	91.0
2006	90.2	89.5	90.6	90.8	91.7	93.2	92.4	92.9	94.0	94.2	95.1	96.9	92.6
2007	93.5	93.1	93.7	93.7	94.4	95.9	94.3	95.2	96.0	98.1	98.5	99.0	95.5
2008	94.2	93.0	92.4	93.9	95.0	94.7	93.8	94.5	93.5	93.3	94.5	96.5	94.1
2009	89.9	88.7	88.6	87.4	87.8	88.1	87.4	88.3	88.4	88.5	89.6	91.1	88.7
2010	86.3	85.7	86.1	86.7	87.2	88.6	87.9	88.7	89.3	90.2	92.2	95.4	88.7
2011	89.4	89.3	90.0	89.9	90.3	91.9	91.9	92.5	93.5	93.6	96.9	98.1	92.3
2012	92.2	92.7	93.0	92.7	93.0	93.5	93.0	93.7	94.1	93.2	94.7	96.6	93.5
2013	91.4	91.0	91.6	91.4	92.0	92.2	91.7	93.0	93.8	92.8	94.4	97.8	92.8
Information													
2002	32.3	32.2	32.2	31.6	31.5	31.6	31.3	31.2	30.9	30.5	30.7	30.8	31.4
2003	30.5	30.6	30.8	30.1	30.2	29.9	29.5	29.3	28.8	29.0	29.0	29.1	29.7
2004	28.9	29.0	29.0	29.0	29.1	29.4	29.3	29.1	28.7	28.9	29.1	29.4	29.1
2005	28.6	28.7	29.0	29.0	29.4	29.6	29.6	29.6	29.3	29.2	29.5	29.7	29.3
2006	29.4	29.5	29.5	29.4	29.6	29.7	29.5	29.4	29.2	29.5	29.6	29.7	29.5
2007	29.6	29.5	29.6	29.9	30.3	30.5	30.3	30.2	30.1	29.9	30.2	30.3	30.0
2008	29.8	29.7	29.7	29.6	29.8	30.1	29.7	29.6	29.1	28.5	28.6	28.3	29.4
2009	27.9	27.7	27.5	27.3	27.3	27.2	27.0	26.9	26.5	26.5	26.6	26.7	27.1
2010	26.2	26.1	26.2	26.2	26.4	26.5	26.1	26.2	26.1	26.2	26.7	27.4	26.4
2011	27.1	26.9	26.8	26.7	26.8	26.8	26.8	26.8	26.5	26.6	27.0	27.2	26.8
2012	26.9	26.7	26.4	26.5	26.5	26.5	26.5	26.5	26.1	26.2	26.4	26.5	26.5
2013	26.4	26.4	26.4	26.2	26.4	26.4	26.3	26.4	26.1	26.0	26.0	26.0	26.3

1. Employment by Industry: Kentucky, Selected Years, 2002–2013—*Continued*

(Numbers in thousands, not seasonally adjusted)

Industry and year	January	February	March	April	May	June	July	August	September	October	November	December	Annual average
Financial Activities													
2002	81.5	81.8	82.0	82.4	83.0	83.5	83.2	83.3	82.8	82.7	82.9	83.3	82.7
2003	82.7	82.6	83.1	83.7	84.3	85.0	84.9	85.7	85.3	85.3	85.4	85.8	84.5
2004	84.4	84.4	84.9	85.2	85.3	85.4	85.3	85.5	84.7	84.4	84.5	85.1	84.9
2005	84.3	84.4	84.5	85.2	85.4	86.3	86.1	86.3	86.1	86.3	86.5	87.1	85.7
2006	86.9	87.2	88.0	88.3	88.9	89.5	89.0	89.2	89.5	89.8	90.2	91.0	89.0
2007	90.2	90.2	90.3	90.8	91.1	91.8	91.9	91.8	91.2	91.4	91.5	92.1	91.2
2008	91.6	92.3	92.3	92.0	92.3	92.0	92.2	92.0	91.0	90.6	90.9	90.9	91.7
2009	89.5	88.9	88.7	88.8	89.0	88.8	88.7	88.2	87.5	87.5	87.1	87.4	88.3
2010	86.3	85.8	85.9	86.1	86.1	86.3	86.1	85.6	84.9	84.9	84.8	85.4	85.7
2011	84.2	84.4	84.6	84.1	84.2	84.8	85.1	85.4	85.5	85.3	85.3	85.9	84.9
2012	85.3	85.3	85.6	85.6	86.0	86.9	87.3	87.4	87.6	87.4	87.8	88.2	86.7
2013	87.7	87.6	88.0	88.1	88.4	88.8	89.1	89.3	88.9	87.9	89.0	87.5	88.4
Professional and Business Services													
2002	151.3	151.3	153.2	154.8	156.7	158.4	157.9	161.6	160.2	160.1	160.8	159.6	157.2
2003	153.1	151.8	153.7	155.6	156.5	156.3	155.2	158.5	158.9	162.2	163.5	164.8	157.5
2004	155.8	156.9	158.6	161.4	162.0	163.4	164.9	167.7	169.0	171.8	172.8	173.2	164.8
2005	166.2	167.8	169.6	172.1	172.0	173.8	172.5	175.8	177.8	179.5	181.1	181.1	174.1
2006	174.2	174.5	179.1	179.2	179.5	181.7	180.1	183.0	183.5	184.7	187.1	189.5	181.3
2007	179.1	179.1	181.7	182.5	184.0	184.7	182.5	184.4	184.0	187.2	189.3	191.8	184.2
2008	182.4	181.7	182.2	184.3	184.4	185.9	183.5	184.1	182.3	181.3	179.9	180.1	182.7
2009	169.5	168.6	167.6	167.8	166.7	167.5	169.0	170.9	171.2	174.6	178.8	180.4	171.1
2010	172.6	170.5	173.0	178.3	178.6	181.4	180.9	181.3	182.0	182.9	184.8	189.6	179.7
2011	179.6	178.8	181.0	184.6	183.3	185.0	186.1	189.7	190.0	190.7	192.6	195.3	186.4
2012	186.2	185.3	186.7	189.3	190.3	192.7	191.1	194.2	193.5	196.4	200.7	203.7	192.5
2013	193.0	191.4	193.2	196.9	198.0	198.2	197.9	202.8	200.7	202.9	208.3	214.1	199.8
Education and Health Services													
2002	217.1	218.1	218.7	222.1	222.4	221.6	221.2	222.8	225.0	226.5	227.9	227.7	222.6
2003	225.6	226.5	227.5	227.8	228.2	227.0	223.8	225.8	229.4	229.9	230.0	229.6	227.6
2004	227.5	229.1	230.1	230.9	230.5	229.6	229.3	230.6	232.4	233.8	234.6	234.5	231.1
2005	231.2	233.6	233.5	235.3	235.9	234.6	234.3	235.4	237.4	237.0	236.8	237.1	235.2
2006	234.9	236.2	237.3	238.3	238.0	237.5	235.6	236.2	238.4	239.7	239.9	240.3	237.7
2007	238.6	239.4	240.5	240.3	241.1	240.6	239.2	240.1	241.4	242.9	243.1	243.2	240.9
2008	240.9	241.3	242.3	244.8	245.0	243.4	242.7	244.3	245.6	247.3	247.6	247.3	244.4
2009	244.1	244.2	245.4	246.9	247.1	246.1	244.8	246.3	248.0	249.6	250.1	249.9	246.9
2010	246.8	247.8	249.6	250.8	251.4	250.4	250.2	250.8	252.9	254.6	255.1	255.1	251.3
2011	252.0	252.6	253.4	254.5	254.3	252.7	252.3	253.7	256.5	256.8	256.9	255.6	254.3
2012	253.9	255.6	256.6	256.4	256.7	256.5	254.8	256.2	257.5	258.7	259.4	259.4	256.8
2013	256.0	257.5	258.4	258.8	258.2	255.6	255.8	257.5	258.7	259.5	259.8	260.0	258.0
Leisure and Hospitality													
2002	141.8	143.5	147.8	153.7	159.7	160.2	160.2	160.3	156.7	155.0	153.1	150.0	153.5
2003	144.1	144.7	149.4	156.7	160.3	163.6	162.6	163.7	160.8	156.7	155.6	154.2	156.0
2004	149.0	149.7	155.0	161.8	164.5	168.1	168.0	167.9	164.8	162.6	160.8	159.3	161.0
2005	152.1	153.6	158.4	166.5	169.1	172.6	171.9	172.0	169.6	165.4	163.5	160.4	164.6
2006	156.6	158.8	163.9	169.8	174.0	175.5	173.3	173.9	171.7	168.8	168.4	166.4	168.4
2007	160.9	161.7	166.9	173.5	178.8	180.2	178.3	179.1	175.2	172.8	171.1	168.5	172.3
2008	162.1	163.7	166.9	174.0	178.6	179.2	179.7	179.7	175.5	171.4	167.4	165.1	171.9
2009	158.3	158.9	164.4	170.8	175.2	176.1	175.4	173.1	170.9	167.0	164.7	160.9	168.0
2010	154.2	155.2	160.5	169.7	172.7	175.0	173.4	173.4	171.6	170.0	168.4	165.0	167.4
2011	157.5	159.1	164.6	173.4	176.2	177.6	175.8	175.8	173.9	170.6	170.0	166.4	170.1
2012	161.3	164.2	169.2	176.1	182.3	182.9	179.8	180.5	177.8	176.3	175.8	172.7	174.9
2013	168.4	169.3	173.8	181.5	186.1	186.1	185.1	184.7	182.5	177.6	174.8	172.5	178.5
Other Services													
2002	74.3	74.5	74.9	75.8	76.1	76.9	76.1	75.9	75.5	75.8	76.0	76.0	75.7
2003	75.5	75.6	76.2	76.7	77.2	78.0	77.4	78.0	77.7	77.8	77.5	77.8	77.1
2004	76.8	77.0	77.6	78.6	78.7	79.4	77.7	77.7	77.4	76.6	76.4	76.7	77.6
2005	75.4	75.9	76.3	76.2	76.6	76.7	76.1	76.1	76.0	75.8	75.9	76.0	76.1
2006	75.1	75.5	76.5	75.9	76.1	76.6	75.7	75.2	75.1	75.0	74.9	75.3	75.6
2007	74.6	74.6	75.5	75.7	76.3	76.8	75.7	75.8	75.7	75.7	75.5	75.6	75.6
2008	74.5	74.7	75.2	75.1	75.6	75.6	74.3	74.1	73.3	73.6	73.1	72.5	74.3
2009	70.4	70.7	71.0	70.5	70.5	71.1	70.6	70.4	69.8	69.4	69.0	68.9	70.2
2010	67.8	67.4	68.6	69.0	69.1	69.3	69.2	68.9	68.5	69.1	68.8	68.7	68.7
2011	67.7	67.8	68.4	67.8	67.8	68.1	68.1	67.7	67.4	67.2	66.8	66.8	67.6
2012	66.4	66.3	66.9	66.7	66.4	66.6	66.1	65.6	65.2	65.0	64.9	64.9	65.9
2013	64.2	64.5	65.0	65.3	65.4	65.6	65.0	65.1	65.0	64.9	65.1	65.1	65.0
Government													
2002	312.3	316.4	318.2	319.4	319.7	314.9	302.7	301.5	315.8	318.4	319.7	318.0	314.8
2003	312.7	317.1	317.8	318.5	320.3	313.3	299.2	300.9	312.1	313.0	313.5	311.6	312.5
2004	309.3	312.7	314.3	315.6	313.8	309.1	298.4	299.2	310.5	312.3	313.3	311.6	310.0
2005	309.6	313.9	315.2	317.3	318.3	313.3	302.9	308.0	315.6	317.6	318.8	317.7	314.0
2006	313.9	318.1	319.6	321.5	322.6	315.2	306.7	312.7	320.5	322.3	323.3	322.8	318.3
2007	317.8	322.0	323.6	326.5	328.2	323.3	313.9	318.2	325.1	325.5	327.2	327.7	323.3
2008	322.6	326.1	327.2	326.7	327.9	321.9	310.8	315.4	319.8	325.3	326.0	325.3	322.9
2009	317.8	319.8	322.7	328.1	329.2	324.6	314.4	318.9	326.1	330.8	331.2	330.1	324.5
2010	324.7	328.0	331.0	334.3	341.6	335.3	319.0	319.6	331.1	334.1	335.1	334.0	330.7
2011	329.1	334.1	336.3	338.1	338.1	334.1	321.8	327.8	336.3	338.2	340.0	340.4	334.5
2012	336.0	340.5	342.6	344.4	343.4	337.6	322.8	327.9	337.0	339.5	340.7	340.5	337.7
2013	334.8	339.8	341.3	341.2	341.5	335.7	323.1	329.5	337.2	339.3	341.3	341.3	337.2

2. Average Weekly Hours by Selected Industry: Kentucky, 2009–2013

(Not seasonally adjusted)

Industry and year	January	February	March	April	May	June	July	August	September	October	November	December	Annual average
Total Private													
2009	35.6	35.9	35.7	35.2	35.2	35.3	35.2	35.5	35.1	35.1	35.7	35.4	35.4
2010	35.1	34.7	35.3	35.4	35.6	35.6	35.4	35.7	35.2	35.4	35.2	34.8	35.3
2011	34.6	34.6	34.8	34.9	35.2	35.2	35.1	35.2	35.0	35.4	34.9	34.8	35.0
2012	34.8	34.7	34.6	34.5	34.5	34.8	34.8	34.6	34.7	34.6	34.6	35.1	34.7
2013	34.4	34.6	34.6	34.5	34.4	34.9	34.7	34.7	34.9	34.9	34.9	35.3	34.7
Goods-Producing													
2009	40.1	40.2	39.8	39.3	39.4	39.5	38.9	39.5	39.3	39.7	41.0	40.9	39.8
2010	40.6	39.4	40.2	40.3	40.3	40.2	39.6	40.4	40.2	40.4	40.3	40.0	40.2
2011	39.6	40.0	40.8	40.3	40.5	40.8	40.5	41.7	40.7	41.1	40.0	40.2	40.5
2012	40.2	40.1	40.4	40.8	40.4	40.8	40.4	40.4	40.5	40.4	40.3	41.1	40.5
2013	40.5	40.5	40.1	40.1	40.0	40.5	40.5	40.5	40.5	40.7	40.8	40.9	40.5
Construction													
2009	38.8	40.0	39.5	39.1	39.1	40.3	40.8	40.8	39.7	38.3	41.9	38.5	39.7
2010	37.6	35.4	37.0	37.7	36.8	37.4	37.5	38.4	37.2	38.8	38.3	36.5	37.4
2011	36.2	36.1	37.8	37.3	39.6	39.8	38.9	40.8	38.4	39.2	39.1	37.7	38.5
2012	36.2	37.0	37.1	38.6	38.2	39.1	38.8	39.2	39.8	39.7	38.6	38.0	38.4
2013	36.5	36.9	36.3	37.7	36.8	37.8	39.3	39.0	38.7	39.8	39.9	38.0	38.1
Manufacturing													
2009	38.6	38.6	38.6	38.3	38.3	38.5	37.6	38.5	38.7	39.4	40.0	40.8	38.8
2010	40.3	39.2	40.1	40.1	40.3	40.2	40.0	40.4	40.4	40.3	40.7	40.9	40.2
2011	40.5	40.8	41.4	40.8	40.3	40.4	40.3	41.5	41.0	41.2	40.0	40.6	40.7
2012	40.9	40.4	41.0	40.9	40.6	40.8	40.3	39.7	39.8	39.9	39.9	41.0	40.4
2013	40.6	40.6	40.7	40.3	40.5	40.9	40.3	40.6	40.6	40.6	40.7	41.2	40.6
Trade, Transportation, and Utilities													
2009	34.6	34.9	34.6	34.1	34.2	34.7	34.6	34.3	34.6	34.4	34.4	34.5	34.5
2010	33.5	33.2	33.9	34.2	34.2	34.9	34.7	34.5	34.4	34.6	34.7	34.6	34.3
2011	34.0	33.9	34.0	34.5	34.8	35.2	35.2	34.9	35.0	35.4	35.0	35.0	34.7
2012	34.8	34.6	34.3	34.3	34.5	35.0	34.8	34.8	34.8	34.8	34.6	34.9	34.7
2013	34.6	34.8	34.9	35.0	35.1	35.2	35.2	35.5	35.5	35.3	35.2	35.6	35.2
Financial Activities													
2009	38.5	39.1	38.9	37.9	37.1	37.4	37.6	37.6	36.3	35.8	37.9	36.3	37.5
2010	37.2	36.9	37.6	36.7	38.8	37.5	37.9	39.7	37.5	38.1	38.5	37.4	37.8
2011	39.4	37.7	38.5	37.8	39.2	37.8	37.9	37.5	37.2	37.7	37.0	36.6	37.9
2012	38.5	36.4	36.4	37.2	36.0	36.3	37.2	35.9	36.9	35.8	36.0	38.2	36.7
2013	36.7	36.1	36.4	36.7	36.0	37.2	36.4	36.5	37.5	36.4	36.1	37.0	36.6
Professional and Business Services													
2009	35.0	35.3	35.4	35.5	35.6	35.4	35.9	36.4	36.0	36.5	36.6	36.7	35.9
2010	36.1	36.9	37.0	37.0	37.1	36.9	36.9	37.5	37.0	37.4	37.1	36.1	36.9
2011	35.2	35.2	35.4	35.9	35.9	35.6	35.5	36.2	35.4	36.2	35.2	35.1	35.6
2012	34.5	34.7	33.9	34.1	34.4	34.6	34.8	35.0	35.2	34.6	34.8	34.3	34.6
2013	32.9	33.8	33.9	33.4	33.3	34.7	34.2	34.0	34.1	34.8	34.5	36.4	34.2
Education and Health Services													
2009	36.1	36.2	36.1	35.6	35.7	35.8	35.7	36.0	35.4	35.5	36.0	35.7	35.8
2010	35.3	35.0	35.1	34.9	35.3	35.1	34.7	35.2	34.5	34.4	34.4	34.4	34.9
2011	34.7	34.8	34.6	34.7	35.2	35.2	35.1	34.9	34.9	34.9	34.6	34.6	34.8
2012	34.6	34.7	34.8	33.9	34.8	34.6	34.7	34.5	34.5	34.3	34.7	34.5	34.5
2013	34.0	33.8	33.9	33.9	33.8	34.2	33.9	34.1	34.3	34.3	34.5	34.4	34.1
Leisure and Hospitality													
2009	26.5	27.4	27.1	27.0	27.2	27.0	27.1	26.8	26.4	25.8	26.0	25.8	26.7
2010	25.0	25.3	25.8	26.2	26.7	27.2	27.2	26.9	26.5	26.4	25.4	24.9	26.2
2011	24.0	24.8	25.0	24.8	25.5	25.5	25.6	25.0	25.1	25.5	25.1	25.2	25.1
2012	25.1	25.8	25.9	25.6	25.6	26.0	25.8	25.4	25.0	25.1	24.6	25.6	25.5
2013	24.2	24.7	24.9	25.0	25.0	25.3	25.2	25.0	24.9	25.0	24.9	24.8	24.9

3. Average Hourly Earnings by Selected Industry: Kentucky, 2009–2013

(Dollars, not seasonally adjusted)

Industry and year	January	February	March	April	May	June	July	August	September	October	November	December	Annual average
Total Private													
2009	18.63	18.77	18.62	18.50	18.75	18.67	18.69	18.71	18.95	19.05	19.25	19.27	18.82
2010	19.52	19.40	19.17	19.21	19.29	19.04	19.42	19.61	19.50	19.45	19.45	19.69	19.40
2011	19.98	20.19	19.81	19.82	19.85	19.62	19.73	19.72	19.68	19.81	19.69	19.79	19.80
2012	20.18	20.15	19.99	20.14	19.92	19.84	20.02	19.93	20.14	20.17	20.02	20.29	20.06
2013	20.43	20.27	20.21	20.32	20.04	19.99	20.06	19.99	20.10	20.03	20.14	20.29	20.16
Goods-Producing													
2009	21.01	21.13	21.15	21.18	21.35	21.45	21.24	21.22	21.73	22.01	22.18	22.54	21.51
2010	22.43	21.98	21.81	21.88	21.92	21.63	21.82	21.68	21.99	21.76	21.52	21.67	21.84
2011	21.58	21.52	21.37	21.10	21.24	21.02	21.41	21.14	21.09	20.94	20.66	20.84	21.15
2012	21.12	21.41	21.06	21.21	21.26	21.22	21.11	21.17	21.29	21.19	21.26	21.27	21.21
2013	21.27	21.18	20.85	21.12	21.09	21.30	21.32	21.30	21.56	21.64	21.77	21.85	21.36
Construction													
2009	20.11	20.43	20.12	20.15	20.37	20.80	20.93	21.01	21.14	21.91	21.54	22.03	20.88
2010	22.55	22.01	22.73	22.65	22.73	21.74	21.90	22.20	22.14	22.52	22.02	22.04	22.27
2011	22.08	22.44	21.96	21.90	21.84	21.86	22.02	22.32	21.95	22.01	21.94	22.21	22.04
2012	22.18	22.03	22.14	22.00	22.04	22.37	22.08	22.45	22.28	22.78	22.79	22.47	22.31
2013	21.26	21.67	21.13	21.58	21.18	21.15	21.26	20.96	20.76	21.19	21.43	21.15	21.22
Manufacturing													
2009	20.60	20.86	21.00	20.85	21.10	21.14	21.53	21.51	22.21	22.18	22.53	22.80	21.52
2010	22.45	22.01	21.47	21.60	21.76	21.75	21.91	21.68	21.89	21.42	21.33	21.49	21.73
2011	21.34	21.19	20.96	20.57	20.81	20.42	20.90	20.34	20.49	20.30	19.90	20.11	20.61
2012	20.40	20.21	20.20	20.36	20.26	20.16	20.22	20.15	20.42	20.12	20.23	20.31	20.25
2013	20.40	20.29	20.08	20.24	20.34	20.67	20.63	20.69	20.92	20.94	21.10	21.24	20.63
Trade, Transportation, and Utilities													
2009	16.35	16.35	16.36	16.37	16.50	16.09	16.36	16.44	16.64	16.37	16.64	16.44	16.41
2010	16.87	16.76	16.64	16.50	16.82	16.72	17.36	17.57	17.57	17.89	17.98	18.04	17.24
2011	18.23	18.21	18.04	17.91	17.83	17.65	17.70	17.64	17.29	17.50	17.43	17.51	17.74
2012	17.85	17.62	17.77	18.06	17.82	17.57	17.76	17.62	17.59	17.45	17.36	17.47	17.66
2013	17.96	17.89	18.09	18.08	18.08	18.33	18.36	18.57	18.55	18.66	18.68	19.33	18.39
Financial Activities													
2009	21.44	21.73	21.92	21.41	21.15	21.45	21.24	21.43	21.42	21.93	22.25	21.56	21.58
2010	20.76	21.20	20.89	21.73	21.62	21.49	22.11	22.59	21.44	21.59	21.43	21.43	21.53
2011	21.57	21.84	20.81	20.89	20.72	20.57	20.22	20.84	20.30	21.06	21.09	20.97	20.91
2012	20.60	21.61	21.28	21.53	21.19	21.32	21.27	21.55	22.10	22.13	22.37	22.50	21.62
2013	22.76	22.95	22.72	22.74	22.55	22.61	22.59	22.82	22.32	22.68	22.47	22.26	22.62
Professional and Business Services													
2009	20.27	20.48	20.13	20.01	20.31	20.21	19.80	20.09	20.29	20.60	21.02	20.84	20.35
2010	21.20	21.53	21.21	21.04	21.25	20.95	21.20	21.99	21.92	22.18	22.24	22.00	21.57
2011	22.16	21.88	21.64	21.25	21.43	21.31	21.51	21.18	20.96	21.21	20.73	20.63	21.31
2012	20.58	20.23	20.45	20.36	20.45	20.61	21.15	20.70	20.79	20.81	20.36	21.02	20.63
2013	20.77	21.03	21.33	21.24	20.74	20.62	20.84	20.51	20.65	20.40	20.19	19.86	20.66
Education and Health Services													
2009	20.44	20.28	19.55	19.80	19.81	19.72	19.76	19.62	19.55	19.64	19.62	20.22	19.83
2010	20.66	20.25	19.92	20.04	20.26	20.10	20.62	20.93	20.66	20.95	20.91	21.05	20.53
2011	21.79	22.31	21.63	22.09	22.68	22.68	22.77	22.95	23.18	23.45	23.58	23.76	22.74
2012	24.91	24.69	24.34	24.73	23.96	24.05	24.67	24.60	25.46	25.83	25.14	25.73	24.84
2013	25.65	25.04	24.98	24.85	24.09	23.90	24.04	23.72	23.59	23.10	23.41	23.25	24.13
Leisure and Hospitality													
2009	10.34	10.38	10.26	10.29	10.63	10.61	10.78	10.70	10.71	10.67	10.77	10.70	10.57
2010	10.68	10.63	10.58	10.65	10.63	10.54	10.40	10.34	10.33	10.53	10.66	10.69	10.55
2011	10.77	10.83	10.74	10.74	10.60	10.66	10.54	10.72	10.65	10.77	10.82	10.87	10.72
2012	10.72	10.67	10.62	10.52	10.61	10.56	10.56	10.54	10.60	10.55	10.45	10.49	10.57
2013	10.41	10.46	10.28	10.31	10.33	10.29	10.27	10.41	10.48	10.58	10.47	10.65	10.41

4. Average Weekly Earnings by Selected Industry: Kentucky, 2009–2013

(Dollars, not seasonally adjusted)

Industry and year	January	February	March	April	May	June	July	August	September	October	November	December	Annual average
Total Private													
2009	663.23	673.84	664.73	651.20	660.00	659.05	657.89	664.21	665.15	668.66	687.23	682.16	666.23
2010	685.15	673.18	676.70	680.03	686.72	677.82	687.47	700.08	686.40	688.53	684.64	685.21	684.82
2011	691.31	698.57	689.39	691.72	698.72	690.62	692.52	694.14	688.80	701.27	687.18	688.69	693.00
2012	702.26	699.21	691.65	694.83	687.24	690.43	696.70	689.58	698.86	697.88	692.69	712.18	696.08
2013	702.79	701.34	699.27	701.04	689.38	697.65	696.08	693.65	701.49	699.05	702.89	716.24	699.55
Goods-Producing													
2009	842.50	849.43	841.77	832.37	841.19	847.28	826.24	838.19	853.99	873.80	909.38	921.89	856.10
2010	910.66	866.01	876.76	881.76	883.38	869.53	864.07	875.87	884.00	879.10	867.26	866.80	877.97
2011	854.57	860.80	871.90	850.33	860.22	857.62	867.11	881.54	858.36	860.63	826.40	837.77	856.58
2012	849.02	858.54	850.82	865.37	858.90	865.78	852.84	855.27	862.25	856.08	856.78	874.20	859.01
2013	861.44	857.79	836.09	846.91	843.60	862.65	863.46	862.65	873.18	880.75	888.22	893.67	865.08
Construction													
2009	780.27	817.20	794.74	787.87	796.47	838.24	853.94	857.21	839.26	839.15	902.53	848.16	828.94
2010	847.88	779.15	841.01	853.91	836.46	813.08	821.25	852.48	823.61	873.78	843.37	804.46	832.90
2011	799.30	810.08	830.09	816.87	864.86	870.03	856.58	910.66	842.88	862.79	857.85	837.32	848.54
2012	802.92	815.11	821.39	849.20	841.93	874.67	856.70	880.04	886.74	904.37	879.69	853.86	856.70
2013	775.99	799.62	767.02	813.57	779.42	799.47	835.52	817.44	803.41	843.36	855.06	803.70	808.48
Manufacturing													
2009	795.16	805.20	810.60	798.56	808.13	813.89	809.53	828.14	859.53	873.89	901.20	930.24	834.98
2010	904.74	862.79	860.95	866.16	876.93	874.35	876.40	875.87	884.36	863.23	868.13	878.94	873.55
2011	864.27	864.55	867.74	839.26	838.64	824.97	842.27	844.11	840.09	836.36	796.00	816.47	838.83
2012	834.36	816.48	828.20	832.72	822.56	822.53	814.87	799.96	812.72	802.79	807.18	832.71	818.10
2013	828.24	823.77	817.26	815.67	823.77	845.40	831.39	840.01	849.35	850.16	858.77	875.09	837.58
Trade, Transportation, and Utilities													
2009	565.71	570.62	566.06	558.22	564.30	558.32	566.06	563.89	575.74	563.13	572.42	567.18	566.15
2010	565.15	556.43	564.10	564.30	575.24	583.53	602.39	606.17	604.41	618.99	623.91	624.18	591.33
2011	619.82	617.32	613.36	617.90	620.48	621.28	623.04	615.64	605.15	619.50	610.05	612.85	615.58
2012	621.18	609.65	609.51	619.46	614.79	614.95	618.05	613.18	612.13	607.26	600.66	609.70	612.80
2013	621.42	622.57	631.34	632.80	634.61	645.22	646.27	659.24	658.53	658.70	657.54	688.15	647.33
Financial Activities													
2009	825.44	849.64	852.69	811.44	784.67	802.23	798.62	805.77	777.55	785.09	843.28	782.63	809.25
2010	772.27	782.28	785.46	797.49	838.86	805.88	837.97	896.82	804.00	822.58	825.06	801.48	813.83
2011	849.86	823.37	801.19	789.64	812.22	777.55	766.34	781.50	755.16	793.96	780.33	767.50	792.49
2012	793.10	786.60	774.59	800.92	762.84	773.92	791.24	773.65	815.49	792.25	805.32	859.50	793.45
2013	835.29	828.50	827.01	834.56	811.80	841.09	822.28	832.93	837.00	825.55	811.17	823.62	827.89
Professional and Business Services													
2009	709.45	722.94	712.60	710.36	723.04	715.43	710.82	731.28	730.44	751.90	769.33	764.83	730.57
2010	765.32	794.46	784.77	778.48	788.38	773.06	782.28	824.63	811.04	829.53	825.10	794.20	795.93
2011	780.03	770.18	766.06	762.88	769.34	758.64	763.61	766.72	741.98	767.80	729.70	724.11	758.64
2012	710.01	701.98	693.26	694.28	703.48	713.11	736.02	724.50	731.81	720.03	708.53	720.99	713.80
2013	683.33	710.81	723.09	709.42	690.64	715.51	712.73	697.34	704.17	709.92	696.56	722.90	706.57
Education and Health Services													
2009	737.88	734.14	705.76	704.88	707.22	705.98	705.43	706.32	692.07	697.22	706.32	721.85	709.91
2010	729.30	708.75	699.19	699.40	715.18	715.51	715.51	736.74	712.77	720.68	719.30	724.12	716.50
2011	756.11	776.39	748.40	766.52	798.34	798.34	799.23	800.96	808.98	818.41	815.87	822.10	791.35
2012	861.89	856.74	847.03	838.35	833.81	832.13	856.05	848.70	878.37	885.97	872.36	887.69	856.98
2013	872.10	846.35	846.82	842.42	814.24	817.38	814.96	808.85	809.14	792.33	807.65	799.80	822.83
Leisure and Hospitality													
2009	274.01	284.41	278.05	277.83	289.14	286.47	292.14	286.76	282.74	275.29	280.02	276.06	282.22
2010	267.00	268.94	272.96	279.03	283.82	286.69	282.88	278.15	273.75	277.99	270.76	266.18	276.41
2011	258.48	268.58	268.50	266.35	270.30	271.83	269.82	268.00	267.32	274.64	271.58	273.92	269.07
2012	269.07	275.29	275.06	269.31	271.62	274.56	272.45	267.72	265.00	264.81	257.07	268.54	269.54
2013	251.92	258.36	255.97	257.75	258.25	260.34	258.80	260.25	260.95	264.50	260.70	264.12	259.21

LOUISIANA
At a Glance

Population:
    2000 census: 4,469,035
    2010 census: 4,533,372
    2013 estimate: 4,395,295

Percent change in population:
    2000–2010: 1.4%
    2010–2013: -3.0%

Percent change in total nonfarm employment:
    2000–2010: -1.7%
    2010–2013: 3.5%

Industry with the largest growth in employment, 2000–2013 (thousands):
    Education and Health Services, 66.1

Industry with the largest decline or smallest growth in employment, 2000–2013 (thousands):
    Manufacturing, -32.9

Civilian labor force:
    2000: 2,031,292
    2010: 2,072,597
    2013: 2,099,428

Unemployment rate and rank among states (lowest to highest):
    2000: 5.0%, 44th
    2010: 7.4%, 13th
    2013: 6.2%, 15th

Over-the-year change in unemployment rates:
    2010–2011: -0.2%
    2011–2012: -0.7%
    2012–2013: -0.3%

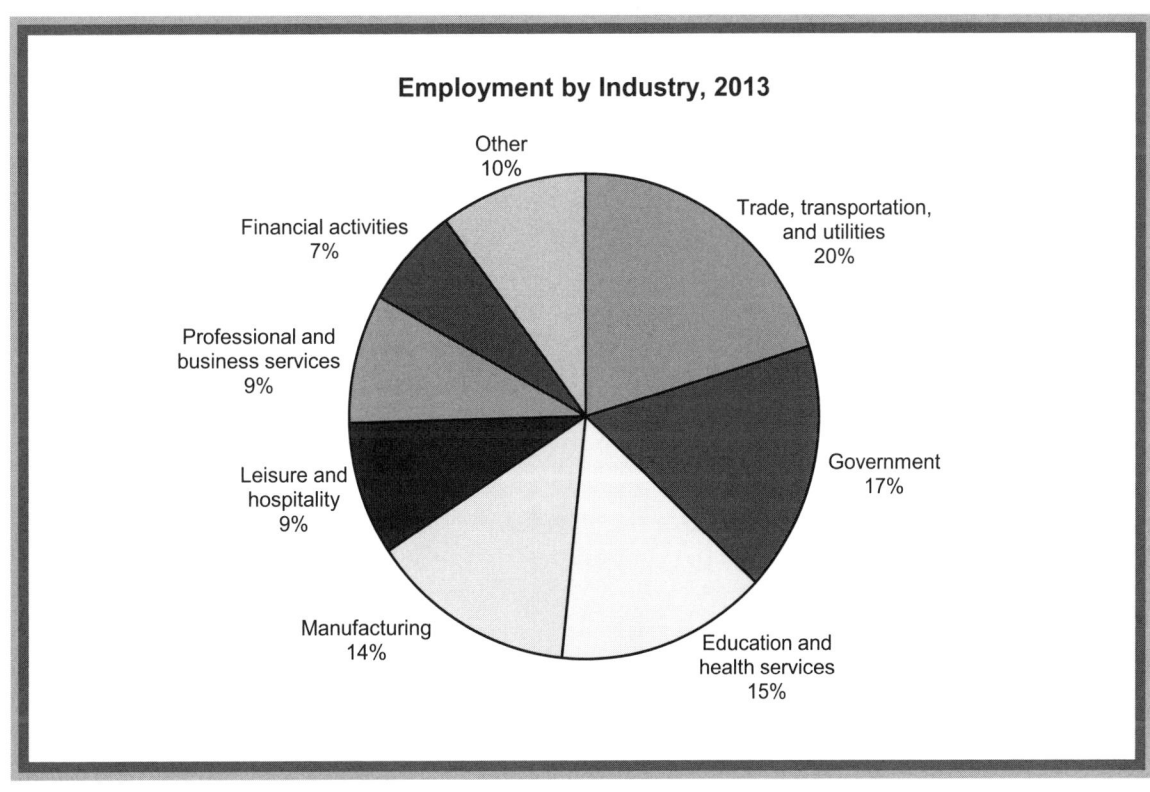

Employment by Industry, 2013

Other 10%
Trade, transportation, and utilities 20%
Financial activities 7%
Professional and business services 9%
Leisure and hospitality 9%
Manufacturing 14%
Education and health services 15%
Government 17%

1. Employment by Industry: Louisiana, Selected Years, 2002–2013

(Numbers in thousands, not seasonally adjusted)

Industry and year	January	February	March	April	May	June	July	August	September	October	November	December	Annual average
Total Nonfarm													
2002	1,872.2	1,880.1	1,890.9	1,903.1	1,907.1	1,907.5	1,883.9	1,888.2	1,899.8	1,897.6	1,908.7	1,908.4	1,895.6
2003	1,882.8	1,893.1	1,899.4	1,906.4	1,913.2	1,911.5	1,890.8	1,895.0	1,908.7	1,916.9	1,923.4	1,925.2	1,905.5
2004	1,891.4	1,902.7	1,919.7	1,924.7	1,923.0	1,924.5	1,905.9	1,908.5	1,913.3	1,922.0	1,935.8	1,939.0	1,917.5
2005	1,904.9	1,913.9	1,930.8	1,948.5	1,951.8	1,953.3	1,937.6	1,941.1	1,823.8	1,776.0	1,801.9	1,817.6	1,891.8
2006	1,789.8	1,813.1	1,839.8	1,841.5	1,854.3	1,859.4	1,835.0	1,852.4	1,874.9	1,880.5	1,892.9	1,904.6	1,853.2
2007	1,876.5	1,895.4	1,915.5	1,904.5	1,911.6	1,917.7	1,894.0	1,911.3	1,922.0	1,936.5	1,947.1	1,953.5	1,915.5
2008	1,910.6	1,928.5	1,937.6	1,939.9	1,945.5	1,940.8	1,919.8	1,938.0	1,922.5	1,950.4	1,957.5	1,958.8	1,937.5
2009	1,910.3	1,917.9	1,918.2	1,909.5	1,912.0	1,897.0	1,881.1	1,885.9	1,890.9	1,894.3	1,901.4	1,895.4	1,901.2
2010	1,855.7	1,864.1	1,881.1	1,889.7	1,897.7	1,895.6	1,873.0	1,876.1	1,885.6	1,895.5	1,900.5	1,902.2	1,884.7
2011	1,871.5	1,885.6	1,897.6	1,906.3	1,908.0	1,896.3	1,887.3	1,894.6	1,909.0	1,917.2	1,924.1	1,923.4	1,901.7
2012	1,893.6	1,907.9	1,919.2	1,933.8	1,940.0	1,930.4	1,906.7	1,916.3	1,920.4	1,937.9	1,950.9	1,950.1	1,925.6
2013	1,917.0	1,935.7	1,944.5	1,951.1	1,954.6	1,952.1	1,932.1	1,945.9	1,951.1	1,973.1	1,979.6	1,974.9	1,951.0
Total Private													
2002	1,502.2	1,504.6	1,513.8	1,525.6	1,529.5	1,531.1	1,517.2	1,523.7	1,524.7	1,518.9	1,527.5	1,529.5	1,520.7
2003	1,508.3	1,511.4	1,516.3	1,523.4	1,531.1	1,531.3	1,519.4	1,527.5	1,529.5	1,534.3	1,539.0	1,543.8	1,526.3
2004	1,514.1	1,518.6	1,533.8	1,539.3	1,539.2	1,542.6	1,532.2	1,536.7	1,530.3	1,535.9	1,548.9	1,553.4	1,535.4
2005	1,528.4	1,530.6	1,547.7	1,564.3	1,569.6	1,573.6	1,567.8	1,570.9	1,445.7	1,415.8	1,441.1	1,458.7	1,517.9
2006	1,446.8	1,463.6	1,488.7	1,492.2	1,504.4	1,517.8	1,501.0	1,513.2	1,522.0	1,526.8	1,536.9	1,549.0	1,505.2
2007	1,527.8	1,538.2	1,556.0	1,550.7	1,558.0	1,566.3	1,553.8	1,565.0	1,561.8	1,573.2	1,582.2	1,588.2	1,560.0
2008	1,553.4	1,563.4	1,573.2	1,573.2	1,578.7	1,579.8	1,566.5	1,578.6	1,557.5	1,579.3	1,583.9	1,587.9	1,573.0
2009	1,545.6	1,546.2	1,546.7	1,536.1	1,539.9	1,531.7	1,525.8	1,528.8	1,521.3	1,517.9	1,523.7	1,520.1	1,532.0
2010	1,489.1	1,492.8	1,507.5	1,516.6	1,519.7	1,525.4	1,520.5	1,522.8	1,524.6	1,530.4	1,534.1	1,537.6	1,518.4
2011	1,513.9	1,523.8	1,535.8	1,544.7	1,548.0	1,542.5	1,544.0	1,549.7	1,552.3	1,556.2	1,562.7	1,565.1	1,544.9
2012	1,543.6	1,553.7	1,565.8	1,579.4	1,586.7	1,583.3	1,571.0	1,579.4	1,574.4	1,586.9	1,599.1	1,599.3	1,576.9
2013	1,576.5	1,590.6	1,599.6	1,606.4	1,610.4	1,613.3	1,603.7	1,616.2	1,611.7	1,629.1	1,634.8	1,631.5	1,610.3
Goods-Producing													
2002	328.4	326.6	327.4	328.7	330.6	330.4	327.2	329.0	328.0	329.4	326.4	324.3	328.0
2003	321.1	320.1	320.4	319.3	324.8	325.6	321.6	322.8	322.9	324.5	320.9	319.1	321.9
2004	313.2	312.9	317.2	315.7	314.3	315.8	314.7	312.6	312.3	314.5	315.1	314.9	314.4
2005	308.9	310.5	314.4	319.9	321.9	323.5	321.6	323.0	307.5	311.6	315.1	317.7	316.3
2006	320.4	322.8	327.9	329.7	331.9	336.2	328.0	332.4	336.5	338.0	338.1	341.0	331.9
2007	332.2	335.5	338.7	340.2	342.7	344.9	342.3	344.3	343.6	345.9	345.2	344.0	341.6
2008	337.0	338.4	339.2	340.4	343.3	345.0	343.2	344.8	341.2	346.9	345.1	344.3	342.4
2009	335.5	332.6	330.5	326.1	326.7	324.4	322.7	320.9	317.9	317.0	315.2	311.3	323.4
2010	305.5	305.1	308.6	309.5	310.5	313.9	314.0	313.9	313.2	314.4	311.7	311.4	311.0
2011	306.7	309.6	312.9	315.5	315.4	315.3	318.2	317.9	319.3	319.1	316.5	315.0	315.1
2012	314.7	318.4	321.3	321.9	324.6	326.5	322.0	324.3	325.2	326.7	326.4	323.6	323.0
2013	319.1	323.7	327.1	327.0	328.7	332.1	330.3	331.5	332.0	337.4	332.9	329.4	329.3
Service-Providing													
2002	1,543.8	1,553.5	1,563.5	1,574.4	1,576.5	1,577.1	1,556.7	1,559.2	1,571.8	1,568.2	1,582.3	1,584.1	1,567.6
2003	1,561.7	1,573.0	1,579.0	1,587.1	1,588.4	1,585.9	1,569.2	1,572.2	1,585.8	1,592.4	1,602.5	1,606.1	1,583.6
2004	1,578.2	1,589.8	1,602.5	1,609.0	1,608.7	1,608.7	1,591.2	1,595.9	1,601.0	1,607.5	1,620.7	1,624.1	1,603.1
2005	1,596.0	1,603.4	1,616.4	1,628.6	1,629.9	1,629.8	1,616.0	1,618.1	1,516.3	1,464.4	1,486.8	1,499.9	1,575.5
2006	1,469.4	1,490.3	1,511.9	1,511.8	1,522.4	1,523.2	1,507.0	1,520.0	1,538.4	1,542.5	1,554.8	1,563.6	1,521.3
2007	1,544.3	1,559.9	1,576.8	1,564.3	1,568.9	1,572.8	1,551.7	1,567.0	1,578.4	1,590.6	1,601.9	1,609.5	1,573.8
2008	1,573.6	1,590.1	1,598.4	1,599.5	1,602.2	1,595.8	1,576.6	1,593.2	1,581.3	1,603.5	1,612.4	1,614.5	1,595.1
2009	1,574.8	1,585.3	1,587.7	1,583.4	1,585.3	1,572.6	1,558.4	1,565.0	1,573.0	1,577.3	1,586.2	1,584.1	1,577.8
2010	1,550.2	1,559.0	1,572.5	1,580.2	1,587.2	1,581.7	1,559.0	1,562.2	1,572.4	1,581.1	1,588.8	1,590.8	1,573.8
2011	1,564.8	1,576.0	1,584.7	1,590.8	1,592.6	1,581.0	1,569.1	1,576.7	1,589.7	1,598.1	1,607.6	1,608.4	1,586.6
2012	1,578.9	1,589.5	1,597.9	1,611.9	1,615.4	1,603.9	1,584.7	1,592.0	1,595.2	1,611.2	1,624.5	1,626.5	1,602.6
2013	1,597.9	1,612.0	1,617.4	1,624.1	1,625.9	1,620.0	1,601.8	1,614.4	1,619.1	1,635.7	1,646.7	1,645.5	1,621.7
Mining and Logging													
2002	49.5	48.8	48.5	48.2	48.6	48.9	48.7	48.8	48.7	47.5	47.4	47.4	48.4
2003	47.3	47.3	47.4	47.2	47.4	48.2	47.3	47.5	47.0	46.8	46.5	45.8	47.1
2004	44.9	44.9	45.4	45.2	44.7	45.0	44.3	44.4	43.9	44.6	44.5	44.5	44.7
2005	44.0	44.2	44.8	45.2	45.5	46.0	45.8	46.0	45.7	45.4	45.1	45.3	45.3
2006	46.4	46.9	47.3	47.2	47.6	48.6	49.1	49.7	50.5	50.1	49.9	50.1	48.6
2007	49.6	49.8	50.0	51.2	51.7	52.1	52.0	53.0	52.4	52.6	53.0	52.9	51.7
2008	53.9	53.7	54.0	54.1	54.4	55.0	55.4	55.5	54.9	56.3	55.9	55.6	54.9
2009	55.0	54.1	53.3	51.2	51.4	51.3	50.1	50.0	49.5	49.6	49.7	50.2	51.3
2010	49.4	50.6	51.1	51.5	52.1	52.6	52.0	52.2	51.8	52.2	51.9	52.0	51.6
2011	51.5	52.0	52.2	53.0	52.9	53.6	54.4	54.6	54.7	54.5	54.5	54.7	53.6
2012	55.9	56.6	56.3	54.9	55.4	55.3	53.6	53.9	53.3	53.3	53.3	52.8	54.6
2013	52.7	53.1	53.3	53.8	54.1	54.8	54.9	55.2	54.9	54.1	53.4	53.2	54.0
Construction													
2002	119.2	117.8	118.4	119.9	120.8	119.1	118.3	119.4	118.9	120.8	118.6	116.9	119.0
2003	117.2	117.3	117.0	118.1	120.9	120.3	119.6	119.9	120.1	121.5	118.7	117.6	119.0
2004	116.8	116.6	120.1	117.9	116.4	116.3	116.7	114.2	114.1	115.7	116.6	115.7	116.4
2005	112.2	113.9	116.2	120.7	121.4	121.6	120.9	121.2	114.5	118.5	121.8	122.8	118.8
2006	125.7	127.3	130.8	132.4	133.3	134.9	127.3	129.0	130.3	131.8	131.6	133.3	130.6
2007	129.1	130.5	132.7	132.2	133.8	134.3	132.3	133.8	133.5	134.7	133.6	132.8	132.8
2008	129.3	131.0	132.0	133.7	135.3	136.1	134.8	136.4	135.3	138.0	137.7	137.1	134.7
2009	132.7	132.9	132.7	130.8	131.9	131.1	131.6	130.3	128.3	127.9	126.9	123.5	130.1
2010	119.5	118.7	120.6	119.5	119.7	122.5	123.9	123.6	123.4	123.5	121.8	121.1	121.5
2011	118.4	120.3	122.8	124.4	123.5	122.5	123.4	122.5	123.1	122.3	120.3	118.8	121.9
2012	119.2	122.1	124.4	125.2	126.5	127.6	125.2	127.0	128.8	130.6	130.1	127.8	126.2
2013	124.5	128.4	131.1	130.3	130.9	132.5	130.9	131.5	132.2	137.5	132.3	130.0	131.0

1. Employment by Industry: Louisiana, Selected Years, 2002–2013—*Continued*

(Numbers in thousands, not seasonally adjusted)

Industry and year	January	February	March	April	May	June	July	August	September	October	November	December	Annual average
Manufacturing													
2002	159.7	160.0	160.5	160.6	161.2	162.4	160.2	160.8	160.4	161.1	160.4	160.0	160.6
2003	156.6	155.5	156.0	154.0	156.5	157.1	154.7	155.4	155.8	156.2	155.7	155.7	155.8
2004	151.5	151.4	151.7	152.6	153.2	154.5	153.7	154.0	154.3	154.2	154.0	154.7	153.3
2005	152.7	152.4	153.4	154.0	155.0	155.9	154.9	155.8	147.3	147.7	148.2	149.6	152.2
2006	148.3	148.6	149.8	150.1	151.0	152.7	151.6	153.7	155.7	156.1	156.6	157.6	152.7
2007	153.5	155.2	156.0	156.8	157.2	158.5	158.0	157.5	157.7	158.6	158.6	158.3	157.2
2008	153.8	153.7	153.2	152.6	153.6	153.9	153.0	152.9	151.0	152.6	151.5	151.6	152.8
2009	147.8	145.6	144.5	144.1	143.4	142.0	141.0	140.6	140.1	139.5	138.6	137.6	142.1
2010	136.6	135.8	136.9	138.5	138.7	138.8	138.1	138.1	138.0	138.7	138.0	138.3	137.9
2011	136.8	137.3	137.9	138.1	139.0	139.2	140.4	140.8	141.5	142.3	141.7	141.5	139.7
2012	139.6	139.7	140.6	141.8	142.7	143.6	143.2	143.4	143.1	142.8	143.0	143.0	142.2
2013	141.9	142.2	142.7	142.9	143.7	144.8	144.5	144.8	144.9	145.8	147.2	146.2	144.3
Trade, Transportation, and Utilities													
2002	379.9	378.4	381.6	383.6	384.8	386.6	383.8	384.3	383.8	381.8	388.2	393.0	384.2
2003	379.1	377.9	379.4	379.5	379.8	380.8	378.0	379.6	378.9	380.7	386.1	390.2	380.8
2004	376.6	376.0	379.1	379.6	380.7	381.3	377.8	377.9	376.0	378.7	383.6	388.5	379.7
2005	375.8	375.1	378.2	381.3	382.9	384.2	385.1	385.1	353.2	348.5	361.8	369.9	373.4
2006	361.1	362.9	369.6	368.9	371.4	374.4	373.2	374.6	375.2	377.0	382.4	388.6	373.3
2007	378.9	377.9	382.4	378.8	380.3	381.3	380.6	382.3	382.7	385.8	391.9	396.2	383.3
2008	383.5	381.9	384.7	382.9	384.0	383.8	381.9	383.8	378.1	382.2	386.9	390.5	383.7
2009	375.5	373.0	373.0	369.2	369.2	369.7	369.5	368.8	367.7	365.2	370.1	371.2	370.2
2010	359.6	358.6	361.7	364.2	365.6	366.4	365.9	366.6	366.1	370.5	376.3	379.9	366.8
2011	369.8	368.9	370.7	373.1	374.0	373.1	373.9	373.9	373.1	374.6	381.3	384.2	374.2
2012	373.6	372.1	374.7	376.3	377.6	377.3	375.6	375.9	374.8	378.7	387.6	389.5	377.8
2013	378.0	376.5	379.7	380.1	380.5	381.5	381.2	382.9	383.4	386.4	394.6	397.3	383.5
Wholesale Trade													
2002	76.5	76.6	76.9	77.6	78.0	78.2	77.4	77.4	77.2	76.6	76.7	76.7	77.2
2003	76.2	76.1	76.3	75.5	75.7	76.1	75.5	75.6	75.5	75.4	75.3	74.9	75.7
2004	75.1	75.1	75.6	75.9	75.9	75.7	75.3	75.4	75.3	74.3	74.4	74.4	75.2
2005	73.6	73.8	74.1	75.0	75.3	75.4	76.3	76.3	71.6	71.0	71.4	71.8	73.8
2006	70.5	71.1	71.8	72.1	72.7	73.5	73.2	73.5	73.5	73.4	73.7	74.1	72.8
2007	74.9	75.2	75.8	74.9	75.3	75.9	76.4	76.8	76.3	76.6	76.6	76.9	76.0
2008	75.6	75.9	76.3	75.9	76.1	76.1	75.8	76.0	75.5	75.4	75.0	75.2	75.7
2009	73.3	73.2	72.8	72.1	72.0	71.7	71.5	71.3	71.0	70.9	70.8	70.4	71.8
2010	69.2	69.4	69.9	70.2	70.5	70.6	70.6	70.8	70.6	71.3	71.2	71.2	70.5
2011	71.6	71.8	72.1	71.5	72.0	72.0	72.5	72.5	72.4	72.6	72.7	72.8	72.2
2012	71.9	72.1	72.4	72.7	72.7	72.8	72.5	72.5	72.1	72.3	72.6	72.6	72.4
2013	72.7	72.8	73.2	73.1	73.3	73.3	73.3	73.7	73.6	74.0	74.4	74.1	73.5
Retail Trade													
2002	223.0	221.6	224.3	225.0	225.1	226.5	224.0	224.2	223.7	221.8	227.9	232.4	225.0
2003	221.6	220.5	222.2	222.1	221.9	222.5	221.0	222.3	221.9	223.4	228.3	232.7	223.4
2004	222.1	221.2	223.1	223.8	224.3	225.0	222.5	222.2	220.6	223.3	228.2	232.2	224.0
2005	222.1	220.9	223.1	224.9	225.8	226.7	226.5	226.6	204.2	201.7	213.4	219.6	219.6
2006	213.8	214.7	219.2	218.1	219.3	220.4	219.3	219.9	219.8	222.1	226.7	230.3	220.3
2007	222.3	221.2	224.8	222.6	223.6	223.6	223.2	223.4	224.3	226.6	232.6	236.1	225.4
2008	226.6	224.5	226.6	224.6	224.9	224.9	224.0	225.0	220.6	223.5	228.5	231.4	225.4
2009	220.7	219.7	220.3	219.8	220.3	221.1	221.3	220.6	220.1	217.7	222.7	223.7	220.7
2010	215.1	214.1	216.2	216.7	217.2	217.2	216.2	216.0	215.6	218.4	224.5	226.8	217.8
2011	218.7	217.7	219.2	221.2	221.4	220.6	220.1	219.5	218.6	219.9	226.4	228.1	221.0
2012	220.4	218.8	220.4	221.2	222.0	221.7	220.9	220.3	219.5	222.9	230.6	231.8	222.5
2013	221.3	219.3	221.4	221.9	222.2	223.3	223.1	223.8	224.3	226.4	233.6	235.5	224.7
Transportation and Utilities													
2002	80.4	80.2	80.4	81.0	81.7	81.9	82.4	82.7	82.9	83.4	83.6	83.9	82.0
2003	81.3	81.3	80.9	81.9	82.2	82.2	81.5	81.7	81.5	81.9	82.5	82.6	81.8
2004	79.4	79.7	80.4	79.9	80.5	80.6	80.0	80.3	80.1	81.1	81.0	81.9	80.4
2005	80.1	80.4	81.0	81.4	81.8	82.1	82.3	82.2	77.4	75.8	77.0	78.5	80.0
2006	76.8	77.1	78.6	78.7	79.4	80.5	80.7	81.2	81.9	81.5	82.0	84.2	80.2
2007	81.7	81.5	81.8	81.3	81.4	81.8	81.0	82.1	82.1	82.6	82.7	83.2	81.9
2008	81.3	81.5	81.8	82.4	83.0	82.8	82.1	82.8	82.0	83.3	83.4	83.9	82.5
2009	81.5	80.1	79.9	77.3	76.9	76.9	76.7	76.9	76.6	76.6	76.6	77.1	77.8
2010	75.3	75.1	75.6	77.3	77.9	78.6	79.1	79.8	79.9	80.8	80.6	81.9	78.5
2011	79.5	79.4	79.4	80.4	80.6	80.5	81.3	81.9	82.1	82.1	82.2	83.3	81.1
2012	81.3	81.2	81.9	82.4	82.9	82.8	82.2	83.1	83.2	83.5	84.4	85.1	82.8
2013	84.0	84.4	85.1	85.1	85.0	84.9	84.8	85.4	85.5	86.0	86.6	87.7	85.4
Information													
2002	29.3	29.3	29.5	29.0	28.9	29.3	29.0	29.0	28.9	28.5	28.8	28.9	29.0
2003	29.2	28.9	29.1	29.0	29.4	29.8	28.4	28.9	28.8	28.7	28.9	29.0	29.0
2004	29.1	29.4	29.3	30.3	30.0	30.7	29.6	31.1	29.9	30.9	33.0	31.5	30.4
2005	31.2	30.3	30.3	29.5	29.3	29.6	30.0	30.4	28.6	26.4	26.9	27.0	29.1
2006	27.2	27.3	29.2	28.2	28.3	27.6	25.9	25.8	25.7	25.8	26.4	26.6	27.0
2007	26.5	27.5	29.6	28.7	28.5	29.0	27.9	27.4	26.2	27.0	26.7	27.1	27.7
2008	26.7	28.5	30.2	30.1	30.8	31.7	26.6	28.0	27.9	26.2	27.1	27.8	28.5
2009	24.9	25.2	25.2	24.5	24.8	24.9	24.5	24.1	23.9	24.2	25.4	24.8	24.7
2010	24.4	24.8	24.5	25.3	25.8	26.4	23.4	23.5	25.6	23.6	24.0	24.7	24.7
2011	23.4	23.5	25.1	23.7	24.6	24.0	22.9	22.9	23.0	23.6	23.5	24.2	23.7
2012	23.2	23.9	23.9	27.1	28.0	25.4	24.8	24.7	24.3	23.9	25.0	25.7	25.0
2013	25.4	26.9	26.3	26.9	27.6	27.8	25.6	25.6	24.6	24.4	25.1	24.3	25.9

1. Employment by Industry: Louisiana, Selected Years, 2002–2013—*Continued*

(Numbers in thousands, not seasonally adjusted)

Industry and year	January	February	March	April	May	June	July	August	September	October	November	December	Annual average
Financial Activities													
2002	96.7	96.6	96.8	97.8	97.9	98.0	97.8	98.1	97.7	98.0	98.4	98.7	97.7
2003	98.6	98.8	98.6	98.8	98.9	99.2	99.5	99.8	99.5	99.8	99.5	100.2	99.3
2004	99.5	99.6	100.0	100.3	100.2	100.6	100.8	100.8	100.1	100.1	99.9	100.4	100.2
2005	98.6	98.9	99.1	98.8	98.9	99.6	100.5	100.7	95.3	96.2	96.8	97.0	98.4
2006	95.2	95.2	95.4	94.8	95.1	95.4	94.8	95.1	95.1	95.6	95.6	96.2	95.3
2007	97.7	98.0	97.1	96.3	96.2	96.4	96.3	96.0	95.4	95.7	95.7	95.8	96.4
2008	94.4	94.8	95.2	94.7	94.7	95.0	94.5	94.2	93.4	95.2	94.3	94.2	94.6
2009	92.1	91.9	92.1	92.8	92.8	93.0	92.8	92.5	92.0	91.4	91.9	92.4	92.3
2010	91.4	91.6	92.2	92.2	92.5	93.3	93.8	93.7	93.4	93.8	93.7	94.1	93.0
2011	93.6	94.0	94.0	93.6	93.7	93.5	93.5	93.2	93.6	93.9	93.7	93.7	93.7
2012	92.8	93.3	93.7	93.5	93.7	93.8	93.6	93.7	93.4	94.0	94.8	95.0	93.8
2013	93.7	93.8	94.0	94.4	94.9	95.3	95.3	95.5	95.8	95.8	96.1	95.9	95.0
Professional and Business Services													
2002	181.7	182.1	183.3	183.7	182.0	182.3	179.3	180.2	179.3	177.7	177.4	177.3	180.5
2003	177.8	178.8	179.7	181.5	180.3	180.2	179.4	180.9	180.4	182.2	183.5	185.3	180.8
2004	181.8	182.9	185.0	186.5	184.8	185.9	183.2	184.2	182.9	184.1	186.1	187.1	184.5
2005	187.0	187.4	189.8	194.1	192.1	191.6	191.8	192.7	175.7	181.0	185.8	188.2	188.1
2006	185.7	188.5	191.4	192.4	193.8	195.6	193.3	195.5	196.8	197.1	197.1	198.1	193.8
2007	197.8	199.7	201.7	200.4	200.9	202.2	199.4	201.6	201.6	205.3	205.8	206.8	201.9
2008	201.7	204.2	204.1	204.5	204.8	204.1	202.6	204.7	203.6	205.9	206.5	206.3	204.4
2009	198.4	198.9	197.8	194.5	194.3	192.7	191.0	191.2	189.4	191.0	191.3	191.3	193.5
2010	187.6	189.2	191.0	193.0	193.6	195.6	196.8	196.0	194.6	195.3	194.7	194.5	193.5
2011	192.2	194.7	194.8	196.3	196.4	195.9	195.7	197.6	197.7	198.9	198.9	199.2	196.5
2012	196.9	199.3	201.0	205.2	205.7	204.4	203.3	203.6	202.9	205.7	206.0	204.8	203.2
2013	202.1	208.1	207.2	206.5	205.8	206.1	206.2	208.2	206.3	209.6	209.0	207.8	206.9
Education and Health Services													
2002	230.1	232.5	232.8	235.5	234.8	232.3	230.7	233.8	240.1	240.5	243.5	242.6	235.8
2003	242.2	243.2	242.7	244.7	244.9	241.0	240.2	242.2	247.7	249.2	251.8	250.7	245.0
2004	248.7	249.8	250.5	252.3	251.7	247.6	247.9	251.4	252.7	253.0	254.7	253.5	251.2
2005	254.9	254.9	256.2	258.1	257.1	254.9	252.3	252.6	239.8	222.7	223.3	223.2	245.8
2006	225.1	226.8	228.8	232.0	233.6	233.0	232.2	234.9	238.4	240.0	242.1	241.2	234.0
2007	241.2	243.1	244.6	246.0	245.6	245.6	243.8	248.2	249.2	251.7	253.0	253.9	247.2
2008	251.2	254.2	255.2	255.9	254.9	253.8	254.4	259.1	257.3	260.7	261.8	262.1	256.7
2009	261.0	263.4	264.1	264.9	265.5	261.0	262.3	266.4	267.3	270.2	271.0	270.8	265.7
2010	267.8	268.8	270.4	272.2	270.2	267.7	268.4	270.3	272.8	274.7	275.1	275.1	271.1
2011	272.5	274.7	275.7	277.1	276.6	273.1	273.5	276.1	279.0	281.2	282.7	282.2	277.0
2012	277.8	280.1	281.6	282.5	283.1	281.4	279.3	283.1	283.4	286.7	287.2	287.2	282.8
2013	287.0	288.8	289.1	290.8	290.6	287.2	284.1	289.4	290.6	293.4	293.5	293.4	289.8
Leisure and Hospitality													
2002	186.8	189.4	192.1	196.2	198.9	200.3	198.4	198.2	195.7	192.1	193.6	193.1	194.6
2003	190.0	193.3	195.5	199.5	201.5	202.9	202.1	203.0	200.9	198.3	197.6	198.6	198.6
2004	195.1	197.6	201.7	203.5	206.1	208.9	206.7	207.3	205.2	204.0	205.9	206.8	204.1
2005	202.0	203.3	208.3	211.0	215.6	218.0	214.3	214.3	180.4	167.3	169.8	171.9	198.0
2006	169.7	176.6	181.8	181.6	184.8	189.5	188.0	189.0	187.6	186.5	188.2	189.9	184.4
2007	186.4	188.7	193.2	192.5	195.5	198.2	195.3	196.2	193.7	192.3	193.4	194.7	193.3
2008	191.1	193.4	196.0	198.9	200.0	200.3	198.2	198.7	191.4	194.2	194.2	194.7	195.9
2009	190.7	193.4	196.1	196.3	198.5	198.2	195.2	196.0	194.0	191.3	191.2	190.6	194.3
2010	187.9	189.6	193.6	195.9	197.1	197.7	194.8	195.3	195.7	194.5	195.3	194.7	194.3
2011	192.6	195.0	198.9	201.6	203.7	203.6	202.2	203.9	202.5	201.1	202.5	203.1	200.9
2012	201.6	203.2	205.9	208.6	209.5	209.6	208.0	209.6	206.1	206.6	207.4	208.7	207.1
2013	206.6	207.6	210.6	215.0	216.3	217.0	215.1	217.3	213.3	215.8	217.7	217.4	214.1
Other Services													
2002	69.3	69.7	70.3	71.1	71.6	71.9	71.0	71.1	71.2	70.9	71.2	71.6	70.9
2003	70.3	70.4	70.9	71.1	71.5	71.8	70.2	70.3	70.4	70.9	70.7	70.7	70.8
2004	70.1	70.4	71.0	71.1	71.4	71.8	71.5	71.4	71.2	70.6	70.6	70.7	71.0
2005	70.0	70.2	71.4	71.6	71.8	72.2	72.2	72.1	65.2	62.1	62.6	63.8	68.8
2006	62.4	63.5	64.6	64.6	65.5	66.1	65.6	65.9	66.7	66.8	67.0	67.4	65.5
2007	67.1	67.8	68.7	67.8	68.3	68.7	68.2	69.0	69.4	69.5	69.5	69.7	68.6
2008	67.8	68.0	68.6	65.8	66.2	66.1	65.1	65.3	64.6	68.0	68.0	68.0	66.8
2009	67.5	67.8	67.9	67.8	68.1	67.8	67.8	68.9	69.1	67.6	67.6	67.7	68.0
2010	64.9	65.1	65.5	64.3	64.4	64.4	63.4	63.5	63.2	63.6	63.3	63.2	64.1
2011	63.1	63.4	63.7	63.8	63.6	64.0	64.1	64.2	64.1	63.8	63.6	63.5	63.7
2012	63.0	63.4	63.7	64.3	64.5	64.9	64.4	64.5	64.3	64.6	64.7	64.8	64.3
2013	64.6	65.2	65.6	65.7	66.0	66.3	65.9	65.8	65.7	66.3	65.9	66.0	65.8
Government													
2002	370.0	375.5	377.1	377.5	377.6	376.4	366.7	364.5	375.1	378.7	381.2	378.9	374.9
2003	374.5	381.7	383.1	383.0	382.1	380.2	371.4	367.5	379.2	382.6	384.4	381.4	379.3
2004	377.3	384.1	385.9	385.4	383.8	381.9	373.7	371.8	383.0	386.1	386.9	385.6	382.1
2005	376.5	383.3	383.1	384.2	382.2	379.7	369.8	370.2	378.1	360.2	360.8	358.9	373.9
2006	343.0	349.5	351.1	349.3	349.9	341.6	334.0	339.2	352.9	353.7	356.0	355.6	348.0
2007	348.7	357.2	359.5	353.8	353.6	351.4	340.2	346.3	360.2	363.3	365.9	365.3	355.5
2008	357.2	365.1	364.4	366.7	366.8	361.0	353.3	359.4	365.0	371.1	373.6	370.9	364.5
2009	364.7	371.7	371.5	373.4	372.1	365.3	355.3	357.1	369.6	376.4	377.7	375.3	369.2
2010	366.6	371.3	373.6	373.1	378.0	370.2	352.5	353.3	361.0	365.1	366.4	364.6	366.3
2011	357.6	361.8	361.8	361.6	360.0	353.8	343.3	344.9	356.7	361.0	361.4	358.3	356.9
2012	350.0	354.2	353.4	354.4	353.3	347.1	335.7	336.9	346.0	351.0	351.8	350.8	348.7
2013	340.5	345.1	344.9	344.7	344.2	338.8	328.4	329.7	339.4	344.0	344.8	343.4	340.7

2. Average Weekly Hours by Selected Industry: Louisiana, 2009–2013

(Not seasonally adjusted)

Industry and year	January	February	March	April	May	June	July	August	September	October	November	December	Annual average
Total Private													
2009	36.2	36.6	36.5	35.7	36.1	36.2	35.9	36.6	35.1	35.7	36.6	35.7	36.1
2010	35.9	35.5	36.1	36.5	37.1	36.8	36.8	37.1	36.4	36.7	36.3	36.7	36.5
2011	36.5	36.2	36.0	36.4	36.7	36.4	36.3	36.2	36.0	36.8	36.1	36.1	36.3
2012	36.1	36.0	36.1	36.6	36.5	36.4	36.4	36.4	36.2	35.8	35.7	35.9	36.2
2013	35.0	35.4	36.0	35.6	35.7	36.4	35.6	35.9	36.1	35.9	35.8	36.1	35.8
Goods-Producing													
2009	41.1	40.8	40.3	39.3	40.9	41.5	40.4	41.1	39.7	41.3	43.3	41.7	40.9
2010	41.8	40.3	42.9	43.4	43.3	42.9	42.3	41.9	41.3	42.3	42.0	42.8	42.3
2011	41.8	41.4	40.9	42.0	42.3	42.0	41.6	42.1	41.6	43.0	42.5	41.9	41.9
2012	41.3	42.6	42.9	43.1	43.9	43.4	41.8	43.0	43.7	43.5	43.3	43.2	43.0
2013	41.1	41.9	42.8	43.3	43.2	43.5	42.8	43.9	44.0	44.5	43.7	44.2	43.2
Construction													
2009	43.4	42.4	41.7	39.7	40.6	40.4	39.5	40.6	38.0	40.8	41.9	40.9	40.8
2010	40.9	40.4	43.6	42.7	43.6	42.0	42.3	41.2	40.5	41.0	41.8	42.7	41.9
2011	42.0	40.8	40.2	41.9	42.4	41.9	40.7	41.8	41.6	41.8	41.3	40.6	41.4
2012	38.9	39.5	41.4	41.4	42.0	41.8	40.7	42.6	42.5	43.0	43.1	42.9	41.7
2013	38.6	41.2	42.6	42.4	42.1	43.5	41.7	43.0	43.6	44.0	41.9	42.1	42.2
Manufacturing													
2009	40.8	40.3	40.1	38.9	40.6	41.7	40.8	41.5	40.9	41.8	43.1	42.2	41.0
2010	41.9	39.9	41.4	42.4	42.2	42.7	41.6	41.9	41.4	41.9	41.0	41.2	41.6
2011	40.8	40.8	40.6	41.0	41.1	41.2	41.2	41.1	40.2	42.8	42.2	41.8	41.2
2012	42.2	44.0	42.9	43.5	44.3	43.6	41.9	42.9	44.3	43.7	43.4	43.8	43.4
2013	42.8	42.1	42.6	43.6	43.7	43.3	43.2	44.4	43.9	44.7	44.8	44.9	43.7
Trade, Transportation, and Utilities													
2009	37.2	37.6	37.6	36.9	37.8	37.6	37.1	37.8	36.2	36.8	37.6	36.7	37.2
2010	36.3	36.3	36.7	37.0	37.4	37.6	37.3	37.9	37.0	37.1	37.2	37.5	37.1
2011	37.0	36.7	36.8	36.8	37.8	37.5	37.5	36.7	36.6	37.0	36.2	36.2	36.9
2012	36.7	35.2	35.6	36.1	36.4	36.3	36.5	36.4	37.4	36.2	35.7	36.0	36.2
2013	35.8	35.9	36.7	36.3	36.7	37.2	36.4	36.2	36.2	35.4	35.1	35.1	36.1
Financial Activities													
2009	36.1	37.4	37.7	36.3	36.5	36.5	36.6	37.1	35.8	36.1	37.5	35.9	36.6
2010	36.5	35.1	35.1	35.9	37.5	36.0	36.5	37.7	36.3	36.7	35.9	35.4	36.2
2011	37.0	36.6	36.7	36.7	38.8	37.4	37.4	37.0	37.8	39.0	37.3	37.3	37.4
2012	38.1	37.7	37.4	38.2	38.1	38.3	39.7	38.5	39.3	38.9	38.7	39.6	38.5
2013	38.7	38.5	38.7	38.1	38.3	39.7	37.6	38.6	38.5	38.5	38.2	38.6	38.5
Professional and Business Services													
2009	37.7	38.8	39.3	37.9	38.0	37.6	37.3	38.7	36.9	37.7	39.0	38.0	38.1
2010	38.1	38.5	38.8	39.0	39.4	39.0	40.1	40.8	40.3	41.1	40.6	40.9	39.7
2011	41.0	39.8	39.3	39.8	39.6	39.0	38.8	38.6	38.1	39.4	38.5	38.7	39.2
2012	38.8	38.7	38.8	39.9	38.4	38.4	39.1	38.6	39.7	38.6	38.4	38.5	38.8
2013	37.1	37.0	37.9	36.0	36.0	37.1	35.5	35.9	36.4	36.2	36.7	36.6	36.5
Education and Health Services													
2009	33.2	33.4	33.3	33.1	32.3	32.3	32.4	32.6	32.0	31.6	32.5	32.3	32.6
2010	32.6	32.0	32.4	32.6	33.0	32.7	32.6	33.0	32.5	32.6	32.8	33.0	32.6
2011	33.5	33.1	32.8	33.4	33.2	32.9	33.2	33.0	33.0	33.3	33.3	33.3	33.2
2012	33.4	33.0	32.8	33.0	33.2	33.3	33.5	33.1	33.2	33.4	33.4	33.6	33.2
2013	33.0	32.8	32.9	33.3	33.0	33.4	33.3	33.2	33.1	32.9	33.0	33.3	33.1
Leisure and Hospitality													
2009	27.0	27.3	27.2	26.7	26.7	27.2	27.1	27.5	26.6	26.5	26.9	26.5	26.9
2010	26.6	27.4	27.3	26.9	27.8	27.6	27.8	27.4	26.7	26.6	26.4	26.5	27.1
2011	25.9	26.8	26.8	26.5	26.7	26.5	26.4	26.6	26.2	26.7	26.4	26.8	26.5
2012	26.7	27.1	27.4	27.1	27.2	27.1	26.9	26.8	26.7	26.9	27.1	27.6	27.0
2013	26.7	27.6	27.8	27.5	27.3	27.6	27.1	26.9	26.8	26.9	27.0	27.6	27.2

3. Average Hourly Earnings Selected Industry: Louisiana, 2009–2013

(Dollars, not seasonally adjusted)

Industry and year	January	February	March	April	May	June	July	August	September	October	November	December	Annual average
Total Private													
2009	19.45	19.57	19.42	19.44	19.44	19.42	19.33	19.44	19.53	19.38	19.49	19.57	19.46
2010	19.52	19.58	19.50	19.52	19.14	19.17	19.40	19.67	19.82	19.73	19.77	19.74	19.55
2011	20.08	20.09	20.05	20.35	20.43	20.43	20.73	20.74	21.07	21.21	21.23	21.10	20.63
2012	21.12	21.03	21.11	21.37	21.05	21.09	21.22	21.26	21.91	21.75	21.59	21.85	21.36
2013	21.81	21.94	21.90	21.99	21.83	22.15	21.95	21.66	22.19	22.00	22.00	22.23	21.97
Goods-Producing													
2009	22.89	22.94	22.84	22.81	22.82	22.33	22.45	23.02	23.21	23.04	22.96	23.27	22.88
2010	23.34	23.39	23.14	22.93	22.85	22.89	23.07	23.33	23.98	23.27	23.33	23.47	23.25
2011	23.69	23.81	23.94	24.12	24.09	24.13	24.55	24.10	24.71	24.58	24.50	24.46	24.23
2012	24.41	24.21	24.51	24.49	24.40	24.42	24.63	24.76	24.67	24.97	24.67	25.17	24.61
2013	25.86	25.80	26.03	26.09	25.72	26.02	25.90	25.14	25.70	25.27	25.51	26.27	25.77
Construction													
2009	21.54	21.08	21.31	21.46	21.32	20.63	19.97	20.59	20.70	21.08	21.09	21.17	21.00
2010	21.26	21.52	20.99	20.74	20.52	20.68	20.76	21.25	21.92	21.60	21.69	21.76	21.22
2011	21.66	21.93	22.03	22.10	22.14	22.01	22.17	22.10	22.47	22.74	22.68	22.82	22.24
2012	22.44	22.56	22.92	23.03	23.19	22.86	23.01	23.43	23.55	23.76	23.56	24.06	23.22
2013	24.74	24.20	24.66	24.39	24.01	23.45	23.56	23.13	23.27	23.77	23.60	24.47	23.92
Manufacturing													
2009	23.41	23.66	23.53	23.47	23.49	23.03	23.73	23.52	23.83	23.47	23.26	23.70	23.51
2010	23.98	23.85	23.78	23.64	23.80	23.62	23.80	23.84	24.62	23.60	23.61	23.51	23.80
2011	24.10	24.32	24.60	25.00	24.82	24.90	25.44	25.02	25.84	25.24	25.14	24.90	24.95
2012	25.18	24.55	24.92	24.86	24.76	24.98	25.34	25.18	24.83	25.26	24.83	25.32	25.00
2013	26.13	26.40	26.46	26.84	26.38	27.05	26.84	25.85	26.29	25.45	25.66	26.33	26.30
Trade, Transportation, and Utilities													
2009	16.36	16.68	16.77	16.62	16.89	16.85	16.74	17.01	16.64	16.50	16.96	16.74	16.73
2010	16.90	17.04	16.91	17.37	17.61	17.47	17.54	18.04	17.77	17.84	18.05	17.68	17.53
2011	18.01	17.56	17.80	18.41	18.62	18.34	19.19	19.16	19.27	19.66	20.16	19.77	18.83
2012	20.30	19.73	19.84	20.63	20.10	20.29	20.32	20.13	20.40	20.14	20.09	20.01	20.17
2013	19.77	19.99	19.96	20.21	20.16	20.54	20.51	20.18	20.62	20.55	20.34	20.51	20.28
Financial Activities													
2009	19.63	20.47	20.10	19.88	20.61	20.19	19.63	19.66	19.65	19.36	19.30	19.29	19.82
2010	19.17	19.63	19.73	19.67	19.10	18.95	19.19	19.11	19.16	19.62	19.34	18.23	19.24
2011	19.59	19.80	18.03	19.16	19.10	20.07	19.43	19.40	19.40	19.85	19.71	18.78	19.36
2012	18.39	18.65	19.44	19.71	19.26	19.54	19.95	19.91	20.17	20.11	19.56	20.18	19.58
2013	20.71	20.55	20.51	21.04	21.06	21.17	21.51	21.06	21.43	21.25	21.59	21.81	21.14
Professional and Business Services													
2009	23.86	23.72	23.84	23.80	23.20	23.43	23.55	22.90	23.52	23.24	23.28	23.67	23.50
2010	23.64	23.76	23.43	23.03	23.72	23.65	23.53	24.19	23.97	24.30	24.36	24.38	23.84
2011	24.39	24.54	24.81	24.34	24.93	24.63	24.54	24.65	25.18	25.33	25.01	25.20	24.80
2012	25.11	25.53	25.46	25.73	25.59	25.25	25.50	25.27	25.55	25.03	24.84	25.73	25.38
2013	25.10	25.77	25.17	25.30	24.81	25.61	25.14	25.21	26.31	25.92	25.93	25.99	25.52
Education and Health Services													
2009	16.84	16.71	16.69	17.14	17.17	17.23	17.40	17.48	17.68	17.45	17.31	17.15	17.19
2010	17.15	17.37	17.78	17.64	16.73	16.69	16.92	17.27	17.11	16.94	16.89	17.09	17.13
2011	17.31	17.68	17.76	18.24	18.30	18.52	18.71	19.00	19.39	19.52	19.63	20.00	18.68
2012	19.76	20.04	19.92	20.04	19.62	19.72	19.88	19.99	19.85	19.61	19.78	19.79	19.83
2013	19.52	19.41	19.48	19.20	19.10	19.24	19.04	19.07	19.33	19.28	19.27	19.43	19.28
Leisure and Hospitality													
2009	11.80	11.93	11.65	11.65	11.72	11.69	11.58	11.62	12.06	11.97	12.10	12.10	11.82
2010	12.18	11.92	11.92	11.92	11.94	11.89	11.82	11.96	12.21	12.24	12.28	12.30	12.05
2011	12.63	12.24	12.34	12.28	12.32	11.89	11.85	11.86	11.89	12.13	12.12	12.14	12.14
2012	12.36	12.18	12.21	12.17	12.21	11.90	11.94	11.90	12.22	12.47	12.46	12.66	12.22
2013	12.49	12.58	12.4	12.42	12.39	12.27	12.16	12.31	12.3	12.71	12.75	12.82	12.47

4. Average Weekly Earnings Selected Industry: Louisiana, 2009–2013

(Dollars, not seasonally adjusted)

Industry and year	January	February	March	April	May	June	July	August	September	October	November	December	Annual average
Total Private													
2009	704.09	716.26	708.83	694.01	701.78	703.00	693.95	711.50	685.50	691.87	713.33	698.65	702.51
2010	700.77	695.09	703.95	712.48	710.09	705.46	713.92	729.76	721.45	724.09	717.65	724.46	713.58
2011	732.92	727.26	721.80	740.74	749.78	743.65	752.50	750.79	758.52	780.53	766.40	761.71	748.87
2012	762.43	757.08	762.07	782.14	768.33	767.68	772.41	773.86	793.14	778.65	770.76	784.42	773.23
2013	763.35	776.68	788.40	782.84	779.33	806.26	781.42	777.59	801.06	789.80	787.60	802.50	786.53
Goods-Producing													
2009	940.78	935.95	920.45	896.43	933.34	926.70	906.98	946.12	921.44	951.55	994.17	970.36	935.79
2010	975.61	942.62	992.71	995.16	989.41	981.98	975.86	977.53	990.37	984.32	979.86	1,004.52	983.48
2011	990.24	985.73	979.15	1,013.04	1,019.01	1,013.46	1,021.28	1,014.61	1,027.94	1,056.94	1,041.25	1,024.87	1,015.24
2012	1,008.13	1,031.35	1,051.48	1,055.52	1,071.16	1,059.83	1,029.53	1,064.68	1,078.08	1,086.20	1,068.21	1,087.34	1,058.23
2013	1,062.85	1,081.02	1,114.08	1,129.70	1,111.10	1,131.87	1,108.52	1,103.65	1,130.80	1,124.52	1,114.79	1,161.13	1,113.26
Construction													
2009	934.84	893.79	888.63	851.96	865.59	833.45	788.82	835.95	786.60	860.06	883.67	865.85	856.80
2010	869.53	869.41	915.16	885.60	894.67	868.56	878.15	875.50	887.76	885.60	906.64	929.15	889.12
2011	909.72	894.74	885.61	925.99	938.74	922.22	902.32	923.78	934.75	950.53	936.68	926.49	920.74
2012	872.92	891.12	948.89	953.44	973.98	955.55	936.51	998.12	1,000.88	1,021.68	1,015.44	1,032.17	968.27
2013	954.96	997.04	1,050.52	1,034.14	1,010.82	1,020.08	982.45	994.59	1,014.57	1,045.88	988.84	1,030.19	1,009.42
Manufacturing													
2009	955.13	953.50	943.55	912.98	953.69	960.35	968.18	976.08	974.65	981.05	1,002.51	1,000.14	963.91
2010	1,004.76	951.62	984.49	1,002.34	1,004.36	1,008.57	990.08	998.90	1,019.27	988.84	968.01	968.61	990.08
2011	983.28	992.26	998.76	1,025.00	1,020.10	1,025.88	1,048.13	1,028.32	1,038.77	1,080.27	1,060.91	1,040.82	1,027.94
2012	1,062.60	1,080.20	1,069.07	1,081.41	1,096.87	1,089.13	1,061.75	1,080.22	1,099.97	1,103.86	1,077.62	1,109.02	1,085.00
2013	1,118.36	1,111.44	1,127.20	1,170.22	1,152.81	1,171.27	1,159.49	1,147.74	1,154.13	1,137.62	1,149.57	1,182.22	1,149.31
Trade, Transportation, and Utilities													
2009	608.59	627.17	630.55	613.28	638.44	633.56	621.05	642.98	602.37	607.20	637.70	614.36	622.36
2010	613.47	618.55	620.60	642.69	658.61	656.87	654.24	683.72	657.49	661.86	671.46	663.00	650.36
2011	666.37	644.45	655.04	677.49	703.84	687.75	719.63	703.17	705.28	727.42	729.79	715.67	694.83
2012	745.01	694.50	706.30	744.74	731.64	736.53	741.68	732.73	762.96	729.07	717.21	720.36	730.15
2013	707.77	717.64	732.53	733.62	739.87	764.09	746.56	730.52	746.44	727.47	713.93	719.90	732.11
Financial Activities													
2009	708.64	765.58	757.77	721.64	752.27	736.94	718.46	729.39	703.47	698.90	723.75	692.51	725.41
2010	699.71	689.01	692.52	706.15	716.25	682.20	700.44	720.45	695.51	720.05	694.31	645.34	696.49
2011	724.83	724.68	661.70	703.17	741.08	750.62	726.68	717.80	733.32	774.15	735.18	700.49	724.06
2012	700.66	703.11	727.06	752.92	733.81	748.38	792.02	766.54	792.68	782.28	756.97	799.13	753.83
2013	801.48	791.18	793.74	801.62	806.60	840.45	808.78	812.92	825.06	818.13	824.74	841.87	813.89
Professional and Business Services													
2009	899.52	920.34	936.91	902.02	881.60	880.97	878.42	886.23	867.89	876.15	907.92	899.46	895.35
2010	900.68	914.76	909.08	898.17	934.57	922.35	943.55	986.95	965.99	998.73	989.02	997.14	946.45
2011	999.99	976.69	975.03	968.73	987.23	960.57	952.15	951.49	959.36	998.00	962.89	975.24	972.16
2012	974.27	988.01	987.85	1,026.63	982.66	969.60	997.05	975.42	1,014.34	966.16	953.86	990.61	984.74
2013	931.21	953.49	953.94	910.80	893.16	950.13	892.47	905.04	957.68	938.30	951.63	951.23	931.48
Education and Health Services													
2009	559.09	558.11	555.78	567.33	554.59	556.53	563.76	569.85	565.76	551.42	562.58	553.95	560.39
2010	559.09	555.84	576.07	575.06	552.09	545.76	551.59	569.91	556.08	552.24	553.99	563.97	558.44
2011	579.89	585.21	582.53	609.22	607.56	609.31	621.17	627.00	639.87	650.02	653.68	666.00	620.18
2012	659.98	661.32	653.38	661.32	651.38	656.68	665.98	661.67	659.02	654.97	660.65	664.94	658.36
2013	644.16	636.65	640.89	639.36	630.30	642.62	634.03	633.12	639.82	634.31	635.91	647.02	638.17
Leisure and Hospitality													
2009	318.60	325.69	316.88	311.06	312.92	317.97	313.82	319.55	320.80	317.21	325.49	320.65	317.96
2010	323.99	326.61	325.42	320.65	331.93	328.16	328.60	327.70	326.01	325.58	324.19	325.95	326.56
2011	327.12	328.03	330.71	325.42	328.94	315.09	312.84	315.48	311.52	323.87	319.97	349.42	321.71
2012	330.01	330.08	334.55	329.81	332.11	322.49	321.19	318.92	326.27	329.64	337.67	353.83	329.94
2013	333.48	347.21	344.72	341.55	338.25	338.65	329.54	331.14	329.64	341.90	344.25	353.83	339.18

MAINE
At a Glance

Population:
    2000 census: 1,274,779
    2010 census: 1,328,361
    2013 estimate: 1,328,302

Percent change in population:
    2000–2010: 4.2%
    2010–2013: 1.5%

Percent change in total nonfarm employment:
    2000–2010: -1.7%
    2010–2013: 1.5%

Industry with the largest growth in employment, 2000–2013 (thousands):
    Education and Health Services, 24.7

Industry with the largest decline or smallest growth in employment, 2000–2013 (thousands):
    Manufacturing, -29.1

Civilian labor force:
    2000: 672,440
    2010: 702,083
    2013: 708,967

Unemployment rate and rank among states (lowest to highest):
    2000: 3.3%, 14th
    2010: 8.2%, 21st
    2013: 6.7%, 23rd

Over-the-year change in unemployment rates:
    2010–2011: -0.5%
    2011–2012: -0.5%
    2012–2013: -0.5%

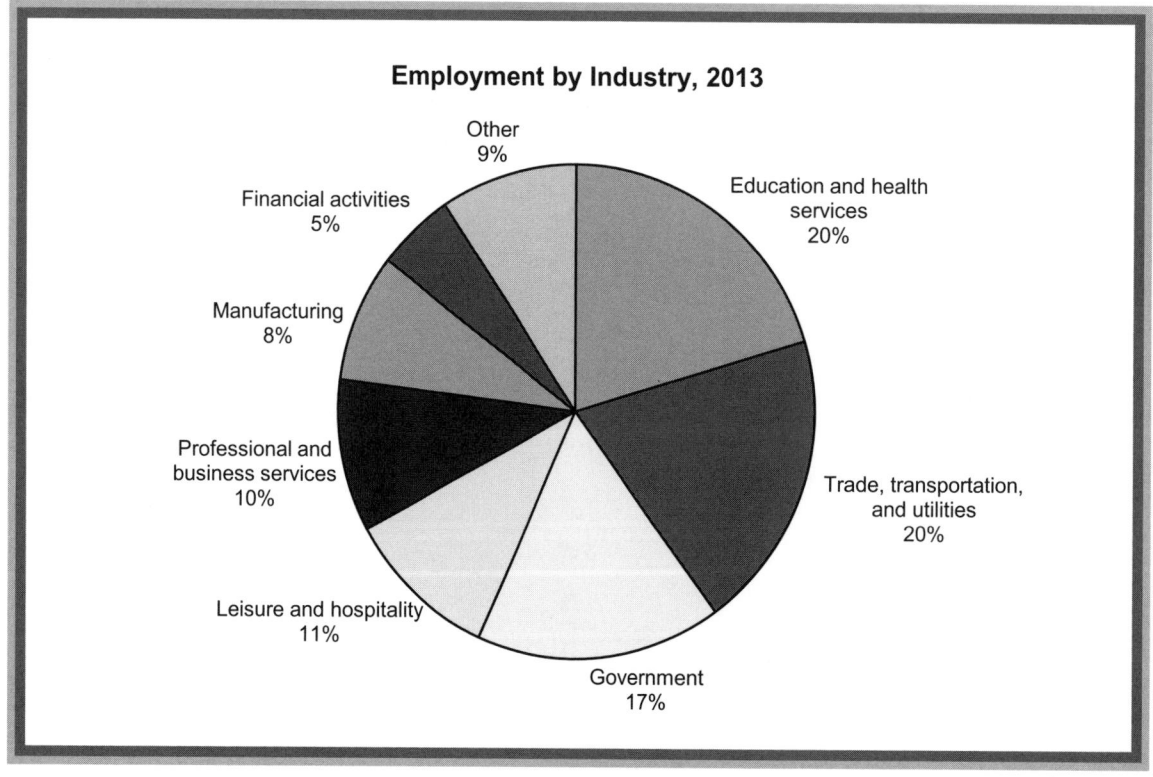

Employment by Industry, 2013

- Other 9%
- Financial activities 5%
- Manufacturing 8%
- Professional and business services 10%
- Leisure and hospitality 11%
- Government 17%
- Education and health services 20%
- Trade, transportation, and utilities 20%

1. Employment by Industry: Maine, Selected Years, 2002–2013

(Numbers in thousands, not seasonally adjusted)

Industry and year	January	February	March	April	May	June	July	August	September	October	November	December	Annual average
Total Nonfarm													
2002	583.7	585.5	588.9	598.3	610.4	622.3	618.5	618.2	617.1	614.2	610.5	609.9	606.5
2003	584.0	585.2	587.8	595.2	608.2	618.7	617.3	619.2	618.8	617.5	615.5	614.0	606.8
2004	588.4	591.6	594.0	601.9	614.0	625.4	622.8	623.5	622.8	620.0	619.6	616.7	611.7
2005	589.5	591.3	592.1	603.0	614.6	625.6	623.2	623.2	623.1	619.2	618.2	617.8	611.7
2006	592.1	592.6	596.1	606.5	617.4	629.9	624.1	626.6	625.1	622.9	621.1	621.4	614.7
2007	596.1	596.2	599.1	604.4	618.2	632.4	629.0	629.0	628.6	627.8	626.6	625.2	617.7
2008	599.7	600.1	601.8	609.6	623.0	633.6	630.0	628.1	625.8	625.0	617.6	612.6	617.2
2009	584.0	582.5	579.9	588.3	601.8	607.6	603.9	603.9	605.3	603.8	598.6	595.8	596.3
2010	572.0	572.9	574.8	583.7	599.2	604.5	602.8	602.6	604.4	603.8	598.7	596.2	593.0
2011	572.5	574.2	575.4	582.9	594.6	605.9	608.6	608.5	608.9	606.3	601.3	597.6	594.7
2012	575.0	577.2	578.7	587.7	602.3	613.4	611.5	611.5	610.7	608.9	601.7	598.8	598.1
2013	577.7	578.1	579.8	588.3	604.7	616.1	617.1	616.4	615.0	614.5	607.5	605.2	601.7
Total Private													
2002	481.8	480.3	482.7	492.8	504.1	517.6	526.8	527.6	514.5	508.1	502.7	501.9	503.4
2003	481.1	478.7	480.8	488.5	501.5	514.2	525.6	527.8	515.5	510.4	507.1	505.3	503.0
2004	484.8	484.3	486.2	494.0	506.3	519.6	529.7	531.0	518.3	511.9	510.2	507.6	507.0
2005	485.5	483.7	484.5	495.4	506.7	519.3	530.2	530.6	518.0	511.5	509.2	508.9	507.0
2006	487.8	485.9	488.8	499.3	509.7	525.3	532.1	533.4	520.7	514.8	512.2	512.7	510.2
2007	492.4	489.9	492.1	497.9	510.5	527.3	536.8	537.6	523.9	519.5	517.8	516.5	513.5
2008	495.8	493.6	494.4	501.9	515.1	528.4	537.9	535.8	521.4	516.8	508.8	504.1	512.8
2009	480.5	476.3	473.3	480.9	494.2	502.9	513.1	513.1	501.4	496.7	490.8	488.3	492.6
2010	468.3	466.6	467.0	476.1	489.1	499.8	510.9	511.7	501.4	496.9	491.3	489.0	489.0
2011	469.4	468.9	469.8	477.9	490.0	504.2	516.4	517.2	506.6	501.8	496.0	493.3	492.6
2012	474.0	473.4	474.5	483.9	497.4	512.4	519.6	519.5	509.1	504.4	497.3	494.5	496.7
2013	476.1	475.1	476.2	485.1	500.8	516.6	526.4	526.4	514.8	511.3	504.1	501.9	501.2
Goods-Producing													
2002	98.0	96.5	96.3	98.5	100.5	102.7	101.5	103.3	101.8	101.3	101.2	99.3	100.1
2003	93.9	92.1	92.6	94.0	97.2	99.2	99.2	100.9	99.8	99.4	99.5	97.6	97.1
2004	93.1	91.7	92.3	93.4	96.4	98.6	99.0	100.2	98.9	97.8	98.3	96.5	96.4
2005	91.3	90.5	90.5	92.8	95.0	97.2	97.6	98.1	96.6	95.6	96.3	94.8	94.7
2006	90.7	89.8	90.3	92.3	94.7	96.8	97.1	97.8	96.1	95.1	94.5	93.3	94.0
2007	89.3	87.7	88.5	89.7	92.3	95.7	96.1	96.5	95.1	95.2	95.2	93.5	92.9
2008	89.1	87.9	87.7	88.8	91.7	94.0	94.2	93.9	92.1	91.8	90.3	87.1	90.7
2009	80.9	78.6	76.8	77.6	80.1	81.3	81.9	82.0	80.9	80.8	80.0	77.6	79.9
2010	73.9	72.9	73.2	74.8	78.0	79.4	80.0	80.9	80.3	80.3	80.0	78.1	77.7
2011	74.7	73.8	74.1	75.3	77.9	80.5	81.5	82.0	81.3	81.0	80.8	79.4	78.5
2012	75.1	74.5	74.6	76.7	79.4	81.5	82.1	82.1	81.3	80.8	79.8	77.9	78.8
2013	74.1	73.5	73.6	75.1	78.2	80.7	81.4	82.0	80.8	81.1	80.6	78.0	78.3
Service-Providing													
2002	485.7	489.0	492.6	499.8	509.9	519.6	517.0	514.9	515.3	512.9	509.3	510.6	506.4
2003	490.1	493.1	495.2	501.2	511.0	519.5	518.1	518.3	519.0	518.1	516.0	516.4	509.7
2004	495.3	499.9	501.7	508.5	517.6	526.8	523.8	523.3	523.9	522.2	521.3	520.2	515.4
2005	498.2	500.8	501.6	510.2	519.6	528.4	525.6	525.1	526.5	523.6	521.9	523.0	517.0
2006	501.4	502.8	505.8	514.2	522.7	533.1	527.0	528.8	529.0	527.8	526.6	528.1	520.6
2007	506.8	508.5	510.6	514.7	525.9	536.7	532.9	532.5	533.5	532.6	531.4	531.7	524.8
2008	510.6	512.2	514.1	520.8	531.3	539.6	535.8	534.2	533.7	533.2	527.3	525.5	526.5
2009	503.1	503.9	503.1	510.7	521.7	526.3	522.0	521.9	524.4	523.0	518.6	518.2	516.4
2010	498.1	500.0	501.6	508.9	521.2	525.1	522.8	521.7	524.1	523.5	518.7	518.1	515.3
2011	497.8	500.4	501.3	507.6	516.7	525.4	527.1	526.5	527.6	525.3	520.5	518.2	516.2
2012	499.9	502.7	504.1	511.0	522.9	531.9	529.4	529.4	529.4	528.1	521.9	520.9	519.3
2013	503.6	504.6	506.2	513.2	526.5	535.4	535.7	534.4	534.2	533.4	526.9	527.2	523.4
Mining and Logging													
2002	2.8	2.8	2.7	2.0	1.9	2.4	2.7	2.8	2.8	2.8	2.8	2.8	2.6
2003	2.7	2.7	2.6	2.0	1.8	2.4	2.7	2.8	2.7	2.7	2.7	2.7	2.5
2004	2.7	2.7	2.7	2.1	2.0	2.4	2.6	2.7	2.7	2.8	2.9	2.9	2.6
2005	2.9	2.9	2.8	2.2	2.0	2.5	2.8	2.8	2.8	2.8	2.9	2.9	2.7
2006	2.9	2.9	2.8	2.1	2.1	2.6	2.9	2.9	2.9	3.0	2.8	2.9	2.7
2007	2.9	2.9	2.9	2.0	1.8	2.5	2.8	2.8	2.8	2.8	2.9	2.8	2.7
2008	2.8	2.8	2.8	2.1	1.8	2.3	2.6	2.6	2.6	2.8	2.8	2.8	2.6
2009	2.8	2.8	2.6	1.5	1.5	1.9	2.4	2.6	2.6	2.7	2.8	2.7	2.4
2010	2.7	2.7	2.6	1.9	2.1	2.5	2.7	2.7	2.7	2.7	2.7	2.7	2.5
2011	2.6	2.6	2.6	1.9	1.8	2.4	2.7	2.7	2.7	2.7	2.7	2.7	2.5
2012	2.6	2.6	2.5	1.8	1.9	2.4	2.6	2.7	2.7	2.7	2.6	2.6	2.5
2013	2.6	2.6	2.4	1.8	1.9	2.3	2.5	2.6	2.6	2.7	2.7	2.6	2.4
Construction													
2002	26.4	25.5	25.6	28.0	30.1	31.2	31.7	31.8	31.3	31.4	30.8	29.5	29.4
2003	27.0	26.0	26.5	28.5	31.3	32.5	33.2	33.2	32.8	32.8	31.8	30.3	30.5
2004	28.0	27.5	28.3	29.4	31.7	32.6	33.3	33.0	32.3	31.9	31.2	29.9	30.8
2005	27.0	26.5	26.7	29.2	31.4	32.8	33.6	33.2	32.7	32.4	31.9	30.4	30.7
2006	28.3	27.5	28.0	30.3	32.3	33.7	33.9	33.9	33.1	32.6	31.6	30.6	31.3
2007	28.1	26.9	27.4	29.1	31.4	33.0	33.2	33.3	32.8	32.7	31.9	30.3	30.8
2008	27.6	26.7	26.6	28.0	30.6	31.8	31.8	31.5	30.8	30.9	29.3	27.1	29.4
2009	24.0	22.8	22.3	23.8	26.0	26.8	27.1	27.0	26.5	26.6	25.2	23.7	25.2
2010	21.3	20.6	20.6	22.8	25.0	25.7	26.2	26.5	26.6	26.6	25.9	24.4	24.4
2011	22.0	21.3	21.4	23.2	25.3	27.0	27.7	27.7	27.6	27.6	26.9	25.6	25.3
2012	22.9	22.2	22.3	24.5	26.6	27.4	27.7	27.8	27.4	27.1	26.1	24.7	25.6
2013	22.3	21.9	21.9	23.8	26.1	27.3	27.5	27.8	27.4	27.6	26.5	24.6	25.4

1. Employment by Industry: Maine, Selected Years, 2002–2013—*Continued*

(Numbers in thousands, not seasonally adjusted)

Industry and year	January	February	March	April	May	June	July	August	September	October	November	December	Annual average
Manufacturing													
2002	68.8	68.2	68.0	68.5	68.5	69.1	67.1	68.7	67.7	67.1	67.6	67.0	68.0
2003	64.2	63.4	63.5	63.5	64.1	64.3	63.3	64.9	64.3	63.9	65.0	64.6	64.1
2004	62.4	61.5	61.3	61.9	62.7	63.6	63.1	64.5	63.9	63.1	64.2	63.7	63.0
2005	61.4	61.1	61.0	61.4	61.6	61.9	61.2	62.1	61.1	60.4	61.5	61.5	61.4
2006	59.5	59.4	59.5	59.9	60.3	60.5	60.3	61.0	60.1	59.5	60.1	59.8	60.0
2007	58.3	57.9	58.2	58.6	59.1	60.2	60.1	60.4	59.5	59.7	60.4	60.4	59.4
2008	58.7	58.4	58.3	58.7	59.3	59.9	59.8	59.8	58.7	58.1	58.2	57.2	58.8
2009	54.1	53.0	51.9	52.3	52.6	52.6	52.4	52.4	51.8	51.5	52.0	51.2	52.3
2010	49.9	49.6	50.0	50.1	50.9	51.2	51.1	51.7	51.0	51.0	51.5	51.1	50.8
2011	50.1	49.9	50.1	50.2	50.8	51.1	51.1	51.6	51.0	50.7	51.2	51.1	50.7
2012	49.6	49.7	49.8	50.4	50.9	51.7	51.8	51.6	51.2	51.0	51.1	51.1	50.8
2013	49.2	49.0	49.3	49.5	50.2	51.1	51.4	51.6	50.8	50.8	51.4	50.8	50.4
Trade, Transportation, and Utilities													
2002	120.3	118.1	118.1	119.6	121.7	125.2	127.1	127.0	124.5	124.0	125.7	127.4	123.2
2003	119.5	116.9	116.8	118.1	120.9	124.2	126.2	127.0	124.7	125.7	128.6	129.4	123.2
2004	121.3	119.8	119.7	120.8	123.4	126.4	128.2	128.3	126.0	127.2	130.0	131.5	125.2
2005	123.1	120.7	119.8	121.3	123.0	126.1	127.7	127.9	126.1	126.4	129.4	130.8	125.2
2006	123.4	119.9	120.3	121.7	123.3	126.7	127.7	128.0	126.2	127.2	131.1	132.2	125.6
2007	123.9	120.7	121.1	121.0	123.8	127.2	129.1	129.2	126.5	127.4	131.1	132.0	126.1
2008	124.7	121.1	120.8	121.7	123.9	126.4	127.7	127.6	124.8	125.3	126.9	127.0	124.8
2009	118.8	115.4	114.3	114.9	117.6	119.6	120.9	121.3	119.3	119.4	121.6	122.4	118.8
2010	114.7	112.2	111.6	112.6	115.1	118.1	119.6	120.1	117.2	118.7	120.2	121.5	116.8
2011	114.5	112.3	111.5	112.8	114.8	118.0	119.6	120.2	118.1	119.2	121.1	121.8	117.0
2012	115.2	112.9	112.3	113.1	115.8	119.1	119.9	120.3	117.9	119.4	121.6	121.8	117.4
2013	114.4	112.0	111.5	112.8	115.8	119.7	121.6	122.0	119.8	120.6	122.5	123.6	118.0
Wholesale Trade													
2002	19.8	19.7	19.7	20.0	20.1	20.4	20.9	20.9	20.8	20.8	20.8	20.8	20.4
2003	20.4	20.2	20.3	20.6	20.9	21.3	21.5	21.6	21.5	21.4	21.5	21.5	21.1
2004	20.9	20.9	21.0	21.2	21.4	21.6	21.9	21.9	21.5	21.5	21.3	21.3	21.4
2005	20.9	20.9	20.9	21.1	21.4	21.7	21.9	21.9	21.7	21.6	21.5	21.6	21.4
2006	21.1	21.0	21.1	21.4	21.5	22.0	22.0	21.9	21.6	21.5	21.3	21.3	21.5
2007	20.8	20.7	20.9	20.9	21.2	21.4	21.6	21.5	21.2	21.1	20.9	21.0	21.1
2008	20.7	20.5	20.5	20.5	20.8	21.1	21.3	21.2	20.9	20.8	20.5	20.5	20.8
2009	19.7	19.4	19.3	19.3	19.5	19.6	19.9	19.8	19.5	19.3	19.2	19.2	19.5
2010	18.5	18.4	18.5	18.6	18.9	19.2	19.4	19.4	19.5	19.2	19.1	19.1	19.0
2011	18.7	18.6	18.5	18.7	18.9	19.3	19.7	19.7	19.5	19.3	19.2	19.3	19.1
2012	18.9	18.8	18.8	19.1	19.4	19.9	20.1	20.0	19.7	19.7	19.5	19.5	19.5
2013	18.8	18.8	18.8	19.0	19.5	20.0	20.3	20.2	20.0	19.8	19.5	19.2	19.5
Retail Trade													
2002	82.4	80.5	80.7	81.8	83.5	86.3	87.5	87.4	84.9	84.4	86.2	87.4	84.4
2003	81.2	79.4	79.4	80.6	82.7	85.0	86.5	87.0	84.7	85.4	87.8	88.3	84.0
2004	82.5	81.5	81.4	82.3	84.3	86.4	87.8	87.7	85.9	86.5	88.7	89.7	85.4
2005	83.6	81.7	81.3	82.8	84.0	86.1	87.2	87.3	85.6	85.5	88.0	89.0	85.2
2006	83.8	80.9	81.4	82.7	83.9	86.1	87.0	87.5	85.8	86.4	89.6	90.2	85.4
2007	84.3	81.6	82.0	82.2	84.5	87.0	88.5	88.4	85.8	86.4	89.7	90.2	85.9
2008	85.4	82.5	82.3	83.4	85.1	86.9	87.9	87.9	85.4	85.8	87.2	87.1	85.6
2009	81.3	79.0	78.2	78.8	81.1	82.9	83.9	84.4	82.7	82.9	84.4	84.8	82.0
2010	79.7	77.6	77.1	77.9	79.8	82.0	83.2	83.7	81.1	82.3	83.8	84.5	81.1
2011	79.4	77.6	77.0	78.0	79.7	81.9	83.1	83.6	81.4	82.6	84.2	84.6	81.1
2012	79.7	77.7	77.4	78.0	80.0	82.3	83.1	83.5	81.1	82.3	84.4	84.2	81.1
2013	79.0	76.8	76.4	77.4	79.6	82.4	84.2	84.5	82.2	83.0	84.7	85.5	81.3
Transportation and Utilities													
2002	18.1	17.9	17.7	17.8	18.1	18.5	18.7	18.7	18.8	18.8	18.7	19.2	18.4
2003	17.9	17.3	17.1	16.9	17.3	17.9	18.2	18.4	18.5	18.9	19.3	19.6	18.1
2004	17.9	17.4	17.3	17.3	17.7	18.4	18.5	18.7	18.6	19.2	20.0	20.5	18.5
2005	18.6	18.1	17.6	17.4	17.6	18.3	18.6	18.7	18.8	19.3	19.9	20.2	18.6
2006	18.5	18.0	17.8	17.6	17.9	18.6	18.7	18.6	18.8	19.3	20.2	20.7	18.7
2007	18.8	18.4	18.2	17.9	18.1	18.8	19.0	19.3	19.5	19.9	20.5	20.8	19.1
2008	18.6	18.1	18.0	17.8	18.0	18.4	18.5	18.5	18.5	18.7	19.2	19.4	18.5
2009	17.8	17.0	16.8	16.8	17.0	17.1	17.1	17.1	17.1	17.2	18.0	18.4	17.3
2010	16.5	16.2	16.0	16.1	16.4	16.9	17.0	16.9	16.9	17.2	17.3	17.9	16.8
2011	16.4	16.1	16.0	16.1	16.2	16.8	16.8	16.9	17.2	17.3	17.7	17.9	16.8
2012	16.6	16.4	16.1	16.0	16.4	16.9	16.7	16.8	17.1	17.4	17.7	18.1	16.9
2013	16.6	16.4	16.3	16.4	16.7	17.3	17.1	17.3	17.6	17.8	18.3	18.9	17.2
Information													
2002	11.8	11.7	11.6	11.6	11.7	11.7	11.6	11.5	11.4	11.3	11.5	11.6	11.6
2003	11.3	11.4	11.3	11.3	11.2	11.3	11.3	11.3	11.2	11.5	11.5	11.6	11.4
2004	11.6	11.4	11.4	11.0	10.9	11.1	11.3	11.2	11.0	11.1	11.3	11.3	11.2
2005	11.2	11.1	11.2	11.1	11.2	11.1	11.2	11.2	11.1	11.1	11.1	11.3	11.2
2006	11.2	11.2	11.1	11.1	11.1	11.3	11.3	11.3	11.1	11.3	11.3	11.4	11.2
2007	11.2	11.4	11.4	11.4	11.3	11.3	11.3	11.2	11.0	11.1	11.1	11.1	11.2
2008	10.9	10.9	10.8	10.7	10.6	10.7	10.6	10.4	10.1	10.2	10.0	9.9	10.5
2009	9.4	9.2	9.0	9.1	9.2	9.1	9.0	8.9	8.8	8.8	8.8	8.7	9.0
2010	8.7	8.8	8.7	8.7	8.8	8.8	8.8	8.7	8.6	8.6	8.6	8.5	8.7
2011	8.4	8.3	8.3	8.3	8.3	8.3	8.3	8.3	8.1	8.1	8.1	8.1	8.2
2012	7.9	8.0	7.9	7.9	7.9	7.9	7.9	7.9	7.8	7.7	7.7	7.8	7.9
2013	7.8	7.7	7.7	7.7	7.7	7.7	7.7	7.6	7.5	7.5	7.5	7.5	7.6

1. Employment by Industry: Maine, Selected Years, 2002–2013—*Continued*

(Numbers in thousands, not seasonally adjusted)

Industry and year	January	February	March	April	May	June	July	August	September	October	November	December	Annual average
Financial Activities													
2002	34.6	34.6	34.8	34.7	34.9	35.5	35.7	35.6	35.2	35.2	35.2	35.4	35.1
2003	34.8	34.8	34.9	35.0	35.0	35.2	35.7	35.5	35.0	34.9	34.9	35.3	35.1
2004	34.9	35.0	34.9	34.8	35.0	35.3	35.5	35.4	34.6	34.5	34.3	34.4	34.9
2005	34.0	33.9	34.0	33.9	34.1	34.3	34.8	34.6	34.0	34.2	34.0	34.1	34.2
2006	33.7	33.6	33.5	33.5	33.5	34.1	34.0	34.1	33.4	33.5	33.2	33.5	33.6
2007	33.0	33.0	33.0	33.1	33.3	33.7	33.9	33.7	33.1	32.8	32.7	32.8	33.2
2008	32.4	32.5	32.5	32.7	33.0	33.3	33.5	33.5	32.6	32.4	32.3	32.1	32.7
2009	31.8	31.8	31.8	31.8	32.2	32.7	32.7	32.6	32.0	31.9	31.7	31.7	32.1
2010	31.2	31.3	31.4	31.5	31.7	32.1	32.1	32.2	31.8	31.6	31.4	31.6	31.7
2011	31.2	31.2	31.3	31.2	31.5	31.9	32.2	32.2	31.6	31.6	31.4	31.7	31.6
2012	31.2	31.0	31.1	31.2	31.5	31.9	32.2	32.1	31.5	31.4	31.2	31.3	31.5
2013	31.1	31.1	31.3	31.4	31.8	32.3	32.6	32.5	32.0	31.9	32.1	32.3	31.9
Professional and Business Services													
2002	49.4	49.4	50.0	51.4	52.0	53.1	52.9	52.8	51.7	51.7	51.3	50.8	51.4
2003	49.2	49.1	49.3	50.1	50.5	51.1	51.4	51.8	51.1	50.5	49.9	49.5	50.3
2004	47.8	48.2	48.4	49.5	50.2	50.7	50.7	50.7	49.7	49.7	49.9	49.3	49.6
2005	47.8	47.8	48.2	49.7	50.6	51.2	51.9	52.1	51.3	51.2	50.9	51.0	50.3
2006	48.9	49.4	49.7	52.3	53.0	54.0	53.5	53.6	52.8	52.3	52.4	52.6	52.0
2007	51.1	51.0	51.3	53.0	54.0	55.4	55.5	55.7	54.8	55.1	55.3	55.2	54.0
2008	54.2	54.5	55.0	56.3	57.1	58.1	58.1	58.1	57.1	57.2	56.4	56.0	56.5
2009	54.2	53.9	53.6	54.7	55.9	56.1	56.2	56.3	55.5	55.9	55.9	55.5	55.3
2010	54.1	53.8	54.0	55.4	56.2	56.6	57.2	57.2	56.6	56.6	56.8	56.2	55.9
2011	54.9	55.2	55.3	56.9	57.6	58.6	59.1	59.3	58.9	58.6	58.5	57.4	57.5
2012	56.0	55.9	56.0	57.7	58.3	59.6	59.4	59.7	59.2	59.3	58.9	58.4	58.2
2013	56.8	57.5	57.2	58.8	60.0	61.4	62.0	62.1	61.5	61.7	60.5	60.0	60.0
Education and Health Services													
2002	101.9	104.2	104.8	105.5	105.3	104.0	104.4	104.0	105.2	106.4	106.8	106.6	104.9
2003	104.3	106.3	107.0	107.2	106.9	106.0	106.7	106.3	108.0	109.5	109.6	109.9	107.3
2004	108.4	110.3	111.0	111.4	110.9	109.9	110.1	110.0	111.2	112.5	113.1	112.1	110.9
2005	110.0	111.6	111.9	112.7	112.8	111.5	111.5	111.3	112.3	113.6	114.1	113.5	112.2
2006	111.6	113.6	114.2	114.4	114.1	113.0	112.9	113.3	114.4	115.5	115.9	115.9	114.1
2007	114.2	116.5	116.6	116.4	116.2	115.1	114.7	115.0	115.9	117.1	117.5	117.7	116.1
2008	115.3	117.4	117.7	117.7	117.8	116.6	116.5	116.2	117.4	119.1	119.3	119.1	117.5
2009	117.2	119.0	119.1	119.6	119.4	117.4	117.4	117.2	117.9	119.7	119.8	119.8	118.6
2010	117.5	119.3	119.3	119.8	119.6	117.5	117.2	117.0	119.3	120.3	120.3	120.2	118.9
2011	117.1	119.3	119.6	120.1	119.9	118.1	118.0	118.2	120.2	122.0	122.1	122.0	119.7
2012	119.5	121.6	121.6	121.9	122.2	119.9	119.6	119.0	121.5	123.1	122.9	122.7	121.3
2013	120.6	122.4	122.4	123.0	122.8	120.5	120.1	119.8	122.3	124.3	124.2	123.9	122.2
Leisure and Hospitality													
2002	46.7	46.7	47.9	51.9	58.2	65.4	73.0	72.8	64.6	58.5	51.3	51.1	57.3
2003	48.0	48.0	48.7	52.5	59.3	66.4	74.3	74.4	65.5	59.0	53.3	52.2	58.5
2004	48.1	48.3	48.9	53.2	59.4	67.4	74.2	74.5	66.6	59.1	53.4	52.6	58.8
2005	48.6	48.6	49.2	53.9	59.8	67.6	74.9	75.0	66.4	59.5	53.6	53.5	59.2
2006	48.9	49.0	50.2	54.5	60.3	69.4	75.3	75.2	67.1	60.2	54.1	54.0	59.9
2007	50.3	50.3	50.8	53.6	59.6	68.7	75.6	75.8	67.4	61.0	55.2	54.5	60.2
2008	49.8	49.8	50.3	54.3	61.0	69.0	76.8	76.0	67.5	60.8	53.7	53.1	60.2
2009	48.8	49.0	49.5	53.7	60.0	66.7	74.7	74.5	67.2	60.4	53.3	52.9	59.2
2010	48.9	49.0	49.5	53.8	60.0	67.4	75.6	75.5	67.7	61.1	54.3	53.4	59.7
2011	49.3	49.5	50.3	53.6	59.9	68.5	77.1	76.6	68.4	61.3	54.2	53.1	60.2
2012	49.6	50.0	51.3	55.5	62.3	72.2	77.8	77.9	69.8	62.6	55.1	54.6	61.6
2013	51.3	50.9	52.3	55.9	63.7	73.2	79.7	79.2	70.1	63.6	56.1	56.2	62.7
Other Services													
2002	19.1	19.1	19.2	19.6	19.8	20.0	20.6	20.6	20.1	19.7	19.7	19.7	19.8
2003	20.1	20.1	20.2	20.3	20.5	20.8	20.8	20.6	20.2	19.9	19.8	19.8	20.3
2004	19.6	19.6	19.6	19.9	20.1	20.2	20.7	20.7	20.3	20.0	19.9	19.9	20.0
2005	19.5	19.5	19.7	20.0	20.2	20.3	20.6	20.4	20.2	19.9	19.8	19.8	20.0
2006	19.4	19.4	19.5	19.5	19.7	20.0	20.3	20.1	19.6	19.7	19.7	19.8	19.7
2007	19.4	19.3	19.4	19.7	20.0	20.2	20.6	20.5	20.1	19.8	19.7	19.7	19.9
2008	19.4	19.5	19.6	19.7	20.0	20.3	20.5	20.1	19.8	20.0	19.9	19.8	19.9
2009	19.4	19.4	19.2	19.5	19.8	20.0	20.3	20.3	19.8	19.8	19.7	19.7	19.7
2010	19.3	19.3	19.3	19.5	19.7	19.9	20.4	20.1	19.9	19.7	19.7	19.5	19.7
2011	19.3	19.3	19.4	19.7	20.1	20.3	20.6	20.4	20.0	20.0	19.8	19.8	19.9
2012	19.5	19.5	19.7	19.9	20.0	20.3	20.7	20.5	20.1	20.1	20.0	20.0	20.0
2013	20.0	20.0	20.2	20.4	20.8	21.1	21.3	21.2	20.8	20.6	20.6	20.4	20.6
Government													
2002	101.9	105.2	106.2	105.5	106.3	104.7	91.7	90.6	102.6	106.1	107.8	108.0	103.1
2003	102.9	106.5	107.0	106.7	106.7	104.5	91.7	91.4	103.3	107.1	108.4	108.7	103.7
2004	103.6	107.3	107.8	107.9	107.7	105.8	93.1	92.5	104.5	108.1	109.4	109.1	104.7
2005	104.0	107.6	107.6	107.6	107.9	106.3	93.0	92.6	105.1	107.7	109.0	108.9	104.8
2006	104.3	106.7	107.3	107.2	107.7	104.6	92.0	93.2	104.4	108.1	108.9	108.7	104.4
2007	103.7	106.3	107.0	106.5	107.7	105.1	92.2	91.4	104.7	108.3	108.8	108.7	104.2
2008	103.9	106.5	107.4	107.7	107.9	105.2	92.1	92.3	104.4	108.2	108.8	108.5	104.4
2009	103.5	106.2	106.6	107.4	107.6	104.7	90.8	90.8	103.9	107.1	107.8	107.5	103.7
2010	103.7	106.3	107.8	107.6	110.1	104.7	91.9	90.9	103.0	106.9	107.4	107.2	104.0
2011	103.1	105.3	105.6	105.0	104.6	101.7	92.2	91.3	102.3	104.5	105.3	104.3	102.1
2012	101.0	103.8	104.2	103.8	104.9	101.0	91.9	92.0	101.6	104.5	104.4	104.3	101.5
2013	101.6	103.0	103.6	103.2	103.9	99.5	90.7	90.0	100.2	103.2	103.4	103.3	100.5

2. Average Weekly Hours by Selected Industry: Maine, 2009–2013

(Not seasonally adjusted)

Industry and year	January	February	March	April	May	June	July	August	September	October	November	December	Annual average
Total Private													
2009	33.1	33.3	33.0	33.3	33.0	33.0	33.7	33.8	33.3	33.7	33.4	33.4	33.3
2010	33.0	33.3	33.2	33.4	33.6	33.8	34.1	34.4	34.1	34.4	33.8	34.3	33.8
2011	33.7	33.9	33.7	33.7	33.8	34.0	34.4	34.4	34.1	34.2	33.9	34.2	34.0
2012	34.0	33.9	33.8	34.2	33.9	34.0	34.4	34.3	34.4	34.1	33.9	34.6	34.1
2013	33.5	33.7	33.9	33.9	34.1	34.0	34.3	34.6	34.2	34.0	33.8	34.4	34.0
Goods-Producing													
2009	39.0	39.1	38.8	38.6	39.1	38.8	38.7	39.7	39.5	40.7	40.4	39.5	39.3
2010	39.4	38.9	39.3	39.7	40.2	39.5	39.8	40.0	40.3	41.4	40.2	39.5	39.9
2011	39.2	39.6	38.9	38.8	39.1	40.1	40.0	39.7	40.2	40.1	39.4	39.4	39.5
2012	39.4	39.2	39.4	39.2	39.1	40.3	39.6	40.0	40.4	40.2	39.9	40.1	39.7
2013	39.5	39.6	39.8	39.7	40.1	40.1	40.0	40.6	40.1	40.5	39.6	40.7	40.0
Construction													
2009	37.1	38.3	37.6	38.8	38.1	37.6	38.5	40.0	38.5	40.0	39.2	38.0	38.5
2010	37.7	38.0	38.1	38.9	40.0	39.2	39.8	40.1	40.0	40.2	39.1	37.7	39.1
2011	36.7	37.4	37.3	37.6	38.5	39.1	39.7	39.0	40.3	39.5	40.2	38.8	38.7
2012	37.6	37.4	38.2	38.3	39.1	39.8	39.4	39.6	40.1	39.3	38.6	38.9	38.9
2013	38.1	37.8	38.4	38.4	39.4	39.0	39.0	40.3	39.0	39.4	38.7	38.4	38.9
Manufacturing													
2009	39.5	39.0	39.0	38.2	39.0	38.7	38.3	39.1	39.5	40.3	41.0	40.3	39.3
2010	40.1	39.2	39.8	40.3	40.6	39.9	40.0	40.1	40.3	41.8	40.6	40.4	40.3
2011	40.2	40.2	39.5	39.5	39.6	40.6	40.1	39.9	40.0	40.3	38.8	38.8	39.8
2012	39.1	38.8	38.9	39.0	38.4	39.6	38.8	39.2	39.7	39.6	39.6	39.7	39.2
2013	39.1	39.3	39.5	39.6	39.8	39.9	39.8	40.0	40.0	40.4	39.5	40.2	39.8
Trade, Transportation, and Utilities													
2009	30.8	32.0	31.3	31.4	30.4	31.1	32.4	32.8	32.0	31.5	30.8	32.3	31.6
2010	31.1	31.9	32.0	31.9	32.7	32.8	33.4	33.6	32.7	33.5	31.6	33.8	32.6
2011	31.5	32.5	32.4	32.3	32.2	32.8	33.4	33.2	32.3	32.2	31.8	33.5	32.5
2012	31.7	32.2	32.5	32.9	32.8	32.9	33.4	33.3	33.2	32.5	31.8	33.6	32.7
2013	31.5	32.5	32.5	32.7	32.7	33.1	33.7	34.2	33.4	33.1	32.3	33.9	33.0
Professional and Business Services													
2009	36.4	36.2	36.1	35.6	35.5	35.3	35.4	35.4	34.7	35.3	35.0	34.9	35.5
2010	34.1	34.6	34.5	34.9	34.8	35.3	35.5	35.4	34.7	35.4	35.1	35.5	35.0
2011	35.0	34.8	35.1	35.0	34.8	34.8	34.6	34.8	34.8	34.6	34.4	34.3	34.7
2012	33.7	34.0	33.9	34.7	34.2	34.1	34.4	34.2	35.1	34.6	33.7	34.2	34.2
2013	32.8	33.3	33.5	33.6	34.1	34.0	33.5	33.6	33.9	33.5	33.5	34.3	33.6
Education and Health Services													
2009	31.8	31.9	31.7	32.0	31.9	32.0	32.0	31.9	32.1	32.5	32.7	32.6	32.1
2010	32.6	32.5	32.2	32.3	32.4	33.1	32.9	33.4	33.5	33.5	33.5	33.7	33.0
2011	33.9	33.3	33.1	33.3	33.8	33.8	33.7	33.7	33.8	33.9	34.0	33.9	33.7
2012	34.9	34.3	34.2	34.4	34.0	34.1	34.3	33.8	34.0	34.0	34.2	34.6	34.2
2013	34.3	34.0	34.2	34.3	34.2	34.0	34.3	34.4	34.4	33.9	34.3	33.9	34.2
Leisure and Hospitality													
2009	22.1	22.9	23.5	23.4	23.8	23.6	27.3	27.2	25.6	25.8	24.2	23.1	24.6
2010	23.3	24.0	23.7	23.6	23.9	24.5	26.0	26.8	26.1	26.0	25.2	24.5	24.9
2011	24.0	25.0	24.6	25.0	25.2	25.4	28.0	28.8	26.5	26.5	25.9	25.1	26.0
2012	24.3	25.6	25.3	25.5	25.6	25.7	27.6	28.3	26.8	26.1	25.0	25.0	26.1
2013	25.0	25.0	25.7	25.6	25.6	25.5	27.6	28.4	26.0	26.2	25.2	24.1	26.0

3. Average Hourly Earnings by Selected Industry: Maine, 2009–2013

(Dollars, not seasonally adjusted)

Industry and year	January	February	March	April	May	June	July	August	September	October	November	December	Annual average
Total Private													
2009	19.30	19.39	19.27	19.25	19.09	19.00	18.76	18.96	19.23	19.05	19.38	19.24	19.16
2010	19.37	19.46	19.57	19.46	19.40	19.25	19.20	19.29	19.49	19.61	19.66	19.67	19.45
2011	19.95	19.78	19.91	20.01	19.89	19.67	19.57	19.58	20.04	20.28	20.33	20.49	19.96
2012	21.15	20.87	21.14	20.92	20.91	20.75	20.66	20.70	20.99	21.17	21.18	21.12	20.96
2013	21.37	21.40	21.22	21.26	20.97	20.87	20.68	20.59	20.98	20.85	21.10	20.92	21.01
Goods-Producing													
2009	20.90	21.13	21.05	21.07	21.15	21.26	21.14	21.27	21.63	21.11	21.33	21.45	21.21
2010	21.43	21.49	21.53	21.56	21.45	21.37	21.38	21.57	21.98	22.11	21.50	21.93	21.61
2011	22.29	22.33	22.43	22.33	22.26	21.92	21.77	22.07	22.34	22.51	22.92	22.72	22.32
2012	23.31	22.96	22.95	23.20	22.84	22.34	22.39	22.58	22.79	22.56	22.64	22.90	22.78
2013	23.20	23.16	22.95	22.87	22.86	22.79	22.70	22.59	23.07	22.91	23.44	23.29	22.98
Construction													
2009	19.71	19.94	19.72	19.95	19.79	19.83	19.71	19.98	19.99	19.82	19.89	19.92	19.86
2010	19.90	20.11	19.87	19.78	19.71	19.55	19.53	19.82	20.14	20.29	20.16	20.46	19.94
2011	20.93	20.98	20.93	20.90	20.81	20.71	20.41	20.87	21.47	21.87	21.68	22.54	21.19
2012	23.21	23.44	23.45	23.41	23.21	22.93	22.64	23.07	22.83	22.53	22.83	22.88	23.01
2013	23.12	22.93	22.72	22.64	22.47	22.23	21.94	21.61	21.98	21.98	21.91	22.31	22.28
Manufacturing													
2009	22.00	22.12	22.02	22.00	22.18	22.38	22.32	22.41	22.79	22.31	22.55	22.59	22.31
2010	22.69	22.50	22.79	22.81	22.79	22.78	22.83	22.85	23.31	23.38	22.52	22.77	22.84
2011	23.08	23.14	23.25	22.90	22.89	22.47	22.51	22.89	23.07	23.16	23.80	23.64	23.06
2012	24.30	23.56	23.46	23.65	23.34	23.02	23.34	23.43	24.01	23.75	23.61	23.88	23.61
2013	24.15	24.27	23.97	23.73	23.81	23.87	23.91	23.85	24.31	24.09	24.92	24.39	24.11
Trade, Transportation, and Utilities													
2009	17.72	17.95	17.77	17.62	17.59	17.30	17.25	17.54	17.65	17.71	17.89	17.37	17.61
2010	17.34	17.44	17.69	17.78	17.82	17.65	17.47	17.59	17.52	17.68	17.67	17.11	17.56
2011	17.45	17.47	17.58	17.87	18.16	17.55	17.62	17.29	17.44	17.58	17.62	17.48	17.59
2012	18.09	18.24	18.44	18.67	18.74	18.56	18.52	18.38	18.61	18.65	18.66	18.19	18.48
2013	19.02	18.78	18.64	18.80	18.70	18.60	18.43	18.53	18.94	18.69	18.88	18.47	18.70
Professional and Business Services													
2009	22.09	22.29	22.55	22.54	22.31	22.12	22.19	22.01	21.75	21.66	21.89	22.19	22.13
2010	22.15	22.11	22.15	22.16	22.62	22.10	22.03	22.28	22.40	22.44	22.90	22.62	22.33
2011	22.94	22.65	22.41	22.31	22.46	22.35	22.16	21.93	21.83	21.94	21.81	22.08	22.23
2012	23.32	23.16	23.14	22.75	23.30	23.14	22.93	23.21	22.80	22.60	23.04	23.01	23.03
2013	23.10	23.14	23.10	23.31	22.60	22.96	22.80	22.55	22.72	22.61	22.87	22.51	22.85
Education and Health Services													
2009	19.17	19.26	19.32	19.54	19.23	19.46	19.40	19.49	19.70	19.55	19.47	19.38	19.41
2010	19.79	19.56	19.78	19.65	19.46	19.64	19.85	19.70	19.97	20.29	20.35	20.36	19.87
2011	20.57	20.23	20.49	20.85	20.19	20.59	20.83	20.94	21.61	21.89	21.78	22.19	21.02
2012	22.58	22.22	22.57	21.64	21.86	22.07	22.46	22.67	22.71	22.65	22.29	22.64	22.36
2013	22.08	22.16	21.96	21.97	21.63	21.75	21.90	21.83	21.38	21.23	20.88	20.88	21.63
Leisure and Hospitality													
2009	12.61	12.87	12.73	12.62	12.45	12.36	11.74	12.05	12.41	12.45	12.56	12.87	12.41
2010	12.51	12.82	12.55	12.85	12.49	12.15	12.17	12.40	12.65	12.56	12.74	12.88	12.54
2011	12.70	12.88	12.75	12.78	12.71	12.54	12.64	12.82	12.89	12.94	12.86	13.01	12.79
2012	12.91	12.65	12.81	12.80	12.78	12.80	12.61	12.71	12.99	13.10	13.02	13.06	12.84
2013	12.94	13.15	12.98	13.12	13.15	12.73	12.73	12.88	13.26	13.43	13.36	13.40	13.07

4. Average Weekly Earnings by Selected Industry: Maine, 2009–2013

(Dollars, not seasonally adjusted)

Industry and year	January	February	March	April	May	June	July	August	September	October	November	December	Annual average
Total Private													
2009	638.83	645.69	635.91	641.03	629.97	627.00	632.21	640.85	640.36	641.99	647.29	642.62	638.03
2010	639.21	648.02	649.72	649.96	651.84	650.65	654.72	663.58	664.61	674.58	664.51	674.68	657.41
2011	672.32	670.54	670.97	674.34	672.28	668.78	673.21	673.55	683.36	693.58	689.19	700.76	678.64
2012	719.10	707.49	714.53	715.46	708.85	705.50	710.70	710.01	722.06	721.90	718.00	730.75	714.74
2013	715.90	721.18	719.36	720.71	715.08	709.58	709.32	712.41	717.52	708.90	713.18	719.65	714.34
Goods-Producing													
2009	815.10	826.18	816.74	813.30	826.97	824.89	818.12	844.42	854.39	859.18	861.73	847.28	833.55
2010	844.34	835.96	846.13	855.93	862.29	844.12	850.92	862.80	885.79	915.35	864.30	866.24	862.24
2011	873.77	884.27	872.53	866.40	870.37	878.99	870.80	876.18	898.07	902.65	903.05	895.17	881.64
2012	918.41	900.03	904.23	909.44	893.04	900.30	886.64	903.20	920.72	906.91	903.34	918.29	904.37
2013	916.40	917.14	913.41	907.94	916.69	913.88	908.00	917.15	925.11	927.86	928.22	947.90	919.20
Construction													
2009	731.24	763.70	741.47	774.06	754.00	745.61	758.84	799.20	769.62	792.80	779.69	756.96	764.61
2010	750.23	764.18	757.05	769.44	788.40	766.36	777.29	794.78	805.60	815.66	788.26	771.34	779.65
2011	768.13	784.65	780.69	785.84	801.19	809.76	810.28	813.93	865.24	863.87	871.54	874.55	820.05
2012	872.70	876.66	895.79	896.60	907.51	912.61	892.02	913.57	915.48	885.43	881.24	890.03	895.09
2013	880.87	866.75	872.45	869.38	885.32	866.97	855.66	870.88	857.22	866.01	847.92	856.70	866.69
Manufacturing													
2009	869.00	862.68	858.78	840.40	865.02	866.11	854.86	876.23	900.21	899.09	924.55	910.38	876.78
2010	909.87	882.00	907.04	919.24	925.27	908.92	913.20	916.29	939.39	977.28	914.31	919.91	920.45
2011	927.82	930.23	918.38	904.55	906.44	912.28	902.65	913.31	922.80	933.35	923.44	917.23	917.79
2012	950.13	914.13	912.59	922.35	896.26	911.59	905.59	918.46	953.20	940.50	934.96	948.04	925.51
2013	944.27	953.81	946.82	939.71	947.64	952.41	951.62	954.00	972.40	973.24	984.34	980.48	959.58
Trade, Transportation, and Utilities													
2009	545.78	574.40	556.20	553.27	534.74	538.03	558.90	575.31	564.80	557.87	551.01	561.05	556.48
2010	539.27	556.34	566.08	567.18	582.71	578.92	583.50	591.02	572.90	592.28	558.37	578.32	572.46
2011	549.68	567.78	569.59	577.20	584.75	575.64	588.51	574.03	563.31	566.08	560.32	585.58	571.68
2012	573.45	587.33	599.30	614.24	614.67	610.62	618.57	612.05	617.85	606.13	593.39	611.18	604.30
2013	599.13	610.35	605.80	614.76	611.49	615.66	621.09	633.73	632.60	618.64	609.82	626.13	617.10
Professional and Business Services													
2009	804.08	806.90	814.06	802.42	792.01	780.84	785.53	779.15	754.73	764.60	766.15	774.43	785.62
2010	755.32	765.01	764.18	773.38	787.18	780.13	782.07	788.71	777.28	794.38	803.79	803.01	781.55
2011	802.90	788.22	786.59	780.85	781.61	777.78	766.74	763.16	759.68	759.12	750.26	757.34	771.38
2012	785.88	787.44	784.45	789.43	796.86	789.07	788.79	793.78	800.28	781.96	776.45	786.94	787.63
2013	757.68	770.56	773.85	783.22	770.66	780.64	763.80	757.68	770.21	757.44	766.15	772.09	767.76
Education and Health Services													
2009	609.61	614.39	612.44	625.28	613.44	622.72	620.80	621.73	632.37	635.38	636.67	631.79	623.06
2010	645.15	635.70	636.92	634.70	630.50	650.08	653.07	657.98	669.00	679.72	681.73	686.13	655.71
2011	697.32	673.66	678.22	694.31	682.42	695.94	701.97	705.68	730.42	742.07	740.52	752.24	708.37
2012	788.04	762.15	771.89	744.42	743.24	752.59	770.38	766.25	772.14	770.10	762.32	783.34	764.71
2013	757.34	753.44	751.03	753.57	739.75	739.50	751.17	750.95	735.47	719.70	716.18	707.83	739.75
Leisure and Hospitality													
2009	278.68	294.72	299.16	295.31	296.31	291.70	320.50	327.76	317.70	321.21	303.95	297.30	305.29
2010	291.48	307.68	297.44	303.26	298.51	297.68	316.42	332.32	330.17	326.56	321.05	315.56	312.25
2011	304.80	322.00	313.65	319.50	320.29	318.52	353.92	369.22	341.59	342.91	333.07	326.55	332.54
2012	313.71	323.84	324.09	326.40	327.17	328.96	348.04	359.69	348.13	341.91	325.50	326.50	335.12
2013	323.50	328.75	333.59	335.87	336.64	324.62	351.35	365.79	344.76	351.87	336.67	322.94	339.82

MARYLAND
At a Glance

Population:
    2000 census: 5,296,647
    2010 census: 5,773,552
    2013 estimate: 5,928,814

Percent change in population:
    2000–2010: 9.0%
    2010–2013: 2.7%

Percent change in total nonfarm employment:
    2000–2010: 2.5%
    2010–2013: 3.2%

Industry with the largest growth in employment, 2000–2013 (thousands):
    Education and Health Services, 111.2

Industry with the largest decline or smallest growth in employment, 2000–2013 (thousands):
    Manufacturing, -66.1

Civilian labor force:
    2000: 2,811,657
    2010: 3,074,202
    2013: 3,127,676

Unemployment rate and rank among states (lowest to highest):
    2000: 3.6%, 20th
    2010: 7.9%, 15th
    2013: 6.6%, 22nd

Over-the-year change in unemployment rates:
    2010–2011: -0.6%
    2011–2012: -0.4%
    2012–2013: -0.3%

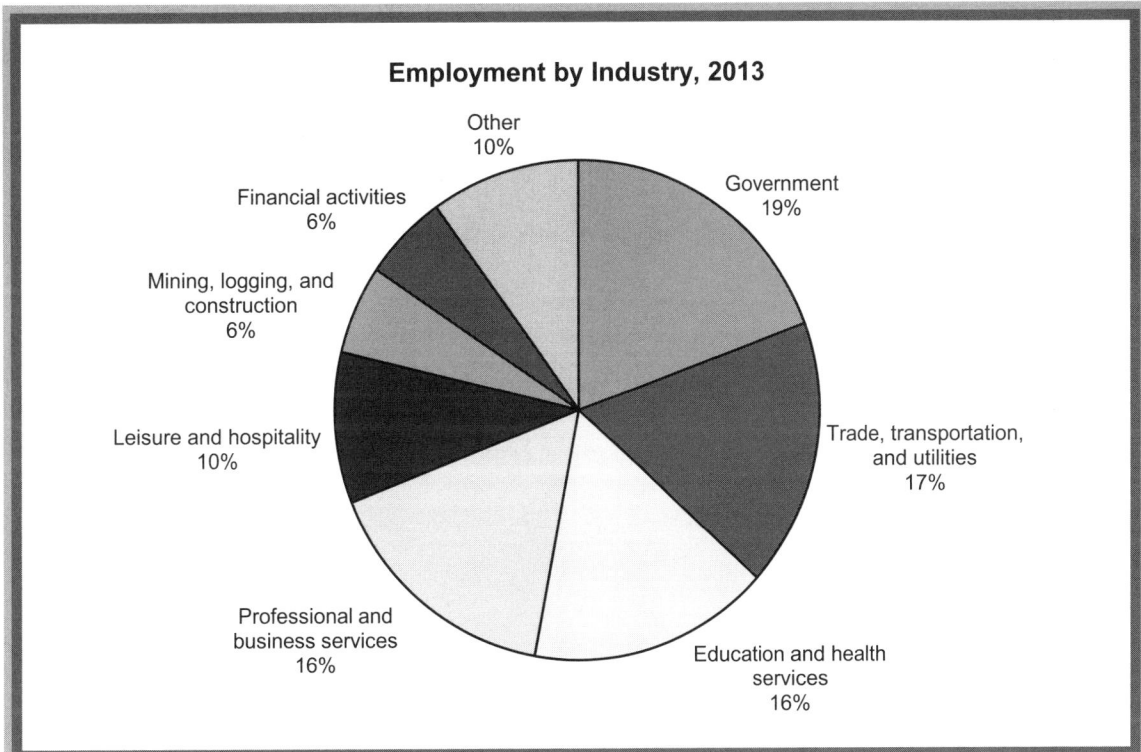

Employment by Industry, 2013

Other 10%
Government 19%
Financial activities 6%
Mining, logging, and construction 6%
Trade, transportation, and utilities 17%
Leisure and hospitality 10%
Professional and business services 16%
Education and health services 16%

1. Employment by Industry: Maryland, Selected Years, 2002–2013

(Numbers in thousands, not seasonally adjusted)

Industry and year	January	February	March	April	May	June	July	August	September	October	November	December	Annual average
Total Nonfarm													
2002	2,420.6	2,436.5	2,462.2	2,472.8	2,494.1	2,512.7	2,490.2	2,489.3	2,490.3	2,490.0	2,499.7	2,501.8	2,480.0
2003	2,428.6	2,426.8	2,452.7	2,477.5	2,499.3	2,518.3	2,497.5	2,494.2	2,503.2	2,505.8	2,513.4	2,520.1	2,486.5
2004	2,447.7	2,451.4	2,485.1	2,501.9	2,524.8	2,545.8	2,531.3	2,530.4	2,531.0	2,543.8	2,551.5	2,560.9	2,517.1
2005	2,480.8	2,494.0	2,513.8	2,544.3	2,564.7	2,579.3	2,569.9	2,568.6	2,579.3	2,577.5	2,589.6	2,597.5	2,554.9
2006	2,522.2	2,535.7	2,568.2	2,583.7	2,601.2	2,617.3	2,595.8	2,593.5	2,598.8	2,604.5	2,614.1	2,626.7	2,588.5
2007	2,549.8	2,553.2	2,587.1	2,599.6	2,621.9	2,634.9	2,618.9	2,616.6	2,620.5	2,629.7	2,638.1	2,607.3
2008	2,558.1	2,569.2	2,588.9	2,610.1	2,624.5	2,626.7	2,611.3	2,605.1	2,598.1	2,607.7	2,597.1	2,592.7	2,598.7
2009	2,497.6	2,498.8	2,512.5	2,529.6	2,543.8	2,551.2	2,525.6	2,515.9	2,514.9	2,524.9	2,526.9	2,525.9	2,522.3
2010	2,445.1	2,424.2	2,480.7	2,520.7	2,542.1	2,552.9	2,532.5	2,527.2	2,528.8	2,544.6	2,548.3	2,553.2	2,516.7
2011	2,473.3	2,490.0	2,517.1	2,543.6	2,554.4	2,565.4	2,556.9	2,543.7	2,553.7	2,565.6	2,571.4	2,577.7	2,542.7
2012	2,507.2	2,523.6	2,554.0	2,568.1	2,585.3	2,598.3	2,578.8	2,578.5	2,587.9	2,596.9	2,604.2	2,609.4	2,574.4
2013	2,533.2	2,551.5	2,573.2	2,592.8	2,614.5	2,621.4	2,602.1	2,601.8	2,604.3	2,613.5	2,622.8	2,621.8	2,596.1
Total Private													
2002	1,963.2	1,969.1	1,990.3	2,004.4	2,024.8	2,048.9	2,042.4	2,042.2	2,026.8	2,017.5	2,025.7	2,029.1	2,015.4
2003	1,969.4	1,958.4	1,981.3	2,007.2	2,029.2	2,055.5	2,052.9	2,056.3	2,042.3	2,038.5	2,045.2	2,052.7	2,024.1
2004	1,988.5	1,986.8	2,015.8	2,034.0	2,054.7	2,085.4	2,087.8	2,087.3	2,074.5	2,073.4	2,089.4	2,054.7
2005	2,023.6	2,027.8	2,045.8	2,074.6	2,092.1	2,118.0	2,120.5	2,119.6	2,113.6	2,102.3	2,109.9	2,119.6	2,089.0
2006	2,062.3	2,063.8	2,091.5	2,106.1	2,122.6	2,151.2	2,142.1	2,141.3	2,129.5	2,123.6	2,130.9	2,142.9	2,117.3
2007	2,082.4	2,074.7	2,102.9	2,116.5	2,136.0	2,161.3	2,157.0	2,155.5	2,141.6	2,133.3	2,138.1	2,146.8	2,128.8
2008	2,082.3	2,080.3	2,096.0	2,116.4	2,130.3	2,144.1	2,138.3	2,132.8	2,114.6	2,106.0	2,097.1	2,093.4	2,111.0
2009	2,016.3	2,004.9	2,013.3	2,027.3	2,041.5	2,060.9	2,046.6	2,040.3	2,027.3	2,020.3	2,020.3	2,020.7	2,028.3
2010	1,958.0	1,926.3	1,974.8	2,011.7	2,026.1	2,048.9	2,045.2	2,042.2	2,032.2	2,036.7	2,035.8	2,043.4	2,015.1
2011	1,980.0	1,981.8	2,003.0	2,030.3	2,041.9	2,062.6	2,067.7	2,060.7	2,053.0	2,051.2	2,059.3	2,065.4	2,038.1
2012	2,012.2	2,013.2	2,037.6	2,054.1	2,072.5	2,099.5	2,095.8	2,097.3	2,086.0	2,083.9	2,090.2	2,096.1	2,069.9
2013	2,038.7	2,042.1	2,060.2	2,078.2	2,100.3	2,119.5	2,119.5	2,120.1	2,103.7	2,103.1	2,110.3	2,109.9	2,092.1
Goods-Producing													
2002	316.6	317.4	320.9	323.2	325.1	328.6	326.4	326.9	324.1	320.2	319.6	316.8	322.2
2003	309.1	305.8	309.5	312.3	315.7	318.8	318.5	319.7	317.8	317.0	316.5	315.5	314.7
2004	306.5	305.1	311.3	315.9	319.2	323.7	325.9	326.3	324.9	323.6	322.7	323.2	319.0
2005	314.6	312.7	315.7	322.4	325.1	328.9	329.7	331.0	330.6	327.2	328.4	327.9	324.5
2006	318.6	317.9	323.1	325.0	326.5	331.2	330.9	331.0	329.2	326.5	325.2	324.9	325.8
2007	316.1	312.0	318.1	320.9	323.8	328.3	328.4	328.6	325.8	323.1	320.7	318.5	322.0
2008	310.3	308.7	310.1	310.9	311.1	313.5	313.1	312.5	309.3	304.8	300.0	294.5	308.2
2009	281.0	277.1	276.0	275.3	275.4	277.3	276.7	274.5	271.8	269.3	266.8	264.3	273.8
2010	253.8	244.3	252.7	259.7	261.7	264.6	265.6	265.1	263.0	261.0	259.9	257.7	259.1
2011	250.7	249.8	252.5	257.4	258.7	261.8	263.4	262.3	259.6	258.7	257.7	256.4	257.4
2012	249.1	247.8	250.0	252.5	253.4	257.9	259.1	258.9	256.3	255.4	254.6	253.7	254.1
2013	246.7	246.3	248.1	252.9	255.1	258.1	259.5	260.2	258.1	258.5	259.4	256.9	255.0
Service-Providing													
2002	2,104.0	2,119.1	2,141.3	2,149.6	2,169.0	2,184.1	2,163.8	2,162.4	2,166.2	2,169.8	2,180.1	2,185.0	2,157.9
2003	2,119.5	2,121.0	2,143.2	2,165.2	2,183.6	2,199.5	2,179.0	2,174.5	2,185.4	2,188.8	2,196.9	2,204.6	2,171.8
2004	2,141.2	2,146.3	2,173.8	2,186.0	2,205.6	2,222.1	2,205.4	2,204.1	2,206.1	2,220.2	2,228.8	2,237.7	2,198.1
2005	2,166.2	2,181.3	2,198.1	2,221.9	2,239.6	2,250.4	2,240.2	2,237.6	2,248.7	2,250.3	2,261.2	2,269.6	2,230.4
2006	2,203.6	2,217.8	2,245.1	2,258.7	2,274.7	2,286.1	2,264.9	2,262.5	2,269.6	2,278.0	2,288.9	2,301.8	2,262.6
2007	2,233.7	2,241.2	2,269.0	2,278.7	2,298.1	2,306.6	2,290.5	2,288.0	2,290.8	2,297.4	2,309.0	2,319.6	2,285.2
2008	2,247.8	2,260.5	2,278.8	2,299.2	2,313.4	2,313.2	2,298.2	2,292.6	2,288.8	2,297.9	2,297.1	2,298.2	2,290.5
2009	2,216.6	2,221.7	2,236.5	2,254.3	2,268.4	2,273.9	2,248.9	2,241.4	2,243.1	2,255.6	2,260.1	2,261.6	2,248.5
2010	2,191.3	2,179.9	2,228.0	2,261.0	2,280.4	2,288.3	2,266.9	2,262.1	2,265.8	2,283.6	2,288.4	2,295.5	2,257.6
2011	2,222.6	2,240.2	2,264.6	2,286.2	2,295.7	2,303.6	2,293.5	2,281.4	2,294.1	2,306.9	2,313.7	2,321.3	2,285.3
2012	2,258.1	2,275.8	2,304.0	2,315.6	2,331.9	2,340.4	2,319.7	2,319.6	2,331.6	2,341.5	2,349.6	2,355.7	2,320.3
2013	2,286.5	2,305.2	2,325.1	2,339.9	2,359.4	2,363.3	2,342.6	2,341.6	2,346.2	2,355.0	2,363.4	2,364.9	2,341.1
Mining, Logging, and Construction													
2002	159.2	160.2	163.8	166.2	168.3	171.4	171.9	172.5	170.5	169.0	168.8	166.4	167.4
2003	160.8	158.3	161.7	165.1	168.8	171.7	173.8	175.5	174.5	174.5	174.0	173.3	169.3
2004	166.1	164.8	170.6	174.7	177.7	181.5	183.4	184.1	183.5	182.4	181.7	181.8	177.7
2005	174.7	173.0	175.8	182.5	185.4	189.0	190.5	191.5	191.7	189.4	190.3	189.7	185.3
2006	183.1	182.6	187.3	189.5	191.2	195.0	195.0	195.2	194.3	192.4	191.4	190.9	190.7
2007	183.9	180.2	186.0	188.9	191.5	195.2	195.6	195.9	194.0	191.5	189.4	187.0	189.9
2008	180.4	178.9	180.7	182.1	182.4	184.3	184.2	183.7	181.6	178.5	174.6	170.0	180.1
2009	158.8	156.3	155.8	156.1	156.5	158.2	158.3	156.5	154.2	151.9	149.6	147.4	155.0
2010	138.4	130.9	138.1	144.4	146.4	148.8	149.9	150.1	149.1	147.9	147.5	145.5	144.8
2011	138.0	137.2	139.5	143.9	145.3	148.0	149.7	149.0	147.5	147.1	146.6	145.7	144.8
2012	139.4	138.7	140.7	142.9	143.8	147.3	148.6	149.0	148.4	148.1	147.5	146.6	145.1
2013	140.6	140.0	141.8	146.5	148.4	150.8	152.2	152.8	151.8	153.1	155.0	153.3	148.9

1. Employment by Industry: Maryland, Selected Years, 2002–2013—*Continued*

(Numbers in thousands, not seasonally adjusted)

Industry and year	January	February	March	April	May	June	July	August	September	October	November	December	Annual average
Manufacturing													
2002	157.4	157.2	157.1	157.0	156.8	157.2	154.5	154.4	153.6	151.2	150.8	150.4	154.8
2003	148.3	147.5	147.8	147.2	146.9	147.1	144.7	144.2	143.3	142.5	142.5	142.2	145.4
2004	140.4	140.3	140.7	141.2	141.5	142.2	142.5	142.2	141.4	141.2	141.0	141.4	141.3
2005	139.9	139.7	139.9	139.9	139.7	139.9	139.2	139.5	138.9	137.8	138.1	138.2	139.2
2006	135.5	135.3	135.8	135.5	135.3	136.2	135.9	135.8	134.9	134.1	133.8	134.0	135.2
2007	132.2	131.8	132.1	132.0	132.3	133.1	132.8	132.7	131.8	131.6	131.3	131.5	132.1
2008	129.9	129.8	129.4	128.8	128.7	129.2	128.9	128.8	127.7	126.3	125.4	124.5	128.1
2009	122.2	120.8	120.2	119.2	118.9	119.1	118.4	118.0	117.6	117.4	117.2	116.9	118.8
2010	115.4	113.4	114.6	115.3	115.3	115.8	115.7	115.0	113.9	113.1	112.4	112.2	114.3
2011	112.7	112.6	113.0	113.5	113.4	113.8	113.7	113.3	112.1	111.6	111.1	110.7	112.6
2012	109.7	109.1	109.3	109.6	109.6	110.6	110.5	109.9	107.9	107.3	107.1	107.1	109.0
2013	106.1	106.3	106.3	106.4	106.7	107.3	107.3	107.4	106.3	105.4	104.4	103.6	106.1
Trade, Transportation, and Utilities													
2002	460.5	455.0	459.4	460.4	463.9	468.6	463.7	463.1	463.4	465.3	472.7	480.0	464.7
2003	455.3	449.4	452.7	454.9	459.2	463.7	460.4	462.4	463.0	466.0	475.9	482.9	462.2
2004	459.8	455.2	459.0	460.4	464.4	471.6	466.4	466.6	466.8	470.6	479.4	487.6	467.3
2005	462.1	459.4	461.7	464.0	467.9	471.8	472.6	472.0	471.8	473.4	482.0	491.8	470.9
2006	470.6	465.1	468.9	469.8	473.5	477.6	473.9	473.7	472.6	476.4	487.5	496.0	475.5
2007	474.8	467.3	471.8	470.2	475.4	479.0	476.2	474.4	473.1	474.6	484.5	493.2	476.2
2008	469.3	462.5	464.2	463.0	465.4	468.6	465.0	464.3	461.5	461.2	465.4	470.0	465.0
2009	445.1	437.6	436.6	436.1	438.9	441.8	436.5	436.4	436.6	436.8	445.6	449.9	439.9
2010	429.5	418.8	427.8	434.4	437.9	441.5	438.8	439.1	437.2	442.5	450.7	457.5	438.0
2011	436.8	432.1	434.9	439.3	442.2	444.9	443.5	444.5	443.8	447.0	456.8	464.0	444.2
2012	444.2	439.5	444.1	445.4	448.9	451.5	448.3	448.4	449.2	451.4	462.6	468.8	450.2
2013	446.4	440.9	443.2	444.9	449.3	452.1	451.5	452.1	450.7	451.4	461.3	467.1	450.9
Wholesale Trade													
2002	93.3	93.2	93.5	93.0	93.2	93.5	93.1	93.2	92.7	92.9	92.9	92.9	93.1
2003	91.1	90.7	91.3	91.0	91.5	91.8	91.4	91.4	91.2	91.1	91.3	91.4	91.3
2004	89.9	90.2	90.9	91.6	91.9	92.9	93.2	93.0	92.9	93.2	93.4	93.6	92.2
2005	92.6	92.9	93.1	93.8	94.4	95.0	95.2	95.1	94.6	94.4	94.4	95.0	94.2
2006	93.7	94.1	94.6	95.3	95.3	95.6	96.2	95.7	95.6	95.2	95.3	95.6	95.2
2007	94.0	94.3	94.7	95.1	95.4	95.7	95.3	95.2	94.9	94.3	94.3	94.7	94.8
2008	93.1	93.1	93.9	93.8	94.0	94.4	93.6	93.4	92.8	92.2	91.4	90.9	93.1
2009	89.2	88.7	88.2	88.2	88.0	87.9	87.2	87.2	86.7	86.3	86.0	85.8	87.5
2010	84.2	83.7	84.6	85.5	86.1	86.3	86.0	86.0	85.1	85.8	85.8	86.0	85.4
2011	84.8	84.8	85.3	85.8	86.4	86.5	86.7	86.6	86.2	86.1	85.9	86.0	85.9
2012	84.7	85.0	85.8	86.1	86.8	87.2	86.8	86.8	86.3	86.3	86.2	86.3	86.2
2013	85.0	85.0	85.3	85.7	86.0	86.4	86.2	86.1	85.7	84.3	83.8	83.7	85.3
Retail Trade													
2002	292.0	287.0	290.8	290.2	292.6	297.1	295.0	294.2	294.0	294.5	302.4	309.6	295.0
2003	289.7	284.5	286.3	288.9	291.7	295.3	293.9	295.5	294.5	295.8	305.4	311.6	294.4
2004	292.2	287.5	289.9	290.3	293.3	298.5	295.6	296.3	295.0	298.5	307.0	313.8	296.5
2005	291.9	288.5	289.9	292.6	295.2	297.7	299.7	299.3	297.7	299.2	307.2	314.4	297.8
2006	298.2	291.8	294.5	294.8	297.5	300.1	298.8	298.5	296.2	299.9	310.7	316.2	299.8
2007	300.2	292.5	295.9	295.2	299.1	301.5	301.0	299.7	297.5	299.6	309.4	315.3	300.6
2008	297.6	290.7	292.1	291.3	292.9	294.9	293.5	292.8	289.7	289.9	294.1	297.2	293.1
2009	279.4	273.0	272.7	272.7	275.4	277.7	275.5	275.5	274.1	275.2	283.1	286.7	276.8
2010	271.7	262.7	269.3	272.7	275.7	278.4	278.0	278.4	275.6	279.6	287.2	291.8	276.8
2011	276.4	272.2	274.1	276.8	278.5	280.8	280.1	281.1	279.2	282.5	291.2	296.5	280.8
2012	281.5	276.8	280.1	280.5	282.8	284.6	283.5	283.5	282.7	285.1	295.0	298.4	284.5
2013	281.9	277.7	279.2	280.7	283.7	286.0	286.9	287.5	284.6	286.7	296.1	299.9	285.9
Transportation and Utilities													
2002	75.2	74.8	75.1	77.2	78.1	78.0	75.6	75.7	76.7	77.9	77.4	77.5	76.6
2003	74.5	74.2	75.1	75.0	76.0	76.6	75.1	75.5	77.3	79.1	79.2	79.9	76.5
2004	77.7	77.5	78.2	78.5	79.2	80.2	77.6	77.3	78.9	78.9	79.0	80.2	78.6
2005	77.6	78.0	78.7	77.6	78.3	79.1	77.7	77.6	79.5	79.8	80.4	82.4	78.9
2006	78.7	79.2	79.8	79.7	80.4	81.3	79.4	79.6	81.2	81.2	81.7	84.2	80.5
2007	80.6	80.5	81.2	79.9	80.9	81.8	79.9	79.5	80.7	80.7	80.8	83.2	80.8
2008	78.6	78.7	78.2	77.9	78.5	79.3	77.9	78.1	79.0	79.1	79.9	81.9	78.9
2009	76.9	75.9	75.7	75.2	75.5	76.2	73.8	73.7	75.8	75.3	76.5	77.4	75.7
2010	73.6	72.4	73.9	76.2	76.1	76.8	74.8	74.7	76.5	77.1	77.7	79.7	75.8
2011	75.6	75.1	75.5	76.7	77.3	77.6	76.7	76.8	78.4	78.4	79.7	81.5	77.4
2012	78.0	77.7	78.2	78.8	79.3	79.7	78.0	78.1	80.2	80.0	81.4	84.1	79.5
2013	79.5	78.2	78.7	78.5	79.6	79.7	78.4	78.5	80.4	80.4	81.4	83.5	79.7
Information													
2002	55.2	54.9	54.8	54.4	54.4	54.0	53.3	53.0	52.2	50.7	51.4	51.1	53.3
2003	50.4	50.5	50.6	51.1	51.7	51.6	51.4	51.1	50.7	50.7	51.4	51.5	51.1
2004	50.3	49.6	50.5	50.2	50.6	51.1	49.9	50.1	49.5	49.3	49.6	49.6	50.0
2005	48.8	49.0	49.1	49.3	49.8	50.1	51.3	51.7	51.6	51.9	51.8	51.9	50.5
2006	50.5	50.8	51.2	50.6	50.9	50.9	50.2	50.2	49.9	49.6	50.2	50.5	50.5
2007	49.3	49.7	50.5	50.5	51.0	51.8	51.4	52.1	51.5	50.0	50.8	51.4	50.8
2008	50.0	50.3	50.6	50.6	50.7	50.1	49.8	49.5	49.3	48.1	49.0	48.8	49.7
2009	46.4	46.6	47.5	46.3	46.0	46.7	45.4	45.7	44.6	43.7	44.0	44.0	45.6
2010	43.2	43.6	45.0	44.8	44.7	45.5	44.1	43.1	43.9	43.4	42.3	44.2	44.0
2011	41.3	41.9	42.1	41.4	41.2	41.1	41.2	38.1	40.2	40.2	40.9	40.7	40.9
2012	39.8	39.9	39.9	38.8	39.1	40.5	40.4	40.5	40.0	39.5	39.8	40.7	39.9
2013	39.7	39.8	40.0	39.6	39.6	39.7	39.5	39.5	38.9	38.6	38.7	38.5	39.3

1. Employment by Industry: Maryland, Selected Years, 2002–2013—*Continued*

(Numbers in thousands, not seasonally adjusted)

Industry and year	January	February	March	April	May	June	July	August	September	October	November	December	Annual average
Financial Activities													
2002	148.7	149.2	149.3	149.8	150.6	152.2	152.5	152.8	152.1	152.0	152.6	153.7	151.3
2003	153.1	153.2	154.2	154.7	156.0	157.6	158.5	158.7	157.5	155.5	155.9	156.3	155.9
2004	153.6	153.7	154.7	154.8	155.4	156.1	157.4	157.7	156.4	157.2	157.1	157.8	156.0
2005	156.2	156.6	156.6	157.7	158.2	160.0	160.8	160.9	160.4	159.3	159.3	160.0	158.8
2006	158.5	159.0	159.6	159.6	159.9	161.6	161.2	161.0	159.8	159.1	159.1	160.1	159.9
2007	157.9	158.0	158.3	157.9	158.5	159.5	159.4	158.8	157.3	156.4	155.9	156.4	157.9
2008	153.5	153.9	154.1	153.8	153.9	154.6	154.1	153.6	151.8	151.5	150.4	150.7	153.0
2009	147.5	146.9	146.3	146.7	146.8	147.6	146.9	146.5	145.3	145.1	144.9	145.2	146.3
2010	142.4	141.8	142.5	142.8	143.3	144.9	145.0	144.8	143.9	144.3	144.4	145.5	143.8
2011	142.6	142.8	143.2	143.5	143.5	144.3	144.4	143.7	142.7	142.9	142.4	142.8	143.2
2012	141.8	141.7	141.8	141.6	142.4	143.9	144.4	144.4	143.8	143.9	143.3	144.7	143.2
2013	143.5	143.5	143.9	144.3	144.8	146.2	146.7	146.2	145.3	146.8	146.4	147.3	145.4
Professional and Business Services													
2002	357.3	360.1	364.2	367.2	370.0	372.5	371.9	374.4	371.0	369.4	369.9	369.8	368.1
2003	358.4	356.6	361.6	368.5	370.8	374.5	373.1	375.5	373.7	375.3	374.4	375.8	369.9
2004	364.5	366.6	373.7	375.2	378.4	382.7	383.8	384.3	382.5	384.4	383.3	384.8	378.7
2005	373.9	377.0	382.6	388.4	390.6	393.9	393.5	394.6	394.3	392.8	391.6	391.4	388.7
2006	383.4	386.3	392.7	396.3	397.4	400.9	400.2	400.9	398.5	396.7	395.5	396.1	395.4
2007	385.5	386.9	392.6	396.9	398.2	402.0	401.3	402.9	400.8	400.6	400.5	401.1	397.4
2008	390.3	391.1	394.3	400.4	400.7	402.2	402.6	403.2	399.9	398.2	395.2	392.6	397.6
2009	380.5	378.3	380.6	384.8	384.7	388.5	386.5	387.1	383.7	384.6	383.3	382.5	383.8
2010	372.7	369.4	378.7	387.3	387.6	393.3	393.2	393.7	391.6	395.5	393.1	394.4	387.5
2011	384.5	385.6	390.1	398.3	397.3	404.0	407.3	407.1	406.8	405.9	407.5	407.8	400.2
2012	396.9	398.1	404.8	407.4	410.1	415.2	414.2	418.5	415.6	415.8	418.1	415.4	410.8
2013	406.4	410.0	415.2	414.9	416.3	420.3	419.3	423.3	419.6	419.3	420.1	418.6	416.9
Education and Health Services													
2002	323.6	328.9	330.0	328.9	329.6	328.8	327.0	325.8	329.0	334.2	337.1	337.8	330.1
2003	332.7	334.9	337.3	338.9	339.1	339.4	338.7	338.9	339.7	342.2	343.9	344.9	339.2
2004	341.9	343.3	345.5	345.5	345.7	346.2	347.9	346.3	346.7	350.3	352.0	352.4	347.0
2005	346.3	350.1	351.4	353.6	352.9	351.2	349.9	348.7	353.3	358.9	360.5	361.8	353.2
2006	355.2	359.3	362.4	362.8	362.6	361.6	358.3	357.3	362.8	368.2	370.2	372.2	362.7
2007	365.9	369.9	372.8	373.0	372.2	370.9	368.4	367.3	372.2	376.8	378.4	380.1	372.3
2008	374.1	378.6	380.7	383.0	382.2	380.0	378.8	377.7	383.5	390.0	391.7	393.6	382.8
2009	386.6	391.1	392.8	395.0	393.2	391.8	388.0	385.9	391.1	397.3	399.0	400.4	392.7
2010	393.7	391.5	398.9	401.3	399.1	396.2	394.6	392.2	397.4	403.7	405.3	406.1	398.3
2011	399.2	404.6	406.3	406.0	403.8	400.1	399.9	398.3	404.1	410.3	411.9	412.6	404.8
2012	407.7	413.2	415.4	416.8	414.7	412.4	411.1	409.0	414.3	420.2	420.5	422.8	414.8
2013	414.2	419.6	420.9	421.8	422.1	416.8	415.2	414.0	418.8	424.5	426.7	425.6	420.0
Leisure and Hospitality													
2002	191.4	192.5	199.1	207.1	216.9	228.0	230.1	230.1	220.6	211.8	208.2	205.1	211.7
2003	197.5	194.7	200.3	210.7	220.1	230.9	233.2	233.1	224.6	216.8	212.7	210.5	215.4
2004	200.5	201.0	207.8	215.7	224.2	236.1	238.4	238.9	231.0	222.0	218.0	217.4	220.9
2005	206.8	207.3	212.1	222.6	230.6	244.0	245.5	243.8	235.4	223.6	220.7	218.8	225.9
2006	210.7	210.2	217.4	225.3	234.6	248.8	249.2	249.3	239.5	230.5	226.4	225.6	230.6
2007	216.7	214.7	221.4	229.5	238.6	249.9	252.0	252.5	242.5	233.5	228.7	227.3	233.9
2008	218.2	218.2	224.5	236.2	247.3	254.9	255.2	253.4	241.3	234.8	228.1	225.8	236.5
2009	213.3	212.5	218.1	227.4	240.1	249.5	249.6	248.1	238.7	228.3	221.4	218.6	230.5
2010	209.2	205.0	214.8	226.8	236.6	246.8	248.1	248.8	240.7	231.9	225.6	223.5	229.8
2011	211.8	212.1	220.4	229.9	240.5	250.6	252.7	252.2	242.7	233.5	229.2	227.6	233.6
2012	220.8	221.7	229.8	239.0	251.1	264.4	264.7	264.7	254.7	246.5	239.3	238.3	244.6
2013	232.2	232.6	239.3	249.2	262.1	274.6	275.8	273.6	261.3	253.9	246.7	245.1	253.9
Other Services													
2002	109.9	111.1	112.6	113.4	114.3	116.2	117.5	116.1	114.4	113.9	114.2	114.8	114.0
2003	112.9	113.3	115.1	116.1	116.6	119.0	119.1	116.9	115.3	115.0	114.5	115.3	115.8
2004	111.4	112.3	113.3	116.3	116.8	117.9	118.1	117.1	116.7	116.0	116.1	116.6	115.7
2005	114.9	115.7	116.6	116.6	117.0	118.1	117.2	116.9	116.2	115.2	115.6	116.0	116.3
2006	114.8	115.2	116.2	116.7	117.2	118.6	118.2	117.9	117.2	116.6	116.8	117.5	116.9
2007	116.2	116.2	117.4	117.6	118.3	119.9	119.9	118.9	118.4	118.3	118.6	118.8	118.2
2008	116.6	117.0	117.5	118.5	119.0	120.2	119.7	118.6	118.0	117.4	117.3	117.4	118.1
2009	115.5	114.8	115.4	115.7	116.4	117.7	117.0	116.1	115.5	115.2	115.3	115.8	115.9
2010	113.5	111.9	114.4	114.6	115.2	116.1	115.8	115.4	114.5	114.4	114.5	114.5	114.6
2011	113.1	112.9	113.5	114.5	114.7	115.8	115.3	114.5	113.1	112.7	112.9	113.5	113.9
2012	111.9	111.3	111.8	112.6	112.8	113.7	113.6	112.9	112.1	111.2	111.0	111.7	112.2
2013	109.6	109.4	109.6	110.6	111.0	111.7	112.0	111.2	111.0	110.1	111.0	110.8	110.7
Government													
2002	457.4	467.4	471.9	468.4	469.3	463.8	447.8	447.1	463.5	472.5	474.0	472.7	464.7
2003	459.2	468.4	471.4	470.3	470.1	462.8	444.6	437.9	460.9	467.3	468.2	467.4	462.4
2004	459.2	464.6	469.3	467.9	470.1	460.4	443.5	443.1	456.5	470.4	473.3	471.5	462.5
2005	457.2	466.2	468.0	469.7	472.6	461.3	449.4	449.0	465.7	475.2	479.7	477.9	466.0
2006	459.9	471.9	476.7	477.6	478.6	466.1	453.7	452.2	469.3	480.9	483.2	483.8	471.2
2007	467.4	478.5	484.2	483.1	485.9	473.6	461.9	461.4	475.0	487.2	491.6	491.3	478.4
2008	475.8	488.9	492.9	493.7	494.2	482.6	473.0	472.3	483.5	496.7	500.0	499.3	487.7
2009	481.3	493.9	499.2	502.3	502.3	490.3	479.0	475.6	487.6	504.6	506.6	505.2	494.0
2010	487.1	497.9	505.9	509.0	516.0	504.0	487.3	485.0	496.6	507.9	512.5	509.8	501.6
2011	493.3	508.2	514.1	513.3	512.5	502.8	489.2	483.0	500.7	514.4	512.1	512.3	504.7
2012	495.0	510.4	516.4	514.0	512.8	498.8	483.0	481.2	501.9	513.0	514.0	513.3	504.5
2013	494.5	509.4	513.0	514.6	514.2	501.9	482.6	481.7	500.6	510.4	512.5	511.9	503.9

2. Average Weekly Hours by Selected Industry: Maryland, 2009–2013

(Not seasonally adjusted)

Industry and year	January	February	March	April	May	June	July	August	September	October	November	December	Annual average
Total Private													
2009	34.3	34.5	34.4	34.1	34.3	34.4	34.6	35.0	34.7	34.4	34.6	34.3	34.5
2010	34.6	33.2	34.4	34.5	33.8	33.9	33.9	34.3	34.0	34.0	34.1	34.1	34.1
2011	34.3	34.2	34.3	34.4	34.8	34.6	34.7	34.3	34.3	34.7	33.9	33.9	34.4
2012	33.9	33.9	33.9	34.2	33.9	34.0	34.0	33.8	34.1	33.8	33.8	34.3	34.0
2013	33.4	33.5	33.5	33.8	33.8	34.1	34.0	34.1	34.6	33.8	34.1	34.1	33.9
Goods-Producing													
2009	38.4	38.6	38.6	38.0	38.2	38.0	38.4	38.5	37.6	38.0	37.5	38.0	38.2
2010	37.9	34.8	37.7	38.6	38.8	38.9	38.3	38.8	38.7	38.3	38.5	38.6	38.2
2011	38.5	38.4	38.8	38.9	39.4	39.5	39.1	39.1	38.0	38.8	39.1	39.4	38.9
2012	38.5	38.6	38.4	38.8	38.5	38.7	38.7	38.9	39.5	39.5	39.0	39.3	38.9
2013	38.2	38.4	38.3	38.3	38.5	37.6	37.8	38.7	39.0	38.7	39.5	38.4	38.5
Mining, Logging, and Construction													
2009	37.9	38.0	38.1	37.6	37.8	37.3	37.5	38.0	36.1	36.6	36.1	36.6	37.3
2010	36.5	33.1	36.0	37.8	37.8	38.2	37.3	38.0	37.9	37.3	37.6	37.3	37.1
2011	36.6	37.0	37.2	37.4	38.3	38.9	38.5	38.4	36.7	37.5	38.5	38.6	37.8
2012	37.6	37.7	36.9	37.5	37.7	37.9	37.8	38.2	39.0	39.0	38.3	38.7	38.0
2013	37.5	37.4	36.6	37.2	37.8	36.3	37.0	38.3	38.4	37.4	38.9	37.4	37.5
Manufacturing													
2009	39.1	39.4	39.2	38.6	38.7	39.0	39.7	39.2	39.6	39.8	39.4	39.8	39.3
2010	39.5	36.8	39.8	39.6	40.0	39.9	39.7	39.8	39.7	39.6	39.6	40.3	39.5
2011	40.8	40.2	40.9	40.8	40.8	40.2	40.0	40.0	39.8	40.6	40.0	40.4	40.4
2012	39.7	39.7	40.2	40.5	39.7	39.8	39.9	39.8	40.2	40.2	39.9	40.2	40.0
2013	39.2	39.7	40.6	39.9	39.4	39.5	39.0	39.3	39.9	40.6	40.5	39.9	39.8
Trade, Transportation, and Utilities													
2009	33.4	33.4	33.7	33.5	33.8	33.8	34.2	34.3	35.2	34.6	34.5	33.9	34.0
2010	33.8	31.9	34.2	34.4	34.7	34.9	34.8	34.9	34.3	34.0	33.4	33.9	34.1
2011	33.2	33.0	33.2	33.5	33.9	33.7	33.8	33.3	33.7	33.5	33.7	33.7	33.5
2012	33.0	33.5	33.7	34.3	34.0	33.8	34.1	33.6	33.9	33.7	33.7	34.5	33.8
2013	33.2	33.3	33.5	33.2	33.5	34.1	33.9	34.0	34.0	33.0	32.8	33.0	33.5
Financial Activities													
2009	36.1	36.3	36.0	35.5	35.8	35.8	36.3	36.6	36.4	36.6	36.9	36.2	36.2
2010	36.8	36.1	36.7	36.4	36.6	36.5	36.0	36.5	36.3	36.9	37.2	37.5	36.6
2011	38.4	38.0	38.3	38.4	38.2	38.3	37.8	37.9	39.0	39.7	39.2	39.1	38.5
2012	39.4	38.6	38.9	38.4	38.2	37.5	37.9	37.3	37.6	36.8	36.8	37.2	37.9
2013	36.1	36.5	36.5	36.6	36.4	37.1	36.7	36.5	37.5	36.8	37.0	36.8	36.7
Professional and Business Services													
2009	35.9	36.2	36.0	36.4	36.7	36.8	36.9	37.4	36.4	36.5	36.8	36.4	36.5
2010	36.7	35.6	37.0	36.7	36.4	36.1	35.8	36.5	36.1	36.5	37.0	37.0	36.5
2011	37.8	37.5	37.4	37.5	38.0	37.9	37.8	37.3	37.5	38.2	37.9	37.5	37.7
2012	37.5	37.2	37.3	37.3	36.5	36.5	36.7	36.2	36.5	35.8	36.2	36.8	36.7
2013	35.4	35.3	35.3	36.3	35.7	36.1	36.3	36.6	37.1	35.8	36.3	36.5	36.1
Education and Health Services													
2009	33.5	33.2	33.2	32.8	32.8	33.1	33.1	33.3	33.3	33.3	33.8	33.3	33.2
2010	33.6	33.5	33.2	33.0	33.3	33.2	33.5	33.7	33.2	33.0	33.3	32.9	33.3
2011	32.9	32.7	32.8	32.9	33.1	32.9	33.0	33.0	32.9	33.1	32.8	32.6	32.9
2012	33.1	32.9	32.8	32.5	32.5	33.1	33.1	33.4	33.4	33.0	32.7	32.8	32.9
2013	33.0	33.3	33.0	33.3	33.3	33.9	33.3	33.1	33.5	33.2	33.2	33.1	33.3
Leisure and Hospitality													
2009	25.3	26.1	26.2	25.8	26.7	27.2	27.4	27.5	26.0	25.4	25.7	25.2	26.2
2010	25.4	24.5	26.2	26.7	26.8	27.3	27.9	28.1	27.4	27.0	27.0	26.3	26.8
2011	26.5	27.0	27.1	27.0	27.4	27.3	27.7	27.4	26.3	26.9	26.3	26.2	26.9
2012	26.5	26.8	26.6	27.0	26.9	27.3	27.4	27.4	26.9	26.6	26.5	26.5	26.9
2013	25.6	26.0	25.8	25.7	25.9	26.5	26.9	26.4	26.2	25.6	25.6	25.3	26.0
Other Services													
2009	30.0	30.7	30.9	30.5	30.4	30.9	30.3	31.7	31.9	31.3	31.4	31.3	30.9
2010	31.4	30.6	32.3	33.2	33.9	34.2	33.6	33.5	34.4	34.6	34.1	34.0	33.3
2011	32.9	33.1	33.6	33.4	33.2	34.3	33.8	33.1	33.9	34.0	34.4	34.4	33.7
2012	34.0	33.5	33.1	33.7	33.2	33.3	33.6	33.2	33.5	33.5	33.3	33.0	33.4
2013	31.8	32.4	32.5	32.8	33.3	32.5	32.5	31.8	33.5	32.2	33.1	33.4	32.7

3. Average Hourly Earnings by Selected Industry: Maryland, 2009–2013

(Dollars, not seasonally adjusted)

Industry and year	January	February	March	April	May	June	July	August	September	October	November	December	Annual average
Total Private													
2009	25.23	25.82	25.24	25.32	24.83	25.00	24.99	25.46	25.49	25.57	25.99	26.06	25.42
2010	26.15	26.99	26.22	26.06	26.08	26.08	26.20	26.39	25.96	25.84	25.97	26.23	26.17
2011	26.54	26.43	25.91	25.78	25.79	25.41	25.47	25.35	25.48	25.79	25.75	25.99	25.80
2012	26.41	26.00	25.85	25.88	25.61	25.49	25.92	25.59	26.11	25.93	26.02	26.54	25.95
2013	26.70	26.36	26.45	26.43	26.34	26.64	26.26	26.44	27.00	26.94	27.00	27.38	26.66
Goods-Producing													
2009	24.51	24.27	24.32	24.26	23.98	24.04	23.89	24.21	24.39	24.67	24.81	24.74	24.34
2010	24.93	26.32	25.35	25.32	25.47	25.05	25.30	25.19	25.13	25.34	25.37	25.83	25.37
2011	25.79	25.67	25.34	25.53	25.54	25.41	25.76	25.57	25.67	25.52	25.34	25.75	25.57
2012	25.75	25.73	25.69	25.05	24.90	24.96	24.88	24.88	24.96	24.65	24.91	24.98	25.11
2013	25.39	25.08	25.53	25.63	25.73	26.25	25.96	26.25	26.24	25.82	26.08	26.71	25.89
Mining, Logging, and Construction													
2009	25.48	25.25	25.04	24.94	24.57	24.74	24.49	24.59	24.83	25.39	25.88	26.12	25.10
2010	26.04	27.62	26.72	26.29	26.07	25.92	26.33	26.02	26.13	26.37	26.49	27.35	26.42
2011	27.83	27.71	27.34	27.43	27.51	27.09	27.54	27.25	27.40	27.30	27.18	27.39	27.41
2012	27.33	27.35	27.53	27.24	27.25	27.26	27.05	27.06	27.22	26.82	27.11	27.24	27.20
2013	26.73	26.69	27.07	27.08	27.19	27.50	27.10	26.97	26.94	27.12	27.03	27.22	27.06
Manufacturing													
2009	23.30	23.04	23.41	23.40	23.22	23.16	23.13	23.72	23.86	23.81	23.55	23.14	23.39
2010	23.70	24.97	23.85	24.16	24.76	23.98	24.04	24.16	23.89	24.07	23.97	24.00	24.12
2011	23.55	23.38	23.10	23.33	23.18	23.29	23.50	23.45	23.58	23.35	23.00	23.70	23.37
2012	23.84	23.78	23.51	22.41	21.96	22.04	22.11	22.05	21.95	21.74	22.01	22.01	22.45
2013	23.68	23.08	23.67	23.77	23.77	24.63	24.43	25.24	25.28	24.07	24.71	26.00	24.36
Trade, Transportation, and Utilities													
2009	18.93	18.90	18.97	18.97	19.08	18.98	19.36	19.34	19.45	19.63	20.17	19.82	19.31
2010	20.31	20.96	20.32	20.34	20.09	19.61	19.94	20.19	20.10	19.62	19.55	19.44	20.03
2011	19.58	19.65	19.38	19.36	19.83	19.52	19.63	19.44	19.69	19.80	19.70	19.81	19.62
2012	19.53	19.15	19.00	18.69	18.50	18.80	19.35	18.86	19.56	19.41	19.14	19.68	19.14
2013	19.84	20.16	19.89	20.28	20.29	20.33	20.15	20.12	20.13	20.42	20.26	20.11	20.17
Financial Activities													
2009	28.97	29.12	28.68	28.03	28.12	27.57	28.69	30.10	29.02	28.86	29.52	28.83	28.80
2010	28.23	28.34	28.48	28.05	28.08	27.16	27.39	28.25	26.74	26.68	27.46	27.21	27.67
2011	26.61	26.72	26.28	25.52	26.04	26.15	25.94	26.30	25.40	26.12	25.88	27.09	26.17
2012	27.65	27.41	27.35	27.10	27.29	27.82	28.62	28.42	28.91	28.91	29.76	31.04	28.35
2013	31.15	31.68	31.45	31.23	31.39	31.43	32.01	32.29	32.49	32.05	32.57	32.96	31.90
Professional and Business Services													
2009	32.44	32.72	32.98	32.82	32.78	33.09	32.84	33.81	33.62	33.16	33.98	33.69	33.16
2010	33.43	34.78	33.54	33.68	34.44	33.77	33.71	34.30	33.97	33.82	34.46	35.06	34.08
2011	35.46	34.94	34.39	34.13	33.96	33.51	33.74	33.26	33.39	34.13	33.48	34.00	34.02
2012	34.84	33.55	32.91	33.20	33.14	32.49	33.39	32.77	33.75	33.63	33.59	34.86	33.51
2013	34.60	33.86	33.87	33.19	31.29	32.42	31.46	31.84	33.06	33.15	33.34	34.26	33.02
Education and Health Services													
2009	26.27	26.12	25.91	25.90	25.69	26.08	26.03	26.03	26.11	26.15	25.78	25.76	25.98
2010	25.73	25.81	25.75	25.89	25.73	25.84	26.09	25.46	25.37	25.54	25.22	25.87	25.69
2011	25.87	26.02	25.87	26.20	26.34	26.46	26.58	26.45	26.62	26.80	26.71	26.90	26.40
2012	27.24	27.25	27.35	27.34	27.37	27.66	27.75	27.83	28.11	27.94	28.03	28.10	27.67
2013	28.32	28.05	28.27	28.27	27.95	27.72	27.72	27.79	27.82	27.82	27.61	27.71	27.92
Leisure and Hospitality													
2009	14.62	14.71	14.43	14.95	14.49	14.10	14.22	13.96	14.34	14.66	14.98	15.37	14.54
2010	15.22	15.69	15.16	14.88	14.69	14.27	13.96	13.87	14.45	14.88	15.11	15.70	14.77
2011	15.55	15.63	15.33	15.14	14.94	14.57	14.28	14.18	14.43	14.55	15.10	14.99	14.86
2012	14.69	14.67	14.62	14.63	14.34	14.07	13.82	13.53	13.98	13.99	14.08	14.22	14.20
2013	13.94	14.07	13.86	13.84	14.05	13.86	13.56	13.64	14.91	14.92	14.97	15.19	14.22
Other Services													
2009	20.50	20.44	20.62	21.13	21.55	21.11	21.68	21.69	22.50	22.44	22.76	22.72	21.60
2010	22.39	22.62	22.55	21.70	21.73	21.60	22.06	21.44	21.29	21.40	22.14	22.47	21.94
2011	22.70	22.23	22.11	21.90	21.82	20.83	20.82	21.03	20.91	20.99	19.94	20.20	21.28
2012	20.21	19.88	20.49	20.67	20.20	20.26	20.48	21.05	21.57	21.04	21.73	21.68	20.77
2013	22.02	22.53	22.49	23.04	22.64	23.92	24.08	23.78	23.62	24.14	23.75	23.65	23.31

4. Average Weekly Earnings by Selected Industry: Maryland, 2009–2013

(Dollars, not seasonally adjusted)

Industry and year	January	February	March	April	May	June	July	August	September	October	November	December	Annual average
Total Private													
2009	865.39	890.79	868.26	863.41	851.67	860.00	864.65	891.10	884.50	879.61	899.25	893.86	876.99
2010	904.79	896.07	901.97	899.07	881.50	884.11	888.18	905.18	882.64	878.56	885.58	894.44	892.40
2011	910.32	903.91	888.71	886.83	897.49	879.19	883.81	869.51	873.96	894.91	872.93	881.06	887.52
2012	895.30	881.40	876.32	885.10	868.18	866.66	881.28	864.94	890.35	876.43	879.48	910.32	882.30
2013	891.78	883.06	886.08	893.33	890.29	908.42	892.84	901.60	934.20	910.57	920.70	933.66	903.77
Goods-Producing													
2009	941.18	936.82	938.75	921.88	916.04	913.52	917.38	932.09	917.06	937.46	930.38	940.12	929.79
2010	944.85	915.94	955.70	977.35	988.24	974.45	968.99	977.37	972.53	970.52	976.75	997.04	969.13
2011	992.92	985.73	983.19	993.12	1,006.28	1,003.70	1,007.22	999.79	975.46	990.18	990.79	1,014.55	994.67
2012	991.38	993.18	986.50	971.94	958.65	965.95	962.86	967.83	985.92	973.68	971.49	981.71	976.78
2013	969.90	963.07	977.80	981.63	990.61	987.00	981.29	1,015.88	1,023.36	999.23	1,030.16	1,025.66	996.77
Mining, Logging, and Construction													
2009	965.69	959.50	954.02	937.74	928.75	922.80	918.38	934.42	896.36	929.27	934.27	955.99	936.23
2010	950.46	914.22	961.92	993.76	985.45	990.14	982.11	988.76	990.33	983.60	996.02	1,020.16	980.18
2011	1,018.58	1,025.27	1,017.05	1,025.88	1,053.63	1,053.80	1,060.29	1,046.40	1,005.58	1,023.75	1,046.43	1,057.25	1,036.10
2012	1,027.61	1,031.10	1,015.86	1,021.50	1,027.33	1,033.15	1,022.49	1,033.69	1,061.58	1,045.98	1,038.31	1,054.19	1,033.60
2013	1,002.38	998.21	990.76	1,007.38	1,027.78	998.25	1,002.70	1,032.95	1,034.50	1,014.29	1,051.47	1,018.03	1,014.75
Manufacturing													
2009	911.03	907.78	917.67	903.24	898.61	903.24	918.26	929.82	944.86	947.64	927.87	920.97	919.23
2010	936.15	918.90	949.23	956.74	990.40	956.80	954.39	961.57	948.43	953.17	949.21	967.20	952.74
2011	960.84	939.88	944.79	951.86	945.74	936.26	940.00	938.00	938.48	948.01	920.00	957.48	944.15
2012	946.45	944.07	945.10	907.61	871.81	877.19	882.19	877.59	882.39	873.95	878.20	884.80	898.00
2013	928.26	916.28	961.00	948.42	936.54	972.89	952.77	991.93	1,008.67	977.24	1,000.76	1,037.40	969.53
Trade, Transportation, and Utilities													
2009	632.26	631.26	639.29	635.50	644.90	641.52	662.11	663.36	684.64	679.20	695.87	671.90	656.54
2010	686.48	668.62	694.94	699.70	697.12	684.39	693.91	704.63	689.43	667.08	652.97	659.02	683.02
2011	650.06	648.45	643.42	648.56	672.24	657.82	663.49	647.35	663.55	663.30	663.89	667.60	657.27
2012	644.49	641.53	640.30	641.07	629.00	635.44	659.84	633.70	663.08	654.12	645.02	678.96	646.93
2013	658.69	671.33	666.32	673.30	679.72	693.25	683.09	684.08	684.42	673.86	664.53	663.63	675.70
Financial Activities													
2009	1,045.82	1,057.06	1,032.48	995.07	1,006.70	987.01	1,041.45	1,101.66	1,056.33	1,056.28	1,089.29	1,043.65	1,042.56
2010	1,038.86	1,023.07	1,045.22	1,021.02	1,027.73	991.34	986.04	1,031.13	970.66	984.49	1,021.51	1,020.38	1,012.72
2011	1,021.82	1,015.36	1,006.52	979.97	994.73	1,001.55	980.53	996.77	990.60	1,036.96	1,014.50	1,059.22	1,007.55
2012	1,089.41	1,058.03	1,063.92	1,040.64	1,042.48	1,043.25	1,084.70	1,060.07	1,087.02	1,063.89	1,095.17	1,154.69	1,074.47
2013	1,124.52	1,156.32	1,147.93	1,143.02	1,142.60	1,166.05	1,174.77	1,178.59	1,218.38	1,179.44	1,205.09	1,212.93	1,170.73
Professional and Business Services													
2009	1,164.60	1,184.46	1,187.28	1,194.65	1,203.03	1,217.71	1,211.80	1,264.49	1,223.77	1,210.34	1,250.46	1,226.32	1,210.34
2010	1,226.88	1,238.17	1,240.98	1,236.06	1,253.62	1,219.10	1,206.82	1,251.95	1,226.32	1,234.43	1,275.02	1,297.22	1,243.92
2011	1,340.39	1,310.25	1,286.19	1,279.88	1,290.48	1,270.03	1,275.37	1,240.60	1,252.13	1,303.77	1,268.89	1,275.00	1,282.55
2012	1,306.50	1,248.06	1,227.54	1,238.36	1,209.61	1,185.89	1,225.41	1,186.27	1,231.88	1,203.95	1,215.96	1,282.85	1,229.82
2013	1,224.84	1,195.26	1,195.61	1,204.80	1,117.05	1,170.36	1,142.00	1,165.34	1,226.53	1,186.77	1,210.24	1,250.49	1,192.02
Education and Health Services													
2009	880.05	867.18	860.21	849.52	842.63	863.25	861.59	866.80	869.46	870.80	871.36	857.81	862.54
2010	864.53	864.64	854.90	854.37	856.81	857.89	874.02	858.00	842.28	842.82	839.83	851.12	855.48
2011	851.12	850.85	848.54	861.98	871.85	870.53	877.14	872.85	875.80	887.08	876.09	876.94	868.56
2012	901.64	896.53	897.08	888.55	889.53	915.55	918.53	929.52	938.87	922.02	916.58	921.68	910.34
2013	934.56	934.07	932.91	941.39	930.74	939.71	923.08	919.85	931.97	923.62	916.65	917.20	929.74
Leisure and Hospitality													
2009	369.89	383.93	378.07	385.71	386.88	383.52	389.63	383.90	372.84	372.36	384.99	387.32	380.95
2010	386.59	384.41	397.19	397.30	393.69	389.57	389.48	389.75	395.93	401.76	407.97	412.91	395.84
2011	412.08	422.01	415.44	408.78	409.36	397.76	395.56	388.53	379.51	391.40	397.13	392.74	399.73
2012	389.29	393.16	388.89	395.01	385.75	384.11	378.67	370.72	376.06	372.13	373.12	376.83	381.98
2013	356.86	365.82	357.59	355.69	363.90	367.29	364.76	360.10	390.64	381.95	383.23	384.31	369.72
Other Services													
2009	615.00	627.51	637.16	644.47	655.12	652.30	656.90	687.57	717.75	702.37	714.66	711.14	667.44
2010	703.05	692.17	728.37	720.44	736.65	738.72	741.22	718.24	732.38	740.44	754.97	763.98	730.60
2011	746.83	735.81	742.90	731.46	724.42	714.47	703.72	696.09	708.85	713.66	685.94	694.88	717.14
2012	687.14	665.98	678.22	696.58	670.64	674.66	688.13	698.86	722.60	704.84	723.61	715.44	693.72
2013	700.24	729.97	730.93	755.71	753.91	777.40	782.60	756.20	791.27	777.31	786.13	789.91	762.24

MASSACHUSETTS
At a Glance

Population:
    2000 census: 6,349,364
    2010 census: 6,547,629
    2013 estimate: 6,692,824

Percent change in population:
    2000–2010: 3.1%
    2010–2013: 2.2%

Percent change in total nonfarm employment:
    2000–2010: -3.3%
    2010–2013: 4.3%

Industry with the largest growth in employment, 2000–2013 (thousands):
    Education and Health Services, 185.3

Industry with the largest decline or smallest growth in employment, 2000–2013 (thousands):
    Manufacturing, -152.8

Civilian labor force:
    2000: 3,362,573
    2010: 3,470,522
    2013: 3,484,105

Unemployment rate and rank among states (lowest to highest):
    2000: 2.7%, 3rd
    2010: 8.3%, 23rd
    2013: 7.1%, 29th

Over-the-year change in unemployment rates:
    2010–2011: -1.0%
    2011–2012: -0.5%
    2012–2013: -0.3%

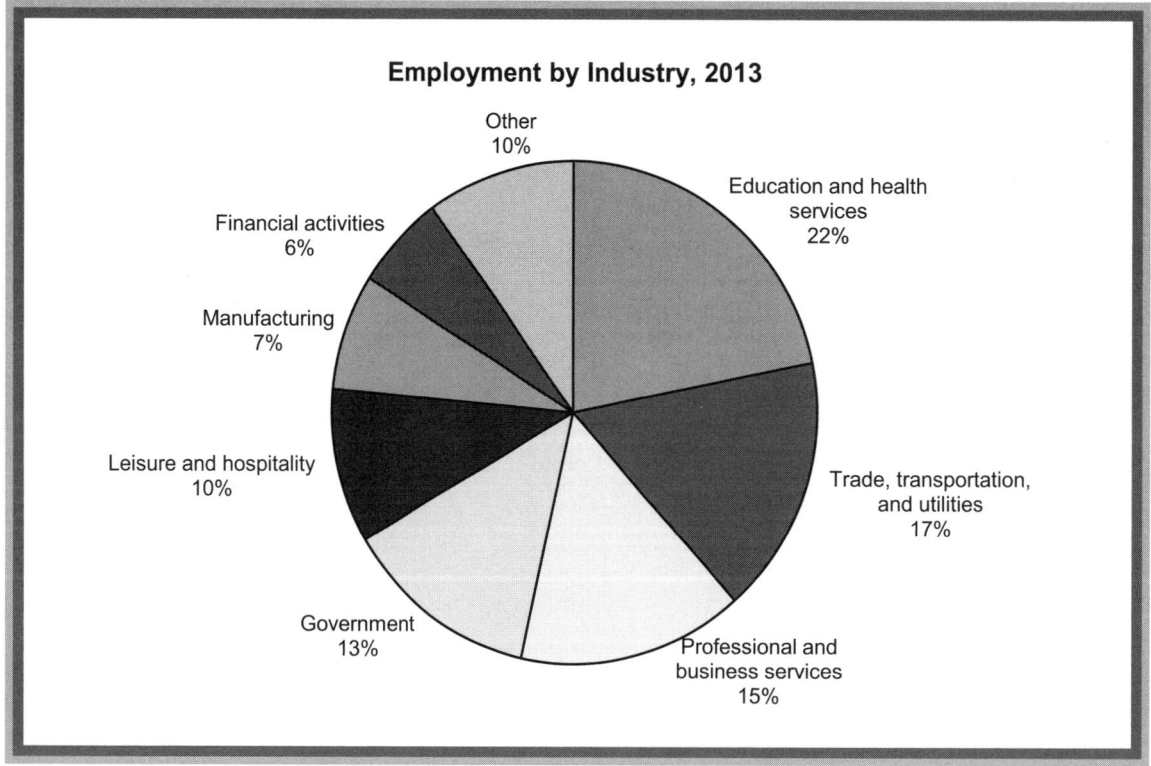

Employment by Industry, 2013

- Other 10%
- Education and health services 22%
- Financial activities 6%
- Manufacturing 7%
- Leisure and hospitality 10%
- Government 13%
- Professional and business services 15%
- Trade, transportation, and utilities 17%

1. Employment by Industry: Massachusetts, Selected Years, 2002–2013

(Numbers in thousands, not seasonally adjusted)

Industry and year	January	February	March	April	May	June	July	August	September	October	November	December	Annual average
Total Nonfarm													
2002	3,225.1	3,223.9	3,243.4	3,269.6	3,292.3	3,306.4	3,266.5	3,257.9	3,281.1	3,281.6	3,283.4	3,281.6	3,267.7
2003	3,168.5	3,158.4	3,171.3	3,206.0	3,232.6	3,244.2	3,209.0	3,199.6	3,229.5	3,230.8	3,232.9	3,227.7	3,209.2
2004	3,125.0	3,135.1	3,158.1	3,201.2	3,224.6	3,245.3	3,220.5	3,207.6	3,235.0	3,243.0	3,245.7	3,248.7	3,207.5
2005	3,138.9	3,156.0	3,164.2	3,218.6	3,241.2	3,262.5	3,238.6	3,229.4	3,257.7	3,258.8	3,269.5	3,273.3	3,225.7
2006	3,173.0	3,184.1	3,204.7	3,248.6	3,271.6	3,301.7	3,273.8	3,265.6	3,290.2	3,301.7	3,307.5	3,312.8	3,261.3
2007	3,215.8	3,223.6	3,238.8	3,280.8	3,315.3	3,345.8	3,313.2	3,306.5	3,324.9	3,337.9	3,344.7	3,342.1	3,299.1
2008	3,246.2	3,258.9	3,274.5	3,314.0	3,341.0	3,357.5	3,329.3	3,317.4	3,330.0	3,339.7	3,320.6	3,304.7	3,311.2
2009	3,181.2	3,180.3	3,177.2	3,209.1	3,225.3	3,232.1	3,200.1	3,184.8	3,207.2	3,223.1	3,217.0	3,219.8	3,204.8
2010	3,140.3	3,143.5	3,156.4	3,210.1	3,245.2	3,247.8	3,232.0	3,217.1	3,235.7	3,263.9	3,261.4	3,261.5	3,217.9
2011	3,162.9	3,176.5	3,191.8	3,248.7	3,268.4	3,283.9	3,278.4	3,262.4	3,291.9	3,306.7	3,304.2	3,304.8	3,256.7
2012	3,215.0	3,227.0	3,254.7	3,292.3	3,319.9	3,355.5	3,324.8	3,316.6	3,338.2	3,355.5	3,360.3	3,353.8	3,309.5
2013	3,257.2	3,273.7	3,299.0	3,344.1	3,377.1	3,398.4	3,368.5	3,364.7	3,379.9	3,408.0	3,403.9	3,397.3	3,356.0
Total Private													
2002	2,783.7	2,775.0	2,793.8	2,822.3	2,844.5	2,868.9	2,859.6	2,856.1	2,843.5	2,844.9	2,843.6	2,843.7	2,831.6
2003	2,738.8	2,721.9	2,734.7	2,769.4	2,795.6	2,816.1	2,811.8	2,808.5	2,799.2	2,802.2	2,803.4	2,798.7	2,783.4
2004	2,705.9	2,706.1	2,727.9	2,769.4	2,792.5	2,821.1	2,829.5	2,823.8	2,810.7	2,813.6	2,813.8	2,817.7	2,786.0
2005	2,717.6	2,722.6	2,730.9	2,784.1	2,805.2	2,835.5	2,843.6	2,841.6	2,831.7	2,824.8	2,832.8	2,838.6	2,800.8
2006	2,747.9	2,748.3	2,767.8	2,810.6	2,831.7	2,869.4	2,874.2	2,873.8	2,860.2	2,863.7	2,866.7	2,873.6	2,832.3
2007	2,785.9	2,783.9	2,798.0	2,838.8	2,870.6	2,909.9	2,911.7	2,911.6	2,891.2	2,896.1	2,900.7	2,898.9	2,866.4
2008	2,812.9	2,814.0	2,828.9	2,866.7	2,892.3	2,918.8	2,922.9	2,917.9	2,892.4	2,892.6	2,872.4	2,857.9	2,874.1
2009	2,745.4	2,732.1	2,729.6	2,756.1	2,775.1	2,793.1	2,794.7	2,787.2	2,772.6	2,775.8	2,770.0	2,770.2	2,766.8
2010	2,701.8	2,697.3	2,709.1	2,758.7	2,785.0	2,805.8	2,826.3	2,819.6	2,799.1	2,817.1	2,810.9	2,812.3	2,778.6
2011	2,730.1	2,731.3	2,746.2	2,803.2	2,821.0	2,847.9	2,876.5	2,869.0	2,855.6	2,863.6	2,860.5	2,859.0	2,822.0
2012	2,783.3	2,783.1	2,807.7	2,845.6	2,871.6	2,916.6	2,921.1	2,918.9	2,898.0	2,908.5	2,908.7	2,904.2	2,872.3
2013	2,823.4	2,822.6	2,846.6	2,888.6	2,920.0	2,956.9	2,964.6	2,966.5	2,942.4	2,960.0	2,953.5	2,946.2	2,915.9
Goods-Producing													
2002	490.0	483.7	485.9	491.6	497.4	501.2	494.2	496.1	493.4	491.5	488.7	481.3	491.3
2003	462.9	453.4	454.4	463.5	469.5	472.7	467.0	468.6	465.4	462.5	461.1	454.1	462.9
2004	436.7	433.5	439.5	450.5	457.8	464.3	462.6	465.0	461.9	457.9	456.7	452.4	453.2
2005	433.9	430.1	430.6	443.3	450.4	456.4	456.0	457.1	455.4	451.2	450.7	446.7	446.8
2006	431.1	428.3	430.8	441.4	446.1	452.5	451.1	451.9	449.0	445.9	442.7	439.8	442.6
2007	425.0	419.4	421.0	428.2	437.3	445.0	443.3	444.6	441.6	437.9	435.8	430.1	434.1
2008	414.3	410.0	412.4	420.0	426.3	431.1	430.7	430.6	425.8	421.6	414.6	405.1	420.2
2009	380.8	372.0	368.2	372.1	374.1	377.4	376.2	374.3	370.9	368.8	366.3	362.2	371.9
2010	348.8	343.9	346.3	355.9	362.4	368.4	371.9	371.0	368.5	368.7	366.9	362.6	361.3
2011	348.3	344.5	347.1	358.9	365.4	372.4	376.4	377.2	373.6	372.2	370.0	366.6	364.4
2012	355.3	352.0	356.1	363.6	368.2	376.5	377.7	378.1	375.1	375.7	374.3	371.1	368.6
2013	358.9	356.3	358.9	366.9	374.9	381.5	383.6	384.6	380.9	380.6	378.7	371.7	373.1
Service-Providing													
2002	2,735.1	2,740.2	2,757.5	2,778.0	2,794.9	2,805.2	2,772.3	2,761.8	2,787.7	2,790.1	2,794.7	2,800.3	2,776.5
2003	2,705.6	2,705.0	2,716.9	2,742.5	2,763.1	2,771.5	2,742.0	2,731.0	2,764.1	2,768.3	2,771.8	2,773.6	2,746.3
2004	2,688.3	2,701.6	2,718.6	2,750.7	2,766.8	2,781.0	2,757.9	2,742.6	2,773.1	2,785.1	2,789.0	2,796.3	2,754.3
2005	2,705.0	2,725.9	2,733.6	2,775.3	2,790.8	2,806.1	2,782.6	2,772.3	2,802.3	2,807.6	2,818.8	2,826.6	2,778.9
2006	2,741.9	2,755.8	2,773.9	2,807.2	2,825.5	2,849.2	2,822.7	2,813.7	2,841.2	2,855.8	2,864.8	2,873.0	2,818.7
2007	2,790.8	2,804.2	2,817.8	2,852.6	2,878.0	2,900.8	2,869.9	2,861.9	2,883.3	2,900.0	2,908.9	2,912.0	2,865.0
2008	2,831.9	2,848.9	2,862.1	2,894.0	2,914.7	2,926.4	2,898.6	2,886.8	2,904.2	2,918.1	2,906.0	2,899.6	2,890.9
2009	2,800.4	2,808.3	2,809.0	2,837.0	2,851.2	2,854.7	2,823.9	2,810.5	2,836.3	2,854.3	2,850.7	2,857.6	2,832.8
2010	2,791.5	2,799.6	2,810.1	2,854.2	2,882.8	2,879.4	2,860.1	2,846.1	2,867.2	2,895.2	2,894.5	2,898.9	2,856.6
2011	2,814.6	2,832.0	2,844.7	2,889.8	2,903.0	2,911.5	2,902.0	2,885.2	2,918.3	2,934.5	2,934.2	2,938.2	2,892.3
2012	2,859.7	2,875.0	2,898.6	2,928.7	2,951.7	2,979.0	2,947.1	2,938.5	2,963.1	2,979.8	2,986.0	2,982.7	2,940.8
2013	2,898.3	2,917.4	2,940.1	2,977.2	3,002.2	3,016.9	2,984.9	2,980.1	2,999.0	3,027.4	3,025.2	3,025.6	2,982.9
Mining and Logging													
2002	1.3	1.3	1.4	1.6	1.7	1.7	1.7	1.7	1.8	1.8	1.8	1.7	1.6
2003	1.5	1.5	1.5	1.7	1.8	1.9	1.9	1.9	2.0	2.0	2.0	1.9	1.8
2004	1.7	1.6	1.6	1.9	2.0	2.0	2.1	2.1	2.0	2.0	2.0	2.0	1.9
2005	1.8	1.7	1.7	2.0	2.1	2.1	2.1	2.1	2.1	2.0	2.0	1.8	2.0
2006	1.6	1.6	1.7	1.8	1.9	1.9	2.0	1.9	1.9	1.9	1.9	1.7	1.8
2007	1.4	1.3	1.4	1.5	1.7	1.8	1.7	1.7	1.7	1.6	1.6	1.5	1.6
2008	1.2	1.2	1.2	1.4	1.5	1.5	1.5	1.4	1.4	1.4	1.4	1.3	1.4
2009	1.1	1.1	1.1	1.3	1.4	1.4	1.4	1.4	1.4	1.4	1.4	1.3	1.3
2010	1.0	1.0	1.0	1.2	1.3	1.3	1.2	1.2	1.2	1.1	1.1	1.1	1.1
2011	0.9	0.9	0.9	1.1	1.2	1.2	1.2	1.2	1.2	1.2	1.1	1.1	1.1
2012	0.9	0.8	0.9	0.9	1.0	1.0	1.0	1.0	1.0	1.0	1.0	1.0	1.0
2013	0.8	0.8	0.9	1.0	1.0	1.0	1.0	1.1	1.1	1.1	1.0	1.0	1.0
Construction													
2002	128.4	125.8	128.8	137.8	144.3	147.0	148.6	149.4	146.6	147.5	145.9	139.3	140.8
2003	126.9	120.6	122.7	133.2	140.5	143.5	145.5	146.0	143.7	142.2	141.0	135.8	136.8
2004	122.5	120.1	124.8	134.6	141.8	146.3	148.6	148.8	146.5	144.6	143.4	139.2	138.4
2005	124.5	120.7	122.3	135.3	141.9	146.4	150.3	150.7	149.3	145.8	145.8	141.4	139.5
2006	129.2	126.6	129.3	140.1	144.4	148.3	150.2	150.4	147.7	145.4	142.5	138.7	141.1
2007	126.7	121.5	123.8	131.8	140.2	145.4	147.5	147.6	145.7	143.9	141.8	135.9	137.7
2008	123.4	120.4	123.1	130.7	136.7	139.9	142.4	141.6	138.7	136.1	131.7	124.8	132.5
2009	109.0	104.3	103.6	110.1	114.0	116.8	118.1	117.2	114.6	113.1	110.4	106.0	111.4
2010	96.1	92.3	94.5	103.3	108.7	112.8	116.3	115.5	114.0	113.2	111.5	107.3	107.1
2011	96.8	94.0	95.8	105.9	111.7	116.6	120.6	121.1	119.3	117.9	116.3	112.6	110.7
2012	103.3	100.4	103.8	111.5	115.5	120.4	123.5	123.9	122.0	122.5	121.3	118.0	115.5
2013	108.8	106.7	108.6	116.4	123.6	127.7	131.3	131.8	129.5	130.0	127.2	120.1	121.8

1. Employment by Industry: Massachusetts, Selected Years, 2002–2013—*Continued*

(Numbers in thousands, not seasonally adjusted)

Industry and year	January	February	March	April	May	June	July	August	September	October	November	December	Annual average
Manufacturing													
2002	360.3	356.6	355.7	352.2	351.4	352.5	343.9	345.0	345.0	342.2	341.0	340.3	348.8
2003	334.5	331.3	330.2	328.6	327.2	327.3	319.6	320.7	319.7	318.3	318.1	316.4	324.3
2004	312.5	311.8	313.1	314.0	314.0	316.0	311.9	314.1	313.4	311.3	311.3	311.2	312.9
2005	307.6	307.7	306.6	306.0	306.4	307.9	303.6	304.3	304.0	303.4	302.9	303.5	305.3
2006	300.3	300.1	299.8	299.5	299.8	302.3	298.9	299.6	299.4	298.6	298.3	299.4	299.7
2007	296.9	296.6	295.8	294.9	295.4	297.8	294.1	295.3	294.2	292.4	292.4	292.7	294.9
2008	289.7	288.4	288.1	287.9	288.1	289.7	286.8	287.6	285.7	284.1	281.5	279.0	286.4
2009	270.7	266.6	263.5	260.7	258.7	259.2	256.7	255.7	254.9	254.3	254.5	254.9	259.2
2010	251.7	250.6	250.8	251.4	252.4	254.3	254.4	254.3	253.3	254.4	254.3	254.2	253.0
2011	250.6	249.6	250.4	251.9	252.5	254.6	254.6	254.9	253.1	253.1	252.6	252.9	252.6
2012	251.1	250.8	251.4	251.2	251.7	255.1	253.2	253.2	252.1	252.2	252.0	252.1	252.2
2013	249.3	248.8	249.4	249.5	250.3	252.8	251.3	251.7	250.3	249.5	250.5	250.6	250.3
Trade, Transportation, and Utilities													
2002	577.4	567.4	569.5	572.3	577.4	586.5	580.5	578.1	579.6	581.0	589.3	598.8	579.8
2003	568.8	560.2	562.2	566.2	571.6	579.6	572.6	571.7	574.2	578.2	587.2	593.5	573.8
2004	568.2	561.4	563.0	564.4	569.4	577.2	571.4	569.1	568.7	575.6	584.2	593.0	572.1
2005	565.2	559.8	559.0	563.7	568.2	575.4	569.6	569.4	568.5	570.9	579.9	590.5	570.0
2006	566.5	555.3	558.0	562.6	566.8	575.1	569.4	569.8	570.4	573.9	584.1	593.3	570.4
2007	567.3	557.2	558.8	560.7	568.5	577.5	571.1	569.3	568.9	574.1	585.7	592.2	570.9
2008	570.9	558.9	560.2	563.1	568.8	576.1	570.2	569.2	566.8	568.6	571.7	576.7	568.4
2009	547.4	536.7	533.1	533.1	539.3	547.4	539.7	538.5	539.6	543.9	550.7	556.8	542.2
2010	537.4	528.3	528.9	535.5	542.0	548.8	545.7	545.4	541.8	548.6	555.6	565.1	543.6
2011	541.7	534.6	534.6	541.0	545.1	552.0	549.6	549.5	548.4	552.6	560.2	567.7	548.1
2012	545.9	535.7	537.9	540.6	548.5	558.4	552.9	552.7	550.8	555.6	565.8	571.2	551.3
2013	548.6	539.7	541.4	546.4	554.2	563.6	558.1	558.6	556.5	561.8	570.6	579.9	556.6
Wholesale Trade													
2002	136.4	135.7	136.2	136.0	136.5	137.7	136.9	136.6	135.8	135.4	135.5	136.3	136.3
2003	135.0	134.5	134.6	134.6	134.9	135.7	135.8	135.5	134.6	134.7	135.3	135.8	135.1
2004	133.6	133.6	134.7	134.3	134.1	135.0	134.4	133.9	132.7	132.6	132.5	132.7	133.7
2005	131.4	131.2	131.1	132.1	133.1	134.2	134.6	135.0	134.6	135.3	136.1	136.8	133.8
2006	134.9	134.5	135.0	136.2	136.6	138.1	138.3	138.7	137.9	138.1	138.2	138.8	137.1
2007	136.7	136.4	136.9	136.9	137.5	139.1	139.1	138.9	137.8	138.4	138.3	138.5	137.9
2008	137.0	135.9	136.3	136.8	137.1	138.1	137.6	136.8	135.6	134.9	134.0	133.6	136.1
2009	130.0	128.5	127.7	127.2	127.0	127.5	126.6	125.8	124.4	124.2	123.5	123.2	126.3
2010	121.4	120.8	121.0	121.5	122.5	123.3	123.7	123.5	122.1	122.9	122.7	122.7	122.3
2011	121.1	120.9	120.7	122.0	122.1	122.5	123.3	122.6	121.2	121.2	120.8	120.8	121.6
2012	119.8	119.5	120.0	121.1	121.7	122.9	123.1	123.2	121.9	122.6	122.5	122.4	121.7
2013	121.2	121.0	121.4	122.2	122.7	123.9	124.6	124.4	123.5	124.2	124.0	124.6	123.1
Retail Trade													
2002	354.8	346.0	347.8	349.5	353.2	360.1	359.3	358.0	355.5	356.6	365.9	375.4	356.8
2003	348.4	341.1	342.7	346.5	350.7	357.3	354.9	355.1	353.3	357.4	366.2	372.4	353.8
2004	352.2	345.8	346.1	346.7	350.9	357.1	356.2	355.4	352.2	357.7	367.1	376.1	355.3
2005	352.3	347.2	346.5	349.5	352.2	357.3	355.1	355.4	351.0	353.4	361.7	370.3	354.3
2006	351.1	340.5	342.3	344.9	347.4	352.5	350.4	350.6	346.5	350.4	360.8	368.1	350.5
2007	347.3	338.1	338.8	340.3	346.2	352.0	350.2	349.3	344.8	349.5	361.7	366.8	348.8
2008	349.8	339.5	340.0	341.8	345.8	351.1	350.4	351.1	344.7	348.0	353.0	357.3	347.7
2009	335.7	327.3	324.6	325.1	330.4	336.9	334.7	335.4	332.1	336.5	344.2	348.9	334.3
2010	334.6	326.6	327.1	331.8	335.9	340.8	341.8	342.8	336.1	341.8	349.2	356.2	338.7
2011	338.7	332.0	331.9	336.1	339.0	344.0	344.9	346.5	341.7	346.2	354.3	360.4	343.0
2012	343.3	333.8	335.1	336.4	342.3	349.3	348.1	348.6	343.1	347.0	357.6	360.8	345.5
2013	343.6	334.9	336.0	339.3	344.9	351.3	349.8	351.4	345.2	349.3	358.5	364.9	347.4
Transportation and Utilities													
2002	86.2	85.7	85.5	86.8	87.7	88.7	84.3	83.5	88.3	89.0	87.9	87.1	86.7
2003	85.4	84.6	84.9	85.1	86.0	86.6	81.9	81.1	86.3	86.1	85.7	85.3	84.9
2004	82.4	82.0	82.2	83.4	84.4	85.1	80.8	79.8	83.8	85.3	84.6	84.2	83.2
2005	81.5	81.4	81.4	82.1	82.9	83.9	79.9	79.0	82.9	82.2	82.1	83.4	81.9
2006	80.5	80.3	80.7	81.5	82.8	84.5	80.7	80.5	86.0	85.4	85.1	86.4	82.9
2007	83.3	82.7	83.1	83.5	84.8	86.4	81.8	81.1	86.3	86.2	85.7	86.9	84.3
2008	84.1	83.5	83.9	84.5	85.9	86.9	82.2	81.3	86.5	85.7	84.7	85.8	84.6
2009	81.7	80.9	80.8	80.8	81.9	83.0	78.4	77.3	83.1	83.2	83.0	84.7	81.6
2010	81.4	80.9	80.8	82.2	83.6	84.7	80.2	79.1	83.6	83.9	83.7	86.2	82.5
2011	81.9	81.7	82.0	82.9	84.0	85.5	81.4	80.4	85.5	85.2	85.1	86.5	83.5
2012	82.8	82.4	82.8	83.1	84.5	86.2	81.7	80.9	85.8	86.0	85.7	88.0	84.2
2013	83.8	83.8	84.0	84.9	86.6	88.4	83.7	82.8	87.8	88.3	88.1	90.4	86.1
Information													
2002	103.5	102.7	102.5	100.4	100.0	99.9	99.5	98.8	96.9	96.9	96.7	96.9	99.6
2003	93.7	93.1	93.0	91.9	91.7	92.4	91.0	90.9	89.7	89.3	89.2	89.2	91.3
2004	87.4	86.8	87.5	86.8	87.2	87.8	87.8	87.7	86.9	87.0	87.6	87.7	87.4
2005	86.5	86.7	86.7	86.4	86.6	87.3	88.0	87.6	86.9	86.2	86.6	87.1	86.9
2006	86.5	86.5	86.5	85.9	86.4	87.3	87.1	87.5	86.5	87.0	87.4	88.0	86.9
2007	86.4	86.7	87.6	88.2	87.9	88.9	89.8	89.9	89.9	88.8	88.8	89.4	88.5
2008	87.7	88.7	89.4	90.7	90.6	90.5	89.7	89.5	88.8	87.7	87.6	87.8	89.1
2009	86.8	85.4	85.5	85.2	85.1	85.8	85.2	86.0	87.0	86.0	86.1	85.9	85.8
2010	84.8	84.8	85.0	85.2	85.7	86.7	85.8	85.4	84.7	83.6	83.8	84.3	85.0
2011	83.3	83.4	83.8	83.8	84.3	85.5	86.8	83.2	85.4	85.5	85.3	85.7	84.7
2012	85.4	85.0	85.3	85.7	86.3	88.1	89.3	88.6	86.0	86.1	85.6	85.5	86.4
2013	84.7	84.7	84.7	85.0	85.4	86.9	87.5	87.3	86.2	86.2	86.7	87.9	86.1

1. Employment by Industry: Massachusetts, Selected Years, 2002–2013—*Continued*

(Numbers in thousands, not seasonally adjusted)

Industry and year	January	February	March	April	May	June	July	August	September	October	November	December	Annual average
Financial Activities													
2002	230.2	228.9	228.3	226.8	227.2	229.7	230.8	230.3	226.9	226.4	225.6	226.4	228.1
2003	224.7	223.2	223.5	223.5	224.0	226.2	226.5	226.4	222.5	221.1	221.0	221.6	223.7
2004	218.8	218.6	218.9	219.3	219.6	222.2	223.3	222.6	219.8	217.9	217.4	218.5	219.7
2005	217.5	217.1	217.6	218.2	219.6	222.9	225.6	225.9	223.7	222.0	222.7	224.4	221.4
2006	220.6	220.4	220.8	221.5	222.8	225.8	227.9	227.4	225.0	224.2	224.3	225.9	223.9
2007	223.9	223.8	223.8	223.9	224.6	227.3	227.9	227.6	223.7	222.4	221.8	222.6	224.4
2008	220.5	220.2	220.5	220.7	221.2	223.7	224.8	224.3	221.1	220.2	219.2	219.3	221.3
2009	216.4	215.0	214.4	213.6	213.7	215.2	215.2	214.4	211.0	209.9	209.6	210.1	213.2
2010	207.4	206.8	206.5	206.6	207.6	209.3	210.6	210.3	207.4	207.1	206.6	207.6	207.8
2011	205.0	204.6	204.6	205.5	205.8	208.1	210.0	210.0	207.3	206.6	205.8	206.3	206.6
2012	204.2	204.3	204.3	204.5	205.7	208.8	209.4	209.6	206.3	206.0	205.7	206.3	206.3
2013	204.0	204.2	204.8	204.7	206.0	208.6	209.7	210.0	206.4	207.5	206.8	207.1	206.7
Professional and Business Services													
2002	448.6	445.3	448.4	455.8	456.9	460.7	458.9	458.5	455.0	453.5	452.2	449.8	453.6
2003	433.5	428.3	429.5	438.9	441.0	444.8	446.3	446.0	443.4	444.6	445.5	445.4	440.6
2004	431.7	431.6	435.6	448.4	450.8	457.7	460.4	461.2	459.3	458.5	458.7	459.3	451.1
2005	443.1	443.3	445.4	459.5	460.8	467.9	468.8	469.5	468.3	466.5	468.5	467.8	460.8
2006	453.0	454.7	458.4	469.1	471.8	480.4	479.3	481.0	477.5	478.2	479.0	478.2	471.7
2007	461.9	463.8	467.2	480.2	484.7	492.4	490.4	492.5	487.5	488.3	489.8	489.5	482.4
2008	475.7	477.0	478.6	488.4	491.6	497.6	496.9	496.0	491.7	490.3	485.4	480.0	487.4
2009	461.5	457.1	455.1	461.1	460.1	462.8	461.6	460.5	456.8	457.0	456.0	455.4	458.8
2010	447.4	447.4	449.5	462.3	464.2	469.1	473.5	472.6	467.2	472.5	471.2	469.8	463.9
2011	460.3	461.2	461.3	477.8	478.0	484.3	489.6	488.1	485.4	488.6	488.5	486.1	479.1
2012	472.2	472.6	478.8	490.0	492.4	501.6	502.6	502.7	498.6	501.0	501.8	497.2	492.6
2013	484.8	487.9	490.4	502.8	506.6	513.9	516.1	517.0	510.7	515.3	514.3	511.6	506.0
Education and Health Services													
2002	565.5	577.0	581.0	583.4	576.7	564.3	561.7	560.3	575.4	587.5	594.1	595.2	576.8
2003	578.0	588.0	591.6	593.6	586.0	572.6	571.8	569.3	585.3	596.9	601.6	601.2	586.3
2004	585.5	596.9	600.3	601.9	594.0	581.3	581.8	578.8	593.0	605.1	609.2	609.1	594.7
2005	592.0	605.1	606.9	610.5	603.1	590.5	591.1	589.1	603.5	616.4	621.8	621.7	604.3
2006	606.8	619.7	624.2	625.7	619.5	609.0	609.0	606.4	621.9	634.4	639.3	640.0	621.3
2007	629.3	640.6	642.4	648.2	642.0	629.2	631.6	630.1	643.2	657.3	661.4	662.2	643.1
2008	647.0	660.6	664.6	667.5	659.7	646.9	649.9	647.8	660.1	674.4	678.3	678.9	661.3
2009	663.8	675.9	679.6	682.6	674.9	660.3	664.5	662.7	675.5	687.7	692.5	693.6	676.1
2010	681.9	693.6	697.0	696.7	690.6	673.3	676.7	675.0	689.9	703.2	707.3	707.2	691.0
2011	692.0	704.4	708.6	710.7	703.2	685.7	691.2	689.2	705.4	716.4	721.5	721.6	704.2
2012	707.8	721.1	725.6	725.1	718.6	703.8	704.1	703.0	718.8	731.6	736.6	737.0	719.4
2013	721.3	731.2	737.3	737.4	730.0	716.2	716.7	714.7	730.4	744.0	746.9	744.5	730.9
Leisure and Hospitality													
2002	254.1	255.4	262.0	275.6	291.3	306.8	312.4	312.7	299.5	291.1	279.9	278.0	284.9
2003	262.2	260.9	264.5	275.6	294.4	308.3	315.6	315.8	302.1	293.6	281.4	277.2	287.6
2004	263.4	262.8	267.5	282.2	296.8	311.6	321.4	319.1	305.1	295.4	283.9	280.9	290.8
2005	265.2	265.9	269.2	285.3	298.8	314.1	322.0	321.3	307.2	294.6	285.3	282.2	292.6
2006	267.6	267.9	272.1	286.7	299.7	317.2	326.8	326.6	311.3	302.0	292.1	289.9	296.7
2007	276.2	276.0	279.8	291.1	305.6	325.4	331.7	332.2	315.6	307.4	297.1	292.4	302.5
2008	279.5	280.7	284.5	297.1	313.8	329.0	334.6	335.2	318.1	310.2	296.4	291.2	305.9
2009	272.9	274.2	276.9	290.5	308.6	321.2	327.9	327.1	313.8	304.7	291.5	288.6	299.8
2010	278.7	277.4	279.9	298.8	313.4	327.6	336.7	335.7	321.2	315.7	302.1	298.2	307.1
2011	284.1	282.8	288.7	306.2	319.0	336.4	346.5	346.2	330.0	322.0	309.6	305.1	314.7
2012	295.2	295.0	300.6	315.4	329.9	352.9	357.3	357.7	340.3	330.9	317.4	314.4	325.6
2013	302.1	299.8	308.3	323.2	339.6	358.9	363.6	365.6	347.5	340.0	324.4	319.1	332.7
Other Services													
2002	114.4	114.6	116.2	116.4	117.6	119.8	121.6	121.3	116.8	117.0	117.1	117.3	117.5
2003	115.0	114.8	116.0	116.2	117.4	119.5	121.0	119.8	116.6	116.0	116.4	116.5	117.1
2004	114.2	114.5	115.6	115.9	116.9	119.0	120.8	120.3	116.0	116.2	116.1	116.8	116.9
2005	114.2	114.6	115.5	117.2	117.7	121.0	122.5	121.7	118.2	117.0	117.3	118.2	117.9
2006	115.8	115.5	117.0	117.7	118.6	122.1	123.6	123.2	118.6	118.1	117.8	118.5	118.9
2007	115.9	116.4	117.4	118.3	120.0	124.2	125.9	125.4	120.8	119.9	120.3	120.5	120.4
2008	117.3	117.9	118.7	119.2	120.3	123.9	126.1	125.3	120.0	119.6	119.2	118.9	120.5
2009	115.8	115.8	116.8	117.9	119.3	123.0	124.4	123.7	118.0	117.8	117.3	117.6	119.0
2010	115.4	115.1	116.0	117.7	119.1	122.6	125.4	124.2	118.4	117.7	117.4	117.5	118.9
2011	115.4	115.8	117.5	119.3	120.2	123.5	126.4	125.6	120.1	119.7	119.6	119.9	120.3
2012	117.3	117.4	119.1	120.7	122.0	126.5	127.8	126.5	122.1	121.6	121.5	121.5	122.0
2013	119.0	118.8	120.8	122.2	123.3	127.3	129.3	128.7	123.8	124.6	125.1	124.4	123.9
Government													
2002	441.4	448.9	449.6	447.3	447.8	437.5	406.9	401.8	437.6	436.7	439.8	437.9	436.1
2003	429.7	436.5	436.6	436.6	437.0	428.1	397.2	391.1	430.3	428.6	429.5	429.0	425.9
2004	419.1	429.0	430.2	431.8	432.1	424.2	391.0	383.8	424.3	429.4	431.9	431.0	421.5
2005	421.3	433.4	433.3	434.5	436.0	427.0	395.0	387.8	426.0	434.0	436.7	434.7	425.0
2006	425.1	435.8	436.9	438.0	439.9	432.3	399.6	391.8	430.0	438.0	440.8	439.2	429.0
2007	429.9	439.7	440.8	442.0	444.7	435.9	401.5	394.9	433.7	441.8	444.0	443.2	432.7
2008	433.3	444.9	445.6	447.3	448.7	438.7	406.4	399.5	437.6	447.1	448.2	446.8	437.0
2009	435.8	448.2	447.6	453.0	450.2	439.0	405.4	397.6	434.6	447.3	447.0	449.6	437.9
2010	438.5	446.2	447.3	451.4	460.2	442.0	405.7	397.5	436.6	446.8	450.5	449.2	439.3
2011	432.8	445.2	445.6	445.5	447.4	436.0	401.9	393.4	436.3	443.1	443.7	445.8	434.7
2012	431.7	443.9	447.0	446.7	448.3	438.9	403.7	397.7	440.2	447.0	451.6	449.6	437.2
2013	433.8	451.1	452.4	455.5	457.1	441.5	403.9	398.2	437.5	448.0	450.4	451.1	440.0

2. Average Weekly Hours by Selected Industry: Massachusetts, 2009–2013

(Not seasonally adjusted)

Industry and year	January	February	March	April	May	June	July	August	September	October	November	December	Annual average
Total Private													
2009	33.4	33.6	33.6	33.4	33.4	33.4	33.6	33.7	33.5	33.4	33.8	33.7	33.5
2010	33.6	33.5	33.6	33.8	33.9	33.8	33.8	34.0	33.5	33.4	33.3	33.4	33.6
2011	32.9	32.9	33.0	33.1	33.2	33.1	33.2	33.2	33.2	33.1	33.1	33.1	33.1
2012	32.9	32.7	32.9	33.1	32.9	33.0	33.3	33.0	33.2	32.8	33.0	33.4	33.0
2013	32.7	33.0	32.9	33.0	33.1	33.3	33.3	33.5	33.7	33.3	33.2	33.6	33.2
Goods-Producing													
2009	38.8	38.7	38.8	38.7	38.5	39.1	38.5	39.0	38.4	39.1	40.0	40.0	39.0
2010	40.0	39.3	39.8	40.0	40.3	40.3	39.8	40.0	39.8	39.6	39.5	40.2	39.9
2011	38.7	39.6	40.1	39.8	40.0	40.2	39.7	39.8	39.9	39.2	39.6	40.0	39.7
2012	39.5	39.3	39.3	39.3	39.0	39.1	39.0	38.8	39.0	38.9	39.2	39.8	39.2
2013	39.3	39.2	39.3	39.3	39.5	39.6	39.2	39.8	39.8	39.9	39.4	40.0	39.5
Construction													
2009	37.6	37.3	37.0	38.0	38.4	38.2	38.8	39.1	37.7	36.8	37.5	37.6	37.9
2010	38.1	37.2	37.5	38.0	38.5	38.2	38.4	38.6	37.8	36.9	36.4	36.1	37.7
2011	34.0	33.2	34.1	34.6	35.7	36.0	36.3	36.4	36.8	35.4	36.7	37.3	35.6
2012	36.3	36.3	36.6	37.0	37.1	37.5	37.8	37.8	38.0	36.8	37.1	38.0	37.2
2013	38.0	37.1	37.3	38.0	38.6	38.2	38.0	38.9	38.3	38.2	37.3	37.7	38.0
Manufacturing													
2009	39.4	39.1	39.4	38.8	38.4	39.4	38.2	38.4	38.1	39.5	40.5	40.5	39.1
2010	40.2	40.0	40.4	40.2	40.4	40.3	39.9	40.2	40.0	40.1	40.2	40.5	40.2
2011	39.9	39.9	40.2	39.9	39.7	40.1	39.4	39.8	39.9	39.7	39.9	40.3	39.9
2012	40.1	39.9	39.9	39.8	39.5	39.4	39.3	39.1	39.3	39.8	40.0	40.5	39.7
2013	39.7	40.0	40.1	39.8	39.8	40.2	39.7	40.1	40.4	40.4	40.2	40.9	40.1
Trade, Transportation, and Utilities													
2009	32.6	32.9	33.1	32.8	33.0	33.0	33.2	33.0	33.1	32.7	33.2	33.4	33.0
2010	32.7	32.9	33.3	33.2	33.4	33.3	33.3	33.6	33.2	32.8	32.7	33.2	33.1
2011	31.6	32.1	32.5	32.5	32.3	32.3	32.4	32.6	33.0	32.4	33.1	33.0	32.5
2012	32.3	32.4	32.7	32.9	32.9	33.2	32.8	32.6	33.1	32.6	33.0	33.0	32.8
2013	32.0	32.3	32.3	32.5	32.9	32.8	33.0	33.3	33.6	33.1	32.7	33.6	32.8
Information													
2009	35.7	36.6	35.6	35.5	34.6	34.1	34.8	35.0	34.6	34.5	35.4	34.0	35.0
2010	34.9	35.9	36.0	36.3	36.0	35.6	36.1	36.4	36.3	36.3	36.7	36.3	36.1
2011	36.2	35.4	35.3	34.9	35.0	34.2	34.9	35.2	35.1	36.2	35.5	35.8	35.3
2012	36.8	35.9	36.0	37.2	35.9	35.5	37.2	36.1	37.5	36.3	36.5	37.4	36.5
2013	35.8	35.6	35.9	35.2	35.1	36.9	36.0	35.9	36.7	35.8	36.1	37.4	36.0
Financial Activities													
2009	37.3	37.0	37.1	36.7	35.8	36.6	36.8	37.6	37.4	36.8	37.4	37.0	37.0
2010	36.8	36.5	36.5	36.3	36.6	36.7	36.4	36.8	35.9	35.8	35.5	36.5	36.4
2011	36.6	35.7	35.6	35.8	36.6	36.0	35.4	35.6	36.0	36.3	35.8	35.6	35.9
2012	36.5	35.4	35.5	35.8	35.6	35.7	36.0	35.6	36.0	35.7	35.5	36.1	35.8
2013	35.4	35.9	36.0	35.9	35.8	36.8	36.1	36.2	37.1	36.2	36.2	36.9	36.2
Professional and Business Services													
2009	35.5	35.9	35.9	35.6	36.0	35.8	35.7	35.8	35.6	35.8	36.2	35.5	35.8
2010	35.8	35.7	35.9	36.0	36.3	35.9	35.8	36.1	35.9	35.5	34.9	34.8	35.7
2011	35.5	34.6	34.9	35.3	35.8	35.4	35.5	35.8	35.7	36.2	35.8	36.0	35.5
2012	35.6	35.5	35.4	36.2	35.6	35.4	36.2	35.4	35.6	34.7	34.9	35.8	35.5
2013	34.7	35.4	35.2	35.4	35.5	36.3	35.7	36.0	36.5	35.9	36.0	36.4	35.8
Education and Health Services													
2009	31.3	31.5	31.5	31.6	31.6	31.6	31.9	32.0	31.9	31.7	31.8	31.8	31.7
2010	31.9	31.8	31.8	31.9	31.8	31.7	31.9	31.9	31.5	31.7	31.7	31.4	31.7
2011	31.4	31.0	31.0	31.1	31.0	31.0	31.2	30.9	30.7	30.5	30.3	30.0	30.8
2012	30.1	30.0	30.2	30.5	30.5	30.5	30.8	31.0	31.1	31.1	31.4	31.8	30.8
2013	31.6	31.8	31.6	31.7	31.7	31.8	31.9	31.9	32.0	31.9	32.0	32.0	31.8
Leisure and Hospitality													
2009	25.8	25.4	25.5	25.5	26.0	26.0	26.7	26.9	26.6	26.2	25.9	25.8	26.1
2010	25.4	25.5	25.4	26.2	26.5	26.5	27.0	26.9	26.0	26.0	25.6	25.6	26.1
2011	24.8	25.7	25.6	26.0	26.1	25.9	26.6	26.6	26.2	26.1	25.8	25.8	26.0
2012	25.6	25.4	26.0	25.8	26.1	26.2	26.8	26.7	26.3	25.7	25.4	25.4	26.0
2013	24.8	24.6	25.1	25.4	25.6	25.5	26.4	26.3	26.0	25.4	24.8	24.4	25.4
Other Services													
2009	32.9	33.3	33.0	33.2	32.7	32.3	32.6	33.0	32.0	32.0	32.2	32.2	32.6
2010	32.1	32.5	32.3	32.5	33.0	32.6	32.9	33.4	32.4	32.4	32.8	32.5	32.6
2011	31.7	31.6	31.2	31.2	31.1	30.8	31.5	31.4	30.7	30.7	30.3	30.6	31.1
2012	30.4	30.3	30.6	30.7	30.2	30.5	31.3	31.0	30.3	29.9	29.6	29.7	30.4
2013	28.8	28.8	28.3	28.0	27.9	27.3	28.3	28.8	27.7	27.5	27.4	27.7	28.0

3. Average Hourly Earnings by Selected Industry: Massachusetts, 2009–2013

(Dollars, not seasonally adjusted)

Industry and year	January	February	March	April	May	June	July	August	September	October	November	December	Annual average
Total Private													
2009	26.81	27.15	27.14	26.98	26.65	26.50	26.46	26.59	26.77	26.67	27.04	27.18	26.83
2010	27.10	27.26	27.30	27.05	26.99	26.86	26.99	27.05	27.07	27.12	27.21	27.37	27.11
2011	27.78	27.49	27.37	27.46	27.52	27.25	27.42	27.21	27.66	28.09	27.98	28.10	27.61
2012	28.45	28.31	28.12	28.43	27.99	27.78	27.91	27.68	28.12	28.01	28.06	28.67	28.12
2013	28.73	28.94	28.86	28.78	28.60	28.82	28.57	28.63	29.18	29.09	29.24	29.51	28.91
Goods-Producing													
2009	28.71	29.12	28.99	28.97	28.53	28.81	28.89	29.54	29.78	29.48	29.68	30.34	29.24
2010	30.47	30.76	31.38	30.25	30.04	29.63	29.76	29.87	29.61	29.41	29.23	29.50	29.98
2011	29.68	29.50	29.24	29.24	29.16	28.76	29.25	29.35	29.38	29.65	29.60	29.74	29.38
2012	29.67	29.34	29.20	29.55	29.43	29.56	29.61	29.57	29.84	29.74	29.44	29.81	29.57
2013	29.45	30.00	29.90	30.08	30.15	29.94	30.15	30.24	30.18	30.13	30.42	30.57	30.11
Construction													
2009	31.99	32.21	32.43	31.97	31.44	31.45	31.27	32.61	31.84	31.97	32.38	33.55	32.07
2010	33.50	34.15	34.11	33.38	32.93	32.79	33.00	33.16	33.12	33.52	33.64	33.98	33.41
2011	33.81	33.77	33.42	33.13	32.98	32.80	33.03	33.03	33.46	33.18	33.33	33.86	33.30
2012	34.62	34.06	33.79	33.46	33.44	33.41	33.52	33.51	33.61	33.57	33.46	33.62	33.65
2013	33.01	34.02	33.67	33.62	33.45	33.35	33.25	33.60	33.44	33.17	33.98	34.43	33.57
Manufacturing													
2009	27.19	27.19	26.89	27.05	26.65	27.10	27.25	27.61	28.39	28.02	28.18	28.66	27.51
2010	28.76	28.76	28.52	28.70	28.63	28.06	28.27	28.00	27.86	27.95	27.95	27.97	28.28
2011	28.17	28.06	27.81	27.78	27.59	27.06	27.64	27.79	27.67	28.31	28.10	28.10	27.84
2012	27.80	27.59	27.46	27.82	27.59	27.72	27.73	27.66	28.03	27.96	27.61	28.11	27.76
2013	27.92	28.01	28.04	28.18	28.33	28.11	28.47	28.44	28.53	28.57	28.69	28.82	28.34
Trade, Transportation, and Utilities													
2009	23.23	23.19	23.13	23.03	22.98	22.53	22.88	22.83	22.68	22.22	22.48	22.49	22.80
2010	22.75	22.82	22.65	22.65	22.70	22.62	23.12	23.13	22.94	22.65	22.72	22.58	22.78
2011	22.77	22.42	22.46	22.50	22.50	22.39	22.43	22.26	22.44	22.47	22.38	21.65	22.38
2012	22.36	22.32	22.37	22.75	22.73	22.60	22.73	22.42	22.54	22.38	22.29	22.61	22.51
2013	23.38	23.32	23.39	23.39	23.18	23.47	23.60	23.46	23.80	24.12	24.07	24.14	23.62
Information													
2009	34.71	35.22	35.06	34.53	34.74	34.63	34.18	34.68	34.22	33.94	34.57	35.41	34.66
2010	35.41	35.91	36.05	35.57	35.68	35.87	35.65	35.71	35.93	35.56	35.74	35.76	35.74
2011	35.58	36.06	36.27	36.05	37.43	36.48	37.21	37.81	39.02	39.85	41.44	40.32	37.82
2012	41.94	41.64	41.25	41.00	39.55	40.15	40.85	40.23	41.07	41.55	41.11	42.17	41.04
2013	42.17	42.65	42.51	41.72	42.38	42.48	42.90	43.79	43.24	42.90	43.41	43.51	42.82
Financial Activities													
2009	30.74	31.28	31.22	31.39	31.32	31.45	31.21	31.29	30.93	31.44	31.92	31.80	31.33
2010	31.78	31.87	31.79	31.77	31.74	31.76	32.39	31.90	32.11	31.81	32.26	32.85	32.00
2011	33.89	33.20	33.21	33.01	32.76	33.11	33.30	33.21	33.76	34.31	34.45	35.00	33.60
2012	34.91	35.08	34.68	35.12	34.76	34.30	34.00	34.49	34.89	34.36	34.64	35.07	34.69
2013	34.66	34.95	33.65	34.19	34.00	35.02	34.14	34.38	35.35	34.67	34.00	34.24	34.44
Professional and Business Services													
2009	34.21	34.75	35.17	34.83	34.35	33.87	33.93	33.96	34.42	34.11	34.73	34.87	34.43
2010	34.35	34.68	34.62	34.39	34.50	34.54	34.75	34.83	34.37	34.86	35.20	35.22	34.69
2011	35.85	35.20	35.08	34.99	34.94	34.47	34.87	34.18	34.80	35.32	35.06	35.76	35.04
2012	36.33	36.09	35.73	36.31	35.86	35.73	36.08	35.24	35.92	35.62	35.81	36.85	35.96
2013	36.54	36.48	36.61	36.46	36.29	36.51	36.37	36.09	37.01	36.88	36.86	37.58	36.64
Education and Health Services													
2009	24.68	25.20	25.19	25.16	24.75	24.84	24.80	24.76	24.96	24.99	25.19	25.32	24.99
2010	24.90	25.07	25.03	25.23	25.12	25.06	25.05	25.24	25.55	25.84	25.83	26.23	25.35
2011	26.22	26.59	26.28	26.85	27.10	27.10	27.38	27.06	27.40	27.92	27.60	27.96	27.12
2012	27.93	27.78	27.62	27.76	27.11	26.93	27.12	27.11	27.45	27.45	27.58	28.31	27.52
2013	28.34	28.49	28.74	28.54	28.34	28.64	28.32	28.61	29.03	28.63	28.99	29.02	28.64
Leisure and Hospitality													
2009	15.74	15.76	15.67	15.47	15.72	15.54	15.39	15.40	15.68	15.62	15.80	15.94	15.64
2010	15.60	15.53	15.48	15.25	15.33	15.12	15.12	15.18	15.17	15.45	15.44	15.41	15.33
2011	15.34	15.02	15.08	15.05	15.09	14.88	14.83	14.85	15.11	15.29	15.17	15.25	15.07
2012	15.08	15.10	15.18	15.14	15.16	14.82	14.62	14.77	14.94	14.90	15.01	15.27	14.99
2013	15.21	15.38	15.39	15.45	15.32	15.21	15.12	15.13	15.44	15.55	15.49	15.73	15.36
Other Services													
2009	21.71	21.80	21.66	21.63	21.44	21.07	20.94	21.00	21.99	22.35	22.20	22.34	21.67
2010	22.30	22.41	22.36	22.31	22.27	22.26	22.07	21.87	22.51	22.09	21.85	22.23	22.21
2011	22.51	22.09	22.12	22.34	22.61	22.03	21.27	21.13	22.09	22.09	22.05	22.24	22.04
2012	22.66	22.73	22.85	22.91	22.73	22.34	21.91	21.84	22.33	22.30	22.22	22.27	22.42
2013	22.48	22.64	22.13	22.04	22.14	21.91	20.93	20.91	22.06	21.94	21.71	22.27	21.92

4. Average Hourly Earnings by Selected Industry: Massachusetts, 2009–2013

(Dollars, not seasonally adjusted)

Industry and year	January	February	March	April	May	June	July	August	September	October	November	December	Annual average
Total Private													
2009	895.45	912.24	911.90	901.13	890.11	885.10	889.06	896.08	896.80	890.78	913.95	915.97	898.81
2010	910.56	913.21	917.28	914.29	914.96	907.87	912.26	919.70	906.85	905.81	906.09	914.16	910.90
2011	913.96	904.42	903.21	908.93	913.66	901.98	910.34	903.37	918.31	929.78	926.24	930.11	913.89
2012	936.01	925.74	925.15	941.03	920.87	916.74	929.40	913.44	933.58	918.73	925.98	957.58	927.96
2013	939.47	955.02	949.49	949.74	946.66	959.71	951.38	959.11	983.37	968.70	970.77	991.54	959.81
Goods-Producing													
2009	1,113.95	1,126.94	1,124.81	1,121.14	1,098.41	1,126.47	1,112.27	1,152.06	1,143.55	1,152.67	1,187.20	1,213.60	1,140.36
2010	1,218.80	1,208.87	1,248.92	1,210.00	1,210.61	1,194.09	1,184.45	1,194.80	1,178.48	1,164.64	1,154.59	1,185.90	1,196.20
2011	1,148.62	1,168.20	1,172.52	1,163.75	1,166.40	1,156.15	1,161.23	1,168.13	1,172.26	1,162.28	1,172.16	1,189.60	1,166.39
2012	1,171.97	1,153.06	1,147.56	1,161.32	1,147.77	1,155.80	1,154.79	1,147.32	1,163.76	1,156.89	1,154.05	1,186.44	1,159.14
2013	1,157.39	1,176.00	1,175.07	1,182.14	1,190.93	1,185.62	1,181.88	1,203.55	1,201.16	1,202.19	1,198.55	1,222.80	1,189.35
Construction													
2009	1,202.82	1,201.43	1,199.91	1,214.86	1,207.30	1,201.39	1,213.28	1,275.05	1,200.37	1,176.50	1,214.25	1,261.48	1,215.45
2010	1,276.35	1,270.38	1,279.13	1,268.44	1,267.81	1,252.58	1,267.20	1,279.98	1,251.94	1,236.89	1,224.50	1,226.68	1,259.56
2011	1,149.54	1,121.16	1,139.62	1,146.30	1,177.39	1,180.80	1,198.99	1,202.29	1,231.33	1,174.57	1,223.21	1,262.98	1,185.48
2012	1,256.71	1,236.38	1,236.71	1,238.02	1,240.62	1,252.88	1,267.06	1,266.68	1,277.18	1,235.38	1,241.37	1,277.56	1,251.78
2013	1,254.38	1,262.14	1,255.89	1,277.56	1,291.17	1,273.97	1,263.50	1,307.04	1,280.75	1,267.09	1,267.45	1,298.01	1,275.66
Manufacturing													
2009	1,071.29	1,063.13	1,059.47	1,049.54	1,023.36	1,067.74	1,040.95	1,060.22	1,081.66	1,106.79	1,141.29	1,160.73	1,075.64
2010	1,156.15	1,150.40	1,152.21	1,153.74	1,156.65	1,130.82	1,127.97	1,125.60	1,114.40	1,120.80	1,123.59	1,132.79	1,136.86
2011	1,123.98	1,119.59	1,117.96	1,108.42	1,095.32	1,085.11	1,089.02	1,106.04	1,104.03	1,123.91	1,121.19	1,132.43	1,110.82
2012	1,114.78	1,100.84	1,095.65	1,107.24	1,089.81	1,092.17	1,089.79	1,081.51	1,101.58	1,112.81	1,104.40	1,138.46	1,102.07
2013	1,108.42	1,120.40	1,124.40	1,121.56	1,127.53	1,130.02	1,130.26	1,140.44	1,152.61	1,154.23	1,153.34	1,178.74	1,136.43
Trade, Transportation, and Utilities													
2009	757.30	762.95	765.60	755.38	758.34	743.49	759.62	753.39	750.71	726.59	746.34	751.17	752.40
2010	743.93	750.78	754.25	751.98	758.18	753.25	769.90	777.17	761.61	742.92	742.94	749.66	754.02
2011	719.53	719.68	729.95	731.25	726.75	723.20	726.73	725.68	740.52	728.03	740.78	714.45	727.35
2012	722.23	723.17	731.50	748.48	747.82	750.32	745.54	730.89	746.07	729.59	735.57	746.13	738.33
2013	748.16	753.24	755.50	760.18	762.62	769.82	778.80	781.22	799.68	798.37	787.09	811.10	774.74
Information													
2009	1,239.15	1,289.05	1,248.14	1,225.82	1,202.00	1,180.88	1,189.46	1,213.80	1,184.01	1,170.93	1,223.78	1,203.94	1,213.10
2010	1,235.81	1,289.17	1,297.80	1,291.19	1,284.48	1,276.97	1,286.97	1,299.84	1,304.26	1,290.83	1,311.66	1,298.09	1,290.21
2011	1,288.00	1,276.52	1,280.33	1,258.15	1,310.05	1,247.62	1,298.63	1,330.91	1,369.60	1,442.57	1,471.12	1,443.46	1,335.05
2012	1,543.39	1,494.88	1,485.00	1,525.20	1,419.85	1,425.33	1,519.62	1,452.30	1,540.13	1,508.27	1,500.52	1,577.16	1,497.96
2013	1,509.69	1,518.34	1,526.11	1,468.54	1,487.54	1,567.51	1,544.40	1,572.06	1,586.91	1,535.82	1,567.10	1,627.27	1,541.52
Financial Activities													
2009	1,146.60	1,157.36	1,158.26	1,152.01	1,121.26	1,151.07	1,148.53	1,176.50	1,156.78	1,156.99	1,193.81	1,176.60	1,159.21
2010	1,169.50	1,163.26	1,160.34	1,153.25	1,161.68	1,165.59	1,179.00	1,173.92	1,152.75	1,138.80	1,145.23	1,199.03	1,164.80
2011	1,240.37	1,185.24	1,182.28	1,181.76	1,199.02	1,191.96	1,178.82	1,182.28	1,215.36	1,245.45	1,233.31	1,246.00	1,206.24
2012	1,274.22	1,241.83	1,231.14	1,257.30	1,237.46	1,224.51	1,224.00	1,227.84	1,256.04	1,226.65	1,229.72	1,266.03	1,241.90
2013	1,226.96	1,254.71	1,211.40	1,227.42	1,217.20	1,288.74	1,232.45	1,244.56	1,311.49	1,255.05	1,230.80	1,263.46	1,246.73
Professional and Business Services													
2009	1,214.46	1,247.53	1,262.60	1,239.95	1,236.60	1,212.55	1,211.30	1,215.77	1,225.35	1,221.14	1,257.23	1,237.89	1,232.59
2010	1,229.73	1,238.08	1,242.86	1,238.04	1,252.35	1,239.99	1,244.05	1,257.36	1,233.88	1,237.53	1,228.48	1,225.66	1,238.43
2011	1,272.68	1,217.92	1,224.29	1,235.15	1,250.85	1,220.24	1,237.89	1,223.64	1,242.36	1,278.58	1,255.15	1,287.36	1,243.92
2012	1,293.35	1,281.20	1,264.84	1,314.42	1,276.62	1,264.84	1,306.10	1,247.50	1,278.75	1,236.01	1,249.77	1,319.23	1,276.58
2013	1,267.94	1,291.39	1,288.67	1,290.68	1,288.30	1,325.31	1,298.41	1,299.24	1,350.87	1,323.99	1,326.96	1,367.91	1,311.71
Education and Health Services													
2009	772.48	793.80	793.49	795.06	782.10	784.94	791.12	792.32	796.22	792.18	801.04	805.18	792.18
2010	794.31	797.23	795.95	804.84	798.82	794.40	799.10	805.16	804.83	819.13	818.81	823.62	803.60
2011	823.31	824.29	814.68	835.04	840.10	840.10	854.26	836.15	841.18	851.56	836.28	838.80	835.30
2012	840.69	833.40	834.12	846.68	826.86	821.37	835.30	840.41	853.70	853.70	866.01	900.26	847.62
2013	895.54	905.98	908.18	904.72	898.38	910.75	903.41	912.66	928.96	913.30	927.68	928.64	910.75
Leisure and Hospitality													
2009	406.09	400.30	399.59	394.49	408.72	404.04	410.91	414.26	417.09	409.24	409.22	411.25	408.20
2010	396.24	396.02	393.19	399.55	406.25	400.68	408.24	408.34	394.42	401.70	395.26	394.50	400.11
2011	380.43	386.01	386.05	391.30	393.85	385.39	394.48	395.01	395.88	399.07	391.39	393.45	391.82
2012	386.05	383.54	394.68	390.61	395.68	388.28	391.82	394.36	392.92	382.93	381.25	387.86	389.74
2013	377.21	378.35	386.29	392.43	392.19	387.86	399.17	397.92	401.44	394.97	384.15	383.81	390.14
Other Services													
2009	714.26	725.94	714.78	718.12	701.09	680.56	682.64	693.00	703.68	715.20	714.84	719.35	706.44
2010	715.83	728.33	722.23	725.08	734.91	725.68	726.10	730.46	729.32	715.72	716.68	722.48	724.05
2011	713.57	698.04	690.14	697.01	703.17	678.52	670.01	663.48	678.16	678.16	668.12	680.54	685.44
2012	688.86	688.72	699.21	703.34	686.45	681.37	685.78	677.04	676.60	666.77	657.71	661.42	681.57
2013	647.42	652.03	626.28	617.12	617.71	598.14	592.32	602.21	611.06	603.35	594.85	616.88	613.76

MICHIGAN
At a Glance

Population:
    2000 census: 9,938,823
    2010 census: 9,883,640
    2013 estimate: 9,895,622

Percent change in population:
    2000–2010: -0.6%
    2010–2013: 0.1%

Percent change in total nonfarm employment:
    2000–2010: -17.4%
    2010–2013: 6.2%

Industry with the largest growth in employment, 2000–2013 (thousands):
    Education and Health Services, 135.4

Industry with the largest decline or smallest growth in employment, 2000–2013 (thousands):
    Manufacturing, -342.0

Civilian labor force:
    2000: 5,143,916
    2010: 4,753,649
    2013: 4,707,124

Unemployment rate and rank among states (lowest to highest):
    2000: 3.7%, 22nd
    2010: 12.7%, 50th
    2013: 8.8%, 47th

Over-the-year change in unemployment rates:
    2010–2011: -2.3%
    2011–2012: -1.3%
    2012–2013: -0.3%

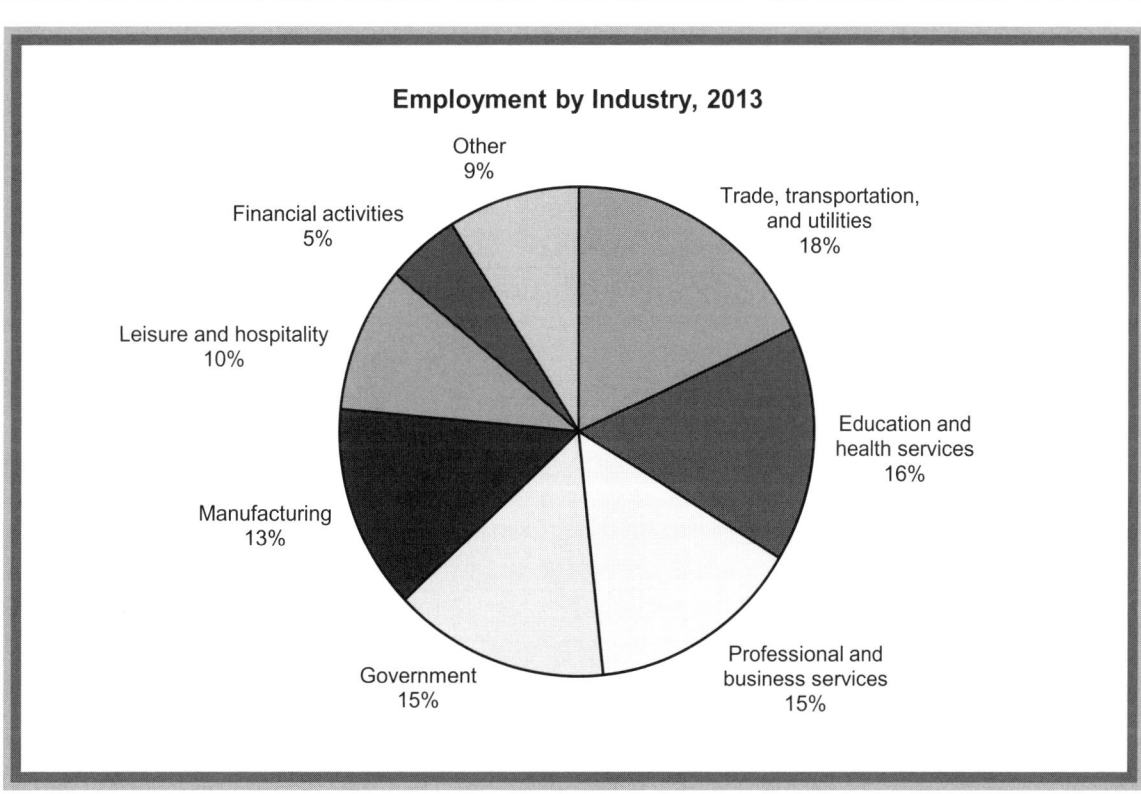

Employment by Industry, 2013

Other
9%

Trade, transportation,
and utilities
18%

Financial activities
5%

Leisure and hospitality
10%

Education and
health services
16%

Manufacturing
13%

Government
15%

Professional and
business services
15%

1. Employment by Industry: Michigan, Selected Years, 2002–2013

(Numbers in thousands, not seasonally adjusted)

Industry and year	January	February	March	April	May	June	July	August	September	October	November	December	Annual average
Total Nonfarm													
2002	4,388.5	4,409.4	4,436.1	4,469.1	4,532.5	4,547.3	4,446.1	4,484.6	4,526.9	4,536.5	4,538.6	4,527.1	4,486.9
2003	4,353.0	4,356.3	4,369.8	4,395.5	4,468.6	4,475.7	4,339.8	4,392.9	4,444.8	4,467.8	4,465.2	4,461.6	4,415.9
2004	4,302.7	4,312.9	4,338.9	4,397.4	4,451.1	4,449.7	4,325.1	4,382.1	4,448.1	4,459.6	4,463.3	4,456.5	4,399.0
2005	4,289.3	4,323.0	4,339.1	4,397.8	4,448.8	4,440.2	4,325.0	4,366.0	4,444.0	4,433.2	4,443.1	4,426.7	4,389.7
2006	4,265.5	4,279.8	4,303.1	4,341.0	4,385.3	4,394.1	4,249.3	4,294.8	4,361.7	4,344.4	4,353.9	4,345.1	4,326.5
2007	4,185.6	4,212.3	4,233.3	4,261.7	4,325.4	4,330.0	4,214.1	4,256.2	4,302.3	4,293.9	4,305.7	4,292.8	4,267.8
2008	4,145.6	4,158.7	4,159.0	4,172.8	4,225.6	4,243.8	4,112.5	4,147.6	4,180.2	4,168.6	4,139.2	4,092.1	4,162.1
2009	3,863.6	3,881.9	3,872.1	3,895.7	3,910.9	3,882.6	3,793.6	3,818.3	3,876.3	3,895.9	3,886.3	3,869.0	3,870.5
2010	3,751.8	3,768.3	3,780.9	3,838.6	3,895.8	3,907.7	3,845.8	3,851.3	3,913.4	3,941.4	3,942.3	3,922.3	3,863.3
2011	3,831.6	3,846.5	3,874.1	3,926.0	3,972.4	3,985.9	3,931.1	3,952.2	4,012.4	4,033.5	4,038.2	4,017.1	3,951.8
2012	3,929.5	3,948.4	3,976.4	4,015.4	4,060.9	4,068.8	4,006.9	4,026.4	4,076.4	4,094.8	4,102.7	4,092.8	4,033.3
2013	4,004.1	4,029.3	4,051.0	4,072.3	4,142.0	4,153.6	4,069.7	4,102.8	4,148.8	4,170.2	4,166.0	4,144.3	4,104.5
Total Private													
2002	3,699.7	3,703.6	3,726.9	3,772.0	3,837.9	3,872.5	3,827.3	3,864.9	3,842.0	3,821.7	3,820.7	3,814.4	3,800.3
2003	3,662.9	3,647.1	3,661.6	3,691.4	3,767.8	3,802.2	3,725.8	3,782.3	3,767.7	3,752.9	3,751.3	3,753.1	3,730.5
2004	3,616.5	3,611.7	3,634.8	3,696.2	3,755.0	3,781.1	3,719.5	3,778.8	3,769.3	3,756.3	3,756.6	3,755.0	3,719.2
2005	3,611.8	3,625.6	3,640.2	3,700.2	3,756.9	3,776.9	3,727.6	3,767.0	3,766.2	3,737.9	3,743.1	3,733.8	3,715.6
2006	3,593.8	3,589.4	3,607.8	3,653.3	3,704.7	3,740.2	3,655.9	3,704.9	3,696.8	3,659.5	3,665.2	3,662.7	3,661.2
2007	3,525.4	3,534.4	3,550.3	3,587.4	3,652.0	3,683.2	3,622.8	3,662.1	3,647.5	3,622.6	3,633.0	3,624.4	3,612.1
2008	3,496.4	3,493.2	3,492.1	3,504.6	3,567.6	3,601.9	3,519.5	3,549.0	3,525.4	3,497.9	3,467.5	3,430.1	3,512.1
2009	3,210.9	3,216.9	3,206.1	3,226.4	3,251.0	3,243.5	3,204.0	3,228.8	3,230.6	3,232.0	3,221.9	3,212.9	3,223.8
2010	3,110.1	3,112.9	3,125.0	3,180.1	3,238.6	3,274.0	3,261.1	3,275.3	3,283.4	3,295.4	3,294.1	3,282.3	3,227.7
2011	3,206.6	3,210.3	3,235.8	3,288.4	3,348.9	3,376.5	3,366.1	3,390.6	3,392.8	3,401.5	3,403.5	3,391.1	3,334.3
2012	3,313.7	3,320.3	3,348.1	3,387.8	3,445.0	3,472.6	3,451.4	3,470.7	3,464.1	3,471.9	3,476.5	3,475.3	3,424.8
2013	3,401.0	3,413.3	3,436.0	3,455.2	3,536.1	3,566.5	3,521.8	3,557.1	3,543.3	3,553.6	3,545.6	3,530.0	3,505.0
Goods-Producing													
2002	947.6	954.3	956.6	963.5	980.2	991.8	973.3	989.5	981.0	974.9	968.2	957.0	969.8
2003	910.4	900.3	902.1	904.7	928.9	942.2	895.5	934.6	928.3	920.9	918.5	912.1	916.5
2004	874.3	869.1	877.1	895.2	910.4	917.2	875.7	920.3	917.9	912.2	908.8	900.8	898.3
2005	852.7	859.9	858.7	871.7	889.5	895.0	861.5	888.0	889.6	885.3	883.6	869.3	875.4
2006	828.4	824.0	826.5	843.5	854.1	862.8	813.9	847.8	842.7	828.4	827.0	816.5	834.6
2007	771.7	780.0	782.7	789.8	804.0	814.4	785.4	810.9	804.3	787.2	790.4	779.2	791.7
2008	744.7	742.2	731.0	729.1	743.1	768.4	722.7	746.8	739.4	727.1	714.6	690.5	733.3
2009	597.5	608.3	602.9	601.8	591.7	586.6	584.9	603.2	604.5	605.2	596.3	588.0	597.6
2010	567.2	564.3	567.2	585.3	600.9	613.5	616.5	617.1	627.1	630.2	625.8	616.1	602.6
2011	601.2	601.7	607.0	623.3	641.2	655.6	655.4	666.4	665.7	666.9	665.7	659.5	642.4
2012	644.0	642.5	649.4	659.2	674.1	685.7	687.2	691.9	690.7	690.2	686.0	682.7	673.6
2013	665.9	667.3	672.5	674.9	696.6	708.5	702.1	716.0	713.5	715.2	711.4	701.4	695.4
Service-Providing													
2002	3,440.9	3,455.1	3,479.5	3,505.6	3,552.3	3,555.5	3,472.8	3,495.1	3,545.9	3,561.6	3,570.4	3,570.1	3,517.1
2003	3,442.6	3,456.0	3,467.7	3,490.8	3,539.7	3,533.5	3,444.3	3,458.3	3,516.5	3,546.9	3,546.7	3,549.5	3,499.4
2004	3,428.4	3,443.8	3,461.8	3,502.2	3,540.7	3,532.5	3,449.4	3,461.8	3,530.2	3,547.4	3,554.5	3,555.7	3,500.7
2005	3,436.6	3,463.1	3,480.4	3,526.1	3,559.3	3,545.2	3,463.5	3,478.0	3,554.4	3,547.9	3,559.5	3,557.4	3,514.3
2006	3,437.1	3,455.8	3,476.6	3,497.5	3,531.2	3,531.3	3,435.4	3,447.0	3,519.0	3,516.0	3,526.9	3,528.6	3,491.9
2007	3,413.9	3,432.3	3,450.6	3,471.9	3,521.4	3,515.6	3,428.7	3,445.3	3,498.0	3,506.7	3,515.3	3,513.6	3,476.1
2008	3,400.9	3,416.5	3,428.0	3,443.7	3,482.5	3,475.4	3,389.8	3,400.8	3,440.8	3,441.5	3,424.6	3,401.6	3,428.8
2009	3,266.1	3,273.6	3,269.2	3,293.9	3,319.2	3,296.0	3,208.7	3,215.1	3,271.8	3,290.7	3,290.0	3,281.0	3,272.9
2010	3,184.6	3,204.0	3,213.7	3,253.3	3,294.9	3,294.2	3,229.3	3,234.2	3,286.3	3,311.2	3,316.5	3,306.2	3,260.7
2011	3,230.4	3,244.8	3,267.1	3,302.7	3,331.2	3,330.3	3,275.7	3,285.8	3,346.7	3,367.2	3,372.5	3,357.6	3,309.3
2012	3,285.5	3,305.9	3,327.0	3,356.2	3,386.8	3,383.1	3,319.7	3,334.5	3,385.7	3,404.6	3,416.7	3,410.1	3,359.7
2013	3,338.2	3,362.0	3,378.5	3,397.4	3,445.4	3,445.1	3,367.6	3,386.8	3,435.3	3,455.0	3,454.6	3,442.9	3,409.1
Mining and Logging													
2002	8.0	8.0	8.1	8.4	8.9	9.0	9.0	8.8	8.9	8.9	8.8	8.5	8.6
2003	7.6	7.6	7.6	7.9	8.6	8.9	8.3	8.3	8.3	8.4	8.2	7.9	8.1
2004	7.4	7.4	7.6	8.0	8.4	8.4	8.6	8.7	8.7	8.5	8.3	7.9	8.2
2005	7.7	7.7	7.7	8.4	8.8	9.0	9.0	8.9	8.6	8.6	8.4	8.0	8.4
2006	7.4	7.5	7.5	7.9	8.2	8.5	8.5	8.5	8.3	8.3	8.1	7.6	8.0
2007	7.2	7.2	7.0	7.3	7.8	8.2	8.2	8.1	8.0	7.9	7.7	7.4	7.7
2008	7.1	7.1	7.1	7.5	8.0	8.2	8.4	8.4	8.3	8.2	8.1	7.8	7.9
2009	6.7	6.9	6.3	6.5	6.8	7.1	7.2	7.2	7.2	7.2	7.0	6.8	6.9
2010	6.6	6.5	6.2	6.8	7.2	7.5	7.6	7.6	7.5	7.5	7.3	7.0	7.1
2011	6.7	6.7	6.7	7.0	7.5	7.8	7.9	7.9	7.8	7.9	7.8	7.6	7.4
2012	7.4	7.5	7.3	7.7	8.0	8.0	8.0	8.1	8.2	8.1	7.9	7.7	7.8
2013	7.5	7.5	7.5	7.4	8.0	8.2	8.3	8.4	8.3	8.3	8.2	7.9	8.0
Construction													
2002	182.5	178.0	180.6	192.5	207.1	213.2	216.2	216.0	210.9	207.8	201.7	190.8	199.8
2003	169.1	163.3	164.8	178.9	196.7	204.8	208.8	208.3	204.8	203.1	197.8	190.5	190.9
2004	167.1	163.7	167.7	183.5	196.0	204.2	208.9	208.1	205.5	204.2	200.8	191.5	191.8
2005	168.3	164.9	167.7	183.4	195.5	203.5	207.0	205.2	201.8	199.1	194.3	182.8	189.5
2006	162.9	159.1	162.1	174.9	185.8	192.9	192.9	191.6	188.1	183.9	177.4	169.1	178.4
2007	151.1	145.6	150.1	158.4	172.0	179.3	180.8	180.8	178.2	174.7	169.1	160.0	166.7
2008	143.2	138.2	139.7	146.8	160.5	166.4	166.6	166.6	163.7	159.8	151.1	138.9	153.5
2009	119.6	116.6	115.8	124.1	133.5	136.8	137.5	136.3	133.0	132.3	127.2	118.5	127.6
2010	102.8	100.0	103.4	114.5	123.7	129.1	133.6	134.5	133.8	134.5	129.2	120.4	121.6
2011	108.0	104.9	107.4	114.5	126.1	133.9	138.9	139.6	137.6	135.7	132.3	124.6	125.3
2012	113.2	110.1	114.0	122.1	129.9	135.4	137.9	138.7	138.5	137.6	133.1	127.9	128.2
2013	118.3	115.4	117.2	120.8	135.4	140.3	143.7	145.1	143.6	143.8	137.4	127.2	132.4

1. Employment by Industry: Michigan, Selected Years, 2002–2013—*Continued*

(Numbers in thousands, not seasonally adjusted)

Industry and year	January	February	March	April	May	June	July	August	September	October	November	December	Annual average
Manufacturing													
2002	757.1	768.3	767.9	762.6	764.2	769.6	748.1	764.7	761.2	758.2	757.7	757.7	761.4
2003	733.7	729.4	729.7	717.9	723.6	728.5	678.4	718.0	715.2	709.4	712.5	713.7	717.5
2004	699.8	698.0	701.8	703.7	706.0	704.6	658.2	703.5	703.7	699.5	699.7	701.4	698.3
2005	676.7	687.3	683.3	679.9	685.2	682.5	645.5	673.9	679.2	677.6	680.9	678.5	677.5
2006	658.1	657.4	656.9	660.7	660.1	661.4	612.5	647.7	646.3	636.2	641.5	639.8	648.2
2007	613.4	627.2	625.6	624.1	624.2	626.9	596.4	622.0	618.1	604.6	613.6	611.8	617.3
2008	594.4	596.9	584.2	574.8	574.6	593.8	547.7	571.8	567.4	559.1	555.4	543.8	572.0
2009	471.2	484.8	480.8	471.2	451.4	442.7	440.2	459.7	464.3	465.7	462.1	462.7	463.1
2010	457.8	457.8	457.6	464.0	470.0	476.9	475.3	475.0	485.8	488.2	489.1	488.7	473.9
2011	486.5	490.1	492.9	501.8	507.6	513.9	508.6	518.9	520.3	522.7	525.6	527.3	509.7
2012	523.4	524.9	528.1	529.4	536.2	542.3	541.3	545.1	544.0	544.5	545.0	547.1	537.6
2013	540.1	544.4	547.8	546.7	553.2	560.0	550.1	562.5	561.6	563.1	565.8	566.3	555.1
Trade, Transportation, and Utilities													
2002	826.1	814.9	820.4	825.6	838.6	843.5	834.7	838.3	836.8	832.8	845.8	854.0	834.3
2003	807.8	798.8	800.7	803.8	816.9	822.8	814.9	820.3	819.5	823.8	833.4	841.8	817.0
2004	796.9	789.9	792.0	800.7	812.7	817.1	811.5	814.1	808.1	813.7	826.4	834.3	809.8
2005	791.0	785.3	788.1	796.9	807.8	811.9	811.0	811.7	806.8	806.1	818.8	825.7	805.1
2006	784.5	776.1	780.3	787.3	797.5	803.6	796.8	798.8	795.0	795.4	809.1	816.0	795.0
2007	779.2	770.1	772.1	777.1	789.4	794.4	789.6	791.1	787.3	787.0	800.6	806.5	787.0
2008	771.9	763.7	765.8	764.6	776.1	780.6	774.1	774.1	769.4	765.2	769.2	769.2	770.3
2009	723.6	714.0	709.8	711.6	720.4	722.6	714.3	717.3	713.0	713.1	721.3	725.4	717.2
2010	695.0	687.9	690.8	699.4	710.3	716.6	717.1	716.8	711.6	719.0	729.6	733.6	710.6
2011	704.7	698.7	700.6	709.5	720.8	727.0	728.8	728.9	725.1	729.2	742.0	746.1	721.8
2012	715.6	708.4	713.0	718.1	729.7	735.5	735.3	735.0	730.7	735.1	751.9	754.2	730.2
2013	726.2	721.7	724.8	729.7	743.2	751.8	750.9	752.4	745.5	749.4	762.0	768.2	743.8
Wholesale Trade													
2002	173.0	173.0	173.6	175.0	177.1	177.8	176.5	176.7	175.4	175.3	175.5	175.9	175.4
2003	171.7	171.7	172.2	172.6	173.5	174.1	173.1	173.2	172.3	172.4	171.8	172.1	172.6
2004	167.2	167.4	168.8	170.2	171.6	172.6	172.3	172.0	171.0	171.1	171.0	171.3	170.5
2005	167.8	168.2	169.1	170.3	172.0	172.5	172.4	172.2	171.1	171.2	170.9	171.2	170.7
2006	167.9	168.1	169.0	171.1	172.2	173.7	172.8	172.0	170.7	170.0	169.5	169.8	170.6
2007	167.2	166.8	167.2	169.0	170.4	171.4	170.5	170.1	169.0	169.1	168.6	169.0	169.0
2008	167.0	167.1	167.7	168.5	170.0	170.6	169.1	169.0	168.1	166.9	165.3	163.8	167.8
2009	158.0	156.4	155.0	154.9	154.9	153.2	150.9	151.3	150.5	150.1	149.8	150.0	152.9
2010	146.8	147.1	147.9	149.8	151.4	152.0	152.0	152.5	151.4	152.0	152.5	152.2	150.7
2011	150.8	151.1	152.1	153.6	155.4	156.5	156.7	157.2	156.4	156.5	156.9	156.9	155.0
2012	155.1	155.6	156.6	158.2	160.0	161.3	161.5	161.5	160.6	160.9	160.8	161.3	159.5
2013	160.1	160.7	161.8	162.8	164.7	166.0	164.7	165.2	164.4	164.2	164.2	163.8	163.6
Retail Trade													
2002	526.7	515.8	519.5	522.8	531.8	534.9	530.1	532.2	532.6	528.2	542.1	551.1	530.7
2003	511.0	503.1	503.9	505.8	516.4	521.0	517.0	520.8	521.2	524.5	535.6	543.7	518.7
2004	507.6	500.1	500.9	506.2	515.6	518.0	513.7	515.4	510.5	513.5	526.9	534.5	513.6
2005	499.0	492.2	493.5	500.1	507.5	509.7	510.5	508.8	505.5	504.9	517.4	523.3	506.0
2006	490.1	481.9	484.6	488.8	496.1	499.4	497.4	497.2	494.9	496.7	510.5	514.8	496.0
2007	486.6	476.7	478.6	481.1	490.0	492.4	492.3	490.9	488.5	489.3	503.2	507.1	489.7
2008	481.0	472.2	473.5	472.4	480.5	482.3	480.7	480.0	476.3	474.8	481.1	482.3	478.1
2009	452.6	443.3	441.4	444.7	453.2	457.1	452.0	453.5	449.3	449.9	458.8	461.2	451.4
2010	437.7	431.1	432.3	438.6	446.5	450.5	451.6	450.2	445.4	450.6	460.4	463.5	446.5
2011	439.4	433.6	434.1	440.6	447.7	451.0	452.8	451.7	448.2	452.3	464.3	467.0	448.6
2012	441.8	434.2	437.4	440.9	448.6	451.7	452.2	451.2	447.5	451.2	467.4	467.6	449.3
2013	444.4	439.1	441.0	444.6	454.1	459.8	461.1	460.8	455.6	458.9	469.1	474.1	455.2
Transportation and Utilities													
2002	126.4	126.1	127.3	127.8	129.7	130.8	128.1	129.4	128.8	129.3	128.2	127.0	128.2
2003	125.1	124.0	124.6	125.4	127.0	127.7	124.8	126.3	126.0	126.9	126.0	126.0	125.8
2004	122.1	122.4	122.3	124.3	125.5	126.5	125.5	126.7	126.6	129.1	128.5	128.5	125.7
2005	124.2	124.9	125.5	126.5	128.3	129.7	128.1	130.7	130.2	130.0	130.5	131.2	128.3
2006	126.5	126.1	126.7	127.4	129.2	130.5	126.6	129.6	129.4	128.7	129.1	131.4	128.4
2007	125.4	126.6	126.3	127.0	129.0	130.6	126.8	130.1	129.8	128.6	128.8	130.4	128.3
2008	123.9	124.4	124.6	123.7	125.6	127.7	124.3	125.1	125.0	123.5	122.8	123.1	124.5
2009	113.0	114.3	113.4	112.0	112.3	112.3	111.4	112.5	113.2	113.1	112.7	114.2	112.9
2010	110.5	109.7	110.6	111.0	112.4	114.1	113.5	114.1	114.8	116.2	116.7	117.9	113.5
2011	114.5	114.0	114.4	115.3	117.7	119.5	119.3	120.0	120.5	120.4	120.8	122.2	118.2
2012	118.7	118.6	119.0	119.0	121.1	122.5	121.6	122.3	122.6	123.0	123.7	125.3	121.5
2013	121.7	121.9	122.0	122.3	124.4	126.0	125.1	126.4	125.5	126.3	128.7	130.3	125.1
Information													
2002	72.5	72.3	72.2	70.8	71.3	71.3	69.9	69.5	68.5	68.5	69.1	69.4	70.4
2003	67.8	67.6	67.9	67.7	67.9	67.9	66.8	66.7	66.0	65.9	66.4	66.8	67.1
2004	65.7	65.3	65.5	65.4	65.8	66.2	66.2	66.0	65.2	65.4	65.9	66.3	65.7
2005	65.5	64.9	65.0	65.0	65.4	65.6	65.3	65.0	64.2	63.9	64.6	64.8	64.9
2006	64.4	64.5	64.1	64.2	64.7	65.1	63.8	63.6	62.8	62.9	63.2	63.3	63.9
2007	63.4	63.4	63.1	63.4	64.1	64.0	63.2	62.9	62.0	61.8	62.0	62.0	62.9
2008	61.2	61.2	60.5	60.0	60.6	60.9	59.9	60.2	60.2	59.0	59.5	59.1	60.2
2009	57.8	57.7	56.7	56.8	57.0	57.0	56.2	55.6	55.0	55.0	55.6	55.7	56.3
2010	54.3	54.2	53.9	54.2	54.8	55.3	54.8	57.0	56.5	54.0	54.0	54.2	54.8
2011	53.8	53.5	53.4	52.1	52.7	52.8	53.1	53.2	52.7	53.6	53.8	53.8	53.2
2012	53.4	53.2	53.1	52.9	53.2	53.2	53.6	54.2	52.9	53.2	53.5	53.6	53.3
2013	54.0	54.2	54.4	55.0	55.3	55.8	55.9	55.9	55.1	56.0	56.3	56.2	55.3

1. Employment by Industry: Michigan, Selected Years, 2002–2013—*Continued*

(Numbers in thousands, not seasonally adjusted)

Industry and year	January	February	March	April	May	June	July	August	September	October	November	December	Annual average
Financial Activities													
2002	210.6	210.7	210.7	212.2	214.1	215.1	215.3	216.1	213.7	213.3	213.8	214.9	213.4
2003	213.1	213.1	213.4	216.4	218.7	220.5	220.4	220.6	217.5	215.9	214.9	215.7	216.7
2004	212.8	212.3	213.4	215.4	217.0	218.7	219.0	218.4	216.1	214.4	214.6	216.0	215.7
2005	214.5	214.5	214.5	215.5	216.9	218.8	218.4	218.4	216.2	215.0	215.0	215.2	216.1
2006	213.4	213.3	213.0	213.5	215.2	217.3	216.0	215.9	213.2	211.6	211.2	212.0	213.8
2007	209.1	209.0	208.8	209.9	211.5	213.2	213.1	211.5	208.0	207.0	206.1	206.5	209.5
2008	204.4	204.4	203.6	203.0	205.0	205.3	203.7	203.0	199.8	198.2	196.8	196.5	202.0
2009	193.1	192.6	191.4	192.4	193.5	194.3	193.2	192.6	189.8	188.4	187.8	187.5	191.4
2010	186.2	185.8	185.0	184.7	186.7	188.9	190.0	190.7	189.2	189.3	189.6	190.7	188.1
2011	190.4	190.9	191.5	191.0	192.2	194.1	195.7	196.5	194.1	193.4	193.6	194.4	193.2
2012	192.2	192.6	193.3	194.6	196.2	198.4	199.9	200.1	197.3	197.3	197.5	198.4	196.5
2013	198.5	199.2	199.5	200.6	202.8	206.1	206.1	206.2	202.3	201.6	200.4	200.7	202.0
Professional and Business Services													
2002	578.0	579.0	582.3	593.9	603.4	608.9	602.0	614.7	610.3	607.9	606.7	604.3	599.3
2003	578.6	577.0	579.2	589.3	597.6	600.6	585.4	596.0	592.4	587.9	588.6	585.9	588.2
2004	565.0	564.9	566.8	583.0	590.4	595.8	587.9	598.8	597.3	597.2	595.3	592.9	586.3
2005	573.7	574.7	576.2	592.1	596.8	599.7	594.7	604.4	606.8	601.1	600.1	597.2	593.1
2006	575.3	572.6	572.9	581.8	587.1	595.4	583.8	594.8	594.6	591.5	592.5	591.4	586.1
2007	565.0	567.7	568.1	577.5	584.5	588.3	575.5	586.3	585.8	589.8	592.1	588.4	580.8
2008	564.6	566.4	567.5	571.3	577.7	574.1	557.9	561.3	558.5	562.6	554.6	545.5	563.5
2009	510.1	509.4	505.2	506.5	506.3	495.2	480.6	484.9	497.1	507.1	509.2	506.5	501.5
2010	490.1	496.1	496.5	508.0	515.7	519.3	509.0	516.6	528.3	538.6	539.7	533.2	515.9
2011	528.2	533.4	540.0	552.1	560.7	555.5	543.7	552.9	566.5	576.6	576.1	566.2	554.3
2012	560.3	565.9	570.4	582.4	591.1	583.7	568.5	577.8	587.4	595.6	595.2	591.3	580.8
2013	585.3	591.4	597.2	598.6	614.5	609.1	584.0	599.5	609.9	615.5	613.0	605.3	601.9
Education and Health Services													
2002	522.4	528.0	531.0	536.4	538.1	538.0	528.9	530.2	536.2	541.7	546.0	544.3	535.1
2003	538.5	544.1	544.8	544.7	546.5	544.7	540.0	540.8	547.9	554.2	558.3	558.2	546.9
2004	548.8	555.2	558.5	562.0	562.1	556.6	553.2	553.4	564.1	569.6	574.0	573.3	560.9
2005	564.1	572.8	576.0	576.1	577.1	570.1	566.4	566.9	579.7	583.8	588.6	588.1	575.8
2006	575.2	580.6	585.4	583.0	586.0	580.6	573.7	573.6	587.6	588.4	592.6	593.2	583.3
2007	584.9	591.3	594.2	596.0	598.4	594.8	588.6	589.3	599.4	605.2	608.6	609.2	596.7
2008	600.0	605.4	607.2	607.2	610.3	606.1	600.1	600.1	607.8	613.8	616.0	614.6	607.4
2009	602.6	609.9	611.4	611.2	613.0	609.5	600.7	600.7	605.8	614.5	616.8	614.6	609.2
2010	603.6	609.4	610.9	611.9	613.8	609.6	605.3	605.6	610.3	618.9	621.8	620.8	611.8
2011	610.8	615.1	618.0	622.0	622.1	618.6	616.0	617.1	623.8	630.4	633.1	633.2	621.7
2012	623.3	630.6	632.7	632.3	632.6	630.6	624.1	626.0	631.5	638.7	641.5	642.6	632.2
2013	630.4	636.9	639.0	640.0	640.2	639.0	629.5	630.9	635.3	643.4	644.9	640.4	637.5
Leisure and Hospitality													
2002	367.9	368.5	376.3	390.8	411.7	421.8	422.0	424.8	415.1	402.9	391.9	390.1	398.7
2003	369.8	368.8	374.3	387.9	413.1	424.5	422.3	422.2	416.2	404.6	391.8	391.9	399.0
2004	376.2	376.9	382.3	396.1	416.5	427.7	425.8	427.3	420.1	403.7	392.4	391.6	403.1
2005	374.2	376.5	383.2	402.7	421.7	432.1	429.0	431.8	423.2	404.3	394.2	394.3	405.6
2006	377.8	382.4	388.1	402.4	421.1	434.3	429.5	431.6	423.0	405.1	393.5	393.3	406.8
2007	379.3	379.2	386.0	398.1	422.4	433.9	429.5	431.8	423.4	408.0	397.1	395.5	407.0
2008	376.3	375.7	381.3	393.4	416.7	426.9	423.6	426.1	414.2	397.1	384.1	382.8	399.9
2009	358.8	357.2	361.1	376.8	398.1	406.0	404.2	405.1	397.0	380.9	367.8	367.1	381.7
2010	349.9	350.7	355.4	371.2	389.7	402.0	400.0	403.3	393.9	379.2	367.8	367.6	377.6
2011	353.6	352.7	359.8	372.0	391.3	403.2	404.1	406.0	397.0	384.2	372.2	370.2	380.5
2012	360.0	361.5	369.2	380.0	398.2	413.2	411.3	413.7	402.7	391.8	381.3	382.7	388.8
2013	372.3	373.7	378.3	386.3	411.6	422.5	419.6	421.9	409.4	401.2	386.0	386.6	397.5
Other Services													
2002	174.6	175.9	177.4	178.8	180.5	182.1	181.2	181.8	180.4	179.7	179.2	180.4	179.3
2003	176.9	177.4	179.2	176.9	178.2	179.0	180.5	181.1	179.9	179.7	179.4	180.7	179.1
2004	176.8	178.1	179.2	178.4	180.1	181.8	180.2	180.5	180.5	180.1	179.2	179.8	179.6
2005	176.1	177.0	178.5	180.2	181.7	183.7	181.3	180.8	179.7	178.4	178.2	179.2	179.6
2006	174.8	175.9	177.5	177.6	179.0	181.1	178.4	178.8	177.9	176.2	176.1	177.0	177.5
2007	172.8	173.7	175.3	175.6	177.7	180.2	177.9	178.3	177.3	176.6	176.1	177.1	176.6
2008	173.3	174.2	175.2	176.0	178.1	179.6	177.5	177.4	176.1	174.9	172.7	171.9	175.6
2009	167.4	167.8	167.6	169.3	171.0	172.3	169.9	169.4	168.4	167.8	167.1	168.1	168.8
2010	163.8	164.5	165.3	165.4	166.7	168.8	168.4	168.2	166.5	166.2	165.8	166.1	166.3
2011	163.9	164.3	165.5	166.4	167.9	169.7	169.3	169.6	167.9	167.8	167.0	167.7	167.3
2012	164.9	165.6	167.0	168.3	169.9	172.3	171.5	172.0	170.9	170.0	169.6	169.8	169.3
2013	168.4	168.9	170.3	170.1	171.9	173.7	173.7	174.3	172.3	171.3	171.6	171.2	171.5
Government													
2002	688.8	705.8	709.2	697.1	694.6	674.8	618.8	619.7	684.9	714.8	717.9	712.7	686.6
2003	690.1	709.2	708.2	704.1	700.8	673.5	614.0	610.6	677.1	714.9	713.9	708.5	685.4
2004	686.2	701.2	704.1	701.2	696.1	668.6	605.6	603.3	678.8	703.3	706.7	701.5	679.7
2005	677.5	697.4	698.9	697.6	691.9	663.3	597.4	599.0	677.8	695.3	700.0	692.9	674.1
2006	671.7	690.4	695.3	687.7	680.6	653.9	593.4	589.9	664.9	684.9	688.7	682.4	665.3
2007	660.2	677.9	683.0	674.3	673.4	646.8	591.3	594.1	654.8	671.3	672.7	668.4	655.7
2008	649.2	665.5	666.9	668.2	658.0	641.9	593.0	598.6	654.8	670.7	671.7	662.0	650.0
2009	652.7	665.0	666.0	669.3	659.9	639.1	589.6	589.5	645.7	663.9	664.4	656.1	646.8
2010	641.7	655.4	655.9	658.5	657.2	633.7	584.7	576.0	630.0	646.0	648.2	640.0	635.6
2011	625.0	636.2	638.3	637.6	623.5	609.4	565.0	561.6	619.6	632.0	634.7	626.0	617.4
2012	615.8	628.1	628.3	627.6	615.9	596.2	555.5	555.7	612.3	622.9	626.2	617.5	608.5
2013	603.1	616.0	615.0	617.1	605.9	587.1	547.9	545.7	605.5	616.6	620.4	614.3	599.6

2. Average Weekly Hours by Selected Industry: Michigan, 2009–2013

(Not seasonally adjusted)

Industry and year	January	February	March	April	May	June	July	August	September	October	November	December	Annual average
Total Private													
2009	32.6	33.5	33.4	33.0	33.1	33.4	33.5	34.0	33.3	33.4	33.5	33.3	33.3
2010	33.0	33.0	33.2	33.4	33.8	33.9	33.9	34.3	33.9	34.1	34.1	34.0	33.7
2011	34.0	33.8	33.8	34.0	34.5	34.2	34.2	34.4	34.3	34.6	34.3	34.2	34.2
2012	34.1	34.1	34.0	34.2	34.0	34.3	34.4	34.3	34.4	34.0	34.0	34.4	34.2
2013	33.6	33.8	33.9	33.8	34.2	34.8	34.3	34.6	34.7	34.3	34.3	34.7	34.3
Goods-Producing													
2009	36.3	38.1	38.3	38.0	37.5	39.2	39.2	40.0	38.3	39.3	39.0	40.0	38.6
2010	39.3	39.2	39.7	40.1	40.6	41.1	40.7	41.4	40.8	40.9	41.0	41.0	40.5
2011	41.3	41.1	41.3	41.1	41.7	41.2	40.5	41.6	41.7	41.6	41.5	41.3	41.3
2012	40.9	40.7	40.3	40.7	40.4	40.8	40.4	41.1	41.3	41.3	40.9	41.8	40.9
2013	41.0	40.9	41.1	40.6	40.9	41.5	41.0	41.9	42.3	41.8	41.5	42.2	41.4
Construction													
2009	36.1	36.8	35.8	35.7	37.5	36.9	38.1	38.4	36.3	38.5	37.4	37.2	37.1
2010	37.0	36.5	36.9	37.7	37.9	38.5	38.2	38.7	38.0	39.5	39.0	38.4	38.1
2011	37.8	37.7	37.7	38.3	39.4	39.5	40.2	40.5	40.8	40.4	39.6	38.7	39.3
2012	37.9	37.7	37.0	38.0	38.8	40.0	39.1	39.4	39.6	40.1	38.8	38.8	38.8
2013	38.0	37.9	37.5	37.4	39.9	39.9	40.5	39.2	39.3	39.4	37.0	37.6	38.7
Manufacturing													
2009	36.8	38.9	39.4	39.1	37.9	40.3	39.9	40.7	39.0	39.6	39.5	40.7	39.3
2010	39.8	39.9	40.5	40.6	41.0	41.3	41.0	41.6	41.3	41.1	41.3	41.5	40.9
2011	41.6	41.4	41.6	41.3	41.8	41.3	40.2	41.3	41.4	41.4	41.5	41.5	41.4
2012	41.2	41.1	40.7	41.1	40.6	41.0	40.8	41.5	41.7	41.6	41.5	42.5	41.3
2013	41.6	41.5	41.8	41.3	41.1	41.8	41.0	42.5	43.0	42.4	42.5	43.1	42.0
Trade, Transportation, and Utilities													
2009	32.2	32.5	32.3	32.1	32.7	32.6	33.0	33.1	33.1	32.6	32.7	32.4	32.6
2010	32.0	32.2	32.2	32.2	32.8	32.9	33.1	33.4	33.0	33.1	32.9	33.2	32.8
2011	32.8	32.9	32.7	33.2	33.4	33.3	33.6	33.5	33.5	33.7	33.1	33.4	33.3
2012	32.8	33.1	33.3	33.5	33.3	33.8	33.7	33.2	33.4	32.9	33.0	33.3	33.3
2013	32.4	32.9	33.0	32.9	33.6	33.8	33.5	33.6	33.8	33.2	33.3	33.6	33.3
Information													
2009	35.8	36.6	36.4	35.8	37.3	36.1	35.4	36.4	36.3	35.5	36.3	35.6	36.1
2010	35.3	34.9	34.9	34.3	34.5	34.9	35.2	35.5	35.2	34.5	34.9	35.2	34.9
2011	35.6	34.7	35.2	34.9	36.5	35.7	36.0	35.8	35.7	36.3	36.0	36.1	35.7
2012	37.6	35.8	35.7	37.0	35.7	35.3	35.8	34.9	35.5	34.5	35.1	35.7	35.7
2013	35.1	35.6	35.0	35.4	35.8	37.3	37.5	36.7	37.9	35.9	36.0	36.6	36.2
Financial Activities													
2009	35.3	36.0	36.1	36.2	36.0	36.0	36.2	36.6	35.8	36.0	36.7	36.2	36.1
2010	36.3	36.1	36.7	36.4	37.2	36.9	36.6	36.9	36.7	36.4	36.2	36.3	36.6
2011	36.2	35.8	35.8	35.6	36.5	36.3	36.5	36.7	36.4	36.8	36.7	37.1	36.4
2012	36.9	37.2	36.7	36.9	36.4	36.9	36.6	36.7	36.3	36.1	35.9	36.2	36.6
2013	35.5	35.7	35.5	35.8	35.9	36.3	35.6	35.7	36.1	35.7	35.5	35.6	35.7
Professional and Business Services													
2009	33.9	34.8	34.9	34.0	34.6	34.6	34.6	35.7	34.6	34.7	35.2	34.4	34.7
2010	34.7	34.3	34.5	35.0	35.6	35.4	35.1	35.9	35.1	36.0	35.9	35.7	35.3
2011	35.7	35.2	35.5	35.8	36.5	35.7	35.7	35.9	35.6	36.5	36.0	35.7	35.8
2012	36.3	36.4	36.4	36.4	35.8	36.0	36.4	36.2	36.6	35.8	35.9	36.6	36.2
2013	34.9	35.5	35.6	35.9	36.2	37.8	36.6	36.4	36.8	36.4	36.4	37.1	36.3
Education and Health Services													
2009	33.7	34.4	34.1	33.7	33.6	33.4	33.4	33.4	33.0	33.0	32.9	32.5	33.4
2010	32.2	32.0	32.0	32.1	32.1	32.1	32.4	32.5	32.5	32.7	32.7	32.3	32.3
2011	32.5	32.1	32.1	32.1	32.3	32.2	32.3	32.0	32.0	32.2	32.0	31.9	32.1
2012	32.2	32.0	32.1	32.4	32.3	32.5	32.5	32.5	32.8	32.4	32.6	32.7	32.4
2013	32.4	32.4	32.3	32.1	32.2	32.7	32.3	32.4	32.7	32.3	32.6	32.9	32.4
Leisure and Hospitality													
2009	22.3	22.9	22.8	22.7	23.5	23.9	24.5	24.7	23.9	23.7	23.4	23.4	23.5
2010	23.0	23.4	23.6	23.8	24.0	24.7	25.4	25.3	24.5	24.4	24.0	24.0	24.2
2011	23.9	23.8	23.9	23.9	24.8	24.8	25.3	25.3	24.7	24.7	24.4	24.3	24.5
2012	23.8	23.9	23.8	23.7	24.0	24.5	25.0	25.0	24.2	23.6	23.4	23.6	24.1
2013	22.5	22.9	23.3	23.3	24.2	24.3	24.3	24.6	24.0	23.7	23.4	23.7	23.7
Other Services													
2009	31.7	31.8	31.5	31.8	31.6	31.2	31.6	32.0	31.0	30.9	31.2	30.7	31.4
2010	30.7	30.8	31.6	31.8	32.3	31.6	31.8	31.9	31.4	31.3	31.9	31.7	31.6
2011	31.8	32.0	31.2	31.8	32.0	32.0	31.9	31.7	31.7	31.8	31.6	31.4	31.7
2012	31.6	31.3	31.3	31.4	31.5	31.4	32.6	31.4	31.0	30.7	30.5	31.1	31.3
2013	31.0	30.8	31.1	30.9	30.9	31.2	31.0	32.2	30.8	30.1	30.2	30.4	30.9

3. Average Hourly Earnings by Selected Industry: Michigan, 2009–2013

(Dollars, not seasonally adjusted)

Industry and year	January	February	March	April	May	June	July	August	September	October	November	December	Annual average
Total Private													
2009	22.01	22.17	22.17	22.03	21.81	21.73	21.71	21.36	21.59	21.91	22.06	22.13	21.89
2010	22.12	22.14	22.15	22.16	22.18	21.97	22.06	22.24	22.35	22.41	22.50	22.79	22.26
2011	22.84	22.66	22.35	22.42	22.52	22.03	22.20	21.98	22.11	22.44	22.27	22.35	22.34
2012	22.74	22.40	22.38	22.62	22.17	22.06	22.45	22.17	22.58	22.47	22.45	22.84	22.44
2013	22.94	22.85	22.82	22.84	22.63	22.97	22.89	22.67	23.20	23.00	23.04	23.27	22.93
Goods-Producing													
2009	25.50	25.70	25.51	25.58	25.20	25.29	25.45	24.11	24.71	25.04	25.06	25.51	25.22
2010	25.06	25.08	25.15	25.10	25.17	25.11	25.33	25.38	25.50	25.30	25.45	25.86	25.30
2011	25.48	25.44	25.40	25.04	25.04	24.59	24.74	24.29	24.45	24.57	24.43	24.57	24.82
2012	24.86	24.72	24.64	24.75	24.37	24.26	24.92	24.47	24.94	24.77	24.82	24.97	24.71
2013	24.93	24.67	24.62	24.56	24.66	24.74	24.87	24.56	24.84	24.61	24.66	24.80	24.71
Construction													
2009	27.08	26.74	26.74	26.65	26.25	26.05	26.02	26.07	26.03	26.02	25.95	26.78	26.34
2010	26.34	26.37	26.35	26.42	26.40	26.29	26.24	26.23	26.25	26.31	26.11	26.72	26.33
2011	26.52	26.71	26.34	26.06	25.30	25.03	25.15	25.03	25.14	25.01	25.38	25.84	25.55
2012	25.96	26.05	25.83	25.72	25.52	24.97	25.13	25.19	25.35	25.26	25.82	26.27	25.56
2013	26.03	25.99	26.03	26.07	25.82	25.45	26.20	26.07	26.07	25.90	26.11	26.77	26.03
Manufacturing													
2009	25.70	24.80	24.66	24.82	24.52	24.72	24.97	23.15	24.09	24.48	24.56	24.73	24.59
2010	24.39	24.46	24.58	24.67	24.66	24.76	24.82	24.88	25.05	24.82	25.11	25.26	24.80
2011	25.43	25.35	25.37	24.95	25.09	24.58	24.75	24.16	24.35	24.55	24.29	24.51	24.77
2012	24.82	24.65	24.55	24.69	24.26	24.19	24.96	24.37	24.90	24.69	24.65	24.92	24.64
2013	24.93	24.62	24.54	24.41	24.46	24.64	24.56	24.23	24.57	24.33	24.40	24.50	24.51
Trade, Transportation, and Utilities													
2009	18.84	18.80	18.76	18.84	18.62	18.66	18.56	18.94	18.85	18.95	19.17	19.03	18.84
2010	19.50	19.23	19.21	19.46	19.46	19.55	19.46	19.65	19.64	19.67	19.78	19.98	19.55
2011	20.17	20.08	19.33	19.44	19.40	19.26	19.22	19.08	19.12	19.40	19.29	19.26	19.41
2012	19.88	19.45	19.55	20.10	19.69	19.59	19.76	19.63	19.95	19.83	19.59	19.86	19.74
2013	20.04	20.19	20.21	20.18	19.89	20.15	20.33	20.19	20.49	20.56	20.71	20.57	20.30
Information													
2009	24.78	25.27	25.29	25.27	26.12	26.25	27.51	27.18	27.11	27.83	28.74	29.16	26.69
2010	28.68	28.79	30.03	30.42	31.10	31.42	32.09	31.07	30.59	31.22	31.45	31.62	30.71
2011	32.35	31.88	31.75	32.43	32.36	31.32	31.02	30.90	30.59	31.41	31.00	30.82	31.48
2012	30.17	29.84	29.63	30.27	29.91	29.66	29.88	29.63	29.94	29.68	29.49	29.94	29.84
2013	29.49	29.95	29.57	29.77	29.23	29.53	29.05	29.09	29.87	29.57	29.76	30.09	29.58
Financial Activities													
2009	23.24	22.77	22.97	23.20	24.08	23.11	23.56	24.24	24.07	24.21	24.49	24.27	23.68
2010	24.51	24.68	24.62	25.19	24.90	24.28	24.71	24.68	24.51	24.69	24.71	25.00	24.71
2011	24.91	24.61	23.97	24.79	24.18	23.46	24.10	23.72	23.76	24.19	24.11	23.89	24.14
2012	24.43	24.04	23.66	23.84	23.57	23.14	23.40	22.69	22.76	22.70	22.57	22.72	23.29
2013	22.87	22.60	22.90	23.04	22.71	22.68	22.42	22.56	22.83	23.31	23.31	23.56	22.90
Professional and Business Services													
2009	28.08	28.99	29.03	28.44	28.13	27.80	27.66	25.96	25.98	26.21	27.05	27.01	27.53
2010	26.81	27.34	27.25	26.76	26.86	26.16	26.57	27.06	26.89	26.91	27.13	27.93	26.97
2011	28.41	27.85	27.41	27.54	28.57	27.32	27.96	27.45	27.48	28.03	27.50	27.96	27.79
2012	28.18	27.46	27.58	27.86	27.04	26.87	27.86	27.31	27.77	27.42	27.42	28.69	27.62
2013	28.69	28.36	28.50	28.39	28.16	29.45	28.78	27.78	29.13	28.40	28.09	29.37	28.60
Education and Health Services													
2009	20.59	20.45	20.51	20.53	20.54	20.80	20.86	21.08	21.49	21.86	21.24	21.27	20.93
2010	21.07	21.07	21.08	21.18	21.18	21.04	21.10	21.14	21.49	21.46	21.30	21.35	21.21
2011	21.13	21.13	20.98	21.26	21.25	21.32	21.69	21.61	21.66	21.75	21.63	21.72	21.43
2012	22.10	21.79	21.79	21.76	21.59	21.84	22.11	21.94	22.13	22.03	22.06	22.14	21.94
2013	22.37	22.44	22.15	22.47	22.36	22.58	22.85	22.78	23.11	22.78	22.87	22.88	22.64
Leisure and Hospitality													
2009	11.50	11.41	11.51	11.50	11.32	11.29	11.21	11.31	11.52	11.52	11.70	11.74	11.45
2010	11.66	11.69	11.70	11.74	11.72	11.69	11.69	11.73	11.77	11.91	11.89	11.94	11.76
2011	11.83	11.83	11.69	11.75	11.65	11.51	11.42	11.36	11.42	11.57	11.47	11.56	11.58
2012	11.43	11.61	11.60	11.73	11.53	11.47	11.40	11.41	11.49	11.64	11.67	11.86	11.56
2013	12.01	11.81	11.77	11.74	11.68	11.59	11.63	11.68	11.84	11.86	11.97	12.18	11.81
Other Services													
2009	20.42	20.02	20.32	19.64	19.64	19.44	19.06	18.78	19.05	19.20	19.03	19.43	19.50
2010	19.83	19.69	19.68	19.49	19.60	19.42	19.39	19.65	19.87	20.01	19.77	20.02	19.70
2011	20.14	19.55	19.61	19.70	19.62	19.31	19.21	19.13	19.39	19.76	19.69	19.58	19.56
2012	19.66	19.38	19.25	19.65	19.68	19.92	19.82	19.76	20.23	20.00	20.35	20.69	19.87
2013	20.58	20.76	20.97	20.94	20.54	19.99	20.50	21.58	21.01	20.42	20.43	19.69	20.62

4. Average Weekly Earnings by Selected Industry: Michigan, 2009–2013

(Dollars, not seasonally adjusted)

Industry and year	January	February	March	April	May	June	July	August	September	October	November	December	Annual average
Total Private													
2009	717.53	742.70	740.48	726.99	721.91	725.78	727.29	726.24	718.95	731.79	739.01	736.93	728.94
2010	729.96	730.62	735.38	740.14	749.68	744.78	747.83	762.83	757.67	764.18	767.25	774.86	750.16
2011	776.56	765.91	755.43	762.28	776.94	753.43	759.24	756.11	758.37	776.42	763.86	764.37	764.03
2012	775.43	763.84	760.92	773.60	753.78	756.66	772.28	760.43	776.75	763.98	763.30	785.70	767.45
2013	770.78	772.33	773.60	771.99	773.95	799.36	785.13	784.38	805.04	788.90	790.27	807.47	786.50
Goods-Producing													
2009	925.65	979.17	977.03	972.04	945.00	991.37	997.64	964.40	946.39	984.07	977.34	1,020.40	973.49
2010	984.86	983.14	998.46	1,006.51	1,021.90	1,032.02	1,030.93	1,050.73	1,040.40	1,034.77	1,043.45	1,060.26	1,024.65
2011	1,052.32	1,045.58	1,049.02	1,029.14	1,044.17	1,013.11	1,001.97	1,010.46	1,019.57	1,022.11	1,013.85	1,014.74	1,025.07
2012	1,016.77	1,006.10	992.99	1,007.33	984.55	989.81	1,006.77	1,005.72	1,030.02	1,023.00	1,015.14	1,043.75	1,010.64
2013	1,022.13	1,009.00	1,011.88	997.14	1,008.59	1,026.71	1,019.67	1,029.06	1,050.73	1,028.70	1,023.39	1,046.56	1,022.99
Construction													
2009	977.59	984.03	957.29	951.41	984.38	961.25	991.36	1,001.09	944.89	1,001.77	970.53	996.22	977.21
2010	974.58	962.51	972.32	996.03	1,000.56	1,012.17	1,002.37	1,015.10	997.50	1,039.25	1,018.29	1,026.05	1,003.17
2011	1,002.46	1,006.97	993.02	998.10	996.82	988.69	1,011.03	1,013.72	1,025.71	1,010.40	1,005.05	1,000.01	1,004.12
2012	983.88	982.09	955.71	977.36	990.18	998.80	982.58	992.49	1,003.86	1,012.93	1,001.82	1,019.28	991.73
2013	989.14	985.02	976.13	975.02	1,030.22	1,015.46	1,061.10	1,021.94	1,024.55	1,020.46	966.07	1,006.55	1,007.36
Manufacturing													
2009	945.76	964.72	971.60	970.46	929.31	996.22	996.30	942.21	939.51	969.41	970.12	1,006.51	966.39
2010	970.72	975.95	995.49	1,001.60	1,011.06	1,022.59	1,017.62	1,035.01	1,034.57	1,020.10	1,037.04	1,048.29	1,014.32
2011	1,057.89	1,049.49	1,055.39	1,030.44	1,048.76	1,015.15	994.95	997.81	1,008.09	1,016.37	1,008.04	1,017.17	1,025.48
2012	1,022.58	1,013.12	999.19	1,014.76	984.96	991.79	1,018.37	1,011.36	1,038.33	1,027.10	1,022.98	1,059.10	1,017.63
2013	1,037.09	1,021.73	1,025.77	1,008.13	1,005.31	1,029.95	1,006.96	1,029.78	1,056.51	1,031.59	1,037.00	1,055.95	1,029.42
Trade, Transportation, and Utilities													
2009	606.65	611.00	605.95	604.76	608.87	608.32	612.48	626.91	623.94	617.77	626.86	616.57	614.18
2010	624.00	619.21	618.56	626.61	638.29	643.20	644.13	656.31	648.12	651.08	650.76	663.34	641.24
2011	661.58	660.63	632.09	645.41	647.96	641.36	645.79	639.18	640.52	653.78	638.50	643.28	646.35
2012	652.06	643.80	651.02	673.35	655.68	662.14	665.91	651.72	666.33	652.41	646.47	661.34	657.34
2013	649.30	664.25	666.93	663.92	668.30	681.07	681.06	678.38	692.56	682.59	689.64	691.15	675.99
Information													
2009	887.12	924.88	920.56	904.67	974.28	947.63	973.85	989.35	984.09	987.97	1,043.26	1,038.10	963.51
2010	1,012.40	1,004.77	1,048.05	1,043.41	1,072.95	1,096.56	1,129.57	1,102.99	1,076.77	1,077.09	1,097.61	1,113.02	1,071.78
2011	1,151.66	1,106.24	1,117.60	1,131.81	1,181.14	1,118.12	1,116.72	1,106.22	1,092.06	1,140.18	1,116.00	1,112.60	1,123.84
2012	1,134.39	1,068.27	1,057.79	1,119.99	1,067.79	1,047.00	1,069.70	1,034.09	1,062.87	1,023.96	1,035.10	1,068.86	1,065.29
2013	1,035.10	1,066.22	1,034.95	1,053.86	1,046.43	1,101.47	1,089.38	1,067.60	1,132.07	1,061.56	1,071.36	1,101.29	1,070.80
Financial Activities													
2009	820.37	819.72	829.22	839.84	866.88	831.96	852.87	887.18	861.71	871.56	898.78	878.57	854.85
2010	889.71	890.95	903.55	916.92	926.28	895.93	904.39	910.69	899.52	898.72	894.50	907.50	904.39
2011	901.74	881.04	858.13	882.52	882.57	851.60	879.65	870.52	864.86	890.19	884.84	886.32	878.70
2012	901.47	894.29	868.32	879.70	857.95	853.87	856.44	832.72	826.19	819.47	810.26	822.46	852.41
2013	811.89	806.82	812.95	824.83	815.29	823.28	798.15	805.39	824.16	832.17	827.51	838.74	817.53
Professional and Business Services													
2009	951.91	1,008.85	1,013.15	966.96	973.30	961.88	957.04	926.77	898.91	909.49	952.16	929.14	955.29
2010	930.31	937.76	940.13	936.60	956.22	926.06	932.61	971.45	943.84	968.76	973.97	997.10	952.04
2011	1,014.24	980.32	973.06	985.93	1,042.81	975.32	998.17	985.46	978.29	1,023.10	990.00	998.17	994.88
2012	1,022.93	999.54	1,003.91	1,014.10	968.03	967.32	1,014.10	988.62	1,016.38	981.64	984.38	1,050.05	999.84
2013	1,001.28	1,006.78	1,014.60	1,019.20	1,019.39	1,113.21	1,053.35	1,011.19	1,071.98	1,033.76	1,022.48	1,089.63	1,038.18
Education and Health Services													
2009	693.88	703.48	699.39	691.86	690.14	694.72	696.72	704.07	709.17	721.38	698.80	691.28	699.06
2010	678.45	674.24	674.56	679.88	679.88	675.38	683.64	687.05	698.43	701.74	696.51	689.61	685.08
2011	686.73	678.27	673.46	682.45	686.38	686.50	700.59	691.52	693.12	700.35	692.16	692.87	687.90
2012	711.62	697.28	699.46	705.02	697.36	709.80	718.58	713.05	725.86	713.77	719.16	723.98	710.86
2013	724.79	727.06	715.45	721.29	719.99	738.37	738.06	738.07	755.70	735.79	745.56	752.75	733.54
Leisure and Hospitality													
2009	256.45	261.29	262.43	261.05	266.02	269.83	274.65	279.36	275.33	273.02	273.78	274.72	269.08
2010	268.18	273.55	276.12	279.41	281.28	288.74	296.93	296.77	288.37	290.60	285.36	286.56	284.59
2011	282.74	281.55	279.39	280.83	288.92	285.45	288.93	287.41	282.07	285.78	279.87	280.91	283.71
2012	272.03	277.48	276.08	278.00	276.72	281.02	285.00	285.25	278.06	274.70	273.08	279.90	278.60
2013	270.23	270.45	274.24	273.54	282.66	281.64	282.61	287.33	284.16	281.08	280.10	288.67	279.90
Other Services													
2009	647.31	636.64	640.08	624.55	620.62	606.53	602.30	600.96	590.55	593.28	593.74	596.50	612.30
2010	608.78	606.45	621.89	619.78	633.08	613.67	616.60	606.42	614.66	626.84	623.92	634.63	622.52
2011	640.45	625.60	611.83	626.46	627.84	617.92	612.80	606.42	614.66	628.37	622.20	614.81	620.05
2012	621.26	606.59	602.53	617.01	619.92	625.49	646.13	620.46	627.13	614.00	620.68	643.46	621.93
2013	637.98	639.41	652.17	647.05	634.69	623.69	635.50	694.88	647.11	614.64	616.99	598.58	637.16

MINNESOTA
At a Glance

Population:
  2000 census: 4,919,631
  2010 census: 5,303,925
  2013 estimate: 5,420,380

Percent change in population:
  2000–2010: 7.8%
  2010–2013: 2.2%

Percent change in total nonfarm employment:
  2000–2010: -1.6
  2010–2013: 5.1%

Industry with the largest growth in employment, 2000–2013 (thousands):
  Education and Health Services, 166.7

Industry with the largest decline or smallest growth in employment, 2000–2013 (thousands):
  Manufacturing, -88.8

Civilian labor force:
  2000: 2,807,668
  2010: 2,866,024
  2013: 2,973,519

Unemployment rate and rank among states (lowest to highest):
  2000: 3.1%, 12th
  2010: 7.4%, 13th
  2013: 5.1%, 9th

Over-the-year change in unemployment rates:
  2010–2011: -0.9%
  2011–2012: -0.9%
  2012–2013: -0.5%

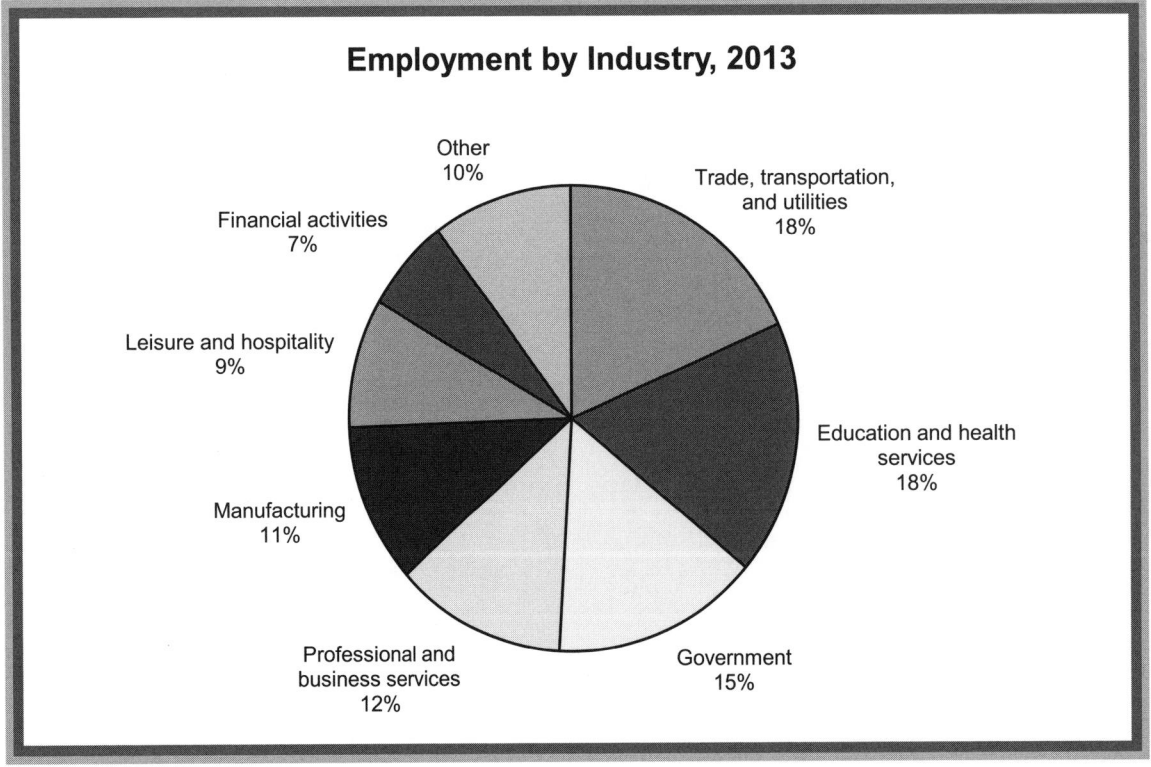

Employment by Industry, 2013

Other 10%
Trade, transportation, and utilities 18%
Financial activities 7%
Leisure and hospitality 9%
Manufacturing 11%
Education and health services 18%
Professional and business services 12%
Government 15%

1. Employment by Industry: Minnesota, Selected Years, 2002–2013

(Numbers in thousands, not seasonally adjusted)

Industry and year	January	February	March	April	May	June	July	August	September	October	November	December	Annual average
Total Nonfarm													
2002	2,612.2	2,610.2	2,617.1	2,641.5	2,681.6	2,706.2	2,673.8	2,673.3	2,690.0	2,690.2	2,693.5	2,684.0	2,664.5
2003	2,605.4	2,607.4	2,613.4	2,646.1	2,685.6	2,703.0	2,663.6	2,671.3	2,681.5	2,686.9	2,680.3	2,679.1	2,660.3
2004	2,598.2	2,601.3	2,612.8	2,668.0	2,705.2	2,727.4	2,690.3	2,693.1	2,707.5	2,724.7	2,720.9	2,722.9	2,681.0
2005	2,629.3	2,634.4	2,648.3	2,705.1	2,746.5	2,768.3	2,737.9	2,743.8	2,757.5	2,769.6	2,769.8	2,768.9	2,723.3
2006	2,701.9	2,700.9	2,715.7	2,737.9	2,775.2	2,810.0	2,766.1	2,767.7	2,775.9	2,781.5	2,783.9	2,781.2	2,758.2
2007	2,711.5	2,711.9	2,722.2	2,746.1	2,793.9	2,823.4	2,784.3	2,786.4	2,788.4	2,798.9	2,799.7	2,789.1	2,771.3
2008	2,719.1	2,721.8	2,729.4	2,747.2	2,792.1	2,814.6	2,775.1	2,779.1	2,777.5	2,787.8	2,768.5	2,744.1	2,763.0
2009	2,654.3	2,640.5	2,632.0	2,653.1	2,683.3	2,690.4	2,650.4	2,646.9	2,639.4	2,665.8	2,658.1	2,647.1	2,655.1
2010	2,570.3	2,571.8	2,581.4	2,628.9	2,663.2	2,683.0	2,649.7	2,654.8	2,657.0	2,685.6	2,681.6	2,667.9	2,641.3
2011	2,607.4	2,614.7	2,624.0	2,673.3	2,710.2	2,730.8	2,680.2	2,710.7	2,728.7	2,734.0	2,729.1	2,720.6	2,688.6
2012	2,652.7	2,658.6	2,674.2	2,716.6	2,746.7	2,769.4	2,729.3	2,746.0	2,760.6	2,775.8	2,775.6	2,764.0	2,730.8
2013	2,702.7	2,714.7	2,722.8	2,747.2	2,795.8	2,819.2	2,772.5	2,792.7	2,804.5	2,826.4	2,818.4	2,809.2	2,777.2
Total Private													
2002	2,197.9	2,189.8	2,197.1	2,223.3	2,261.5	2,285.3	2,282.4	2,293.5	2,279.6	2,270.3	2,266.1	2,259.0	2,250.5
2003	2,192.6	2,185.8	2,192.0	2,223.5	2,263.4	2,285.0	2,278.8	2,288.5	2,277.0	2,269.5	2,260.6	2,257.4	2,247.8
2004	2,186.6	2,182.4	2,193.9	2,247.5	2,282.8	2,312.6	2,306.6	2,313.9	2,300.4	2,305.5	2,297.5	2,298.0	2,269.0
2005	2,212.9	2,212.3	2,225.4	2,280.5	2,321.6	2,348.3	2,346.8	2,359.1	2,348.8	2,349.0	2,349.6	2,346.7	2,308.4
2006	2,286.7	2,279.4	2,293.2	2,314.9	2,351.7	2,388.3	2,374.9	2,381.3	2,365.0	2,359.1	2,358.1	2,354.2	2,342.2
2007	2,297.3	2,291.4	2,302.6	2,325.9	2,369.9	2,401.3	2,394.8	2,402.4	2,380.8	2,376.4	2,373.8	2,364.1	2,356.7
2008	2,302.0	2,297.9	2,305.0	2,323.3	2,363.9	2,388.1	2,383.0	2,390.5	2,363.6	2,360.5	2,337.9	2,314.1	2,344.2
2009	2,236.9	2,215.5	2,206.8	2,226.4	2,254.8	2,264.7	2,257.3	2,261.6	2,235.3	2,242.1	2,231.6	2,221.0	2,237.8
2010	2,153.6	2,148.3	2,156.0	2,202.6	2,232.6	2,257.2	2,260.4	2,271.6	2,252.2	2,263.3	2,255.8	2,243.1	2,224.7
2011	2,193.8	2,193.4	2,203.0	2,251.2	2,288.6	2,311.8	2,318.2	2,332.3	2,323.1	2,314.5	2,307.6	2,298.9	2,278.0
2012	2,242.6	2,240.4	2,255.5	2,295.6	2,326.2	2,350.6	2,351.7	2,365.1	2,352.3	2,352.9	2,348.0	2,338.5	2,318.3
2013	2,289.3	2,291.8	2,301.4	2,325.5	2,372.3	2,399.7	2,398.0	2,414.0	2,395.7	2,404.5	2,395.5	2,386.6	2,364.5
Goods-Producing													
2002	470.1	464.8	466.9	474.5	489.1	501.5	503.6	508.2	501.7	494.4	486.5	474.4	486.3
2003	455.7	450.3	451.6	461.9	477.3	489.6	491.1	494.8	489.1	485.2	477.3	467.4	474.3
2004	446.5	443.6	446.4	465.0	477.9	492.1	496.4	500.1	496.0	495.6	487.4	479.5	477.2
2005	454.7	452.5	455.7	470.7	487.2	499.4	502.9	506.4	500.7	494.2	488.6	477.6	482.6
2006	461.5	457.6	460.7	469.3	482.6	497.6	496.8	498.5	492.1	487.4	477.0	467.7	479.1
2007	452.0	446.6	449.4	454.9	471.9	485.5	485.0	486.9	479.0	474.8	468.0	456.5	467.5
2008	440.4	436.6	437.5	442.2	458.9	470.0	471.1	472.3	463.7	459.9	445.9	429.5	452.3
2009	406.2	395.5	389.5	391.1	399.1	406.7	407.8	407.9	402.8	400.3	392.6	381.3	398.4
2010	362.9	358.3	359.7	375.3	386.4	397.5	404.3	405.8	402.5	402.0	395.1	385.0	386.2
2011	372.9	371.2	373.6	386.1	399.4	411.2	417.1	420.5	416.1	414.6	407.1	397.9	399.0
2012	383.1	381.0	386.5	398.8	409.3	421.6	424.9	427.3	422.5	420.1	412.4	404.1	407.6
2013	390.0	388.8	392.6	399.4	416.2	428.7	432.0	435.9	431.3	433.1	427.3	415.5	415.9
Service-Providing													
2002	2,142.1	2,145.4	2,150.2	2,167.0	2,192.5	2,204.7	2,170.2	2,165.1	2,188.3	2,195.8	2,207.0	2,209.6	2,178.2
2003	2,149.7	2,157.1	2,161.8	2,184.2	2,208.3	2,213.4	2,172.5	2,176.5	2,192.4	2,201.7	2,203.0	2,211.7	2,186.0
2004	2,151.7	2,157.7	2,166.4	2,203.0	2,227.3	2,235.3	2,193.9	2,193.0	2,211.5	2,229.1	2,233.5	2,243.4	2,203.8
2005	2,174.6	2,181.9	2,192.6	2,234.4	2,259.3	2,268.9	2,235.0	2,237.4	2,256.8	2,275.4	2,281.2	2,291.3	2,240.7
2006	2,240.4	2,243.3	2,255.0	2,268.6	2,292.6	2,312.4	2,269.3	2,269.2	2,283.8	2,294.1	2,306.9	2,313.5	2,279.1
2007	2,259.5	2,265.3	2,272.8	2,291.2	2,322.0	2,337.9	2,299.3	2,299.5	2,309.4	2,324.1	2,331.7	2,332.6	2,303.8
2008	2,278.7	2,285.2	2,291.9	2,305.0	2,333.2	2,344.6	2,304.0	2,306.8	2,313.8	2,327.9	2,322.6	2,314.6	2,310.7
2009	2,248.1	2,245.0	2,242.5	2,262.0	2,284.2	2,283.7	2,242.6	2,239.0	2,236.6	2,265.5	2,265.5	2,265.8	2,256.7
2010	2,207.4	2,213.5	2,221.7	2,253.6	2,276.8	2,285.5	2,245.4	2,249.0	2,254.5	2,283.6	2,286.5	2,282.9	2,255.0
2011	2,234.5	2,243.5	2,250.4	2,287.2	2,310.8	2,319.6	2,263.1	2,290.2	2,312.6	2,319.4	2,322.0	2,322.7	2,289.7
2012	2,269.6	2,277.6	2,287.7	2,317.8	2,337.4	2,347.8	2,304.4	2,318.7	2,338.1	2,355.7	2,363.2	2,359.9	2,323.2
2013	2,312.7	2,325.9	2,330.2	2,347.8	2,379.6	2,390.5	2,340.5	2,356.8	2,373.2	2,393.3	2,391.1	2,393.7	2,361.3
Mining and Logging													
2002	6.2	5.6	6.2	6.1	6.4	6.7	6.7	6.8	6.7	6.7	6.6	6.3	6.4
2003	6.1	6.0	6.0	5.9	6.3	6.4	6.5	6.1	5.9	6.0	5.8	5.6	6.1
2004	5.6	5.6	5.6	5.8	6.1	6.3	6.4	6.5	6.4	6.2	6.1	6.0	6.1
2005	5.6	5.7	5.7	5.8	6.1	6.3	6.3	6.3	6.2	6.1	6.0	5.7	6.0
2006	5.7	5.8	5.8	5.8	5.9	6.3	6.4	6.4	6.2	6.2	6.0	5.8	6.0
2007	5.6	5.6	5.6	5.6	5.9	6.1	6.3	6.4	6.2	6.2	6.2	6.0	6.0
2008	5.9	5.9	5.9	5.9	6.3	6.4	6.7	6.7	6.5	6.5	6.3	6.0	6.3
2009	5.8	5.6	5.3	5.1	4.6	4.4	5.3	5.0	4.6	5.7	5.4	5.0	5.2
2010	5.3	5.4	5.4	5.7	6.0	5.6	6.5	6.5	6.4	6.5	6.3	6.0	6.0
2011	6.0	6.2	6.1	6.1	6.5	6.8	7.0	7.1	6.9	7.0	6.9	6.6	6.6
2012	6.6	6.6	6.6	6.8	7.0	7.3	7.4	7.5	7.2	7.2	7.1	6.8	7.0
2013	6.6	6.6	6.7	6.6	6.9	7.2	7.2	7.4	7.2	7.2	7.1	6.7	7.0
Construction													
2002	106.1	103.2	104.1	113.0	126.5	134.5	139.6	141.2	138.1	134.5	128.6	119.3	124.1
2003	106.0	102.6	103.6	113.3	127.2	136.1	140.2	141.9	138.9	137.1	130.7	121.4	124.9
2004	105.5	103.5	105.8	120.3	131.4	138.7	143.4	144.0	141.5	140.7	136.5	127.3	128.2
2005	108.3	106.5	108.5	120.6	132.7	140.9	145.5	146.1	143.2	139.0	135.1	126.4	129.4
2006	114.6	112.8	114.2	120.8	131.6	139.7	139.7	139.3	136.7	133.7	127.7	118.8	127.5
2007	108.0	104.0	106.5	110.3	124.9	132.6	132.7	133.4	129.2	126.7	121.6	111.3	120.1
2008	100.3	97.4	98.4	102.3	115.7	122.6	123.8	123.9	119.5	116.6	107.9	97.4	110.5
2009	82.1	79.6	79.6	86.5	97.7	102.4	103.9	103.8	102.3	100.0	95.2	87.3	93.4
2010	73.3	69.5	70.2	81.9	89.4	95.6	99.2	99.8	98.0	97.9	92.8	83.4	87.6
2011	74.2	72.7	74.5	83.3	93.6	101.1	103.8	105.6	103.8	102.5	97.3	88.8	91.8
2012	77.4	75.9	79.7	90.0	98.0	104.4	106.9	108.2	105.2	104.0	98.2	91.4	94.9
2013	80.5	80.0	82.4	89.0	102.7	110.3	113.6	116.3	114.2	115.5	110.2	99.0	101.1

1. Employment by Industry: Minnesota, Selected Years, 2002–2013—*Continued*

(Numbers in thousands, not seasonally adjusted)

Industry and year	January	February	March	April	May	June	July	August	September	October	November	December	Annual average
Manufacturing													
2002	357.8	356.0	356.6	355.4	356.2	360.3	357.3	360.2	356.9	353.2	351.3	348.8	355.8
2003	343.6	341.7	342.0	342.7	343.8	347.1	344.4	346.8	344.3	342.1	340.8	340.4	343.3
2004	335.4	334.5	335.0	338.9	340.4	347.1	346.7	349.6	348.1	348.7	344.8	346.2	343.0
2005	340.8	340.3	341.5	344.3	348.4	352.2	351.1	354.0	351.3	349.1	347.5	345.5	347.2
2006	341.2	339.0	340.7	342.7	345.1	351.6	350.7	352.8	349.2	347.5	343.3	343.1	345.6
2007	338.4	337.0	337.3	339.0	341.1	346.6	346.0	347.1	343.6	341.9	340.2	339.2	341.5
2008	334.2	333.3	333.2	334.0	336.9	341.0	340.6	341.7	337.7	336.8	331.7	326.1	335.6
2009	318.3	310.3	304.6	299.5	296.8	299.9	298.6	299.1	295.9	294.6	292.0	289.0	299.9
2010	284.3	283.4	284.1	287.7	291.0	296.3	298.6	299.5	298.1	297.6	296.0	295.6	292.7
2011	292.7	292.3	293.0	296.7	299.3	303.3	306.3	307.8	305.4	305.1	302.9	302.5	300.6
2012	299.1	298.5	300.2	302.0	304.3	309.9	310.6	311.6	310.1	308.9	307.1	305.9	305.7
2013	302.9	302.2	303.5	303.8	306.6	311.2	311.2	312.2	309.9	310.4	310.0	309.8	307.8
Trade, Transportation, and Utilities													
2002	525.2	516.0	516.8	521.8	527.7	529.1	523.4	523.1	521.7	524.5	534.3	538.9	525.2
2003	518.6	511.2	511.4	517.4	523.9	524.8	518.4	520.2	518.9	522.9	528.9	532.2	520.7
2004	511.5	506.0	507.0	517.3	524.6	528.9	525.4	526.0	524.6	530.0	537.8	542.6	523.5
2005	517.6	512.7	514.4	522.6	528.3	531.1	527.6	528.7	526.9	531.9	540.0	545.0	527.2
2006	525.7	519.4	520.5	523.7	529.4	534.1	527.1	527.0	526.2	527.8	538.3	541.1	528.4
2007	523.7	518.8	519.3	523.2	530.7	534.4	529.4	529.8	528.2	531.7	539.6	543.0	529.3
2008	523.6	516.8	518.2	519.9	526.7	527.2	522.4	522.2	519.0	520.7	524.1	523.7	522.0
2009	502.9	495.2	492.5	494.1	500.0	501.2	494.7	494.5	490.6	493.0	499.6	500.5	496.6
2010	482.3	476.6	477.5	486.4	491.6	496.1	491.6	491.5	489.5	494.1	500.7	503.1	490.1
2011	484.7	480.9	482.3	492.2	499.0	500.9	499.5	500.4	500.7	502.3	509.6	513.0	497.1
2012	495.4	488.6	491.4	498.4	504.9	506.9	503.4	505.1	503.4	507.8	517.1	517.5	503.3
2013	502.3	497.0	498.2	501.5	510.9	515.3	511.9	514.9	512.3	516.5	523.1	527.9	511.0
Wholesale Trade													
2002	126.6	126.4	126.2	127.4	128.1	128.6	128.7	128.1	126.5	127.0	126.6	126.3	127.2
2003	126.6	126.7	126.7	128.1	128.8	129.6	129.6	129.2	127.8	127.8	127.2	127.1	127.9
2004	125.0	125.0	125.5	129.1	130.0	131.3	131.3	131.1	129.3	129.8	129.8	129.9	128.9
2005	127.3	127.4	127.5	131.1	131.4	133.3	132.8	133.1	132.0	132.2	132.3	132.4	131.1
2006	131.3	131.4	132.2	133.1	134.0	135.1	134.6	134.5	133.1	133.0	133.0	132.7	133.2
2007	131.1	131.0	131.6	132.9	134.5	135.5	135.2	135.2	133.2	133.6	133.7	133.6	133.4
2008	131.7	131.5	132.1	132.8	134.3	134.9	135.0	134.9	132.9	132.6	132.1	131.2	133.0
2009	128.2	127.0	126.1	127.3	127.5	127.6	127.2	126.5	124.0	123.9	124.0	123.5	126.1
2010	120.8	120.4	120.8	123.0	123.6	124.9	125.1	124.8	123.0	124.3	124.2	123.6	123.2
2011	122.1	122.3	122.8	125.4	127.0	127.2	128.0	128.0	126.6	126.7	126.6	126.4	125.8
2012	125.2	125.2	126.2	128.6	129.5	130.7	131.1	130.5	128.9	129.3	129.4	129.4	128.7
2013	127.9	127.8	128.3	129.4	131.6	132.6	132.5	132.3	130.5	132.4	132.5	131.6	130.8
Retail Trade													
2002	302.5	294.6	295.8	298.4	302.6	304.8	302.7	303.4	300.7	301.4	311.7	317.5	303.0
2003	299.0	292.2	292.5	296.7	302.1	303.7	299.5	302.0	299.2	301.4	308.4	312.3	300.8
2004	296.1	290.7	291.1	295.8	301.1	304.5	302.4	303.0	299.5	302.0	309.8	314.5	300.9
2005	296.0	290.7	291.9	296.0	300.7	303.2	300.3	301.8	299.8	303.8	311.9	316.5	301.1
2006	300.3	294.7	294.8	297.4	301.4	305.2	301.5	302.2	298.5	300.0	309.0	312.5	301.5
2007	299.2	293.7	294.4	296.3	301.5	304.9	302.3	302.7	299.2	301.2	309.2	311.6	301.4
2008	297.2	290.2	290.9	292.1	296.4	297.5	295.4	295.5	290.7	291.7	296.1	296.1	294.2
2009	282.8	276.8	274.8	275.9	281.3	283.6	280.4	281.6	276.1	278.0	284.1	285.3	280.1
2010	272.8	267.9	268.2	273.7	277.8	281.2	279.3	280.5	276.2	278.0	283.9	286.1	277.1
2011	272.6	268.4	269.0	275.5	280.0	282.9	282.5	284.1	281.6	282.2	289.5	292.1	280.0
2012	279.3	272.7	274.4	277.7	282.3	284.9	283.0	284.6	281.6	284.6	293.4	293.5	282.7
2013	282.0	276.5	277.4	279.4	285.2	290.0	288.9	291.1	287.5	289.9	296.2	300.6	287.1
Transportation and Utilities													
2002	96.1	95.0	94.8	96.0	97.0	95.7	92.0	91.6	94.5	96.1	96.0	95.1	95.0
2003	93.0	92.3	92.2	92.6	93.0	91.5	89.3	89.0	91.9	93.7	93.3	92.8	92.1
2004	90.4	90.3	90.4	92.4	93.5	93.1	91.7	91.9	95.8	98.2	98.2	98.2	93.7
2005	94.3	94.6	95.0	95.5	96.2	94.6	94.5	93.8	95.1	95.9	95.8	96.1	95.1
2006	94.1	93.3	93.5	93.2	94.0	93.8	91.0	90.3	94.6	94.8	96.3	95.9	93.7
2007	93.4	94.1	93.3	94.0	94.7	94.0	91.9	91.9	95.8	96.9	96.7	97.8	94.5
2008	94.7	95.1	95.2	95.0	96.0	94.8	92.0	91.8	95.4	96.4	95.9	96.4	94.9
2009	91.9	91.4	91.6	90.9	91.2	90.0	87.1	86.4	90.5	91.1	91.5	91.7	90.4
2010	88.7	88.3	88.5	89.7	90.2	90.0	87.2	86.2	90.3	91.8	92.6	93.4	89.7
2011	90.0	90.2	90.5	91.3	92.0	90.8	89.0	88.3	92.5	93.4	93.5	94.5	91.3
2012	90.9	90.7	90.8	92.1	93.1	91.3	89.3	90.0	92.9	93.9	94.3	94.6	92.0
2013	92.4	92.7	92.5	92.7	94.1	92.7	90.5	91.5	94.3	94.2	94.4	95.7	93.1
Information													
2002	67.5	67.2	67.2	67.4	67.3	67.7	67.2	66.1	64.9	64.4	64.5	64.3	66.3
2003	62.5	62.3	62.3	62.7	62.9	62.6	62.0	61.7	60.8	60.6	61.1	61.4	61.9
2004	60.6	60.5	60.7	61.1	61.3	61.0	60.1	59.5	58.8	58.6	59.2	59.2	60.1
2005	58.7	58.6	58.7	59.7	59.8	60.0	59.6	59.0	58.5	58.4	58.7	59.0	59.1
2006	58.3	58.1	58.4	57.8	58.3	58.7	58.2	58.3	57.5	57.3	57.7	57.8	58.0
2007	57.9	57.9	58.2	58.2	58.3	58.6	58.2	58.2	57.6	57.3	57.4	57.8	58.0
2008	57.6	57.4	57.6	57.8	57.7	57.9	58.0	58.0	57.6	57.0	57.1	56.4	57.5
2009	56.1	55.9	55.7	55.1	55.2	55.3	55.6	55.5	54.9	54.7	55.0	54.8	55.3
2010	54.4	54.4	54.3	54.1	54.0	54.2	54.4	54.4	53.7	53.8	53.9	53.7	54.1
2011	53.7	53.3	53.1	53.8	53.8	54.1	54.3	54.6	54.0	53.8	53.8	53.8	53.8
2012	52.9	53.0	53.0	53.5	53.9	54.0	54.0	54.0	53.6	53.7	53.6	53.8	53.6
2013	53.1	53.2	53.1	53.1	53.4	53.4	53.9	53.7	52.9	53.4	54.6	55.6	53.6

1. Employment by Industry: Minnesota, Selected Years, 2002–2013—*Continued*

(Numbers in thousands, not seasonally adjusted)

Industry and year	January	February	March	April	May	June	July	August	September	October	November	December	Annual average
Financial Activities													
2002	168.3	168.6	168.6	169.6	170.4	171.5	173.3	173.9	173.1	173.0	173.8	174.8	171.6
2003	172.0	172.6	173.2	174.9	176.1	178.1	178.3	178.7	177.3	175.3	175.1	175.9	175.6
2004	174.9	174.6	174.6	176.6	177.0	178.8	177.7	177.9	176.4	176.4	176.5	177.3	176.6
2005	175.2	175.1	175.7	179.9	180.6	182.5	181.5	182.1	180.8	180.0	180.2	181.2	179.6
2006	179.8	179.7	180.2	179.5	180.7	182.4	181.7	181.5	180.0	179.8	180.1	181.0	180.5
2007	178.6	179.2	179.3	178.9	178.9	181.1	180.8	180.6	178.9	178.8	178.9	179.4	179.5
2008	176.7	176.8	177.0	176.6	177.0	178.4	178.8	178.5	176.5	176.0	175.7	176.4	177.0
2009	173.8	173.2	172.6	172.5	173.2	174.1	174.4	173.8	172.5	172.7	172.5	173.1	173.2
2010	170.7	170.5	170.4	170.9	171.5	173.2	173.7	174.0	172.8	174.2	174.0	175.1	172.6
2011	172.9	173.1	173.0	173.3	173.9	174.7	175.7	176.0	174.4	174.5	174.3	174.8	174.2
2012	174.4	174.8	175.0	177.1	178.2	178.8	179.5	179.7	178.5	179.3	179.4	180.1	177.9
2013	179.5	179.8	179.9	180.3	181.1	182.8	183.0	183.0	180.9	181.4	180.4	181.0	181.1
Professional and Business Services													
2002	290.1	289.8	290.4	292.7	295.5	299.7	301.3	304.4	302.2	302.9	300.3	297.7	297.3
2003	287.8	288.1	288.9	292.3	294.5	298.0	298.1	299.8	299.4	301.2	299.7	300.6	295.7
2004	288.7	290.6	292.8	299.7	302.2	306.6	306.2	307.3	304.7	306.9	305.4	304.1	301.3
2005	291.1	292.0	294.8	304.1	307.3	311.6	310.5	314.5	315.1	319.5	319.2	319.0	308.2
2006	313.2	313.6	315.3	319.8	322.9	329.0	327.0	329.5	328.1	329.6	329.5	328.6	323.8
2007	319.9	321.1	323.2	326.1	329.5	333.8	334.4	337.9	334.0	334.1	333.3	331.9	329.9
2008	322.7	323.5	323.3	326.3	329.5	332.9	333.8	336.2	332.5	332.7	328.3	324.3	328.8
2009	308.3	304.0	301.7	305.3	306.9	307.8	307.3	310.9	305.7	311.7	311.2	311.4	307.7
2010	300.1	301.0	300.9	309.7	312.0	315.9	319.5	319.6	323.6	318.2	322.7	323.1	321.4	314.0
2011	314.4	315.1	316.9	325.5	327.5	330.8	335.2	339.4	337.9	339.2	338.0	336.1	329.7
2012	324.8	324.8	326.4	333.5	335.0	338.7	341.4	345.0	341.6	344.5	342.9	342.4	336.8
2013	333.2	336.4	337.3	341.1	343.9	348.7	349.2	352.7	349.0	352.0	346.7	347.6	344.8
Education and Health Services													
2002	346.3	353.1	355.2	357.1	359.4	352.9	349.9	351.0	356.7	363.2	365.5	365.9	356.4
2003	361.7	368.3	369.8	370.1	371.5	365.7	364.0	363.3	369.0	373.3	374.8	374.0	368.8
2004	369.6	374.1	375.7	377.9	379.0	374.4	372.3	371.8	375.6	381.9	383.3	385.7	376.8
2005	377.6	384.1	385.9	388.3	392.1	387.1	388.8	389.8	394.8	399.8	402.2	403.8	391.2
2006	399.2	402.1	404.4	407.0	408.3	406.3	407.7	407.9	411.4	415.2	419.0	420.6	409.1
2007	418.0	421.1	422.9	426.1	428.1	426.3	425.6	426.0	429.4	435.1	438.4	437.6	427.9
2008	433.0	437.8	439.8	442.9	442.4	439.6	438.6	439.8	443.2	450.5	452.7	452.9	442.8
2009	448.2	452.1	453.8	458.1	457.5	450.3	448.6	448.6	448.1	458.0	458.5	458.8	453.4
2010	451.3	456.4	458.3	460.4	460.7	456.4	451.5	454.1	457.3	464.0	466.2	464.5	458.4
2011	461.7	466.4	466.7	471.8	472.3	467.6	464.8	466.2	471.1	473.7	475.0	475.5	469.4
2012	470.1	475.5	475.9	478.2	478.1	472.1	470.0	473.1	480.4	485.4	487.5	486.7	477.8
2013	482.9	488.4	488.3	492.4	492.8	486.2	482.7	486.5	492.0	499.7	502.3	499.8	491.2
Leisure and Hospitality													
2002	213.8	213.6	215.0	222.3	233.9	243.6	244.2	246.9	240.1	228.7	221.7	222.8	228.9
2003	216.6	215.1	216.4	225.8	238.5	246.5	246.4	249.4	242.4	232.0	224.6	226.1	231.7
2004	217.8	216.9	219.4	231.0	242.2	251.0	250.5	252.6	246.5	238.1	230.3	231.2	235.6
2005	223.0	222.3	224.6	237.0	247.3	256.9	256.8	259.0	252.7	246.0	241.7	241.3	242.4
2006	233.5	233.5	236.4	239.8	250.9	260.3	257.7	259.8	251.4	243.4	237.7	238.1	245.2
2007	232.1	231.9	234.0	241.6	254.8	263.3	263.6	265.1	257.0	248.1	241.3	240.5	247.8
2008	232.9	232.4	234.9	239.5	253.2	261.9	260.9	263.8	253.2	245.2	236.4	234.6	245.7
2009	226.7	224.9	225.8	234.2	246.5	252.1	252.4	254.0	245.3	237.2	228.3	227.0	237.9
2010	219.5	218.5	221.3	232.1	242.3	248.5	250.2	252.6	244.5	237.7	228.8	226.4	235.2
2011	220.8	220.4	223.8	233.7	247.5	255.9	255.1	258.3	252.7	241.1	234.6	232.3	239.7
2012	227.7	228.4	232.5	240.6	251.0	260.6	261.4	263.7	256.6	246.2	239.3	238.0	245.5
2013	233.3	232.9	235.9	241.1	256.0	265.3	266.7	268.0	259.2	250.0	242.0	239.9	249.2
Other Services													
2002	116.6	116.7	117.0	117.9	118.2	119.3	119.5	119.9	119.2	119.2	119.5	120.2	118.6
2003	117.7	117.9	118.4	118.4	118.7	119.7	120.5	120.6	120.1	119.0	119.1	119.8	119.2
2004	117.0	116.1	117.3	118.9	118.6	119.8	118.0	118.7	117.8	118.0	117.6	118.4	118.0
2005	115.0	115.0	115.6	118.2	119.0	119.7	119.1	119.6	119.3	119.2	119.0	119.8	118.2
2006	115.5	115.4	117.3	118.0	118.6	119.9	118.7	118.8	118.3	118.6	118.8	119.3	118.1
2007	115.1	114.8	116.3	116.9	117.7	118.3	117.8	117.9	116.7	116.5	116.9	117.4	116.9
2008	115.1	116.6	116.7	118.1	118.5	120.2	119.4	119.7	119.7	117.9	117.7	116.3	117.9
2009	114.7	114.7	115.2	116.0	116.4	117.2	116.5	116.4	115.4	114.5	113.9	114.1	115.4
2010	112.4	112.6	113.6	113.7	114.1	115.4	115.2	115.6	113.7	114.8	114.0	113.9	114.1
2011	112.7	113.0	113.6	114.8	115.2	116.6	116.5	116.9	116.2	115.3	115.2	115.5	115.1
2012	114.2	114.3	114.8	115.5	115.8	117.9	117.1	117.2	115.7	115.9	115.8	115.9	115.8
2013	115.0	115.3	116.1	116.6	118.0	119.3	118.6	119.3	118.1	118.4	119.1	119.3	117.8
Government													
2002	414.3	420.4	420.0	418.2	420.1	420.9	391.4	379.8	410.4	419.9	427.4	425.0	414.0
2003	412.8	421.6	421.4	422.6	422.2	418.0	384.8	382.8	404.5	417.4	419.7	421.7	412.5
2004	411.6	418.9	418.9	420.5	422.4	414.8	383.7	379.2	407.1	419.2	423.4	424.9	412.1
2005	416.4	422.1	422.9	424.6	424.9	420.0	391.1	384.7	408.7	420.6	422.2	422.2	414.9
2006	415.2	421.5	422.5	423.0	423.5	421.7	391.2	386.4	410.9	422.4	425.8	427.0	415.9
2007	414.2	420.5	419.6	420.2	424.0	422.1	389.5	384.0	407.6	422.5	425.9	425.0	414.6
2008	417.1	423.9	424.4	423.9	428.2	426.5	392.1	388.6	413.9	427.3	430.6	430.0	418.9
2009	417.4	425.0	425.2	426.7	428.5	425.7	393.1	385.3	404.1	423.7	426.5	426.1	417.3
2010	416.7	423.5	425.4	426.3	430.6	425.8	389.3	383.2	404.8	422.3	425.8	424.8	416.5
2011	413.6	421.3	421.0	422.1	421.6	419.0	362.0	378.4	405.6	419.5	421.5	421.7	410.6
2012	410.1	418.2	418.7	421.0	420.5	418.8	377.6	380.9	408.3	422.9	427.6	425.5	412.5
2013	413.4	422.9	421.4	421.7	423.5	419.5	374.5	378.7	408.8	421.9	422.9	422.6	412.7

2.　Average Weekly Hours by Selected Industry: Minnesota, 2009–2013

(Not seasonally adjusted)

Industry and year	January	February	March	April	May	June	July	August	September	October	November	December	Annual average
Total Private													
2009	32.5	32.8	32.7	32.7	32.3	32.3	32.5	33.1	32.2	32.6	33.1	32.6	32.6
2010	32.7	32.7	32.7	32.7	33.1	32.8	33.0	33.5	33.1	33.2	33.0	33.0	33.0
2011	33.3	32.9	32.9	33.1	33.4	33.1	33.2	33.3	33.5	33.8	33.3	33.5	33.3
2012	33.7	33.2	33.2	33.9	33.2	33.5	33.9	33.7	34.3	33.5	33.2	33.7	33.6
2013	33.1	33.2	33.4	33.2	33.4	34.3	33.4	33.7	34.3	33.8	33.7	34.0	33.7
Goods-Producing													
2009	37.6	38.0	37.8	37.7	38.7	38.1	38.3	38.8	37.7	38.0	38.2	38.0	38.1
2010	38.1	38.0	38.1	38.8	38.8	38.1	38.8	39.2	38.8	39.4	38.6	38.6	38.6
2011	38.0	37.9	38.3	38.7	38.8	38.9	38.8	40.0	40.8	40.4	39.4	40.0	39.2
2012	39.8	39.6	39.7	40.3	40.0	40.6	40.5	40.7	41.1	40.6	39.8	39.8	40.2
2013	39.8	39.8	40.0	40.1	40.1	41.0	40.5	41.2	41.3	41.3	40.5	40.3	40.5
Construction													
2009	33.3	34.9	34.2	36.1	38.1	37.8	38.3	38.4	35.5	35.8	36.2	33.0	36.1
2010	34.7	32.7	33.0	33.9	33.9	33.3	36.4	36.7	35.4	37.8	35.6	35.9	35.1
2011	35.6	34.6	35.6	36.6	37.4	37.3	37.5	41.1	41.5	40.3	38.5	37.8	38.1
2012	37.6	36.8	38.6	39.3	39.5	40.6	40.7	41.3	42.0	41.3	38.8	38.8	39.8
2013	38.9	38.4	38.7	38.4	39.1	41.1	40.2	41.2	41.2	41.5	39.4	37.8	39.8
Manufacturing													
2009	38.6	38.8	38.8	38.2	38.5	37.9	37.8	38.2	37.9	38.4	38.4	38.8	38.4
2010	38.8	39.3	39.3	40.0	40.1	39.5	39.4	39.8	39.6	39.8	39.6	39.5	39.6
2011	39.0	39.0	39.2	39.5	39.4	39.5	39.3	40.0	40.4	40.3	39.5	40.3	39.6
2012	40.0	39.9	39.7	40.3	39.8	40.2	40.0	40.2	40.6	40.3	40.1	40.1	40.1
2013	40.0	40.1	40.3	40.6	40.4	40.8	40.4	41.0	41.2	41.2	40.9	41.0	40.7
Trade, Transportation, and Utilities													
2009	31.0	31.4	31.5	31.3	31.2	31.2	31.4	32.1	31.5	31.8	32.5	32.2	31.6
2010	31.5	31.7	31.7	31.6	32.0	31.9	32.5	33.1	32.7	32.1	31.4	31.6	32.0
2011	31.5	31.4	31.4	31.5	32.3	32.0	32.2	31.9	32.7	33.0	32.5	32.9	32.1
2012	32.5	32.1	32.0	32.5	32.3	32.3	33.1	32.7	33.3	32.4	32.1	33.0	32.5
2013	31.9	32.3	32.6	32.4	33.2	33.6	33.2	32.9	33.6	33.0	33.0	33.7	33.0
Financial Activities													
2009	37.1	36.7	36.4	35.9	35.7	35.4	35.7	36.6	35.5	35.9	37.0	36.0	36.2
2010	37.7	36.5	36.3	36.4	37.7	36.4	36.2	37.6	37.0	36.9	37.4	37.4	37.0
2011	39.2	38.0	37.6	37.5	38.4	37.3	37.5	37.8	37.7	39.0	38.3	38.2	38.0
2012	39.8	38.1	38.0	39.1	37.5	37.5	38.8	37.5	39.0	37.4	37.6	38.7	38.2
2013	37.2	37.5	37.2	37.2	37.1	38.6	36.1	36.5	38.1	36.4	36.8	37.8	37.2
Professional and Business Services													
2009	35.2	36.2	36.4	36.1	35.9	36.2	35.7	36.6	35.4	35.6	36.2	35.3	35.9
2010	34.8	35.2	35.5	35.7	36.4	35.7	36.0	36.5	35.9	36.2	36.0	35.9	35.8
2011	36.6	36.1	35.9	35.9	36.7	36.0	35.9	35.7	35.2	36.0	34.7	35.3	35.8
2012	36.2	35.6	35.7	36.8	35.7	35.9	36.2	35.3	36.8	35.2	35.0	35.7	35.8
2013	34.8	35.4	35.5	35.1	35.0	36.5	34.3	34.8	36.3	35.1	35.3	35.7	35.3
Education and Health Services													
2009	32.2	31.9	31.5	31.2	31.2	31.2	31.2	31.5	30.7	30.8	31.1	30.8	31.3
2010	30.8	30.6	30.7	30.7	30.7	30.7	30.8	31.0	30.6	30.7	30.8	30.7	30.7
2011	30.9	30.7	30.7	30.6	30.7	30.6	30.8	30.7	30.7	31.0	31.0	30.9	30.8
2012	30.9	30.8	30.7	31.1	30.7	30.7	30.9	30.9	31.2	30.9	30.9	31.0	30.9
2013	31.1	30.9	31.0	30.8	30.8	31.2	31.0	31.2	31.3	31.1	31.1	31.3	31.1
Leisure and Hospitality													
2009	22.0	22.9	22.8	22.2	22.2	22.5	23.0	23.3	22.3	22.0	22.1	21.7	22.4
2010	21.8	22.4	22.2	21.7	22.0	22.1	22.2	22.9	21.7	21.8	21.6	21.3	22.0
2011	22.1	22.1	22.1	21.9	22.0	22.4	22.7	22.9	22.3	22.8	22.4	22.7	22.4
2012	22.3	22.5	22.8	22.8	22.8	23.5	23.7	24.0	23.5	22.9	22.4	22.7	23.0
2013	22.0	22.6	23.2	22.4	22.9	23.9	24.2	24.4	24.0	23.3	23.0	22.9	23.3
Other Services													
2009	26.4	27.5	26.2	25.8	26.9	27.5	27.8	28.5	27.3	27.9	28.4	27.2	27.3
2010	28.3	27.9	27.8	27.2	27.8	28.0	27.7	28.4	27.9	27.6	27.7	27.2	27.8
2011	27.8	27.2	27.3	28.0	29.1	29.1	29.1	28.4	28.8	29.5	29.3	29.7	28.6
2012	30.1	29.4	29.5	29.8	29.5	29.8	29.9	29.9	29.5	28.9	29.3	29.1	29.6
2013	28.4	28.7	29.5	29.2	29.5	30.1	29.1	29.5	30.0	30.2	30.5	31.5	29.7

3. Average Hourly Earnings by Selected Industry: Minnesota, 2009–2013

(Dollars, not seasonally adjusted)

Industry and year	January	February	March	April	May	June	July	August	September	October	November	December	Annual average
Total Private													
2009	23.70	23.83	23.57	23.23	23.67	23.36	23.75	22.69	22.95	23.19	23.43	23.51	23.41
2010	23.64	24.02	23.70	23.67	23.71	23.23	23.63	23.65	23.88	24.19	24.28	24.61	23.85
2011	24.45	24.33	24.55	24.58	24.59	24.17	24.31	24.31	24.61	24.90	24.74	24.89	24.54
2012	24.69	24.51	24.49	24.89	24.69	24.70	25.00	24.81	25.44	25.20	25.27	25.67	24.95
2013	25.71	25.55	25.55	25.68	25.52	25.55	25.57	25.40	25.77	25.75	25.74	25.94	25.64
Goods-Producing													
2009	24.48	23.04	23.28	23.62	24.31	24.27	24.40	24.34	24.25	24.36	24.78	24.93	24.17
2010	25.04	24.81	24.55	24.82	24.72	24.58	25.13	24.68	24.97	25.67	25.58	25.70	25.03
2011	26.09	25.61	25.75	25.79	25.58	25.36	25.42	25.45	25.81	25.79	25.76	26.17	25.71
2012	25.71	25.33	25.39	25.56	25.60	25.53	25.74	25.54	26.09	26.07	26.06	26.20	25.74
2013	26.23	26.11	26.25	26.59	26.51	26.46	26.51	26.25	26.45	26.40	26.40	26.61	26.40
Construction													
2009	25.72	25.59	25.12	25.24	26.49	26.11	25.59	26.17	26.14	26.48	26.30	26.81	26.01
2010	26.37	26.98	27.43	27.53	27.38	27.24	28.10	27.63	27.46	28.11	27.59	28.21	27.55
2011	28.49	28.19	28.64	28.56	28.02	27.49	27.24	27.86	29.00	27.93	28.05	28.57	28.14
2012	28.34	28.48	28.53	28.41	28.22	27.95	28.08	28.12	29.16	29.10	28.86	29.01	28.52
2013	29.14	28.69	29.45	29.86	28.97	28.58	28.27	28.24	28.30	28.38	28.15	28.54	28.65
Manufacturing													
2009	24.47	24.24	24.00	24.18	24.30	24.02	24.47	24.60	24.34	24.57	25.16	25.09	24.45
2010	25.48	25.01	24.65	24.80	24.59	24.26	24.26	24.06	24.26	24.86	25.01	24.98	24.68
2011	25.40	24.90	24.89	24.92	24.72	24.51	24.68	24.38	24.48	24.80	24.85	25.37	24.82
2012	25.32	24.87	24.85	25.01	25.00	24.75	25.01	24.66	24.93	24.91	25.05	25.30	24.97
2013	25.28	25.34	25.23	25.44	25.55	25.55	25.70	25.32	25.57	25.50	25.59	25.81	25.49
Trade, Transportation, and Utilities													
2009	20.04	21.02	21.04	20.25	20.27	20.25	20.76	20.83	20.95	20.76	21.19	20.87	20.69
2010	21.07	21.77	20.98	21.44	21.41	20.94	21.01	21.04	22.66	21.51	21.52	21.61	21.41
2011	22.12	21.75	21.88	21.95	21.82	21.28	21.30	21.08	21.44	21.80	21.27	21.07	21.56
2012	21.62	21.04	20.98	21.66	21.50	21.55	21.75	21.64	22.28	21.75	21.86	22.13	21.65
2013	22.39	22.49	22.40	22.57	22.32	22.56	22.50	22.46	22.94	22.73	22.75	22.34	22.54
Financial Activities													
2009	26.71	28.45	27.01	26.61	27.07	25.93	26.26	27.35	26.94	27.27	27.60	27.74	27.08
2010	26.52	27.43	26.37	26.08	26.49	26.47	27.06	27.52	26.37	27.10	27.73	27.49	26.89
2011	26.51	26.96	28.65	28.36	28.66	28.61	28.55	29.02	28.86	29.55	30.20	29.90	28.65
2012	29.80	29.61	29.63	30.21	30.31	30.65	30.99	31.62	32.09	31.39	31.94	32.40	30.89
2013	32.83	33.50	33.80	33.43	33.47	33.87	34.23	34.01	33.53	33.62	33.43	33.56	33.61
Professional and Business Services													
2009	28.90	29.54	29.53	29.83	29.95	28.98	29.27	30.03	30.07	30.17	30.23	30.85	29.78
2010	30.20	30.18	30.38	30.23	30.35	29.78	30.04	29.90	29.51	29.64	29.69	30.30	30.01
2011	31.08	30.65	30.72	30.86	31.44	30.84	31.15	30.83	30.79	30.90	30.18	30.49	30.83
2012	30.61	29.93	29.60	29.98	29.00	28.74	29.44	28.80	29.01	28.59	28.86	29.50	29.33
2013	29.04	28.84	28.91	28.52	28.39	28.36	28.37	28.05	28.40	27.94	27.95	28.70	28.45
Education and Health Services													
2009	23.79	23.82	23.59	23.58	23.32	23.59	24.23	23.93	24.50	24.54	24.18	23.77	23.90
2010	23.81	23.88	23.90	23.63	23.83	22.90	23.06	23.41	24.06	23.99	23.88	24.22	23.72
2011	23.93	24.30	24.35	24.57	24.44	24.02	24.37	24.39	24.69	25.01	24.83	25.05	24.50
2012	25.22	25.25	25.38	25.50	25.53	25.73	25.87	25.69	25.93	26.08	25.98	26.33	25.71
2013	26.16	26.10	26.07	26.23	26.24	26.06	26.27	26.06	26.41	26.61	26.48	26.64	26.28
Leisure and Hospitality													
2009	13.41	13.27	13.26	13.03	12.97	12.68	12.33	12.77	13.12	13.38	13.50	13.58	13.09
2010	13.70	13.64	13.53	14.13	13.97	13.53	13.59	13.57	13.80	13.99	14.04	14.21	13.80
2011	13.97	13.95	13.69	13.69	13.47	12.98	12.95	12.81	13.01	12.99	13.25	13.20	13.31
2012	13.19	13.25	13.16	13.15	13.06	12.81	12.86	12.70	13.01	13.24	13.28	13.51	13.09
2013	13.44	13.51	13.45	13.46	13.31	13.02	13.03	12.97	13.29	13.50	13.70	13.83	13.36
Other Services													
2009	17.36	16.80	17.04	17.54	16.79	16.62	17.47	17.18	17.20	17.05	17.49	17.73	17.19
2010	18.53	18.58	18.33	18.39	18.14	18.36	18.78	18.50	18.89	19.02	18.80	19.07	18.61
2011	19.00	19.18	19.91	19.71	19.97	20.11	20.07	20.23	19.81	19.89	19.71	20.26	19.83
2012	20.86	20.38	20.20	20.18	20.47	20.52	21.02	21.19	21.45	21.54	21.42	21.90	20.93
2013	22.48	22.20	22.39	22.59	22.84	23.20	23.57	22.97	23.37	23.10	23.04	23.93	22.99

4. Average Weekly Earnings by Selected Industry: Minnesota, 2009–2013

(Dollars, not seasonally adjusted)

Industry and year	January	February	March	April	May	June	July	August	September	October	November	December	Annual average
Total Private													
2009	770.25	781.62	770.74	759.62	764.54	754.53	771.88	751.04	738.99	755.99	775.53	766.43	763.17
2010	773.03	785.45	774.99	774.01	784.80	761.94	779.79	792.28	790.43	803.11	801.24	812.13	787.05
2011	814.19	800.46	807.70	813.60	821.31	800.03	807.09	809.52	824.44	841.62	823.84	833.82	817.18
2012	832.05	813.73	813.07	843.77	819.71	827.45	847.50	836.10	872.59	844.20	838.96	865.08	838.32
2013	851.00	848.26	853.37	852.58	852.37	876.37	854.04	855.98	883.91	870.35	867.44	881.96	864.07
Goods-Producing													
2009	920.45	875.52	879.98	890.47	940.80	924.69	934.52	944.39	914.23	925.68	946.60	947.34	920.88
2010	954.02	942.78	935.36	963.02	959.14	936.50	975.04	967.46	968.84	1,011.40	987.39	992.02	966.16
2011	991.42	970.62	986.23	998.07	992.50	986.50	986.30	1,018.00	1,053.05	1,041.92	1,014.94	1,046.80	1,007.83
2012	1,023.26	1,003.07	1,007.98	1,030.07	1,024.00	1,036.52	1,042.47	1,039.48	1,072.30	1,058.44	1,037.19	1,042.76	1,034.75
2013	1,043.95	1,039.18	1,050.00	1,066.26	1,063.05	1,084.86	1,073.66	1,081.50	1,092.39	1,090.32	1,069.20	1,072.38	1,069.20
Construction													
2009	856.48	893.09	859.10	911.16	1,009.27	986.96	980.10	1,004.93	927.97	947.98	952.06	884.73	938.96
2010	915.04	882.25	905.19	933.27	928.18	907.09	1,022.84	1,014.02	972.08	1,062.56	982.20	1,012.74	967.01
2011	1,014.24	975.37	1,019.58	1,045.30	1,047.95	1,025.38	1,021.50	1,145.05	1,203.50	1,125.58	1,079.93	1,079.95	1,072.13
2012	1,065.58	1,048.06	1,101.26	1,116.51	1,114.69	1,134.77	1,142.86	1,161.36	1,224.72	1,201.83	1,119.77	1,125.59	1,135.10
2013	1,133.55	1,101.70	1,139.72	1,146.62	1,132.73	1,174.64	1,136.45	1,163.49	1,165.96	1,177.77	1,109.11	1,078.81	1,140.27
Manufacturing													
2009	944.54	940.51	931.20	923.68	935.55	910.36	924.97	939.72	922.49	943.49	966.14	973.49	938.88
2010	988.62	982.89	968.75	992.00	986.06	958.27	955.84	957.59	960.70	989.43	990.40	986.71	977.33
2011	990.60	971.10	975.69	984.34	973.97	968.15	969.92	975.20	988.99	999.44	981.58	1,022.41	982.87
2012	1,012.80	992.31	986.55	1,007.90	995.00	994.95	1,000.40	991.33	1,012.16	1,003.87	1,004.51	1,014.53	1,001.30
2013	1,011.20	1,016.13	1,016.77	1,032.86	1,032.22	1,042.44	1,038.28	1,038.12	1,053.48	1,050.60	1,046.63	1,058.21	1,037.44
Trade, Transportation, and Utilities													
2009	621.24	660.03	662.76	633.83	632.42	631.80	651.86	668.64	659.93	660.17	688.68	672.01	653.80
2010	663.71	690.11	665.07	677.50	685.12	667.99	682.83	696.42	740.98	690.47	675.73	682.88	685.12
2011	696.78	682.95	687.03	691.43	704.79	680.96	685.86	672.45	701.09	719.40	691.28	693.20	692.08
2012	702.65	675.38	671.36	703.95	694.45	696.07	719.93	707.63	741.92	704.70	701.71	730.29	703.63
2013	714.24	726.43	730.24	731.27	741.02	758.02	747.00	738.93	770.78	750.09	750.75	752.86	743.82
Financial Activities													
2009	990.94	1,044.12	983.16	955.30	966.40	917.92	937.48	1,001.01	956.37	978.99	1,021.20	998.64	980.30
2010	999.80	1,001.20	957.23	949.31	998.67	963.51	979.57	1,034.75	975.69	999.99	1,037.10	1,028.13	994.93
2011	1,039.19	1,024.48	1,077.24	1,063.50	1,100.54	1,067.15	1,070.63	1,096.96	1,088.02	1,152.45	1,156.66	1,142.18	1,088.70
2012	1,186.04	1,128.14	1,125.94	1,181.21	1,136.63	1,149.38	1,202.41	1,185.75	1,251.51	1,173.99	1,200.94	1,253.88	1,180.00
2013	1,221.28	1,256.25	1,257.36	1,243.60	1,241.74	1,307.38	1,235.70	1,241.37	1,277.49	1,223.77	1,230.22	1,268.57	1,250.29
Professional and Business Services													
2009	1,017.28	1,069.35	1,074.89	1,076.86	1,075.21	1,049.08	1,044.94	1,099.10	1,064.48	1,074.05	1,094.33	1,089.01	1,069.10
2010	1,050.96	1,062.34	1,078.49	1,079.21	1,104.74	1,063.15	1,081.44	1,091.35	1,059.41	1,072.97	1,068.84	1,087.77	1,074.36
2011	1,137.53	1,106.47	1,102.85	1,107.87	1,153.85	1,110.24	1,118.29	1,100.63	1,083.81	1,112.40	1,047.25	1,076.30	1,103.71
2012	1,108.08	1,065.51	1,056.72	1,103.26	1,035.30	1,031.77	1,065.73	1,016.64	1,067.57	1,006.37	1,010.10	1,053.15	1,050.01
2013	1,010.59	1,020.94	1,026.31	1,001.05	993.65	1,035.14	973.09	976.14	1,030.92	980.69	986.64	1,024.59	1,004.29
Education and Health Services													
2009	766.04	759.86	743.09	735.70	727.58	736.01	755.98	753.80	752.15	755.83	752.00	732.12	748.07
2010	733.35	730.73	733.73	725.44	731.58	703.03	710.25	725.71	736.24	736.49	735.50	743.55	728.20
2011	739.44	746.01	747.55	751.84	750.31	735.01	750.60	748.77	757.98	775.31	769.73	774.05	754.60
2012	779.30	777.70	779.17	793.05	783.77	789.91	799.38	793.82	809.02	805.87	802.78	816.23	794.44
2013	813.58	806.49	808.17	807.88	808.19	813.07	814.37	813.07	826.63	827.57	823.53	833.83	817.31
Leisure and Hospitality													
2009	295.02	303.88	302.33	289.27	287.93	285.30	283.59	297.54	292.58	294.36	298.35	294.69	293.22
2010	298.66	305.54	300.37	306.62	307.34	299.01	301.70	310.75	299.46	304.98	303.26	302.67	303.60
2011	308.74	308.30	302.55	299.81	296.34	290.75	293.97	293.35	290.12	296.17	296.80	299.64	298.14
2012	294.14	298.13	300.05	299.82	297.77	301.04	304.78	304.80	305.74	303.20	297.47	306.68	301.07
2013	295.68	305.33	312.04	301.50	304.80	311.18	315.33	316.47	318.96	314.55	315.10	316.71	311.29
Other Services													
2009	458.30	462.00	446.45	452.53	451.65	457.05	485.67	489.63	469.56	475.70	496.72	482.26	469.29
2010	524.40	518.38	509.57	500.21	504.29	514.08	520.21	525.40	527.03	524.95	520.76	518.70	517.36
2011	528.20	521.70	543.54	551.88	581.13	585.20	584.04	574.53	570.53	586.76	577.50	601.72	567.14
2012	627.89	599.17	595.90	601.36	603.87	611.50	628.50	633.58	632.78	622.51	627.61	637.29	619.53
2013	638.43	637.14	660.51	659.63	673.78	698.32	685.89	677.62	701.10	697.62	702.72	753.80	682.80

MISSISSIPPI
At a Glance

Population:
    2000 census: 2,844,754
    2010 census: 2,967,297
    2013 estimate: 2,991,207

Percent change in population:
    2000–2010: 4.3%
    2010–2013: 0.8%

Percent change in total nonfarm employment:
    2000–2010: -5.3%
    2010–2013: 1.8%

Industry with the largest growth in employment, 2000–2013 (thousands):
    Education and Health Services, 29.0

Industry with the largest decline or smallest growth in employment, 2000–2013 (thousands):
    Manufacturing, -85.7

Civilian labor force:
    2000: 1,314,154
    2010: 1,309,903
    2013: 1,286,423

Unemployment rate and rank among states (lowest to highest):
    2000: 5.7%, 49th
    2010: 10.6%, 43rd
    2013: 8.6%, 46th

Over-the-year change in unemployment rates:
    2010–2011: 0.0%
    2011–2012: -1.4%
    2012–2013: -0.6%

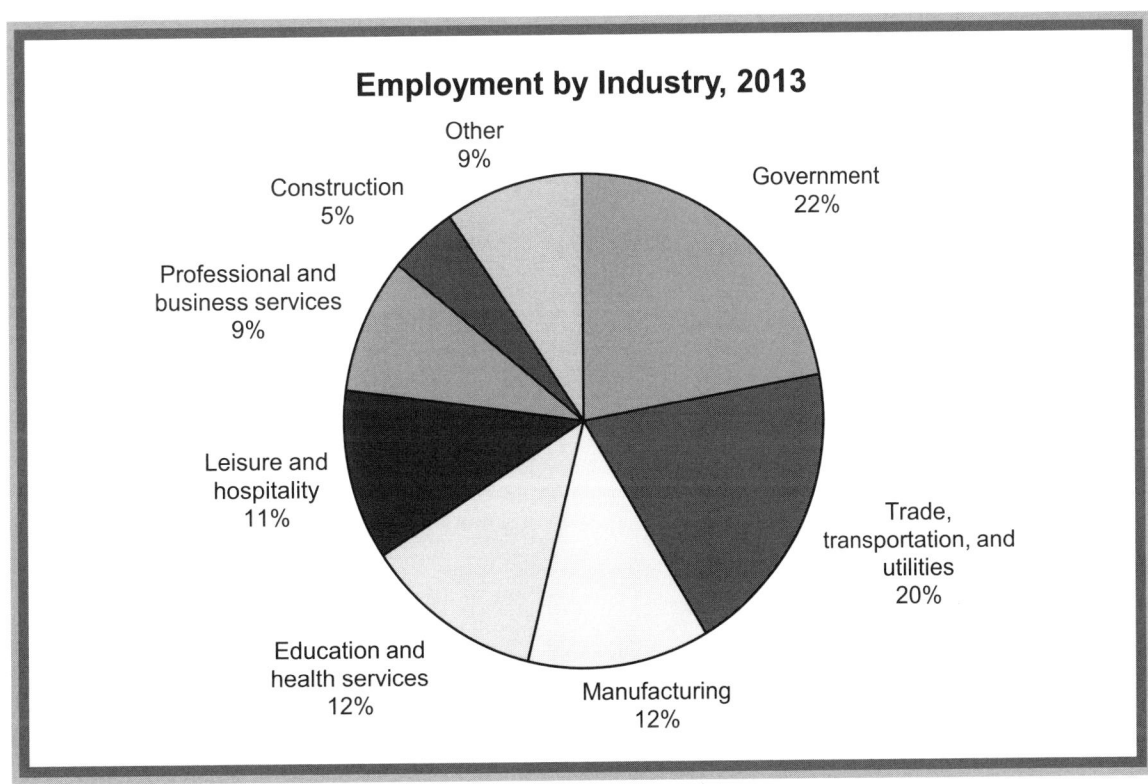

Employment by Industry, 2013

Other 9%
Construction 5%
Professional and business services 9%
Leisure and hospitality 11%
Education and health services 12%
Manufacturing 12%
Trade, transportation, and utilities 20%
Government 22%

1. Employment by Industry: Mississippi, Selected Years, 2002–2013

(Numbers in thousands, not seasonally adjusted)

Industry and year	January	February	March	April	May	June	July	August	September	October	November	December	Annual average
Total Nonfarm													
2002	1,112.4	1,115.3	1,121.7	1,129.3	1,133.1	1,134.7	1,121.1	1,129.8	1,132.1	1,123.6	1,123.0	1,124.7	1,125.1
2003	1,108.7	1,110.2	1,113.7	1,117.9	1,118.1	1,112.3	1,105.9	1,113.2	1,120.9	1,124.6	1,126.2	1,124.7	1,116.4
2004	1,109.6	1,115.0	1,122.6	1,131.5	1,130.7	1,126.6	1,115.9	1,125.5	1,134.1	1,132.4	1,134.8	1,134.1	1,126.1
2005	1,119.7	1,127.9	1,135.9	1,140.7	1,140.0	1,134.6	1,124.4	1,135.4	1,122.0	1,127.1	1,139.7	1,133.1	1,131.7
2006	1,117.5	1,127.8	1,138.9	1,142.8	1,146.2	1,145.0	1,126.2	1,144.9	1,154.8	1,152.1	1,157.8	1,157.1	1,142.6
2007	1,139.7	1,146.3	1,150.0	1,155.5	1,157.5	1,153.9	1,138.1	1,154.9	1,163.0	1,160.4	1,166.1	1,165.3	1,154.2
2008	1,148.6	1,155.2	1,159.3	1,163.3	1,162.3	1,153.6	1,130.5	1,144.9	1,149.0	1,145.6	1,143.1	1,132.7	1,149.0
2009	1,107.9	1,107.8	1,107.0	1,105.5	1,105.6	1,097.8	1,080.6	1,088.6	1,095.5	1,091.3	1,094.1	1,090.0	1,097.6
2010	1,072.2	1,077.9	1,087.9	1,097.9	1,104.8	1,100.6	1,083.5	1,089.6	1,098.4	1,100.2	1,099.5	1,098.0	1,092.5
2011	1,078.3	1,084.0	1,094.4	1,099.9	1,100.2	1,093.6	1,078.4	1,088.8	1,099.0	1,099.0	1,101.7	1,097.6	1,092.9
2012	1,085.2	1,095.4	1,103.7	1,107.3	1,108.2	1,100.4	1,086.6	1,102.0	1,107.8	1,107.5	1,112.5	1,110.7	1,102.3
2013	1,092.7	1,104.7	1,110.1	1,114.6	1,115.1	1,109.8	1,093.6	1,108.6	1,117.9	1,123.8	1,127.2	1,125.0	1,111.9
Total Private													
2002	874.2	876.0	882.1	888.6	892.0	895.2	887.5	890.9	889.9	880.9	880.2	881.9	885.0
2003	867.4	868.0	870.6	874.5	876.8	875.2	873.4	877.4	877.8	880.3	881.8	883.9	875.6
2004	868.9	871.4	877.6	885.7	886.8	886.9	884.0	887.7	889.6	886.9	889.2	892.7	884.0
2005	879.3	883.7	891.3	896.1	896.5	894.6	892.6	897.9	880.7	885.7	897.6	895.0	890.9
2006	879.6	886.8	897.8	901.8	906.3	907.4	898.8	908.3	911.5	909.0	914.0	916.8	903.2
2007	898.9	901.7	905.2	909.5	912.2	911.9	905.1	913.7	915.8	911.8	917.5	919.8	910.3
2008	902.8	905.8	909.5	912.5	912.9	908.1	895.6	900.7	898.8	893.5	890.6	883.3	901.2
2009	859.4	856.5	855.5	852.9	852.8	848.8	841.3	843.7	843.7	838.4	841.8	840.7	848.0
2010	823.9	826.2	834.4	845.6	849.3	849.8	844.9	847.8	850.6	849.7	850.1	849.7	843.5
2011	833.1	836.5	846.1	851.1	852.1	849.5	841.7	847.0	851.5	849.9	853.1	852.5	847.0
2012	839.8	847.0	854.5	858.5	859.6	856.6	851.3	860.3	860.8	858.6	863.6	865.0	856.3
2013	848.0	856.4	861.4	865.8	867.2	866.5	859.1	867.7	870.7	874.8	878.6	878.9	866.3
Goods-Producing													
2002	252.8	253.2	254.0	253.0	253.7	255.0	251.5	251.2	250.3	246.6	244.3	243.1	250.7
2003	239.8	239.6	239.3	239.2	239.1	238.2	236.6	236.4	237.2	238.6	237.9	237.5	238.3
2004	233.7	233.9	235.6	238.1	238.3	240.1	237.6	239.1	238.9	238.2	238.7	238.7	237.6
2005	235.9	235.8	238.0	239.7	240.2	240.7	239.4	239.8	236.0	239.8	241.9	243.7	239.2
2006	239.5	239.5	241.7	242.8	244.6	247.1	244.0	244.0	242.8	242.3	243.0	243.1	242.9
2007	239.0	238.2	235.0	239.3	238.9	238.7	236.5	237.5	238.0	236.5	236.9	237.8	237.7
2008	234.3	233.9	234.1	236.1	236.4	235.1	228.5	227.7	225.7	224.4	221.2	217.1	229.5
2009	209.3	206.5	204.8	202.8	202.8	202.2	199.9	198.6	197.4	194.3	194.3	193.9	200.6
2010	190.1	189.5	192.0	196.5	197.0	196.7	195.8	195.5	194.8	194.6	193.8	193.4	194.1
2011	190.0	190.3	193.4	193.7	195.3	195.4	193.4	193.1	193.9	193.4	192.6	192.5	193.1
2012	191.1	193.0	194.5	195.9	195.9	195.6	194.4	195.3	195.2	195.0	194.5	194.8	194.6
2013	191.5	194.0	194.5	195.5	197.6	198.5	197.6	198.3	199.2	201.6	201.0	200.5	197.5
Service-Providing													
2002	859.6	862.1	867.7	876.3	879.4	879.7	869.6	878.6	881.8	877.0	878.7	881.6	874.3
2003	868.9	870.6	874.4	878.7	879.0	874.1	869.3	876.8	883.7	886.0	888.3	887.2	878.1
2004	875.9	881.1	887.0	893.4	892.4	886.5	878.3	886.4	895.2	894.2	896.1	895.4	888.5
2005	883.8	892.1	897.9	901.0	899.8	893.9	885.0	895.6	886.0	887.3	897.8	889.4	892.5
2006	878.0	888.3	897.2	900.0	901.6	897.9	882.2	900.9	912.0	909.8	914.8	914.0	899.7
2007	900.7	908.1	915.0	916.2	918.6	915.2	901.6	917.4	925.0	923.9	929.2	927.5	916.5
2008	914.3	921.3	925.2	927.2	925.9	918.5	902.0	917.2	923.3	921.2	921.9	915.6	919.5
2009	898.6	901.3	902.2	902.7	902.8	895.6	880.7	890.0	898.1	897.0	899.8	896.1	897.1
2010	882.1	888.4	895.9	901.4	907.8	903.9	887.7	894.1	903.6	905.6	905.7	904.6	898.4
2011	888.3	893.7	901.0	906.2	904.9	898.2	885.0	895.7	905.1	905.6	909.1	905.1	899.8
2012	894.1	902.4	909.2	911.4	912.3	904.8	892.2	906.7	912.6	912.5	918.0	915.9	907.7
2013	901.2	910.7	915.6	919.1	917.5	911.3	896.0	910.3	918.7	922.2	926.2	924.5	914.4
Mining and Logging													
2002	8.9	8.9	9.0	8.9	9.0	9.0	9.0	9.0	9.0	8.8	8.7	8.5	8.9
2003	8.3	8.3	8.5	8.7	8.8	8.8	8.9	9.0	9.1	8.9	8.9	8.9	8.8
2004	8.6	8.5	8.8	8.7	8.8	8.9	9.0	9.0	8.8	8.9	9.0	8.9	8.8
2005	8.5	8.4	8.6	8.8	8.8	8.8	8.8	8.9	8.8	8.9	8.9	8.9	8.8
2006	8.9	9.0	9.2	9.6	9.6	9.5	9.5	9.7	9.6	9.7	9.8	9.6	9.5
2007	9.2	9.3	9.4	9.6	9.7	9.5	9.5	9.6	9.6	9.5	9.7	9.6	9.5
2008	9.4	9.1	9.2	9.4	9.5	9.5	9.4	9.5	9.5	10.0	10.0	9.8	9.5
2009	9.2	9.0	8.8	8.5	8.4	8.3	8.3	8.2	8.2	8.1	8.1	8.1	8.4
2010	8.1	8.1	8.4	8.8	8.9	8.9	8.9	9.0	9.0	9.0	8.9	8.8	8.7
2011	8.8	8.8	9.0	9.0	9.1	9.1	9.3	9.3	9.2	9.1	9.1	9.0	9.1
2012	9.0	9.1	9.2	9.3	9.3	9.3	9.4	9.4	9.4	9.2	9.3	9.2	9.3
2013	8.9	9.0	9.0	9.1	9.2	9.2	9.3	9.3	9.3	9.2	9.3	9.2	9.2
Construction													
2002	53.3	53.2	53.9	53.6	54.3	55.7	54.8	54.9	54.7	53.3	52.7	52.4	53.9
2003	51.0	51.1	50.8	51.1	50.9	50.9	50.6	50.6	50.7	50.4	49.6	49.2	50.6
2004	47.2	47.0	47.7	48.9	49.2	50.1	50.0	50.3	50.6	49.8	49.7	49.0	49.1
2005	47.4	47.5	49.0	50.5	51.5	52.1	52.3	52.6	54.5	55.6	56.4	57.3	52.2
2006	54.7	54.3	55.6	56.8	58.6	60.7	58.9	59.1	58.9	58.3	58.3	58.3	57.7
2007	56.9	56.6	58.4	58.0	58.2	58.7	58.5	59.0	59.4	59.5	60.2	61.2	58.7
2008	59.7	60.0	61.0	63.5	64.5	63.9	60.8	59.4	59.1	59.3	57.3	55.8	60.4
2009	52.5	52.1	52.1	52.0	53.1	53.9	52.3	51.3	49.8	48.4	48.3	47.4	51.1
2010	45.6	45.7	47.6	50.6	50.8	50.7	50.5	50.7	50.8	50.6	50.3	49.5	49.5
2011	46.9	47.2	49.1	49.3	50.3	50.5	49.3	48.8	49.5	49.1	48.2	47.2	48.8
2012	46.0	47.6	48.8	50.0	49.8	48.9	47.9	48.4	48.7	48.4	47.9	47.6	48.3
2013	46.2	48.6	49.3	50.0	51.9	52.6	52.6	52.5	53.0	54.7	53.4	52.9	51.5

1. Employment by Industry: Mississippi, Selected Years, 2002–2013—*Continued*

(Numbers in thousands, not seasonally adjusted)

Industry and year	January	February	March	April	May	June	July	August	September	October	November	December	Annual average
Manufacturing													
2002	190.6	191.1	191.1	190.5	190.4	190.3	187.7	187.3	186.6	184.5	182.9	182.2	187.9
2003	180.5	180.2	180.0	179.4	179.4	178.5	177.1	176.8	177.4	179.3	179.4	179.4	179.0
2004	177.9	178.4	179.1	180.5	180.3	181.1	178.6	179.8	179.5	179.5	180.0	180.8	179.6
2005	180.0	179.9	180.4	180.4	179.9	179.8	178.3	178.3	172.7	175.3	176.6	177.5	178.3
2006	175.9	176.2	176.9	176.4	176.4	176.9	175.6	175.2	174.3	174.3	174.9	175.2	175.7
2007	172.9	172.3	167.2	171.7	171.0	170.5	168.5	168.9	169.0	167.5	167.0	167.0	169.5
2008	165.2	164.8	163.9	163.2	162.4	161.7	158.3	158.8	157.1	155.1	153.9	151.5	159.7
2009	147.6	145.4	143.9	142.3	141.3	140.0	139.3	139.1	139.4	137.8	137.9	138.4	141.0
2010	136.4	135.7	136.0	137.1	137.3	137.1	136.4	135.8	135.0	135.0	134.6	135.1	136.0
2011	134.3	134.3	135.3	135.4	135.9	135.8	134.8	135.0	135.2	135.2	135.3	136.3	135.2
2012	136.1	136.3	136.5	136.6	136.8	137.4	137.1	137.5	137.1	137.4	137.3	138.0	137.0
2013	136.4	136.4	136.2	136.4	136.5	136.6	135.7	136.5	136.9	137.7	138.3	138.4	136.8
Trade, Transportation, and Utilities													
2002	217.9	217.1	218.1	219.7	220.9	222.6	221.2	221.6	221.7	220.6	223.1	225.6	220.8
2003	217.3	216.7	216.5	216.3	217.8	218.3	218.1	218.9	218.8	220.0	222.6	224.7	218.8
2004	217.2	216.4	218.0	218.7	219.9	220.2	219.2	219.7	219.4	220.6	223.1	226.4	219.9
2005	218.1	217.3	219.4	220.1	220.3	220.5	220.8	222.4	217.1	218.3	224.0	228.2	220.5
2006	221.3	221.5	224.7	224.7	225.8	226.1	224.8	226.1	226.2	225.7	228.7	231.8	225.6
2007	224.2	223.3	226.1	225.7	227.2	227.7	225.6	226.7	227.0	226.9	230.6	232.4	227.0
2008	225.1	224.4	226.1	224.5	224.4	224.0	222.9	224.2	223.2	221.7	224.1	225.3	224.2
2009	216.9	215.3	214.8	213.9	214.7	214.6	213.5	213.2	213.7	213.4	216.2	217.0	214.8
2010	210.3	209.6	211.3	212.9	213.8	213.5	212.7	213.3	212.8	214.3	217.3	219.8	213.5
2011	212.5	212.2	214.2	215.1	215.3	214.6	213.8	214.6	214.2	214.4	218.5	220.7	215.0
2012	213.9	213.3	214.2	214.8	215.8	215.5	215.1	215.5	215.1	214.7	219.1	220.9	215.7
2013	213.2	212.5	213.3	214.2	215.3	216.3	215.4	217.1	216.9	218.7	223.0	225.9	216.8
Wholesale Trade													
2002	34.9	34.9	34.9	34.9	34.8	35.1	35.1	35.5	35.4	35.0	34.8	35.1	35.0
2003	34.7	34.6	34.5	34.6	34.8	35.2	34.9	35.1	35.0	34.9	34.9	35.1	34.9
2004	34.8	34.7	34.7	34.9	34.8	35.0	35.1	35.2	35.1	34.9	34.9	35.2	34.9
2005	34.6	34.7	34.9	35.2	35.4	35.5	35.6	35.9	35.3	35.2	35.3	35.8	35.3
2006	35.7	35.9	36.1	35.9	36.2	36.5	36.4	37.0	36.7	36.6	36.6	37.1	36.4
2007	36.6	36.6	36.6	36.6	36.7	36.8	36.8	37.2	37.0	36.7	36.5	37.2	36.8
2008	36.8	36.7	36.6	36.5	36.5	36.6	36.3	36.4	36.0	36.1	35.7	36.0	36.4
2009	35.5	35.4	35.1	34.8	34.7	34.7	34.6	34.7	34.4	34.3	34.1	34.5	34.7
2010	34.0	34.0	33.9	34.2	34.2	34.3	34.2	34.6	34.2	34.3	34.1	34.7	34.2
2011	34.2	34.3	34.2	34.2	34.3	34.1	34.2	34.6	34.5	34.2	34.2	34.7	34.3
2012	34.5	34.6	34.3	34.1	34.2	34.3	34.2	34.5	34.3	33.9	33.9	34.2	34.3
2013	34.3	34.2	34.0	34.0	34.2	34.2	33.9	34.4	34.2	34.6	34.7	35.7	34.4
Retail Trade													
2002	138.3	137.5	138.7	139.8	140.4	141.5	140.3	139.7	139.9	139.0	141.8	144.3	140.1
2003	137.1	136.4	136.7	136.2	137.2	137.2	137.4	138.0	137.9	139.1	141.6	143.7	138.2
2004	136.8	136.0	137.2	137.5	138.2	138.3	137.6	137.4	137.2	138.3	140.9	143.3	138.2
2005	137.0	136.1	137.4	137.8	137.8	137.9	138.1	138.9	134.8	136.4	141.7	144.9	138.2
2006	139.1	138.8	141.5	141.5	142.0	142.0	141.2	141.4	141.3	141.0	143.9	145.9	141.6
2007	139.9	139.2	141.5	141.0	142.0	142.5	140.5	140.7	141.0	141.2	144.8	146.1	141.7
2008	140.2	139.5	141.2	140.0	139.7	139.1	138.3	138.7	138.1	137.0	139.6	140.8	139.4
2009	133.8	132.6	132.8	132.7	133.5	133.6	132.6	132.6	131.7	132.3	132.2	135.1	133.2
2010	130.3	129.7	131.3	132.1	133.0	132.6	131.9	131.7	131.2	132.2	135.4	136.9	132.4
2011	131.2	130.8	132.4	133.4	133.5	133.1	132.4	132.3	131.7	132.4	136.3	137.7	133.1
2012	132.4	131.7	132.6	133.3	133.8	133.5	133.2	132.7	132.1	132.6	136.8	137.7	133.5
2013	130.8	130.2	131.1	131.8	132.4	133.4	133.1	133.7	133.5	134.6	138.1	139.4	133.5
Transportation and Utilities													
2002	44.7	44.7	44.5	45.0	45.7	46.0	45.8	46.4	46.4	46.6	46.5	46.2	45.7
2003	45.5	45.7	45.3	45.5	45.8	45.9	45.8	45.8	45.9	46.0	46.1	45.9	45.8
2004	45.6	45.7	46.1	46.3	46.9	46.9	46.5	47.1	47.1	47.4	47.3	47.9	46.7
2005	46.5	46.5	47.1	47.1	47.1	47.1	47.1	47.6	47.0	46.7	47.0	47.5	47.0
2006	46.5	46.8	47.1	47.3	47.6	47.6	47.2	47.7	48.2	48.1	48.2	48.8	47.6
2007	47.7	47.5	48.0	48.1	48.5	48.4	48.3	48.8	49.0	49.0	49.3	49.1	48.5
2008	48.1	48.2	48.3	48.0	48.2	48.3	48.3	49.1	49.1	48.6	48.8	48.5	48.5
2009	47.6	47.3	46.9	46.4	46.5	46.3	46.3	46.8	47.0	46.9	47.0	46.8	46.8
2010	46.0	45.9	46.1	46.6	46.6	46.6	46.6	47.0	47.4	47.8	47.8	48.2	46.9
2011	47.1	47.1	47.6	47.5	47.5	47.4	47.2	47.7	48.0	47.8	48.0	48.3	47.6
2012	47.0	47.0	47.3	47.4	47.8	47.7	47.7	48.3	48.7	48.2	48.4	49.0	47.9
2013	48.1	48.1	48.2	48.4	48.7	48.7	48.4	49.0	49.2	49.5	50.2	50.8	48.9
Information													
2002	16.5	16.4	16.3	16.3	16.3	16.2	16.1	16.0	15.8	15.7	15.8	15.7	16.1
2003	15.5	15.3	15.3	15.1	15.1	15.0	15.0	15.0	15.0	14.9	14.9	15.0	15.1
2004	14.9	14.8	14.8	14.6	14.6	14.7	14.6	14.5	14.4	14.3	14.5	14.5	14.6
2005	14.5	14.5	14.5	14.4	14.4	14.6	14.3	14.3	14.0	14.0	14.0	14.1	14.3
2006	14.0	13.9	13.9	13.8	13.8	13.9	13.7	13.6	13.4	13.3	13.3	13.4	13.7
2007	13.2	13.3	13.3	13.3	13.3	13.5	13.6	13.5	13.5	13.4	13.5	13.5	13.4
2008	13.4	13.5	13.5	13.5	13.5	13.6	13.6	13.5	13.4	13.2	13.4	13.4	13.5
2009	13.3	13.2	13.1	13.0	12.9	12.9	12.6	12.6	12.6	12.4	12.4	12.3	12.8
2010	12.2	12.2	12.3	12.1	12.2	12.3	12.3	12.3	12.6	12.7	12.3	12.2	12.3
2011	12.0	12.0	12.0	11.9	12.0	12.1	12.1	12.1	12.1	12.1	12.2	12.4	12.1
2012	12.5	12.5	12.5	12.5	12.5	12.5	12.6	12.4	12.4	12.4	12.7	12.7	12.5
2013	12.8	12.8	12.7	12.7	12.6	12.8	12.7	12.7	12.8	12.8	12.7	12.8	12.7

1. Employment by Industry: Mississippi, Selected Years, 2002–2013—*Continued*

(Numbers in thousands, not seasonally adjusted)

Industry and year	January	February	March	April	May	June	July	August	September	October	November	December	Annual average
Financial Activities													
2002	45.1	44.9	45.0	45.2	45.2	45.6	45.3	45.3	45.1	45.2	45.5	45.5	45.2
2003	45.3	45.2	45.3	45.2	45.5	45.6	45.7	45.6	45.5	45.2	45.2	45.5	45.4
2004	45.0	44.9	45.1	45.4	45.4	45.8	45.8	45.8	45.6	45.6	45.6	46.0	45.5
2005	45.4	45.4	45.6	45.5	45.7	45.8	46.2	46.1	45.3	46.1	46.3	46.4	45.8
2006	45.1	45.8	45.8	45.7	45.8	46.2	46.3	46.3	46.2	46.0	46.3	46.6	46.0
2007	46.0	46.2	46.3	46.4	46.6	46.8	46.6	46.8	46.5	46.7	46.7	46.9	46.5
2008	46.5	46.5	46.7	46.5	46.6	46.6	46.5	46.4	46.2	46.5	46.3	46.5	46.5
2009	46.0	45.7	45.6	45.4	45.6	45.4	45.0	45.0	44.9	44.8	44.8	45.0	45.3
2010	44.5	44.4	44.5	44.5	44.7	44.8	44.7	44.5	44.4	44.2	44.2	44.4	44.5
2011	43.9	44.0	44.0	44.3	44.1	44.4	44.2	44.3	44.2	44.1	44.2	44.2	44.2
2012	43.9	43.9	44.0	44.1	44.3	44.3	44.3	44.4	44.2	44.1	44.2	44.2	44.2
2013	43.6	43.8	43.9	43.9	43.8	43.8	43.8	43.8	43.7	43.9	43.8	43.8	43.8
Professional and Business Services													
2002	76.0	76.7	77.3	78.7	78.2	79.3	78.6	79.7	78.9	77.5	76.8	77.4	77.9
2003	77.3	77.5	77.4	79.1	78.7	78.8	79.0	79.9	80.2	81.0	81.1	81.8	79.3
2004	80.7	81.4	81.9	83.4	82.8	83.1	83.2	83.0	83.6	82.9	82.9	84.4	82.8
2005	84.6	86.7	87.0	87.1	85.7	85.8	86.2	87.1	87.5	89.9	91.6	91.3	87.5
2006	90.1	92.0	93.7	94.2	94.4	93.6	91.5	92.8	92.7	92.0	92.8	92.5	92.7
2007	91.0	92.3	93.4	92.4	92.2	92.3	91.9	93.2	93.9	94.0	95.0	95.8	93.1
2008	94.5	95.4	95.5	96.3	96.1	95.7	94.1	94.6	95.2	94.6	94.1	92.2	94.9
2009	89.8	89.5	89.0	87.8	87.0	86.7	85.3	86.2	85.9	86.3	87.0	87.3	87.3
2010	85.7	87.3	87.9	90.2	92.4	95.8	95.3	93.7	95.1	94.2	93.6	93.6	92.1
2011	91.9	92.8	94.2	94.9	94.4	93.8	91.8	92.9	94.0	94.2	94.5	93.5	93.6
2012	91.9	94.3	96.3	96.3	96.5	95.8	93.9	97.2	97.7	98.1	99.0	99.1	96.3
2013	97.0	100.0	100.7	99.9	99.2	98.2	95.5	98.8	98.0	97.4	99.0	98.4	98.5
Education and Health Services													
2002	109.7	110.0	110.7	111.6	111.7	108.7	108.0	109.9	112.3	112.7	113.0	113.3	111.0
2003	112.4	112.8	113.3	114.2	114.3	111.7	111.0	113.3	114.8	116.1	116.5	116.4	113.9
2004	116.2	117.3	117.6	118.0	117.5	113.8	114.0	115.7	119.6	119.9	120.2	119.5	117.4
2005	119.2	120.3	120.6	120.9	120.3	116.5	116.1	118.6	120.5	120.7	120.8	120.7	119.6
2006	119.8	121.2	122.1	122.3	122.3	118.2	117.9	121.2	124.8	125.1	125.6	125.1	122.1
2007	124.4	125.5	126.2	126.2	126.2	123.1	122.0	126.2	128.3	128.6	128.4	127.5	126.1
2008	125.9	127.0	126.9	126.9	125.7	123.2	122.2	125.8	128.4	129.2	128.9	128.1	126.5
2009	127.0	127.7	127.9	128.3	127.3	124.4	124.6	127.7	130.5	131.3	131.5	130.7	128.2
2010	129.6	130.3	130.7	131.1	130.0	126.8	125.9	129.1	132.7	133.6	133.6	132.4	130.5
2011	131.7	132.5	132.7	133.0	131.3	128.9	127.6	130.2	134.5	134.9	134.6	133.6	132.1
2012	132.7	134.1	134.4	134.2	132.2	129.7	129.0	132.0	134.5	135.4	135.3	134.5	133.2
2013	133.4	134.7	135.0	135.8	133.7	130.4	129.1	131.3	135.4	136.9	136.6	136.5	134.1
Leisure and Hospitality													
2002	115.7	117.1	119.7	122.9	124.7	126.1	125.6	126.2	124.8	121.8	120.9	120.5	122.2
2003	118.9	119.9	121.8	123.8	124.8	125.9	126.4	127.0	125.1	123.4	122.6	121.9	123.5
2004	120.0	121.2	123.2	125.8	126.7	127.4	128.3	128.8	127.0	124.6	123.5	122.5	124.9
2005	120.9	122.4	125.0	126.9	128.4	129.2	128.5	128.6	120.1	116.8	118.8	110.4	123.0
2006	109.8	112.2	115.2	117.6	118.9	121.1	119.7	123.5	124.8	124.3	124.1	124.1	119.6
2007	120.6	122.1	123.8	125.4	126.9	128.6	127.9	128.9	127.8	125.3	125.8	125.3	125.7
2008	122.6	124.2	125.5	127.5	128.7	128.6	126.9	127.7	125.8	123.4	122.6	121.0	125.4
2009	118.0	119.6	121.2	122.4	123.3	123.3	121.3	121.6	119.9	117.5	117.3	116.3	120.1
2010	113.4	114.8	117.3	119.5	120.4	121.2	119.7	121.0	119.7	117.8	117.4	116.2	118.2
2011	113.8	115.4	118.1	120.6	121.8	122.2	121.0	122.2	121.0	119.1	118.9	118.1	119.4
2012	116.3	118.4	120.8	122.7	124.2	124.7	123.5	124.9	123.1	120.8	120.6	120.5	121.7
2013	118.2	120.0	122.5	125.0	126.1	127.1	125.9	126.7	125.8	125.1	124.0	122.9	124.1
Other Services													
2002	40.5	40.6	41.0	41.2	41.3	41.7	41.2	41.0	41.0	40.8	40.8	40.8	41.0
2003	40.9	41.0	41.7	41.6	41.5	41.7	41.6	41.3	41.2	41.1	41.0	41.1	41.3
2004	41.2	41.5	41.4	41.7	41.6	41.8	41.3	41.1	41.1	40.8	40.7	40.7	41.2
2005	40.7	41.3	41.2	41.5	41.5	41.5	41.1	41.0	40.2	40.1	40.2	40.2	40.9
2006	40.0	40.7	40.7	40.7	40.7	41.2	40.9	40.8	40.6	40.3	40.2	40.2	40.6
2007	40.5	40.8	41.1	40.8	40.9	41.2	41.0	40.9	40.9	40.5	40.6	40.6	40.8
2008	40.5	40.9	41.2	41.2	41.5	41.3	40.9	40.8	40.9	40.5	40.0	39.7	40.8
2009	39.1	39.0	39.1	39.3	39.2	39.3	39.1	38.8	38.8	38.4	38.3	38.2	38.9
2010	38.1	38.1	38.4	38.8	38.8	38.7	38.5	38.4	38.5	38.3	37.9	37.7	38.4
2011	37.3	37.3	37.5	37.6	37.9	38.1	37.8	37.6	37.6	37.7	37.6	37.5	37.6
2012	37.5	37.5	37.8	38.0	38.2	38.5	38.5	38.6	38.6	38.3	38.4	38.5	38.2
2013	38.3	38.6	38.8	38.8	38.9	39.4	39.1	39.0	38.9	38.4	38.5	38.1	38.7
Government													
2002	238.2	239.3	239.6	240.7	241.1	239.5	233.6	238.9	242.2	242.7	242.8	242.8	240.1
2003	241.3	242.2	243.1	243.4	241.3	237.1	232.5	235.8	243.1	244.3	244.4	240.8	240.8
2004	240.7	243.6	245.0	245.8	243.9	239.7	231.9	237.8	244.5	245.5	245.6	241.4	242.1
2005	240.4	244.2	244.6	244.6	243.5	240.0	231.8	237.5	241.3	241.4	242.1	238.1	240.8
2006	237.9	241.0	241.1	241.0	239.9	237.6	227.0	236.6	243.3	243.1	243.8	240.3	239.4
2007	240.8	244.6	244.8	246.0	245.3	242.0	233.0	241.2	247.2	248.6	248.6	245.5	244.0
2008	245.8	249.4	249.8	250.8	249.4	245.5	234.9	244.2	250.2	252.1	252.5	249.4	247.8
2009	248.5	251.3	251.5	252.6	252.8	249.0	239.3	244.9	251.8	252.9	252.3	249.3	249.7
2010	248.3	251.7	253.5	252.3	255.5	250.8	238.6	241.8	247.8	250.5	249.4	248.3	249.0
2011	245.2	247.5	248.3	248.8	248.1	244.1	236.7	241.8	247.5	249.1	248.6	245.1	245.9
2012	245.4	248.4	249.2	248.8	248.6	243.8	235.3	241.7	247.0	248.9	248.9	245.7	246.0
2013	244.7	248.3	248.7	248.8	247.9	243.3	234.5	240.9	247.2	249.0	248.6	246.1	245.7

2. Average Weekly Hours by Selected Industry: Mississippi, 2009–2013

(Not seasonally adjusted)

Industry and year	January	February	March	April	May	June	July	August	September	October	November	December	Annual average
Total Private													
2009	35.6	35.6	35.5	35.0	35.2	35.7	35.8	36.0	34.9	34.9	35.7	35.5	35.4
2010	35.4	34.8	35.5	36.2	36.2	36.1	36.1	36.3	35.9	35.9	36.0	36.1	35.9
2011	35.5	35.5	35.7	36.1	36.6	36.0	36.2	36.1	36.0	36.3	35.7	35.9	36.0
2012	35.7	35.6	35.5	36.0	35.2	35.4	35.6	35.5	36.0	35.5	35.3	36.0	35.6
2013	35.0	35.2	35.4	34.9	34.7	35.5	35.1	35.5	36.2	35.7	35.6	36.1	35.4
Goods-Producing													
2009	40.7	40.2	39.8	39.8	40.1	41.4	41.7	41.3	39.6	39.8	40.5	40.3	40.4
2010	40.4	38.6	41.0	42.1	41.6	41.5	41.8	40.9	40.8	40.5	41.1	40.8	40.9
2011	39.0	39.2	39.9	40.5	41.0	40.5	40.7	41.3	41.3	41.4	40.6	41.4	40.6
2012	40.1	40.7	40.8	41.2	40.5	40.6	40.8	41.2	42.0	41.3	41.2	42.3	41.1
2013	40.7	40.4	41.6	41.1	40.3	41.4	41.0	42.0	43.1	42.2	42.2	43.3	41.6
Construction													
2009	38.8	38.3	37.8	38.1	38.3	39.7	38.8	39.9	36.4	35.2	38.3	35.3	37.9
2010	37.7	35.1	38.1	42.1	41.4	41.4	42.0	40.5	40.7	40.5	40.7	39.8	40.1
2011	38.7	39.1	39.4	40.8	41.5	41.2	41.2	41.2	39.5	39.3	37.9	38.5	39.9
2012	37.0	39.7	39.6	40.4	39.5	39.7	39.4	42.1	42.3	42.2	40.7	40.0	40.2
2013	37.4	38.3	41.5	40.6	40.1	41.2	41.0	41.3	44.6	44.9	43.2	41.1	41.3
Manufacturing													
2009	40.8	40.4	40.1	39.1	39.3	40.6	40.4	40.4	39.8	40.3	40.5	40.9	40.2
2010	40.2	38.7	41.1	41.1	40.6	40.5	40.7	40.7	40.5	40.0	40.7	40.9	40.5
2011	39.1	39.2	40.0	40.4	40.9	40.2	40.5	41.1	41.5	41.6	41.1	42.0	40.6
2012	40.8	40.4	40.6	40.9	40.2	40.4	40.8	40.5	41.6	40.5	41.0	42.6	40.9
2013	41.2	40.7	41.1	40.6	40.0	41.1	40.7	41.9	42.3	41.0	41.5	43.6	41.3
Trade, Transportation, and Utilities													
2009	34.7	35.0	34.9	34.5	34.5	34.7	34.2	34.9	34.1	34.0	34.0	34.6	34.5
2010	34.9	34.7	35.0	35.3	35.7	35.6	35.8	36.1	36.3	35.9	36.2	36.4	35.7
2011	35.8	35.9	35.7	36.4	37.0	36.5	36.4	36.3	36.4	36.3	36.1	36.3	36.3
2012	36.0	35.9	35.9	36.3	35.6	35.8	35.8	35.8	35.9	35.7	35.4	36.0	35.8
2013	34.9	35.5	35.9	35.1	35.6	36.2	36.0	36.0	36.6	35.8	35.3	35.8	35.7
Financial Activities													
2009	37.9	39.2	38.9	37.5	37.1	37.7	36.2	38.8	35.8	35.8	37.8	35.4	37.3
2010	35.2	35.4	35.3	36.1	37.8	36.0	35.9	37.5	36.5	36.6	36.6	36.5	36.3
2011	37.4	37.2	37.2	37.0	38.8	37.4	38.0	37.4	37.4	38.8	37.0	37.2	37.6
2012	39.5	37.9	38.0	39.5	37.4	37.5	40.0	38.7	40.7	38.6	37.9	40.3	38.8
2013	38.2	38.4	37.6	37.5	37.1	40.3	37.5	37.4	40.2	37.2	37.4	39.6	38.2
Professional and Business Services													
2009	35.3	35.0	35.4	34.9	35.6	35.5	34.6	36.1	34.0	34.4	35.9	35.8	35.2
2010	35.5	35.3	35.4	35.9	35.4	35.9	35.3	36.0	34.8	34.9	34.9	35.0	35.4
2011	35.0	34.7	35.8	36.2	36.5	35.9	35.8	36.1	35.1	36.3	35.2	35.5	35.7
2012	35.1	34.7	34.3	35.3	33.9	34.1	33.5	33.9	34.4	34.4	34.2	35.0	34.4
2013	34.0	34.9	35.0	33.4	33.3	34.0	33.3	34.5	34.7	34.5	35.0	35.1	34.3
Education and Health Services													
2009	33.8	33.2	33.8	33.9	34.1	34.3	34.2	34.3	34.5	34.5	34.9	34.7	34.2
2010	34.7	34.3	34.1	34.7	34.8	34.6	34.4	34.7	34.5	34.0	34.3	34.2	34.4
2011	34.3	33.5	33.2	33.8	34.2	33.7	34.0	33.8	33.8	33.9	33.8	33.5	33.8
2012	34.2	33.4	33.2	33.9	33.5	33.3	34.1	33.6	34.1	33.3	33.5	33.5	33.6
2013	33.3	33.5	32.9	33.2	33.0	33.3	33.0	33.0	33.7	33.5	33.4		33.3
Leisure and Hospitality													
2009	28.7	29.3	29.0	28.7	29.3	29.7	32.3	31.9	30.8	30.8	31.4	30.8	30.2
2010	30.4	30.3	30.5	30.5	30.4	30.6	30.4	30.0	28.8	29.3	28.7	29.0	29.9
2011	29.0	29.4	29.3	28.8	28.8	28.9	29.1	28.5	28.0	28.7	28.1	27.5	28.7
2012	27.1	27.9	28.3	28.1	27.6	27.9	28.3	27.6	27.9	27.9	27.7	28.4	27.9
2013	27.3	27.5	27.5	27.5	27.4	28.1	28.1	27.7	27.4	27.6	27.3	27.5	27.6

3. Average Hourly Earnings by Selected Industry: Mississippi, 2009–2013

(Dollars, not seasonally adjusted)

Industry and year	January	February	March	April	May	June	July	August	September	October	November	December	Annual average
Total Private													
2009	17.06	17.42	17.64	17.62	17.78	17.78	17.94	18.13	18.24	18.19	18.39	18.25	17.87
2010	18.29	18.25	18.19	17.98	18.14	17.93	17.95	17.95	17.92	17.98	17.96	18.08	18.05
2011	18.31	18.19	18.12	18.06	18.06	17.94	17.91	17.98	18.07	18.36	18.14	18.43	18.13
2012	18.33	18.75	18.80	18.86	18.63	18.67	18.89	18.80	19.12	18.90	19.03	19.20	18.83
2013	19.16	19.42	19.29	19.36	19.24	19.27	19.26	19.41	19.68	19.69	19.62	19.74	19.43
Goods-Producing													
2009	17.10	17.51	18.07	18.07	18.40	18.64	18.87	18.84	18.61	18.47	18.59	18.63	18.31
2010	18.65	18.55	18.60	18.40	18.57	18.49	18.68	18.23	18.26	18.17	18.22	18.22	18.42
2011	18.26	18.18	18.39	18.46	18.39	18.27	18.38	18.42	18.38	18.32	18.38	19.24	18.42
2012	19.41	20.55	20.97	21.00	20.73	20.52	20.68	20.67	20.86	20.53	20.62	20.82	20.62
2013	20.40	20.48	20.35	20.16	20.04	20.08	20.12	20.30	20.68	21.02	20.63	20.47	20.40
Construction													
2009	18.37	18.60	18.86	18.71	18.75	18.73	18.60	18.66	17.59	17.89	17.68	18.45	18.43
2010	18.84	18.97	18.69	18.46	18.37	18.52	18.76	18.69	18.84	18.70	18.79	18.77	18.69
2011	18.88	18.83	19.30	19.21	19.31	18.79	18.80	19.11	18.70	18.68	18.64	20.25	19.04
2012	20.53	22.00	22.81	22.42	22.41	22.05	22.00	21.41	21.22	21.30	21.12	21.16	21.71
2013	20.90	21.24	21.04	21.14	20.76	20.53	20.27	20.40	20.98	21.32	21.05	21.07	20.89
Manufacturing													
2009	16.32	16.83	17.37	17.26	17.46	17.65	17.49	17.57	17.69	17.48	17.78	17.62	17.37
2010	17.48	17.36	17.53	17.33	17.55	17.48	17.44	17.18	17.27	17.32	17.44	17.49	17.41
2011	17.37	17.38	17.51	17.66	17.53	17.59	17.74	17.75	17.90	17.82	17.95	17.96	17.68
2012	18.06	19.23	19.07	19.24	19.02	18.95	19.28	19.51	19.91	19.55	19.69	20.12	19.31
2013	19.66	19.69	19.59	19.39	19.37	19.52	19.66	19.95	20.29	20.68	20.27	20.06	19.85
Trade, Transportation, and Utilities													
2009	14.90	15.46	15.18	15.25	15.29	15.01	14.95	15.02	15.28	15.42	15.58	15.41	15.23
2010	15.52	15.48	15.39	15.58	15.83	15.93	15.90	16.03	16.12	16.15	16.25	16.22	15.87
2011	16.15	16.28	16.12	16.37	16.35	16.02	15.94	16.18	16.33	16.53	16.19	16.30	16.23
2012	15.54	15.80	15.80	16.10	16.13	16.17	16.21	16.15	16.45	16.35	16.43	16.69	16.15
2013	17.18	17.45	17.47	17.80	17.65	17.68	17.83	17.77	17.87	17.94	18.04	18.44	17.77
Financial Activities													
2009	19.06	18.99	19.14	19.29	19.23	19.39	19.56	19.60	19.58	19.64	19.82	20.06	19.44
2010	20.03	20.02	19.87	19.71	19.92	19.64	19.67	19.90	19.87	19.73	19.86	20.17	19.87
2011	20.30	20.23	20.31	20.40	20.61	20.40	20.28	20.26	20.46	20.89	20.53	20.72	20.45
2012	20.66	20.79	21.29	22.04	21.74	22.37	22.31	22.30	22.98	22.67	23.66	23.06	22.16
2013	22.84	23.54	23.48	23.25	25.05	24.18	24.06	24.97	25.20	24.93	25.63	24.85	24.33
Professional and Business Services													
2009	18.81	19.68	19.84	19.90	19.86	19.99	19.98	19.87	19.97	20.45	20.66	20.72	19.97
2010	20.68	20.58	20.48	20.29	20.31	19.72	19.56	19.69	19.79	19.81	19.77	19.42	20.00
2011	19.58	19.52	19.42	18.96	19.47	19.56	19.77	19.62	19.70	20.12	19.61	19.95	19.61
2012	19.71	20.64	20.39	20.56	20.34	20.44	21.16	20.68	21.02	20.93	20.97	21.02	20.66
2013	20.92	21.49	21.44	22.34	22.08	22.19	22.19	21.81	22.37	22.06	22.00	22.49	21.95
Education and Health Services													
2009	18.82	19.04	19.02	19.15	19.27	19.27	19.47	19.63	19.82	19.75	19.96	19.75	19.42
2010	19.79	19.84	19.83	19.64	19.54	19.54	19.72	19.74	19.58	19.62	19.47	19.40	19.64
2011	19.44	19.33	19.22	19.21	19.00	19.33	19.18	19.17	19.26	19.59	19.34	19.33	19.28
2012	19.36	19.53	19.51	19.62	19.37	19.68	19.79	19.58	19.54	19.57	19.65	19.31	19.54
2013	19.65	19.88	19.87	20.09	19.74	20.02	20.02	20.21	20.14	20.14	19.82	19.90	19.96
Leisure and Hospitality													
2009	11.23	11.75	11.59	11.57	11.50	11.42	11.42	11.56	11.69	11.70	11.74	11.96	11.59
2010	12.06	12.19	12.10	12.14	12.03	11.94	12.01	12.24	12.22	12.31	12.39	12.28	12.16
2011	12.39	12.42	12.27	12.27	12.31	12.19	12.22	12.36	12.37	12.47	12.47	12.48	12.35
2012	12.60	12.69	12.43	12.35	12.21	12.22	12.17	12.12	12.24	12.25	12.32	12.38	12.33
2013	12.48	12.62	12.29	12.04	11.96	11.89	11.95	12.13	12.07	12.07	12.06	12.15	12.14

4. Average Hourly Earnings by Selected Industry: Mississippi, 2009–2013

(Dollars, not seasonally adjusted)

Industry and year	January	February	March	April	May	June	July	August	September	October	November	December	Annual average
Total Private													
2009	607.34	620.15	626.22	616.70	625.86	634.75	642.25	652.68	636.58	634.83	656.52	647.88	632.60
2010	647.47	635.10	645.75	650.88	656.67	647.27	648.00	651.59	643.33	645.48	646.56	652.69	648.00
2011	650.01	645.75	646.88	651.97	661.00	645.84	648.34	649.08	650.52	666.47	647.60	661.64	652.68
2012	654.38	667.50	667.40	678.96	655.78	660.92	672.48	667.40	688.32	670.95	671.76	691.20	670.35
2013	670.60	683.58	682.87	675.66	667.63	684.09	676.03	689.06	712.42	702.93	698.47	712.61	687.82
Goods-Producing													
2009	695.97	703.90	719.19	719.19	737.84	771.70	786.88	778.09	736.96	735.11	752.90	750.79	739.72
2010	753.46	716.03	762.60	774.64	772.51	767.34	780.82	745.61	745.01	735.89	748.84	743.38	753.38
2011	712.14	712.66	733.76	747.63	753.99	739.94	748.07	760.75	759.09	758.45	746.23	796.54	747.85
2012	778.34	836.39	855.58	865.20	839.57	833.11	843.74	851.60	876.12	847.89	849.54	880.69	847.48
2013	830.28	827.39	846.56	828.58	807.61	831.31	824.92	852.60	891.31	887.04	870.59	886.35	848.64
Construction													
2009	712.76	712.38	712.91	712.85	718.13	743.58	721.68	744.53	640.28	629.73	677.14	651.29	698.50
2010	710.27	665.85	712.09	777.17	760.52	766.73	787.92	756.95	766.79	757.35	764.75	747.05	749.47
2011	730.66	736.25	760.42	783.77	801.37	774.15	774.56	787.33	738.65	734.12	706.46	779.63	759.70
2012	759.61	873.40	903.28	905.77	885.20	875.39	866.80	901.36	897.61	898.86	859.58	846.40	872.74
2013	781.66	813.49	873.16	858.28	832.48	845.84	831.07	842.52	935.71	957.27	909.36	865.98	862.76
Manufacturing													
2009	665.86	679.93	696.54	674.87	686.18	716.59	706.60	709.83	704.06	704.44	720.09	720.66	698.27
2010	702.70	671.83	720.48	712.26	712.53	707.94	709.81	699.23	699.44	692.80	709.81	715.34	705.11
2011	679.17	681.30	700.40	713.46	716.98	707.12	718.47	729.53	742.85	741.31	737.75	754.32	717.81
2012	736.85	776.89	774.24	786.92	764.60	765.58	786.62	790.16	828.26	791.78	807.29	857.11	789.78
2013	809.99	801.38	805.15	787.23	774.80	802.27	800.16	835.91	858.27	847.88	841.21	874.62	819.81
Trade, Transportation, and Utilities													
2009	517.03	541.10	529.78	526.13	527.51	520.85	511.29	524.20	521.05	524.28	529.72	533.19	525.44
2010	541.65	537.16	538.65	549.97	565.13	567.11	569.22	578.68	585.16	579.79	588.25	590.41	566.56
2011	578.17	584.45	575.48	595.87	604.95	584.73	580.22	587.33	594.41	600.04	584.46	591.69	589.15
2012	559.44	567.22	567.22	584.43	574.23	578.89	580.32	578.17	590.56	583.70	581.62	600.84	578.17
2013	599.58	619.48	627.17	624.78	628.34	640.02	641.88	639.72	654.04	642.25	636.81	660.15	634.39
Financial Activities													
2009	722.37	744.41	744.55	723.38	713.43	731.00	708.07	760.48	700.96	703.11	749.20	710.12	725.11
2010	705.05	708.71	701.41	711.53	752.98	707.04	706.15	746.25	725.26	722.12	726.88	736.21	721.28
2011	759.22	752.56	755.53	754.80	799.67	762.96	770.64	757.72	765.20	810.53	759.61	770.78	768.92
2012	816.07	787.94	809.02	870.58	813.08	838.88	892.40	863.01	935.29	875.06	896.71	929.32	859.81
2013	872.49	903.94	882.85	871.88	929.36	974.45	902.25	933.88	1,013.04	927.40	958.56	984.06	929.41
Professional and Business Services													
2009	663.99	688.80	702.34	694.51	707.02	709.65	691.31	717.31	678.98	703.48	741.69	741.78	702.94
2010	734.14	726.47	724.99	728.41	718.97	707.95	690.47	708.84	688.69	691.37	689.97	679.70	708.00
2011	685.30	677.34	695.24	686.35	710.66	702.20	707.77	708.28	691.47	730.36	690.27	708.23	700.08
2012	691.82	716.21	699.38	725.77	689.53	697.00	708.86	701.05	723.09	719.99	717.17	735.70	710.70
2013	711.28	750.00	750.40	746.16	735.26	754.46	738.93	752.45	776.24	761.07	770.00	789.40	752.89
Education and Health Services													
2009	636.12	632.13	642.88	649.19	657.11	660.96	665.87	673.31	683.79	681.38	696.60	685.33	664.16
2010	686.71	680.51	676.20	681.51	679.99	676.08	678.37	684.98	675.51	667.08	667.82	663.48	675.62
2011	666.79	647.56	638.10	649.30	649.80	651.42	652.12	647.95	650.99	664.10	653.69	647.56	651.66
2012	662.11	652.30	647.73	665.12	648.90	655.34	674.84	657.89	666.31	651.68	654.35	646.89	656.54
2013	654.35	665.98	653.72	666.99	651.42	666.67	660.66	666.93	678.72	674.69	663.97	664.66	664.67
Leisure and Hospitality													
2009	322.30	344.28	336.11	332.06	336.95	339.17	368.87	368.76	360.05	360.36	368.64	368.37	350.02
2010	366.62	369.36	369.05	370.27	365.71	365.36	365.10	367.20	351.94	360.68	355.59	356.12	363.58
2011	359.31	365.15	359.51	353.38	354.53	352.29	355.60	352.26	346.36	357.89	350.41	343.20	354.45
2012	341.46	354.05	351.77	347.04	337.00	340.94	344.41	334.51	341.50	341.78	341.26	351.59	344.01
2013	340.70	347.05	337.98	331.10	327.70	334.11	335.80	336.00	330.72	333.13	329.24	334.13	335.06

MISSOURI
At a Glance

Population:
    2000 census: 5,596,564
    2010 census: 5,988,927
    2013 estimate: 6,044,171

Percent change in population:
    2000–2010: 7.0%
    2010–2013: 0.9%

Percent change in total nonfarm employment:
    2000–2010: -3.3%
    2010–2013: 2.7%

Industry with the largest growth in employment, 2000–2013 (thousands):
    Education and Health Services, 98.9

Industry with the largest decline or smallest growth in employment, 2000–2013 (thousands):
    Manufacturing, -112.3

Civilian labor force:
    2000: 2,973,092
    2010: 3,034,651
    2013: 3,018,056

Unemployment rate and rank among states (lowest to highest):
    2000: 3.3%, 14th
    2010: 9.3%, 31st
    2013: 6.5%, 18th

Over-the-year change in unemployment rates:
    2010–2011: -0.8%
    2011–2012: -1.5%
    2012–2013: -0.5%

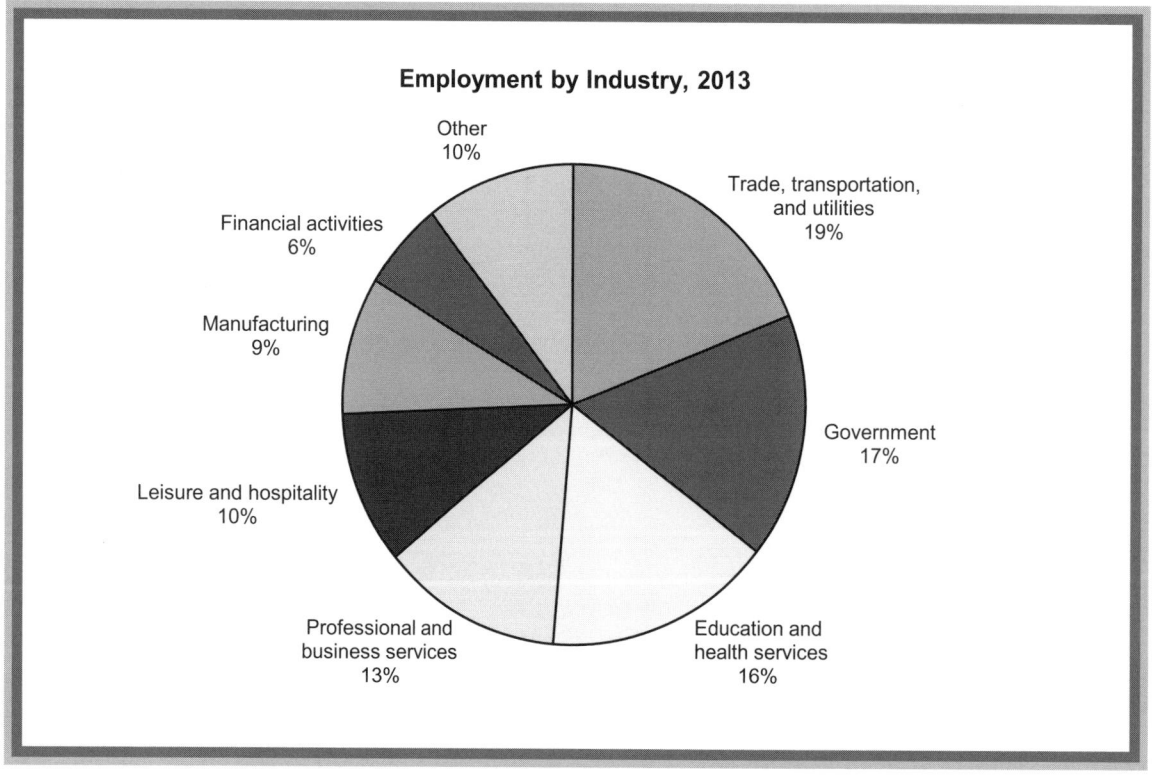

Employment by Industry, 2013

Other 10%
Trade, transportation, and utilities 19%
Financial activities 6%
Government 17%
Manufacturing 9%
Education and health services 16%
Leisure and hospitality 10%
Professional and business services 13%

1. Employment by Industry: Missouri, Selected Years, 2002–2013

(Numbers in thousands, not seasonally adjusted)

Industry and year	January	February	March	April	May	June	July	August	September	October	November	December	Annual average
Total Nonfarm													
2002	2,661.2	2,668.0	2,691.5	2,706.5	2,721.0	2,728.8	2,662.0	2,678.5	2,720.1	2,717.0	2,721.4	2,721.0	2,699.8
2003	2,641.4	2,644.3	2,665.9	2,691.1	2,704.7	2,710.8	2,655.9	2,663.9	2,696.3	2,705.5	2,700.5	2,699.9	2,681.7
2004	2,631.0	2,632.2	2,668.3	2,703.9	2,714.6	2,725.6	2,674.6	2,685.8	2,719.5	2,731.8	2,731.9	2,732.6	2,696.0
2005	2,657.8	2,673.4	2,705.2	2,751.2	2,760.2	2,766.0	2,723.5	2,737.7	2,763.0	2,765.3	2,771.0	2,773.6	2,737.3
2006	2,708.6	2,725.1	2,757.8	2,787.0	2,800.6	2,807.1	2,754.1	2,763.5	2,796.0	2,800.0	2,808.2	2,812.2	2,776.7
2007	2,731.9	2,744.6	2,788.3	2,806.5	2,827.5	2,828.7	2,771.2	2,789.1	2,818.5	2,818.7	2,825.9	2,823.3	2,797.8
2008	2,751.5	2,764.9	2,786.1	2,813.8	2,832.7	2,832.5	2,772.8	2,784.2	2,807.4	2,805.1	2,791.4	2,776.4	2,793.2
2009	2,686.0	2,684.2	2,698.0	2,714.4	2,721.7	2,714.8	2,656.0	2,664.2	2,687.7	2,687.4	2,684.0	2,678.2	2,689.7
2010	2,596.9	2,609.1	2,639.3	2,672.6	2,691.3	2,681.4	2,631.0	2,658.7	2,675.9	2,683.9	2,682.8	2,677.4	2,658.4
2011	2,606.7	2,612.3	2,646.6	2,687.0	2,698.2	2,689.4	2,646.4	2,654.3	2,685.0	2,690.2	2,692.9	2,691.3	2,666.7
2012	2,625.3	2,637.0	2,667.3	2,694.7	2,713.0	2,711.0	2,663.6	2,681.6	2,707.0	2,722.2	2,729.2	2,728.1	2,690.0
2013	2,659.2	2,678.9	2,700.6	2,738.5	2,758.9	2,751.7	2,701.4	2,720.3	2,746.3	2,763.9	2,772.4	2,765.2	2,729.8
Total Private													
2002	2,225.3	2,228.9	2,250.8	2,265.5	2,278.0	2,295.1	2,272.1	2,287.9	2,288.6	2,276.8	2,278.2	2,276.9	2,268.7
2003	2,204.0	2,201.7	2,222.5	2,243.9	2,256.2	2,270.2	2,266.3	2,274.3	2,264.3	2,267.5	2,261.6	2,261.8	2,249.5
2004	2,199.7	2,194.8	2,227.5	2,261.8	2,275.1	2,296.3	2,284.0	2,293.1	2,287.4	2,294.0	2,291.6	2,293.7	2,266.6
2005	2,230.0	2,236.9	2,266.2	2,310.9	2,320.9	2,337.1	2,326.9	2,337.0	2,333.5	2,329.4	2,331.8	2,334.0	2,307.9
2006	2,276.9	2,283.6	2,313.2	2,342.1	2,354.6	2,376.2	2,358.5	2,364.5	2,360.0	2,356.6	2,361.6	2,366.0	2,342.8
2007	2,295.3	2,298.2	2,339.2	2,356.0	2,375.1	2,390.6	2,373.9	2,384.9	2,375.6	2,366.8	2,371.2	2,368.9	2,358.0
2008	2,310.0	2,311.7	2,331.6	2,356.8	2,374.1	2,385.6	2,369.9	2,372.0	2,358.5	2,345.9	2,330.7	2,316.4	2,346.9
2009	2,237.1	2,226.6	2,238.1	2,247.8	2,255.2	2,261.6	2,246.8	2,248.9	2,231.5	2,223.5	2,220.5	2,216.1	2,237.8
2010	2,147.0	2,149.8	2,176.8	2,209.6	2,220.3	2,234.8	2,232.8	2,238.6	2,227.9	2,232.5	2,230.3	2,227.4	2,210.7
2011	2,164.1	2,164.5	2,196.5	2,233.1	2,243.1	2,253.3	2,252.4	2,253.0	2,244.2	2,243.0	2,243.5	2,242.4	2,227.8
2012	2,188.4	2,189.9	2,218.0	2,241.8	2,258.4	2,272.1	2,266.3	2,270.8	2,258.1	2,264.8	2,269.5	2,268.4	2,247.2
2013	2,209.9	2,218.4	2,236.6	2,271.9	2,291.6	2,302.3	2,299.7	2,307.2	2,294.8	2,303.5	2,308.5	2,301.5	2,278.8
Goods-Producing													
2002	461.9	462.5	465.8	464.5	465.6	470.8	458.1	471.2	469.8	465.5	462.9	461.2	465.0
2003	449.8	446.8	450.9	453.0	456.4	460.5	454.3	461.2	458.2	459.8	456.6	454.0	455.1
2004	441.8	437.8	447.6	455.1	457.9	464.3	455.5	464.7	462.2	459.9	457.5	456.4	455.1
2005	442.8	444.2	451.4	460.3	464.2	468.4	458.8	468.8	466.8	466.4	465.0	463.4	460.0
2006	452.6	453.9	460.5	464.9	466.3	473.2	467.0	468.3	465.4	462.7	461.7	460.3	463.1
2007	446.7	443.8	455.0	456.9	461.7	465.9	459.5	464.1	461.5	457.0	455.2	450.6	456.5
2008	437.2	435.9	437.8	441.6	446.5	449.5	445.0	443.2	440.3	434.2	426.1	416.8	437.8
2009	395.0	389.6	389.6	385.9	382.8	384.4	382.7	378.5	374.5	369.4	365.7	359.6	379.8
2010	344.1	342.1	349.2	355.4	356.6	362.5	361.9	363.7	361.8	362.8	360.1	357.2	356.5
2011	342.1	341.1	349.1	356.0	359.2	364.4	366.4	363.6	364.0	361.4	358.9	357.3	357.0
2012	349.9	349.1	355.6	359.1	361.6	366.7	366.9	367.3	364.2	363.2	361.0	359.4	360.3
2013	350.5	352.3	354.7	360.7	366.1	371.5	370.5	372.4	370.8	369.7	367.4	361.3	364.0
Service-Providing													
2002	2,199.3	2,205.5	2,225.7	2,242.0	2,255.4	2,258.0	2,203.9	2,207.3	2,250.3	2,251.5	2,258.5	2,259.8	2,234.8
2003	2,191.6	2,197.5	2,215.0	2,238.1	2,248.3	2,250.3	2,201.6	2,202.7	2,238.1	2,245.7	2,243.9	2,245.9	2,226.6
2004	2,189.2	2,194.4	2,220.7	2,248.8	2,256.7	2,261.3	2,219.1	2,221.1	2,257.3	2,271.9	2,274.4	2,276.2	2,240.9
2005	2,215.0	2,229.2	2,253.8	2,290.9	2,296.0	2,297.6	2,264.7	2,268.9	2,296.2	2,298.9	2,306.0	2,310.2	2,277.3
2006	2,256.0	2,271.2	2,297.3	2,322.1	2,334.3	2,333.9	2,287.1	2,295.2	2,330.6	2,337.3	2,346.5	2,351.9	2,313.6
2007	2,285.2	2,300.8	2,333.3	2,349.6	2,365.8	2,362.8	2,311.7	2,325.0	2,357.0	2,361.7	2,370.7	2,371.7	2,341.3
2008	2,314.3	2,329.0	2,348.3	2,372.2	2,386.2	2,383.0	2,327.8	2,341.0	2,367.1	2,370.9	2,365.3	2,359.6	2,355.4
2009	2,291.0	2,294.6	2,308.4	2,328.5	2,338.9	2,330.4	2,273.3	2,285.7	2,313.2	2,318.0	2,318.3	2,318.6	2,309.9
2010	2,252.8	2,267.0	2,290.1	2,317.2	2,334.7	2,318.9	2,269.1	2,295.0	2,314.1	2,321.1	2,322.7	2,320.2	2,301.9
2011	2,264.6	2,271.2	2,297.5	2,331.0	2,339.0	2,325.0	2,280.0	2,290.7	2,321.0	2,328.8	2,334.0	2,334.0	2,309.7
2012	2,275.4	2,287.9	2,311.7	2,335.6	2,351.4	2,344.3	2,296.7	2,314.3	2,342.8	2,359.0	2,368.2	2,368.7	2,329.7
2013	2,308.7	2,326.6	2,345.9	2,377.8	2,392.8	2,380.2	2,330.9	2,347.9	2,375.5	2,394.2	2,405.0	2,403.9	2,365.8
Mining and Logging													
2002	4.5	4.5	4.5	4.5	4.6	4.7	4.7	4.7	4.7	4.6	4.6	4.5	4.6
2003	4.4	4.4	4.4	4.5	4.6	4.7	4.6	4.7	4.6	4.6	4.5	4.5	4.5
2004	4.6	4.5	4.6	4.8	4.8	4.9	5.0	5.0	5.0	4.9	4.8	4.7	4.8
2005	4.9	4.9	5.1	5.3	5.4	5.5	5.5	5.5	5.4	5.4	5.4	5.4	5.3
2006	5.3	5.3	5.4	5.4	5.5	5.6	5.6	5.5	5.5	5.4	5.3	5.2	5.4
2007	5.1	5.0	5.2	5.2	5.2	5.4	5.7	6.2	6.1	6.0	6.0	5.7	5.6
2008	5.4	5.2	5.1	5.0	4.9	5.0	5.1	5.3	5.4	5.4	4.9	4.7	5.1
2009	4.4	4.3	4.3	4.3	4.2	4.3	4.3	4.4	4.3	4.3	4.2	4.1	4.3
2010	3.8	3.9	4.1	4.3	4.3	4.4	4.4	4.4	4.3	4.3	4.3	4.2	4.2
2011	3.9	3.8	4.2	4.3	4.3	4.4	4.4	4.4	4.4	4.3	4.3	4.1	4.2
2012	3.9	3.9	4.1	4.2	4.2	4.3	4.2	4.2	4.2	4.2	4.1	4.1	4.1
2013	3.8	3.9	3.9	4.1	4.2	4.2	4.3	4.3	4.2	4.2	4.2	4.1	4.1
Construction													
2002	129.8	129.0	132.1	131.8	134.0	138.9	141.7	141.0	138.8	137.4	135.1	133.8	135.3
2003	125.3	123.1	126.4	131.7	134.9	138.5	141.2	141.0	139.1	139.4	136.6	133.3	134.2
2004	126.2	122.3	130.3	136.5	139.0	142.7	145.2	144.2	142.3	141.3	139.1	137.7	137.2
2005	126.5	127.6	133.9	142.0	145.6	148.6	150.9	151.1	149.9	148.8	147.0	144.8	143.1
2006	139.1	139.5	143.6	147.8	149.2	153.9	153.6	153.4	151.1	149.3	146.9	145.1	147.7
2007	138.2	133.1	143.4	146.4	150.7	155.2	154.7	154.9	152.0	150.2	147.7	143.0	147.5
2008	136.0	132.5	137.4	140.4	144.3	146.6	147.3	147.2	143.9	141.0	136.8	130.7	140.3
2009	117.9	116.7	119.0	119.7	121.6	123.4	124.4	121.8	119.3	116.2	114.2	108.9	118.6
2010	97.7	95.6	101.0	106.7	106.8	110.7	112.1	111.4	110.2	109.9	107.6	104.1	106.2
2011	91.6	90.5	96.9	102.8	105.2	108.4	110.4	109.7	108.6	107.3	104.9	102.8	103.3
2012	96.1	94.9	99.7	102.6	105.6	108.4	109.2	109.6	108.2	107.3	105.8	104.7	104.3
2013	96.8	97.5	99.4	104.1	108.6	112.4	114.6	113.8	113.1	112.6	110.7	104.3	107.3

1. Employment by Industry: Missouri, Selected Years, 2002–2013—*Continued*

(Numbers in thousands, not seasonally adjusted)

Industry and year	January	February	March	April	May	June	July	August	September	October	November	December	Annual average
Manufacturing													
2002	327.6	329.0	329.2	328.2	327.0	327.2	311.7	325.5	326.3	323.5	323.2	322.9	325.1
2003	320.1	319.3	320.1	316.8	316.9	317.3	308.5	315.5	314.5	315.8	315.5	316.2	316.4
2004	311.0	311.0	312.7	313.8	314.1	316.7	305.3	315.5	314.9	313.7	313.6	314.0	313.0
2005	311.4	311.7	312.4	313.0	313.2	314.3	302.4	312.2	311.5	312.2	312.6	313.2	311.7
2006	308.2	309.1	311.5	311.7	311.6	313.7	307.8	309.4	308.8	308.0	309.5	310.0	309.9
2007	303.4	305.7	306.4	305.3	305.8	305.3	299.1	303.0	303.4	300.8	301.5	301.9	303.5
2008	295.8	298.2	295.3	296.2	297.3	297.9	292.6	290.7	291.0	287.8	284.4	281.4	292.4
2009	272.7	268.6	266.3	261.9	257.0	256.7	254.0	252.3	250.9	248.9	247.3	246.6	256.9
2010	242.6	242.6	244.1	244.4	245.5	247.4	245.4	247.9	247.3	248.6	248.2	248.9	246.1
2011	246.6	246.8	248.0	248.9	249.7	251.6	251.6	249.5	251.0	249.8	249.7	250.4	249.5
2012	249.9	250.3	251.8	252.3	251.8	254.0	253.5	253.5	251.8	251.7	251.1	250.6	251.9
2013	249.9	250.9	251.4	252.5	253.3	254.9	251.6	254.3	253.5	252.9	252.5	252.9	252.6
Trade, Transportation, and Utilities													
2002	535.9	530.9	535.1	533.6	537.9	539.2	537.6	537.1	542.4	540.7	549.8	554.0	539.5
2003	529.4	524.8	527.6	528.8	530.7	530.4	529.1	530.1	530.4	538.0	543.8	547.3	532.5
2004	525.1	519.7	524.7	527.6	531.6	533.2	530.0	530.1	532.2	537.2	545.8	551.0	532.4
2005	530.4	526.0	531.2	538.0	540.8	541.5	540.4	541.2	541.0	542.8	551.9	556.3	540.1
2006	538.3	534.1	538.8	541.2	544.4	545.7	541.3	543.3	544.7	547.1	555.6	561.0	544.6
2007	542.1	538.4	546.0	546.5	550.2	549.9	545.7	546.0	547.3	548.8	559.4	562.1	548.5
2008	542.4	537.1	540.4	542.7	545.7	546.0	542.0	542.1	540.9	540.2	544.2	545.1	542.4
2009	522.6	516.9	516.8	517.9	520.0	519.8	515.8	517.1	516.7	514.0	523.4	525.2	519.1
2010	506.4	502.3	506.7	510.6	514.4	515.1	512.5	514.4	511.9	514.0	521.4	524.9	512.9
2011	506.9	503.5	507.9	515.3	516.8	516.5	513.5	514.2	513.2	514.3	522.9	526.2	514.3
2012	507.6	502.7	506.2	509.1	513.2	513.6	511.1	512.5	512.2	514.9	525.3	527.5	513.0
2013	507.1	503.0	505.3	511.3	515.3	516.8	515.7	517.8	516.3	518.8	527.3	529.7	515.4
Wholesale Trade													
2002	119.3	119.2	119.8	119.4	119.5	120.2	120.4	119.4	119.5	118.8	118.8	118.7	119.4
2003	117.8	117.9	118.1	118.4	118.6	118.9	119.1	119.2	118.2	118.3	118.4	118.6	118.5
2004	117.7	117.6	118.6	119.6	119.8	121.2	120.9	120.1	121.0	120.4	120.4	121.1	119.9
2005	121.7	120.9	121.5	121.6	121.7	122.6	122.5	122.4	121.3	120.9	121.3	121.8	121.7
2006	120.7	120.5	121.5	122.3	123.0	124.0	123.1	123.4	123.3	123.5	123.8	124.8	122.8
2007	123.0	123.7	124.8	124.6	124.9	125.9	125.5	125.5	125.2	125.3	125.6	126.1	125.0
2008	124.7	124.6	125.2	125.6	125.7	126.3	125.9	125.7	125.0	124.5	123.6	123.4	125.0
2009	120.5	119.8	119.2	118.9	118.4	118.6	118.0	117.5	116.6	117.2	116.6	117.1	118.2
2010	115.2	115.1	115.9	116.4	116.7	116.9	116.6	116.1	115.5	115.9	115.6	116.1	116.0
2011	114.2	114.3	115.1	116.4	116.4	117.1	117.1	116.6	116.2	116.4	116.5	117.2	116.1
2012	116.0	116.2	117.0	117.5	117.9	118.6	118.2	118.2	117.8	117.6	117.7	118.0	117.6
2013	115.9	116.3	116.8	118.3	119.0	119.4	119.4	119.3	119.0	118.7	119.4	120.8	118.5
Retail Trade													
2002	308.6	304.1	307.3	306.0	309.2	310.7	308.3	308.6	312.8	311.5	320.9	326.4	311.2
2003	305.3	300.7	303.7	305.3	307.3	308.0	307.2	308.6	309.1	315.8	322.6	326.1	310.0
2004	306.7	301.4	304.6	305.8	309.1	310.7	308.9	308.8	308.9	313.6	322.0	326.1	310.6
2005	309.2	305.7	309.5	313.8	316.0	316.3	316.8	316.4	315.3	317.5	325.8	328.7	315.9
2006	313.3	309.3	312.7	314.1	316.0	316.7	314.5	314.6	314.4	316.8	324.8	328.0	316.3
2007	312.9	308.6	314.0	315.4	317.9	318.2	315.4	314.4	314.3	315.9	325.5	327.2	316.6
2008	312.7	307.3	309.6	311.2	313.5	314.7	311.8	311.3	309.6	310.1	315.2	316.4	312.0
2009	300.5	296.3	297.4	298.6	301.1	302.6	300.3	300.9	300.6	301.1	307.8	309.3	301.4
2010	294.9	291.5	294.5	296.1	299.1	301.0	299.9	300.2	297.6	299.4	306.8	309.2	299.2
2011	295.9	292.3	295.4	300.1	301.9	302.8	301.3	301.5	300.2	301.6	310.2	312.2	301.3
2012	298.2	294.1	296.8	298.8	301.6	302.3	301.3	300.4	299.9	302.3	312.3	313.0	301.8
2013	297.3	293.2	294.6	298.0	300.8	302.9	302.0	302.4	300.7	303.9	309.9	309.6	301.3
Transportation and Utilities													
2002	108.0	107.6	108.0	108.2	109.2	108.3	108.9	109.1	110.1	110.4	110.1	108.9	108.9
2003	106.3	106.2	105.8	105.1	104.8	103.5	102.8	102.3	103.1	103.9	102.8	102.6	104.1
2004	100.7	100.7	101.5	102.2	102.7	101.3	100.2	101.2	102.3	103.2	103.4	103.8	101.9
2005	99.5	99.4	100.2	102.6	103.1	102.6	101.1	102.4	104.4	104.4	104.8	105.8	102.5
2006	104.3	104.3	104.6	104.8	105.4	105.0	103.7	105.3	107.0	106.8	107.0	108.2	105.5
2007	106.2	106.1	107.2	106.5	107.4	105.8	104.8	106.1	107.8	107.6	108.3	108.8	106.9
2008	105.0	105.2	105.6	105.9	106.5	105.0	104.3	105.1	106.3	105.6	105.4	105.3	105.4
2009	101.6	100.8	100.2	100.4	100.5	98.6	97.5	98.7	99.5	99.1	99.0	98.8	99.6
2010	96.3	95.7	96.3	98.1	98.6	97.2	96.0	98.1	98.8	98.7	99.0	99.6	97.7
2011	96.8	96.9	97.4	98.8	98.5	96.6	95.1	96.1	96.8	96.3	96.2	96.8	96.9
2012	93.4	92.4	92.4	92.8	93.7	92.7	91.6	93.9	94.5	95.0	95.3	96.5	93.7
2013	93.9	93.5	93.9	95.0	95.5	94.5	94.3	96.1	96.6	96.2	98.0	99.3	95.6
Information													
2002	72.8	72.8	72.4	70.9	71.1	71.1	69.2	69.1	68.7	66.9	67.4	67.6	70.0
2003	68.0	68.5	68.6	67.1	66.6	67.0	66.0	65.5	65.0	64.5	64.6	65.0	66.4
2004	65.1	65.2	65.3	64.8	64.6	64.7	63.9	63.2	62.8	63.6	64.1	63.6	64.2
2005	62.8	62.9	63.2	64.2	64.3	64.5	64.4	64.0	63.8	63.9	63.9	64.0	63.8
2006	63.0	63.0	63.2	62.9	63.0	63.4	62.9	62.8	62.8	62.7	63.1	63.5	63.0
2007	62.2	62.4	62.9	62.6	63.1	63.7	63.4	63.6	63.7	64.0	64.4	64.6	63.4
2008	64.3	64.0	64.2	63.8	64.4	64.9	64.6	64.5	64.1	64.2	64.0	64.5	64.3
2009	64.0	64.0	63.7	64.4	64.5	64.9	63.6	63.6	63.2	61.1	61.0	61.4	63.3
2010	58.9	58.6	58.8	61.3	61.0	61.4	60.5	60.5	60.3	60.2	60.1	60.0	60.1
2011	58.5	58.3	58.2	59.2	59.5	59.7	60.0	59.8	59.8	59.4	59.4	59.4	59.3
2012	58.7	58.4	58.3	58.4	58.7	58.7	59.0	58.7	58.4	58.1	58.0	58.0	58.5
2013	57.5	57.8	57.9	58.1	58.3	58.6	58.4	58.2	57.9	58.8	58.5	58.2	58.2

1. Employment by Industry: Missouri, Selected Years, 2002–2013—*Continued*

(Numbers in thousands, not seasonally adjusted)

Industry and year	January	February	March	April	May	June	July	August	September	October	November	December	Annual average
Financial Activities													
2002	158.5	158.4	160.7	160.3	160.8	161.5	161.3	161.6	160.8	160.8	161.1	162.0	160.7
2003	160.5	160.4	160.8	161.8	162.5	163.9	165.4	165.7	164.1	163.4	162.7	162.9	162.8
2004	160.1	159.8	160.4	161.8	162.2	164.1	164.5	164.8	163.1	163.2	162.7	163.1	162.5
2005	160.8	161.6	162.2	162.7	162.7	164.1	165.4	165.0	164.3	163.9	163.9	164.3	163.4
2006	162.1	162.5	163.2	164.5	165.6	167.0	166.9	167.2	166.4	165.1	165.0	165.6	165.1
2007	164.5	164.9	165.6	165.3	166.2	167.6	167.8	167.6	166.2	166.2	165.6	166.0	166.1
2008	165.3	165.6	165.3	165.3	166.2	166.8	167.3	167.3	165.8	165.7	165.3	165.1	165.9
2009	163.8	163.4	163.8	163.9	164.2	164.9	163.9	163.6	161.7	162.4	161.7	161.6	163.2
2010	160.9	160.8	161.1	162.1	162.6	163.6	163.7	162.9	161.9	162.5	162.5	162.3	162.2
2011	159.8	160.1	160.3	160.8	161.1	161.4	162.3	162.6	161.7	162.7	162.9	163.0	161.6
2012	161.4	162.1	162.8	162.6	163.3	164.0	164.5	164.7	163.5	164.6	164.9	164.5	163.6
2013	161.9	162.3	162.4	163.5	163.9	164.6	165.2	164.9	163.7	164.8	165.4	165.3	164.0
Professional and Business Services													
2002	299.4	302.5	304.7	306.3	304.8	305.9	303.7	305.2	305.5	307.0	307.5	306.7	304.9
2003	294.5	295.1	297.7	299.3	298.0	300.5	299.5	301.3	301.3	301.3	299.6	300.9	299.1
2004	294.6	294.9	300.5	304.6	303.4	308.6	308.1	309.8	308.9	310.4	309.9	311.6	305.4
2005	306.6	309.1	313.2	319.0	316.4	320.0	320.4	320.3	321.9	320.7	321.3	322.5	317.6
2006	315.8	319.3	324.3	328.7	327.6	332.5	329.8	331.5	331.3	333.7	333.9	336.2	328.7
2007	324.3	325.5	331.5	334.1	333.9	337.5	336.6	338.7	336.9	336.4	336.7	337.8	334.2
2008	331.8	333.9	337.7	343.9	340.8	342.5	340.6	341.1	339.0	335.9	332.2	329.6	337.4
2009	318.4	316.5	316.1	316.1	313.7	314.4	312.2	313.1	310.4	311.5	312.3	313.5	314.0
2010	306.5	309.4	312.4	318.9	317.0	319.3	321.6	323.0	321.0	323.4	322.6	323.6	318.2
2011	318.0	319.7	324.5	330.6	328.8	330.7	329.1	329.3	329.3	330.5	331.0	332.1	327.8
2012	325.2	326.5	331.3	335.5	335.5	338.4	336.7	337.4	336.6	339.6	341.3	341.5	335.5
2013	332.2	336.2	341.0	346.1	346.9	349.1	349.4	351.7	349.2	354.5	354.7	356.0	347.3
Education and Health Services													
2002	346.3	349.2	349.6	350.5	351.3	350.6	349.0	349.6	354.3	353.7	355.0	355.4	351.2
2003	350.7	353.1	354.2	354.3	353.5	352.5	353.5	353.4	356.1	356.8	357.5	358.1	354.5
2004	353.6	357.3	358.3	359.5	359.5	358.7	358.9	358.6	362.0	365.1	365.5	365.9	360.2
2005	361.4	365.0	366.3	370.6	370.1	369.2	369.2	369.4	373.7	376.7	377.5	378.3	370.6
2006	371.7	376.2	377.5	379.5	379.4	378.0	376.4	376.7	382.2	384.8	387.7	386.9	379.8
2007	379.2	384.1	386.2	387.5	387.5	385.8	385.6	386.7	390.9	392.7	394.1	395.1	388.0
2008	388.5	393.6	393.8	396.2	395.7	394.7	394.7	395.8	399.4	404.1	405.5	406.2	397.4
2009	399.9	403.3	404.2	405.2	405.5	403.4	403.8	405.5	409.0	412.8	414.1	415.0	406.8
2010	406.9	411.0	412.3	414.7	414.9	412.7	412.3	413.1	417.7	422.5	424.0	424.1	415.5
2011	419.3	422.8	424.3	425.5	423.7	419.8	419.6	420.3	424.1	426.2	427.6	426.9	423.3
2012	422.2	425.9	425.9	426.3	426.0	423.0	423.4	425.4	428.4	431.9	432.5	433.4	427.0
2013	427.7	433.0	431.3	435.6	433.7	428.1	429.7	430.7	432.7	435.4	438.7	438.3	432.9
Leisure and Hospitality													
2002	234.9	236.5	245.6	261.8	268.6	276.8	274.9	276.0	269.4	264.6	257.2	252.7	259.9
2003	235.5	237.0	245.8	262.1	270.6	276.4	277.6	276.7	270.4	265.0	258.5	255.0	260.9
2004	242.6	243.0	252.5	268.7	276.1	281.7	282.1	281.3	276.0	274.2	266.3	262.6	267.3
2005	247.2	249.7	259.9	276.2	282.6	288.3	287.6	288.0	282.5	276.0	269.8	266.2	272.8
2006	254.3	256.5	266.6	280.2	288.0	294.6	292.9	293.8	286.9	280.4	274.4	272.2	278.4
2007	257.7	260.1	271.7	282.6	291.3	298.3	293.9	297.2	288.9	281.8	276.0	272.9	281.0
2008	260.5	261.3	271.4	282.1	293.0	298.5	293.3	295.8	287.4	280.0	273.2	269.6	280.5
2009	255.2	254.6	265.1	275.6	285.4	290.1	285.4	288.9	278.4	271.6	265.3	262.8	273.2
2010	248.2	250.3	260.5	274.4	281.3	286.9	286.9	287.9	281.2	274.5	267.3	263.2	271.9
2011	248.7	248.2	260.1	271.2	279.3	285.4	286.0	288.0	277.8	274.1	266.6	263.4	270.7
2012	251.0	252.5	264.2	276.0	284.6	291.4	288.6	289.2	280.1	277.6	271.6	269.3	274.7
2013	258.7	259.0	268.7	281.4	291.6	296.8	294.5	295.2	288.9	285.5	279.9	276.5	281.4
Other Services													
2002	115.6	116.1	116.9	117.6	117.9	119.2	118.3	118.1	117.7	117.6	117.3	117.3	117.5
2003	115.6	116.0	116.9	117.5	117.9	119.0	120.9	120.4	118.8	118.7	118.3	118.6	118.2
2004	116.8	117.1	118.2	119.7	119.8	121.0	121.0	120.6	120.2	120.4	119.8	119.5	119.5
2005	118.0	118.4	118.8	119.9	119.8	121.1	120.7	120.3	119.5	119.0	118.5	119.0	119.4
2006	119.1	118.1	119.0	120.2	120.3	121.8	121.3	120.9	120.3	120.1	120.2	120.3	120.1
2007	118.6	119.0	120.3	120.5	121.2	121.9	121.4	121.0	120.2	119.9	119.8	119.8	120.3
2008	120.0	120.3	121.0	121.2	121.8	122.7	122.4	122.2	121.6	121.6	120.2	119.5	121.2
2009	118.2	118.3	118.8	118.8	119.1	119.7	119.4	118.6	117.6	117.3	117.0	117.0	118.3
2010	115.1	115.3	115.8	112.2	112.5	113.3	113.4	113.1	112.1	112.6	112.3	112.1	113.3
2011	110.8	110.8	112.1	114.5	114.7	115.4	115.5	115.2	114.3	114.4	114.2	114.1	113.8
2012	112.4	112.7	113.7	114.8	115.5	116.3	116.1	115.6	114.7	114.9	114.9	114.8	114.7
2013	114.3	114.8	115.3	115.2	115.8	116.8	116.3	116.3	115.3	116.0	116.6	116.2	115.7
Government													
2002	435.9	439.1	440.7	441.0	443.0	433.7	389.9	390.6	431.5	440.2	443.2	444.1	431.1
2003	437.4	442.6	443.4	447.2	448.5	440.6	389.6	389.6	432.0	438.0	438.9	438.1	432.2
2004	431.3	437.4	440.8	442.1	439.5	429.3	390.6	392.7	432.1	437.8	440.3	438.9	429.4
2005	427.8	436.5	439.0	440.3	439.3	428.9	396.6	400.7	429.5	435.9	439.2	439.6	429.4
2006	431.7	441.5	444.6	444.9	446.0	430.9	395.6	399.0	436.0	443.4	446.6	446.2	433.9
2007	436.6	446.4	449.1	450.5	452.4	438.1	397.3	404.2	442.9	451.9	454.7	453.4	439.8
2008	441.5	453.2	454.5	457.0	458.6	446.9	402.9	412.2	448.9	459.2	460.7	460.0	446.3
2009	448.9	457.6	459.9	466.6	466.5	453.2	409.2	415.3	456.2	463.9	463.5	462.1	451.9
2010	449.9	459.3	462.5	463.0	471.0	446.6	398.2	420.1	448.0	451.4	452.5	450.0	447.7
2011	442.6	447.8	450.1	453.9	455.1	436.1	394.0	401.3	440.8	447.2	449.4	448.9	438.9
2012	436.9	447.1	449.3	452.9	454.6	438.9	397.3	410.8	448.9	457.4	459.7	459.7	442.8
2013	449.3	460.5	464.0	466.6	467.3	449.4	401.7	413.1	451.5	460.4	463.9	463.7	451.0

2. Average Weekly Hours by Selected Industry: Missouri, 2009–2013

(Not seasonally adjusted)

Industry and year	January	February	March	April	May	June	July	August	September	October	November	December	Annual average
Total Private													
2009	33.7	34.4	33.9	33.4	33.6	33.3	33.8	34.4	33.9	33.7	34.5	33.8	33.9
2010	33.7	33.9	33.8	33.9	34.1	33.9	33.8	34.3	33.8	33.8	33.9	34.1	33.9
2011	34.6	34.3	34.5	34.6	35.0	34.9	34.8	34.7	34.9	35.3	34.5	34.5	34.7
2012	34.7	34.3	34.5	34.7	34.4	34.6	34.9	34.4	35.1	34.4	34.5	35.0	34.6
2013	34.1	34.3	34.3	34.2	34.3	35.2	34.3	34.6	34.9	34.2	34.1	34.4	34.4
Goods-Producing													
2009	36.7	37.7	37.5	36.9	37.9	37.9	38.9	39.7	38.7	38.8	39.4	38.7	38.2
2010	38.4	38.9	38.8	39.4	38.7	39.3	38.7	39.2	38.7	39.2	38.4	38.4	38.8
2011	37.6	38.4	38.0	38.3	38.7	39.1	39.4	39.2	39.7	39.7	38.5	38.9	38.8
2012	38.2	38.5	39.0	39.2	39.4	39.3	39.6	39.3	39.3	39.3	39.4	39.5	39.1
2013	39.0	39.4	39.7	39.1	39.4	40.2	39.3	39.5	39.9	39.7	38.7	38.6	39.4
Construction													
2009	35.6	35.8	35.3	35.2	37.0	37.9	39.0	38.5	36.5	37.1	37.1	35.3	36.7
2010	34.3	34.6	35.7	36.5	34.6	36.2	36.0	37.0	36.2	37.0	35.0	35.6	35.8
2011	34.7	35.3	35.0	35.2	36.3	36.8	37.0	37.3	37.5	37.7	35.6	36.0	36.3
2012	35.1	35.6	37.7	37.6	37.7	36.8	37.5	37.6	38.1	37.7	35.6	36.3	37.0
2013	35.9	37.1	37.7	36.2	37.2	37.9	37.0	37.8	37.8	37.5	34.9	34.4	36.8
Manufacturing													
2009	37.4	38.0	37.8	37.2	37.9	37.4	38.2	38.9	38.5	38.5	39.4	39.4	38.2
2010	39.4	40.0	39.5	40.0	39.9	40.1	39.5	39.8	39.7	39.5	39.5	39.2	39.7
2011	38.4	39.3	39.0	39.4	39.6	39.9	40.4	40.0	40.7	40.6	40.1	40.7	39.8
2012	40.1	40.2	40.2	40.4	40.6	40.7	40.8	40.3	40.1	40.4	40.2	40.8	40.4
2013	40.2	40.3	40.6	40.5	40.6	41.4	40.5	40.4	41.1	40.9	40.7	40.9	40.7
Trade, Transportation, and Utilities													
2009	33.7	34.8	34.4	34.4	34.9	34.0	34.6	34.8	34.7	34.1	34.5	33.9	34.4
2010	33.2	33.6	33.9	34.2	34.2	33.8	34.3	34.4	34.7	34.3	34.1	34.5	34.1
2011	33.8	33.9	34.3	34.7	35.3	35.3	35.2	35.4	35.6	35.7	35.0	35.6	35.0
2012	35.0	35.1	35.5	35.6	35.6	35.7	35.7	35.5	35.9	35.1	35.3	35.6	35.5
2013	34.7	34.7	34.4	34.7	34.9	35.1	34.8	34.9	34.8	34.4	34.3	34.4	34.7
Financial Activities													
2009	37.4	37.9	37.9	36.9	36.5	36.8	36.7	38.1	37.6	37.3	38.8	37.5	37.4
2010	37.9	37.6	37.3	37.3	38.2	37.2	37.2	37.9	37.5	38.3	38.0	37.2	37.6
2011	37.6	37.1	37.5	37.5	37.7	37.3	37.2	36.9	37.4	38.3	37.3	37.1	37.4
2012	38.1	37.3	37.0	37.2	36.6	36.8	37.1	36.2	37.8	36.5	37.1	37.9	37.1
2013	36.8	37.2	37.3	37.1	36.9	38.3	37.0	37.9	38.1	37.1	36.8	37.5	37.3
Professional and Business Services													
2009	34.7	35.4	35.1	34.8	34.5	34.2	34.4	35.7	34.3	35.0	35.9	34.9	34.9
2010	35.0	35.6	35.4	35.7	35.5	34.7	34.5	35.3	34.9	35.4	35.3	35.4	35.2
2011	35.8	35.0	35.2	35.4	35.9	35.6	35.1	35.1	35.1	35.8	34.7	34.7	35.3
2012	35.6	34.9	35.4	36.3	35.4	35.5	36.3	35.6	36.8	36.1	36.1	36.5	35.9
2013	35.5	36.3	35.8	36.1	35.6	37.1	35.2	36.5	37.1	35.8	35.8	36.4	36.1
Education and Health Services													
2009	32.3	32.7	32.4	32.0	31.9	32.3	32.2	32.2	32.3	31.8	32.5	31.9	32.2
2010	31.9	31.8	31.9	31.9	32.1	32.3	31.7	32.4	32.5	32.1	32.6	32.9	32.2
2011	33.8	33.1	33.5	33.4	34.1	34.1	33.9	33.9	33.8	34.3	33.8	33.7	33.8
2012	34.8	33.5	33.4	33.9	33.2	33.6	34.0	33.0	34.3	33.1	33.1	33.8	33.6
2013	32.6	32.5	32.5	32.5	32.3	33.5	32.9	32.7	33.3	32.5	32.7	32.9	32.7
Leisure and Hospitality													
2009	23.5	24.1	24.1	23.8	24.4	24.4	25.5	25.0	24.4	24.4	24.4	24.6	24.4
2010	23.8	24.1	24.3	24.1	24.5	24.8	24.9	24.9	24.4	24.5	25.2	25.3	24.6
2011	25.7	25.6	26.4	26.0	26.2	26.5	26.4	26.0	25.7	26.6	25.8	25.6	26.1
2012	24.9	25.6	25.7	25.3	25.5	25.6	25.8	25.3	25.5	25.6	25.4	25.6	25.5
2013	24.2	25.0	25.4	25.1	25.5	26.2	25.9	25.5	25.5	25.6	25.2	24.8	25.3

3. Average Hourly Earnings by Selected Industry: Missouri, 2009–2013

(Dollars, not seasonally adjusted)

Industry and year	January	February	March	April	May	June	July	August	September	October	November	December	Annual average
Total Private													
2009	21.18	21.07	21.01	20.76	20.94	20.92	20.78	20.96	20.86	20.81	21.06	20.97	20.94
2010	21.05	21.16	21.13	21.02	21.34	21.01	21.26	21.03	21.25	21.31	21.37	21.43	21.20
2011	20.78	20.86	20.63	20.79	20.84	20.54	20.78	20.66	20.69	20.93	20.95	21.05	20.79
2012	21.23	21.37	21.33	21.53	21.41	21.53	21.55	21.41	21.71	21.39	21.60	21.66	21.48
2013	21.78	22.00	21.76	21.72	21.70	21.77	21.63	21.81	22.04	21.82	22.16	22.21	21.87
Goods-Producing													
2009	24.95	25.92	25.61	25.40	25.52	25.47	25.25	24.92	24.92	24.94	25.28	24.66	25.24
2010	24.44	23.88	24.40	24.27	24.15	24.08	24.40	24.51	24.68	24.77	24.71	24.81	24.43
2011	24.59	24.01	23.95	23.77	23.65	22.99	23.14	22.90	22.83	22.88	23.13	22.83	23.37
2012	22.77	22.63	23.20	23.19	23.08	23.04	23.54	23.52	23.95	23.93	23.92	23.87	23.39
2013	24.10	24.22	24.46	24.50	24.61	24.89	25.04	25.43	25.76	25.45	26.35	26.05	25.08
Construction													
2009	27.11	27.84	26.01	26.34	26.84	26.25	26.49	26.68	27.10	27.70	28.33	27.34	26.99
2010	28.09	27.48	27.11	26.84	26.60	26.59	26.78	26.63	26.92	27.26	27.04	27.28	27.03
2011	27.99	27.45	27.43	27.19	27.06	26.63	26.83	26.98	27.29	26.86	28.31	28.48	27.35
2012	28.40	28.51	28.46	28.55	28.17	27.91	28.23	28.53	28.44	28.54	28.08	27.76	28.30
2013	27.62	27.59	27.55	27.77	27.60	27.91	28.29	28.41	28.17	27.96	27.75	26.87	27.81
Manufacturing													
2009	24.30	25.05	25.48	24.99	24.80	25.04	24.63	24.46	24.36	24.11	24.41	24.05	24.64
2010	23.54	22.91	23.62	23.47	23.39	23.26	23.59	23.78	23.76	23.69	23.75	23.83	23.55
2011	23.40	22.83	22.62	22.37	22.14	21.71	21.80	21.36	21.11	21.36	20.98	20.57	21.84
2012	20.60	20.42	21.03	21.04	21.02	21.10	21.65	21.55	22.15	22.10	22.40	22.46	21.46
2013	22.83	22.93	23.28	23.25	23.40	23.62	23.59	24.01	24.63	24.29	24.73	24.96	23.80
Trade, Transportation, and Utilities													
2009	18.65	18.38	18.28	18.13	17.94	18.10	18.46	18.40	18.40	18.19	18.19	18.01	18.26
2010	18.91	18.74	18.94	19.08	19.30	18.96	18.90	19.22	19.37	18.96	18.98	18.94	19.03
2011	19.05	18.74	18.56	18.94	18.82	18.64	19.10	18.67	18.57	19.14	18.93	18.89	18.84
2012	19.61	19.48	19.52	19.94	19.62	19.88	20.01	19.52	19.97	19.57	19.60	19.78	19.71
2013	19.95	20.47	20.15	20.12	20.04	20.09	19.74	19.91	20.33	19.88	20.01	20.13	20.07
Financial Activities													
2009	22.91	23.15	22.20	21.92	22.56	22.08	22.21	22.58	22.26	22.17	22.38	22.37	22.40
2010	21.57	22.28	22.11	22.08	22.62	21.75	22.25	22.49	22.69	22.69	22.69	22.19	22.29
2011	22.40	23.31	22.16	22.20	21.89	21.16	21.60	21.63	21.65	21.90	21.89	21.93	21.97
2012	22.02	24.23	23.78	24.23	25.09	26.09	24.77	25.27	25.35	25.07	26.59	26.09	24.88
2013	26.13	27.95	26.49	26.44	26.63	26.38	25.99	26.46	26.05	25.75	26.98	27.25	26.54
Professional and Business Services													
2009	25.61	26.06	25.71	25.50	26.29	26.77	26.35	26.42	26.31	25.96	26.23	26.51	26.14
2010	25.94	25.93	25.17	24.30	25.09	24.65	24.84	24.80	24.77	24.60	24.88	25.58	25.04
2011	25.67	26.08	25.90	25.44	25.48	25.24	25.50	25.83	26.13	26.28	26.48	26.69	25.89
2012	26.63	26.91	26.68	26.41	26.53	26.69	26.32	26.15	26.62	25.64	26.12	26.23	26.41
2013	25.92	25.78	25.69	25.43	25.59	25.87	25.85	25.69	25.93	25.60	25.72	25.30	25.70
Education and Health Services													
2009	20.17	19.82	20.34	20.07	20.67	20.47	20.01	20.07	19.54	19.68	19.94	19.73	20.04
2010	20.25	20.85	20.52	21.23	21.46	21.43	21.42	21.27	21.40	21.56	21.53	21.51	21.21
2011	21.50	21.38	21.01	21.32	21.22	21.43	21.43	21.02	20.94	21.02	20.69	21.06	21.17
2012	20.69	20.46	20.39	20.24	20.08	19.91	19.97	20.00	19.81	19.67	19.53	19.66	20.03
2013	19.71	19.57	19.48	19.60	19.51	19.52	19.46	19.43	19.54	19.48	19.38	19.55	19.52
Leisure and Hospitality													
2009	12.92	12.82	12.86	12.47	12.53	12.59	12.59	12.51	12.64	12.57	12.76	13.05	12.69
2010	12.90	12.76	12.53	12.21	12.21	12.13	12.13	12.13	12.34	12.28	12.30	12.60	12.36
2011	11.76	11.91	11.74	11.74	11.57	11.57	11.70	11.73	11.99	11.83	12.07	12.26	11.82
2012	12.27	12.25	12.11	12.02	12.14	11.94	11.99	12.07	12.16	12.10	12.22	12.46	12.14
2013	12.52	12.49	12.41	12.46	12.16	11.99	12.09	12.23	12.49	12.50	12.59	12.68	12.38

4. Average Weekly Earnings by Selected Industry: Missouri, 2009–2013

(Dollars, not seasonally adjusted)

Industry and year	January	February	March	April	May	June	July	August	September	October	November	December	Annual average
Total Private													
2009	713.77	724.81	712.24	693.38	703.58	696.64	702.36	721.02	707.15	701.30	726.57	708.79	709.87
2010	709.39	717.32	714.19	712.58	727.69	712.24	718.59	721.33	718.25	720.28	724.44	730.76	718.68
2011	718.99	715.50	711.74	719.33	729.40	716.85	723.14	716.90	722.08	738.83	722.78	726.23	721.41
2012	736.68	732.99	735.89	747.09	736.50	744.94	752.10	736.50	762.02	735.82	745.20	758.10	743.21
2013	742.70	754.60	746.37	742.82	744.31	766.30	741.91	754.63	769.20	746.24	755.66	764.02	752.33
Goods-Producing													
2009	915.67	977.18	960.38	937.26	967.21	965.31	982.23	989.32	964.40	967.67	996.03	954.34	964.17
2010	938.50	928.93	946.72	956.24	934.61	946.34	944.28	960.79	955.12	970.98	948.86	952.70	947.88
2011	924.58	921.98	910.10	910.39	915.26	898.91	911.72	897.68	906.35	908.34	890.51	888.09	906.76
2012	869.81	871.26	904.80	909.05	909.35	905.47	932.18	924.34	941.24	942.84	928.10	942.87	914.55
2013	939.90	954.27	971.06	957.95	969.63	1,000.58	984.07	1,004.49	1,027.82	1,010.37	1,019.75	1,005.53	988.15
Construction													
2009	965.12	996.67	918.15	927.17	993.08	994.88	1,033.11	1,027.18	989.15	1,027.67	1,051.04	965.10	990.53
2010	963.49	950.81	967.83	979.66	920.36	962.56	964.08	985.31	974.50	1,008.62	946.40	971.17	967.67
2011	971.25	968.99	960.05	957.09	982.28	979.98	992.71	1,006.35	1,023.38	1,012.62	1,007.84	1,025.28	992.81
2012	996.84	1,014.96	1,072.94	1,073.48	1,062.01	1,027.09	1,058.63	1,072.73	1,083.56	1,075.96	999.65	1,007.69	1,047.10
2013	991.56	1,023.59	1,038.64	1,005.27	1,026.72	1,057.79	1,046.73	1,073.90	1,064.83	1,048.50	968.48	924.33	1,023.41
Manufacturing													
2009	908.82	951.90	963.14	929.63	939.92	936.50	940.87	951.49	937.86	928.24	961.75	947.57	941.25
2010	927.48	916.40	932.99	938.80	933.26	932.73	931.81	946.44	943.27	935.76	938.13	934.14	934.94
2011	898.56	897.22	882.18	881.38	876.74	866.23	880.72	854.40	859.18	867.22	841.30	837.20	869.23
2012	826.06	820.88	845.41	850.02	853.41	858.77	883.32	868.47	888.22	892.84	900.48	916.37	866.98
2013	917.77	924.08	945.17	941.63	950.04	977.87	955.40	970.00	1,012.29	993.46	1,006.51	1,020.86	968.66
Trade, Transportation, and Utilities													
2009	628.51	639.62	628.83	623.67	626.11	615.40	638.72	640.32	638.48	620.28	627.56	610.54	628.14
2010	627.81	629.66	642.07	652.54	660.06	640.85	648.27	661.17	672.14	650.33	647.22	653.43	648.92
2011	643.89	635.29	636.61	657.22	664.35	657.99	672.32	660.92	661.09	683.30	662.55	672.48	659.40
2012	686.35	683.75	692.96	709.86	698.47	709.72	714.36	692.96	716.92	686.91	691.88	704.17	699.71
2013	692.27	710.31	693.16	698.16	699.40	705.16	686.95	694.86	707.48	683.87	686.34	692.47	696.43
Financial Activities													
2009	856.83	877.39	841.38	808.85	823.44	812.54	815.11	860.30	836.98	826.94	868.34	838.88	837.76
2010	817.50	837.73	824.70	823.58	864.08	809.10	827.70	852.37	851.25	869.03	862.22	825.47	838.10
2011	842.24	864.80	831.00	832.50	825.25	789.27	803.52	798.15	809.71	838.77	816.50	813.60	821.68
2012	838.96	903.78	879.86	901.36	918.29	960.11	918.97	914.77	958.23	915.06	986.49	988.81	923.05
2013	961.58	1,039.74	988.08	980.92	982.65	1,010.35	961.63	1,002.83	992.51	955.33	992.86	1,021.88	989.94
Professional and Business Services													
2009	888.67	922.52	902.42	887.40	907.01	915.53	906.44	943.19	902.43	908.60	941.66	925.20	912.29
2010	907.90	923.11	891.02	867.51	890.70	855.36	856.98	875.44	864.47	870.84	878.26	905.53	881.41
2011	918.99	912.80	911.68	900.58	914.73	898.54	895.05	906.63	917.16	940.82	918.86	926.14	913.92
2012	948.03	939.16	944.47	958.68	939.16	947.50	955.42	930.94	979.62	925.60	942.93	957.40	948.12
2013	920.16	935.81	919.70	918.02	911.00	959.78	909.92	937.69	962.00	916.48	920.78	920.92	927.77
Education and Health Services													
2009	651.49	648.11	659.02	642.24	659.37	661.18	644.32	646.25	631.14	625.82	648.05	629.39	645.29
2010	645.98	663.03	654.59	677.24	688.87	692.19	679.01	689.15	695.50	692.08	701.88	707.68	682.96
2011	726.70	707.68	703.84	712.09	723.60	730.76	726.48	712.58	707.77	720.99	699.32	709.72	715.55
2012	720.01	685.41	681.03	686.14	666.66	668.98	678.98	660.00	679.48	651.08	646.44	664.51	673.01
2013	642.55	636.03	633.10	637.00	630.17	653.92	640.23	635.36	650.68	633.10	633.73	643.20	638.30
Leisure and Hospitality													
2009	303.62	308.96	309.93	296.79	305.73	307.20	321.05	312.75	308.42	306.71	311.34	321.03	309.64
2010	307.02	307.52	304.48	294.26	299.15	300.82	302.04	302.04	301.10	300.86	309.96	318.78	304.06
2011	302.23	304.90	309.94	305.24	303.13	306.61	308.88	304.98	308.14	314.68	311.41	313.86	308.50
2012	305.52	313.60	311.23	304.11	309.57	305.66	309.34	305.37	310.08	309.76	310.39	318.98	309.57
2013	302.98	312.25	315.21	312.75	310.08	314.14	313.13	311.87	318.50	320.00	317.27	314.46	313.21

MONTANA
At a Glance

Population:
2000 census: 902,200
2010 census: 989,415
2013 estimate: 1,015,165

Percent change in population:
2000–2010: 9.7%
2010–2013: 2.6%

Percent change in total nonfarm employment:
2000–2010: 9.4%
2010–2013: 4.8%

Industry with the largest growth in employment, 2000–2013 (thousands):
Education and Health Services, 20.1

Industry with the largest decline or smallest growth in employment, 2000–2013 (thousands):
Manufacturing, -4.2

Civilian labor force:
2000: 468,865
2010: 496,207
2013: 513,638

Unemployment rate and rank among states (lowest to highest):
2000: 4.8%, 42nd
2010: 6.7%, 7th
2013: 5.6%, 14th

Over-the-year change in unemployment rates:
2010–2011: -0.2%
2011–2012: -0.5%
2012–2013: -0.4%

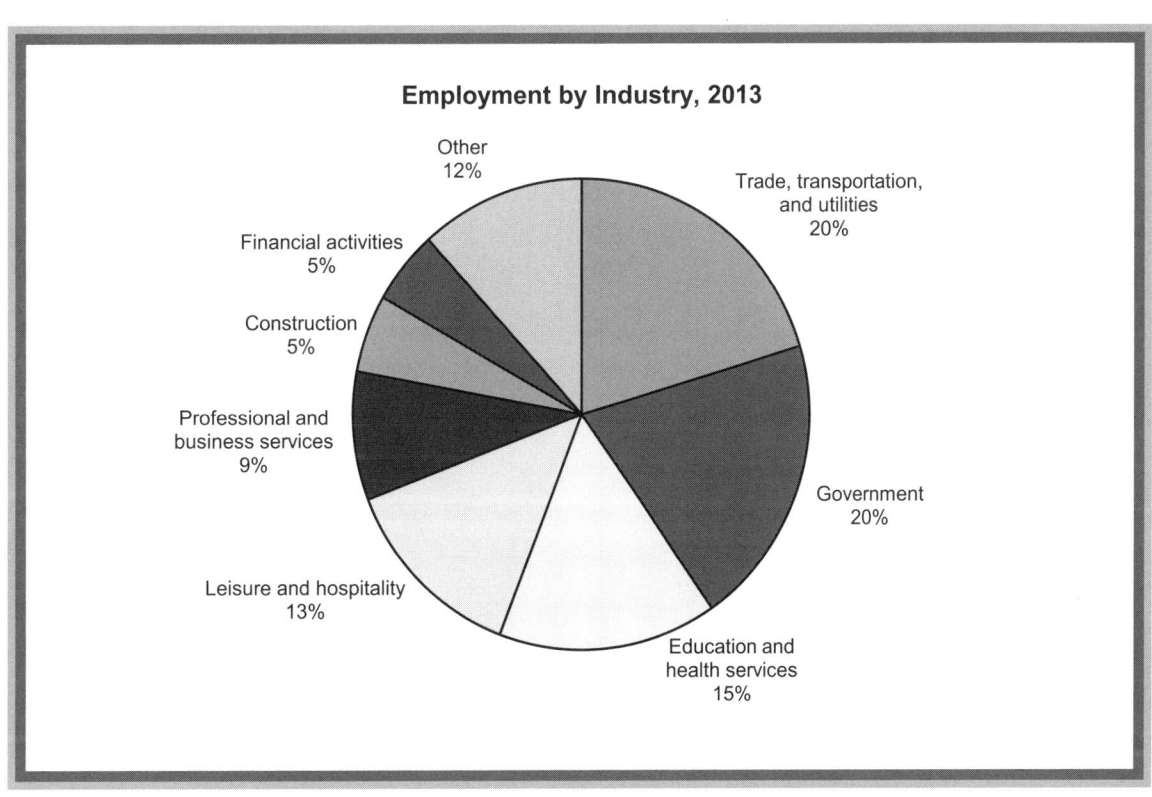

Employment by Industry, 2013

Other 12%
Trade, transportation, and utilities 20%
Financial activities 5%
Construction 5%
Professional and business services 9%
Government 20%
Leisure and hospitality 13%
Education and health services 15%

1. Employment by Industry: Montana, Selected Years, 2002–2013

(Numbers in thousands, not seasonally adjusted)

Industry and year	January	February	March	April	May	June	July	August	September	October	November	December	Annual average
Total Nonfarm													
2002	381.4	383.0	385.3	390.4	398.6	404.4	400.0	401.6	403.7	401.1	399.3	399.3	395.7
2003	386.0	388.3	390.0	396.7	403.7	406.7	404.0	407.2	407.8	406.6	403.1	403.4	400.3
2004	390.0	393.8	398.9	408.6	413.9	420.8	418.5	417.8	418.6	417.1	415.6	416.0	410.8
2005	400.1	405.3	410.0	414.1	420.7	427.8	427.6	427.8	429.0	428.1	426.9	426.1	420.3
2006	413.9	418.4	423.2	429.0	436.9	446.5	445.9	442.3	439.8	438.4	436.9	438.4	434.1
2007	426.2	429.3	435.7	439.1	446.9	453.3	452.1	452.9	449.4	449.6	447.1	447.1	444.1
2008	432.7	435.5	439.2	441.4	449.8	454.0	452.4	453.3	450.3	447.1	442.5	439.8	444.8
2009	420.1	420.0	419.7	425.4	431.6	438.2	435.5	435.6	433.6	432.0	428.7	426.8	428.9
2010	413.3	414.0	418.6	423.8	432.2	437.4	436.7	437.5	435.6	433.0	428.0	427.4	428.1
2011	413.7	415.7	419.7	425.5	433.6	438.8	437.4	440.3	441.2	438.2	434.7	434.7	431.1
2012	422.8	424.0	427.9	434.5	443.6	448.5	448.3	450.2	449.9	447.2	443.2	443.8	440.3
2013	432.4	435.8	439.1	445.1	452.8	456.9	456.4	458.3	457.2	453.0	450.1	448.7	448.8
Total Private													
2002	297.8	297.9	299.6	304.6	311.0	319.3	320.7	322.5	318.2	314.8	311.9	311.6	310.8
2003	302.9	302.6	304.0	308.6	314.6	322.0	323.8	325.8	320.7	318.2	314.9	315.4	314.5
2004	305.9	306.8	311.3	320.0	324.5	333.1	336.5	336.7	331.6	328.5	326.2	327.4	324.0
2005	315.3	318.1	322.4	326.5	332.4	341.6	346.3	347.6	342.9	339.8	337.9	337.7	334.0
2006	329.1	330.8	334.8	340.2	346.6	357.4	357.6	359.0	353.3	349.6	347.2	349.9	346.3
2007	340.5	341.3	346.7	351.0	357.6	366.3	368.6	370.0	363.8	359.5	357.5	358.4	356.8
2008	347.3	347.6	350.7	353.3	359.0	365.9	368.7	369.3	362.3	355.9	350.7	349.7	356.7
2009	333.3	331.1	330.1	335.2	339.5	347.9	350.1	349.7	344.5	339.2	336.1	334.5	339.3
2010	323.1	322.6	325.4	331.1	336.2	344.3	348.0	348.8	343.9	339.8	335.2	334.9	336.1
2011	324.3	324.7	327.8	333.9	340.3	347.8	352.9	354.5	350.4	347.0	343.9	344.1	341.0
2012	334.1	334.4	337.5	344.2	351.2	359.4	362.1	364.6	359.6	356.2	352.2	353.3	350.7
2013	342.2	344.3	347.2	353.6	360.8	367.8	370.7	372.4	366.5	361.9	359.1	358.2	358.7
Goods-Producing													
2002	44.0	43.5	43.4	45.3	47.8	50.1	50.9	51.6	50.6	50.5	49.0	47.5	47.9
2003	44.3	43.7	43.9	46.6	49.0	50.8	51.2	51.2	50.6	50.9	48.9	47.6	48.2
2004	45.0	45.0	46.4	50.0	51.2	53.4	54.7	54.8	53.9	54.3	53.2	52.2	51.2
2005	48.0	49.4	50.6	52.8	54.7	56.6	58.4	59.2	58.1	58.7	57.5	55.1	54.9
2006	52.7	52.8	53.8	55.8	58.9	62.0	62.4	62.5	61.5	61.4	60.1	59.2	58.6
2007	56.1	55.8	57.8	59.8	62.2	64.4	64.3	64.9	63.2	63.0	61.8	59.8	61.1
2008	55.6	55.1	56.0	57.0	59.1	60.5	61.4	61.2	59.5	58.8	56.5	53.8	57.9
2009	47.8	46.1	45.1	47.3	48.6	50.5	50.9	51.1	50.0	49.8	48.3	45.7	48.4
2010	42.2	41.6	42.4	44.9	46.7	48.3	49.5	50.0	49.5	49.8	47.9	45.1	46.5
2011	41.6	41.6	42.5	45.4	47.3	49.3	50.9	51.7	51.4	51.5	49.9	48.1	47.6
2012	44.8	44.5	45.4	48.5	50.5	52.0	52.8	53.5	53.3	53.5	51.7	50.6	50.1
2013	46.3	46.8	47.7	50.2	53.4	54.1	54.6	55.2	54.4	54.3	52.6	49.8	51.6
Service-Providing													
2002	337.4	339.5	341.9	345.1	350.8	354.3	349.1	350.0	353.1	350.6	350.3	351.8	347.8
2003	341.7	344.6	346.1	350.1	354.7	355.9	352.8	356.0	357.2	355.7	354.2	355.8	352.1
2004	345.0	348.8	352.5	358.6	362.7	367.4	363.8	363.0	364.7	362.8	362.4	363.8	359.6
2005	352.1	355.9	359.4	361.3	366.0	371.2	369.2	368.6	370.9	369.4	369.4	371.0	365.4
2006	361.2	365.6	369.4	373.2	378.0	384.5	383.5	379.8	378.3	377.0	376.8	379.2	375.5
2007	370.1	373.5	377.9	379.3	384.7	388.9	387.8	388.0	386.2	386.6	385.3	387.3	383.0
2008	377.1	380.4	383.2	384.4	390.7	393.5	391.0	392.1	390.8	388.3	386.0	386.0	387.0
2009	372.3	373.9	374.6	378.1	383.0	387.7	384.6	384.5	383.6	382.2	380.4	381.1	380.5
2010	371.1	372.4	376.2	378.9	385.5	389.1	387.2	387.5	386.1	383.2	380.1	382.3	381.6
2011	372.1	374.1	377.2	380.1	386.3	389.5	386.5	388.6	389.8	386.7	384.8	386.6	383.5
2012	378.0	379.5	382.5	386.0	393.1	396.5	395.5	396.7	396.6	393.7	391.5	393.2	390.2
2013	386.1	389.0	391.4	394.9	399.4	402.8	401.8	403.1	402.8	398.7	397.5	398.9	397.2
Mining and Logging													
2002	5.9	5.9	5.8	5.8	6.0	6.3	6.4	6.5	6.4	6.5	6.3	6.3	6.2
2003	6.0	5.9	5.7	5.4	5.8	6.2	6.3	6.3	6.3	6.6	6.7	6.7	6.2
2004	6.6	6.5	6.6	6.8	7.0	7.3	7.6	7.5	7.4	7.4	7.5	7.4	7.1
2005	7.3	7.5	7.4	7.2	7.5	7.9	8.1	8.2	8.0	8.0	7.9	7.9	7.7
2006	7.8	7.8	7.9	7.8	8.2	8.6	8.7	8.6	8.4	8.4	8.4	8.3	8.2
2007	8.1	8.1	8.3	8.1	8.2	8.6	8.7	8.7	8.4	8.4	8.3	8.3	8.4
2008	7.9	7.9	7.9	7.8	8.0	8.4	8.6	8.8	8.8	8.8	8.8	8.4	8.3
2009	7.7	7.1	6.9	6.8	6.8	6.9	7.2	7.2	7.0	7.1	7.0	7.0	7.1
2010	6.9	6.9	7.0	7.1	7.3	7.5	7.7	7.9	7.8	7.8	7.7	7.5	7.4
2011	7.4	7.5	7.6	7.6	7.8	8.0	8.5	8.8	8.6	8.7	8.8	8.7	8.2
2012	8.7	8.8	8.7	8.8	9.0	9.4	9.7	9.9	9.7	9.8	9.7	9.8	9.3
2013	9.1	9.3	9.3	9.1	9.4	9.7	9.6	9.7	9.6	9.6	9.7	9.5	9.5
Construction													
2002	18.2	18.0	18.1	19.9	21.9	23.5	24.1	24.5	24.0	23.7	22.7	21.5	21.7
2003	19.2	19.0	19.4	22.4	24.1	25.4	25.7	25.9	25.5	25.4	23.3	21.9	23.1
2004	19.8	19.9	21.1	24.4	25.2	26.8	27.6	27.8	27.1	27.4	26.2	25.2	24.9
2005	21.7	22.8	24.0	26.3	27.8	29.0	30.5	31.1	30.6	30.7	29.6	27.2	27.6
2006	25.3	25.3	26.2	28.2	30.6	32.9	33.2	33.5	32.8	32.5	31.1	30.2	30.2
2007	27.8	27.6	29.1	31.5	33.7	35.1	35.0	35.6	34.4	34.0	32.8	30.9	32.3
2008	27.6	27.2	28.1	29.1	30.8	31.7	32.5	32.2	31.0	30.1	28.3	26.3	29.6
2009	22.1	21.5	21.2	23.2	24.3	26.0	26.3	26.5	25.8	25.2	24.0	21.5	24.0
2010	18.9	18.4	19.3	21.7	23.1	24.3	25.2	25.4	25.1	25.2	23.3	20.8	22.6
2011	17.9	17.8	18.5	21.3	22.9	24.5	25.5	25.9	25.9	25.6	24.0	22.1	22.7
2012	19.3	19.0	20.0	22.5	24.0	24.9	25.2	25.6	25.7	25.4	23.7	22.4	23.1
2013	19.6	19.8	20.7	23.2	25.9	26.1	26.4	26.8	26.3	26.0	24.2	21.8	23.9

1. Employment by Industry: Montana, Selected Years, 2002–2013—*Continued*

(Numbers in thousands, not seasonally adjusted)

Industry and year	January	February	March	April	May	June	July	August	September	October	November	December	Annual average
Manufacturing													
2002	19.9	19.6	19.5	19.6	19.9	20.3	20.4	20.6	20.2	20.3	20.0	19.7	20.0
2003	19.1	18.8	18.8	18.8	19.1	19.2	19.2	19.0	18.8	18.9	18.9	19.0	19.0
2004	18.6	18.6	18.7	18.8	19.0	19.3	19.5	19.5	19.4	19.5	19.5	19.6	19.2
2005	19.0	19.1	19.2	19.3	19.4	19.7	19.8	19.9	19.5	20.0	20.0	20.0	19.6
2006	19.6	19.7	19.7	19.8	20.1	20.5	20.5	20.4	20.3	20.5	20.6	20.7	20.2
2007	20.2	20.1	20.4	20.2	20.3	20.7	20.6	20.6	20.4	20.6	20.7	20.6	20.5
2008	20.1	20.0	20.0	20.1	20.3	20.4	20.3	20.2	19.7	19.9	19.4	19.1	20.0
2009	18.0	17.5	17.0	17.3	17.5	17.6	17.4	17.4	17.2	17.5	17.3	17.2	17.4
2010	16.4	16.3	16.1	16.1	16.3	16.5	16.6	16.7	16.6	16.8	16.9	16.8	16.5
2011	16.3	16.3	16.4	16.5	16.6	16.8	16.9	17.0	16.9	17.2	17.1	17.3	16.8
2012	16.8	16.7	16.7	17.2	17.5	17.7	17.9	18.0	17.9	18.3	18.3	18.4	17.6
2013	17.6	17.7	17.7	17.9	18.1	18.3	18.6	18.7	18.5	18.7	18.7	18.5	18.3
Trade, Transportation, and Utilities													
2002	82.3	81.8	82.3	83.6	84.9	85.7	85.9	85.7	85.0	84.9	85.4	86.0	84.5
2003	82.1	81.4	81.8	82.4	84.0	84.8	84.5	85.0	84.8	85.1	86.0	86.5	84.0
2004	83.4	83.1	83.8	85.0	86.2	86.9	86.8	86.4	85.6	86.1	87.2	87.9	85.7
2005	84.4	84.0	84.9	85.7	86.8	87.9	88.3	88.2	87.5	87.6	88.3	89.5	86.9
2006	86.0	85.8	86.4	87.4	88.7	89.9	89.5	89.7	89.1	89.3	90.6	91.7	88.7
2007	88.8	88.6	89.4	89.8	91.4	92.0	92.9	92.5	92.2	92.5	93.9	94.6	91.6
2008	91.0	90.1	90.6	90.8	91.4	92.1	91.9	92.1	91.4	90.9	91.1	91.4	91.2
2009	86.9	85.7	85.1	86.2	87.1	88.0	87.9	87.9	87.2	86.7	87.3	87.7	87.0
2010	84.3	83.6	84.1	85.0	86.0	86.9	86.7	86.8	86.0	85.9	86.5	87.2	85.8
2011	84.1	83.6	83.7	85.0	86.2	87.2	87.5	87.8	87.1	87.2	88.3	88.9	86.4
2012	85.9	85.5	85.9	87.0	88.6	89.9	89.8	90.2	89.8	90.2	91.2	91.8	88.8
2013	88.4	88.2	88.6	90.2	91.7	92.4	92.2	92.6	91.6	91.8	93.6	94.9	91.4
Wholesale Trade													
2002	14.9	14.8	14.9	15.3	15.5	15.6	15.7	15.6	15.4	15.4	15.4	15.5	15.3
2003	15.0	14.9	15.0	15.4	15.6	15.7	15.6	15.6	15.5	15.5	15.6	15.7	15.4
2004	15.5	15.5	15.7	16.0	16.1	16.3	16.5	16.4	16.2	16.1	16.3	16.3	16.1
2005	15.8	15.9	16.1	16.3	16.5	16.6	16.6	16.6	16.5	16.3	16.2	16.4	16.3
2006	16.0	16.1	16.3	16.3	16.6	16.8	16.8	16.8	16.7	16.7	16.8	16.8	16.6
2007	16.4	16.6	16.7	16.8	17.1	17.1	17.3	17.1	17.1	17.0	17.0	17.1	16.9
2008	16.5	16.5	16.7	16.8	16.9	17.0	16.9	16.9	16.7	16.6	16.5	16.5	16.7
2009	16.0	15.9	15.8	16.1	16.1	16.2	16.2	16.0	15.8	15.7	15.7	15.7	15.9
2010	15.3	15.3	15.5	15.7	15.7	15.8	15.8	15.8	15.6	15.5	15.5	15.5	15.6
2011	15.2	15.2	15.3	15.6	15.8	15.9	16.0	16.0	15.9	15.9	15.9	16.0	15.7
2012	15.8	15.8	16.1	16.3	16.4	16.6	16.6	16.7	16.6	16.6	16.5	16.5	16.4
2013	16.5	16.6	16.9	17.2	17.4	17.4	17.3	17.3	17.1	17.1	17.3	17.2	17.1
Retail Trade													
2002	52.0	51.6	51.9	52.8	53.7	54.4	54.7	54.6	54.1	53.9	54.7	55.1	53.6
2003	52.2	51.7	52.0	52.3	53.4	54.1	54.3	54.6	54.1	54.3	55.2	55.7	53.7
2004	53.2	53.0	53.4	54.1	55.1	55.6	55.6	55.3	54.5	54.7	55.6	56.2	54.7
2005	53.6	53.1	53.7	54.3	55.1	56.0	56.4	56.4	55.7	55.8	56.5	57.2	55.3
2006	54.5	54.1	54.4	55.2	56.1	57.0	57.0	57.1	56.2	56.5	57.8	58.6	56.2
2007	56.5	56.0	56.7	56.9	58.0	58.8	59.5	59.4	58.9	59.1	60.5	60.9	58.4
2008	58.7	57.9	58.1	58.1	58.7	59.3	59.5	59.6	58.7	58.4	58.7	58.8	58.7
2009	55.5	54.5	54.1	54.7	55.5	56.4	56.6	56.7	55.8	55.3	56.0	56.1	55.6
2010	53.7	53.0	53.2	53.9	54.7	55.6	55.5	55.6	54.6	54.7	55.3	55.6	54.6
2011	53.2	52.7	52.8	53.7	54.5	55.3	55.7	55.8	55.1	55.1	56.1	56.3	54.7
2012	53.9	53.3	53.4	54.1	55.3	56.2	56.3	56.2	55.6	56.0	57.1	57.2	55.4
2013	54.1	53.6	53.7	55.0	56.0	56.8	57.1	57.2	56.3	56.8	58.2	59.2	56.2
Transportation and Utilities													
2002	15.4	15.4	15.5	15.5	15.7	15.7	15.5	15.5	15.5	15.6	15.3	15.4	15.5
2003	14.9	14.8	14.8	14.7	15.0	15.0	14.6	14.8	15.2	15.3	15.2	15.1	15.0
2004	14.7	14.6	14.7	14.9	15.0	15.0	14.7	14.7	14.9	15.3	15.3	15.4	14.9
2005	15.0	15.0	15.1	15.1	15.2	15.3	15.3	15.3	15.5	15.6	15.6	15.9	15.3
2006	15.5	15.6	15.7	15.9	16.0	16.1	15.7	15.8	16.2	16.1	16.0	16.3	15.9
2007	15.9	16.0	16.0	16.1	16.3	16.1	16.1	16.0	16.2	16.4	16.4	16.6	16.2
2008	15.8	15.7	15.8	15.9	15.8	15.8	15.5	15.6	16.0	15.9	15.9	16.1	15.8
2009	15.4	15.3	15.2	15.4	15.5	15.4	15.1	15.2	15.6	15.7	15.6	15.9	15.4
2010	15.3	15.3	15.4	15.4	15.6	15.5	15.4	15.4	15.8	15.7	15.7	16.1	15.6
2011	15.7	15.7	15.6	15.7	15.9	16.0	15.8	16.0	16.1	16.2	16.3	16.6	16.0
2012	16.2	16.4	16.4	16.6	16.9	17.1	16.9	17.3	17.6	17.6	17.6	18.1	17.1
2013	17.8	18.0	18.0	18.0	18.3	18.2	17.8	18.1	18.2	17.9	18.1	18.5	18.1
Information													
2002	7.8	7.8	7.8	7.8	7.9	7.9	8.0	7.9	7.8	7.7	7.8	7.8	7.8
2003	7.7	7.8	7.7	7.6	7.6	7.6	7.6	7.7	7.6	7.7	7.7	7.6	7.7
2004	7.6	7.6	7.7	7.7	7.8	7.9	8.0	8.1	7.8	7.7	7.8	7.8	7.8
2005	7.7	7.8	7.8	7.7	7.8	7.9	7.9	7.9	7.7	7.7	7.7	7.8	7.8
2006	7.7	7.8	7.7	7.7	7.8	7.9	7.8	7.8	7.7	7.6	7.6	7.7	7.7
2007	7.4	7.5	7.5	7.5	7.6	7.6	7.6	7.7	7.6	7.5	7.6	7.6	7.6
2008	7.6	7.6	7.6	7.7	7.7	7.8	7.7	7.7	7.8	7.7	7.7	7.8	7.7
2009	7.5	7.6	7.5	7.4	7.5	7.6	7.5	7.4	7.4	7.3	7.3	7.3	7.4
2010	7.3	7.4	7.4	7.3	7.3	7.5	7.4	7.3	7.2	7.2	7.2	7.2	7.3
2011	7.1	7.2	7.2	7.2	7.2	7.3	7.3	7.3	7.2	7.2	7.2	7.1	7.2
2012	6.9	7.0	6.9	6.8	6.9	6.9	6.9	7.0	6.9	6.9	7.0	7.0	6.9
2013	6.8	7.0	6.9	6.9	7.0	6.9	6.9	6.9	6.9	6.9	6.8	6.9	6.9

1. Employment by Industry: Montana, Selected Years, 2002–2013—*Continued*

(Numbers in thousands, not seasonally adjusted)

Industry and year	January	February	March	April	May	June	July	August	September	October	November	December	Annual average
Financial Activities													
2002	18.8	18.9	19.0	19.2	19.4	19.6	19.3	19.3	19.1	19.6	19.6	19.9	19.3
2003	19.9	19.9	20.0	19.9	20.0	20.4	20.6	20.8	20.5	20.5	20.5	20.7	20.3
2004	20.7	20.7	20.8	20.8	21.0	21.3	21.5	21.5	21.2	21.1	21.0	21.3	21.1
2005	20.8	20.8	20.8	21.0	21.2	21.5	21.8	21.8	21.7	21.8	21.9	22.2	21.4
2006	21.7	21.8	21.9	22.0	21.9	22.3	22.3	22.2	21.9	21.8	21.7	21.9	22.0
2007	21.4	21.4	21.6	21.5	21.7	21.9	22.0	22.1	21.8	21.9	21.8	22.2	21.8
2008	21.7	21.7	21.7	21.8	21.8	22.1	22.1	22.2	21.7	21.8	21.7	21.7	21.8
2009	21.1	21.0	21.0	21.1	21.3	21.6	21.8	21.8	21.6	21.6	21.6	22.0	21.5
2010	21.0	21.0	21.1	21.0	21.1	21.4	21.5	21.4	21.1	21.2	20.9	21.2	21.2
2011	20.7	20.7	20.8	20.7	20.8	21.2	21.4	21.3	21.2	21.6	21.6	21.9	21.2
2012	20.9	20.9	20.9	21.0	21.3	21.7	21.9	22.0	21.9	22.0	22.0	22.4	21.6
2013	21.9	22.1	22.2	22.5	22.5	22.8	23.1	23.1	22.8	22.9	23.4	23.3	22.7
Professional and Business Services													
2002	31.3	31.6	31.7	31.9	32.0	32.8	33.0	33.4	33.3	32.9	32.3	31.7	32.3
2003	31.2	31.3	31.7	32.6	32.9	33.4	33.6	33.8	32.9	32.9	32.1	32.0	32.5
2004	30.4	31.0	31.6	33.2	33.8	34.7	34.9	34.9	34.3	34.2	33.9	33.3	33.4
2005	32.1	32.7	33.3	34.4	34.7	35.8	36.6	36.8	36.2	36.4	36.5	36.2	35.1
2006	35.5	35.9	36.6	37.5	38.2	39.6	39.4	40.2	39.2	39.0	38.5	38.6	38.2
2007	38.1	38.5	39.3	40.3	41.0	42.1	42.0	42.5	41.2	41.5	40.8	40.3	40.6
2008	39.1	39.6	39.7	40.8	41.6	41.8	42.2	42.2	40.9	40.4	39.5	39.3	40.6
2009	37.9	37.7	37.9	38.7	38.8	39.5	39.9	39.6	38.9	38.9	39.0	38.0	38.7
2010	37.1	37.4	37.7	38.9	39.2	40.0	40.6	40.6	39.8	40.5	39.7	39.7	39.3
2011	38.6	38.8	39.3	40.4	40.8	41.3	41.8	41.9	40.9	40.5	40.1	39.4	40.3
2012	38.7	38.8	39.4	40.7	41.1	41.6	41.9	41.8	40.6	40.5	39.8	39.4	40.4
2013	37.9	38.1	38.4	39.5	40.0	40.8	41.4	41.0	40.1	40.2	39.0	38.7	39.6
Education and Health Services													
2002	51.4	51.6	51.9	52.2	52.4	51.9	50.6	50.9	51.8	52.8	53.3	53.3	52.0
2003	53.2	53.6	53.5	53.3	53.4	52.6	51.5	52.2	52.6	53.5	53.9	54.1	53.1
2004	53.5	53.7	54.3	54.5	54.4	54.0	53.1	53.3	54.6	55.1	55.7	56.1	54.4
2005	55.5	55.7	56.1	55.5	55.7	55.8	54.9	55.0	56.1	56.5	56.9	56.9	55.9
2006	56.4	56.9	57.3	57.7	57.6	57.2	56.4	56.8	57.9	58.0	58.4	58.7	57.4
2007	58.2	58.7	59.0	58.9	59.0	58.5	57.6	58.0	59.3	59.4	59.5	60.0	58.8
2008	60.0	60.6	60.9	60.9	61.0	60.3	59.6	60.2	61.3	61.7	62.0	62.5	60.9
2009	61.8	62.3	62.3	62.5	62.4	62.2	61.4	61.6	62.5	63.2	63.4	63.8	62.5
2010	63.1	63.3	63.5	63.9	63.9	63.8	63.1	63.2	64.0	64.3	64.4	64.6	63.8
2011	63.9	64.2	64.3	64.2	64.8	64.6	63.9	64.5	65.6	66.4	66.5	67.1	65.0
2012	66.8	67.3	67.3	67.5	67.8	67.3	66.6	67.2	67.7	68.2	68.4	68.8	67.6
2013	68.3	68.6	68.8	68.9	69.2	68.8	68.0	68.6	69.5	69.6	70.2	70.1	69.1
Leisure and Hospitality													
2002	46.7	47.1	47.8	48.7	50.5	55.0	56.7	57.4	54.3	50.2	48.3	49.1	51.0
2003	48.6	49.0	49.4	49.8	51.3	56.0	58.4	58.8	55.2	51.0	49.3	50.2	52.3
2004	49.0	49.3	50.1	52.1	53.3	58.0	60.5	60.6	57.2	53.1	50.6	51.9	53.8
2005	50.4	51.1	52.2	52.7	54.7	59.1	61.7	61.9	58.8	54.5	52.5	53.2	55.2
2006	52.6	53.2	54.2	55.1	56.4	61.2	62.7	62.7	58.9	55.4	53.3	55.0	56.7
2007	53.7	54.0	54.9	55.9	57.5	62.3	65.0	65.2	61.4	56.5	54.9	56.7	58.2
2008	55.2	55.6	56.6	56.7	58.8	63.5	66.1	66.1	62.2	57.0	54.7	55.9	59.0
2009	53.5	53.7	54.2	55.0	56.7	61.3	63.5	63.4	59.9	54.7	52.3	53.1	56.8
2010	51.5	51.7	52.4	53.4	55.2	59.4	62.4	62.8	59.6	54.2	52.0	53.3	55.7
2011	51.9	52.1	53.3	54.2	56.2	59.8	62.9	63.0	60.0	55.6	53.4	54.5	56.4
2012	53.4	53.5	54.7	55.4	57.5	62.3	64.6	65.2	61.7	57.1	54.6	55.9	58.0
2013	55.4	56.1	57.1	57.8	59.2	64.1	66.7	67.1	63.5	58.6	55.8	56.8	59.9
Other Services													
2002	15.5	15.6	15.7	15.9	16.1	16.3	16.3	16.3	16.3	16.2	16.2	16.3	16.1
2003	15.9	15.9	16.0	16.4	16.4	16.4	16.4	16.3	16.5	16.6	16.5	16.7	16.3
2004	16.3	16.4	16.6	16.7	16.8	16.9	17.0	17.1	17.0	16.9	16.8	16.9	16.8
2005	16.4	16.6	16.7	16.7	16.8	17.0	16.7	16.8	16.8	16.6	16.6	16.8	16.7
2006	16.5	16.6	16.9	17.0	17.1	17.3	17.1	17.1	17.1	17.1	17.0	17.1	17.0
2007	16.8	16.8	17.2	17.3	17.2	17.5	17.2	17.1	17.1	17.2	17.2	17.2	17.2
2008	17.1	17.3	17.6	17.6	17.6	17.8	17.7	17.6	17.5	17.6	17.5	17.3	17.5
2009	16.8	17.0	17.0	17.0	17.1	17.2	17.2	16.9	17.0	17.0	16.9	16.9	17.0
2010	16.6	16.6	16.8	16.7	16.8	17.0	16.8	16.7	16.7	16.7	16.6	16.6	16.7
2011	16.4	16.5	16.7	16.8	17.0	17.1	17.2	17.0	17.0	17.0	16.9	17.1	16.9
2012	16.7	16.9	17.0	17.3	17.5	17.7	17.6	17.7	17.7	17.8	17.5	17.4	17.4
2013	17.2	17.4	17.5	17.6	17.8	17.9	17.8	17.9	17.9	17.7	17.6	17.7	17.7
Government													
2002	83.6	85.1	85.7	85.8	87.6	85.1	79.3	79.1	85.5	86.3	87.4	87.7	84.9
2003	83.1	85.7	86.0	88.1	89.1	84.7	80.2	81.4	87.1	88.4	88.2	88.0	85.8
2004	84.1	87.0	87.6	88.6	89.4	87.7	82.0	81.1	87.0	88.6	89.4	88.6	86.8
2005	84.8	87.2	87.6	87.6	88.3	86.2	81.3	80.2	86.1	88.3	89.0	88.4	86.3
2006	84.8	87.6	88.4	88.8	90.3	89.1	88.3	83.3	86.5	88.8	89.7	88.5	87.8
2007	85.7	88.0	89.0	88.1	89.3	87.0	83.5	82.9	85.6	90.1	89.6	89.7	87.3
2008	85.4	87.9	88.5	88.1	90.8	88.1	83.7	84.0	88.0	91.2	91.8	90.1	88.1
2009	86.8	88.9	89.6	90.2	92.1	90.3	85.4	85.9	89.1	92.8	92.6	92.3	89.7
2010	90.2	91.4	93.2	92.7	96.0	93.1	88.7	88.7	91.7	93.2	92.8	92.5	92.0
2011	89.4	91.0	91.9	91.6	93.3	91.0	84.5	85.8	90.8	91.2	90.8	90.6	90.2
2012	88.7	89.6	90.4	90.3	92.4	89.1	86.2	85.6	90.3	90.3	91.0	90.5	89.6
2013	90.2	91.5	91.9	91.5	92.0	89.1	85.7	85.9	90.7	91.1	91.0	90.5	90.1

2. Average Weekly Hours by Selected Industry: Montana, 2009–2013

(Not seasonally adjusted)

Industry and year	January	February	March	April	May	June	July	August	September	October	November	December	Annual average
Total Private													
2009	30.0	30.7	30.5	30.4	30.9	31.0	31.3	32.1	31.6	31.8	32.2	31.4	31.2
2010	31.5	31.7	31.8	32.1	33.1	32.6	32.9	33.9	33.2	32.9	32.7	32.8	32.6
2011	33.0	32.7	32.6	33.1	33.6	33.1	33.1	33.2	32.9	33.4	32.4	32.3	32.9
2012	32.7	32.3	32.4	33.4	32.9	33.1	34.0	33.4	34.0	33.0	32.7	33.9	33.2
2013	32.7	33.2	33.0	33.1	33.3	34.1	33.3	33.6	33.9	33.3	33.0	33.2	33.3
Goods-Producing													
2009	36.1	36.1	35.4	36.4	36.3	38.1	38.1	39.4	37.2	38.1	37.9	35.5	37.1
2010	36.7	36.2	36.9	37.4	38.9	37.8	38.6	39.3	38.3	38.9	38.2	39.4	38.1
2011	39.8	38.7	38.7	39.9	40.0	40.1	39.9	39.9	39.0	39.4	37.6	37.7	39.2
2012	37.6	36.9	37.7	39.3	38.8	39.7	40.1	38.9	38.4	38.4	37.3	37.3	38.4
2013	36.2	37.0	37.0	37.4	38.4	39.4	38.1	38.4	38.5	38.0	37.3	37.1	37.8
Construction													
2009	33.1	33.1	32.0	32.8	33.6	35.5	35.0	38.3	33.4	34.6	34.7	29.6	34.0
2010	31.9	31.7	33.0	33.3	36.6	34.5	36.2	38.0	36.8	37.5	36.6	30.6	35.0
2011	31.6	31.3	32.4	34.8	34.9	36.2	36.7	37.1	36.3	36.6	34.4	33.2	34.9
2012	32.9	32.9	34.8	37.2	38.8	39.3	38.6	38.6	36.0	37.2	34.6	34.2	36.4
2013	32.4	34.3	35.1	35.7	37.6	39.4	37.3	38.5	38.5	38.3	36.0	35.8	36.8
Trade, Transportation, and Utilities													
2009	33.2	32.3	32.1	32.3	32.9	32.8	32.4	33.3	32.9	32.8	32.9	32.9	32.7
2010	32.7	33.1	33.1	32.2	33.8	33.4	33.9	34.6	33.8	34.1	34.1	34.5	33.6
2011	34.8	34.3	34.3	34.9	34.5	34.7	34.3	34.4	33.7	33.5	32.6	33.4	34.1
2012	33.5	33.3	33.3	33.9	33.2	32.9	33.7	33.5	34.0	32.7	32.4	35.4	33.5
2013	34.0	34.4	34.1	34.3	34.4	35.5	34.6	34.8	34.7	33.4	32.9	33.4	34.2
Financial Activities													
2009	37.0	38.2	38.4	38.5	37.7	37.6	36.6	36.8	36.5	36.5	37.2	35.8	37.2
2010	36.6	36.5	37.0	37.4	37.7	37.7	37.6	38.0	37.0	36.9	36.7	35.9	37.1
2011	37.1	36.3	36.4	36.7	37.6	36.6	36.7	36.8	37.3	38.3	36.7	35.8	36.9
2012	38.1	36.3	35.9	38.6	37.6	37.2	38.9	37.6	38.9	37.1	37.5	38.9	37.7
2013	37.3	37.7	37.6	37.6	37.6	38.9	37.3	37.8	38.6	38.2	38.3	38.8	38.0
Professional and Business Services													
2009	18.8	20.5	22.0	22.6	23.1	24.0	25.7	26.0	26.5	27.0	28.1	27.3	24.3
2010	28.5	29.3	29.5	30.4	31.6	30.9	30.3	33.3	32.0	32.9	32.5	32.4	31.2
2011	33.5	33.0	33.0	33.5	34.2	33.0	32.8	32.7	33.6	34.2	33.8	33.3	33.4
2012	32.9	33.5	33.5	33.9	34.2	34.6	34.3	34.4	35.1	34.2	33.8	34.1	34.0
2013	32.6	33.8	34.1	34.0	34.3	35.5	33.4	34.5	34.4	34.1	33.9	33.6	34.0
Education and Health Services													
2009	32.2	33.0	33.1	32.4	33.0	32.3	32.8	32.7	32.9	32.9	33.4	33.0	32.8
2010	32.7	32.9	32.9	32.9	33.5	33.1	33.1	33.6	33.4	33.6	33.7	34.1	33.3
2011	33.8	33.9	33.7	33.7	34.0	32.9	33.1	32.6	33.0	33.5	33.2	32.9	33.4
2012	33.3	32.9	33.0	33.5	33.0	33.2	34.2	33.5	34.2	33.6	33.6	34.1	33.5
2013	33.4	33.4	33.5	33.5	33.1	33.0	33.4	33.4	34.1	33.9	33.8	34.5	33.6
Leisure and Hospitality													
2009	23.4	24.4	24.0	22.9	24.4	24.1	25.2	27.0	25.3	25.0	25.7	24.5	24.7
2010	24.1	24.4	24.5	24.8	25.5	25.4	26.8	27.9	26.0	21.9	21.3	21.4	24.6
2011	21.3	21.4	21.3	21.7	22.8	22.7	24.2	24.9	23.4	23.8	22.4	22.4	22.8
2012	23.3	22.6	22.8	23.6	23.7	24.4	26.6	25.8	25.7	23.6	22.9	24.2	24.2
2013	22.7	23.7	23.2	22.7	23.4	25.1	24.8	24.8	24.5	23.5	22.9	23.2	23.8

3. Average Hourly Earnings by Selected Industry: Montana, 2009–2013

(Dollars, not seasonally adjusted)

Industry and year	January	February	March	April	May	June	July	August	September	October	November	December	Annual average
Total Private													
2009	20.27	20.26	20.00	19.98	19.58	19.57	19.49	19.74	19.61	19.77	20.26	19.89	19.86
2010	20.05	19.93	19.83	20.28	20.47	19.67	19.68	20.29	20.46	20.50	20.80	20.32	20.19
2011	20.54	20.44	20.58	20.74	20.83	20.40	20.61	20.32	20.81	21.06	21.15	20.55	20.67
2012	20.61	20.67	20.69	20.93	20.91	20.48	20.69	20.48	20.57	20.76	20.56	21.06	20.70
2013	21.20	21.37	20.87	21.01	20.79	20.82	20.86	20.63	20.99	20.95	20.97	21.15	20.96
Goods-Producing													
2009	22.70	23.34	22.65	23.37	22.18	22.54	22.36	23.12	23.06	22.69	23.42	22.96	22.86
2010	23.04	23.71	23.75	24.33	24.45	23.49	23.80	24.81	25.50	24.37	24.57	24.87	24.26
2011	24.90	24.98	25.77	24.63	24.69	24.30	24.55	23.84	24.03	24.13	24.02	23.61	24.42
2012	22.88	23.66	23.69	24.35	24.14	23.48	23.86	23.80	23.92	24.10	23.60	23.95	23.80
2013	23.83	23.87	23.04	23.70	23.83	23.93	23.21	23.16	22.88	22.78	22.97	23.20	23.36
Construction													
2009	22.65	22.59	22.47	24.48	23.24	23.61	23.73	24.55	22.62	23.44	23.96	24.20	23.50
2010	23.34	23.74	23.39	24.33	24.12	22.70	21.83	23.03	23.51	24.23	23.99	24.32	23.51
2011	24.37	24.15	23.76	24.56	24.77	24.34	24.37	24.45	24.90	24.67	23.96	24.04	24.39
2012	23.48	23.61	24.05	24.83	24.38	23.20	23.13	23.35	23.71	24.03	23.25	24.22	23.76
2013	24.33	23.58	23.49	23.84	24.52	24.75	23.67	23.66	23.46	23.55	24.07	24.32	23.94
Trade, Transportation, and Utilities													
2009	17.68	17.54	17.53	17.47	17.78	17.88	17.48	18.44	17.93	18.33	17.97	18.02	17.84
2010	18.64	18.30	18.32	18.70	18.55	18.07	18.24	18.24	18.24	18.23	18.34	18.24	18.34
2011	18.51	18.50	18.55	19.03	18.87	18.65	18.50	18.34	18.44	18.51	18.30	18.36	18.55
2012	19.17	19.11	19.36	19.84	19.43	19.53	19.38	19.13	19.41	19.13	19.06	20.78	19.46
2013	20.94	20.81	20.49	20.54	20.25	20.26	20.15	20.03	20.10	19.89	19.86	19.84	20.26
Financial Activities													
2009	20.92	20.24	20.44	19.80	19.95	20.11	20.50	20.80	19.99	20.46	20.33	21.10	20.38
2010	21.03	20.85	20.47	21.66	21.03	20.50	20.25	20.92	21.87	21.39	20.84	20.52	20.94
2011	20.52	21.09	21.12	22.00	21.77	20.96	22.00	21.86	22.92	23.48	22.50	20.44	21.74
2012	20.44	20.61	20.73	20.70	20.34	20.38	22.28	21.33	21.46	21.42	21.37	21.53	21.07
2013	22.09	22.11	22.09	21.90	21.50	21.75	21.52	21.47	21.82	22.15	22.31	22.00	21.89
Professional and Business Services													
2009	26.15	26.21	25.65	24.73	24.27	23.28	23.05	23.15	22.73	22.58	22.63	22.39	23.73
2010	21.10	21.45	20.94	20.72	20.77	20.64	20.64	20.51	20.55	20.80	20.94	21.21	20.83
2011	21.62	21.19	21.10	21.36	21.29	20.97	21.09	21.25	21.51	22.04	21.85	22.45	21.48
2012	22.93	23.23	22.85	22.87	22.36	22.29	23.31	22.70	22.77	22.68	22.49	22.95	22.78
2013	22.80	22.68	22.57	22.45	22.14	22.29	22.41	22.29	23.86	23.11	23.40	24.15	22.84
Education and Health Services													
2009	20.01	19.61	19.76	19.81	19.54	19.82	20.13	20.18	19.99	20.15	20.06	18.75	19.81
2010	19.81	19.22	19.54	20.19	21.76	20.35	20.48	22.21	21.35	20.97	22.38	20.95	20.78
2011	21.78	21.34	21.48	22.14	23.20	22.91	23.60	23.59	23.69	23.78	25.03	23.08	22.97
2012	23.14	22.53	22.62	22.61	23.59	22.43	22.16	22.58	21.90	22.33	21.72	22.05	22.47
2013	22.33	23.26	22.04	22.27	21.83	22.16	23.10	22.26	22.44	22.43	21.98	22.47	22.38
Leisure and Hospitality													
2009	13.38	13.40	13.07	13.50	13.49	13.27	13.45	13.58	14.35	14.80	14.90	15.67	13.89
2010	15.27	15.11	14.64	14.41	14.10	13.67	13.58	13.44	13.57	13.67	13.63	13.11	13.99
2011	13.35	13.48	13.31	13.06	12.86	12.59	12.54	12.28	12.52	12.45	12.45	12.63	12.76
2012	12.55	12.49	12.35	12.41	12.35	12.19	12.03	12.04	12.28	12.12	12.26	12.31	12.27
2013	12.35	12.26	12.23	12.09	12.04	11.77	11.92	11.88	12.07	12.14	12.08	12.30	12.08

4. Average Hourly Earnings by Selected Industry: Montana, 2009–2013

(Dollars, not seasonally adjusted)

Industry and year	January	February	March	April	May	June	July	August	September	October	November	December	Annual average
Total Private													
2009	608.10	621.98	610.00	607.39	605.02	606.67	610.04	633.65	619.68	628.69	652.37	624.55	619.63
2010	631.58	631.78	630.59	650.99	677.56	641.24	647.47	687.83	679.27	674.45	680.16	666.50	658.19
2011	677.82	668.39	670.91	686.49	699.89	675.24	682.19	674.62	684.65	703.40	685.26	663.77	680.04
2012	673.95	667.64	670.36	699.06	687.94	677.89	703.46	684.03	699.38	685.08	672.31	713.93	687.24
2013	693.24	709.48	688.71	695.43	692.31	709.96	694.64	693.17	711.56	697.64	692.01	702.18	697.97
Goods-Producing													
2009	819.47	842.57	801.81	850.67	805.13	858.77	851.92	910.93	857.83	864.49	887.62	815.08	848.11
2010	845.57	858.30	876.38	909.94	951.11	887.92	918.68	975.03	976.65	947.99	938.57	979.88	924.31
2011	991.02	966.73	997.30	982.74	987.60	974.43	979.55	951.22	937.17	950.72	903.15	890.10	957.26
2012	860.29	873.05	893.11	956.96	936.63	932.16	956.79	925.82	918.53	925.44	880.28	893.34	913.92
2013	862.65	883.19	852.48	886.38	915.07	942.84	884.30	889.34	880.88	865.64	856.78	860.72	883.01
Construction													
2009	749.72	747.73	719.04	802.94	780.86	838.16	830.55	940.27	755.51	811.02	831.41	716.32	799.00
2010	744.55	752.56	771.87	810.19	882.79	783.15	790.25	875.14	865.17	908.63	878.03	744.19	822.85
2011	770.09	755.90	769.82	854.69	864.47	881.11	894.38	907.10	903.87	902.92	824.22	798.13	851.21
2012	772.49	776.77	836.94	923.68	945.94	911.76	892.82	901.31	853.56	893.92	804.45	828.32	864.86
2013	788.29	808.79	824.50	851.09	921.95	975.15	882.89	910.91	903.21	901.97	866.52	870.66	880.99
Trade, Transportation, and Utilities													
2009	586.98	566.54	562.71	564.28	584.96	586.46	566.35	614.05	589.90	601.22	591.21	592.86	583.37
2010	609.53	605.73	606.39	602.14	626.99	603.54	618.34	631.10	616.51	621.64	625.39	629.28	616.22
2011	644.15	634.55	636.27	664.15	651.02	647.16	634.55	630.90	621.43	620.09	596.58	613.22	632.56
2012	642.20	636.36	644.69	672.58	645.08	642.54	653.11	640.86	659.94	625.55	617.54	735.61	651.91
2013	711.96	715.86	698.71	704.52	696.60	719.23	697.19	697.04	697.47	664.33	653.39	662.66	692.89
Financial Activities													
2009	774.04	773.17	784.90	762.30	752.12	756.14	750.30	765.44	729.64	746.79	756.28	755.38	758.14
2010	769.70	761.03	757.39	810.08	792.83	772.85	761.40	794.96	809.19	789.29	764.83	736.67	776.87
2011	761.29	765.57	768.77	807.40	818.55	767.14	807.40	804.45	854.92	899.28	825.75	731.75	802.21
2012	778.76	748.14	744.21	799.02	764.78	758.14	866.69	802.01	834.79	794.68	801.38	837.52	794.34
2013	823.96	833.55	830.58	823.44	808.40	846.08	802.70	811.57	842.25	846.13	854.47	853.60	831.82
Professional and Business Services													
2009	491.62	537.31	564.30	558.90	560.64	558.72	592.39	601.90	602.35	609.66	635.90	611.25	576.64
2010	601.35	628.49	617.73	629.89	656.33	630.67	625.39	682.98	657.60	684.32	680.55	687.20	649.90
2011	724.27	699.27	696.30	715.56	728.12	692.01	691.75	694.88	722.74	753.77	738.53	747.59	717.43
2012	754.40	778.21	765.48	775.29	764.71	771.23	799.53	780.88	799.23	775.66	760.16	782.60	774.52
2013	743.28	766.58	769.64	763.30	759.40	791.30	748.49	769.01	820.78	788.05	793.26	811.44	776.56
Education and Health Services													
2009	644.32	647.13	654.06	641.84	644.82	640.19	660.26	659.89	657.67	662.94	670.00	618.75	649.77
2010	647.79	632.34	642.87	664.25	728.96	673.59	677.89	746.26	713.09	704.59	754.21	714.40	691.97
2011	736.16	723.43	723.88	746.12	788.80	753.74	781.16	769.03	781.77	796.63	831.00	759.33	767.20
2012	770.56	741.24	746.46	757.44	778.47	744.68	757.87	756.43	748.98	750.29	729.79	751.91	752.75
2013	745.82	776.88	738.34	746.05	722.57	731.28	771.54	743.48	765.20	760.38	742.92	775.22	751.97
Leisure and Hospitality													
2009	313.09	326.96	313.68	309.15	329.16	319.81	338.94	366.66	363.06	370.00	382.93	383.92	343.08
2010	368.01	368.68	358.68	357.37	359.55	347.22	363.94	374.98	352.82	299.37	290.32	280.55	344.15
2011	284.36	288.47	283.50	283.40	293.21	285.79	303.47	305.77	292.97	296.31	278.88	282.91	290.93
2012	292.42	282.27	281.58	292.88	292.70	297.44	320.00	310.63	315.60	286.03	280.75	297.90	296.93
2013	280.35	290.56	283.74	274.44	281.74	295.43	295.62	294.62	295.72	285.29	276.63	285.36	287.50

NEBRASKA
At a Glance

Population:
    2000 census: 1,711,230
    2010 census: 1,826,341
    2013 estimate: 1,826,516

Percent change in population:
    2000–2010: 6.7%
    2010–2013: 2.3%

Percent change in total nonfarm employment:
    2000–2010: 3.8%
    2010–2013: 3.5%

Industry with the largest growth in employment, 2000–2013 (thousands):
    Education and Health Services, 40.0

Industry with the largest decline or smallest growth in employment, 2000–2013 (thousands):
    Manufacturing, -17.8

Civilian labor force:
    2000: 949,762
    2010: 990,199
    2013: 1,025,340

Unemployment rate and rank among states (lowest to highest):
    2000: 2.8%, 8th
    2010: 4.7%, 2nd
    2013: 3.9%, 3rd

Over-the-year change in unemployment rates:
    2010–2011: -0.2%
    2011–2012: -0.5%
    2012–2013: -0.1%

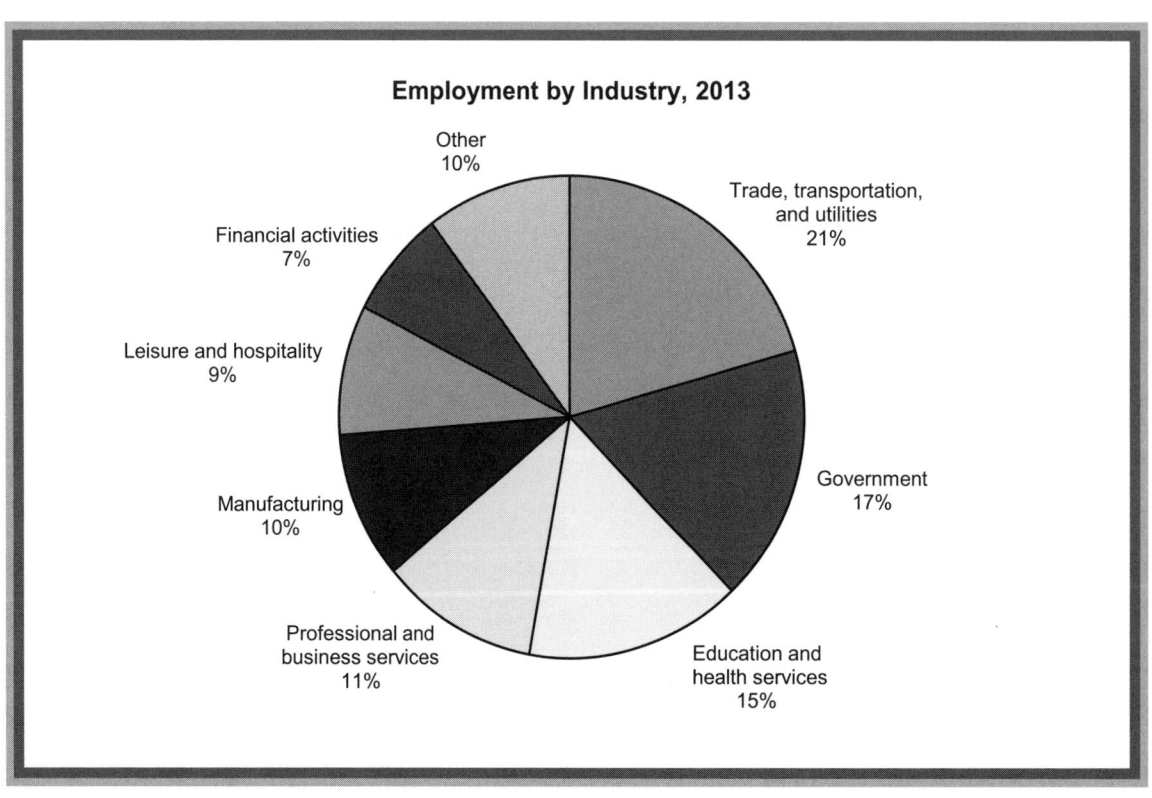

Employment by Industry, 2013

Other 10%
Financial activities 7%
Leisure and hospitality 9%
Manufacturing 10%
Professional and business services 11%
Education and health services 15%
Government 17%
Trade, transportation, and utilities 21%

1. Employment by Industry: Nebraska, Selected Years, 2002–2013

(Numbers in thousands, not seasonally adjusted)

Industry and year	January	February	March	April	May	June	July	August	September	October	November	December	Annual average
Total Nonfarm													
2002	892.7	896.0	902.1	912.3	919.8	925.0	910.4	910.8	914.5	914.4	916.9	917.5	911.0
2003	898.7	898.6	902.7	915.2	922.3	926.8	910.3	911.4	915.4	919.8	921.3	922.0	913.7
2004	899.4	897.5	906.5	919.4	928.5	933.8	922.3	923.3	928.2	929.8	933.0	933.6	921.3
2005	909.3	914.4	923.0	932.8	940.7	946.1	934.6	934.5	940.2	942.4	946.1	944.4	934.0
2006	922.8	928.1	934.8	941.5	951.2	958.2	943.8	944.8	951.5	953.1	958.3	957.9	945.5
2007	936.4	939.5	946.3	956.5	968.6	974.1	961.5	965.5	970.0	972.6	975.5	973.6	961.7
2008	953.5	955.0	961.3	969.7	979.9	979.5	966.7	969.5	972.6	978.3	976.0	972.0	969.5
2009	944.8	943.9	946.3	951.1	959.1	957.2	947.9	946.2	948.1	951.2	951.3	944.8	949.3
2010	921.7	925.1	931.3	944.6	954.4	956.7	947.0	947.9	948.1	955.8	954.9	953.9	945.1
2011	928.5	931.7	939.0	953.5	960.9	959.7	950.4	953.1	957.5	964.5	966.6	965.8	952.6
2012	944.8	947.7	957.6	967.7	977.9	977.1	967.2	969.4	973.7	979.4	981.6	981.7	968.8
2013	955.9	959.8	965.9	974.5	988.2	986.3	977.3	981.7	985.2	990.5	989.1	985.7	978.3
Total Private													
2002	736.3	736.5	741.9	751.8	757.0	763.3	758.8	759.9	756.6	752.8	754.7	755.9	752.1
2003	739.0	737.9	742.0	751.7	757.3	763.0	759.0	761.8	759.0	758.3	759.8	760.7	754.1
2004	741.3	737.9	746.0	757.7	765.2	771.5	769.3	770.8	767.7	767.6	770.4	771.1	761.4
2005	750.3	753.4	761.1	770.2	776.1	782.8	780.9	781.4	778.4	778.5	781.9	781.1	773.0
2006	762.3	765.6	771.5	777.7	785.2	793.0	790.1	790.7	788.8	788.6	793.1	793.6	783.4
2007	774.7	776.2	782.6	792.3	801.6	808.4	808.6	811.4	807.8	807.8	810.2	809.5	799.3
2008	790.6	791.7	797.7	804.2	811.9	813.8	811.3	813.7	808.5	810.7	808.1	804.7	805.6
2009	779.1	775.9	777.6	780.4	786.6	787.4	784.4	784.0	780.1	780.3	779.6	774.9	780.9
2010	754.7	755.6	759.9	772.6	779.1	784.6	784.6	785.4	780.3	783.9	782.9	782.7	775.5
2011	761.2	762.2	769.2	782.1	788.7	791.7	791.3	792.3	790.9	793.2	795.2	795.2	784.4
2012	777.7	778.0	787.8	796.8	804.4	810.0	807.4	808.0	805.5	808.4	810.0	811.0	800.4
2013	788.8	790.3	796.3	803.9	814.2	817.6	816.9	820.1	816.9	818.6	816.8	815.0	809.6
Goods-Producing													
2002	148.2	147.4	148.5	151.1	153.2	155.6	155.9	155.6	154.3	153.4	152.2	151.0	152.2
2003	145.7	144.5	145.1	148.4	150.8	152.9	153.2	153.4	151.6	151.8	150.7	149.8	149.8
2004	144.6	143.2	145.8	148.6	150.9	153.2	153.6	153.0	151.0	150.5	149.8	148.9	149.4
2005	142.7	143.2	145.7	148.3	150.0	152.7	153.3	152.8	151.5	150.9	150.3	148.3	149.1
2006	144.9	145.2	146.6	148.9	150.2	153.0	153.1	152.7	152.1	151.5	150.5	149.2	149.8
2007	144.7	144.4	146.6	149.7	152.1	155.0	156.7	156.9	155.8	155.0	153.9	151.7	151.9
2008	147.4	147.2	149.0	151.9	154.1	155.2	155.2	155.2	153.2	152.6	150.1	146.6	151.5
2009	140.2	138.7	138.9	140.3	142.3	143.2	143.5	142.9	141.7	139.8	138.2	134.2	140.3
2010	128.9	128.9	129.5	133.9	135.6	138.0	137.9	137.5	136.6	136.2	135.4	133.3	134.3
2011	128.6	128.3	130.7	134.0	136.0	137.8	138.1	137.4	137.1	137.0	137.1	135.9	134.8
2012	132.4	131.5	134.1	136.6	138.9	141.4	141.4	141.4	140.8	140.9	140.5	139.7	138.3
2013	134.9	135.4	136.6	139.6	142.8	144.7	145.2	145.4	144.7	144.4	143.2	141.0	141.5
Service-Providing													
2002	744.5	748.6	753.6	761.2	766.6	769.4	754.5	755.2	760.2	761.0	764.7	766.5	758.8
2003	753.0	754.1	757.6	766.8	771.5	773.9	757.1	758.0	763.8	768.0	770.6	772.2	763.9
2004	754.8	754.3	760.7	770.8	777.6	780.6	768.7	770.3	777.2	779.3	783.2	784.7	771.9
2005	766.6	771.2	777.3	784.5	790.7	793.4	781.3	781.7	788.7	791.5	795.8	796.1	784.9
2006	777.9	782.9	788.2	792.6	801.0	805.2	790.7	792.1	799.4	801.6	807.8	808.7	795.7
2007	791.7	795.1	799.7	806.8	816.5	819.1	804.8	808.6	814.2	817.6	821.6	821.9	809.8
2008	806.1	807.8	812.3	817.8	825.8	824.3	811.5	814.3	819.4	825.7	825.9	825.4	818.0
2009	804.6	805.2	807.4	810.8	816.8	814.0	804.4	803.3	806.4	811.4	813.1	810.6	809.0
2010	792.8	796.2	801.8	810.7	818.8	818.7	809.1	810.4	811.5	819.6	819.5	820.6	810.8
2011	799.9	803.4	808.3	819.5	824.9	821.9	812.3	815.7	820.4	827.5	829.5	829.9	817.8
2012	812.4	816.2	823.5	831.1	839.0	835.7	825.8	828.0	832.9	838.5	841.1	842.0	830.5
2013	821.0	824.4	829.3	834.9	845.4	841.6	832.1	836.3	840.5	846.1	845.9	844.7	836.9
Mining, Logging, and Construction													
2002	41.2	40.8	42.4	45.3	47.2	48.8	49.3	49.1	48.3	47.9	46.9	45.8	46.1
2003	42.7	41.8	42.7	46.0	48.3	50.2	51.0	51.2	49.8	49.6	48.6	47.3	47.4
2004	43.6	42.4	44.9	48.3	50.1	51.8	52.2	51.7	50.2	49.7	48.7	47.3	48.4
2005	43.0	42.7	44.7	47.1	49.0	50.9	51.4	51.1	50.1	49.2	48.5	46.2	47.8
2006	43.4	43.5	44.9	47.4	49.2	51.2	51.3	51.1	50.8	50.1	49.4	48.0	48.4
2007	44.7	44.0	46.2	49.1	50.9	53.0	54.7	55.0	54.1	53.2	51.7	49.2	50.5
2008	45.5	45.0	46.7	49.9	51.9	53.1	53.5	53.4	52.3	51.7	49.9	48.0	50.1
2009	43.4	43.0	44.1	46.5	48.7	50.1	51.3	50.9	49.8	48.2	46.4	42.8	47.1
2010	38.4	38.1	38.6	42.5	43.8	45.8	45.7	45.5	44.6	44.2	43.0	40.7	42.6
2011	36.8	36.4	38.3	41.1	42.7	44.0	44.2	43.9	43.5	43.3	42.5	40.9	41.5
2012	38.6	37.8	40.0	42.5	44.3	45.8	45.7	46.0	45.3	45.7	44.7	43.6	43.3
2013	39.8	39.8	40.9	43.7	46.4	47.8	48.7	48.6	47.9	48.1	47.4	45.2	45.4

1. Employment by Industry: Nebraska, Selected Years, 2002–2013—*Continued*

(Numbers in thousands, not seasonally adjusted)

Industry and year	January	February	March	April	May	June	July	August	September	October	November	December	Annual average
Manufacturing													
2002	107.0	106.6	106.1	105.8	106.0	106.8	106.6	106.5	106.0	105.5	105.3	105.2	106.1
2003	103.0	102.7	102.4	102.4	102.5	102.7	102.2	102.2	101.8	102.2	102.1	102.5	102.4
2004	101.0	100.8	100.9	100.3	100.8	101.4	101.4	101.3	100.8	100.8	101.1	101.6	101.0
2005	99.7	100.5	101.0	101.2	101.0	101.8	101.9	101.7	101.4	101.7	101.8	102.1	101.3
2006	101.5	101.7	101.7	101.5	101.0	101.8	101.8	101.6	101.3	101.4	101.1	101.2	101.5
2007	100.0	100.4	100.4	100.6	101.2	102.0	102.0	101.9	101.7	101.8	102.2	102.5	101.4
2008	101.9	102.2	102.3	102.0	102.2	102.1	101.7	101.8	100.9	100.9	100.2	98.6	101.4
2009	96.8	95.7	94.8	93.8	93.6	93.1	92.2	92.0	91.9	91.6	91.8	91.4	93.2
2010	90.5	90.8	90.9	91.4	91.8	92.2	92.2	92.0	92.0	92.0	92.4	92.6	91.7
2011	91.8	91.9	92.4	92.9	93.3	93.8	93.9	93.5	93.6	93.7	94.6	95.0	93.4
2012	93.8	93.7	94.1	94.1	94.6	95.6	95.7	95.4	95.5	95.2	95.8	96.1	95.0
2013	95.1	95.6	95.7	95.9	96.4	96.9	96.5	96.8	96.8	96.3	95.8	95.8	96.1
Trade, Transportation, and Utilities													
2002	194.9	192.4	193.1	194.3	196.0	196.1	194.8	194.8	195.1	194.4	198.1	200.1	195.3
2003	193.0	191.5	192.5	193.6	194.8	195.2	193.4	194.1	194.1	195.4	197.9	199.9	194.6
2004	192.8	190.3	191.7	194.3	196.6	197.5	196.8	197.7	197.8	199.2	201.6	203.7	196.7
2005	197.1	196.5	198.1	198.6	200.9	201.0	200.1	200.1	199.7	200.4	203.4	205.1	200.1
2006	196.8	196.0	197.1	197.9	200.3	200.7	200.0	200.5	200.8	202.1	206.0	208.1	200.5
2007	200.9	199.9	201.1	202.4	205.0	205.4	204.9	205.3	205.1	205.9	209.5	211.1	204.7
2008	203.9	202.2	203.7	203.3	205.4	205.5	203.9	204.4	203.5	206.4	208.6	210.0	205.1
2009	200.6	198.1	198.1	197.4	198.8	198.1	196.6	196.5	195.8	197.6	199.8	200.5	198.2
2010	192.8	191.4	192.5	194.6	196.3	196.3	195.7	195.6	194.5	197.5	200.1	202.6	195.8
2011	193.8	192.7	193.8	196.4	197.6	197.8	197.6	198.4	198.1	199.3	203.2	204.8	197.8
2012	197.2	195.2	196.5	198.4	200.0	200.2	199.3	198.9	198.9	200.7	204.8	206.8	199.7
2013	198.1	196.4	197.4	198.4	200.9	201.4	200.9	201.6	200.5	202.9	205.3	208.1	201.0
Wholesale Trade													
2002	41.1	40.9	41.3	41.6	42.0	42.2	42.5	42.0	41.6	41.0	41.0	41.1	41.5
2003	40.4	40.3	40.5	41.0	41.3	41.6	41.5	41.4	41.2	41.2	40.8	41.0	41.0
2004	40.0	39.9	40.3	41.0	41.2	41.3	41.6	41.1	40.8	40.9	40.7	40.7	40.8
2005	40.0	40.0	40.4	40.5	40.9	41.0	41.3	40.8	40.4	40.5	40.4	40.5	40.6
2006	40.2	40.2	40.4	40.8	41.2	41.4	41.3	40.9	40.7	40.6	40.6	40.9	40.8
2007	39.9	39.8	40.2	40.8	41.2	41.7	41.7	41.2	41.2	41.5	41.6	41.8	41.1
2008	41.2	41.2	41.5	41.9	42.5	42.8	42.5	42.1	41.9	42.3	42.1	42.1	42.0
2009	41.2	40.9	41.0	41.2	41.5	41.6	41.5	41.0	40.8	41.4	41.2	41.3	41.2
2010	39.9	39.8	40.1	40.9	41.2	41.4	41.4	40.7	40.4	40.7	40.4	40.5	40.6
2011	39.8	39.8	40.1	40.7	41.1	41.3	41.3	41.0	40.9	41.1	41.2	41.3	40.8
2012	40.6	40.5	41.0	41.5	41.8	42.1	41.8	41.4	41.1	41.3	41.3	41.6	41.3
2013	40.9	40.9	41.3	41.8	42.5	42.7	42.5	42.1	41.7	42.1	41.9	41.9	41.9
Retail Trade													
2002	108.5	106.3	106.6	107.4	108.7	108.8	107.8	108.0	108.9	109.0	112.3	114.2	108.9
2003	106.7	104.9	105.6	106.2	106.8	106.9	105.9	106.2	106.3	107.7	110.7	112.3	107.2
2004	106.3	104.2	104.5	105.3	106.7	107.1	106.1	106.5	106.1	107.5	110.6	112.4	106.9
2005	106.0	105.0	105.9	106.5	107.7	107.4	106.8	106.8	106.3	107.2	109.8	111.1	107.2
2006	105.0	103.8	104.4	104.8	106.1	106.1	105.7	105.9	105.7	107.0	110.5	111.9	106.4
2007	105.6	104.5	105.2	106.1	107.9	107.7	107.2	107.5	106.9	107.7	110.9	112.4	107.5
2008	107.3	105.7	106.5	105.9	106.8	106.9	106.0	106.1	105.4	107.1	109.5	110.9	107.0
2009	105.0	103.2	103.3	103.5	104.6	104.4	103.7	103.9	103.2	104.1	106.6	106.8	104.4
2010	102.4	101.2	101.9	102.8	104.1	104.2	103.7	103.6	102.5	104.7	107.1	108.5	103.9
2011	102.8	101.9	102.4	103.9	104.6	104.6	104.3	104.8	104.2	105.2	108.7	109.7	104.8
2012	104.1	102.4	103.1	104.2	105.2	105.3	104.9	104.7	104.6	106.3	109.8	110.5	105.4
2013	104.3	103.3	103.9	104.4	105.6	106.0	106.0	106.4	105.8	107.2	110.5	112.2	106.3
Transportation and Utilities													
2002	45.3	45.2	45.2	45.3	45.3	45.1	44.5	44.8	44.6	44.4	44.8	44.8	44.9
2003	45.9	46.3	46.4	46.4	46.7	46.7	46.0	46.5	46.6	46.5	46.4	46.6	46.4
2004	46.5	46.2	46.9	48.0	48.7	49.1	49.1	50.1	50.9	50.8	50.3	50.6	48.9
2005	51.1	51.5	51.8	51.6	52.3	52.6	52.0	52.5	53.0	52.7	53.2	53.5	52.3
2006	51.6	52.0	52.3	52.3	53.0	53.2	53.0	53.7	54.4	54.5	54.9	55.3	53.4
2007	55.4	55.6	55.7	55.5	55.9	56.0	56.0	56.6	57.0	56.7	57.0	56.9	56.2
2008	55.4	55.3	55.7	55.5	56.1	55.8	55.4	56.2	56.2	57.0	57.0	57.0	56.1
2009	54.4	54.0	53.8	52.7	52.7	52.1	51.4	51.6	51.8	52.1	52.0	52.4	52.6
2010	50.5	50.4	50.5	50.9	51.0	50.7	50.8	51.3	51.6	52.1	52.6	53.6	51.3
2011	51.2	51.0	51.3	51.8	51.9	51.9	52.0	52.6	53.0	53.0	53.3	53.8	52.2
2012	52.5	52.3	52.4	52.7	53.0	52.8	52.6	52.8	53.2	53.1	53.7	54.7	53.0
2013	52.9	52.2	52.2	52.2	52.8	52.7	52.4	53.1	53.0	53.6	52.9	54.0	52.8
Information													
2002	24.5	24.3	24.0	23.8	23.5	23.3	23.0	22.8	22.5	22.3	22.0	21.8	23.2
2003	21.5	21.5	21.5	21.4	21.4	21.6	21.5	21.3	21.2	21.4	21.5	21.7	21.5
2004	21.3	21.3	21.3	21.2	21.1	21.2	21.2	21.0	20.9	20.8	20.9	20.7	21.1
2005	20.4	20.5	20.4	20.3	20.0	20.3	20.2	20.2	20.0	20.0	20.0	20.1	20.2
2006	19.7	19.6	19.6	19.6	19.5	19.7	19.6	19.5	19.3	19.1	19.2	19.3	19.5
2007	19.1	19.1	19.1	19.4	19.3	19.6	19.6	19.6	19.4	19.4	19.5	19.4	19.4
2008	19.2	19.2	19.1	19.1	18.8	18.8	18.7	18.5	18.2	18.2	18.2	18.1	18.7
2009	17.7	17.7	17.6	17.4	17.3	17.6	17.5	17.5	17.3	17.2	17.4	17.4	17.5
2010	17.2	17.1	17.0	16.9	17.0	17.1	17.0	17.0	17.0	16.9	16.9	17.1	17.0
2011	16.9	16.9	16.8	16.8	16.8	16.9	17.3	17.2	17.1	17.2	17.2	17.3	17.0
2012	17.2	17.3	17.3	17.2	17.1	17.2	17.2	17.2	17.1	17.2	17.2	17.2	17.2
2013	17.1	17.2	17.2	17.1	17.1	17.0	17.1	17.1	17.1	17.2	17.1	16.6	17.1

1. Employment by Industry: Nebraska, Selected Years, 2002–2013—*Continued*

(Numbers in thousands, not seasonally adjusted)

Industry and year	January	February	March	April	May	June	July	August	September	October	November	December	Annual average
Financial Activities													
2002	60.6	60.7	60.9	61.0	61.3	61.9	61.9	61.8	61.4	61.6	61.7	62.2	61.4
2003	61.8	61.9	62.0	62.0	62.3	62.9	63.0	62.9	62.3	62.3	62.3	62.8	62.4
2004	62.2	62.1	62.6	62.8	63.1	63.6	63.7	63.8	63.4	63.5	63.8	64.2	63.2
2005	63.5	63.8	63.9	64.1	64.5	64.9	64.9	65.0	64.7	64.8	64.7	65.0	64.5
2006	64.6	64.9	65.2	65.7	66.4	67.2	67.4	67.6	67.2	67.4	67.8	68.5	66.7
2007	67.7	68.2	68.4	68.4	69.1	69.4	69.4	69.1	68.7	68.6	68.6	68.8	68.7
2008	68.5	68.9	69.0	69.0	69.3	69.7	69.7	69.6	69.0	69.2	69.1	69.5	69.2
2009	68.6	68.8	68.8	68.4	68.5	68.7	68.4	68.4	67.9	68.1	68.2	68.5	68.4
2010	68.0	68.1	68.3	68.4	68.6	69.3	69.5	69.6	69.1	69.4	69.4	69.6	68.9
2011	69.3	69.2	69.4	69.9	70.1	70.4	70.4	70.4	70.3	70.4	70.6	71.0	70.1
2012	70.3	70.2	70.4	70.7	71.0	71.4	71.4	71.3	71.0	71.2	71.4	71.8	71.0
2013	71.0	71.2	71.2	71.3	71.7	72.1	72.0	72.1	71.7	71.7	71.6	71.6	71.6
Professional and Business Services													
2002	89.0	89.8	91.4	92.9	92.7	93.1	91.3	91.2	90.8	90.9	90.9	90.5	91.2
2003	88.3	89.0	89.7	92.0	91.8	92.9	92.9	93.8	94.4	94.2	93.7	93.8	92.2
2004	91.1	91.1	92.3	94.7	94.8	96.0	95.2	95.7	94.7	95.3	95.4	95.1	94.3
2005	93.9	94.5	95.7	97.3	97.5	98.5	98.5	99.0	98.9	100.3	100.5	100.5	97.9
2006	97.9	98.7	100.4	101.2	102.3	104.4	103.8	103.4	102.9	102.5	102.5	102.1	101.8
2007	100.5	101.2	102.0	103.2	103.8	105.7	105.8	106.2	105.5	105.2	105.8	106.4	104.3
2008	103.8	104.4	105.2	106.6	106.8	107.2	106.7	106.7	106.5	106.6	105.3	104.2	105.8
2009	101.1	100.7	100.3	100.8	100.5	101.4	100.5	100.0	99.1	100.1	99.4	99.2	100.3
2010	97.5	97.7	98.0	100.6	100.7	102.0	103.0	102.7	102.7	103.3	102.5	102.8	101.1
2011	99.5	100.1	100.8	102.8	102.9	103.7	104.8	105.0	105.6	105.7	105.2	105.1	103.4
2012	103.8	104.7	105.2	106.7	107.1	109.1	109.0	108.6	108.7	108.8	108.4	108.2	107.4
2013	106.2	106.6	107.4	108.5	109.2	110.3	110.6	110.4	110.6	109.1	108.5	109.1	108.9
Education and Health Services													
2002	115.1	116.8	117.7	118.4	118.1	118.9	118.0	118.7	119.9	120.0	120.8	121.2	118.6
2003	121.2	121.8	121.9	122.7	122.4	122.6	121.3	121.9	123.0	122.7	124.2	124.0	122.5
2004	123.0	123.7	124.1	125.2	124.7	124.7	123.7	124.3	125.7	125.9	127.3	127.0	124.9
2005	125.0	126.2	126.6	127.8	127.0	127.3	126.5	126.6	128.1	128.4	130.0	129.7	127.4
2006	127.6	129.2	129.4	129.3	129.5	129.6	128.4	129.4	130.6	130.5	132.6	131.6	129.8
2007	129.9	131.3	131.5	132.2	132.8	132.6	132.2	133.5	134.6	135.4	136.1	136.3	133.2
2008	134.7	136.5	136.6	136.7	137.3	136.0	136.2	137.7	138.5	138.8	139.8	139.7	137.4
2009	137.8	138.6	138.5	138.5	138.7	136.9	137.1	137.4	139.0	140.1	140.6	140.7	138.7
2010	138.7	140.2	140.4	140.5	140.8	140.4	140.2	140.9	140.8	141.8	141.9	142.0	140.7
2011	141.0	142.0	142.1	143.1	143.5	142.1	141.3	142.0	143.0	144.7	145.0	145.2	142.9
2012	143.1	144.5	146.1	145.9	146.0	144.9	144.3	145.6	146.6	147.9	148.0	148.2	145.9
2013	145.5	146.6	147.3	147.7	147.9	146.1	145.5	146.5	147.1	148.2	148.9	148.5	147.2
Leisure and Hospitality													
2002	71.9	72.6	73.8	76.8	78.7	80.8	80.2	81.6	79.4	77.0	76.0	76.0	77.1
2003	73.9	74.0	75.3	77.5	79.7	80.6	79.7	80.6	78.7	76.9	75.9	75.2	77.3
2004	72.9	72.7	74.5	77.0	79.9	80.9	80.6	80.9	79.7	77.8	77.0	76.6	77.5
2005	73.9	74.4	76.3	79.3	81.5	83.2	82.5	83.1	81.1	79.4	78.8	78.2	79.3
2006	76.8	77.8	78.7	80.5	82.5	83.6	83.0	83.3	81.6	80.9	80.0	80.4	80.8
2007	77.7	77.8	79.2	82.1	84.4	85.6	85.1	86.1	84.1	83.3	81.8	80.8	82.3
2008	78.5	78.5	80.1	82.4	84.7	85.8	85.6	86.4	84.6	83.1	81.4	80.8	82.7
2009	77.8	77.9	79.9	81.7	84.3	84.9	84.2	84.7	82.8	80.9	79.2	77.6	81.3
2010	75.3	75.8	77.3	80.7	83.0	84.3	84.1	85.1	83.1	82.2	80.1	78.7	80.8
2011	76.1	76.8	79.0	82.4	85.0	86.1	85.1	85.5	83.4	82.6	80.7	79.6	81.9
2012	77.7	78.5	81.7	84.7	87.4	88.6	87.8	88.1	85.6	85.0	83.0	82.4	84.2
2013	79.8	80.5	82.2	84.3	87.4	88.5	88.2	89.6	87.9	87.5	84.5	82.1	85.2
Other Services													
2002	32.1	32.5	32.5	33.5	33.5	33.6	33.7	33.4	33.2	33.2	33.0	33.1	33.1
2003	33.6	33.7	34.0	34.1	34.1	34.3	34.0	33.8	33.7	33.6	33.6	33.5	33.8
2004	33.4	33.5	33.7	33.9	34.1	34.4	34.5	34.4	34.5	34.6	34.6	34.9	34.2
2005	33.8	34.3	34.4	34.5	34.7	34.9	34.9	34.6	34.4	34.3	34.2	34.2	34.4
2006	34.0	34.2	34.5	34.6	34.5	34.8	34.8	34.3	34.3	34.6	34.5	34.4	34.5
2007	34.2	34.3	34.7	34.9	35.1	35.1	34.9	34.7	34.6	35.0	35.0	35.0	34.8
2008	34.6	34.8	35.0	35.2	35.5	35.6	35.3	35.2	35.0	35.8	35.6	35.8	35.3
2009	35.3	35.4	35.5	35.9	36.2	36.6	36.6	36.6	36.5	36.5	36.8	36.8	36.2
2010	36.3	36.4	36.9	37.0	37.1	37.2	37.2	37.0	36.6	36.6	36.5	36.6	36.8
2011	36.0	36.2	36.6	36.7	36.8	36.9	36.7	36.4	36.3	36.3	36.2	36.3	36.5
2012	36.0	36.1	36.5	36.6	36.9	37.2	37.0	36.9	36.8	36.7	36.7	36.7	36.7
2013	36.2	36.4	37.0	37.0	37.2	37.5	37.4	37.4	37.3	37.6	37.7	38.0	37.2
Government													
2002	156.4	159.5	160.2	160.5	162.8	161.7	151.6	150.9	157.9	161.6	162.2	161.6	158.9
2003	159.7	160.7	160.7	163.5	165.0	163.8	151.3	149.6	156.4	161.5	161.5	161.3	159.6
2004	158.1	159.6	160.5	161.7	163.3	162.3	153.0	152.5	160.5	162.2	162.6	162.5	159.9
2005	159.0	161.0	161.9	162.6	164.6	163.3	153.7	153.1	161.8	163.9	164.2	163.3	161.0
2006	160.5	162.5	163.3	163.8	166.0	165.2	153.7	154.1	162.7	164.5	165.2	164.3	162.2
2007	161.7	163.3	163.7	164.2	167.0	165.7	152.9	154.1	162.2	164.8	165.3	164.1	162.4
2008	162.9	163.3	163.6	165.5	168.0	165.7	155.4	155.8	164.1	167.6	167.9	167.3	163.9
2009	165.7	168.0	168.7	170.7	172.5	169.8	163.5	162.2	168.0	170.9	171.7	169.9	168.5
2010	167.0	169.5	171.4	172.0	175.3	172.1	162.4	162.5	167.8	171.9	172.0	171.2	169.6
2011	167.3	169.5	169.8	171.4	172.2	168.0	159.1	160.8	166.6	171.3	171.4	170.6	168.2
2012	167.1	169.7	169.8	170.9	173.5	167.1	159.8	161.4	168.2	171.0	171.6	170.7	168.4
2013	167.1	169.5	169.6	170.6	174.0	168.7	160.4	161.6	168.3	171.9	172.3	170.7	168.7

2. Average Weekly Hours by Selected Industry: Nebraska, 2009–2013

(Not seasonally adjusted)

Industry and year	January	February	March	April	May	June	July	August	September	October	November	December	Annual average
Total Private													
2009	33.3	33.7	33.8	33.4	33.7	33.9	33.9	34.3	33.3	33.7	34.1	33.1	33.7
2010	33.6	33.7	33.7	33.9	34.4	34.3	34.3	34.8	34.3	34.3	34.1	33.8	34.1
2011	34.0	33.8	33.9	34.0	34.5	34.3	34.2	34.1	34.0	34.7	34.0	33.8	34.1
2012	34.2	33.8	33.7	34.3	33.7	34.0	34.2	33.8	34.6	34.2	33.8	34.3	34.0
2013	33.5	33.9	33.9	33.9	34.2	35.2	34.3	34.3	34.6	34.1	33.9	34.1	34.2
Goods-Producing													
2009	38.5	38.4	38.7	38.5	39.6	39.5	40.4	40.6	39.6	40.7	40.6	38.7	39.5
2010	40.0	39.8	40.1	40.4	40.4	40.9	40.7	41.2	40.2	41.1	40.8	39.6	40.4
2011	39.5	39.7	40.2	40.5	40.3	41.0	41.1	40.8	41.2	41.1	40.4	39.9	40.5
2012	39.9	39.9	39.7	40.2	40.8	40.5	40.0	40.7	40.5	40.8	40.2	40.4	40.3
2013	39.4	39.9	39.8	39.8	40.6	41.4	40.7	40.7	40.8	40.9	40.4	40.4	40.4
Mining, Logging, and Construction													
2009	38.3	38.5	37.7	39.7	40.6	40.5	42.5	42.3	40.9	41.9	42.2	37.0	40.3
2010	38.9	38.8	38.8	40.4	40.0	40.8	41.5	41.3	40.0	40.8	39.3	38.3	40.0
2011	37.4	37.5	37.8	38.7	38.7	39.8	40.4	39.3	40.4	41.2	39.9	38.5	39.2
2012	38.8	37.5	38.9	39.2	41.6	41.0	41.5	41.9	40.4	40.1	40.3	39.9	40.2
2013	38.5	38.4	37.7	38.7	40.9	42.1	41.6	40.0	40.5	40.4	39.0	38.4	39.8
Manufacturing													
2009	38.6	38.3	39.2	37.9	39.0	39.0	39.2	39.7	38.9	40.0	39.8	39.5	39.1
2010	40.4	40.3	40.6	40.4	40.5	40.9	40.3	41.2	40.3	41.2	41.5	40.2	40.7
2011	40.4	40.6	41.2	41.2	41.0	41.6	41.4	41.5	41.6	41.0	40.6	40.5	41.1
2012	40.4	40.8	40.1	40.6	40.4	40.2	39.3	40.1	40.6	41.2	40.2	40.6	40.4
2013	39.8	40.6	40.6	40.3	40.5	41.0	40.3	41.0	40.9	41.1	41.1	41.4	40.7
Trade, Transportation, and Utilities													
2009	31.6	32.0	32.3	31.9	32.0	32.5	32.1	32.7	31.6	32.0	32.1	32.1	32.1
2010	32.5	32.8	32.3	33.0	33.4	33.6	33.1	33.2	32.9	33.3	32.9	33.0	33.0
2011	32.2	32.1	32.5	32.6	33.3	33.4	33.2	33.1	33.2	34.2	33.5	33.8	33.1
2012	33.2	33.5	33.9	34.1	33.8	33.9	33.9	33.6	34.5	33.8	33.7	34.2	33.8
2013	33.9	34.4	34.5	34.3	34.9	35.3	34.6	34.6	34.8	34.2	33.6	34.0	34.4
Financial Activities													
2009	36.8	38.3	38.0	36.2	36.1	36.4	36.4	37.7	36.2	36.4	38.1	36.5	36.9
2010	36.6	36.6	36.8	36.4	38.1	36.7	36.8	38.4	36.9	36.9	36.8	36.9	37.0
2011	39.1	37.3	36.7	37.8	38.2	36.8	37.6	38.3	36.9	39.4	36.9	36.6	37.6
2012	39.4	36.6	36.7	39.1	36.1	36.9	38.5	36.6	38.2	37.4	36.3	37.9	37.5
2013	36.6	37.0	36.8	36.9	36.9	38.6	37.1	37.5	38.4	37.0	37.7	38.6	37.4
Professional and Business Services													
2009	34.6	34.9	34.9	35.0	35.1	35.7	35.5	36.0	35.1	35.2	35.5	34.4	35.2
2010	34.8	34.5	34.9	35.0	35.2	35.0	34.9	35.3	34.9	35.0	34.8	34.6	34.9
2011	34.9	34.6	34.3	34.3	34.8	34.5	34.5	34.5	34.6	35.6	34.8	35.1	34.7
2012	35.7	35.6	35.5	35.8	35.2	35.7	35.7	35.4	36.4	36.1	35.4	35.9	35.7
2013	34.2	34.9	34.9	34.9	35.4	36.3	34.7	35.1	35.1	34.8	34.9	34.7	35.0
Education and Health Services													
2009	33.0	32.7	32.6	32.8	33.1	32.4	32.3	32.4	32.1	32.2	32.5	31.8	32.5
2010	32.1	32.1	32.4	32.8	33.1	33.4	32.9	33.3	32.5	32.3	32.5	32.2	32.6
2011	32.1	32.2	32.3	32.5	32.9	32.7	32.2	31.6	31.6	31.9	31.8	31.5	32.1
2012	31.9	31.4	31.4	32.3	31.4	31.8	32.1	31.5	31.7	31.5	31.1	31.8	31.7
2013	31.5	31.7	31.9	32.2	32.1	33.1	32.1	32.0	32.8	32.2	31.9	32.3	32.2
Leisure and Hospitality													
2009	21.3	22.4	22.1	21.1	21.5	22.4	22.4	22.6	20.4	21.1	21.4	20.6	21.6
2010	21.1	21.8	22.0	21.9	22.6	22.5	22.6	22.7	22.5	22.6	22.3	22.0	22.2
2011	21.8	22.6	22.5	22.3	22.6	22.9	22.5	22.5	22.4	22.4	22.4	22.2	22.4
2012	22.2	22.8	22.8	22.5	22.7	23.4	23.6	22.8	23.1	22.3	22.3	22.4	22.7
2013	21.7	22.2	22.2	21.5	22.0	23.4	22.7	22.7	22.3	21.9	22.1	22.0	22.2

3. Average Hourly Earnings by Selected Industry: Nebraska, 2009–2013

(Dollars, not seasonally adjusted)

Industry and year	January	February	March	April	May	June	July	August	September	October	November	December	Annual average
Total Private													
2009	20.08	20.40	20.27	20.25	19.80	19.86	19.82	20.24	20.25	20.23	20.48	20.61	20.19
2010	20.63	20.67	20.81	20.99	21.09	20.87	20.83	20.99	20.97	20.94	20.89	20.93	20.89
2011	21.08	21.06	20.82	20.70	20.74	20.55	20.55	20.66	20.90	21.10	20.84	21.13	20.84
2012	21.30	21.16	20.92	20.86	20.91	20.59	20.85	20.84	20.97	20.78	20.97	21.24	20.95
2013	21.09	21.09	21.13	21.05	20.66	20.72	20.63	20.74	20.98	20.84	21.03	21.12	20.92
Goods-Producing													
2009	19.84	20.27	19.94	19.97	19.58	19.73	19.66	19.70	19.68	19.67	20.01	20.09	19.84
2010	20.00	20.02	19.95	19.71	19.78	19.72	19.78	19.75	19.90	19.84	19.89	20.10	19.87
2011	20.04	20.08	20.12	19.76	19.64	19.51	19.58	19.61	19.65	19.83	19.74	20.08	19.80
2012	20.16	20.05	20.02	19.90	20.10	20.01	20.04	20.16	20.37	20.12	20.09	20.12	20.10
2013	20.18	20.09	20.23	20.06	19.95	19.88	20.02	20.35	20.32	20.25	20.39	20.29	20.17
Mining, Logging, and Construction													
2009	20.49	21.14	20.58	19.50	19.29	19.40	19.19	19.37	19.43	19.59	19.84	20.37	19.79
2010	20.87	20.99	21.34	20.56	20.71	20.41	20.34	20.47	20.49	20.55	20.70	21.33	20.70
2011	21.34	21.64	21.55	20.66	20.35	20.28	20.27	20.41	20.18	20.50	20.42	21.42	20.71
2012	20.95	21.54	21.50	21.06	21.58	21.34	21.37	21.52	21.82	21.35	21.21	21.65	21.41
2013	21.43	21.55	21.60	21.25	20.96	20.45	20.86	21.33	21.24	21.62	21.61	21.75	21.28
Manufacturing													
2009	19.55	19.87	19.66	20.21	19.74	19.92	19.95	19.90	19.83	19.71	20.10	19.97	19.87
2010	19.65	19.63	19.39	19.31	19.34	19.38	19.49	19.40	19.61	19.50	19.53	19.59	19.48
2011	19.56	19.51	19.57	19.39	19.34	19.16	19.27	19.25	19.41	19.52	19.44	19.53	19.41
2012	19.85	19.49	19.41	19.40	19.38	19.36	19.37	19.48	19.68	19.54	19.56	19.44	19.50
2013	19.68	19.51	19.69	19.54	19.46	19.59	19.58	19.87	19.87	19.57	19.82	19.65	19.65
Trade, Transportation, and Utilities													
2009	17.31	17.26	17.18	17.44	17.34	17.15	17.26	17.86	17.75	17.71	17.90	18.10	17.52
2010	17.87	17.91	17.83	18.16	18.35	18.15	18.11	18.14	18.13	18.04	17.87	17.66	18.02
2011	18.05	18.03	17.91	17.82	17.99	18.55	18.33	18.53	19.02	18.56	18.22	18.25	18.28
2012	18.99	18.82	18.62	18.30	18.15	18.08	18.23	18.38	18.41	18.25	18.12	18.29	18.38
2013	18.44	18.75	18.68	18.56	18.28	18.33	18.16	18.20	18.31	18.29	18.48	18.47	18.41
Financial Activities													
2009	26.20	26.51	26.91	26.81	26.39	26.58	26.28	27.71	27.19	26.71	26.98	26.65	26.75
2010	26.42	26.41	26.33	26.94	27.10	26.79	26.57	26.86	26.33	26.27	26.05	26.08	26.51
2011	26.24	26.16	25.67	26.03	26.57	25.85	25.68	25.52	26.00	26.29	26.07	26.52	26.05
2012	26.06	25.95	25.92	26.19	26.47	25.73	26.40	25.62	25.66	25.09	25.49	25.09	25.81
2013	24.51	24.85	25.07	25.19	25.50	25.83	25.23	25.46	26.04	25.63	25.75	27.02	25.52
Professional and Business Services													
2009	22.65	24.11	23.81	23.45	22.15	22.10	22.06	22.42	22.57	22.93	23.36	23.43	22.91
2010	23.68	23.90	23.49	23.81	24.29	23.90	23.96	24.29	24.27	24.25	24.37	24.23	24.04
2011	24.22	24.06	24.07	24.13	24.15	23.79	23.62	23.91	24.02	24.61	24.70	25.02	24.20
2012	25.29	25.39	25.39	25.48	25.42	25.17	25.40	25.42	25.10	25.36	25.41	26.55	25.45
2013	26.22	25.92	25.82	25.96	25.07	25.60	25.58	25.27	25.60	25.47	25.67	25.86	25.66
Education and Health Services													
2009	20.79	20.48	20.25	20.19	19.90	20.20	20.10	20.32	20.30	20.00	20.01	20.16	20.22
2010	20.38	20.59	20.41	20.67	20.68	20.57	20.62	20.53	20.63	20.84	20.79	20.76	20.62
2011	20.52	20.50	20.15	19.98	20.04	19.99	20.37	20.46	20.73	21.00	20.57	20.89	20.43
2012	20.93	20.50	20.49	20.66	20.58	20.82	21.08	21.01	21.22	20.75	20.95	21.41	20.87
2013	21.39	21.20	21.40	21.31	21.25	21.24	21.37	21.57	21.78	21.65	21.96	22.06	21.52
Leisure and Hospitality													
2009	10.81	10.82	10.77	10.80	10.75	10.57	10.48	10.82	11.22	11.36	11.45	11.40	10.92
2010	11.45	11.37	11.43	11.48	11.54	11.41	11.44	11.62	11.46	11.41	11.43	11.48	11.46
2011	11.42	11.47	11.28	11.40	11.43	11.17	11.31	11.41	11.74	11.74	11.76	12.33	11.53
2012	12.09	12.35	12.44	12.43	12.22	12.06	12.01	12.00	11.94	12.11	12.00	12.32	12.16
2013	12.00	12.03	11.98	11.98	11.80	11.61	11.46	11.48	11.70	11.63	11.66	11.65	11.74

4. Average Weekly Earnings by Selected Industry: Nebraska, 2009–2013

(Dollars, not seasonally adjusted)

Industry and year	January	February	March	April	May	June	July	August	September	October	November	December	Annual average
Total Private													
2009	668.66	687.48	685.13	676.35	667.26	673.25	671.90	694.23	674.33	681.75	698.37	682.19	680.40
2010	693.17	696.58	701.30	711.56	725.50	715.84	714.47	730.45	719.27	718.24	712.35	707.43	712.35
2011	716.72	711.83	705.80	703.80	715.53	704.87	702.81	704.51	710.60	732.17	708.56	714.19	710.64
2012	728.46	715.21	705.00	715.50	704.67	700.06	713.07	704.39	725.56	710.68	708.79	728.53	712.30
2013	706.52	714.95	716.31	713.60	706.57	729.34	707.61	711.38	725.91	710.64	712.92	720.19	715.46
Goods-Producing													
2009	763.84	778.37	771.68	768.85	775.37	779.34	794.26	799.82	779.33	800.57	812.41	777.48	783.68
2010	800.00	796.80	800.00	796.28	799.11	806.55	805.05	813.70	799.98	815.42	811.51	795.96	802.75
2011	791.58	797.18	808.82	800.28	791.49	799.91	804.74	800.09	809.58	815.01	797.50	801.19	801.90
2012	804.38	800.00	794.79	799.98	820.08	810.41	801.60	820.51	824.99	820.90	807.62	812.85	810.03
2013	795.09	801.59	805.15	798.39	809.97	823.03	814.81	828.25	829.06	828.23	823.76	819.72	814.87
Mining, Logging, and Construction													
2009	784.77	813.89	775.87	774.15	783.17	785.70	815.58	819.35	794.69	820.82	837.25	753.69	797.54
2010	811.84	814.41	827.99	830.62	828.40	832.73	844.11	845.41	819.60	838.44	813.51	816.94	828.00
2011	798.12	811.50	814.59	799.54	787.55	807.14	818.91	802.11	815.27	844.60	814.76	824.67	811.83
2012	812.86	807.75	836.35	825.55	897.73	874.94	886.86	901.69	881.53	856.14	854.76	863.84	860.68
2013	825.06	827.52	814.32	822.38	857.26	860.95	867.78	853.20	860.22	873.45	842.79	835.20	846.94
Manufacturing													
2009	754.63	761.02	770.67	765.96	769.86	776.88	782.04	790.03	771.39	788.40	799.98	788.82	776.92
2010	793.86	791.09	787.23	780.12	783.27	792.64	785.45	799.28	790.28	803.40	810.50	787.52	792.84
2011	790.22	792.11	806.28	798.87	792.94	797.06	797.78	798.88	807.46	800.32	789.26	790.97	797.75
2012	801.94	795.19	778.34	787.64	782.95	778.27	761.24	781.15	799.01	805.05	786.31	789.26	787.80
2013	783.26	792.11	799.41	787.46	788.13	803.19	789.07	814.67	812.68	804.33	814.60	813.51	799.76
Trade, Transportation, and Utilities													
2009	547.00	552.32	554.91	556.34	554.88	557.38	554.05	584.02	560.90	566.72	574.59	581.01	562.39
2010	580.78	587.45	575.91	599.28	612.89	609.84	599.44	602.25	596.48	600.73	587.92	582.78	594.66
2011	581.21	578.76	582.08	580.93	599.07	619.57	608.56	613.34	631.46	634.75	610.37	616.85	605.07
2012	630.47	630.47	631.22	624.03	613.47	612.91	618.00	617.57	635.15	616.85	610.64	625.52	621.24
2013	625.12	645.00	644.46	636.61	637.97	647.05	628.34	629.72	637.19	625.52	620.93	627.98	633.30
Financial Activities													
2009	964.16	1,015.33	1,022.58	970.52	952.68	967.51	956.59	1,044.67	984.28	972.24	1,027.94	972.73	987.08
2010	966.97	966.61	968.94	980.62	1,032.51	983.19	977.78	1,031.42	971.58	969.36	958.64	962.35	980.87
2011	1,025.98	975.77	942.09	983.93	1,014.97	951.28	965.57	977.42	959.40	1,035.83	961.98	970.63	979.48
2012	1,026.76	949.77	951.26	1,024.03	955.57	949.44	1,016.40	937.69	980.21	938.37	925.29	950.91	967.88
2013	897.07	919.45	922.58	929.51	940.95	997.04	936.03	954.75	999.94	948.31	970.78	1,042.97	954.45
Professional and Business Services													
2009	783.69	841.44	830.97	820.75	777.47	788.97	783.13	807.12	792.21	807.14	829.28	805.99	806.43
2010	824.06	824.55	819.80	833.35	855.01	836.50	836.20	857.44	847.02	848.75	848.08	838.36	839.00
2011	845.28	832.48	825.60	827.66	840.42	820.76	814.89	824.90	831.09	876.12	859.56	878.20	839.74
2012	902.85	903.88	901.35	912.19	894.78	898.57	906.78	899.87	913.64	915.50	899.51	953.15	908.57
2013	896.72	904.61	901.12	906.00	887.48	929.28	887.63	886.98	898.56	886.36	895.88	897.34	898.45
Education and Health Services													
2009	686.07	669.70	660.15	662.23	658.69	654.48	649.23	658.37	651.63	644.00	650.33	641.09	657.15
2010	654.20	660.94	661.28	677.98	684.51	687.04	678.40	683.65	670.48	673.13	675.68	668.47	672.21
2011	658.69	660.10	650.85	649.35	659.32	653.67	655.91	646.54	655.07	669.90	654.13	658.04	655.80
2012	667.67	643.70	643.39	667.32	646.21	662.08	676.67	661.82	672.67	653.63	651.55	680.84	661.58
2013	673.79	672.04	682.66	686.18	682.13	703.04	685.98	690.24	714.38	697.13	700.52	712.54	692.94
Leisure and Hospitality													
2009	230.25	242.37	238.02	227.88	231.13	236.77	234.75	244.53	228.89	239.70	245.03	234.84	235.87
2010	241.60	247.87	251.46	251.41	260.80	256.73	258.54	263.77	257.85	257.87	254.89	252.56	254.41
2011	248.96	259.22	253.80	254.22	258.32	255.79	254.48	256.73	262.98	262.98	263.42	273.73	258.27
2012	268.40	281.58	283.63	279.68	277.39	282.20	283.44	273.60	275.81	270.05	267.60	275.97	276.03
2013	260.40	267.07	265.96	257.57	259.60	271.67	260.14	260.60	260.91	254.70	257.69	256.30	260.63

NEVADA
At a Glance

Population:
  2000 census: 1,998,250
  2010 census: 2,700,551
  2013 estimate: 2,790,136

Percent change in population:
  2000–2010: 35.1%
  2010–2013: 3.3%

Percent change in total nonfarm employment:
  2000–2010: 8.9%
  2010–2013: 5.2%

Industry with the largest growth in employment, 2000–2013 (thousands):
  Education and Health Services, 48.5

Industry with the largest decline or smallest growth in employment, 2000–2013 (thousands):
  Construction, -32.4

Civilian labor force:
  2000: 1,062,845
  2010: 1,392,109
  2013: 1,372,996

Unemployment rate and rank among states (lowest to highest):
  2000: 4.5%, 38th
  2010: 13.8%, 51st
  2013: 9.8%, 51st

Over-the-year change in unemployment rates:
  2010–2011: -0.6%
  2011–2012: -1.7%
  2012–2013: -1.7%

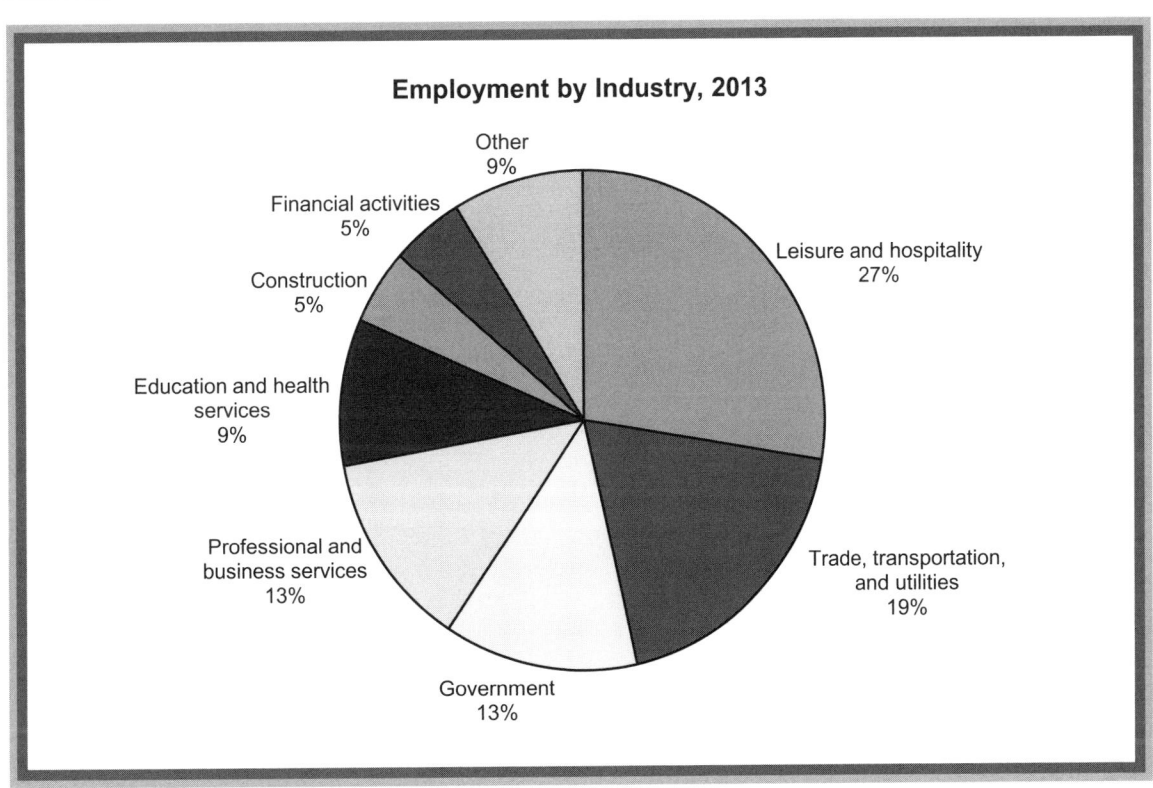

Employment by Industry, 2013

- Other 9%
- Financial activities 5%
- Construction 5%
- Education and health services 9%
- Professional and business services 13%
- Government 13%
- Leisure and hospitality 27%
- Trade, transportation, and utilities 19%

1. Employment by Industry: Nevada, Selected Years, 2002–2013

(Numbers in thousands, not seasonally adjusted)

Industry and year	January	February	March	April	May	June	July	August	September	October	November	December	Annual average
Total Nonfarm													
2002	1,019.1	1,025.9	1,037.4	1,046.2	1,055.6	1,053.6	1,049.2	1,057.5	1,063.6	1,070.5	1,072.2	1,072.7	1,052.0
2003	1,053.5	1,062.9	1,071.8	1,074.1	1,084.1	1,083.6	1,083.2	1,093.2	1,103.9	1,114.3	1,115.2	1,119.9	1,088.3
2004	1,101.5	1,108.3	1,122.0	1,140.2	1,148.3	1,153.7	1,153.6	1,158.8	1,174.0	1,189.2	1,189.4	1,193.0	1,152.7
2005	1,166.7	1,179.5	1,195.0	1,216.5	1,221.8	1,226.7	1,225.7	1,229.5	1,246.4	1,250.3	1,256.3	1,261.5	1,223.0
2006	1,239.8	1,255.0	1,268.3	1,276.3	1,286.3	1,291.2	1,279.8	1,282.9	1,292.6	1,292.0	1,294.8	1,295.6	1,279.6
2007	1,268.2	1,283.3	1,290.9	1,294.5	1,303.8	1,302.1	1,287.2	1,288.1	1,292.3	1,297.7	1,301.0	1,300.4	1,292.5
2008	1,269.1	1,272.9	1,275.8	1,281.0	1,286.2	1,279.5	1,265.2	1,260.6	1,261.6	1,252.5	1,238.1	1,221.1	1,263.6
2009	1,180.8	1,171.7	1,163.3	1,158.5	1,155.9	1,147.6	1,133.5	1,128.1	1,135.5	1,135.5	1,134.6	1,134.1	1,148.3
2010	1,104.2	1,105.7	1,109.0	1,120.8	1,128.3	1,124.0	1,116.7	1,114.1	1,116.0	1,124.0	1,125.7	1,124.7	1,117.8
2011	1,107.1	1,109.6	1,114.7	1,126.6	1,130.4	1,128.6	1,122.8	1,122.4	1,132.3	1,138.0	1,139.3	1,136.8	1,125.7
2012	1,120.3	1,123.5	1,131.1	1,139.5	1,148.1	1,150.1	1,139.5	1,145.3	1,153.7	1,160.7	1,165.7	1,160.5	1,144.8
2013	1,145.0	1,148.9	1,158.3	1,168.2	1,176.0	1,177.3	1,170.3	1,179.5	1,184.7	1,193.7	1,203.2	1,203.1	1,175.7
Total Private													
2002	893.2	895.0	906.4	915.4	923.9	925.3	927.5	935.5	933.5	935.3	936.4	936.5	922.0
2003	923.1	927.4	935.5	938.0	947.1	950.9	957.5	967.7	970.0	977.0	977.6	981.7	954.5
2004	968.8	971.3	982.7	1,000.9	1,007.9	1,018.2	1,024.7	1,030.4	1,035.2	1,046.0	1,045.8	1,049.1	1,015.1
2005	1,028.6	1,036.3	1,049.7	1,071.3	1,075.7	1,085.2	1,090.8	1,095.7	1,102.9	1,102.1	1,107.0	1,111.9	1,079.8
2006	1,096.6	1,105.9	1,118.3	1,125.0	1,134.5	1,144.0	1,139.6	1,143.2	1,143.0	1,136.9	1,138.5	1,139.2	1,130.4
2007	1,117.8	1,126.4	1,133.4	1,135.4	1,144.2	1,147.4	1,140.0	1,142.1	1,136.8	1,137.0	1,139.4	1,138.1	1,136.5
2008	1,112.8	1,110.6	1,112.6	1,116.7	1,121.2	1,119.7	1,111.7	1,108.3	1,100.7	1,086.8	1,072.2	1,055.6	1,102.4
2009	1,022.5	1,009.5	1,001.1	996.6	994.7	991.7	983.8	979.9	979.2	977.4	976.8	976.8	990.8
2010	951.9	948.7	951.2	962.9	967.1	970.3	969.1	969.3	964.1	970.5	971.8	970.9	964.0
2011	956.0	955.0	960.3	971.9	976.1	981.0	980.5	980.0	983.7	987.4	988.5	985.1	975.5
2012	973.3	973.3	979.3	987.7	995.8	1,002.6	997.0	1,003.1	1,003.9	1,009.0	1,013.2	1,007.2	995.5
2013	995.5	997.0	1,005.2	1,015.0	1,022.5	1,028.1	1,027.7	1,034.0	1,032.9	1,040.4	1,049.7	1,048.9	1,024.7
Goods-Producing													
2002	136.1	136.6	139.0	141.9	144.1	144.7	147.1	149.6	148.2	148.2	147.0	145.6	144.0
2003	142.4	144.0	146.7	148.0	150.9	153.3	155.3	157.9	157.9	160.3	158.9	159.0	152.9
2004	155.8	158.8	161.6	168.2	170.8	174.7	178.5	180.6	182.5	185.4	183.8	183.9	173.7
2005	176.8	181.1	185.5	190.0	191.0	193.7	197.8	199.7	201.9	201.2	200.5	201.1	193.4
2006	196.3	200.1	202.5	205.6	208.7	211.5	210.0	210.5	208.5	204.4	201.3	198.9	204.9
2007	191.9	193.5	196.9	197.1	200.2	200.8	199.7	200.5	197.1	193.9	191.1	187.8	195.9
2008	179.8	179.9	179.3	179.7	181.6	182.5	182.8	181.2	177.6	173.1	165.6	158.5	176.8
2009	149.4	144.9	141.6	138.5	134.4	133.2	131.3	129.7	127.6	126.1	122.4	117.3	133.0
2010	108.6	107.1	107.1	109.7	110.6	111.5	111.3	111.3	109.6	110.1	109.0	107.1	109.4
2011	102.7	102.7	101.3	102.7	103.8	105.4	106.4	106.8	106.4	106.5	105.2	104.0	104.5
2012	100.8	100.6	101.8	103.4	105.5	107.7	108.6	110.4	110.3	110.5	110.2	109.5	106.6
2013	106.6	107.5	108.8	110.7	111.2	113.3	114.4	116.2	115.9	118.0	116.5	115.7	112.9
Service-Providing													
2002	883.0	889.3	898.4	904.3	911.5	908.9	902.1	907.9	915.4	922.3	925.2	927.1	908.0
2003	911.1	918.9	925.1	926.1	933.2	930.3	927.9	935.3	946.0	954.0	956.3	960.9	935.4
2004	945.7	949.5	960.4	972.0	977.5	979.0	975.1	978.2	991.5	1,003.8	1,005.6	1,009.1	979.0
2005	989.9	998.4	1,009.5	1,026.5	1,030.8	1,033.0	1,027.9	1,029.8	1,044.5	1,049.1	1,055.8	1,060.4	1,029.6
2006	1,043.5	1,054.9	1,065.8	1,070.7	1,077.6	1,079.7	1,069.8	1,072.4	1,084.1	1,087.6	1,093.5	1,096.7	1,074.7
2007	1,076.3	1,089.8	1,094.0	1,097.4	1,103.6	1,101.3	1,087.5	1,087.6	1,095.2	1,103.8	1,109.9	1,112.6	1,096.6
2008	1,089.3	1,093.0	1,096.5	1,101.3	1,104.6	1,097.0	1,082.4	1,079.4	1,084.0	1,079.4	1,072.5	1,062.6	1,086.8
2009	1,031.4	1,026.8	1,021.7	1,020.0	1,021.5	1,014.4	1,002.2	998.4	1,007.9	1,009.4	1,012.2	1,016.8	1,015.2
2010	995.6	998.6	1,001.9	1,011.1	1,017.7	1,012.5	1,005.4	1,002.8	1,006.4	1,013.9	1,016.7	1,017.6	1,008.4
2011	1,004.4	1,006.9	1,013.4	1,023.9	1,026.6	1,023.2	1,016.4	1,015.6	1,025.9	1,031.5	1,034.1	1,032.8	1,021.2
2012	1,019.5	1,022.9	1,029.3	1,036.1	1,042.6	1,042.4	1,030.9	1,034.9	1,043.4	1,050.2	1,055.5	1,051.0	1,038.2
2013	1,038.4	1,041.4	1,049.5	1,057.5	1,064.8	1,064.0	1,055.9	1,063.3	1,068.8	1,075.7	1,086.7	1,087.4	1,062.8
Mining and Logging													
2002	9.0	8.9	8.8	8.8	8.8	8.9	8.9	8.9	8.8	8.8	8.6	8.7	8.8
2003	8.2	8.6	8.7	8.6	8.7	8.9	9.1	9.1	8.9	9.1	9.1	9.2	8.9
2004	9.0	9.1	9.2	9.2	9.3	9.5	9.9	10.0	10.0	9.9	9.8	9.8	9.6
2005	9.8	9.8	10.1	10.5	10.4	10.8	11.1	11.2	11.1	11.2	11.0	11.0	10.7
2006	11.0	10.9	11.1	11.3	11.5	11.7	11.9	12.0	11.9	11.8	11.8	11.8	11.6
2007	11.8	11.7	11.9	11.9	12.0	12.3	12.3	12.4	12.1	11.9	12.0	11.9	12.0
2008	11.9	11.9	11.9	11.9	12.0	12.2	12.5	12.6	12.5	12.2	12.2	12.0	12.2
2009	11.6	11.5	11.5	11.4	11.5	11.9	11.9	11.9	11.7	11.7	11.6	11.6	11.7
2010	11.5	11.5	11.7	11.7	12.0	12.4	12.7	12.7	12.4	12.4	12.7	12.8	12.2
2011	12.8	13.0	13.2	13.4	13.7	14.3	14.6	14.6	14.5	14.5	14.6	14.7	14.0
2012	14.4	14.6	15.0	15.2	15.4	15.8	16.1	16.1	15.9	15.7	15.6	15.6	15.5
2013	15.4	15.5	15.4	15.3	15.3	15.5	15.8	15.7	15.2	15.1	15.3	15.2	15.4
Construction													
2002	85.0	85.6	88.1	90.8	92.6	92.9	94.8	97.3	96.1	95.7	94.7	93.3	92.2
2003	91.2	92.4	94.9	96.3	98.7	100.8	102.3	104.6	105.0	106.8	105.4	105.4	100.3
2004	102.8	105.2	107.5	113.6	115.6	118.9	122.2	123.9	126.1	128.8	127.1	127.3	118.3
2005	120.2	124.3	128.1	131.8	132.9	134.8	138.4	140.3	142.2	141.4	141.0	141.5	134.7
2006	136.9	140.2	141.9	144.2	146.7	148.8	146.9	147.3	145.3	141.9	138.8	136.3	142.9
2007	130.3	132.0	134.7	134.7	137.5	137.6	136.7	137.5	134.6	132.1	129.4	126.7	133.7
2008	118.9	119.2	118.7	119.0	120.6	121.2	121.3	119.8	117.0	113.3	107.1	101.3	116.5
2009	94.4	91.2	88.6	86.2	82.7	81.5	79.8	78.5	76.7	75.4	71.9	67.0	81.2
2010	59.3	57.9	57.7	60.0	60.6	60.9	60.5	60.6	59.2	59.9	58.5	56.4	59.3
2011	52.4	52.1	50.2	51.3	51.9	52.6	53.3	53.5	53.1	53.1	51.9	50.6	52.2
2012	48.0	47.6	48.1	49.3	51.0	52.4	52.9	54.6	54.8	55.2	55.1	54.4	52.0
2013	51.9	52.4	53.6	55.3	55.6	57.1	57.8	59.5	59.6	61.8	60.2	59.6	57.0

1. Employment by Industry: Nevada, Selected Years, 2002–2013—*Continued*

(Numbers in thousands, not seasonally adjusted)

Industry and year	January	February	March	April	May	June	July	August	September	October	November	December	Annual average
Manufacturing													
2002	42.1	42.1	42.1	42.3	42.7	42.9	43.4	43.4	43.3	43.7	43.7	43.6	42.9
2003	43.0	43.0	43.1	43.1	43.5	43.6	43.9	44.2	44.0	44.4	44.4	44.4	43.7
2004	44.0	44.5	44.9	45.4	45.9	46.3	46.4	46.7	46.4	46.7	46.9	46.8	45.9
2005	46.8	47.0	47.3	47.7	47.7	48.1	48.3	48.2	48.6	48.6	48.5	48.6	48.0
2006	48.4	49.0	49.5	50.1	50.5	51.0	51.2	51.2	51.3	50.7	50.7	50.8	50.4
2007	49.8	49.8	50.3	50.5	50.7	50.9	50.7	50.6	50.4	49.9	49.7	49.2	50.2
2008	49.0	48.8	48.7	48.8	49.0	49.1	49.0	48.8	48.1	47.6	46.3	45.2	48.2
2009	43.4	42.2	41.5	40.9	40.2	39.8	39.6	39.3	39.2	39.0	38.9	38.7	40.2
2010	37.8	37.7	37.7	38.0	38.0	38.2	38.1	38.0	38.0	37.8	37.8	37.9	37.9
2011	37.5	37.6	37.9	38.0	38.2	38.5	38.5	38.7	38.8	38.9	38.7	38.7	38.3
2012	38.4	38.4	38.7	38.9	39.1	39.5	39.6	39.7	39.6	39.6	39.5	39.5	39.2
2013	39.3	39.6	39.8	40.1	40.3	40.7	40.8	41.0	41.1	41.1	41.0	40.9	40.5
Trade, Transportation, and Utilities													
2002	187.5	185.6	186.4	188.9	190.1	190.7	191.4	191.4	192.0	194.6	197.0	199.3	191.2
2003	190.2	189.7	191.3	190.5	191.8	193.0	193.7	195.9	197.6	201.3	204.8	207.9	195.6
2004	197.9	197.5	199.1	200.7	202.0	204.2	204.7	205.3	205.8	209.2	213.1	215.6	204.6
2005	207.6	207.5	208.9	211.0	211.9	213.5	215.1	215.8	217.9	219.4	223.6	226.2	214.9
2006	220.4	220.2	222.6	223.0	224.2	225.4	225.1	226.1	226.9	228.6	233.1	235.9	226.0
2007	228.6	227.5	228.8	229.6	231.1	232.1	231.6	232.8	232.9	234.1	239.7	242.6	232.6
2008	233.7	231.3	231.8	231.3	231.3	232.1	232.2	232.3	231.1	230.2	231.2	230.1	231.5
2009	219.2	215.0	213.6	211.8	211.8	212.1	211.5	211.0	211.4	212.2	216.0	217.0	213.6
2010	208.6	206.3	206.5	207.1	208.2	209.1	209.9	210.3	209.8	211.8	216.0	217.5	210.1
2011	209.1	207.5	208.0	209.5	210.5	211.2	212.1	212.9	213.2	215.4	221.2	222.0	212.7
2012	215.0	212.8	213.9	214.9	216.1	217.2	217.1	217.6	218.4	219.8	226.9	226.7	218.0
2013	218.2	216.3	215.7	216.8	219.5	220.8	221.7	222.4	223.0	227.6	235.5	236.5	222.8
Wholesale Trade													
2002	34.4	34.6	35.0	35.0	35.0	35.1	34.9	34.9	34.7	34.7	34.6	34.7	34.8
2003	34.0	34.2	34.2	34.1	34.1	34.2	34.4	34.3	34.3	34.6	34.6	34.7	34.3
2004	34.4	34.5	34.7	34.9	35.1	35.4	35.9	35.8	35.9	36.2	36.1	36.3	35.4
2005	36.1	36.5	36.7	37.0	37.2	37.4	37.6	37.6	37.8	37.7	37.8	38.0	37.3
2006	37.8	38.1	38.4	38.5	38.7	38.9	38.9	39.0	39.1	39.1	39.1	39.3	38.7
2007	38.9	39.1	39.3	39.3	39.4	39.6	39.5	39.6	39.5	39.4	39.4	39.4	39.4
2008	39.0	39.1	39.1	39.1	39.2	39.2	39.2	39.1	38.9	38.5	37.9	37.4	38.8
2009	36.5	36.0	35.6	35.0	34.7	34.4	34.2	34.0	33.7	33.6	33.4	33.3	34.5
2010	32.7	32.6	32.7	32.9	33.1	33.1	33.0	33.0	32.9	33.1	32.9	33.0	32.9
2011	32.5	32.6	32.7	32.7	32.8	32.9	32.9	32.8	32.7	32.7	32.7	32.7	32.7
2012	32.3	32.3	32.5	32.5	32.6	32.7	32.8	32.7	32.6	32.7	32.7	32.8	32.6
2013	32.3	32.4	32.5	32.7	32.8	33.0	33.1	33.2	33.2	33.8	33.4	33.7	33.0
Retail Trade													
2002	112.3	110.6	111.1	112.5	113.7	114.3	114.3	114.1	114.9	117.0	120.7	123.2	114.9
2003	115.4	114.5	115.8	115.2	116.4	117.4	118.0	120.0	121.2	123.9	127.3	129.9	119.6
2004	120.9	120.4	121.4	122.9	123.9	125.5	125.1	125.7	126.1	128.2	132.2	134.6	125.6
2005	127.3	126.5	127.3	128.1	128.5	129.5	130.8	131.2	132.5	134.0	137.5	139.3	131.0
2006	134.1	133.6	135.2	135.2	135.8	136.1	135.7	136.2	136.6	138.1	141.7	143.5	136.8
2007	137.5	136.3	137.0	137.8	138.8	139.1	139.2	139.7	139.5	140.1	145.0	147.4	139.8
2008	140.4	138.3	138.7	138.2	137.8	138.1	138.3	138.3	137.6	137.3	139.0	138.7	138.4
2009	130.9	127.7	126.9	125.9	126.2	126.7	126.6	126.4	127.2	128.2	132.0	133.0	128.1
2010	126.1	124.1	124.3	124.8	125.4	126.0	126.7	127.1	126.8	128.5	132.7	133.5	127.2
2011	126.8	125.1	125.4	126.1	126.9	127.2	127.6	128.3	128.4	130.2	135.7	136.0	128.6
2012	130.4	128.4	129.2	129.7	130.5	131.2	130.9	131.4	132.1	133.5	140.3	139.7	132.3
2013	132.6	130.8	130.9	131.7	133.2	134.0	134.6	135.3	135.5	138.7	146.2	146.3	135.8
Transportation and Utilities													
2002	40.8	40.4	40.3	41.4	41.4	41.3	42.2	42.4	42.4	42.9	41.7	41.4	41.6
2003	40.8	41.0	41.3	41.2	41.3	41.4	41.3	41.6	42.1	42.8	42.9	43.3	41.8
2004	42.6	42.6	43.0	42.9	43.0	43.3	43.7	43.8	43.8	44.8	44.8	44.7	43.6
2005	44.2	44.5	44.9	45.9	46.2	46.6	46.7	47.0	47.6	47.7	48.3	48.9	46.5
2006	48.5	48.5	49.0	49.3	49.7	50.4	50.5	50.9	51.2	51.4	52.3	53.1	50.4
2007	52.2	52.1	52.5	52.5	52.9	53.4	52.9	53.5	53.9	54.6	55.3	55.8	53.5
2008	54.3	53.9	54.0	54.0	54.3	54.3	54.7	54.9	54.6	54.4	54.3	54.0	54.3
2009	51.8	51.3	51.1	50.9	50.9	51.0	50.7	50.6	50.5	50.4	50.6	50.7	50.9
2010	49.8	49.6	49.5	49.4	49.7	50.0	50.2	50.2	50.1	50.2	50.4	51.0	50.0
2011	49.8	49.8	49.9	50.7	50.8	51.1	51.6	51.8	52.1	52.5	52.8	53.3	51.4
2012	52.3	52.1	52.2	52.7	53.0	53.3	53.4	53.5	53.7	53.6	53.9	54.2	53.2
2013	53.3	53.1	52.3	52.4	53.5	53.8	54.0	53.9	54.3	55.1	55.9	56.5	54.0
Information													
2002	17.5	17.3	17.1	17.1	17.3	16.9	16.7	16.8	16.7	16.4	16.5	16.5	16.9
2003	16.1	16.0	15.8	15.8	15.9	15.8	15.4	15.2	15.1	15.0	15.1	15.2	15.5
2004	14.9	14.6	14.5	15.7	15.0	14.9	14.8	14.6	14.5	14.8	14.8	14.6	14.8
2005	15.0	14.4	14.4	15.0	15.4	14.7	14.5	14.4	14.2	14.7	14.6	14.5	14.7
2006	14.8	15.2	14.7	15.1	15.2	15.2	15.6	15.7	15.2	15.2	15.1	15.0	15.2
2007	15.3	15.8	15.6	15.7	16.0	15.8	15.2	15.6	15.2	15.5	15.6	15.3	15.6
2008	15.2	15.2	15.1	15.4	15.9	15.2	14.8	14.8	14.5	14.9	14.4	14.1	15.0
2009	13.5	13.6	13.6	13.0	13.2	13.1	13.1	13.2	12.8	12.8	12.9	12.9	13.1
2010	12.3	12.4	12.3	12.6	12.6	12.5	12.8	12.5	12.3	12.4	12.6	12.5	12.5
2011	12.4	12.3	12.4	12.6	12.7	12.7	12.5	12.4	12.6	13.0	12.3	12.8	12.6
2012	12.2	12.3	12.5	12.3	12.6	12.6	12.6	12.3	12.7	13.3	14.4	12.9	12.7
2013	12.0	12.3	12.5	12.6	12.9	13.8	13.0	12.8	12.7	12.9	12.8	12.8	12.8

1. Employment by Industry: Nevada, Selected Years, 2002–2013—*Continued*

(Numbers in thousands, not seasonally adjusted)

Industry and year	January	February	March	April	May	June	July	August	September	October	November	December	Annual average
Financial Activities													
2002	54.4	55.1	55.4	55.5	55.6	55.8	55.9	56.3	56.0	56.5	57.0	57.2	55.9
2003	56.6	56.9	57.0	57.6	58.4	58.5	59.2	59.3	59.6	59.7	59.6	60.0	58.5
2004	59.5	59.7	60.1	60.5	60.7	61.4	62.0	62.2	62.3	63.1	63.2	64.0	61.6
2005	63.0	63.0	63.6	63.7	64.0	64.5	64.3	64.8	65.0	64.8	65.0	65.3	64.3
2006	64.2	64.2	64.8	64.8	65.2	65.7	65.7	65.8	66.1	65.5	65.8	66.2	65.3
2007	65.0	65.1	65.5	65.0	65.3	65.4	64.7	64.5	64.4	63.9	63.4	63.5	64.6
2008	62.2	62.3	62.4	62.2	62.0	61.9	61.5	61.0	60.8	60.5	59.9	59.3	61.3
2009	57.3	57.0	56.6	56.3	55.8	55.8	54.7	54.8	54.2	54.2	53.8	53.6	55.3
2010	52.9	52.5	52.5	53.3	53.0	52.9	53.0	52.7	52.5	53.1	52.8	53.0	52.9
2011	52.4	52.1	52.1	52.5	52.4	52.6	52.7	52.3	52.7	52.9	52.7	53.0	52.5
2012	52.6	52.7	53.0	53.9	54.2	54.6	54.5	54.8	54.9	55.7	55.7	55.8	54.4
2013	55.4	56.1	56.7	56.7	57.2	57.0	56.7	56.7	56.7	57.0	56.7	56.8	56.6
Professional and Business Services													
2002	110.7	110.7	112.6	112.5	113.5	112.6	112.5	116.3	116.8	116.5	117.5	116.2	114.0
2003	117.4	117.8	118.1	118.7	119.2	118.2	120.2	123.8	124.2	126.7	126.4	126.3	121.4
2004	128.0	126.4	127.8	130.5	131.4	132.3	132.7	134.9	136.2	140.9	139.1	138.2	133.2
2005	139.4	140.1	141.9	144.4	144.4	145.4	145.5	147.8	148.9	150.9	153.4	154.3	146.4
2006	153.6	154.8	157.3	157.8	158.8	159.8	157.4	159.0	158.6	158.9	159.8	159.1	157.9
2007	158.4	161.3	159.6	160.3	160.4	159.7	156.9	158.5	156.8	159.8	159.2	157.4	159.0
2008	156.5	155.2	155.4	156.0	156.8	154.4	150.7	150.7	151.0	147.6	146.1	143.3	152.0
2009	141.7	139.3	137.1	134.9	135.3	134.1	130.7	131.4	133.8	133.9	136.1	136.6	135.4
2010	134.8	133.2	133.4	135.3	135.8	136.2	134.8	137.0	134.9	137.6	138.0	137.9	135.7
2011	138.6	137.0	137.4	138.9	138.6	139.5	138.7	139.2	141.3	142.9	142.7	141.8	139.7
2012	144.5	143.6	142.3	143.4	144.0	145.4	141.7	145.4	146.2	147.8	147.4	145.2	144.7
2013	148.8	147.1	148.7	150.1	151.1	150.3	147.5	150.6	148.9	150.8	152.5	153.5	150.0
Education and Health Services													
2002	69.1	70.0	71.7	72.5	73.1	73.0	72.6	73.3	73.6	74.4	74.8	75.0	72.8
2003	74.5	75.4	75.7	75.9	76.3	76.1	75.9	76.4	77.3	77.6	78.3	78.5	76.5
2004	78.2	79.0	79.9	80.4	80.3	80.4	81.0	81.1	82.5	82.8	83.1	83.6	81.0
2005	82.9	83.9	84.7	85.5	85.6	85.8	85.2	85.2	85.8	85.6	86.1	86.9	85.3
2006	86.0	87.1	87.8	87.7	88.1	88.7	87.8	88.4	89.6	90.3	91.0	91.6	88.7
2007	90.7	92.2	92.6	92.2	92.9	92.9	92.6	92.9	93.4	94.2	94.5	94.2	92.9
2008	94.2	95.3	95.6	96.8	97.0	96.9	96.7	96.8	97.1	97.9	98.2	98.2	96.7
2009	97.1	97.4	97.4	97.8	98.1	98.2	98.3	98.5	98.5	100.3	100.2	100.2	98.5
2010	99.7	100.1	100.6	101.5	101.7	101.4	101.1	101.1	101.4	103.0	103.3	103.6	101.5
2011	103.1	104.0	104.7	105.3	105.3	105.5	104.9	105.4	105.9	106.5	107.1	107.5	105.4
2012	106.9	107.8	108.1	108.6	109.1	108.6	107.4	108.7	108.5	109.1	109.2	109.6	108.5
2013	108.7	110.1	110.6	110.9	111.3	111.4	111.0	111.8	112.4	112.6	114.3	115.0	111.7
Leisure and Hospitality													
2002	288.9	290.3	294.3	297.1	300.0	301.1	301.6	302.0	300.8	299.4	297.4	297.6	297.5
2003	296.5	298.0	300.9	301.8	304.6	305.3	307.1	308.4	307.6	305.8	303.7	303.7	303.6
2004	303.1	303.2	306.5	311.4	313.7	315.5	317.3	318.0	317.6	315.4	314.7	315.1	312.6
2005	311.5	313.6	317.5	328.5	329.9	333.5	334.2	333.6	334.6	331.0	329.1	328.5	327.1
2006	327.4	330.0	333.6	336.0	338.8	341.8	342.0	341.4	341.7	337.9	336.4	336.6	337.0
2007	332.7	335.7	338.4	339.4	341.8	343.6	342.3	340.2	340.0	338.9	339.0	340.1	339.3
2008	334.6	334.9	336.2	338.7	339.4	340.0	336.1	334.4	331.6	326.1	321.0	317.0	332.5
2009	310.6	308.9	307.6	310.4	311.9	310.9	310.1	310.1	307.2	306.9	304.5	306.2	308.1
2010	302.4	304.4	305.8	310.4	312.1	313.6	312.8	311.2	310.6	309.5	307.8	307.3	309.0
2011	306.1	307.6	312.4	317.9	320.1	321.2	320.2	318.1	319.0	317.9	315.1	311.7	315.6
2012	309.2	311.3	315.1	318.2	320.8	322.6	321.6	319.6	319.0	318.5	316.3	314.7	317.2
2013	313.4	315.0	319.3	323.8	325.6	327.5	329.5	329.7	329.7	327.6	328.9	326.7	324.7
Other Services													
2002	29.0	29.4	29.9	29.9	30.2	30.5	29.7	29.8	29.4	29.3	29.2	29.1	29.6
2003	29.4	29.6	30.0	29.7	30.0	30.7	30.7	30.8	30.7	30.6	30.8	31.1	30.3
2004	31.4	32.1	33.2	33.5	34.0	34.8	33.7	33.7	33.8	34.4	34.0	34.1	33.6
2005	32.4	32.7	33.2	33.2	33.5	34.1	34.2	34.4	34.6	34.5	34.7	35.1	33.9
2006	33.9	34.3	35.0	35.0	35.5	35.9	36.0	36.3	36.4	36.1	36.0	35.9	35.5
2007	35.2	35.3	36.0	36.1	36.5	37.1	37.0	37.1	37.0	36.7	36.9	37.2	36.5
2008	36.6	36.5	36.8	36.6	37.2	37.2	36.9	37.1	37.0	36.5	35.8	35.1	36.6
2009	33.7	33.4	33.6	33.9	34.2	34.3	34.1	34.1	34.0	33.4	33.2	33.0	33.7
2010	32.6	32.7	33.0	33.0	33.1	33.1	33.4	33.2	33.0	33.0	32.3	32.0	32.9
2011	31.6	31.8	32.0	32.5	32.7	32.9	33.0	32.9	32.6	32.3	32.2	32.3	32.4
2012	32.1	32.2	32.6	33.0	33.5	33.9	33.8	33.9	33.9	34.3	33.1	32.8	33.3
2013	32.4	32.6	32.9	33.4	33.7	34.0	33.9	33.8	33.6	33.9	32.5	31.9	33.2
Government													
2002	125.9	130.9	131.0	130.8	131.7	128.3	121.7	122.0	130.1	135.2	135.8	136.2	130.0
2003	130.4	135.5	136.3	136.1	137.0	132.7	125.7	125.5	133.9	137.3	137.6	138.2	133.9
2004	132.7	137.0	139.3	139.3	140.4	135.5	128.9	128.4	138.8	143.2	143.6	143.9	137.6
2005	138.1	143.2	145.3	145.2	146.1	141.5	134.9	133.8	143.5	148.2	149.3	149.6	143.2
2006	143.2	149.1	150.0	151.3	151.8	147.2	140.2	139.7	149.6	155.1	156.3	156.4	149.2
2007	150.4	156.9	157.5	159.1	159.6	154.7	147.2	146.0	155.5	160.7	161.6	162.3	156.0
2008	156.3	162.3	163.2	164.3	165.0	159.8	153.5	152.3	160.9	165.7	165.9	165.5	161.2
2009	158.3	162.2	162.2	161.9	161.2	155.9	149.7	148.2	156.3	158.1	157.8	157.3	157.4
2010	152.3	157.0	157.8	157.9	161.2	153.7	147.6	144.8	151.9	153.5	153.9	153.8	153.8
2011	151.1	154.6	154.4	154.7	154.3	147.6	142.3	142.4	148.6	150.6	150.8	151.7	150.3
2012	147.0	150.2	151.8	151.8	152.3	147.5	142.5	142.2	149.8	151.7	152.5	153.3	149.4
2013	149.5	151.9	153.1	153.2	153.5	149.2	142.6	145.5	151.8	153.3	153.5	154.2	150.9

2. Average Weekly Hours by Selected Industry: Nevada, 2009–2013

(Not seasonally adjusted)

Industry and year	January	February	March	April	May	June	July	August	September	October	November	December	Annual average
Total Private													
2009	36.4	36.3	36.3	36.2	36.1	35.8	35.8	35.7	35.7	35.2	35.3	35.1	35.8
2010	34.9	34.8	34.7	34.6	34.6	34.5	34.5	34.4	34.3	34.2	34.3	34.6	34.5
2011	34.6	34.6	34.6	34.7	34.8	34.3	34.1	34.5	34.4	34.7	34.0	33.5	34.4
2012	33.8	33.6	33.7	34.0	33.8	34.0	34.4	34.1	34.5	34.2	34.1	34.0	34.0
2013	33.5	33.3	33.5	33.3	33.3	33.8	33.4	33.7	33.7	33.6	33.3	33.6	33.5
Goods-Producing													
2009	38.0	37.7	37.7	37.5	37.8	37.7	37.7	37.7	37.3	36.8	36.9	37.0	37.5
2010	36.6	36.3	36.2	36.2	36.2	36.2	36.2	36.2	36.1	36.0	36.1	36.0	36.2
2011	35.7	35.8	36.4	36.6	36.6	36.8	37.2	37.8	37.8	39.0	36.4	36.7	36.9
2012	36.2	35.5	35.6	35.9	36.5	36.3	36.5	36.9	37.1	36.5	36.1	36.4	36.3
2013	36.8	35.8	36.6	37.3	37.6	38.2	37.7	38.7	38.0	38.5	38.5	39.0	37.8
Construction													
2009	36.7	36.4	36.5	36.2	36.4	36.1	35.9	36.0	35.4	35.2	34.8	34.9	35.9
2010	34.7	34.5	34.3	34.3	34.4	34.3	34.1	34.2	34.0	33.8	33.6	33.4	34.1
2011	33.2	33.3	33.9	34.8	34.7	35.9	36.0	36.3	35.6	35.7	34.8	35.2	35.0
2012	34.5	33.9	34.6	34.9	35.0	35.2	35.1	35.5	34.9	34.5	34.3	34.7	34.8
2013	35.0	33.7	34.6	35.3	35.6	37.6	37.1	38.0	36.9	37.3	37.5	37.3	36.4
Trade, Transportation, and Utilities													
2009	37.2	37.1	37.1	37.1	37.0	36.9	36.8	36.7	37.1	36.5	36.6	36.8	36.9
2010	36.1	36.0	35.7	35.7	35.9	35.9	35.9	35.9	36.0	35.7	35.8	36.1	35.9
2011	35.5	35.3	34.7	35.9	35.4	34.9	34.6	35.3	35.2	34.6	34.4	34.3	35.0
2012	33.7	34.0	34.4	34.1	34.5	34.4	34.5	34.3	34.9	34.2	34.4	34.3	34.3
2013	33.5	33.8	34.1	33.8	34.0	34.4	34.2	34.1	34.1	33.6	33.0	33.7	33.9
Financial Activities													
2009	37.2	37.3	37.2	37.0	37.0	36.9	37.1	36.6	37.5	37.3	36.9	37.1	37.1
2010	37.3	37.2	37.0	37.0	37.1	36.9	36.8	36.7	36.8	36.7	36.5	36.5	36.9
2011	36.6	36.5	36.8	36.4	38.2	37.8	37.3	37.7	38.5	38.7	37.3	36.3	37.3
2012	36.7	36.1	36.7	37.5	37.3	37.3	37.9	36.8	39.5	39.1	39.4	40.2	37.9
2013	39.6	39.3	39.5	39.1	39.4	39.9	38.6	38.3	38.8	38.0	38.4	38.7	39.0
Professional and Business Services													
2009	35.9	35.7	35.7	35.5	35.4	35.0	34.7	34.7	33.5	33.2	33.7	33.3	34.7
2010	32.8	32.6	32.6	32.4	32.2	32.2	32.0	32.0	32.1	32.2	32.4	32.6	32.3
2011	32.4	32.2	33.0	32.9	33.0	32.2	32.3	33.5	32.9	34.0	33.4	33.7	33.0
2012	34.3	34.1	34.2	34.5	34.2	35.1	35.4	34.9	35.1	35.3	35.5	36.0	34.9
2013	34.9	34.6	34.4	34.4	34.6	35.6	34.8	35.5	36.0	35.4	35.3	35.2	35.1
Leisure and Hospitality													
2009	34.2	34.3	34.3	34.3	34.2	34.0	34.0	34.0	33.7	33.2	33.3	32.5	33.8
2010	32.5	32.5	32.3	32.3	32.3	32.2	32.2	32.2	32.1	31.8	31.7	31.4	32.1
2011	31.5	31.6	31.5	31.3	31.4	30.9	30.7	31.0	31.1	31.4	30.9	29.5	31.1
2012	29.6	29.3	29.4	29.8	29.3	29.7	29.8	30.0	30.1	30.4	30.1	30.1	29.8
2013	29.8	29.7	30.0	29.7	29.6	29.9	29.8	30.0	29.8	30.3	29.8	29.5	29.8

3. Average Hourly Earnings by Selected Industry: Nevada, 2009–2013

(Dollars, not seasonally adjusted)

Industry and year	January	February	March	April	May	June	July	August	September	October	November	December	Annual average
Total Private													
2009	19.76	19.74	19.71	19.67	19.65	19.66	19.57	19.56	19.37	19.36	19.34	19.30	19.56
2010	19.20	19.16	19.14	19.14	19.14	19.13	19.12	19.12	19.10	19.09	19.09	19.11	19.13
2011	19.11	19.10	19.12	19.27	19.57	19.23	19.44	19.56	19.49	19.63	19.34	19.36	19.35
2012	19.66	19.67	19.73	19.97	19.62	19.53	19.82	19.84	19.84	19.92	20.11	20.20	19.83
2013	20.07	20.08	20.14	20.13	20.05	20.23	20.00	20.13	20.35	20.19	20.47	20.65	20.21
Goods-Producing													
2009	24.37	24.40	24.39	24.41	24.39	24.49	24.50	24.47	23.94	23.99	24.00	23.62	24.26
2010	23.58	23.55	23.57	23.58	23.59	23.56	23.57	23.55	23.59	23.60	23.61	23.62	23.58
2011	23.59	23.60	23.80	24.81	24.64	24.78	25.20	25.32	25.15	25.38	24.70	23.99	24.60
2012	24.08	24.08	24.75	24.84	24.33	24.68	25.00	24.86	24.34	24.56	24.96	25.48	24.67
2013	23.99	24.23	24.87	24.33	24.82	24.88	25.02	24.72	25.08	24.66	25.06	25.11	24.74
Construction													
2009	25.94	25.99	25.96	25.98	25.99	26.08	26.05	26.01	25.50	25.79	25.78	24.92	25.86
2010	24.88	24.84	24.83	24.83	24.79	24.79	24.77	24.74	24.78	24.77	24.76	24.73	24.79
2011	24.70	24.71	24.55	26.00	25.78	25.52	26.28	26.40	25.17	25.61	25.48	26.10	25.54
2012	26.18	26.07	26.60	26.40	26.12	26.42	27.16	27.24	26.90	27.14	26.73	27.78	26.75
2013	27.25	27.54	27.28	25.95	26.34	26.16	25.80	25.45	25.56	25.17	25.53	25.90	26.10
Trade, Transportation, and Utilities													
2009	17.67	17.68	17.67	17.65	17.69	17.73	17.69	17.64	17.48	17.35	17.36	17.38	17.58
2010	17.35	17.33	17.31	17.30	17.31	17.28	17.25	17.21	17.17	17.13	17.14	17.16	17.24
2011	17.13	17.11	17.19	17.24	17.38	16.84	17.44	17.21	17.11	17.19	17.09	17.15	17.17
2012	17.53	17.54	17.43	17.81	17.42	17.61	18.05	18.27	18.33	18.56	18.64	18.70	18.00
2013	18.86	18.81	19.02	19.31	18.76	18.85	18.47	18.42	18.70	18.93	19.05	18.90	18.84
Financial Activities													
2009	23.45	23.43	23.41	23.39	23.39	23.39	23.47	23.46	22.24	22.10	22.14	22.11	23.01
2010	21.97	21.98	21.97	21.99	21.95	21.95	21.95	21.95	21.93	21.91	21.91	21.91	21.95
2011	21.92	21.91	22.05	21.67	21.48	21.21	21.03	20.94	20.59	20.87	20.83	20.91	21.28
2012	21.25	21.50	21.50	21.70	20.84	20.49	20.79	20.86	20.71	20.92	21.00	20.85	21.02
2013	21.28	21.58	21.74	21.62	22.40	23.03	22.35	22.52	21.55	21.62	21.85	21.57	21.93
Professional and Business Services													
2009	26.29	26.20	26.19	26.00	25.94	25.74	25.63	25.64	25.30	25.43	25.40	25.35	25.77
2010	25.41	25.38	25.33	25.32	25.32	25.29	25.28	25.29	25.27	25.29	25.30	25.35	25.32
2011	25.33	25.30	24.89	24.62	25.05	24.21	23.82	23.87	23.58	23.79	23.52	23.45	24.27
2012	23.08	23.00	22.82	22.78	22.31	21.91	22.00	21.94	21.80	21.73	22.19	22.35	22.32
2013	22.34	22.86	22.64	22.88	22.71	22.93	23.25	23.40	23.85	23.62	24.31	25.02	23.33
Leisure and Hospitality													
2009	14.61	14.65	14.65	14.63	14.62	14.53	14.42	14.33	14.19	14.14	14.03	14.01	14.41
2010	13.93	13.91	13.88	13.86	13.84	13.83	13.83	13.81	13.81	13.79	13.77	13.70	13.83
2011	13.66	13.68	13.62	13.60	13.82	13.50	13.62	13.67	13.83	14.01	14.14	14.14	13.77
2012	14.51	14.39	14.30	14.21	14.17	14.15	14.20	14.29	14.34	14.46	14.57	14.53	14.34
2013	14.71	14.58	14.52	14.46	14.37	14.42	14.55	14.75	15.06	14.82	15.03	15.08	14.70

4. Average Weekly Earnings by Selected Industry: Nevada, 2009–2013

(Dollars, not seasonally adjusted)

Industry and year	January	February	March	April	May	June	July	August	September	October	November	December	Annual average
Total Private													
2009	719.26	716.56	715.47	712.05	709.37	703.83	700.61	698.29	691.51	681.47	682.70	677.43	700.25
2010	670.08	666.77	664.16	662.24	662.24	659.99	659.64	657.73	655.13	652.88	654.79	661.21	659.99
2011	661.21	660.86	661.55	668.67	681.04	659.59	662.90	674.82	670.46	681.16	657.56	648.56	665.64
2012	664.51	660.91	664.90	678.98	663.16	664.02	681.81	676.54	684.48	681.26	685.75	686.80	674.22
2013	672.35	668.66	674.69	670.33	667.67	683.77	668.00	678.38	685.80	678.38	681.65	693.84	677.04
Goods-Producing													
2009	926.06	919.88	919.50	915.38	921.94	923.27	923.65	922.52	892.96	882.83	885.60	873.94	909.75
2010	863.03	854.87	853.23	853.60	853.96	852.87	853.23	852.51	851.60	849.60	852.32	850.32	853.60
2011	842.16	844.88	866.32	908.05	901.82	911.90	937.44	957.10	950.67	989.82	899.08	880.43	907.74
2012	871.70	854.84	881.10	891.76	888.05	895.88	912.50	917.33	903.01	896.44	901.06	927.47	895.52
2013	882.83	867.43	910.24	907.51	933.23	950.42	943.25	956.66	953.04	949.41	964.81	979.29	935.17
Construction													
2009	952.00	946.04	947.54	940.48	946.04	941.49	935.20	936.36	902.70	907.81	897.14	869.71	928.37
2010	863.34	856.98	851.67	851.67	852.78	850.30	844.66	846.11	842.52	837.23	831.94	825.98	845.34
2011	820.04	822.84	832.25	904.80	894.57	916.17	946.08	958.32	896.05	914.28	886.70	918.72	893.90
2012	903.21	883.77	920.36	921.36	914.20	929.98	953.32	967.02	938.81	936.33	916.84	963.97	930.90
2013	953.75	928.10	943.89	916.04	937.70	983.62	957.18	967.10	943.16	938.84	957.38	966.07	950.04
Trade, Transportation, and Utilities													
2009	657.32	655.93	655.56	654.82	654.53	654.24	650.99	647.39	648.51	633.28	635.38	639.58	648.70
2010	626.34	623.88	617.97	617.61	621.43	620.35	619.28	617.84	618.12	611.54	613.61	619.48	618.92
2011	608.12	603.98	596.49	618.92	615.25	587.72	603.42	607.51	602.27	594.77	587.90	588.25	600.95
2012	590.76	596.36	599.59	607.32	600.99	605.78	622.73	626.66	639.72	634.75	641.22	641.41	617.40
2013	631.81	635.78	648.58	652.68	637.84	648.44	631.67	628.12	637.67	636.05	628.65	636.93	638.68
Financial Activities													
2009	872.34	873.94	870.85	865.43	865.43	863.09	870.74	858.64	834.00	824.33	816.97	820.28	853.67
2010	819.48	817.66	812.89	813.63	814.35	809.96	807.76	805.57	807.02	804.10	799.72	799.72	809.96
2011	802.27	799.72	811.44	788.79	820.54	801.74	784.42	789.44	792.72	807.67	776.96	759.03	793.74
2012	779.88	776.15	789.05	813.75	777.33	764.28	787.94	767.65	818.05	817.97	827.40	838.17	796.66
2013	842.69	848.09	858.73	845.34	882.56	918.90	862.71	862.52	836.14	821.56	839.04	834.76	855.27
Professional and Business Services													
2009	943.81	935.34	934.98	923.00	918.28	900.90	889.36	889.71	847.55	844.28	855.98	844.16	894.22
2010	833.45	827.39	825.76	820.37	814.34	814.34	808.96	809.28	811.17	814.34	819.72	826.41	817.84
2011	820.69	814.66	821.37	810.00	826.65	779.56	769.39	799.65	775.78	808.86	785.57	790.27	800.91
2012	791.64	784.30	780.44	785.91	763.00	769.04	778.80	765.71	765.18	767.07	787.75	804.60	778.97
2013	779.67	790.96	778.82	787.07	785.77	816.31	809.10	830.70	858.60	836.15	858.14	880.70	818.88
Leisure and Hospitality													
2009	499.66	502.50	502.50	501.81	500.00	494.02	490.28	487.22	478.20	469.45	467.20	455.33	487.06
2010	452.73	452.08	448.32	447.68	447.03	445.33	445.33	444.68	443.30	438.52	436.51	430.18	443.94
2011	430.29	432.29	429.03	425.68	433.95	417.15	418.13	423.77	430.11	439.91	436.93	417.13	428.25
2012	429.50	421.63	420.42	423.46	415.18	420.26	423.16	428.70	431.63	439.58	438.56	437.35	427.33
2013	438.36	433.03	435.60	429.46	425.35	431.16	433.59	442.50	448.79	449.05	447.89	444.86	438.06

NEW HAMPSHIRE
At a Glance

Population:
  2000 census: 1,235,807
  2010 census: 1,316,470
  2013 estimate: 1,323,459

Percent change in population:
  2000–2010: 6.5%
  2010–2013: 0.5%

Percent change in total nonfarm employment:
  2000–2010: 0.4%
  2010–2013: 2.4%

Industry with the largest growth in employment, 2000–2013 (thousands):
  Education and Health Services, 31.9

Industry with the largest decline or smallest growth in employment, 2000–2013 (thousands):
  Manufacturing, -36.7

Civilian labor force:
  2000: 694,254
  2010: 739,288
  2013: 742,071

Unemployment rate and rank among states (lowest to highest):
  2000: 2.7%, 3rd
  2010: 6.2%, 4th
  2013: 5.3%, 10th

Over-the-year change in unemployment rates:
  2010–2011: -0.7%
  2011–2012: 0.0%
  2012–2013: -0.2%

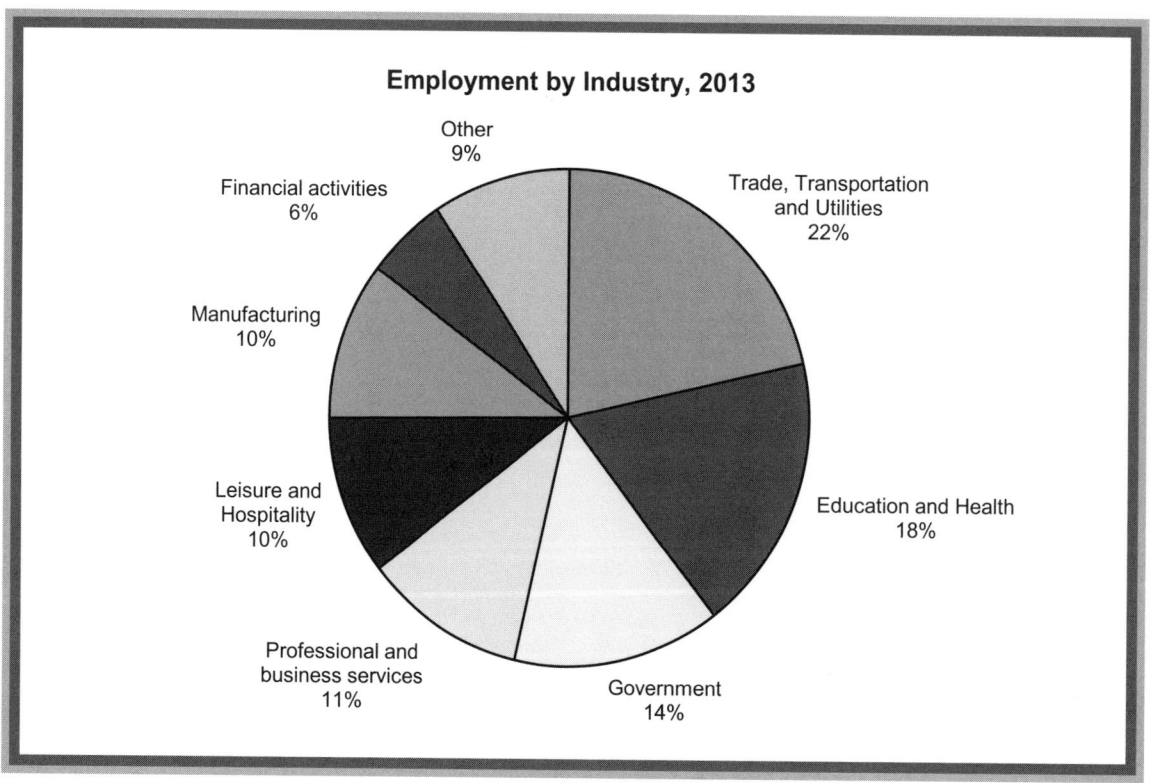

Employment by Industry, 2013

Other 9%
Financial activities 6%
Manufacturing 10%
Leisure and Hospitality 10%
Professional and business services 11%
Government 14%
Trade, Transportation and Utilities 22%
Education and Health 18%

1. Employment by Industry: New Hampshire, Selected Years, 2002–2013

(Numbers in thousands, not seasonally adjusted)

Industry and year	January	February	March	April	May	June	July	August	September	October	November	December	Annual average
Total Nonfarm													
2002	607.8	607.7	610.7	613.9	620.7	626.4	620.6	621.4	623.7	621.0	620.4	624.2	618.2
2003	603.0	602.7	605.1	608.9	617.4	624.9	620.6	623.8	624.6	625.8	626.0	629.4	617.7
2004	607.5	609.2	615.4	621.4	630.1	634.9	631.8	631.7	635.9	635.7	634.8	638.2	627.2
2005	620.9	620.3	622.1	631.0	638.4	643.8	640.7	639.5	645.6	642.9	643.9	649.0	636.5
2006	625.5	627.8	631.2	639.3	644.5	651.9	646.9	645.6	650.7	649.2	648.7	654.1	643.0
2007	633.1	635.6	637.6	640.4	650.7	658.1	652.0	651.2	654.2	652.9	653.7	657.9	648.1
2008	640.0	639.9	641.1	644.6	653.7	659.9	653.0	653.7	655.6	654.3	650.4	649.5	649.6
2009	628.1	625.4	622.3	624.1	633.3	635.9	624.8	625.2	630.6	631.5	628.5	631.6	628.4
2010	609.6	612.7	615.4	619.6	629.8	633.0	625.3	625.3	630.5	631.8	630.5	634.4	624.8
2011	613.9	617.1	619.1	624.8	631.0	634.6	628.5	627.6	634.8	635.1	635.7	638.4	628.4
2012	620.5	620.9	624.6	627.7	635.7	642.7	636.7	638.4	642.4	642.4	641.7	643.8	634.8
2013	625.3	628.3	628.8	634.0	644.3	649.3	641.8	643.9	644.5	647.2	646.0	648.3	640.1
Total Private													
2002	520.9	517.4	519.6	523.9	531.6	539.7	541.4	543.2	535.1	528.7	526.8	530.5	529.9
2003	514.3	510.5	512.4	516.4	526.3	535.8	539.6	543.9	534.5	531.8	531.3	534.2	527.6
2004	518.4	517.4	521.8	528.3	536.9	547.1	551.9	553.1	545.0	541.1	539.9	543.1	537.0
2005	528.0	526.2	527.2	536.9	543.5	555.4	560.7	560.6	552.8	548.3	548.3	553.2	545.1
2006	535.3	533.0	535.8	543.9	549.2	562.9	565.4	565.9	556.1	552.8	552.2	556.8	550.8
2007	541.0	539.2	540.9	543.9	554.6	567.2	570.0	570.1	559.9	555.2	555.9	559.9	554.8
2008	546.3	542.8	542.8	546.8	556.0	566.1	569.8	569.7	558.0	554.6	549.3	548.5	554.2
2009	531.8	526.3	522.8	524.6	533.3	540.1	541.1	541.3	533.7	530.9	527.1	530.2	531.9
2010	514.4	512.4	513.9	519.4	528.2	538.3	542.4	542.9	534.6	533.6	531.4	535.5	528.9
2011	521.9	520.3	522.0	528.9	534.5	544.6	550.1	550.6	542.6	539.9	539.5	542.0	536.4
2012	529.2	526.4	529.2	532.9	541.1	554.8	556.7	558.8	549.0	547.3	545.9	547.2	543.2
2013	535.1	533.8	534.9	539.8	550.0	560.9	564.2	565.2	554.2	554.4	553.0	554.4	550.0
Goods-Producing													
2002	114.5	113.2	113.2	114.4	115.5	115.5	114.4	114.9	113.7	112.8	111.6	112.2	113.8
2003	108.3	106.7	107.3	108.9	110.9	112.2	111.0	112.7	111.6	111.7	111.3	110.5	110.3
2004	106.7	105.8	106.7	109.6	111.3	112.9	112.9	113.2	112.6	111.7	110.8	110.3	110.4
2005	107.1	106.6	106.9	110.1	111.4	112.9	112.2	112.9	111.9	112.0	112.2	111.3	110.6
2006	106.5	105.4	106.2	108.8	109.8	111.0	110.0	111.1	110.2	109.8	108.6	107.4	108.7
2007	104.1	102.9	103.4	105.0	107.2	108.4	108.2	108.6	107.2	106.9	106.5	105.4	106.2
2008	102.2	101.3	101.6	102.6	104.0	105.2	105.2	105.5	103.8	103.2	101.6	99.2	103.0
2009	94.1	92.1	90.6	91.3	92.2	92.3	91.4	92.1	91.7	91.4	89.6	88.4	91.4
2010	84.5	83.7	84.3	86.6	88.4	89.4	90.1	90.7	90.0	90.3	89.7	89.1	88.1
2011	86.2	85.7	86.6	88.9	89.9	91.0	91.6	91.9	91.2	90.9	90.6	89.7	89.5
2012	86.7	86.0	86.7	88.6	89.4	90.6	90.7	91.0	90.6	90.5	89.5	88.7	89.1
2013	86.5	86.0	86.4	88.0	89.7	91.2	90.9	91.2	90.5	90.1	89.9	88.7	89.1
Service-Providing													
2002	493.3	494.5	497.5	499.5	505.2	510.9	506.2	506.5	510.0	508.2	508.8	512.0	504.4
2003	494.7	496.0	497.8	500.0	506.5	512.7	509.6	511.1	513.0	514.1	514.7	518.9	507.4
2004	500.8	503.4	508.7	511.8	518.8	522.0	518.6	518.3	523.3	524.0	524.0	527.9	516.8
2005	513.8	513.7	515.2	520.9	527.0	530.9	528.5	526.6	533.7	530.9	531.7	537.7	525.9
2006	519.0	522.4	525.0	530.5	534.7	540.9	536.9	534.5	540.5	539.4	540.1	546.7	534.2
2007	529.0	532.7	534.2	535.4	543.5	549.7	543.8	542.6	547.0	546.0	547.2	552.5	542.0
2008	537.8	538.6	539.5	542.0	549.7	554.1	547.8	548.2	551.8	551.1	548.8	550.3	546.6
2009	534.0	533.3	531.7	532.8	541.1	543.6	533.4	533.1	538.9	540.1	538.9	543.2	537.0
2010	525.1	529.0	531.1	533.0	541.4	543.6	535.2	534.6	540.5	541.5	540.8	545.3	536.8
2011	527.7	531.4	532.5	535.9	541.1	543.6	536.9	535.7	543.6	544.2	545.1	548.7	538.9
2012	533.8	534.9	537.9	539.1	546.3	552.1	546.0	547.4	551.8	551.9	552.2	555.1	545.7
2013	538.8	542.3	542.4	546.0	554.6	558.1	550.9	552.7	554.0	557.1	556.1	559.6	551.1
Mining and Logging													
2002	0.9	0.9	0.9	0.9	0.9	1.0	1.0	1.0	1.0	1.0	0.9	0.9	0.9
2003	0.9	0.8	0.9	0.9	0.9	1.0	1.0	1.0	1.0	1.0	1.0	0.9	0.9
2004	0.8	0.9	0.9	1.0	1.0	1.0	1.0	1.0	1.0	1.1	1.1	1.0	1.0
2005	0.9	0.9	1.0	1.0	1.0	1.1	1.1	1.1	1.1	1.1	1.1	1.1	1.0
2006	0.9	0.9	1.0	1.0	1.1	1.1	1.2	1.2	1.2	1.2	1.1	1.1	1.1
2007	1.0	1.0	1.0	1.1	1.1	1.2	1.2	1.2	1.2	1.2	1.2	1.1	1.1
2008	1.0	1.0	1.0	1.0	1.0	1.1	1.1	1.1	1.1	1.1	1.0	0.9	1.0
2009	0.8	0.8	0.8	0.8	0.9	1.0	1.0	1.0	1.0	1.0	1.0	0.9	0.9
2010	0.8	0.8	0.8	0.9	0.9	1.0	1.0	1.0	1.0	1.0	0.9	0.9	0.9
2011	0.8	0.8	0.8	0.8	0.9	0.9	1.0	1.0	1.0	1.0	1.0	0.9	0.9
2012	0.8	0.8	0.8	0.9	0.9	1.0	1.0	1.0	1.0	1.0	1.0	0.9	0.9
2013	0.8	0.8	0.8	0.9	0.9	1.0	1.0	1.0	1.0	1.0	1.0	1.0	0.9
Construction													
2002	26.2	25.4	25.7	27.4	28.9	29.0	28.8	29.4	28.8	28.9	28.2	28.0	27.9
2003	25.7	24.9	25.2	27.4	29.4	30.5	31.2	31.4	30.8	30.9	30.2	29.4	28.9
2004	26.4	25.7	26.2	28.8	30.3	31.2	31.8	31.6	31.0	30.5	29.7	29.0	29.4
2005	26.3	25.8	26.0	28.9	30.1	31.0	31.5	31.5	30.9	30.7	30.7	29.8	29.4
2006	27.2	26.5	27.1	29.2	30.2	31.3	31.3	31.3	30.9	30.3	29.2	28.0	29.4
2007	25.6	24.6	24.8	26.2	28.4	29.1	29.5	29.4	28.7	28.2	27.8	26.6	27.4
2008	24.2	23.6	23.9	25.5	26.7	27.3	28.2	28.0	27.2	27.0	26.0	24.5	26.0
2009	21.5	20.6	20.3	21.6	22.9	23.4	23.7	23.9	24.3	24.1	22.9	21.9	22.6
2010	18.9	18.2	18.6	20.4	21.7	22.2	23.0	23.2	22.9	23.1	22.6	21.7	21.4
2011	19.6	19.1	19.7	21.7	22.5	23.1	23.6	23.6	23.5	23.7	23.2	22.4	22.1
2012	20.0	19.5	20.1	21.8	22.6	23.2	23.5	23.7	23.7	23.6	22.8	21.9	22.2
2013	20.3	19.8	20.2	21.7	23.2	23.8	23.7	23.8	23.6	23.0	23.0	21.7	22.3

1. Employment by Industry: New Hampshire, Selected Years, 2002–2013—*Continued*

(Numbers in thousands, not seasonally adjusted)

Industry and year	January	February	March	April	May	June	July	August	September	October	November	December	Annual average
Manufacturing													
2002	87.4	86.9	86.6	86.1	85.7	85.5	84.6	84.5	83.9	82.9	82.5	83.3	85.0
2003	81.7	81.0	81.2	80.6	80.6	80.7	78.8	80.3	79.8	79.8	80.1	80.2	80.4
2004	79.5	79.2	79.6	79.9	80.0	80.7	80.4	80.8	80.5	80.1	80.1	80.3	80.1
2005	79.9	79.9	79.9	80.2	80.3	80.8	79.6	80.3	79.9	80.2	80.4	80.4	80.2
2006	78.4	78.0	78.1	78.6	78.5	78.6	77.5	78.6	78.1	78.3	78.3	78.3	78.3
2007	77.5	77.3	77.6	77.7	77.7	78.1	77.5	78.0	77.3	77.5	77.5	77.7	77.6
2008	77.0	76.7	76.7	76.1	76.3	76.8	75.9	76.4	75.5	75.1	74.6	73.8	75.9
2009	71.8	70.7	69.5	68.9	68.4	67.9	66.7	67.2	66.4	66.3	65.7	65.6	67.9
2010	64.8	64.7	64.9	65.3	65.8	66.2	66.1	66.5	66.1	66.3	66.2	66.5	65.8
2011	65.8	65.8	66.1	66.4	66.5	67.0	67.0	67.3	66.7	66.4	66.4	66.4	66.5
2012	65.9	65.7	65.8	65.9	65.9	66.4	66.2	66.3	65.9	65.9	65.8	65.9	66.0
2013	65.4	65.4	65.4	65.4	65.6	66.4	66.2	66.4	65.9	66.1	65.9	66.0	65.8
Trade, Transportation, and Utilities													
2002	137.1	133.6	134.3	135.9	137.3	139.5	138.6	139.2	138.9	138.7	141.0	144.6	138.2
2003	136.0	133.3	134.3	135.2	136.9	139.2	139.2	140.0	138.9	140.3	142.9	144.7	138.4
2004	137.1	135.2	136.3	137.5	139.2	140.9	140.5	140.1	139.5	140.6	143.0	145.7	139.6
2005	139.2	136.7	136.6	137.8	139.5	141.8	141.5	141.7	140.2	141.7	144.2	146.8	140.6
2006	140.2	137.5	138.3	140.1	141.1	143.0	142.2	142.3	140.7	141.5	144.9	147.7	141.6
2007	141.5	138.0	138.5	138.9	140.9	142.9	142.6	142.0	139.7	140.5	144.2	146.5	141.4
2008	140.9	137.6	137.4	137.2	139.4	141.4	141.0	140.8	138.6	139.8	141.4	142.7	139.9
2009	136.1	132.8	131.6	131.7	134.0	135.4	133.6	133.2	132.5	133.2	135.5	137.3	133.9
2010	131.5	129.2	129.3	130.1	132.3	134.3	133.6	133.5	131.8	133.5	136.2	138.8	132.8
2011	132.7	130.3	130.5	131.7	133.1	135.1	134.4	134.4	133.7	134.7	137.3	140.0	134.0
2012	134.4	131.8	132.4	132.7	134.4	137.9	137.0	137.3	135.5	136.0	139.6	140.8	135.8
2013	134.8	132.5	132.9	134.0	136.3	138.2	137.6	137.8	135.9	136.8	140.2	144.2	136.8
Wholesale Trade													
2002	26.5	26.4	26.5	26.4	26.4	26.7	26.7	26.7	26.6	26.8	26.6	26.8	26.6
2003	26.2	26.1	26.0	26.4	26.6	27.0	27.2	27.3	26.9	26.9	26.9	26.9	26.7
2004	26.6	26.6	26.9	27.2	27.3	27.5	27.7	27.8	27.4	27.3	27.1	27.2	27.2
2005	27.1	26.9	27.0	27.4	27.6	27.7	27.8	27.7	27.4	27.8	27.7	27.7	27.5
2006	27.5	27.4	27.6	27.9	28.2	28.4	28.3	28.4	28.2	28.2	28.1	28.3	28.0
2007	28.2	28.0	28.2	28.3	28.4	28.5	28.5	28.4	28.2	28.1	28.1	28.1	28.3
2008	28.0	27.9	27.9	28.1	28.3	28.4	28.4	28.3	28.0	28.0	27.8	27.6	28.1
2009	27.1	26.7	26.5	26.6	26.7	26.6	26.4	26.4	26.1	26.2	26.1	26.1	26.5
2010	25.6	25.6	25.6	25.7	25.9	26.0	26.1	26.1	25.8	26.0	26.1	26.0	25.9
2011	25.8	25.9	26.0	26.1	26.3	26.3	26.4	26.3	26.2	26.3	26.2	26.4	26.2
2012	26.3	26.2	26.3	26.5	26.6	26.9	26.9	26.9	26.8	26.7	26.7	26.7	26.6
2013	26.4	26.4	26.5	26.6	26.8	27.0	27.0	27.1	26.9	26.8	26.5	26.1	26.7
Retail Trade													
2002	95.3	92.0	92.5	93.7	94.9	96.6	96.2	96.9	96.3	95.8	98.4	101.6	95.9
2003	94.1	91.8	92.7	93.2	94.4	96.2	96.5	97.4	96.0	97.2	99.9	101.7	95.9
2004	95.1	93.4	94.2	95.0	96.3	97.6	97.8	97.6	96.4	97.3	100.2	102.8	97.0
2005	96.6	94.4	94.2	95.0	96.3	98.1	98.3	98.6	96.9	98.1	100.7	103.0	97.5
2006	97.5	94.9	95.4	96.7	97.2	98.6	98.5	98.6	96.6	97.6	101.1	103.2	98.0
2007	98.0	94.9	95.1	95.3	97.0	98.6	98.8	98.4	95.8	96.9	100.9	102.5	97.7
2008	97.9	95.0	94.8	94.3	95.8	97.6	97.7	97.6	95.3	96.6	98.6	99.6	96.7
2009	94.4	91.6	90.7	90.8	92.7	93.9	93.4	93.2	91.7	92.3	94.8	96.1	93.0
2010	91.7	89.4	89.5	90.2	91.8	93.4	93.6	93.6	91.2	92.5	95.1	97.2	92.4
2011	92.3	90.0	90.0	90.9	91.8	93.6	93.7	93.9	92.4	93.4	96.2	98.2	93.0
2012	93.6	91.2	91.5	91.6	92.9	95.8	95.8	95.8	93.5	94.2	97.9	98.5	94.4
2013	93.7	91.5	91.7	92.7	94.4	95.9	96.1	96.0	93.7	94.6	98.3	101.9	95.0
Transportation and Utilities													
2002	15.3	15.2	15.3	15.8	16.0	16.2	15.7	15.6	16.0	16.1	16.0	16.2	15.8
2003	15.7	15.4	15.6	15.6	15.9	16.0	15.5	15.3	16.0	16.2	16.1	16.1	15.8
2004	15.4	15.2	15.2	15.3	15.6	15.8	15.0	14.7	15.7	16.0	15.7	15.7	15.4
2005	15.5	15.4	15.4	15.4	15.6	16.0	15.4	15.4	15.9	15.8	15.8	16.1	15.6
2006	15.2	15.2	15.3	15.5	15.7	16.0	15.4	15.3	15.9	15.7	15.7	16.2	15.6
2007	15.3	15.1	15.2	15.3	15.5	15.8	15.3	15.2	15.7	15.5	15.2	15.9	15.4
2008	15.0	14.7	14.7	14.8	15.3	15.4	14.9	14.9	15.3	15.2	15.0	15.5	15.1
2009	14.6	14.5	14.4	14.3	14.6	14.9	13.8	13.6	14.7	14.7	14.6	15.1	14.5
2010	14.2	14.2	14.2	14.2	14.6	14.9	13.9	13.8	14.8	15.0	15.0	15.6	14.5
2011	14.6	14.4	14.5	14.7	15.0	15.2	14.3	14.2	15.1	15.0	14.9	15.4	14.8
2012	14.5	14.4	14.6	14.6	14.9	15.2	14.3	14.6	15.2	15.1	15.0	15.6	14.8
2013	14.7	14.6	14.7	14.7	15.1	15.3	14.5	14.7	15.3	15.4	15.4	16.2	15.1
Information													
2002	13.4	13.3	13.1	13.0	12.9	12.9	12.8	12.7	12.7	12.7	12.7	12.6	12.9
2003	12.4	12.2	12.2	12.1	12.1	12.2	12.2	12.1	11.9	12.0	12.2	12.3	12.2
2004	12.1	12.3	12.4	12.6	12.6	12.6	12.7	12.7	12.5	12.6	12.7	12.8	12.6
2005	12.5	12.5	12.5	12.7	12.8	12.8	12.9	12.9	12.7	12.7	12.9	12.9	12.7
2006	12.8	12.6	12.7	12.7	12.6	12.7	12.6	12.5	12.3	12.1	12.1	12.2	12.5
2007	12.3	12.2	12.1	12.3	12.3	12.5	12.6	12.8	12.4	12.4	12.5	12.5	12.4
2008	12.7	12.6	12.5	12.6	12.6	12.8	12.8	12.8	12.5	12.5	12.5	12.5	12.6
2009	12.5	12.4	12.3	12.7	12.6	12.5	12.4	12.3	12.2	12.1	12.0	12.0	12.3
2010	11.8	11.7	11.6	11.5	11.4	11.5	11.4	11.3	11.1	11.1	11.0	11.0	11.4
2011	11.0	10.9	11.0	11.1	11.2	11.4	11.6	11.6	11.6	11.6	11.8	11.8	11.4
2012	11.8	11.8	12.0	12.0	12.1	12.1	12.2	12.2	12.0	12.0	12.0	12.1	12.0
2013	11.9	11.8	11.8	11.8	11.8	12.0	12.0	12.0	11.9	11.9	12.0	11.9	11.9

1. Employment by Industry: New Hampshire, Selected Years, 2002–2013—*Continued*

(Numbers in thousands, not seasonally adjusted)

Industry and year	January	February	March	April	May	June	July	August	September	October	November	December	Annual average
Financial Activities													
2002	36.3	36.2	36.2	36.1	36.3	36.7	36.8	37.0	36.8	36.7	36.7	36.8	36.6
2003	36.8	36.8	36.7	37.1	37.3	37.5	37.5	37.5	36.8	36.6	36.6	36.8	37.0
2004	36.7	36.7	37.1	37.1	37.3	37.7	37.8	38.0	37.4	37.6	37.6	38.0	37.4
2005	38.2	38.1	38.3	38.9	39.1	39.8	40.3	40.4	40.0	39.7	39.6	40.0	39.4
2006	39.1	39.2	39.3	39.3	39.2	39.8	40.0	39.7	39.3	39.2	39.0	39.2	39.4
2007	38.1	38.1	38.2	38.1	38.4	38.8	39.1	39.1	38.4	38.1	38.2	38.4	38.4
2008	38.0	38.0	38.0	38.1	38.2	38.6	38.6	38.5	37.8	37.8	37.6	37.7	38.1
2009	37.3	36.9	36.7	36.7	36.8	37.2	36.9	36.5	36.1	35.9	35.8	35.8	36.6
2010	35.6	35.2	35.2	35.2	35.1	35.5	35.6	35.4	34.9	34.8	34.7	34.8	35.2
2011	34.4	34.2	34.2	34.3	34.2	34.4	34.6	34.5	34.4	34.2	34.2	34.2	34.3
2012	34.1	34.1	34.2	34.3	34.7	35.4	35.4	35.6	35.2	35.3	35.2	35.2	34.9
2013	34.9	35.0	35.0	35.2	35.4	35.9	36.0	36.1	35.6	35.3	35.1	35.2	35.4
Professional and Business Services													
2002	53.0	52.8	53.1	53.9	54.7	55.0	55.4	55.7	55.0	54.5	54.6	53.9	54.3
2003	52.5	52.3	52.3	54.0	54.5	55.5	55.6	56.3	55.7	55.7	56.0	56.0	54.7
2004	54.3	54.6	55.6	57.2	57.6	58.0	58.2	59.2	58.0	58.3	58.5	58.5	57.3
2005	56.6	56.7	56.9	58.9	59.0	60.0	60.4	60.6	60.1	60.0	60.4	60.3	59.2
2006	58.3	58.8	58.8	61.6	61.7	63.4	63.2	63.4	63.0	63.2	63.1	63.4	61.8
2007	62.4	63.2	63.1	64.7	65.6	66.6	66.5	67.1	66.3	66.6	66.5	67.3	65.5
2008	65.4	65.0	64.8	67.3	67.7	67.9	67.3	67.5	67.0	66.4	65.8	64.6	66.4
2009	63.2	62.2	61.6	62.5	62.6	63.1	63.0	62.9	62.6	63.2	63.6	63.6	62.8
2010	61.3	61.3	61.7	64.1	64.5	64.9	65.2	65.4	64.6	65.7	65.9	65.4	64.2
2011	64.1	64.1	63.9	66.4	66.3	67.4	67.4	67.6	67.3	67.5	68.6	67.7	66.5
2012	66.0	65.4	66.0	67.7	68.3	69.1	68.8	69.7	69.1	69.5	69.8	69.1	68.2
2013	67.4	68.2	67.8	69.0	70.3	71.0	71.6	71.8	71.0	71.2	71.6	70.8	70.1
Education and Health Services													
2002	89.9	91.5	92.2	92.1	92.4	91.6	90.5	90.5	92.4	91.8	92.4	92.3	91.6
2003	91.6	92.9	93.2	92.8	92.9	92.3	91.4	91.8	93.4	93.7	94.4	94.3	92.9
2004	93.1	94.5	94.9	95.1	95.0	94.3	93.5	93.5	95.4	96.0	96.5	96.2	94.8
2005	95.2	96.7	97.0	98.0	97.9	97.4	97.2	97.1	99.3	99.3	99.6	100.3	97.9
2006	98.8	100.1	100.5	100.7	100.7	100.6	100.0	100.0	101.7	102.3	102.9	103.7	101.0
2007	101.7	103.9	104.4	104.3	104.5	104.6	103.5	103.2	105.4	105.8	106.3	106.7	104.5
2008	105.1	106.4	107.1	107.5	107.8	107.3	107.3	107.0	108.9	109.7	110.2	110.8	107.9
2009	109.2	110.6	110.8	110.8	111.0	109.9	109.3	109.2	110.8	111.6	111.9	112.5	110.6
2010	110.8	112.0	112.5	112.2	112.4	111.7	110.9	110.6	112.5	112.9	113.3	113.7	112.1
2011	112.3	113.7	114.2	114.0	113.8	112.7	112.1	111.7	113.4	114.4	114.1	114.5	113.4
2012	113.6	114.6	114.8	114.3	114.4	113.8	112.7	112.8	114.5	115.1	115.4	116.0	114.3
2013	115.0	115.9	116.1	116.0	116.0	115.2	114.2	114.4	115.6	117.3	118.2	116.3	115.9
Leisure and Hospitality													
2002	54.8	54.9	55.7	56.6	60.4	66.3	70.9	71.1	64.1	60.6	57.1	57.5	60.8
2003	56.3	56.0	55.9	55.9	61.1	66.2	71.4	72.2	65.4	61.3	57.3	58.9	61.5
2004	57.8	57.9	58.2	58.5	62.9	69.3	74.3	74.6	68.2	63.3	59.7	60.5	63.8
2005	58.5	58.2	58.1	59.0	62.3	69.0	74.3	73.1	67.0	61.6	58.1	60.1	63.3
2006	58.5	58.3	58.8	59.1	62.3	70.1	74.8	74.3	67.0	62.9	59.6	61.2	63.9
2007	59.2	59.1	59.2	58.7	63.3	70.3	74.2	74.1	67.9	62.3	59.2	60.4	64.0
2008	59.4	59.5	59.1	59.2	63.7	69.8	74.4	74.3	66.6	62.5	57.9	58.8	63.8
2009	57.5	57.5	57.3	56.9	61.8	67.2	71.9	72.3	65.6	61.4	56.7	58.4	62.0
2010	56.9	57.2	57.1	57.4	61.5	67.9	72.2	72.6	66.8	62.2	57.4	59.5	62.4
2011	58.0	58.1	58.0	58.9	62.1	68.2	73.7	74.1	66.8	62.6	58.8	60.0	63.3
2012	58.7	58.9	59.2	59.3	63.5	71.0	75.0	75.2	67.7	64.4	60.0	61.0	64.5
2013	60.4	60.3	60.6	61.4	65.8	72.3	76.7	76.6	68.9	67.1	61.6	62.6	66.2
Other Services													
2002	21.9	21.9	21.8	21.9	22.1	22.2	22.0	22.1	21.5	20.9	20.7	20.6	21.6
2003	20.4	20.3	20.5	20.4	20.6	20.7	21.3	21.3	20.8	20.5	20.6	20.7	20.7
2004	20.6	20.4	20.6	20.7	21.0	21.4	21.7	21.6	21.4	21.0	21.1	21.1	21.1
2005	20.7	20.7	20.9	21.5	21.5	21.7	21.9	21.9	21.6	21.3	21.3	21.5	21.4
2006	21.1	21.1	21.2	21.6	21.8	22.3	22.6	22.6	21.9	21.8	22.0	22.0	21.8
2007	21.7	21.8	22.0	21.9	22.4	23.1	23.3	23.2	22.6	22.6	22.5	22.7	22.5
2008	22.6	22.4	22.3	22.3	22.6	23.1	23.2	23.3	22.8	22.7	22.3	22.2	22.7
2009	21.9	21.8	21.9	22.0	22.3	22.5	22.6	22.8	22.2	22.1	22.0	22.2	22.2
2010	22.0	22.1	22.2	22.3	22.6	23.1	23.4	23.4	22.9	23.1	23.2	23.2	22.8
2011	23.2	23.3	23.6	23.6	23.9	24.4	24.7	24.8	24.2	24.0	24.1	24.1	24.0
2012	23.9	23.8	23.9	24.0	24.3	24.9	24.9	25.0	24.4	24.5	24.4	24.3	24.4
2013	24.2	24.1	24.3	24.4	24.7	25.1	25.2	25.3	24.8	24.7	24.4	24.7	24.7
Government													
2002	86.9	90.3	91.1	90.0	89.1	86.7	79.2	78.2	88.6	92.3	93.6	93.7	88.3
2003	88.7	92.2	92.7	92.5	91.1	89.1	81.0	79.9	90.1	94.0	94.7	95.2	90.1
2004	89.1	91.8	93.6	93.1	93.2	87.8	79.9	78.6	90.9	94.6	94.9	95.1	90.2
2005	92.9	94.1	94.9	94.1	94.9	88.4	80.0	78.9	92.8	94.6	95.6	95.8	91.4
2006	90.2	94.8	95.4	95.4	95.3	89.0	81.5	79.7	94.6	96.4	96.5	97.3	92.2
2007	92.1	96.4	96.7	96.5	96.1	90.9	82.0	81.1	94.3	97.7	97.8	98.0	93.3
2008	93.7	97.1	98.3	97.8	97.7	93.2	83.2	84.0	97.6	99.7	101.1	101.0	95.4
2009	96.3	99.1	99.5	99.5	100.0	95.8	83.7	83.9	96.9	100.6	101.4	101.4	96.5
2010	95.2	100.3	101.5	100.2	101.6	94.7	82.9	82.4	95.9	98.2	99.1	98.9	95.9
2011	92.0	96.8	97.1	95.9	96.5	90.0	78.4	77.0	92.2	95.2	96.2	96.4	92.0
2012	91.3	94.5	95.4	94.8	94.6	87.9	80.0	79.6	93.4	95.1	95.8	96.6	91.6
2013	90.2	94.5	93.9	94.2	94.3	88.4	77.6	78.7	90.3	92.8	93.0	93.9	90.2

2. Average Weekly Hours by Selected Industry: New Hampshire, 2009–2013

(Not seasonally adjusted)

Industry and year	January	February	March	April	May	June	July	August	September	October	November	December	Annual average
Total Private													
2009	32.5	32.6	32.5	32.7	32.7	32.0	32.8	33.1	32.6	33.0	33.1	33.1	32.7
2010	32.8	32.7	32.8	33.1	33.4	32.6	33.3	33.4	33.0	33.4	33.6	33.5	33.1
2011	32.8	32.9	33.1	33.2	33.2	32.9	33.3	33.6	33.3	33.4	33.2	33.2	33.2
2012	32.7	32.8	32.7	33.0	32.8	32.8	33.5	33.4	33.4	33.1	33.0	33.4	33.1
2013	32.9	33.0	33.2	33.6	33.5	33.5	33.6	33.9	33.9	33.7	33.4	33.5	33.5
Goods-Producing													
2009	39.4	38.3	38.2	38.4	38.3	38.4	38.7	38.4	37.8	39.2	39.2	39.8	38.7
2010	39.9	37.9	39.6	40.0	40.2	39.4	39.0	38.7	38.9	39.0	39.3	39.6	39.3
2011	38.8	38.3	38.6	38.8	39.0	39.1	38.9	39.3	39.5	38.2	39.9	39.6	39.0
2012	38.4	38.5	38.5	38.7	38.4	38.6	38.8	39.9	39.6	39.4	39.5	40.1	39.0
2013	39.4	39.5	39.8	39.5	39.8	39.9	39.7	40.0	40.4	40.1	39.8	40.3	39.9
Manufacturing													
2009	40.6	39.0	39.2	39.2	38.9	39.1	39.1	38.8	38.1	39.4	39.6	40.4	39.3
2010	41.1	39.1	41.1	41.5	41.2	40.5	39.7	39.4	38.9	39.0	39.4	39.7	40.0
2011	39.0	38.2	38.8	38.8	38.7	38.9	38.8	39.3	39.3	38.4	40.2	40.4	39.1
2012	39.1	39.1	39.2	39.3	39.2	39.2	39.3	40.4	40.3	40.1	40.4	40.7	39.7
2013	40.3	40.0	40.5	40.0	40.3	40.9	40.7	40.5	41.3	41.1	41.1	41.8	40.7
Trade, Transportation, and Utilities													
2009	30.0	30.5	30.9	31.9	31.9	31.1	32.1	32.0	32.5	32.2	32.4	32.4	31.7
2010	31.7	32.6	32.5	32.7	32.5	32.2	32.9	32.5	32.3	32.6	32.8	33.0	32.5
2011	32.2	33.2	33.4	33.7	34.0	33.9	34.4	34.4	34.2	35.1	34.3	34.5	34.0
2012	33.8	33.4	33.1	33.3	33.1	33.4	33.8	33.3	34.1	33.3	32.7	33.8	33.4
2013	32.7	32.7	33.1	33.3	33.5	33.3	33.7	33.8	33.9	33.4	32.4	32.8	33.2
Professional and Business Services													
2009	35.7	36.4	36.0	36.5	35.6	34.9	34.5	35.4	34.9	35.3	35.0	35.1	35.4
2010	35.1	34.5	34.9	34.8	36.0	35.0	35.0	35.2	35.2	35.5	36.1	34.8	35.2
2011	34.6	33.3	33.7	33.9	33.3	32.9	32.7	32.9	32.9	33.6	33.5	32.9	33.3
2012	32.4	32.9	33.5	33.9	33.8	33.7	34.3	34.2	34.9	34.2	35.1	35.1	34.0
2013	35.5	35.1	35.0	36.0	35.9	35.6	34.9	35.2	35.9	36.1	36.2	36.5	35.7
Education and Health Services													
2009	31.7	31.6	31.7	31.5	31.5	31.1	32.0	32.2	31.8	32.2	32.3	32.3	31.8
2010	32.3	32.6	31.9	32.0	31.9	32.0	32.3	32.7	32.4	32.7	33.2	32.6	32.4
2011	32.3	32.5	32.7	32.4	32.7	32.3	32.0	32.8	32.8	32.9	33.0	32.9	32.6
2012	32.7	33.3	32.9	32.8	32.9	32.7	33.8	33.6	33.2	33.2	32.8	32.8	33.1
2013	32.7	33.0	32.9	33.3	33.2	33.1	33.2	33.4	33.3	33.5	33.6	33.4	33.2
Leisure and Hospitality													
2009	22.5	23.7	22.9	23.2	23.1	23.3	25.2	26.1	24.3	24.3	24.6	23.3	23.9
2010	23.4	23.1	22.5	23.3	24.0	24.1	26.1	26.7	24.7	24.6	24.2	23.3	24.3
2011	23.1	23.4	23.4	23.6	23.8	23.9	26.5	26.6	24.3	24.3	22.9	22.4	24.1
2012	22.4	22.5	22.9	23.2	23.4	24.0	25.6	25.6	24.1	23.6	22.8	22.8	23.7
2013	22.3	22.6	23.1	24.0	23.1	24.2	25.2	25.8	23.4	23.3	22.6	21.9	23.5

3. Average Hourly Earnings by Selected Industry: New Hampshire, 2009–2013

(Dollars, not seasonally adjusted)

Industry and year	January	February	March	April	May	June	July	August	September	October	November	December	Annual average
Total Private													
2009	23.11	22.98	22.85	22.75	22.67	22.56	22.35	22.30	22.50	22.64	22.74	22.92	22.70
2010	22.91	22.75	22.91	23.07	23.24	23.04	22.87	22.76	22.98	23.17	23.05	23.03	22.98
2011	23.23	23.08	23.08	23.39	23.02	22.72	22.46	22.33	23.19	23.12	23.25	23.18	23.00
2012	23.57	23.65	23.66	23.82	23.71	23.57	23.46	23.27	23.86	23.80	24.11	23.99	23.70
2013	24.21	24.27	24.24	24.56	24.16	24.08	23.74	23.79	24.43	24.36	24.69	24.55	24.25
Goods-Producing													
2009	25.55	25.47	25.56	25.76	25.56	25.48	25.33	25.44	25.59	25.50	25.44	25.64	25.53
2010	25.44	25.64	25.44	25.39	25.58	25.39	25.56	25.42	25.62	25.82	26.02	26.06	25.62
2011	26.26	26.43	26.10	26.50	26.25	25.56	25.64	26.02	26.35	26.34	25.94	25.79	26.09
2012	26.12	26.60	26.07	25.97	25.90	25.80	25.76	25.42	25.59	25.34	25.77	25.62	25.82
2013	25.75	26.00	25.65	26.14	25.65	25.66	25.41	25.58	25.90	25.90	26.25	26.27	25.85
Manufacturing													
2009	25.26	25.21	25.22	25.08	25.01	25.08	25.12	25.32	25.50	25.53	25.73	25.83	25.32
2010	25.74	25.94	25.74	25.76	25.96	25.78	25.98	26.02	26.22	26.42	26.62	26.73	26.07
2011	26.93	27.08	26.66	27.30	27.01	26.12	26.28	26.51	26.95	26.89	26.43	26.09	26.68
2012	26.62	27.08	26.44	26.27	26.16	25.85	26.05	25.67	25.70	25.38	25.82	25.80	26.06
2013	25.96	25.88	25.79	26.31	25.59	25.76	25.33	25.33	25.58	25.48	25.78	25.76	25.71
Trade, Transportation, and Utilities													
2009	19.02	19.21	19.01	19.17	19.19	19.33	19.50	19.68	19.88	19.99	20.13	19.93	19.51
2010	20.13	19.93	19.94	20.14	20.17	19.97	19.81	19.67	19.67	19.68	19.48	18.61	19.76
2011	18.81	18.71	19.09	19.44	19.11	19.00	19.14	18.95	19.79	19.64	19.74	19.34	19.24
2012	20.27	20.11	20.67	21.05	21.17	20.94	20.88	20.57	21.16	21.10	21.42	20.87	20.85
2013	21.57	21.46	20.92	21.18	20.91	21.02	20.84	20.87	21.38	21.19	21.33	20.86	21.12
Professional and Business Services													
2009	29.99	29.79	29.82	29.62	29.47	29.66	29.66	29.46	29.26	29.06	28.86	28.79	29.45
2010	28.92	28.72	28.52	28.36	28.47	28.32	28.26	28.46	28.32	28.35	28.15	28.35	28.43
2011	28.37	28.17	28.37	28.53	27.69	27.75	27.26	26.87	27.22	27.07	27.13	27.44	27.65
2012	27.94	27.73	27.87	28.32	28.08	28.12	28.68	28.14	29.23	28.83	28.72	29.26	28.43
2013	29.16	28.78	29.24	29.22	28.75	28.94	28.56	28.97	28.73	28.68	28.80	29.26	28.92
Education and Health Services													
2009	21.78	21.76	21.81	21.87	21.99	22.00	21.95	21.87	22.02	22.17	22.01	22.21	21.95
2010	22.04	22.09	22.29	22.41	22.60	22.52	22.46	22.29	22.49	22.57	22.79	22.99	22.46
2011	22.98	23.18	23.34	23.73	23.83	24.29	24.67	24.10	24.74	24.91	25.01	25.18	24.17
2012	25.05	25.19	25.29	25.31	25.25	25.33	25.58	25.52	25.56	25.40	25.49	25.61	25.38
2013	25.59	25.61	26.18	26.73	26.71	26.76	26.96	27.03	27.11	27.04	26.98	26.85	26.63
Leisure and Hospitality													
2009	13.21	13.16	13.32	13.41	13.54	13.34	13.34	13.23	13.43	13.44	13.62	13.47	13.37
2010	13.42	13.27	13.24	13.44	13.45	13.25	13.10	13.25	13.44	13.40	13.20	13.38	13.31
2011	13.23	13.34	13.30	13.45	13.35	13.16	12.69	12.82	13.44	13.66	13.83	13.57	13.29
2012	13.63	13.78	13.56	13.65	13.51	13.11	12.89	13.07	13.39	13.55	13.75	13.84	13.44
2013	13.53	13.92	13.60	13.64	13.69	13.50	12.99	13.07	13.82	14.09	14.17	14.11	13.64

4. Average Weekly Earnings by Selected Industry: New Hampshire, 2009–2013

(Dollars, not seasonally adjusted)

Industry and year	January	February	March	April	May	June	July	August	September	October	November	December	Annual average
Total Private													
2009	751.08	749.15	742.63	743.93	741.31	721.92	733.08	738.13	733.50	747.12	752.69	758.65	742.29
2010	751.45	743.93	751.45	763.62	776.22	751.10	761.57	760.18	758.34	773.88	774.48	771.51	760.64
2011	761.94	759.33	763.95	776.55	764.26	747.49	747.92	750.29	772.23	772.21	771.90	769.58	763.60
2012	770.74	775.72	773.68	786.06	777.69	773.10	785.91	777.22	796.92	787.78	795.63	801.27	784.47
2013	796.51	800.91	804.77	825.22	809.36	806.68	797.66	806.48	828.18	820.93	824.65	822.43	812.38
Goods-Producing													
2009	1,006.67	975.50	976.39	989.18	978.95	978.43	980.27	976.90	967.30	999.60	997.25	1,020.47	988.01
2010	1,015.06	971.76	1,007.42	1,015.60	1,028.32	1,000.37	996.84	983.75	996.62	1,006.98	1,022.59	1,031.98	1,006.87
2011	1,018.89	1,012.27	1,007.46	1,028.20	1,023.75	999.40	997.40	1,022.59	1,040.83	1,006.19	1,035.01	1,021.28	1,017.51
2012	1,003.01	1,024.10	1,003.70	1,005.04	994.56	995.88	999.49	1,014.26	1,013.36	998.40	1,017.92	1,027.36	1,006.98
2013	1,014.55	1,027.00	1,020.87	1,032.53	1,020.87	1,023.83	1,008.78	1,023.20	1,046.36	1,038.59	1,044.75	1,058.68	1,031.42
Manufacturing													
2009	1,025.56	983.19	988.62	983.14	972.89	980.63	982.19	982.42	971.55	1,005.88	1,018.91	1,043.53	995.08
2010	1,057.91	1,014.25	1,057.91	1,069.04	1,069.55	1,044.09	1,031.42	1,025.19	1,019.96	1,030.38	1,048.83	1,061.18	1,042.80
2011	1,050.27	1,034.46	1,034.41	1,059.24	1,045.29	1,016.07	1,019.66	1,041.84	1,059.14	1,032.58	1,062.49	1,054.04	1,043.19
2012	1,040.84	1,058.83	1,036.45	1,032.41	1,025.47	1,013.32	1,023.77	1,037.07	1,035.71	1,017.74	1,043.13	1,050.06	1,034.58
2013	1,046.19	1,035.20	1,044.50	1,052.40	1,031.28	1,053.58	1,030.93	1,025.87	1,056.45	1,047.23	1,059.56	1,076.77	1,046.40
Trade, Transportation, and Utilities													
2009	570.60	585.91	587.41	611.52	612.16	601.16	625.95	629.76	646.10	643.68	652.21	645.73	618.47
2010	638.12	649.72	648.05	658.58	655.53	643.03	651.75	639.28	635.34	641.57	638.94	614.13	642.20
2011	605.68	621.17	637.61	655.13	649.74	644.10	658.42	651.88	676.82	689.36	677.08	667.23	654.16
2012	685.13	671.67	684.18	700.97	700.73	699.40	705.74	684.98	721.56	702.63	700.43	705.41	696.39
2013	705.34	701.74	692.45	705.29	700.49	699.97	702.31	705.41	724.78	707.75	691.09	684.21	701.18
Professional and Business Services													
2009	1,070.64	1,084.36	1,073.52	1,081.13	1,049.13	1,035.13	1,023.27	1,042.88	1,021.17	1,025.82	1,010.10	1,010.53	1,042.53
2010	1,015.09	990.84	995.35	986.93	1,024.92	991.20	989.10	1,001.79	996.86	1,006.43	1,016.22	986.58	1,000.74
2011	981.60	938.06	956.07	967.17	922.08	912.98	891.40	884.02	895.54	909.55	908.86	902.78	920.75
2012	905.26	912.32	933.65	960.05	949.10	947.64	983.72	962.39	1,020.13	985.99	1,008.07	1,027.03	966.62
2013	1,035.18	1,010.18	1,023.40	1,051.92	1,032.13	1,030.26	996.74	1,019.74	1,031.41	1,035.35	1,042.56	1,067.99	1,032.44
Education and Health Services													
2009	690.43	687.62	691.38	688.91	692.69	684.20	702.40	704.21	700.24	713.87	710.92	717.38	698.01
2010	711.89	720.13	711.05	717.12	720.94	720.64	725.46	728.88	728.68	738.04	756.63	749.47	727.70
2011	742.25	753.35	763.22	768.85	779.24	784.57	789.44	790.48	811.47	819.54	825.33	828.42	787.94
2012	819.14	838.83	832.04	830.17	830.73	828.29	864.60	857.47	848.59	843.28	836.07	840.01	840.08
2013	836.79	845.13	861.32	890.11	886.77	885.76	895.07	902.80	902.76	905.84	906.53	896.79	884.12
Leisure and Hospitality													
2009	297.23	311.89	305.03	311.11	312.77	310.82	336.17	345.30	326.35	326.59	335.05	313.85	319.54
2010	314.03	306.54	297.90	313.15	322.80	319.33	341.91	353.78	331.97	329.64	319.44	311.75	323.43
2011	305.61	312.16	311.22	317.42	317.73	314.52	336.29	341.01	326.59	331.94	316.71	303.97	320.29
2012	305.31	310.05	310.52	316.68	316.13	314.64	329.98	334.59	322.70	319.78	313.50	315.55	318.53
2013	301.72	314.59	314.16	327.36	316.24	326.70	327.35	337.21	323.39	328.30	320.24	309.01	320.54

NEW JERSEY
At a Glance

Population:
  2000 census: 8,414,764
  2010 census: 8,791,894
  2013 estimate: 8,899,339

Percent change in population:
  2000–2010: 4.5%
  2010–2013: 1.2%

Percent change in total nonfarm employment:
  2000–2010: -3.7%
  2010–2013: 2.2%

Industry with the largest growth in employment, 2000–2013 (thousands):
  Education and Health Services, 135.4

Industry with the largest decline or smallest growth in employment, 2000–2013 (thousands):
  Manufacturing, -178.2

Civilian labor force:
  2000: 4,287,783
  2010: 4,545,580
  2013: 4,537,820

Unemployment rate and rank among states (lowest to highest):
  2000: 3.7%, 22nd
  2010: 9.6%, 33rd
  2013: 8.2%, 41st

Over-the-year change in unemployment rates:
  2010–2011: -0.3%
  2011–2012: 0.0%
  2012–2013: -1.1%

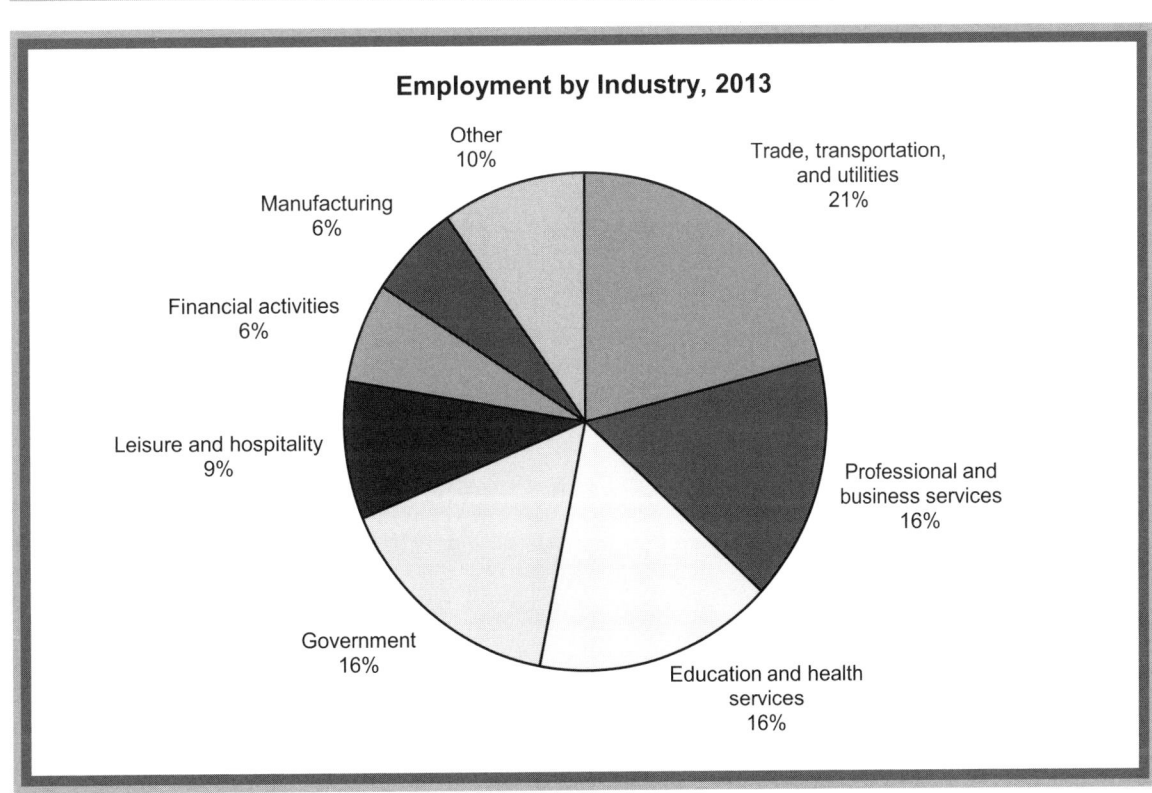

Employment by Industry, 2013

Other 10%

Manufacturing 6%

Financial activities 6%

Leisure and hospitality 9%

Government 16%

Trade, transportation, and utilities 21%

Professional and business services 16%

Education and health services 16%

1. Employment by Industry: New Jersey, Selected Years, 2002–2013

(Numbers in thousands, not seasonally adjusted)

Industry and year	January	February	March	April	May	June	July	August	September	October	November	December	Annual average
Total Nonfarm													
2002	3,931.5	3,940.2	3,968.8	3,982.7	4,007.4	4,041.8	3,981.6	3,969.7	3,974.7	3,983.2	4,006.5	4,014.4	3,983.5
2003	3,906.4	3,897.5	3,921.3	3,955.7	3,992.3	4,030.1	4,000.9	3,983.3	3,989.8	4,004.8	4,017.8	4,025.4	3,977.1
2004	3,902.0	3,907.2	3,943.8	3,969.5	4,014.1	4,061.5	4,020.5	4,003.2	4,014.1	4,025.9	4,048.9	4,062.3	3,997.8
2005	3,943.2	3,950.2	3,974.1	4,023.6	4,058.2	4,111.4	4,065.1	4,046.9	4,054.0	4,058.6	4,081.7	4,091.5	4,038.2
2006	3,983.1	3,991.5	4,027.4	4,049.8	4,090.2	4,141.3	4,088.7	4,074.8	4,074.1	4,086.8	4,106.0	4,120.7	4,069.5
2007	3,995.9	3,991.6	4,024.5	4,052.9	4,104.2	4,156.6	4,098.5	4,083.0	4,074.2	4,100.9	4,115.4	4,125.2	4,076.9
2008	4,013.2	4,015.7	4,041.4	4,060.7	4,091.7	4,135.8	4,069.9	4,041.0	4,036.3	4,033.7	4,024.0	4,015.3	4,048.2
2009	3,880.1	3,868.6	3,874.0	3,889.7	3,928.6	3,963.3	3,893.0	3,871.5	3,877.6	3,882.4	3,894.6	3,903.1	3,893.9
2010	3,774.6	3,766.7	3,797.4	3,848.3	3,893.6	3,936.7	3,865.3	3,840.4	3,841.6	3,861.6	3,874.2	3,879.9	3,848.4
2011	3,754.0	3,763.7	3,793.3	3,836.6	3,866.2	3,916.6	3,862.0	3,838.5	3,862.6	3,875.9	3,895.7	3,904.7	3,847.5
2012	3,793.8	3,812.1	3,850.2	3,862.0	3,910.2	3,972.4	3,895.7	3,887.7	3,908.6	3,922.0	3,926.0	3,949.0	3,890.8
2013	3,836.7	3,855.2	3,888.2	3,914.4	3,955.7	4,015.5	3,947.9	3,942.2	3,955.8	3,964.0	3,980.7	3,961.6	3,934.8
Total Private													
2002	3,319.5	3,317.8	3,343.0	3,358.9	3,384.4	3,420.8	3,396.5	3,394.2	3,376.2	3,362.9	3,378.7	3,387.3	3,370.0
2003	3,290.0	3,270.1	3,290.5	3,324.3	3,361.6	3,400.2	3,401.6	3,397.9	3,381.9	3,374.0	3,380.8	3,389.3	3,355.2
2004	3,277.2	3,270.9	3,302.7	3,329.2	3,374.6	3,420.5	3,411.6	3,404.8	3,390.7	3,380.9	3,398.1	3,410.9	3,364.3
2005	3,307.0	3,301.6	3,324.1	3,371.8	3,409.6	3,460.5	3,449.1	3,441.2	3,425.7	3,408.8	3,425.0	3,435.0	3,396.6
2006	3,339.2	3,335.1	3,369.0	3,391.0	3,434.8	3,484.0	3,466.6	3,463.8	3,443.9	3,431.7	3,446.2	3,461.2	3,422.2
2007	3,350.7	3,335.0	3,364.7	3,393.6	3,446.3	3,496.1	3,482.0	3,473.3	3,444.4	3,445.3	3,454.5	3,464.4	3,429.2
2008	3,364.5	3,356.2	3,379.4	3,399.6	3,430.5	3,473.6	3,445.9	3,432.8	3,403.8	3,379.9	3,365.3	3,357.0	3,399.0
2009	3,230.5	3,209.0	3,211.0	3,225.1	3,264.1	3,298.7	3,267.1	3,256.8	3,240.4	3,224.7	3,230.6	3,240.3	3,241.5
2010	3,127.3	3,112.5	3,140.1	3,189.4	3,224.5	3,273.0	3,247.3	3,244.1	3,229.5	3,230.4	3,236.5	3,246.3	3,208.4
2011	3,136.8	3,134.9	3,162.3	3,203.1	3,236.9	3,288.3	3,272.3	3,263.6	3,259.2	3,248.4	3,263.0	3,274.8	3,228.6
2012	3,180.7	3,185.8	3,219.5	3,234.8	3,286.4	3,344.7	3,309.8	3,313.3	3,306.4	3,295.7	3,298.6	3,321.6	3,274.8
2013	3,220.3	3,224.5	3,257.1	3,291.4	3,336.0	3,392.0	3,365.2	3,367.1	3,354.2	3,339.6	3,352.0	3,334.3	3,319.5
Goods-Producing													
2002	527.3	526.6	529.5	534.1	537.7	540.0	532.7	535.9	533.9	530.2	528.0	523.7	531.6
2003	503.7	498.3	501.0	511.0	517.3	521.4	518.6	520.3	519.0	515.6	513.2	509.9	512.4
2004	490.6	487.4	495.3	501.6	508.7	514.5	513.9	514.9	514.8	511.2	509.0	506.9	505.7
2005	487.8	484.1	488.5	498.4	504.7	509.5	507.4	509.4	510.2	505.7	506.6	502.7	501.3
2006	489.5	488.7	494.8	501.9	505.9	509.2	506.5	507.0	505.3	501.1	498.7	495.9	500.4
2007	477.3	470.4	475.8	483.9	489.6	494.7	493.4	493.6	490.3	488.4	485.2	480.1	485.2
2008	463.7	460.3	464.3	469.8	472.4	475.6	472.3	471.4	467.6	462.0	454.8	445.0	464.9
2009	416.6	409.4	408.3	408.3	410.8	411.9	407.8	406.5	403.0	400.8	398.2	395.2	406.4
2010	377.6	373.6	377.7	387.2	391.7	395.1	394.6	393.9	392.8	392.5	392.1	387.4	388.0
2011	369.0	366.7	373.1	380.9	384.8	389.4	390.0	391.2	388.8	387.7	387.0	383.5	382.7
2012	369.6	367.7	370.7	374.3	377.2	381.2	379.8	381.0	380.2	380.5	380.4	381.2	377.0
2013	368.3	367.0	371.8	379.7	383.7	388.0	386.9	389.6	388.7	387.3	386.5	377.0	381.2
Service-Providing													
2002	3,404.2	3,413.6	3,439.3	3,448.6	3,469.7	3,501.8	3,448.9	3,433.8	3,440.8	3,453.0	3,478.5	3,490.7	3,451.9
2003	3,402.7	3,399.2	3,420.3	3,444.7	3,475.0	3,508.7	3,482.3	3,463.0	3,470.8	3,489.2	3,504.6	3,515.5	3,464.7
2004	3,411.4	3,419.8	3,448.5	3,467.9	3,505.4	3,547.0	3,506.6	3,488.3	3,499.3	3,514.7	3,539.9	3,555.4	3,492.0
2005	3,455.4	3,466.1	3,485.6	3,525.2	3,553.5	3,601.9	3,557.7	3,537.5	3,543.8	3,552.9	3,575.1	3,588.8	3,537.0
2006	3,493.6	3,502.8	3,532.6	3,547.9	3,584.3	3,632.1	3,582.2	3,567.8	3,568.8	3,585.7	3,607.3	3,624.8	3,569.2
2007	3,518.6	3,521.2	3,548.7	3,569.0	3,614.6	3,661.9	3,605.1	3,589.4	3,583.9	3,612.5	3,630.2	3,645.1	3,591.7
2008	3,549.5	3,555.4	3,577.1	3,590.9	3,619.3	3,660.2	3,597.6	3,569.6	3,568.7	3,571.7	3,569.2	3,570.3	3,583.3
2009	3,463.5	3,459.2	3,465.7	3,481.4	3,517.8	3,551.4	3,485.2	3,465.0	3,474.6	3,481.6	3,496.4	3,507.9	3,487.5
2010	3,397.0	3,393.1	3,419.7	3,461.1	3,501.9	3,541.6	3,470.7	3,446.5	3,448.8	3,469.1	3,482.1	3,492.5	3,460.3
2011	3,385.0	3,397.0	3,420.2	3,455.7	3,481.4	3,527.2	3,472.0	3,447.3	3,473.8	3,488.2	3,508.7	3,521.2	3,464.8
2012	3,424.2	3,444.4	3,479.5	3,487.7	3,533.0	3,591.2	3,515.9	3,506.7	3,528.4	3,541.5	3,545.6	3,567.8	3,513.8
2013	3,468.4	3,488.2	3,516.4	3,534.7	3,572.0	3,627.5	3,561.0	3,552.6	3,567.1	3,576.7	3,594.2	3,584.6	3,553.6
Mining and Logging													
2002	1.6	1.6	1.7	1.5	1.5	1.6	1.5	1.5	1.5	1.6	1.7	1.7	1.6
2003	1.4	1.4	1.5	1.5	1.6	1.6	1.6	1.6	1.6	1.6	1.6	1.6	1.6
2004	1.5	1.4	1.5	1.6	1.7	1.7	1.7	1.7	1.7	1.7	1.7	1.7	1.6
2005	1.6	1.5	1.6	1.7	1.8	1.8	1.8	1.8	1.8	1.8	1.8	1.8	1.7
2006	1.6	1.6	1.7	1.8	1.8	1.8	1.8	1.7	1.7	1.7	1.7	1.6	1.7
2007	1.6	1.5	1.6	1.7	1.7	1.7	1.7	1.7	1.7	1.7	1.7	1.7	1.7
2008	1.6	1.5	1.6	1.6	1.7	1.7	1.7	1.7	1.7	1.7	1.7	1.6	1.7
2009	1.4	1.4	1.4	1.4	1.5	1.5	1.5	1.6	1.6	1.6	1.5	1.5	1.5
2010	1.2	1.3	1.3	1.4	1.4	1.4	1.4	1.4	1.4	1.4	1.4	1.4	1.4
2011	1.2	1.2	1.2	1.3	1.3	1.4	1.3	1.3	1.3	1.3	1.3	1.3	1.3
2012	1.2	1.2	1.2	1.3	1.3	1.3	1.3	1.3	1.3	1.3	1.3	1.3	1.3
2013	1.2	1.1	1.2	1.3	1.3	1.4	1.4	1.4	1.4	1.4	1.4	1.4	1.3
Construction													
2002	153.0	152.2	155.2	160.7	164.1	166.9	167.5	169.2	167.5	166.9	165.7	161.8	162.6
2003	149.1	144.3	147.1	157.1	162.9	165.8	168.2	169.1	167.8	167.1	165.3	162.0	160.5
2004	151.0	148.0	154.9	162.4	167.8	171.4	173.4	174.7	173.9	173.0	171.2	169.0	165.9
2005	155.4	151.4	154.7	166.0	171.6	174.8	176.6	178.0	178.5	174.7	176.0	172.0	169.1
2006	161.5	161.2	166.5	175.4	178.8	180.9	181.0	182.2	181.1	178.3	176.7	175.2	174.9
2007	161.2	155.4	160.7	169.9	175.7	179.5	179.6	181.0	179.1	178.1	175.5	171.5	172.3
2008	158.7	156.7	160.1	165.4	168.8	171.1	171.1	170.8	168.5	166.2	161.4	154.9	164.5
2009	137.2	134.1	135.7	139.0	141.9	143.0	142.7	142.5	139.8	138.1	136.3	133.4	138.6
2010	119.8	116.7	120.8	129.2	132.4	134.2	135.2	134.8	133.7	134.2	133.9	128.8	129.5
2011	114.2	112.4	118.3	126.9	130.9	134.3	137.2	138.3	137.4	137.5	137.2	134.2	129.9
2012	123.6	122.1	123.3	127.9	129.8	132.5	133.3	134.4	133.7	134.3	134.7	135.3	130.4
2013	125.8	124.6	128.0	136.0	139.5	141.9	142.7	144.4	143.7	141.8	139.1	130.4	136.5

1. Employment by Industry: New Jersey, Selected Years, 2002–2013—*Continued*

(Numbers in thousands, not seasonally adjusted)

Industry and year	January	February	March	April	May	June	July	August	September	October	November	December	Annual average
Manufacturing													
2002	372.7	372.8	372.6	371.9	372.1	371.5	363.7	365.2	364.9	361.7	360.6	360.2	367.5
2003	353.2	352.6	352.4	352.4	352.8	354.0	348.8	349.6	349.6	346.9	346.3	346.3	350.4
2004	338.1	338.0	338.9	337.6	339.2	341.4	338.8	338.5	339.2	336.5	336.1	336.2	338.2
2005	330.8	331.2	332.2	330.7	331.3	332.9	329.0	329.6	329.9	329.2	328.8	328.9	330.4
2006	326.4	325.9	326.6	324.7	325.3	326.5	323.7	323.1	322.5	321.1	320.3	319.1	323.8
2007	314.5	313.5	313.5	312.3	312.2	313.5	312.1	310.9	309.5	308.6	308.0	306.9	311.3
2008	303.4	302.1	302.6	302.8	301.9	302.8	299.5	298.9	297.4	294.1	291.7	288.5	298.8
2009	278.0	273.9	271.2	267.9	267.4	267.4	263.6	262.4	261.6	261.1	260.4	260.3	266.3
2010	256.6	255.6	255.6	256.6	257.9	259.5	258.0	257.7	257.7	256.9	256.8	257.2	257.2
2011	253.6	253.1	253.6	252.7	252.6	253.7	251.5	251.6	250.1	248.9	248.5	248.0	251.5
2012	244.8	244.4	246.2	245.1	246.1	247.4	245.2	245.3	245.2	244.9	244.4	244.6	245.3
2013	241.3	241.3	242.6	242.4	242.9	244.7	242.8	243.8	243.6	244.1	246.0	245.2	243.4
Trade, Transportation, and Utilities													
2002	879.3	869.5	874.8	873.0	877.3	887.4	875.1	873.2	877.8	882.3	896.1	910.7	881.4
2003	873.5	862.9	864.3	866.3	872.9	880.1	869.8	867.5	871.8	878.2	889.4	902.1	874.9
2004	864.4	858.9	862.8	860.3	871.6	881.4	870.2	868.8	871.2	878.7	891.9	905.3	873.8
2005	869.4	861.2	863.7	867.2	876.3	886.3	877.5	873.0	875.0	876.6	890.3	905.8	876.9
2006	870.6	857.6	862.1	861.4	871.1	879.7	870.4	867.8	869.6	876.1	892.6	907.2	873.9
2007	870.2	855.1	859.4	859.7	872.1	883.1	871.9	867.7	868.4	873.0	889.6	904.0	872.9
2008	867.1	854.7	857.3	854.7	862.7	871.0	859.6	855.6	855.1	855.2	861.4	868.4	860.2
2009	827.6	814.9	811.5	806.9	816.5	824.3	811.8	807.6	811.7	812.7	826.0	836.9	817.4
2010	799.8	788.0	790.7	798.3	805.8	816.0	807.1	806.6	806.4	813.1	825.9	839.8	808.1
2011	804.6	797.4	800.1	804.5	810.1	820.4	812.7	812.3	813.9	817.7	834.5	847.1	814.6
2012	815.5	806.2	810.9	807.7	820.9	831.5	819.2	817.0	820.0	822.9	838.4	850.3	821.7
2013	815.3	806.6	810.4	814.2	823.1	834.7	828.1	827.7	828.5	834.4	849.2	859.9	827.7
Wholesale Trade													
2002	238.5	238.2	239.3	237.8	237.7	238.1	235.6	234.8	234.4	234.8	234.5	234.9	236.6
2003	232.0	231.0	231.2	232.7	232.8	233.5	232.8	231.1	230.4	229.7	229.5	229.8	231.4
2004	226.3	228.5	230.1	229.7	230.4	231.7	232.1	232.7	232.2	232.7	232.2	233.1	231.0
2005	231.3	232.1	232.0	232.6	234.9	236.7	235.5	234.3	233.7	232.4	232.4	232.9	233.4
2006	230.4	229.9	230.4	230.8	232.7	234.0	233.3	232.7	231.8	231.5	232.0	232.8	231.9
2007	230.8	228.7	230.7	230.8	231.7	233.6	232.4	232.0	230.9	231.3	231.0	231.4	231.3
2008	228.0	229.0	229.3	228.6	230.1	231.0	229.7	228.4	227.1	226.0	224.2	223.2	227.9
2009	219.6	219.2	217.8	217.3	217.2	217.7	215.4	214.1	213.3	213.1	213.0	213.2	215.9
2010	208.0	206.5	206.6	207.5	207.8	209.1	208.6	208.1	207.5	207.7	207.9	208.0	207.8
2011	205.4	206.8	207.9	209.2	210.2	211.7	212.1	212.3	211.0	211.0	211.4	212.9	210.2
2012	210.4	211.0	212.2	211.8	212.9	214.8	213.8	213.6	213.3	212.6	213.1	213.6	212.8
2013	210.7	210.7	211.4	211.9	212.9	214.5	214.7	214.8	214.2	215.6	213.9	213.3	213.2
Retail Trade													
2002	461.2	451.7	455.7	455.1	459.4	468.1	464.3	464.4	461.9	462.8	•477.1	491.9	464.5
2003	461.9	453.3	454.1	456.5	462.3	468.5	465.3	466.1	462.7	467.9	479.6	491.1	465.8
2004	461.5	453.8	455.3	455.1	463.3	471.1	468.5	468.2	463.0	468.7	481.9	494.2	467.1
2005	466.1	457.3	457.7	460.8	466.7	473.3	472.5	470.7	465.1	467.2	479.7	492.3	469.1
2006	465.7	452.9	456.7	456.3	462.1	469.1	466.7	465.7	459.9	466.0	481.0	491.9	466.2
2007	464.8	452.7	454.2	455.5	463.4	470.9	469.1	466.6	459.7	463.3	479.3	489.9	465.8
2008	463.7	450.0	451.3	449.7	455.3	462.5	460.5	458.3	452.2	454.5	462.4	469.5	457.5
2009	439.4	427.9	426.7	425.0	432.7	439.2	436.5	435.7	432.6	434.9	447.0	456.1	436.1
2010	430.7	421.1	423.7	427.5	434.1	441.9	440.6	441.3	434.5	440.3	451.6	461.9	437.4
2011	435.8	427.7	428.7	431.8	435.6	443.3	442.2	442.5	437.5	440.8	455.1	464.1	440.4
2012	441.3	430.9	433.8	433.3	441.0	448.3	444.7	444.2	439.6	443.0	457.3	465.3	443.6
2013	439.8	431.4	433.6	436.5	443.4	452.9	452.7	453.5	447.9	451.1	463.2	470.8	448.1
Transportation and Utilities													
2002	179.6	179.6	179.8	180.1	180.2	181.2	175.2	174.0	181.5	184.7	184.5	183.9	180.4
2003	179.6	178.6	179.0	177.1	177.8	178.1	171.7	170.3	178.7	180.6	180.3	181.2	177.8
2004	176.6	176.6	177.4	175.5	177.9	178.6	169.6	167.9	176.0	177.3	177.8	178.0	175.8
2005	172.0	171.8	174.0	173.8	174.7	176.3	169.5	168.0	176.2	177.0	178.2	180.6	174.3
2006	174.5	174.8	175.0	174.3	176.3	176.6	170.4	169.4	177.9	178.6	179.6	182.5	175.8
2007	174.6	173.7	174.5	173.4	177.0	178.6	170.4	169.1	177.8	178.4	179.3	182.7	175.8
2008	175.4	175.7	176.7	176.4	177.3	177.5	169.4	168.9	175.8	174.7	174.8	175.7	174.9
2009	168.6	167.8	167.0	164.6	166.6	167.4	159.9	157.8	165.8	164.7	166.0	167.6	165.3
2010	161.1	160.4	160.4	163.3	163.9	165.0	157.9	157.2	164.4	165.1	166.4	169.9	162.9
2011	163.4	162.9	163.5	163.5	164.3	165.4	158.4	157.5	165.4	165.9	168.0	170.1	164.0
2012	163.8	164.3	164.9	162.6	167.0	168.4	160.7	159.2	167.1	167.3	168.0	171.4	165.4
2013	164.8	164.5	165.4	165.8	166.8	167.3	160.7	159.4	166.4	167.7	172.1	175.8	166.4
Information													
2002	121.0	120.3	120.3	116.3	116.5	115.7	111.4	111.0	109.4	104.6	106.1	105.6	113.2
2003	102.8	102.4	102.8	102.0	102.1	102.5	102.3	102.9	101.0	101.1	101.4	101.2	102.0
2004	100.1	98.7	99.6	98.2	98.0	97.9	97.3	97.1	96.2	96.9	97.5	97.9	98.0
2005	96.7	96.4	97.0	96.2	96.6	97.8	97.4	97.2	96.7	96.9	97.8	98.3	97.1
2006	97.4	98.1	98.2	97.0	97.4	98.3	97.6	98.0	97.8	96.3	96.1	96.4	97.4
2007	96.3	97.1	97.5	96.7	96.5	96.7	96.5	97.2	95.4	94.0	94.3	93.9	96.0
2008	93.7	94.2	94.2	92.8	92.2	92.7	91.0	90.8	89.7	88.4	88.3	87.8	91.3
2009	86.5	85.9	86.1	84.5	84.8	85.0	84.0	84.7	83.1	82.0	82.1	82.4	84.3
2010	80.4	80.3	80.5	79.5	79.4	80.3	78.7	78.8	78.7	78.4	76.6	79.0	79.2
2011	75.5	75.3	75.4	76.3	76.5	77.7	78.9	73.0	78.6	76.3	77.0	78.6	76.6
2012	76.5	77.8	79.0	76.3	77.3	78.5	77.6	78.9	76.8	75.9	77.5	76.0	77.3
2013	74.7	76.6	76.1	75.3	75.2	75.9	75.5	75.7	74.1	73.2	76.0	75.3	75.3

1. Employment by Industry: New Jersey, Selected Years, 2002–2013—*Continued*

(Numbers in thousands, not seasonally adjusted)

Industry and year	January	February	March	April	May	June	July	August	September	October	November	December	Annual average
Financial Activities													
2002	277.3	276.2	275.1	275.7	276.1	277.7	279.4	278.9	276.6	275.1	275.8	276.4	276.7
2003	274.5	273.8	274.3	274.0	275.0	278.2	279.5	279.6	276.9	276.3	276.1	275.8	276.2
2004	273.1	272.7	273.6	275.6	276.9	279.5	280.9	280.4	277.0	277.2	277.7	278.1	276.9
2005	275.8	275.1	275.9	277.5	278.7	281.8	284.0	284.4	281.7	279.6	280.8	281.0	279.7
2006	276.8	276.5	277.3	278.3	279.6	281.9	283.6	283.0	279.1	278.4	278.1	278.3	279.2
2007	274.9	274.3	274.3	274.8	276.1	278.7	279.9	279.0	274.7	274.0	274.0	273.9	275.7
2008	272.0	271.9	272.3	271.7	272.4	274.2	273.5	272.7	268.4	265.7	264.6	264.0	270.3
2009	258.6	257.7	256.8	257.1	257.3	258.2	257.5	256.1	253.8	252.0	251.5	251.7	255.7
2010	250.4	250.0	250.5	250.6	251.1	254.1	253.7	253.7	251.7	250.7	250.7	251.4	251.6
2011	248.6	248.4	248.9	249.0	249.7	252.6	252.0	252.2	250.0	247.3	247.4	247.9	249.5
2012	246.4	246.3	247.4	248.5	250.1	253.4	252.8	252.9	250.7	250.1	250.1	251.9	250.1
2013	253.1	253.4	253.9	254.2	255.0	257.8	257.5	257.2	254.6	252.7	252.9	251.9	254.5
Professional and Business Services													
2002	569.0	570.8	581.0	584.2	583.6	588.2	584.9	587.8	582.2	580.1	581.9	579.9	581.1
2003	562.2	559.0	565.2	572.0	575.1	581.0	585.4	589.1	587.6	586.8	586.8	587.6	578.2
2004	564.0	562.7	572.1	582.0	585.3	592.1	592.1	593.0	591.5	592.3	593.9	592.8	584.5
2005	570.0	571.5	577.0	593.0	594.2	604.3	600.3	601.6	599.8	600.7	600.3	597.4	592.5
2006	577.8	583.3	592.3	598.2	603.9	613.7	611.9	616.0	613.1	614.2	615.6	615.1	604.6
2007	588.8	590.1	599.1	610.3	616.5	626.5	628.0	630.7	626.3	627.6	628.9	626.9	616.6
2008	605.5	606.8	612.7	618.9	620.0	626.5	625.5	626.2	620.4	615.0	611.1	605.5	616.2
2009	583.3	578.3	578.1	585.3	586.3	591.5	587.9	588.4	585.5	584.1	584.0	582.4	584.6
2010	559.9	562.3	569.6	582.9	586.5	596.6	593.3	595.8	594.3	596.5	597.6	596.9	586.0
2011	579.8	580.8	586.8	597.5	600.6	609.6	608.9	611.1	611.2	613.1	614.8	611.9	602.2
2012	591.0	594.7	602.9	610.2	616.4	626.6	621.1	628.2	630.2	628.5	633.7	634.9	618.2
2013	607.6	610.9	620.1	625.8	633.3	642.8	639.0	643.8	642.5	640.3	637.0	631.3	631.2
Education and Health Services													
2002	516.3	522.9	524.4	526.2	528.8	528.5	523.4	520.9	526.6	531.3	535.6	536.0	526.7
2003	531.0	532.5	536.2	537.3	540.9	539.1	535.4	530.2	537.3	541.6	544.1	544.6	537.5
2004	536.0	539.9	543.6	544.5	548.9	548.9	541.5	538.9	545.6	552.5	554.7	555.9	545.9
2005	547.9	552.9	555.3	556.9	561.3	559.8	553.6	550.0	557.1	565.0	567.6	568.1	558.0
2006	559.6	563.2	567.1	566.1	571.1	570.0	562.0	561.4	567.3	572.7	575.9	579.1	568.0
2007	570.5	575.6	580.1	576.9	585.0	580.3	573.7	570.5	577.2	586.7	585.5	589.6	579.3
2008	582.7	587.7	590.5	590.3	592.0	592.8	583.0	580.9	587.8	593.1	595.3	599.8	589.7
2009	589.3	594.5	597.0	597.7	600.4	601.0	588.7	586.6	594.7	602.6	605.3	609.9	597.3
2010	598.6	599.9	603.8	603.8	604.8	603.0	590.7	587.7	596.0	605.7	607.4	607.0	600.7
2011	597.8	603.1	607.0	607.3	609.0	608.6	596.4	593.3	605.7	611.4	614.4	618.6	606.1
2012	610.6	619.0	623.8	620.3	625.7	624.4	609.2	607.1	620.0	627.4	625.2	630.9	620.3
2013	622.0	628.4	633.6	634.9	638.0	634.6	618.5	617.0	628.9	636.1	643.3	638.9	631.2
Leisure and Hospitality													
2002	283.3	285.0	290.8	302.2	316.0	333.2	338.8	336.5	322.4	310.8	306.8	306.0	311.0
2003	293.7	292.7	297.3	310.3	325.8	342.8	354.8	352.9	334.9	321.0	316.2	314.0	321.4
2004	298.1	299.2	303.5	314.0	330.3	349.5	358.5	355.3	340.5	318.1	319.3	319.5	325.5
2005	305.1	305.3	311.3	324.2	338.8	359.8	367.5	364.9	348.2	327.7	324.5	323.9	333.4
2006	310.7	310.8	319.0	327.5	343.7	366.5	371.5	368.7	352.7	333.2	329.2	328.1	338.5
2007	313.2	312.8	318.2	328.0	345.6	367.9	371.9	369.2	349.7	337.9	333.4	332.1	340.0
2008	317.3	317.9	325.0	336.2	352.2	371.7	373.4	368.9	351.7	337.7	327.5	324.4	342.0
2009	309.1	308.3	313.0	323.8	344.8	361.3	365.7	363.7	348.7	330.3	323.1	321.6	334.5
2010	303.4	302.0	309.6	326.7	343.4	362.7	365.7	364.5	349.7	333.1	325.9	323.5	334.2
2011	303.7	305.2	311.7	326.9	344.2	364.1	368.7	367.1	350.5	334.2	327.4	325.8	335.8
2012	311.1	314.0	323.2	334.6	353.8	379.9	382.2	381.2	363.8	346.3	329.9	331.6	346.0
2013	317.8	319.6	328.2	342.1	361.2	387.3	389.8	387.1	371.0	351.0	341.6	335.2	352.7
Other Services													
2002	146.0	146.5	147.1	147.2	148.4	150.1	150.8	150.0	147.3	148.5	148.4	149.0	148.3
2003	148.6	148.5	149.4	151.4	152.5	155.1	155.8	155.4	153.4	153.4	153.6	154.1	152.6
2004	150.9	151.4	152.2	153.0	154.9	156.7	157.2	156.4	153.9	154.0	154.1	154.5	154.1
2005	154.3	155.1	155.4	158.4	159.0	161.2	161.4	160.7	157.0	156.6	157.1	157.8	157.8
2006	156.8	156.9	158.2	160.6	162.1	164.7	163.1	161.9	159.0	159.7	160.0	161.1	160.3
2007	159.5	159.6	160.3	163.3	164.9	168.2	166.7	165.4	162.4	163.7	163.6	163.9	163.5
2008	162.5	162.7	163.1	165.2	166.6	169.1	167.6	166.3	163.1	162.8	162.3	162.1	164.5
2009	159.5	160.0	160.2	161.5	163.2	165.5	163.7	163.2	159.9	160.2	160.4	160.2	161.5
2010	157.2	156.4	157.7	160.4	161.8	165.2	163.5	163.1	159.9	160.4	160.3	161.3	160.6
2011	157.8	158.0	159.3	160.7	162.0	165.9	164.7	163.4	160.5	160.7	160.5	161.4	161.2
2012	160.0	160.1	161.6	162.9	165.0	169.2	167.9	167.0	164.7	164.1	163.4	164.8	164.2
2013	161.5	162.0	163.0	165.2	166.5	170.9	169.9	169.0	165.9	164.6	165.5	164.8	165.7
Government													
2002	612.0	622.4	625.8	623.8	623.0	621.0	585.1	575.5	598.5	620.3	627.8	627.1	613.5
2003	616.4	627.4	630.8	631.4	630.7	629.9	599.3	585.4	607.9	630.8	637.0	636.1	621.9
2004	624.8	636.3	641.4	640.3	639.5	641.0	608.9	598.4	623.4	645.0	650.8	651.4	633.4
2005	636.2	648.6	650.0	651.8	648.6	650.9	616.0	605.7	628.3	649.8	656.7	656.5	641.6
2006	643.9	656.4	658.4	658.8	655.4	657.3	622.1	611.0	630.2	655.1	659.8	659.5	647.3
2007	645.2	656.6	658.9	659.3	657.9	660.5	616.5	609.7	629.8	655.6	660.9	660.8	647.7
2008	648.7	659.5	662.0	661.1	661.2	662.2	624.0	608.2	632.5	653.8	658.7	658.3	649.2
2009	649.6	659.6	663.0	664.6	664.5	664.6	625.9	614.7	637.2	657.7	664.0	662.8	652.4
2010	647.3	654.2	657.3	658.9	669.1	663.7	618.0	596.3	612.1	631.2	637.7	633.6	640.0
2011	617.2	628.8	631.0	633.5	629.3	628.3	589.7	574.9	603.4	627.5	632.7	629.9	618.9
2012	613.1	626.3	630.7	627.2	623.8	627.7	585.9	574.4	602.2	626.3	627.4	627.4	616.0
2013	616.4	630.7	631.1	623.0	619.7	623.5	582.7	575.1	601.6	624.4	628.7	627.3	615.4

2. Average Weekly Hours by Selected Industry: New Jersey, 2009–2013

(Not seasonally adjusted)

Industry and year	January	February	March	April	May	June	July	August	September	October	November	December	Annual average
Total Private													
2009	33.0	33.4	33.3	33.1	33.5	33.5	33.7	33.9	33.7	33.9	33.9	33.9	33.6
2010	33.5	32.9	33.3	33.6	33.9	33.7	33.8	34.4	34.0	34.2	34.3	34.3	33.8
2011	34.3	34.4	34.2	34.4	34.6	33.5	33.6	33.5	33.5	33.8	33.5	33.8	33.9
2012	33.6	33.5	33.6	33.7	33.2	33.4	33.7	33.3	33.7	33.4	33.9	34.2	33.6
2013	33.3	33.4	33.6	33.4	33.6	33.8	33.5	33.5	34.0	33.6	33.6	33.8	33.6
Goods-Producing													
2009	38.3	38.1	38.4	37.6	38.6	38.2	38.3	36.9	36.5	36.8	37.4	37.9	37.8
2010	37.2	35.1	38.0	38.6	38.4	38.5	38.3	38.6	38.7	38.7	38.5	38.8	38.1
2011	38.3	38.6	38.5	38.4	38.7	38.9	38.5	38.5	38.5	39.1	38.7	39.4	38.7
2012	38.3	38.7	38.7	38.6	36.5	37.0	36.9	37.4	37.9	38.4	38.9	39.3	38.0
2013	38.5	38.2	38.5	38.4	38.9	38.6	38.4	38.5	38.8	38.7	39.4	39.3	38.7
Construction													
2009	35.8	36.3	36.7	35.6	37.5	36.1	37.1	36.5	35.3	35.3	35.6	36.2	36.2
2010	35.4	33.8	35.1	35.7	35.3	35.9	35.4	35.7	35.8	35.9	35.7	35.6	35.5
2011	35.2	35.5	35.9	35.4	36.0	36.3	36.1	36.3	36.2	37.0	36.3	37.4	36.2
2012	35.8	36.4	36.8	36.2	30.6	31.2	32.1	33.1	33.9	34.5	35.0	36.1	34.3
2013	35.9	35.5	35.7	35.4	36.5	35.9	36.5	36.3	36.4	36.5	37.3	36.0	36.2
Manufacturing													
2009	39.6	39.1	39.4	38.8	39.3	39.5	39.0	39.4	39.3	39.5	39.7	40.0	39.4
2010	39.2	37.8	39.0	39.1	39.1	39.0	39.2	39.3	39.5	39.4	39.3	39.4	39.1
2011	39.0	39.2	39.0	39.2	39.3	39.6	39.2	39.2	39.4	40.0	39.9	40.5	39.5
2012	39.7	39.9	39.8	40.0	39.8	40.3	39.6	39.8	40.0	40.4	40.7	40.8	40.1
2013	39.7	39.4	39.7	39.7	40.0	39.9	39.3	39.7	40.1	39.9	40.6	40.9	39.9
Trade, Transportation, and Utilities													
2009	32.5	32.9	33.0	32.3	32.8	33.3	33.7	33.8	33.3	33.7	33.8	34.0	33.3
2010	33.4	32.9	33.6	33.6	34.0	34.1	34.1	34.3	33.8	34.1	34.2	34.5	33.9
2011	33.8	34.1	34.0	34.5	34.4	34.1	34.5	34.5	34.7	34.5	34.0	34.7	34.3
2012	34.1	34.0	34.1	34.3	34.4	34.4	34.7	33.8	34.1	33.7	34.3	34.3	34.2
2013	33.3	33.6	34.0	33.9	34.1	34.2	34.3	34.0	34.6	34.0	33.8	34.2	34.0
Financial Activities													
2009	36.9	37.1	37.0	37.3	36.5	36.3	36.2	36.5	36.4	36.0	36.9	36.4	36.6
2010	36.7	37.0	37.6	36.9	37.8	36.9	36.9	37.2	37.3	37.8	37.8	37.7	37.3
2011	38.4	37.8	37.4	37.2	37.7	37.0	36.5	36.3	36.6	37.6	36.4	36.0	37.1
2012	37.3	36.6	36.3	36.9	35.8	36.0	37.2	35.8	37.2	35.8	36.0	37.1	36.5
2013	36.1	36.2	36.1	35.6	35.5	37.0	35.4	35.9	36.9	35.5	35.3	36.7	36.0
Professional and Business Services													
2009	33.9	34.9	34.9	34.8	36.3	35.7	35.0	36.2	36.0	36.3	36.5	35.7	35.5
2010	35.7	34.6	35.7	35.9	36.3	35.6	35.5	36.0	34.8	35.4	35.3	35.4	35.5
2011	35.1	35.4	35.1	35.4	36.2	35.5	35.3	35.4	35.4	35.7	35.4	35.7	35.5
2012	35.8	35.7	36.2	36.4	35.6	36.0	36.1	35.6	36.0	35.5	35.8	36.4	35.9
2013	35.2	35.9	36.3	36.1	36.2	36.8	35.8	35.9	36.7	35.9	36.2	36.0	36.1
Education and Health Services													
2009	31.1	31.3	30.9	31.1	31.1	31.1	31.7	31.8	31.3	32.5	32.7	32.3	31.6
2010	32.2	32.0	32.2	32.3	32.8	32.5	32.6	32.9	32.7	32.8	33.0	32.9	32.6
2011	32.6	32.5	32.3	32.4	32.2	31.8	31.5	31.7	31.4	31.5	31.6	31.6	31.9
2012	31.7	31.3	31.3	31.2	31.2	31.3	31.2	31.1	31.2	31.0	31.1	31.2	31.2
2013	31.2	31.2	31.0	30.6	30.7	31.0	30.9	30.6	30.8	30.6	30.7	30.5	30.8
Leisure and Hospitality													
2009	26.3	26.7	26.1	26.0	26.7	26.8	28.2	28.3	27.9	26.7	26.5	25.9	26.9
2010	25.8	25.6	26.3	26.6	26.8	26.6	28.0	28.1	26.6	25.9	26.1	25.3	26.5
2011	25.2	25.7	25.8	26.1	26.3	25.8	26.1	26.2	25.3	26.2	26.4	26.1	25.9
2012	26.1	26.1	26.1	26.3	26.1	26.2	27.0	26.9	26.3	26.0	25.9	26.3	26.3
2013	25.4	25.7	26.0	26.1	26.5	26.6	27.0	27.4	27.3	26.9	27.0	26.8	26.6
Other Services													
2009	32.8	33.0	32.9	32.4	32.4	32.3	32.5	33.8	33.9	33.2	33.4	33.3	33.0
2010	33.0	31.6	32.6	32.4	32.6	32.4	32.2	32.8	32.3	31.9	32.1	32.0	32.3
2011	32.1	31.6	31.3	31.5	32.0	31.2	31.8	31.6	31.9	31.9	31.1	31.6	31.6
2012	31.8	31.2	31.4	31.7	31.5	31.8	32.8	33.0	33.4	33.4	33.1	33.1	32.4
2013	31.8	31.1	31.8	31.3	30.7	31.2	31.2	31.9	30.7	30.1	29.7	30.2	31.0

3. Average Hourly Earnings by Selected Industry: New Jersey, 2009–2013

(Dollars, not seasonally adjusted)

Industry and year	January	February	March	April	May	June	July	August	September	October	November	December	Annual average
Total Private													
2009	25.56	25.71	26.05	25.83	25.63	25.49	25.53	25.63	26.09	26.05	26.84	26.66	25.92
2010	26.56	26.89	26.29	26.19	26.04	25.78	25.68	25.45	25.63	25.65	25.67	25.80	25.96
2011	26.03	25.82	25.73	25.72	25.68	25.39	25.20	25.19	25.58	25.99	25.71	25.59	25.64
2012	26.38	26.14	26.17	26.64	26.37	26.17	26.61	26.19	26.70	26.42	26.69	26.91	26.45
2013	26.83	26.87	26.77	27.08	26.69	26.94	26.42	26.43	27.03	26.85	26.84	26.85	26.80
Goods-Producing													
2009	27.42	28.16	28.22	27.63	27.61	27.66	27.18	28.06	28.04	27.84	27.86	28.64	27.85
2010	28.32	29.38	28.40	28.49	28.84	28.91	28.84	28.46	28.39	28.41	28.54	28.60	28.63
2011	28.64	28.52	28.56	28.46	28.33	28.41	28.56	28.29	28.32	28.08	28.02	28.06	28.35
2012	27.80	27.93	28.14	28.57	29.59	29.69	29.68	29.88	29.51	29.07	28.98	29.44	29.02
2013	28.87	28.76	28.75	29.16	28.83	28.99	28.67	28.86	28.95	28.54	28.24	27.42	28.67
Construction													
2009	33.62	34.51	34.19	33.62	33.25	33.83	33.34	33.19	33.28	33.18	33.73	33.96	33.64
2010	34.02	34.30	34.10	34.09	33.96	33.87	33.84	33.64	33.69	33.68	33.68	33.76	33.88
2011	33.53	33.72	33.51	33.32	33.05	33.44	33.81	34.05	33.59	33.11	32.93	32.78	33.40
2012	32.34	32.59	33.41	33.77	37.46	37.09	36.41	36.40	36.09	35.81	35.34	35.71	35.17
2013	34.55	34.67	34.84	35.30	34.29	33.98	33.58	33.83	33.81	33.38	33.46	33.24	34.06
Manufacturing													
2009	24.53	25.19	25.25	24.63	24.79	24.60	23.85	23.87	23.82	23.67	23.69	24.03	24.33
2010	23.98	24.78	23.99	23.88	24.60	24.72	24.75	24.73	24.60	24.64	24.72	24.77	24.51
2011	24.90	24.76	24.65	24.68	24.61	24.50	24.48	23.90	24.38	24.41	24.53	24.82	24.55
2012	24.95	25.10	24.90	25.18	24.95	25.22	25.52	25.71	25.44	24.87	25.19	25.75	25.23
2013	25.63	25.60	25.54	25.85	25.75	26.16	25.89	26.18	26.19	25.80	25.42	25.83	25.82
Trade, Transportation, and Utilities													
2009	24.52	24.01	24.35	23.93	23.98	23.44	23.69	23.57	23.59	23.35	24.11	23.26	23.81
2010	23.00	22.98	22.44	22.48	22.56	21.82	22.46	22.66	22.83	22.74	22.67	22.51	22.59
2011	22.98	22.82	22.53	22.53	22.44	21.96	22.03	21.96	22.53	22.65	22.45	22.08	22.41
2012	23.02	22.71	22.86	23.39	22.96	22.78	23.14	22.71	22.97	22.80	23.33	22.69	22.95
2013	22.79	23.02	23.09	23.61	23.02	23.09	23.07	22.92	23.27	23.17	23.09	22.93	23.09
Financial Activities													
2009	28.21	28.57	30.80	32.35	31.43	31.35	33.03	34.30	33.08	32.99	33.00	32.55	31.79
2010	32.32	33.00	32.90	32.34	34.20	33.81	33.26	33.06	32.92	32.31	32.30	32.71	33.03
2011	33.86	33.25	33.29	34.04	34.31	33.51	33.29	33.51	33.77	37.04	35.71	35.37	34.24
2012	36.77	36.08	36.83	38.28	36.22	35.64	37.49	36.16	36.34	35.64	35.10	36.55	36.43
2013	36.33	35.95	35.57	36.13	35.50	36.72	34.32	34.13	34.39	34.14	34.11	33.57	35.08
Professional and Business Services													
2009	29.66	30.50	30.41	29.79	28.79	28.72	29.09	28.77	28.78	29.03	30.36	30.46	29.52
2010	30.84	32.00	31.74	31.05	30.86	30.31	30.32	30.57	30.96	30.99	30.90	31.18	30.97
2011	32.83	31.94	31.94	31.96	31.96	31.56	31.72	31.40	31.23	32.13	31.09	30.85	31.71
2012	32.83	32.49	31.98	32.28	32.30	32.07	33.09	32.02	33.19	32.86	32.81	33.19	32.60
2013	33.14	33.26	33.06	33.05	32.79	33.10	32.63	32.93	33.90	33.40	33.57	34.19	33.25
Education and Health Services													
2009	25.25	25.17	25.55	25.46	25.51	25.37	25.31	25.50	25.61	25.27	25.70	25.93	25.47
2010	25.81	25.43	25.17	25.06	24.87	24.80	24.87	24.61	25.24	25.39	25.34	25.53	25.18
2011	24.92	24.88	24.75	24.87	24.61	24.64	24.59	24.57	24.88	24.42	24.66	24.74	24.71
2012	24.79	25.04	24.98	25.10	24.81	24.84	25.37	25.14	25.26	25.00	25.56	25.82	25.14
2013	25.77	25.73	25.75	26.18	25.92	26.11	25.96	25.55	25.81	25.76	25.92	26.08	25.88
Leisure and Hospitality													
2009	15.33	15.52	15.29	15.68	16.84	17.97	17.35	16.96	16.65	16.42	16.63	16.33	16.47
2010	15.99	15.74	15.58	15.53	15.41	15.28	14.77	14.72	14.77	14.87	14.77	15.08	15.18
2011	14.71	14.47	14.52	14.35	15.18	16.34	14.28	15.98	15.27	14.26	14.33	14.32	14.86
2012	14.04	14.02	14.05	13.95	14.20	13.77	13.46	13.51	13.81	13.91	14.06	14.15	13.90
2013	14.00	14.12	13.91	14.10	14.18	14.15	13.96	13.97	13.99	14.18	14.19	14.54	14.11
Other Services													
2009	20.33	21.02	21.16	21.63	21.63	21.97	21.59	22.27	22.67	23.43	23.61	23.13	22.04
2010	24.06	24.11	23.54	24.31	23.20	23.66	22.76	22.92	23.60	23.54	24.08	24.08	23.59
2011	24.23	24.05	23.89	23.34	23.16	23.01	21.97	21.84	22.20	22.29	22.66	22.45	22.92
2012	21.94	21.65	21.84	21.83	22.27	21.81	21.20	21.03	21.63	21.19	21.34	22.42	21.67
2013	22.26	22.71	21.76	22.17	22.58	22.38	21.61	21.61	22.78	22.76	22.46	23.22	22.35

4. Average Weekly Earnings by Selected Industry: New Jersey, 2009–2013

(Dollars, not seasonally adjusted)

Industry and year	January	February	March	April	May	June	July	August	September	October	November	December	Annual average
Total Private													
2009	843.48	858.71	867.47	854.97	858.61	853.92	860.36	868.86	879.23	883.10	909.88	903.77	870.91
2010	889.76	884.68	875.46	879.98	882.76	868.79	867.98	875.48	871.42	877.23	880.48	884.94	877.45
2011	892.83	888.21	879.97	884.77	888.53	850.57	846.72	843.87	856.93	878.46	861.29	864.94	869.20
2012	886.37	875.69	879.31	897.77	875.48	874.08	896.76	872.13	899.79	882.43	904.79	920.32	888.72
2013	893.44	897.46	899.47	904.47	896.78	910.57	885.07	885.41	919.02	902.16	901.82	907.53	900.48
Goods-Producing													
2009	1,050.19	1,072.90	1,083.65	1,038.89	1,065.75	1,056.61	1,040.99	1,035.41	1,023.46	1,024.51	1,041.96	1,085.46	1,052.73
2010	1,053.50	1,031.24	1,079.20	1,099.71	1,107.46	1,113.04	1,104.57	1,098.56	1,098.69	1,099.47	1,098.79	1,109.68	1,090.80
2011	1,096.91	1,100.87	1,099.56	1,092.86	1,096.37	1,105.15	1,099.56	1,089.17	1,090.32	1,097.93	1,084.37	1,105.56	1,097.15
2012	1,064.74	1,080.89	1,089.02	1,102.80	1,080.04	1,098.53	1,095.19	1,117.51	1,118.43	1,116.29	1,127.32	1,156.99	1,102.76
2013	1,111.50	1,098.63	1,106.88	1,119.74	1,121.49	1,119.01	1,100.93	1,111.11	1,123.26	1,104.50	1,112.66	1,077.61	1,109.53
Construction													
2009	1,203.60	1,252.71	1,254.77	1,196.87	1,246.88	1,221.26	1,236.91	1,211.44	1,174.78	1,171.25	1,200.79	1,229.35	1,217.77
2010	1,204.31	1,159.34	1,196.91	1,217.01	1,198.79	1,215.93	1,197.94	1,200.95	1,206.10	1,209.11	1,202.38	1,201.86	1,202.74
2011	1,180.26	1,197.06	1,203.01	1,179.53	1,189.80	1,213.87	1,220.54	1,236.02	1,215.96	1,225.07	1,195.36	1,225.97	1,209.08
2012	1,157.77	1,186.28	1,229.49	1,222.47	1,146.28	1,157.21	1,168.76	1,204.84	1,223.45	1,235.45	1,236.90	1,289.13	1,206.33
2013	1,240.35	1,230.79	1,243.79	1,249.62	1,251.59	1,219.88	1,225.67	1,228.03	1,230.68	1,218.37	1,248.06	1,196.64	1,232.97
Manufacturing													
2009	971.39	984.93	994.85	955.64	974.25	971.70	930.15	940.48	936.13	934.97	940.49	961.20	958.60
2010	940.02	936.68	935.61	933.71	961.86	964.08	970.20	971.89	971.70	970.82	971.50	975.94	958.34
2011	971.10	970.59	961.35	967.46	967.17	970.20	959.62	936.88	960.57	976.40	978.75	1,005.21	969.73
2012	990.52	1,001.49	991.02	1,007.20	993.01	1,016.37	1,010.59	1,023.26	1,017.60	1,004.75	1,025.23	1,050.60	1,011.72
2013	1,017.51	1,008.64	1,013.94	1,026.25	1,030.00	1,043.78	1,017.48	1,039.35	1,050.22	1,029.42	1,032.05	1,056.45	1,030.22
Trade, Transportation, and Utilities													
2009	796.90	789.93	803.55	772.94	786.54	780.55	798.35	796.67	785.55	786.90	814.92	790.84	792.87
2010	768.20	756.04	753.98	755.33	767.04	744.06	765.89	777.24	771.65	775.43	775.31	776.60	765.80
2011	776.72	778.16	766.02	777.29	771.94	748.84	760.04	757.62	781.79	781.43	763.30	766.18	768.66
2012	784.98	772.14	779.53	802.28	789.82	783.63	802.96	767.60	783.28	768.36	800.22	778.27	784.89
2013	758.91	773.47	785.06	800.38	784.98	789.68	791.30	779.28	805.14	787.78	780.44	784.21	785.06
Financial Activities													
2009	1,040.95	1,059.95	1,139.60	1,206.66	1,147.20	1,138.01	1,195.69	1,251.95	1,204.11	1,187.64	1,217.70	1,184.82	1,163.51
2010	1,186.14	1,221.00	1,237.04	1,237.63	1,292.76	1,247.59	1,227.29	1,229.83	1,227.92	1,221.32	1,220.94	1,233.17	1,232.02
2011	1,300.22	1,256.85	1,245.05	1,266.29	1,293.49	1,239.87	1,215.09	1,216.41	1,235.98	1,392.70	1,299.84	1,273.32	1,270.30
2012	1,371.52	1,320.53	1,336.93	1,412.53	1,296.68	1,283.04	1,394.63	1,294.53	1,351.85	1,275.91	1,263.60	1,356.01	1,329.70
2013	1,311.51	1,301.39	1,284.08	1,286.23	1,260.25	1,358.64	1,214.93	1,225.27	1,268.99	1,211.97	1,204.08	1,232.02	1,262.88
Professional and Business Services													
2009	1,005.47	1,064.45	1,061.31	1,036.69	1,045.08	1,025.30	1,018.15	1,041.47	1,036.08	1,053.79	1,108.14	1,087.42	1,047.96
2010	1,100.99	1,107.20	1,133.12	1,114.70	1,120.22	1,079.04	1,076.36	1,100.52	1,077.41	1,097.05	1,090.77	1,103.77	1,099.44
2011	1,152.33	1,130.68	1,121.09	1,132.45	1,156.95	1,120.38	1,119.72	1,111.56	1,105.54	1,147.04	1,100.59	1,101.35	1,125.71
2012	1,175.31	1,159.89	1,157.68	1,174.99	1,149.88	1,154.52	1,194.55	1,139.91	1,194.84	1,166.53	1,174.60	1,208.12	1,170.34
2013	1,166.53	1,194.03	1,200.08	1,193.11	1,187.00	1,218.08	1,168.15	1,182.19	1,244.13	1,199.06	1,215.23	1,230.84	1,200.33
Education and Health Services													
2009	785.28	787.82	789.50	791.81	793.36	789.01	802.33	810.90	801.59	821.28	840.39	837.54	804.85
2010	831.08	813.76	810.47	809.44	815.74	806.00	810.76	809.67	825.35	832.79	836.22	839.94	820.87
2011	812.39	808.60	799.43	805.79	792.44	783.55	774.59	778.87	781.23	769.23	779.26	781.78	788.25
2012	785.84	783.75	781.87	783.12	774.07	777.49	791.54	781.85	788.11	775.00	794.92	805.58	784.37
2013	804.02	802.78	798.25	801.11	795.74	809.41	802.16	781.83	794.95	788.26	795.74	795.44	797.10
Leisure and Hospitality													
2009	403.18	414.38	399.07	407.68	449.63	481.60	489.27	479.97	464.54	438.41	440.70	422.95	443.04
2010	412.54	402.94	409.75	413.10	412.99	406.45	413.56	413.63	392.88	385.13	385.50	381.52	402.27
2011	370.69	371.88	374.62	374.54	399.23	421.57	372.71	418.68	386.33	373.61	378.31	373.75	384.87
2012	366.44	365.92	366.71	366.89	370.62	360.77	363.42	363.42	363.20	361.66	364.15	372.15	365.57
2013	355.60	362.88	361.66	368.01	375.77	376.39	376.92	382.78	381.93	381.44	383.13	389.67	375.33
Other Services													
2009	666.82	693.66	696.16	700.81	700.81	709.63	701.68	752.73	768.51	777.88	788.57	770.23	727.32
2010	793.98	761.88	767.40	787.64	756.32	766.58	732.87	751.78	762.28	750.93	748.57	770.56	761.96
2011	777.78	759.98	747.76	735.21	741.12	717.91	698.65	690.14	708.18	711.05	704.73	709.42	724.27
2012	697.69	675.48	685.78	692.01	701.51	693.56	695.36	693.99	722.44	707.75	706.35	742.10	702.11
2013	707.87	706.28	691.97	693.92	693.21	698.26	674.23	689.36	699.35	685.08	667.06	701.24	692.85

NEW MEXICO
At a Glance

Population:
2000 census: 1,819,017
2010 census: 2,059,179
2013 estimate: 2,085,287

Percent change in population:
2000–2010: 13.2%
2010–2013: 1.3%

Percent change in total nonfarm employment:
2000–2010: 7.8%
2010–2013: 1.0%

Industry with the largest growth in employment, 2000–2013 (thousands):
Education and Health Services, 41.4

Industry with the largest decline or smallest growth in employment, 2000–2013 (thousands):
Manufacturing, -12.8

Civilian labor force:
2000: 852,293
2010: 930,293
2013: 926,242

Unemployment rate and rank among states (lowest to highest):
2000: 5.0%, 44th
2010: 8.0%, 17th
2013: 6.9%, 27th

Over-the-year change in unemployment rates:
2010–2011: -0.4%
2011–2012: -0.5%
2012–2013: -0.2%

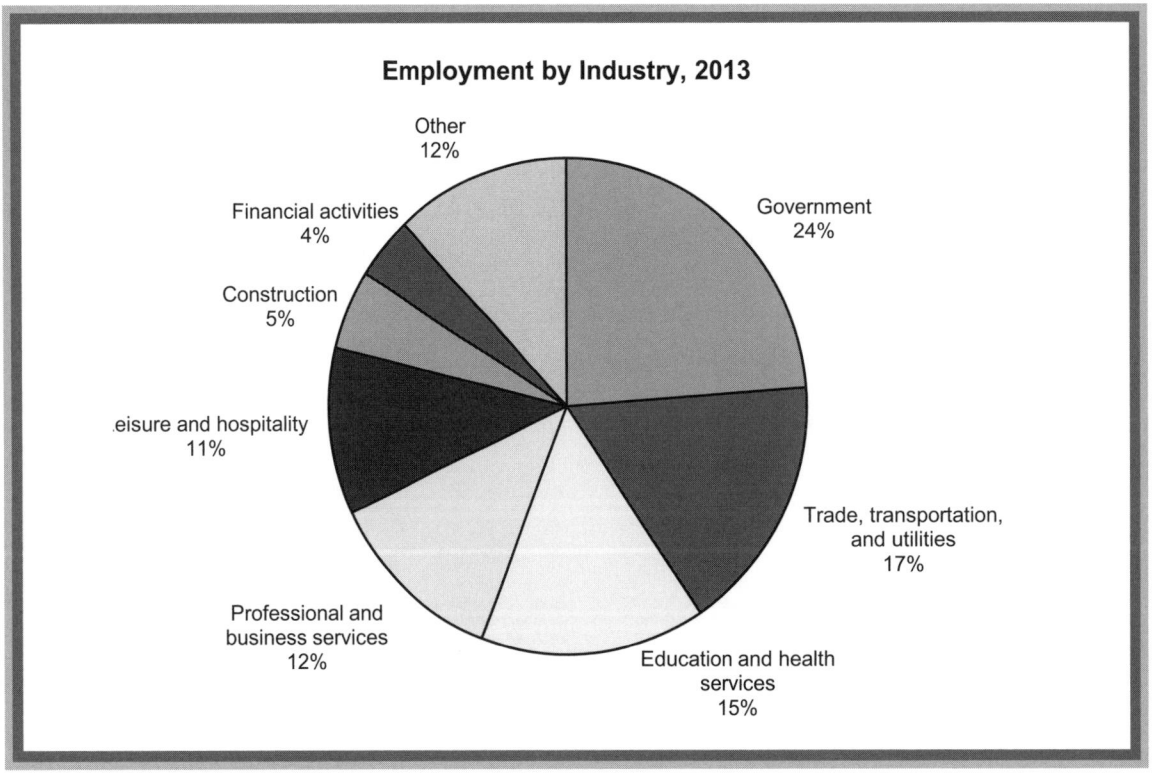

Employment by Industry, 2013

Other 12%
Financial activities 4%
Construction 5%
Leisure and hospitality 11%
Professional and business services 12%
Education and health services 15%
Trade, transportation, and utilities 17%
Government 24%

1. Employment by Industry: New Mexico, Selected Years, 2002–2013

(Numbers in thousands, not seasonally adjusted)

Industry and year	January	February	March	April	May	June	July	August	September	October	November	December	Annual average
Total Nonfarm													
2002	748.5	754.1	760.9	764.2	770.0	769.4	763.7	768.3	774.1	770.6	773.7	776.2	766.1
2003	759.5	765.2	769.9	772.6	777.2	776.5	772.1	776.7	781.4	783.8	784.8	787.4	775.6
2004	769.8	778.0	783.8	788.7	792.6	791.1	787.0	789.5	795.3	801.5	802.5	805.2	790.4
2005	786.5	793.6	799.1	806.9	810.1	808.6	805.2	809.7	818.8	818.5	822.3	824.5	808.7
2006	809.2	819.7	827.1	828.6	835.2	837.3	828.0	832.0	842.5	839.5	842.9	844.3	832.2
2007	824.4	833.9	842.3	840.2	845.6	845.9	837.8	843.2	850.2	851.9	853.9	855.3	843.7
2008	834.0	843.3	847.5	848.8	852.8	850.2	841.7	846.8	854.7	852.2	847.2	842.4	846.8
2009	816.9	818.2	816.7	816.0	817.0	811.7	803.5	807.6	812.4	811.3	808.8	808.5	812.4
2010	789.4	795.8	801.1	807.2	810.5	807.2	799.8	801.7	803.6	807.8	806.2	807.1	803.1
2011	787.9	795.7	800.4	808.0	808.2	805.6	797.4	801.6	809.6	808.8	808.2	807.0	803.2
2012	790.1	798.2	803.8	805.8	807.7	805.9	795.7	802.3	809.8	821.6	821.2	818.4	806.7
2013	801.5	808.1	809.9	816.1	817.6	807.7	802.2	810.2	814.4	816.6	815.7	815.0	811.3
Total Private													
2002	563.4	563.4	568.8	572.1	576.9	579.1	579.2	582.5	580.3	576.7	579.0	581.0	575.2
2003	569.0	569.9	573.4	575.3	580.6	582.8	583.8	587.4	584.6	584.6	585.8	588.3	580.5
2004	576.8	578.5	583.1	587.9	592.3	594.5	595.7	597.5	595.9	599.3	599.7	602.8	592.1
2005	590.3	591.5	595.7	603.2	606.0	609.1	611.4	614.9	615.4	613.9	617.3	620.1	607.4
2006	610.4	614.1	620.8	623.2	629.3	645.7	642.5	645.1	647.0	642.8	645.9	647.4	634.5
2007	633.8	637.9	644.6	643.4	648.9	653.2	651.3	655.5	653.9	653.7	654.7	655.9	648.9
2008	640.8	644.6	647.8	649.3	652.4	654.5	652.4	656.3	654.9	650.8	645.3	640.8	649.2
2009	621.2	617.3	615.0	613.4	614.8	614.3	612.5	615.6	613.4	609.7	606.8	606.7	613.4
2010	595.0	595.2	597.8	602.1	603.7	606.9	606.8	609.0	606.4	606.5	605.3	607.0	603.5
2011	595.4	597.3	600.5	607.2	608.8	610.9	612.2	613.8	612.9	610.2	609.6	608.5	607.3
2012	598.4	600.9	605.3	608.8	610.6	614.8	613.2	615.9	614.1	622.8	622.1	620.0	612.2
2013	609.7	611.0	611.8	617.6	620.1	620.2	622.6	625.4	619.6	620.5	619.4	620.3	618.2
Goods-Producing													
2002	97.6	96.6	97.5	98.0	98.8	99.2	99.4	100.5	98.9	98.5	97.2	96.3	98.2
2003	94.4	94.1	94.9	95.9	97.4	99.0	99.7	100.9	99.6	100.1	99.2	98.4	97.8
2004	96.1	96.0	97.2	99.0	100.6	102.1	104.2	104.4	103.9	104.8	103.6	104.1	101.3
2005	101.4	101.4	103.0	104.5	105.7	107.4	109.8	110.7	111.2	111.3	111.6	111.4	107.5
2006	110.1	111.7	113.1	113.8	115.3	117.2	117.5	118.3	118.4	118.3	116.5	115.7	115.5
2007	112.5	113.1	114.4	114.5	115.9	117.6	117.2	118.1	117.0	117.1	115.8	114.9	115.7
2008	112.0	112.5	113.1	114.2	114.9	115.9	115.1	116.6	115.9	114.3	111.6	108.3	113.7
2009	102.2	99.6	97.4	95.8	95.3	95.5	95.0	95.5	93.9	93.9	92.1	90.7	95.6
2010	88.6	88.2	88.4	89.9	90.7	91.7	92.6	93.3	93.1	93.7	92.6	91.8	91.2
2011	89.5	89.3	91.1	92.4	93.1	94.2	95.1	96.0	95.7	95.4	94.4	93.3	93.3
2012	91.3	91.7	92.7	93.4	94.2	95.6	95.7	96.4	96.2	99.0	97.2	96.1	95.0
2013	94.1	94.7	95.1	96.0	96.4	97.3	98.0	99.5	98.7	99.8	97.5	96.6	97.0
Service-Providing													
2002	650.9	657.5	663.4	666.2	671.2	670.2	664.3	667.8	675.2	672.1	676.5	679.9	667.9
2003	665.1	671.1	675.0	676.7	679.8	677.5	672.4	675.8	681.8	683.7	685.6	689.0	677.8
2004	673.7	682.0	686.6	689.7	692.0	689.0	682.8	685.1	691.4	696.7	698.9	701.1	689.1
2005	685.1	692.2	696.1	702.4	704.4	701.2	695.4	699.0	707.6	707.2	710.7	713.1	701.2
2006	699.1	708.0	714.0	714.8	719.9	720.1	710.5	713.7	724.1	721.2	726.4	728.6	716.7
2007	711.9	720.8	727.9	725.7	729.7	728.3	720.6	725.1	733.2	734.8	738.1	740.4	728.0
2008	722.0	730.8	734.4	734.6	737.9	734.3	726.6	730.2	738.8	737.9	735.6	734.1	733.1
2009	714.7	718.6	719.3	720.2	721.7	716.2	708.5	712.1	718.5	717.4	716.7	717.8	716.8
2010	700.8	707.6	712.7	717.3	719.8	715.5	707.2	708.4	710.5	714.1	713.6	715.3	711.9
2011	698.4	706.4	709.3	715.6	715.1	711.4	702.3	705.6	713.9	713.4	713.8	713.7	709.9
2012	698.8	706.5	711.1	712.4	713.5	710.3	700.0	705.9	713.6	722.6	724.0	722.3	711.8
2013	707.4	713.4	714.8	720.1	721.2	710.4	704.2	710.7	715.7	716.8	718.2	718.4	714.3
Mining and Logging													
2002	14.6	14.4	14.3	14.0	14.0	13.9	13.8	13.9	13.7	13.9	13.8	13.8	14.0
2003	13.8	13.9	14.0	14.1	14.3	14.4	14.4	14.4	14.4	14.6	14.7	14.8	14.3
2004	14.4	14.3	14.5	14.7	14.8	15.0	15.1	15.4	15.4	15.6	15.7	16.1	15.1
2005	15.9	15.9	16.1	16.2	16.4	16.6	17.2	17.4	17.8	17.8	17.7	17.7	16.9
2006	17.8	18.0	18.1	18.3	18.5	18.8	18.8	19.1	19.1	19.2	19.1	19.2	18.7
2007	19.3	19.0	19.1	19.2	19.4	19.7	19.9	20.0	19.6	19.7	19.9	19.9	19.6
2008	19.8	19.8	20.0	20.6	21.0	21.3	21.5	22.1	22.1	22.1	21.9	21.3	21.1
2009	19.9	19.1	18.3	17.8	17.5	17.5	17.5	17.5	17.1	17.3	17.5	17.5	17.9
2010	17.4	17.6	17.6	17.9	18.3	18.7	18.9	18.9	18.8	19.2	19.3	19.6	18.5
2011	19.7	20.0	20.2	20.6	21.0	21.4	21.7	22.1	22.3	22.6	22.9	23.2	21.5
2012	23.2	23.4	23.3	23.5	23.8	24.2	24.4	24.5	24.6	25.1	24.9	24.9	24.2
2013	25.2	25.4	25.5	25.8	25.9	26.1	26.4	26.5	26.2	26.4	26.2	26.7	26.0
Construction													
2002	44.7	44.3	45.1	45.8	46.3	46.5	46.1	46.8	45.8	46.2	46.0	45.6	45.8
2003	44.4	44.2	44.9	46.0	47.1	48.0	48.4	48.9	47.8	48.4	48.0	47.7	47.0
2004	46.7	46.8	47.7	48.9	50.0	50.9	52.6	52.1	51.5	52.3	51.7	51.9	50.3
2005	50.2	50.3	51.6	52.8	53.7	55.0	56.5	56.6	56.5	56.4	56.9	56.8	54.4
2006	55.9	56.8	58.1	58.5	59.8	60.9	60.4	60.4	60.4	60.4	59.4	58.7	59.1
2007	56.0	56.8	58.1	58.6	59.6	60.8	60.2	60.5	59.9	60.6	59.7	59.0	59.2
2008	57.0	57.5	58.1	58.5	58.6	59.1	58.0	58.3	57.6	57.2	55.7	53.6	57.4
2009	50.7	49.6	48.9	48.1	48.1	48.1	47.7	47.9	46.9	46.6	45.4	44.0	47.7
2010	42.7	42.2	42.3	43.4	43.5	43.9	44.6	44.6	44.3	44.4	43.9	43.0	43.6
2011	40.9	40.5	41.9	42.7	43.0	43.4	43.8	43.4	42.7	42.2	41.6	40.5	42.2
2012	38.9	39.2	40.2	40.5	40.9	41.8	41.5	41.6	41.1	43.2	42.5	41.8	41.1
2013	40.1	40.5	40.9	41.4	41.6	42.0	42.4	43.1	42.9	43.7	42.7	41.8	41.9

1. Employment by Industry: New Mexico, Selected Years, 2002–2013—*Continued*

(Numbers in thousands, not seasonally adjusted)

Industry and year	January	February	March	April	May	June	July	August	September	October	November	December	Annual average
Manufacturing													
2002	38.3	37.9	38.1	38.2	38.5	38.8	39.5	39.8	39.4	38.4	37.4	36.9	38.4
2003	36.2	36.0	36.0	35.8	36.0	36.6	36.9	37.6	37.4	37.1	36.5	35.9	36.5
2004	35.0	34.9	35.0	35.4	35.8	36.2	36.5	36.9	37.0	36.9	36.2	36.1	36.0
2005	35.3	35.2	35.3	35.5	35.6	35.8	36.1	36.7	36.9	37.1	37.0	36.9	36.1
2006	36.4	36.9	36.9	37.0	37.0	37.5	38.3	38.8	38.9	38.7	38.0	37.8	37.7
2007	37.2	37.3	37.2	36.7	36.9	37.1	37.1	37.6	37.5	36.8	36.2	36.0	37.0
2008	35.2	35.2	35.0	35.1	35.3	35.5	35.6	36.2	36.2	35.0	34.0	33.4	35.1
2009	31.6	30.9	30.2	29.9	29.7	29.9	29.8	30.1	29.9	30.0	29.2	29.2	30.0
2010	28.5	28.4	28.5	28.6	28.9	29.1	29.1	29.8	30.0	30.1	29.4	29.2	29.1
2011	28.9	28.8	29.0	29.1	29.1	29.4	29.6	30.5	30.7	30.6	29.9	29.6	29.6
2012	29.2	29.1	29.2	29.4	29.5	29.6	29.8	30.3	30.5	30.7	29.8	29.4	29.7
2013	28.8	28.8	28.7	28.8	28.9	29.2	29.2	29.9	29.6	29.7	28.6	28.1	29.0
Trade, Transportation, and Utilities													
2002	133.9	132.7	133.1	133.7	135.3	135.7	135.0	136.0	135.8	135.9	138.2	139.9	135.4
2003	134.1	133.3	134.1	134.1	135.2	134.8	134.7	135.9	135.8	136.9	139.0	140.6	135.7
2004	135.9	135.4	136.2	136.5	137.4	137.2	137.1	137.3	136.9	138.5	140.7	142.2	137.6
2005	137.5	136.9	137.4	138.0	139.2	138.9	139.5	140.4	140.0	140.5	143.0	144.5	139.7
2006	139.6	138.5	139.8	140.0	141.3	141.4	141.6	142.3	142.0	142.0	144.9	146.3	141.6
2007	142.3	141.8	143.2	142.4	144.1	143.8	144.3	145.2	145.0	146.3	149.1	150.5	144.8
2008	145.8	145.1	145.8	144.9	145.0	144.3	144.1	144.5	143.7	143.3	143.7	144.2	144.5
2009	138.7	136.5	136.3	134.8	135.3	135.2	134.7	135.1	135.0	134.8	135.7	136.6	135.7
2010	132.0	131.0	131.8	132.0	132.6	132.7	133.0	133.7	132.5	133.6	135.2	136.2	133.0
2011	131.9	131.0	131.3	132.7	133.5	133.4	133.1	133.6	133.6	134.8	137.0	137.6	133.6
2012	134.0	133.3	133.9	134.2	134.9	135.0	135.0	135.2	135.3	137.4	139.4	139.9	135.6
2013	135.3	134.5	134.2	135.1	135.8	136.0	136.7	137.1	136.2	136.5	139.0	141.0	136.5
Wholesale Trade													
2002	22.5	22.5	22.5	22.5	22.6	22.8	22.9	22.8	22.5	22.5	22.5	22.5	22.6
2003	21.9	21.9	22.2	22.2	22.1	22.2	22.2	22.2	22.0	22.0	21.9	22.0	22.1
2004	21.7	21.8	22.1	22.3	22.3	22.4	22.5	22.3	22.2	22.3	22.2	22.4	22.2
2005	22.2	22.4	22.5	22.6	22.8	22.9	23.0	22.9	22.8	22.8	22.9	23.0	22.7
2006	22.6	22.7	22.9	23.1	23.3	23.6	23.7	23.7	23.6	23.5	23.5	23.5	23.3
2007	23.4	23.4	23.4	23.5	23.6	23.9	24.1	24.0	23.9	24.1	24.1	24.2	23.8
2008	23.9	23.8	23.8	23.9	23.9	23.9	23.9	23.8	23.4	23.3	23.0	22.7	23.6
2009	22.3	22.1	22.0	21.7	21.7	22.0	21.8	21.6	21.5	21.7	21.6	21.8	21.8
2010	21.5	21.5	21.6	21.7	21.7	21.9	21.8	21.6	21.2	21.2	21.0	21.0	21.5
2011	20.7	20.6	20.7	20.8	21.1	21.3	21.4	21.3	21.2	21.1	21.0	21.0	21.0
2012	20.8	21.0	21.2	21.2	21.4	21.7	21.8	21.6	21.5	21.7	21.6	21.7	21.4
2013	21.3	21.4	21.4	21.5	21.6	21.7	21.8	21.9	21.5	21.4	21.3	21.3	21.5
Retail Trade													
2002	88.7	87.6	88.2	88.5	89.9	90.0	90.1	90.4	90.2	90.1	92.4	94.1	90.1
2003	89.5	88.7	89.2	89.2	90.3	90.4	90.4	91.1	90.7	91.6	93.9	95.3	90.9
2004	90.9	90.4	90.8	91.1	91.9	92.2	92.1	92.0	91.4	92.7	95.1	96.3	92.2
2005	92.3	91.5	91.6	92.2	93.1	93.4	93.9	94.2	93.6	94.1	96.4	97.3	93.6
2006	93.1	91.9	93.1	93.1	94.0	94.2	94.3	94.6	94.1	94.3	97.0	97.8	94.3
2007	94.2	93.6	95.0	94.2	95.6	95.7	96.2	96.3	95.8	96.6	99.3	100.2	96.1
2008	96.5	96.1	96.7	96.1	96.0	96.5	96.6	96.5	96.0	95.9	96.7	97.3	96.4
2009	92.7	90.9	91.1	90.5	90.9	91.4	91.4	91.7	91.7	91.2	92.2	92.7	91.5
2010	88.9	88.0	88.7	88.7	89.2	89.6	89.8	90.3	89.2	90.1	91.9	92.6	89.8
2011	89.0	88.1	88.5	89.6	90.0	89.9	89.6	89.9	89.8	90.8	93.1	93.4	90.1
2012	90.2	89.2	89.5	89.9	90.2	90.3	90.3	90.3	90.4	91.9	94.0	94.2	90.9
2013	90.4	89.6	89.5	90.5	90.8	91.3	91.8	91.9	91.2	91.5	94.0	95.7	91.5
Transportation and Utilities													
2002	22.7	22.6	22.4	22.7	22.8	21.1	22.0	22.8	23.1	23.3	23.3	23.3	22.8
2003	22.7	22.7	22.7	22.7	22.8	22.2	22.1	22.6	23.1	23.3	23.2	23.3	22.8
2004	23.3	23.2	23.3	23.1	23.2	22.6	22.5	23.0	23.3	23.5	23.4	23.5	23.2
2005	23.0	23.0	23.3	23.2	23.3	22.6	22.6	23.3	23.6	23.6	23.7	24.2	23.3
2006	23.9	23.9	23.8	23.8	24.0	23.6	23.6	24.0	24.3	24.2	24.4	25.0	24.0
2007	24.7	24.8	24.8	24.7	24.9	24.2	24.0	24.9	25.3	25.6	25.7	26.1	25.0
2008	25.4	25.2	25.3	24.9	25.1	23.9	23.6	24.2	24.3	24.1	24.0	24.2	24.5
2009	23.7	23.5	23.2	22.6	22.8	21.8	21.5	21.8	21.8	21.9	21.9	22.1	22.4
2010	21.6	21.5	21.5	21.6	21.7	21.2	21.4	21.8	22.1	22.3	22.3	22.6	21.8
2011	22.2	22.3	22.1	22.3	22.4	22.2	22.1	22.4	22.6	22.9	22.9	23.2	22.5
2012	23.0	23.1	23.2	23.1	23.3	23.0	22.9	23.3	23.4	23.8	23.8	24.0	23.3
2013	23.6	23.5	23.3	23.1	23.4	23.0	23.1	23.3	23.5	23.6	23.7	24.0	23.4
Information													
2002	16.8	17.1	17.2	17.0	17.0	16.8	17.0	16.8	16.6	16.4	16.8	16.8	16.9
2003	16.3	16.1	16.3	15.8	16.0	16.0	15.7	15.5	15.5	15.2	15.3	15.3	15.8
2004	14.9	15.2	15.0	14.7	15.0	14.9	14.7	14.7	14.3	14.9	15.1	15.0	14.9
2005	13.9	14.1	14.1	14.1	15.1	14.7	14.8	14.8	14.5	14.9	15.0	15.4	14.7
2006	14.5	15.4	15.9	15.0	15.6	17.4	15.1	15.9	17.1	14.9	15.9	16.9	15.8
2007	14.5	15.5	15.8	14.4	14.8	16.3	15.3	16.5	17.4	16.8	17.1	17.1	16.0
2008	15.6	16.3	16.1	15.1	15.4	16.2	16.0	15.8	16.5	16.3	16.3	15.6	15.9
2009	14.0	14.4	14.3	14.5	14.8	15.1	14.6	15.0	15.5	15.0	15.0	14.4	14.7
2010	14.2	14.6	14.7	15.3	14.7	15.0	13.8	14.1	14.1	13.7	14.0	14.3	14.4
2011	13.8	13.4	13.6	14.4	14.6	14.3	13.6	13.1	12.4	12.6	13.0	12.6	13.5
2012	13.2	13.7	14.3	13.9	13.6	13.1	13.3	14.0	13.2	13.0	14.0	13.1	13.5
2013	13.1	13.6	12.9	13.7	14.3	13.7	13.2	12.8	12.3	12.3	12.8	12.3	13.1

1. Employment by Industry: New Mexico, Selected Years, 2002–2013—*Continued*

(Numbers in thousands, not seasonally adjusted)

Industry and year	January	February	March	April	May	June	July	August	September	October	November	December	Annual average
Financial Activities													
2002	33.4	33.3	33.4	33.3	33.3	33.4	33.7	33.9	33.6	33.4	33.5	33.8	33.5
2003	33.3	33.4	33.4	33.5	33.8	34.0	34.2	34.5	34.2	34.1	34.0	34.4	33.9
2004	34.3	34.1	34.4	34.1	34.1	34.4	34.5	34.4	34.4	34.5	34.5	34.9	34.4
2005	34.7	34.6	34.6	34.7	34.8	35.1	35.2	35.1	35.0	34.9	35.0	35.6	34.9
2006	35.2	35.2	35.2	35.1	35.2	35.3	35.2	35.1	35.0	34.9	34.9	35.3	35.1
2007	34.9	35.0	35.3	35.1	35.2	35.4	35.5	35.5	35.2	35.2	35.1	35.3	35.2
2008	34.7	34.8	34.8	34.7	34.7	34.8	34.9	34.8	34.7	34.4	34.1	34.3	34.6
2009	33.7	33.5	33.2	33.8	33.9	33.7	33.7	33.6	33.5	33.9	33.5	33.8	33.7
2010	33.3	33.1	33.3	32.9	33.7	33.0	33.0	32.9	32.6	32.7	32.7	33.0	33.0
2011	32.5	32.4	32.4	32.6	32.5	32.5	32.7	32.6	32.5	32.5	32.5	32.7	32.5
2012	32.3	32.5	32.7	32.6	32.6	32.8	32.9	32.8	32.6	33.3	33.3	33.3	32.8
2013	33.0	32.9	32.9	33.0	33.1	33.2	33.4	33.4	33.3	33.8	34.3	34.7	33.4
Professional and Business Services													
2002	87.7	87.8	88.9	88.6	89.0	89.2	90.1	90.0	89.9	89.3	89.7	90.2	89.2
2003	87.7	88.6	88.8	88.6	88.6	88.4	88.5	88.8	88.2	88.6	88.2	88.7	88.5
2004	87.0	87.6	88.6	89.6	90.0	90.2	90.5	90.8	91.0	92.1	91.3	91.7	90.0
2005	90.2	90.5	90.7	92.8	92.4	93.3	93.2	93.6	94.0	93.5	94.3	94.3	92.7
2006	93.6	94.5	95.2	96.0	96.6	108.1	107.3	107.6	107.5	107.7	107.6	107.9	102.5
2007	106.3	107.6	108.3	108.3	108.7	109.3	109.5	110.3	109.2	108.6	108.4	108.2	108.6
2008	106.5	107.5	107.4	108.1	108.5	109.0	109.2	110.3	109.7	109.1	107.5	107.0	108.3
2009	104.1	103.4	102.4	102.4	102.0	102.4	102.8	103.5	102.7	101.8	101.1	101.1	102.5
2010	99.3	99.6	99.1	100.3	99.5	100.6	101.1	101.4	101.0	101.1	100.5	100.7	100.4
2011	98.8	101.0	99.6	100.3	99.9	100.4	101.4	101.2	101.5	99.7	99.0	98.6	100.1
2012	96.5	96.7	97.2	98.5	97.8	99.1	97.9	98.1	98.2	99.2	99.2	98.2	98.1
2013	98.0	98.3	98.1	99.2	99.0	98.7	99.5	99.6	98.4	98.2	97.9	97.0	98.5
Education and Health Services													
2002	91.7	92.6	93.5	94.6	94.6	91.3	90.4	91.7	95.9	96.4	97.6	97.3	94.0
2003	97.7	98.5	98.6	99.2	99.2	95.8	95.9	96.7	100.5	100.8	101.9	102.0	98.9
2004	101.6	102.4	102.4	103.1	103.0	99.7	99.0	100.0	103.5	104.1	105.4	104.8	102.4
2005	104.0	104.6	105.1	105.4	105.6	102.0	101.5	102.7	106.7	107.1	107.6	107.6	105.0
2006	106.9	107.4	108.4	108.3	108.7	105.6	104.5	105.2	109.4	109.7	110.8	110.6	108.0
2007	110.1	110.9	111.8	112.4	112.8	109.2	107.9	108.6	112.0	113.2	113.8	114.2	111.4
2008	112.6	114.1	114.8	115.8	116.3	113.0	111.9	113.2	116.9	117.8	118.3	118.7	115.3
2009	117.8	118.9	119.4	119.3	119.6	115.5	114.6	115.9	119.2	119.5	120.0	120.0	118.3
2010	119.4	119.9	120.4	120.1	120.1	117.8	117.0	117.0	120.3	120.9	121.4	121.6	119.7
2011	120.5	121.0	121.6	122.2	122.2	119.4	119.3	119.8	122.9	123.1	123.1	122.6	121.5
2012	121.8	122.8	122.7	122.9	122.9	120.5	120.1	120.2	123.3	124.5	124.8	125.0	122.6
2013	123.8	124.3	124.7	125.0	124.7	121.7	120.5	121.3	123.9	124.4	124.0	124.1	123.5
Leisure and Hospitality													
2002	75.7	76.3	78.0	79.6	81.3	83.6	83.6	83.9	81.9	79.1	78.4	79.1	80.0
2003	78.0	78.3	79.6	80.7	82.5	84.6	84.7	85.0	82.6	80.8	80.1	80.7	81.5
2004	79.1	79.7	81.1	82.8	83.8	85.3	85.4	85.3	83.4	82.0	80.8	81.8	82.5
2005	80.6	81.1	82.5	84.1	84.6	86.7	86.3	86.7	85.2	83.3	82.3	82.7	83.8
2006	82.6	83.0	84.6	86.3	87.6	89.3	89.9	89.7	88.4	86.3	86.3	86.0	86.7
2007	84.9	85.3	86.9	87.6	88.4	90.2	90.3	90.6	89.2	87.5	86.5	86.7	87.8
2008	84.9	85.1	86.5	87.2	87.9	89.0	89.1	89.4	87.8	85.7	84.3	83.9	86.7
2009	82.4	82.5	83.5	84.5	85.4	86.2	86.5	86.8	85.3	82.9	81.5	82.1	84.1
2010	80.7	81.1	82.4	83.8	84.6	86.2	86.1	86.3	84.9	83.3	81.8	82.4	83.6
2011	81.4	82.0	83.5	84.9	85.2	86.4	86.5	87.3	86.2	84.7	83.3	83.8	84.6
2012	82.0	82.6	84.0	85.4	86.6	88.4	88.3	89.4	87.3	87.9	86.1	86.4	86.2
2013	84.9	85.1	86.2	87.9	88.9	89.6	91.2	91.7	89.1	87.7	86.1	87.0	88.0
Other Services													
2002	26.6	27.0	27.2	27.3	27.6	29.9	30.0	29.7	27.7	27.7	27.6	27.6	28.0
2003	27.5	27.6	27.7	27.5	27.9	30.2	30.4	30.1	28.2	28.1	28.1	28.2	28.5
2004	27.9	28.1	28.2	28.1	28.4	30.7	30.9	30.6	28.5	28.4	28.3	28.3	28.9
2005	28.0	28.3	28.3	28.4	28.6	31.0	31.1	30.9	28.8	28.4	28.5	28.6	29.1
2006	27.9	28.4	28.6	28.7	29.0	31.4	31.4	31.0	29.2	29.0	29.0	28.7	29.4
2007	28.3	28.7	28.9	28.7	29.0	31.4	31.3	30.7	28.9	29.0	28.9	29.0	29.4
2008	28.7	29.2	29.3	29.3	29.7	32.3	32.1	31.7	29.7	29.9	29.5	28.8	30.0
2009	28.3	28.5	28.5	28.3	28.5	30.7	30.6	30.2	28.3	27.9	27.9	28.0	28.8
2010	27.5	27.7	27.7	27.8	27.8	29.9	30.2	30.3	27.9	27.5	27.1	27.0	28.2
2011	27.0	27.2	27.4	27.7	27.8	30.3	30.5	30.2	28.1	27.4	27.3	27.3	28.2
2012	27.3	27.6	27.8	27.9	28.0	30.3	30.0	29.8	28.0	28.5	28.1	28.0	28.4
2013	27.5	27.6	27.7	27.7	27.9	30.0	30.1	30.0	27.7	27.8	27.8	27.6	28.3
Government													
2002	185.1	190.7	192.1	192.1	193.1	190.3	184.5	185.8	193.8	193.9	194.7	195.2	190.9
2003	190.5	195.3	196.5	197.3	196.6	193.7	188.3	189.3	196.8	199.2	199.0	199.1	195.1
2004	193.0	199.5	200.7	200.8	200.3	196.6	190.7	192.0	199.4	202.2	202.8	202.4	198.4
2005	196.2	202.1	203.4	203.7	204.1	199.5	193.8	194.8	203.4	204.6	205.0	204.4	201.3
2006	198.8	205.6	206.3	205.4	205.9	191.6	185.5	186.9	195.5	196.7	197.0	196.9	197.7
2007	190.6	196.0	197.7	196.8	196.7	192.7	186.5	187.7	196.3	198.2	199.2	199.4	194.8
2008	193.2	198.7	199.7	199.5	200.4	195.7	189.3	190.5	199.8	201.4	201.9	201.6	197.6
2009	195.7	200.9	201.7	202.6	202.2	197.4	191.0	192.0	199.0	201.6	202.0	201.8	199.0
2010	194.4	200.6	203.3	205.1	206.8	200.3	193.0	192.7	197.2	201.3	200.9	200.1	199.6
2011	192.5	198.4	199.9	200.8	199.4	194.7	185.2	187.8	196.7	198.6	198.6	198.5	195.9
2012	191.7	197.3	198.5	197.0	197.1	191.1	182.5	186.4	195.7	198.8	199.1	198.4	194.5
2013	191.8	197.1	198.1	198.5	197.5	187.5	179.6	184.8	194.8	196.1	196.3	194.7	193.1

2. Average Weekly Hours by Selected Industry: New Mexico, 2009–2013

(Not seasonally adjusted)

Industry and year	January	February	March	April	May	June	July	August	September	October	November	December	Annual average
Total Private													
2009	35.7	35.5	35.0	34.8	34.9	35.2	35.2	35.4	34.7	34.9	35.4	34.7	35.1
2010	34.4	34.4	34.8	34.9	35.4	34.8	34.7	35.9	35.1	35.2	35.4	35.1	35.0
2011	35.7	35.0	34.9	34.9	35.2	35.2	35.2	35.1	34.8	35.7	34.9	34.1	35.1
2012	34.6	34.5	34.5	34.6	34.4	34.9	35.2	35.0	35.2	34.9	34.4	34.7	34.8
2013	34.0	34.3	34.3	34.7	34.9	35.4	34.9	35.2	35.2	35.0	34.9	35.0	34.8
Goods-Producing													
2009	42.5	39.8	38.3	38.4	39.6	39.2	39.3	39.8	38.0	39.2	39.7	39.2	39.4
2010	39.8	38.7	39.1	39.6	39.6	40.2	40.3	41.2	40.2	41.3	40.6	39.6	40.0
2011	40.6	40.4	40.3	41.2	41.2	41.9	41.8	42.4	41.9	42.1	42.3	41.3	41.5
2012	41.7	42.0	42.1	42.4	42.4	42.6	42.5	43.7	42.1	42.9	41.9	41.5	42.3
2013	40.8	41.9	41.6	43.1	43.4	43.3	43.0	45.0	43.4	44.1	43.9	41.9	43.0
Construction													
2009	39.5	39.0	38.3	38.4	39.2	39.1	39.2	39.6	36.9	39.2	40.1	38.8	39.0
2010	39.5	37.8	37.9	38.5	38.5	39.7	39.7	40.4	39.0	40.4	39.4	38.9	39.2
2011	40.2	38.8	39.1	40.1	39.6	40.5	40.4	41.0	40.4	40.7	40.8	39.0	40.1
2012	39.8	40.5	41.2	40.8	41.4	41.5	40.2	41.6	38.6	39.7	38.9	37.7	40.2
2013	37.0	38.9	38.4	39.6	40.5	40.7	39.0	41.4	39.3	40.9	41.1	39.0	39.7
Trade, Transportation, and Utilities													
2009	35.8	35.2	34.2	34.1	34.0	35.3	34.8	35.4	34.5	34.8	35.1	34.8	34.8
2010	34.3	34.3	34.3	34.4	35.3	34.9	35.1	35.3	34.7	34.5	34.8	35.0	34.7
2011	35.3	33.6	34.6	34.3	34.9	34.5	34.7	34.7	34.6	35.2	33.8	32.4	34.4
2012	32.1	32.8	33.1	33.6	33.1	34.4	34.8	34.7	35.2	35.1	34.7	35.2	34.1
2013	34.8	34.8	35.0	35.6	35.5	35.6	35.1	35.0	35.1	34.9	34.3	34.8	35.0
Professional and Business Services													
2009	35.9	36.5	35.8	36.1	36.0	36.7	35.6	35.9	35.7	36.0	36.8	36.0	36.1
2010	35.1	35.9	36.2	36.1	36.3	36.4	35.4	35.8	36.0	36.2	37.0	36.7	36.1
2011	36.8	36.6	36.6	37.0	37.1	36.8	36.2	36.0	36.0	37.1	36.4	35.8	36.5
2012	36.4	36.4	36.1	36.4	35.8	36.4	36.2	36.4	36.6	35.8	36.0	36.1	36.2
2013	34.8	35.0	35.2	35.7	35.7	36.2	35.6	36.1	36.1	36.0	35.8	36.9	35.8
Education and Health Services													
2009	36.0	37.1	36.5	35.7	35.7	36.2	36.5	36.2	36.0	35.7	36.3	35.7	36.1
2010	36.2	36.2	36.0	35.8	36.4	35.9	35.6	36.4	35.1	35.7	35.6	35.9	35.9
2011	36.6	35.2	34.7	34.9	35.0	34.9	34.9	34.8	34.0	35.0	35.2	34.1	34.9
2012	34.4	34.1	33.8	33.8	33.3	33.4	33.8	33.1	34.1	33.6	33.2	33.4	33.7
2013	33.2	33.0	32.8	32.7	32.9	33.2	32.8	32.9	33.2	32.7	33.4	33.4	33.0
Leisure and Hospitality													
2009	26.2	27.0	26.7	25.8	26.8	26.3	27.1	27.2	26.6	26.2	26.5	25.9	26.5
2010	25.8	25.7	26.5	26.7	27.5	26.8	27.5	28.2	27.4	26.7	26.6	25.4	26.7
2011	25.3	25.9	25.5	25.0	25.6	26.3	26.7	26.6	25.8	26.5	25.2	25.1	25.8
2012	25.8	25.9	26.3	25.9	26.6	26.7	27.5	27.0	27.1	26.7	26.3	26.8	26.6
2013	26.3	26.4	27.2	26.8	27.3	27.8	27.6	27.1	26.8	27.4	26.9	27.1	27.1

3. Average Hourly Earnings by Selected Industry: New Mexico, 2009–2013

(Dollars, not seasonally adjusted)

Industry and year	January	February	March	April	May	June	July	August	September	October	November	December	Annual average
Total Private													
2009	18.77	18.80	18.73	18.66	18.83	18.69	18.83	18.91	19.19	19.12	19.32	19.19	18.92
2010	19.51	19.76	19.72	19.59	19.46	19.38	19.25	19.68	19.49	19.40	19.81	19.79	19.57
2011	19.96	19.84	19.79	19.74	19.82	19.65	19.78	19.44	19.69	19.47	19.50	19.78	19.70
2012	19.88	19.73	19.74	19.93	19.79	19.56	19.77	19.74	19.92	19.76	19.95	20.06	19.82
2013	19.86	19.88	19.96	20.08	19.99	20.08	19.94	20.08	20.47	20.60	20.62	20.63	20.19
Goods-Producing													
2009	21.73	21.90	21.53	21.02	21.59	21.21	21.40	21.30	21.16	21.54	21.80	21.52	21.48
2010	21.85	21.60	21.25	21.18	21.29	21.28	21.27	21.37	20.99	21.53	21.80	22.53	21.49
2011	21.78	22.25	22.30	22.15	21.96	21.80	22.01	21.90	22.23	22.40	22.17	23.69	22.22
2012	23.46	23.20	23.35	23.15	22.80	22.39	22.47	22.90	22.89	22.80	22.81	23.46	22.97
2013	23.42	22.86	22.54	22.79	22.76	22.91	22.54	22.35	22.69	23.63	24.53	24.33	23.11
Construction													
2009	20.94	21.00	21.07	20.71	20.98	20.72	21.41	21.22	21.09	21.52	21.58	21.61	21.15
2010	22.04	21.59	21.34	21.00	20.97	20.98	21.06	21.37	21.33	21.94	21.72	22.43	21.48
2011	21.18	21.67	21.77	21.80	21.36	21.07	21.07	21.19	21.45	21.42	21.26	21.06	21.36
2012	20.56	20.22	20.31	20.00	19.90	19.73	19.93	20.66	21.03	21.36	20.81	21.21	20.47
2013	21.22	20.35	20.41	20.57	20.33	20.47	20.48	20.10	20.57	20.47	20.92	21.12	20.58
Trade, Transportation, and Utilities													
2009	17.22	17.85	17.24	17.10	17.31	17.46	17.93	18.07	18.46	17.70	18.07	17.75	17.68
2010	17.15	17.44	17.50	17.85	17.48	17.28	17.26	17.88	17.51	16.86	17.07	16.59	17.32
2011	16.86	17.01	16.61	16.33	16.65	16.67	17.05	16.47	16.73	16.64	17.02	16.47	16.71
2012	17.04	17.17	17.39	17.77	17.76	18.44	18.24	18.43	18.50	18.40	18.59	18.57	18.05
2013	18.47	18.60	18.87	18.88	18.55	18.64	18.50	18.32	18.86	18.75	18.78	18.75	18.66
Professional and Business Services													
2009	23.28	23.05	22.74	22.96	22.52	21.95	21.93	22.12	22.35	22.14	22.03	21.84	22.41
2010	21.95	22.72	23.12	21.91	22.18	22.16	22.69	22.60	22.18	21.52	23.61	23.71	22.53
2011	23.92	23.82	23.79	24.10	24.65	24.59	24.94	24.01	24.43	22.95	22.95	23.65	23.99
2012	24.37	24.06	24.19	24.50	24.09	23.99	24.33	24.08	24.73	24.30	24.74	25.33	24.39
2013	25.26	25.45	25.40	25.03	25.48	25.66	25.65	25.69	26.34	25.84	25.50	26.02	25.61
Education and Health Services													
2009	16.79	16.60	17.03	17.50	17.22	17.72	18.00	18.05	18.61	18.97	18.90	19.18	17.88
2010	21.04	21.06	21.04	20.99	20.88	21.20	20.88	21.13	20.70	20.54	20.91	20.52	20.91
2011	20.23	20.21	20.07	20.02	19.86	19.94	20.01	19.95	19.89	19.73	19.61	19.74	19.94
2012	19.37	19.03	19.04	18.90	19.62	18.73	19.32	18.95	18.92	18.67	18.94	18.70	19.02
2013	18.60	18.89	19.29	19.32	19.54	19.24	19.07	20.05	20.09	20.53	20.32	20.54	19.63
Leisure and Hospitality													
2009	11.53	11.55	11.60	11.19	11.75	11.61	11.62	11.48	12.19	11.98	12.24	12.00	11.73
2010	11.85	11.99	11.84	11.74	11.60	11.83	11.93	12.05	11.98	12.23	12.27	12.48	11.98
2011	12.28	11.97	12.26	12.09	11.92	11.80	11.83	11.52	11.60	11.73	11.70	11.61	11.85
2012	11.57	11.47	11.38	11.70	11.56	11.88	12.13	11.76	11.72	11.68	11.52	11.54	11.67
2013	11.57	11.67	11.59	11.58	11.63	11.87	12.06	12.13	11.87	11.62	11.69	11.97	11.78

4. Average Weekly Earnings by Selected Industry: New Mexico, 2009–2013

(Dollars, not seasonally adjusted)

Industry and year	January	February	March	April	May	June	July	August	September	October	November	December	Annual average
Total Private													
2009	670.09	667.40	655.55	649.37	657.17	657.89	662.82	669.41	665.89	667.29	683.93	665.89	664.09
2010	671.14	679.74	686.26	683.69	688.88	674.42	667.98	706.51	684.10	682.88	701.27	694.63	684.95
2011	712.57	694.40	690.67	688.93	697.66	691.68	696.26	682.34	685.21	695.08	680.55	674.50	691.47
2012	687.85	680.69	681.03	689.58	680.78	682.64	695.90	690.90	701.18	689.62	686.28	696.08	689.74
2013	675.24	681.88	684.63	696.78	697.65	710.83	695.91	706.82	720.54	721.00	719.64	722.05	702.61
Goods-Producing													
2009	923.53	871.62	824.60	807.17	854.96	831.43	841.02	847.74	804.08	844.37	865.46	843.58	846.31
2010	869.63	835.92	830.88	838.73	843.08	855.46	857.18	880.44	843.80	889.19	885.08	892.19	859.60
2011	884.27	898.90	898.69	912.58	904.75	913.42	920.02	928.56	931.44	943.04	937.79	978.40	922.13
2012	978.28	974.40	983.04	981.56	966.72	953.81	954.98	1,000.73	963.67	978.12	955.74	973.59	971.63
2013	955.54	957.83	937.66	982.25	987.78	992.00	969.22	1,005.75	984.75	1,042.08	1,076.87	1,019.43	993.73
Construction													
2009	827.13	819.00	806.98	795.26	822.42	810.15	839.27	840.31	778.22	843.58	865.36	838.47	824.85
2010	870.58	816.10	808.79	808.50	807.35	832.91	836.08	863.35	831.87	886.38	855.77	872.53	842.02
2011	851.44	840.80	851.21	874.18	845.86	853.34	851.23	868.79	866.58	871.79	867.41	821.34	856.54
2012	818.29	818.91	836.77	816.00	823.86	818.80	801.19	859.46	811.76	847.99	809.51	799.62	822.89
2013	785.14	791.62	783.74	814.57	823.37	833.13	798.72	832.14	808.40	837.22	859.81	823.68	817.03
Trade, Transportation, and Utilities													
2009	616.48	628.32	589.61	583.11	588.54	616.34	623.96	639.68	636.87	615.96	634.26	617.70	615.26
2010	588.25	598.19	600.25	614.04	617.04	603.07	605.83	631.16	607.60	581.67	594.04	580.65	601.00
2011	595.16	571.54	574.71	560.12	581.09	575.12	591.64	571.51	578.86	585.73	575.28	533.63	574.82
2012	546.98	563.18	575.61	597.07	587.86	634.34	634.75	639.52	651.20	645.84	645.07	653.66	615.51
2013	642.76	647.28	660.45	672.13	658.53	663.58	649.35	641.20	661.99	654.38	644.15	652.50	653.10
Professional and Business Services													
2009	835.75	841.33	814.09	828.86	810.72	805.57	780.71	794.11	797.90	797.04	810.70	786.24	809.00
2010	770.45	815.65	836.94	790.95	805.13	806.62	803.23	809.08	798.48	779.02	873.57	870.16	813.33
2011	880.26	871.81	870.71	891.70	914.52	904.91	902.83	864.36	879.48	851.45	835.38	846.67	875.64
2012	887.07	875.78	873.26	891.80	862.42	873.24	880.75	876.51	905.12	869.94	890.64	914.41	882.92
2013	879.05	890.75	894.08	893.57	909.64	928.89	913.14	927.41	950.87	930.24	912.90	960.14	916.84
Education and Health Services													
2009	604.44	615.86	621.60	624.75	614.75	641.46	657.00	653.41	669.96	677.23	686.07	684.73	645.47
2010	761.65	762.37	757.44	751.44	760.03	761.08	743.33	769.13	726.57	733.28	744.40	736.67	750.67
2011	740.42	711.39	696.43	698.70	695.10	695.91	698.35	694.26	676.26	690.55	690.27	673.13	695.91
2012	666.33	648.92	643.55	638.82	653.35	625.58	653.02	627.25	645.17	627.31	628.81	624.58	640.97
2013	617.52	623.37	632.71	631.76	642.87	638.77	625.50	659.65	666.99	671.33	678.69	686.04	647.79
Leisure and Hospitality													
2009	302.09	311.85	309.72	288.70	314.90	305.34	314.90	312.26	324.25	313.88	324.36	310.80	310.85
2010	305.73	308.14	313.76	313.46	319.00	317.04	328.08	339.81	328.25	326.54	326.38	316.99	319.87
2011	310.68	310.02	312.63	302.25	305.15	310.34	315.86	306.43	299.28	310.85	294.84	291.41	305.73
2012	298.51	297.07	299.29	303.03	307.50	317.20	333.58	317.52	317.61	311.86	302.98	309.27	310.42
2013	304.29	308.09	315.25	310.34	317.50	329.99	332.86	328.72	318.12	318.39	314.46	324.39	319.24

NEW YORK
At a Glance

Population:
2000 census: 18,977,026
2010 census: 19,378,102
2013 estimate: 19,651,127

Percent change in population:
2000–2010: 2.1%
2010–2013: 1.4%

Percent change in total nonfarm employment:
2000–2010: -0.9%
2010–2013: 4.1%

Industry with the largest growth in employment, 2000–2013 (thousands):
Education and Health Services, 409.4

Industry with the largest decline or smallest growth in employment, 2000–2013 (thousands):
Manufacturing, -294.4

Civilian labor force:
2000: 9,166,972
2010: 9,594,249
2013: 9,636,025

Unemployment rate and rank among states (lowest to highest):
2000: 4.5%, 38th
2010: 8.6%, 27th
2013: 7.7%, 36th

Over-the-year change in unemployment rates:
2010–2011: -0.4%
2011–2012: 0.3%
2012–2013: -0.8%

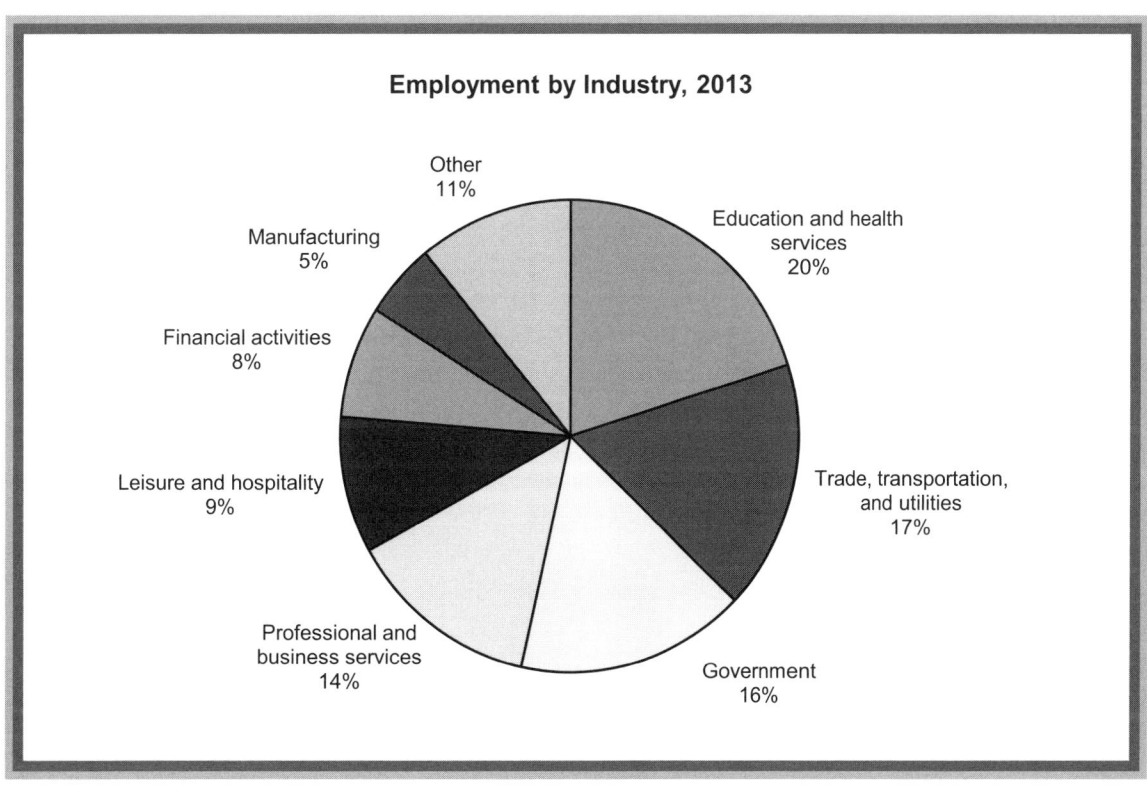

Employment by Industry, 2013

Other 11%
Manufacturing 5%
Financial activities 8%
Leisure and hospitality 9%
Professional and business services 14%
Government 16%
Trade, transportation, and utilities 17%
Education and health services 20%

1. Employment by Industry: New York, Selected Years, 2002–2013

(Numbers in thousands, not seasonally adjusted)

Industry and year	January	February	March	April	May	June	July	August	September	October	November	December	Annual average
Total Nonfarm													
2002	8,284.1	8,331.9	8,385.1	8,420.3	8,500.4	8,529.9	8,448.9	8,433.8	8,436.0	8,518.4	8,553.1	8,575.6	8,451.5
2003	8,256.8	8,289.9	8,333.7	8,357.6	8,436.5	8,469.1	8,377.1	8,355.2	8,389.5	8,473.5	8,513.5	8,540.5	8,399.4
2004	8,225.3	8,281.8	8,355.4	8,390.8	8,489.3	8,533.5	8,470.6	8,442.9	8,474.8	8,560.9	8,596.7	8,632.0	8,454.5
2005	8,321.9	8,361.8	8,406.9	8,502.0	8,556.7	8,607.0	8,530.6	8,516.2	8,558.3	8,603.8	8,656.2	8,699.5	8,526.7
2006	8,395.0	8,436.4	8,501.4	8,558.3	8,637.2	8,694.5	8,598.2	8,574.8	8,624.0	8,704.8	8,761.6	8,811.7	8,608.2
2007	8,522.7	8,561.3	8,617.7	8,653.4	8,750.7	8,815.6	8,722.2	8,692.1	8,729.0	8,832.3	8,878.0	8,911.3	8,723.9
2008	8,625.7	8,669.6	8,710.0	8,775.8	8,839.2	8,881.5	8,809.2	8,770.7	8,785.3	8,846.1	8,841.8	8,835.7	8,782.6
2009	8,495.7	8,512.6	8,514.9	8,520.7	8,583.7	8,592.6	8,547.7	8,499.6	8,494.5	8,574.8	8,596.3	8,613.7	8,545.6
2010	8,329.7	8,378.5	8,434.1	8,547.7	8,635.7	8,650.2	8,552.6	8,519.7	8,558.4	8,665.2	8,700.0	8,709.9	8,556.8
2011	8,443.1	8,505.4	8,549.8	8,665.6	8,711.1	8,741.7	8,689.8	8,660.1	8,716.3	8,787.0	8,825.3	8,842.5	8,678.1
2012	8,564.5	8,645.7	8,700.2	8,758.4	8,845.8	8,871.7	8,780.7	8,768.5	8,821.2	8,922.3	8,922.3	8,973.5	8,797.9
2013	8,660.8	8,736.6	8,794.4	8,889.2	8,960.6	8,980.9	8,922.9	8,893.4	8,935.8	9,022.5	9,059.4	9,045.3	8,908.5
Total Private													
2002	6,807.5	6,830.2	6,875.2	6,919.2	6,991.0	7,024.5	6,978.7	6,985.7	6,982.7	7,021.2	7,039.0	7,057.4	6,959.4
2003	6,778.0	6,787.5	6,827.1	6,855.7	6,931.5	6,965.8	6,923.9	6,922.9	6,938.4	6,981.4	7,005.9	7,027.5	6,912.1
2004	6,754.4	6,788.8	6,855.5	6,894.5	6,981.0	7,029.9	7,016.3	7,010.5	7,026.3	7,070.7	7,093.0	7,127.3	6,970.7
2005	6,842.7	6,864.3	6,907.8	6,996.9	7,047.5	7,098.4	7,069.0	7,075.0	7,097.1	7,111.0	7,151.3	7,188.9	7,037.5
2006	6,919.7	6,943.2	7,005.8	7,059.5	7,133.2	7,193.4	7,146.3	7,144.4	7,166.4	7,210.0	7,255.2	7,297.2	7,122.9
2007	7,033.2	7,052.3	7,106.6	7,144.1	7,233.0	7,298.6	7,255.6	7,241.8	7,254.1	7,319.5	7,355.2	7,380.1	7,222.8
2008	7,130.3	7,153.7	7,190.2	7,246.0	7,305.6	7,348.1	7,309.9	7,299.6	7,297.6	7,319.9	7,306.7	7,296.6	7,267.0
2009	6,988.6	6,981.1	6,980.5	6,982.8	7,041.1	7,061.6	7,016.5	6,995.9	7,019.2	7,050.8	7,064.0	7,079.7	7,021.8
2010	6,828.8	6,853.9	6,904.4	7,011.6	7,058.1	7,096.1	7,080.0	7,078.8	7,095.3	7,158.5	7,184.2	7,198.0	7,045.6
2011	6,967.4	7,007.9	7,049.7	7,158.7	7,209.3	7,252.1	7,236.7	7,218.3	7,266.6	7,299.3	7,332.6	7,351.7	7,195.9
2012	7,119.9	7,168.1	7,219.7	7,278.2	7,361.7	7,400.9	7,355.5	7,361.0	7,394.1	7,455.6	7,455.0	7,500.4	7,339.2
2013	7,234.4	7,279.2	7,334.3	7,428.5	7,493.8	7,527.2	7,508.5	7,495.2	7,524.9	7,572.1	7,595.5	7,578.6	7,464.4
Goods-Producing													
2002	954.6	951.1	959.0	970.9	986.0	995.9	989.6	998.5	992.4	988.7	980.3	965.3	977.7
2003	917.3	910.3	919.6	926.6	943.6	954.1	946.7	954.1	951.7	945.8	939.9	926.8	936.4
2004	882.3	881.6	896.3	908.1	927.3	941.5	940.3	948.4	946.0	942.9	938.3	927.4	923.4
2005	879.8	873.7	881.3	900.1	914.8	928.2	926.5	934.2	931.1	923.5	922.8	910.6	910.6
2006	874.0	870.5	879.6	899.1	915.6	930.9	925.6	932.8	929.1	927.5	921.7	913.3	910.0
2007	877.1	867.8	877.5	894.1	915.9	931.2	928.8	933.1	928.8	929.1	924.1	912.2	910.0
2008	876.4	869.9	876.3	891.0	908.4	919.2	920.7	924.7	916.4	910.0	892.8	868.0	897.8
2009	815.2	801.0	798.7	803.1	812.8	817.7	818.2	817.8	810.0	803.9	793.4	777.9	805.8
2010	737.3	729.9	739.5	762.1	773.0	783.6	789.2	793.9	789.3	786.2	779.9	764.4	769.0
2011	729.1	726.6	736.4	757.7	774.0	787.9	796.5	802.1	796.5	793.4	787.9	776.2	772.0
2012	746.5	743.1	752.7	767.4	780.2	794.3	797.9	801.1	796.6	796.1	787.2	783.8	778.9
2013	754.9	749.5	757.5	775.8	791.4	800.3	805.0	809.5	804.1	799.1	790.7	775.5	784.4
Service-Providing													
2002	7,329.5	7,380.8	7,426.1	7,449.4	7,514.4	7,534.0	7,459.3	7,435.3	7,443.6	7,529.7	7,572.8	7,610.3	7,473.8
2003	7,339.5	7,379.6	7,414.1	7,431.0	7,492.9	7,515.0	7,430.4	7,401.1	7,437.8	7,527.7	7,573.6	7,613.7	7,463.0
2004	7,343.0	7,400.2	7,459.1	7,482.7	7,562.0	7,592.0	7,530.3	7,494.5	7,528.8	7,618.0	7,658.4	7,704.6	7,531.1
2005	7,442.1	7,488.1	7,525.6	7,601.9	7,641.9	7,678.8	7,604.1	7,582.0	7,627.2	7,680.3	7,733.4	7,788.9	7,616.2
2006	7,521.0	7,565.9	7,621.8	7,659.2	7,721.6	7,763.6	7,672.6	7,642.0	7,694.9	7,777.3	7,839.9	7,898.4	7,698.2
2007	7,645.6	7,693.5	7,740.2	7,759.3	7,834.8	7,884.4	7,793.4	7,759.0	7,800.2	7,903.2	7,953.9	7,999.1	7,813.9
2008	7,749.3	7,799.7	7,833.7	7,884.8	7,930.8	7,962.3	7,888.5	7,846.0	7,868.9	7,936.1	7,949.0	7,967.7	7,884.7
2009	7,680.5	7,711.6	7,716.2	7,717.6	7,770.9	7,774.9	7,729.5	7,681.8	7,684.5	7,770.9	7,802.9	7,835.8	7,739.8
2010	7,592.4	7,648.6	7,694.6	7,785.6	7,862.7	7,866.6	7,763.4	7,725.8	7,769.1	7,879.0	7,920.1	7,945.5	7,787.8
2011	7,714.0	7,778.8	7,813.4	7,907.9	7,937.1	7,953.8	7,893.3	7,858.0	7,919.8	7,993.6	8,037.4	8,066.3	7,906.1
2012	7,818.0	7,902.6	7,947.5	7,991.0	8,065.6	8,077.4	7,982.8	7,967.4	8,024.6	8,126.2	8,135.1	8,189.7	8,019.0
2013	7,905.9	7,987.1	8,036.9	8,113.4	8,169.2	8,180.6	8,117.9	8,083.9	8,131.7	8,223.4	8,268.7	8,269.8	8,124.0
Mining and Logging													
2002	4.4	4.4	4.6	5.0	5.4	5.4	5.5	5.5	5.4	5.4	5.3	4.9	5.1
2003	4.4	4.4	4.6	5.0	5.5	5.6	5.7	5.8	5.8	5.7	5.6	5.4	5.3
2004	4.7	4.6	5.0	5.4	5.8	6.0	6.1	6.2	6.2	6.1	6.0	5.7	5.7
2005	4.9	4.8	5.0	5.7	6.0	6.3	6.4	6.5	6.4	6.4	6.2	5.9	5.9
2006	5.0	5.1	5.4	6.1	6.4	6.6	6.7	6.7	6.7	6.8	6.6	6.1	6.2
2007	5.2	5.3	5.5	5.9	6.4	6.7	6.8	6.7	6.7	6.7	6.6	6.2	6.2
2008	5.3	5.2	5.5	6.0	6.6	6.9	7.1	7.0	6.9	6.8	6.3	5.8	6.3
2009	4.8	4.8	4.9	5.2	5.6	5.8	5.9	5.8	5.7	5.7	5.6	5.2	5.4
2010	4.4	4.5	4.7	5.3	5.6	5.7	5.7	5.8	5.8	5.6	5.5	5.1	5.3
2011	4.3	4.4	4.5	5.1	5.4	5.6	5.7	5.8	5.8	5.8	5.6	5.4	5.3
2012	4.5	4.6	4.9	5.3	5.5	5.6	5.7	5.6	5.6	5.6	5.3	5.0	5.3
2013	4.3	4.3	4.5	5.0	5.3	5.3	5.3	5.3	5.4	5.4	5.2	4.9	5.0
Construction													
2002	293.8	291.5	297.1	311.3	323.9	332.0	338.4	342.7	338.5	337.4	332.7	323.2	321.9
2003	291.4	286.3	293.2	307.3	323.0	331.2	337.9	340.1	336.9	333.9	328.9	319.6	319.1
2004	285.6	283.7	293.6	309.8	325.3	334.6	341.6	344.5	342.4	340.4	336.9	327.9	322.2
2005	295.0	290.1	294.8	314.6	328.6	337.8	341.7	346.8	345.1	339.4	340.0	329.1	325.3
2006	303.3	300.3	308.0	326.3	340.6	350.8	353.1	358.6	356.2	356.0	351.1	344.9	337.4
2007	318.8	310.5	318.8	336.9	355.9	367.7	370.5	374.2	371.7	373.1	369.5	358.8	352.2
2008	334.9	330.1	335.9	351.3	366.3	373.1	379.8	383.3	377.3	374.5	363.6	345.8	359.7
2009	310.8	305.3	307.9	318.0	329.7	335.7	342.3	342.6	335.5	331.3	324.5	310.5	324.5
2010	280.1	273.2	281.2	302.4	310.7	317.5	325.5	329.4	324.2	320.1	315.1	300.3	306.6
2011	273.4	270.6	278.9	296.0	310.0	319.5	329.7	333.6	328.7	325.8	321.2	310.1	308.1
2012	288.0	283.9	291.6	305.4	315.0	324.9	330.4	333.1	328.7	328.8	323.4	319.9	314.4
2013	299.0	294.3	300.6	316.2	329.9	335.9	342.4	345.7	341.5	337.6	333.4	317.8	324.5

1. Employment by Industry: New York, Selected Years, 2002–2013—*Continued*

(Numbers in thousands, not seasonally adjusted)

Industry and year	January	February	March	April	May	June	July	August	September	October	November	December	Annual average
Manufacturing													
2002	656.4	655.2	657.3	654.6	656.7	658.5	645.7	650.3	648.5	645.9	642.3	637.2	650.7
2003	621.5	619.6	621.8	614.3	615.1	617.3	603.1	608.2	609.0	606.2	605.4	601.8	611.9
2004	592.0	593.3	597.7	592.9	596.2	600.9	592.6	597.7	597.4	596.4	595.4	593.8	595.5
2005	579.9	578.8	581.5	579.8	580.2	584.1	578.4	580.9	579.6	577.7	576.6	575.6	579.4
2006	565.7	565.1	566.2	566.7	568.6	573.5	565.8	567.5	566.2	564.7	564.0	562.3	566.4
2007	553.1	552.0	553.2	551.3	553.6	556.8	551.5	552.2	550.4	549.3	548.0	547.2	551.6
2008	536.2	534.6	534.9	533.7	535.5	539.2	533.8	534.4	532.2	528.7	522.9	516.4	531.9
2009	499.6	490.9	485.9	479.9	477.5	476.2	470.0	469.4	468.8	466.9	463.3	462.0	475.9
2010	452.8	452.2	453.6	454.4	456.7	460.4	458.0	458.7	459.3	460.5	459.3	459.0	457.1
2011	451.4	451.6	453.0	456.6	458.6	462.8	461.1	462.7	462.0	461.8	461.1	460.7	458.6
2012	454.0	454.6	456.2	456.7	459.7	463.8	461.8	462.4	462.3	461.7	458.5	458.9	459.2
2013	451.6	450.9	452.4	454.6	456.2	459.1	457.3	458.5	457.2	456.1	452.1	452.8	454.9
Trade, Transportation, and Utilities													
2002	1,466.6	1,446.3	1,455.0	1,456.3	1,471.3	1,488.4	1,465.5	1,466.6	1,480.3	1,490.4	1,514.1	1,540.9	1,478.5
2003	1,463.8	1,445.0	1,448.8	1,448.4	1,464.7	1,479.9	1,459.5	1,461.9	1,473.9	1,490.9	1,514.6	1,538.0	1,474.1
2004	1,456.4	1,442.5	1,450.6	1,452.4	1,475.5	1,493.5	1,480.6	1,480.8	1,492.5	1,511.5	1,535.4	1,561.3	1,486.1
2005	1,479.6	1,462.4	1,467.4	1,478.4	1,491.9	1,508.5	1,491.6	1,493.4	1,502.7	1,509.8	1,536.7	1,567.9	1,499.2
2006	1,492.3	1,468.9	1,476.9	1,482.4	1,498.0	1,518.9	1,497.1	1,495.5	1,505.6	1,523.1	1,555.5	1,582.2	1,508.0
2007	1,512.1	1,488.4	1,495.3	1,493.6	1,516.6	1,537.3	1,516.4	1,509.1	1,520.8	1,534.6	1,568.7	1,592.4	1,523.8
2008	1,525.0	1,501.0	1,506.3	1,507.6	1,519.6	1,535.6	1,514.0	1,511.2	1,520.1	1,524.8	1,540.1	1,555.7	1,521.8
2009	1,470.3	1,446.6	1,440.3	1,431.9	1,449.6	1,464.0	1,441.2	1,439.8	1,449.5	1,458.5	1,482.8	1,503.3	1,456.5
2010	1,436.6	1,417.6	1,424.6	1,441.1	1,454.4	1,473.7	1,455.5	1,456.4	1,464.1	1,481.6	1,506.6	1,526.3	1,461.5
2011	1,466.0	1,448.7	1,451.3	1,463.1	1,475.6	1,495.0	1,475.6	1,479.7	1,489.6	1,502.0	1,532.6	1,555.7	1,486.2
2012	1,495.5	1,475.4	1,480.1	1,482.7	1,504.3	1,521.5	1,493.2	1,498.2	1,509.4	1,524.4	1,553.8	1,575.5	1,509.5
2013	1,502.9	1,479.8	1,490.5	1,500.5	1,516.2	1,536.4	1,520.8	1,517.8	1,531.3	1,538.7	1,575.1	1,597.6	1,525.6
Wholesale Trade													
2002	352.1	352.3	353.3	352.8	354.6	356.1	353.0	354.8	354.2	356.5	357.2	358.1	354.6
2003	349.8	349.6	351.0	349.8	352.7	354.7	353.6	353.8	353.3	354.0	355.4	356.7	352.9
2004	347.1	347.5	349.6	350.5	352.7	355.1	355.2	354.7	353.5	355.9	356.5	358.3	353.1
2005	347.3	348.1	349.1	350.5	351.9	353.6	353.6	354.5	354.1	354.3	355.4	357.7	352.5
2006	348.0	347.9	349.9	351.2	353.0	356.0	354.5	355.2	354.1	355.2	355.6	358.9	353.3
2007	352.0	351.8	353.1	353.0	354.9	358.0	356.9	355.9	354.9	357.4	357.2	358.7	355.3
2008	351.3	351.0	351.4	351.3	352.0	353.8	352.3	351.2	350.0	348.9	347.2	346.0	350.5
2009	337.4	334.1	332.3	328.9	329.0	329.7	326.7	326.2	324.8	324.6	324.5	325.3	328.6
2010	318.6	318.1	319.9	322.0	323.9	326.5	327.2	327.1	326.5	328.2	329.2	330.3	324.8
2011	324.6	324.1	325.7	328.3	330.1	332.6	332.8	333.2	331.9	332.7	332.7	334.3	330.3
2012	329.4	330.1	331.3	332.5	334.0	336.4	335.4	334.9	333.1	335.2	334.6	336.6	333.6
2013	330.9	331.0	331.8	333.6	335.4	338.7	338.6	338.3	337.2	334.4	336.9	339.1	335.5
Retail Trade													
2002	850.1	830.7	837.7	837.8	847.9	862.1	854.2	856.8	857.1	862.0	886.5	912.0	857.9
2003	848.6	830.9	832.1	836.0	846.6	859.1	851.2	854.4	854.0	867.1	890.1	911.4	856.8
2004	849.0	835.3	840.0	841.0	856.8	870.7	867.6	869.1	870.1	881.6	905.6	928.9	868.0
2005	868.4	850.7	853.8	862.2	870.8	882.8	878.3	880.3	876.0	883.8	907.7	932.0	878.9
2006	875.6	853.2	857.8	862.4	871.5	886.0	881.3	880.5	875.8	891.8	921.1	940.4	883.2
2007	889.1	866.1	870.7	869.9	885.2	899.7	894.9	891.6	887.9	897.6	930.6	948.7	894.3
2008	899.6	876.8	880.4	879.7	888.2	899.9	896.0	895.4	891.0	897.7	914.2	926.3	895.4
2009	865.2	846.3	843.2	839.4	854.0	867.0	860.9	861.7	860.2	868.8	891.3	906.8	863.7
2010	859.5	843.2	847.4	856.5	866.0	881.0	877.3	879.1	872.2	886.6	908.4	923.3	875.0
2011	877.6	862.9	863.1	873.1	881.3	895.5	892.5	896.8	892.1	904.2	931.8	948.9	893.3
2012	905.2	885.2	887.5	890.9	904.7	916.5	911.8	912.5	908.6	921.1	949.5	961.7	912.9
2013	908.6	892.4	896.1	903.0	914.7	929.5	928.0	929.0	925.1	936.0	963.0	979.5	925.4
Transportation and Utilities													
2002	264.4	263.3	264.0	265.7	268.8	270.2	258.3	255.0	269.0	271.9	270.4	270.8	266.0
2003	265.4	264.5	265.7	262.6	265.4	266.1	254.7	253.7	266.6	269.8	269.1	269.9	264.5
2004	260.3	259.7	261.0	260.9	266.0	267.7	257.8	257.0	268.9	274.0	273.3	274.1	265.1
2005	263.9	263.6	264.5	265.7	269.2	272.1	259.7	258.6	272.6	271.7	273.6	278.2	267.8
2006	268.7	267.8	269.2	268.8	273.5	276.9	261.3	259.8	275.7	276.1	277.8	282.9	271.5
2007	271.0	270.5	271.5	270.7	276.5	279.6	264.6	261.6	278.0	279.6	280.9	285.0	274.1
2008	274.1	273.2	274.5	276.6	279.4	281.9	265.7	264.6	279.1	278.2	278.7	283.4	275.8
2009	267.7	266.2	264.8	263.6	266.6	267.3	253.6	251.9	264.5	265.1	267.0	271.2	264.1
2010	258.5	256.3	257.3	262.6	264.5	266.2	251.0	250.2	265.4	266.8	269.0	272.7	261.7
2011	263.8	261.7	262.5	261.7	264.2	266.9	250.3	249.7	265.6	265.1	268.1	272.5	262.7
2012	260.9	260.1	261.3	259.3	265.6	268.6	246.0	250.8	267.7	268.1	269.7	277.2	262.9
2013	263.4	256.4	262.6	263.9	266.1	268.2	254.2	250.5	269.0	268.3	275.2	279.0	264.7
Information													
2002	300.0	303.9	299.7	299.1	306.0	303.5	293.1	295.4	289.9	291.1	293.3	291.8	297.2
2003	278.2	282.3	279.5	276.5	281.9	278.2	273.8	277.6	274.1	276.5	280.5	279.3	278.2
2004	269.6	271.2	272.7	271.6	272.1	271.7	271.3	273.0	273.2	272.5	275.3	273.4	272.3
2005	267.1	269.3	270.2	270.6	272.4	276.6	273.9	274.9	274.6	275.5	276.7	280.0	273.5
2006	271.3	271.4	272.8	270.0	272.1	274.7	272.4	272.8	270.7	268.8	270.8	272.5	271.7
2007	265.6	267.2	267.6	267.3	270.0	272.6	271.2	271.8	270.4	268.9	271.2	272.5	269.7
2008	265.8	267.7	268.2	266.8	269.6	272.9	270.8	271.6	271.1	269.9	270.8	272.1	269.8
2009	263.3	261.2	261.8	260.5	260.9	260.8	259.5	258.4	257.1	256.1	256.6	257.3	259.5
2010	249.2	249.4	250.8	250.1	251.6	253.2	254.5	254.9	253.8	255.7	256.6	258.6	253.2
2011	251.4	252.1	253.5	255.8	256.3	257.7	258.7	243.4	258.2	257.3	258.3	259.5	255.2
2012	254.5	255.4	256.1	258.3	260.6	262.3	260.1	259.9	258.7	260.2	261.3	261.6	259.1
2013	253.6	255.1	256.8	258.4	259.9	262.2	262.4	263.4	262.4	263.6	263.7	263.0	260.4

1. Employment by Industry: New York, Selected Years, 2002–2013—*Continued*

(Numbers in thousands, not seasonally adjusted)

Industry and year	January	February	March	April	May	June	July	August	September	October	November	December	Annual average
Financial Activities													
2002	705.5	705.5	705.4	703.4	703.7	710.2	710.5	709.5	699.6	700.3	700.7	703.4	704.8
2003	692.2	690.1	689.7	689.9	693.5	701.6	704.7	704.0	696.7	695.6	696.8	702.8	696.5
2004	692.0	692.7	695.5	694.2	695.8	705.1	711.5	710.5	702.5	705.0	705.6	712.5	701.9
2005	701.0	701.2	703.4	707.1	707.2	717.6	723.6	723.6	716.3	716.4	718.2	723.8	713.3
2006	712.8	714.7	717.8	719.4	722.6	732.5	736.7	737.3	728.6	727.7	729.8	735.1	726.3
2007	723.0	724.4	726.4	725.2	726.0	737.9	741.3	739.0	729.3	731.9	733.3	735.8	731.1
2008	723.3	723.0	723.6	720.9	720.9	728.5	730.6	729.6	715.6	711.5	708.5	708.7	720.4
2009	692.9	687.5	683.9	677.7	676.3	678.8	678.9	675.7	669.2	667.2	665.8	668.3	676.9
2010	657.1	657.9	659.8	664.8	666.0	675.3	678.7	678.7	671.5	672.2	673.9	678.4	669.5
2011	672.4	673.3	674.6	677.4	678.6	688.6	693.3	694.5	684.9	683.8	684.0	686.8	682.7
2012	677.5	679.4	679.3	679.1	679.5	689.1	691.7	690.8	680.8	683.4	683.2	688.0	683.5
2013	672.5	674.2	675.1	677.1	677.5	687.6	692.4	690.9	681.3	682.5	681.2	682.9	681.3
Professional and Business Services													
2002	1,033.7	1,037.6	1,043.2	1,052.7	1,056.7	1,067.0	1,063.8	1,064.1	1,058.6	1,062.2	1,063.4	1,063.9	1,055.6
2003	1,020.0	1,019.6	1,029.2	1,039.2	1,042.1	1,053.3	1,049.5	1,049.5	1,046.7	1,052.8	1,055.3	1,059.8	1,043.1
2004	1,017.2	1,025.1	1,037.6	1,051.8	1,057.7	1,072.9	1,070.6	1,070.5	1,065.4	1,069.8	1,074.1	1,081.8	1,057.9
2005	1,044.4	1,046.0	1,052.0	1,075.3	1,076.4	1,091.2	1,094.3	1,096.6	1,095.5	1,094.9	1,101.9	1,108.7	1,081.4
2006	1,068.9	1,073.4	1,086.7	1,098.1	1,101.8	1,119.9	1,117.4	1,121.0	1,114.7	1,119.1	1,127.7	1,135.3	1,107.0
2007	1,097.5	1,102.8	1,114.5	1,122.6	1,129.8	1,150.0	1,149.9	1,152.7	1,140.2	1,152.6	1,156.8	1,162.5	1,136.0
2008	1,126.6	1,133.2	1,139.8	1,154.6	1,155.5	1,170.3	1,171.6	1,169.2	1,156.1	1,154.5	1,149.1	1,144.7	1,152.1
2009	1,096.2	1,091.9	1,091.1	1,091.7	1,090.1	1,100.4	1,096.1	1,091.0	1,084.6	1,088.0	1,090.6	1,092.7	1,092.0
2010	1,059.8	1,065.6	1,073.1	1,096.6	1,097.1	1,111.6	1,116.0	1,115.2	1,105.5	1,117.2	1,119.4	1,120.6	1,099.8
2011	1,092.6	1,098.4	1,106.8	1,130.5	1,130.9	1,149.3	1,155.1	1,153.7	1,149.4	1,150.5	1,157.1	1,157.2	1,136.0
2012	1,127.4	1,133.4	1,144.3	1,160.2	1,165.5	1,183.8	1,184.1	1,186.8	1,179.3	1,193.2	1,196.4	1,198.8	1,171.1
2013	1,161.7	1,168.1	1,176.6	1,196.1	1,200.7	1,216.8	1,222.3	1,221.0	1,211.8	1,218.9	1,218.5	1,213.4	1,202.2
Education and Health Services													
2002	1,422.5	1,450.6	1,464.0	1,466.6	1,465.0	1,435.3	1,424.0	1,418.1	1,459.2	1,492.4	1,500.6	1,502.1	1,458.4
2003	1,463.2	1,491.1	1,502.0	1,500.7	1,497.1	1,467.9	1,446.4	1,437.0	1,481.6	1,515.1	1,523.8	1,524.2	1,487.5
2004	1,483.2	1,515.6	1,528.4	1,525.2	1,525.2	1,490.7	1,472.7	1,461.9	1,503.9	1,542.8	1,550.4	1,553.3	1,512.8
2005	1,504.1	1,537.4	1,546.4	1,551.7	1,542.6	1,507.2	1,486.5	1,480.1	1,529.5	1,562.8	1,573.2	1,574.9	1,533.0
2006	1,530.2	1,565.2	1,576.0	1,578.4	1,573.6	1,538.2	1,510.6	1,502.2	1,560.4	1,597.3	1,607.4	1,613.1	1,562.7
2007	1,561.0	1,594.2	1,605.2	1,602.6	1,595.2	1,562.0	1,534.4	1,526.8	1,584.0	1,626.2	1,632.9	1,636.5	1,588.4
2008	1,589.2	1,626.4	1,633.2	1,636.6	1,627.8	1,595.9	1,565.2	1,560.2	1,616.3	1,654.5	1,666.9	1,673.1	1,620.4
2009	1,626.8	1,664.0	1,669.4	1,668.0	1,659.5	1,626.8	1,598.6	1,592.8	1,646.6	1,688.7	1,700.1	1,706.7	1,654.0
2010	1,661.5	1,698.8	1,709.8	1,716.3	1,704.0	1,663.5	1,633.7	1,627.8	1,684.3	1,726.1	1,740.2	1,743.3	1,692.4
2011	1,691.2	1,733.7	1,740.1	1,753.8	1,742.0	1,691.9	1,664.4	1,656.6	1,720.9	1,754.1	1,763.8	1,768.6	1,723.4
2012	1,715.5	1,761.4	1,772.2	1,774.5	1,772.1	1,718.4	1,690.7	1,686.3	1,758.6	1,793.0	1,793.3	1,805.2	1,753.4
2013	1,750.6	1,800.4	1,811.3	1,822.8	1,809.1	1,752.7	1,730.4	1,722.9	1,791.2	1,834.8	1,847.1	1,840.6	1,792.8
Leisure and Hospitality													
2002	584.3	592.8	603.8	624.0	653.4	674.0	683.3	686.0	656.9	646.2	635.2	638.0	639.8
2003	598.7	603.4	610.1	625.7	657.0	678.0	692.4	690.0	666.4	654.7	644.4	644.8	647.1
2004	608.7	613.3	624.3	640.0	672.5	697.8	714.6	712.7	690.3	670.5	657.8	659.5	663.5
2005	617.5	623.5	634.1	656.6	683.3	708.6	714.9	716.8	692.0	671.8	664.0	663.3	670.5
2006	620.7	628.4	641.7	656.6	690.7	717.5	728.6	727.1	700.3	686.7	681.6	682.4	680.2
2007	640.9	649.8	659.8	677.3	713.5	739.7	750.3	748.2	719.4	711.0	702.0	700.9	701.1
2008	662.3	669.8	678.2	701.8	733.7	754.4	767.4	765.0	734.9	724.7	708.8	704.8	717.2
2009	662.2	666.1	671.2	686.6	725.2	745.5	757.8	756.5	739.7	723.5	709.1	707.3	712.6
2010	670.4	677.4	687.3	717.8	746.5	768.6	784.3	784.9	762.6	751.1	739.1	736.9	735.6
2011	701.2	709.8	719.9	747.9	776.5	804.9	817.7	815.1	792.9	782.9	773.1	770.4	767.7
2012	731.7	747.2	759.1	778.5	817.8	846.5	856.0	858.1	830.5	821.6	797.7	803.3	804.0
2013	761.1	773.2	786.0	813.9	851.9	881.6	887.6	882.8	858.0	845.6	830.5	818.1	832.5
Other Services													
2002	340.3	342.4	345.1	346.2	348.9	350.2	348.9	347.5	345.8	349.9	351.4	352.0	347.4
2003	344.6	345.7	348.2	348.7	351.6	352.8	350.9	348.8	347.3	350.0	350.6	351.8	349.3
2004	345.0	346.8	350.1	351.2	354.9	356.7	354.7	352.7	352.5	355.7	356.1	358.1	352.9
2005	349.2	350.8	353.0	357.4	358.9	360.5	357.7	355.4	355.4	356.3	357.8	359.7	356.0
2006	349.5	350.7	354.3	355.5	358.8	360.8	357.9	355.7	357.0	359.8	360.7	363.3	357.0
2007	356.0	357.7	360.3	361.4	366.0	367.9	363.3	361.1	361.2	365.2	366.2	367.3	362.8
2008	361.7	362.7	364.6	366.7	370.1	371.3	369.6	368.1	367.1	370.0	369.7	369.5	367.6
2009	361.7	362.8	364.1	363.3	366.7	367.6	366.2	363.9	362.5	364.9	365.6	366.2	364.6
2010	356.9	357.3	359.5	362.8	365.5	366.6	368.1	367.0	364.2	368.4	368.5	369.5	364.5
2011	363.5	365.3	367.1	372.5	375.4	376.8	375.4	373.2	374.2	375.3	375.8	377.3	372.7
2012	371.3	372.8	375.9	377.5	381.7	385.0	381.8	379.8	380.2	383.7	382.1	384.2	379.7
2013	377.1	378.9	380.5	383.9	387.1	389.6	387.6	386.9	384.8	388.9	388.7	387.5	385.1
Government													
2002	1,476.6	1,501.7	1,509.9	1,501.1	1,509.4	1,505.4	1,470.2	1,448.1	1,453.3	1,497.2	1,514.1	1,518.2	1,492.1
2003	1,478.8	1,502.4	1,506.6	1,501.9	1,505.0	1,503.3	1,453.2	1,432.3	1,451.1	1,492.1	1,507.6	1,513.0	1,487.3
2004	1,470.9	1,493.0	1,499.9	1,496.3	1,508.3	1,503.6	1,454.3	1,432.4	1,448.5	1,490.2	1,503.7	1,504.7	1,483.8
2005	1,479.2	1,497.5	1,499.1	1,505.1	1,509.2	1,508.6	1,461.6	1,441.2	1,461.2	1,492.8	1,504.9	1,510.6	1,489.3
2006	1,475.3	1,493.2	1,495.6	1,498.8	1,504.0	1,501.1	1,451.9	1,430.4	1,457.6	1,494.8	1,506.4	1,514.5	1,485.3
2007	1,489.5	1,509.0	1,511.1	1,509.3	1,517.7	1,517.0	1,466.6	1,450.3	1,474.9	1,512.8	1,522.8	1,531.2	1,501.0
2008	1,495.4	1,515.9	1,519.8	1,529.8	1,533.6	1,533.4	1,499.3	1,471.1	1,487.7	1,526.2	1,535.1	1,539.1	1,515.5
2009	1,507.1	1,531.5	1,534.4	1,537.9	1,542.6	1,531.0	1,531.2	1,503.7	1,475.3	1,524.0	1,532.3	1,534.0	1,523.8
2010	1,500.9	1,524.6	1,529.7	1,536.1	1,577.6	1,554.1	1,472.6	1,440.9	1,463.1	1,506.7	1,515.8	1,511.9	1,511.2
2011	1,475.7	1,497.5	1,500.1	1,506.9	1,501.8	1,489.6	1,453.1	1,441.8	1,449.7	1,487.7	1,492.7	1,490.8	1,482.3
2012	1,444.6	1,477.6	1,480.5	1,480.2	1,484.1	1,470.8	1,425.2	1,407.5	1,427.1	1,466.7	1,467.3	1,473.1	1,458.7
2013	1,426.4	1,457.4	1,460.1	1,460.7	1,466.8	1,453.7	1,414.4	1,398.2	1,410.9	1,450.4	1,463.9	1,466.7	1,444.1

2. Average Weekly Hours by Selected Industry: New York, 2009–2013

(Not seasonally adjusted)

Industry and year	January	February	March	April	May	June	July	August	September	October	November	December	Annual average
Total Private													
2009	33.6	34.0	33.8	33.5	33.7	33.6	33.7	34.1	33.7	33.7	34.0	33.7	33.7
2010	33.6	33.5	33.7	33.8	34.0	33.9	34.1	34.4	34.0	34.0	34.1	34.1	33.9
2011	33.9	33.8	33.7	34.0	34.2	34.2	34.4	34.3	34.2	34.3	34.1	34.2	34.1
2012	34.1	33.8	33.7	34.0	33.8	33.9	34.2	34.0	34.3	33.7	33.8	34.3	34.0
2013	33.5	33.6	33.6	33.6	33.6	34.2	33.9	34.0	34.1	33.7	33.7	33.9	33.8
Goods-Producing													
2009	36.8	36.9	37.0	36.3	37.2	37.5	37.3	37.8	37.2	37.7	38.1	37.9	37.3
2010	37.6	36.6	37.7	38.0	38.2	38.5	38.2	38.6	38.0	38.6	39.1	38.7	38.2
2011	37.8	38.4	38.4	38.8	39.0	39.0	39.0	38.9	38.9	38.9	39.1	39.1	38.8
2012	38.3	38.5	38.6	38.5	38.4	38.9	38.6	38.6	39.1	38.8	38.6	39.1	38.7
2013	38.2	37.7	37.6	38.0	38.1	38.1	38.4	38.4	38.7	38.5	38.3	38.4	38.2
Construction													
2009	36.1	36.0	36.3	35.7	36.4	36.2	36.6	36.7	35.3	36.0	36.8	36.1	36.2
2010	36.2	34.0	35.8	36.0	36.3	36.8	36.4	37.1	36.3	36.9	37.3	36.9	36.4
2011	35.6	36.8	37.0	37.5	38.0	38.2	38.4	37.9	37.8	37.9	38.1	37.5	37.6
2012	36.7	37.3	37.5	37.1	36.9	37.6	37.3	37.2	37.8	37.5	37.0	37.3	37.3
2013	37.0	35.5	35.4	36.6	36.9	36.2	37.5	36.7	37.2	36.7	36.7	36.1	36.6
Manufacturing													
2009	37.1	37.3	37.3	36.8	37.7	38.3	37.6	38.3	38.3	38.5	38.6	39.0	37.9
2010	38.4	38.1	38.8	39.2	39.3	39.5	39.2	39.4	39.0	39.5	39.8	39.7	39.2
2011	39.0	39.4	39.4	39.8	39.9	39.8	39.6	39.8	39.8	39.8	39.9	40.3	39.7
2012	39.5	39.3	39.3	39.4	39.3	39.7	39.4	39.5	40.0	39.7	39.7	40.2	39.6
2013	38.8	38.8	38.8	38.6	38.7	39.2	38.7	39.3	39.5	39.4	39.2	39.6	39.1
Trade, Transportation, and Utilities													
2009	33.4	33.7	33.7	33.6	33.9	33.8	34.0	34.2	34.1	33.9	34.3	34.3	33.9
2010	33.7	33.9	34.4	34.4	34.8	34.5	34.7	34.8	34.3	34.4	34.5	34.6	34.4
2011	33.8	33.8	34.0	34.3	34.5	34.9	34.8	34.9	35.2	35.1	34.9	35.5	34.6
2012	34.9	34.6	34.6	34.6	34.8	34.9	35.1	35.0	35.2	34.4	34.8	35.3	34.9
2013	34.2	34.3	34.6	34.6	34.7	35.0	34.8	34.8	34.6	34.2	34.2	34.5	34.5
Information													
2009	33.7	34.8	34.2	33.9	33.9	33.9	33.8	34.7	33.9	33.8	34.8	32.7	34.0
2010	32.7	32.9	32.9	33.3	33.6	33.3	33.3	34.5	33.9	33.7	34.0	34.0	33.5
2011	34.4	34.4	34.2	34.6	35.3	34.9	34.9	34.9	35.0	35.3	35.3	35.0	34.9
2012	35.7	34.9	35.0	35.3	34.8	34.5	35.4	35.0	35.5	35.1	35.5	35.9	35.2
2013	35.3	35.1	34.9	35.2	34.8	35.8	34.9	35.0	35.3	34.9	34.8	35.0	35.1
Financial Activities													
2009	36.7	37.7	37.0	36.5	36.4	36.6	36.6	37.2	36.8	36.9	36.9	36.4	36.8
2010	36.6	37.0	36.9	36.8	37.2	37.0	36.8	37.5	36.8	37.1	36.8	36.6	36.9
2011	37.0	36.6	36.6	36.9	37.3	37.2	37.4	37.6	37.6	37.9	37.3	37.0	37.2
2012	37.6	36.9	36.4	37.1	36.4	36.7	37.4	36.4	37.4	36.6	37.0	37.9	37.0
2013	36.5	36.7	36.6	36.8	36.6	38.0	36.8	37.1	37.8	36.7	37.0	37.7	37.0
Professional and Business Services													
2009	35.0	35.7	35.4	34.6	34.8	34.7	34.3	34.9	34.3	34.5	35.2	34.6	34.8
2010	34.9	34.7	34.7	34.8	35.5	34.7	34.8	35.4	34.9	35.1	35.1	35.2	35.0
2011	35.3	35.0	34.8	35.1	35.4	35.0	35.0	34.9	34.8	35.5	35.0	35.1	35.1
2012	35.4	34.8	34.9	35.6	34.8	35.2	35.8	35.3	36.4	34.9	35.0	35.7	35.3
2013	34.4	34.8	34.8	34.7	34.7	35.8	35.0	35.0	35.8	34.8	34.8	35.2	35.0
Education and Health Services													
2009	33.4	33.4	33.2	33.1	33.1	33.0	33.2	33.1	33.1	32.9	32.9	32.7	33.1
2010	32.8	32.5	32.4	32.5	32.5	32.5	32.8	32.9	32.9	32.6	32.9	32.6	32.7
2011	33.1	32.8	32.8	32.9	33.0	32.8	33.1	32.8	32.7	32.8	32.6	32.6	32.8
2012	32.7	32.5	32.2	32.3	32.2	32.4	32.5	32.4	32.5	32.3	32.2	32.5	32.4
2013	32.4	32.3	32.2	32.1	32.1	32.5	32.5	32.4	32.4	32.3	32.3	32.4	32.3
Leisure and Hospitality													
2009	26.9	27.4	27.2	27.5	28.1	27.5	28.3	28.6	27.9	28.1	28.1	28.0	27.8
2010	27.6	27.7	27.8	28.1	28.0	28.0	28.8	28.7	27.8	28.1	28.0	27.6	28.0
2011	26.9	27.2	27.0	27.3	27.5	28.4	29.0	28.8	27.6	27.7	27.5	27.5	27.7
2012	26.8	26.8	27.0	27.4	27.7	27.7	28.1	28.0	27.7	27.7	27.4	27.7	27.5
2013	26.9	26.9	27.1	27.1	27.4	27.7	28.2	28.6	27.8	27.8	27.7	27.7	27.6
Other Services													
2009	29.9	30.2	30.2	30.3	30.6	30.9	31.5	31.8	30.6	30.8	30.9	31.0	30.7
2010	31.3	31.0	31.2	31.6	31.9	31.7	33.1	34.0	33.4	33.2	32.7	32.9	32.3
2011	32.6	32.6	32.3	32.6	32.8	32.2	32.3	32.1	32.0	31.9	31.7	32.0	32.3
2012	31.9	31.3	31.4	31.8	31.8	31.5	31.9	31.4	31.5	30.4	30.1	31.5	31.4
2013	31.1	31.4	31.5	31.6	31.8	32.2	31.8	32.2	32.6	31.3	31.0	31.6	31.7

3. Average Hourly Earnings by Selected Industry: New York, 2009–2013

(Dollars, not seasonally adjusted)

Industry and year	January	February	March	April	May	June	July	August	September	October	November	December	Annual average
Total Private													
2009	25.67	25.80	25.73	25.53	25.35	25.61	25.57	25.72	25.80	25.76	25.98	25.96	25.71
2010	26.10	26.11	26.05	26.13	26.19	25.83	25.83	25.94	25.93	26.14	26.23	26.35	26.07
2011	26.75	26.37	26.43	26.36	26.55	26.10	26.21	26.10	26.56	26.92	26.72	26.70	26.48
2012	27.39	27.09	27.08	27.47	26.88	26.81	27.11	26.77	27.33	27.15	27.28	27.81	27.18
2013	27.83	27.78	27.72	27.81	27.63	27.87	27.68	27.63	28.06	27.78	27.87	28.12	27.82
Goods-Producing													
2009	25.48	25.52	25.84	26.00	25.91	25.81	26.37	26.31	26.61	26.36	26.40	26.45	26.09
2010	26.54	26.59	26.71	26.67	26.70	26.28	26.85	27.10	26.91	27.04	26.90	26.92	26.77
2011	26.72	26.51	27.08	27.01	27.15	27.07	27.64	27.57	27.75	28.02	28.49	28.39	27.47
2012	28.16	28.32	28.53	28.49	28.42	28.49	28.70	28.54	28.59	28.62	28.73	28.70	28.53
2013	28.94	28.84	29.05	29.05	28.73	28.63	28.93	28.99	28.80	28.69	28.81	28.78	28.85
Construction													
2009	30.60	30.45	30.54	30.42	30.31	30.42	31.08	31.02	31.69	31.27	31.23	31.80	30.91
2010	32.20	32.26	32.60	32.41	32.20	31.73	32.60	33.09	32.81	32.94	32.93	33.03	32.58
2011	32.71	32.11	32.75	31.89	31.43	31.27	31.65	31.70	32.02	32.18	32.69	32.74	32.07
2012	32.75	32.94	33.36	33.30	33.21	33.15	33.28	33.54	33.90	34.00	34.90	34.94	33.62
2013	34.67	35.30	35.27	35.01	34.66	34.35	34.53	35.00	34.50	34.16	34.68	34.94	34.74
Manufacturing													
2009	23.00	23.07	23.24	23.46	23.23	22.96	23.27	23.20	23.48	23.32	23.39	23.36	23.25
2010	23.43	23.78	23.50	23.37	23.50	23.12	23.34	23.32	23.30	23.45	23.23	23.39	23.39
2011	23.59	23.54	23.81	23.93	24.36	24.33	25.00	24.91	25.10	25.39	25.86	25.85	24.65
2012	25.73	25.87	25.95	25.90	25.79	25.85	26.07	25.64	25.57	25.59	25.42	25.40	25.73
2013	25.88	25.57	25.80	25.78	25.34	25.37	25.45	25.33	25.37	25.45	25.35	25.65	25.53
Trade, Transportation, and Utilities													
2009	21.57	21.57	21.53	21.53	21.26	21.40	21.29	21.59	21.50	21.55	21.45	21.55	21.48
2010	21.64	21.63	21.40	21.66	21.64	21.35	21.41	21.19	21.48	21.46	21.42	21.54	21.48
2011	22.12	22.01	22.04	21.96	22.02	21.59	21.62	21.55	21.93	21.91	21.66	21.51	21.82
2012	21.93	21.78	21.89	22.36	21.70	21.59	21.77	21.23	21.83	21.68	21.59	22.02	21.78
2013	22.30	22.20	22.21	22.35	22.18	22.28	22.42	22.44	22.99	22.69	22.82	22.90	22.49
Information													
2009	34.87	35.05	34.67	34.07	34.76	35.47	35.81	35.38	35.66	35.80	35.86	36.02	35.28
2010	36.43	36.65	36.67	36.54	37.59	37.21	37.59	37.64	38.99	38.94	38.91	38.73	37.68
2011	40.67	39.07	39.03	39.11	39.22	39.05	39.09	38.80	39.22	39.99	39.81	40.01	39.43
2012	41.20	41.32	40.64	41.47	41.35	41.03	40.95	40.29	41.23	40.91	40.80	42.22	41.12
2013	42.07	42.16	42.51	42.59	43.06	43.73	42.61	41.86	41.99	41.62	41.72	41.74	42.31
Financial Activities													
2009	34.13	34.33	34.79	34.59	34.53	34.56	34.47	34.98	34.71	34.78	35.85	35.49	34.76
2010	35.12	35.47	35.63	35.86	35.86	34.97	34.72	34.76	34.03	34.66	34.96	35.16	35.10
2011	35.86	34.83	34.75	34.61	35.04	34.62	34.33	34.14	34.75	35.81	35.08	34.84	34.89
2012	36.63	35.97	36.30	37.48	36.36	36.41	36.75	36.65	37.59	37.38	37.15	37.94	36.89
2013	38.18	38.31	38.53	39.09	39.25	40.05	39.22	39.63	40.12	39.83	40.11	40.66	39.43
Professional and Business Services													
2009	33.30	33.86	33.50	33.07	32.59	33.17	33.43	33.59	33.42	33.75	33.94	34.04	33.47
2010	34.49	34.19	34.18	34.39	34.38	33.78	34.01	34.49	33.94	34.31	34.34	34.48	34.25
2011	35.11	34.41	34.32	34.07	34.56	33.74	33.79	33.53	33.97	34.45	33.84	34.06	34.15
2012	35.50	34.83	34.44	34.86	34.19	33.89	34.39	33.72	34.44	34.03	34.31	35.35	34.49
2013	35.29	34.96	34.50	34.57	34.34	34.69	34.27	33.83	34.23	33.83	33.81	34.44	34.39
Education and Health Services													
2009	22.11	22.10	21.95	22.00	22.05	22.09	22.09	21.99	22.23	22.10	22.28	22.28	22.11
2010	22.32	22.43	22.36	22.44	22.50	22.56	22.76	22.65	22.72	22.90	23.10	23.17	22.66
2011	23.19	23.11	23.18	23.23	23.32	23.45	23.83	23.72	23.92	24.17	24.07	24.10	23.61
2012	24.47	24.24	24.29	24.42	24.20	24.30	24.63	24.51	24.78	24.66	24.94	25.33	24.57
2013	25.10	25.08	25.08	25.06	24.98	24.93	25.11	25.08	25.38	25.12	25.17	25.19	25.11
Leisure and Hospitality													
2009	17.53	17.54	17.38	16.95	16.96	18.00	17.39	17.38	18.03	17.43	17.76	18.15	17.54
2010	17.92	17.59	17.52	17.30	17.42	16.86	16.41	16.50	17.02	17.33	17.61	17.99	17.26
2011	17.27	17.24	17.29	17.21	17.31	15.79	15.57	15.78	16.87	17.36	17.33	17.65	16.85
2012	17.15	17.08	16.98	16.89	16.66	16.21	16.19	16.10	16.62	16.84	16.97	17.22	16.72
2013	16.97	16.93	17.00	16.94	16.95	16.65	16.51	16.54	17.13	17.56	17.73	18.10	17.08
Other Services													
2009	21.66	21.44	21.39	21.08	21.20	21.07	20.19	20.86	21.75	21.60	21.84	21.74	21.31
2010	21.55	21.91	21.88	21.78	21.69	21.75	20.13	20.30	21.00	20.99	21.42	21.57	21.31
2011	21.61	21.57	21.68	21.80	22.01	21.73	21.41	21.35	21.89	21.87	22.24	22.60	21.81
2012	22.48	22.38	22.56	23.03	22.50	22.47	22.55	22.73	23.23	23.14	23.42	23.93	22.87
2013	23.63	23.93	23.72	23.78	23.57	24.32	23.80	23.69	24.43	23.90	23.85	24.18	23.90

4. Average Weekly Earnings by Selected Industry: New York, 2009–2013

(Dollars, not seasonally adjusted)

Industry and year	January	February	March	April	May	June	July	August	September	October	November	December	Annual average
Total Private													
2009	862.51	877.20	869.67	855.26	854.30	860.50	861.71	877.05	869.46	868.11	883.32	874.85	866.43
2010	876.96	874.69	877.89	883.19	890.46	875.64	880.80	892.34	881.62	888.76	894.44	898.54	883.77
2011	906.83	891.31	890.69	896.24	908.01	892.62	901.62	895.23	908.35	923.36	911.15	913.14	902.97
2012	934.00	915.64	912.60	933.98	908.54	908.86	927.16	910.18	937.42	914.96	922.06	953.88	924.12
2013	932.31	933.41	931.39	934.42	928.37	953.15	938.35	939.42	956.85	936.19	939.22	953.27	940.32
Goods-Producing													
2009	937.66	941.69	956.08	943.80	963.85	967.88	983.60	994.52	989.89	993.77	1,005.84	1,002.46	973.16
2010	997.90	973.19	1,006.97	1,013.46	1,019.94	1,011.78	1,025.67	1,046.06	1,022.58	1,043.74	1,051.79	1,041.80	1,022.61
2011	1,010.02	1,017.98	1,039.87	1,047.99	1,058.85	1,055.73	1,077.96	1,072.47	1,079.48	1,089.98	1,113.96	1,110.05	1,065.84
2012	1,078.53	1,090.32	1,101.26	1,096.87	1,091.33	1,108.26	1,107.82	1,101.64	1,117.87	1,110.46	1,108.98	1,122.17	1,104.11
2013	1,105.51	1,087.27	1,092.28	1,103.90	1,094.61	1,090.80	1,110.91	1,113.22	1,114.56	1,104.57	1,103.42	1,105.15	1,102.07
Construction													
2009	1,104.66	1,096.20	1,108.60	1,085.99	1,103.28	1,101.20	1,137.53	1,138.43	1,118.66	1,125.72	1,149.26	1,147.98	1,118.94
2010	1,165.64	1,096.84	1,167.08	1,166.76	1,168.86	1,167.66	1,186.64	1,227.64	1,191.00	1,215.49	1,228.29	1,218.81	1,185.91
2011	1,164.48	1,181.65	1,211.75	1,195.88	1,194.34	1,194.51	1,215.36	1,201.43	1,210.36	1,219.62	1,245.49	1,227.75	1,205.83
2012	1,201.93	1,228.66	1,251.00	1,235.43	1,225.45	1,246.44	1,241.34	1,247.69	1,281.42	1,275.00	1,291.30	1,303.26	1,254.03
2013	1,282.79	1,253.15	1,248.56	1,281.37	1,278.95	1,243.47	1,294.88	1,284.50	1,283.40	1,253.67	1,272.76	1,261.33	1,271.48
Manufacturing													
2009	853.30	860.51	866.85	863.33	875.77	879.37	874.95	888.56	899.28	897.82	902.85	911.04	881.18
2010	899.71	906.02	911.80	916.10	923.55	913.24	914.93	918.81	908.70	926.28	929.20	928.58	916.89
2011	920.01	927.48	938.11	952.41	971.96	968.33	990.00	991.42	998.98	1,010.52	1,031.81	1,041.76	978.61
2012	1,016.34	1,016.69	1,019.84	1,020.46	1,013.55	1,026.25	1,027.16	1,012.78	1,022.80	1,015.92	1,009.17	1,021.08	1,018.91
2013	1,004.14	992.12	1,001.04	995.11	980.66	994.50	984.92	995.47	1,002.12	1,002.73	993.72	1,015.74	998.22
Trade, Transportation, and Utilities													
2009	720.44	726.91	725.56	723.41	720.71	723.32	723.86	738.38	733.15	730.55	735.74	739.17	728.17
2010	729.27	733.26	736.16	745.10	753.07	736.58	742.93	737.41	736.76	738.22	738.99	745.28	738.91
2011	747.66	743.94	749.36	753.23	759.69	753.49	752.38	752.10	771.94	769.04	755.93	763.61	754.97
2012	765.36	753.59	757.39	773.66	755.16	753.49	764.13	743.05	768.42	745.79	751.33	777.31	760.12
2013	762.66	761.46	768.47	773.31	769.65	779.80	780.22	780.91	795.45	776.00	780.44	790.05	775.91
Information													
2009	1,175.12	1,219.74	1,185.71	1,154.97	1,178.36	1,202.43	1,210.38	1,227.69	1,208.87	1,210.04	1,247.93	1,177.85	1,199.52
2010	1,191.26	1,205.79	1,206.44	1,216.78	1,263.02	1,239.09	1,251.75	1,298.58	1,321.76	1,312.28	1,322.94	1,316.82	1,262.28
2011	1,399.05	1,344.01	1,334.83	1,353.21	1,384.47	1,362.85	1,364.24	1,354.12	1,372.70	1,411.65	1,405.29	1,400.35	1,376.11
2012	1,470.84	1,442.07	1,422.40	1,463.89	1,438.98	1,415.54	1,449.63	1,410.15	1,463.67	1,435.94	1,448.40	1,515.70	1,447.42
2013	1,485.07	1,479.82	1,483.60	1,499.17	1,498.49	1,565.53	1,487.09	1,465.10	1,482.25	1,452.54	1,451.86	1,460.90	1,485.08
Financial Activities													
2009	1,252.57	1,294.24	1,287.23	1,262.54	1,256.89	1,264.90	1,261.60	1,301.26	1,277.33	1,283.38	1,322.87	1,291.84	1,279.17
2010	1,285.39	1,312.39	1,314.75	1,319.65	1,333.99	1,293.89	1,277.70	1,303.50	1,252.30	1,285.89	1,286.53	1,286.86	1,295.19
2011	1,326.82	1,274.78	1,271.85	1,277.11	1,306.99	1,287.86	1,283.94	1,283.66	1,306.60	1,357.20	1,308.48	1,289.08	1,297.91
2012	1,377.29	1,327.29	1,321.32	1,390.51	1,323.50	1,336.25	1,374.45	1,334.06	1,405.87	1,368.11	1,374.55	1,437.93	1,364.93
2013	1,393.57	1,405.98	1,410.20	1,438.51	1,436.55	1,521.90	1,443.30	1,470.27	1,516.54	1,461.76	1,484.07	1,532.88	1,458.91
Professional and Business Services													
2009	1,165.50	1,208.80	1,185.90	1,144.22	1,134.13	1,151.00	1,146.65	1,172.29	1,146.31	1,164.38	1,194.69	1,177.78	1,164.76
2010	1,203.70	1,186.39	1,186.05	1,196.77	1,220.49	1,172.17	1,183.55	1,220.95	1,184.51	1,204.28	1,205.33	1,213.70	1,198.75
2011	1,239.38	1,204.35	1,194.34	1,195.86	1,223.42	1,180.90	1,182.65	1,170.20	1,182.16	1,222.98	1,184.40	1,195.51	1,198.67
2012	1,256.70	1,212.08	1,201.96	1,241.02	1,189.81	1,192.93	1,231.16	1,190.32	1,253.62	1,187.65	1,200.85	1,262.00	1,217.50
2013	1,213.98	1,216.61	1,200.60	1,199.58	1,191.60	1,241.90	1,199.45	1,184.05	1,225.43	1,177.28	1,176.59	1,212.29	1,203.65
Education and Health Services													
2009	738.47	738.14	728.74	728.20	729.86	728.97	733.39	727.87	735.81	727.09	733.01	728.56	731.84
2010	732.10	728.98	724.46	729.30	731.25	733.20	746.53	745.19	747.49	746.54	759.99	762.29	740.98
2011	767.59	758.01	760.30	764.27	769.56	769.16	788.77	778.02	782.18	792.78	784.68	785.66	774.41
2012	800.17	787.80	782.14	788.77	779.24	787.32	800.48	794.12	805.35	796.52	803.07	823.23	796.07
2013	813.24	810.08	807.58	804.43	801.86	810.23	816.08	812.59	822.31	811.38	812.99	816.16	811.05
Leisure and Hospitality													
2009	471.56	480.60	472.74	466.13	476.58	495.00	492.14	497.07	503.04	489.78	499.06	508.20	487.61
2010	494.59	487.24	487.06	486.13	487.76	472.08	472.61	473.55	454.46	465.61	486.97	496.52	483.28
2011	464.56	468.93	466.83	469.83	476.03	448.44	451.53	454.46	465.61	480.87	476.58	485.38	466.75
2012	459.62	457.74	458.46	462.79	461.48	449.02	454.94	450.80	460.37	466.47	464.98	476.99	459.80
2013	456.49	455.42	460.70	459.07	464.43	461.21	465.58	473.04	476.21	488.17	491.12	501.37	471.41
Other Services													
2009	647.63	647.49	645.98	638.72	648.72	651.06	635.99	663.35	665.55	665.28	674.86	673.94	654.22
2010	674.52	679.21	682.66	688.25	691.91	689.48	666.30	690.20	701.40	696.87	700.43	709.65	688.31
2011	704.49	703.18	700.26	710.68	721.93	699.71	691.54	685.34	700.48	697.65	705.01	723.20	704.46
2012	717.11	700.49	708.38	732.35	715.50	707.81	719.35	713.72	731.75	703.46	704.94	753.80	718.12
2013	734.89	751.40	747.18	751.45	749.53	783.10	756.84	762.82	796.42	748.07	739.35	764.09	757.63

NORTH CAROLINA
At a Glance

Population:
    2000 census: 8,046,346
    2010 census: 9,535,483
    2013 estimate: 9,848,060

Percent change in population:
    2000–2010: 18.5%
    2010–2013: 3.3%

Percent change in total nonfarm employment:
    2000–2010: -1.3%
    2010–2013: 4.8%

Industry with the largest growth in employment, 2000–2013 (thousands):
    Education and Health Services, 137.7

Industry with the largest decline or smallest growth in employment, 2000–2013 (thousands):
    Manufacturing, -315.5

Civilian labor force:
    2000: 4,123,812
    2010: 4,586,094
    2013: 4,694,939

Unemployment rate and rank among states (lowest to highest):
    2000: 3.7%, 22nd
    2010: 10.8%, 44th
    2013: 8.0%, 39th

Over-the-year change in unemployment rates:
    2010–2011: -0.6%
    2011–2012: -1.0%
    2012–2013: -1.2%

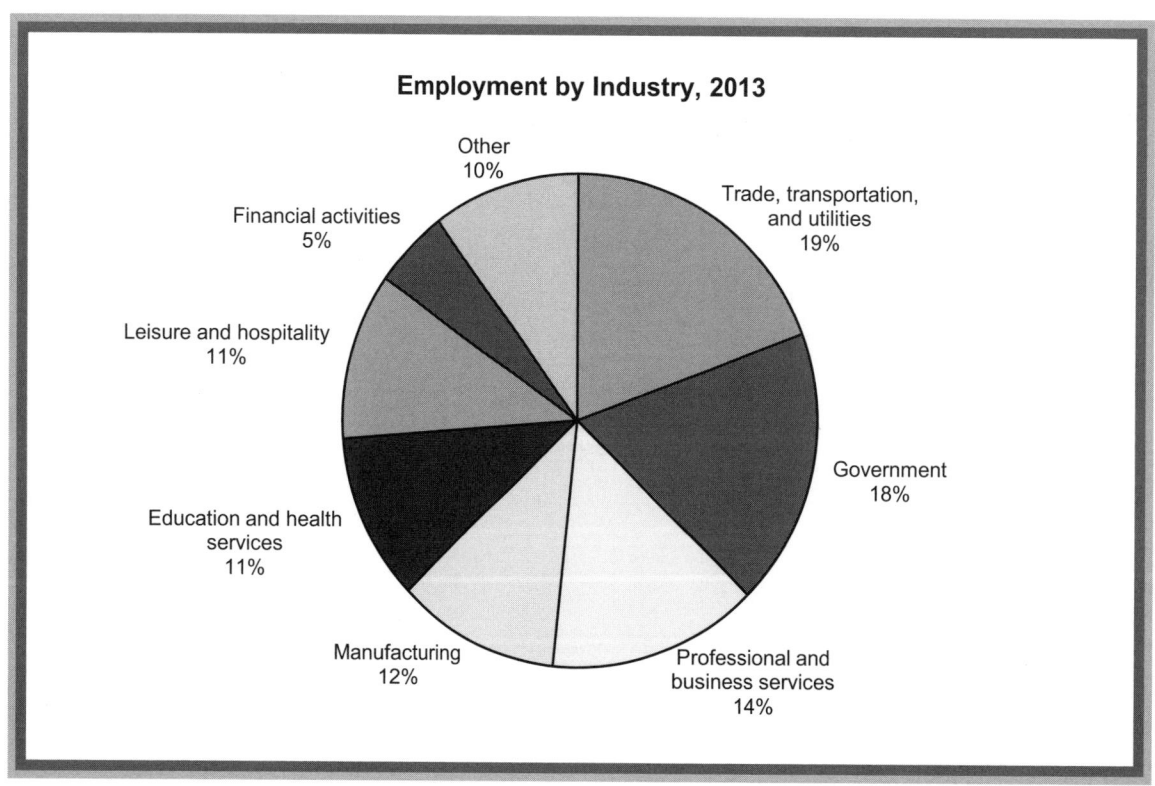

Employment by Industry, 2013

Other 10%
Financial activities 5%
Leisure and hospitality 11%
Education and health services 11%
Manufacturing 12%
Professional and business services 14%
Government 18%
Trade, transportation, and utilities 19%

1. Employment by Industry: North Carolina, Selected Years, 2002–2013

(Numbers in thousands, not seasonally adjusted)

Industry and year	January	February	March	April	May	June	July	August	September	October	November	December	Annual average
Total Nonfarm													
2002	3,781.4	3,797.8	3,826.6	3,851.0	3,873.4	3,856.1	3,790.7	3,840.9	3,850.9	3,856.2	3,851.5	3,844.4	3,835.1
2003	3,748.2	3,751.0	3,774.4	3,794.9	3,822.4	3,806.8	3,714.9	3,775.0	3,799.1	3,820.1	3,815.7	3,820.0	3,786.9
2004	3,736.7	3,747.0	3,783.4	3,816.6	3,848.9	3,842.1	3,795.1	3,856.4	3,885.0	3,888.9	3,898.4	3,907.6	3,833.8
2005	3,829.2	3,845.4	3,876.3	3,902.6	3,922.5	3,906.7	3,850.9	3,922.6	3,958.5	3,965.9	3,980.6	3,983.1	3,912.0
2006	3,918.7	3,933.6	3,969.6	4,016.4	4,048.3	4,045.3	3,988.0	4,060.3	4,085.7	4,107.8	4,134.4	4,139.8	4,037.3
2007	4,050.2	4,073.3	4,113.5	4,123.0	4,160.6	4,164.1	4,077.2	4,155.9	4,182.3	4,185.2	4,203.4	4,206.4	4,141.3
2008	4,109.4	4,129.0	4,149.8	4,152.3	4,177.8	4,159.5	4,067.3	4,135.4	4,154.7	4,131.0	4,112.3	4,089.5	4,130.7
2009	3,947.3	3,935.9	3,928.9	3,921.9	3,937.0	3,909.7	3,818.6	3,879.7	3,902.9	3,889.8	3,893.4	3,882.7	3,904.0
2010	3,791.9	3,797.4	3,833.2	3,866.4	3,907.1	3,886.4	3,810.2	3,876.9	3,893.0	3,920.9	3,930.6	3,920.6	3,869.6
2011	3,825.9	3,861.1	3,891.0	3,922.6	3,942.3	3,928.0	3,852.5	3,925.4	3,946.0	3,960.1	3,974.8	3,969.4	3,916.6
2012	3,899.5	3,923.8	3,957.3	3,983.0	4,014.9	3,988.3	3,910.7	3,993.7	4,016.9	4,037.7	4,056.8	4,052.5	3,986.3
2013	3,964.8	3,994.2	4,023.3	4,051.2	4,077.4	4,057.1	3,980.9	4,062.4	4,089.5	4,124.6	4,132.3	4,125.6	4,056.9
Total Private													
2002	3,127.9	3,137.3	3,161.7	3,188.3	3,209.2	3,224.9	3,205.1	3,216.8	3,199.4	3,188.0	3,186.1	3,183.5	3,185.7
2003	3,098.3	3,095.7	3,114.7	3,136.9	3,161.2	3,176.1	3,137.3	3,152.9	3,141.8	3,141.1	3,144.3	3,150.9	3,137.6
2004	3,078.3	3,083.6	3,115.3	3,149.5	3,179.1	3,204.0	3,209.0	3,219.0	3,207.3	3,213.4	3,224.5	3,224.5	3,174.2
2005	3,155.2	3,165.0	3,191.8	3,218.6	3,236.3	3,257.2	3,263.9	3,277.0	3,273.5	3,276.6	3,288.2	3,292.7	3,241.3
2006	3,233.5	3,242.1	3,272.8	3,317.2	3,345.4	3,371.8	3,386.1	3,398.7	3,388.2	3,401.8	3,417.9	3,425.1	3,350.1
2007	3,348.5	3,364.9	3,399.9	3,409.5	3,443.0	3,474.6	3,461.1	3,475.1	3,463.2	3,465.3	3,476.1	3,480.4	3,438.5
2008	3,392.3	3,404.2	3,419.8	3,420.6	3,441.5	3,451.1	3,437.6	3,439.9	3,414.1	3,388.7	3,365.1	3,344.3	3,409.9
2009	3,214.8	3,199.6	3,187.4	3,176.5	3,192.2	3,196.0	3,184.1	3,182.5	3,165.6	3,157.1	3,157.4	3,149.3	3,180.2
2010	3,068.7	3,068.4	3,097.9	3,125.6	3,148.0	3,168.6	3,180.5	3,187.5	3,172.5	3,188.0	3,192.8	3,186.3	3,148.7
2011	3,102.8	3,131.5	3,157.0	3,187.2	3,207.1	3,228.3	3,232.3	3,243.0	3,233.3	3,233.8	3,242.3	3,242.7	3,203.4
2012	3,180.4	3,196.8	3,226.9	3,251.6	3,280.5	3,299.2	3,299.8	3,309.6	3,298.9	3,303.5	3,316.3	3,318.2	3,273.5
2013	3,239.9	3,260.4	3,286.1	3,314.2	3,340.6	3,365.7	3,365.5	3,379.0	3,369.7	3,390.4	3,391.9	3,390.1	3,341.1
Goods-Producing													
2002	879.4	878.8	879.3	876.8	877.6	875.7	870.2	871.8	866.5	860.9	855.0	850.1	870.2
2003	834.6	829.2	830.0	829.1	828.9	827.9	810.4	810.5	808.0	806.2	802.4	799.9	818.1
2004	787.7	786.4	792.9	798.9	803.3	809.3	810.6	810.1	809.3	808.3	806.8	800.8	802.5
2005	794.6	795.6	798.5	800.7	803.8	807.7	805.9	807.7	808.2	802.8	802.6	800.8	802.4
2006	789.2	788.7	793.6	805.2	807.8	812.8	813.0	815.0	812.8	810.7	808.9	809.8	805.6
2007	797.6	797.8	801.5	796.8	799.6	807.4	801.9	804.1	802.5	799.0	797.5	795.7	800.1
2008	776.2	775.2	775.0	767.5	768.3	766.8	762.7	759.4	755.0	743.9	732.4	720.8	758.6
2009	685.1	673.9	662.2	651.9	646.9	644.8	639.3	636.8	634.5	629.8	625.5	622.7	646.1
2010	606.3	603.0	608.0	612.0	614.6	618.5	620.8	620.4	620.4	618.3	616.0	613.7	614.3
2011	597.4	603.2	608.0	610.5	614.6	617.8	618.6	619.6	619.0	615.1	614.0	613.2	612.6
2012	605.5	608.2	613.6	614.7	618.5	621.1	621.6	621.8	622.3	621.0	621.3	621.5	617.6
2013	609.8	612.4	615.5	617.8	621.2	626.0	625.8	625.5	626.3	626.7	626.0	623.3	621.4
Service-Providing													
2002	2,902.0	2,919.0	2,947.3	2,974.2	2,995.8	2,980.4	2,920.5	2,969.1	2,984.4	2,995.3	2,996.5	2,994.3	2,964.9
2003	2,913.6	2,921.8	2,944.4	2,965.8	2,993.5	2,978.9	2,904.5	2,964.5	2,991.1	3,013.9	3,013.3	3,020.1	2,968.8
2004	2,949.0	2,960.6	2,990.5	3,017.7	3,045.6	3,032.8	2,984.5	3,046.3	3,075.7	3,080.6	3,091.6	3,100.8	3,031.3
2005	3,034.6	3,049.8	3,077.8	3,101.9	3,118.7	3,099.0	3,045.0	3,114.9	3,150.3	3,163.1	3,178.0	3,182.3	3,109.6
2006	3,129.5	3,144.9	3,176.0	3,211.2	3,240.5	3,232.5	3,175.0	3,245.3	3,272.9	3,297.1	3,325.5	3,330.0	3,231.7
2007	3,252.6	3,275.5	3,312.0	3,326.2	3,361.0	3,356.7	3,275.3	3,351.8	3,379.8	3,386.2	3,405.9	3,410.7	3,341.1
2008	3,333.2	3,353.8	3,374.8	3,384.8	3,409.5	3,392.7	3,304.6	3,376.0	3,399.7	3,387.1	3,379.9	3,368.7	3,372.1
2009	3,262.2	3,262.0	3,266.7	3,270.0	3,290.1	3,264.9	3,179.3	3,242.9	3,268.4	3,260.0	3,267.9	3,260.0	3,257.9
2010	3,185.6	3,194.4	3,225.2	3,254.4	3,292.5	3,267.9	3,189.4	3,256.5	3,272.6	3,302.6	3,314.6	3,306.9	3,255.2
2011	3,228.5	3,257.9	3,283.0	3,312.1	3,327.7	3,310.2	3,233.9	3,305.8	3,327.0	3,345.0	3,360.8	3,356.2	3,304.0
2012	3,294.0	3,315.6	3,343.7	3,368.3	3,396.4	3,367.2	3,289.1	3,371.9	3,394.6	3,416.7	3,435.5	3,431.0	3,368.7
2013	3,355.0	3,381.8	3,407.8	3,433.4	3,456.2	3,431.1	3,355.1	3,436.9	3,463.2	3,497.9	3,506.3	3,502.3	3,435.6
Mining and Logging													
2002	8.0	8.0	8.1	8.0	8.0	7.9	7.8	7.8	7.8	7.8	7.7	7.7	7.9
2003	7.6	7.5	7.6	7.6	7.6	7.6	7.1	7.2	7.1	7.2	7.0	7.0	7.3
2004	6.8	6.8	6.9	6.9	6.9	7.0	6.9	7.0	7.1	6.9	6.9	6.9	6.9
2005	6.8	6.8	6.8	6.7	6.6	6.7	6.6	6.6	6.6	6.7	6.7	6.6	6.7
2006	6.6	6.6	6.7	6.7	6.7	6.8	6.9	7.0	7.0	6.9	6.9	6.9	6.8
2007	6.9	6.9	7.0	7.1	7.1	7.1	7.0	7.1	7.0	6.9	6.9	6.9	7.0
2008	6.8	6.8	6.7	6.6	6.6	6.6	6.6	6.6	6.6	6.5	6.5	6.4	6.6
2009	6.1	6.0	6.0	5.8	5.8	5.9	5.9	5.9	5.9	5.8	5.7	5.6	5.9
2010	5.6	5.5	5.6	5.6	5.6	5.6	5.8	5.7	5.7	5.7	5.6	5.6	5.6
2011	5.5	5.6	5.6	5.5	5.5	5.6	5.7	5.7	5.7	5.6	5.6	5.6	5.6
2012	5.5	5.5	5.6	5.5	5.5	5.6	5.6	5.6	5.6	5.6	5.6	5.5	5.6
2013	5.4	5.4	5.4	5.5	5.5	5.5	5.5	5.5	5.5	5.6	5.5	5.5	5.5
Construction													
2002	214.4	214.4	216.9	221.0	223.3	224.1	222.7	223.3	220.1	217.2	214.5	213.7	218.8
2003	206.1	204.6	206.8	209.7	214.2	215.4	212.5	212.8	212.2	215.3	214.0	213.3	211.4
2004	206.0	205.0	210.1	214.9	218.2	221.0	223.7	223.9	222.9	224.3	223.9	224.6	218.2
2005	219.3	220.2	223.4	227.2	230.4	233.5	237.2	238.0	238.5	235.6	235.5	234.5	231.1
2006	230.2	231.2	236.4	242.1	244.7	248.7	251.5	253.5	252.5	251.9	252.5	252.7	245.7
2007	246.5	247.0	252.0	253.7	256.0	259.8	258.6	259.2	258.4	256.6	255.0	253.0	254.7
2008	242.1	241.6	242.3	239.9	241.0	240.6	240.2	237.3	234.7	229.9	223.9	218.4	236.0
2009	202.2	199.6	197.5	193.6	193.7	194.1	193.7	191.9	189.8	186.6	183.6	182.1	192.4
2010	171.8	169.7	173.8	177.3	178.5	179.9	180.7	180.2	178.5	177.7	176.2	173.5	176.5
2011	162.5	167.2	170.7	172.9	175.2	176.8	177.7	177.7	174.3	173.6	172.9	172.3	173.3
2012	166.5	167.5	171.2	172.1	173.4	175.5	174.0	174.3	176.7	176.6	172.3	172.1	172.0
2013	165.6	166.6	169.5	172.3	174.3	175.9	176.3	176.7	176.6	176.8	177.0	174.2	173.5

1. Employment by Industry: North Carolina, Selected Years, 2002–2013—*Continued*

(Numbers in thousands, not seasonally adjusted)

Industry and year	January	February	March	April	May	June	July	August	September	October	November	December	Annual average
Manufacturing													
2002	657.0	656.4	654.3	647.8	646.3	643.7	639.7	640.7	638.6	635.9	632.8	628.7	643.5
2003	620.9	617.1	615.6	611.8	607.1	604.9	590.8	590.5	588.7	583.7	581.4	579.6	599.3
2004	574.9	574.6	575.9	577.1	578.2	581.3	580.0	579.2	579.3	577.1	576.0	575.3	577.4
2005	568.5	568.6	568.3	566.8	566.8	567.5	562.1	563.1	563.1	560.5	560.4	559.7	564.6
2006	552.4	550.9	550.5	556.4	556.4	557.3	554.6	554.5	553.3	551.9	549.5	550.2	553.2
2007	544.2	543.9	542.5	536.0	536.5	540.5	536.3	537.8	537.1	535.5	535.6	535.8	538.5
2008	527.3	526.8	526.0	521.0	520.7	519.6	515.9	515.5	513.7	507.5	502.0	496.0	516.0
2009	476.8	468.3	458.7	452.5	447.4	444.8	439.7	439.0	438.8	437.4	436.2	435.0	447.9
2010	428.9	427.8	428.6	429.1	430.5	433.0	434.3	434.5	436.2	434.9	434.2	434.6	432.2
2011	429.4	430.4	431.7	432.1	433.9	435.4	435.2	436.2	436.2	434.7	434.7	434.8	433.7
2012	433.5	435.2	436.8	437.1	439.6	442.0	442.0	441.9	443.1	442.5	443.4	443.9	440.1
2013	438.8	440.4	440.6	440.0	441.4	444.6	444.0	443.3	444.1	444.4	443.5	443.6	442.4
Trade, Transportation, and Utilities													
2002	715.6	710.5	716.9	720.4	724.1	728.7	725.3	727.7	725.2	725.5	738.5	745.3	725.3
2003	711.1	708.2	710.8	712.3	716.3	720.9	714.7	717.7	716.6	721.5	732.2	739.3	718.5
2004	710.5	707.2	712.9	719.0	725.0	728.7	728.0	730.2	728.8	731.8	743.5	752.2	726.5
2005	723.3	723.2	728.0	733.5	736.8	738.9	741.5	742.0	739.8	748.7	761.5	769.5	740.6
2006	739.8	734.7	740.7	750.1	755.3	756.4	761.9	763.7	761.7	768.2	784.8	791.7	759.1
2007	765.9	762.1	770.8	770.7	777.6	780.2	779.3	779.4	776.7	780.3	795.4	802.4	778.4
2008	771.3	768.3	772.9	769.4	772.0	773.6	770.9	769.2	763.3	763.6	767.8	769.2	769.3
2009	729.7	721.3	720.4	715.9	720.7	722.5	719.2	717.9	714.0	716.1	724.1	727.2	720.8
2010	700.2	696.8	703.3	706.8	712.4	715.2	716.0	717.3	712.4	718.0	730.5	736.2	713.8
2011	709.8	710.1	715.2	720.4	724.1	726.8	730.8	731.9	728.7	733.4	746.5	753.0	727.6
2012	729.6	725.5	731.6	735.4	741.7	744.7	745.6	744.4	743.4	746.8	763.4	767.7	743.3
2013	738.7	737.2	741.9	745.5	751.7	756.4	758.5	760.4	758.1	761.1	775.7	782.8	755.7
Wholesale Trade													
2002	162.1	162.1	162.8	161.6	162.0	162.8	163.0	162.8	162.8	162.6	161.9	162.0	162.4
2003	160.1	160.1	160.7	162.3	162.7	163.6	163.4	163.4	163.6	164.0	164.2	164.2	162.7
2004	162.0	161.9	162.8	163.2	163.6	164.6	163.8	164.3	163.8	165.1	165.5	166.1	163.9
2005	164.5	164.2	165.3	165.6	166.2	167.0	167.0	167.6	167.7	167.9	168.0	168.8	166.7
2006	166.3	166.9	166.8	168.9	169.9	170.2	171.2	171.6	171.8	173.4	174.3	174.8	170.5
2007	171.7	172.1	172.9	175.5	176.3	176.7	177.7	177.7	177.7	177.7	178.6	179.1	176.1
2008	179.1	180.0	181.3	181.7	182.4	183.7	183.6	183.1	182.8	183.0	183.2	183.6	182.3
2009	181.3	182.1	182.8	180.8	181.4	181.3	180.4	179.8	178.4	178.3	176.7	175.2	179.9
2010	170.6	169.9	168.8	167.4	166.9	166.4	165.4	165.0	164.1	164.6	164.2	164.0	166.4
2011	164.2	165.3	166.0	167.1	167.4	168.0	168.9	168.8	168.7	168.7	169.2	169.4	167.6
2012	167.6	168.5	170.0	170.9	171.9	172.3	172.6	172.7	172.5	172.6	172.8	172.7	171.4
2013	170.2	171.4	172.3	172.5	173.3	174.1	174.4	175.1	175.0	174.2	176.5	175.5	173.7
Retail Trade													
2002	431.0	426.5	431.8	433.6	436.2	438.6	434.9	436.5	434.7	433.7	446.4	453.4	436.4
2003	424.7	421.2	423.6	425.0	428.2	431.5	427.0	428.7	427.0	430.6	441.5	446.9	429.7
2004	423.3	419.4	423.4	427.4	432.1	434.2	432.6	434.2	432.5	435.4	446.6	453.5	432.9
2005	430.7	429.7	434.0	437.0	438.9	439.9	442.6	442.3	439.5	445.6	456.5	462.9	441.6
2006	440.1	434.5	438.6	445.3	448.9	448.9	452.3	453.4	450.9	457.0	472.3	478.1	451.7
2007	456.3	452.3	458.7	458.7	464.4	465.7	465.8	466.3	464.1	468.2	482.7	488.0	465.9
2008	463.4	459.7	463.6	462.1	463.4	465.0	464.0	462.7	459.0	459.4	465.3	467.0	462.9
2009	438.4	432.4	433.2	431.8	437.1	439.0	437.9	437.4	434.4	436.5	444.7	447.0	437.5
2010	426.7	423.0	427.4	429.3	433.4	435.7	435.4	436.4	432.0	436.1	447.4	452.2	434.6
2011	430.1	428.9	432.3	435.5	438.8	440.1	442.8	443.5	439.7	444.3	456.4	460.8	441.1
2012	442.9	438.2	441.7	444.9	449.9	452.1	452.8	451.5	449.9	453.0	468.7	470.9	451.4
2013	447.5	446.1	449.0	452.3	456.9	460.2	461.9	462.2	459.7	463.5	474.8	480.0	459.5
Transportation and Utilities													
2002	124.5	123.9	124.4	124.5	125.2	126.5	127.0	127.8	126.9	127.8	127.9	127.7	126.2
2003	124.4	125.1	124.4	124.1	124.5	124.8	123.9	124.7	125.8	125.8	125.2	126.3	124.9
2004	122.7	123.6	124.2	126.0	126.7	127.5	128.4	128.4	128.6	128.5	128.9	129.9	127.0
2005	126.3	126.6	127.2	127.6	128.0	128.8	127.7	128.1	128.5	129.7	130.7	131.8	128.4
2006	128.0	128.1	129.2	129.3	130.1	130.8	131.9	132.6	133.1	133.5	133.9	134.5	131.3
2007	130.5	129.8	130.8	130.3	130.8	130.8	129.9	130.0	129.8	129.1	129.5	130.8	130.2
2008	126.6	126.5	126.5	126.5	127.2	127.3	126.5	126.7	125.9	125.9	125.8	127.0	126.5
2009	120.7	119.0	118.4	116.7	116.7	117.1	115.9	115.5	115.5	115.0	115.2	116.2	116.8
2010	111.8	111.6	112.5	113.4	114.5	115.1	115.6	115.7	116.0	116.4	117.1	117.9	114.8
2011	115.5	115.9	116.9	117.8	117.9	118.7	119.1	119.6	120.3	120.4	120.9	122.8	118.8
2012	119.1	118.8	119.9	119.6	119.9	120.3	120.2	120.2	121.0	121.2	121.9	124.1	120.5
2013	121.0	119.7	120.6	120.7	121.5	122.1	122.2	123.1	123.4	123.4	124.4	127.3	122.5
Information													
2002	73.8	73.6	73.8	73.5	73.7	73.6	72.8	72.4	71.7	71.9	71.9	72.1	72.9
2003	70.4	70.3	70.0	68.6	69.0	69.4	68.9	68.9	67.8	67.7	67.8	67.9	68.9
2004	67.2	66.7	67.0	66.4	66.3	67.1	67.1	67.2	66.7	68.1	69.3	69.7	67.4
2005	69.6	69.4	69.6	70.1	70.4	71.0	71.4	72.1	72.5	72.8	73.2	74.5	71.4
2006	74.1	74.0	73.9	72.7	72.9	73.5	72.6	72.7	72.3	72.5	72.5	72.9	73.1
2007	72.2	72.6	72.4	72.5	72.7	73.1	73.0	72.7	72.4	72.7	72.9	72.8	72.7
2008	72.0	72.3	72.2	72.2	72.4	72.4	72.2	72.2	71.5	72.2	72.5	72.4	72.2
2009	71.3	71.1	70.6	70.4	70.3	70.1	69.6	69.1	68.5	68.6	68.8	68.7	69.8
2010	67.7	67.7	67.9	67.8	68.3	68.6	68.7	68.6	68.4	68.3	68.7	68.8	68.3
2011	67.9	67.9	67.9	68.4	68.4	68.9	69.3	69.5	69.2	69.3	69.6	69.5	68.8
2012	69.1	69.2	69.0	69.1	69.0	69.5	69.6	69.3	68.6	68.8	69.1	69.3	69.1
2013	69.2	69.5	69.4	68.9	69.4	69.5	70.0	69.9	69.1	70.2	69.9	70.6	69.6

1. Employment by Industry: North Carolina, Selected Years, 2002–2013—*Continued*

(Numbers in thousands, not seasonally adjusted)

Industry and year	January	February	March	April	May	June	July	August	September	October	November	December	Annual average
Financial Activities													
2002	186.4	187.0	188.2	187.6	188.3	190.6	191.6	192.1	191.2	191.5	190.7	191.2	189.7
2003	188.2	188.8	190.0	191.1	192.4	194.2	191.9	193.1	192.4	193.0	191.0	192.4	191.5
2004	190.5	190.9	191.6	192.8	193.1	195.3	197.0	197.3	196.6	194.7	194.3	194.9	194.1
2005	192.5	193.3	194.0	196.9	197.7	200.0	201.7	201.9	201.0	200.7	200.1	200.9	198.4
2006	197.7	199.1	200.5	204.6	205.8	208.0	211.7	212.1	210.3	210.5	209.9	210.2	206.7
2007	207.7	208.8	210.2	212.2	213.3	215.6	215.2	215.3	213.6	213.4	212.4	212.9	212.6
2008	210.2	211.4	212.0	213.7	213.8	215.7	214.7	214.7	212.2	211.4	209.6	209.7	212.4
2009	205.3	204.7	203.9	203.3	204.0	204.4	204.5	203.6	201.1	200.1	199.9	200.1	202.9
2010	197.7	197.9	198.7	198.3	198.8	200.6	201.8	202.0	200.8	200.7	200.5	200.7	199.9
2011	198.5	199.0	199.3	199.9	201.3	203.2	203.7	204.1	201.8	201.6	201.1	201.3	201.2
2012	198.7	199.5	201.0	201.6	202.4	204.5	204.5	204.8	203.4	204.3	203.9	204.1	202.7
2013	201.8	202.3	203.0	205.1	206.2	208.7	209.4	209.8	208.5	206.9	204.4	205.1	205.9
Professional and Business Services													
2002	405.6	411.9	416.4	421.7	425.6	428.8	422.9	429.6	429.5	427.1	424.4	423.8	422.3
2003	412.6	414.2	419.4	424.6	427.9	428.9	418.3	423.7	423.4	427.6	427.9	427.1	423.0
2004	417.8	421.7	426.5	429.6	432.8	435.8	437.0	441.3	440.0	444.7	442.6	442.7	434.4
2005	435.6	437.4	441.4	446.8	443.5	445.4	450.1	454.4	457.2	460.9	460.0	458.9	449.3
2006	455.4	458.7	463.4	470.3	473.7	479.8	483.4	488.7	489.8	493.9	493.9	492.6	478.6
2007	477.4	484.4	490.1	495.1	498.6	505.6	502.4	507.1	508.7	510.9	508.7	508.7	499.8
2008	497.3	501.1	502.8	505.7	506.8	508.9	504.2	508.4	504.2	502.2	492.4	486.0	501.7
2009	470.5	467.8	463.5	461.3	459.8	460.2	461.5	464.8	466.4	472.6	474.2	473.3	466.3
2010	461.7	464.7	469.7	477.9	477.8	482.6	489.2	493.3	494.4	505.5	503.9	503.1	485.3
2011	490.4	500.2	503.6	509.5	508.6	513.2	516.2	520.6	524.3	526.2	526.1	525.5	513.7
2012	514.7	522.3	526.4	530.7	532.3	535.5	533.3	539.4	538.7	541.6	541.6	541.3	533.2
2013	526.0	535.1	538.9	544.0	545.6	549.2	548.0	556.5	558.0	567.4	565.0	563.0	549.7
Education and Health Services													
2002	413.6	417.5	419.2	424.2	424.9	423.4	420.4	423.8	425.7	429.0	430.2	430.2	423.5
2003	425.9	428.9	430.9	432.3	433.4	432.6	432.1	436.5	438.9	440.5	441.6	443.4	434.8
2004	437.7	440.6	443.7	448.1	449.6	449.0	449.3	453.1	456.3	457.6	459.9	461.3	450.5
2005	457.6	461.0	464.6	465.6	467.1	465.5	467.0	471.8	476.1	476.8	479.5	479.3	469.3
2006	479.2	483.3	485.9	487.5	489.5	489.6	489.9	494.6	498.1	502.4	505.8	507.4	492.8
2007	502.4	508.7	512.4	515.0	517.8	517.4	514.7	520.4	523.6	528.1	530.9	531.9	518.6
2008	523.9	528.9	529.4	529.1	531.5	529.3	526.3	530.0	533.3	534.1	537.8	537.9	531.0
2009	532.1	536.6	536.4	537.0	538.7	536.4	532.6	535.9	537.1	539.5	541.0	539.7	536.9
2010	533.8	535.7	537.3	538.0	538.4	533.9	532.7	534.5	533.0	541.0	542.5	540.2	536.8
2011	532.3	538.5	538.7	541.3	540.7	536.6	533.1	536.1	540.6	544.9	546.7	546.0	539.6
2012	541.3	546.1	546.4	546.9	549.0	545.8	543.2	546.3	551.0	555.9	557.3	558.1	548.9
2013	550.6	556.2	557.5	557.9	558.6	554.8	552.8	556.0	560.3	570.4	570.1	570.2	559.6
Leisure and Hospitality													
2002	311.4	315.1	324.0	338.2	348.3	356.1	356.3	356.4	348.8	340.1	334.8	332.7	338.5
2003	319.0	319.3	326.6	339.0	351.3	357.9	356.5	358.5	350.8	344.9	342.2	340.6	342.2
2004	326.0	328.0	336.7	350.8	362.2	369.1	372.7	373.7	365.4	357.2	353.1	351.8	353.9
2005	337.9	339.8	349.4	358.9	368.7	377.4	377.7	378.4	371.3	365.1	362.0	359.3	362.2
2006	349.3	353.1	362.3	377.0	388.3	396.3	401.2	400.9	394.2	390.7	388.8	386.9	382.4
2007	372.8	376.6	386.8	394.6	408.4	417.2	415.6	417.6	409.3	402.6	400.0	397.5	399.9
2008	384.7	389.2	397.6	403.3	415.3	420.7	422.6	423.0	414.3	402.8	395.0	391.7	405.0
2009	374.3	376.8	382.9	390.4	404.7	409.9	410.1	408.9	401.6	389.7	384.2	379.4	392.7
2010	364.3	365.4	374.8	387.3	399.0	408.7	410.7	411.6	404.8	397.0	391.8	385.5	391.7
2011	369.8	375.0	385.9	398.9	410.3	419.9	418.7	420.3	410.6	403.5	399.0	394.8	400.6
2012	383.1	387.1	399.0	412.1	424.6	432.9	436.0	437.8	426.1	419.9	414.2	410.8	415.3
2013	399.1	401.6	412.0	426.6	438.7	450.0	450.2	450.5	440.0	436.7	430.9	423.9	430.0
Other Services													
2002	142.1	142.9	143.9	145.9	146.7	148.0	145.6	143.0	140.8	142.0	140.6	138.1	143.3
2003	136.5	136.8	137.0	139.9	142.0	144.3	144.5	144.0	143.9	139.7	139.2	140.3	140.7
2004	140.9	142.1	144.0	143.9	146.8	151.3	147.3	146.1	144.2	144.6	144.8	145.1	145.0
2005	144.1	145.3	146.3	146.1	148.3	151.3	148.6	148.7	147.4	148.8	149.3	149.5	147.8
2006	148.8	150.5	152.5	149.8	152.1	155.4	152.4	151.0	149.0	152.9	153.3	153.6	151.8
2007	152.5	153.9	155.7	152.6	155.0	158.1	159.0	158.5	156.4	158.3	158.3	158.5	156.4
2008	156.7	157.8	157.9	159.7	161.4	163.5	164.0	163.0	160.3	158.5	157.6	156.6	159.8
2009	146.5	147.4	147.5	146.3	147.1	147.7	147.3	145.5	142.4	140.7	139.7	138.2	144.7
2010	137.0	137.2	138.2	137.5	138.7	140.5	140.6	139.8	138.3	139.2	138.9	138.1	138.7
2011	136.7	137.6	138.4	138.3	139.1	141.9	141.9	140.9	139.1	139.8	139.3	139.4	139.4
2012	138.4	138.9	139.9	141.1	143.0	145.2	146.0	145.8	145.4	145.2	145.5	145.4	143.3
2013	144.7	146.1	147.9	148.4	149.2	151.1	150.8	150.4	149.4	151.0	149.9	151.2	149.2
Government													
2002	653.5	660.5	664.9	662.7	664.2	631.2	585.6	624.1	651.5	668.2	665.4	660.9	649.4
2003	649.9	655.3	659.7	658.0	661.2	630.7	577.6	622.1	657.3	679.0	671.4	669.1	649.3
2004	658.4	663.4	668.1	667.1	669.8	638.1	586.1	637.4	677.7	681.9	684.1	683.1	659.6
2005	674.0	680.4	684.5	684.0	686.2	649.5	587.0	645.6	685.0	689.3	692.4	690.4	670.7
2006	685.2	691.5	696.8	699.2	702.9	673.5	601.9	661.6	697.5	706.0	716.5	714.7	687.3
2007	701.7	708.4	713.6	713.5	717.6	689.5	616.1	680.8	719.1	719.9	727.3	726.0	702.8
2008	717.1	724.8	730.0	731.7	736.3	708.4	629.7	695.5	740.6	742.3	747.2	745.2	720.7
2009	732.5	736.3	741.5	745.4	744.8	713.7	634.5	697.2	737.3	732.7	736.0	733.4	723.8
2010	723.2	729.0	735.3	740.8	759.1	717.8	629.7	689.4	720.5	732.9	737.8	734.3	720.8
2011	723.1	729.6	734.0	735.4	735.2	699.7	620.2	682.4	712.7	726.3	732.5	726.7	713.2
2012	719.1	727.0	730.4	731.4	734.4	689.1	610.9	684.1	718.0	734.2	740.5	734.3	712.8
2013	724.9	733.8	737.2	737.0	736.8	691.4	615.4	683.4	719.8	734.2	740.4	735.5	715.8

2. Average Weekly Hours by Selected Industry: North Carolina, 2009–2013

(Not seasonally adjusted)

Industry and year	January	February	March	April	May	June	July	August	September	October	November	December	Annual average
Total Private													
2009	33.6	34.0	33.7	33.6	33.8	33.8	33.9	34.0	33.9	34.1	34.0	33.8	33.8
2010	33.4	33.5	33.5	33.9	34.2	34.3	34.1	34.5	34.2	34.4	34.4	34.3	34.1
2011	33.8	34.1	34.1	34.4	34.6	34.3	34.3	34.2	34.2	34.6	34.3	34.4	34.3
2012	34.4	34.3	34.4	34.7	34.3	34.4	34.5	34.3	34.9	34.4	34.5	34.9	34.5
2013	34.0	34.4	34.5	34.4	34.3	34.9	34.2	34.6	35.0	34.4	34.6	34.7	34.5
Goods-Producing													
2009	37.5	37.6	37.5	37.1	38.0	38.4	38.7	38.7	38.6	38.6	38.5	38.5	38.1
2010	38.3	37.9	38.2	39.5	40.0	40.0	39.2	39.9	39.8	40.2	40.1	39.8	39.4
2011	39.2	38.8	39.2	39.8	39.9	40.1	39.8	39.7	39.8	40.0	40.1	40.3	39.7
2012	39.8	39.8	40.2	40.6	40.0	40.0	39.6	39.8	40.3	39.7	40.0	40.2	40.0
2013	39.4	39.5	39.9	39.9	39.9	40.4	39.8	40.7	41.0	40.1	40.8	40.7	40.2
Construction													
2009	36.9	37.6	37.3	37.2	37.8	38.4	38.5	38.0	37.7	37.1	36.1	36.1	37.4
2010	35.8	35.6	36.4	38.9	39.6	39.8	39.2	39.6	39.1	39.0	38.7	38.7	38.4
2011	37.8	38.0	38.2	39.7	39.4	39.4	39.6	39.1	39.0	38.8	38.9	39.1	38.9
2012	37.4	38.0	38.8	39.1	38.8	38.8	38.4	38.5	39.0	38.3	38.6	38.6	38.5
2013	37.8	37.3	38.7	38.9	38.9	39.0	38.7	39.8	40.1	38.9	39.8	38.4	38.9
Manufacturing													
2009	37.9	37.8	37.7	37.2	38.2	38.5	38.6	38.9	39.1	39.3	39.7	40.0	38.6
2010	39.8	39.3	39.4	40.2	40.6	40.5	39.6	40.4	40.4	41.0	40.9	41.0	40.3
2011	40.5	40.3	40.6	40.7	40.9	41.1	40.6	40.5	40.6	40.9	40.9	41.0	40.7
2012	41.0	40.7	40.9	41.3	40.5	40.5	40.0	40.3	40.9	40.4	40.7	41.0	40.7
2013	40.2	40.5	40.5	40.5	40.4	41.1	40.4	41.2	41.5	40.7	41.3	41.8	40.8
Trade, Transportation, and Utilities													
2009	34.6	34.5	34.3	33.9	34.4	34.7	34.8	35.1	35.0	35.3	34.7	34.8	34.7
2010	34.9	35.0	35.1	35.3	35.4	36.1	35.8	35.9	35.6	35.7	35.6	35.7	35.5
2011	34.8	35.3	35.1	35.1	35.1	34.8	34.7	34.6	34.8	34.8	34.2	34.5	34.8
2012	34.3	34.7	34.7	35.1	34.7	34.7	35.0	34.7	35.3	34.8	34.8	34.8	34.8
2013	34.0	34.5	34.7	34.6	34.5	35.0	34.7	34.8	35.1	34.5	34.4	34.7	34.6
Information													
2009	35.6	34.8	35.3	35.0	34.7	34.7	35.0	35.1	35.0	35.2	35.8	35.8	35.2
2010	35.3	35.5	36.1	36.3	35.6	36.3	36.3	36.5	35.4	35.6	36.2	36.3	35.9
2011	36.0	36.0	36.4	35.9	36.7	36.5	36.8	36.5	36.9	37.9	37.0	36.7	36.6
2012	37.5	37.0	36.8	37.0	36.6	36.5	37.2	36.5	37.3	36.6	37.2	37.6	37.0
2013	36.1	36.3	36.1	36.5	37.1	38.9	36.5	36.7	36.8	35.7	36.9	37.2	36.7
Financial Activities													
2009	38.0	38.4	37.9	37.2	36.8	36.7	36.0	36.1	35.8	35.8	36.5	35.6	36.7
2010	36.3	36.8	36.1	36.7	38.0	37.2	37.1	38.2	37.5	37.9	37.8	36.8	37.2
2011	37.4	37.9	37.3	37.4	37.9	37.2	37.4	36.8	37.1	39.0	37.7	37.7	37.6
2012	38.4	37.4	37.4	37.5	36.4	36.7	37.3	36.4	37.8	36.7	36.9	37.9	37.2
2013	36.1	37.0	36.5	36.5	36.6	37.6	36.0	36.1	36.9	36.0	36.2	36.7	36.5
Professional and Business Services													
2009	34.8	35.8	35.5	35.6	35.4	35.0	34.7	35.0	34.9	35.3	35.7	35.1	35.2
2010	32.0	32.5	32.8	33.2	33.7	33.8	33.3	34.3	34.0	34.1	34.2	34.4	33.5
2011	33.5	34.1	34.1	35.3	36.1	35.6	35.3	35.5	35.4	36.1	35.7	35.9	35.2
2012	35.5	35.4	35.5	36.2	35.7	36.2	36.1	36.0	36.5	35.8	36.0	36.9	36.0
2013	35.7	36.2	36.1	36.2	36.4	36.9	35.8	36.6	37.2	36.4	36.5	36.5	36.4
Education and Health Services													
2009	31.8	32.2	31.9	31.9	32.3	31.9	31.9	32.0	31.9	32.1	32.1	31.6	32.0
2010	31.9	31.8	31.7	31.8	32.3	31.9	32.1	32.3	32.1	32.3	32.3	32.1	32.0
2011	32.0	32.3	32.2	32.3	32.7	32.2	32.2	32.1	32.1	32.4	32.2	32.3	32.3
2012	32.8	32.3	32.5	32.8	32.5	32.7	33.1	32.9	33.4	33.0	33.0	33.2	32.8
2013	32.9	33.0	32.8	32.8	32.7	33.4	32.7	32.7	33.2	32.8	32.8	33.0	32.9
Leisure and Hospitality													
2009	24.5	26.2	25.7	26.3	26.3	26.6	26.6	26.7	26.4	26.3	26.1	26.0	26.2
2010	25.6	26.3	26.3	26.4	26.2	26.2	26.6	26.6	25.6	25.9	25.8	25.7	26.1
2011	25.1	26.0	25.9	26.1	25.9	25.7	26.0	25.9	25.2	25.8	25.4	25.1	25.7
2012	25.1	25.5	25.5	25.5	25.6	25.6	25.9	25.7	25.4	25.4	25.1	25.4	25.5
2013	24.5	25.5	25.9	25.8	25.6	25.9	25.8	25.7	25.7	25.7	25.7	25.6	25.6
Other Services													
2009	29.1	29.6	29.1	29.3	29.0	28.9	29.3	29.5	29.5	29.5	29.6	29.5	29.3
2010	29.7	30.3	29.0	29.1	29.2	29.9	30.5	30.2	29.6	29.8	29.8	29.7	29.7
2011	29.6	30.7	30.5	30.6	30.9	30.6	31.3	31.3	31.3	31.1	32.0	31.8	31.0
2012	31.5	31.0	31.1	31.5	31.1	30.8	31.0	30.4	31.3	31.0	31.7	32.1	31.2
2013	30.9	31.1	31.3	30.7	30.3	31.3	30.5	30.8	31.9	30.9	31.4	30.8	31.0

3. Average Hourly Earnings by Selected Industry: North Carolina, 2009–2013

(Dollars, not seasonally adjusted)

Industry and year	January	February	March	April	May	June	July	August	September	October	November	December	Annual average
Total Private													
2009	20.87	20.72	20.72	20.62	20.38	20.47	20.41	20.48	20.54	20.57	20.84	20.68	20.61
2010	21.01	21.06	20.97	20.80	20.62	20.32	20.46	20.49	20.41	20.45	20.42	20.55	20.63
2011	20.86	20.76	20.57	20.68	20.78	20.61	20.79	20.78	21.11	21.39	21.28	21.35	20.91
2012	21.64	21.63	21.53	21.78	21.50	21.67	21.74	21.56	21.90	21.65	21.78	22.10	21.71
2013	21.93	21.85	21.75	21.63	21.55	21.67	21.52	21.51	21.68	21.55	21.64	21.85	21.68
Goods-Producing													
2009	19.76	19.83	19.95	20.09	19.90	19.89	19.83	19.90	19.89	19.77	19.93	19.90	19.89
2010	20.41	20.58	20.35	20.22	19.98	19.61	20.21	20.01	19.69	19.53	19.72	19.96	20.01
2011	20.16	20.33	20.04	20.13	20.28	20.14	20.22	20.09	20.32	20.46	20.52	20.65	20.28
2012	20.68	20.65	20.62	20.58	20.42	20.41	20.66	20.39	20.66	20.58	20.91	21.05	20.63
2013	21.06	20.91	20.96	20.98	20.85	20.79	20.88	20.76	20.81	20.81	20.90	21.15	20.90
Construction													
2009	20.42	20.34	20.48	20.64	20.51	20.25	19.99	20.12	20.22	20.23	20.56	20.66	20.36
2010	20.64	20.82	20.51	20.15	19.64	19.70	19.91	19.75	19.69	19.96	19.88	19.91	20.03
2011	20.17	20.36	20.36	20.31	20.43	20.11	20.14	20.03	20.05	20.55	20.77	20.66	20.33
2012	20.49	20.56	20.46	20.23	20.29	20.25	20.63	20.30	20.53	20.39	20.84	21.10	20.50
2013	21.14	21.05	20.89	20.66	20.70	20.50	20.35	20.59	20.59	20.85	20.64	21.08	20.75
Manufacturing													
2009	19.50	19.62	19.75	19.75	19.55	19.54	19.56	19.62	19.60	19.42	19.53	19.49	19.58
2010	20.23	20.39	20.20	20.16	20.05	19.64	20.41	20.19	19.77	19.43	19.72	19.70	19.99
2011	20.40	20.23	19.83	19.98	20.15	20.08	20.17	20.05	20.38	20.40	20.40	20.62	20.22
2012	20.74	20.65	20.64	20.68	20.43	20.42	20.61	20.36	20.63	20.58	20.86	20.96	20.63
2013	20.97	20.79	20.92	21.04	20.85	20.84	21.03	20.80	20.87	20.79	20.96	21.14	20.92
Trade, Transportation, and Utilities													
2009	20.16	19.90	20.04	19.39	19.03	19.44	19.17	19.32	19.42	19.42	19.49	19.13	19.49
2010	19.60	19.55	19.73	19.29	18.79	18.83	18.89	18.85	18.79	18.98	18.87	19.01	19.09
2011	19.51	19.46	19.14	19.60	19.47	19.46	19.54	19.42	19.67	20.00	19.87	19.71	19.57
2012	20.30	20.47	20.40	20.63	20.36	20.75	20.69	20.70	20.91	20.70	20.70	21.06	20.64
2013	20.92	20.70	20.72	20.70	20.54	20.82	20.82	20.71	21.07	20.90	20.85	20.96	20.81
Information													
2009	28.16	28.00	28.16	27.36	27.78	27.54	27.55	27.66	27.48	28.35	29.07	28.12	27.94
2010	28.37	29.26	28.06	28.07	28.68	28.70	27.68	27.53	28.32	29.10	28.70	28.27	28.31
2011	28.55	29.08	28.19	28.86	28.96	28.53	29.79	29.29	29.82	30.39	30.66	30.29	29.38
2012	31.21	30.52	29.94	31.34	30.95	31.47	31.60	30.72	32.50	30.92	30.50	31.47	31.10
2013	31.20	30.99	31.25	30.93	30.37	31.53	30.73	31.00	31.72	31.29	32.08	31.92	31.25
Financial Activities													
2009	25.50	25.07	25.00	24.97	25.29	25.42	25.93	25.99	25.88	25.66	26.36	25.51	25.54
2010	25.34	25.78	25.81	25.52	25.54	25.75	25.99	25.86	25.72	26.16	26.15	26.28	25.83
2011	26.19	26.34	26.01	25.90	25.75	25.19	25.69	26.50	26.84	26.79	26.83	26.91	26.25
2012	27.41	27.51	27.33	27.96	27.78	27.53	27.83	27.85	28.11	28.05	27.96	27.84	27.76
2013	27.73	28.29	27.77	27.46	28.17	28.19	28.02	28.10	27.62	27.27	27.56	27.75	27.83
Professional and Business Services													
2009	26.65	26.41	26.57	26.91	26.59	26.85	26.88	26.89	26.90	26.80	27.38	27.43	26.86
2010	29.04	28.82	28.68	28.20	27.80	26.73	26.84	26.96	26.95	26.80	26.38	26.53	27.43
2011	27.69	26.88	26.48	26.11	26.56	26.06	26.52	26.27	26.45	26.73	26.33	26.45	26.53
2012	26.67	26.70	26.42	26.89	26.43	26.56	26.85	26.27	26.66	25.76	26.00	26.68	26.49
2013	26.32	26.35	26.30	25.84	25.54	25.90	25.44	25.29	25.68	25.24	25.54	26.01	25.78
Education and Health Services													
2009	20.73	20.74	20.69	20.50	20.32	20.42	20.39	20.29	20.37	20.39	20.47	20.56	20.49
2010	20.31	20.27	20.14	20.31	20.41	20.35	20.37	20.34	20.03	20.04	20.13	20.21	20.24
2011	20.01	19.94	20.40	20.44	20.35	20.52	20.56	20.67	21.08	21.49	21.42	21.47	20.70
2012	21.69	21.71	21.75	22.06	21.89	22.18	22.13	22.11	22.28	22.21	22.34	22.47	22.07
2013	22.08	22.00	21.88	21.89	21.94	21.89	21.88	21.98	21.94	22.05	22.05	22.06	21.97
Leisure and Hospitality													
2009	11.90	11.98	11.30	11.84	11.71	11.57	11.58	11.66	11.77	11.87	11.89	11.84	11.74
2010	11.64	11.64	11.52	11.67	11.82	11.63	11.47	11.67	11.88	11.65	11.66	11.58	11.65
2011	11.24	11.39	11.54	11.64	11.85	11.90	11.96	12.19	12.43	12.61	12.56	12.93	12.03
2012	12.75	12.67	12.75	12.68	12.73	12.85	12.63	12.69	12.97	12.98	13.10	13.21	12.83
2013	13.02	12.96	12.80	12.70	12.68	12.62	12.50	12.54	12.52	12.56	12.57	12.60	12.67
Other Services													
2009	16.50	16.43	16.30	16.33	16.38	15.94	15.92	15.99	16.01	16.05	16.16	16.37	16.20
2010	16.19	16.33	16.43	16.74	17.07	16.78	16.48	16.82	16.71	16.73	16.70	16.74	16.64
2011	16.64	16.30	16.15	16.39	16.95	16.47	16.45	16.53	16.90	16.83	16.58	16.84	16.59
2012	17.09	16.99	17.08	17.44	17.11	17.26	17.14	16.95	17.25	17.63	17.25	17.71	17.25
2013	18.17	17.96	17.90	18.07	17.97	18.03	17.91	18.15	18.10	18.17	17.82	18.12	18.03

4. Average Weekly Earnings by Selected Industry: North Carolina, 2009–2013

(Dollars, not seasonally adjusted)

Industry and year	January	February	March	April	May	June	July	August	September	October	November	December	Annual average
Total Private													
2009	701.23	704.48	698.26	692.83	688.84	691.89	691.90	696.32	696.31	701.44	708.56	698.98	696.62
2010	701.73	705.51	702.50	705.12	705.20	696.98	697.69	706.91	698.02	703.48	702.45	704.87	703.48
2011	705.07	707.92	701.44	711.39	718.99	706.92	713.10	710.68	721.96	740.09	729.90	734.44	717.21
2012	744.42	741.91	740.63	755.77	737.45	745.45	750.03	739.51	764.31	744.76	751.41	771.29	749.00
2013	745.62	751.64	750.38	744.07	739.17	756.28	735.98	744.25	758.80	741.32	748.74	758.20	747.96
Goods-Producing													
2009	741.00	745.61	748.13	745.34	756.20	763.78	767.42	770.13	767.75	763.12	767.31	766.15	757.81
2010	781.70	779.98	777.37	798.69	799.20	784.40	792.23	798.40	783.66	785.11	790.77	794.41	788.39
2011	790.27	788.80	785.57	801.17	809.17	807.61	804.76	797.57	808.74	818.40	822.85	832.20	805.12
2012	823.06	821.87	828.92	835.55	816.80	816.40	818.14	811.52	832.60	817.03	836.40	846.21	825.20
2013	829.76	825.95	836.30	837.10	831.92	839.92	831.02	844.93	853.21	834.48	852.72	860.81	840.18
Construction													
2009	753.50	764.78	763.90	767.81	775.28	777.60	769.62	764.56	762.29	750.53	742.22	745.83	761.46
2010	738.91	741.19	746.56	783.84	777.74	784.06	780.47	782.10	769.88	778.44	769.36	770.52	769.15
2011	762.43	773.68	777.75	806.31	804.94	792.33	797.54	783.17	781.95	797.34	807.95	807.81	790.84
2012	766.33	781.28	793.85	790.99	787.25	785.70	792.19	781.55	800.67	780.94	804.42	814.46	789.25
2013	799.09	785.17	808.44	803.67	805.23	799.50	787.55	819.48	825.66	811.07	821.47	809.47	807.18
Manufacturing													
2009	739.05	741.64	744.58	734.70	746.81	752.29	755.02	763.22	766.36	763.21	775.34	779.60	755.79
2010	805.15	801.33	795.88	810.43	814.03	795.42	808.24	815.68	798.71	796.63	806.55	807.70	805.60
2011	826.20	815.27	805.10	813.19	824.14	825.29	818.90	812.03	827.43	834.36	834.36	845.42	822.95
2012	850.34	840.46	844.18	854.08	827.42	827.01	824.40	820.51	843.77	831.43	849.00	859.36	839.64
2013	842.99	842.00	847.26	852.12	842.34	856.52	849.61	856.96	866.11	846.15	865.65	883.65	853.54
Trade, Transportation, and Utilities													
2009	697.54	686.55	687.37	657.32	654.63	674.57	667.12	678.13	679.70	685.53	676.30	665.72	676.30
2010	684.04	684.25	692.52	680.94	665.17	679.76	676.26	676.72	668.92	677.59	671.77	678.66	677.70
2011	678.95	686.94	671.81	687.96	683.40	677.21	678.04	671.93	684.52	696.00	679.55	680.00	681.04
2012	696.29	710.31	707.88	724.11	706.49	720.03	724.15	718.29	738.12	720.36	720.36	732.89	718.27
2013	711.28	714.15	718.98	716.22	708.63	728.70	722.45	720.71	739.56	721.05	717.24	727.31	720.03
Information													
2009	1,002.50	974.40	994.05	957.60	963.97	955.64	964.25	970.87	961.80	997.92	1,040.71	1,006.70	983.49
2010	1,001.46	1,038.73	1,012.97	1,018.94	1,021.01	1,009.14	1,004.78	1,004.85	1,002.53	1,035.96	1,038.94	1,026.20	1,016.33
2011	1,027.80	1,046.88	1,026.12	1,036.07	1,062.83	1,041.35	1,096.27	1,069.09	1,100.36	1,151.78	1,134.42	1,111.64	1,075.31
2012	1,170.38	1,129.24	1,101.79	1,159.58	1,132.77	1,148.66	1,175.52	1,121.28	1,212.25	1,131.67	1,134.60	1,183.27	1,150.70
2013	1,126.32	1,124.94	1,128.13	1,128.95	1,126.73	1,226.52	1,121.65	1,137.70	1,167.30	1,117.05	1,183.75	1,187.42	1,146.88
Financial Activities													
2009	969.00	962.69	947.50	928.88	930.67	932.91	933.48	938.24	926.50	918.63	962.14	908.16	937.32
2010	919.84	948.70	931.74	936.58	970.52	957.90	964.23	987.85	964.50	991.46	988.47	967.10	960.88
2011	979.51	998.29	970.17	968.66	975.93	937.07	960.81	975.20	995.76	1,044.81	1,011.49	1,014.51	987.00
2012	1,052.54	1,028.87	1,022.14	1,048.50	1,011.19	1,010.35	1,038.06	1,013.74	1,062.56	1,029.44	1,031.72	1,055.14	1,032.67
2013	1,001.05	1,046.73	1,013.61	1,002.29	1,031.02	1,059.94	1,008.72	1,014.41	1,019.18	981.72	997.67	1,018.43	1,015.80
Professional and Business Services													
2009	927.42	945.48	943.24	958.00	941.29	939.75	932.74	941.15	938.81	946.04	977.47	962.79	945.47
2010	929.28	936.65	940.70	936.24	936.86	903.47	893.77	924.73	916.30	913.88	902.20	912.63	918.91
2011	927.62	916.61	902.97	921.68	958.82	927.74	936.16	932.59	936.33	964.95	939.98	949.56	933.86
2012	946.79	945.18	937.91	973.42	943.55	961.47	969.29	945.72	973.09	922.21	936.00	984.49	953.64
2013	939.62	953.87	949.43	935.41	929.66	955.71	910.75	925.61	955.30	918.74	932.21	949.37	938.39
Education and Health Services													
2009	659.21	667.83	660.01	653.95	656.34	651.40	650.44	649.28	649.80	654.52	657.09	649.70	655.68
2010	647.89	644.59	638.44	645.86	659.24	649.17	653.88	656.98	642.96	647.29	650.20	648.74	647.68
2011	640.32	644.06	656.88	660.21	665.45	660.74	662.03	663.51	676.67	696.28	689.72	693.48	668.61
2012	711.43	701.23	706.88	723.57	711.43	725.29	732.50	727.42	744.15	732.93	737.22	746.00	723.90
2013	726.43	726.00	717.66	717.99	717.44	731.13	715.48	718.75	728.41	723.24	723.24	727.98	722.81
Leisure and Hospitality													
2009	291.55	313.88	290.41	311.39	307.97	307.76	308.03	311.32	310.73	312.18	310.33	307.84	307.59
2010	297.98	306.13	302.98	308.09	309.68	304.71	305.10	310.42	304.13	301.74	300.83	297.61	304.07
2011	282.12	296.14	298.89	303.80	306.92	305.83	310.96	315.72	313.24	325.34	319.02	324.54	309.17
2012	320.03	323.09	325.13	323.34	325.89	328.96	327.12	326.13	329.44	329.69	328.81	335.53	327.17
2013	318.99	330.48	331.52	327.66	324.61	326.86	322.50	322.28	321.76	322.79	323.05	322.56	324.35
Other Services													
2009	480.15	486.33	474.33	478.47	475.02	460.67	466.46	471.71	472.30	473.48	478.34	482.92	474.66
2010	480.84	494.80	476.47	487.13	498.44	501.72	502.64	507.96	494.62	498.55	497.66	497.18	494.21
2011	492.54	500.41	492.58	501.53	523.76	503.98	514.89	517.39	528.97	523.41	530.56	535.51	514.29
2012	538.34	526.69	531.19	549.36	532.12	531.61	531.34	515.28	539.93	546.53	546.83	568.49	538.20
2013	561.45	558.56	560.27	554.75	544.49	564.34	546.26	559.02	577.39	561.45	559.55	558.10	558.93

NORTH DAKOTA
At a Glance

Population:
2000 census: 642,237
2010 census: 672,591
2013 estimate: 723,393

Percent change in population:
2000–2010: 4.7%
2010–2013: 7.6%

Percent change in total nonfarm employment:
2000–2010: 14.7%
2010–2013: 18.2%

Industry with the largest growth in employment, 2000–2013 (thousands):
Trade, Transportation, and Utilities, 29.6

Industry with the largest decline or smallest growth in employment, 2000–2013 (thousands):
Information, -1.6

Civilian labor force:
2000: 345,881
2010: 377,516
2013: 400,588

Unemployment rate and rank among states (lowest to highest):
2000: 2.9%, 10th
2010: 3.8%, 1st
2013: 2.9%, 1st

Over-the-year change in unemployment rates:
2010–2011: -0.4%
2011–2012: -0.4%
2012–2013: -0.1%

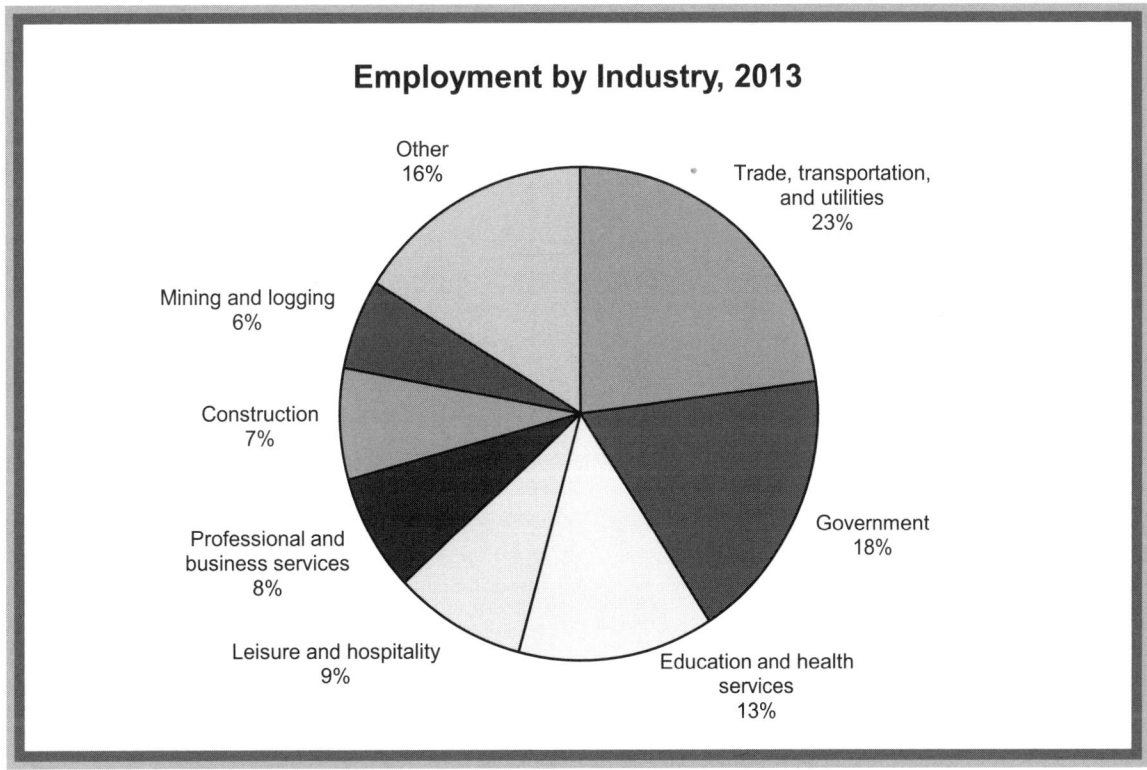

Employment by Industry, 2013

Other
16%

Trade, transportation,
and utilities
23%

Mining and logging
6%

Construction
7%

Professional and
business services
8%

Government
18%

Leisure and hospitality
9%

Education and health
services
13%

1. Employment by Industry: North Dakota, Selected Years, 2002–2013

(Numbers in thousands, not seasonally adjusted)

Industry and year	January	February	March	April	May	June	July	August	September	October	November	December	Annual average
Total Nonfarm													
2002	322.6	323.9	323.9	328.6	333.8	333.4	325.1	327.0	334.2	335.5	334.5	334.5	329.8
2003	323.9	325.3	327.2	331.7	336.9	335.4	326.7	330.9	338.7	340.1	337.7	337.2	332.6
2004	326.5	328.2	330.6	337.1	342.0	341.2	334.9	336.2	343.7	346.1	344.8	343.9	337.9
2005	333.4	336.1	338.3	345.7	349.7	348.3	339.5	342.3	351.4	350.7	350.5	350.8	344.7
2006	341.1	343.7	347.0	352.2	357.0	356.2	345.6	349.1	358.6	358.8	358.3	359.0	352.2
2007	348.5	349.6	352.6	356.2	362.7	362.7	352.9	354.2	364.2	365.8	365.8	365.6	358.4
2008	356.9	359.0	361.6	365.9	371.8	371.2	363.0	364.0	373.7	374.9	373.6	372.1	367.3
2009	358.7	359.8	360.5	362.9	370.7	372.0	361.8	362.4	372.6	374.2	372.6	372.1	366.7
2010	360.1	362.6	365.9	374.2	379.0	379.8	371.2	373.1	383.0	388.3	387.4	387.5	376.0
2011	377.5	379.1	382.7	389.2	396.0	397.8	391.8	395.4	408.2	412.1	413.6	415.2	396.6
2012	408.2	411.4	416.3	424.2	432.2	436.0	428.9	430.7	439.3	441.9	439.1	439.2	429.0
2013	428.0	431.1	433.5	436.3	446.4	449.8	441.5	444.1	453.2	456.8	456.4	454.0	444.3
Total Private													
2002	247.5	247.8	247.9	252.3	257.3	261.3	260.7	261.0	258.6	258.3	257.2	256.2	255.5
2003	248.5	247.8	249.3	253.4	258.4	262.5	262.0	263.9	261.8	259.8	259.0	259.0	257.4
2004	251.0	251.6	253.8	259.9	265.0	268.9	270.6	270.2	267.5	268.3	267.2	266.0	263.3
2005	257.8	258.4	260.4	267.3	271.6	275.2	275.5	276.2	274.7	273.1	272.8	272.8	269.7
2006	264.9	266.0	268.8	273.7	278.6	282.5	281.4	282.8	281.7	280.3	279.8	280.1	276.7
2007	272.0	271.8	274.6	277.8	284.2	288.0	287.7	287.9	287.2	287.5	287.1	286.8	282.7
2008	279.9	280.6	283.4	287.4	292.5	296.4	296.9	297.0	296.0	295.6	294.3	292.5	291.0
2009	281.2	281.1	281.4	283.2	290.0	294.0	293.5	293.3	292.3	292.9	291.3	290.3	288.8
2010	280.7	281.6	284.0	292.1	296.1	299.8	301.0	302.5	302.5	306.1	305.2	305.1	296.4
2011	297.3	297.7	301.2	307.7	314.2	318.4	322.5	325.7	328.2	330.6	332.3	333.3	317.4
2012	328.5	330.4	335.0	342.7	350.5	356.6	358.6	360.7	358.6	359.5	356.7	356.7	349.5
2013	347.5	349.4	351.8	354.6	364.1	369.4	370.6	373.3	372.3	373.8	373.7	370.9	364.3
Goods-Producing													
2002	38.4	38.2	38.4	40.2	42.7	44.4	45.0	45.3	44.2	43.7	42.4	40.9	42.0
2003	38.5	38.0	38.4	40.2	43.2	45.4	45.9	46.7	46.2	45.7	43.6	42.1	42.8
2004	39.5	39.5	40.5	43.6	46.1	48.6	49.5	49.4	48.6	48.1	46.6	44.6	45.4
2005	42.0	42.3	43.2	45.8	48.2	50.1	51.1	51.2	50.4	49.6	48.8	47.3	47.5
2006	44.4	44.4	45.1	48.0	50.1	52.0	52.4	52.7	52.0	50.9	50.1	49.0	49.3
2007	45.9	45.3	46.4	48.2	50.9	52.9	53.7	53.6	53.2	53.1	52.1	50.4	50.5
2008	48.1	48.3	49.6	51.4	54.3	57.0	58.0	58.0	57.7	57.1	55.3	53.0	54.0
2009	47.6	47.7	47.7	48.5	51.2	53.7	54.6	54.9	54.7	54.1	52.4	50.2	51.4
2010	46.6	47.1	48.1	52.0	54.7	56.3	58.0	59.0	59.4	60.2	59.2	58.0	54.9
2011	54.9	55.0	56.5	59.9	63.4	66.0	68.7	70.4	71.6	72.8	72.8	71.4	65.3
2012	69.4	70.5	72.6	76.7	80.4	83.6	85.3	86.0	85.0	84.5	81.3	79.6	79.6
2013	76.2	76.6	77.5	79.3	84.6	87.9	88.7	90.1	89.4	89.3	86.5	82.9	84.1
Service-Providing													
2002	284.2	285.7	285.5	288.4	291.1	289.0	280.1	281.7	290.0	291.8	292.1	293.6	287.8
2003	285.4	287.3	288.8	291.5	293.7	290.0	280.8	284.2	292.5	294.4	294.1	295.1	289.8
2004	287.0	288.7	290.1	293.5	295.9	292.6	285.4	286.8	295.1	298.0	298.2	299.3	292.6
2005	291.4	293.8	295.1	299.9	301.5	298.2	288.4	291.1	301.0	301.1	301.7	303.5	297.2
2006	296.7	299.3	301.9	304.2	306.9	304.2	293.2	296.4	306.6	307.9	308.2	310.0	303.0
2007	302.6	304.3	306.2	308.0	311.8	309.8	299.2	300.6	311.0	312.7	313.7	315.2	307.9
2008	308.8	310.7	312.0	314.5	317.5	314.2	305.0	306.0	316.0	317.8	318.3	319.1	313.3
2009	311.1	312.1	312.8	314.4	319.5	318.3	307.2	307.5	317.9	320.1	320.2	321.9	315.3
2010	313.5	315.5	317.8	322.2	324.3	323.5	313.2	314.1	323.6	328.1	328.2	329.5	321.1
2011	322.6	324.1	326.2	329.3	332.6	331.8	323.1	325.0	336.6	339.3	340.8	343.8	331.3
2012	338.8	340.9	343.7	347.5	351.8	352.4	343.6	344.7	354.3	357.4	357.8	359.6	349.4
2013	351.8	354.5	356.0	357.0	361.8	361.9	352.8	354.0	363.8	367.5	369.9	371.1	360.2
Mining and Logging													
2002	2.9	2.8	2.9	3.1	3.3	3.4	3.4	3.4	3.3	3.4	3.3	3.1	3.2
2003	2.9	2.9	3.0	3.2	3.5	3.6	3.6	3.6	3.5	3.6	3.4	3.3	3.3
2004	3.2	3.2	3.3	3.4	3.5	3.6	3.7	3.8	3.8	3.7	3.7	3.6	3.5
2005	3.6	3.7	3.7	3.9	4.1	4.2	4.3	4.5	4.4	4.3	4.4	4.4	4.1
2006	4.1	4.3	4.3	4.6	4.8	4.7	4.7	4.9	5.0	5.1	5.1	5.0	4.7
2007	4.8	4.7	4.8	4.9	5.1	5.2	5.3	5.3	5.3	5.3	5.3	5.5	5.1
2008	5.4	5.6	5.9	6.2	6.5	6.8	6.9	7.3	7.5	7.8	8.0	7.9	6.8
2009	7.4	7.2	7.1	6.7	6.8	6.9	6.7	6.7	6.8	6.9	7.1	7.4	7.0
2010	7.6	8.3	8.8	9.4	10.0	10.6	11.2	11.7	12.1	12.5	12.7	13.2	10.7
2011	13.5	14.0	14.5	15.2	15.9	16.3	17.1	17.7	18.3	19.0	20.2	21.0	16.9
2012	21.3	22.2	23.2	23.9	24.6	25.4	26.1	26.1	25.6	25.2	24.9	24.8	24.4
2013	24.6	25.1	25.5	25.5	26.0	26.4	26.3	26.6	26.6	27.0	27.4	27.5	26.2
Construction													
2002	12.4	12.2	12.2	13.6	15.7	16.9	17.6	17.8	17.1	16.4	15.3	14.2	15.1
2003	12.4	12.2	12.4	13.9	16.3	17.9	18.4	19.1	18.9	18.2	16.6	15.1	16.0
2004	13.1	13.0	13.7	16.3	18.2	19.8	20.4	20.1	19.5	19.0	17.6	15.9	17.2
2005	13.6	13.6	14.1	16.3	18.2	19.5	20.4	20.3	19.7	19.0	18.1	16.6	17.5
2006	14.8	14.7	15.2	17.6	19.4	20.9	21.0	21.2	20.6	20.2	18.8	17.6	18.5
2007	15.6	15.3	16.1	17.7	19.9	21.2	21.8	22.0	21.6	21.4	20.4	18.6	19.3
2008	16.7	16.6	17.5	18.9	21.4	23.3	24.3	24.2	23.7	22.7	21.0	19.3	20.8
2009	16.7	16.3	16.5	17.9	20.8	23.2	24.4	24.8	24.6	23.9	22.2	20.0	20.9
2010	17.2	16.9	17.4	20.4	22.4	23.1	24.1	24.6	24.2	24.4	23.2	21.5	21.6
2011	18.5	18.1	18.9	21.1	23.8	25.7	27.6	28.8	29.2	29.4	28.1	25.8	24.6
2012	23.7	23.7	24.5	27.9	30.6	32.6	33.6	34.1	33.7	33.6	31.1	29.8	29.9
2013	27.1	26.9	27.3	28.9	33.0	35.6	36.5	37.6	37.0	36.1	33.2	29.8	32.4

1. Employment by Industry: North Dakota, Selected Years, 2002–2013—*Continued*

(Numbers in thousands, not seasonally adjusted)

Industry and year	January	February	March	April	May	June	July	August	September	October	November	December	Annual average
Manufacturing													
2002	23.1	23.2	23.3	23.5	23.7	24.1	24.0	24.1	23.8	23.9	23.8	23.6	23.7
2003	23.2	22.9	23.0	23.1	23.4	23.9	23.9	24.0	23.8	23.9	23.6	23.7	23.5
2004	23.2	23.3	23.5	23.9	24.4	25.2	25.4	25.5	25.3	25.4	25.3	25.1	24.6
2005	24.8	25.0	25.4	25.6	25.9	26.4	26.4	26.4	26.3	26.3	26.3	26.3	25.9
2006	25.5	25.4	25.6	25.8	25.9	26.4	26.7	26.6	26.4	25.6	26.2	26.4	26.0
2007	25.5	25.3	25.5	25.6	25.9	26.5	26.6	26.3	26.3	26.4	26.4	26.3	26.1
2008	26.0	26.1	26.2	26.3	26.4	26.9	26.8	26.5	26.6	26.3	25.8	26.4	26.4
2009	23.5	24.2	24.1	23.9	23.6	23.6	23.5	23.4	23.3	23.3	23.1	22.8	23.5
2010	21.8	21.9	21.9	22.2	22.3	22.6	22.7	22.7	23.1	23.3	23.3	23.3	22.6
2011	22.9	22.9	23.1	23.6	23.7	24.0	24.0	23.9	24.1	24.4	24.5	24.6	23.8
2012	24.4	24.6	24.9	24.9	25.2	25.6	25.6	25.8	25.7	25.7	25.3	25.0	25.2
2013	24.5	24.6	24.7	24.9	25.6	25.9	25.9	25.9	25.8	26.2	25.9	25.6	25.5
Trade, Transportation, and Utilities													
2002	71.0	70.3	70.3	70.9	72.2	72.4	71.7	71.5	71.2	71.8	72.9	73.6	71.7
2003	70.9	70.2	70.4	71.5	72.3	72.3	71.5	72.0	71.6	72.6	73.5	74.1	71.9
2004	71.3	71.0	71.3	72.4	73.5	73.4	73.0	72.9	72.5	73.5	74.8	75.6	72.9
2005	72.3	72.3	72.8	74.3	75.0	74.9	74.4	74.2	74.4	74.8	75.7	76.5	74.3
2006	74.0	73.9	74.6	76.0	76.9	76.9	76.1	76.3	76.2	76.4	77.4	78.0	76.1
2007	75.4	75.0	75.1	75.9	77.0	76.8	76.7	76.4	76.2	77.1	78.3	78.9	76.6
2008	76.6	76.3	76.7	77.4	78.1	78.0	78.1	77.9	77.9	78.4	79.3	79.7	77.9
2009	77.0	76.5	76.6	76.9	78.5	78.5	78.2	77.8	77.8	78.7	79.8	80.1	78.0
2010	77.7	77.6	77.8	79.7	80.6	80.9	80.9	81.1	81.0	82.4	83.5	84.2	80.6
2011	82.2	82.2	82.6	84.3	85.7	86.2	86.9	87.6	88.0	89.8	91.8	93.2	86.7
2012	91.8	92.0	93.0	95.0	96.8	97.6	97.9	98.2	97.9	99.2	100.3	100.8	96.7
2013	98.3	98.4	98.7	99.4	101.4	101.7	101.8	102.5	102.5	104.0	105.8	107.2	101.8
Wholesale Trade													
2002	17.8	17.7	17.7	18.0	18.4	18.6	18.2	18.1	17.8	18.0	17.9	17.8	18.0
2003	17.5	17.3	17.4	18.1	18.4	18.4	18.2	18.1	17.8	18.1	18.0	18.0	17.9
2004	17.8	17.8	18.0	18.6	18.8	18.8	18.7	18.6	18.2	18.4	18.5	18.6	18.4
2005	18.1	18.1	18.3	19.0	19.3	19.3	19.1	19.0	18.8	19.0	18.9	19.0	18.8
2006	18.6	18.6	18.8	19.3	19.6	19.6	19.2	19.2	19.0	19.1	19.0	19.0	19.1
2007	18.8	18.7	18.9	19.4	19.8	19.8	19.5	19.4	19.2	19.5	19.5	19.4	19.3
2008	19.1	19.2	19.4	19.9	20.3	20.2	20.2	20.1	19.9	20.0	20.0	20.0	19.9
2009	19.7	19.7	19.8	20.0	20.7	20.8	20.5	20.4	20.1	20.3	20.4	20.4	20.2
2010	20.1	20.2	20.3	21.1	21.3	21.4	21.4	21.4	21.3	21.5	21.6	21.8	21.1
2011	21.5	21.5	21.8	22.3	22.9	23.1	22.9	22.8	22.7	23.1	23.3	23.6	22.6
2012	23.5	23.7	24.2	24.9	25.5	25.7	25.6	25.6	25.4	25.5	25.7	25.8	25.1
2013	25.4	25.5	25.7	26.1	27.0	27.1	26.9	26.9	26.5	27.0	27.1	27.6	26.6
Retail Trade													
2002	40.3	39.8	39.8	40.0	40.8	40.8	40.5	40.5	40.4	40.7	41.9	42.6	40.7
2003	40.3	39.9	39.9	40.3	40.9	41.0	40.5	41.0	40.7	41.2	42.2	42.8	40.9
2004	40.6	40.2	40.4	40.8	41.5	41.5	41.2	41.2	41.0	41.5	42.7	43.3	41.3
2005	41.1	41.0	41.2	41.9	42.3	42.3	42.1	42.0	42.1	42.3	43.3	43.8	42.1
2006	41.9	41.7	42.1	43.0	43.6	43.6	43.3	43.3	43.3	43.4	44.5	44.9	43.2
2007	42.9	42.5	42.4	42.6	43.1	43.1	43.2	42.9	42.7	43.1	44.2	44.8	43.1
2008	43.0	42.5	42.6	42.8	43.0	43.0	43.2	42.9	42.9	43.1	44.0	44.3	43.1
2009	42.4	41.9	41.9	42.0	42.7	42.7	42.8	42.6	42.7	43.2	44.2	44.4	42.8
2010	42.7	42.4	42.4	42.9	43.4	43.5	43.5	43.4	43.2	44.0	44.9	45.2	43.5
2011	43.5	43.3	43.2	43.9	44.3	44.2	44.6	44.7	44.8	45.5	47.0	47.3	44.7
2012	45.7	45.4	45.4	46.2	46.7	47.0	47.2	47.2	47.2	48.1	49.3	49.7	47.1
2013	48.0	47.8	47.7	47.8	48.5	48.6	48.9	49.3	49.5	50.1	51.5	52.3	49.2
Transportation and Utilities													
2002	12.9	12.8	12.8	12.9	13.0	13.0	13.0	12.9	13.0	13.1	13.1	13.2	13.0
2003	13.1	13.0	13.1	13.1	13.0	12.9	12.8	12.9	13.1	13.3	13.3	13.3	13.1
2004	12.9	13.0	12.9	13.0	13.2	13.1	13.1	13.1	13.3	13.6	13.6	13.7	13.2
2005	13.1	13.2	13.3	13.4	13.4	13.3	13.2	13.2	13.5	13.5	13.5	13.7	13.4
2006	13.5	13.6	13.7	13.7	13.7	13.7	13.6	13.8	13.9	13.9	13.9	14.1	13.8
2007	13.7	13.8	13.8	13.9	14.1	13.9	14.0	14.1	14.3	14.5	14.6	14.7	14.1
2008	14.5	14.6	14.7	14.7	14.8	14.8	14.7	14.9	15.1	15.3	15.3	15.4	14.9
2009	14.9	14.9	14.9	14.9	15.1	15.0	14.9	14.8	15.0	15.2	15.2	15.3	15.0
2010	14.9	15.0	15.1	15.7	15.9	16.0	16.0	16.3	16.5	16.9	17.0	17.2	16.0
2011	17.2	17.4	17.6	18.1	18.5	18.9	19.4	20.1	20.5	21.2	21.5	22.3	19.4
2012	22.6	22.9	23.4	23.9	24.6	24.9	25.1	25.4	25.3	25.6	25.3	25.3	24.5
2013	24.9	25.1	25.3	25.5	25.9	26.0	26.0	26.3	26.5	26.9	27.2	27.3	26.1
Information													
2002	8.0	8.0	7.9	7.9	8.0	8.0	8.0	7.9	7.8	7.8	7.8	7.9	7.9
2003	7.7	7.6	7.7	7.7	7.7	7.7	7.7	7.7	7.7	7.7	7.7	7.7	7.7
2004	7.6	7.6	7.6	7.6	7.7	7.7	7.8	7.8	7.7	7.8	7.8	7.7	7.7
2005	7.6	7.6	7.5	7.6	7.6	7.6	7.6	7.6	7.6	7.4	7.4	7.5	7.6
2006	7.4	7.4	7.4	7.4	7.4	7.5	7.5	7.6	7.5	7.5	7.6	7.6	7.5
2007	7.6	7.6	7.6	7.6	7.7	7.6	7.6	7.7	7.5	7.5	7.5	7.5	7.6
2008	7.4	7.4	7.4	7.4	7.5	7.6	7.6	7.6	7.6	7.6	7.6	7.6	7.5
2009	7.7	7.7	7.6	7.5	7.5	7.5	7.5	7.5	7.4	7.3	7.3	7.3	7.5
2010	7.3	7.3	7.3	7.3	7.3	7.4	7.3	7.3	7.2	7.2	7.2	7.2	7.3
2011	7.1	7.1	7.1	7.1	7.1	7.2	7.2	7.2	7.1	7.0	7.1	7.1	7.1
2012	7.0	6.9	6.9	6.9	6.9	7.0	7.0	7.0	6.9	6.9	6.9	6.9	6.9
2013	6.9	6.8	6.7	6.7	6.8	6.9	6.9	6.9	6.8	6.8	6.8	6.7	6.8

1. Employment by Industry: North Dakota, Selected Years, 2002–2013—*Continued*

(Numbers in thousands, not seasonally adjusted)

Industry and year	January	February	March	April	May	June	July	August	September	October	November	December	Annual average
Financial Activities													
2002	17.7	17.8	17.8	17.8	17.9	18.1	18.1	18.3	18.1	18.3	18.3	18.4	18.1
2003	18.2	18.1	18.3	18.2	18.3	18.4	18.5	18.6	18.5	18.4	18.4	18.5	18.4
2004	18.5	18.6	18.7	18.5	18.6	18.7	18.7	18.6	18.6	18.6	18.7	18.8	18.6
2005	18.6	18.6	18.7	18.7	18.8	18.8	18.9	19.1	18.8	18.9	18.8	19.1	18.8
2006	18.9	19.0	19.1	19.0	19.1	19.3	19.4	19.4	19.3	19.2	19.3	19.6	19.2
2007	19.3	19.4	19.5	19.5	19.8	19.9	20.0	20.0	19.9	20.0	19.9	20.2	19.8
2008	19.9	20.0	20.1	20.1	20.2	20.4	20.5	20.5	20.4	20.5	20.5	20.7	20.3
2009	20.2	20.1	20.1	20.1	20.1	20.2	20.3	20.3	20.1	20.2	20.1	20.5	20.2
2010	20.1	20.1	20.1	20.4	20.5	20.7	20.7	20.8	20.7	20.8	20.8	21.2	20.6
2011	20.8	20.8	20.8	21.0	21.2	21.2	21.3	21.3	21.3	21.3	21.4	21.5	21.2
2012	21.2	21.3	21.4	21.6	21.8	22.0	22.1	22.1	22.0	22.2	22.2	22.5	21.9
2013	22.2	22.3	22.5	22.6	22.7	22.9	23.0	23.1	23.0	23.3	23.4	23.5	22.9
Professional and Business Services													
2002	23.1	23.5	23.6	24.1	24.1	25.0	24.6	24.7	24.7	24.4	24.0	23.8	24.1
2003	23.2	23.5	23.3	23.5	23.5	24.1	23.8	24.3	24.1	23.9	23.8	23.6	23.7
2004	22.9	23.3	23.4	24.2	24.5	25.0	25.0	25.1	24.7	25.6	25.1	25.2	24.5
2005	24.5	24.7	24.7	26.4	26.6	27.1	27.4	27.7	27.4	27.3	27.2	27.3	26.5
2006	26.8	27.1	27.5	27.8	28.4	29.1	28.9	28.9	29.1	29.0	28.7	28.6	28.3
2007	28.1	28.3	28.8	29.0	29.5	29.9	29.7	29.9	30.0	29.9	29.7	29.8	29.4
2008	29.3	29.5	29.8	30.3	30.6	31.0	30.8	30.9	30.7	30.4	30.0	29.7	30.3
2009	28.8	28.8	28.7	28.7	29.2	29.7	29.3	29.2	29.8	29.0	28.8	28.5	29.0
2010	27.5	27.8	27.9	28.4	28.1	28.8	28.4	28.6	28.6	29.2	28.8	28.7	28.4
2011	28.0	28.1	28.6	29.2	29.2	29.9	30.8	31.2	31.1	31.0	30.4	30.6	29.8
2012	30.3	30.4	31.0	31.7	32.4	33.3	33.5	34.0	33.7	33.8	33.5	33.4	32.6
2013	32.6	33.2	33.3	33.7	34.2	34.8	35.1	35.2	35.1	34.6	34.6	33.8	34.2
Education and Health Services													
2002	46.2	46.3	46.0	46.4	46.6	46.9	46.9	46.9	46.7	47.0	47.1	47.2	46.7
2003	46.9	47.0	47.1	47.4	47.5	48.1	48.1	47.9	47.7	47.8	48.0	48.3	47.7
2004	47.9	47.9	48.1	48.5	48.5	48.7	48.8	48.7	48.3	48.3	48.4	48.5	48.4
2005	48.2	48.2	48.2	48.5	48.4	49.1	48.9	49.0	49.0	49.0	49.1	49.4	48.8
2006	49.1	49.3	49.7	49.6	49.4	50.0	49.8	49.9	49.8	50.0	50.0	50.3	49.7
2007	50.0	50.1	50.3	50.3	50.6	51.2	51.0	51.2	51.3	51.4	51.4	51.7	50.9
2008	51.3	51.6	51.6	52.1	52.1	52.2	52.2	52.1	52.2	52.6	52.5	52.8	52.1
2009	52.3	52.7	52.6	52.8	53.1	53.6	53.2	53.2	53.5	54.2	53.8	54.4	53.3
2010	54.1	54.1	54.5	54.8	54.6	55.1	55.2	55.1	55.1	55.7	55.5	55.7	55.0
2011	55.6	55.6	55.8	56.0	56.1	56.1	56.1	56.1	56.6	56.6	56.8	57.1	56.2
2012	56.8	57.1	57.2	57.3	57.6	57.9	57.6	57.9	58.0	58.1	58.1	58.6	57.7
2013	58.1	58.4	58.6	58.7	58.8	58.8	58.8	58.8	58.9	59.5	59.8	59.8	58.9
Leisure and Hospitality													
2002	28.0	28.4	28.6	29.6	30.4	31.1	31.2	31.2	30.7	30.1	29.4	29.2	29.8
2003	28.1	28.2	28.9	29.6	30.6	31.3	31.4	31.5	30.6	30.4	29.6	29.4	30.0
2004	28.5	28.7	29.2	30.0	31.0	31.6	32.7	32.6	32.1	31.3	30.7	30.5	30.7
2005	29.7	29.7	30.1	30.8	31.8	32.5	32.3	32.5	32.2	31.2	30.9	30.7	31.2
2006	29.5	30.0	30.4	30.9	32.2	32.8	32.4	32.9	32.8	32.2	31.4	31.6	31.6
2007	30.7	31.1	31.7	32.1	33.5	34.4	33.9	34.1	33.9	33.3	32.9	33.0	32.9
2008	32.1	32.2	32.7	33.2	34.1	34.7	34.4	34.7	34.2	33.7	33.7	33.6	33.6
2009	32.4	32.4	32.8	33.2	34.8	35.4	35.0	35.2	34.8	34.1	33.8	33.8	34.0
2010	32.3	32.4	33.0	34.1	34.9	35.2	35.1	35.3	35.1	35.0	34.6	34.6	34.3
2011	33.4	33.5	34.2	34.5	35.8	36.3	36.0	36.4	36.8	36.3	36.3	36.7	35.5
2012	36.1	36.3	36.9	37.4	38.5	39.1	39.0	39.4	39.1	38.7	38.2	38.7	38.1
2013	37.3	37.6	38.2	38.0	39.1	40.0	40.1	40.4	40.3	40.0	40.4	40.5	39.3
Other Services													
2002	15.1	15.3	15.3	15.4	15.4	15.4	15.2	15.2	15.2	15.2	15.3	15.2	15.3
2003	15.0	15.2	15.2	15.3	15.3	15.2	15.1	15.2	15.4	15.3	15.2	15.3	15.2
2004	14.8	15.0	15.0	15.1	15.1	15.2	15.1	15.1	15.0	15.1	15.1	15.1	15.1
2005	14.9	15.0	15.2	15.2	15.2	15.1	14.9	14.9	14.9	14.9	14.9	15.0	15.0
2006	14.8	14.9	15.0	15.0	15.1	14.9	14.9	15.1	15.0	15.1	15.3	15.4	15.0
2007	15.0	15.0	15.2	15.2	15.2	15.3	15.1	15.0	15.2	15.2	15.3	15.3	15.2
2008	15.2	15.3	15.5	15.5	15.6	15.5	15.3	15.3	15.3	15.3	15.4	15.4	15.4
2009	15.2	15.2	15.3	15.5	15.6	15.4	15.4	15.2	15.1	15.3	15.3	15.5	15.3
2010	15.1	15.2	15.3	15.4	15.4	15.4	15.4	15.3	15.4	15.6	15.6	15.5	15.4
2011	15.3	15.4	15.6	15.7	15.7	15.5	15.5	15.5	15.7	15.8	15.7	15.7	15.6
2012	15.9	15.9	16.0	16.1	16.1	16.1	16.2	16.1	16.0	16.1	16.2	16.2	16.1
2013	15.9	16.1	16.3	16.2	16.5	16.4	16.2	16.3	16.3	16.3	16.4	16.5	16.3
Government													
2002	75.1	76.1	76.0	76.3	76.5	72.1	64.4	66.0	75.6	77.2	77.3	78.3	74.2
2003	75.4	77.5	77.9	78.3	78.5	72.9	64.7	67.0	76.9	78.3	77.9	78.2	75.3
2004	75.5	76.6	76.8	77.2	77.0	72.3	64.3	66.0	76.2	77.8	77.6	77.9	74.6
2005	75.6	77.7	77.9	78.4	78.1	73.1	64.0	66.1	76.7	77.6	77.7	78.0	75.1
2006	76.2	77.7	78.2	78.5	78.4	73.7	64.2	66.3	76.9	78.5	78.5	78.9	75.5
2007	76.5	77.8	78.0	78.4	78.5	74.7	65.2	66.3	77.0	78.3	78.7	78.8	75.7
2008	77.0	78.4	78.2	78.5	79.3	74.8	66.1	67.0	77.7	79.3	79.3	79.6	76.3
2009	77.5	78.7	79.1	79.7	80.7	78.0	68.3	69.1	79.4	81.3	81.3	81.8	77.9
2010	79.4	81.0	81.9	82.1	82.9	80.0	70.2	70.6	80.5	82.2	82.2	82.4	79.6
2011	80.2	81.4	81.5	81.5	81.8	79.4	69.3	69.7	80.0	81.5	81.3	81.9	79.1
2012	79.7	81.0	81.3	81.5	81.7	79.4	70.3	70.0	80.7	82.4	82.4	82.5	79.4
2013	80.5	81.7	81.7	81.7	82.3	80.4	70.9	70.8	80.9	83.0	82.7	83.1	80.0

2. Average Weekly Hours by Selected Industry: North Dakota, 2009–2013

(Not seasonally adjusted)

Industry and year	January	February	March	April	May	June	July	August	September	October	November	December	Annual average
Total Private													
2009	31.4	31.9	31.3	31.3	31.9	32.5	32.5	33.1	32.1	31.9	32.4	31.6	32.0
2010	31.3	31.3	31.6	32.1	32.9	33.0	33.2	34.1	33.3	33.1	32.9	32.7	32.7
2011	33.1	33.0	32.8	33.2	34.2	34.4	34.7	35.3	34.5	35.2	34.3	34.1	34.1
2012	34.3	34.1	34.0	34.9	35.0	35.4	35.8	35.4	35.9	35.5	34.7	35.5	35.1
2013	34.3	34.8	34.5	34.6	35.5	37.0	35.8	36.7	36.6	35.6	35.7	35.6	35.6
Goods-Producing													
2009	35.4	35.8	35.1	36.7	38.5	39.9	39.3	40.4	38.9	38.9	39.3	38.0	38.1
2010	36.5	35.9	37.2	37.9	39.0	39.8	40.8	41.0	40.4	40.5	39.1	37.8	38.9
2011	36.5	37.5	37.8	38.3	39.1	39.4	40.2	42.4	42.9	43.2	41.9	41.0	40.2
2012	40.5	41.0	41.1	41.6	42.2	42.5	42.3	42.4	42.3	42.6	40.1	40.8	41.6
2013	38.9	40.0	39.8	40.0	41.2	43.4	41.7	43.9	43.5	42.7	43.2	42.6	41.8
Construction													
2009	32.4	32.7	32.2	34.7	38.8	41.6	41.2	42.6	40.6	40.7	42.0	37.6	38.7
2010	34.0	33.3	35.0	36.0	37.6	40.8	42.6	41.8	41.6	42.2	40.5	36.5	38.9
2011	35.3	36.2	35.6	37.7	39.0	40.4	42.8	45.2	45.6	44.6	42.8	40.7	41.1
2012	39.2	40.2	39.9	41.3	43.3	44.3	44.4	44.0	44.7	43.7	39.7	40.6	42.3
2013	38.3	38.5	38.0	39.1	41.7	44.7	43.2	44.5	42.8	42.1	42.6	43.0	41.8
Manufacturing													
2009	35.8	36.0	35.0	36.4	37.4	37.8	37.4	38.3	37.7	37.8	37.5	37.8	37.1
2010	36.9	36.8	37.7	38.1	38.7	38.2	38.4	39.2	39.1	39.7	38.5	38.8	38.3
2011	38.3	38.8	39.3	39.2	39.1	38.6	37.7	40.1	40.6	41.6	41.3	40.8	39.6
2012	40.8	41.0	41.6	42.0	41.6	40.2	40.1	41.2	39.9	41.5	40.6	40.8	40.9
2013	38.6	40.0	40.9	41.0	40.8	42.3	40.1	43.1	42.5	41.8	41.9	39.3	41.1
Trade, Transportation, and Utilities													
2009	32.7	33.3	33.1	32.8	33.7	34.9	34.3	35.2	34.5	34.1	34.8	33.9	34.0
2010	33.7	33.8	33.9	34.6	34.7	34.5	34.4	35.3	34.2	33.8	33.2	33.4	34.1
2011	33.9	33.2	33.5	33.7	35.4	35.7	35.0	35.2	33.0	34.3	33.7	33.2	34.2
2012	33.5	33.3	33.6	34.6	34.8	35.4	35.3	35.2	36.0	35.8	34.9	36.0	34.9
2013	34.9	35.9	35.4	35.2	36.9	37.5	36.1	36.9	36.8	36.0	36.8	36.8	36.3
Financial Activities													
2009	39.3	39.6	37.4	36.4	35.8	35.9	35.7	37.6	35.2	34.9	36.7	35.1	36.6
2010	37.7	35.3	34.5	35.9	37.7	36.3	36.1	38.9	36.8	35.6	35.1	35.5	36.3
2011	38.1	36.0	35.0	34.3	35.1	35.8	36.2	37.2	37.0	36.6	33.7	35.6	35.9
2012	39.4	35.6	35.2	37.8	35.7	36.5	38.1	36.0	38.5	35.5	35.9	38.3	36.9
2013	36.2	36.3	35.9	36.4	36.2	38.1	36.5	37.1	38.7	36.9	37.3	38.0	37.0
Professional and Business Services													
2009	32.2	33.0	33.3	32.5	31.7	32.8	33.6	33.3	31.5	32.0	32.7	31.9	32.6
2010	32.3	32.0	32.0	32.2	34.0	34.1	34.4	35.0	33.2	34.0	34.4	34.5	33.5
2011	35.4	36.0	35.2	35.0	37.0	36.8	36.4	37.2	37.7	38.3	37.4	37.9	36.7
2012	38.4	38.0	38.1	38.9	38.0	37.9	38.6	37.6	37.8	38.3	37.4	38.9	38.2
2013	37.4	37.5	37.7	37.3	39.0	40.1	39.4	40.1	39.4	38.5	38.0	37.7	38.5
Education and Health Services													
2009	30.6	30.9	30.5	30.4	30.5	30.9	30.8	30.9	30.7	30.8	31.3	31.3	30.8
2010	30.7	31.0	31.6	31.2	31.3	31.5	31.3	31.6	31.8	32.0	32.8	32.5	31.6
2011	33.1	32.8	32.5	32.8	33.2	33.1	34.1	33.3	32.9	33.3	33.4	33.5	33.2
2012	33.9	33.4	33.2	33.7	33.1	33.7	33.6	33.6	33.8	33.1	33.5	33.7	33.5
2013	33.7	33.6	33.0	33.2	33.1	33.8	32.6	33.0	33.1	32.5	32.5	32.6	33.0
Leisure and Hospitality													
2009	20.5	20.8	20.5	20.5	21.2	21.5	21.9	22.9	20.8	20.3	20.5	20.0	21.0
2010	19.6	20.5	20.9	21.0	22.1	22.0	22.4	23.5	21.8	21.1	21.0	20.7	21.4
2011	21.4	21.0	20.7	21.6	22.4	22.6	23.3	23.9	22.2	22.6	21.9	21.9	22.1
2012	21.7	22.1	22.1	22.5	23.3	24.0	24.9	24.5	24.1	23.0	22.6	23.5	23.2
2013	22.0	22.5	22.9	22.8	23.4	25.1	24.6	24.4	24.1	23.2	22.7	23.2	23.4
Other Services													
2009	22.7	23.3	22.8	23.2	24.1	25.0	24.5	24.4	23.8	23.5	23.9	23.1	23.7
2010	23.7	23.8	22.9	24.6	25.6	25.3	24.2	26.2	25.1	24.6	24.4	24.4	24.6
2011	25.1	25.4	24.2	24.9	25.3	26.1	25.7	26.6	26.0	26.7	25.6	25.4	25.6
2012	25.1	25.9	24.5	24.8	26.0	25.1	25.8	25.0	25.2	25.4	25.9	27.0	25.5
2013	25.0	24.9	24.3	25.4	24.3	29.9	28.2	30.5	29.9	26.5	27.1	27.2	27.0

3. Average Hourly Earnings by Selected Industry: North Dakota, 2009–2013

(Dollars, not seasonally adjusted)

Industry and year	January	February	March	April	May	June	July	August	September	October	November	December	Annual average
Total Private													
2009	19.21	19.11	19.18	19.11	19.02	18.89	19.09	19.32	19.47	19.40	19.42	19.28	19.21
2010	19.50	19.65	19.39	20.04	20.20	19.78	20.05	20.20	20.59	20.69	20.94	21.03	20.19
2011	20.85	21.05	20.93	21.35	21.29	21.12	21.25	21.47	21.79	21.90	21.90	22.25	21.45
2012	22.26	22.35	22.54	22.55	22.48	22.49	22.68	22.63	23.39	22.96	23.25	23.53	22.77
2013	23.63	23.64	23.58	23.69	23.51	23.81	23.74	23.69	24.08	24.07	24.32	24.67	23.88
Goods-Producing													
2009	21.41	21.45	21.91	21.70	21.39	21.24	21.18	21.24	20.89	21.27	21.42	21.24	21.34
2010	21.22	21.05	21.14	21.48	21.89	21.70	21.93	21.78	22.18	22.35	22.21	22.33	21.82
2011	22.79	22.61	22.60	23.04	23.27	23.22	23.07	23.20	23.75	23.67	23.44	23.79	23.26
2012	23.98	23.68	24.12	23.88	24.12	24.57	24.48	24.34	24.95	24.74	25.61	26.01	24.56
2013	25.98	25.95	26.17	26.01	25.86	26.46	26.00	26.15	26.19	26.34	27.21	28.20	26.39
Construction													
2009	20.59	20.29	20.70	19.98	20.01	19.91	20.27	20.34	19.29	19.94	20.41	20.41	20.13
2010	19.46	19.68	19.82	19.78	20.21	20.65	20.92	20.88	21.45	21.90	21.77	21.77	20.83
2011	22.13	22.56	22.72	22.88	23.59	23.75	23.71	24.82	24.89	24.48	24.33	24.52	23.91
2012	24.70	24.08	24.95	24.51	25.10	25.24	24.55	25.04	25.73	25.58	26.79	27.09	25.32
2013	26.64	27.23	27.48	27.48	27.25	28.05	26.86	26.92	27.36	27.15	27.80	29.03	27.44
Manufacturing													
2009	19.44	19.46	20.06	20.07	19.54	19.43	19.31	19.36	19.70	19.66	19.59	19.61	19.60
2010	19.77	19.54	19.53	19.73	20.11	19.35	19.49	19.36	19.73	19.67	19.12	19.42	19.57
2011	19.69	19.28	19.29	19.73	19.99	19.93	20.51	19.89	20.29	20.59	20.29	20.86	20.05
2012	21.22	20.84	21.13	21.35	21.42	21.53	22.00	21.46	22.10	21.68	22.06	22.62	21.62
2013	22.97	22.38	22.44	22.27	22.25	22.41	22.17	22.28	22.45	22.55	22.57	23.91	22.55
Trade, Transportation, and Utilities													
2009	19.08	19.10	18.81	18.76	18.86	19.01	19.15	20.12	20.42	20.67	20.33	19.89	19.53
2010	20.38	20.00	20.09	20.25	19.96	19.59	19.67	19.60	20.03	20.19	20.06	20.08	19.99
2011	20.33	20.56	20.57	21.46	20.98	20.73	21.45	21.33	21.04	21.42	21.41	22.05	21.13
2012	22.09	22.09	22.62	22.54	22.04	21.85	22.31	22.11	22.96	22.60	22.54	22.84	22.39
2013	23.13	23.06	22.75	23.54	22.85	23.43	23.13	22.88	23.64	23.46	23.19	23.54	23.22
Financial Activities													
2009	17.07	17.26	17.34	17.41	17.82	17.82	18.22	18.82	18.46	18.58	18.89	18.78	18.02
2010	18.00	19.86	19.37	19.23	19.41	19.38	19.33	19.29	19.30	19.66	20.06	19.50	19.36
2011	18.97	20.52	19.77	19.96	19.80	19.58	19.36	19.45	19.72	19.90	20.64	20.01	19.80
2012	19.26	21.18	20.40	20.04	20.15	20.12	20.62	20.90	22.33	20.79	21.38	21.40	20.72
2013	22.80	22.91	22.74	22.28	22.49	22.29	22.08	22.24	22.67	22.82	23.37	23.84	22.72
Professional and Business Services													
2009	21.81	21.85	22.23	22.70	22.60	21.92	21.78	22.80	23.10	22.48	23.15	23.10	22.45
2010	22.84	22.84	23.03	23.04	23.39	22.56	22.62	23.09	23.05	23.00	22.91	23.41	22.98
2011	23.34	23.72	24.05	23.47	24.25	23.61	24.41	24.41	25.29	25.72	25.92	27.79	24.72
2012	26.35	26.43	26.18	27.25	26.87	26.97	27.15	26.24	27.52	26.95	27.63	28.79	27.04
2013	28.21	28.12	27.95	27.66	27.46	28.18	27.81	27.69	29.35	29.23	29.57	29.91	28.43
Education and Health Services													
2009	19.44	19.08	19.23	19.32	19.05	19.02	19.54	19.48	19.89	19.62	19.49	19.54	19.39
2010	20.08	20.57	19.99	21.19	21.49	20.62	21.22	22.03	22.28	22.25	23.52	23.48	21.59
2011	23.95	24.05	23.43	23.41	23.12	22.91	22.40	23.12	23.06	23.00	22.84	22.68	23.16
2012	23.48	23.36	23.02	22.95	23.17	22.76	23.04	23.56	24.05	23.31	23.22	23.10	23.25
2013	23.39	23.33	23.17	23.06	23.07	22.79	23.66	23.38	23.28	23.40	23.44	23.33	23.27
Leisure and Hospitality													
2009	10.44	10.47	10.66	10.63	10.57	10.43	10.68	10.72	10.88	11.01	11.02	11.24	10.73
2010	11.20	11.23	11.08	10.87	11.02	10.73	10.75	10.58	10.85	10.89	11.02	11.28	10.95
2011	11.21	11.24	11.21	11.29	11.26	11.26	11.20	11.37	11.74	11.82	12.08	12.25	11.50
2012	11.98	11.95	12.01	11.96	12.09	12.25	12.12	11.98	12.40	12.28	12.41	12.77	12.19
2013	12.53	12.81	12.72	12.79	12.88	12.57	12.66	12.62	12.90	12.79	12.85	13.05	12.76
Other Services													
2009	14.04	13.95	14.69	14.66	15.11	15.56	15.72	16.18	16.00	15.98	16.00	16.18	15.35
2010	16.15	16.15	15.77	15.91	16.02	15.96	16.08	16.17	16.33	16.19	15.90	16.05	16.06
2011	16.04	16.08	16.51	17.25	17.49	17.19	17.61	17.96	17.96	17.81	17.61	17.65	17.28
2012	17.26	17.59	18.47	18.04	18.65	18.92	19.77	19.60	19.06	19.85	19.99	19.47	18.90
2013	18.18	20.20	20.53	21.10	20.48	20.92	21.77	21.83	22.75	22.41	22.49	22.63	21.34

4. Average Weekly Earnings by Selected Industry: North Dakota, 2009–2013

(Dollars, not seasonally adjusted)

Industry and year	January	February	March	April	May	June	July	August	September	October	November	December	Annual average
Total Private													
2009	603.19	609.61	600.33	598.14	606.74	613.93	620.43	639.49	624.99	618.86	629.21	609.25	614.72
2010	610.35	615.05	612.72	643.28	664.58	652.74	665.66	688.82	685.65	684.84	688.93	687.68	660.21
2011	690.14	694.65	686.50	708.82	728.12	726.53	737.38	757.89	751.76	770.88	751.17	758.73	731.45
2012	763.52	762.14	766.36	787.00	786.80	796.15	811.94	801.10	839.70	815.08	806.78	835.32	799.23
2013	810.51	822.67	813.51	819.67	834.61	880.97	849.89	869.42	881.33	856.89	868.22	878.25	850.13
Goods-Producing													
2009	757.91	767.91	769.04	796.39	823.52	847.48	832.37	858.10	812.62	827.40	841.81	807.12	813.05
2010	774.53	755.70	786.41	814.09	853.71	863.66	894.74	892.98	896.07	905.18	868.41	844.07	848.80
2011	831.84	847.88	854.28	882.43	909.86	914.87	927.41	983.68	1,018.88	1,022.54	982.14	975.39	935.05
2012	971.19	970.88	991.33	993.41	1,017.86	1,044.23	1,035.50	1,032.02	1,055.39	1,053.92	1,026.96	1,061.21	1,021.70
2013	1,010.62	1,038.00	1,041.57	1,040.40	1,065.43	1,148.36	1,084.20	1,147.99	1,139.27	1,124.72	1,175.47	1,201.32	1,103.10
Construction													
2009	667.12	663.48	666.54	693.31	776.39	828.26	835.12	866.48	783.17	811.56	857.22	767.42	779.03
2010	661.64	655.34	693.70	712.08	759.90	842.52	891.19	872.78	892.32	924.18	881.69	794.61	810.29
2011	781.19	816.67	808.83	862.58	920.01	959.50	1,014.79	1,121.86	1,134.98	1,091.81	1,041.32	997.96	982.70
2012	968.24	968.02	995.51	1,012.26	1,086.83	1,118.13	1,090.02	1,101.76	1,150.13	1,117.85	1,063.56	1,099.85	1,071.04
2013	1,020.31	1,048.36	1,044.24	1,074.47	1,136.33	1,253.84	1,160.35	1,197.94	1,171.01	1,143.02	1,184.28	1,248.29	1,146.99
Manufacturing													
2009	695.95	700.56	702.10	730.55	730.80	734.45	722.19	741.49	742.69	743.15	734.63	741.26	727.16
2010	729.51	719.07	736.28	751.71	778.26	739.17	748.42	758.91	771.44	780.90	736.12	753.50	749.53
2011	754.13	748.06	758.10	773.42	781.61	769.30	773.23	797.59	823.77	856.54	837.98	851.09	793.98
2012	865.78	854.44	879.01	896.70	891.07	865.51	882.20	884.15	881.79	899.72	895.64	922.90	884.26
2013	886.64	895.20	917.80	913.07	907.80	947.94	889.02	960.27	954.13	942.59	945.68	939.66	926.81
Trade, Transportation, and Utilities													
2009	623.92	636.03	622.61	615.33	635.58	663.45	656.85	708.22	704.49	704.85	707.48	674.27	664.02
2010	686.81	676.00	681.05	700.65	692.61	675.86	676.65	691.88	685.03	682.42	665.99	670.67	681.66
2011	689.19	682.59	689.10	723.20	742.69	740.06	750.75	750.82	694.32	734.71	721.52	732.06	722.65
2012	740.02	735.60	760.03	779.88	766.99	773.49	787.54	778.27	826.56	809.08	786.65	822.24	781.41
2013	807.24	827.85	805.35	828.61	843.17	878.63	834.99	844.27	869.95	844.56	853.39	866.27	842.89
Financial Activities													
2009	670.85	683.50	648.52	633.72	637.96	639.74	650.45	707.63	649.79	648.44	693.26	659.18	659.53
2010	678.60	701.06	668.27	690.36	731.76	703.49	697.81	750.38	710.24	699.90	704.11	692.25	702.77
2011	722.76	738.72	691.95	684.63	694.98	700.96	700.83	723.54	729.64	728.34	695.57	712.36	710.82
2012	758.84	754.01	718.08	757.51	719.36	734.38	785.62	752.40	859.71	738.05	767.54	819.62	764.57
2013	825.36	831.63	816.37	810.99	814.14	849.25	805.92	825.10	877.33	842.06	871.70	905.92	840.64
Professional and Business Services													
2009	702.28	721.05	740.26	737.75	716.42	718.98	731.81	759.24	727.65	719.36	757.01	736.89	731.87
2010	737.73	730.88	736.96	741.89	795.26	769.30	778.13	808.15	765.26	782.00	788.10	807.65	769.83
2011	826.24	853.92	846.56	821.45	897.25	868.85	888.52	908.05	953.43	985.08	969.41	1,053.24	907.22
2012	1,011.84	1,004.34	997.46	1,060.03	1,021.06	1,022.16	1,047.99	986.62	1,040.26	1,032.19	1,033.36	1,119.93	1,032.93
2013	1,055.05	1,054.50	1,053.72	1,031.72	1,070.94	1,130.02	1,095.71	1,110.37	1,156.39	1,125.36	1,123.66	1,127.61	1,094.56
Education and Health Services													
2009	594.86	589.57	586.52	587.33	581.03	587.72	601.83	601.93	610.62	604.30	610.04	611.60	597.21
2010	616.46	637.67	631.68	661.13	672.64	649.53	664.19	696.15	708.50	712.00	771.46	763.10	682.24
2011	792.75	788.84	761.48	767.85	767.58	758.32	763.84	769.90	758.67	765.90	762.86	759.78	768.91
2012	795.97	780.22	764.26	773.42	766.93	767.01	774.14	791.62	812.89	771.56	777.87	778.47	778.88
2013	788.24	783.89	764.61	765.59	763.62	770.30	771.32	771.54	770.57	760.50	761.80	760.56	767.91
Leisure and Hospitality													
2009	214.02	217.78	218.53	217.92	224.08	224.25	233.89	245.49	226.30	223.50	225.91	224.80	225.33
2010	219.52	230.22	231.57	228.27	243.54	236.06	240.80	248.63	236.53	229.78	231.42	233.50	234.33
2011	239.89	236.04	232.05	243.86	252.22	253.80	260.96	271.74	260.63	267.13	264.55	268.28	254.15
2012	259.97	264.10	265.42	269.10	281.70	294.00	301.79	293.51	298.84	282.44	280.47	300.10	282.81
2013	275.66	288.23	291.29	291.61	301.39	315.51	311.44	307.93	310.89	296.73	291.70	302.76	298.58
Other Services													
2009	318.71	325.04	334.93	340.11	364.15	389.00	385.14	394.79	380.80	375.53	382.40	373.76	363.80
2010	382.76	384.37	361.13	391.39	410.11	403.79	389.14	423.65	409.88	398.27	387.96	391.62	395.08
2011	402.60	408.43	399.54	429.53	442.50	448.66	452.58	477.74	466.96	475.53	450.82	448.31	442.37
2012	433.23	455.58	452.52	447.39	484.90	474.89	510.07	490.00	480.31	504.19	517.74	525.69	481.95
2013	454.50	502.98	498.88	535.94	497.66	625.51	613.91	665.82	680.23	593.87	609.48	615.54	576.18

OHIO
At a Glance

Population:
    2000 census: 11,353,336
    2010 census: 11,536,504
    2013 estimate: 11,570,808

Percent change in population:
    2000–2010: 1.6%
    2010–2013: 0.3%

Percent change in total nonfarm employment:
    2000–2010: -10.6%
    2010–2013: 4.4%

Industry with the largest growth in employment, 2000–2013 (thousands):
    Education and Health Services, 197.6

Industry with the largest decline or smallest growth in employment, 2000–2013 (thousands):
    Manufacturing, -359.0

Civilian labor force:
    2000: 5,807,036
    2010: 5,845,369
    2013: 5,765,704

Unemployment rate and rank among states (lowest to highest):
    2000: 4.0%, 28th
    2010: 10.0%, 36th
    2013: 7.4%, 31st

Over-the-year change in unemployment rates:
    2010–2011: -1.3%
    2011–2012: -1.3%
    2012–2013: -0.0%

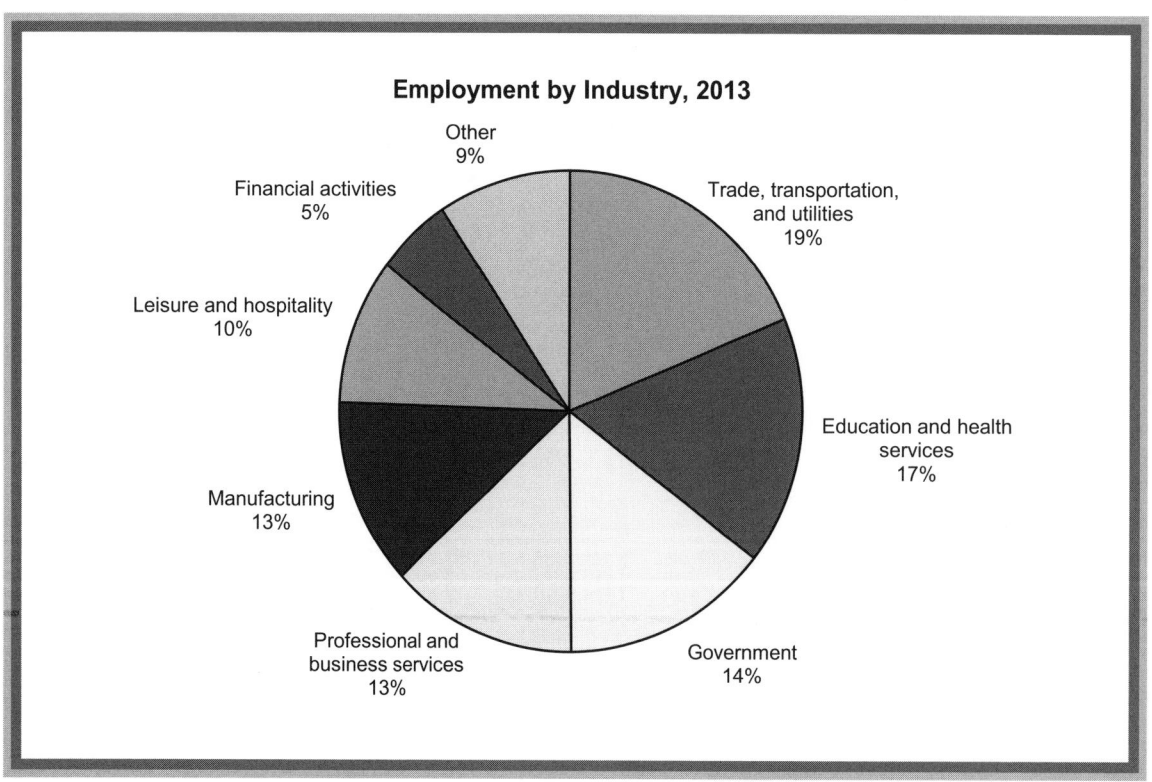

Employment by Industry, 2013

Other 9%
Financial activities 5%
Leisure and hospitality 10%
Manufacturing 13%
Professional and business services 13%
Government 14%
Education and health services 17%
Trade, transportation, and utilities 19%

1. Employment by Industry: Ohio, Selected Years, 2002–2013

(Numbers in thousands, not seasonally adjusted)

Industry and year	January	February	March	April	May	June	July	August	September	October	November	December	Annual average
Total Nonfarm													
2002	5,348.7	5,363.6	5,398.0	5,429.2	5,480.1	5,492.5	5,443.4	5,456.6	5,469.5	5,479.1	5,492.6	5,486.2	5,445.0
2003	5,309.8	5,307.0	5,338.5	5,390.0	5,439.9	5,440.2	5,389.2	5,405.0	5,414.5	5,441.1	5,446.5	5,450.7	5,397.7
2004	5,277.0	5,292.7	5,342.6	5,395.2	5,438.4	5,454.9	5,417.2	5,423.5	5,439.9	5,466.1	5,476.4	5,476.5	5,408.4
2005	5,287.2	5,313.9	5,354.0	5,424.3	5,465.4	5,472.4	5,431.2	5,440.1	5,469.1	5,476.8	5,494.6	5,491.3	5,426.7
2006	5,326.3	5,347.0	5,389.7	5,434.7	5,478.4	5,494.0	5,428.5	5,440.8	5,461.0	5,465.7	5,479.2	5,480.0	5,435.4
2007	5,323.1	5,319.8	5,367.7	5,416.0	5,473.4	5,492.1	5,422.6	5,436.8	5,450.3	5,463.3	5,480.6	5,470.2	5,426.3
2008	5,314.4	5,323.5	5,323.2	5,382.0	5,432.5	5,425.6	5,365.8	5,369.4	5,373.0	5,367.4	5,337.9	5,299.7	5,359.5
2009	5,096.4	5,081.0	5,074.7	5,090.0	5,115.1	5,087.6	5,032.3	5,029.5	5,049.4	5,062.3	5,058.8	5,045.9	5,068.6
2010	4,900.2	4,905.6	4,940.2	5,017.6	5,075.6	5,071.4	5,038.1	5,041.7	5,063.6	5,100.5	5,110.4	5,100.6	5,030.5
2011	4,952.9	4,974.8	5,008.5	5,085.7	5,126.2	5,123.4	5,105.9	5,121.8	5,143.5	5,162.9	5,184.4	5,179.2	5,097.4
2012	5,041.9	5,071.7	5,118.0	5,175.7	5,234.3	5,244.6	5,184.5	5,203.4	5,224.9	5,256.4	5,266.2	5,253.5	5,189.6
2013	5,107.6	5,134.7	5,162.4	5,238.9	5,305.4	5,305.8	5,260.5	5,287.4	5,298.8	5,320.9	5,314.1	5,292.4	5,252.4
Total Private													
2002	4,553.9	4,550.4	4,580.5	4,615.3	4,663.4	4,697.5	4,684.8	4,704.0	4,677.7	4,667.0	4,673.4	4,668.8	4,644.7
2003	4,511.5	4,493.9	4,520.9	4,573.2	4,619.6	4,642.1	4,625.4	4,648.1	4,621.8	4,627.1	4,627.3	4,630.3	4,595.1
2004	4,481.7	4,477.4	4,522.3	4,577.3	4,618.2	4,654.6	4,654.9	4,666.9	4,650.1	4,653.7	4,660.3	4,662.2	4,606.6
2005	4,494.9	4,501.5	4,539.6	4,611.7	4,646.7	4,677.6	4,672.1	4,683.9	4,677.7	4,664.1	4,676.8	4,678.1	4,627.1
2006	4,530.8	4,536.0	4,575.6	4,622.6	4,659.6	4,697.6	4,669.5	4,683.9	4,668.3	4,652.8	4,662.2	4,665.7	4,635.4
2007	4,529.3	4,512.1	4,556.4	4,605.3	4,659.0	4,696.0	4,665.7	4,681.7	4,661.0	4,654.0	4,667.3	4,663.5	4,629.3
2008	4,521.6	4,512.8	4,514.2	4,572.1	4,617.8	4,633.4	4,611.5	4,616.4	4,585.5	4,557.5	4,523.2	4,493.8	4,563.3
2009	4,306.2	4,275.9	4,269.3	4,282.3	4,306.4	4,302.7	4,287.3	4,287.8	4,271.2	4,263.2	4,258.3	4,254.8	4,280.5
2010	4,121.7	4,114.9	4,147.2	4,220.4	4,260.8	4,288.5	4,300.7	4,310.1	4,298.3	4,311.2	4,317.8	4,312.0	4,250.3
2011	4,188.0	4,195.4	4,226.6	4,303.9	4,345.2	4,365.9	4,382.6	4,400.9	4,386.1	4,388.1	4,405.5	4,404.2	4,332.7
2012	4,290.1	4,301.4	4,345.0	4,401.0	4,452.5	4,486.2	4,468.5	4,482.7	4,462.3	4,480.2	4,489.4	4,483.1	4,428.5
2013	4,354.0	4,366.5	4,395.6	4,465.9	4,528.9	4,555.6	4,546.2	4,564.8	4,537.6	4,548.1	4,539.5	4,524.8	4,494.0
Goods-Producing													
2002	1,117.8	1,113.3	1,118.0	1,125.1	1,137.5	1,150.8	1,143.4	1,155.9	1,147.0	1,138.8	1,131.9	1,119.6	1,133.3
2003	1,080.0	1,069.0	1,073.5	1,082.7	1,096.8	1,103.5	1,089.1	1,099.7	1,092.0	1,088.9	1,081.9	1,075.1	1,086.0
2004	1,037.2	1,034.8	1,047.9	1,063.5	1,074.5	1,086.1	1,083.6	1,089.1	1,083.2	1,079.8	1,073.5	1,066.3	1,068.3
2005	1,025.7	1,024.2	1,032.4	1,052.7	1,062.5	1,074.1	1,071.5	1,075.6	1,071.7	1,066.2	1,062.3	1,050.5	1,055.8
2006	1,018.1	1,016.0	1,024.1	1,039.4	1,046.3	1,059.4	1,049.0	1,054.1	1,048.8	1,039.3	1,032.4	1,024.5	1,037.6
2007	990.4	982.2	993.7	1,003.5	1,017.5	1,028.9	1,016.4	1,027.0	1,019.7	1,009.6	1,007.2	996.9	1,007.8
2008	962.1	957.8	952.7	964.4	976.3	986.1	978.0	978.8	971.5	960.6	940.5	915.9	962.1
2009	855.4	842.4	832.9	826.4	824.2	819.8	814.9	819.9	816.0	813.1	803.7	797.9	822.2
2010	765.2	760.9	768.4	787.8	801.3	812.6	818.3	821.8	819.6	821.9	819.2	810.1	800.6
2011	785.2	784.1	793.8	810.9	821.5	833.4	843.2	851.5	848.5	848.9	848.9	842.4	826.0
2012	817.8	818.4	828.1	841.0	852.5	864.7	862.5	866.9	862.8	859.9	858.4	851.6	848.7
2013	828.5	828.4	834.6	847.7	863.1	875.3	873.0	880.8	877.0	874.6	867.5	859.5	859.2
Service-Providing													
2002	4,230.9	4,250.3	4,280.0	4,304.1	4,342.6	4,341.7	4,300.0	4,300.7	4,322.5	4,340.3	4,360.7	4,366.6	4,311.7
2003	4,229.8	4,238.0	4,265.0	4,307.3	4,343.1	4,336.7	4,300.1	4,305.3	4,322.5	4,352.2	4,364.6	4,375.6	4,311.7
2004	4,239.8	4,257.9	4,294.7	4,331.7	4,363.9	4,368.8	4,333.6	4,334.4	4,356.7	4,386.3	4,402.9	4,410.2	4,340.1
2005	4,261.5	4,289.7	4,321.6	4,371.6	4,402.9	4,398.3	4,359.7	4,364.5	4,397.4	4,410.6	4,432.3	4,440.8	4,370.9
2006	4,308.2	4,331.0	4,365.6	4,395.3	4,432.1	4,434.6	4,379.5	4,386.7	4,412.2	4,426.4	4,446.8	4,455.5	4,397.8
2007	4,332.7	4,337.6	4,374.0	4,412.5	4,455.9	4,463.2	4,406.2	4,409.8	4,430.6	4,453.7	4,473.4	4,473.3	4,418.6
2008	4,352.3	4,365.7	4,370.5	4,417.6	4,456.2	4,439.5	4,387.8	4,390.6	4,401.5	4,406.8	4,397.4	4,383.8	4,397.5
2009	4,241.0	4,238.6	4,241.8	4,263.6	4,290.9	4,267.8	4,217.4	4,209.6	4,233.4	4,249.2	4,255.1	4,248.0	4,246.4
2010	4,135.0	4,144.7	4,171.8	4,229.8	4,274.3	4,258.8	4,219.8	4,219.9	4,244.0	4,278.6	4,291.2	4,290.5	4,229.9
2011	4,167.7	4,190.7	4,214.7	4,274.8	4,304.7	4,290.0	4,262.7	4,270.3	4,295.0	4,314.0	4,335.5	4,336.8	4,271.4
2012	4,224.1	4,253.3	4,289.9	4,334.7	4,381.8	4,379.9	4,322.0	4,336.5	4,362.1	4,396.5	4,407.8	4,401.9	4,340.9
2013	4,279.1	4,306.3	4,327.8	4,391.2	4,442.3	4,430.5	4,387.5	4,406.6	4,421.8	4,446.3	4,446.6	4,432.9	4,393.2
Mining and Logging													
2002	12.0	12.0	12.1	12.4	12.0	12.3	12.2	12.3	12.2	12.2	12.0	11.9	12.1
2003	11.5	11.3	11.4	11.6	11.7	11.8	11.8	11.9	11.8	11.8	11.8	11.6	11.7
2004	11.3	11.3	11.5	11.6	11.8	11.9	11.9	11.9	11.9	11.7	11.6	11.6	11.7
2005	10.8	10.8	10.9	11.3	11.4	11.5	11.7	11.6	11.6	11.7	11.7	11.5	11.4
2006	11.0	11.0	11.2	11.6	11.6	11.8	11.8	11.9	11.7	11.7	11.7	11.6	11.6
2007	11.3	11.0	11.2	11.6	11.8	11.9	12.0	12.1	11.9	11.8	11.9	11.7	11.7
2008	11.3	11.2	11.1	11.5	11.9	12.0	12.4	12.5	12.4	12.5	12.5	12.1	12.0
2009	11.6	11.4	11.5	11.8	12.0	12.0	12.1	12.0	11.8	11.6	11.5	11.3	11.7
2010	10.5	10.5	10.5	11.2	11.4	11.5	11.7	11.6	11.7	11.6	11.5	11.3	11.3
2011	10.7	10.7	10.9	11.2	11.3	11.4	11.6	11.7	11.7	11.7	11.6	11.4	11.3
2012	11.0	10.8	11.0	11.4	11.6	11.7	11.8	11.7	11.6	11.5	11.6	11.4	11.4
2013	11.3	11.3	11.8	12.3	12.5	12.6	12.7	12.8	12.8	12.8	12.8	12.6	12.4
Construction													
2002	212.2	210.4	216.8	226.3	236.9	246.5	253.8	255.7	250.8	249.0	243.4	232.2	236.2
2003	207.5	200.8	207.5	224.0	234.2	242.6	246.0	248.7	245.2	245.5	240.1	232.8	231.2
2004	208.5	205.6	216.0	229.0	238.3	246.8	252.0	250.7	247.6	246.4	241.1	232.8	234.6
2005	204.9	203.9	209.5	228.3	237.6	246.0	250.4	250.3	247.3	244.9	241.4	230.0	232.9
2006	208.1	207.5	215.2	227.2	234.9	241.5	243.4	244.0	240.5	237.2	232.4	225.0	229.7
2007	204.3	195.6	206.1	219.2	231.3	238.7	239.7	240.2	237.2	235.9	230.7	218.6	224.8
2008	196.4	192.2	194.6	208.3	218.3	223.7	226.0	225.9	221.3	219.6	210.8	196.8	211.2
2009	173.5	168.9	172.0	175.8	185.9	190.9	193.9	192.1	187.1	185.4	179.3	168.8	181.1
2010	147.4	142.8	149.6	162.8	170.2	176.7	183.1	183.4	181.0	182.5	178.6	167.9	168.8
2011	150.1	147.9	154.2	167.0	175.1	183.0	190.7	193.6	192.6	190.8	187.7	180.8	176.1
2012	162.9	160.3	165.8	176.1	184.0	189.6	191.9	192.4	191.1	191.5	187.3	179.9	181.1
2013	163.0	161.7	166.0	176.1	188.1	194.9	198.3	200.2	198.8	199.1	190.5	180.8	184.8

1. Employment by Industry: Ohio, Selected Years, 2002–2013—*Continued*

(Numbers in thousands, not seasonally adjusted)

Industry and year	January	February	March	April	May	June	July	August	September	October	November	December	Annual average
Manufacturing													
2002	893.6	890.9	889.1	886.4	888.6	892.0	877.4	887.9	884.0	877.6	876.5	875.5	885.0
2003	861.0	856.9	854.6	847.1	850.9	849.1	831.3	839.1	835.0	831.6	830.0	830.7	843.1
2004	817.4	817.9	820.4	822.9	824.4	827.4	819.7	826.5	823.7	821.7	820.8	821.9	822.1
2005	810.0	809.5	812.0	813.1	813.5	816.6	809.4	813.7	812.8	809.6	809.2	809.0	811.5
2006	799.0	797.5	797.7	800.6	799.8	806.1	793.8	798.2	796.6	790.4	788.3	787.9	796.3
2007	774.8	775.6	776.4	772.7	774.4	778.3	764.7	774.7	770.6	761.9	764.6	766.6	771.3
2008	754.4	754.4	747.0	744.6	746.1	750.4	739.6	740.4	737.8	728.5	717.2	707.0	739.0
2009	670.3	662.1	649.4	638.8	626.3	616.9	608.9	615.8	617.1	616.1	612.9	617.8	629.4
2010	607.3	607.6	608.3	613.8	619.7	624.4	623.5	626.8	626.9	627.8	629.1	630.9	620.5
2011	624.4	625.5	628.7	632.7	635.1	639.0	640.9	646.2	644.2	646.4	649.6	650.2	638.6
2012	643.9	647.3	651.3	653.5	656.9	663.4	658.8	662.8	660.1	656.9	659.5	660.3	656.2
2013	654.2	655.4	656.8	659.3	662.5	667.8	662.0	667.8	665.4	662.7	664.2	666.1	662.0
Trade, Transportation, and Utilities													
2002	1,058.2	1,045.3	1,050.2	1,053.2	1,060.1	1,064.7	1,061.5	1,061.5	1,053.5	1,057.7	1,077.5	1,089.2	1,061.1
2003	1,034.7	1,023.7	1,026.8	1,035.9	1,042.4	1,044.6	1,040.2	1,042.7	1,039.2	1,051.1	1,067.2	1,078.6	1,043.9
2004	1,026.0	1,015.1	1,021.0	1,025.4	1,033.0	1,039.8	1,039.7	1,041.7	1,036.1	1,049.2	1,068.6	1,080.9	1,039.7
2005	1,028.2	1,020.4	1,027.2	1,035.0	1,041.3	1,043.1	1,042.8	1,042.2	1,038.5	1,044.5	1,066.3	1,082.4	1,042.7
2006	1,034.4	1,024.5	1,029.7	1,034.6	1,043.6	1,047.5	1,043.7	1,044.9	1,041.5	1,047.3	1,071.5	1,085.1	1,045.7
2007	1,038.6	1,024.8	1,033.8	1,038.8	1,050.5	1,054.8	1,052.5	1,051.1	1,047.2	1,053.2	1,076.6	1,088.0	1,050.8
2008	1,038.7	1,024.4	1,025.5	1,032.1	1,039.9	1,040.2	1,036.6	1,037.2	1,028.3	1,028.0	1,035.5	1,041.0	1,034.0
2009	985.6	970.0	966.3	963.5	968.6	967.7	962.8	960.1	953.3	957.3	971.6	979.3	967.2
2010	934.4	924.6	929.8	937.6	945.9	950.2	949.1	950.2	944.0	954.4	970.7	980.8	947.6
2011	936.7	931.3	934.4	947.3	953.3	957.7	959.5	962.4	957.6	967.0	987.7	997.8	957.7
2012	956.6	949.7	957.0	962.0	972.1	975.7	971.4	972.3	968.8	979.3	1,001.8	1,007.6	972.9
2013	964.4	956.4	960.5	968.2	980.1	984.8	982.9	984.6	979.3	989.2	1,009.9	1,015.0	981.3
Wholesale Trade													
2002	238.4	237.7	238.6	239.3	240.2	240.9	240.7	240.2	238.3	237.7	237.6	238.3	239.0
2003	233.7	233.5	234.1	234.4	235.1	235.3	235.1	234.7	232.5	232.9	232.4	232.4	233.8
2004	228.1	228.0	229.0	229.9	231.5	233.1	234.5	234.7	233.0	234.8	235.4	236.4	232.4
2005	232.0	232.1	232.9	234.9	235.7	237.0	238.1	237.6	236.2	235.9	236.6	237.4	235.5
2006	234.7	235.1	235.7	237.0	238.2	239.9	239.5	239.3	237.6	237.5	237.9	238.8	237.6
2007	236.5	236.1	237.1	237.7	239.1	240.3	240.2	239.6	237.8	238.0	237.9	238.5	238.2
2008	235.5	235.2	235.2	236.8	238.2	238.8	238.5	238.0	235.7	235.1	233.1	231.7	236.0
2009	226.8	224.6	223.3	221.7	221.1	220.7	220.2	219.0	217.0	216.9	216.6	216.7	220.4
2010	213.3	213.1	213.6	214.9	215.5	216.5	217.2	216.9	215.1	215.5	215.1	214.8	215.1
2011	212.7	213.1	213.8	216.2	217.6	218.8	220.4	220.8	219.8	220.8	221.0	221.6	218.1
2012	220.0	220.8	221.9	222.7	224.2	225.9	225.7	225.7	224.2	225.1	225.4	225.7	223.9
2013	222.9	223.1	223.9	225.7	227.6	228.6	228.9	229.0	227.7	229.6	229.4	227.3	227.0
Retail Trade													
2002	637.4	626.1	630.3	631.1	635.8	639.8	635.8	634.9	629.4	631.3	650.7	662.9	637.1
2003	618.8	609.4	612.3	619.4	623.8	626.1	622.5	624.4	622.5	629.8	646.2	657.5	626.1
2004	616.4	607.0	611.2	612.4	616.9	621.1	617.8	618.5	613.7	619.1	637.0	647.6	619.9
2005	607.0	598.8	603.4	608.7	613.0	613.0	609.7	608.7	604.3	607.2	624.6	637.6	611.3
2006	599.9	589.8	593.6	596.1	602.0	603.4	600.6	600.4	595.9	601.1	621.4	630.8	602.9
2007	594.7	583.3	590.4	592.8	601.0	602.6	601.2	598.7	595.2	599.2	619.1	627.5	600.5
2008	592.2	579.7	581.1	585.5	590.8	592.2	591.2	591.0	584.9	586.0	595.8	603.5	589.5
2009	563.3	552.4	552.2	554.7	561.0	561.6	558.4	557.3	553.5	556.6	570.8	577.6	560.0
2010	543.0	534.9	539.1	544.4	550.4	552.7	552.0	552.5	547.4	555.9	571.2	579.1	551.9
2011	544.0	538.5	540.6	549.2	552.6	555.2	555.1	556.1	550.7	558.5	576.8	583.8	555.1
2012	551.0	543.4	549.0	552.7	559.1	560.0	556.5	556.3	553.8	561.7	581.4	583.9	559.1
2013	552.7	545.5	548.6	554.2	562.1	564.6	562.8	563.3	559.0	565.6	582.4	588.1	562.4
Transportation and Utilities													
2002	182.4	181.5	181.3	182.8	184.1	184.0	185.0	186.4	185.8	188.7	189.2	188.0	184.9
2003	182.2	180.8	180.4	182.1	183.5	183.2	182.6	183.6	184.2	188.4	188.6	188.7	184.0
2004	181.5	180.1	180.8	183.1	184.6	185.6	187.4	188.5	189.4	195.3	196.2	196.9	187.5
2005	189.2	189.5	190.9	191.4	192.6	193.1	195.0	195.9	198.0	201.4	205.1	207.4	195.8
2006	199.8	199.6	200.4	201.5	203.4	204.2	203.6	205.2	208.0	208.7	212.2	215.5	205.2
2007	207.4	205.4	206.3	208.3	210.4	211.9	211.1	212.8	214.2	216.0	219.6	222.0	212.1
2008	211.0	209.5	209.2	209.8	210.9	209.2	206.9	208.2	207.7	206.9	206.6	205.8	208.5
2009	195.5	193.0	190.8	187.1	186.5	185.4	184.2	183.8	182.8	183.8	184.2	185.0	186.8
2010	178.1	176.6	177.1	178.3	180.0	181.0	179.9	180.8	181.5	183.0	184.4	186.9	180.6
2011	180.0	179.7	180.0	181.9	183.1	183.7	184.0	185.5	187.1	187.7	189.9	192.4	184.6
2012	185.6	185.5	186.1	186.6	188.8	189.8	189.2	190.3	190.8	192.5	195.0	198.0	189.9
2013	188.8	187.8	188.0	188.3	190.4	191.6	191.2	192.3	192.6	194.0	198.1	199.6	191.9
Information													
2002	103.5	102.5	102.2	101.9	101.7	101.9	101.3	100.8	99.5	98.4	99.1	99.2	101.0
2003	98.2	97.7	97.7	97.4	97.6	97.4	97.0	96.5	94.8	94.4	94.5	94.6	96.5
2004	93.4	93.0	92.9	92.4	92.6	93.3	92.9	92.3	90.8	90.5	91.5	91.1	92.2
2005	89.9	89.5	89.5	90.0	90.6	90.8	90.6	90.3	89.7	89.0	89.4	89.8	89.9
2006	88.8	88.6	88.7	88.3	88.6	88.9	88.8	88.6	87.8	87.5	87.8	88.0	88.4
2007	87.3	87.4	87.0	87.8	88.4	88.9	88.8	88.5	87.3	86.9	87.1	87.4	87.7
2008	86.3	86.2	86.1	86.4	86.4	86.4	86.5	86.4	84.8	84.5	84.9	84.8	85.8
2009	83.6	83.1	82.2	81.2	81.3	81.1	80.9	80.4	79.1	78.5	78.7	79.0	80.8
2010	78.5	78.1	77.9	77.4	77.6	77.5	77.9	77.9	77.0	76.8	77.1	77.2	77.6
2011	76.1	75.8	75.3	75.9	76.3	76.4	76.8	76.7	76.2	75.8	76.1	76.0	76.1
2012	75.0	74.8	74.7	74.6	75.0	75.4	75.5	75.0	74.6	74.8	75.1	75.4	75.0
2013	74.9	75.3	75.5	74.1	74.1	74.5	75.8	75.5	74.6	74.1	74.4	74.5	74.8

1. Employment by Industry: Ohio, Selected Years, 2002–2013—*Continued*

(Numbers in thousands, not seasonally adjusted)

Industry and year	January	February	March	April	May	June	July	August	September	October	November	December	Annual average
Financial Activities													
2002	305.6	306.9	307.5	306.4	307.5	309.6	310.7	310.3	307.9	308.0	309.6	311.1	308.4
2003	307.9	308.7	309.6	309.4	311.5	314.1	314.3	315.2	312.8	311.9	311.9	313.8	311.8
2004	309.8	310.5	311.3	310.4	311.1	313.5	313.5	313.3	309.6	308.8	308.8	309.9	310.9
2005	305.7	305.8	305.9	306.8	308.0	310.6	310.9	311.2	309.2	309.0	309.1	309.8	308.5
2006	305.6	305.5	306.3	306.1	306.5	307.9	307.3	306.1	304.2	304.5	304.1	303.5	305.6
2007	301.5	301.2	300.0	301.8	302.3	301.7	301.5	301.0	297.9	297.1	295.5	295.8	299.8
2008	292.1	291.6	291.3	291.4	292.1	292.5	291.7	291.2	288.3	287.4	286.9	286.8	290.3
2009	282.9	281.5	280.8	280.4	281.1	281.7	281.5	280.1	277.8	277.2	277.2	277.0	279.9
2010	274.4	273.9	273.6	274.9	275.8	277.3	278.9	278.8	277.1	278.2	278.6	279.3	276.7
2011	277.4	277.5	277.4	277.9	278.6	278.8	278.9	278.7	277.8	277.4	277.5	277.7	278.0
2012	275.7	275.6	276.3	277.9	279.6	281.5	282.5	282.3	280.4	281.6	282.7	282.8	279.9
2013	279.5	280.1	280.1	282.5	284.3	286.3	286.9	286.9	284.8	283.8	281.6	281.4	283.2
Professional and Business Services													
2002	596.8	597.0	603.2	610.5	613.8	618.9	621.4	626.3	625.4	627.1	625.2	621.5	615.6
2003	597.8	597.4	602.2	609.5	611.2	614.1	615.2	620.7	616.6	619.9	619.9	615.8	611.7
2004	600.5	601.1	608.6	620.0	622.0	631.1	634.0	639.7	640.2	641.9	640.4	638.8	626.5
2005	615.1	619.0	625.2	639.8	640.5	646.4	649.6	656.4	658.5	659.4	657.1	657.2	643.7
2006	633.4	636.0	644.2	653.4	654.9	663.6	661.2	668.9	666.4	666.0	664.3	664.4	656.4
2007	645.1	646.7	653.4	664.2	667.4	676.8	674.1	677.7	676.0	680.2	680.6	678.8	668.4
2008	660.5	662.1	661.9	673.3	674.0	677.2	678.2	680.1	674.1	668.9	660.4	652.6	668.6
2009	625.8	619.0	614.1	617.0	615.5	614.6	613.7	616.2	613.9	616.0	618.4	614.5	616.6
2010	596.2	598.1	603.0	621.6	622.6	630.1	634.4	639.4	636.6	642.5	643.6	641.8	625.8
2011	624.6	628.1	634.2	649.8	648.6	652.4	659.0	663.6	662.5	664.9	667.1	666.6	651.8
2012	648.8	652.6	658.8	670.5	673.0	677.8	678.2	683.6	680.6	688.9	688.1	683.7	673.7
2013	657.1	662.3	667.1	685.1	690.7	694.8	693.2	700.6	699.8	705.7	702.1	695.6	687.8
Education and Health Services													
2002	698.2	708.9	709.8	711.8	710.6	703.2	697.2	700.2	714.0	724.7	728.7	728.9	711.4
2003	719.1	725.2	727.2	730.1	726.9	719.6	717.7	719.9	734.4	743.8	746.9	747.2	729.8
2004	734.7	741.5	744.1	748.3	744.0	736.3	734.6	732.9	749.7	760.0	763.2	766.2	746.3
2005	748.6	757.1	760.2	763.3	759.8	753.3	748.7	750.2	768.6	775.8	780.0	781.4	762.3
2006	766.8	777.6	781.0	782.0	778.5	769.8	763.5	765.6	783.1	789.3	792.3	792.1	778.5
2007	779.9	785.2	789.5	792.5	791.6	785.0	780.7	783.9	801.7	809.2	814.0	814.1	793.9
2008	803.9	811.5	812.6	815.1	813.3	803.7	799.2	802.1	818.9	826.5	829.9	829.9	813.9
2009	818.6	825.7	827.3	829.5	826.8	817.0	815.4	817.0	832.6	841.7	844.5	844.4	828.4
2010	833.6	839.1	842.4	843.2	839.1	827.2	826.6	828.0	845.1	853.7	856.0	853.6	840.6
2011	841.5	849.7	850.6	856.0	857.9	843.6	840.0	841.3	854.9	862.4	864.5	864.9	852.3
2012	856.0	864.2	865.9	869.2	869.2	860.8	851.3	855.3	866.5	876.4	878.2	876.6	865.8
2013	865.4	876.2	875.6	881.2	880.6	871.5	868.2	872.2	876.4	885.5	893.3	889.0	877.9
Leisure and Hospitality													
2002	448.2	449.9	461.1	477.9	502.0	516.7	519.4	518.4	502.5	484.5	473.9	471.2	485.5
2003	449.1	447.1	456.7	480.5	504.2	519.3	523.1	524.7	506.0	490.3	479.5	479.3	488.3
2004	457.4	457.8	470.1	489.8	512.1	524.4	527.0	529.2	513.9	496.3	487.9	484.0	495.8
2005	460.6	463.2	475.1	498.4	517.5	531.8	531.7	532.0	517.8	496.6	488.7	483.7	499.8
2006	463.8	467.4	479.5	496.2	517.2	533.9	531.9	532.6	514.9	497.6	489.1	486.8	500.9
2007	468.3	466.4	478.4	495.9	519.4	535.5	529.3	530.9	512.5	498.5	487.6	483.9	500.6
2008	462.6	463.3	467.8	491.8	516.6	527.1	522.3	522.2	503.7	485.8	471.1	469.6	492.0
2009	445.5	445.2	455.9	474.4	497.9	509.7	507.8	505.4	491.8	472.8	458.9	457.0	476.9
2010	436.7	437.3	448.5	472.0	492.3	505.5	506.7	506.1	492.6	476.8	466.2	462.4	475.3
2011	442.6	444.6	455.6	479.5	500.9	514.4	515.0	517.1	500.8	484.0	476.1	471.2	483.5
2012	454.0	459.2	474.2	495.0	518.5	535.0	532.0	533.3	516.4	505.9	492.7	492.7	500.7
2013	474.1	477.2	490.3	513.2	540.7	552.1	550.8	549.1	532.7	520.8	497.1	496.1	516.2
Other Services													
2002	225.6	226.6	228.5	228.5	230.2	231.7	229.9	230.6	227.9	227.8	227.5	228.1	228.6
2003	224.7	225.1	227.2	227.7	229.0	229.5	228.8	228.7	226.0	226.8	225.5	225.9	227.1
2004	222.7	223.6	226.4	227.5	228.9	230.1	229.6	228.7	226.6	227.2	226.4	225.0	226.9
2005	221.1	222.3	224.1	225.7	226.5	227.5	226.3	226.0	223.7	223.6	223.9	223.3	224.5
2006	219.9	220.4	222.1	222.6	224.0	226.6	224.1	223.1	221.6	221.3	220.7	221.3	222.3
2007	218.2	218.2	220.6	220.8	221.9	224.4	222.4	222.4	221.6	218.7	219.3	218.7	220.3
2008	215.4	215.9	216.3	217.6	219.2	220.2	219.0	218.4	215.9	215.8	214.0	213.2	216.7
2009	208.8	209.0	209.8	209.9	211.0	211.1	210.3	208.7	206.7	206.6	205.3	205.7	208.6
2010	202.7	202.9	203.6	205.9	206.2	208.1	208.8	207.9	206.3	206.9	206.4	206.8	206.0
2011	203.9	204.3	205.3	206.6	208.1	209.2	210.2	209.6	207.8	207.7	207.6	207.6	207.3
2012	206.2	206.9	210.0	210.8	212.6	215.3	215.1	214.0	212.3	213.4	212.4	212.7	211.8
2013	210.1	210.6	211.9	213.9	215.3	216.3	215.4	215.1	213.0	214.4	213.6	213.7	213.6
Government													
2002	794.8	813.2	817.5	813.9	816.7	795.0	758.6	752.6	791.8	812.1	819.2	817.4	800.2
2003	798.3	813.1	817.6	816.8	820.3	798.1	763.8	756.9	792.7	814.0	819.2	820.4	802.6
2004	795.3	815.3	820.3	817.9	820.2	800.3	762.3	756.6	789.8	812.4	816.1	814.3	801.7
2005	792.3	812.4	814.4	812.6	818.7	794.8	759.1	756.2	791.4	812.7	817.8	813.2	799.6
2006	795.5	811.0	814.1	812.1	818.8	796.4	759.0	756.9	792.7	812.9	817.0	814.3	800.1
2007	793.8	807.7	811.3	810.7	814.4	796.1	756.9	755.1	789.3	809.3	813.3	806.7	797.1
2008	792.8	810.7	809.0	809.9	814.7	792.2	754.3	753.0	787.5	809.9	814.7	805.9	796.2
2009	790.2	805.1	805.4	807.7	808.7	784.9	745.0	741.7	778.2	799.1	800.5	791.1	788.1
2010	778.5	790.7	793.0	797.2	814.8	782.9	737.4	731.6	765.3	789.3	792.6	788.6	780.2
2011	764.9	779.4	781.9	781.8	781.0	757.5	723.3	720.9	757.4	774.8	778.9	775.0	764.7
2012	751.8	770.3	773.0	774.7	781.8	758.4	716.0	720.7	762.6	776.2	776.8	770.4	761.1
2013	753.6	768.2	766.8	773.0	776.5	750.2	714.3	722.6	761.2	772.8	774.6	767.6	758.5

2. Average Weekly Hours by Selected Industry: Ohio, 2009–2013

(Not seasonally adjusted)

Industry and year	January	February	March	April	May	June	July	August	September	October	November	December	Annual average
Total Private													
2009	32.5	33.0	32.9	32.5	32.8	32.9	32.9	33.3	33.0	33.0	33.5	33.2	33.0
2010	33.1	32.9	33.4	33.5	33.5	33.4	33.5	33.8	33.4	33.8	33.7	33.5	33.5
2011	33.4	33.4	33.4	33.7	33.9	33.7	33.6	33.6	33.8	34.3	34.0	33.9	33.7
2012	34.0	33.9	33.9	34.4	34.0	34.0	34.2	34.0	34.3	34.1	34.2	34.6	34.1
2013	34.1	34.2	34.2	34.2	34.1	34.4	33.9	34.2	34.5	34.0	34.1	34.3	34.2
Goods-Producing													
2009	36.2	36.7	36.5	36.5	37.2	37.7	37.5	38.2	37.6	37.9	38.5	38.8	37.4
2010	38.8	38.7	39.4	39.8	39.8	40.0	39.5	40.1	39.6	40.4	40.3	39.8	39.7
2011	39.3	39.7	39.7	39.9	39.9	39.9	39.7	40.5	40.3	40.4	40.6	40.5	40.0
2012	40.1	40.2	40.1	40.4	40.3	40.3	40.4	40.2	40.7	40.6	40.5	41.0	40.4
2013	40.3	40.4	40.5	40.4	40.7	40.9	40.0	41.0	41.1	40.9	41.4	41.3	40.7
Construction													
2009	35.3	36.3	35.8	35.1	36.5	37.3	38.0	38.8	38.3	37.7	38.1	37.5	37.1
2010	37.2	37.1	37.2	37.8	37.2	37.7	37.8	38.4	37.6	38.8	38.5	37.6	37.8
2011	37.4	37.6	37.2	38.1	38.4	39.1	40.1	40.4	40.0	39.1	39.8	38.4	38.9
2012	37.4	37.3	36.6	37.5	37.3	38.0	39.2	39.1	39.9	40.1	40.3	39.0	38.5
2013	38.1	38.0	38.1	38.8	39.4	39.6	39.2	40.9	39.9	40.7	40.1	38.8	39.4
Manufacturing													
2009	37.6	37.7	37.8	37.9	38.1	38.4	37.9	38.9	38.5	38.8	39.2	39.6	38.4
2010	39.5	39.5	39.8	40.1	40.5	40.4	39.7	40.3	40.0	40.8	40.7	40.3	40.1
2011	39.5	40.0	40.0	40.1	40.1	40.0	39.4	40.4	40.2	40.6	40.6	40.8	40.1
2012	40.5	40.6	40.7	40.9	40.9	40.6	40.4	40.6	41.1	40.9	40.7	41.7	40.8
2013	41.1	41.2	41.2	41.0	41.3	41.6	40.5	41.3	41.7	41.2	41.9	42.0	41.3
Trade, Transportation, and Utilities													
2009	33.1	33.5	33.3	33.1	33.6	33.7	33.6	33.9	33.9	33.6	33.6	33.6	33.5
2010	33.3	33.5	33.8	33.6	33.9	33.9	34.3	34.6	34.6	34.7	34.5	35.0	34.1
2011	34.6	34.1	34.2	34.6	34.8	34.7	34.6	34.3	34.8	35.3	34.6	35.0	34.6
2012	34.8	34.5	34.4	35.0	34.7	34.7	34.7	34.5	34.9	34.6	34.4	34.5	34.6
2013	34.4	34.6	34.6	34.8	34.9	34.8	34.6	34.8	35.1	34.6	34.3	34.9	34.7
Financial Activities													
2009	36.8	37.3	36.7	36.1	36.4	36.5	36.1	36.7	36.4	36.1	36.9	36.5	36.5
2010	36.2	36.2	36.1	36.4	36.5	36.2	35.8	36.7	36.5	36.7	36.7	36.5	36.4
2011	37.1	36.0	36.1	36.6	37.7	37.1	36.8	36.6	36.9	37.5	36.8	36.9	36.8
2012	38.2	36.7	36.7	37.8	36.2	36.2	38.0	36.4	37.8	36.3	36.3	38.2	37.1
2013	37.1	36.9	37.2	36.8	36.7	37.9	36.2	35.9	37.4	35.8	36.0	37.4	36.8
Professional and Business Services													
2009	34.7	34.8	34.7	34.7	34.5	34.4	34.2	34.6	34.2	34.0	34.6	34.2	34.5
2010	34.4	34.3	34.6	34.8	35.0	34.7	35.0	35.3	34.6	35.2	34.8	34.8	34.8
2011	34.9	34.5	34.6	34.6	34.9	34.1	33.9	34.3	34.1	35.4	34.5	34.3	34.5
2012	34.5	34.5	34.9	36.0	35.1	35.3	35.3	35.3	35.6	35.6	35.9	36.5	35.4
2013	35.6	35.9	36.1	36.4	36.2	36.6	35.9	36.2	36.5	36.0	36.4	36.5	36.2
Education and Health Services													
2009	32.2	32.7	32.8	32.1	32.9	32.6	32.7	33.0	32.9	32.8	33.2	32.8	32.7
2010	32.6	32.3	32.6	32.5	32.2	32.0	32.2	32.1	32.1	32.3	32.3	32.2	32.3
2011	32.4	32.4	32.4	32.6	32.5	32.3	32.7	32.2	32.4	32.6	32.6	32.5	32.5
2012	32.6	32.3	32.2	32.4	32.2	32.1	32.2	32.2	32.5	32.4	32.3	32.4	32.3
2013	32.2	32.1	32.0	31.9	31.5	31.7	31.5	31.6	31.9	31.4	31.4	31.6	31.7
Leisure and Hospitality													
2009	22.3	22.4	22.5	22.2	22.8	23.3	23.6	23.6	23.3	23.2	23.4	23.6	23.0
2010	23.1	23.4	23.9	23.8	24.0	24.3	24.4	24.7	23.8	24.1	24.0	23.6	23.9
2011	22.8	23.5	23.6	23.9	23.8	24.1	24.0	23.9	23.6	24.0	23.9	23.6	23.7
2012	22.8	23.5	23.5	23.7	24.0	24.4	24.5	24.3	23.6	23.7	23.6	24.2	23.8
2013	23.3	24.0	24.0	24.0	24.2	24.3	24.2	24.4	23.7	23.4	23.3	23.1	23.8
Other Services													
2009	31.2	30.6	30.4	29.7	29.9	29.7	29.9	30.3	29.9	30.3	30.3	30.2	30.2
2010	30.4	30.2	30.4	30.2	30.4	29.7	29.6	29.9	29.8	29.9	30.8	30.3	30.1
2011	30.8	30.5	30.5	30.4	30.6	30.4	30.1	29.7	29.9	30.2	29.8	29.8	30.2
2012	29.6	28.6	28.5	28.8	28.4	28.0	28.2	28.0	28.5	28.0	28.4	28.5	28.5
2013	27.8	28.1	28.1	28.6	28.9	29.2	28.8	29.0	29.6	29.4	29.7	30.1	28.9

3. Average Hourly Earnings by Selected Industry: Ohio, 2009–2013

(Dollars, not seasonally adjusted)

Industry and year	January	February	March	April	May	June	July	August	September	October	November	December	Annual average
Total Private													
2009	20.02	20.01	19.95	19.98	19.86	19.76	19.73	19.74	19.95	20.03	20.11	20.24	19.95
2010	20.11	20.17	20.06	20.19	20.14	20.01	20.11	20.20	20.25	20.31	20.39	20.62	20.22
2011	20.85	20.94	20.83	20.85	21.03	20.77	20.93	21.11	21.30	21.43	21.38	21.40	21.07
2012	21.97	21.83	21.86	22.11	21.81	21.69	21.87	21.82	22.32	22.13	22.26	22.48	22.01
2013	22.40	22.32	22.17	22.18	22.01	22.19	22.11	22.08	22.44	22.24	22.33	22.45	22.24
Goods-Producing													
2009	21.80	22.11	21.92	21.93	21.86	21.82	21.80	21.47	21.65	21.54	21.67	21.56	21.76
2010	21.42	21.45	21.49	21.56	21.73	21.69	21.84	21.82	21.93	21.90	21.86	22.07	21.74
2011	22.19	22.43	22.65	22.81	22.85	22.91	22.99	23.21	23.58	23.51	23.57	23.90	23.07
2012	23.92	23.63	23.85	23.95	23.47	23.36	23.55	23.54	23.98	23.94	24.19	24.23	23.80
2013	24.04	23.89	23.80	23.79	23.87	23.86	24.07	24.16	24.28	24.12	24.20	24.66	24.07
Construction													
2009	24.64	24.88	24.93	24.78	25.19	24.91	24.70	24.68	24.79	24.90	25.00	25.12	24.87
2010	25.09	25.14	25.09	24.95	25.07	25.10	25.00	25.04	24.87	24.84	24.67	24.89	24.97
2011	24.95	25.09	25.57	25.14	25.02	25.16	25.10	25.42	25.64	25.61	25.81	26.07	25.40
2012	25.86	26.03	26.68	26.35	26.22	25.81	25.83	25.94	26.66	26.91	26.73	26.76	26.32
2013	26.13	26.18	26.01	25.67	25.43	25.23	25.49	25.66	25.68	25.60	25.45	25.98	25.69
Manufacturing													
2009	21.89	21.93	21.86	21.85	21.63	21.56	21.54	21.13	21.28	21.17	21.36	21.22	21.54
2010	21.16	21.16	21.15	21.26	21.36	21.37	21.37	21.32	21.47	21.40	21.46	22.13	21.37
2011	22.20	22.34	22.51	22.70	22.79	22.73	22.77	22.93	23.23	23.20	23.19	23.38	22.84
2012	23.48	23.27	23.38	23.55	23.04	22.97	23.14	23.09	23.42	23.28	23.64	23.76	23.34
2013	23.70	23.50	23.40	23.46	23.58	23.60	23.81	23.89	24.02	23.84	23.97	24.32	23.76
Trade, Transportation, and Utilities													
2009	18.30	18.46	18.49	18.40	18.41	18.34	18.48	18.56	18.50	18.44	18.46	18.29	18.43
2010	18.37	18.46	18.41	18.52	18.33	18.47	18.56	18.66	18.68	18.83	18.62	18.81	18.56
2011	19.00	19.02	18.91	18.38	18.52	18.55	19.00	19.03	19.09	19.09	19.01	18.69	18.86
2012	19.40	19.24	19.36	19.94	19.59	19.81	20.25	19.94	20.09	20.22	19.95	20.23	19.84
2013	20.48	20.45	20.43	20.51	20.23	20.56	20.39	20.17	20.60	20.16	20.28	20.08	20.36
Financial Activities													
2009	23.50	23.75	23.55	23.71	23.54	23.31	23.49	23.42	23.42	23.35	23.27	23.35	23.47
2010	23.25	24.33	24.38	24.41	24.48	24.35	24.34	24.31	24.35	24.54	24.74	24.99	24.38
2011	24.80	24.53	24.08	24.37	24.66	24.26	24.80	24.56	24.68	25.10	24.92	25.27	24.67
2012	26.84	26.64	26.74	27.78	27.25	27.20	27.18	27.36	27.90	27.36	27.87	27.94	27.34
2013	27.90	27.10	27.00	27.62	27.52	27.45	27.56	27.53	27.79	27.90	27.88	27.64	27.57
Professional and Business Services													
2009	24.42	24.07	24.08	23.92	23.60	23.67	23.61	23.72	23.56	23.78	23.89	24.00	23.86
2010	24.14	24.17	24.06	23.90	24.01	23.85	23.72	23.81	23.79	23.74	24.00	23.94	23.92
2011	24.20	24.11	23.74	24.35	24.33	24.04	24.24	24.02	24.23	24.83	24.69	24.60	24.29
2012	25.41	25.10	25.19	25.64	25.37	25.31	25.52	25.07	25.89	25.37	25.72	26.10	25.48
2013	25.94	25.72	25.46	25.44	25.13	25.58	25.30	25.42	25.89	25.63	25.61	26.00	25.59
Education and Health Services													
2009	19.47	19.41	19.67	19.89	20.19	20.25	20.06	20.03	20.23	20.34	20.29	20.44	20.03
2010	20.44	20.32	20.41	20.57	20.46	20.47	20.66	20.62	20.72	21.01	20.65	20.90	20.60
2011	21.11	21.32	21.30	21.33	21.71	21.23	21.14	21.34	21.34	21.51	21.51	21.47	21.36
2012	21.42	21.66	21.47	21.28	21.44	21.16	21.28	21.15	21.41	21.20	21.27	21.44	21.35
2013	21.19	21.50	21.29	21.34	21.27	21.47	21.38	21.26	21.58	21.65	21.67	21.72	21.44
Leisure and Hospitality													
2009	11.12	11.10	11.05	10.99	10.90	10.84	10.86	10.88	10.99	11.13	11.28	11.26	11.03
2010	11.32	11.30	11.20	11.30	11.21	11.16	11.00	10.94	11.13	11.15	11.87	11.96	11.29
2011	11.78	11.77	11.67	11.72	11.74	11.60	11.56	11.66	11.65	11.66	11.81	11.95	11.71
2012	11.97	12.15	11.96	11.96	11.87	11.74	11.71	11.75	12.03	11.94	12.01	12.07	11.92
2013	12.10	12.20	12.14	12.17	12.11	12.06	12.12	12.09	12.35	12.46	12.57	12.69	12.25
Other Services													
2009	16.32	16.39	16.19	15.86	15.72	15.79	15.63	16.29	16.35	16.17	16.19	16.22	16.09
2010	16.12	16.31	16.23	16.30	16.36	16.21	16.29	16.37	16.24	16.40	16.26	16.49	16.30
2011	16.83	17.03	17.17	17.01	17.42	17.38	17.64	17.76	17.97	17.91	18.03	18.41	17.54
2012	18.66	18.70	18.91	19.25	19.08	18.74	19.18	19.05	19.57	19.36	19.63	19.71	19.15
2013	19.34	19.38	19.36	19.06	19.02	18.95	19.07	19.08	19.17	19.08	19.44	19.49	19.20

4. Average Weekly Earnings by Selected Industry: Ohio, 2009–2013

(Dollars, not seasonally adjusted)

Industry and year	January	February	March	April	May	June	July	August	September	October	November	December	Annual average
Total Private													
2009	650.65	660.33	656.36	649.35	651.41	650.10	649.12	657.34	658.35	660.99	673.69	671.97	658.35
2010	665.64	663.59	670.00	676.37	674.69	668.33	673.69	682.76	676.35	686.48	687.14	690.77	677.37
2011	696.39	699.40	695.72	702.65	712.92	699.95	703.25	709.30	719.94	735.05	726.92	725.46	710.06
2012	746.98	740.04	741.05	760.58	741.54	737.46	747.95	741.88	765.58	754.63	761.29	777.81	750.54
2013	763.84	763.34	758.21	758.56	750.54	763.34	749.53	755.14	774.18	756.16	761.45	770.04	760.61
Goods-Producing													
2009	789.16	811.44	800.08	800.45	813.19	822.61	817.50	820.15	814.04	816.37	834.30	836.53	813.82
2010	831.10	830.12	846.71	858.09	864.85	867.60	862.68	874.98	868.43	884.76	880.96	878.39	863.08
2011	872.07	890.47	899.21	910.12	911.72	914.11	912.70	940.01	950.27	949.80	956.94	967.95	922.80
2012	959.19	949.93	956.39	967.58	945.84	941.41	951.42	946.31	975.99	971.96	979.70	993.43	961.52
2013	968.81	965.16	963.90	961.12	971.51	975.87	962.80	990.56	997.91	986.51	1,001.88	1,018.46	979.65
Construction													
2009	869.79	903.14	892.49	869.78	919.44	929.14	938.60	957.58	949.46	938.73	952.50	942.00	922.68
2010	933.35	932.69	933.35	943.11	932.60	946.27	945.00	961.54	935.11	963.79	949.80	935.86	943.87
2011	933.13	943.38	951.20	957.83	960.77	983.76	1,006.51	1,026.97	1,025.60	1,001.35	1,027.24	1,001.09	988.06
2012	967.16	970.92	976.49	988.13	978.01	980.78	1,012.54	1,014.25	1,063.73	1,079.09	1,077.22	1,043.64	1,013.32
2013	995.55	994.84	990.98	996.00	1,001.94	999.11	999.21	1,049.49	1,024.63	1,041.92	1,020.55	1,008.02	1,012.19
Manufacturing													
2009	823.06	826.76	826.31	828.12	824.10	827.90	816.37	821.96	819.28	821.40	837.31	840.31	827.14
2010	835.82	835.82	841.77	852.53	865.08	856.08	848.39	859.20	858.80	873.12	873.42	891.84	856.94
2011	876.90	893.60	900.40	910.27	913.88	909.20	897.14	926.37	933.85	941.92	941.51	953.90	915.88
2012	950.94	944.76	951.57	963.20	942.34	932.58	934.86	937.45	962.56	952.15	962.15	990.79	952.27
2013	974.07	968.20	964.08	961.86	973.85	981.76	964.31	986.66	1,001.63	982.21	1,004.34	1,021.44	981.29
Trade, Transportation, and Utilities													
2009	605.73	618.41	615.72	609.04	618.58	618.06	620.93	629.18	627.15	619.58	620.26	614.54	617.41
2010	611.72	618.41	622.26	622.27	621.39	626.13	636.61	645.64	646.33	653.40	642.39	658.35	632.90
2011	657.40	648.58	646.72	635.95	644.50	643.69	657.40	652.73	664.33	673.88	657.75	654.15	652.56
2012	675.12	663.78	665.98	697.90	679.77	687.41	702.68	687.93	701.14	699.61	686.28	697.94	686.46
2013	704.51	707.57	706.88	713.75	706.03	715.49	705.49	701.92	723.06	697.54	695.60	700.79	706.49
Financial Activities													
2009	864.80	885.88	864.29	855.93	856.86	850.82	847.99	859.51	852.49	842.94	858.66	852.28	856.66
2010	841.65	880.75	880.12	888.52	893.52	881.47	871.37	892.18	888.78	900.62	907.96	912.14	887.43
2011	920.08	883.08	869.29	891.94	929.68	900.05	912.64	898.90	910.69	941.25	917.06	932.46	907.86
2012	1,025.29	977.69	981.36	1,050.08	986.45	984.64	1,032.84	995.90	1,054.62	993.17	1,011.68	1,067.31	1,014.31
2013	1,035.09	999.99	1,004.40	1,016.42	1,009.98	1,040.36	997.67	988.33	1,039.35	998.82	1,003.68	1,033.74	1,014.58
Professional and Business Services													
2009	847.37	837.64	835.58	830.02	814.20	814.25	807.46	820.71	805.75	808.52	826.59	820.80	823.17
2010	830.42	829.03	832.48	831.72	840.35	827.60	830.20	840.49	823.13	835.65	835.20	833.11	832.42
2011	844.58	831.80	821.40	842.51	849.12	819.76	821.74	823.89	826.24	878.98	851.81	843.78	838.01
2012	876.65	865.95	879.13	923.04	890.49	893.44	900.86	884.97	921.68	903.17	923.35	952.65	901.99
2013	923.46	923.35	919.11	926.02	909.71	936.23	908.27	920.20	944.99	922.68	932.20	949.00	926.36
Education and Health Services													
2009	626.93	634.71	645.18	638.47	664.25	660.15	655.96	660.99	665.57	667.15	673.63	670.43	654.98
2010	666.34	656.34	665.37	668.53	658.81	655.04	665.25	661.90	665.11	678.62	667.00	672.98	665.38
2011	683.96	690.77	690.12	695.36	705.58	685.73	691.28	687.15	691.42	701.23	701.23	697.78	694.20
2012	698.29	699.62	691.33	689.47	690.37	679.24	685.22	681.03	695.83	686.88	687.02	694.66	689.61
2013	682.32	690.15	681.28	680.75	670.01	680.60	673.47	671.82	688.40	679.81	680.44	686.35	679.65
Leisure and Hospitality													
2009	247.98	248.64	248.63	243.98	248.52	252.57	256.30	256.77	256.07	258.22	263.95	265.74	253.69
2010	261.49	264.42	267.68	268.94	269.04	271.19	268.40	270.22	264.89	268.72	284.88	282.26	269.83
2011	268.58	276.60	275.41	280.11	279.41	279.56	277.44	278.67	274.94	279.84	282.26	282.02	277.53
2012	272.92	285.53	281.06	283.45	284.88	286.46	286.90	285.53	283.91	282.98	283.44	292.09	283.70
2013	281.93	292.80	291.36	292.08	293.06	293.06	293.30	295.00	292.70	291.56	292.88	293.14	291.55
Other Services													
2009	509.18	501.53	492.18	471.04	470.03	468.96	467.34	493.59	488.87	489.95	490.56	489.84	485.92
2010	490.05	492.56	493.39	492.26	497.34	481.44	482.18	489.46	483.95	490.36	500.81	499.65	490.63
2011	518.36	519.42	523.69	517.10	533.05	528.35	530.96	527.47	537.30	540.88	537.29	548.62	529.71
2012	552.34	534.82	538.94	554.40	541.87	524.72	540.88	533.40	557.75	542.08	557.49	561.74	545.78
2013	537.65	544.58	544.02	545.12	549.68	553.34	549.22	553.32	567.43	560.95	577.37	586.65	554.88

OKLAHOMA
At a Glance

Population:
    2000 census: 3,450,451
    2010 census: 3,751,351
    2013 estimate: 3,850,568

Percent change in population:
    2000–2010: 8.7%
    2010–2013: 2.6%

Percent change in total nonfarm employment:
    2000–2010: 5.4%
    2010–2013: 5.0%

Industry with the largest growth in employment, 2000–2013 (thousands):
    Education and Health Services, 64.7

Industry with the largest decline or smallest growth in employment, 2000–2013 (thousands):
    Manufacturing, -40.4

Civilian labor force:
    2000: 1,661,045
    2010: 1,775,398
    2013: 1,816,794

Unemployment rate and rank among states (lowest to highest):
    2000: 3.1%, 12th
    2010: 6.9%, 9th
    2013: 5.4%, 11th

Over-the-year change in unemployment rates:
    2010–2011: -1.0%
    2011–2012: -0.5%
    2012–2013: 0.0%

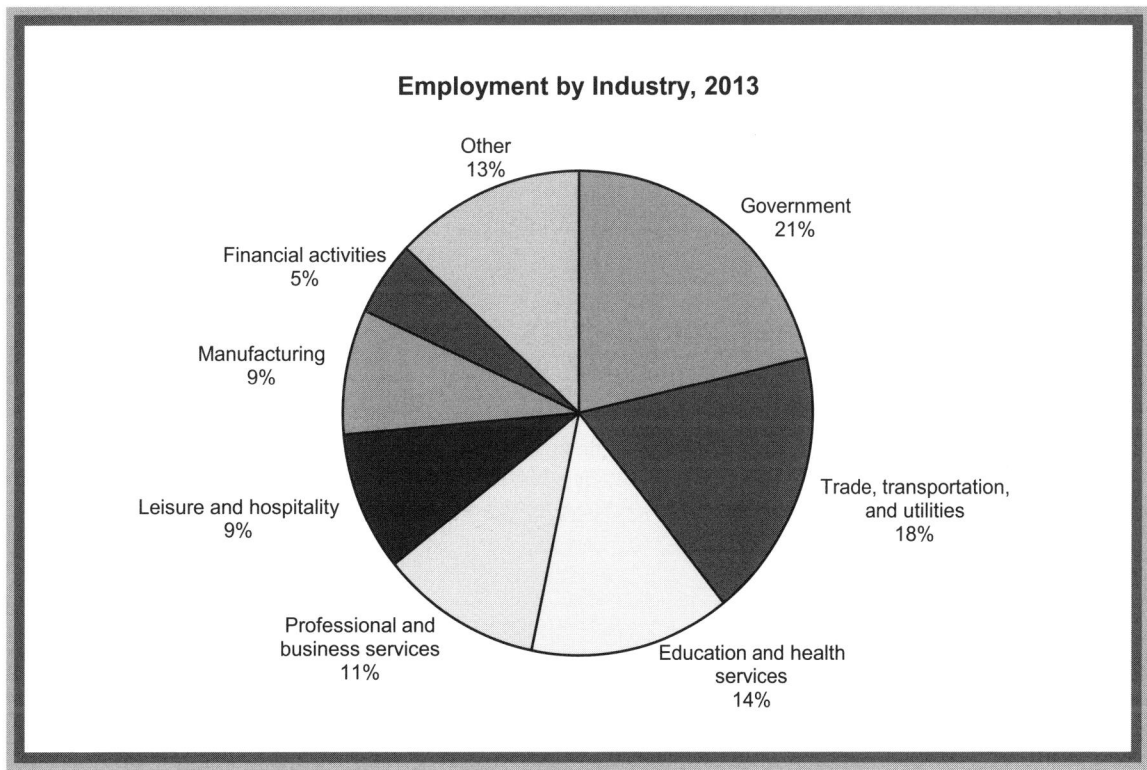

Employment by Industry, 2013

Other
13%

Government
21%

Financial activities
5%

Manufacturing
9%

Trade, transportation,
and utilities
18%

Leisure and hospitality
9%

Professional and
business services
11%

Education and health
services
14%

1. Employment by Industry: Oklahoma, Selected Years, 2002–2013

(Numbers in thousands, not seasonally adjusted)

Industry and year	January	February	March	April	May	June	July	August	September	October	November	December	Annual average
Total Nonfarm													
2002	1,481.3	1,489.6	1,500.4	1,509.5	1,521.6	1,506.5	1,486.9	1,495.6	1,501.2	1,497.3	1,502.1	1,499.5	1,499.3
2003	1,460.9	1,464.9	1,468.3	1,473.9	1,483.2	1,466.1	1,454.9	1,461.4	1,473.7	1,479.0	1,482.1	1,483.4	1,471.0
2004	1,452.5	1,461.1	1,476.0	1,485.8	1,493.1	1,484.6	1,476.4	1,483.8	1,498.3	1,506.6	1,511.0	1,516.3	1,487.1
2005	1,478.3	1,492.7	1,509.6	1,523.5	1,532.2	1,526.0	1,512.0	1,523.3	1,540.0	1,545.7	1,556.8	1,562.2	1,525.2
2006	1,529.0	1,543.2	1,559.7	1,559.5	1,573.2	1,571.1	1,551.1	1,565.2	1,579.9	1,579.7	1,585.6	1,591.3	1,565.7
2007	1,554.5	1,569.5	1,590.7	1,589.0	1,599.9	1,598.9	1,579.0	1,594.9	1,607.9	1,613.9	1,622.4	1,617.9	1,594.9
2008	1,592.0	1,606.9	1,618.2	1,622.2	1,632.2	1,618.0	1,603.7	1,615.2	1,627.0	1,629.3	1,629.1	1,627.2	1,618.4
2009	1,581.3	1,582.2	1,585.1	1,579.9	1,579.8	1,568.2	1,550.5	1,550.6	1,557.5	1,558.1	1,559.6	1,557.9	1,567.6
2010	1,521.7	1,528.6	1,543.8	1,557.2	1,569.6	1,564.0	1,549.8	1,550.8	1,558.4	1,571.9	1,576.1	1,580.2	1,556.0
2011	1,541.8	1,541.5	1,565.0	1,580.7	1,584.5	1,578.4	1,565.0	1,573.1	1,594.6	1,597.7	1,602.3	1,607.4	1,577.7
2012	1,575.0	1,590.0	1,602.8	1,614.6	1,622.8	1,617.3	1,596.0	1,608.3	1,621.0	1,634.2	1,642.3	1,644.5	1,614.1
2013	1,600.9	1,614.5	1,626.3	1,632.6	1,643.2	1,633.2	1,615.6	1,628.2	1,640.8	1,648.3	1,658.1	1,655.3	1,633.1
Total Private													
2002	1,174.5	1,177.1	1,186.2	1,195.1	1,203.6	1,202.5	1,194.1	1,200.3	1,192.9	1,182.2	1,186.3	1,183.8	1,189.9
2003	1,157.3	1,155.3	1,159.0	1,165.2	1,172.5	1,168.5	1,167.9	1,173.3	1,169.6	1,168.9	1,171.1	1,171.7	1,166.7
2004	1,149.5	1,150.8	1,163.9	1,173.3	1,178.5	1,183.3	1,183.5	1,184.7	1,183.3	1,186.7	1,191.0	1,194.8	1,176.8
2005	1,164.6	1,171.6	1,186.3	1,198.5	1,204.7	1,210.7	1,210.7	1,216.2	1,217.1	1,215.3	1,225.0	1,230.4	1,204.3
2006	1,205.7	1,211.8	1,226.8	1,227.3	1,238.0	1,248.0	1,240.5	1,247.6	1,246.9	1,241.2	1,246.6	1,252.7	1,236.1
2007	1,224.0	1,232.3	1,251.7	1,251.4	1,260.3	1,271.1	1,266.6	1,275.1	1,270.8	1,272.3	1,279.7	1,277.0	1,261.0
2008	1,262.4	1,269.8	1,279.4	1,280.6	1,287.3	1,289.8	1,286.8	1,290.9	1,286.8	1,281.5	1,280.3	1,278.3	1,281.2
2009	1,241.1	1,235.1	1,235.0	1,227.7	1,225.5	1,227.2	1,216.4	1,212.9	1,207.1	1,200.5	1,201.7	1,200.8	1,219.3
2010	1,175.4	1,176.7	1,189.0	1,202.2	1,208.7	1,215.5	1,213.4	1,217.1	1,215.5	1,221.7	1,225.5	1,229.2	1,207.5
2011	1,200.5	1,195.3	1,216.8	1,230.8	1,234.5	1,240.3	1,241.2	1,245.8	1,248.3	1,247.2	1,250.9	1,254.0	1,233.8
2012	1,232.2	1,239.6	1,250.8	1,262.5	1,269.9	1,277.5	1,268.6	1,274.3	1,272.7	1,279.9	1,286.2	1,289.1	1,266.9
2013	1,255.4	1,261.0	1,271.6	1,277.8	1,286.7	1,291.5	1,287.3	1,294.4	1,293.2	1,294.6	1,303.0	1,300.7	1,284.8
Goods-Producing													
2002	246.6	246.3	246.7	245.8	248.1	248.7	247.1	246.8	243.7	241.2	240.1	239.6	245.1
2003	237.2	235.6	236.0	236.0	236.6	235.6	238.0	239.2	237.8	236.8	235.0	235.2	236.6
2004	231.8	230.9	233.9	234.8	236.9	237.5	241.0	240.8	240.2	241.3	240.5	242.2	237.7
2005	236.8	238.3	241.7	243.9	244.7	246.3	249.6	250.4	250.5	251.7	252.8	255.9	246.9
2006	253.8	255.4	258.7	256.7	259.7	263.8	263.3	265.6	265.0	264.5	264.4	266.0	261.4
2007	260.7	261.2	265.1	264.9	266.9	271.4	272.0	273.9	271.8	273.4	275.1	274.6	269.3
2008	272.3	273.7	275.6	276.8	279.0	280.9	281.5	281.7	280.1	277.9	275.2	273.2	277.3
2009	263.8	258.3	253.7	246.5	243.2	242.1	238.3	235.4	232.4	229.9	228.3	227.7	241.6
2010	224.2	223.9	226.6	230.2	232.4	235.4	236.8	237.7	237.7	240.8	240.7	242.6	234.1
2011	237.8	237.1	242.2	246.4	247.6	251.4	253.2	253.9	255.2	256.1	256.5	257.8	249.6
2012	254.8	256.3	259.1	260.8	263.2	266.6	266.0	266.6	266.1	269.3	270.1	270.5	264.1
2013	264.3	265.4	267.5	268.3	269.7	272.5	271.7	273.3	272.4	274.1	274.7	272.5	270.5
Service-Providing													
2002	1,234.7	1,243.3	1,253.7	1,263.7	1,273.5	1,257.8	1,239.8	1,248.8	1,257.5	1,256.1	1,262.0	1,259.9	1,254.2
2003	1,223.7	1,229.3	1,232.3	1,237.9	1,246.6	1,230.5	1,216.9	1,222.2	1,235.9	1,242.2	1,247.1	1,248.2	1,234.4
2004	1,220.7	1,230.2	1,242.1	1,251.0	1,256.2	1,247.1	1,235.4	1,243.0	1,258.1	1,265.3	1,270.5	1,274.1	1,249.5
2005	1,241.5	1,254.4	1,267.9	1,279.6	1,287.5	1,279.7	1,262.4	1,272.9	1,289.5	1,294.0	1,304.0	1,306.3	1,278.3
2006	1,275.2	1,287.8	1,301.0	1,302.8	1,313.5	1,307.3	1,287.8	1,299.6	1,314.9	1,315.2	1,321.2	1,325.3	1,304.3
2007	1,293.8	1,308.3	1,325.6	1,324.1	1,333.0	1,327.5	1,307.0	1,321.0	1,336.1	1,340.5	1,347.3	1,343.3	1,325.6
2008	1,319.7	1,333.2	1,342.6	1,345.4	1,353.2	1,337.1	1,322.2	1,333.5	1,346.9	1,351.4	1,353.9	1,354.0	1,341.1
2009	1,317.5	1,323.9	1,331.4	1,333.4	1,336.6	1,326.1	1,312.2	1,315.2	1,325.1	1,328.2	1,331.3	1,330.2	1,325.9
2010	1,297.5	1,304.7	1,317.2	1,327.0	1,337.2	1,328.6	1,313.0	1,313.1	1,320.7	1,331.1	1,335.4	1,337.6	1,321.9
2011	1,304.0	1,304.4	1,322.8	1,334.3	1,336.9	1,327.0	1,311.8	1,319.2	1,339.4	1,341.6	1,345.8	1,349.6	1,328.1
2012	1,320.2	1,333.7	1,343.7	1,353.8	1,359.6	1,350.7	1,330.0	1,341.7	1,354.9	1,364.9	1,372.2	1,374.0	1,350.0
2013	1,336.6	1,349.1	1,358.8	1,364.3	1,373.5	1,360.7	1,343.9	1,354.9	1,368.4	1,374.2	1,383.4	1,382.8	1,362.6
Mining and Logging													
2002	28.1	28.1	28.1	28.2	28.7	29.0	28.9	28.9	28.3	27.9	27.8	27.9	28.3
2003	28.7	28.8	28.9	28.9	29.3	29.9	30.0	30.4	30.5	30.5	30.5	30.8	29.8
2004	30.8	30.9	31.3	31.6	32.1	32.8	32.9	33.0	32.9	33.5	33.9	34.4	32.5
2005	34.4	34.5	34.8	34.8	35.3	35.8	36.1	36.5	36.8	37.2	37.5	37.9	36.0
2006	38.4	39.2	40.0	40.7	41.3	42.4	42.5	43.5	43.6	43.4	43.9	44.5	42.0
2007	44.3	44.2	44.8	44.9	45.3	46.4	47.2	47.9	47.6	48.6	49.2	49.3	46.6
2008	49.6	49.9	50.2	50.5	51.4	52.5	52.9	53.5	53.3	53.8	53.3	52.7	52.0
2009	50.4	48.9	47.3	44.7	43.4	42.8	41.9	41.3	40.4	39.8	39.9	40.3	43.4
2010	40.5	40.6	41.3	42.2	42.8	43.9	44.4	45.0	45.1	46.0	46.1	47.1	43.8
2011	47.3	47.8	48.6	49.3	50.0	51.3	52.6	53.0	53.6	54.3	54.8	55.6	51.5
2012	55.4	56.0	56.9	57.2	58.0	59.0	59.4	59.4	58.9	58.9	59.3	59.1	58.1
2013	58.5	58.7	58.8	59.3	59.6	60.3	59.9	60.1	59.8	59.9	59.8	60.5	59.6
Construction													
2002	63.1	63.3	63.7	63.6	65.2	65.9	66.5	66.4	64.8	64.0	63.3	63.1	64.4
2003	62.0	61.3	61.8	63.7	64.6	65.9	65.9	65.7	64.3	63.6	62.1	62.3	63.6
2004	59.7	59.2	61.3	61.7	62.6	64.0	65.2	64.8	64.5	64.3	63.1	63.4	62.8
2005	61.1	61.4	63.6	65.5	65.3	66.9	68.1	68.1	68.0	68.1	68.0	68.8	66.1
2006	67.7	68.1	69.7	69.6	70.1	72.1	71.1	71.5	71.3	71.0	70.4	70.5	70.3
2007	67.5	67.7	70.2	70.0	70.7	73.0	72.4	73.5	72.4	72.8	73.3	72.2	71.3
2008	71.6	72.3	73.8	74.8	76.2	77.0	78.0	78.0	77.7	76.8	75.7	74.7	75.6
2009	71.4	70.7	70.7	69.4	69.3	70.4	69.8	69.0	68.0	67.0	65.9	65.2	68.9
2010	62.9	62.5	64.2	65.9	66.9	68.0	68.4	68.6	68.6	70.0	69.0	69.1	67.0
2011	65.1	63.7	66.8	68.5	68.6	70.0	69.5	69.6	69.8	69.6	69.0	68.8	68.3
2012	66.6	66.8	67.9	68.8	69.9	71.1	70.6	70.9	70.8	72.8	74.0	74.1	70.4
2013	69.6	70.5	72.2	72.8	73.9	75.3	75.1	76.6	76.6	77.8	78.2	74.9	74.5

1. Employment by Industry: Oklahoma, Selected Years, 2002–2013—*Continued*

(Numbers in thousands, not seasonally adjusted)

Industry and year	January	February	March	April	May	June	July	August	September	October	November	December	Annual average
Manufacturing													
2002	155.4	154.9	154.9	154.0	154.2	153.8	151.7	151.5	150.6	149.3	149.0	148.6	152.3
2003	146.5	145.5	145.3	143.4	142.7	139.8	142.1	143.1	143.0	142.7	142.4	142.1	143.2
2004	141.3	140.8	141.3	141.5	142.2	140.7	142.9	143.0	142.8	143.5	143.5	144.4	142.3
2005	141.3	142.4	143.3	143.6	144.1	143.6	145.4	145.8	145.7	146.4	147.3	149.2	144.8
2006	147.7	148.1	149.0	146.4	148.3	149.3	149.7	150.6	150.1	150.1	150.1	151.0	149.2
2007	148.9	149.3	150.1	150.0	150.9	152.0	152.4	152.5	151.8	152.0	152.6	153.1	151.3
2008	151.1	151.5	151.6	151.5	151.4	151.4	150.6	150.2	149.1	147.3	146.2	145.8	149.8
2009	142.0	138.7	135.7	132.4	130.5	128.9	126.6	125.1	124.0	123.1	122.5	122.2	129.3
2010	120.8	120.8	121.1	122.1	122.7	123.5	124.0	124.1	124.0	124.8	125.6	126.4	123.3
2011	125.4	125.6	126.8	128.6	129.0	130.1	131.1	131.3	131.8	132.2	132.7	133.4	129.8
2012	132.8	133.5	134.3	134.8	135.3	136.5	136.0	136.3	136.4	137.2	137.0	137.5	135.6
2013	136.2	136.2	136.5	136.2	136.2	136.9	136.7	136.6	136.0	136.4	136.7	137.1	136.5
Trade, Transportation, and Utilities													
2002	283.5	281.3	283.9	283.9	285.1	284.9	282.5	283.1	281.8	280.7	285.5	287.3	283.6
2003	275.9	273.8	274.9	275.4	277.0	276.1	274.6	276.0	275.2	277.0	281.5	284.5	276.8
2004	273.3	271.1	274.0	274.1	275.7	276.0	273.6	273.4	272.1	274.1	279.1	282.4	274.9
2005	272.1	271.8	274.3	276.7	278.1	278.5	279.0	280.3	280.5	282.3	287.6	290.6	279.3
2006	278.1	278.1	280.3	281.8	284.4	284.9	282.8	283.8	283.7	284.0	288.8	292.8	283.6
2007	282.8	282.6	288.3	285.2	287.3	288.2	286.7	287.3	286.4	287.8	293.1	294.1	287.5
2008	285.8	285.2	287.9	287.8	288.9	289.4	289.3	290.0	289.3	289.9	293.4	295.0	289.3
2009	284.2	282.2	282.7	282.3	282.8	282.5	279.9	279.4	278.5	277.8	281.2	282.5	281.3
2010	272.8	271.3	274.0	275.4	277.3	278.5	277.9	277.8	275.8	278.3	282.9	285.2	277.3
2011	275.8	274.2	278.4	281.2	282.0	282.7	282.6	284.1	283.7	285.0	290.0	292.3	282.7
2012	284.6	283.4	286.3	288.0	289.9	291.2	289.8	289.8	289.8	292.8	298.6	300.9	290.4
2013	287.8	287.8	289.7	291.5	294.0	295.1	294.7	295.9	295.8	295.7	301.4	303.7	294.4
Wholesale Trade													
2002	56.4	56.1	56.5	56.2	56.6	57.0	56.8	56.9	56.6	56.0	56.1	56.1	56.4
2003	54.9	54.5	54.9	54.6	55.0	55.3	54.6	54.5	54.6	54.9	54.6	54.7	54.8
2004	54.1	53.7	53.9	54.0	54.7	55.3	55.1	55.1	54.8	55.2	55.4	55.7	54.8
2005	54.9	55.1	55.5	56.0	56.3	56.9	57.1	57.2	57.0	57.3	57.4	57.7	56.5
2006	57.2	57.6	58.0	57.8	58.4	58.9	58.7	58.8	58.8	58.6	58.7	58.9	58.4
2007	58.4	58.6	59.4	59.3	59.5	60.3	59.5	59.2	59.0	59.6	59.7	59.7	59.4
2008	59.2	59.1	59.3	59.2	59.5	59.9	59.6	59.3	59.1	59.1	59.1	58.9	59.3
2009	58.0	57.8	57.5	57.1	56.6	56.5	56.0	55.4	55.0	55.0	54.7	54.7	56.2
2010	54.2	54.2	54.6	55.1	55.6	56.1	55.9	55.8	55.9	56.6	56.8	56.8	55.6
2011	56.2	56.4	57.3	57.5	57.6	58.0	58.3	58.3	58.3	58.7	58.7	58.9	57.9
2012	58.4	58.9	59.6	60.0	60.5	60.9	60.5	60.5	60.5	61.1	61.3	61.6	60.3
2013	60.8	61.0	61.3	61.4	61.9	62.4	62.0	62.2	62.2	62.2	62.3	63.0	61.9
Retail Trade													
2002	172.0	170.2	172.2	172.5	173.2	172.5	170.2	170.9	170.1	169.7	174.7	176.9	172.1
2003	167.6	165.8	166.6	167.9	169.1	168.5	167.8	169.1	168.7	170.0	174.8	177.6	169.5
2004	167.6	165.9	168.2	168.7	169.4	168.8	166.5	166.3	165.3	166.7	171.5	173.9	168.2
2005	165.5	164.9	166.7	168.1	169.0	168.5	168.6	169.5	170.0	171.6	176.4	178.5	169.8
2006	167.6	167.2	168.7	169.7	171.1	170.8	168.9	169.3	168.8	169.1	173.5	176.3	170.1
2007	167.8	167.1	171.7	169.5	171.0	170.7	169.9	170.9	170.5	171.6	176.7	177.3	171.2
2008	170.7	170.3	172.6	172.1	172.5	172.3	172.3	173.1	172.5	172.9	176.4	177.7	173.0
2009	169.8	168.4	169.4	169.3	170.6	170.4	168.9	169.4	169.2	168.3	171.9	172.8	169.9
2010	166.0	164.5	166.7	167.4	168.7	169.3	168.9	169.0	166.8	168.7	172.9	174.3	168.6
2011	167.2	165.3	168.2	170.1	170.4	170.1	169.6	170.9	170.4	171.1	175.8	177.0	170.5
2012	170.3	168.6	170.6	171.7	172.7	173.1	172.2	172.1	172.1	174.1	179.4	180.9	173.2
2013	170.0	169.3	170.8	172.4	173.9	174.3	174.2	175.3	175.3	175.3	180.6	181.0	174.4
Transportation and Utilities													
2002	55.1	55.0	55.2	55.2	55.3	55.4	55.5	55.3	55.1	55.0	54.7	54.3	55.1
2003	53.4	53.5	53.4	52.9	52.9	52.3	52.2	52.4	51.9	52.1	52.1	52.2	52.6
2004	51.6	51.5	51.9	51.4	51.6	51.9	52.0	52.0	52.0	52.2	52.2	52.8	51.9
2005	51.7	51.8	52.1	52.6	52.8	53.1	53.3	53.6	53.5	53.4	53.8	54.4	53.0
2006	53.3	53.3	53.6	54.3	54.9	55.2	55.2	55.7	56.1	56.3	56.6	57.6	55.2
2007	56.6	56.9	57.2	56.4	56.8	57.2	57.3	57.2	56.9	56.6	56.7	57.1	56.9
2008	55.9	55.8	56.0	56.5	56.9	57.2	57.4	57.6	57.7	57.9	57.9	58.4	57.1
2009	56.4	56.0	55.8	55.9	55.6	55.6	55.0	54.6	54.3	54.5	54.6	55.0	55.3
2010	52.6	52.6	52.7	52.9	53.0	53.1	53.1	53.0	53.1	53.0	53.2	54.1	53.0
2011	52.4	52.5	52.9	53.6	54.0	54.6	54.7	54.9	55.0	55.2	55.5	56.4	54.3
2012	55.9	55.9	56.1	56.3	56.7	57.2	57.1	57.2	57.2	57.6	57.9	58.4	57.0
2013	57.0	57.5	57.6	57.7	58.2	58.4	58.5	58.4	58.3	58.2	58.5	59.7	58.2
Information													
2002	36.8	36.9	36.4	35.6	35.4	35.1	35.0	34.9	34.5	34.3	34.4	34.0	35.3
2003	33.5	33.2	32.9	32.7	32.8	32.4	32.0	31.6	31.3	31.7	31.9	32.2	32.4
2004	31.6	31.6	31.4	31.2	31.1	31.4	31.4	30.9	30.1	30.5	30.4	30.5	31.0
2005	30.2	30.4	30.1	30.4	30.4	30.4	30.5	30.2	29.9	29.8	30.0	30.3	30.2
2006	30.0	30.0	30.0	29.7	29.8	29.8	29.9	29.8	29.6	29.3	29.3	30.2	29.8
2007	29.2	29.0	28.6	28.6	28.8	28.8	28.8	28.8	28.6	28.8	28.9	29.0	28.8
2008	28.7	28.9	28.8	29.0	29.1	29.0	29.1	28.8	28.4	28.2	28.2	28.2	28.7
2009	27.8	27.8	27.7	27.5	27.4	27.2	27.0	26.5	25.9	25.7	25.6	25.5	26.8
2010	25.1	24.8	24.5	24.7	24.6	24.3	24.4	24.0	23.8	23.6	23.7	23.7	24.3
2011	23.3	23.1	22.9	23.0	23.1	23.1	23.2	23.1	22.8	22.9	23.0	23.0	23.0
2012	22.8	22.7	22.7	22.6	22.6	22.5	22.6	22.3	22.1	22.2	22.2	22.3	22.5
2013	21.8	21.7	21.6	21.8	21.9	22.0	22.1	21.9	21.6	21.6	21.7	21.6	21.8

1. Employment by Industry: Oklahoma, Selected Years, 2002–2013—*Continued*

(Numbers in thousands, not seasonally adjusted)

Industry and year	January	February	March	April	May	June	July	August	September	October	November	December	Annual average
Financial Activities													
2002	82.9	82.6	82.6	82.7	83.3	84.0	83.8	83.8	82.9	82.4	82.5	82.5	83.0
2003	81.6	81.7	82.0	82.7	83.2	83.8	83.7	84.0	83.6	83.8	83.8	84.0	83.2
2004	83.1	83.3	83.9	84.1	84.1	84.7	84.2	84.2	83.6	83.7	83.7	84.0	83.9
2005	82.3	82.4	82.8	82.4	83.0	83.7	83.8	83.8	83.4	82.8	83.0	84.0	83.1
2006	83.5	83.5	84.0	83.0	83.5	84.0	83.4	83.5	83.1	82.9	82.9	83.0	83.4
2007	82.8	83.3	83.5	82.4	82.6	83.1	83.0	83.1	82.7	82.9	82.9	83.0	82.9
2008	83.0	83.0	83.1	83.1	83.4	83.5	83.8	83.3	83.0	82.8	82.8	83.2	83.2
2009	81.7	81.4	81.5	81.8	82.0	82.2	82.0	81.7	81.1	80.7	80.6	80.9	81.5
2010	79.8	79.8	79.9	79.9	80.2	80.5	80.1	80.0	79.5	79.6	79.6	80.0	79.9
2011	78.7	78.5	79.1	79.3	79.3	79.7	79.7	79.9	79.5	79.6	79.6	79.9	79.4
2012	79.0	79.4	79.4	79.6	80.1	80.5	80.4	80.4	79.9	80.2	80.2	80.9	80.0
2013	79.9	80.2	80.3	80.2	80.8	81.0	81.3	81.2	80.8	80.8	81.1	81.5	80.8
Professional and Business Services													
2002	156.5	158.3	160.7	163.9	165.6	165.1	162.2	164.2	163.5	161.4	160.7	160.5	161.9
2003	154.3	154.8	154.8	156.6	158.1	157.9	158.3	158.8	159.0	158.5	158.3	157.7	157.3
2004	154.2	155.8	157.0	161.3	161.3	162.5	165.0	165.8	166.3	167.9	168.4	168.1	162.8
2005	162.2	164.9	166.9	169.7	170.1	171.6	171.2	173.2	174.4	172.7	174.6	173.8	170.4
2006	170.1	172.1	174.8	174.7	175.8	178.0	176.5	178.4	178.9	176.5	177.3	176.6	175.8
2007	173.6	176.4	179.7	180.3	181.3	182.9	182.0	184.9	184.6	184.2	184.6	184.2	181.6
2008	181.6	183.9	184.8	185.0	184.8	184.9	183.2	184.8	184.2	182.7	181.4	179.3	183.4
2009	171.0	171.1	170.0	168.0	166.7	167.7	166.1	166.2	166.3	167.0	167.0	167.4	167.9
2010	163.3	164.6	166.4	169.0	169.4	171.4	172.7	173.7	173.6	175.1	174.7	174.2	170.7
2011	169.7	168.9	172.1	174.8	174.4	174.5	175.6	176.4	176.8	176.9	175.5	175.5	174.3
2012	171.4	174.7	175.5	177.0	177.4	179.6	178.4	180.5	179.4	181.2	181.0	179.1	177.9
2013	174.6	176.0	178.5	178.8	179.6	180.7	180.5	181.9	181.7	182.9	183.0	182.3	180.0
Education and Health Services													
2002	186.4	188.0	188.3	190.3	189.8	188.4	188.8	192.0	193.5	192.5	195.6	194.5	190.7
2003	192.4	193.1	192.9	193.5	193.1	190.8	190.5	191.9	193.6	193.0	194.6	192.9	192.7
2004	193.9	195.1	196.0	197.4	196.3	194.3	194.8	195.5	197.7	198.1	199.0	198.6	196.4
2005	195.8	196.6	198.3	200.2	200.7	200.6	199.8	201.4	203.2	202.9	204.6	204.9	200.8
2006	201.2	201.9	203.5	204.0	204.9	205.5	203.6	204.9	206.8	206.5	207.8	207.5	204.8
2007	204.0	205.8	207.2	209.7	210.2	210.9	209.5	211.2	212.4	213.5	213.6	213.1	210.1
2008	211.6	213.8	214.4	214.9	215.5	213.7	213.0	214.7	215.6	216.1	216.9	216.9	214.8
2009	215.4	215.7	216.7	217.3	217.8	218.5	218.5	219.5	220.4	220.7	221.3	221.1	218.6
2010	219.0	219.7	220.5	221.8	221.7	221.1	219.9	221.1	222.5	224.1	224.4	224.7	221.7
2011	220.5	219.6	221.6	222.5	222.9	222.7	222.0	223.3	225.2	225.3	225.7	226.1	223.1
2012	223.3	224.4	225.1	226.4	226.6	225.8	223.4	225.8	227.4	228.2	228.8	229.6	226.2
2013	226.3	227.2	227.8	227.7	227.9	226.7	224.2	226.1	227.6	227.7	228.3	228.3	227.2
Leisure and Hospitality													
2002	120.2	121.8	125.2	128.1	131.3	131.1	130.2	131.3	129.4	127.4	125.4	123.5	127.1
2003	120.9	121.4	123.8	127.6	130.5	130.1	129.4	130.6	128.3	127.6	125.7	124.5	126.7
2004	121.5	122.6	126.5	129.1	131.5	132.6	131.9	132.8	132.5	130.6	129.4	128.3	129.1
2005	124.9	126.5	130.9	134.2	136.5	138.0	135.1	135.6	134.1	132.1	131.4	129.9	132.4
2006	128.7	130.2	134.3	136.2	138.0	139.2	138.7	139.4	137.8	135.6	134.1	134.4	135.6
2007	129.4	131.9	136.6	137.2	139.8	141.3	140.8	142.1	140.6	138.7	138.5	136.3	137.8
2008	136.8	138.2	141.3	140.2	142.7	144.2	142.9	143.6	142.7	140.3	139.4	139.7	141.0
2009	135.3	136.7	140.5	142.4	143.5	144.6	142.6	142.7	141.2	137.9	136.9	135.3	140.0
2010	131.4	132.7	136.7	140.5	142.1	142.8	141.0	142.0	141.9	139.6	139.0	138.4	139.0
2011	135.2	134.5	140.4	144.5	146.1	146.8	146.0	146.8	146.8	143.5	142.7	141.7	142.9
2012	139.1	141.2	145.1	148.6	150.4	151.3	148.6	149.8	149.4	147.6	147.2	147.8	147.2
2013	143.4	145.2	148.5	151.5	154.4	154.5	154.1	155.7	155.1	153.4	154.5	152.6	151.9
Other Services													
2002	61.6	61.9	62.4	64.8	65.0	65.2	64.5	64.2	63.6	62.3	62.1	61.9	63.3
2003	61.5	61.7	61.7	60.7	61.2	61.8	61.4	61.2	60.8	60.5	60.3	60.7	61.1
2004	60.1	60.4	61.2	61.3	61.6	62.3	61.6	61.3	60.8	60.5	60.5	60.7	61.0
2005	60.3	60.7	61.3	61.0	61.2	61.6	61.7	61.3	61.1	61.0	61.0	61.0	61.1
2006	60.3	60.6	61.2	61.2	61.9	62.8	62.3	62.2	62.0	61.9	62.0	62.2	61.7
2007	61.5	62.1	62.7	63.1	63.4	64.5	63.8	63.8	63.7	63.0	63.0	62.7	63.1
2008	62.6	63.1	63.5	63.8	63.9	64.2	64.0	64.0	63.5	63.6	63.0	62.8	63.5
2009	61.9	61.9	62.2	61.9	62.1	62.4	62.0	61.5	61.3	60.8	60.8	60.4	61.6
2010	59.8	59.9	60.4	60.7	61.0	61.5	60.6	60.8	60.7	60.6	60.5	60.4	60.6
2011	59.5	59.4	60.1	59.1	59.1	59.4	58.9	58.3	58.3	57.9	57.9	57.7	58.8
2012	57.2	57.5	57.6	59.5	59.7	60.0	59.4	59.1	58.6	58.4	58.1	58.0	58.6
2013	57.3	57.5	57.7	58.0	58.4	59.0	58.7	58.4	58.2	58.4	58.3	58.2	58.2
Government													
2002	306.8	312.5	314.2	314.4	318.0	304.0	292.8	295.3	308.3	315.1	315.8	315.7	309.4
2003	303.6	309.6	309.3	308.7	310.7	297.6	287.0	288.1	304.1	310.1	311.0	311.7	304.3
2004	303.0	310.3	312.1	312.5	314.6	303.3	292.9	299.1	315.0	319.9	320.0	321.5	310.4
2005	313.7	321.1	323.3	325.0	327.5	315.3	301.3	307.1	322.9	330.4	331.8	331.8	320.9
2006	323.3	331.4	332.9	332.2	335.2	323.1	310.6	317.6	333.0	338.5	339.0	338.6	329.6
2007	330.5	337.2	339.0	337.6	339.6	327.8	312.4	319.8	337.1	341.6	342.7	340.9	333.9
2008	329.6	337.1	338.8	341.6	344.9	328.2	316.9	324.3	340.2	347.8	348.8	348.9	337.3
2009	340.2	347.1	350.1	352.2	354.3	341.0	334.1	337.7	350.4	357.6	357.9	357.1	348.3
2010	346.3	351.9	354.8	355.0	360.9	348.5	336.4	333.7	342.9	350.2	350.6	351.0	348.5
2011	341.3	346.2	348.2	349.9	350.0	338.1	323.8	327.3	346.3	350.5	351.4	353.4	343.9
2012	342.8	350.4	352.0	352.1	352.9	339.8	327.4	334.0	348.3	354.3	356.1	355.4	347.1
2013	345.5	353.5	354.7	354.8	356.5	341.7	328.3	333.8	347.6	353.7	355.1	354.6	348.3

2. Average Weekly Hours by Selected Industry: Oklahoma, 2009–2013

(Not seasonally adjusted)

Industry and year	January	February	March	April	May	June	July	August	September	October	November	December	Annual average
Total Private													
2009	34.7	35.3	35.0	34.2	34.2	35.0	35.2	35.9	35.1	34.9	36.1	35.4	35.1
2010	35.2	35.3	35.5	36.0	36.0	35.8	36.1	36.3	35.1	35.2	34.9	35.3	35.6
2011	35.5	34.1	35.5	35.6	36.2	35.6	35.4	35.4	35.3	36.0	35.1	35.2	35.4
2012	35.6	35.0	35.4	35.8	35.2	35.3	35.6	35.1	35.9	35.3	35.6	35.6	35.4
2013	34.5	34.7	35.1	34.8	34.8	35.8	34.8	35.1	35.5	34.9	35.0	35.3	35.0
Goods-Producing													
2009	40.1	40.6	40.0	40.4	39.4	41.3	42.3	41.9	40.9	40.4	42.2	41.8	40.9
2010	40.5	40.3	41.0	42.5	40.5	41.3	42.1	42.5	42.0	41.9	41.1	41.7	41.5
2011	40.8	39.8	43.1	43.4	42.6	42.5	41.7	42.0	41.7	41.9	41.1	41.2	41.8
2012	40.8	39.9	41.3	40.8	41.6	41.5	40.9	41.1	40.9	41.2	41.5	41.4	41.1
2013	40.6	40.5	40.7	39.6	39.8	40.8	39.3	40.1	40.9	40.4	40.7	40.8	40.3
Construction													
2009	39.0	39.2	39.0	39.9	39.3	40.7	40.8	41.5	39.5	39.7	41.6	40.0	40.0
2010	39.1	38.1	39.9	41.5	39.5	40.5	40.9	42.0	41.5	42.0	40.1	42.1	40.6
2011	40.0	38.0	44.0	45.1	43.5	43.0	42.9	41.3	41.3	41.0	40.4	40.9	41.8
2012	40.6	38.2	40.2	40.3	40.7	41.3	42.3	42.5	41.2	41.6	41.6	41.5	41.0
2013	40.2	40.7	41.4	39.9	40.8	41.9	39.5	39.7	41.6	41.4	41.3	40.3	40.7
Manufacturing													
2009	39.8	40.6	40.2	40.5	38.8	40.6	41.8	39.8	40.6	40.2	41.5	42.6	40.6
2010	40.5	41.2	41.9	42.7	41.3	42.1	42.1	41.8	41.6	41.2	41.2	40.9	41.5
2011	39.4	40.4	42.2	42.0	42.1	42.2	41.7	42.1	41.9	42.1	41.4	41.7	41.6
2012	40.8	40.8	41.9	40.6	41.8	41.4	41.0	40.9	41.4	41.3	41.8	41.7	41.3
2013	40.6	40.3	40.5	39.1	40.0	40.6	39.8	40.7	40.8	40.5	41.0	41.3	40.4
Trade, Transportation, and Utilities													
2009	34.7	34.8	34.4	34.2	34.6	34.9	35.0	35.8	35.9	35.8	35.7	35.9	35.1
2010	35.8	36.6	36.7	37.2	37.0	36.6	35.9	36.7	35.0	35.5	34.8	35.4	36.1
2011	35.9	34.4	35.2	35.9	36.6	36.3	35.7	35.2	35.2	36.0	35.1	35.2	35.6
2012	35.8	35.8	35.8	36.2	34.9	35.2	35.6	35.5	36.2	35.6	35.7	34.8	35.6
2013	33.7	34.2	34.6	34.3	34.3	35.3	34.8	34.8	35.2	34.7	34.7	34.5	34.6
Financial Activities													
2009	36.4	38.1	38.1	36.4	36.6	37.6	37.1	38.1	37.0	35.6	37.1	35.7	37.0
2010	35.0	35.0	35.0	35.3	37.0	35.4	35.6	37.3	35.5	34.8	35.3	35.0	35.5
2011	36.7	34.9	35.8	36.1	38.2	36.0	36.3	36.1	37.0	38.8	36.9	37.1	36.7
2012	38.9	36.8	37.0	37.7	36.0	35.6	37.7	36.2	38.0	35.7	35.9	38.0	37.0
2013	35.9	36.5	36.5	36.5	36.1	37.1	36.1	36.1	37.3	35.9	36.1	37.2	36.4
Professional and Business Services													
2009	36.7	38.5	38.3	36.6	37.2	38.4	37.0	38.4	36.8	37.4	38.4	37.1	37.6
2010	37.3	36.8	37.1	37.6	38.0	37.3	37.5	38.2	37.1	37.7	37.1	37.0	37.4
2011	37.8	36.5	37.3	37.0	37.9	37.5	37.5	37.7	37.4	37.7	36.6	36.8	37.3
2012	37.4	36.8	37.4	37.8	36.4	36.7	37.3	36.2	38.7	37.0	37.3	36.3	37.1
2013	35.0	35.3	36.2	36.2	36.2	37.6	36.4	36.8	37.7	36.7	36.5	36.8	36.5
Education and Health Services													
2009	32.5	32.5	32.6	31.6	31.6	31.8	32.6	33.9	32.4	32.2	33.8	32.2	32.5
2010	32.4	32.7	32.6	33.2	33.6	33.1	34.3	32.8	32.0	31.9	31.9	32.5	32.7
2011	33.0	31.4	32.6	33.0	33.8	33.0	33.1	33.2	33.5	34.0	33.4	33.4	33.1
2012	33.8	33.1	33.3	34.6	33.5	33.7	34.3	33.5	34.5	33.9	34.0	34.7	33.9
2013	33.8	33.8	33.7	33.6	33.7	34.6	33.7	33.8	34.3	33.5	33.7	33.8	33.8
Leisure and Hospitality													
2009	26.5	27.3	27.1	26.3	26.1	26.7	26.7	26.7	25.6	25.8	26.4	25.8	26.4
2010	25.2	26.2	26.6	25.8	26.3	27.4	26.8	26.7	25.5	26.6	26.8	26.4	26.4
2011	25.9	24.7	26.0	25.9	26.4	26.5	25.6	25.6	25.2	25.9	25.2	25.1	25.7
2012	25.1	25.6	26.1	26.3	26.3	27.1	27.1	26.2	26.4	25.8	26.0	26.9	26.2
2013	25.6	26.3	26.6	26.8	26.4	27.3	26.3	26.5	26.3	26.1	25.9	25.7	26.3

3. Average Hourly Earnings by Selected Industry: Oklahoma, 2009–2013

(Dollars, not seasonally adjusted)

Industry and year	January	February	March	April	May	June	July	August	September	October	November	December	Annual average
Total Private													
2009	17.78	17.93	17.85	17.88	18.02	17.86	18.02	18.18	18.24	18.28	18.39	18.33	18.06
2010	18.76	18.55	18.37	18.87	18.83	18.61	18.81	19.48	19.95	19.85	20.03	20.05	19.18
2011	20.07	20.75	20.40	20.42	20.19	20.12	20.32	20.14	20.31	20.19	20.38	20.96	20.35
2012	21.02	20.80	20.66	20.66	20.61	20.64	20.77	20.95	21.19	21.07	21.05	21.41	20.90
2013	21.19	21.10	21.00	21.09	21.11	21.20	21.09	21.22	21.33	21.39	21.32	21.51	21.21
Goods-Producing													
2009	20.66	20.77	20.57	20.43	21.25	20.70	20.78	21.34	20.92	21.02	21.15	20.88	20.87
2010	21.55	21.52	21.08	20.97	21.58	21.26	21.84	22.50	23.27	22.18	22.71	22.46	21.93
2011	22.56	23.19	22.41	22.00	21.83	21.97	22.17	22.07	21.89	21.97	22.45	22.56	22.24
2012	22.60	22.36	22.25	22.34	22.01	22.32	21.95	22.01	22.17	22.11	22.29	22.51	22.24
2013	22.39	22.56	22.41	22.57	22.97	22.99	22.85	23.16	23.23	23.06	22.85	23.13	22.85
Construction													
2009	19.63	20.11	19.78	19.91	20.47	19.64	19.87	19.93	20.06	20.37	19.72	20.03	19.96
2010	20.73	21.03	20.49	20.36	20.47	20.01	20.52	20.62	20.39	20.70	21.07	20.62	20.58
2011	20.64	21.03	20.27	19.68	19.75	19.43	19.70	19.92	19.76	20.00	19.77	20.08	19.98
2012	20.27	20.44	20.20	20.12	19.69	19.82	19.92	20.11	20.05	20.20	20.42	20.46	20.14
2013	20.54	20.68	20.87	20.79	21.45	20.99	21.09	20.70	21.10	21.01	20.83	21.12	20.94
Manufacturing													
2009	19.25	18.85	18.52	18.30	19.21	18.60	18.49	19.36	18.74	18.74	19.67	18.93	18.88
2010	18.86	18.65	18.36	18.47	19.21	18.39	18.21	18.39	18.26	18.19	18.11	18.18	18.44
2011	18.71	18.89	18.58	18.49	18.19	18.14	18.75	18.85	18.83	18.77	19.13	19.46	18.73
2012	19.55	19.09	19.19	19.54	19.37	19.36	19.53	19.52	19.93	19.78	20.20	20.34	19.62
2013	20.02	20.30	20.19	20.72	20.78	21.04	20.94	21.18	21.25	20.95	21.00	21.42	20.82
Trade, Transportation, and Utilities													
2009	17.47	17.58	17.60	17.74	17.55	17.68	17.79	17.99	17.93	17.98	18.21	17.89	17.79
2010	18.26	18.44	17.86	18.17	17.44	17.20	18.04	18.46	18.27	18.61	19.32	18.97	18.25
2011	18.53	19.45	18.07	18.47	18.43	18.47	18.93	18.66	19.29	18.69	18.81	19.86	18.80
2012	20.67	20.30	19.84	20.30	20.36	20.50	21.31	21.02	21.06	21.01	20.64	21.25	20.69
2013	21.07	20.52	20.37	20.31	20.67	20.55	20.07	20.05	20.10	19.94	19.76	19.41	20.23
Financial Activities													
2009	17.55	17.93	17.83	17.61	18.03	18.33	18.26	18.70	18.79	18.57	18.98	18.78	18.28
2010	19.47	19.15	18.95	19.88	20.32	20.42	20.76	20.35	20.80	20.74	20.61	21.63	20.26
2011	22.24	21.97	20.58	21.45	20.68	20.85	21.57	21.43	21.70	21.43	21.79	21.81	21.46
2012	21.62	22.45	22.34	22.86	22.45	22.51	22.74	22.90	23.71	23.31	23.57	23.90	22.86
2013	23.15	23.59	23.71	23.54	23.71	24.08	23.36	23.56	24.19	23.89	24.00	24.15	23.75
Professional and Business Services													
2009	19.91	20.50	20.60	20.85	20.42	19.84	20.01	20.29	20.01	19.72	20.12	20.12	20.20
2010	20.85	20.58	20.31	20.61	20.92	20.99	20.63	21.02	21.10	21.92	21.58	21.41	21.00
2011	21.49	21.38	21.04	21.29	21.12	20.86	20.64	20.44	20.54	20.94	21.17	22.06	21.08
2012	21.26	20.72	21.05	20.97	21.12	20.96	20.75	20.49	20.81	21.07	21.05	21.55	20.98
2013	21.60	22.10	21.69	21.54	21.27	21.78	21.52	21.88	22.21	22.39	22.71	23.30	22.01
Education and Health Services													
2009	16.71	16.97	17.07	17.24	17.49	17.45	17.87	17.09	17.87	17.93	17.54	17.83	17.42
2010	17.94	17.19	17.71	18.10	17.57	17.35	16.85	17.60	18.17	18.23	18.46	18.30	17.78
2011	18.27	19.18	18.29	18.59	18.51	19.01	19.27	19.38	19.90	19.60	19.78	20.83	19.23
2012	20.85	20.99	20.90	20.29	20.76	21.06	21.21	21.29	21.34	21.23	21.41	21.80	21.10
2013	21.81	21.54	21.63	22.07	21.73	21.75	22.41	22.50	22.34	22.27	22.19	22.55	22.07
Leisure and Hospitality													
2009	10.56	10.41	10.42	10.53	10.52	10.39	10.28	10.53	10.53	11.05	10.69	10.78	10.55
2010	10.87	10.91	10.82	10.94	11.08	10.79	10.87	10.93	11.24	11.12	11.14	11.16	10.99
2011	11.12	11.26	10.87	10.87	10.93	10.59	10.64	10.76	10.87	10.94	10.87	11.02	10.89
2012	11.00	10.91	10.86	11.01	10.99	10.83	11.00	10.95	11.21	11.10	10.98	11.15	11.00
2013	10.73	10.72	10.79	10.85	10.84	10.67	10.69	10.77	10.89	10.81	10.91	11.13	10.82

4. Average Weekly Earnings by Selected Industry: Oklahoma, 2009–2013

(Dollars, not seasonally adjusted)

Industry and year	January	February	March	April	May	June	July	August	September	October	November	December	Annual average
Total Private													
2009	616.97	632.93	624.75	611.50	616.28	625.10	634.30	652.66	640.22	637.97	663.88	648.88	633.91
2010	660.35	654.82	652.14	679.32	677.88	666.24	679.04	707.12	700.25	698.72	699.05	707.77	682.81
2011	712.49	707.58	724.20	726.95	730.88	716.27	719.33	712.96	716.94	726.84	715.34	737.79	720.39
2012	748.31	728.00	731.36	739.63	725.47	728.59	739.41	735.35	760.72	743.77	749.38	762.20	739.86
2013	731.06	732.17	737.10	733.93	734.63	758.96	733.93	744.82	757.22	746.51	746.20	759.30	742.35
Goods-Producing													
2009	828.47	843.26	822.80	825.37	837.25	854.91	878.99	894.15	855.63	849.21	892.53	872.78	853.58
2010	872.78	867.26	864.28	891.23	873.99	878.04	919.46	956.25	977.34	929.34	933.38	936.58	910.10
2011	920.45	922.96	965.87	954.80	929.96	933.73	924.49	926.94	912.81	920.54	922.70	929.47	929.63
2012	922.08	892.16	918.93	911.47	915.62	926.28	897.76	904.61	906.75	910.93	925.04	931.91	914.06
2013	909.03	913.68	912.09	893.77	914.21	937.99	898.01	928.72	950.11	931.62	930.00	943.70	920.86
Construction													
2009	765.57	788.31	771.42	794.41	804.47	799.35	810.70	827.10	792.37	808.69	820.35	801.20	798.40
2010	810.54	801.24	817.55	844.94	808.57	810.41	839.27	866.04	846.19	869.40	844.91	868.10	835.55
2011	825.60	799.14	891.88	887.57	859.13	835.49	845.13	822.70	816.09	820.00	798.71	821.27	835.16
2012	822.96	780.81	812.04	810.84	801.38	818.57	842.62	854.68	826.06	840.32	849.47	849.09	825.74
2013	825.71	841.68	864.02	829.52	875.16	879.48	833.06	821.79	877.76	869.81	860.28	851.14	852.26
Manufacturing													
2009	766.15	765.31	744.50	741.15	745.35	755.16	772.88	770.53	760.84	753.35	816.31	806.42	766.53
2010	763.83	768.38	769.28	788.67	793.37	774.22	766.64	768.70	759.62	749.45	746.13	743.56	765.26
2011	737.17	763.16	784.08	776.58	765.80	765.51	781.88	793.59	788.98	790.22	791.98	811.48	779.17
2012	797.64	778.87	804.06	793.32	809.67	801.50	800.73	798.37	825.10	816.91	844.36	848.18	810.31
2013	812.81	818.09	817.70	810.15	831.20	854.22	833.41	862.03	867.00	848.48	861.00	884.65	841.13
Trade, Transportation, and Utilities													
2009	606.21	611.78	605.44	606.71	607.23	617.03	622.65	644.04	643.69	643.68	650.10	642.25	624.43
2010	653.71	674.90	655.46	675.92	645.28	629.52	647.64	677.48	639.45	660.66	672.34	671.54	658.83
2011	665.23	669.08	636.06	663.07	674.54	670.46	675.80	656.83	679.01	672.84	660.23	699.07	669.28
2012	739.99	726.74	710.27	734.86	710.56	721.60	758.64	746.21	762.37	747.96	736.85	739.50	736.56
2013	710.06	701.78	704.80	696.63	708.98	725.42	698.44	697.74	707.52	691.92	685.67	669.65	699.96
Financial Activities													
2009	638.82	683.13	679.32	641.00	659.90	689.21	677.45	712.47	695.23	661.09	704.16	670.45	676.36
2010	681.45	670.25	663.25	701.76	751.84	722.87	739.06	759.06	738.40	721.75	727.53	757.05	719.23
2011	816.21	766.75	736.76	774.35	789.98	750.60	782.99	773.62	802.90	831.48	804.05	809.15	787.58
2012	841.02	826.16	826.58	861.82	808.20	801.36	857.30	828.98	900.98	832.17	846.16	908.20	845.82
2013	831.09	861.04	865.42	859.21	855.93	893.37	843.30	850.52	902.29	857.65	866.40	898.38	864.50
Professional and Business Services													
2009	730.70	789.25	788.98	763.11	759.62	761.86	740.37	779.14	736.37	737.53	772.61	746.45	759.52
2010	777.71	757.34	753.50	774.94	794.96	782.93	773.63	802.96	782.81	826.38	800.62	792.17	785.40
2011	812.32	780.37	784.79	787.73	800.45	782.25	774.00	770.59	768.20	789.44	774.82	811.81	786.28
2012	795.12	762.50	787.27	792.67	768.77	769.23	773.98	741.74	805.35	779.59	785.17	782.27	778.36
2013	756.00	780.13	785.18	779.75	769.97	818.93	783.33	805.18	837.32	821.71	828.92	857.44	803.37
Education and Health Services													
2009	543.08	551.53	556.48	544.78	552.68	554.91	582.56	579.35	578.99	577.35	592.85	574.13	566.15
2010	581.26	562.11	577.35	600.92	590.35	574.29	577.96	577.28	581.44	581.54	588.87	594.75	581.41
2011	602.91	602.25	596.25	613.47	625.64	627.33	637.84	643.42	666.65	666.40	660.65	695.72	636.51
2012	704.73	694.77	695.97	702.03	695.46	709.72	727.50	713.22	736.23	719.70	727.94	756.46	715.29
2013	737.18	728.05	728.93	741.55	732.30	752.55	755.22	760.50	766.26	746.05	747.80	762.19	745.97
Leisure and Hospitality													
2009	279.84	284.19	282.38	276.94	274.57	277.41	274.48	281.15	269.57	285.09	282.22	278.12	278.52
2010	273.92	285.84	287.81	282.25	291.40	295.65	291.32	291.83	286.62	295.79	298.55	294.62	290.14
2011	288.01	278.12	282.62	281.53	288.55	280.64	272.38	275.46	273.92	283.35	273.92	276.60	279.87
2012	276.10	279.30	283.45	289.56	289.04	293.49	298.10	286.89	295.94	286.38	285.48	299.94	288.20
2013	274.69	281.94	287.01	290.78	286.18	291.29	281.15	285.41	286.41	282.14	282.57	286.04	284.57

OREGON
At a Glance

Population:
    2000 census: 3,421,524
    2010 census: 3,831,074
    2013 estimate: 3,930,065

Percent change in population:
    2000–2010: 12.0%
    2010–2013: 2.6%

Percent change in total nonfarm employment:
    2000–2010: -1.0%
    2010–2013: 4.5%

Industry with the largest growth in employment, 2000–2013 (thousands):
    Education and Health Services, 70.3

Industry with the largest decline or smallest growth in employment, 2000–2013 (thousands):
    Manufacturing, -40.1

Civilian labor force:
    2000: 1,810,150
    2010: 1,968,730
    2013: 1,924,604

Unemployment rate and rank among states (lowest to highest):
    2000: 5.1%, 47th
    2010: 10.8%, 44th
    2013: 7.7%, 36th

Over-the-year change in unemployment rates:
    2010–2011: -1.1%
    2011–2012: -0.9%
    2012–2013: -1.1%

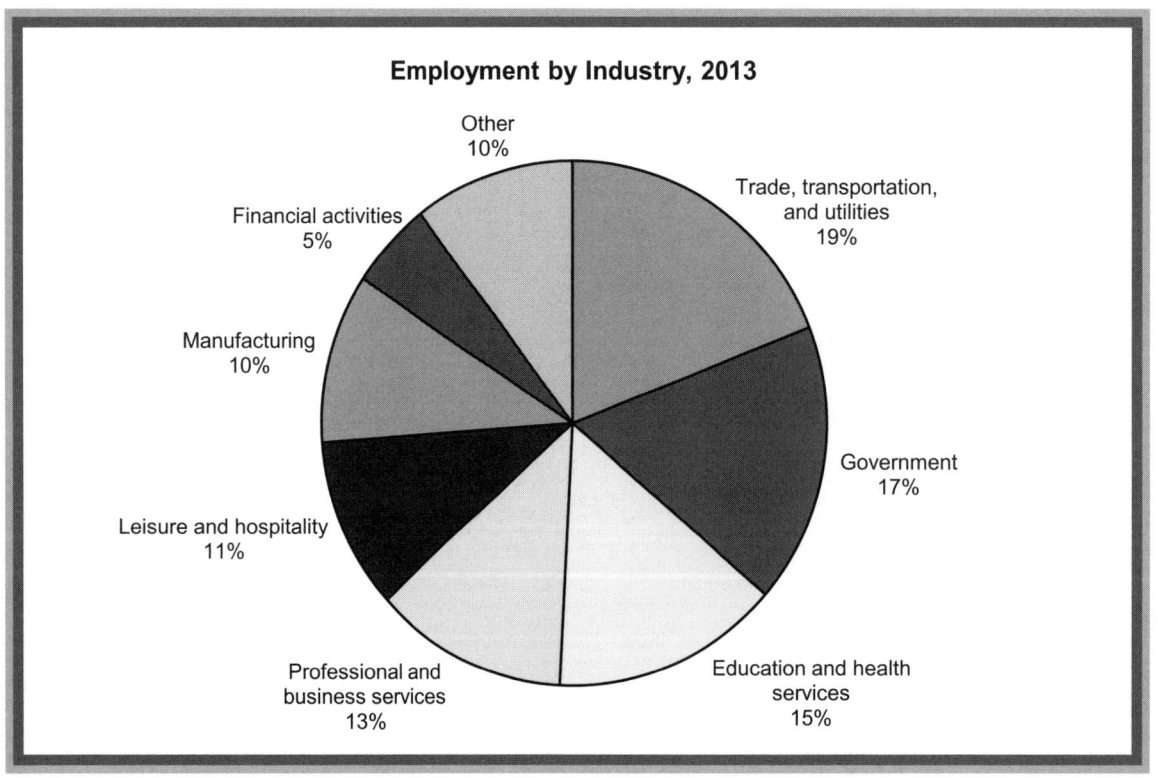

Employment by Industry, 2013

- Other 10%
- Trade, transportation, and utilities 19%
- Financial activities 5%
- Manufacturing 10%
- Government 17%
- Leisure and hospitality 11%
- Education and health services 15%
- Professional and business services 13%

1. Employment by Industry: Oregon, Selected Years, 2002–2013

(Numbers in thousands, not seasonally adjusted)

Industry and year	January	February	March	April	May	June	July	August	September	October	November	December	Annual average
Total Nonfarm													
2002	1,547.9	1,558.6	1,567.0	1,575.7	1,589.3	1,602.2	1,584.5	1,591.4	1,599.6	1,606.8	1,603.4	1,595.0	1,585.1
2003	1,552.6	1,557.5	1,561.4	1,561.0	1,572.1	1,582.3	1,561.2	1,570.7	1,581.8	1,597.6	1,595.6	1,595.4	1,574.1
2004	1,542.2	1,558.5	1,574.4	1,591.3	1,604.7	1,622.2	1,609.9	1,615.7	1,628.3	1,642.3	1,643.5	1,644.3	1,606.4
2005	1,598.6	1,613.5	1,628.1	1,640.0	1,650.9	1,667.7	1,651.0	1,658.3	1,672.7	1,683.3	1,691.4	1,694.5	1,654.2
2006	1,647.9	1,664.9	1,677.8	1,690.3	1,707.0	1,722.4	1,700.1	1,706.8	1,720.4	1,732.0	1,735.2	1,734.0	1,703.2
2007	1,687.9	1,704.2	1,717.4	1,720.7	1,736.0	1,748.6	1,722.9	1,732.1	1,740.5	1,754.7	1,755.6	1,751.4	1,731.0
2008	1,702.6	1,714.5	1,721.4	1,727.9	1,735.3	1,740.2	1,717.9	1,718.5	1,724.3	1,724.3	1,705.9	1,684.2	1,718.1
2009	1,625.6	1,620.9	1,612.8	1,614.8	1,619.9	1,623.3	1,600.5	1,594.9	1,605.6	1,614.7	1,609.9	1,603.5	1,612.2
2010	1,562.5	1,570.5	1,578.9	1,596.4	1,611.3	1,621.1	1,597.4	1,598.3	1,607.2	1,629.0	1,626.7	1,621.0	1,601.7
2011	1,583.3	1,596.3	1,603.1	1,618.0	1,625.1	1,635.0	1,611.2	1,615.2	1,628.6	1,641.0	1,642.5	1,638.8	1,619.8
2012	1,599.5	1,612.7	1,620.4	1,632.2	1,646.3	1,654.5	1,632.3	1,639.8	1,649.5	1,665.9	1,666.6	1,661.4	1,640.1
2013	1,622.5	1,639.7	1,648.4	1,664.3	1,679.4	1,685.2	1,665.8	1,673.8	1,688.7	1,704.2	1,707.1	1,704.9	1,673.7
Total Private													
2002	1,262.5	1,267.6	1,274.1	1,284.2	1,294.9	1,306.9	1,317.8	1,326.6	1,323.4	1,317.0	1,311.7	1,306.4	1,299.4
2003	1,267.0	1,269.1	1,273.2	1,274.4	1,283.7	1,295.1	1,305.1	1,314.0	1,314.4	1,313.6	1,309.7	1,311.9	1,294.3
2004	1,263.2	1,273.5	1,286.5	1,304.4	1,315.2	1,329.9	1,346.2	1,352.9	1,354.5	1,354.3	1,352.9	1,355.8	1,324.1
2005	1,312.5	1,323.1	1,336.7	1,348.1	1,357.4	1,372.3	1,386.8	1,394.6	1,398.4	1,394.8	1,399.2	1,405.3	1,369.1
2006	1,363.4	1,374.3	1,385.7	1,399.1	1,411.9	1,425.9	1,434.8	1,442.1	1,444.3	1,440.6	1,439.9	1,443.2	1,417.1
2007	1,401.3	1,412.1	1,423.2	1,426.4	1,436.8	1,448.1	1,454.1	1,464.0	1,462.0	1,458.1	1,455.6	1,453.3	1,441.3
2008	1,407.8	1,414.4	1,419.4	1,425.5	1,429.6	1,433.4	1,438.1	1,440.2	1,436.0	1,420.0	1,397.9	1,379.0	1,420.1
2009	1,324.6	1,315.0	1,306.1	1,307.1	1,309.7	1,314.4	1,319.6	1,317.2	1,320.8	1,312.1	1,305.0	1,301.2	1,312.7
2010	1,263.8	1,267.1	1,274.0	1,288.9	1,296.4	1,306.7	1,316.0	1,320.6	1,323.6	1,326.2	1,320.5	1,319.5	1,301.9
2011	1,283.7	1,292.7	1,299.3	1,313.5	1,318.2	1,327.8	1,339.3	1,345.6	1,349.6	1,343.8	1,342.6	1,341.8	1,324.8
2012	1,307.0	1,315.0	1,322.0	1,334.4	1,344.8	1,353.3	1,363.7	1,372.5	1,371.4	1,370.4	1,368.4	1,366.5	1,349.1
2013	1,332.8	1,344.2	1,352.8	1,368.9	1,380.6	1,387.4	1,401.2	1,409.8	1,411.7	1,409.7	1,409.1	1,408.4	1,384.7
Goods-Producing													
2002	280.5	280.5	281.6	283.7	287.0	292.7	299.6	301.3	298.3	294.0	287.7	283.5	289.2
2003	276.2	275.7	275.0	272.9	275.7	281.5	286.2	290.0	288.7	287.8	283.4	281.4	282.1
2004	272.1	275.4	278.4	284.2	288.3	295.0	304.0	306.2	304.9	303.4	298.4	296.3	292.2
2005	289.2	291.4	294.4	296.8	300.1	305.9	313.4	315.9	314.8	313.2	309.2	307.9	304.4
2006	302.3	305.4	308.0	311.1	315.0	321.4	328.6	330.2	328.3	325.1	319.5	316.8	317.6
2007	309.7	311.2	312.9	312.1	315.4	319.9	325.6	328.9	325.5	322.1	316.0	311.3	317.6
2008	301.1	300.7	299.7	299.6	300.5	302.4	306.0	306.4	302.2	296.3	284.7	274.7	297.9
2009	259.8	252.2	247.3	245.3	245.0	248.0	253.1	251.9	250.8	246.9	239.6	235.7	248.0
2010	229.2	228.2	229.5	232.3	235.3	239.6	246.4	247.6	247.2	246.2	240.3	236.4	238.2
2011	230.8	232.9	234.5	238.6	241.0	245.2	251.5	255.0	253.6	250.6	246.9	244.3	243.7
2012	238.3	239.3	240.0	242.5	247.1	251.4	257.6	260.9	257.4	255.9	250.1	246.6	248.9
2013	242.1	244.3	246.1	250.3	254.6	258.7	264.9	267.4	266.0	264.4	260.0	256.6	256.3
Service-Providing													
2002	1,267.4	1,278.1	1,285.4	1,292.0	1,302.3	1,309.5	1,284.9	1,290.1	1,301.3	1,312.8	1,315.7	1,311.5	1,295.9
2003	1,276.4	1,281.8	1,286.4	1,288.1	1,296.4	1,300.8	1,275.0	1,280.7	1,293.1	1,309.8	1,312.2	1,314.0	1,292.9
2004	1,270.1	1,283.1	1,296.0	1,307.1	1,316.4	1,327.2	1,305.9	1,309.5	1,323.4	1,338.9	1,345.1	1,348.0	1,314.2
2005	1,309.4	1,322.1	1,333.7	1,343.2	1,350.8	1,361.8	1,337.6	1,342.4	1,357.9	1,370.1	1,382.2	1,386.6	1,349.8
2006	1,345.6	1,359.5	1,369.8	1,379.2	1,392.0	1,401.0	1,371.5	1,376.6	1,392.1	1,406.9	1,415.7	1,417.2	1,385.6
2007	1,378.2	1,393.0	1,404.5	1,408.6	1,420.6	1,428.7	1,397.3	1,403.2	1,415.0	1,432.6	1,439.6	1,440.1	1,413.5
2008	1,401.5	1,413.8	1,421.7	1,428.3	1,434.8	1,437.8	1,411.9	1,412.1	1,422.1	1,428.0	1,421.2	1,409.5	1,420.2
2009	1,365.8	1,368.7	1,365.5	1,369.5	1,374.9	1,375.3	1,347.4	1,343.0	1,354.8	1,367.8	1,370.3	1,367.8	1,364.2
2010	1,333.3	1,342.3	1,349.4	1,364.1	1,376.0	1,381.5	1,351.0	1,350.7	1,360.0	1,382.8	1,386.4	1,384.6	1,363.5
2011	1,352.5	1,363.4	1,368.6	1,379.4	1,384.1	1,389.8	1,359.7	1,360.2	1,375.0	1,390.4	1,395.6	1,394.5	1,376.1
2012	1,361.2	1,373.4	1,380.4	1,389.7	1,399.2	1,403.1	1,374.7	1,378.9	1,392.1	1,410.0	1,416.5	1,414.8	1,391.2
2013	1,380.4	1,395.4	1,402.3	1,414.0	1,424.8	1,426.5	1,400.9	1,406.4	1,422.7	1,439.8	1,447.1	1,448.3	1,417.4
Mining and Logging													
2002	8.7	8.7	8.7	8.6	9.0	9.5	9.9	9.9	9.8	9.8	9.7	9.5	9.3
2003	8.9	8.9	8.8	8.9	9.1	9.6	9.9	9.9	9.8	9.8	9.5	9.3	9.4
2004	8.8	9.0	9.2	9.4	9.6	10.0	10.2	10.2	10.1	10.0	9.7	9.7	9.7
2005	9.2	9.4	9.3	9.1	9.2	9.6	10.1	10.1	9.9	9.8	9.6	9.4	9.6
2006	8.8	9.0	8.9	9.0	9.3	9.7	9.9	10.0	9.9	9.8	9.4	9.2	9.4
2007	8.7	8.9	8.9	9.1	9.3	9.6	9.7	9.7	9.6	9.4	9.2	8.8	9.2
2008	8.4	8.4	8.3	8.3	8.5	8.8	9.1	9.3	9.2	9.0	8.7	8.1	8.7
2009	7.1	7.0	6.7	6.7	6.6	6.9	7.0	7.0	7.0	6.9	6.6	6.3	6.8
2010	6.2	6.2	6.3	6.4	6.6	6.9	7.3	7.2	7.2	7.0	6.7	6.5	6.7
2011	6.2	6.5	6.4	6.6	6.8	7.0	7.4	7.5	7.6	7.5	7.4	7.3	7.0
2012	6.7	6.8	6.8	6.8	7.1	7.4	7.5	7.7	7.6	7.6	7.5	7.3	7.2
2013	6.9	7.1	7.1	7.3	7.6	7.8	8.0	8.1	8.0	7.9	7.7	7.5	7.6
Construction													
2002	72.6	72.9	73.9	75.0	77.2	79.9	82.6	84.9	83.3	81.8	79.1	76.5	78.3
2003	72.1	72.0	72.1	72.6	74.6	76.9	79.9	82.4	81.7	81.6	79.5	78.1	77.0
2004	72.4	74.2	76.2	79.2	81.4	84.2	87.9	89.0	88.9	88.1	85.9	85.2	82.7
2005	80.8	82.0	84.0	86.1	88.5	91.4	95.2	97.3	98.0	96.9	95.3	95.1	90.9
2006	91.3	93.3	94.7	97.2	100.2	103.2	105.7	107.2	106.9	105.7	103.5	101.9	100.9
2007	97.4	98.9	100.5	101.5	104.2	105.8	109.4	110.8	109.2	107.4	104.5	101.3	104.2
2008	94.4	94.3	94.2	94.7	95.8	96.9	98.7	98.6	96.9	93.1	87.9	83.4	94.1
2009	76.9	74.2	72.6	72.4	73.1	75.0	77.1	77.1	76.3	74.4	70.5	68.1	74.0
2010	63.4	62.7	63.4	65.0	66.6	68.4	71.8	72.6	72.1	71.5	68.1	66.1	67.6
2011	62.1	62.9	63.6	66.4	67.8	70.0	72.4	73.5	73.6	72.2	70.2	68.6	68.6
2012	65.0	65.4	65.4	67.1	69.6	70.9	73.9	75.7	74.0	73.1	70.0	67.9	69.8
2013	64.9	66.2	67.9	70.6	73.6	75.1	78.4	79.8	79.1	79.2	76.5	74.0	73.8

1. Employment by Industry: Oregon, Selected Years, 2002–2013—*Continued*

(Numbers in thousands, not seasonally adjusted)

Industry and year	January	February	March	April	May	June	July	August	September	October	November	December	Annual average
Manufacturing													
2002	199.2	198.9	199.0	200.1	200.8	203.3	207.1	206.5	205.2	202.4	198.9	197.5	201.6
2003	195.2	194.8	194.1	191.4	192.0	195.0	196.4	197.7	197.2	196.4	194.4	194.0	194.9
2004	190.9	192.2	193.0	195.6	197.3	200.8	205.9	207.0	205.9	205.3	202.8	201.4	199.8
2005	199.2	200.0	201.1	201.6	202.4	204.9	208.1	208.5	206.9	206.5	204.3	203.4	203.9
2006	202.2	203.1	204.4	204.9	205.5	208.5	213.0	213.0	211.5	209.6	206.6	205.7	207.3
2007	203.6	203.4	203.5	201.5	201.9	204.5	206.5	208.4	206.7	205.3	202.3	201.2	204.1
2008	198.3	198.0	197.2	196.6	196.2	196.7	198.2	198.5	196.1	194.2	188.1	183.2	195.1
2009	175.8	171.0	168.0	166.2	165.3	166.1	169.0	167.8	167.5	165.6	162.5	161.3	167.2
2010	159.6	159.3	159.8	160.9	162.1	164.3	167.3	167.8	167.9	167.7	165.5	163.8	163.8
2011	162.5	163.5	164.5	165.6	166.4	168.2	171.7	174.0	172.4	170.9	169.3	168.4	168.1
2012	166.6	167.1	167.8	168.6	170.4	173.1	176.2	177.5	175.8	175.2	172.6	171.4	171.9
2013	170.3	171.0	171.1	172.4	173.4	175.8	178.5	179.5	178.9	177.3	175.8	175.1	174.9
Trade, Transportation, and Utilities													
2002	306.0	303.7	304.9	306.8	308.7	311.1	313.0	313.4	313.9	314.5	319.3	322.4	311.5
2003	306.4	304.3	304.4	304.6	306.8	308.8	310.7	311.8	312.3	315.2	320.5	322.3	310.7
2004	307.4	304.8	306.6	309.4	311.9	314.8	318.0	318.8	319.4	321.4	327.4	330.6	315.9
2005	314.5	313.2	315.9	317.0	318.4	322.3	324.5	326.6	328.1	329.3	336.4	340.7	323.9
2006	323.5	322.0	323.4	324.5	327.7	330.0	330.9	332.2	333.3	334.2	340.5	344.5	330.6
2007	329.2	327.1	328.6	329.1	331.0	333.9	335.0	336.8	338.1	338.6	345.3	347.4	335.0
2008	331.4	329.1	329.5	329.7	329.8	330.5	331.6	331.9	331.5	329.7	329.6	328.8	330.3
2009	311.9	307.1	304.1	303.1	304.6	304.6	304.9	304.9	306.3	305.2	307.9	310.3	306.2
2010	297.1	294.7	295.0	297.6	298.9	300.9	302.7	304.3	305.1	306.9	311.2	314.3	302.4
2011	300.7	298.7	299.0	301.4	303.2	304.9	306.4	307.2	308.4	309.2	314.7	316.7	305.9
2012	304.1	301.8	302.6	304.4	307.5	309.8	309.9	311.6	312.4	313.9	320.1	322.1	310.0
2013	309.8	309.1	309.6	312.4	315.5	317.0	318.9	321.3	322.4	324.1	330.6	332.7	318.6
Wholesale Trade													
2002	69.0	69.1	69.1	69.4	69.4	69.9	70.9	70.9	70.7	71.1	70.8	70.8	70.1
2003	69.7	70.0	70.0	70.0	70.1	70.3	71.5	71.0	71.2	71.0	70.9	70.7	70.5
2004	69.4	69.8	70.0	70.3	70.6	71.1	72.3	72.3	72.2	72.0	72.2	72.4	71.2
2005	71.5	72.0	72.3	72.5	72.2	73.0	73.8	73.9	74.3	73.9	74.1	74.1	73.1
2006	73.2	74.0	74.1	74.2	74.8	75.1	75.4	75.3	75.3	75.7	75.7	75.5	74.9
2007	74.9	75.4	75.3	75.1	75.2	75.5	76.1	75.8	75.6	75.9	75.8	75.5	75.5
2008	74.5	75.1	75.2	74.9	75.1	75.1	75.7	75.3	75.2	75.1	74.2	73.3	74.9
2009	71.6	71.1	70.3	69.9	69.9	69.5	69.5	68.9	68.6	68.1	67.6	67.3	69.4
2010	66.1	66.2	66.0	66.8	67.1	67.0	67.6	67.4	67.7	67.9	67.5	67.4	67.1
2011	66.3	66.8	66.9	67.5	67.8	67.9	68.2	68.4	68.2	68.5	68.1	67.9	67.7
2012	66.8	67.4	67.7	68.4	69.1	68.9	69.4	69.7	69.6	69.8	69.6	69.4	68.8
2013	69.9	70.5	70.4	70.9	71.3	71.3	72.3	72.5	72.6	73.0	73.0	73.2	71.7
Retail Trade													
2002	181.7	179.3	180.5	181.7	183.3	184.9	186.3	186.1	186.6	186.8	192.2	195.4	185.4
2003	181.2	179.0	179.4	179.7	181.6	183.1	184.1	184.8	184.7	187.3	192.9	195.0	184.4
2004	182.4	179.6	180.9	183.0	185.0	187.3	189.1	189.6	189.2	190.7	196.8	199.9	187.8
2005	186.8	184.8	186.7	187.9	189.6	192.3	194.2	195.7	195.7	197.5	204.3	207.4	193.6
2006	193.2	190.5	191.7	192.7	194.9	196.1	197.7	198.8	198.8	199.3	205.6	208.8	197.3
2007	196.6	193.9	195.3	195.9	197.5	199.3	201.0	202.6	202.9	202.9	209.3	210.9	200.7
2008	198.3	195.2	195.6	195.6	195.4	196.2	197.7	197.9	197.1	195.8	197.9	197.9	196.7
2009	185.1	181.6	180.0	179.9	181.2	181.8	183.0	183.4	183.8	183.8	187.6	189.5	183.4
2010	179.6	177.3	177.8	179.0	180.0	181.6	183.6	184.9	184.4	185.9	190.8	193.1	183.2
2011	182.0	179.6	179.7	181.2	182.3	183.7	185.4	185.8	185.9	186.6	192.1	193.5	184.8
2012	183.9	180.9	181.2	182.5	184.6	186.7	187.6	188.4	188.0	189.5	195.6	196.8	187.1
2013	186.3	184.6	184.9	186.8	189.4	190.6	192.9	194.4	194.2	195.5	201.2	201.8	191.9
Transportation and Utilities													
2002	55.3	55.3	55.3	55.7	56.0	56.3	55.8	56.4	56.6	56.6	56.3	56.2	56.0
2003	55.5	55.3	55.0	54.9	55.1	55.4	55.1	56.0	56.4	56.9	56.7	56.6	55.7
2004	55.6	55.4	55.7	56.1	56.3	56.4	56.6	56.9	58.0	58.7	58.4	58.3	56.9
2005	56.2	56.4	56.9	56.6	56.6	57.0	56.5	57.0	58.1	57.9	58.0	59.2	57.2
2006	57.1	57.5	57.6	57.6	58.0	58.8	57.8	58.1	59.2	59.2	59.2	60.2	58.4
2007	57.7	57.8	58.0	58.1	58.3	59.1	57.9	58.4	59.6	59.8	60.2	61.0	58.8
2008	58.6	58.8	58.7	59.2	59.3	59.2	58.2	58.7	59.2	58.8	57.5	57.6	58.7
2009	55.2	54.4	53.8	53.3	53.5	53.3	52.4	52.6	53.9	53.3	52.7	53.5	53.5
2010	51.4	51.2	51.2	51.8	51.8	52.3	51.5	52.0	53.0	53.1	52.9	53.8	52.2
2011	52.4	52.3	52.4	52.7	53.1	53.3	52.8	53.0	54.3	54.1	54.5	55.3	53.4
2012	53.4	53.5	53.7	53.5	53.8	54.2	52.9	53.5	54.8	54.6	54.9	55.9	54.1
2013	53.6	54.0	54.3	54.7	54.8	55.1	53.7	54.4	55.6	55.6	56.4	57.7	55.0
Information													
2002	37.9	38.0	37.3	35.8	35.8	35.7	35.5	35.5	35.2	35.2	35.1	35.8	36.1
2003	34.8	34.5	34.3	33.5	33.7	33.2	32.7	32.9	32.5	32.7	33.1	32.9	33.4
2004	32.5	32.6	32.4	32.6	32.9	33.0	32.9	33.0	32.7	32.9	32.8	32.8	32.7
2005	32.3	32.7	32.6	32.9	33.2	33.3	33.4	33.3	33.5	33.8	34.1	34.8	33.3
2006	33.8	34.2	34.2	33.9	34.2	34.5	34.7	34.8	34.8	35.0	35.0	35.6	34.6
2007	34.6	35.0	35.5	35.6	35.9	36.2	35.7	35.9	35.7	35.5	35.9	36.9	35.7
2008	35.8	36.0	36.0	35.6	35.8	36.0	35.3	35.4	35.1	34.5	34.2	33.9	35.3
2009	33.0	33.1	33.0	32.5	32.9	33.9	32.8	32.7	32.2	31.7	32.3	32.5	32.7
2010	31.3	31.4	31.6	31.5	31.9	32.3	31.6	32.0	31.8	31.5	31.9	31.9	31.7
2011	31.5	31.6	32.0	31.8	31.6	31.6	31.8	31.9	31.7	31.5	31.6	31.6	31.7
2012	31.2	31.3	31.9	32.3	32.1	32.5	32.7	32.5	32.1	32.4	32.5	32.3	32.2
2013	32.0	32.1	32.2	32.1	32.0	31.8	32.1	32.3	32.5	32.8	33.1	32.9	32.3

1. Employment by Industry: Oregon, Selected Years, 2002–2013—*Continued*

(Numbers in thousands, not seasonally adjusted)

Industry and year	January	February	March	April	May	June	July	August	September	October	November	December	Annual average
Financial Activities													
2002	93.7	94.1	93.9	93.6	94.1	94.5	96.5	96.9	96.5	96.4	96.3	97.1	95.3
2003	95.2	95.5	96.2	96.9	97.1	98.0	98.8	99.1	98.1	97.0	96.3	96.4	97.1
2004	94.1	94.4	94.9	95.9	96.9	98.0	98.7	99.2	98.8	99.1	99.1	99.9	97.4
2005	98.0	98.8	99.5	100.4	101.1	102.0	103.9	104.3	103.9	103.8	104.3	105.1	102.1
2006	103.2	103.8	104.3	105.1	105.8	106.8	107.4	107.9	107.6	107.0	106.9	107.6	106.1
2007	105.8	106.5	107.1	106.4	106.8	107.4	107.9	107.5	105.8	105.6	105.1	105.3	106.4
2008	102.5	102.8	102.6	102.9	102.8	102.5	102.5	102.4	101.2	100.7	99.7	99.5	101.8
2009	96.4	96.2	95.7	95.7	95.5	95.3	96.1	96.0	95.3	95.6	94.9	95.2	95.7
2010	92.4	92.1	92.1	93.1	93.2	93.8	94.2	94.1	93.5	93.4	92.8	93.5	93.2
2011	91.3	91.7	91.4	91.7	91.8	92.4	92.6	92.3	91.5	91.3	90.8	91.3	91.7
2012	89.4	89.6	89.3	89.9	89.9	90.2	91.6	91.7	91.0	91.1	90.9	91.1	90.5
2013	89.7	89.9	90.0	90.9	91.4	91.6	92.7	92.7	92.1	91.2	90.5	90.9	91.1
Professional and Business Services													
2002	168.3	170.4	172.1	174.1	175.5	177.8	179.9	183.2	181.4	180.3	178.0	174.9	176.3
2003	168.4	169.7	170.7	171.8	173.5	174.8	177.4	179.3	179.7	178.8	176.4	178.0	174.9
2004	169.8	172.4	175.3	178.2	178.9	181.4	184.2	185.6	185.0	185.7	185.0	186.3	180.7
2005	179.4	182.5	184.6	187.4	187.8	190.8	193.6	195.2	195.4	194.8	195.1	196.8	190.3
2006	189.1	191.9	193.8	196.6	198.0	201.2	202.8	204.6	204.8	204.6	203.1	202.5	199.4
2007	195.7	198.2	200.5	201.4	201.9	204.2	204.5	206.6	205.6	205.9	203.4	202.6	202.5
2008	196.9	199.4	200.8	203.0	203.4	204.1	206.2	207.2	205.3	202.4	197.7	194.3	201.7
2009	187.9	186.6	185.0	186.0	184.9	185.8	187.1	186.1	186.1	185.7	185.2	185.2	186.0
2010	179.7	181.8	183.4	187.4	187.6	189.0	191.7	192.8	192.1	193.4	192.3	192.1	188.6
2011	186.5	188.6	190.2	193.5	193.0	194.7	199.0	199.7	200.0	199.3	198.8	198.9	195.2
2012	194.9	196.8	197.8	200.3	200.6	202.4	204.9	206.4	204.9	205.3	205.3	205.7	202.1
2013	199.0	201.1	203.5	206.6	207.5	209.6	213.3	214.7	213.6	212.4	211.5	213.0	208.8
Education and Health Services													
2002	180.5	184.0	185.1	186.6	186.4	183.4	180.4	180.9	185.2	189.5	190.7	190.1	185.2
2003	186.7	189.4	190.1	189.9	189.7	186.1	183.3	183.3	188.2	192.3	193.0	193.6	188.8
2004	187.0	191.8	193.1	193.8	193.0	190.2	187.5	187.7	193.9	197.5	198.9	199.1	192.8
2005	193.9	197.8	199.0	199.7	199.8	196.1	194.0	193.8	199.8	202.7	204.4	204.0	198.8
2006	200.1	204.1	205.5	206.8	206.7	202.7	198.5	199.0	205.2	208.9	210.9	211.0	205.0
2007	206.3	211.3	212.4	212.8	212.7	209.3	205.2	206.2	212.3	217.1	218.0	218.0	211.8
2008	213.7	218.8	219.8	220.8	220.1	217.3	213.8	214.2	220.7	224.7	225.3	225.4	219.6
2009	219.7	223.8	224.1	225.3	224.5	221.2	217.5	217.5	224.3	228.1	228.9	228.2	223.6
2010	225.0	228.4	229.5	230.3	229.5	226.2	222.2	222.3	229.1	234.3	235.5	235.1	229.0
2011	230.9	234.6	235.8	236.3	235.0	231.3	227.0	227.7	234.7	238.7	240.0	239.3	234.3
2012	233.8	238.9	240.2	241.0	239.2	234.2	230.4	231.5	238.4	242.1	243.4	243.2	238.0
2013	238.5	243.8	244.3	245.3	243.4	238.1	234.7	236.0	243.1	247.4	248.2	248.2	242.6
Leisure and Hospitality													
2002	140.8	141.6	143.6	147.4	150.8	155.1	156.6	159.0	156.3	150.5	148.1	146.4	149.7
2003	143.7	144.1	146.2	148.4	150.3	156.0	159.2	160.6	157.3	152.7	150.2	150.4	151.6
2004	144.9	145.9	148.8	153.1	156.0	159.5	162.9	164.6	161.6	156.0	154.0	154.0	155.1
2005	149.4	150.1	153.9	156.7	159.5	164.1	166.4	167.9	165.2	159.6	158.2	158.4	159.1
2006	154.6	155.5	158.4	162.5	165.2	169.4	172.6	173.9	170.8	166.2	164.6	165.6	164.9
2007	161.5	163.2	166.2	169.0	172.4	176.1	179.8	181.4	178.4	172.5	171.2	171.1	171.9
2008	166.6	167.2	170.2	172.8	175.5	178.9	181.6	181.7	178.6	171.1	167.0	163.3	172.9
2009	158.1	158.1	159.2	161.4	164.2	167.7	170.0	170.2	168.0	161.7	159.1	157.3	162.9
2010	153.2	154.4	156.5	160.3	163.1	167.4	170.2	170.9	167.9	163.6	160.2	160.0	162.3
2011	156.2	158.3	159.9	163.4	165.6	170.5	173.8	174.6	172.3	166.2	163.0	162.9	165.6
2012	159.1	160.7	163.4	166.7	170.4	174.9	178.7	180.1	177.6	171.9	168.9	168.5	170.1
2013	164.9	166.6	169.5	173.5	177.6	182.2	185.9	186.6	183.5	178.6	176.3	174.7	176.7
Other Services													
2002	54.8	55.3	55.6	56.2	56.6	56.6	56.3	56.4	56.6	56.6	56.5	56.2	56.1
2003	55.6	55.9	56.3	56.4	56.9	56.7	56.8	57.0	57.6	57.1	56.8	56.9	56.7
2004	55.4	56.2	57.0	57.2	57.3	58.0	58.0	57.8	58.2	58.7	57.2	56.8	57.3
2005	55.8	56.6	56.8	57.2	57.2	57.5	57.8	57.6	57.6	57.7	57.6	57.5	57.3
2006	56.8	57.4	58.1	58.6	59.3	59.9	59.3	59.5	59.5	59.6	59.4	59.6	58.9
2007	58.5	59.6	60.0	60.0	60.7	61.1	60.4	60.7	60.6	60.8	60.7	60.7	60.3
2008	59.8	60.4	60.8	61.1	61.7	61.7	61.1	61.0	61.4	60.6	59.7	59.1	60.7
2009	57.8	57.9	57.7	57.8	58.1	57.9	58.1	57.9	57.8	57.2	57.1	56.8	57.7
2010	55.9	56.1	56.4	56.4	56.9	57.5	57.0	56.6	56.9	56.9	56.3	56.2	56.6
2011	55.8	56.3	56.5	56.8	57.0	57.2	57.2	57.2	57.4	57.0	56.8	56.8	56.8
2012	56.2	56.6	56.8	57.3	58.0	57.9	57.9	57.8	57.6	57.8	57.2	57.0	57.3
2013	56.8	57.3	57.6	57.8	58.6	58.4	58.7	58.8	58.5	58.8	58.9	59.4	58.3
Government													
2002	285.4	291.0	292.9	291.5	294.4	295.3	266.7	264.8	276.2	289.8	291.7	288.6	285.7
2003	285.6	288.4	288.2	286.6	288.4	287.2	256.1	256.7	267.4	284.0	285.9	283.5	279.8
2004	279.0	285.0	287.9	286.9	289.5	292.3	263.7	262.8	273.8	288.0	290.6	288.5	282.3
2005	286.1	290.4	291.4	291.9	293.5	295.4	264.2	263.7	274.3	288.5	292.2	289.2	285.1
2006	284.5	290.6	292.1	291.2	295.1	296.5	265.3	264.7	276.1	291.4	295.3	290.8	286.1
2007	286.6	292.1	294.2	294.3	299.2	300.5	268.8	268.1	278.5	296.6	300.0	298.1	289.8
2008	294.8	300.1	302.0	302.4	305.7	306.8	279.8	278.3	288.3	304.3	308.0	305.2	298.0
2009	301.0	305.9	306.7	307.7	310.2	308.9	280.9	277.7	284.8	302.6	304.9	302.3	299.5
2010	298.7	303.4	304.9	307.5	314.9	314.4	281.4	277.7	283.6	302.8	306.2	301.5	299.8
2011	299.6	303.6	303.8	304.5	306.9	307.2	271.9	269.6	279.0	297.2	299.9	297.0	295.0
2012	292.5	297.7	298.4	297.8	301.5	301.2	268.6	267.3	278.1	295.5	298.2	294.9	291.0
2013	289.7	295.5	295.6	295.4	298.8	297.8	264.6	264.0	277.0	294.5	298.0	296.5	289.0

2. Average Weekly Hours by Selected Industry: Oregon, 2009–2013

(Not seasonally adjusted)

Industry and year	January	February	March	April	May	June	July	August	September	October	November	December	Annual average
Total Private													
2009	32.8	33.7	33.4	32.9	32.7	33.0	32.9	34.1	33.3	33.3	34.0	33.0	33.2
2010	33.0	33.4	33.1	33.4	34.3	33.4	33.6	34.8	33.6	33.7	33.3	33.6	33.6
2011	34.1	33.6	33.3	33.8	34.4	33.6	33.8	33.9	33.9	34.1	33.6	33.6	33.8
2012	33.7	33.3	33.1	34.3	33.3	33.7	34.4	33.8	34.6	33.4	33.2	34.1	33.8
2013	32.8	33.6	33.5	33.6	33.5	34.7	33.4	33.9	34.7	33.6	33.5	33.9	33.7
Goods-Producing													
2009	36.7	36.9	37.1	37.0	37.4	38.0	37.4	38.0	37.0	37.5	37.3	37.2	37.3
2010	37.3	37.3	37.1	37.6	38.0	37.6	37.7	38.5	38.0	38.6	37.6	37.5	37.7
2011	37.0	37.3	37.2	37.6	38.1	37.9	37.7	38.5	38.7	38.8	38.6	38.9	38.0
2012	38.3	38.4	38.3	39.0	38.7	39.1	39.0	38.6	38.8	38.7	38.2	38.4	38.6
2013	37.8	39.0	39.0	39.4	39.1	40.1	38.5	39.5	40.0	39.5	39.3	39.1	39.2
Construction													
2009	36.4	35.8	35.0	35.0	34.9	35.5	35.9	36.3	34.8	35.3	35.3	34.6	35.4
2010	34.9	34.8	34.2	34.8	35.2	35.8	36.8	37.3	35.5	35.9	34.7	35.0	35.4
2011	34.5	34.5	34.1	34.7	35.8	35.3	35.7	36.4	36.8	36.1	36.1	36.3	35.6
2012	36.1	36.0	36.0	37.3	37.0	37.6	37.1	36.9	36.9	36.3	35.0	34.9	36.4
2013	34.2	35.7	36.2	36.7	36.7	37.2	37.3	38.1	38.5	37.8	36.5	36.0	36.8
Manufacturing													
2009	37.2	37.4	38.1	38.0	38.5	39.1	38.3	38.9	38.0	38.6	38.4	38.3	38.2
2010	38.2	38.3	38.4	39.0	39.4	38.7	38.2	39.2	39.4	40.0	39.0	38.8	38.9
2011	38.2	38.6	38.5	38.8	39.1	39.0	38.7	39.5	39.8	40.0	39.9	40.1	39.2
2012	39.2	39.3	39.4	39.7	39.3	39.6	39.7	39.2	39.5	39.6	39.4	39.7	39.5
2013	39.0	39.9	39.9	40.2	39.9	40.8	38.7	39.6	40.2	39.7	40.1	40.2	39.8
Trade, Transportation, and Utilities													
2009	33.8	34.5	34.1	33.7	33.5	34.0	34.2	35.1	34.7	33.9	34.1	33.8	34.1
2010	33.4	34.0	33.8	34.2	35.2	34.5	34.7	35.7	34.8	34.6	34.2	35.1	34.5
2011	35.3	34.5	34.4	35.1	36.0	35.1	35.3	35.5	35.4	35.5	34.8	35.0	35.2
2012	34.2	33.9	33.9	35.0	34.3	34.5	35.2	34.8	35.4	34.1	34.1	34.6	34.5
2013	33.2	33.9	34.2	34.2	34.4	35.4	34.7	35.0	35.3	34.4	34.3	34.7	34.5
Financial Activities													
2009	36.7	37.9	37.2	35.8	35.5	35.3	35.1	37.4	35.7	35.8	37.9	35.7	36.3
2010	36.6	36.1	36.2	35.6	37.8	35.6	35.6	37.6	35.2	36.0	35.9	34.9	36.1
2011	37.8	36.0	35.9	35.8	37.3	35.7	35.5	36.7	36.7	37.8	37.4	37.3	36.7
2012	39.7	37.9	37.8	39.5	37.2	37.7	38.7	37.5	38.9	36.6	36.1	38.4	38.0
2013	36.0	36.3	36.1	36.0	36.1	38.2	36.2	36.3	38.5	35.9	36.6	37.9	36.7
Professional and Business Services													
2009	33.9	35.2	35.0	34.3	33.8	34.0	34.1	35.2	33.1	33.6	34.9	34.2	34.3
2010	34.5	35.1	34.6	34.9	35.3	34.5	34.9	36.1	34.8	34.9	34.7	34.6	34.9
2011	35.6	35.3	34.5	35.3	35.3	34.3	34.6	34.1	34.2	35.0	34.4	34.2	34.7
2012	34.6	34.3	34.2	35.2	34.2	34.6	34.7	34.5	35.4	34.6	34.5	35.5	34.7
2013	33.9	34.8	34.7	35.0	34.6	35.9	34.1	34.6	35.8	34.8	34.9	35.2	34.9
Education and Health Services													
2009	30.4	31.3	30.9	30.4	30.0	30.0	29.7	30.8	30.2	30.1	31.2	29.8	30.4
2010	30.0	30.4	30.0	30.4	31.3	30.5	30.6	31.3	30.7	30.6	30.5	30.5	30.6
2011	31.8	30.8	30.7	31.1	31.6	30.9	31.3	31.1	31.3	31.4	30.9	30.5	31.1
2012	31.2	30.5	30.2	31.6	30.6	30.8	31.5	30.8	32.2	30.9	31.1	32.0	31.1
2013	31.5	32.2	31.5	31.5	31.2	32.2	30.7	31.2	32.0	31.0	31.5	31.8	31.5
Leisure and Hospitality													
2009	23.6	25.1	25.0	24.5	24.7	25.0	25.3	27.2	24.9	24.7	25.1	23.9	24.9
2010	23.3	24.2	23.9	24.5	26.2	24.9	25.4	27.6	25.3	24.9	24.3	24.9	25.0
2011	25.4	25.0	24.9	26.0	26.7	25.6	26.6	26.2	25.7	25.7	24.9	24.4	25.6
2012	24.9	24.6	24.5	26.2	24.7	25.4	27.0	26.3	26.8	24.8	24.1	25.9	25.5
2013	23.9	24.9	24.9	24.9	25.1	26.8	25.5	26.2	26.9	24.5	24.0	25.1	25.2
Other Services													
2009	27.2	28.7	28.3	27.7	28.0	28.3	28.4	30.4	34.1	34.6	35.1	33.3	30.3
2010	33.3	33.3	32.1	31.9	32.5	31.6	31.8	32.7	30.2	30.4	30.8	31.0	31.8
2011	31.3	30.6	29.0	30.3	30.7	29.8	29.8	29.7	29.8	30.0	29.3	29.9	30.0
2012	30.3	30.1	29.2	30.2	28.7	29.4	30.3	29.7	30.3	28.7	28.6	29.8	29.6
2013	28.5	29.3	29.1	28.9	29.3	30.3	29.5	30.0	30.0	29.1	29.0	29.7	29.4

3. Average Hourly Earnings by Selected Industry: Oregon, 2009–2013

(Dollars, not seasonally adjusted)

Industry and year	January	February	March	April	May	June	July	August	September	October	November	December	Annual average
Total Private													
2009	21.42	21.68	21.63	21.31	21.27	21.06	20.95	21.21	21.25	21.21	21.39	21.52	21.33
2010	21.52	21.56	21.74	21.64	21.59	21.42	21.55	21.47	21.49	21.55	21.54	21.66	21.56
2011	21.95	21.75	21.68	21.69	21.57	21.53	21.66	21.52	21.69	21.91	21.90	22.15	21.75
2012	22.40	22.27	22.17	22.30	22.11	22.05	22.09	21.92	22.25	22.23	22.29	22.65	22.23
2013	22.41	22.41	22.31	22.39	22.27	22.37	22.34	22.34	22.65	22.68	22.83	23.21	22.52
Goods-Producing													
2009	22.32	22.40	22.55	22.43	22.53	22.23	22.44	22.47	22.26	22.37	22.50	22.42	22.41
2010	22.39	22.58	22.71	22.76	22.88	22.93	23.20	23.19	23.00	23.09	23.07	23.10	22.92
2011	23.31	23.11	23.14	23.47	23.36	23.41	23.66	23.47	23.69	23.96	23.91	24.30	23.58
2012	24.50	24.17	24.34	24.62	24.35	24.28	24.15	24.00	24.24	23.97	24.09	24.55	24.27
2013	24.05	23.95	23.96	24.08	23.98	23.95	24.03	24.05	24.26	24.28	24.17	24.59	24.11
Construction													
2009	25.24	25.33	25.71	25.62	25.92	25.54	25.70	25.84	26.01	25.95	26.04	26.40	25.77
2010	26.30	26.57	26.76	26.13	26.33	26.71	26.64	27.28	27.19	27.06	26.85	27.27	26.77
2011	26.96	27.02	27.09	27.20	26.96	27.18	27.01	27.08	27.16	27.47	27.29	28.37	27.24
2012	28.89	28.78	29.05	29.37	28.78	28.65	27.84	28.14	28.11	27.68	27.53	28.40	28.42
2013	27.86	27.79	28.30	28.55	28.21	27.91	27.90	28.04	28.00	28.12	27.92	28.76	28.11
Manufacturing													
2009	21.02	21.17	21.13	21.09	21.15	20.80	20.96	21.01	20.71	20.90	21.11	21.07	21.01
2010	21.17	21.38	21.46	21.49	21.71	21.54	21.85	21.56	21.39	21.55	21.72	21.65	21.54
2011	22.14	21.84	21.92	22.30	22.22	22.20	22.61	22.13	22.42	22.65	22.69	22.78	22.33
2012	23.00	22.63	22.76	22.87	22.75	22.65	22.76	22.30	22.71	22.52	22.78	23.19	22.74
2013	22.74	22.54	22.42	22.49	22.49	22.49	22.55	22.46	22.78	22.75	22.75	23.08	22.63
Trade, Transportation, and Utilities													
2009	19.34	19.51	20.32	19.51	19.57	19.24	19.36	19.50	19.22	19.11	19.24	19.49	19.45
2010	19.67	19.30	19.67	19.32	19.32	19.18	19.29	19.16	19.16	19.34	19.11	19.22	19.31
2011	19.91	19.71	19.79	19.53	19.50	19.53	19.70	19.42	19.58	19.78	19.35	19.13	19.57
2012	19.90	19.68	19.61	19.97	19.80	19.79	19.88	19.49	19.88	19.75	19.70	20.06	19.79
2013	20.25	20.23	20.21	20.08	20.03	20.11	20.02	20.01	20.07	19.89	19.92	20.13	20.08
Financial Activities													
2009	23.93	25.51	24.41	24.37	24.82	24.64	25.46	25.60	25.42	25.35	25.66	26.38	25.13
2010	25.60	27.68	26.20	27.20	26.37	26.36	26.62	26.57	26.57	26.17	26.07	26.15	26.46
2011	25.52	25.31	25.20	25.16	24.84	24.41	24.55	24.49	24.67	24.44	24.96	24.72	24.86
2012	24.37	24.59	23.99	24.00	23.83	23.46	23.68	24.16	24.22	24.49	24.54	25.13	24.20
2013	24.36	24.23	23.78	24.42	24.25	24.63	24.60	24.22	24.97	24.86	24.74	25.01	24.51
Professional and Business Services													
2009	25.29	25.33	24.62	24.55	24.04	23.94	23.92	24.08	24.18	24.05	24.45	24.44	24.41
2010	24.43	24.35	24.62	24.81	25.18	24.50	24.53	24.79	24.48	24.61	24.62	25.03	24.67
2011	25.18	25.02	24.71	24.79	24.92	24.60	24.36	24.52	24.36	24.82	24.97	24.98	24.77
2012	25.07	25.18	25.17	25.34	24.82	24.81	25.10	24.77	25.43	25.40	25.53	25.77	25.20
2013	25.23	25.44	25.25	25.38	25.38	25.72	25.36	25.29	25.87	25.75	26.18	26.72	25.64
Education and Health Services													
2009	21.87	21.62	21.61	21.47	21.61	21.67	21.77	21.74	22.09	21.93	21.63	21.78	21.73
2010	21.82	21.60	21.86	21.77	21.65	21.62	21.89	21.69	21.72	21.61	21.80	22.07	21.76
2011	22.31	22.20	22.25	22.49	22.26	22.32	22.75	22.47	22.57	22.54	22.60	22.68	22.45
2012	22.64	22.80	22.54	22.62	22.69	22.86	22.96	22.82	22.98	23.11	23.16	23.35	22.88
2013	23.03	23.00	23.21	23.39	23.24	23.71	24.19	24.44	24.59	24.53	24.86	25.18	23.95
Leisure and Hospitality													
2009	13.08	13.10	13.06	12.84	12.84	12.62	12.59	12.57	12.78	13.04	13.10	13.17	12.89
2010	13.19	12.97	13.03	12.80	12.80	12.62	12.55	12.45	12.77	13.03	13.03	13.34	12.87
2011	13.14	13.27	13.00	13.03	12.92	12.88	13.01	13.00	13.16	13.20	13.26	13.36	13.10
2012	13.46	13.32	13.42	13.23	13.41	13.27	13.20	13.18	13.39	13.42	13.46	13.58	13.36
2013	13.63	13.55	13.43	13.48	13.44	13.31	13.26	13.34	13.46	13.70	13.76	13.96	13.52
Other Services													
2009	17.99	18.08	18.02	17.84	17.78	17.89	17.72	17.76	17.95	17.63	18.13	18.19	17.92
2010	18.12	18.07	18.44	18.41	18.80	18.15	18.05	18.42	18.10	17.99	18.21	18.37	18.26
2011	18.50	18.75	19.00	18.96	19.44	19.45	19.49	19.22	19.64	19.95	20.25	19.33	
2012	20.37	20.73	20.44	20.62	20.50	20.50	20.74	20.51	20.68	20.28	20.40	20.77	20.55
2013	20.16	20.36	20.38	20.40	20.32	20.42	20.19	20.35	20.94	20.73	21.07	21.40	20.56

4. Average Weekly Earnings by Selected Industry: Oregon, 2009–2013

(Dollars, not seasonally adjusted)

Industry and year	January	February	March	April	May	June	July	August	September	October	November	December	Annual average
Total Private													
2009	702.58	730.62	722.44	701.10	695.53	694.98	689.26	723.26	707.63	706.29	727.26	710.16	708.16
2010	710.16	720.10	719.59	722.78	740.54	715.43	724.08	747.16	722.06	726.24	717.28	727.78	724.42
2011	748.50	730.80	721.94	733.12	742.01	723.41	732.11	729.53	735.29	747.13	735.84	744.24	735.15
2012	754.88	741.59	733.83	764.89	736.26	743.09	759.90	740.90	769.85	742.48	740.03	772.37	751.37
2013	735.05	752.98	747.39	752.30	746.05	776.24	746.16	757.33	785.96	762.05	764.81	786.82	758.92
Goods-Producing													
2009	819.14	826.56	836.61	829.91	842.62	844.74	839.26	853.86	823.62	838.88	839.25	834.02	835.89
2010	835.15	842.23	842.54	855.78	869.44	862.17	874.64	892.82	874.00	891.27	867.43	866.25	864.08
2011	862.47	862.00	860.81	882.47	890.02	887.24	891.98	903.60	916.80	929.65	922.93	945.27	896.04
2012	938.35	928.13	932.22	960.18	942.35	949.35	941.85	926.40	940.51	927.64	920.24	942.72	936.82
2013	909.09	934.05	934.44	948.75	937.62	960.40	925.16	949.98	970.40	959.06	949.88	961.47	945.11
Construction													
2009	918.74	906.81	899.85	896.70	904.61	906.67	922.63	937.99	905.15	916.04	919.21	913.44	912.26
2010	917.87	924.64	915.19	909.32	926.82	956.22	980.35	1,017.54	965.25	971.45	931.70	954.45	947.66
2011	930.12	932.19	923.77	943.84	965.17	959.45	964.26	985.71	999.49	991.67	985.17	1,029.83	969.74
2012	1,042.93	1,036.08	1,045.80	1,095.50	1,064.86	1,077.24	1,032.86	1,038.37	1,037.26	1,004.78	963.55	991.16	1,034.49
2013	952.81	992.10	1,024.46	1,047.79	1,035.31	1,038.25	1,040.67	1,068.32	1,078.00	1,062.94	1,019.08	1,035.36	1,034.45
Manufacturing													
2009	781.94	791.76	805.05	801.42	814.28	813.28	802.77	817.29	786.98	806.74	810.62	806.98	802.58
2010	808.69	818.85	824.06	838.11	855.37	833.60	834.67	845.15	842.77	862.00	847.08	840.02	837.91
2011	845.75	843.02	843.92	865.24	868.80	865.80	875.01	874.14	892.32	906.00	905.33	913.48	875.34
2012	901.60	889.36	896.74	907.94	894.08	896.94	903.57	874.16	897.05	891.79	897.53	920.64	898.23
2013	886.86	899.35	894.56	904.10	897.35	917.59	872.69	889.42	915.76	903.18	912.28	927.82	900.67
Trade, Transportation, and Utilities													
2009	653.69	673.10	692.91	657.49	655.60	654.16	662.11	684.45	666.93	647.83	656.08	658.76	663.25
2010	656.98	656.20	664.85	660.74	680.06	661.71	669.36	684.01	666.77	669.16	653.56	674.62	666.20
2011	702.82	680.00	680.78	685.50	702.00	685.50	695.41	689.41	693.13	702.19	673.38	669.55	688.86
2012	680.58	667.15	664.78	698.95	679.14	682.76	699.78	678.25	703.75	673.48	671.77	694.08	682.76
2013	672.30	685.80	691.18	686.74	689.03	711.89	694.69	700.35	708.47	684.22	683.26	698.51	692.76
Financial Activities													
2009	878.23	966.83	908.05	872.45	881.11	869.79	893.65	957.44	907.49	907.53	972.51	941.77	912.22
2010	936.96	999.25	948.44	968.32	996.79	938.42	947.67	999.03	935.26	942.12	935.91	912.64	955.21
2011	964.66	911.16	904.68	900.73	926.53	871.44	871.53	898.78	905.39	923.83	933.50	922.06	912.36
2012	967.49	931.96	906.82	948.00	886.48	884.44	916.42	906.00	942.16	896.33	885.89	964.99	919.60
2013	876.96	879.55	858.46	879.12	875.43	940.87	890.52	879.19	961.35	892.47	905.48	947.88	899.52
Professional and Business Services													
2009	857.33	891.62	861.70	842.07	812.55	813.96	815.67	847.62	800.36	808.08	853.31	835.85	837.26
2010	842.84	854.69	851.85	865.87	888.85	845.25	856.10	894.92	851.90	858.89	854.31	866.04	860.98
2011	896.41	883.21	852.50	875.09	879.68	843.78	842.86	836.13	833.11	868.70	858.97	854.32	859.52
2012	867.42	863.67	860.81	891.97	848.84	858.43	870.97	854.57	900.22	878.84	880.79	914.84	874.44
2013	855.30	885.31	876.18	888.30	878.15	923.35	864.78	875.03	926.15	896.10	913.68	940.54	894.84
Education and Health Services													
2009	664.85	676.71	667.75	652.69	648.30	650.10	646.57	669.59	667.12	660.09	674.86	649.04	660.59
2010	654.60	656.64	655.80	661.81	677.65	659.41	669.83	678.90	666.80	661.27	664.90	673.14	665.86
2011	709.46	683.76	683.08	699.44	703.42	689.69	712.08	698.82	706.44	707.76	698.34	691.74	698.20
2012	706.37	695.40	680.71	714.79	694.31	704.09	723.24	702.86	739.96	714.10	720.28	747.20	711.57
2013	725.45	740.60	731.12	736.79	725.09	763.46	742.63	762.53	786.88	760.43	783.09	800.72	754.43
Leisure and Hospitality													
2009	308.69	328.81	326.50	314.58	317.15	315.50	318.53	341.90	318.22	322.09	328.81	314.76	320.96
2010	307.33	313.87	311.42	313.60	335.36	314.24	318.77	343.62	323.08	324.45	316.63	332.17	321.75
2011	333.76	331.75	323.70	338.78	344.96	329.73	346.07	340.60	338.21	339.24	330.17	325.98	335.36
2012	335.15	327.67	328.79	346.63	331.23	337.06	356.40	346.63	358.85	332.82	324.39	351.72	340.68
2013	325.76	337.40	334.41	335.65	337.34	356.71	338.13	349.51	362.07	335.65	330.24	350.40	340.70
Other Services													
2009	489.33	518.90	509.97	494.17	497.84	506.29	503.25	539.90	612.10	610.00	636.36	605.73	542.98
2010	603.40	601.73	591.92	587.28	611.00	573.54	573.99	602.33	546.62	546.90	560.87	569.47	580.67
2011	579.05	573.75	551.00	574.49	596.81	579.61	580.80	570.83	574.84	589.20	584.54	605.48	579.90
2012	617.21	623.97	596.85	622.72	588.35	602.70	628.42	609.15	626.60	582.04	583.44	618.95	608.28
2013	574.56	596.55	593.06	589.56	595.38	618.73	595.61	610.50	628.20	603.24	611.03	635.58	604.46

PENNSYLVANIA
At a Glance

Population:
2000 census: 12,280,548
2010 census: 12,702,379
2013 estimate: 12,773,801

Percent change in population:
2000–2010: 3.4%
2010–2013: 0.6%

Percent change in total nonfarm employment:
2000–2010: -1.3%
2010–2013: 2.1%

Industry with the largest growth in employment, 2000–2013 (thousands):
Education and Health Services, 238.8

Industry with the largest decline or smallest growth in employment, 2000–2013 (thousands):
Manufacturing, -300.7

Civilian labor force:
2000: 6,085,833
2010: 6,391,522
2013: 6,460,354

Unemployment rate and rank among states (lowest to highest):
2000: 4.2%, 33rd
2010: 8.5%, 24th
2013: 7.4%, 31st

Over-the-year change in unemployment rates:
2010–2011: -0.5%
2011–2012: -0.1%
2012–2013: -0.5%

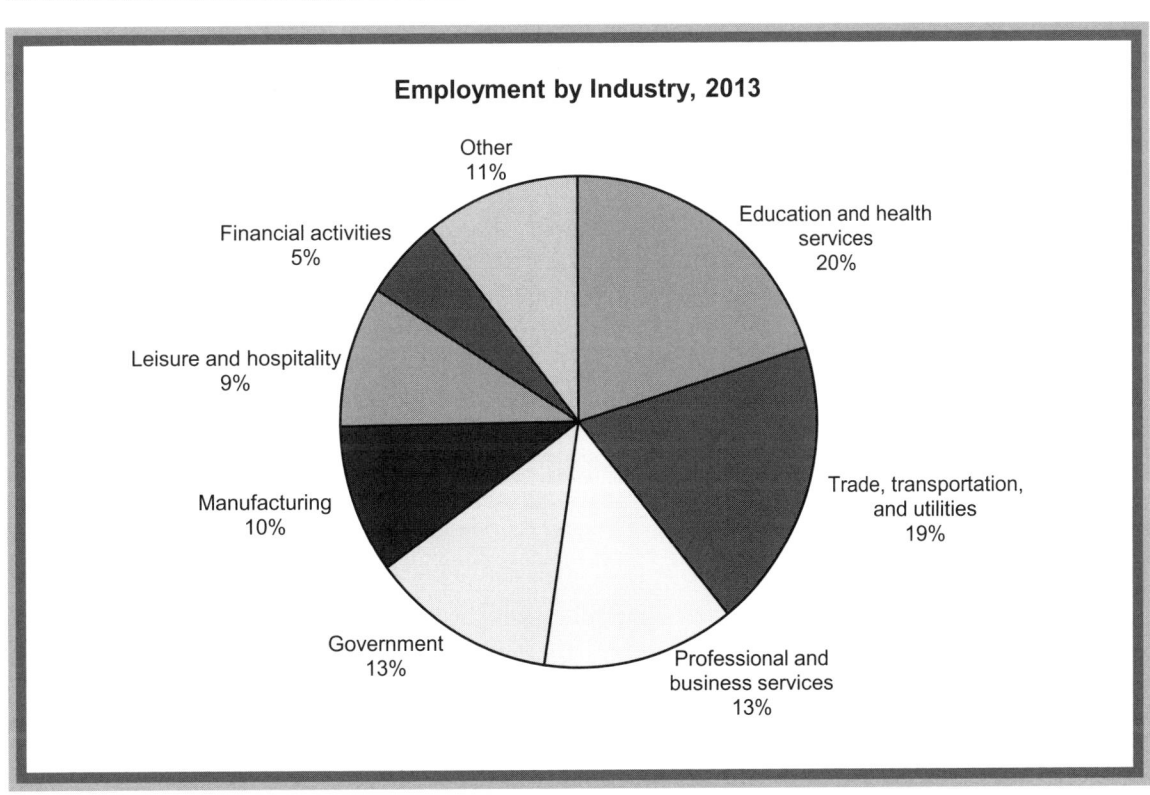

Employment by Industry, 2013

Other
11%

Financial activities
5%

Education and health
services
20%

Leisure and hospitality
9%

Trade, transportation,
and utilities
19%

Manufacturing
10%

Government
13%

Professional and
business services
13%

1. Employment by Industry: Pennsylvania, Selected Years, 2002–2013

(Numbers in thousands, not seasonally adjusted)

Industry and year	January	February	March	April	May	June	July	August	September	October	November	December	Annual average
Total Nonfarm													
2002	5,552.3	5,577.7	5,616.5	5,649.7	5,683.5	5,695.1	5,617.0	5,616.9	5,664.5	5,683.7	5,691.9	5,672.7	5,643.5
2003	5,525.2	5,533.1	5,572.0	5,612.0	5,650.9	5,659.6	5,578.6	5,582.2	5,631.0	5,671.3	5,678.7	5,673.9	5,614.0
2004	5,509.8	5,533.1	5,585.0	5,636.6	5,677.5	5,694.6	5,631.1	5,624.8	5,681.9	5,721.7	5,735.1	5,731.4	5,646.9
2005	5,571.0	5,600.9	5,631.5	5,710.9	5,742.5	5,750.3	5,694.8	5,687.3	5,744.4	5,767.0	5,784.3	5,774.2	5,704.9
2006	5,624.6	5,658.7	5,703.4	5,762.9	5,797.9	5,803.0	5,734.2	5,732.3	5,790.0	5,823.8	5,837.8	5,836.9	5,758.8
2007	5,681.8	5,693.0	5,744.4	5,795.5	5,840.2	5,855.9	5,787.6	5,779.3	5,821.1	5,863.5	5,877.9	5,867.8	5,800.7
2008	5,714.6	5,734.8	5,763.2	5,829.5	5,864.8	5,858.5	5,786.1	5,780.0	5,822.1	5,848.0	5,825.6	5,797.4	5,802.1
2009	5,603.4	5,607.3	5,606.6	5,636.7	5,662.5	5,643.7	5,570.1	5,551.2	5,600.0	5,647.5	5,652.6	5,634.3	5,618.0
2010	5,473.4	5,484.6	5,541.8	5,623.3	5,678.3	5,673.8	5,606.2	5,601.9	5,651.5	5,703.8	5,722.9	5,712.5	5,622.8
2011	5,555.6	5,588.1	5,631.1	5,700.7	5,730.7	5,729.8	5,654.9	5,648.4	5,713.3	5,748.5	5,772.8	5,759.0	5,686.1
2012	5,600.9	5,647.6	5,702.0	5,742.0	5,774.3	5,760.0	5,687.4	5,687.8	5,748.8	5,780.6	5,797.9	5,781.6	5,725.9
2013	5,619.7	5,664.0	5,702.0	5,745.6	5,784.9	5,770.9	5,706.7	5,712.7	5,766.9	5,809.3	5,830.8	5,796.8	5,742.5
Total Private													
2002	4,812.0	4,817.4	4,854.4	4,885.1	4,924.2	4,958.0	4,930.1	4,936.7	4,922.6	4,921.7	4,922.1	4,909.4	4,899.5
2003	4,780.0	4,765.3	4,800.2	4,839.8	4,883.3	4,907.6	4,882.7	4,890.8	4,885.2	4,902.6	4,905.9	4,907.2	4,862.6
2004	4,760.7	4,765.0	4,811.8	4,860.8	4,905.7	4,942.4	4,938.3	4,937.6	4,933.3	4,953.9	4,960.1	4,964.7	4,894.5
2005	4,819.1	4,829.8	4,856.6	4,932.8	4,973.1	4,999.4	4,998.0	4,997.1	4,994.7	4,998.5	5,010.3	5,006.3	4,951.3
2006	4,875.2	4,887.8	4,929.6	4,987.3	5,024.2	5,051.4	5,038.2	5,038.3	5,037.3	5,052.8	5,059.0	5,064.3	5,003.8
2007	4,929.8	4,921.7	4,969.8	5,020.1	5,068.9	5,103.8	5,089.2	5,083.9	5,071.3	5,093.2	5,102.3	5,096.7	5,045.9
2008	4,961.1	4,962.7	4,987.8	5,051.2	5,093.6	5,103.1	5,088.5	5,079.8	5,059.5	5,065.3	5,038.6	5,017.0	5,042.4
2009	4,842.8	4,826.0	4,823.1	4,846.3	4,881.5	4,879.2	4,856.4	4,843.7	4,832.2	4,859.7	4,858.9	4,847.4	4,849.8
2010	4,712.9	4,702.8	4,754.1	4,829.9	4,876.4	4,894.5	4,891.5	4,893.2	4,887.5	4,920.4	4,933.4	4,930.1	4,852.2
2011	4,793.4	4,808.7	4,850.1	4,919.4	4,960.1	4,977.8	4,966.2	4,964.6	4,973.1	4,992.7	5,010.0	5,000.6	4,934.7
2012	4,870.5	4,893.5	4,946.5	4,986.8	5,021.8	5,036.5	5,014.4	5,013.4	5,018.8	5,036.0	5,048.9	5,036.7	4,993.7
2013	4,897.5	4,922.5	4,960.6	5,003.4	5,041.5	5,061.9	5,045.2	5,046.6	5,049.1	5,077.1	5,090.2	5,061.4	5,021.4
Goods-Producing													
2002	1,017.1	1,012.9	1,019.0	1,027.7	1,036.0	1,048.0	1,043.2	1,045.1	1,035.1	1,027.3	1,014.5	999.1	1,027.1
2003	972.6	959.4	965.5	975.1	985.1	992.8	989.3	989.0	982.4	977.7	969.0	957.8	976.3
2004	928.9	922.5	935.8	950.6	963.6	977.5	981.6	981.1	976.3	972.4	965.9	958.2	959.5
2005	928.9	921.9	928.3	948.9	961.6	973.7	975.6	976.2	969.3	964.4	961.4	947.7	954.8
2006	924.4	921.9	934.4	948.8	958.0	969.8	969.5	971.8	965.6	959.8	952.1	944.1	951.7
2007	921.6	906.3	922.4	936.4	948.7	962.5	962.5	961.8	955.2	953.5	945.6	933.0	942.5
2008	910.1	901.9	909.4	923.2	934.9	943.3	941.0	939.6	930.2	922.3	905.7	885.8	920.6
2009	844.8	828.2	822.9	824.5	825.5	828.2	824.0	821.3	816.3	815.3	807.0	793.8	821.0
2010	766.8	759.2	773.7	797.2	807.8	818.8	823.4	823.5	819.2	818.8	816.2	804.7	802.4
2011	781.5	778.9	793.4	811.6	823.7	835.8	842.4	844.0	840.3	840.9	837.9	827.9	821.5
2012	806.2	805.9	816.3	826.5	833.4	845.7	846.4	845.7	842.6	839.6	830.8	820.8	830.0
2013	798.9	797.6	807.1	819.2	829.9	840.3	841.4	842.6	838.9	839.5	834.6	816.9	825.6
Service-Providing													
2002	4,535.2	4,564.8	4,597.5	4,622.0	4,647.5	4,647.1	4,573.8	4,571.8	4,629.4	4,656.4	4,677.4	4,673.6	4,616.4
2003	4,552.6	4,573.7	4,606.5	4,636.9	4,665.8	4,666.8	4,589.3	4,593.2	4,648.6	4,693.6	4,709.7	4,716.1	4,637.7
2004	4,580.9	4,610.6	4,649.2	4,686.0	4,713.9	4,717.1	4,649.5	4,643.7	4,705.6	4,749.3	4,769.2	4,773.2	4,687.4
2005	4,642.1	4,679.0	4,703.2	4,762.0	4,780.9	4,776.6	4,719.2	4,711.1	4,775.1	4,802.6	4,822.9	4,826.5	4,750.1
2006	4,700.2	4,736.8	4,769.0	4,814.1	4,839.9	4,833.2	4,764.7	4,760.5	4,824.4	4,864.0	4,885.7	4,892.8	4,807.1
2007	4,760.2	4,786.7	4,822.0	4,859.1	4,891.5	4,893.4	4,825.1	4,817.5	4,865.9	4,910.0	4,932.3	4,934.8	4,858.2
2008	4,804.5	4,832.9	4,853.8	4,906.3	4,929.9	4,915.2	4,845.1	4,840.4	4,891.9	4,925.7	4,919.9	4,911.6	4,881.4
2009	4,758.6	4,779.1	4,783.7	4,812.2	4,837.0	4,815.5	4,746.1	4,729.9	4,783.7	4,832.2	4,845.6	4,840.5	4,797.0
2010	4,706.6	4,725.4	4,768.1	4,826.1	4,870.5	4,855.0	4,782.8	4,778.4	4,832.3	4,885.0	4,906.7	4,907.8	4,820.4
2011	4,774.1	4,809.2	4,837.7	4,889.1	4,907.0	4,894.0	4,812.5	4,804.4	4,873.0	4,907.6	4,934.9	4,931.1	4,864.6
2012	4,794.7	4,841.7	4,885.7	4,915.5	4,940.9	4,914.3	4,841.0	4,842.1	4,906.2	4,941.0	4,967.1	4,960.8	4,895.9
2013	4,820.8	4,866.4	4,894.9	4,926.4	4,955.0	4,930.6	4,865.3	4,870.1	4,928.0	4,969.8	4,996.2	4,979.9	4,917.0
Mining and Logging													
2002	18.7	18.7	18.8	18.9	19.2	19.4	18.9	19.3	18.9	18.8	18.4	17.8	18.8
2003	17.2	17.1	17.3	17.5	17.8	18.1	18.3	18.3	18.4	18.4	18.3	17.9	17.9
2004	17.2	17.2	17.7	18.4	18.7	19.2	19.5	19.5	19.3	19.3	19.3	19.1	18.7
2005	18.6	18.6	18.6	19.6	19.8	20.3	20.5	20.4	20.4	20.2	20.1	19.6	19.7
2006	19.2	19.3	19.7	20.3	20.6	20.9	21.0	20.9	20.8	20.7	20.7	20.3	20.4
2007	19.9	19.8	20.2	20.8	21.2	21.7	21.9	21.9	21.6	21.5	21.4	21.0	21.1
2008	20.6	20.5	20.9	21.6	22.2	22.8	22.9	23.1	23.1	23.4	23.3	22.5	22.2
2009	21.8	21.5	21.2	21.7	21.9	22.4	22.6	22.6	22.7	22.9	23.1	22.7	22.3
2010	22.4	22.8	23.6	25.3	26.0	26.8	27.5	27.9	28.6	28.9	29.6	29.4	26.6
2011	29.4	30.2	30.8	32.0	32.9	34.0	34.6	35.1	35.5	36.2	37.0	37.3	33.8
2012	36.9	37.7	37.9	37.7	37.8	37.9	37.4	37.0	36.6	36.3	35.9	35.3	37.0
2013	34.7	34.8	35.4	35.8	36.3	36.5	36.6	36.3	36.2	35.5	36.0	35.9	35.8
Construction													
2002	225.3	224.8	231.9	243.9	253.4	260.8	264.0	265.8	260.4	258.6	252.2	240.7	248.5
2003	224.1	218.6	226.4	239.4	250.6	256.5	261.7	263.1	259.2	258.0	252.7	242.2	246.0
2004	223.8	219.9	231.3	243.7	254.1	262.0	266.7	266.5	264.9	262.4	257.1	249.5	250.2
2005	229.3	225.4	230.6	250.9	260.8	268.2	272.7	273.7	270.8	267.8	265.3	253.4	255.7
2006	237.2	236.4	245.3	258.1	265.9	272.3	274.8	276.6	274.2	270.4	263.7	256.6	261.0
2007	241.8	232.9	244.0	257.3	267.9	275.9	278.1	278.7	276.0	274.3	266.5	253.9	262.3
2008	239.1	234.0	240.3	255.2	264.3	269.3	270.2	269.8	264.7	260.9	250.5	236.9	254.6
2009	215.4	211.8	215.9	224.5	230.6	234.3	235.5	234.3	230.8	229.9	222.1	210.6	224.6
2010	191.4	185.5	196.3	215.2	222.2	227.4	231.3	231.2	227.9	226.9	223.3	212.1	215.9
2011	194.7	192.5	203.5	217.6	225.9	232.7	237.5	238.4	236.7	237.4	233.7	222.7	222.8
2012	206.1	205.7	213.8	223.0	228.0	235.0	236.7	237.1	237.7	236.7	229.4	220.2	225.8
2013	203.6	202.9	210.9	222.0	230.3	235.4	238.2	240.2	238.9	239.8	234.8	220.1	226.4

1. Employment by Industry: Pennsylvania, Selected Years, 2002–2013—*Continued*

(Numbers in thousands, not seasonally adjusted)

Industry and year	January	February	March	April	May	June	July	August	September	October	November	December	Annual average
Manufacturing													
2002	773.1	769.4	768.3	764.9	763.4	767.8	760.3	760.0	755.8	749.9	743.9	740.6	759.8
2003	731.3	723.7	721.8	718.2	716.7	718.2	709.3	707.6	704.8	701.3	698.0	697.7	712.4
2004	687.9	685.4	686.8	688.5	690.8	696.3	695.4	695.1	692.1	690.7	689.5	689.6	690.7
2005	681.0	677.9	679.1	678.4	681.0	685.2	682.4	682.1	678.1	676.4	676.0	674.7	679.4
2006	668.0	666.2	669.4	670.4	671.5	676.6	673.7	674.3	670.6	668.7	667.7	667.2	670.4
2007	659.9	653.6	658.2	658.3	659.6	664.9	662.5	661.2	657.6	657.7	657.7	658.1	659.1
2008	650.4	647.4	648.2	646.4	648.4	651.2	647.9	646.7	642.4	638.0	631.9	626.4	643.8
2009	607.6	594.9	585.8	578.3	573.0	571.5	565.9	564.4	562.8	562.5	561.8	560.5	574.1
2010	553.0	550.9	553.8	556.7	559.6	564.6	564.6	564.4	562.7	563.0	563.3	563.2	560.0
2011	557.4	556.2	559.1	562.0	564.9	569.1	570.3	570.5	568.1	567.3	567.2	567.9	565.0
2012	563.2	562.5	564.6	565.8	567.6	572.8	572.3	571.6	568.3	566.6	565.5	565.3	567.2
2013	560.6	559.9	560.8	561.4	563.3	568.4	566.6	566.1	563.8	564.2	563.8	560.9	563.3
Trade, Transportation, and Utilities													
2002	1,111.4	1,094.5	1,101.1	1,101.7	1,111.9	1,115.5	1,102.3	1,104.8	1,109.1	1,117.9	1,135.7	1,148.5	1,112.9
2003	1,101.4	1,085.7	1,090.7	1,096.8	1,105.6	1,110.6	1,095.6	1,098.9	1,105.5	1,120.6	1,137.1	1,150.4	1,108.2
2004	1,102.3	1,091.8	1,097.7	1,101.9	1,111.3	1,115.4	1,104.6	1,105.2	1,110.1	1,123.9	1,142.2	1,157.3	1,113.6
2005	1,108.9	1,097.7	1,102.0	1,110.1	1,119.2	1,121.5	1,113.6	1,113.9	1,118.5	1,127.7	1,147.6	1,162.9	1,120.3
2006	1,119.6	1,103.2	1,110.5	1,115.2	1,122.7	1,123.7	1,113.6	1,115.2	1,122.2	1,135.0	1,156.5	1,172.3	1,125.8
2007	1,130.6	1,110.6	1,119.1	1,122.9	1,134.2	1,137.3	1,126.6	1,123.9	1,127.6	1,137.1	1,162.1	1,174.4	1,133.9
2008	1,133.4	1,114.2	1,118.3	1,121.9	1,130.8	1,130.3	1,117.6	1,115.4	1,119.4	1,126.7	1,136.3	1,146.5	1,125.9
2009	1,093.5	1,077.3	1,072.5	1,071.9	1,082.5	1,081.8	1,065.4	1,064.2	1,070.9	1,081.1	1,099.3	1,109.5	1,080.8
2010	1,068.1	1,049.8	1,059.9	1,066.8	1,078.8	1,083.5	1,070.7	1,071.9	1,077.2	1,090.0	1,109.3	1,124.6	1,079.2
2011	1,082.4	1,071.8	1,074.8	1,084.1	1,091.6	1,091.4	1,080.4	1,081.1	1,087.7	1,097.0	1,119.2	1,132.0	1,091.1
2012	1,089.9	1,078.4	1,087.4	1,090.2	1,099.9	1,099.5	1,088.6	1,089.4	1,095.3	1,105.0	1,131.3	1,139.9	1,099.6
2013	1,094.2	1,083.8	1,088.1	1,092.3	1,101.5	1,103.9	1,091.0	1,095.0	1,098.9	1,106.2	1,128.8	1,145.7	1,102.5
Wholesale Trade													
2002	225.4	224.3	225.2	225.3	226.8	228.3	227.9	227.3	225.9	226.5	226.8	227.5	226.4
2003	225.4	225.2	226.7	226.9	228.2	228.7	228.2	228.1	227.0	227.3	227.7	228.6	227.3
2004	225.7	225.4	227.1	227.9	229.0	231.1	231.8	231.8	230.5	231.1	231.3	232.4	229.6
2005	229.9	230.0	231.2	233.2	234.6	235.7	236.2	236.2	235.2	235.3	235.5	236.5	234.1
2006	233.3	233.8	235.0	236.7	238.2	239.9	239.7	239.9	238.6	239.0	239.0	239.3	237.7
2007	236.5	235.6	237.2	238.3	239.3	241.2	241.5	240.7	239.2	239.7	240.6	240.8	239.2
2008	237.8	237.7	238.4	239.3	240.5	241.2	241.2	240.3	238.1	237.7	235.6	234.5	238.5
2009	230.0	228.0	227.1	226.3	226.7	226.8	225.5	224.7	223.0	223.1	222.6	222.7	225.5
2010	219.6	218.4	219.9	221.3	222.9	224.0	224.5	224.7	223.2	224.2	224.0	224.2	222.6
2011	222.1	222.1	223.1	224.7	225.6	226.1	226.2	226.0	224.7	225.0	224.7	224.9	224.6
2012	222.4	222.6	224.1	224.7	225.8	227.3	226.4	225.9	224.8	224.6	224.4	225.2	224.9
2013	222.4	222.6	223.8	224.7	226.0	227.2	226.6	226.8	226.5	226.1	225.6	228.4	225.6
Retail Trade													
2002	666.2	651.2	656.1	655.1	662.5	666.8	661.7	664.4	659.9	663.1	682.0	695.3	665.4
2003	657.1	642.8	646.4	650.7	656.7	662.4	657.3	660.4	657.8	667.2	683.7	697.0	661.6
2004	657.9	647.9	650.8	652.7	659.8	663.0	660.9	661.6	656.4	666.6	684.3	696.8	663.2
2005	658.2	647.0	648.6	652.9	658.7	661.2	661.3	660.9	653.5	661.0	678.4	690.0	661.0
2006	655.8	639.6	643.9	646.6	650.0	652.6	649.8	650.3	645.6	656.0	676.7	688.2	654.6
2007	655.7	637.7	642.8	644.6	653.1	655.7	655.1	653.3	646.6	655.6	678.2	687.9	655.5
2008	656.7	638.4	641.7	642.6	648.8	650.1	647.2	645.8	639.5	646.6	658.1	667.6	648.6
2009	628.5	616.0	613.4	613.8	623.3	625.4	621.8	621.8	616.5	624.9	642.3	649.7	624.8
2010	620.1	604.1	611.2	615.3	623.5	627.3	625.0	625.4	618.0	628.2	646.1	656.4	625.1
2011	624.4	613.5	614.7	620.9	626.2	627.8	626.4	628.0	621.2	629.3	649.4	658.3	628.3
2012	627.9	615.5	621.2	623.2	630.2	632.8	631.3	632.6	625.6	634.0	658.5	662.4	632.9
2013	628.1	617.8	619.8	622.5	628.8	633.7	631.5	633.3	625.2	631.1	650.8	660.2	631.9
Transportation and Utilities													
2002	219.8	219.0	219.8	221.3	222.6	220.4	212.7	213.1	223.3	228.3	226.9	225.7	221.1
2003	218.9	217.7	217.6	219.2	220.7	219.5	210.1	210.4	220.7	226.1	225.7	224.8	219.3
2004	218.7	218.5	219.8	221.3	222.5	221.3	211.9	211.8	223.2	226.2	226.6	228.1	220.8
2005	220.8	220.7	222.2	224.0	225.9	224.6	216.1	216.8	229.8	231.4	233.7	236.4	225.2
2006	230.5	229.8	231.6	231.9	234.5	231.2	224.1	225.0	238.0	240.0	240.8	244.8	233.5
2007	238.4	237.3	239.1	240.0	241.8	240.4	230.0	229.9	241.8	241.8	243.3	245.7	239.1
2008	238.9	238.1	238.2	240.0	241.5	239.0	229.2	229.3	241.8	242.4	242.6	244.4	238.8
2009	235.0	233.3	232.0	231.8	232.5	229.6	218.1	217.7	231.4	233.1	234.4	237.1	230.5
2010	228.4	227.3	228.8	230.2	232.4	232.2	221.2	221.8	236.0	237.6	239.2	244.0	231.6
2011	235.9	236.2	237.0	238.5	239.8	237.5	227.8	227.1	241.8	242.7	245.1	248.8	238.2
2012	239.6	240.3	242.1	242.3	243.9	239.4	230.9	230.9	244.9	246.4	248.4	252.3	241.8
2013	243.7	243.4	244.5	245.1	246.7	243.0	232.9	234.9	247.2	249.0	252.4	257.1	245.0
Information													
2002	130.6	130.2	130.9	129.3	129.9	129.6	128.3	127.9	126.3	125.7	126.0	125.9	128.4
2003	124.3	123.7	124.5	122.8	122.4	122.1	120.6	119.8	118.1	116.7	116.6	115.6	120.6
2004	114.1	113.4	113.4	112.7	112.8	113.2	113.1	112.2	110.8	110.4	110.3	110.2	112.2
2005	109.1	108.8	109.0	109.4	110.0	110.5	109.6	109.4	111.6	108.1	108.8	109.1	109.5
2006	107.6	108.0	107.7	108.1	108.7	108.9	108.6	108.4	108.3	108.0	107.5	108.3	108.2
2007	106.8	106.5	106.4	106.6	107.3	109.0	108.1	108.0	108.1	107.0	107.6	108.9	107.5
2008	107.2	106.8	106.5	108.1	108.3	107.8	106.2	105.3	103.9	103.7	103.4	103.2	105.9
2009	101.6	101.0	100.8	100.5	100.3	100.4	99.8	98.7	97.9	98.5	97.8	98.2	99.6
2010	94.1	93.3	93.3	93.3	93.6	94.7	94.7	93.6	93.3	91.5	91.8	92.0	93.3
2011	90.6	90.6	90.7	91.4	92.0	92.5	92.1	87.6	91.2	91.7	92.5	90.6	91.1
2012	89.9	89.4	90.4	89.9	91.1	90.9	90.8	91.2	90.2	89.7	90.6	89.9	90.3
2013	88.8	88.4	88.3	88.0	88.4	88.4	88.6	88.3	87.4	88.0	89.4	88.2	88.4

1. Employment by Industry: Pennsylvania, Selected Years, 2002–2013—*Continued*

(Numbers in thousands, not seasonally adjusted)

Industry and year	January	February	March	April	May	June	July	August	September	October	November	December	Annual average
Financial Activities													
2002	334.7	334.5	335.5	335.1	336.3	339.7	340.1	340.6	337.4	335.4	335.7	337.1	336.8
2003	335.9	335.8	336.7	336.9	338.9	341.4	342.2	342.2	338.6	337.5	337.5	338.5	338.5
2004	336.5	335.4	336.4	335.4	337.0	339.0	339.8	338.6	334.3	333.4	333.2	335.2	336.2
2005	332.3	332.4	332.9	333.9	335.5	338.2	339.4	339.9	336.0	335.0	335.6	337.1	335.7
2006	333.9	333.7	334.1	334.9	335.9	339.3	338.9	337.4	333.6	332.7	332.6	333.2	335.0
2007	330.4	330.4	330.6	331.0	332.3	335.9	337.2	336.4	332.5	331.8	332.3	332.3	332.8
2008	328.2	328.7	329.3	329.9	331.1	333.7	334.2	333.6	328.5	327.0	326.5	326.6	329.8
2009	321.5	320.4	319.9	319.3	319.9	321.3	321.0	319.0	315.5	314.8	314.1	313.9	318.4
2010	311.4	310.2	310.9	310.5	311.9	313.3	313.0	312.5	308.8	309.5	309.5	310.0	311.0
2011	308.1	306.9	307.2	307.4	308.3	310.5	311.1	311.1	308.2	307.9	308.1	308.7	308.6
2012	306.7	306.7	307.4	307.3	309.0	312.1	312.6	312.4	309.5	309.4	310.0	310.5	309.5
2013	308.8	309.4	309.9	310.9	312.0	315.2	315.6	315.7	312.1	313.1	314.0	313.5	312.5
Professional and Business Services													
2002	589.0	589.9	596.7	604.8	607.0	613.3	611.6	615.5	611.1	610.6	610.4	608.4	605.7
2003	589.6	587.3	592.9	603.1	607.3	611.7	612.7	620.1	621.2	624.8	627.1	627.7	610.5
2004	610.1	611.8	620.1	631.1	634.9	644.3	645.4	649.1	647.9	654.0	654.3	653.6	638.1
2005	634.3	638.1	642.4	657.9	659.1	666.6	668.6	671.3	669.9	672.9	673.0	671.3	660.5
2006	653.8	658.9	666.9	679.1	682.6	692.3	693.0	697.3	696.1	701.4	701.8	700.4	685.3
2007	679.9	681.6	688.1	701.8	706.3	716.3	715.2	717.4	713.7	715.8	716.8	715.8	705.7
2008	695.7	695.5	699.7	713.3	714.8	719.0	720.0	721.0	713.8	713.1	706.8	699.5	709.4
2009	675.9	671.1	669.7	674.4	675.8	675.8	672.8	674.3	670.5	679.5	680.9	679.3	674.8
2010	661.4	662.9	669.3	686.8	689.0	694.8	696.0	698.7	696.4	705.3	709.1	709.0	689.9
2011	690.8	692.7	699.1	714.2	717.4	722.6	721.6	724.9	725.7	730.2	732.6	729.5	716.8
2012	709.5	712.3	721.2	731.8	734.7	739.6	737.6	739.0	738.5	744.5	746.2	742.5	733.1
2013	723.1	729.3	736.3	746.8	750.4	757.3	757.3	759.7	754.7	761.8	759.1	753.7	749.1
Education and Health Services													
2002	946.8	969.0	972.7	969.3	961.1	950.7	943.4	940.6	962.7	977.6	982.8	973.9	962.6
2003	962.6	982.5	986.8	985.7	976.6	964.7	955.3	951.4	974.5	994.5	998.4	994.9	977.3
2004	969.8	992.1	998.1	999.7	991.3	978.6	976.3	971.0	995.5	1,015.7	1,021.2	1,018.3	994.0
2005	999.3	1,023.7	1,024.3	1,032.0	1,021.7	1,004.6	1,005.4	1,001.5	1,028.4	1,048.8	1,052.4	1,048.0	1,024.2
2006	1,025.8	1,050.8	1,051.9	1,057.3	1,049.2	1,030.1	1,027.0	1,023.6	1,050.6	1,067.5	1,071.0	1,066.6	1,047.6
2007	1,045.0	1,068.7	1,073.9	1,075.2	1,067.5	1,049.5	1,046.9	1,044.5	1,068.8	1,092.2	1,093.6	1,088.6	1,067.9
2008	1,066.7	1,095.2	1,095.2	1,102.4	1,092.2	1,073.0	1,071.9	1,070.9	1,095.4	1,116.8	1,121.0	1,118.2	1,093.2
2009	1,096.2	1,119.8	1,118.6	1,121.8	1,112.2	1,092.1	1,090.7	1,084.4	1,106.2	1,128.8	1,133.4	1,127.5	1,111.0
2010	1,105.8	1,126.6	1,130.0	1,133.8	1,127.4	1,106.3	1,104.0	1,100.1	1,124.5	1,149.0	1,151.6	1,147.1	1,125.5
2011	1,120.8	1,148.1	1,150.3	1,151.5	1,143.3	1,123.1	1,116.1	1,112.9	1,142.6	1,160.5	1,165.7	1,160.7	1,141.3
2012	1,135.3	1,164.4	1,169.9	1,169.1	1,156.9	1,130.9	1,122.8	1,117.6	1,153.6	1,172.2	1,175.6	1,168.7	1,153.1
2013	1,142.5	1,171.8	1,173.7	1,171.4	1,155.6	1,133.7	1,126.9	1,121.6	1,159.9	1,178.7	1,183.3	1,169.2	1,157.4
Leisure and Hospitality													
2002	428.0	430.6	440.8	458.6	481.8	497.6	497.9	499.8	482.0	468.3	458.3	457.0	466.7
2003	437.4	435.1	444.7	460.4	486.3	500.4	502.9	506.4	485.2	470.9	460.7	461.8	471.0
2004	441.1	440.1	449.1	467.6	491.1	506.5	508.9	512.9	493.9	479.6	469.0	467.6	477.3
2005	446.1	446.5	455.6	477.9	502.4	518.3	519.6	521.4	501.6	483.0	473.1	472.5	484.8
2006	454.4	455.5	466.8	485.0	506.9	524.6	525.0	524.0	503.4	491.4	481.2	483.1	491.8
2007	463.0	464.8	474.9	490.6	515.5	533.5	532.3	533.6	510.5	501.2	489.6	489.4	499.9
2008	468.5	469.5	478.2	498.6	525.8	537.7	538.8	536.7	513.5	501.7	485.9	485.0	503.3
2009	461.4	460.2	469.5	484.8	515.9	525.6	528.7	529.7	506.9	493.4	478.5	477.0	494.3
2010	459.4	456.1	469.6	492.9	516.8	529.2	535.1	538.7	517.5	505.2	494.7	491.9	500.6
2011	471.4	471.2	484.4	506.7	529.9	544.3	544.8	546.4	524.5	511.6	501.4	498.2	511.2
2012	482.6	485.4	500.5	518.0	541.2	558.6	557.2	561.2	535.9	523.1	512.8	512.9	524.1
2013	492.7	493.6	507.3	523.8	550.2	565.7	568.3	568.2	545.0	537.0	526.1	521.1	533.3
Other Services													
2002	254.4	255.8	257.7	258.6	260.2	263.6	263.3	262.4	258.9	258.9	258.7	259.5	259.3
2003	256.2	255.8	258.4	259.0	261.1	263.9	264.1	263.0	259.7	259.9	259.5	260.5	260.1
2004	257.9	257.9	261.2	261.8	263.7	267.9	268.6	267.5	264.5	264.5	264.0	264.3	263.7
2005	260.2	260.7	262.1	262.7	263.6	266.0	266.2	263.5	259.4	258.6	258.4	257.7	261.6
2006	255.7	255.8	257.3	258.9	260.2	262.7	262.6	260.6	257.5	257.0	256.3	256.3	258.4
2007	252.5	252.8	254.4	255.6	257.1	259.8	260.4	258.3	254.9	254.6	254.7	254.3	255.8
2008	251.3	250.9	251.2	253.8	255.7	258.3	258.8	257.3	254.8	254.0	253.0	252.2	254.3
2009	247.9	248.0	249.2	249.1	251.7	254.0	254.0	252.1	248.0	248.3	247.9	248.2	249.9
2010	245.9	244.7	247.4	248.6	251.1	253.9	254.6	254.2	250.6	251.1	251.2	250.8	250.3
2011	247.8	248.5	250.2	252.5	253.9	257.6	257.7	256.6	252.9	252.9	252.6	253.0	253.0
2012	250.4	251.0	253.4	254.0	255.6	259.2	258.4	256.9	253.2	252.5	251.6	251.5	254.0
2013	248.5	248.6	249.9	251.0	253.5	257.4	256.1	255.5	252.2	252.8	254.9	253.1	252.8
Government													
2002	740.3	760.3	762.1	764.6	759.3	737.1	686.9	680.2	741.9	762.0	769.8	763.3	744.0
2003	745.2	767.8	771.8	772.2	767.6	752.0	695.9	691.4	745.8	768.7	772.8	766.7	751.5
2004	749.1	768.1	773.2	775.8	771.8	752.2	692.8	687.2	748.6	767.8	775.0	766.7	752.4
2005	751.9	771.3	774.9	778.1	769.4	750.9	696.8	690.2	749.7	768.5	774.0	767.9	753.6
2006	749.4	770.9	773.8	775.6	773.7	751.6	696.0	694.0	752.7	771.0	778.8	772.6	755.0
2007	752.0	771.3	774.6	775.4	771.3	752.1	698.4	695.4	749.8	770.3	775.6	771.1	754.8
2008	753.5	772.1	775.4	778.3	771.2	755.4	697.6	700.2	762.6	782.7	787.0	780.4	759.7
2009	760.6	781.3	783.5	790.4	781.0	764.5	713.7	707.5	767.8	787.8	793.7	786.9	768.2
2010	760.5	781.8	787.7	793.4	801.9	779.3	714.7	708.7	764.0	783.4	789.5	782.4	770.6
2011	762.2	779.4	781.0	781.3	770.6	752.0	688.7	683.8	740.2	755.8	762.8	758.4	751.4
2012	730.4	754.1	755.5	755.2	752.5	723.5	673.0	674.4	730.0	744.6	749.0	744.9	732.3
2013	722.2	741.5	741.4	742.2	743.4	709.0	661.5	666.1	717.8	732.2	740.6	735.4	721.1

2. Average Weekly Hours by Selected Industry: Pennsylvania, 2009–2013

(Not seasonally adjusted)

Industry and year	January	February	March	April	May	June	July	August	September	October	November	December	Annual average
Total Private													
2009	33.0	33.4	33.1	32.9	33.0	32.9	33.0	33.2	32.9	32.9	33.3	33.1	33.0
2010	33.0	32.2	33.1	33.3	33.5	33.3	33.4	33.7	33.5	33.6	33.7	33.6	33.3
2011	33.5	33.3	33.4	33.6	33.7	33.5	33.5	33.4	33.4	33.6	33.6	33.6	33.5
2012	33.3	33.1	33.1	33.3	33.1	33.2	33.3	33.0	33.4	33.0	33.0	33.4	33.2
2013	32.9	33.1	33.2	33.3	33.3	33.6	33.6	33.6	33.9	33.6	33.8	33.6	33.5
Goods-Producing													
2009	37.7	37.8	37.8	37.1	37.6	38.0	37.9	38.5	37.8	38.2	38.6	38.4	37.9
2010	38.8	36.4	39.0	39.3	39.5	39.2	38.9	39.6	39.5	39.6	40.0	39.1	39.1
2011	39.0	38.9	38.9	39.2	39.4	39.3	39.3	39.2	39.2	39.5	39.6	39.3	39.2
2012	38.7	38.6	38.2	38.9	38.8	39.3	39.0	38.8	39.2	39.1	38.9	39.2	38.9
2013	38.5	38.7	39.1	39.2	39.2	39.2	39.2	39.3	39.5	39.3	39.5	39.0	39.1
Construction													
2009	36.1	36.5	37.4	36.8	37.6	37.3	37.9	37.9	36.5	36.9	36.8	36.6	37.0
2010	36.5	33.4	36.6	37.7	37.2	37.3	37.8	38.4	37.8	37.7	38.2	36.9	37.2
2011	36.9	37.0	37.0	37.5	38.8	39.3	38.9	38.8	38.1	38.4	38.7	38.1	38.2
2012	36.6	36.8	36.9	37.7	37.6	38.4	38.6	38.6	39.3	39.4	38.5	37.9	38.1
2013	37.4	37.5	38.2	39.1	38.9	38.2	38.7	38.9	39.4	38.6	39.3	37.9	38.5
Manufacturing													
2009	39.2	39.0	38.7	38.0	38.5	39.0	38.6	39.3	38.7	39.0	39.5	39.3	38.9
2010	39.8	37.5	39.9	39.7	40.2	39.7	39.0	39.8	39.9	40.1	40.3	39.5	39.6
2011	39.4	39.3	39.5	39.6	39.4	39.1	39.2	39.2	39.6	39.8	39.8	39.6	39.5
2012	39.2	39.1	39.1	39.1	39.2	39.3	38.8	39.0	39.3	39.1	39.4	40.1	39.2
2013	39.4	39.5	39.6	39.4	39.5	39.7	39.5	39.6	39.7	39.8	39.8	39.7	39.6
Trade, Transportation, and Utilities													
2009	33.2	33.4	33.1	33.3	33.7	33.6	33.5	33.6	33.9	33.5	33.6	33.7	33.5
2010	33.2	32.2	33.1	33.5	33.9	33.9	33.9	34.0	34.0	33.9	33.8	34.4	33.7
2011	33.6	33.8	34.0	34.3	34.3	34.4	34.2	34.1	34.0	34.1	34.0	34.2	34.1
2012	33.7	33.6	33.7	33.8	33.8	34.0	33.9	33.6	33.7	33.1	33.2	33.5	33.6
2013	32.7	33.1	33.4	33.5	33.6	33.7	34.0	34.1	34.3	33.8	34.0	33.8	33.7
Information													
2009	32.1	32.0	32.1	31.6	31.4	31.9	31.9	32.2	31.4	31.1	31.9	31.5	31.8
2010	31.5	31.4	32.6	32.3	32.6	32.7	32.5	32.7	32.9	32.9	33.1	33.3	32.5
2011	33.3	32.5	32.9	33.0	32.0	32.3	32.8	31.6	32.0	31.3	31.7	31.2	32.2
2012	31.9	31.8	31.4	32.0	31.9	32.3	32.2	31.6	32.3	31.7	32.0	32.2	31.9
2013	31.5	30.8	31.7	31.4	31.7	32.6	32.3	32.6	33.3	32.9	34.3	32.2	32.3
Financial Activities													
2009	36.0	36.3	36.3	35.3	35.8	35.4	35.3	35.5	35.0	35.2	36.0	35.6	35.6
2010	35.4	35.5	35.9	35.5	35.9	35.5	35.5	36.0	35.4	35.6	35.6	35.8	35.6
2011	36.5	36.1	36.1	36.5	36.6	36.2	36.2	36.1	36.4	36.8	36.5	36.3	36.4
2012	37.1	36.6	36.8	37.1	36.5	36.7	37.2	36.7	37.2	36.5	36.6	37.2	36.9
2013	36.2	36.7	37.0	36.9	36.6	37.1	36.4	36.4	37.0	36.5	36.5	37.0	36.7
Professional and Business Services													
2009	34.0	34.8	34.5	34.0	34.3	34.0	34.1	34.6	33.7	34.1	34.6	34.2	34.2
2010	34.2	33.6	34.3	34.6	34.9	34.6	34.9	35.5	35.0	35.6	35.7	35.7	34.9
2011	35.8	35.3	35.3	35.4	35.7	35.2	34.9	35.1	35.0	35.6	35.3	35.4	35.3
2012	35.7	35.4	35.4	36.0	35.2	35.1	35.3	34.9	35.8	35.3	35.4	36.4	35.5
2013	35.8	35.8	35.9	36.1	36.1	36.7	36.3	36.2	36.9	36.3	36.4	36.5	36.3
Education and Health Services													
2009	32.0	32.4	32.4	32.4	32.0	31.7	32.1	32.2	31.8	31.8	32.1	32.0	32.1
2010	31.9	31.6	31.8	32.1	32.1	32.0	32.1	32.0	32.0	32.0	32.0	31.9	32.0
2011	32.1	31.9	32.0	32.0	32.1	31.8	31.7	31.6	31.7	31.8	31.7	31.9	31.9
2012	31.4	31.1	31.2	31.2	31.2	31.3	31.4	31.2	31.7	31.5	31.4	31.6	31.4
2013	31.4	31.6	31.4	31.5	31.5	31.9	31.8	31.7	32.1	31.9	32.1	32.1	31.8
Leisure and Hospitality													
2009	23.6	24.8	24.0	24.1	24.3	24.0	24.2	24.3	23.8	23.7	23.7	23.6	24.0
2010	23.3	23.2	23.9	24.2	24.1	24.0	24.8	24.8	24.3	24.4	24.3	24.0	24.1
2011	23.5	23.9	23.9	24.1	24.2	24.5	24.6	24.5	24.2	24.4	24.5	24.2	24.2
2012	23.6	24.0	24.0	23.9	24.1	24.1	24.6	24.6	24.2	23.9	23.8	24.3	24.1
2013	23.6	24.3	24.3	24.4	24.6	25.0	25.2	25.3	25.0	24.9	25.0	24.4	24.7
Other Services													
2009	31.6	31.3	30.7	30.5	30.4	30.5	30.9	31.4	30.9	31.4	31.8	31.3	31.1
2010	31.4	31.0	31.2	31.4	31.6	31.2	31.4	31.6	31.2	30.8	30.6	30.3	31.1
2011	30.5	29.6	30.0	30.2	30.4	30.4	30.4	30.2	30.6	30.8	30.4	30.1	30.3
2012	30.1	29.8	29.6	29.7	29.1	29.2	29.7	28.8	29.0	28.4	28.4	28.7	29.2
2013	28.5	28.6	28.2	28.5	28.0	28.4	28.6	28.8	29.0	28.6	28.4	28.3	28.5

3. Average Hourly Earnings by Selected Industry: Pennsylvania, 2009–2013

(Dollars, not seasonally adjusted)

Industry and year	January	February	March	April	May	June	July	August	September	October	November	December	Annual average
Total Private													
2009	20.65	20.65	20.70	20.68	20.64	20.62	20.65	20.76	20.82	20.88	20.95	20.96	20.75
2010	21.07	21.15	21.12	21.16	21.15	21.09	21.14	21.21	21.26	21.35	21.37	21.44	21.21
2011	21.61	21.61	21.70	21.77	21.81	21.65	21.79	21.79	21.96	22.09	22.13	22.28	21.85
2012	22.43	22.37	22.41	22.57	22.40	22.42	22.61	22.43	22.92	22.84	22.88	23.14	22.62
2013	23.11	23.18	23.19	23.24	23.15	23.21	23.12	23.15	23.43	23.36	23.44	23.73	23.28
Goods-Producing													
2009	22.15	22.25	22.37	22.42	22.38	22.39	22.49	22.60	22.62	22.74	22.79	22.91	22.51
2010	22.93	22.96	22.84	22.92	22.88	22.83	22.93	22.94	22.85	22.80	22.87	23.00	22.89
2011	23.18	23.26	23.37	23.46	23.65	23.55	23.66	23.81	23.87	23.89	24.03	24.13	23.66
2012	24.03	24.30	24.35	24.34	24.22	24.19	24.51	24.41	24.64	24.66	24.76	24.97	24.45
2013	24.86	25.07	25.09	25.12	25.18	25.10	25.18	25.19	25.28	25.26	25.22	25.48	25.17
Construction													
2009	24.18	24.32	24.28	24.26	24.43	24.51	24.53	24.79	24.75	24.89	24.89	24.99	24.57
2010	25.07	25.09	25.04	25.02	25.12	25.12	25.22	25.32	25.15	25.26	25.24	25.37	25.17
2011	25.49	25.57	25.59	25.62	25.62	25.51	25.80	26.19	26.01	25.92	26.02	26.03	25.79
2012	26.21	26.36	26.27	26.09	25.90	26.13	26.37	26.41	26.51	26.46	26.83	27.05	26.39
2013	27.08	27.32	27.37	27.41	27.30	27.27	27.77	27.65	27.84	28.16	27.56	28.11	27.58
Manufacturing													
2009	21.42	21.49	21.62	21.70	21.64	21.64	21.77	21.74	21.80	21.81	21.90	22.06	21.71
2010	22.06	22.09	21.91	22.04	21.92	21.84	21.97	21.94	21.97	21.83	21.90	22.06	21.96
2011	22.30	22.30	22.42	22.56	22.72	22.61	22.63	22.68	22.86	22.97	23.13	23.30	22.71
2012	23.19	23.18	23.42	23.74	23.62	23.55	23.60	23.49	23.78	23.89	23.90	24.13	23.63
2013	23.96	24.20	24.16	24.13	24.20	24.09	23.88	23.97	24.04	23.87	24.10	24.34	24.08
Trade, Transportation, and Utilities													
2009	18.34	18.39	18.46	18.46	18.50	18.39	18.39	18.58	18.69	18.61	18.67	18.59	18.51
2010	18.73	18.81	18.86	18.98	18.87	18.78	18.91	18.93	18.98	19.10	18.91	18.87	18.90
2011	19.01	19.12	19.31	19.12	19.05	18.98	19.06	19.00	19.05	19.14	19.09	19.18	19.09
2012	19.38	19.39	19.47	19.53	19.37	19.50	19.91	19.42	19.95	19.79	19.67	19.76	19.60
2013	19.78	19.86	20.03	20.23	20.21	20.23	20.19	20.19	20.37	20.10	20.13	20.18	20.13
Information													
2009	22.79	22.58	22.51	22.61	22.26	22.45	22.35	22.25	22.14	22.23	22.18	22.16	22.38
2010	22.27	22.40	22.33	22.43	22.57	22.60	22.67	22.87	22.83	22.93	23.06	23.12	22.68
2011	23.13	22.96	22.66	22.24	22.38	21.93	21.71	21.70	21.84	21.74	21.38	21.52	22.11
2012	21.81	21.48	21.56	21.85	22.68	23.01	22.63	21.99	22.56	22.78	23.18	23.35	22.41
2013	23.80	24.12	24.71	25.01	24.96	25.89	26.11	26.30	26.94	27.35	28.16	27.54	25.94
Financial Activities													
2009	26.62	26.78	26.74	26.88	26.68	26.69	26.78	26.87	26.88	26.89	27.04	27.11	26.83
2010	27.26	27.42	27.32	27.46	27.53	27.64	27.73	27.82	27.88	27.98	27.86	28.01	27.66
2011	28.16	28.09	28.15	28.34	28.51	27.98	28.02	27.83	27.89	28.12	28.31	28.54	28.16
2012	29.09	29.08	28.89	29.31	29.56	29.30	29.50	29.50	30.18	29.89	29.58	30.38	29.52
2013	30.20	30.24	30.12	30.54	30.37	30.55	30.50	30.50	30.48	30.20	30.61	30.88	30.43
Professional and Business Services													
2009	25.50	25.69	25.73	25.76	25.94	25.89	25.89	26.10	26.15	26.24	26.35	26.42	25.97
2010	26.51	26.64	26.68	26.58	26.76	26.71	26.62	26.78	26.83	26.97	27.07	27.24	26.79
2011	27.33	27.14	27.25	27.34	27.38	27.03	27.27	27.24	27.49	27.85	28.09	28.34	27.48
2012	28.27	27.90	27.94	28.23	27.97	28.04	28.39	28.20	28.81	28.56	28.74	29.22	28.36
2013	28.83	29.15	28.98	28.77	28.75	29.12	28.49	28.64	29.06	28.89	29.10	29.82	28.97
Education and Health Services													
2009	19.31	19.14	19.16	19.16	19.17	19.23	19.31	19.36	19.47	19.43	19.40	19.43	19.30
2010	19.57	19.69	19.63	19.71	19.73	19.65	19.79	19.87	19.98	20.00	20.06	20.13	19.82
2011	20.23	20.35	20.49	20.82	20.88	21.03	21.37	21.26	21.53	21.52	21.44	21.61	21.04
2012	21.80	21.64	21.71	21.86	21.82	21.78	21.78	21.71	21.97	21.88	22.00	22.19	21.85
2013	22.20	22.06	22.01	22.08	21.90	21.91	22.12	22.13	22.32	22.35	22.34	22.52	22.16
Leisure and Hospitality													
2009	12.75	12.60	12.55	12.53	12.40	12.33	12.25	12.23	12.39	12.51	12.53	12.54	12.46
2010	12.45	12.40	12.35	12.37	12.44	12.33	12.32	12.25	12.32	12.47	12.51	12.69	12.41
2011	12.57	12.62	12.65	12.62	12.59	12.20	12.19	12.25	12.39	12.45	12.45	12.63	12.46
2012	12.53	12.66	12.62	12.70	12.66	12.53	12.50	12.53	12.87	13.03	13.01	13.15	12.73
2013	13.56	13.53	13.63	13.60	13.61	13.50	13.46	13.56	14.06	14.24	14.37	14.85	13.83
Other Services													
2009	18.39	18.39	18.49	18.62	18.48	18.39	18.32	18.21	18.24	18.28	18.32	18.38	18.37
2010	18.28	18.39	18.35	18.34	18.39	18.33	18.32	18.25	18.34	18.27	18.35	18.39	18.33
2011	18.50	18.53	18.30	18.52	18.65	18.64	18.50	18.65	18.84	18.97	19.03	19.27	18.70
2012	19.19	19.14	19.41	19.77	19.19	19.65	19.25	19.57	20.17	20.05	20.23	20.65	19.68
2013	20.15	20.19	20.36	20.10	20.13	19.77	19.48	19.36	20.04	20.05	20.18	20.73	20.04

4. Average Weekly Earnings by Selected Industry: Pennsylvania, 2009–2013

(Dollars, not seasonally adjusted)

Industry and year	January	February	March	April	May	June	July	August	September	October	November	December	Annual average
Total Private													
2009	681.45	689.71	685.17	680.37	681.12	678.40	681.45	689.23	684.98	686.95	697.64	693.78	684.75
2010	695.31	681.03	699.07	704.63	708.53	702.30	706.08	714.78	712.21	717.36	720.17	720.38	706.29
2011	723.94	719.61	724.78	731.47	735.00	725.28	729.97	727.79	733.46	742.22	743.57	748.61	731.98
2012	746.92	740.45	741.77	751.58	741.44	744.34	752.91	740.19	765.53	753.72	755.04	772.88	750.98
2013	760.32	767.26	769.91	773.89	770.90	779.86	776.83	777.84	794.28	784.90	792.27	797.33	779.88
Goods-Producing													
2009	835.06	841.05	845.59	831.78	841.49	850.82	852.37	870.10	855.04	868.67	879.69	879.74	853.13
2010	889.68	835.74	890.76	900.76	903.76	894.94	891.98	908.42	902.58	902.88	914.80	899.30	895.00
2011	904.02	904.81	909.09	919.63	931.81	925.52	929.84	933.35	935.70	943.66	951.59	948.31	927.47
2012	929.96	937.98	930.17	946.83	939.74	950.67	955.89	947.11	965.89	964.21	963.16	978.82	951.11
2013	957.11	970.21	981.02	984.70	987.06	983.92	987.06	989.97	998.56	992.72	996.19	993.72	984.15
Construction													
2009	872.90	887.68	908.07	892.77	918.57	914.22	929.69	939.54	903.38	918.44	915.95	914.63	909.09
2010	915.06	838.01	916.46	943.25	934.46	936.98	953.32	972.29	950.67	952.30	964.17	936.15	936.32
2011	940.58	946.09	946.83	960.75	994.06	1,002.54	1,003.62	1,016.17	990.98	995.33	1,006.97	991.74	985.18
2012	959.29	970.05	969.36	983.59	973.84	1,003.39	1,017.88	1,019.43	1,041.84	1,042.52	1,032.96	1,025.20	1,005.46
2013	1,012.79	1,024.50	1,045.53	1,071.73	1,061.97	1,041.71	1,074.70	1,075.59	1,096.90	1,086.98	1,083.11	1,065.37	1,061.83
Manufacturing													
2009	839.66	838.11	836.69	824.60	833.14	843.96	840.32	854.38	843.66	850.59	865.05	866.96	844.52
2010	877.99	828.38	874.21	874.99	881.18	867.05	856.83	873.21	876.60	875.38	882.57	871.37	869.62
2011	878.62	876.39	885.59	893.38	895.17	884.05	887.10	889.06	905.26	914.21	920.57	922.68	897.05
2012	909.05	906.34	915.72	928.23	925.90	925.52	915.68	916.11	934.55	934.10	941.66	967.61	926.30
2013	944.02	955.90	956.74	950.72	955.90	956.37	943.26	949.21	954.39	950.03	959.18	966.30	953.57
Trade, Transportation, and Utilities													
2009	608.89	614.23	611.03	614.72	623.45	617.90	616.07	624.29	633.59	623.44	627.31	626.48	620.09
2010	621.84	605.68	624.27	635.83	639.69	636.64	641.05	643.62	645.32	647.49	639.16	649.13	636.93
2011	638.74	646.26	656.54	655.82	653.42	652.91	651.85	647.90	647.70	652.67	649.06	655.96	650.97
2012	653.11	651.50	656.14	660.11	654.71	663.00	674.95	652.51	672.32	655.05	653.04	661.96	658.56
2013	646.81	657.37	669.00	677.71	679.06	681.75	686.46	688.48	698.69	679.38	684.42	682.08	678.38
Information													
2009	731.56	722.56	722.57	714.48	698.96	716.16	712.97	716.45	695.20	691.35	707.54	698.04	711.68
2010	701.51	703.36	727.96	724.49	735.78	739.02	736.78	747.85	751.11	754.40	763.29	769.90	737.10
2011	770.23	746.20	745.51	733.92	716.16	708.34	712.09	685.72	698.88	680.46	677.75	671.42	711.94
2012	695.74	683.06	676.98	699.20	723.49	743.22	728.69	694.88	728.69	722.13	741.76	751.87	714.88
2013	749.70	742.90	783.31	785.31	791.23	844.01	843.35	857.38	897.10	899.82	965.89	886.79	837.86
Financial Activities													
2009	958.32	972.11	970.66	948.86	955.14	944.83	945.33	953.89	940.80	946.53	973.44	965.12	955.15
2010	965.00	973.41	980.79	974.83	988.33	981.22	984.42	1,001.52	986.95	996.09	991.82	1,002.76	984.70
2011	1,027.84	1,014.05	1,016.22	1,034.41	1,043.47	1,012.88	1,014.32	1,004.66	1,015.20	1,034.82	1,033.32	1,036.00	1,025.02
2012	1,079.24	1,064.33	1,063.15	1,087.40	1,078.94	1,075.31	1,097.40	1,082.65	1,122.70	1,090.99	1,082.63	1,130.14	1,089.29
2013	1,093.24	1,109.81	1,114.44	1,126.93	1,111.54	1,133.41	1,110.20	1,110.20	1,127.76	1,102.30	1,117.27	1,142.56	1,116.78
Professional and Business Services													
2009	867.00	894.01	887.69	875.84	889.74	880.26	882.85	903.06	881.26	894.78	911.71	903.56	888.17
2010	906.64	895.10	915.12	919.67	933.92	924.17	929.04	950.69	939.05	960.13	966.40	972.47	934.97
2011	978.41	958.04	961.93	967.84	977.47	951.46	951.72	956.12	962.15	991.46	991.58	1,003.24	970.04
2012	1,009.24	987.66	989.08	1,016.28	984.54	984.20	1,002.17	984.18	1,031.40	1,008.17	1,017.40	1,063.61	1,006.78
2013	1,032.11	1,043.57	1,040.38	1,038.60	1,037.88	1,068.70	1,034.19	1,036.77	1,072.31	1,048.71	1,059.24	1,088.43	1,051.61
Education and Health Services													
2009	617.92	620.14	620.78	620.78	613.44	609.59	619.85	623.39	619.15	617.87	622.74	621.76	619.53
2010	624.28	622.20	624.23	632.69	633.33	628.80	635.26	635.84	639.36	640.00	641.92	642.15	634.24
2011	649.38	649.17	655.68	666.24	670.25	668.75	677.43	671.82	682.50	684.34	679.65	689.36	671.18
2012	684.52	673.00	677.35	682.03	680.78	681.71	683.89	677.35	696.45	689.22	690.80	701.20	686.09
2013	697.08	697.10	691.11	695.52	689.85	698.93	703.42	701.52	716.47	712.97	717.11	722.89	704.69
Leisure and Hospitality													
2009	300.90	312.48	301.20	301.97	301.32	295.92	296.45	297.19	294.88	296.49	296.96	295.94	299.04
2010	290.09	287.68	295.17	299.35	299.80	295.92	305.54	303.80	299.38	304.27	303.99	304.56	299.08
2011	295.40	301.62	302.34	304.14	304.68	298.90	299.87	300.13	299.84	303.78	305.03	305.65	301.53
2012	295.71	303.84	302.88	303.53	305.11	301.97	307.50	308.24	311.45	311.42	309.64	319.55	306.79
2013	320.02	328.78	331.21	331.84	334.81	337.50	339.19	343.07	351.50	354.58	359.25	362.34	341.60
Other Services													
2009	581.12	575.61	567.64	567.91	561.79	560.90	566.09	571.79	563.62	573.99	582.58	575.29	571.31
2010	573.99	570.09	572.52	575.88	581.12	571.90	575.25	576.70	572.21	562.72	561.51	557.22	570.06
2011	564.25	548.49	549.00	559.30	566.96	566.66	562.40	563.23	576.50	584.28	578.51	580.03	566.61
2012	577.62	570.37	574.54	587.17	558.43	573.78	571.73	563.62	584.93	569.42	574.53	592.66	574.66
2013	574.28	577.43	574.15	572.85	563.64	561.47	557.13	557.57	581.16	573.43	573.11	586.66	571.14

RHODE ISLAND
At a Glance

Population:
    2000 census: 1,048,259
    2010 census: 1,052,567
    2013 estimate: 1,051,511

Percent change in population:
    2000–2010: 0.4%
    2010–2013: -0.1%

Percent change in total nonfarm employment:
    2000–2010: -3.9%
    2010–2013: 2.8%

Industry with the largest growth in employment, 2000–2013 (thousands):
    Education and Health Services, 21.3

Industry with the largest decline or smallest growth in employment, 2000–2013 (thousands):
    Manufacturing, -31.2

Civilian labor force:
    2000: 543,404
    2010: 572,300
    2013: 555,578

Unemployment rate and rank among states (lowest to highest):
    2000: 4.2%, 33rd
    2010: 11.7%, 48th
    2013: 9.5%, 50th

Over-the-year change in unemployment rates:
    2010–2011: -0.5%
    2011–2012: -0.9%
    2012–2013: -0.8%

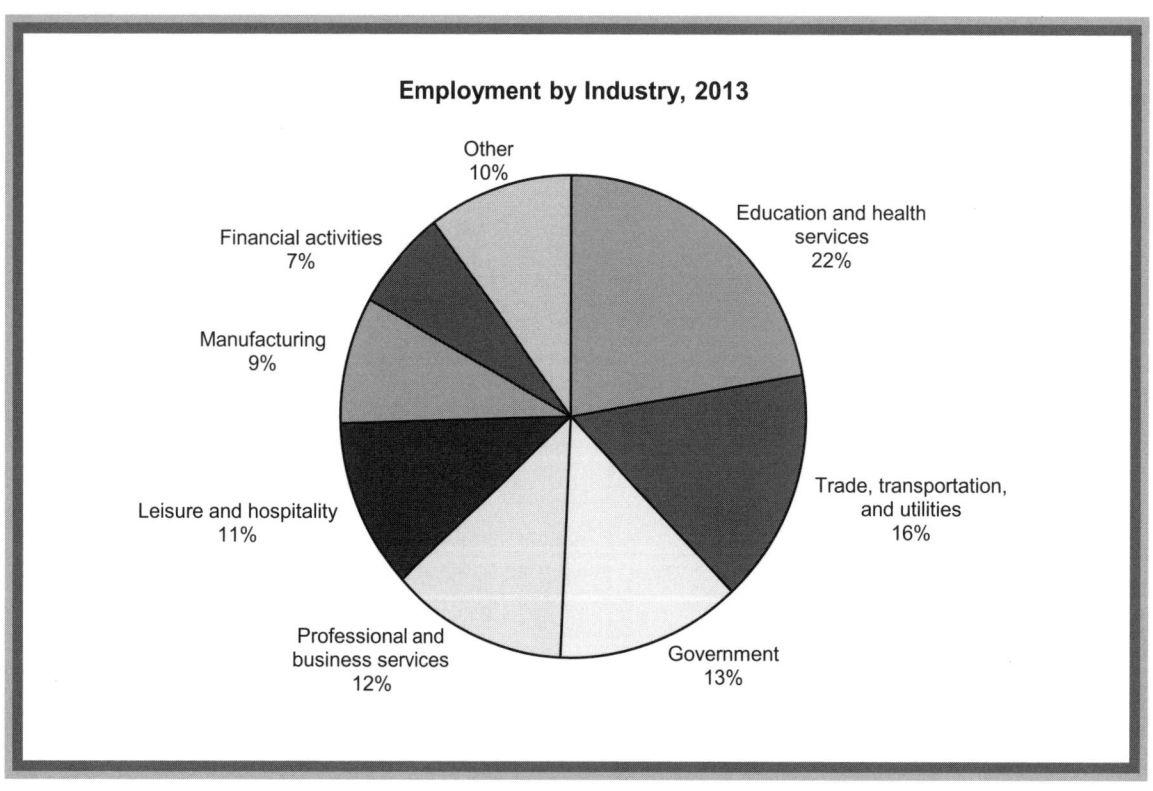

Employment by Industry, 2013

Other 10%
Financial activities 7%
Manufacturing 9%
Leisure and hospitality 11%
Professional and business services 12%
Government 13%
Trade, transportation, and utilities 16%
Education and health services 22%

1. Employment by Industry: Rhode Island, Selected Years, 2002–2013

(Numbers in thousands, not seasonally adjusted)

Industry and year	January	February	March	April	May	June	July	August	September	October	November	December	Annual average
Total Nonfarm													
2002	466.0	467.1	471.4	478.6	484.3	485.3	475.4	479.5	484.7	486.0	487.1	487.2	479.4
2003	469.9	469.9	473.5	482.0	489.4	490.7	482.7	485.1	490.5	492.1	492.8	492.4	484.3
2004	473.2	475.5	478.5	486.0	494.4	494.7	487.7	489.3	494.7	496.4	496.5	495.3	488.5
2005	475.8	478.6	481.0	491.0	495.7	498.1	491.2	492.8	497.5	496.7	497.8	496.1	491.0
2006	475.5	478.5	482.9	494.0	497.3	500.1	490.6	493.2	500.0	500.7	501.1	500.5	492.9
2007	481.0	482.8	485.2	492.4	498.9	500.7	491.9	492.0	495.3	495.1	494.1	492.5	491.8
2008	473.5	475.5	477.4	484.0	489.2	489.5	479.2	480.2	484.4	482.7	479.9	476.2	481.0
2009	454.3	455.4	454.8	458.7	465.1	465.3	456.2	456.1	461.5	463.2	462.4	460.3	459.4
2010	443.6	445.7	449.1	456.0	463.5	463.6	459.3	460.1	463.9	464.1	464.5	462.3	458.0
2011	444.6	447.8	450.8	460.2	465.8	467.9	461.7	461.1	466.1	467.4	467.2	464.9	460.5
2012	449.0	454.0	457.2	463.4	470.2	472.1	464.4	466.6	472.8	472.1	471.2	471.9	465.4
2013	455.1	457.4	461.3	468.6	475.3	478.9	471.8	472.4	478.1	479.2	478.2	473.0	470.8
Total Private													
2002	399.3	400.3	404.3	411.4	416.6	418.6	413.5	417.8	419.4	419.1	419.7	419.6	413.3
2003	402.8	402.8	406.1	414.8	421.7	422.9	420.7	423.0	424.8	425.4	426.0	425.5	418.0
2004	407.1	409.2	411.6	419.8	427.4	428.0	425.7	427.5	429.5	430.5	430.0	429.5	423.0
2005	410.3	412.8	415.1	425.2	429.6	432.2	429.7	432.1	433.4	430.9	431.7	430.2	426.1
2006	410.1	412.6	417.0	428.4	431.5	434.5	429.3	432.2	435.3	435.0	434.7	434.5	427.9
2007	415.8	417.4	419.9	427.1	432.9	435.8	430.4	430.8	431.4	430.4	429.3	427.5	427.4
2008	408.9	411.0	412.5	419.2	423.7	425.0	419.0	420.7	422.0	419.6	415.9	412.5	417.5
2009	391.3	392.1	391.6	395.3	401.4	402.3	398.4	398.6	400.2	400.4	399.4	397.5	397.4
2010	381.3	383.4	386.4	393.3	398.7	400.5	400.8	401.9	403.4	402.5	402.4	400.4	396.3
2011	383.2	386.4	389.0	398.4	403.8	406.3	405.1	404.3	406.2	406.4	406.0	403.7	399.9
2012	388.4	393.1	396.2	402.2	408.4	411.6	408.2	410.0	413.1	411.3	410.1	410.8	405.3
2013	394.6	396.9	400.3	407.6	413.5	418.1	414.9	415.6	418.3	418.3	417.0	411.9	410.6
Goods-Producing													
2002	81.1	81.0	81.9	82.1	83.0	83.6	79.4	82.8	82.7	82.2	82.0	80.9	81.9
2003	77.5	76.3	77.0	79.2	80.3	81.0	78.5	81.3	81.8	81.3	81.1	79.9	79.6
2004	75.5	75.0	75.4	77.5	78.5	79.5	77.8	79.8	79.9	80.3	79.9	79.1	78.2
2005	74.8	74.2	74.5	77.1	78.0	79.1	76.4	78.7	78.6	77.6	77.8	76.8	77.0
2006	73.1	72.8	73.4	76.0	76.7	77.8	75.5	77.5	77.3	76.9	76.4	76.0	75.8
2007	72.6	71.6	71.9	73.0	74.2	74.8	72.7	74.3	74.1	73.8	73.1	71.7	73.2
2008	68.4	67.4	67.9	69.3	70.2	70.8	68.4	70.0	69.8	68.5	67.2	65.5	68.6
2009	60.9	59.0	58.5	59.3	59.7	59.9	58.7	59.5	59.2	59.1	58.5	57.5	59.2
2010	54.2	53.7	54.0	55.5	56.8	57.7	57.1	58.2	57.9	57.9	57.8	56.8	56.5
2011	54.0	53.4	53.9	55.6	56.5	57.4	56.9	57.4	57.0	56.9	56.8	56.1	56.0
2012	53.4	53.2	54.0	55.3	55.9	57.1	56.2	57.2	56.9	57.1	56.9	56.6	55.8
2013	53.9	53.2	54.2	55.5	56.6	57.3	56.5	57.7	57.7	58.2	58.2	56.8	56.3
Service-Providing													
2002	384.9	386.1	389.5	396.5	401.3	401.7	396.0	396.7	402.0	403.8	405.1	406.3	397.5
2003	392.4	393.6	396.5	402.8	409.1	409.7	404.2	403.8	408.7	410.8	411.7	412.5	404.7
2004	397.7	400.5	403.1	408.5	415.9	415.2	409.9	409.5	414.8	416.1	416.6	416.2	410.3
2005	401.0	404.4	406.5	413.9	417.7	419.0	414.8	414.1	418.9	419.1	420.0	419.3	414.1
2006	402.4	405.7	409.5	418.0	420.6	422.3	415.1	415.7	422.7	423.8	424.7	424.5	417.1
2007	408.4	411.2	413.3	419.4	424.7	425.9	419.2	417.7	421.2	421.3	421.0	420.8	418.7
2008	405.1	408.1	409.5	414.7	419.0	418.7	410.8	410.2	414.6	414.2	412.7	410.7	412.4
2009	393.4	396.4	396.3	399.4	405.4	405.4	397.5	396.6	402.3	404.1	403.9	402.8	400.3
2010	389.4	392.0	395.1	400.5	406.7	405.9	402.2	401.9	406.0	406.2	406.7	405.5	401.5
2011	390.6	394.4	396.9	404.6	409.3	410.5	404.8	403.7	409.1	410.5	410.4	408.8	404.5
2012	395.6	400.8	403.2	408.1	414.3	415.0	408.2	409.4	415.9	415.0	414.3	415.3	409.6
2013	401.2	404.2	407.1	413.1	418.7	421.6	415.3	414.7	420.4	421.0	420.0	416.2	414.5
Mining and Logging													
2002	0.2	0.2	0.2	0.2	0.2	0.2	0.3	0.2	0.2	0.2	0.2	0.2	0.2
2003	0.2	0.1	0.2	0.2	0.2	0.2	0.2	0.2	0.2	0.2	0.2	0.2	0.2
2004	0.2	0.2	0.2	0.2	0.2	0.2	0.2	0.2	0.3	0.3	0.3	0.3	0.2
2005	0.2	0.2	0.2	0.3	0.3	0.3	0.3	0.3	0.3	0.3	0.3	0.3	0.3
2006	0.2	0.2	0.2	0.3	0.3	0.3	0.3	0.3	0.3	0.3	0.3	0.3	0.3
2007	0.2	0.2	0.2	0.3	0.3	0.3	0.3	0.3	0.3	0.3	0.3	0.2	0.3
2008	0.2	0.2	0.2	0.2	0.3	0.3	0.3	0.3	0.3	0.3	0.2	0.2	0.3
2009	0.2	0.1	0.2	0.2	0.2	0.2	0.2	0.2	0.2	0.2	0.2	0.2	0.2
2010	0.1	0.1	0.1	0.2	0.2	0.2	0.2	0.2	0.2	0.2	0.2	0.2	0.2
2011	0.1	0.1	0.1	0.2	0.2	0.2	0.2	0.2	0.2	0.2	0.2	0.2	0.2
2012	0.1	0.1	0.2	0.2	0.2	0.2	0.2	0.2	0.2	0.2	0.2	0.2	0.2
2013	0.2	0.1	0.2	0.2	0.2	0.2	0.2	0.2	0.2	0.2	0.2	0.2	0.2
Construction													
2002	17.4	17.3	18.0	19.1	19.9	20.4	20.4	20.6	20.5	20.1	19.9	19.4	19.4
2003	17.2	16.6	17.3	19.6	21.1	21.8	22.8	23.0	23.0	22.7	22.4	21.5	20.8
2004	18.6	18.0	18.4	20.3	21.1	21.8	22.5	22.4	22.3	22.4	22.2	21.6	21.0
2005	18.8	18.3	18.6	21.3	22.3	23.4	23.5	23.6	23.5	22.8	23.1	22.2	21.8
2006	19.8	19.4	20.0	22.5	23.3	24.3	24.4	24.7	24.4	24.0	23.7	23.3	22.8
2007	21.0	19.9	20.4	21.6	22.8	23.4	23.6	23.4	23.0	22.8	22.5	21.4	22.2
2008	18.8	18.3	18.7	20.3	21.3	21.9	22.0	21.9	21.7	20.9	20.2	19.0	20.4
2009	16.4	15.9	15.9	17.1	17.8	18.0	18.2	18.2	17.8	17.6	17.1	16.3	17.2
2010	13.9	13.5	13.9	15.5	16.4	16.9	17.3	17.5	17.0	16.9	16.7	15.8	15.9
2011	13.6	13.0	13.4	15.0	15.9	16.6	17.2	17.1	16.8	16.8	16.8	16.2	15.7
2012	14.3	13.8	14.5	15.7	16.1	16.9	17.2	17.1	16.8	16.8	16.7	16.3	16.0
2013	14.1	13.7	14.3	15.5	16.5	16.9	17.3	17.3	17.2	17.4	17.2	15.9	16.1

1. Employment by Industry: Rhode Island, Selected Years, 2002–2013—*Continued*

(Numbers in thousands, not seasonally adjusted)

Industry and year	January	February	March	April	May	June	July	August	September	October	November	December	Annual average
Manufacturing													
2002	63.5	63.5	63.7	62.8	62.9	63.0	58.7	62.0	62.0	61.9	61.9	61.3	62.3
2003	60.1	59.6	59.5	59.4	59.0	59.0	55.5	58.1	58.6	58.4	58.5	58.2	58.7
2004	56.7	56.8	56.8	57.0	57.2	57.5	55.1	57.2	57.3	57.6	57.4	57.2	57.0
2005	55.8	55.7	55.7	55.5	55.4	55.4	52.6	54.8	54.8	54.5	54.4	54.3	54.9
2006	53.1	53.2	53.2	53.2	53.1	53.2	50.8	52.5	52.6	52.6	52.4	52.4	52.7
2007	51.4	51.5	51.3	51.1	51.1	51.1	48.8	50.6	50.8	50.7	50.3	50.1	50.7
2008	49.4	48.9	49.0	48.8	48.6	48.6	46.1	47.8	47.8	47.3	46.7	46.3	47.9
2009	44.3	43.0	42.4	42.0	41.7	41.7	40.3	41.1	41.2	41.3	41.2	41.0	41.8
2010	40.2	40.1	40.0	39.8	40.2	40.6	39.6	40.5	40.7	40.8	40.9	40.8	40.4
2011	40.3	40.3	40.4	40.4	40.4	40.6	39.5	40.1	40.0	39.9	39.8	39.7	40.1
2012	39.0	39.3	39.3	39.4	39.6	40.0	38.8	39.9	39.9	40.1	40.0	40.1	39.6
2013	39.6	39.4	39.7	39.8	39.9	40.2	39.0	40.2	40.3	40.6	40.8	40.7	40.0
Trade, Transportation, and Utilities													
2002	79.0	77.7	77.9	79.1	79.9	81.0	80.0	80.1	81.2	82.0	83.3	84.5	80.5
2003	79.6	78.5	78.6	79.3	80.4	81.3	80.2	80.4	81.3	81.9	83.4	84.3	80.8
2004	79.7	78.9	78.8	78.3	80.2	80.8	79.8	79.6	80.2	81.1	82.2	83.1	80.2
2005	78.9	78.3	78.3	79.3	79.9	80.7	79.8	80.0	80.1	80.7	82.1	83.1	80.1
2006	78.6	77.7	78.0	79.2	79.5	80.2	79.0	79.0	79.9	80.6	82.1	83.2	79.8
2007	79.1	78.0	78.2	78.9	79.8	80.7	79.8	79.6	79.7	79.8	81.2	82.2	79.8
2008	77.8	76.7	76.6	77.0	77.4	78.3	77.2	77.3	77.3	77.4	77.6	78.0	77.4
2009	73.8	72.8	72.4	71.8	73.1	73.7	72.8	72.6	73.3	73.5	74.4	75.0	73.3
2010	72.0	71.5	71.9	71.4	71.8	72.9	72.3	72.4	73.0	73.5	74.5	75.2	72.7
2011	72.2	71.7	71.9	72.8	73.7	74.4	73.5	73.7	74.5	74.9	76.2	77.1	73.9
2012	73.8	73.1	73.3	73.6	74.6	75.6	74.1	74.2	74.9	75.2	76.4	76.8	74.6
2013	72.7	72.2	72.0	72.7	73.8	74.5	73.9	74.0	74.6	74.6	75.5	76.6	73.9
Wholesale Trade													
2002	16.5	16.3	16.4	16.5	16.6	16.7	16.4	16.4	16.3	16.4	16.5	16.4	16.5
2003	16.4	16.2	16.3	16.4	16.6	16.7	16.5	16.4	16.4	16.4	16.4	16.3	16.4
2004	16.1	16.0	16.1	16.3	16.4	16.6	16.6	16.6	16.5	16.6	16.6	16.7	16.4
2005	16.3	16.4	16.5	16.8	16.9	17.0	16.9	17.0	16.9	16.9	16.9	17.0	16.8
2006	16.7	16.7	16.8	17.0	17.0	17.1	17.1	17.1	17.1	17.2	17.2	17.2	17.0
2007	17.0	16.9	16.9	17.2	17.3	17.4	17.4	17.3	17.1	17.2	17.3	17.4	17.2
2008	16.9	16.9	16.9	16.9	17.0	17.1	17.0	16.9	16.9	16.9	16.8	16.7	16.9
2009	16.3	16.2	16.1	16.0	16.0	16.1	15.9	15.9	15.9	16.0	15.9	16.0	16.0
2010	15.6	15.6	15.7	15.6	15.9	16.0	15.9	16.0	16.0	16.0	16.0	16.1	15.9
2011	15.8	15.8	15.9	16.1	16.3	16.5	16.5	16.6	16.7	16.7	16.8	16.9	16.4
2012	16.7	16.8	16.9	16.8	17.0	17.1	17.0	17.0	16.9	16.9	16.9	16.8	16.9
2013	16.5	16.4	16.5	16.5	16.7	16.7	16.7	16.8	16.8	16.8	16.7	16.9	16.7
Retail Trade													
2002	51.7	50.9	51.0	51.8	52.4	53.1	53.1	53.3	53.7	54.2	55.5	56.8	53.1
2003	52.4	51.5	51.3	51.8	52.4	53.1	52.9	53.3	53.3	54.0	55.5	56.5	53.2
2004	52.6	52.0	51.8	51.7	52.5	53.0	52.9	52.8	52.5	53.5	54.7	55.4	53.0
2005	52.1	51.4	51.3	51.7	52.0	52.5	52.2	52.2	51.9	52.6	54.0	54.8	52.4
2006	51.3	50.4	50.6	51.3	51.4	51.8	51.4	51.3	51.4	52.1	53.6	54.6	51.8
2007	51.3	50.5	50.7	50.7	51.3	51.9	51.7	51.6	51.1	51.2	52.5	53.2	51.5
2008	50.1	49.1	49.0	49.1	49.3	49.9	49.6	49.6	49.1	49.5	50.0	50.2	49.5
2009	47.3	46.5	46.3	45.9	46.9	47.3	47.3	47.0	46.9	47.2	48.1	48.5	47.1
2010	46.5	46.0	46.3	45.6	45.6	46.3	46.5	46.6	46.2	46.7	47.7	48.0	46.5
2011	46.0	45.5	45.6	46.1	46.6	46.9	46.8	47.1	46.7	47.2	48.4	48.8	46.8
2012	46.4	45.7	45.8	46.1	46.7	47.3	46.9	46.9	46.8	47.2	48.3	48.5	46.9
2013	45.8	45.3	45.0	45.5	46.2	46.8	46.9	46.8	46.6	46.7	47.6	48.1	46.4
Transportation and Utilities													
2002	10.8	10.5	10.5	10.8	10.9	11.2	10.5	10.4	11.2	11.4	11.3	11.3	10.9
2003	10.8	10.8	11.0	11.1	11.4	11.5	10.8	10.7	11.6	11.5	11.5	11.5	11.2
2004	11.0	10.9	10.9	10.3	11.3	11.2	10.3	10.2	11.2	11.0	10.9	11.0	10.9
2005	10.5	10.5	10.5	10.8	11.0	11.2	10.7	10.8	11.3	11.2	11.2	11.3	10.9
2006	10.6	10.6	10.6	10.9	11.1	11.3	10.5	10.6	11.4	11.3	11.3	11.4	11.0
2007	10.8	10.6	10.6	11.0	11.2	11.4	10.7	10.7	11.5	11.4	11.4	11.6	11.1
2008	10.8	10.7	10.7	11.0	11.1	11.3	10.6	10.8	11.3	11.0	10.8	11.1	10.9
2009	10.2	10.1	10.0	9.9	10.2	10.3	9.6	9.7	10.5	10.3	10.4	10.5	10.1
2010	9.9	9.9	9.9	10.2	10.3	10.6	9.9	9.8	10.8	10.8	10.8	11.1	10.3
2011	10.4	10.4	10.4	10.6	10.8	11.0	10.2	10.0	11.1	11.0	11.0	11.4	10.7
2012	10.7	10.6	10.6	10.7	10.9	11.2	10.2	10.3	11.2	11.1	11.2	11.5	10.9
2013	10.4	10.5	10.5	10.7	10.9	11.0	10.3	10.4	11.2	11.1	11.2	11.6	10.8
Information													
2002	11.3	11.2	11.3	11.2	11.2	11.3	11.3	11.2	11.2	10.9	11.1	11.2	11.2
2003	11.1	11.1	11.1	11.0	11.0	11.2	11.0	11.0	10.8	11.0	11.0	10.9	11.0
2004	11.1	11.0	11.1	11.1	11.0	10.9	10.7	10.7	10.6	10.6	10.6	10.6	10.8
2005	10.8	10.8	10.7	10.7	10.7	10.7	10.8	10.8	10.7	10.8	10.9	11.0	10.8
2006	11.0	10.9	11.0	11.3	11.3	11.4	10.8	10.7	10.7	10.6	10.8	10.9	11.0
2007	10.5	10.4	10.5	10.5	10.6	10.6	10.6	10.7	10.6	10.5	10.8	10.8	10.6
2008	10.6	10.9	10.9	10.8	10.6	10.9	10.6	11.0	10.8	10.8	10.5	10.4	10.7
2009	10.4	10.3	10.2	10.3	10.4	10.4	10.0	10.0	9.9	9.7	9.9	9.9	10.1
2010	9.8	9.8	9.9	9.9	9.8	9.8	9.8	9.9	10.2	10.2	10.2	10.2	10.0
2011	9.8	9.8	10.0	10.5	10.7	10.5	10.4	9.5	10.1	10.0	10.0	10.2	10.1
2012	9.9	9.9	10.0	9.8	9.6	9.7	9.5	9.6	9.3	9.2	9.2	9.3	9.6
2013	9.2	9.3	9.1	8.9	9.1	9.1	9.0	9.1	8.9	8.8	8.9	8.8	9.0

1. Employment by Industry: Rhode Island, Selected Years, 2002–2013—*Continued*

(Numbers in thousands, not seasonally adjusted)

Industry and year	January	February	March	April	May	June	July	August	September	October	November	December	Annual average
Financial Activities													
2002	32.3	32.3	32.2	32.6	32.6	32.9	33.3	33.2	33.1	33.2	33.3	33.6	32.9
2003	33.1	33.2	33.5	33.2	33.5	33.9	34.0	34.0	33.8	33.8	33.9	34.1	33.7
2004	33.8	33.8	33.8	33.9	34.2	34.3	34.2	34.2	34.0	34.1	34.1	34.1	34.0
2005	33.7	33.8	33.8	34.3	34.3	34.5	34.7	34.7	34.5	34.2	34.3	34.6	34.3
2006	34.2	34.1	34.4	34.5	34.8	34.9	35.2	35.6	35.7	35.6	35.7	36.1	35.1
2007	35.2	35.3	35.2	35.3	35.4	35.3	35.0	34.7	34.6	34.1	34.1	34.0	34.9
2008	33.6	33.7	33.5	33.4	33.5	33.5	33.3	33.2	33.3	32.4	32.3	32.3	33.2
2009	31.9	31.9	31.6	31.2	31.3	31.5	31.3	30.9	30.7	30.7	30.9	30.8	31.2
2010	30.3	30.4	30.6	30.4	30.5	30.6	30.8	30.7	30.8	31.0	31.0	31.1	30.7
2011	30.5	30.6	30.6	30.7	30.6	31.2	30.8	30.8	30.9	30.8	31.1	31.0	30.8
2012	30.8	31.0	31.2	31.3	31.6	31.8	31.8	31.8	31.8	31.9	31.9	32.0	31.6
2013	31.7	31.9	32.2	32.3	32.3	32.6	32.7	32.5	32.3	32.1	32.1	32.1	32.2
Professional and Business Services													
2002	47.2	47.0	47.7	49.4	49.4	50.1	48.9	49.3	49.7	49.7	49.4	48.8	48.9
2003	46.4	46.5	47.0	49.2	49.8	50.9	50.9	51.5	51.4	52.2	52.0	52.0	50.0
2004	49.9	50.3	50.9	53.2	53.7	54.5	54.3	55.0	55.4	55.6	55.2	54.7	53.6
2005	51.8	52.2	52.7	55.2	55.3	55.9	56.2	56.9	57.2	56.2	56.2	55.8	55.1
2006	52.6	53.0	53.6	56.6	56.8	57.9	56.9	57.8	58.7	58.4	57.8	57.3	56.5
2007	54.3	54.0	54.3	56.4	56.9	58.0	56.8	56.8	56.6	56.2	56.0	55.7	56.0
2008	53.2	52.9	53.1	55.2	55.3	56.2	55.4	55.5	55.9	55.5	54.8	53.6	54.7
2009	51.1	51.0	51.1	52.5	52.7	53.5	53.0	53.2	53.4	53.3	53.2	52.5	52.5
2010	50.1	50.2	51.1	54.0	54.2	54.9	54.4	54.5	54.6	54.8	54.6	53.6	53.4
2011	51.5	51.8	52.2	54.2	54.6	55.2	54.9	55.3	55.7	55.9	55.7	54.5	54.3
2012	52.8	53.1	54.1	56.1	56.6	57.5	56.9	57.2	57.2	57.1	57.2	57.1	56.1
2013	55.0	55.6	56.1	58.4	59.0	60.3	59.5	60.0	60.1	60.4	60.2	59.2	58.7
Education and Health Services													
2002	85.6	87.7	88.7	88.9	89.1	84.6	84.0	85.1	88.4	90.3	91.5	92.2	88.0
2003	89.6	91.6	92.6	93.0	93.2	88.0	87.1	86.6	90.3	92.6	93.4	93.7	91.0
2004	90.8	93.3	94.4	95.0	95.2	89.9	89.1	88.9	92.7	94.6	95.4	95.9	92.9
2005	92.7	95.2	96.2	96.7	96.6	92.5	92.0	91.7	96.0	97.9	98.5	97.8	95.3
2006	94.0	97.4	98.6	99.2	98.2	93.9	92.6	92.5	96.2	98.9	99.7	99.2	96.7
2007	96.0	99.4	100.3	100.4	100.3	96.1	94.6	94.4	98.2	100.3	101.0	100.4	98.5
2008	97.0	100.5	101.3	101.1	100.8	96.3	94.8	95.0	98.5	101.1	101.5	101.5	99.1
2009	97.8	101.1	101.5	101.3	101.0	97.2	96.0	95.8	99.5	102.4	103.1	102.7	100.0
2010	99.8	102.2	102.9	102.8	102.8	98.1	97.8	97.8	101.6	103.1	103.8	104.1	101.4
2011	99.7	102.8	103.7	104.4	104.3	99.7	98.8	98.3	101.7	104.7	104.9	104.2	102.3
2012	100.7	104.7	104.9	104.1	104.6	100.0	98.7	99.0	104.7	105.8	105.6	106.4	103.3
2013	103.3	105.5	106.3	106.0	105.5	102.3	100.2	99.7	104.9	107.5	107.8	105.0	104.5
Leisure and Hospitality													
2002	41.7	42.3	43.4	46.6	49.6	52.7	53.9	53.5	51.0	48.5	46.8	45.8	48.0
2003	43.3	43.4	44.0	47.1	50.4	53.1	55.2	54.6	52.3	49.6	47.9	47.2	49.0
2004	43.6	44.1	44.3	47.7	51.2	54.4	55.8	55.5	53.4	50.7	49.0	48.5	49.9
2005	44.7	45.4	45.8	48.8	51.4	55.1	55.8	55.3	53.2	50.5	48.8	48.1	50.2
2006	44.4	44.5	45.6	48.7	51.1	54.8	55.6	55.5	53.7	50.7	48.9	48.6	50.2
2007	45.5	46.0	46.7	49.6	52.4	56.4	57.1	56.7	54.6	52.6	50.0	49.5	51.4
2008	45.9	46.4	46.7	49.7	53.0	55.8	55.9	55.5	53.7	51.2	49.4	48.7	51.0
2009	43.6	44.1	44.4	46.8	51.0	53.6	53.8	54.0	52.3	49.5	47.2	47.0	48.9
2010	43.6	44.0	44.4	47.6	50.8	54.3	55.5	55.2	53.1	50.0	48.3	47.3	49.5
2011	44.0	44.6	45.0	48.1	51.1	55.0	56.1	55.8	53.8	50.9	48.9	48.2	50.1
2012	45.2	46.2	46.8	49.8	53.1	56.9	57.6	57.6	55.4	52.5	50.4	49.9	51.8
2013	46.8	47.2	48.2	51.4	54.6	58.9	59.7	59.4	57.2	54.2	51.9	51.5	53.4
Other Services													
2002	21.1	21.1	21.2	21.5	21.8	22.4	22.7	22.6	22.1	22.3	22.3	22.6	22.0
2003	22.2	22.2	22.4	22.8	23.1	23.5	23.8	23.6	23.1	23.0	23.3	23.4	23.0
2004	22.7	22.8	22.9	23.1	23.4	23.7	24.0	23.8	23.3	23.5	23.6	23.5	23.4
2005	22.9	22.9	23.1	23.1	23.4	23.7	24.0	24.0	23.1	23.0	23.1	23.0	23.3
2006	22.2	22.2	22.4	22.9	23.1	23.6	23.7	23.6	23.1	23.3	23.3	23.2	23.1
2007	22.6	22.7	22.8	23.0	23.3	23.9	23.8	23.6	23.0	23.1	23.1	23.2	23.2
2008	22.4	22.5	22.5	22.7	22.9	23.2	23.4	23.2	22.7	22.7	22.6	22.5	22.8
2009	21.8	21.9	21.9	22.1	22.2	22.5	22.8	22.6	21.9	22.2	22.2	22.1	22.2
2010	21.5	21.6	21.6	21.7	22.0	22.2	23.0	22.9	22.1	22.0	22.2	22.1	22.1
2011	21.5	21.7	21.7	22.1	22.3	22.9	23.7	23.5	22.5	22.3	22.4	22.4	22.4
2012	21.8	21.9	21.9	22.2	22.4	23.0	23.4	23.4	22.9	22.5	22.5	22.7	22.6
2013	22.0	22.0	22.2	22.4	22.6	23.1	23.4	23.2	22.6	22.5	22.4	21.9	22.5
Government													
2002	66.7	66.8	67.1	67.2	67.7	66.7	61.9	61.7	65.3	66.9	67.4	67.6	66.1
2003	67.1	67.1	67.4	67.2	67.7	67.8	62.0	62.1	65.7	66.7	66.8	66.9	66.2
2004	66.1	66.3	66.9	66.2	67.0	66.7	62.0	61.8	65.2	65.9	66.5	65.8	65.5
2005	65.5	65.8	65.9	65.8	66.1	65.9	61.5	60.7	64.1	65.8	66.1	65.9	64.9
2006	65.4	65.9	65.9	65.6	65.8	65.6	61.3	61.0	64.7	65.7	66.4	66.0	64.9
2007	65.2	65.4	65.3	65.3	66.0	64.9	61.5	61.2	63.9	64.7	64.8	65.0	64.4
2008	64.6	64.5	64.9	64.8	65.5	64.5	60.2	59.5	62.4	63.1	64.0	63.7	63.5
2009	63.0	63.3	63.2	63.4	63.7	63.0	57.8	57.5	61.3	62.8	62.8	62.8	62.1
2010	62.3	62.3	62.7	62.7	64.8	63.1	58.5	58.2	60.5	61.6	62.1	61.9	61.7
2011	61.4	61.4	61.8	61.8	62.0	61.6	56.6	56.8	59.9	61.0	61.2	61.2	60.6
2012	60.6	60.9	61.0	61.2	61.8	60.5	56.2	56.6	59.7	60.8	61.1	61.1	60.1
2013	60.5	60.5	61.0	61.0	61.8	60.8	56.9	56.8	59.8	60.9	61.2	61.1	60.2

2. Average Weekly Hours by Selected Industry: Rhode Island, 2009–2013

(Not seasonally adjusted)

Industry and year	January	February	March	April	May	June	July	August	September	October	November	December	Annual average
Total Private													
2009	33.5	33.8	33.6	33.8	33.7	33.6	33.9	34.0	34.0	34.0	34.1	34.1	33.9
2010	33.9	33.6	34.1	34.2	34.4	34.0	34.2	34.0	33.8	33.7	33.4	33.7	33.9
2011	33.0	33.3	33.2	33.1	33.3	32.9	33.1	32.9	33.0	33.0	32.9	32.9	33.0
2012	33.1	32.9	33.1	33.1	33.2	33.2	33.4	33.1	33.4	32.9	32.7	33.1	33.1
2013	32.7	32.5	32.9	33.0	33.1	33.1	33.2	33.0	33.1	32.7	32.8	32.9	32.9
Goods-Producing													
2009	36.4	36.3	36.0	35.9	35.7	35.6	36.0	35.9	35.8	36.1	35.7	36.7	36.0
2010	35.6	35.1	36.3	36.4	37.2	36.9	37.0	36.8	37.0	37.0	37.0	37.4	36.7
2011	36.6	36.4	36.7	36.9	37.3	37.1	36.8	36.3	36.5	36.5	37.1	38.2	36.9
2012	37.9	38.1	37.8	38.4	38.0	38.6	38.2	37.8	39.4	38.5	38.5	39.9	38.4
2013	38.7	38.3	38.8	39.2	39.3	39.6	39.3	38.7	39.6	38.7	38.6	38.9	39.0
Construction													
2009	33.9	34.0	34.3	35.1	35.9	34.8	36.8	36.4	36.2	35.6	35.5	36.0	35.4
2010	34.9	34.4	35.0	34.9	36.1	35.9	36.4	36.0	35.6	35.6	35.3	35.6	35.5
2011	34.9	35.1	35.4	35.0	35.9	36.0	36.6	35.7	36.3	36.1	37.3	38.5	36.1
2012	35.6	36.8	37.5	37.5	36.8	38.0	38.6	37.3	38.1	35.4	36.6	36.9	37.1
2013	35.2	34.4	36.1	37.0	37.0	36.7	37.1	36.3	37.1	37.4	36.5	36.4	36.5
Manufacturing													
2009	38.7	38.3	38.0	37.3	36.9	37.4	37.4	38.4	38.2	38.5	37.9	38.6	38.0
2010	37.5	37.1	38.5	38.5	38.9	38.4	38.2	38.2	38.6	38.6	38.6	38.5	38.3
2011	38.1	38.4	38.5	38.8	38.9	38.6	37.9	37.5	37.5	38.0	38.3	38.9	38.3
2012	39.2	39.0	38.3	39.0	38.6	39.0	38.3	38.2	39.3	39.0	38.7	40.4	38.9
2013	39.4	39.1	39.1	39.3	39.5	40.1	39.5	39.0	40.0	40.1	40.2	40.5	39.7
Trade, Transportation, and Utilities													
2009	34.2	34.6	34.0	34.2	34.5	34.5	34.9	35.6	34.6	35.1	35.7	35.2	34.8
2010	34.9	35.3	35.5	36.6	36.8	36.2	36.3	36.0	35.3	35.4	35.2	35.4	35.7
2011	34.8	35.2	35.4	34.9	35.2	34.9	34.9	34.7	34.7	33.8	33.4	34.4	34.7
2012	33.5	33.5	34.4	34.4	34.6	35.1	35.0	34.5	34.4	34.1	34.1	34.6	34.3
2013	33.4	33.4	34.6	34.6	34.6	34.2	34.7	34.5	34.1	34.1	34.2	34.4	34.2
Professional and Business Services													
2009	36.1	36.1	35.7	36.4	36.5	36.7	37.1	37.2	37.2	37.3	36.9	36.0	36.6
2010	35.7	35.3	35.6	36.1	36.6	36.4	36.0	36.0	36.1	36.3	36.3	36.1	36.1
2011	35.6	35.9	36.0	35.8	35.7	36.0	36.0	36.1	36.0	35.6	35.2	35.7	35.8
2012	35.4	35.6	35.9	35.0	36.0	35.7	35.6	36.3	36.2	35.8	36.1	36.0	35.8
2013	35.8	35.5	35.0	35.0	35.0	34.6	34.5	34.1	34.5	33.7	33.6	33.3	34.5
Education and Health Services													
2009	32.2	32.8	33.2	33.4	33.8	34.2	34.1	33.9	33.9	33.7	34.1	32.9	33.5
2010	32.9	32.6	32.2	32.0	32.0	31.4	31.9	31.4	31.5	31.8	31.7	31.4	31.9
2011	31.1	31.7	31.5	31.3	31.2	31.1	31.0	30.7	30.5	31.2	31.3	30.7	31.1
2012	30.4	30.4	30.3	30.5	30.4	30.0	30.2	29.9	30.1	30.4	29.7	29.9	30.2
2013	30.3	30.1	30.2	30.4	30.7	30.5	31.0	31.2	30.9	31.1	31.3	31.3	30.8
Leisure and Hospitality													
2009	24.4	24.7	24.9	26.0	26.1	25.9	26.8	27.3	26.6	26.1	26.2	26.3	26.0
2010	26.4	25.9	26.1	26.5	26.5	26.2	26.9	26.3	25.6	25.7	25.6	25.8	26.1
2011	25.3	25.8	25.4	25.9	26.1	25.8	26.8	26.8	25.7	25.6	25.4	25.3	25.9
2012	25.2	25.0	24.3	25.2	25.5	25.8	27.1	26.9	26.4	25.4	24.9	24.8	25.6
2013	24.1	24.1	25.1	25.2	25.5	25.7	26.7	26.7	25.7	25.5	25.6	24.8	25.4

3. Average Hourly Earnings by Selected Industry: Rhode Island, 2009–2013

(Dollars, not seasonally adjusted)

Industry and year	January	February	March	April	May	June	July	August	September	October	November	December	Annual average
Total Private													
2009	22.81	22.63	22.98	22.64	22.49	22.35	22.19	22.31	22.36	22.44	22.58	22.52	22.52
2010	22.42	22.66	22.50	22.41	22.52	22.64	22.60	22.70	22.78	22.90	22.90	22.95	22.67
2011	23.04	22.96	23.13	23.06	23.40	23.41	23.88	24.02	24.12	24.49	24.66	24.46	23.73
2012	25.34	24.99	25.14	25.21	25.01	24.63	24.95	24.62	24.91	24.82	24.89	25.53	25.00
2013	25.66	25.76	25.62	25.56	25.29	25.06	25.13	25.07	25.40	25.37	25.45	25.70	25.42
Goods-Producing													
2009	22.74	22.51	22.54	23.19	23.33	23.28	23.79	24.04	23.75	23.80	23.93	23.74	23.38
2010	24.04	24.08	23.94	24.13	24.23	24.33	24.35	24.45	24.42	24.52	24.51	24.38	24.29
2011	24.42	24.41	24.58	24.55	24.69	24.79	25.64	25.78	25.40	25.42	25.48	25.74	25.09
2012	25.56	25.11	25.16	25.10	25.04	24.68	25.31	25.00	25.06	24.89	25.22	25.08	25.10
2013	25.22	25.35	25.64	25.60	25.51	25.54	26.01	26.28	26.17	27.00	27.25	26.71	26.04
Construction													
2009	26.06	26.54	27.05	27.29	27.38	26.95	27.27	27.63	27.56	27.54	27.40	27.42	27.20
2010	27.64	27.73	27.76	27.61	27.67	27.56	27.59	27.67	27.73	27.83	27.78	27.70	27.69
2011	27.70	27.73	28.33	28.42	28.02	28.02	28.17	28.62	28.03	28.17	28.69	28.77	28.24
2012	28.65	28.89	28.54	28.67	28.56	27.95	28.49	28.13	29.05	28.43	29.07	28.75	28.59
2013	29.26	29.25	28.93	28.96	28.87	29.08	29.24	29.60	29.35	29.66	29.86	30.21	29.37
Manufacturing													
2009	20.96	21.15	21.00	21.56	21.80	21.63	22.13	22.19	22.20	22.28	22.36	22.04	21.76
2010	22.08	21.97	21.80	22.00	22.09	22.17	22.18	22.20	22.03	22.08	22.13	22.17	22.08
2011	22.26	22.20	22.41	22.61	22.94	23.08	23.98	24.14	24.19	24.27	24.16	24.48	23.38
2012	24.63	24.14	24.11	23.84	23.83	23.46	24.00	23.70	23.52	23.65	23.92	24.00	23.90
2013	24.10	24.29	24.68	24.58	24.45	24.42	24.93	25.15	25.08	25.21	25.60	25.27	24.82
Trade, Transportation, and Utilities													
2009	19.51	19.81	20.24	19.68	19.51	19.46	19.19	19.70	20.04	20.07	20.26	20.04	19.79
2010	19.56	19.87	19.80	19.65	19.76	19.70	19.74	19.78	19.87	19.94	19.90	19.86	19.79
2011	19.95	19.96	20.41	20.02	20.23	20.41	20.29	20.72	20.74	21.23	20.99	20.86	20.49
2012	20.74	20.67	20.54	20.64	20.74	20.61	20.82	20.93	20.69	20.59	20.97	21.12	20.76
2013	21.16	21.24	21.50	21.52	21.27	21.23	21.35	21.38	21.19	20.91	21.32	20.92	21.25
Professional and Business Services													
2009	29.10	29.13	28.50	27.88	27.72	27.56	27.00	26.88	26.79	26.83	26.86	27.03	27.58
2010	27.06	27.12	27.27	27.13	27.20	27.27	27.32	27.45	27.44	27.50	27.54	27.59	27.33
2011	27.69	27.64	27.66	27.31	28.08	28.24	29.85	29.48	29.64	29.95	30.65	30.32	28.90
2012	31.28	30.53	30.87	30.68	30.14	29.52	30.29	30.25	30.72	30.33	29.82	30.26	30.38
2013	30.63	30.52	30.42	30.01	30.10	29.15	29.71	29.44	29.42	29.56	29.60	30.32	29.90
Education and Health Services													
2009	23.41	23.91	23.73	23.69	23.70	23.24	23.04	23.17	23.26	23.34	23.40	24.08	23.50
2010	23.26	23.39	23.14	23.06	23.24	23.32	23.25	23.21	23.20	23.23	23.25	23.35	23.24
2011	23.34	23.36	23.37	23.51	23.34	23.16	23.29	23.24	23.51	23.27	23.55	23.51	23.37
2012	23.78	23.51	23.22	23.10	22.95	23.32	23.56	23.58	23.24	23.25	23.42	23.89	23.40
2013	23.55	23.36	23.30	23.16	22.83	23.02	23.18	22.99	23.35	23.04	22.93	23.47	23.18
Leisure and Hospitality													
2009	15.39	15.49	15.63	15.23	15.25	15.06	14.59	14.42	14.49	14.42	14.47	14.57	14.89
2010	14.50	14.41	14.43	14.16	14.09	14.03	13.98	13.93	13.87	13.91	13.88	13.89	14.08
2011	13.92	13.90	13.99	13.97	13.98	13.89	13.62	13.77	13.92	13.96	14.32	14.09	13.94
2012	13.83	13.78	14.01	13.96	13.98	13.62	13.42	13.29	14.14	14.04	13.91	14.03	13.82
2013	13.87	14.19	14.03	14.06	14.14	13.88	13.77	13.67	14.08	14.22	14.03	14.23	14.00

4. Average Weekly Earnings by Selected Industry: Rhode Island, 2009–2013

(Dollars, not seasonally adjusted)

Industry and year	January	February	March	April	May	June	July	August	September	October	November	December	Annual average
Total Private													
2009	764.14	764.89	772.13	765.23	757.91	750.96	752.24	758.54	760.24	762.96	769.98	767.93	763.43
2010	760.04	761.38	767.25	766.42	774.69	769.76	772.92	771.80	769.96	771.73	764.86	773.42	768.51
2011	760.32	764.57	767.92	763.29	779.22	770.19	790.43	790.26	795.96	808.17	811.31	804.73	783.09
2012	838.75	822.17	832.13	834.45	830.33	817.72	833.33	814.92	831.99	816.58	813.90	845.04	827.50
2013	839.08	837.20	842.90	843.48	837.10	829.49	834.32	827.31	840.74	829.60	834.76	845.53	836.32
Goods-Producing													
2009	827.74	817.11	811.44	832.52	832.88	828.77	856.44	863.04	850.25	859.18	854.30	871.26	841.68
2010	855.82	845.21	869.02	878.33	901.36	897.78	900.95	899.76	903.54	907.24	906.87	911.81	891.44
2011	893.77	888.52	902.09	905.90	920.94	919.71	943.55	935.81	927.10	927.83	945.31	983.27	925.82
2012	968.72	956.69	951.05	963.84	951.52	952.65	966.84	945.00	987.36	958.27	970.97	1,000.69	963.84
2013	976.01	970.91	994.83	1,003.52	1,002.54	1,011.38	1,022.19	1,017.04	1,036.33	1,044.90	1,051.85	1,039.02	1,015.56
Construction													
2009	883.43	902.36	927.82	957.88	982.94	937.86	1,003.54	1,005.73	997.67	980.42	972.70	987.12	962.88
2010	964.64	953.91	971.60	963.59	998.89	989.40	1,004.28	996.12	987.19	990.75	980.63	986.12	983.00
2011	966.73	973.32	1,002.88	994.70	1,005.92	1,008.72	1,031.02	1,021.73	1,017.49	1,016.94	1,070.14	1,107.65	1,019.46
2012	1,019.94	1,063.15	1,070.25	1,075.13	1,051.01	1,062.10	1,099.71	1,049.25	1,106.81	1,006.42	1,063.96	1,060.88	1,060.69
2013	1,029.95	1,006.20	1,044.37	1,071.52	1,068.19	1,067.24	1,084.80	1,074.48	1,088.89	1,109.28	1,089.89	1,099.64	1,072.01
Manufacturing													
2009	811.15	810.05	798.00	804.19	804.42	808.96	827.66	852.10	848.04	857.78	847.44	850.74	826.88
2010	828.00	815.09	839.30	847.00	859.30	851.33	847.28	848.04	850.36	852.29	854.22	853.55	845.66
2011	848.11	852.48	862.79	877.27	892.37	890.89	908.84	905.25	907.13	922.26	925.33	952.27	895.45
2012	965.50	941.46	923.41	929.76	919.84	914.94	919.20	905.34	924.34	922.35	925.70	969.60	929.71
2013	949.54	949.74	964.99	965.99	965.78	979.24	984.74	980.85	1,003.20	1,010.92	1,029.12	1,023.44	985.35
Trade, Transportation, and Utilities													
2009	667.24	685.43	688.16	673.06	673.10	671.37	669.73	701.32	693.38	704.46	723.28	705.41	688.69
2010	682.64	701.41	702.90	719.19	727.17	713.14	716.56	712.08	701.41	705.88	700.48	703.04	706.50
2011	694.26	702.59	722.51	698.70	712.10	712.31	708.12	718.98	719.68	717.57	701.07	717.58	711.00
2012	694.79	692.45	706.58	710.02	717.60	723.41	728.70	722.09	711.74	702.12	715.08	730.75	712.07
2013	706.74	709.42	743.90	744.59	735.94	726.07	740.85	737.61	722.58	713.03	729.14	719.65	726.75
Professional and Business Services													
2009	1,050.51	1,051.59	1,017.45	1,014.83	1,011.78	1,011.45	1,001.70	999.94	996.59	1,000.76	991.13	973.08	1,009.43
2010	966.04	957.34	970.81	979.39	995.52	992.63	983.52	988.20	990.58	998.25	999.70	996.00	986.61
2011	985.76	992.28	995.76	977.70	1,002.46	1,016.64	1,074.60	1,064.23	1,067.04	1,066.22	1,078.88	1,082.42	1,034.62
2012	1,107.31	1,086.87	1,108.23	1,073.80	1,085.04	1,053.86	1,078.32	1,098.08	1,112.06	1,085.81	1,076.50	1,089.36	1,087.60
2013	1,096.55	1,083.46	1,064.70	1,050.35	1,053.50	1,008.59	1,025.00	1,003.90	1,014.99	996.17	994.56	1,009.66	1,031.55
Education and Health Services													
2009	753.80	784.25	787.84	791.25	801.06	794.81	785.66	785.46	788.51	786.56	797.94	792.23	787.25
2010	765.25	762.51	745.11	737.92	743.68	732.25	741.68	728.79	730.80	738.71	737.03	733.19	741.36
2011	725.87	740.51	736.16	735.86	728.21	720.28	721.99	713.47	717.06	726.02	737.12	721.76	726.81
2012	722.91	714.70	703.57	704.55	697.68	699.60	711.51	705.04	699.52	706.80	695.57	714.31	706.68
2013	713.57	703.14	703.66	704.06	700.88	702.11	718.58	717.29	721.52	716.54	717.71	734.61	713.94
Leisure and Hospitality													
2009	375.52	382.60	389.19	395.98	398.03	390.05	391.01	393.67	385.43	376.36	379.11	383.19	387.14
2010	382.80	373.22	376.62	375.24	373.39	367.59	376.06	366.36	355.07	357.49	355.33	358.36	367.49
2011	352.18	358.62	355.35	361.82	364.88	358.36	365.02	369.04	357.74	357.38	363.73	356.48	361.05
2012	348.52	344.50	340.44	351.79	356.49	351.40	363.68	357.50	373.30	356.62	346.36	347.94	353.79
2013	334.27	341.98	352.15	354.31	360.57	356.72	367.66	364.99	361.86	362.61	359.17	352.90	355.60

SOUTH CAROLINA
At a Glance

Population:
  2000 census: 4,012,023
  2010 census: 4,625,364
  2013 estimate: 4,774,839

Percent change in population:
  2000–2010: 15.3%
  2010–2013: 3.2%

Percent change in total nonfarm employment:
  2000–2010: -3.0%
  2010–2013: 5.0%

Industry with the largest growth in employment, 2000–2013 (thousands):
  Education and Health Services, 62.2

Industry with the largest decline or smallest growth in employment, 2000–2013 (thousands):
  Manufacturing, -111.3

Civilian labor force:
  2000: 1,988,159
  2010: 2,165,665
  2013: 2,181,639

Unemployment rate and rank among states (lowest to highest):
  2000: 3.6%, 20th
  2010: 11.1%, 46th
  2013: 7.6%, 35th

Over-the-year change in unemployment rates:
  2010–2011: -0.8%
  2011–2012: -1.3%
  2012–2013: -1.4%

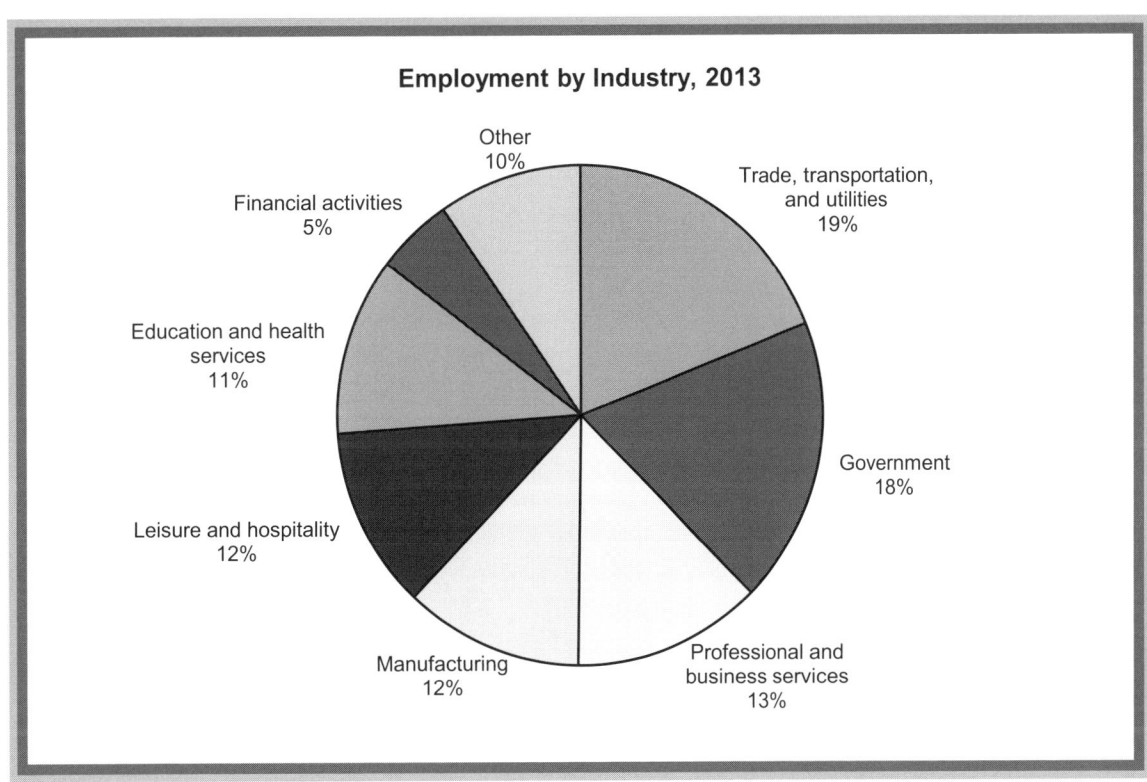

Employment by Industry, 2013

Other 10%
Financial activities 5%
Education and health services 11%
Leisure and hospitality 12%
Manufacturing 12%
Professional and business services 13%
Government 18%
Trade, transportation, and utilities 19%

1. Employment by Industry: South Carolina, Selected Years, 2002–2013

(Numbers in thousands, not seasonally adjusted)

Industry and year	January	February	March	April	May	June	July	August	September	October	November	December	Annual average
Total Nonfarm													
2002	1,759.3	1,767.4	1,790.8	1,809.3	1,820.4	1,820.0	1,792.1	1,804.2	1,811.9	1,812.6	1,812.0	1,812.9	1,801.1
2003	1,774.4	1,784.0	1,802.7	1,809.5	1,818.9	1,812.0	1,792.7	1,802.3	1,812.5	1,812.4	1,812.3	1,816.5	1,804.2
2004	1,778.7	1,785.1	1,812.3	1,832.4	1,844.6	1,841.8	1,824.3	1,833.0	1,844.2	1,850.8	1,855.9	1,856.6	1,830.0
2005	1,818.2	1,828.3	1,842.4	1,866.3	1,876.6	1,859.8	1,859.8	1,871.2	1,877.0	1,884.9	1,893.5	1,883.9	1,863.5
2006	1,857.1	1,872.2	1,895.2	1,912.8	1,921.7	1,896.2	1,883.4	1,893.0	1,908.1	1,930.1	1,933.9	1,942.2	1,903.8
2007	1,902.0	1,910.6	1,936.1	1,944.2	1,957.3	1,959.3	1,932.4	1,941.5	1,954.6	1,952.9	1,957.6	1,956.6	1,942.1
2008	1,916.6	1,923.8	1,941.0	1,944.5	1,957.9	1,946.3	1,912.1	1,912.9	1,922.3	1,911.4	1,903.4	1,888.6	1,923.4
2009	1,825.5	1,817.0	1,823.3	1,827.2	1,831.8	1,818.2	1,794.8	1,796.0	1,799.5	1,798.9	1,800.3	1,794.7	1,810.6
2010	1,758.1	1,764.9	1,785.1	1,813.1	1,833.8	1,824.2	1,808.5	1,812.4	1,815.4	1,818.7	1,822.4	1,822.6	1,806.6
2011	1,775.3	1,791.0	1,813.3	1,837.1	1,846.4	1,841.1	1,824.3	1,830.9	1,837.8	1,837.7	1,844.8	1,842.3	1,826.8
2012	1,808.4	1,824.3	1,849.4	1,863.1	1,875.2	1,872.9	1,850.9	1,857.2	1,867.0	1,870.8	1,886.8	1,883.2	1,859.1
2013	1,842.0	1,857.3	1,877.7	1,897.1	1,911.8	1,908.0	1,891.0	1,896.7	1,911.2	1,919.2	1,923.9	1,923.2	1,896.6
Total Private													
2002	1,431.8	1,439.8	1,459.9	1,478.0	1,488.8	1,500.7	1,489.1	1,490.3	1,481.0	1,479.0	1,476.0	1,475.7	1,474.2
2003	1,444.1	1,452.2	1,468.2	1,474.9	1,485.5	1,492.5	1,487.4	1,491.3	1,482.3	1,480.6	1,479.2	1,481.4	1,476.6
2004	1,450.2	1,458.2	1,481.6	1,500.6	1,513.3	1,523.8	1,522.8	1,522.3	1,514.5	1,517.8	1,521.6	1,521.1	1,504.0
2005	1,489.1	1,499.2	1,509.9	1,533.0	1,543.6	1,538.5	1,554.3	1,558.8	1,542.0	1,546.9	1,553.1	1,542.3	1,534.2
2006	1,524.1	1,538.2	1,555.2	1,572.8	1,581.8	1,574.9	1,576.8	1,579.9	1,574.1	1,589.1	1,592.4	1,598.5	1,571.5
2007	1,563.9	1,572.6	1,593.7	1,603.0	1,615.4	1,627.6	1,617.4	1,618.6	1,610.4	1,604.2	1,605.9	1,604.6	1,603.1
2008	1,568.8	1,576.0	1,590.0	1,592.4	1,603.9	1,603.1	1,588.4	1,587.5	1,570.3	1,554.7	1,544.6	1,529.5	1,575.8
2009	1,474.2	1,467.4	1,470.9	1,472.8	1,478.0	1,476.3	1,467.4	1,464.2	1,452.0	1,446.3	1,446.5	1,440.3	1,463.0
2010	1,409.1	1,416.4	1,432.7	1,459.6	1,470.3	1,477.9	1,478.4	1,479.2	1,469.8	1,470.7	1,473.8	1,473.4	1,459.3
2011	1,432.3	1,448.6	1,467.6	1,490.2	1,500.0	1,504.9	1,502.2	1,504.8	1,493.4	1,489.3	1,494.9	1,494.0	1,485.2
2012	1,465.6	1,476.4	1,496.9	1,511.2	1,522.8	1,529.3	1,521.8	1,527.1	1,517.7	1,517.2	1,529.3	1,528.1	1,512.0
2013	1,491.9	1,503.6	1,519.6	1,537.9	1,553.0	1,562.3	1,559.8	1,564.4	1,557.1	1,561.3	1,564.1	1,564.2	1,544.9
Goods-Producing													
2002	405.9	405.7	406.8	408.4	409.6	410.6	406.8	407.0	404.6	403.1	399.6	398.4	405.6
2003	396.4	396.9	397.6	395.3	394.1	392.7	391.5	390.7	390.0	389.4	387.0	386.2	392.3
2004	382.0	381.7	385.6	386.9	388.1	389.8	389.6	388.8	388.1	386.5	385.4	384.9	386.5
2005	381.6	382.2	383.3	383.6	384.3	382.3	382.1	382.5	379.6	380.2	380.2	377.2	381.6
2006	376.7	378.0	380.0	382.4	384.1	382.3	381.1	380.8	379.4	382.3	381.8	383.6	381.0
2007	377.9	378.8	381.8	380.2	381.5	383.7	380.1	379.4	378.3	374.9	373.9	373.4	378.7
2008	367.3	365.7	366.0	361.1	361.6	360.3	356.2	354.1	351.8	345.8	341.7	336.3	355.6
2009	325.6	320.0	316.0	309.3	306.3	304.8	299.7	297.7	296.2	293.1	292.5	291.6	304.4
2010	286.3	286.1	287.4	290.0	291.4	292.5	292.2	291.6	291.5	291.1	291.6	293.0	290.4
2011	287.3	291.0	294.2	295.9	297.0	298.5	298.0	298.5	298.2	297.9	298.8	299.7	296.3
2012	296.5	298.6	301.0	300.5	302.1	302.8	301.1	302.3	302.0	302.6	303.4	304.2	301.4
2013	301.9	303.5	306.1	306.4	308.2	309.3	308.0	309.3	310.1	314.7	315.1	314.6	308.9
Service-Providing													
2002	1,353.4	1,361.7	1,384.0	1,400.9	1,410.8	1,409.4	1,385.3	1,397.2	1,407.3	1,409.5	1,412.2	1,414.5	1,395.5
2003	1,378.0	1,387.1	1,405.1	1,414.2	1,424.8	1,419.3	1,401.2	1,411.6	1,422.5	1,423.0	1,425.3	1,430.3	1,411.9
2004	1,396.7	1,403.4	1,426.7	1,445.5	1,456.5	1,452.0	1,434.7	1,444.2	1,456.1	1,464.3	1,470.5	1,471.7	1,443.5
2005	1,436.6	1,446.1	1,459.1	1,482.7	1,492.3	1,477.5	1,477.7	1,488.7	1,497.4	1,504.7	1,513.3	1,506.7	1,481.9
2006	1,480.4	1,494.2	1,515.2	1,530.4	1,537.6	1,513.9	1,502.3	1,512.2	1,528.7	1,547.8	1,552.1	1,558.6	1,522.8
2007	1,524.1	1,531.8	1,554.3	1,564.0	1,575.8	1,575.6	1,552.3	1,562.1	1,576.3	1,578.0	1,583.7	1,583.2	1,563.4
2008	1,549.3	1,558.1	1,575.0	1,583.4	1,596.3	1,586.0	1,555.9	1,558.8	1,570.5	1,565.6	1,561.7	1,552.3	1,567.8
2009	1,499.9	1,497.0	1,507.3	1,517.9	1,525.5	1,513.4	1,495.1	1,498.3	1,503.3	1,505.8	1,507.8	1,503.1	1,506.2
2010	1,471.8	1,478.8	1,497.7	1,523.1	1,542.4	1,531.7	1,516.3	1,520.8	1,523.9	1,527.6	1,530.8	1,529.6	1,516.2
2011	1,488.0	1,500.0	1,519.1	1,541.2	1,549.4	1,542.6	1,526.3	1,532.4	1,539.6	1,539.8	1,546.0	1,542.6	1,530.6
2012	1,511.9	1,525.7	1,548.4	1,562.6	1,573.1	1,570.1	1,549.8	1,554.9	1,565.0	1,568.2	1,583.4	1,579.0	1,557.7
2013	1,540.1	1,553.8	1,571.6	1,590.7	1,603.6	1,598.7	1,583.0	1,587.4	1,601.1	1,604.5	1,608.8	1,608.6	1,587.7
Mining and Logging													
2002	5.1	5.1	5.1	5.1	5.1	5.1	5.0	5.0	5.0	5.0	5.0	5.0	5.1
2003	5.1	5.1	5.1	5.0	5.0	5.0	5.0	5.0	5.0	5.0	5.0	5.0	5.0
2004	5.1	5.1	5.1	5.1	5.1	5.1	5.1	5.1	5.1	5.0	5.0	5.0	5.1
2005	4.9	4.9	4.9	4.9	4.9	4.9	4.8	4.8	4.7	4.7	4.7	4.7	4.8
2006	4.7	4.7	4.7	4.7	4.7	4.7	4.7	4.7	4.7	4.7	4.7	4.8	4.7
2007	4.7	4.7	4.7	4.6	4.6	4.7	4.6	4.6	4.6	4.6	4.6	4.6	4.6
2008	4.5	4.5	4.5	4.4	4.4	4.3	4.3	4.3	4.3	4.3	4.3	4.3	4.4
2009	4.2	4.1	4.1	4.1	4.1	4.1	4.1	4.1	4.1	4.0	4.0	4.0	4.1
2010	4.0	4.0	4.0	4.0	4.0	4.0	4.0	4.0	4.0	4.0	3.9	3.9	4.0
2011	3.9	3.9	4.0	4.0	4.0	4.0	3.9	3.9	3.9	3.9	3.9	3.9	3.9
2012	3.9	3.9	3.9	3.9	3.9	3.9	3.8	3.8	3.8	3.8	3.8	3.8	3.9
2013	3.8	3.8	3.8	3.8	3.8	3.8	3.7	3.7	3.8	3.7	3.8	3.7	3.8
Construction													
2002	107.5	108.8	110.4	112.0	113.4	114.2	113.9	113.8	112.8	112.5	111.8	111.0	111.8
2003	110.7	111.1	112.3	110.9	111.7	112.6	112.5	113.0	113.3	114.5	113.4	113.0	112.4
2004	110.8	110.9	113.2	114.4	115.3	115.7	116.4	116.0	115.6	115.5	114.7	113.8	114.4
2005	112.5	112.9	114.0	115.1	117.4	116.8	118.7	119.4	118.2	119.5	120.4	118.2	116.9
2006	119.3	120.8	122.5	123.8	125.4	123.9	125.7	126.2	125.8	128.1	127.7	127.6	124.7
2007	124.2	124.4	126.7	125.8	126.6	127.7	126.7	126.7	125.6	122.9	121.8	120.8	125.0
2008	116.3	115.7	116.0	112.5	112.6	112.5	109.9	109.0	107.3	104.4	102.1	99.4	109.8
2009	94.6	92.4	92.5	89.7	89.3	88.9	86.9	85.5	84.2	82.7	81.8	81.3	87.5
2010	77.6	77.1	78.2	80.1	80.6	81.2	81.2	80.3	79.8	79.4	79.1	78.5	79.4
2011	74.0	75.6	76.7	77.2	77.9	78.3	78.0	77.7	77.4	77.3	77.4	76.9	77.0
2012	75.0	76.2	77.5	76.6	77.7	78.4	78.0	78.5	78.2	78.1	78.0	78.0	77.5
2013	77.0	76.9	78.6	79.0	79.9	80.5	80.7	80.8	80.8	83.1	82.7	82.2	80.2

1. Employment by Industry: South Carolina, Selected Years, 2002–2013—*Continued*

(Numbers in thousands, not seasonally adjusted)

Industry and year	January	February	March	April	May	June	July	August	September	October	November	December	Annual average
Manufacturing													
2002	293.3	291.8	291.3	291.3	291.1	291.3	287.9	288.2	286.8	285.6	283.0	282.4	288.7
2003	280.6	280.7	280.2	279.4	277.4	275.1	274.0	272.7	271.7	269.9	268.6	268.2	274.9
2004	266.1	265.7	267.3	267.4	267.7	269.0	268.1	267.7	267.4	266.0	265.7	266.1	267.0
2005	264.2	264.4	264.4	263.6	262.0	260.6	258.6	258.3	256.7	256.0	255.1	254.3	259.9
2006	252.7	252.5	252.8	253.9	254.0	253.7	250.7	249.9	248.9	249.5	249.4	251.2	251.6
2007	249.0	249.7	250.4	249.8	250.3	251.3	248.8	248.1	248.1	247.4	247.5	248.0	249.0
2008	246.5	245.5	245.5	244.2	244.6	243.5	242.0	240.8	239.7	237.1	235.3	232.6	241.4
2009	226.8	223.5	219.4	215.5	212.9	211.8	208.7	208.1	207.9	206.4	206.7	206.3	212.8
2010	204.7	205.0	205.2	205.9	206.8	207.3	207.0	207.3	207.7	207.7	208.6	210.6	207.0
2011	209.4	211.5	213.5	214.7	215.1	216.2	216.1	216.9	216.9	216.7	217.5	218.9	215.3
2012	217.6	218.5	219.6	220.0	220.5	220.5	219.3	220.0	220.0	220.7	221.6	222.4	220.1
2013	221.1	222.8	223.7	223.6	224.5	225.0	223.6	224.8	225.5	227.9	228.6	228.7	225.0
Trade, Transportation, and Utilities													
2002	340.9	340.0	344.3	346.8	348.6	350.5	347.8	347.5	346.3	347.1	352.5	356.1	347.4
2003	342.7	341.9	344.5	344.5	347.2	349.9	348.3	349.2	347.8	348.6	353.2	357.5	347.9
2004	346.1	345.4	349.8	351.0	354.2	354.8	357.0	357.2	355.7	358.2	364.0	367.7	355.1
2005	355.2	355.0	356.5	359.7	363.4	361.1	364.5	365.2	360.7	364.9	370.7	373.1	362.5
2006	361.4	364.7	368.7	368.8	368.9	367.5	367.5	369.0	368.6	374.1	382.0	385.0	370.5
2007	370.1	369.4	374.9	374.8	377.8	380.0	379.5	379.0	378.2	379.5	385.9	388.9	378.2
2008	375.5	374.4	377.1	375.9	375.8	376.0	374.0	373.2	370.5	368.5	370.5	371.2	373.6
2009	353.0	348.4	348.6	349.4	350.9	351.3	348.9	348.3	346.0	345.0	349.1	350.6	349.1
2010	339.0	337.9	341.5	343.6	345.8	347.4	347.2	347.8	345.3	347.7	353.1	355.8	346.0
2011	341.7	342.5	345.0	348.4	349.9	351.9	351.6	351.5	349.0	350.5	355.9	358.4	349.7
2012	347.5	346.4	349.5	351.1	353.8	356.0	355.4	355.3	354.1	356.5	364.6	365.7	354.7
2013	351.4	351.3	354.7	357.1	360.1	363.7	364.6	365.4	362.9	364.4	369.9	374.0	361.6
Wholesale Trade													
2002	61.7	62.4	63.1	63.3	63.3	64.0	63.5	63.1	62.8	63.5	63.6	63.4	63.1
2003	62.7	63.1	63.3	63.3	63.7	63.9	63.6	63.6	63.4	63.5	63.5	63.9	63.5
2004	63.5	63.7	64.4	64.8	65.3	65.6	66.2	66.5	66.4	66.6	67.0	67.0	65.6
2005	67.6	68.0	68.0	67.7	68.7	67.9	68.3	68.5	68.2	68.8	68.9	68.6	68.3
2006	69.0	69.5	69.7	70.6	70.7	70.5	69.4	69.8	70.2	71.4	71.6	71.7	70.3
2007	70.7	71.1	71.8	71.9	71.9	72.4	72.1	71.9	71.9	72.2	72.1	72.5	71.9
2008	71.9	72.4	72.6	72.6	72.3	72.4	72.5	72.3	72.2	71.9	71.5	70.8	72.1
2009	68.5	67.8	67.2	67.0	66.8	66.2	65.7	65.6	65.0	65.1	65.0	64.8	66.2
2010	64.0	64.0	64.2	64.5	64.7	64.7	64.7	64.8	64.2	64.4	64.4	64.3	64.4
2011	63.4	64.1	64.2	64.5	64.6	64.7	64.7	64.7	64.5	64.4	64.4	64.7	64.4
2012	64.9	65.3	65.6	65.6	65.8	66.3	65.9	65.9	65.6	65.7	65.7	65.8	65.7
2013	65.5	65.8	66.2	66.4	66.7	66.9	66.6	66.8	66.5	67.0	66.0	66.6	66.4
Retail Trade													
2002	219.1	216.9	220.5	222.1	223.7	225.4	223.7	223.3	222.4	221.8	226.6	230.7	223.0
2003	218.9	217.4	219.6	220.1	222.0	224.3	223.4	224.0	222.9	223.1	227.5	231.1	222.9
2004	221.6	220.4	223.8	225.2	227.1	227.2	227.9	227.2	226.1	228.1	233.3	237.1	227.1
2005	225.8	225.0	226.3	229.1	230.9	229.8	232.0	232.2	228.1	231.7	237.1	239.3	230.6
2006	228.5	230.7	234.4	233.7	233.4	231.8	233.3	234.0	233.1	236.8	244.3	246.4	235.0
2007	234.5	232.8	237.3	236.9	239.4	240.7	241.0	240.3	239.5	240.1	246.0	248.0	239.7
2008	237.7	235.8	238.6	237.5	237.5	237.8	236.6	235.7	234.1	231.6	234.3	235.4	236.1
2009	222.4	219.2	220.2	221.9	223.7	224.6	223.9	223.3	221.6	221.0	225.8	226.8	222.9
2010	217.5	216.4	219.1	220.7	222.5	223.6	223.1	223.5	221.6	223.3	228.3	230.5	222.5
2011	219.1	219.2	221.2	224.4	225.2	226.3	226.3	225.7	223.4	224.3	229.1	230.5	224.6
2012	221.2	219.7	222.3	223.7	225.7	226.8	226.9	226.5	225.4	227.0	234.5	234.5	226.2
2013	222.7	222.2	224.9	227.1	229.4	232.0	233.2	233.6	231.6	233.0	238.6	240.6	230.7
Transportation and Utilities													
2002	60.1	60.7	60.7	61.4	61.6	61.1	60.6	61.1	61.1	61.8	62.3	62.0	61.2
2003	61.1	61.4	61.6	61.1	61.5	61.7	61.3	61.6	61.5	62.0	62.2	62.5	61.6
2004	61.0	61.3	61.6	61.0	61.8	62.0	62.9	63.5	63.2	63.5	63.7	63.6	62.4
2005	61.8	62.0	62.2	62.9	63.8	63.4	64.2	64.5	64.4	64.4	64.7	65.2	63.6
2006	63.9	64.5	64.6	64.5	64.8	65.2	64.8	65.2	65.3	65.9	66.1	66.9	65.1
2007	64.9	65.5	65.8	66.0	66.5	66.9	66.4	66.8	66.8	67.2	67.8	68.4	66.6
2008	65.9	66.2	65.9	66.1	65.9	65.7	65.1	65.3	64.5	64.9	64.7	65.0	65.4
2009	62.1	61.4	61.2	60.5	60.4	60.5	59.3	59.4	59.4	58.9	58.3	59.0	60.0
2010	57.5	57.5	58.2	58.4	58.6	59.1	59.4	59.5	59.5	60.0	60.4	61.0	59.1
2011	59.2	59.2	59.6	59.5	60.1	60.9	60.6	61.1	61.1	61.8	62.4	63.2	60.7
2012	61.4	61.4	61.6	61.8	62.3	62.9	62.6	62.9	63.1	63.8	64.4	65.4	62.8
2013	63.2	63.3	63.6	63.6	64.0	64.8	64.8	65.0	64.8	64.4	65.3	66.8	64.5
Information													
2002	27.7	27.6	27.8	27.5	28.0	28.1	27.8	27.9	27.4	27.9	28.3	28.3	27.9
2003	27.5	27.6	27.5	26.7	26.9	26.9	27.1	27.1	26.9	26.7	26.8	26.9	27.1
2004	26.8	26.5	26.5	26.5	26.9	27.0	27.0	26.9	26.6	26.8	26.7	27.2	26.8
2005	26.6	26.7	26.6	27.0	27.3	27.2	27.2	27.1	26.9	26.9	27.1	27.4	27.0
2006	27.2	27.6	27.4	27.5	27.6	27.7	27.5	27.4	27.1	27.3	27.8	27.9	27.5
2007	27.1	27.2	27.4	27.6	27.9	28.5	28.7	28.5	28.0	28.1	28.2	28.4	28.0
2008	28.1	28.2	28.2	28.6	28.8	29.0	29.1	28.9	28.4	28.2	28.2	28.4	28.5
2009	27.9	27.7	27.9	27.5	27.4	27.4	27.6	26.9	26.5	26.5	26.4	26.3	27.2
2010	26.3	26.3	26.3	25.5	25.6	26.0	26.3	25.7	25.4	25.5	25.7	26.1	25.9
2011	26.0	25.7	25.9	25.7	25.7	25.8	25.8	25.7	25.3	26.0	26.1	26.1	25.8
2012	25.5	25.8	25.6	25.7	26.0	26.1	25.8	25.6	25.4	25.6	25.9	26.3	25.8
2013	26.1	26.4	26.4	26.7	26.7	26.4	26.6	26.3	26.1	26.3	26.3	26.2	26.4

1. Employment by Industry: South Carolina, Selected Years, 2002–2013—*Continued*

(Numbers in thousands, not seasonally adjusted)

Industry and year	January	February	March	April	May	June	July	August	September	October	November	December	Annual average
Financial Activities													
2002	81.0	81.3	82.1	83.5	84.3	85.4	85.0	84.6	83.9	83.8	83.8	84.2	83.6
2003	83.4	83.4	84.1	85.7	86.9	88.0	87.4	88.2	86.5	86.5	86.1	86.5	86.1
2004	84.9	85.6	86.6	87.7	88.4	90.0	89.6	89.8	89.5	89.8	89.9	90.5	88.5
2005	90.0	90.3	90.5	91.5	92.7	93.0	94.3	94.4	93.7	93.0	93.1	93.6	92.5
2006	94.0	94.6	94.9	96.6	97.2	97.8	98.6	99.1	98.6	99.1	98.9	99.4	97.4
2007	98.7	98.7	99.6	100.0	100.8	101.8	101.5	101.5	100.8	100.8	100.8	101.2	100.5
2008	99.8	100.6	100.9	100.8	101.3	102.2	101.5	101.3	99.8	99.3	98.7	98.6	100.4
2009	96.3	96.2	96.2	96.0	96.4	96.7	96.8	96.1	94.6	93.5	92.9	92.7	95.4
2010	91.2	91.2	91.6	92.0	92.4	93.1	93.3	92.8	91.4	91.4	91.2	90.9	91.9
2011	89.5	89.5	89.8	90.5	91.3	91.9	92.3	92.3	91.4	91.4	91.7	91.7	91.1
2012	91.0	91.4	91.9	93.1	93.5	94.6	94.5	94.8	94.0	93.7	94.1	94.5	93.4
2013	93.0	93.6	94.4	95.1	95.9	96.6	96.9	97.1	96.0	96.8	95.9	95.8	95.6
Professional and Business Services													
2002	175.4	177.7	180.4	184.7	185.4	187.6	185.3	188.2	187.5	188.8	186.9	186.4	184.5
2003	181.4	184.0	187.7	188.2	188.6	188.7	187.2	189.4	188.5	191.8	192.1	192.2	188.3
2004	186.1	188.4	192.8	196.5	196.3	198.8	198.9	200.3	199.2	201.9	201.8	200.4	196.8
2005	196.5	198.6	198.7	204.3	205.1	204.4	206.8	210.3	210.4	213.3	214.6	211.6	206.2
2006	212.6	214.6	216.1	218.9	220.2	218.0	217.3	219.3	220.7	223.7	221.7	224.3	219.0
2007	220.9	223.6	225.2	227.0	228.5	230.0	226.7	229.2	229.2	227.9	227.5	226.5	226.9
2008	220.7	223.3	224.6	225.3	227.5	225.5	221.2	223.5	220.7	218.6	216.6	210.6	221.5
2009	201.0	199.9	200.2	199.2	199.0	198.2	198.5	199.9	199.5	203.8	205.3	203.5	200.7
2010	200.0	202.8	205.5	214.4	216.0	218.0	219.2	221.2	221.0	222.6	223.1	223.0	215.6
2011	217.8	222.0	225.1	230.1	230.4	230.8	231.1	233.1	231.7	230.6	231.4	231.5	228.8
2012	227.4	230.3	234.0	237.2	238.5	239.6	236.7	239.1	236.0	235.6	239.7	240.0	236.2
2013	232.9	234.8	236.2	237.9	240.5	242.7	242.0	243.5	242.2	240.1	239.1	239.7	239.3
Education and Health Services													
2002	168.9	170.2	172.1	171.8	172.4	171.6	171.6	172.5	174.1	174.1	175.2	174.9	172.5
2003	173.2	174.5	175.4	176.4	176.9	176.2	175.6	177.4	179.6	179.0	179.2	179.6	176.9
2004	178.3	179.5	180.2	181.1	181.8	180.5	179.8	181.0	182.2	183.0	184.1	184.3	181.3
2005	182.6	184.3	184.7	187.5	187.8	184.7	187.2	187.8	189.2	190.5	191.0	189.9	187.3
2006	189.2	191.4	191.8	192.7	193.0	189.6	189.9	191.5	193.8	197.9	198.2	199.0	193.2
2007	196.0	198.1	199.1	199.7	200.2	199.7	199.6	200.6	202.6	203.4	204.1	204.0	200.6
2008	204.1	206.2	207.2	205.8	207.2	206.1	205.2	206.5	208.1	209.1	209.5	209.1	207.0
2009	206.0	207.5	207.4	208.0	208.7	207.0	207.0	208.4	208.8	210.3	211.2	210.5	208.4
2010	209.8	211.7	211.9	214.3	214.5	212.5	212.2	213.4	213.9	216.2	216.4	216.0	213.6
2011	212.3	215.0	215.3	216.0	215.7	213.5	212.2	213.1	214.7	215.1	215.6	214.9	214.5
2012	212.6	214.6	215.1	214.5	215.0	211.1	210.3	211.8	216.3	217.5	218.1	217.9	214.6
2013	214.6	217.5	217.6	218.4	219.1	215.4	214.5	216.4	219.8	222.1	223.2	222.8	218.5
Leisure and Hospitality													
2002	169.4	173.9	181.7	191.1	195.6	201.3	200.6	197.9	191.9	190.5	185.7	183.4	188.6
2003	176.1	180.0	186.7	194.0	200.1	204.8	205.4	204.1	197.7	193.3	189.2	186.5	193.2
2004	181.0	185.5	193.6	202.0	207.6	211.4	211.8	209.0	203.5	201.0	197.9	194.1	199.9
2005	185.5	189.7	196.5	206.7	209.7	212.9	217.3	215.9	206.1	202.7	200.7	194.6	203.2
2006	191.1	194.7	200.1	209.8	214.5	216.1	218.7	217.0	210.6	210.0	207.7	205.0	207.9
2007	199.8	203.0	211.3	219.4	224.1	229.3	227.9	227.4	220.9	217.9	214.0	210.6	217.1
2008	203.1	207.2	214.7	223.2	229.3	231.5	229.0	228.0	219.9	214.0	208.5	204.8	217.8
2009	195.0	198.1	204.8	213.5	219.1	220.8	219.1	217.7	211.2	205.1	200.5	196.7	208.5
2010	189.1	192.7	200.1	211.0	215.6	219.2	219.3	218.3	212.7	207.5	204.2	200.3	207.5
2011	190.2	195.0	203.7	214.7	221.0	223.5	222.1	222.1	214.8	209.9	207.6	204.1	210.7
2012	197.4	201.4	210.8	220.1	224.4	229.2	228.1	228.5	220.5	216.1	213.7	209.8	216.7
2013	202.6	206.8	213.5	225.4	231.3	236.5	235.8	234.8	228.1	225.0	222.9	218.5	223.4
Other Services													
2002	62.6	63.4	64.7	64.2	64.9	65.6	64.2	64.7	65.3	63.7	63.8	64.0	64.3
2003	63.4	63.9	64.7	64.1	64.8	65.3	64.9	65.2	65.3	65.3	65.6	66.0	64.9
2004	65.0	65.6	66.5	68.9	70.0	71.5	69.1	69.3	69.7	70.6	71.8	72.0	69.2
2005	71.1	72.4	73.1	72.7	73.3	72.9	74.9	75.6	75.4	75.4	75.7	74.9	74.0
2006	71.9	72.6	76.2	76.1	76.3	75.9	76.2	75.8	75.3	74.7	74.3	74.3	75.0
2007	73.4	73.8	74.4	74.3	74.6	74.6	73.4	73.0	72.4	71.7	71.5	71.6	73.2
2008	70.2	70.4	71.3	71.7	72.4	72.5	72.2	72.0	71.6	71.2	70.9	70.5	71.4
2009	69.4	69.6	69.8	69.9	70.2	70.1	69.8	69.2	69.2	69.0	68.6	68.4	69.4
2010	67.4	67.7	68.4	68.8	69.0	69.2	68.7	68.4	68.6	68.7	68.5	68.3	68.5
2011	67.5	67.9	68.6	68.9	69.0	69.0	69.1	68.5	68.3	67.9	67.8	67.6	68.3
2012	67.7	67.9	69.0	69.0	69.5	69.9	69.9	69.7	69.4	69.6	69.8	69.7	69.3
2013	69.4	69.7	70.7	70.9	71.2	71.7	71.4	71.6	71.9	71.9	71.7	72.6	71.2
Government													
2002	327.5	327.6	330.9	331.3	331.6	319.3	303.0	313.9	330.9	333.6	336.0	337.2	326.9
2003	330.3	331.8	334.5	334.6	333.4	319.5	305.3	311.0	330.2	331.8	333.1	335.1	327.6
2004	328.5	326.9	330.7	331.8	331.3	318.0	301.5	310.7	329.7	333.0	334.3	335.5	326.0
2005	329.1	329.1	332.5	333.3	333.0	321.3	305.5	312.4	335.0	338.0	340.4	341.6	329.3
2006	333.0	334.0	340.0	340.0	339.9	321.3	306.6	313.1	334.0	341.0	341.5	343.7	332.3
2007	338.1	338.0	342.4	341.2	341.9	331.7	315.0	322.9	344.2	348.7	351.7	352.0	339.0
2008	347.8	347.8	351.0	352.1	354.0	343.2	323.7	325.4	352.0	356.7	358.8	359.1	347.6
2009	351.3	349.6	352.4	354.4	353.8	341.9	327.4	331.8	347.5	352.6	353.8	354.4	347.6
2010	349.0	348.5	352.4	353.5	363.5	346.3	330.1	333.2	345.6	348.0	348.6	349.2	347.3
2011	343.0	342.4	345.7	346.9	346.4	336.2	322.1	326.1	344.4	348.4	349.9	348.3	341.7
2012	342.8	347.9	352.5	351.9	352.4	343.6	329.1	330.1	349.3	353.6	357.5	355.1	347.2
2013	350.1	353.7	358.1	359.2	358.8	345.7	331.2	332.3	354.1	357.9	359.8	359.0	351.7

2. Average Weekly Hours by Selected Industry: South Carolina, 2009–2013

(Not seasonally adjusted)

Industry and year	January	February	March	April	May	June	July	August	September	October	November	December	Annual average
Total Private													
2009	34.8	34.9	35.0	34.6	34.8	34.8	34.6	34.9	34.3	34.4	34.7	35.0	34.7
2010	34.7	34.4	34.5	34.8	34.9	34.7	34.9	35.3	34.7	34.9	34.8	34.7	34.8
2011	33.6	34.8	34.8	35.0	35.1	35.1	34.9	34.8	34.7	35.0	34.7	34.8	34.8
2012	34.9	35.1	35.1	35.4	34.9	35.0	35.3	35.1	35.4	35.0	34.9	35.2	35.1
2013	34.5	34.6	35.0	35.0	34.8	35.1	34.6	34.9	35.3	34.8	34.8	35.1	34.9
Goods-Producing													
2009	39.9	40.0	40.2	39.4	40.9	40.9	40.7	41.0	40.3	40.2	40.5	41.1	40.4
2010	41.5	40.6	40.8	41.3	41.6	41.3	40.8	41.7	40.9	40.9	41.2	41.2	41.1
2011	38.2	40.4	40.6	40.8	41.1	41.5	40.7	41.1	41.0	40.9	41.3	41.2	40.7
2012	40.9	41.2	41.4	41.5	41.2	41.7	41.4	41.4	41.7	41.2	40.9	41.8	41.4
2013	40.4	40.3	40.7	41.0	41.1	41.3	39.8	41.2	41.5	41.5	41.4	41.6	41.0
Construction													
2009	37.3	37.4	36.6	36.0	36.5	37.5	37.7	37.6	36.3	35.9	36.6	37.3	36.9
2010	39.1	37.8	36.4	37.0	36.8	37.5	37.9	38.8	37.3	38.9	38.8	37.6	37.8
2011	34.3	36.7	37.1	37.8	39.0	39.2	38.4	39.2	37.7	37.1	40.0	39.2	38.0
2012	38.6	39.1	39.9	39.6	39.7	39.7	39.9	40.3	40.1	40.1	39.5	40.2	39.7
2013	39.8	38.3	40.3	40.1	40.9	40.7	39.3	39.6	40.1	40.2	40.6	40.0	40.0
Manufacturing													
2009	41.6	41.6	41.9	40.6	42.7	42.1	42.0	42.5	42.1	42.2	42.5	42.8	42.0
2010	41.2	40.3	41.3	41.6	42.1	41.6	40.7	41.5	41.2	40.7	41.3	41.5	41.2
2011	39.2	40.9	41.1	41.2	41.2	41.7	40.9	41.3	41.7	41.8	41.5	41.6	41.2
2012	41.3	41.5	41.5	41.7	41.3	42.0	41.6	41.6	42.0	41.4	41.2	42.3	41.6
2013	40.4	40.9	40.7	41.2	41.0	41.4	39.9	41.6	41.9	41.9	41.6	42.1	41.2
Trade, Transportation, and Utilities													
2009	34.1	34.2	34.4	34.4	34.8	34.7	34.4	34.5	34.2	34.5	34.5	34.8	34.5
2010	34.7	34.7	35.1	35.1	35.2	34.9	35.3	35.3	35.2	35.2	34.9	34.6	35.0
2011	34.0	34.9	35.1	35.0	34.9	34.7	34.5	34.7	34.2	34.4	33.7	34.2	34.5
2012	34.2	34.1	34.1	34.6	34.0	34.2	34.5	34.2	34.3	34.1	34.5	34.5	34.3
2013	33.5	33.8	34.2	34.3	34.5	34.5	34.6	34.7	34.5	34.1	34.1	34.8	34.3
Financial Activities													
2009	35.8	36.7	36.5	36.4	36.9	36.6	36.9	37.6	35.7	36.7	37.5	36.7	36.7
2010	36.5	36.2	36.6	36.4	36.6	36.1	36.8	37.2	36.6	36.8	37.1	37.0	36.7
2011	37.8	37.4	37.3	37.9	38.0	37.6	38.2	34.6	35.1	35.8	35.3	36.2	36.8
2012	36.9	36.6	36.3	37.0	36.6	36.0	37.3	36.6	37.5	36.7	36.9	37.7	36.8
2013	37.0	37.5	37.4	37.2	37.2	38.4	37.9	37.7	39.2	38.1	38.0	38.5	37.8
Professional and Business Services													
2009	38.3	37.5	38.4	37.1	36.7	37.6	37.1	37.4	37.0	36.3	36.2	37.4	37.2
2010	35.6	34.9	34.5	35.5	35.9	35.5	35.1	36.2	34.9	34.9	34.6	35.5	35.3
2011	34.0	35.4	35.6	36.8	37.0	36.7	36.8	36.9	36.6	36.6	35.7	35.8	36.2
2012	35.8	36.6	36.4	36.8	36.6	36.8	37.0	36.7	37.4	37.0	37.3	37.9	36.9
2013	36.9	36.7	37.1	37.2	37.1	37.6	36.6	36.7	38.1	36.8	37.2	37.6	37.1
Education and Health Services													
2009	32.4	33.1	32.9	32.6	31.8	31.9	32.0	32.1	31.7	31.7	32.8	33.0	32.3
2010	34.5	34.3	33.7	33.7	34.1	33.7	33.7	33.9	34.0	34.0	33.6	33.4	33.9
2011	32.7	33.6	32.2	32.4	32.5	32.6	32.3	32.8	32.8	33.6	33.8	33.8	32.9
2012	34.4	34.3	34.3	34.6	34.3	34.6	34.7	34.6	35.0	34.4	34.4	34.3	34.5
2013	34.1	34.1	34.3	34.2	33.8	34.0	33.5	33.4	33.6	33.5	33.3	32.9	33.7
Leisure and Hospitality													
2009	24.7	25.4	25.9	26.4	26.4	26.9	27.0	27.0	25.2	25.4	25.3	25.0	25.9
2010	24.9	25.0	25.5	26.2	25.9	26.5	27.3	27.2	26.3	26.2	26.2	25.7	26.1
2011	24.6	25.8	26.1	26.5	26.4	26.6	27.0	27.2	26.4	26.7	26.2	25.6	26.3
2012	25.5	26.4	26.7	27.4	26.3	26.5	26.9	26.9	26.1	25.9	25.2	25.4	26.3
2013	25.0	25.4	26.1	26.2	25.9	26.4	26.6	26.9	25.8	25.5	25.1	25.0	25.8
Other Services													
2009	31.9	31.8	31.9	32.3	31.2	30.2	30.6	30.8	30.9	30.8	30.8	31.2	31.2
2010	31.5	30.8	32.2	32.3	32.3	32.5	32.3	32.3	31.8	32.6	31.8	31.4	32.0
2011	30.6	32.3	32.5	32.9	33.9	34.0	34.0	33.4	33.9	34.5	33.2	32.8	33.2
2012	33.9	33.6	33.3	32.8	32.1	32.5	33.0	31.7	33.1	33.0	32.9	32.9	32.9
2013	34.0	32.6	33.3	33.7	33.1	32.9	31.8	31.6	32.3	31.6	31.3	31.5	32.5

3. Average Hourly Earnings by Selected Industry: South Carolina, 2009–2013

(Dollars, not seasonally adjusted)

Industry and year	January	February	March	April	May	June	July	August	September	October	November	December	Annual average
Total Private													
2009	19.16	19.33	18.75	18.74	18.70	18.67	18.78	19.41	19.70	19.41	19.72	19.77	19.17
2010	19.98	20.11	19.63	19.56	19.65	19.44	19.56	19.81	20.03	20.19	20.25	20.54	19.89
2011	21.00	20.80	20.90	20.90	20.71	20.44	20.54	20.25	20.53	20.37	20.28	20.29	20.58
2012	20.42	20.32	20.17	19.96	19.79	19.78	19.94	19.92	20.22	20.09	20.17	20.37	20.09
2013	20.27	20.57	20.72	20.23	20.15	20.34	20.26	20.40	20.64	20.69	20.92	21.05	20.52
Goods-Producing													
2009	20.26	20.07	20.29	20.43	20.22	20.09	20.16	20.06	20.08	20.13	20.81	20.70	20.27
2010	20.75	21.23	20.80	20.74	20.48	20.27	20.68	20.39	20.83	20.84	20.81	21.29	20.76
2011	21.73	21.22	21.21	21.23	20.98	20.73	20.84	20.74	20.98	20.68	20.64	21.01	20.99
2012	20.76	20.53	20.68	20.77	20.64	20.71	20.95	20.83	21.12	20.89	21.04	21.13	20.84
2013	20.96	20.72	20.85	20.92	20.89	21.14	21.25	21.36	21.69	21.67	21.97	22.24	21.31
Construction													
2009	20.98	20.15	20.24	20.35	21.42	21.46	21.29	21.20	21.18	21.19	21.56	21.39	21.02
2010	21.25	22.11	21.37	21.24	20.97	20.52	20.34	20.19	20.49	20.41	20.79	21.12	20.89
2011	21.77	21.25	21.58	21.65	21.36	21.06	21.01	21.07	21.43	21.44	21.37	21.41	21.36
2012	20.97	20.94	20.57	20.41	20.05	20.25	20.40	20.23	20.27	20.36	20.57	20.16	20.43
2013	19.90	20.38	20.76	20.22	19.99	20.11	19.81	19.90	19.99	19.91	19.86	20.20	20.08
Manufacturing													
2009	19.67	19.67	19.98	20.18	19.89	19.68	19.88	19.70	19.73	19.77	20.26	20.21	19.88
2010	20.40	20.67	20.38	20.36	20.23	20.22	20.85	20.74	21.15	21.22	20.96	21.29	20.71
2011	21.72	21.16	21.04	21.06	20.82	20.56	20.74	20.59	20.78	20.37	20.32	20.83	20.82
2012	20.63	20.34	20.70	20.91	20.84	20.85	21.14	21.03	21.40	21.08	21.21	21.48	20.97
2013	21.37	20.84	21.06	21.33	21.37	21.66	21.95	22.02	22.43	22.43	22.78	23.00	21.87
Trade, Transportation, and Utilities													
2009	17.57	17.66	18.01	17.28	17.17	17.30	17.34	17.70	17.65	17.71	17.90	17.76	17.59
2010	18.04	18.25	18.10	17.44	17.38	17.51	17.76	17.97	18.18	18.35	18.16	18.43	17.96
2011	18.88	18.74	18.48	18.33	18.44	18.21	18.09	18.13	18.61	18.68	18.52	17.90	18.41
2012	18.52	18.53	18.65	17.93	17.86	17.80	18.25	18.50	18.54	18.46	18.63	18.88	18.38
2013	19.01	19.05	19.47	19.06	19.07	19.33	19.34	19.37	19.82	19.80	19.98	19.92	19.44
Financial Activities													
2009	22.26	22.37	20.55	20.56	20.70	20.98	21.34	21.62	21.96	22.03	22.49	22.26	21.59
2010	22.80	22.81	22.68	22.90	23.57	23.87	23.39	23.88	24.00	24.37	24.08	25.37	23.65
2011	24.89	25.30	23.75	23.80	23.40	22.99	22.80	22.49	22.72	22.73	22.76	22.30	23.34
2012	23.11	24.32	22.73	23.00	22.80	22.60	22.73	22.90	23.20	23.18	22.97	23.05	23.05
2013	22.95	22.77	20.16	20.69	20.64	20.69	20.80	21.09	19.87	20.45	20.82	21.32	21.01
Professional and Business Services													
2009	23.27	24.46	23.56	23.94	23.88	23.37	23.01	25.41	25.64	23.62	23.65	23.49	23.94
2010	22.45	22.65	21.93	21.06	21.44	20.97	21.08	21.54	21.77	22.12	22.13	21.62	21.72
2011	22.82	22.42	21.74	22.33	22.05	21.87	22.23	21.90	22.26	22.56	22.09	22.36	22.21
2012	22.54	22.46	22.19	22.09	21.91	22.22	22.32	22.22	23.07	22.63	22.74	23.50	22.50
2013	22.93	23.64	23.42	23.10	22.99	23.41	22.85	22.98	23.23	23.25	23.44	23.54	23.23
Education and Health Services													
2009	19.75	20.48	20.80	20.77	21.22	21.22	21.87	21.79	22.19	22.16	22.03	22.90	21.43
2010	22.03	23.24	22.98	22.93	23.46	23.12	23.39	23.23	23.09	23.38	24.08	23.93	23.24
2011	24.46	24.63	25.50	25.50	25.49	25.34	25.94	25.24	25.02	24.27	24.52	24.02	24.98
2012	23.93	23.87	24.02	23.87	23.42	23.45	23.31	23.02	23.01	23.34	23.25	23.05	23.46
2013	22.80	22.85	22.79	22.81	22.77	23.14	23.33	23.94	23.76	23.73	24.09	24.14	23.34
Leisure and Hospitality													
2009	10.79	10.96	10.87	10.90	10.80	10.76	10.90	11.05	11.16	11.00	11.09	11.11	10.95
2010	11.10	11.19	11.20	11.31	11.37	11.26	11.21	11.31	11.30	11.51	11.80	11.87	11.37
2011	12.13	11.89	11.87	11.93	11.80	11.77	11.91	11.90	11.99	11.93	11.85	12.05	11.91
2012	11.96	11.92	11.84	11.69	11.62	11.63	11.59	11.52	11.55	11.43	11.49	11.35	11.63
2013	11.54	11.75	11.57	11.43	11.56	11.46	11.49	11.36	11.61	11.60	11.70	11.77	11.56
Other Services													
2009	16.63	17.03	16.44	16.14	15.91	15.90	15.68	16.00	16.08	15.74	16.04	16.04	16.14
2010	16.09	16.38	16.27	16.57	16.41	16.35	16.28	16.72	16.98	16.59	17.09	17.25	16.58
2011	17.43	17.63	16.76	17.45	17.59	17.96	18.56	18.29	18.41	18.22	17.77	18.16	17.86
2012	18.16	18.15	18.06	18.21	17.76	17.44	17.64	17.79	17.18	17.23	17.21	17.28	17.67
2013	16.96	17.25	16.85	16.71	16.57	16.63	16.50	16.33	16.21	16.11	16.37	16.25	16.56

4. Average Weekly Earnings by Selected Industry: South Carolina, 2009–2013

(Dollars, not seasonally adjusted)

Industry and year	January	February	March	April	May	June	July	August	September	October	November	December	Annual average
Total Private													
2009	666.77	674.62	656.25	648.40	650.76	649.72	649.79	677.41	675.71	667.70	684.28	691.95	665.20
2010	693.31	691.78	677.24	680.69	685.79	674.57	682.64	699.29	695.04	704.63	704.70	712.74	692.17
2011	705.60	723.84	727.32	731.50	726.92	717.44	716.85	704.70	712.39	712.95	703.72	706.09	716.18
2012	712.66	713.23	707.97	706.58	690.67	692.30	703.88	699.19	715.79	703.15	703.93	717.02	705.16
2013	699.32	711.72	725.20	708.05	701.22	713.93	701.00	711.96	728.59	720.01	728.02	738.86	716.15
Goods-Producing													
2009	808.37	802.80	815.66	804.94	827.00	821.68	820.51	822.46	809.22	809.23	842.81	850.77	818.91
2010	861.13	861.94	848.64	856.56	851.97	837.15	843.74	850.26	851.95	852.36	857.37	877.15	853.24
2011	830.09	857.29	861.13	866.18	862.28	860.30	848.19	852.41	860.18	845.81	852.43	865.61	854.29
2012	849.08	845.84	856.15	861.96	850.37	863.61	867.33	862.36	880.70	860.67	860.54	883.23	862.78
2013	846.78	835.02	848.60	857.72	858.58	873.08	845.75	880.03	900.14	899.31	909.56	925.18	873.71
Construction													
2009	782.55	753.61	740.78	732.60	781.83	804.75	802.63	797.12	768.83	760.72	789.10	797.85	775.64
2010	830.88	835.76	777.87	785.88	771.70	769.50	770.89	783.37	764.28	793.95	806.65	794.11	789.64
2011	746.71	779.88	800.62	818.37	833.04	825.55	806.78	825.94	807.91	795.42	854.80	839.27	811.68
2012	809.44	818.75	820.74	808.24	795.99	803.93	813.96	815.27	812.83	816.44	812.52	810.43	811.07
2013	792.02	780.55	836.63	810.82	817.59	818.48	778.53	788.04	801.60	800.38	806.32	808.00	803.20
Manufacturing													
2009	818.27	818.27	837.16	819.31	849.30	828.53	834.96	837.25	830.63	834.29	861.05	864.99	834.96
2010	840.48	833.00	841.69	846.98	851.68	841.15	848.60	860.71	871.38	863.65	865.65	883.54	853.25
2011	851.42	865.44	864.74	867.67	857.78	857.35	848.27	850.37	866.53	851.47	843.28	866.53	857.78
2012	852.02	844.11	859.05	871.95	860.69	875.70	879.42	874.85	898.80	872.71	873.85	908.60	872.35
2013	863.35	852.36	857.14	878.80	876.17	896.72	875.81	916.03	939.82	939.82	947.65	968.30	901.04
Trade, Transportation, and Utilities													
2009	599.14	603.97	619.54	594.43	597.52	600.31	596.50	610.65	603.63	611.00	617.55	618.05	606.86
2010	625.99	633.28	635.31	612.14	611.78	611.10	626.93	634.34	639.94	645.92	633.78	637.68	628.60
2011	641.92	654.03	648.65	641.55	643.56	631.89	624.11	629.11	636.46	642.59	624.12	612.18	635.15
2012	633.38	631.87	635.97	620.38	607.24	608.76	629.63	632.70	635.92	629.49	642.74	651.36	630.43
2013	636.84	643.89	665.87	653.76	657.92	666.89	669.16	672.14	683.79	675.18	681.32	693.22	666.79
Financial Activities													
2009	796.91	820.98	750.08	748.38	763.83	767.87	787.45	812.91	783.97	808.50	843.38	816.94	792.35
2010	832.20	825.72	830.09	833.56	862.66	861.71	860.75	888.34	878.40	896.82	893.37	938.69	867.96
2011	940.84	946.22	885.88	902.02	889.20	864.42	870.96	778.15	797.47	813.73	803.43	807.26	858.91
2012	852.76	890.11	825.10	851.00	834.48	813.60	847.83	838.14	870.00	850.71	847.59	868.99	848.24
2013	849.15	853.88	753.98	769.67	767.81	794.50	788.32	795.09	778.90	779.15	791.16	820.82	794.18
Professional and Business Services													
2009	891.24	917.25	904.70	888.17	876.40	878.71	853.67	950.33	948.68	857.41	856.13	878.53	890.57
2010	799.22	790.49	756.59	747.63	769.70	744.44	739.91	779.75	759.77	771.99	765.70	767.51	766.72
2011	775.88	793.67	773.94	821.74	815.85	802.63	818.06	808.11	814.72	825.70	788.61	800.49	804.00
2012	806.93	822.04	807.72	812.91	801.91	817.70	825.84	815.47	862.82	837.31	848.20	890.65	830.25
2013	846.12	867.59	868.88	859.32	852.93	880.22	836.31	843.37	885.06	855.60	871.97	885.10	861.83
Education and Health Services													
2009	639.90	677.89	684.32	677.10	674.80	676.92	699.84	699.46	703.42	702.47	722.58	755.70	692.19
2010	760.04	797.13	774.43	772.74	799.99	779.14	788.24	787.50	785.06	794.92	809.09	799.26	787.84
2011	799.84	827.57	821.10	826.20	828.43	826.08	837.86	827.87	820.66	815.47	828.78	811.88	821.84
2012	823.19	818.74	823.89	825.90	803.31	811.37	808.86	796.49	805.35	802.90	799.80	790.62	809.37
2013	777.48	779.19	781.70	780.10	769.63	786.76	781.56	799.60	798.34	794.96	802.20	794.21	786.56
Leisure and Hospitality													
2009	266.51	278.38	281.53	287.76	285.12	289.44	294.30	298.35	281.23	279.40	280.58	277.75	283.61
2010	276.39	279.75	285.60	296.32	294.48	298.39	306.03	307.63	297.19	301.56	309.16	305.06	296.76
2011	298.40	306.76	309.81	316.15	311.52	313.08	321.57	323.68	316.54	318.53	310.47	308.48	313.23
2012	304.98	314.69	316.13	320.31	305.61	308.20	311.77	309.89	301.46	296.04	289.55	288.29	305.87
2013	288.50	298.45	301.98	299.47	299.40	302.54	305.63	305.58	299.54	295.80	293.67	294.25	298.25
Other Services													
2009	530.50	541.55	524.44	521.32	496.39	480.18	479.81	492.80	496.87	484.79	494.03	500.45	503.57
2010	506.84	504.50	523.89	535.21	530.04	531.38	525.84	540.06	539.96	540.83	543.46	541.65	530.56
2011	533.36	569.45	544.70	574.11	596.30	610.64	631.04	610.89	624.10	628.59	589.96	595.65	592.95
2012	615.62	609.84	601.40	597.29	570.10	566.80	582.12	563.94	568.66	568.59	566.21	568.51	581.34
2013	576.64	562.35	561.11	563.13	548.47	547.13	524.70	516.03	523.58	509.08	512.38	511.88	538.20

SOUTH DAKOTA
At a Glance

Population:
  2000 census: 754,858
  2010 census: 814,180
  2013 estimate: 844,877

Percent change in population:
  2000–2010: 7.9%
  2010–2013: 3.8%

Percent change in total nonfarm employment:
  2000–2010: 6.7%
  2010–2013: 3.4%

Industry with the largest growth in employment, 2000–2013 (thousands):
  Education and Health Services, 16.7

Industry with the largest decline or smallest growth in employment, 2000–2013 (thousands):
  Manufacturing, -2.2

Civilian labor force:
  2000: 408,685
  2010: 443,014
  2013: 448,361

Unemployment rate and rank among states (lowest to highest):
  2000: 2.7%, 3rd
  2010: 5.1%, 3rd
  2013: 3.8%, 2nd

Over-the-year change in unemployment rates:
  2010–2011: -0.4%
  2011–2012: -0.5%
  2012–2013: -0.4%

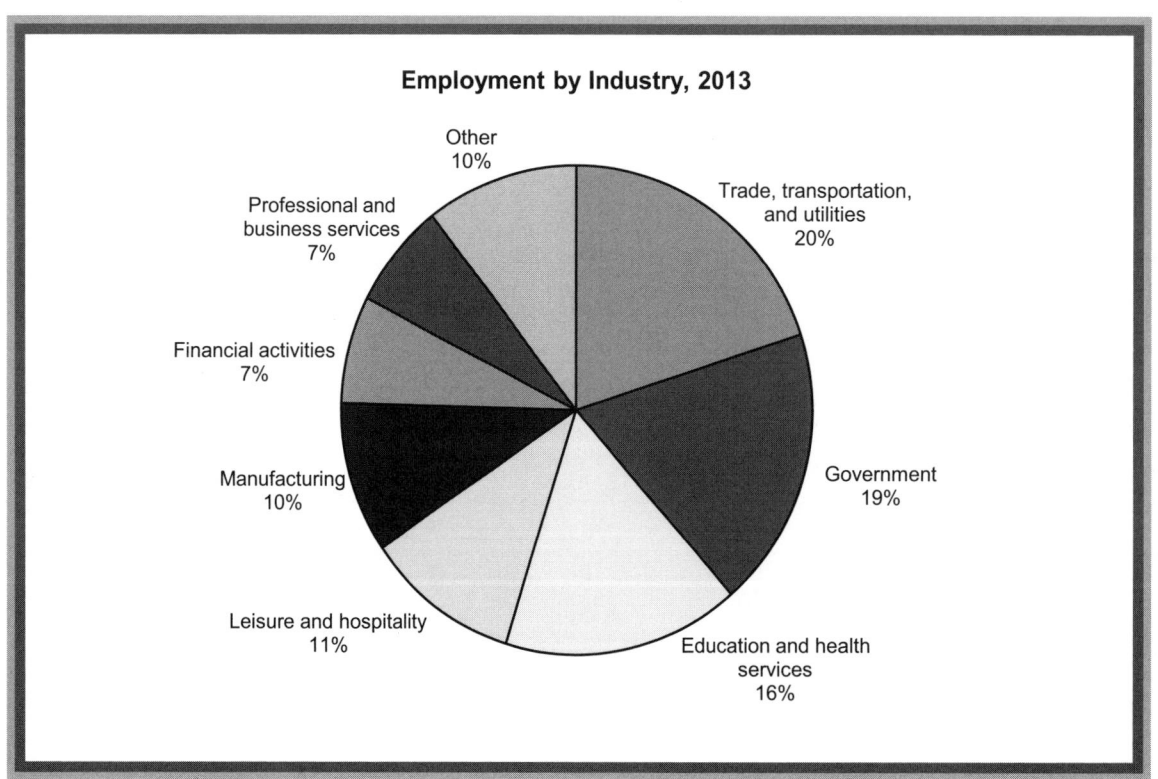

Employment by Industry, 2013

- Other 10%
- Professional and business services 7%
- Financial activities 7%
- Manufacturing 10%
- Leisure and hospitality 11%
- Education and health services 16%
- Government 19%
- Trade, transportation, and utilities 20%

1. Employment by Industry: South Dakota, Selected Years, 2002–2013

(Numbers in thousands, not seasonally adjusted)

Industry and year	January	February	March	April	May	June	July	August	September	October	November	December	Annual average
Total Nonfarm													
2002	365.7	365.7	367.3	373.6	382.9	388.1	383.2	384.7	381.1	380.9	378.7	378.6	377.5
2003	367.9	367.2	368.9	375.0	383.0	387.8	383.4	386.0	381.2	381.1	380.2	379.5	378.4
2004	369.7	370.0	372.1	381.0	388.9	394.1	388.4	391.2	388.9	388.0	386.3	385.4	383.7
2005	375.3	376.3	379.6	386.8	393.9	399.8	395.6	398.2	395.7	393.7	393.2	393.5	390.1
2006	384.0	385.0	388.1	393.3	402.7	408.8	404.0	407.4	403.4	402.6	401.8	401.9	398.6
2007	391.9	392.8	396.4	401.5	411.6	416.7	413.3	415.8	411.0	410.4	409.1	407.8	406.5
2008	399.6	401.1	403.5	407.1	416.5	420.9	416.6	420.1	415.3	414.8	411.6	409.7	411.4
2009	397.5	396.9	397.2	399.0	409.2	413.0	408.9	409.1	406.2	404.4	402.8	399.9	403.7
2010	388.2	389.1	392.1	399.4	407.5	413.1	409.1	411.6	407.9	408.8	406.8	405.0	403.2
2011	393.0	394.4	396.8	403.2	411.1	417.1	412.7	414.9	412.2	412.9	410.9	411.0	407.5
2012	399.8	400.6	404.6	411.1	418.7	424.5	419.1	420.8	418.5	417.9	417.0	415.4	414.0
2013	404.4	405.7	408.6	411.3	422.9	427.3	422.3	425.0	422.5	420.1	418.7	416.3	417.1
Total Private													
2002	292.4	291.6	293.1	299.3	306.8	311.8	312.0	313.2	307.1	305.9	303.5	303.0	303.3
2003	294.0	292.4	293.8	299.7	306.5	311.6	312.4	314.2	306.9	305.7	304.9	304.0	303.8
2004	295.4	295.1	297.0	304.9	311.7	317.3	317.2	320.1	313.8	312.1	310.1	309.1	308.7
2005	300.4	300.9	303.7	310.7	316.6	322.8	323.8	326.7	320.4	317.7	317.0	317.5	314.9
2006	309.6	309.5	312.3	317.4	325.2	331.5	332.1	335.4	328.5	326.5	325.4	325.8	323.3
2007	317.7	317.0	320.6	325.7	334.0	339.9	340.7	343.0	335.7	334.0	332.5	331.5	331.0
2008	324.9	324.6	327.0	330.5	338.1	344.0	344.5	346.8	339.3	337.2	333.9	332.1	335.2
2009	321.4	319.6	319.4	320.4	328.8	334.2	334.1	334.4	328.1	325.3	323.5	321.5	325.9
2010	311.1	310.7	312.7	319.6	326.3	332.8	333.9	336.3	329.2	329.1	327.0	325.6	324.5
2011	315.4	315.4	317.7	323.8	331.3	337.2	338.4	341.4	335.0	334.1	332.2	332.1	329.5
2012	323.0	322.9	326.2	332.4	339.8	345.9	345.6	347.8	341.1	338.9	337.8	336.7	336.5
2013	327.5	327.5	330.2	333.1	344.0	349.6	349.5	351.5	344.4	341.5	340.0	338.1	339.7
Goods-Producing													
2002	55.0	54.0	54.2	56.3	58.8	60.6	61.3	60.9	59.6	59.3	58.0	56.9	57.9
2003	54.3	53.6	54.2	56.7	59.1	60.6	61.0	61.0	59.5	59.3	58.4	56.9	57.9
2004	54.7	54.4	55.3	58.7	60.6	62.4	63.1	62.8	61.7	61.5	60.7	59.5	59.6
2005	56.9	56.8	57.7	60.5	62.3	64.3	64.9	64.7	63.7	63.7	63.0	61.5	61.7
2006	59.9	59.6	60.5	62.8	65.1	67.1	67.8	67.6	66.4	65.9	64.9	64.1	64.3
2007	61.5	60.6	61.9	63.6	65.9	67.8	68.4	68.1	67.2	66.9	66.1	64.6	65.2
2008	62.7	62.3	63.2	64.8	67.4	68.8	69.1	68.7	67.7	67.3	65.9	63.4	65.9
2009	59.6	58.4	57.8	57.7	60.3	62.1	62.2	61.2	60.1	59.7	58.4	56.2	59.5
2010	53.1	52.7	53.3	56.2	58.1	60.2	61.2	61.3	60.6	60.7	59.8	57.9	57.9
2011	54.9	54.6	55.4	58.1	60.9	62.8	63.5	63.6	62.9	63.2	62.1	60.7	60.2
2012	58.4	58.3	59.2	61.5	63.3	65.1	65.1	65.0	63.9	63.6	62.8	61.4	62.3
2013	59.0	58.6	59.3	60.6	64.0	65.9	66.1	66.1	64.9	64.2	63.8	62.0	62.9
Service-Providing													
2002	310.7	311.7	313.1	317.3	324.1	327.5	321.9	323.8	321.5	321.6	320.7	321.7	319.6
2003	313.6	313.6	314.7	318.3	323.9	327.2	322.4	325.0	321.7	321.8	321.8	322.6	320.6
2004	315.0	315.6	316.8	322.3	328.3	331.7	325.3	328.4	327.2	326.5	325.6	325.9	324.1
2005	318.4	319.5	321.9	326.3	331.6	335.5	330.7	333.5	332.0	330.0	330.2	332.0	328.5
2006	324.1	325.4	327.6	330.5	337.6	341.7	336.2	339.8	337.0	336.7	336.9	337.8	334.3
2007	330.4	332.2	334.5	337.9	345.7	348.9	344.9	347.7	343.8	343.5	343.0	343.2	341.3
2008	336.9	338.8	340.3	342.3	349.1	352.1	347.5	351.4	347.6	347.5	345.7	346.3	345.5
2009	337.9	338.5	339.4	341.3	348.9	350.9	346.7	347.9	346.1	344.7	344.4	343.7	344.2
2010	335.1	336.4	338.8	343.2	349.4	352.9	347.9	350.3	347.3	348.1	347.0	347.1	345.3
2011	338.1	339.8	341.4	345.1	350.2	354.3	349.2	351.3	349.3	349.7	348.8	350.3	347.3
2012	341.4	342.3	345.4	349.6	355.4	359.4	354.0	355.8	354.6	354.3	354.2	354.0	351.7
2013	345.4	347.1	349.3	350.7	358.9	361.4	356.2	358.9	357.6	355.9	354.9	354.3	354.2
Mining, Logging, and Construction													
2002	16.4	16.1	16.3	18.1	20.5	21.9	22.2	22.1	21.2	20.9	19.9	19.0	19.6
2003	16.8	16.4	16.8	19.1	21.4	22.7	23.1	23.0	22.0	21.6	20.5	19.3	20.2
2004	17.1	16.7	17.4	20.0	21.7	22.9	23.5	23.4	22.4	22.2	21.4	20.5	20.8
2005	18.1	17.9	18.6	21.0	22.7	24.2	24.7	24.7	23.7	23.5	22.7	21.2	21.9
2006	19.5	19.3	19.8	21.8	23.7	25.1	25.7	25.5	24.4	23.7	22.7	21.8	22.8
2007	19.7	19.0	20.0	21.5	23.9	25.4	26.1	26.0	25.2	24.6	23.9	22.5	23.2
2008	20.6	20.0	20.5	22.2	24.5	25.6	25.9	25.7	24.9	24.4	23.3	21.6	23.3
2009	19.0	18.7	18.9	19.9	22.6	24.4	25.3	24.3	23.2	22.9	21.9	20.0	21.8
2010	17.3	16.8	17.2	19.9	21.4	23.1	23.7	23.9	23.2	23.2	22.3	20.3	21.0
2011	17.4	16.9	17.4	19.6	21.7	23.3	23.9	23.8	23.2	23.1	21.8	20.5	21.1
2012	18.5	18.0	18.8	20.6	22.0	23.3	23.2	23.2	22.3	21.8	21.0	20.0	21.1
2013	17.8	17.5	18.0	19.3	22.3	23.7	24.2	24.3	23.4	22.8	22.2	20.2	21.3

1. Employment by Industry: South Dakota, Selected Years, 2002–2013—*Continued*

(Numbers in thousands, not seasonally adjusted)

Industry and year	January	February	March	April	May	June	July	August	September	October	November	December	Annual average
Manufacturing													
2002	38.6	37.9	37.9	38.2	38.3	38.7	39.1	38.8	38.4	38.4	38.1	37.9	38.4
2003	37.5	37.2	37.4	37.6	37.7	37.9	37.9	38.0	37.5	37.7	37.9	37.6	37.7
2004	37.6	37.7	37.9	38.7	38.9	39.5	39.6	39.4	39.3	39.3	39.3	39.0	38.9
2005	38.8	38.9	39.1	39.5	39.6	40.1	40.2	40.0	40.0	40.2	40.3	40.3	39.8
2006	40.4	40.3	40.7	41.0	41.4	42.0	42.1	42.1	42.0	42.2	42.2	42.3	41.6
2007	41.8	41.6	41.9	42.1	42.0	42.4	42.3	42.1	42.0	42.3	42.2	42.1	42.1
2008	42.1	42.3	42.7	42.6	42.9	43.2	43.2	43.0	42.8	42.9	42.6	41.8	42.7
2009	40.6	39.7	38.9	37.8	37.7	37.7	36.9	36.9	36.9	36.8	36.5	36.2	37.7
2010	35.8	35.9	36.1	36.3	36.7	37.1	37.5	37.4	37.4	37.5	37.5	37.6	36.9
2011	37.5	37.7	38.0	38.5	39.2	39.5	39.6	39.8	39.7	40.1	40.3	40.2	39.2
2012	39.9	40.3	40.4	40.9	41.3	41.8	41.9	41.8	41.6	41.8	41.8	41.4	41.2
2013	41.2	41.1	41.3	41.3	41.7	42.2	41.9	41.8	41.5	41.4	41.6	41.8	41.6
Trade, Transportation, and Utilities													
2002	75.0	74.3	74.3	75.9	77.2	77.8	77.0	77.4	76.4	77.1	77.7	78.2	76.5
2003	75.1	74.3	74.5	76.0	77.0	77.4	77.0	77.2	75.9	76.5	77.3	78.0	76.4
2004	75.2	74.4	74.7	76.2	77.7	78.2	77.8	78.7	77.1	77.8	78.7	79.3	77.2
2005	76.4	76.4	76.9	78.3	79.4	79.6	79.6	80.5	79.2	79.2	80.2	81.0	78.9
2006	78.3	77.7	78.3	79.0	80.4	81.2	80.7	81.6	80.1	80.5	81.4	82.2	80.1
2007	79.5	78.7	79.5	80.2	81.7	82.3	82.3	82.6	81.2	81.6	82.4	82.9	81.2
2008	81.0	80.3	80.6	81.1	82.3	83.0	83.3	83.7	82.2	82.6	82.6	83.1	82.2
2009	80.0	79.2	79.1	79.4	81.1	81.6	81.4	81.8	80.5	80.6	81.5	81.7	80.7
2010	78.8	78.1	78.6	79.7	80.9	81.7	81.6	82.0	80.4	81.2	82.0	82.3	80.6
2011	79.7	79.3	79.6	80.9	82.1	82.7	82.6	83.2	81.7	82.1	83.2	83.7	81.7
2012	81.2	80.4	81.0	82.0	83.5	84.2	83.8	84.3	83.1	83.2	84.4	84.6	83.0
2013	81.7	81.1	81.6	82.2	84.1	84.8	84.5	84.7	83.4	83.1	83.9	84.3	83.3
Wholesale Trade													
2002	16.6	16.6	16.6	16.9	16.9	17.0	16.7	16.6	16.3	16.6	16.6	16.6	16.7
2003	16.4	16.3	16.4	16.8	16.9	16.8	16.7	16.6	16.6	16.9	16.9	16.9	16.7
2004	16.6	16.6	16.9	17.2	17.3	17.3	17.1	17.1	16.9	17.4	17.3	17.4	17.1
2005	17.1	17.1	17.1	17.5	17.7	17.7	17.6	17.8	17.6	17.8	17.8	17.8	17.6
2006	18.0	18.0	18.1	18.3	18.6	18.6	18.3	18.3	18.0	18.2	18.1	18.1	18.2
2007	18.0	17.9	18.1	18.3	18.6	18.6	18.5	18.6	18.4	18.5	18.6	18.6	18.4
2008	18.6	18.6	18.7	18.8	19.0	19.0	18.9	18.9	18.6	18.8	18.4	18.6	18.7
2009	18.1	18.1	18.1	18.2	18.6	18.5	18.5	18.5	18.1	18.4	18.4	18.3	18.3
2010	18.1	18.1	18.2	18.6	18.8	18.8	18.8	18.8	18.6	18.8	18.8	18.7	18.6
2011	18.5	18.5	18.7	18.9	19.2	19.3	19.2	19.2	18.9	19.1	19.2	19.2	19.0
2012	19.2	19.1	19.3	19.6	19.8	19.9	19.7	19.6	19.3	19.5	19.5	19.5	19.5
2013	19.4	19.3	19.6	19.7	20.3	20.3	20.2	20.0	19.7	19.8	19.7	19.8	19.8
Retail Trade													
2002	46.8	46.1	46.1	47.2	48.3	48.9	48.7	49.1	48.2	48.7	49.4	49.8	48.1
2003	47.2	46.6	46.7	47.8	48.5	49.0	48.8	49.1	47.8	48.1	48.9	49.6	48.2
2004	47.4	46.7	46.7	47.7	48.9	49.3	49.2	50.0	48.4	48.5	49.5	50.1	48.5
2005	47.7	47.7	48.2	49.0	49.7	49.9	49.9	50.5	49.2	49.0	50.0	50.6	49.3
2006	48.0	47.4	47.8	48.2	49.0	49.8	49.7	50.3	49.1	49.3	50.4	51.0	49.2
2007	48.8	48.2	48.8	49.1	50.1	50.7	50.9	51.0	49.6	49.9	50.7	51.2	49.9
2008	49.4	48.7	48.9	49.2	50.0	50.7	51.1	51.5	50.2	50.4	50.9	51.2	50.2
2009	48.9	48.2	48.2	48.5	49.6	50.2	50.3	50.6	49.6	49.5	50.5	50.8	49.6
2010	48.5	47.9	48.2	48.7	49.5	50.2	50.3	50.6	49.1	49.7	50.5	50.9	49.5
2011	48.9	48.5	48.6	49.4	50.2	50.7	50.9	51.3	50.1	50.4	51.4	51.8	50.2
2012	49.8	49.1	49.4	50.2	51.2	51.7	51.6	52.2	51.0	51.0	52.2	52.4	51.0
2013	50.0	49.5	49.7	50.1	51.1	51.8	51.7	52.1	51.1	50.7	51.8	51.9	51.0
Transportation and Utilities													
2002	11.6	11.6	11.6	11.8	12.0	11.9	11.6	11.7	11.9	11.8	11.7	11.8	11.8
2003	11.5	11.4	11.4	11.4	11.6	11.6	11.5	11.5	11.5	11.5	11.5	11.5	11.5
2004	11.2	11.1	11.1	11.3	11.5	11.6	11.5	11.6	11.8	11.9	11.9	11.8	11.5
2005	11.6	11.6	11.6	11.8	12.0	12.0	12.1	12.2	12.4	12.4	12.4	12.6	12.1
2006	12.3	12.3	12.4	12.5	12.8	12.8	12.7	13.0	13.0	13.0	12.9	13.1	12.7
2007	12.7	12.6	12.6	12.8	13.0	13.0	12.9	13.0	13.2	13.2	13.1	13.1	12.9
2008	13.0	13.0	13.0	13.1	13.3	13.3	13.3	13.3	13.4	13.4	13.3	13.3	13.2
2009	13.0	12.9	12.8	12.7	12.9	12.9	12.6	12.7	12.8	12.7	12.6	12.6	12.8
2010	12.2	12.1	12.2	12.4	12.6	12.7	12.5	12.6	12.7	12.7	12.7	12.7	12.5
2011	12.3	12.3	12.3	12.6	12.7	12.7	12.5	12.7	12.7	12.6	12.6	12.7	12.6
2012	12.2	12.2	12.3	12.2	12.5	12.6	12.5	12.5	12.8	12.7	12.7	12.7	12.5
2013	12.3	12.3	12.3	12.4	12.7	12.7	12.6	12.6	12.6	12.6	12.4	12.6	12.5
Information													
2002	6.8	6.7	6.8	6.7	6.8	6.9	6.9	6.8	6.7	6.9	6.9	6.9	6.8
2003	6.8	6.7	6.7	6.6	6.7	6.8	6.7	6.8	6.7	6.8	6.9	6.9	6.8
2004	6.8	6.8	6.8	6.7	6.8	6.7	6.8	6.8	6.7	6.6	6.6	6.6	6.7
2005	6.6	6.6	6.5	6.5	6.7	6.8	6.9	6.9	6.9	6.9	6.9	6.9	6.8
2006	6.8	6.9	6.9	6.8	6.9	7.0	7.1	7.1	7.0	6.9	6.9	7.0	6.9
2007	7.0	7.1	7.0	7.3	7.4	7.5	7.1	7.2	7.0	7.0	7.0	7.0	7.1
2008	7.0	7.0	6.9	6.8	6.9	7.0	7.0	7.1	6.9	6.9	6.9	6.9	6.9
2009	6.8	6.8	6.7	6.6	6.8	6.7	6.7	6.7	6.7	6.7	6.7	6.7	6.7
2010	6.6	6.6	6.5	6.5	6.5	6.6	6.6	6.6	6.5	6.4	6.5	6.5	6.5
2011	6.4	6.4	6.4	6.3	6.4	6.5	6.5	6.5	6.4	6.4	6.3	6.3	6.4
2012	6.2	6.3	6.2	6.2	6.3	6.3	6.3	6.3	6.1	6.1	6.1	6.1	6.2
2013	6.0	6.0	6.0	6.0	6.1	6.1	6.1	6.2	6.0	6.1	6.2	6.2	6.1

1. Employment by Industry: South Dakota, Selected Years, 2002–2013—*Continued*

(Numbers in thousands, not seasonally adjusted)

Industry and year	January	February	March	April	May	June	July	August	September	October	November	December	Annual average
Financial Activities													
2002	28.0	28.0	27.9	27.9	27.9	28.1	28.0	28.0	27.7	27.6	27.7	28.0	27.9
2003	27.6	27.6	27.8	27.5	27.4	27.6	27.8	27.8	27.6	27.7	27.7	28.0	27.7
2004	27.7	27.6	27.8	27.5	27.7	28.0	27.9	28.0	27.9	27.8	27.8	28.1	27.8
2005	28.2	28.0	28.2	27.9	28.2	28.8	28.6	28.6	28.7	28.5	28.6	29.2	28.5
2006	29.0	29.0	29.1	29.0	29.2	29.5	29.7	29.9	29.8	29.8	29.9	30.2	29.5
2007	30.2	30.4	30.7	30.6	30.8	31.3	31.3	31.2	31.1	31.2	31.2	31.2	30.9
2008	31.0	31.0	31.3	30.9	31.2	31.5	31.4	31.1	31.0	30.6	30.6	30.7	31.0
2009	30.7	30.8	30.9	30.7	30.6	30.9	30.6	30.3	30.0	29.9	29.8	29.9	30.4
2010	29.3	29.1	28.9	28.8	28.9	29.0	29.0	28.9	28.5	28.6	28.6	28.7	28.9
2011	28.3	28.3	28.3	28.1	28.1	28.3	28.1	28.1	27.9	27.9	27.9	28.2	28.1
2012	27.9	27.9	28.1	28.3	28.6	29.0	29.0	29.0	28.8	28.8	29.0	29.2	28.6
2013	29.1	29.3	29.4	29.4	29.7	30.2	30.0	30.0	29.8	29.9	29.8	30.0	29.7
Professional and Business Services													
2002	24.2	24.6	24.7	25.1	25.1	25.5	25.1	25.4	24.7	24.9	25.0	24.9	24.9
2003	24.2	24.4	24.2	24.2	24.3	24.5	24.5	24.6	24.0	24.2	24.5	24.2	24.3
2004	23.2	23.8	23.4	24.3	24.5	24.5	24.5	25.2	24.7	24.5	24.1	24.0	24.2
2005	23.2	23.7	23.9	24.6	24.4	24.7	25.0	25.2	24.6	24.6	24.8	25.3	24.5
2006	24.6	25.0	25.0	25.5	25.7	26.0	26.1	26.1	25.8	26.1	26.1	26.4	25.7
2007	26.0	26.4	26.6	27.4	28.0	28.5	28.5	28.6	27.9	27.6	27.5	27.8	27.6
2008	27.4	27.6	27.8	28.2	28.2	28.6	28.5	28.8	28.1	27.8	27.7	27.8	28.0
2009	27.1	27.0	26.7	26.7	27.0	27.2	27.2	27.1	26.6	26.5	26.5	26.6	26.9
2010	26.2	26.4	26.6	27.6	27.6	27.9	28.2	28.2	27.7	28.1	27.8	28.0	27.5
2011	27.4	27.6	27.8	28.6	28.8	29.1	29.4	29.3	29.0	29.1	29.0	29.3	28.7
2012	28.3	28.4	28.7	29.1	29.2	29.6	29.9	30.0	29.5	29.3	29.2	29.1	29.2
2013	28.5	28.6	28.8	29.1	29.8	30.0	30.1	30.1	29.7	29.8	29.4	29.3	29.4
Education and Health Services													
2002	53.1	53.5	53.8	54.2	54.1	53.7	53.2	53.4	54.1	54.7	54.9	55.0	54.0
2003	54.9	54.8	54.9	55.2	55.3	54.9	55.0	55.2	55.4	56.2	56.4	56.5	55.4
2004	55.8	56.2	56.4	56.6	56.5	56.4	55.8	55.7	56.4	57.0	57.3	57.5	56.5
2005	56.8	57.0	57.3	57.5	57.3	57.2	56.6	57.0	57.6	57.9	58.2	58.4	57.4
2006	57.8	58.0	58.3	58.4	58.4	58.2	57.9	58.2	58.9	59.0	59.5	59.6	58.5
2007	58.9	59.1	59.5	59.8	60.1	59.8	59.6	59.9	60.5	60.9	61.2	61.3	60.1
2008	61.2	61.5	61.7	61.6	62.0	61.9	61.4	61.9	62.2	62.7	63.0	63.4	62.0
2009	62.6	62.7	62.9	63.0	63.2	63.2	62.7	62.6	63.1	63.7	64.1	64.5	63.2
2010	63.5	63.8	64.1	64.2	64.6	64.5	64.3	64.1	64.5	65.0	65.2	65.6	64.5
2011	64.5	64.7	65.0	64.9	65.5	65.4	64.9	65.2	65.3	65.9	66.2	66.5	65.3
2012	65.6	65.9	66.3	67.1	67.5	67.6	66.9	66.9	67.3	67.6	68.0	68.1	67.1
2013	67.2	67.7	68.0	67.8	68.4	67.9	67.4	67.5	67.6	68.5	68.8	68.8	68.0
Leisure and Hospitality													
2002	34.7	34.9	35.7	37.4	40.8	43.1	44.3	45.2	41.9	39.4	37.5	37.4	39.4
2003	35.6	35.5	36.0	37.8	40.9	43.9	44.5	45.7	42.0	39.3	38.0	37.7	39.7
2004	36.4	36.3	36.9	39.0	41.8	45.0	45.2	46.8	43.3	40.7	38.8	38.5	40.7
2005	37.0	37.0	37.8	39.9	42.7	45.7	46.5	48.1	44.1	41.5	39.8	39.7	41.7
2006	37.9	38.0	38.8	40.4	43.8	46.7	46.9	49.0	44.7	42.6	41.0	40.6	42.5
2007	39.0	39.1	39.7	41.1	44.2	46.7	47.5	49.5	45.0	43.1	41.5	41.0	43.1
2008	39.1	39.3	39.9	41.3	44.1	47.1	47.6	49.3	45.2	43.3	41.4	41.0	43.2
2009	39.0	39.1	39.8	40.7	44.0	46.6	47.4	48.9	45.5	42.6	41.0	40.3	42.9
2010	38.2	38.6	39.2	41.0	44.0	47.0	47.1	49.4	45.4	43.5	41.7	41.1	43.0
2011	38.9	39.2	39.8	41.4	43.9	46.5	47.5	49.6	46.2	43.9	42.0	41.7	43.4
2012	39.8	40.2	41.1	42.5	45.5	48.0	48.4	50.2	46.6	44.5	42.6	42.4	44.3
2013	40.4	40.5	41.4	42.1	45.7	48.4	49.0	50.7	47.0	44.0	42.2	41.6	44.4
Other Services													
2002	15.6	15.6	15.7	15.8	16.1	16.1	16.2	16.1	16.0	16.0	15.8	15.7	15.9
2003	15.5	15.5	15.5	15.7	15.8	15.9	15.9	15.9	15.8	15.7	15.7	15.8	15.7
2004	15.6	15.6	15.7	15.9	16.1	16.1	16.1	16.1	16.0	16.2	16.1	15.6	15.9
2005	15.3	15.4	15.4	15.5	15.6	15.7	15.7	15.7	15.6	15.4	15.5	15.5	15.5
2006	15.3	15.3	15.4	15.5	15.7	15.8	15.9	15.9	15.8	15.7	15.7	15.7	15.6
2007	15.6	15.6	15.7	15.7	15.9	16.0	16.0	15.9	15.8	15.7	15.6	15.7	15.8
2008	15.5	15.6	15.6	15.8	16.0	16.1	16.2	16.2	16.0	16.0	15.8	15.8	15.9
2009	15.6	15.6	15.5	15.6	15.8	15.9	15.9	15.8	15.6	15.6	15.5	15.6	15.7
2010	15.4	15.4	15.5	15.6	15.7	15.9	15.9	15.8	15.6	15.6	15.4	15.5	15.6
2011	15.3	15.3	15.4	15.5	15.6	15.9	15.9	15.9	15.6	15.6	15.5	15.7	15.6
2012	15.6	15.5	15.6	15.7	15.9	16.1	16.2	16.1	15.8	15.8	15.7	15.8	15.8
2013	15.6	15.7	15.7	15.9	16.2	16.3	16.3	16.2	16.0	15.9	15.9	15.9	16.0
Government													
2002	73.3	74.1	74.2	74.3	76.1	76.3	71.2	71.5	74.0	75.0	75.2	75.6	74.2
2003	73.9	74.8	75.1	75.3	76.5	76.2	71.0	71.8	74.3	75.4	75.3	75.5	74.6
2004	74.3	74.9	75.1	76.1	77.2	76.8	71.2	71.1	75.1	75.9	76.2	76.3	75.0
2005	74.9	75.4	75.9	76.1	77.3	77.0	71.8	71.5	75.3	76.0	76.2	76.0	75.3
2006	74.4	75.5	75.8	75.9	77.5	77.3	71.9	72.0	74.9	76.1	76.4	76.1	75.3
2007	74.2	75.8	75.8	75.8	77.6	76.8	72.6	72.8	75.3	76.4	76.6	76.3	75.5
2008	74.7	76.5	76.5	76.6	78.4	76.9	72.1	73.3	76.0	77.6	77.7	77.6	76.2
2009	76.1	77.3	77.8	78.6	80.4	78.8	74.8	74.7	78.1	79.1	79.3	78.4	77.8
2010	77.1	78.4	79.4	79.8	81.2	80.3	75.2	75.3	78.7	79.7	79.8	79.4	78.7
2011	77.6	79.0	79.1	79.4	79.8	79.9	74.3	73.5	77.2	78.8	78.7	78.9	78.0
2012	76.8	77.7	78.4	78.7	78.9	78.6	73.5	73.0	77.4	79.0	79.2	78.7	77.5
2013	76.9	78.2	78.4	78.2	78.9	77.7	72.8	73.5	78.1	78.6	78.7	78.2	77.4

2. Average Weekly Hours by Selected Industry: South Dakota, 2009–2013

(Not seasonally adjusted)

Industry and year	January	February	March	April	May	June	July	August	September	October	November	December	Annual average
Total Private													
2009	32.4	32.8	32.9	32.3	33.2	33.1	33.9	34.5	34.1	33.1	33.9	33.5	33.3
2010	33.2	33.7	33.3	33.6	33.8	34.0	34.2	34.5	33.8	33.9	34.2	33.7	33.8
2011	33.8	33.7	33.7	33.9	34.1	34.1	34.0	33.8	33.9	34.3	34.0	33.8	33.9
2012	34.3	34.1	34.1	34.6	34.6	35.5	35.5	35.1	35.3	34.6	34.3	34.5	34.7
2013	33.9	33.9	34.0	33.3	34.3	35.5	34.6	35.0	35.3	34.4	34.6	34.8	34.5
Goods-Producing													
2009	36.3	36.6	35.6	34.8	37.3	36.3	37.7	38.6	37.7	37.5	38.7	37.6	37.1
2010	37.1	37.3	36.9	39.1	37.7	38.4	39.0	39.2	39.3	39.8	39.7	38.8	38.6
2011	38.2	38.1	39.2	39.6	40.0	39.7	39.6	39.7	40.1	40.5	40.2	39.8	39.6
2012	39.2	39.3	39.6	40.7	41.0	41.1	41.1	41.3	41.2	41.4	40.7	39.9	40.6
2013	38.7	39.4	39.9	38.4	40.4	41.8	41.5	42.0	42.7	41.5	41.9	40.8	40.8
Mining, Logging, and Construction													
2009	36.6	37.2	37.6	37.9	40.4	39.1	41.6	41.8	40.3	38.6	39.9	37.0	39.2
2010	36.7	36.2	35.6	40.4	36.6	38.5	40.2	41.1	40.0	41.9	40.5	37.4	38.9
2011	36.8	36.7	37.7	38.9	38.9	40.1	39.9	40.2	40.0	41.1	41.0	38.6	39.3
2012	37.9	38.2	38.6	39.9	41.9	42.9	42.6	42.7	42.6	42.9	41.2	39.8	41.1
2013	38.0	38.7	37.8	35.8	40.7	42.6	42.1	43.1	43.5	41.0	41.4	37.2	40.4
Manufacturing													
2009	36.1	36.3	34.6	33.2	35.5	34.5	35.1	36.4	36.0	36.9	37.9	38.0	35.8
2010	37.4	37.7	37.6	38.4	38.4	38.3	38.2	38.0	38.9	38.5	39.2	39.5	38.4
2011	38.9	38.7	39.9	39.9	40.6	39.4	39.4	39.5	40.2	40.1	39.7	40.4	39.7
2012	39.8	39.9	40.1	41.2	40.4	40.1	40.2	40.6	40.5	40.6	40.4	40.0	40.3
2013	38.9	39.7	40.8	39.6	40.2	41.3	41.1	41.5	42.2	41.7	42.1	42.6	41.0
Trade, Transportation, and Utilities													
2009	31.5	32.3	32.2	31.6	33.3	33.0	33.1	33.1	32.9	32.7	33.5	33.4	32.7
2010	32.8	33.6	33.4	33.2	34.0	34.1	34.2	34.6	33.7	33.8	33.5	32.6	33.6
2011	33.2	33.1	32.9	33.0	33.6	33.5	33.2	33.0	32.9	33.3	32.7	32.5	33.1
2012	33.2	33.2	33.3	34.1	34.1	34.7	34.5	34.2	33.6	33.5	33.2	33.2	33.7
2013	32.7	33.0	33.0	32.4	34.3	34.9	34.2	34.3	33.9	33.9	33.5	33.2	33.6
Professional and Business Services													
2009	32.8	33.4	34.5	33.1	32.2	33.1	33.5	34.3	33.5	33.7	34.4	34.1	33.5
2010	34.6	35.7	35.4	36.0	35.9	37.2	36.8	37.0	36.1	36.6	37.2	36.3	36.2
2011	37.5	37.2	37.2	37.6	38.7	38.4	37.7	38.3	37.6	39.2	38.1	37.8	38.0
2012	38.3	38.1	37.5	37.7	37.7	38.4	37.0	37.3	37.5	37.9	36.7	37.4	37.6
2013	37.1	37.0	36.8	36.1	36.7	38.1	36.8	37.4	37.3	36.3	37.1	37.0	37.0
Education and Health Services													
2009	33.8	33.0	35.4	35.2	34.9	35.2	37.1	37.0	37.2	33.5	34.0	34.5	35.1
2010	32.7	32.9	32.2	32.2	32.7	32.6	33.5	32.3	32.0	32.3	32.6	32.3	32.5
2011	32.0	31.7	31.3	31.3	30.6	31.2	31.6	30.9	31.5	30.9	31.4	30.6	31.2
2012	30.9	30.6	31.4	31.0	31.6	33.3	32.8	32.4	33.6	31.8	31.9	33.0	32.0
2013	32.8	33.0	33.1	33.0	32.8	33.7	32.2	32.2	32.5	31.6	32.3	32.7	32.7
Leisure and Hospitality													
2009	21.9	23.5	22.9	22.2	23.1	24.1	25.0	25.5	23.9	22.7	23.2	22.3	23.4
2010	22.5	22.7	23.0	22.6	23.8	24.1	24.6	26.4	23.9	23.1	22.8	22.5	23.6
2011	22.9	22.7	23.1	22.7	23.3	23.8	24.5	25.3	23.0	23.4	22.8	22.7	23.4
2012	23.6	23.8	23.6	23.5	23.2	24.8	26.8	26.2	25.2	24.3	24.0	24.2	24.5
2013	23.6	24.0	23.8	22.9	23.9	25.5	25.9	25.6	25.0	23.9	23.3	23.5	24.3

3. Average Hourly Earnings by Selected Industry: South Dakota, 2009–2013

(Dollars, not seasonally adjusted)

Industry and year	January	February	March	April	May	June	July	August	September	October	November	December	Annual average
Total Private													
2009	17.72	17.78	17.89	17.69	17.80	17.60	18.10	17.78	18.10	18.13	18.30	18.43	17.94
2010	18.78	18.63	18.53	18.68	18.41	18.14	18.55	18.16	18.65	18.64	18.73	18.75	18.55
2011	19.20	19.14	19.14	19.21	18.96	18.66	18.72	18.74	18.98	19.19	19.26	19.45	19.05
2012	19.50	19.41	19.34	19.53	19.27	19.14	19.28	19.13	19.63	19.64	19.51	19.74	19.42
2013	19.40	19.61	19.42	19.89	19.56	19.40	19.41	19.52	19.89	19.54	19.75	20.04	19.62
Goods-Producing													
2009	17.73	18.31	18.35	18.28	17.86	18.13	18.16	17.95	18.09	18.15	17.82	17.88	18.06
2010	18.32	18.73	18.32	18.94	18.55	18.39	18.70	18.74	18.81	18.85	18.82	19.47	18.73
2011	19.75	19.68	19.55	19.44	19.12	19.02	18.97	18.99	19.09	19.11	18.80	18.96	19.19
2012	19.25	18.97	19.01	19.01	18.77	18.72	18.96	18.83	19.06	19.08	18.74	19.40	18.98
2013	19.42	19.68	19.34	19.54	19.35	19.13	19.17	19.13	19.61	19.58	19.56	19.95	19.45
Mining, Logging, and Construction													
2009	20.40	21.09	20.43	19.88	19.56	19.25	19.32	19.31	19.05	19.28	19.64	19.63	19.67
2010	20.53	21.17	20.89	21.14	20.22	19.76	20.15	20.15	20.15	20.16	20.47	21.29	20.45
2011	21.15	21.16	21.23	20.71	20.38	19.82	19.68	19.36	19.48	19.39	19.41	19.93	20.04
2012	20.32	20.14	20.05	19.96	19.38	19.10	19.34	19.22	19.39	19.42	19.43	19.96	19.59
2013	20.06	20.27	19.85	20.12	19.65	19.41	19.11	19.44	19.96	20.05	20.02	20.35	19.81
Manufacturing													
2009	16.47	16.96	17.25	17.32	16.70	17.31	17.22	16.93	17.42	17.41	16.66	16.94	17.04
2010	17.27	17.63	17.17	17.67	17.62	17.54	17.73	17.77	17.95	17.96	17.80	18.53	17.73
2011	19.13	19.05	18.83	18.81	18.46	18.54	18.53	18.76	18.87	18.95	18.46	18.49	18.73
2012	18.78	18.47	18.54	18.54	18.44	18.50	18.73	18.60	18.87	18.90	18.38	19.13	18.66
2013	19.15	19.44	19.13	19.29	19.19	18.96	19.21	18.95	19.40	19.32	19.32	19.78	19.26
Trade, Transportation, and Utilities													
2009	17.50	17.71	18.13	17.98	18.41	18.25	18.50	18.51	19.37	19.60	20.34	20.13	18.72
2010	20.57	19.98	19.77	20.23	19.58	19.18	19.73	19.08	19.74	19.78	19.60	19.16	19.69
2011	19.20	19.40	19.43	19.83	19.54	18.70	18.82	18.97	19.00	19.22	19.10	18.96	19.18
2012	19.27	19.55	19.29	19.55	19.11	19.08	19.24	18.96	19.82	19.68	19.64	19.87	19.42
2013	19.60	19.51	19.27	19.75	19.42	19.06	18.69	18.64	18.83	19.01	19.30	19.03	19.17
Professional and Business Services													
2009	22.42	21.94	21.32	20.68	21.38	20.63	20.78	21.46	20.81	21.02	21.13	21.23	21.23
2010	20.95	20.56	20.50	19.88	20.08	19.63	20.09	20.32	20.81	20.90	21.04	21.16	20.49
2011	23.46	22.89	23.01	22.93	22.70	22.34	22.79	22.63	23.54	23.95	24.19	23.98	23.20
2012	23.32	22.42	22.82	23.45	23.13	22.45	23.52	22.95	23.74	23.37	22.97	23.55	23.14
2013	23.15	23.47	23.43	23.74	23.76	23.55	23.65	23.37	24.22	23.84	24.47	24.26	23.74
Education and Health Services													
2009	17.25	17.03	17.78	17.98	17.67	18.01	19.02	18.58	18.67	18.21	18.22	18.38	18.08
2010	18.52	18.51	18.84	19.05	18.99	19.54	19.25	18.27	18.96	19.16	19.04	18.34	18.87
2011	18.65	18.52	18.50	18.44	18.00	17.80	18.28	18.04	18.00	18.09	18.31	18.05	18.22
2012	18.46	18.35	18.17	18.34	18.46	18.93	18.86	18.89	18.87	18.67	18.73	18.85	18.64
2013	18.20	18.51	18.63	19.53	18.94	19.36	19.76	20.52	20.48	20.59	20.43	20.47	19.61
Leisure and Hospitality													
2009	11.58	11.56	11.30	11.43	11.29	10.94	10.78	11.26	10.00	10.23	10.47	10.83	10.96
2010	10.68	10.90	10.88	10.88	10.56	10.26	10.34	10.45	10.75	10.73	10.72	11.17	10.67
2011	11.05	10.99	10.90	10.81	10.74	10.42	10.47	10.91	10.89	10.85	11.18	11.30	10.86
2012	11.46	11.47	11.69	11.72	11.61	11.26	11.21	11.38	11.66	11.80	11.84	12.01	11.58
2013	11.97	12.09	11.89	11.93	11.70	11.41	11.46	11.48	11.80	12.09	12.23	12.44	11.84

4. Average Weekly Earnings by Selected Industry: South Dakota, 2009–2013

(Dollars, not seasonally adjusted)

Industry and year	January	February	March	April	May	June	July	August	September	October	November	December	Annual average
Total Private													
2009	574.13	583.18	588.58	571.39	590.96	582.56	613.59	613.41	617.21	600.10	620.37	617.41	597.40
2010	623.50	627.83	617.05	627.65	622.26	616.76	634.41	626.52	630.37	631.90	640.57	631.88	626.99
2011	648.96	645.02	645.02	651.22	646.54	636.31	636.48	633.41	643.42	658.22	654.84	657.41	645.80
2012	668.85	661.88	659.49	675.74	666.74	679.47	684.44	671.46	692.94	679.54	669.19	681.03	673.87
2013	657.66	664.78	660.28	662.34	670.91	688.70	671.59	683.20	702.12	672.18	683.35	697.39	676.89
Goods-Producing													
2009	643.60	670.15	653.26	636.14	666.18	658.12	684.63	692.87	681.99	680.63	689.63	672.29	670.03
2010	679.67	698.63	676.01	740.55	699.34	706.18	729.30	734.61	739.23	750.23	747.15	755.44	722.98
2011	754.45	749.81	766.36	769.82	764.80	755.09	751.21	753.90	765.51	773.96	755.76	754.61	759.92
2012	754.60	745.52	752.80	773.71	769.57	769.39	779.26	777.68	785.27	789.91	762.72	774.06	770.59
2013	751.55	775.39	771.67	750.34	781.74	799.63	795.56	803.46	837.35	812.57	819.56	813.96	793.56
Mining, Logging, and Construction													
2009	746.64	784.55	768.17	753.45	790.22	752.68	803.71	807.16	767.72	744.21	783.64	726.31	771.06
2010	753.45	766.35	743.68	854.06	740.05	760.76	810.03	828.17	806.00	844.70	829.04	796.25	795.51
2011	778.32	776.57	800.37	805.62	792.78	794.78	785.23	778.27	779.20	796.93	795.81	769.30	787.57
2012	770.13	769.35	773.93	796.40	812.02	819.39	823.88	820.69	826.01	833.12	800.52	794.41	805.15
2013	762.28	784.45	750.33	720.30	799.76	826.87	804.53	837.86	868.26	822.05	828.83	757.02	800.32
Manufacturing													
2009	594.57	615.65	596.85	575.02	592.85	597.20	604.42	616.25	627.12	642.43	631.41	643.72	610.03
2010	645.90	664.65	645.59	678.53	676.61	671.78	677.29	675.26	698.26	691.46	697.76	731.94	680.83
2011	744.16	737.24	751.32	750.52	749.48	730.48	730.08	741.02	758.57	759.90	732.86	747.00	743.58
2012	747.44	736.95	743.45	763.85	744.98	741.85	752.95	755.16	764.24	767.34	742.55	765.20	752.00
2013	744.94	771.77	780.50	763.88	771.44	783.05	789.53	786.43	818.68	805.64	813.37	842.63	789.66
Trade, Transportation, and Utilities													
2009	551.25	572.03	583.79	568.17	613.05	602.25	612.35	612.68	637.27	640.92	681.39	672.34	612.14
2010	674.70	671.33	660.32	671.64	665.72	654.04	674.77	660.17	665.24	668.56	656.60	624.62	661.58
2011	637.44	642.14	639.25	654.39	656.54	626.45	624.82	626.01	625.10	640.03	624.57	616.20	634.86
2012	639.76	649.06	642.36	666.66	651.65	662.08	663.78	648.43	665.95	659.28	652.05	659.68	654.45
2013	640.92	643.83	635.91	639.90	666.11	665.19	639.20	639.35	638.34	644.44	646.55	631.80	644.11
Professional and Business Services													
2009	735.38	732.80	735.54	684.51	688.44	682.85	696.13	736.08	697.14	708.37	726.87	723.94	711.21
2010	724.87	733.99	725.70	715.68	720.87	730.24	739.31	751.84	751.24	764.94	782.69	768.11	741.74
2011	879.75	851.51	855.97	862.17	878.49	857.86	859.18	866.73	885.10	938.84	921.64	906.44	881.60
2012	893.16	854.20	855.75	884.07	872.00	862.08	870.24	856.04	890.25	885.72	843.00	880.77	870.06
2013	858.87	868.39	862.22	857.01	871.99	897.26	870.32	874.04	903.41	865.39	907.84	897.62	878.38
Education and Health Services													
2009	583.05	561.99	629.41	632.90	616.68	633.95	705.64	687.46	694.52	610.04	619.48	634.11	634.61
2010	605.60	608.98	606.65	613.41	620.97	637.00	644.88	590.12	606.72	618.87	620.70	592.38	613.28
2011	596.80	587.08	579.05	577.17	550.80	555.36	577.65	557.44	567.00	558.98	574.93	552.33	568.46
2012	570.41	561.51	570.54	568.54	583.34	630.37	618.61	612.04	634.03	593.71	597.49	622.05	596.48
2013	596.96	610.83	616.65	644.49	621.23	652.43	636.27	660.74	665.60	650.64	659.89	669.37	641.25
Leisure and Hospitality													
2009	253.60	271.66	258.77	253.75	260.80	263.65	269.50	287.13	239.00	232.22	242.90	241.51	256.46
2010	240.30	247.43	250.24	245.89	251.33	247.27	254.36	275.88	256.93	247.86	244.42	251.33	251.81
2011	253.05	249.47	251.79	245.39	250.24	248.00	256.52	276.02	250.47	253.89	254.90	256.51	254.12
2012	270.46	272.99	275.88	275.42	269.35	279.25	300.43	298.16	293.83	286.74	284.16	290.64	283.71
2013	282.49	290.16	282.98	273.20	279.63	290.96	296.81	293.89	295.00	288.95	284.96	292.34	287.71

TENNESSEE
At a Glance

Population:
    2000 census: 5,689,427
    2010 census: 6,346,105
    2013 estimate: 6,495,978

Percent change in population:
    2000–2010: 11.5%
    2010–2013: 2.4%

Percent change in total nonfarm employment:
    2000–2010: -4.3%
    2010–2013: 5.1%

Industry with the largest growth in employment, 2000–2013 (thousands):
    Education and Health Services, 114.8

Industry with the largest decline or smallest growth in employment, 2000–2013 (thousands):
    Manufacturing, -178.4

Civilian labor force:
    2000: 2,871,539
    2010: 3,082,645
    2013: 3,070,271

Unemployment rate and rank among states (lowest to highest):
    2000: 4.0%, 28th
    2010: 9.9%, 34th
    2013: 8.2%, 41st

Over-the-year change in unemployment rates:
    2010–2011: -0.6%
    2011–2012: -1.1%
    2012–2013: 0.0%

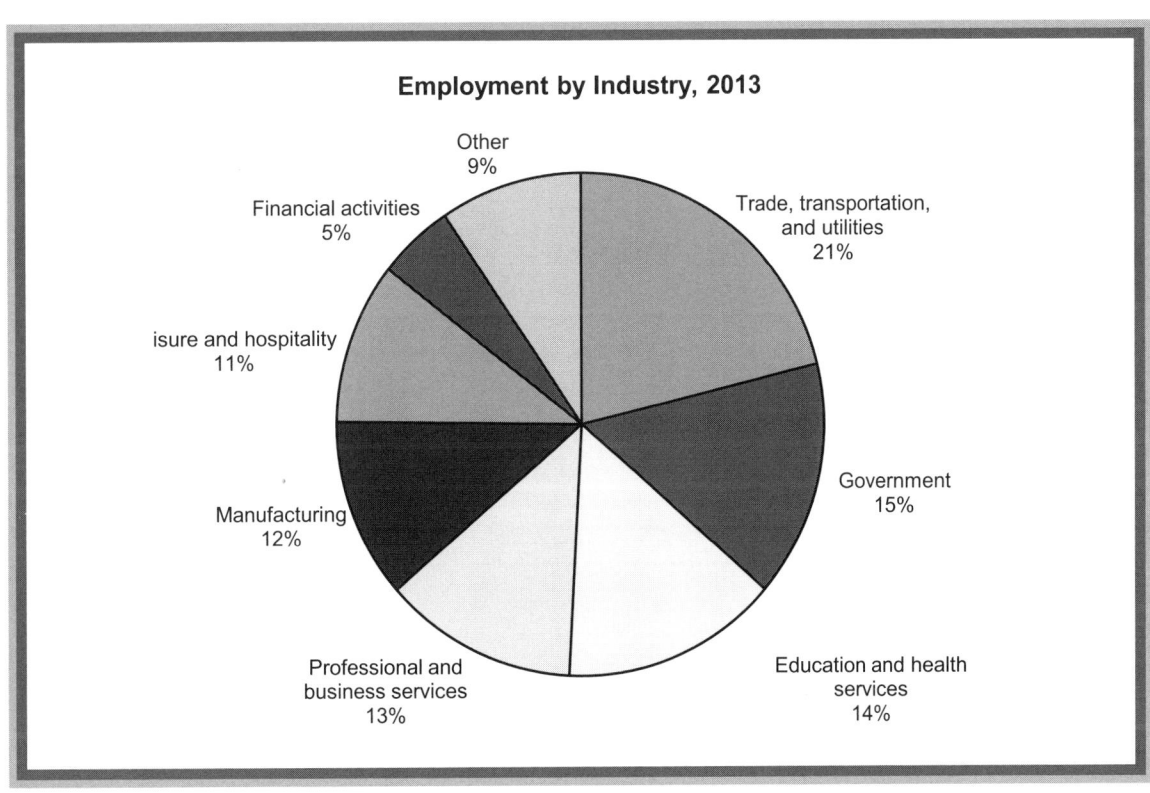

Employment by Industry, 2013

Other 9%
Financial activities 5%
Trade, transportation, and utilities 21%
isure and hospitality 11%
Manufacturing 12%
Government 15%
Professional and business services 13%
Education and health services 14%

1. Employment by Industry: Tennessee, Selected Years, 2002–2013

(Numbers in thousands, not seasonally adjusted)

Industry and year	January	February	March	April	May	June	July	August	September	October	November	December	Annual average
Total Nonfarm													
2002	2,611.9	2,622.8	2,643.7	2,660.0	2,670.2	2,672.0	2,657.2	2,674.7	2,684.2	2,684.6	2,693.5	2,698.1	2,664.4
2003	2,619.8	2,627.9	2,646.0	2,662.8	2,671.8	2,668.1	2,637.3	2,661.8	2,675.7	2,683.5	2,694.7	2,702.4	2,662.7
2004	2,637.4	2,668.4	2,678.9	2,700.4	2,706.7	2,710.6	2,693.6	2,716.3	2,725.5	2,732.6	2,746.2	2,756.2	2,706.1
2005	2,671.3	2,696.1	2,718.4	2,739.5	2,746.5	2,743.7	2,731.8	2,753.6	2,776.3	2,767.1	2,784.7	2,788.3	2,743.1
2006	2,727.1	2,734.8	2,765.3	2,781.4	2,791.6	2,791.4	2,769.8	2,796.8	2,810.2	2,793.8	2,811.4	2,818.6	2,782.7
2007	2,744.9	2,753.7	2,784.0	2,787.9	2,799.3	2,798.0	2,782.4	2,811.2	2,821.7	2,815.9	2,833.6	2,836.4	2,797.4
2008	2,762.4	2,771.9	2,790.1	2,797.1	2,805.4	2,784.3	2,758.6	2,779.0	2,779.4	2,766.1	2,758.6	2,745.1	2,774.8
2009	2,647.6	2,636.8	2,634.6	2,629.9	2,630.3	2,599.3	2,582.6	2,600.2	2,609.6	2,616.2	2,629.0	2,621.9	2,619.8
2010	2,556.9	2,562.4	2,585.2	2,614.9	2,638.0	2,613.2	2,600.4	2,619.4	2,635.4	2,645.7	2,657.1	2,655.6	2,615.4
2011	2,587.5	2,609.6	2,632.1	2,660.6	2,669.3	2,646.1	2,643.0	2,670.7	2,688.2	2,697.4	2,716.7	2,715.5	2,661.4
2012	2,648.9	2,667.6	2,698.8	2,715.1	2,724.6	2,704.8	2,686.5	2,713.4	2,732.5	2,743.7	2,764.7	2,766.9	2,714.0
2013	2,688.8	2,708.4	2,730.4	2,747.7	2,756.7	2,737.0	2,722.2	2,749.6	2,769.9	2,782.7	2,805.3	2,798.2	2,749.7
Total Private													
2002	2,205.5	2,208.0	2,226.9	2,240.8	2,255.1	2,266.4	2,271.0	2,278.9	2,275.1	2,268.9	2,274.5	2,278.7	2,254.2
2003	2,211.4	2,212.6	2,228.4	2,242.6	2,254.1	2,263.6	2,248.4	2,263.4	2,264.1	2,267.5	2,277.7	2,284.7	2,251.5
2004	2,226.3	2,235.3	2,257.8	2,279.7	2,289.2	2,303.1	2,301.8	2,313.8	2,310.2	2,313.6	2,325.0	2,334.3	2,290.8
2005	2,261.1	2,278.4	2,299.4	2,322.9	2,331.4	2,343.9	2,339.8	2,352.1	2,358.0	2,347.1	2,363.1	2,367.6	2,330.4
2006	2,315.1	2,317.2	2,345.0	2,359.3	2,371.0	2,387.0	2,371.8	2,386.7	2,387.4	2,370.0	2,385.1	2,393.4	2,365.8
2007	2,326.8	2,331.2	2,358.7	2,365.2	2,376.0	2,392.8	2,382.1	2,396.7	2,394.0	2,384.5	2,400.3	2,405.3	2,376.1
2008	2,337.7	2,341.8	2,357.7	2,363.8	2,371.5	2,378.6	2,352.7	2,360.0	2,348.8	2,327.3	2,318.6	2,306.5	2,347.1
2009	2,219.7	2,204.1	2,200.1	2,193.8	2,195.1	2,195.6	2,178.0	2,183.1	2,178.0	2,176.2	2,187.9	2,184.2	2,191.3
2010	2,126.3	2,127.5	2,148.4	2,174.1	2,188.2	2,199.6	2,191.4	2,198.3	2,197.1	2,205.2	2,215.9	2,217.5	2,182.5
2011	2,156.3	2,173.1	2,194.5	2,223.6	2,234.1	2,243.8	2,244.7	2,254.1	2,256.4	2,261.5	2,280.0	2,281.6	2,233.6
2012	2,224.5	2,234.9	2,263.0	2,280.2	2,295.4	2,306.9	2,291.8	2,306.3	2,304.9	2,310.0	2,329.0	2,332.2	2,289.9
2013	2,268.4	2,278.9	2,299.2	2,315.7	2,329.6	2,342.1	2,330.1	2,345.9	2,345.5	2,354.6	2,376.5	2,371.9	2,329.9
Goods-Producing													
2002	544.6	543.1	544.3	546.3	551.1	554.0	552.0	554.1	552.4	547.8	543.1	543.2	548.0
2003	530.3	528.2	530.3	532.4	534.7	537.0	532.0	534.9	534.5	533.6	532.3	533.5	532.8
2004	522.0	522.8	526.7	531.8	536.5	539.8	537.3	539.1	538.9	534.1	533.2	533.0	532.9
2005	526.0	527.4	531.2	532.4	535.0	538.4	534.3	538.1	539.7	535.6	536.5	533.3	534.0
2006	530.3	529.7	535.0	536.7	538.4	541.8	535.4	538.5	537.7	529.6	527.4	525.2	533.8
2007	517.8	517.4	522.1	520.0	518.2	522.0	517.1	519.4	518.5	515.5	513.6	512.2	517.8
2008	502.0	502.2	503.6	501.9	502.8	503.9	494.7	496.3	491.5	482.8	473.2	464.9	493.3
2009	443.7	435.5	430.9	423.0	418.3	415.5	413.5	413.9	413.2	409.6	408.1	403.8	419.0
2010	393.2	391.5	396.4	402.6	404.6	409.3	408.2	409.8	409.9	408.7	407.8	406.5	404.0
2011	397.2	400.6	404.9	409.6	412.1	416.8	417.8	418.6	419.8	420.7	421.4	417.7	413.1
2012	409.9	412.1	417.3	419.8	422.7	427.0	425.0	428.4	427.4	426.2	426.2	425.1	422.3
2013	417.1	418.9	421.9	424.1	426.9	430.1	427.9	430.8	431.2	431.6	432.9	429.7	426.9
Service-Providing													
2002	2,067.3	2,079.7	2,099.4	2,113.7	2,119.1	2,118.0	2,105.2	2,120.6	2,131.8	2,136.8	2,150.4	2,154.9	2,116.4
2003	2,089.5	2,099.7	2,115.7	2,130.4	2,137.1	2,131.1	2,105.3	2,126.9	2,141.2	2,149.9	2,162.4	2,168.9	2,129.8
2004	2,115.4	2,145.6	2,152.2	2,168.6	2,170.2	2,170.8	2,156.3	2,177.2	2,186.6	2,198.5	2,213.0	2,223.2	2,173.1
2005	2,145.3	2,168.7	2,187.2	2,207.1	2,211.5	2,205.3	2,197.5	2,215.5	2,236.6	2,231.5	2,248.2	2,255.0	2,209.1
2006	2,196.8	2,205.1	2,230.3	2,244.7	2,253.2	2,249.6	2,234.4	2,258.3	2,272.5	2,264.2	2,284.0	2,293.4	2,248.9
2007	2,227.1	2,236.3	2,261.9	2,267.9	2,281.1	2,276.0	2,265.3	2,291.8	2,303.2	2,300.4	2,320.0	2,324.2	2,279.6
2008	2,260.4	2,269.7	2,286.5	2,295.2	2,302.6	2,280.4	2,263.9	2,282.7	2,287.9	2,283.3	2,285.4	2,280.2	2,281.5
2009	2,203.9	2,201.3	2,203.7	2,206.9	2,212.0	2,184.3	2,169.1	2,186.3	2,196.4	2,206.6	2,220.9	2,218.1	2,200.8
2010	2,163.7	2,170.9	2,188.8	2,212.3	2,233.4	2,203.9	2,192.2	2,209.6	2,225.5	2,237.0	2,249.3	2,249.1	2,211.3
2011	2,190.3	2,209.0	2,227.2	2,251.0	2,257.2	2,229.3	2,225.2	2,252.1	2,268.4	2,276.7	2,295.3	2,297.8	2,248.3
2012	2,239.0	2,255.5	2,281.5	2,295.3	2,301.9	2,277.8	2,261.5	2,285.0	2,305.1	2,317.5	2,338.5	2,341.8	2,291.7
2013	2,271.7	2,289.5	2,308.5	2,323.6	2,329.8	2,306.9	2,294.3	2,318.8	2,338.7	2,351.1	2,372.4	2,368.5	2,322.8
Mining, Logging, and Construction													
2002	114.5	114.3	115.9	117.9	120.5	122.5	122.4	122.7	122.3	121.1	119.9	120.1	119.5
2003	113.6	112.4	115.0	118.5	120.9	122.5	122.5	123.3	123.2	121.8	120.7	120.8	119.6
2004	115.3	115.2	117.8	120.2	122.8	124.8	124.8	124.4	123.8	122.0	121.8	120.9	121.2
2005	117.0	117.6	120.3	121.4	124.2	127.0	128.1	129.4	130.1	129.4	129.2	129.1	125.2
2006	126.4	126.9	131.6	133.3	135.2	138.3	137.4	138.4	138.6	136.5	135.5	134.8	134.4
2007	129.9	130.1	135.0	136.5	138.6	141.5	140.3	141.6	141.5	141.0	139.9	138.5	137.9
2008	132.7	132.6	134.0	134.3	135.6	136.3	134.7	134.7	133.0	130.2	127.1	123.2	132.4
2009	113.2	111.1	111.4	110.3	110.1	111.1	110.7	110.1	110.1	108.2	107.0	104.9	109.9
2010	97.5	96.8	100.1	104.8	105.6	108.2	108.5	108.8	108.9	108.9	107.3	105.9	105.1
2011	97.8	99.8	103.1	107.0	108.3	111.3	112.1	113.1	114.3	113.8	112.8	110.7	108.7
2012	104.3	104.9	107.7	107.8	109.3	110.9	110.5	111.6	111.9	110.4	109.4	107.9	108.9
2013	102.2	103.4	105.1	106.4	108.5	110.0	110.1	110.7	111.0	110.8	110.6	108.5	108.1

1. Employment by Industry: Tennessee, Selected Years, 2002–2013—*Continued*

(Numbers in thousands, not seasonally adjusted)

Industry and year	January	February	March	April	May	June	July	August	September	October	November	December	Annual average
Manufacturing													
2002	430.1	428.8	428.4	428.4	430.6	431.5	429.6	431.4	430.1	426.7	423.2	423.1	428.5
2003	416.7	415.8	415.3	413.9	413.8	414.5	409.5	411.6	411.3	411.8	411.6	412.7	413.2
2004	406.7	407.6	408.9	411.6	413.7	415.0	412.5	414.7	415.1	412.1	411.4	412.1	411.8
2005	409.0	409.8	410.9	411.0	410.8	411.4	406.2	408.7	409.6	406.2	407.3	404.2	408.8
2006	403.9	402.8	403.4	403.4	403.2	403.5	398.0	400.1	399.1	393.1	391.9	390.4	399.4
2007	387.9	387.3	387.1	383.5	379.6	380.5	376.8	377.8	377.0	374.5	373.7	373.7	380.0
2008	369.3	369.6	369.6	367.6	367.2	367.6	360.0	361.6	358.5	352.6	346.1	341.7	361.0
2009	330.5	324.4	319.5	312.7	308.2	303.9	302.8	303.8	303.1	301.4	301.1	298.9	309.2
2010	295.7	294.7	296.3	297.8	299.0	301.1	299.7	301.0	301.0	299.8	300.5	300.6	298.9
2011	299.4	300.8	301.8	302.6	303.8	305.5	305.7	305.5	305.5	306.9	308.6	307.0	304.4
2012	305.6	307.2	309.6	312.0	313.4	316.1	314.5	316.8	315.5	315.8	316.8	317.2	313.4
2013	314.9	315.5	316.8	317.7	318.4	320.1	317.8	320.1	320.2	320.8	322.3	321.2	318.8
Trade, Transportation, and Utilities													
2002	569.4	566.1	570.1	570.3	572.3	573.6	576.6	576.6	577.5	581.3	590.2	597.1	576.8
2003	571.2	569.0	572.1	573.4	574.5	576.4	574.4	578.0	579.5	584.7	593.3	598.1	578.7
2004	575.9	574.8	580.0	582.0	583.1	586.0	584.9	587.3	587.6	594.5	604.9	613.0	587.8
2005	578.4	585.4	590.5	593.6	595.8	595.8	599.5	600.2	601.7	602.0	613.5	620.0	598.0
2006	598.3	596.2	602.2	603.5	606.1	607.0	604.2	607.7	608.6	607.4	619.4	626.6	607.3
2007	603.8	600.6	607.1	606.3	609.1	609.6	606.8	609.5	610.3	611.2	623.5	628.4	610.5
2008	605.4	602.4	606.1	602.9	602.5	601.5	598.3	599.3	596.7	591.7	596.4	598.1	600.1
2009	571.7	564.4	561.8	557.0	557.7	557.1	553.8	555.1	553.1	554.2	562.0	565.8	559.5
2010	546.5	543.9	547.4	550.4	552.5	554.2	554.7	556.1	554.5	558.8	568.5	573.2	555.1
2011	550.4	550.2	553.9	559.9	561.7	563.4	562.9	564.3	563.9	568.4	579.7	583.7	563.5
2012	564.9	561.5	568.0	570.4	573.3	574.0	572.4	574.2	575.9	578.8	592.0	595.7	575.1
2013	573.1	571.7	573.3	577.1	579.9	582.5	582.3	583.5	582.1	584.8	596.8	600.6	582.3
Wholesale Trade													
2002	124.7	125.0	125.2	125.4	125.8	126.1	127.0	127.2	127.0	127.8	128.1	128.9	126.5
2003	126.7	127.0	127.2	127.2	127.4	127.2	125.9	126.0	125.9	125.8	126.2	126.1	126.6
2004	124.9	125.4	126.6	127.2	127.5	128.4	128.7	129.1	129.0	129.5	129.9	130.2	128.0
2005	128.4	128.8	129.7	130.1	130.7	130.4	130.5	130.6	131.0	130.7	131.1	131.4	130.3
2006	130.0	130.6	131.4	131.7	132.3	132.5	132.6	132.9	133.0	132.4	132.5	132.5	132.0
2007	131.0	131.4	132.3	132.7	133.0	133.4	133.1	133.3	133.8	134.0	133.7	133.9	133.0
2008	132.5	132.9	133.1	132.8	133.1	132.5	131.8	131.9	131.7	130.5	129.3	128.2	131.7
2009	124.9	123.9	123.0	122.0	121.4	121.0	119.8	119.3	118.6	118.7	118.3	118.1	120.8
2010	116.6	116.5	117.2	117.2	117.3	117.2	116.9	116.8	116.3	116.6	116.5	116.3	116.8
2011	115.4	116.0	116.5	117.5	118.1	118.4	118.4	118.5	118.6	118.7	119.2	119.2	117.9
2012	118.1	118.9	119.6	120.1	120.8	121.1	120.7	121.1	121.0	121.4	121.5	121.6	120.5
2013	120.0	120.4	121.1	121.8	122.3	122.8	122.8	123.1	123.1	123.0	124.0	124.2	122.4
Retail Trade													
2002	307.8	304.8	307.5	307.7	309.0	310.0	311.2	310.6	312.4	313.9	322.3	328.9	312.2
2003	307.3	304.9	307.0	308.1	308.7	310.2	309.5	312.0	313.5	318.6	326.5	331.9	313.2
2004	313.7	312.2	314.8	315.5	316.3	317.9	316.3	317.4	317.5	322.7	332.4	337.0	319.5
2005	311.7	318.1	321.0	322.2	323.5	323.7	324.1	323.7	324.1	324.8	334.9	339.7	324.3
2006	323.2	320.8	324.7	325.9	327.0	327.4	325.7	327.1	326.7	327.6	338.6	343.7	328.2
2007	327.1	323.5	328.3	327.1	329.0	329.1	327.3	328.0	328.3	330.0	342.3	346.5	330.5
2008	328.7	325.9	329.6	326.5	325.5	325.2	323.6	323.6	321.3	320.4	325.9	327.6	325.3
2009	310.6	305.9	305.1	303.7	305.1	305.4	304.5	305.5	304.2	305.1	313.1	316.2	307.0
2010	301.9	299.7	302.2	304.6	306.0	307.0	306.0	306.8	304.0	307.5	316.1	319.0	306.7
2011	303.3	302.1	304.5	307.5	308.1	309.0	308.7	308.9	307.6	309.6	319.1	321.8	309.2
2012	308.2	304.6	309.2	310.7	312.1	312.6	311.7	311.2	310.4	313.4	324.5	325.5	312.8
2013	309.7	307.5	308.8	310.8	313.1	314.6	314.9	315.1	314.2	315.9	325.5	328.0	314.8
Transportation and Utilities													
2002	136.9	136.3	137.4	137.2	137.5	137.5	138.4	138.8	138.1	139.6	139.8	139.3	138.1
2003	137.2	137.1	137.9	138.1	138.4	139.0	139.0	140.0	140.1	140.3	140.6	140.1	139.0
2004	137.3	137.2	138.6	139.3	139.3	139.7	139.9	140.8	141.1	142.3	142.6	145.8	140.3
2005	138.3	138.5	139.8	141.3	141.6	141.7	144.9	145.9	146.6	146.5	147.5	148.9	143.5
2006	145.1	144.8	146.1	145.9	146.8	147.1	145.9	147.7	148.9	147.4	148.3	150.4	147.0
2007	145.7	145.7	146.5	146.5	147.1	147.1	146.4	148.2	148.2	147.2	147.5	148.0	147.0
2008	144.2	143.6	143.4	143.6	143.9	143.8	142.9	143.8	143.7	140.8	141.2	142.3	143.1
2009	136.2	134.6	133.7	131.3	131.2	130.7	129.5	130.3	130.3	130.4	130.6	131.5	131.7
2010	128.0	127.7	128.0	128.6	129.2	130.0	131.8	132.5	134.2	134.7	135.9	137.9	131.5
2011	131.7	132.1	132.9	134.9	135.5	136.0	135.8	136.9	137.7	140.1	141.4	142.7	136.5
2012	138.6	138.0	139.2	139.6	140.4	140.3	140.0	141.9	144.5	144.0	146.0	148.6	141.8
2013	143.4	143.8	143.4	144.5	144.5	145.1	144.6	145.3	144.8	145.9	147.3	148.4	145.1
Information													
2002	54.1	53.9	54.4	53.6	53.8	53.3	52.9	53.0	52.4	52.7	53.1	52.9	53.3
2003	52.1	51.9	51.8	51.7	51.4	51.1	50.5	50.4	49.9	50.6	51.3	51.4	51.2
2004	50.1	49.9	49.7	49.7	49.4	49.6	49.5	49.5	48.3	49.0	49.3	50.0	49.5
2005	49.7	49.7	49.6	49.5	49.7	49.9	49.4	49.2	48.8	48.8	49.3	49.3	49.4
2006	49.1	49.2	49.4	49.9	50.1	50.2	49.3	49.2	49.4	49.4	49.8	50.0	49.6
2007	49.1	49.3	49.2	49.6	50.1	50.4	50.7	50.6	50.6	50.6	51.2	51.8	50.3
2008	51.0	51.0	51.2	50.9	51.1	51.2	50.7	50.3	49.9	49.7	49.5	49.7	50.5
2009	49.1	48.8	48.3	47.6	47.3	46.8	46.2	46.1	45.8	45.5	45.9	45.7	46.9
2010	45.4	46.3	45.5	44.8	44.7	44.8	44.7	44.3	44.3	44.9	45.1	45.3	45.0
2011	44.3	44.1	44.1	44.1	44.1	43.9	43.7	43.9	43.3	43.0	43.3	43.2	43.8
2012	42.8	43.1	42.9	43.2	43.9	43.9	42.7	42.9	42.4	43.1	43.4	44.1	43.2
2013	43.5	43.8	44.0	43.9	44.2	44.9	44.1	44.0	43.4	43.4	44.0	44.0	43.9

1. Employment by Industry: Tennessee, Selected Years, 2002–2013—*Continued*

(Numbers in thousands, not seasonally adjusted)

Industry and year	January	February	March	April	May	June	July	August	September	October	November	December	Annual average
Financial Activities													
2002	137.2	137.6	137.9	137.7	138.2	138.9	138.2	138.5	137.6	138.0	138.8	139.1	138.1
2003	137.9	137.9	138.5	138.8	139.4	140.1	140.5	140.9	140.2	140.4	141.2	142.0	139.8
2004	140.6	140.4	140.8	141.0	141.5	142.0	142.3	142.5	142.1	142.8	143.1	144.0	141.9
2005	141.3	141.7	142.4	142.9	143.4	144.3	143.9	144.1	144.0	143.5	143.7	144.1	143.3
2006	142.5	142.8	143.5	143.1	143.6	144.3	143.7	144.2	143.7	143.2	143.5	144.2	143.5
2007	142.0	142.8	143.8	143.8	145.0	146.1	145.8	146.0	145.5	145.2	145.6	146.3	144.8
2008	144.5	144.9	145.2	145.1	145.6	146.3	145.8	145.7	144.9	144.3	144.1	144.0	145.0
2009	141.8	141.6	141.1	141.1	141.5	141.2	140.3	140.6	139.6	139.1	139.4	139.6	140.6
2010	137.7	137.6	137.5	138.6	138.5	137.9	137.5	137.3	135.9	135.6	135.7	135.6	137.1
2011	134.8	134.7	134.7	136.2	136.9	136.8	137.3	137.6	137.1	137.1	137.6	137.7	136.5
2012	136.4	136.9	137.0	137.0	137.5	137.5	137.5	137.4	136.7	136.8	137.1	137.5	137.1
2013	136.0	135.9	136.2	136.5	137.0	137.6	138.5	138.6	138.3	138.5	138.3	138.1	137.5
Professional and Business Services													
2002	292.3	293.4	297.3	297.4	297.4	297.6	297.8	300.4	298.6	296.2	295.8	293.4	296.5
2003	281.3	282.2	284.0	284.0	286.0	286.7	282.8	288.9	290.9	292.6	294.8	295.5	287.5
2004	288.5	291.8	294.5	299.2	298.9	301.7	301.5	306.5	307.4	312.4	313.6	314.4	302.5
2005	300.6	304.4	306.5	309.9	308.7	310.6	308.3	315.1	319.6	319.8	322.6	325.6	312.6
2006	310.9	311.3	314.9	316.2	316.0	319.6	315.4	321.6	324.3	321.9	327.2	329.1	319.0
2007	310.8	312.6	316.0	318.0	319.3	322.6	321.9	326.5	328.6	328.2	332.7	333.7	322.6
2008	318.1	319.3	321.2	325.0	324.1	327.4	317.8	321.2	322.1	321.3	319.4	316.2	321.1
2009	297.9	296.8	294.1	291.0	291.0	290.6	284.5	289.4	291.3	297.2	301.8	300.9	293.9
2010	291.4	293.7	297.1	300.0	307.7	306.3	301.0	304.8	307.6	311.5	313.9	314.7	304.1
2011	304.9	311.7	316.0	319.5	319.2	320.6	320.9	325.9	328.0	331.4	336.4	338.9	322.8
2012	323.3	327.5	331.5	334.9	338.1	340.3	334.7	340.8	342.3	345.5	351.0	351.5	338.5
2013	337.3	340.7	344.2	345.0	347.1	348.9	343.2	352.5	356.3	360.9	366.9	366.4	350.8
Education and Health Services													
2002	288.7	291.2	293.8	296.3	297.8	297.6	299.7	301.8	306.3	307.7	309.6	310.5	300.1
2003	307.2	310.5	311.3	312.7	312.3	311.3	310.1	311.6	314.8	316.9	316.9	317.5	312.8
2004	313.6	316.5	318.6	319.4	318.8	318.5	320.7	322.2	323.5	324.9	326.0	326.6	320.8
2005	323.1	325.2	325.9	329.6	329.5	329.1	330.0	331.7	334.0	334.3	335.2	335.8	330.3
2006	332.6	334.3	336.5	338.9	339.6	339.9	340.1	341.9	344.7	345.5	346.6	347.2	340.7
2007	342.7	345.7	347.4	347.4	348.0	347.6	349.4	352.1	354.9	353.9	354.3	355.0	349.9
2008	351.1	353.3	354.4	356.6	357.2	356.8	357.2	360.0	362.4	364.3	365.5	366.2	358.8
2009	361.0	362.3	362.3	365.5	364.8	365.4	364.9	365.3	368.4	369.7	370.5	371.0	365.9
2010	366.4	368.2	370.1	374.1	371.8	370.4	372.0	373.5	377.3	380.6	381.2	381.4	373.9
2011	376.0	379.9	380.7	384.6	384.1	380.4	381.8	383.6	388.2	390.1	391.1	390.7	384.3
2012	387.2	391.1	392.8	393.0	391.5	389.4	388.3	391.2	395.9	397.2	397.8	397.5	392.7
2013	392.2	395.9	397.2	397.5	396.1	392.6	390.4	393.2	397.4	400.6	402.6	401.1	396.4
Leisure and Hospitality													
2002	220.6	223.1	228.9	239.0	243.1	248.7	250.8	252.3	247.4	242.3	241.2	239.7	239.8
2003	229.9	231.6	238.2	247.0	252.6	257.6	255.6	256.6	252.2	247.0	246.2	245.0	246.6
2004	234.8	237.6	244.7	254.6	259.0	262.7	263.2	264.7	261.0	254.9	253.9	252.7	253.7
2005	243.0	244.8	252.0	263.6	268.0	273.4	272.9	272.9	269.3	263.1	261.8	259.6	262.0
2006	252.7	254.3	262.7	270.2	275.3	280.2	280.8	280.8	276.1	270.9	269.0	268.6	270.1
2007	258.9	260.5	268.9	276.2	281.2	288.3	285.9	288.2	281.7	276.0	275.5	274.1	276.3
2008	262.4	264.3	270.7	276.6	282.2	285.1	283.1	282.5	277.4	269.3	267.2	264.4	273.8
2009	253.2	253.0	259.1	266.0	271.8	275.5	271.8	270.6	265.4	259.7	258.8	256.9	263.5
2010	247.2	247.4	254.5	263.7	267.7	274.2	270.9	270.3	265.8	262.7	261.3	258.0	262.0
2011	249.0	251.5	259.0	268.2	273.7	278.0	276.8	277.0	273.8	268.8	268.2	267.4	267.6
2012	258.2	260.1	269.6	277.8	283.4	288.5	285.3	286.6	279.9	278.2	277.4	277.0	276.8
2013	266.2	268.3	277.8	286.2	292.4	298.2	296.8	297.1	291.1	289.9	289.9	286.7	286.7
Other Services													
2002	98.6	99.6	100.2	100.2	101.4	102.7	103.0	102.2	102.9	102.9	102.7	102.8	101.6
2003	101.5	101.3	102.2	102.6	103.2	103.4	102.5	102.1	102.1	101.7	101.7	101.7	102.2
2004	100.8	101.5	102.8	102.0	102.0	102.8	102.4	102.0	101.4	101.0	101.0	100.6	101.7
2005	99.0	99.8	101.3	101.4	101.3	102.4	101.5	100.8	100.9	100.0	100.5	99.9	100.7
2006	98.7	99.4	100.8	100.8	101.9	104.0	102.9	102.8	102.9	102.1	102.2	102.5	101.8
2007	101.7	102.3	104.2	103.9	105.1	106.2	104.5	104.4	103.9	103.9	103.9	103.8	104.0
2008	103.2	104.4	105.3	104.8	106.0	106.4	105.1	104.7	103.9	103.9	103.3	103.0	104.5
2009	101.3	101.7	102.5	102.6	102.7	104.0	103.0	102.1	101.2	101.2	101.4	100.5	102.0
2010	98.5	98.9	99.9	99.9	100.7	102.5	102.4	102.2	101.8	102.4	102.4	102.8	101.2
2011	99.7	100.4	101.2	101.5	102.3	103.9	103.5	103.2	102.3	102.0	102.3	102.3	102.1
2012	101.8	102.6	103.9	104.1	105.0	106.3	105.9	104.8	104.4	104.2	104.1	103.8	104.2
2013	103.0	103.7	104.6	105.4	106.0	107.3	106.9	106.2	105.7	104.9	105.1	105.3	105.3
Government													
2002	406.4	414.8	416.8	419.2	415.1	405.6	386.2	395.8	409.1	415.7	419.0	419.4	410.3
2003	408.4	415.3	417.6	420.2	417.7	404.5	388.9	398.4	411.6	416.0	417.0	417.7	411.1
2004	411.1	433.1	421.1	420.7	417.5	407.5	391.8	402.5	415.3	419.0	421.2	421.9	415.2
2005	410.2	417.7	419.0	416.6	415.1	399.8	392.0	401.5	418.3	420.0	421.6	420.7	412.7
2006	412.0	417.6	420.3	422.1	420.6	404.4	398.0	410.1	422.8	423.8	426.3	425.2	416.9
2007	418.1	422.5	425.3	422.7	423.3	405.2	400.3	414.5	427.7	431.4	433.3	431.1	421.3
2008	424.7	430.1	432.4	433.3	433.9	405.7	405.9	419.0	430.6	438.8	440.0	438.6	427.8
2009	427.9	432.7	434.5	436.1	435.2	403.7	404.6	417.1	431.6	440.0	441.1	437.7	428.5
2010	430.6	434.9	436.8	440.8	449.8	413.6	409.0	421.1	438.3	440.5	441.2	438.1	432.9
2011	431.2	436.5	437.6	437.0	435.2	402.3	398.3	416.6	431.8	435.9	436.7	433.9	427.8
2012	424.4	432.7	435.8	434.9	429.2	397.9	394.7	407.1	427.6	433.7	435.7	434.7	424.0
2013	420.4	429.5	431.2	432.0	427.1	394.9	392.1	403.7	424.4	428.1	428.8	426.3	419.9

2. Average Weekly Hours by Selected Industry: Tennessee, 2009–2013

(Not seasonally adjusted)

Industry and year	January	February	March	April	May	June	July	August	September	October	November	December	Annual average
Total Private													
2009	34.6	35.2	34.9	34.7	35.0	35.3	35.1	35.7	35.1	35.5	35.8	35.4	35.2
2010	35.0	35.0	35.2	35.5	35.7	35.5	35.5	35.6	35.0	35.2	35.2	35.0	35.3
2011	34.5	34.8	35.3	35.2	35.5	35.3	35.1	35.3	35.0	35.6	35.0	35.2	35.2
2012	35.2	35.1	35.0	35.6	35.2	35.5	35.6	35.5	35.8	35.2	35.4	35.6	35.4
2013	34.7	35.2	35.2	35.2	35.2	35.9	35.2	35.4	35.7	35.3	35.3	35.7	35.3
Goods-Producing													
2009	37.9	38.6	38.4	38.7	38.9	40.0	39.8	40.6	40.0	40.5	41.0	40.7	39.6
2010	40.7	40.2	40.9	41.8	41.6	41.6	41.0	41.6	41.2	41.8	41.8	41.0	41.3
2011	39.7	40.6	41.5	41.0	40.9	41.3	40.3	41.3	41.1	41.4	41.3	41.4	41.0
2012	41.0	41.2	41.2	41.8	41.3	41.7	40.9	41.3	41.6	40.5	41.3	40.5	41.2
2013	39.6	40.4	40.6	40.6	40.4	41.0	40.3	41.3	41.5	41.3	41.2	41.1	40.8
Mining, Logging, and Construction													
2009	36.3	36.4	36.6	36.4	36.4	37.4	37.5	38.0	36.3	35.9	36.8	36.4	36.7
2010	35.5	34.3	35.9	37.1	37.4	37.8	37.2	38.5	37.5	38.3	38.2	36.9	37.1
2011	35.1	36.9	37.6	38.6	39.6	39.9	39.4	40.0	39.0	39.4	39.3	38.9	38.7
2012	37.4	37.7	38.4	39.3	39.2	39.6	38.8	39.8	40.3	38.8	40.2	39.8	39.1
2013	37.9	39.0	40.0	40.7	40.9	40.9	41.1	41.7	41.0	41.8	41.4	40.0	40.6
Manufacturing													
2009	38.5	39.3	39.0	39.5	39.8	41.0	40.7	41.6	41.3	42.1	42.5	42.2	40.6
2010	42.4	42.2	42.6	43.5	43.1	43.0	42.4	42.8	42.5	43.0	43.1	42.4	42.7
2011	41.2	41.9	42.8	41.8	41.4	41.8	40.6	41.8	41.8	42.2	42.1	42.3	41.8
2012	42.2	42.4	42.1	42.7	42.1	42.4	41.6	41.9	42.0	41.1	41.7	40.8	41.9
2013	40.2	40.9	40.8	40.6	40.3	41.1	40.1	41.2	41.6	41.2	41.1	41.5	40.9
Trade, Transportation, and Utilities													
2009	34.9	35.7	35.3	34.7	35.0	34.9	34.5	35.0	35.4	36.2	35.9	36.0	35.3
2010	35.5	35.6	35.5	35.6	35.8	35.6	35.8	36.1	35.6	35.4	35.6	35.6	35.6
2011	34.6	35.1	35.5	35.5	35.8	35.8	35.6	35.7	34.5	34.7	34.2	34.8	35.1
2012	34.4	34.4	34.2	34.5	34.5	34.7	34.9	34.9	35.3	34.9	35.1	35.1	34.7
2013	34.2	34.7	34.7	34.6	35.0	35.3	35.3	35.4	35.4	35.1	35.1	35.3	35.0
Information													
2009	35.9	37.2	37.0	36.4	36.6	36.6	36.8	37.8	36.8	36.5	37.1	36.7	36.8
2010	36.0	36.5	36.0	36.2	36.8	36.9	37.0	37.3	36.9	36.9	37.0	37.0	36.7
2011	37.2	37.5	37.0	37.6	38.0	37.5	37.2	37.5	37.4	38.1	37.1	36.9	37.4
2012	37.9	37.4	37.2	38.5	38.2	38.0	39.6	39.1	40.3	38.0	38.1	38.4	38.4
2013	37.5	36.7	36.8	36.8	37.4	38.2	37.7	37.1	37.7	36.6	36.5	37.4	37.2
Financial Activities													
2009	37.1	37.5	37.3	36.5	36.9	37.0	37.1	38.1	36.8	37.0	37.4	36.7	37.1
2010	36.4	36.2	36.2	36.6	37.8	37.0	37.4	38.6	37.5	37.4	37.1	37.1	37.1
2011	37.7	36.7	36.4	36.6	37.5	37.0	36.9	37.1	37.0	38.3	37.2	37.1	37.1
2012	38.1	37.4	37.0	38.0	37.1	37.6	38.4	37.2	38.1	37.3	37.3	38.3	37.7
2013	37.3	37.2	37.2	36.8	37.2	38.6	37.0	37.0	38.2	37.5	37.0	38.9	37.5
Professional and Business Services													
2009	36.2	36.9	36.3	35.9	37.6	37.8	36.9	37.9	36.7	36.7	37.5	36.6	36.9
2010	36.0	36.3	36.3	36.7	36.9	36.2	36.4	36.9	36.2	36.4	36.4	36.1	36.4
2011	36.0	36.0	36.4	36.4	36.8	36.3	35.9	36.1	36.4	36.5	35.5	35.6	36.2
2012	36.0	35.8	35.9	36.6	35.8	36.4	36.5	36.5	36.6	36.0	36.5	37.9	36.4
2013	36.2	37.0	36.5	36.7	36.3	37.4	36.1	36.5	37.0	36.4	36.4	36.9	36.6
Education and Health Services													
2009	34.3	34.3	34.4	34.2	34.0	34.2	34.6	35.0	34.4	34.6	34.6	33.8	34.4
2010	33.7	33.3	33.6	34.0	34.5	34.3	34.6	32.9	32.8	33.0	33.0	33.0	33.6
2011	33.4	33.1	33.5	33.9	34.4	34.0	34.5	34.1	34.2	34.9	34.3	34.5	34.1
2012	35.1	34.2	34.2	34.9	34.6	34.5	35.4	34.7	35.2	34.7	34.6	35.1	34.8
2013	34.7	35.1	34.8	34.8	34.9	35.2	34.4	34.3	34.7	34.0	34.5	34.8	34.7
Leisure and Hospitality													
2009	25.7	26.8	26.7	26.6	26.7	27.4	27.2	27.1	26.4	26.6	26.6	26.3	26.7
2010	25.6	26.4	26.7	26.6	26.3	26.8	26.8	26.7	25.6	25.8	25.6	25.2	26.2
2011	24.6	25.8	26.2	26.4	26.1	26.2	26.1	26.3	25.9	27.1	26.2	26.3	26.1
2012	26.2	26.4	26.9	27.2	26.8	27.2	27.5	27.3	27.1	27.1	26.3	26.1	26.9
2013	25.2	25.9	26.3	26.5	26.5	27.3	26.9	26.9	26.8	26.8	26.6	26.7	26.5
Other Services													
2009	33.5	33.5	33.4	33.6	33.1	33.2	32.8	34.2	32.1	32.5	33.4	33.0	33.2
2010	33.0	32.7	33.1	33.3	33.6	33.2	32.9	33.1	32.8	33.3	33.2	32.5	33.1
2011	32.2	32.3	32.9	32.4	32.9	32.1	32.4	32.1	31.8	33.6	32.8	33.3	32.6
2012	33.1	33.1	32.6	34.1	33.1	33.5	33.1	33.5	33.7	33.1	32.7	33.6	33.3
2013	32.9	33.1	33.2	33.4	33.6	34.6	33.8	33.4	34.4	33.7	32.9	34.1	33.6

3. Average Hourly Earnings by Selected Industry: Tennessee, 2009–2013

(Dollars, not seasonally adjusted)

Industry and year	January	February	March	April	May	June	July	August	September	October	November	December	Annual average
Total Private													
2009	19.41	19.65	19.59	19.50	19.39	19.39	19.47	19.60	19.65	19.53	19.59	19.50	19.52
2010	19.54	19.78	19.74	19.79	19.84	19.74	19.88	20.06	20.18	20.23	20.18	20.26	19.94
2011	20.52	20.34	20.15	20.13	20.09	19.92	20.13	20.05	20.23	20.47	20.17	20.22	20.20
2012	20.50	20.34	19.99	20.14	19.89	19.94	20.05	19.93	20.26	20.01	20.20	20.31	20.13
2013	20.15	20.30	20.39	20.21	20.03	20.15	20.23	20.03	20.33	20.27	20.47	20.69	20.27
Goods-Producing													
2009	20.04	20.51	20.51	20.69	20.56	20.86	20.98	21.24	21.42	21.30	21.25	21.01	20.86
2010	21.15	21.44	21.45	21.34	21.52	21.45	21.63	21.54	21.76	21.73	21.73	22.17	21.58
2011	22.33	22.00	21.98	21.45	21.43	21.28	21.14	21.09	20.85	20.74	20.79	20.95	21.32
2012	20.84	20.48	20.50	20.41	20.47	20.64	20.68	20.73	20.82	20.80	20.73	20.91	20.67
2013	20.63	20.60	20.65	20.56	20.54	20.55	20.89	20.83	20.98	20.98	21.14	21.25	20.80
Mining, Logging, and Construction													
2009	19.71	19.78	20.00	20.12	20.18	20.01	19.95	20.29	20.24	20.49	20.07	20.37	20.10
2010	20.62	20.71	20.38	19.99	20.24	20.17	20.01	19.99	20.21	20.30	20.15	20.56	20.26
2011	21.01	20.76	20.63	20.45	20.15	20.34	20.34	20.19	20.23	20.37	20.67	20.84	20.48
2012	20.99	20.79	20.79	20.61	20.74	20.67	21.08	20.87	21.04	20.93	20.96	21.38	20.91
2013	21.24	21.53	21.46	21.04	20.93	20.89	21.02	20.98	21.36	21.53	21.31	22.06	21.28
Manufacturing													
2009	20.15	20.74	20.68	20.87	20.69	21.15	21.33	21.55	21.79	21.55	21.61	21.21	21.11
2010	21.29	21.63	21.75	21.75	21.91	21.85	22.14	22.04	22.25	22.19	22.23	22.66	21.98
2011	22.70	22.36	22.39	21.78	21.87	21.61	21.43	21.41	21.07	20.87	20.83	20.99	21.60
2012	20.79	20.38	20.41	20.34	20.38	20.63	20.55	20.68	20.75	20.76	20.66	20.75	20.59
2013	20.44	20.31	20.38	20.40	20.40	20.43	20.84	20.78	20.85	20.79	21.08	20.99	20.64
Trade, Transportation, and Utilities													
2009	19.01	19.10	19.06	19.01	18.67	18.54	18.60	18.60	18.35	17.99	18.05	17.96	18.58
2010	17.76	18.20	18.41	18.60	18.52	18.45	18.64	18.55	18.50	18.53	18.41	18.34	18.41
2011	18.77	18.28	18.24	18.38	18.22	18.00	18.50	18.30	18.55	18.76	18.20	18.27	18.37
2012	18.61	18.49	18.37	18.51	18.25	18.23	18.42	18.21	18.56	18.43	18.36	18.57	18.42
2013	18.47	18.75	19.15	19.11	18.57	18.84	19.00	18.47	18.82	18.68	18.51	18.82	18.77
Information													
2009	22.46	23.05	22.82	22.35	22.86	22.70	22.43	23.53	23.18	23.36	23.51	23.24	22.95
2010	23.12	23.45	23.28	23.32	24.06	23.53	23.90	24.10	24.61	24.45	24.65	24.61	23.93
2011	24.68	24.31	23.72	23.40	23.61	23.48	23.93	23.23	23.04	23.89	24.11	23.19	23.72
2012	23.75	23.28	22.69	22.55	22.23	23.22	22.76	22.67	23.26	23.27	23.68	24.00	23.11
2013	24.59	25.24	25.49	24.86	25.26	25.10	25.47	25.53	26.10	25.39	25.60	25.88	25.38
Financial Activities													
2009	21.35	21.89	21.63	21.24	21.26	21.24	21.20	21.25	21.17	21.39	21.43	21.33	21.37
2010	21.46	21.71	21.74	22.19	22.01	22.24	22.09	22.65	22.51	22.78	22.59	22.57	22.21
2011	22.88	23.11	22.86	22.91	22.96	22.77	23.37	23.55	23.36	23.67	23.28	23.47	23.19
2012	23.76	23.28	22.65	23.49	22.73	22.93	23.42	22.84	23.26	23.13	23.00	23.52	23.17
2013	23.51	24.23	23.71	24.27	24.01	24.37	23.84	23.46	23.31	23.08	23.66	23.98	23.79
Professional and Business Services													
2009	22.39	22.92	22.79	22.52	22.33	22.29	22.63	22.26	22.47	22.28	22.35	22.55	22.48
2010	22.74	22.96	22.70	22.65	22.98	22.75	23.10	23.03	23.13	23.13	23.17	23.18	22.96
2011	23.36	23.80	23.43	23.96	24.24	24.04	24.23	24.02	24.55	25.38	24.86	24.76	24.23
2012	25.95	25.53	24.83	25.51	25.00	24.91	25.36	24.71	25.53	24.43	25.12	24.31	25.09
2013	24.14	24.13	24.51	23.71	23.75	24.12	24.40	23.83	24.61	24.61	25.60	25.93	24.46
Education and Health Services													
2009	20.38	20.48	20.67	20.59	20.65	20.69	20.58	20.77	21.06	20.98	21.03	21.00	20.74
2010	21.07	21.21	21.05	21.24	20.83	20.96	21.01	22.04	22.25	22.35	22.09	22.02	21.51
2011	21.99	21.90	21.60	21.65	21.31	21.29	21.49	21.36	21.64	21.54	21.15	21.22	21.51
2012	21.08	21.37	20.74	20.71	20.54	20.81	20.57	20.82	20.90	20.81	21.04	21.43	20.90
2013	20.96	21.21	21.21	21.00	20.89	20.90	20.86	21.04	21.06	21.06	21.01	21.04	21.02
Leisure and Hospitality													
2009	11.27	11.33	11.27	11.22	11.42	11.35	11.46	11.95	11.87	11.89	11.98	11.87	11.57
2010	11.87	11.86	11.60	11.40	11.63	11.46	11.55	11.65	11.55	11.51	11.67	11.65	11.61
2011	11.94	11.73	11.56	11.51	11.54	11.44	11.57	11.69	11.80	12.14	12.07	12.04	11.75
2012	12.09	12.27	11.95	11.96	11.95	11.75	11.71	11.77	11.87	11.81	11.90	12.03	11.92
2013	12.03	11.96	11.85	11.81	11.75	11.66	11.59	11.52	11.55	11.62	11.59	11.75	11.72
Other Services													
2009	16.61	16.49	16.25	16.41	16.27	16.19	16.38	16.26	16.16	16.34	16.46	16.51	16.36
2010	16.26	16.35	16.54	16.22	16.67	16.55	16.40	16.53	16.56	16.60	16.80	17.11	16.55
2011	16.99	17.21	17.07	16.99	17.17	17.24	17.05	17.45	17.49	18.47	18.20	18.64	17.50
2012	18.82	18.68	18.64	18.40	18.14	17.60	17.96	17.92	18.15	17.99	18.54	18.62	18.28
2013	18.81	18.92	18.92	19.17	19.26	19.16	19.00	19.21	19.26	19.24	19.63	19.52	19.18

4. Average Weekly Earnings by Selected Industry: Tennessee, 2009–2013

(Dollars, not seasonally adjusted)

Industry and year	January	February	March	April	May	June	July	August	September	October	November	December	Annual average
Total Private													
2009	671.59	691.68	683.69	676.65	678.65	684.47	683.40	699.72	689.72	693.32	701.32	690.30	687.10
2010	683.90	692.30	694.85	702.55	708.29	700.77	705.74	714.14	706.30	712.10	710.34	709.10	703.88
2011	707.94	707.83	711.30	708.58	713.20	703.18	706.56	707.77	708.05	728.73	705.95	711.74	711.04
2012	721.60	713.93	699.65	716.98	700.13	707.87	713.78	707.52	725.31	704.35	715.08	723.04	712.60
2013	699.21	714.56	717.73	711.39	705.06	723.39	712.10	709.06	725.78	715.53	722.59	738.63	715.53
Goods-Producing													
2009	759.52	791.69	787.58	800.70	799.78	834.40	835.00	862.34	856.80	862.65	871.25	855.11	826.06
2010	860.81	861.89	877.31	892.01	895.23	892.32	886.83	896.06	896.51	908.31	908.31	908.97	891.25
2011	886.50	893.20	912.17	879.45	876.49	878.86	851.94	871.02	856.94	858.64	858.63	867.33	874.12
2012	854.44	843.78	844.60	853.14	845.41	860.69	845.81	856.15	866.11	842.40	856.15	846.86	851.60
2013	816.95	832.24	838.39	834.74	829.82	842.55	841.87	860.28	870.67	866.47	870.97	873.38	848.64
Mining, Logging, and Construction													
2009	715.47	719.99	732.00	732.37	734.55	748.37	748.13	771.02	734.71	735.59	738.58	741.47	737.67
2010	732.01	710.35	731.64	741.63	756.98	762.43	744.37	769.62	757.88	777.49	769.73	758.66	751.65
2011	737.45	766.04	775.69	789.37	797.94	811.57	801.40	807.60	788.97	802.58	812.33	810.68	792.58
2012	785.03	783.78	798.34	809.97	813.01	818.53	817.90	830.63	847.91	812.08	842.59	850.92	817.58
2013	805.00	839.67	858.40	856.33	856.04	854.40	863.92	874.87	875.76	899.95	882.23	882.40	863.97
Manufacturing													
2009	775.78	815.08	806.52	824.37	823.46	867.15	868.13	896.48	899.93	907.26	918.43	895.06	857.07
2010	902.70	912.79	926.55	946.13	944.32	939.55	938.74	943.31	945.63	954.17	958.11	960.78	938.55
2011	935.24	936.88	958.29	910.40	905.42	903.30	870.06	894.94	880.73	880.71	876.94	887.88	902.88
2012	877.34	864.11	859.26	868.52	858.00	874.71	854.88	866.49	871.50	853.24	861.52	846.60	862.72
2013	821.69	830.68	831.50	828.24	822.12	839.67	835.68	856.14	867.36	856.55	866.39	871.09	844.18
Trade, Transportation, and Utilities													
2009	663.45	681.87	672.82	659.65	653.45	647.05	641.70	651.00	649.59	651.24	648.00	646.56	655.87
2010	630.48	647.92	653.56	662.16	663.02	656.82	667.31	669.66	658.60	655.96	655.40	652.90	655.40
2011	649.44	641.63	647.52	652.49	652.28	644.40	658.60	653.31	639.98	650.97	622.44	635.80	644.79
2012	640.18	636.06	628.25	638.60	629.63	632.58	642.86	635.53	655.17	643.21	644.44	651.81	639.17
2013	631.67	650.63	664.51	661.21	649.95	665.05	670.70	653.84	666.23	655.67	649.70	664.35	656.95
Information													
2009	806.31	857.46	844.34	813.54	836.68	830.82	825.42	889.43	853.02	852.64	872.22	852.91	844.56
2010	832.32	855.93	838.08	844.18	885.41	868.26	884.30	898.93	908.11	902.21	912.05	910.57	878.23
2011	918.10	911.63	877.64	879.84	897.18	880.50	890.20	871.13	861.70	910.21	894.48	855.71	887.13
2012	900.13	870.67	844.07	868.18	849.19	882.36	901.30	886.40	937.38	884.26	902.21	921.60	887.42
2013	922.13	926.31	938.03	914.85	944.72	958.82	960.22	947.16	983.97	929.27	934.40	967.91	944.14
Financial Activities													
2009	792.09	820.88	806.80	775.26	784.49	785.88	786.52	809.63	779.06	791.43	801.48	782.81	792.83
2010	781.14	785.90	786.99	812.15	831.98	822.88	826.17	874.29	844.13	851.97	838.09	837.35	823.99
2011	862.58	848.14	832.10	838.51	861.00	842.49	862.35	873.71	864.32	906.56	866.02	870.74	860.35
2012	905.26	870.67	838.05	892.62	843.28	862.17	899.33	849.65	886.21	862.75	857.90	900.82	873.51
2013	876.92	901.36	882.01	893.14	893.17	940.68	882.08	868.02	890.44	865.50	875.42	932.82	892.13
Professional and Business Services													
2009	810.52	845.75	827.28	808.47	839.61	842.56	835.05	843.65	824.65	817.68	838.13	825.33	829.51
2010	818.64	833.45	824.01	831.26	847.96	823.55	840.84	849.81	837.31	841.93	843.39	836.80	835.74
2011	840.96	856.80	852.85	872.14	892.03	872.65	869.86	867.12	893.62	926.37	882.53	881.46	877.13
2012	934.20	913.97	891.40	933.67	895.00	906.72	925.64	901.92	934.40	879.48	916.88	921.35	913.28
2013	873.87	892.81	894.62	870.16	862.13	902.09	880.84	869.80	910.57	895.80	931.84	956.82	895.24
Education and Health Services													
2009	699.03	702.46	711.05	704.18	702.10	707.60	712.07	726.95	724.46	725.91	727.64	709.80	713.46
2010	710.06	706.29	707.28	722.16	718.64	718.93	726.95	725.12	729.80	737.55	728.97	726.66	722.74
2011	734.47	724.89	723.60	733.94	733.06	723.86	741.41	728.38	740.09	751.75	725.45	732.09	733.49
2012	739.91	730.85	709.31	722.78	710.68	717.95	728.18	722.45	735.68	722.11	727.98	752.19	727.32
2013	727.31	744.47	738.11	730.80	729.06	735.68	717.58	721.67	730.78	716.04	724.85	732.19	729.39
Leisure and Hospitality													
2009	289.64	303.64	300.91	298.45	304.91	310.99	311.71	323.85	313.37	316.27	318.67	312.18	308.92
2010	303.87	313.10	309.72	303.24	305.87	307.13	309.54	311.06	295.68	296.96	298.75	293.58	304.18
2011	293.72	302.63	302.87	303.86	301.19	299.73	301.98	307.45	305.62	328.99	316.23	316.65	306.68
2012	316.76	323.93	321.46	325.31	320.26	319.60	322.03	321.32	321.68	320.05	312.97	313.98	320.65
2013	303.16	309.76	311.66	312.97	311.38	318.32	311.77	309.89	309.54	311.42	308.29	313.73	310.58
Other Services													
2009	556.44	552.42	542.75	551.38	538.54	537.51	537.26	556.09	518.74	531.05	549.76	544.83	543.15
2010	536.58	534.65	547.47	540.13	560.11	549.46	539.56	547.14	543.17	552.78	557.76	556.08	547.81
2011	547.08	555.88	561.60	550.48	564.89	553.40	552.42	560.15	556.18	620.59	596.96	620.71	570.50
2012	622.94	618.31	607.66	627.44	600.43	589.60	594.48	600.32	611.66	595.47	606.26	625.63	608.72
2013	618.85	626.25	628.14	640.28	647.14	662.94	642.20	641.61	662.54	648.39	645.83	665.63	644.45

TEXAS
At a Glance

Population:
  2000 census: 20,851,028
  2010 census: 25,145,561
  2013 estimate: 26,448,193

Percent change in population:
  2000–2010: 20.6%
  2010–2013: 5.2%

Percent change in total nonfarm employment:
  2000–2010: 9.6%
  2010–2013: 8.3%

Industry with the largest growth in employment, 2000–2013 (thousands):
  Education and Health Services, 481.3

Industry with the largest decline or smallest growth in employment, 2000–2013 (thousands):
  Manufacturing, -195.7

Civilian labor force:
  2000: 10,347,847
  2010: 12,287,566
  2013: 12,819,871

Unemployment rate and rank among states (lowest to highest):
  2000: 4.4%, 37th
  2010: 8.2%, 21st
  2013: 6.3%, 17th

Over-the-year change in unemployment rates:
  2010–2011: -0.3%
  2011–2012: -1.1%
  2012–2013: -0.5%

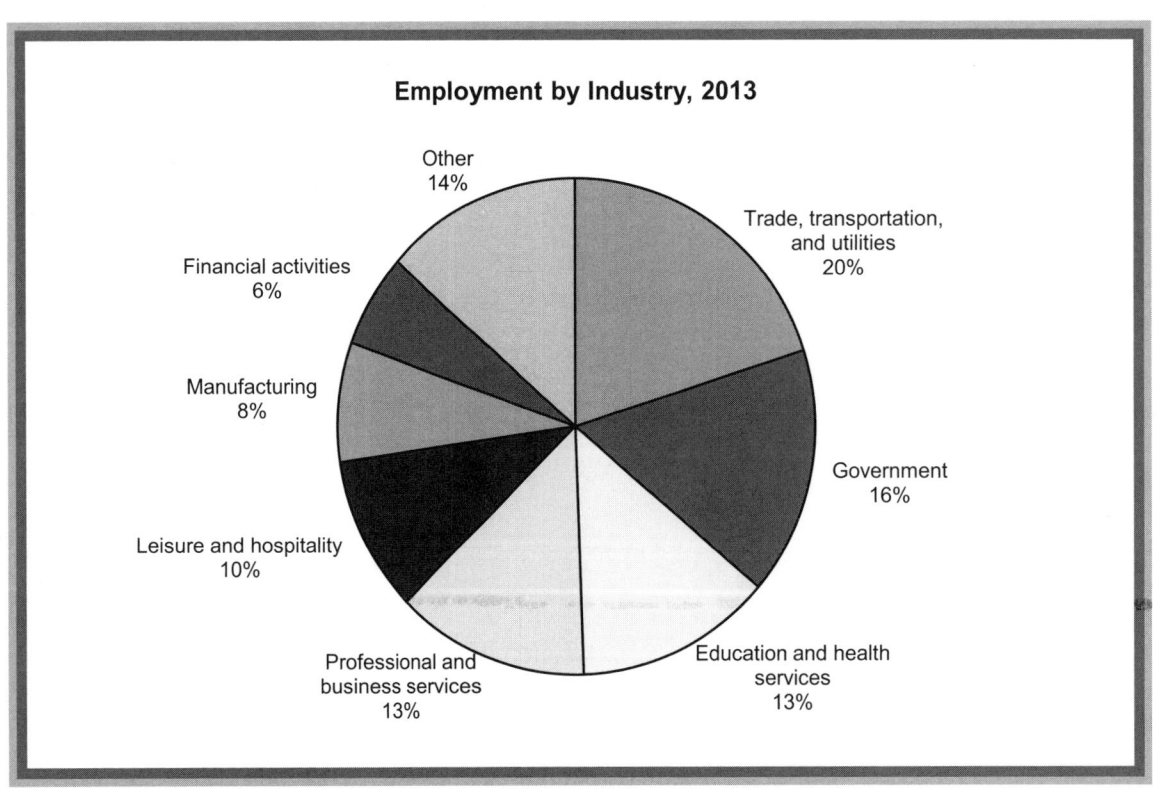

Employment by Industry, 2013

Other 14%
Trade, transportation, and utilities 20%
Financial activities 6%
Manufacturing 8%
Government 16%
Leisure and hospitality 10%
Education and health services 13%
Professional and business services 13%

1. Employment by Industry: Texas, Selected Years, 2002–2013

(Numbers in thousands, not seasonally adjusted)

Industry and year	January	February	March	April	May	June	July	August	September	October	November	December	Annual average
Total Nonfarm													
2002	9,303.1	9,356.7	9,413.7	9,419.5	9,465.5	9,450.2	9,345.6	9,398.9	9,447.3	9,424.8	9,457.6	9,469.3	9,412.7
2003	9,277.9	9,323.3	9,357.2	9,370.7	9,398.6	9,378.0	9,279.2	9,335.1	9,392.0	9,400.2	9,428.8	9,461.8	9,366.9
2004	9,304.2	9,368.2	9,430.3	9,476.9	9,503.4	9,505.5	9,448.8	9,494.6	9,542.8	9,581.7	9,618.0	9,655.4	9,494.2
2005	9,490.3	9,560.5	9,630.5	9,697.4	9,727.6	9,735.0	9,696.1	9,749.7	9,831.1	9,843.5	9,923.2	9,965.5	9,737.5
2006	9,807.4	9,889.4	9,977.8	10,002.5	10,057.8	10,089.0	9,993.0	10,072.3	10,155.7	10,174.7	10,246.3	10,296.1	10,063.5
2007	10,109.2	10,209.5	10,304.8	10,336.5	10,395.1	10,435.0	10,351.5	10,403.7	10,457.0	10,511.6	10,582.0	10,616.7	10,392.7
2008	10,437.9	10,533.0	10,577.5	10,607.9	10,655.1	10,657.6	10,573.9	10,612.8	10,608.7	10,660.4	10,681.3	10,669.6	10,606.3
2009	10,402.1	10,397.2	10,392.4	10,352.0	10,352.6	10,320.2	10,198.2	10,189.7	10,214.1	10,253.1	10,283.4	10,295.9	10,304.2
2010	10,113.4	10,172.8	10,261.0	10,311.5	10,392.7	10,390.4	10,291.0	10,316.5	10,359.4	10,438.6	10,483.9	10,512.1	10,336.9
2011	10,319.3	10,384.0	10,479.7	10,553.6	10,580.8	10,609.8	10,544.6	10,577.6	10,634.6	10,657.6	10,718.7	10,749.7	10,567.5
2012	10,579.8	10,677.2	10,762.9	10,816.0	10,875.4	10,913.4	10,831.8	10,893.2	10,939.3	11,004.5	11,090.5	11,116.1	10,875.0
2013	10,893.9	11,028.6	11,095.7	11,140.3	11,188.1	11,223.6	11,159.6	11,203.4	11,251.8	11,331.6	11,378.2	11,387.0	11,190.2
Total Private													
2002	7,700.7	7,722.1	7,772.2	7,778.4	7,821.7	7,852.5	7,817.6	7,850.2	7,818.2	7,760.8	7,783.6	7,801.5	7,790.0
2003	7,638.0	7,649.2	7,685.0	7,697.2	7,725.2	7,748.0	7,726.1	7,766.7	7,752.7	7,740.1	7,759.4	7,801.9	7,724.1
2004	7,667.0	7,697.5	7,758.1	7,804.0	7,828.5	7,870.9	7,883.1	7,910.6	7,884.2	7,900.8	7,928.1	7,970.7	7,842.0
2005	7,826.9	7,863.5	7,931.3	7,996.1	8,024.4	8,076.7	8,100.9	8,133.6	8,144.3	8,131.7	8,199.6	8,254.0	8,056.9
2006	8,114.1	8,164.3	8,251.8	8,279.7	8,334.6	8,407.1	8,386.2	8,439.7	8,448.2	8,437.7	8,500.5	8,557.7	8,360.1
2007	8,396.5	8,465.3	8,554.4	8,586.5	8,642.6	8,719.9	8,707.5	8,750.8	8,729.2	8,744.9	8,800.4	8,839.4	8,661.5
2008	8,679.8	8,743.5	8,779.9	8,816.5	8,859.8	8,895.5	8,881.9	8,913.3	8,838.3	8,853.8	8,855.7	8,849.2	8,830.6
2009	8,601.6	8,568.7	8,557.1	8,507.4	8,508.5	8,510.6	8,464.8	8,460.4	8,409.3	8,397.4	8,415.0	8,435.6	8,486.4
2010	8,280.8	8,307.9	8,383.6	8,422.5	8,469.2	8,516.3	8,509.3	8,544.0	8,527.8	8,563.9	8,598.5	8,639.9	8,480.3
2011	8,478.7	8,518.9	8,614.0	8,687.0	8,718.9	8,779.6	8,791.9	8,841.7	8,846.7	8,844.9	8,898.8	8,940.4	8,746.8
2012	8,799.0	8,860.8	8,942.9	8,996.1	9,057.1	9,129.0	9,105.1	9,176.3	9,161.4	9,188.9	9,263.9	9,290.8	9,080.9
2013	9,107.6	9,202.8	9,265.0	9,307.2	9,357.6	9,422.3	9,411.4	9,469.0	9,450.7	9,493.5	9,522.2	9,539.1	9,379.0
Goods-Producing													
2002	1,672.4	1,673.1	1,679.6	1,668.8	1,673.4	1,680.3	1,667.4	1,670.0	1,657.8	1,639.3	1,630.0	1,621.5	1,661.1
2003	1,600.5	1,600.7	1,600.3	1,600.0	1,605.3	1,609.0	1,600.1	1,603.2	1,600.0	1,589.5	1,580.5	1,582.1	1,597.6
2004	1,565.5	1,568.7	1,577.3	1,580.6	1,583.1	1,593.7	1,596.5	1,598.8	1,596.1	1,597.9	1,596.6	1,599.7	1,587.9
2005	1,583.7	1,591.8	1,605.5	1,615.9	1,620.9	1,635.0	1,642.4	1,645.4	1,650.9	1,648.1	1,655.0	1,664.2	1,629.9
2006	1,654.1	1,670.3	1,690.4	1,690.8	1,706.9	1,731.2	1,725.9	1,735.3	1,742.7	1,739.6	1,745.6	1,751.9	1,715.4
2007	1,733.0	1,750.5	1,766.9	1,772.3	1,783.5	1,807.1	1,799.9	1,808.6	1,807.0	1,812.6	1,818.0	1,819.0	1,789.9
2008	1,799.2	1,817.6	1,822.7	1,825.7	1,835.0	1,843.8	1,840.9	1,846.0	1,836.4	1,838.4	1,825.4	1,806.3	1,828.1
2009	1,750.9	1,727.1	1,700.5	1,661.6	1,645.9	1,633.6	1,615.2	1,608.6	1,594.7	1,582.2	1,571.9	1,569.0	1,638.4
2010	1,553.3	1,552.9	1,565.4	1,569.5	1,576.2	1,586.6	1,594.5	1,600.2	1,598.0	1,601.3	1,597.2	1,598.9	1,582.8
2011	1,578.2	1,590.0	1,605.4	1,613.8	1,619.8	1,640.0	1,653.4	1,663.5	1,668.6	1,668.9	1,670.5	1,673.7	1,637.2
2012	1,662.4	1,677.8	1,693.0	1,702.1	1,713.2	1,729.7	1,731.9	1,743.3	1,742.2	1,749.4	1,748.8	1,747.0	1,720.1
2013	1,727.7	1,750.0	1,759.5	1,761.0	1,767.9	1,783.6	1,783.5	1,792.6	1,790.3	1,796.1	1,781.1	1,784.1	1,773.1
Service-Providing													
2002	7,630.7	7,683.6	7,734.1	7,750.7	7,792.1	7,769.9	7,678.2	7,728.9	7,789.5	7,785.5	7,827.6	7,847.8	7,751.6
2003	7,677.4	7,722.6	7,756.9	7,770.7	7,793.3	7,769.0	7,679.1	7,731.9	7,792.0	7,810.7	7,848.3	7,879.7	7,769.3
2004	7,738.7	7,799.5	7,853.0	7,896.3	7,920.3	7,911.8	7,852.3	7,895.8	7,946.7	7,983.8	8,021.4	8,055.7	7,906.3
2005	7,906.6	7,968.7	8,025.0	8,081.5	8,106.7	8,100.0	8,053.7	8,104.3	8,180.2	8,195.4	8,268.2	8,301.3	8,107.6
2006	8,153.3	8,219.1	8,287.4	8,311.7	8,350.9	8,357.8	8,267.1	8,337.0	8,413.0	8,435.1	8,500.7	8,544.2	8,348.1
2007	8,376.2	8,459.0	8,537.9	8,564.2	8,611.6	8,627.9	8,551.6	8,595.1	8,650.0	8,699.0	8,764.0	8,797.7	8,602.9
2008	8,638.7	8,715.4	8,754.8	8,782.2	8,820.1	8,813.8	8,733.0	8,766.8	8,772.3	8,822.0	8,855.9	8,863.3	8,778.2
2009	8,651.2	8,670.1	8,691.9	8,690.4	8,706.7	8,686.6	8,583.0	8,581.1	8,619.4	8,670.9	8,711.5	8,726.9	8,665.8
2010	8,560.1	8,619.9	8,695.6	8,742.0	8,816.5	8,803.8	8,696.5	8,716.3	8,761.4	8,837.3	8,886.7	8,913.2	8,754.1
2011	8,741.1	8,794.0	8,874.3	8,939.8	8,961.0	8,969.8	8,891.2	8,914.1	8,966.0	8,988.7	9,048.2	9,076.0	8,930.4
2012	8,917.4	8,999.4	9,069.9	9,113.9	9,162.2	9,183.7	9,099.9	9,149.9	9,197.1	9,255.1	9,341.7	9,369.1	9,154.9
2013	9,166.2	9,278.6	9,336.2	9,379.3	9,420.2	9,440.0	9,376.1	9,410.8	9,461.5	9,535.5	9,597.1	9,602.9	9,417.0
Mining and Logging													
2002	147.7	146.8	146.0	144.5	145.3	146.2	144.9	145.5	145.5	143.7	143.8	144.1	145.3
2003	142.6	143.3	144.4	144.6	145.9	147.3	148.2	149.3	148.8	147.8	147.8	149.5	146.6
2004	149.2	149.3	150.6	150.2	151.2	152.9	153.8	154.6	154.6	155.6	156.3	157.5	153.0
2005	158.4	159.1	160.1	161.6	163.1	165.9	168.1	169.1	169.7	170.9	172.0	174.0	166.0
2006	173.2	175.6	177.5	179.3	181.4	185.9	188.0	190.3	192.5	194.3	195.5	197.1	185.9
2007	197.6	199.3	201.4	202.6	204.3	208.2	209.9	211.9	211.2	213.3	215.1	216.9	207.6
2008	218.6	221.6	222.9	224.4	226.5	230.7	233.6	235.9	236.0	238.8	237.8	235.8	230.2
2009	227.7	221.5	215.4	205.3	200.3	197.7	195.5	193.9	192.2	191.0	191.5	193.2	202.1
2010	193.2	195.4	197.6	200.6	203.1	206.9	208.6	210.9	211.7	213.9	215.0	217.7	206.2
2011	218.3	220.9	223.9	227.7	229.9	235.7	240.7	244.7	246.7	251.0	253.2	256.7	237.5
2012	257.2	260.4	263.6	265.9	269.4	273.4	276.5	277.6	276.9	279.5	280.3	281.9	271.9
2013	280.6	283.0	284.6	286.9	288.4	292.0	294.1	295.9	295.5	295.0	291.7	293.2	290.1
Construction													
2002	556.3	562.9	572.5	569.4	575.2	579.5	574.0	577.4	571.0	563.7	558.7	552.8	567.8
2003	545.5	547.1	549.7	551.0	557.9	559.4	555.5	558.5	556.3	551.9	543.5	543.4	551.6
2004	534.1	535.4	541.8	543.6	543.1	548.1	548.9	549.5	548.5	548.9	545.9	546.6	544.5
2005	540.1	545.5	555.3	564.6	565.9	570.6	573.6	574.8	579.3	576.6	577.9	581.1	567.1
2006	575.8	586.0	599.5	594.7	602.9	614.8	609.3	613.4	617.4	615.6	617.5	619.8	605.6
2007	609.2	622.2	635.2	637.7	644.9	657.9	652.2	658.7	659.4	665.3	668.5	666.3	648.1
2008	653.8	667.0	672.5	675.3	679.8	681.8	678.0	681.4	676.6	680.2	671.7	661.4	673.3
2009	634.0	627.8	620.5	606.9	603.8	602.1	595.6	591.0	582.0	576.2	569.3	565.0	597.9
2010	554.6	552.4	560.6	563.9	565.0	568.1	572.2	573.6	570.8	569.8	562.7	559.4	564.4
2011	543.5	549.4	557.6	559.0	560.1	567.3	571.6	574.7	576.5	572.2	569.0	565.5	563.9
2012	557.0	564.4	573.1	576.4	584.0	589.7	585.7	594.5	594.8	600.7	597.9	593.2	584.3
2013	583.0	599.1	606.6	606.8	611.0	618.0	616.7	623.0	621.8	625.8	615.0	610.9	611.5

1. Employment by Industry: Texas, Selected Years, 2002–2013—*Continued*

(Numbers in thousands, not seasonally adjusted)

Industry and year	January	February	March	April	May	June	July	August	September	October	November	December	Annual average
Manufacturing													
2002	968.4	963.4	961.1	954.9	952.9	954.6	948.5	947.1	941.3	931.9	927.5	924.6	948.0
2003	912.4	910.3	906.2	904.4	901.5	902.3	896.4	895.4	894.9	889.8	889.2	889.2	899.3
2004	882.2	884.0	884.9	886.8	888.8	892.7	893.8	894.7	893.0	893.4	894.4	895.6	890.4
2005	885.2	887.2	890.1	889.7	891.9	898.5	900.7	901.5	901.9	900.6	905.1	909.1	896.8
2006	905.1	908.7	913.4	916.8	922.6	930.5	928.6	931.6	932.8	929.7	932.6	935.0	924.0
2007	926.2	929.0	930.3	932.0	934.3	941.0	937.8	938.0	936.4	934.0	934.4	935.8	934.1
2008	926.8	929.0	927.3	926.0	928.7	931.3	929.3	928.7	923.8	919.4	915.9	909.1	924.6
2009	889.2	877.8	864.6	849.4	841.8	833.8	824.1	823.7	820.5	815.0	811.1	810.8	838.5
2010	805.5	805.1	807.2	805.0	808.1	811.6	813.7	815.7	815.5	817.6	819.5	821.8	812.2
2011	816.4	819.7	823.9	827.1	829.8	837.0	841.1	844.1	845.4	845.7	848.3	851.5	835.8
2012	848.2	853.0	856.3	859.8	859.8	866.6	869.7	871.2	870.5	869.2	870.6	871.9	863.9
2013	864.1	867.9	868.3	867.3	868.5	873.6	872.7	873.7	873.0	875.3	874.4	880.0	871.6
Trade, Transportation, and Utilities													
2002	1,944.8	1,932.4	1,939.5	1,937.8	1,945.6	1,950.2	1,945.3	1,950.0	1,942.4	1,937.5	1,964.9	1,989.7	1,948.3
2003	1,910.7	1,896.0	1,898.8	1,896.9	1,897.7	1,903.4	1,900.7	1,915.7	1,914.0	1,922.6	1,951.5	1,978.6	1,915.6
2004	1,913.6	1,907.7	1,917.9	1,925.5	1,931.9	1,935.8	1,941.6	1,956.1	1,945.8	1,956.9	1,990.0	2,018.0	1,945.1
2005	1,954.1	1,942.7	1,954.5	1,964.7	1,973.4	1,983.5	1,992.8	2,007.1	2,003.3	2,006.5	2,055.0	2,086.1	1,993.7
2006	2,013.7	2,004.8	2,022.0	2,022.9	2,031.7	2,040.4	2,039.5	2,056.4	2,054.2	2,062.6	2,104.0	2,135.6	2,049.0
2007	2,071.9	2,064.4	2,084.8	2,084.7	2,095.3	2,107.8	2,111.1	2,121.9	2,118.8	2,130.9	2,171.2	2,198.5	2,113.4
2008	2,129.7	2,124.1	2,130.0	2,127.5	2,133.2	2,142.1	2,143.8	2,157.0	2,136.7	2,142.2	2,166.1	2,182.6	2,143.1
2009	2,098.3	2,072.7	2,070.5	2,054.5	2,052.9	2,051.2	2,044.1	2,050.0	2,041.6	2,041.3	2,064.4	2,085.9	2,060.6
2010	2,019.8	2,009.1	2,023.8	2,027.6	2,038.0	2,047.0	2,048.1	2,060.0	2,052.8	2,067.5	2,101.3	2,129.3	2,052.0
2011	2,063.8	2,055.0	2,071.5	2,088.0	2,093.8	2,103.1	2,108.8	2,124.5	2,117.1	2,129.2	2,168.9	2,197.4	2,110.1
2012	2,134.4	2,126.5	2,138.0	2,146.7	2,159.1	2,173.2	2,174.8	2,189.8	2,180.9	2,195.1	2,248.5	2,267.5	2,177.9
2013	2,196.3	2,194.7	2,199.8	2,211.3	2,221.4	2,236.0	2,239.5	2,257.3	2,251.6	2,262.7	2,310.7	2,336.4	2,243.1
Wholesale Trade													
2002	460.6	460.4	463.0	461.4	463.0	465.1	465.0	465.6	464.7	462.6	463.5	464.4	463.3
2003	456.9	456.5	457.7	456.9	457.9	460.1	459.0	459.5	459.4	458.0	458.5	460.2	458.4
2004	454.7	455.4	457.9	460.1	461.6	463.9	466.1	466.5	466.1	467.7	468.3	469.7	463.2
2005	465.1	466.1	468.7	472.7	474.9	477.7	480.9	481.8	483.8	482.9	485.1	488.8	477.4
2006	485.4	488.2	492.1	492.6	495.5	499.9	499.1	501.3	503.1	503.1	505.9	509.2	498.0
2007	504.7	508.1	511.4	513.1	516.2	521.7	521.8	523.5	523.3	526.4	527.0	530.2	519.0
2008	525.0	527.4	527.6	529.0	530.4	532.6	531.6	532.2	529.2	529.1	527.2	526.2	529.0
2009	515.7	510.5	507.1	501.6	499.8	498.4	496.3	495.0	492.6	492.2	490.8	491.7	499.3
2010	489.3	489.6	490.9	492.7	495.2	498.1	499.0	500.0	499.7	500.9	501.7	503.8	496.7
2011	500.2	503.5	506.5	510.6	513.9	517.2	518.6	520.7	522.7	524.6	525.9	529.2	516.1
2012	526.4	530.2	533.9	535.5	539.4	543.9	543.3	545.6	545.1	546.1	548.2	551.0	540.7
2013	547.6	551.6	554.1	554.2	556.3	560.2	561.1	563.4	564.8	565.7	568.9	568.4	559.7
Retail Trade													
2002	1,093.7	1,082.7	1,087.6	1,087.9	1,092.0	1,093.5	1,087.3	1,089.3	1,084.8	1,080.1	1,107.4	1,130.7	1,093.1
2003	1,065.8	1,053.0	1,055.0	1,054.5	1,055.7	1,058.6	1,056.9	1,067.8	1,066.2	1,073.3	1,101.1	1,122.2	1,069.2
2004	1,068.7	1,060.4	1,067.1	1,070.6	1,074.4	1,075.5	1,076.1	1,089.6	1,079.9	1,087.0	1,118.0	1,139.1	1,083.9
2005	1,088.2	1,077.6	1,085.3	1,090.2	1,094.9	1,102.1	1,106.1	1,115.9	1,109.7	1,111.9	1,154.2	1,176.0	1,109.3
2006	1,118.6	1,106.5	1,117.1	1,116.8	1,120.5	1,122.5	1,122.5	1,134.1	1,127.9	1,135.3	1,172.0	1,191.0	1,132.1
2007	1,142.8	1,130.4	1,144.0	1,142.9	1,148.3	1,152.4	1,156.9	1,162.8	1,158.4	1,167.5	1,206.5	1,224.5	1,161.5
2008	1,171.3	1,161.4	1,169.0	1,162.1	1,163.4	1,168.7	1,171.2	1,180.6	1,164.8	1,171.7	1,197.3	1,210.6	1,174.3
2009	1,152.4	1,136.8	1,138.1	1,132.8	1,134.2	1,134.6	1,132.1	1,139.6	1,133.4	1,133.9	1,157.8	1,172.2	1,141.5
2010	1,119.7	1,108.9	1,119.9	1,120.9	1,127.1	1,131.0	1,129.7	1,138.7	1,130.2	1,142.9	1,174.1	1,193.8	1,136.4
2011	1,140.3	1,127.4	1,138.0	1,148.3	1,149.7	1,154.6	1,155.8	1,166.9	1,155.1	1,166.6	1,202.5	1,219.4	1,160.4
2012	1,169.2	1,155.1	1,159.5	1,166.0	1,172.1	1,178.3	1,180.8	1,190.0	1,181.3	1,194.8	1,242.0	1,251.9	1,186.8
2013	1,192.9	1,187.4	1,188.0	1,198.1	1,203.7	1,211.6	1,214.7	1,227.5	1,220.4	1,229.6	1,268.3	1,283.1	1,218.8
Transportation and Utilities													
2002	390.5	389.3	388.9	388.5	390.6	391.6	393.0	395.1	392.9	394.8	394.0	394.6	392.0
2003	388.0	386.5	386.1	385.5	384.1	384.7	384.8	388.4	388.4	391.3	391.9	396.2	388.0
2004	390.2	391.9	392.9	394.8	395.9	396.4	399.4	400.0	399.8	402.2	403.7	409.2	398.0
2005	400.8	399.0	400.5	401.8	403.6	403.7	405.8	409.4	410.8	411.7	415.7	421.3	407.0
2006	409.7	410.1	412.8	413.5	415.7	418.0	417.9	421.0	423.2	424.2	426.1	435.4	419.0
2007	424.4	425.9	429.4	428.7	430.8	433.7	432.4	435.6	437.1	437.0	437.7	443.8	433.0
2008	433.4	435.3	435.4	436.4	439.4	440.8	441.0	444.2	442.7	441.4	441.6	445.8	439.8
2009	430.2	425.4	425.3	420.1	418.9	418.2	415.7	415.4	415.6	415.2	415.8	422.0	419.8
2010	410.8	410.6	413.0	414.0	415.7	417.9	419.4	421.3	422.9	423.7	425.5	431.7	418.9
2011	423.3	424.1	427.0	429.1	430.2	431.3	434.4	436.9	439.3	438.0	440.5	448.8	433.6
2012	438.8	441.2	444.6	445.2	447.6	451.0	450.7	454.2	454.5	454.2	458.3	464.6	450.4
2013	455.8	455.7	457.7	459.0	461.4	464.2	463.7	466.4	466.4	467.4	473.5	484.9	464.7
Information													
2002	258.1	256.0	255.0	251.7	251.5	251.2	247.7	246.5	244.2	243.7	243.0	242.4	249.3
2003	238.4	237.7	237.3	235.2	235.1	235.1	234.1	232.9	230.3	229.2	229.6	229.2	233.7
2004	227.4	225.5	227.2	225.8	226.1	226.8	225.2	224.2	223.2	222.4	222.6	223.2	224.9
2005	221.8	222.1	222.5	222.8	223.1	224.6	224.1	223.9	223.9	222.0	223.1	223.7	223.1
2006	221.2	222.1	222.3	221.9	222.7	223.9	221.7	221.4	221.0	219.9	220.6	221.3	221.7
2007	219.4	220.7	220.7	220.0	221.9	222.4	221.9	222.2	220.4	220.0	221.1	221.0	221.0
2008	219.0	219.2	219.2	218.3	219.3	219.3	218.2	217.3	214.4	213.8	214.3	214.3	217.2
2009	211.2	210.2	209.2	207.0	206.1	205.3	203.2	201.5	198.9	198.9	199.3	199.7	204.2
2010	196.8	195.9	196.0	196.5	196.2	197.5	195.6	195.4	193.9	193.8	195.1	195.3	195.7
2011	194.6	194.2	194.6	194.9	195.8	196.5	197.6	196.6	195.3	195.2	195.8	197.1	195.7
2012	196.4	196.1	196.7	196.8	196.8	197.3	198.5	198.3	197.6	196.3	198.8	199.2	197.4
2013	197.1	197.5	198.4	199.2	200.5	202.0	202.8	202.9	200.6	202.1	201.8	203.7	200.7

1. Employment by Industry: Texas, Selected Years, 2002–2013—*Continued*

(Numbers in thousands, not seasonally adjusted)

Industry and year	January	February	March	April	May	June	July	August	September	October	November	December	Annual average
Financial Activities													
2002	574.8	575.5	576.8	576.2	579.6	582.4	582.7	583.3	580.4	579.9	581.5	582.7	579.7
2003	577.4	579.4	580.8	582.2	584.8	587.5	589.0	590.9	587.8	587.8	587.6	590.2	585.5
2004	586.1	587.0	588.5	591.2	592.0	596.1	599.4	600.4	599.1	600.2	600.1	604.3	595.4
2005	597.0	598.7	600.2	602.4	603.7	608.2	613.9	616.1	616.8	617.1	618.7	621.6	609.5
2006	614.2	616.8	620.7	624.0	626.6	631.9	630.5	633.4	633.2	633.5	634.4	638.9	628.2
2007	633.7	636.8	639.8	640.1	643.6	648.1	648.3	649.7	646.4	645.6	646.7	648.4	643.9
2008	641.7	645.2	644.7	647.8	650.6	652.9	652.4	651.7	646.9	644.3	642.4	643.2	647.0
2009	632.9	632.4	630.9	628.8	629.1	629.9	629.1	627.6	624.0	622.9	622.9	624.5	627.9
2010	618.3	619.9	621.4	621.0	623.7	626.6	626.8	627.0	625.0	629.3	631.4	634.1	625.4
2011	629.0	631.4	634.3	636.1	637.4	641.3	644.0	644.9	645.5	647.0	647.8	651.1	640.8
2012	646.9	650.0	652.5	654.3	657.5	663.0	664.3	666.3	665.6	670.4	672.5	675.5	661.6
2013	668.4	673.0	675.6	676.2	679.0	684.6	688.5	690.3	688.8	686.3	684.1	686.1	681.7
Professional and Business Services													
2002	1,048.5	1,053.4	1,061.0	1,066.7	1,068.5	1,072.8	1,070.7	1,080.7	1,075.2	1,067.2	1,066.7	1,064.5	1,066.3
2003	1,039.3	1,043.6	1,049.9	1,055.6	1,056.0	1,057.0	1,056.1	1,064.9	1,065.5	1,067.2	1,070.3	1,078.9	1,058.7
2004	1,060.7	1,069.5	1,078.1	1,094.1	1,095.1	1,104.2	1,110.4	1,116.0	1,112.3	1,120.1	1,122.0	1,125.4	1,100.7
2005	1,108.5	1,122.3	1,131.7	1,150.6	1,148.1	1,157.8	1,163.1	1,172.9	1,183.6	1,193.1	1,200.3	1,208.5	1,161.7
2006	1,189.0	1,204.1	1,219.6	1,225.8	1,231.8	1,244.4	1,245.8	1,257.2	1,261.9	1,261.7	1,272.2	1,279.6	1,241.1
2007	1,250.9	1,269.0	1,283.0	1,287.8	1,292.6	1,307.3	1,307.0	1,319.3	1,319.4	1,326.1	1,330.0	1,335.8	1,302.4
2008	1,313.4	1,327.2	1,330.8	1,338.7	1,339.8	1,345.3	1,341.7	1,351.3	1,338.9	1,345.3	1,336.4	1,327.3	1,336.3
2009	1,280.1	1,272.3	1,266.4	1,254.4	1,249.2	1,250.6	1,241.2	1,240.5	1,232.9	1,242.7	1,249.0	1,249.2	1,252.4
2010	1,231.0	1,240.6	1,253.0	1,264.0	1,265.5	1,275.5	1,279.3	1,287.7	1,288.5	1,301.7	1,304.8	1,310.9	1,275.2
2011	1,288.3	1,301.9	1,318.0	1,334.1	1,330.9	1,342.0	1,345.2	1,357.8	1,363.5	1,362.0	1,368.2	1,373.4	1,340.4
2012	1,353.9	1,370.3	1,385.6	1,396.4	1,402.6	1,413.0	1,410.0	1,430.5	1,428.0	1,434.6	1,445.6	1,442.3	1,409.4
2013	1,411.0	1,431.9	1,443.4	1,446.6	1,449.0	1,459.9	1,458.0	1,473.3	1,473.4	1,485.4	1,488.2	1,476.7	1,458.1
Education and Health Services													
2002	1,054.1	1,065.5	1,070.3	1,073.8	1,079.7	1,076.5	1,077.0	1,089.5	1,100.6	1,096.4	1,102.4	1,105.1	1,082.6
2003	1,098.2	1,107.2	1,111.8	1,113.4	1,116.6	1,109.0	1,110.8	1,121.2	1,133.3	1,135.2	1,136.9	1,136.7	1,119.2
2004	1,124.5	1,135.5	1,140.8	1,144.3	1,145.9	1,141.7	1,143.6	1,150.6	1,159.7	1,169.7	1,171.4	1,174.4	1,150.2
2005	1,157.4	1,167.7	1,174.0	1,177.3	1,179.5	1,176.6	1,181.0	1,189.2	1,200.7	1,199.0	1,204.0	1,207.1	1,184.5
2006	1,193.3	1,201.9	1,206.1	1,206.8	1,210.2	1,210.3	1,208.1	1,221.4	1,231.4	1,232.8	1,236.8	1,240.6	1,216.6
2007	1,223.0	1,238.1	1,246.4	1,247.4	1,252.8	1,252.5	1,252.2	1,261.4	1,268.7	1,270.1	1,275.1	1,276.6	1,255.4
2008	1,260.0	1,274.5	1,275.2	1,280.9	1,288.3	1,284.2	1,284.2	1,293.4	1,298.2	1,306.6	1,311.3	1,316.7	1,289.5
2009	1,298.4	1,308.5	1,314.7	1,325.0	1,332.6	1,332.7	1,337.8	1,344.2	1,350.9	1,361.8	1,363.8	1,366.2	1,336.4
2010	1,351.2	1,362.0	1,371.2	1,376.3	1,382.1	1,380.4	1,375.6	1,383.4	1,390.5	1,398.0	1,399.5	1,401.8	1,381.0
2011	1,384.5	1,390.4	1,398.5	1,408.2	1,411.5	1,409.2	1,409.2	1,418.8	1,430.3	1,430.6	1,434.5	1,437.9	1,413.6
2012	1,417.6	1,430.2	1,436.4	1,435.8	1,441.3	1,439.8	1,432.0	1,448.9	1,458.1	1,464.2	1,469.2	1,473.4	1,445.6
2013	1,449.8	1,467.8	1,473.4	1,478.6	1,482.5	1,477.4	1,472.7	1,487.8	1,494.6	1,508.0	1,507.5	1,507.0	1,483.9
Leisure and Hospitality													
2002	800.6	815.4	834.4	847.4	864.2	876.2	868.4	871.4	859.7	842.4	839.2	839.8	846.6
2003	820.9	830.9	847.7	857.4	872.2	885.0	877.0	880.4	867.0	858.2	852.7	854.4	858.7
2004	838.3	850.4	869.8	884.3	897.3	912.2	908.8	909.7	897.7	886.1	880.1	880.4	884.6
2005	861.4	874.1	893.6	912.2	925.0	936.6	930.7	928.6	916.1	902.1	899.7	898.7	906.6
2006	887.8	901.8	923.9	938.3	954.4	970.3	964.3	965.5	955.8	940.7	939.2	942.0	940.3
2007	919.8	937.3	960.9	980.6	996.6	1,013.0	1,007.7	1,008.7	991.8	982.7	980.8	982.6	980.2
2008	961.6	977.8	995.7	1,014.8	1,028.8	1,039.2	1,032.4	1,028.8	1,004.9	999.4	996.4	996.3	1,006.3
2009	971.2	984.8	1,003.7	1,014.6	1,029.4	1,040.3	1,029.2	1,025.7	1,008.3	990.2	985.3	983.6	1,005.5
2010	956.3	971.8	994.5	1,007.9	1,025.1	1,036.5	1,025.3	1,027.0	1,018.5	1,011.8	1,009.5	1,009.2	1,007.8
2011	983.4	996.8	1,028.7	1,045.8	1,061.4	1,074.3	1,061.4	1,064.2	1,055.5	1,043.0	1,042.9	1,039.8	1,041.4
2012	1,017.9	1,038.1	1,065.8	1,084.5	1,103.3	1,123.1	1,106.3	1,112.3	1,104.3	1,091.7	1,093.1	1,097.7	1,086.5
2013	1,072.2	1,097.9	1,122.3	1,141.0	1,160.3	1,176.3	1,165.0	1,164.8	1,153.4	1,152.4	1,149.7	1,147.1	1,141.9
Other Services													
2002	347.4	350.8	355.6	356.0	359.2	362.9	358.4	358.8	357.9	354.4	355.9	355.8	356.1
2003	352.6	353.7	358.4	356.5	357.5	362.0	358.3	357.5	354.8	350.4	350.3	351.8	355.3
2004	350.9	353.2	358.5	358.2	357.1	360.4	357.6	354.8	351.2	347.5	345.3	345.3	353.3
2005	343.0	344.1	349.3	350.2	350.7	354.4	352.9	350.4	348.0	343.8	343.8	344.1	347.9
2006	340.8	342.5	346.8	349.2	350.3	354.7	350.4	349.1	348.0	346.9	347.7	347.8	347.9
2007	344.8	348.5	351.9	353.6	356.3	361.7	359.4	359.0	356.7	356.9	357.5	357.5	355.3
2008	355.2	357.9	359.6	362.8	364.8	368.7	368.3	367.8	361.9	363.8	363.4	362.5	363.1
2009	358.6	360.7	361.2	361.5	363.3	367.0	365.0	362.3	358.0	357.4	358.4	357.5	360.9
2010	354.1	355.7	358.3	359.7	362.4	366.2	364.1	363.3	360.6	360.5	359.7	360.4	360.4
2011	356.9	359.2	363.0	366.1	368.3	373.2	372.3	371.4	370.9	369.0	369.6	369.9	367.5
2012	369.5	371.8	374.9	379.5	382.8	388.7	387.5	387.6	386.0	386.7	387.2	388.2	382.5
2013	385.1	390.0	392.6	393.3	397.0	402.5	401.4	400.0	398.0	400.5	399.1	398.0	396.5
Government													
2002	1,602.4	1,634.6	1,641.5	1,641.1	1,643.8	1,597.7	1,528.0	1,548.7	1,629.1	1,664.0	1,674.0	1,667.8	1,622.7
2003	1,639.9	1,674.1	1,672.2	1,673.5	1,673.4	1,630.0	1,553.1	1,568.4	1,639.3	1,660.1	1,669.4	1,659.9	1,642.8
2004	1,637.2	1,670.7	1,672.2	1,672.9	1,674.9	1,634.6	1,565.7	1,584.0	1,658.6	1,680.9	1,689.9	1,684.7	1,652.2
2005	1,663.4	1,697.0	1,699.2	1,701.3	1,703.2	1,658.3	1,595.2	1,616.1	1,686.8	1,711.8	1,723.6	1,711.5	1,680.6
2006	1,693.3	1,725.1	1,726.0	1,722.8	1,723.2	1,681.9	1,606.8	1,632.6	1,707.5	1,737.0	1,745.8	1,738.4	1,703.4
2007	1,712.7	1,744.2	1,750.4	1,750.0	1,752.5	1,715.1	1,644.0	1,652.9	1,727.8	1,766.7	1,781.6	1,777.3	1,731.3
2008	1,758.1	1,789.5	1,797.6	1,791.4	1,795.3	1,762.1	1,692.0	1,699.5	1,770.4	1,806.6	1,825.6	1,820.4	1,775.7
2009	1,800.5	1,828.5	1,835.3	1,844.6	1,844.1	1,809.6	1,733.4	1,729.3	1,804.8	1,855.7	1,868.4	1,860.3	1,817.9
2010	1,832.6	1,864.9	1,877.4	1,889.0	1,923.5	1,874.1	1,781.7	1,772.5	1,831.6	1,874.7	1,885.4	1,872.2	1,856.6
2011	1,840.6	1,865.1	1,865.7	1,866.6	1,861.9	1,830.2	1,752.7	1,735.9	1,787.9	1,812.7	1,819.9	1,809.3	1,820.7
2012	1,780.8	1,816.4	1,820.0	1,819.9	1,818.3	1,784.4	1,726.7	1,716.9	1,777.9	1,815.6	1,826.6	1,825.3	1,794.1
2013	1,786.3	1,825.8	1,830.7	1,833.1	1,830.5	1,801.3	1,748.2	1,734.4	1,801.1	1,838.1	1,856.0	1,847.9	1,811.1

2. Average Weekly Hours by Selected Industry: Texas, 2009–2013

(Not seasonally adjusted)

Industry and year	January	February	March	April	May	June	July	August	September	October	November	December	Annual average
Total Private													
2009	35.4	35.5	35.3	35.0	35.0	35.1	35.0	35.5	34.8	35.1	35.8	35.4	35.2
2010	35.1	35.0	35.7	35.7	36.4	35.9	36.1	36.8	35.7	36.1	36.0	36.4	35.9
2011	36.8	36.1	36.7	36.6	37.0	36.8	36.6	36.7	36.7	37.4	37.0	36.9	36.8
2012	37.3	35.9	36.0	36.4	35.7	36.1	36.6	36.3	36.8	36.3	36.3	37.1	36.4
2013	35.6	36.3	36.4	36.2	36.1	36.9	36.2	36.3	36.7	36.1	36.1	36.5	36.3
Goods-Producing													
2009	41.1	40.0	39.1	39.6	40.5	40.6	40.7	40.8	39.9	40.5	41.8	41.0	40.5
2010	40.5	39.0	40.8	41.1	41.5	41.5	41.9	42.7	41.2	42.0	41.6	42.8	41.4
2011	43.1	42.4	44.0	43.9	43.2	43.7	43.1	43.2	43.1	43.2	43.3	42.7	43.2
2012	42.9	42.5	42.9	43.0	42.7	43.1	42.8	42.8	42.8	42.9	42.9	43.4	42.9
2013	40.5	42.4	42.9	42.4	42.3	43.0	42.8	42.9	43.1	43.2	43.2	42.8	42.6
Construction													
2009	41.7	40.1	38.3	39.3	40.9	41.3	42.1	41.5	41.0	42.0	42.0	41.0	40.9
2010	40.1	39.6	40.6	41.1	41.3	42.1	42.2	42.9	42.1	44.1	42.7	42.8	41.8
2011	43.2	42.7	44.5	44.4	43.2	44.5	43.8	44.1	43.8	43.4	43.5	42.2	43.6
2012	42.6	42.1	43.6	43.4	42.9	44.3	43.1	44.3	43.8	44.7	44.2	44.1	43.6
2013	42.4	44.7	45.6	44.3	43.9	44.8	44.1	44.2	44.0	44.0	43.8	42.4	44.0
Manufacturing													
2009	40.5	38.9	38.9	39.2	39.7	39.7	39.1	39.7	39.4	39.6	40.3	39.9	39.6
2010	39.8	38.7	38.8	39.4	39.9	39.8	39.6	40.5	40.3	40.2	40.4	41.2	39.9
2011	40.9	40.3	40.8	40.9	40.6	40.9	40.5	40.6	40.9	41.3	41.8	41.8	40.9
2012	41.8	41.6	41.4	41.6	41.6	41.6	41.6	40.9	41.3	41.2	41.5	42.4	41.5
2013	40.9	41.9	42.1	42.0	41.7	42.0	42.2	42.4	42.7	42.9	42.9	43.1	42.2
Trade, Transportation, and Utilities													
2009	38.4	38.5	38.0	37.5	37.3	37.3	37.0	37.0	36.9	36.3	36.8	36.8	37.3
2010	36.2	36.1	36.1	36.2	36.5	36.9	37.2	37.3	36.0	36.4	36.6	37.2	36.6
2011	36.7	36.6	36.8	37.1	37.3	36.9	36.9	37.3	37.2	37.6	37.0	37.2	37.1
2012	37.4	37.3	37.3	37.8	37.5	37.8	37.8	37.8	38.4	37.3	37.3	38.2	37.7
2013	37.0	37.4	37.6	37.4	37.2	37.6	37.2	37.2	37.3	36.7	36.6	37.2	37.2
Financial Activities													
2009	37.8	38.3	37.8	37.9	36.8	36.9	37.2	38.0	37.1	37.9	38.4	37.7	37.7
2010	38.1	38.2	38.4	37.8	38.9	38.5	38.2	39.1	38.6	38.3	38.3	38.4	38.4
2011	38.8	38.7	38.8	39.0	40.3	38.7	38.9	38.1	38.6	40.1	39.4	39.5	39.1
2012	40.2	39.7	39.7	40.5	38.8	39.1	40.4	39.1	40.1	39.1	39.1	40.3	39.7
2013	38.5	38.4	38.4	38.4	38.1	39.4	37.7	37.7	39.0	37.5	37.8	38.9	38.3
Professional and Business Services													
2009	34.6	35.1	35.0	34.7	34.6	35.2	34.5	35.2	34.2	34.5	35.5	34.7	34.8
2010	34.5	34.4	35.1	35.4	36.5	36.6	36.8	37.8	37.2	38.1	37.8	37.5	36.5
2011	37.6	37.3	37.9	37.7	38.4	38.6	38.2	38.1	37.9	38.8	38.0	37.6	38.0
2012	38.4	38.0	38.0	39.0	37.9	38.1	38.4	38.0	38.4	37.7	37.9	38.7	38.2
2013	37.2	37.6	37.8	37.7	37.5	38.3	37.2	37.6	37.9	36.9	37.3	37.9	37.6
Education and Health Services													
2009	34.8	35.4	35.8	35.0	35.0	34.8	34.9	35.0	34.8	34.5	35.2	34.6	35.0
2010	34.5	34.5	34.1	34.3	34.6	33.9	34.0	34.5	34.2	34.0	33.7	33.9	34.2
2011	34.6	34.0	34.2	34.2	34.1	34.6	33.9	34.0	33.6	33.9	34.4	33.6	34.1
2012	34.3	33.5	33.4	34.1	33.2	33.7	34.3	33.8	34.4	33.6	33.6	34.2	33.8
2013	33.4	33.7	33.2	33.1	33.3	34.1	33.0	33.2	33.9	32.9	33.0	33.7	33.4
Leisure and Hospitality													
2009	26.3	27.2	27.3	26.5	26.3	26.6	26.3	27.0	25.9	26.8	26.5	26.8	26.6
2010	26.2	27.3	27.4	27.4	28.0	27.8	27.8	28.0	27.1	27.8	27.7	28.2	27.6
2011	27.8	28.0	28.7	27.9	28.8	28.1	28.2	28.1	27.6	28.4	27.7	27.9	28.1
2012	28.0	27.9	28.3	28.3	27.7	28.1	28.5	28.1	27.8	27.5	27.5	28.3	28.0
2013	27.2	28.3	28.7	27.8	28.1	28.8	28.0	28.1	27.7	27.6	27.7	27.8	28.0
Other Services													
2009	32.7	33.5	33.2	32.9	33.1	33.4	33.9	34.1	33.6	34.5	34.9	34.3	33.7
2010	34.0	33.6	34.7	33.9	35.0	34.5	34.1	35.1	34.3	34.4	34.1	34.3	34.3
2011	34.8	34.1	35.5	35.1	35.9	35.1	35.3	35.8	36.0	36.6	35.4	35.9	35.5
2012	36.7	35.9	34.8	35.3	34.5	34.7	35.5	34.9	34.9	34.9	34.8	35.2	35.2
2013	33.8	34.8	34.7	34.2	34.1	34.2	33.1	33.1	33.4	32.7	32.9	33.9	33.7

3. Average Hourly Earnings by Selected Industry: Texas, 2009–2013

(Dollars, not seasonally adjusted)

Industry and year	January	February	March	April	May	June	July	August	September	October	November	December	Annual average
Total Private													
2009	21.32	21.37	21.26	21.22	21.30	21.26	21.39	21.47	21.50	21.47	21.76	21.41	21.39
2010	21.31	21.41	21.31	21.42	21.39	21.17	21.29	21.37	21.43	21.44	21.48	21.32	21.36
2011	21.95	22.00	21.84	21.92	22.02	21.74	21.90	21.86	21.94	22.22	22.15	22.10	21.97
2012	22.36	22.15	21.98	22.28	21.97	21.89	22.18	21.94	22.37	22.25	22.37	22.70	22.21
2013	22.73	22.69	22.60	22.81	22.73	22.88	22.79	22.79	23.15	23.11	23.19	23.43	22.91
Goods-Producing													
2009	22.68	22.63	22.65	22.60	22.70	22.74	22.85	22.88	22.80	23.04	23.12	23.06	22.81
2010	22.80	22.90	22.68	22.61	22.69	22.61	22.88	22.90	22.86	23.03	22.86	21.25	22.67
2011	22.70	22.76	22.33	22.79	22.82	22.48	22.74	22.79	22.99	23.39	23.43	23.64	22.91
2012	23.57	23.60	23.42	23.36	22.97	23.02	23.14	23.08	23.48	23.40	23.59	24.21	23.40
2013	24.44	24.08	23.94	24.13	24.12	24.15	24.31	24.35	24.63	24.61	24.56	24.98	24.36
Construction													
2009	19.19	19.36	19.72	19.60	19.48	19.50	19.48	19.52	19.77	19.86	19.63	19.66	19.56
2010	19.49	19.56	19.55	19.45	19.66	19.81	19.78	19.85	19.89	19.67	19.70	19.78	19.69
2011	19.70	19.74	19.18	19.35	19.86	19.76	19.55	20.03	20.38	20.80	20.99	21.19	20.04
2012	21.07	21.39	21.33	21.38	21.51	21.42	21.73	21.72	22.08	22.21	22.40	22.97	21.78
2013	22.94	22.55	22.13	22.12	22.26	22.22	22.31	22.59	22.80	22.71	22.78	23.41	22.56
Manufacturing													
2009	22.92	22.96	23.14	23.21	23.28	23.40	23.30	23.40	23.45	23.51	23.54	23.57	23.30
2010	23.53	23.51	23.56	23.73	23.87	23.82	23.77	23.74	23.67	23.79	23.87	23.82	23.73
2011	23.69	23.71	23.23	23.87	24.39	23.96	24.36	23.91	23.91	24.15	24.12	24.32	23.97
2012	24.16	24.04	23.78	23.49	22.86	23.09	22.74	23.14	23.47	23.37	23.38	23.97	23.46
2013	24.34	24.17	24.30	24.62	24.55	24.59	24.76	24.62	24.96	25.02	24.94	25.08	24.67
Trade, Transportation, and Utilities													
2009	27.65	27.60	27.55	27.58	27.64	27.60	27.73	27.68	27.60	27.64	27.41	27.47	27.60
2010	27.68	27.43	27.87	27.74	27.68	27.97	27.94	27.92	27.82	27.86	27.88	27.90	27.81
2011	27.84	27.87	27.24	26.50	26.18	25.58	25.22	24.67	24.15	24.40	23.56	23.52	25.53
2012	23.57	22.81	22.68	22.92	22.24	22.18	22.47	21.98	22.12	21.73	21.45	21.39	22.28
2013	21.62	21.35	21.39	21.69	21.25	21.63	21.25	21.26	21.70	21.24	21.10	21.06	21.38
Financial Activities													
2009	25.32	25.54	25.37	25.24	25.47	25.48	25.59	25.42	25.47	25.20	25.34	25.20	25.39
2010	25.36	25.42	25.32	25.53	25.73	25.53	25.73	25.81	25.77	25.57	25.37	25.17	25.53
2011	25.37	25.11	25.14	25.00	25.18	24.68	24.50	24.81	24.61	25.23	24.73	24.41	24.90
2012	25.02	24.83	24.67	25.56	24.87	24.30	24.04	23.61	23.91	23.50	23.76	23.92	24.33
2013	24.24	24.87	24.66	24.93	25.03	25.37	25.35	25.10	25.53	25.44	25.66	26.07	25.19
Professional and Business Services													
2009	25.86	26.18	26.32	26.53	26.26	26.00	26.25	26.39	26.45	26.27	26.22	26.14	26.24
2010	26.12	26.40	26.20	26.34	26.46	26.26	26.12	26.32	26.13	26.17	26.20	26.31	26.25
2011	26.39	26.33	26.00	25.85	26.00	25.15	25.20	25.05	25.34	25.56	25.48	25.74	25.67
2012	25.90	25.59	25.09	25.44	25.19	25.37	25.68	25.33	25.80	25.67	25.79	26.63	25.63
2013	26.39	26.37	26.33	26.24	26.41	26.63	26.30	26.42	26.92	26.60	26.77	27.29	26.56
Education and Health Services													
2009	21.81	21.64	21.60	21.74	21.74	21.62	21.76	21.82	21.85	21.95	21.85	21.97	21.78
2010	21.87	21.98	21.91	22.00	21.97	22.07	21.97	21.97	21.95	22.02	22.10	22.08	21.99
2011	21.91	22.02	21.84	21.77	21.80	21.87	22.36	22.37	22.43	22.48	22.58	22.57	22.17
2012	22.80	23.00	23.04	23.22	23.23	23.00	23.07	22.80	23.11	23.30	23.57	23.62	23.15
2013	23.51	23.79	23.78	23.82	23.70	23.53	23.95	23.77	23.66	24.19	24.31	24.14	23.85
Leisure and Hospitality													
2009	11.60	11.69	11.71	11.65	11.58	11.48	11.58	11.50	11.69	11.73	11.88	11.93	11.67
2010	11.80	11.75	11.63	11.76	11.69	11.59	11.62	11.70	11.76	11.73	11.77	11.91	11.72
2011	11.98	11.95	11.89	11.86	11.82	11.91	11.85	11.91	11.89	11.95	12.08	12.07	11.93
2012	12.02	12.05	11.91	11.93	11.94	11.77	11.88	11.84	11.86	11.92	11.95	12.04	11.92
2013	11.92	11.82	11.77	11.86	11.91	11.78	11.74	11.89	12.06	12.09	12.11	12.42	11.95
Other Services													
2009	16.65	16.78	16.90	16.84	16.70	16.71	16.76	16.74	16.82	16.89	16.75	16.84	16.78
2010	16.83	16.83	16.97	17.06	17.11	17.19	17.30	17.41	17.52	17.64	17.77	17.85	17.29
2011	18.00	17.93	18.40	18.56	19.05	19.16	19.12	20.26	20.21	21.00	20.84	20.87	19.47
2012	21.52	20.71	21.07	20.90	20.96	20.98	20.60	20.53	21.32	21.26	20.76	21.49	21.01
2013	21.43	21.58	21.66	21.65	21.42	21.51	20.62	20.44	20.78	20.84	20.59	20.69	21.11

4. Average Weekly Earnings by Selected Industry: Texas, 2009–2013

(Dollars, not seasonally adjusted)

Industry and year	January	February	March	April	May	June	July	August	September	October	November	December	Annual average
Total Private													
2009	754.73	758.64	750.48	742.70	745.50	746.23	748.65	762.19	748.20	753.60	779.01	757.91	752.93
2010	747.98	749.35	760.77	764.69	778.60	760.00	768.57	786.42	765.05	773.98	773.28	776.05	766.82
2011	807.76	794.20	801.53	802.27	814.74	800.03	801.54	802.26	805.20	831.03	819.55	815.49	808.50
2012	834.03	795.19	791.28	810.99	784.33	790.23	811.79	796.42	823.22	807.68	812.03	842.17	808.44
2013	809.19	823.65	822.64	825.72	820.55	844.27	825.00	827.28	849.61	834.27	837.16	855.20	831.63
Goods-Producing													
2009	932.15	905.20	885.62	894.96	919.35	923.24	930.00	933.50	909.72	933.12	966.42	945.46	923.81
2010	923.40	893.10	925.34	929.27	941.64	938.32	958.67	977.83	941.83	967.26	950.98	909.50	938.54
2011	978.37	965.02	982.52	1,000.48	985.82	982.38	980.09	984.53	990.87	1,010.45	1,014.52	1,009.43	989.71
2012	1,011.15	1,003.00	1,004.72	1,004.48	980.82	992.16	990.39	987.82	1,004.94	1,003.86	1,012.01	1,050.71	1,003.86
2013	989.82	1,020.99	1,027.03	1,023.11	1,020.28	1,038.45	1,040.47	1,044.62	1,061.55	1,063.15	1,060.99	1,069.14	1,037.74
Construction													
2009	800.22	776.34	755.28	770.28	796.73	805.35	820.11	810.08	810.57	834.12	824.46	806.06	800.00
2010	781.55	774.58	793.73	799.40	811.96	834.00	834.72	851.57	837.37	867.45	841.19	846.58	823.04
2011	851.04	842.90	853.51	859.14	857.95	879.32	856.29	883.32	892.64	902.72	913.07	894.22	873.74
2012	897.58	900.52	929.99	927.89	922.78	948.91	936.56	962.20	967.10	992.79	990.08	1,012.98	949.61
2013	972.66	1,007.99	1,009.13	979.92	977.21	995.46	983.87	998.48	1,003.20	999.24	997.76	992.58	992.64
Manufacturing													
2009	928.26	893.14	900.15	909.83	924.22	928.98	911.03	928.98	923.93	931.00	948.66	940.44	922.68
2010	936.49	909.84	914.13	934.96	952.41	948.04	941.29	961.47	953.90	956.36	964.35	981.38	946.83
2011	968.92	955.51	947.78	976.28	990.23	979.96	986.58	970.75	977.92	997.40	1,008.22	1,016.58	980.37
2012	1,009.89	1,000.06	984.49	977.18	950.98	960.54	945.98	946.43	969.31	962.84	970.27	1,016.33	973.59
2013	995.51	1,012.72	1,023.03	1,034.04	1,023.74	1,032.78	1,044.87	1,043.89	1,065.79	1,073.36	1,069.93	1,080.95	1,041.07
Trade, Transportation, and Utilities													
2009	1,061.76	1,062.60	1,046.90	1,034.25	1,030.97	1,029.48	1,026.01	1,024.16	1,018.44	1,003.33	1,008.69	1,010.90	1,029.48
2010	1,002.02	990.22	1,006.11	1,004.19	1,010.32	1,032.09	1,039.37	1,041.42	1,001.52	1,014.10	1,020.41	1,037.88	1,017.85
2011	1,021.73	1,020.04	1,002.43	983.15	976.51	943.90	930.62	920.19	898.38	917.44	871.72	874.94	947.16
2012	881.52	850.81	845.96	866.38	834.00	838.40	849.37	830.84	849.41	810.53	800.09	817.10	839.96
2013	799.94	798.49	804.26	811.21	790.50	813.29	790.50	790.87	809.41	779.51	772.26	783.43	795.34
Financial Activities													
2009	957.10	978.18	958.99	956.60	937.30	940.21	951.95	965.96	944.94	955.08	973.06	950.04	957.20
2010	966.22	971.04	972.29	965.03	1,000.90	982.91	982.89	1,009.17	994.72	979.33	971.67	966.53	980.35
2011	984.36	971.76	975.43	975.00	1,014.75	955.12	953.05	945.26	949.95	1,011.72	974.36	964.20	973.59
2012	1,005.80	985.75	979.40	1,035.18	964.96	950.13	971.22	923.15	958.79	918.85	929.02	963.98	965.90
2013	933.24	955.01	946.94	957.31	953.64	999.58	955.70	946.27	995.67	954.00	969.95	1,014.12	964.78
Professional and Business Services													
2009	894.76	918.92	921.20	920.59	908.60	915.20	905.63	928.93	904.59	906.32	930.81	907.06	913.15
2010	901.14	908.16	919.62	932.44	965.79	961.12	961.22	994.90	972.04	997.08	990.36	986.63	958.13
2011	992.26	982.11	985.40	974.55	998.40	970.79	962.64	954.41	960.39	991.73	968.24	967.82	975.46
2012	994.56	972.42	953.42	992.16	954.70	966.60	986.11	962.54	990.72	967.76	977.44	1,030.58	979.07
2013	981.71	991.51	995.27	989.25	990.38	1,019.93	978.36	993.39	1,020.27	981.54	998.52	1,034.29	998.66
Education and Health Services													
2009	758.99	766.06	773.28	760.90	760.90	752.38	759.42	763.70	760.38	757.28	769.12	760.16	762.30
2010	754.52	758.31	747.13	754.60	760.16	748.17	746.98	757.97	750.69	748.68	744.77	748.51	752.06
2011	758.09	748.68	746.93	742.36	754.28	741.39	760.24	751.63	760.38	773.31	758.69	765.12	756.00
2012	782.04	770.50	769.54	791.80	771.24	775.10	791.30	770.64	794.98	782.88	791.95	807.80	782.47
2013	785.23	801.72	789.50	788.44	789.21	802.37	790.35	789.16	802.07	795.85	802.23	813.52	796.59
Leisure and Hospitality													
2009	305.08	317.97	319.68	308.73	304.55	305.37	304.55	310.50	302.77	314.36	314.82	319.72	310.42
2010	309.16	320.78	318.66	322.22	327.32	322.20	323.04	327.60	318.70	326.09	326.03	335.86	323.47
2011	333.04	334.60	341.24	330.89	340.42	334.67	334.17	334.67	328.16	339.38	334.62	336.75	335.23
2012	336.56	336.20	337.05	337.62	330.74	330.74	338.58	332.70	329.71	327.80	328.63	340.73	333.76
2013	324.22	334.51	337.80	329.71	334.67	339.26	328.72	334.11	334.06	333.68	335.45	345.28	334.60
Other Services													
2009	544.46	562.13	561.08	554.04	552.77	558.11	568.16	570.83	565.15	582.71	584.58	577.61	565.49
2010	572.22	565.49	588.86	578.33	598.85	593.06	589.93	611.09	600.94	606.82	605.96	612.26	593.05
2011	626.40	611.41	653.20	651.46	683.90	672.52	674.94	725.31	727.56	768.60	737.74	749.23	691.19
2012	789.78	743.49	733.24	737.77	723.12	728.01	731.30	716.50	744.07	741.97	722.45	756.45	739.55
2013	724.33	750.98	751.60	740.43	730.42	735.64	682.52	676.56	694.05	681.47	677.41	701.39	711.41

UTAH
At a Glance

Population:
    2000 census: 2,233,183
    2010 census: 2,763,885
    2013 estimate: 2,900,872

Percent change in population:
    2000–2010: 23.8%
    2010–2013: 5.0%

Percent change in total nonfarm employment:
    2000–2010: 10.0%
    2010–2013: 9.1%

Industry with the largest growth in employment, 2000–2013 (thousands):
    Education and Health Services, 66.8

Industry with the largest decline or smallest growth in employment, 2000–2013 (thousands):
    Manufacturing, -6.4

Civilian labor force:
    2000: 1,136,036
    2010: 1,362,489
    2013: 1,418,522

Unemployment rate and rank among states (lowest to highest):
    2000: 3.4%, 17th
    2010: 8.1%, 20th
    2013: 4.4%, 4th

Over-the-year change in unemployment rates:
    2010–2011: -1.3%
    2011–2012: -1.4%
    2012–2013: -1.0%

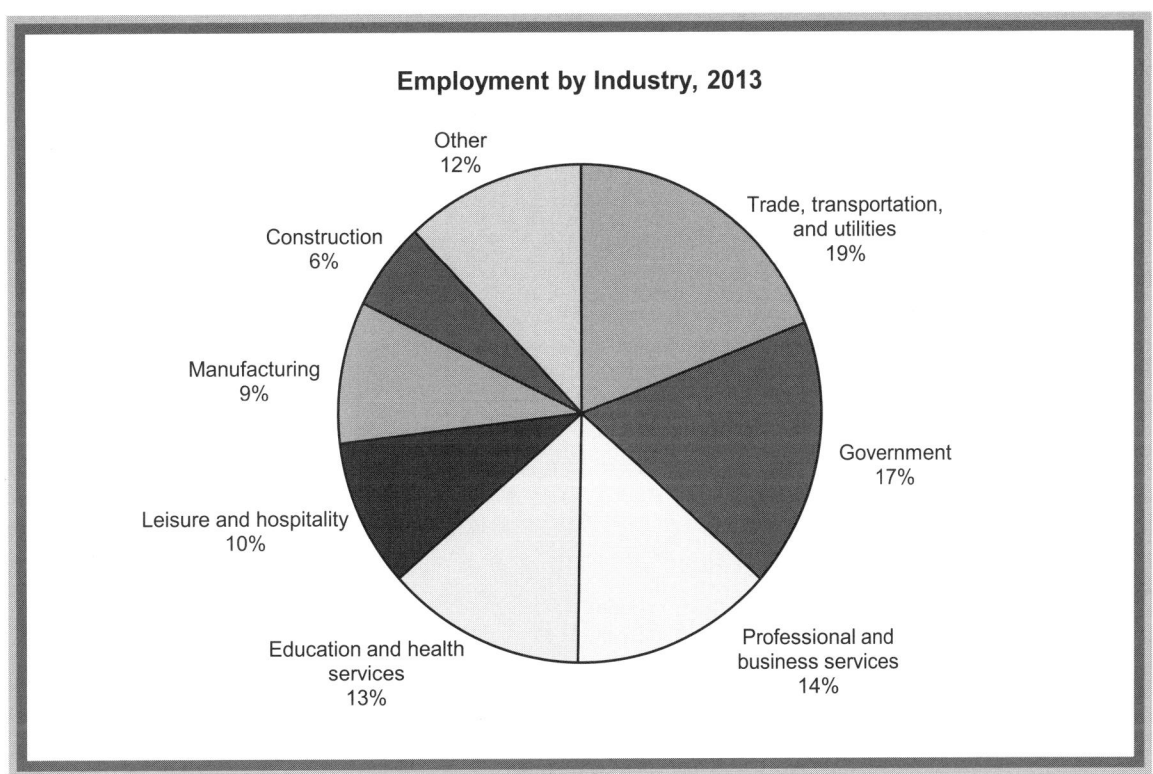

Employment by Industry, 2013

Other 12%
Construction 6%
Manufacturing 9%
Leisure and hospitality 10%
Education and health services 13%
Trade, transportation, and utilities 19%
Government 17%
Professional and business services 14%

1. Employment by Industry: Utah, Selected Years, 2002–2013

(Numbers in thousands, not seasonally adjusted)

Industry and year	January	February	March	April	May	June	July	August	September	October	November	December	Annual average
Total Nonfarm													
2002	1,062.8	1,069.6	1,065.7	1,073.4	1,072.0	1,077.1	1,063.3	1,066.5	1,079.1	1,080.3	1,084.4	1,087.1	1,073.4
2003	1,058.2	1,059.0	1,062.3	1,069.2	1,069.9	1,076.0	1,062.8	1,070.0	1,082.4	1,087.8	1,092.2	1,099.2	1,074.1
2004	1,072.3	1,077.7	1,086.2	1,098.8	1,100.1	1,109.8	1,096.9	1,102.9	1,117.1	1,123.1	1,130.3	1,136.4	1,104.3
2005	1,110.8	1,118.0	1,126.8	1,138.4	1,139.7	1,149.0	1,140.1	1,152.1	1,168.0	1,170.0	1,177.9	1,185.3	1,148.0
2006	1,162.9	1,171.5	1,182.5	1,192.9	1,196.1	1,211.1	1,196.1	1,208.2	1,222.5	1,222.8	1,234.6	1,243.3	1,203.7
2007	1,219.2	1,226.7	1,238.5	1,247.0	1,250.3	1,261.9	1,244.6	1,256.2	1,266.5	1,270.5	1,276.6	1,281.0	1,253.3
2008	1,244.5	1,248.0	1,253.3	1,259.1	1,256.6	1,261.4	1,242.8	1,252.3	1,261.4	1,254.9	1,249.1	1,246.7	1,252.5
2009	1,203.3	1,197.0	1,195.9	1,194.2	1,189.7	1,190.4	1,168.5	1,174.4	1,187.3	1,187.8	1,187.5	1,190.0	1,188.8
2010	1,159.7	1,159.9	1,168.9	1,182.2	1,183.9	1,187.1	1,171.9	1,179.1	1,193.1	1,198.2	1,201.4	1,204.7	1,182.5
2011	1,177.1	1,182.2	1,190.7	1,204.9	1,203.0	1,209.8	1,197.1	1,207.7	1,224.2	1,227.1	1,231.6	1,236.9	1,207.7
2012	1,212.1	1,218.7	1,229.2	1,246.4	1,251.3	1,257.6	1,237.2	1,249.1	1,265.0	1,272.3	1,281.7	1,283.8	1,250.4
2013	1,257.6	1,265.1	1,274.4	1,286.6	1,288.1	1,291.3	1,279.4	1,288.2	1,302.1	1,312.1	1,317.4	1,316.0	1,289.9
Total Private													
2002	868.5	874.6	867.7	874.5	874.4	879.3	878.9	883.6	883.3	882.5	885.9	888.7	878.5
2003	860.1	859.3	862.4	868.1	870.1	878.0	879.3	886.3	885.7	888.4	892.8	899.9	877.5
2004	873.9	877.7	885.1	895.8	898.6	909.4	911.4	915.8	916.8	920.1	926.9	933.5	905.4
2005	908.5	914.0	922.1	932.4	934.7	944.7	951.3	960.4	964.3	964.5	971.8	979.8	945.7
2006	958.9	965.3	975.6	985.2	989.5	1,004.0	1,004.8	1,014.0	1,016.5	1,015.3	1,026.2	1,035.7	999.3
2007	1,013.2	1,018.7	1,029.8	1,037.0	1,040.8	1,052.3	1,052.3	1,060.2	1,057.9	1,059.5	1,064.7	1,070.0	1,046.4
2008	1,034.4	1,035.9	1,040.3	1,044.7	1,042.3	1,047.8	1,046.5	1,051.3	1,046.7	1,038.0	1,031.6	1,030.1	1,040.8
2009	988.9	980.7	979.4	974.9	971.2	973.8	969.7	971.6	970.7	968.8	968.5	971.8	974.2
2010	943.4	942.2	950.2	961.2	959.2	966.5	969.6	973.1	973.3	975.9	979.2	983.8	964.8
2011	958.1	961.0	968.0	980.6	978.4	987.0	992.4	999.1	1,001.9	1,003.0	1,007.6	1,013.4	987.5
2012	989.6	994.3	1,004.1	1,017.9	1,023.3	1,031.3	1,029.3	1,039.2	1,040.2	1,044.0	1,053.6	1,057.5	1,027.0
2013	1,033.0	1,038.7	1,047.8	1,057.9	1,057.5	1,063.9	1,068.5	1,075.7	1,073.7	1,081.4	1,086.6	1,085.6	1,064.2
Goods-Producing													
2002	185.4	182.0	183.2	185.6	188.6	190.8	191.9	192.8	192.5	192.3	191.2	188.9	188.8
2003	181.3	179.8	180.4	182.8	186.2	188.7	189.4	191.0	190.2	191.2	190.1	189.0	186.7
2004	182.4	182.5	185.3	190.1	194.1	197.6	199.9	200.9	200.6	200.3	200.0	199.5	194.4
2005	194.0	195.4	196.9	202.8	206.4	210.4	213.3	215.6	216.4	215.3	216.4	216.0	208.2
2006	212.0	214.5	218.1	222.0	227.1	232.0	233.0	235.6	236.3	236.1	237.1	237.2	228.4
2007	231.6	232.8	236.7	239.8	243.9	248.6	248.5	250.3	248.2	247.9	244.7	241.6	242.9
2008	231.0	228.9	229.8	230.1	231.7	233.6	233.1	233.0	230.5	226.7	221.5	215.8	228.8
2009	202.1	196.4	194.8	192.3	194.2	195.5	195.3	195.1	193.7	192.9	190.4	187.7	194.2
2010	180.2	178.4	179.6	183.3	186.0	188.3	190.0	191.5	191.6	191.8	190.6	188.4	186.6
2011	181.4	181.2	182.9	186.4	188.3	191.8	195.9	197.5	196.7	196.0	195.3	193.4	190.6
2012	188.6	189.5	191.8	195.0	199.6	202.1	202.6	204.4	203.2	203.0	202.3	201.2	198.6
2013	195.6	195.9	198.7	201.7	204.7	206.9	208.8	209.9	208.5	210.5	210.8	207.1	204.9
Service-Providing													
2002	877.4	887.6	882.5	887.8	883.4	886.3	871.4	873.7	886.6	888.0	893.2	898.2	884.7
2003	876.9	879.2	881.9	886.4	883.7	887.3	873.4	879.0	892.2	896.6	902.1	910.2	887.4
2004	889.9	895.2	900.9	908.7	906.0	912.2	897.0	902.0	916.5	922.8	930.3	936.9	909.9
2005	916.8	922.6	929.9	935.6	933.3	938.6	926.8	936.5	951.6	954.7	961.5	969.3	939.8
2006	950.9	957.0	964.4	970.9	969.0	979.1	963.1	972.6	986.2	986.7	997.5	1,006.1	975.3
2007	987.6	993.9	1,001.8	1,007.2	1,006.4	1,013.3	996.1	1,005.9	1,018.3	1,022.6	1,031.9	1,039.4	1,010.4
2008	1,013.5	1,019.1	1,023.5	1,029.0	1,024.9	1,027.8	1,009.7	1,019.3	1,030.9	1,028.2	1,027.6	1,030.9	1,023.7
2009	1,001.2	1,000.6	1,001.1	1,001.9	995.5	994.9	973.2	979.3	993.6	994.9	997.1	1,002.3	994.6
2010	979.5	981.5	989.3	998.9	997.9	998.8	981.9	987.6	1,001.5	1,006.4	1,010.8	1,016.3	995.9
2011	995.7	1,001.0	1,007.8	1,018.5	1,014.7	1,018.0	1,001.2	1,010.2	1,027.5	1,031.1	1,036.3	1,043.5	1,017.1
2012	1,023.5	1,029.2	1,037.4	1,051.4	1,051.7	1,055.5	1,034.6	1,044.7	1,061.8	1,069.3	1,079.4	1,082.6	1,051.8
2013	1,062.0	1,069.2	1,075.7	1,084.9	1,083.4	1,084.4	1,070.6	1,078.3	1,093.6	1,101.6	1,106.6	1,108.9	1,084.9
Mining and Logging													
2002	6.7	6.7	6.7	6.9	7.0	7.1	7.1	7.1	7.2	7.1	7.1	7.0	7.0
2003	6.6	6.5	6.6	6.7	6.8	6.9	6.9	6.8	6.8	6.9	6.8	6.8	6.8
2004	6.7	6.6	6.6	6.9	7.1	7.3	7.4	7.4	7.5	7.6	7.6	7.7	7.2
2005	7.6	7.8	7.8	8.2	8.4	8.6	8.8	8.9	9.0	9.0	9.2	9.2	8.5
2006	9.0	9.2	9.4	9.7	9.9	10.2	10.4	10.5	10.5	10.6	10.7	10.8	10.1
2007	10.6	10.6	10.8	10.9	11.1	11.2	11.3	11.4	11.1	11.4	11.4	11.4	11.1
2008	11.4	11.4	11.5	11.8	12.3	12.6	12.8	13.4	13.5	13.6	13.5	13.2	12.6
2009	12.1	11.8	11.5	10.9	10.6	10.6	10.5	10.3	10.3	10.1	10.1	10.0	10.7
2010	9.8	9.8	10.0	10.2	10.4	10.6	10.6	10.8	10.8	11.0	11.0	11.0	10.5
2011	10.8	10.9	11.1	11.3	11.4	11.7	12.0	12.1	12.3	12.3	12.2	12.2	11.7
2012	12.1	12.3	12.5	12.6	12.8	12.8	12.8	12.9	12.8	12.7	12.6	12.4	12.6
2013	12.1	12.0	12.1	12.2	12.3	12.4	12.3	12.3	12.3	12.3	12.2	12.2	12.2
Construction													
2002	63.9	61.5	62.9	65.1	67.6	69.5	70.8	71.6	71.4	71.3	70.4	68.3	67.9
2003	62.6	62.0	62.5	64.4	67.2	69.1	70.2	71.7	71.1	71.4	70.1	68.8	67.6
2004	63.9	63.8	66.1	69.8	72.5	75.2	77.1	77.9	77.6	77.1	76.1	75.2	72.7
2005	71.1	72.1	73.7	78.1	80.5	83.3	85.5	86.9	87.5	86.8	86.9	86.0	81.5
2006	83.0	84.5	87.3	90.4	94.6	98.4	99.1	101.1	101.6	100.9	100.9	100.3	95.2
2007	96.0	96.5	99.3	102.1	105.2	108.6	108.3	109.7	108.0	107.2	103.2	99.7	103.7
2008	91.2	89.3	90.3	91.1	92.6	94.0	93.6	93.9	92.0	89.1	85.3	81.7	90.3
2009	72.1	69.3	69.1	68.4	70.9	72.0	72.5	72.6	71.9	71.2	69.2	66.4	70.5
2010	60.5	59.3	60.4	62.6	64.9	66.2	67.4	68.4	68.8	69.1	67.6	65.1	65.0
2011	59.4	58.8	60.0	62.5	64.0	66.5	69.3	70.5	69.7	68.8	68.0	66.0	65.3
2012	62.1	62.6	64.2	66.8	70.2	71.9	72.2	73.6	72.6	72.3	71.6	70.5	69.2
2013	66.2	66.6	68.8	71.2	73.9	75.4	77.3	78.0	77.0	77.5	77.3	74.0	73.6

1. Employment by Industry: Utah, Selected Years, 2002–2013—*Continued*

(Numbers in thousands, not seasonally adjusted)

Industry and year	January	February	March	April	May	June	July	August	September	October	November	December	Annual average
Manufacturing													
2002	114.8	113.8	113.6	113.6	114.0	114.2	114.0	114.1	113.9	113.9	113.7	113.6	113.9
2003	112.1	111.3	111.3	111.7	112.2	112.7	112.3	112.5	112.3	112.9	113.2	113.4	112.3
2004	111.8	112.1	112.6	113.4	114.5	115.1	115.4	115.6	115.5	115.6	116.3	116.6	114.5
2005	115.3	115.5	115.4	116.5	117.5	118.5	119.0	119.8	119.9	119.5	120.3	120.8	118.2
2006	120.0	120.8	121.4	121.9	122.6	123.4	123.5	124.0	124.2	124.6	125.5	126.1	123.2
2007	125.0	125.7	126.6	126.8	127.6	128.8	128.9	129.2	129.1	129.3	130.1	130.5	128.1
2008	128.4	128.2	128.0	127.2	126.8	127.0	126.7	125.7	125.0	124.0	122.7	120.9	125.9
2009	117.9	115.3	114.2	113.0	112.7	112.9	112.3	112.2	111.5	111.6	111.1	111.3	113.0
2010	109.9	109.3	109.2	110.5	110.7	111.5	112.0	112.3	112.0	111.7	112.0	112.3	111.1
2011	111.2	111.5	111.8	112.6	112.9	113.6	114.6	114.9	114.7	114.9	115.1	115.2	113.6
2012	114.4	114.6	115.1	115.6	116.6	117.4	117.6	117.9	117.8	118.0	118.1	118.3	116.8
2013	117.3	117.3	117.8	118.3	118.5	119.1	119.2	119.6	119.2	120.7	121.3	120.9	119.1
Trade, Transportation, and Utilities													
2002	214.2	212.5	211.7	213.5	215.2	215.5	215.3	216.1	215.1	216.2	220.0	221.8	215.6
2003	211.1	209.6	210.0	210.6	212.1	212.8	212.9	214.5	213.9	215.8	220.5	223.4	213.9
2004	214.6	213.1	213.6	215.5	217.5	218.5	218.5	219.4	219.3	221.3	226.3	228.7	218.9
2005	219.7	218.8	221.2	221.8	223.0	223.8	225.1	227.5	227.6	229.7	234.2	237.3	225.8
2006	228.6	228.1	229.6	230.0	231.7	234.2	234.8	237.2	237.6	238.3	244.8	248.6	235.3
2007	240.4	239.9	241.8	241.8	243.4	244.3	245.2	246.8	247.0	248.1	253.5	256.4	245.7
2008	246.9	245.5	246.3	247.0	247.8	248.8	248.2	249.1	248.0	247.5	250.1	251.0	248.0
2009	238.6	236.0	235.1	233.2	233.9	233.6	231.6	231.8	231.8	231.8	235.4	237.1	234.2
2010	226.3	225.0	225.9	226.8	227.8	228.5	228.6	229.8	228.9	230.1	234.8	236.7	229.1
2011	227.5	226.5	227.8	230.8	231.6	232.6	233.5	234.7	234.5	235.7	241.3	243.3	233.3
2012	234.9	233.9	235.6	237.8	239.7	241.2	240.9	241.7	242.0	243.5	250.6	251.3	241.1
2013	242.0	241.2	241.6	243.1	245.1	245.9	247.3	248.4	247.2	249.1	253.4	255.5	246.7
Wholesale Trade													
2002	39.9	40.0	40.0	40.1	40.6	40.5	40.5	40.6	40.4	40.5	40.4	40.5	40.3
2003	39.8	39.8	39.9	40.1	40.4	40.5	40.2	40.3	40.2	40.3	40.4	40.5	40.2
2004	40.1	40.2	40.4	40.8	41.1	41.5	41.4	41.4	41.5	41.7	42.0	42.2	41.2
2005	41.8	42.0	42.2	42.4	42.9	43.1	43.1	43.3	43.3	43.5	43.7	43.8	42.9
2006	43.3	43.6	43.8	44.1	44.6	45.2	45.1	45.3	45.5	45.7	46.0	46.4	44.9
2007	46.2	46.4	46.6	46.6	47.2	47.5	47.6	47.9	47.8	48.0	48.2	48.5	47.4
2008	47.7	47.8	48.0	48.2	48.5	48.6	48.5	48.6	48.5	48.2	47.9	48.0	48.2
2009	46.6	46.4	46.0	45.3	45.1	45.0	44.7	44.6	44.5	44.5	44.3	44.4	45.1
2010	43.6	43.4	43.6	43.9	44.3	44.3	44.5	44.6	44.5	44.7	44.9	45.3	44.3
2011	44.8	45.1	45.4	45.7	46.0	46.2	46.3	46.5	46.4	46.5	46.7	46.8	46.0
2012	46.4	46.6	46.9	47.1	47.4	47.5	47.4	47.6	47.5	47.6	47.6	47.7	47.3
2013	47.6	47.7	47.7	48.1	48.4	48.4	48.5	48.6	48.5	48.8	49.5	49.7	48.5
Retail Trade													
2002	129.6	127.5	127.5	129.0	130.1	130.6	130.3	131.0	130.5	130.9	135.0	137.1	130.8
2003	127.7	126.3	126.7	127.1	128.1	128.8	128.9	130.2	129.8	131.1	135.8	138.5	129.9
2004	130.1	128.5	128.8	130.2	131.7	132.2	132.3	133.1	132.9	134.2	138.7	140.6	132.8
2005	132.4	130.8	132.8	132.4	133.0	133.5	134.6	136.6	136.4	137.9	142.0	144.3	135.6
2006	137.0	135.9	137.1	137.1	138.3	139.9	140.5	142.3	142.2	142.9	148.6	151.2	141.1
2007	144.3	143.4	144.7	144.8	145.6	145.9	146.5	147.5	147.3	147.8	152.7	154.5	147.1
2008	148.3	146.7	147.2	147.5	148.1	149.1	148.6	149.2	148.3	148.2	151.1	151.8	148.7
2009	142.0	140.2	140.2	139.5	140.5	140.7	139.1	139.7	139.8	139.9	143.7	144.9	140.9
2010	136.4	135.2	135.7	136.3	136.9	137.2	136.9	137.6	136.7	137.5	141.4	142.1	137.5
2011	134.8	133.6	134.4	136.8	137.3	137.7	138.5	139.3	139.0	140.3	145.2	146.2	138.6
2012	139.1	138.0	139.1	140.4	141.7	142.9	143.4	143.7	143.6	145.0	151.7	151.5	143.3
2013	143.4	142.6	143.2	145.1	146.5	147.2	148.0	148.9	147.9	149.4	152.3	153.5	147.3
Transportation and Utilities													
2002	44.7	45.0	44.2	44.4	44.5	44.4	44.5	44.5	44.2	44.8	44.6	44.2	44.5
2003	43.6	43.5	43.4	43.4	43.6	43.5	43.8	44.0	43.9	44.4	44.3	44.4	43.8
2004	44.4	44.4	44.4	44.5	44.7	44.8	44.8	44.9	44.9	45.4	45.6	45.9	44.9
2005	45.5	46.0	46.2	47.0	47.1	47.2	47.4	47.6	47.9	48.3	48.5	49.2	47.3
2006	48.3	48.6	48.7	48.8	48.8	49.1	49.2	49.6	49.9	49.7	50.2	51.0	49.3
2007	49.9	50.1	50.5	50.4	50.6	50.9	51.1	51.4	51.9	52.3	52.6	53.4	51.3
2008	50.9	51.0	51.1	51.3	51.2	51.1	51.1	51.3	51.2	51.1	51.1	51.2	51.1
2009	50.0	49.4	48.9	48.4	48.3	47.9	47.8	47.5	47.5	47.4	47.4	47.8	48.2
2010	46.3	46.4	46.6	46.6	46.6	47.0	47.2	47.6	47.7	47.9	48.5	49.3	47.3
2011	47.9	47.8	48.0	48.3	48.3	48.7	48.7	48.9	49.1	48.9	49.4	50.3	48.7
2012	49.4	49.3	49.6	50.3	50.6	50.8	50.1	50.4	50.9	50.9	51.3	52.1	50.5
2013	51.0	50.9	50.7	49.9	50.2	50.3	50.8	50.9	50.8	50.9	51.6	52.3	50.9
Information													
2002	31.8	31.7	31.1	30.9	31.3	31.1	31.0	30.7	30.5	30.5	30.8	30.7	31.0
2003	30.1	30.0	29.9	29.4	30.1	30.2	29.8	30.0	29.8	30.2	30.1	30.6	30.0
2004	29.4	30.0	30.1	30.3	30.2	30.7	30.1	30.3	30.2	30.5	31.3	31.3	30.4
2005	31.0	31.5	31.8	31.6	31.7	31.7	32.4	33.0	32.7	32.2	32.5	32.3	32.0
2006	31.7	31.5	31.5	31.9	32.8	33.0	32.1	32.5	32.2	32.0	32.5	32.0	32.1
2007	32.0	32.0	32.2	30.9	31.1	31.0	30.9	31.0	30.4	30.4	30.5	30.5	31.1
2008	29.8	30.5	30.6	30.9	31.4	31.5	31.1	31.1	30.8	30.5	30.7	30.8	30.8
2009	29.9	30.0	29.9	29.5	29.8	29.9	29.5	29.3	29.3	29.0	29.4	29.7	29.6
2010	28.7	28.9	29.3	29.4	29.3	29.4	29.3	29.0	29.0	29.0	29.8	29.9	29.3
2011	28.9	29.2	29.2	29.2	29.5	29.6	29.6	29.8	29.6	29.8	30.7	30.8	29.7
2012	30.2	30.5	30.6	32.0	32.7	32.7	31.3	31.5	31.1	31.3	32.3	32.5	31.6
2013	33.2	33.3	33.3	32.0	32.3	32.4	32.5	32.8	32.2	33.2	33.1	33.8	32.8

1. Employment by Industry: Utah, Selected Years, 2002–2013—*Continued*

(Numbers in thousands, not seasonally adjusted)

Industry and year	January	February	March	April	May	June	July	August	September	October	November	December	Annual average
Financial Activities													
2002	63.4	63.4	62.9	63.0	63.3	63.4	63.0	63.3	62.9	63.7	63.8	64.6	63.4
2003	64.1	64.8	64.4	64.6	64.9	64.6	65.1	65.2	64.6	64.4	64.3	64.9	64.7
2004	63.7	64.2	64.2	64.7	64.7	64.7	65.0	64.9	65.0	65.3	65.7	66.6	64.9
2005	65.5	66.0	65.5	66.8	66.7	67.2	67.9	68.1	68.1	68.7	69.0	70.3	67.5
2006	69.2	69.9	70.1	70.7	70.9	71.4	71.8	72.1	72.0	72.9	73.5	74.6	71.6
2007	73.7	74.4	74.6	75.0	75.2	75.6	75.6	75.7	75.2	75.7	75.9	76.6	75.3
2008	74.2	74.9	74.6	74.5	74.3	74.2	74.1	74.1	73.4	73.1	72.9	73.8	74.0
2009	72.5	72.5	72.4	71.7	71.4	71.2	70.3	70.3	69.8	69.7	69.6	70.5	71.0
2010	68.5	67.9	68.1	67.8	67.6	67.7	67.6	67.9	67.7	68.2	68.3	68.8	68.0
2011	67.4	67.6	67.7	68.0	67.8	68.2	68.2	68.4	68.0	68.4	68.5	69.3	68.1
2012	67.9	68.2	68.2	68.6	68.6	69.2	69.5	70.3	70.1	70.6	71.0	71.9	69.5
2013	70.6	71.1	71.3	71.8	71.9	72.9	73.6	74.2	73.6	73.8	74.2	74.6	72.8
Professional and Business Services													
2002	129.5	132.7	129.6	131.2	132.4	132.6	132.1	133.4	133.3	132.9	133.1	132.0	132.1
2003	126.5	126.4	127.0	129.3	131.0	132.0	132.8	134.6	134.2	135.7	136.1	136.4	131.8
2004	132.2	133.6	134.7	137.1	138.5	139.9	139.5	140.6	139.3	142.1	142.1	142.8	138.5
2005	138.2	139.5	140.9	143.4	145.3	146.1	147.4	149.0	149.1	150.1	150.5	151.1	145.9
2006	147.1	148.5	149.8	152.2	153.8	156.2	156.6	157.5	157.1	156.9	158.1	158.6	154.4
2007	153.5	154.5	156.4	160.0	163.0	164.7	164.1	165.8	165.0	167.0	168.2	167.8	162.5
2008	159.0	159.8	160.6	162.2	164.2	164.4	164.4	165.8	164.6	162.6	160.0	158.9	162.2
2009	150.5	149.6	148.8	149.1	149.5	149.4	149.0	149.0	148.9	149.9	148.9	149.0	149.3
2010	144.2	145.0	147.9	150.9	152.8	154.3	155.4	155.0	154.4	156.1	156.1	156.5	152.4
2011	151.8	153.2	155.0	157.7	158.5	159.3	160.4	161.6	162.2	164.8	165.0	164.9	159.5
2012	158.9	160.7	162.7	165.4	167.4	168.5	168.9	171.5	171.1	173.9	174.2	173.7	168.1
2013	168.0	170.1	172.2	175.6	176.1	176.3	177.9	179.4	179.8	180.5	179.5	178.2	176.1
Education and Health Services													
2002	111.7	112.9	113.4	114.5	110.8	110.7	110.0	111.6	116.3	117.6	118.1	119.2	113.9
2003	117.4	118.4	119.1	119.0	115.0	115.6	114.6	115.5	120.1	121.6	122.1	123.3	118.5
2004	121.4	122.9	123.8	123.7	120.2	121.0	120.0	120.9	125.5	126.8	127.8	128.3	123.5
2005	126.8	128.0	128.7	129.0	125.0	125.9	124.5	125.9	130.7	132.0	133.1	133.6	128.6
2006	132.6	133.5	134.6	134.8	131.2	131.6	130.2	131.9	136.5	137.6	138.6	139.1	134.4
2007	137.7	139.1	139.8	140.5	136.7	136.6	135.7	137.7	142.6	144.1	145.2	146.1	140.2
2008	145.0	146.3	146.8	147.2	143.1	142.6	141.7	143.4	148.7	150.4	151.7	152.1	146.6
2009	150.4	150.9	151.7	151.5	147.5	146.8	146.0	147.6	152.6	154.5	155.7	155.7	150.9
2010	154.6	155.3	156.0	156.4	152.1	151.4	150.7	151.7	157.1	158.6	158.9	158.4	155.1
2011	157.6	158.8	159.0	159.7	155.9	155.1	153.5	155.1	160.9	162.5	163.2	163.4	158.7
2012	162.2	163.2	164.0	165.7	161.6	161.0	158.9	161.4	166.8	168.9	170.3	170.4	164.5
2013	169.4	170.9	171.5	173.0	168.2	166.5	164.3	166.5	171.7	174.4	176.9	175.0	170.7
Leisure and Hospitality													
2002	100.5	106.3	103.3	103.1	100.0	102.1	102.1	102.2	99.9	96.8	96.1	99.0	101.0
2003	97.7	98.4	99.5	100.1	98.4	101.3	101.7	102.3	100.6	97.6	97.6	100.2	99.6
2004	98.4	99.4	100.9	101.8	100.5	103.9	104.4	104.9	103.9	101.0	100.9	103.5	102.0
2005	100.9	102.2	104.0	103.7	103.2	106.0	106.1	106.8	105.8	103.1	102.5	105.4	104.1
2006	104.5	105.8	107.8	109.5	107.4	110.4	110.8	111.6	109.6	106.9	107.0	110.6	108.5
2007	109.9	111.2	113.3	113.8	111.6	115.2	115.7	116.0	113.6	110.6	111.1	115.4	113.1
2008	113.7	114.9	116.3	117.4	114.2	116.8	117.3	117.7	114.9	112.2	109.9	112.9	114.9
2009	111.0	111.3	112.6	113.5	110.7	112.9	113.0	113.6	111.1	107.4	105.7	108.7	111.0
2010	107.8	108.5	109.8	113.1	110.0	113.0	113.4	113.9	111.2	108.7	107.4	111.8	110.7
2011	110.5	111.2	113.0	115.1	112.7	116.0	116.4	116.9	115.4	111.5	109.4	114.1	113.5
2012	113.1	114.3	116.8	118.8	118.7	121.3	121.5	122.6	120.5	117.4	117.5	120.9	118.6
2013	119.0	120.5	123.1	124.1	122.1	126.4	127.0	127.4	124.4	123.2	122.4	124.7	123.7
Other Services													
2002	32.0	33.1	32.5	32.7	32.8	33.1	33.5	33.5	32.8	32.5	32.8	32.5	32.8
2003	31.9	31.9	32.1	32.3	32.4	32.8	33.0	33.2	32.3	31.9	32.0	32.1	32.3
2004	31.8	32.0	32.5	32.6	32.9	33.1	34.0	33.9	33.0	32.8	32.8	32.8	32.9
2005	32.4	32.6	33.1	33.3	33.4	33.6	34.6	34.5	33.9	33.4	33.6	33.8	33.5
2006	33.2	33.5	34.1	34.1	34.6	35.2	35.5	35.6	35.2	34.6	34.6	35.0	34.6
2007	34.4	34.8	35.0	35.2	35.9	36.3	36.6	36.9	35.9	35.7	35.6	35.6	35.7
2008	34.8	35.1	35.3	35.4	35.6	35.9	36.6	37.1	35.8	35.0	34.8	34.8	35.5
2009	33.9	34.0	34.1	34.1	34.2	34.5	35.0	34.9	33.8	33.6	33.4	33.4	34.1
2010	33.1	33.2	33.6	33.5	33.6	33.9	34.6	34.3	33.4	33.4	33.3	33.3	33.6
2011	33.0	33.3	33.4	33.7	34.1	34.4	34.9	35.1	34.6	34.3	34.2	34.2	34.1
2012	33.8	34.0	34.4	34.6	35.0	35.3	35.7	35.8	35.4	35.4	35.4	35.6	35.0
2013	35.2	35.7	36.1	36.6	37.1	36.6	37.1	37.1	36.3	36.7	36.3	36.7	36.5
Government													
2002	194.3	195.0	198.0	198.9	197.6	197.8	184.4	182.9	195.8	197.8	198.5	198.4	195.0
2003	198.1	199.7	199.9	201.1	199.8	198.0	183.5	183.7	196.7	199.4	199.4	199.3	196.6
2004	198.4	200.0	201.1	203.0	201.5	200.4	185.5	187.1	200.3	203.0	203.4	202.9	198.9
2005	202.3	204.0	204.7	206.0	205.0	204.3	188.8	191.7	203.7	205.5	206.1	205.5	202.3
2006	204.0	206.2	206.9	207.7	206.6	207.1	191.3	194.2	206.0	207.5	208.4	207.6	204.5
2007	206.0	208.0	208.7	210.0	209.5	209.6	192.3	196.0	208.6	211.0	211.9	211.0	206.9
2008	210.1	212.1	213.0	214.4	214.3	213.6	196.3	201.0	214.7	216.9	217.5	216.6	211.7
2009	214.4	216.3	216.5	219.3	218.5	216.6	198.8	202.8	216.6	219.0	219.0	218.2	214.7
2010	216.3	217.7	218.7	221.0	224.7	220.6	202.3	206.0	219.8	222.3	222.2	220.9	217.7
2011	219.0	221.2	222.7	224.3	224.6	222.8	204.7	208.6	222.3	224.1	224.0	223.5	220.2
2012	222.5	224.4	225.1	228.5	228.0	226.3	207.9	209.9	224.8	228.3	228.1	226.3	223.3
2013	224.6	226.4	226.6	228.7	230.6	227.4	210.9	212.5	228.4	230.7	230.8	230.4	225.7

2. Average Weekly Hours by Selected Industry: Utah, 2009–2013

(Not seasonally adjusted)

Industry and year	January	February	March	April	May	June	July	August	September	October	November	December	Annual average
Total Private													
2009	34.1	34.9	34.9	35.9	36.0	36.1	36.2	36.7	36.1	36.1	36.6	36.1	35.8
2010	35.9	36.0	35.3	34.7	35.6	35.4	35.4	36.3	35.4	35.4	35.1	35.3	35.5
2011	35.1	34.8	34.8	34.8	35.3	35.0	34.9	35.0	34.7	35.7	34.9	34.7	35.0
2012	35.1	34.7	34.9	35.2	34.8	35.1	35.7	35.2	35.8	35.3	34.9	35.6	35.2
2013	34.6	34.9	34.8	34.5	35.1	35.7	34.7	35.1	35.5	34.7	34.8	35.3	35.0
Goods-Producing													
2009	36.8	37.1	37.5	37.0	37.8	37.3	37.9	38.5	37.1	39.1	39.4	38.5	37.8
2010	40.4	40.7	40.9	38.3	39.2	38.3	38.3	39.5	38.7	40.9	39.5	40.0	39.6
2011	39.6	39.2	39.2	39.3	39.7	39.4	38.9	39.6	38.9	39.7	40.1	39.5	39.4
2012	39.6	39.7	39.9	39.6	40.4	39.9	40.0	39.7	40.4	40.7	40.1	40.5	40.0
2013	39.2	39.3	39.1	39.4	39.9	39.9	39.6	40.2	40.1	39.7	40.4	40.1	39.7
Construction													
2009	35.2	34.6	35.0	35.1	36.9	36.4	36.9	37.5	35.2	38.5	38.0	35.4	36.2
2010	36.9	35.7	37.1	36.8	37.0	37.3	37.0	37.7	36.5	38.9	37.5	38.2	37.2
2011	36.9	37.4	37.7	38.4	38.4	38.8	38.2	38.5	38.2	38.4	38.7	37.3	38.1
2012	37.2	37.7	38.2	37.3	39.2	39.4	39.7	40.1	40.5	41.3	40.1	39.1	39.2
2013	37.2	38.4	38.0	39.2	39.4	39.5	39.3	40.0	39.8	40.0	39.8	39.1	39.2
Manufacturing													
2009	36.6	37.9	38.1	37.3	37.6	37.1	37.8	38.4	37.8	39.1	39.8	39.9	38.1
2010	40.3	40.2	40.3	40.3	40.7	40.0	39.2	39.2	39.0	39.0	39.7	39.5	39.8
2011	39.5	39.1	39.0	38.9	39.6	39.0	38.7	39.5	38.5	39.7	40.1	39.9	39.3
2012	39.8	39.8	40.0	40.0	40.2	39.4	39.3	39.1	40.0	40.1	39.9	40.8	39.9
2013	39.1	39.8	39.7	39.5	40.2	40.1	39.7	40.2	40.2	39.3	40.4	40.4	39.9
Trade, Transportation, and Utilities													
2009	30.5	31.3	31.8	31.1	31.4	31.5	31.9	32.6	31.8	31.8	31.9	32.2	31.6
2010	31.2	32.2	31.1	31.6	32.3	32.5	32.6	33.3	32.9	33.0	33.0	33.5	32.4
2011	33.6	33.5	34.0	34.1	34.2	34.2	34.1	34.0	33.6	34.4	33.4	33.6	33.9
2012	33.3	33.0	33.4	33.6	33.3	33.8	34.1	33.8	34.1	33.5	33.5	34.4	33.7
2013	32.9	33.3	33.3	33.3	33.5	34.3	33.5	33.6	33.7	32.7	33.0	33.5	33.4
Information													
2009	33.3	36.3	35.9	34.2	34.5	34.5	34.4	35.4	33.7	33.6	34.5	32.8	34.4
2010	32.7	32.8	32.7	32.3	32.9	31.3	32.3	33.1	32.1	31.7	31.9	32.3	32.3
2011	32.6	32.1	32.4	31.8	33.6	32.2	33.1	33.1	33.5	34.8	34.2	34.1	33.1
2012	34.9	33.0	33.4	34.4	33.2	32.8	34.9	32.9	34.6	32.8	32.9	33.2	33.6
2013	31.1	31.7	32.4	32.1	32.6	34.3	31.9	31.4	33.4	32.1	32.7	34.0	32.5
Financial Activities													
2009	34.1	34.6	34.0	34.0	34.1	35.8	34.1	34.9	34.5	34.6	36.6	35.3	34.7
2010	35.0	35.0	35.0	35.0	35.3	34.9	34.6	35.0	34.7	34.3	34.6	34.9	34.9
2011	35.1	34.9	34.8	35.4	36.1	35.3	35.2	35.1	35.3	36.1	35.4	35.7	35.4
2012	35.7	34.7	34.8	35.3	34.2	35.1	35.4	34.8	36.1	35.2	35.5	36.0	35.2
2013	35.1	35.3	35.8	35.5	35.8	36.9	35.8	36.2	37.0	36.0	36.1	37.0	36.0
Professional and Business Services													
2009	33.4	35.3	34.9	36.0	36.2	36.7	36.2	36.9	35.7	35.5	36.3	36.5	35.8
2010	37.3	36.9	35.8	36.4	37.3	37.3	37.0	37.8	36.2	35.7	35.6	35.5	36.6
2011	35.2	35.9	35.8	35.8	36.5	36.2	35.4	35.9	35.8	36.7	35.3	34.7	35.8
2012	35.7	35.1	35.3	36.4	33.7	34.3	35.8	35.5	36.0	35.3	35.0	35.7	35.3
2013	34.5	35.0	35.1	34.7	35.0	36.1	34.3	35.0	35.7	35.0	34.9	35.6	35.1
Education and Health Services													
2009	39.7	40.0	39.6	39.3	39.1	39.0	39.3	39.6	41.0	39.5	39.8	39.9	39.7
2010	39.7	39.8	39.0	38.5	39.1	39.4	39.2	39.7	41.0	40.3	40.7	40.6	39.8
2011	40.2	40.2	39.8	39.5	39.8	39.3	39.3	39.0	38.8	39.4	39.0	39.1	39.4
2012	40.0	39.3	38.3	38.6	38.3	38.6	38.8	38.7	39.1	38.4	38.3	39.3	38.8
2013	39.3	38.9	38.5	37.9	38.4	38.5	37.8	38.1	38.7	37.9	37.9	38.3	38.3
Leisure and Hospitality													
2009	23.9	24.4	24.7	22.8	23.6	24.3	24.5	26.4	24.5	24.5	24.3	23.4	24.3
2010	24.5	25.2	24.7	25.0	26.0	26.7	27.1	27.2	25.1	25.2	24.2	24.3	25.4
2011	26.0	25.9	25.4	25.3	25.5	24.7	25.5	25.2	24.4	26.0	24.2	23.8	25.2
2012	24.4	24.6	24.6	24.8	24.9	25.2	26.3	25.6	26.0	24.9	23.6	24.7	25.0
2013	23.8	25.0	24.8	24.2	24.8	26.5	25.3	25.8	25.8	24.8	23.9	25.5	25.0

3. Average Hourly Earnings by Selected Industry: Utah, 2009–2013

(Dollars, not seasonally adjusted)

Industry and year	January	February	March	April	May	June	July	August	September	October	November	December	Annual average
Total Private													
2009	21.48	22.01	22.14	22.69	22.46	22.44	22.09	22.16	22.20	21.95	22.11	25.96	22.48
2010	25.51	25.55	24.64	24.48	24.13	24.08	23.92	23.88	23.86	23.80	24.12	23.76	24.31
2011	23.90	23.85	24.68	23.31	23.03	22.58	22.75	22.44	22.63	22.70	22.73	22.80	23.11
2012	23.11	23.18	23.00	21.89	21.50	21.47	21.94	21.83	22.19	22.24	22.85	22.21	22.28
2013	22.38	22.47	22.57	23.17	22.82	23.28	22.96	22.85	23.19	23.14	23.70	23.42	23.00
Goods-Producing													
2009	23.61	23.95	23.94	24.06	23.80	23.72	23.39	23.64	24.01	23.61	23.47	23.68	23.74
2010	23.52	23.95	23.39	23.63	23.41	23.25	22.85	23.45	23.36	23.16	23.78	23.22	23.41
2011	23.64	23.47	23.27	23.47	23.41	22.90	23.11	22.91	22.99	23.14	22.99	23.21	23.20
2012	23.46	23.36	22.86	23.11	23.38	23.23	23.76	23.80	23.69	23.65	23.65	23.77	23.48
2013	24.03	23.96	24.02	24.06	23.59	23.59	23.37	23.32	23.46	23.54	23.45	23.99	23.69
Construction													
2009	24.01	24.09	24.09	24.48	24.29	24.21	23.32	23.62	23.81	23.95	23.47	24.75	23.99
2010	24.27	24.66	24.24	23.94	24.17	23.66	23.29	24.19	24.02	24.21	24.50	24.07	24.09
2011	24.37	23.94	23.62	23.50	24.00	23.36	23.30	23.58	23.11	23.27	23.12	23.03	23.50
2012	22.97	23.18	22.44	22.84	24.04	23.75	23.84	24.43	24.41	24.05	24.62	24.85	23.84
2013	24.83	25.33	25.28	25.01	24.50	24.06	24.05	23.71	23.47	23.36	23.30	23.83	24.18
Manufacturing													
2009	20.80	20.28	21.55	21.76	21.69	21.84	21.91	22.30	22.94	22.31	22.50	21.98	21.82
2010	22.32	22.90	22.32	22.86	22.71	23.02	22.66	23.01	22.97	22.50	22.77	22.05	22.67
2011	22.27	21.99	21.84	22.40	21.97	21.53	21.94	21.49	21.88	21.91	21.79	22.21	21.93
2012	22.62	22.45	22.06	22.28	22.12	22.05	22.32	22.17	22.09	22.14	21.93	21.85	22.17
2013	22.29	21.92	22.16	22.50	22.04	22.31	22.00	22.10	22.52	22.67	22.54	23.08	22.35
Trade, Transportation, and Utilities													
2009	18.85	20.31	19.41	20.24	19.42	19.43	18.55	19.13	18.91	19.09	19.46	19.29	19.34
2010	19.49	19.46	18.37	19.36	19.38	19.06	19.08	19.03	19.05	19.23	19.65	19.70	19.24
2011	19.91	20.74	20.66	20.64	20.53	20.32	20.84	20.40	20.65	20.89	20.69	20.58	20.57
2012	21.28	21.06	21.27	22.16	21.84	21.91	22.55	22.12	22.60	22.80	22.23	21.61	21.96
2013	21.19	21.34	21.87	22.98	22.48	22.89	22.53	22.32	22.63	22.34	22.25	22.46	22.28
Information													
2009	26.62	26.78	26.63	26.78	26.32	26.26	26.68	28.11	27.31	27.69	28.15	27.60	27.07
2010	27.65	26.51	26.91	28.23	27.64	27.55	27.85	27.66	26.92	27.57	27.41	27.92	27.49
2011	27.67	26.73	26.70	26.77	25.96	25.65	26.50	26.06	27.42	28.69	28.09	27.94	27.04
2012	27.72	26.85	25.44	25.14	24.84	24.32	25.04	24.78	26.31	25.35	25.80	26.31	25.65
2013	26.75	26.66	28.45	29.70	28.17	32.22	28.63	28.47	29.81	29.23	29.40	29.69	28.96
Financial Activities													
2009	25.58	25.30	25.77	26.06	25.77	25.87	28.09	26.55	26.20	25.95	25.38	25.48	25.99
2010	26.40	26.06	25.67	26.26	26.16	25.26	25.49	25.23	25.02	24.86	24.49	24.59	25.46
2011	24.97	25.11	24.95	24.88	24.66	25.12	25.61	25.90	26.24	25.64	25.98	26.30	25.45
2012	27.23	27.70	27.52	27.36	26.74	26.36	26.17	26.08	26.11	25.94	26.36	26.10	26.63
2013	25.73	26.25	25.85	26.76	26.07	26.81	26.62	26.60	27.11	26.65	27.05	27.66	26.61
Professional and Business Services													
2009	32.25	31.54	31.33	31.44	31.33	31.12	29.43	30.50	30.02	29.04	29.57	27.93	30.44
2010	29.12	30.58	29.71	29.14	29.26	27.83	27.26	26.10	26.02	26.33	26.78	27.49	27.94
2011	27.30	26.43	26.16	26.01	25.82	25.41	25.14	24.67	25.13	25.84	25.60	25.80	25.76
2012	26.71	25.93	26.23	26.72	24.29	24.22	25.59	24.85	25.80	25.06	25.53	26.16	25.59
2013	26.76	26.98	26.82	27.28	27.23	27.79	27.79	27.76	28.77	28.50	28.65	29.38	27.83
Education and Health Services													
2009	18.85	19.01	19.16	19.33	19.22	19.39	19.25	19.22	19.65	19.23	19.31	19.11	19.23
2010	18.45	19.47	19.36	19.71	19.68	19.37	19.55	19.64	19.86	20.02	20.11	19.79	19.59
2011	19.00	20.01	19.65	17.67	17.77	17.47	18.24	18.29	18.39	18.85	18.77	19.49	18.64
2012	19.38	20.90	20.57	20.71	20.45	20.38	20.53	20.78	20.74	21.06	21.78	21.00	20.69
2013	21.29	21.34	21.45	22.05	21.60	22.48	21.74	21.57	21.76	21.76	23.97	21.67	21.89
Leisure and Hospitality													
2009	12.26	11.64	11.92	11.47	11.47	11.49	11.43	11.75	12.01	12.07	12.32	12.63	11.87
2010	12.79	12.60	12.51	12.02	11.69	11.73	11.83	11.65	11.91	11.90	12.21	12.62	12.11
2011	12.83	12.73	12.87	12.25	12.03	11.84	11.75	11.73	11.84	11.68	12.01	12.25	12.15
2012	12.09	12.21	12.23	12.09	12.09	11.95	11.92	12.05	12.07	12.20	12.58	12.66	12.17
2013	12.76	12.94	12.93	12.65	12.44	12.30	12.35	12.44	12.65	12.57	12.72	12.76	12.62

4. Average Weekly Earnings by Selected Industry: Utah, 2009–2013

(Dollars, not seasonally adjusted)

Industry and year	January	February	March	April	May	June	July	August	September	October	November	December	Annual average
Total Private													
2009	732.47	768.15	772.69	814.57	808.56	810.08	799.66	813.27	801.42	792.40	809.23	937.16	804.78
2010	915.81	919.80	869.79	849.46	859.03	852.43	846.77	866.84	844.64	842.52	846.61	838.73	863.01
2011	838.89	829.98	858.86	811.19	812.96	790.30	793.98	785.40	785.26	810.39	793.28	791.16	808.85
2012	811.16	804.35	802.70	770.53	748.20	753.60	783.26	768.42	794.40	785.07	797.47	790.68	784.26
2013	774.35	784.20	785.44	799.37	800.98	831.10	796.71	802.04	823.25	802.96	824.76	826.73	805.00
Goods-Producing													
2009	868.85	888.55	897.75	890.22	899.64	884.76	886.48	910.14	890.77	923.15	924.72	911.68	897.37
2010	950.21	974.77	956.65	905.03	917.67	890.48	875.16	926.28	904.03	947.24	939.31	928.80	927.04
2011	936.14	920.02	912.18	922.37	929.38	902.26	898.98	907.24	894.31	918.66	921.90	916.80	914.08
2012	929.02	927.39	912.11	915.16	944.55	926.88	950.40	944.86	957.08	962.56	948.37	962.69	939.20
2013	941.98	941.63	939.18	947.96	941.24	941.24	925.45	937.46	940.75	934.54	947.38	962.00	940.49
Construction													
2009	845.15	833.51	843.15	859.25	896.30	881.24	860.51	885.75	838.11	922.08	891.86	876.15	868.44
2010	895.56	880.36	899.30	880.99	894.29	882.52	861.73	911.96	876.73	941.77	918.75	919.47	896.15
2011	899.25	895.36	890.47	902.40	921.60	906.37	890.06	907.83	882.80	893.57	894.74	859.02	895.35
2012	854.48	873.89	857.21	851.93	942.37	935.75	946.45	979.64	988.61	993.27	987.26	971.64	934.53
2013	923.68	972.67	960.64	980.39	965.30	950.37	945.17	948.40	934.11	934.40	927.34	931.75	947.86
Manufacturing													
2009	761.28	768.61	821.06	811.65	815.54	810.26	828.20	856.32	867.13	872.32	895.50	877.00	831.34
2010	899.50	920.58	899.50	921.26	924.30	920.80	888.27	901.99	895.83	877.50	903.97	870.98	902.27
2011	879.67	859.81	851.76	871.36	870.01	839.67	849.08	848.86	842.38	869.83	873.78	886.18	861.85
2012	900.28	893.51	882.40	891.20	889.22	868.77	877.18	866.85	883.60	887.81	875.01	891.48	884.58
2013	871.54	872.42	879.75	888.75	886.01	894.63	873.40	888.42	905.30	890.93	910.62	932.43	891.77
Trade, Transportation, and Utilities													
2009	574.93	635.70	617.24	629.46	609.79	612.05	591.75	623.64	601.34	607.06	620.77	621.14	611.14
2010	608.09	626.61	571.31	611.78	625.97	619.45	622.01	633.70	626.75	634.59	648.45	659.95	623.38
2011	668.98	694.79	702.44	703.82	702.13	694.94	710.64	693.60	693.84	718.62	691.05	691.49	697.32
2012	708.62	694.98	710.42	744.58	727.27	740.56	768.96	747.66	770.66	763.80	744.71	743.38	740.05
2013	697.15	710.62	728.27	765.23	753.08	785.13	754.76	749.95	762.63	730.52	734.25	752.41	744.15
Information													
2009	886.45	972.11	956.02	915.88	908.04	905.97	917.79	995.09	920.35	930.38	971.18	905.28	931.21
2010	904.16	869.53	879.96	911.83	909.36	862.32	899.56	915.55	864.13	873.97	874.38	901.82	887.93
2011	902.04	858.03	865.08	851.29	872.26	825.93	877.15	862.59	918.57	998.41	960.68	952.75	895.02
2012	967.43	886.05	849.70	864.82	824.69	797.70	873.90	815.26	910.33	831.48	848.82	873.49	861.84
2013	831.93	845.12	921.78	953.37	918.34	1,105.15	913.30	893.96	995.65	938.28	961.38	1,009.46	941.20
Financial Activities													
2009	872.28	875.38	876.18	886.04	878.76	926.15	957.87	926.60	903.90	897.87	928.91	899.44	901.85
2010	924.00	912.10	898.45	919.10	923.45	881.57	881.95	883.05	868.19	852.70	847.35	858.19	888.55
2011	876.45	876.34	868.26	880.75	890.23	886.74	901.47	909.09	926.27	925.60	919.69	938.91	900.93
2012	972.11	961.19	957.70	965.81	914.51	925.24	926.42	907.58	942.57	913.09	935.78	939.60	937.38
2013	903.12	926.63	925.43	949.98	933.31	989.29	953.00	962.92	1,003.07	959.40	976.51	1,023.42	957.96
Professional and Business Services													
2009	1,077.15	1,113.36	1,093.42	1,131.84	1,134.15	1,142.10	1,065.37	1,125.45	1,071.71	1,030.92	1,073.39	1,019.45	1,089.75
2010	1,086.18	1,128.40	1,063.62	1,060.70	1,091.40	1,038.06	1,008.62	986.58	941.92	939.98	953.37	975.90	1,022.60
2011	960.96	948.84	936.53	931.16	942.43	919.84	889.96	885.65	899.65	948.33	903.68	895.26	922.21
2012	953.55	910.14	925.92	972.61	818.57	830.75	916.12	882.18	928.80	884.62	893.55	933.91	903.33
2013	923.22	944.30	941.38	946.62	953.05	1,003.22	953.20	971.60	1,027.09	997.50	999.89	1,045.93	976.83
Education and Health Services													
2009	748.35	760.40	758.74	759.67	751.50	756.21	756.53	761.11	805.65	759.59	768.54	762.49	763.43
2010	732.47	774.91	755.04	758.84	769.49	763.18	766.36	779.71	814.26	806.81	818.48	803.47	779.68
2011	763.80	804.40	782.07	697.97	707.25	686.57	716.83	713.31	713.53	742.69	732.03	762.06	734.42
2012	775.20	821.37	787.83	799.41	783.24	786.67	796.56	804.19	810.93	808.70	834.17	825.30	802.77
2013	836.70	830.13	825.83	835.70	829.44	865.48	821.77	821.82	842.11	824.70	908.46	829.96	838.39
Leisure and Hospitality													
2009	293.01	284.02	294.42	261.52	270.69	279.21	280.04	310.20	294.25	295.72	299.38	295.54	288.44
2010	313.36	317.52	309.00	300.50	303.94	313.19	320.59	316.88	298.94	299.88	295.48	306.67	307.59
2011	333.58	329.71	326.90	309.93	306.77	292.45	299.63	295.60	288.90	303.68	290.64	291.55	306.18
2012	295.00	300.37	300.86	299.83	301.04	301.14	313.50	308.48	313.82	303.78	296.89	312.70	304.25
2013	303.69	323.50	320.66	306.13	308.51	325.95	312.46	320.95	326.37	311.74	304.01	325.38	315.50

VERMONT
At a Glance

Population:
    2000 census: 606,613
    2010 census: 625,741
    2013 estimate: 626,630

Percent change in population:
    2000–2010: 3.2%
    2010–2013: 0.1%

Percent change in total nonfarm employment:
    2000–2010: -0.3%
    2010–2013: 2.7%

Industry with the largest growth in employment, 2000–2013 (thousands):
    Education and Health Services, 15.7

Industry with the largest decline or smallest growth in employment, 2000–2013 (thousands):
    Manufacturing, -14.6

Civilian labor force:
    2000: 335,798
    2010: 359,798
    2013: 351,330

Unemployment rate and rank among states (lowest to highest):
    2000: 2.7%, 3rd
    2010: 6.4%, 6th
    2013: 4.4%, 4th

Over-the-year change in unemployment rates:
    2010–2011: -0.8%
    2011–2012: -0.7%
    2012–2013: -0.5%

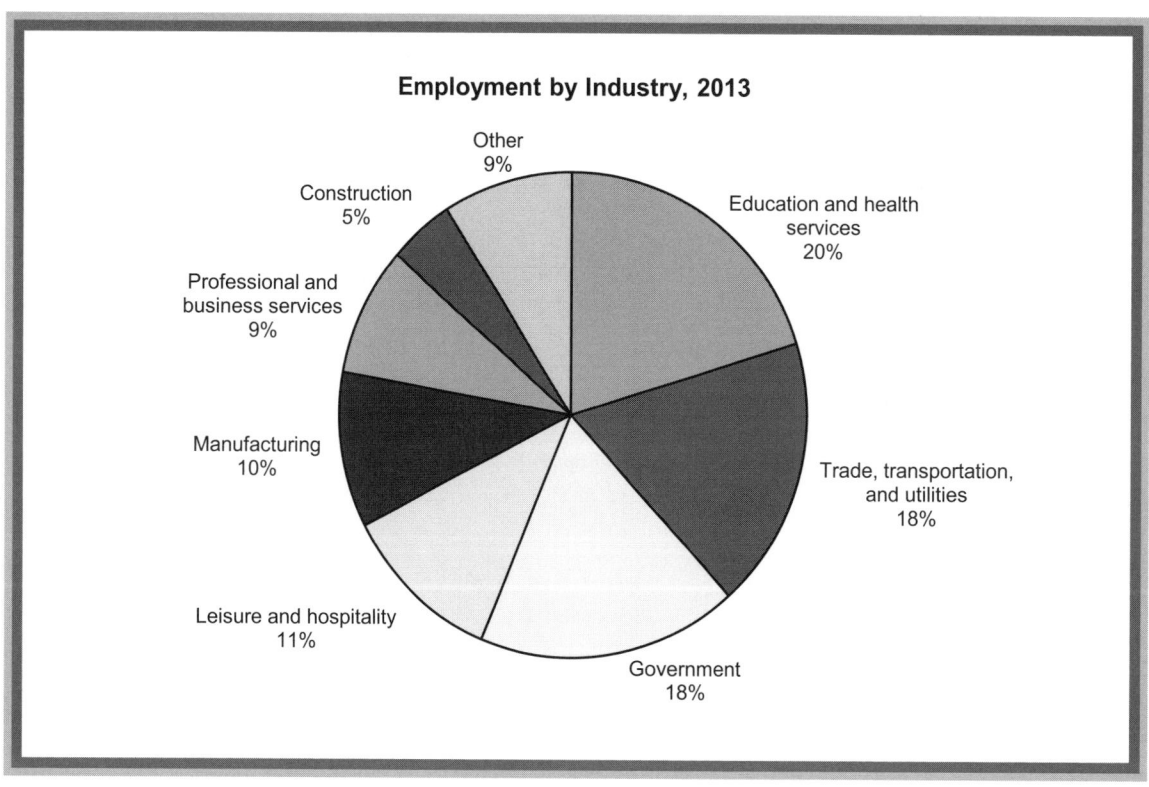

Employment by Industry, 2013

Other 9%
Construction 5%
Professional and business services 9%
Manufacturing 10%
Leisure and hospitality 11%
Government 18%
Trade, transportation, and utilities 18%
Education and health services 20%

1. Employment by Industry: Vermont, Selected Years, 2002–2013

(Numbers in thousands, not seasonally adjusted)

Industry and year	January	February	March	April	May	June	July	August	September	October	November	December	Annual average
Total Nonfarm													
2002	299.4	299.4	299.1	297.1	299.4	302.1	294.0	293.9	300.8	302.6	300.2	304.1	299.3
2003	297.2	297.8	296.9	293.6	298.0	301.1	294.2	294.9	301.7	304.4	302.5	307.9	299.2
2004	298.7	300.6	300.1	298.8	302.8	305.2	298.8	298.9	306.9	308.2	306.3	310.3	303.0
2005	302.9	304.0	303.5	302.4	305.1	307.1	300.7	301.1	308.4	309.5	308.1	313.6	305.5
2006	305.3	306.4	306.1	303.5	306.8	310.5	301.9	302.6	310.6	312.6	311.5	314.9	307.7
2007	306.2	307.2	306.8	303.3	308.2	311.6	303.7	303.5	310.8	312.1	311.3	315.5	308.4
2008	307.0	308.4	306.6	304.5	308.6	309.0	301.7	301.5	309.2	311.9	307.9	310.3	307.2
2009	299.0	300.9	297.3	293.8	297.7	297.3	290.1	290.8	297.5	301.6	298.4	302.4	297.2
2010	293.6	296.1	295.2	295.6	297.5	297.5	294.8	292.7	299.7	305.3	301.5	305.6	297.9
2011	297.0	299.9	298.5	295.9	299.1	300.6	294.5	295.0	303.2	306.8	304.5	310.4	300.5
2012	300.8	303.0	303.5	299.1	304.0	305.2	299.2	300.8	307.6	308.3	307.9	312.5	304.3
2013	303.5	304.9	305.6	302.7	305.9	306.9	300.1	300.1	307.6	310.2	310.7	314.0	306.0
Total Private													
2002	248.1	246.8	246.4	244.2	246.7	251.1	252.2	251.8	249.6	248.6	245.8	250.7	248.5
2003	245.1	243.9	243.1	239.7	244.1	249.2	250.9	252.0	248.9	249.5	247.3	252.8	247.2
2004	246.2	246.3	245.8	244.3	248.5	254.1	255.6	255.6	253.4	252.8	250.3	254.7	250.6
2005	249.5	248.9	248.3	247.3	250.1	255.2	257.3	256.9	254.3	253.3	251.6	257.3	252.5
2006	250.9	250.4	250.1	247.5	251.1	257.3	258.1	258.6	256.1	255.9	254.5	258.1	254.1
2007	251.4	250.8	250.4	247.3	252.0	257.9	259.4	259.4	256.2	255.6	254.7	258.7	254.5
2008	251.5	252.0	250.3	248.2	252.4	255.6	257.1	256.9	254.3	254.6	250.3	252.9	253.0
2009	244.0	243.9	240.7	236.3	240.0	243.2	245.2	245.8	242.8	243.9	240.8	245.5	242.7
2010	238.3	239.1	237.6	238.1	238.7	242.7	249.4	247.7	245.0	247.8	244.0	248.4	243.1
2011	241.8	242.9	241.5	238.8	241.5	246.4	250.2	250.8	248.0	249.1	246.7	252.3	245.8
2012	245.4	245.6	246.0	241.4	246.0	251.3	254.7	254.9	251.4	250.6	249.8	254.5	249.3
2013	247.3	247.6	248.0	245.2	247.9	252.7	255.2	255.7	252.0	252.3	252.7	257.1	251.1
Goods-Producing													
2002	56.5	55.3	55.1	56.2	57.6	58.4	58.1	57.0	56.4	56.2	55.3	54.0	56.3
2003	51.7	51.0	51.1	52.2	54.4	55.5	55.9	56.1	54.6	55.0	54.5	53.7	53.8
2004	51.1	51.1	51.0	53.1	55.2	56.6	57.0	57.0	56.3	56.0	55.3	54.5	54.5
2005	51.6	51.1	51.0	52.9	54.9	56.4	57.1	57.1	56.2	56.1	55.4	54.3	54.5
2006	51.7	51.1	51.1	53.3	54.9	56.2	56.8	56.8	56.0	55.9	55.4	54.6	54.5
2007	51.7	50.8	50.9	51.9	54.6	55.7	55.9	55.7	54.7	54.4	53.6	52.7	53.6
2008	50.0	49.6	49.2	50.1	52.2	53.4	53.9	53.5	52.9	52.7	51.4	49.2	51.5
2009	45.6	44.7	43.7	44.2	45.6	46.4	46.9	47.4	46.8	46.7	45.9	44.8	45.7
2010	41.9	41.7	41.6	43.8	45.5	46.1	47.1	47.0	46.4	46.7	45.9	44.7	44.9
2011	42.4	42.5	42.0	43.4	45.4	47.1	48.1	48.4	48.1	48.7	47.8	47.2	45.9
2012	44.3	44.0	44.4	45.8	47.4	48.4	48.9	48.7	48.3	48.0	47.3	46.7	46.9
2013	44.2	44.2	44.4	45.2	46.9	47.9	48.3	47.9	47.7	47.8	47.6	46.3	46.5
Service-Providing													
2002	242.9	244.1	244.0	240.9	241.8	243.7	235.9	236.9	244.4	246.4	244.9	250.1	243.0
2003	245.5	246.8	245.8	241.4	243.6	245.6	238.3	238.8	247.1	249.4	248.0	254.2	245.4
2004	247.6	249.5	249.1	245.7	247.6	248.6	241.8	241.9	250.6	252.2	251.0	255.8	248.5
2005	251.3	252.9	252.5	249.5	250.2	250.7	243.6	244.0	252.2	253.4	252.7	259.3	251.0
2006	253.6	255.3	255.0	250.2	251.9	254.3	245.1	245.8	254.6	256.7	256.1	260.3	253.2
2007	254.5	256.4	255.9	251.4	253.6	255.9	247.8	247.8	256.1	257.7	257.7	262.8	254.8
2008	257.0	258.8	257.4	254.4	256.4	255.6	247.8	248.0	256.3	259.2	256.5	261.1	255.7
2009	253.4	256.2	253.6	249.6	252.1	250.9	243.2	243.4	250.7	254.9	252.5	257.6	251.5
2010	251.7	254.4	253.6	251.8	252.0	251.4	247.7	245.7	253.3	258.6	255.6	260.9	253.1
2011	254.6	257.4	256.5	252.5	253.7	253.5	246.4	246.6	255.1	258.1	256.7	263.2	254.5
2012	256.5	259.0	259.1	253.3	256.6	256.8	250.3	252.1	259.3	260.3	260.6	265.8	257.5
2013	259.3	260.7	261.2	257.5	259.0	259.0	251.8	252.2	259.9	262.4	263.1	267.7	259.5
Mining and Logging													
2002	0.9	0.9	0.9	1.0	1.0	1.1	1.1	1.1	1.1	1.0	1.0	0.9	1.0
2003	0.8	0.8	0.9	0.9	1.0	1.0	1.0	1.0	1.0	1.0	1.0	0.9	0.9
2004	0.8	0.8	0.8	0.9	1.0	1.0	0.9	0.9	0.9	0.9	0.9	0.9	0.9
2005	0.7	0.7	0.8	0.8	0.8	0.9	0.9	0.9	0.9	0.9	0.9	0.8	0.8
2006	0.8	0.7	0.8	0.9	0.9	0.9	0.9	0.9	0.9	0.9	0.9	0.9	0.9
2007	0.8	0.8	0.8	0.8	0.9	0.9	0.9	0.9	0.9	0.8	0.8	0.8	0.8
2008	0.8	0.8	0.8	0.8	0.9	0.9	0.9	0.9	0.9	0.9	0.9	0.8	0.9
2009	0.7	0.7	0.7	0.8	0.8	0.8	0.8	0.8	0.8	0.8	0.8	0.7	0.8
2010	0.7	0.7	0.7	0.7	0.8	0.8	0.8	0.8	0.8	0.8	0.8	0.7	0.8
2011	0.7	0.7	0.7	0.7	0.8	0.8	0.8	0.8	0.8	0.8	0.8	0.8	0.8
2012	0.7	0.7	0.7	0.8	0.8	0.8	0.9	0.9	0.9	0.9	0.8	0.8	0.8
2013	0.7	0.7	0.7	0.7	0.8	0.8	0.8	0.8	0.8	0.8	0.8	0.8	0.8
Construction													
2002	13.4	12.9	12.8	13.9	15.3	15.8	16.3	16.3	15.8	15.8	15.3	14.3	14.8
2003	13.0	12.4	12.5	13.7	15.6	16.6	17.2	17.4	16.9	17.0	16.5	15.8	15.4
2004	14.1	13.8	13.9	15.7	17.3	18.3	18.8	18.7	18.2	17.9	17.3	16.2	16.7
2005	14.4	13.8	13.8	15.4	17.3	18.3	19.2	19.1	18.5	18.3	17.6	16.6	16.9
2006	14.9	14.5	14.7	16.4	17.8	18.8	19.4	19.4	18.9	18.6	18.0	17.1	17.4
2007	15.1	14.2	14.4	15.3	17.7	18.5	18.8	18.7	18.1	17.8	17.0	16.0	16.8
2008	14.1	13.5	13.3	14.2	16.2	17.1	17.5	17.3	16.9	16.9	15.9	14.3	15.6
2009	12.3	11.6	11.4	12.4	14.0	14.9	15.3	15.6	15.2	15.1	14.4	13.2	13.8
2010	11.4	10.9	10.9	12.8	14.2	14.4	15.2	15.2	14.9	15.0	14.3	13.1	13.5
2011	11.5	11.1	11.0	12.2	13.8	15.0	15.9	16.0	16.0	16.4	15.5	14.5	14.1
2012	12.5	11.9	12.1	13.4	14.6	15.4	15.9	15.8	15.4	15.2	14.6	13.6	14.2
2013	12.1	11.7	12.0	12.7	14.2	14.9	15.4	15.4	15.4	15.8	15.3	14.3	14.1

1. Employment by Industry: Vermont, Selected Years, 2002–2013—*Continued*

(Numbers in thousands, not seasonally adjusted)

Industry and year	January	February	March	April	May	June	July	August	September	October	November	December	Annual average
Manufacturing													
2002	42.2	41.5	41.4	41.3	41.3	41.5	40.7	39.6	39.5	39.4	39.0	38.8	40.5
2003	37.9	37.8	37.7	37.6	37.8	37.9	37.7	37.7	36.7	37.0	37.0	37.0	37.5
2004	36.2	36.5	36.3	36.5	36.9	37.3	37.3	37.4	37.2	37.2	37.1	37.4	36.9
2005	36.5	36.6	36.4	36.7	36.8	37.2	37.0	37.1	36.8	36.9	36.9	36.9	36.8
2006	36.0	35.9	35.6	36.0	36.2	36.5	36.5	36.5	36.2	36.4	36.5	36.6	36.2
2007	35.8	35.8	35.7	35.8	36.0	36.3	36.2	36.1	35.7	35.8	35.8	35.9	35.9
2008	35.1	35.3	35.1	35.1	35.1	35.4	35.5	35.3	35.1	34.9	34.6	34.1	35.1
2009	32.6	32.4	31.6	31.0	30.8	30.7	30.8	31.0	30.8	30.8	30.7	30.9	31.2
2010	29.8	30.1	30.0	30.3	30.5	30.9	31.1	31.0	30.7	30.9	30.8	30.9	30.6
2011	30.2	30.7	30.3	30.5	30.8	31.3	31.4	31.6	31.3	31.5	31.5	31.9	31.1
2012	31.1	31.4	31.6	31.6	32.0	32.2	32.1	32.0	32.0	31.9	31.9	32.3	31.8
2013	31.4	31.8	31.7	31.8	31.9	32.2	32.1	31.7	31.5	31.2	31.5	31.2	31.7
Trade, Transportation, and Utilities													
2002	58.3	57.7	57.9	57.9	58.7	59.2	59.1	59.2	58.7	59.1	59.7	60.5	58.8
2003	57.9	57.4	56.8	57.0	57.6	58.4	57.9	58.1	57.8	59.1	59.9	61.1	58.3
2004	57.9	57.4	57.5	57.8	58.7	59.3	59.1	59.0	58.6	59.8	60.8	61.4	58.9
2005	59.0	58.6	58.1	58.6	59.1	59.7	59.4	59.4	59.2	59.8	60.6	61.6	59.4
2006	58.9	58.3	58.2	58.4	59.4	59.9	59.4	59.5	59.4	60.1	61.1	61.9	59.5
2007	59.2	58.4	58.0	57.8	58.9	59.7	59.3	59.0	58.9	59.9	61.2	61.8	59.3
2008	59.0	58.7	58.1	58.2	59.1	59.6	58.8	58.9	58.3	58.9	59.3	59.8	58.9
2009	56.5	56.1	55.1	55.0	56.0	56.5	55.8	56.0	55.5	56.3	56.8	57.8	56.1
2010	54.8	54.5	54.0	54.7	54.9	55.7	56.6	56.4	56.0	57.2	57.7	58.4	55.9
2011	55.6	55.3	54.9	54.8	55.3	56.0	55.8	55.9	55.5	56.3	57.0	57.9	55.9
2012	54.7	54.4	54.1	54.4	55.1	56.0	55.8	55.8	55.6	55.8	56.7	57.6	55.5
2013	54.8	54.3	54.3	54.3	55.2	56.0	55.5	55.6	55.4	55.8	56.9	57.8	55.5
Wholesale Trade													
2002	9.9	9.9	10.0	10.0	10.1	10.1	10.2	10.2	10.3	10.2	10.3	10.4	10.1
2003	10.1	10.1	10.1	10.1	10.2	10.3	10.3	10.3	10.3	10.5	10.4	10.4	10.3
2004	10.1	10.1	10.2	10.2	10.3	10.2	10.4	10.1	10.0	10.1	10.2	9.9	10.2
2005	9.9	9.9	9.8	10.0	10.0	10.1	10.2	10.3	10.2	10.2	10.3	10.3	10.1
2006	10.2	10.1	10.2	10.2	10.3	10.2	10.4	10.5	10.5	10.5	10.5	10.6	10.4
2007	10.4	10.3	10.3	10.3	10.4	10.4	10.4	10.4	10.4	10.4	10.5	10.5	10.4
2008	10.2	10.2	10.3	10.3	10.3	10.3	10.2	10.2	10.1	10.0	10.0	9.9	10.2
2009	9.8	9.7	9.7	9.7	9.7	9.7	9.6	9.6	9.5	9.5	9.5	9.5	9.6
2010	9.2	9.2	9.2	9.3	9.3	9.4	9.6	9.6	9.5	9.7	9.7	9.6	9.4
2011	9.4	9.4	9.4	9.4	9.4	9.4	9.6	9.6	9.5	9.5	9.5	9.3	9.5
2012	9.1	9.1	9.1	9.2	9.2	9.3	9.3	9.3	9.2	9.2	9.3	9.2	9.2
2013	9.0	9.0	9.0	9.0	9.1	9.3	9.3	9.3	9.2	9.4	9.3	9.3	9.2
Retail Trade													
2002	39.7	39.2	39.3	39.2	39.8	40.3	40.5	40.5	39.7	40.0	40.5	41.2	40.0
2003	39.2	38.8	38.3	38.4	38.9	39.4	39.6	39.7	39.0	39.9	40.9	42.0	39.5
2004	39.2	38.7	38.8	39.1	39.8	40.3	40.3	40.4	39.8	40.6	41.5	42.4	40.1
2005	40.1	39.8	39.4	39.8	40.3	40.7	40.8	40.7	40.2	40.6	41.2	42.1	40.5
2006	39.9	39.5	39.3	39.5	40.3	40.9	40.7	40.7	40.1	40.7	41.6	42.2	40.5
2007	40.0	39.4	39.1	39.0	39.7	40.4	40.5	40.2	39.6	40.4	41.5	42.0	40.2
2008	40.1	39.9	39.3	39.4	40.0	40.4	40.2	40.2	39.4	40.1	40.4	40.8	40.0
2009	38.3	38.0	37.2	37.2	38.0	38.5	38.2	38.3	37.6	38.2	38.6	39.3	38.1
2010	37.3	37.0	36.5	37.2	37.2	37.8	38.6	38.4	37.7	38.6	39.1	39.5	37.9
2011	37.5	37.3	36.9	37.0	37.4	37.9	38.0	38.2	37.2	37.8	38.4	39.3	37.7
2012	37.1	36.9	36.6	36.7	37.3	38.0	38.3	38.2	37.6	37.7	38.5	39.1	37.7
2013	37.1	36.8	36.6	36.9	37.5	38.1	38.1	38.2	37.5	37.7	38.7	39.3	37.7
Transportation and Utilities													
2002	8.7	8.6	8.6	8.7	8.8	8.8	8.4	8.5	8.7	8.9	8.9	8.9	8.7
2003	8.6	8.5	8.4	8.5	8.5	8.7	8.0	8.1	8.5	8.7	8.6	8.7	8.5
2004	8.6	8.6	8.5	8.5	8.6	8.8	8.4	8.5	8.8	9.1	9.1	9.1	8.7
2005	9.0	8.9	8.9	8.8	8.8	8.9	8.4	8.4	8.8	9.0	9.1	9.2	8.9
2006	8.8	8.7	8.7	8.7	8.8	8.8	8.3	8.3	8.8	8.9	9.0	9.1	8.7
2007	8.8	8.7	8.6	8.5	8.8	8.9	8.4	8.4	8.9	9.1	9.2	9.3	8.8
2008	8.7	8.6	8.5	8.5	8.8	8.9	8.4	8.5	8.8	8.8	8.9	9.1	8.7
2009	8.4	8.4	8.2	8.1	8.3	8.3	8.0	8.1	8.4	8.6	8.7	9.0	8.4
2010	8.3	8.3	8.3	8.2	8.4	8.5	8.4	8.4	8.8	8.9	8.9	9.3	8.6
2011	8.7	8.6	8.6	8.4	8.5	8.7	8.2	8.1	8.8	9.0	9.1	9.3	8.7
2012	8.5	8.4	8.4	8.5	8.6	8.7	8.2	8.3	8.8	8.9	8.9	9.3	8.6
2013	8.7	8.5	8.7	8.4	8.6	8.6	8.1	8.1	8.7	8.7	8.9	9.2	8.6
Information													
2002	6.7	6.7	6.7	6.8	6.7	6.7	6.7	6.7	6.6	6.5	6.6	6.6	6.7
2003	6.5	6.4	6.5	6.4	6.5	6.6	6.5	6.5	6.5	6.5	6.5	6.5	6.5
2004	6.4	6.4	6.4	6.4	6.4	6.4	6.4	6.4	6.2	6.3	6.3	6.3	6.4
2005	6.3	6.2	6.2	6.2	6.2	6.2	6.3	6.2	6.2	6.2	6.2	6.3	6.2
2006	6.1	6.1	6.2	6.0	6.0	6.0	6.0	6.0	6.0	5.9	6.0	6.0	6.0
2007	6.0	5.9	5.9	5.9	5.9	5.9	6.0	6.0	5.9	5.8	5.8	5.8	5.9
2008	5.8	5.8	5.8	5.8	5.8	5.7	5.8	5.8	5.8	5.7	5.7	5.7	5.8
2009	5.6	5.6	5.6	5.6	5.5	5.6	5.5	5.5	5.4	5.4	5.4	5.4	5.5
2010	5.4	5.4	5.4	5.4	5.4	5.4	5.3	5.3	5.3	5.3	5.3	5.3	5.4
2011	5.2	5.3	5.2	5.0	4.9	5.0	4.9	4.9	4.8	4.8	4.8	4.8	5.0
2012	4.7	4.7	4.7	4.6	4.7	4.7	4.7	4.7	4.7	4.7	4.7	4.8	4.7
2013	4.7	4.7	4.7	4.7	4.7	4.8	4.7	4.7	4.6	4.5	4.6	4.5	4.7

1. Employment by Industry: Vermont, Selected Years, 2002–2013—*Continued*

(Numbers in thousands, not seasonally adjusted)

Industry and year	January	February	March	April	May	June	July	August	September	October	November	December	Annual average
Financial Activities													
2002	13.0	13.0	13.0	12.9	13.1	13.3	13.5	13.5	13.2	13.2	13.0	13.2	13.2
2003	13.0	13.0	13.0	13.0	13.2	13.4	13.5	13.5	13.3	13.3	13.2	13.5	13.2
2004	13.3	13.1	13.1	13.1	13.3	13.4	13.5	13.5	13.3	13.1	13.1	13.4	13.3
2005	13.1	13.1	13.1	13.0	13.1	13.4	13.4	13.4	13.2	13.2	13.1	13.3	13.2
2006	13.2	13.2	13.2	13.1	13.2	13.4	13.4	13.4	13.2	13.1	13.1	13.2	13.2
2007	13.2	13.1	13.2	13.1	13.2	13.4	13.4	13.3	13.1	13.0	13.0	13.0	13.2
2008	12.8	12.8	12.8	12.8	12.9	13.0	13.1	13.0	12.8	12.7	12.6	12.7	12.8
2009	12.5	12.4	12.4	12.2	12.4	12.5	12.6	12.5	12.3	12.3	12.2	12.2	12.4
2010	12.1	12.1	12.0	12.1	12.0	12.3	12.4	12.4	12.1	12.2	12.1	12.2	12.2
2011	12.1	12.0	12.0	11.9	12.0	12.3	12.3	12.3	12.1	12.1	12.0	12.1	12.1
2012	12.0	11.9	12.0	11.8	12.1	12.2	12.3	12.2	12.0	11.9	11.9	12.0	12.0
2013	11.8	11.8	11.8	11.8	12.1	12.3	12.3	12.3	12.1	12.1	12.1	12.1	12.1
Professional and Business Services													
2002	19.2	19.2	19.3	20.0	20.5	20.6	20.7	20.9	21.0	20.9	20.4	20.3	20.3
2003	19.3	19.4	19.3	20.0	20.6	21.0	21.0	21.0	20.7	20.7	20.6	20.7	20.4
2004	20.0	20.0	20.3	21.4	21.2	21.7	21.8	21.9	21.8	21.8	21.6	21.8	21.3
2005	20.8	20.9	21.2	21.7	22.0	22.3	22.4	22.4	22.1	22.2	22.1	22.2	21.9
2006	21.5	21.5	21.6	22.0	22.3	22.8	22.8	22.9	22.5	22.4	21.9	22.0	22.2
2007	21.2	21.3	21.6	22.1	22.6	23.1	23.1	23.2	22.9	22.8	22.5	22.7	22.4
2008	21.8	21.9	21.7	22.4	23.3	23.5	23.5	23.3	23.1	23.3	22.7	22.4	22.7
2009	21.3	21.3	21.1	21.8	22.4	22.8	22.9	23.0	22.4	22.9	22.9	22.6	22.3
2010	21.8	21.8	22.0	23.1	23.2	23.6	24.3	24.4	24.1	24.4	24.0	23.6	23.4
2011	23.0	23.2	23.4	24.1	24.9	25.4	25.7	25.9	25.9	25.9	25.6	25.5	24.9
2012	24.6	24.8	25.1	26.0	26.2	26.9	26.9	27.0	26.5	26.4	26.1	26.0	26.0
2013	25.0	25.1	25.5	26.1	26.8	27.3	27.1	27.2	26.8	27.1	26.7	26.2	26.4
Education and Health Services													
2002	49.0	49.7	50.0	50.1	50.3	49.5	49.5	49.2	50.7	50.9	51.3	51.5	50.1
2003	50.9	51.4	51.8	52.0	52.2	51.7	51.8	51.7	53.0	53.0	52.9	53.3	52.1
2004	51.9	52.7	53.1	53.1	53.5	52.9	52.5	52.1	53.8	53.4	53.7	53.8	53.0
2005	53.3	53.9	54.2	54.5	54.6	53.7	53.5	53.2	54.7	54.3	54.6	55.2	54.1
2006	54.2	55.1	55.3	55.0	55.1	55.0	55.0	54.8	56.1	56.1	56.3	56.8	55.4
2007	55.7	56.7	56.8	57.1	57.0	57.1	57.1	56.8	58.1	58.0	58.6	58.4	57.3
2008	57.3	58.2	58.6	58.7	59.1	58.0	58.3	58.2	59.3	59.6	59.5	59.6	58.7
2009	58.0	59.5	59.8	59.5	60.0	59.0	59.4	58.8	59.4	59.5	59.1	59.2	59.3
2010	58.1	59.0	59.2	59.7	58.9	58.2	59.5	58.5	59.4	60.0	59.5	59.7	59.1
2011	58.5	59.7	59.8	59.9	59.5	58.5	59.5	59.1	59.8	59.7	59.8	60.1	59.5
2012	59.5	60.2	60.8	60.4	60.2	59.6	61.0	61.0	60.7	61.5	61.4	61.8	60.7
2013	60.7	61.3	61.9	61.6	61.3	60.8	62.1	61.8	61.6	62.5	62.6	62.7	61.7
Leisure and Hospitality													
2002	35.6	35.5	34.6	30.4	29.8	33.0	34.1	34.9	32.7	31.7	29.5	34.4	33.0
2003	35.9	35.4	34.6	29.1	29.5	32.2	34.0	34.8	32.8	31.7	29.6	33.7	32.8
2004	35.5	35.5	34.4	29.3	30.0	33.4	35.0	35.5	33.3	32.3	29.6	33.5	33.1
2005	35.6	35.3	34.7	30.4	30.1	33.2	35.0	35.1	32.8	31.7	29.8	34.5	33.2
2006	35.6	35.4	34.8	29.9	30.3	33.9	34.5	35.1	32.9	32.4	30.8	33.7	33.3
2007	34.6	34.8	34.2	29.7	29.9	32.9	34.5	35.3	32.7	31.7	30.1	34.3	32.9
2008	35.1	35.3	34.4	30.4	30.1	32.4	33.8	34.4	32.3	31.9	29.4	33.8	32.8
2009	35.0	34.8	33.6	28.5	28.5	30.6	32.3	32.9	31.3	31.0	28.8	33.7	31.8
2010	34.5	34.9	33.7	29.4	29.0	31.5	34.0	33.6	31.7	32.0	29.7	34.7	32.4
2011	35.3	35.2	34.5	29.8	29.5	32.0	33.7	34.2	31.7	31.5	29.7	34.6	32.6
2012	35.6	35.6	34.8	28.5	30.3	33.4	34.9	35.3	33.5	32.2	31.7	35.6	33.5
2013	36.3	36.4	35.6	31.6	30.9	33.4	35.1	36.1	33.8	32.8	32.4	37.6	34.3
Other Services													
2002	9.8	9.7	9.8	9.9	10.0	10.4	10.5	10.4	10.3	10.1	10.0	10.2	10.1
2003	9.9	9.9	10.0	10.0	10.1	10.4	10.3	10.3	10.2	10.2	10.1	10.3	10.1
2004	10.1	10.1	10.0	10.1	10.2	10.4	10.3	10.2	10.1	10.1	9.9	10.0	10.1
2005	9.8	9.8	9.8	10.0	10.1	10.3	10.2	10.1	9.9	9.8	9.8	9.9	10.0
2006	9.7	9.7	9.7	9.8	9.9	10.1	10.2	10.1	10.0	10.0	9.9	9.9	9.9
2007	9.8	9.8	9.8	9.7	9.9	10.1	10.1	10.1	9.9	10.0	9.9	10.0	9.9
2008	9.7	9.7	9.7	9.8	9.9	10.0	9.9	9.8	9.8	9.8	9.7	9.7	9.8
2009	9.5	9.5	9.4	9.5	9.6	9.8	9.8	9.7	9.7	9.8	9.7	9.8	9.7
2010	9.7	9.7	9.7	9.9	9.8	9.9	10.2	10.1	10.0	10.0	9.8	9.8	9.9
2011	9.7	9.7	9.7	9.9	10.0	10.1	10.2	10.1	10.1	10.1	10.0	10.1	10.0
2012	10.0	10.0	10.1	9.9	10.0	10.1	10.2	10.2	10.1	10.1	10.0	10.0	10.1
2013	9.8	9.8	9.8	9.9	10.0	10.2	10.1	10.1	10.0	9.7	9.8	9.9	9.9
Government													
2002	51.3	52.6	52.7	52.9	52.7	51.0	41.8	42.1	51.2	54.0	54.4	53.4	50.8
2003	52.1	53.9	53.8	53.9	53.9	51.9	43.3	42.9	52.8	54.9	55.2	55.1	52.0
2004	52.5	54.3	54.3	54.5	54.3	51.1	43.2	43.3	53.5	55.4	56.0	55.6	52.3
2005	53.4	55.1	55.2	55.1	55.0	51.9	43.4	44.2	54.1	56.2	56.5	56.3	53.0
2006	54.4	56.0	56.0	56.0	55.7	53.2	43.8	44.0	54.5	56.7	57.0	56.8	53.7
2007	54.8	56.4	56.4	56.0	56.2	53.7	44.3	44.1	54.6	56.5	56.6	56.8	53.9
2008	55.5	56.4	56.3	56.3	56.2	53.4	44.6	44.6	54.9	57.3	57.6	57.4	54.2
2009	55.0	57.0	56.6	57.5	57.7	54.1	44.9	45.0	54.7	57.7	57.6	56.9	54.6
2010	55.3	57.0	57.6	57.5	58.8	54.8	45.4	45.0	54.7	57.5	57.5	57.2	54.9
2011	55.2	57.0	57.0	57.1	57.6	54.2	44.3	44.2	55.2	57.7	57.8	58.1	54.6
2012	55.4	57.4	57.5	57.7	58.0	53.9	44.5	45.9	56.2	57.7	58.1	58.0	55.0
2013	56.2	57.3	57.6	57.5	58.0	54.2	44.9	44.4	55.6	57.9	58.0	56.9	54.9

2. Average Weekly Hours by Selected Industry: Vermont, 2009–2013

(Not seasonally adjusted)

Industry and year	January	February	March	April	May	June	July	August	September	October	November	December	Annual average
Total Private													
2009	34.1	33.8	33.5	33.7	34.1	34.2	34.3	34.9	34.4	34.5	34.4	33.5	34.1
2010	33.5	33.7	33.1	33.8	34.6	34.4	34.9	34.8	34.8	34.5	34.0	33.9	34.2
2011	33.6	33.5	33.3	33.2	33.9	33.7	34.2	34.0	33.9	34.2	33.8	33.6	33.7
2012	33.5	33.3	33.3	33.9	33.7	33.7	34.2	34.0	34.3	34.1	33.4	33.7	33.8
2013	33.2	33.5	33.5	33.4	34.0	34.0	34.0	34.3	34.2	34.0	33.6	33.6	33.8
Goods-Producing													
2009	37.4	36.9	36.7	35.8	36.8	37.4	37.5	38.4	37.7	38.4	37.6	36.6	37.3
2010	37.5	38.1	37.1	37.7	38.4	38.6	38.9	39.2	39.3	39.1	38.6	38.5	38.5
2011	37.7	38.2	37.6	38.5	38.7	38.2	38.9	38.6	39.0	38.4	38.6	38.6	38.4
2012	38.2	37.8	38.1	38.5	39.0	39.5	39.1	39.5	39.9	39.9	38.6	39.0	39.0
2013	38.0	38.2	38.3	38.4	39.3	39.0	39.0	39.3	39.1	39.1	38.6	38.9	38.8
Construction													
2009	36.9	36.9	36.1	36.6	39.8	40.2	40.4	41.0	40.2	41.2	40.4	39.8	39.3
2010	40.0	39.2	39.9	40.4	40.7	40.6	40.6	41.0	41.5	40.7	40.0	39.1	40.4
2011	38.2	38.1	37.0	38.8	40.3	39.1	40.4	40.2	40.8	39.8	40.1	39.9	39.5
2012	39.5	38.5	38.2	38.8	39.7	40.9	40.2	41.3	41.4	41.5	39.7	38.6	40.0
2013	37.1	37.5	37.1	37.5	39.9	38.7	39.6	39.8	39.5	39.9	38.4	38.1	38.7
Manufacturing													
2009	37.9	37.0	37.0	35.6	35.8	36.5	36.1	36.9	36.3	37.2	36.9	36.4	36.6
2010	37.1	37.9	37.2	37.7	38.5	38.7	39.1	39.3	39.1	39.1	38.8	38.9	38.5
2011	38.4	39.0	38.7	39.1	38.6	38.3	38.5	38.4	38.7	38.2	38.6	38.7	38.6
2012	38.2	38.1	38.7	38.8	39.0	38.9	38.6	38.5	39.0	39.0	38.0	39.3	38.7
2013	38.6	38.6	38.9	38.8	38.9	39.3	38.6	39.0	38.9	38.7	38.8	39.5	38.9
Trade, Transportation, and Utilities													
2009	32.9	31.5	31.6	32.2	32.6	32.9	32.9	33.6	33.3	33.3	33.2	33.4	32.8
2010	32.6	32.8	32.4	32.6	32.4	32.3	33.0	32.9	33.0	32.5	32.2	33.2	32.7
2011	32.5	32.3	32.3	32.4	32.6	32.9	33.6	33.6	33.2	33.6	33.4	33.8	33.0
2012	32.3	32.0	32.6	32.7	32.8	32.4	33.2	33.3	33.3	33.2	32.7	33.5	32.9
2013	32.5	33.0	33.3	33.3	33.8	33.6	33.8	33.8	34.0	33.4	32.8	33.7	33.4
Professional and Business Services													
2009	37.4	39.5	39.2	39.2	37.7	37.9	37.1	37.6	36.9	36.9	36.9	36.2	37.7
2010	37.2	36.7	36.7	37.7	37.1	36.4	35.9	35.0	35.7	36.1	36.5	35.7	36.4
2011	36.0	35.2	35.1	34.9	36.2	36.0	36.5	35.3	35.1	36.4	35.6	35.8	35.7
2012	36.7	35.7	35.4	36.6	35.3	35.2	35.9	35.3	36.3	35.4	35.1	36.0	35.8
2013	35.8	35.5	35.4	35.6	36.1	36.5	35.6	36.0	36.6	35.9	36.4	36.5	36.0
Education and Health Services													
2009	33.7	33.3	32.8	32.8	33.1	32.7	32.9	32.8	32.8	32.6	32.8	33.1	33.0
2010	32.8	32.8	32.9	32.7	32.8	33.2	33.2	33.4	33.3	33.4	32.9	33.1	33.0
2011	33.2	32.8	32.8	32.6	32.9	32.9	33.0	33.4	33.4	33.2	33.1	33.2	33.0
2012	33.2	33.3	33.2	33.0	33.3	33.4	33.4	32.9	33.2	33.2	32.9	32.9	33.2
2013	33.0	33.1	32.7	32.6	32.6	32.9	33.0	33.1	33.3	32.9	32.8	32.9	32.9
Leisure and Hospitality													
2009	24.7	25.0	23.7	23.8	25.3	25.8	26.7	27.1	26.2	27.0	26.2	25.2	25.6
2010	26.3	26.9	25.9	26.2	26.8	26.3	27.3	27.0	26.1	26.2	25.8	25.7	26.4
2011	26.2	26.2	25.1	24.5	25.9	25.8	27.5	27.6	25.7	26.3	24.6	24.4	25.9
2012	25.4	25.7	24.9	25.5	25.1	25.6	27.3	27.6	26.2	26.6	24.8	24.3	25.7
2013	25.7	25.9	26.1	25.0	26.5	26.9	27.6	27.9	26.4	26.7	25.2	24.4	26.2

3. Average Hourly Earnings by Selected Industry: Vermont, 2009–2013

(Dollars, not seasonally adjusted)

Industry and year	January	February	March	April	May	June	July	August	September	October	November	December	Annual average
Total Private													
2009	21.54	22.11	22.49	22.32	22.23	22.37	22.34	22.29	22.51	22.93	23.17	22.66	22.41
2010	23.04	22.91	23.10	23.39	23.32	22.75	22.76	22.71	22.73	23.09	22.93	23.46	23.01
2011	23.65	23.14	23.23	23.53	23.32	22.80	22.57	22.53	22.93	23.07	23.02	22.66	23.03
2012	23.10	22.83	22.97	23.23	22.79	22.47	22.30	22.40	22.59	23.07	22.83	22.99	22.79
2013	22.73	22.68	22.69	22.87	22.72	22.72	22.53	22.58	22.91	23.03	22.91	22.85	22.77
Goods-Producing													
2009	21.40	21.83	21.87	21.48	22.23	21.39	21.42	21.33	21.30	21.59	21.60	22.14	21.62
2010	21.87	22.43	22.75	22.45	22.11	21.85	21.99	22.32	22.09	22.39	22.41	22.43	22.25
2011	22.67	21.91	22.10	21.94	21.90	21.76	21.93	22.00	22.53	22.64	22.35	22.39	22.18
2012	22.77	22.68	22.93	22.81	22.18	22.18	22.04	22.17	22.20	22.22	22.31	22.45	22.40
2013	22.72	22.57	22.51	22.47	21.88	21.95	21.95	21.81	21.88	21.89	21.76	22.02	22.10
Construction													
2009	23.29	23.00	23.22	22.41	21.81	21.95	21.93	21.40	20.83	21.24	21.48	22.16	21.96
2010	21.59	21.88	21.91	21.30	20.64	20.35	20.81	20.77	20.67	21.16	21.71	21.64	21.15
2011	21.65	21.37	21.23	20.92	20.83	20.73	20.69	20.96	21.75	21.61	21.57	22.40	21.31
2012	22.69	23.05	23.36	22.71	21.85	21.96	21.43	21.74	21.70	21.74	21.84	22.42	22.14
2013	22.57	22.75	22.54	22.50	21.57	21.66	21.65	21.57	21.81	21.63	21.82	21.82	21.94
Manufacturing													
2009	20.69	21.28	21.23	21.12	21.69	21.53	21.58	21.67	21.95	22.11	21.88	22.22	21.57
2010	22.05	22.64	23.10	22.98	22.89	22.64	22.67	23.16	22.87	22.52	22.34	22.44	22.69
2011	22.88	22.49	22.80	22.70	22.74	22.57	22.89	22.81	23.04	23.30	22.94	22.60	22.81
2012	22.86	22.54	22.73	22.87	22.39	22.31	22.45	22.49	22.58	22.57	22.61	22.44	22.57
2013	22.81	22.49	22.51	22.47	22.09	22.15	22.18	22.00	21.94	22.08	21.75	22.18	22.22
Trade, Transportation, and Utilities													
2009	18.61	19.50	19.56	18.94	18.95	18.90	18.78	18.92	19.01	19.07	18.99	19.40	19.05
2010	19.90	19.36	19.68	19.78	19.27	18.80	18.74	18.83	18.66	18.77	18.37	18.50	19.04
2011	18.77	18.51	19.04	19.00	18.88	18.52	18.31	18.10	18.38	18.27	18.15	18.00	18.48
2012	18.47	18.41	18.58	18.56	18.24	18.18	18.05	18.08	18.15	18.03	17.88	17.77	18.19
2013	18.41	18.47	18.54	18.56	18.69	18.72	18.78	18.80	19.39	19.27	18.94	18.88	18.79
Professional and Business Services													
2009	21.82	22.92	23.76	23.80	24.21	25.03	25.48	25.43	26.04	26.56	26.57	26.34	24.84
2010	25.91	26.50	26.51	26.10	26.94	26.04	26.94	26.31	26.24	26.89	26.75	27.61	26.56
2011	28.14	27.68	27.70	29.04	29.02	28.71	28.43	29.35	29.54	29.35	29.99	28.99	28.85
2012	29.82	29.96	30.46	30.81	30.46	30.04	30.42	29.91	30.01	30.95	30.28	30.73	30.32
2013	30.50	30.70	30.96	30.44	30.73	30.62	30.11	31.07	30.96	31.07	31.06	31.45	30.81
Education and Health Services													
2009	25.93	26.12	26.17	25.88	25.37	25.63	25.39	25.63	25.96	25.77	26.60	25.66	25.84
2010	26.42	26.45	26.32	26.53	26.87	26.73	26.76	26.72	26.69	27.56	27.06	27.95	26.84
2011	27.16	27.06	26.83	26.69	26.10	25.98	25.78	25.25	25.57	25.82	25.80	25.29	26.11
2012	25.12	24.85	24.61	24.78	24.46	24.24	23.99	24.12	24.16	25.29	24.23	25.09	24.58
2013	23.95	23.98	24.10	24.49	24.43	24.80	24.69	24.55	25.04	25.79	25.24	25.13	24.69
Leisure and Hospitality													
2009	14.51	14.63	14.59	15.23	14.80	15.67	15.24	14.96	15.38	15.40	15.21	14.51	15.00
2010	14.19	13.97	14.14	15.15	14.21	14.93	13.93	14.17	14.80	15.06	14.93	14.23	14.45
2011	14.02	14.14	14.44	14.43	14.35	14.30	14.00	14.08	14.57	15.05	15.04	14.98	14.43
2012	14.63	14.80	14.79	15.25	14.96	14.66	14.41	14.53	14.84	14.98	15.24	14.79	14.81
2013	14.44	14.63	14.37	14.47	14.45	14.35	14.19	14.21	14.80	15.14	15.07	15.09	14.59

4. Average Weekly Earnings by Selected Industry: Vermont, 2009–2013

(Dollars, not seasonally adjusted)

Industry and year	January	February	March	April	May	June	July	August	September	October	November	December	Annual average
Total Private													
2009	734.51	747.32	753.42	752.18	758.04	765.05	766.26	777.92	774.34	791.09	797.05	759.11	764.18
2010	771.84	772.07	764.61	790.58	806.87	782.60	794.32	790.31	791.00	796.61	779.62	795.29	786.94
2011	794.64	775.19	773.56	781.20	790.55	768.36	771.89	766.02	777.33	788.99	778.08	761.38	776.11
2012	773.85	760.24	764.90	787.50	768.02	757.24	762.66	761.60	774.84	786.69	762.52	774.76	770.30
2013	754.64	759.78	760.12	763.86	772.48	772.48	766.02	774.49	783.52	783.02	769.78	767.76	769.63
Goods-Producing													
2009	800.36	805.53	802.63	768.98	818.06	799.99	803.25	819.07	803.01	829.06	812.16	810.32	806.43
2010	820.13	854.58	844.03	846.37	849.02	843.41	855.41	874.94	868.14	875.45	865.03	863.56	856.63
2011	854.66	836.96	830.96	844.69	847.53	831.23	853.08	849.20	878.67	869.38	862.71	864.25	851.71
2012	869.81	857.30	873.63	878.19	865.02	876.11	861.76	875.72	885.78	886.58	861.17	875.55	873.60
2013	863.36	862.17	862.13	862.85	859.88	856.05	856.05	857.13	855.51	855.90	839.94	856.58	857.48
Construction													
2009	859.40	848.70	838.24	820.21	868.04	882.39	885.97	877.40	837.37	875.09	867.79	881.97	863.03
2010	863.60	857.70	874.21	860.52	840.05	826.21	844.89	851.57	857.81	861.21	868.40	846.12	854.46
2011	827.03	814.20	785.51	811.70	839.45	810.54	835.88	842.59	887.40	860.08	864.96	893.76	841.75
2012	896.26	887.43	892.35	881.15	867.45	898.16	861.49	897.86	898.38	902.21	867.05	865.41	885.60
2013	837.35	853.13	836.23	843.75	860.64	838.24	857.34	858.49	861.50	863.04	837.89	831.34	849.08
Manufacturing													
2009	784.15	787.36	785.51	751.87	776.50	785.85	779.04	799.62	796.79	822.49	807.37	808.81	789.46
2010	818.06	858.06	859.32	866.35	881.27	876.17	886.40	910.19	894.22	880.53	866.79	872.92	873.57
2011	878.59	877.11	882.36	887.57	877.76	864.43	881.27	875.90	891.65	890.06	885.48	874.62	880.47
2012	873.25	858.77	879.65	887.36	873.21	867.86	866.57	865.87	880.62	880.23	859.18	881.89	873.46
2013	880.47	868.11	875.64	871.84	859.30	870.50	856.15	858.00	853.47	854.50	843.90	876.11	864.36
Trade, Transportation, and Utilities													
2009	612.27	614.25	618.10	609.87	617.77	621.81	617.86	635.71	633.03	635.03	630.47	647.96	624.84
2010	648.74	635.01	637.63	644.83	624.35	607.24	618.42	619.51	615.78	610.03	591.51	614.20	622.61
2011	610.03	597.87	614.99	615.60	615.49	609.31	615.22	608.16	610.22	613.87	606.21	608.40	609.84
2012	596.58	589.12	605.71	606.91	598.27	589.03	599.26	602.06	604.40	598.60	584.68	595.30	598.45
2013	598.33	609.51	617.38	618.05	631.72	628.99	634.76	635.44	659.26	643.62	621.23	636.26	627.59
Professional and Business Services													
2009	816.07	905.34	931.39	932.96	912.72	948.64	945.31	956.17	960.88	980.06	980.43	953.51	936.47
2010	963.85	972.55	972.92	983.97	999.47	947.86	967.15	920.85	936.77	970.73	976.38	985.68	966.78
2011	1,013.04	974.34	972.27	1,013.50	1,050.52	1,033.56	1,037.70	1,036.06	1,036.85	1,068.34	1,067.64	1,037.84	1,029.95
2012	1,094.39	1,069.57	1,078.28	1,127.65	1,075.24	1,057.41	1,092.08	1,055.82	1,089.36	1,095.63	1,062.83	1,106.28	1,085.46
2013	1,091.90	1,089.85	1,095.98	1,083.66	1,109.35	1,117.63	1,071.92	1,118.52	1,133.14	1,115.41	1,130.58	1,147.93	1,109.16
Education and Health Services													
2009	873.84	869.80	858.38	848.86	839.75	838.10	835.33	840.66	851.49	840.10	872.48	849.35	852.72
2010	866.58	867.56	865.93	867.53	881.34	887.44	888.43	892.45	888.78	920.50	890.27	925.15	885.72
2011	901.71	887.57	880.02	870.09	858.69	854.74	850.74	843.35	854.04	857.22	853.98	839.63	861.63
2012	833.98	827.51	817.05	817.74	814.52	809.62	801.27	793.55	802.11	839.63	797.17	825.46	816.06
2013	790.35	793.74	788.07	798.37	796.42	815.92	814.77	812.61	833.83	848.49	827.87	826.78	812.30
Leisure and Hospitality													
2009	358.40	365.75	345.78	362.47	374.44	404.29	406.91	405.42	402.96	415.80	398.50	365.65	384.00
2010	373.20	375.79	366.23	396.93	380.83	392.66	380.29	382.59	386.28	394.57	385.19	365.71	381.48
2011	367.32	370.47	362.44	353.54	371.67	368.94	385.00	388.61	374.45	395.82	369.98	365.51	373.74
2012	371.60	380.36	368.27	388.88	375.50	375.30	393.39	401.03	388.81	398.47	377.95	359.40	380.62
2013	371.11	378.92	375.06	361.75	382.93	386.02	391.64	396.46	390.72	404.24	379.76	368.20	382.26

VIRGINIA
At a Glance

Population:
    2000 census: 7,079,057
    2010 census: 8,001,024
    2013 estimate: 8,260,405

Percent change in population:
    2000–2010: 13.0%
    2010–2013: 3.2%

Percent change in total nonfarm employment:
    2000–2010: 3.8%
    2010–2013: 3.1%

Industry with the largest growth in employment, 2000–2013 (thousands):
    Education and Health Services, 164.8

Industry with the largest decline or smallest growth in employment, 2000–2013 (thousands):
    Manufacturing, -133.0

Civilian labor force:
    2000: 3,584,037
    2010: 4,139,160
    2013: 4,240,111

Unemployment rate and rank among states (lowest to highest):
    2000: 2.3%, 1st
    2010: 7.1%, 11th
    2013: 5.5%, 13th

Over-the-year change in unemployment rates:
    2010–2011: -0.7%
    2011–2012: -0.5%
    2012–2013: -0.5%

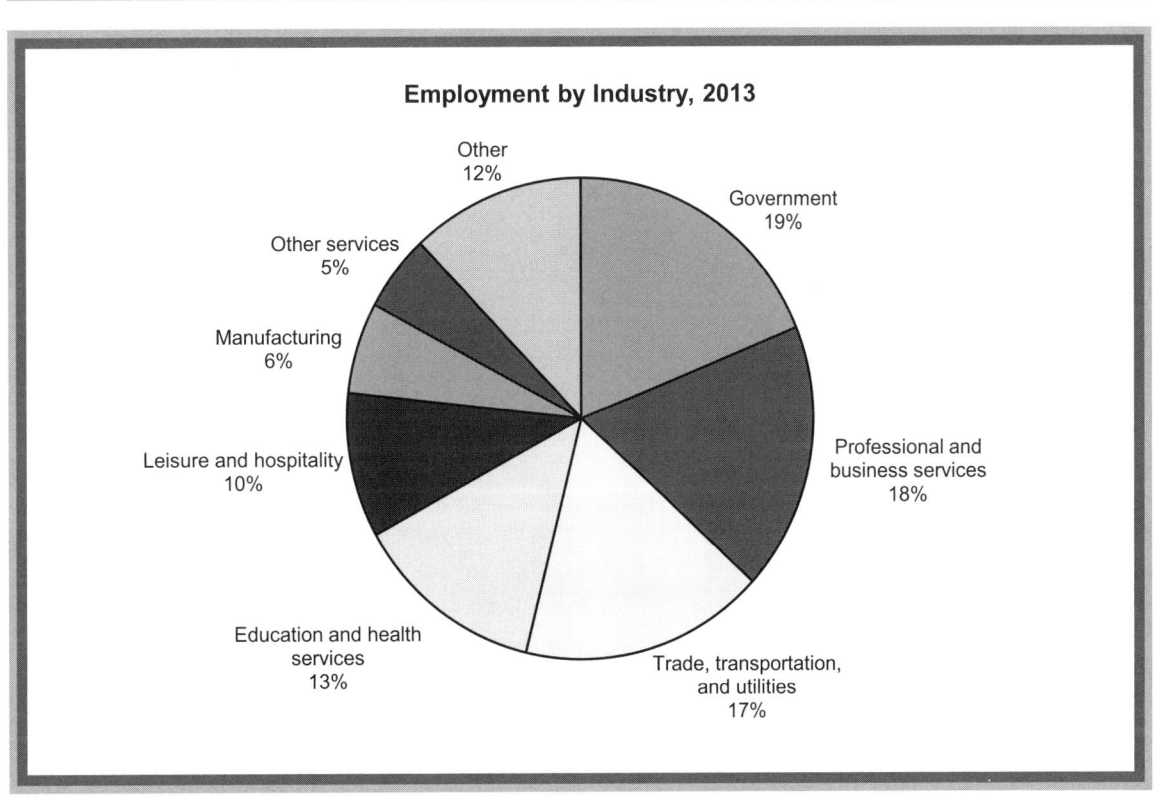

Employment by Industry, 2013

Other 12%
Government 19%
Other services 5%
Manufacturing 6%
Leisure and hospitality 10%
Professional and business services 18%
Education and health services 13%
Trade, transportation, and utilities 17%

1. Employment by Industry: Virginia, Selected Years, 2002–2013

(Numbers in thousands, not seasonally adjusted)

Industry and year	January	February	March	April	May	June	July	August	September	October	November	December	Annual average
Total Nonfarm													
2002	3,437.7	3,448.6	3,476.9	3,494.8	3,514.4	3,542.7	3,506.3	3,508.4	3,508.5	3,512.9	3,527.7	3,533.5	3,501.0
2003	3,442.7	3,439.4	3,464.5	3,480.4	3,506.3	3,532.8	3,505.7	3,512.2	3,517.0	3,531.7	3,553.0	3,562.6	3,504.0
2004	3,487.6	3,500.1	3,539.6	3,570.0	3,592.4	3,625.7	3,606.8	3,605.8	3,609.5	3,630.0	3,649.9	3,662.4	3,590.0
2005	3,575.9	3,591.3	3,616.9	3,653.5	3,674.2	3,704.0	3,685.5	3,686.3	3,703.4	3,699.9	3,721.9	3,730.8	3,670.3
2006	3,659.1	3,669.7	3,705.8	3,719.1	3,748.4	3,782.8	3,749.7	3,745.2	3,742.0	3,751.9	3,770.7	3,782.5	3,735.6
2007	3,707.2	3,713.1	3,744.5	3,760.6	3,785.3	3,816.3	3,785.1	3,777.4	3,780.7	3,787.6	3,806.0	3,810.2	3,772.8
2008	3,730.3	3,738.9	3,759.8	3,783.7	3,801.0	3,821.9	3,789.3	3,784.1	3,776.7	3,779.9	3,774.2	3,765.6	3,775.5
2009	3,652.4	3,641.2	3,647.8	3,657.6	3,676.1	3,689.0	3,643.5	3,634.4	3,634.7	3,647.5	3,658.2	3,655.5	3,653.2
2010	3,565.4	3,550.5	3,593.1	3,648.8	3,680.1	3,697.4	3,665.3	3,654.3	3,663.7	3,684.1	3,694.1	3,694.6	3,649.3
2011	3,614.0	3,631.9	3,658.6	3,694.6	3,699.7	3,719.3	3,703.3	3,696.4	3,718.0	3,725.9	3,742.8	3,736.5	3,695.1
2012	3,661.3	3,678.5	3,706.0	3,730.0	3,740.0	3,760.1	3,725.6	3,738.6	3,751.5	3,773.4	3,790.2	3,788.0	3,736.9
2013	3,700.1	3,719.4	3,740.0	3,768.6	3,776.0	3,789.6	3,765.3	3,768.0	3,772.8	3,784.1	3,797.0	3,785.3	3,763.9
Total Private													
2002	2,807.4	2,811.3	2,836.5	2,853.3	2,874.7	2,902.8	2,891.9	2,898.4	2,879.1	2,868.7	2,880.3	2,889.2	2,866.1
2003	2,808.8	2,799.3	2,822.8	2,837.3	2,865.1	2,890.4	2,890.4	2,900.9	2,880.6	2,888.2	2,901.0	2,913.4	2,866.5
2004	2,845.1	2,849.4	2,884.2	2,911.5	2,938.0	2,971.2	2,978.2	2,981.6	2,962.3	2,969.5	2,981.5	2,996.2	2,939.1
2005	2,922.0	2,930.0	2,952.8	2,983.1	3,006.0	3,036.5	3,045.3	3,051.2	3,042.1	3,030.2	3,045.0	3,057.1	3,008.4
2006	2,993.1	2,994.9	3,025.5	3,037.0	3,066.7	3,101.6	3,095.0	3,095.9	3,072.8	3,069.3	3,082.3	3,095.5	3,060.8
2007	3,028.1	3,025.3	3,055.2	3,069.0	3,096.7	3,129.3	3,123.1	3,122.5	3,103.4	3,099.6	3,109.2	3,116.9	3,089.9
2008	3,043.9	3,042.1	3,058.7	3,084.2	3,102.4	3,125.5	3,119.0	3,114.8	3,087.2	3,075.2	3,063.3	3,056.6	3,081.1
2009	2,956.2	2,937.3	2,939.6	2,947.2	2,967.2	2,982.5	2,972.8	2,965.5	2,941.3	2,940.4	2,942.4	2,945.0	2,953.1
2010	2,865.3	2,845.5	2,882.1	2,932.3	2,956.4	2,978.5	2,987.9	2,985.1	2,962.7	2,975.0	2,980.8	2,982.9	2,944.5
2011	2,910.3	2,916.0	2,939.3	2,974.3	2,984.9	3,007.3	3,023.3	3,020.2	3,007.7	3,005.2	3,016.8	3,011.7	2,984.8
2012	2,953.2	2,959.0	2,984.9	3,009.6	3,024.5	3,047.7	3,051.8	3,062.0	3,044.5	3,054.9	3,066.4	3,065.0	3,027.0
2013	2,994.2	3,001.2	3,020.6	3,046.7	3,058.5	3,078.4	3,083.2	3,090.4	3,066.4	3,066.4	3,074.4	3,066.0	3,053.9
Goods-Producing													
2002	539.1	538.5	542.5	544.4	547.9	551.4	546.9	550.1	547.5	545.6	543.4	541.2	544.9
2003	528.3	525.1	529.1	528.9	534.0	535.5	534.9	537.8	535.4	534.9	534.3	532.4	532.6
2004	522.6	522.4	529.6	536.0	539.8	545.8	546.4	547.5	546.9	547.5	546.9	547.0	539.9
2005	538.0	537.4	539.8	546.3	549.4	555.3	557.8	560.2	557.3	553.9	553.6	552.8	550.2
2006	543.1	543.0	547.4	549.9	553.7	558.6	554.9	554.9	548.8	543.6	540.4	539.2	548.1
2007	526.8	525.1	529.8	531.2	532.9	537.0	534.0	533.2	529.3	524.1	521.0	518.3	528.6
2008	504.5	500.1	500.4	505.0	504.4	506.5	504.8	503.2	498.7	493.7	486.3	478.9	498.9
2009	456.4	446.7	443.8	441.3	440.0	441.0	440.3	438.5	435.9	434.3	430.7	429.4	439.9
2010	414.1	407.8	415.2	424.5	428.1	429.3	431.6	430.5	429.0	428.0	425.8	423.0	423.9
2011	409.7	410.3	414.1	418.9	421.0	424.4	428.5	427.8	424.7	422.8	421.6	420.2	420.3
2012	411.4	410.8	414.6	416.4	418.3	421.7	424.9	424.5	422.7	421.5	420.3	419.5	418.9
2013	409.4	410.2	412.7	416.8	418.9	422.9	424.2	424.3	422.1	417.8	419.3	417.0	418.0
Service-Providing													
2002	2,898.6	2,910.1	2,934.4	2,950.4	2,966.5	2,991.3	2,959.4	2,958.3	2,961.0	2,967.3	2,984.3	2,992.3	2,956.2
2003	2,914.4	2,914.3	2,935.4	2,951.5	2,972.3	2,997.3	2,970.8	2,974.4	2,981.6	2,996.8	3,018.7	3,030.2	2,971.5
2004	2,965.0	2,977.7	3,010.0	3,034.0	3,052.6	3,079.9	3,060.4	3,058.3	3,062.6	3,082.5	3,103.0	3,115.4	3,050.1
2005	3,037.9	3,053.9	3,077.1	3,107.2	3,124.8	3,148.7	3,127.7	3,126.1	3,146.1	3,146.0	3,168.3	3,178.0	3,120.2
2006	3,116.0	3,126.7	3,158.4	3,169.2	3,194.7	3,224.2	3,194.8	3,190.3	3,193.2	3,208.3	3,230.3	3,243.3	3,187.5
2007	3,180.4	3,188.0	3,214.7	3,229.4	3,252.4	3,279.3	3,251.1	3,244.2	3,251.4	3,263.5	3,285.0	3,291.9	3,244.3
2008	3,225.8	3,238.8	3,259.4	3,278.7	3,296.6	3,315.4	3,284.5	3,280.9	3,278.0	3,286.2	3,287.9	3,286.7	3,276.6
2009	3,196.0	3,194.5	3,204.0	3,216.3	3,236.1	3,248.0	3,203.2	3,195.9	3,198.8	3,213.2	3,227.5	3,226.1	3,213.3
2010	3,151.3	3,142.7	3,177.9	3,224.3	3,252.0	3,268.1	3,233.7	3,223.8	3,234.7	3,256.1	3,268.3	3,271.6	3,225.4
2011	3,204.3	3,221.6	3,244.5	3,275.7	3,278.7	3,294.9	3,274.8	3,268.6	3,293.3	3,303.1	3,321.2	3,316.3	3,274.8
2012	3,249.9	3,267.7	3,291.4	3,313.6	3,321.7	3,338.4	3,300.7	3,314.1	3,328.8	3,351.9	3,369.9	3,368.5	3,318.1
2013	3,290.7	3,309.2	3,327.3	3,351.8	3,357.1	3,366.7	3,341.1	3,343.7	3,350.7	3,366.3	3,377.7	3,368.3	3,345.9
Mining and Logging													
2002	11.0	10.9	11.0	10.7	10.8	10.7	10.5	10.4	10.4	10.2	10.2	10.2	10.6
2003	10.0	9.9	10.1	9.9	10.1	10.2	10.2	10.2	10.1	10.2	10.2	10.3	10.1
2004	10.0	10.1	10.2	10.2	10.3	10.4	10.3	10.3	10.3	10.3	10.4	10.4	10.3
2005	10.4	10.4	10.1	10.3	10.4	10.8	10.9	10.9	10.9	10.9	11.0	11.1	10.7
2006	11.0	11.0	11.2	11.0	11.2	11.5	11.5	11.5	11.3	11.2	11.3	11.3	11.3
2007	11.3	11.2	11.4	10.7	10.8	10.8	11.0	11.0	10.6	10.7	10.6	10.8	10.9
2008	10.6	10.9	10.8	10.9	11.0	11.1	11.2	11.2	11.3	11.5	11.5	11.4	11.1
2009	10.8	10.5	10.4	10.2	10.1	10.1	10.0	10.1	10.1	10.2	10.2	10.2	10.2
2010	9.9	9.8	10.0	10.3	10.3	10.4	10.5	10.6	10.6	10.7	10.7	10.6	10.4
2011	10.7	10.6	10.7	10.7	10.8	10.9	11.0	11.1	11.2	11.1	11.2	11.2	10.9
2012	11.1	11.1	11.1	11.0	11.0	11.1	11.0	11.0	10.8	10.3	10.5	10.4	10.9
2013	10.2	10.1	10.1	10.2	10.2	10.2	10.0	10.0	9.9	10.0	10.1	9.9	10.1
Construction													
2002	205.0	206.0	210.0	213.0	216.4	218.9	219.7	220.5	217.7	216.5	214.5	212.9	214.3
2003	204.4	202.6	208.1	211.6	218.3	220.2	224.2	225.7	223.7	225.0	223.5	222.8	217.5
2004	215.3	215.4	221.4	227.3	231.4	235.6	238.6	238.0	236.7	237.6	237.0	236.6	230.9
2005	230.5	230.1	232.9	239.6	242.7	247.5	252.5	253.1	250.9	248.5	248.2	247.1	243.6
2006	240.8	241.7	246.8	248.5	252.1	256.0	254.8	254.0	251.1	247.9	246.0	245.3	248.8
2007	236.1	233.3	237.6	240.9	243.3	246.0	244.9	245.2	242.6	238.7	236.1	233.6	239.9
2008	223.7	222.0	223.9	226.2	226.8	228.6	228.3	227.1	223.8	220.4	214.9	209.6	222.9
2009	195.4	190.8	190.2	190.6	191.1	192.4	192.9	192.2	189.9	188.4	185.6	184.0	190.3
2010	173.9	168.6	175.5	184.1	186.4	187.6	190.2	189.4	187.9	186.4	185.0	181.7	183.1
2011	171.7	171.9	174.5	178.1	179.5	181.4	184.3	183.7	180.8	179.7	178.5	177.3	178.5
2012	169.7	169.0	172.3	174.8	177.1	180.4	181.4	181.0	179.2	179.2	177.9	176.9	176.6
2013	169.6	170.3	172.7	176.2	178.0	180.9	182.0	182.3	180.7	177.9	179.3	177.5	177.3

1. Employment by Industry: Virginia, Selected Years, 2002–2013—*Continued*

(Numbers in thousands, not seasonally adjusted)

Industry and year	January	February	March	April	May	June	July	August	September	October	November	December	Annual average
Manufacturing													
2002	323.1	321.6	321.5	320.7	320.7	321.8	316.7	319.2	319.4	318.9	318.7	318.1	320.0
2003	313.9	312.6	310.9	307.4	305.6	305.1	300.5	301.9	301.6	299.7	300.6	299.3	304.9
2004	297.3	296.9	298.0	298.5	298.1	299.8	297.5	299.2	299.9	299.6	299.5	300.0	298.7
2005	297.1	296.9	296.8	296.4	296.3	297.0	294.4	296.2	295.5	294.5	294.4	294.6	295.8
2006	291.3	290.3	289.4	290.4	290.4	291.1	288.6	289.4	286.4	284.5	283.1	282.6	288.1
2007	279.4	280.6	280.8	279.6	278.8	280.2	278.1	277.0	276.1	274.7	274.3	273.9	277.8
2008	270.2	267.2	265.7	267.9	266.6	266.8	265.3	264.9	263.6	261.8	259.9	257.9	264.8
2009	250.2	245.4	243.2	240.5	238.8	238.5	237.4	236.2	235.9	235.7	234.9	235.2	239.3
2010	230.3	229.4	229.7	230.1	231.4	231.3	230.9	230.5	230.5	230.9	230.1	230.7	230.5
2011	227.3	227.8	228.9	230.1	230.7	232.1	233.2	233.0	232.7	232.0	231.9	231.7	231.0
2012	230.6	230.7	231.2	230.6	230.2	230.2	232.5	232.5	232.7	232.0	231.9	232.2	231.4
2013	229.6	229.8	229.9	230.4	230.7	231.8	232.2	232.0	231.5	229.9	229.9	229.6	230.6
Trade, Transportation, and Utilities													
2002	632.9	623.7	625.5	626.3	630.8	636.2	634.6	636.3	634.8	639.2	652.9	663.7	636.4
2003	625.3	618.4	621.0	622.9	628.5	632.7	632.8	634.0	634.0	643.7	657.8	669.2	635.2
2004	635.8	630.2	633.3	636.0	641.4	646.4	646.3	647.6	644.4	652.5	666.4	676.5	646.4
2005	646.9	640.6	643.6	648.1	651.6	655.1	656.1	657.2	655.6	662.7	678.4	689.4	657.1
2006	659.2	648.1	653.4	652.9	659.0	663.6	660.3	661.0	658.1	665.9	682.0	692.1	663.0
2007	663.5	654.2	658.5	657.6	664.4	668.4	668.2	667.2	665.7	669.1	686.2	694.4	668.1
2008	663.4	653.3	655.3	654.2	658.0	661.5	660.0	659.4	655.7	654.8	663.8	669.7	659.1
2009	633.3	622.3	619.7	618.1	623.6	624.9	620.9	619.8	617.9	620.1	631.9	638.8	624.3
2010	611.2	601.0	607.0	614.2	620.3	623.6	622.6	623.6	618.6	625.9	638.2	647.3	621.1
2011	619.6	614.5	616.8	623.1	626.3	629.1	629.4	630.5	626.6	630.2	644.6	653.1	628.7
2012	626.8	619.9	623.9	625.7	631.5	633.2	631.0	631.2	629.1	636.3	652.4	660.8	633.5
2013	627.8	621.5	623.6	628.7	633.6	637.7	638.9	640.3	637.4	645.4	653.9	659.6	637.4
Wholesale Trade													
2002	112.4	112.2	112.6	112.8	113.0	113.4	112.8	113.0	112.6	112.7	113.1	113.5	112.8
2003	112.3	112.3	112.6	112.5	113.3	113.5	113.5	113.7	113.1	113.6	113.8	114.5	113.2
2004	113.0	113.1	113.9	114.1	114.4	115.1	115.5	115.2	114.5	115.2	115.4	115.9	114.6
2005	114.7	115.0	115.6	116.8	117.2	117.4	117.9	118.2	117.8	118.1	118.7	119.1	117.2
2006	117.4	117.8	118.5	119.1	119.7	120.5	119.9	120.1	119.8	120.5	120.8	121.2	119.6
2007	120.0	120.4	121.1	120.7	121.2	121.8	121.2	121.4	120.9	120.7	120.6	121.0	120.9
2008	119.6	119.7	119.7	120.0	120.4	120.6	120.3	120.1	119.2	119.0	118.1	117.6	119.5
2009	115.4	114.7	114.2	113.8	113.6	113.1	112.2	112.0	111.1	110.6	110.2	110.2	112.6
2010	107.9	107.6	108.2	109.5	110.0	110.2	110.7	110.9	110.5	111.2	111.5	111.7	110.0
2011	110.6	110.7	111.1	111.7	111.8	112.1	112.3	112.1	111.2	110.9	111.0	111.2	111.4
2012	110.0	110.3	110.9	111.1	111.7	112.1	112.0	112.2	111.7	111.7	111.8	111.8	111.4
2013	110.6	110.8	111.2	111.3	111.5	111.8	111.7	111.8	111.5	111.9	110.3	110.4	111.2
Retail Trade													
2002	402.8	394.7	396.1	396.4	400.1	403.6	401.6	402.8	402.2	405.3	418.1	428.6	404.4
2003	395.8	389.6	391.3	392.8	397.1	400.4	398.9	402.1	401.6	409.4	424.2	434.5	403.1
2004	407.6	401.7	403.5	405.1	409.3	412.6	410.7	411.5	409.2	415.5	428.9	437.0	412.7
2005	412.3	405.9	407.3	410.4	413.3	416.1	416.8	417.7	417.1	422.6	436.5	445.5	418.5
2006	422.2	412.9	416.6	415.8	420.6	423.1	421.2	421.5	418.6	425.3	440.7	447.6	423.8
2007	425.5	416.2	419.2	418.7	424.3	426.4	426.5	425.4	424.4	428.1	444.5	450.3	427.5
2008	425.9	415.8	418.1	415.8	418.5	421.0	420.0	419.2	417.1	417.4	426.7	431.5	420.6
2009	403.5	394.4	392.8	392.4	397.4	399.0	396.2	395.6	394.3	397.3	408.6	414.0	398.8
2010	393.1	383.8	388.5	393.3	398.0	400.0	398.3	398.9	394.4	400.0	410.9	417.9	398.1
2011	396.1	391.4	392.9	397.8	400.3	402.0	401.2	402.2	399.8	403.8	417.4	423.9	402.4
2012	403.4	395.9	399.3	400.0	403.9	404.5	402.4	402.3	400.9	407.6	423.2	429.0	406.0
2013	402.2	396.9	398.1	402.6	406.6	409.6	410.2	411.3	409.0	416.9	425.6	430.0	409.9
Transportation and Utilities													
2002	117.7	116.8	116.8	117.1	117.7	119.2	120.2	120.5	120.0	121.2	121.7	121.6	119.2
2003	117.2	116.5	117.1	117.6	118.1	118.8	120.4	120.2	119.3	120.7	119.8	120.2	118.8
2004	115.2	115.4	115.9	116.8	117.7	118.7	120.1	120.9	120.7	121.8	122.1	123.6	119.1
2005	119.9	119.7	120.7	120.9	121.1	121.6	121.4	121.3	120.7	122.0	123.2	124.8	121.4
2006	119.6	117.4	118.3	118.0	118.7	120.0	119.2	119.4	119.7	120.1	120.5	123.3	119.5
2007	118.0	117.6	118.2	118.2	118.9	120.2	120.5	120.4	120.4	120.3	121.1	123.1	119.7
2008	117.9	117.8	117.5	118.4	119.1	119.9	119.7	120.1	119.4	118.4	119.0	120.6	119.0
2009	114.4	113.2	112.7	111.9	112.6	112.8	112.5	112.2	112.5	112.2	113.1	114.6	112.9
2010	110.2	109.6	110.3	111.4	112.3	113.4	113.6	113.8	113.7	114.7	115.8	117.7	113.0
2011	112.9	112.4	112.8	113.6	114.2	115.0	115.9	116.2	115.6	115.5	116.2	118.0	114.9
2012	113.4	113.7	113.7	114.6	115.9	116.6	116.6	116.7	116.5	117.0	117.4	120.0	116.0
2013	115.0	113.8	114.3	114.8	115.5	116.3	117.0	117.2	116.9	116.6	118.0	119.2	116.2
Information													
2002	109.9	109.4	108.8	107.4	107.5	107.3	104.9	104.4	102.6	102.2	102.9	102.6	105.8
2003	101.3	101.6	101.5	100.7	101.2	102.2	102.2	101.8	100.9	100.5	101.3	101.5	101.4
2004	101.1	100.7	101.2	99.4	99.1	99.1	98.8	97.7	96.2	95.4	95.5	95.0	98.3
2005	93.5	93.4	93.4	93.0	93.0	93.3	92.9	92.6	91.8	91.6	91.9	92.0	92.7
2006	91.3	91.7	91.8	91.1	93.4	91.8	92.9	91.8	91.3	90.4	90.8	90.8	91.6
2007	91.9	91.3	90.7	90.5	91.0	90.9	90.3	89.8	89.7	89.6	89.7	89.5	90.4
2008	88.7	88.7	88.5	88.1	88.2	88.2	88.4	88.0	87.5	86.4	85.6	84.9	87.4
2009	84.0	83.8	83.1	82.1	81.9	81.8	81.1	80.1	79.1	79.0	78.7	78.5	81.1
2010	77.4	76.7	76.7	75.7	75.7	76.0	75.8	75.8	75.5	75.5	75.5	75.7	76.0
2011	74.7	74.5	74.6	74.0	74.2	74.4	74.8	70.1	73.5	72.7	73.3	74.1	73.7
2012	71.3	72.0	72.6	71.1	71.8	72.8	71.6	72.9	70.3	70.5	72.1	70.9	71.7
2013	70.3	72.1	72.0	71.1	71.1	71.3	71.3	72.4	70.1	70.6	70.0	70.3	71.1

1. Employment by Industry: Virginia, Selected Years, 2002–2013—*Continued*

(Numbers in thousands, not seasonally adjusted)

Industry and year	January	February	March	April	May	June	July	August	September	October	November	December	Annual average
Financial Activities													
2002	179.0	179.7	180.4	180.3	181.6	184.0	183.9	183.9	182.6	182.4	183.4	184.4	182.1
2003	182.6	183.3	184.2	184.9	186.4	188.9	190.0	190.3	188.1	186.3	185.6	186.7	186.4
2004	184.8	185.0	186.0	188.2	189.0	191.1	191.9	191.9	190.0	189.5	189.8	190.8	189.0
2005	188.7	189.4	189.9	191.2	192.2	194.5	195.9	195.9	194.2	192.3	192.1	193.5	192.5
2006	191.9	192.6	193.6	193.6	195.0	197.6	197.0	197.1	194.8	194.4	194.3	195.5	194.8
2007	193.7	193.9	194.7	194.0	195.1	196.6	196.0	195.1	193.0	191.3	190.2	190.3	193.7
2008	189.3	189.5	189.6	189.1	189.1	190.5	191.1	190.1	187.7	186.7	185.5	185.6	188.7
2009	182.1	181.1	181.1	181.0	180.6	181.6	181.0	180.8	178.4	177.4	177.0	177.5	180.0
2010	176.3	175.6	176.4	177.4	178.3	180.8	181.7	181.6	179.9	180.1	180.2	180.7	179.1
2011	178.4	178.6	179.0	180.9	182.0	183.7	185.4	185.4	184.2	183.8	184.2	185.3	182.6
2012	183.2	184.0	184.8	186.8	187.3	189.6	190.7	190.8	189.9	190.3	190.7	191.4	188.3
2013	189.2	189.7	190.4	191.1	191.8	193.4	194.4	194.1	192.4	193.3	193.0	192.8	192.1
Professional and Business Services													
2002	537.1	541.5	547.3	548.4	548.5	552.0	550.3	551.7	548.1	545.7	546.1	546.9	547.0
2003	535.9	535.9	541.4	544.3	545.7	549.9	550.4	554.8	552.8	557.9	560.5	562.6	549.3
2004	551.7	556.7	563.7	570.0	573.5	581.0	586.0	590.5	587.7	592.1	592.9	596.4	578.5
2005	584.8	590.4	595.1	599.4	600.7	607.0	612.8	615.8	616.5	616.1	616.3	618.7	606.1
2006	610.5	615.0	621.1	622.3	625.4	632.4	633.2	636.0	634.3	636.1	637.2	639.0	628.5
2007	628.4	631.9	638.2	642.1	643.6	650.6	650.9	653.7	649.9	655.0	655.3	656.4	646.3
2008	644.9	647.3	650.3	656.4	657.0	662.5	663.2	665.6	661.1	662.0	658.3	655.8	657.0
2009	640.3	639.0	639.2	638.0	636.7	639.7	639.5	640.8	636.9	642.4	644.6	643.7	640.1
2010	631.2	631.1	636.0	648.7	648.4	652.4	657.5	658.3	655.1	661.7	662.5	661.7	650.4
2011	652.7	655.3	659.5	665.5	663.9	666.2	672.6	674.7	673.7	675.3	677.2	673.1	667.5
2012	664.4	666.9	671.0	675.8	675.7	679.1	681.9	685.4	682.0	687.7	686.6	685.1	678.5
2013	674.2	677.1	679.4	683.3	681.5	683.7	681.6	683.8	677.1	674.0	674.9	668.1	678.2
Education and Health Services													
2002	360.0	364.3	366.3	368.0	367.7	367.3	365.5	366.8	371.0	374.4	376.6	376.9	368.7
2003	373.9	374.0	373.7	376.5	376.1	375.5	372.7	374.1	377.7	379.8	381.7	382.7	376.5
2004	380.7	383.4	387.3	386.9	387.4	386.1	384.5	385.1	388.1	392.0	394.1	395.4	387.6
2005	389.8	393.8	395.5	397.8	399.5	398.1	395.2	396.0	406.6	405.5	407.7	408.1	399.5
2006	405.4	408.8	411.2	411.1	412.9	413.7	412.7	412.3	417.9	420.2	423.0	424.1	414.4
2007	419.4	422.3	425.1	427.8	430.3	431.4	429.0	430.6	437.2	441.1	443.6	445.7	432.0
2008	440.8	446.9	448.2	452.8	453.6	452.4	448.0	448.7	454.6	458.1	459.3	459.9	451.9
2009	454.9	457.1	458.4	460.7	462.7	460.6	458.2	457.6	459.9	463.1	464.8	465.4	460.3
2010	459.5	459.3	463.3	466.8	468.0	465.1	467.4	466.3	469.2	476.3	477.8	476.4	468.0
2011	472.3	475.3	477.1	477.1	470.0	467.3	469.2	470.9	479.0	481.9	483.4	474.8	474.9
2012	479.1	482.4	484.2	486.1	478.3	476.9	476.9	482.6	490.5	495.6	496.9	491.0	485.0
2013	492.0	496.1	498.3	498.9	491.9	488.0	487.6	492.6	499.6	504.1	507.6	508.0	497.1
Leisure and Hospitality													
2002	275.8	279.2	289.3	301.5	312.3	324.5	326.4	326.2	314.4	302.7	298.5	296.2	303.9
2003	283.5	282.7	292.0	303.2	316.9	328.4	330.4	329.7	316.7	310.2	304.8	303.0	308.5
2004	292.4	294.4	304.8	316.3	328.3	340.4	341.9	340.4	329.6	321.0	316.2	314.9	320.1
2005	302.3	305.9	315.6	326.2	337.6	349.9	350.8	350.6	338.4	328.1	324.9	322.2	329.4
2006	313.2	316.7	326.7	335.3	345.4	360.2	360.4	359.4	345.7	336.8	332.7	332.3	338.7
2007	322.3	323.9	333.7	341.0	353.3	367.0	367.2	366.3	353.1	343.2	337.0	335.4	345.3
2008	327.2	329.7	339.2	349.7	362.1	372.7	372.9	369.6	354.3	344.6	336.2	333.6	349.3
2009	320.2	321.9	328.4	339.7	355.0	364.9	364.0	361.1	348.3	339.0	330.3	327.2	341.7
2010	313.3	312.5	323.8	339.8	351.6	364.2	364.5	363.0	351.2	342.7	336.4	334.0	341.4
2011	319.9	323.5	333.0	346.9	359.2	371.8	372.0	370.7	357.4	350.0	344.0	342.4	349.2
2012	330.2	335.2	344.8	355.2	368.3	379.5	379.3	380.4	367.2	359.4	354.2	353.3	358.9
2013	340.4	342.9	351.7	363.6	375.6	385.7	388.2	387.2	373.8	367.1	361.5	356.2	366.2
Other Services													
2002	173.6	175.0	176.4	177.0	178.4	180.1	179.4	179.0	178.1	176.5	176.5	177.3	177.3
2003	178.0	178.3	179.9	175.9	176.3	177.3	177.0	176.4	175.0	174.9	175.0	175.3	176.6
2004	176.0	176.6	178.3	178.7	179.5	181.3	182.4	180.9	179.4	179.5	179.7	180.2	179.4
2005	178.0	179.1	179.9	181.1	182.0	183.3	183.8	182.9	181.7	180.0	180.1	180.4	181.0
2006	178.5	179.0	180.3	180.8	181.9	183.7	183.6	183.4	181.9	181.9	181.9	182.5	181.6
2007	182.1	182.7	184.5	184.8	186.1	187.4	187.5	186.6	185.5	186.2	186.2	186.9	185.5
2008	185.1	186.6	187.2	188.9	190.0	191.0	191.0	190.7	188.7	189.7	188.5	188.2	188.8
2009	185.0	185.4	185.9	186.3	186.7	188.0	187.8	186.8	184.9	185.1	184.4	184.5	185.9
2010	182.3	181.5	183.7	185.2	186.0	187.1	186.8	186.0	184.2	184.8	184.4	184.1	184.7
2011	183.0	184.0	185.2	187.9	188.3	190.4	191.4	190.1	188.6	188.5	188.5	188.7	187.9
2012	186.8	187.8	189.0	192.5	193.3	194.9	195.5	194.2	192.8	193.6	193.2	193.0	192.2
2013	190.9	191.6	192.5	193.2	194.1	195.7	197.0	195.7	193.9	194.1	194.2	194.0	193.9
Government													
2002	630.3	637.3	640.4	641.5	639.7	639.9	614.4	610.0	629.4	644.2	647.4	644.3	634.9
2003	633.9	640.1	641.7	643.1	641.2	642.4	615.3	611.3	636.4	643.5	652.0	649.2	637.5
2004	642.5	650.7	655.4	658.5	654.4	654.5	628.6	624.2	647.2	660.5	668.4	666.2	650.9
2005	653.9	661.3	664.1	670.4	668.2	667.5	640.2	635.1	661.3	669.7	676.9	673.7	661.9
2006	666.0	674.8	680.3	682.1	681.7	681.2	654.7	649.3	669.2	682.6	688.4	687.0	674.8
2007	679.1	687.8	689.3	691.6	688.6	687.0	662.0	654.9	677.3	688.0	696.8	693.3	683.0
2008	686.4	696.8	701.1	699.5	698.6	696.4	670.3	669.3	689.5	704.7	710.9	709.0	694.4
2009	696.2	703.9	708.2	710.4	708.9	706.5	670.7	668.9	693.4	707.1	715.8	710.5	700.0
2010	700.1	705.0	711.0	716.5	723.7	718.9	677.4	669.2	701.0	709.1	713.3	711.7	704.7
2011	703.7	715.9	719.3	720.3	714.8	712.0	680.0	676.2	710.3	720.7	726.0	724.8	710.3
2012	708.1	719.5	721.1	720.4	715.5	712.4	673.8	676.6	707.0	718.5	723.8	723.0	710.0
2013	705.9	718.2	719.4	721.9	717.5	711.2	682.1	677.6	706.4	717.7	722.6	719.3	710.0

2. Average Weekly Hours by Selected Industry: Virginia, 2009–2013

(Not seasonally adjusted)

Industry and year	January	February	March	April	May	June	July	August	September	October	November	December	Annual average
Total Private													
2009	34.6	34.7	34.6	34.3	34.5	34.3	34.5	35.1	34.3	34.8	35.0	34.6	34.6
2010	34.4	34.0	35.1	35.6	36.1	35.5	35.5	36.0	35.5	35.5	35.6	35.6	35.4
2011	35.8	35.3	35.2	35.5	35.9	35.5	35.6	35.5	35.3	35.5	34.9	35.0	35.4
2012	35.0	34.8	34.9	35.2	34.7	35.0	35.2	35.1	35.4	34.7	34.8	35.3	35.0
2013	34.1	34.5	34.5	34.7	34.6	34.9	34.5	34.6	34.9	33.9	34.3	34.6	34.5
Goods-Producing													
2009	38.3	38.7	37.9	38.5	38.5	39.1	39.6	39.5	38.6	39.7	39.5	39.4	38.9
2010	38.7	36.8	38.7	39.8	40.0	39.8	39.2	39.7	39.9	40.4	40.7	39.7	39.5
2011	39.0	39.0	39.2	39.9	40.6	40.4	39.5	39.6	39.6	38.6	39.7	39.5	39.6
2012	38.1	38.2	39.2	39.7	39.1	39.5	39.0	39.7	40.2	39.7	39.5	40.0	39.3
2013	38.2	38.5	38.4	39.3	39.3	38.7	39.0	40.1	40.2	38.4	40.3	38.5	39.1
Construction													
2009	37.5	37.6	37.1	37.5	37.5	37.9	38.6	38.7	37.2	37.7	36.4	37.4	37.6
2010	37.1	35.0	37.0	39.2	38.7	38.8	38.2	38.8	38.7	38.6	39.7	38.2	38.2
2011	37.2	37.9	37.1	38.5	39.7	39.5	39.3	39.0	38.9	37.9	39.5	39.1	38.6
2012	37.1	36.8	38.2	39.2	38.3	38.6	38.4	39.1	39.9	39.2	39.0	39.4	38.6
2013	37.2	37.3	37.1	38.9	38.5	38.1	38.1	39.6	39.9	37.1	40.1	37.4	38.3
Manufacturing													
2009	37.8	38.6	38.0	38.8	38.9	39.8	40.3	40.0	39.4	40.2	40.3	40.8	39.4
2010	39.7	38.1	40.0	40.1	41.1	40.7	40.4	40.7	40.6	41.6	41.2	40.4	40.4
2011	40.2	39.6	40.8	40.7	41.0	40.9	39.2	39.7	39.9	39.1	39.7	39.7	40.0
2012	38.9	39.2	39.8	39.8	39.4	40.0	39.2	39.9	40.2	39.9	39.8	40.4	39.7
2013	39.2	39.7	39.8	39.7	40.2	39.5	40.1	40.7	40.9	40.1	40.6	40.8	40.1
Trade, Transportation, and Utilities													
2009	33.9	34.7	34.7	34.4	34.5	34.2	34.4	34.8	34.9	35.1	34.9	34.8	34.6
2010	34.6	34.4	34.5	35.0	34.7	34.4	34.7	34.6	34.1	34.2	33.4	34.1	34.4
2011	33.4	33.1	33.2	34.1	34.3	34.6	34.9	34.7	34.7	34.9	34.4	34.9	34.3
2012	34.1	34.2	34.2	34.7	34.3	34.7	34.8	34.6	35.0	34.2	34.5	34.8	34.5
2013	33.6	34.1	34.1	34.2	34.3	34.5	34.6	34.6	34.9	33.8	33.9	34.3	34.2
Financial Activities													
2009	35.5	35.9	35.9	34.6	34.8	35.5	35.9	36.9	36.2	36.3	37.2	36.0	35.9
2010	36.7	36.5	36.7	36.6	38.0	37.1	37.1	38.1	37.2	37.2	37.3	37.3	37.2
2011	39.7	39.3	38.3	38.7	39.5	37.9	38.5	37.9	38.3	39.4	38.0	38.3	38.6
2012	39.4	38.3	37.8	38.7	38.3	38.6	39.4	38.6	40.0	38.8	38.9	40.2	38.9
2013	38.6	38.6	38.6	38.1	37.7	38.7	37.5	37.4	37.4	36.7	36.8	37.5	37.8
Professional and Business Services													
2009	37.5	38.2	38.1	37.8	37.8	36.8	36.7	37.7	36.7	37.2	37.6	36.9	37.4
2010	36.9	36.6	37.2	37.5	38.1	37.1	36.9	38.0	36.9	36.7	37.0	36.8	37.1
2011	38.1	37.6	37.4	37.7	38.1	37.2	37.1	37.1	37.3	37.2	35.6	36.0	37.2
2012	36.9	36.6	36.6	36.6	35.7	36.0	36.5	36.3	36.9	35.6	35.9	36.7	36.4
2013	35.7	36.3	36.2	36.2	36.2	37.3	36.4	36.3	36.9	35.4	35.9	36.9	36.3
Education and Health Services													
2009	33.6	33.6	33.8	33.6	33.7	33.6	33.2	33.6	33.3	33.5	33.8	33.9	33.6
2010	33.8	34.2	34.1	34.2	34.2	33.9	34.2	34.7	34.2	34.2	34.2	34.3	34.2
2011	35.1	34.3	34.3	34.4	34.8	34.9	35.1	35.1	34.9	35.3	34.8	34.7	34.8
2012	35.0	34.4	34.8	34.9	34.8	35.1	35.1	34.8	35.1	34.7	34.4	34.7	34.8
2013	34.1	34.0	34.0	33.9	33.9	34.2	33.9	33.8	34.1	33.8	33.8	34.1	34.0
Leisure and Hospitality													
2009	25.4	26.3	26.1	25.9	25.9	25.8	26.3	26.1	25.6	25.8	26.1	25.5	25.9
2010	25.6	25.1	26.1	26.8	26.7	27.3	28.7	28.3	27.5	27.6	27.3	26.6	27.0
2011	26.6	26.3	26.2	26.3	26.4	26.1	27.2	26.7	26.1	26.6	26.3	26.0	26.4
2012	25.8	25.7	26.1	26.8	26.7	27.6	27.8	27.6	27.2	27.6	27.6	27.5	27.0
2013	26.6	27.1	27.0	27.5	27.1	27.1	26.7	26.5	26.1	25.9	26.0	25.9	26.6
Other Services													
2009	33.2	33.1	32.7	32.4	32.5	32.8	33.5	33.8	33.4	33.5	33.4	32.4	33.1
2010	31.9	30.9	32.2	32.4	32.9	32.4	31.8	32.2	32.6	31.9	32.6	31.8	32.1
2011	32.1	31.8	32.2	32.1	32.9	32.3	32.3	31.8	32.4	33.8	31.8	31.4	32.2
2012	31.7	31.7	31.5	32.7	32.0	32.0	33.0	32.3	33.3	31.6	31.7	32.4	32.2
2013	31.4	32.1	31.9	32.7	32.4	32.6	32.4	31.5	32.7	31.7	31.4	32.8	32.1

3. Average Hourly Earnings by Selected Industry: Virginia, 2009–2013

(Dollars, not seasonally adjusted)

Industry and year	January	February	March	April	May	June	July	August	September	October	November	December	Annual average
Total Private													
2009	22.19	22.24	22.46	22.17	22.20	22.38	22.42	22.72	22.62	22.86	23.31	23.39	22.58
2010	23.54	23.97	23.42	23.24	23.63	22.89	23.05	23.52	23.58	23.68	23.73	24.33	23.55
2011	24.46	24.54	24.36	24.49	24.53	24.32	24.47	24.39	24.72	25.39	25.10	25.12	24.66
2012	25.17	25.09	25.03	25.30	24.86	24.66	24.99	24.56	25.09	24.79	24.77	25.49	24.98
2013	25.14	25.08	25.25	25.05	25.04	25.28	24.96	24.98	25.50	25.25	25.32	25.90	25.23
Goods-Producing													
2009	20.54	20.53	20.97	20.78	20.79	20.94	20.82	21.01	20.90	20.91	21.12	21.08	20.86
2010	21.19	21.61	21.28	21.04	21.01	21.01	21.18	21.11	21.05	21.15	21.20	21.64	21.20
2011	21.58	21.50	21.47	21.68	21.77	21.66	21.80	21.75	21.79	22.01	22.04	22.11	21.76
2012	22.19	22.01	21.73	21.86	22.03	21.94	22.16	21.85	22.06	22.09	22.42	22.69	22.09
2013	22.34	22.49	22.82	22.60	22.56	22.90	22.79	22.73	22.77	22.84	22.76	23.11	22.73
Construction													
2009	20.94	20.89	21.33	21.30	21.30	21.29	21.11	21.54	21.60	21.64	21.81	21.98	21.39
2010	22.08	22.64	21.99	21.54	21.58	21.38	21.63	21.55	21.43	21.96	21.60	22.15	21.77
2011	22.06	22.00	22.06	22.19	22.04	21.93	22.18	22.13	22.23	22.62	22.53	22.42	22.20
2012	22.29	22.41	22.17	21.99	22.16	22.25	22.48	22.06	22.41	22.48	22.95	23.15	22.40
2013	22.71	23.14	23.56	23.35	23.43	23.55	23.64	23.89	23.88	23.94	23.57	24.39	23.60
Manufacturing													
2009	19.91	20.02	20.26	20.03	20.11	20.32	20.46	20.38	20.37	20.35	20.68	20.92	20.32
2010	20.94	21.21	20.97	20.84	20.77	20.86	21.01	20.85	20.90	20.51	20.89	21.24	20.91
2011	21.17	20.99	20.93	21.19	21.55	21.64	22.31	22.13	22.06	21.99	22.10	22.30	21.70
2012	22.54	22.06	21.64	22.01	22.15	21.84	22.04	21.80	21.85	21.79	21.96	22.32	22.00
2013	22.03	21.87	22.10	21.80	21.63	22.12	21.88	21.44	21.44	21.62	21.77	21.81	21.79
Trade, Transportation, and Utilities													
2009	19.24	19.67	19.53	18.64	18.81	18.87	19.03	19.34	19.61	19.08	19.45	19.32	19.22
2010	19.86	20.03	19.53	19.69	19.58	19.28	19.57	19.68	19.68	19.78	19.88	20.27	19.74
2011	20.56	20.56	20.48	20.73	20.57	20.77	20.85	20.58	20.44	20.70	20.60	20.11	20.58
2012	20.27	19.90	19.72	20.00	19.43	19.90	20.24	19.66	20.31	19.81	19.67	20.13	19.92
2013	20.07	19.76	19.72	19.68	19.76	20.16	19.72	19.92	19.97	19.90	19.82	20.02	19.88
Financial Activities													
2009	21.03	21.44	21.32	21.65	21.71	21.91	21.76	21.96	21.42	22.63	22.45	22.97	21.85
2010	22.99	23.45	23.31	25.45	25.89	24.68	24.76	24.95	25.58	25.96	25.64	25.96	24.90
2011	24.55	25.05	24.91	26.07	25.35	25.59	25.83	25.37	26.56	27.72	27.56	26.90	25.96
2012	25.90	26.01	26.41	26.42	26.18	25.99	26.11	26.09	26.43	26.21	26.36	26.34	26.21
2013	26.15	26.55	26.91	27.21	26.72	26.65	27.22	26.82	27.04	26.54	26.56	27.24	26.80
Professional and Business Services													
2009	33.03	33.74	33.70	33.68	33.38	33.69	33.73	33.44	33.49	33.51	33.78	33.62	33.57
2010	33.71	34.10	33.45	33.60	34.09	33.37	33.41	33.91	33.54	33.60	33.79	34.20	33.73
2011	34.36	34.52	34.19	33.79	34.17	33.45	33.80	33.81	33.58	34.84	34.60	35.08	34.18
2012	35.29	35.53	35.45	36.18	35.31	35.05	35.51	34.96	35.58	35.30	35.08	36.10	35.45
2013	35.29	35.06	35.42	35.20	34.81	34.89	34.12	34.07	34.92	34.49	34.49	35.46	34.85
Education and Health Services													
2009	20.35	20.58	20.65	20.62	20.43	20.25	20.48	20.57	20.87	20.93	21.14	21.14	20.67
2010	20.96	21.15	21.13	21.39	21.44	21.25	21.53	21.46	21.56	21.65	21.60	21.72	21.41
2011	21.42	21.93	21.76	22.10	22.47	22.45	23.00	22.99	23.44	23.82	23.94	23.96	22.78
2012	23.08	23.28	23.48	23.88	23.65	23.49	23.74	23.60	24.22	23.86	23.62	23.86	23.65
2013	23.66	23.84	24.49	24.04	24.47	24.62	24.57	24.59	24.91	24.35	24.52	24.92	24.42
Leisure and Hospitality													
2009	12.04	11.86	11.95	12.09	12.17	12.15	11.83	12.14	12.40	12.55	12.66	12.70	12.21
2010	12.79	13.02	13.15	12.94	12.82	13.41	13.06	12.98	13.35	13.50	13.46	13.58	13.18
2011	13.36	13.34	13.19	13.31	13.04	12.87	12.62	12.62	13.06	13.00	12.99	13.08	13.03
2012	13.02	12.99	12.85	12.76	12.83	12.43	12.37	12.44	12.80	12.76	12.89	13.18	12.76
2013	12.98	12.95	12.84	12.72	12.79	12.78	12.74	12.76	12.90	12.98	13.02	13.22	12.88
Other Services													
2009	21.51	21.41	21.60	21.66	21.66	21.50	21.60	21.67	21.66	21.47	21.69	21.60	21.59
2010	21.79	22.24	21.92	22.24	22.43	22.42	22.54	22.70	22.55	22.42	22.83	23.03	22.43
2011	23.48	23.62	23.39	24.10	24.15	24.07	24.36	24.48	24.38	25.37	24.20	25.35	24.25
2012	24.86	24.89	24.81	25.50	25.01	25.23	25.41	25.35	25.93	25.02	25.27	26.21	25.30
2013	25.43	25.63	26.00	25.24	25.41	25.39	24.95	24.74	25.78	25.51	26.14	25.90	25.51

4. Average Weekly Earnings by Selected Industry: Virginia, 2009–2013

(Dollars, not seasonally adjusted)

Industry and year	January	February	March	April	May	June	July	August	September	October	November	December	Annual average
Total Private													
2009	767.77	771.73	777.12	760.43	765.90	767.63	773.49	797.47	775.87	795.53	815.85	809.29	781.27
2010	809.78	814.98	822.04	827.34	853.04	812.60	818.28	846.72	837.09	840.64	844.79	866.15	833.67
2011	875.67	866.26	857.47	869.40	880.63	863.36	871.13	865.85	872.62	901.35	875.99	879.20	872.96
2012	880.95	873.13	873.55	890.56	862.64	863.10	879.65	862.06	888.19	860.21	862.00	899.80	874.30
2013	857.27	865.26	871.13	869.24	866.38	882.27	861.12	864.31	889.95	855.98	868.48	896.14	870.44
Goods-Producing													
2009	786.68	794.51	794.76	800.03	800.42	818.75	824.47	829.90	806.74	830.13	834.24	830.55	811.45
2010	820.05	795.25	823.54	837.39	840.40	836.20	830.26	838.07	839.90	854.46	862.84	859.11	837.40
2011	841.62	838.50	841.62	865.03	883.86	875.06	861.10	861.30	862.88	849.59	874.99	873.35	861.70
2012	845.44	840.78	851.82	867.84	861.37	866.63	864.24	867.45	886.81	876.97	885.59	907.60	868.14
2013	853.39	865.87	876.29	888.18	886.61	886.23	888.81	911.47	915.35	877.06	917.23	889.74	888.74
Construction													
2009	785.25	785.46	791.34	798.75	798.75	806.89	814.85	833.60	803.52	815.83	793.88	822.05	804.26
2010	819.17	792.40	813.63	844.37	835.15	829.54	826.27	836.14	829.34	847.66	857.52	846.13	831.61
2011	820.63	833.80	818.43	854.32	874.99	866.24	871.67	863.07	864.75	857.30	889.94	876.62	856.92
2012	826.96	824.69	846.89	862.01	848.73	858.85	863.23	862.55	894.16	881.22	895.05	912.11	864.64
2013	844.81	863.12	874.08	908.32	902.06	897.26	900.68	946.04	952.81	888.17	945.16	912.19	903.88
Manufacturing													
2009	752.60	772.77	769.88	777.16	782.28	808.74	824.54	815.20	802.58	818.07	833.40	853.54	800.61
2010	831.32	808.10	838.80	835.68	853.65	849.00	848.80	848.60	848.54	853.22	860.67	858.10	844.76
2011	851.03	831.20	853.94	862.43	883.55	885.08	874.55	878.56	880.19	859.81	877.37	885.31	868.00
2012	876.81	864.75	861.27	876.00	872.71	873.60	863.97	869.82	878.37	869.42	874.01	901.73	873.40
2013	863.58	868.24	879.58	865.46	869.53	873.74	877.39	872.61	876.90	866.96	883.86	889.85	873.78
Trade, Transportation, and Utilities													
2009	652.24	682.55	677.69	641.22	648.95	645.35	654.63	673.03	684.39	669.71	678.81	672.34	665.01
2010	687.16	689.03	673.79	689.15	679.43	663.23	679.08	680.93	671.09	676.48	663.99	691.21	679.06
2011	686.70	680.54	679.94	706.89	705.55	718.64	727.67	714.13	709.27	722.43	708.64	701.84	705.89
2012	691.21	680.58	674.42	694.00	666.45	690.53	704.35	680.24	710.85	677.50	678.62	700.52	687.24
2013	674.35	673.82	672.45	673.06	677.77	695.52	682.31	689.23	696.95	672.62	671.90	686.69	679.90
Financial Activities													
2009	746.57	769.70	765.39	749.09	755.51	777.81	781.18	810.32	775.40	821.47	835.14	826.92	784.42
2010	843.73	855.93	855.48	931.47	983.82	915.63	918.60	950.60	951.58	965.71	956.37	968.31	926.28
2011	974.64	984.47	954.05	1,008.91	1,001.33	969.86	994.46	961.52	1,017.25	1,092.17	1,047.28	1,030.27	1,002.06
2012	1,020.46	996.18	998.30	1,022.45	1,002.69	1,003.21	1,028.73	1,007.07	1,057.20	1,016.95	1,025.40	1,058.87	1,019.57
2013	1,009.39	1,024.83	1,038.73	1,036.70	1,007.34	1,031.36	1,020.75	1,003.07	1,011.30	974.02	977.41	1,021.50	1,013.04
Professional and Business Services													
2009	1,238.63	1,288.87	1,283.97	1,273.10	1,261.76	1,239.79	1,237.89	1,260.69	1,229.08	1,246.57	1,270.13	1,240.58	1,255.52
2010	1,243.90	1,248.06	1,244.34	1,260.00	1,298.83	1,238.03	1,232.83	1,288.58	1,237.63	1,233.12	1,250.23	1,258.56	1,251.38
2011	1,309.12	1,297.95	1,278.71	1,273.88	1,301.88	1,244.34	1,253.98	1,254.35	1,252.53	1,296.05	1,231.76	1,262.88	1,271.50
2012	1,302.20	1,300.40	1,297.47	1,324.19	1,260.57	1,261.80	1,296.12	1,269.05	1,312.90	1,256.68	1,259.37	1,324.87	1,290.38
2013	1,259.85	1,272.68	1,282.20	1,274.24	1,260.12	1,301.40	1,241.97	1,236.74	1,288.55	1,220.95	1,238.19	1,308.47	1,265.06
Education and Health Services													
2009	683.76	691.49	697.97	692.83	688.49	680.40	679.94	691.15	694.97	701.16	714.53	716.65	694.51
2010	708.45	723.33	720.53	731.54	733.25	720.38	736.33	744.66	737.35	740.43	738.72	745.00	732.22
2011	751.84	752.20	746.37	760.24	781.96	783.51	807.30	806.95	818.06	840.85	833.11	831.41	792.74
2012	807.80	800.83	817.10	833.41	823.02	824.50	833.27	821.28	850.12	827.94	812.53	827.94	823.02
2013	806.81	810.56	832.66	814.96	829.53	842.00	832.92	831.14	849.43	823.03	828.78	849.77	830.28
Leisure and Hospitality													
2009	305.82	311.92	311.90	313.13	315.20	313.47	311.13	316.85	317.44	323.79	330.43	323.85	316.24
2010	327.42	326.80	343.22	346.79	342.29	366.09	374.82	367.33	367.13	372.60	367.46	361.23	355.86
2011	355.38	350.84	345.58	350.05	344.26	335.91	343.26	336.95	340.87	345.80	341.64	340.08	343.99
2012	335.92	333.84	335.39	341.97	342.56	343.07	343.89	343.34	348.16	352.18	355.76	362.45	344.52
2013	345.27	350.95	346.68	349.80	346.61	346.34	340.16	338.14	336.69	336.18	338.52	342.40	342.61
Other Services													
2009	714.13	708.67	706.32	701.78	703.95	705.20	723.60	732.45	723.44	719.25	724.45	699.84	714.63
2010	695.10	687.22	705.82	720.58	737.95	726.41	716.77	730.94	735.13	715.20	744.26	732.35	720.00
2011	753.71	751.12	753.16	773.61	794.54	777.46	786.83	778.46	789.91	857.51	769.56	795.99	780.85
2012	788.06	789.01	781.52	833.85	800.32	807.36	838.53	818.81	863.47	790.63	801.06	849.20	814.66
2013	798.50	822.72	829.40	825.35	823.28	827.71	808.38	779.31	843.01	808.67	820.80	849.52	818.87

WASHINGTON
At a Glance

Population:
    2000 census: 5,894,281
    2010 census: 6,724,540
    2013 estimate: 6,971,406

Percent change in population:
    2000–2010: 14.1%
    2010–2013: 3.7%

Percent change in total nonfarm employment:
    2000–2010: 4.6%
    2010–2013: 5.3%

Industry with the largest growth in employment, 2000–2013 (thousands):
    Education and Health Services, 146.8

Industry with the largest decline or smallest growth in employment, 2000–2013 (thousands):
    Manufacturing, -45.7

Civilian labor force:
    2000: 3,050,021
    2010: 3,515,195
    2013: 3,461,123

Unemployment rate and rank among states (lowest to highest):
    2000: 5.0%, 48th
    2010: 9.9%, 34th
    2013: 7.0%, 28th

Over-the-year change in unemployment rates:
    2010–2011: -0.7%
    2011–2012: -1.1%
    2012–2013: -1.1%

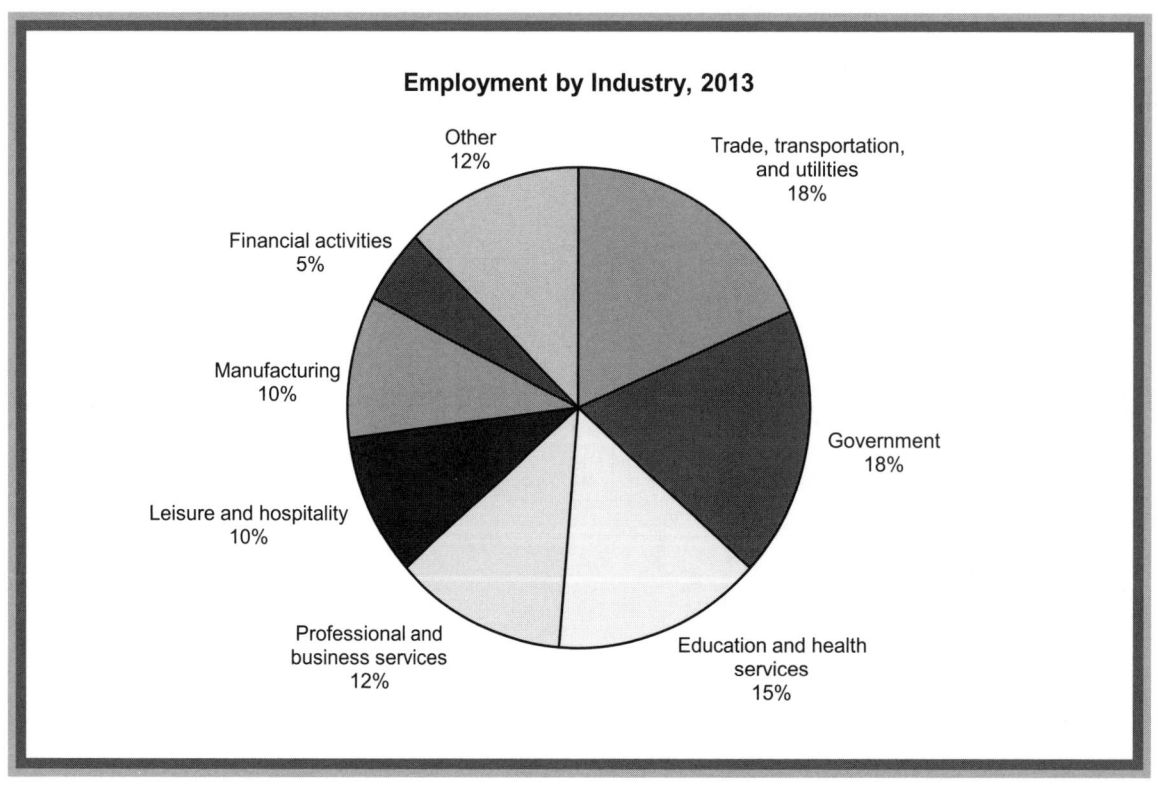

Employment by Industry, 2013

- Other 12%
- Trade, transportation, and utilities 18%
- Financial activities 5%
- Government 18%
- Manufacturing 10%
- Education and health services 15%
- Leisure and hospitality 10%
- Professional and business services 12%

1. Employment by Industry: Washington, Selected Years, 2002–2013

(Numbers in thousands, not seasonally adjusted)

Industry and year	January	February	March	April	May	June	July	August	September	October	November	December	Annual average
Total Nonfarm													
2002	2,644.4	2,649.3	2,661.0	2,675.5	2,701.8	2,717.7	2,699.6	2,698.8	2,713.5	2,717.7	2,723.3	2,710.1	2,692.7
2003	2,650.7	2,660.7	2,667.9	2,682.0	2,707.7	2,723.1	2,703.6	2,703.1	2,720.5	2,728.7	2,731.1	2,726.6	2,700.5
2004	2,654.1	2,672.9	2,698.1	2,720.3	2,742.4	2,764.7	2,747.8	2,742.7	2,762.4	2,780.7	2,789.3	2,784.8	2,738.4
2005	2,723.0	2,738.6	2,763.9	2,789.2	2,814.2	2,834.5	2,821.2	2,821.3	2,834.3	2,854.5	2,868.3	2,869.1	2,811.0
2006	2,809.7	2,830.2	2,850.9	2,866.5	2,896.5	2,927.5	2,897.2	2,901.3	2,928.0	2,930.9	2,940.3	2,936.9	2,893.0
2007	2,877.5	2,908.0	2,925.8	2,944.0	2,973.4	2,999.7	2,978.1	2,979.2	2,994.8	3,005.1	3,018.9	3,009.5	2,967.8
2008	2,951.2	2,971.0	2,983.4	2,994.4	3,015.8	3,028.4	3,013.4	3,009.5	3,015.1	2,990.1	2,993.8	2,960.7	2,993.9
2009	2,886.6	2,880.2	2,871.9	2,868.1	2,881.6	2,881.7	2,858.3	2,837.5	2,851.3	2,860.3	2,850.3	2,833.5	2,863.4
2010	2,778.5	2,786.4	2,803.2	2,828.3	2,854.7	2,860.5	2,848.2	2,830.3	2,849.9	2,872.7	2,871.7	2,860.2	2,837.1
2011	2,808.5	2,821.3	2,833.3	2,864.1	2,881.3	2,894.4	2,889.7	2,879.1	2,896.6	2,906.9	2,909.6	2,896.2	2,873.4
2012	2,841.6	2,856.2	2,878.1	2,899.5	2,928.0	2,947.6	2,934.0	2,930.9	2,945.6	2,967.4	2,972.7	2,959.3	2,921.7
2013	2,911.6	2,929.9	2,944.7	2,965.8	2,995.3	3,007.6	3,001.8	3,002.9	3,018.3	3,026.0	3,023.3	3,016.5	2,987.0
Total Private													
2002	2,132.1	2,130.2	2,140.0	2,153.8	2,177.3	2,193.0	2,201.4	2,213.8	2,209.4	2,194.1	2,190.4	2,183.5	2,176.6
2003	2,130.0	2,134.4	2,140.6	2,154.7	2,174.8	2,192.7	2,202.5	2,213.5	2,213.5	2,204.1	2,198.9	2,199.0	2,179.9
2004	2,132.4	2,145.3	2,167.8	2,190.0	2,210.2	2,231.0	2,241.4	2,250.2	2,250.6	2,252.0	2,251.7	2,253.9	2,214.7
2005	2,196.7	2,207.8	2,230.0	2,254.7	2,278.3	2,296.9	2,312.6	2,326.7	2,320.2	2,322.5	2,328.5	2,336.5	2,284.3
2006	2,280.1	2,293.7	2,312.7	2,329.7	2,357.4	2,385.6	2,387.9	2,404.5	2,410.1	2,395.8	2,397.7	2,400.6	2,363.0
2007	2,346.8	2,370.4	2,389.0	2,404.3	2,431.4	2,458.2	2,460.6	2,474.7	2,473.0	2,463.9	2,469.5	2,467.0	2,434.1
2008	2,409.9	2,421.3	2,434.2	2,444.5	2,463.0	2,475.2	2,482.4	2,490.0	2,481.3	2,434.2	2,429.6	2,405.4	2,447.6
2009	2,334.9	2,323.8	2,313.3	2,303.2	2,316.7	2,326.2	2,325.8	2,323.6	2,321.0	2,304.3	2,290.7	2,283.6	2,313.9
2010	2,227.1	2,231.3	2,246.5	2,267.1	2,282.3	2,300.0	2,312.5	2,314.9	2,319.6	2,318.6	2,313.4	2,311.7	2,287.1
2011	2,258.9	2,268.2	2,279.9	2,308.5	2,324.2	2,345.0	2,360.7	2,368.4	2,373.2	2,358.9	2,358.6	2,354.8	2,329.9
2012	2,299.1	2,310.5	2,329.5	2,348.6	2,375.6	2,401.1	2,408.0	2,422.0	2,420.4	2,417.8	2,419.0	2,415.5	2,380.6
2013	2,365.7	2,379.9	2,393.9	2,412.6	2,440.9	2,459.7	2,476.9	2,491.4	2,490.7	2,475.4	2,468.1	2,469.0	2,443.7
Goods-Producing													
2002	443.7	440.2	440.6	443.5	450.4	454.1	458.8	462.7	457.4	452.3	443.4	435.5	448.6
2003	422.4	421.7	421.3	424.8	430.2	436.0	440.5	444.2	442.8	439.0	432.1	427.7	431.9
2004	413.0	416.8	422.7	428.5	434.3	440.0	448.5	450.7	450.5	451.1	445.7	442.0	437.0
2005	431.1	435.0	442.1	448.8	455.7	462.6	472.4	476.2	464.1	477.3	472.0	470.2	459.0
2006	461.8	467.9	472.7	476.9	485.6	496.5	502.2	506.3	508.3	504.7	498.1	493.6	489.6
2007	484.5	490.4	494.5	499.8	508.0	518.5	522.5	526.8	525.9	521.8	515.4	508.1	509.7
2008	496.9	498.7	500.4	500.6	505.4	509.3	513.6	515.6	511.2	479.7	487.0	471.7	499.2
2009	451.0	444.4	436.5	430.8	431.7	433.8	434.9	434.5	432.0	424.8	412.8	404.5	431.0
2010	393.4	392.5	394.1	397.4	401.4	406.8	414.4	416.7	417.9	415.2	406.9	400.2	404.7
2011	390.4	393.2	395.9	401.6	406.8	413.6	421.6	426.3	428.5	424.4	417.9	412.0	411.0
2012	402.0	403.8	409.2	413.5	420.0	429.2	435.9	441.7	441.4	440.7	435.6	430.1	425.3
2013	422.4	425.9	429.2	431.6	438.5	445.2	452.0	456.8	456.8	450.3	440.5	433.4	440.2
Service-Providing													
2002	2,200.7	2,209.1	2,220.4	2,232.0	2,251.4	2,263.6	2,240.8	2,236.1	2,256.1	2,265.4	2,279.9	2,274.6	2,244.2
2003	2,228.3	2,239.0	2,246.6	2,257.2	2,277.5	2,287.1	2,263.1	2,258.9	2,277.7	2,289.7	2,299.0	2,298.9	2,268.6
2004	2,241.1	2,256.1	2,275.4	2,291.8	2,308.1	2,324.7	2,299.3	2,292.0	2,311.9	2,329.6	2,343.6	2,342.8	2,301.4
2005	2,291.9	2,303.6	2,321.8	2,340.4	2,358.5	2,371.9	2,348.8	2,345.1	2,370.2	2,377.2	2,396.3	2,398.9	2,352.1
2006	2,347.9	2,362.3	2,378.2	2,389.6	2,410.9	2,431.0	2,395.0	2,395.0	2,419.7	2,426.2	2,442.2	2,443.3	2,403.4
2007	2,393.0	2,417.6	2,431.3	2,444.2	2,465.4	2,481.2	2,455.6	2,452.4	2,468.9	2,483.3	2,503.5	2,501.4	2,458.2
2008	2,454.3	2,472.3	2,483.0	2,493.8	2,510.4	2,519.1	2,499.8	2,493.9	2,503.9	2,510.4	2,506.8	2,489.0	2,494.7
2009	2,435.6	2,435.8	2,435.4	2,437.3	2,449.9	2,447.9	2,423.4	2,403.0	2,419.3	2,435.5	2,437.5	2,429.0	2,432.5
2010	2,385.1	2,393.9	2,409.1	2,430.9	2,453.3	2,453.7	2,433.8	2,413.6	2,432.0	2,457.5	2,464.8	2,460.0	2,432.3
2011	2,418.1	2,428.1	2,437.4	2,462.5	2,474.5	2,480.8	2,468.1	2,452.8	2,468.1	2,482.5	2,491.7	2,484.2	2,462.4
2012	2,439.6	2,452.4	2,468.9	2,486.0	2,508.0	2,518.4	2,498.1	2,489.2	2,504.2	2,526.7	2,537.1	2,529.2	2,496.5
2013	2,489.2	2,504.0	2,515.5	2,534.2	2,556.8	2,562.4	2,549.8	2,546.1	2,561.5	2,575.7	2,582.8	2,583.1	2,546.8
Mining and Logging													
2002	9.0	9.1	8.9	8.9	9.3	9.5	9.7	9.7	9.8	9.7	9.4	9.3	9.4
2003	8.7	8.7	8.5	8.3	8.5	8.7	8.8	8.8	8.7	8.7	8.5	8.6	8.6
2004	8.5	8.7	8.6	8.8	9.0	9.2	9.5	9.6	9.7	9.5	9.3	9.2	9.1
2005	8.8	8.9	8.8	8.8	9.1	9.2	9.2	9.1	9.1	8.9	8.8	8.8	9.0
2006	8.4	8.5	8.5	8.4	8.8	9.0	9.0	8.9	8.8	8.7	8.6	8.6	8.7
2007	8.4	7.9	7.6	7.9	8.2	8.5	8.5	8.4	8.3	8.3	8.0	7.9	8.2
2008	7.4	7.4	7.3	7.3	7.5	7.6	7.9	7.9	7.8	7.8	7.4	7.2	7.5
2009	6.5	6.4	5.8	5.6	5.8	6.2	6.3	6.3	6.3	6.1	5.7	5.5	6.0
2010	5.4	5.5	5.5	5.6	5.9	6.1	6.2	6.3	6.3	6.2	5.9	5.7	5.9
2011	5.6	5.7	5.7	5.7	5.8	6.1	6.2	6.3	6.2	6.3	6.1	6.0	6.0
2012	5.7	5.6	5.6	5.6	5.7	6.0	6.1	6.2	6.2	6.2	6.0	5.9	5.9
2013	5.7	5.8	5.8	5.7	6.0	6.2	6.3	6.4	6.5	6.4	6.2	6.1	6.1
Construction													
2002	143.2	143.5	144.6	148.4	153.6	156.6	161.3	166.0	163.9	161.2	156.5	151.6	154.2
2003	144.9	145.2	145.8	149.8	154.6	158.6	163.0	166.6	165.4	164.2	160.1	156.4	156.2
2004	147.3	151.0	155.5	158.8	163.1	166.5	172.0	174.0	172.7	172.9	170.2	166.6	164.2
2005	158.4	162.0	167.0	170.8	175.0	178.7	184.5	188.2	189.3	187.7	184.5	182.8	177.4
2006	175.6	179.5	184.2	187.7	193.8	200.1	203.3	206.9	207.1	204.6	200.0	196.4	194.9
2007	190.3	194.4	199.6	203.5	210.2	215.3	216.5	220.4	218.0	214.6	210.3	205.2	208.2
2008	196.6	197.3	200.3	201.6	204.6	206.9	209.1	210.1	206.5	200.9	190.6	181.1	200.5
2009	168.4	163.7	162.4	159.9	161.8	162.8	162.6	162.3	160.6	156.7	148.9	143.3	159.5
2010	134.7	133.9	135.5	137.2	140.0	142.2	146.8	148.6	147.7	146.2	140.4	135.2	140.7
2011	127.2	127.8	129.3	132.8	136.3	139.3	142.5	144.5	144.5	142.0	137.2	133.4	136.4
2012	125.5	126.9	130.2	133.7	137.6	141.6	144.7	148.1	147.4	147.5	144.2	141.5	139.1
2013	135.2	137.4	139.9	142.8	147.6	150.6	155.3	159.0	158.7	154.6	149.0	144.8	147.9

1. Employment by Industry: Washington, Selected Years, 2002–2013—*Continued*

(Numbers in thousands, not seasonally adjusted)

Industry and year	January	February	March	April	May	June	July	August	September	October	November	December	Annual average
Manufacturing													
2002	291.5	287.6	287.1	286.2	287.5	288.0	287.8	287.0	283.7	281.4	277.5	274.6	285.0
2003	268.8	267.8	267.0	266.7	267.1	268.7	268.7	268.8	268.7	266.1	263.5	262.7	267.1
2004	257.2	257.1	258.6	260.9	262.2	264.3	267.0	267.1	268.1	268.7	266.2	266.2	263.6
2005	263.9	264.1	266.3	269.2	271.6	274.7	278.7	278.9	265.7	280.7	278.7	278.6	272.6
2006	277.8	279.9	280.0	280.8	283.0	287.4	289.9	290.5	292.4	291.4	289.5	288.6	285.9
2007	285.8	288.1	287.3	288.4	289.6	294.7	297.5	298.0	299.6	298.9	297.1	295.0	293.3
2008	292.9	294.0	292.8	291.7	293.3	294.8	296.6	297.6	296.9	271.0	289.0	283.4	291.2
2009	276.1	274.3	268.3	265.3	264.1	264.8	266.0	265.9	265.1	262.0	258.2	255.7	265.5
2010	253.3	253.1	253.1	254.6	255.5	258.5	261.4	261.8	263.9	262.8	260.6	259.3	258.2
2011	257.6	259.7	260.9	263.1	264.7	268.2	272.9	275.5	277.8	276.1	274.6	272.6	268.6
2012	270.8	271.3	273.4	274.2	276.7	281.6	285.1	287.4	287.8	287.0	285.4	282.7	280.3
2013	281.5	282.7	283.5	283.1	284.9	288.4	290.4	291.4	291.6	289.3	285.3	282.5	286.2
Trade, Transportation, and Utilities													
2002	505.1	498.9	500.1	501.2	505.7	510.0	512.4	512.0	512.7	512.6	518.3	522.1	509.3
2003	502.1	497.9	498.3	499.7	504.2	509.2	513.2	513.5	514.3	515.7	522.0	527.0	509.8
2004	501.9	500.9	504.1	509.0	513.6	519.4	521.0	523.9	523.6	527.3	535.4	540.6	518.4
2005	517.2	515.2	517.9	520.5	525.8	530.4	531.7	535.3	535.7	536.0	546.3	553.4	530.5
2006	530.4	527.2	530.4	531.4	537.4	543.5	543.0	546.0	546.0	546.2	556.2	561.5	541.6
2007	540.5	539.1	541.9	544.0	549.0	554.2	555.8	557.5	556.2	558.3	570.5	573.5	553.4
2008	552.4	548.2	549.7	549.6	552.6	554.6	557.1	557.5	554.3	553.7	555.1	555.7	553.4
2009	531.2	523.0	518.9	515.6	519.5	520.8	522.8	521.8	521.4	520.8	525.6	527.9	522.4
2010	507.7	504.0	506.3	510.4	514.0	517.6	519.5	519.1	518.6	522.7	529.9	533.8	517.0
2011	512.7	510.0	512.3	515.9	520.4	524.9	530.4	531.3	530.4	531.1	539.9	542.6	525.2
2012	522.1	519.0	521.8	524.0	531.3	537.7	540.8	542.4	541.3	543.8	553.3	555.1	536.1
2013	535.6	533.7	534.5	537.6	545.3	549.7	554.6	557.5	556.3	558.7	566.7	572.4	550.2
Wholesale Trade													
2002	114.8	115.0	115.3	114.9	115.8	116.3	116.3	116.4	116.3	116.1	115.5	114.4	115.6
2003	113.5	113.7	114.3	114.9	115.3	116.3	117.3	117.2	117.4	117.8	117.5	116.5	116.0
2004	114.9	115.7	116.9	118.6	118.8	119.8	120.7	120.7	120.8	121.6	121.4	121.1	119.3
2005	119.2	119.8	120.6	120.2	121.2	122.7	122.8	123.3	123.5	124.0	124.5	124.4	122.2
2006	123.7	124.2	125.0	124.8	126.0	127.9	128.1	127.8	127.9	128.3	128.1	127.1	126.6
2007	125.9	126.6	127.3	128.0	128.9	130.3	130.7	130.6	130.2	131.2	131.4	130.9	129.3
2008	129.0	129.6	130.0	130.1	130.7	130.7	131.4	130.8	130.7	131.3	129.4	127.7	130.1
2009	125.6	124.7	123.8	122.7	122.7	122.8	122.9	121.9	121.6	122.5	121.2	120.1	122.7
2010	118.0	118.4	118.9	120.3	120.6	120.8	121.0	120.6	120.4	121.4	121.3	120.1	120.2
2011	119.0	119.4	120.1	120.7	121.9	122.3	123.1	122.8	122.6	123.3	123.1	122.2	121.7
2012	121.0	121.4	122.1	122.8	123.9	124.9	125.1	125.6	125.0	125.8	125.5	124.9	124.0
2013	123.4	124.6	125.0	125.7	126.6	127.4	128.6	128.7	128.7	130.4	129.2	129.5	127.3
Retail Trade													
2002	303.2	297.2	298.3	299.3	302.1	304.8	306.6	306.3	306.4	306.1	314.1	319.5	305.3
2003	301.7	297.8	298.0	298.7	302.1	305.2	307.4	307.7	307.0	308.0	316.1	321.1	305.9
2004	300.9	299.2	300.5	302.9	306.6	309.0	309.8	312.5	310.7	312.2	321.6	326.7	309.4
2005	308.7	305.5	307.1	309.1	312.4	314.6	316.5	319.2	318.3	319.1	328.6	334.2	316.1
2006	315.4	311.5	313.3	314.2	317.9	320.4	320.6	323.2	322.0	322.7	333.6	337.8	321.1
2007	321.2	318.9	320.3	321.1	324.4	326.8	328.8	329.7	328.3	329.6	341.9	344.4	328.0
2008	328.7	323.5	324.8	324.3	325.7	327.2	328.8	329.7	326.6	326.3	330.6	332.2	327.4
2009	312.3	307.1	305.0	303.4	306.6	307.7	309.0	309.6	308.7	308.5	315.1	317.6	309.2
2010	303.0	299.4	300.7	302.8	305.4	308.0	308.7	309.2	308.0	311.0	319.0	322.7	308.2
2011	306.3	303.3	303.8	306.0	308.9	312.1	314.1	315.6	314.0	316.3	325.2	327.4	312.8
2012	311.3	307.6	309.2	310.5	315.1	319.1	321.8	322.6	321.7	324.2	334.0	335.3	319.4
2013	320.2	317.0	317.9	320.1	325.7	328.7	331.6	333.6	331.9	333.3	342.6	347.0	329.1
Transportation and Utilities													
2002	87.1	86.7	86.5	87.0	87.8	88.9	89.5	89.3	90.0	90.4	88.7	88.2	88.3
2003	86.9	86.4	86.0	86.1	86.8	87.7	88.5	88.6	89.9	89.9	88.4	89.4	87.9
2004	86.1	86.0	86.7	87.5	88.2	90.6	90.5	90.7	92.1	93.5	92.4	92.8	89.8
2005	89.3	89.9	90.2	91.2	92.2	93.1	92.4	92.8	93.9	92.9	93.2	94.8	92.2
2006	91.3	91.5	92.1	92.4	93.5	95.2	94.3	95.0	96.1	95.2	94.5	96.6	94.0
2007	93.4	93.6	94.3	94.9	95.7	97.1	96.3	97.2	97.7	97.5	97.2	98.2	96.1
2008	94.7	95.1	94.9	95.2	96.2	96.7	96.9	97.0	97.0	96.1	95.1	95.8	95.9
2009	93.3	91.2	90.1	89.5	90.2	90.3	90.9	90.3	91.1	89.8	89.3	90.2	90.5
2010	86.7	86.2	86.7	87.3	88.0	88.8	89.8	89.3	90.2	90.3	89.6	91.0	88.7
2011	87.4	87.3	88.4	89.2	89.6	90.5	93.2	92.9	93.8	91.5	91.6	93.0	90.7
2012	89.8	90.0	90.5	90.7	92.3	93.7	93.9	94.2	94.6	93.8	93.8	94.9	92.7
2013	92.0	92.1	91.6	91.8	93.0	93.6	94.4	95.2	95.7	95.0	94.9	95.9	93.8
Information													
2002	94.2	93.9	93.5	93.2	93.3	93.8	93.9	94.0	93.1	93.3	93.4	93.3	93.6
2003	92.2	92.0	91.5	91.0	91.6	92.1	92.2	93.1	92.4	92.6	93.0	93.6	92.3
2004	91.7	91.7	92.1	92.1	92.8	93.2	93.4	93.7	92.7	93.0	93.7	94.2	92.9
2005	92.7	93.5	93.4	94.1	94.5	94.9	95.7	96.4	95.4	94.6	95.5	96.1	94.7
2006	94.8	95.2	95.9	96.2	96.9	99.5	100.0	100.7	100.6	99.7	100.6	101.1	98.4
2007	100.4	101.3	101.0	101.5	102.4	103.5	103.7	104.0	103.3	102.0	103.1	103.3	102.5
2008	102.7	103.8	104.0	104.2	104.9	106.0	107.2	107.9	106.8	105.9	107.0	107.0	105.6
2009	104.9	105.4	105.0	103.7	104.2	104.5	104.8	104.2	102.9	102.2	102.5	102.4	103.9
2010	102.2	102.4	102.3	101.7	102.5	103.6	103.8	104.2	103.7	102.8	103.3	103.8	103.0
2011	102.8	103.4	103.1	103.3	103.6	104.7	105.7	106.0	104.9	104.0	104.5	104.3	104.2
2012	104.0	104.4	104.0	103.8	104.6	105.9	106.0	106.0	104.5	103.9	104.5	105.0	104.7
2013	104.1	104.8	104.5	104.9	105.7	106.6	108.0	108.5	107.4	106.7	107.0	106.2	106.2

1. Employment by Industry: Washington, Selected Years, 2002–2013—*Continued*

(Numbers in thousands, not seasonally adjusted)

Industry and year	January	February	March	April	May	June	July	August	September	October	November	December	Annual average
Financial Activities													
2002	145.7	146.3	146.7	147.4	148.3	148.9	149.8	150.8	150.5	149.8	150.8	151.4	148.9
2003	150.9	151.6	152.4	153.5	154.7	155.6	156.9	157.5	156.6	155.7	155.0	154.8	154.6
2004	152.6	152.9	154.1	153.7	154.3	155.0	155.5	155.7	155.0	154.9	154.6	156.0	154.5
2005	153.2	153.9	154.1	155.2	156.3	157.3	159.1	160.2	159.7	159.1	159.1	159.9	157.3
2006	157.9	158.1	158.5	158.7	159.4	160.2	160.4	160.2	159.3	158.3	157.8	158.2	158.9
2007	156.6	157.2	157.9	158.4	158.8	159.8	159.8	159.8	157.9	157.3	157.5	157.4	158.2
2008	156.0	156.2	156.2	155.9	156.9	156.7	155.9	156.1	154.5	153.0	152.1	151.2	155.1
2009	148.5	148.1	146.6	146.4	146.5	147.1	146.1	145.6	144.6	143.0	142.1	142.0	145.6
2010	139.8	139.5	139.7	140.0	140.0	140.6	141.5	141.6	141.1	140.8	140.5	141.0	140.5
2011	139.1	139.2	139.3	140.4	140.3	141.5	141.9	142.1	142.0	140.9	141.2	141.3	140.8
2012	140.0	140.7	141.3	142.1	143.4	144.6	146.2	146.4	145.8	145.9	146.3	146.9	144.1
2013	146.5	147.2	148.0	148.5	149.6	150.5	151.9	152.0	151.0	150.7	151.4	150.9	149.9
Professional and Business Services													
2002	279.8	282.3	284.6	287.1	288.6	291.5	293.2	297.2	297.1	295.3	294.9	291.3	290.2
2003	282.2	284.5	285.4	287.8	288.3	289.7	292.1	295.6	295.5	295.4	294.3	293.2	290.3
2004	286.0	289.8	294.2	298.8	299.9	303.0	306.2	308.6	308.1	309.6	309.3	307.4	301.7
2005	300.0	304.7	308.3	312.4	314.9	317.0	320.8	323.0	324.8	322.7	322.5	321.8	316.1
2006	313.6	317.4	320.6	325.6	328.5	333.3	335.1	338.8	339.2	338.3	338.6	338.0	330.6
2007	329.4	335.6	339.9	340.8	343.4	347.2	348.5	351.2	350.8	349.3	349.2	349.7	344.6
2008	340.5	344.2	346.9	351.0	352.4	353.6	354.9	355.5	353.6	349.5	342.8	337.7	348.6
2009	330.0	327.5	325.6	323.4	322.8	324.9	324.4	324.1	323.7	323.2	321.5	321.6	324.4
2010	313.2	315.3	319.1	323.3	324.0	326.9	331.6	331.0	332.0	333.8	333.0	333.6	326.4
2011	326.3	329.4	331.9	338.9	338.4	340.8	344.9	345.0	346.3	344.9	344.3	342.7	339.5
2012	335.4	338.6	341.3	346.7	349.0	353.0	352.4	356.6	356.4	358.1	357.4	355.4	350.0
2013	348.9	351.9	354.1	357.9	359.4	361.8	363.6	367.5	367.6	366.8	363.3	362.3	360.4
Education and Health Services													
2002	337.2	341.0	342.6	343.0	344.8	341.7	336.5	337.3	342.8	347.6	350.0	350.1	342.9
2003	347.0	351.6	353.7	355.6	356.4	353.5	349.1	348.3	352.7	356.4	357.3	356.7	353.2
2004	350.5	353.6	354.5	356.1	356.7	354.8	348.3	348.0	353.3	358.5	359.4	358.5	354.4
2005	354.2	357.2	359.6	362.4	363.3	359.4	353.9	354.6	362.1	365.8	367.4	366.7	360.6
2006	362.6	366.7	369.1	370.0	371.3	367.3	360.2	361.6	368.9	373.2	374.4	374.0	368.3
2007	370.4	376.3	378.6	379.3	381.8	378.4	372.2	373.6	380.9	387.6	389.8	389.2	379.8
2008	384.6	390.1	391.2	393.1	395.3	392.1	388.0	389.9	396.7	403.4	404.7	403.8	394.4
2009	402.0	406.8	409.4	410.1	412.3	409.2	403.9	404.4	411.6	418.6	420.7	421.1	410.8
2010	416.9	421.8	423.8	425.3	426.1	422.8	416.6	415.7	422.4	429.7	430.8	429.4	423.4
2011	426.3	430.0	431.6	431.8	431.8	428.9	423.9	423.1	428.9	433.8	435.2	434.7	430.0
2012	427.9	432.8	435.0	434.7	435.9	432.1	425.2	425.2	430.3	435.5	437.1	436.5	432.4
2013	431.2	437.3	438.6	439.4	440.2	435.7	433.0	432.6	439.4	444.5	445.8	446.3	438.7
Leisure and Hospitality													
2002	231.4	232.2	236.0	241.2	248.1	253.7	256.7	259.7	257.0	245.4	241.8	242.1	245.4
2003	235.7	237.2	239.6	243.7	249.9	256.2	258.4	261.3	259.8	250.7	247.1	247.6	248.9
2004	239.6	241.6	247.0	252.1	257.9	263.8	266.2	267.5	266.0	256.9	253.5	254.8	255.6
2005	248.1	247.2	252.4	259.2	265.1	271.2	274.7	276.7	274.9	264.4	263.1	265.4	263.5
2006	257.6	258.9	262.3	267.4	273.9	279.7	281.5	285.4	282.7	271.7	268.4	270.3	271.7
2007	262.9	266.7	270.5	275.9	282.5	289.8	291.5	294.8	292.0	282.1	278.3	280.1	280.6
2008	271.8	274.0	278.5	282.7	287.2	293.7	295.6	297.5	295.2	281.4	274.0	272.3	283.7
2009	261.7	262.5	264.5	266.5	272.7	278.4	281.1	281.6	278.8	266.4	260.9	259.7	269.6
2010	251.2	252.7	257.4	264.6	269.2	275.1	277.5	278.9	277.6	267.4	262.6	263.7	266.5
2011	256.1	257.0	259.5	268.7	274.1	280.3	281.6	283.9	282.7	270.7	267.1	268.3	270.8
2012	260.3	262.8	267.3	273.2	280.0	286.2	288.3	290.8	288.9	278.5	274.0	276.0	277.2
2013	268.9	270.3	275.3	282.3	290.6	297.9	300.0	302.7	299.9	285.6	282.1	284.9	286.7
Other Services													
2002	95.0	95.4	95.9	97.2	98.1	99.3	100.1	100.1	98.8	97.8	97.8	97.7	97.8
2003	97.5	97.9	98.4	98.6	99.5	100.4	100.1	100.0	99.4	98.6	98.1	98.4	98.9
2004	97.1	98.0	99.1	99.7	100.7	101.8	102.3	102.1	101.4	100.7	100.1	100.4	100.3
2005	100.2	101.1	102.2	102.1	102.7	104.1	104.3	104.3	103.5	102.6	102.6	103.0	102.7
2006	101.4	102.3	103.2	103.5	104.4	105.6	105.5	105.5	105.1	103.7	103.6	103.9	104.0
2007	102.1	103.8	104.7	104.6	105.5	106.8	106.6	107.0	106.0	105.5	105.7	105.7	105.3
2008	105.0	106.1	107.3	107.4	108.3	109.2	110.1	110.0	109.0	107.6	106.9	106.0	107.7
2009	105.6	106.1	106.8	106.7	107.0	107.5	107.8	107.4	106.0	105.3	104.6	104.4	106.3
2010	102.7	103.1	103.8	104.4	105.1	106.6	107.6	107.7	106.3	106.2	106.4	106.2	105.5
2011	105.2	106.0	106.3	107.9	108.8	110.3	110.7	110.7	109.5	109.1	108.5	108.9	108.5
2012	107.4	108.4	109.6	110.6	111.4	112.4	113.2	112.9	111.8	111.4	110.8	110.5	110.9
2013	108.1	108.8	109.7	110.4	111.6	112.3	113.8	113.8	112.3	112.1	111.3	112.6	111.4
Government													
2002	512.3	519.1	521.0	521.7	524.5	524.7	498.2	485.0	504.1	523.6	532.9	526.6	516.1
2003	520.7	526.3	527.3	527.3	532.9	530.4	501.1	489.6	507.0	524.6	532.2	527.6	520.6
2004	521.7	527.6	530.3	530.3	532.2	533.7	506.4	492.5	511.8	528.7	537.6	530.9	523.6
2005	526.3	530.8	533.9	534.5	535.9	537.6	508.6	494.6	514.1	532.0	539.8	532.6	526.7
2006	529.6	536.5	538.2	536.8	539.1	541.9	509.3	496.8	517.9	535.1	542.6	536.3	530.0
2007	530.7	537.6	536.8	539.7	542.0	541.5	517.5	504.5	521.8	541.2	549.4	542.5	533.8
2008	541.3	549.7	549.2	549.9	552.8	553.2	531.0	519.5	533.8	555.9	564.2	555.3	546.3
2009	551.7	556.4	558.6	564.9	564.9	555.5	532.5	513.9	530.3	556.0	559.6	549.9	549.5
2010	551.4	555.1	556.7	561.2	572.4	560.5	535.7	515.4	530.3	554.1	558.3	548.5	550.0
2011	549.6	553.1	553.4	555.6	557.1	549.4	529.0	510.7	523.4	548.0	551.0	541.4	543.5
2012	542.5	545.7	548.6	550.9	552.4	546.5	526.0	508.9	525.2	549.6	553.7	543.8	541.2
2013	545.9	550.0	550.8	553.2	554.4	547.9	524.9	511.5	527.6	550.6	555.2	547.5	543.3

2. Average Weekly Hours by Selected Industry: Washington, 2009–2013

(Not seasonally adjusted)

Industry and year	January	February	March	April	May	June	July	August	September	October	November	December	Annual average
Total Private													
2009	33.8	34.9	34.9	34.1	34.2	34.3	34.2	35.3	34.0	33.9	34.7	33.5	34.3
2010	33.5	33.8	33.7	33.9	35.0	33.9	34.1	35.3	34.1	34.2	33.9	34.0	34.1
2011	34.9	34.1	34.0	34.3	35.1	34.4	34.5	34.5	34.5	34.5	35.4	34.2	34.5
2012	34.4	34.1	34.0	35.1	34.1	34.2	35.2	34.4	35.4	34.2	34.1	35.1	34.5
2013	33.6	34.2	34.1	34.1	34.0	35.1	34.0	34.4	35.1	34.0	34.0	34.6	34.3
Goods-Producing													
2009	40.3	40.6	39.3	39.5	39.4	39.8	39.5	40.1	39.1	39.7	39.7	38.6	39.6
2010	37.9	38.3	38.7	38.7	39.5	39.0	39.1	39.9	39.2	39.2	39.0	39.4	39.0
2011	39.1	39.0	39.2	39.6	40.1	39.7	39.8	40.0	40.0	40.3	40.2	40.0	39.8
2012	39.1	40.0	40.1	40.1	39.9	39.9	39.7	39.9	40.4	40.4	40.1	40.4	40.0
2013	39.6	39.9	40.1	40.0	39.8	40.2	39.5	40.2	40.0	39.9	39.9	39.8	39.9
Construction													
2009	36.8	37.2	35.8	36.0	36.2	36.5	36.1	37.3	35.0	35.5	34.8	32.3	35.8
2010	32.3	32.3	32.9	33.6	34.6	34.7	35.0	36.2	34.5	33.8	33.1	33.7	33.9
2011	32.8	33.4	33.2	34.2	34.8	34.6	35.3	36.5	36.1	35.5	35.3	35.2	34.8
2012	34.2	34.8	35.3	36.0	35.6	35.7	36.4	36.3	36.9	36.4	35.5	36.1	35.8
2013	34.8	35.7	36.3	36.4	36.4	37.4	36.4	38.0	37.7	37.2	36.7	36.2	36.6
Manufacturing													
2009	41.9	42.0	40.8	41.1	41.0	41.3	41.1	41.5	41.2	41.8	41.6	41.7	41.4
2010	40.6	41.0	41.3	41.1	41.7	41.0	41.1	41.7	41.4	41.8	41.7	41.8	41.4
2011	41.5	41.1	41.5	41.6	42.1	41.7	41.6	41.4	41.6	42.1	42.0	41.7	41.7
2012	40.7	41.7	41.6	41.3	41.3	41.2	40.8	41.1	41.6	41.8	41.6	41.8	41.4
2013	41.2	41.3	41.5	41.3	41.0	41.2	40.6	41.0	40.9	41.1	41.3	41.4	41.1
Trade, Transportation, and Utilities													
2009	33.9	35.4	37.2	36.4	36.4	36.4	36.1	37.4	36.7	35.8	35.8	35.0	36.0
2010	34.5	34.9	34.7	35.0	36.0	35.2	35.6	36.8	35.8	35.5	35.0	35.3	35.4
2011	35.9	35.4	35.4	35.8	36.5	36.2	36.3	35.9	36.0	36.5	35.1	35.1	35.8
2012	34.8	34.7	34.5	35.2	34.8	34.9	35.8	35.3	36.2	34.8	34.7	35.7	35.1
2013	34.0	34.7	34.6	34.3	34.6	35.7	34.9	35.1	35.6	34.4	34.3	34.9	34.8
Information													
2009	38.4	41.7	41.7	38.4	38.3	38.3	39.0	41.6	38.3	38.4	41.9	38.5	39.5
2010	38.5	38.7	38.0	38.4	41.3	38.3	38.3	41.1	38.1	38.0	38.1	38.3	38.8
2011	41.3	38.2	38.0	38.3	40.8	38.3	37.9	37.8	37.9	40.8	38.0	37.9	38.8
2012	41.0	38.2	38.0	41.2	38.2	38.3	41.3	38.4	41.5	38.2	38.4	40.7	39.4
2013	37.9	38.3	38.2	38.4	38.3	40.9	37.9	37.6	40.7	39.2	39.2	42.1	39.1
Financial Activities													
2009	36.7	38.1	38.0	36.3	36.3	35.6	35.7	37.5	34.9	35.6	37.5	35.5	36.5
2010	38.6	38.7	38.6	38.2	40.2	37.2	37.6	38.7	36.8	36.9	37.0	35.5	37.8
2011	38.4	36.2	34.9	35.6	36.6	35.2	35.3	35.5	35.6	37.5	34.7	34.8	35.9
2012	37.5	35.2	34.8	36.7	34.5	34.9	36.8	34.9	36.7	34.5	34.2	36.3	35.6
2013	34.8	35.6	35.1	35.0	34.6	36.2	34.5	34.8	35.8	34.2	34.5	35.7	35.1
Professional and Business Services													
2009	34.0	34.8	34.5	34.1	34.2	34.5	34.2	35.0	33.6	33.8	34.5	33.5	34.2
2010	33.6	34.1	34.1	34.4	35.5	34.2	34.3	35.5	34.8	35.3	35.2	35.1	34.7
2011	35.9	35.3	35.2	35.6	36.5	35.8	35.7	35.7	35.5	37.0	35.5	35.6	35.8
2012	36.1	35.5	35.4	37.1	35.8	35.7	36.7	35.7	36.9	35.3	35.2	36.5	36.0
2013	35.1	35.8	35.6	36.0	35.7	37.0	35.3	36.0	36.9	35.6	35.4	36.0	35.9
Education and Health Services													
2009	31.1	31.9	31.9	31.3	31.3	31.5	31.6	32.8	31.8	31.6	32.6	31.9	31.8
2010	32.0	31.8	31.6	32.0	32.9	32.0	31.9	32.7	32.1	32.0	32.1	32.0	32.1
2011	33.3	32.1	32.0	31.9	32.5	31.8	31.7	31.8	32.2	32.8	32.1	32.2	32.2
2012	32.5	32.0	31.9	32.8	31.8	32.0	32.9	31.8	33.2	31.9	32.1	32.9	32.3
2013	31.6	31.8	31.6	31.7	31.6	32.8	31.7	31.8	33.0	31.9	32.1	32.6	32.0
Leisure and Hospitality													
2009	23.9	25.2	24.8	24.0	24.6	24.6	24.7	26.1	24.5	24.4	25.3	24.1	24.7
2010	23.6	24.4	24.2	24.2	25.6	24.5	24.9	26.3	24.4	24.6	24.0	23.9	24.6
2011	24.7	24.9	24.6	25.1	25.8	25.2	25.7	25.9	25.5	26.2	24.8	24.8	25.3
2012	24.8	25.0	25.1	26.2	25.5	25.5	26.8	26.3	26.4	25.3	24.8	26.3	25.7
2013	24.1	25.1	25.0	25.0	25.1	26.3	25.1	26.0	26.2	24.7	24.4	25.4	25.2
Other Services													
2009	31.0	32.3	32.2	30.9	30.8	31.0	31.5	31.0	29.0	28.4	30.1	29.0	30.6
2010	29.7	30.2	29.2	29.9	31.5	29.8	30.6	32.3	29.3	30.1	29.5	29.6	30.1
2011	31.2	30.5	29.7	30.7	31.4	30.3	31.0	30.7	30.5	30.8	29.6	29.7	30.5
2012	30.7	30.3	30.0	31.9	30.2	30.3	32.0	30.9	31.8	30.0	30.4	31.2	30.8
2013	30.0	30.9	30.7	30.5	31.1	32.2	30.8	31.4	32.5	30.7	31.2	32.2	31.2

3. Average Hourly Earnings by Selected Industry: Washington, 2009–2013

(Dollars, not seasonally adjusted)

Industry and year	January	February	March	April	May	June	July	August	September	October	November	December	Annual average
Total Private													
2009	26.22	26.46	26.45	26.24	26.08	25.93	26.49	26.05	26.05	26.24	26.63	26.82	26.30
2010	26.62	26.80	26.84	26.79	26.79	26.71	26.70	26.70	26.94	27.18	27.24	27.91	26.94
2011	27.61	27.48	27.37	27.38	27.33	27.09	27.02	26.69	27.00	27.31	27.26	27.50	27.25
2012	27.85	27.38	27.34	27.49	27.06	27.11	27.18	26.87	27.31	27.27	27.45	27.56	27.32
2013	27.66	27.77	27.76	27.71	27.51	27.65	27.44	27.33	27.79	27.80	27.93	27.97	27.69
Goods-Producing													
2009	29.69	30.09	30.99	30.69	30.55	30.27	30.14	30.00	30.43	30.20	31.48	31.67	30.50
2010	30.70	31.34	31.37	31.02	30.66	30.69	30.55	30.42	30.19	30.48	30.80	31.68	30.82
2011	30.90	30.59	31.23	31.02	30.87	30.92	30.91	30.55	30.65	30.71	30.77	31.16	30.85
2012	31.29	31.10	31.47	31.33	31.27	31.20	31.08	30.79	30.97	31.02	31.25	31.51	31.19
2013	31.58	31.65	31.65	31.66	31.52	31.47	31.38	31.39	31.49	31.72	31.96	32.53	31.66
Construction													
2009	30.08	30.10	31.73	30.90	30.38	30.31	30.28	30.20	30.88	30.53	30.65	31.09	30.58
2010	29.85	29.94	29.81	29.76	30.15	30.12	30.29	30.35	30.60	32.46	32.53	32.69	30.72
2011	31.25	30.90	30.67	30.51	30.06	30.17	29.86	29.78	29.73	29.48	29.36	29.81	30.10
2012	29.92	29.64	29.67	29.52	29.68	29.37	29.52	29.29	29.32	29.39	29.33	29.67	29.52
2013	29.72	30.10	30.17	30.03	30.20	30.11	29.44	29.78	29.50	29.50	30.03	30.09	29.88
Manufacturing													
2009	29.59	30.19	30.80	30.72	30.77	30.42	30.33	30.15	30.48	30.26	32.16	32.23	30.66
2010	32.16	32.90	32.72	32.08	31.54	31.55	31.22	30.98	31.22	30.96	31.19	31.42	31.65
2011	31.00	30.72	31.41	31.35	31.27	31.29	31.27	30.91	31.15	31.25	31.34	31.68	31.22
2012	31.77	31.61	32.08	31.99	31.88	31.89	31.72	31.43	31.64	31.65	31.94	32.16	31.81
2013	32.19	32.19	32.17	32.26	32.04	32.03	32.16	32.08	32.32	32.59	32.74	33.49	32.35
Trade, Transportation, and Utilities													
2009	21.16	21.62	20.93	20.70	20.58	20.46	20.71	20.79	20.53	20.57	20.80	21.15	20.83
2010	21.02	21.40	21.82	21.73	21.79	21.73	21.56	21.79	22.19	22.06	22.29	22.92	21.87
2011	22.26	22.21	22.06	22.28	22.26	22.06	21.98	21.62	21.82	21.85	21.84	22.02	22.02
2012	22.50	21.81	21.62	21.80	21.42	21.63	21.76	21.58	22.09	21.98	22.09	22.03	21.86
2013	22.37	22.55	22.72	22.75	22.56	22.77	22.48	22.37	22.75	22.36	22.32	21.58	22.46
Information													
2009	47.78	48.51	47.79	47.33	47.17	47.17	52.18	47.31	46.88	46.95	47.23	46.75	47.77
2010	47.03	46.92	47.20	47.51	47.90	47.28	47.05	47.97	48.80	48.79	48.75	48.58	47.82
2011	49.20	49.03	48.27	48.38	49.15	47.46	46.81	45.67	48.17	49.21	48.85	49.21	48.29
2012	50.01	49.80	50.20	51.02	50.56	50.68	51.24	50.42	52.03	52.14	52.05	52.42	51.06
2013	52.40	52.51	52.89	52.63	53.13	53.46	52.51	52.62	56.24	54.26	54.05	54.90	53.50
Financial Activities													
2009	24.69	25.55	26.55	25.80	26.11	25.88	26.14	26.69	26.15	26.81	26.63	26.63	26.13
2010	27.64	27.80	27.71	27.00	27.36	26.61	26.51	27.00	27.10	27.15	26.47	27.72	27.17
2011	27.75	28.23	27.77	28.09	28.26	27.70	27.51	27.90	27.64	28.42	28.46	28.58	28.03
2012	28.70	28.56	28.44	29.05	28.56	28.03	28.29	28.36	28.74	28.63	28.91	28.94	28.60
2013	28.70	29.28	29.34	28.77	28.54	28.45	28.88	28.27	28.34	28.54	28.75	28.54	28.70
Professional and Business Services													
2009	29.94	30.66	30.94	30.55	30.38	29.87	30.11	30.90	30.79	30.34	30.72	31.14	30.53
2010	31.21	30.93	30.72	30.84	30.95	31.33	31.11	31.55	31.85	32.29	32.30	33.33	31.55
2011	33.16	33.31	32.84	32.87	32.75	32.65	32.81	32.34	32.94	33.49	33.27	33.45	32.99
2012	33.67	33.03	32.77	32.93	32.07	32.23	32.65	31.82	32.33	32.15	32.42	32.59	32.55
2013	32.42	32.79	32.57	32.48	32.17	32.67	31.87	31.66	32.29	32.48	32.72	32.86	32.41
Education and Health Services													
2009	25.76	24.55	24.35	25.14	25.03	25.07	25.97	24.63	25.03	25.84	25.60	25.90	25.24
2010	25.59	25.59	25.44	26.07	26.03	26.15	27.06	25.97	26.10	27.23	26.68	27.14	26.26
2011	27.02	27.01	26.76	26.92	26.50	26.59	26.63	26.32	26.43	26.52	26.38	26.75	26.65
2012	26.64	26.16	25.95	26.02	25.74	25.86	25.74	25.68	25.56	25.51	25.70	25.72	25.86
2013	25.65	25.41	25.26	25.27	25.06	25.16	25.30	25.50	25.31	25.39	25.74	25.81	25.41
Leisure and Hospitality													
2009	15.12	15.01	15.09	14.96	14.87	14.79	14.60	14.62	14.52	14.73	14.80	15.29	14.86
2010	14.80	14.75	14.65	14.51	14.22	14.12	13.98	13.90	13.92	12.96	13.10	13.77	14.05
2011	13.37	13.30	13.28	13.19	13.31	13.35	13.43	13.38	13.44	13.50	13.71	14.17	13.45
2012	14.23	14.32	14.23	14.15	14.15	14.26	14.15	14.18	14.33	14.44	14.63	14.92	14.33
2013	14.78	14.90	14.85	14.85	14.92	14.92	14.77	14.66	14.94	15.19	15.27	15.54	14.96
Other Services													
2009	21.13	22.04	22.47	21.76	21.59	22.16	24.22	21.76	22.60	22.91	22.92	23.28	22.39
2010	22.35	22.76	22.86	22.60	23.10	22.59	22.32	22.74	24.00	23.88	24.76	24.66	23.21
2011	24.22	23.76	23.27	22.92	22.95	22.36	21.77	21.45	21.36	21.25	21.14	21.23	22.30
2012	21.30	21.35	21.48	21.44	21.17	21.06	20.69	20.83	21.61	21.46	21.52	21.79	21.31
2013	21.70	22.06	21.92	22.08	21.81	21.84	22.59	22.33	22.60	22.56	22.54	23.29	22.29

4. Average Weekly Earnings by Selected Industry: Washington, 2009–2013

(Dollars, not seasonally adjusted)

Industry and year	January	February	March	April	May	June	July	August	September	October	November	December	Annual average
Total Private													
2009	886.24	923.45	923.11	894.78	891.94	889.40	905.96	919.57	885.70	889.54	924.06	898.47	902.09
2010	891.77	905.84	904.51	908.18	937.65	905.47	910.47	942.51	918.65	929.56	923.44	948.94	918.65
2011	963.59	937.07	930.58	939.13	959.28	931.90	932.19	920.81	931.50	966.77	932.29	940.50	940.13
2012	958.04	933.66	929.56	964.90	922.75	927.16	956.74	924.33	966.77	932.63	936.05	967.36	942.54
2013	929.38	949.73	946.62	944.91	935.34	970.52	932.96	940.15	975.43	945.20	949.62	967.76	949.77
Goods-Producing													
2009	1,196.51	1,221.65	1,217.91	1,212.26	1,203.67	1,204.75	1,190.53	1,203.00	1,189.81	1,198.94	1,249.76	1,222.46	1,207.80
2010	1,163.53	1,200.32	1,214.02	1,200.47	1,211.07	1,196.91	1,194.51	1,213.76	1,183.45	1,194.82	1,201.20	1,248.19	1,201.98
2011	1,208.19	1,193.01	1,224.22	1,228.39	1,237.89	1,227.52	1,230.22	1,222.00	1,226.00	1,237.61	1,236.95	1,246.40	1,227.83
2012	1,223.44	1,244.00	1,261.95	1,256.33	1,247.67	1,244.88	1,233.88	1,228.52	1,251.19	1,253.21	1,253.13	1,273.00	1,247.60
2013	1,250.57	1,262.84	1,269.17	1,266.40	1,254.50	1,265.09	1,239.51	1,261.88	1,259.60	1,265.63	1,275.20	1,294.69	1,263.23
Construction													
2009	1,106.94	1,119.72	1,135.93	1,112.40	1,099.76	1,106.32	1,093.11	1,126.46	1,080.80	1,083.82	1,066.62	1,004.21	1,094.76
2010	964.16	967.06	980.75	999.94	1,043.19	1,045.16	1,060.15	1,098.67	1,055.70	1,097.15	1,076.74	1,101.65	1,041.41
2011	1,025.00	1,032.06	1,018.24	1,043.44	1,046.09	1,043.88	1,054.06	1,086.97	1,073.25	1,046.54	1,036.41	1,049.31	1,047.48
2012	1,023.26	1,031.47	1,047.35	1,062.72	1,056.61	1,048.51	1,074.53	1,063.23	1,081.91	1,069.80	1,041.22	1,071.09	1,056.82
2013	1,034.26	1,074.57	1,095.17	1,093.09	1,099.28	1,126.11	1,071.62	1,131.64	1,112.15	1,097.40	1,102.10	1,089.26	1,093.61
Manufacturing													
2009	1,239.82	1,267.98	1,256.64	1,262.59	1,261.57	1,256.35	1,246.56	1,251.23	1,255.78	1,264.87	1,337.86	1,343.99	1,269.32
2010	1,305.70	1,348.90	1,351.34	1,318.49	1,315.22	1,293.55	1,283.14	1,291.87	1,292.51	1,294.13	1,300.62	1,313.36	1,310.31
2011	1,286.50	1,262.59	1,303.52	1,304.16	1,316.47	1,304.79	1,300.83	1,279.67	1,295.84	1,315.63	1,316.28	1,321.06	1,301.87
2012	1,293.04	1,318.14	1,334.53	1,321.19	1,316.64	1,313.87	1,294.18	1,291.77	1,316.22	1,322.97	1,328.70	1,344.29	1,316.93
2013	1,326.23	1,329.45	1,335.06	1,332.34	1,313.64	1,319.64	1,305.70	1,315.28	1,321.89	1,339.45	1,352.16	1,386.49	1,329.59
Trade, Transportation, and Utilities													
2009	717.32	765.35	778.60	753.48	749.11	744.74	747.63	777.55	753.45	736.41	744.64	740.25	749.88
2010	725.19	746.86	757.15	760.55	784.44	764.90	767.54	801.87	794.40	783.13	780.15	809.08	774.20
2011	799.13	786.23	780.92	797.62	812.49	798.57	797.87	776.16	785.52	797.53	766.58	772.90	788.32
2012	783.00	756.81	745.89	767.36	745.42	754.89	779.01	761.77	799.66	764.90	766.52	786.47	767.29
2013	760.58	782.49	786.11	780.33	780.58	812.89	784.55	785.19	809.90	769.18	765.58	753.14	781.61
Information													
2009	1,834.75	2,022.87	1,992.84	1,817.47	1,806.61	1,806.61	2,035.02	1,968.10	1,795.50	1,802.88	1,978.94	1,799.88	1,886.92
2010	1,810.66	1,815.80	1,793.60	1,824.38	1,978.27	1,810.82	1,802.02	1,971.57	1,859.28	1,854.02	1,857.38	1,860.61	1,855.42
2011	2,031.96	1,872.95	1,834.26	1,852.95	2,005.32	1,817.72	1,774.10	1,726.33	1,825.64	2,007.77	1,856.30	1,865.06	1,873.65
2012	2,050.41	1,902.36	1,907.60	2,102.02	1,931.39	1,941.04	2,116.21	1,936.13	2,159.25	1,991.75	1,998.72	2,133.49	2,011.76
2013	1,985.96	2,011.13	2,020.40	2,020.99	2,034.88	2,186.51	1,990.13	1,978.51	2,288.97	2,126.99	2,118.76	2,311.29	2,091.85
Financial Activities													
2009	906.12	973.46	1,008.90	936.54	947.79	921.33	933.20	1,000.88	912.64	954.44	998.63	945.37	953.75
2010	1,066.90	1,075.86	1,069.61	1,031.40	1,099.87	989.89	996.78	1,044.90	997.28	1,001.84	979.39	984.06	1,027.03
2011	1,065.60	1,021.93	969.17	1,000.00	1,034.32	975.04	971.10	990.45	983.98	1,065.75	987.56	994.58	1,006.28
2012	1,076.25	1,005.31	989.71	1,066.14	985.32	978.25	1,041.07	989.76	1,054.76	987.74	988.72	1,050.52	1,018.16
2013	998.76	1,042.37	1,029.83	1,006.95	987.48	1,029.89	996.36	983.80	1,014.57	976.07	991.88	1,018.88	1,007.37
Professional and Business Services													
2009	1,017.96	1,066.97	1,067.43	1,041.76	1,039.00	1,030.52	1,029.76	1,081.50	1,034.54	1,025.49	1,059.84	1,043.19	1,044.13
2010	1,048.66	1,054.71	1,047.55	1,060.90	1,098.73	1,071.49	1,067.07	1,120.03	1,108.38	1,139.84	1,136.96	1,169.88	1,094.79
2011	1,190.44	1,175.84	1,155.97	1,170.17	1,195.38	1,168.87	1,171.32	1,154.54	1,169.37	1,239.13	1,181.09	1,190.82	1,181.04
2012	1,215.49	1,172.57	1,160.06	1,221.70	1,148.11	1,150.61	1,198.26	1,135.97	1,192.98	1,134.90	1,141.18	1,189.54	1,171.80
2013	1,137.94	1,173.88	1,159.49	1,169.28	1,148.47	1,208.79	1,125.01	1,139.76	1,191.50	1,156.29	1,158.29	1,182.96	1,163.52
Education and Health Services													
2009	801.14	783.15	776.77	786.88	783.44	789.71	820.65	807.86	795.95	816.54	834.56	826.21	802.63
2010	818.88	813.76	803.90	834.24	856.39	836.80	863.21	849.22	837.81	871.36	856.43	868.48	842.95
2011	899.77	867.02	856.32	858.75	861.25	845.56	844.17	836.98	851.05	869.86	846.80	861.35	858.13
2012	865.80	837.12	827.81	853.46	818.53	827.52	846.85	816.62	848.59	813.77	824.97	846.19	835.28
2013	810.54	808.04	798.22	801.06	791.90	825.25	802.01	810.90	835.23	809.94	826.25	841.41	813.12
Leisure and Hospitality													
2009	361.37	378.25	374.23	359.04	365.80	363.83	360.62	381.58	355.74	359.41	374.44	368.49	367.04
2010	349.28	359.90	354.53	351.14	364.03	345.94	348.10	365.57	339.65	318.82	314.40	329.10	345.63
2011	330.24	331.17	326.69	331.07	343.40	336.42	345.15	346.54	342.72	353.70	340.01	351.42	340.29
2012	352.90	358.00	357.17	370.73	360.83	363.63	379.22	372.93	378.31	365.33	362.82	392.40	368.28
2013	356.20	373.99	371.25	371.25	374.49	392.40	370.73	381.16	391.43	375.19	372.59	394.72	376.99
Other Services													
2009	655.03	711.89	723.53	672.38	664.97	686.96	762.93	674.56	655.40	650.64	689.89	675.12	685.13
2010	663.80	687.35	667.51	675.74	727.65	673.18	682.99	734.50	703.20	718.79	730.42	729.94	698.62
2011	755.66	724.68	691.12	703.64	720.63	677.51	674.87	658.52	651.48	654.50	625.74	630.53	680.15
2012	653.91	646.91	644.40	683.94	639.33	638.12	662.08	643.65	687.20	643.80	654.21	679.85	656.35
2013	651.00	681.65	672.94	673.44	678.29	703.25	695.77	701.16	734.50	692.59	703.25	749.94	695.45

WEST VIRGINIA
At a Glance

Population:
  2000 census: 1,808,193
  2010 census: 1,852,994
  2013 estimate: 1,854,304

Percent change in population:
  2000–2010: 2.5%
  2010–2013: 0.1%

Percent change in total nonfarm employment:
  2000–2010: 1.6%
  2010–2013: 2.1%

Industry with the largest growth in employment, 2000–2013 (thousands):
  Education and Health Services, 26.4

Industry with the largest decline or smallest growth in employment, 2000–2013 (thousands):
  Manufacturing, -27.5

Civilian labor force:
  2000: 808,861
  2010: 807,291
  2013: 796,242

Unemployment rate and rank among states (lowest to highest):
  2000: 5.5%, 48th
  2010: 8.5%, 24th
  2013: 6.5%, 18th

Over-the-year change in unemployment rates:
  2010–2011: -0.7%
  2011–2012: -0.6%
  2012–2013: -0.7%

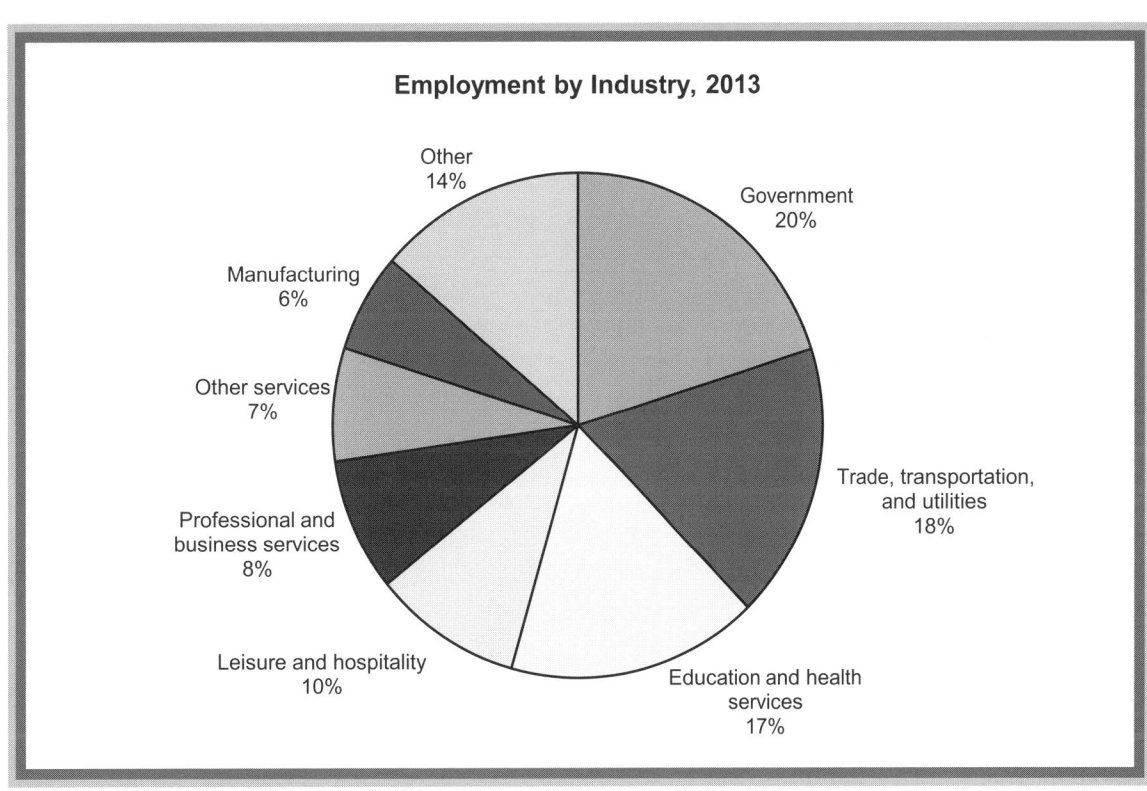

Employment by Industry, 2013

Other 14%
Government 20%
Manufacturing 6%
Other services 7%
Professional and business services 8%
Leisure and hospitality 10%
Education and health services 17%
Trade, transportation, and utilities 18%

1. Employment by Industry: West Virginia, Selected Years, 2002–2013

(Numbers in thousands, not seasonally adjusted)

Industry and year	January	February	March	April	May	June	July	August	September	October	November	December	Annual average
Total Nonfarm													
2002	716.7	719.9	727.5	731.5	747.3	736.6	730.2	731.8	735.6	735.9	738.2	737.2	732.4
2003	713.9	711.1	719.6	726.9	731.8	732.2	725.2	726.8	730.5	734.7	733.2	737.3	726.9
2004	715.6	717.4	728.0	736.8	753.0	740.6	735.7	736.2	742.1	746.2	745.9	747.3	737.1
2005	726.5	728.5	734.9	745.1	751.4	752.1	744.9	746.9	753.7	751.0	756.2	758.4	745.8
2006	737.6	741.3	750.4	754.3	770.0	761.9	749.8	753.7	761.6	762.1	766.4	766.1	756.3
2007	739.9	741.5	752.0	755.9	761.8	763.4	753.0	757.5	764.3	765.9	769.2	768.6	757.8
2008	746.1	750.6	754.9	760.4	777.2	762.7	758.9	760.8	768.7	770.4	770.0	767.8	762.4
2009	740.0	740.9	744.9	747.1	752.1	752.5	741.0	741.9	744.7	747.0	748.5	750.0	745.9
2010	724.6	725.6	737.9	745.4	762.7	753.2	747.7	748.1	754.8	756.5	758.5	755.1	747.5
2011	729.9	736.5	745.2	755.1	759.2	753.7	748.8	753.6	766.2	768.4	771.8	771.2	755.0
2012	748.7	754.5	762.6	768.1	782.3	763.6	755.7	758.6	770.7	771.9	772.5	772.0	765.1
2013	747.3	752.8	758.9	764.8	770.6	764.2	757.3	760.2	766.4	771.1	774.0	770.1	763.1
Total Private													
2002	577.6	578.9	583.8	588.1	592.8	594.4	595.5	596.5	595.0	592.6	593.1	592.3	590.1
2003	573.1	568.8	575.6	581.9	586.7	590.0	589.2	590.5	590.8	591.2	588.5	592.5	584.9
2004	575.2	575.4	583.3	591.6	597.1	597.3	598.7	599.4	600.3	600.4	600.5	602.2	593.5
2005	584.0	584.9	589.7	599.5	605.6	608.8	608.4	610.4	611.1	607.5	609.9	611.8	602.6
2006	596.3	596.5	603.9	607.9	612.8	618.3	613.0	615.2	617.5	615.1	618.5	618.1	611.1
2007	597.5	595.7	604.6	608.7	613.7	619.0	615.2	618.5	619.7	618.9	621.3	620.9	612.8
2008	602.8	604.1	607.0	612.3	616.3	618.2	618.6	619.5	621.4	620.6	619.6	617.3	614.8
2009	594.7	592.0	593.9	596.7	599.6	598.5	595.3	595.6	596.2	594.7	595.8	597.1	595.8
2010	575.5	573.9	582.9	590.9	593.8	599.0	600.8	601.7	602.8	602.9	603.9	600.7	594.1
2011	583.1	585.5	591.7	600.3	604.2	606.6	608.1	611.2	611.7	612.5	615.7	615.2	603.8
2012	597.9	599.7	606.0	612.1	615.4	616.2	614.0	615.8	616.9	615.8	615.1	614.8	611.6
2013	596.8	597.9	602.8	608.6	613.1	612.3	612.3	613.9	612.9	614.0	615.9	612.3	609.4
Goods-Producing													
2002	123.8	123.5	123.9	126.0	126.2	127.0	126.7	127.2	127.0	125.6	124.4	121.3	125.2
2003	116.0	113.6	116.3	118.4	119.8	121.1	121.5	121.1	121.4	121.3	120.6	118.9	119.2
2004	114.5	114.2	117.0	121.6	123.7	123.3	124.1	124.3	124.2	124.2	123.3	122.3	121.4
2005	118.3	118.8	119.9	123.4	125.6	127.3	127.1	127.9	129.0	128.7	128.1	126.8	125.1
2006	122.7	122.7	125.5	128.1	129.9	131.6	130.1	130.5	130.5	130.2	130.0	129.2	128.4
2007	123.4	121.0	124.3	125.9	127.3	129.4	128.6	128.7	128.2	128.4	127.8	125.5	126.5
2008	120.9	119.8	121.1	124.9	126.3	127.7	128.5	129.4	130.4	132.0	130.4	127.4	126.6
2009	118.9	116.8	116.8	116.3	115.9	114.3	112.7	112.7	112.0	112.7	112.1	111.6	114.4
2010	104.7	104.0	107.5	110.8	111.6	113.6	115.2	115.8	116.3	116.5	115.6	112.2	112.0
2011	107.7	108.4	110.6	114.1	115.8	117.9	118.9	119.7	120.0	120.3	120.5	119.6	116.1
2012	115.8	115.8	117.4	119.0	119.6	121.0	119.8	119.4	119.3	119.1	116.9	115.5	118.2
2013	110.7	110.5	111.7	114.3	116.3	116.0	116.8	117.0	116.3	116.9	116.4	112.1	114.6
Service-Providing													
2002	592.9	596.4	603.6	605.5	621.1	609.6	603.5	604.6	608.6	610.3	613.8	615.9	607.2
2003	597.9	597.5	603.3	608.5	612.0	611.1	603.7	605.7	609.1	613.4	612.6	618.4	607.8
2004	601.1	603.2	611.0	615.2	629.3	617.3	611.6	611.9	617.9	622.0	622.6	625.0	615.7
2005	608.2	609.7	615.0	621.7	625.8	624.8	617.8	619.0	624.7	622.3	628.1	631.6	620.7
2006	614.9	618.6	624.9	626.2	640.1	630.3	619.7	623.2	631.1	631.9	636.4	636.9	627.9
2007	616.5	620.5	627.7	630.0	634.5	634.0	624.4	628.8	636.1	637.5	641.4	643.1	631.2
2008	625.2	630.8	633.8	635.5	650.9	635.0	630.4	631.4	638.3	638.4	639.6	640.4	635.8
2009	621.1	624.1	628.1	630.8	636.2	638.2	628.3	629.2	632.7	634.3	636.4	638.4	631.5
2010	619.9	621.6	630.4	634.6	651.1	639.6	632.5	632.3	638.5	640.0	642.9	642.9	635.5
2011	622.2	628.1	634.6	641.0	643.4	635.8	629.9	633.9	646.2	648.1	651.3	651.6	638.8
2012	632.9	638.7	645.2	649.1	662.7	642.6	635.9	639.2	651.4	652.8	655.6	656.5	646.9
2013	636.6	642.3	647.2	650.5	654.3	648.2	640.5	643.2	650.1	654.2	657.6	658.0	648.6
Mining and Logging													
2002	24.4	24.1	23.6	23.3	22.9	22.9	22.6	22.8	22.8	22.7	22.9	22.5	23.1
2003	22.1	21.6	22.1	22.1	22.0	22.1	22.1	21.7	21.8	21.8	22.0	22.2	22.0
2004	22.4	22.1	22.5	23.4	23.9	24.1	24.2	24.2	24.5	24.6	24.6	24.7	23.8
2005	24.4	24.7	25.0	25.4	26.0	26.2	26.2	26.4	26.7	26.8	27.2	27.4	26.0
2006	27.2	27.4	27.7	27.8	27.9	28.3	28.3	28.2	28.3	28.0	28.3	28.4	28.0
2007	28.1	27.9	27.9	28.2	28.2	28.9	28.9	29.2	28.9	28.9	29.1	29.1	28.6
2008	28.7	28.8	29.2	29.8	30.5	31.1	31.3	31.7	32.5	33.3	33.4	33.4	31.1
2009	32.7	32.0	31.8	30.9	29.9	29.3	28.5	28.5	28.4	28.5	28.5	28.9	29.8
2010	28.2	28.4	28.8	29.2	29.4	30.1	30.5	30.9	31.1	31.2	31.6	31.6	30.1
2011	31.6	32.0	32.2	32.6	32.9	33.7	33.8	34.4	34.8	35.0	35.3	35.7	33.7
2012	35.2	34.9	34.7	34.0	33.7	33.7	33.1	33.0	32.8	32.6	32.5	32.2	33.5
2013	31.6	31.6	31.7	31.8	32.1	32.2	31.9	32.0	31.6	31.3	32.0	32.0	31.8
Construction													
2002	29.7	30.0	31.0	33.4	34.0	34.9	35.4	35.8	35.7	35.2	34.3	31.8	33.4
2003	28.4	27.1	29.3	31.3	32.9	34.1	34.6	34.9	35.3	35.5	34.9	33.6	32.7
2004	29.1	29.2	31.7	34.7	36.0	36.2	36.8	37.0	36.6	36.9	36.2	34.9	34.6
2005	31.9	32.2	33.0	35.9	37.2	38.3	38.3	38.9	39.6	39.8	39.1	37.5	36.8
2006	34.3	34.0	36.2	39.1	40.8	42.0	40.8	41.3	41.2	41.8	41.3	40.3	39.4
2007	36.2	34.2	37.2	38.7	39.9	40.8	40.2	40.3	40.2	40.9	40.3	38.3	38.9
2008	34.9	34.2	35.3	38.2	39.0	39.6	40.4	41.0	41.6	42.5	41.5	38.7	38.9
2009	32.6	32.6	33.9	33.8	35.1	34.6	34.8	34.5	34.2	34.9	34.4	33.5	34.1
2010	28.3	27.5	30.3	32.8	33.0	34.0	35.0	35.1	35.8	36.0	34.6	31.1	32.8
2011	27.4	27.7	29.2	32.2	33.4	34.2	35.1	35.5	35.6	35.8	35.6	34.3	33.0
2012	31.3	31.6	33.3	35.6	36.4	37.6	37.3	37.9	38.2	37.7	35.9	34.3	35.6
2013	31.0	30.9	32.0	34.4	35.8	35.1	36.1	36.3	36.0	37.0	35.7	31.8	34.3

1. Employment by Industry: West Virginia, Selected Years, 2002–2013—*Continued*

(Numbers in thousands, not seasonally adjusted)

Industry and year	January	February	March	April	May	June	July	August	September	October	November	December	Annual average
Manufacturing													
2002	69.7	69.4	69.3	69.3	69.3	69.2	68.7	68.6	68.5	67.7	67.2	67.0	68.7
2003	65.5	64.9	64.9	65.0	64.9	64.9	64.8	64.5	64.3	64.0	63.7	63.1	64.5
2004	63.0	62.9	62.8	63.5	63.8	63.0	63.1	63.1	63.1	62.7	62.5	62.7	63.0
2005	62.0	61.9	61.9	62.1	62.4	62.8	62.6	62.6	62.7	62.1	61.8	61.9	62.2
2006	61.2	61.3	61.6	61.2	61.2	61.3	61.0	61.0	61.0	60.4	60.4	60.5	61.0
2007	59.1	58.9	59.2	59.0	59.2	59.7	59.5	59.2	59.1	58.6	58.4	58.1	59.0
2008	57.3	56.8	56.6	56.9	56.8	57.0	56.8	56.7	56.3	56.2	55.5	55.3	56.5
2009	53.6	52.2	51.1	51.6	50.9	50.4	49.4	49.7	49.4	49.3	49.2	49.2	50.5
2010	48.2	48.1	48.4	48.8	49.2	49.5	49.7	49.8	49.4	49.3	49.4	49.5	49.1
2011	48.7	48.7	49.2	49.3	49.5	50.0	50.0	49.8	49.6	49.5	49.6	49.6	49.5
2012	49.3	49.3	49.4	49.4	49.5	49.7	49.4	48.5	48.3	48.8	48.5	49.0	49.1
2013	48.1	48.0	48.0	48.1	48.4	48.7	48.8	48.7	48.7	48.6	48.7	48.3	48.4
Trade, Transportation, and Utilities													
2002	136.1	134.9	135.9	136.2	137.4	137.7	137.1	136.9	136.2	136.6	138.6	139.7	136.9
2003	133.5	131.7	132.9	134.3	135.5	136.1	135.8	136.3	136.2	136.8	136.7	140.2	135.5
2004	134.7	133.3	134.2	135.3	136.5	137.0	137.4	137.9	138.0	139.0	141.4	142.3	137.3
2005	136.9	136.1	136.7	138.1	139.6	139.7	139.6	139.8	139.9	140.3	143.2	144.6	139.5
2006	139.0	138.1	139.6	140.3	141.1	142.1	141.2	141.6	142.2	143.2	146.5	147.2	141.8
2007	141.3	140.1	141.6	141.4	142.6	143.3	142.7	143.4	143.6	144.4	147.2	147.8	143.3
2008	141.7	140.8	141.5	140.9	141.4	141.9	141.7	141.5	141.5	141.0	142.6	143.3	141.7
2009	136.5	134.6	134.6	135.0	135.8	136.3	135.5	135.5	135.8	135.6	137.6	138.2	135.9
2010	132.5	131.1	132.5	133.2	134.4	134.8	134.8	134.7	134.1	135.8	138.8	139.1	134.7
2011	133.4	132.5	133.2	134.4	134.8	135.2	135.3	135.8	135.5	136.1	139.1	139.7	135.4
2012	134.4	132.9	133.8	134.0	134.7	135.0	134.9	135.4	135.6	136.4	139.7	140.2	135.6
2013	134.3	133.2	133.4	134.1	134.7	135.5	135.5	135.4	135.4	135.3	137.8	139.1	135.3
Wholesale Trade													
2002	23.0	23.2	23.4	23.5	23.5	23.4	23.3	23.2	23.1	23.0	23.0	23.0	23.2
2003	22.4	22.3	22.6	22.7	22.9	23.0	22.9	22.9	22.8	22.8	22.8	22.8	22.7
2004	22.7	22.8	23.0	23.2	23.2	23.2	23.2	23.1	23.3	23.5	23.6	23.7	23.2
2005	23.6	23.6	23.8	24.1	24.3	24.4	24.4	24.3	24.3	24.3	24.4	24.6	24.2
2006	24.3	24.3	24.5	24.7	24.8	25.3	24.9	25.0	25.1	25.2	25.5	25.6	24.9
2007	24.8	24.7	24.9	24.8	24.8	24.9	25.0	25.1	25.2	25.5	25.6	25.7	25.1
2008	24.5	24.5	24.6	24.6	24.8	24.8	24.6	24.6	24.7	24.5	24.4	24.4	24.6
2009	23.8	23.5	23.5	23.4	23.5	23.4	23.3	23.1	23.1	23.0	22.9	22.8	23.3
2010	22.4	22.3	22.5	22.7	22.7	22.8	23.0	22.9	23.0	23.3	23.4	23.3	22.9
2011	22.7	22.6	22.9	23.1	23.2	23.2	23.2	23.3	23.3	23.4	23.6	23.7	23.2
2012	23.1	22.9	23.2	23.1	23.1	23.1	23.0	23.0	23.2	23.4	23.7	23.5	23.2
2013	22.8	22.7	22.6	22.7	22.7	22.9	23.0	23.1	23.1	22.8	23.2	23.2	22.9
Retail Trade													
2002	87.2	86.0	86.9	87.1	88.1	88.3	88.2	88.1	87.8	88.2	90.4	91.5	88.2
2003	86.0	84.5	85.3	86.6	87.4	87.9	87.8	88.2	88.2	89.0	89.0	92.5	87.7
2004	87.4	85.9	86.4	87.0	88.1	88.4	88.7	89.1	88.9	89.6	92.0	92.7	88.7
2005	88.0	87.0	87.3	88.3	89.4	89.2	89.2	89.3	89.3	89.7	92.5	93.5	89.4
2006	88.8	87.9	89.0	89.2	89.7	90.0	89.7	89.9	90.4	91.3	94.2	94.6	90.4
2007	90.0	89.0	90.2	89.9	90.8	91.2	90.7	91.2	91.2	91.9	94.5	94.9	91.3
2008	90.4	89.4	90.1	89.1	89.3	89.6	89.6	89.4	89.3	89.1	90.9	91.5	89.8
2009	86.4	84.8	85.0	85.6	86.4	87.0	86.6	86.8	87.1	87.2	89.4	90.0	86.9
2010	85.3	84.0	84.9	85.4	86.3	86.5	86.5	86.5	85.9	87.2	90.1	90.2	86.6
2011	85.7	84.8	85.3	86.5	86.8	87.1	87.1	87.5	87.1	87.6	90.4	90.7	87.2
2012	86.7	85.4	86.1	86.4	87.1	87.3	87.4	87.8	87.6	88.2	91.1	91.4	87.7
2013	86.9	85.9	86.2	86.7	87.3	87.8	87.6	87.3	87.2	87.2	89.0	89.6	87.4
Transportation and Utilities													
2002	25.9	25.7	25.6	25.6	25.8	26.0	25.6	25.6	25.3	25.4	25.2	25.2	25.6
2003	25.1	24.9	25.0	25.0	25.2	25.2	25.1	25.2	25.2	25.0	24.9	24.9	25.1
2004	24.6	24.6	24.8	25.1	25.2	25.4	25.5	25.7	25.8	25.9	25.8	25.9	25.4
2005	25.3	25.5	25.6	25.7	25.9	26.1	26.0	26.2	26.3	26.3	26.3	26.5	26.0
2006	25.9	25.9	26.1	26.4	26.6	26.8	26.6	26.7	26.7	26.7	26.8	27.0	26.5
2007	26.5	26.4	26.5	26.7	27.0	27.2	27.0	27.1	27.2	27.0	27.1	27.2	26.9
2008	26.8	26.9	26.8	27.2	27.3	27.5	27.5	27.5	27.5	27.4	27.3	27.4	27.3
2009	26.3	26.3	26.1	26.0	25.9	25.9	25.6	25.6	25.6	25.4	25.3	25.4	25.8
2010	24.8	24.8	25.1	25.1	25.4	25.5	25.3	25.3	25.2	25.3	25.3	25.6	25.2
2011	25.0	25.1	25.0	24.8	24.8	24.9	25.0	25.0	25.1	25.1	25.1	25.3	25.0
2012	24.6	24.6	24.5	24.5	24.5	24.6	24.5	24.6	24.8	24.8	24.9	25.3	24.7
2013	24.6	24.6	24.6	24.7	24.7	24.8	24.9	25.0	25.1	25.3	25.6	26.3	25.0
Information													
2002	13.4	13.4	13.4	13.2	13.3	13.3	13.3	13.3	13.2	13.2	13.4	13.4	13.3
2003	12.9	12.8	12.8	12.7	12.6	12.6	12.6	12.6	12.5	12.3	12.2	12.0	12.5
2004	11.8	11.7	12.0	11.9	11.9	12.0	12.0	12.0	12.0	11.8	11.7	11.8	11.9
2005	11.6	11.4	11.5	11.5	11.7	11.8	11.9	12.0	11.8	11.8	11.9	12.0	11.7
2006	11.7	11.5	11.5	11.4	11.5	11.6	11.5	11.6	11.6	11.5	11.4	11.4	11.5
2007	11.3	11.3	11.2	11.3	11.4	11.5	11.6	11.5	11.5	11.4	11.4	11.5	11.4
2008	11.3	11.3	11.2	11.2	11.2	11.2	11.2	11.2	11.1	11.1	11.0	10.9	11.2
2009	10.9	10.7	10.7	10.6	10.5	10.4	10.3	10.2	10.3	10.2	10.2	10.4	10.4
2010	10.1	10.0	10.0	9.8	10.1	10.3	10.7	10.6	10.5	10.5	10.5	10.6	10.3
2011	10.4	10.4	10.4	10.3	10.2	10.2	10.2	10.2	10.0	10.0	9.9	9.9	10.2
2012	9.5	9.5	9.5	9.6	9.6	9.7	9.6	9.6	9.6	9.6	9.6	9.5	9.6
2013	9.3	9.4	9.5	9.5	9.5	9.5	9.5	9.5	9.5	9.4	9.6	9.6	9.5

1. Employment by Industry: West Virginia, Selected Years, 2002–2013—*Continued*

(Numbers in thousands, not seasonally adjusted)

Industry and year	January	February	March	April	May	June	July	August	September	October	November	December	Annual average
Financial Activities													
2002	30.2	30.4	30.7	30.8	31.0	31.3	31.5	31.7	31.5	31.6	31.6	31.8	31.2
2003	30.8	30.8	30.8	30.9	30.7	31.0	30.6	30.6	30.7	30.7	30.7	30.8	30.8
2004	30.3	30.1	30.4	30.5	30.5	30.7	30.7	30.4	30.1	30.1	29.9	30.0	30.3
2005	29.6	29.5	29.5	29.7	29.7	29.8	29.8	29.8	29.7	29.6	29.7	29.7	29.7
2006	29.9	29.9	30.0	30.1	30.3	30.7	30.1	30.1	30.0	30.0	29.9	30.0	30.1
2007	29.5	29.5	29.6	29.8	30.0	30.2	30.0	30.1	30.0	29.9	29.9	30.1	29.9
2008	29.8	29.8	29.7	29.9	29.8	29.9	29.9	29.7	29.6	29.6	29.6	29.6	29.7
2009	28.9	28.7	28.7	28.9	29.1	29.1	29.0	28.8	28.6	28.6	28.4	28.4	28.8
2010	28.1	28.1	28.4	28.5	28.5	28.8	28.5	28.4	28.3	28.5	28.5	28.4	28.4
2011	27.9	27.6	27.6	27.7	27.8	27.8	28.0	27.9	27.9	28.0	27.9	28.1	27.9
2012	27.7	27.9	28.0	28.2	28.3	28.4	28.4	28.6	28.6	28.3	28.3	28.6	28.3
2013	28.2	28.4	28.6	28.8	28.7	28.7	28.7	28.7	28.6	28.7	29.3	29.6	28.8
Professional and Business Services													
2002	54.5	54.8	55.6	56.5	56.6	57.4	57.8	58.4	57.7	56.8	57.0	57.5	56.7
2003	55.5	55.4	55.8	56.3	56.3	57.0	56.7	57.1	57.0	57.5	57.4	58.7	56.7
2004	57.3	57.2	57.6	57.7	57.6	58.4	59.0	59.2	59.0	59.1	58.5	60.1	58.4
2005	57.6	57.1	57.5	58.6	58.4	59.1	59.2	59.7	59.2	59.3	59.8	60.8	58.9
2006	59.4	59.5	59.7	60.0	59.5	60.6	60.2	60.3	60.2	59.4	59.8	59.6	59.9
2007	59.1	58.8	59.7	60.7	60.7	61.1	60.9	61.4	61.2	61.1	61.4	62.4	60.7
2008	60.2	60.4	60.4	61.4	61.3	61.5	61.4	61.3	60.8	61.1	61.1	61.4	61.0
2009	60.1	60.0	59.7	60.3	60.0	60.1	59.8	60.1	60.0	60.2	60.7	61.7	60.2
2010	59.7	59.5	60.2	61.3	60.4	61.0	61.8	61.7	61.5	61.8	61.9	62.0	61.1
2011	61.3	61.9	62.5	63.4	62.8	63.2	63.7	64.2	64.4	64.6	65.2	65.2	63.5
2012	63.4	63.7	63.9	65.2	65.0	65.1	64.7	65.1	64.8	65.0	64.6	64.7	64.6
2013	63.4	63.9	64.5	64.9	65.1	65.2	65.4	65.9	65.1	65.6	66.2	65.7	65.1
Education and Health Services													
2002	104.9	106.7	107.4	106.9	107.3	105.5	105.8	105.4	107.0	108.5	109.3	109.7	107.0
2003	107.9	108.2	108.7	108.6	109.0	107.4	106.5	107.1	108.6	110.3	110.5	110.8	108.6
2004	107.9	110.0	111.0	110.9	111.0	109.3	108.9	109.1	111.2	112.4	112.8	112.7	110.6
2005	110.3	112.1	112.6	113.0	113.1	112.5	112.2	112.6	114.1	113.3	113.9	114.3	112.8
2006	112.1	113.1	113.6	113.4	113.3	111.5	110.5	110.9	113.2	113.6	114.1	114.1	112.8
2007	110.7	112.7	113.5	113.1	113.6	112.9	112.0	112.9	115.5	116.2	116.8	116.4	113.9
2008	114.3	116.6	116.5	116.4	116.4	115.2	114.7	115.0	117.4	117.1	117.6	117.4	116.2
2009	115.0	117.0	117.7	118.5	119.0	118.0	117.7	118.1	120.4	120.7	121.2	121.4	118.7
2010	118.0	119.4	120.4	120.8	120.5	119.8	119.5	119.7	122.2	121.9	122.4	122.4	120.6
2011	119.7	121.5	122.3	123.2	123.5	121.6	121.1	122.0	124.0	124.9	125.6	125.6	122.9
2012	122.5	124.4	125.3	126.2	126.5	124.3	123.7	124.5	127.4	127.2	127.5	127.7	125.6
2013	124.3	126.1	126.5	126.6	126.9	124.5	123.6	124.6	127.0	127.8	128.0	127.9	126.2
Leisure and Hospitality													
2002	59.8	60.2	61.7	63.0	65.3	66.6	67.9	68.2	67.1	65.2	63.8	63.7	64.4
2003	61.8	61.7	63.3	65.4	67.6	69.3	70.0	70.4	68.9	66.9	65.4	66.0	66.4
2004	64.1	64.3	65.8	67.8	69.6	70.8	71.2	71.5	70.3	68.3	67.1	67.4	68.2
2005	65.1	65.3	66.6	68.5	70.6	72.0	72.7	73.0	71.7	69.2	68.1	68.3	69.3
2006	66.9	67.0	68.7	69.3	71.7	74.1	73.8	74.4	73.7	70.9	70.5	70.5	71.0
2007	67.0	66.9	69.0	70.9	72.6	74.6	74.0	75.3	74.3	72.1	71.3	71.9	71.7
2008	69.3	69.9	70.9	72.2	74.1	75.0	75.6	76.0	75.2	73.2	71.6	71.6	72.9
2009	68.8	68.7	70.3	71.3	73.4	74.5	74.8	75.1	73.9	71.4	70.2	70.2	71.9
2010	67.7	67.4	69.3	71.5	73.0	75.0	75.1	75.8	74.8	72.9	71.4	71.2	72.1
2011	68.6	68.9	70.5	72.4	74.3	75.5	75.6	76.3	74.8	73.2	72.1	72.0	72.9
2012	69.9	70.7	72.7	74.0	75.7	76.7	77.1	77.6	76.2	74.6	73.0	73.2	74.3
2013	71.7	71.5	72.9	74.3	76.3	77.3	77.2	77.3	75.6	75.1	73.4	73.3	74.7
Other Services													
2002	54.9	55.0	55.2	55.5	55.7	55.6	55.4	55.4	55.3	55.1	55.0	55.2	55.3
2003	54.7	54.6	55.0	55.3	55.2	55.5	55.5	55.4	55.7	55.5	55.0	55.1	55.2
2004	54.6	54.6	55.3	55.9	56.3	55.8	55.4	55.0	55.7	55.6	55.7	55.6	55.5
2005	54.6	54.6	55.4	56.7	56.9	56.6	55.9	55.6	55.7	55.3	55.2	55.3	55.7
2006	54.6	54.7	55.3	55.3	55.5	56.1	55.6	55.8	56.2	56.3	56.3	56.1	55.7
2007	55.2	55.4	55.7	55.6	55.5	56.0	55.4	55.2	55.4	55.4	55.5	55.3	55.5
2008	55.3	55.5	55.7	55.4	55.8	55.8	55.6	55.4	55.4	55.5	55.7	55.7	55.6
2009	55.6	55.5	55.4	55.8	55.9	55.8	55.5	55.1	55.2	55.3	55.4	55.4	55.5
2010	54.7	54.4	54.6	55.0	55.3	55.7	55.2	55.0	55.1	55.0	54.8	54.8	55.0
2011	54.1	54.3	54.6	54.8	55.0	55.2	55.3	55.1	55.1	55.4	55.4	55.1	55.0
2012	54.7	54.8	55.4	55.9	56.0	56.0	55.8	55.6	55.4	55.6	55.5	55.4	55.5
2013	54.9	54.9	55.7	56.1	55.6	55.6	55.6	55.5	55.4	55.2	55.2	55.0	55.4
Government													
2002	139.1	141.0	143.7	143.4	154.5	142.2	134.7	135.3	140.6	143.3	145.1	144.9	142.3
2003	140.8	142.3	144.0	145.0	145.1	142.2	136.0	136.3	139.7	143.5	144.7	144.8	142.0
2004	140.4	142.0	144.7	145.2	155.9	143.3	137.0	136.8	141.8	145.8	145.4	145.1	143.6
2005	142.5	143.6	145.2	145.6	145.8	143.3	136.5	136.5	142.6	143.5	146.3	146.6	143.2
2006	141.3	144.8	146.5	146.4	157.2	143.6	136.8	138.5	144.1	147.0	147.9	148.0	145.2
2007	142.4	145.8	147.4	147.2	148.1	144.4	137.8	139.0	144.6	147.0	147.9	147.7	144.9
2008	143.3	146.5	147.9	148.1	160.9	144.5	140.3	141.3	147.3	149.8	150.4	150.5	147.6
2009	145.3	148.9	151.0	150.4	152.5	154.0	145.7	146.3	148.5	152.3	152.7	152.9	150.0
2010	149.1	151.7	155.0	154.5	168.9	154.2	146.9	146.4	152.0	153.6	154.6	154.4	153.4
2011	146.8	151.0	153.5	154.8	155.0	147.1	140.7	142.4	154.5	155.9	156.1	156.0	151.2
2012	150.8	154.8	156.6	156.0	166.9	147.4	141.7	142.8	153.8	156.1	157.4	157.2	153.5
2013	150.5	154.9	156.1	156.2	157.5	151.9	145.0	146.3	153.5	157.1	158.1	157.8	153.7

2. Average Weekly Hours by Selected Industry: West Virginia, 2009–2013

(Not seasonally adjusted)

Industry and year	January	February	March	April	May	June	July	August	September	October	November	December	Annual average
Total Private													
2009	34.0	34.1	34.1	34.0	34.3	34.3	34.4	34.6	34.6	34.6	35.1	35.1	34.4
2010	34.4	34.2	34.6	35.2	35.3	35.1	35.0	35.1	35.1	35.2	35.1	34.8	34.9
2011	34.8	34.5	34.3	34.7	35.1	34.9	34.5	34.4	34.6	34.4	34.2	34.1	34.5
2012	34.1	34.0	34.1	34.5	34.3	34.7	34.9	34.5	34.8	34.5	34.5	34.5	34.4
2013	33.9	34.0	34.4	34.3	34.6	34.9	34.4	34.7	35.0	34.8	35.0	34.5	34.5
Goods-Producing													
2009	40.6	40.3	40.1	40.1	40.4	40.9	40.6	41.6	41.0	41.0	41.5	41.4	40.8
2010	40.7	40.0	40.6	41.5	41.3	41.6	41.2	41.6	41.1	41.2	41.2	40.7	41.1
2011	40.8	40.4	39.9	40.1	40.8	40.6	40.3	40.3	40.1	40.4	40.6	40.5	40.4
2012	40.9	40.1	40.0	40.1	39.7	40.7	39.2	39.5	40.4	39.7	39.7	39.6	40.0
2013	39.2	39.4	39.9	39.7	41.1	40.7	40.0	41.0	41.6	41.6	41.4	39.5	40.4
Mining and Logging													
2009	45.7	45.1	44.9	45.0	44.2	45.8	45.3	46.1	45.3	45.1	46.0	45.9	45.4
2010	46.4	45.6	46.0	45.5	46.3	46.8	45.5	46.6	47.0	47.4	47.0	46.1	46.4
2011	48.7	47.4	46.9	46.3	45.9	45.4	44.0	45.3	44.2	44.0	44.0	44.5	45.5
2012	47.1	42.8	42.9	42.4	42.2	42.9	41.4	42.1	43.6	42.2	39.8	41.5	42.6
2013	41.7	41.0	43.6	42.4	42.6	43.6	42.2	43.1	43.7	45.5	43.9	41.8	43.0
Construction													
2009	36.5	36.7	36.4	36.5	38.2	38.5	39.1	39.8	39.1	39.5	40.0	39.7	38.4
2010	38.1	36.4	38.2	41.3	38.9	40.2	40.0	40.5	39.9	40.0	39.1	37.4	39.3
2011	37.0	36.7	36.7	38.8	40.4	40.3	40.2	40.1	39.2	39.9	40.5	39.2	39.2
2012	37.3	38.0	38.2	39.0	38.7	40.4	39.6	39.7	39.7	39.8	40.1	38.8	39.2
2013	37.9	38.5	38.2	39.6	41.3	40.5	39.9	40.8	41.2	40.0	40.0	38.1	39.7
Manufacturing													
2009	40.1	39.7	39.5	39.5	39.6	39.7	39.0	40.2	39.9	39.7	39.9	39.9	39.7
2010	38.9	38.8	38.9	39.2	40.0	39.4	39.4	39.2	38.2	38.2	39.0	39.3	39.0
2011	37.9	37.9	37.3	36.8	37.6	37.5	38.0	37.0	37.9	38.2	38.2	38.5	37.7
2012	38.8	39.5	39.2	39.4	38.8	39.3	37.3	37.7	38.7	37.9	39.3	38.9	38.7
2013	38.4	38.9	38.5	38.0	39.9	39.0	38.5	39.8	40.6	40.3	40.7	38.9	39.3
Trade, Transportation, and Utilities													
2009	34.8	34.5	34.5	34.4	34.8	34.6	34.4	34.2	34.1	34.6	34.6	35.0	34.5
2010	34.5	34.9	35.2	36.7	36.4	36.8	36.4	36.6	36.4	36.5	36.2	35.5	36.0
2011	35.2	34.7	35.2	35.4	35.8	35.6	35.6	35.4	35.6	35.2	34.7	34.8	35.3
2012	33.8	33.9	34.5	35.1	35.2	34.9	35.5	35.4	35.4	34.8	34.8	35.3	34.9
2013	34.3	34.7	35.0	35.0	34.9	35.3	35.1	35.0	34.9	34.7	34.6	34.5	34.8
Financial Activities													
2009	35.3	35.4	35.3	35.4	35.9	35.9	35.9	36.0	35.9	36.0	36.1	35.3	35.7
2010	36.1	36.0	35.4	35.2	36.3	36.0	35.9	36.1	36.3	36.0	35.8	36.0	36.0
2011	36.3	36.2	36.0	36.5	36.8	36.3	36.0	35.5	36.7	37.4	35.6	35.1	36.2
2012	36.2	36.1	35.4	36.5	35.5	35.5	36.0	34.9	35.9	35.2	35.5	35.8	35.7
2013	34.4	34.4	35.5	36.0	35.9	37.3	35.3	36.7	37.2	37.2	37.4	37.5	36.3
Professional and Business Services													
2009	34.8	35.0	35.4	35.5	35.8	35.3	35.2	36.0	35.6	35.4	36.5	36.5	35.6
2010	36.2	36.4	36.8	36.4	37.1	36.5	36.1	37.4	36.8	36.6	36.6	36.7	36.6
2011	37.0	37.1	37.0	37.6	38.2	37.6	37.0	37.4	37.2	37.5	37.7	36.6	37.3
2012	36.6	35.7	36.1	37.0	36.6	37.0	38.0	36.7	37.5	36.7	37.2	36.6	36.8
2013	35.4	35.4	36.1	36.1	35.9	36.5	35.9	36.1	36.1	36.1	35.4	35.6	35.9
Education and Health Services													
2009	34.4	34.7	34.7	34.5	34.4	34.2	34.2	34.2	34.5	34.5	34.7	34.4	34.5
2010	34.2	34.4	34.7	34.8	35.0	34.7	34.6	34.2	34.3	34.5	34.4	34.0	34.5
2011	34.3	34.3	34.0	34.2	34.2	34.4	34.2	34.1	33.8	34.2	33.8	33.8	34.1
2012	34.1	34.0	33.8	34.0	33.6	34.3	34.3	34.0	34.3	34.1	34.3	34.1	34.1
2013	34.1	33.9	34.1	34.2	34.2	34.3	34.0	33.9	34.5	34.4	35.1	34.8	34.3
Leisure and Hospitality													
2009	26.7	27.1	27.0	27.3	27.8	28.2	28.5	27.9	27.6	27.2	27.2	26.7	27.5
2010	26.5	26.4	27.2	27.4	27.4	27.9	28.1	28.3	27.6	27.5	26.8	26.4	27.3
2011	26.4	27.0	26.7	26.5	26.8	26.9	27.4	27.1	26.4	26.7	26.1	26.0	26.7
2012	25.2	25.9	26.3	26.6	26.9	26.8	27.6	27.3	26.2	26.4	26.1	26.1	26.5
2013	25.3	26.0	26.2	25.8	26.1	26.3	26.5	26.5	26.2	26.0	26.0	25.6	26.0
Other Services													
2009	31.4	31.5	31.8	31.6	31.6	31.6	31.3	32.1	32.1	32.2	32.5	32.4	31.8
2010	31.4	31.7	31.8	33.0	32.3	32.0	32.2	31.7	31.7	31.5	31.6	31.5	31.9
2011	31.2	30.9	30.7	31.1	31.0	31.0	30.9	31.2	30.4	31.4	31.3	31.3	31.0
2012	31.1	32.1	32.0	30.9	31.6	31.8	32.0	32.3	32.5	32.8	32.7	33.1	32.1
2013	32.9	32.3	31.9	32.5	32.0	32.7	31.8	32.9	32.9	31.4	32.0	31.7	32.3

3. Average Hourly Earnings by Selected Industry: West Virginia, 2009–2013

(Dollars, not seasonally adjusted)

Industry and year	January	February	March	April	May	June	July	August	September	October	November	December	Annual average
Total Private													
2009	18.19	18.10	18.13	18.17	17.90	17.85	17.96	18.01	18.12	18.15	18.23	18.28	18.09
2010	18.41	18.63	18.49	18.52	18.72	18.69	18.78	18.83	18.68	18.58	18.62	18.88	18.65
2011	18.82	18.66	18.74	18.86	18.87	18.84	18.96	18.90	19.05	19.12	19.23	19.18	18.94
2012	19.43	19.39	19.33	19.56	19.33	19.37	19.43	19.45	19.85	19.73	19.79	20.05	19.56
2013	20.09	20.26	20.13	20.34	20.29	20.44	20.49	20.40	20.56	20.45	20.44	20.41	20.36
Goods-Producing													
2009	22.96	22.83	23.02	23.07	22.75	22.81	22.88	22.94	22.86	22.83	23.04	22.89	22.91
2010	22.93	22.74	22.67	22.65	22.74	22.82	22.75	22.85	22.83	22.66	22.70	23.20	22.79
2011	22.81	22.60	22.60	22.78	22.82	22.67	22.73	22.82	22.82	23.16	23.31	23.52	22.89
2012	23.51	23.08	23.32	23.25	23.11	23.53	23.53	23.77	24.11	23.87	24.06	24.32	23.62
2013	24.48	24.64	24.95	25.08	25.16	25.32	25.39	25.11	25.38	25.28	25.52	25.45	25.15
Mining and Logging													
2009	26.10	26.01	26.26	26.41	26.47	26.26	26.16	27.00	27.03	26.90	26.99	26.59	26.50
2010	27.01	26.77	26.76	26.66	26.73	26.24	25.88	26.04	25.60	25.42	25.52	26.26	26.22
2011	25.68	25.78	26.05	26.11	26.11	25.60	25.26	25.69	25.80	26.51	26.54	26.86	26.00
2012	27.18	27.06	27.73	27.49	27.21	27.60	27.95	27.94	28.69	27.89	28.49	28.85	27.82
2013	29.40	29.51	30.00	30.41	30.65	31.40	31.73	31.31	31.43	31.80	32.05	32.07	30.99
Construction													
2009	22.18	22.21	23.02	23.10	22.55	22.49	22.89	22.97	22.76	22.93	23.15	22.71	22.75
2010	23.12	22.64	22.63	22.36	22.30	22.60	22.61	22.96	23.14	22.89	23.12	23.77	22.84
2011	23.29	22.69	22.53	22.98	23.14	23.36	23.93	23.75	23.58	23.77	24.42	24.48	23.55
2012	23.52	23.46	23.73	23.10	23.24	23.21	23.27	24.14	23.96	24.33	24.42	24.39	23.74
2013	24.74	24.65	25.12	25.02	25.13	24.90	24.83	24.66	24.91	24.58	24.57	24.58	24.81
Manufacturing													
2009	21.21	20.98	20.74	20.78	20.44	20.71	20.68	20.25	20.22	20.09	20.32	20.51	20.58
2010	19.98	20.00	19.82	20.06	20.26	20.51	20.63	20.42	20.44	20.32	20.24	20.56	20.27
2011	20.16	19.93	19.81	19.88	19.92	19.77	19.85	19.66	19.81	19.96	19.81	20.07	19.89
2012	20.31	19.78	19.66	20.21	19.99	20.76	20.46	20.29	20.74	20.51	20.79	21.09	20.38
2013	20.79	21.24	21.05	21.18	21.30	21.14	21.27	21.04	21.49	21.06	21.57	21.30	21.21
Trade, Transportation, and Utilities													
2009	15.40	15.36	15.45	15.43	15.12	15.11	15.09	15.24	15.30	15.37	15.28	15.29	15.29
2010	15.63	16.30	16.33	16.35	16.63	16.61	16.56	16.75	16.69	16.42	16.16	16.14	16.39
2011	16.52	16.54	16.61	16.88	16.79	16.76	17.02	16.87	17.48	17.11	17.10	16.83	16.88
2012	17.30	17.41	17.59	17.92	17.52	17.59	17.42	17.29	17.80	17.28	17.47	17.20	17.48
2013	17.20	17.29	17.17	17.32	17.40	17.67	17.68	17.59	17.66	17.72	17.77	17.96	17.54
Financial Activities													
2009	17.15	17.13	17.16	17.23	17.08	17.07	17.03	16.81	16.74	16.90	17.00	17.00	17.02
2010	17.22	17.27	17.07	17.34	17.48	17.49	17.57	17.96	17.09	17.25	17.39	17.32	17.37
2011	17.23	17.18	17.33	17.41	17.48	17.14	17.63	17.95	17.80	18.16	18.28	17.86	17.62
2012	17.79	17.96	18.15	18.50	18.01	17.67	18.04	17.99	17.25	17.32	17.11	17.10	17.74
2013	17.39	17.53	17.94	18.49	18.30	18.57	18.88	19.11	19.63	19.23	18.96	20.03	18.70
Professional and Business Services													
2009	19.89	20.08	20.04	20.18	19.99	19.90	19.92	19.76	19.58	19.49	19.40	19.44	19.80
2010	20.16	20.04	20.12	19.91	20.18	19.74	19.77	19.47	19.47	19.48	19.59	19.88	19.81
2011	19.71	19.83	19.90	19.71	19.78	19.81	19.98	20.05	20.23	20.85	20.63	20.72	20.11
2012	21.76	21.52	21.52	22.39	21.91	21.44	22.09	21.90	22.11	21.92	21.77	22.56	21.91
2013	22.08	22.36	22.26	22.58	22.18	22.08	21.38	21.36	21.41	20.73	21.32	21.15	21.74
Education and Health Services													
2009	18.22	18.52	18.41	18.39	18.44	18.37	18.42	18.21	18.48	18.59	18.66	18.87	18.47
2010	18.83	18.73	18.65	18.66	18.90	19.00	19.39	19.24	19.19	18.92	19.08	19.22	18.98
2011	19.42	19.62	19.56	19.50	19.39	19.63	19.94	19.78	19.60	19.50	19.70	19.67	19.61
2012	19.66	20.11	19.81	19.92	20.02	20.00	20.10	20.01	20.41	20.60	20.56	21.12	20.20
2013	21.27	21.61	21.08	21.31	21.26	21.53	21.96	21.79	21.76	21.63	21.15	21.12	21.45
Leisure and Hospitality													
2009	10.34	10.34	10.54	10.66	10.47	10.51	10.45	10.71	10.57	10.43	10.36	10.62	10.50
2010	10.54	10.66	10.57	10.34	10.49	10.45	10.47	10.52	10.46	10.55	10.75	11.07	10.57
2011	10.92	10.85	10.68	10.56	10.61	10.55	10.51	10.54	10.51	10.59	10.64	10.67	10.63
2012	10.71	10.59	10.59	10.45	10.40	10.26	10.31	10.26	10.39	10.42	10.40	10.58	10.44
2013	10.41	10.43	10.31	10.46	10.32	10.37	10.36	10.41	10.50	10.51	10.56	10.71	10.44
Other Services													
2009	16.84	16.88	17.00	16.93	16.54	16.54	16.36	16.58	16.54	16.54	16.69	16.64	16.67
2010	16.64	16.98	16.90	16.70	16.75	16.32	16.19	16.47	16.25	16.13	15.93	16.25	16.46
2011	16.23	16.40	16.21	15.76	15.77	15.74	15.63	15.59	15.67	15.80	15.84	16.14	15.90
2012	16.06	15.77	16.15	16.13	16.05	16.01	15.86	16.17	16.49	16.51	17.01	17.11	16.28
2013	17.06	17.42	17.51	17.56	17.53	17.43	17.48	17.56	18.22	18.63	18.45	18.94	17.81

4. Average Weekly Earnings by Selected Industry: West Virginia, 2009–2013

(Dollars, not seasonally adjusted)

Industry and year	January	February	March	April	May	June	July	August	September	October	November	December	Annual average
Total Private													
2009	618.46	617.21	618.23	617.78	613.97	612.26	617.82	623.15	626.95	627.99	639.87	641.63	622.30
2010	633.30	637.15	639.75	651.90	660.82	656.02	657.30	660.93	655.67	654.02	653.56	657.02	650.89
2011	654.94	643.77	642.78	654.44	662.34	657.52	654.12	650.16	659.13	657.73	657.67	654.04	653.43
2012	662.56	659.26	659.15	674.82	663.02	672.14	678.11	671.03	690.78	680.69	682.76	691.73	672.86
2013	681.05	688.84	692.47	697.66	702.03	713.36	704.86	707.88	719.60	711.66	715.40	704.15	702.42
Goods-Producing													
2009	932.18	920.05	923.10	925.11	919.10	932.93	928.93	954.30	937.26	936.03	956.16	947.65	934.73
2010	933.25	909.60	920.40	939.98	939.16	949.31	937.30	950.56	938.31	933.59	935.24	944.24	936.67
2011	930.65	913.04	901.74	913.48	931.06	920.40	916.02	919.65	915.08	935.66	946.39	952.56	924.76
2012	961.56	925.51	932.80	932.33	917.47	957.67	922.38	938.92	974.04	947.64	955.18	963.07	944.80
2013	959.62	970.82	995.51	995.68	1,034.08	1,030.52	1,015.60	1,029.51	1,055.81	1,051.65	1,056.53	1,005.28	1,016.06
Mining and Logging													
2009	1,192.77	1,173.05	1,179.07	1,188.45	1,169.97	1,202.71	1,185.05	1,244.70	1,224.46	1,213.19	1,241.54	1,220.48	1,203.10
2010	1,253.26	1,220.71	1,230.96	1,213.03	1,237.60	1,228.03	1,177.54	1,163.76	1,203.20	1,204.91	1,199.44	1,210.59	1,216.61
2011	1,250.62	1,221.97	1,221.75	1,208.89	1,198.45	1,162.24	1,111.44	1,163.76	1,140.36	1,166.44	1,167.76	1,195.27	1,183.00
2012	1,280.18	1,158.17	1,189.62	1,165.58	1,148.26	1,184.04	1,157.13	1,176.27	1,250.88	1,176.96	1,133.90	1,197.28	1,185.13
2013	1,225.98	1,209.91	1,308.00	1,289.38	1,305.69	1,369.04	1,339.01	1,349.46	1,373.49	1,446.90	1,407.00	1,340.53	1,332.57
Construction													
2009	809.57	815.11	837.93	843.15	861.41	865.87	895.00	914.21	889.92	905.74	926.00	901.59	873.60
2010	880.87	824.10	864.47	923.47	867.47	908.52	904.40	929.88	923.29	915.60	903.99	889.00	897.61
2011	861.73	832.72	826.85	891.62	934.86	941.41	961.99	952.38	924.34	948.42	989.01	959.62	923.16
2012	877.30	891.48	906.49	900.90	899.39	937.68	921.49	958.36	951.21	968.33	979.24	946.33	930.61
2013	937.65	949.03	959.58	990.79	1,037.87	1,008.45	990.72	1,006.13	1,026.29	983.20	982.80	936.50	984.96
Manufacturing													
2009	850.52	832.91	819.23	820.81	809.42	822.19	806.52	814.05	806.78	797.57	810.77	818.35	817.03
2010	777.22	776.00	771.00	786.35	810.40	808.09	812.82	800.46	780.81	776.22	789.36	808.01	790.53
2011	764.06	755.35	738.91	731.58	748.99	741.38	754.30	727.42	750.80	762.47	756.74	772.70	749.85
2012	788.03	781.31	770.67	796.27	775.61	815.87	763.16	764.93	802.64	777.33	817.05	820.40	788.71
2013	798.34	826.24	810.43	804.84	849.87	824.46	818.90	837.39	872.49	848.72	877.90	828.57	833.55
Trade, Transportation, and Utilities													
2009	535.92	529.92	533.03	530.79	526.18	522.81	519.10	521.21	521.73	531.80	528.69	535.15	527.51
2010	539.24	568.87	574.82	600.05	605.33	611.25	602.78	613.05	607.52	599.33	584.99	572.97	590.04
2011	581.50	573.94	584.67	597.55	601.08	596.66	605.91	597.20	622.29	602.27	593.37	585.68	595.86
2012	584.74	590.20	606.86	628.99	616.70	613.89	618.41	612.07	630.12	601.34	607.96	607.16	610.05
2013	589.96	599.96	600.95	606.20	607.26	623.75	620.57	615.65	616.33	614.88	614.84	619.62	610.39
Financial Activities													
2009	605.40	606.40	605.75	609.94	613.17	612.81	611.38	605.16	600.97	608.40	613.70	600.10	607.61
2010	621.64	621.72	604.28	610.37	634.52	629.64	630.76	648.36	620.37	621.00	622.56	623.52	625.32
2011	625.45	621.92	623.88	635.47	643.26	622.18	634.68	637.23	653.26	679.18	650.77	626.89	637.84
2012	644.00	648.36	642.51	675.25	639.36	627.29	649.44	627.85	619.28	609.66	607.41	612.18	633.32
2013	598.22	603.03	636.87	665.64	656.97	692.66	666.46	701.34	730.24	715.36	709.10	751.13	678.81
Professional and Business Services													
2009	692.17	702.80	709.42	716.39	715.64	702.47	701.18	711.36	697.05	689.95	708.10	709.56	704.88
2010	729.79	729.46	740.42	724.72	748.68	720.51	713.70	728.18	716.50	712.97	716.99	729.60	725.05
2011	729.27	735.69	736.30	741.10	755.60	744.86	739.26	749.87	752.56	781.88	777.75	758.35	750.10
2012	796.42	768.26	776.87	828.43	801.91	793.28	839.42	803.73	829.13	804.46	809.84	825.70	806.29
2013	781.63	791.54	803.59	815.14	796.26	805.92	767.54	771.10	772.90	748.35	754.73	752.94	780.47
Education and Health Services													
2009	626.77	642.64	638.83	634.46	634.34	628.25	629.96	622.78	637.56	641.36	647.50	649.13	637.22
2010	643.99	644.31	647.16	649.37	661.50	659.30	670.89	658.01	652.74	656.35	653.48	654.81
2011	666.11	672.97	665.04	666.90	667.02	671.35	679.95	668.56	670.32	659.10	671.77	664.85	668.70
2012	670.41	683.74	669.58	677.28	672.67	686.00	689.43	680.34	700.06	702.46	705.21	720.19	688.82
2013	725.31	732.58	718.83	728.80	727.09	738.48	746.64	738.68	750.72	744.07	742.37	734.98	735.74
Leisure and Hospitality													
2009	276.08	280.21	284.58	291.02	291.07	296.38	297.83	298.81	291.73	283.70	281.79	283.55	288.75
2010	279.31	281.42	287.50	283.32	287.43	291.56	294.21	297.72	288.70	290.13	288.10	292.25	288.56
2011	288.29	292.95	285.16	279.84	284.35	283.80	287.97	285.63	277.46	282.75	277.70	277.42	283.82
2012	269.89	274.28	278.52	277.97	279.76	274.97	284.56	280.10	272.22	275.09	271.44	276.14	276.66
2013	263.37	271.18	270.12	269.87	269.35	272.73	274.54	275.87	275.10	273.26	274.56	274.18	271.44
Other Services													
2009	528.78	531.72	540.60	534.99	522.66	522.66	512.07	532.22	530.93	532.59	542.43	539.14	530.11
2010	522.50	538.27	537.42	551.10	541.03	522.24	521.32	522.10	515.13	508.10	503.39	511.88	525.07
2011	506.38	506.76	497.65	490.14	488.87	487.94	482.97	486.41	476.37	496.12	495.79	505.18	492.90
2012	499.47	506.22	516.80	498.42	507.18	509.12	507.52	522.29	535.93	541.53	556.23	566.34	522.59
2013	561.27	562.67	558.57	570.70	560.96	569.96	555.86	577.72	599.44	584.98	590.40	600.40	575.26

WISCONSIN
At a Glance

Population:
    2000 census: 5,363,757
    2010 census: 5,686,986
    2013 estimate: 5,742,713

Percent change in population:
    2000–2010: 6.0%
    2010–2013: 1.0%

Percent change in total nonfarm employment:
    2000–2010: -3.7%
    2010–2013: 3.3%

Industry with the largest growth in employment, 2000–2013 (thousands):
    Education and Health Services, 84.4

Industry with the largest decline or smallest growth in employment, 2000–2013 (thousands):
    Manufacturing, -136.1

Civilian labor force:
    2000: 2,996,091
    2010: 3,084,557
    2013: 3,074,588

Unemployment rate and rank among states (lowest to highest):
    2000: 3.4%, 17th
    2010: 8.5%, 24th
    2013: 6.7%, 23rd

Over-the-year change in unemployment rates:
    2010–2011: -1.0%
    2011–2012: -0.6%
    2012–2013: -0.2%

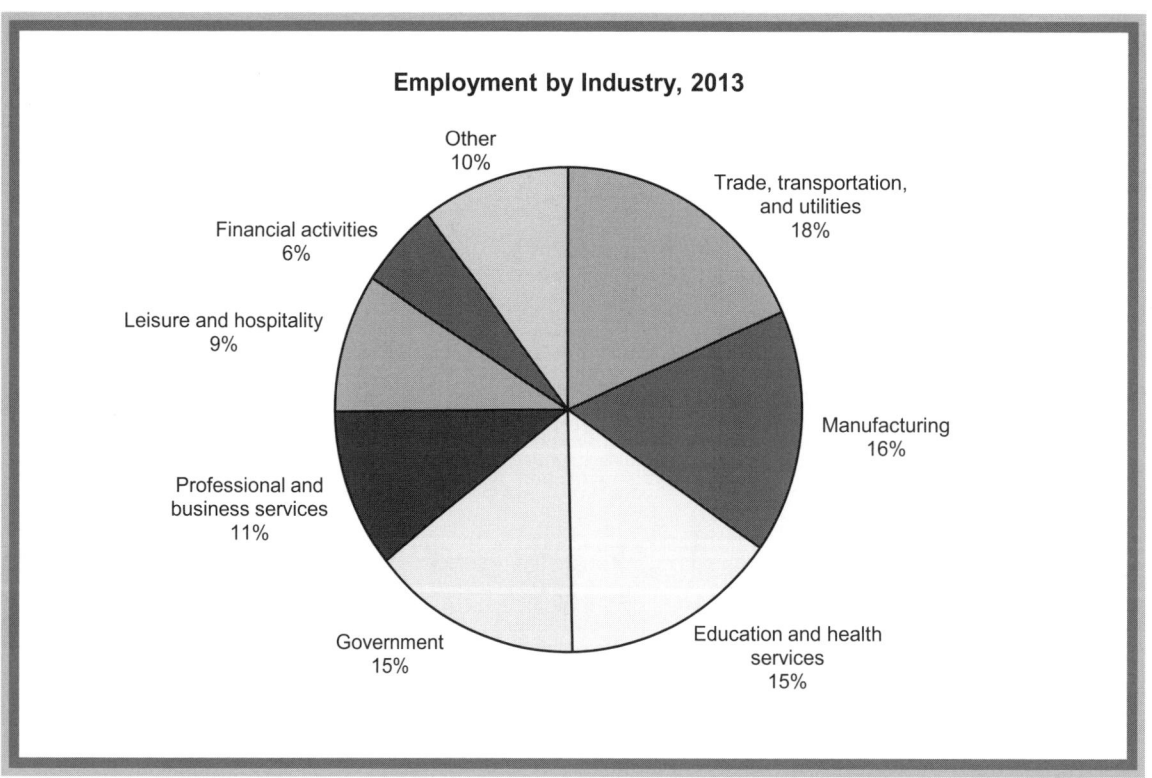

Employment by Industry, 2013

- Other 10%
- Financial activities 6%
- Leisure and hospitality 9%
- Professional and business services 11%
- Government 15%
- Education and health services 15%
- Manufacturing 16%
- Trade, transportation, and utilities 18%

1. Employment by Industry: Wisconsin, Selected Years, 2002–2013

(Numbers in thousands, not seasonally adjusted)

Industry and year	January	February	March	April	May	June	July	August	September	October	November	December	Annual average
Total Nonfarm													
2002	2,719.4	2,717.6	2,735.9	2,766.0	2,799.2	2,822.8	2,795.0	2,800.0	2,797.9	2,813.5	2,815.7	2,800.9	2,782.0
2003	2,709.5	2,717.4	2,725.5	2,760.3	2,794.5	2,816.8	2,780.3	2,782.3	2,791.3	2,808.5	2,801.5	2,798.1	2,773.8
2004	2,716.0	2,725.1	2,742.0	2,781.5	2,814.8	2,845.2	2,831.8	2,836.1	2,833.9	2,844.7	2,844.1	2,838.4	2,804.5
2005	2,754.0	2,765.5	2,780.1	2,827.2	2,851.3	2,876.7	2,858.0	2,860.2	2,873.0	2,870.0	2,871.8	2,872.0	2,838.3
2006	2,785.6	2,789.4	2,807.2	2,846.9	2,875.8	2,912.2	2,880.9	2,882.0	2,891.0	2,889.9	2,889.9	2,887.7	2,861.5
2007	2,808.9	2,804.4	2,824.3	2,856.6	2,898.4	2,936.8	2,900.2	2,901.5	2,901.7	2,902.8	2,904.0	2,900.3	2,878.3
2008	2,821.6	2,817.3	2,830.1	2,858.6	2,900.8	2,921.9	2,890.3	2,889.1	2,892.3	2,892.4	2,879.9	2,857.4	2,871.0
2009	2,747.3	2,734.3	2,726.4	2,738.5	2,767.9	2,778.2	2,741.3	2,735.2	2,734.9	2,747.1	2,742.8	2,734.9	2,744.1
2010	2,649.3	2,654.0	2,668.4	2,713.8	2,746.5	2,765.3	2,744.4	2,748.9	2,751.2	2,772.0	2,772.8	2,758.1	2,728.7
2011	2,681.6	2,688.9	2,705.0	2,743.4	2,773.3	2,791.3	2,778.0	2,778.4	2,790.0	2,793.7	2,794.0	2,785.6	2,758.6
2012	2,698.7	2,713.2	2,741.7	2,777.6	2,811.2	2,829.0	2,796.7	2,803.3	2,814.3	2,828.0	2,835.9	2,823.4	2,789.4
2013	2,725.8	2,755.2	2,769.3	2,787.6	2,828.6	2,850.4	2,828.0	2,836.7	2,848.0	2,870.1	2,864.9	2,852.5	2,818.1
Total Private													
2002	2,310.8	2,296.1	2,309.7	2,337.8	2,373.1	2,409.5	2,411.3	2,419.9	2,393.9	2,386.8	2,382.9	2,374.7	2,367.2
2003	2,305.2	2,292.5	2,299.3	2,331.4	2,369.5	2,396.5	2,397.3	2,402.4	2,392.1	2,388.1	2,379.2	2,377.9	2,361.0
2004	2,312.8	2,304.8	2,320.0	2,358.8	2,392.6	2,430.6	2,447.2	2,454.3	2,427.9	2,424.0	2,417.9	2,416.9	2,392.3
2005	2,343.1	2,340.9	2,356.3	2,400.0	2,425.3	2,462.4	2,472.3	2,478.7	2,458.7	2,446.9	2,446.4	2,445.0	2,423.0
2006	2,375.5	2,369.7	2,382.6	2,419.4	2,449.8	2,493.6	2,493.6	2,498.7	2,477.1	2,468.5	2,465.0	2,462.2	2,446.3
2007	2,398.7	2,387.6	2,401.8	2,429.6	2,471.3	2,514.7	2,511.9	2,516.7	2,487.7	2,479.0	2,477.7	2,471.5	2,462.4
2008	2,404.9	2,395.1	2,402.9	2,429.0	2,468.3	2,499.7	2,497.9	2,501.1	2,469.3	2,459.9	2,438.5	2,421.4	2,449.1
2009	2,328.7	2,303.0	2,293.7	2,303.6	2,332.2	2,356.4	2,348.9	2,350.1	2,326.4	2,321.0	2,311.6	2,303.1	2,323.2
2010	2,234.0	2,228.9	2,240.9	2,278.3	2,309.0	2,343.9	2,354.4	2,364.6	2,340.1	2,343.2	2,338.9	2,331.6	2,309.0
2011	2,269.5	2,262.3	2,276.9	2,312.7	2,344.7	2,379.8	2,391.1	2,397.7	2,381.4	2,374.6	2,372.0	2,363.4	2,343.8
2012	2,302.8	2,301.8	2,321.9	2,350.4	2,382.5	2,420.4	2,418.4	2,424.7	2,407.6	2,405.6	2,406.2	2,400.5	2,378.6
2013	2,331.0	2,334.9	2,349.7	2,365.1	2,412.0	2,445.8	2,448.9	2,459.5	2,436.9	2,441.3	2,436.2	2,424.9	2,407.2
Goods-Producing													
2002	643.5	634.9	638.6	646.8	658.0	671.8	673.1	675.7	667.4	662.4	657.0	645.7	656.2
2003	621.1	613.0	614.0	623.2	635.8	646.3	647.7	648.2	640.8	637.2	631.1	623.9	631.9
2004	607.0	603.4	608.7	623.3	634.0	646.1	654.6	655.8	648.5	644.1	640.0	634.3	633.3
2005	612.0	611.3	615.0	628.4	637.1	652.2	656.4	657.0	649.0	644.4	640.5	633.2	636.4
2006	618.8	613.9	617.2	629.7	638.8	656.0	656.7	656.9	648.4	642.9	636.5	630.2	637.2
2007	614.4	607.4	612.2	620.8	633.6	649.2	650.1	650.0	640.9	636.2	632.3	623.2	630.9
2008	606.8	601.7	603.6	610.3	621.3	633.8	633.5	632.1	621.9	616.0	605.5	590.1	614.7
2009	561.4	546.8	538.3	536.2	540.5	546.9	546.2	545.7	541.8	536.5	531.3	521.7	541.1
2010	504.3	500.9	504.7	517.5	526.3	540.1	546.2	548.7	542.8	540.1	536.7	527.8	528.0
2011	515.0	512.5	517.3	529.2	539.9	554.4	561.0	562.0	555.3	551.6	549.2	541.3	540.7
2012	529.3	527.1	533.0	544.3	551.5	566.8	571.5	571.6	563.8	562.1	558.0	552.9	552.7
2013	539.4	537.6	541.0	545.2	559.3	572.5	577.1	578.8	570.3	568.5	568.1	556.9	559.6
Service-Providing													
2002	2,075.9	2,082.7	2,097.3	2,119.2	2,141.2	2,151.0	2,121.9	2,124.3	2,130.5	2,151.1	2,158.7	2,155.2	2,125.8
2003	2,088.4	2,104.4	2,111.5	2,137.1	2,158.7	2,170.5	2,132.6	2,134.1	2,150.5	2,171.3	2,170.4	2,174.2	2,142.0
2004	2,109.0	2,121.7	2,133.3	2,158.2	2,180.8	2,199.1	2,177.2	2,180.3	2,185.4	2,200.6	2,204.1	2,204.1	2,171.2
2005	2,142.0	2,154.2	2,165.1	2,198.8	2,214.2	2,224.5	2,201.6	2,203.2	2,224.0	2,225.6	2,231.3	2,238.8	2,201.9
2006	2,166.8	2,175.5	2,190.0	2,217.2	2,237.0	2,256.2	2,224.2	2,225.1	2,242.6	2,247.0	2,253.4	2,257.5	2,224.4
2007	2,194.5	2,197.0	2,212.1	2,235.8	2,264.8	2,287.6	2,250.1	2,251.5	2,260.8	2,266.6	2,271.7	2,277.1	2,247.5
2008	2,214.8	2,215.6	2,226.5	2,248.3	2,279.5	2,288.1	2,256.8	2,257.0	2,270.4	2,276.4	2,274.4	2,267.3	2,256.3
2009	2,185.9	2,187.5	2,188.1	2,202.3	2,227.4	2,231.3	2,195.1	2,189.5	2,193.1	2,210.6	2,211.5	2,213.2	2,203.0
2010	2,145.0	2,153.1	2,163.7	2,196.3	2,220.2	2,225.2	2,198.2	2,200.2	2,208.4	2,231.9	2,236.1	2,230.3	2,200.7
2011	2,166.6	2,176.4	2,187.7	2,214.2	2,233.4	2,236.9	2,217.0	2,216.4	2,234.7	2,242.1	2,244.8	2,244.3	2,217.9
2012	2,169.4	2,186.1	2,208.7	2,233.3	2,259.7	2,262.2	2,225.2	2,231.7	2,250.5	2,265.9	2,277.9	2,270.5	2,236.8
2013	2,186.4	2,217.6	2,228.3	2,242.4	2,269.3	2,277.9	2,250.9	2,257.9	2,277.7	2,301.6	2,296.8	2,295.6	2,258.5
Mining and Logging													
2002	3.2	3.2	3.3	3.6	4.1	4.2	4.2	4.2	4.2	4.1	3.9	3.6	3.8
2003	3.2	3.1	3.2	3.5	4.0	4.1	4.1	4.1	4.1	4.0	3.9	3.7	3.8
2004	3.1	3.2	3.3	3.7	4.0	4.1	4.2	4.2	4.1	4.2	4.1	3.9	3.8
2005	3.3	3.3	3.5	3.8	4.1	4.3	4.4	4.4	4.3	4.2	4.1	3.8	4.0
2006	3.4	3.4	3.5	3.8	4.2	4.3	4.3	4.3	4.2	4.1	3.9	3.7	3.9
2007	3.2	3.2	3.3	3.5	3.9	3.9	4.0	4.0	3.9	3.8	3.7	3.3	3.6
2008	3.0	2.9	3.0	3.1	3.5	3.7	3.7	3.8	3.7	3.6	3.5	3.1	3.4
2009	2.6	2.6	2.6	2.7	3.1	3.2	3.3	3.3	3.3	3.3	3.1	2.8	3.0
2010	2.4	2.4	2.5	2.8	3.1	3.2	3.3	3.3	3.2	3.2	3.1	2.7	2.9
2011	2.5	2.5	2.6	2.7	3.0	3.3	3.3	3.3	3.4	3.4	3.4	3.1	3.0
2012	2.9	2.9	3.1	3.4	3.6	3.7	3.8	3.8	3.8	3.7	3.6	3.4	3.5
2013	3.2	3.2	3.2	3.4	3.8	3.9	4.0	4.1	4.0	4.0	3.9	3.5	3.7
Construction													
2002	108.7	105.7	108.0	117.9	127.2	133.4	136.7	136.7	133.1	132.0	129.2	120.9	124.1
2003	108.6	105.0	106.6	116.2	127.8	133.6	136.0	136.5	133.3	132.8	129.1	123.4	124.1
2004	110.4	107.6	110.9	122.2	129.6	135.4	139.7	138.7	135.7	134.0	131.4	125.4	126.8
2005	112.1	109.5	111.8	123.2	130.5	137.8	139.5	138.9	136.2	134.6	132.2	125.2	127.5
2006	114.3	111.9	113.4	124.0	131.1	137.8	138.5	138.1	134.9	132.9	129.3	123.6	127.5
2007	112.5	107.9	113.0	120.0	130.2	135.7	137.0	136.9	133.8	132.8	130.0	121.2	125.9
2008	108.0	104.9	106.8	113.8	123.9	127.9	129.4	129.0	125.6	124.1	118.4	108.9	118.4
2009	93.9	91.4	91.0	98.0	105.7	109.5	110.8	109.5	107.6	106.2	102.7	94.3	101.7
2010	82.1	79.9	81.6	92.1	97.1	101.7	103.6	103.9	102.1	102.3	98.5	90.0	94.6
2011	79.2	76.8	79.5	87.7	95.1	100.5	102.8	103.0	101.0	100.3	97.3	89.6	92.7
2012	79.7	78.0	81.5	90.4	95.3	100.6	101.9	102.3	100.5	101.2	98.3	93.1	93.6
2013	83.6	82.9	85.2	89.2	100.7	105.9	108.5	109.8	107.2	106.1	103.4	92.0	97.9

1. Employment by Industry: Wisconsin, Selected Years, 2002–2013—*Continued*

(Numbers in thousands, not seasonally adjusted)

Industry and year	January	February	March	April	May	June	July	August	September	October	November	December	Annual average
Manufacturing													
2002	531.6	526.0	527.3	525.3	526.7	534.2	532.2	534.8	530.1	526.3	523.9	521.2	528.3
2003	509.3	504.9	504.2	503.5	504.0	508.6	507.6	507.6	503.4	500.4	498.1	496.8	504.0
2004	493.5	492.6	494.5	497.4	500.4	506.6	510.7	512.9	508.7	505.9	504.5	505.0	502.7
2005	496.6	498.5	499.7	501.4	502.5	511.4	512.5	513.7	508.5	505.6	504.2	504.2	504.9
2006	501.1	498.6	500.3	501.9	503.5	513.9	513.9	514.5	509.3	505.9	503.3	502.9	505.8
2007	498.7	496.3	495.9	497.3	499.5	509.6	509.1	509.1	503.2	499.6	498.6	498.7	501.3
2008	495.8	493.9	493.8	493.4	493.9	502.2	500.4	499.3	492.6	488.3	483.6	478.1	492.9
2009	464.9	452.8	444.7	435.5	431.7	434.2	432.1	432.9	430.9	427.0	425.5	424.6	436.4
2010	419.8	418.6	420.6	422.6	426.1	435.2	439.3	441.5	437.5	434.6	435.1	435.1	430.5
2011	433.3	433.2	435.2	438.8	441.8	450.6	454.9	455.7	450.9	447.9	448.5	448.6	445.0
2012	446.7	446.2	448.4	450.5	452.6	462.5	465.8	465.5	459.5	457.2	456.1	456.4	455.6
2013	452.6	451.5	452.6	452.6	454.8	462.7	464.6	464.9	459.1	458.4	460.8	461.4	458.0
Trade, Transportation, and Utilities													
2002	533.0	524.7	527.4	528.9	535.8	538.2	533.5	534.9	535.4	540.8	552.4	555.9	536.7
2003	528.3	521.9	521.8	528.4	535.8	540.1	533.3	535.6	537.7	543.7	551.8	557.7	536.3
2004	529.5	522.5	524.7	529.2	537.1	543.0	539.9	540.6	540.0	545.7	555.6	559.5	538.9
2005	532.0	526.7	529.0	535.4	541.3	543.8	542.1	543.9	544.1	551.7	561.4	566.8	543.2
2006	536.0	529.6	532.7	536.8	542.9	548.0	542.9	544.3	544.4	549.3	561.4	565.8	544.5
2007	541.3	533.5	536.3	538.3	547.7	552.3	547.5	547.2	546.5	550.0	561.0	563.0	547.1
2008	539.9	531.4	533.2	536.6	543.2	546.3	541.6	542.1	538.8	541.5	546.4	547.7	540.7
2009	520.6	511.9	510.2	512.3	519.0	523.1	515.9	515.7	513.6	517.8	523.2	524.6	517.3
2010	501.3	494.4	496.4	501.7	507.6	512.1	508.0	509.0	507.2	514.7	521.6	524.0	508.2
2011	502.1	495.6	497.8	503.9	508.7	512.1	511.5	512.7	512.2	516.8	525.5	527.8	510.6
2012	505.5	498.6	500.7	503.3	511.2	514.7	511.5	513.2	511.8	517.2	528.9	530.4	512.3
2013	507.6	502.5	504.4	508.4	517.1	522.5	518.8	520.7	517.7	525.4	531.7	534.0	517.6
Wholesale Trade													
2002	113.2	112.7	113.2	113.9	114.8	115.5	116.1	115.6	114.4	113.6	113.7	113.6	114.2
2003	111.3	111.1	111.3	112.5	113.2	114.4	114.1	114.1	113.2	113.7	113.2	113.9	113.0
2004	112.3	111.8	112.4	112.9	113.6	114.9	116.6	117.0	115.0	115.7	116.0	116.5	114.6
2005	115.0	114.7	114.9	116.9	117.8	119.3	119.8	119.6	118.4	118.9	119.1	119.8	117.9
2006	118.5	118.1	118.8	119.9	120.6	122.6	122.8	122.5	121.2	121.3	121.4	121.9	120.8
2007	120.0	119.7	120.0	121.1	122.2	124.1	124.3	123.5	122.3	122.2	122.6	122.9	122.1
2008	121.1	120.4	120.9	122.0	123.2	124.3	124.2	123.6	121.5	121.1	120.7	120.1	121.9
2009	117.6	116.5	116.0	115.6	116.2	117.0	116.3	115.3	113.4	113.8	113.3	113.1	115.3
2010	110.6	110.0	110.3	112.0	112.7	114.0	114.7	114.5	112.4	113.3	113.4	113.4	112.6
2011	111.8	111.6	112.1	113.7	114.8	116.2	117.3	116.8	115.5	115.8	115.9	116.0	114.8
2012	114.6	114.4	115.2	116.5	117.2	118.7	118.6	118.0	116.5	116.8	117.0	117.2	116.7
2013	116.8	116.6	116.9	118.1	119.6	121.1	121.1	120.6	118.7	119.7	119.1	118.2	118.9
Retail Trade													
2002	317.1	309.9	311.3	310.5	314.5	317.6	315.8	317.4	315.0	319.8	331.5	336.4	318.1
2003	314.2	308.0	307.2	310.7	315.6	318.3	315.9	318.3	316.7	321.2	330.6	336.6	317.8
2004	313.8	307.3	308.1	310.4	315.6	319.7	317.9	318.5	316.1	318.9	329.1	333.4	317.4
2005	311.7	306.2	307.4	310.2	314.0	315.4	315.7	317.7	315.1	321.9	331.5	336.1	316.9
2006	310.4	303.9	305.5	307.6	311.4	314.4	312.5	314.0	311.2	315.5	328.0	331.4	313.8
2007	313.5	305.6	307.6	307.9	314.4	316.1	315.7	315.0	311.9	314.9	325.6	327.4	314.6
2008	310.3	302.5	303.8	305.9	309.9	312.0	311.2	312.0	307.9	310.7	316.8	319.1	310.2
2009	299.4	292.4	291.4	292.5	296.9	299.8	297.8	298.4	294.7	298.5	305.4	307.1	297.9
2010	290.3	283.9	285.3	287.3	291.7	294.5	293.3	294.8	291.6	297.4	304.7	307.0	293.5
2011	290.6	284.6	286.0	289.5	292.2	295.0	295.5	297.1	294.2	298.2	307.0	309.0	294.9
2012	292.0	285.4	286.7	288.1	292.6	295.4	294.5	296.4	293.2	298.0	309.5	310.2	295.2
2013	292.0	287.0	288.2	290.9	296.2	300.5	300.0	301.4	297.5	304.9	311.4	315.6	298.8
Transportation and Utilities													
2002	102.7	102.1	102.9	104.5	106.5	105.1	101.6	101.9	106.0	107.4	107.2	105.9	104.5
2003	102.8	102.8	102.3	105.2	107.0	107.4	103.3	103.2	107.8	108.8	108.0	107.2	105.6
2004	103.4	103.4	104.2	105.9	107.9	108.4	105.4	105.1	108.9	111.1	110.5	109.6	107.0
2005	105.3	105.8	106.7	108.3	109.5	109.1	106.6	106.6	110.6	110.9	110.8	110.9	108.4
2006	107.1	107.6	108.4	109.3	110.9	111.0	107.6	107.8	112.0	112.5	112.0	112.5	109.9
2007	107.8	108.2	108.7	109.3	111.5	112.1	107.5	108.7	112.3	112.9	112.8	112.7	110.4
2008	108.5	108.5	108.5	108.7	110.1	110.0	106.2	106.5	109.4	109.7	108.9	108.5	108.6
2009	103.6	103.0	102.8	104.2	105.9	106.3	101.8	102.0	105.5	105.5	104.5	104.4	104.1
2010	100.4	100.5	100.8	102.4	103.2	103.6	100.0	99.7	103.2	104.0	103.5	103.6	102.1
2011	99.7	99.4	99.7	100.7	101.7	100.9	98.7	98.8	102.5	102.8	102.6	102.8	100.9
2012	98.9	98.8	98.8	98.7	101.4	100.6	98.4	98.8	102.1	102.4	102.4	103.0	100.4
2013	98.8	98.9	99.3	99.4	101.3	100.9	97.7	98.7	101.5	100.8	101.2	100.2	99.9
Information													
2002	51.8	51.3	51.2	51.1	51.0	51.1	51.1	51.2	50.6	50.8	51.2	51.4	51.2
2003	50.7	50.1	50.1	49.9	49.9	50.2	50.2	50.4	50.4	50.3	50.8	51.0	50.3
2004	50.2	49.8	49.9	49.6	49.6	49.7	50.2	50.3	49.7	49.6	50.0	50.1	49.9
2005	49.6	49.4	49.3	49.6	49.7	50.1	49.8	50.0	49.6	49.6	50.0	50.1	49.7
2006	49.6	49.3	49.1	48.9	48.9	49.1	49.2	49.4	48.9	49.3	49.8	50.0	49.3
2007	49.8	49.5	49.4	49.7	49.9	50.4	50.6	50.8	50.3	50.6	50.8	50.9	50.2
2008	50.3	50.0	49.9	50.1	50.9	50.7	50.5	50.5	49.8	49.7	49.9	49.9	50.2
2009	49.1	48.9	48.3	48.0	48.1	48.1	48.1	48.0	47.4	46.9	47.4	47.6	48.0
2010	46.6	46.2	46.1	45.9	46.1	46.7	47.1	47.2	46.8	46.5	47.4	47.4	46.7
2011	46.9	46.6	46.4	46.5	46.5	46.4	47.1	47.2	46.8	46.7	47.2	47.1	46.8
2012	46.4	46.0	45.8	45.9	45.9	46.5	46.8	47.1	46.5	46.6	47.1	46.9	46.5
2013	46.9	46.7	46.5	46.5	46.9	46.9	47.4	47.6	47.1	47.0	47.2	47.0	47.0

1. Employment by Industry: Wisconsin, Selected Years, 2002–2013—*Continued*

(Numbers in thousands, not seasonally adjusted)

Industry and year	January	February	March	April	May	June	July	August	September	October	November	December	Annual average
Financial Activities													
2002	151.4	151.7	151.7	152.4	153.1	154.8	155.6	156.0	154.5	154.2	154.8	155.5	153.8
2003	154.3	154.9	155.0	155.9	157.1	158.7	158.7	158.8	157.2	156.9	156.9	157.8	156.9
2004	156.7	156.5	156.7	157.7	158.3	159.9	160.8	161.0	158.9	159.1	159.1	160.4	158.8
2005	158.3	157.7	158.1	158.8	159.3	161.0	161.8	161.8	160.4	159.9	159.9	161.0	159.8
2006	159.5	159.2	159.2	160.6	161.7	163.2	164.2	163.9	162.6	162.3	162.3	163.3	161.8
2007	162.1	161.9	161.5	162.3	162.7	164.6	164.5	164.0	162.3	163.5	163.4	164.3	163.1
2008	163.1	163.4	163.0	163.8	164.9	165.7	166.4	166.0	163.5	163.0	162.8	163.3	164.1
2009	162.1	161.5	160.8	161.6	161.9	162.7	162.6	162.4	159.9	159.7	159.4	159.7	161.2
2010	157.9	157.6	157.8	157.9	158.4	159.6	160.1	160.0	158.6	158.8	158.8	159.7	158.8
2011	158.1	157.9	158.3	159.7	160.2	161.7	162.4	162.4	161.6	161.3	161.3	162.1	160.6
2012	161.5	161.5	161.9	162.0	162.6	163.9	164.2	164.2	162.5	162.4	162.1	162.6	162.6
2013	161.0	160.6	161.3	161.0	161.7	163.1	163.9	163.9	162.3	160.8	161.4	159.8	161.7
Professional and Business Services													
2002	228.8	229.5	233.1	239.8	241.5	244.2	245.1	247.1	244.6	244.5	240.8	238.7	239.8
2003	234.9	236.4	238.3	243.1	243.6	245.9	247.6	248.8	249.3	249.5	247.3	247.1	244.3
2004	240.0	241.0	243.3	249.5	250.8	256.3	258.4	262.6	258.7	260.7	257.8	257.2	253.0
2005	249.6	251.6	254.7	262.3	261.4	265.3	268.5	271.2	270.2	267.7	267.1	267.5	263.1
2006	257.2	260.2	261.6	270.1	270.7	275.4	275.1	277.5	276.6	276.9	275.4	273.6	270.9
2007	265.5	267.2	269.2	275.8	278.1	284.0	283.8	286.8	284.1	284.0	283.6	284.5	278.9
2008	274.4	276.8	276.0	280.6	282.4	285.9	286.6	289.7	286.5	283.6	278.5	276.0	281.4
2009	260.0	255.6	252.7	255.1	255.8	257.5	258.6	260.3	258.7	262.1	262.6	262.9	258.5
2010	253.2	256.6	257.0	266.3	268.1	271.9	276.1	280.3	278.7	282.8	283.1	283.3	271.5
2011	274.4	274.7	277.6	280.9	281.9	287.7	288.3	290.8	291.0	291.0	290.8	288.1	284.8
2012	279.9	281.4	285.2	288.8	290.1	295.4	294.4	295.9	296.1	297.6	298.8	294.9	291.5
2013	285.0	288.8	292.0	292.0	296.7	301.4	303.0	305.6	304.1	305.4	304.3	303.5	298.5
Education and Health Services													
2002	350.3	352.3	353.0	355.5	355.9	358.4	356.1	357.4	357.5	360.2	362.7	362.1	356.8
2003	358.8	360.6	360.8	362.7	362.6	358.1	358.8	359.0	366.3	370.1	370.1	369.5	363.1
2004	366.5	369.1	369.7	372.4	371.9	372.6	372.2	372.0	372.7	374.7	376.6	377.0	372.3
2005	373.9	375.8	376.9	379.2	378.8	380.3	378.7	379.0	381.1	382.3	384.4	384.4	379.6
2006	381.5	383.9	384.2	385.3	386.4	387.4	386.3	386.7	388.5	390.8	392.3	392.1	387.1
2007	387.6	389.8	390.7	391.2	392.7	393.5	392.3	393.5	394.7	394.5	395.2	396.2	392.7
2008	392.3	394.3	395.7	396.5	398.1	398.5	397.8	399.5	400.8	405.3	406.5	408.4	399.5
2009	403.7	405.7	407.4	405.9	406.3	406.1	404.4	405.0	405.2	408.9	409.0	409.3	406.4
2010	405.4	407.5	409.3	406.5	407.1	406.1	405.5	406.0	406.2	409.5	410.5	411.0	407.6
2011	405.2	407.5	408.4	410.4	411.6	408.2	406.9	407.4	412.8	415.9	416.7	418.1	410.8
2012	410.1	415.6	418.2	418.4	419.3	416.2	410.6	413.3	420.2	425.1	425.8	427.1	418.3
2013	416.7	423.4	424.8	425.2	424.3	420.7	416.4	418.9	425.1	429.5	431.0	431.8	424.0
Leisure and Hospitality													
2002	221.0	220.7	222.5	231.4	245.8	256.9	264.2	265.0	251.9	241.7	232.0	232.1	240.4
2003	225.6	224.0	226.6	235.8	252.2	262.6	267.5	268.2	257.5	248.3	239.5	237.9	245.5
2004	230.3	229.4	232.6	242.7	256.2	265.9	275.0	275.6	263.4	252.9	243.4	242.6	250.8
2005	233.8	233.9	237.7	250.3	261.5	271.9	278.0	278.8	267.7	255.2	247.7	245.6	255.2
2006	239.0	239.6	243.4	252.6	264.4	276.5	282.1	283.1	271.0	260.6	251.4	250.2	259.5
2007	242.9	242.8	246.0	254.2	268.6	281.0	284.1	286.1	271.4	261.9	253.6	251.0	262.0
2008	242.2	241.1	244.2	252.7	268.3	277.9	281.2	282.2	268.7	259.6	249.2	246.1	259.5
2009	235.1	235.6	237.9	246.3	262.0	271.9	274.0	274.3	262.2	251.5	241.5	239.6	252.7
2010	230.8	230.7	233.6	245.4	258.1	268.8	273.1	275.4	262.8	253.0	244.1	241.2	251.4
2011	232.7	232.4	235.0	245.1	258.4	270.3	275.1	276.7	264.3	253.8	244.3	241.0	252.4
2012	234.4	235.4	240.4	250.2	263.9	276.5	280.2	280.6	269.0	256.6	247.8	247.6	256.9
2013	238.8	239.6	243.2	250.0	268.3	279.3	283.5	285.3	272.1	264.5	253.9	252.6	260.9
Other Services													
2002	131.0	131.0	132.2	131.9	132.0	134.1	132.6	132.6	132.0	132.2	132.0	133.3	132.2
2003	131.5	131.6	132.7	132.4	132.5	134.6	133.5	133.4	132.9	132.1	131.7	133.0	132.7
2004	132.6	133.1	134.4	134.4	134.7	137.1	136.1	136.4	136.0	137.2	135.4	135.8	135.3
2005	133.9	134.5	135.6	136.0	136.2	137.8	137.0	137.0	136.6	136.1	135.4	136.4	136.0
2006	133.9	134.0	135.2	135.4	136.0	138.0	137.1	136.9	136.7	136.4	135.9	137.0	136.0
2007	135.1	135.5	136.5	137.3	138.0	139.7	139.0	138.3	137.5	138.3	137.8	138.4	137.6
2008	135.9	136.4	137.3	138.4	139.2	140.9	140.3	140.0	139.3	141.2	139.7	139.9	139.0
2009	136.7	137.0	138.1	138.2	138.6	140.1	139.1	138.7	137.6	137.6	137.2	137.7	138.1
2010	134.5	135.0	136.0	137.1	137.3	138.6	138.3	138.0	137.0	137.8	136.7	137.2	137.0
2011	135.1	135.1	136.1	137.0	137.5	139.0	138.8	138.5	137.4	137.5	137.0	137.9	137.2
2012	135.7	136.2	136.7	137.5	138.0	140.4	139.2	138.8	137.7	138.0	137.7	138.1	137.8
2013	135.6	135.7	136.5	136.8	137.7	139.4	138.8	138.7	138.2	140.2	138.6	139.3	138.0
Government													
2002	408.6	421.5	426.2	428.2	426.1	413.3	383.7	380.1	404.0	426.7	432.8	426.2	414.8
2003	404.3	424.9	426.2	428.9	425.0	420.3	383.0	379.9	399.2	420.4	423.3	420.2	412.9
2004	403.2	420.3	422.0	422.7	422.2	414.6	384.6	381.8	406.0	420.7	426.2	421.5	412.2
2005	410.9	424.6	423.8	427.2	426.0	414.3	385.7	381.5	414.3	423.1	425.4	427.0	415.3
2006	410.1	419.7	424.6	427.5	426.0	418.6	387.3	383.3	413.9	421.4	424.9	425.5	415.2
2007	410.2	416.8	422.5	427.0	427.1	422.1	388.3	384.8	414.0	423.8	426.3	428.8	416.0
2008	416.7	422.2	427.2	429.6	432.5	422.2	392.4	387.0	423.0	432.5	441.4	436.0	421.9
2009	418.6	431.3	432.7	434.9	435.7	421.8	392.4	385.1	408.5	426.1	431.2	431.8	420.8
2010	415.3	425.1	427.5	435.5	437.5	421.4	390.0	384.3	411.1	428.8	433.9	426.5	419.7
2011	412.1	426.6	428.1	430.7	428.6	411.5	386.9	380.7	408.6	419.1	422.0	422.2	414.8
2012	395.9	411.4	419.8	427.2	428.7	408.6	378.3	378.6	406.7	422.4	429.7	422.9	410.9
2013	394.8	420.3	419.6	422.5	416.6	404.6	379.1	377.2	411.1	428.8	428.7	427.6	410.9

2. Average Weekly Hours by Selected Industry: Wisconsin, 2009–2013

(Not seasonally adjusted)

Industry and year	January	February	March	April	May	June	July	August	September	October	November	December	Annual average
Total Private													
2009	31.8	32.2	31.9	31.6	31.8	32.0	32.4	32.8	32.2	32.4	33.2	32.3	32.2
2010	32.4	32.4	32.5	32.6	32.9	32.8	32.9	33.4	32.8	33.0	32.9	32.6	32.8
2011	32.9	32.4	32.8	32.9	33.3	33.1	33.2	33.3	33.3	33.7	33.2	33.3	33.1
2012	33.3	33.1	33.0	33.5	33.1	33.5	33.9	33.6	33.9	33.5	33.3	33.7	33.5
2013	33.2	33.4	33.4	33.3	33.3	33.8	33.6	33.7	33.8	33.5	33.4	33.6	33.5
Goods-Producing													
2009	36.8	37.3	36.9	37.0	37.6	37.7	37.8	38.0	37.6	38.6	39.4	38.3	37.7
2010	38.4	38.2	38.5	38.6	38.6	39.0	38.9	39.2	38.8	39.4	39.4	38.8	38.8
2011	38.8	38.4	39.1	39.3	39.6	39.8	39.6	40.1	40.7	40.3	40.0	40.2	39.7
2012	39.9	39.7	39.4	39.6	39.7	39.8	39.5	39.6	39.6	39.5	38.9	39.4	39.5
2013	39.5	39.4	39.6	39.5	39.5	40.2	39.9	40.1	40.0	40.1	40.0	39.8	39.8
Construction													
2009	34.4	35.6	34.7	36.2	37.6	36.7	38.2	38.3	37.8	38.0	38.4	35.0	36.8
2010	37.5	37.2	37.1	37.9	36.7	37.4	38.2	38.2	38.0	39.4	38.3	35.3	37.7
2011	35.7	34.8	35.5	36.8	37.9	38.0	38.3	38.1	38.1	37.6	35.6	36.6	37.0
2012	35.2	35.1	35.3	36.2	36.9	37.9	37.3	37.9	38.2	38.6	37.2	37.5	37.0
2013	37.1	36.0	37.1	36.2	39.1	40.0	40.0	40.3	39.7	40.0	38.8	37.2	38.6
Manufacturing													
2009	37.3	37.2	36.8	36.6	37.0	37.5	37.3	37.6	37.2	38.2	38.8	38.8	37.5
2010	38.3	38.2	38.7	38.6	38.9	39.3	38.9	39.6	39.1	39.5	39.8	39.7	39.1
2011	39.6	39.2	39.9	39.8	39.9	40.2	39.5	40.3	40.8	40.4	40.6	40.5	40.1
2012	40.4	40.3	39.9	40.1	40.1	40.0	39.8	39.8	39.8	39.5	39.1	39.6	39.9
2013	39.8	40.1	40.1	40.2	39.5	40.1	39.7	39.9	39.9	40.0	40.2	40.3	40.0
Trade, Transportation, and Utilities													
2009	31.6	32.4	32.3	31.7	31.9	32.5	32.7	33.1	32.5	32.7	33.8	32.6	32.5
2010	31.9	32.1	32.7	32.7	33.0	32.7	33.1	33.8	33.1	33.5	32.8	32.6	32.8
2011	32.0	31.6	31.9	32.1	32.6	32.7	32.6	32.5	32.7	32.7	32.5	32.6	32.4
2012	31.6	32.0	31.7	32.0	31.7	32.3	32.4	32.3	32.6	32.7	32.3	32.6	32.2
2013	31.8	32.0	32.7	32.3	32.5	32.8	32.7	32.8	33.0	32.3	32.0	32.5	32.5
Financial Activities													
2009	36.6	37.3	36.8	35.9	35.7	35.8	35.6	37.5	35.5	35.9	37.0	36.0	36.3
2010	36.8	36.0	35.9	36.2	37.3	36.7	36.9	38.0	36.3	36.5	36.2	36.4	36.6
2011	36.8	34.8	34.8	35.3	36.8	35.2	35.8	35.6	36.0	37.1	35.8	35.6	35.8
2012	37.1	36.1	36.3	37.5	35.9	36.4	37.6	36.6	37.8	36.4	36.5	38.0	36.8
2013	36.5	36.9	36.6	36.6	36.4	37.5	36.4	36.6	37.5	36.6	36.6	38.0	36.8
Professional and Business Services													
2009	31.9	32.2	32.1	31.7	31.6	31.5	31.0	32.3	31.0	31.9	32.5	31.6	31.8
2010	31.9	33.0	32.5	32.8	33.2	33.1	33.1	33.5	33.4	33.1	33.3	33.4	33.0
2011	34.2	33.2	33.3	33.6	34.2	33.6	33.2	33.5	33.2	34.1	33.4	33.0	33.5
2012	33.2	33.1	33.3	34.1	33.8	33.8	34.7	33.9	34.6	34.1	33.8	34.2	33.9
2013	33.4	34.5	34.0	33.8	33.7	34.7	34.0	34.6	34.6	34.6	34.5	34.8	34.3
Education and Health Services													
2009	31.0	31.3	31.1	30.9	31.3	31.3	31.3	31.6	31.4	31.1	31.6	31.0	31.2
2010	31.0	31.0	30.9	31.1	31.2	31.2	31.0	31.4	31.2	30.9	30.7	30.6	31.0
2011	30.9	30.7	30.5	30.6	30.8	30.9	31.2	31.0	31.1	31.8	31.5	31.9	31.1
2012	32.0	31.7	31.3	31.6	31.5	31.8	32.3	32.0	32.3	31.9	32.1	32.1	31.9
2013	32.0	31.8	31.7	31.7	31.6	31.8	31.6	31.4	31.7	31.3	31.5	31.7	31.6
Leisure and Hospitality													
2009	20.4	21.2	20.6	20.1	20.4	20.8	22.6	22.8	21.4	20.6	21.1	20.8	21.1
2010	20.8	21.5	21.4	21.7	22.1	22.0	22.8	23.0	21.9	22.1	21.4	21.4	21.9
2011	21.3	22.0	22.1	22.2	22.6	23.7	24.6	23.6	22.7	22.8	22.0	21.9	22.7
2012	21.7	22.1	21.9	22.1	21.9	23.2	24.0	23.4	23.1	22.5	22.1	22.0	22.5
2013	21.5	22.4	22.3	21.9	22.5	23.2	23.4	23.2	22.8	22.6	22.2	22.2	22.5
Other Services													
2009	26.1	26.0	26.2	25.9	25.3	25.7	27.0	26.6	25.0	25.5	26.2	25.3	25.9
2010	26.0	25.7	25.8	25.6	26.0	25.8	27.1	27.5	25.9	25.7	26.0	25.3	26.0
2011	26.7	26.2	27.4	26.9	27.5	26.6	27.6	28.6	26.7	28.3	27.7	27.6	27.3
2012	28.2	28.1	29.1	28.7	28.1	29.6	30.4	29.4	28.2	28.2	28.8	29.7	28.9
2013	29.5	29.6	29.0	29.4	28.9	30.1	29.9	30.5	29.3	29.4	29.4	30.6	29.6

3. Average Hourly Earnings by Selected Industry: Wisconsin, 2009–2013

(Dollars, not seasonally adjusted)

Industry and year	January	February	March	April	May	June	July	August	September	October	November	December	Annual average
Total Private													
2009	21.04	21.37	21.23	21.17	20.99	20.90	21.03	20.95	20.96	21.23	21.17	21.48	21.13
2010	21.37	21.39	21.26	21.38	21.38	21.06	21.23	21.06	21.30	21.53	21.48	21.79	21.35
2011	21.98	22.05	21.78	21.94	21.92	21.50	21.76	21.61	21.75	22.07	21.86	21.94	21.85
2012	22.29	22.14	22.20	22.47	22.18	22.01	22.30	22.03	22.63	22.51	22.66	23.14	22.38
2013	23.10	23.22	23.00	23.26	23.04	22.89	22.92	22.83	23.35	23.10	23.19	23.39	23.11
Goods-Producing													
2009	22.99	23.34	23.20	22.97	23.07	22.83	22.89	22.60	22.82	22.78	22.86	23.08	22.95
2010	23.13	22.62	22.77	22.83	23.04	22.66	22.73	22.64	22.99	23.03	22.65	23.16	22.85
2011	23.04	23.06	22.69	22.96	22.86	22.49	22.89	22.46	22.58	22.78	22.53	22.57	22.74
2012	22.47	22.42	22.63	22.65	22.67	22.58	22.63	22.72	22.86	23.14	23.40	23.53	22.81
2013	23.11	23.21	23.17	23.33	23.37	23.40	23.33	23.23	23.68	23.54	23.55	23.81	23.40
Construction													
2009	27.63	28.33	28.34	28.37	28.50	28.19	28.25	28.21	27.81	28.61	27.92	28.86	28.25
2010	28.36	27.65	27.86	27.80	27.51	27.43	27.37	27.83	27.92	27.89	27.60	28.55	27.80
2011	28.50	29.11	29.01	28.44	27.73	27.27	27.91	27.55	27.79	27.90	27.47	28.21	28.01
2012	26.98	26.81	27.24	26.64	26.68	26.29	26.24	26.51	26.26	26.43	26.31	26.49	26.54
2013	25.96	25.95	26.05	26.40	25.68	25.76	26.06	25.89	26.56	26.47	26.72	27.19	26.22
Manufacturing													
2009	21.78	22.05	21.85	21.52	21.49	21.28	21.28	20.92	21.38	21.08	21.45	21.78	21.49
2010	21.97	21.44	21.55	21.49	21.71	21.23	21.32	21.13	21.59	21.60	21.35	22.05	21.53
2011	21.96	21.93	21.53	21.78	21.68	21.29	21.63	21.23	21.31	21.55	21.43	21.39	21.55
2012	21.60	21.57	21.75	21.85	21.80	21.72	21.79	21.79	22.02	22.30	22.58	22.75	21.96
2013	22.40	22.44	22.36	22.50	22.59	22.59	22.38	22.32	22.72	22.58	22.56	22.91	22.53
Trade, Transportation, and Utilities													
2009	19.00	18.81	18.93	18.97	18.77	18.63	18.51	18.55	18.45	18.39	18.26	18.59	18.65
2010	18.79	18.64	18.46	18.73	18.51	18.36	18.55	18.12	18.29	18.88	18.26	18.58	18.51
2011	19.36	19.11	18.90	19.20	19.05	18.75	19.17	19.07	19.17	19.76	19.22	19.06	19.15
2012	19.84	19.82	19.67	20.19	19.67	19.40	19.92	19.51	20.08	19.62	19.60	20.04	19.78
2013	20.38	20.49	19.82	20.31	20.06	20.03	19.85	19.94	20.31	19.92	19.75	19.58	20.03
Financial Activities													
2009	24.02	26.44	25.21	24.62	24.72	25.21	25.75	26.75	25.55	26.01	25.99	26.17	25.54
2010	25.16	27.00	26.23	25.89	26.26	25.46	25.37	25.99	26.07	25.96	26.39	26.38	26.01
2011	26.23	27.96	27.64	27.30	27.35	27.40	27.73	27.93	27.67	28.52	28.38	28.65	27.73
2012	28.84	29.47	28.95	29.43	28.84	28.54	28.89	28.34	28.78	28.57	28.48	28.83	28.83
2013	29.46	29.09	28.92	29.77	29.04	28.57	28.61	28.28	28.62	28.20	28.37	28.33	28.77
Professional and Business Services													
2009	23.62	24.45	24.64	24.25	24.36	24.10	23.54	23.06	23.69	24.01	24.43	25.82	24.17
2010	25.22	24.70	24.57	25.26	25.06	24.34	24.67	24.58	24.86	25.14	25.30	26.05	24.98
2011	26.31	26.16	26.02	26.04	26.07	25.82	26.01	25.55	25.97	26.05	26.01	26.64	26.05
2012	26.99	26.02	26.26	26.54	26.01	25.87	26.60	26.00	26.75	26.61	26.72	27.77	26.52
2013	27.61	28.58	28.35	28.58	28.79	28.92	29.95	29.66	29.75	29.28	29.49	29.51	29.06
Education and Health Services													
2009	20.59	20.67	20.67	21.29	20.81	21.24	21.67	21.65	21.40	21.88	21.54	21.66	21.26
2010	21.40	21.73	21.62	21.81	21.76	21.69	21.99	21.54	21.48	21.65	22.02	22.01	21.72
2011	21.95	22.27	22.03	22.27	22.40	22.30	22.63	22.57	22.38	22.55	22.48	22.63	22.37
2012	22.82	22.75	22.95	23.19	23.19	23.22	23.40	23.07	23.52	23.34	23.49	23.86	23.24
2013	23.76	23.53	23.50	23.56	23.44	23.18	23.09	23.15	23.90	23.47	23.80	24.39	23.57
Leisure and Hospitality													
2009	11.36	11.37	11.66	11.60	11.52	11.18	11.27	11.16	11.32	11.82	11.82	11.85	11.48
2010	11.95	11.75	11.72	11.56	11.62	11.36	11.42	11.25	11.54	11.72	12.14	12.28	11.67
2011	12.02	12.07	11.94	11.95	11.96	11.70	11.61	11.58	11.82	11.80	11.92	11.94	11.84
2012	11.90	11.92	11.96	11.92	11.80	11.63	11.59	11.59	11.85	11.89	11.89	11.92	11.81
2013	11.86	11.81	11.85	11.93	11.71	11.48	11.49	11.55	11.75	11.98	12.06	12.16	11.79
Other Services													
2009	17.52	17.57	17.45	17.60	17.56	17.10	16.68	17.09	17.60	17.46	17.60	17.90	17.42
2010	17.75	17.80	17.74	17.89	18.08	18.15	17.62	17.77	18.29	18.30	18.35	19.19	18.07
2011	18.95	18.66	18.68	18.53	18.55	18.25	18.41	18.23	18.51	18.42	18.59	19.06	18.57
2012	19.18	19.40	19.39	19.17	18.82	18.55	18.70	18.75	19.44	19.36	19.66	20.00	19.20
2013	19.79	19.95	20.08	19.77	19.71	19.42	19.19	19.11	20.53	20.89	19.77	21.02	19.94

4. Average Weekly Earnings by Selected Industry: Wisconsin, 2009–2013

(Dollars, not seasonally adjusted)

Industry and year	January	February	March	April	May	June	July	August	September	October	November	December	Annual average
Total Private													
2009	669.07	688.11	677.24	668.97	667.48	668.80	681.37	687.16	674.91	687.85	702.84	693.80	680.39
2010	692.39	693.04	690.95	696.99	703.40	690.77	698.47	703.40	698.64	710.49	706.69	710.35	700.28
2011	723.14	714.42	714.38	721.83	729.94	711.65	722.43	719.61	724.28	743.76	725.75	730.60	723.24
2012	742.26	732.83	732.60	752.75	734.16	737.34	755.97	740.21	767.16	754.09	754.58	779.82	749.73
2013	766.92	775.55	768.20	774.56	767.23	773.68	770.11	769.37	789.23	773.85	774.55	785.90	774.19
Goods-Producing													
2009	846.03	870.58	856.08	849.89	867.43	860.69	865.24	858.80	858.03	879.31	900.68	883.96	865.22
2010	888.19	864.08	876.65	881.24	889.34	883.74	884.20	887.49	892.01	907.38	892.41	898.61	886.58
2011	893.95	885.50	887.18	902.33	905.26	895.10	906.44	900.65	919.01	918.03	901.20	907.31	902.78
2012	896.55	890.07	891.62	896.94	900.00	898.68	893.89	899.71	905.26	914.03	910.26	927.08	901.00
2013	912.85	914.47	917.53	921.54	923.12	940.68	930.87	931.52	947.20	943.95	942.00	947.64	931.32
Construction													
2009	950.47	1,008.55	983.40	1,026.99	1,071.60	1,034.57	1,079.15	1,080.44	1,051.22	1,087.18	1,072.13	1,010.10	1,039.60
2010	1,063.50	1,028.58	1,033.61	1,053.62	1,009.62	1,025.88	1,045.53	1,063.11	1,060.96	1,098.87	1,057.08	1,007.82	1,048.06
2011	1,017.45	1,013.03	1,029.86	1,046.59	1,050.97	1,036.26	1,068.95	1,049.66	1,058.80	1,049.04	977.93	1,032.49	1,036.37
2012	949.70	941.03	961.57	964.37	984.49	996.39	978.75	1,004.73	1,003.13	1,020.20	978.73	993.38	981.98
2013	963.12	934.20	966.46	955.68	1,004.09	1,030.40	1,042.40	1,043.37	1,054.43	1,058.80	1,036.74	1,011.47	1,012.09
Manufacturing													
2009	812.39	820.26	804.08	787.63	795.13	798.00	793.74	786.59	795.34	805.26	832.26	845.06	805.88
2010	841.45	819.01	833.99	829.51	844.52	834.34	829.35	836.75	844.17	853.20	849.73	875.39	841.82
2011	869.62	859.66	859.05	866.84	865.03	855.86	854.39	855.57	869.45	870.62	870.06	866.30	864.16
2012	872.64	869.27	867.83	876.19	874.18	868.80	867.24	867.24	876.40	880.85	882.88	900.90	876.20
2013	891.52	899.84	896.64	904.50	892.31	905.86	888.49	890.57	906.53	903.20	906.91	923.27	901.20
Trade, Transportation, and Utilities													
2009	600.40	609.44	611.44	601.35	598.76	605.48	605.28	614.01	599.63	601.35	617.19	606.03	606.13
2010	599.40	598.34	603.64	612.47	610.83	600.37	614.01	612.46	605.40	632.48	598.93	605.71	607.13
2011	619.52	603.88	602.91	616.32	621.03	613.13	624.94	619.78	626.86	646.15	624.65	621.36	620.46
2012	626.94	634.24	623.54	646.08	623.54	626.62	645.41	630.17	654.61	641.57	633.08	653.30	636.92
2013	648.08	655.68	648.11	656.01	651.95	656.98	649.10	654.03	670.23	643.42	632.00	636.35	650.98
Financial Activities													
2009	879.13	986.21	927.73	883.86	882.50	902.52	916.70	1,003.13	907.03	933.76	961.63	942.12	927.10
2010	925.89	972.00	941.66	937.22	979.50	934.38	936.15	987.62	946.34	947.54	955.32	960.23	951.97
2011	965.26	973.01	961.87	963.69	1,006.48	964.48	992.73	994.31	996.12	1,058.09	1,016.00	1,019.94	992.73
2012	1,069.96	1,063.87	1,050.89	1,103.63	1,035.36	1,038.86	1,086.26	1,037.24	1,087.88	1,039.95	1,039.52	1,095.54	1,060.94
2013	1,075.29	1,073.42	1,058.47	1,089.58	1,057.06	1,071.38	1,041.40	1,035.05	1,073.25	1,032.12	1,038.34	1,076.54	1,058.74
Professional and Business Services													
2009	753.48	787.29	790.94	768.73	769.78	759.15	729.74	744.84	734.39	765.92	793.98	815.91	768.61
2010	804.52	815.10	798.53	828.53	831.99	805.65	816.58	823.43	830.32	832.13	842.49	870.07	824.34
2011	899.80	868.51	866.47	874.94	891.59	867.55	863.53	855.93	862.20	888.31	868.73	879.12	872.68
2012	896.07	861.26	874.46	905.01	879.14	874.41	923.02	881.40	925.55	907.40	903.14	949.73	899.03
2013	922.17	986.01	963.90	966.00	970.22	1,003.52	1,018.30	1,026.24	1,029.35	1,013.09	1,017.41	1,026.95	996.76
Education and Health Services													
2009	638.29	646.97	642.84	657.86	651.35	664.81	678.27	684.14	671.96	680.47	680.66	671.46	663.31
2010	663.40	673.63	668.06	678.29	678.91	676.73	681.69	676.36	670.18	668.99	676.01	673.51	673.32
2011	678.26	683.69	671.92	681.46	689.92	689.07	706.06	699.67	696.02	717.09	708.12	721.90	695.71
2012	730.24	721.18	718.34	732.80	730.49	738.40	755.82	738.24	759.70	744.55	754.03	765.91	741.36
2013	760.32	748.25	744.95	746.85	740.70	737.12	729.64	726.91	757.63	734.61	749.70	773.16	744.81
Leisure and Hospitality													
2009	231.74	241.04	240.20	233.16	235.01	232.54	254.70	254.45	242.25	243.49	249.40	246.48	242.23
2010	248.56	252.63	250.81	250.85	256.80	249.92	260.38	258.75	252.73	259.01	259.80	262.79	255.57
2011	256.03	265.54	263.87	265.29	270.30	277.29	285.61	273.29	268.31	269.04	262.24	261.49	268.77
2012	258.23	263.43	261.92	263.43	258.42	269.82	278.16	271.21	273.74	267.53	262.77	262.24	265.73
2013	254.99	264.54	264.26	261.27	263.48	266.34	268.87	267.96	267.90	270.75	267.73	269.95	265.28
Other Services													
2009	457.27	456.82	457.19	455.84	444.27	439.47	450.36	454.59	440.00	445.23	461.12	452.87	451.18
2010	461.50	457.46	457.69	457.98	470.08	468.27	477.50	488.68	473.71	470.31	477.10	485.51	469.82
2011	505.97	488.89	511.83	498.46	510.13	485.45	508.12	521.38	494.22	521.29	514.94	526.06	506.96
2012	540.88	545.14	564.25	550.18	528.84	549.08	568.48	551.25	548.21	545.95	566.21	594.00	554.88
2013	583.81	590.52	582.32	581.24	569.62	584.54	573.78	582.86	601.53	614.17	581.24	643.21	590.22

WYOMING
At a Glance

Population:
    2000 census: 493,786
    2010 census: 563,626
    2013 estimate: 582,658

Percent change in population:
    2000–2010: 14.1%
    2010–2013: 3.4%

Percent change in total nonfarm employment:
    2000–2010: 17.8%
    2010–2013: 3.1%

Industry with the largest growth in employment, 2000–2013 (thousands):
    Government, 11.4

Industry with the largest decline or smallest growth in employment, 2000–2013 (thousands):
    Manufacturing, -0.9

Civilian labor force:
    2000: 266,882
    2010: 302,192
    2013: 306,315

Unemployment rate and rank among states (lowest to highest):
    2000: 3.8%, 25th
    2010: 7.0%, 10th
    2013: 4.6%, 6th

Over-the-year change in unemployment rates:
    2010–2011: -0.9%
    2011–2012: -0.7%
    2012–2013: -0.8%

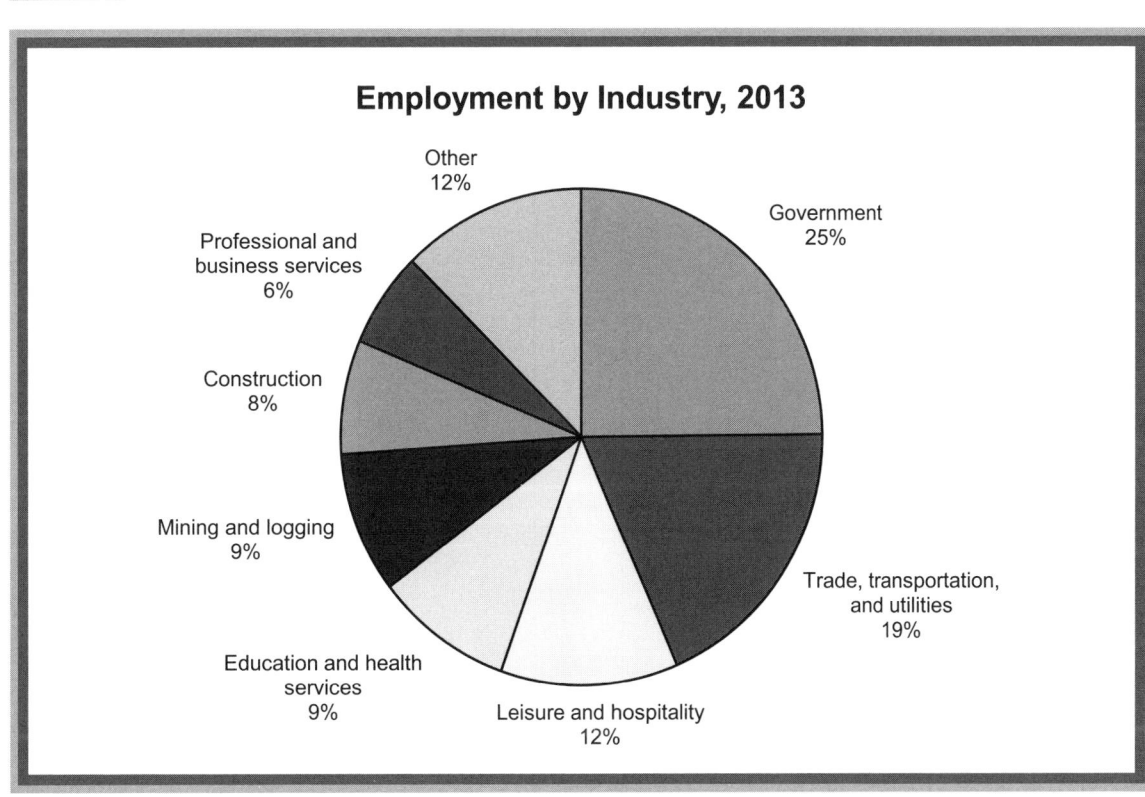

Employment by Industry, 2013

Other 12%

Professional and business services 6%

Construction 8%

Mining and logging 9%

Education and health services 9%

Leisure and hospitality 12%

Government 25%

Trade, transportation, and utilities 19%

1. Employment by Industry: Wyoming, Selected Years, 2002–2013

(Numbers in thousands, not seasonally adjusted)

Industry and year	January	February	March	April	May	June	July	August	September	October	November	December	Annual average
Total Nonfarm													
2002	238.1	237.9	240.4	242.5	250.3	257.8	255.2	255.0	254.4	250.7	246.6	246.2	247.9
2003	239.1	238.7	240.2	243.3	250.9	259.9	257.0	258.3	257.4	255.2	250.0	250.5	250.0
2004	244.1	244.6	247.2	250.9	256.5	265.6	262.7	262.4	260.3	258.6	255.5	256.1	255.4
2005	249.8	251.0	254.3	257.2	264.1	273.1	271.1	271.7	271.7	269.6	266.1	267.5	263.9
2006	262.7	264.6	267.8	269.9	277.9	288.2	283.7	284.1	284.9	282.1	279.4	282.0	277.3
2007	275.4	277.2	280.6	280.7	289.4	298.5	294.8	295.3	296.1	293.9	291.7	292.5	288.8
2008	286.4	288.2	290.0	290.5	299.2	306.5	304.1	303.8	305.4	302.9	297.3	296.0	297.5
2009	286.0	284.1	284.0	281.9	289.2	292.9	287.8	286.8	289.2	283.6	278.8	278.2	285.2
2010	270.4	271.3	273.5	276.1	283.9	290.4	286.4	287.9	290.6	287.8	281.4	281.7	281.8
2011	273.2	274.7	277.1	278.2	285.7	293.6	293.7	294.1	295.9	292.2	287.0	288.4	286.2
2012	279.8	281.2	283.2	284.5	290.7	297.3	295.8	295.7	295.6	292.6	287.5	288.3	289.4
2013	280.2	281.0	283.4	283.9	291.6	299.1	297.9	297.2	296.3	294.7	290.3	290.0	290.5
Total Private													
2002	176.2	175.6	177.0	179.5	186.2	193.7	196.7	196.6	191.7	186.5	182.3	181.1	185.3
2003	175.8	175.0	175.7	179.1	185.7	194.7	197.8	199.2	194.5	190.3	185.5	185.4	186.6
2004	179.9	180.0	181.9	185.4	190.0	199.2	201.9	202.0	196.6	193.0	190.0	190.4	190.9
2005	185.1	185.8	188.5	191.4	197.0	206.5	210.1	210.6	206.6	203.1	199.9	201.1	198.8
2006	197.9	199.0	201.6	203.8	210.8	220.8	222.4	223.2	219.4	215.2	212.9	215.0	211.8
2007	209.3	210.3	213.2	213.3	220.6	229.8	232.3	232.8	228.1	224.8	222.6	223.5	221.7
2008	219.0	219.5	220.7	221.0	227.8	236.3	240.3	240.5	235.9	232.3	226.8	225.3	228.8
2009	217.0	213.5	212.8	210.2	216.0	220.8	222.9	222.0	217.8	211.6	207.1	206.4	214.8
2010	200.3	199.8	200.8	203.9	208.9	216.6	220.5	222.2	218.8	215.0	209.1	209.2	210.4
2011	202.6	202.6	204.3	205.5	211.6	220.3	224.5	225.7	223.4	218.9	214.2	215.4	214.1
2012	208.5	208.2	209.8	211.8	216.5	224.2	226.2	227.4	223.0	219.1	214.4	215.0	217.0
2013	208.7	208.2	210.1	210.7	217.2	225.7	229.2	228.8	223.9	221.6	217.5	217.2	218.2
Goods-Producing													
2002	45.5	44.2	44.7	45.9	48.2	49.0	49.4	50.2	49.4	48.7	47.0	45.1	47.3
2003	42.9	42.3	42.6	44.5	46.8	48.3	49.4	50.9	50.5	50.4	48.8	47.6	47.1
2004	44.6	44.6	45.4	47.1	48.9	50.7	51.4	51.5	50.6	51.0	50.5	49.5	48.8
2005	47.6	47.8	49.0	50.8	52.6	54.4	55.6	56.2	56.0	56.5	56.1	55.3	53.2
2006	54.6	54.8	55.7	58.2	60.8	62.8	62.8	64.1	63.8	63.9	63.3	62.9	60.6
2007	59.7	59.4	60.6	61.7	63.8	65.8	66.3	67.0	65.9	66.5	66.9	65.6	64.1
2008	63.9	63.6	63.9	64.6	66.9	68.7	70.3	71.1	70.2	70.4	69.0	66.2	67.4
2009	61.6	59.3	58.3	57.7	59.0	58.9	59.4	59.2	58.3	57.6	56.7	55.0	58.4
2010	52.3	51.9	52.5	54.2	55.8	56.9	58.3	59.7	59.3	59.7	57.9	56.1	56.2
2011	52.9	52.7	53.2	54.5	56.5	58.5	59.9	60.7	61.3	61.6	60.7	59.4	57.7
2012	56.1	55.7	56.4	58.3	59.2	59.8	59.9	60.6	60.4	60.1	58.8	57.4	58.6
2013	55.1	54.6	55.2	55.9	58.1	59.3	60.1	60.4	59.2	59.4	58.6	56.9	57.7
Service-Providing													
2002	192.6	193.7	195.7	196.6	202.1	208.8	205.8	204.8	205.0	202.0	199.6	201.1	200.7
2003	196.2	196.4	197.6	198.8	204.1	211.6	207.6	207.4	206.9	204.8	201.2	202.9	203.0
2004	199.5	200.0	201.8	203.8	207.6	214.9	211.3	210.9	209.7	207.6	205.0	206.6	206.6
2005	202.2	203.2	205.3	206.4	211.5	218.7	215.5	215.5	215.7	213.1	210.0	212.2	210.8
2006	208.1	209.8	212.1	211.7	217.1	225.4	220.9	220.0	221.1	218.2	216.1	219.1	216.6
2007	215.7	217.8	220.0	219.0	225.6	232.7	228.5	228.3	230.2	227.4	224.8	226.9	224.7
2008	222.5	224.6	226.1	225.9	232.3	237.8	233.8	232.7	235.2	232.5	228.3	229.8	230.1
2009	224.4	224.8	225.7	224.2	230.2	234.0	228.4	227.6	230.9	226.0	222.1	223.2	226.8
2010	218.1	219.4	221.0	221.9	228.1	233.5	228.1	228.2	231.3	228.1	223.5	225.6	225.6
2011	220.3	222.0	223.9	223.7	229.2	235.1	233.8	233.4	234.6	230.6	226.3	229.0	228.5
2012	223.7	225.5	226.8	226.2	231.5	237.5	235.9	235.1	235.2	232.5	228.7	230.9	230.8
2013	225.1	226.4	228.2	228.0	233.5	239.8	237.8	236.8	237.1	235.3	231.7	233.1	232.7
Mining and Logging													
2002	18.4	18.1	17.9	17.4	17.7	18.0	18.3	18.4	18.0	17.8	17.5	17.3	17.9
2003	17.1	17.2	17.2	17.4	17.8	18.3	18.9	19.1	18.9	19.1	19.0	19.2	18.3
2004	18.9	19.0	19.1	19.2	19.4	20.2	20.6	20.9	20.9	21.0	21.3	21.3	20.2
2005	21.0	21.3	21.6	21.8	22.1	22.9	23.2	23.4	23.5	23.6	23.9	24.3	22.7
2006	24.6	25.0	25.4	25.8	26.2	27.0	27.3	27.6	27.5	27.5	27.4	27.6	26.6
2007	27.0	26.9	26.8	26.8	27.2	27.7	27.6	27.7	27.5	27.6	27.8	27.9	27.4
2008	28.1	28.1	28.1	28.0	28.6	29.3	29.8	30.2	30.2	30.5	30.5	30.3	29.3
2009	29.2	28.1	27.2	25.8	25.2	24.8	24.6	24.4	24.2	24.1	24.2	24.2	25.5
2010	24.0	24.0	24.1	24.2	24.6	25.1	25.6	25.9	25.8	26.1	26.3	26.5	25.2
2011	26.2	26.2	26.3	26.4	26.7	27.3	27.8	28.1	28.2	28.5	28.6	28.8	27.4
2012	28.3	28.3	28.1	27.8	27.8	28.1	27.8	27.7	27.3	27.3	27.4	27.3	27.8
2013	26.6	26.5	26.5	26.3	26.3	26.6	26.8	26.9	26.7	27.0	26.9	26.8	26.7
Construction													
2002	17.6	17.0	17.5	19.2	21.1	21.5	21.6	22.2	21.9	21.2	19.8	18.2	19.9
2003	16.6	16.2	16.6	18.1	19.9	20.7	21.1	22.3	22.2	21.6	20.1	18.7	19.5
2004	16.5	16.6	17.2	18.7	20.3	20.9	21.2	21.0	20.2	20.2	19.5	18.5	19.2
2005	17.0	17.2	18.0	19.5	21.0	21.8	22.7	23.0	22.7	22.8	22.1	21.0	20.7
2006	20.2	20.1	20.6	22.6	24.6	25.5	25.1	26.2	26.0	25.9	25.4	24.8	23.9
2007	22.4	22.4	23.6	24.9	26.5	28.0	28.6	29.2	28.3	28.6	28.7	27.4	26.6
2008	25.8	25.6	26.2	26.8	28.5	29.4	30.5	30.9	30.1	29.6	28.2	25.9	28.1
2009	22.8	22.0	22.1	23.0	24.9	25.2	25.8	25.8	25.0	24.4	23.5	21.9	23.9
2010	19.7	19.5	19.9	21.6	22.8	23.2	24.0	24.9	24.6	24.5	22.4	20.5	22.3
2011	17.9	17.8	18.3	19.3	20.9	22.1	23.0	23.3	23.8	23.5	22.5	21.0	21.1
2012	18.6	18.2	19.2	21.5	22.3	22.4	22.7	23.6	23.7	23.1	21.8	20.6	21.5
2013	19.1	18.8	19.6	20.5	22.6	23.3	23.8	23.9	22.9	22.4	21.7	20.2	21.6

1. Employment by Industry: Wyoming, Selected Years, 2002–2013—*Continued*

(Numbers in thousands, not seasonally adjusted)

Industry and year	January	February	March	April	May	June	July	August	September	October	November	December	Annual average
Manufacturing													
2002	9.5	9.1	9.3	9.3	9.4	9.5	9.5	9.6	9.5	9.7	9.7	9.6	9.5
2003	9.2	8.9	8.8	9.0	9.1	9.3	9.4	9.5	9.4	9.7	9.7	9.7	9.3
2004	9.2	9.0	9.1	9.2	9.2	9.6	9.6	9.6	9.5	9.8	9.7	9.7	9.4
2005	9.6	9.3	9.4	9.5	9.5	9.7	9.7	9.8	9.8	10.1	10.1	10.0	9.7
2006	9.8	9.7	9.7	9.8	10.0	10.3	10.4	10.3	10.3	10.5	10.5	10.5	10.2
2007	10.3	10.1	10.2	10.0	10.1	10.1	10.1	10.1	10.1	10.1	10.3	10.4	10.3	10.2
2008	10.0	9.9	9.6	9.8	9.8	10.0	10.0	10.0	9.9	10.3	10.3	10.0	10.0
2009	9.6	9.2	9.0	8.9	8.9	8.9	9.0	9.0	9.1	9.1	9.0	8.9	9.1
2010	8.6	8.4	8.5	8.4	8.4	8.6	8.7	8.9	8.9	9.1	9.2	9.1	8.7
2011	8.8	8.7	8.6	8.8	8.9	9.1	9.1	9.3	9.3	9.6	9.6	9.6	9.1
2012	9.2	9.2	9.1	9.0	9.1	9.3	9.4	9.3	9.4	9.7	9.6	9.5	9.3
2013	9.4	9.3	9.1	9.1	9.2	9.4	9.5	9.6	9.6	10.0	10.0	9.9	9.5
Trade, Transportation, and Utilities													
2002	47.0	46.4	46.7	47.2	48.5	49.7	50.0	50.0	49.1	48.7	49.0	49.2	48.5
2003	47.1	46.5	46.5	47.2	48.2	49.5	50.1	50.2	49.4	48.9	48.6	49.1	48.4
2004	47.5	47.4	47.6	48.3	49.1	50.5	51.0	50.8	49.9	49.4	49.5	50.0	49.3
2005	48.2	48.2	48.7	49.3	50.4	52.0	52.4	52.5	51.8	51.5	51.5	52.2	50.7
2006	50.7	50.6	51.1	51.0	52.1	53.9	54.2	54.0	53.3	52.8	53.4	54.0	52.6
2007	53.0	53.2	53.8	53.4	54.7	56.3	56.8	56.9	56.1	55.7	56.0	56.7	55.2
2008	55.0	54.7	54.8	54.8	55.8	56.9	57.4	57.3	56.7	56.0	56.0	56.4	56.0
2009	54.1	53.5	53.3	52.8	53.5	54.5	54.5	54.4	53.6	52.5	52.4	52.6	53.5
2010	50.6	50.3	50.3	50.9	51.6	52.9	53.2	53.1	52.5	52.1	52.2	52.7	51.9
2011	50.8	50.7	51.0	51.4	52.3	53.5	54.1	54.1	53.6	52.9	53.2	53.6	52.6
2012	52.1	51.8	52.1	52.5	53.4	54.4	54.7	54.7	53.8	53.5	53.8	54.4	53.4
2013	52.3	52.2	52.5	52.7	54.0	55.4	55.9	55.8	54.7	54.8	55.7	55.9	54.3
Wholesale Trade													
2002	7.0	7.0	7.0	7.0	7.0	7.1	7.1	7.1	7.0	7.0	7.0	7.0	7.0
2003	6.9	6.8	6.8	6.9	6.9	7.0	7.1	7.1	7.0	7.0	7.0	7.1	7.0
2004	7.1	7.2	7.2	7.3	7.4	7.4	7.5	7.4	7.4	7.3	7.4	7.4	7.3
2005	7.3	7.4	7.5	7.6	7.8	7.9	7.9	7.9	7.9	7.9	7.9	8.0	7.8
2006	7.8	7.9	8.0	8.0	8.2	8.4	8.3	8.3	8.3	8.3	8.4	8.4	8.2
2007	8.4	8.5	8.6	8.7	8.8	9.0	8.8	8.9	8.8	8.7	8.8	8.9	8.7
2008	8.8	8.8	8.9	9.0	9.2	9.2	9.2	9.2	9.2	9.2	9.2	9.2	9.1
2009	9.0	9.0	8.9	8.8	8.8	8.9	8.7	8.6	8.5	8.4	8.4	8.4	8.7
2010	8.3	8.3	8.4	8.4	8.5	8.6	8.5	8.5	8.5	8.5	8.6	8.6	8.5
2011	8.5	8.6	8.7	8.7	8.8	8.9	8.9	8.9	8.9	8.9	9.0	9.0	8.8
2012	9.0	9.0	9.1	9.3	9.3	9.3	9.2	9.2	9.1	9.1	9.1	9.2	9.2
2013	9.0	9.0	9.1	9.2	9.2	9.3	9.3	9.3	9.3	9.5	9.7	9.4	9.3
Retail Trade													
2002	28.9	28.4	28.7	29.1	30.3	31.2	31.5	31.4	30.7	30.1	30.4	30.6	30.1
2003	28.8	28.3	28.3	28.9	29.7	30.7	31.2	31.2	30.6	30.1	30.1	30.4	29.9
2004	28.8	28.6	28.8	29.2	29.9	31.0	31.3	31.2	30.4	30.0	30.1	30.4	30.0
2005	28.9	28.7	29.0	29.2	30.1	31.4	31.7	31.7	31.1	30.7	30.7	31.0	30.4
2006	29.8	29.5	29.8	29.7	30.5	31.8	32.2	32.0	31.3	30.9	31.4	31.7	30.9
2007	30.8	30.8	31.2	30.7	31.7	32.6	33.3	33.1	32.4	32.2	32.4	32.8	32.0
2008	31.6	31.3	31.3	31.2	31.8	32.8	33.3	33.1	32.7	32.2	32.2	32.4	32.2
2009	30.7	30.1	30.1	30.0	30.7	31.4	31.7	31.6	31.0	30.3	30.2	30.3	30.7
2010	28.8	28.7	28.7	28.9	29.5	30.3	30.5	30.2	29.6	29.3	29.3	29.6	29.5
2011	28.2	27.9	28.1	28.4	29.0	29.9	30.4	30.3	29.8	29.3	29.5	29.7	29.2
2012	28.5	28.2	28.3	28.5	29.3	30.3	30.6	30.5	29.8	29.6	29.9	30.1	29.5
2013	28.5	28.3	28.5	28.6	29.7	30.7	31.2	31.0	30.1	30.3	30.9	31.2	29.9
Transportation and Utilities													
2002	11.1	11.0	11.0	11.1	11.2	11.4	11.4	11.5	11.4	11.6	11.6	11.6	11.3
2003	11.4	11.4	11.4	11.4	11.6	11.8	11.8	11.9	11.8	11.8	11.5	11.6	11.6
2004	11.6	11.6	11.6	11.8	11.8	12.1	12.2	12.2	12.1	12.1	12.0	12.2	11.9
2005	12.0	12.1	12.2	12.5	12.5	12.7	12.8	12.9	12.8	12.9	12.9	13.2	12.6
2006	13.1	13.2	13.3	13.3	13.4	13.7	13.7	13.7	13.7	13.6	13.6	13.9	13.5
2007	13.8	13.9	14.0	14.0	14.2	14.7	14.7	14.9	14.9	14.8	14.8	15.0	14.5
2008	14.6	14.6	14.6	14.6	14.8	14.9	14.9	15.0	14.8	14.6	14.6	14.8	14.7
2009	14.4	14.4	14.3	14.0	14.0	14.2	14.1	14.2	14.1	13.8	13.8	13.9	14.1
2010	13.5	13.3	13.2	13.6	13.6	14.0	14.2	14.4	14.4	14.3	14.3	14.5	13.9
2011	14.1	14.2	14.2	14.3	14.5	14.7	14.8	14.9	14.9	14.7	14.7	14.9	14.6
2012	14.6	14.6	14.7	14.7	14.8	14.8	14.9	15.0	14.9	14.8	14.8	15.1	14.8
2013	14.8	14.9	14.9	14.9	15.1	15.4	15.4	15.5	15.3	15.0	15.1	15.3	15.1
Information													
2002	4.2	4.2	4.2	4.2	4.1	4.2	4.2	4.1	4.1	4.0	4.1	4.1	4.1
2003	4.1	4.1	4.2	4.1	4.2	4.3	4.3	4.3	4.2	4.3	4.3	4.3	4.2
2004	4.3	4.3	4.3	4.2	4.2	4.3	4.4	4.4	4.4	4.2	4.3	4.3	4.3
2005	4.3	4.3	4.3	4.3	4.3	4.4	4.3	4.3	4.3	4.2	4.3	4.3	4.3
2006	4.3	4.3	4.2	4.1	4.1	4.2	4.1	4.1	4.1	4.0	4.0	4.1	4.1
2007	4.0	4.0	4.0	4.0	4.0	4.1	4.1	4.1	4.0	4.0	4.0	4.0	4.0
2008	4.0	4.0	4.0	4.0	4.0	4.0	4.1	4.1	4.0	4.0	4.0	4.0	4.0
2009	4.0	4.0	4.0	3.9	4.0	4.0	4.0	4.0	3.9	3.9	3.9	3.9	4.0
2010	3.9	3.9	3.9	3.9	3.9	3.9	3.9	3.9	3.9	3.8	3.8	3.8	3.9
2011	3.8	3.8	3.8	3.8	3.9	3.9	3.9	3.9	3.8	3.8	3.8	3.9	3.8
2012	3.9	3.9	3.9	3.9	3.9	4.0	4.0	4.0	3.9	3.8	3.9	3.9	3.9
2013	3.8	3.8	3.8	3.7	3.9	3.8	3.8	3.8	3.8	3.8	3.8	3.8	3.8

1. Employment by Industry: Wyoming, Selected Years, 2002–2013—*Continued*

(Numbers in thousands, not seasonally adjusted)

Industry and year	January	February	March	April	May	June	July	August	September	October	November	December	Annual average
Financial Activities													
2002	9.6	9.7	9.7	9.8	10.0	10.3	10.4	10.4	10.3	10.0	9.9	9.9	10.0
2003	9.8	9.8	10.0	10.0	10.1	10.4	10.3	10.4	10.3	10.3	10.2	10.2	10.2
2004	10.2	10.2	10.3	10.3	10.5	10.6	10.6	10.7	10.5	10.4	10.5	10.6	10.5
2005	10.5	10.4	10.6	10.6	10.8	11.0	11.0	11.0	10.9	10.8	10.8	11.0	10.8
2006	10.9	10.9	11.0	11.0	11.1	11.3	11.3	11.3	11.2	11.1	11.2	11.3	11.1
2007	11.0	11.0	11.1	11.2	11.3	11.6	11.6	11.6	11.5	11.5	11.4	11.5	11.4
2008	11.4	11.4	11.4	11.5	11.6	11.8	11.9	11.9	11.7	11.7	11.6	11.6	11.6
2009	11.3	11.3	11.2	11.2	11.3	11.4	11.3	11.3	11.1	11.0	10.9	11.0	11.2
2010	10.7	10.7	10.7	10.8	10.9	10.9	10.9	10.8	10.7	10.8	10.7	10.8	10.8
2011	10.7	10.6	10.6	10.7	10.7	10.8	10.8	10.9	10.8	10.7	10.7	10.7	10.7
2012	10.6	10.6	10.7	10.6	10.7	10.9	10.9	11.0	10.8	10.9	10.8	10.8	10.8
2013	10.9	10.9	10.9	11.0	11.1	11.2	11.4	11.4	11.3	11.4	11.3	11.5	11.2
Professional and Business Services													
2002	14.5	14.8	15.0	15.5	15.7	16.2	16.6	16.4	15.7	15.8	15.5	15.2	15.6
2003	14.3	14.5	14.5	15.3	15.7	16.5	16.7	16.8	16.0	16.1	15.2	14.9	15.5
2004	14.3	14.3	14.4	15.2	15.4	16.2	16.4	16.5	15.7	15.6	15.1	14.8	15.3
2005	14.5	14.6	14.9	15.5	15.8	16.6	16.8	17.0	16.4	16.3	15.9	15.6	15.8
2006	15.4	15.7	15.9	16.7	17.3	17.9	18.0	18.1	17.8	17.4	17.2	17.3	17.1
2007	16.8	17.1	17.5	17.9	18.8	19.6	19.5	19.5	19.0	18.8	18.0	17.8	18.4
2008	17.3	17.5	17.7	18.2	18.9	19.7	19.8	19.8	19.2	19.0	18.3	18.0	18.6
2009	17.3	17.0	17.0	17.1	17.6	17.9	18.0	18.0	17.5	17.2	16.7	16.3	17.3
2010	16.0	15.8	16.1	16.8	17.2	17.9	18.3	18.6	18.0	17.5	17.0	16.7	17.2
2011	16.4	16.4	16.6	17.1	17.8	18.5	18.8	19.2	18.5	18.2	17.9	17.7	17.8
2012	17.1	17.2	17.3	17.7	18.0	18.9	18.7	19.0	18.4	18.2	17.7	17.6	18.0
2013	16.9	17.0	17.2	17.8	18.3	19.0	19.2	18.9	18.5	18.4	18.1	18.0	18.1
Education and Health Services													
2002	19.5	19.9	20.0	19.8	20.0	19.6	19.5	19.7	20.2	20.1	20.2	20.3	19.9
2003	20.6	20.8	20.6	20.8	20.8	20.5	20.4	20.4	21.1	21.0	21.2	21.2	20.8
2004	21.4	21.4	21.5	21.4	21.3	21.1	21.0	21.3	21.8	21.7	22.1	22.1	21.5
2005	21.9	22.0	22.2	21.9	22.0	21.6	21.6	21.7	22.3	22.4	22.6	22.5	22.1
2006	22.4	22.5	22.8	22.4	22.7	22.3	22.1	22.3	22.9	22.9	23.1	22.9	22.6
2007	23.0	23.2	23.3	23.0	23.3	22.9	22.8	23.0	23.7	23.8	24.1	23.9	23.3
2008	24.0	24.4	24.4	24.3	24.3	24.1	24.1	24.2	25.0	25.3	25.2	25.1	24.5
2009	25.5	25.6	25.8	25.5	25.9	25.1	25.1	25.2	25.9	26.1	26.4	26.4	25.7
2010	26.1	26.3	26.4	26.4	26.4	25.8	25.7	25.9	26.7	27.0	27.1	26.9	26.4
2011	26.9	27.2	27.4	27.0	27.1	26.1	25.8	26.1	26.9	26.9	26.6	26.9	26.7
2012	26.5	26.7	26.7	26.6	26.7	26.0	25.8	26.2	26.9	26.9	27.0	27.1	26.6
2013	26.8	26.8	27.2	27.0	27.0	26.3	26.0	26.3	26.9	27.4	27.4	27.3	26.9
Leisure and Hospitality													
2002	26.6	27.0	27.2	27.5	29.9	34.9	36.7	35.9	33.2	29.6	27.1	27.7	30.3
2003	27.5	27.5	27.7	27.8	30.3	35.5	36.8	36.4	33.5	29.8	27.7	28.5	30.8
2004	28.1	28.2	28.8	29.2	30.8	36.0	37.1	36.8	34.0	31.1	28.4	29.4	31.5
2005	28.7	28.9	29.2	29.3	31.3	36.5	38.1	37.6	34.8	31.4	28.7	30.0	32.0
2006	29.3	29.8	30.2	29.6	31.6	37.0	38.4	37.8	35.0	31.8	29.4	31.0	32.6
2007	30.5	31.0	31.3	30.5	32.6	37.4	39.1	38.6	36.0	32.6	30.4	31.9	33.5
2008	31.6	32.0	32.5	31.6	34.1	38.8	40.3	39.7	36.9	33.8	30.6	31.9	34.5
2009	31.1	30.8	31.2	30.1	32.5	36.8	38.5	38.0	35.8	31.8	28.7	29.8	32.9
2010	29.4	29.6	29.6	29.4	31.6	36.7	38.5	38.5	36.1	32.6	28.9	30.8	32.6
2011	29.8	29.8	30.2	29.3	31.7	37.1	39.1	38.9	36.7	33.1	29.6	31.5	33.1
2012	30.6	30.7	31.1	30.4	32.7	38.1	40.1	39.8	36.8	33.9	30.7	32.1	33.9
2013	31.3	31.3	31.7	31.1	33.4	38.8	40.8	40.4	37.9	34.8	31.1	32.4	34.6
Other Services													
2002	9.3	9.4	9.5	9.6	9.8	9.8	9.9	9.9	9.7	9.6	9.5	9.6	9.6
2003	9.5	9.5	9.6	9.4	9.6	9.7	9.8	9.8	9.5	9.5	9.5	9.6	9.6
2004	9.5	9.6	9.6	9.7	9.8	9.8	10.0	10.0	9.7	9.6	9.6	9.7	9.7
2005	9.4	9.6	9.6	9.7	9.8	10.0	10.3	10.3	10.1	10.0	10.0	10.2	9.9
2006	10.3	10.4	10.7	10.8	11.1	11.4	11.5	11.5	11.3	11.3	11.3	11.5	11.1
2007	11.3	11.4	11.6	11.6	12.1	12.1	12.1	12.1	11.9	11.9	11.8	12.0	11.8
2008	11.8	11.9	12.0	12.0	12.2	12.3	12.4	12.4	12.2	12.1	12.1	12.1	12.1
2009	12.1	12.0	12.0	11.9	12.2	12.2	12.1	11.9	11.7	11.5	11.4	11.4	11.9
2010	11.3	11.3	11.3	11.5	11.5	11.6	11.7	11.7	11.6	11.5	11.5	11.4	11.5
2011	11.3	11.4	11.5	11.7	11.6	11.9	12.1	11.9	11.8	11.7	11.7	11.7	11.7
2012	11.6	11.6	11.6	11.8	11.9	12.1	12.1	12.1	12.0	11.8	11.7	11.7	11.8
2013	11.6	11.6	11.6	11.5	11.5	11.9	12.0	11.8	11.6	11.6	11.5	11.4	11.6
Government													
2002	61.9	62.3	63.4	63.0	64.1	64.1	58.5	58.4	62.7	64.2	64.3	65.1	62.7
2003	63.3	63.7	64.5	64.2	65.2	65.2	59.2	59.1	62.9	64.9	64.5	65.1	63.5
2004	64.2	64.6	65.3	65.5	66.5	66.4	60.8	60.4	63.7	65.6	65.5	65.7	64.5
2005	64.7	65.2	65.8	65.8	67.1	66.6	61.0	61.1	65.1	66.5	66.2	66.4	65.1
2006	64.8	65.6	66.2	66.1	67.1	67.4	61.3	60.9	65.5	66.9	66.5	67.0	65.4
2007	66.1	66.9	67.4	67.4	68.8	68.7	62.5	62.5	68.0	69.1	69.1	69.0	67.1
2008	67.4	68.7	69.3	69.5	71.4	70.2	63.8	63.3	69.5	70.6	70.5	70.7	68.7
2009	69.0	70.6	71.2	71.7	73.2	72.1	64.9	64.8	71.4	72.0	71.7	71.8	70.4
2010	70.1	71.5	72.7	72.2	75.0	73.8	65.9	65.7	71.8	72.8	72.3	72.5	71.4
2011	70.6	72.1	72.8	72.7	74.1	73.3	69.2	68.4	72.5	73.3	72.8	73.0	72.1
2012	71.3	73.0	73.4	72.7	74.2	73.1	69.6	68.3	72.6	73.5	73.1	73.3	72.3
2013	71.5	72.8	73.3	73.2	74.4	73.4	68.7	68.4	72.4	73.1	72.8	72.8	72.2

2. Average Weekly Hours by Selected Industry: Wyoming, 2009–2013

(Not seasonally adjusted)

Industry and year	January	February	March	April	May	June	July	August	September	October	November	December	Annual average
Total Private													
2009	35.8	36.3	35.5	35.1	35.3	35.2	35.5	36.7	35.2	35.1	36.1	34.9	35.5
2010	35.4	35.5	35.2	35.3	35.7	36.0	36.6	37.2	36.1	36.1	36.1	35.3	35.9
2011	35.8	35.3	35.1	36.4	36.3	36.4	36.6	36.5	36.4	37.1	36.0	35.5	36.1
2012	35.9	35.4	35.0	36.3	35.8	36.6	37.1	36.2	37.5	36.6	36.6	37.4	36.4
2013	35.8	36.4	35.7	35.0	35.9	36.8	35.4	36.0	36.5	35.6	35.9	35.7	35.9
Goods-Producing													
2009	41.9	41.9	41.0	40.8	41.2	39.8	41.3	42.9	40.9	40.8	41.8	41.1	41.3
2010	42.1	41.1	40.8	41.4	41.6	42.5	43.4	44.2	43.3	43.5	43.5	42.6	42.6
2011	42.2	41.9	41.9	42.9	42.8	43.4	43.4	43.5	43.2	43.9	43.3	42.2	42.9
2012	41.6	42.4	40.9	42.7	43.2	43.2	42.8	42.3	43.5	43.8	44.1	43.1	42.8
2013	41.7	42.1	41.4	39.8	42.3	42.4	40.8	42.1	41.9	41.1	42.3	41.8	41.7
Mining and Logging													
2009	44.4	43.5	42.8	42.6	41.6	41.4	42.6	43.7	44.2	44.2	44.7	44.8	43.4
2010	45.6	45.3	44.1	43.7	44.0	44.1	44.7	46.1	46.3	46.4	46.8	46.5	45.3
2011	46.3	45.4	44.0	45.0	43.9	45.0	45.2	46.1	46.2	48.0	47.1	45.5	45.6
2012	44.2	45.7	44.1	45.0	44.0	44.2	44.7	43.9	44.6	44.7	43.2	43.9	44.3
2013	42.9	42.1	42.9	41.7	42.9	43.9	43.2	44.2	45.3	43.1	45.0	45.0	43.5
Construction													
2009	41.0	41.6	39.9	40.0	41.2	38.8	41.0	42.9	39.8	39.5	40.8	39.2	40.5
2010	40.5	39.6	40.0	41.4	41.0	41.9	42.7	43.7	42.0	42.3	41.9	41.0	41.6
2011	39.9	40.0	41.7	42.8	42.7	44.3	44.3	44.3	43.4	43.3	42.7	41.4	42.7
2012	40.9	41.4	39.6	42.5	44.5	44.7	43.4	42.8	43.8	44.8	45.8	43.8	43.3
2013	42.0	41.8	41.8	38.9	43.5	42.7	41.0	41.8	40.4	40.5	41.2	41.1	41.4
Trade, Transportation, and Utilities													
2009	35.7	36.6	36.7	37.1	36.5	36.6	36.0	37.3	36.0	36.0	37.2	35.7	36.4
2010	36.1	36.5	36.3	36.3	36.9	37.0	37.1	37.1	36.8	36.9	36.9	35.8	36.6
2011	36.4	36.1	35.7	36.7	36.5	36.1	36.5	36.0	35.7	37.0	35.5	35.1	36.1
2012	36.4	35.0	35.1	36.1	35.8	36.4	37.6	36.4	38.0	36.4	36.3	37.8	36.4
2013	36.0	36.9	36.5	35.6	36.6	36.6	35.4	35.6	36.8	36.1	36.2	36.6	36.2
Professional and Business Services													
2009	34.9	34.7	33.9	34.1	34.5	34.9	35.2	35.8	34.8	34.4	35.1	33.9	34.7
2010	33.8	34.6	33.5	34.6	34.1	34.3	34.5	35.4	34.6	34.0	33.6	33.3	34.2
2011	34.2	33.7	32.8	37.3	37.5	36.5	36.8	36.8	36.4	37.9	34.4	34.8	35.8
2012	34.9	35.0	34.6	36.0	34.1	36.1	36.1	34.5	35.8	35.5	35.3	35.4	35.3
2013	34.5	35.3	34.3	34.2	34.2	35.4	33.1	34.1	35.0	34.2	34.8	35.0	34.5
Education and Health Services													
2009	32.4	33.1	32.9	31.9	33.2	33.9	33.5	34.6	33.8	33.7	34.5	33.5	33.4
2010	33.6	33.6	33.4	33.8	33.9	34.1	34.5	35.1	34.2	33.6	34.1	34.1	34.0
2011	35.1	34.3	33.9	35.2	34.9	35.4	35.3	34.9	35.9	35.6	35.4	35.2	35.1
2012	35.8	35.0	35.0	36.2	34.7	35.9	36.2	34.6	36.3	35.1	34.9	36.1	35.5
2013	33.4	34.5	34.2	33.8	33.8	35.5	33.7	34.7	35.3	33.6	34.6	34.3	34.3
Leisure and Hospitality													
2009	25.5	25.8	25.0	24.7	25.5	27.4	27.7	29.2	27.3	26.7	26.6	25.9	26.5
2010	26.4	27.1	27.2	26.3	26.7	27.6	29.1	29.9	27.7	27.0	25.8	25.6	27.3
2011	26.6	25.8	25.8	25.6	25.7	26.8	27.4	27.8	26.5	25.7	24.1	23.5	26.0
2012	24.2	23.6	23.7	24.4	24.0	25.9	27.2	26.4	27.0	24.2	23.7	24.7	25.0
2013	23.9	24.4	24.3	24.3	24.7	27.8	27.7	27.6	27.1	25.6	24.7	24.8	25.7
Other Services													
2009	29.9	29.5	29.8	30.2	30.4	29.5	28.9	29.8	27.3	27.8	29.1	28.0	29.2
2010	28.0	28.0	28.6	27.4	28.3	28.0	28.3	29.0	26.9	27.2	27.7	28.5	28.0
2011	29.8	29.3	30.0	31.4	31.8	33.5	33.1	33.3	33.7	33.8	32.2	33.9	32.2
2012	35.4	34.6	34.0	35.8	34.9	35.1	36.1	36.2	35.7	36.7	36.7	38.0	35.8
2013	36.8	35.4	33.9	34.1	35.0	36.7	34.3	34.5	36.0	36.2	35.4	35.6	35.3

3. Average Hourly Earnings by Selected Industry: Wyoming, 2009–2013

(Dollars, not seasonally adjusted)

Industry and year	January	February	March	April	May	June	July	August	September	October	November	December	Annual average
Total Private													
2009	21.27	21.26	21.25	21.25	21.09	20.51	20.46	20.69	20.83	21.22	21.35	21.69	21.06
2010	21.49	21.41	21.44	21.68	21.68	21.10	21.11	21.11	21.43	21.62	21.63	21.81	21.45
2011	22.00	21.83	21.76	22.69	22.68	21.98	22.05	21.81	22.13	22.36	22.27	22.55	22.18
2012	22.56	22.59	22.66	22.98	22.55	22.16	22.13	22.10	22.64	22.55	22.66	23.06	22.55
2013	22.94	23.00	23.22	23.34	23.04	22.64	22.55	22.52	23.02	22.87	22.95	23.14	22.93
Goods-Producing													
2009	25.17	25.14	25.72	25.89	25.55	25.32	24.96	25.39	25.29	25.57	25.66	26.03	25.47
2010	25.80	25.75	25.63	25.90	25.99	25.49	25.69	25.52	25.68	25.41	25.29	25.84	25.66
2011	26.33	26.05	26.09	26.10	26.52	25.84	25.86	25.48	25.73	25.43	25.42	26.02	25.89
2012	25.79	26.09	26.48	26.64	26.27	25.93	25.90	26.00	26.33	25.97	25.69	26.47	26.13
2013	26.57	26.73	27.24	27.91	27.46	27.21	27.04	27.13	27.59	27.02	27.02	27.47	27.20
Mining and Logging													
2009	28.04	28.26	28.46	29.10	28.96	28.99	28.83	29.00	29.02	28.77	28.96	28.64	28.73
2010	28.57	28.49	28.70	28.99	29.34	28.87	29.05	29.02	28.74	28.31	27.62	28.05	28.63
2011	28.58	27.74	27.60	27.50	27.79	27.63	27.99	27.35	27.48	27.84	27.52	28.23	27.77
2012	27.97	28.49	29.18	28.98	29.02	29.02	29.13	29.30	29.26	29.55	29.35	29.76	29.05
2013	29.82	30.01	30.79	31.90	31.80	32.25	32.42	32.69	33.73	33.73	33.50	34.08	32.26
Construction													
2009	24.29	24.07	24.44	24.56	24.26	23.84	23.22	23.84	23.54	24.10	24.01	24.23	24.02
2010	24.08	24.15	24.08	24.52	24.74	23.89	24.17	23.92	24.17	23.84	24.02	24.65	24.18
2011	25.19	25.21	25.35	24.99	25.75	24.48	24.08	23.91	24.61	23.94	23.98	24.63	24.62
2012	24.27	24.55	24.61	25.07	24.31	23.60	23.24	23.34	23.62	23.56	23.76	24.47	23.99
2013	24.43	25.15	24.96	26.18	25.64	24.81	24.54	24.65	25.12	24.56	24.85	25.48	25.02
Trade, Transportation, and Utilities													
2009	20.39	20.38	20.41	21.07	20.64	19.64	19.79	20.29	20.12	20.84	20.29	20.55	20.36
2010	20.69	20.67	21.19	21.28	20.98	20.15	19.95	20.05	20.13	20.43	20.56	20.58	20.55
2011	20.95	20.73	20.77	21.38	20.96	20.63	20.81	20.99	21.05	21.65	21.10	21.71	21.06
2012	22.52	22.14	22.40	23.37	22.45	22.42	22.60	22.36	23.10	22.77	22.84	23.18	22.69
2013	22.82	22.59	22.73	22.95	22.58	22.53	22.12	21.94	22.48	22.16	22.05	22.06	22.41
Professional and Business Services													
2009	24.37	24.74	24.87	24.42	23.92	23.84	23.41	23.81	23.79	24.33	24.45	24.58	24.20
2010	24.71	24.56	24.96	24.78	24.97	24.53	24.75	24.93	25.76	26.49	26.78	27.06	25.35
2011	26.36	26.25	25.87	29.65	28.51	27.02	26.37	26.72	26.68	27.30	27.93	28.02	27.25
2012	27.45	27.10	26.40	26.37	25.46	24.56	24.45	24.16	25.10	25.15	25.33	25.50	25.55
2013	25.23	25.19	25.63	25.52	25.17	25.33	25.84	25.53	25.92	26.05	25.75	26.32	25.63
Education and Health Services													
2009	19.36	19.11	18.83	18.97	19.09	18.83	18.98	19.37	19.48	19.59	19.67	20.08	19.29
2010	20.05	19.88	19.47	19.49	19.66	19.24	19.53	19.45	19.38	19.62	19.51	19.74	19.58
2011	20.03	20.06	19.74	19.83	20.43	19.81	19.87	20.02	20.57	20.32	20.03	20.25	20.08
2012	20.14	20.17	20.28	20.19	20.05	20.08	20.21	20.14	20.52	20.04	20.73	21.15	20.31
2013	21.60	22.00	22.11	21.84	21.49	21.13	21.65	21.56	21.93	21.82	21.60	22.02	21.73
Leisure and Hospitality													
2009	12.18	12.47	12.42	12.48	12.34	11.92	12.11	12.37	12.92	12.73	12.91	13.24	12.49
2010	13.33	13.57	13.35	13.17	13.14	12.77	12.60	12.77	13.22	13.07	12.97	13.06	13.06
2011	12.87	12.75	12.68	12.28	12.40	11.90	11.87	11.77	12.09	11.98	12.00	12.35	12.21
2012	12.41	12.49	12.35	12.28	12.17	11.90	11.85	11.83	12.10	12.10	12.21	12.41	12.14
2013	12.47	12.45	12.43	12.28	12.23	12.09	12.49	12.18	12.49	12.53	12.64	12.72	12.40
Other Services													
2009	19.03	18.80	19.26	19.28	19.41	19.40	18.85	18.81	18.50	18.98	19.52	19.99	19.15
2010	19.30	19.37	19.20	19.28	19.31	19.33	19.24	19.12	19.42	19.21	19.52	19.57	19.32
2011	19.91	19.71	20.61	20.59	20.17	20.47	20.33	21.48	21.28	21.72	22.06	21.52	20.85
2012	21.38	21.50	21.23	20.32	20.71	21.29	21.29	21.18	20.98	20.79	20.79	21.07	21.04
2013	20.47	21.06	21.24	20.29	20.26	19.61	19.39	19.30	18.98	19.30	19.63	19.84	19.94

4. Average Weekly Earnings by Selected Industry: Wyoming, 2009–2013

(Dollars, not seasonally adjusted)

Industry and year	January	February	March	April	May	June	July	August	September	October	November	December	Annual average
Total Private													
2009	761.47	771.74	754.38	745.88	744.48	721.95	726.33	759.32	733.22	744.82	770.74	756.98	747.63
2010	760.75	760.06	754.69	765.30	773.98	759.60	772.63	785.29	773.62	780.48	780.84	769.89	770.06
2011	787.60	770.60	763.78	825.92	823.28	800.07	807.03	796.07	805.53	829.56	801.72	800.53	800.70
2012	809.90	799.69	793.10	834.17	807.29	811.06	821.02	800.02	849.00	825.33	829.36	862.44	820.82
2013	821.25	837.20	828.95	816.90	827.14	833.15	798.27	810.72	840.23	814.17	823.91	826.10	823.19
Goods-Producing													
2009	1,054.62	1,053.37	1,054.52	1,056.31	1,052.66	1,007.74	1,030.85	1,089.23	1,034.36	1,043.26	1,072.59	1,069.83	1,051.91
2010	1,086.18	1,058.33	1,045.70	1,072.26	1,081.18	1,083.33	1,114.95	1,127.98	1,111.94	1,105.34	1,100.12	1,100.78	1,093.12
2011	1,111.13	1,091.50	1,093.17	1,119.69	1,135.06	1,121.46	1,122.32	1,108.38	1,111.54	1,116.38	1,100.69	1,098.04	1,110.68
2012	1,072.86	1,106.22	1,083.03	1,137.53	1,134.86	1,120.18	1,108.52	1,099.80	1,145.36	1,137.49	1,132.93	1,140.86	1,118.36
2013	1,107.97	1,125.33	1,127.74	1,110.82	1,161.56	1,153.70	1,103.23	1,142.17	1,156.02	1,110.52	1,142.95	1,148.25	1,134.24
Mining and Logging													
2009	1,244.98	1,229.31	1,218.09	1,239.66	1,204.74	1,200.19	1,228.16	1,267.30	1,282.68	1,271.63	1,294.51	1,283.07	1,246.88
2010	1,302.79	1,290.60	1,265.67	1,266.86	1,290.96	1,273.17	1,298.54	1,337.82	1,330.66	1,313.58	1,292.62	1,304.33	1,296.94
2011	1,323.25	1,259.40	1,214.40	1,237.50	1,219.98	1,243.35	1,265.15	1,260.84	1,269.58	1,336.32	1,296.19	1,284.47	1,266.31
2012	1,236.27	1,301.99	1,286.84	1,304.10	1,276.88	1,287.55	1,309.71	1,284.51	1,317.93	1,311.95	1,235.95	1,306.46	1,286.92
2013	1,279.28	1,263.42	1,320.89	1,330.23	1,364.22	1,415.78	1,400.54	1,444.90	1,527.97	1,453.76	1,507.50	1,533.60	1,403.31
Construction													
2009	995.89	1,001.31	975.16	982.40	999.51	924.99	952.02	1,022.74	936.89	951.95	979.61	949.82	972.81
2010	975.24	956.34	963.20	1,015.13	1,014.34	1,000.99	1,032.06	1,045.30	1,015.14	1,008.43	1,006.44	1,010.65	1,005.89
2011	1,005.08	1,008.40	1,057.10	1,069.57	1,099.53	1,084.46	1,066.74	1,059.21	1,068.07	1,036.60	1,023.95	1,019.68	1,051.27
2012	992.64	1,016.37	974.56	1,065.48	1,081.80	1,054.92	1,008.62	998.95	1,034.56	1,055.49	1,088.21	1,071.79	1,038.77
2013	1,026.06	1,051.27	1,043.33	1,018.40	1,115.34	1,059.39	1,006.14	1,030.37	1,014.85	994.68	1,023.82	1,047.23	1,035.83
Trade, Transportation, and Utilities													
2009	727.92	745.91	749.05	781.70	753.36	718.82	712.44	756.82	724.32	750.24	754.79	733.64	741.10
2010	746.91	754.46	769.20	772.46	774.16	745.55	740.15	743.86	740.78	753.87	758.66	736.76	752.13
2011	762.58	748.35	741.49	784.65	765.04	744.74	759.57	755.64	751.49	801.05	749.05	762.02	760.27
2012	819.73	774.90	786.24	843.66	803.71	816.09	849.76	813.90	877.80	828.83	829.09	876.20	825.92
2013	821.52	833.57	829.65	817.02	826.43	824.60	783.05	781.06	827.26	799.98	798.21	807.40	811.24
Professional and Business Services													
2009	850.51	858.48	843.09	832.72	825.24	832.02	824.03	852.40	827.89	836.95	858.20	833.26	839.74
2010	835.20	849.78	836.16	857.39	851.48	841.38	853.88	882.52	891.30	900.66	899.81	901.10	866.97
2011	901.51	884.63	848.54	1,105.95	1,069.13	986.23	970.42	983.30	971.15	1,034.67	960.79	975.10	975.55
2012	958.01	948.50	913.44	949.32	868.19	886.62	882.65	833.52	898.58	892.83	894.15	902.70	901.92
2013	870.44	889.21	879.11	872.78	860.81	896.68	855.30	870.57	907.20	890.91	896.10	921.20	884.24
Education and Health Services													
2009	627.26	632.54	619.51	605.14	633.79	638.34	635.83	670.20	658.42	660.18	678.62	672.68	644.29
2010	673.68	667.97	650.30	658.76	666.47	656.08	673.79	682.70	662.80	659.23	665.29	673.13	665.72
2011	703.05	688.06	669.19	698.02	713.01	701.27	701.41	698.70	738.46	723.39	709.06	712.80	704.81
2012	721.01	705.95	709.80	730.88	695.74	720.87	731.60	696.84	744.88	703.40	723.48	763.52	721.01
2013	721.44	759.00	756.16	738.19	726.36	750.12	729.61	748.13	774.13	733.15	747.36	755.29	745.34
Leisure and Hospitality													
2009	310.59	321.73	310.50	308.26	314.67	326.61	335.45	361.20	352.72	339.89	343.41	342.92	330.99
2010	351.91	367.75	363.12	346.37	350.84	352.45	366.66	381.82	366.19	352.89	334.63	334.34	356.54
2011	342.34	328.95	327.14	314.37	318.68	318.92	325.24	327.21	320.39	307.89	289.20	290.23	317.46
2012	300.32	294.76	292.70	299.63	292.08	308.21	322.32	312.31	326.70	292.82	289.38	306.53	303.50
2013	298.03	303.78	302.05	298.40	302.08	336.10	345.97	336.17	338.48	320.77	312.21	315.46	318.68
Other Services													
2009	569.00	554.60	573.95	582.26	590.06	572.30	544.77	560.54	505.05	527.64	568.03	559.72	559.18
2010	540.40	542.36	549.12	528.27	546.47	541.24	544.49	554.48	522.40	522.51	540.70	557.75	540.96
2011	593.32	577.50	618.30	646.53	641.41	685.75	672.92	715.28	717.14	734.14	710.33	729.53	671.37
2012	756.85	743.90	721.82	727.46	722.78	747.28	768.57	766.72	748.99	762.99	762.99	800.66	753.23
2013	753.30	745.52	720.04	691.89	709.10	719.69	665.08	665.85	683.28	698.66	694.90	706.30	703.88

PART B

METROPOLITAN STATISTICAL AREA (MSA) DATA

METROPOLITAN STATISTICAL AREA (MSA) NOTES

Part B provides employment data for the 75 largest (of the 380) metropolitan statistical areas (MSAs) and New England city and town areas (NECTAs) in the United States from 2002 through 2013. As mentioned in the technical notes, all employment data are for MSAs unless otherwise noted. NECTAs are similar to MSAs but are defined by cities and towns rather than counties in the region.

According to the 2010 Census and the 2013 estimates from the Census Bureau, New York–Newark–Jersey City, NY–NJ–PA, has remained the largest MSA in the United States—with a population of 19,949,502. Los Angeles–Long Beach–Anaheim, CA, again followed with a population of 13,131,431. Although the New York area was the most populated MSA, it was not among the fastest growing. Between 2012 and 2013 Austin–Round Rock–San Marcos, TX, again grew most, increasing population 2.6 percent, followed by Houston–The Woodlands–Sugar Land, TX, which grew 2.2 percent. New Haven–Milford, CT, experienced the highest reduction in population, decreasing 0.2 percent.

According to the 2013 unemployment ratings from the Bureau of Labor Statistics, the rate of unemployment decreased between 2012 and 2013 in all but 9 of the 75 largest MSAs. In these 9 areas, the unemployment rate increased less than 0.3 percent. Unemployment rates ranged between 4.2 percent in Salt Lake City, UT, to a high of 12.9 percent in Fresno, CA (although this rate was 2.1 percent lower than Fresno's rate in 2012). Of the MSAs with population of 1,000,000 or more, four areas reported the lowest unemployment rates—below 5 percent; Salt Lake City, UT, at 4.2 percent; Urban Honolulu, HI, and Omaha–Council Bluffs, NE–IA, both at 4.3 percent; and Minneapolis–St. Paul–Bloomington, MN–WI, at 4.8 percent.

When compared with the years 1990–2013, total nonfarm employment, although increasing, has increased at a moderate pace between 2002 and 2013. In McAllen–Edinburg–Mission, TX, total nonfarm employment increased 68.4 percent from 2002 to 2013; however the change in employment in this MSA was higher than in all the 75 largest MSAs, by more than 37 percentage points. Austin–Round Rock–San Marcos, TX, was the closest follower with a 31.3 percent increase in nonfarm employment from 2002 through 2013.

Although nonfarm employment increased in most MSAs from 2002 to 2013, it decreased in several areas, most significantly in Detroit–Warren–Livonia, MI; New Orleans–Metairie–Kenner, LA; and Dayton, OH, where nonfarm employment declined between 10 percent and 45 percent in these areas. All other declines in employment among these largest seventy-five MSAs were below 5.2 percent.

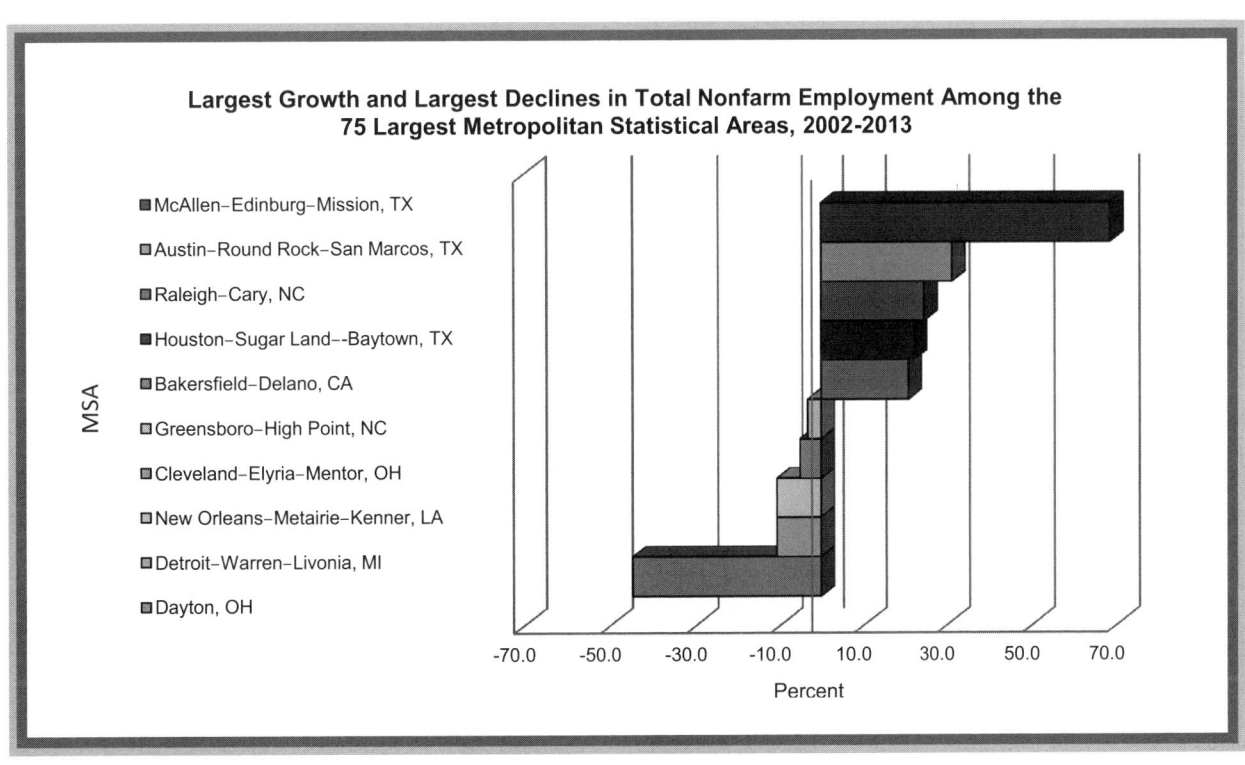

Metropolitan Statistical Areas: Employment and Unemployment Rates

Seventy-five largest MSAs; ranked by population

Rank	Metropolitan statistical area	2013 Census population estimates[1]	Total nonfarm employment		Percent change in total nonfarm employment, 2002–2013	Unemployment rate[2]		
			2002	2013		2011	2012	2013
1	New York–Newark–Jersey City, NY–NJ–PA	19,949,502	8,275.5	8,692.0	5.0	8.6	8.8	7.8
2	Los Angeles–Long Beach–Santa Ana, CA	13,131,431	5,492.2	5,566.8	1.4	11.4	10.1	9.0
3	Chicago–Joliet–Naperville, IL–IN–WI	9,537,289	4,453.8	4,439.1	-0.3	9.8	8.9	9.1
4	Dallas–Fort Worth–Arlington, TX	6,810,913	2,702.9	3,089.8	14.3	7.8	6.8	6.2
5	Houston–Sugar Land–Baytown, TX	6,313,158	2,284.5	2,788.4	22.1	8.1	6.8	6.2
6	Philadelphia–Camden–Wilmington, PA–NJ–DE–MD	6,034,678	2,739.5	2,748.6	0.3	8.6	8.5	7.8
7	Washington–Arlington–Alexandria, DC–VA–MD–WV	5,949,859	2,176.5	2,507.2	15.2	6.0	5.6	5.4
8	Miami–Fort Lauderdale–Pompano Beach, FL	5,828,191	2,199.5	2,347.2	6.7	10.3	8.7	7.4
9	Atlanta–Sandy Springs–Marietta, GA	5,522,942	2,262.8	2,404.9	6.3	9.8	8.8	7.9
10	Boston–Cambridge–Quincy, MA–NH	4,684,299	2,469.4	2,554.0	3.4	6.6	6.1	6.4
11	San Francisco–Oakland–Fremont, CA	4,516,276	2,041.5	2,103.9	3.1	9.4	8.1	7.0
12	Phoenix–Mesa–Glendale, AZ	4,398,762	1,598.5	1,811.4	13.3	8.6	7.4	6.9
13	Riverside–San Bernardino–Ontario, CA	4,380,878	1,072.5	1,226.4	14.3	13.6	12.0	10.2
14	Detroit–Warren–Livonia, MI	4,294,983	2,087.5	1,864.2	-10.7	11.6	10.3	9.4
15	Seattle–Tacoma–Bellevue, WA	3,610,105	1,603.3	1,784.6	11.3	8.7	7.4	5.9
16	Minneapolis–St. Paul–Bloomington, MN–WI	3,459,146	1,721.4	1,796.4	4.4	6.3	5.5	4.8
17	San Diego–Carlsbad–San Marcos, CA	3,211,252	1,235.7	1,312.0	6.2	10.0	8.9	7.5
18	Tampa–St. Petersburg–Clearwater, FL	2,870,569	1,128.9	1,176.8	4.2	10.6	8.8	7.3
19	St. Louis, MO–IL	2,801,056	1,332.6	1,315.2	-1.3	8.8	7.6	7.2
20	Baltimore–Towson, MD	2,770,738	1,250.8	1,332.9	6.6	7.6	7.2	6.8
21	Denver–Aurora–Broomfield, CO	2,697,476	1,172.3	1,294.1	10.4	8.6	7.8	6.6
22	Pittsburgh, PA	2,360,867	1,142.1	1,157.8	1.4	7.3	7.2	6.8
23	Charlotte–Gastonia–Rock Hill, NC–SC	2,335,358	769.7	873.8	13.5	10.7	9.3	8.1
24	Portland–Vancouver–Hillsboro, OR–WA	2,314,554	946.2	1,035.9	9.5	9.3	8.2	7.3
25	San Antonio, New Braunfels, TX	2,277,550	754.1	906.3	20.2	7.5	6.5	6.0
26	Orlando–Kissimmee–Sanford, FL	2,267,846	897.9	1,065.0	18.6	10.2	8.7	6.9
27	Sacramento–Arden-Arcade–Roseville, CA	2,215,770	839.1	864.4	3.0	11.9	10.3	8.6
28	Cincinnati—Middletown, OH–KY–IN	2,137,406	1,008.6	1,023.9	1.5	8.6	7.3	7.1
29	Cleveland–Elyria—Mentor, OH	2,064,725	1,082.3	1,026.3	-5.2	7.9	7.4	7.5
30	Kansas City, MO–KS	2,054,473	964.7	1,006.9	4.4	8.0	6.7	6.4
31	Las Vegas—Paradise, NV	2,027,868	730.9	848.9	16.1	13.6	11.7	10.0
32	Columbus, OH	1,967,066	913.6	979.3	7.2	7.5	6.3	6.2
33	Indianapolis–Carmel, IN	1,953,961	857.8	933.9	8.9	8.3	7.6	6.9
34	San Jose–Sunnyvale–Santa Clara, CA	1,919,641	919.4	961.8	4.6	10.0	8.6	7.0
35	Austin—Round Rock—San Marcos, TX	1,883,051	658.4	864.2	31.3	6.8	5.8	5.2
36	Nashville–Davidson–Murfreesboro–Franklin, TN	1,757,912	689.6	808.3	17.2	8.1	6.8	6.5
37	Virginia Beach–Norfolk–Newport News, VA–NC	1,707,369	734.8	752.7	2.4	7.1	6.6	6.0
38	Providence—Fall River—Warwick, RI–MA	1,604,291	574.9	556.5	-3.2	11.2	10.2	9.7
39	Milwaukee–Waukesha–West Allis, WI	1,569,659	839.5	825.8	-1.6	8.0	7.5	7.3
40	Jacksonville, FL	1,394,624	557.9	608.5	9.1	9.9	8.4	6.9
41	Memphis, TN–MS–AR	1,341,746	613.1	605.1	-1.3	10.1	9.1	9.3
42	Oklahoma City, OK	1,319,677	546.8	607.2	11.0	5.5	5.0	5.1
43	Louisville/Jefferson County, KY–IN	1,262,261	597.1	625.9	4.8	9.6	8.2	7.8
44	Richmond, VA	1,245,764	587.6	632.9	7.7	7.1	6.4	5.9
45	New Orleans–Metairie–Kenner, LA	1,240,977	610.9	545.6	-10.7	7.2	6.5	6.1
46	Hartford–West Hartford–East Hartford, CT NECTA	1,215,211	544.6	549.1	0.8	9.0	8.3	7.8
47	Raleigh–Cary, NC	1,214,516	434.3	541.2	24.6	8.4	7.6	6.4
48	Salt Lake City, UT	1,140,483	563.3	662.2	17.6	6.7	5.5	4.2
49	Birmingham–Hoover, AL	1,140,300	509.4	507.3	-0.4	7.7	6.2	5.7
50	Buffalo—Niagara Falls, NY	1,134,115	547.1	547.9	0.1	8.0	8.3	7.5
51	Rochester, NY	1,083,278	512.1	514.5	0.5	7.7	7.9	7.1
52	Grand Rapids–Wyoming, MI	1,016,603	392.5	402.4	2.5	8..5	7.9	7.1
53	Tucson, AZ	996,554	342.8	361.2	5.4	8.3	7.3	7.0
54	Urban Honolulu, Hi	983,429	412.9	455.7	10.4	5.6	5.2	4.3
55	Fresno, CA	955,272	287.8	305.3	6.1	16.4	15.0	12.9
56	Tulsa, OK	961,561	410.1	431.3	5.2	6.6	5.6	5.7
57	Bridgeport–Stamford–Norwalk, CT	939,904	414.4	411.0	-0.8	8.3	7.7	7.2
58	Worcester, MA–CT	926,710	244.2	248.1	1.6	7.8	7.4	7.7
59	Albuquerque, NM	902,797	361.7	370.3	2.4	8.0	7.5	7.2
60	Omaha–Council Bluffs, NE–IA	895,151	440.2	475.7	8.1	5.0	4.5	4.3
61	Albany–Schenectady–Troy, NY	877,905	437.8	447.7	2.3	7.3	7.4	6.4
62	Bakersfield–Delano, CA	864,124	207.0	249.9	20.7	15.0	13.3	11.8
63	New Haven, CT NECTA	862,287	274.5	274.3	-0.1	9.3	8.6	8.1
64	Knoxville, TN	852,715	313.2	332.1	6.0	7.5	6.7	6.9
65	Greenville–Mauldin–Easley, SC	850,965	293.9	312.2	6.2	8.5	7.5	6.2
66	Oxnard–Thousand Oaks–Ventura, CA	839,620	282.5	286.6	1.5	10.2	9.1	7.8
67	El Paso, TX	831,036	256.1	286.9	12.0	10.4	9.4	8.8
68	Allentown–Bethlehem–Easton, PA–NJ	827,048	324.5	346.9	6.9	8.7	8.5	7.7
69	Baton Rouge, LA	820,159	336.1	384.9	14.5	7.3	6.4	5.9
70	McAllen–Edinburg–Mission, TX	815,996	168.0	282.9	68.4	12.1	11.1	10.8
71	Dayton, OH	802,489	422.2	233.9	-44.6	9.2	7.7	7.7
72	Columbia, SC	793,779	337.4	361.1	7.0	8.9	7.9	6.7
73	Greensboro–High Point, NC	741,065	357.7	345.9	-3.3	10.6	9.7	8.4
74	North Port–Sarasota–Bradenton, FL	732,535	444.5	467.4	5.2	10.6	8.8	7.0
75	Little Rock–North Little Rock–Conway, AR	717,666	324.3	342.4	5.6	7.0	6.5	6.8

1. Population estimates are from July 1, 2012, to July 1, 2013.
2. Data include revised inputs, model reestimations, and adjustments to new state control totals.

Employment by Industry: Albany–Schenectady–Troy, NY, Selected Years, 2002–2013

(Numbers in thousands, not seasonally adjusted)

Industry and year	January	February	March	April	May	June	July	August	September	October	November	December	Annual average
Total Nonfarm													
2002	426.4	431.1	434.6	438.5	440.6	441.6	434.9	437.6	439.8	442.1	443.5	442.4	437.8
2003	427.1	430.7	431.7	434.8	439.1	439.4	434.5	437.0	438.0	441.7	444.4	444.0	436.9
2004	430.0	433.4	436.3	439.7	446.8	445.6	440.7	441.2	442.7	446.0	447.5	448.4	441.5
2005	434.3	437.1	437.5	444.4	445.8	447.1	442.6	443.6	445.3	448.0	449.7	449.1	443.7
2006	434.1	438.4	441.5	445.6	447.8	448.7	441.9	442.5	444.8	449.8	451.9	453.0	445.0
2007	436.9	439.7	442.2	443.6	449.5	451.9	443.9	445.0	447.9	453.0	455.2	455.4	447.0
2008	440.2	443.9	444.8	450.1	455.4	456.5	449.6	449.5	450.3	454.8	455.1	452.8	450.3
2009	435.9	440.1	440.1	442.7	445.3	445.0	437.2	436.3	438.2	442.8	444.0	441.9	440.8
2010	426.5	430.9	432.2	438.5	441.9	440.9	433.0	431.7	434.6	438.6	440.9	439.0	435.7
2011	423.3	429.7	430.3	437.8	439.5	439.4	435.0	434.1	438.3	443.0	445.3	443.3	436.6
2012	430.2	436.5	437.7	444.0	447.6	447.7	439.7	440.0	444.0	450.0	452.9	450.0	443.4
2013	435.2	442.5	443.8	448.6	452.4	453.0	445.6	443.9	448.2	453.3	454.2	451.2	447.7
Total Private													
2002	319.2	320.8	324.3	327.8	330.0	331.7	331.1	334.4	331.2	332.2	333.0	332.1	329.0
2003	319.1	320.5	322.1	325.8	330.1	331.2	331.6	334.8	331.2	333.2	335.7	335.2	329.2
2004	323.9	325.1	327.9	330.6	337.3	336.3	337.2	338.5	336.5	337.8	338.9	339.9	334.2
2005	327.1	328.6	328.9	335.3	336.7	338.7	339.8	341.5	339.4	339.7	341.2	340.5	336.5
2006	328.0	330.3	333.4	337.0	339.3	341.1	339.6	341.2	339.9	341.9	343.8	343.8	338.2
2007	330.0	330.8	333.6	334.8	340.1	342.7	341.4	342.3	341.8	343.6	345.4	344.5	339.3
2008	333.1	334.7	335.8	339.6	344.1	345.7	344.4	345.4	343.1	344.4	344.6	341.8	341.4
2009	328.6	330.0	330.5	331.6	334.3	334.8	332.9	333.5	332.4	333.7	334.3	332.0	332.4
2010	319.3	322.0	323.7	329.4	331.0	330.7	331.7	332.6	332.4	334.4	336.1	334.4	329.8
2011	322.6	326.4	327.2	333.5	334.9	335.3	336.3	336.9	338.8	340.1	342.0	339.9	334.5
2012	329.5	333.5	335.4	340.8	343.8	345.0	343.3	344.2	345.0	348.0	349.9	347.5	342.2
2013	334.5	339.0	340.7	345.3	348.3	349.5	348.3	347.7	349.5	351.4	351.4	348.6	346.2
Goods-Producing													
2002	40.4	39.7	40.3	41.5	42.7	43.4	43.9	44.1	43.6	43.0	42.4	40.8	42.2
2003	38.6	37.8	37.9	38.9	40.5	41.4	41.8	42.4	41.9	42.0	41.3	40.2	40.4
2004	38.0	37.5	37.9	39.6	41.1	41.8	42.7	42.9	42.3	42.0	41.7	40.4	40.7
2005	38.8	38.1	38.3	40.5	41.8	42.6	43.3	43.4	42.8	42.4	42.3	40.9	41.3
2006	39.1	38.5	39.1	40.9	42.1	42.9	43.0	43.3	42.7	42.7	42.0	40.8	41.4
2007	38.8	37.8	38.6	39.9	41.9	42.8	43.4	43.4	42.9	43.0	42.2	40.9	41.3
2008	38.7	37.8	38.1	39.5	41.3	42.3	42.7	42.9	42.4	42.3	41.3	39.6	40.7
2009	36.7	35.8	35.7	36.8	37.8	38.8	39.3	39.5	38.9	38.7	38.3	36.9	37.8
2010	34.7	34.0	34.4	36.1	37.0	37.9	38.0	38.2	38.5	38.1	37.7	36.8	36.8
2011	35.2	34.8	35.1	37.1	38.2	39.4	40.4	40.8	40.4	40.2	39.9	38.5	38.3
2012	37.0	36.4	37.0	39.0	40.1	41.3	41.8	42.0	41.6	41.3	40.9	40.3	39.9
2013	38.7	38.5	38.9	40.2	41.9	42.7	43.3	43.4	42.9	43.0	42.4	42.1	41.5
Service-Providing													
2002	386.0	391.4	394.3	397.0	397.9	398.2	391.0	393.5	396.2	399.1	401.1	401.6	395.6
2003	388.5	392.9	393.8	395.9	398.6	398.0	392.7	394.6	396.1	399.7	403.1	403.8	396.5
2004	392.0	395.9	398.4	400.1	405.7	403.8	398.0	398.3	400.4	404.0	405.8	408.0	400.9
2005	395.5	399.0	399.2	403.9	404.0	404.5	399.3	400.2	402.5	405.6	407.4	408.2	402.4
2006	395.0	399.9	402.4	404.7	405.7	405.8	398.9	399.2	402.1	407.1	409.9	412.2	403.6
2007	398.1	401.9	403.6	403.7	407.6	409.1	400.5	401.6	405.0	410.0	413.0	414.5	405.7
2008	401.5	406.1	406.7	410.6	414.1	414.2	406.9	406.6	407.9	412.5	413.8	413.2	409.5
2009	399.2	404.3	404.4	405.9	407.5	406.2	397.9	396.8	399.3	404.1	405.7	405.0	403.0
2010	391.8	396.9	397.8	402.4	404.9	403.0	395.0	393.5	396.1	400.5	403.2	402.2	398.9
2011	388.1	394.9	395.2	400.7	401.3	400.0	394.6	393.3	397.9	402.8	405.4	404.8	398.3
2012	393.2	400.1	400.7	405.0	407.5	406.4	397.9	398.0	402.4	408.7	412.0	409.7	403.5
2013	396.5	404.0	404.9	408.4	410.5	410.3	402.3	400.5	405.3	410.3	411.8	409.1	406.2
Mining, Logging, and Construction													
2002	15.3	14.8	15.3	16.7	17.9	18.4	19.1	19.3	18.9	18.5	18.3	17.1	17.5
2003	15.5	14.9	15.0	16.1	17.7	18.6	19.5	19.8	19.3	19.3	18.6	17.6	17.7
2004	15.8	15.4	15.7	17.1	18.5	19.0	19.6	19.5	19.2	19.0	18.6	17.4	17.9
2005	16.0	15.4	15.5	17.4	18.6	19.3	20.0	20.0	19.6	19.4	19.2	17.9	18.2
2006	16.1	15.6	16.1	17.6	18.7	19.4	19.6	19.8	19.4	19.4	18.6	17.6	18.2
2007	16.0	15.1	15.7	16.8	18.8	19.4	20.0	20.1	19.8	19.9	19.2	17.9	18.2
2008	16.1	15.5	15.7	17.2	18.7	19.4	20.0	20.2	19.9	19.9	19.0	17.5	18.3
2009	15.3	14.7	14.9	16.1	17.2	18.0	18.7	18.9	18.3	18.1	17.7	16.4	17.0
2010	14.5	14.0	14.3	15.9	16.7	17.4	18.1	18.4	18.1	17.6	17.0	16.2	16.5
2011	14.7	14.2	14.4	15.9	16.9	17.8	18.6	19.0	18.6	18.2	17.8	16.5	16.9
2012	15.2	14.5	14.8	16.7	17.6	18.5	18.8	18.9	18.5	18.2	17.7	17.1	17.2
2013	15.2	14.9	15.2	16.3	17.9	18.3	19.1	19.2	18.9	19.0	18.4	18.0	17.5
Manufacturing													
2002	25.1	24.9	25.0	24.8	24.8	25.0	24.8	24.8	24.7	24.5	24.1	23.7	24.7
2003	23.1	22.9	22.9	22.8	22.8	22.8	22.3	22.6	22.6	22.7	22.7	22.6	22.7
2004	22.2	22.1	22.2	22.5	22.6	22.8	23.1	23.4	23.1	23.0	23.1	23.0	22.8
2005	22.8	22.7	22.8	23.1	23.2	23.3	23.3	23.4	23.2	23.0	23.1	23.0	23.1
2006	23.0	22.9	23.0	23.3	23.4	23.5	23.4	23.5	23.3	23.3	23.4	23.2	23.3
2007	22.8	22.7	22.9	23.1	23.1	23.4	23.4	23.3	23.1	23.1	23.0	23.0	23.1
2008	22.6	22.3	22.4	22.3	22.6	22.9	22.7	22.7	22.5	22.4	22.3	22.1	22.5
2009	21.4	21.1	20.8	20.7	20.6	20.8	20.6	20.6	20.6	20.6	20.6	20.5	20.7
2010	20.2	20.0	20.1	20.2	20.3	20.5	19.9	19.8	20.4	20.5	20.7	20.6	20.3
2011	20.5	20.6	20.7	21.2	21.3	21.6	21.8	21.8	21.8	22.0	22.1	22.0	21.5
2012	21.8	21.9	22.2	22.3	22.5	22.8	23.0	23.1	23.1	23.1	23.2	23.2	22.7
2013	23.5	23.6	23.7	23.9	24.0	24.4	24.2	24.2	24.0	24.0	24.0	24.1	24.0

Employment by Industry: Albany–Schenectady–Troy, NY, Selected Years, 2002–2013—*Continued*

(Numbers in thousands, not seasonally adjusted)

Industry and year	January	February	March	April	May	June	July	August	September	October	November	December	Annual average
Trade, Transportation, and Utilities													
2002	76.8	75.6	76.0	76.4	76.8	77.7	77.1	77.2	77.0	77.4	79.3	80.9	77.4
2003	77.4	76.4	76.5	76.4	77.3	78.4	77.5	78.0	78.1	79.5	81.8	83.2	78.4
2004	78.7	78.0	78.2	77.8	79.0	79.8	78.8	79.0	79.0	80.4	82.3	83.7	79.6
2005	79.4	78.0	77.9	78.6	79.1	79.7	79.8	80.1	79.6	80.2	82.0	83.5	79.8
2006	78.8	77.4	77.7	78.0	79.0	79.6	78.4	78.5	77.8	78.9	81.1	82.4	79.0
2007	77.9	76.1	76.8	75.9	77.2	77.8	77.1	76.8	76.7	77.6	79.4	80.3	77.5
2008	76.4	74.9	75.0	75.2	76.1	76.8	76.1	76.2	75.8	76.5	77.4	78.5	76.2
2009	74.1	72.9	72.5	72.4	73.3	74.1	73.0	73.1	72.6	73.1	74.6	75.6	73.4
2010	71.7	70.2	70.7	71.3	71.8	72.6	72.0	72.5	71.8	72.4	73.9	75.0	72.2
2011	71.3	70.2	70.4	71.3	71.8	72.5	72.0	72.6	72.2	72.7	74.5	75.9	72.3
2012	72.6	71.4	71.5	72.2	73.3	74.0	73.5	73.6	73.1	73.9	75.7	76.3	73.4
2013	72.4	71.4	71.6	72.3	73.1	74.2	73.8	73.8	73.5	73.6	75.1	76.5	73.4
Wholesale Trade													
2002	16.3	16.2	16.2	16.2	16.3	16.3	16.4	16.3	16.2	16.1	16.2	16.2	16.2
2003	16.5	16.5	16.5	16.4	16.5	16.6	16.6	16.6	16.6	16.6	16.8	17.0	16.6
2004	16.7	16.9	16.9	16.9	16.8	16.7	16.4	16.4	16.3	16.2	16.2	16.2	16.6
2005	15.9	15.7	15.7	15.7	15.6	15.6	15.9	15.8	15.6	15.6	15.7	15.7	15.7
2006	15.3	15.2	15.2	14.9	14.9	15.0	14.9	14.9	14.7	14.7	14.6	14.8	14.9
2007	14.7	14.6	14.8	14.7	14.7	14.8	14.6	14.5	14.2	14.2	14.1	14.1	14.5
2008	13.7	13.7	13.7	13.7	13.8	13.9	14.0	14.0	13.9	13.9	13.9	14.0	13.9
2009	13.6	13.6	13.5	13.5	13.4	13.4	13.4	13.4	13.2	13.1	13.1	13.2	13.4
2010	12.7	12.7	12.7	12.9	13.0	13.0	13.0	13.1	13.1	13.2	13.3	13.2	13.0
2011	13.1	13.1	13.1	13.3	13.3	13.3	13.3	13.4	13.2	13.1	13.2	13.2	13.2
2012	13.1	13.1	13.2	13.4	13.6	13.7	13.8	13.7	13.6	13.6	13.6	13.6	13.5
2013	13.5	13.4	13.5	13.5	13.6	13.7	13.8	13.8	13.7	13.7	13.7	13.8	13.6
Retail Trade													
2002	47.8	46.8	47.2	47.5	47.7	48.5	48.2	48.3	47.9	48.2	50.0	51.6	48.3
2003	48.1	47.0	47.1	47.3	48.0	49.0	48.6	49.0	48.8	50.1	52.2	53.5	49.1
2004	49.9	48.8	48.9	48.5	49.4	50.2	49.8	50.1	49.8	51.0	52.9	54.3	50.3
2005	50.6	49.3	49.2	49.5	49.9	50.3	50.3	50.5	49.8	50.5	52.0	53.5	50.5
2006	49.8	48.5	48.7	49.4	50.2	50.7	50.1	50.0	49.2	50.2	52.6	53.6	50.3
2007	50.0	48.4	48.7	48.1	49.1	49.6	49.3	49.2	49.0	49.8	51.6	52.4	49.6
2008	49.6	48.2	48.2	48.3	48.8	49.3	48.8	48.9	48.3	48.8	49.7	50.6	49.0
2009	47.3	46.2	45.9	45.8	46.6	47.4	46.7	46.8	46.2	46.8	48.2	49.0	46.9
2010	46.2	44.8	45.1	45.5	45.9	46.7	46.2	46.6	45.9	46.5	47.8	48.9	46.3
2011	46.1	45.0	45.3	45.9	46.2	46.9	46.5	46.9	46.5	47.1	48.7	49.8	46.7
2012	47.3	46.2	46.2	46.7	47.5	48.0	47.5	47.7	47.1	47.9	49.7	50.0	47.7
2013	47.0	45.9	46.1	46.6	47.2	48.1	47.8	47.8	47.4	47.4	48.8	49.9	47.5
Transportation and Utilities													
2002	12.7	12.6	12.6	12.7	12.8	12.9	12.5	12.6	12.9	13.1	13.1	13.1	12.8
2003	12.8	12.9	12.9	12.7	12.8	12.8	12.3	12.4	12.7	12.8	12.8	12.7	12.7
2004	12.1	12.3	12.4	12.4	12.8	12.9	12.6	12.5	12.9	13.2	13.2	13.2	12.7
2005	12.9	13.0	13.0	13.4	13.6	13.8	13.6	13.8	14.2	14.1	14.3	14.3	13.7
2006	13.7	13.7	13.8	13.7	13.9	13.9	13.4	13.6	13.9	14.0	13.9	14.0	13.8
2007	13.2	13.1	13.3	13.1	13.4	13.4	13.2	13.1	13.5	13.6	13.7	13.8	13.4
2008	13.1	13.0	13.1	13.2	13.5	13.6	13.3	13.3	13.6	13.8	13.8	13.9	13.4
2009	13.2	13.1	13.1	13.1	13.3	13.3	12.9	12.9	13.2	13.2	13.3	13.4	13.2
2010	12.8	12.7	12.9	12.9	12.9	12.9	12.8	12.8	12.8	12.7	12.8	12.9	12.8
2011	12.1	12.1	12.0	12.1	12.3	12.3	12.2	12.3	12.5	12.5	12.6	12.9	12.3
2012	12.2	12.1	12.1	12.1	12.2	12.3	12.2	12.2	12.4	12.4	12.4	12.7	12.3
2013	11.9	12.1	12.0	12.2	12.3	12.4	12.2	12.2	12.4	12.5	12.6	12.8	12.3
Information													
2002	11.9	11.9	12.0	12.0	12.1	12.1	11.9	11.9	11.8	11.9	12.0	12.0	12.0
2003	11.6	11.7	12.0	12.0	11.8	11.5	11.2	11.1	10.8	10.6	10.4	10.2	11.2
2004	11.1	11.1	11.5	11.0	10.7	10.7	10.8	10.8	10.8	10.6	10.7	10.5	10.9
2005	10.5	10.6	10.8	11.1	11.0	11.1	11.0	11.1	10.9	10.9	10.8	10.9	10.9
2006	10.8	10.7	10.7	10.6	10.6	10.6	10.5	10.4	10.1	10.2	10.2	10.2	10.5
2007	10.1	10.0	10.0	9.9	10.0	10.0	10.0	10.0	9.8	9.7	9.7	9.8	9.9
2008	9.4	9.4	9.4	9.5	9.8	9.9	9.9	9.9	9.7	9.8	9.8	9.8	9.7
2009	9.8	9.7	9.6	9.6	9.6	9.7	9.6	9.6	9.4	9.2	9.3	9.3	9.5
2010	9.0	9.0	9.0	8.8	8.9	8.9	9.0	9.0	8.8	8.8	8.8	8.8	8.9
2011	8.8	8.7	8.7	8.8	8.8	8.9	9.0	8.2	8.8	8.8	8.8	8.8	8.8
2012	8.7	8.7	8.7	8.7	8.7	8.7	8.7	8.6	8.5	8.6	8.6	8.5	8.6
2013	8.5	8.5	8.5	8.5	8.4	8.4	8.4	8.5	8.3	8.3	8.3	8.3	8.4
Financial Activities													
2002	24.4	24.7	24.9	24.8	25.1	25.4	25.0	25.3	24.8	25.2	25.3	25.4	25.0
2003	25.3	25.3	25.4	25.5	25.8	26.3	26.3	26.3	25.9	26.0	26.1	26.1	25.9
2004	25.8	25.6	25.9	25.7	25.8	26.5	26.6	26.5	26.4	26.3	26.1	26.3	26.1
2005	25.9	25.9	26.0	26.1	26.2	26.6	26.8	26.8	26.5	26.5	26.4	26.6	26.4
2006	26.2	26.3	26.5	26.7	26.6	27.0	27.1	27.0	26.6	26.7	26.7	26.7	26.7
2007	26.3	26.0	26.0	26.1	26.2	26.7	26.5	26.4	26.0	26.0	26.1	26.1	26.2
2008	25.9	25.8	25.9	25.9	26.0	26.4	26.4	26.3	25.8	25.6	25.5	25.4	25.9
2009	25.3	25.2	25.2	24.9	25.0	25.3	25.1	25.1	24.6	24.5	24.4	24.4	24.9
2010	24.3	24.2	24.3	24.3	24.3	24.7	24.8	24.7	24.3	24.5	24.4	24.6	24.5
2011	24.3	24.3	24.3	24.4	24.4	24.8	25.0	25.1	24.7	24.6	24.6	24.7	24.6
2012	24.7	24.7	24.8	24.9	24.9	25.5	25.6	25.5	25.2	25.3	25.4	25.5	25.2
2013	25.0	25.0	25.1	25.2	25.3	25.8	25.7	25.7	25.2	25.7	25.4	25.4	25.4

Employment by Industry: Albany–Schenectady–Troy, NY, Selected Years, 2002–2013—*Continued*

(Numbers in thousands, not seasonally adjusted)

Industry and year	January	February	March	April	May	June	July	August	September	October	November	December	Annual average
Professional and Business Services													
2002	47.7	47.5	48.0	48.7	48.4	49.2	49.0	49.3	48.7	48.6	48.0	47.6	48.4
2003	45.9	45.8	46.1	47.2	47.9	48.7	48.9	49.2	48.4	48.3	48.8	49.0	47.9
2004	47.6	47.6	48.1	49.3	49.9	50.8	50.9	51.0	50.3	49.6	49.8	49.8	49.6
2005	49.5	49.7	49.6	50.7	50.5	51.7	52.2	51.9	52.0	51.3	51.5	50.8	51.0
2006	50.6	50.8	51.4	52.3	51.7	52.5	53.0	53.0	52.8	52.4	52.9	53.0	52.2
2007	51.3	51.8	52.1	52.4	52.5	54.0	54.2	54.2	53.6	53.5	53.9	54.0	53.1
2008	54.0	54.1	54.4	55.1	54.9	56.0	55.8	56.0	55.0	54.8	54.5	54.1	54.9
2009	52.9	52.3	52.6	52.3	51.7	51.8	51.6	51.2	50.9	51.2	50.8	50.5	51.7
2010	49.1	49.2	49.5	50.5	50.6	51.0	51.9	51.5	50.7	51.1	51.2	50.9	50.6
2011	50.0	50.2	50.3	51.4	51.2	51.8	52.1	51.8	51.7	51.8	52.4	51.6	51.4
2012	51.4	51.4	51.8	52.7	52.8	53.3	53.2	53.2	52.3	52.6	53.2	52.0	52.5
2013	51.8	51.8	51.9	52.8	52.9	53.6	53.6	53.3	52.8	52.7	52.7	51.0	52.6
Education and Health Services													
2002	72.2	75.1	75.8	76.0	74.7	72.8	73.0	73.0	75.5	76.7	76.9	76.9	74.9
2003	74.1	76.9	77.1	77.5	76.9	74.4	73.7	73.4	75.9	77.2	78.0	77.6	76.1
2004	75.2	77.7	77.8	78.3	79.6	74.6	74.8	74.2	77.1	78.7	78.8	79.5	77.2
2005	75.6	78.5	78.1	78.8	77.5	75.2	74.9	74.3	76.7	78.3	78.5	78.1	77.0
2006	75.6	78.7	78.8	79.2	78.3	76.0	75.2	74.9	78.7	80.1	80.4	80.5	78.0
2007	77.2	80.3	80.4	80.5	79.9	77.7	76.6	76.3	80.4	81.7	82.7	82.5	79.7
2008	79.6	83.0	82.6	82.9	82.6	80.1	78.4	77.8	81.5	82.8	84.2	83.5	81.6
2009	80.8	84.6	84.8	84.8	83.7	81.1	79.7	79.4	83.3	85.0	85.7	84.5	83.1
2010	82.2	86.3	86.4	87.1	85.6	82.4	81.3	81.0	85.4	87.0	88.0	86.7	85.0
2011	83.6	88.1	88.0	88.5	87.2	83.8	82.5	81.9	86.6	88.8	89.3	88.1	86.4
2012	85.1	89.8	90.1	90.3	89.2	85.9	83.8	83.2	88.7	91.2	91.7	91.1	88.3
2013	87.3	92.0	92.0	92.9	91.1	87.3	85.8	85.2	90.3	92.7	93.2	91.8	90.1
Leisure and Hospitality													
2002	28.5	28.8	29.6	30.5	32.3	33.2	33.4	35.8	32.0	31.3	30.7	30.2	31.4
2003	28.0	28.4	28.9	30.1	31.7	32.3	33.8	36.0	32.0	31.2	30.8	30.5	31.1
2004	29.2	29.2	30.0	30.4	32.6	33.7	34.2	35.8	32.5	31.6	30.9	31.2	31.8
2005	29.1	29.3	29.8	31.1	32.3	33.6	33.8	35.9	32.9	31.9	31.4	31.5	31.9
2006	29.2	29.9	30.9	31.1	32.7	34.2	34.2	36.0	33.1	32.5	31.7	31.7	32.3
2007	30.2	30.4	31.2	31.8	33.9	35.2	35.6	37.2	34.4	33.8	33.0	32.4	33.3
2008	30.7	31.2	31.9	33.1	34.9	35.7	36.5	37.7	34.6	33.9	33.1	32.2	33.8
2009	30.4	30.7	31.2	32.2	34.4	35.3	36.0	37.3	34.6	33.7	33.0	32.6	33.5
2010	30.7	31.4	31.7	33.5	34.9	35.5	36.8	37.7	35.3	34.8	34.4	33.7	34.2
2011	31.8	32.4	32.7	34.1	35.3	36.4	37.3	38.5	36.4	35.5	34.8	34.5	35.0
2012	32.5	33.5	33.6	35.1	36.9	38.3	38.7	40.2	37.8	37.2	36.5	36.0	36.4
2013	33.3	34.1	34.8	35.7	37.8	39.5	39.7	39.8	38.8	37.6	36.5	35.7	36.9
Other Services													
2002	17.3	17.5	17.7	17.9	17.9	17.9	17.8	17.8	17.8	18.1	18.4	18.3	17.9
2003	18.2	18.2	18.2	18.2	18.2	18.2	18.4	18.4	18.2	18.4	18.5	18.4	18.3
2004	18.3	18.4	18.5	18.5	18.6	18.4	18.4	18.3	18.1	18.6	18.6	18.5	18.4
2005	18.3	18.5	18.4	18.4	18.3	18.2	18.0	18.0	18.0	18.2	18.3	18.2	18.2
2006	17.7	18.0	18.3	18.2	18.3	18.3	18.2	18.1	18.1	18.4	18.4	18.5	18.2
2007	18.2	18.4	18.5	18.5	18.5	18.5	18.0	18.0	18.0	18.3	18.4	18.5	18.3
2008	18.4	18.5	18.5	18.4	18.5	18.5	18.6	18.6	18.3	18.7	18.8	18.7	18.5
2009	18.6	18.8	18.9	18.6	18.8	18.7	18.6	18.3	18.1	18.3	18.2	18.2	18.5
2010	17.6	17.7	17.7	17.8	17.9	17.7	17.9	18.0	17.6	17.7	17.7	17.9	17.8
2011	17.6	17.7	17.7	17.9	18.0	17.7	18.0	18.0	18.0	17.7	17.7	17.8	17.8
2012	17.5	17.6	17.9	17.9	17.9	18.0	18.0	17.9	17.8	17.9	17.9	17.8	17.8
2013	17.5	17.7	17.9	17.7	17.8	18.0	18.0	18.0	17.7	17.8	17.8	17.8	17.8
Government													
2002	107.2	110.3	110.3	110.7	110.6	109.9	103.8	103.2	108.6	109.9	110.5	110.3	108.8
2003	108.0	110.2	109.6	109.0	109.0	108.2	102.9	102.2	106.8	108.5	108.7	108.8	107.7
2004	106.1	108.3	108.4	109.1	109.5	109.3	103.5	102.7	106.2	108.2	108.6	108.5	107.4
2005	107.2	108.5	108.6	109.1	109.1	108.4	102.8	102.1	105.9	108.3	108.5	108.6	107.3
2006	106.1	108.1	108.1	108.6	108.5	107.6	102.3	101.3	104.9	107.9	108.5	109.2	106.8
2007	106.9	108.9	108.6	108.8	109.4	109.2	102.5	102.7	106.1	109.8	110.9	110.7	107.8
2008	107.1	109.2	109.0	110.5	111.3	110.8	105.2	104.1	107.2	110.4	110.5	111.0	108.9
2009	107.3	110.1	109.6	111.1	111.0	110.2	104.3	102.8	105.8	109.1	109.7	109.9	108.4
2010	107.2	108.9	108.5	109.1	110.9	110.2	101.3	99.1	102.2	104.2	104.8	104.6	105.9
2011	100.7	103.3	103.1	104.3	104.6	104.1	98.7	97.2	99.5	102.9	103.3	103.4	102.1
2012	100.7	103.0	102.3	103.2	103.8	102.7	96.4	95.8	99.0	102.0	103.0	102.5	101.2
2013	100.7	103.5	103.1	103.3	104.1	103.5	97.3	96.2	98.7	101.9	102.8	102.6	101.5

Employment by Industry: Albuquerque, NM, Selected Years, 2002–2013

(Numbers in thousands, not seasonally adjusted)

Industry and year	January	February	March	April	May	June	July	August	September	October	November	December	Annual average
Total Nonfarm													
2002	355.5	357.2	359.9	360.7	363.3	364.0	361.4	361.7	364.7	362.1	364.0	366.1	361.7
2003	356.6	359.5	362.0	362.5	364.0	364.4	361.9	363.5	365.0	364.5	365.6	368.0	363.1
2004	360.2	364.5	367.5	369.6	371.3	371.1	369.1	369.4	371.4	375.1	376.0	376.9	370.2
2005	367.5	370.5	373.0	376.4	377.9	378.4	376.5	378.4	381.6	382.2	385.0	387.0	377.9
2006	381.5	385.2	389.6	389.8	391.8	393.8	390.1	391.2	394.8	395.2	397.2	397.8	391.5
2007	388.0	391.6	395.9	395.4	397.7	397.5	393.9	396.0	397.2	398.0	399.1	399.5	395.8
2008	390.1	392.8	394.6	396.7	398.0	396.3	394.0	396.7	398.3	396.9	393.2	390.7	394.9
2009	380.5	379.5	379.3	379.8	379.6	377.1	374.3	376.7	378.2	377.6	376.5	376.4	378.0
2010	367.7	368.7	370.3	373.5	374.3	372.8	369.2	370.0	371.4	373.8	373.7	374.3	371.6
2011	365.6	369.8	370.1	373.0	372.8	370.1	367.5	367.9	371.5	371.5	370.5	369.5	370.0
2012	361.6	364.4	367.2	368.0	368.7	365.2	363.6	365.7	369.7	374.8	374.8	373.7	368.1
2013	365.9	369.0	369.3	372.7	373.0	369.7	368.9	370.3	371.4	371.3	371.4	371.0	370.3
Total Private													
2002	285.6	284.7	287.1	287.9	290.5	290.8	290.2	290.9	291.3	289.3	290.8	292.3	289.3
2003	285.8	286.1	288.1	288.7	290.4	290.9	290.0	291.6	291.0	290.5	291.3	292.9	289.8
2004	288.6	289.5	292.0	294.3	296.1	296.6	296.7	297.0	296.3	298.9	299.4	300.0	295.5
2005	293.7	294.1	296.4	300.0	301.7	302.7	302.8	304.4	304.8	304.4	307.1	308.5	301.7
2006	305.1	306.7	310.7	311.2	313.3	316.0	314.2	314.1	315.4	315.4	317.1	317.4	313.1
2007	310.6	312.1	315.4	315.7	318.1	319.0	317.4	318.2	316.8	316.9	317.6	318.0	316.3
2008	311.4	311.8	313.1	315.2	315.9	315.9	315.5	316.9	315.9	313.8	310.2	307.7	313.6
2009	299.3	296.3	295.6	296.0	296.4	295.6	295.3	296.4	295.4	293.5	292.5	292.1	295.4
2010	286.2	285.1	286.1	288.5	288.9	289.8	289.2	289.4	288.4	289.4	289.3	289.7	288.3
2011	283.7	285.8	285.5	288.5	289.0	287.5	287.4	287.3	288.1	287.0	286.0	284.7	286.7
2012	280.6	281.1	283.4	285.0	285.9	286.7	285.6	286.1	287.0	290.8	290.6	289.3	286.0
2013	284.8	285.6	285.7	289.2	290.1	288.4	289.7	290.2	288.7	287.7	287.6	287.1	287.9
Goods-Producing													
2002	48.4	47.9	48.2	48.2	48.3	48.8	49.1	49.1	48.4	47.7	47.2	47.3	48.2
2003	46.8	46.7	46.9	47.0	47.5	47.9	48.3	48.6	48.0	47.5	47.1	47.1	47.5
2004	46.2	46.4	46.9	47.5	48.1	49.1	50.1	50.0	49.6	49.8	49.6	49.6	48.6
2005	48.9	49.1	49.6	50.5	51.0	51.5	52.2	52.3	52.4	52.8	53.3	53.6	51.4
2006	53.5	54.3	55.0	54.9	55.5	56.4	56.4	56.4	56.2	56.2	55.4	55.5	55.5
2007	53.6	54.0	54.6	54.6	55.1	55.4	54.9	54.8	53.9	53.6	53.1	52.2	54.2
2008	50.9	50.9	51.1	51.3	51.4	51.9	51.3	51.0	50.5	49.2	48.1	46.9	50.4
2009	44.6	43.3	42.5	42.4	42.1	42.3	42.2	42.3	41.6	41.2	40.5	39.8	42.1
2010	38.8	38.3	38.2	38.6	39.0	39.2	39.9	39.6	39.3	39.0	38.7	38.3	38.9
2011	37.3	37.1	37.8	38.2	38.3	38.6	38.6	38.3	37.7	37.5	36.8	36.4	37.7
2012	35.9	35.9	36.2	36.3	36.6	37.0	36.8	36.8	36.4	37.4	37.1	36.9	36.6
2013	35.9	36.1	36.4	36.9	37.0	37.3	37.5	37.3	36.9	37.0	36.6	35.9	36.7
Service-Providing													
2002	307.1	309.3	311.7	312.5	315.0	315.2	312.3	312.6	316.3	314.4	316.8	318.8	313.5
2003	309.8	312.8	315.1	315.5	316.5	316.5	313.6	314.9	317.0	317.0	318.5	320.9	315.7
2004	314.0	318.1	320.6	322.1	323.2	322.0	319.0	319.4	321.8	325.3	326.4	327.3	321.6
2005	318.6	321.4	323.4	325.9	326.9	326.9	324.3	326.1	329.2	329.4	331.7	333.4	326.4
2006	328.0	330.9	334.6	334.9	336.3	337.4	333.7	334.8	338.6	339.0	341.8	342.3	336.0
2007	334.4	337.6	341.3	340.8	342.6	342.1	339.0	341.2	343.3	344.4	346.0	347.3	341.7
2008	339.2	341.9	343.5	345.4	346.6	344.4	342.7	345.7	347.8	347.7	345.1	343.8	344.5
2009	335.9	336.2	336.8	337.4	337.5	334.8	332.1	334.4	336.6	336.4	336.0	336.6	335.9
2010	328.9	330.4	332.1	334.9	335.3	333.6	329.3	330.4	332.1	334.8	335.0	336.0	332.7
2011	328.3	332.7	332.3	334.8	334.5	331.5	328.9	329.6	333.8	334.0	333.7	333.1	332.3
2012	325.7	328.5	331.0	331.7	332.1	328.2	326.8	328.9	333.3	337.4	337.7	336.8	331.5
2013	330.0	332.9	332.9	335.8	336.0	332.4	331.4	333.0	334.5	334.3	334.8	335.1	333.6
Mining, Logging, and Construction													
2002	23.4	23.1	23.4	23.3	23.4	23.7	23.8	23.9	23.4	23.2	23.1	23.2	23.4
2003	23.1	23.0	23.2	23.5	24.1	24.5	24.8	25.0	24.6	24.4	24.4	24.5	24.1
2004	24.0	24.3	24.7	25.0	25.4	26.3	27.1	27.0	26.7	27.0	26.9	26.9	25.9
2005	26.3	26.6	27.1	27.8	28.2	28.8	29.5	29.5	29.5	29.6	30.0	30.2	28.6
2006	30.2	30.5	31.2	31.0	31.6	32.2	32.0	32.0	31.7	31.7	31.3	31.4	31.4
2007	29.8	29.9	30.6	30.8	31.2	31.4	30.9	30.8	30.3	30.5	30.1	29.4	30.5
2008	28.6	28.6	28.8	29.0	29.0	29.4	28.9	28.5	28.1	27.8	27.1	26.2	28.3
2009	24.7	24.0	23.8	24.0	24.0	24.2	24.2	24.5	24.1	23.8	23.2	22.4	23.9
2010	21.5	21.0	20.9	21.1	21.3	21.5	22.1	21.9	21.6	21.3	21.1	20.7	21.3
2011	19.8	19.7	20.3	20.5	20.6	20.8	20.8	20.4	19.9	19.6	19.1	18.7	20.0
2012	18.3	18.3	18.5	18.6	18.8	19.2	18.9	18.9	18.7	19.5	19.4	19.3	18.9
2013	18.5	18.7	19.1	19.5	19.7	19.9	20.1	19.9	19.7	19.7	19.7	19.1	19.5
Manufacturing													
2002	25.0	24.8	24.8	24.9	24.9	25.1	25.3	25.2	25.0	24.5	24.1	24.1	24.8
2003	23.7	23.7	23.7	23.5	23.4	23.4	23.5	23.6	23.4	23.1	22.7	22.6	23.4
2004	22.2	22.1	22.2	22.5	22.7	22.8	23.0	23.0	22.9	22.8	22.7	22.7	22.6
2005	22.6	22.5	22.5	22.7	22.8	22.7	22.7	22.8	22.9	23.2	23.3	23.4	22.8
2006	23.3	23.8	23.8	23.9	23.9	24.2	24.4	24.4	24.5	24.5	24.1	24.1	24.1
2007	23.8	24.1	24.0	23.8	23.9	24.0	24.0	24.0	23.6	23.1	23.0	22.8	23.7
2008	22.3	22.3	22.3	22.3	22.4	22.5	22.4	22.5	22.4	21.4	21.0	20.7	22.0
2009	19.9	19.3	18.7	18.4	18.1	18.1	18.0	17.8	17.5	17.4	17.3	17.4	18.2
2010	17.3	17.3	17.3	17.5	17.7	17.7	17.8	17.7	17.7	17.7	17.6	17.6	17.6
2011	17.5	17.4	17.5	17.7	17.7	17.8	17.8	17.9	17.8	17.9	17.7	17.7	17.7
2012	17.6	17.6	17.7	17.7	17.8	17.8	17.9	17.9	17.7	17.9	17.7	17.6	17.7
2013	17.4	17.4	17.3	17.4	17.3	17.4	17.4	17.4	17.2	17.3	16.9	16.8	17.3

Employment by Industry: Albuquerque, NM, Selected Years, 2002–2013—*Continued*

(Numbers in thousands, not seasonally adjusted)

Industry and year	January	February	March	April	May	June	July	August	September	October	November	December	Annual average
Trade, Transportation, and Utilities													
2002	65.6	64.5	64.5	64.9	65.8	65.5	65.3	65.7	65.9	66.1	67.8	68.9	65.9
2003	65.6	64.8	65.4	65.2	65.4	65.0	64.7	65.3	65.2	65.7	67.2	68.3	65.7
2004	65.8	65.4	65.6	65.8	65.8	65.5	65.6	65.8	65.6	66.6	68.1	68.8	66.2
2005	66.2	65.9	65.9	66.0	66.6	66.0	66.4	67.1	66.9	67.4	68.8	69.7	66.9
2006	66.7	66.0	66.5	66.6	67.2	66.9	67.1	67.5	67.6	67.8	69.5	70.2	67.5
2007	68.2	67.7	67.9	67.7	68.5	68.4	68.4	68.8	68.7	69.2	70.9	72.0	68.9
2008	69.5	68.6	68.6	68.4	68.3	67.9	68.0	68.2	68.0	67.8	67.9	68.2	68.3
2009	64.9	63.5	63.2	62.6	62.7	62.7	62.8	62.8	63.0	63.1	63.9	64.5	63.3
2010	62.0	61.2	61.5	61.2	61.6	61.5	61.7	62.1	61.5	62.2	63.3	63.9	62.0
2011	61.6	61.2	61.1	61.8	62.1	61.2	61.0	61.0	61.2	61.6	62.8	63.1	61.6
2012	61.5	61.0	61.3	61.2	61.4	61.2	61.1	61.4	61.6	62.4	63.6	63.7	61.8
2013	61.6	61.2	60.9	61.6	61.7	61.5	61.8	62.3	61.8	61.9	63.1	64.1	62.0
Wholesale Trade													
2002	13.6	13.5	13.5	13.4	13.5	13.4	13.5	13.4	13.4	13.4	13.4	13.3	13.4
2003	13.0	12.9	13.3	13.2	13.0	13.0	12.9	13.0	13.0	12.8	12.8	12.9	13.0
2004	12.8	12.8	13.0	13.2	12.9	12.8	12.9	12.7	12.7	12.7	12.7	12.7	12.8
2005	12.7	12.9	12.9	12.9	13.0	12.9	13.0	13.0	13.0	13.0	13.1	13.1	13.0
2006	12.9	13.0	13.1	13.2	13.3	13.3	13.3	13.3	13.4	13.4	13.3	13.4	13.2
2007	13.3	13.2	13.2	13.2	13.2	13.3	13.4	13.4	13.4	13.5	13.4	13.6	13.3
2008	13.5	13.3	13.2	13.2	13.2	13.1	13.2	13.1	12.9	12.8	12.6	12.5	13.1
2009	12.2	12.1	12.0	11.9	11.8	11.8	12.0	11.9	12.0	12.0	12.0	12.0	12.0
2010	11.9	11.8	11.8	11.8	11.8	11.8	11.8	11.7	11.6	11.6	11.5	11.5	11.7
2011	11.4	11.4	11.4	11.5	11.6	11.4	11.5	11.4	11.4	11.3	11.3	11.3	11.4
2012	11.3	11.4	11.5	11.5	11.6	11.6	11.6	11.6	11.5	11.6	11.6	11.6	11.5
2013	11.4	11.4	11.3	11.4	11.4	11.3	11.3	11.4	11.2	11.3	11.2	11.2	11.3
Retail Trade													
2002	41.4	40.4	40.6	41.0	41.8	41.8	41.5	41.6	41.8	41.9	43.5	44.6	41.8
2003	42.0	41.4	41.6	41.5	41.9	41.7	41.6	41.8	41.7	42.3	43.8	44.8	42.2
2004	42.4	41.9	42.0	42.0	42.3	42.5	42.5	42.6	42.4	43.3	44.9	45.5	42.9
2005	43.1	42.6	42.6	42.8	43.2	43.2	43.4	43.7	43.4	43.9	45.3	45.9	43.6
2006	43.3	42.6	43.0	43.0	43.4	43.3	43.5	43.6	43.6	43.8	45.5	45.8	43.7
2007	44.1	43.6	43.9	43.7	44.4	44.5	44.5	44.5	44.3	44.6	46.4	47.0	44.6
2008	44.9	44.3	44.5	44.3	44.2	44.4	44.4	44.4	44.4	44.6	44.9	45.2	44.5
2009	42.4	41.2	41.2	41.0	41.1	41.4	41.5	41.5	41.6	41.6	42.4	42.9	41.7
2010	40.7	40.0	40.3	40.1	40.4	40.4	40.6	41.0	40.4	41.0	42.1	42.6	40.8
2011	40.6	40.2	40.3	40.8	41.0	40.5	40.2	40.3	40.3	40.7	41.9	42.1	40.7
2012	40.7	40.1	40.2	40.3	40.4	40.4	40.2	40.3	40.5	41.1	42.2	42.2	40.7
2013	40.5	40.1	40.0	40.6	40.7	40.7	41.0	41.2	40.9	40.8	42.1	42.9	41.0
Transportation and Utilities													
2002	10.6	10.6	10.4	10.5	10.5	10.3	10.3	10.7	10.7	10.8	10.9	11.0	10.6
2003	10.6	10.5	10.5	10.5	10.5	10.3	10.2	10.5	10.5	10.6	10.6	10.6	10.5
2004	10.6	10.7	10.6	10.6	10.6	10.2	10.2	10.5	10.5	10.6	10.5	10.6	10.5
2005	10.4	10.4	10.4	10.3	10.4	9.9	10.0	10.4	10.5	10.5	10.4	10.7	10.4
2006	10.5	10.4	10.4	10.4	10.5	10.3	10.3	10.6	10.6	10.6	10.7	11.0	10.5
2007	10.8	10.9	10.8	10.8	10.9	10.6	10.5	10.9	11.0	11.1	11.1	11.4	10.9
2008	11.1	11.0	10.9	10.9	10.9	10.4	10.4	10.7	10.7	10.4	10.4	10.5	10.7
2009	10.3	10.2	10.0	9.7	9.8	9.5	9.3	9.4	9.4	9.5	9.5	9.6	9.7
2010	9.4	9.4	9.4	9.3	9.4	9.3	9.3	9.4	9.5	9.6	9.7	9.8	9.5
2011	9.6	9.6	9.4	9.5	9.5	9.3	9.3	9.3	9.5	9.6	9.6	9.7	9.5
2012	9.5	9.5	9.6	9.4	9.4	9.2	9.3	9.5	9.6	9.7	9.8	9.9	9.5
2013	9.7	9.7	9.6	9.6	9.6	9.5	9.5	9.7	9.7	9.8	9.8	10.0	9.7
Information													
2002	11.2	11.4	11.5	11.3	11.4	11.1	10.9	10.7	10.4	10.5	10.8	10.8	11.0
2003	10.5	10.5	10.5	10.3	10.3	10.3	10.2	10.0	10.1	9.9	9.9	10.0	10.2
2004	9.9	9.9	9.9	9.6	9.8	9.6	9.4	9.3	9.0	9.4	9.5	9.5	9.6
2005	8.5	8.5	8.6	8.7	8.8	8.7	8.7	8.7	8.5	8.7	8.8	9.0	8.7
2006	8.7	9.3	9.5	9.1	9.2	9.9	9.2	9.3	9.7	9.4	9.9	10.0	9.4
2007	8.7	8.9	9.2	9.1	9.3	9.8	9.1	9.1	9.1	9.3	9.3	9.3	9.2
2008	9.4	9.4	9.3	9.1	9.0	9.0	9.7	9.6	9.6	9.4	9.4	9.3	9.4
2009	8.8	8.7	8.7	8.9	8.8	8.9	9.2	9.4	9.4	9.0	9.1	9.1	9.0
2010	8.9	8.6	8.3	9.2	8.7	9.2	8.7	8.8	8.3	8.3	8.6	8.6	8.7
2011	8.4	8.4	8.4	8.5	8.8	8.5	8.2	7.9	7.7	7.8	7.9	7.7	8.2
2012	7.9	8.1	8.5	8.3	7.7	7.8	8.1	8.3	8.5	8.2	8.3	8.1	8.2
2013	7.8	8.4	7.9	8.1	8.5	8.1	7.8	7.7	7.4	7.4	7.5	7.4	7.8
Financial Activities													
2002	18.7	18.6	18.7	18.7	18.8	18.9	19.0	19.1	19.0	19.0	18.9	19.0	18.9
2003	18.5	18.6	18.7	18.7	18.8	18.9	19.0	19.2	19.0	18.8	18.8	18.9	18.8
2004	18.8	18.8	19.0	19.0	19.0	19.1	19.1	19.1	19.1	19.1	19.2	19.3	19.1
2005	19.1	19.1	19.2	19.2	19.3	19.5	19.5	19.4	19.3	19.4	19.4	19.6	19.3
2006	19.3	19.3	19.3	19.3	19.3	19.4	19.3	19.2	19.1	19.1	19.1	19.2	19.2
2007	19.0	19.1	19.2	19.2	19.2	19.3	19.3	19.3	19.3	19.2	19.3	19.1	19.2
2008	18.8	18.8	18.7	18.8	18.7	18.7	18.9	18.9	18.8	18.6	18.4	18.4	18.7
2009	18.0	18.0	17.9	18.1	18.2	18.3	18.3	18.3	18.3	18.3	18.3	18.4	18.2
2010	18.1	18.0	18.1	17.8	17.8	17.9	17.8	17.8	17.6	17.6	17.5	17.6	17.8
2011	17.3	17.3	17.2	17.4	17.4	17.4	17.5	17.5	17.5	17.5	17.4	17.5	17.4
2012	17.3	17.4	17.6	17.4	17.5	17.5	17.6	17.5	17.4	17.7	17.6	17.6	17.5
2013	17.6	17.5	17.5	17.6	17.7	17.7	17.9	18.0	17.9	18.0	18.0	18.2	17.8

Employment by Industry: Albuquerque, NM, Selected Years, 2002–2013—*Continued*

(Numbers in thousands, not seasonally adjusted)

Industry and year	January	February	March	April	May	June	July	August	September	October	November	December	Annual average
Professional and Business Services													
2002	57.2	57.1	57.8	57.1	57.7	57.9	58.0	58.0	58.5	57.8	57.9	58.4	57.8
2003	56.8	57.3	57.6	57.0	57.1	57.5	57.4	57.7	57.6	57.8	57.8	57.9	57.5
2004	57.4	57.8	58.5	58.6	59.0	59.3	59.4	59.6	59.7	60.8	60.1	60.1	59.2
2005	59.3	59.3	59.5	60.6	60.3	61.2	61.1	61.4	61.6	60.8	61.5	61.4	60.7
2006	61.7	62.2	62.7	62.9	62.8	63.8	62.8	62.8	62.9	63.3	63.3	63.6	62.9
2007	62.8	63.6	64.0	63.8	64.2	64.8	64.9	65.6	64.7	64.3	64.2	64.4	64.3
2008	63.5	63.9	63.8	64.0	64.3	64.4	64.8	66.1	65.4	65.1	63.6	63.2	64.3
2009	61.9	61.2	60.6	60.5	60.2	60.1	60.1	60.5	59.7	59.0	58.3	58.2	60.0
2010	57.0	57.1	56.7	57.3	56.8	57.6	57.4	57.6	57.7	58.1	57.7	57.8	57.4
2011	56.4	58.5	56.8	56.9	56.8	57.1	57.2	57.3	57.7	56.6	56.2	55.7	56.9
2012	54.2	54.2	54.6	54.8	54.8	55.6	55.2	55.1	55.1	55.8	55.9	55.2	55.0
2013	55.2	55.4	55.0	55.7	55.6	55.3	56.2	56.1	55.4	54.9	55.0	54.3	55.3
Education and Health Services													
2002	40.8	41.1	41.4	41.4	41.6	40.8	40.2	40.5	41.8	41.8	42.1	41.9	41.3
2003	42.4	42.7	42.9	43.0	43.0	42.2	41.5	41.9	43.2	43.2	43.4	43.5	42.7
2004	44.2	44.4	44.7	45.3	45.3	44.5	43.9	44.4	45.4	45.7	46.1	45.9	45.0
2005	45.7	45.9	46.5	46.5	46.7	45.8	45.2	45.6	46.7	46.9	47.1	47.1	46.3
2006	47.2	47.2	48.4	48.0	48.3	47.6	47.2	47.0	48.5	48.3	48.5	48.4	47.9
2007	48.5	48.8	49.5	49.6	49.7	48.5	48.1	47.9	48.8	49.4	49.7	49.8	49.0
2008	49.4	50.0	50.7	51.5	51.8	51.0	50.3	50.6	51.7	52.3	52.5	52.6	51.2
2009	53.0	53.5	54.1	54.0	54.2	52.9	52.5	52.8	53.8	54.0	54.2	54.1	53.6
2010	54.2	54.4	54.9	55.0	55.1	54.2	53.7	53.6	54.9	55.3	55.5	55.6	54.7
2011	55.4	55.5	55.7	55.8	55.7	54.3	54.7	54.8	56.2	56.4	56.1	55.9	55.5
2012	56.0	56.2	56.1	56.5	56.5	55.6	55.2	55.2	56.8	57.5	57.6	57.7	56.4
2013	57.4	57.6	57.9	58.0	57.8	56.5	56.0	56.3	57.7	58.3	57.9	57.9	57.4
Leisure and Hospitality													
2002	32.8	33.0	33.8	34.9	35.5	36.0	35.9	36.0	35.7	34.9	34.6	34.5	34.8
2003	33.7	34.0	34.5	36.0	36.7	37.2	36.9	37.0	36.2	35.9	35.5	35.6	35.8
2004	34.7	35.2	35.8	36.9	37.3	37.4	37.0	36.7	36.1	35.8	35.1	35.2	36.1
2005	34.4	34.7	35.4	36.8	37.2	37.8	37.4	37.7	37.5	36.6	36.4	36.3	36.5
2006	36.3	36.6	37.4	38.3	38.9	39.5	39.7	39.6	39.3	39.0	39.2	38.6	38.5
2007	37.9	38.0	38.8	39.6	39.9	40.3	40.2	40.5	40.3	39.6	39.1	39.0	39.4
2008	37.8	37.9	38.6	39.8	40.0	40.1	39.7	39.9	39.4	38.7	37.8	37.1	38.9
2009	36.2	36.1	36.6	37.6	38.2	38.1	38.1	38.3	37.9	37.2	36.5	36.2	37.3
2010	35.5	35.8	36.7	37.7	38.2	38.1	38.0	37.9	37.4	37.1	36.5	36.4	37.1
2011	35.8	36.1	36.8	38.1	38.2	38.4	38.2	38.6	38.5	38.1	37.3	36.9	37.6
2012	36.3	36.6	37.3	38.7	39.6	39.9	39.7	40.0	39.4	39.7	38.8	38.4	38.7
2013	37.8	37.8	38.5	39.7	40.3	40.5	40.8	41.0	40.1	38.7	38.1	37.9	39.3
Other Services													
2002	10.9	11.1	11.2	11.4	11.4	11.8	11.8	11.8	11.6	11.5	11.5	11.5	11.5
2003	11.5	11.5	11.6	11.5	11.6	11.9	12.0	11.9	11.7	11.7	11.6	11.6	11.7
2004	11.6	11.6	11.6	11.6	11.8	12.1	12.2	12.1	11.8	11.7	11.7	11.6	11.8
2005	11.6	11.6	11.7	11.7	11.8	12.2	12.3	12.2	11.9	11.8	11.8	11.8	11.9
2006	11.7	11.8	11.9	12.1	12.1	12.5	12.5	12.3	12.1	12.3	12.2	11.9	12.1
2007	11.9	12.0	12.2	12.1	12.2	12.5	12.5	12.2	12.1	12.2	12.2	12.2	12.2
2008	12.1	12.3	12.3	12.3	12.4	12.9	12.8	12.6	12.5	12.7	12.5	12.0	12.5
2009	11.9	12.0	12.0	11.9	12.0	12.3	12.1	12.0	11.7	11.7	11.7	11.8	11.9
2010	11.7	11.7	11.7	11.7	11.7	12.1	12.0	12.0	11.7	11.8	11.5	11.5	11.8
2011	11.5	11.7	11.7	11.8	11.7	12.0	12.0	11.9	11.6	11.5	11.5	11.5	11.7
2012	11.5	11.7	11.8	11.8	11.8	12.1	11.9	11.8	11.8	12.1	11.7	11.7	11.8
2013	11.5	11.6	11.6	11.6	11.5	11.5	11.7	11.5	11.5	11.5	11.5	11.4	11.5
Government													
2002	69.9	72.5	72.8	72.8	72.8	73.2	71.2	70.8	73.4	72.8	73.2	73.8	72.4
2003	70.8	73.4	73.9	73.8	73.6	73.5	71.9	71.9	74.0	74.0	74.3	75.1	73.4
2004	71.6	75.0	75.5	75.3	75.2	74.5	72.4	72.4	75.1	76.2	76.6	76.9	74.7
2005	73.8	76.4	76.6	76.4	76.2	75.7	73.7	74.0	76.8	77.8	77.9	78.5	76.2
2006	76.4	78.5	78.9	78.6	78.5	77.8	75.9	77.1	79.4	79.8	80.1	80.4	78.5
2007	77.4	79.5	80.5	79.7	79.6	78.5	76.5	77.8	80.4	81.1	81.5	81.5	79.5
2008	78.7	81.0	81.5	81.5	82.1	80.4	78.5	79.8	82.4	83.1	83.0	83.0	81.3
2009	81.2	83.2	83.7	83.8	83.2	81.5	79.0	80.3	82.8	84.1	84.0	84.3	82.6
2010	81.5	83.6	84.2	85.0	85.4	83.0	80.0	80.6	83.0	84.4	84.4	84.6	83.3
2011	81.9	84.0	84.6	84.5	83.8	82.6	80.1	80.6	83.4	84.5	84.5	84.8	83.3
2012	81.0	83.3	83.8	83.0	82.8	78.5	78.0	79.6	82.7	84.0	84.2	84.4	82.1
2013	81.1	83.4	83.6	83.5	82.9	81.3	79.2	80.1	82.7	83.6	83.8	83.9	82.4

Employment by Industry: Allentown–Bethlehem–Easton, PA–NJ, Selected Years, 2002–2013

(Numbers in thousands, not seasonally adjusted)

Industry and year	January	February	March	April	May	June	July	August	September	October	November	December	Annual average
Total Nonfarm													
2002	318.9	319.2	323.1	322.7	326.4	327.4	323.0	324.1	327.1	327.4	327.1	327.4	324.5
2003	320.7	319.8	322.8	324.9	329.0	329.9	321.4	322.1	328.4	330.3	330.9	330.8	325.9
2004	321.6	323.1	327.2	329.6	333.1	334.9	326.5	326.5	331.1	335.0	334.9	334.2	329.8
2005	325.8	328.1	331.1	336.7	339.5	340.7	334.9	334.1	339.1	340.6	341.4	341.1	336.1
2006	332.7	334.4	339.3	341.6	344.2	346.0	338.4	340.2	344.9	347.0	346.4	346.7	341.8
2007	336.7	337.0	341.8	343.3	348.0	350.2	342.5	342.4	346.5	350.0	349.5	349.4	344.8
2008	338.6	339.3	342.5	344.8	348.7	349.7	342.6	342.4	344.8	346.7	343.7	343.6	344.0
2009	331.0	331.0	332.5	333.4	337.9	337.4	330.3	330.1	332.9	335.5	335.8	335.2	333.6
2010	324.7	325.9	329.9	334.2	338.4	338.6	330.4	330.8	335.2	337.9	339.1	341.2	333.9
2011	328.9	331.1	334.9	340.0	343.7	345.1	338.0	338.2	343.0	344.4	345.3	346.7	339.9
2012	337.1	339.9	343.1	346.3	349.0	349.2	340.7	341.0	346.6	347.9	349.3	349.1	344.9
2013	340.5	341.4	344.1	347.8	351.3	352.6	344.5	345.0	349.6	350.1	348.6	347.0	346.9
Total Private													
2002	280.2	279.7	283.3	283.0	286.3	288.2	287.4	288.9	288.6	287.6	287.2	287.4	285.7
2003	281.3	279.2	281.9	284.0	287.7	289.0	286.7	287.9	288.5	289.4	289.3	289.5	286.2
2004	281.6	281.8	285.6	288.1	291.0	293.2	290.9	291.2	290.9	293.4	293.2	292.6	289.5
2005	285.5	286.3	289.2	293.9	297.0	299.2	299.2	299.2	298.5	299.0	299.4	299.0	295.5
2006	291.5	292.3	296.9	299.2	301.5	304.1	302.6	304.1	303.8	304.8	303.5	303.9	300.7
2007	295.2	294.3	298.9	300.3	304.3	307.0	305.2	305.3	304.4	306.8	305.8	305.6	302.8
2008	296.6	296.0	299.0	301.3	304.9	305.6	304.2	304.0	302.2	302.7	299.3	299.3	301.3
2009	288.8	287.1	288.2	288.7	293.0	293.3	291.7	291.5	290.3	291.4	291.2	290.7	290.5
2010	282.0	281.9	285.6	289.5	292.6	293.7	292.3	293.4	293.5	295.5	296.2	298.5	291.2
2011	287.7	288.6	292.1	297.1	300.7	302.2	301.1	302.0	302.5	302.7	303.1	304.5	298.7
2012	296.1	298.1	301.3	304.2	306.4	308.0	305.3	305.9	306.5	306.5	307.8	307.3	304.5
2013	299.7	300.1	302.5	306.2	309.4	311.7	309.2	309.5	309.5	309.3	307.6	306.1	306.7
Goods-Producing													
2002	64.5	64.2	64.7	64.6	65.1	65.5	64.6	64.6	63.7	62.6	61.9	61.1	63.9
2003	59.2	58.2	58.4	58.7	59.2	59.7	58.8	58.8	58.3	58.2	57.7	57.1	58.5
2004	56.0	55.7	56.5	57.0	57.7	58.7	58.6	59.1	58.7	58.5	58.6	58.3	57.8
2005	56.8	56.4	56.8	58.1	58.7	59.6	59.2	59.3	59.0	58.6	58.4	57.8	58.2
2006	56.1	56.1	56.8	57.2	57.2	58.4	57.6	58.2	57.5	57.4	56.8	56.6	57.2
2007	55.5	54.9	55.7	56.2	57.0	57.8	57.4	57.5	57.3	57.0	56.6	55.7	56.6
2008	54.4	54.1	54.8	55.4	56.2	56.8	56.1	56.2	55.9	55.4	54.1	53.0	55.2
2009	50.9	49.8	49.6	49.6	49.7	49.7	49.6	49.2	48.7	48.2	48.1	47.4	49.2
2010	45.7	45.0	45.7	46.7	47.4	48.2	48.2	48.2	48.1	48.0	47.8	47.3	47.2
2011	45.7	45.3	46.3	47.1	47.8	48.7	48.5	48.9	48.5	47.9	47.5	47.0	47.4
2012	45.8	45.8	46.5	47.0	47.2	48.0	48.0	47.8	47.7	47.5	47.3	46.9	47.1
2013	45.8	45.5	46.0	46.8	47.6	48.1	48.0	48.0	47.8	47.7	47.4	46.7	47.1
Service-Providing													
2002	254.4	255.0	258.4	258.1	261.3	261.9	258.4	259.5	263.4	264.8	265.2	266.3	260.6
2003	261.5	261.6	264.4	266.2	269.8	270.2	262.6	263.3	270.1	272.1	273.2	273.7	267.4
2004	265.6	267.4	270.7	272.6	275.4	276.2	267.9	267.4	272.4	276.5	276.3	275.9	272.0
2005	269.0	271.7	274.3	278.6	280.8	281.1	275.7	274.8	280.1	282.0	283.0	283.3	277.9
2006	276.6	278.3	282.5	284.4	287.0	287.6	280.8	282.0	287.4	289.6	289.6	290.1	284.7
2007	281.2	282.1	286.1	287.1	291.0	292.4	285.1	284.9	289.2	293.0	292.9	293.7	288.2
2008	284.2	285.2	287.7	289.4	292.5	292.9	286.5	286.2	288.9	291.3	289.6	290.6	288.8
2009	280.1	281.2	282.9	283.8	288.2	287.7	280.7	280.9	284.2	287.3	287.7	287.8	284.4
2010	279.0	280.9	284.2	287.5	291.0	290.4	282.2	282.6	287.1	289.9	291.3	293.9	286.7
2011	283.2	285.8	288.6	292.9	295.9	296.4	289.5	289.3	294.5	296.5	297.8	299.7	292.5
2012	291.3	294.1	296.6	299.3	301.8	301.2	292.7	293.2	298.9	300.4	302.0	302.2	297.8
2013	294.7	295.9	298.1	301.0	303.7	304.5	296.5	297.0	301.8	302.4	301.2	300.3	299.8
Mining, Logging, and Construction													
2002	13.5	13.5	14.0	14.9	15.3	15.8	16.0	15.7	15.3	15.0	15.0	14.6	14.9
2003	13.4	13.0	13.4	14.3	15.0	15.6	15.9	16.0	15.7	15.7	15.5	15.1	14.9
2004	14.5	14.3	15.0	15.5	16.2	16.7	16.9	17.0	16.8	16.6	16.5	16.4	16.0
2005	15.3	15.1	15.3	16.6	17.1	17.8	18.0	17.9	17.6	17.3	17.4	16.9	16.9
2006	15.8	15.8	16.2	16.9	17.1	17.7	17.7	17.9	17.5	17.3	16.9	16.7	17.0
2007	15.6	14.9	15.4	16.2	17.0	17.5	17.7	17.8	17.4	17.0	16.6	15.8	16.6
2008	14.9	14.6	15.0	15.6	16.4	16.9	16.8	16.5	16.2	15.9	15.1	14.3	15.7
2009	13.0	12.6	12.8	13.3	13.6	13.6	13.6	13.4	13.1	13.0	12.7	12.1	13.1
2010	10.8	10.5	11.0	12.0	12.5	12.9	13.0	13.1	13.1	13.0	12.7	12.1	12.2
2011	10.9	10.7	11.4	12.2	12.8	13.1	13.2	13.2	13.2	13.0	12.8	12.2	12.4
2012	11.3	11.3	11.7	12.2	12.4	12.8	12.7	12.6	12.6	12.6	12.4	11.9	12.2
2013	11.1	10.9	11.4	12.1	12.8	13.0	13.0	13.1	13.2	13.2	12.8	12.2	12.4
Manufacturing													
2002	51.0	50.7	50.7	49.7	49.8	49.7	48.6	48.9	48.4	47.6	46.9	46.5	49.0
2003	45.8	45.2	45.0	44.4	44.2	44.1	42.9	42.8	42.6	42.5	42.2	42.0	43.6
2004	41.5	41.4	41.5	41.5	41.5	42.0	41.7	42.1	41.9	41.9	42.1	41.9	41.8
2005	41.5	41.3	41.5	41.5	41.6	41.8	41.2	41.4	41.4	41.3	41.0	40.9	41.4
2006	40.3	40.3	40.6	40.3	40.1	40.7	39.9	40.3	40.0	40.1	39.9	39.9	40.2
2007	39.9	40.0	40.3	40.0	40.0	40.3	39.7	39.7	39.9	40.0	40.0	39.9	40.0
2008	39.5	39.5	39.8	39.8	39.8	39.9	39.3	39.7	39.7	39.5	39.0	38.7	39.5
2009	37.9	37.2	36.8	36.3	36.1	36.1	36.0	35.8	35.6	35.2	35.4	35.3	36.1
2010	34.9	34.5	34.7	34.7	34.9	35.3	35.2	35.1	35.0	35.0	35.1	35.2	35.0
2011	34.8	34.6	34.9	34.9	35.0	35.6	35.3	35.7	35.3	34.9	34.7	34.8	35.0
2012	34.5	34.5	34.8	34.8	34.8	35.2	35.3	35.2	35.1	34.9	34.9	35.0	34.9
2013	34.7	34.6	34.6	34.7	34.8	35.1	35.0	34.9	34.6	34.5	34.6	34.5	34.7

Employment by Industry: Allentown–Bethlehem–Easton, PA–NJ, Selected Years, 2002–2013—*Continued*

(Numbers in thousands, not seasonally adjusted)

Industry and year	January	February	March	April	May	June	July	August	September	October	November	December	Annual average
Trade, Transportation, and Utilities													
2002	63.2	62.2	62.9	62.2	63.0	63.1	63.3	63.9	64.8	64.9	66.3	67.4	63.9
2003	65.0	63.7	64.1	64.4	65.1	65.6	64.3	64.5	64.9	65.8	66.7	67.7	65.2
2004	64.5	63.6	64.5	64.6	64.9	65.2	64.1	64.2	64.4	65.2	66.5	68.1	65.0
2005	66.1	65.5	65.9	66.7	67.5	68.0	67.6	67.7	67.6	68.3	70.0	70.9	67.7
2006	68.9	68.0	68.5	69.3	69.7	70.3	69.9	70.3	70.5	71.1	72.4	73.2	70.2
2007	70.3	68.9	69.3	69.3	70.2	70.7	70.2	70.1	69.9	71.0	72.8	73.5	70.5
2008	70.9	69.3	69.5	69.4	70.1	70.4	69.6	69.5	69.5	70.0	70.7	71.2	70.0
2009	67.9	66.8	66.5	65.9	67.0	67.3	66.6	66.4	66.4	67.3	68.2	68.7	67.1
2010	66.1	64.9	65.6	65.9	66.4	67.0	67.1	67.5	67.7	68.7	69.9	71.0	67.3
2011	68.1	67.3	67.7	68.1	68.9	69.8	69.8	70.1	70.5	71.6	73.1	74.4	70.0
2012	71.9	71.3	71.9	72.0	72.2	72.6	72.0	72.1	72.2	72.9	74.6	75.3	72.6
2013	72.5	71.6	71.7	72.0	72.6	73.1	72.0	72.5	72.5	72.9	75.0	75.7	72.8
Wholesale Trade													
2002	11.3	11.1	11.2	11.1	11.2	11.3	11.3	11.2	11.1	11.0	11.1	11.2	11.2
2003	11.2	11.1	11.2	11.1	11.2	11.3	11.3	11.4	11.3	11.4	11.5	11.6	11.3
2004	11.3	11.2	11.4	11.6	11.6	11.8	11.7	11.6	11.7	11.8	11.9	12.1	11.6
2005	12.1	12.1	12.3	12.6	12.6	12.6	12.6	12.5	12.3	12.3	12.3	12.3	12.4
2006	12.5	12.7	12.9	13.3	13.5	13.7	13.7	13.8	13.7	13.8	13.8	13.9	13.4
2007	13.4	13.4	13.5	13.6	13.8	14.0	14.1	14.0	13.9	14.1	14.1	14.1	13.8
2008	13.8	13.8	13.8	14.0	14.1	14.2	14.3	14.2	14.0	14.0	13.9	13.8	14.0
2009	13.4	13.3	13.3	13.4	13.4	13.5	13.4	13.3	13.3	13.5	13.4	13.4	13.4
2010	13.0	12.9	13.0	13.3	13.3	13.5	13.5	13.5	13.5	13.6	13.6	13.6	13.4
2011	13.2	13.2	13.4	13.4	13.5	13.6	13.8	13.8	13.7	13.9	13.8	13.8	13.6
2012	13.7	13.7	13.8	13.9	13.8	14.0	13.8	13.7	13.7	13.6	13.5	13.5	13.7
2013	13.2	13.2	13.2	13.3	13.4	13.5	13.4	13.3	13.4	13.4	13.4	13.4	13.3
Retail Trade													
2002	39.6	38.8	39.1	38.7	39.3	39.5	40.0	40.5	40.4	40.4	41.7	42.7	40.1
2003	40.4	39.4	39.6	39.8	40.3	40.7	40.3	40.5	40.4	41.0	41.9	42.9	40.6
2004	40.4	39.6	40.1	40.1	40.8	41.0	40.3	40.5	40.0	40.7	41.8	43.1	40.7
2005	41.2	40.6	40.6	40.8	41.4	41.8	41.6	41.6	40.9	41.2	42.5	43.3	41.5
2006	41.3	40.1	40.4	40.5	40.8	41.3	41.3	41.5	41.2	41.7	43.0	43.7	41.4
2007	41.5	40.2	40.4	40.2	40.8	41.2	41.1	41.1	40.5	41.2	42.9	43.6	41.2
2008	41.8	40.4	40.5	40.3	40.8	41.0	40.5	40.4	40.1	40.5	41.3	42.0	40.8
2009	39.5	38.8	38.6	38.2	38.9	39.3	39.1	39.1	38.5	38.9	40.0	40.5	39.1
2010	38.9	37.9	38.3	38.3	38.7	39.1	39.0	39.0	38.6	39.3	40.4	41.4	39.1
2011	39.3	38.5	38.7	38.9	39.3	39.7	39.4	39.6	39.0	39.5	40.8	41.9	39.6
2012	39.9	39.1	39.3	39.4	39.7	39.9	39.8	40.0	39.3	40.0	41.6	42.0	40.0
2013	40.1	39.3	39.3	39.4	39.8	40.2	39.7	39.9	39.4	39.6	41.5	42.1	40.0
Transportation and Utilities													
2002	12.3	12.3	12.6	12.4	12.5	12.3	12.0	12.2	13.3	13.5	13.5	13.5	12.7
2003	13.4	13.2	13.3	13.5	13.6	13.6	12.7	12.6	13.2	13.4	13.3	13.2	13.3
2004	12.8	12.8	13.0	12.9	12.5	12.4	12.1	12.1	12.7	12.7	12.8	12.9	12.6
2005	12.8	12.8	13.0	13.3	13.5	13.6	13.4	13.6	14.4	14.8	15.2	15.3	13.8
2006	15.1	15.2	15.2	15.5	15.4	15.3	14.9	15.0	15.6	15.6	15.6	15.6	15.3
2007	15.4	15.3	15.4	15.5	15.6	15.5	15.0	15.0	15.5	15.7	15.8	15.8	15.5
2008	15.3	15.1	15.2	15.1	15.2	15.2	14.8	14.9	15.4	15.5	15.5	15.4	15.2
2009	15.0	14.7	14.6	14.3	14.7	14.5	14.1	14.0	14.6	14.9	14.8	14.8	14.6
2010	14.2	14.1	14.3	14.3	14.4	14.4	14.6	15.0	15.6	15.8	15.9	16.0	14.9
2011	15.6	15.6	15.6	15.8	16.1	16.5	16.6	16.7	17.8	18.2	18.5	18.7	16.8
2012	18.3	18.5	18.8	18.7	18.7	18.7	18.4	18.4	19.2	19.3	19.5	19.8	18.9
2013	19.2	19.1	19.2	19.3	19.4	19.4	18.9	19.3	19.7	19.9	20.1	20.2	19.5
Information													
2002	7.8	7.8	7.8	7.8	7.8	7.9	7.8	7.7	7.6	7.6	7.6	7.7	7.7
2003	7.6	7.7	7.8	7.8	7.8	7.9	7.7	7.7	7.6	7.6	7.7	7.8	7.7
2004	7.6	7.6	7.6	7.7	7.7	7.8	7.8	7.7	7.6	7.7	7.7	7.8	7.7
2005	7.6	7.6	7.6	7.6	7.6	7.6	7.6	7.6	7.4	7.4	7.4	7.4	7.5
2006	7.4	7.4	7.4	7.4	7.5	7.6	7.5	7.5	7.5	7.4	7.4	7.5	7.5
2007	7.4	7.3	7.3	7.3	7.4	7.5	7.5	7.5	7.4	7.4	7.4	7.5	7.4
2008	7.4	7.4	7.4	7.5	7.6	7.5	7.5	7.4	7.3	7.3	7.1	7.2	7.4
2009	7.1	7.0	6.9	6.7	6.7	6.6	6.5	6.3	6.2	6.1	5.9	5.9	6.5
2010	5.6	5.5	5.5	5.6	5.6	5.7	5.7	5.7	5.7	5.6	5.6	5.6	5.6
2011	5.5	5.6	5.6	5.7	5.8	5.8	5.9	5.7	5.8	5.8	5.9	5.8	5.7
2012	5.7	5.8	5.9	6.0	6.0	6.1	6.0	6.1	6.1	6.0	6.1	6.1	6.0
2013	6.1	6.1	6.2	6.1	6.2	6.2	6.2	6.2	6.1	6.2	6.3	6.2	6.2
Financial Activities													
2002	16.6	16.6	16.6	16.6	16.5	16.8	16.9	17.0	16.8	16.5	16.5	16.8	16.7
2003	16.7	16.7	16.7	16.6	16.7	16.8	16.8	16.8	16.5	16.5	16.5	16.6	16.7
2004	16.3	16.1	16.2	16.3	16.5	16.5	16.4	16.4	16.2	16.4	16.4	16.5	16.4
2005	16.3	16.3	16.3	16.5	16.6	16.7	16.7	16.8	16.6	16.5	16.6	16.6	16.5
2006	16.4	16.5	16.6	16.6	16.6	16.8	16.7	16.7	16.6	16.4	16.4	16.5	16.6
2007	16.3	16.4	16.4	16.2	16.2	16.3	16.2	16.2	16.0	16.0	15.9	15.8	16.2
2008	15.7	15.8	15.8	15.9	15.9	15.9	16.0	15.9	15.7	15.6	15.7	15.7	15.8
2009	15.5	15.6	15.5	15.6	15.7	15.8	15.8	15.7	15.6	15.6	15.6	15.6	15.6
2010	15.6	15.6	15.5	15.4	15.4	15.4	15.4	15.4	15.2	15.3	15.3	15.4	15.4
2011	15.2	15.2	15.2	15.2	15.2	15.3	15.1	15.0	15.0	15.0	15.0	15.1	15.1
2012	15.2	15.2	15.2	15.1	15.1	15.1	15.1	15.1	14.9	14.8	14.8	14.9	15.0
2013	14.9	15.0	15.0	15.0	15.1	15.2	15.2	15.1	15.0	15.0	15.0	15.0	15.0

Employment by Industry: Allentown–Bethlehem–Easton, PA–NJ, Selected Years, 2002–2013—*Continued*

(Numbers in thousands, not seasonally adjusted)

Industry and year	January	February	March	April	May	June	July	August	September	October	November	December	Annual average
Professional and Business Services													
2002	36.1	35.9	36.6	37.0	36.8	37.3	37.5	38.0	37.7	38.1	37.9	37.9	37.2
2003	36.7	36.6	37.1	38.0	38.6	39.1	39.4	40.4	40.9	41.0	41.3	41.5	39.2
2004	40.1	39.9	40.4	41.1	41.1	41.4	41.4	41.6	41.3	42.2	41.9	41.5	41.2
2005	40.0	40.4	40.4	41.3	41.4	42.0	42.5	42.7	42.6	43.3	43.5	43.1	41.9
2006	41.4	41.6	42.3	42.6	43.0	43.7	44.0	44.5	44.3	44.9	44.4	44.1	43.4
2007	42.7	42.6	43.1	43.6	43.7	44.3	44.0	43.6	43.8	44.6	44.2	44.0	43.7
2008	42.2	41.5	41.9	42.6	42.7	42.7	43.2	43.2	42.7	42.9	42.4	42.7	42.6
2009	40.5	39.9	40.0	40.1	40.3	41.0	40.4	41.2	41.2	41.6	42.3	42.5	40.9
2010	41.1	40.9	41.7	42.7	42.8	43.0	42.4	42.6	42.9	44.2	45.5	47.0	43.1
2011	43.8	44.0	44.8	46.1	46.4	46.0	45.8	46.5	46.8	46.2	46.5	47.6	45.9
2012	45.3	45.2	45.4	46.1	46.1	46.4	45.8	46.0	46.5	46.7	47.1	47.5	46.2
2013	46.1	45.4	45.8	46.8	46.8	47.6	47.6	48.1	47.6	48.6	47.4	46.9	47.1
Education and Health Services													
2002	51.9	52.8	53.7	53.4	53.5	52.1	52.2	52.2	54.5	55.6	56.1	55.0	53.6
2003	54.5	55.0	55.9	56.0	55.8	54.3	54.1	54.2	56.3	57.4	57.9	57.5	55.7
2004	55.6	57.3	58.3	58.0	57.9	56.7	56.2	56.0	57.6	59.3	59.4	58.1	57.5
2005	57.4	58.1	59.3	59.6	59.2	57.8	58.1	57.7	59.5	60.8	60.9	60.5	59.1
2006	59.2	60.2	61.8	61.5	60.9	59.2	59.2	59.3	61.4	62.9	62.6	62.3	60.9
2007	60.6	61.6	63.3	63.2	63.0	61.3	61.2	62.0	63.5	65.0	64.7	64.5	62.8
2008	62.6	64.3	65.3	65.3	64.0	62.9	62.9	63.4	64.6	65.8	66.1	65.9	64.4
2009	64.6	65.6	66.6	66.4	65.6	64.0	64.0	64.3	65.8	67.3	67.6	67.2	65.8
2010	65.0	67.5	68.2	67.8	67.8	65.9	65.4	66.0	67.3	68.2	68.4	68.2	67.1
2011	66.6	68.0	68.6	68.5	68.6	67.1	66.6	66.4	68.4	69.7	70.1	69.4	68.2
2012	67.9	70.2	71.1	71.1	70.6	69.1	68.2	68.0	70.7	71.5	71.6	71.0	70.1
2013	69.0	71.3	71.8	71.6	71.1	69.6	68.9	68.6	71.2	72.0	72.4	71.1	70.7
Leisure and Hospitality													
2002	25.4	25.5	26.2	26.5	28.6	30.3	29.8	30.3	28.7	27.6	26.2	26.6	27.6
2003	27.0	26.7	27.1	27.7	29.5	30.4	30.3	30.4	29.1	28.0	26.6	26.4	28.3
2004	26.8	26.8	27.2	28.3	30.0	31.4	30.9	30.9	30.0	28.9	27.5	27.0	28.8
2005	26.2	26.7	27.5	28.9	30.6	31.9	31.9	32.0	30.6	29.2	27.7	27.7	29.2
2006	27.4	27.7	28.6	29.5	31.3	32.7	32.3	32.3	30.9	29.8	28.6	28.6	30.0
2007	27.6	27.8	28.7	29.4	31.5	33.7	33.2	33.0	31.3	30.8	29.2	29.4	30.5
2008	28.5	28.6	29.3	30.1	33.2	33.9	33.5	33.2	31.5	30.8	28.4	28.7	30.8
2009	27.8	27.8	28.5	29.7	33.2	34.0	34.0	33.7	32.1	31.0	29.2	29.1	30.8
2010	28.9	28.6	29.3	31.2	33.0	34.1	33.8	33.7	32.6	31.5	29.7	29.9	31.4
2011	29.0	29.4	30.0	32.3	33.8	35.0	34.9	35.1	33.5	32.5	30.9	31.0	32.3
2012	30.2	30.5	31.1	32.8	34.9	36.3	36.0	36.6	34.5	33.2	32.5	31.7	33.4
2013	31.7	31.6	32.3	34.1	36.1	37.8	37.2	37.0	35.7	33.3	30.5	30.9	34.0
Other Services													
2002	14.7	14.7	14.8	14.9	15.0	15.2	15.3	15.2	14.8	14.7	14.7	14.9	14.9
2003	14.6	14.6	14.8	14.8	15.0	15.2	15.3	15.1	14.9	14.9	14.9	14.9	14.9
2004	14.7	14.8	14.9	15.1	15.2	15.5	15.5	15.3	15.1	15.2	15.2	15.3	15.2
2005	15.1	15.3	15.4	15.2	15.4	15.6	15.6	15.4	15.2	14.9	14.9	15.0	15.3
2006	14.7	14.8	14.9	15.1	15.3	15.4	15.4	15.3	15.1	14.9	14.9	15.1	15.1
2007	14.8	14.8	15.1	15.1	15.3	15.4	15.5	15.4	15.2	15.0	15.0	15.2	15.2
2008	14.9	15.0	15.0	15.1	15.2	15.5	15.4	15.2	15.0	14.9	14.8	14.9	15.1
2009	14.5	14.6	14.6	14.7	14.8	14.9	14.8	14.7	14.3	14.3	14.3	14.3	14.6
2010	14.0	13.9	14.1	14.2	14.2	14.4	14.3	14.3	14.0	14.0	14.0	14.1	14.1
2011	13.8	13.8	13.9	14.1	14.2	14.5	14.5	14.3	14.0	14.0	14.1	14.2	14.1
2012	14.1	14.1	14.2	14.1	14.3	14.4	14.2	14.2	13.9	13.9	13.8	13.9	14.1
2013	13.6	13.6	13.7	13.8	13.9	14.1	14.1	14.0	13.6	13.6	13.6	13.6	13.8
Government													
2002	38.7	39.5	39.8	39.7	40.1	39.2	35.6	35.2	38.5	39.8	39.9	40.0	38.8
2003	39.4	40.6	40.9	40.9	41.3	40.9	34.7	34.2	39.9	40.9	41.6	41.3	39.7
2004	40.0	41.3	41.6	41.5	42.1	41.7	35.6	35.3	40.2	41.6	41.7	41.6	40.4
2005	40.3	41.8	41.9	42.8	42.5	41.5	35.7	34.9	40.6	41.6	42.0	42.1	40.6
2006	41.2	42.1	42.4	42.4	42.7	41.9	35.8	36.1	41.1	42.2	42.9	42.8	41.1
2007	41.5	42.7	42.9	43.0	43.7	43.2	37.3	37.1	42.1	43.2	43.7	43.8	42.0
2008	42.0	43.3	43.5	43.5	43.8	44.1	38.4	38.4	42.6	44.0	44.4	44.3	42.7
2009	42.2	43.9	44.3	44.7	44.9	44.1	38.6	38.6	42.6	44.1	44.6	44.5	43.1
2010	42.7	44.0	44.3	44.7	45.8	44.9	38.1	37.4	41.7	42.4	42.9	42.7	42.6
2011	41.2	42.5	42.8	42.9	43.0	42.9	36.9	36.2	40.5	41.7	42.2	42.2	41.3
2012	41.0	41.8	41.8	42.1	42.6	41.2	35.4	35.1	40.1	41.4	41.5	41.8	40.5
2013	40.8	41.3	41.6	41.6	41.9	40.9	35.3	35.5	40.1	40.8	41.0	40.9	40.1

Employment by Industry: Atlanta–Sandy Springs–Marietta, GA, Selected Years, 2002–2013

(Numbers in thousands, not seasonally adjusted)

Industry and year	January	February	March	April	May	June	July	August	September	October	November	December	Annual average
Total Nonfarm													
2002	2,237.5	2,239.8	2,258.8	2,270.2	2,277.4	2,279.8	2,246.8	2,267.6	2,266.5	2,260.9	2,271.8	2,275.9	2,262.8
2003	2,211.3	2,221.3	2,234.7	2,231.5	2,238.8	2,235.0	2,223.7	2,248.1	2,250.7	2,250.3	2,263.2	2,271.5	2,240.0
2004	2,219.8	2,232.1	2,249.3	2,260.1	2,265.7	2,261.6	2,264.1	2,284.4	2,276.5	2,297.4	2,309.1	2,315.9	2,269.7
2005	2,280.6	2,292.1	2,299.2	2,329.4	2,341.3	2,331.8	2,330.5	2,355.0	2,356.3	2,369.5	2,386.9	2,391.8	2,338.7
2006	2,354.9	2,364.6	2,377.9	2,389.7	2,401.7	2,403.1	2,388.3	2,411.3	2,414.2	2,438.6	2,453.1	2,459.8	2,404.8
2007	2,421.0	2,433.6	2,445.5	2,443.6	2,455.3	2,449.1	2,444.7	2,468.0	2,463.5	2,463.9	2,476.3	2,478.3	2,453.6
2008	2,433.4	2,444.6	2,446.1	2,446.3	2,453.8	2,438.8	2,415.3	2,428.7	2,413.6	2,409.4	2,403.0	2,390.7	2,427.0
2009	2,331.4	2,325.5	2,315.7	2,309.3	2,306.8	2,288.4	2,265.7	2,268.8	2,262.8	2,268.5	2,275.2	2,273.0	2,290.9
2010	2,230.4	2,237.9	2,249.5	2,267.1	2,285.2	2,276.5	2,268.8	2,274.3	2,267.1	2,289.9	2,299.2	2,295.5	2,270.1
2011	2,242.6	2,277.5	2,293.8	2,308.7	2,316.8	2,305.1	2,299.6	2,312.4	2,311.7	2,324.7	2,337.4	2,336.9	2,305.6
2012	2,299.0	2,310.8	2,325.6	2,343.4	2,356.5	2,354.0	2,336.9	2,354.8	2,347.5	2,369.8	2,390.9	2,386.2	2,348.0
2013	2,351.0	2,366.4	2,375.6	2,396.7	2,405.8	2,402.6	2,397.3	2,419.2	2,416.7	2,431.3	2,446.8	2,449.3	2,404.9
Total Private													
2002	1,941.0	1,943.5	1,957.9	1,966.7	1,973.8	1,981.5	1,960.7	1,968.0	1,959.9	1,955.2	1,964.3	1,970.9	1,962.0
2003	1,906.3	1,914.7	1,926.4	1,924.3	1,933.6	1,939.2	1,937.4	1,950.8	1,945.9	1,944.0	1,956.7	1,965.5	1,937.1
2004	1,914.0	1,920.9	1,937.5	1,948.9	1,956.4	1,963.0	1,973.1	1,977.9	1,964.2	1,985.9	1,995.9	2,005.4	1,961.9
2005	1,970.6	1,977.7	1,984.2	2,013.8	2,026.1	2,027.3	2,034.5	2,042.0	2,040.1	2,050.2	2,066.7	2,072.3	2,025.5
2006	2,036.1	2,042.2	2,053.8	2,067.3	2,080.1	2,086.8	2,084.7	2,091.3	2,087.9	2,109.4	2,121.5	2,128.7	2,082.5
2007	2,092.1	2,100.4	2,111.1	2,110.4	2,122.8	2,125.0	2,126.9	2,136.2	2,126.8	2,127.8	2,138.5	2,140.6	2,121.6
2008	2,095.7	2,101.6	2,101.4	2,102.3	2,110.5	2,102.9	2,091.2	2,091.5	2,075.4	2,064.5	2,054.9	2,045.2	2,086.4
2009	1,986.2	1,976.9	1,966.2	1,960.7	1,962.2	1,951.3	1,944.0	1,938.8	1,924.3	1,930.5	1,937.1	1,936.3	1,951.4
2010	1,894.9	1,900.3	1,911.1	1,927.8	1,940.6	1,940.7	1,947.3	1,950.5	1,941.2	1,962.7	1,967.9	1,968.5	1,937.8
2011	1,919.3	1,950.8	1,965.4	1,982.3	1,990.2	1,985.3	1,989.6	1,996.9	1,991.2	2,002.6	2,012.4	2,013.6	1,983.3
2012	1,978.4	1,987.8	1,999.2	2,018.2	2,032.6	2,034.1	2,030.9	2,040.7	2,029.4	2,049.5	2,065.7	2,065.1	2,027.6
2013	2,031.6	2,044.8	2,053.5	2,073.5	2,084.9	2,088.2	2,094.1	2,107.5	2,100.1	2,113.4	2,126.9	2,130.2	2,087.4
Goods-Producing													
2002	311.0	311.0	313.4	314.3	314.0	315.4	314.4	314.5	312.4	308.7	307.7	305.3	311.8
2003	299.1	301.7	303.0	300.1	302.1	302.9	302.2	303.8	303.4	304.2	303.0	303.8	302.4
2004	297.6	300.7	302.3	303.2	303.4	306.0	308.1	308.6	307.1	308.2	308.5	308.7	305.2
2005	304.5	306.0	305.8	310.3	312.6	312.9	312.9	314.0	315.8	314.0	316.3	315.5	311.7
2006	312.3	314.1	314.5	314.7	316.9	319.5	319.3	322.1	321.2	322.5	319.3	317.8	317.9
2007	316.0	317.6	318.3	317.1	317.9	318.6	317.2	318.1	315.7	315.2	314.4	312.5	316.6
2008	306.9	307.2	305.7	302.3	302.1	301.1	298.2	296.0	292.8	289.2	284.3	278.6	297.0
2009	266.9	263.7	259.5	255.1	253.0	249.9	244.3	242.4	240.6	239.5	238.2	236.4	249.1
2010	233.6	233.5	233.7	234.5	236.0	236.5	238.2	237.9	237.2	238.2	237.3	235.5	236.0
2011	228.1	234.3	236.2	238.5	239.1	239.9	240.8	240.1	238.5	238.9	238.1	236.5	237.4
2012	233.0	233.9	234.2	235.4	236.2	236.7	237.5	237.7	237.4	238.8	239.3	238.2	236.5
2013	235.6	236.8	238.5	238.2	240.5	242.1	244.0	244.8	245.4	247.9	248.3	247.5	242.5
Service-Providing													
2002	1,926.5	1,928.8	1,945.4	1,955.9	1,963.4	1,964.4	1,932.4	1,953.1	1,954.1	1,952.2	1,964.1	1,970.6	1,950.9
2003	1,912.2	1,919.6	1,931.7	1,931.4	1,936.7	1,932.1	1,921.5	1,944.3	1,947.3	1,946.1	1,960.2	1,967.7	1,937.6
2004	1,922.2	1,931.4	1,947.0	1,956.9	1,962.3	1,955.6	1,956.0	1,975.8	1,969.4	1,989.2	2,000.6	2,007.2	1,964.5
2005	1,976.1	1,986.1	1,993.4	2,019.1	2,028.7	2,018.9	2,017.6	2,041.0	2,040.5	2,055.5	2,070.6	2,076.3	2,027.0
2006	2,042.6	2,050.5	2,063.4	2,075.0	2,084.8	2,083.6	2,069.0	2,089.2	2,093.0	2,116.1	2,133.8	2,142.0	2,086.9
2007	2,105.0	2,116.0	2,127.2	2,126.5	2,137.4	2,130.5	2,127.5	2,149.9	2,147.8	2,148.7	2,161.9	2,165.8	2,137.0
2008	2,126.5	2,137.4	2,140.4	2,144.0	2,151.7	2,137.7	2,117.1	2,132.7	2,120.8	2,120.2	2,118.7	2,112.1	2,129.9
2009	2,064.5	2,061.8	2,056.2	2,054.2	2,053.8	2,038.5	2,021.4	2,026.4	2,022.2	2,029.0	2,037.0	2,036.6	2,041.8
2010	1,996.8	2,004.4	2,015.8	2,032.6	2,049.2	2,040.0	2,030.6	2,036.4	2,029.9	2,051.7	2,061.9	2,060.0	2,034.1
2011	2,014.5	2,043.2	2,057.6	2,070.2	2,077.7	2,065.2	2,058.8	2,072.3	2,073.2	2,085.8	2,099.3	2,100.4	2,068.2
2012	2,066.0	2,076.9	2,091.4	2,108.0	2,120.3	2,117.3	2,099.4	2,117.1	2,110.1	2,131.0	2,151.6	2,148.0	2,111.4
2013	2,115.4	2,129.6	2,137.1	2,158.5	2,165.3	2,160.5	2,153.3	2,174.4	2,171.3	2,183.4	2,198.5	2,201.8	2,162.4
Mining and Logging													
2002	2.2	2.1	2.1	2.1	2.1	2.1	2.1	2.2	2.2	2.1	2.1	2.0	2.1
2003	2.0	2.0	2.0	2.0	2.0	2.0	2.0	2.0	2.0	2.1	2.0	2.0	2.0
2004	2.0	2.0	2.0	2.0	2.0	2.1	2.1	2.1	2.1	2.0	2.1	2.1	2.1
2005	1.9	1.9	1.9	2.1	2.1	2.1	2.1	2.1	2.1	2.1	2.1	2.1	2.1
2006	2.2	2.1	2.1	2.1	2.1	2.1	2.1	2.1	2.0	2.1	2.1	2.1	2.1
2007	2.1	2.0	2.1	2.0	2.0	2.0	2.0	2.0	2.0	2.0	2.0	1.9	2.0
2008	1.8	1.8	1.8	1.7	1.6	1.6	1.5	1.5	1.5	1.5	1.5	1.5	1.6
2009	1.3	1.4	1.3	1.3	1.3	1.3	1.3	1.3	1.3	1.3	1.3	1.3	1.3
2010	1.3	1.3	1.3	1.3	1.3	1.3	1.3	1.3	1.4	1.4	1.3	1.3	1.3
2011	1.3	1.3	1.3	1.3	1.3	1.3	1.3	1.3	1.3	1.3	1.3	1.3	1.3
2012	1.2	1.2	1.2	1.2	1.2	1.2	1.2	1.2	1.1	1.1	1.1	1.1	1.2
2013	1.1	1.1	1.1	1.2	1.2	1.2	1.2	1.2	1.2	1.2	1.2	1.2	1.2
Construction													
2002	122.7	123.7	125.0	125.1	124.8	125.1	124.7	124.7	123.8	122.7	122.1	120.6	123.8
2003	117.4	118.0	119.3	119.1	120.1	121.2	122.1	123.2	123.6	123.6	123.4	123.8	121.2
2004	121.0	121.2	122.6	124.1	124.1	126.5	129.0	128.2	127.2	127.9	128.1	128.2	125.7
2005	125.9	127.1	127.0	130.1	132.1	132.5	133.3	134.1	135.0	134.5	135.0	133.8	131.7
2006	131.2	132.8	133.5	134.7	136.5	138.4	140.5	141.4	141.2	141.7	141.2	139.7	137.7
2007	137.0	138.7	139.6	139.1	139.9	140.4	139.8	140.5	139.1	139.1	138.4	136.7	139.0
2008	132.7	133.3	133.2	130.4	130.6	130.0	128.9	127.5	125.7	123.3	120.2	116.9	127.6
2009	110.5	109.3	106.9	104.9	104.2	102.7	99.7	97.8	96.6	96.0	95.4	93.7	101.5
2010	91.1	91.4	91.3	92.2	92.7	92.6	93.2	93.0	92.5	92.6	91.8	89.6	92.0
2011	84.1	88.2	89.8	91.5	91.4	91.8	92.1	91.7	91.1	91.2	89.9	88.4	90.1
2012	85.4	86.2	86.3	87.0	86.8	87.1	87.7	87.9	87.7	88.6	89.1	87.8	87.3
2013	85.6	86.8	88.3	88.6	90.5	91.8	93.5	94.3	94.6	95.5	96.3	95.3	91.8

Employment by Industry: Atlanta–Sandy Springs–Marietta, GA, Selected Years, 2002–2013—*Continued*

(Numbers in thousands, not seasonally adjusted)

Industry and year	January	February	March	April	May	June	July	August	September	October	November	December	Annual average
Manufacturing													
2002	186.1	185.2	186.3	187.1	187.1	188.2	187.6	187.6	186.4	183.9	183.5	182.7	186.0
2003	179.7	181.7	181.7	179.0	180.0	179.7	178.1	178.6	177.8	178.5	177.6	178.0	179.2
2004	174.6	177.5	177.7	177.1	177.3	177.4	177.0	178.3	177.8	178.3	178.3	178.4	177.5
2005	176.7	177.0	176.9	178.1	178.4	178.3	177.5	177.8	178.7	177.4	179.2	179.6	178.0
2006	178.9	179.2	178.9	177.9	178.3	179.0	176.7	178.6	178.0	178.7	176.0	176.0	178.0
2007	176.9	176.9	176.6	176.0	176.0	176.2	175.4	175.6	174.6	174.1	174.0	173.9	175.5
2008	172.4	172.1	171.7	170.2	169.9	169.5	167.8	167.0	165.6	164.4	162.6	160.2	167.8
2009	155.1	153.0	151.3	148.9	147.5	145.9	143.3	143.3	142.7	142.2	141.5	141.4	146.3
2010	141.2	140.8	141.1	141.0	142.0	142.6	143.7	143.6	143.3	144.2	144.2	144.6	142.7
2011	142.7	144.8	145.1	145.7	146.4	146.8	147.4	147.1	146.1	146.4	146.9	146.8	146.0
2012	146.4	146.5	146.7	147.2	148.2	148.4	148.6	148.6	148.6	149.1	149.1	149.3	148.1
2013	148.9	148.9	149.1	148.4	148.8	149.1	149.3	149.3	149.6	151.2	150.8	151.0	149.5
Trade, Transportation, and Utilities													
2002	530.8	525.8	528.1	528.9	530.8	533.1	525.1	526.5	526.0	529.2	538.3	546.1	530.7
2003	516.7	513.6	514.9	511.7	514.0	514.1	514.2	516.8	516.1	518.2	528.2	533.5	517.7
2004	513.1	509.8	512.6	511.4	513.6	514.9	517.7	518.5	515.3	522.1	531.9	538.3	518.3
2005	522.1	521.0	522.7	529.7	532.3	532.6	538.3	537.0	535.1	541.2	553.0	559.8	535.4
2006	540.4	537.8	540.9	545.2	548.5	549.5	547.7	548.9	550.5	559.7	572.4	580.1	551.8
2007	560.4	556.4	557.1	557.4	560.8	561.0	561.4	561.2	561.2	563.4	573.8	578.4	562.7
2008	560.2	557.9	558.1	554.5	555.7	553.6	553.2	552.0	549.6	546.8	549.8	551.4	553.6
2009	529.7	523.8	520.2	515.8	516.2	514.9	513.2	513.1	510.8	509.9	517.7	521.2	517.2
2010	507.2	505.4	506.4	507.3	510.6	511.4	512.3	513.2	509.8	518.2	525.9	530.2	513.2
2011	509.7	513.6	516.0	519.3	521.3	520.8	521.7	522.5	520.1	525.3	534.5	537.5	521.9
2012	522.1	520.0	521.8	525.0	528.0	527.5	527.6	527.6	525.3	530.4	543.1	544.4	528.6
2013	527.6	526.1	526.0	529.7	532.3	532.7	536.3	538.2	536.3	541.1	549.6	555.4	535.9
Wholesale Trade													
2002	155.0	154.7	155.5	155.0	154.7	154.5	151.9	151.8	150.9	152.4	152.1	152.1	153.4
2003	151.1	151.4	151.9	150.9	151.3	151.3	151.3	151.1	150.5	150.1	151.0	151.7	151.1
2004	149.9	150.1	150.8	151.4	151.2	151.5	152.7	152.6	151.3	152.0	152.3	152.8	151.6
2005	153.2	154.0	154.4	155.3	155.2	155.2	155.8	156.2	155.9	155.4	155.5	156.1	155.2
2006	154.6	155.3	155.6	157.2	158.1	158.3	159.3	159.2	159.3	160.7	160.0	161.2	158.2
2007	159.2	159.6	159.6	160.1	159.9	159.7	160.6	160.6	160.1	160.1	160.0	160.4	160.0
2008	159.7	160.2	159.9	159.6	159.7	159.1	159.4	159.2	158.6	157.6	156.2	155.0	158.7
2009	152.3	150.7	148.9	147.7	146.5	145.5	145.2	144.6	144.0	144.0	143.8	143.7	146.4
2010	143.0	143.4	143.3	144.0	144.5	144.4	144.4	144.3	143.2	144.7	144.7	144.1	144.0
2011	142.8	144.1	144.2	144.9	145.5	144.9	145.9	146.2	145.3	146.2	146.6	146.2	145.2
2012	145.1	146.0	146.0	146.8	147.6	147.3	148.2	148.1	146.6	147.9	148.1	147.9	147.1
2013	146.3	146.9	146.6	147.5	148.0	148.0	148.3	148.5	147.8	148.9	150.3	150.8	148.2
Retail Trade													
2002	256.8	252.7	254.3	253.9	255.4	256.3	252.8	253.5	254.3	254.8	263.7	271.6	256.7
2003	246.8	243.8	244.8	244.2	246.1	246.3	245.7	248.0	248.0	250.1	258.7	263.5	248.8
2004	245.9	242.6	244.0	241.6	243.5	244.7	245.2	245.9	244.7	250.0	259.0	264.7	247.7
2005	249.3	246.2	247.3	253.9	256.2	256.8	259.3	258.2	256.3	262.5	272.1	277.3	258.0
2006	263.2	259.8	261.7	263.7	265.3	265.6	262.2	263.0	263.3	271.2	283.8	288.0	267.6
2007	275.2	270.4	270.6	270.3	271.6	270.8	271.5	271.0	270.9	273.3	283.4	286.3	273.8
2008	271.6	268.4	268.7	265.7	266.2	264.8	264.7	263.8	262.4	261.6	266.3	267.7	266.0
2009	251.9	248.6	247.1	245.9	247.0	246.6	245.2	245.8	244.0	243.5	251.0	253.6	247.5
2010	242.0	240.0	240.9	242.1	243.8	244.2	244.6	244.9	242.7	247.8	254.8	257.8	245.5
2011	243.5	244.7	246.0	248.6	249.2	249.0	249.0	249.3	247.9	252.0	260.0	262.1	250.1
2012	250.9	248.5	249.9	251.1	252.8	252.5	252.0	251.9	251.2	254.7	266.0	266.0	254.0
2013	253.5	252.4	252.9	254.4	256.4	257.4	259.3	261.1	260.3	263.3	268.0	272.1	259.3
Transportation and Utilities													
2002	119.0	118.4	118.3	120.0	120.7	122.3	120.4	121.2	120.8	122.0	122.5	122.4	120.7
2003	118.8	118.4	118.2	116.6	116.6	116.5	117.2	117.7	117.6	118.0	118.5	118.3	117.7
2004	117.3	117.1	117.8	118.4	118.9	118.7	119.8	120.0	119.3	120.1	120.6	120.8	119.1
2005	119.6	120.8	121.0	120.5	120.9	120.6	123.2	122.6	122.9	123.3	125.4	126.4	122.3
2006	122.6	122.7	123.6	124.3	125.1	125.6	126.2	126.7	127.9	127.8	128.6	130.9	126.0
2007	126.0	126.4	126.9	127.0	129.3	130.5	129.3	129.6	130.2	130.0	130.4	131.7	128.9
2008	128.9	129.3	129.5	129.2	129.8	129.7	129.1	129.0	128.6	127.6	127.3	128.7	128.9
2009	125.5	124.5	124.2	122.2	122.7	122.8	122.8	122.7	122.8	122.4	122.9	123.9	123.3
2010	122.2	122.0	122.2	121.2	122.3	122.8	123.3	124.0	123.9	125.7	126.4	128.3	123.7
2011	123.4	124.8	125.8	125.8	126.6	126.9	126.8	127.0	126.9	127.1	127.9	129.2	126.5
2012	126.1	125.5	125.9	127.1	127.6	127.7	127.4	127.6	127.5	127.8	129.0	130.5	127.5
2013	127.8	126.8	126.5	127.8	127.9	127.3	128.7	128.6	128.2	128.9	131.3	132.5	128.5
Information													
2002	104.4	103.5	104.6	101.2	100.2	100.1	99.6	99.1	98.0	98.0	97.5	97.4	100.3
2003	92.5	92.6	92.8	91.2	90.7	91.1	90.5	91.1	90.0	90.2	91.2	91.2	91.3
2004	88.9	88.4	88.9	88.4	88.1	88.5	88.0	87.6	87.0	86.5	87.2	87.1	87.9
2005	85.3	85.3	85.8	85.8	84.8	86.3	85.7	84.4	85.0	85.4	86.2	86.6	85.6
2006	85.0	85.4	85.8	85.4	85.9	85.5	85.0	84.7	84.6	84.8	85.7	85.9	85.3
2007	86.3	86.1	86.1	85.3	85.8	85.8	85.5	85.6	85.7	84.7	85.1	85.2	85.6
2008	83.2	83.7	84.0	84.0	84.5	84.7	83.9	83.7	83.1	82.3	82.5	82.4	83.5
2009	82.3	82.2	81.7	81.3	81.1	80.7	80.0	79.7	79.2	78.4	78.5	79.0	80.3
2010	77.7	77.6	77.8	78.3	78.8	78.5	78.7	78.5	77.9	77.9	78.4	78.6	78.2
2011	79.8	79.9	80.4	80.4	80.3	79.6	80.7	80.9	80.6	81.0	82.4	80.7	80.6
2012	80.2	81.4	81.2	80.7	81.6	81.5	82.1	82.7	82.7	83.7	84.3	84.2	82.2
2013	83.1	84.1	84.1	84.4	84.8	84.3	84.8	85.2	84.9	84.6	85.2	85.0	84.5

Employment by Industry: Atlanta–Sandy Springs–Marietta, GA, Selected Years, 2002–2013—*Continued*

(Numbers in thousands, not seasonally adjusted)

Industry and year	January	February	March	April	May	June	July	August	September	October	November	December	Annual average
Financial Activities													
2002	156.5	156.7	156.4	157.1	157.5	157.8	157.6	158.3	157.3	157.0	157.4	157.9	157.3
2003	155.7	156.3	156.9	157.0	158.1	158.9	159.2	159.9	159.5	156.7	157.0	157.4	157.7
2004	155.7	156.3	156.7	158.3	158.6	158.2	159.2	159.4	158.8	160.7	160.7	161.4	158.7
2005	161.6	162.0	162.0	162.7	163.6	163.9	163.3	164.3	164.3	166.5	166.7	168.0	164.1
2006	164.8	165.7	166.2	168.1	168.7	169.1	169.0	169.8	169.7	171.2	171.0	171.7	168.8
2007	168.7	170.2	170.5	169.8	169.7	169.5	169.6	169.5	168.2	168.0	167.9	167.6	169.1
2008	163.9	164.4	163.9	163.6	163.6	162.9	162.9	161.9	160.1	160.6	159.0	158.3	162.1
2009	155.9	155.1	154.2	153.4	153.7	153.3	152.7	151.8	150.5	150.1	149.9	150.0	152.6
2010	148.1	148.0	147.9	147.6	148.0	148.0	147.8	148.3	147.7	149.2	149.4	149.8	148.3
2011	149.0	149.5	149.8	150.3	150.5	150.5	150.7	151.3	151.1	152.0	152.1	152.3	150.8
2012	152.3	152.7	153.1	153.0	152.8	153.2	153.5	153.5	152.5	153.9	155.0	155.0	153.4
2013	153.1	153.7	154.2	155.3	155.9	156.4	157.3	157.9	157.0	158.2	158.2	159.0	156.4
Professional and Business Services													
2002	362.8	366.4	367.4	371.5	372.9	373.6	370.5	372.8	370.8	369.6	369.4	368.7	369.7
2003	357.6	361.3	361.9	363.6	361.4	362.6	362.5	365.9	365.1	366.8	367.7	368.8	363.8
2004	358.1	361.7	366.1	370.4	370.7	371.0	376.5	376.3	373.3	383.0	382.3	383.1	372.7
2005	377.8	381.3	382.0	385.6	386.2	386.7	391.4	394.7	396.1	397.9	399.0	397.4	389.7
2006	393.0	394.4	396.8	399.5	399.7	402.8	403.2	402.8	401.7	405.6	405.9	407.1	401.0
2007	401.3	404.8	408.5	405.2	407.4	408.9	412.7	416.1	415.3	415.5	416.8	417.7	410.9
2008	409.5	410.2	407.9	412.4	411.5	412.4	407.3	408.3	405.0	405.1	401.0	398.4	407.4
2009	381.0	378.4	375.4	374.2	373.0	374.1	375.8	372.9	370.5	379.5	381.3	381.8	376.5
2010	371.2	374.0	377.3	384.3	385.3	386.9	389.2	388.7	387.1	393.8	393.5	393.5	385.4
2011	387.3	397.7	400.8	401.0	400.3	400.6	401.6	404.8	405.4	408.1	409.1	410.8	402.3
2012	401.1	405.1	408.0	412.7	415.8	419.9	416.8	420.1	417.0	423.8	426.8	426.8	416.2
2013	419.7	426.7	428.5	432.7	433.2	436.5	436.1	439.8	439.5	440.7	442.2	441.9	434.8
Education and Health Services													
2002	193.5	196.3	198.7	198.3	199.0	199.0	198.3	201.2	202.2	203.3	205.0	205.1	200.0
2003	202.1	204.3	205.7	205.6	206.8	205.7	204.9	207.7	208.4	209.4	210.8	211.6	206.9
2004	209.8	211.1	212.0	213.1	214.0	212.5	213.3	215.8	215.7	219.5	220.4	221.1	214.9
2005	219.6	220.6	218.6	223.5	224.9	221.1	223.5	226.2	227.0	229.6	230.2	230.4	224.7
2006	230.7	232.2	232.2	232.6	233.3	230.7	231.5	233.8	235.5	240.3	240.9	240.9	234.6
2007	238.7	241.0	241.1	242.4	242.5	240.4	241.2	245.2	246.5	249.0	249.9	250.0	244.0
2008	246.9	250.1	250.2	251.1	252.5	247.9	248.6	253.0	253.1	255.0	256.0	256.4	251.7
2009	254.4	255.8	254.7	255.5	256.8	252.3	251.2	254.6	254.1	258.2	259.1	259.0	255.5
2010	256.6	259.2	260.3	261.0	262.6	259.2	260.8	264.0	264.1	268.3	268.4	268.0	262.7
2011	263.4	267.4	268.4	273.3	273.1	268.5	269.0	273.1	274.7	278.6	278.7	279.6	272.3
2012	277.8	280.7	282.0	284.0	284.8	280.7	279.7	285.3	286.4	289.5	289.8	290.1	284.2
2013	289.4	292.1	292.7	294.9	295.2	290.8	289.1	294.5	295.4	298.6	299.8	299.3	294.3
Leisure and Hospitality													
2002	189.7	191.7	196.8	203.1	207.2	209.6	203.4	203.8	201.7	199.5	199.4	201.0	200.6
2003	191.7	193.7	199.3	203.6	208.1	210.8	210.7	212.2	210.5	206.1	206.3	206.9	205.0
2004	199.3	201.5	206.1	211.6	215.1	218.4	216.6	218.0	214.5	213.9	212.8	213.7	211.8
2005	206.4	207.5	212.9	220.7	225.6	226.8	223.0	223.8	221.1	220.2	219.9	219.1	218.9
2006	214.6	217.1	221.8	224.8	229.4	231.7	230.6	231.4	228.1	228.7	229.7	229.1	226.4
2007	224.5	227.8	232.6	235.2	240.0	241.7	240.0	241.3	236.6	234.1	233.0	232.2	234.9
2008	227.8	229.8	233.4	236.3	241.4	241.2	238.6	238.1	234.3	228.8	226.1	224.2	233.3
2009	217.4	219.0	222.3	226.3	229.5	230.1	228.3	227.3	223.6	220.0	218.4	216.1	223.2
2010	208.9	210.6	215.6	221.7	225.4	226.9	226.2	226.2	224.1	222.9	220.9	219.9	220.8
2011	210.8	215.5	220.8	227.3	232.6	232.5	232.2	231.6	228.7	226.6	225.5	225.0	225.8
2012	221.2	222.8	227.6	234.9	240.3	241.1	240.0	240.5	235.5	235.9	233.9	234.0	234.0
2013	231.0	232.8	237.2	244.8	249.1	251.2	252.2	252.9	247.9	248.4	249.8	249.5	245.6
Other Services													
2002	92.3	92.1	92.5	92.3	92.2	92.9	91.8	91.8	91.5	89.9	89.6	89.4	91.5
2003	90.9	91.2	91.9	91.5	92.4	93.1	93.2	93.4	92.9	92.4	92.5	92.3	92.3
2004	91.5	91.4	92.8	92.5	92.9	93.5	93.7	93.7	92.5	92.0	92.1	92.0	92.6
2005	93.3	94.0	94.4	95.5	96.1	96.0	96.4	97.6	95.7	95.4	95.4	95.5	95.4
2006	95.3	95.5	95.6	97.0	97.7	98.0	98.4	97.8	96.6	96.6	96.6	96.1	96.8
2007	96.2	96.5	96.9	98.0	98.7	99.1	99.3	99.2	97.6	97.9	97.6	97.0	97.8
2008	97.3	98.3	98.2	98.1	99.2	99.1	98.5	98.5	97.4	96.7	96.2	95.5	97.8
2009	98.6	98.9	98.2	99.1	98.9	98.3	98.5	97.0	95.0	94.9	94.0	92.8	97.0
2010	91.6	92.0	92.1	93.1	93.9	93.3	94.1	93.7	93.3	93.3	94.2	94.1	93.2
2011	91.2	92.9	93.0	92.2	93.0	92.9	92.9	92.6	92.1	92.1	92.0	91.2	92.3
2012	90.7	91.2	91.3	92.5	93.1	93.5	93.7	93.3	92.6	93.5	93.5	92.4	92.6
2013	92.1	92.5	92.3	93.5	93.9	94.2	94.3	94.2	93.7	93.9	93.8	92.6	93.4
Government													
2002	296.5	296.3	300.9	303.5	303.6	298.3	286.1	299.6	306.6	305.7	307.5	305.0	300.8
2003	305.0	306.6	308.3	307.2	305.2	295.8	286.3	297.3	304.8	306.3	306.5	306.0	302.9
2004	305.8	311.2	311.8	311.2	309.3	298.6	291.0	306.5	312.3	311.5	313.2	310.5	307.7
2005	310.0	314.4	315.0	315.6	315.2	304.5	296.0	313.0	316.2	319.3	320.2	319.5	313.2
2006	318.8	322.4	324.1	322.4	321.6	316.3	303.6	320.0	326.3	329.2	331.6	331.1	322.3
2007	328.9	333.2	334.4	333.2	332.5	324.1	317.8	331.8	336.7	336.1	337.8	337.7	332.0
2008	337.7	343.0	344.7	344.0	343.3	335.9	324.1	337.2	338.2	344.9	348.1	345.5	340.6
2009	345.2	348.6	349.5	348.6	344.6	334.8	321.7	330.0	338.5	338.0	338.1	336.7	339.5
2010	335.5	337.6	338.4	339.3	344.6	335.8	321.5	323.8	325.9	327.2	331.3	327.0	332.3
2011	323.3	326.7	328.4	326.4	326.6	319.8	310.0	315.5	320.5	322.1	325.0	323.3	322.3
2012	320.6	323.0	326.4	325.2	323.9	319.9	306.0	314.1	318.1	320.3	325.2	321.1	320.3
2013	319.4	321.6	322.1	323.2	320.9	314.4	303.2	311.7	316.6	317.9	319.9	319.1	317.5

Employment by Industry: Austin–Round Rock–San Marcos, TX, Selected Years, 2002–2013

(Numbers in thousands, not seasonally adjusted)

Industry and year	January	February	March	April	May	June	July	August	September	October	November	December	Annual average
Total Nonfarm													
2002	652.4	656.5	659.8	661.0	662.5	656.9	652.2	658.1	659.1	658.9	662.7	660.4	658.4
2003	646.5	648.7	649.4	653.6	654.8	653.2	649.3	652.8	654.3	656.3	658.0	659.1	653.0
2004	648.5	655.5	661.0	665.5	667.1	666.9	664.2	669.3	671.5	676.9	680.8	681.8	667.4
2005	672.2	679.2	684.4	690.3	692.8	693.4	690.1	693.7	698.4	699.1	705.7	706.9	692.2
2006	696.4	704.2	710.8	717.0	720.8	723.5	715.9	724.1	734.8	737.7	744.6	748.6	723.2
2007	732.3	744.1	752.1	755.3	759.4	762.2	754.5	758.6	763.4	768.5	773.8	774.1	758.2
2008	764.6	772.5	774.6	777.2	779.9	779.4	770.7	775.0	779.0	781.4	784.1	779.7	776.5
2009	760.9	761.3	761.5	763.4	764.5	761.9	751.7	753.2	755.0	759.2	763.2	761.4	759.8
2010	750.6	756.0	764.5	768.2	772.5	774.0	765.0	768.5	770.2	781.4	786.8	785.5	770.3
2011	773.5	781.1	788.0	796.4	797.2	798.3	791.1	796.2	800.6	804.9	811.2	811.6	795.8
2012	802.8	808.9	815.4	820.4	824.4	828.1	821.2	826.6	832.6	841.3	852.2	850.1	827.0
2013	837.0	846.4	853.0	860.5	864.3	868.5	860.7	863.9	869.9	876.8	884.4	884.9	864.2
Total Private													
2002	509.7	510.9	513.0	513.9	516.4	517.8	514.4	516.7	514.1	510.7	512.9	512.8	513.6
2003	499.9	499.6	500.8	503.8	506.2	508.5	508.2	510.7	510.4	511.7	513.1	515.6	507.4
2004	504.8	508.5	512.9	516.7	519.0	523.1	525.8	528.0	526.8	528.6	531.1	534.5	521.7
2005	525.3	528.5	533.5	538.6	541.1	545.8	546.9	549.3	550.6	548.6	553.5	557.2	543.2
2006	547.0	551.1	557.1	562.6	566.9	573.3	573.9	578.2	580.2	581.6	588.6	594.2	571.2
2007	578.3	586.7	593.5	596.4	600.6	606.6	605.4	607.7	607.3	608.4	612.6	615.2	601.6
2008	604.6	609.1	608.8	614.0	616.9	618.3	616.2	619.2	616.3	617.1	617.5	615.1	614.4
2009	596.3	593.4	592.7	593.2	594.5	594.3	592.4	593.3	588.9	590.5	591.9	592.5	592.8
2010	582.0	585.2	590.6	594.9	598.0	601.3	601.9	605.0	603.8	610.1	614.1	615.8	600.2
2011	605.4	609.7	616.2	623.9	625.7	628.5	630.3	635.5	636.2	638.1	642.9	645.9	628.2
2012	636.5	640.7	646.8	651.1	655.7	661.5	661.3	667.3	668.1	673.2	681.5	682.5	660.5
2013	669.0	676.1	681.8	687.8	692.4	698.0	696.6	701.8	702.7	706.7	711.5	715.0	695.0
Goods-Producing													
2002	105.4	104.7	104.7	103.0	103.0	103.7	102.1	101.4	99.5	98.6	97.5	96.8	101.7
2003	96.0	95.2	95.2	95.2	95.4	96.0	95.7	95.4	94.8	94.5	94.1	94.0	95.1
2004	92.4	92.6	93.2	94.1	94.4	95.6	96.6	96.7	96.3	96.7	96.4	96.1	95.1
2005	95.1	95.4	96.0	96.4	96.7	98.0	98.7	98.6	98.4	98.1	98.5	99.0	97.4
2006	98.5	99.5	101.0	101.5	102.4	104.5	105.2	105.5	105.3	105.3	105.9	106.9	103.5
2007	104.9	106.2	107.2	108.2	108.9	110.3	110.0	110.2	109.3	109.6	109.7	109.0	108.6
2008	106.8	107.4	107.0	106.6	106.7	106.8	105.9	105.2	103.5	101.4	99.7	98.0	104.6
2009	93.1	91.5	89.6	90.3	89.9	90.0	89.5	88.6	88.0	87.2	86.5	86.8	89.3
2010	85.0	85.1	85.8	86.8	86.7	87.8	88.5	89.3	88.8	89.2	89.0	88.9	87.6
2011	87.6	87.9	88.4	88.6	88.7	89.8	90.2	90.3	90.1	89.8	89.7	89.9	89.3
2012	89.2	90.2	91.0	91.3	92.0	93.7	94.2	95.0	94.8	94.7	94.7	94.7	93.0
2013	93.9	94.9	95.8	96.2	97.2	98.1	98.6	99.0	99.0	98.6	98.5	98.6	97.4
Service-Providing													
2002	547.0	551.8	555.1	558.0	559.5	553.2	550.1	556.7	559.6	560.3	565.2	563.6	556.7
2003	550.5	553.5	554.2	558.4	559.4	557.2	553.6	557.4	559.5	561.8	563.9	565.1	557.9
2004	556.1	562.9	567.8	571.4	572.7	571.3	567.6	572.6	575.2	580.2	584.4	585.7	572.3
2005	577.1	583.8	588.4	593.9	596.1	595.4	591.4	595.1	600.0	601.0	607.2	607.9	594.8
2006	597.9	604.7	609.8	615.5	618.4	619.0	610.7	618.6	629.5	632.4	638.7	641.7	619.7
2007	627.4	637.9	644.9	647.1	650.5	651.9	644.5	648.4	654.1	658.9	664.1	665.1	649.6
2008	657.8	665.1	667.6	670.6	673.2	672.6	664.8	669.8	675.5	680.0	684.4	681.7	671.9
2009	667.8	669.8	671.9	673.1	674.6	671.9	662.2	664.6	667.0	672.0	676.7	674.6	670.5
2010	665.6	670.9	678.7	681.4	685.8	686.2	676.5	679.2	681.4	692.2	697.8	696.6	682.7
2011	685.9	693.2	699.6	707.8	708.5	708.5	700.9	705.9	710.5	715.1	721.5	721.7	706.6
2012	713.6	718.7	724.4	729.1	732.4	734.4	727.0	731.6	737.8	746.6	757.5	755.4	734.0
2013	743.1	751.5	757.2	764.3	767.1	770.4	762.1	764.9	770.9	778.2	785.9	786.3	766.8
Mining, Logging, and Construction													
2002	37.6	38.0	38.7	38.5	38.8	39.4	39.2	39.0	37.9	37.6	37.1	36.5	38.2
2003	36.6	36.5	36.6	37.3	37.8	38.3	38.3	38.3	37.9	37.5	37.1	36.9	37.4
2004	35.9	36.1	36.4	37.2	37.2	37.9	38.8	38.7	38.5	38.9	38.5	38.2	37.7
2005	37.8	38.2	38.8	39.3	39.8	40.5	41.2	41.1	41.3	41.0	41.3	41.5	40.2
2006	41.2	41.9	42.9	43.5	44.1	45.3	45.7	45.9	46.0	45.7	46.1	46.8	44.6
2007	45.7	46.7	47.5	48.2	48.9	49.9	49.8	50.2	49.9	50.3	50.7	49.9	49.0
2008	48.0	48.4	48.3	48.3	48.5	48.6	48.1	48.0	47.2	46.0	44.9	44.0	47.4
2009	42.4	42.0	41.4	40.7	40.8	41.4	41.2	40.5	40.2	39.6	39.6	39.7	40.8
2010	38.2	38.0	38.7	39.7	39.6	40.3	41.0	41.5	40.9	41.0	40.6	40.3	40.0
2011	39.3	39.3	39.5	39.2	39.1	39.7	39.8	39.8	39.9	39.6	39.5	39.6	39.5
2012	39.5	40.0	40.7	41.0	41.5	42.6	42.8	43.4	43.4	43.3	43.2	43.3	42.1
2013	42.8	43.5	44.2	44.6	45.3	45.5	45.8	46.2	46.3	45.9	45.8	45.6	45.1
Manufacturing													
2002	67.8	66.7	66.0	64.5	64.2	64.3	62.9	62.4	61.6	61.0	60.4	60.3	63.5
2003	59.4	58.7	58.6	57.9	57.6	57.7	57.4	57.1	56.9	57.0	57.0	57.1	57.7
2004	56.5	56.5	56.8	56.9	57.2	57.7	57.8	58.0	57.8	57.8	57.9	57.9	57.4
2005	57.3	57.2	57.2	57.1	56.9	57.5	57.5	57.5	57.1	57.1	57.2	57.5	57.3
2006	57.3	57.6	58.1	58.0	58.3	59.2	59.5	59.6	59.3	59.6	59.8	60.1	58.9
2007	59.2	59.5	59.7	60.0	60.0	60.4	60.2	60.0	59.4	59.3	59.0	59.1	59.7
2008	58.8	59.0	58.7	58.3	58.2	58.2	57.8	57.2	56.3	55.4	54.8	54.0	57.2
2009	50.7	49.5	48.2	49.6	49.1	48.6	48.3	48.1	47.8	47.6	46.9	47.1	48.5
2010	46.8	47.1	47.1	47.1	47.1	47.5	47.5	47.8	47.9	48.2	48.4	48.6	47.6
2011	48.3	48.6	48.9	49.4	49.6	50.1	50.4	50.5	50.2	50.2	50.2	50.3	49.7
2012	49.7	50.2	50.3	50.3	50.5	51.1	51.4	51.6	51.4	51.4	51.5	51.4	50.9
2013	51.1	51.4	51.6	51.6	51.9	52.6	52.8	52.8	52.7	52.7	52.7	53.0	52.2

Employment by Industry: Austin–Round Rock–San Marcos, TX, Selected Years, 2002–2013—*Continued*

(Numbers in thousands, not seasonally adjusted)

Industry and year	January	February	March	April	May	June	July	August	September	October	November	December	Annual average
Trade, Transportation, and Utilities													
2002	113.8	112.7	112.7	112.9	113.0	113.1	112.6	113.0	112.2	112.4	114.7	116.6	113.3
2003	110.9	109.7	109.6	109.7	109.9	110.4	111.6	112.7	112.8	113.8	116.1	117.9	112.1
2004	113.5	113.1	113.5	113.0	113.3	113.8	115.1	116.1	115.9	117.0	119.6	121.9	115.5
2005	117.8	117.7	118.6	119.1	120.2	121.4	122.4	123.4	123.1	123.0	126.1	128.3	121.8
2006	123.2	122.7	123.4	124.4	125.2	126.5	127.3	128.4	128.2	129.4	133.4	136.5	127.4
2007	131.9	132.2	133.3	134.0	134.5	136.1	136.4	136.6	136.4	137.8	140.0	143.0	136.0
2008	138.4	137.8	137.5	137.8	137.7	138.3	138.5	139.7	138.9	140.0	141.7	142.5	139.1
2009	136.9	133.0	133.0	131.1	131.2	131.0	131.2	132.2	131.3	132.2	134.4	136.0	132.8
2010	133.0	131.9	132.4	133.4	133.8	134.2	134.4	135.5	135.2	136.8	140.0	142.2	135.2
2011	137.5	137.2	138.2	138.9	139.3	139.1	140.2	141.7	141.3	143.0	146.1	148.4	140.9
2012	143.6	142.9	143.2	144.1	144.9	145.6	145.8	147.2	146.5	147.9	152.6	153.9	146.5
2013	149.0	148.7	148.5	149.6	150.1	151.5	152.0	153.2	152.8	154.6	158.4	160.1	152.4
Wholesale Trade													
2002	33.9	33.9	34.0	33.9	33.9	34.2	34.2	34.1	34.0	33.8	33.7	33.7	33.9
2003	33.4	33.4	33.3	33.3	33.5	33.7	33.9	33.9	33.8	33.8	34.1	34.5	33.7
2004	34.4	34.7	34.8	34.8	34.9	35.3	35.7	35.8	35.8	35.9	36.1	36.5	35.4
2005	36.5	36.8	36.8	37.0	37.3	37.5	38.0	38.1	38.0	37.5	37.4	37.4	37.4
2006	37.1	37.3	37.5	37.6	37.8	38.3	38.6	38.7	38.8	39.1	40.0	40.8	38.5
2007	40.4	40.7	40.9	41.0	41.4	42.4	42.1	41.8	41.4	41.5	40.4	41.6	41.3
2008	41.3	41.3	41.2	41.1	41.1	41.5	41.6	41.7	41.6	41.7	41.7	41.6	41.5
2009	41.2	38.2	38.2	37.3	37.1	36.9	37.5	37.4	37.1	37.1	37.2	37.3	37.7
2010	39.1	39.0	39.1	39.5	39.6	39.8	39.9	40.0	39.9	40.5	40.7	40.8	39.8
2011	40.7	41.1	41.4	41.6	41.8	42.0	42.3	42.5	42.8	43.6	43.9	44.1	42.3
2012	43.6	43.7	43.8	44.0	44.3	44.6	44.5	44.6	44.3	44.2	44.3	44.5	44.2
2013	44.7	44.9	45.0	45.1	44.8	45.4	45.4	45.6	45.3	45.4	45.6	45.6	45.2
Retail Trade													
2002	68.7	67.7	67.6	67.9	68.0	67.9	67.3	67.7	67.2	67.5	69.9	71.8	68.3
2003	67.0	65.9	65.9	66.0	66.0	66.3	67.2	68.2	68.4	69.2	71.2	72.6	67.8
2004	68.6	67.8	68.1	67.5	67.7	67.8	68.4	69.1	68.8	69.7	72.0	73.7	69.1
2005	69.9	69.5	70.2	70.6	71.3	72.3	72.9	73.6	73.2	73.7	76.7	78.5	72.7
2006	74.2	73.4	73.7	74.5	74.9	75.8	76.2	77.0	76.5	77.3	80.3	82.2	76.3
2007	78.6	78.5	79.1	79.9	79.9	80.5	81.2	81.4	81.5	82.7	85.9	87.5	81.4
2008	83.7	83.0	82.8	83.4	83.3	83.5	83.9	84.7	83.9	85.0	86.6	87.4	84.3
2009	82.8	82.0	82.1	81.1	81.4	81.4	81.2	82.1	81.4	82.1	84.1	85.2	82.2
2010	81.2	80.2	80.5	81.2	81.4	81.7	82.0	82.8	82.3	83.4	86.2	87.8	82.6
2011	83.5	82.8	83.5	84.0	84.0	84.1	84.7	85.5	84.7	85.8	88.5	90.1	85.1
2012	86.3	85.4	85.6	86.4	86.8	87.3	87.7	88.6	88.1	89.7	94.0	94.7	88.4
2013	90.2	89.9	89.7	90.5	91.1	91.8	92.4	93.1	92.9	94.6	98.0	99.5	92.8
Transportation and Utilities													
2002	11.2	11.1	11.1	11.1	11.1	11.0	11.1	11.2	11.0	11.1	11.1	11.1	11.1
2003	10.5	10.4	10.4	10.4	10.4	10.4	10.5	10.6	10.6	10.8	10.8	10.8	10.6
2004	10.5	10.6	10.6	10.7	10.7	10.7	11.0	11.2	11.3	11.4	11.5	11.7	11.0
2005	11.4	11.4	11.6	11.5	11.6	11.6	11.5	11.7	11.9	11.8	12.0	12.4	11.7
2006	11.9	12.0	12.2	12.3	12.5	12.4	12.5	12.7	12.9	13.0	13.1	13.5	12.6
2007	12.9	13.0	13.3	13.1	13.2	13.2	13.1	13.4	13.5	13.6	13.7	13.9	13.3
2008	13.4	13.5	13.5	13.3	13.3	13.3	13.0	13.3	13.4	13.3	13.4	13.5	13.4
2009	12.9	12.8	12.7	12.7	12.7	12.7	12.5	12.7	12.8	13.0	13.1	13.5	12.8
2010	12.7	12.7	12.8	12.7	12.8	12.7	12.5	12.7	13.0	12.9	13.1	13.6	12.9
2011	13.3	13.3	13.3	13.3	13.5	13.0	13.2	13.7	13.8	13.6	13.7	14.2	13.5
2012	13.7	13.8	13.8	13.7	13.8	13.7	13.6	14.0	14.1	14.0	14.3	14.7	13.9
2013	14.1	13.9	13.8	14.0	14.2	14.3	14.2	14.5	14.6	14.6	14.8	15.0	14.3
Information													
2002	23.0	22.9	23.0	22.9	22.8	23.0	22.7	22.5	22.3	22.1	22.0	21.8	22.6
2003	21.5	21.4	21.3	20.9	20.9	21.1	20.8	20.7	20.5	20.4	20.2	20.2	20.8
2004	20.1	20.1	20.3	20.2	20.4	20.7	20.6	20.7	20.6	20.9	21.0	21.0	20.5
2005	21.0	21.1	21.3	21.2	21.4	21.6	21.7	21.5	22.1	21.5	21.7	21.9	21.5
2006	21.8	21.8	21.8	21.8	21.7	21.7	21.5	21.6	21.6	21.8	22.1	22.2	21.8
2007	21.9	22.1	22.1	22.2	22.3	22.3	21.7	21.6	21.6	21.5	21.8	21.6	21.9
2008	21.3	21.0	20.9	20.8	21.0	21.1	21.1	21.1	20.8	20.8	21.0	20.9	21.0
2009	20.4	20.3	20.2	19.9	19.9	19.6	19.6	19.6	19.4	19.2	19.3	19.4	19.7
2010	19.2	19.2	19.2	19.2	19.3	19.4	19.5	19.6	19.5	19.8	19.9	20.0	19.5
2011	19.7	19.8	19.9	20.0	20.2	20.4	20.9	20.9	21.0	21.0	21.3	21.5	20.6
2012	21.5	21.4	21.6	21.6	21.8	22.1	22.6	22.6	22.5	22.8	23.1	23.3	22.2
2013	22.6	22.7	23.1	22.9	22.9	23.3	23.5	23.6	23.5	23.6	23.6	23.8	23.3
Financial Activities													
2002	36.7	36.9	37.0	37.4	37.7	38.1	38.2	38.4	38.5	38.7	38.9	39.1	38.0
2003	38.5	38.6	38.7	39.1	39.4	39.6	39.8	40.0	39.9	40.0	40.1	40.2	39.5
2004	39.3	39.4	39.5	39.7	39.7	40.0	40.0	40.1	40.1	40.4	40.5	40.8	40.0
2005	40.0	40.3	40.5	40.6	40.8	41.1	41.4	41.7	41.7	41.9	41.9	42.4	41.2
2006	41.9	42.2	42.5	42.6	42.9	43.3	43.4	43.7	43.9	44.1	44.1	44.6	43.3
2007	43.8	44.1	44.5	44.5	44.9	45.1	45.0	45.0	44.8	44.6	44.9	45.2	44.7
2008	44.5	44.9	44.8	45.1	45.2	45.4	45.4	45.4	45.2	44.9	45.0	45.2	45.1
2009	43.8	43.9	43.7	43.8	43.8	43.9	43.7	43.6	43.3	43.3	43.2	43.3	43.6
2010	42.2	42.3	42.4	42.4	42.6	42.6	42.6	42.6	42.3	42.7	42.8	42.8	42.5
2011	42.7	42.9	43.3	43.7	44.0	44.2	44.4	44.5	44.4	44.6	44.8	45.2	44.1
2012	44.9	45.1	45.3	45.5	45.8	46.2	46.2	46.5	46.5	47.0	47.2	47.4	46.1
2013	46.9	47.2	47.3	47.6	47.8	48.1	48.4	48.5	48.5	49.4	49.5	49.7	48.2

Employment by Industry: Austin–Round Rock–San Marcos, TX, Selected Years, 2002–2013—*Continued*

(Numbers in thousands, not seasonally adjusted)

Industry and year	January	February	March	April	May	June	July	August	September	October	November	December	Annual average
Professional and Business Services													
2002	86.3	86.4	86.7	87.0	87.4	88.0	87.6	88.8	87.7	86.9	87.1	86.6	87.2
2003	84.6	84.6	84.8	85.4	86.0	86.1	86.1	86.0	86.0	86.2	85.6	86.0	85.6
2004	84.9	86.1	87.1	88.0	88.5	89.4	90.4	91.2	90.9	90.9	90.8	91.4	89.1
2005	90.3	91.2	92.1	93.1	93.2	94.4	95.2	95.8	95.8	95.4	96.2	96.6	94.1
2006	94.7	95.6	96.9	97.5	98.6	99.7	100.2	101.1	101.4	102.1	103.5	103.7	99.6
2007	100.8	102.9	104.4	103.9	104.8	106.3	106.8	108.0	108.0	108.3	108.8	108.7	106.0
2008	108.7	109.5	109.1	111.0	111.8	112.0	111.4	112.3	111.7	112.3	111.6	110.7	111.0
2009	108.2	107.8	107.7	107.5	107.5	107.7	106.5	106.8	105.5	107.0	107.0	106.4	107.1
2010	105.1	106.1	107.7	107.9	108.6	109.7	109.9	110.2	110.2	112.4	112.5	112.9	109.4
2011	112.1	113.6	115.1	116.4	116.1	117.3	117.7	118.9	119.7	120.0	120.5	121.3	117.4
2012	120.0	120.9	122.8	122.8	123.4	124.8	125.7	127.5	127.9	129.3	130.4	129.8	125.4
2013	126.9	128.9	130.6	131.9	132.8	134.1	134.9	136.8	137.5	138.7	139.7	139.3	134.3
Education and Health Services													
2002	62.7	63.9	64.0	64.7	64.9	64.1	64.0	64.7	65.7	65.7	66.1	65.8	64.7
2003	64.6	65.4	65.1	65.9	65.9	65.2	65.0	65.8	66.9	67.3	67.3	67.2	66.0
2004	66.2	67.3	67.5	68.5	68.4	67.9	67.7	68.0	68.8	70.0	70.4	70.3	68.4
2005	69.4	70.3	70.8	71.2	71.3	70.5	69.9	70.4	72.1	72.1	72.2	72.5	71.1
2006	71.5	72.5	72.8	73.3	73.4	73.0	72.8	73.8	75.0	75.8	75.7	75.6	73.8
2007	73.6	75.5	76.3	76.2	76.9	76.5	76.8	77.3	78.8	79.2	79.6	79.8	77.2
2008	78.8	80.2	80.1	80.7	81.1	80.1	79.8	80.7	81.6	82.3	82.6	82.8	80.9
2009	80.7	82.0	82.6	83.3	83.7	82.9	83.0	83.7	83.7	84.7	84.9	85.0	83.4
2010	84.2	85.7	86.2	87.2	87.6	87.1	87.5	87.9	88.4	89.5	89.8	89.5	87.6
2011	88.4	89.5	89.8	91.9	92.2	91.7	92.3	94.0	94.6	95.1	95.8	95.6	92.6
2012	94.7	96.1	96.7	96.8	97.3	97.0	96.4	97.7	98.7	99.5	100.0	99.8	97.6
2013	98.9	100.4	100.4	101.6	101.7	101.1	99.1	100.4	101.2	102.0	100.6	100.7	100.7
Leisure and Hospitality													
2002	58.8	60.1	61.4	62.4	63.5	63.6	63.1	63.6	63.6	62.3	62.4	62.3	62.3
2003	60.3	61.0	62.2	63.7	64.6	65.4	64.7	65.3	64.8	64.3	64.3	64.6	63.8
2004	62.8	63.9	65.4	67.1	68.2	69.4	69.4	69.1	68.4	67.5	66.8	67.1	67.1
2005	65.8	66.5	68.0	70.3	70.9	71.7	70.9	71.1	70.6	70.4	70.6	70.1	69.7
2006	69.3	70.4	72.0	74.0	74.9	76.4	75.3	75.9	76.4	75.1	75.7	76.3	74.3
2007	74.3	75.9	77.6	79.2	79.8	81.1	80.4	80.8	80.2	79.2	79.3	79.3	78.9
2008	77.9	79.4	80.5	82.2	83.1	83.8	82.8	83.1	82.6	83.3	83.5	82.3	82.0
2009	80.5	81.5	82.5	83.8	84.8	85.0	85.2	85.3	84.6	83.9	83.6	82.7	83.6
2010	80.6	81.9	83.7	85.2	86.4	87.2	86.2	86.4	86.3	86.6	87.1	86.7	85.4
2011	84.7	85.9	88.3	91.0	91.6	92.0	90.7	91.3	91.5	90.9	91.0	90.5	90.0
2012	88.7	90.0	92.0	94.0	95.2	96.1	94.3	94.7	95.1	95.7	97.0	97.0	94.2
2013	94.4	96.4	99.0	100.6	102.1	103.4	101.8	102.0	102.3	101.8	103.2	104.8	101.0
Other Services													
2002	23.0	23.3	23.5	23.6	24.1	24.2	24.1	24.3	24.6	24.0	24.2	23.8	23.9
2003	23.5	23.7	23.9	23.9	24.1	24.7	24.5	24.8	24.7	25.2	25.4	25.5	24.5
2004	25.6	26.0	26.4	26.1	26.1	26.3	26.0	26.1	25.8	25.5	25.7	25.9	26.0
2005	25.9	26.0	26.2	26.7	26.6	27.1	26.7	26.8	26.8	26.2	26.3	26.4	26.5
2006	26.1	26.4	26.7	27.5	27.8	28.2	28.2	28.2	28.4	28.0	28.2	28.4	27.7
2007	27.1	27.8	28.1	28.2	28.5	28.9	28.3	28.2	28.2	28.2	28.5	28.6	28.2
2008	28.2	28.9	28.9	29.8	30.3	30.8	31.3	31.7	32.0	32.1	32.4	32.7	30.8
2009	32.7	33.4	33.4	33.5	33.7	34.2	33.7	33.5	33.1	33.0	33.0	32.9	33.3
2010	32.7	33.0	33.2	32.8	33.0	33.3	33.3	33.5	33.1	33.1	33.0	32.8	33.1
2011	32.7	32.9	33.2	33.4	33.6	34.0	33.9	33.9	33.6	33.7	33.7	33.5	33.5
2012	33.9	34.1	34.2	35.0	35.3	36.0	36.1	36.1	36.1	36.3	36.5	36.6	35.5
2013	36.4	36.9	37.1	37.4	37.8	38.4	38.3	38.3	37.9	38.0	38.0	38.0	37.7
Government													
2002	142.7	145.6	146.8	147.1	146.1	139.1	137.8	141.4	145.0	148.2	149.8	147.6	144.8
2003	146.6	149.1	148.6	149.8	148.6	144.7	141.1	142.1	143.9	144.6	144.9	143.5	145.6
2004	143.7	147.0	148.1	148.8	148.1	143.8	138.4	141.3	144.7	148.3	149.7	147.3	145.8
2005	146.9	150.7	150.9	151.7	151.7	147.6	143.2	144.4	147.8	150.5	152.2	149.7	148.9
2006	149.4	153.1	153.7	154.4	153.9	150.2	142.0	145.9	154.6	156.1	156.0	154.4	152.0
2007	154.0	157.4	158.6	158.9	158.8	155.6	149.1	150.9	156.1	160.1	161.2	158.9	156.6
2008	160.0	163.4	165.8	163.2	163.0	161.1	154.5	155.8	162.7	164.3	166.6	164.6	162.1
2009	164.6	167.9	168.8	170.2	170.0	167.6	159.3	159.9	166.1	168.7	171.3	168.9	166.9
2010	168.6	170.8	173.9	173.3	174.5	172.7	163.1	163.5	166.4	171.3	172.7	169.7	170.0
2011	168.1	171.4	171.8	172.5	171.5	169.8	160.8	160.7	164.4	166.8	168.3	165.7	167.7
2012	166.3	168.2	168.6	169.3	168.7	166.6	159.9	159.3	164.5	168.1	170.7	167.6	166.5
2013	168.0	170.3	171.2	172.7	171.9	170.5	164.1	162.1	167.2	170.1	172.9	169.9	169.2

Employment by Industry: Bakersfield–Delano, CA, Selected Years, 2002–2013

(Numbers in thousands, not seasonally adjusted)

Industry and year	January	February	March	April	May	June	July	August	September	October	November	December	Annual average
Total Nonfarm													
2002	204.0	204.7	207.3	207.7	208.6	210.1	203.7	204.3	205.1	208.0	209.8	210.4	207.0
2003	207.0	207.3	210.0	209.2	210.2	210.2	207.1	207.5	208.5	210.5	211.3	212.1	209.2
2004	207.5	208.6	210.7	214.1	214.9	218.1	212.5	212.5	214.3	217.4	219.0	219.7	214.1
2005	217.3	218.5	220.0	222.9	225.1	226.5	223.3	224.5	227.4	229.3	230.9	232.0	224.8
2006	230.2	231.7	232.8	233.9	236.5	237.8	233.6	235.9	238.3	240.6	241.5	241.7	236.2
2007	238.4	239.5	240.8	243.0	243.6	243.8	237.9	239.8	242.2	243.0	243.8	244.1	241.7
2008	239.1	240.7	241.5	243.1	244.0	244.7	238.9	238.6	240.5	242.7	243.5	242.2	241.6
2009	236.4	235.8	235.5	235.0	234.9	235.1	223.7	226.8	228.5	227.9	228.7	228.2	231.4
2010	224.9	225.1	228.3	232.6	232.6	232.9	223.3	226.3	229.4	231.1	232.1	233.4	229.3
2011	229.6	231.1	232.8	235.4	237.3	237.2	234.6	236.8	237.6	238.5	239.6	240.1	235.9
2012	237.4	239.8	242.6	244.4	246.9	248.0	242.5	244.1	246.0	249.2	250.2	250.0	245.1
2013	245.2	246.9	248.3	250.4	251.7	249.7	246.1	248.3	250.6	252.0	254.0	255.4	249.9
Total Private													
2002	148.9	149.4	150.8	151.1	152.3	153.0	151.9	152.6	152.2	152.3	152.9	153.6	151.8
2003	150.5	151.2	153.2	153.2	154.6	154.9	155.7	156.1	156.3	156.8	156.5	157.5	154.7
2004	153.8	154.6	156.4	159.4	160.3	161.1	161.2	162.2	161.9	162.6	163.5	164.2	160.1
2005	162.0	162.5	163.7	166.7	168.7	169.8	171.3	171.2	172.8	171.9	173.4	174.7	169.1
2006	172.7	174.0	174.9	175.9	178.7	179.7	179.7	180.8	181.3	180.9	181.7	182.1	178.5
2007	178.9	179.9	181.1	181.2	182.0	182.1	182.4	183.4	183.6	181.7	182.0	182.2	181.7
2008	177.6	178.5	179.0	180.7	181.7	182.0	180.7	181.3	180.9	180.0	179.9	179.3	180.1
2009	174.1	172.9	172.3	171.9	172.3	172.1	169.6	170.4	169.1	167.8	167.6	167.2	170.6
2010	164.7	164.3	165.8	168.4	168.5	169.4	169.9	170.5	170.6	170.1	170.6	171.7	168.7
2011	169.1	170.0	171.0	173.7	175.5	175.6	177.8	179.1	179.5	178.5	179.2	179.8	175.7
2012	178.3	180.0	182.2	184.8	187.1	188.1	188.0	188.9	188.5	189.4	190.3	190.1	186.3
2013	186.7	187.6	188.5	190.8	192.6	192.5	191.9	193.2	193.0	192.7	194.5	195.7	191.6
Goods-Producing													
2002	31.9	31.9	32.2	32.2	32.4	32.8	33.0	33.2	33.3	33.5	33.5	33.6	32.8
2003	33.5	33.7	33.8	33.6	33.8	33.9	34.5	34.7	34.9	34.7	34.3	34.6	34.2
2004	34.5	34.7	35.3	36.1	36.2	36.8	36.8	36.9	37.2	37.2	36.7	37.2	36.3
2005	36.6	37.0	37.4	38.1	38.5	39.2	40.0	39.7	40.7	40.5	40.6	40.7	39.1
2006	40.6	41.2	41.5	41.5	42.3	42.8	43.2	43.2	43.5	43.1	42.6	42.5	42.3
2007	41.0	41.3	41.6	41.0	41.2	41.4	42.0	42.3	42.2	41.7	41.2	40.9	41.5
2008	40.0	40.0	39.9	40.5	40.7	41.4	41.5	41.5	41.7	41.5	41.1	41.2	40.9
2009	39.0	37.8	37.5	36.6	36.1	36.1	35.5	35.4	35.3	34.7	34.6	34.4	36.1
2010	34.2	33.7	34.3	35.0	35.7	35.9	36.5	36.7	37.1	37.1	36.9	37.4	35.9
2011	36.9	37.1	37.3	38.3	38.6	39.4	39.7	40.1	40.4	40.1	39.9	40.5	39.0
2012	40.8	41.4	42.1	42.9	43.2	43.8	44.5	44.8	44.9	44.5	44.3	43.8	43.4
2013	42.7	42.8	43.2	43.6	43.8	44.2	44.3	44.8	45.0	44.9	44.8	45.0	44.1
Service-Providing													
2002	172.1	172.8	175.1	175.5	176.2	177.3	170.7	171.1	171.8	174.5	176.3	176.8	174.2
2003	173.5	173.6	176.2	175.6	176.4	176.3	172.6	172.8	173.6	175.8	177.0	177.5	175.1
2004	173.0	173.9	175.4	178.0	178.7	181.3	175.7	175.6	177.1	180.2	182.3	182.5	177.8
2005	180.7	181.5	182.6	184.8	186.6	187.3	183.3	184.8	186.7	188.8	190.3	191.3	185.7
2006	189.6	190.5	191.3	192.4	194.2	195.0	190.4	192.7	194.8	197.5	198.9	199.2	193.9
2007	197.4	198.2	199.2	202.0	202.4	202.4	195.9	197.5	200.0	201.3	202.6	203.2	200.2
2008	199.1	200.7	201.6	202.6	203.3	203.3	197.4	197.1	198.8	201.2	202.4	201.0	200.7
2009	197.4	198.0	198.0	198.4	198.8	199.0	188.2	191.4	193.2	193.2	194.1	193.8	195.3
2010	190.7	191.4	194.0	197.6	196.9	197.0	186.8	189.6	192.3	194.0	195.2	196.0	193.5
2011	192.7	194.0	195.5	197.1	198.7	197.8	194.9	196.7	197.2	198.4	199.7	199.6	196.9
2012	196.6	198.4	200.5	201.5	203.7	204.2	198.0	199.3	201.1	204.7	205.9	206.2	201.7
2013	202.5	204.1	205.1	206.8	207.9	205.5	201.8	203.5	205.6	207.1	209.2	210.4	205.8
Mining and Logging													
2002	8.2	8.0	7.9	7.8	7.7	7.8	7.9	7.9	7.9	7.9	7.9	7.9	7.9
2003	7.8	7.9	7.9	7.9	8.0	7.9	8.1	8.1	8.0	8.1	8.0	8.2	8.0
2004	8.0	8.1	8.2	8.1	8.2	8.3	8.1	8.2	8.1	8.1	8.1	8.2	8.1
2005	8.1	8.2	8.3	8.4	8.4	8.4	8.5	8.6	8.7	8.7	8.7	8.8	8.5
2006	8.9	8.9	9.0	9.1	9.2	9.4	9.4	9.6	9.6	9.7	9.7	9.7	9.4
2007	9.5	9.6	9.6	9.6	9.6	9.6	9.9	10.0	9.9	9.9	9.9	10.0	9.8
2008	10.1	10.2	10.3	10.3	10.4	10.5	10.9	10.9	10.9	11.2	11.3	11.2	10.7
2009	10.7	10.4	10.2	10.0	9.9	10.0	9.7	9.5	9.5	9.3	9.3	9.5	9.8
2010	9.4	9.1	9.2	9.5	10.2	10.2	10.6	10.7	10.8	10.7	10.8	11.1	10.2
2011	11.1	11.2	11.4	11.7	11.9	12.0	12.1	12.3	12.4	12.5	12.6	12.7	12.0
2012	12.8	12.9	13.0	13.0	13.1	13.4	13.6	13.7	13.6	13.5	13.5	13.4	13.3
2013	12.8	13.0	13.0	13.1	13.2	13.3	12.9	12.9	12.8	12.8	12.8	12.9	13.0
Construction													
2002	12.9	13.1	13.4	13.3	13.4	13.5	13.4	13.5	13.3	13.3	13.5	13.4	13.3
2003	13.2	13.2	13.3	13.2	13.3	13.4	13.7	13.9	13.9	13.9	13.9	14.0	13.6
2004	14.0	14.1	14.6	15.2	15.2	15.8	15.9	16.0	15.8	16.1	16.0	16.3	15.4
2005	15.9	16.3	16.8	17.4	17.8	18.5	19.0	18.7	19.2	19.3	19.5	19.5	18.2
2006	19.0	19.5	19.7	19.8	20.4	20.7	20.8	20.4	20.4	20.0	19.8	19.7	20.0
2007	18.8	18.9	19.1	18.5	18.7	18.7	18.5	18.6	18.2	18.2	17.7	17.4	18.4
2008	16.5	16.4	16.2	16.6	16.6	16.9	16.9	16.8	16.7	16.5	16.0	16.1	16.5
2009	14.8	14.0	14.0	13.4	13.1	13.1	12.7	12.6	12.4	12.3	12.4	12.2	13.1
2010	12.1	12.0	12.4	12.6	12.7	12.9	12.9	13.0	12.8	12.9	12.9	13.1	12.7
2011	12.8	13.0	13.0	13.6	13.8	14.2	14.5	14.6	14.4	14.4	14.3	14.7	13.9
2012	15.2	15.6	16.1	16.8	17.0	17.0	17.2	17.3	17.1	17.1	17.1	16.7	16.7
2013	16.5	16.4	16.6	16.7	16.9	16.9	17.3	17.7	17.6	17.8	17.7	17.8	17.2

Employment by Industry: Bakersfield–Delano, CA, Selected Years, 2002–2013—*Continued*

(Numbers in thousands, not seasonally adjusted)

Industry and year	January	February	March	April	May	June	July	August	September	October	November	December	Annual average
Manufacturing													
2002	10.8	10.8	10.9	11.1	11.3	11.5	11.7	11.8	12.1	12.3	12.1	12.3	11.6
2003	12.5	12.6	12.6	12.5	12.5	12.6	12.7	12.7	13.0	12.7	12.4	12.4	12.6
2004	12.5	12.5	12.5	12.8	12.8	12.7	12.8	12.7	13.3	13.0	12.6	12.7	12.7
2005	12.6	12.5	12.3	12.3	12.3	12.3	12.5	12.4	12.8	12.5	12.4	12.4	12.4
2006	12.7	12.8	12.8	12.6	12.7	12.7	13.0	13.2	13.5	13.4	13.1	13.1	13.0
2007	12.7	12.8	12.9	12.9	12.9	13.1	13.6	13.7	14.1	13.6	13.6	13.5	13.3
2008	13.4	13.4	13.4	13.6	13.7	14.0	13.7	13.8	14.1	13.8	13.8	13.9	13.7
2009	13.5	13.4	13.3	13.2	13.1	13.0	13.1	13.3	13.4	13.1	12.9	12.7	13.2
2010	12.7	12.6	12.7	12.9	12.8	12.8	13.0	13.0	13.5	13.5	13.2	13.2	13.0
2011	13.0	12.9	12.9	13.0	12.9	13.2	13.1	13.2	13.6	13.2	13.0	13.1	13.1
2012	12.8	12.9	13.0	13.1	13.1	13.4	13.7	13.8	14.2	13.9	13.7	13.7	13.4
2013	13.4	13.4	13.6	13.8	13.7	14.0	14.1	14.2	14.6	14.3	14.3	14.3	14.0
Trade, Transportation, and Utilities													
2002	38.2	38.0	38.4	38.7	38.9	39.2	39.4	39.4	39.5	39.3	39.9	40.5	39.1
2003	38.9	38.9	39.5	39.6	39.7	39.8	40.0	39.8	39.7	40.4	40.5	41.2	39.8
2004	39.5	39.2	39.7	40.7	41.1	41.3	41.7	42.1	41.7	42.2	42.9	42.9	41.3
2005	41.9	41.9	42.2	42.8	43.6	43.5	43.8	44.0	44.4	44.7	45.7	46.8	43.8
2006	45.5	45.2	45.4	45.4	46.5	46.4	46.4	46.7	46.8	46.7	47.9	48.3	46.4
2007	46.3	46.0	46.4	46.6	47.1	46.8	46.7	46.8	46.7	46.7	47.5	47.7	46.8
2008	45.8	45.4	45.5	45.6	46.3	45.9	45.2	45.2	45.1	44.6	45.0	45.0	45.4
2009	43.2	43.1	42.6	43.0	43.5	43.0	43.2	43.7	42.7	42.5	42.5	42.7	43.0
2010	41.7	41.5	41.4	41.9	42.0	42.0	42.8	43.2	43.1	42.2	42.8	43.6	42.4
2011	42.4	42.2	42.2	43.1	43.9	43.6	44.5	44.7	44.6	44.2	44.8	45.1	43.8
2012	43.6	43.4	43.6	44.7	45.3	45.7	45.8	45.8	45.6	45.9	47.2	47.7	45.4
2013	46.0	45.9	46.1	47.0	47.3	47.5	47.5	47.7	47.9	47.9	49.6	50.3	47.6
Wholesale Trade													
2002	6.0	6.0	6.0	6.0	6.0	6.1	6.3	6.3	6.3	6.2	6.0	6.1	6.1
2003	5.9	5.9	6.0	6.1	6.2	6.2	6.3	6.2	6.2	6.3	6.4	6.5	6.2
2004	6.2	6.2	6.2	6.3	6.4	6.5	6.7	6.7	6.6	6.6	6.6	6.6	6.5
2005	6.6	6.6	6.6	6.8	6.8	6.9	6.9	6.9	6.9	7.0	7.0	7.1	6.8
2006	7.2	7.3	7.4	7.4	7.6	7.7	7.7	7.7	7.8	7.8	7.9	7.9	7.6
2007	7.8	7.8	7.9	8.0	8.0	8.1	8.2	8.1	8.1	8.2	8.1	8.0	8.0
2008	8.0	8.0	8.0	8.1	8.2	8.3	8.3	8.3	8.4	8.2	8.2	8.0	8.2
2009	8.1	8.3	8.0	8.1	8.3	8.1	9.0	9.5	8.3	7.9	7.5	7.2	8.2
2010	7.4	7.4	7.1	7.6	7.6	8.0	8.9	9.1	9.1	7.8	7.7	7.7	8.0
2011	7.7	7.6	7.4	7.8	7.9	8.0	8.9	8.8	8.8	8.4	8.0	7.9	8.1
2012	7.9	7.8	7.8	8.3	8.5	8.7	8.6	8.6	8.6	8.6	8.6	8.7	8.4
2013	8.8	8.9	9.0	9.1	9.1	9.2	9.1	9.1	9.2	9.1	9.1	9.2	9.1
Retail Trade													
2002	24.2	23.9	24.3	24.6	24.7	24.9	24.6	24.6	24.7	24.6	25.4	26.0	24.7
2003	24.7	24.6	24.8	24.6	24.7	24.7	24.7	24.6	24.6	25.3	25.5	26.2	24.9
2004	25.1	24.8	25.2	25.9	26.0	26.0	25.9	26.1	26.0	26.4	27.3	27.4	26.0
2005	26.7	26.5	26.8	27.2	27.3	27.4	27.6	27.8	28.1	28.2	29.4	30.4	27.8
2006	29.3	28.8	28.9	28.9	29.2	29.2	29.2	29.5	29.5	29.5	30.6	30.9	29.5
2007	29.4	29.0	29.1	29.2	29.2	29.0	28.8	28.9	28.8	28.6	29.7	30.0	29.1
2008	28.5	28.1	28.2	28.0	28.1	27.9	27.4	27.3	27.0	26.7	27.2	27.5	27.7
2009	25.9	25.7	25.6	25.9	26.0	25.8	25.2	25.2	25.4	25.9	26.5	27.0	25.8
2010	26.0	25.8	26.0	26.0	25.8	25.6	25.4	25.6	25.5	25.8	26.6	27.6	26.0
2011	26.5	26.3	26.5	26.8	27.1	27.0	26.9	27.0	26.8	26.9	28.0	28.4	27.0
2012	27.3	27.0	27.2	27.7	27.8	27.8	27.7	27.7	27.5	27.8	29.2	29.5	27.9
2013	28.1	27.9	28.0	28.6	28.8	28.7	28.9	29.0	28.8	29.0	30.6	31.2	29.0
Transportation and Utilities													
2002	8.0	8.1	8.1	8.1	8.2	8.2	8.5	8.5	8.5	8.5	8.5	8.4	8.3
2003	8.3	8.4	8.7	8.9	8.8	8.9	9.0	9.0	8.9	8.8	8.6	8.5	8.7
2004	8.2	8.2	8.3	8.5	8.7	8.8	9.1	9.3	9.1	9.2	9.0	8.9	8.8
2005	8.6	8.8	8.8	8.8	9.5	9.2	9.3	9.3	9.4	9.5	9.3	9.3	9.2
2006	9.0	9.1	9.1	9.1	9.7	9.5	9.5	9.5	9.5	9.4	9.4	9.5	9.4
2007	9.1	9.2	9.4	9.4	9.9	9.7	9.7	9.8	9.8	9.9	9.7	9.7	9.6
2008	9.3	9.3	9.3	9.5	10.0	9.7	9.5	9.6	9.7	9.7	9.6	9.5	9.6
2009	9.2	9.1	9.0	9.0	9.2	9.1	9.0	9.0	9.0	8.7	8.5	8.5	8.9
2010	8.3	8.3	8.3	8.3	8.6	8.4	8.5	8.5	8.5	8.6	8.5	8.3	8.4
2011	8.2	8.3	8.3	8.5	8.9	8.6	8.7	8.9	9.0	8.9	8.8	8.8	8.7
2012	8.4	8.6	8.6	8.7	9.0	9.2	9.5	9.5	9.5	9.5	9.4	9.5	9.1
2013	9.1	9.1	9.1	9.3	9.4	9.6	9.5	9.6	9.9	9.8	9.9	9.9	9.5
Information													
2002	2.6	2.6	2.6	2.6	2.6	2.6	2.5	2.4	2.4	2.5	2.5	2.5	2.5
2003	2.6	2.6	2.6	2.6	2.6	2.5	2.5	2.5	2.5	2.5	2.5	2.5	2.5
2004	2.5	2.5	2.5	2.5	2.5	2.6	2.6	2.5	2.5	2.5	2.5	2.6	2.5
2005	2.5	2.5	2.5	2.5	2.5	2.5	2.6	2.5	2.6	2.5	2.6	2.6	2.5
2006	2.6	2.7	2.6	2.6	2.7	2.7	2.7	2.7	2.6	2.6	2.7	2.7	2.7
2007	2.8	2.8	2.7	2.8	2.8	2.9	2.8	2.9	2.8	2.8	2.9	2.9	2.8
2008	2.9	3.0	3.0	3.1	3.1	3.1	3.0	3.0	3.0	3.0	3.0	2.9	3.0
2009	2.8	2.8	2.8	2.8	2.8	2.8	2.8	2.7	2.7	2.7	2.7	2.7	2.8
2010	2.7	2.6	2.6	2.6	2.6	2.6	2.9	2.8	2.7	2.7	2.7	2.8	2.7
2011	2.7	2.6	2.6	2.6	2.6	2.6	2.7	2.6	2.6	2.6	2.6	2.6	2.6
2012	2.7	2.7	2.7	2.7	2.7	2.8	2.6	2.6	2.6	2.6	2.7	2.7	2.7
2013	2.7	2.6	2.5	2.6	2.6	2.6	2.6	2.5	2.5	2.5	2.5	2.5	2.6

Employment by Industry: Bakersfield–Delano, CA, Selected Years, 2002–2013—*Continued*

(Numbers in thousands, not seasonally adjusted)

Industry and year	January	February	March	April	May	June	July	August	September	October	November	December	Annual average
Financial Activities													
2002	7.7	7.8	7.9	8.0	8.0	8.0	8.0	8.0	8.0	8.0	8.1	8.2	8.0
2003	8.1	8.1	8.2	8.2	8.3	8.4	8.4	8.5	8.4	8.4	8.4	8.4	8.3
2004	8.4	8.4	8.5	8.7	8.6	8.6	8.7	8.7	8.7	8.6	8.6	8.6	8.6
2005	8.6	8.5	8.6	8.6	8.7	8.8	8.9	8.9	8.8	8.7	8.8	8.8	8.7
2006	8.9	8.9	8.9	8.9	9.1	9.1	9.0	9.0	8.9	9.0	9.0	9.0	9.0
2007	9.1	9.2	9.2	9.1	9.1	9.2	9.1	9.1	9.0	9.0	8.9	8.9	9.1
2008	8.8	8.8	8.9	9.0	9.0	8.9	8.9	8.9	8.9	8.8	8.8	8.8	8.9
2009	8.7	8.7	8.5	8.5	8.5	8.5	8.5	8.5	8.4	8.4	8.2	8.3	8.5
2010	8.2	8.3	8.3	8.3	8.3	8.3	8.2	8.1	8.1	8.0	7.9	7.9	8.2
2011	7.8	8.0	8.0	8.1	8.3	8.2	8.5	8.6	8.5	8.5	8.5	8.4	8.3
2012	8.4	8.5	8.5	8.8	9.0	8.9	8.9	8.9	8.8	8.8	8.7	8.7	8.7
2013	8.8	8.8	8.7	8.9	9.0	8.9	8.9	8.9	8.8	8.8	8.8	8.8	8.8
Professional and Business Services													
2002	23.2	23.3	23.4	22.8	22.6	22.6	21.9	22.3	21.9	21.6	21.4	21.3	22.4
2003	20.7	20.7	21.2	21.3	21.5	21.8	21.8	22.1	22.3	22.1	22.3	22.3	21.7
2004	21.1	21.5	21.6	21.8	21.8	21.7	21.5	21.9	21.6	21.9	22.1	22.2	21.7
2005	22.1	22.1	22.0	22.8	22.8	23.0	23.4	23.6	23.9	23.4	23.8	23.6	23.0
2006	23.7	24.0	24.1	24.3	24.8	25.0	25.3	25.6	25.9	26.0	25.8	25.7	25.0
2007	26.0	26.3	26.2	26.5	26.5	26.3	26.2	26.5	26.7	25.3	25.3	25.4	26.1
2008	24.7	25.2	25.2	25.4	25.1	25.1	25.0	25.1	25.1	25.0	24.9	24.5	25.0
2009	24.6	24.0	24.0	23.7	23.8	23.9	23.3	23.5	23.6	23.2	23.7	23.3	23.7
2010	23.3	23.1	23.5	24.4	24.0	24.3	23.6	23.6	23.6	24.1	24.5	24.4	23.9
2011	24.3	24.7	25.1	25.2	25.0	24.9	25.5	25.6	26.0	25.7	25.9	25.6	25.3
2012	25.4	26.1	26.8	26.4	26.8	26.9	26.9	26.9	26.8	26.6	26.4	26.2	26.5
2013	25.9	26.3	26.3	26.3	26.7	26.6	26.2	26.5	26.1	26.0	26.4	26.8	26.3
Education and Health Services													
2002	21.7	22.0	22.1	22.4	22.7	22.8	22.4	22.6	22.6	22.7	22.8	22.9	22.5
2003	22.7	23.0	23.1	23.1	23.4	23.3	23.3	23.4	23.4	23.4	23.4	23.6	23.3
2004	23.3	23.3	23.5	23.6	23.7	23.8	23.8	24.0	23.9	23.9	24.0	24.2	23.8
2005	24.0	24.2	24.3	24.6	24.8	24.7	25.0	25.0	24.9	25.0	25.0	25.1	24.7
2006	25.1	25.3	25.3	25.3	25.3	25.6	25.4	25.7	25.8	26.2	26.4	26.5	25.7
2007	26.7	27.1	27.1	26.9	26.8	26.9	27.2	27.3	27.5	27.5	27.6	27.8	27.2
2008	27.8	28.0	28.2	28.3	28.3	28.3	28.3	28.7	28.6	28.7	28.8	28.9	28.4
2009	28.5	28.8	29.0	29.0	29.1	29.4	28.8	29.1	28.9	29.1	28.8	28.8	28.9
2010	28.3	28.4	28.5	28.6	28.4	28.5	28.7	28.9	28.7	29.0	28.9	29.0	28.7
2011	28.7	28.8	28.8	29.0	29.2	29.0	29.2	29.5	29.7	29.6	29.6	29.8	29.2
2012	29.8	30.0	30.2	30.5	30.8	30.6	30.3	30.7	30.8	31.8	31.7	31.8	30.8
2013	31.4	31.8	31.9	32.1	32.3	31.8	31.8	32.1	32.1	32.0	31.8	31.8	31.9
Leisure and Hospitality													
2002	16.8	16.9	17.3	17.6	18.1	18.2	17.9	17.9	17.8	17.7	17.6	17.7	17.6
2003	17.3	17.4	17.9	17.9	18.3	18.3	18.4	18.3	18.1	18.3	18.2	18.0	18.0
2004	17.6	18.1	18.4	19.0	19.4	19.4	19.3	19.3	19.3	19.1	19.3	19.4	19.0
2005	19.3	19.3	19.6	20.1	20.5	20.9	20.6	20.5	20.3	20.0	20.1	20.3	20.1
2006	19.6	19.9	20.2	20.9	21.0	21.3	21.0	20.9	20.9	20.6	20.7	20.9	20.7
2007	20.5	20.7	21.2	21.7	21.9	22.1	21.7	21.7	21.8	21.7	21.6	21.6	21.5
2008	20.9	21.2	21.4	21.8	22.0	22.1	22.0	21.9	21.5	21.2	21.2	21.0	21.5
2009	20.6	20.9	21.2	21.5	21.7	21.7	21.0	20.8	20.8	20.4	20.4	20.4	21.0
2010	19.7	20.0	20.4	20.8	20.8	21.1	20.8	20.6	20.7	20.4	20.4	20.1	20.5
2011	19.8	20.1	20.4	20.7	21.1	21.2	21.0	21.0	20.7	20.9	20.9	20.8	20.7
2012	20.6	20.8	21.2	21.6	22.0	22.2	22.0	21.9	21.7	21.8	21.9	21.9	21.6
2013	21.9	22.0	22.3	22.7	23.2	23.5	23.3	23.1	23.0	23.0	23.0	23.0	22.8
Other Services													
2002	6.8	6.9	6.9	6.8	7.0	6.8	6.8	6.8	6.7	7.0	7.1	6.9	6.9
2003	6.7	6.8	6.9	6.9	7.0	6.9	6.8	6.8	7.0	7.0	6.9	6.9	6.9
2004	6.9	6.9	6.9	7.0	7.0	6.9	6.8	6.8	7.0	7.2	7.4	7.1	7.0
2005	7.0	7.0	7.1	7.2	7.3	7.2	7.0	7.0	7.2	7.1	6.8	6.8	7.1
2006	6.7	6.8	6.9	7.0	7.0	6.8	6.7	7.0	6.9	6.7	6.6	6.5	6.8
2007	6.5	6.5	6.7	6.6	6.6	6.5	6.7	6.8	6.9	7.0	7.0	7.0	6.7
2008	6.7	6.9	6.9	7.0	7.2	7.2	6.8	7.0	7.0	7.2	7.1	7.0	7.0
2009	6.7	6.8	6.7	6.8	6.8	6.7	6.5	6.7	6.7	6.8	6.7	6.6	6.7
2010	6.6	6.7	6.8	6.8	6.7	6.7	6.4	6.6	6.6	6.6	6.5	6.5	6.6
2011	6.5	6.5	6.6	6.7	6.8	6.7	6.7	7.0	7.0	6.9	7.0	7.0	6.8
2012	7.0	7.1	7.1	7.2	7.3	7.2	7.0	7.3	7.3	7.4	7.4	7.3	7.2
2013	7.3	7.4	7.5	7.6	7.7	7.4	7.3	7.6	7.6	7.6	7.6	7.5	7.5
Government													
2002	55.1	55.3	56.5	56.6	56.3	57.1	51.8	51.7	52.9	55.7	56.9	56.8	55.2
2003	56.5	56.1	56.8	56.0	55.6	55.3	51.4	51.4	52.2	53.7	54.8	54.6	54.5
2004	53.7	54.0	54.3	54.7	54.6	57.0	51.3	50.3	52.4	54.8	55.5	55.5	54.0
2005	55.3	56.0	56.3	56.2	56.4	56.7	52.0	53.3	54.6	57.4	57.5	57.3	55.8
2006	57.5	57.7	57.9	58.0	57.8	58.1	53.9	55.1	57.0	59.7	59.8	59.6	57.7
2007	59.5	59.6	59.7	61.8	61.6	61.7	55.5	56.4	58.6	61.3	61.8	61.9	60.0
2008	61.5	62.2	62.5	62.4	62.3	62.7	58.2	57.3	59.6	62.7	63.6	62.9	61.5
2009	62.3	62.9	63.2	63.1	62.6	63.0	54.1	56.4	59.4	60.1	61.1	61.0	60.8
2010	60.2	60.8	62.5	64.2	64.1	63.5	53.4	55.8	58.8	61.0	61.5	61.7	60.6
2011	60.5	61.1	61.8	61.7	61.8	61.6	56.8	57.7	58.1	60.0	60.4	60.3	60.2
2012	59.1	59.8	60.4	59.6	59.8	59.9	54.5	55.2	57.5	59.8	59.9	59.9	58.8
2013	58.5	59.3	59.8	59.6	59.1	57.2	54.2	55.1	57.6	59.3	59.5	59.7	58.2

Employment by Industry: Baltimore–Towson, MD, Selected Years, 2002–2013

(Numbers in thousands, not seasonally adjusted)

Industry and year	January	February	March	April	May	June	July	August	September	October	November	December	Annual average
Total Nonfarm													
2002	1,227.4	1,234.3	1,246.7	1,248.7	1,258.7	1,265.0	1,252.5	1,249.5	1,251.3	1,254.2	1,260.2	1,261.2	1,250.8
2003	1,225.0	1,222.6	1,235.1	1,247.5	1,256.4	1,251.6	1,240.6	1,251.9	1,255.0	1,260.2	1,266.2	1,269.6	1,248.5
2004	1,233.6	1,234.8	1,250.8	1,258.3	1,266.1	1,276.1	1,266.1	1,265.3	1,266.0	1,275.7	1,281.7	1,285.1	1,263.3
2005	1,247.7	1,255.1	1,263.3	1,278.6	1,286.7	1,293.2	1,290.8	1,286.0	1,299.1	1,300.4	1,306.6	1,311.5	1,284.9
2006	1,274.0	1,280.2	1,295.2	1,304.0	1,311.5	1,316.7	1,305.5	1,304.0	1,308.6	1,317.0	1,323.2	1,330.3	1,305.9
2007	1,291.2	1,292.8	1,309.0	1,315.2	1,324.3	1,328.2	1,318.2	1,317.9	1,319.2	1,323.9	1,330.3	1,334.2	1,317.0
2008	1,297.0	1,301.6	1,311.4	1,320.6	1,325.2	1,325.0	1,316.2	1,313.2	1,311.2	1,316.8	1,313.1	1,311.7	1,313.6
2009	1,264.3	1,263.5	1,268.4	1,276.9	1,282.2	1,284.5	1,269.1	1,263.9	1,268.6	1,277.2	1,278.0	1,278.6	1,272.9
2010	1,240.8	1,229.6	1,259.4	1,278.4	1,284.8	1,288.0	1,274.4	1,272.0	1,273.6	1,287.8	1,290.7	1,291.9	1,272.6
2011	1,257.6	1,264.7	1,279.2	1,294.7	1,298.4	1,300.5	1,292.6	1,290.9	1,297.4	1,307.1	1,312.3	1,315.5	1,292.6
2012	1,284.6	1,290.9	1,304.0	1,312.5	1,319.6	1,321.9	1,311.2	1,311.7	1,320.2	1,328.4	1,334.0	1,337.1	1,314.7
2013	1,302.1	1,310.3	1,322.5	1,331.5	1,341.0	1,341.1	1,325.5	1,324.9	1,336.2	1,349.5	1,356.3	1,353.3	1,332.9
Total Private													
2002	1,006.9	1,010.1	1,020.4	1,025.4	1,034.9	1,044.0	1,037.2	1,037.6	1,031.3	1,029.6	1,035.1	1,037.6	1,029.2
2003	1,006.6	1,000.4	1,011.0	1,024.1	1,033.8	1,036.2	1,030.8	1,035.2	1,037.6	1,039.5	1,044.8	1,049.5	1,029.1
2004	1,018.8	1,018.5	1,031.6	1,038.3	1,047.0	1,059.1	1,058.4	1,058.0	1,053.2	1,057.7	1,061.5	1,065.7	1,047.3
2005	1,034.1	1,037.0	1,045.2	1,058.7	1,065.9	1,075.1	1,080.7	1,080.2	1,082.0	1,078.4	1,082.6	1,088.1	1,067.3
2006	1,058.8	1,060.1	1,073.1	1,080.6	1,087.9	1,097.3	1,092.2	1,091.5	1,089.9	1,092.2	1,096.5	1,103.2	1,085.3
2007	1,072.1	1,068.9	1,082.6	1,089.9	1,098.3	1,106.7	1,103.6	1,103.6	1,099.8	1,098.6	1,103.2	1,107.6	1,094.6
2008	1,077.7	1,076.7	1,084.9	1,092.1	1,096.5	1,101.0	1,097.4	1,095.5	1,088.2	1,086.8	1,082.5	1,081.1	1,088.4
2009	1,041.1	1,035.1	1,038.2	1,044.8	1,050.3	1,056.5	1,047.2	1,044.7	1,043.8	1,042.6	1,043.6	1,044.8	1,044.4
2010	1,014.0	998.1	1,024.0	1,040.8	1,046.0	1,052.7	1,047.9	1,047.0	1,044.9	1,051.6	1,052.8	1,056.4	1,039.7
2011	1,028.1	1,029.6	1,040.0	1,055.2	1,061.1	1,066.9	1,068.6	1,066.8	1,067.0	1,069.1	1,075.5	1,078.8	1,058.9
2012	1,054.7	1,055.1	1,065.0	1,074.8	1,083.4	1,091.9	1,088.1	1,090.0	1,090.1	1,091.5	1,097.0	1,100.7	1,081.9
2013	1,073.5	1,076.1	1,086.2	1,094.9	1,105.3	1,111.6	1,110.1	1,110.9	1,108.5	1,117.0	1,123.0	1,120.3	1,103.1
Goods-Producing													
2002	156.2	157.2	158.4	159.6	160.4	162.1	160.3	160.8	159.3	157.8	157.5	156.4	158.8
2003	152.9	150.9	151.9	153.2	154.3	155.9	155.4	156.1	155.4	154.9	154.8	154.6	154.2
2004	150.0	149.0	152.0	154.1	155.4	157.4	158.5	159.1	158.2	158.1	158.1	158.6	155.7
2005	154.2	153.6	154.9	158.0	159.1	160.9	161.1	161.7	161.7	160.3	160.8	160.9	158.9
2006	157.0	156.5	158.6	159.3	159.9	161.9	161.8	161.8	160.9	159.1	158.4	158.1	159.4
2007	154.4	152.5	155.0	155.9	157.4	159.3	159.8	159.9	158.5	156.8	156.2	155.3	156.8
2008	152.4	151.3	151.9	151.8	151.9	153.3	153.8	153.5	151.7	149.6	147.8	145.6	151.2
2009	138.7	136.6	135.9	135.3	135.8	137.1	136.7	136.1	134.8	133.8	132.8	132.1	135.5
2010	127.6	123.1	126.7	130.1	131.0	132.6	132.5	132.5	131.5	130.9	130.4	130.0	129.9
2011	126.8	126.2	127.5	130.2	130.9	132.3	133.0	132.6	131.1	130.6	130.0	129.7	130.1
2012	126.5	125.4	126.4	127.3	127.6	129.4	129.9	129.9	128.2	127.6	127.8	127.6	127.8
2013	124.5	123.7	124.7	127.0	127.9	129.6	130.6	131.0	130.0	132.5	131.5	130.2	128.6
Service-Providing													
2002	1,071.2	1,077.1	1,088.3	1,089.1	1,098.3	1,102.9	1,092.2	1,088.7	1,092.0	1,096.4	1,102.7	1,104.8	1,092.0
2003	1,072.1	1,071.7	1,083.2	1,094.3	1,102.1	1,095.7	1,085.2	1,095.8	1,099.6	1,105.3	1,111.4	1,115.0	1,094.3
2004	1,083.6	1,085.8	1,098.8	1,104.2	1,110.7	1,118.7	1,107.6	1,106.2	1,107.8	1,117.6	1,123.6	1,126.5	1,107.6
2005	1,093.5	1,101.5	1,108.4	1,120.6	1,127.6	1,132.3	1,129.7	1,124.3	1,137.4	1,140.1	1,145.8	1,150.6	1,126.0
2006	1,117.0	1,123.7	1,136.6	1,144.7	1,151.6	1,154.8	1,143.7	1,142.2	1,147.7	1,157.9	1,164.8	1,172.2	1,146.4
2007	1,136.8	1,140.3	1,154.0	1,159.3	1,166.9	1,168.9	1,158.4	1,158.0	1,160.7	1,167.1	1,174.1	1,178.9	1,160.3
2008	1,144.6	1,150.3	1,159.5	1,168.8	1,173.3	1,171.7	1,162.4	1,159.7	1,159.5	1,167.2	1,165.3	1,166.1	1,162.4
2009	1,125.6	1,126.9	1,132.5	1,141.6	1,146.4	1,147.4	1,132.4	1,127.8	1,133.8	1,143.4	1,145.2	1,146.5	1,137.5
2010	1,113.2	1,106.5	1,132.7	1,148.3	1,153.8	1,155.4	1,141.9	1,139.5	1,142.1	1,156.9	1,160.3	1,161.9	1,142.7
2011	1,130.8	1,138.5	1,151.7	1,164.5	1,167.5	1,168.2	1,159.6	1,158.3	1,166.3	1,176.5	1,182.3	1,185.8	1,162.5
2012	1,158.1	1,165.5	1,177.6	1,185.2	1,192.0	1,192.5	1,181.3	1,181.8	1,192.0	1,200.8	1,206.2	1,209.5	1,186.9
2013	1,177.6	1,186.6	1,197.8	1,204.5	1,213.1	1,211.5	1,194.9	1,193.9	1,206.2	1,217.0	1,224.8	1,223.1	1,204.3
Mining, Logging, and Construction													
2002	69.6	70.1	71.7	73.1	74.1	75.5	76.0	76.4	75.5	75.2	75.0	74.1	73.9
2003	71.3	69.6	70.6	72.2	73.9	75.4	76.6	77.5	77.3	77.3	77.4	77.4	74.7
2004	74.0	73.1	76.0	77.9	79.1	80.9	81.8	82.4	81.9	81.9	81.9	82.2	79.4
2005	78.9	78.1	79.4	82.3	83.6	85.3	85.9	86.3	86.3	85.6	86.0	85.9	83.6
2006	83.2	82.9	84.7	85.8	86.7	88.4	88.4	88.6	88.0	87.1	86.6	86.3	86.4
2007	83.2	81.5	83.9	84.9	86.2	87.7	88.2	88.4	87.4	86.0	85.5	84.3	85.6
2008	82.1	81.1	81.9	82.4	82.5	83.6	84.4	84.2	83.0	81.8	80.5	78.5	82.2
2009	73.2	72.0	71.6	71.7	72.2	73.4	73.5	72.9	71.7	70.8	70.0	69.2	71.9
2010	65.2	61.7	64.9	68.1	68.9	70.1	69.9	69.9	69.4	69.2	69.1	68.5	67.9
2011	64.8	64.2	65.4	67.6	68.5	69.8	70.7	70.5	69.8	69.8	69.5	69.2	68.3
2012	66.4	65.6	66.7	67.7	68.1	69.4	69.8	70.0	69.9	69.6	69.8	69.4	68.5
2013	66.9	66.1	67.1	69.5	70.4	71.7	72.5	72.9	72.5	75.1	74.7	73.8	71.1
Manufacturing													
2002	86.6	87.1	86.7	86.5	86.3	86.6	84.3	84.4	83.8	82.6	82.5	82.3	85.0
2003	81.6	81.3	81.3	81.0	80.4	80.5	78.8	78.6	78.1	77.6	77.4	77.2	79.5
2004	76.0	75.9	76.0	76.2	76.3	76.5	76.7	76.7	76.3	76.2	76.2	76.4	76.3
2005	75.3	75.5	75.5	75.7	75.5	75.6	75.2	75.4	75.4	74.7	74.8	75.0	75.3
2006	73.8	73.6	73.9	73.5	73.2	73.5	73.4	73.2	72.9	72.0	71.8	71.8	73.1
2007	71.2	71.0	71.1	71.0	71.2	71.6	71.6	71.5	71.1	70.8	70.7	71.0	71.2
2008	70.3	70.2	70.0	69.4	69.4	69.7	69.4	69.3	68.7	67.8	67.3	67.1	69.1
2009	65.5	64.6	64.3	63.6	63.6	63.7	63.2	63.2	63.1	63.0	62.8	62.9	63.6
2010	62.4	61.4	61.8	62.0	62.1	62.5	62.6	62.6	62.1	61.7	61.3	61.5	62.0
2011	62.0	62.0	62.1	62.6	62.4	62.5	62.3	62.1	61.3	60.8	60.5	60.5	61.8
2012	60.1	59.8	59.7	59.6	59.5	60.0	60.1	59.9	58.3	58.0	58.0	58.2	59.3
2013	57.6	57.6	57.6	57.5	57.5	57.9	58.1	58.1	57.5	57.4	56.8	56.4	57.5

Employment by Industry: Baltimore–Towson, MD, Selected Years, 2002–2013—*Continued*

(Numbers in thousands, not seasonally adjusted)

Industry and year	January	February	March	April	May	June	July	August	September	October	November	December	Annual average
Trade, Transportation, and Utilities													
2002	236.5	233.4	235.4	236.2	238.1	239.9	236.4	236.3	237.3	237.8	241.3	245.6	237.9
2003	234.2	231.2	233.0	234.0	236.5	238.3	236.1	237.8	238.9	241.1	246.2	250.1	238.1
2004	239.5	237.6	239.2	239.0	240.4	242.8	239.8	239.8	239.9	242.0	246.2	249.9	241.3
2005	239.1	237.1	238.1	239.2	240.9	242.7	242.8	242.2	243.4	244.4	248.4	253.1	242.6
2006	243.7	241.4	243.3	243.6	245.2	246.8	244.2	244.0	243.8	246.6	251.9	256.5	245.9
2007	246.3	242.3	244.4	243.7	246.9	247.9	246.2	245.3	244.8	246.1	251.2	255.7	246.7
2008	244.1	240.4	241.4	240.2	241.2	242.4	240.5	239.9	238.6	238.8	240.4	242.7	240.9
2009	231.5	227.5	226.8	226.5	227.4	229.0	225.0	224.8	225.6	226.2	230.3	231.8	227.7
2010	221.5	216.1	220.9	224.7	225.7	226.4	224.8	224.8	224.4	228.1	231.7	235.0	225.3
2011	226.1	224.2	225.7	228.4	229.7	230.5	229.4	230.0	230.0	231.4	236.7	240.4	230.2
2012	230.6	228.1	230.0	231.2	232.8	233.3	231.4	231.5	232.7	233.8	239.5	242.3	233.1
2013	234.3	231.6	232.7	233.2	235.1	236.0	234.4	234.3	234.6	236.9	242.8	243.8	235.8
Wholesale Trade													
2002	54.6	54.6	54.6	54.2	54.3	54.4	54.3	54.5	54.4	54.2	54.1	54.3	54.4
2003	53.3	52.9	53.3	53.2	53.4	53.6	53.3	53.3	53.3	53.1	53.1	53.2	53.3
2004	52.6	52.9	53.3	53.5	53.6	53.9	53.9	53.9	53.8	54.1	54.0	54.2	53.6
2005	54.3	54.4	54.5	54.8	55.1	55.6	55.9	55.7	55.8	56.0	56.1	56.5	55.4
2006	56.0	56.3	56.4	56.7	56.7	57.0	56.8	56.8	56.7	56.7	56.6	56.9	56.6
2007	55.9	56.0	56.0	56.2	56.4	56.5	56.4	56.3	56.1	55.8	55.8	56.1	56.1
2008	55.5	55.3	55.7	55.7	55.9	56.0	55.5	55.3	55.0	54.8	54.4	54.2	55.3
2009	53.6	53.3	52.9	52.7	52.5	52.4	51.8	51.7	51.6	51.6	51.4	51.3	52.2
2010	50.3	50.1	50.5	51.0	51.2	51.1	51.2	51.0	50.6	51.1	51.2	51.3	50.9
2011	50.9	51.1	51.3	51.7	51.9	52.0	52.0	51.9	51.6	51.4	51.4	51.5	51.6
2012	51.0	51.1	51.5	52.2	52.6	52.8	52.6	52.6	52.3	52.4	52.4	52.6	52.2
2013	51.9	52.1	52.2	52.6	52.7	52.9	52.8	52.7	52.6	52.0	51.7	51.5	52.3
Retail Trade													
2002	141.0	138.2	140.1	139.7	140.8	142.6	141.3	140.9	141.0	141.3	145.3	148.9	141.8
2003	140.1	137.7	138.4	139.8	141.2	142.8	142.2	143.7	143.5	144.8	149.9	153.3	143.1
2004	144.4	142.3	143.4	142.3	143.2	145.1	143.0	143.2	142.2	143.9	148.2	151.3	144.4
2005	140.7	138.7	139.3	140.6	141.6	142.5	143.2	143.2	142.9	143.7	147.7	151.2	142.9
2006	143.6	140.6	142.1	141.9	143.1	144.0	142.8	142.6	141.6	144.4	149.8	153.1	144.1
2007	145.1	141.2	142.8	142.1	144.4	144.9	144.4	144.1	143.0	144.6	149.7	153.2	145.0
2008	143.8	140.3	141.1	140.6	141.0	141.8	141.0	140.7	139.0	139.6	141.7	143.4	141.2
2009	135.0	131.8	131.7	131.8	132.9	133.7	132.4	132.3	131.8	132.7	136.5	138.2	133.4
2010	130.1	125.7	129.0	130.5	131.7	132.3	131.9	132.1	130.9	133.4	137.1	139.7	132.0
2011	132.4	130.5	131.6	132.5	133.5	134.2	133.4	134.0	133.3	135.4	140.0	143.0	134.5
2012	135.1	132.5	133.9	133.9	134.9	135.1	134.4	134.5	134.4	135.6	140.4	142.2	135.6
2013	136.9	134.7	135.3	135.5	136.6	137.4	137.5	137.6	136.4	139.6	145.2	146.1	138.2
Transportation and Utilities													
2002	40.9	40.6	40.7	42.3	43.0	42.9	40.8	40.9	41.9	42.3	41.9	42.4	41.7
2003	40.8	40.6	41.3	41.0	41.9	41.9	40.6	40.8	42.1	43.2	43.2	43.6	41.8
2004	42.5	42.4	42.5	43.2	43.6	43.8	42.9	42.7	43.9	44.0	44.0	44.4	43.3
2005	44.1	44.0	44.3	43.8	44.2	44.6	43.7	43.3	44.7	44.7	44.6	45.4	44.3
2006	44.1	44.5	44.8	45.0	45.4	45.8	44.6	44.6	45.5	45.5	45.5	46.5	45.2
2007	45.3	45.1	45.6	45.4	46.1	46.5	45.4	44.9	45.7	45.7	45.7	46.4	45.7
2008	44.8	44.8	44.6	43.9	44.3	44.6	44.0	43.9	44.6	44.4	44.3	45.1	44.4
2009	42.9	42.4	42.2	42.0	42.0	42.9	40.8	40.8	42.2	41.9	42.4	42.3	42.1
2010	41.1	40.3	41.4	43.2	42.8	43.0	41.7	41.7	42.9	43.6	43.4	44.0	42.4
2011	42.8	42.6	42.8	44.2	44.3	44.3	44.0	44.1	45.1	44.6	45.3	45.9	44.2
2012	44.5	44.5	44.6	45.1	45.3	45.4	44.4	44.4	46.0	45.8	46.7	47.5	45.4
2013	45.5	44.8	45.2	45.1	45.8	45.7	44.1	44.0	45.6	45.3	45.9	46.2	45.3
Information													
2002	22.5	22.5	22.4	22.3	22.3	22.2	21.7	21.8	21.2	20.6	21.1	20.8	21.8
2003	20.8	20.8	20.8	21.1	21.4	21.2	21.2	21.0	20.7	20.7	21.2	21.3	21.0
2004	21.2	20.8	21.1	21.0	21.2	21.5	21.0	21.3	21.0	21.0	21.2	21.0	21.1
2005	20.8	20.9	21.0	21.2	21.3	21.6	22.2	22.6	22.2	22.2	22.2	22.2	21.7
2006	21.6	21.8	21.9	21.9	22.1	22.3	22.1	22.2	22.3	22.2	22.7	22.9	22.2
2007	22.4	22.6	23.1	23.1	23.3	24.0	23.7	24.1	24.1	23.1	23.6	23.6	23.4
2008	23.1	23.1	23.4	23.2	23.3	22.9	22.7	23.0	22.8	22.1	22.4	22.3	22.9
2009	21.3	21.3	21.5	20.6	20.5	20.8	20.1	20.3	19.9	19.5	19.7	19.6	20.4
2010	19.4	19.8	21.1	20.8	20.9	21.3	20.0	19.3	19.3	18.9	18.5	19.3	19.9
2011	17.7	18.1	18.2	17.7	17.8	17.5	17.5	16.6	17.1	17.2	17.6	17.3	17.5
2012	17.1	17.1	17.1	16.7	16.7	17.2	17.2	17.2	17.1	16.8	16.9	17.6	17.1
2013	17.0	16.9	16.9	16.7	16.7	16.8	16.8	16.8	16.6	16.5	16.6	16.5	16.7
Financial Activities													
2002	79.0	79.1	79.3	79.5	79.8	80.6	80.6	80.7	80.8	80.5	81.0	81.3	80.2
2003	81.0	81.0	81.5	81.8	82.3	83.2	83.4	83.7	83.1	82.0	82.3	82.5	82.3
2004	81.4	81.6	82.1	82.1	82.2	82.4	82.2	82.3	81.7	82.0	81.9	82.0	82.0
2005	81.0	81.7	81.7	82.3	82.4	83.0	83.7	84.1	83.7	83.0	83.2	83.6	82.8
2006	82.8	82.9	83.2	82.9	82.7	83.3	83.1	82.8	82.4	82.0	81.8	82.4	82.7
2007	81.6	81.6	81.7	81.7	81.8	82.2	82.1	81.7	80.8	80.4	80.2	80.5	81.4
2008	79.2	79.5	79.7	79.2	79.3	79.7	79.1	78.8	78.1	78.2	77.5	77.7	78.8
2009	75.9	75.7	75.4	75.3	75.2	75.5	74.8	74.8	74.4	74.5	74.6	74.6	75.1
2010	73.4	72.9	73.3	73.2	73.4	74.0	74.2	74.3	74.0	74.4	74.5	75.0	73.9
2011	73.9	74.0	74.5	74.6	74.6	74.9	74.8	74.5	74.1	74.2	74.1	74.0	74.4
2012	74.0	73.9	73.7	73.7	74.1	74.6	75.1	75.4	75.2	75.2	75.7	75.9	74.7
2013	75.4	75.5	75.5	75.8	75.9	76.4	76.9	76.8	76.4	76.4	76.4	76.8	76.2

Employment by Industry: Baltimore–Towson, MD, Selected Years, 2002–2013—*Continued*

(Numbers in thousands, not seasonally adjusted)

Industry and year	January	February	March	April	May	June	July	August	September	October	November	December	Annual average
Professional and Business Services													
2002	171.2	171.8	174.0	174.4	176.5	177.5	177.2	178.7	176.1	175.1	175.3	175.0	175.2
2003	168.8	166.8	169.5	173.9	175.2	176.1	174.1	175.9	174.9	177.1	176.5	177.0	173.8
2004	171.4	172.0	174.9	175.8	178.3	180.4	181.8	181.9	180.0	181.8	181.8	181.7	178.5
2005	177.3	178.5	181.2	183.0	184.6	185.7	189.8	190.4	190.5	189.5	188.8	188.3	185.6
2006	182.0	183.5	186.6	188.9	190.1	191.5	191.6	192.0	191.4	191.3	190.8	191.3	189.3
2007	185.5	185.5	188.1	191.1	191.7	193.5	193.1	194.9	194.5	194.6	195.1	195.1	191.9
2008	190.4	190.6	192.4	194.7	195.6	195.9	196.1	196.8	194.7	193.5	191.0	188.9	193.4
2009	182.0	180.0	180.4	183.1	182.9	184.7	184.8	185.4	184.2	184.6	183.7	183.3	183.3
2010	177.9	175.6	180.7	184.6	185.0	188.0	186.9	188.0	187.0	189.7	189.1	189.0	185.1
2011	184.2	184.2	186.7	192.4	193.7	196.5	198.5	200.2	201.0	202.4	203.9	204.3	195.7
2012	200.1	199.8	202.0	204.2	206.8	208.6	208.2	211.6	211.9	212.0	213.7	212.7	207.6
2013	207.7	208.9	211.8	212.5	214.3	217.5	216.2	218.7	218.8	218.4	219.2	220.7	215.4
Education and Health Services													
2002	191.7	195.7	196.5	195.3	195.2	194.4	193.4	192.3	194.4	198.0	200.2	200.3	195.6
2003	195.4	197.6	198.8	199.5	199.3	192.1	191.7	191.8	199.4	201.8	203.0	203.7	197.8
2004	200.8	202.1	203.2	203.3	203.1	203.2	203.7	202.1	204.1	206.9	208.2	208.1	204.1
2005	203.5	206.7	207.0	208.5	208.1	206.7	206.7	206.0	209.8	213.6	215.0	216.2	209.0
2006	211.3	214.3	215.8	216.3	215.7	213.8	212.1	211.6	215.4	220.1	221.2	222.5	215.8
2007	217.1	220.4	222.1	222.9	221.7	219.9	218.9	218.0	221.4	225.3	225.8	226.8	221.7
2008	222.7	226.0	227.4	229.2	227.6	225.7	224.8	224.2	228.6	232.8	234.0	235.2	228.2
2009	230.2	233.2	234.3	235.9	234.0	232.1	229.6	228.3	232.5	236.9	238.0	239.2	233.7
2010	234.9	234.4	238.7	239.9	237.9	235.3	234.4	232.7	236.4	241.4	242.5	243.0	237.6
2011	240.3	243.2	243.4	242.8	240.5	237.8	237.4	236.0	240.2	244.8	245.5	245.8	241.5
2012	242.1	245.7	246.8	248.0	245.7	244.0	242.6	241.4	245.3	249.9	250.2	252.0	246.1
2013	245.9	250.2	251.6	251.8	252.0	247.5	246.8	246.0	249.2	255.7	256.9	255.9	250.8
Leisure and Hospitality													
2002	97.0	97.2	100.5	103.8	107.8	111.9	111.9	112.1	107.5	105.2	103.9	103.3	105.2
2003	99.7	98.2	100.7	106.1	109.9	113.7	113.7	114.4	111.2	107.9	106.9	106.3	107.4
2004	101.7	101.9	105.1	108.3	111.4	115.8	115.9	116.5	113.5	111.5	109.6	109.6	110.1
2005	104.4	104.3	106.6	111.4	114.2	118.6	118.9	117.9	115.8	110.8	109.5	108.8	111.8
2006	105.9	105.0	108.5	111.7	115.8	120.8	120.5	120.4	117.1	114.6	113.2	112.9	113.9
2007	108.7	108.0	111.5	115.4	119.0	122.7	122.4	123.0	119.3	115.9	114.5	113.9	116.2
2008	110.0	109.7	112.2	117.1	120.8	123.7	123.4	122.6	117.3	115.5	113.2	112.7	116.5
2009	106.4	105.8	108.5	112.7	118.7	121.2	120.2	119.2	116.9	111.5	108.9	108.5	113.2
2010	104.8	102.5	107.4	112.1	116.3	119.1	119.0	119.6	116.7	112.8	110.6	109.8	112.6
2011	104.5	105.0	108.8	113.4	118.1	121.1	121.9	121.1	118.5	113.7	113.0	112.4	114.3
2012	110.1	111.0	114.5	118.6	124.6	129.1	128.2	128.1	125.2	122.0	119.3	118.6	120.8
2013	115.4	115.7	119.1	123.6	129.0	133.0	133.5	133.1	128.6	126.0	124.3	122.2	125.3
Other Services													
2002	52.8	53.2	53.9	54.3	54.8	55.4	55.7	54.9	54.7	54.6	54.8	54.9	54.5
2003	53.8	53.9	54.8	54.5	54.9	55.7	55.2	54.5	54.0	54.0	53.9	54.0	54.4
2004	52.8	53.5	54.0	54.7	55.0	55.6	55.5	55.0	54.8	54.4	54.5	54.8	54.6
2005	53.8	54.2	54.7	55.1	55.3	55.9	55.5	55.3	54.9	54.6	54.7	55.0	54.9
2006	54.5	54.7	55.2	56.0	56.4	56.9	56.8	56.7	56.6	56.3	56.5	56.6	56.1
2007	56.1	56.0	56.7	56.7	56.5	57.2	57.4	56.7	56.4	56.4	56.6	56.7	56.6
2008	55.8	56.1	56.5	56.7	56.8	57.4	57.0	56.7	56.4	56.3	56.2	56.0	56.5
2009	55.1	55.0	55.4	55.4	55.8	56.1	56.0	55.8	55.5	55.6	55.6	55.7	55.6
2010	54.5	53.7	55.2	55.4	55.8	56.0	56.1	55.8	55.6	55.4	55.5	55.3	55.4
2011	54.6	54.7	55.2	55.7	55.8	56.3	56.1	55.8	55.0	54.8	54.7	54.9	55.3
2012	54.2	54.1	54.5	55.1	55.1	55.7	55.5	54.9	54.5	54.2	53.9	54.0	54.6
2013	53.3	53.6	53.9	54.3	54.4	54.8	54.9	54.2	54.3	54.6	55.3	54.2	54.3
Government													
2002	220.5	224.2	226.3	223.3	223.8	221.0	215.3	211.9	220.0	224.6	225.1	223.6	221.6
2003	218.4	222.2	224.1	223.4	222.6	215.4	209.8	216.7	217.4	220.7	221.4	220.1	219.4
2004	214.8	216.3	219.2	220.0	219.1	217.0	207.7	207.3	212.8	218.0	220.2	219.4	216.0
2005	213.6	218.1	218.1	219.9	220.8	218.1	210.1	205.8	217.1	222.0	224.0	223.4	217.6
2006	215.2	220.1	222.1	223.4	223.6	219.4	213.3	212.5	218.7	224.8	226.7	227.1	220.6
2007	219.1	223.9	226.4	225.3	226.0	221.5	214.6	214.3	219.4	225.3	227.1	226.6	222.5
2008	219.3	224.9	226.5	228.5	228.7	224.0	218.8	217.7	223.0	230.0	230.6	230.6	225.2
2009	223.2	228.4	230.2	232.1	231.9	228.0	221.9	219.2	224.8	234.6	234.4	233.8	228.5
2010	226.8	231.5	235.4	237.6	238.8	235.3	226.5	225.0	228.7	236.2	237.9	235.5	232.9
2011	229.5	235.1	239.2	239.5	237.3	233.6	224.0	224.1	230.4	238.0	236.8	236.7	233.7
2012	229.9	235.8	239.0	237.7	236.2	230.0	223.1	221.7	230.1	236.9	237.0	236.4	232.8
2013	228.6	234.2	236.3	236.6	235.7	229.5	215.4	214.0	227.7	232.5	233.3	233.0	229.7

Employment by Industry: Baton Rouge, LA, Selected Years, 2002–2013

(Numbers in thousands, not seasonally adjusted)

Industry and year	January	February	March	April	May	June	July	August	September	October	November	December	Annual average
Total Nonfarm													
2002	333.1	334.1	335.0	337.0	338.6	337.7	330.2	332.5	337.1	339.2	340.0	338.9	336.1
2003	332.2	336.0	336.9	340.3	341.4	339.8	337.1	337.3	341.0	344.3	343.5	341.7	339.3
2004	337.4	341.4	345.3	345.7	343.2	344.4	340.7	339.6	341.9	343.1	346.5	345.3	342.9
2005	338.5	343.8	346.9	353.4	351.7	351.3	351.1	352.6	359.0	361.1	365.6	364.9	353.3
2006	357.0	362.4	365.6	364.0	364.1	359.8	350.8	357.4	362.3	363.1	364.8	367.1	361.5
2007	361.0	366.4	370.5	371.6	372.5	373.3	371.7	374.9	379.3	379.9	381.9	383.3	373.9
2008	370.7	375.7	377.1	375.2	375.0	375.6	370.8	373.6	370.5	378.3	381.3	381.9	375.5
2009	369.8	373.2	374.5	374.3	373.8	370.4	368.5	369.4	372.5	370.3	371.6	369.5	371.5
2010	359.2	361.2	364.1	364.2	365.4	364.9	360.5	363.4	364.6	367.5	368.2	367.6	364.2
2011	363.7	367.8	369.5	371.1	370.5	367.1	364.9	365.5	371.0	373.6	373.5	372.9	369.3
2012	368.1	372.9	375.2	376.0	375.9	373.7	367.4	373.4	376.7	379.2	381.4	380.1	375.0
2013	374.3	380.4	383.2	384.5	385.5	383.6	379.1	383.7	387.4	391.9	392.4	392.3	384.9
Total Private													
2002	264.7	264.6	265.2	267.2	268.2	267.6	267.5	269.2	268.2	269.2	269.1	268.4	267.4
2003	260.9	261.9	262.6	266.5	267.5	267.0	266.2	267.0	267.3	269.8	269.0	269.2	266.2
2004	266.3	267.3	271.0	271.0	269.7	270.9	268.1	267.3	267.0	267.4	270.7	271.1	269.0
2005	265.9	268.6	271.5	278.1	278.0	277.8	279.6	280.0	283.5	284.2	288.2	288.8	278.7
2006	284.5	287.2	290.2	290.1	290.7	291.4	284.1	285.7	288.3	288.9	290.2	293.5	288.7
2007	288.5	291.2	294.6	294.8	296.5	297.7	298.5	299.0	300.1	301.5	302.9	304.9	297.5
2008	295.2	297.2	298.9	297.1	297.8	299.0	295.9	298.3	294.5	299.1	301.6	303.1	298.1
2009	293.5	294.1	295.3	295.4	296.0	293.6	293.7	294.8	293.7	291.2	292.3	291.1	293.7
2010	282.9	283.4	286.0	286.4	287.3	288.5	287.5	287.9	287.0	289.4	290.0	290.2	287.2
2011	288.8	290.8	292.8	294.1	293.7	292.0	291.9	293.0	294.2	296.0	295.7	295.7	293.2
2012	293.2	296.9	299.6	300.7	301.0	300.5	297.3	300.9	302.1	304.8	306.8	306.1	300.8
2013	302.4	306.8	309.6	311.1	312.3	311.9	310.5	312.6	313.6	318.9	319.2	319.9	312.4
Goods-Producing													
2002	64.1	63.2	62.4	63.4	63.5	62.3	62.6	63.3	63.2	65.4	63.3	61.8	63.2
2003	61.0	61.4	61.2	61.8	62.8	62.1	62.0	61.9	62.4	63.4	61.6	61.0	61.9
2004	62.7	62.7	64.9	62.3	61.2	61.1	58.9	58.2	58.9	59.9	61.0	60.7	61.0
2005	58.4	60.5	61.5	65.1	65.1	64.3	63.7	63.8	64.2	63.5	64.8	64.5	63.3
2006	65.6	66.1	67.0	67.4	66.9	66.7	62.6	63.2	64.4	65.4	65.4	66.8	65.6
2007	65.5	66.7	67.5	68.3	69.2	69.2	69.2	68.6	68.8	70.6	70.7	71.3	68.8
2008	66.2	67.0	67.5	67.3	67.7	68.2	67.1	68.3	67.8	69.0	69.5	69.9	68.0
2009	67.6	68.0	68.4	68.3	68.6	67.4	68.4	68.7	68.3	66.2	65.7	64.1	67.5
2010	63.6	63.5	63.6	62.9	62.8	64.0	64.6	64.9	64.7	64.9	64.2	64.2	64.0
2011	64.7	65.9	66.7	66.6	65.8	65.0	65.0	64.8	65.8	66.7	65.4	64.7	65.6
2012	65.4	67.3	68.2	67.9	67.8	67.6	66.9	68.3	69.3	70.6	71.0	70.0	68.4
2013	69.6	72.0	73.2	72.5	73.0	73.3	72.6	73.1	74.2	77.1	75.5	75.5	73.5
Service-Providing													
2002	269.0	270.9	272.6	273.6	275.1	275.4	267.6	269.2	273.9	273.8	276.7	277.1	272.9
2003	271.2	274.6	275.7	278.5	278.6	277.7	275.1	275.4	278.6	280.9	281.9	280.7	277.4
2004	274.7	278.7	280.4	283.4	282.0	283.3	281.8	281.4	283.0	283.2	285.5	284.6	281.8
2005	280.1	283.3	285.4	288.3	286.6	287.0	287.4	288.8	294.8	297.6	300.8	300.4	290.0
2006	291.4	296.3	298.6	296.6	297.2	293.1	288.2	294.2	297.9	297.7	299.4	300.3	295.9
2007	295.5	299.7	303.0	303.3	303.3	304.1	302.5	306.3	310.5	309.3	311.2	312.0	305.1
2008	304.5	308.7	309.6	307.9	307.3	307.4	303.7	305.3	302.7	309.3	311.8	312.0	307.5
2009	302.2	305.2	306.1	306.0	305.2	303.0	300.1	300.7	304.2	304.1	305.9	305.4	304.0
2010	295.6	297.7	300.5	301.3	302.6	300.9	295.9	298.5	299.9	302.6	304.0	303.4	300.2
2011	299.0	301.9	302.8	304.5	304.7	302.1	299.9	300.7	305.2	306.9	308.1	308.2	303.7
2012	302.7	305.6	307.0	308.1	308.1	306.1	300.5	305.1	307.4	308.6	310.4	310.1	306.6
2013	304.7	308.4	310.0	312.0	312.5	310.3	306.5	310.6	313.2	314.8	316.9	316.8	311.4
Mining and Logging													
2005	1.5	1.5	1.5	1.6	1.5	1.6	1.5	1.5	1.6	1.8	1.8	1.8	1.6
2006	1.6	1.6	1.6	1.5	1.5	1.5	1.5	1.4	1.5	1.4	1.4	1.4	1.5
2007	1.6	1.7	1.7	1.8	1.9	1.9	1.8	1.9	1.9	1.9	1.9	1.9	1.8
2008	1.6	1.6	1.7	1.7	1.7	1.7	1.6	1.6	1.6	1.6	1.6	1.6	1.6
2009	1.6	1.5	1.5	1.6	1.5	1.5	1.4	1.5	1.5	1.5	1.4	1.6	1.5
2010	1.6	1.8	1.8	2.0	1.9	1.9	1.8	1.9	1.9	1.9	1.9	1.8	1.9
2011	1.9	2.0	2.1	1.9	1.6	1.7	1.6	1.6	1.6	1.7	1.6	1.6	1.7
2012	1.5	1.6	1.6	1.5	1.6	1.4	1.3	1.4	1.4	1.4	1.4	1.3	1.5
2013	1.3	1.3	1.3	1.2	1.2	1.2	1.3	1.3	1.3	1.4	1.3	1.3	1.3
Construction													
2005	31.4	33.4	34.2	37.5	37.6	36.9	36.2	36.4	36.8	36.0	37.3	36.9	35.9
2006	38.5	39.0	39.7	40.4	39.9	39.5	36.0	36.6	37.5	38.5	38.4	39.7	38.6
2007	38.1	39.1	39.8	40.4	41.0	40.6	40.6	40.6	40.8	42.1	42.0	42.5	40.6
2008	38.8	39.4	39.8	39.6	39.9	40.4	39.5	40.7	40.4	41.3	41.8	42.0	40.3
2009	40.4	40.9	41.4	41.1	41.5	40.5	42.0	42.3	42.1	40.1	39.8	38.0	40.8
2010	37.4	37.0	37.1	36.3	36.1	37.2	37.9	38.1	37.9	37.9	37.2	37.2	37.3
2011	37.6	38.7	39.4	39.5	38.8	37.9	37.5	37.0	37.8	38.5	37.4	36.6	38.1
2012	37.7	39.5	40.1	39.9	39.5	39.2	38.7	40.0	41.0	42.3	42.6	41.7	40.2
2013	41.5	43.9	45.0	44.5	44.8	44.9	44.0	44.3	45.2	47.9	46.3	46.3	44.9

Employment by Industry: Baton Rouge, LA, Selected Years, 2002–2013—*Continued*

(Numbers in thousands, not seasonally adjusted)

Industry and year	January	February	March	April	May	June	July	August	September	October	November	December	Annual average
Manufacturing													
2002	28.5	28.1	28.2	27.9	27.9	28.1	27.8	27.9	27.8	28.0	27.8	27.7	28.0
2003	27.5	27.4	27.5	27.4	27.5	27.5	26.9	26.8	26.8	27.1	27.0	27.0	27.2
2004	26.8	26.8	26.8	26.6	26.5	26.6	26.2	26.1	26.1	26.0	26.0	26.1	26.4
2005	25.5	25.6	25.8	26.0	26.0	25.8	26.0	25.9	25.8	25.7	25.7	25.8	25.8
2006	25.5	25.5	25.7	25.5	25.5	25.7	25.1	25.2	25.4	25.5	25.6	25.7	25.5
2007	25.8	25.9	26.0	26.1	26.3	26.7	26.8	26.1	26.1	26.6	26.8	26.9	26.3
2008	25.8	26.0	26.0	26.0	26.1	26.1	26.0	26.0	25.8	26.1	26.1	26.3	26.0
2009	25.6	25.6	25.5	25.6	25.6	25.4	25.0	24.9	24.7	24.6	24.5	24.5	25.1
2010	24.6	24.7	24.7	24.6	24.8	24.9	24.9	24.9	24.9	25.1	25.1	25.2	24.9
2011	25.2	25.2	25.2	25.2	25.4	25.4	25.9	26.2	26.4	26.5	26.4	26.5	25.8
2012	26.2	26.2	26.5	26.5	26.7	27.0	26.9	26.9	26.9	26.9	27.0	27.0	26.7
2013	26.8	26.8	26.9	26.8	27.0	27.2	27.3	27.5	27.7	27.8	27.9	27.9	27.3
Trade, Transportation, and Utilities													
2002	65.1	65.1	65.3	65.8	65.9	66.0	65.5	65.9	65.8	65.4	67.1	67.9	65.9
2003	63.1	62.9	63.1	64.0	63.9	64.0	63.5	63.7	63.7	64.1	65.1	65.9	63.9
2004	63.3	63.2	63.5	63.6	63.7	64.0	63.3	63.4	63.2	63.2	64.3	64.9	63.6
2005	62.3	62.3	62.8	63.1	63.6	63.7	64.7	64.9	65.7	66.5	68.6	69.4	64.8
2006	66.4	66.2	67.0	66.1	66.5	66.3	65.6	65.6	65.8	65.9	67.2	68.2	66.4
2007	65.7	65.5	66.3	65.4	65.9	66.1	66.7	67.2	67.6	67.7	69.4	70.2	67.0
2008	67.7	67.1	67.7	66.7	66.8	66.9	66.8	67.3	66.4	66.8	67.9	68.8	67.2
2009	66.1	65.5	65.6	65.8	65.7	65.3	65.3	65.3	64.9	64.9	66.0	66.6	65.6
2010	64.0	63.9	64.5	64.9	65.0	64.9	64.4	64.5	64.3	65.2	66.5	67.2	64.9
2011	65.0	64.8	65.0	65.5	65.6	65.4	65.0	65.2	65.0	65.7	66.8	67.7	65.6
2012	65.8	65.8	66.4	66.5	66.7	66.4	66.0	66.3	65.8	66.8	68.7	69.1	66.7
2013	66.5	66.4	66.8	67.2	67.3	67.3	67.2	67.7	67.8	68.8	70.3	70.6	67.8
Wholesale Trade													
2002	13.7	13.7	13.7	13.6	13.7	13.8	13.7	13.7	13.7	13.5	13.6	13.6	13.7
2003	13.5	13.4	13.5	13.4	13.4	13.5	13.4	13.4	13.4	13.3	13.3	13.2	13.4
2004	13.2	13.2	13.3	13.3	13.2	13.2	12.9	13.0	12.9	12.6	12.7	12.8	13.0
2005	12.6	12.5	12.6	12.7	12.8	12.8	13.1	13.1	13.1	12.9	12.9	13.0	12.8
2006	12.7	12.7	12.8	12.8	12.9	13.0	12.9	12.8	12.9	12.9	13.0	13.0	12.9
2007	13.2	13.2	13.3	13.2	13.3	13.5	13.7	13.7	13.8	13.8	13.9	14.0	13.6
2008	13.6	13.6	13.7	13.4	13.5	13.4	13.4	13.4	13.5	13.5	13.4	13.4	13.5
2009	13.2	13.2	13.1	13.3	13.2	13.1	12.7	12.6	12.7	12.6	12.7	12.7	12.9
2010	12.4	12.4	12.4	12.5	12.5	12.4	12.4	12.5	12.4	12.7	12.6	12.6	12.5
2011	12.7	12.7	12.7	12.8	12.9	12.9	12.9	12.9	12.9	13.0	13.0	13.0	12.9
2012	13.1	13.1	13.2	13.2	13.2	13.2	13.1	13.1	13.1	13.3	13.4	13.4	13.2
2013	13.6	13.7	13.8	13.9	13.9	13.8	13.8	13.9	13.9	14.0	14.0	14.0	13.9
Retail Trade													
2002	38.7	38.4	38.4	38.5	38.4	38.3	38.0	38.2	38.2	38.0	39.5	40.3	38.6
2003	36.4	36.2	36.3	37.1	36.9	37.0	36.7	36.8	36.7	37.2	38.1	39.0	37.0
2004	37.0	36.8	37.0	37.2	37.4	37.8	37.5	37.5	37.5	37.8	38.9	39.5	37.7
2005	37.5	37.5	37.9	37.9	38.2	38.4	39.1	39.3	40.1	41.1	43.0	43.6	39.5
2006	41.5	41.2	41.9	41.1	41.2	40.9	40.2	40.3	40.3	40.5	41.6	42.4	41.1
2007	40.3	40.0	40.8	40.0	40.3	40.3	40.6	40.7	41.0	41.4	42.9	43.6	41.0
2008	41.5	40.9	41.4	40.8	40.7	41.0	40.9	41.1	40.2	40.9	42.1	42.9	41.2
2009	40.6	40.3	40.5	40.8	40.8	40.8	41.1	41.0	40.9	40.4	41.5	41.9	40.9
2010	40.0	39.9	40.4	40.5	40.6	40.6	40.2	40.1	40.0	40.5	41.9	42.3	40.6
2011	40.2	39.9	40.2	40.6	40.6	40.4	40.2	40.0	39.9	40.3	41.6	42.2	40.5
2012	40.5	40.5	40.9	41.0	41.0	41.0	40.9	40.8	40.5	41.3	43.0	43.2	41.2
2013	40.5	40.2	40.4	40.7	40.6	40.9	40.8	40.9	41.1	42.0	43.5	43.6	41.3
Transportation and Utilities													
2002	12.7	13.0	13.2	13.7	13.8	13.9	13.8	14.0	13.9	13.9	14.0	14.0	13.7
2003	13.2	13.3	13.3	13.5	13.6	13.5	13.4	13.5	13.6	13.6	13.7	13.7	13.5
2004	13.1	13.2	13.2	13.1	13.1	13.0	12.9	12.9	12.8	12.8	12.7	12.6	13.0
2005	12.2	12.3	12.3	12.5	12.6	12.5	12.5	12.5	12.5	12.5	12.7	12.8	12.5
2006	12.2	12.3	12.3	12.2	12.4	12.4	12.5	12.5	12.6	12.5	12.6	12.8	12.4
2007	12.2	12.3	12.2	12.2	12.3	12.3	12.4	12.7	12.8	12.5	12.6	12.6	12.4
2008	12.6	12.6	12.6	12.5	12.6	12.5	12.5	12.8	12.7	12.4	12.4	12.5	12.6
2009	12.3	12.0	12.0	11.7	11.7	11.4	11.5	11.7	11.7	11.9	11.8	12.0	11.8
2010	11.6	11.6	11.7	11.9	11.9	11.9	11.8	11.9	11.9	12.0	12.0	12.3	11.9
2011	12.1	12.2	12.1	12.1	12.1	12.1	11.9	12.3	12.2	12.4	12.2	12.5	12.2
2012	12.2	12.2	12.3	12.3	12.5	12.2	12.0	12.4	12.2	12.2	12.3	12.5	12.3
2013	12.4	12.5	12.6	12.6	12.8	12.6	12.6	12.9	12.8	12.8	12.8	13.0	12.7
Information													
2002	5.2	5.2	5.3	5.0	5.1	5.1	5.2	5.2	5.2	5.0	5.0	5.0	5.1
2003	4.9	4.9	5.0	5.2	5.3	5.3	5.4	5.6	5.6	5.6	5.6	5.7	5.3
2004	5.6	5.6	5.6	5.6	5.6	5.6	5.5	5.5	5.4	5.4	5.5	5.5	5.5
2005	5.8	5.7	5.7	5.9	5.6	5.5	5.6	5.5	5.4	5.4	5.6	5.5	5.6
2006	5.6	5.6	5.7	5.7	5.6	5.5	5.4	5.3	5.2	5.4	5.5	5.4	5.5
2007	5.5	5.5	5.5	5.7	5.8	5.6	6.0	5.9	5.8	6.6	5.9	5.8	5.8
2008	5.6	6.0	5.8	6.4	6.2	6.4	5.8	5.8	5.6	5.6	6.0	6.0	5.9
2009	5.5	5.4	5.2	5.1	5.0	4.9	4.7	4.8	4.6	4.7	4.7	4.7	4.9
2010	4.6	4.6	4.6	4.8	4.8	4.8	4.7	4.6	4.4	4.7	4.7	5.0	4.7
2011	4.8	4.9	4.8	4.9	4.8	4.8	4.8	4.9	4.8	5.0	4.9	5.0	4.9
2012	4.8	5.0	4.9	5.4	4.8	5.0	4.9	4.7	5.3	4.7	4.9	5.2	5.0
2013	5.5	5.9	6.3	6.6	6.7	6.6	6.4	5.9	5.7	5.5	5.6	5.6	6.0

Employment by Industry: Baton Rouge, LA, Selected Years, 2002–2013—*Continued*

(Numbers in thousands, not seasonally adjusted)

Industry and year	January	February	March	April	May	June	July	August	September	October	November	December	Annual average
Financial Activities													
2002	16.7	16.7	16.5	17.0	17.0	17.0	17.1	17.2	17.0	17.3	17.2	17.4	17.0
2003	16.7	16.8	16.8	17.4	17.3	17.4	17.5	17.6	17.6	17.9	17.9	18.0	17.4
2004	17.9	17.9	18.0	18.2	18.2	18.2	18.1	18.1	17.9	17.8	17.8	18.0	18.0
2005	17.9	18.0	18.0	18.1	18.2	18.2	18.5	18.5	18.5	18.5	18.6	18.7	18.3
2006	18.5	18.5	18.6	18.6	18.6	18.6	18.4	18.5	18.5	18.7	18.7	18.8	18.6
2007	19.1	19.2	18.9	18.9	18.8	18.8	18.7	18.7	18.5	18.4	18.5	18.6	18.8
2008	18.3	18.3	18.4	18.2	18.2	18.3	18.1	18.1	17.9	18.0	17.9	17.9	18.1
2009	17.5	17.4	17.4	17.6	17.7	17.6	17.4	17.4	17.2	17.2	17.5	17.5	17.5
2010	17.3	17.3	17.4	17.3	17.3	17.3	17.0	17.1	16.9	17.0	17.1	17.1	17.2
2011	17.1	17.2	17.1	17.0	17.0	16.9	17.0	17.0	17.0	17.1	17.0	17.2	17.1
2012	17.1	17.1	17.2	17.2	17.2	17.2	17.1	17.3	17.1	17.3	17.5	17.5	17.2
2013	17.2	17.3	17.3	17.4	17.5	17.7	17.6	17.7	17.7	17.8	17.9	17.9	17.6
Professional and Business Services													
2002	39.0	39.0	39.2	39.1	38.9	38.9	38.7	38.8	38.4	38.6	38.6	38.7	38.8
2003	37.6	37.2	37.6	38.3	37.9	37.9	37.2	37.3	36.7	36.8	36.9	37.0	37.4
2004	36.8	37.2	37.5	38.1	37.3	37.6	37.6	37.4	36.9	36.6	36.8	36.8	37.2
2005	37.6	37.7	38.1	39.7	38.5	38.4	38.8	39.1	40.5	41.3	42.0	42.4	39.5
2006	41.1	41.8	42.3	42.7	42.7	43.0	42.5	42.6	43.1	43.4	43.0	43.8	42.7
2007	43.8	44.2	44.9	45.1	44.4	45.0	45.4	45.8	46.3	46.7	47.0	47.3	45.5
2008	47.0	46.7	46.7	45.9	45.8	45.8	44.9	45.2	45.6	46.3	46.3	46.4	46.1
2009	44.8	44.7	44.7	44.6	44.5	44.1	43.0	43.3	42.7	42.3	42.3	42.4	43.6
2010	41.0	41.1	41.5	41.7	41.8	41.9	41.8	41.9	41.5	41.9	41.6	41.7	41.6
2011	41.6	41.9	42.3	42.8	42.6	42.4	42.2	42.8	43.3	43.0	42.7	42.8	42.5
2012	42.9	43.4	43.9	44.8	45.0	44.7	43.6	43.9	44.4	44.8	44.3	44.0	44.1
2013	44.0	44.8	45.0	45.2	44.6	44.3	44.5	45.1	45.1	45.8	45.3	44.9	44.9
Education and Health Services													
2002	34.9	35.1	35.5	35.2	35.4	35.6	35.5	36.0	36.4	36.0	36.3	36.4	35.7
2003	35.8	36.1	36.1	36.2	36.4	36.5	37.2	37.4	37.7	38.1	38.1	38.2	37.0
2004	37.7	38.0	38.0	38.5	38.5	38.5	38.9	39.0	39.2	39.4	39.5	39.5	38.7
2005	39.4	39.6	39.7	40.1	40.4	40.4	41.3	41.2	41.6	42.4	42.4	42.0	40.9
2006	41.7	42.1	42.4	42.8	43.0	43.2	42.8	43.3	43.7	43.9	43.8	43.7	43.0
2007	42.9	43.3	43.5	44.0	44.6	44.5	44.3	44.8	44.7	44.3	44.4	44.8	44.2
2008	44.2	44.8	45.0	45.2	45.3	45.6	45.6	46.2	45.3	46.0	46.1	46.3	45.5
2009	45.7	46.2	46.4	46.7	46.6	46.3	47.4	47.5	47.8	48.5	48.6	48.6	47.2
2010	47.7	47.9	48.4	48.9	49.2	48.8	48.8	48.8	49.2	49.6	49.8	49.5	48.9
2011	49.6	49.9	50.0	49.4	49.4	49.2	49.7	49.6	50.0	50.2	50.5	50.4	49.8
2012	49.9	50.6	50.8	50.3	50.3	50.4	49.9	50.6	50.5	51.1	51.1	51.2	50.6
2013	50.9	51.3	51.3	51.7	52.0	51.6	51.3	52.2	52.2	52.6	52.8	53.3	51.9
Leisure and Hospitality													
2002	26.8	27.3	27.9	28.3	28.8	29.0	29.0	29.1	28.6	27.9	28.0	27.7	28.2
2003	28.3	29.1	29.3	29.9	30.1	30.0	29.8	29.9	30.0	30.0	30.0	29.7	29.7
2004	28.9	29.2	29.9	30.2	30.7	31.1	30.9	30.9	30.7	30.6	31.2	31.2	30.5
2005	30.2	30.5	31.1	31.5	31.9	32.4	32.0	32.0	32.6	32.0	31.7	31.7	31.6
2006	31.3	32.4	32.7	32.3	32.8	33.2	32.1	32.5	32.7	31.7	32.0	32.1	32.3
2007	31.3	32.0	33.0	32.5	33.0	33.4	32.9	32.8	33.2	32.3	32.3	32.1	32.6
2008	31.7	32.5	32.9	33.3	33.6	33.5	33.2	33.3	32.1	32.9	33.4	33.4	33.0
2009	32.0	32.6	33.3	33.0	33.5	33.4	32.8	33.2	33.0	32.4	32.5	32.1	32.8
2010	31.0	31.3	32.2	32.4	32.9	33.1	32.7	32.8	32.8	32.4	32.6	32.1	32.4
2011	32.5	32.6	33.3	34.1	34.8	34.4	34.1	34.6	34.3	34.4	34.5	34.2	34.0
2012	33.7	33.9	34.5	34.7	35.3	35.2	35.2	36.1	36.0	35.8	35.6	35.5	35.1
2013	35.1	35.3	35.7	36.6	37.3	37.1	37.1	37.0	37.0	37.3	37.9	38.2	36.8
Other Services													
2002	12.9	13.0	13.1	13.4	13.6	13.7	13.9	13.7	13.6	13.6	13.6	13.5	13.5
2003	13.5	13.5	13.5	13.7	13.8	13.8	13.6	13.6	13.6	13.9	13.8	13.7	13.7
2004	13.4	13.5	13.6	14.5	14.5	14.8	14.9	14.8	14.8	14.5	14.6	14.5	14.4
2005	14.3	14.3	14.6	14.6	14.7	14.9	15.0	15.0	15.0	14.6	14.5	14.6	14.7
2006	14.3	14.5	14.5	14.5	14.6	14.9	14.7	14.7	14.9	14.5	14.6	14.7	14.6
2007	14.7	14.8	15.0	14.9	14.8	15.1	15.3	15.2	15.2	14.9	14.7	14.8	15.0
2008	14.5	14.8	14.9	14.1	14.2	14.3	14.4	14.1	13.8	14.5	14.5	14.4	14.4
2009	14.3	14.3	14.3	14.3	14.4	14.6	14.7	14.6	14.8	15.0	15.0	15.1	14.6
2010	13.7	13.8	13.8	13.5	13.5	13.7	13.5	13.3	13.2	13.7	13.5	13.4	13.6
2011	13.5	13.6	13.6	13.8	13.7	13.9	14.1	14.1	14.0	13.9	13.9	13.7	13.8
2012	13.6	13.8	13.7	13.9	13.9	14.0	13.7	13.7	13.7	13.7	13.7	13.6	13.8
2013	13.6	13.8	14.0	13.9	13.9	14.0	13.8	13.9	13.9	14.0	13.9	13.9	13.9
Government													
2002	68.4	69.5	69.8	69.8	70.4	70.1	62.7	63.3	68.9	70.0	70.9	70.5	68.7
2003	71.3	74.1	74.3	73.8	73.9	72.8	70.9	70.3	73.7	74.5	74.5	72.5	73.1
2004	71.1	74.1	74.3	74.7	73.5	73.5	72.6	72.3	74.9	75.7	75.8	74.2	73.9
2005	72.6	75.2	75.4	75.3	73.7	73.5	71.5	72.6	75.5	76.9	77.4	76.1	74.6
2006	72.5	75.2	75.4	73.9	73.4	68.4	66.7	71.7	74.0	74.2	74.6	73.6	72.8
2007	72.5	75.2	75.9	76.8	76.0	75.6	73.2	75.9	79.2	78.4	79.0	78.4	76.3
2008	75.5	78.5	78.2	78.1	77.2	76.6	74.9	75.3	76.0	79.2	79.7	78.8	77.3
2009	76.3	79.1	79.2	78.9	77.8	76.8	74.8	74.6	78.8	79.1	79.3	78.4	77.8
2010	76.3	77.8	78.1	77.8	78.1	76.4	73.0	75.5	77.6	78.1	78.2	77.4	77.0
2011	74.9	77.0	76.7	77.0	76.8	75.1	73.0	72.5	76.8	77.6	77.8	77.2	76.0
2012	74.9	76.0	75.6	75.3	74.9	73.2	70.1	72.5	74.6	74.4	74.6	74.0	74.2
2013	71.9	73.6	73.6	73.4	73.2	71.7	68.6	71.1	73.8	73.0	73.2	72.4	72.5

Employment by Industry: Birmingham–Hoover, AL, Selected Years, 2002–2013

(Numbers in thousands, not seasonally adjusted)

Industry and year	January	February	March	April	May	June	July	August	September	October	November	December	Annual average
Total Nonfarm													
2002	507.0	507.6	510.7	510.2	510.7	509.9	508.1	507.0	508.7	509.2	512.2	511.8	509.4
2003	499.6	501.7	504.2	505.2	506.1	505.6	504.2	505.6	506.8	509.1	512.0	514.0	506.2
2004	504.4	506.3	509.1	510.9	511.6	512.6	511.2	510.8	511.3	514.3	517.6	518.8	511.6
2005	510.2	512.2	515.2	518.9	519.5	520.3	518.9	519.5	521.6	522.8	525.7	526.6	519.3
2006	519.1	521.4	524.5	527.0	529.0	533.2	528.4	529.8	531.8	531.7	534.6	535.6	528.8
2007	528.0	530.5	533.8	530.7	533.7	536.2	531.2	532.9	533.9	534.2	537.3	538.7	533.4
2008	527.2	528.7	529.5	531.3	533.7	534.9	529.4	529.4	528.0	527.7	526.2	525.3	529.3
2009	507.7	506.0	504.4	502.7	503.0	501.5	496.0	494.0	494.4	494.7	496.8	496.3	499.8
2010	487.3	488.0	489.4	492.2	495.7	495.1	491.4	490.0	489.4	492.9	495.3	495.4	491.8
2011	484.9	487.2	490.1	492.4	493.9	496.1	493.2	493.4	496.2	495.8	499.2	500.3	493.6
2012	493.4	495.5	499.9	502.9	503.8	505.5	499.7	500.9	503.0	503.7	507.3	507.0	501.9
2013	498.2	501.5	503.7	506.8	508.8	510.1	505.8	506.4	507.8	510.4	513.3	514.9	507.3
Total Private													
2002	431.0	431.3	434.1	433.5	433.6	434.0	434.8	434.1	432.3	431.5	434.0	433.6	433.2
2003	422.1	423.6	425.8	426.2	427.0	428.4	428.8	430.1	428.5	430.3	432.9	434.6	428.2
2004	425.4	427.2	430.2	431.4	432.5	434.3	434.7	434.3	432.6	435.2	438.0	439.3	432.9
2005	431.4	432.9	435.7	439.1	439.6	440.9	442.0	442.0	441.9	442.1	444.8	445.9	439.9
2006	437.7	439.8	442.8	444.8	446.6	450.9	449.3	450.2	449.5	448.7	451.4	452.3	447.0
2007	445.1	447.2	450.3	447.2	449.9	452.6	451.2	452.2	450.6	450.3	453.2	454.7	450.4
2008	443.6	444.7	445.3	446.9	449.0	450.2	448.3	447.8	444.4	442.7	441.3	440.1	445.4
2009	423.2	421.4	419.8	417.7	418.2	416.7	415.4	413.1	411.3	410.8	412.5	412.1	416.0
2010	403.4	403.9	404.8	407.2	408.4	409.1	409.5	408.8	406.4	409.0	411.4	411.4	407.8
2011	401.2	403.4	406.2	408.4	409.7	412.2	412.6	413.3	413.8	413.8	417.1	418.1	410.8
2012	411.8	413.3	417.3	420.4	421.3	423.6	421.3	422.3	422.5	422.1	425.4	425.0	420.5
2013	416.7	419.7	421.9	425.0	427.3	428.9	427.3	427.9	427.5	429.6	432.5	434.2	426.5
Goods-Producing													
2002	80.1	79.4	80.1	80.7	80.4	80.3	80.2	80.3	79.9	80.4	80.1	79.2	80.1
2003	77.7	77.7	78.4	78.4	78.3	78.2	78.2	78.7	78.5	79.9	80.1	80.0	78.7
2004	78.4	79.0	79.5	79.3	79.1	78.9	79.0	78.9	79.0	80.0	80.0	79.8	79.2
2005	78.4	78.4	78.7	79.7	79.4	79.3	80.1	80.4	80.5	80.9	81.1	80.6	79.8
2006	79.7	79.9	80.6	81.3	82.0	82.9	82.8	82.5	82.9	82.5	82.1	81.8	81.8
2007	81.1	81.7	82.2	81.4	81.5	82.2	81.5	81.8	81.7	81.2	80.7	80.5	81.5
2008	79.0	79.0	78.6	78.9	79.2	79.3	79.4	78.6	78.2	76.6	75.5	74.5	78.1
2009	70.4	69.3	68.6	67.0	66.9	66.0	65.9	65.3	64.9	64.0	63.9	63.9	66.3
2010	62.2	61.8	61.6	62.1	62.0	61.9	62.3	62.3	61.7	61.3	61.5	61.4	61.8
2011	60.3	60.8	61.8	61.9	62.6	63.3	62.9	63.3	63.8	63.9	64.3	64.7	62.8
2012	63.9	63.8	64.5	64.9	65.3	65.5	65.6	65.5	65.5	65.7	65.6	65.7	65.1
2013	65.2	64.8	65.6	65.9	66.2	66.4	66.1	66.3	66.1	66.2	65.7	66.5	65.9
Service-Providing													
2002	426.9	428.2	430.6	429.5	430.3	429.6	427.9	426.7	428.8	428.8	432.1	432.6	429.3
2003	421.9	424.0	425.8	426.8	427.8	427.4	426.0	426.9	428.3	429.2	431.9	434.0	427.5
2004	426.0	427.3	429.6	431.6	432.5	433.7	432.2	431.9	432.3	434.3	437.6	439.0	432.3
2005	431.8	433.8	436.5	439.2	440.1	441.0	438.8	439.1	441.1	441.9	444.6	446.0	439.5
2006	439.4	441.5	443.9	445.7	447.0	450.3	445.6	447.3	448.9	449.2	452.5	453.8	447.1
2007	446.9	448.8	451.6	449.3	452.2	454.0	449.7	451.1	452.2	453.0	456.6	458.2	452.0
2008	448.2	449.7	450.9	452.4	454.5	455.6	450.0	450.8	449.8	451.1	450.7	450.8	451.2
2009	437.3	436.7	435.8	435.7	436.1	435.5	430.1	428.7	429.5	430.7	432.9	432.4	433.5
2010	425.1	426.2	427.8	430.1	433.7	433.2	429.1	427.7	427.7	431.6	433.8	434.0	430.0
2011	424.6	426.4	428.3	430.5	431.3	432.8	430.3	430.1	432.4	431.9	434.9	435.6	430.8
2012	429.5	431.7	435.4	438.0	438.5	440.0	434.1	435.4	437.5	438.0	441.7	441.3	436.8
2013	433.0	436.7	438.1	440.9	442.6	443.7	439.7	440.1	441.7	444.2	447.6	448.4	441.4
Mining and Logging													
2002	3.0	3.0	3.1	3.2	3.2	3.2	3.1	3.2	3.2	3.4	3.4	3.2	3.2
2003	3.1	3.0	3.0	3.0	3.0	3.0	2.9	2.8	2.8	2.8	2.8	2.8	2.9
2004	2.7	2.7	2.7	2.8	2.8	2.9	2.9	3.0	3.0	3.0	3.0	3.1	2.9
2005	3.0	3.0	3.1	3.1	3.2	3.2	3.3	3.3	3.3	3.3	3.3	3.3	3.2
2006	3.1	3.1	3.1	3.0	3.1	3.1	3.2	3.1	3.2	3.1	3.1	3.2	3.1
2007	3.1	3.1	3.1	3.0	3.0	2.9	2.9	3.0	3.0	3.0	3.0	3.1	3.0
2008	3.0	3.0	3.0	3.0	3.0	3.0	3.1	3.1	3.1	3.1	3.1	3.1	3.1
2009	2.9	2.9	2.9	2.9	2.9	2.8	2.8	2.7	2.8	2.8	2.8	2.8	2.8
2010	2.8	2.8	2.8	2.9	2.9	3.0	3.0	3.1	2.9	3.1	3.1	3.1	3.0
2011	3.1	3.1	3.2	3.4	3.4	3.5	3.4	3.5	3.6	3.6	3.7	3.7	3.4
2012	3.6	3.6	3.6	3.6	3.6	3.5	3.5	3.5	3.5	3.5	3.4	3.4	3.5
2013	3.4	3.2	3.3	3.2	3.2	3.2	3.3	3.2	3.2	3.2	3.3	3.2	3.2
Construction													
2002	30.3	30.6	31.0	31.7	31.6	31.4	31.8	31.8	31.7	32.2	32.0	31.5	31.5
2003	31.1	31.3	32.0	32.1	31.9	31.9	32.6	33.3	33.3	34.8	34.8	34.5	32.8
2004	34.0	34.5	34.9	34.3	33.8	33.3	33.3	33.1	33.2	33.9	33.6	33.1	33.8
2005	32.4	32.6	32.6	33.6	32.9	32.7	33.3	33.3	33.3	34.1	34.0	33.4	33.2
2006	33.0	33.0	33.7	34.3	34.6	35.2	34.8	34.9	35.0	34.9	34.7	34.2	34.4
2007	33.8	34.3	34.8	34.1	34.1	34.4	34.2	34.4	34.7	34.7	34.2	33.9	34.3
2008	33.2	33.0	32.9	33.4	33.8	33.5	33.7	33.2	32.8	31.7	31.0	30.6	32.7
2009	28.5	28.0	28.0	27.1	27.2	27.3	27.1	26.7	26.4	25.2	25.1	25.0	26.8
2010	24.1	23.9	24.0	24.2	24.3	24.4	24.6	24.7	24.3	23.9	23.7	24.2	24.2
2011	22.8	23.2	23.9	23.9	24.0	24.6	24.5	24.5	24.9	24.7	24.8	25.0	24.3
2012	24.2	24.1	24.4	24.5	24.7	24.7	24.9	24.7	24.5	24.9	24.7	24.6	24.6
2013	24.2	23.9	24.6	24.7	24.9	24.9	24.9	25.0	24.7	24.1	23.4	24.3	24.5

Employment by Industry: Birmingham–Hoover, AL, Selected Years, 2002–2013—*Continued*

(Numbers in thousands, not seasonally adjusted)

Industry and year	January	February	March	April	May	June	July	August	September	October	November	December	Annual average
Manufacturing													
2002	46.8	45.8	46.0	45.8	45.6	45.7	45.3	45.3	45.0	44.8	44.7	44.5	45.4
2003	43.5	43.4	43.4	43.3	43.4	43.3	42.7	42.6	42.4	42.3	42.5	42.7	43.0
2004	41.7	41.8	41.9	42.2	42.5	42.7	42.8	42.8	42.8	43.1	43.4	43.6	42.6
2005	43.0	42.8	43.0	43.0	43.3	43.4	43.5	43.8	43.9	43.5	43.8	43.9	43.4
2006	43.6	43.8	43.8	44.0	44.3	44.6	44.8	44.5	44.7	44.5	44.3	44.4	44.3
2007	44.2	44.3	44.3	44.3	44.4	44.9	44.4	44.4	44.0	43.5	43.5	43.5	44.1
2008	42.8	43.0	42.7	42.5	42.4	42.8	42.6	42.3	42.3	41.8	41.4	40.8	42.3
2009	39.0	38.4	37.7	37.0	36.8	35.9	36.0	35.9	35.7	36.0	36.0	36.1	36.7
2010	35.3	35.1	34.8	35.0	34.8	34.5	34.7	34.5	34.5	34.3	34.7	34.6	34.7
2011	34.4	34.5	34.7	34.6	34.9	35.2	35.0	35.3	35.3	35.6	35.8	36.0	35.1
2012	36.1	36.1	36.5	36.8	37.0	37.3	37.2	37.3	37.5	37.4	37.5	37.7	37.0
2013	37.6	37.7	37.7	38.0	38.1	38.3	37.9	38.1	38.2	38.9	39.0	39.0	38.2
Trade, Transportation, and Utilities													
2002	110.9	110.2	110.7	109.3	109.7	109.6	109.9	109.8	108.9	109.6	112.0	113.5	110.3
2003	108.9	108.5	109.0	108.8	109.2	109.8	110.4	110.5	110.3	111.0	112.9	114.4	110.3
2004	110.9	110.8	111.5	111.3	111.6	111.6	111.2	111.1	110.7	111.3	113.4	115.3	111.7
2005	110.5	110.2	110.6	111.0	111.3	111.7	111.4	111.8	111.6	112.2	114.0	115.7	111.8
2006	112.4	112.1	112.9	112.9	113.3	114.0	113.5	114.0	113.8	115.0	117.2	118.7	114.2
2007	114.7	114.4	115.5	114.5	115.5	116.4	116.2	115.8	115.9	116.1	118.4	119.7	116.1
2008	115.7	115.1	115.5	115.2	115.2	115.3	114.9	115.0	114.4	114.2	115.2	115.9	115.1
2009	110.4	109.4	108.8	107.9	107.9	107.3	106.8	106.3	106.0	106.1	107.0	107.8	107.6
2010	104.3	104.1	104.6	104.5	105.1	105.2	105.2	105.3	105.0	106.3	107.9	108.8	105.5
2011	104.9	104.9	105.1	104.9	105.1	105.3	105.4	105.7	105.7	106.3	108.1	109.3	105.9
2012	106.4	106.2	107.2	106.9	107.6	107.5	107.1	106.9	106.8	107.3	109.8	110.5	107.5
2013	106.8	107.0	107.6	107.7	108.0	108.2	108.7	108.8	108.6	110.1	112.2	113.6	108.9
Wholesale Trade													
2002	30.0	29.9	29.9	29.7	29.6	29.6	29.6	29.7	29.4	29.3	29.4	29.4	29.6
2003	29.1	29.1	29.1	29.1	29.2	29.3	29.5	29.4	29.5	29.7	29.9	30.1	29.4
2004	29.8	29.9	30.0	30.0	30.2	30.2	30.3	30.4	30.2	30.3	30.4	30.5	30.2
2005	30.1	30.2	30.2	30.3	30.2	30.3	30.4	30.5	30.6	30.4	30.4	30.6	30.4
2006	30.6	30.8	31.0	31.1	31.2	31.5	31.5	31.6	31.5	31.5	31.6	31.7	31.3
2007	31.4	31.6	31.8	31.4	31.4	31.7	31.5	31.5	31.6	31.6	31.7	31.8	31.6
2008	31.5	31.6	31.6	31.6	31.6	31.5	31.4	31.5	31.5	31.5	31.2	31.2	31.5
2009	30.4	30.2	30.0	29.7	29.6	29.4	29.4	29.3	29.2	29.3	28.9	28.9	29.5
2010	28.3	28.3	28.3	28.3	28.4	28.3	28.3	28.4	28.2	28.5	28.4	28.4	28.3
2011	27.9	28.1	28.0	28.2	28.2	28.1	28.4	28.4	28.5	28.7	28.7	28.9	28.3
2012	28.5	28.8	29.0	28.8	29.1	29.1	29.0	29.0	29.0	29.1	29.1	29.3	29.0
2013	29.1	29.3	29.3	29.3	29.2	29.1	29.4	29.5	29.5	30.2	29.8	29.8	29.5
Retail Trade													
2002	61.4	60.9	61.3	60.4	60.6	60.6	60.9	60.6	60.1	61.0	63.2	64.6	61.3
2003	60.7	60.3	60.8	60.8	61.0	61.4	61.8	62.2	62.1	62.4	64.1	65.4	61.9
2004	62.3	62.1	62.6	62.4	62.5	62.4	61.8	61.6	61.5	62.0	64.0	65.6	62.6
2005	61.5	61.0	61.2	61.5	61.8	62.0	61.7	62.0	61.6	62.2	64.1	65.5	62.2
2006	62.3	61.8	62.3	62.0	62.2	62.3	61.7	62.0	61.8	62.7	64.8	66.0	62.7
2007	62.8	62.2	62.9	62.4	63.2	63.6	63.4	62.9	62.8	63.1	65.2	66.2	63.4
2008	63.0	62.4	62.8	62.3	62.3	62.5	62.1	61.9	61.4	61.5	62.9	63.6	62.4
2009	59.3	58.6	58.4	58.0	58.1	57.8	57.4	56.9	56.7	56.7	58.0	58.5	57.9
2010	55.9	55.6	56.1	56.0	56.2	56.3	55.9	55.9	55.7	56.7	58.4	59.2	56.5
2011	56.1	55.7	55.9	56.1	56.2	56.5	56.2	56.5	56.3	56.7	58.5	59.3	56.7
2012	56.5	55.8	56.2	56.2	56.7	56.6	56.3	56.1	55.9	56.5	59.0	59.4	56.8
2013	55.5	55.4	55.8	56.1	56.4	56.7	56.8	56.7	56.5	57.3	59.8	60.9	57.0
Transportation and Utilities													
2002	19.5	19.4	19.5	19.2	19.5	19.4	19.4	19.5	19.4	19.3	19.4	19.5	19.4
2003	19.1	19.1	19.1	18.9	19.0	19.1	19.1	18.9	18.7	18.9	18.9	18.9	19.0
2004	18.8	18.8	18.9	18.9	18.9	19.0	19.1	19.1	19.0	19.0	19.0	19.2	19.0
2005	18.9	19.0	19.2	19.2	19.3	19.4	19.3	19.3	19.4	19.6	19.5	19.6	19.3
2006	19.5	19.5	19.6	19.8	19.9	20.2	20.3	20.4	20.5	20.8	20.8	21.0	20.2
2007	20.5	20.6	20.8	20.7	20.9	21.1	21.3	21.4	21.5	21.4	21.5	21.7	21.1
2008	21.2	21.1	21.1	21.3	21.3	21.3	21.4	21.6	21.5	21.2	21.1	21.1	21.3
2009	20.7	20.6	20.4	20.2	20.2	20.1	20.0	20.1	20.1	20.1	20.1	20.4	20.3
2010	20.1	20.2	20.2	20.2	20.5	20.6	21.0	21.0	21.1	21.1	21.1	21.2	20.7
2011	20.9	21.1	21.2	20.6	20.7	20.7	20.8	20.8	20.9	20.9	20.9	21.1	20.9
2012	21.4	21.6	22.0	21.9	21.8	21.8	21.8	21.8	21.9	21.7	21.7	21.8	21.8
2013	22.2	22.3	22.5	22.3	22.4	22.4	22.5	22.6	22.6	22.6	22.6	22.9	22.5
Information													
2002	15.1	15.0	15.2	15.0	14.9	14.9	15.0	14.8	14.6	14.8	14.7	14.5	14.9
2003	14.1	14.1	14.0	13.2	13.1	13.2	13.2	13.1	13.1	13.1	13.2	13.2	13.4
2004	13.2	13.0	13.1	13.1	13.1	13.2	13.2	13.0	12.8	12.9	13.0	12.9	13.0
2005	12.9	12.8	12.8	12.8	12.7	12.7	12.7	12.6	12.7	12.6	12.5	12.5	12.7
2006	12.2	12.1	12.2	12.0	12.0	12.0	11.9	11.8	11.7	11.7	11.7	11.7	11.9
2007	11.6	11.6	11.6	11.5	11.5	11.5	11.4	11.5	11.4	11.3	11.4	11.4	11.5
2008	11.1	11.1	11.2	11.2	11.2	11.1	11.0	11.1	10.9	10.9	10.8	10.8	11.0
2009	10.5	10.4	10.4	10.3	10.2	10.2	10.1	10.0	9.9	9.9	9.8	9.9	10.1
2010	9.8	9.7	9.7	9.5	9.5	9.6	9.4	9.4	9.3	9.3	9.3	9.3	9.5
2011	9.2	9.1	9.1	9.0	9.0	9.0	9.0	9.0	9.0	8.9	8.9	8.9	9.0
2012	8.9	8.9	9.0	8.8	8.8	8.9	8.9	8.9	8.9	8.8	8.8	8.9	8.9
2013	8.9	8.9	8.8	8.9	9.0	9.0	9.1	9.0	8.9	8.8	8.8	8.8	8.9

Employment by Industry: Birmingham–Hoover, AL, Selected Years, 2002–2013—*Continued*

(Numbers in thousands, not seasonally adjusted)

Industry and year	January	February	March	April	May	June	July	August	September	October	November	December	Annual average
Financial Activities													
2002	41.5	41.3	41.2	41.3	41.5	41.6	41.6	41.6	41.4	41.5	41.6	41.9	41.5
2003	40.8	40.7	40.6	40.9	41.0	41.2	41.3	41.1	41.0	41.0	41.2	41.3	41.0
2004	40.9	41.0	41.0	41.1	41.2	41.4	41.3	41.3	41.1	41.5	41.5	41.6	41.2
2005	41.0	41.2	41.5	41.6	41.5	41.6	41.6	41.5	41.5	41.7	41.8	42.0	41.5
2006	41.2	41.4	41.4	41.4	41.4	41.5	41.6	41.5	41.3	41.5	41.7	41.9	41.5
2007	41.7	41.8	42.0	41.0	41.2	41.5	41.4	41.4	41.5	41.5	41.7	41.9	41.6
2008	41.3	41.4	41.5	41.5	41.5	41.5	41.7	41.8	41.3	41.3	41.2	41.2	41.4
2009	40.8	40.9	40.7	40.6	40.5	40.5	40.3	40.1	39.9	39.8	39.6	39.5	40.3
2010	39.1	39.1	39.2	39.2	39.3	39.3	39.3	39.3	39.3	40.0	40.2	40.4	39.5
2011	40.0	40.1	40.0	40.2	40.1	39.7	40.1	39.9	39.8	39.8	39.9	40.0	40.0
2012	39.9	40.0	40.2	40.4	40.6	40.6	40.7	40.7	40.7	41.0	41.1	41.1	40.6
2013	40.6	40.8	40.8	40.9	41.1	41.1	41.4	41.6	41.4	41.4	41.9	42.2	41.3
Professional and Business Services													
2002	62.8	63.0	63.8	63.6	63.2	63.4	62.4	62.6	62.1	61.5	61.3	61.0	62.6
2003	59.6	60.2	60.5	60.3	60.4	60.7	60.8	61.3	60.8	61.0	60.8	61.0	60.6
2004	59.7	59.9	60.1	60.8	61.2	61.8	62.7	62.8	62.6	63.4	63.5	63.6	61.8
2005	63.7	64.5	64.8	65.2	65.2	65.4	66.4	66.2	66.7	67.1	67.5	67.5	65.9
2006	66.8	67.2	67.7	67.9	67.7	69.0	68.6	69.1	69.2	68.9	69.0	69.1	68.4
2007	68.1	68.8	68.7	68.0	68.1	68.3	67.5	67.9	67.7	67.8	68.5	68.1	68.1
2008	66.3	66.6	66.2	66.5	66.7	67.0	65.9	65.9	65.6	65.6	65.4	64.9	66.1
2009	62.0	61.6	61.0	60.5	60.1	59.8	59.3	59.0	58.6	59.4	59.6	59.1	60.0
2010	58.9	59.1	59.2	60.0	59.8	59.4	60.2	60.0	59.3	59.9	59.7	59.5	59.6
2011	58.6	59.2	59.4	60.3	60.3	61.0	61.2	61.3	61.9	61.5	61.6	62.0	60.7
2012	61.1	61.8	62.4	63.4	63.0	63.9	63.6	64.2	63.9	63.7	63.4	62.9	63.1
2013	61.5	62.9	63.1	62.9	62.7	63.3	63.0	62.9	62.5	63.0	62.7	62.3	62.7
Education and Health Services													
2002	57.1	58.3	58.5	58.7	58.4	58.2	59.6	59.1	60.2	59.9	60.2	59.7	59.0
2003	59.0	59.8	60.1	60.1	59.8	59.4	59.4	59.5	59.7	60.1	60.7	60.5	59.8
2004	59.8	60.4	60.7	60.8	60.6	60.5	60.5	60.6	61.0	61.1	61.5	61.4	60.7
2005	60.9	61.4	61.7	62.0	62.1	61.9	62.2	62.1	62.1	62.4	62.5	62.5	62.0
2006	61.2	61.9	61.9	62.2	62.2	62.1	62.1	62.3	62.5	62.8	63.5	63.0	62.3
2007	62.2	62.7	62.8	63.3	63.6	63.7	64.0	64.5	64.3	64.6	64.7	64.9	63.8
2008	64.0	64.5	64.7	64.6	65.1	65.0	65.0	65.1	65.2	65.8	65.2	65.1	64.9
2009	63.9	64.1	64.1	64.5	64.6	64.2	65.1	65.0	65.1	65.4	66.3	65.6	64.8
2010	65.0	65.6	65.3	65.6	65.7	65.6	65.7	65.6	65.6	65.9	66.2	65.6	65.6
2011	64.6	64.9	65.5	65.4	65.5	65.2	65.4	65.6	66.2	66.0	66.7	66.1	65.6
2012	65.9	66.2	66.5	67.0	66.6	66.8	66.3	67.1	67.9	67.5	68.4	68.3	67.0
2013	67.3	68.5	68.0	68.5	68.9	68.7	67.8	68.5	69.0	68.9	69.3	69.3	68.6
Leisure and Hospitality													
2002	38.0	38.4	38.9	39.4	39.9	40.3	40.2	40.1	39.7	38.5	38.7	38.6	39.2
2003	37.4	38.0	38.6	39.7	40.3	40.8	40.5	40.9	40.5	39.8	39.8	40.1	39.7
2004	38.7	39.2	40.3	41.1	41.8	42.7	42.5	42.4	41.6	41.3	41.3	40.9	41.2
2005	40.5	40.9	42.1	43.2	43.8	44.5	43.8	43.8	43.5	42.0	42.2	42.0	42.7
2006	41.2	42.1	42.9	43.8	44.7	45.5	45.1	45.4	44.7	43.2	42.9	42.8	43.7
2007	42.4	42.9	43.9	43.8	44.7	45.1	45.1	45.3	44.4	44.0	43.9	44.2	44.1
2008	42.2	42.8	43.4	44.7	45.8	46.3	45.6	45.7	44.6	44.2	44.0	43.8	44.4
2009	41.4	41.9	42.4	43.2	44.1	44.3	43.5	43.3	43.4	42.7	42.8	42.8	43.0
2010	40.7	41.0	41.6	42.7	43.3	43.8	43.0	42.8	42.7	42.5	43.0	43.0	42.5
2011	40.7	41.3	42.1	43.3	43.7	45.0	44.8	45.0	44.1	44.0	44.1	43.8	43.5
2012	42.3	42.9	43.7	45.3	45.6	46.1	44.9	45.0	45.2	44.4	44.8	44.2	44.5
2013	43.1	43.5	44.5	46.6	47.7	48.1	47.1	46.7	47.0	47.2	47.9	47.6	46.4
Other Services													
2002	25.5	25.7	25.7	25.5	25.6	25.7	25.9	25.8	25.5	25.3	25.4	25.2	25.6
2003	24.6	24.6	24.6	24.8	24.9	25.1	25.0	25.0	24.6	24.4	24.2	24.1	24.7
2004	23.8	23.9	24.0	23.9	23.9	24.2	24.3	24.2	23.8	23.7	23.8	23.8	23.9
2005	23.5	23.5	23.5	23.6	23.6	23.8	23.8	23.6	23.3	23.2	23.2	23.1	23.5
2006	23.0	23.1	23.2	23.3	23.3	23.9	23.7	23.6	23.4	23.1	23.3	23.3	23.4
2007	23.3	23.3	23.6	23.7	23.8	23.9	24.1	24.0	23.7	23.8	23.9	24.0	23.8
2008	24.0	24.2	24.2	24.3	24.3	24.7	24.8	24.6	24.2	24.1	24.0	23.9	24.3
2009	23.8	23.8	23.8	23.7	23.9	24.4	24.4	24.1	23.5	23.5	23.5	23.5	23.8
2010	23.4	23.5	23.6	23.6	23.7	24.3	24.4	24.1	23.5	23.8	23.6	23.4	23.7
2011	22.9	23.1	23.2	23.4	23.4	23.7	23.8	23.5	23.3	23.4	23.5	23.3	23.4
2012	23.4	23.5	23.8	23.7	23.8	24.3	24.2	24.0	23.6	23.7	23.5	23.4	23.7
2013	23.3	23.3	23.5	23.6	23.7	24.1	24.1	24.1	24.0	24.0	24.0	23.9	23.8
Government													
2002	76.0	76.3	76.6	76.7	77.1	75.9	73.3	72.9	76.4	77.7	78.2	78.2	76.3
2003	77.5	78.1	78.4	79.0	79.1	77.2	75.4	75.5	78.3	78.8	79.1	79.4	78.0
2004	79.0	79.1	78.9	79.5	79.1	78.3	76.5	76.5	78.7	79.1	79.6	79.5	78.7
2005	78.8	79.3	79.5	79.8	79.9	79.4	76.9	77.5	79.7	80.7	80.9	80.7	79.4
2006	81.4	81.6	81.7	82.2	82.4	82.3	79.1	79.6	82.3	83.0	83.2	83.3	81.8
2007	82.9	83.3	83.5	83.5	83.8	83.6	80.0	80.7	83.3	83.9	84.1	84.0	83.1
2008	83.6	84.0	84.2	84.4	84.7	84.7	81.1	81.6	83.6	85.0	84.9	85.2	83.9
2009	84.5	84.6	84.6	85.0	84.8	84.8	80.6	80.9	83.1	83.9	84.3	84.2	83.8
2010	83.9	84.1	84.6	85.0	87.3	86.0	81.9	81.2	83.0	83.9	83.9	84.0	84.1
2011	83.7	83.8	83.9	84.0	84.2	83.9	80.6	80.1	82.4	82.0	82.1	82.2	82.7
2012	81.6	82.2	82.6	82.5	82.5	81.9	78.4	78.6	80.5	81.6	81.9	82.0	81.4
2013	81.5	81.8	81.8	81.8	81.5	81.2	78.5	78.5	80.3	80.8	80.8	80.7	80.8

Employment by Industry: Boston–Cambridge–Quincy, MA–NH, NECTA, Selected Years, 2002–2013

(Numbers in thousands, not seasonally adjusted)

Industry and year	January	February	March	April	May	June	July	August	September	October	November	December	Annual average
Total Nonfarm													
2002	2,454.7	2,448.5	2,460.6	2,475.8	2,484.3	2,490.8	2,454.5	2,447.7	2,468.1	2,476.5	2,484.8	2,486.5	2,469.4
2003	2,398.5	2,388.5	2,396.8	2,417.9	2,428.1	2,434.9	2,406.4	2,396.2	2,418.8	2,424.6	2,434.3	2,431.4	2,414.7
2004	2,358.8	2,364.1	2,378.7	2,406.3	2,418.0	2,428.9	2,410.6	2,400.0	2,421.9	2,435.0	2,443.3	2,448.9	2,409.5
2005	2,375.8	2,385.0	2,391.0	2,426.9	2,436.6	2,448.9	2,428.4	2,421.6	2,445.0	2,453.8	2,468.1	2,474.4	2,429.6
2006	2,404.5	2,409.8	2,424.1	2,448.2	2,458.2	2,478.2	2,455.2	2,449.4	2,475.0	2,486.9	2,497.3	2,505.0	2,457.7
2007	2,442.1	2,443.4	2,453.4	2,481.8	2,500.9	2,517.8	2,491.7	2,486.1	2,505.3	2,520.2	2,532.5	2,533.3	2,492.4
2008	2,472.5	2,475.8	2,485.0	2,508.7	2,522.3	2,533.3	2,506.6	2,497.4	2,513.7	2,526.2	2,519.6	2,509.5	2,505.9
2009	2,423.2	2,417.3	2,412.6	2,434.0	2,438.8	2,440.0	2,407.3	2,399.4	2,422.1	2,441.3	2,444.4	2,447.3	2,427.3
2010	2,395.9	2,395.7	2,405.6	2,435.0	2,452.3	2,451.6	2,433.2	2,426.5	2,443.5	2,470.8	2,474.9	2,479.5	2,438.7
2011	2,410.5	2,417.5	2,429.4	2,467.0	2,473.9	2,482.4	2,474.9	2,462.7	2,488.3	2,504.0	2,510.5	2,514.1	2,469.6
2012	2,452.5	2,457.5	2,476.6	2,497.7	2,513.1	2,537.4	2,512.3	2,507.9	2,528.9	2,549.4	2,560.9	2,560.8	2,512.9
2013	2,493.6	2,501.3	2,518.8	2,545.5	2,564.4	2,581.1	2,554.6	2,551.8	2,568.1	2,589.5	2,590.8	2,588.7	2,554.0
Total Private													
2002	2,150.2	2,141.6	2,153.3	2,169.4	2,177.6	2,185.6	2,171.1	2,167.9	2,163.0	2,173.9	2,179.6	2,181.6	2,167.9
2003	2,097.7	2,085.3	2,093.9	2,114.6	2,125.2	2,133.4	2,123.6	2,119.9	2,119.1	2,126.7	2,135.3	2,133.0	2,117.3
2004	2,064.4	2,065.7	2,080.0	2,106.9	2,119.4	2,132.5	2,136.3	2,131.9	2,127.0	2,138.2	2,144.8	2,150.7	2,116.5
2005	2,080.4	2,084.8	2,090.9	2,126.1	2,135.6	2,151.5	2,152.4	2,151.5	2,149.0	2,154.2	2,166.4	2,173.9	2,134.7
2006	2,107.0	2,107.8	2,121.8	2,145.6	2,155.2	2,178.2	2,176.2	2,177.1	2,176.2	2,184.9	2,193.6	2,202.0	2,160.5
2007	2,141.6	2,139.5	2,149.0	2,176.5	2,194.6	2,215.5	2,212.9	2,213.5	2,204.5	2,215.3	2,225.6	2,227.1	2,193.0
2008	2,168.8	2,167.9	2,176.8	2,199.2	2,212.3	2,226.0	2,223.5	2,220.4	2,208.8	2,217.0	2,209.0	2,199.4	2,202.4
2009	2,117.4	2,106.0	2,101.8	2,119.5	2,126.6	2,132.2	2,126.8	2,121.8	2,117.5	2,131.5	2,134.2	2,135.8	2,122.6
2010	2,088.6	2,085.9	2,095.1	2,122.9	2,134.8	2,142.4	2,151.0	2,147.1	2,138.7	2,162.6	2,164.4	2,169.0	2,133.5
2011	2,108.2	2,109.4	2,121.0	2,159.1	2,165.5	2,177.7	2,193.3	2,187.2	2,185.3	2,198.3	2,203.7	2,205.5	2,167.9
2012	2,150.0	2,150.3	2,167.9	2,190.7	2,205.6	2,231.6	2,231.3	2,230.8	2,224.4	2,242.7	2,250.5	2,251.8	2,210.6
2013	2,192.8	2,192.3	2,209.7	2,234.6	2,252.2	2,274.2	2,274.7	2,276.4	2,266.4	2,285.1	2,283.0	2,281.7	2,251.9
Goods-Producing													
2002	362.4	356.6	357.9	362.0	365.7	367.2	362.6	363.0	360.5	360.1	358.0	352.8	360.7
2003	340.7	333.4	334.0	339.6	343.4	345.7	342.4	342.9	340.4	337.9	337.0	332.5	339.2
2004	319.9	318.2	322.2	329.7	335.3	340.0	339.7	340.9	338.3	335.2	334.1	331.6	332.1
2005	320.1	317.7	318.3	326.2	330.3	335.1	335.6	336.7	334.7	332.3	332.0	329.2	329.0
2006	318.9	316.5	317.8	324.2	327.3	331.7	332.1	333.4	331.6	329.6	327.2	325.1	326.3
2007	315.8	311.9	313.5	317.8	323.8	328.9	329.2	329.6	327.2	325.2	323.6	319.7	322.2
2008	309.7	306.9	308.4	312.7	316.7	320.1	320.6	320.4	317.0	314.0	309.6	302.9	313.3
2009	286.3	280.1	277.1	279.5	280.5	282.4	282.1	281.6	279.1	278.5	276.8	273.8	279.8
2010	264.9	261.9	263.3	268.3	272.8	276.7	279.6	279.4	277.6	278.6	277.5	275.2	273.0
2011	265.6	263.3	265.1	272.7	275.8	280.2	283.1	283.4	280.2	278.8	277.5	275.4	275.1
2012	267.9	265.7	268.2	273.5	277.2	283.1	285.1	285.6	283.7	284.2	283.0	281.3	278.2
2013	273.5	271.3	273.0	278.2	283.9	288.8	290.5	290.6	288.4	288.7	286.3	281.8	282.9
Service-Providing													
2002	2,092.3	2,091.9	2,102.7	2,113.8	2,118.6	2,123.6	2,091.9	2,084.7	2,107.6	2,116.4	2,126.8	2,133.7	2,108.7
2003	2,057.8	2,055.1	2,062.8	2,078.3	2,084.7	2,089.2	2,064.0	2,053.3	2,078.4	2,086.7	2,097.3	2,098.9	2,075.5
2004	2,038.9	2,045.9	2,056.5	2,076.6	2,082.7	2,088.9	2,070.9	2,059.1	2,083.6	2,099.8	2,109.2	2,117.3	2,077.5
2005	2,055.7	2,067.3	2,072.7	2,100.7	2,106.3	2,113.8	2,092.8	2,084.9	2,110.3	2,121.5	2,136.1	2,145.2	2,100.6
2006	2,085.6	2,093.3	2,106.3	2,124.0	2,130.9	2,146.5	2,123.1	2,116.0	2,143.4	2,157.3	2,170.1	2,179.9	2,131.4
2007	2,126.3	2,131.5	2,139.9	2,164.0	2,177.1	2,188.9	2,162.5	2,156.5	2,178.1	2,195.0	2,208.9	2,213.6	2,170.2
2008	2,162.8	2,168.9	2,176.6	2,196.0	2,205.6	2,213.2	2,186.0	2,177.0	2,196.7	2,212.2	2,210.0	2,206.6	2,192.6
2009	2,136.9	2,137.2	2,135.5	2,154.5	2,158.3	2,157.6	2,125.2	2,117.8	2,143.0	2,162.8	2,167.6	2,173.5	2,147.5
2010	2,131.0	2,133.8	2,142.3	2,166.7	2,179.5	2,174.9	2,153.6	2,147.1	2,165.9	2,192.2	2,197.4	2,204.3	2,165.7
2011	2,144.9	2,154.2	2,164.3	2,194.3	2,198.1	2,202.2	2,191.8	2,179.3	2,208.1	2,225.2	2,233.0	2,238.7	2,194.5
2012	2,184.6	2,191.8	2,208.4	2,224.2	2,235.9	2,254.3	2,227.2	2,222.3	2,245.2	2,265.2	2,277.9	2,279.5	2,234.7
2013	2,220.1	2,230.0	2,245.8	2,267.3	2,280.5	2,292.3	2,264.1	2,261.2	2,279.7	2,300.8	2,304.5	2,306.9	2,271.1
Mining and Logging													
2002	0.8	0.8	0.9	1.0	1.1	1.1	1.1	1.1	1.1	1.1	1.1	1.1	1.0
2003	1.0	0.9	0.9	1.1	1.2	1.2	1.3	1.2	1.3	1.3	1.3	1.2	1.2
2004	1.0	1.0	1.0	1.2	1.3	1.3	1.3	1.3	1.3	1.3	1.3	1.3	1.2
2005	1.1	1.0	1.0	1.3	1.3	1.4	1.4	1.3	1.3	1.3	1.3	1.1	1.2
2006	1.0	1.0	1.0	1.1	1.2	1.2	1.3	1.2	1.2	1.2	1.2	1.1	1.1
2007	0.9	0.8	0.9	1.0	1.1	1.1	1.1	1.1	1.1	1.0	1.0	0.9	1.0
2008	0.7	0.7	0.7	0.8	0.9	0.9	0.9	0.8	0.8	0.8	0.8	0.7	0.8
2009	0.7	0.6	0.6	0.7	0.8	0.8	0.8	0.8	0.8	0.8	0.8	0.7	0.7
2010	0.6	0.5	0.6	0.7	0.7	0.7	0.6	0.6	0.6	0.6	0.6	0.5	0.6
2011	0.4	0.4	0.4	0.5	0.6	0.6	0.6	0.6	0.6	0.6	0.6	0.5	0.5
2012	0.4	0.4	0.5	0.5	0.5	0.5	0.5	0.5	0.5	0.5	0.5	0.5	0.5
2013	0.4	0.4	0.4	0.5	0.5	0.6	0.6	0.6	0.6	0.6	0.5	0.5	0.5
Construction													
2002	96.7	93.9	95.9	102.6	106.8	108.1	109.1	109.3	107.6	108.9	107.8	102.9	104.1
2003	95.0	90.5	91.6	98.6	103.0	104.8	105.8	106.0	104.5	103.2	102.4	98.9	100.4
2004	90.0	88.6	91.6	97.9	103.0	106.0	107.5	107.6	105.9	104.4	103.7	101.1	100.6
2005	91.5	89.2	90.3	98.5	102.4	105.7	108.2	108.6	107.7	105.5	105.4	102.5	101.3
2006	94.4	92.5	94.0	100.9	103.6	106.3	107.7	108.1	106.6	105.2	102.9	100.2	101.9
2007	92.4	88.9	90.5	95.5	100.8	104.3	106.1	106.3	105.1	104.1	102.9	98.9	99.7
2008	90.8	88.7	90.5	95.3	98.9	100.9	102.7	102.3	100.3	98.7	95.6	91.0	96.3
2009	80.1	76.6	75.9	80.0	82.4	84.1	85.1	84.9	83.5	83.0	80.8	77.7	81.2
2010	71.1	68.8	70.0	75.1	78.6	81.2	83.7	83.5	82.2	82.0	80.9	78.5	78.0
2011	71.7	69.9	71.3	77.8	81.1	84.1	86.7	87.2	85.6	84.6	83.6	81.4	80.4
2012	75.4	73.5	75.6	80.5	83.3	86.7	89.4	90.0	89.3	89.6	88.5	86.4	84.0
2013	80.5	78.8	80.2	85.4	90.2	93.0	95.5	95.8	94.4	94.3	91.6	86.8	88.9

Employment by Industry: Boston–Cambridge–Quincy, MA–NH, NECTA, Selected Years, 2002–2013—*Continued*

(Numbers in thousands, not seasonally adjusted)

Industry and year	January	February	March	April	May	June	July	August	September	October	November	December	Annual average
Manufacturing													
2002	264.9	261.9	261.1	258.4	257.8	258.0	252.4	252.6	251.8	250.1	249.1	248.8	255.6
2003	244.7	242.0	241.5	239.9	239.2	239.7	235.3	235.7	234.6	233.4	233.3	232.4	237.6
2004	228.9	228.6	229.6	230.6	231.0	232.7	230.9	232.0	231.1	229.5	229.1	229.2	230.3
2005	227.5	227.5	227.0	226.4	226.6	228.0	226.0	226.8	225.7	225.5	225.3	225.6	226.5
2006	223.5	223.0	222.8	222.2	222.5	224.2	223.1	224.1	223.8	223.2	223.1	223.8	223.3
2007	222.5	222.2	222.1	221.3	221.9	223.5	222.0	222.2	221.0	220.1	219.7	219.9	221.5
2008	218.2	217.5	217.2	216.6	216.9	218.3	217.0	217.3	215.9	214.5	213.2	211.2	216.2
2009	205.5	202.9	200.6	198.8	197.3	197.5	196.2	195.9	194.8	194.7	195.2	195.4	197.9
2010	193.2	192.6	192.7	192.5	193.5	194.8	195.3	195.3	194.8	196.0	196.0	196.2	194.4
2011	193.5	193.0	193.4	194.4	194.1	195.5	195.8	195.6	194.0	193.6	193.3	193.5	194.1
2012	192.1	191.8	192.1	192.5	193.4	195.9	195.2	195.1	193.9	194.1	194.0	194.4	193.7
2013	192.6	192.1	192.4	192.3	193.2	195.2	194.4	194.2	193.4	193.8	194.2	194.5	193.5
Trade, Transportation, and Utilities													
2002	434.4	426.5	427.5	428.5	431.2	436.0	430.0	428.5	430.6	433.3	441.0	449.4	433.1
2003	426.0	419.3	420.7	421.5	423.9	428.5	422.7	422.2	424.3	428.5	436.7	442.0	426.4
2004	422.9	417.4	417.9	417.8	420.4	424.8	419.8	418.4	417.9	425.5	433.0	440.5	423.0
2005	420.1	415.8	414.8	417.6	420.2	423.8	418.8	418.5	417.7	420.9	428.5	437.5	421.2
2006	419.6	411.2	413.1	414.5	416.7	421.8	416.1	416.2	417.3	421.4	430.1	438.4	419.7
2007	419.3	411.1	411.9	412.0	417.1	422.4	416.8	415.9	415.7	420.3	430.1	435.9	419.0
2008	421.1	411.6	412.0	413.2	416.9	420.9	416.4	415.9	414.4	417.3	421.1	425.9	417.2
2009	404.2	395.8	392.7	392.3	395.7	399.9	393.9	392.6	394.3	399.5	406.0	411.1	398.2
2010	397.2	390.3	390.6	393.3	396.8	400.7	397.4	396.8	394.8	401.5	407.6	415.6	398.6
2011	399.2	393.6	393.8	398.1	400.0	404.1	402.0	401.4	401.1	405.3	412.2	419.0	402.5
2012	402.8	394.9	396.5	397.0	402.0	408.5	404.0	403.6	402.6	408.2	416.9	422.1	404.9
2013	406.1	398.9	399.8	402.5	407.0	413.0	409.0	409.5	408.2	412.5	419.9	429.8	409.7
Wholesale Trade													
2002	107.1	106.6	106.9	105.9	106.0	106.7	105.7	105.2	104.4	104.7	104.7	105.2	105.8
2003	104.7	104.2	104.1	103.7	103.9	104.4	104.5	104.4	103.6	103.8	104.2	104.7	104.2
2004	102.8	102.6	103.2	102.9	102.6	103.2	102.8	102.5	101.3	101.3	101.2	101.3	102.3
2005	100.8	100.6	100.2	100.9	101.5	102.1	102.8	102.8	102.3	103.1	103.4	104.1	102.1
2006	103.0	102.6	102.8	103.4	103.5	104.7	104.9	105.2	104.5	104.8	104.9	105.4	104.1
2007	104.3	103.9	104.2	103.8	104.1	105.1	104.9	104.6	103.7	103.8	103.5	103.6	104.1
2008	102.6	101.6	101.5	101.9	101.9	102.6	102.5	101.9	100.8	100.3	99.7	99.4	101.4
2009	97.0	95.6	94.9	94.2	93.8	94.0	93.3	92.8	91.6	92.2	91.8	91.7	93.6
2010	90.5	90.2	90.3	90.4	91.0	91.5	91.9	91.7	90.8	91.2	91.1	91.2	91.0
2011	90.5	90.3	90.5	91.2	91.1	91.3	92.1	91.6	90.6	90.7	90.4	90.5	90.9
2012	89.9	89.8	90.1	90.7	91.1	91.9	92.2	92.3	91.2	91.9	91.9	92.0	91.3
2013	91.0	90.7	90.9	91.5	91.7	92.5	93.3	93.2	92.5	92.9	93.0	93.5	92.2
Retail Trade													
2002	259.7	252.6	253.5	255.1	257.0	260.6	258.3	257.8	257.8	259.5	267.5	276.0	259.6
2003	255.0	249.2	250.5	251.7	253.2	257.1	254.3	254.4	254.2	258.5	266.3	271.5	256.3
2004	256.6	251.8	251.7	251.1	253.4	257.1	254.9	254.5	253.2	259.6	267.5	275.3	257.2
2005	257.2	253.1	252.6	254.3	255.7	258.3	254.8	255.0	252.9	256.4	263.8	271.4	257.1
2006	256.7	248.8	250.2	250.7	252.0	254.8	251.0	251.3	249.5	253.8	262.5	269.3	254.2
2007	253.2	245.9	246.1	246.5	250.4	253.6	251.1	250.8	248.5	253.2	263.7	268.6	252.6
2008	256.7	248.7	248.8	249.2	251.4	254.3	252.6	253.4	249.9	253.9	258.9	263.1	253.4
2009	246.9	240.3	238.1	238.1	241.3	244.8	242.5	242.8	241.7	246.3	253.2	257.2	244.4
2010	246.6	240.4	240.5	242.5	244.6	247.5	246.9	247.4	243.4	249.4	255.8	262.1	247.3
2011	249.2	244.0	243.7	246.4	247.7	250.6	250.2	251.1	248.4	252.9	260.1	265.7	250.8
2012	252.7	245.0	246.1	246.2	250.0	254.6	252.5	252.8	249.6	254.4	263.4	266.8	252.8
2013	255.1	248.1	248.7	250.1	253.3	257.1	255.2	256.4	252.6	256.5	264.1	271.6	255.7
Transportation and Utilities													
2002	67.6	67.3	67.1	67.5	68.2	68.7	66.0	65.5	68.4	69.1	68.8	68.2	67.7
2003	66.3	65.9	66.1	66.1	66.8	67.0	63.9	63.4	66.5	66.2	66.2	65.8	65.9
2004	63.5	63.0	63.0	63.8	64.4	64.5	62.1	61.4	63.4	64.6	64.3	63.9	63.5
2005	62.1	62.1	62.0	62.4	63.0	63.4	61.2	60.7	62.5	61.4	61.3	62.0	62.0
2006	59.9	59.8	60.1	60.4	61.2	62.3	60.2	59.7	63.3	62.8	62.7	63.7	61.3
2007	61.8	61.3	61.6	61.6	61.7	62.6	63.7	60.8	60.5	63.5	62.9	63.7	62.3
2008	61.8	61.3	61.7	62.1	63.3	64.0	61.3	60.6	63.7	63.1	62.5	63.4	62.4
2009	60.3	59.9	59.7	60.0	60.6	61.1	58.1	57.0	61.0	61.0	61.0	62.2	60.2
2010	60.1	59.7	59.8	60.4	61.2	61.7	58.6	57.7	60.6	60.9	60.7	62.3	60.3
2011	59.5	59.3	59.6	60.5	61.2	62.2	59.7	58.7	62.1	61.7	61.7	62.8	60.8
2012	60.2	60.1	60.3	60.1	60.9	62.0	59.3	58.5	61.8	61.9	61.6	63.3	60.8
2013	60.0	60.1	60.2	60.9	62.0	63.4	60.5	59.9	63.1	63.1	62.8	64.7	61.7
Information													
2002	88.2	87.5	87.2	85.6	84.9	84.7	84.1	84.3	82.0	82.0	81.8	81.9	84.5
2003	79.5	79.1	79.0	78.0	77.6	78.0	76.9	76.5	75.7	75.4	75.2	75.2	77.2
2004	73.8	73.4	73.4	74.0	73.3	73.5	73.7	73.9	73.9	73.5	73.4	73.8	73.7
2005	73.4	73.6	73.6	73.7	73.8	74.4	74.6	74.3	73.7	73.8	74.0	74.3	73.9
2006	74.0	74.1	74.1	73.7	74.0	74.6	74.4	74.5	73.6	74.6	74.6	74.9	74.3
2007	73.6	73.8	74.0	74.2	74.5	75.3	75.5	75.5	75.0	74.5	74.7	74.9	74.6
2008	74.8	75.2	75.4	75.1	75.1	76.0	76.4	76.5	75.7	75.3	75.0	75.0	75.5
2009	74.8	73.6	73.3	72.7	72.6	72.8	72.7	72.9	72.6	72.9	72.9	73.1	73.1
2010	73.3	73.2	73.1	73.3	73.4	74.1	73.4	73.4	72.6	71.8	72.0	72.2	73.0
2011	71.5	71.6	71.8	72.1	72.6	73.5	75.0	72.0	72.0	74.2	74.4	74.8	73.2
2012	74.3	74.2	74.4	74.7	74.8	76.3	77.4	76.5	74.4	74.8	74.7	74.6	75.1
2013	73.8	73.6	73.5	73.8	73.9	75.2	75.7	75.3	74.3	74.7	74.9	75.9	74.6

Employment by Industry: Boston–Cambridge–Quincy, MA–NH, NECTA, Selected Years, 2002–2013—*Continued*
(Numbers in thousands, not seasonally adjusted)

Industry and year	January	February	March	April	May	June	July	August	September	October	November	December	Annual average
Financial Activities													
2002	195.0	193.7	193.1	190.6	190.9	192.7	193.1	192.6	189.8	190.4	189.8	190.5	191.9
2003	188.5	187.3	187.2	187.1	187.3	188.4	188.3	188.2	184.9	183.7	184.0	184.4	186.6
2004	181.8	182.1	182.3	182.5	182.7	184.9	186.1	185.5	183.4	182.1	182.1	183.1	183.2
2005	182.5	182.4	182.6	183.2	184.1	186.9	189.7	189.9	188.6	187.0	187.8	189.4	186.2
2006	185.7	185.6	185.9	186.1	186.8	189.3	191.6	191.1	189.4	188.9	189.4	190.9	188.4
2007	188.5	188.5	188.5	188.5	189.0	191.3	191.8	191.8	188.7	187.5	187.2	188.2	189.1
2008	186.0	185.6	185.8	185.6	185.9	187.7	188.7	188.4	185.6	184.9	184.3	184.4	186.1
2009	181.8	180.6	179.9	178.9	178.8	179.8	179.6	178.7	176.2	175.8	175.8	176.0	178.5
2010	174.1	173.3	173.0	172.8	173.6	175.0	175.9	175.7	173.4	173.3	173.0	174.1	173.9
2011	171.9	171.6	171.6	172.2	172.4	174.0	175.6	175.5	173.3	172.5	171.9	172.2	172.9
2012	170.7	170.9	171.0	171.1	171.9	174.4	174.9	175.2	172.4	172.5	172.4	173.0	172.5
2013	170.9	171.3	171.6	171.1	171.9	173.9	174.9	175.2	172.3	172.6	172.0	172.2	172.5
Professional and Business Services													
2002	382.0	378.7	380.0	385.3	384.9	387.5	385.2	384.4	381.1	381.2	380.2	379.0	382.5
2003	363.4	359.4	359.7	367.0	367.7	370.5	371.8	371.6	369.9	371.2	372.4	371.9	368.0
2004	361.4	361.4	364.1	373.5	374.7	380.0	383.2	383.9	382.8	383.4	383.7	385.0	376.4
2005	372.6	373.1	374.8	384.2	384.9	390.2	391.4	392.2	390.9	390.9	393.3	393.4	386.0
2006	382.5	383.8	386.3	393.5	395.2	402.6	402.1	403.1	401.2	402.4	403.4	403.9	396.7
2007	393.5	395.3	397.6	406.9	409.8	415.4	415.2	417.2	412.9	415.0	416.5	417.0	409.4
2008	408.1	408.9	409.8	415.9	417.9	422.1	421.2	419.9	416.6	416.9	413.3	409.0	415.0
2009	395.4	391.0	389.3	393.0	391.4	393.7	392.2	391.1	387.9	389.8	389.7	390.2	391.2
2010	384.1	384.3	386.0	394.7	395.1	398.0	401.4	400.7	396.2	401.0	400.6	399.8	395.2
2011	392.5	392.4	392.8	404.4	404.3	408.7	412.6	411.0	409.1	412.2	413.2	412.8	405.5
2012	403.4	403.0	407.8	416.2	418.1	425.6	426.4	426.7	424.4	427.6	428.7	426.9	419.6
2013	417.2	419.6	421.6	430.3	433.2	439.3	441.0	441.4	437.2	440.9	441.2	438.9	433.5
Education and Health Services													
2002	415.9	425.7	428.7	429.8	423.6	412.9	411.6	410.5	422.8	432.8	437.9	437.8	424.2
2003	422.3	430.6	433.6	434.8	428.3	418.1	416.6	414.4	427.5	436.4	440.2	439.8	428.6
2004	427.5	436.9	439.2	440.8	434.4	424.1	424.5	421.7	432.6	442.6	445.4	445.4	434.6
2005	432.8	442.8	444.1	447.9	441.1	430.6	430.8	429.3	441.0	451.7	455.8	456.0	442.0
2006	443.8	454.3	457.7	458.5	453.1	445.2	443.3	442.0	455.2	464.0	467.8	468.1	454.4
2007	460.9	469.3	470.5	476.5	470.5	460.1	461.0	459.3	470.4	481.4	484.8	485.2	470.8
2008	473.5	483.7	486.3	488.9	482.6	472.9	473.3	471.6	482.3	493.6	496.6	497.0	483.5
2009	485.1	494.8	497.0	500.9	493.9	482.4	484.9	483.8	495.1	505.0	508.6	509.2	495.1
2010	499.7	509.4	512.0	509.8	503.3	489.8	492.2	490.9	503.6	514.7	518.0	517.7	505.1
2011	505.1	515.8	518.8	518.7	512.2	498.7	501.7	500.5	514.3	524.4	528.7	528.5	514.0
2012	516.7	527.9	530.5	528.8	522.6	510.7	511.3	510.8	524.9	536.4	541.4	542.6	525.4
2013	530.0	538.9	543.4	541.3	534.5	524.1	524.3	522.8	536.5	547.4	549.0	546.5	536.6
Leisure and Hospitality													
2002	185.9	186.4	191.4	200.0	207.9	215.2	214.7	215.0	208.7	206.1	202.6	201.6	203.0
2003	190.5	189.6	192.2	199.3	209.1	215.5	215.8	215.7	209.4	206.9	202.5	199.9	203.9
2004	190.8	190.2	193.3	202.3	210.8	217.3	220.5	219.3	212.2	209.7	205.6	203.9	206.3
2005	193.2	193.5	196.1	205.6	213.3	221.4	221.7	221.2	214.4	210.4	207.4	205.7	208.7
2006	195.4	195.7	199.1	207.0	213.7	223.2	226.0	226.1	219.3	215.4	212.5	211.7	212.1
2007	202.3	201.5	204.2	211.3	219.3	229.6	230.1	230.9	223.7	220.9	217.5	215.0	217.2
2008	206.1	206.4	209.0	217.2	226.2	233.4	232.7	233.6	225.8	223.8	218.0	214.4	220.6
2009	200.7	201.2	202.8	211.3	221.9	226.8	226.6	226.6	221.2	219.3	213.7	211.6	215.3
2010	205.8	204.2	207.0	219.4	227.1	232.8	233.7	233.6	227.5	228.8	222.7	220.8	222.0
2011	210.6	208.8	213.4	225.6	232.3	240.1	243.1	243.5	237.1	234.8	229.6	226.7	228.8
2012	219.8	219.2	223.6	233.7	242.2	252.9	251.7	252.7	245.2	242.4	236.9	234.7	237.9
2013	226.4	223.9	230.3	240.0	249.5	258.8	257.5	259.8	251.0	249.9	241.0	237.5	243.8
Other Services													
2002	86.4	86.5	87.5	87.6	88.5	89.4	89.8	89.6	87.5	88.0	88.3	88.6	88.1
2003	86.8	86.6	87.5	87.3	87.9	88.7	89.1	88.4	87.0	86.7	87.3	87.3	87.6
2004	86.3	86.1	87.0	87.0	87.6	87.7	88.6	88.3	86.3	86.3	86.7	87.1	87.1
2005	85.7	85.9	86.6	87.7	87.9	89.1	89.8	89.4	88.0	87.2	87.6	88.4	87.8
2006	87.1	86.6	87.8	88.1	88.4	89.8	90.6	90.7	88.6	88.7	88.6	89.0	88.7
2007	87.7	88.1	88.8	89.3	90.6	92.5	93.3	93.3	90.9	90.5	91.2	91.2	90.6
2008	89.5	89.6	90.1	90.6	91.3	92.9	94.2	94.1	91.4	91.2	91.1	90.8	91.4
2009	89.1	88.9	89.7	90.9	91.8	94.4	94.8	94.5	91.1	90.8	90.7	90.8	91.5
2010	89.5	89.3	90.1	91.3	92.7	95.3	97.1	96.6	93.0	92.9	93.0	93.6	92.9
2011	91.8	92.3	93.7	95.3	95.9	98.4	100.2	99.9	96.0	95.9	96.1	96.1	96.0
2012	94.4	94.5	95.9	95.7	96.8	100.1	100.5	99.7	96.8	96.6	96.5	96.6	97.0
2013	94.9	94.8	96.5	97.4	98.3	101.1	101.8	101.8	98.5	98.4	98.7	99.1	98.4
Government													
2002	304.5	306.9	307.3	306.4	306.7	305.2	283.4	279.8	305.1	302.6	305.2	304.9	301.5
2003	300.8	303.2	302.9	303.3	302.9	301.5	282.8	276.3	299.7	297.9	299.0	298.4	297.4
2004	294.4	298.4	298.7	299.4	298.6	296.4	274.3	268.1	294.9	296.8	298.5	298.2	293.1
2005	295.4	300.2	300.1	300.8	301.0	297.4	276.0	270.1	296.0	299.6	301.7	300.5	294.9
2006	297.5	302.0	302.3	302.6	303.0	300.0	279.0	272.3	298.8	302.0	303.7	303.0	297.2
2007	300.5	303.9	304.4	305.3	306.3	302.3	278.8	272.6	300.8	304.9	306.9	306.2	299.4
2008	303.7	307.9	308.2	309.5	310.0	307.3	283.1	277.0	304.9	309.2	310.6	310.1	303.5
2009	305.8	311.3	310.8	314.5	312.2	307.8	280.5	277.6	304.6	309.8	310.2	311.5	304.7
2010	307.3	309.8	310.5	312.1	317.5	309.2	282.2	279.4	304.8	308.2	310.5	310.5	305.2
2011	302.3	308.1	308.4	307.9	308.4	304.7	281.6	275.5	303.0	305.7	306.8	308.6	301.8
2012	302.5	307.2	308.7	307.0	307.5	305.8	281.0	277.1	304.5	306.7	310.4	309.0	302.3
2013	300.8	309.0	309.1	310.9	312.2	306.9	279.9	275.4	301.7	304.4	307.8	307.0	302.1

Employment by Industry: Bridgeport–Stamford–Norwalk, CT, NECTA, Selected Years, 2002–2013

(Numbers in thousands, not seasonally adjusted)

Industry and year	January	February	March	April	May	June	July	August	September	October	November	December	Annual average
Total Nonfarm													
2002	410.6	409.5	412.5	416.8	418.9	421.5	410.7	408.9	412.0	414.7	417.8	418.9	414.4
2003	406.0	404.8	407.1	409.8	413.0	415.5	411.6	406.7	409.7	412.5	413.6	414.1	410.4
2004	402.5	402.1	405.8	407.2	411.4	415.2	412.1	408.2	410.5	412.9	415.1	416.3	409.9
2005	402.0	402.9	404.7	411.0	413.8	417.2	414.2	410.1	411.8	413.1	415.8	418.4	411.3
2006	408.4	408.9	408.8	415.6	418.9	422.1	417.8	414.3	416.0	418.1	421.4	425.2	416.3
2007	412.1	411.7	413.3	417.1	422.0	425.7	424.1	419.6	419.2	421.5	424.0	426.8	419.8
2008	414.3	413.1	415.6	418.0	421.4	424.6	419.2	415.1	415.6	416.3	417.1	416.9	417.3
2009	402.0	399.3	399.2	396.8	400.9	403.2	398.2	394.2	396.3	396.6	398.2	399.8	398.7
2010	385.5	384.1	386.7	392.8	401.0	403.7	403.3	399.3	398.4	399.7	400.8	403.3	396.6
2011	391.2	392.2	394.1	399.6	403.0	405.5	405.4	401.4	402.4	403.7	405.3	407.6	401.0
2012	398.1	397.5	400.9	403.7	408.0	412.2	410.8	406.8	406.7	407.6	409.7	412.8	406.2
2013	401.4	399.3	403.0	408.6	412.5	418.2	416.3	412.8	412.5	413.2	416.0	418.1	411.0
Total Private													
2002	362.9	361.4	364.2	368.0	369.9	372.4	369.8	367.5	365.1	366.3	368.6	369.9	367.2
2003	357.9	356.5	358.6	361.8	364.7	367.1	366.5	364.1	363.5	365.4	365.9	366.6	363.2
2004	355.0	354.1	357.3	359.7	363.8	367.7	367.6	365.2	363.8	365.1	366.9	368.8	362.9
2005	355.4	355.9	357.6	363.0	365.5	368.8	368.7	366.1	364.9	365.7	368.3	370.6	364.2
2006	361.1	361.1	360.8	367.8	370.9	375.2	373.5	371.4	369.5	370.9	373.7	377.7	369.5
2007	365.2	364.1	365.7	369.6	373.5	378.4	377.8	374.9	372.4	373.5	375.6	378.7	372.5
2008	366.5	364.5	367.2	370.0	372.6	376.9	374.2	371.5	368.4	368.1	368.0	368.4	369.7
2009	354.5	351.4	351.1	349.9	352.5	355.1	353.5	350.6	349.4	349.4	350.5	352.6	351.7
2010	339.0	337.5	340.1	347.1	352.0	356.6	357.9	355.8	352.8	354.0	354.7	356.9	350.4
2011	345.6	346.0	347.9	353.1	356.1	360.0	362.5	360.0	357.3	357.9	359.2	361.5	355.6
2012	352.8	352.1	355.3	358.0	361.9	367.0	367.1	364.3	361.5	362.1	363.5	366.8	361.0
2013	355.7	353.5	357.1	362.6	366.3	371.7	372.1	369.9	367.0	367.3	369.5	371.7	365.4
Goods-Producing													
2002	59.6	59.2	59.5	60.4	60.5	60.9	59.9	60.0	59.7	59.2	58.9	58.3	59.7
2003	56.7	56.2	56.3	56.9	57.5	57.8	56.8	57.2	56.9	57.0	56.8	56.4	56.9
2004	54.8	54.4	55.0	56.2	56.6	57.2	56.8	56.8	56.9	57.2	56.9	56.8	56.3
2005	55.2	54.9	54.9	56.3	56.7	57.2	57.1	56.7	56.3	56.4	56.4	55.9	56.2
2006	54.9	55.1	52.3	56.4	56.6	57.2	57.2	57.1	56.8	56.7	56.5	56.3	56.1
2007	55.0	54.7	55.1	55.7	56.1	57.0	57.0	56.8	56.5	56.1	55.9	55.7	56.0
2008	54.1	53.5	54.0	54.7	55.4	55.7	55.3	55.1	54.9	54.2	53.7	52.8	54.5
2009	50.8	49.8	49.5	49.6	49.5	49.8	49.2	48.6	48.4	48.0	47.7	47.3	49.0
2010	45.3	44.9	45.2	46.4	46.9	47.8	48.0	47.9	47.5	47.2	46.8	46.5	46.7
2011	45.3	45.3	45.5	46.5	47.1	47.5	47.6	47.4	47.1	46.9	46.8	46.6	46.6
2012	45.4	45.3	45.2	45.4	45.8	46.6	46.5	46.3	45.7	45.7	45.6	45.6	45.8
2013	44.4	44.2	44.2	45.2	45.8	46.4	46.1	46.2	45.9	45.5	45.9	45.7	45.5
Service-Providing													
2002	351.0	350.3	353.0	356.4	358.4	360.6	350.8	348.9	352.3	355.5	358.9	360.6	354.7
2003	349.3	348.6	350.8	352.9	355.5	357.7	354.8	349.5	352.8	355.5	356.8	357.7	353.5
2004	347.7	347.7	350.8	351.0	354.8	358.0	355.3	351.4	353.6	355.7	358.2	359.5	353.6
2005	346.8	348.0	349.8	354.7	357.1	360.0	357.1	353.4	355.5	356.7	359.4	362.5	355.1
2006	353.5	353.8	356.5	359.2	362.3	364.9	360.6	357.2	359.2	361.4	364.9	368.9	360.2
2007	357.1	357.0	358.2	361.4	365.9	368.7	367.1	362.8	362.7	365.4	368.1	371.1	363.8
2008	360.2	359.6	361.6	363.3	366.0	368.9	363.9	360.0	360.7	362.1	363.4	364.1	362.8
2009	351.2	349.5	349.7	347.2	351.4	353.4	349.0	345.6	347.9	348.6	350.5	352.5	349.7
2010	340.2	339.2	341.5	346.4	354.1	355.9	355.3	351.4	350.9	352.5	354.0	356.8	349.9
2011	345.9	346.9	348.6	353.1	355.9	358.0	357.8	354.0	355.3	356.8	358.5	361.0	354.3
2012	352.7	352.2	355.7	358.3	362.2	365.6	364.3	360.5	361.0	361.9	364.1	367.2	360.5
2013	357.0	355.1	358.8	363.4	366.7	371.8	370.2	366.6	366.6	367.7	370.1	372.4	365.5
Mining, Logging, and Construction													
2002	13.6	13.4	13.8	14.5	14.8	15.2	15.2	15.2	15.0	14.7	14.6	14.0	14.5
2003	13.0	12.7	12.9	13.9	14.6	14.7	15.0	15.1	14.9	14.9	14.7	14.2	14.2
2004	12.9	12.5	12.9	14.2	14.7	15.0	15.3	15.4	15.2	15.3	15.1	14.8	14.4
2005	13.6	13.4	13.5	15.1	15.5	15.7	16.0	15.9	15.6	15.6	15.6	15.0	15.0
2006	14.3	14.2	14.6	15.5	15.8	16.0	16.4	16.3	16.1	16.0	15.8	15.5	15.5
2007	14.6	14.1	14.4	15.6	16.0	16.4	16.6	16.6	16.3	16.2	16.0	15.7	15.7
2008	14.3	14.1	14.3	15.2	15.7	15.8	15.8	15.8	15.6	15.1	14.7	14.0	15.0
2009	12.6	12.2	12.0	12.3	12.5	12.6	12.6	12.3	12.1	12.0	11.8	11.4	12.2
2010	9.7	9.5	9.7	11.0	11.3	11.7	11.9	12.0	11.8	11.6	11.5	11.1	11.1
2011	9.9	9.9	10.0	11.1	11.6	11.9	12.1	12.1	12.1	12.0	12.0	11.7	11.4
2012	10.8	10.6	10.8	11.5	11.8	12.2	12.4	12.2	12.0	12.0	11.9	11.8	11.7
2013	10.8	10.5	10.6	11.6	12.1	12.3	12.5	12.6	12.5	12.5	12.5	12.0	11.9
Manufacturing													
2002	46.0	45.8	45.7	45.9	45.7	45.7	44.7	44.8	44.7	44.5	44.3	44.3	45.2
2003	43.7	43.5	43.4	43.0	42.9	43.1	41.8	42.1	42.0	42.1	42.1	42.2	42.7
2004	41.9	41.9	42.1	42.0	41.9	42.2	41.5	41.4	41.7	41.9	41.8	42.0	41.9
2005	41.6	41.5	41.4	41.2	41.2	41.5	41.1	40.8	40.7	40.8	40.8	40.9	41.1
2006	40.6	40.9	37.7	40.9	40.8	41.2	40.8	40.8	40.7	40.7	40.7	40.8	40.6
2007	40.4	40.6	40.7	40.1	40.1	40.6	40.4	40.2	40.2	39.9	39.9	40.0	40.3
2008	39.8	39.4	39.7	39.5	39.7	39.9	39.5	39.3	39.3	39.1	39.0	38.8	39.4
2009	38.2	37.6	37.5	37.3	37.0	37.2	36.6	36.3	36.3	36.0	35.9	35.9	36.8
2010	35.6	35.4	35.5	35.4	35.6	36.1	36.1	35.9	35.7	35.6	35.3	35.4	35.6
2011	35.4	35.4	35.5	35.4	35.5	35.6	35.5	35.3	35.0	34.9	34.8	34.9	35.3
2012	34.6	34.7	34.4	33.9	34.0	34.4	34.1	34.1	33.7	33.7	33.7	33.8	34.1
2013	33.6	33.7	33.6	33.6	33.7	34.1	33.6	33.6	33.4	33.0	33.4	33.7	33.6

Employment by Industry: Bridgeport–Stamford–Norwalk, CT, NECTA, Selected Years, 2002–2013—*Continued*

(Numbers in thousands, not seasonally adjusted)

Industry and year	January	February	March	April	May	June	July	August	September	October	November	December	Annual average
Trade, Transportation, and Utilities													
2002	77.4	75.9	76.4	76.9	77.3	78.3	76.4	75.7	76.4	75.5	78.1	79.6	77.0
2003	75.5	74.1	74.5	74.1	74.7	75.3	74.2	73.4	74.4	75.1	76.5	78.0	75.0
2004	74.8	73.6	73.7	73.6	74.5	75.3	74.3	73.5	74.4	75.2	77.1	78.5	74.9
2005	75.3	74.1	74.2	74.2	74.7	75.3	74.1	73.8	74.7	75.5	77.4	79.5	75.2
2006	76.4	75.1	75.3	75.3	75.7	76.6	75.1	74.6	74.9	75.8	78.1	80.0	76.1
2007	76.1	74.3	74.6	74.6	75.8	77.0	75.6	75.3	75.6	76.1	78.6	80.8	76.2
2008	77.1	75.3	75.5	75.1	75.7	76.5	74.9	74.6	74.9	74.7	76.1	77.4	75.7
2009	73.2	71.5	71.2	69.9	70.7	71.4	69.8	69.2	69.7	70.2	71.9	73.5	71.0
2010	69.6	68.3	68.6	68.7	70.3	71.5	70.5	70.2	70.2	71.0	72.8	74.6	70.5
2011	71.0	69.9	69.9	70.7	71.1	72.0	71.1	70.7	70.6	71.2	72.9	74.8	71.3
2012	72.1	70.5	71.0	70.7	71.6	72.6	71.3	70.8	70.9	71.6	73.5	74.9	71.8
2013	72.2	70.5	71.2	71.4	71.8	72.8	71.8	71.6	71.7	72.2	73.8	75.9	72.2
Wholesale Trade													
2002	15.8	15.6	15.7	15.6	15.6	15.5	15.5	15.5	15.4	15.4	15.4	15.5	15.5
2003	15.1	15.0	15.0	14.9	14.9	15.0	15.0	14.9	14.9	14.8	14.9	15.0	15.0
2004	14.9	14.8	14.8	14.7	14.8	15.0	14.9	14.9	14.7	14.7	14.8	14.8	14.8
2005	14.7	14.7	14.7	14.6	14.7	14.8	14.7	14.7	14.6	14.7	14.6	14.8	14.7
2006	14.6	14.7	14.7	14.6	14.6	14.6	14.6	14.4	14.4	14.4	14.5	14.6	14.6
2007	14.4	14.4	14.5	14.4	14.4	14.6	14.6	14.7	14.6	14.6	14.7	14.9	14.6
2008	14.8	14.7	14.8	14.8	14.8	14.9	14.8	14.8	14.7	14.7	14.7	14.8	14.8
2009	14.4	14.3	14.2	13.9	13.8	13.9	13.8	13.6	13.6	13.6	13.4	13.5	13.8
2010	13.1	13.1	13.2	13.3	13.4	13.6	13.5	13.5	13.4	13.4	13.5	13.6	13.4
2011	13.5	13.4	13.5	13.6	13.6	13.8	13.8	13.8	13.6	13.6	13.5	13.6	13.6
2012	13.5	13.4	13.5	13.5	13.5	13.7	13.7	13.6	13.5	13.6	13.6	13.6	13.6
2013	13.6	13.5	13.6	13.6	13.6	13.8	13.8	13.7	13.6	13.7	13.7	13.8	13.7
Retail Trade													
2002	50.7	49.4	49.8	50.2	50.6	51.6	50.5	50.1	50.0	49.9	51.5	52.9	50.6
2003	49.6	48.3	48.6	48.8	49.3	49.7	49.4	49.0	49.0	49.6	50.9	52.3	49.5
2004	49.5	48.5	48.6	48.5	49.2	49.7	49.5	49.1	49.3	49.8	51.6	53.0	49.7
2005	50.1	49.0	49.0	49.1	49.5	50.0	49.6	49.6	49.6	50.1	52.0	53.7	50.1
2006	51.1	49.7	49.9	49.9	50.1	50.9	50.2	50.0	49.4	50.0	52.2	53.6	50.6
2007	50.3	48.6	48.8	48.8	49.9	50.7	50.2	50.0	49.6	50.1	52.3	54.0	50.3
2008	51.0	49.3	49.4	48.9	49.4	50.0	49.4	49.4	49.1	49.1	50.4	51.4	49.7
2009	47.9	46.4	46.2	45.7	46.4	47.0	46.2	46.1	45.8	46.3	48.2	49.3	46.8
2010	46.5	45.2	45.4	45.6	46.7	47.5	47.3	47.1	46.5	47.3	48.8	50.1	47.0
2011	47.2	46.2	46.1	46.6	47.0	47.6	47.3	47.1	46.5	47.1	48.8	50.2	47.3
2012	48.0	46.5	46.9	46.7	47.4	48.2	47.7	47.5	47.0	47.5	49.3	50.3	47.8
2013	48.2	46.9	47.2	47.4	47.8	48.5	48.2	48.2	47.5	47.8	49.1	50.8	48.1
Transportation and Utilities													
2002	10.9	10.9	10.9	11.1	11.1	11.2	10.4	10.1	11.0	10.2	11.2	11.2	10.9
2003	10.8	10.8	10.9	10.4	10.5	10.6	9.8	9.5	10.5	10.7	10.7	10.7	10.5
2004	10.4	10.3	10.3	10.4	10.5	10.6	9.9	9.5	10.4	10.7	10.7	10.7	10.4
2005	10.5	10.4	10.5	10.5	10.5	10.5	9.8	9.5	10.5	10.7	10.8	11.0	10.4
2006	10.7	10.7	10.7	10.8	11.0	11.1	10.3	10.2	11.1	11.3	11.4	11.8	10.9
2007	11.4	11.3	11.3	11.4	11.5	11.7	10.8	10.6	11.4	11.4	11.6	11.9	11.4
2008	11.3	11.3	11.3	11.4	11.5	11.6	10.7	10.4	11.1	10.9	11.0	11.2	11.1
2009	10.9	10.8	10.8	10.3	10.5	10.5	9.8	9.5	10.3	10.3	10.3	10.7	10.4
2010	10.0	10.0	10.0	9.8	10.2	10.4	9.7	9.6	10.3	10.3	10.5	10.9	10.1
2011	10.3	10.3	10.3	10.5	10.5	10.6	10.0	9.8	10.5	10.5	10.6	11.0	10.4
2012	10.6	10.6	10.6	10.5	10.7	10.7	9.9	9.7	10.4	10.5	10.6	11.0	10.5
2013	10.4	10.1	10.4	10.4	10.4	10.5	9.8	9.7	10.6	10.7	11.0	11.3	10.4
Information													
2002	13.2	13.0	13.0	12.8	12.7	12.7	12.7	12.6	12.4	12.4	12.4	12.4	12.7
2003	12.3	12.2	12.3	12.2	12.2	12.2	12.2	12.2	12.0	12.0	12.1	12.1	12.2
2004	12.2	12.1	12.0	12.0	12.1	12.2	12.1	12.1	11.9	11.7	11.8	11.7	12.0
2005	11.6	11.6	11.6	11.6	11.6	11.6	11.5	11.5	11.3	11.4	11.4	11.4	11.5
2006	11.3	11.2	11.4	11.3	11.4	11.4	11.3	11.2	11.2	11.1	11.2	11.4	11.3
2007	11.3	11.4	11.5	11.3	11.5	11.5	11.8	11.8	12.1	11.8	11.2	11.3	11.5
2008	11.3	11.3	11.4	11.3	11.3	11.5	11.5	11.6	11.5	11.5	11.6	11.7	11.5
2009	11.8	11.7	11.6	11.5	11.4	11.4	11.3	11.2	11.1	10.9	11.0	11.0	11.3
2010	10.8	10.8	10.8	10.9	11.0	10.9	10.8	10.8	10.7	10.7	10.8	10.9	10.8
2011	10.8	10.8	10.8	10.8	10.8	10.9	11.0	11.0	10.9	10.9	11.0	11.2	10.9
2012	11.1	11.1	11.0	11.0	11.0	11.0	11.1	11.2	11.1	11.1	11.2	11.4	11.1
2013	11.4	11.7	11.8	11.6	11.8	12.0	12.2	12.1	12.0	12.0	12.0	12.0	11.9
Financial Activities													
2002	40.0	40.1	39.8	40.3	40.4	40.8	41.0	41.1	40.7	41.0	41.2	41.7	40.7
2003	41.1	41.1	41.3	41.3	41.5	41.8	42.0	41.9	41.3	41.2	41.2	41.4	41.4
2004	40.9	41.0	41.2	41.0	41.3	41.8	42.2	42.2	41.9	42.0	42.1	42.3	41.7
2005	42.1	42.3	42.6	42.7	42.7	43.1	43.4	43.3	42.8	42.9	43.0	43.2	42.8
2006	43.1	43.1	43.4	43.3	43.7	44.2	44.4	44.8	44.4	44.6	45.0	45.2	44.1
2007	45.0	45.0	45.1	45.0	45.3	45.9	46.3	46.1	45.4	45.6	45.6	45.8	45.5
2008	45.2	45.3	45.5	45.4	45.4	46.0	45.8	45.9	45.1	45.0	44.9	45.0	45.4
2009	44.0	44.0	44.0	43.0	42.9	43.3	43.5	43.4	42.9	43.0	43.0	43.2	43.4
2010	42.3	42.3	42.4	42.4	42.5	43.2	43.4	43.5	42.8	42.6	42.7	43.0	42.8
2011	42.7	42.7	42.7	42.7	42.6	42.6	43.5	43.3	42.5	42.4	42.4	42.5	42.7
2012	42.0	41.9	41.9	41.8	41.9	42.5	42.6	42.3	41.7	41.8	41.7	41.8	42.0
2013	41.7	41.5	41.5	41.4	41.6	42.3	42.5	42.3	41.8	41.8	42.2	42.2	41.9

Employment by Industry: Bridgeport–Stamford–Norwalk, CT, NECTA, Selected Years, 2002–2013—*Continued*

(Numbers in thousands, not seasonally adjusted)

Industry and year	January	February	March	April	May	June	July	August	September	October	November	December	Annual average
Professional and Business Services													
2002	70.4	70.3	71.1	71.8	71.7	72.2	70.9	71.0	70.5	71.1	70.8	70.5	71.0
2003	68.8	68.8	68.9	70.7	70.6	71.0	70.6	71.0	71.4	71.2	70.8	70.5	70.4
2004	67.7	67.8	68.8	69.3	70.1	71.1	70.5	70.4	69.9	69.6	69.8	70.2	69.6
2005	66.6	67.1	67.9	69.4	69.6	70.4	70.2	70.3	71.0	70.7	71.2	71.4	69.7
2006	68.6	69.3	70.5	71.5	71.7	72.6	71.1	71.2	71.2	70.9	71.1	72.0	71.0
2007	68.6	68.5	68.7	70.6	71.0	71.7	70.4	70.2	69.9	70.4	70.3	70.4	70.1
2008	67.5	66.8	67.4	68.8	68.7	69.2	68.5	68.2	67.3	67.1	66.5	66.1	67.7
2009	63.7	63.0	63.0	63.3	63.1	63.6	63.0	62.9	62.6	62.7	62.5	62.5	63.0
2010	60.0	60.3	61.3	63.8	64.1	64.8	65.3	65.2	64.9	65.3	64.8	64.6	63.7
2011	62.4	63.2	63.7	65.2	65.6	66.1	66.7	66.4	66.0	66.3	66.3	66.1	65.3
2012	64.5	64.6	66.0	67.5	67.7	68.3	68.5	68.2	67.8	67.3	67.2	66.9	67.0
2013	64.1	64.3	64.8	66.8	67.3	68.1	68.4	68.6	67.9	68.1	68.2	67.9	67.0
Education and Health Services													
2002	56.6	57.6	58.3	58.3	58.3	57.2	57.2	56.4	57.4	59.4	59.8	59.7	58.0
2003	58.0	58.7	59.1	58.9	58.8	57.9	58.3	57.2	58.5	60.1	60.2	60.0	58.8
2004	58.4	59.1	59.8	59.4	59.2	58.5	58.7	58.2	58.9	60.2	60.5	60.1	59.3
2005	58.4	59.6	59.4	59.8	59.8	58.7	59.1	58.2	59.0	59.9	60.3	60.3	59.4
2006	59.6	60.3	60.2	60.6	60.8	59.9	60.0	59.1	60.0	61.2	61.8	62.2	60.5
2007	60.6	62.0	61.9	62.3	61.9	61.5	61.3	60.4	61.5	62.8	63.3	63.7	61.9
2008	62.3	63.6	64.0	64.0	63.5	63.5	63.1	62.1	63.4	64.7	65.2	65.4	63.7
2009	63.8	64.6	64.6	64.4	64.7	63.7	63.8	63.2	64.3	65.2	65.7	66.1	64.5
2010	64.8	65.0	65.2	66.1	66.2	65.4	65.7	64.8	65.8	66.8	67.1	67.3	65.9
2011	66.2	66.7	67.1	67.3	67.2	66.8	66.8	66.1	67.1	67.5	68.1	68.3	67.1
2012	67.8	68.5	68.8	68.8	68.9	68.4	68.3	67.6	68.9	69.4	69.8	70.7	68.8
2013	69.3	69.3	70.0	70.6	70.6	70.2	69.9	69.0	70.1	71.1	71.2	71.2	70.2
Leisure and Hospitality													
2002	28.8	28.4	29.2	30.5	31.8	33.0	34.2	33.4	31.3	30.9	30.5	30.7	31.1
2003	29.0	28.9	29.6	31.0	32.7	34.3	35.2	34.3	32.5	32.2	31.8	31.7	31.9
2004	29.8	29.7	30.3	31.6	33.3	34.7	35.6	34.8	33.3	32.6	32.1	32.5	32.5
2005	29.8	29.8	30.3	32.1	33.4	35.3	35.8	35.2	33.1	32.2	31.8	31.9	32.6
2006	30.4	30.3	30.9	32.5	34.0	36.1	36.6	36.0	34.1	33.5	32.9	33.4	33.4
2007	31.5	31.2	31.7	33.0	34.7	36.4	37.5	36.8	34.4	33.9	34.2	34.2	34.1
2008	32.3	32.2	32.8	34.0	35.8	37.3	37.6	36.7	34.6	34.2	33.3	33.3	34.5
2009	31.0	30.7	31.0	32.1	33.9	35.3	36.0	35.4	34.2	33.2	32.4	32.6	33.2
2010	30.3	30.1	30.7	32.7	34.6	36.2	37.1	36.3	34.6	34.1	33.3	33.6	33.6
2011	31.2	31.3	32.0	33.6	35.2	37.4	38.6	38.1	36.7	36.4	35.3	35.5	35.1
2012	33.5	33.7	34.9	36.2	38.1	40.4	41.3	40.6	38.6	38.4	37.7	38.5	37.7
2013	36.1	35.5	37.0	38.7	40.4	42.7	43.6	42.7	40.7	39.9	39.3	39.4	39.7
Other Services													
2002	16.9	16.9	16.9	17.0	17.2	17.3	17.5	17.3	16.7	16.8	16.9	17.0	17.0
2003	16.5	16.5	16.6	16.7	16.7	16.8	17.2	16.9	16.5	16.6	16.5	16.5	16.7
2004	16.4	16.4	16.5	16.6	16.7	16.9	17.4	17.2	16.6	16.6	16.6	16.7	16.7
2005	16.4	16.5	16.7	16.9	17.0	17.2	17.5	17.1	16.7	16.7	16.8	17.0	16.9
2006	16.8	16.7	16.8	16.9	17.0	17.2	17.8	17.4	16.9	17.1	17.1	17.2	17.1
2007	17.1	17.0	17.1	17.1	17.2	17.4	17.9	17.5	17.0	16.8	16.8	16.8	17.1
2008	16.7	16.5	16.6	16.7	16.8	17.2	17.5	17.3	16.7	16.7	16.7	16.7	16.8
2009	16.2	16.1	16.2	16.1	16.3	16.6	16.9	16.7	16.2	16.2	16.3	16.4	16.4
2010	15.9	15.8	15.9	16.1	16.4	16.8	17.1	17.1	16.3	16.3	16.4	16.4	16.4
2011	16.0	16.1	16.2	16.3	16.5	16.7	17.2	17.0	16.4	16.3	16.4	16.5	16.5
2012	16.4	16.5	16.5	16.6	16.9	17.2	17.5	17.3	16.8	16.8	16.8	17.0	16.9
2013	16.5	16.5	16.6	16.9	17.0	17.2	17.6	17.4	16.9	16.7	16.9	17.4	17.0
Government													
2002	47.7	48.1	48.3	48.8	49.0	49.1	40.9	41.4	46.9	48.4	49.2	49.0	47.2
2003	48.1	48.3	48.5	48.0	48.3	48.4	45.1	42.6	46.2	47.1	47.7	47.5	47.2
2004	47.5	48.0	48.5	47.5	47.6	47.5	44.5	43.0	46.7	47.8	48.2	47.5	47.0
2005	46.6	47.0	47.1	48.0	48.3	48.4	45.5	44.0	46.9	47.4	47.5	47.8	47.0
2006	47.3	47.8	48.0	47.8	48.0	46.9	44.3	42.9	46.5	47.2	47.7	47.5	46.8
2007	46.9	47.6	47.6	47.5	48.5	47.3	46.3	44.7	46.8	48.0	48.4	48.1	47.3
2008	47.8	48.6	48.4	48.0	48.8	47.7	45.0	43.6	47.2	48.2	49.1	48.5	47.6
2009	47.5	47.9	48.1	46.9	48.4	48.1	44.7	43.6	46.9	47.2	47.7	47.2	47.0
2010	46.5	46.6	46.6	45.7	49.0	47.1	45.4	43.5	45.6	45.7	46.1	46.4	46.2
2011	45.6	46.2	46.2	46.5	46.9	45.5	42.9	41.4	45.1	45.8	46.1	46.1	45.4
2012	45.3	45.4	45.6	45.7	46.1	45.2	43.7	42.5	45.2	45.5	46.2	46.0	45.2
2013	45.7	45.8	45.9	46.0	46.2	46.5	44.2	42.9	45.5	45.9	46.5	46.4	45.6

Employment by Industry: Buffalo–Niagara Falls, NY, Selected Years, 2002–2013

(Numbers in thousands, not seasonally adjusted)

Industry and year	January	February	March	April	May	June	July	August	September	October	November	December	Annual average
Total Nonfarm													
2002	536.5	538.5	540.5	542.4	550.2	552.7	545.5	547.4	548.5	553.8	554.1	555.0	547.1
2003	535.0	536.8	539.5	541.4	546.9	549.6	540.3	541.1	547.3	551.0	554.4	554.7	544.8
2004	534.5	538.4	543.1	541.9	551.0	551.2	542.9	544.7	550.8	555.7	556.4	557.7	547.4
2005	534.3	537.3	538.2	544.5	549.4	550.4	540.1	543.3	551.4	554.9	555.5	554.8	546.2
2006	533.6	536.8	539.6	544.1	550.3	551.5	540.9	544.1	547.4	548.0	554.2	555.7	545.5
2007	534.0	536.9	540.6	540.2	550.2	551.4	541.9	544.8	549.8	556.7	558.2	558.3	546.9
2008	538.4	540.7	542.2	548.8	555.7	558.4	550.4	551.7	555.6	561.0	558.4	555.5	551.4
2009	531.1	531.5	532.4	534.3	539.5	540.1	535.2	535.7	538.5	544.3	544.4	542.3	537.4
2010	523.9	525.9	528.7	536.3	542.3	541.7	532.4	534.9	539.8	547.6	548.4	547.7	537.5
2011	529.6	532.1	533.0	541.0	545.3	547.5	539.4	540.5	549.4	551.3	552.0	551.8	542.7
2012	533.1	537.8	539.7	542.2	549.1	550.7	542.0	544.6	548.5	554.2	554.1	554.2	545.9
2013	534.8	538.3	540.8	543.7	550.1	551.1	546.0	546.6	551.9	558.8	558.9	553.9	547.9
Total Private													
2002	444.7	444.5	446.0	449.6	456.3	460.1	456.3	458.1	458.1	459.5	459.6	460.3	454.4
2003	441.9	441.2	442.5	445.5	450.7	454.2	450.0	451.2	454.3	456.1	456.3	456.5	450.0
2004	438.9	440.5	444.5	446.1	453.2	456.6	453.3	455.3	458.4	459.8	459.1	461.0	452.2
2005	439.7	440.6	442.8	449.2	453.7	457.1	452.1	455.5	458.8	459.6	459.8	459.3	452.4
2006	441.0	442.3	445.2	449.5	455.3	457.5	452.1	455.5	455.2	453.2	458.8	460.1	452.1
2007	440.4	441.7	445.1	445.3	454.6	456.6	453.1	454.7	456.8	460.5	461.7	461.7	452.7
2008	444.6	444.8	446.0	452.2	459.0	462.4	459.7	460.5	461.3	463.7	460.5	458.0	456.1
2009	436.3	435.3	435.9	437.6	442.2	444.4	443.3	443.8	444.6	447.1	446.8	445.2	441.9
2010	428.7	429.1	431.4	439.2	443.3	445.1	444.3	446.4	448.3	451.4	451.5	451.0	442.5
2011	435.1	436.5	437.8	445.3	450.0	453.9	450.5	451.5	458.0	457.2	457.7	457.5	449.3
2012	441.4	443.8	445.8	448.9	455.5	458.8	454.9	457.9	459.3	461.8	461.3	461.4	454.2
2013	444.7	446.0	448.4	452.0	458.5	461.0	460.2	460.6	463.4	466.0	465.8	460.8	457.3
Goods-Producing													
2002	89.2	88.7	89.2	91.4	93.4	94.4	94.4	94.2	93.3	93.6	93.1	90.8	92.1
2003	87.0	85.6	86.4	86.2	88.0	89.2	88.3	89.0	89.2	88.7	87.7	86.3	87.6
2004	82.5	82.2	83.7	84.9	86.8	88.0	87.4	88.6	88.5	87.9	87.4	86.3	86.2
2005	81.8	80.9	81.0	82.3	83.9	84.8	83.8	85.4	84.8	84.5	84.3	82.3	83.3
2006	79.8	79.0	79.5	81.5	83.1	84.3	83.3	84.3	83.5	82.1	82.2	80.8	82.0
2007	77.7	76.5	77.3	78.2	81.0	82.4	81.6	82.3	81.6	81.1	80.5	79.0	79.9
2008	75.2	74.7	74.3	76.4	79.3	80.8	80.9	81.6	80.8	80.3	78.3	76.1	78.2
2009	70.6	69.0	68.4	69.6	70.7	70.5	70.8	71.2	70.9	70.4	69.7	67.9	70.0
2010	64.5	63.8	64.2	66.9	68.7	69.8	70.8	71.3	71.1	71.2	70.6	69.0	68.5
2011	66.7	66.4	67.0	69.4	71.2	72.9	73.4	74.1	73.5	73.1	72.4	70.5	70.9
2012	68.0	67.5	68.3	69.8	71.6	72.9	73.1	73.4	72.6	72.3	71.3	70.2	70.9
2013	67.3	66.7	67.3	68.4	70.9	71.9	71.9	72.4	71.8	71.6	70.6	68.6	70.0
Service-Providing													
2002	447.3	449.8	451.3	451.0	456.8	458.3	451.1	453.2	455.2	460.2	461.0	464.2	455.0
2003	448.0	451.2	453.1	455.2	458.9	460.4	452.0	452.1	458.1	462.3	466.7	468.4	457.2
2004	452.0	456.2	459.4	457.0	464.2	463.2	455.5	456.1	462.3	467.8	469.0	471.4	461.2
2005	452.5	456.4	457.2	462.2	465.5	465.6	456.3	457.9	466.6	470.4	471.2	472.5	462.9
2006	453.8	457.8	460.1	462.6	467.2	467.2	457.6	459.8	463.9	465.9	472.0	474.9	463.6
2007	456.3	460.4	463.3	462.0	469.2	469.0	460.3	462.5	468.2	475.6	477.7	479.3	467.0
2008	463.2	466.0	467.9	472.4	476.4	477.6	469.5	470.1	474.8	481.1	480.1	479.4	473.2
2009	460.5	462.5	464.0	464.7	468.8	469.6	464.4	464.5	467.6	473.9	474.7	474.4	467.5
2010	459.4	462.1	464.5	469.4	473.6	471.9	461.6	463.6	468.7	476.4	477.8	478.7	469.0
2011	462.9	465.7	466.0	471.6	474.1	474.6	466.0	466.4	475.9	478.2	479.6	481.3	471.9
2012	465.1	470.3	471.4	472.4	477.5	477.8	468.9	471.2	475.9	481.9	482.8	484.0	474.9
2013	467.5	471.6	473.5	475.3	479.2	479.2	474.1	474.2	480.1	487.2	488.3	485.3	478.0
Mining, Logging, and Construction													
2002	17.1	16.7	17.4	19.4	21.2	22.0	22.9	23.1	22.4	22.4	21.7	20.2	20.5
2003	17.3	16.6	16.9	18.2	20.1	20.9	21.9	22.5	22.0	22.0	20.8	19.8	19.9
2004	16.7	16.6	17.4	19.1	21.0	21.9	22.7	22.9	22.6	22.8	22.1	20.6	20.5
2005	17.4	17.0	16.7	18.7	20.2	21.2	21.7	22.3	21.7	21.6	21.3	19.6	20.0
2006	17.2	16.7	17.1	19.2	20.8	21.8	21.9	22.3	21.7	21.3	21.1	19.9	20.1
2007	17.6	16.3	17.2	18.3	20.8	21.9	22.1	22.4	21.7	21.6	20.8	19.6	20.0
2008	17.3	16.5	16.9	19.0	21.4	22.3	23.5	23.8	23.3	23.1	21.6	20.0	20.7
2009	17.1	16.6	17.0	18.3	19.9	20.5	21.2	21.5	20.8	20.5	19.8	17.9	19.3
2010	15.5	15.0	15.3	18.1	19.5	20.2	21.1	21.3	20.9	21.0	20.5	18.5	18.9
2011	16.5	16.1	16.7	18.6	20.3	21.4	22.2	22.5	22.2	21.8	21.0	19.1	19.9
2012	17.1	16.6	17.4	18.9	20.3	21.3	21.5	21.7	21.1	20.8	19.9	18.7	19.6
2013	16.6	16.2	16.5	17.6	20.0	20.8	21.3	21.5	21.1	21.1	20.1	18.1	19.2
Manufacturing													
2002	72.1	72.0	71.8	72.0	72.2	72.4	71.5	71.1	70.9	71.2	71.4	70.6	71.6
2003	69.7	69.0	69.5	68.0	67.9	68.3	66.4	66.5	67.2	66.7	66.9	66.5	67.7
2004	65.8	65.6	66.3	65.8	65.8	66.1	64.7	65.7	65.9	65.1	65.3	65.7	65.7
2005	64.4	63.9	64.3	63.6	63.7	63.6	62.1	63.1	63.1	62.9	63.0	62.7	63.4
2006	62.6	62.3	62.4	62.3	62.3	62.5	61.4	62.0	61.8	60.8	61.1	60.9	61.9
2007	60.1	60.2	60.1	59.9	60.2	60.5	59.5	59.9	59.9	59.5	59.7	59.4	59.9
2008	57.9	58.2	57.4	57.4	57.9	58.5	57.4	57.8	57.5	57.2	56.7	56.1	57.5
2009	53.5	52.4	51.4	51.3	50.8	50.0	49.6	49.7	50.1	49.9	49.9	50.0	50.7
2010	49.0	48.8	48.9	48.8	49.2	49.6	49.7	50.0	50.2	50.2	50.1	50.5	49.6
2011	50.2	50.3	50.3	50.8	50.9	51.5	51.2	51.6	51.3	51.3	51.4	51.4	51.0
2012	50.9	50.9	50.9	50.9	51.3	51.6	51.6	51.7	51.5	51.5	51.4	51.5	51.3
2013	50.7	50.5	50.8	50.8	50.9	51.1	50.6	50.9	50.7	50.5	50.5	50.5	50.7

Employment by Industry: Buffalo–Niagara Falls, NY, Selected Years, 2002–2013—*Continued*

(Numbers in thousands, not seasonally adjusted)

Industry and year	January	February	March	April	May	June	July	August	September	October	November	December	Annual average
Trade, Transportation, and Utilities													
2002	105.2	103.1	103.2	103.1	104.3	105.9	103.9	104.0	104.4	105.2	106.6	108.0	104.7
2003	102.4	100.4	100.5	100.7	102.1	103.2	102.1	102.3	102.9	103.7	105.4	106.7	102.7
2004	100.8	99.4	99.7	99.9	102.0	102.9	101.9	102.5	103.1	103.9	105.8	107.5	102.5
2005	102.0	100.7	101.8	102.4	103.3	104.3	103.1	103.3	103.6	103.9	105.2	107.1	103.4
2006	102.1	99.5	100.0	100.9	102.2	103.7	102.2	102.7	102.8	103.7	106.1	107.5	102.8
2007	102.7	100.9	101.2	100.8	102.9	104.1	102.9	103.0	104.3	104.9	107.0	108.9	103.6
2008	103.4	101.1	101.2	101.8	103.1	104.4	102.5	102.5	103.3	103.7	104.3	105.0	103.0
2009	98.4	96.9	96.6	96.1	97.6	98.4	97.7	97.7	98.2	98.8	100.4	101.2	98.2
2010	96.4	95.0	95.1	96.1	97.4	98.4	96.9	97.3	98.3	99.3	101.3	101.9	97.8
2011	97.3	95.8	96.0	97.1	98.2	99.6	98.3	99.1	99.9	100.8	103.2	104.0	99.1
2012	99.5	97.5	98.1	98.1	100.1	101.3	99.9	100.4	101.2	101.5	103.3	104.4	100.4
2013	99.2	97.5	98.0	98.2	99.6	100.6	99.5	99.4	100.3	101.1	103.1	104.4	100.1
Wholesale Trade													
2002	23.2	23.2	23.1	23.0	23.1	23.3	23.2	23.1	23.1	23.3	23.3	23.3	23.2
2003	22.5	22.4	22.5	22.4	22.8	22.7	23.0	23.0	22.9	22.9	23.0	23.1	22.8
2004	22.8	22.7	22.8	22.9	23.1	23.2	23.3	23.4	23.2	23.4	23.6	23.8	23.2
2005	23.4	23.4	23.5	23.6	23.6	23.7	23.8	23.6	23.5	23.3	23.5	23.5	23.5
2006	23.3	23.2	23.3	23.3	23.4	23.6	23.3	23.3	23.1	23.3	23.4	23.6	23.3
2007	23.6	23.5	23.5	23.5	23.6	23.9	23.9	23.8	23.7	23.8	23.8	24.0	23.7
2008	23.4	23.2	23.2	23.1	23.1	23.2	23.2	23.0	22.7	22.6	22.5	22.4	23.0
2009	22.1	21.8	21.7	21.5	21.5	21.5	21.4	21.2	21.2	21.1	21.1	21.1	21.4
2010	20.9	20.8	20.8	21.0	21.1	21.2	21.3	21.3	21.2	21.3	21.4	21.4	21.1
2011	21.2	21.0	21.1	21.3	21.5	21.7	21.8	21.8	21.7	21.7	21.9	21.9	21.6
2012	21.6	21.6	21.6	21.6	21.7	22.0	21.9	22.1	21.9	21.9	21.8	22.0	21.8
2013	21.7	21.6	21.7	21.6	21.6	21.7	21.8	21.8	21.7	21.6	21.7	21.9	21.7
Retail Trade													
2002	62.9	61.2	61.6	61.3	62.0	63.1	62.2	62.3	61.9	62.5	64.0	65.4	62.5
2003	61.2	59.6	59.6	60.0	60.8	61.9	61.4	61.7	61.5	62.3	64.1	65.5	61.6
2004	60.8	59.5	59.7	59.6	61.1	62.0	61.6	62.1	61.9	62.6	64.4	65.8	61.8
2005	61.4	60.2	61.1	61.5	62.0	62.7	62.3	62.6	62.4	62.8	64.2	65.8	62.4
2006	61.8	59.6	59.8	60.5	61.2	62.1	61.6	61.9	61.2	62.0	64.3	65.2	61.8
2007	61.2	59.6	59.8	59.2	60.8	61.5	61.3	61.6	61.7	62.3	64.5	65.9	61.6
2008	62.0	60.1	60.2	60.4	61.4	62.3	62.1	62.2	62.1	62.8	63.6	64.3	62.0
2009	59.7	58.6	58.6	58.4	59.6	60.4	60.2	60.6	60.7	61.3	62.9	63.5	60.4
2010	59.8	58.7	58.8	59.4	60.3	60.9	60.4	60.8	60.8	61.8	63.5	64.0	60.8
2011	60.4	59.3	59.5	60.3	60.8	61.7	61.4	62.3	62.0	62.9	65.0	65.5	61.8
2012	62.1	60.5	61.0	61.1	62.3	62.9	62.8	63.1	63.0	63.4	65.3	65.8	62.8
2013	61.7	60.3	60.6	60.9	61.8	62.6	62.3	62.3	62.1	63.1	64.9	65.7	62.4
Transportation and Utilities													
2002	19.1	18.7	18.5	18.8	19.2	19.5	18.5	18.6	19.4	19.4	19.3	19.3	19.0
2003	18.7	18.4	18.4	18.3	18.5	18.6	17.7	17.6	18.5	18.5	18.3	18.1	18.3
2004	17.2	17.2	17.2	17.4	17.8	17.7	17.0	17.0	18.0	17.9	17.8	17.9	17.5
2005	17.2	17.1	17.2	17.3	17.7	17.9	17.0	17.1	17.7	17.8	17.5	17.8	17.4
2006	17.0	16.7	16.9	17.1	17.6	18.0	17.3	17.5	18.5	18.4	18.4	18.7	17.7
2007	17.9	17.8	17.9	18.1	18.5	18.7	17.7	17.6	18.9	18.8	18.7	19.0	18.3
2008	18.0	17.8	17.8	18.3	18.6	18.9	17.2	17.3	18.5	18.3	18.2	18.3	18.1
2009	16.6	16.5	16.3	16.2	16.5	16.5	16.1	15.9	16.3	16.4	16.4	16.6	16.4
2010	15.7	15.5	15.5	15.7	16.0	16.3	15.2	15.2	16.3	16.2	16.4	16.5	15.9
2011	15.7	15.5	15.4	15.5	15.9	16.2	15.1	15.0	16.2	16.2	16.3	16.6	15.8
2012	15.8	15.4	15.5	15.4	16.1	16.4	15.2	15.2	16.3	16.2	16.2	16.6	15.9
2013	15.8	15.6	15.7	15.7	16.2	16.3	15.4	15.3	16.5	16.4	16.5	16.8	16.0
Information													
2002	10.4	10.5	10.6	10.6	10.9	10.9	10.7	10.9	10.9	10.8	10.2	10.3	10.6
2003	9.8	9.9	9.9	9.9	9.9	9.8	9.8	10.1	9.8	9.9	9.9	10.0	9.9
2004	9.8	9.8	9.9	9.9	9.9	9.9	9.8	9.9	9.7	9.7	9.6	9.6	9.8
2005	9.5	9.4	9.4	9.5	9.5	9.5	9.7	9.7	9.6	9.6	9.6	9.7	9.6
2006	9.4	9.3	9.3	9.2	9.3	9.3	9.2	9.1	8.9	8.6	8.6	8.6	9.1
2007	8.5	8.5	8.5	8.4	8.6	8.6	8.6	8.5	8.4	8.3	8.4	8.4	8.5
2008	8.3	8.3	8.3	8.3	8.6	8.6	8.6	8.7	8.5	8.4	8.4	8.5	8.5
2009	8.3	8.2	8.3	8.4	8.4	8.5	8.4	8.3	8.1	8.2	8.1	8.1	8.3
2010	7.9	7.8	7.9	7.7	7.7	7.8	7.9	7.9	7.8	7.8	7.8	7.7	7.8
2011	7.6	7.6	7.6	7.7	7.7	7.8	7.8	6.9	7.7	7.6	7.6	7.7	7.6
2012	7.6	7.6	7.6	7.6	7.7	7.8	7.7	7.6	7.6	7.6	7.5	7.6	7.6
2013	7.5	7.5	7.5	7.5	7.5	7.6	7.6	7.6	7.6	7.5	7.5	7.5	7.5
Financial Activities													
2002	33.1	33.1	32.9	32.8	32.9	33.3	33.4	33.3	32.9	33.4	33.7	33.8	33.2
2003	33.2	32.8	32.4	33.7	33.8	34.2	34.2	34.4	34.3	34.4	34.5	34.6	33.9
2004	34.4	34.4	34.7	34.1	34.1	34.2	34.5	34.3	34.0	34.0	34.0	34.1	34.2
2005	33.4	33.3	33.3	34.0	34.1	34.7	34.8	34.9	34.8	34.8	35.0	35.2	34.4
2006	35.0	35.1	35.2	34.9	35.1	35.2	35.1	35.0	34.5	34.0	34.0	34.3	34.8
2007	33.3	33.4	33.6	32.9	33.0	33.5	33.5	33.4	33.0	33.3	33.4	33.9	33.4
2008	32.8	32.7	32.6	32.7	32.9	33.1	33.0	32.9	32.5	32.5	32.5	32.8	32.8
2009	31.4	31.3	31.3	31.4	31.5	31.7	31.7	31.4	31.0	31.0	30.9	31.1	31.3
2010	30.3	30.3	30.4	30.4	30.4	30.6	30.7	30.5	30.2	30.5	30.6	31.1	30.5
2011	31.1	31.1	31.2	31.5	31.1	31.4	31.4	31.7	31.5	31.4	31.5	32.2	31.4
2012	31.5	31.6	31.5	31.8	31.8	32.3	32.3	32.3	31.9	32.2	32.3	32.4	32.0
2013	31.9	31.9	32.0	32.0	32.0	32.3	33.0	31.8	31.4	31.4	31.4	31.5	31.9

Employment by Industry: Buffalo–Niagara Falls, NY, Selected Years, 2002–2013—*Continued*

(Numbers in thousands, not seasonally adjusted)

Industry and year	January	February	March	April	May	June	July	August	September	October	November	December	Annual average
Professional and Business Services													
2002	60.3	60.4	60.3	60.9	61.9	63.0	63.4	64.2	64.3	64.0	63.9	63.7	62.5
2003	61.3	62.0	61.9	62.9	63.0	64.0	64.6	64.4	64.4	64.4	64.2	64.2	63.4
2004	62.0	62.5	63.1	64.3	65.0	66.6	66.4	66.6	66.2	66.3	66.0	65.9	65.1
2005	63.4	63.7	63.8	65.7	66.0	67.8	67.5	68.2	68.9	68.8	68.1	67.8	66.6
2006	65.7	66.1	66.4	67.9	68.2	69.4	68.8	69.9	68.9	69.1	70.5	70.4	68.4
2007	67.1	67.6	68.3	68.9	69.6	70.9	70.8	71.5	71.0	71.4	71.5	71.3	70.0
2008	69.4	70.0	70.4	72.9	73.3	74.6	74.8	74.6	73.7	73.2	72.4	71.6	72.6
2009	69.4	69.3	69.7	69.9	70.4	72.1	72.2	72.0	71.2	71.5	71.2	70.5	70.8
2010	69.2	68.9	69.4	71.6	71.7	72.5	73.5	73.5	72.8	72.6	71.5	71.5	71.6
2011	70.1	70.3	70.1	72.0	72.5	73.7	74.4	73.9	73.8	73.7	72.8	72.6	72.5
2012	71.0	71.2	71.3	72.4	72.9	74.3	74.6	74.8	73.6	74.4	73.9	73.2	73.1
2013	71.2	71.6	71.9	73.0	73.8	75.3	76.3	76.1	76.1	75.6	75.9	74.2	74.3
Education and Health Services													
2002	79.8	81.0	81.3	81.2	81.1	79.8	78.3	78.3	81.4	82.7	83.0	83.2	80.9
2003	80.8	82.5	83.1	82.8	82.5	81.1	79.2	79.1	83.0	84.5	84.9	85.0	82.4
2004	82.3	84.2	84.5	84.1	83.8	82.6	81.5	80.7	84.3	86.6	86.7	86.9	84.0
2005	82.7	85.5	85.4	85.9	85.4	83.2	80.9	80.5	84.7	86.1	86.5	86.1	84.4
2006	82.2	85.3	85.8	85.5	85.4	83.0	81.5	81.6	85.1	86.1	86.7	86.8	84.6
2007	82.9	85.4	86.2	85.8	85.7	83.1	81.5	81.3	85.2	87.3	87.4	87.4	84.9
2008	85.1	87.0	87.6	87.9	86.9	85.0	83.9	83.6	87.2	89.5	89.8	89.9	87.0
2009	87.3	89.5	90.0	89.2	88.8	86.8	85.3	85.0	88.6	91.2	91.6	91.8	88.8
2010	88.9	91.1	91.5	91.9	91.3	88.9	86.7	86.7	90.3	92.4	92.9	92.6	90.4
2011	89.8	92.1	92.2	92.6	91.9	89.2	87.1	87.0	91.1	92.3	92.9	92.9	90.9
2012	90.4	93.2	93.0	92.9	92.5	89.2	87.5	87.7	91.9	93.9	94.0	94.4	91.7
2013	91.5	93.8	94.3	94.6	93.6	90.9	89.6	89.6	93.8	96.2	95.6	94.9	93.2
Leisure and Hospitality													
2002	43.9	44.6	45.1	46.3	48.5	49.5	49.1	50.1	48.2	47.1	46.2	47.5	47.2
2003	44.7	45.1	45.2	45.9	48.0	49.2	48.5	49.0	47.8	47.6	46.8	46.7	47.0
2004	44.7	45.2	45.7	45.8	48.1	49.3	49.0	49.8	49.5	48.3	46.4	47.3	47.4
2005	44.2	44.4	44.8	46.4	48.3	49.7	49.5	50.7	49.6	49.0	48.2	48.0	47.7
2006	44.5	45.6	46.1	46.8	48.9	49.6	49.2	49.9	48.6	46.6	47.6	48.3	47.6
2007	45.6	46.5	46.8	47.2	50.5	50.6	50.8	51.2	50.1	50.6	49.8	49.2	49.1
2008	47.1	47.6	47.9	48.5	51.0	52.0	51.9	52.4	51.5	51.8	50.8	50.1	50.2
2009	47.5	47.5	47.8	49.0	50.8	52.4	53.2	54.2	52.9	52.0	51.0	51.0	50.8
2010	48.6	49.2	49.8	51.4	52.9	53.8	53.6	54.7	54.7	54.3	53.5	53.8	52.5
2011	49.7	50.2	50.7	51.8	54.1	55.8	54.8	55.5	57.1	55.2	54.2	54.3	53.6
2012	50.4	52.2	52.8	53.1	55.4	57.3	56.3	58.2	57.2	56.5	55.4	55.6	55.0
2013	52.5	53.4	53.7	54.7	57.2	58.5	58.5	59.6	58.6	58.6	57.7	55.6	56.6
Other Services													
2002	22.8	23.1	23.4	23.3	23.3	23.3	23.1	23.1	22.7	22.7	22.9	23.0	23.1
2003	22.7	22.9	23.1	23.4	23.4	23.5	23.3	22.9	22.9	22.9	22.9	23.0	23.1
2004	22.4	22.8	23.2	23.1	23.5	23.1	22.8	22.9	23.1	23.1	23.2	23.4	23.1
2005	22.7	22.7	23.3	23.0	23.2	23.1	22.8	22.8	22.8	22.9	22.9	23.1	22.9
2006	22.3	22.4	22.9	22.8	23.1	23.0	22.8	23.0	22.9	23.0	23.1	23.4	22.9
2007	22.6	22.9	23.2	23.1	23.3	23.4	23.4	23.5	23.2	23.6	23.5	23.6	23.3
2008	23.3	23.4	23.7	23.7	23.9	23.9	24.1	24.2	23.8	24.3	24.0	24.0	23.9
2009	23.4	23.6	23.8	24.0	24.0	24.0	24.0	24.0	23.7	24.0	23.9	23.6	23.8
2010	22.9	23.0	23.1	23.2	23.2	23.3	24.2	24.5	23.1	23.3	23.3	23.4	23.4
2011	22.8	23.0	23.0	23.2	23.3	23.5	23.3	23.3	23.4	23.1	23.1	23.3	23.2
2012	23.0	23.0	23.2	23.2	23.5	23.7	23.5	23.5	23.3	23.5	23.5	23.6	23.4
2013	23.6	23.6	23.7	23.6	23.9	23.9	23.8	24.1	23.9	24.0	24.0	24.1	23.9
Government													
2002	91.8	94.0	94.5	92.8	93.9	92.6	89.2	89.3	90.4	94.3	94.5	94.7	92.7
2003	93.1	95.6	97.0	95.9	96.2	95.4	90.3	89.9	93.0	94.9	98.1	98.2	94.8
2004	95.6	97.9	98.6	95.8	97.8	94.6	89.6	89.4	92.4	95.9	97.3	96.7	95.1
2005	94.6	96.7	95.4	95.3	95.7	93.3	88.0	87.8	92.6	95.3	95.7	95.5	93.8
2006	92.6	94.5	94.4	94.6	95.0	94.0	88.8	88.6	92.2	94.8	95.4	95.6	93.4
2007	93.6	95.2	95.5	94.9	95.6	94.8	88.8	90.1	93.0	96.2	96.7	96.6	94.3
2008	93.8	95.9	96.2	96.6	96.7	96.0	90.7	91.2	94.3	97.7	97.9	97.5	95.4
2009	94.8	96.2	96.5	96.7	97.3	95.7	91.9	91.9	93.9	97.2	97.6	97.1	95.6
2010	95.2	96.8	97.3	97.1	99.0	96.6	88.1	88.5	91.5	96.2	96.9	96.7	95.0
2011	94.5	95.6	95.2	95.7	95.3	93.6	88.9	89.0	91.4	94.1	94.3	94.3	93.5
2012	91.7	94.0	93.9	93.3	93.6	91.9	87.1	86.7	89.2	92.4	92.8	92.8	91.6
2013	90.1	92.3	92.4	91.7	91.6	90.1	85.8	86.0	88.5	92.8	93.1	93.1	90.6

Employment by Industry: Charlotte-Gastonia-Rock Hill, NC–SC, Selected Years, 2002–2013

(Numbers in thousands, not seasonally adjusted)

Industry and year	January	February	March	April	May	June	July	August	September	October	November	December	Annual average
Total Nonfarm													
2002	758.5	762.5	768.7	768.9	771.8	773.8	761.0	770.2	774.3	775.7	776.3	774.4	769.7
2003	757.8	758.4	764.7	766.1	772.6	769.9	743.3	755.3	765.3	772.3	773.3	773.8	764.4
2004	755.4	757.4	763.6	766.4	773.1	772.3	756.1	770.7	779.5	787.2	789.1	788.8	771.6
2005	771.4	775.5	781.6	786.0	790.4	787.2	772.4	789.4	798.5	807.8	809.5	809.8	790.0
2006	801.4	804.8	812.8	822.2	828.2	823.3	808.9	829.1	838.1	846.3	852.7	853.9	826.8
2007	838.4	843.7	852.9	856.4	863.4	858.2	841.0	862.9	867.9	875.6	878.2	880.0	859.9
2008	857.7	862.7	868.1	866.3	870.9	863.8	841.0	862.3	865.3	863.5	857.8	855.6	861.3
2009	825.2	822.3	821.2	815.4	816.6	808.1	787.0	806.2	806.6	806.0	806.8	806.2	810.6
2010	791.6	793.7	801.8	807.4	815.9	807.5	788.1	808.7	810.8	822.6	825.1	826.4	808.3
2011	807.6	816.6	823.4	828.9	832.0	826.0	809.7	832.1	834.8	839.5	845.9	846.8	828.6
2012	833.4	837.8	846.1	849.8	857.9	847.5	833.9	853.4	857.2	867.9	872.3	873.6	852.6
2013	854.7	860.4	867.1	872.1	877.9	868.2	856.7	874.4	877.5	890.4	892.0	893.6	873.8
Total Private													
2002	664.8	667.3	672.7	673.7	676.7	681.5	678.5	682.0	680.1	677.5	677.7	677.3	675.8
2003	662.4	662.1	667.7	669.2	675.1	676.4	666.7	669.8	669.3	670.4	671.8	673.4	669.5
2004	656.9	657.9	664.0	666.7	673.2	676.5	678.3	682.8	679.8	684.3	685.7	686.6	674.4
2005	671.1	674.3	679.9	683.5	688.2	689.7	693.3	695.8	695.9	702.5	704.1	704.9	690.3
2006	697.4	700.2	707.8	716.9	722.8	726.5	729.2	733.1	732.2	739.1	743.7	744.9	724.5
2007	730.5	734.3	743.4	747.7	754.0	758.3	757.5	759.8	758.1	763.8	765.0	766.5	753.2
2008	744.6	748.4	753.3	751.5	755.7	756.3	751.3	752.4	747.6	746.1	739.1	736.2	748.5
2009	707.4	704.0	702.3	696.4	698.3	695.6	693.2	692.3	689.0	688.1	688.3	687.4	695.2
2010	671.6	672.4	679.6	685.1	690.4	693.1	693.3	695.8	695.4	701.7	703.8	704.8	690.6
2011	688.5	696.5	702.5	707.4	710.5	713.8	714.6	717.4	718.5	719.4	723.0	724.1	711.4
2012	712.6	715.8	723.2	726.0	733.4	738.0	736.8	738.5	737.7	742.5	745.7	747.3	733.1
2013	730.3	734.9	740.9	746.2	751.9	757.3	757.1	760.1	759.1	766.0	766.4	768.2	753.2
Goods Producing													
2002	150.3	149.9	150.3	149.7	150.5	151.3	150.2	150.5	149.7	148.4	147.4	145.4	149.5
2003	143.3	142.6	143.3	141.5	141.7	141.5	137.2	136.8	136.3	136.5	135.9	135.4	139.3
2004	132.6	132.7	133.8	134.7	135.9	136.8	137.2	137.7	137.2	137.3	136.8	136.5	135.8
2005	134.9	135.6	136.3	135.8	136.7	137.5	137.9	138.1	138.0	137.8	137.8	137.6	137.0
2006	136.4	136.6	138.1	139.7	140.3	141.2	142.0	143.0	142.4	142.6	142.2	142.8	140.6
2007	141.0	141.4	141.8	142.5	142.5	143.3	143.4	143.6	143.1	142.5	141.8	141.3	142.4
2008	138.2	138.0	138.0	136.8	136.9	136.5	135.8	135.3	134.1	131.9	129.2	126.5	134.8
2009	120.1	118.3	116.8	114.0	113.1	112.3	111.9	110.8	110.1	108.7	108.0	107.7	112.7
2010	104.4	104.0	104.6	105.5	105.2	105.7	105.6	105.1	104.8	104.5	104.4	104.1	104.8
2011	101.3	102.9	103.5	104.8	105.6	106.4	107.6	108.0	108.2	108.0	108.3	108.2	106.1
2012	108.2	108.8	109.7	110.2	111.2	112.2	112.1	112.5	112.1	112.2	112.5	112.9	111.2
2013	111.4	112.4	113.5	113.9	114.0	115.3	115.2	115.4	115.2	116.1	115.8	115.7	114.5
Service-Providing													
2002	608.2	612.6	618.4	619.2	621.3	622.5	610.8	619.7	624.6	627.3	628.9	629.0	620.2
2003	614.5	615.8	621.4	624.6	630.9	628.4	606.1	618.5	629.0	635.8	637.4	638.4	625.1
2004	622.8	624.7	629.8	631.7	637.2	635.5	618.9	633.0	642.3	649.9	652.3	652.3	635.9
2005	636.5	639.9	645.3	650.2	653.7	649.7	634.5	651.3	660.5	670.0	671.7	672.2	653.0
2006	665.0	668.2	674.7	682.5	687.9	682.1	666.9	686.1	695.7	703.7	710.5	711.1	686.2
2007	697.4	702.3	711.1	713.9	720.9	714.9	697.6	719.3	724.8	733.1	736.4	738.7	717.5
2008	719.5	724.7	730.1	729.5	734.0	727.3	705.2	727.0	731.2	731.6	728.6	729.1	726.5
2009	705.1	704.0	704.4	701.4	703.5	695.8	675.1	695.4	696.5	697.3	698.8	698.5	698.0
2010	687.2	689.7	697.2	701.9	710.7	701.8	682.5	703.6	706.0	718.1	720.7	722.3	703.5
2011	706.3	713.7	719.9	724.1	726.4	719.6	702.1	724.1	726.6	731.5	737.6	738.6	722.5
2012	725.2	729.0	736.4	739.6	746.7	735.3	721.8	740.9	745.1	755.7	759.8	760.7	741.4
2013	743.3	748.0	753.6	758.2	763.9	752.9	741.5	759.0	762.3	774.3	776.2	777.9	759.3
Mining, Logging, and Construction													
2002	50.0	49.8	50.7	50.9	51.6	51.9	52.1	52.2	51.2	50.2	49.7	49.4	50.8
2003	47.8	47.5	47.9	47.1	47.9	48.3	48.4	48.6	48.6	49.1	49.1	49.0	48.3
2004	47.4	47.3	48.1	48.9	49.8	50.3	50.7	51.0	50.5	51.4	51.3	51.3	49.8
2005	50.5	50.7	51.3	51.1	51.7	52.6	54.0	54.4	54.5	53.9	54.1	54.0	52.7
2006	53.3	53.6	54.8	56.0	56.5	57.4	58.1	58.8	58.5	58.7	58.5	58.7	56.9
2007	57.6	58.1	58.9	59.6	59.7	60.6	60.7	60.8	60.4	60.0	59.3	58.6	59.5
2008	56.3	56.1	56.0	55.6	55.8	55.6	55.1	54.6	53.8	52.3	50.7	49.3	54.3
2009	45.9	45.1	44.3	43.1	43.0	43.0	43.0	42.4	41.7	40.6	40.0	39.7	42.7
2010	37.3	37.0	37.6	38.2	38.0	38.5	38.4	38.1	37.7	37.6	37.4	36.9	37.7
2011	34.4	35.7	36.2	36.8	37.1	37.5	38.1	38.0	37.9	37.7	37.6	37.3	37.0
2012	37.1	37.3	38.1	38.5	38.9	39.6	39.4	39.6	39.3	39.4	39.6	39.6	38.9
2013	38.7	39.2	40.1	40.9	41.0	41.4	41.6	41.9	42.0	43.1	42.8	42.3	41.3
Manufacturing													
2002	100.3	100.1	99.6	98.8	98.9	99.4	98.1	98.3	98.5	98.2	97.7	96.0	98.7
2003	95.5	95.1	95.4	94.4	93.8	93.2	88.8	88.2	87.7	87.4	86.8	86.4	91.1
2004	85.2	85.4	85.7	85.8	86.1	86.5	86.5	86.7	86.7	85.9	85.5	85.2	85.9
2005	84.4	84.9	85.0	84.7	85.0	84.9	83.9	83.7	83.5	83.9	83.7	83.6	84.3
2006	83.1	83.0	83.3	83.7	83.8	83.8	83.9	84.2	83.9	83.9	83.7	84.1	83.7
2007	83.4	83.3	82.9	82.9	82.8	82.7	82.7	82.8	82.7	82.5	82.5	82.7	82.8
2008	81.9	81.9	82.0	81.2	81.1	80.9	80.7	80.7	80.3	79.6	78.5	77.2	80.5
2009	74.2	73.2	72.5	70.9	70.1	69.3	68.9	68.4	68.4	68.1	68.0	68.0	70.0
2010	67.1	67.0	67.0	67.3	67.2	67.2	67.2	67.0	67.1	66.9	67.0	67.2	67.1
2011	66.9	67.2	67.3	68.0	68.5	68.9	69.5	70.0	70.3	70.3	70.7	70.9	69.0
2012	71.1	71.5	71.6	71.7	72.3	72.6	72.7	72.9	72.8	72.8	72.9	73.3	72.4
2013	72.7	73.2	73.4	73.0	73.0	73.9	73.6	73.5	73.2	73.0	73.0	73.4	73.2

Employment by Industry: Charlotte-Gastonia-Rock Hill, NC–SC, Selected Years, 2002–2013—*Continued*

(Numbers in thousands, not seasonally adjusted)

Industry and year	January	February	March	April	May	June	July	August	September	October	November	December	Annual average
Trade, Transportation, and Utilities													
2002	165.7	164.6	165.7	164.7	164.7	165.4	165.0	165.8	165.2	165.2	168.5	170.2	165.9
2003	162.6	162.3	162.4	162.6	162.9	163.6	162.0	162.8	163.3	164.5	167.4	169.2	163.8
2004	163.5	163.4	163.5	165.2	166.6	166.6	166.3	167.6	167.0	167.8	170.2	172.0	166.6
2005	167.1	167.7	168.7	169.1	169.1	168.5	168.4	168.5	167.8	171.2	173.9	176.2	169.7
2006	170.5	169.5	170.6	172.9	174.0	173.9	174.2	174.6	174.3	176.9	181.3	182.7	174.6
2007	178.0	177.3	179.4	180.0	181.1	181.3	181.9	182.1	182.0	183.7	187.6	189.1	182.0
2008	182.5	181.5	182.4	180.8	181.1	180.9	179.4	179.4	178.1	178.7	179.8	180.2	180.4
2009	174.6	172.3	171.6	169.2	169.9	169.4	168.6	168.6	167.6	168.2	169.9	170.7	170.1
2010	165.3	164.4	165.8	166.0	167.2	167.3	167.3	167.9	166.9	168.7	171.8	173.5	167.7
2011	167.4	167.4	168.6	168.9	169.4	169.3	170.4	170.6	170.0	171.7	175.1	176.5	170.4
2012	171.9	170.9	172.1	172.9	174.1	175.0	175.3	175.4	175.5	176.6	181.2	182.5	175.3
2013	175.9	175.5	176.7	176.8	178.2	179.1	179.8	180.8	180.5	181.8	185.7	187.8	179.9
Wholesale Trade													
2002	46.8	46.7	46.9	46.8	46.5	46.4	46.5	46.5	46.5	46.4	46.5	46.4	46.6
2003	46.0	46.0	45.9	46.2	46.1	46.1	45.8	45.7	45.6	46.5	46.6	46.7	46.1
2004	47.3	47.4	47.5	46.9	46.9	46.8	47.1	47.1	46.9	46.0	45.7	45.6	46.8
2005	46.0	46.0	46.1	46.7	46.8	46.4	46.5	46.5	46.4	47.0	47.3	47.3	46.6
2006	47.5	47.6	47.8	48.2	48.3	48.2	47.5	47.5	47.3	47.3	47.4	47.5	47.7
2007	47.7	48.0	48.5	49.0	48.9	49.1	49.4	49.3	49.2	49.8	49.7	49.7	49.0
2008	49.2	49.5	50.0	49.2	49.2	49.0	48.3	48.5	48.2	48.3	48.0	48.0	48.8
2009	47.2	47.1	46.6	45.6	45.2	44.8	44.5	44.3	43.8	44.1	43.8	43.7	45.1
2010	43.3	43.5	43.8	43.6	43.7	43.5	43.7	43.8	43.6	44.0	43.9	44.1	43.7
2011	43.5	43.8	44.0	43.8	43.9	43.8	44.3	44.3	44.3	44.5	44.7	44.8	44.1
2012	44.4	44.5	44.7	44.8	45.0	45.2	45.3	45.3	45.2	45.2	45.3	45.5	45.0
2013	44.8	45.2	45.4	45.4	45.7	45.8	46.1	46.4	46.4	46.5	47.2	47.2	46.0
Retail Trade													
2002	82.1	81.2	82.1	81.7	81.8	82.2	81.4	81.8	81.5	81.8	85.0	86.6	82.4
2003	80.5	79.8	80.5	80.7	80.9	81.5	80.7	81.2	81.2	81.8	84.6	85.7	81.6
2004	81.0	80.3	80.7	81.7	82.8	82.9	81.8	82.8	82.6	84.3	86.8	88.4	83.0
2005	83.8	84.2	85.0	84.8	84.6	84.1	84.6	84.7	84.3	86.7	89.0	90.7	85.5
2006	85.9	84.7	85.4	87.2	88.1	87.9	88.7	88.9	89.0	91.5	95.7	96.8	89.2
2007	92.8	91.8	93.1	93.2	94.3	94.3	94.6	95.0	95.0	96.2	100.3	101.5	95.2
2008	95.9	94.7	95.4	94.1	94.2	94.3	93.7	93.4	92.7	93.2	94.7	94.9	94.3
2009	91.3	89.8	89.4	88.5	89.6	89.5	89.2	89.6	89.0	89.7	91.8	92.4	90.0
2010	88.4	87.4	88.3	88.5	89.3	89.5	89.3	89.9	89.0	90.3	93.1	94.4	89.8
2011	89.4	89.0	89.7	90.0	90.3	90.2	90.8	90.9	90.2	91.6	94.6	95.6	91.0
2012	92.2	91.1	91.9	92.4	93.4	93.8	93.9	94.0	94.0	95.1	99.2	99.8	94.2
2013	94.7	94.1	94.7	95.0	95.7	96.3	96.7	97.2	96.8	97.1	100.0	101.7	96.7
Transportation and Utilities													
2002	36.8	36.7	36.7	36.2	36.4	36.8	37.1	37.5	37.2	37.0	37.0	37.2	36.9
2003	36.1	36.5	36.0	35.7	35.9	36.0	35.5	35.9	36.5	36.2	36.2	36.8	36.1
2004	35.2	35.7	35.3	36.6	36.9	36.9	37.4	37.7	37.5	37.5	37.7	38.0	36.9
2005	37.3	37.5	37.6	37.6	37.7	38.0	37.3	37.3	37.1	37.5	37.6	38.2	37.6
2006	37.1	37.2	37.4	37.5	37.6	37.8	38.0	38.2	38.0	38.1	38.2	38.4	37.8
2007	37.5	37.5	37.8	37.8	37.9	37.9	37.9	37.8	37.8	37.7	37.6	37.9	37.8
2008	37.4	37.3	37.0	37.5	37.7	37.6	37.4	37.5	37.2	37.2	37.1	37.3	37.4
2009	36.1	35.4	35.6	35.1	35.1	35.1	34.9	34.7	34.8	34.4	34.3	34.6	35.0
2010	33.6	33.5	33.7	33.9	34.2	34.3	34.3	34.2	34.3	34.4	34.8	35.0	34.2
2011	34.5	34.6	34.9	35.1	35.2	35.3	35.3	35.4	35.5	35.6	35.8	36.1	35.3
2012	35.3	35.3	35.5	35.7	35.7	36.0	36.1	36.1	36.3	36.3	36.7	37.2	36.0
2013	36.4	36.2	36.6	36.4	36.8	37.0	37.0	37.2	37.3	38.2	38.5	38.9	37.2
Information													
2002	23.1	23.0	23.2	22.8	22.8	23.0	22.9	22.8	22.7	23.0	23.0	23.2	23.0
2003	22.5	22.3	22.4	22.1	22.0	22.3	22.0	21.9	21.8	21.9	21.9	22.0	22.1
2004	22.0	21.9	22.0	21.8	21.6	21.8	21.1	20.9	20.6	21.0	21.1	20.8	21.4
2005	20.5	20.4	20.5	20.8	21.0	21.1	21.2	21.2	21.2	21.3	21.7	22.1	21.1
2006	22.2	22.2	22.2	21.9	22.0	22.1	21.7	22.1	22.0	21.9	22.1	22.3	22.1
2007	22.0	22.0	21.9	21.9	22.0	22.4	22.3	22.3	22.2	22.1	22.3	22.4	22.2
2008	21.8	22.0	22.1	22.0	22.1	22.2	22.1	22.0	22.0	22.3	22.3	22.4	22.1
2009	21.6	21.5	21.5	21.5	21.4	21.3	21.2	21.1	21.0	20.9	21.0	21.0	21.3
2010	20.9	20.9	21.0	20.9	21.0	21.1	21.1	21.2	21.3	21.4	21.5	21.6	21.2
2011	21.3	21.4	21.4	21.5	21.3	21.5	21.6	21.8	22.0	21.9	21.9	21.8	21.6
2012	21.7	21.9	21.9	21.9	21.9	22.0	22.2	22.1	22.0	21.8	21.9	21.9	21.9
2013	22.0	22.0	22.0	22.0	22.3	22.2	22.2	22.3	22.1	22.3	22.3	22.3	22.2
Financial Activities													
2002	63.3	63.8	64.3	64.1	64.0	64.4	65.0	65.2	64.8	65.1	65.2	65.1	64.5
2003	66.1	66.4	66.6	66.3	66.5	66.9	65.9	66.2	66.1	66.9	66.7	67.1	66.5
2004	66.7	66.9	67.0	67.7	68.0	68.5	69.6	70.0	70.0	70.3	70.7	71.0	68.9
2005	68.6	69.0	69.1	69.4	69.9	70.6	71.5	71.3	71.2	71.9	72.1	72.7	70.6
2006	73.8	74.6	75.1	77.2	77.6	78.1	78.4	78.5	78.2	79.6	79.7	80.0	77.6
2007	76.4	77.0	77.2	77.5	77.8	78.0	77.7	77.6	77.2	77.6	77.6	77.8	77.5
2008	75.4	75.7	75.8	76.5	75.8	75.9	75.0	75.0	74.3	74.2	73.7	74.0	75.1
2009	72.4	72.3	72.0	71.4	71.4	71.0	70.6	70.1	69.3	69.3	69.3	69.5	70.7
2010	69.1	69.7	69.8	69.5	69.7	70.0	70.0	70.0	70.3	70.7	71.2	71.7	70.3
2011	71.9	72.3	72.2	71.5	72.0	72.3	71.4	71.7	71.2	71.9	71.9	72.4	71.9
2012	72.0	72.5	72.6	72.2	72.3	72.8	72.7	72.9	72.8	73.0	73.4	73.6	72.7
2013	73.3	73.7	73.4	73.9	74.2	74.6	75.2	75.2	75.2	75.7	75.2	75.3	74.6

Employment by Industry: Charlotte-Gastonia-Rock Hill, NC–SC, Selected Years, 2002–2013—*Continued*

(Numbers in thousands, not seasonally adjusted)

Industry and year	January	February	March	April	May	June	July	August	September	October	November	December	Annual average
Professional and Business Services													
2002	110.2	112.2	112.9	113.3	114.4	114.9	114.0	116.1	116.2	114.9	113.7	112.8	113.8
2003	111.9	111.5	113.0	114.0	114.9	114.4	113.9	115.9	116.2	115.4	114.9	114.1	114.2
2004	110.1	111.9	113.5	111.3	111.5	113.1	113.8	115.3	115.1	117.5	117.1	115.2	113.8
2005	112.9	113.5	114.2	115.7	116.3	115.8	117.8	118.5	120.4	121.9	121.0	119.3	117.3
2006	117.5	118.7	120.1	122.5	123.9	124.5	125.9	127.3	128.4	129.8	130.2	128.1	124.7
2007	125.5	127.2	129.9	131.7	133.2	134.3	134.1	135.7	136.4	138.2	137.3	136.8	133.4
2008	133.5	136.0	137.1	137.2	138.6	138.9	137.2	137.7	137.2	136.1	133.0	131.6	136.2
2009	126.5	126.3	125.8	124.8	123.9	123.2	123.6	123.9	124.4	126.1	126.6	126.5	125.1
2010	123.6	124.2	126.6	128.3	128.9	129.6	130.3	131.6	132.1	135.4	135.0	135.1	130.1
2011	131.7	135.5	136.6	138.3	137.5	138.1	138.1	138.6	140.4	140.1	140.3	139.9	137.9
2012	136.6	138.1	139.4	140.3	141.2	141.8	139.9	140.8	141.6	144.1	142.8	142.3	140.7
2013	137.6	139.1	140.1	142.5	142.7	143.7	144.4	146.0	146.7	149.6	148.0	148.5	144.1
Education and Health Services													
2002	57.8	58.7	58.8	58.4	59.0	59.5	59.8	60.7	61.4	62.0	62.4	63.4	60.2
2003	62.6	63.3	63.8	63.9	64.4	64.5	63.9	64.7	64.7	65.5	65.7	66.4	64.5
2004	65.1	63.5	63.8	64.5	64.6	64.2	64.9	65.4	65.5	66.2	66.5	67.6	65.2
2005	66.2	66.3	67.0	67.5	67.4	67.2	67.6	68.3	68.7	69.5	69.7	69.7	67.9
2006	71.0	71.6	71.9	71.3	71.3	72.0	72.2	72.9	73.5	74.8	75.2	75.8	72.8
2007	75.1	76.0	76.4	77.0	77.2	77.4	77.4	78.0	78.2	79.6	79.5	80.0	77.7
2008	77.9	78.6	78.8	78.5	78.6	78.6	78.4	79.3	79.7	81.5	82.1	82.6	79.6
2009	80.6	81.1	81.0	81.2	81.5	81.1	80.7	81.6	81.6	82.2	82.8	82.7	81.5
2010	81.6	82.2	82.2	83.4	83.6	82.7	83.1	83.7	83.7	85.3	85.8	85.8	83.6
2011	85.0	86.0	85.9	85.9	85.7	84.6	84.8	85.5	86.3	86.9	87.3	87.9	86.0
2012	87.2	88.0	87.8	86.8	87.2	86.9	86.5	86.8	87.3	89.3	89.4	90.0	87.8
2013	88.2	89.3	88.9	89.0	89.2	88.6	87.9	88.3	89.4	90.8	90.7	91.1	89.2
Leisure and Hospitality													
2002	62.9	63.5	65.6	68.8	69.8	71.2	70.7	70.5	69.7	68.5	67.2	67.6	68.0
2003	64.8	65.3	67.7	69.7	73.3	73.8	72.3	72.2	71.3	71.2	70.8	70.7	70.3
2004	68.0	68.7	71.0	72.5	75.5	75.6	75.7	76.4	75.2	74.3	73.4	73.3	73.3
2005	71.1	71.9	73.9	75.3	77.3	78.2	78.2	79.3	78.0	78.2	77.3	76.7	76.3
2006	75.3	75.8	78.3	80.6	82.3	82.7	83.7	83.6	82.5	82.4	81.9	81.9	80.9
2007	81.3	81.9	84.7	86.1	88.8	89.9	89.0	88.8	87.5	87.8	86.6	86.7	86.6
2008	84.4	85.7	88.3	89.6	91.9	92.6	92.9	93.2	92.4	91.8	89.6	89.7	90.2
2009	83.5	83.9	85.4	86.5	89.2	89.6	88.9	88.7	88.0	86.0	84.0	83.0	86.4
2010	80.7	80.9	83.2	85.3	88.3	89.9	89.0	88.8	88.6	87.7	86.1	85.2	86.1
2011	82.2	82.9	86.0	88.1	90.5	92.9	91.9	92.4	91.8	90.2	89.2	88.6	88.9
2012	86.5	87.0	90.8	92.6	96.1	97.8	98.2	98.0	96.2	95.3	94.1	93.6	93.9
2013	91.3	91.9	94.4	96.3	99.8	102.4	101.0	100.6	98.6	98.3	97.1	96.5	97.4
Other Services													
2002	31.5	31.6	31.9	31.9	31.5	31.8	30.9	30.4	30.4	30.4	30.3	29.6	31.0
2003	28.6	28.4	28.5	29.1	29.4	29.4	29.5	29.3	29.6	28.5	28.5	28.5	28.9
2004	28.9	28.9	29.4	29.0	29.5	29.9	29.7	29.5	29.2	29.9	29.9	30.2	29.5
2005	29.8	29.9	30.2	29.9	30.5	30.8	30.7	30.6	30.6	30.7	30.6	30.6	30.4
2006	30.7	31.2	31.5	30.8	31.4	32.0	31.1	31.1	30.9	31.1	31.1	31.3	31.2
2007	31.2	31.5	32.1	31.0	31.4	31.7	31.7	31.7	31.5	32.3	32.3	32.4	31.7
2008	30.9	30.9	30.8	30.1	30.7	30.7	30.5	30.5	29.8	29.6	29.4	29.2	30.3
2009	28.1	28.3	28.2	27.8	27.9	27.7	27.7	27.5	27.0	26.7	26.7	26.3	27.5
2010	26.0	26.1	26.4	26.2	26.5	26.8	26.9	27.2	27.3	27.5	27.7	27.8	26.9
2011	27.7	28.1	28.3	28.4	28.5	28.7	28.8	28.8	28.6	28.7	28.7	28.8	28.5
2012	28.5	28.6	28.9	29.1	29.4	29.5	29.9	30.0	30.2	30.2	30.4	30.5	29.6
2013	30.6	31.0	31.9	31.8	31.5	31.4	31.4	31.5	31.4	31.4	31.6	32.0	31.5
Government													
2002	93.7	95.2	96.0	95.2	95.1	92.3	82.5	88.2	94.2	98.2	98.6	97.1	93.9
2003	95.4	96.3	97.0	96.9	97.5	93.5	76.6	85.5	96.0	101.9	101.5	100.4	94.9
2004	98.5	99.5	99.6	99.7	99.9	95.8	77.8	87.9	99.7	102.9	103.4	102.2	97.2
2005	100.3	101.2	101.7	102.5	102.2	97.5	79.1	93.6	102.6	105.3	105.4	104.9	99.7
2006	104.0	104.6	105.0	105.3	105.4	96.8	79.7	96.0	105.9	107.2	109.0	109.0	102.3
2007	107.9	109.4	109.5	108.7	109.4	99.9	83.5	103.1	109.8	111.8	113.2	113.5	106.6
2008	113.1	114.3	114.8	114.8	115.2	107.5	89.7	109.9	117.7	117.4	118.7	119.4	112.7
2009	117.8	118.3	118.9	119.0	118.3	112.5	93.8	113.9	117.6	117.9	118.5	118.8	115.4
2010	120.0	121.3	122.2	122.3	125.5	114.4	94.8	112.9	115.4	120.9	121.3	121.6	117.7
2011	119.1	120.1	120.9	121.5	121.5	112.2	95.1	114.7	116.3	120.1	122.9	122.7	117.3
2012	120.8	122.0	122.9	123.8	124.5	109.5	97.1	114.9	119.5	125.4	126.6	126.3	119.4
2013	124.4	125.5	126.2	125.9	126.0	110.9	99.6	114.3	118.4	124.4	125.6	125.4	120.6

Employment by Industry: Chicago-Joliet-Naperville, IL–IN–WI, Selected Years, 2002–2013

(Numbers in thousands, not seasonally adjusted)

Industry and year	January	February	March	April	May	June	July	August	September	October	November	December	Annual average
Total Nonfarm													
2002	4,377.2	4,372.5	4,395.3	4,436.4	4,471.8	4,501.6	4,477.9	4,489.7	4,475.4	4,476.2	4,487.2	4,484.5	4,453.8
2003	4,342.1	4,338.0	4,359.0	4,392.0	4,432.9	4,461.7	4,447.9	4,451.7	4,437.1	4,428.7	4,427.4	4,437.1	4,413.0
2004	4,296.5	4,299.2	4,334.5	4,383.3	4,431.5	4,465.8	4,450.2	4,450.7	4,447.1	4,464.7	4,475.0	4,479.5	4,414.8
2005	4,339.5	4,347.2	4,372.8	4,440.5	4,474.7	4,496.9	4,498.1	4,497.4	4,505.1	4,510.7	4,526.5	4,527.0	4,461.4
2006	4,401.0	4,413.7	4,446.4	4,495.0	4,533.5	4,577.3	4,549.4	4,554.0	4,557.2	4,560.6	4,574.5	4,576.1	4,519.9
2007	4,451.8	4,450.3	4,490.0	4,531.2	4,580.0	4,614.5	4,588.7	4,590.8	4,583.8	4,591.7	4,606.9	4,605.4	4,557.1
2008	4,472.5	4,469.4	4,489.7	4,536.3	4,576.2	4,594.2	4,568.3	4,565.2	4,541.0	4,536.8	4,514.2	4,484.2	4,529.0
2009	4,316.5	4,294.0	4,285.3	4,296.1	4,321.5	4,327.8	4,287.5	4,276.0	4,270.5	4,280.4	4,281.5	4,268.1	4,292.1
2010	4,141.1	4,149.2	4,170.2	4,223.6	4,278.8	4,294.0	4,253.5	4,264.2	4,269.6	4,302.3	4,313.9	4,306.2	4,247.2
2011	4,184.1	4,192.0	4,223.2	4,281.9	4,316.1	4,343.6	4,329.8	4,340.0	4,350.1	4,360.5	4,373.3	4,365.3	4,305.0
2012	4,252.0	4,261.2	4,295.2	4,343.5	4,387.1	4,421.1	4,394.1	4,409.8	4,419.4	4,428.1	4,446.5	4,442.0	4,375.0
2013	4,313.7	4,334.4	4,363.2	4,401.1	4,457.7	4,491.0	4,456.0	4,472.3	4,473.6	4,498.7	4,509.4	4,497.7	4,439.1
Total Private													
2002	3,821.9	3,806.5	3,826.7	3,864.6	3,895.8	3,927.7	3,915.4	3,930.1	3,915.2	3,903.1	3,911.8	3,908.9	3,885.6
2003	3,778.7	3,764.3	3,782.8	3,818.6	3,855.6	3,886.2	3,875.2	3,880.1	3,875.1	3,862.7	3,861.4	3,873.6	3,843.5
2004	3,742.5	3,736.5	3,769.5	3,816.9	3,861.1	3,897.7	3,897.9	3,903.6	3,892.5	3,896.7	3,904.4	3,914.7	3,852.8
2005	3,783.2	3,780.6	3,802.0	3,868.9	3,900.1	3,927.7	3,941.2	3,947.2	3,943.9	3,943.4	3,956.0	3,961.3	3,896.3
2006	3,844.8	3,847.2	3,877.7	3,923.7	3,958.5	4,003.8	3,995.6	4,004.9	3,992.0	3,991.8	4,002.9	4,008.8	3,954.3
2007	3,894.0	3,881.7	3,918.8	3,958.6	4,005.0	4,042.6	4,033.9	4,038.5	4,018.6	4,022.6	4,035.7	4,037.9	3,990.7
2008	3,912.8	3,899.4	3,917.0	3,962.0	3,996.4	4,018.5	4,008.2	4,008.9	3,971.5	3,960.2	3,937.3	3,910.7	3,958.6
2009	3,754.1	3,724.4	3,712.6	3,718.6	3,740.3	3,752.9	3,731.0	3,725.9	3,703.1	3,703.1	3,703.8	3,696.2	3,722.2
2010	3,578.5	3,579.1	3,599.7	3,648.5	3,686.1	3,715.5	3,703.7	3,721.0	3,711.2	3,735.6	3,745.8	3,746.1	3,680.9
2011	3,634.4	3,634.5	3,663.6	3,720.3	3,751.6	3,786.4	3,786.2	3,803.3	3,797.2	3,803.5	3,813.7	3,810.8	3,750.5
2012	3,709.3	3,709.5	3,740.4	3,788.0	3,827.7	3,866.0	3,857.9	3,875.3	3,869.8	3,873.5	3,890.6	3,889.9	3,824.8
2013	3,773.2	3,784.4	3,810.7	3,847.8	3,898.9	3,935.8	3,918.5	3,937.0	3,924.0	3,943.3	3,952.0	3,940.3	3,888.8
Goods Producing													
2002	754.9	750.8	755.5	765.6	771.1	778.3	773.0	777.0	775.8	772.5	768.7	758.9	766.8
2003	725.4	720.7	725.1	735.9	744.3	749.5	743.8	748.3	745.7	737.3	730.9	723.9	735.9
2004	691.4	687.1	696.5	709.1	719.0	726.5	727.3	728.8	728.6	727.2	724.4	717.9	715.3
2005	686.9	686.6	691.8	708.6	715.2	721.8	721.9	723.8	723.9	723.3	721.1	711.4	711.4
2006	688.8	688.7	692.6	709.1	715.2	724.5	720.1	721.9	721.0	720.0	715.6	708.8	710.5
2007	682.3	673.7	686.0	697.8	706.9	716.3	712.7	712.4	710.5	708.9	704.5	696.0	700.7
2008	667.2	660.6	666.3	677.3	685.2	690.0	688.2	688.0	682.1	675.9	662.7	642.8	673.9
2009	601.8	593.3	588.6	586.3	585.3	588.1	582.3	581.3	577.4	573.6	567.2	555.3	581.7
2010	528.2	527.0	533.5	546.6	554.3	560.5	555.9	565.5	563.0	567.3	563.7	553.1	551.6
2011	533.2	531.7	540.4	554.3	563.2	570.0	572.6	574.2	570.5	569.5	566.8	557.6	558.7
2012	538.2	536.7	545.1	555.8	562.8	571.2	573.9	575.0	573.8	571.5	567.3	562.1	561.1
2013	539.7	540.9	546.5	553.0	563.8	571.8	571.9	573.2	570.5	571.4	565.9	553.9	560.2
Service-Providing													
2002	3,622.3	3,621.7	3,639.8	3,670.8	3,700.7	3,723.3	3,704.9	3,712.7	3,699.6	3,703.7	3,718.5	3,725.6	3,687.0
2003	3,616.7	3,617.3	3,633.9	3,656.1	3,688.6	3,712.2	3,704.1	3,703.4	3,691.4	3,691.4	3,696.5	3,713.2	3,677.1
2004	3,605.1	3,612.1	3,638.0	3,674.2	3,712.5	3,739.3	3,722.9	3,721.9	3,718.5	3,737.5	3,750.6	3,761.6	3,699.5
2005	3,652.6	3,660.6	3,681.0	3,731.9	3,759.5	3,775.1	3,776.2	3,773.6	3,781.2	3,787.4	3,805.4	3,815.6	3,750.0
2006	3,712.2	3,725.0	3,753.8	3,785.9	3,818.3	3,852.8	3,829.3	3,832.1	3,836.2	3,840.6	3,858.9	3,867.3	3,809.4
2007	3,769.5	3,776.6	3,804.0	3,833.4	3,873.1	3,898.2	3,876.0	3,878.4	3,873.3	3,882.8	3,902.4	3,909.4	3,856.4
2008	3,805.3	3,808.8	3,823.4	3,859.0	3,891.0	3,904.2	3,880.1	3,877.2	3,858.9	3,860.9	3,851.5	3,841.4	3,855.1
2009	3,714.7	3,700.7	3,696.7	3,709.8	3,736.2	3,739.7	3,705.2	3,694.7	3,693.1	3,706.8	3,714.3	3,712.8	3,710.4
2010	3,612.9	3,622.2	3,636.7	3,677.0	3,724.5	3,733.5	3,697.6	3,698.7	3,706.6	3,735.0	3,750.2	3,753.1	3,695.7
2011	3,650.9	3,660.3	3,682.8	3,727.6	3,752.9	3,773.6	3,757.2	3,765.8	3,779.6	3,791.0	3,806.5	3,807.7	3,746.3
2012	3,713.8	3,724.5	3,750.1	3,787.7	3,824.3	3,849.9	3,820.2	3,834.8	3,845.6	3,856.6	3,879.2	3,879.9	3,813.9
2013	3,774.0	3,793.5	3,816.7	3,848.1	3,893.9	3,919.2	3,884.1	3,899.1	3,903.1	3,927.3	3,943.5	3,943.8	3,878.9
Mining and Logging													
2004	1.8	1.9	2.1	2.2	2.2	2.2	2.2	2.3	2.3	2.2	2.3	2.2	2.2
2005	2.0	2.0	2.1	2.3	2.3	2.4	2.5	2.4	2.4	2.5	2.4	2.3	2.3
2006	2.0	2.0	2.1	2.4	2.5	2.6	2.6	2.6	2.6	2.5	2.6	2.4	2.4
2007	2.3	2.1	2.4	2.3	2.4	2.4	2.4	2.4	2.3	2.3	2.3	2.1	2.3
2008	1.9	1.8	1.9	2.1	2.1	2.2	2.2	2.2	2.1	2.0	1.9	1.8	2.0
2009	1.4	1.5	1.6	1.8	1.8	1.8	1.8	1.8	1.8	1.7	1.7	1.6	1.7
2010	1.3	1.3	1.3	1.5	1.6	1.6	1.6	1.6	1.6	1.6	1.6	1.5	1.5
2011	1.2	1.2	1.3	1.5	1.6	1.6	1.7	1.5	1.6	1.5	1.5	1.3	1.5
2012	1.2	1.2	1.2	1.3	1.4	1.5	1.5	1.5	1.6	1.5	1.5	1.4	1.4
2013	1.2	1.2	1.2	1.3	1.6	1.6	1.5	1.6	1.5	1.4	1.4	1.3	1.4
Construction													
2004	189.5	186.1	193.6	206.8	214.6	220.1	224.7	224.5	223.8	223.9	221.6	215.2	212.0
2005	189.3	188.8	192.9	209.0	215.2	220.3	224.3	225.5	226.0	226.2	223.8	214.1	213.0
2006	197.9	197.5	203.2	216.6	223.9	229.7	229.0	230.9	228.2	227.8	223.9	216.6	218.8
2007	196.3	188.3	199.4	211.9	220.9	227.1	227.2	227.2	225.6	224.1	221.1	210.7	215.0
2008	188.1	184.6	189.7	201.2	209.3	212.7	215.2	215.9	212.3	209.3	200.0	185.6	202.0
2009	157.4	155.6	157.1	163.4	167.2	170.7	171.1	170.9	167.6	166.1	161.1	149.4	163.1
2010	128.2	126.7	132.3	144.1	149.8	153.6	150.0	157.4	155.4	157.2	152.9	141.9	145.8
2011	125.8	124.1	130.4	142.2	150.1	154.3	157.7	159.5	157.2	155.7	155.7	144.3	146.2
2012	128.6	126.7	133.3	142.7	148.5	154.0	157.4	158.4	158.3	158.1	153.4	146.9	147.2
2013	129.8	130.5	135.4	142.7	152.2	156.9	159.9	160.4	159.7	161.1	156.4	143.1	149.0

Employment by Industry: Chicago-Joliet-Naperville, IL–IN–WI, Selected Years, 2002–2013—*Continued*

(Numbers in thousands, not seasonally adjusted)

Industry and year	January	February	March	April	May	June	July	August	September	October	November	December	Annual average
Manufacturing													
2002	558.6	555.8	555.1	553.5	551.6	552.7	543.2	545.2	544.8	542.2	540.6	539.5	548.6
2003	527.3	525.9	524.9	523.1	521.0	520.6	511.8	513.2	512.3	509.2	507.8	507.2	517.0
2004	500.1	499.1	500.8	500.1	502.2	504.2	500.4	502.0	502.5	501.1	500.5	500.5	501.1
2005	495.6	495.8	496.8	497.3	497.7	499.1	495.1	495.9	495.5	494.6	494.9	495.0	496.1
2006	488.9	489.2	487.3	490.1	488.8	492.2	488.5	488.4	490.2	489.7	489.1	489.8	489.4
2007	483.7	483.3	484.2	483.6	483.6	486.8	483.1	482.8	482.6	482.5	481.1	483.2	483.4
2008	477.2	474.2	474.7	474.0	473.8	475.1	470.8	469.9	467.7	464.6	460.8	455.4	469.9
2009	443.0	436.2	429.9	421.1	416.3	415.6	409.4	408.6	408.0	405.8	404.4	404.3	416.9
2010	398.7	399.0	399.9	401.0	402.9	405.3	404.3	406.5	406.0	408.5	409.2	409.7	404.3
2011	406.2	406.4	408.7	410.6	411.5	414.1	413.2	413.2	411.7	412.3	412.0	412.0	411.0
2012	408.4	408.8	410.6	411.8	412.9	415.7	415.0	415.1	413.9	411.9	412.4	413.8	412.5
2013	408.7	409.2	409.9	409.0	410.0	413.3	410.5	411.2	409.3	408.9	408.1	409.5	409.8
Trade, Transportation, and Utilities													
2002	921.2	907.3	910.3	913.1	918.1	922.1	916.8	918.8	918.3	921.6	938.0	949.5	921.3
2003	904.3	895.3	897.3	897.3	903.5	908.0	900.1	902.3	904.0	907.8	921.7	935.3	906.4
2004	895.3	886.8	891.3	895.7	905.8	911.8	907.0	908.4	909.4	915.7	930.8	944.8	908.6
2005	902.6	892.9	896.2	902.3	909.3	913.9	911.6	913.8	915.0	918.9	934.5	949.5	913.4
2006	911.6	903.0	908.2	911.1	918.3	925.1	919.3	920.1	919.0	922.8	942.0	954.7	921.3
2007	923.9	912.0	918.3	916.4	926.9	934.1	928.5	928.4	927.4	931.8	954.1	966.0	930.7
2008	931.5	918.2	920.7	921.0	927.6	930.7	923.7	922.7	917.5	918.9	927.1	931.9	924.3
2009	890.1	875.7	870.2	863.7	868.5	869.7	859.9	859.5	855.8	858.4	869.3	876.6	868.1
2010	843.0	835.6	838.0	843.9	851.5	856.6	853.5	855.7	853.0	861.7	877.1	889.0	854.9
2011	857.4	849.3	852.3	860.5	866.4	872.3	869.6	873.8	874.0	880.2	896.4	907.3	871.6
2012	874.6	864.5	869.4	872.1	879.9	885.0	883.7	885.9	885.2	892.6	913.9	920.2	885.6
2013	884.0	876.2	879.6	882.0	891.7	899.4	896.5	900.1	897.1	903.9	926.3	938.3	897.9
Wholesale Trade													
2002	250.8	250.7	251.0	251.2	251.4	252.9	251.2	251.1	250.1	250.0	250.6	250.6	251.0
2003	248.6	248.5	249.0	247.5	247.9	248.6	247.2	246.2	245.1	243.2	243.9	244.6	246.7
2004	240.9	240.4	241.5	242.4	243.9	245.3	244.7	244.6	243.8	244.5	245.1	246.3	243.6
2005	241.1	240.9	241.7	243.4	244.5	246.2	246.4	245.9	246.0	246.3	247.5	249.1	244.9
2006	246.0	246.0	247.2	247.7	248.8	250.8	249.7	249.3	248.4	248.5	248.6	250.1	248.4
2007	247.7	247.7	248.8	248.9	250.2	252.4	252.0	251.3	250.5	251.7	252.0	253.4	250.6
2008	250.3	249.7	250.4	250.8	251.9	252.9	251.0	250.4	249.1	248.6	247.6	247.0	250.0
2009	241.3	239.2	237.7	235.1	234.2	233.8	231.2	230.7	228.7	229.1	228.3	228.6	233.2
2010	225.5	225.1	226.3	227.6	229.0	230.0	230.2	230.3	228.9	229.9	230.1	230.8	228.6
2011	229.0	229.2	230.0	231.4	232.3	234.1	234.3	234.4	233.4	233.5	233.8	235.2	232.6
2012	233.9	233.8	235.1	236.1	237.4	239.5	238.8	238.8	238.1	238.7	239.2	240.0	237.5
2013	237.7	238.1	239.5	239.1	240.5	243.1	243.6	243.2	242.6	242.3	243.1	243.3	241.3
Retail Trade													
2002	469.7	457.6	461.1	461.3	466.1	470.6	466.9	467.9	466.8	469.2	485.8	497.6	470.1
2003	459.5	452.1	453.7	454.6	459.1	463.9	459.2	461.2	460.5	464.7	477.7	490.2	463.0
2004	458.7	451.4	454.1	455.5	462.2	468.5	463.9	465.0	463.6	467.3	481.8	494.2	465.5
2005	462.9	453.2	454.8	458.1	463.3	467.2	467.9	469.7	467.5	470.0	483.5	495.2	467.8
2006	466.8	457.6	460.1	461.7	466.0	471.6	469.2	469.9	465.1	469.8	487.8	496.6	470.2
2007	474.5	462.6	466.7	465.6	472.5	478.0	475.8	475.3	471.3	474.2	495.0	502.9	476.2
2008	477.9	465.2	466.3	466.4	470.2	474.2	471.8	469.7	463.5	465.8	475.3	479.7	470.5
2009	452.6	441.8	439.1	437.2	442.1	445.1	441.9	441.4	436.9	439.1	450.9	456.3	443.7
2010	431.7	424.5	425.6	428.2	433.1	437.8	436.9	437.1	432.3	438.6	452.6	461.0	436.6
2011	437.0	428.6	430.2	435.0	438.7	443.3	442.3	444.7	442.1	447.8	463.0	470.4	443.6
2012	444.5	434.9	437.2	437.1	441.7	446.2	445.8	445.7	442.8	449.0	468.6	471.4	447.1
2013	445.5	437.1	438.5	440.2	447.2	453.8	451.7	452.4	449.0	453.7	473.2	482.5	452.1
Transportation and Utilities													
2002	200.7	199.0	198.2	200.6	200.6	198.6	198.7	199.8	201.4	202.4	201.6	201.3	200.2
2003	196.2	194.7	194.6	195.2	196.5	195.5	193.7	194.9	198.4	199.9	200.1	200.5	196.7
2004	195.7	195.0	195.7	197.8	199.7	198.0	198.4	198.8	202.0	203.9	203.9	204.3	199.4
2005	198.6	198.8	199.7	200.8	201.5	200.5	197.3	198.2	201.5	202.6	203.5	205.2	200.7
2006	198.8	199.4	200.9	201.7	203.5	202.7	200.4	200.9	205.5	204.5	205.6	208.0	202.7
2007	201.7	201.7	202.8	201.9	204.2	203.7	200.7	201.8	205.6	205.9	207.1	209.7	203.9
2008	203.3	203.3	204.0	203.8	205.5	203.6	200.9	202.6	204.9	204.5	204.2	205.2	203.8
2009	196.2	194.7	193.4	191.4	192.2	190.8	186.8	187.4	190.2	190.2	190.1	191.7	191.3
2010	185.8	186.0	186.1	188.1	189.4	188.8	186.4	188.3	191.8	193.2	194.4	197.2	189.6
2011	191.4	191.5	192.1	194.1	195.4	194.9	193.0	194.7	198.5	198.9	199.6	201.7	195.5
2012	196.2	195.8	197.1	198.9	200.8	199.3	199.1	201.4	204.3	204.9	206.1	208.8	201.1
2013	200.8	201.0	201.6	202.7	204.0	202.5	201.2	204.5	205.5	207.9	210.0	212.5	204.5
Information													
2002	111.3	110.7	110.5	110.0	110.1	110.1	107.9	107.6	105.9	105.5	105.0	104.7	108.3
2003	102.1	102.2	101.2	100.3	100.2	100.4	99.8	98.9	97.8	97.5	97.1	96.9	99.5
2004	96.1	96.0	95.8	95.4	95.4	95.7	95.2	94.7	93.5	93.9	93.8	94.5	95.0
2005	93.4	93.1	93.1	93.4	93.1	93.4	93.6	92.8	92.0	91.8	91.7	91.7	92.8
2006	91.4	91.2	91.2	91.3	91.6	92.0	91.7	91.4	90.6	90.8	90.7	91.0	91.2
2007	90.4	90.8	90.5	90.5	90.8	91.3	91.6	91.7	91.0	91.0	91.0	91.1	91.0
2008	90.7	90.9	90.9	90.8	91.1	91.0	90.9	90.7	89.0	88.4	88.0	87.9	90.0
2009	86.6	85.8	84.8	84.1	83.9	83.8	83.4	83.2	82.6	82.4	82.1	82.3	83.8
2010	81.5	80.8	80.5	80.4	80.5	81.0	80.8	80.7	79.8	80.2	80.1	79.9	80.5
2011	79.5	79.2	79.0	79.4	79.8	80.5	81.3	81.0	80.1	80.3	80.8	80.6	80.1
2012	80.6	80.4	80.3	80.8	81.5	81.3	81.3	80.9	80.4	81.2	81.1	81.1	80.9
2013	80.0	80.0	79.6	80.3	81.1	81.5	81.2	80.7	79.5	80.1	80.4	81.2	80.5

Employment by Industry: Chicago-Joliet-Naperville, IL–IN–WI, Selected Years, 2002–2013—*Continued*

(Numbers in thousands, not seasonally adjusted)

Industry and year	January	February	March	April	May	June	July	August	September	October	November	December	Annual average
Financial Activities													
2002	320.5	319.9	320.6	319.8	320.9	324.4	323.9	324.2	322.0	322.5	323.7	325.7	322.3
2003	323.9	323.6	324.6	325.3	326.7	330.4	330.7	330.9	328.3	324.9	325.2	326.6	326.8
2004	321.8	321.5	323.0	322.3	323.5	326.7	327.5	327.5	324.1	323.7	323.5	325.7	324.2
2005	323.1	322.8	323.4	325.2	326.2	329.1	331.4	331.4	329.6	329.7	330.0	332.1	327.8
2006	327.6	327.9	328.9	329.8	330.7	333.8	334.7	334.7	333.1	332.1	331.8	333.2	331.5
2007	329.8	329.5	329.3	329.4	330.0	332.2	331.2	329.8	325.7	324.8	323.9	324.2	328.3
2008	318.7	318.6	318.6	318.0	318.5	320.0	318.4	317.8	313.6	312.4	310.7	310.6	316.3
2009	304.4	302.4	300.7	299.8	299.4	300.1	298.6	297.6	294.4	293.6	293.0	293.5	298.1
2010	288.8	288.4	288.4	288.0	288.2	290.1	289.3	289.1	286.0	287.3	286.7	287.1	288.1
2011	283.1	282.8	282.6	283.0	283.6	286.0	287.3	287.5	285.5	286.5	286.1	286.3	285.0
2012	283.2	283.6	284.1	284.8	286.0	289.0	290.0	290.3	288.3	287.8	287.3	288.5	286.9
2013	285.8	286.2	286.0	287.4	288.6	292.4	292.3	291.9	290.5	290.2	288.9	289.9	289.2
Professional and Business Services													
2002	662.1	660.9	662.9	676.0	678.9	684.9	685.5	692.3	690.0	683.8	680.7	673.5	677.6
2003	647.0	644.9	646.9	659.1	663.4	668.0	667.7	673.2	675.7	676.4	671.0	671.8	663.8
2004	645.8	648.7	655.3	671.8	680.2	691.8	690.9	695.9	696.6	703.1	700.8	696.9	681.5
2005	672.0	675.2	680.8	698.7	702.5	711.7	714.5	719.5	721.8	728.2	727.7	723.5	706.3
2006	695.2	698.7	707.9	722.2	726.7	738.8	739.0	745.8	744.2	747.8	745.2	740.0	729.3
2007	711.4	713.9	721.1	739.0	744.9	753.1	754.2	760.1	755.0	757.8	755.4	753.0	743.2
2008	723.5	725.2	724.9	739.4	743.2	746.4	744.5	747.8	739.3	736.9	727.3	717.5	734.7
2009	681.9	674.2	666.8	672.1	675.4	677.3	675.5	676.5	672.4	677.3	678.0	674.5	675.2
2010	652.8	656.0	657.1	677.5	681.8	690.9	693.2	698.6	696.7	704.7	704.5	702.8	684.7
2011	677.3	681.2	685.7	704.2	705.0	715.2	719.6	724.9	724.8	728.5	728.9	723.0	709.9
2012	703.1	704.6	711.9	730.2	737.7	749.0	748.0	755.9	757.4	759.0	762.4	757.8	739.8
2013	731.2	737.7	743.7	757.6	768.3	777.7	772.4	780.4	780.1	788.0	783.5	775.6	766.4
Education and Health Services													
2002	518.9	524.0	526.9	528.3	530.3	527.1	521.5	523.0	529.9	533.9	537.0	537.4	528.2
2003	529.7	532.6	535.5	536.6	538.4	534.9	533.2	534.0	540.1	545.0	547.2	548.5	538.0
2004	539.9	543.7	545.9	549.5	549.6	545.1	542.4	542.2	548.6	554.1	556.9	560.1	548.2
2005	552.9	556.2	556.6	562.1	562.7	556.2	555.9	554.7	561.9	566.3	569.0	570.1	560.4
2006	563.0	569.8	572.3	573.1	574.8	571.7	568.6	569.9	578.1	581.9	585.3	585.3	574.5
2007	578.7	586.2	588.8	589.1	591.9	588.8	585.1	584.1	592.7	599.5	603.0	603.8	591.0
2008	596.8	602.4	603.2	608.0	609.0	606.6	604.1	604.7	612.3	618.4	622.6	623.3	609.3
2009	614.0	620.5	622.2	622.8	623.4	618.7	615.7	614.6	621.3	628.8	631.8	632.5	622.2
2010	624.1	630.8	633.9	636.4	638.7	633.9	630.0	629.4	637.4	645.6	650.0	651.2	636.8
2011	642.2	648.9	651.7	651.6	652.2	648.3	643.3	644.5	655.6	660.7	662.9	666.1	652.3
2012	654.1	662.7	662.9	665.7	666.1	663.2	656.1	657.9	668.9	672.2	675.0	676.2	665.1
2013	665.3	675.7	677.6	678.6	679.4	673.8	664.6	670.3	678.3	685.3	691.4	688.7	677.4
Leisure and Hospitality													
2002	345.8	345.7	351.6	363.0	376.9	387.9	389.8	389.9	382.4	373.0	367.9	367.8	370.1
2003	351.6	350.2	355.5	369.0	382.7	395.4	394.7	394.6	387.4	377.7	372.8	374.2	375.5
2004	358.1	357.8	365.3	377.3	390.8	400.8	403.3	402.8	395.3	382.9	378.1	377.1	382.5
2005	360.6	361.6	367.0	384.2	396.4	404.7	408.7	408.0	402.6	389.7	385.6	385.1	387.9
2006	370.8	372.6	379.4	392.3	405.1	418.9	419.7	418.5	409.6	399.9	395.6	397.1	398.3
2007	382.9	381.1	387.8	400.4	415.6	426.0	425.5	426.9	417.8	410.8	405.4	404.4	407.1
2008	387.9	386.3	394.0	409.1	421.8	431.5	430.5	429.5	417.9	409.7	399.9	397.4	409.6
2009	380.9	378.0	383.8	395.1	408.3	416.8	414.5	412.8	405.7	394.7	387.9	386.4	397.1
2010	369.4	369.9	376.6	389.4	403.7	413.2	412.6	413.8	408.1	400.3	394.9	393.7	395.5
2011	375.5	374.7	383.6	398.3	410.7	421.2	420.4	426.0	416.6	408.4	403.1	399.9	403.2
2012	388.1	389.1	397.6	410.1	423.6	434.2	433.3	438.7	426.1	420.2	414.2	414.4	415.8
2013	400.0	399.7	408.6	419.8	435.5	446.8	445.7	446.5	436.1	432.0	424.4	421.6	426.4
Other Services													
2002	187.2	187.2	188.4	188.8	189.5	192.9	197.0	197.3	190.9	190.3	190.8	191.4	191.0
2003	194.7	194.8	196.7	195.1	196.4	199.6	205.2	205.9	196.1	196.1	195.5	196.4	197.7
2004	194.1	194.9	196.4	195.8	196.8	199.3	204.3	203.3	196.4	196.1	196.1	197.7	197.6
2005	191.7	192.2	193.1	194.4	194.7	196.9	203.6	203.2	197.1	195.5	196.4	197.9	196.4
2006	196.4	195.3	197.2	194.8	196.1	199.0	202.5	202.6	196.4	196.5	196.7	198.7	197.7
2007	194.6	194.5	197.0	196.0	198.0	200.8	205.1	205.1	198.5	198.0	198.4	199.4	198.8
2008	196.5	197.2	198.4	198.4	200.0	202.3	207.9	207.7	199.8	199.6	199.0	199.3	200.5
2009	194.4	194.5	195.5	194.7	196.1	198.4	201.1	200.4	193.5	194.3	194.5	195.1	196.0
2010	190.7	190.6	191.7	186.3	187.4	189.3	188.4	188.2	187.2	188.5	188.8	189.3	188.9
2011	186.2	186.7	188.3	189.0	190.7	192.9	192.1	191.4	190.1	189.4	188.7	190.0	189.6
2012	187.4	187.9	189.1	188.5	190.1	193.1	191.6	190.7	189.7	189.0	189.4	189.6	189.7
2013	187.2	188.0	189.1	189.1	190.5	192.4	193.9	193.9	191.9	192.4	191.2	191.1	190.9
Government													
2002	555.3	566.0	568.6	571.8	576.0	573.9	562.5	559.6	560.2	573.1	575.4	575.6	568.2
2003	563.4	573.7	576.2	573.4	577.3	575.5	572.7	563.6	562.0	566.0	566.0	563.5	569.4
2004	554.0	562.7	565.0	566.4	570.4	568.1	552.3	547.1	554.6	568.0	570.6	564.8	562.0
2005	556.3	566.6	570.8	571.6	574.6	569.2	556.9	550.2	561.2	567.3	570.5	565.7	565.1
2006	556.2	566.5	568.7	571.3	575.0	573.5	553.8	549.1	565.2	568.8	571.6	567.3	565.6
2007	557.8	568.6	571.2	572.6	575.0	571.9	554.8	552.3	565.2	569.1	571.2	567.5	566.4
2008	559.7	570.0	572.7	574.3	579.8	575.7	560.1	556.3	569.5	576.6	576.9	573.5	570.4
2009	562.4	569.6	572.7	575.5	581.2	574.9	556.5	550.1	567.4	577.3	577.7	571.9	569.9
2010	562.6	570.1	570.5	575.1	592.7	578.5	549.8	543.2	558.4	566.7	568.1	560.1	566.3
2011	549.7	557.5	559.6	561.6	564.5	557.2	543.6	536.7	552.9	557.0	559.6	554.5	554.5
2012	542.7	551.7	554.8	555.5	559.4	555.1	536.2	534.5	549.6	554.6	555.9	552.1	550.2
2013	540.5	550.0	552.5	553.3	558.8	555.2	537.5	535.3	549.6	555.4	557.4	557.4	550.2

Employment by Industry: Cincinnati-Middletown, OH–KY–IN, Selected Years, 2002–2013

(Numbers in thousands, not seasonally adjusted)

Industry and year	January	February	March	April	May	June	July	August	September	October	November	December	Annual average
Total Nonfarm													
2002	988.2	991.4	998.7	1,004.3	1,013.3	1,014.3	1,009.0	1,012.8	1,014.4	1,015.6	1,019.8	1,021.9	1,008.6
2003	998.9	998.0	1,007.4	1,017.6	1,023.6	1,024.0	1,013.9	1,020.9	1,019.1	1,020.8	1,022.9	1,026.0	1,016.1
2004	997.8	999.8	1,012.1	1,022.3	1,029.9	1,034.2	1,029.4	1,033.7	1,033.1	1,034.4	1,037.7	1,039.4	1,025.3
2005	1,004.3	1,010.2	1,021.1	1,033.7	1,041.7	1,044.5	1,037.1	1,039.2	1,044.3	1,041.0	1,045.8	1,048.7	1,034.3
2006	1,017.3	1,020.9	1,028.1	1,036.5	1,043.9	1,046.8	1,036.4	1,041.7	1,043.1	1,040.5	1,044.4	1,047.1	1,037.2
2007	1,022.8	1,023.1	1,036.3	1,045.6	1,057.9	1,059.8	1,045.9	1,050.0	1,050.9	1,055.3	1,058.4	1,060.4	1,047.2
2008	1,032.9	1,034.4	1,037.1	1,051.2	1,059.6	1,055.1	1,046.7	1,048.1	1,041.6	1,042.1	1,037.3	1,034.7	1,043.4
2009	997.2	993.4	993.1	995.4	1,002.3	998.4	985.6	988.5	987.2	987.8	989.4	989.2	992.3
2010	959.1	959.3	969.6	984.8	995.5	993.5	980.5	981.5	982.0	988.6	990.3	988.3	981.1
2011	962.7	965.9	975.7	991.0	998.3	996.9	994.1	997.8	999.4	1,000.1	1,003.7	1,005.7	990.9
2012	980.3	984.4	993.9	1,006.3	1,017.3	1,020.1	1,004.0	1,011.7	1,015.7	1,020.0	1,019.7	1,019.3	1,007.7
2013	992.7	999.0	1,006.0	1,023.1	1,033.5	1,034.6	1,023.3	1,031.2	1,033.5	1,039.2	1,037.1	1,033.0	1,023.9
Total Private													
2002	858.9	858.6	864.7	870.5	878.8	885.6	886.9	888.7	885.2	882.9	886.5	889.2	878.0
2003	866.9	863.4	871.5	881.1	886.9	892.8	890.3	894.2	886.9	884.9	886.6	890.0	883.0
2004	865.7	864.4	875.3	885.2	892.4	901.6	905.9	907.9	901.5	899.2	902.0	904.6	892.1
2005	873.2	876.2	886.1	898.3	905.8	912.8	913.8	914.1	912.7	906.1	910.4	914.0	902.0
2006	886.0	886.4	892.3	900.5	907.1	915.4	913.4	916.6	911.1	905.5	909.1	912.0	904.6
2007	890.6	887.9	899.8	909.4	920.6	926.7	921.9	924.1	919.4	920.8	921.9	924.7	914.0
2008	901.5	898.8	901.6	915.5	922.5	923.9	922.8	922.2	910.4	907.4	900.8	899.1	910.5
2009	865.0	858.7	858.6	859.9	866.5	867.0	863.9	864.6	857.2	855.0	856.3	857.1	860.8
2010	829.6	827.6	836.9	851.0	858.4	862.8	861.5	861.7	856.1	860.1	860.1	858.7	852.0
2011	836.9	837.8	846.7	861.8	869.5	873.0	876.8	878.0	873.6	872.6	875.6	877.8	865.0
2012	856.0	856.7	865.3	877.2	887.5	894.1	890.7	893.1	889.6	891.6	890.8	891.3	882.0
2013	866.5	869.9	877.3	893.0	903.9	908.7	906.8	909.2	905.7	909.4	906.4	902.8	896.6
Goods Producing													
2002	178.2	177.3	177.7	177.8	178.7	180.2	180.5	181.4	180.7	180.2	179.6	177.7	179.2
2003	174.2	172.8	174.9	177.4	178.4	179.3	178.0	178.8	177.5	176.6	175.8	175.5	176.6
2004	171.3	170.9	173.4	176.2	177.8	180.1	179.6	179.4	178.6	177.8	177.2	176.2	176.5
2005	169.7	170.1	172.3	174.6	176.8	178.0	178.5	178.6	178.5	177.4	177.1	175.7	175.6
2006	170.4	170.5	169.4	173.3	174.8	176.5	175.7	176.7	175.2	172.9	172.3	172.1	173.3
2007	167.8	166.8	170.0	172.1	174.0	174.8	174.0	174.3	173.2	172.3	171.2	169.9	171.7
2008	165.5	164.7	165.0	167.9	169.2	169.9	169.3	169.0	166.8	165.5	162.9	160.1	166.3
2009	151.8	149.2	148.2	146.4	147.0	146.7	145.5	146.3	144.8	144.2	143.3	141.9	146.3
2010	135.4	134.0	136.1	139.0	140.1	140.9	142.2	142.1	141.9	142.7	142.0	139.7	139.7
2011	135.9	136.1	137.7	140.6	142.3	143.6	145.1	145.2	145.1	145.1	144.7	144.3	142.1
2012	140.1	139.8	141.1	143.1	144.6	146.5	146.6	146.5	145.9	145.2	144.9	143.9	144.0
2013	139.8	139.2	139.8	142.8	145.1	146.7	147.5	147.5	147.6	148.3	145.3	145.1	144.6
Service-Providing													
2002	810.0	814.1	821.0	826.5	834.6	834.1	828.5	831.4	833.7	835.4	840.2	844.2	829.5
2003	824.7	825.2	832.5	840.2	845.2	844.7	835.9	842.1	841.6	844.2	847.1	850.5	839.5
2004	826.5	828.9	838.7	846.1	852.1	854.1	849.8	854.3	854.5	856.6	860.5	863.2	848.8
2005	834.6	840.1	848.8	859.1	864.9	866.5	858.6	860.6	865.8	863.6	868.7	873.0	858.7
2006	846.9	850.4	858.7	863.2	869.1	870.3	860.7	865.0	867.9	867.6	872.1	875.0	863.9
2007	855.0	856.3	866.3	873.5	883.9	885.0	871.9	875.7	877.7	883.0	887.2	890.5	875.5
2008	867.4	869.7	872.1	883.3	890.4	885.2	877.4	879.1	874.8	876.6	874.4	874.6	877.1
2009	845.4	844.2	844.9	849.0	855.3	851.7	840.1	842.2	842.4	843.6	846.1	847.3	846.0
2010	823.7	825.3	833.5	845.8	855.4	852.6	838.3	839.4	840.1	845.9	848.3	848.6	841.4
2011	826.8	829.8	838.0	850.4	856.0	853.3	849.0	852.6	854.3	855.0	859.0	861.4	848.8
2012	840.2	844.6	852.8	863.2	872.7	873.6	857.4	865.2	869.8	874.8	874.8	875.4	863.7
2013	852.9	859.8	866.2	880.3	888.4	887.9	875.8	883.7	885.9	890.9	891.8	887.9	879.3
Mining, Logging, and Construction													
2002	46.1	46.0	46.8	47.7	48.9	50.6	51.2	51.6	51.0	50.8	50.4	48.7	49.2
2003	45.3	44.4	46.1	49.0	50.2	51.5	51.4	52.3	51.6	51.6	50.9	50.4	49.6
2004	48.3	48.0	49.9	51.7	53.0	54.8	55.2	55.1	54.4	53.6	52.9	51.8	52.4
2005	47.4	48.1	49.6	51.6	53.2	54.3	55.1	55.1	54.9	54.1	53.7	52.1	52.4
2006	48.5	48.8	49.9	52.0	53.0	54.1	54.2	54.8	53.6	52.1	51.4	50.5	51.9
2007	47.3	45.8	48.0	50.4	52.0	52.7	53.0	53.0	52.4	52.2	51.2	49.6	50.6
2008	45.4	44.6	45.1	47.3	48.7	49.4	49.7	49.5	48.2	47.9	46.6	44.7	47.3
2009	40.0	39.1	39.4	39.2	40.7	40.9	40.9	41.1	40.2	39.8	39.1	37.8	39.9
2010	33.0	31.9	33.4	35.9	36.7	37.4	38.3	38.4	38.0	38.9	38.3	36.5	36.4
2011	33.4	33.4	34.7	37.0	38.1	38.9	40.0	40.2	40.0	40.0	39.2	38.6	37.8
2012	35.5	35.0	36.2	38.0	38.9	39.7	39.8	40.0	40.0	39.5	39.2	38.1	38.3
2013	35.3	34.9	35.5	37.4	38.7	39.7	40.3	40.6	41.1	40.3	39.0	38.3	38.4
Manufacturing													
2002	132.1	131.3	130.9	130.1	129.8	129.6	129.3	129.8	129.7	129.4	129.2	129.0	130.0
2003	128.9	128.4	128.8	128.4	128.2	127.8	126.6	126.5	125.9	125.0	124.9	125.1	127.0
2004	123.0	122.9	123.5	124.5	124.8	125.3	124.4	124.3	124.2	124.2	124.3	124.4	124.2
2005	122.3	122.0	122.7	123.0	123.6	123.7	123.4	123.5	123.6	123.3	123.4	123.6	123.2
2006	121.9	121.7	119.5	121.3	121.8	122.4	121.5	121.9	121.6	120.8	120.9	121.6	121.4
2007	120.5	121.0	122.0	121.7	122.0	122.1	121.0	121.3	120.8	120.1	120.0	120.3	121.1
2008	120.1	120.1	119.9	120.6	120.5	120.5	119.6	119.5	118.6	117.6	116.3	115.4	119.1
2009	111.8	110.1	108.8	107.2	106.3	105.8	104.6	105.2	104.6	104.4	104.2	104.1	106.4
2010	102.4	102.1	102.7	103.1	103.4	103.5	103.9	103.7	103.9	103.8	103.7	103.2	103.3
2011	102.5	102.7	103.0	103.6	104.2	104.7	105.1	105.0	105.1	105.1	105.5	105.7	104.4
2012	104.6	104.8	104.9	105.1	105.7	106.8	106.8	106.5	105.9	105.7	105.7	105.8	105.7
2013	104.5	104.3	104.3	105.4	106.4	107.0	107.2	106.9	106.5	108.0	106.3	106.8	106.1

Employment by Industry: Cincinnati-Middletown, OH–KY–IN, Selected Years, 2002–2013—*Continued*

(Numbers in thousands, not seasonally adjusted)

Industry and year	January	February	March	April	May	June	July	August	September	October	November	December	Annual average
Trade, Transportation, and Utilities													
2002	212.5	210.9	211.7	212.1	213.1	213.6	213.0	212.9	213.0	212.5	217.3	221.2	213.7
2003	210.3	208.6	209.5	209.7	210.5	210.6	209.1	210.2	209.4	211.1	214.7	217.4	210.9
2004	207.3	205.3	206.5	207.2	208.3	209.4	210.5	212.2	210.5	211.9	216.1	218.8	210.3
2005	208.2	206.7	208.1	209.1	210.4	210.5	211.5	210.6	210.9	209.9	213.5	217.0	210.5
2006	208.6	206.3	207.0	207.2	209.0	209.5	208.7	209.2	209.6	210.5	214.9	217.5	209.8
2007	210.3	208.3	210.1	210.5	212.9	213.3	212.8	212.6	212.9	214.3	218.5	221.2	213.1
2008	212.2	209.9	210.2	210.9	212.4	211.8	210.9	211.3	209.5	209.4	211.2	212.8	211.0
2009	202.2	199.5	198.2	196.1	197.4	196.6	195.6	196.7	195.8	197.7	200.8	202.5	198.3
2010	193.3	192.6	193.5	194.6	196.2	196.3	194.7	194.7	193.8	196.2	200.2	201.4	195.6
2011	193.0	191.9	192.9	194.7	195.5	196.0	196.8	197.7	197.7	199.7	204.6	206.1	197.2
2012	197.0	195.8	197.1	198.3	200.5	200.6	199.5	200.3	200.1	201.9	205.7	206.2	200.3
2013	198.6	197.4	198.6	200.2	202.0	202.4	200.8	201.8	200.5	203.3	206.3	207.5	201.6
Wholesale Trade													
2002	57.6	57.7	57.7	57.9	58.0	58.2	58.7	58.4	58.5	58.7	58.8	59.0	58.3
2003	57.8	57.7	57.9	57.5	57.6	57.9	56.9	56.9	56.3	56.4	56.6	56.8	57.2
2004	55.6	55.5	55.6	55.6	55.8	56.2	57.8	57.9	57.7	57.1	57.4	57.9	56.7
2005	56.7	56.6	56.8	57.2	57.5	58.0	58.6	58.9	59.4	58.6	58.9	59.2	58.0
2006	58.9	58.9	59.0	59.1	59.3	59.8	59.6	59.8	59.5	59.4	59.5	59.9	59.4
2007	60.5	60.4	60.6	60.7	60.8	61.3	61.1	61.1	61.2	61.3	61.3	61.7	61.0
2008	61.3	61.4	61.5	61.3	61.5	61.8	61.6	61.3	60.7	60.8	60.6	60.4	61.2
2009	59.1	58.6	58.0	56.4	56.3	55.8	55.6	55.4	55.0	55.2	55.2	55.4	56.3
2010	54.8	54.8	54.8	54.7	54.8	55.1	54.9	54.7	54.3	54.5	54.6	54.5	54.7
2011	54.5	54.6	54.9	55.4	55.6	55.7	56.0	56.1	56.2	56.0	56.2	56.1	55.6
2012	56.2	56.3	56.6	57.2	57.6	58.2	57.9	58.1	57.9	58.2	58.1	58.4	57.6
2013	58.6	58.8	59.1	59.6	60.0	60.3	60.0	60.1	60.0	60.8	60.2	59.9	59.8
Retail Trade													
2002	111.9	110.5	111.2	111.4	112.2	113.2	112.1	112.1	111.7	111.1	115.3	118.6	112.6
2003	109.4	107.7	108.2	109.0	109.8	110.4	110.0	110.6	110.3	111.0	114.4	116.7	110.6
2004	109.5	107.9	108.9	109.3	109.9	110.9	110.3	111.3	109.7	111.0	116.7	116.7	110.8
2005	108.8	107.0	107.9	108.5	109.3	109.1	109.7	108.6	108.1	108.4	111.6	114.9	109.3
2006	108.1	106.2	106.9	107.4	108.7	108.8	108.6	108.8	108.4	109.2	112.8	114.4	109.0
2007	108.1	106.4	108.0	108.5	110.0	110.9	110.9	109.3	108.7	109.5	113.0	114.5	109.7
2008	108.5	106.4	106.7	107.6	108.6	108.4	108.2	108.3	107.1	107.0	108.9	110.3	108.0
2009	103.3	101.7	101.5	101.5	102.8	102.8	101.9	102.0	101.6	102.8	105.4	106.5	102.8
2010	100.0	99.4	100.3	101.3	102.4	102.0	101.9	101.7	100.9	102.6	105.8	106.6	102.1
2011	100.4	99.5	99.9	101.0	101.4	101.9	102.0	101.9	100.8	102.5	106.0	107.1	102.0
2012	100.8	99.5	100.5	101.4	102.7	102.7	102.3	102.2	101.9	103.8	107.5	107.7	102.8
2013	101.8	100.6	101.4	102.5	103.7	104.0	103.2	103.6	102.2	104.2	107.0	107.6	103.5
Transportation and Utilities													
2002	43.0	42.7	42.8	42.8	42.9	42.2	42.2	42.4	42.8	42.7	43.2	43.6	42.8
2003	43.1	43.2	43.4	43.2	43.1	42.3	42.2	42.7	42.8	43.7	43.7	43.9	43.1
2004	42.2	41.9	42.0	42.3	42.6	42.3	42.4	43.0	43.1	43.8	44.1	44.2	42.8
2005	42.7	43.1	43.4	43.4	43.6	43.4	43.2	43.1	43.4	42.9	43.0	42.9	43.2
2006	41.6	41.2	41.1	40.7	41.0	40.9	40.5	40.6	41.7	41.9	42.6	43.2	41.4
2007	41.7	41.5	41.5	41.3	42.1	42.1	41.8	42.2	43.0	43.5	44.2	45.0	42.5
2008	42.4	42.1	42.0	42.0	42.3	41.6	41.1	41.7	41.7	41.6	41.7	42.1	41.9
2009	39.8	39.2	38.7	38.2	38.3	38.0	38.1	39.3	39.2	39.7	40.2	40.6	39.1
2010	38.5	38.4	38.4	38.6	39.0	39.2	37.9	38.3	38.6	39.1	39.8	40.3	38.8
2011	38.1	37.8	38.1	38.3	38.5	38.4	38.8	39.7	40.7	41.2	42.4	42.9	39.6
2012	40.0	40.0	40.0	39.7	40.2	39.7	39.3	40.0	40.3	39.9	40.1	40.1	39.9
2013	38.2	38.0	38.1	38.1	38.3	38.1	37.6	38.1	38.3	38.3	39.1	40.0	38.4
Information													
2002	18.4	18.1	18.1	17.9	17.9	18.2	18.1	17.8	17.4	16.9	17.1	17.1	17.8
2003	16.4	16.2	16.3	16.3	16.5	16.4	16.5	16.3	16.0	15.7	15.9	16.0	16.2
2004	15.9	15.7	15.7	16.0	16.1	16.2	16.2	16.2	16.0	16.1	16.1	16.1	16.0
2005	15.9	15.9	15.9	15.8	16.0	15.9	15.9	15.8	15.7	15.8	15.9	16.1	15.9
2006	15.7	15.6	15.7	15.8	15.7	15.8	15.8	15.8	15.5	15.5	15.6	15.6	15.7
2007	15.3	15.4	15.3	15.5	15.6	15.7	15.7	15.7	15.3	15.2	15.2	15.2	15.4
2008	15.1	15.1	15.2	15.1	15.1	15.2	15.3	15.3	15.1	15.2	15.1	15.1	15.2
2009	15.0	14.9	14.9	14.8	14.8	14.8	14.8	14.6	14.4	14.3	14.4	14.3	14.7
2010	14.2	14.0	14.0	14.0	14.1	14.1	14.2	14.2	14.1	14.0	14.1	14.0	14.1
2011	14.0	13.9	13.9	13.9	14.0	14.0	14.1	14.1	14.0	13.8	14.0	14.0	14.0
2012	13.9	13.9	13.8	13.7	13.8	13.9	13.9	13.9	13.7	14.0	14.1	14.2	13.9
2013	14.1	14.2	14.2	14.1	14.2	14.2	14.1	14.1	13.9	13.9	14.0	14.0	14.1
Financial Activities													
2002	62.4	62.9	62.9	63.3	63.9	64.4	64.5	64.7	64.3	64.7	65.1	65.7	64.1
2003	65.6	65.9	65.9	65.6	65.9	66.2	66.3	66.6	66.1	65.9	65.8	66.0	66.0
2004	64.8	64.9	65.0	65.0	65.0	65.5	65.5	65.5	64.8	64.5	64.6	65.0	65.0
2005	64.7	64.8	64.8	65.0	65.2	65.8	65.6	65.6	65.0	64.9	65.0	65.5	65.2
2006	64.6	64.7	64.9	65.2	65.5	65.7	65.4	65.4	64.9	64.9	64.9	65.2	65.1
2007	65.0	65.2	65.3	65.4	65.7	66.0	66.3	66.0	65.5	65.3	65.6	65.6	65.5
2008	65.2	65.1	65.2	65.7	65.9	66.1	66.2	66.0	65.3	65.1	65.1	64.9	65.5
2009	64.1	63.8	63.7	63.5	63.9	63.8	63.8	63.1	62.6	62.6	62.5	62.3	63.3
2010	61.9	61.7	61.7	62.5	62.7	63.0	63.7	63.6	63.4	63.5	63.6	63.8	62.9
2011	63.6	63.6	63.7	63.6	63.7	63.8	63.5	63.5	63.2	63.1	63.4	63.7	63.5
2012	63.7	63.6	63.7	63.8	64.2	64.7	64.8	64.7	64.6	64.7	64.9	65.3	64.4
2013	64.6	64.8	65.0	65.3	65.6	66.2	66.5	66.7	66.2	66.3	66.0	65.6	65.7

Employment by Industry: Cincinnati-Middletown, OH–KY–IN, Selected Years, 2002–2013—*Continued*

(Numbers in thousands, not seasonally adjusted)

Industry and year	January	February	March	April	May	June	July	August	September	October	November	December	Annual average
Professional and Business Services													
2002	134.9	134.3	135.4	137.0	137.9	139.6	140.5	142.1	142.5	144.2	144.1	143.1	139.6
2003	141.7	141.3	142.7	144.3	144.0	144.7	143.8	144.8	144.5	146.3	145.6	145.2	144.1
2004	142.6	141.3	143.3	144.1	144.2	146.7	149.2	150.3	150.6	150.2	150.6	150.8	147.0
2005	145.0	146.3	148.3	150.5	150.9	153.5	153.9	155.7	157.2	156.8	157.3	158.0	152.8
2006	151.3	151.8	153.8	154.3	153.5	154.6	155.9	156.6	156.3	154.9	154.9	154.7	154.4
2007	150.8	151.0	153.8	155.7	155.8	157.7	156.6	157.7	157.7	160.5	161.3	161.3	156.7
2008	157.8	157.1	157.2	159.3	158.5	159.2	160.3	160.5	159.0	159.6	157.6	156.5	158.6
2009	149.9	148.7	147.9	147.2	146.3	146.1	146.0	146.7	145.8	146.0	147.2	147.9	147.1
2010	143.9	143.7	145.4	148.5	148.2	149.7	149.6	150.3	149.8	151.8	151.6	151.1	148.6
2011	149.1	149.5	151.3	154.2	153.3	153.8	156.4	157.2	157.1	157.8	158.9	158.9	154.8
2012	156.3	155.9	157.5	160.3	160.4	161.3	161.5	163.2	163.3	163.9	162.8	162.5	160.7
2013	156.8	157.8	159.1	162.6	162.6	163.7	164.1	165.8	166.1	167.9	168.8	165.9	163.4
Education and Health Services													
2002	121.4	122.6	122.8	123.9	124.4	123.5	123.4	124.4	126.0	127.2	127.8	128.4	124.7
2003	125.5	125.7	125.8	126.2	126.2	125.5	126.4	127.2	128.4	128.9	130.0	130.3	127.2
2004	128.8	129.7	130.3	131.0	130.9	130.4	130.8	130.6	131.6	132.5	133.4	133.6	131.1
2005	131.5	132.8	133.3	135.1	134.8	134.2	133.3	134.1	134.9	135.7	136.3	136.5	134.4
2006	135.1	136.2	137.0	138.1	138.1	137.7	136.6	137.6	138.9	140.1	140.8	141.0	138.1
2007	139.3	139.9	140.9	141.6	142.2	141.0	139.7	140.3	142.9	144.0	145.0	144.9	141.8
2008	143.3	144.2	144.9	146.1	146.5	144.0	144.4	144.6	145.4	146.2	146.8	146.6	145.3
2009	144.2	144.7	145.3	147.0	147.2	145.4	145.7	145.5	146.0	147.3	148.3	147.9	146.2
2010	145.2	146.1	147.1	148.8	149.0	147.1	146.5	146.6	147.6	149.1	149.7	149.6	147.7
2011	146.8	148.0	148.6	150.5	151.6	149.8	149.0	149.2	150.5	151.1	151.4	151.6	149.8
2012	149.9	151.4	152.1	153.0	153.8	152.4	150.6	151.2	153.3	154.6	155.2	155.0	152.7
2013	152.8	154.6	155.2	156.5	157.4	155.8	155.0	155.3	157.3	158.6	160.0	159.1	156.5
Leisure and Hospitality													
2002	90.7	91.8	95.1	97.4	101.5	104.2	105.3	104.0	100.7	96.8	95.1	95.6	98.2
2003	92.1	91.5	94.4	99.4	102.8	107.3	107.6	107.8	103.0	98.4	96.9	97.5	99.9
2004	93.4	94.7	98.6	102.7	106.8	109.7	110.7	110.2	106.1	103.2	101.2	101.2	103.2
2005	96.2	97.3	100.7	105.0	108.4	111.5	111.9	110.7	107.8	102.9	102.7	102.5	104.8
2006	98.5	99.5	102.3	104.3	107.8	112.5	112.1	112.1	107.7	104.0	103.1	103.1	105.6
2007	99.8	99.0	101.4	105.4	110.8	113.9	112.9	113.4	108.6	105.5	101.9	102.9	106.3
2008	99.1	99.4	100.3	106.7	110.9	113.3	112.4	111.7	106.3	103.1	99.1	100.0	105.2
2009	95.4	95.5	97.7	102.4	107.1	110.7	109.6	109.0	105.5	100.5	97.8	98.1	102.4
2010	94.3	94.3	97.5	102.7	107.3	110.6	109.4	109.1	104.9	102.2	98.6	98.9	102.5
2011	94.6	95.1	98.5	104.0	108.5	111.7	111.7	111.2	106.6	103.1	100.0	100.8	103.8
2012	97.2	98.7	102.0	106.4	111.3	115.0	114.2	113.7	109.4	107.8	103.7	104.5	107.0
2013	100.5	102.4	105.7	111.5	116.8	119.3	118.6	117.9	114.2	110.8	106.0	105.7	110.8
Other Services													
2002	40.4	40.7	41.0	41.1	41.4	41.9	41.6	41.4	40.6	40.4	40.4	40.4	40.9
2003	41.1	41.4	42.0	42.2	42.6	42.8	42.6	42.5	42.0	42.0	41.9	42.1	42.1
2004	41.6	41.9	42.5	43.0	43.3	43.6	43.4	43.5	43.3	43.0	42.8	42.9	42.9
2005	42.0	42.3	42.7	43.2	43.3	43.4	43.2	43.0	42.7	42.7	42.6	42.7	42.8
2006	41.8	41.8	42.2	42.3	42.7	43.1	43.2	43.2	43.0	42.7	42.6	42.8	42.6
2007	42.3	42.3	43.0	43.2	43.6	44.3	43.9	44.1	43.3	43.7	43.7	43.7	43.4
2008	43.3	43.3	43.6	43.8	44.0	44.4	44.0	43.8	43.0	43.3	43.0	43.1	43.6
2009	42.4	42.4	42.7	42.5	42.8	42.9	42.9	42.7	42.3	42.4	42.0	42.2	42.5
2010	41.4	41.2	41.6	40.9	40.8	41.1	41.2	41.1	40.6	40.6	40.3	40.2	40.9
2011	39.9	39.7	40.1	40.3	40.6	40.3	40.2	39.9	39.4	38.9	38.6	38.4	39.7
2012	37.9	37.6	38.0	38.6	38.9	39.7	39.6	39.6	39.3	39.5	39.5	39.7	39.0
2013	39.3	39.5	39.7	40.0	40.2	40.4	40.2	40.1	39.9	40.3	40.0	39.9	40.0
Government													
2002	129.3	132.8	134.0	133.8	134.5	128.7	122.1	124.1	129.2	132.7	133.3	132.7	130.6
2003	132.0	134.6	135.9	136.5	136.7	131.2	123.6	126.7	132.2	135.9	136.3	136.0	133.1
2004	132.1	135.4	136.8	137.1	137.5	132.6	123.5	125.8	131.6	135.2	135.7	134.8	133.2
2005	131.1	134.0	135.0	135.4	135.9	131.7	123.3	125.1	131.6	134.9	135.4	134.7	132.3
2006	131.3	134.5	135.8	136.0	136.8	131.4	123.0	125.1	132.0	135.0	135.3	135.1	132.6
2007	132.2	135.2	136.5	136.2	137.3	133.1	124.0	125.9	131.5	134.5	136.5	135.7	133.2
2008	131.4	135.6	135.5	135.7	137.1	131.2	123.9	125.9	131.2	134.7	136.5	135.6	132.9
2009	132.2	134.7	134.5	135.5	135.8	131.4	121.7	123.9	130.0	132.8	133.1	132.1	131.5
2010	129.5	131.7	132.7	133.8	137.1	130.7	119.0	119.8	125.9	128.5	130.2	129.6	129.0
2011	125.8	128.1	129.0	129.2	128.8	123.9	117.3	119.8	125.8	127.5	128.1	127.9	125.9
2012	124.3	127.7	128.6	129.1	129.8	126.0	113.3	118.6	126.1	128.4	128.9	128.0	125.7
2013	126.2	129.1	128.7	130.1	129.6	125.9	116.5	122.0	127.8	129.8	130.7	130.2	127.2

Employment by Industry: Cleveland-Elyria-Mentor, OH, Selected Years, 2002–2013

(Numbers in thousands, not seasonally adjusted)

Industry and year	January	February	March	April	May	June	July	August	September	October	November	December	Annual average
Total Nonfarm													
2002	1,069.6	1,072.2	1,078.5	1,078.7	1,087.5	1,091.2	1,081.7	1,084.1	1,084.5	1,087.0	1,086.8	1,085.9	1,082.3
2003	1,057.1	1,058.1	1,063.8	1,072.1	1,083.4	1,085.0	1,076.1	1,076.3	1,077.1	1,079.8	1,080.4	1,081.1	1,074.2
2004	1,047.3	1,050.5	1,059.9	1,067.7	1,076.8	1,082.6	1,076.2	1,076.4	1,077.1	1,082.0	1,084.8	1,084.0	1,072.1
2005	1,044.9	1,051.2	1,058.1	1,068.6	1,075.5	1,082.0	1,075.4	1,077.2	1,079.8	1,082.7	1,085.3	1,085.3	1,072.2
2006	1,053.6	1,057.6	1,065.4	1,074.8	1,082.1	1,088.9	1,076.9	1,078.4	1,079.1	1,080.2	1,081.1	1,081.3	1,075.0
2007	1,052.8	1,052.6	1,061.5	1,070.4	1,080.2	1,090.2	1,075.6	1,076.9	1,073.8	1,076.6	1,079.4	1,077.4	1,072.3
2008	1,049.9	1,050.4	1,048.2	1,060.9	1,072.8	1,075.8	1,064.3	1,062.6	1,060.8	1,058.9	1,052.6	1,044.9	1,058.5
2009	1,009.3	1,006.1	1,003.4	1,004.9	1,008.6	1,006.7	995.9	992.4	994.1	995.8	997.2	994.7	1,000.8
2010	969.1	969.8	973.0	986.3	998.5	1,000.1	996.2	995.7	995.4	1,002.2	1,003.4	1,001.4	990.9
2011	971.4	977.3	981.8	998.6	1,006.1	1,007.9	1,008.9	1,011.6	1,006.6	1,009.4	1,016.1	1,014.7	1,000.9
2012	986.6	994.1	1,002.7	1,016.0	1,026.9	1,032.0	1,024.5	1,025.2	1,023.4	1,030.9	1,034.4	1,031.5	1,019.0
2013	1,002.1	1,004.3	1,009.4	1,022.4	1,035.0	1,040.6	1,031.8	1,038.3	1,030.8	1,033.7	1,035.7	1,031.3	1,026.3
Total Private													
2002	927.5	926.0	931.4	932.8	940.4	946.4	945.3	946.6	940.7	940.6	940.0	939.6	938.1
2003	914.7	912.8	917.4	926.2	937.4	941.5	939.8	942.5	935.9	935.1	934.9	935.3	931.1
2004	906.0	905.8	914.1	922.0	930.4	938.6	941.0	942.6	937.7	939.0	940.9	940.6	929.9
2005	905.8	908.4	914.7	924.9	931.1	938.8	940.7	943.7	940.9	940.5	943.0	942.7	931.3
2006	914.8	915.8	922.3	931.7	938.1	946.6	943.0	945.3	940.3	938.2	937.9	938.2	934.4
2007	913.0	909.3	916.8	925.2	934.3	942.9	936.1	938.6	933.7	932.9	935.1	934.1	929.3
2008	908.6	906.2	904.8	916.9	926.3	928.6	924.8	924.7	920.6	915.3	909.0	902.6	915.7
2009	868.9	863.4	860.8	861.8	864.5	863.9	860.0	857.9	855.9	854.7	855.9	854.8	860.2
2010	831.4	829.4	833.1	845.8	853.9	859.1	861.7	863.6	860.4	863.3	864.4	863.3	852.5
2011	838.9	840.4	844.4	860.3	868.1	870.7	877.5	881.6	873.9	875.1	880.4	879.3	865.9
2012	855.2	858.6	866.5	879.6	889.4	896.4	894.3	895.2	889.6	895.8	899.3	897.3	884.8
2013	868.9	870.7	876.2	888.5	899.5	906.6	903.9	908.6	898.9	900.3	901.5	897.5	893.4
Goods Producing													
2002	203.0	201.5	202.4	202.4	204.4	206.7	206.8	207.2	205.4	204.8	203.4	200.8	204.1
2003	195.1	194.0	195.0	195.8	199.5	200.5	198.5	199.0	197.4	197.5	196.7	194.5	197.0
2004	187.3	187.5	189.9	193.0	195.7	198.0	198.0	198.1	197.4	197.4	196.4	194.2	194.4
2005	185.8	185.4	187.1	191.6	193.4	195.9	195.3	195.8	195.4	194.7	194.1	191.2	192.1
2006	185.5	184.3	185.3	189.0	190.1	193.0	192.6	192.8	191.9	190.9	188.7	184.7	189.1
2007	180.8	178.8	181.1	182.9	186.4	188.5	184.2	186.8	185.5	184.8	184.4	181.9	183.8
2008	176.1	175.3	174.9	177.8	180.3	181.7	181.5	179.6	179.4	178.1	173.4	167.8	177.2
2009	158.6	156.9	154.6	152.9	151.9	151.5	149.8	149.5	149.4	148.6	149.1	147.1	151.7
2010	142.1	141.6	143.1	145.1	148.4	150.9	150.6	151.8	151.2	151.9	151.1	149.0	148.1
2011	145.2	145.2	146.4	149.7	152.0	152.9	156.3	158.4	156.2	156.8	158.4	157.3	152.9
2012	150.4	151.6	153.4	156.1	158.1	160.2	159.4	160.0	159.4	158.5	159.5	158.5	157.1
2013	153.6	153.4	154.3	156.4	158.6	160.4	158.4	161.4	160.5	158.8	160.6	158.4	157.9
Service-Providing													
2002	866.6	870.7	876.1	876.3	883.1	884.5	874.9	876.9	879.1	882.2	883.4	885.1	878.2
2003	862.0	864.1	868.8	876.3	883.9	884.5	877.6	877.3	879.7	882.3	883.7	886.6	877.2
2004	860.0	863.0	870.0	874.7	881.1	884.6	878.2	878.3	879.7	884.6	888.4	889.8	877.7
2005	859.1	865.8	871.0	877.0	882.1	886.1	880.1	881.4	884.4	888.0	891.2	894.1	880.0
2006	868.1	873.3	880.1	885.8	892.0	895.9	884.3	885.6	887.2	889.3	892.4	896.6	885.9
2007	872.0	873.8	880.4	887.5	893.8	901.7	891.4	890.1	888.3	891.8	895.0	895.5	888.4
2008	873.8	875.1	873.3	883.1	892.5	894.1	882.8	883.0	881.4	880.8	879.2	877.1	881.4
2009	850.7	849.2	848.8	852.0	856.7	855.2	846.1	842.9	844.7	847.2	848.1	847.6	849.1
2010	827.0	828.2	829.9	841.2	850.1	849.2	845.6	843.9	844.2	850.3	852.3	852.4	842.9
2011	826.2	832.1	835.4	848.9	854.1	855.0	852.6	853.2	850.4	852.6	857.7	857.4	848.0
2012	836.2	842.5	849.3	859.9	868.8	871.8	865.1	865.2	864.0	872.4	874.9	873.0	861.9
2013	848.5	850.9	855.1	866.0	876.4	880.2	873.4	876.9	870.3	874.9	875.1	872.9	868.4
Mining, Logging, and Construction													
2002	37.8	37.2	38.3	40.3	42.6	44.5	45.9	46.3	45.5	45.5	44.3	42.0	42.5
2003	38.0	37.1	38.4	41.4	44.1	45.9	46.3	46.9	46.1	46.5	45.4	43.3	43.3
2004	38.3	38.4	40.1	42.4	44.8	46.4	47.3	47.0	46.6	46.7	45.6	43.5	43.9
2005	37.1	37.0	37.8	42.2	44.0	45.9	46.4	46.5	45.9	45.7	44.5	41.5	42.9
2006	37.0	36.5	37.5	40.7	42.5	43.7	44.7	44.8	44.3	44.0	43.0	40.7	41.6
2007	36.6	34.9	36.6	39.6	43.0	44.4	43.9	44.2	43.5	43.3	42.4	39.9	41.0
2008	35.1	34.4	34.5	37.1	39.7	40.9	42.0	41.9	40.9	40.6	38.5	35.6	38.4
2009	30.6	29.9	30.6	31.9	34.0	35.2	35.8	35.5	34.9	34.9	33.6	31.6	33.2
2010	27.3	26.6	27.9	30.2	31.9	33.4	34.7	34.6	34.1	34.2	33.3	30.8	31.6
2011	27.6	27.2	28.1	30.3	32.1	33.6	35.8	36.3	36.2	36.1	35.7	34.4	32.8
2012	30.0	29.3	30.4	32.6	34.4	35.4	36.1	35.7	35.0	35.5	35.2	33.9	33.6
2013	30.0	29.7	30.4	32.4	34.6	35.7	36.3	36.8	36.6	36.4	35.9	33.9	34.1
Manufacturing													
2002	165.2	164.3	164.1	162.1	161.8	162.2	160.9	160.9	159.9	159.3	159.1	158.8	161.6
2003	157.1	156.9	156.6	154.4	155.4	154.6	152.2	152.1	151.3	151.0	151.3	151.2	153.7
2004	149.0	149.1	149.8	150.6	150.9	151.6	150.7	151.1	150.8	150.7	150.8	150.7	150.5
2005	148.7	148.4	149.3	149.4	149.4	150.0	148.9	149.3	149.5	149.0	149.6	149.7	149.3
2006	148.5	147.8	147.8	148.3	147.6	149.3	147.9	148.0	147.6	146.9	145.7	144.0	147.5
2007	144.2	143.9	144.5	143.3	143.4	144.1	140.3	142.6	142.0	141.5	142.0	142.0	142.8
2008	141.0	140.9	140.4	140.7	140.6	140.8	139.5	137.7	138.5	137.5	134.9	132.2	138.7
2009	128.0	127.0	124.0	121.0	117.9	116.3	114.0	114.0	114.5	113.7	115.5	115.5	118.5
2010	114.8	115.0	115.2	114.9	116.5	117.5	115.9	117.2	117.1	117.7	117.8	118.2	116.5
2011	117.6	118.0	118.3	119.4	119.9	119.3	120.5	122.1	120.0	120.7	122.7	122.9	120.1
2012	120.4	122.3	123.0	123.5	123.7	124.8	123.3	124.3	124.4	123.0	124.3	124.6	123.5
2013	123.6	123.7	123.9	124.0	124.0	124.7	122.1	124.6	123.9	122.4	124.7	124.5	123.8

Employment by Industry: Cleveland-Elyria-Mentor, OH, Selected Years, 2002–2013—*Continued*

(Numbers in thousands, not seasonally adjusted)

Industry and year	January	February	March	April	May	June	July	August	September	October	November	December	Annual average
Trade, Transportation, and Utilities													
2002	204.6	201.3	202.6	200.9	202.5	203.3	202.9	202.9	200.9	202.6	204.9	207.5	203.1
2003	200.4	197.9	197.4	200.2	201.9	202.7	202.1	201.9	200.6	202.8	205.5	208.7	201.8
2004	199.3	197.2	198.0	197.8	199.0	200.4	199.6	199.6	197.5	199.8	203.7	206.1	199.8
2005	197.0	195.5	196.3	196.5	198.0	198.8	199.1	199.0	197.7	198.7	202.0	205.2	198.7
2006	197.6	196.0	197.1	198.5	199.6	200.4	198.9	199.3	198.2	199.3	203.1	206.5	199.5
2007	198.2	195.4	196.8	197.4	198.6	199.8	199.0	198.1	196.6	197.6	201.3	204.0	198.6
2008	196.5	193.2	192.6	193.9	195.4	195.4	194.9	195.2	192.9	192.7	193.9	195.7	194.4
2009	185.7	182.9	182.2	180.7	181.3	181.4	179.9	179.0	177.1	177.6	179.6	181.5	180.7
2010	174.3	172.3	172.6	173.6	175.0	176.4	176.8	177.3	175.5	176.9	179.5	182.1	176.0
2011	174.0	172.9	173.5	175.7	176.7	177.7	177.8	178.3	176.4	178.3	182.0	184.6	177.3
2012	177.8	176.4	177.8	179.0	181.2	181.8	181.2	180.7	179.7	181.5	185.4	187.1	180.8
2013	179.1	177.2	177.8	179.3	181.9	183.0	181.7	182.2	180.5	181.4	186.4	187.6	181.5
Wholesale Trade													
2002	55.5	55.1	55.4	54.9	54.9	54.6	54.6	54.3	53.6	53.5	53.2	53.5	54.4
2003	54.6	54.5	54.4	54.7	55.1	55.1	55.1	55.0	54.6	54.7	54.8	55.0	54.8
2004	54.1	54.1	54.3	54.2	54.5	54.9	54.9	54.9	54.3	54.9	55.1	55.4	54.6
2005	54.6	54.6	54.8	54.9	55.0	55.5	55.7	55.8	55.6	55.3	55.4	55.8	55.3
2006	55.5	55.6	55.9	56.2	56.3	56.6	56.5	56.3	56.1	55.8	55.9	56.2	56.1
2007	55.4	55.4	55.5	55.3	55.3	55.4	55.2	54.8	54.1	53.9	53.8	53.8	54.8
2008	53.7	53.5	53.3	53.7	53.9	53.8	53.5	53.3	52.7	52.5	52.0	51.5	53.1
2009	50.6	50.0	49.5	48.9	48.7	48.4	48.0	47.7	47.2	47.1	46.9	46.6	48.3
2010	46.2	46.1	46.0	46.2	46.3	46.5	47.1	47.1	46.8	46.8	46.7	46.8	46.6
2011	47.1	47.1	47.2	47.6	47.8	48.1	48.4	48.4	47.9	48.3	48.5	48.8	47.9
2012	48.6	48.6	48.8	49.1	49.5	49.8	49.8	49.6	49.3	49.5	49.6	49.7	49.3
2013	48.9	48.8	49.0	49.1	49.5	49.9	49.6	49.7	49.3	49.5	49.8	49.9	49.4
Retail Trade													
2002	115.9	112.9	114.0	112.4	113.6	114.5	114.1	114.2	113.0	114.0	116.8	119.5	114.6
2003	113.4	111.5	111.5	113.4	114.3	115.1	114.6	114.7	114.0	115.1	117.8	120.9	114.7
2004	113.5	111.5	111.9	111.8	112.6	113.3	112.4	112.2	110.6	111.6	115.1	117.4	112.8
2005	110.2	108.5	108.9	109.2	110.3	110.7	110.5	110.3	109.2	110.1	113.1	115.5	110.5
2006	109.0	107.4	108.0	108.7	109.6	109.9	108.9	109.1	107.8	109.3	112.8	115.4	109.7
2007	108.9	106.3	107.3	107.5	109.0	110.0	109.8	109.2	108.1	109.1	112.8	115.2	109.4
2008	108.9	106.1	105.9	106.4	107.4	107.9	107.8	108.1	106.6	106.8	108.7	110.6	107.6
2009	103.1	100.9	101.1	100.9	101.9	102.4	101.8	101.4	100.1	100.7	103.2	105.0	101.9
2010	99.1	97.3	97.7	98.4	99.6	100.5	100.4	100.7	99.3	100.6	103.4	105.5	100.2
2011	98.3	97.3	97.7	99.2	99.8	100.4	100.3	100.6	99.1	100.4	103.9	105.6	100.2
2012	100.2	98.7	99.8	100.4	101.8	102.0	101.4	100.8	100.1	101.6	104.9	106.0	101.5
2013	100.4	98.7	99.2	100.2	102.0	102.6	102.1	102.1	100.8	101.5	105.3	106.7	101.8
Transportation and Utilities													
2002	33.2	33.3	33.2	33.6	34.0	34.2	34.2	34.4	34.3	35.1	34.9	34.5	34.1
2003	32.4	31.9	31.5	32.1	32.5	32.5	32.4	32.2	32.0	33.0	32.9	32.8	32.4
2004	31.7	31.6	31.8	31.8	31.9	32.2	32.3	32.5	32.6	33.3	33.5	33.3	32.4
2005	32.2	32.4	32.6	32.4	32.7	32.6	32.9	32.9	32.9	33.3	33.5	33.9	32.9
2006	33.1	33.0	33.2	33.6	33.7	33.9	33.5	33.9	34.3	34.2	34.4	34.9	33.8
2007	33.9	33.7	34.0	34.6	34.3	34.4	34.0	34.1	34.4	34.6	34.7	35.0	34.3
2008	33.9	33.6	33.4	33.8	34.1	33.7	33.6	33.8	33.6	33.4	33.2	33.6	33.6
2009	32.0	32.0	31.6	30.9	30.7	30.6	30.1	29.9	29.8	29.8	29.5	29.9	30.6
2010	29.0	28.9	28.9	29.0	29.1	29.4	29.4	29.5	29.4	29.5	29.4	29.8	29.3
2011	28.6	28.5	28.6	28.9	29.1	29.2	29.1	29.3	29.4	29.6	29.6	30.2	29.2
2012	29.0	29.1	29.2	29.5	29.9	30.0	30.0	30.3	30.3	30.4	30.9	31.4	30.0
2013	29.8	29.7	29.6	30.0	30.4	30.5	30.0	30.4	30.4	30.4	31.3	31.0	30.3
Information													
2002	23.3	23.0	22.9	22.1	21.9	21.9	21.6	21.4	21.2	21.1	21.1	21.0	21.9
2003	21.3	21.2	21.2	21.0	21.0	20.9	20.7	20.5	20.2	20.2	20.2	20.4	20.7
2004	20.1	20.0	20.1	20.0	20.0	20.1	20.1	20.0	19.7	19.7	19.8	19.6	19.9
2005	19.5	19.5	19.4	19.7	19.7	19.6	19.5	19.5	19.2	19.2	19.3	19.2	19.4
2006	19.2	19.1	19.1	18.8	18.9	18.9	18.9	18.9	18.7	18.6	18.7	18.7	18.9
2007	18.4	18.5	18.3	18.5	18.6	18.6	18.7	18.5	18.4	18.3	18.4	18.4	18.5
2008	18.2	18.0	18.0	18.0	18.0	17.9	17.8	17.7	17.2	17.2	17.3	17.3	17.7
2009	17.1	17.0	16.7	16.5	16.5	16.6	16.5	16.4	16.1	16.1	16.2	16.2	16.5
2010	16.0	15.9	15.8	15.8	15.9	15.9	15.8	15.8	15.9	15.5	15.6	15.7	15.8
2011	15.4	15.3	15.2	15.3	15.4	15.4	15.5	15.5	15.5	15.4	15.5	15.5	15.4
2012	15.5	15.3	15.3	15.3	15.3	15.4	15.5	15.4	15.2	15.2	15.3	15.2	15.3
2013	14.9	15.0	15.0	14.9	15.1	15.3	15.3	15.2	15.1	15.1	15.1	15.2	15.1
Financial Activities													
2002	75.7	76.0	76.0	75.9	75.8	75.7	75.6	75.4	74.6	74.4	75.1	75.5	75.5
2003	75.8	75.9	76.2	76.0	76.5	77.5	77.7	77.9	77.2	76.6	76.9	77.6	76.8
2004	76.7	76.9	77.1	76.6	76.8	77.8	77.7	77.7	76.7	76.3	76.3	76.4	76.9
2005	75.5	75.4	75.2	74.4	74.3	75.3	75.1	75.0	74.2	74.9	74.7	74.6	74.9
2006	73.6	73.7	73.8	73.5	73.5	74.0	74.4	74.2	73.7	73.5	73.7	73.8	73.8
2007	73.1	73.0	72.9	72.8	72.9	72.8	72.7	72.3	71.3	71.0	70.7	70.5	72.2
2008	69.7	69.3	69.3	69.1	69.2	69.2	69.4	69.2	68.2	67.9	67.9	67.7	68.8
2009	66.9	66.5	66.2	65.9	65.9	66.1	66.1	65.8	65.3	64.9	64.9	64.9	65.8
2010	64.4	64.3	64.1	64.5	64.6	64.8	65.1	65.0	64.3	64.7	64.6	64.6	64.6
2011	64.4	64.3	64.0	64.1	63.9	63.7	63.5	63.2	62.7	62.5	62.4	62.2	63.4
2012	61.8	61.8	61.9	62.2	62.4	62.7	63.1	63.1	62.6	62.8	63.0	63.0	62.5
2013	62.4	62.5	62.4	62.9	62.8	63.3	63.6	63.7	63.0	62.4	62.4	62.5	62.8

Employment by Industry: Cleveland-Elyria-Mentor, OH, Selected Years, 2002–2013—*Continued*

(Numbers in thousands, not seasonally adjusted)

Industry and year	January	February	March	April	May	June	July	August	September	October	November	December	Annual average
Professional and Business Services													
2002	132.5	132.8	134.1	134.3	134.3	135.7	135.2	136.0	134.1	135.7	134.3	133.6	134.4
2003	131.5	131.6	132.9	134.5	135.3	136.6	137.1	138.7	136.5	135.5	134.6	133.1	134.8
2004	129.3	129.8	131.3	135.8	136.9	139.1	140.1	141.7	141.1	140.9	139.8	139.0	137.1
2005	133.2	134.9	136.2	139.4	139.5	141.3	143.0	144.3	144.2	144.6	144.3	143.1	140.7
2006	138.6	139.4	140.8	143.4	143.8	145.8	145.8	147.2	146.4	146.1	145.3	145.3	144.0
2007	140.2	140.4	141.0	143.3	144.1	146.4	146.2	147.0	146.0	146.1	146.0	145.3	144.3
2008	142.1	142.2	141.5	144.3	145.6	146.5	146.6	147.5	145.9	143.3	141.7	139.0	143.9
2009	134.1	132.3	131.3	131.4	131.5	132.0	131.5	131.7	131.1	131.7	131.6	129.9	131.7
2010	126.4	126.1	126.5	131.3	132.1	133.9	134.7	135.0	134.4	134.8	135.0	134.7	132.1
2011	131.2	132.5	133.6	138.5	139.2	140.5	143.1	144.3	142.9	143.2	143.0	141.9	139.5
2012	137.5	138.6	140.1	142.3	143.6	145.0	145.9	146.4	144.1	147.1	147.0	144.3	143.5
2013	138.2	139.6	141.3	145.1	147.0	148.7	148.3	150.1	146.7	148.6	147.0	145.8	145.5
Education and Health Services													
2002	158.8	162.2	162.5	162.6	162.4	161.1	160.3	160.7	164.3	165.9	166.8	167.1	162.9
2003	161.5	163.6	164.1	164.1	163.9	161.5	161.5	161.1	164.4	166.0	166.4	165.5	163.6
2004	163.0	165.1	165.7	164.2	163.5	161.5	162.9	161.8	166.0	168.2	168.7	169.3	165.0
2005	164.9	167.5	167.8	166.6	166.2	165.4	164.6	164.9	169.2	170.1	171.3	172.0	167.5
2006	168.5	171.7	172.2	171.3	170.7	169.9	168.0	167.7	170.8	172.5	173.4	173.3	170.8
2007	171.3	172.8	173.9	174.7	174.0	173.2	172.1	172.3	176.6	178.4	179.2	179.5	174.8
2008	176.9	179.2	179.0	179.8	179.0	177.3	174.7	175.4	180.6	183.4	184.1	184.3	179.5
2009	182.1	184.1	184.5	184.8	183.7	181.4	180.8	181.0	185.6	187.6	188.2	188.1	184.3
2010	186.9	188.3	188.4	188.1	187.1	184.3	184.7	184.2	188.8	190.5	191.0	190.3	187.7
2011	187.0	188.7	188.6	189.9	190.2	187.5	186.7	186.6	189.2	191.0	191.6	191.4	189.0
2012	189.3	192.4	192.5	194.2	194.7	193.3	191.2	191.4	195.0	197.7	197.7	196.8	193.9
2013	193.5	195.9	195.9	195.9	195.0	194.4	194.1	194.5	195.7	197.7	198.8	198.2	195.8
Leisure and Hospitality													
2002	84.1	83.6	85.0	88.8	93.0	95.4	96.4	96.7	94.2	90.7	89.1	88.8	90.5
2003	85.0	84.5	86.2	90.2	94.7	96.8	97.7	98.8	95.4	92.5	90.8	91.5	92.0
2004	86.6	85.6	87.6	90.1	93.8	96.6	97.5	98.9	94.9	92.3	91.8	91.7	92.3
2005	86.3	86.4	88.6	92.3	95.6	97.8	99.3	100.6	96.8	94.2	93.1	93.0	93.7
2006	88.1	87.9	90.2	93.5	97.4	99.7	99.8	101.0	96.7	93.5	91.3	91.8	94.2
2007	87.6	87.0	89.0	91.6	95.5	98.7	98.3	99.0	95.2	92.8	91.2	90.5	93.0
2008	85.7	85.4	86.0	90.6	95.1	96.7	96.2	96.5	93.2	89.7	87.8	87.8	90.9
2009	82.1	81.4	82.9	87.1	91.1	92.4	92.8	92.2	89.4	86.3	84.6	85.2	87.3
2010	80.2	80.0	81.4	86.0	89.5	91.4	92.3	92.9	89.5	87.5	86.3	85.4	86.9
2011	80.8	80.7	82.3	86.3	89.9	92.2	93.4	94.3	90.6	87.4	87.2	86.3	87.6
2012	83.2	82.7	85.4	90.4	93.8	97.2	97.3	97.7	93.7	93.2	91.7	92.6	91.6
2013	87.9	88.0	90.3	94.3	99.1	101.5	102.6	101.5	97.9	95.8	90.7	89.8	95.0
Other Services													
2002	45.5	45.6	45.9	45.8	46.1	46.6	46.5	46.3	46.0	45.4	45.3	45.3	45.9
2003	44.1	44.1	44.4	44.4	44.6	45.0	44.5	44.6	44.2	44.0	43.8	44.0	44.3
2004	43.7	43.7	44.4	44.5	44.7	45.1	45.1	44.8	44.4	44.4	44.4	44.3	44.5
2005	43.6	43.8	44.1	44.4	44.4	44.7	44.8	44.6	44.2	44.1	44.2	44.4	44.3
2006	43.7	43.7	43.8	43.7	44.1	44.9	44.6	44.2	43.9	43.8	43.7	44.1	44.0
2007	43.4	43.4	43.8	44.0	44.2	44.9	44.9	44.6	44.1	43.9	43.9	44.0	44.1
2008	43.4	43.6	43.5	43.4	43.7	43.9	43.7	43.6	43.2	43.0	42.9	43.0	43.4
2009	42.3	42.3	42.4	42.5	42.6	42.5	42.6	42.3	41.9	41.9	41.7	41.9	42.2
2010	41.1	40.9	41.2	41.4	41.3	41.6	41.7	41.5	41.2	41.4	41.3	41.5	41.3
2011	40.9	40.8	40.8	40.8	40.8	40.8	41.2	41.0	40.4	40.5	40.3	40.1	40.7
2012	39.7	39.8	40.1	40.1	40.3	40.8	40.7	40.5	39.9	39.8	39.7	39.8	40.1
2013	39.3	39.1	39.2	39.7	40.0	40.0	39.9	40.0	39.5	40.5	40.5	40.0	39.8
Government													
2002	142.1	146.2	147.1	145.9	147.1	144.8	136.4	137.5	143.8	146.4	146.8	146.3	144.2
2003	142.4	145.3	146.4	145.9	146.0	143.5	136.3	133.8	141.2	144.7	145.5	145.8	143.1
2004	141.3	144.7	145.8	145.7	146.4	144.0	135.2	133.8	139.4	143.0	143.9	143.4	142.2
2005	139.1	142.8	143.4	143.7	144.4	143.2	134.7	133.5	138.9	142.2	142.3	142.6	140.9
2006	138.8	141.8	143.1	143.1	144.0	142.3	133.9	133.1	138.8	142.0	143.2	143.1	140.6
2007	139.8	143.3	144.7	145.2	145.9	147.3	139.5	138.3	140.1	143.7	144.3	143.3	143.0
2008	141.3	144.2	143.4	144.0	146.5	147.2	139.5	137.9	140.2	143.6	143.6	142.3	142.8
2009	140.4	142.7	142.6	143.1	144.1	142.8	135.9	134.5	138.2	141.1	141.3	139.9	140.6
2010	137.7	140.4	139.9	140.5	144.6	141.0	134.5	132.1	135.0	138.9	139.0	138.1	138.5
2011	132.5	136.9	137.4	138.3	138.0	137.2	131.4	130.0	132.7	134.3	135.7	135.4	135.0
2012	131.4	135.5	136.2	136.4	137.5	135.6	130.2	130.0	133.8	135.1	135.1	134.2	134.3
2013	133.2	133.6	133.2	133.9	135.5	134.0	127.9	129.7	131.9	133.4	134.2	133.8	132.9

Employment by Industry: Columbia, SC, Selected Years, 2002–2013

(Numbers in thousands, not seasonally adjusted)

Industry and year	January	February	March	April	May	June	July	August	September	October	November	December	Annual average
Total Nonfarm													
2002	330.9	332.3	334.9	336.8	338.7	337.0	333.9	336.6	339.6	342.3	342.3	344.0	337.4
2003	334.7	335.8	336.8	337.1	339.1	336.4	332.1	336.0	339.1	342.2	342.5	344.8	338.1
2004	337.6	338.1	341.0	344.4	345.9	345.0	341.6	344.5	348.2	350.7	350.4	352.7	345.0
2005	347.8	350.4	350.6	351.9	351.9	347.7	348.1	352.6	353.9	356.3	358.7	359.6	352.5
2006	354.9	356.9	358.4	359.9	361.8	356.7	353.2	357.5	360.9	361.9	364.1	366.8	359.4
2007	359.4	361.7	363.6	365.6	368.5	367.7	363.4	365.0	368.5	369.3	369.5	370.5	366.1
2008	364.6	366.0	366.5	367.0	368.7	364.8	360.0	362.7	363.8	362.6	362.5	361.9	364.3
2009	350.0	349.0	349.2	348.1	348.4	344.8	341.5	341.4	343.7	345.4	346.0	345.4	346.1
2010	340.2	341.8	343.3	345.4	347.6	345.1	340.9	341.2	344.1	347.1	348.5	347.6	344.4
2011	338.7	342.7	344.7	348.5	348.8	345.9	342.2	344.8	348.2	351.6	355.0	354.3	347.1
2012	347.7	351.2	353.4	353.9	355.6	353.0	350.8	353.0	355.9	358.6	365.5	365.4	355.3
2013	354.5	357.1	358.6	361.6	363.1	359.6	357.2	358.2	363.9	365.3	367.1	366.8	361.1
Total Private													
2002	254.0	255.1	257.4	259.8	261.4	263.3	262.2	262.9	262.4	264.8	264.6	265.8	261.1
2003	257.3	257.9	258.7	259.7	261.7	262.5	261.0	263.1	262.5	265.3	265.4	267.1	261.9
2004	260.4	261.3	263.7	267.1	268.4	270.7	269.8	270.8	271.0	273.6	273.4	275.1	268.8
2005	271.6	273.7	273.6	274.4	274.5	273.8	276.5	278.0	276.1	278.1	280.4	281.1	276.0
2006	277.4	278.8	279.8	282.0	283.9	282.3	281.2	283.4	283.6	284.4	286.3	288.6	282.6
2007	282.2	283.7	285.3	287.5	290.0	291.7	289.3	290.0	289.9	289.7	289.5	290.2	288.3
2008	284.5	285.6	286.0	285.9	287.4	286.7	284.6	285.4	282.4	280.8	280.4	279.6	284.1
2009	269.2	267.7	267.9	266.5	267.1	266.6	264.7	264.3	263.7	264.6	265.0	264.1	266.0
2010	260.2	261.3	262.4	264.0	264.8	265.2	264.0	264.7	264.5	266.7	267.8	266.9	264.4
2011	259.3	262.6	264.3	268.1	269.3	269.1	267.9	269.5	268.9	270.7	273.9	274.9	268.2
2012	269.5	270.3	272.3	272.5	274.2	274.0	273.8	275.7	275.8	277.4	283.8	283.8	275.3
2013	274.4	275.7	276.9	279.9	281.6	281.1	281.0	283.3	283.7	284.2	285.5	285.2	281.0
Goods Producing													
2002	53.3	53.3	53.3	53.7	54.5	54.5	54.4	54.7	54.2	54.0	53.5	53.4	53.9
2003	53.0	52.7	53.2	52.8	53.2	53.2	53.0	53.0	52.5	52.6	52.2	52.0	52.8
2004	51.0	51.0	51.3	51.9	51.9	52.3	52.3	52.4	52.5	52.4	52.3	52.5	52.0
2005	52.1	52.2	52.1	52.3	52.9	52.2	52.2	52.2	51.7	51.8	52.0	51.7	52.1
2006	51.7	52.0	52.2	53.3	53.7	53.9	53.4	53.5	53.2	52.9	53.0	52.6	53.0
2007	52.1	52.4	52.6	52.9	53.4	53.8	53.7	53.8	53.2	52.9	52.8	52.7	53.0
2008	51.6	51.2	51.0	50.4	50.4	50.8	50.5	50.4	49.8	49.0	48.8	48.3	50.2
2009	46.4	45.6	45.0	44.5	44.5	44.4	44.0	43.5	43.1	42.9	42.8	42.6	44.1
2010	42.1	42.1	42.0	41.8	41.9	42.3	42.3	41.9	42.0	42.1	42.2	42.0	42.1
2011	41.1	41.6	42.0	42.2	42.4	42.5	42.7	42.8	42.4	42.4	42.4	42.6	42.3
2012	41.9	42.1	42.4	41.9	42.1	42.5	42.7	42.7	42.6	42.8	42.8	42.7	42.4
2013	41.9	42.0	42.3	42.3	42.5	42.7	42.9	42.9	43.0	43.5	43.5	43.3	42.7
Service-Providing													
2002	277.6	279.0	281.6	283.1	284.2	282.5	279.5	281.9	285.4	288.3	288.8	290.6	283.5
2003	281.7	283.1	283.6	284.3	285.9	283.2	279.1	283.0	286.6	289.6	290.3	292.8	285.3
2004	286.6	287.1	289.7	292.5	294.0	292.7	289.3	292.1	295.7	298.3	298.1	300.2	293.0
2005	295.7	298.2	298.5	299.6	299.0	295.5	295.9	300.4	302.2	304.5	306.7	307.9	300.3
2006	303.2	304.9	306.2	306.6	308.1	302.8	299.8	304.0	307.7	309.0	311.1	314.2	306.5
2007	307.3	309.3	311.0	312.7	315.1	313.9	309.7	311.2	315.3	316.4	316.7	317.8	313.0
2008	313.0	314.8	315.5	316.6	318.3	314.0	309.5	312.3	314.0	313.6	313.7	313.6	314.1
2009	303.6	303.4	304.2	303.6	303.9	300.4	297.5	297.9	300.6	302.5	303.2	302.8	302.0
2010	298.1	299.7	301.3	303.6	305.7	302.8	298.6	299.3	302.1	305.0	306.3	305.6	302.3
2011	297.6	301.1	302.7	306.3	306.4	303.4	299.5	302.0	305.8	309.2	312.6	311.7	304.9
2012	305.8	309.1	311.0	312.0	313.5	310.5	308.1	310.3	313.3	315.8	322.7	322.7	312.9
2013	312.6	315.1	316.3	319.3	320.6	316.9	314.3	315.3	320.9	321.8	323.6	323.5	318.4
Mining, Logging, and Construction													
2002	18.8	18.9	19.1	19.5	19.8	20.0	19.8	19.9	19.7	19.6	19.7	19.7	19.5
2003	20.0	20.0	20.2	19.7	20.1	20.3	20.5	20.6	20.6	20.8	20.5	20.5	20.3
2004	20.1	20.1	20.3	20.6	20.8	21.0	20.7	20.7	20.9	20.8	20.7	20.7	20.6
2005	20.2	20.2	20.0	20.6	21.1	20.5	20.7	20.7	20.4	20.6	20.8	20.6	20.5
2006	20.7	20.9	21.1	22.1	22.4	22.4	22.4	22.5	22.3	22.1	22.2	21.7	21.9
2007	21.0	21.2	21.4	21.6	21.9	22.1	22.1	22.0	21.7	21.4	21.3	21.2	21.6
2008	20.3	20.3	20.2	19.6	19.6	19.9	19.7	19.7	19.4	18.9	18.7	18.4	19.6
2009	17.6	17.2	17.1	17.1	17.1	17.0	16.7	16.4	16.0	15.9	15.8	15.6	16.6
2010	15.3	15.2	15.3	15.1	15.0	15.2	15.2	14.9	14.8	14.8	14.7	14.6	15.0
2011	13.9	14.2	14.5	14.5	14.5	14.6	14.8	14.8	14.6	14.8	14.8	14.8	14.6
2012	14.2	14.2	14.4	14.0	14.2	14.4	14.6	14.5	14.5	14.5	14.5	14.6	14.4
2013	14.3	14.3	14.5	14.6	14.7	14.9	15.1	15.0	15.0	15.2	15.1	14.9	14.8
Manufacturing													
2002	34.5	34.4	34.2	34.2	34.7	34.5	34.6	34.8	34.5	34.4	33.8	33.7	34.4
2003	33.0	32.7	33.0	33.1	33.1	32.9	32.5	32.4	31.9	31.8	31.7	31.5	32.5
2004	30.9	30.9	31.0	31.3	31.1	31.3	31.6	31.7	31.6	31.6	31.6	31.8	31.4
2005	31.9	32.0	32.1	31.7	31.8	31.7	31.5	31.5	31.3	31.2	31.2	31.1	31.6
2006	31.0	31.1	31.1	31.2	31.3	31.5	31.0	31.0	30.9	30.8	30.8	30.9	31.1
2007	31.1	31.2	31.2	31.3	31.5	31.7	31.6	31.8	31.5	31.5	31.5	31.5	31.5
2008	31.3	30.9	30.8	30.8	30.8	30.9	30.8	30.7	30.4	30.1	30.1	29.9	30.6
2009	28.8	28.4	27.9	27.4	27.4	27.4	27.3	27.1	27.1	27.0	27.0	27.0	27.5
2010	26.8	26.9	26.7	26.7	26.9	27.1	27.1	27.0	27.2	27.3	27.5	27.4	27.1
2011	27.2	27.4	27.5	27.7	27.9	27.9	27.9	28.0	27.8	27.6	27.6	27.8	27.7
2012	27.7	27.9	28.0	27.9	27.9	28.1	28.1	28.2	28.1	28.3	28.3	28.1	28.1
2013	27.6	27.7	27.8	27.7	27.8	27.8	27.8	27.9	28.0	28.3	28.4	28.4	27.9

Employment by Industry: Columbia, SC, Selected Years, 2002–2013—*Continued*

(Numbers in thousands, not seasonally adjusted)

Industry and year	January	February	March	April	May	June	July	August	September	October	November	December	Annual average
Trade, Transportation, and Utilities													
2002	61.7	61.9	62.4	63.2	63.6	64.2	63.6	63.4	63.5	63.8	65.2	66.2	63.6
2003	61.0	61.5	61.9	62.3	62.7	63.5	62.4	62.8	63.2	64.0	65.2	66.3	63.1
2004	63.4	63.0	63.5	63.5	64.2	64.1	64.8	65.0	64.6	65.2	66.2	67.5	64.6
2005	65.4	65.2	65.5	65.9	65.8	65.4	66.1	66.2	65.7	66.8	68.2	69.1	66.3
2006	66.8	66.8	67.4	67.1	67.5	67.1	66.8	67.2	67.6	68.2	69.8	71.2	67.8
2007	68.8	68.9	69.1	69.3	69.8	69.9	69.5	69.6	69.4	69.8	70.8	71.4	69.7
2008	69.6	69.6	69.6	69.7	69.5	69.4	69.0	68.6	68.0	66.8	67.3	68.1	68.8
2009	64.6	63.6	63.2	63.1	63.4	63.3	63.2	63.1	63.0	62.9	63.7	64.5	63.5
2010	62.5	62.1	62.3	62.4	62.4	62.4	62.2	62.5	61.8	62.3	63.2	64.0	62.5
2011	61.4	61.7	61.8	62.3	62.4	62.8	62.3	62.5	62.5	62.9	64.3	64.9	62.7
2012	63.1	62.5	62.9	62.7	63.2	63.0	63.2	63.9	63.9	64.5	66.3	66.7	63.8
2013	63.9	64.0	64.3	64.7	65.0	65.2	65.5	65.9	65.8	66.1	67.1	67.3	65.4
Wholesale Trade													
2002	14.4	14.8	14.9	15.1	15.1	15.2	15.0	14.9	14.8	14.6	14.6	14.6	14.8
2003	13.6	13.6	13.6	13.9	14.0	14.2	13.9	14.0	14.1	14.1	14.2	14.3	14.0
2004	14.4	14.4	14.6	14.6	14.8	14.8	15.1	15.2	15.0	15.0	15.1	15.2	14.9
2005	16.0	15.9	16.0	15.9	16.0	15.9	16.2	16.2	16.1	16.2	16.2	16.3	16.1
2006	16.5	16.6	16.8	16.9	16.9	16.8	16.9	16.9	17.1	17.0	17.0	17.1	16.9
2007	17.4	17.9	17.7	17.3	17.1	17.1	16.9	16.8	16.7	16.7	16.6	16.6	17.1
2008	16.8	16.9	16.7	16.8	16.9	16.8	16.7	16.3	16.0	15.9	15.8	15.9	16.5
2009	15.2	15.0	14.9	14.8	14.8	14.7	14.5	14.4	14.4	14.4	14.3	14.3	14.6
2010	14.0	14.0	14.0	14.0	13.9	13.9	13.8	13.7	13.5	13.7	13.7	13.7	13.8
2011	13.5	13.6	13.6	13.7	13.7	13.7	13.6	13.6	13.6	13.5	13.6	13.6	13.6
2012	13.7	13.8	13.8	13.7	13.9	13.9	14.1	14.1	14.0	14.0	14.0	14.0	13.9
2013	13.8	13.9	14.0	14.0	14.1	14.1	14.0	14.0	14.0	14.1	14.1	14.1	14.0
Retail Trade													
2002	37.2	36.9	37.2	37.7	38.1	38.4	37.8	37.8	38.0	38.3	39.7	40.7	38.2
2003	37.3	37.8	38.1	38.1	38.3	38.8	38.1	38.3	38.5	39.0	40.1	40.9	38.6
2004	38.3	37.8	38.1	38.2	38.5	38.2	38.4	38.4	38.2	38.9	39.6	40.6	38.6
2005	38.2	38.1	38.1	38.7	38.4	38.1	38.4	38.4	38.0	38.8	40.0	40.6	38.7
2006	38.7	38.5	38.8	38.5	38.8	38.5	38.2	38.4	38.5	39.5	40.8	41.7	39.1
2007	39.7	39.3	39.7	40.2	40.7	40.6	40.5	40.7	40.5	40.9	41.8	42.1	40.6
2008	41.2	41.0	41.2	41.2	40.9	40.9	40.5	40.7	40.6	39.8	40.3	40.7	40.8
2009	38.7	37.9	37.8	37.9	38.1	38.1	38.1	38.2	38.1	38.0	39.0	39.5	38.3
2010	38.0	37.6	37.8	38.2	38.3	38.2	37.9	38.3	37.9	38.1	39.0	39.7	38.3
2011	37.5	37.6	37.7	38.0	38.1	38.3	38.2	38.3	38.2	38.3	39.3	39.8	38.3
2012	38.2	37.6	38.0	37.8	38.0	37.7	37.7	38.0	37.9	38.2	39.6	39.8	38.2
2013	37.8	37.7	37.9	38.2	38.4	38.4	38.6	39.0	38.8	39.0	39.9	39.9	38.6
Transportation and Utilities													
2002	10.1	10.2	10.3	10.4	10.4	10.6	10.8	10.7	10.7	10.9	10.9	10.9	10.6
2003	10.1	10.1	10.2	10.3	10.4	10.5	10.4	10.5	10.6	10.9	10.9	11.1	10.5
2004	10.7	10.8	10.8	10.7	10.9	11.1	11.3	11.4	11.4	11.3	11.5	11.7	11.1
2005	11.2	11.2	11.4	11.3	11.4	11.4	11.5	11.6	11.6	11.8	12.0	12.2	11.6
2006	11.6	11.7	11.8	11.7	11.8	11.8	11.7	11.9	12.0	11.7	12.0	12.4	11.8
2007	11.7	11.7	11.7	11.8	12.0	12.2	12.1	12.1	12.2	12.2	12.4	12.7	12.1
2008	11.6	11.7	11.7	11.7	11.7	11.7	11.8	11.6	11.4	11.1	11.2	11.5	11.6
2009	10.7	10.7	10.5	10.4	10.5	10.5	10.6	10.5	10.5	10.5	10.4	10.7	10.5
2010	10.5	10.5	10.5	10.2	10.2	10.3	10.5	10.5	10.4	10.5	10.5	10.6	10.4
2011	10.4	10.5	10.5	10.6	10.6	10.8	10.5	10.6	10.7	11.1	11.4	11.5	10.8
2012	11.2	11.1	11.1	11.2	11.3	11.4	11.4	11.8	12.0	12.3	12.7	12.9	11.7
2013	12.3	12.4	12.4	12.5	12.5	12.7	12.9	12.9	13.0	13.0	13.1	13.3	12.8
Information													
2002	6.4	6.3	6.4	6.3	6.4	6.5	6.4	6.5	6.3	6.5	6.6	6.6	6.4
2003	6.2	6.1	6.2	6.1	6.3	6.2	6.4	6.3	6.3	6.2	6.2	6.3	6.2
2004	6.1	6.1	6.1	6.0	6.0	6.0	6.1	6.0	6.0	6.0	5.9	6.0	6.0
2005	6.0	6.1	6.0	6.1	6.1	6.2	6.2	6.1	6.0	6.1	6.1	6.1	6.1
2006	6.2	6.2	6.2	6.2	6.2	6.2	6.2	6.1	6.1	6.1	6.3	6.4	6.2
2007	6.1	6.1	6.1	6.1	6.2	6.2	6.1	6.0	6.0	6.2	6.1	6.2	6.1
2008	5.8	5.9	5.9	5.9	5.9	6.0	6.0	6.0	5.9	5.9	5.9	5.9	5.9
2009	5.9	5.8	5.9	5.8	5.8	5.8	5.7	5.7	5.7	5.7	5.7	5.6	5.8
2010	5.6	5.6	5.6	5.6	5.6	5.5	5.6	5.7	5.6	5.6	5.7	5.6	5.6
2011	5.4	5.4	5.4	5.3	5.4	5.4	5.4	5.4	5.3	5.3	5.4	5.4	5.4
2012	5.4	5.4	5.4	5.2	5.2	5.2	5.2	5.2	5.2	5.3	5.4	5.4	5.3
2013	5.5	5.8	5.8	5.8	5.5	5.3	5.3	5.3	5.3	5.3	5.4	5.4	5.5
Financial Activities													
2002	25.4	25.6	25.7	25.2	25.3	25.5	25.8	25.8	26.0	26.6	26.7	26.7	25.9
2003	26.3	26.0	26.6	26.2	26.5	26.6	26.2	26.6	26.3	26.5	26.6	26.7	26.4
2004	26.3	26.5	26.6	26.7	26.8	27.1	26.9	27.0	27.3	27.8	27.8	28.1	27.1
2005	28.5	28.9	28.7	28.5	28.9	29.0	29.2	29.2	29.2	29.1	29.3	29.7	29.0
2006	29.4	29.5	29.5	29.3	29.6	29.6	29.7	29.7	29.8	29.9	30.0	30.5	29.7
2007	30.4	30.4	30.3	30.4	30.5	30.6	30.2	29.8	30.0	30.0	30.2	30.3	30.3
2008	30.0	30.1	30.2	30.1	30.1	30.2	29.8	29.8	29.7	29.8	29.9	30.0	30.0
2009	29.3	29.5	29.5	29.0	29.1	28.9	28.8	28.6	28.3	27.9	27.8	27.6	28.7
2010	27.4	27.4	27.3	27.0	27.0	27.0	26.7	26.7	26.5	26.7	26.7	26.7	26.9
2011	26.6	26.6	26.7	26.7	26.9	27.1	27.0	27.2	27.2	27.5	27.7	27.9	27.1
2012	27.9	28.0	28.1	28.1	28.3	28.4	28.5	28.6	28.7	28.7	28.9	28.9	28.4
2013	28.8	29.0	29.3	29.3	29.5	29.6	29.8	29.8	29.9	30.0	30.0	29.9	29.6

Employment by Industry: Columbia, SC, Selected Years, 2002–2013—*Continued*

(Numbers in thousands, not seasonally adjusted)

Industry and year	January	February	March	April	May	June	July	August	September	October	November	December	Annual average
Professional and Business Services													
2002	34.4	34.4	35.1	36.4	36.2	36.7	36.3	36.8	36.5	36.7	36.2	36.3	36.0
2003	35.2	35.4	33.8	35.8	35.8	35.9	35.8	36.3	36.0	37.0	37.0	37.1	35.9
2004	36.1	36.6	37.2	39.5	39.3	41.0	40.1	40.4	40.5	40.8	40.3	40.0	39.3
2005	39.5	40.2	39.5	40.0	39.3	40.5	40.9	42.1	42.3	42.5	43.2	43.3	41.1
2006	42.6	42.4	42.2	43.4	43.9	42.8	43.0	44.3	43.9	43.0	43.4	43.2	43.2
2007	42.5	42.8	43.0	43.2	43.4	43.8	43.4	44.1	44.4	44.2	43.5	43.4	43.5
2008	41.9	42.3	41.9	41.6	42.8	41.4	41.2	42.5	41.0	41.3	41.2	40.2	41.6
2009	38.3	37.7	37.9	37.6	37.4	37.4	37.0	37.3	37.1	38.8	38.9	38.4	37.8
2010	38.1	38.8	39.1	39.8	40.0	40.4	40.2	40.6	40.9	41.5	41.2	40.9	40.1
2011	40.1	41.1	41.3	42.4	42.3	42.2	42.0	42.5	42.1	42.5	43.3	44.1	42.2
2012	42.8	43.0	43.3	44.0	44.5	44.5	44.4	44.4	43.9	44.4	47.8	48.3	44.6
2013	45.0	44.0	43.8	44.5	45.0	45.1	45.2	45.7	45.9	44.8	45.7	45.4	45.0
Education and Health Services													
2002	34.8	35.1	35.4	35.6	35.7	35.7	36.1	36.2	36.5	36.4	36.7	37.1	35.9
2003	37.1	37.2	37.5	37.2	37.2	37.2	37.2	37.5	37.9	38.1	38.2	38.5	37.6
2004	37.7	37.9	38.2	38.2	38.2	38.0	38.0	38.1	38.3	38.3	38.6	38.6	38.2
2005	39.0	39.3	39.6	38.8	38.8	37.9	38.7	38.7	38.6	39.3	39.4	39.3	39.0
2006	39.2	39.9	39.8	39.5	39.5	39.3	39.3	39.4	39.7	41.0	41.0	41.1	39.9
2007	40.4	40.8	41.0	41.7	42.1	42.5	42.1	41.9	42.4	42.2	42.2	42.1	41.8
2008	42.7	43.1	43.3	43.2	43.3	43.3	43.1	43.0	43.3	43.2	43.3	43.3	43.2
2009	42.1	42.4	42.5	42.3	42.4	42.1	42.2	42.3	42.7	42.6	42.8	42.6	42.4
2010	42.3	42.6	42.6	42.8	43.0	42.9	42.8	42.8	42.9	43.5	43.5	43.3	42.9
2011	42.5	43.1	43.1	44.2	44.2	43.8	43.6	43.3	43.7	43.9	44.0	43.8	43.6
2012	43.3	43.6	43.7	43.6	43.6	42.9	42.8	43.0	43.7	43.9	44.1	43.9	43.5
2013	42.9	43.6	43.6	43.9	44.1	43.5	43.4	43.7	44.1	44.2	44.4	44.8	43.9
Leisure and Hospitality													
2002	26.5	27.1	27.5	27.5	27.8	28.1	28.0	27.9	27.8	28.8	27.8	27.6	27.7
2003	27.0	27.5	27.8	27.7	28.2	28.1	28.4	28.9	28.6	29.1	28.3	28.4	28.2
2004	28.2	28.5	29.1	29.4	29.9	29.9	29.3	29.5	29.4	30.5	29.7	29.7	29.4
2005	28.8	29.2	29.4	30.1	30.0	29.8	30.2	30.3	29.6	30.0	29.6	29.3	29.7
2006	28.8	29.2	29.8	30.4	30.5	30.4	30.2	30.4	30.3	30.7	30.5	30.7	30.2
2007	29.3	29.7	30.3	31.2	31.7	32.0	31.5	31.9	31.8	31.7	31.2	31.1	31.1
2008	30.0	30.5	31.0	31.9	32.3	32.6	31.9	32.0	31.8	31.8	31.1	31.0	31.5
2009	29.8	30.4	31.1	31.5	31.8	32.0	31.1	31.2	31.3	31.3	30.8	30.4	31.1
2010	29.7	30.2	30.8	31.9	32.1	31.8	31.5	31.9	32.1	32.1	32.6	31.7	31.5
2011	29.8	30.7	31.5	32.3	32.8	32.2	31.7	32.6	32.5	33.1	33.6	32.8	32.1
2012	31.4	31.9	32.5	33.0	33.2	33.1	32.7	33.6	33.5	33.5	34.1	33.4	33.0
2013	31.9	32.8	33.1	34.6	35.1	34.8	34.3	35.0	34.8	35.4	34.6	34.2	34.2
Other Services													
2002	11.5	11.4	11.6	11.9	11.9	12.1	11.6	11.6	11.6	12.0	11.9	11.9	11.8
2003	11.5	11.5	11.7	11.6	11.8	11.8	11.6	11.7	11.7	11.8	11.7	11.8	11.7
2004	11.6	11.7	11.7	11.9	12.1	12.3	12.3	12.4	12.4	12.6	12.6	12.7	12.2
2005	12.3	12.6	12.8	12.7	12.7	12.8	13.0	13.2	13.0	12.5	12.6	12.6	12.7
2006	12.7	12.8	12.7	12.8	13.0	13.0	12.6	12.8	13.0	12.6	12.7	12.7	12.8
2007	12.6	12.6	12.9	12.7	12.9	12.9	12.8	12.9	12.7	12.7	12.7	13.0	12.8
2008	12.9	12.9	13.1	13.1	13.1	13.0	13.1	13.1	12.9	13.0	12.9	12.8	13.0
2009	12.8	12.7	12.8	12.7	12.7	12.7	12.7	12.6	12.5	12.5	12.5	12.4	12.6
2010	12.5	12.5	12.7	12.7	12.8	12.9	12.7	12.6	12.7	12.9	12.7	12.7	12.7
2011	12.4	12.4	12.5	12.7	12.9	13.1	13.2	13.2	13.2	13.1	13.2	13.4	12.9
2012	13.7	13.8	14.0	14.0	14.1	14.4	14.3	14.3	14.3	14.3	14.4	14.5	14.2
2013	14.5	14.5	14.7	14.8	14.9	14.9	14.8	15.0	14.9	14.9	14.8	14.9	14.8
Government													
2002	76.9	77.2	77.5	77.0	77.3	73.7	71.7	73.7	77.2	77.5	77.7	78.2	76.3
2003	77.4	77.9	78.1	77.4	77.4	73.9	71.1	72.9	76.6	76.9	77.1	77.7	76.2
2004	77.2	76.8	77.3	77.3	77.5	74.3	71.8	73.7	77.2	77.1	77.0	77.6	76.2
2005	76.2	76.7	77.0	77.5	77.4	73.9	71.6	74.6	77.8	78.2	78.3	78.5	76.5
2006	77.5	78.1	78.6	77.9	77.9	74.4	72.0	74.1	77.3	77.5	77.8	78.2	76.8
2007	77.2	78.0	78.3	78.1	78.5	76.0	74.1	75.0	78.6	79.6	80.0	80.3	77.8
2008	80.1	80.4	80.5	81.1	81.3	78.1	75.4	77.3	81.4	81.8	82.1	82.3	80.2
2009	80.8	81.3	81.3	81.6	81.3	78.2	76.8	77.1	80.0	80.8	81.0	81.3	80.1
2010	80.0	80.5	80.9	81.4	82.8	79.9	76.9	76.5	79.6	80.4	80.7	80.7	80.0
2011	79.4	80.1	80.4	80.4	79.5	76.8	74.3	75.3	79.3	80.9	81.1	79.4	78.9
2012	78.2	80.9	81.1	81.4	81.4	79.0	77.0	77.3	80.1	81.2	81.7	81.6	80.1
2013	80.1	81.4	81.7	81.7	81.5	78.5	76.2	74.9	80.2	81.1	81.6	81.6	80.0

Employment by Industry: Columbus, OH, Selected Years, 2002–2013

(Numbers in thousands, not seasonally adjusted)

Industry and year	January	February	March	April	May	June	July	August	September	October	November	December	Annual average
Total Nonfarm													
2002	903.9	904.7	909.3	911.3	916.3	919.8	913.4	913.4	911.7	917.0	921.5	921.1	913.6
2003	901.3	898.8	902.2	907.5	912.0	914.4	910.8	911.8	908.0	916.8	921.8	922.6	910.7
2004	894.5	895.1	902.8	909.5	916.8	921.5	917.4	920.0	917.0	928.8	934.2	934.8	916.0
2005	902.7	903.7	909.3	917.7	923.4	926.9	923.2	925.2	925.8	933.9	939.8	940.5	922.7
2006	911.9	915.2	921.8	927.8	934.0	937.8	931.5	933.1	932.5	940.5	946.9	949.5	931.9
2007	926.1	922.5	929.5	938.4	947.1	951.9	943.9	943.8	943.1	950.6	957.2	956.2	942.5
2008	932.1	931.8	931.0	939.9	946.1	946.7	942.5	942.1	938.4	945.0	943.0	939.3	939.8
2009	911.2	905.9	905.3	908.0	912.0	909.7	901.0	900.9	898.3	906.6	907.7	905.1	906.0
2010	884.3	884.0	888.6	899.8	907.8	908.0	903.3	905.8	904.5	915.2	919.7	919.0	903.3
2011	897.7	901.0	905.6	920.5	927.3	926.1	927.9	932.2	935.4	943.6	950.8	949.6	926.5
2012	928.5	934.5	939.7	948.3	957.9	962.0	951.5	955.4	963.2	975.8	982.7	979.4	956.6
2013	958.0	958.7	961.9	974.9	984.5	985.7	979.4	985.1	988.8	988.5	993.5	992.6	979.3
Total Private													
2002	753.4	753.6	758.1	760.6	765.2	767.7	766.1	767.0	763.7	766.2	768.9	768.1	763.2
2003	749.3	746.2	749.6	755.2	759.0	761.0	761.2	763.6	759.1	764.7	768.5	768.8	758.9
2004	741.9	741.8	749.0	756.3	762.6	766.3	766.2	768.9	765.6	773.4	777.6	778.4	762.3
2005	748.2	747.5	752.8	761.4	766.4	769.1	769.4	771.4	772.8	776.6	781.8	782.8	766.7
2006	755.8	757.7	763.9	770.5	775.6	780.3	777.9	779.2	779.2	782.9	788.5	791.0	775.2
2007	769.1	765.0	771.6	780.5	788.2	792.5	790.6	791.5	788.1	791.4	797.0	796.5	785.2
2008	773.5	771.9	771.6	780.9	785.5	786.6	787.5	787.8	783.0	784.7	782.8	780.0	781.3
2009	753.2	747.0	746.3	748.6	752.0	751.1	748.6	749.4	743.6	746.8	747.8	746.8	748.4
2010	727.0	725.8	730.6	740.6	745.0	748.1	751.3	754.3	750.0	755.8	759.9	758.9	745.6
2011	740.0	742.8	747.3	760.7	766.3	767.9	773.7	776.3	776.8	781.4	787.3	787.9	767.4
2012	768.3	772.3	777.8	786.8	793.7	799.6	798.4	801.1	799.1	809.3	815.7	815.4	794.8
2013	794.9	794.9	798.4	810.6	819.2	824.0	824.0	827.8	823.6	822.1	826.4	826.7	816.1
Goods Producing													
2002	128.2	127.8	128.5	129.2	130.9	132.6	131.9	133.1	132.5	131.2	129.7	127.9	130.3
2003	123.1	121.5	122.0	124.2	125.1	126.2	126.4	126.8	126.1	125.9	125.0	124.2	124.7
2004	118.6	118.0	119.2	121.8	123.5	123.8	123.7	123.8	123.1	122.1	121.5	120.7	121.7
2005	114.5	114.0	114.8	117.7	119.3	121.0	121.8	121.9	121.7	120.8	120.6	119.3	119.0
2006	114.2	114.3	115.3	117.4	118.3	119.9	119.6	119.9	119.6	118.5	117.2	116.6	117.6
2007	113.0	111.1	112.5	114.1	115.9	117.2	117.5	117.6	116.8	115.2	114.6	113.2	114.9
2008	109.4	108.5	108.1	109.5	111.0	112.2	112.1	111.7	111.1	109.6	107.8	105.4	109.7
2009	99.8	97.4	96.7	96.6	96.9	97.3	96.1	96.2	94.7	93.5	92.4	91.1	95.7
2010	87.4	86.5	87.4	89.5	91.1	92.2	92.9	93.1	92.6	93.3	92.8	91.3	90.8
2011	88.2	88.4	89.4	91.8	92.9	94.3	95.8	96.1	95.6	95.7	95.5	94.4	93.2
2012	91.7	92.3	93.1	94.8	96.2	97.5	98.5	98.5	97.9	97.9	97.7	96.7	96.1
2013	94.7	94.7	95.6	97.8	99.6	101.3	101.5	101.8	101.4	101.2	101.5	99.4	99.2
Service-Providing													
2002	775.7	776.9	780.8	782.1	785.4	787.2	781.5	780.3	779.2	785.8	791.8	793.2	783.3
2003	778.2	777.3	780.2	783.3	786.9	788.2	784.4	785.0	781.9	790.9	796.8	798.4	786.0
2004	775.9	777.1	783.6	787.7	793.3	797.7	793.7	796.2	793.9	806.7	812.7	814.1	794.4
2005	788.2	789.7	794.5	800.0	804.1	805.9	801.4	803.3	804.1	813.1	819.2	821.2	803.7
2006	797.7	800.9	806.5	810.4	815.7	817.9	811.9	813.2	812.9	822.0	829.7	832.9	814.3
2007	813.1	811.4	817.0	824.3	831.2	834.3	826.4	826.2	826.3	835.4	842.6	843.0	827.6
2008	822.7	823.3	822.9	830.4	835.1	834.5	830.4	830.4	827.3	835.4	835.2	833.9	830.1
2009	811.4	808.5	808.6	811.4	815.1	812.4	804.9	804.7	803.6	813.1	815.3	814.0	810.3
2010	796.9	797.5	801.2	810.3	816.7	815.8	810.4	812.7	811.9	821.9	826.9	827.7	812.5
2011	809.5	812.6	816.2	828.7	834.4	831.8	832.1	836.1	839.8	847.9	855.3	855.2	833.3
2012	836.8	842.2	846.6	853.5	861.7	864.5	853.0	856.9	865.3	877.9	885.0	882.7	860.5
2013	863.3	864.0	866.3	877.1	884.9	884.4	877.9	883.3	887.4	887.3	892.0	893.2	880.1
Mining, Logging, and Construction													
2002	37.7	37.4	38.4	39.8	41.2	42.4	43.3	43.5	43.0	42.5	41.9	40.5	41.0
2003	37.1	36.1	36.8	39.6	40.8	42.0	42.7	43.0	42.6	42.5	41.9	41.1	40.5
2004	37.1	36.5	37.5	40.1	41.7	42.4	43.1	42.9	42.5	41.8	41.3	40.3	40.6
2005	35.7	35.3	36.2	39.1	40.7	41.8	42.9	43.0	42.6	41.8	41.5	40.1	40.1
2006	36.6	36.5	37.4	39.3	40.3	41.2	41.6	41.6	41.3	40.7	39.8	38.9	39.6
2007	35.9	34.4	35.8	37.2	38.9	40.3	40.5	40.4	39.8	39.2	38.3	36.7	38.1
2008	33.8	32.9	33.0	35.2	36.6	37.3	36.9	36.7	36.2	35.7	34.2	32.3	35.1
2009	28.9	28.2	28.7	29.1	30.2	31.3	31.6	31.6	30.5	29.3	28.5	27.1	29.6
2010	24.7	23.8	24.6	26.5	27.8	28.7	29.4	29.5	29.3	29.5	28.9	27.4	27.5
2011	25.1	25.1	25.9	27.6	28.7	29.7	31.0	31.1	30.8	30.5	30.0	28.9	28.7
2012	26.9	27.0	27.7	29.0	30.1	30.9	31.6	31.7	31.2	31.1	30.4	29.4	29.8
2013	27.7	27.6	28.4	30.1	31.8	32.9	33.3	33.7	33.4	33.9	34.4	32.1	31.6
Manufacturing													
2002	90.5	90.4	90.1	89.4	89.7	90.2	88.6	89.6	89.5	88.7	87.8	87.4	89.3
2003	86.0	85.4	85.2	84.6	84.3	84.2	83.7	83.8	83.5	83.4	83.1	83.1	84.2
2004	81.5	81.5	81.7	81.7	81.8	81.4	80.6	80.9	80.6	80.3	80.2	80.4	81.1
2005	78.8	78.7	78.6	78.6	78.6	79.2	78.9	78.9	79.1	79.0	79.1	79.2	78.9
2006	77.6	77.8	77.9	78.1	78.0	78.7	78.0	78.3	78.3	77.8	77.4	77.7	78.0
2007	77.1	76.7	76.7	76.9	77.0	77.3	77.0	77.2	77.0	76.0	76.3	76.5	76.8
2008	75.6	75.6	75.1	74.3	74.4	74.9	75.2	75.0	74.9	73.9	73.6	73.1	74.6
2009	70.9	69.2	68.0	67.5	66.7	66.0	64.5	64.6	64.2	64.2	63.9	64.0	66.1
2010	62.7	62.7	62.8	63.0	63.3	63.5	63.5	63.6	63.3	63.8	63.9	63.9	63.3
2011	63.1	63.3	63.5	64.2	64.2	64.6	64.8	65.0	64.8	65.2	65.5	65.5	64.5
2012	64.8	65.3	65.4	65.8	66.1	66.6	66.9	66.8	66.7	66.8	67.3	67.3	66.3
2013	67.0	67.1	67.2	67.7	67.8	68.4	68.2	68.1	68.0	67.3	67.1	67.3	67.6

Employment by Industry: Columbus, OH, Selected Years, 2002–2013—*Continued*

(Numbers in thousands, not seasonally adjusted)

Industry and year	January	February	March	April	May	June	July	August	September	October	November	December	Annual average
Trade, Transportation, and Utilities													
2002	191.0	189.0	189.9	189.5	190.0	189.5	189.2	188.9	188.0	189.2	192.1	194.4	190.1
2003	185.1	182.8	183.4	184.2	184.6	184.6	184.3	185.2	184.5	187.1	191.1	193.6	185.9
2004	182.4	179.9	181.4	180.4	181.7	183.6	184.2	184.6	184.2	188.6	193.9	197.3	185.2
2005	185.8	183.2	184.1	184.2	184.8	184.3	184.1	184.2	184.7	187.8	193.3	197.2	186.5
2006	185.8	183.8	184.1	184.4	186.1	186.0	185.9	185.7	185.8	189.1	196.1	199.3	187.7
2007	189.2	185.9	187.1	187.7	189.7	189.9	190.5	190.6	190.8	193.6	199.7	201.7	191.4
2008	190.8	187.6	187.4	188.7	189.7	189.1	190.0	190.6	189.7	191.5	194.2	196.0	190.4
2009	183.5	179.7	178.4	178.7	179.2	178.4	178.0	178.3	177.2	178.9	182.7	184.7	179.8
2010	175.3	173.1	173.1	173.9	175.4	175.7	174.9	175.6	174.8	177.9	181.5	183.7	176.2
2011	176.1	175.7	175.7	178.1	178.9	178.9	179.7	180.2	179.7	182.6	186.8	189.6	180.2
2012	181.1	179.6	179.8	180.5	182.0	182.6	182.3	182.5	182.2	185.6	190.7	192.3	183.4
2013	183.1	181.2	181.1	182.5	184.0	185.0	185.6	185.9	185.4	188.4	193.2	195.4	185.9
Wholesale Trade													
2002	39.1	39.1	39.3	38.8	38.8	38.7	38.8	38.8	38.6	38.6	38.6	38.7	38.8
2003	38.1	38.1	38.3	38.2	38.1	37.8	37.8	37.8	37.2	37.4	37.3	37.3	37.8
2004	36.8	36.6	36.4	36.5	36.8	36.9	37.3	37.5	37.2	37.4	37.5	37.4	37.0
2005	37.0	37.0	37.0	37.3	37.3	37.2	37.7	37.5	37.5	37.4	37.7	37.7	37.4
2006	37.4	37.6	37.5	37.6	37.8	37.8	37.8	37.7	37.6	37.7	38.1	38.1	37.7
2007	37.8	37.8	38.0	38.2	38.7	38.8	38.8	38.8	38.7	38.8	38.8	38.8	38.5
2008	38.9	38.9	38.9	39.2	39.4	39.4	39.5	39.6	39.3	39.0	38.8	38.6	39.1
2009	38.4	38.2	38.2	37.7	37.5	37.4	37.4	37.2	36.7	36.6	36.6	36.5	37.4
2010	36.9	37.1	36.9	37.3	37.4	37.5	37.4	37.5	37.1	37.2	37.3	37.1	37.2
2011	37.1	37.2	37.2	37.5	37.7	37.6	37.7	37.7	37.4	37.7	37.6	37.7	37.5
2012	37.8	38.0	38.0	38.3	38.4	38.6	38.8	38.8	38.6	38.7	38.8	38.7	38.5
2013	38.5	38.7	38.7	39.1	39.3	39.2	39.5	39.8	39.6	39.9	40.4	40.1	39.4
Retail Trade													
2002	116.5	114.8	115.6	115.8	116.3	115.7	114.4	113.7	113.2	113.8	116.5	118.8	115.4
2003	110.7	108.4	108.9	109.4	109.7	109.9	109.4	109.9	109.5	111.2	115.0	117.4	110.8
2004	108.0	106.1	107.3	105.9	106.7	108.0	107.6	107.8	107.6	109.6	114.3	117.6	108.9
2005	108.4	106.1	106.8	106.6	107.0	106.5	105.4	105.4	105.4	106.7	110.5	114.3	107.4
2006	104.7	102.7	103.0	102.8	103.9	103.5	103.1	102.6	101.8	103.4	108.3	110.7	104.2
2007	102.2	99.9	100.9	101.2	102.1	101.8	102.4	102.2	101.8	103.0	107.2	108.9	102.8
2008	101.4	99.2	98.9	100.2	101.4	101.3	102.5	102.9	101.8	103.3	105.5	107.7	102.2
2009	98.9	96.6	95.9	96.7	97.5	97.1	96.7	96.9	96.3	97.7	100.9	102.9	97.8
2010	95.0	93.3	93.6	94.6	95.5	95.8	95.6	96.2	95.5	98.0	100.7	102.5	96.4
2011	95.9	95.4	95.4	97.0	97.3	97.4	98.1	98.6	97.9	99.9	103.2	105.4	98.5
2012	98.3	96.9	97.1	97.8	98.7	98.7	98.1	98.3	97.9	100.2	104.2	104.9	99.3
2013	98.6	97.0	96.9	98.1	99.0	99.4	99.7	99.8	99.3	101.9	104.6	106.1	100.0
Transportation and Utilities													
2002	35.4	35.1	35.0	34.9	34.9	35.1	36.0	36.4	36.2	36.8	37.0	36.9	35.8
2003	36.3	36.3	36.2	36.6	36.8	36.9	37.1	37.5	37.8	38.5	38.8	38.9	37.3
2004	37.6	37.2	37.7	38.0	38.2	38.7	39.3	39.3	39.4	41.6	42.1	42.3	39.3
2005	40.4	40.1	40.3	40.3	40.5	40.6	41.0	41.3	41.8	43.7	45.1	45.2	41.7
2006	43.7	43.5	43.6	44.0	44.4	44.7	45.0	45.4	46.4	48.0	49.7	50.5	45.7
2007	49.2	48.2	48.2	48.3	48.9	49.3	49.3	49.6	50.3	51.8	53.7	54.0	50.1
2008	50.5	49.5	49.6	49.3	48.9	48.4	48.0	48.1	48.6	49.2	49.9	49.7	49.1
2009	46.2	44.9	44.3	44.3	44.2	43.9	43.9	44.2	44.2	44.6	45.2	45.3	44.6
2010	43.4	42.7	42.6	42.0	42.5	42.4	41.9	41.9	42.2	42.7	43.5	44.1	42.7
2011	43.1	43.1	43.1	43.6	43.9	43.9	43.9	43.9	44.4	45.0	46.0	46.5	44.2
2012	45.0	44.7	44.7	44.4	44.9	45.3	45.4	45.4	45.7	46.7	47.7	48.7	45.7
2013	46.0	45.5	45.5	45.3	45.7	46.4	46.4	46.3	46.5	46.6	48.2	49.2	46.5
Information													
2002	21.8	21.5	21.5	21.1	21.1	21.2	21.3	21.4	21.3	21.1	21.2	21.2	21.3
2003	21.1	21.1	20.8	20.7	20.6	20.6	20.4	20.4	20.1	20.2	20.2	20.1	20.5
2004	19.8	19.8	19.6	19.5	19.6	19.8	19.9	19.7	19.7	19.6	19.6	19.5	19.7
2005	19.4	19.2	19.3	19.3	19.4	19.4	19.4	19.5	19.6	19.2	19.2	19.2	19.3
2006	19.1	19.0	19.0	18.8	18.9	18.9	18.8	18.7	18.5	18.4	18.5	18.5	18.8
2007	18.7	18.8	18.7	18.8	18.8	18.8	18.8	18.6	18.3	18.0	18.0	18.0	18.5
2008	17.6	17.7	17.7	17.8	17.7	17.7	17.7	17.7	17.5	17.5	17.6	17.6	17.7
2009	17.6	17.5	17.3	17.1	17.1	17.0	17.1	16.9	16.6	16.5	16.5	16.7	17.0
2010	16.8	16.8	16.7	16.5	16.6	16.6	16.7	16.7	16.6	16.5	16.8	16.8	16.7
2011	16.6	16.6	16.5	16.9	16.9	17.0	17.1	17.0	16.7	16.8	16.8	16.9	16.8
2012	16.6	16.7	16.7	16.8	16.9	17.2	17.3	17.2	17.2	17.3	17.5	17.7	17.1
2013	17.9	18.2	18.4	18.1	18.0	18.0	18.4	18.4	18.2	18.1	18.2	18.3	18.2
Financial Activities													
2002	76.7	77.1	77.3	77.3	77.1	76.9	77.0	77.0	76.8	77.4	77.9	78.1	77.2
2003	76.1	76.6	76.6	75.9	75.9	76.1	75.8	75.9	75.4	74.9	75.0	75.1	75.8
2004	74.3	74.4	74.4	74.3	74.1	74.3	74.1	73.9	73.2	73.3	73.2	73.1	73.9
2005	72.3	72.3	72.3	72.3	72.5	72.8	73.1	73.2	73.3	73.3	73.5	73.8	72.9
2006	73.1	73.0	73.1	73.2	73.3	73.8	74.3	73.9	74.0	74.6	74.7	74.5	73.8
2007	74.1	74.0	73.4	74.2	73.7	73.0	72.9	72.9	72.2	72.2	71.8	71.8	73.0
2008	71.2	71.4	71.2	71.0	71.1	71.0	70.6	70.7	70.3	70.5	70.2	70.3	70.8
2009	69.6	69.5	69.5	69.1	69.1	68.9	69.1	68.9	68.5	68.7	69.1	69.0	69.1
2010	68.2	68.2	68.1	68.8	68.7	68.9	69.3	69.2	68.9	69.4	69.5	69.6	68.9
2011	69.7	69.7	69.8	69.6	70.1	70.2	70.5	70.9	71.4	71.6	71.7	71.6	70.6
2012	71.8	72.0	72.4	72.4	73.0	73.4	73.6	73.8	73.5	73.8	74.3	74.4	73.2
2013	74.3	74.6	74.8	74.9	75.5	75.8	75.9	76.0	75.5	75.0	75.3	75.5	75.3

Employment by Industry: Columbus, OH, Selected Years, 2002–2013—*Continued*

(Numbers in thousands, not seasonally adjusted)

Industry and year	January	February	March	April	May	June	July	August	September	October	November	December	Annual average
Professional and Business Services													
2002	129.1	129.2	129.5	129.4	128.4	128.8	128.8	129.0	128.5	129.5	130.1	129.6	129.2
2003	131.4	130.6	131.3	130.9	130.4	129.8	130.5	131.1	130.3	132.2	133.1	132.0	131.1
2004	129.1	129.9	131.4	133.5	133.6	134.5	134.2	136.3	136.2	139.1	138.9	139.1	134.7
2005	134.3	135.0	136.0	136.9	137.0	137.4	137.8	139.6	140.4	142.0	141.7	141.9	138.3
2006	137.5	138.4	140.0	142.2	142.2	144.1	143.7	145.2	145.1	146.1	146.6	147.7	143.2
2007	143.9	144.1	145.9	148.5	149.2	151.0	151.0	151.5	151.2	152.9	153.7	154.2	149.8
2008	151.3	151.6	151.8	154.3	153.6	153.9	155.3	155.0	153.6	153.9	152.9	152.1	153.3
2009	149.0	147.0	146.1	146.4	145.9	145.1	144.8	145.6	143.6	145.1	144.8	143.2	145.6
2010	141.3	141.5	142.4	145.9	145.2	146.4	148.1	149.5	147.5	149.1	149.9	149.9	146.4
2011	145.8	146.3	147.7	150.0	149.4	150.2	152.4	153.2	153.6	154.9	156.8	157.0	151.4
2012	153.0	153.8	155.2	157.0	156.8	158.3	158.4	159.7	159.2	162.9	165.0	165.3	158.7
2013	159.6	159.0	159.2	162.2	163.2	164.5	165.7	167.3	167.1	164.2	163.8	164.2	163.3
Education and Health Services													
2002	92.4	93.7	94.1	94.3	94.5	93.7	93.2	93.2	94.4	96.7	97.2	97.3	94.6
2003	95.6	96.7	97.0	97.9	98.0	96.9	96.5	96.7	98.1	100.2	101.0	100.9	98.0
2004	98.4	100.0	100.7	102.1	102.2	100.8	100.6	100.4	101.9	104.0	104.4	104.5	101.7
2005	102.0	103.4	103.9	105.4	104.8	103.5	103.5	103.5	105.5	107.2	107.9	107.7	104.9
2006	105.7	107.6	108.4	108.8	108.1	106.4	105.4	105.6	108.4	109.6	110.1	109.8	107.8
2007	108.5	109.4	110.2	111.2	111.4	110.5	109.8	110.1	111.7	113.0	113.9	113.5	111.1
2008	112.6	114.3	114.1	114.5	114.3	113.2	112.9	113.2	115.0	116.4	117.2	117.2	114.6
2009	116.4	117.8	118.0	118.6	118.7	117.9	118.0	118.6	120.7	122.5	122.9	123.4	119.5
2010	122.5	123.6	124.8	125.1	124.9	123.0	123.8	124.9	126.5	127.5	128.0	127.4	125.2
2011	126.5	128.1	128.3	130.7	131.3	128.4	129.2	129.9	133.1	134.1	134.7	134.7	130.8
2012	133.5	135.8	136.0	137.8	137.4	135.9	133.7	134.6	135.7	138.1	138.5	137.9	136.2
2013	137.1	138.2	137.6	139.7	139.7	138.1	136.6	138.2	137.7	136.8	138.9	138.8	138.1
Leisure and Hospitality													
2002	78.8	79.4	81.2	83.2	86.1	87.6	87.4	87.0	85.1	84.1	83.5	82.3	83.8
2003	79.7	79.5	80.9	83.7	86.5	88.5	89.1	89.3	86.9	86.5	85.4	85.0	85.1
2004	81.6	81.8	83.7	86.1	89.3	90.6	90.5	91.3	88.9	88.0	87.0	86.5	87.1
2005	82.8	83.0	84.7	88.0	90.8	92.8	92.2	91.8	90.4	88.7	87.5	86.5	88.3
2006	83.4	84.4	86.5	88.1	91.0	92.9	92.3	92.3	90.3	89.0	87.8	87.3	88.8
2007	84.7	84.6	86.5	89.0	92.1	94.1	92.7	93.0	90.6	89.8	88.7	87.7	89.5
2008	84.7	84.8	85.2	88.7	91.5	92.6	91.8	91.7	89.0	87.8	86.1	85.4	88.3
2009	81.8	82.2	84.3	86.1	88.7	90.2	89.5	89.1	87.1	86.2	84.2	83.5	86.1
2010	80.4	80.9	82.7	85.6	87.8	89.7	89.7	89.5	87.8	86.6	86.0	84.8	86.0
2011	82.4	83.2	85.1	88.4	91.5	93.3	93.1	93.2	91.3	89.9	89.4	88.4	89.1
2012	85.3	86.6	88.9	91.3	94.9	97.5	96.8	97.5	96.1	95.2	94.2	93.4	93.1
2013	91.3	91.9	94.4	97.6	101.2	103.1	102.2	102.3	100.7	100.8	98.0	97.5	98.4
Other Services													
2002	35.4	35.9	36.1	36.6	37.1	37.4	37.3	37.4	37.1	37.0	37.2	37.3	36.8
2003	37.2	37.4	37.6	37.7	37.9	38.3	38.2	38.2	37.7	37.7	37.7	37.9	37.8
2004	37.7	38.0	38.6	38.6	38.6	38.9	39.0	38.9	38.4	38.7	39.1	37.7	38.5
2005	37.1	37.4	37.7	37.6	37.8	37.9	37.5	37.7	37.2	37.6	38.1	37.2	37.6
2006	37.0	37.2	37.5	37.6	37.7	38.3	37.9	37.9	37.5	37.6	37.5	37.3	37.6
2007	37.0	37.1	37.3	37.0	37.4	37.6	37.4	37.2	36.5	36.7	36.6	36.4	37.0
2008	35.9	36.0	36.1	36.4	36.6	36.9	37.1	37.2	36.8	37.5	36.8	36.0	36.6
2009	35.5	35.9	36.0	36.0	36.4	36.3	36.0	35.8	35.2	35.4	35.2	35.2	35.7
2010	35.1	35.2	35.4	35.3	35.3	35.6	35.9	35.8	35.3	35.5	35.4	35.4	35.4
2011	34.7	34.8	34.8	35.2	35.3	35.6	35.9	35.8	35.4	35.8	35.6	35.3	35.4
2012	35.3	35.5	35.7	36.2	36.5	37.2	37.8	37.3	37.3	38.5	37.8	37.7	36.9
2013	36.9	37.1	37.3	37.8	38.0	38.2	38.1	37.9	37.6	37.6	37.5	37.6	37.6
Government													
2002	150.5	151.1	151.2	150.7	151.1	152.1	147.3	146.4	148.0	150.8	152.6	153.0	150.4
2003	152.0	152.6	152.6	152.3	153.0	153.4	149.6	148.2	148.9	152.1	153.3	153.8	151.8
2004	152.6	153.3	153.8	153.2	154.2	155.2	151.2	151.1	151.4	155.4	156.6	156.4	153.7
2005	154.5	156.2	156.5	156.3	157.0	157.8	153.8	153.8	153.0	157.3	158.0	157.7	156.0
2006	156.1	157.5	157.9	157.3	158.4	157.5	153.6	153.9	153.3	157.6	158.4	158.5	156.7
2007	157.0	157.5	157.9	157.9	158.9	159.4	153.3	152.3	155.0	159.2	160.2	159.7	157.4
2008	158.6	159.9	159.4	159.0	160.6	160.1	155.0	154.3	155.4	160.3	160.2	159.3	158.5
2009	158.0	158.9	159.0	159.4	160.0	158.6	152.4	151.5	154.7	159.8	159.9	158.3	157.5
2010	157.3	158.2	158.0	159.2	162.8	159.9	152.0	151.5	154.5	159.4	159.8	160.1	157.7
2011	157.7	158.2	158.3	159.8	161.0	158.2	154.2	155.9	158.6	162.2	163.5	161.7	159.1
2012	160.2	162.2	161.9	161.5	164.2	162.4	153.1	154.3	164.1	166.5	167.0	164.0	161.8
2013	163.1	163.8	163.5	164.3	165.3	161.7	155.4	157.3	165.2	166.4	167.1	165.9	163.3

Employment by Industry: Dallas-Fort Worth-Arlington, TX, Selected Years, 2002–2013

(Numbers in thousands, not seasonally adjusted)

Industry and year	January	February	March	April	May	June	July	August	September	October	November	December	Annual average
Total Nonfarm													
2002	2,687.5	2,694.2	2,708.7	2,709.0	2,718.4	2,718.6	2,689.8	2,700.9	2,704.1	2,696.3	2,703.3	2,704.2	2,702.9
2003	2,644.5	2,652.1	2,658.0	2,663.2	2,668.3	2,666.5	2,644.6	2,656.2	2,666.5	2,674.0	2,682.0	2,685.8	2,663.5
2004	2,638.6	2,652.4	2,670.7	2,688.5	2,695.5	2,694.8	2,688.7	2,702.9	2,712.2	2,727.8	2,735.8	2,745.7	2,696.1
2005	2,687.1	2,705.0	2,723.5	2,749.0	2,758.1	2,763.7	2,761.9	2,777.3	2,794.9	2,802.7	2,822.2	2,828.1	2,764.5
2006	2,780.6	2,800.3	2,821.5	2,837.9	2,852.9	2,866.2	2,843.5	2,867.5	2,881.9	2,886.8	2,910.3	2,923.3	2,856.1
2007	2,860.0	2,887.7	2,915.5	2,922.0	2,937.6	2,950.9	2,926.0	2,946.0	2,956.5	2,971.6	2,990.8	2,999.8	2,938.7
2008	2,942.2	2,964.0	2,974.4	2,980.1	2,997.0	2,995.4	2,972.0	2,978.6	2,974.7	2,976.0	2,970.9	2,968.6	2,974.5
2009	2,889.4	2,883.5	2,881.8	2,876.8	2,879.3	2,870.5	2,843.5	2,845.1	2,840.9	2,851.7	2,855.8	2,861.1	2,865.0
2010	2,803.8	2,814.8	2,837.5	2,850.1	2,873.0	2,879.8	2,856.9	2,864.3	2,868.2	2,894.1	2,902.9	2,913.9	2,863.3
2011	2,861.6	2,874.3	2,901.1	2,924.4	2,934.8	2,948.1	2,934.6	2,946.3	2,958.6	2,963.3	2,977.2	2,985.6	2,934.2
2012	2,935.8	2,957.8	2,980.3	2,995.7	3,010.8	3,024.8	2,997.9	3,018.5	3,027.1	3,041.1	3,065.7	3,074.6	3,010.8
2013	3,005.4	3,033.7	3,053.0	3,064.0	3,083.4	3,100.5	3,086.5	3,107.5	3,118.9	3,133.2	3,149.1	3,142.5	3,089.8
Total Private													
2002	2,359.9	2,358.2	2,371.8	2,374.2	2,382.0	2,387.7	2,377.3	2,381.7	2,369.1	2,353.4	2,356.6	2,358.5	2,369.2
2003	2,307.6	2,305.9	2,312.6	2,317.2	2,320.9	2,324.3	2,322.2	2,332.8	2,324.4	2,328.0	2,333.2	2,340.1	2,322.4
2004	2,297.5	2,304.3	2,324.3	2,340.1	2,345.1	2,351.5	2,360.4	2,366.8	2,358.6	2,373.2	2,378.0	2,388.6	2,349.0
2005	2,335.2	2,345.8	2,365.2	2,389.7	2,397.7	2,412.1	2,426.2	2,433.1	2,434.5	2,438.7	2,454.9	2,466.9	2,408.3
2006	2,421.6	2,434.2	2,456.7	2,472.2	2,486.3	2,507.7	2,498.3	2,515.5	2,517.0	2,515.8	2,537.0	2,552.6	2,492.9
2007	2,493.3	2,514.2	2,541.2	2,549.5	2,563.1	2,584.0	2,576.2	2,592.0	2,585.9	2,592.7	2,608.7	2,619.0	2,568.3
2008	2,566.0	2,580.3	2,589.5	2,595.5	2,610.5	2,616.3	2,606.9	2,611.3	2,593.5	2,585.9	2,577.3	2,574.8	2,592.3
2009	2,502.8	2,490.0	2,487.4	2,481.9	2,483.9	2,483.9	2,472.3	2,473.8	2,457.2	2,456.7	2,458.3	2,467.2	2,476.3
2010	2,414.5	2,418.1	2,439.5	2,452.1	2,464.3	2,478.6	2,476.0	2,486.7	2,481.7	2,496.9	2,503.9	2,515.6	2,469.0
2011	2,468.5	2,477.0	2,503.4	2,524.8	2,534.7	2,552.9	2,556.5	2,569.8	2,571.1	2,572.4	2,585.0	2,594.8	2,542.6
2012	2,551.1	2,567.6	2,589.8	2,605.2	2,618.9	2,640.3	2,628.7	2,648.3	2,642.2	2,650.0	2,673.1	2,680.4	2,624.6
2013	2,618.8	2,640.5	2,658.4	2,668.6	2,687.8	2,709.1	2,708.8	2,728.5	2,728.2	2,735.3	2,747.1	2,741.0	2,697.7
Goods Producing													
2002	473.5	472.4	474.0	472.7	474.0	477.3	475.0	474.0	469.4	461.9	459.7	456.2	470.0
2003	448.0	448.2	448.0	448.6	450.3	452.5	451.3	451.9	449.9	447.4	446.0	445.2	448.9
2004	441.2	442.6	446.0	448.7	449.9	452.2	455.1	454.6	453.3	451.4	449.4	449.4	449.5
2005	443.0	446.8	450.4	453.8	456.4	461.9	465.6	466.0	465.4	464.4	464.3	465.1	458.6
2006	459.2	463.4	468.0	469.5	474.2	480.7	477.7	480.5	482.1	478.8	480.5	480.9	474.6
2007	473.3	478.1	483.1	481.7	483.9	490.2	486.6	488.8	489.2	485.8	486.0	486.6	484.4
2008	479.4	483.8	485.0	482.8	484.9	487.2	484.8	485.4	482.5	478.1	472.5	468.5	481.2
2009	454.2	449.5	444.3	437.6	433.9	430.3	423.9	424.5	419.4	411.9	408.8	407.2	428.8
2010	401.9	399.6	403.2	404.8	406.9	410.9	411.4	412.5	410.8	409.7	408.8	409.1	407.5
2011	401.8	403.8	407.7	409.6	411.1	416.0	418.6	419.9	419.2	417.1	417.7	418.1	413.4
2012	414.5	417.7	420.5	421.7	422.0	426.9	429.6	430.9	429.4	428.2	429.1	429.4	425.0
2013	423.4	426.2	429.2	428.7	431.3	435.4	437.6	439.1	438.7	438.9	436.0	433.7	433.2
Service-Providing													
2002	2,214.0	2,221.8	2,234.7	2,236.3	2,244.4	2,241.3	2,214.8	2,226.9	2,234.7	2,234.4	2,243.6	2,248.0	2,232.9
2003	2,196.5	2,203.9	2,210.0	2,214.6	2,218.0	2,214.0	2,193.3	2,204.3	2,216.6	2,226.6	2,236.0	2,240.6	2,214.5
2004	2,197.4	2,209.8	2,224.7	2,239.8	2,245.6	2,242.6	2,233.6	2,248.3	2,258.9	2,276.4	2,286.4	2,296.3	2,246.7
2005	2,244.1	2,258.2	2,273.1	2,295.2	2,301.7	2,301.8	2,296.3	2,311.3	2,329.5	2,338.3	2,357.9	2,363.0	2,305.9
2006	2,321.4	2,336.9	2,353.5	2,368.4	2,378.7	2,385.5	2,365.8	2,387.0	2,399.8	2,408.0	2,429.8	2,442.4	2,381.4
2007	2,386.7	2,409.6	2,432.4	2,440.3	2,453.7	2,460.7	2,439.4	2,457.2	2,467.3	2,485.8	2,504.8	2,513.2	2,454.3
2008	2,462.8	2,480.2	2,489.4	2,497.3	2,512.1	2,508.2	2,487.2	2,493.2	2,492.2	2,497.9	2,498.4	2,500.1	2,493.3
2009	2,435.2	2,434.0	2,437.5	2,439.2	2,445.4	2,440.2	2,419.6	2,420.6	2,421.5	2,439.8	2,447.0	2,453.9	2,436.2
2010	2,401.9	2,415.2	2,434.3	2,445.3	2,466.1	2,468.9	2,445.5	2,451.8	2,457.4	2,484.4	2,494.1	2,504.8	2,455.8
2011	2,459.8	2,470.5	2,493.4	2,514.8	2,523.7	2,532.1	2,516.0	2,526.4	2,539.4	2,546.2	2,559.5	2,567.5	2,520.8
2012	2,521.3	2,540.1	2,559.8	2,574.0	2,588.8	2,597.9	2,568.3	2,587.6	2,597.7	2,612.9	2,636.6	2,645.2	2,585.9
2013	2,582.0	2,607.5	2,623.8	2,635.3	2,652.1	2,665.1	2,648.9	2,668.4	2,680.2	2,694.3	2,713.1	2,708.8	2,656.6
Mining, Logging, and Construction													
2002	157.7	158.2	160.2	160.4	161.9	164.5	163.5	163.9	160.7	156.9	156.3	154.3	159.9
2003	150.0	150.2	151.0	152.2	154.2	156.2	157.4	157.8	156.4	154.8	153.9	153.2	153.9
2004	150.8	151.0	153.7	155.6	156.6	158.2	160.6	160.9	160.3	158.9	157.7	157.6	156.8
2005	155.8	157.4	160.1	163.1	165.0	168.4	169.6	169.9	170.5	169.6	168.8	169.0	165.6
2006	165.6	167.8	171.2	171.6	174.9	179.0	177.2	178.9	180.4	179.4	180.4	181.4	175.7
2007	176.9	179.9	184.3	184.7	186.4	191.1	188.9	191.9	192.9	192.0	192.9	192.9	187.9
2008	189.0	192.9	195.2	194.6	196.2	198.7	197.0	197.5	195.9	193.2	189.7	187.2	193.9
2009	179.0	177.6	175.5	172.2	171.0	171.2	169.1	167.3	163.2	157.8	156.3	155.5	168.0
2010	151.6	150.7	153.9	155.1	156.1	158.6	159.4	160.1	158.8	157.9	156.7	156.5	156.3
2011	152.1	153.0	155.7	156.6	157.5	160.3	162.1	163.0	162.0	160.1	160.4	160.7	158.6
2012	158.7	160.7	163.0	164.1	166.9	170.0	169.9	171.0	170.1	169.6	170.5	170.2	167.1
2013	166.9	168.9	171.4	171.7	173.8	176.4	178.9	180.5	180.2	180.6	178.2	176.3	175.3
Manufacturing													
2002	315.8	314.2	313.8	312.3	312.1	312.8	311.5	310.1	308.7	305.0	303.4	301.9	310.1
2003	298.0	298.0	297.0	296.4	296.1	296.3	293.9	294.1	293.5	292.6	292.1	292.0	295.0
2004	290.4	291.6	292.3	293.1	293.3	294.0	294.5	293.7	293.0	292.5	291.7	291.8	292.7
2005	287.2	289.4	290.3	290.7	291.4	293.5	296.0	296.1	294.9	294.8	295.5	296.1	293.0
2006	293.6	295.6	296.8	297.9	299.3	301.7	300.5	301.6	301.7	299.4	300.1	299.5	299.0
2007	296.4	298.2	298.8	297.0	297.5	299.1	297.7	296.9	296.3	293.8	293.1	293.7	296.5
2008	290.4	290.9	289.8	288.2	288.7	288.5	287.8	287.9	286.6	284.9	282.8	281.3	287.3
2009	275.2	271.9	268.8	265.4	262.9	259.1	254.8	257.2	256.2	254.1	252.5	251.7	260.8
2010	250.3	248.9	249.3	249.7	250.8	252.3	252.0	252.4	252.0	251.8	252.1	252.6	251.2
2011	249.7	250.8	252.0	253.0	253.6	255.7	256.5	256.9	257.2	257.0	257.3	257.4	254.8
2012	255.8	257.0	257.5	257.6	255.1	256.9	259.7	259.9	259.3	258.6	258.6	259.2	257.9
2013	256.5	257.3	257.8	257.0	257.5	259.0	258.7	258.6	258.5	258.3	257.8	257.4	257.9

Employment by Industry: Dallas-Fort Worth-Arlington, TX, Selected Years, 2002–2013—*Continued*

(Numbers in thousands, not seasonally adjusted)

Industry and year	January	February	March	April	May	June	July	August	September	October	November	December	Annual average
Trade, Transportation, and Utilities													
2002	618.2	613.7	615.4	613.6	614.1	614.9	615.3	615.7	612.3	610.4	616.8	624.0	615.4
2003	598.5	592.7	592.3	588.8	587.0	585.8	583.2	588.1	586.0	588.8	596.1	601.2	590.7
2004	582.5	580.1	583.3	583.8	586.5	587.2	590.0	594.8	591.6	595.2	604.7	611.5	590.9
2005	591.7	586.6	590.7	591.6	593.8	596.9	600.1	604.3	604.1	605.0	618.8	626.6	600.9
2006	604.4	601.1	605.2	606.5	608.9	611.0	609.6	614.0	611.7	613.8	626.6	635.3	612.3
2007	614.5	612.1	617.3	616.4	618.4	621.8	622.0	624.0	622.7	628.0	640.2	647.2	623.7
2008	627.3	624.6	626.4	623.9	625.6	626.9	626.2	629.2	624.1	623.9	628.1	632.6	626.6
2009	609.2	601.3	599.9	594.4	593.9	591.8	590.6	591.0	588.3	589.2	595.3	601.6	595.5
2010	582.3	578.9	583.0	583.8	587.3	589.3	589.6	591.9	589.7	594.6	604.6	610.9	590.5
2011	592.1	589.7	594.3	599.0	600.3	602.7	604.6	608.6	607.2	610.4	621.0	627.9	604.8
2012	609.3	607.5	610.8	612.1	616.0	620.0	620.0	624.1	621.7	625.6	640.9	646.0	621.2
2013	623.7	622.2	623.7	625.9	629.7	634.5	637.0	643.2	643.1	645.1	659.3	665.3	637.7
Wholesale Trade													
2002	166.3	166.1	167.1	166.0	166.0	166.5	166.6	166.5	166.2	165.2	165.3	165.7	166.1
2003	162.6	162.1	162.6	161.9	161.3	161.5	160.9	160.6	159.9	159.6	159.1	159.3	161.0
2004	157.7	157.7	158.5	158.1	158.3	158.4	159.1	159.0	158.4	159.2	159.0	159.3	158.6
2005	157.2	157.5	158.2	159.3	159.7	160.2	161.6	162.0	162.4	161.8	162.4	163.5	160.5
2006	162.3	162.8	163.7	164.3	165.0	166.0	166.1	166.9	167.3	167.6	168.5	169.2	165.8
2007	166.9	168.0	168.9	168.8	169.5	171.0	170.8	171.1	171.0	173.1	174.0	174.3	170.6
2008	172.5	173.0	172.8	172.6	172.7	172.7	171.9	171.9	170.9	170.3	169.6	169.0	171.7
2009	165.8	164.9	163.2	161.3	160.7	159.6	159.1	158.4	157.6	157.2	156.3	156.6	160.1
2010	154.8	154.7	155.0	154.5	155.2	155.6	156.5	156.5	156.1	156.7	156.8	157.3	155.8
2011	155.7	156.8	157.2	158.0	158.9	159.6	159.6	159.9	160.0	160.4	160.6	161.4	159.0
2012	159.9	161.0	161.7	162.4	163.6	164.6	164.7	165.2	164.9	164.6	165.4	165.9	163.7
2013	164.6	165.3	166.0	166.2	167.0	168.2	169.0	169.8	170.9	171.3	173.6	172.7	168.7
Retail Trade													
2002	316.7	313.1	313.2	312.2	312.0	311.9	312.0	312.0	309.5	307.9	315.1	322.4	313.2
2003	302.2	297.6	296.9	294.3	293.7	293.3	292.2	296.3	295.1	297.1	304.7	309.5	297.7
2004	293.4	290.9	292.9	293.6	295.9	296.3	297.3	301.6	298.9	301.5	311.7	317.4	299.3
2005	300.8	297.1	299.0	300.1	301.3	303.8	304.8	307.4	306.0	307.5	319.7	325.7	306.1
2006	308.0	303.9	306.4	306.6	307.5	307.9	306.3	308.7	305.2	306.4	317.6	323.1	309.0
2007	307.8	303.9	307.4	306.7	307.3	308.4	309.6	310.4	308.5	311.6	322.7	328.1	311.0
2008	313.1	309.8	311.9	308.9	309.9	311.3	311.9	313.5	309.2	310.5	315.5	319.4	312.1
2009	303.1	298.0	298.2	296.2	296.8	296.3	296.0	297.4	295.3	297.0	303.6	308.5	298.9
2010	294.7	291.5	294.7	296.5	298.7	299.7	298.8	300.6	298.2	302.2	311.0	316.0	300.2
2011	300.7	296.6	299.8	303.3	303.6	305.2	306.8	309.9	307.3	311.0	320.5	325.3	307.5
2012	310.6	306.7	308.3	308.7	310.5	312.4	312.2	314.7	311.8	316.2	329.5	331.5	314.4
2013	315.4	313.2	313.4	315.0	316.9	319.6	321.0	325.7	324.0	325.1	334.4	337.8	321.8
Transportation and Utilities													
2002	135.2	134.5	135.1	135.4	136.1	136.5	136.7	137.2	136.6	137.3	136.4	135.9	136.1
2003	133.7	133.0	132.8	132.6	132.0	131.0	130.1	131.2	131.0	132.1	132.3	132.4	132.0
2004	131.4	131.5	131.9	132.1	132.3	132.5	133.6	134.2	134.3	134.5	134.0	134.8	133.1
2005	133.7	132.0	133.5	132.2	132.8	132.9	133.7	134.9	135.7	135.7	136.7	137.4	134.3
2006	134.1	134.4	135.1	135.6	136.4	137.1	137.2	138.4	139.2	139.8	140.5	143.0	137.6
2007	139.8	140.2	141.0	140.9	141.6	142.4	141.6	142.5	143.2	143.3	143.5	144.8	142.1
2008	141.7	141.8	141.7	142.4	143.0	142.9	142.4	143.8	144.0	143.1	143.0	144.2	142.8
2009	140.3	138.4	138.5	136.9	136.4	135.9	135.5	135.2	135.4	135.0	135.4	136.5	136.6
2010	132.8	132.7	133.3	132.8	133.4	134.0	134.3	134.8	135.4	135.7	136.8	137.6	134.5
2011	135.7	136.3	137.3	137.7	137.8	137.9	138.2	138.8	139.9	139.0	139.9	141.2	138.3
2012	138.8	139.8	140.8	141.0	141.9	143.0	143.1	144.2	145.0	144.8	146.0	148.6	143.1
2013	143.7	143.7	144.3	144.7	145.8	146.7	147.0	147.7	148.2	148.7	151.3	154.8	147.2
Information													
2002	114.2	113.0	112.6	110.1	109.3	108.6	106.2	105.3	104.1	103.5	103.0	102.4	107.7
2003	100.6	100.4	100.1	98.9	98.5	98.2	98.0	97.5	96.4	96.7	96.3	96.3	98.2
2004	96.1	94.7	96.1	94.8	94.9	94.7	94.0	93.4	92.7	92.9	92.8	93.0	94.2
2005	92.5	92.5	92.7	92.4	92.2	92.5	92.8	92.5	92.7	92.2	92.4	92.2	92.5
2006	91.5	92.4	92.3	91.0	90.3	90.3	89.4	88.5	87.9	86.6	86.1	85.8	89.3
2007	87.8	88.4	88.5	88.2	88.8	88.9	89.4	90.0	89.5	89.9	90.3	89.8	89.1
2008	89.1	89.2	89.2	88.9	88.8	88.6	88.2	87.8	86.4	86.0	86.1	86.0	87.9
2009	85.4	84.8	84.1	83.6	83.4	83.2	82.3	81.6	80.7	80.8	80.9	81.0	82.7
2010	79.6	79.1	79.2	79.8	79.4	79.8	79.4	79.3	78.7	78.5	78.7	78.7	79.2
2011	78.9	78.6	78.6	78.4	78.8	79.1	79.2	78.8	78.4	78.6	78.9	79.1	78.8
2012	78.0	77.9	77.8	77.9	78.0	78.3	77.9	77.6	77.1	77.7	78.5	78.4	77.9
2013	78.0	78.3	78.2	78.5	79.1	79.4	79.9	80.2	79.3	79.8	79.8	80.3	79.2
Financial Activities													
2002	212.3	212.4	212.8	212.2	212.8	213.3	213.2	213.4	212.4	211.7	212.3	212.1	212.6
2003	210.4	211.2	210.7	211.1	211.9	212.7	213.4	214.2	213.4	213.0	212.9	213.7	212.4
2004	212.0	212.0	212.7	213.6	214.6	214.6	216.2	216.8	216.1	217.5	217.6	218.7	215.1
2005	216.5	217.0	217.3	218.3	218.8	220.4	222.5	223.6	224.2	224.3	225.2	226.4	221.2
2006	224.3	225.4	227.4	229.0	229.4	230.7	229.5	230.6	230.3	230.4	231.1	232.5	229.2
2007	229.3	230.3	231.6	232.4	233.2	235.1	234.3	235.4	234.3	233.7	233.9	234.3	233.2
2008	231.7	232.8	233.0	234.5	235.5	236.1	234.7	234.5	232.6	231.4	230.3	229.9	233.1
2009	227.0	226.8	226.6	228.8	229.4	229.5	228.9	228.9	227.2	227.1	227.3	228.3	228.0
2010	226.1	226.7	227.2	227.3	227.9	229.0	229.7	229.7	229.5	231.2	231.3	232.6	229.0
2011	231.6	232.3	233.4	234.1	234.2	235.9	237.1	237.8	237.9	238.6	239.2	240.7	236.1
2012	238.9	240.4	241.4	242.0	243.1	245.2	245.1	245.5	245.6	246.9	248.2	249.6	244.3
2013	247.6	249.4	251.2	250.8	252.1	254.3	256.0	256.4	255.8	253.1	251.0	251.5	252.4

Employment by Industry: Dallas-Fort Worth-Arlington, TX, Selected Years, 2002–2013—*Continued*

(Numbers in thousands, not seasonally adjusted)

Industry and year	January	February	March	April	May	June	July	August	September	October	November	December	Annual average
Professional and Business Services													
2002	352.2	351.7	354.0	355.4	356.6	357.3	356.1	359.6	357.8	355.4	355.2	353.8	355.4
2003	344.0	343.5	345.4	349.3	349.8	351.5	353.7	356.6	357.3	358.5	361.0	364.5	352.9
2004	354.8	357.3	360.5	366.3	366.3	368.3	371.5	373.1	371.2	376.6	376.4	377.3	368.3
2005	366.4	370.4	373.7	383.0	382.2	385.1	389.7	392.3	395.5	400.1	402.9	405.3	387.2
2006	395.9	399.9	404.4	409.4	411.3	415.3	416.3	421.9	424.1	426.2	431.4	433.9	415.8
2007	422.3	428.3	433.2	435.2	436.2	441.5	440.7	446.8	447.7	451.8	453.8	456.6	441.2
2008	444.1	446.4	448.5	449.9	451.8	453.9	452.2	454.3	450.5	449.2	445.1	440.0	448.8
2009	422.9	418.3	416.3	413.5	413.5	415.5	415.3	415.9	412.7	417.4	418.6	418.7	416.6
2010	409.9	412.3	415.7	420.6	421.4	424.5	426.6	430.5	431.8	436.3	437.6	439.2	425.5
2011	431.8	435.4	440.0	445.2	445.0	448.8	450.2	454.4	457.1	457.1	459.2	458.7	448.6
2012	451.9	456.8	462.5	466.7	470.0	473.0	468.0	476.1	475.6	479.9	484.1	480.3	470.4
2013	468.0	473.9	477.1	476.4	479.5	483.7	483.2	489.7	491.5	496.8	496.4	493.0	484.1
Education and Health Services													
2002	256.0	258.5	259.3	260.7	262.2	260.9	261.0	263.8	265.5	265.2	266.6	266.9	262.2
2003	266.5	268.3	269.0	269.6	270.1	268.0	269.7	270.8	272.3	274.3	274.5	272.7	270.5
2004	268.6	272.3	273.3	274.6	274.6	271.7	274.2	275.1	277.5	283.2	283.4	284.3	276.1
2005	277.8	281.0	282.1	285.2	285.6	284.9	288.8	289.3	291.2	294.0	294.5	295.0	287.5
2006	293.2	295.4	296.0	296.9	297.5	298.5	298.3	302.6	305.2	306.8	308.1	310.5	300.8
2007	303.8	308.9	312.0	313.0	314.4	314.3	314.0	317.1	319.4	321.0	322.7	323.2	315.3
2008	319.4	324.3	325.1	325.6	328.4	326.2	327.0	329.1	331.2	332.4	333.9	336.4	328.3
2009	331.7	334.3	337.2	339.3	341.3	340.8	342.8	344.9	347.6	351.2	351.6	353.0	343.0
2010	345.7	348.6	352.2	354.7	356.0	355.1	354.2	356.7	358.2	361.6	361.9	363.6	355.7
2011	358.9	359.8	363.6	366.1	367.7	367.7	367.5	369.5	372.9	373.1	373.8	375.8	368.0
2012	370.3	373.9	376.1	376.1	376.3	375.5	374.0	377.2	378.7	379.6	380.7	382.0	376.7
2013	374.7	379.4	380.9	382.2	383.6	382.3	379.9	384.2	386.5	388.5	389.2	387.5	383.2
Leisure and Hospitality													
2002	232.5	234.6	239.7	244.6	247.8	249.3	246.0	245.6	243.6	241.9	239.2	239.3	242.0
2003	234.9	236.1	239.1	243.7	246.2	247.6	245.3	246.5	242.8	244.6	241.7	241.0	242.5
2004	237.1	239.0	243.4	250.6	252.3	255.0	253.5	254.2	252.7	254.1	251.5	251.5	249.6
2005	244.9	248.0	251.9	258.6	261.1	262.2	261.3	260.2	257.2	256.3	254.1	253.1	255.7
2006	250.4	253.1	257.4	262.5	267.2	272.0	268.7	268.9	267.2	265.7	264.8	265.0	263.6
2007	258.9	262.9	268.9	277.0	281.6	283.7	283.0	283.8	278.1	279.2	278.5	278.2	276.2
2008	272.3	275.8	279.0	286.0	290.6	291.5	289.4	286.6	282.2	282.2	278.7	278.8	282.8
2009	271.4	273.3	277.3	282.5	286.0	289.2	286.3	285.1	280.5	278.6	274.6	276.3	280.1
2010	268.9	272.3	277.5	280.2	284.2	287.5	283.7	284.7	282.3	284.3	280.3	280.5	280.5
2011	273.4	276.6	283.9	289.5	294.1	297.9	294.4	295.8	292.9	293.0	290.6	289.5	289.3
2012	283.3	288.0	294.4	301.7	305.8	312.0	305.6	308.2	306.2	303.8	302.9	305.4	301.4
2013	295.6	302.1	308.3	315.7	321.2	326.6	323.0	323.1	320.8	320.5	322.6	316.8	316.4
Other Services													
2002	101.0	101.9	104.0	104.9	105.2	106.1	104.5	104.3	104.0	103.4	103.8	103.8	103.9
2003	104.7	105.5	108.0	107.2	107.1	108.0	107.6	107.2	106.3	104.7	104.7	105.5	106.4
2004	105.2	106.3	109.0	107.7	106.9	107.8	105.9	104.8	103.5	102.3	102.2	102.9	105.4
2005	102.4	103.5	106.4	106.8	107.6	108.2	105.4	104.9	104.2	102.4	102.7	103.2	104.8
2006	102.7	103.5	106.0	107.4	107.5	109.2	108.8	108.5	108.5	107.5	108.4	108.7	107.2
2007	103.4	105.2	106.6	105.6	106.6	108.5	106.2	106.1	105.0	103.3	103.3	103.1	105.2
2008	102.7	103.4	103.3	103.9	104.9	105.9	104.4	104.4	104.0	102.7	102.6	102.6	103.7
2009	101.0	101.7	101.7	102.2	102.5	103.6	102.2	101.9	100.8	100.5	101.2	101.1	101.7
2010	100.1	100.6	101.5	100.9	101.2	102.5	101.4	101.4	100.7	100.7	100.7	101.0	101.1
2011	100.0	100.8	101.9	102.9	103.5	104.8	104.9	105.0	105.5	104.5	104.6	105.0	103.6
2012	104.9	105.4	106.3	107.0	107.7	109.4	108.5	108.7	107.9	108.3	108.7	109.3	107.7
2013	107.8	109.0	109.8	110.4	111.3	112.9	112.2	112.6	112.5	112.6	112.8	112.9	111.4
Government													
2002	327.6	336.0	336.9	334.8	336.4	330.9	312.5	319.2	335.0	342.9	346.7	345.7	333.7
2003	336.9	346.2	345.4	346.0	347.4	342.2	322.4	323.4	342.1	346.0	348.8	345.7	341.0
2004	341.1	348.1	346.4	348.4	350.4	343.3	328.3	336.1	353.6	354.6	357.8	357.1	347.1
2005	351.9	359.2	358.3	359.3	360.4	351.6	335.7	344.2	360.4	364.0	367.3	361.2	356.1
2006	359.0	366.1	364.8	365.7	366.6	358.5	345.2	352.0	364.9	371.0	373.3	370.7	363.2
2007	366.7	373.5	374.3	372.5	374.5	366.9	349.8	354.0	370.6	378.9	382.1	380.8	370.4
2008	376.2	383.7	384.9	384.6	386.5	379.1	365.1	367.3	381.2	390.1	393.6	393.8	382.2
2009	386.6	393.5	394.4	394.9	395.4	386.6	371.2	371.3	383.7	395.0	397.5	393.9	388.7
2010	389.3	396.7	398.0	398.0	408.7	401.2	380.9	377.6	386.5	397.2	399.0	398.3	394.3
2011	393.1	397.3	397.7	399.6	400.1	395.2	378.1	376.5	387.5	390.9	392.2	390.8	391.6
2012	384.7	390.2	390.5	390.5	391.9	384.5	369.2	370.2	384.9	391.1	392.6	394.2	386.2
2013	386.6	393.2	394.6	395.4	395.6	391.4	377.7	379.0	390.7	397.9	402.0	401.5	392.1

Employment by Industry: Dayton, OH, Selected Years, 2002–2013

(Numbers in thousands, not seasonally adjusted)

Industry and year	January	February	March	April	May	June	July	August	September	October	November	December	Annual average
Total Nonfarm													
2002	418.1	420.4	421.8	421.4	422.2	422.1	417.3	418.3	421.2	420.6	422.3	421.4	420.6
2003	411.5	410.6	413.2	416.8	417.2	418.0	412.8	414.1	416.1	418.1	418.8	418.9	415.5
2004	406.0	406.8	409.1	413.3	413.5	414.6	410.2	411.8	413.8	414.2	414.2	414.4	411.8
2005	404.1	405.6	408.0	412.1	412.3	411.5	407.0	408.9	412.7	412.3	413.0	413.0	410.0
2006	401.9	404.4	407.9	410.1	412.2	412.0	404.5	406.2	408.3	408.5	410.1	411.2	408.1
2007	396.6	399.3	402.4	404.9	406.4	407.0	400.4	402.2	404.7	405.7	406.1	404.7	403.4
2008	394.7	395.4	393.7	395.8	397.3	397.9	392.7	394.2	395.3	394.3	392.3	390.1	394.5
2009	375.5	374.5	374.4	373.3	374.5	372.1	367.6	368.1	371.9	372.7	373.2	372.3	372.5
2010	363.1	363.6	366.6	370.7	373.1	371.7	367.1	368.7	372.5	374.3	376.0	376.0	370.3
2011	367.0	368.5	371.2	376.1	377.4	375.7	371.1	372.4	377.4	378.5	380.3	380.2	374.7
2012	372.2	374.7	377.0	379.3	380.4	381.9	374.9	375.7	378.7	379.3	381.2	380.8	378.0
2013	369.8	372.7	374.6	377.2	380.9	379.8	375.1	376.9	378.7	377.0	379.0	376.4	376.5
Total Private													
2002	351.3	352.2	353.7	353.9	353.8	354.3	352.3	353.8	354.5	352.7	354.0	353.4	353.3
2003	346.3	344.3	347.1	350.9	350.5	351.7	349.6	351.5	351.7	352.2	352.8	352.8	350.1
2004	341.3	341.2	343.3	347.6	347.0	348.7	347.3	349.2	349.4	348.6	348.4	348.8	346.7
2005	339.8	339.9	342.5	346.6	346.1	346.8	344.4	346.6	348.1	347.1	347.7	348.4	345.3
2006	337.9	338.9	342.4	344.7	345.8	346.2	341.6	343.6	344.5	343.1	344.7	345.8	343.3
2007	332.5	334.5	337.4	340.1	340.8	342.1	338.7	340.5	340.8	340.7	342.0	341.6	339.3
2008	331.9	330.9	329.1	331.1	331.5	333.7	331.1	332.6	331.1	329.0	326.6	325.5	330.3
2009	311.0	309.4	308.9	307.5	307.2	306.1	305.1	305.6	306.5	305.9	306.6	307.0	307.2
2010	297.8	297.6	300.1	303.8	304.4	304.9	304.5	305.8	307.3	307.5	309.4	309.5	304.4
2011	301.6	302.2	304.5	309.3	309.7	309.6	308.7	309.9	312.3	312.6	314.3	315.7	309.2
2012	308.4	309.4	311.6	313.7	314.5	316.8	314.5	314.6	314.4	314.3	316.2	316.3	313.7
2013	307.4	308.4	310.1	312.8	315.7	316.6	314.8	316.0	314.8	312.5	314.3	312.2	313.0
Goods Producing													
2002	81.4	81.6	81.1	81.7	81.9	82.7	81.6	82.3	81.4	80.8	80.3	79.9	81.4
2003	77.9	76.5	76.6	77.7	78.3	78.8	76.6	77.8	76.9	76.7	76.4	76.0	77.2
2004	73.7	73.2	73.6	74.2	74.6	75.4	74.8	75.5	74.9	74.5	73.8	73.8	74.3
2005	71.4	71.1	71.3	72.7	72.9	74.1	73.4	74.1	73.8	73.2	72.5	71.9	72.7
2006	69.4	69.7	70.5	71.1	71.4	72.3	70.1	71.0	70.4	69.7	69.2	69.3	70.3
2007	63.8	65.6	66.2	66.9	67.3	68.3	67.0	68.0	67.4	66.5	66.6	65.9	66.6
2008	63.5	62.9	60.5	60.5	61.1	63.9	63.3	64.0	62.5	61.8	60.0	58.5	61.9
2009	53.3	52.4	51.7	50.9	50.6	50.1	50.0	50.4	50.0	50.0	49.4	49.4	50.7
2010	47.3	47.0	47.6	48.8	49.6	50.2	50.7	51.2	51.0	50.7	50.7	50.5	49.6
2011	49.3	49.3	50.1	50.7	51.4	52.1	52.5	52.7	52.7	52.7	52.6	52.7	51.6
2012	51.4	51.3	51.8	52.1	52.7	53.4	53.2	53.2	53.2	52.9	52.9	52.9	52.6
2013	51.4	51.5	52.0	52.1	53.0	53.6	53.3	53.7	53.3	53.1	53.0	52.9	52.7
Service-Providing													
2002	336.7	338.8	340.7	339.7	340.3	339.4	335.7	336.0	339.8	339.8	342.0	341.5	339.2
2003	333.6	334.1	336.6	339.1	338.9	339.2	336.2	336.3	339.2	341.4	342.4	342.9	338.3
2004	332.3	333.6	335.5	339.1	338.9	339.2	335.4	336.3	338.9	339.7	340.4	340.6	337.5
2005	332.7	334.5	336.7	339.4	339.4	337.4	333.6	334.8	338.9	339.1	340.5	341.1	337.3
2006	332.5	334.7	337.4	339.0	340.8	339.7	334.4	335.2	337.9	338.8	340.9	341.9	337.8
2007	332.8	333.7	336.2	338.0	339.1	338.7	333.4	334.2	337.3	339.2	339.5	338.8	336.7
2008	331.2	332.5	333.2	335.3	336.2	334.0	329.4	330.2	332.8	332.5	332.3	331.6	332.6
2009	322.2	322.1	322.7	322.4	323.9	322.0	317.6	317.7	321.9	322.7	323.8	322.9	321.8
2010	315.8	316.6	319.0	321.9	323.5	321.5	316.4	317.5	321.5	323.6	325.3	325.5	320.7
2011	317.7	319.2	321.1	325.4	326.0	323.6	318.6	319.7	324.7	325.8	327.7	327.5	323.1
2012	320.8	323.4	325.2	327.2	327.7	328.5	321.7	322.5	325.5	326.4	328.3	327.9	325.4
2013	318.4	321.2	322.6	325.1	327.9	326.2	321.8	323.2	325.4	323.9	326.0	323.5	323.8
Mining, Logging, and Construction													
2002	14.1	14.1	14.4	14.9	15.3	15.8	16.2	16.2	15.8	15.9	15.4	15.0	15.3
2003	13.8	13.3	13.7	14.7	15.3	15.8	16.1	16.3	15.9	16.1	15.9	15.6	15.2
2004	14.5	14.1	14.5	15.2	15.7	16.3	16.8	16.5	16.2	16.0	15.7	15.5	15.6
2005	14.0	13.7	14.2	15.2	15.7	16.3	16.6	16.3	16.1	15.7	15.6	15.0	15.4
2006	14.1	14.0	14.4	15.0	15.4	16.1	16.2	16.2	15.7	15.1	14.8	14.5	15.1
2007	13.4	12.8	13.5	14.5	15.2	15.9	15.9	15.7	15.2	14.9	15.0	14.3	14.7
2008	13.0	12.8	12.9	13.6	14.3	14.5	14.7	14.5	14.0	13.7	13.1	12.5	13.6
2009	11.2	11.1	11.3	11.4	11.9	12.2	12.5	12.2	11.8	11.8	11.5	11.2	11.7
2010	10.0	9.6	10.1	10.8	11.1	11.5	11.8	11.8	11.5	11.3	11.2	10.7	11.0
2011	9.8	9.7	10.1	10.7	11.4	11.8	12.2	12.2	12.1	11.8	11.7	11.4	11.2
2012	10.7	10.5	10.8	11.2	11.7	11.9	11.8	11.7	11.7	11.5	11.4	11.2	11.3
2013	10.3	10.4	10.9	11.1	11.8	12.1	11.9	12.0	11.8	11.6	11.7	11.2	11.4
Manufacturing													
2002	67.3	67.5	66.7	66.8	66.6	66.9	65.4	66.1	65.6	64.9	64.9	64.9	66.1
2003	64.1	63.2	62.9	63.0	63.0	63.0	60.5	61.5	61.0	60.6	60.5	60.4	62.0
2004	59.2	59.1	59.1	59.0	58.9	59.1	58.0	59.0	58.7	58.5	58.1	58.3	58.8
2005	57.4	57.4	57.1	57.5	57.2	57.8	56.8	57.8	57.7	57.5	56.9	56.9	57.3
2006	55.3	55.7	56.1	56.1	56.1	56.2	53.9	54.8	54.7	54.6	54.4	54.8	55.2
2007	50.4	52.8	52.7	52.4	52.1	52.4	51.1	52.3	52.2	51.6	51.6	51.6	51.9
2008	50.5	50.1	47.6	46.9	46.8	49.4	48.6	49.5	48.5	48.1	46.9	46.0	48.2
2009	42.1	41.3	40.4	39.5	38.7	37.9	37.5	38.2	38.2	38.2	37.9	38.2	39.0
2010	37.3	37.4	37.5	38.0	38.5	38.7	38.9	39.4	39.5	39.4	39.5	39.8	38.7
2011	39.5	39.6	40.0	40.0	40.0	40.3	40.3	40.5	40.6	40.9	40.9	41.3	40.3
2012	40.7	40.8	41.0	40.9	41.0	41.5	41.4	41.5	41.5	41.4	41.5	41.7	41.2
2013	41.1	41.1	41.1	41.0	41.2	41.5	41.4	41.7	41.5	41.5	41.3	41.7	41.3

Employment by Industry: Dayton, OH, Selected Years, 2002–2013—*Continued*

(Numbers in thousands, not seasonally adjusted)

Industry and year	January	February	March	April	May	June	July	August	September	October	November	December	Annual average
Trade, Transportation, and Utilities													
2002	75.9	75.2	75.4	74.8	75.1	75.5	74.8	74.2	74.0	73.6	75.2	76.0	75.0
2003	72.7	71.5	71.9	72.6	72.8	72.4	72.0	72.1	72.2	72.7	74.1	74.7	72.6
2004	70.4	69.9	70.4	71.3	71.6	72.0	71.5	71.4	71.5	72.2	73.3	73.9	71.6
2005	70.3	70.2	70.8	71.5	71.5	71.5	71.0	70.9	70.7	70.8	72.2	73.1	71.2
2006	69.6	69.1	69.8	69.9	70.6	70.4	69.7	69.9	69.0	69.2	70.7	71.5	70.0
2007	68.1	67.3	68.1	68.7	69.0	69.0	68.9	68.5	68.4	68.6	70.0	70.6	68.8
2008	67.3	66.4	66.6	67.0	67.2	67.5	66.7	66.9	66.5	66.1	66.7	67.5	66.9
2009	63.9	63.1	63.2	63.1	63.5	63.3	62.7	62.6	62.3	62.4	63.5	64.2	63.2
2010	61.1	60.5	61.0	61.5	61.7	61.9	61.3	61.5	61.3	62.0	63.7	64.7	61.9
2011	61.8	61.0	61.5	62.4	62.8	62.9	62.7	63.0	63.0	63.9	65.7	66.7	63.1
2012	63.6	63.2	64.0	64.1	64.6	64.6	64.3	64.3	64.4	65.0	66.7	67.2	64.7
2013	64.0	63.6	64.0	64.3	65.0	65.0	65.0	65.0	64.9	65.3	66.2	66.7	64.9
Wholesale Trade													
2002	15.3	15.4	15.3	15.3	15.2	15.1	15.2	15.0	15.1	15.3	15.2	15.2	15.2
2003	14.8	14.7	14.7	14.6	14.6	14.6	14.6	14.6	14.5	14.4	14.5	14.4	14.6
2004	14.1	14.0	14.1	14.2	14.3	14.4	14.5	14.4	14.4	14.5	14.4	14.4	14.3
2005	14.0	14.1	14.1	14.2	14.2	14.3	14.3	14.2	14.1	14.1	14.0	14.1	14.1
2006	13.8	13.8	13.9	13.9	14.1	14.1	14.1	14.0	14.0	14.0	14.0	14.1	14.0
2007	13.9	13.9	14.0	14.0	14.0	14.1	14.2	14.1	14.0	14.1	14.0	14.1	14.0
2008	14.0	13.9	14.0	14.0	14.0	13.9	13.8	13.7	13.6	13.4	13.3	13.2	13.7
2009	13.1	13.0	12.9	12.8	12.6	12.6	12.5	12.4	12.2	12.0	12.0	12.1	12.5
2010	12.0	12.0	12.0	12.0	12.0	12.1	12.1	12.1	12.0	12.0	12.0	12.1	12.0
2011	12.2	12.2	12.3	12.4	12.5	12.5	12.7	12.7	12.7	12.9	12.8	12.9	12.6
2012	12.9	13.1	13.2	12.9	13.0	13.0	13.2	13.2	13.1	13.2	13.1	13.2	13.1
2013	13.0	12.9	12.9	12.9	13.0	13.1	13.0	12.9	12.9	12.9	12.9	12.9	12.9
Retail Trade													
2002	47.1	46.4	46.8	46.3	46.6	47.0	46.3	46.0	45.8	45.5	47.0	47.9	46.6
2003	45.4	44.4	45.0	45.7	45.8	45.5	45.2	45.4	45.6	45.8	47.1	47.7	45.7
2004	44.6	44.0	44.4	45.1	45.2	45.3	44.8	44.7	44.8	45.2	46.3	46.9	45.1
2005	44.1	43.8	44.3	45.0	44.9	44.7	44.0	43.9	43.8	44.0	45.3	46.0	44.5
2006	43.3	42.6	43.1	43.0	43.4	43.1	42.7	42.9	42.8	43.1	44.6	45.2	43.3
2007	42.6	41.8	42.4	43.0	43.2	43.0	42.8	42.5	42.5	42.7	44.2	44.6	42.9
2008	42.0	41.2	41.5	41.9	41.9	42.0	41.4	41.5	41.3	41.2	41.9	42.7	41.7
2009	39.9	39.2	39.5	39.8	40.4	40.2	39.6	39.6	39.4	39.6	40.6	41.1	39.9
2010	38.7	38.1	38.6	39.0	39.2	39.2	38.7	38.8	38.6	39.1	40.6	41.1	39.1
2011	38.8	38.1	38.5	39.1	39.3	39.4	39.0	39.2	39.1	40.0	41.7	42.3	39.5
2012	39.7	39.0	39.7	40.0	40.3	40.1	39.7	39.7	39.7	40.2	41.8	41.9	40.2
2013	39.6	39.1	39.6	40.0	40.5	40.3	40.2	40.2	40.0	40.4	41.1	41.5	40.2
Transportation and Utilities													
2002	13.5	13.4	13.3	13.2	13.3	13.4	13.3	13.2	13.1	12.8	13.0	12.9	13.2
2003	12.5	12.4	12.2	12.3	12.4	12.3	12.2	12.2	12.2	12.4	12.5	12.6	12.4
2004	11.7	11.9	11.9	12.0	12.1	12.3	12.2	12.3	12.3	12.5	12.6	12.6	12.2
2005	12.2	12.3	12.4	12.3	12.4	12.5	12.7	12.8	12.8	12.7	12.9	13.0	12.6
2006	12.5	12.7	12.8	13.0	13.1	13.2	12.9	13.0	12.2	12.1	12.1	12.2	12.7
2007	11.6	11.6	11.7	11.7	11.8	11.9	11.9	11.9	11.9	11.8	11.8	11.9	11.8
2008	11.3	11.3	11.1	11.1	11.3	11.6	11.5	11.7	11.6	11.5	11.5	11.6	11.4
2009	10.9	10.9	10.8	10.5	10.5	10.5	10.6	10.6	10.7	10.8	10.9	11.0	10.7
2010	10.4	10.4	10.4	10.5	10.5	10.6	10.5	10.6	10.7	10.9	11.1	11.5	10.7
2011	10.8	10.7	10.7	10.9	11.0	11.0	11.0	11.1	11.2	11.0	11.2	11.5	11.0
2012	11.0	11.1	11.1	11.2	11.3	11.5	11.4	11.4	11.6	11.6	11.8	12.1	11.4
2013	11.4	11.6	11.5	11.4	11.5	11.6	11.8	11.9	12.0	12.0	12.2	12.3	11.8
Information													
2002	12.8	12.7	12.7	12.6	12.6	12.6	12.6	12.7	12.7	12.7	12.6	12.6	12.7
2003	12.8	12.7	12.7	12.6	12.5	12.6	12.6	12.5	12.3	12.4	12.4	12.4	12.5
2004	12.2	12.0	12.0	12.1	12.0	12.3	12.4	12.5	12.3	12.3	12.4	12.4	12.2
2005	12.3	12.2	12.2	12.2	12.2	12.3	12.2	12.0	11.8	11.7	11.7	11.8	12.1
2006	11.7	11.7	11.7	11.7	11.7	11.8	11.9	12.0	11.9	12.0	12.0	12.1	11.9
2007	12.1	12.1	12.0	12.1	12.2	12.2	12.1	12.1	12.0	12.0	12.1	12.1	12.1
2008	12.2	12.1	12.1	12.1	12.0	11.9	12.2	12.1	11.7	11.6	11.6	11.5	11.9
2009	11.4	11.4	11.2	11.0	11.0	10.9	10.8	10.8	10.7	10.7	10.7	10.8	11.0
2010	10.7	10.7	10.7	10.5	10.4	10.4	10.3	10.2	10.2	10.0	9.9	9.9	10.3
2011	9.8	9.9	9.8	9.8	9.8	9.8	9.8	9.7	9.7	9.5	9.4	9.4	9.7
2012	9.2	9.2	9.0	9.0	8.9	9.0	9.0	8.9	8.8	8.7	8.8	8.8	8.9
2013	8.8	8.8	8.8	8.8	8.7	8.8	8.8	8.8	8.6	8.5	8.5	8.5	8.7
Financial Activities													
2002	18.0	18.1	18.2	18.3	18.3	18.4	18.5	18.6	18.5	18.4	18.4	18.4	18.3
2003	18.4	18.5	18.6	18.7	18.9	19.1	19.1	19.1	18.9	18.8	18.8	18.8	18.8
2004	18.6	18.6	18.8	18.9	19.1	19.2	19.3	19.3	19.1	19.2	19.1	19.2	19.0
2005	18.8	18.9	18.8	19.1	19.2	19.4	19.5	19.6	19.6	19.7	19.7	19.8	19.3
2006	19.7	19.9	20.0	20.1	20.1	20.2	20.2	20.2	20.1	20.2	20.2	20.2	20.1
2007	19.9	20.0	20.0	20.1	20.1	19.9	19.8	19.7	19.4	19.3	19.2	19.1	19.7
2008	19.0	18.7	18.6	18.5	18.4	18.3	18.1	18.0	17.7	17.5	17.4	17.4	18.1
2009	17.3	17.1	16.9	16.9	16.9	17.0	17.0	16.8	16.6	16.7	16.7	16.6	16.9
2010	16.6	16.6	16.6	16.8	16.9	16.9	16.9	16.8	16.7	16.9	16.9	16.9	16.8
2011	16.6	16.6	16.5	16.7	16.8	16.8	16.8	16.8	16.7	16.7	16.8	16.9	16.7
2012	16.7	16.7	16.8	17.0	17.0	17.2	17.3	17.4	17.3	17.3	17.4	17.4	17.1
2013	17.1	17.1	17.1	17.2	17.5	17.4	17.4	17.4	17.3	17.3	17.3	17.2	17.3

Employment by Industry: Dayton, OH, Selected Years, 2002–2013—*Continued*

(Numbers in thousands, not seasonally adjusted)

Industry and year	January	February	March	April	May	June	July	August	September	October	November	December	Annual average
Professional and Business Services													
2002	53.1	53.1	53.6	53.3	53.0	52.9	52.7	52.6	52.7	51.8	52.0	51.3	52.7
2003	52.7	52.3	52.9	54.0	53.9	54.2	54.6	54.8	54.3	54.7	54.4	54.3	53.9
2004	52.5	52.4	52.5	53.6	53.7	54.0	53.4	53.5	54.1	53.3	52.9	52.8	53.2
2005	52.0	51.6	52.0	52.2	52.1	52.0	51.8	52.4	52.4	53.0	52.7	52.9	52.3
2006	51.2	51.1	51.6	52.3	52.7	53.1	52.7	52.9	52.6	52.4	52.4	52.6	52.3
2007	51.6	51.8	52.0	52.2	52.1	52.7	52.3	52.5	52.4	52.9	52.6	52.6	52.3
2008	51.2	51.5	51.6	51.8	51.5	51.7	51.1	50.9	50.4	49.9	48.9	48.8	50.8
2009	46.7	45.9	45.5	45.4	45.0	45.3	45.5	45.6	45.4	45.3	45.4	45.4	45.5
2010	44.0	44.3	44.5	45.8	45.8	46.4	46.3	47.1	46.7	46.6	46.9	46.6	45.9
2011	46.1	46.2	46.6	47.4	47.0	47.2	47.4	47.9	47.9	47.7	47.8	48.1	47.3
2012	47.4	47.6	47.7	48.1	47.9	48.4	48.5	48.2	47.9	48.2	47.9	47.8	48.0
2013	46.8	46.9	46.6	47.8	47.9	48.1	48.2	48.2	47.8	47.8	47.9	46.5	47.5
Education and Health Services													
2002	60.2	61.2	61.4	61.3	59.9	58.6	58.3	58.8	61.9	63.0	63.4	63.2	60.9
2003	61.2	62.0	62.4	62.5	60.1	59.4	59.2	59.4	62.8	63.8	64.1	63.6	61.7
2004	62.3	63.1	63.0	63.7	61.1	60.7	60.5	60.9	62.6	64.0	63.9	64.0	62.5
2005	63.4	64.1	64.5	64.8	63.3	61.9	61.7	61.9	65.2	65.7	66.1	66.1	64.1
2006	64.7	65.5	65.8	65.7	64.5	62.7	61.9	62.5	65.8	66.6	67.1	66.9	65.0
2007	65.5	66.2	66.5	66.5	65.6	64.7	64.0	64.8	67.5	68.4	68.7	68.9	66.4
2008	67.8	68.5	68.6	68.5	67.5	66.4	66.0	66.7	69.3	69.9	70.2	70.3	68.3
2009	68.7	69.7	69.8	69.0	68.0	66.8	66.4	66.7	69.6	70.1	70.3	70.1	68.8
2010	68.9	69.5	69.8	69.2	68.1	66.5	66.4	66.5	69.5	70.5	70.7	70.8	68.9
2011	69.4	70.3	70.5	71.0	69.7	67.8	66.9	67.2	70.7	71.3	71.3	71.5	69.8
2012	70.3	71.3	71.2	71.0	70.0	69.7	68.4	68.8	70.2	70.6	71.0	70.7	70.3
2013	69.1	70.0	70.2	70.3	69.9	69.1	68.2	68.7	70.1	70.2	71.4	70.7	69.8
Leisure and Hospitality													
2002	33.7	33.8	34.6	35.4	36.4	37.0	37.0	37.2	36.6	35.8	35.4	35.3	35.7
2003	34.2	34.3	35.2	36.0	37.2	38.1	38.4	38.3	37.4	36.3	36.0	36.3	36.5
2004	35.3	35.5	36.3	37.0	38.0	38.2	38.5	38.8	38.1	36.5	36.4	36.2	37.1
2005	35.2	35.4	36.3	37.4	38.1	38.7	38.2	38.6	38.0	36.7	36.6	36.6	37.2
2006	35.6	35.8	36.8	37.4	38.3	39.0	38.7	38.8	38.3	36.9	37.0	37.1	37.5
2007	35.7	35.7	36.5	37.5	38.4	39.0	38.6	38.9	37.8	37.1	36.9	36.6	37.4
2008	35.4	35.3	35.6	37.2	38.2	38.5	38.2	38.5	37.6	36.9	36.5	36.2	37.0
2009	34.8	34.9	35.7	36.3	37.2	37.8	37.8	37.7	36.9	35.8	35.6	35.4	36.3
2010	34.2	34.1	34.8	36.1	36.8	37.4	37.5	37.5	36.9	35.9	35.7	35.4	36.0
2011	34.1	34.3	34.9	36.5	37.3	38.0	37.7	37.8	36.9	36.3	36.1	35.8	36.3
2012	35.2	35.4	36.4	37.5	38.3	39.2	38.8	38.8	37.8	36.7	36.6	36.6	37.3
2013	35.5	35.6	36.4	37.2	38.4	39.2	38.8	39.0	37.8	35.3	35.0	34.7	36.9
Other Services													
2002	16.2	16.5	16.7	16.5	16.6	16.6	16.8	17.4	16.7	16.6	16.7	16.7	16.7
2003	16.4	16.5	16.8	16.8	16.8	17.1	17.1	17.5	16.9	16.8	16.6	16.7	16.8
2004	16.3	16.5	16.7	16.8	16.9	16.9	16.9	17.3	16.8	16.6	16.6	16.5	16.7
2005	16.4	16.4	16.6	16.7	16.8	16.9	16.6	17.1	16.6	16.3	16.2	16.2	16.6
2006	16.0	16.1	16.2	16.5	16.5	16.7	16.4	16.3	16.4	16.1	16.1	16.1	16.3
2007	15.8	15.8	16.1	16.1	16.1	16.3	16.0	16.0	15.9	15.9	15.9	15.8	16.0
2008	15.5	15.5	15.5	15.5	15.6	15.5	15.5	15.5	15.4	15.3	15.3	15.3	15.5
2009	14.9	14.9	14.9	14.9	15.0	14.9	14.9	15.0	15.0	14.9	15.0	15.1	15.0
2010	15.0	14.9	15.1	15.1	15.1	15.2	15.1	15.0	15.0	14.9	14.9	14.7	15.0
2011	14.5	14.6	14.6	14.8	14.9	15.0	14.9	14.8	14.7	14.5	14.6	14.6	14.7
2012	14.6	14.7	14.7	14.9	15.1	15.3	15.0	15.0	14.8	14.9	14.9	14.9	14.9
2013	14.7	14.9	15.0	15.1	15.3	15.4	15.1	15.2	15.0	15.0	15.0	15.0	15.1
Government													
2002	66.8	68.2	68.1	67.5	68.4	67.8	65.0	64.5	66.7	67.9	68.3	68.0	67.3
2003	65.2	66.3	66.1	65.9	66.7	66.3	63.2	62.6	64.4	65.9	66.0	66.1	65.4
2004	64.7	65.6	65.8	65.7	66.5	65.9	62.9	62.6	64.4	65.6	65.8	65.6	65.1
2005	64.3	65.7	65.5	65.5	66.2	64.7	62.6	62.3	64.6	65.2	65.3	64.6	64.7
2006	64.0	65.5	65.5	65.4	66.4	65.8	62.9	62.6	63.8	65.4	65.4	65.4	64.8
2007	64.1	64.8	65.0	64.8	65.6	64.9	61.7	61.7	63.9	65.0	64.1	63.1	64.1
2008	62.8	64.5	64.6	64.7	65.8	64.2	61.6	61.6	64.2	65.3	65.7	64.6	64.1
2009	64.5	65.1	65.5	65.8	67.3	66.0	62.5	62.5	65.4	66.8	66.6	65.3	65.3
2010	65.3	66.0	66.5	66.9	68.7	66.8	62.6	62.9	65.2	66.8	66.6	66.5	65.9
2011	65.4	66.3	66.7	66.8	67.7	66.1	62.4	62.5	65.1	65.9	66.0	64.5	65.5
2012	63.8	65.3	65.4	65.6	65.9	65.1	60.4	61.1	64.3	65.0	65.0	64.5	64.3
2013	62.4	64.3	64.5	64.4	65.2	63.2	60.3	60.9	63.9	64.5	64.7	64.2	63.5

Employment by Industry: Denver-Aurora-Broomfield, CO, Selected Years, 2002–2013

(Numbers in thousands, not seasonally adjusted)

Industry and year	January	February	March	April	May	June	July	August	September	October	November	December	Annual average
Total Nonfarm													
2002	1,152.5	1,155.8	1,159.9	1,170.2	1,181.1	1,188.8	1,177.7	1,182.1	1,175.0	1,172.1	1,175.3	1,177.4	1,172.3
2003	1,148.6	1,148.1	1,147.2	1,151.4	1,160.4	1,168.5	1,160.7	1,164.9	1,159.6	1,161.1	1,161.6	1,165.0	1,158.1
2004	1,135.2	1,138.3	1,148.1	1,162.3	1,170.2	1,180.8	1,175.3	1,177.3	1,176.0	1,177.6	1,180.8	1,186.2	1,167.3
2005	1,154.5	1,161.8	1,170.6	1,180.2	1,190.2	1,201.5	1,198.9	1,199.0	1,203.6	1,202.6	1,206.2	1,212.1	1,190.1
2006	1,182.1	1,187.7	1,196.4	1,204.2	1,217.1	1,231.8	1,222.3	1,225.8	1,225.3	1,225.3	1,229.6	1,234.1	1,215.1
2007	1,202.6	1,209.0	1,221.4	1,230.3	1,244.0	1,257.7	1,249.5	1,252.7	1,252.9	1,254.2	1,258.6	1,261.1	1,241.2
2008	1,231.3	1,237.3	1,244.5	1,252.3	1,261.9	1,271.6	1,261.8	1,265.9	1,259.4	1,256.2	1,251.2	1,244.5	1,253.2
2009	1,206.6	1,198.4	1,197.4	1,199.1	1,206.8	1,210.6	1,199.9	1,197.9	1,194.7	1,197.1	1,195.7	1,193.8	1,199.8
2010	1,162.1	1,167.2	1,174.6	1,185.9	1,199.7	1,206.8	1,202.5	1,203.1	1,199.7	1,206.4	1,207.9	1,207.3	1,193.6
2011	1,180.6	1,184.1	1,191.7	1,208.0	1,217.6	1,226.8	1,219.2	1,224.1	1,224.8	1,226.3	1,231.2	1,233.0	1,214.0
2012	1,207.6	1,213.0	1,224.6	1,236.4	1,248.8	1,262.6	1,256.4	1,258.6	1,259.6	1,269.5	1,275.9	1,276.7	1,249.1
2013	1,250.7	1,259.7	1,269.9	1,281.6	1,294.2	1,306.7	1,302.2	1,310.2	1,308.8	1,315.6	1,315.5	1,313.7	1,294.1
Total Private													
2002	993.0	993.1	995.8	1,005.8	1,015.4	1,024.2	1,018.8	1,021.7	1,010.7	1,006.0	1,008.4	1,010.9	1,008.7
2003	986.8	983.1	981.7	986.0	993.0	1,002.6	1,001.7	1,005.0	995.4	996.8	997.0	1,001.3	994.2
2004	976.1	975.7	984.2	997.0	1,004.3	1,016.0	1,017.4	1,019.1	1,011.8	1,012.1	1,014.6	1,020.2	1,004.0
2005	994.1	997.3	1,005.7	1,013.7	1,023.0	1,035.9	1,039.3	1,040.3	1,037.4	1,035.9	1,039.1	1,045.1	1,025.6
2006	1,019.5	1,021.2	1,028.8	1,037.1	1,048.4	1,063.5	1,061.2	1,063.9	1,057.5	1,057.3	1,060.7	1,064.9	1,048.7
2007	1,038.7	1,040.0	1,051.1	1,059.6	1,072.2	1,086.9	1,086.1	1,088.4	1,081.2	1,081.7	1,085.2	1,088.1	1,071.6
2008	1,063.4	1,065.0	1,070.9	1,078.1	1,085.6	1,097.1	1,094.1	1,095.4	1,084.0	1,078.8	1,072.9	1,067.2	1,079.4
2009	1,033.8	1,022.5	1,020.1	1,020.8	1,026.5	1,032.8	1,030.9	1,027.8	1,017.5	1,017.5	1,016.8	1,016.1	1,023.6
2010	990.2	989.6	995.8	1,006.1	1,014.5	1,026.6	1,029.7	1,031.7	1,021.1	1,025.3	1,026.4	1,027.8	1,015.4
2011	1,006.7	1,004.8	1,011.7	1,026.6	1,034.7	1,046.3	1,047.6	1,052.7	1,046.2	1,046.1	1,050.7	1,053.5	1,035.6
2012	1,033.7	1,033.8	1,043.7	1,054.6	1,065.4	1,080.1	1,083.0	1,086.2	1,079.7	1,088.0	1,092.7	1,095.1	1,069.7
2013	1,074.5	1,077.7	1,086.7	1,096.7	1,108.2	1,122.0	1,125.6	1,132.0	1,122.0	1,125.3	1,125.5	1,125.5	1,110.1
Goods Producing													
2002	163.3	164.0	165.9	167.5	169.9	171.4	171.0	170.6	167.7	166.4	163.6	161.1	166.9
2003	157.9	156.7	156.1	156.5	158.4	160.6	160.0	159.5	157.5	157.4	155.7	154.1	157.5
2004	151.0	150.7	153.2	155.6	157.2	160.1	161.1	161.2	160.1	160.8	159.7	158.5	157.4
2005	154.3	155.7	158.1	158.9	160.8	164.6	166.8	167.3	166.8	166.2	165.6	164.3	162.5
2006	161.4	162.6	164.8	165.8	167.9	171.0	170.1	169.8	169.0	167.6	165.8	163.9	166.6
2007	157.3	158.0	161.1	162.5	164.7	168.0	168.6	168.7	167.2	167.6	166.2	163.3	164.4
2008	159.7	159.7	160.9	161.5	163.0	165.6	164.9	165.0	162.8	161.7	158.1	153.9	161.4
2009	146.7	143.2	141.4	140.0	140.0	141.5	141.3	139.7	137.9	136.9	135.6	132.7	139.7
2010	127.8	127.2	128.0	129.9	131.1	133.3	134.4	133.8	133.2	132.3	131.1	130.2	130.9
2011	126.1	125.4	127.4	130.6	131.0	133.9	134.9	135.5	134.8	134.7	134.1	132.8	131.8
2012	130.0	130.0	131.7	133.5	135.5	138.6	139.4	139.9	139.5	140.7	140.2	139.3	136.5
2013	136.6	137.3	139.2	140.3	143.3	146.3	147.2	148.4	147.3	148.0	147.4	144.8	143.8
Service-Providing													
2002	989.2	991.8	994.0	1,002.7	1,011.2	1,017.4	1,006.7	1,011.5	1,007.3	1,005.7	1,011.7	1,016.3	1,005.5
2003	990.7	991.4	991.1	994.9	1,002.0	1,007.9	1,000.7	1,005.4	1,002.1	1,003.7	1,005.9	1,010.9	1,000.6
2004	984.2	987.6	994.9	1,006.7	1,013.0	1,020.7	1,014.2	1,016.1	1,015.9	1,016.8	1,021.1	1,027.7	1,009.9
2005	1,000.2	1,006.1	1,012.5	1,021.3	1,029.4	1,036.9	1,032.1	1,031.7	1,036.8	1,036.4	1,040.6	1,047.8	1,027.7
2006	1,020.7	1,025.1	1,031.6	1,038.4	1,049.2	1,060.8	1,052.2	1,056.0	1,056.3	1,057.7	1,063.8	1,070.2	1,048.5
2007	1,045.3	1,051.0	1,060.3	1,067.8	1,079.3	1,089.7	1,080.9	1,084.0	1,085.7	1,086.6	1,092.4	1,097.8	1,076.7
2008	1,071.6	1,077.6	1,083.6	1,090.8	1,098.9	1,106.0	1,096.9	1,100.9	1,096.6	1,094.5	1,093.1	1,090.6	1,091.8
2009	1,059.9	1,055.2	1,056.0	1,059.1	1,066.8	1,069.1	1,058.6	1,058.2	1,056.8	1,060.2	1,060.1	1,061.1	1,060.1
2010	1,034.3	1,040.0	1,046.6	1,056.0	1,068.6	1,073.5	1,068.1	1,069.3	1,067.5	1,074.1	1,076.8	1,077.1	1,062.7
2011	1,054.5	1,058.7	1,064.3	1,077.4	1,086.6	1,092.9	1,084.3	1,088.6	1,090.0	1,091.6	1,097.1	1,100.2	1,082.2
2012	1,077.6	1,083.0	1,092.9	1,102.9	1,113.3	1,124.0	1,117.0	1,118.7	1,120.1	1,128.8	1,135.7	1,137.4	1,112.6
2013	1,114.1	1,122.4	1,130.7	1,141.3	1,150.9	1,160.4	1,155.0	1,161.8	1,161.5	1,167.6	1,168.1	1,168.9	1,150.2
Mining, Logging, and Construction													
2002	88.3	89.2	91.1	93.2	95.5	96.9	96.8	96.6	94.1	92.9	90.8	88.5	92.8
2003	85.4	84.4	84.3	84.9	86.9	89.0	88.8	88.5	86.8	86.8	85.0	83.4	86.2
2004	80.6	80.1	82.3	84.3	85.8	88.1	88.7	88.5	87.9	88.4	87.3	86.2	85.7
2005	82.8	83.9	86.1	87.0	88.8	92.3	94.1	94.7	94.4	93.6	93.2	91.9	90.2
2006	89.7	90.8	92.7	93.7	95.7	98.4	97.4	97.1	96.5	95.3	93.6	92.0	94.4
2007	86.1	87.1	90.1	91.7	93.4	96.1	96.7	96.8	95.4	95.7	94.3	91.5	92.9
2008	88.7	89.3	90.5	91.4	92.9	95.1	94.5	94.8	93.0	92.3	89.7	86.2	91.5
2009	80.7	78.5	77.3	76.4	76.9	78.5	78.4	77.2	76.0	75.1	73.8	71.2	76.7
2010	67.5	66.9	67.6	69.4	70.0	71.7	72.7	72.1	70.7	70.8	69.6	68.7	69.8
2011	64.9	64.3	66.0	68.8	68.9	71.4	72.3	72.7	72.0	72.3	71.6	70.4	69.6
2012	68.1	67.9	69.2	70.8	72.5	75.0	75.5	76.1	75.7	76.8	76.3	75.5	73.3
2013	73.3	73.9	75.4	76.7	79.6	82.1	83.1	84.3	83.6	84.0	83.0	80.7	80.0
Manufacturing													
2002	75.0	74.8	74.8	74.3	74.4	74.5	74.2	74.0	73.6	73.5	72.8	72.6	74.0
2003	72.5	72.3	71.8	71.6	71.5	71.6	71.2	71.0	70.7	70.6	70.7	70.7	71.4
2004	70.4	70.6	70.9	71.3	71.4	72.0	72.4	72.7	72.2	72.4	72.4	72.3	71.8
2005	71.5	71.8	72.0	71.9	72.0	72.3	72.7	72.6	72.4	72.6	72.4	72.4	72.2
2006	71.7	71.8	72.1	72.1	72.2	72.6	72.7	72.7	72.5	72.3	72.2	71.9	72.2
2007	71.2	70.9	71.0	70.8	71.3	71.9	71.9	71.9	71.8	71.9	71.9	71.8	71.5
2008	71.0	70.4	70.4	70.1	70.1	70.5	70.4	70.2	69.8	69.4	68.4	67.7	69.9
2009	66.0	64.7	64.1	63.6	63.1	63.0	62.9	62.5	61.9	61.8	61.8	61.5	63.1
2010	60.3	60.3	60.4	60.5	61.1	61.6	61.7	61.7	61.5	61.5	61.5	61.5	61.1
2011	61.2	61.1	61.4	61.8	62.1	62.5	62.6	62.8	62.8	62.4	62.5	62.4	62.1
2012	61.9	62.1	62.5	62.7	63.0	63.6	63.9	63.8	63.8	63.9	63.9	63.8	63.2
2013	63.3	63.4	63.8	63.6	63.7	64.2	64.1	64.1	63.7	64.0	64.4	64.1	63.9

Employment by Industry: Denver-Aurora-Broomfield, CO, Selected Years, 2002–2013—*Continued*

(Numbers in thousands, not seasonally adjusted)

Industry and year	January	February	March	April	May	June	July	August	September	October	November	December	Annual average
Trade, Transportation, and Utilities													
2002	233.5	231.1	230.7	232.5	235.5	237.6	236.7	236.8	235.0	235.7	241.6	245.2	236.0
2003	235.2	232.9	231.6	229.8	230.0	230.7	230.5	231.2	230.5	232.2	236.6	239.6	232.6
2004	229.6	227.3	228.3	229.7	231.3	232.7	233.0	233.2	231.8	233.8	238.6	242.4	232.6
2005	232.4	231.3	232.2	232.5	234.3	236.1	236.6	236.3	237.8	239.6	244.2	247.2	236.7
2006	236.6	233.5	234.3	235.3	236.8	238.8	238.4	239.0	238.6	241.4	246.8	250.8	239.2
2007	242.2	239.4	240.1	241.0	242.8	244.3	244.5	244.5	243.8	245.6	251.2	253.8	244.4
2008	245.8	243.0	244.1	244.3	245.0	246.2	245.9	245.5	243.5	243.0	244.7	246.3	244.8
2009	235.7	231.7	229.8	229.1	229.9	230.7	229.5	229.1	227.9	229.3	231.7	234.1	230.7
2010	225.0	223.9	224.0	224.9	226.5	228.2	228.8	229.2	227.7	229.6	232.9	235.3	228.0
2011	226.4	224.6	225.4	227.5	228.8	230.1	230.8	231.2	230.0	231.8	236.1	238.1	230.1
2012	231.0	229.0	229.9	231.1	232.8	235.0	235.7	235.8	235.5	238.3	243.9	246.5	235.4
2013	238.2	236.9	237.7	238.6	240.4	242.2	243.0	244.5	243.4	243.4	245.7	248.7	241.9
Wholesale Trade													
2002	65.4	65.3	65.3	65.1	65.2	65.2	64.9	64.5	64.0	63.9	63.7	63.8	64.7
2003	63.7	63.4	63.3	63.0	62.9	62.9	62.6	62.3	61.9	62.1	61.9	62.0	62.7
2004	61.3	61.5	61.9	62.0	62.1	62.4	62.2	62.2	61.9	62.0	62.1	62.3	62.0
2005	61.6	61.9	62.2	62.4	62.6	63.0	63.1	63.2	63.3	63.3	63.5	63.8	62.8
2006	63.3	63.6	64.0	64.3	64.7	65.4	65.3	65.5	65.3	65.6	65.9	66.4	64.9
2007	65.0	65.4	65.8	65.8	66.3	66.7	66.6	66.7	66.4	66.8	66.9	66.8	66.3
2008	66.5	66.7	66.8	67.0	67.2	67.4	67.4	67.1	66.8	66.4	66.1	66.0	66.8
2009	64.8	64.2	63.5	62.8	62.6	62.5	62.1	61.8	61.3	61.4	61.2	61.4	62.5
2010	60.9	60.7	60.8	60.9	61.1	61.5	61.7	61.7	61.5	61.7	61.7	61.8	61.3
2011	61.3	61.4	61.7	62.0	62.2	62.4	62.6	62.7	62.5	62.4	62.4	62.4	62.2
2012	62.0	62.2	62.6	63.0	63.2	63.7	64.0	64.1	64.0	64.3	64.3	64.7	63.5
2013	63.9	64.3	64.6	64.8	65.0	65.6	65.5	65.8	65.6	65.6	65.7	65.2	65.1
Retail Trade													
2002	121.1	118.5	118.7	119.9	121.5	123.2	122.4	122.5	121.3	121.8	127.0	129.8	122.3
2003	121.3	119.3	118.3	118.1	119.0	120.0	119.7	120.6	120.4	121.4	125.3	127.8	120.9
2004	119.8	117.3	117.7	118.5	119.7	120.5	120.7	121.2	120.3	122.3	126.9	129.7	121.2
2005	121.9	120.3	121.0	121.2	122.9	123.9	124.1	123.7	125.2	126.7	131.0	133.2	124.6
2006	124.4	121.1	121.3	122.3	123.2	123.9	123.9	124.3	124.0	126.4	131.3	133.4	125.0
2007	127.0	124.2	124.5	125.1	126.3	127.2	127.5	127.2	126.8	127.7	132.4	134.0	127.5
2008	127.7	125.3	126.2	126.3	126.7	127.6	127.3	127.7	126.7	127.1	128.8	129.6	127.3
2009	122.5	119.8	118.9	118.3	119.6	120.5	119.8	119.8	119.4	120.6	123.5	124.7	120.6
2010	118.3	117.1	117.4	118.6	120.0	121.2	121.8	122.1	120.8	122.1	125.1	126.3	120.9
2011	119.8	118.4	118.8	120.3	121.4	122.3	122.6	123.1	122.3	123.7	127.6	128.9	122.4
2012	123.2	120.9	121.6	122.3	123.8	125.1	125.2	125.2	125.0	126.2	131.1	132.4	125.2
2013	125.8	124.2	124.6	125.3	126.9	128.2	128.9	129.8	128.9	128.6	131.3	133.3	128.0
Transportation and Utilities													
2002	47.0	47.3	46.7	47.5	48.8	49.2	49.4	49.8	49.7	50.0	50.9	51.6	49.0
2003	50.2	50.2	50.0	48.7	48.1	47.8	48.2	48.3	48.2	48.7	49.4	49.8	49.0
2004	48.5	48.5	48.7	49.2	49.5	49.8	50.1	49.8	49.6	49.5	49.6	50.4	49.4
2005	48.9	49.1	49.0	48.9	48.8	49.2	49.4	49.4	49.3	49.6	49.7	50.2	49.3
2006	48.9	48.8	49.0	48.7	48.9	49.5	49.2	49.2	49.3	49.4	49.6	51.0	49.3
2007	50.2	49.8	49.8	50.1	50.2	50.4	50.4	50.6	50.6	51.1	51.9	53.0	50.7
2008	51.6	51.0	51.1	51.0	51.1	51.2	51.2	50.7	50.0	49.5	49.8	50.7	50.7
2009	48.4	47.7	47.4	48.0	47.7	47.7	47.6	47.5	47.2	47.3	47.0	48.0	47.6
2010	45.8	46.1	45.8	45.4	45.4	45.5	45.3	45.4	45.4	45.8	46.1	47.2	45.8
2011	45.3	44.8	44.9	45.2	45.2	45.4	45.6	45.4	45.2	45.7	46.1	46.8	45.5
2012	45.8	45.9	45.7	45.8	45.8	46.2	46.5	46.5	46.5	47.8	48.5	49.4	46.7
2013	48.5	48.4	48.5	48.5	48.5	48.4	48.6	48.9	48.9	49.2	48.7	50.2	48.8
Information													
2002	62.3	62.0	61.3	60.6	59.6	59.3	58.2	57.9	57.2	56.9	56.9	56.6	59.1
2003	56.1	55.9	55.4	54.7	54.5	54.2	54.0	53.8	53.5	53.2	53.3	53.2	54.3
2004	52.5	52.6	52.3	51.9	52.0	51.9	51.3	51.1	50.4	50.1	50.2	50.0	51.4
2005	49.2	49.0	48.9	48.4	48.4	48.2	47.9	47.7	47.5	47.4	47.7	47.9	48.2
2006	47.7	47.8	48.0	47.7	47.9	48.0	47.8	47.4	47.1	47.2	47.5	47.4	47.6
2007	47.0	47.2	47.2	47.9	48.1	48.5	48.3	48.0	47.5	47.5	47.7	47.6	47.7
2008	47.0	47.1	47.0	47.0	46.8	46.9	47.0	46.8	46.3	46.3	46.4	46.5	46.8
2009	45.8	45.6	45.5	45.1	44.9	44.8	44.7	44.3	44.0	43.8	43.9	43.9	44.7
2010	43.6	43.3	43.4	43.1	43.2	43.5	43.4	43.5	43.4	43.5	43.9	43.9	43.5
2011	43.6	43.6	43.3	43.5	43.5	43.5	43.3	43.3	43.1	43.1	43.2	43.1	43.3
2012	42.9	43.1	43.0	42.8	43.0	43.1	43.0	43.0	42.9	43.0	43.2	43.3	43.0
2013	43.4	43.8	43.9	43.9	44.0	44.5	44.5	44.5	44.1	43.3	43.4	43.5	43.9
Financial Activities													
2002	93.5	93.9	93.9	93.5	93.8	94.6	94.5	95.1	95.0	95.8	96.7	97.4	94.8
2003	96.5	96.8	96.9	97.5	98.0	98.7	99.1	99.5	98.9	98.5	98.1	98.6	98.1
2004	97.1	97.4	97.5	97.7	97.9	98.5	98.5	98.4	98.2	98.1	98.0	98.6	98.0
2005	97.3	97.9	98.5	98.8	99.2	99.7	100.3	100.5	100.7	100.6	101.0	101.8	99.7
2006	99.6	99.8	100.0	100.1	100.8	101.4	101.3	101.3	100.9	100.5	100.5	101.1	100.6
2007	99.4	99.9	99.9	100.0	100.1	100.5	100.4	100.0	99.1	98.8	98.7	98.8	99.6
2008	97.5	97.7	98.1	97.8	97.6	98.0	97.9	97.3	96.4	96.0	95.5	95.6	97.1
2009	93.7	93.5	93.0	93.2	93.3	93.0	92.9	92.6	92.0	92.0	91.7	92.1	92.8
2010	90.5	90.4	90.4	90.5	90.5	90.9	91.2	91.2	90.8	91.0	90.9	91.4	90.8
2011	90.2	90.1	90.1	90.2	90.3	90.9	90.9	91.1	90.8	90.6	91.1	91.7	90.7
2012	90.7	90.8	91.3	91.5	92.0	92.8	93.0	93.4	93.2	94.1	94.1	94.9	92.7
2013	93.9	94.5	94.9	95.3	95.6	96.3	96.5	96.7	96.3	96.6	96.0	95.8	95.7

Employment by Industry: Denver-Aurora-Broomfield, CO, Selected Years, 2002–2013—*Continued*

(Numbers in thousands, not seasonally adjusted)

Industry and year	January	February	March	April	May	June	July	August	September	October	November	December	Annual average
Professional and Business Services													
2002	178.9	179.8	180.3	183.5	184.6	185.3	183.6	185.4	183.3	181.2	180.1	180.3	182.2
2003	175.3	175.2	175.5	177.6	178.8	181.1	181.1	182.8	180.7	181.6	180.2	182.1	179.3
2004	176.1	177.8	179.8	184.7	184.9	187.7	188.9	189.2	188.3	187.7	187.0	188.9	185.1
2005	184.3	184.8	186.7	191.1	191.8	194.5	195.9	196.5	195.8	195.1	194.8	196.9	192.4
2006	190.2	192.2	193.8	197.0	199.6	203.5	203.4	204.7	203.9	203.8	203.3	204.6	200.0
2007	201.6	202.7	205.5	208.3	211.1	215.3	215.3	216.9	217.0	216.1	215.3	216.8	211.8
2008	211.2	213.2	213.9	218.0	218.0	220.5	219.8	221.5	219.5	217.9	216.0	214.5	217.0
2009	207.4	204.5	204.2	204.9	205.0	205.7	204.9	204.1	202.5	202.8	203.0	202.8	204.3
2010	197.1	198.0	199.9	203.4	205.0	207.3	208.2	208.6	205.5	207.3	207.3	206.5	204.5
2011	204.2	204.4	205.1	210.5	212.4	213.8	214.3	215.9	214.8	215.1	216.7	217.0	212.0
2012	212.5	213.3	216.2	220.0	222.1	225.3	226.3	227.8	226.5	229.3	229.1	228.3	223.1
2013	223.8	225.4	227.5	230.6	232.4	235.1	235.8	237.8	235.4	237.9	237.6	236.9	233.0
Education and Health Services													
2002	108.0	108.6	109.0	109.8	110.0	109.7	109.6	110.2	110.4	111.0	111.4	111.8	110.0
2003	111.3	112.2	112.3	113.1	113.1	113.1	113.0	113.1	113.4	114.1	114.4	114.6	113.1
2004	114.2	115.2	115.7	115.9	116.2	116.1	115.6	116.2	117.0	117.9	118.3	118.5	116.4
2005	117.0	118.6	119.1	119.2	119.8	119.6	118.8	119.3	119.7	119.9	120.6	120.9	119.4
2006	120.3	121.7	122.0	122.7	123.1	123.0	122.3	122.9	123.5	124.7	125.1	125.5	123.1
2007	124.5	126.0	126.8	127.2	127.9	127.8	127.3	127.9	128.5	129.6	130.7	131.5	128.0
2008	130.0	131.8	132.0	132.5	133.4	133.3	132.8	133.8	134.5	136.1	137.1	136.8	133.7
2009	135.7	136.8	136.9	137.3	137.7	137.7	137.5	137.9	138.1	139.5	140.3	140.7	138.0
2010	139.6	140.8	141.7	142.1	142.7	142.7	142.1	143.0	143.4	144.5	145.4	145.7	142.8
2011	144.8	145.9	146.4	147.0	147.5	147.4	146.9	148.4	148.8	150.0	150.5	151.9	148.0
2012	150.5	152.0	152.4	152.8	153.0	152.8	152.7	153.2	153.7	155.2	156.0	156.9	153.4
2013	155.8	157.2	157.7	159.0	159.1	158.7	159.0	160.2	160.9	161.7	163.9	163.6	159.7
Leisure and Hospitality													
2002	109.8	110.0	110.8	114.3	117.8	121.6	120.4	120.9	118.0	115.2	114.2	114.6	115.6
2003	110.4	109.7	110.3	112.9	116.1	119.4	119.4	120.6	117.2	116.0	114.8	115.0	115.2
2004	111.4	110.8	113.2	117.1	120.0	123.5	123.4	124.0	120.5	118.2	117.5	117.9	118.1
2005	114.2	114.9	116.9	119.5	123.3	127.3	127.4	127.1	123.9	122.1	120.5	121.1	121.5
2006	118.0	118.1	120.0	122.4	126.0	130.7	131.2	132.0	128.1	125.9	125.5	125.2	125.3
2007	120.4	120.5	123.7	125.8	130.4	134.8	134.3	134.9	130.9	129.2	128.2	128.8	128.5
2008	124.4	124.6	126.7	129.1	133.5	137.9	136.8	136.4	132.1	129.1	126.8	125.8	130.3
2009	120.9	119.9	121.9	124.2	128.2	131.6	132.2	132.3	127.8	125.9	123.5	122.7	125.9
2010	119.5	119.1	121.4	125.3	128.2	132.9	133.6	134.3	130.6	129.8	127.4	127.4	127.5
2011	124.0	123.5	126.4	129.2	132.7	137.7	137.6	138.1	135.2	132.4	130.6	130.3	131.5
2012	127.5	127.0	130.2	133.7	137.6	142.3	142.7	142.8	138.4	137.2	136.2	136.0	136.0
2013	132.7	132.9	135.7	138.9	142.6	147.8	148.5	148.8	144.0	144.0	140.7	140.9	141.5
Other Services													
2002	43.7	43.7	43.9	44.1	44.2	44.7	44.8	44.8	44.1	43.8	43.9	43.9	44.1
2003	44.1	43.7	43.6	43.9	44.1	44.8	44.6	44.5	43.7	43.8	43.9	44.1	44.1
2004	44.2	43.9	44.2	44.4	44.8	45.5	45.6	45.8	45.5	45.5	45.3	45.4	45.0
2005	45.4	45.1	45.3	45.3	45.4	45.9	45.6	45.6	45.2	45.0	44.7	45.0	45.3
2006	45.7	45.5	45.9	46.1	46.3	47.1	46.7	46.8	46.4	46.2	46.2	46.4	46.3
2007	46.3	46.3	46.8	46.9	47.1	47.7	47.4	47.5	47.2	47.3	47.2	47.5	47.1
2008	47.8	47.9	48.2	47.9	48.3	48.7	49.0	49.1	48.9	48.7	48.3	47.8	48.4
2009	47.9	47.3	47.4	47.0	47.5	47.8	47.9	47.8	47.3	47.3	47.1	47.1	47.5
2010	47.1	46.9	47.0	46.9	47.3	47.8	48.0	48.1	47.5	47.3	47.5	47.4	47.4
2011	47.4	47.3	47.6	48.1	48.5	49.0	48.9	49.2	48.7	48.4	48.4	48.6	48.3
2012	48.6	48.6	49.0	49.2	49.4	50.2	50.2	50.3	50.0	50.2	50.0	49.9	49.6
2013	50.1	49.7	50.1	50.1	50.8	51.1	51.1	51.1	50.6	50.4	50.8	51.3	50.6
Government													
2002	159.5	162.7	164.1	164.4	165.7	164.6	158.9	160.4	164.3	166.1	166.9	166.5	163.7
2003	161.8	165.0	165.5	165.4	167.4	165.9	159.0	159.9	164.2	164.3	164.6	163.7	163.9
2004	159.1	162.6	163.9	165.3	165.9	164.8	157.9	158.2	164.2	165.5	166.2	166.0	163.3
2005	160.4	164.5	164.9	166.5	167.2	165.6	159.6	158.7	166.2	166.7	167.1	167.0	164.5
2006	162.6	166.5	167.6	167.1	168.7	168.3	161.1	161.9	167.8	168.0	168.9	169.2	166.5
2007	163.9	169.0	170.3	170.7	171.8	170.8	163.4	164.3	171.7	172.5	173.4	173.0	169.6
2008	167.9	172.3	173.6	174.2	176.3	174.5	167.7	170.5	175.4	177.4	178.3	177.3	173.8
2009	172.8	175.9	177.3	178.3	180.3	177.8	169.0	170.1	177.2	179.6	178.9	177.7	176.2
2010	171.9	177.6	178.8	179.8	185.2	180.2	172.8	171.4	178.6	181.1	181.5	179.5	178.2
2011	173.9	179.3	180.0	181.4	182.9	180.5	171.6	171.4	178.6	180.2	180.5	179.5	178.3
2012	173.9	179.2	180.9	181.8	183.4	182.5	173.4	172.4	179.9	181.5	183.2	181.6	179.5
2013	176.2	182.0	183.2	184.9	186.0	184.7	176.6	178.2	186.8	190.3	190.0	188.2	183.9

Employment by Industry: Detroit-Warren-Livonia, MI, Selected Years, 2002–2013

(Numbers in thousands, not seasonally adjusted)

Industry and year	January	February	March	April	May	June	July	August	September	October	November	December	Annual average
Total Nonfarm													
2002	2,047.1	2,057.0	2,069.1	2,086.4	2,112.1	2,119.4	2,058.3	2,078.4	2,091.7	2,103.2	2,112.1	2,114.8	2,087.5
2003	2,050.5	2,050.2	2,060.0	2,065.5	2,092.3	2,101.0	2,016.9	2,045.7	2,060.8	2,071.4	2,078.9	2,081.1	2,064.5
2004	2,009.4	2,010.4	2,022.6	2,046.2	2,069.7	2,072.6	1,991.3	2,033.8	2,059.0	2,070.0	2,080.7	2,079.3	2,045.4
2005	2,005.2	2,020.3	2,020.9	2,046.7	2,071.2	2,072.6	2,000.4	2,029.6	2,059.9	2,058.7	2,072.5	2,063.3	2,043.7
2006	1,987.9	1,991.2	1,999.2	2,011.2	2,029.6	2,035.1	1,953.2	1,981.7	2,000.9	1,994.6	2,009.8	2,006.7	2,000.1
2007	1,935.7	1,948.2	1,952.1	1,965.1	1,990.0	1,993.6	1,928.1	1,956.7	1,966.6	1,959.8	1,977.2	1,969.9	1,961.9
2008	1,907.4	1,908.9	1,904.6	1,908.4	1,928.6	1,937.0	1,866.5	1,886.8	1,893.9	1,893.6	1,885.3	1,866.1	1,898.9
2009	1,751.6	1,760.6	1,757.3	1,757.3	1,749.3	1,738.7	1,706.0	1,716.4	1,733.8	1,744.2	1,743.4	1,739.5	1,741.5
2010	1,694.4	1,698.5	1,702.0	1,725.9	1,750.3	1,758.0	1,723.8	1,727.7	1,750.6	1,767.4	1,770.9	1,767.7	1,736.4
2011	1,731.3	1,739.6	1,751.5	1,775.6	1,793.9	1,800.5	1,770.7	1,786.5	1,806.4	1,820.9	1,827.9	1,822.4	1,785.6
2012	1,791.2	1,798.0	1,812.4	1,818.3	1,841.0	1,849.5	1,822.3	1,835.3	1,843.2	1,855.9	1,864.0	1,863.2	1,832.9
2013	1,825.8	1,834.7	1,845.3	1,854.8	1,882.6	1,892.2	1,846.5	1,867.8	1,875.2	1,883.9	1,886.1	1,875.4	1,864.2
Total Private													
2002	1,812.9	1,817.9	1,828.3	1,846.9	1,870.5	1,882.3	1,852.8	1,876.1	1,863.6	1,860.7	1,868.7	1,872.0	1,854.4
2003	1,811.0	1,806.2	1,816.0	1,820.3	1,846.5	1,857.3	1,802.1	1,834.2	1,831.8	1,822.2	1,829.8	1,832.8	1,825.9
2004	1,770.1	1,767.1	1,778.0	1,802.7	1,824.7	1,832.5	1,780.5	1,826.1	1,824.6	1,828.0	1,836.4	1,837.7	1,809.0
2005	1,770.2	1,779.4	1,779.9	1,805.2	1,827.9	1,834.6	1,793.3	1,824.0	1,826.6	1,820.6	1,831.9	1,828.8	1,810.2
2006	1,756.6	1,754.3	1,761.1	1,773.6	1,790.9	1,800.8	1,745.8	1,778.0	1,774.1	1,760.9	1,774.3	1,774.0	1,770.4
2007	1,707.2	1,716.4	1,718.0	1,732.4	1,754.6	1,762.4	1,723.2	1,753.0	1,746.4	1,733.8	1,750.7	1,744.8	1,736.9
2008	1,687.5	1,685.0	1,680.2	1,684.4	1,702.9	1,714.3	1,664.1	1,683.3	1,676.5	1,670.4	1,661.2	1,645.1	1,679.6
2009	1,535.0	1,540.2	1,535.9	1,534.3	1,527.9	1,519.7	1,508.4	1,519.1	1,522.2	1,527.4	1,526.3	1,524.8	1,526.8
2010	1,484.8	1,484.8	1,487.7	1,510.0	1,531.4	1,544.3	1,529.8	1,538.6	1,547.7	1,560.1	1,564.2	1,562.6	1,528.8
2011	1,532.1	1,536.1	1,547.9	1,572.0	1,592.9	1,600.9	1,587.4	1,604.3	1,608.9	1,620.3	1,626.3	1,623.0	1,587.7
2012	1,596.8	1,599.8	1,613.9	1,620.3	1,644.8	1,653.7	1,643.6	1,656.8	1,650.0	1,661.4	1,668.4	1,669.4	1,639.9
2013	1,637.2	1,642.6	1,653.3	1,662.4	1,692.0	1,702.1	1,672.8	1,695.6	1,687.9	1,692.7	1,694.6	1,686.3	1,676.6
Goods Producing													
2002	408.8	414.7	415.8	421.3	425.8	430.6	419.4	429.5	425.9	424.1	423.3	420.1	421.6
2003	399.2	395.3	397.4	394.4	403.0	408.3	378.0	402.5	401.6	395.0	397.0	394.4	397.2
2004	376.3	374.8	379.8	385.5	390.9	391.0	356.3	392.1	392.2	390.9	390.8	385.0	383.8
2005	362.7	368.8	364.0	368.0	378.8	380.6	352.6	374.3	378.3	375.8	378.3	370.5	371.1
2006	344.7	345.1	348.7	354.9	360.7	360.7	325.2	349.6	348.9	340.9	346.1	339.9	347.1
2007	315.2	326.7	326.9	329.6	334.7	337.1	316.3	336.2	333.6	320.8	327.3	322.0	327.2
2008	304.9	306.2	300.3	297.2	301.0	312.5	282.0	299.0	298.2	295.1	291.9	280.4	297.4
2009	232.5	241.9	242.2	239.5	227.4	224.8	225.2	234.8	238.5	239.6	234.7	231.4	234.4
2010	225.0	222.9	223.0	230.5	236.6	242.1	240.8	239.7	248.9	250.0	248.7	245.9	237.8
2011	240.6	242.1	244.4	252.8	259.5	265.4	262.1	268.7	270.1	270.8	271.6	270.0	259.8
2012	264.8	263.8	266.8	267.5	274.9	278.9	278.6	281.5	281.6	282.8	281.8	279.9	275.2
2013	274.9	275.9	277.9	279.4	288.1	292.3	286.7	294.9	294.6	295.0	294.4	290.1	287.0
Service-Providing													
2002	1,638.3	1,642.3	1,653.3	1,665.1	1,686.3	1,688.8	1,638.9	1,648.9	1,665.8	1,679.1	1,688.8	1,694.7	1,665.9
2003	1,651.3	1,654.9	1,662.6	1,671.1	1,689.3	1,692.7	1,638.9	1,643.2	1,659.2	1,676.4	1,681.9	1,686.7	1,667.4
2004	1,633.1	1,635.6	1,642.8	1,660.7	1,678.8	1,681.6	1,635.0	1,641.7	1,666.8	1,679.1	1,689.9	1,694.3	1,661.6
2005	1,642.5	1,651.5	1,656.9	1,678.7	1,692.4	1,692.0	1,647.8	1,655.3	1,681.6	1,682.9	1,694.2	1,695.8	1,672.6
2006	1,643.2	1,646.1	1,650.5	1,656.3	1,668.9	1,674.4	1,628.0	1,632.1	1,652.0	1,653.7	1,663.7	1,666.8	1,653.0
2007	1,620.5	1,621.5	1,625.2	1,635.5	1,655.3	1,656.5	1,611.8	1,620.5	1,633.0	1,639.0	1,649.9	1,647.9	1,634.7
2008	1,602.5	1,602.7	1,604.3	1,611.2	1,627.6	1,624.5	1,584.5	1,587.8	1,595.7	1,598.5	1,593.4	1,585.7	1,601.5
2009	1,519.1	1,518.7	1,515.1	1,517.8	1,521.9	1,513.9	1,480.8	1,481.6	1,495.3	1,504.6	1,508.7	1,508.1	1,507.1
2010	1,469.4	1,475.6	1,479.0	1,495.4	1,513.7	1,515.9	1,483.0	1,488.0	1,501.7	1,517.4	1,522.2	1,521.8	1,498.6
2011	1,490.7	1,497.5	1,507.1	1,522.8	1,534.4	1,535.1	1,508.6	1,517.8	1,536.3	1,550.1	1,556.3	1,552.4	1,525.8
2012	1,526.4	1,534.2	1,545.6	1,550.8	1,566.1	1,570.6	1,543.7	1,553.8	1,561.6	1,573.1	1,582.2	1,583.3	1,557.6
2013	1,550.9	1,558.8	1,567.4	1,575.4	1,594.5	1,599.9	1,559.8	1,572.9	1,580.6	1,588.9	1,591.7	1,585.3	1,577.2
Mining, Logging, and Construction													
2002	83.5	81.8	82.7	87.0	92.3	94.9	95.8	95.4	93.1	92.0	89.9	86.2	89.6
2003	76.0	73.8	74.3	79.5	87.8	91.9	93.0	91.9	90.8	90.3	88.4	85.3	85.3
2004	75.2	74.0	75.8	82.0	87.2	90.8	93.2	92.3	91.0	90.7	89.5	85.7	85.6
2005	76.6	74.8	75.8	81.2	86.5	89.9	92.0	90.4	88.9	87.6	85.9	80.7	84.2
2006	71.5	70.1	70.9	74.6	80.0	82.6	82.8	81.8	79.8	78.5	76.8	72.8	76.9
2007	64.9	62.4	64.4	67.1	72.7	75.5	77.9	77.7	76.4	74.0	71.8	68.1	71.1
2008	61.0	58.6	58.6	61.6	66.8	68.9	69.2	68.9	67.4	66.5	63.3	57.8	64.1
2009	50.0	48.4	48.3	49.8	53.9	55.1	55.5	55.0	54.0	54.4	52.6	49.4	52.2
2010	43.9	42.6	44.3	47.9	51.6	53.7	56.2	56.8	56.2	56.6	55.3	52.3	51.5
2011	47.4	46.2	47.3	50.3	54.7	58.6	60.4	60.6	59.7	59.0	57.8	55.2	54.8
2012	51.0	49.1	50.3	52.9	56.4	59.1	59.9	60.0	60.0	59.7	58.4	55.8	56.1
2013	52.2	50.7	51.8	53.2	59.5	61.1	62.6	62.4	61.6	61.6	59.3	55.1	57.6
Manufacturing													
2002	325.3	332.9	333.1	334.3	333.5	335.7	323.6	334.1	332.8	332.1	333.4	333.9	332.1
2003	323.2	321.5	323.1	314.9	315.2	316.4	285.0	310.6	310.8	304.7	308.6	309.1	311.9
2004	301.1	300.8	304.0	303.5	303.7	300.2	263.1	299.8	301.2	300.2	301.3	299.3	298.2
2005	286.1	294.0	288.2	286.8	292.3	290.7	260.6	283.9	289.4	288.2	292.4	289.8	286.9
2006	273.2	275.0	277.8	280.3	280.7	278.1	242.4	267.8	269.1	262.4	269.3	267.1	270.3
2007	250.3	264.3	262.5	262.5	262.0	261.6	238.4	258.5	257.2	246.8	255.5	253.9	256.1
2008	243.9	247.6	241.7	235.6	234.2	243.6	212.8	230.1	230.8	228.6	228.6	222.6	233.3
2009	182.5	193.5	193.9	189.7	173.5	169.7	169.7	179.8	184.5	185.2	182.1	182.0	182.2
2010	181.1	180.3	178.7	182.6	185.0	188.4	184.6	182.9	192.7	193.4	193.4	193.6	186.4
2011	193.2	195.9	197.1	202.5	204.8	206.8	201.7	208.1	210.4	211.8	213.8	214.8	205.1
2012	213.8	214.7	216.5	214.6	218.5	219.8	218.7	221.5	221.6	223.1	223.4	224.1	219.2
2013	222.7	225.2	226.1	226.2	228.6	231.2	224.1	232.5	233.0	233.4	235.1	235.0	229.4

Employment by Industry: Detroit-Warren-Livonia, MI, Selected Years, 2002–2013—*Continued*

(Numbers in thousands, not seasonally adjusted)

Industry and year	January	February	March	April	May	June	July	August	September	October	November	December	Annual average
Trade, Transportation, and Utilities													
2002	394.6	389.4	392.0	390.9	396.3	398.2	393.0	394.8	395.3	394.2	402.6	408.2	395.8
2003	388.7	385.1	385.4	384.3	387.4	388.8	381.6	384.3	384.8	388.4	394.2	399.5	387.7
2004	379.9	376.8	376.9	378.9	383.7	385.1	378.8	380.8	378.7	383.2	391.4	396.9	382.6
2005	376.0	373.5	374.8	376.4	380.0	380.8	378.2	379.5	376.9	379.3	387.1	391.1	379.5
2006	371.8	367.6	368.7	369.7	372.8	374.4	368.8	370.9	369.4	371.5	379.6	384.1	372.4
2007	366.2	361.7	361.5	362.2	366.6	366.8	362.1	365.2	364.4	366.5	375.2	378.7	366.4
2008	363.3	358.3	358.9	357.0	359.7	360.5	356.2	356.4	355.5	354.4	357.2	358.3	358.0
2009	336.6	332.8	330.2	326.1	328.4	327.6	323.6	324.1	324.0	326.3	331.8	335.2	328.9
2010	321.0	318.0	319.6	322.6	326.8	328.7	327.0	328.6	326.9	333.3	339.0	342.7	327.9
2011	329.3	326.4	327.4	330.3	334.3	335.9	335.1	336.5	336.2	339.6	347.5	350.6	335.8
2012	339.5	336.2	337.9	337.0	341.9	343.4	341.4	342.7	341.6	345.5	355.4	357.0	343.3
2013	343.5	341.0	341.9	342.9	347.9	350.9	348.5	350.5	347.9	349.1	356.5	359.8	348.4
Wholesale Trade													
2002	98.1	98.5	98.6	98.5	99.1	99.6	98.5	98.8	98.4	97.4	97.7	98.3	98.5
2003	97.3	97.4	97.6	97.6	97.1	97.7	96.1	96.2	95.7	96.0	95.5	95.9	96.7
2004	93.5	93.5	93.9	94.3	94.7	95.0	94.7	94.4	93.7	93.9	93.9	94.1	94.1
2005	93.2	93.2	93.5	93.7	94.2	94.1	93.8	93.5	93.0	93.7	93.4	93.7	93.6
2006	92.4	92.5	92.7	93.0	93.3	93.3	93.8	93.0	92.7	91.9	91.8	91.7	91.9	92.6
2007	90.5	90.0	89.8	89.9	90.5	90.4	90.2	89.9	89.4	89.9	89.3	89.7	90.0
2008	89.2	88.8	88.9	89.0	89.3	89.2	88.7	88.5	88.2	87.7	86.7	86.0	88.4
2009	84.1	83.1	81.9	80.8	80.2	78.7	77.7	77.9	77.5	77.6	77.5	77.8	79.6
2010	76.3	76.6	76.9	77.5	78.3	78.7	78.7	79.3	78.9	79.9	80.1	80.5	78.5
2011	79.5	79.6	80.0	80.9	81.5	81.6	82.1	82.3	81.8	82.2	82.7	82.7	81.4
2012	82.5	82.8	83.1	83.3	84.2	84.5	84.6	84.8	84.4	84.8	85.0	85.3	84.1
2013	84.9	84.9	85.3	85.2	85.9	86.3	85.9	85.9	85.5	85.0	85.7	85.5	85.5
Retail Trade													
2002	230.8	225.3	226.9	225.9	229.9	231.0	228.0	228.5	229.4	228.9	237.2	242.9	230.4
2003	223.4	220.0	220.2	219.5	223.1	224.0	220.2	221.9	222.8	225.8	232.3	237.1	224.2
2004	221.9	218.6	218.7	219.9	224.3	225.1	220.3	221.6	220.1	223.1	231.3	236.3	223.4
2005	218.7	215.5	216.3	218.7	221.3	222.1	219.8	219.7	218.2	219.9	227.2	230.8	220.7
2006	215.1	210.9	211.5	212.3	214.7	215.7	213.8	214.4	213.5	216.2	223.8	226.6	215.7
2007	212.2	207.0	207.3	207.7	210.7	210.6	209.1	210.2	209.9	212.2	220.7	223.0	211.7
2008	211.3	206.4	206.6	205.6	208.0	207.8	206.6	206.7	205.7	206.3	210.0	211.4	207.7
2009	197.5	193.5	192.4	191.0	194.7	196.1	193.4	193.0	192.3	194.6	200.1	202.1	195.1
2010	191.0	187.9	188.7	191.4	194.4	195.3	194.3	194.8	192.9	197.3	202.4	204.8	194.6
2011	193.6	190.8	191.3	193.4	195.7	196.3	195.9	196.7	196.3	199.4	206.2	208.5	197.0
2012	198.2	194.5	195.7	195.2	198.4	199.2	197.9	198.6	197.3	200.3	209.6	210.1	199.6
2013	198.6	195.8	196.4	197.5	201.2	203.3	202.2	203.3	201.4	202.6	207.5	210.1	201.7
Transportation and Utilities													
2002	65.7	65.6	66.5	66.5	67.3	67.6	66.5	67.5	67.5	67.9	67.7	67.0	66.9
2003	68.0	67.7	67.6	67.2	67.2	67.1	65.3	66.2	66.3	66.6	66.4	66.5	66.8
2004	64.5	64.7	64.3	64.7	64.7	65.0	63.8	64.8	64.9	66.2	66.2	66.5	65.0
2005	64.1	64.8	65.0	64.0	64.5	64.6	64.6	66.3	65.7	65.7	66.5	66.6	65.2
2006	64.3	64.2	64.5	64.4	64.8	64.9	62.0	63.8	64.0	63.5	64.1	65.6	64.2
2007	63.5	64.7	64.4	64.6	65.4	65.8	62.8	65.1	65.1	64.4	65.2	66.0	64.8
2008	62.8	63.1	63.4	62.4	62.4	63.5	60.9	61.2	61.6	60.4	60.5	60.9	61.9
2009	55.0	56.2	55.9	54.3	53.5	52.8	52.5	53.2	54.2	54.1	54.2	55.3	54.3
2010	53.7	53.5	54.0	53.7	54.1	54.7	54.0	54.5	55.1	56.1	56.5	57.4	54.8
2011	56.2	56.0	56.1	56.0	57.1	58.0	57.1	57.5	58.1	58.0	58.6	59.4	57.3
2012	58.8	58.9	59.1	58.5	59.3	59.7	58.9	59.3	59.9	60.4	60.8	61.6	59.6
2013	60.0	60.3	60.2	60.2	60.8	61.3	60.4	61.3	61.0	61.5	63.3	64.2	61.2
Information													
2002	34.5	34.3	34.3	33.6	33.9	33.8	34.1	33.8	33.2	32.7	32.8	33.5	33.7
2003	33.2	33.3	33.4	32.7	32.9	33.2	32.6	32.4	32.0	32.1	32.4	32.4	32.7
2004	31.9	31.8	31.7	31.9	32.1	32.4	32.2	32.1	31.8	31.8	32.1	32.2	32.0
2005	31.9	31.5	31.5	31.4	31.6	31.6	31.5	31.3	30.9	30.5	30.8	30.9	31.3
2006	30.5	30.7	30.3	30.1	30.4	30.4	30.2	30.1	29.6	29.7	29.8	29.9	30.1
2007	30.1	29.9	29.7	30.0	30.3	30.2	30.0	29.9	29.6	29.6	29.7	29.6	29.9
2008	29.7	29.7	29.3	29.2	29.4	29.5	29.2	29.5	29.8	29.0	29.2	28.8	29.4
2009	28.2	28.3	27.7	27.5	27.6	27.7	27.5	27.2	27.0	27.1	27.5	27.7	27.6
2010	26.9	26.8	26.7	26.8	27.0	27.2	26.8	28.6	28.4	26.4	26.3	26.5	27.0
2011	26.4	26.1	26.1	25.8	26.0	26.0	26.1	26.2	26.0	26.7	26.7	26.6	26.2
2012	26.8	26.6	26.7	26.3	26.5	26.3	26.6	27.0	26.2	26.4	26.6	26.6	26.6
2013	26.7	26.7	26.8	27.1	27.4	27.6	27.3	27.4	26.8	27.1	27.2	27.2	27.1
Financial Activities													
2002	115.7	115.7	115.3	115.6	116.2	116.4	116.5	117.2	115.6	115.1	115.7	116.3	115.9
2003	116.7	116.7	116.7	118.7	119.8	120.7	120.3	120.2	118.2	116.9	116.3	116.9	118.2
2004	114.7	114.5	115.0	116.3	117.0	118.0	117.8	117.5	116.4	115.8	115.9	116.7	116.3
2005	116.1	116.2	116.2	116.7	116.9	118.1	117.4	117.4	116.1	115.7	115.7	115.7	116.5
2006	114.0	113.9	113.4	113.2	113.9	114.8	114.1	114.0	112.4	111.7	111.5	112.2	113.3
2007	111.0	110.8	110.5	111.1	111.4	112.2	112.1	111.1	109.0	108.0	107.6	107.5	110.2
2008	106.8	106.7	106.2	105.8	106.7	106.7	105.9	105.0	103.5	102.7	101.9	101.6	105.0
2009	99.9	99.4	98.8	98.8	99.2	99.2	98.8	98.3	97.0	96.0	95.6	95.6	98.1
2010	95.1	94.9	94.2	93.8	95.0	96.1	96.4	96.8	95.7	96.0	96.3	96.9	95.6
2011	96.5	96.7	97.3	98.0	98.1	98.8	99.2	99.5	98.1	97.6	97.6	97.8	97.9
2012	97.2	97.4	97.8	97.8	98.6	99.8	101.0	101.3	99.6	99.8	100.1	100.9	99.3
2013	100.7	101.1	101.5	102.1	102.9	105.1	104.4	104.5	102.1	101.2	100.3	99.9	102.2

Employment by Industry: Detroit-Warren-Livonia, MI, Selected Years, 2002–2013—*Continued*

(Numbers in thousands, not seasonally adjusted)

Industry and year	January	February	March	April	May	June	July	August	September	October	November	December	Annual average
Professional and Business Services													
2002	361.6	362.6	364.0	367.7	371.3	373.1	363.9	372.5	370.1	371.5	371.5	370.5	368.4
2003	361.6	360.2	361.3	365.9	370.2	372.1	361.9	368.2	367.0	360.4	362.0	361.7	364.4
2004	350.4	349.4	349.9	358.4	363.7	367.0	361.8	368.7	369.0	372.7	373.1	373.5	363.1
2005	363.2	363.7	363.0	371.2	373.7	375.7	370.1	375.7	377.4	373.8	374.3	373.6	371.3
2006	361.2	357.7	356.6	358.8	360.4	364.6	358.1	363.9	362.4	361.5	363.2	362.2	360.9
2007	349.0	349.0	346.4	353.2	354.9	357.0	351.5	357.7	355.7	356.3	359.2	355.1	353.8
2008	343.3	343.0	341.6	346.6	348.5	346.7	337.0	338.3	335.7	338.2	333.4	329.0	340.1
2009	307.1	305.8	302.1	301.3	297.4	293.3	292.0	293.2	296.9	299.7	300.0	299.2	299.0
2010	293.8	296.5	295.8	302.4	305.4	307.6	302.2	306.7	312.0	317.1	318.2	315.2	306.1
2011	314.1	316.4	320.3	326.3	329.9	327.7	321.4	328.5	334.2	340.5	340.9	335.4	328.0
2012	333.8	337.5	340.5	345.3	350.2	347.9	343.4	349.0	350.0	355.0	354.6	353.1	346.7
2013	348.9	351.5	355.0	356.3	363.3	362.7	350.1	360.2	362.0	365.4	366.9	362.2	358.7
Education and Health Services													
2002	243.4	245.4	246.3	250.0	250.5	252.2	247.9	248.1	247.6	251.1	252.8	252.3	249.0
2003	250.9	253.5	253.7	252.0	252.1	250.7	249.5	249.0	251.9	254.5	256.3	255.7	252.5
2004	252.6	255.0	255.8	258.0	258.1	255.9	256.5	256.0	258.9	261.7	263.4	263.8	258.0
2005	259.5	262.7	263.8	265.5	265.5	263.4	262.2	262.9	267.1	270.8	272.7	273.3	265.8
2006	269.0	271.0	272.8	270.7	272.0	271.0	268.2	267.9	273.1	272.7	274.2	275.2	271.5
2007	272.5	275.2	276.4	275.9	277.3	277.8	273.4	273.3	277.4	278.9	280.7	280.8	276.6
2008	277.8	279.9	280.2	280.5	282.2	280.8	278.3	278.1	281.0	283.3	284.1	284.1	280.9
2009	279.8	283.0	283.9	283.3	284.7	284.2	280.2	280.5	281.6	284.6	286.4	285.6	283.2
2010	281.3	283.9	284.7	283.9	284.8	283.7	282.2	282.2	283.5	288.4	289.4	289.3	284.8
2011	285.8	287.8	288.8	291.4	291.9	290.3	289.5	289.9	291.8	294.7	295.7	296.4	291.2
2012	292.2	295.5	296.7	295.3	296.1	295.5	293.8	294.4	294.6	297.9	298.8	299.9	295.9
2013	295.4	298.2	298.8	298.3	298.5	297.7	293.9	294.6	296.1	300.0	299.4	298.4	297.4
Leisure and Hospitality													
2002	166.4	167.3	170.6	176.2	183.3	183.9	184.5	185.7	182.4	181.4	179.6	179.5	178.4
2003	172.7	172.3	175.6	181.0	188.9	191.5	186.2	184.9	184.4	183.8	180.9	181.3	182.0
2004	174.1	174.2	177.1	182.6	188.9	191.3	189.0	190.0	187.6	183.6	180.4	180.1	183.2
2005	173.1	174.6	177.6	185.3	191.0	192.7	189.8	191.3	188.5	183.6	181.7	181.8	184.3
2006	175.9	178.6	180.4	186.0	190.0	193.6	191.2	191.5	188.6	184.0	180.9	181.3	185.2
2007	175.9	175.5	178.6	182.8	191.0	192.3	189.5	191.0	188.6	185.9	183.4	183.2	184.8
2008	175.9	175.2	177.5	181.5	187.9	189.9	187.8	189.4	185.7	181.3	178.0	177.8	182.3
2009	167.8	166.1	168.4	175.2	180.1	179.7	178.7	179.0	176.5	173.2	169.7	169.4	173.7
2010	162.8	163.0	164.9	171.8	177.1	179.9	176.6	178.8	176.0	173.2	171.1	171.0	172.2
2011	165.5	166.9	169.7	173.4	178.6	181.5	179.2	180.0	177.9	175.7	172.0	171.5	174.3
2012	168.6	168.7	172.5	175.3	180.2	184.3	181.7	183.1	179.1	177.1	174.6	175.6	176.7
2013	171.1	171.7	174.2	179.1	185.9	187.1	184.1	185.2	180.7	177.8	172.4	171.3	178.4
Other Services													
2002	87.9	88.5	90.0	91.6	93.2	94.1	93.5	94.5	93.5	90.6	90.4	91.6	91.6
2003	88.0	89.8	92.5	91.3	92.2	92.0	92.0	92.7	91.9	91.1	90.7	90.9	91.3
2004	90.2	90.6	91.8	91.1	90.3	91.8	88.1	88.9	90.0	88.3	89.3	89.5	90.0
2005	87.7	88.4	89.0	90.7	90.4	91.7	91.5	91.6	91.4	91.1	91.3	91.9	90.6
2006	89.5	89.7	90.2	90.2	90.7	91.3	90.0	90.1	89.7	88.9	89.0	89.2	89.9
2007	87.3	87.6	88.0	87.6	88.4	89.0	88.3	88.6	88.1	87.8	87.6	87.9	88.0
2008	85.8	86.0	86.2	86.6	87.5	87.7	87.7	87.6	87.1	86.4	85.5	85.1	86.6
2009	83.1	82.9	82.6	82.6	83.1	83.2	82.4	82.0	80.7	80.9	80.6	80.7	82.1
2010	78.9	78.8	78.8	78.2	78.7	79.0	77.8	77.2	76.3	75.7	75.2	75.1	77.5
2011	73.9	73.7	73.9	74.0	74.6	75.3	74.8	75.0	74.6	74.7	74.3	74.7	74.5
2012	73.9	74.1	75.0	75.8	76.4	77.6	77.1	77.8	77.3	76.9	76.5	76.4	76.2
2013	76.0	76.5	77.2	77.2	78.0	78.7	77.8	78.3	77.7	77.1	77.5	77.4	77.5
Government													
2002	234.2	239.1	240.8	239.5	241.6	237.1	205.5	202.3	228.1	242.5	243.4	242.8	233.1
2003	239.5	244.0	244.0	245.2	245.8	243.7	214.8	211.5	229.0	249.2	249.1	248.3	238.7
2004	239.3	243.3	244.6	243.5	245.0	240.1	210.8	207.7	234.4	242.0	244.3	241.6	236.4
2005	235.0	240.9	241.0	241.5	243.3	238.0	207.1	205.6	233.3	238.1	240.6	237.5	233.5
2006	231.3	236.9	238.1	237.6	238.7	234.3	207.4	203.7	226.8	233.7	235.5	232.7	229.7
2007	228.5	231.8	234.1	232.7	235.4	231.2	204.9	203.7	220.2	226.0	226.5	225.1	225.0
2008	219.9	223.9	224.4	224.0	225.7	222.7	202.4	203.5	217.4	223.2	224.1	221.0	219.4
2009	216.6	220.4	221.4	223.0	221.4	219.0	197.6	197.3	211.6	216.8	217.1	214.7	214.7
2010	209.6	213.7	214.3	215.9	218.9	213.7	194.0	189.1	202.9	207.3	206.7	205.1	207.6
2011	199.2	203.5	203.6	203.6	201.0	199.6	183.3	182.2	197.5	200.6	201.6	199.4	197.9
2012	194.4	198.2	198.5	198.0	196.2	195.8	178.7	178.5	193.2	194.5	195.6	193.8	193.0
2013	188.6	192.1	192.0	192.4	190.6	190.1	173.7	172.2	187.3	191.2	191.5	189.1	187.6

Employment by Industry: El Paso, TX, Selected Years, 2002–2013

(Numbers in thousands, not seasonally adjusted)

Industry and year	January	February	March	April	May	June	July	August	September	October	November	December	Annual average
Total Nonfarm													
2002	251.6	251.9	254.7	255.3	255.7	254.7	251.7	256.1	261.0	258.6	260.2	261.1	256.1
2003	254.3	255.1	255.4	255.7	254.8	251.2	249.9	253.4	257.4	257.0	258.0	258.3	255.0
2004	254.3	255.8	256.0	256.1	257.3	255.5	255.3	255.7	258.9	259.8	260.7	260.5	257.2
2005	255.2	256.6	258.3	260.1	260.9	260.5	257.3	259.5	264.2	264.2	265.4	266.0	260.7
2006	261.2	262.9	265.4	263.9	264.8	263.5	259.8	262.6	267.7	267.7	269.4	271.3	265.0
2007	265.5	267.0	269.0	270.1	271.5	269.7	266.9	269.0	274.5	277.5	279.0	281.2	271.7
2008	277.4	279.2	279.8	278.3	279.8	276.8	272.5	274.9	277.5	280.5	280.5	280.3	278.1
2009	274.9	274.1	273.9	274.7	273.9	273.1	268.0	269.2	272.7	274.8	275.9	276.9	273.5
2010	272.9	274.4	277.2	278.5	279.9	279.0	271.9	273.9	278.2	278.7	280.2	281.5	277.2
2011	277.5	278.0	279.3	281.0	280.9	280.1	277.0	278.4	281.8	279.3	281.5	282.7	279.8
2012	279.3	281.1	282.3	284.2	285.3	282.9	280.4	282.6	284.8	286.5	288.3	289.0	283.9
2013	283.2	285.5	286.1	286.8	288.1	285.2	282.8	285.6	288.2	289.6	290.6	290.5	286.9
Total Private													
2002	193.2	192.5	195.5	196.6	197.9	199.0	198.3	201.1	201.6	198.4	199.8	201.7	198.0
2003	195.0	194.4	194.8	195.2	195.3	194.6	194.4	196.4	196.9	196.6	197.4	198.8	195.8
2004	194.2	194.7	195.0	195.2	195.9	197.0	197.8	198.8	198.3	197.9	198.9	199.6	196.9
2005	194.0	194.6	196.3	198.3	199.0	201.2	200.8	202.5	203.6	202.5	203.9	205.3	200.2
2006	200.2	200.9	203.3	202.2	203.0	205.1	203.8	206.1	206.3	204.9	206.4	208.2	204.2
2007	202.4	203.3	205.2	205.2	206.4	207.6	207.4	209.4	209.6	211.1	212.4	214.7	207.9
2008	211.4	211.8	212.5	213.1	213.8	213.4	213.2	215.5	213.2	213.7	213.7	213.5	213.2
2009	207.9	206.6	206.5	205.8	205.4	206.3	206.1	207.2	205.5	205.1	206.2	207.4	206.3
2010	203.5	204.2	207.0	207.8	208.5	210.0	207.9	209.3	208.9	209.1	210.3	211.7	208.2
2011	208.2	208.5	209.9	211.2	211.3	211.4	211.9	213.0	212.3	210.2	212.2	213.7	211.2
2012	209.8	211.6	213.0	214.7	215.5	216.1	215.4	217.2	216.6	216.8	218.3	219.3	215.4
2013	213.8	215.4	216.3	217.0	218.4	218.6	217.8	220.0	219.6	220.0	220.7	220.8	218.2
Goods Producing													
2002	42.9	41.6	42.4	42.1	41.7	42.0	41.6	43.1	43.2	41.5	40.9	40.8	42.0
2003	39.7	39.6	39.4	39.0	38.3	37.8	37.3	37.7	37.8	36.8	36.4	36.1	38.0
2004	35.3	35.5	35.4	35.4	35.6	35.7	35.6	36.0	36.1	36.3	36.0	35.3	35.7
2005	34.2	34.3	34.6	34.7	35.2	35.3	34.7	35.0	35.6	34.8	34.8	34.7	34.8
2006	34.3	34.2	34.4	34.4	34.7	35.5	34.8	34.8	34.7	34.3	34.1	34.4	34.6
2007	33.7	33.9	34.2	34.4	34.5	34.8	34.7	35.4	35.5	35.7	35.8	35.8	34.9
2008	35.3	35.3	35.2	35.6	35.7	35.5	35.4	35.6	35.4	35.0	34.8	34.3	35.3
2009	33.7	33.2	32.6	32.7	32.6	32.2	32.3	32.9	32.4	32.6	32.2	32.3	32.6
2010	31.8	31.9	32.0	32.2	32.1	32.1	32.3	33.1	32.7	32.0	31.8	31.5	32.1
2011	31.0	30.9	31.2	31.2	31.2	31.1	31.0	31.7	31.4	30.5	30.5	30.4	31.0
2012	30.0	30.2	30.2	30.3	30.5	30.9	30.7	31.5	31.3	31.3	31.1	30.9	30.7
2013	30.2	30.8	30.7	30.7	30.8	30.8	30.7	31.5	31.3	31.0	30.3	30.0	30.7
Service-Providing													
2002	208.7	210.3	212.3	213.2	214.0	212.7	210.1	213.0	217.8	217.1	219.3	220.3	214.1
2003	214.6	215.5	216.0	216.7	216.5	213.4	212.6	215.7	219.6	220.2	221.6	222.2	217.1
2004	219.0	220.3	220.6	220.7	221.7	219.8	219.7	219.7	222.8	223.5	224.7	225.2	221.5
2005	221.0	222.3	223.7	225.4	225.7	225.2	222.6	224.5	228.6	229.4	230.6	231.3	225.9
2006	226.9	228.7	231.0	229.5	230.1	228.0	225.0	227.8	233.0	233.4	235.3	236.9	230.5
2007	231.8	233.1	234.8	235.7	237.0	234.9	232.2	233.6	239.0	241.8	243.2	245.4	236.9
2008	242.1	243.9	244.6	242.7	244.1	241.3	237.1	239.3	242.1	245.5	245.7	246.0	242.9
2009	241.2	240.9	241.3	242.0	241.3	240.9	235.7	236.3	240.3	242.2	243.7	244.6	240.9
2010	241.1	242.5	245.2	246.3	247.8	246.9	239.6	240.8	245.5	246.7	248.4	250.0	245.1
2011	246.5	247.1	248.1	249.8	249.7	249.0	246.0	246.7	250.4	248.8	251.0	252.3	248.8
2012	249.3	250.9	252.1	253.9	254.8	252.0	249.7	251.1	253.5	255.2	257.2	258.1	253.2
2013	253.0	254.7	255.4	256.1	257.3	254.4	252.1	254.1	256.9	258.6	260.3	260.5	256.1
Mining, Logging, and Construction													
2002	11.7	11.7	12.0	11.6	11.5	11.8	11.7	12.0	12.0	11.7	11.7	11.6	11.8
2003	11.9	11.9	11.9	11.8	11.8	11.8	11.6	11.7	11.7	11.6	11.5	11.5	11.7
2004	11.1	11.2	11.3	11.3	11.4	11.6	11.7	11.6	11.6	11.9	11.8	11.8	11.5
2005	11.5	11.6	11.6	11.7	12.0	12.1	12.0	12.1	12.5	12.3	12.3	12.2	12.0
2006	12.2	12.2	12.4	12.5	12.6	12.9	12.8	12.8	12.9	12.9	13.0	13.2	12.7
2007	13.3	13.6	14.0	14.2	14.3	14.6	14.5	15.0	15.1	15.5	15.6	15.6	14.6
2008	15.2	15.2	15.3	15.7	15.8	15.6	15.7	15.9	15.9	15.8	15.7	15.6	15.6
2009	15.3	15.2	15.4	15.3	15.4	15.1	15.4	15.6	15.3	15.7	15.5	15.6	15.4
2010	15.5	15.6	15.7	15.8	15.7	15.6	15.5	15.6	15.3	14.7	14.6	14.3	15.3
2011	14.0	13.9	14.0	13.9	13.8	13.6	13.7	13.9	13.8	13.0	13.0	12.9	13.6
2012	12.7	12.7	12.6	12.6	12.7	13.0	12.9	13.2	13.0	13.1	13.0	12.9	12.9
2013	12.3	12.7	12.6	12.5	12.7	12.8	12.9	13.2	13.1	13.0	12.7	12.5	12.8
Manufacturing													
2002	31.2	29.9	30.4	30.5	30.2	30.2	29.9	31.1	31.2	29.8	29.2	29.2	30.2
2003	27.8	27.7	27.5	27.2	26.5	26.0	25.7	26.0	26.1	25.2	24.9	24.6	26.3
2004	24.2	24.3	24.1	24.1	24.2	24.1	23.9	24.4	24.5	24.4	24.2	23.5	24.2
2005	22.7	22.7	23.0	23.0	23.2	23.2	22.7	22.9	23.1	22.5	22.5	22.5	22.8
2006	22.1	22.0	22.0	21.9	22.1	22.6	22.0	22.0	21.8	21.4	21.1	21.2	21.9
2007	20.4	20.3	20.2	20.2	20.2	20.2	20.2	20.4	20.4	20.2	20.2	20.2	20.3
2008	20.1	20.1	19.9	19.9	19.9	19.9	19.7	19.7	19.5	19.2	19.1	18.7	19.6
2009	18.4	18.0	17.2	17.4	17.2	17.1	16.9	17.3	17.1	16.9	16.7	16.7	17.2
2010	16.3	16.3	16.3	16.4	16.4	16.5	16.8	17.5	17.4	17.3	17.2	17.2	16.8
2011	17.0	17.0	17.2	17.3	17.4	17.5	17.3	17.8	17.6	17.5	17.5	17.5	17.4
2012	17.3	17.5	17.6	17.7	17.8	17.9	17.8	18.3	18.3	18.2	18.1	18.0	17.9
2013	17.9	18.1	18.1	18.2	18.1	18.0	17.8	18.3	18.2	18.0	17.6	17.5	18.0

Employment by Industry: El Paso, TX, Selected Years, 2002–2013—*Continued*

(Numbers in thousands, not seasonally adjusted)

Industry and year	January	February	March	April	May	June	July	August	September	October	November	December	Annual average
Trade, Transportation, and Utilities													
2002	53.0	52.2	53.0	53.2	53.8	54.1	53.7	54.1	54.4	54.6	55.6	56.7	54.0
2003	54.3	53.4	53.9	54.5	54.6	54.6	54.8	55.6	55.6	56.0	57.3	58.1	55.2
2004	55.7	55.4	55.6	54.8	54.9	55.1	55.1	55.3	54.9	55.5	56.8	57.5	55.6
2005	54.9	54.5	54.9	55.3	55.4	55.8	56.1	56.7	56.9	57.0	58.7	59.2	56.3
2006	56.9	56.8	57.6	57.3	57.5	57.7	57.7	58.4	58.5	58.3	59.7	60.4	58.1
2007	58.0	57.6	58.2	58.4	58.6	58.7	58.7	59.2	59.6	60.3	61.4	62.2	59.2
2008	59.9	59.2	59.3	58.9	58.8	58.8	58.9	59.5	58.7	59.0	59.4	59.6	59.2
2009	56.5	55.4	55.4	54.6	54.4	54.6	54.6	54.7	54.8	54.7	55.6	56.4	55.1
2010	54.3	54.2	54.7	55.1	55.3	55.2	55.5	55.8	55.8	56.4	57.6	58.8	55.7
2011	56.2	55.7	56.0	56.6	56.7	56.8	57.1	57.5	57.0	57.1	58.8	59.7	57.1
2012	57.5	57.1	57.3	58.2	58.7	59.0	58.5	58.8	58.4	58.8	60.6	61.2	58.7
2013	58.6	58.5	58.9	59.5	60.1	60.1	60.3	60.8	60.5	60.8	62.6	63.5	60.4
Wholesale Trade													
2002	9.7	9.7	9.8	9.8	9.9	9.9	9.8	9.9	9.8	9.7	9.6	9.7	9.8
2003	9.6	9.5	9.6	9.7	9.8	9.8	9.9	10.0	10.0	10.1	10.2	10.3	9.9
2004	10.4	10.3	10.4	10.2	10.2	10.3	10.4	10.4	10.3	10.5	10.5	10.4	10.4
2005	10.1	10.1	10.2	10.2	10.3	10.3	10.3	10.4	10.5	10.4	10.5	10.6	10.3
2006	10.5	10.5	10.6	10.5	10.6	10.6	10.6	10.6	10.6	10.5	10.5	10.5	10.6
2007	10.5	10.5	10.6	10.8	10.8	10.9	10.8	10.9	10.9	11.0	11.0	11.1	10.8
2008	10.8	10.8	10.6	10.9	10.7	10.6	10.8	10.8	10.6	10.6	10.2	10.1	10.6
2009	9.8	9.7	9.6	9.4	9.3	9.3	9.4	9.3	9.3	9.3	9.3	9.4	9.4
2010	9.4	9.4	9.5	9.6	9.6	9.6	9.7	9.7	9.6	9.6	9.6	9.6	9.6
2011	9.5	9.5	9.6	9.6	9.7	9.7	9.9	9.9	9.8	9.7	9.7	9.7	9.7
2012	9.6	9.8	9.8	9.8	9.8	9.9	9.8	9.7	9.7	9.8	9.8	9.9	9.8
2013	9.7	9.7	9.8	9.8	9.9	10.0	10.0	10.1	10.0	10.1	10.1	10.0	9.9
Retail Trade													
2002	31.7	30.9	31.5	31.6	32.0	32.3	31.8	32.1	32.5	32.6	33.6	34.5	32.3
2003	32.6	31.9	32.2	32.6	32.6	32.6	32.7	33.4	33.3	33.6	34.8	35.5	33.2
2004	33.1	32.8	32.8	32.2	32.2	32.2	32.0	32.3	31.9	32.1	33.2	34.0	32.6
2005	31.9	31.4	31.6	31.9	31.9	32.2	32.4	32.8	32.8	33.2	34.6	35.1	32.7
2006	33.1	32.9	33.5	33.4	33.4	33.4	33.4	34.0	34.1	34.0	35.4	36.0	33.9
2007	34.0	33.5	34.0	33.9	34.1	34.1	34.2	34.6	35.0	35.8	36.8	37.4	34.8
2008	35.7	35.0	35.3	34.6	34.6	34.8	34.8	35.2	34.9	35.1	35.9	36.2	35.2
2009	33.9	33.0	33.1	32.7	32.6	32.8	32.6	32.9	33.0	33.0	33.9	34.4	33.2
2010	32.7	32.5	32.9	33.1	33.3	33.2	33.4	33.7	33.8	34.3	35.6	36.6	33.8
2011	34.3	33.7	33.9	34.5	34.6	34.7	34.6	34.9	34.5	34.8	36.4	37.1	34.8
2012	35.2	34.6	34.7	35.5	35.8	35.9	35.5	35.8	35.4	35.7	37.4	37.9	35.8
2013	35.7	35.6	35.6	36.1	36.5	36.4	36.8	37.1	36.9	37.1	38.8	39.5	36.8
Transportation and Utilities													
2002	11.6	11.6	11.7	11.8	11.9	11.9	12.1	12.1	12.1	12.3	12.4	12.5	12.0
2003	12.1	12.0	12.1	12.2	12.2	12.2	12.2	12.2	12.3	12.3	12.3	12.3	12.2
2004	12.2	12.3	12.4	12.4	12.5	12.6	12.7	12.6	12.7	12.9	13.1	13.1	12.6
2005	12.9	13.0	13.1	13.2	13.2	13.3	13.4	13.5	13.6	13.4	13.6	13.5	13.3
2006	13.3	13.4	13.5	13.4	13.5	13.7	13.7	13.8	13.8	13.8	13.8	13.9	13.6
2007	13.5	13.6	13.6	13.7	13.7	13.7	13.7	13.7	13.7	13.5	13.6	13.7	13.6
2008	13.4	13.4	13.4	13.4	13.5	13.4	13.3	13.5	13.2	13.3	13.3	13.3	13.4
2009	12.8	12.7	12.7	12.5	12.5	12.5	12.6	12.5	12.5	12.4	12.4	12.6	12.6
2010	12.2	12.3	12.3	12.4	12.4	12.4	12.4	12.4	12.4	12.5	12.4	12.6	12.4
2011	12.4	12.5	12.5	12.5	12.4	12.4	12.6	12.7	12.7	12.6	12.7	12.9	12.6
2012	12.7	12.7	12.8	12.9	13.1	13.2	13.2	13.3	13.3	13.3	13.4	13.4	13.1
2013	13.2	13.2	13.5	13.6	13.7	13.7	13.5	13.6	13.6	13.6	13.7	14.0	13.6
Information													
2002	5.0	4.9	4.9	5.0	5.0	5.0	5.1	5.2	5.2	5.2	5.3	5.5	5.1
2003	5.5	5.5	5.4	5.5	5.5	5.4	5.4	5.4	5.3	5.5	5.6	5.3	5.4
2004	5.1	5.1	5.0	4.9	4.9	4.9	4.9	4.9	4.8	4.9	4.8	4.9	4.9
2005	4.7	4.7	4.7	4.8	4.8	4.9	4.8	4.8	4.7	4.7	4.8	4.7	4.8
2006	4.7	4.7	4.9	4.6	4.7	4.9	4.6	4.6	4.7	4.8	4.8	5.0	4.8
2007	4.9	5.0	5.0	5.0	5.0	5.0	5.3	5.3	5.2	5.5	5.5	5.5	5.2
2008	5.7	5.7	5.7	5.6	5.8	5.8	5.5	5.5	5.4	5.4	5.4	5.4	5.6
2009	5.3	5.4	5.3	5.3	5.2	5.2	5.1	5.0	4.9	4.8	4.8	4.9	5.1
2010	5.0	5.1	5.1	5.2	5.3	5.5	5.4	5.3	5.3	5.3	5.3	5.3	5.3
2011	5.3	5.3	5.3	5.3	5.3	5.4	5.4	5.4	5.4	5.3	5.4	5.4	5.4
2012	5.6	5.6	5.6	5.6	5.7	5.7	5.7	5.8	5.8	5.9	5.9	6.0	5.7
2013	6.0	5.9	6.0	6.0	6.0	6.0	5.9	5.9	5.8	5.9	5.9	5.8	5.9
Financial Activities													
2002	11.8	11.9	12.0	11.8	11.8	11.8	11.8	11.7	11.7	11.8	12.0	12.0	11.8
2003	12.0	12.0	12.1	11.9	11.9	11.9	12.0	11.9	11.8	11.7	11.7	11.6	11.9
2004	11.5	11.6	11.6	11.4	11.3	11.4	11.4	11.4	11.4	11.4	11.3	11.4	11.4
2005	11.2	11.2	11.3	11.4	11.4	11.4	11.5	11.5	11.5	11.5	11.4	11.5	11.4
2006	11.2	11.3	11.3	11.0	11.0	11.1	11.1	11.2	11.3	11.3	11.4	11.5	11.2
2007	11.3	11.3	11.4	11.5	11.6	11.6	11.6	11.7	11.7	11.7	11.8	12.1	11.6
2008	12.1	12.2	12.2	11.9	12.0	12.1	12.2	12.3	12.2	12.3	12.2	12.2	12.2
2009	12.1	12.1	12.1	12.0	12.0	11.8	11.8	11.9	11.9	11.9	11.9	11.9	12.0
2010	11.5	11.5	11.5	11.6	11.6	11.6	11.8	11.8	11.7	11.9	11.9	12.0	11.7
2011	12.0	12.0	12.0	12.2	12.3	12.3	12.3	12.3	12.3	12.3	12.3	12.4	12.2
2012	12.2	12.4	12.4	12.4	12.4	12.5	12.5	12.5	12.4	12.4	12.3	12.4	12.4
2013	12.2	12.1	12.1	12.2	12.2	12.3	12.1	12.1	12.1	12.1	12.1	12.1	12.1

Employment by Industry: El Paso, TX, Selected Years, 2002–2013—*Continued*

(Numbers in thousands, not seasonally adjusted)

Industry and year	January	February	March	April	May	June	July	August	September	October	November	December	Annual average
Professional and Business Services													
2002	24.9	25.5	25.8	26.1	26.1	26.3	26.5	26.8	27.1	27.4	27.3	27.9	26.5
2003	25.6	25.5	24.8	25.0	25.0	24.5	24.8	25.3	26.0	26.6	26.5	27.4	25.6
2004	26.6	26.5	26.1	27.2	27.1	27.4	28.0	28.1	27.8	26.9	26.9	26.9	27.1
2005	25.6	25.8	25.9	26.2	25.8	26.4	26.8	27.3	27.8	27.9	28.1	28.7	26.9
2006	28.2	28.3	28.6	28.6	28.7	29.2	29.3	30.7	30.9	31.0	31.4	31.6	29.7
2007	30.5	30.9	30.8	30.1	29.9	29.8	29.8	30.3	30.2	30.9	30.8	31.4	30.5
2008	30.7	31.0	31.0	31.1	30.8	30.7	31.2	32.4	31.6	32.1	31.8	31.8	31.4
2009	31.2	30.7	30.7	30.8	29.7	29.9	29.7	30.1	30.0	30.3	30.6	30.6	30.4
2010	30.4	30.4	31.2	30.5	30.2	29.9	30.0	30.0	30.0	30.4	30.4	30.3	30.3
2011	29.9	30.2	30.0	30.0	29.4	28.9	29.2	29.1	29.3	28.8	28.9	29.4	29.4
2012	29.0	29.2	29.6	29.7	29.2	28.9	29.2	29.4	29.5	29.6	29.5	29.7	29.4
2013	29.3	29.8	29.6	29.1	28.8	28.8	28.9	29.5	29.8	30.4	30.2	29.8	29.5
Education and Health Services													
2002	26.3	26.6	26.8	27.2	27.6	27.7	28.1	28.5	28.5	27.6	27.8	28.0	27.6
2003	27.7	28.0	28.3	28.5	28.6	28.7	28.7	29.0	29.2	29.1	29.2	29.3	28.7
2004	28.8	29.1	29.4	29.6	29.9	30.0	30.4	30.6	31.0	31.5	31.7	32.0	30.3
2005	31.8	32.1	32.3	32.4	32.5	32.9	33.0	33.1	33.2	33.2	33.3	33.5	32.8
2006	33.3	33.5	33.6	32.9	32.4	32.2	32.0	32.4	32.0	31.3	31.5	31.4	32.4
2007	31.0	31.3	31.5	31.5	31.8	32.2	32.1	32.4	32.3	32.1	32.3	32.7	31.9
2008	32.3	32.7	32.9	32.6	32.9	32.9	32.7	33.0	33.1	33.2	33.5	33.7	33.0
2009	33.5	33.9	34.0	34.0	34.2	35.3	35.9	35.9	35.2	35.2	35.3	36.7	34.8
2010	35.2	35.1	35.7	35.9	36.1	37.7	35.8	36.0	36.2	36.2	36.4	36.7	36.1
2011	36.6	36.8	36.9	37.3	37.4	37.4	37.5	37.6	37.8	37.7	37.8	37.8	37.4
2012	37.5	38.2	38.6	38.4	38.5	38.5	38.3	38.6	38.8	39.3	39.3	39.4	38.6
2013	38.6	39.0	39.1	39.3	39.4	39.2	39.1	39.3	39.6	39.8	39.6	39.5	39.3
Leisure and Hospitality													
2002	21.6	22.0	22.6	23.2	23.8	24.0	23.6	23.8	23.7	22.6	23.1	23.1	23.1
2003	22.7	22.8	23.3	23.3	23.9	24.1	23.9	24.0	23.8	23.2	23.2	23.5	23.5
2004	23.6	23.7	24.0	24.6	24.8	25.0	25.0	25.0	24.9	24.0	24.0	24.1	24.4
2005	24.2	24.6	25.0	25.7	26.0	26.5	26.2	26.3	26.1	25.6	25.2	25.5	25.6
2006	24.5	24.9	25.6	25.8	26.3	26.7	26.4	26.2	26.4	25.9	25.6	26.0	25.9
2007	25.6	25.8	26.5	26.6	27.1	27.4	27.1	26.9	26.8	26.6	26.4	26.5	26.6
2008	26.8	26.8	27.2	27.9	28.2	28.0	27.8	27.7	27.3	27.3	27.2	27.1	27.4
2009	26.4	26.7	27.1	27.1	28.0	27.9	27.4	27.5	27.1	26.3	26.6	26.8	27.1
2010	26.2	26.8	27.5	28.1	28.7	28.7	28.0	28.1	28.0	27.6	27.7	27.8	27.8
2011	28.0	28.3	29.1	29.1	29.6	29.9	29.9	29.8	29.5	28.9	29.0	29.1	29.2
2012	28.6	29.4	29.7	30.4	30.8	30.8	30.7	30.8	30.7	29.9	30.0	30.2	30.2
2013	29.5	29.9	30.5	30.8	31.6	31.7	31.2	31.3	30.9	30.4	30.4	30.5	30.7
Other Services													
2002	7.7	7.8	8.0	8.0	8.1	8.1	7.9	7.9	7.8	7.7	7.8	7.7	7.9
2003	7.5	7.6	7.6	7.5	7.5	7.6	7.5	7.5	7.4	7.7	7.5	7.5	7.5
2004	7.6	7.8	7.9	7.3	7.4	7.5	7.4	7.5	7.4	7.4	7.4	7.5	7.5
2005	7.4	7.4	7.6	7.8	7.9	8.0	7.7	7.8	7.8	7.8	7.6	7.5	7.7
2006	7.1	7.2	7.3	7.6	7.7	7.8	7.9	7.8	7.8	8.0	7.9	7.9	7.7
2007	7.4	7.5	7.6	7.7	7.9	8.1	8.1	8.2	8.3	8.3	8.4	8.5	8.0
2008	8.6	8.9	9.0	9.5	9.6	9.6	9.5	9.5	9.5	9.4	9.4	9.4	9.3
2009	9.2	9.2	9.3	9.3	9.3	9.4	9.3	9.2	9.2	9.3	9.3	9.2	9.3
2010	9.1	9.2	9.3	9.2	9.2	9.2	9.1	9.2	9.2	9.3	9.2	9.3	9.2
2011	9.2	9.3	9.4	9.5	9.4	9.6	9.5	9.6	9.6	9.6	9.5	9.5	9.5
2012	9.4	9.5	9.6	9.7	9.7	9.8	9.8	9.8	9.7	9.6	9.6	9.5	9.6
2013	9.4	9.4	9.4	9.4	9.5	9.7	9.6	9.6	9.6	9.6	9.6	9.6	9.5
Government													
2002	58.4	59.4	59.2	58.7	57.8	55.7	53.4	55.0	59.4	60.2	60.4	59.4	58.1
2003	59.3	60.7	60.6	60.5	59.5	56.6	55.5	57.0	60.5	60.4	60.6	59.5	59.2
2004	60.1	61.1	61.0	60.9	61.4	58.5	57.5	56.9	60.6	61.9	61.8	60.9	60.2
2005	61.2	62.0	62.0	61.8	61.9	59.3	56.5	57.0	60.6	61.7	61.5	60.7	60.5
2006	61.0	62.0	62.1	61.7	61.8	58.4	56.0	56.5	61.4	62.8	63.0	63.1	60.8
2007	63.1	63.7	63.8	64.9	65.1	62.1	59.5	59.6	64.9	66.4	66.6	66.5	63.9
2008	66.0	67.4	67.3	65.2	66.0	63.4	59.3	59.4	64.3	66.8	66.8	66.8	64.9
2009	67.0	67.5	67.4	68.9	68.5	66.8	61.9	62.0	67.2	69.7	69.7	69.5	67.2
2010	69.4	70.2	70.2	70.7	71.4	69.0	64.0	64.6	69.3	69.6	69.9	69.8	69.0
2011	69.3	69.5	69.4	69.8	69.6	68.7	65.1	65.4	69.5	69.1	69.3	69.0	68.6
2012	69.5	69.5	69.3	69.5	69.8	66.8	65.0	65.4	68.2	69.7	70.0	69.7	68.5
2013	69.4	70.1	69.8	69.8	69.7	66.6	65.0	65.6	68.6	69.6	69.9	69.7	68.7

Employment by Industry: Fresno, CA, Selected Years, 2002–2013

(Numbers in thousands, not seasonally adjusted)

Industry and year	January	February	March	April	May	June	July	August	September	October	November	December	Annual average
Total Nonfarm													
2002	277.3	280.8	283.6	286.3	289.6	290.3	289.0	291.5	292.0	291.0	292.1	290.2	287.8
2003	281.7	283.2	286.0	286.6	290.8	293.4	289.1	289.9	291.8	292.6	292.3	291.4	289.1
2004	285.3	288.7	289.4	292.9	296.1	295.0	294.3	296.9	299.0	299.3	299.1	297.6	294.5
2005	292.0	295.1	297.1	301.6	302.7	302.8	300.8	303.2	304.2	306.9	307.5	309.2	301.9
2006	301.2	305.2	308.5	309.1	312.2	311.1	308.2	310.4	313.7	313.6	313.9	313.8	310.1
2007	307.0	310.5	313.7	315.8	316.7	316.4	314.7	316.3	316.3	314.8	314.1	313.3	314.1
2008	306.4	310.1	311.7	314.0	316.6	314.9	308.9	310.2	312.1	312.3	310.1	307.9	311.3
2009	297.9	298.9	299.6	299.9	300.9	296.9	291.1	290.5	292.3	293.1	292.3	290.1	295.3
2010	282.1	285.5	287.6	289.2	292.5	291.6	283.6	285.4	288.0	292.3	290.4	288.7	288.1
2011	282.8	287.1	289.6	291.1	292.1	290.1	286.9	286.9	290.2	291.0	290.0	288.0	288.8
2012	283.5	286.1	288.8	290.5	294.2	295.6	291.3	292.0	293.3	298.9	299.4	297.1	292.6
2013	294.8	299.1	301.9	302.9	305.1	306.0	303.6	305.6	308.8	312.3	312.2	311.7	305.3
Total Private													
2002	209.1	211.2	213.1	215.2	217.9	219.7	222.1	225.3	225.1	221.8	222.1	221.5	218.7
2003	213.4	213.9	216.5	216.7	221.1	223.6	223.2	226.5	227.3	225.4	225.0	225.2	221.5
2004	218.9	220.7	221.2	224.0	228.3	228.2	230.8	233.5	233.8	232.1	231.7	231.0	227.9
2005	225.5	227.1	228.0	232.2	233.4	234.5	236.9	239.7	239.2	239.8	240.2	242.5	234.9
2006	234.7	237.0	238.5	239.2	241.9	243.3	244.5	246.8	247.7	245.1	245.4	245.9	242.5
2007	239.4	240.7	242.5	243.8	245.2	246.4	248.9	250.8	249.0	245.0	244.2	243.8	245.0
2008	237.4	238.4	239.0	240.7	244.0	243.2	243.9	244.9	244.0	242.0	239.8	238.5	241.3
2009	229.7	228.6	228.3	227.3	229.1	227.7	225.3	226.3	225.3	224.1	224.2	222.9	226.6
2010	215.7	215.9	216.9	218.8	222.0	222.8	221.5	223.6	223.7	224.8	223.7	222.7	221.0
2011	217.4	219.0	220.5	221.4	223.1	223.5	224.1	225.9	227.5	225.7	224.8	224.1	223.1
2012	220.0	220.8	222.6	224.1	227.8	229.9	229.7	232.4	231.7	234.1	235.0	233.5	228.5
2013	231.7	233.5	235.5	236.4	238.9	240.1	243.4	245.8	246.6	247.4	246.9	247.0	241.1
Goods Producing													
2002	40.9	41.2	41.8	42.0	43.5	44.1	45.5	48.0	48.2	45.2	44.3	43.4	44.0
2003	42.0	42.0	42.8	42.6	44.9	46.6	46.5	49.1	49.5	47.6	45.8	45.2	45.4
2004	43.7	43.9	44.2	45.8	48.4	47.4	50.5	52.0	51.5	49.2	48.0	47.3	47.7
2005	45.3	46.0	46.1	47.1	47.6	48.4	51.5	52.7	51.6	50.7	50.0	50.5	49.0
2006	48.7	49.3	49.3	49.3	50.6	51.2	52.6	53.8	53.6	51.6	50.4	49.8	50.9
2007	48.2	48.1	48.6	48.7	49.3	49.7	52.9	53.6	51.7	48.3	46.7	45.9	49.3
2008	44.1	44.2	44.3	44.7	46.4	46.2	47.1	47.3	46.7	45.0	42.9	41.8	45.1
2009	39.8	38.8	38.8	38.5	40.0	39.2	40.2	40.9	39.9	38.0	37.2	36.3	39.0
2010	34.8	34.3	34.6	35.2	36.9	37.4	37.5	38.2	38.2	37.7	36.0	35.2	36.3
2011	33.9	34.0	34.1	34.3	35.5	36.2	36.9	37.4	37.7	36.5	34.8	34.3	35.5
2012	33.9	33.6	34.0	34.1	36.4	37.7	38.3	39.0	37.6	37.0	35.7	35.2	36.0
2013	34.6	34.4	34.7	34.9	35.9	36.7	38.2	38.7	38.6	37.6	35.9	35.7	36.3
Service-Providing													
2002	236.4	239.6	241.8	244.3	246.1	246.2	243.5	243.5	243.8	245.8	247.8	246.8	243.8
2003	239.7	241.2	243.2	244.0	245.9	246.8	242.6	240.8	242.3	245.0	246.5	246.2	243.7
2004	241.6	244.8	245.2	247.1	247.7	247.6	243.8	244.9	247.5	250.1	251.1	250.3	246.8
2005	246.7	249.1	251.0	254.5	255.1	254.4	249.3	250.5	252.6	256.2	257.5	258.7	253.0
2006	252.5	255.9	259.2	259.8	261.6	259.9	255.6	256.6	260.1	262.0	263.5	264.0	259.2
2007	258.8	262.4	265.1	267.1	267.4	266.7	261.8	262.7	264.6	266.5	267.4	267.4	264.8
2008	262.3	265.9	267.4	269.3	270.2	268.7	261.8	262.9	265.4	267.3	267.2	266.1	266.2
2009	258.1	260.1	260.8	261.4	260.9	257.7	250.9	249.6	252.4	255.1	255.1	253.8	256.3
2010	247.3	251.2	253.0	254.0	255.6	254.2	246.1	247.2	249.8	254.6	254.4	253.5	251.7
2011	248.9	253.1	255.5	256.8	256.6	253.9	250.0	249.5	252.5	254.5	255.2	253.7	253.4
2012	249.6	252.5	254.8	256.4	257.8	257.9	253.0	253.0	255.7	261.9	263.7	261.9	256.5
2013	260.2	264.7	267.2	268.0	269.2	269.3	265.4	266.9	270.2	274.7	276.3	276.0	269.0
Mining and Logging													
2002	0.3	0.3	0.2	0.3	0.3	0.3	0.2	0.3	0.3	0.2	0.3	0.2	0.3
2003	0.2	0.2	0.2	0.2	0.2	0.2	0.2	0.2	0.2	0.2	0.2	0.2	0.2
2004	0.2	0.2	0.2	0.2	0.2	0.2	0.2	0.2	0.2	0.2	0.2	0.2	0.2
2005	0.2	0.2	0.2	0.2	0.2	0.2	0.2	0.2	0.2	0.2	0.2	0.2	0.2
2006	0.2	0.2	0.2	0.2	0.2	0.2	0.2	0.2	0.2	0.2	0.2	0.1	0.2
2007	0.1	0.1	0.1	0.1	0.1	0.1	0.2	0.2	0.2	0.2	0.2	0.1	0.1
2008	0.1	0.1	0.1	0.1	0.1	0.1	0.2	0.1	0.1	0.2	0.2	0.1	0.1
2009	0.2	0.2	0.2	0.2	0.2	0.2	0.2	0.2	0.2	0.3	0.3	0.2	0.2
2010	0.2	0.2	0.2	0.2	0.2	0.2	0.2	0.2	0.2	0.2	0.2	0.2	0.2
2011	0.2	0.2	0.2	0.2	0.2	0.2	0.2	0.2	0.2	0.2	0.2	0.2	0.2
2012	0.2	0.2	0.2	0.2	0.2	0.3	0.3	0.3	0.3	0.3	0.3	0.2	0.3
2013	0.2	0.2	0.3	0.2	0.3	0.3	0.3	0.3	0.3	0.3	0.3	0.3	0.3
Construction													
2002	16.0	16.2	16.6	16.7	17.1	17.1	17.2	17.4	17.1	17.1	17.2	17.0	16.9
2003	16.5	16.5	17.2	17.6	18.1	18.8	18.6	18.8	18.8	18.8	18.5	18.4	18.1
2004	18.4	18.7	19.0	19.7	19.8	20.1	20.5	20.8	20.8	20.7	20.3	20.3	19.9
2005	19.3	19.8	20.2	20.7	20.9	21.6	22.4	22.7	22.7	22.7	22.9	23.1	21.6
2006	22.3	22.6	22.6	22.8	23.4	23.7	23.8	24.0	23.6	23.3	23.0	22.9	23.2
2007	21.7	21.5	21.9	21.8	21.7	21.9	21.7	21.4	20.4	20.0	19.7	19.0	21.1
2008	17.9	18.1	18.1	18.6	18.6	18.4	18.5	18.3	17.7	17.4	16.7	16.0	17.9
2009	14.6	14.1	14.3	14.1	14.2	14.1	14.1	13.9	13.4	12.8	12.6	12.0	13.7
2010	11.7	11.5	11.7	11.9	12.3	12.4	12.5	12.4	12.2	12.1	11.8	11.6	12.0
2011	11.0	11.1	11.4	11.4	11.5	11.7	12.1	12.1	11.9	11.6	11.2	11.2	11.5
2012	11.2	11.1	11.4	11.5	12.0	12.6	12.9	13.0	12.5	12.7	12.5	12.4	12.2
2013	12.2	12.1	12.5	12.8	13.2	13.5	13.8	13.7	13.7	13.5	13.3	13.3	13.1

Employment by Industry: Fresno, CA, Selected Years, 2002–2013—*Continued*

(Numbers in thousands, not seasonally adjusted)

Industry and year	January	February	March	April	May	June	July	August	September	October	November	December	Annual average
Manufacturing													
2002	24.6	24.7	25.0	25.0	26.1	26.7	28.1	30.3	30.8	27.9	26.8	26.2	26.9
2003	25.3	25.3	25.4	24.8	26.6	27.6	27.7	30.1	30.5	28.6	27.1	26.6	27.1
2004	25.1	25.0	25.0	25.9	28.4	27.1	29.8	31.0	30.5	28.3	27.5	26.8	27.5
2005	25.8	26.0	25.7	26.2	26.5	26.6	28.9	29.8	28.7	27.8	26.9	27.2	27.2
2006	26.2	26.5	26.5	26.3	27.0	27.3	28.6	29.6	29.8	28.1	27.2	26.8	27.5
2007	26.4	26.5	26.6	26.8	27.5	27.7	31.0	32.0	31.1	28.1	26.8	26.8	28.1
2008	26.1	26.0	26.1	26.0	27.7	27.7	28.4	28.9	28.9	27.4	26.0	25.7	27.1
2009	25.0	24.5	24.3	24.2	25.6	24.9	25.9	26.8	26.3	24.9	24.3	24.1	25.1
2010	22.9	22.6	22.7	23.1	24.4	24.8	24.8	25.6	25.8	25.4	24.0	23.4	24.1
2011	22.7	22.7	22.5	22.7	23.8	24.3	24.6	25.1	25.6	24.7	23.4	22.9	23.8
2012	22.5	22.3	22.4	22.4	24.2	24.8	25.1	25.7	24.8	24.0	22.9	22.6	23.6
2013	22.2	22.1	21.9	21.9	22.4	22.9	24.1	24.7	24.6	23.8	22.3	22.1	22.9
Trade, Transportation, and Utilities													
2002	53.0	52.7	52.7	53.5	53.5	54.6	55.2	55.7	55.8	56.1	57.5	57.9	54.9
2003	54.3	53.9	54.3	55.1	55.6	56.5	56.4	56.5	56.5	56.5	57.3	57.9	55.9
2004	54.5	54.3	54.0	54.6	55.4	56.2	56.0	56.1	56.4	56.5	57.3	57.6	55.7
2005	55.7	55.1	55.3	55.8	56.2	56.9	57.3	57.9	58.0	58.4	59.1	60.0	57.1
2006	56.8	56.4	57.0	56.9	57.5	58.4	58.7	59.0	59.5	59.6	60.8	60.9	58.5
2007	58.7	58.2	58.8	59.1	59.9	60.6	61.1	61.4	61.3	61.1	62.0	62.6	60.4
2008	58.8	58.0	58.0	57.8	59.2	59.3	59.4	59.7	60.0	59.8	60.1	60.0	59.2
2009	56.4	55.6	55.1	54.7	55.3	55.4	54.6	55.0	55.9	55.8	56.8	56.9	55.6
2010	53.6	53.3	53.3	53.7	54.1	54.8	54.7	55.6	56.1	56.7	57.7	58.0	55.1
2011	55.6	55.5	55.2	55.9	56.2	56.4	57.3	57.9	58.8	59.1	60.1	60.0	57.3
2012	56.3	55.6	55.7	56.3	57.1	57.8	58.0	58.6	59.4	59.9	61.3	61.1	58.1
2013	58.2	58.7	59.1	59.4	60.5	60.3	61.2	62.1	62.3	62.5	64.1	64.5	61.1
Wholesale Trade													
2002	11.8	11.8	11.9	12.3	12.3	12.7	12.8	12.9	12.8	13.0	12.9	12.9	12.5
2003	12.2	12.2	12.3	12.6	12.7	12.9	12.7	12.7	12.6	12.6	12.3	12.2	12.5
2004	11.6	11.8	11.7	11.9	12.2	12.4	12.6	12.7	12.7	12.6	12.3	12.2	12.2
2005	12.0	12.0	12.1	12.3	12.4	12.8	13.0	13.1	13.2	13.1	13.0	12.9	12.7
2006	12.7	12.8	12.9	12.9	13.1	13.7	13.6	13.6	13.6	13.6	13.3	13.0	13.2
2007	12.9	13.0	13.3	13.3	13.6	14.0	14.0	14.0	13.8	13.5	13.3	13.0	13.5
2008	12.5	12.5	12.6	12.9	13.1	13.4	13.3	13.2	13.1	12.8	12.6	12.3	12.9
2009	11.9	11.8	11.7	11.7	11.8	12.1	11.9	11.9	12.0	11.9	11.9	11.6	11.9
2010	11.1	11.1	11.1	11.1	11.2	11.6	11.7	11.8	11.7	12.0	11.8	11.6	11.5
2011	12.1	12.2	12.2	12.2	12.3	12.4	12.7	12.7	12.9	12.8	12.8	12.6	12.5
2012	12.2	12.3	12.3	12.4	12.6	12.9	13.0	13.1	13.1	13.2	13.1	13.0	12.8
2013	12.9	13.1	13.2	13.4	13.8	13.7	14.0	13.9	14.0	14.0	13.9	14.0	13.7
Retail Trade													
2002	32.4	32.1	32.0	32.1	32.2	32.7	32.7	32.9	33.0	33.2	34.6	35.2	32.9
2003	33.0	32.6	32.7	33.0	33.2	33.7	33.8	33.8	34.0	34.0	35.4	36.1	33.8
2004	33.6	33.2	32.9	33.2	33.6	34.0	33.7	33.7	34.0	34.2	35.4	35.8	33.9
2005	34.6	34.0	34.0	34.4	34.5	34.6	34.7	35.1	35.1	35.6	36.6	37.7	35.1
2006	35.0	34.5	34.8	34.6	34.7	34.7	34.8	35.1	35.2	35.5	36.7	37.3	35.2
2007	35.7	35.1	35.3	35.5	35.9	36.0	36.2	36.4	36.4	36.6	37.7	38.5	36.3
2008	35.8	35.1	35.0	35.0	35.0	34.8	34.9	35.0	35.2	35.6	36.3	36.6	35.4
2009	33.8	33.2	32.9	32.5	32.8	32.6	32.3	32.5	33.0	33.1	34.2	34.8	33.1
2010	32.3	32.0	32.0	32.2	32.3	32.4	32.2	32.6	33.1	33.4	34.4	35.0	32.8
2011	32.7	32.5	32.2	32.7	32.8	32.8	33.0	33.3	33.8	34.1	35.3	35.7	33.4
2012	33.0	32.3	32.3	32.7	33.0	33.2	33.3	33.6	34.3	34.8	36.5	36.3	33.8
2013	34.0	34.0	34.2	34.3	34.6	34.6	34.8	35.5	35.6	35.8	37.4	37.7	35.2
Transportation and Utilities													
2002	8.8	8.8	8.8	9.1	9.0	9.2	9.7	9.9	10.0	9.9	10.0	9.8	9.4
2003	9.1	9.1	9.3	9.5	9.7	9.9	9.9	10.0	9.9	9.9	9.6	9.6	9.6
2004	9.3	9.3	9.4	9.5	9.6	9.8	9.7	9.7	9.7	9.7	9.6	9.6	9.6
2005	9.1	9.1	9.2	9.1	9.3	9.5	9.6	9.7	9.7	9.7	9.5	9.4	9.4
2006	9.1	9.1	9.3	9.4	9.7	10.0	10.3	10.3	10.7	10.5	10.8	10.6	10.0
2007	10.1	10.1	10.2	10.3	10.4	10.6	10.9	11.0	11.1	11.0	11.0	11.1	10.7
2008	10.5	10.4	10.4	9.9	11.1	11.1	11.2	11.5	11.7	11.4	11.2	11.1	11.0
2009	10.7	10.6	10.5	10.5	10.7	10.7	10.4	10.6	10.9	10.8	10.7	10.5	10.6
2010	10.2	10.2	10.2	10.4	10.6	10.8	10.8	11.2	11.3	11.3	11.5	11.4	10.8
2011	10.8	10.8	10.8	11.0	11.1	11.2	11.6	11.9	12.1	12.2	12.0	11.7	11.4
2012	11.1	11.0	11.1	11.2	11.5	11.7	11.7	11.9	12.0	11.9	11.7	11.8	11.6
2013	11.3	11.6	11.7	11.7	12.1	12.0	12.4	12.7	12.7	12.7	12.8	12.8	12.2
Information													
2002	4.9	4.8	4.9	4.8	4.7	4.7	4.6	4.6	4.5	4.6	4.6	4.5	4.7
2003	4.0	4.1	4.0	4.0	4.0	4.1	4.2	4.3	4.2	4.4	4.5	4.6	4.2
2004	4.5	4.5	4.5	4.5	4.6	4.6	4.6	4.6	4.6	4.7	4.5	4.5	4.6
2005	4.4	4.5	4.4	4.4	4.4	4.4	4.3	4.3	4.3	4.2	4.3	4.2	4.3
2006	4.2	4.2	4.2	4.2	4.2	4.2	4.2	4.2	4.2	4.2	4.2	4.2	4.2
2007	4.1	4.2	4.1	4.1	4.2	4.2	4.2	4.2	4.2	4.2	4.2	4.2	4.2
2008	4.5	4.5	4.4	4.8	4.8	4.8	4.9	4.9	4.8	4.8	4.8	4.8	4.7
2009	4.6	4.6	4.5	4.3	4.2	4.3	4.0	4.0	3.9	3.9	3.9	3.8	4.2
2010	3.8	3.7	3.7	3.5	3.5	3.5	3.6	3.5	3.5	3.5	3.5	3.5	3.6
2011	3.4	3.4	3.4	3.4	3.5	3.5	3.5	3.5	3.6	3.6	3.7	3.6	3.5
2012	3.8	3.7	3.7	3.8	3.8	3.9	3.8	3.8	3.8	3.8	3.8	3.8	3.8
2013	3.8	3.8	3.8	3.8	3.8	3.8	3.9	3.8	3.8	3.8	3.8	3.8	3.8

Employment by Industry: Fresno, CA, Selected Years, 2002–2013—*Continued*

(Numbers in thousands, not seasonally adjusted)

Industry and year	January	February	March	April	May	June	July	August	September	October	November	December	Annual average
Financial Activities													
2002	13.7	13.7	13.8	14.1	14.2	14.2	14.5	14.5	14.4	14.1	14.2	14.2	14.1
2003	13.7	13.7	13.8	13.8	13.9	13.9	13.7	13.7	13.6	13.6	13.5	13.5	13.7
2004	13.5	13.6	13.7	13.7	13.9	14.0	14.0	14.0	14.1	14.2	14.2	14.3	13.9
2005	14.3	14.2	14.3	14.5	14.5	14.6	14.8	14.8	15.0	15.1	15.2	15.3	14.7
2006	15.2	15.3	15.3	15.5	15.6	15.6	15.7	15.7	15.7	15.5	15.5	15.6	15.5
2007	15.3	15.4	15.4	15.5	15.5	15.6	15.4	15.3	15.3	14.9	15.0	15.0	15.3
2008	14.9	14.9	14.9	14.8	14.9	14.9	14.7	14.8	14.6	14.6	14.6	14.5	14.8
2009	14.3	14.2	14.0	14.0	13.9	13.8	13.6	13.6	13.5	13.5	13.5	13.5	13.8
2010	13.5	13.4	13.3	13.4	13.4	13.4	13.4	13.4	13.4	13.3	13.4	13.3	13.4
2011	13.2	13.2	13.2	13.2	13.1	13.1	13.0	13.0	12.7	12.6	12.6	12.6	13.0
2012	12.6	12.5	12.6	12.8	12.9	12.9	13.0	13.0	13.0	12.9	12.9	12.9	12.8
2013	12.8	12.8	12.9	12.9	12.9	12.9	12.9	12.9	12.9	12.9	12.8	12.9	12.9
Professional and Business Services													
2002	23.8	24.3	24.2	25.0	25.2	25.3	25.2	25.6	25.5	26.1	26.1	26.1	25.2
2003	26.2	26.0	26.3	25.8	26.2	26.0	26.2	26.6	26.8	26.6	26.9	26.8	26.4
2004	26.7	27.1	27.2	27.4	27.4	27.4	27.6	28.1	28.1	28.3	28.6	28.2	27.7
2005	27.7	28.4	28.6	29.2	29.3	29.0	28.6	28.9	28.6	29.0	29.0	29.3	28.8
2006	28.7	29.1	29.4	29.8	29.5	29.4	29.3	29.9	29.8	29.9	29.7	29.7	29.5
2007	29.3	29.6	29.9	30.0	29.8	30.0	30.2	30.2	30.3	30.6	30.1	29.9	30.0
2008	30.3	30.6	30.4	30.8	30.4	30.3	31.2	31.2	31.1	30.7	30.3	30.5	30.7
2009	29.6	29.4	29.3	28.8	28.3	28.0	28.0	27.5	27.2	27.5	27.2	27.0	28.2
2010	26.0	26.3	26.6	27.3	27.3	27.2	26.8	26.8	26.3	26.7	26.7	26.4	26.7
2011	26.7	27.4	27.4	27.4	27.4	27.0	26.9	27.0	27.4	27.3	26.9	27.1	27.2
2012	27.1	27.6	27.9	27.7	27.3	27.3	27.4	27.8	28.1	28.8	30.1	28.8	28.0
2013	29.6	29.9	29.8	30.3	30.0	30.9	31.5	32.2	32.8	33.5	33.2	32.9	31.4
Education and Health Services													
2002	38.1	39.0	39.6	39.9	39.9	39.9	40.1	39.8	40.2	40.0	40.1	40.0	39.7
2003	39.4	39.9	40.5	40.9	41.1	41.2	41.1	41.2	41.9	42.6	43.0	43.2	41.3
2004	42.6	43.3	43.3	43.2	42.8	42.6	42.7	43.0	43.5	44.2	44.2	44.2	43.3
2005	43.4	43.6	43.7	44.4	44.1	43.9	43.7	43.9	44.7	45.1	45.1	45.1	44.2
2006	44.2	44.8	44.8	44.7	44.7	44.6	44.5	44.5	45.2	45.4	45.9	46.2	45.0
2007	45.7	46.4	46.5	46.7	46.3	46.3	46.0	46.4	46.9	47.4	47.5	47.6	46.6
2008	47.0	47.8	48.2	48.9	48.8	48.4	47.7	48.0	48.1	48.9	49.1	49.3	48.4
2009	48.6	49.2	49.6	49.8	49.4	49.1	48.0	48.1	48.6	49.4	49.7	49.5	49.1
2010	48.6	48.9	49.0	49.5	49.3	49.0	48.4	48.7	49.3	49.6	49.7	49.7	49.1
2011	48.9	49.0	50.0	50.1	49.8	49.3	48.6	48.8	49.6	49.4	49.8	49.9	49.4
2012	49.7	50.6	50.9	51.0	50.9	50.6	49.7	50.2	50.7	52.9	52.8	53.2	51.1
2013	54.5	55.4	55.8	55.6	55.5	55.0	54.9	55.4	55.7	56.8	56.8	57.0	55.7
Leisure and Hospitality													
2002	23.7	23.9	24.3	23.8	24.6	25.0	25.0	24.7	24.2	23.9	23.6	23.5	24.2
2003	22.6	23.0	23.3	23.2	24.0	24.3	24.5	24.3	23.8	23.3	23.4	23.2	23.6
2004	23.0	23.3	23.5	23.8	24.7	25.2	24.9	24.9	24.7	24.6	24.6	24.5	24.3
2005	24.4	24.8	25.1	25.8	26.3	26.3	26.1	26.1	26.0	26.3	26.5	27.0	25.9
2006	26.5	27.1	27.5	27.8	28.5	28.9	28.7	28.7	28.7	28.1	28.2	28.6	28.1
2007	27.5	27.9	28.3	28.6	28.9	29.1	28.3	28.5	28.2	27.6	27.7	27.7	28.2
2008	27.3	27.7	28.0	28.1	28.7	28.5	28.5	28.4	28.1	27.6	27.5	27.1	28.0
2009	26.2	26.5	26.6	26.9	27.5	27.4	27.2	27.1	26.3	26.0	25.9	25.9	26.6
2010	25.5	25.9	26.3	26.2	27.4	27.4	27.4	27.5	27.1	27.2	26.8	26.7	26.8
2011	26.0	26.6	27.3	27.1	27.6	27.9	27.9	28.0	27.3	26.8	26.5	26.3	27.1
2012	26.5	27.0	27.5	27.8	28.6	28.8	29.0	29.2	28.4	28.0	27.6	27.7	28.0
2013	27.5	27.6	28.4	28.5	29.2	29.6	30.0	29.7	29.4	29.1	29.1	29.1	28.9
Other Services													
2002	11.0	11.6	11.8	12.1	12.3	11.9	12.0	12.4	12.3	11.8	11.7	11.9	11.9
2003	11.2	11.3	11.5	11.3	11.4	11.0	10.6	10.8	11.0	10.8	10.6	10.8	11.0
2004	10.4	10.7	10.8	11.0	11.1	10.8	10.5	10.8	10.9	10.4	10.3	10.4	10.7
2005	10.3	10.5	10.5	11.0	11.0	11.0	10.6	11.1	11.0	11.0	11.0	11.1	10.8
2006	10.4	10.8	11.0	11.0	11.3	11.0	10.8	11.0	11.0	10.8	10.7	10.9	10.9
2007	10.6	10.9	10.9	11.1	11.3	10.9	10.8	11.2	11.1	10.9	11.0	10.9	11.0
2008	10.5	10.7	10.8	10.8	10.8	10.8	10.4	10.6	10.6	10.6	10.5	10.5	10.6
2009	10.2	10.3	10.4	10.3	10.5	10.5	9.7	10.1	10.0	10.0	10.0	10.0	10.2
2010	9.9	10.1	10.1	10.0	10.1	10.1	9.7	9.9	9.9	10.0	10.0	9.9	10.0
2011	9.7	9.9	9.9	10.0	10.0	10.1	10.3	10.4	10.4	10.4	10.4	10.3	10.1
2012	10.1	10.2	10.3	10.6	10.8	10.9	10.5	10.8	10.7	10.8	10.8	10.8	10.6
2013	10.7	10.9	11.0	11.0	11.1	10.9	10.8	11.0	11.1	11.2	11.2	11.1	11.0
Government													
2002	68.2	69.6	70.5	71.1	71.7	70.6	66.9	66.2	66.9	69.2	70.0	68.7	69.1
2003	68.3	69.3	69.5	69.9	69.7	69.8	65.9	63.4	64.5	67.2	67.3	66.2	67.6
2004	66.4	68.0	68.2	68.9	67.8	66.8	63.5	63.4	65.2	67.2	67.4	66.6	66.6
2005	66.5	68.0	69.1	69.4	69.3	68.3	63.9	63.5	65.0	67.1	67.3	66.7	67.0
2006	66.5	68.2	70.0	69.9	70.3	67.8	63.7	63.6	66.0	68.5	68.5	67.9	67.6
2007	67.6	69.8	71.2	72.0	71.5	70.0	65.8	65.5	67.3	69.8	69.9	69.5	69.2
2008	69.0	71.7	72.7	73.3	72.6	71.7	65.0	65.3	68.1	70.3	70.3	69.4	70.0
2009	68.2	70.3	71.3	72.6	71.8	69.2	65.8	64.2	67.0	69.0	68.1	67.2	68.7
2010	66.4	69.6	70.7	70.4	70.5	68.8	62.1	61.8	64.3	67.5	66.7	66.0	67.1
2011	65.4	68.1	69.1	69.7	69.0	66.6	62.8	61.0	62.7	65.3	65.2	63.9	65.7
2012	63.5	65.3	66.2	66.4	66.4	65.7	61.6	59.6	61.6	64.8	64.4	63.6	64.1
2013	63.1	65.6	66.4	66.5	66.2	65.9	60.2	59.8	62.2	64.9	65.3	64.7	64.2

Employment by Industry: Grand Rapids-Wyoming, MI, Selected Years, 2002–2013

(Numbers in thousands, not seasonally adjusted)

Industry and year	January	February	March	April	May	June	July	August	September	October	November	December	Annual average
Total Nonfarm													
2002	385.1	386.1	388.2	391.3	397.1	396.0	387.3	390.1	395.5	397.4	398.2	398.0	392.5
2003	376.4	376.9	376.6	377.2	386.7	384.0	375.1	379.9	384.7	389.2	391.7	392.9	382.6
2004	378.6	379.1	379.8	386.2	390.9	388.4	379.6	382.7	388.4	390.6	392.2	391.6	385.7
2005	378.5	381.0	383.8	388.1	392.9	390.1	385.1	388.0	394.0	394.2	395.5	395.0	388.9
2006	379.9	382.0	384.3	389.0	394.2	391.9	381.2	384.9	391.1	390.5	392.1	392.3	387.8
2007	379.5	381.7	383.4	385.9	391.8	391.5	382.9	386.0	391.3	391.8	393.8	394.6	387.9
2008	382.7	383.5	383.9	386.3	392.3	390.0	377.3	381.2	384.0	383.5	382.2	379.4	383.9
2009	359.8	360.7	360.0	364.3	368.6	361.8	349.2	351.3	359.6	361.9	363.5	363.1	360.3
2010	351.4	354.1	354.4	359.2	366.1	366.3	359.7	360.5	367.8	369.2	370.6	370.2	362.5
2011	361.0	363.0	365.5	370.8	376.7	374.8	369.9	370.7	380.4	383.5	385.5	385.6	374.0
2012	379.1	381.0	382.1	388.7	394.2	391.0	381.8	384.4	394.1	398.8	400.4	400.2	389.7
2013	393.1	396.1	398.4	397.7	407.4	405.9	393.2	397.3	406.0	410.0	411.8	411.6	402.4
Total Private													
2002	346.7	347.0	348.9	352.9	357.8	359.4	355.6	358.6	358.2	357.6	358.0	357.6	354.9
2003	337.2	337.1	336.8	338.1	346.5	346.2	342.1	346.2	346.9	349.6	351.9	353.0	344.3
2004	339.4	339.6	340.0	346.9	350.9	351.9	347.8	350.5	350.9	351.4	352.9	352.2	347.9
2005	340.5	341.7	344.4	348.8	352.8	352.3	352.9	355.5	357.0	355.2	356.4	356.3	351.2
2006	342.1	342.9	345.1	350.0	354.4	354.4	349.2	352.5	354.8	352.3	354.1	354.3	350.5
2007	343.1	344.5	346.1	348.8	354.3	355.1	351.1	353.5	355.3	355.1	357.2	357.9	351.8
2008	347.0	347.1	347.3	349.7	355.5	353.8	345.7	348.4	348.1	346.5	345.5	342.9	348.1
2009	323.5	324.1	323.2	327.3	331.4	326.1	317.5	319.7	324.2	325.9	327.4	327.3	324.8
2010	316.0	318.6	318.9	323.6	329.5	330.8	328.3	329.6	333.5	333.8	335.0	335.2	327.7
2011	326.5	328.5	330.6	336.1	341.8	340.7	340.1	341.3	346.8	349.2	351.3	351.7	340.4
2012	345.3	347.0	348.0	355.0	360.0	359.1	352.3	355.1	361.0	365.0	366.5	366.7	356.8
2013	360.2	362.4	364.8	364.0	373.5	373.2	364.2	367.9	373.1	376.8	378.7	378.2	369.8
Goods Producing													
2002	98.5	97.8	97.7	98.7	100.2	100.7	99.4	99.9	99.2	99.2	98.4	97.8	99.0
2003	93.7	92.8	92.5	91.3	94.9	95.0	92.9	95.0	94.5	94.4	94.2	94.2	93.8
2004	92.1	91.1	91.2	92.8	93.6	94.5	92.9	94.4	94.1	94.0	93.2	93.2	93.1
2005	91.2	90.5	91.5	91.6	92.5	93.4	92.6	93.7	93.3	93.4	93.1	92.7	92.5
2006	90.1	89.5	89.8	91.5	92.6	93.4	91.1	92.7	92.1	90.8	90.0	89.7	91.1
2007	86.8	86.5	86.5	87.8	88.9	90.0	88.6	90.0	89.4	88.8	88.8	88.4	88.4
2008	86.2	85.3	84.8	84.7	86.0	87.4	84.2	86.0	85.0	83.1	81.6	79.7	84.5
2009	72.0	71.5	70.7	70.8	70.7	70.8	69.7	71.6	72.1	71.5	70.6	70.3	71.0
2010	67.7	67.8	68.4	70.3	71.6	72.9	73.4	73.9	73.9	73.6	73.2	73.2	71.7
2011	71.9	72.0	72.3	74.1	75.5	76.8	76.4	77.4	77.2	77.2	77.2	77.2	75.4
2012	76.1	76.2	76.6	77.8	79.0	80.5	80.7	81.1	80.6	80.6	80.2	80.3	79.1
2013	79.6	79.7	80.2	80.4	82.0	83.0	83.0	83.8	83.4	84.1	84.7	84.5	82.4
Service-Providing													
2002	286.6	288.3	290.5	292.6	296.9	295.3	287.9	290.2	296.3	298.2	299.8	300.2	293.6
2003	282.7	284.1	284.1	285.9	291.8	289.0	282.2	284.9	290.2	294.8	297.5	298.7	288.8
2004	286.5	288.0	288.6	293.4	297.3	293.9	286.7	288.3	294.3	296.6	299.0	298.4	292.6
2005	287.3	290.5	292.3	296.5	300.4	296.7	292.5	294.3	300.7	300.8	302.4	302.3	296.4
2006	289.8	292.5	294.5	297.5	301.6	298.5	290.1	292.2	299.0	299.7	302.1	302.6	296.7
2007	292.7	295.2	296.9	298.1	302.9	301.5	294.3	296.0	301.9	303.0	305.0	306.2	299.5
2008	296.5	298.2	299.1	301.6	306.3	302.6	293.1	295.2	299.0	300.4	300.6	299.7	299.4
2009	287.8	289.2	289.3	293.5	297.9	291.0	279.5	279.7	287.5	290.4	292.9	292.8	289.3
2010	283.7	286.3	286.0	288.9	294.5	293.4	286.3	286.6	293.9	295.6	297.4	297.0	290.8
2011	289.1	291.0	293.2	296.7	301.2	298.0	293.5	293.3	303.2	306.3	308.3	308.4	298.5
2012	303.0	304.8	305.5	310.9	315.2	310.5	301.1	303.3	313.5	318.2	320.2	319.9	310.5
2013	313.5	316.4	318.2	317.3	325.4	322.9	310.2	313.5	322.6	325.9	327.1	327.1	320.0
Mining, Logging, and Construction													
2002	19.0	18.8	19.1	20.0	21.2	21.5	21.8	21.7	21.1	20.9	20.3	19.6	20.4
2003	17.2	16.8	16.8	18.1	19.0	19.7	20.3	20.4	19.9	19.6	19.3	19.1	18.9
2004	17.4	16.9	17.2	19.0	19.6	20.2	20.4	20.2	19.9	19.5	19.0	18.7	19.0
2005	17.1	16.6	16.9	18.3	19.0	19.5	19.8	19.8	19.5	19.1	18.7	18.0	18.5
2006	16.5	16.2	16.5	17.9	18.8	19.5	19.3	19.3	18.9	18.4	17.9	17.4	18.1
2007	15.9	15.5	15.7	16.7	17.6	18.2	18.3	18.3	18.0	17.6	17.2	16.7	17.1
2008	15.6	15.3	15.5	16.1	17.1	17.6	17.5	17.6	17.1	16.4	15.7	14.9	16.4
2009	13.2	12.9	12.9	13.6	14.2	14.4	14.6	14.5	14.2	13.9	13.3	12.8	13.7
2010	11.6	11.6	11.9	12.7	13.3	13.7	14.0	14.1	13.7	13.4	13.0	12.5	13.0
2011	11.7	11.5	11.7	12.5	13.3	13.9	14.3	14.3	14.0	13.9	13.6	13.2	13.2
2012	12.3	12.2	12.5	13.2	13.7	14.2	14.5	14.7	14.4	14.4	13.9	13.8	13.7
2013	13.1	12.9	13.1	13.4	14.5	15.1	15.5	15.7	15.5	15.5	15.7	14.9	14.6
Manufacturing													
2002	79.5	79.0	78.6	78.7	79.0	79.2	77.6	78.2	78.1	78.3	78.1	78.2	78.5
2003	76.5	76.0	75.7	73.2	75.9	75.3	72.6	74.6	74.6	74.8	74.9	75.1	74.9
2004	74.7	74.2	74.0	73.8	74.0	74.3	72.5	74.2	74.2	74.5	74.2	74.5	74.1
2005	74.1	73.9	74.6	73.3	73.5	73.9	72.8	73.9	73.8	74.3	74.4	74.7	73.9
2006	73.6	73.3	73.3	73.6	73.8	73.9	71.8	73.4	73.2	72.4	72.1	72.3	73.1
2007	70.9	71.0	70.8	71.1	71.3	71.8	70.3	71.7	71.4	71.2	71.6	71.7	71.2
2008	70.6	70.0	69.3	68.6	68.9	69.8	66.7	68.4	67.9	66.7	65.9	64.8	68.1
2009	58.8	58.6	57.8	57.2	56.5	56.4	55.1	57.1	57.9	57.6	57.3	57.5	57.3
2010	56.1	56.2	56.5	57.6	58.3	59.2	59.4	59.8	60.2	60.2	60.2	60.7	58.7
2011	60.2	60.5	60.6	61.6	62.2	62.9	62.1	63.1	63.2	63.3	63.6	64.0	62.3
2012	63.8	64.0	64.1	64.6	65.3	66.3	66.2	66.4	66.2	66.2	66.3	66.5	65.5
2013	66.5	66.8	67.1	67.0	67.5	67.9	67.5	68.1	67.9	68.6	69.0	69.6	67.8

Employment by Industry: Grand Rapids-Wyoming, MI, Selected Years, 2002–2013—*Continued*

(Numbers in thousands, not seasonally adjusted)

Industry and year	January	February	March	April	May	June	July	August	September	October	November	December	Annual average
Trade, Transportation, and Utilities													
2002	76.9	76.3	76.4	76.5	77.1	77.5	77.0	77.5	77.3	77.4	78.2	79.3	77.3
2003	75.5	74.4	74.3	74.8	75.8	76.3	75.5	75.4	75.4	76.1	77.4	78.1	75.8
2004	74.3	73.3	73.1	74.6	75.1	75.3	74.9	74.9	74.6	75.2	76.6	77.0	74.9
2005	73.7	73.2	73.5	74.6	75.5	75.8	75.8	75.8	75.4	75.4	76.5	76.9	75.2
2006	73.2	72.6	72.7	73.2	73.8	73.9	73.6	73.4	73.3	73.7	75.1	75.7	73.7
2007	73.4	72.4	72.6	73.0	73.9	74.2	73.8	73.6	73.6	73.9	75.1	75.4	73.7
2008	72.8	72.0	72.1	71.9	72.8	73.0	72.0	72.0	71.3	71.1	71.6	71.6	72.0
2009	68.5	67.5	67.1	68.0	68.5	68.5	67.5	67.4	67.1	67.8	68.3	68.5	67.9
2010	66.0	65.5	65.5	66.3	67.0	67.5	66.9	66.8	66.5	67.6	68.5	68.7	66.9
2011	66.1	65.7	65.5	66.8	67.6	67.7	67.6	67.9	67.7	68.0	69.1	69.5	67.4
2012	66.6	66.1	66.4	67.9	68.8	69.1	68.6	68.9	68.7	69.8	71.2	71.5	68.6
2013	69.0	68.8	69.3	69.9	71.0	71.7	71.4	71.9	71.6	71.7	73.0	73.5	71.1
Wholesale Trade													
2002	23.2	22.9	22.9	22.9	23.1	23.2	23.0	23.0	22.7	22.9	22.8	22.9	23.0
2003	22.6	22.4	22.3	22.4	22.6	22.5	22.2	22.1	22.0	22.3	22.3	22.3	22.3
2004	21.7	21.7	21.6	22.1	22.2	22.4	22.3	22.1	22.1	22.1	22.2	22.2	22.1
2005	21.7	21.7	21.8	22.0	22.3	22.4	22.4	22.4	22.3	22.4	22.3	22.4	22.2
2006	22.0	22.0	22.0	22.2	22.4	22.5	22.5	22.4	22.4	22.5	22.4	22.4	22.3
2007	22.2	22.1	22.2	22.5	22.6	22.7	22.8	22.7	22.7	22.7	22.6	22.6	22.5
2008	22.2	22.2	22.3	22.3	22.4	22.5	22.3	22.4	22.3	22.0	21.8	21.6	22.2
2009	21.0	20.8	20.6	20.7	20.8	20.7	20.6	20.6	20.5	20.6	20.6	20.6	20.7
2010	20.2	20.2	20.3	20.4	20.5	20.7	20.6	20.6	20.5	20.6	20.5	20.6	20.5
2011	20.3	20.3	20.2	20.6	20.9	21.1	21.1	21.3	21.2	21.2	21.2	21.3	20.9
2012	20.9	20.9	21.1	21.5	21.8	22.0	21.9	22.0	22.0	22.3	22.3	22.3	21.8
2013	21.9	21.8	21.9	22.3	22.6	22.8	22.8	22.9	22.9	22.9	23.0	23.0	22.6
Retail Trade													
2002	42.5	42.2	42.2	42.4	42.8	43.1	42.9	43.3	43.5	43.2	44.2	45.2	43.1
2003	42.7	42.0	42.0	42.1	42.8	43.3	43.1	43.2	43.3	43.6	45.0	45.6	43.2
2004	42.6	41.7	41.5	42.0	42.4	42.4	42.2	42.3	41.8	42.1	43.5	44.0	42.4
2005	41.6	41.1	41.2	41.9	42.4	42.4	42.4	42.3	42.0	42.0	43.2	43.4	42.2
2006	40.5	40.0	40.1	40.4	40.7	40.6	40.3	40.3	40.1	40.4	41.9	42.4	40.6
2007	40.6	39.8	39.8	39.9	40.5	40.5	40.1	40.1	40.1	40.5	41.7	42.0	40.5
2008	40.2	39.5	39.6	39.2	39.8	39.8	39.2	39.1	38.6	38.7	39.6	39.8	39.4
2009	37.7	37.1	37.0	37.5	37.8	37.9	37.3	37.2	37.1	37.6	38.2	38.4	37.6
2010	36.4	36.0	35.9	36.4	36.9	37.1	36.7	36.8	36.4	37.4	38.3	38.5	36.9
2011	36.4	36.0	35.9	36.6	37.1	37.0	36.8	36.9	36.7	37.1	38.2	38.4	36.9
2012	36.2	35.6	35.8	36.6	37.1	37.1	36.8	36.9	36.7	37.4	38.7	38.7	37.0
2013	36.9	36.7	37.1	37.2	37.8	38.2	38.1	38.4	38.1	38.2	39.3	39.8	38.0
Transportation and Utilities													
2002	11.2	11.2	11.3	11.2	11.2	11.2	11.1	11.2	11.1	11.3	11.2	11.2	11.2
2003	10.2	10.0	10.0	10.3	10.4	10.5	10.2	10.1	10.1	10.2	10.1	10.2	10.2
2004	10.0	9.9	10.0	10.5	10.5	10.5	10.4	10.5	10.7	11.0	10.9	10.8	10.5
2005	10.4	10.4	10.5	10.7	10.8	11.0	11.0	11.1	11.1	11.0	11.0	11.1	10.8
2006	10.7	10.6	10.6	10.6	10.7	10.8	10.8	10.7	10.8	10.8	10.8	10.9	10.7
2007	10.6	10.5	10.6	10.6	10.8	11.0	10.9	10.8	10.8	10.7	10.8	10.8	10.7
2008	10.4	10.3	10.2	10.4	10.6	10.7	10.5	10.5	10.4	10.4	10.2	10.2	10.4
2009	9.8	9.6	9.5	9.8	9.9	9.9	9.6	9.6	9.5	9.6	9.5	9.5	9.7
2010	9.4	9.3	9.3	9.5	9.6	9.7	9.6	9.4	9.6	9.6	9.7	9.6	9.5
2011	9.4	9.4	9.4	9.6	9.6	9.6	9.7	9.7	9.8	9.7	9.7	9.8	9.6
2012	9.5	9.6	9.5	9.8	9.9	10.0	9.9	10.0	10.0	10.1	10.2	10.5	9.9
2013	10.2	10.3	10.3	10.4	10.6	10.7	10.5	10.6	10.6	10.6	10.7	10.7	10.5
Information													
2002	6.5	6.5	6.6	6.1	6.1	6.1	6.0	6.0	5.9	6.1	6.1	6.2	6.2
2003	6.1	6.0	6.0	5.9	6.0	5.9	5.5	5.5	5.4	5.5	5.5	5.5	5.7
2004	5.6	5.6	5.6	5.6	5.5	5.6	5.6	5.5	5.4	5.3	5.4	5.4	5.5
2005	5.5	5.6	5.6	5.7	5.6	5.7	5.6	5.6	5.5	5.7	5.9	5.9	5.7
2006	5.7	5.7	5.7	5.6	5.6	5.7	5.5	5.5	5.4	5.4	5.4	5.4	5.6
2007	5.3	5.3	5.2	5.2	5.3	5.3	5.2	5.2	5.0	5.0	5.1	5.1	5.2
2008	5.0	4.9	4.8	4.8	4.9	4.9	4.9	4.9	4.8	4.8	4.8	4.8	4.9
2009	4.7	4.7	4.6	4.6	4.6	4.6	4.6	4.4	4.4	4.4	4.4	4.4	4.5
2010	4.3	4.2	4.2	4.3	4.4	4.5	4.5	4.5	4.5	4.3	4.3	4.3	4.4
2011	4.2	4.2	4.2	4.1	4.2	4.3	4.2	4.3	4.2	4.2	4.2	4.3	4.2
2012	4.2	4.2	4.1	4.2	4.2	4.3	4.3	4.3	4.2	4.2	4.2	4.2	4.2
2013	4.3	4.3	4.3	4.4	4.4	4.5	4.4	4.4	4.3	4.4	4.4	4.4	4.4
Financial Activities													
2002	19.7	19.9	20.1	19.7	19.7	19.5	19.4	19.5	19.3	19.7	19.5	19.6	19.6
2003	19.6	19.5	19.5	19.7	19.7	19.7	19.8	19.8	19.8	20.0	19.9	20.1	19.8
2004	20.1	20.0	20.2	20.3	20.4	20.4	20.3	20.3	20.2	19.9	20.0	20.1	20.2
2005	20.1	20.4	20.1	20.3	20.4	20.5	20.6	20.6	20.5	20.6	20.6	20.7	20.5
2006	20.9	20.9	20.8	20.9	20.9	20.9	20.8	20.8	20.7	20.5	20.5	20.4	20.8
2007	20.1	20.1	20.0	20.5	20.6	20.4	20.5	20.1	19.9	20.4	20.2	20.3	20.3
2008	20.3	20.4	20.2	20.3	20.4	20.0	19.9	20.0	19.8	19.9	19.9	19.7	20.1
2009	19.4	19.4	19.2	19.6	19.6	19.5	19.4	19.4	18.8	19.0	19.0	18.8	19.3
2010	19.0	19.0	18.8	18.9	19.1	19.1	19.4	19.4	19.5	19.7	19.8	20.1	19.3
2011	19.6	19.8	19.8	19.9	20.0	20.1	20.4	20.6	20.6	20.7	21.0	21.2	20.3
2012	20.8	20.8	21.0	21.1	21.2	21.2	21.1	20.9	20.9	21.3	21.4	21.3	21.1
2013	21.5	21.7	21.6	21.5	21.6	21.9	21.5	21.5	21.6	21.5	21.5	21.5	21.6

Employment by Industry: Grand Rapids-Wyoming, MI, Selected Years, 2002–2013—*Continued*

(Numbers in thousands, not seasonally adjusted)

Industry and year	January	February	March	April	May	June	July	August	September	October	November	December	Annual average
Professional and Business Services													
2002	49.7	50.0	50.4	52.6	54.0	54.5	54.5	55.7	54.8	54.2	54.4	53.8	53.2
2003	46.6	46.3	45.9	47.5	49.0	49.3	50.4	52.1	51.4	52.1	52.9	52.8	49.7
2004	47.9	48.7	48.5	51.0	52.3	52.6	52.1	53.6	52.7	52.2	52.0	51.3	51.2
2005	48.2	48.3	49.0	51.0	52.1	52.6	54.8	55.8	55.9	54.5	54.6	53.8	52.6
2006	50.1	50.9	50.7	52.6	53.9	55.2	54.7	56.1	56.5	55.5	56.2	56.6	54.1
2007	53.3	54.6	55.4	55.3	57.1	57.7	57.1	58.3	59.5	58.6	59.4	59.6	57.2
2008	57.6	58.1	58.3	58.5	59.7	57.7	55.9	56.5	57.7	58.3	58.0	57.6	57.8
2009	52.7	53.4	53.6	54.0	55.9	52.1	47.0	47.6	51.7	51.9	53.9	54.3	52.3
2010	50.5	52.8	52.0	53.5	55.7	56.0	53.9	54.7	58.7	58.0	59.0	58.9	55.3
2011	56.4	58.2	59.3	60.8	62.9	61.0	60.9	60.0	64.8	66.3	66.7	66.3	62.0
2012	66.6	67.3	66.4	69.2	70.5	67.7	62.1	63.1	68.9	71.1	71.1	70.5	67.9
2013	70.0	71.2	71.5	69.0	73.7	70.3	62.7	64.4	69.9	70.8	69.9	68.4	69.3
Education and Health Services													
2002	49.2	50.1	50.8	51.0	51.1	50.9	49.4	49.7	50.7	51.1	52.0	51.4	50.6
2003	49.1	51.5	51.4	51.3	51.9	50.2	49.2	49.3	50.9	52.8	53.7	53.7	51.3
2004	52.4	53.6	53.7	54.3	54.2	53.3	51.9	52.0	54.4	55.6	56.7	56.3	54.0
2005	54.0	55.5	56.0	56.5	56.2	53.4	53.4	53.4	55.7	56.4	56.7	56.7	55.3
2006	54.8	55.4	56.8	57.0	56.9	54.6	53.3	53.7	56.6	57.1	58.1	58.0	56.0
2007	57.0	58.2	58.5	58.9	58.8	57.3	56.3	56.6	58.4	59.3	59.9	60.0	58.3
2008	58.5	59.7	60.0	60.6	61.0	59.7	58.9	59.0	60.2	61.1	62.1	61.7	60.2
2009	60.1	61.1	61.1	62.2	62.3	60.4	59.7	60.0	61.1	62.9	63.4	63.2	61.5
2010	61.8	62.5	62.6	62.3	62.3	60.9	60.9	60.9	61.4	62.4	62.9	62.4	61.9
2011	61.9	62.3	62.7	63.0	62.7	61.7	61.8	61.9	63.6	64.7	65.3	65.2	63.1
2012	64.0	64.9	65.4	65.8	65.8	64.9	64.7	65.3	66.7	67.5	68.3	68.3	66.0
2013	66.4	67.4	68.0	68.4	68.2	68.1	67.8	68.5	69.6	71.1	71.6	71.1	68.9
Leisure and Hospitality													
2002	29.9	30.0	30.4	31.6	32.8	33.2	32.7	33.2	33.8	32.7	32.3	32.3	32.1
2003	29.7	29.6	29.9	30.8	32.2	32.6	31.7	31.9	32.1	31.6	31.2	31.2	31.2
2004	30.0	30.1	30.3	31.3	32.7	33.0	32.8	32.7	32.5	32.1	32.0	31.9	31.8
2005	30.6	30.8	31.2	32.4	33.7	33.9	33.2	33.8	34.1	33.0	32.7	33.3	32.7
2006	31.2	31.6	32.2	32.4	33.8	33.6	33.4	33.6	33.7	32.8	32.4	32.0	32.7
2007	31.1	31.3	31.6	31.7	33.2	33.5	33.0	33.2	33.2	32.7	32.3	32.6	32.5
2008	30.4	30.5	30.8	32.1	33.8	33.9	32.9	33.0	32.5	31.2	30.5	30.7	31.9
2009	29.1	29.4	29.6	30.3	32.0	32.3	31.9	31.8	31.7	31.0	30.5	30.4	30.8
2010	29.6	29.7	30.2	31.0	32.4	32.7	32.2	32.5	32.4	31.5	30.7	30.9	31.3
2011	29.9	30.0	30.4	31.1	32.4	32.8	32.5	32.8	32.5	32.0	31.7	31.8	31.7
2012	31.4	31.7	32.2	32.8	34.0	34.6	34.1	34.8	34.3	33.8	33.3	33.6	33.4
2013	32.4	32.4	32.8	33.2	35.3	36.0	35.7	35.9	35.3	35.8	36.2	37.4	34.9
Other Services													
2002	16.3	16.4	16.5	16.7	16.8	17.0	17.2	17.1	17.2	17.2	17.1	17.2	16.9
2003	16.9	17.0	17.3	16.8	17.0	17.2	17.1	17.2	17.4	17.1	17.1	17.4	17.1
2004	17.0	17.2	17.4	17.0	17.1	17.2	17.3	17.1	17.0	17.1	17.0	17.0	17.1
2005	17.2	17.4	17.5	16.7	16.8	17.0	16.9	16.8	16.6	16.2	16.3	16.3	16.8
2006	16.1	16.3	16.4	16.8	16.9	17.1	16.8	16.7	16.5	16.5	16.4	16.5	16.6
2007	16.1	16.1	16.3	16.4	16.5	16.7	16.6	16.5	16.3	16.4	16.4	16.5	16.4
2008	16.2	16.2	16.3	16.8	16.9	17.2	17.0	17.0	16.8	17.0	17.0	17.1	16.8
2009	17.0	17.1	17.3	17.8	17.8	17.9	17.7	17.5	17.3	17.4	17.3	17.4	17.5
2010	17.1	17.1	17.2	17.0	17.0	17.2	17.1	16.9	16.6	16.7	16.6	16.7	16.9
2011	16.5	16.3	16.4	16.3	16.5	16.3	16.3	16.4	16.2	16.1	16.1	16.2	16.3
2012	15.6	15.8	15.9	16.2	16.5	16.8	16.7	16.7	16.7	16.7	16.8	17.0	16.5
2013	17.0	16.9	17.1	17.2	17.3	17.7	17.7	17.5	17.4	17.4	17.4	17.4	17.3
Government													
2002	38.4	39.1	39.3	38.4	39.3	36.6	31.7	31.5	37.3	39.8	40.2	40.4	37.7
2003	39.2	39.8	39.8	39.1	40.2	37.8	33.0	33.7	37.8	39.6	39.8	39.9	38.3
2004	39.2	39.5	39.8	39.3	40.0	36.5	31.8	32.2	37.5	39.2	39.3	39.4	37.8
2005	38.0	39.3	39.4	39.3	40.1	37.8	32.2	32.5	37.0	39.0	39.1	38.7	37.7
2006	37.8	39.1	39.2	39.0	39.8	37.5	32.0	32.4	36.3	38.2	38.0	38.0	37.3
2007	36.4	37.2	37.3	37.1	37.5	36.4	31.8	32.5	36.0	36.7	36.6	36.7	36.0
2008	35.7	36.4	36.6	36.6	36.8	36.2	31.6	32.8	35.9	37.0	36.7	36.5	35.7
2009	36.3	36.6	36.8	37.0	37.2	35.7	31.7	31.6	35.4	36.0	36.1	35.8	35.5
2010	35.4	35.5	35.5	35.6	36.6	35.5	31.4	30.9	34.3	35.4	35.6	35.0	34.7
2011	34.5	34.5	34.9	34.7	34.9	34.1	29.8	29.4	33.6	34.3	34.2	33.9	33.6
2012	33.8	34.0	34.1	33.7	34.2	31.9	29.5	29.3	33.1	33.8	33.9	33.5	32.9
2013	32.9	33.7	33.6	33.7	33.9	32.7	29.0	29.4	32.9	33.2	33.1	33.4	32.6

Employment by Industry: Greensboro-High Point, NC, Selected Years, 2002–2013

(Numbers in thousands, not seasonally adjusted)

Industry and year	January	February	March	April	May	June	July	August	September	October	November	December	Annual average
Total Nonfarm													
2002	350.9	352.0	353.8	358.6	359.5	360.0	353.6	357.9	359.5	361.5	362.9	362.4	357.7
2003	354.2	354.7	356.7	356.6	356.0	355.0	344.3	347.9	350.0	353.1	352.2	351.6	352.7
2004	345.4	346.5	349.9	355.9	357.6	357.7	350.6	354.6	357.3	359.3	359.8	361.1	354.6
2005	354.8	357.3	360.0	362.2	362.1	361.4	355.1	360.3	361.5	362.9	363.8	364.4	360.5
2006	359.6	361.0	364.2	367.9	370.7	368.8	362.2	367.7	368.1	371.8	373.6	375.0	367.5
2007	365.3	366.5	370.1	370.8	372.3	370.8	363.7	369.4	370.4	373.1	373.5	373.9	370.0
2008	367.1	367.6	369.0	367.5	367.7	364.9	358.0	364.0	365.9	366.0	364.2	359.2	365.1
2009	347.6	346.5	343.4	342.6	341.7	339.8	333.0	337.5	340.1	339.5	339.2	338.2	340.8
2010	331.5	331.7	334.5	336.0	337.8	337.7	333.5	337.3	337.8	341.8	340.0	340.0	336.6
2011	333.0	335.7	337.7	340.7	341.3	338.8	333.8	338.6	341.5	342.6	343.1	342.5	339.1
2012	337.2	339.5	341.2	342.6	343.8	339.1	330.7	340.7	342.7	345.7	347.5	347.9	341.6
2013	341.0	343.1	344.4	346.8	347.3	343.8	336.6	346.0	348.1	351.0	351.9	350.9	345.9
Total Private													
2002	309.1	309.9	311.2	315.5	316.5	318.1	317.6	318.8	317.7	318.4	318.8	318.8	315.9
2003	311.7	311.7	313.5	313.0	312.1	312.9	307.7	308.5	307.6	308.5	308.4	307.8	310.3
2004	302.6	303.5	306.4	312.0	313.6	315.1	313.9	314.7	314.6	315.2	315.9	316.8	312.0
2005	311.3	313.4	315.8	317.8	317.5	318.6	317.9	318.8	317.8	317.5	318.9	319.3	317.1
2006	315.4	316.4	319.0	322.3	324.9	324.5	324.2	325.5	323.7	326.2	327.5	328.5	323.2
2007	320.2	321.2	324.3	324.8	326.1	327.0	325.0	326.5	325.3	326.6	326.6	327.4	325.1
2008	320.6	320.7	321.7	320.0	319.8	319.6	318.0	319.9	318.4	318.2	316.2	311.7	318.7
2009	300.4	298.9	295.5	294.2	293.5	292.9	292.1	292.7	291.6	291.9	291.5	290.9	293.8
2010	284.3	284.4	286.7	287.6	288.2	290.2	291.9	292.9	291.1	294.1	292.7	293.0	289.8
2011	286.6	289.0	290.7	293.7	294.4	295.5	295.1	296.1	295.8	295.9	296.1	295.7	293.7
2012	291.7	293.5	294.8	296.0	296.8	297.1	297.1	298.1	297.4	299.0	300.5	301.4	297.0
2013	295.0	296.8	297.6	300.2	300.6	301.0	300.9	303.3	302.8	304.7	305.2	305.2	301.1
Goods Producing													
2002	88.9	88.4	88.7	89.4	89.7	90.3	90.5	91.0	90.7	89.9	89.1	88.5	89.6
2003	88.2	88.0	87.8	86.9	86.8	86.8	84.5	84.6	84.4	83.7	83.5	83.7	85.7
2004	82.4	82.1	82.7	83.5	84.0	84.8	84.3	84.8	85.1	84.6	84.8	84.9	84.0
2005	84.7	84.8	84.9	85.4	85.5	85.7	84.9	84.7	84.2	83.4	83.3	83.4	84.6
2006	82.1	82.3	82.6	83.2	83.3	83.1	82.4	82.9	82.5	82.6	82.5	82.7	82.7
2007	81.7	81.4	81.8	81.9	81.6	81.9	81.2	81.2	80.8	81.0	80.9	81.3	81.4
2008	79.8	79.6	79.6	78.4	78.5	78.2	77.6	77.5	77.2	76.2	75.5	74.0	77.7
2009	70.6	69.4	67.7	67.2	66.2	65.9	65.4	65.3	65.1	64.4	64.0	64.1	66.3
2010	62.4	62.3	62.8	63.2	63.2	63.8	64.0	64.1	63.9	63.8	63.4	63.6	63.4
2011	62.6	63.1	63.5	64.4	64.7	65.2	65.3	65.6	65.3	64.9	64.6	64.6	64.5
2012	64.6	64.9	64.9	64.5	64.7	64.9	64.9	64.8	65.1	65.1	65.2	65.7	64.9
2013	64.7	64.4	64.8	65.3	65.4	66.0	65.8	65.7	65.8	65.7	65.5	65.1	65.4
Service-Providing													
2002	262.0	263.6	265.1	269.2	269.8	269.7	263.1	266.9	268.8	271.6	273.8	273.9	268.1
2003	266.0	266.7	268.9	269.7	269.2	268.2	259.8	263.3	265.6	269.4	268.7	267.9	267.0
2004	263.0	264.4	267.2	272.4	273.6	272.9	266.3	269.8	272.2	274.7	275.0	276.2	270.6
2005	270.1	272.5	275.1	276.8	276.6	275.7	270.2	275.6	277.3	279.5	280.5	281.0	275.9
2006	277.5	278.7	281.6	284.7	287.4	284.7	279.8	284.8	285.6	289.2	291.1	292.3	284.8
2007	283.6	285.1	288.3	288.9	290.7	288.9	282.5	288.2	289.6	292.1	292.6	292.6	288.6
2008	287.3	288.0	289.4	289.1	289.2	286.7	280.4	286.5	288.7	289.8	288.7	285.2	287.4
2009	277.0	277.1	275.7	275.4	275.5	273.9	267.6	272.2	275.0	275.1	275.2	274.1	274.5
2010	269.1	269.4	271.7	272.8	274.6	273.9	269.5	273.2	273.9	278.0	276.6	276.4	273.3
2011	270.4	272.6	274.2	276.3	276.6	273.6	268.5	273.0	276.2	277.7	278.5	277.9	274.6
2012	272.6	274.6	276.3	278.1	279.1	274.2	265.8	275.9	277.6	280.6	282.3	282.2	276.6
2013	276.3	278.7	279.6	281.5	281.9	277.8	270.8	280.3	282.3	285.3	286.4	285.8	280.6
Mining, Logging, and Construction													
2002	16.9	16.9	17.1	17.2	17.2	17.4	17.6	17.6	17.4	17.0	16.8	16.6	17.1
2003	16.7	16.7	16.9	17.1	17.4	17.5	17.3	17.4	17.6	17.8	17.8	18.0	17.4
2004	17.2	16.9	17.3	17.7	17.9	18.3	18.2	18.4	18.4	18.3	18.3	18.3	17.9
2005	18.0	17.9	18.0	18.5	18.7	18.8	18.8	18.8	18.8	18.5	18.5	18.4	18.5
2006	17.9	17.9	18.2	18.5	18.6	18.8	18.9	19.0	18.9	18.8	18.8	18.8	18.6
2007	18.3	18.2	18.6	18.6	18.6	18.8	18.8	18.7	18.5	18.5	18.5	18.5	18.6
2008	17.7	17.7	17.9	17.5	17.5	17.5	17.5	17.3	17.3	17.1	16.9	16.3	17.4
2009	15.1	14.8	14.5	14.4	14.1	14.1	14.0	13.9	13.7	13.3	13.1	13.1	14.0
2010	12.1	12.0	12.3	12.6	12.5	12.7	12.6	12.6	12.5	12.7	12.6	12.5	12.5
2011	11.7	12.1	12.4	12.8	12.9	13.1	13.1	13.1	13.1	12.9	12.7	12.7	12.7
2012	12.5	12.4	12.5	12.2	12.2	12.3	12.4	12.4	12.3	12.3	12.2	12.2	12.3
2013	11.9	11.9	12.2	12.4	12.5	12.7	12.8	12.9	13.0	13.0	12.8	12.4	12.5
Manufacturing													
2002	72.0	71.5	71.6	72.2	72.5	72.9	72.9	73.4	73.3	72.9	72.3	71.9	72.5
2003	71.5	71.3	70.9	69.8	69.4	69.3	67.2	67.2	66.8	65.9	65.7	65.7	68.4
2004	65.2	65.2	65.4	65.8	66.1	66.5	66.1	66.4	66.7	66.3	66.5	66.6	66.1
2005	66.7	66.9	66.9	66.9	66.8	66.9	66.1	65.9	65.4	64.9	64.8	65.0	66.1
2006	64.2	64.4	64.4	64.7	64.7	64.3	63.5	63.9	63.6	63.8	63.7	63.9	64.1
2007	63.4	63.2	63.2	63.3	63.0	63.1	62.4	62.5	62.3	62.5	62.4	62.8	62.8
2008	62.1	61.9	61.7	60.9	61.0	60.7	60.1	60.2	59.9	59.1	58.6	57.7	60.3
2009	55.5	54.6	53.2	52.8	52.1	51.8	51.4	51.4	51.4	51.1	50.9	51.0	52.3
2010	50.3	50.3	50.5	50.6	50.7	51.1	51.4	51.5	51.4	51.1	50.8	51.1	50.9
2011	50.9	51.0	51.1	51.6	51.8	52.1	52.2	52.5	52.2	52.0	51.9	51.9	51.8
2012	52.1	52.5	52.4	52.3	52.5	52.6	52.5	52.4	52.8	52.8	53.0	53.5	52.6
2013	52.8	52.5	52.6	52.9	52.9	53.3	53.0	52.8	52.8	52.7	52.7	52.7	52.8

Employment by Industry: Greensboro-High Point, NC, Selected Years, 2002–2013—*Continued*

(Numbers in thousands, not seasonally adjusted)

Industry and year	January	February	March	April	May	June	July	August	September	October	November	December	Annual average
Trade, Transportation, and Utilities													
2002	74.9	74.3	74.5	75.0	75.1	75.1	74.2	74.4	73.9	74.3	75.7	76.4	74.8
2003	73.5	73.3	73.7	73.5	73.0	73.4	72.1	72.1	72.0	72.4	73.5	73.8	73.0
2004	71.8	71.2	71.8	72.0	72.3	72.3	72.5	72.6	72.3	72.9	74.3	75.4	72.6
2005	72.1	72.2	72.6	73.0	73.1	73.2	73.5	73.7	73.3	74.8	76.1	76.9	73.7
2006	75.4	75.0	75.1	75.8	76.2	75.4	75.6	75.7	75.7	76.3	78.1	78.9	76.1
2007	76.1	75.7	76.5	76.3	76.8	76.6	76.5	76.9	76.7	77.0	78.0	78.9	76.8
2008	75.3	74.8	74.8	74.6	74.8	74.7	73.8	73.8	73.7	74.0	74.2	74.4	74.4
2009	70.9	70.2	70.0	69.1	69.2	68.9	68.5	68.6	68.6	68.5	69.3	69.6	69.3
2010	67.4	67.2	67.5	67.9	68.1	68.1	68.1	68.2	68.1	68.8	69.5	70.3	68.3
2011	67.9	68.1	68.3	68.7	68.9	68.8	68.8	68.8	68.7	69.0	69.9	70.5	68.9
2012	69.0	68.9	69.0	69.8	70.2	69.8	69.8	69.8	69.9	70.3	71.7	72.2	70.0
2013	69.9	70.0	70.1	70.7	70.7	70.4	70.7	70.9	70.9	72.1	73.1	73.8	71.1
Wholesale Trade													
2002	18.8	19.0	18.9	19.2	19.1	19.2	19.3	19.3	19.3	19.3	19.4	19.4	19.2
2003	18.9	19.0	19.1	19.0	18.8	18.9	18.5	18.5	18.4	18.5	18.5	18.5	18.7
2004	18.6	18.5	18.6	18.9	18.8	18.8	18.5	18.5	18.3	18.3	18.3	18.3	18.5
2005	18.5	18.5	18.5	18.5	18.6	18.5	18.8	18.9	18.8	18.8	18.8	18.8	18.7
2006	18.9	19.1	19.1	19.4	19.6	19.5	19.5	19.6	19.7	19.8	19.9	20.0	19.5
2007	20.1	20.1	20.3	20.3	20.4	20.5	20.6	20.6	20.6	20.6	20.6	20.7	20.5
2008	20.4	20.4	20.4	20.2	20.3	20.2	20.0	19.9	19.9	19.8	19.6	19.3	20.0
2009	18.8	18.7	18.5	18.5	18.5	18.3	18.2	18.4	18.2	18.2	18.2	18.2	18.4
2010	18.0	18.0	18.2	18.2	18.2	18.1	18.1	18.2	18.0	18.0	18.0	18.0	18.1
2011	17.8	18.0	18.0	18.0	18.0	17.9	17.9	17.8	17.7	17.5	17.4	17.4	17.8
2012	17.5	17.6	17.8	18.0	18.0	18.0	18.0	18.0	18.1	18.1	18.2	18.4	18.0
2013	18.2	18.4	18.5	18.6	18.6	18.6	18.6	18.7	18.8	18.7	18.9	18.9	18.6
Retail Trade													
2002	38.2	37.7	38.0	38.1	38.3	38.3	37.7	37.9	37.5	37.6	38.8	39.5	38.1
2003	37.3	36.8	37.0	36.8	36.7	36.6	36.1	36.1	35.9	36.3	37.4	37.7	36.7
2004	35.9	35.5	35.8	36.2	36.6	36.5	36.4	36.6	36.5	37.0	38.3	39.2	36.7
2005	36.6	36.7	37.0	37.3	37.2	37.3	37.4	37.3	36.9	38.4	39.5	40.4	37.7
2006	39.4	38.9	38.9	39.2	39.4	38.8	38.9	39.1	38.9	39.5	41.2	41.8	39.5
2007	39.6	39.3	39.7	39.6	39.9	39.7	39.5	39.6	39.4	39.7	40.6	40.9	39.8
2008	38.7	38.2	38.1	38.1	38.0	37.9	37.7	37.7	37.5	37.9	38.2	38.5	38.0
2009	36.5	36.1	36.2	35.6	35.8	35.7	35.6	35.5	35.6	35.6	36.2	36.4	35.9
2010	34.8	34.6	34.7	34.9	35.0	34.9	34.8	34.8	34.7	35.1	35.9	36.3	35.0
2011	34.6	34.5	34.7	34.9	35.1	35.1	35.1	35.2	35.0	35.4	36.4	36.8	35.2
2012	35.6	35.4	35.2	35.7	36.1	35.8	35.9	35.8	35.8	36.0	37.4	37.5	36.0
2013	35.8	35.8	35.9	36.2	36.3	36.1	36.3	36.2	36.1	37.3	38.0	38.5	36.5
Transportation and Utilities													
2002	17.9	17.6	17.6	17.7	17.7	17.6	17.2	17.2	17.1	17.4	17.5	17.5	17.5
2003	17.3	17.5	17.6	17.7	17.5	17.9	17.5	17.5	17.7	17.6	17.6	17.6	17.6
2004	17.3	17.2	17.4	16.9	16.9	17.0	17.6	17.5	17.5	17.6	17.7	17.9	17.4
2005	17.0	17.0	17.1	17.2	17.3	17.4	17.3	17.5	17.6	17.6	17.8	17.7	17.4
2006	17.1	17.0	17.1	17.2	17.2	17.1	17.2	17.0	17.1	17.0	17.0	17.1	17.1
2007	16.4	16.3	16.5	16.4	16.5	16.4	16.4	16.7	16.7	16.7	16.8	17.3	16.6
2008	16.2	16.2	16.3	16.3	16.5	16.6	16.1	16.2	16.3	16.3	16.4	16.6	16.3
2009	15.6	15.4	15.3	15.0	14.9	14.9	14.7	14.7	14.8	14.7	14.9	15.0	15.0
2010	14.6	14.6	14.6	14.8	14.9	15.1	15.2	15.2	15.4	15.7	15.6	16.0	15.1
2011	15.5	15.6	15.6	15.8	15.8	15.8	15.8	15.8	16.0	16.1	16.1	16.3	15.9
2012	15.9	15.9	16.0	16.1	16.1	16.0	15.9	16.0	16.0	16.0	16.2	16.1	16.3	16.0
2013	15.9	15.8	15.7	15.9	15.8	15.7	15.8	16.0	16.0	16.0	16.1	16.2	16.4	15.9
Information													
2002	7.8	7.7	7.6	7.7	7.9	7.8	7.8	7.7	7.6	7.6	7.7	7.7	7.7
2003	7.5	7.4	7.4	7.4	7.6	7.5	7.5	7.6	7.5	7.4	7.5	7.5	7.5
2004	7.1	6.9	6.9	6.8	6.8	6.7	6.7	6.6	6.5	6.5	6.5	6.5	6.7
2005	6.5	6.4	6.5	6.6	6.6	6.6	6.6	6.6	6.6	6.5	6.5	6.6	6.6
2006	6.6	6.5	6.5	6.3	6.4	6.3	6.3	6.3	6.3	6.4	6.4	6.5	6.4
2007	6.3	6.3	6.2	6.3	6.2	6.2	6.2	6.2	6.2	6.2	6.3	6.3	6.2
2008	6.2	6.1	6.2	6.2	6.2	6.3	6.2	6.1	6.0	6.0	6.2	6.2	6.2
2009	5.9	5.8	5.8	5.8	5.8	5.7	5.6	5.6	5.5	5.5	5.5	5.6	5.7
2010	5.6	5.5	5.5	5.5	5.5	5.5	5.6	5.6	5.5	5.5	5.5	5.6	5.5
2011	5.5	5.5	5.5	5.5	5.5	5.5	5.5	5.5	5.5	5.5	5.4	5.4	5.5
2012	5.4	5.5	5.4	5.4	5.4	5.4	5.4	5.3	5.3	5.3	5.3	5.3	5.4
2013	5.2	5.2	5.1	5.0	5.0	5.0	5.0	4.9	4.9	4.9	4.9	4.9	5.0
Financial Activities													
2002	20.8	20.8	20.7	20.8	20.7	20.8	21.0	21.0	20.9	21.2	20.9	21.0	20.9
2003	21.4	21.4	21.6	21.2	20.9	20.7	20.5	20.3	20.1	19.9	19.6	19.5	20.6
2004	19.6	19.7	19.7	20.7	20.5	20.6	21.0	20.9	20.9	21.0	21.0	21.1	20.6
2005	20.9	21.0	21.1	21.2	21.2	21.3	21.5	21.5	21.5	21.2	21.3	21.3	21.3
2006	21.3	21.4	21.6	21.6	21.8	21.9	22.1	22.2	22.2	22.3	22.3	22.4	21.9
2007	22.1	22.3	22.3	22.3	22.2	22.4	22.2	22.1	22.2	22.2	22.2	22.0	22.2
2008	21.7	21.8	21.8	21.9	22.0	22.1	22.0	22.0	21.9	21.9	22.0	21.9	21.9
2009	21.5	21.4	21.2	21.2	21.2	21.2	21.0	21.0	20.9	20.9	20.8	20.6	21.1
2010	20.3	20.2	20.2	20.0	19.8	19.8	19.9	19.9	19.9	19.9	19.8	19.9	20.0
2011	19.6	19.6	19.7	19.7	19.6	19.6	19.6	19.5	19.4	19.0	18.9	18.8	19.4
2012	18.3	18.4	18.4	18.4	18.3	18.4	18.4	18.5	18.5	18.5	18.7	18.8	18.5
2013	18.3	18.4	18.4	18.4	18.4	18.5	18.3	18.4	18.1	18.1	18.0	18.1	18.3

Employment by Industry: Greensboro-High Point, NC, Selected Years, 2002–2013—*Continued*

(Numbers in thousands, not seasonally adjusted)

Industry and year	January	February	March	April	May	June	July	August	September	October	November	December	Annual average
Professional and Business Services													
2002	38.2	39.2	39.4	40.1	40.3	40.2	40.0	40.8	41.0	41.0	41.1	41.0	40.2
2003	38.9	39.3	40.2	40.4	40.3	40.4	39.8	40.4	40.8	41.9	41.5	40.7	40.4
2004	40.3	41.0	41.6	42.9	43.2	43.1	43.1	43.4	43.8	44.0	43.6	43.5	42.8
2005	43.7	44.7	45.1	44.8	43.9	44.0	44.1	44.5	44.9	44.2	44.3	44.1	44.4
2006	43.1	43.4	44.5	46.3	47.1	46.8	47.0	47.4	46.7	47.9	47.6	47.2	46.3
2007	44.2	45.1	45.9	45.9	46.1	46.3	45.9	47.1	47.4	47.6	47.0	46.7	46.3
2008	46.1	46.2	46.6	46.5	45.7	45.4	46.0	47.5	47.5	48.0	43.8	43.8	46.3
2009	41.7	41.5	40.5	40.1	39.6	40.1	40.6	41.5	42.0	43.4	42.6	42.3	41.3
2010	42.0	42.3	42.9	42.9	42.8	43.6	44.9	45.4	45.3	46.5	45.5	45.1	44.1
2011	44.2	45.1	45.7	46.1	45.9	46.1	46.4	46.7	47.3	47.6	47.6	47.1	46.3
2012	46.6	47.0	47.7	47.5	47.1	47.1	46.6	47.2	46.8	47.4	47.6	47.6	47.2
2013	46.2	47.0	46.9	47.6	47.4	47.3	47.4	48.7	49.3	50.6	50.7	50.6	48.3
Education and Health Services													
2002	39.5	39.9	40.2	40.4	40.4	40.6	40.4	40.5	40.7	41.4	41.5	41.4	40.6
2003	40.8	41.2	41.3	41.1	41.0	40.9	40.7	40.9	41.1	41.6	41.5	41.4	41.1
2004	41.2	41.7	41.7	42.2	42.2	42.2	41.9	42.3	42.5	43.2	43.3	43.4	42.3
2005	42.9	43.4	43.8	44.0	44.0	43.9	44.1	44.4	44.7	44.9	45.1	45.0	44.2
2006	45.2	45.5	45.6	45.5	45.4	45.4	45.3	45.6	45.6	45.9	46.0	46.1	45.6
2007	46.1	46.5	46.6	46.3	46.5	46.2	45.8	45.9	45.6	46.4	46.2	46.2	46.2
2008	45.8	46.0	46.0	46.5	46.4	46.4	46.0	46.5	46.5	47.4	47.9	47.5	46.6
2009	47.2	47.6	47.0	47.3	47.2	46.8	46.6	46.7	46.1	47.0	47.2	47.0	47.0
2010	46.4	46.3	46.5	46.5	46.5	46.3	46.3	46.5	45.9	47.1	47.0	46.9	46.5
2011	46.1	46.4	46.2	46.7	46.6	46.4	45.9	46.2	46.7	47.4	47.5	47.3	46.6
2012	46.5	47.1	47.0	47.2	47.1	46.6	47.0	47.4	48.0	48.2	48.5	48.4	47.4
2013	47.9	48.5	48.5	48.4	48.4	47.7	47.7	48.3	48.7	49.3	49.3	49.3	48.5
Leisure and Hospitality													
2002	25.5	25.9	26.4	28.3	28.7	29.3	29.7	29.6	29.4	29.3	29.1	29.2	28.4
2003	27.8	27.5	28.0	28.8	29.0	29.6	29.1	29.4	28.5	28.6	28.3	28.2	28.6
2004	27.2	27.8	28.7	29.9	30.5	31.2	30.8	30.9	30.4	29.7	29.4	29.0	29.6
2005	27.7	27.9	28.8	29.7	30.2	30.8	30.2	30.5	29.8	29.6	29.4	29.0	29.5
2006	28.9	29.4	30.0	30.8	31.6	32.6	32.8	32.9	32.3	32.0	31.9	31.9	31.4
2007	31.0	31.2	32.1	32.6	33.4	34.0	33.6	33.7	33.1	32.6	32.5	32.5	32.7
2008	32.3	32.7	33.2	32.5	33.0	33.2	32.9	33.1	32.4	31.5	31.2	30.7	32.4
2009	29.6	29.9	30.2	30.5	31.4	31.5	31.6	31.3	30.8	29.7	29.7	29.3	30.5
2010	28.1	28.4	29.1	29.5	30.2	30.9	30.9	31.1	30.6	30.5	30.1	29.8	29.9
2011	28.8	29.3	30.0	30.7	31.3	31.8	31.5	31.8	31.0	30.6	30.3	30.0	30.6
2012	29.4	29.8	30.5	31.1	31.7	32.3	32.5	32.7	31.6	31.7	31.2	31.0	31.3
2013	30.5	30.9	31.4	32.4	32.8	33.3	33.2	33.6	32.5	31.3	31.2	30.8	32.0
Other Services													
2002	13.5	13.7	13.7	13.8	13.7	14.0	14.0	13.8	13.5	13.7	13.7	13.6	13.7
2003	13.6	13.6	13.5	13.7	13.5	13.5	13.6	13.5	13.2	13.2	13.0	13.0	13.4
2004	13.0	13.1	13.3	14.0	14.1	14.2	13.6	13.2	13.1	13.3	13.0	13.0	13.4
2005	12.8	13.0	13.0	13.1	13.0	13.1	13.0	12.9	12.8	12.9	12.9	13.0	13.0
2006	12.8	12.9	13.1	12.8	13.1	13.0	12.7	12.5	12.4	12.8	12.7	12.8	12.8
2007	12.7	12.7	12.9	13.2	13.3	13.4	13.6	13.4	13.3	13.6	13.4	13.5	13.3
2008	13.4	13.5	13.5	13.4	13.2	13.3	13.5	13.4	13.2	13.2	13.2	13.2	13.3
2009	13.0	13.1	13.1	13.0	12.9	12.8	12.8	12.7	12.6	12.5	12.4	12.4	12.8
2010	12.1	12.2	12.2	12.1	12.1	12.2	12.2	12.1	11.9	12.0	11.9	11.8	12.1
2011	11.9	11.9	11.8	11.9	11.9	12.1	12.1	12.0	11.9	11.9	11.9	12.0	11.9
2012	11.9	11.9	11.9	12.1	12.3	12.6	12.5	12.4	12.2	12.3	12.3	12.4	12.2
2013	12.3	12.4	12.4	12.4	12.5	12.8	12.8	12.8	12.6	12.7	12.5	12.6	12.6
Government													
2002	41.8	42.1	42.6	43.1	43.0	41.9	36.0	39.1	41.8	43.1	44.1	43.6	41.9
2003	42.5	43.0	43.2	43.6	43.9	42.1	36.6	39.4	42.4	44.6	43.8	43.8	42.4
2004	42.8	43.0	43.5	43.9	44.0	42.6	36.7	39.9	42.7	44.1	43.9	44.3	42.6
2005	43.5	43.9	44.2	44.4	44.6	42.8	37.2	41.5	43.7	45.4	44.9	45.1	43.4
2006	44.2	44.6	45.2	45.6	45.8	43.3	38.0	42.2	44.4	45.6	46.1	46.5	44.3
2007	45.1	45.3	45.8	46.0	46.2	43.8	38.7	42.9	45.1	46.5	46.9	46.5	44.9
2008	46.5	46.9	47.3	47.5	47.9	45.3	40.0	44.1	47.5	47.8	48.0	47.5	46.4
2009	47.2	47.6	47.9	48.4	48.2	46.9	40.9	44.8	48.5	47.6	47.7	47.3	46.9
2010	47.2	47.3	47.8	48.4	49.6	47.5	41.6	44.4	46.7	47.7	47.3	47.0	46.9
2011	46.4	46.7	47.0	47.0	46.9	43.3	38.7	42.5	45.7	46.7	47.0	46.8	45.4
2012	45.5	46.0	46.4	46.6	47.0	42.0	33.6	42.6	45.3	46.7	47.0	46.5	44.6
2013	46.0	46.3	46.8	46.6	46.7	42.8	35.7	42.7	45.3	46.3	46.7	45.7	44.8

Employment by Industry: Greenville-Mauldin-Easley, SC, Selected Years, 2002–2013

(Numbers in thousands, not seasonally adjusted)

Industry and year	January	February	March	April	May	June	July	August	September	October	November	December	Annual average
Total Nonfarm													
2002	288.0	289.3	292.1	290.4	292.5	292.7	292.9	296.2	297.9	297.3	298.7	299.0	293.9
2003	286.6	287.9	289.8	291.2	291.8	291.9	288.1	288.2	291.0	291.7	293.5	293.5	290.4
2004	287.7	287.2	290.3	292.8	294.2	294.4	292.9	292.6	294.3	295.8	298.6	298.1	293.2
2005	293.0	294.8	295.2	297.9	300.1	296.5	296.0	297.5	301.1	302.9	305.6	302.7	298.6
2006	299.6	301.8	303.0	304.5	306.3	304.0	300.5	302.2	305.9	309.9	310.9	311.3	305.0
2007	306.0	308.6	311.3	313.4	315.8	314.6	311.3	311.7	314.8	315.4	318.8	318.3	313.3
2008	313.3	315.3	316.8	315.9	318.6	314.8	310.7	310.7	313.1	311.4	310.2	306.8	313.1
2009	296.0	295.4	295.2	292.4	294.1	289.3	287.5	286.9	288.8	290.1	291.5	290.6	291.5
2010	284.8	286.7	289.0	291.9	295.8	293.0	291.7	292.6	294.3	296.1	297.8	298.4	292.7
2011	290.0	295.1	298.0	299.8	300.7	297.8	297.6	300.3	301.0	302.1	303.7	303.7	299.2
2012	298.2	300.2	302.7	303.8	306.7	305.0	301.0	303.4	305.9	306.4	309.6	309.9	304.4
2013	304.6	307.2	309.0	310.5	313.0	313.7	310.1	311.8	314.6	316.7	317.1	318.4	312.2
Total Private													
2002	249.4	250.3	252.9	250.7	252.8	254.6	256.0	258.5	258.2	257.4	258.2	258.9	254.8
2003	246.7	247.7	249.4	250.7	251.5	252.7	250.7	250.7	251.3	251.7	253.1	253.6	250.8
2004	247.9	247.3	250.2	252.2	253.7	255.3	254.9	255.3	254.7	255.2	258.0	257.7	253.5
2005	253.3	254.7	255.0	257.6	259.4	257.3	258.7	260.5	260.4	261.8	264.2	261.6	258.7
2006	259.0	260.4	261.6	263.1	264.6	263.8	262.3	264.2	264.5	267.1	268.6	269.0	264.0
2007	264.0	266.2	268.6	270.7	272.6	272.9	271.3	272.6	271.7	271.7	274.4	274.4	270.9
2008	269.7	271.1	272.3	271.5	273.4	271.3	269.0	269.8	268.5	266.1	265.0	262.0	269.1
2009	251.7	250.9	250.6	247.6	248.8	245.9	245.9	245.8	244.9	245.6	246.8	246.2	247.6
2010	241.7	243.5	245.7	248.3	250.8	250.2	251.2	252.8	251.7	253.1	254.7	255.6	249.9
2011	248.1	252.9	255.7	257.2	258.2	256.8	257.0	259.5	258.5	258.9	260.3	260.3	257.0
2012	254.8	256.5	258.8	259.9	262.4	262.4	260.1	262.2	262.2	261.9	264.9	265.4	261.0
2013	260.3	262.8	264.2	265.1	267.9	269.4	267.8	269.3	269.5	270.8	271.0	272.3	267.5
Goods Producing													
2002	66.3	66.1	66.4	65.8	65.9	66.4	67.3	67.3	66.7	66.7	65.9	66.0	66.4
2003	63.6	63.7	63.7	64.3	64.0	64.2	64.5	63.8	64.2	63.8	63.2	63.0	63.8
2004	61.4	60.7	61.8	61.5	62.2	62.5	62.5	62.3	62.5	61.9	61.7	61.2	61.9
2005	60.4	60.8	61.0	61.2	61.2	60.6	60.3	60.2	59.5	59.9	59.7	59.0	60.3
2006	58.6	58.7	58.6	58.7	59.3	59.0	59.0	58.3	58.4	58.5	58.8	59.2	58.8
2007	58.7	59.1	59.6	59.8	60.1	60.4	60.2	60.5	60.3	60.2	60.2	60.0	59.9
2008	59.8	60.0	60.1	59.7	59.8	59.9	58.9	58.7	58.2	57.5	56.8	56.1	58.8
2009	55.1	54.4	53.6	52.5	52.4	52.2	52.2	51.5	51.0	50.6	50.0	49.5	51.9
2010	48.4	48.2	48.3	48.6	49.0	49.1	49.1	49.3	49.0	48.9	49.1	49.4	48.9
2011	47.7	49.1	49.3	49.4	49.6	49.8	49.9	50.0	49.6	49.6	49.8	49.6	49.5
2012	49.3	49.7	50.0	50.0	50.5	50.4	50.4	50.7	50.5	50.7	50.9	51.0	50.3
2013	50.8	51.4	51.9	51.9	52.1	52.4	52.1	52.4	52.5	53.5	52.9	52.9	52.2
Service-Providing													
2002	221.7	223.2	225.7	224.6	226.6	226.3	225.6	228.9	231.2	230.6	232.8	233.0	227.5
2003	223.0	224.2	226.1	226.9	227.8	227.7	223.6	224.4	226.8	227.9	230.3	230.5	226.6
2004	226.3	226.5	228.5	231.3	232.0	231.9	230.4	230.3	231.8	233.9	236.9	236.9	231.4
2005	232.6	234.0	234.2	236.7	238.9	235.9	235.7	237.3	241.6	243.0	245.9	243.7	238.3
2006	241.0	243.1	244.4	245.8	247.0	245.0	242.2	243.8	247.4	251.1	251.7	252.1	246.2
2007	247.3	249.5	251.7	253.6	255.7	254.2	251.1	251.2	254.5	255.2	258.6	258.3	253.4
2008	253.5	255.3	256.7	256.2	258.8	254.9	251.8	252.0	254.9	253.9	253.4	250.7	254.3
2009	240.9	241.0	241.6	239.9	241.7	237.1	236.0	235.9	238.2	240.1	242.0	241.0	239.6
2010	236.4	238.5	240.7	243.3	246.8	243.9	242.6	243.3	245.3	247.2	248.7	249.0	243.8
2011	242.3	246.0	248.7	250.4	251.1	248.0	247.7	250.3	251.4	252.5	253.9	254.1	249.7
2012	248.9	250.5	252.7	253.8	256.2	254.6	250.6	252.7	255.4	255.7	258.7	258.9	254.1
2013	253.8	255.8	257.1	258.6	260.9	261.3	258.0	259.4	262.1	263.2	264.2	265.5	260.0
Mining, Logging, and Construction													
2002	16.1	16.3	16.3	16.6	16.8	17.1	17.2	17.2	17.1	17.5	17.3	17.2	16.9
2003	16.1	16.0	16.0	16.4	16.6	17.0	17.2	17.1	17.3	17.3	17.2	17.2	16.8
2004	16.5	16.4	16.8	16.6	17.1	17.4	17.5	17.5	17.4	17.3	17.2	17.1	17.1
2005	16.9	17.0	17.1	17.4	17.6	17.7	18.1	18.1	18.0	18.0	18.2	17.9	17.7
2006	17.7	17.5	17.4	17.6	17.8	17.7	17.9	18.1	18.3	18.1	18.5	18.4	17.9
2007	18.0	18.0	18.5	18.7	18.9	19.1	19.2	19.2	18.9	18.6	18.4	18.2	18.6
2008	17.8	17.9	17.9	17.7	17.9	17.9	17.3	17.1	16.8	16.5	16.2	15.9	17.2
2009	15.0	14.7	14.4	14.1	14.0	13.9	13.5	13.2	12.8	12.5	12.3	12.4	13.6
2010	11.7	11.6	11.7	11.9	12.1	12.1	12.1	12.0	11.8	11.6	11.7	11.8	11.8
2011	10.8	11.5	11.5	11.6	11.7	11.7	11.6	11.6	11.4	11.3	11.5	11.4	11.5
2012	11.3	11.5	11.8	11.5	11.8	11.7	11.7	11.7	11.5	11.6	11.7	11.6	11.6
2013	11.4	11.4	11.7	11.8	11.9	12.0	11.9	12.0	12.0	12.0	12.0	11.9	11.8
Manufacturing													
2002	50.2	49.8	50.1	49.2	49.1	49.3	50.1	50.1	49.6	49.2	48.6	48.8	49.5
2003	47.5	47.7	47.7	47.9	47.4	47.2	47.3	46.7	46.9	46.5	46.0	45.8	47.1
2004	44.9	44.3	45.0	44.9	45.1	45.1	45.0	44.8	45.1	44.6	44.5	44.1	44.8
2005	43.5	43.8	43.9	43.8	43.6	42.9	42.2	42.1	41.5	41.9	41.5	41.1	42.7
2006	40.9	41.2	41.2	41.1	41.5	41.3	40.4	40.3	40.2	40.7	40.7	40.8	40.9
2007	40.7	41.1	41.1	41.1	41.2	41.3	41.0	41.3	41.4	41.6	41.8	41.8	41.3
2008	42.0	42.1	42.2	42.0	41.9	42.0	41.6	41.6	41.4	41.0	40.6	40.2	41.6
2009	40.1	39.7	39.2	38.4	38.4	38.3	38.0	37.8	37.8	37.5	37.2	37.2	38.3
2010	36.7	36.6	36.6	36.7	36.9	37.0	37.0	37.3	37.2	37.3	37.4	37.6	37.0
2011	36.9	37.6	37.8	37.8	37.9	38.1	38.3	38.4	38.2	38.3	38.3	38.2	38.0
2012	38.0	38.2	38.2	38.5	38.7	38.7	38.7	39.0	39.0	39.1	39.2	39.4	38.7
2013	39.4	40.0	40.2	40.1	40.2	40.4	40.2	40.4	40.5	41.5	40.9	41.0	40.4

Employment by Industry: Greenville-Mauldin-Easley, SC, Selected Years, 2002–2013—*Continued*

(Numbers in thousands, not seasonally adjusted)

Industry and year	January	February	March	April	May	June	July	August	September	October	November	December	Annual average
Trade, Transportation, and Utilities													
2002	62.4	62.0	62.3	62.0	62.2	62.5	61.2	61.5	60.6	60.2	61.7	62.4	61.8
2003	57.4	57.3	57.2	57.9	58.0	58.7	58.1	58.1	57.9	58.2	59.4	60.0	58.2
2004	57.5	57.2	58.0	58.0	58.4	59.0	59.4	59.8	59.6	60.8	62.4	63.3	59.5
2005	60.5	60.5	60.8	61.5	62.0	61.0	61.9	62.4	61.9	62.7	64.5	65.1	62.1
2006	63.1	63.0	63.4	63.4	63.4	63.5	63.2	63.6	63.4	64.3	65.6	66.1	63.8
2007	63.8	64.0	64.3	64.6	64.9	64.9	64.5	64.1	63.6	63.7	65.4	65.8	64.5
2008	64.0	63.8	64.0	62.3	62.4	62.1	62.2	62.0	61.6	60.9	61.4	61.5	62.4
2009	57.5	56.7	56.3	56.1	56.1	55.4	55.4	55.2	55.0	54.8	55.3	55.5	55.8
2010	53.6	53.6	53.9	54.7	55.3	55.3	55.2	55.4	55.0	55.8	57.0	57.4	55.2
2011	55.3	55.6	56.0	56.0	56.3	56.2	56.3	56.5	56.0	56.2	57.0	57.5	56.2
2012	55.7	55.6	55.8	56.1	56.4	56.4	56.4	56.4	56.3	56.5	57.8	57.9	56.4
2013	55.7	55.6	56.0	56.3	56.7	57.1	56.9	57.3	57.1	57.1	58.0	58.4	56.9
Wholesale Trade													
2002	13.5	13.6	13.5	13.6	13.6	14.0	13.6	13.5	13.2	13.1	13.1	13.2	13.5
2003	12.4	12.5	12.5	12.6	12.7	12.8	12.4	12.4	12.3	12.3	12.3	12.3	12.5
2004	11.7	11.8	11.8	11.9	12.1	12.4	12.7	12.8	12.9	13.3	13.4	13.6	12.5
2005	13.3	13.5	13.5	14.0	14.2	14.0	14.2	14.2	14.2	14.5	14.6	14.8	14.1
2006	14.7	14.7	14.7	15.0	14.9	14.9	14.7	14.7	14.7	15.1	15.2	15.3	14.9
2007	15.2	15.5	15.3	15.4	15.4	15.6	15.6	15.5	15.2	15.4	15.6	15.6	15.4
2008	15.4	15.6	15.6	15.5	15.5	15.4	15.4	15.3	15.1	15.0	14.9	14.7	15.3
2009	14.4	14.2	14.1	13.9	13.8	13.6	13.7	13.6	13.6	13.7	13.6	13.5	13.8
2010	13.6	13.7	13.7	14.2	14.4	14.4	14.4	14.5	14.4	14.6	14.6	14.6	14.3
2011	14.7	14.7	14.8	14.7	14.8	14.8	14.9	15.0	14.9	15.0	15.0	15.1	14.9
2012	14.9	14.9	14.9	15.0	15.0	15.1	15.1	15.2	14.9	15.0	15.0	15.1	15.0
2013	15.0	15.0	15.0	15.1	15.2	15.2	15.2	15.4	15.3	15.4	15.4	15.4	15.2
Retail Trade													
2002	37.4	36.8	37.2	36.5	36.6	36.7	36.1	36.4	35.8	35.1	36.4	37.0	36.5
2003	33.9	33.6	33.6	33.7	33.9	34.3	34.2	34.4	34.4	34.8	36.1	36.8	34.5
2004	35.4	35.0	35.8	35.7	35.9	36.1	36.2	36.5	36.4	37.1	38.6	39.3	36.5
2005	37.0	36.6	36.8	37.2	37.4	36.7	37.1	37.5	37.0	37.7	39.2	39.8	37.5
2006	37.8	37.6	38.0	37.6	37.7	37.7	37.7	37.9	37.6	38.3	39.6	40.1	38.1
2007	37.8	37.4	37.9	38.2	38.4	38.2	38.0	37.8	37.6	37.4	38.6	39.0	38.0
2008	37.6	37.1	37.3	35.7	35.8	35.6	35.6	35.7	35.6	35.2	35.8	36.0	36.1
2009	32.9	32.6	32.3	32.4	32.5	32.1	32.1	32.0	31.9	31.9	32.6	32.9	32.4
2010	31.3	31.2	31.5	31.8	32.1	32.1	32.0	32.1	31.9	32.4	33.5	33.9	32.2
2011	31.9	32.1	32.4	32.5	32.5	32.4	32.5	32.6	32.3	32.5	33.3	33.7	32.6
2012	32.2	32.2	32.3	32.3	32.6	32.5	32.5	32.5	32.5	32.6	33.9	33.9	32.7
2013	32.2	32.0	32.5	32.6	32.9	33.2	33.1	33.3	33.3	33.3	34.1	34.5	33.1
Transportation and Utilities													
2002	11.5	11.6	11.6	11.9	12.0	11.8	11.5	11.6	11.6	12.0	12.2	12.2	11.8
2003	11.1	11.2	11.1	11.6	11.4	11.6	11.5	11.3	11.2	11.1	11.0	10.9	11.3
2004	10.4	10.4	10.4	10.4	10.4	10.5	10.5	10.5	10.3	10.4	10.4	10.4	10.4
2005	10.2	10.4	10.5	10.3	10.4	10.3	10.6	10.7	10.7	10.5	10.7	10.5	10.5
2006	10.6	10.7	10.7	10.8	10.8	10.9	10.8	11.0	11.1	10.9	10.8	10.7	10.8
2007	10.8	11.1	11.1	11.0	11.1	11.1	10.9	10.8	10.8	10.9	11.2	11.2	11.0
2008	11.0	11.1	11.1	11.1	11.1	11.1	11.2	11.0	10.9	10.7	10.7	10.8	11.0
2009	10.2	9.9	9.9	9.8	9.8	9.7	9.6	9.6	9.5	9.2	9.1	9.1	9.6
2010	8.7	8.7	8.7	8.7	8.8	8.8	8.8	8.8	8.7	8.8	8.9	8.9	8.8
2011	8.7	8.8	8.8	8.8	9.0	9.0	8.9	8.9	8.8	8.7	8.7	8.7	8.8
2012	8.6	8.5	8.6	8.8	8.8	8.8	8.8	8.7	8.9	8.9	8.9	8.9	8.8
2013	8.5	8.6	8.5	8.6	8.6	8.7	8.6	8.6	8.5	8.4	8.5	8.5	8.6
Information													
2002	7.0	7.0	7.0	6.5	6.6	6.6	6.8	6.9	6.9	7.4	7.4	7.4	7.0
2003	6.9	6.9	6.9	6.9	6.8	6.8	7.0	7.0	7.0	7.0	7.1	7.1	7.0
2004	7.2	7.1	7.0	7.0	7.0	7.0	6.9	6.9	6.7	6.8	6.8	6.8	6.9
2005	6.5	6.6	6.6	6.7	6.7	6.7	6.6	6.6	6.6	6.5	6.4	6.6	6.6
2006	6.5	6.7	6.6	6.7	6.7	6.6	6.6	6.6	6.4	6.4	6.4	6.4	6.6
2007	6.3	6.4	6.4	6.4	6.5	6.6	6.9	6.8	6.5	6.5	6.6	6.6	6.5
2008	6.5	6.7	6.7	7.1	7.2	7.1	7.2	7.1	7.0	7.0	6.9	7.0	7.0
2009	6.7	6.8	7.0	6.7	6.7	6.7	6.9	6.6	6.4	6.3	6.3	6.2	6.6
2010	6.3	6.6	6.5	6.1	6.2	6.6	6.7	6.1	6.0	6.1	6.1	6.5	6.3
2011	6.6	6.5	6.8	6.6	6.4	6.5	6.3	6.3	6.2	7.0	7.0	7.0	6.6
2012	6.9	7.2	7.0	7.2	7.3	7.4	6.7	6.6	6.6	6.6	6.6	6.8	6.9
2013	6.8	6.9	6.8	6.8	6.9	6.8	6.9	6.7	6.6	6.7	6.7	6.7	6.8
Financial Activities													
2002	12.5	12.5	12.5	12.5	12.6	12.8	13.0	13.2	13.2	13.0	13.1	13.1	12.8
2003	12.7	12.7	12.9	13.1	13.1	13.2	13.1	13.3	13.3	13.5	13.4	13.5	13.2
2004	13.3	13.4	13.4	13.5	13.5	13.7	13.7	13.7	13.7	13.9	14.0	14.1	13.7
2005	14.4	14.5	14.7	14.6	14.5	14.5	14.5	14.5	14.5	14.1	14.2	13.9	14.4
2006	13.8	13.7	13.9	13.8	13.7	13.6	13.6	13.6	13.5	12.9	12.8	12.6	13.5
2007	12.8	12.8	13.0	13.0	13.3	13.3	13.4	13.7	13.8	14.1	14.2	14.4	13.5
2008	14.4	14.5	14.6	14.4	14.3	14.3	14.1	14.3	14.1	14.0	14.1	14.0	14.3
2009	13.8	13.8	13.8	13.4	13.6	13.3	13.5	13.5	13.5	13.7	13.8	13.8	13.6
2010	13.5	13.6	13.6	13.5	13.6	13.5	13.4	13.5	13.2	13.5	13.6	13.5	13.5
2011	13.3	13.3	13.3	13.3	13.3	13.1	13.3	13.3	13.3	13.3	13.3	13.3	13.3
2012	13.0	13.0	13.1	13.1	13.2	13.2	13.3	13.4	13.4	13.4	13.5	13.7	13.3
2013	13.7	13.8	13.9	14.1	14.2	14.2	14.3	14.2	14.2	14.3	14.2	14.2	14.1

Employment by Industry: Greenville-Mauldin-Easley, SC, Selected Years, 2002–2013—*Continued*

(Numbers in thousands, not seasonally adjusted)

Industry and year	January	February	March	April	May	June	July	August	September	October	November	December	Annual average
Professional and Business Services													
2002	40.8	41.7	42.5	42.0	42.5	42.8	43.7	44.5	45.0	45.8	45.7	45.7	43.6
2003	43.0	43.4	44.4	43.9	44.1	44.1	42.5	43.1	43.1	44.3	45.0	45.1	43.8
2004	43.8	43.9	44.4	44.7	44.7	44.6	44.4	45.1	44.8	44.6	44.5	44.8	44.5
2005	44.9	44.9	44.0	45.6	46.4	45.9	46.2	47.4	48.4	49.4	49.6	48.0	46.7
2006	48.0	48.7	49.4	50.1	50.4	50.7	49.6	50.6	51.3	52.3	52.1	51.9	50.4
2007	50.8	51.8	52.8	53.3	54.1	54.2	53.3	53.8	53.8	53.6	54.4	54.3	53.4
2008	53.1	53.4	53.5	54.4	55.3	54.5	53.4	53.9	53.8	52.9	52.1	50.2	53.4
2009	47.0	47.1	47.2	45.5	45.7	45.0	45.8	46.0	46.3	47.9	49.0	48.4	46.7
2010	48.0	48.9	49.9	50.7	51.1	51.0	52.0	52.9	52.6	53.3	53.6	53.6	51.5
2011	51.8	53.5	54.4	55.2	55.3	55.3	55.9	57.2	57.4	57.3	57.5	57.6	55.7
2012	55.9	56.1	57.2	57.2	57.6	58.1	57.6	58.4	57.8	57.6	58.6	58.8	57.6
2013	57.2	58.0	58.3	58.0	59.0	60.1	59.2	59.8	59.8	60.2	59.3	60.6	59.1
Education and Health Services													
2002	25.6	25.7	26.0	26.2	26.5	26.5	26.6	27.4	28.1	27.7	27.8	27.8	26.8
2003	27.5	27.7	27.8	28.2	28.6	28.5	28.2	28.3	28.7	28.4	28.4	28.5	28.2
2004	28.3	28.4	28.5	28.7	28.8	29.1	29.2	29.1	29.1	29.1	29.3	29.4	28.9
2005	29.3	29.5	29.6	29.5	29.7	29.8	29.8	29.8	30.0	30.0	30.2	30.0	29.8
2006	30.2	30.3	30.2	30.3	30.5	30.1	30.0	30.3	30.4	31.0	30.8	30.8	30.4
2007	30.5	30.7	30.7	31.2	31.3	31.4	31.5	31.8	31.7	31.3	31.3	31.2	31.2
2008	31.5	31.9	31.9	31.7	32.2	32.0	32.2	32.3	32.1	32.2	32.3	32.3	32.1
2009	31.9	32.0	32.1	32.4	32.8	32.9	32.8	33.0	32.5	32.8	32.9	32.9	32.6
2010	33.7	34.1	34.3	34.8	35.2	35.0	34.9	35.1	35.0	35.4	35.5	35.5	34.9
2011	35.0	35.7	35.7	35.3	35.4	35.3	35.0	35.1	34.8	34.7	34.7	34.7	35.1
2012	34.3	34.7	34.8	34.7	35.1	34.2	33.7	34.1	35.2	35.2	35.4	35.3	34.7
2013	34.9	35.4	35.4	35.3	35.7	35.2	34.9	35.2	35.7	35.9	36.0	36.0	35.5
Leisure and Hospitality													
2002	25.2	25.5	26.0	25.8	26.4	26.8	27.7	28.0	27.6	27.0	27.0	26.9	26.7
2003	26.2	26.6	27.0	26.9	27.3	27.7	27.8	27.7	27.4	26.8	26.9	26.6	27.1
2004	26.5	26.7	27.1	28.1	28.3	28.4	28.4	28.2	27.9	27.6	28.6	27.4	27.8
2005	26.7	27.1	27.4	27.9	28.2	28.2	28.6	28.7	28.4	28.7	29.0	28.4	28.1
2006	28.3	28.6	28.7	29.2	29.6	29.3	29.9	29.9	29.7	30.1	30.3	30.5	29.5
2007	29.5	29.8	30.0	30.7	30.6	30.4	30.1	30.6	30.6	31.1	31.1	30.9	30.5
2008	29.9	30.1	30.6	30.9	31.0	30.3	30.2	30.6	30.6	30.8	30.5	30.1	30.5
2009	29.1	29.4	29.9	30.4	30.8	29.8	29.6	30.2	30.0	29.7	29.7	29.4	29.8
2010	28.3	28.5	29.1	29.8	30.2	29.6	30.0	30.6	30.7	30.0	29.7	29.6	29.7
2011	28.4	29.0	29.9	30.8	31.2	30.1	29.8	30.6	30.5	30.1	30.3	29.9	30.1
2012	28.8	29.2	29.8	30.1	30.8	31.1	30.5	31.1	31.0	30.5	30.7	30.5	30.3
2013	29.9	30.3	30.4	31.2	31.8	32.0	32.0	32.2	32.1	31.6	32.4	32.0	31.5
Other Services													
2002	9.6	9.8	10.2	9.9	10.1	10.2	9.7	9.7	10.1	9.6	9.6	9.6	9.8
2003	9.4	9.4	9.5	9.5	9.6	9.5	9.5	9.4	9.7	9.7	9.7	9.8	9.6
2004	9.9	9.9	10.0	10.7	10.8	11.0	10.4	10.2	10.4	10.5	10.7	10.7	10.4
2005	10.6	10.8	10.9	10.6	10.7	10.6	10.8	10.9	11.1	10.5	10.6	10.6	10.7
2006	10.5	10.7	10.8	10.9	11.0	11.0	11.1	11.2	11.3	11.3	11.4	11.5	11.1
2007	11.6	11.6	11.8	11.7	11.8	11.7	11.4	11.3	11.4	11.2	11.2	11.2	11.5
2008	10.5	10.7	10.9	11.0	11.2	11.1	10.8	10.9	11.1	10.8	10.9	10.8	10.9
2009	10.6	10.7	10.7	10.6	10.7	10.6	10.4	10.3	10.6	10.4	10.3	10.4	10.5
2010	9.9	10.0	10.1	10.1	10.2	10.1	9.9	9.9	10.2	10.1	10.1	10.1	10.1
2011	10.0	10.2	10.3	10.6	10.7	10.5	10.5	10.5	10.7	10.7	10.7	10.7	10.5
2012	10.9	11.0	11.1	11.5	11.5	11.6	11.5	11.5	11.4	11.4	11.4	11.4	11.4
2013	11.3	11.4	11.5	11.5	11.5	11.6	11.5	11.5	11.5	11.5	11.5	11.5	11.5
Government													
2002	38.6	39.0	39.2	39.7	39.7	38.1	36.9	37.7	39.7	39.9	40.5	40.1	39.1
2003	39.9	40.2	40.4	40.5	40.3	39.2	37.4	37.5	39.7	40.0	40.4	39.9	39.6
2004	39.8	39.9	40.1	40.6	40.5	39.1	38.0	37.3	39.6	40.6	40.6	40.4	39.7
2005	39.7	40.1	40.2	40.3	40.7	39.2	37.3	37.0	40.7	41.1	41.4	41.1	39.9
2006	40.6	41.4	41.4	41.4	41.7	40.2	38.2	38.0	41.4	42.8	42.3	42.3	41.0
2007	42.0	42.4	42.7	42.7	43.2	41.7	40.0	39.1	43.1	43.7	44.4	43.9	42.4
2008	43.6	44.2	44.5	44.4	45.2	43.5	41.7	40.9	44.6	45.3	45.2	44.8	44.0
2009	44.3	44.5	44.6	44.8	45.3	43.4	41.6	41.1	43.9	44.5	44.7	44.4	43.9
2010	43.1	43.2	43.3	43.6	45.0	42.8	40.5	39.8	42.6	43.0	43.1	42.8	42.7
2011	41.9	42.2	42.3	42.6	42.5	41.0	40.6	40.8	42.5	43.2	43.4	43.4	42.2
2012	43.4	43.7	43.9	43.9	44.3	42.6	40.9	41.2	43.7	44.5	44.7	44.5	43.4
2013	44.3	44.4	44.8	45.4	45.1	44.3	42.3	42.5	45.1	45.9	46.1	46.1	44.7

Employment by Industry: Hartford-West Hartford-East Hartford, CT, NECTA, Selected Years, 2002–2013

(Numbers in thousands, not seasonally adjusted)

Industry and year	January	February	March	April	May	June	July	August	September	October	November	December	Annual average
Total Nonfarm													
2002	542.7	544.0	545.8	546.3	549.3	549.6	539.2	536.3	543.2	544.3	546.9	547.9	544.6
2003	534.3	533.2	533.3	536.5	539.0	538.1	529.2	526.4	533.5	539.0	540.9	541.3	535.4
2004	528.3	529.2	531.3	537.5	540.0	541.0	534.0	531.0	539.8	543.3	546.4	548.6	537.5
2005	535.0	536.2	537.3	545.0	546.6	548.8	539.9	538.0	546.8	547.7	552.4	553.2	543.9
2006	541.2	541.8	543.7	549.7	551.8	553.0	547.5	545.4	552.6	557.2	559.5	560.4	550.3
2007	547.0	548.7	550.2	554.8	558.5	561.9	553.3	551.0	558.2	561.2	565.1	564.5	556.2
2008	552.2	555.1	557.1	560.7	562.2	565.1	555.7	551.9	559.9	561.8	560.4	556.7	558.2
2009	541.3	543.2	540.8	541.6	543.2	542.5	533.3	529.9	538.6	541.3	541.7	540.8	539.9
2010	521.5	523.4	525.9	533.5	535.5	535.6	528.9	526.6	537.3	542.2	544.4	544.0	533.2
2011	530.8	533.3	533.7	541.0	540.3	540.5	534.8	530.5	541.4	542.9	543.6	545.4	538.2
2012	532.5	536.3	538.9	542.6	542.9	545.2	538.6	536.7	547.1	551.7	555.0	553.7	543.4
2013	540.3	540.7	543.4	548.7	550.5	554.4	545.8	542.6	550.6	554.9	558.3	558.5	549.1
Total Private													
2002	454.8	452.8	454.4	455.5	458.9	462.0	458.2	455.4	454.7	454.6	456.0	457.2	456.2
2003	447.3	443.2	443.8	447.5	451.1	452.7	450.6	448.6	449.9	452.2	453.7	454.2	449.6
2004	444.5	442.2	444.2	449.7	453.4	456.8	455.9	453.8	455.7	456.3	458.4	461.0	452.7
2005	450.6	449.0	450.5	456.8	459.3	464.0	460.4	459.4	460.0	459.3	462.1	464.6	458.0
2006	455.8	454.0	456.0	460.5	463.3	467.6	466.7	465.5	464.9	466.7	467.8	470.2	463.3
2007	459.6	458.6	460.2	464.3	470.6	476.3	472.5	471.1	470.7	470.9	473.9	475.2	468.7
2008	465.8	464.9	466.9	469.9	474.0	479.0	474.3	471.5	472.2	471.6	470.2	468.8	470.8
2009	456.0	452.8	450.7	450.5	455.1	456.8	453.5	450.9	451.2	450.6	450.6	451.0	452.5
2010	437.0	436.1	438.3	445.6	449.5	453.1	451.0	450.0	451.9	454.0	456.1	456.8	448.3
2011	445.9	446.2	446.8	453.5	456.5	459.7	457.9	455.1	456.3	455.6	456.3	458.7	454.0
2012	449.8	449.9	452.7	456.3	460.7	464.6	461.6	460.8	461.8	464.3	466.8	466.5	459.7
2013	455.8	454.8	457.3	462.4	466.9	470.6	466.7	465.9	466.1	468.1	471.0	471.9	464.8
Goods Producing													
2002	89.6	88.7	89.2	90.2	90.8	91.2	90.0	89.7	89.4	88.8	88.1	87.3	89.4
2003	84.5	83.0	83.2	84.5	85.1	85.6	85.6	85.6	85.6	85.5	85.6	85.1	84.9
2004	82.4	81.8	82.6	84.5	85.4	86.6	86.9	86.8	86.9	86.6	86.7	86.3	85.3
2005	83.8	83.1	83.5	85.4	86.2	87.7	87.1	86.9	86.6	86.3	86.4	85.9	85.7
2006	84.1	83.8	84.2	86.1	86.8	88.1	88.6	88.6	88.1	88.0	87.8	87.6	86.8
2007	85.2	84.5	84.9	86.5	87.9	88.9	88.9	88.9	88.0	87.8	87.7	86.9	87.2
2008	84.4	84.0	83.9	85.6	86.1	87.2	86.8	86.5	86.1	85.2	83.9	82.5	85.2
2009	79.8	78.2	77.3	77.1	77.5	77.8	77.4	76.9	76.9	75.7	75.2	74.8	77.1
2010	71.4	70.4	70.6	72.6	73.6	74.7	74.7	74.7	75.0	75.2	75.3	75.0	73.6
2011	72.4	72.2	72.5	73.6	74.6	76.0	76.4	76.0	75.9	75.5	75.7	75.0	74.7
2012	73.2	72.8	73.2	74.2	74.9	75.9	76.3	76.2	75.5	75.6	75.6	75.2	74.9
2013	73.2	72.8	72.8	74.3	75.5	76.3	76.7	76.1	75.9	75.8	75.5	75.4	75.0
Service-Providing													
2002	453.1	455.3	456.6	456.1	458.5	458.4	449.2	446.6	453.8	455.5	458.8	460.6	455.2
2003	449.8	450.2	450.1	452.0	453.9	452.5	443.6	440.8	447.9	453.5	455.3	456.2	450.5
2004	445.9	447.4	448.7	453.0	454.6	454.4	447.1	444.2	452.9	456.7	459.7	462.3	452.2
2005	451.2	453.1	453.8	459.6	460.4	461.1	452.8	451.1	460.2	461.4	466.0	467.3	458.2
2006	457.1	458.0	459.5	463.6	465.0	464.9	458.9	456.8	464.5	469.2	471.7	472.8	463.5
2007	461.8	464.2	465.3	468.3	470.6	473.0	464.4	462.1	470.2	473.4	477.4	477.6	469.0
2008	467.8	471.1	473.2	475.1	476.1	477.9	468.9	465.4	473.8	476.6	476.5	474.2	473.1
2009	461.5	465.0	463.5	464.5	465.7	464.7	455.9	453.0	461.7	465.6	466.5	466.0	462.8
2010	450.1	453.0	455.3	460.9	461.9	460.9	454.2	451.9	462.3	467.0	469.1	469.0	459.6
2011	458.4	461.1	461.2	467.4	465.7	464.5	458.4	454.5	465.5	467.4	467.9	470.4	463.5
2012	459.3	463.5	465.7	468.4	468.0	469.3	462.3	460.5	471.6	476.1	479.4	478.5	468.6
2013	467.1	467.9	470.6	474.4	475.0	478.1	469.1	466.5	474.7	479.1	482.8	483.1	474.0
Mining, Logging, and Construction													
2002	19.6	19.3	19.7	20.9	21.6	21.9	21.8	21.8	21.4	21.2	20.9	20.1	20.9
2003	18.5	17.7	17.9	19.2	20.1	20.6	21.5	21.6	21.4	21.3	21.4	20.7	20.2
2004	18.5	18.1	18.6	20.5	21.3	22.0	22.6	23.0	22.8	22.7	22.6	22.1	21.2
2005	20.1	19.5	19.8	21.3	22.0	23.0	23.1	23.2	22.8	22.4	22.4	21.7	21.8
2006	20.3	19.9	20.2	21.6	22.3	22.9	23.5	23.8	23.3	23.2	23.0	22.5	22.2
2007	20.8	20.1	20.5	22.1	23.4	23.9	24.1	24.2	23.8	23.6	23.3	22.4	22.7
2008	20.4	20.1	20.2	21.4	21.9	22.4	22.5	22.3	21.9	21.4	20.6	19.6	21.2
2009	17.7	17.1	17.1	17.9	18.7	19.1	19.3	19.4	19.2	18.7	18.4	17.9	18.4
2010	15.3	14.5	14.6	16.6	17.3	17.9	18.1	18.3	18.1	18.2	18.1	17.5	17.0
2011	15.6	15.3	15.4	16.6	17.4	18.2	18.6	18.5	18.3	18.1	18.3	17.5	17.3
2012	15.9	15.5	15.9	16.9	17.4	17.9	18.4	18.5	18.4	18.4	18.3	17.8	17.4
2013	16.2	16.0	16.2	17.6	18.7	19.1	19.6	19.6	19.6	19.2	19.0	18.8	18.3
Manufacturing													
2002	70.0	69.4	69.5	69.3	69.2	69.3	68.2	67.9	68.0	67.6	67.2	67.2	68.6
2003	66.0	65.3	65.3	65.3	65.0	65.0	64.1	64.0	64.2	64.2	64.2	64.4	64.8
2004	63.9	63.7	64.0	64.0	64.1	64.6	64.3	63.8	64.1	63.9	64.1	64.2	64.1
2005	63.7	63.6	63.7	64.1	64.2	64.7	64.0	63.7	63.8	63.9	64.0	64.2	64.0
2006	63.8	63.9	64.0	64.5	64.5	65.2	65.1	64.8	64.8	64.8	64.8	65.1	64.6
2007	64.4	64.4	64.4	64.4	64.5	65.0	64.8	64.7	64.2	64.2	64.4	64.5	64.5
2008	64.0	63.9	63.7	64.2	64.2	64.8	64.3	64.2	64.2	63.8	63.3	62.9	64.0
2009	62.1	61.1	60.2	59.2	58.8	58.7	58.1	57.5	57.7	57.0	56.8	56.9	58.7
2010	56.1	55.9	56.0	56.0	56.3	56.8	56.6	56.4	56.9	57.0	57.2	57.5	56.6
2011	56.8	56.9	57.1	57.0	57.2	57.8	57.8	57.5	57.6	57.4	57.4	57.5	57.3
2012	57.3	57.3	57.3	57.3	57.5	58.0	57.9	57.7	57.1	57.2	57.3	57.4	57.4
2013	57.0	56.8	56.6	56.7	56.8	57.2	57.1	56.5	56.3	56.6	56.5	56.6	56.7

Employment by Industry: Hartford-West Hartford-East Hartford, CT, NECTA, Selected Years, 2002–2013—*Continued*

(Numbers in thousands, not seasonally adjusted)

Industry and year	January	February	March	April	May	June	July	August	September	October	November	December	Annual average
Trade, Transportation, and Utilities													
2002	91.0	89.6	89.8	89.1	89.4	90.6	88.2	87.7	88.6	88.3	89.8	91.3	89.5
2003	88.1	86.7	87.0	86.8	87.3	87.7	86.3	86.0	87.5	88.7	90.0	90.8	87.7
2004	88.0	87.1	87.3	88.0	88.6	89.2	88.0	87.5	89.1	90.0	92.3	94.0	89.1
2005	90.2	89.1	89.3	90.1	90.2	90.8	88.4	88.2	89.8	89.7	92.0	93.6	90.1
2006	90.1	88.1	88.6	89.4	89.7	89.9	87.8	87.6	89.0	89.6	91.4	93.0	89.5
2007	89.1	87.6	88.1	87.9	89.6	90.6	88.8	88.3	89.8	90.9	93.1	94.8	89.9
2008	91.3	89.9	90.2	90.1	90.9	91.6	89.3	88.8	90.2	90.5	91.4	92.4	90.6
2009	88.2	86.4	85.8	84.6	86.0	86.4	84.6	84.2	85.6	86.0	87.4	88.3	86.1
2010	84.7	83.4	83.8	83.9	85.1	86.1	84.5	84.2	84.8	86.0	87.6	89.2	85.3
2011	85.5	84.8	84.8	86.0	86.3	87.0	85.2	84.9	85.7	85.9	87.7	89.2	86.1
2012	86.3	85.0	85.6	85.8	87.1	87.5	85.4	85.2	86.5	87.5	89.5	90.3	86.8
2013	87.7	86.1	87.0	87.5	88.5	89.2	87.2	87.3	88.6	89.3	92.0	92.2	88.6
Wholesale Trade													
2002	19.7	19.6	19.6	19.4	19.3	19.3	19.4	19.3	19.2	19.1	19.0	19.1	19.3
2003	19.5	19.4	19.6	19.5	19.5	19.6	19.4	19.4	19.3	19.2	19.2	18.9	19.4
2004	18.7	18.6	18.7	18.9	18.9	19.1	19.2	19.2	19.1	19.0	19.1	19.2	19.0
2005	19.1	19.0	19.1	19.4	19.5	19.7	19.5	19.5	19.6	19.5	19.6	19.6	19.4
2006	19.6	19.5	19.6	19.8	19.7	19.9	19.7	19.7	19.6	19.6	19.5	19.5	19.6
2007	19.5	19.5	19.6	19.6	19.8	19.9	20.1	20.0	20.0	20.0	20.2	20.2	19.9
2008	20.0	20.0	20.2	20.1	20.3	20.4	20.2	20.1	20.0	19.9	19.7	19.5	20.0
2009	19.4	19.1	19.0	18.8	18.8	18.8	18.8	18.7	18.6	18.4	18.4	18.4	18.8
2010	18.0	17.9	18.0	18.2	18.3	18.4	18.5	18.5	18.3	18.3	18.4	18.4	18.3
2011	18.0	18.0	18.1	18.3	18.3	18.5	18.4	18.4	18.2	18.0	18.0	17.9	18.2
2012	17.8	17.8	17.8	17.9	18.0	18.1	18.1	18.0	18.0	18.2	18.0	18.1	18.0
2013	17.9	17.8	17.9	18.0	18.1	18.2	18.1	18.1	18.0	18.0	18.0	18.1	18.0
Retail Trade													
2002	56.4	55.2	55.6	55.5	55.8	57.0	55.7	55.7	55.4	54.8	56.4	57.8	55.9
2003	54.6	53.4	53.5	53.6	54.0	54.3	53.9	54.0	54.2	55.0	56.2	57.4	54.5
2004	55.2	54.4	54.5	54.7	55.2	55.5	55.2	55.0	55.3	55.7	57.8	59.4	55.7
2005	56.2	55.4	55.4	55.8	55.8	56.0	55.0	55.1	55.3	55.3	57.2	58.5	55.9
2006	55.8	54.0	54.5	55.1	55.3	55.3	54.5	54.4	54.6	55.1	56.9	58.1	55.3
2007	54.9	53.5	53.9	54.0	55.3	56.0	55.1	55.2	55.1	55.9	58.0	59.2	55.5
2008	56.4	54.9	55.0	55.0	55.4	55.9	54.8	54.9	54.6	54.8	55.8	56.7	55.4
2009	53.4	52.0	51.6	51.3	52.0	52.5	51.9	51.9	51.9	52.4	53.8	54.6	52.4
2010	51.9	50.8	51.0	51.3	51.9	52.7	52.3	52.1	51.6	52.7	54.0	55.4	52.3
2011	52.8	51.9	51.8	52.7	52.8	53.2	52.6	52.6	52.2	52.6	54.3	55.7	52.9
2012	53.5	52.3	52.7	52.9	53.6	53.8	53.0	53.1	52.7	53.4	55.5	55.9	53.5
2013	54.0	52.8	53.2	53.7	54.2	54.7	54.2	54.5	54.1	54.6	56.9	56.7	54.5
Transportation and Utilities													
2002	14.9	14.8	14.6	14.2	14.3	14.3	13.1	12.7	14.0	14.4	14.4	14.4	14.2
2003	14.0	13.9	13.9	13.7	13.8	13.8	13.0	12.6	14.0	14.5	14.6	14.5	13.9
2004	14.1	14.1	14.1	14.4	14.5	14.6	13.6	13.3	14.7	15.3	15.4	15.4	14.5
2005	14.9	14.7	14.8	14.9	14.9	15.1	13.9	13.6	14.9	14.9	15.2	15.5	14.8
2006	14.7	14.6	14.5	14.5	14.7	14.7	13.6	13.5	14.8	14.9	15.0	15.4	14.6
2007	14.7	14.6	14.6	14.3	14.5	14.7	13.6	13.1	14.7	15.0	15.1	15.4	14.5
2008	14.9	15.0	15.0	15.0	15.2	15.3	14.3	13.8	15.6	15.8	15.9	16.2	15.2
2009	15.4	15.3	15.2	14.5	15.2	15.1	13.9	13.6	15.1	15.2	15.2	15.3	14.9
2010	14.8	14.7	14.8	14.4	14.9	15.0	13.7	13.6	14.9	15.0	15.2	15.4	14.7
2011	14.7	14.9	14.9	15.0	15.2	15.3	14.2	13.9	15.3	15.3	15.4	15.6	15.0
2012	15.0	14.9	15.1	15.0	15.5	15.6	14.3	14.1	15.8	15.9	16.0	16.3	15.3
2013	15.8	15.5	15.9	15.8	16.2	16.3	14.9	14.7	16.5	16.7	17.1	17.4	16.1
Information													
2002	11.4	11.3	11.3	11.4	11.4	11.5	11.4	11.3	11.2	11.2	11.2	11.2	11.3
2003	11.3	11.3	11.3	11.1	11.1	11.3	11.2	11.2	11.0	11.0	11.0	11.0	11.2
2004	11.3	11.2	11.3	11.3	11.3	11.4	11.4	11.4	11.3	11.3	11.4	11.4	11.3
2005	11.5	11.4	11.4	11.4	11.5	11.6	11.6	11.6	11.5	11.6	11.7	11.8	11.6
2006	12.0	12.0	12.0	11.9	11.9	12.1	12.1	12.0	11.8	11.9	11.9	11.9	12.0
2007	11.9	12.0	12.0	12.1	12.1	12.3	12.4	12.3	12.2	12.1	12.2	12.3	12.2
2008	12.4	12.4	12.4	12.4	12.4	12.6	12.6	12.4	12.1	12.1	12.2	12.1	12.3
2009	12.0	12.0	11.8	11.8	11.7	11.7	11.7	11.6	11.5	11.3	11.2	11.2	11.6
2010	11.1	11.0	11.0	11.0	11.0	11.1	11.1	11.2	11.2	11.2	11.3	11.3	11.1
2011	11.3	11.3	11.3	11.1	11.1	11.1	11.1	11.1	11.1	11.0	10.9	10.9	10.8	11.1
2012	10.8	10.9	10.7	11.0	11.0	11.0	11.0	11.0	11.1	11.1	11.1	11.4	11.1	11.0
2013	11.3	11.5	11.4	11.2	11.3	11.3	11.3	11.4	11.0	11.0	11.0	11.0	11.2
Financial Activities													
2002	70.2	69.7	69.7	69.3	69.6	70.3	70.6	70.5	69.9	69.5	69.7	69.7	69.9
2003	69.4	68.9	68.6	69.7	69.9	70.6	70.1	69.7	69.1	68.7	68.7	68.8	69.4
2004	68.2	67.6	67.4	67.4	67.3	68.2	68.8	68.7	68.2	67.8	68.0	68.2	68.0
2005	68.1	67.8	67.0	67.9	67.6	68.4	68.4	68.4	67.8	67.5	67.4	67.7	67.8
2006	67.8	67.6	67.5	67.1	67.2	67.9	68.2	68.0	67.4	67.3	67.4	67.6	67.6
2007	67.6	67.1	66.9	66.6	66.7	67.5	67.2	67.1	66.4	66.1	66.1	66.2	66.8
2008	65.9	66.0	66.6	65.9	66.0	66.8	66.8	66.7	65.7	65.3	65.4	65.2	66.0
2009	64.7	64.5	64.4	63.9	63.9	64.2	63.8	63.4	62.6	62.2	62.1	61.9	63.5
2010	61.6	61.6	62.0	61.3	61.3	62.3	62.3	62.5	61.8	62.0	62.1	62.2	61.9
2011	62.1	61.8	62.0	61.6	61.7	62.2	62.4	62.2	61.6	61.4	61.3	61.4	61.8
2012	61.0	61.0	61.2	60.6	60.6	61.5	61.5	61.0	60.4	60.2	60.0	60.0	60.8
2013	59.9	59.4	59.3	59.1	59.0	60.0	60.0	59.5	58.6	59.0	59.1	59.0	59.3

Employment by Industry: Hartford-West Hartford-East Hartford, CT, NECTA, Selected Years, 2002–2013—*Continued*

(Numbers in thousands, not seasonally adjusted)

Industry and year	January	February	March	April	May	June	July	August	September	October	November	December	Annual average
Professional and Business Services													
2002	56.5	56.6	57.5	57.7	57.6	57.9	57.1	57.0	56.7	56.9	57.0	56.8	57.1
2003	55.5	55.1	55.2	56.0	55.9	56.1	55.9	56.0	56.2	56.3	56.7	56.3	55.9
2004	55.7	55.4	55.8	57.1	56.9	57.5	57.5	57.7	57.8	57.8	58.0	58.1	57.1
2005	56.8	56.8	57.5	58.2	58.1	59.3	59.5	59.5	59.6	59.0	59.3	59.6	58.6
2006	58.3	58.6	58.9	60.0	59.8	60.7	60.7	60.8	60.6	60.7	60.5	60.6	60.0
2007	58.8	59.1	59.4	61.0	61.3	62.4	61.7	61.9	61.4	61.0	61.4	62.1	61.0
2008	61.3	61.5	61.8	62.1	62.4	63.3	62.9	62.6	62.1	61.6	61.3	60.5	62.0
2009	59.2	58.7	58.1	58.7	58.9	58.9	58.2	58.4	57.9	58.3	58.2	58.0	58.5
2010	56.1	56.8	56.8	59.3	59.4	59.8	59.6	59.4	59.2	59.7	59.6	59.3	58.8
2011	58.4	58.6	58.2	60.1	60.2	61.0	61.0	60.8	60.8	61.5	61.3	62.0	60.3
2012	60.6	61.1	61.7	62.8	63.2	63.9	63.9	64.2	63.9	64.2	64.4	63.8	63.1
2013	61.7	62.3	62.3	63.7	64.0	64.8	64.6	65.2	65.1	65.3	65.3	65.1	64.1
Education and Health Services													
2002	81.3	82.0	82.0	81.6	82.2	81.5	81.1	80.4	81.7	82.8	83.6	83.9	82.0
2003	82.6	82.7	82.5	82.5	82.7	81.7	81.5	80.5	82.3	83.7	84.2	84.3	82.6
2004	82.9	83.2	83.5	83.6	84.3	83.2	82.4	81.6	83.4	84.4	84.7	85.0	83.5
2005	83.6	84.1	84.2	84.6	84.8	83.9	83.3	83.0	84.4	85.9	86.1	86.3	84.5
2006	85.3	85.8	85.8	86.2	86.4	85.7	86.1	85.7	86.7	88.1	88.6	88.7	86.6
2007	88.2	89.2	89.6	89.8	89.9	89.6	88.9	88.1	90.1	91.0	91.8	91.5	89.8
2008	91.1	91.6	91.9	92.4	92.2	92.3	91.9	91.1	93.2	94.3	94.9	94.9	92.7
2009	93.8	94.5	94.8	95.1	94.7	94.3	95.1	94.4	95.5	96.5	96.5	96.7	95.2
2010	95.5	95.9	96.6	97.3	96.7	96.0	95.1	94.7	96.8	97.9	98.5	98.5	96.6
2011	97.9	98.4	98.8	99.5	98.8	97.5	96.7	95.8	97.8	97.5	97.3	97.8	97.8
2012	96.9	97.8	98.3	98.2	97.9	97.1	96.6	96.3	98.7	99.8	100.5	101.1	98.3
2013	99.1	99.8	100.5	100.7	100.0	99.5	98.2	98.4	100.8	101.4	102.7	103.5	100.4
Leisure and Hospitality													
2002	33.5	33.6	33.4	34.7	36.3	37.3	38.1	37.5	36.2	35.9	35.3	35.6	35.6
2003	35.2	34.8	35.1	36.0	38.1	38.5	38.8	38.7	37.5	37.6	36.9	37.2	37.0
2004	35.5	35.4	35.7	37.1	38.9	39.7	39.9	39.3	38.4	37.7	36.6	37.3	37.6
2005	36.2	36.3	37.1	38.4	40.2	41.2	41.2	41.1	39.8	38.7	38.6	39.0	39.0
2006	37.7	37.6	38.4	39.0	40.6	42.1	42.1	41.9	40.5	40.2	39.4	40.0	40.0
2007	38.1	38.4	38.6	39.5	42.2	43.7	43.6	43.6	42.0	41.1	40.8	40.6	41.0
2008	38.8	38.8	39.3	40.5	43.0	44.0	43.4	42.9	42.1	41.9	40.4	40.7	41.3
2009	37.9	38.4	38.4	39.1	42.1	43.1	42.6	42.0	41.2	40.5	40.0	39.9	40.4
2010	36.7	37.2	37.7	40.3	42.2	42.7	43.4	43.1	42.8	41.7	41.3	41.1	40.9
2011	38.3	39.1	39.1	41.4	43.3	44.0	44.6	44.0	43.4	42.8	41.9	42.2	42.0
2012	40.6	41.0	41.8	43.4	45.3	46.6	45.9	45.7	44.6	44.5	43.8	44.0	43.9
2013	42.1	41.9	42.9	45.1	47.6	48.1	47.5	47.0	45.3	45.5	44.6	44.9	45.2
Other Services													
2002	21.3	21.3	21.5	21.5	21.6	21.7	21.7	21.3	21.0	21.2	21.3	21.4	21.4
2003	20.7	20.7	20.9	20.9	21.0	21.2	21.2	20.9	20.7	20.7	20.6	20.7	20.9
2004	20.5	20.5	20.6	20.7	20.7	21.0	21.0	20.8	20.6	20.7	20.7	20.7	20.7
2005	20.4	20.4	20.5	20.8	20.7	21.1	20.9	20.7	20.5	20.6	20.6	20.7	20.7
2006	20.5	20.5	20.6	20.8	20.9	21.1	21.1	20.9	20.8	20.9	20.8	20.8	20.8
2007	20.7	20.7	20.7	20.9	20.9	21.3	21.0	20.9	20.8	20.9	20.8	20.8	20.9
2008	20.6	20.7	20.8	20.9	21.0	21.2	20.6	20.5	20.7	20.7	20.7	20.5	20.7
2009	20.4	20.1	20.1	20.2	20.3	20.4	20.1	20.0	20.0	20.1	20.0	20.2	20.2
2010	19.9	19.8	19.8	19.9	20.2	20.4	20.3	20.2	20.3	20.3	20.4	20.2	20.1
2011	20.0	20.0	20.1	20.2	20.5	20.9	20.5	20.3	20.1	20.1	20.2	20.3	20.3
2012	20.4	20.3	20.2	20.3	20.7	21.1	21.0	21.1	21.1	21.4	21.6	21.0	20.9
2013	20.8	21.0	21.1	20.8	21.0	21.4	21.2	21.0	20.8	20.8	20.8	20.8	21.0
Government													
2002	87.9	91.2	91.4	90.8	90.4	87.6	81.0	80.9	88.5	89.7	90.9	90.7	88.4
2003	87.0	90.0	89.5	89.0	87.9	85.4	78.6	77.8	83.6	86.8	87.2	87.1	85.8
2004	83.8	87.0	87.1	87.8	86.6	84.2	78.1	77.2	84.1	87.0	88.0	87.6	84.9
2005	84.4	87.2	86.8	88.2	87.3	84.8	79.5	78.6	86.8	88.4	90.3	88.6	85.9
2006	85.4	87.8	87.7	89.2	88.5	85.4	80.8	79.9	87.7	90.5	91.7	90.2	87.1
2007	87.4	90.1	90.0	90.5	87.9	85.6	80.8	79.9	87.5	90.3	91.2	89.3	87.5
2008	86.4	90.2	90.2	90.8	88.2	86.1	81.4	80.4	87.7	90.2	90.2	87.9	87.5
2009	85.3	90.4	90.1	91.1	88.1	85.7	79.8	79.0	87.4	90.7	91.1	89.8	87.4
2010	84.5	87.3	87.6	87.9	86.0	82.5	77.9	76.6	85.4	88.2	88.3	87.2	85.0
2011	84.9	87.1	86.9	87.5	83.8	80.8	76.9	75.4	85.1	87.3	87.3	86.7	84.1
2012	82.7	86.4	86.2	86.3	82.2	80.6	77.0	75.9	85.3	87.4	88.2	87.2	83.8
2013	84.5	85.9	86.1	86.3	83.6	83.8	79.1	76.7	84.5	86.8	87.3	86.6	84.3

Employment by Industry: Houston-Sugar Land-Baytown, TX, Selected Years, 2002–2013

(Numbers in thousands, not seasonally adjusted)

Industry and year	January	February	March	April	May	June	July	August	September	October	November	December	Annual average
Total Nonfarm													
2002	2,259.2	2,274.7	2,284.6	2,282.1	2,294.5	2,294.4	2,272.8	2,283.0	2,290.1	2,287.2	2,292.7	2,299.0	2,284.5
2003	2,257.2	2,266.7	2,274.3	2,271.1	2,277.2	2,278.0	2,250.2	2,262.6	2,273.1	2,271.6	2,274.8	2,287.7	2,270.4
2004	2,253.1	2,264.5	2,275.8	2,279.9	2,283.7	2,289.4	2,276.1	2,283.4	2,291.1	2,300.1	2,310.5	2,325.3	2,286.1
2005	2,292.9	2,305.3	2,324.3	2,335.4	2,342.7	2,346.9	2,341.6	2,354.9	2,370.1	2,376.3	2,397.8	2,414.5	2,350.2
2006	2,375.4	2,396.3	2,420.6	2,420.5	2,438.1	2,449.8	2,439.7	2,456.9	2,474.6	2,481.4	2,501.8	2,520.5	2,448.0
2007	2,475.4	2,498.8	2,522.7	2,528.1	2,546.9	2,563.6	2,546.1	2,554.8	2,563.1	2,577.1	2,596.0	2,609.6	2,548.5
2008	2,557.8	2,579.8	2,591.1	2,597.2	2,608.9	2,616.4	2,604.5	2,612.2	2,593.3	2,612.9	2,627.8	2,629.5	2,602.6
2009	2,566.0	2,566.0	2,562.6	2,546.5	2,546.6	2,541.0	2,511.3	2,504.4	2,507.8	2,511.2	2,515.0	2,520.7	2,533.3
2010	2,475.7	2,490.3	2,507.9	2,520.5	2,539.2	2,539.2	2,523.7	2,526.3	2,533.6	2,548.0	2,558.7	2,568.0	2,527.6
2011	2,526.3	2,541.8	2,565.2	2,583.6	2,588.8	2,601.1	2,588.9	2,595.4	2,612.0	2,617.7	2,633.2	2,648.5	2,591.9
2012	2,608.3	2,632.2	2,659.0	2,669.3	2,689.3	2,703.7	2,688.8	2,703.3	2,718.7	2,734.2	2,753.4	2,763.9	2,693.7
2013	2,713.7	2,749.9	2,767.1	2,777.0	2,789.7	2,799.0	2,783.5	2,789.0	2,802.3	2,818.9	2,830.6	2,840.1	2,788.4
Total Private													
2002	1,938.9	1,947.2	1,956.0	1,953.6	1,965.0	1,973.7	1,963.4	1,970.7	1,960.2	1,949.7	1,955.0	1,961.7	1,957.9
2003	1,925.6	1,928.3	1,935.5	1,932.6	1,938.9	1,947.9	1,935.5	1,943.7	1,939.6	1,933.4	1,935.5	1,949.6	1,937.2
2004	1,917.9	1,924.5	1,935.4	1,940.5	1,944.6	1,957.0	1,958.3	1,963.0	1,954.9	1,960.7	1,970.3	1,985.1	1,951.0
2005	1,957.6	1,964.0	1,981.7	1,992.2	1,999.6	2,015.1	2,017.2	2,027.5	2,029.2	2,030.5	2,048.8	2,066.4	2,010.8
2006	2,032.0	2,046.8	2,070.4	2,073.1	2,090.3	2,111.8	2,114.0	2,126.1	2,127.9	2,128.9	2,147.5	2,167.5	2,103.0
2007	2,128.8	2,144.9	2,167.3	2,171.4	2,190.0	2,216.9	2,212.3	2,219.0	2,210.8	2,216.6	2,231.7	2,245.6	2,196.3
2008	2,196.6	2,214.2	2,223.9	2,231.1	2,243.2	2,259.9	2,257.1	2,265.8	2,230.7	2,246.7	2,256.7	2,259.3	2,240.4
2009	2,199.7	2,194.1	2,189.1	2,170.1	2,171.4	2,174.2	2,158.9	2,155.4	2,139.9	2,131.3	2,133.0	2,139.9	2,163.1
2010	2,103.3	2,109.0	2,124.4	2,134.8	2,145.2	2,158.7	2,159.7	2,165.8	2,158.9	2,165.3	2,174.4	2,186.7	2,148.9
2011	2,148.6	2,160.1	2,182.3	2,200.8	2,208.9	2,230.3	2,232.8	2,245.8	2,247.4	2,247.4	2,262.9	2,280.0	2,220.6
2012	2,247.6	2,264.0	2,289.4	2,300.1	2,319.9	2,344.3	2,340.8	2,358.1	2,356.5	2,364.2	2,381.7	2,392.3	2,329.9
2013	2,352.3	2,378.5	2,394.4	2,403.8	2,416.3	2,434.5	2,430.9	2,443.0	2,433.1	2,441.0	2,449.6	2,461.7	2,419.9
Goods Producing													
2002	462.0	464.8	466.3	463.5	464.1	464.6	461.4	462.3	460.1	458.8	455.4	453.2	461.4
2003	449.0	448.9	448.1	446.1	446.9	448.1	442.9	443.4	444.3	441.8	437.4	438.0	444.6
2004	435.4	435.6	436.7	436.7	434.8	437.0	436.3	436.6	435.0	437.8	439.0	440.1	436.8
2005	442.5	444.8	448.9	449.7	449.1	453.2	454.2	456.0	458.2	458.4	461.2	464.3	453.4
2006	463.7	469.8	475.6	474.6	480.3	487.2	486.6	490.0	493.3	496.5	499.9	502.5	485.0
2007	500.5	506.3	510.3	509.7	515.4	522.6	521.1	521.0	520.6	526.4	529.3	530.4	517.8
2008	520.6	527.6	528.5	531.6	534.5	536.9	537.0	538.7	535.3	541.8	541.1	536.7	534.2
2009	523.1	518.3	508.9	496.5	492.7	488.9	483.1	480.1	476.1	472.5	467.7	466.4	489.5
2010	463.6	463.7	465.1	466.1	468.1	470.6	472.0	473.6	473.2	474.7	473.0	473.1	469.7
2011	467.4	473.4	476.5	479.2	479.7	487.4	491.7	495.3	498.9	501.1	501.5	503.7	488.0
2012	499.0	505.1	511.5	513.0	518.2	523.9	524.0	528.1	530.4	536.2	535.1	535.9	521.7
2013	531.0	540.6	542.3	544.5	545.8	550.9	550.0	552.2	550.8	556.0	550.4	551.9	547.2
Service-Providing													
2002	1,797.2	1,809.9	1,818.3	1,818.6	1,830.4	1,829.8	1,811.4	1,820.7	1,830.0	1,828.4	1,837.3	1,845.8	1,823.2
2003	1,808.2	1,817.8	1,826.2	1,825.0	1,830.3	1,829.9	1,807.3	1,819.2	1,828.8	1,829.8	1,837.4	1,849.7	1,825.8
2004	1,817.7	1,828.9	1,839.1	1,843.2	1,848.9	1,852.4	1,839.8	1,846.8	1,856.1	1,862.3	1,871.5	1,885.2	1,849.3
2005	1,850.4	1,860.5	1,875.4	1,885.7	1,893.6	1,893.7	1,887.4	1,898.9	1,911.9	1,917.9	1,936.6	1,950.2	1,896.9
2006	1,911.7	1,926.5	1,945.0	1,945.9	1,957.8	1,962.6	1,953.1	1,966.9	1,981.3	1,984.9	2,001.9	2,018.0	1,963.0
2007	1,974.9	1,992.5	2,012.4	2,018.4	2,031.5	2,041.0	2,025.0	2,033.8	2,042.5	2,050.7	2,066.7	2,079.2	2,030.7
2008	2,037.2	2,052.2	2,062.6	2,065.6	2,074.4	2,079.5	2,067.5	2,073.5	2,058.0	2,071.1	2,086.7	2,092.8	2,068.4
2009	2,042.9	2,047.7	2,053.7	2,050.0	2,053.9	2,052.1	2,028.2	2,024.3	2,031.7	2,038.7	2,047.3	2,054.3	2,043.7
2010	2,012.1	2,026.6	2,042.8	2,054.4	2,071.1	2,068.6	2,051.7	2,052.7	2,060.4	2,073.3	2,085.7	2,094.9	2,057.9
2011	2,058.9	2,068.4	2,088.7	2,104.4	2,109.1	2,113.7	2,097.2	2,100.1	2,113.1	2,116.6	2,131.7	2,144.8	2,103.9
2012	2,109.3	2,127.1	2,147.5	2,156.3	2,171.1	2,179.8	2,164.8	2,175.2	2,188.3	2,198.0	2,218.3	2,228.0	2,172.0
2013	2,182.7	2,209.3	2,224.8	2,232.5	2,243.9	2,248.1	2,233.5	2,236.8	2,251.5	2,262.9	2,280.2	2,288.2	2,241.2
Mining and Logging													
2002	59.1	58.7	58.3	58.5	58.7	59.4	59.7	59.8	59.4	59.6	59.8	59.8	59.2
2003	59.5	59.5	59.8	60.0	60.4	60.9	61.7	61.9	61.5	61.4	61.3	62.4	60.9
2004	62.0	61.8	62.3	62.7	62.9	63.2	64.2	64.3	64.0	64.9	65.2	65.5	63.6
2005	65.5	65.9	66.2	65.3	65.7	67.0	67.6	67.8	68.0	68.7	68.9	68.9	67.1
2006	69.6	70.2	70.2	71.2	71.8	73.4	74.6	75.5	76.2	77.6	77.9	78.7	73.9
2007	78.6	79.0	79.3	78.9	79.6	80.8	81.0	81.0	80.3	81.3	81.8	82.1	80.3
2008	82.0	83.0	83.2	83.7	84.5	86.4	87.3	87.8	87.4	88.6	88.5	88.3	85.9
2009	86.7	85.2	84.0	81.4	80.3	80.0	80.1	79.5	78.7	78.1	77.5	77.8	80.8
2010	77.5	77.9	78.1	79.3	80.1	81.6	81.9	82.4	82.2	82.8	83.3	83.7	80.9
2011	83.4	84.5	84.9	85.9	86.1	88.9	90.6	91.9	92.1	93.5	94.1	95.4	89.3
2012	94.2	95.0	96.1	96.6	97.9	99.3	101.0	101.0	101.1	102.0	102.1	103.1	99.1
2013	102.9	103.6	104.1	105.4	105.8	107.4	108.5	108.9	108.3	108.1	106.9	107.4	106.4
Construction													
2002	177.5	180.8	183.4	181.8	182.9	182.2	180.2	181.1	180.8	180.9	178.4	176.4	180.5
2003	175.4	176.4	176.1	174.8	176.4	175.8	171.8	173.0	173.9	173.4	168.6	168.2	173.7
2004	166.0	166.4	166.7	166.9	164.8	165.3	163.3	163.4	163.6	165.8	165.3	165.7	165.3
2005	169.4	170.8	173.7	174.6	172.7	172.9	172.9	174.2	176.0	176.0	177.0	179.0	174.1
2006	178.2	183.0	187.3	183.1	185.8	188.6	187.0	188.3	191.0	192.5	193.8	194.3	187.7
2007	193.5	198.5	200.9	200.5	203.6	207.1	204.9	204.9	205.3	209.3	210.1	210.0	204.1
2008	201.4	206.6	207.0	207.9	208.3	206.8	205.1	206.3	203.8	208.7	207.3	203.3	206.0
2009	196.3	194.9	191.2	185.9	185.4	183.5	180.3	179.4	177.3	176.9	173.6	171.8	183.0
2010	170.6	169.8	170.7	171.3	172.0	172.1	172.6	173.2	173.0	173.3	170.4	169.0	171.5
2011	163.9	167.5	168.7	169.0	168.6	170.9	172.1	173.5	175.6	175.3	173.8	172.2	170.9
2012	169.8	173.1	176.1	175.7	178.2	179.4	177.3	181.4	182.5	187.4	185.4	184.2	179.2
2013	181.1	188.1	188.7	189.1	189.5	190.7	189.0	190.5	189.6	192.9	189.2	188.9	188.9

Employment by Industry: Houston-Sugar Land-Baytown, TX, Selected Years, 2002–2013—*Continued*

(Numbers in thousands, not seasonally adjusted)

Industry and year	January	February	March	April	May	June	July	August	September	October	November	December	Annual average
Manufacturing													
2002	225.4	225.3	224.6	223.2	222.5	223.0	221.5	221.4	219.9	218.3	217.2	217.0	221.6
2003	214.1	213.0	212.2	211.3	210.1	211.4	209.4	208.5	208.9	207.0	207.5	207.4	210.1
2004	207.4	207.4	207.7	207.1	207.1	208.5	208.8	208.9	207.4	207.1	208.5	208.9	207.9
2005	207.6	208.1	209.0	209.8	210.7	213.3	213.7	214.0	214.2	213.7	215.3	216.4	212.2
2006	215.9	216.6	218.1	220.3	222.7	225.2	225.0	226.2	226.1	226.4	228.2	229.5	223.4
2007	228.4	228.8	230.1	230.3	232.2	234.7	235.2	235.1	235.0	235.8	237.4	238.3	233.4
2008	237.2	238.0	238.3	240.0	241.7	243.7	244.6	244.6	244.1	244.5	245.3	245.1	242.3
2009	240.1	238.2	233.7	229.2	227.0	225.4	222.7	221.2	220.1	217.5	216.6	216.8	225.7
2010	215.5	216.0	216.3	215.5	216.0	216.9	217.5	218.0	218.0	218.6	219.3	220.4	217.3
2011	220.1	221.4	222.9	224.3	225.0	227.6	229.0	229.9	231.2	232.3	233.6	236.1	227.8
2012	235.0	237.0	239.3	240.7	242.1	245.2	245.7	245.7	246.8	246.8	247.6	248.6	243.4
2013	247.0	248.9	249.5	250.0	250.5	252.8	252.5	252.8	252.9	255.0	254.3	255.6	251.8
Trade, Transportation, and Utilities													
2002	484.0	482.3	483.4	481.2	482.9	484.2	482.3	483.5	481.0	480.2	487.2	494.7	483.9
2003	473.2	468.1	468.2	467.2	466.0	468.9	468.4	470.7	469.0	469.3	476.4	484.8	470.9
2004	466.6	464.5	467.0	469.9	469.9	472.1	472.5	475.2	471.6	474.1	482.5	491.8	473.1
2005	473.6	470.7	472.5	476.6	478.8	482.0	483.9	487.4	485.8	488.0	500.0	511.2	484.2
2006	491.0	489.2	493.5	493.5	495.0	498.4	499.1	502.5	501.9	504.1	513.0	522.8	500.3
2007	506.2	504.4	509.7	510.1	513.7	519.6	520.4	523.3	522.5	525.6	535.6	544.3	519.6
2008	525.9	525.5	528.1	526.8	528.7	532.8	533.7	536.9	529.3	530.7	540.8	548.2	532.3
2009	525.7	521.3	521.0	517.6	516.9	517.4	514.7	516.2	513.7	512.7	517.9	525.7	518.4
2010	509.1	506.7	509.6	509.9	511.7	515.2	515.7	518.6	516.1	519.2	527.9	537.3	516.4
2011	520.3	517.8	522.0	525.8	526.7	530.7	531.0	535.0	532.0	534.8	545.9	556.0	531.5
2012	537.8	535.6	538.5	540.7	543.6	547.6	547.8	552.0	548.7	552.5	566.1	571.5	548.5
2013	554.6	553.4	555.4	558.7	560.7	564.3	566.4	570.8	567.0	567.7	580.9	587.2	565.6
Wholesale Trade													
2002	117.6	118.0	118.6	117.8	118.2	118.4	118.2	118.5	118.5	118.1	118.5	118.4	118.2
2003	117.1	116.9	117.1	116.4	117.0	117.7	117.8	118.0	118.5	118.1	118.3	118.9	117.7
2004	116.8	117.0	117.8	118.2	118.6	119.4	119.4	119.4	119.6	120.0	120.2	120.8	118.9
2005	119.9	120.1	120.8	121.8	122.2	123.2	123.3	123.6	124.4	124.7	124.9	126.0	122.9
2006	125.3	126.5	127.8	127.5	128.1	129.3	129.3	129.8	130.5	130.7	131.0	131.6	129.0
2007	130.0	131.3	132.3	132.5	133.3	134.8	134.9	135.6	135.7	136.2	136.4	137.1	134.2
2008	136.2	137.5	137.8	138.2	138.9	139.9	139.5	139.9	139.2	139.0	138.9	138.9	138.7
2009	135.5	135.4	134.6	132.9	132.3	132.1	131.0	130.8	130.4	130.1	130.0	130.4	132.1
2010	129.8	129.9	130.3	130.2	130.7	131.5	131.9	132.1	132.0	131.7	131.8	132.3	131.2
2011	132.2	132.9	133.7	134.8	135.5	136.6	137.3	138.0	138.6	138.8	139.6	140.8	136.6
2012	140.2	141.2	142.1	142.3	143.5	145.1	145.1	146.0	145.9	146.4	147.1	147.5	144.4
2013	146.6	147.9	148.8	148.6	149.2	150.3	151.3	152.2	152.2	152.8	154.4	153.8	150.7
Retail Trade													
2002	247.4	245.7	247.5	246.4	247.4	247.8	245.3	245.9	244.4	244.0	250.9	257.2	247.5
2003	240.0	236.9	237.5	237.3	237.4	239.1	238.0	240.0	239.1	240.1	247.0	252.4	240.4
2004	239.7	236.8	238.6	241.3	240.1	241.2	240.4	243.6	240.9	241.9	248.7	254.8	242.3
2005	240.7	237.0	238.3	240.8	241.9	244.0	245.1	247.4	245.6	246.9	257.1	263.6	245.7
2006	248.8	245.8	247.9	248.4	248.6	249.9	250.6	252.8	251.2	252.4	260.8	265.6	251.9
2007	255.4	251.6	255.2	255.4	257.6	260.7	261.2	262.6	261.4	264.0	273.5	278.1	261.4
2008	264.2	261.8	264.2	262.8	263.1	265.1	265.6	268.0	262.5	263.9	273.6	278.3	266.1
2009	264.8	261.2	261.7	260.8	261.2	262.0	261.3	263.1	261.5	261.3	266.7	271.0	263.1
2010	258.5	256.1	258.2	258.1	259.3	261.2	260.6	262.9	260.3	263.7	272.0	277.3	262.4
2011	264.7	261.6	264.4	266.7	267.0	269.5	268.2	271.2	267.3	270.5	280.0	284.7	269.7
2012	272.1	268.5	269.4	270.8	272.5	274.3	274.6	277.3	274.6	278.1	289.5	292.9	276.2
2013	278.1	276.1	276.8	280.1	281.2	283.3	284.1	286.7	283.4	283.4	293.7	298.4	283.8
Transportation and Utilities													
2002	119.0	118.6	117.3	117.0	117.3	118.0	118.8	119.1	118.1	118.1	117.8	119.1	118.2
2003	116.1	114.3	113.6	113.5	111.6	112.1	112.6	112.7	111.4	111.1	111.1	113.5	112.8
2004	110.1	110.7	110.6	110.4	111.2	111.5	112.7	112.2	111.1	112.2	113.6	116.2	111.9
2005	113.0	113.6	113.4	114.0	114.7	114.8	115.5	116.4	115.8	116.4	118.0	121.6	115.6
2006	116.9	116.9	117.8	117.6	118.3	119.2	119.2	119.9	120.2	121.0	121.2	125.6	119.5
2007	120.8	121.5	122.2	122.2	122.8	124.1	124.3	125.1	125.4	125.4	125.7	129.1	124.1
2008	125.5	126.2	126.1	125.8	126.7	127.8	128.6	129.0	127.6	127.8	128.3	131.0	127.5
2009	125.4	124.7	124.7	123.9	123.4	123.3	122.4	122.3	121.8	121.3	121.2	124.3	123.2
2010	120.8	120.7	121.1	121.6	121.7	122.5	123.2	123.6	123.8	123.8	124.1	127.7	122.9
2011	123.4	123.3	123.9	124.3	124.2	124.6	125.5	125.8	126.1	125.5	126.3	130.5	125.3
2012	125.5	125.9	127.0	127.6	127.6	128.2	128.1	128.7	128.2	128.0	129.5	131.1	128.0
2013	129.9	129.4	129.8	130.0	130.3	130.7	131.0	131.9	131.4	131.5	132.8	135.0	131.1
Information													
2002	42.6	42.2	42.0	41.1	41.1	41.3	40.8	40.5	40.1	39.9	39.6	39.5	40.9
2003	39.3	39.2	39.2	38.9	38.8	38.8	38.9	38.6	38.2	37.8	37.8	37.8	38.6
2004	37.7	37.7	37.6	37.5	37.6	38.0	37.4	37.3	36.9	36.5	36.5	36.5	37.3
2005	36.9	36.9	37.1	36.2	36.2	36.5	36.1	36.2	35.8	35.4	35.6	35.7	36.2
2006	35.4	35.5	35.5	35.9	36.2	36.5	36.5	36.5	36.2	36.3	36.5	36.6	36.1
2007	36.6	36.8	36.7	36.5	36.9	37.2	37.1	37.2	36.9	36.7	36.8	36.8	36.9
2008	36.6	36.8	36.7	36.5	36.7	36.7	36.8	36.5	35.9	35.8	35.8	35.9	36.4
2009	35.2	35.2	35.2	34.7	34.5	34.6	34.1	33.9	33.4	33.5	33.5	33.5	34.3
2010	32.7	32.4	32.2	32.1	32.0	32.5	32.0	31.9	31.5	31.6	31.8	31.9	32.1
2011	31.9	31.8	31.7	31.7	31.8	31.9	31.8	31.6	31.4	31.3	31.2	31.3	31.6
2012	31.2	31.2	31.2	31.2	31.3	31.8	32.1	32.3	32.2	31.6	31.9	32.0	31.7
2013	31.5	31.6	31.8	32.0	32.2	32.7	32.8	32.8	32.4	32.5	32.6	32.9	32.3

Employment by Industry: Houston-Sugar Land-Baytown, TX, Selected Years, 2002–2013—*Continued*

(Numbers in thousands, not seasonally adjusted)

Industry and year	January	February	March	April	May	June	July	August	September	October	November	December	Annual average
Financial Activities													
2002	132.1	132.3	132.3	132.2	132.7	133.4	133.2	133.2	132.2	132.6	132.6	132.7	132.6
2003	131.0	131.4	132.0	132.9	133.7	134.4	134.5	135.4	134.6	135.7	135.5	135.9	133.9
2004	134.8	135.2	135.5	136.2	136.5	137.3	137.9	137.9	137.4	137.7	137.0	137.9	136.8
2005	136.3	136.7	137.1	137.3	137.4	138.4	139.8	140.4	140.3	139.5	139.9	139.9	138.6
2006	138.4	138.7	139.5	139.2	139.7	140.9	141.2	141.8	141.6	141.8	141.6	142.5	140.6
2007	141.4	142.3	143.0	142.3	143.1	144.6	145.0	145.5	144.8	145.0	145.1	145.3	144.0
2008	143.3	144.5	144.2	144.0	144.6	145.2	145.1	145.3	143.8	143.0	142.9	143.0	144.1
2009	140.5	140.4	140.1	139.5	139.6	139.9	139.4	138.9	138.1	136.8	136.6	136.7	138.9
2010	135.2	135.5	135.8	135.5	135.7	136.3	136.4	136.4	135.7	136.4	136.6	137.0	136.0
2011	135.9	136.0	136.5	136.7	136.9	137.4	137.9	138.0	138.6	139.0	138.6	138.6	137.5
2012	137.5	138.0	138.5	138.9	139.8	140.7	140.9	140.9	140.4	141.4	141.5	142.0	140.0
2013	139.8	140.9	140.7	141.4	141.9	143.2	144.1	144.4	144.1	143.0	142.1	141.2	142.2
Professional and Business Services													
2002	308.5	309.5	311.7	311.9	312.9	313.9	312.2	314.7	312.2	309.6	309.4	309.1	311.3
2003	305.2	306.4	307.3	307.9	306.5	306.9	304.8	306.7	306.8	306.0	306.0	309.2	306.6
2004	303.2	306.1	307.7	311.4	312.0	315.3	317.7	319.0	319.0	321.1	322.9	324.3	315.0
2005	321.1	324.9	328.4	330.8	331.3	333.8	335.7	337.8	341.0	345.1	346.7	348.2	335.4
2006	342.3	346.8	351.7	351.2	354.4	359.5	361.2	363.4	363.9	363.9	367.8	370.1	358.0
2007	362.6	366.6	370.7	374.0	376.1	381.3	382.1	382.5	380.5	380.9	380.7	381.8	376.7
2008	374.8	379.4	381.4	382.9	383.2	387.2	386.5	388.1	381.4	387.2	384.4	381.4	383.2
2009	368.9	366.2	364.6	360.1	358.6	359.1	357.4	355.7	353.4	353.9	353.9	354.1	358.8
2010	347.3	349.7	352.8	357.7	359.0	362.9	365.1	365.8	364.7	366.1	366.7	368.5	360.5
2011	364.1	368.2	372.8	378.7	379.2	384.5	386.8	389.5	390.0	388.5	389.6	393.2	382.1
2012	391.1	395.3	401.1	404.3	406.8	413.1	414.3	418.0	417.6	416.3	418.9	420.8	409.8
2013	413.7	419.1	424.1	424.8	425.3	429.7	429.1	431.6	430.0	431.2	431.8	431.0	426.8
Education and Health Services													
2002	237.1	239.4	240.2	241.0	241.9	242.2	241.7	244.3	245.4	243.9	245.4	245.6	242.3
2003	243.7	246.5	248.1	247.8	249.2	247.8	247.4	249.7	252.0	252.1	252.2	252.7	249.1
2004	250.4	252.3	253.0	252.0	252.9	252.1	252.1	254.4	256.3	258.7	259.1	260.2	254.5
2005	256.7	258.1	259.8	260.3	261.2	260.5	260.7	263.5	265.5	265.6	267.0	267.9	262.2
2006	265.0	267.0	268.2	269.4	270.6	270.2	269.8	272.1	274.0	274.3	274.9	276.6	271.0
2007	274.7	277.1	278.5	279.6	281.0	280.6	280.0	281.9	282.9	283.9	284.5	284.9	280.8
2008	280.6	282.5	281.8	283.9	284.9	285.6	285.2	288.0	285.5	288.9	290.5	291.6	285.8
2009	288.4	291.0	292.1	293.9	295.9	296.9	297.4	299.5	300.1	302.1	302.7	303.0	296.9
2010	301.9	304.1	305.7	307.6	309.0	308.1	308.2	309.8	311.0	312.4	313.0	313.3	308.7
2011	309.2	310.4	311.7	313.5	314.4	314.1	313.8	315.7	317.6	317.8	319.9	320.8	314.9
2012	317.3	320.1	322.1	323.0	325.0	325.4	324.5	328.1	330.1	332.1	332.9	334.0	326.2
2013	329.8	333.7	334.6	334.8	336.6	335.9	331.2	335.4	336.4	338.2	338.6	340.1	335.4
Leisure and Hospitality													
2002	181.4	184.7	187.5	190.5	196.1	199.8	198.0	198.5	195.8	191.7	192.1	193.3	192.5
2003	188.6	191.9	195.6	196.3	201.6	205.5	202.5	203.2	199.1	197.0	196.6	197.1	197.9
2004	195.5	198.1	201.5	202.3	206.3	209.7	210.0	209.5	206.0	203.7	202.4	203.0	204.0
2005	198.8	199.9	204.8	208.0	212.1	215.8	213.7	214.0	211.0	208.1	207.9	208.7	208.6
2006	206.4	209.3	215.1	216.6	220.7	223.7	224.8	225.2	222.6	217.9	219.3	221.2	218.6
2007	215.5	219.0	224.9	227.0	230.9	236.6	233.8	234.9	230.6	227.0	228.4	230.5	228.3
2008	224.6	227.2	232.3	233.9	238.2	241.7	239.1	238.5	228.5	227.3	229.0	230.6	232.6
2009	226.4	229.7	235.0	235.5	240.5	243.8	240.0	239.5	234.5	229.8	230.0	230.0	234.6
2010	223.6	226.4	232.2	235.6	238.5	241.2	238.4	238.7	236.3	234.4	234.9	235.1	234.6
2011	230.1	232.3	240.1	243.5	247.3	250.2	246.2	247.7	246.2	242.4	243.7	243.6	242.8
2012	241.3	245.6	252.9	254.5	259.5	264.8	260.5	262.0	260.5	257.4	258.9	259.4	256.4
2013	255.5	261.9	267.4	269.7	274.8	277.5	277.0	276.9	273.4	272.1	273.2	277.9	271.4
Other Services													
2002	91.2	92.0	92.6	92.2	93.3	94.3	93.8	93.7	93.4	93.0	93.3	93.6	93.0
2003	95.6	95.9	97.0	95.5	96.2	97.5	96.1	96.0	95.6	93.7	93.6	94.1	95.6
2004	94.3	95.0	96.4	94.5	94.6	95.5	94.4	93.1	92.7	91.1	90.9	91.3	93.7
2005	91.7	92.0	93.1	93.3	93.5	94.9	93.1	92.2	91.6	90.4	90.5	90.5	92.2
2006	89.8	90.5	91.3	92.7	93.4	95.4	94.8	94.6	94.4	94.1	94.5	95.2	93.4
2007	91.3	92.4	93.5	92.2	92.9	94.4	92.8	92.7	92.0	91.1	91.3	91.6	92.4
2008	90.2	90.7	90.9	91.5	92.4	93.8	93.7	93.8	91.0	92.0	92.2	91.9	92.0
2009	91.5	92.0	92.2	92.3	92.7	93.6	92.8	91.6	90.6	90.5	90.7	90.5	91.8
2010	89.9	90.5	91.0	90.3	91.2	91.9	91.9	91.0	90.4	90.5	90.5	90.5	90.8
2011	89.7	90.2	91.0	91.7	92.9	94.1	93.6	93.0	92.7	92.5	92.5	92.8	92.2
2012	92.4	93.1	93.6	94.5	95.7	97.0	96.7	96.7	96.6	96.7	96.4	96.7	95.5
2013	96.4	97.3	98.1	97.9	99.0	100.3	100.3	98.9	99.0	100.3	100.0	99.5	98.9
Government													
2002	320.3	327.5	328.6	328.5	329.5	320.7	309.4	312.3	329.9	337.5	337.7	337.3	326.6
2003	331.6	338.4	338.8	338.5	338.3	330.1	314.7	318.9	333.5	338.2	339.3	338.1	333.2
2004	335.2	340.0	340.4	339.4	339.1	332.4	317.8	320.4	336.2	339.4	340.2	340.2	335.1
2005	335.3	341.3	342.6	343.2	343.1	331.8	324.4	327.4	340.9	345.8	349.0	348.1	339.4
2006	343.4	349.5	350.2	347.4	347.8	338.0	325.7	330.8	346.7	352.5	354.3	353.0	344.9
2007	346.6	353.9	355.4	356.7	356.9	346.7	333.8	335.8	352.3	360.5	364.3	364.0	352.2
2008	361.2	365.6	367.2	366.1	365.7	356.5	347.4	346.4	362.6	366.2	371.1	370.2	362.2
2009	366.3	371.9	373.5	376.4	375.2	366.8	352.4	349.0	367.9	379.9	382.0	380.8	370.2
2010	372.4	381.3	383.5	385.7	394.0	380.5	364.0	360.5	374.7	382.7	384.3	381.3	378.7
2011	377.7	381.7	382.9	382.8	379.9	370.8	356.1	349.6	364.6	370.3	370.3	368.5	371.3
2012	360.7	368.2	369.6	369.2	369.4	359.4	348.0	345.2	362.2	370.0	371.7	371.6	363.8
2013	361.4	371.4	372.7	373.2	373.4	364.5	352.6	346.0	369.2	377.9	381.0	378.4	368.5

Employment by Industry: Indianapolis-Carmel, IN, Selected Years, 2002–2013

(Numbers in thousands, not seasonally adjusted)

Industry and year	January	February	March	April	May	June	July	August	September	October	November	December	Annual average
Total Nonfarm													
2002	838.6	841.5	847.1	854.1	865.1	865.1	852.8	862.1	863.4	866.1	868.6	868.5	857.8
2003	845.4	844.3	849.6	864.3	873.8	869.9	861.1	869.8	872.1	880.4	882.0	879.6	866.0
2004	852.2	852.0	863.1	875.3	884.6	883.1	879.9	883.3	888.2	892.6	895.2	893.8	878.6
2005	863.9	869.3	876.7	887.4	897.8	894.1	888.2	892.6	900.9	898.1	902.4	898.7	889.2
2006	876.6	882.5	891.7	900.3	913.2	909.8	898.2	905.6	913.4	916.2	920.9	920.0	904.0
2007	893.4	892.1	906.9	914.4	926.9	925.9	911.7	921.4	927.2	931.3	934.7	933.0	918.2
2008	900.0	903.6	909.9	916.0	929.6	924.6	916.7	925.9	923.4	923.2	918.0	909.5	916.7
2009	876.9	874.0	874.6	875.2	881.1	875.8	865.2	873.8	875.8	876.7	880.2	877.0	875.5
2010	852.5	851.4	860.1	874.3	882.4	878.5	870.6	880.7	878.0	886.6	888.4	885.8	874.1
2011	864.4	864.8	875.4	887.6	894.5	884.9	885.0	897.4	903.3	906.8	909.6	911.8	890.5
2012	888.1	898.9	904.1	909.5	919.1	917.4	907.6	924.4	926.7	929.2	933.3	932.3	915.9
2013	904.8	912.4	919.2	928.4	936.2	935.7	928.1	944.9	947.4	949.4	952.0	948.7	933.9
Total Private													
2002	729.5	728.5	733.8	740.7	750.7	756.3	751.9	756.3	749.4	750.3	752.0	751.9	745.9
2003	731.8	728.7	733.4	748.6	757.6	759.7	756.2	760.0	756.8	764.4	766.3	763.9	752.3
2004	737.6	735.8	746.5	759.5	768.3	773.5	778.0	777.1	772.0	775.1	777.7	776.3	764.8
2005	748.2	750.6	758.6	770.8	780.9	785.7	786.1	786.5	784.3	782.0	786.0	782.5	775.2
2006	761.4	763.7	772.5	781.1	792.9	799.5	794.0	796.7	794.5	795.4	799.8	798.4	787.5
2007	775.8	771.0	784.9	793.1	804.4	810.7	804.2	806.6	804.3	807.5	810.1	808.1	798.4
2008	779.0	778.2	783.6	790.6	802.2	804.7	800.9	803.3	797.3	795.9	790.5	782.1	792.4
2009	752.4	746.8	747.1	749.5	754.6	758.8	752.6	753.6	751.4	751.2	754.8	751.4	752.0
2010	728.4	725.3	734.1	748.0	753.3	759.0	757.9	761.4	755.3	761.8	763.5	761.6	750.8
2011	741.2	740.8	751.1	763.3	769.9	770.5	775.5	779.9	781.4	784.0	786.7	788.6	769.4
2012	767.0	775.2	781.3	787.3	795.9	801.2	798.6	803.4	804.2	806.8	810.8	810.1	795.2
2013	786.2	789.9	796.4	806.1	813.4	819.1	818.5	824.7	825.1	827.1	829.6	826.0	813.5
Goods Producing													
2002	150.5	149.6	150.6	151.9	154.1	156.3	156.6	157.4	155.9	154.1	153.4	152.0	153.5
2003	148.0	146.9	147.6	150.0	152.0	153.6	153.3	153.7	152.6	153.5	153.1	151.6	151.3
2004	147.1	146.4	148.7	151.6	154.8	156.6	155.4	156.3	155.5	155.4	154.3	153.2	152.9
2005	148.1	147.7	149.4	151.9	153.1	155.3	154.4	155.7	155.0	154.4	154.5	152.8	152.7
2006	148.7	148.8	150.5	153.5	154.7	157.6	155.6	157.1	155.6	154.9	154.3	152.6	153.7
2007	147.6	144.7	148.0	150.4	152.4	154.3	153.9	154.7	153.8	152.0	151.0	149.5	151.0
2008	145.2	145.0	145.7	146.2	148.2	149.3	148.4	148.0	145.2	143.8	141.1	137.2	145.3
2009	130.4	127.6	126.5	125.9	125.5	125.9	125.6	125.9	124.6	123.5	122.7	120.7	125.4
2010	116.7	115.5	117.5	120.5	121.7	123.6	124.1	123.6	122.3	122.2	120.8	118.7	120.6
2011	114.2	113.8	116.0	118.6	120.3	123.0	123.8	124.4	124.5	124.7	123.6	122.6	120.8
2012	120.2	119.9	121.9	124.2	126.0	128.5	128.8	128.9	127.4	126.9	125.6	124.7	125.3
2013	122.2	122.3	122.7	124.6	126.4	128.6	129.0	129.0	128.6	127.4	128.0	126.5	126.3
Service-Providing													
2002	688.1	691.9	696.5	702.2	711.0	708.8	696.2	704.7	707.5	712.0	715.2	716.5	704.2
2003	697.4	697.4	702.0	714.3	721.8	716.3	707.8	716.1	719.5	726.9	728.9	728.0	714.7
2004	705.1	705.6	714.4	723.7	729.8	726.5	724.5	727.0	732.7	737.2	740.9	740.6	725.7
2005	715.8	721.6	727.3	735.5	744.7	738.8	733.8	736.9	745.9	743.7	747.9	745.9	736.5
2006	727.9	733.7	741.2	746.8	758.5	752.2	742.6	748.5	757.8	761.3	766.6	767.4	750.4
2007	745.8	747.4	758.9	764.0	774.5	771.6	757.8	766.7	773.4	779.3	783.7	783.5	767.2
2008	754.8	758.6	764.2	769.8	781.4	775.3	768.3	777.9	778.2	779.4	776.9	772.3	771.4
2009	746.5	746.4	748.1	749.3	755.6	749.9	739.6	747.9	751.2	753.2	757.5	756.3	750.1
2010	735.8	735.9	742.6	753.8	760.7	754.9	746.5	757.1	755.7	764.4	767.6	767.1	753.5
2011	750.2	751.0	759.4	769.0	774.2	761.9	761.2	773.0	778.8	782.1	786.0	789.2	769.7
2012	767.9	779.0	782.2	785.3	793.1	788.9	778.8	795.5	799.3	802.3	807.7	807.6	790.6
2013	782.6	790.1	796.5	803.8	809.8	807.1	799.1	815.9	818.8	822.0	824.0	822.2	807.7
Mining and Logging													
2005	0.8	0.8	0.8	0.8	0.8	0.8	0.8	0.8	0.8	0.8	0.8	0.8	0.8
2006	0.8	0.8	0.8	0.8	0.8	0.8	0.8	0.8	0.8	0.8	0.8	0.8	0.8
2007	0.8	0.8	0.7	0.8	0.8	0.8	0.8	0.8	0.8	0.8	0.8	0.8	0.8
2008	0.7	0.7	0.8	0.8	0.8	0.8	0.8	0.8	0.8	0.8	0.8	0.8	0.8
2009	0.7	0.7	0.7	0.7	0.7	0.7	0.7	0.7	0.7	0.7	0.7	0.7	0.7
2010	0.6	0.6	0.6	0.7	0.7	0.7	0.7	0.7	0.7	0.7	0.7	0.7	0.7
2011	0.5	0.5	0.5	0.6	0.6	0.6	0.6	0.6	0.6	0.6	0.6	0.6	0.6
2012	0.6	0.5	0.6	0.6	0.6	0.6	0.6	0.6	0.6	0.6	0.6	0.6	0.6
2013	0.6	0.6	0.6	0.6	0.6	0.6	0.6	0.6	0.6	0.6	0.6	0.6	0.6
Construction													
2005	46.3	46.1	47.7	50.1	51.0	52.5	53.2	53.3	53.1	53.2	52.9	51.4	50.9
2006	47.7	48.0	49.4	52.0	53.2	54.9	54.8	55.0	54.5	54.2	53.5	52.5	52.5
2007	48.6	46.5	49.4	51.9	53.9	55.2	55.5	55.9	55.1	54.6	53.8	51.4	52.7
2008	47.7	47.4	48.3	49.8	51.1	51.4	52.0	51.2	50.1	48.8	47.6	44.9	49.2
2009	40.2	39.4	39.8	40.5	41.0	41.5	41.9	41.6	40.9	40.3	39.6	37.5	40.4
2010	34.2	33.2	34.9	37.8	38.9	40.2	40.9	40.7	39.7	39.7	38.9	36.8	38.0
2011	33.8	33.5	35.3	37.5	39.0	41.0	41.9	42.6	42.6	42.7	42.0	40.8	39.4
2012	38.2	38.1	39.3	41.2	42.5	43.7	44.1	44.1	43.2	43.0	42.2	41.3	41.7
2013	38.3	38.3	38.7	40.5	42.2	43.7	44.4	44.4	44.4	43.1	43.7	41.9	42.0

Employment by Industry: Indianapolis-Carmel, IN, Selected Years, 2002–2013—*Continued*

(Numbers in thousands, not seasonally adjusted)

Industry and year	January	February	March	April	May	June	July	August	September	October	November	December	Annual average
Manufacturing													
2002	104.5	104.0	104.2	103.5	104.2	105.4	104.6	105.4	104.8	103.9	103.8	103.5	104.3
2003	102.5	102.4	102.2	102.0	102.4	102.8	101.7	101.8	101.0	101.5	101.4	101.1	101.9
2004	100.1	100.0	100.3	100.3	101.2	102.2	101.2	102.4	102.0	101.9	102.0	102.1	101.3
2005	101.0	100.8	100.9	101.0	101.3	102.0	100.4	101.6	101.1	100.4	100.8	100.6	101.0
2006	100.2	100.0	100.3	100.7	100.7	101.9	100.0	101.3	100.3	99.9	100.0	99.3	100.4
2007	98.2	97.5	97.8	97.7	97.7	98.3	97.6	98.0	97.9	96.6	96.4	97.3	97.6
2008	96.8	96.9	96.6	95.6	96.3	97.1	95.6	96.0	94.3	94.2	92.7	91.5	95.3
2009	89.5	87.5	86.0	84.7	83.8	83.7	83.0	83.6	83.0	82.5	82.4	82.5	84.4
2010	81.9	81.7	82.0	82.0	82.1	82.7	82.5	82.2	81.9	81.8	81.2	81.2	81.9
2011	79.9	79.8	80.2	80.5	80.7	81.4	81.3	81.2	81.3	81.4	81.0	81.2	80.8
2012	81.4	81.3	82.0	82.4	82.9	84.2	84.1	84.2	83.6	83.3	82.8	82.8	82.9
2013	83.3	83.4	83.4	83.5	83.6	84.3	84.0	84.0	83.6	83.7	83.7	84.0	83.7
Trade, Transportation, and Utilities													
2002	191.4	189.5	190.0	190.5	191.7	192.4	191.1	191.6	190.6	190.7	194.7	196.9	191.8
2003	189.6	186.6	188.1	189.2	189.3	189.5	188.6	189.1	188.4	190.1	193.9	195.4	189.8
2004	185.7	183.7	185.2	186.7	188.3	189.4	190.4	190.9	188.9	192.3	196.2	198.2	189.7
2005	189.1	189.0	190.4	192.3	193.6	193.9	194.6	195.2	194.6	196.3	199.9	201.0	194.2
2006	192.8	191.4	193.0	192.7	194.3	195.2	195.0	194.8	194.3	195.7	200.2	202.1	195.1
2007	193.5	190.9	193.9	193.8	196.3	197.8	196.8	196.1	195.7	196.3	200.9	202.6	196.2
2008	193.7	192.2	193.4	193.5	196.4	196.7	195.7	196.3	194.9	195.8	196.9	197.3	195.2
2009	187.9	185.4	185.1	184.3	186.1	186.4	185.3	185.0	183.7	185.0	187.8	188.3	185.9
2010	181.4	179.6	181.3	182.8	184.6	185.4	185.7	186.2	184.4	186.9	190.2	191.4	185.0
2011	184.6	183.7	184.5	186.6	188.4	189.0	189.5	190.0	188.8	191.0	194.5	195.6	188.9
2012	188.8	187.9	189.1	190.3	192.7	194.0	193.6	193.5	193.6	195.8	200.4	201.7	193.5
2013	193.3	193.2	194.1	196.1	198.2	199.9	198.9	199.5	199.8	202.1	205.0	205.7	198.8
Wholesale Trade													
2002	47.4	47.7	47.5	47.4	47.7	47.7	47.3	47.2	46.8	46.8	46.7	46.8	47.3
2003	46.3	46.2	46.2	45.8	45.9	46.0	45.7	45.6	45.4	45.6	45.7	45.8	45.9
2004	45.4	45.6	46.0	46.0	46.2	46.6	46.9	46.7	46.3	46.6	46.6	46.5	46.3
2005	46.2	46.4	46.6	46.8	46.8	47.0	47.2	47.2	47.0	47.1	47.1	47.3	46.9
2006	46.9	46.9	47.0	47.1	47.4	47.4	47.5	47.3	47.2	47.5	47.4	47.6	47.3
2007	47.2	47.2	47.6	47.5	47.7	48.1	48.5	48.0	47.8	47.8	48.1	48.2	47.8
2008	47.8	47.9	48.2	48.2	48.5	48.5	48.4	48.1	47.9	47.9	47.8	47.6	48.1
2009	46.4	46.0	45.7	45.2	45.1	45.0	45.1	44.6	44.1	44.3	44.2	44.2	45.0
2010	43.8	43.6	44.0	44.0	44.1	44.1	44.6	44.5	44.2	44.3	44.2	44.1	44.1
2011	44.3	44.5	44.6	45.0	45.3	45.4	45.6	45.6	45.4	45.5	45.6	45.5	45.2
2012	45.0	45.0	45.1	45.4	45.7	45.8	46.0	45.7	45.6	45.7	45.5	45.7	45.5
2013	45.0	45.3	45.6	45.9	46.1	46.4	46.7	46.4	46.2	46.5	46.8	45.8	46.1
Retail Trade													
2002	97.8	96.2	96.9	96.4	97.4	98.1	96.8	96.8	96.4	96.0	99.3	101.4	97.5
2003	96.1	94.2	95.4	95.5	96.6	97.0	95.8	96.4	95.8	96.6	100.2	101.8	96.8
2004	95.2	93.0	93.6	94.2	95.4	96.0	95.9	96.2	95.0	97.1	100.9	102.5	96.3
2005	95.2	94.5	95.4	96.4	97.6	97.4	97.5	97.4	96.8	98.1	101.0	102.4	97.5
2006	96.1	94.7	95.8	95.4	96.2	96.5	96.6	96.3	95.6	96.4	100.1	101.6	96.8
2007	95.3	93.1	94.7	94.6	96.3	97.0	96.2	95.7	95.1	95.6	98.9	100.3	96.1
2008	93.9	92.4	92.7	92.6	94.7	94.9	94.9	95.1	94.3	95.1	96.1	96.5	94.4
2009	90.4	88.7	88.9	89.2	90.7	91.2	90.3	90.1	89.1	89.9	92.5	92.9	90.3
2010	88.5	87.1	88.0	88.8	90.1	90.6	90.4	90.5	88.9	90.7	93.5	94.2	90.1
2011	89.7	88.4	89.2	90.3	91.5	91.7	91.9	92.3	91.5	93.4	96.1	96.9	91.9
2012	92.4	91.5	92.5	93.0	94.5	94.8	94.2	93.9	93.9	95.5	99.3	99.3	94.6
2013	93.7	93.0	93.1	94.4	95.7	96.6	95.8	96.2	96.3	98.1	100.7	101.8	96.3
Transportation and Utilities													
2002	46.2	45.6	45.6	46.7	46.6	46.6	47.0	47.6	47.4	47.9	48.7	48.7	47.1
2003	47.2	46.2	46.5	47.9	46.8	46.5	47.1	47.1	47.2	47.9	48.0	47.8	47.2
2004	45.1	45.1	45.6	46.5	46.7	46.8	47.6	48.0	47.6	48.6	48.7	49.2	47.1
2005	47.7	48.1	48.4	49.1	49.2	49.5	49.9	50.6	50.8	51.1	51.8	51.3	49.8
2006	49.8	49.8	50.2	50.2	50.7	51.0	50.9	51.2	51.5	51.8	52.7	52.9	51.1
2007	51.0	50.6	51.6	51.7	52.3	52.7	52.1	52.4	52.8	52.9	53.9	54.1	52.3
2008	52.0	51.9	52.5	52.7	53.2	53.3	52.4	53.1	52.7	52.8	53.0	53.2	52.7
2009	51.1	50.7	50.5	49.9	50.3	50.2	49.9	50.3	50.5	50.8	51.1	51.2	50.5
2010	49.1	48.9	49.3	50.0	50.4	50.7	50.7	51.2	51.3	51.9	52.5	53.1	50.8
2011	50.6	50.8	50.7	51.3	51.6	51.9	52.0	52.1	51.9	52.1	52.8	53.2	51.8
2012	51.4	51.4	51.5	51.9	52.5	53.4	53.4	53.9	54.1	54.6	55.6	56.7	53.4
2013	54.6	54.9	55.4	55.8	56.4	56.9	56.4	56.9	57.3	57.5	57.5	58.1	56.5
Information													
2002	16.5	16.4	16.6	16.4	16.6	16.7	16.6	16.6	16.4	16.3	16.2	16.2	16.5
2003	16.0	15.9	16.1	15.9	16.2	16.6	16.6	16.8	16.5	16.3	16.4	16.4	16.3
2004	16.3	16.3	16.3	16.2	16.5	16.8	16.8	16.8	16.4	16.6	16.5	16.6	16.5
2005	16.1	16.3	16.3	16.3	16.3	16.5	16.7	16.6	16.6	16.2	16.1	16.2	16.4
2006	15.8	16.0	16.0	16.2	16.3	16.4	16.4	16.3	16.1	16.0	16.1	16.1	16.1
2007	16.1	16.2	16.1	16.2	16.4	16.6	16.7	16.7	16.6	16.5	16.5	16.7	16.4
2008	16.7	16.7	16.7	16.7	16.9	17.0	17.0	16.9	16.6	16.4	16.3	16.3	16.7
2009	16.1	16.1	15.9	15.7	15.8	16.0	15.7	15.7	15.5	15.3	15.2	15.3	15.7
2010	15.0	14.9	14.9	14.9	15.1	15.3	15.1	15.1	14.8	14.6	14.6	14.7	14.9
2011	14.3	14.2	14.3	14.3	14.5	14.7	14.6	14.7	14.7	14.8	14.8	14.9	14.6
2012	15.3	15.4	15.5	15.4	15.5	15.8	15.7	15.7	15.6	15.9	15.9	15.8	15.6
2013	15.8	15.9	16.0	16.0	16.0	16.3	16.4	16.3	16.1	16.1	16.1	16.1	16.1

Employment by Industry: Indianapolis-Carmel, IN, Selected Years, 2002–2013—*Continued*

(Numbers in thousands, not seasonally adjusted)

Industry and year	January	February	March	April	May	June	July	August	September	October	November	December	Annual average
Financial Activities													
2002	62.0	62.0	61.8	61.9	62.2	62.8	62.5	62.6	62.2	62.6	62.8	62.9	62.4
2003	62.7	62.8	62.9	63.2	63.6	64.2	64.2	64.2	63.9	63.9	63.7	63.7	63.6
2004	62.9	63.2	63.2	63.1	63.5	63.9	63.8	63.8	63.1	63.1	63.0	63.4	63.3
2005	62.4	62.5	62.4	62.8	62.8	63.3	63.8	63.8	63.4	63.3	63.2	63.4	63.1
2006	62.5	62.6	62.6	62.7	63.1	63.5	63.4	63.5	62.9	62.7	62.5	62.7	62.9
2007	61.5	61.9	62.0	62.3	62.4	63.0	63.3	63.1	62.7	62.4	62.2	62.3	62.4
2008	60.6	60.7	60.6	60.5	60.7	61.1	61.3	60.8	60.0	59.9	59.3	59.4	60.4
2009	58.8	58.8	58.6	58.5	58.5	58.6	58.5	58.3	57.6	57.6	57.4	57.6	58.2
2010	57.5	57.3	57.4	57.5	57.7	58.2	58.7	58.6	58.1	58.5	58.5	58.6	58.1
2011	58.2	58.3	58.5	58.4	58.7	59.1	59.2	59.0	58.6	58.8	58.7	58.9	58.7
2012	58.5	58.6	58.6	58.6	58.9	59.2	59.3	59.1	58.6	58.6	58.5	58.7	58.8
2013	58.2	58.2	58.2	58.5	59.1	59.8	59.9	60.0	59.6	59.7	60.2	60.6	59.3
Professional and Business Services													
2002	104.1	104.4	105.3	107.2	108.2	108.8	108.9	109.2	108.2	109.3	108.5	107.7	107.5
2003	105.0	105.1	105.2	107.8	110.1	110.7	111.2	111.9	111.5	113.7	114.6	113.1	110.0
2004	106.9	107.3	110.4	115.2	116.4	117.5	122.3	121.5	120.5	119.8	120.5	119.3	116.5
2005	115.4	115.8	117.2	118.9	119.5	120.1	121.8	121.2	121.1	122.2	122.2	120.3	119.6
2006	116.8	117.6	119.5	122.1	124.1	125.0	124.7	127.0	126.4	126.6	127.5	126.0	123.6
2007	123.9	123.3	126.5	129.2	131.1	130.7	130.1	131.8	131.8	134.3	134.1	132.0	129.9
2008	127.2	126.3	127.3	129.5	130.4	130.6	129.9	131.9	130.7	132.2	129.6	125.9	129.3
2009	118.3	117.1	116.8	117.5	117.1	118.8	116.6	118.6	119.3	121.7	123.7	123.3	119.1
2010	115.1	114.4	116.3	121.3	121.1	122.4	123.0	124.6	122.6	126.2	126.6	127.5	121.8
2011	122.6	121.9	124.3	127.9	128.0	127.1	129.7	131.9	132.4	133.5	134.0	135.7	129.1
2012	128.3	132.0	132.2	133.7	135.0	138.0	137.4	139.9	139.7	140.6	141.7	140.7	136.6
2013	135.0	134.4	136.6	139.2	139.8	141.7	143.8	147.0	146.5	147.1	146.9	145.7	142.0
Education and Health Services													
2002	96.4	96.9	97.5	97.5	97.8	96.8	96.0	96.8	98.8	100.0	100.8	101.0	98.0
2003	99.5	100.1	100.4	105.7	104.8	101.5	101.0	100.8	105.0	107.5	107.5	107.4	103.4
2004	107.1	107.1	107.9	107.6	105.6	103.9	104.6	102.0	105.5	107.3	107.3	106.4	106.0
2005	102.8	104.1	104.9	105.8	108.7	107.2	106.8	104.3	109.1	106.5	107.0	106.2	106.1
2006	106.1	107.6	108.6	108.3	111.1	110.2	109.3	107.0	111.6	113.5	113.7	113.5	110.0
2007	112.2	113.3	114.2	115.1	115.0	115.0	113.6	112.2	116.3	118.3	118.9	119.3	115.3
2008	113.8	115.1	115.7	116.7	117.3	116.8	116.9	115.6	119.2	120.6	121.2	121.5	117.5
2009	120.7	121.5	121.4	122.9	122.9	122.9	122.5	121.6	125.2	125.4	126.2	126.0	123.3
2010	125.7	126.4	126.7	127.7	126.6	125.7	124.2	124.6	127.9	129.0	129.4	128.7	126.9
2011	128.5	129.5	130.6	131.6	130.6	127.6	128.2	128.7	133.8	133.7	134.2	134.4	131.0
2012	131.8	135.5	135.9	134.6	133.5	129.9	129.1	130.3	136.2	136.7	137.0	137.2	134.0
2013	133.8	137.5	137.8	138.2	136.3	133.4	132.2	134.1	138.3	138.7	139.6	137.5	136.5
Leisure and Hospitality													
2002	76.2	76.9	78.8	81.6	85.7	87.4	85.3	87.4	83.4	83.4	81.6	81.2	82.4
2003	77.4	77.4	79.0	82.5	86.9	88.4	86.1	88.5	84.6	85.0	82.8	82.2	83.4
2004	77.6	77.5	80.1	84.0	87.6	89.5	88.6	89.7	86.5	85.2	84.7	84.0	84.6
2005	79.3	79.9	82.2	86.8	90.3	92.5	91.2	92.7	88.7	86.9	86.8	86.2	87.0
2006	82.8	83.5	85.8	88.7	92.0	93.6	92.0	93.3	90.4	89.0	88.4	88.3	89.0
2007	84.2	83.8	86.8	88.4	92.6	94.4	91.0	93.7	89.6	89.8	88.8	88.0	89.3
2008	84.5	84.6	86.6	89.2	94.0	94.1	92.5	94.9	92.3	89.1	88.0	86.8	89.7
2009	82.9	83.2	85.4	87.3	90.9	91.9	90.4	91.0	88.7	85.8	85.0	83.5	87.2
2010	80.5	80.7	82.9	86.2	89.1	90.3	89.1	90.9	87.7	86.8	85.8	84.7	86.2
2011	81.7	82.2	85.2	88.0	91.3	91.4	91.5	92.3	90.2	89.2	88.6	88.3	88.3
2012	86.1	87.5	89.5	91.8	95.2	96.0	94.9	96.2	94.0	92.9	92.3	92.0	92.4
2013	88.7	89.0	91.2	93.7	97.5	98.2	97.5	98.4	96.4	96.1	94.0	94.1	94.6
Other Services													
2002	32.4	32.8	33.2	33.7	34.4	35.1	34.9	34.7	33.9	33.9	34.0	34.0	33.9
2003	33.6	33.9	34.1	34.3	34.7	35.2	35.2	35.0	34.3	34.4	34.3	34.1	34.4
2004	34.0	34.3	34.7	35.1	35.6	35.9	36.1	36.1	35.6	35.4	35.2	35.2	35.3
2005	35.0	35.3	35.8	36.0	36.4	36.7	36.9	37.0	36.2	36.3	36.2	36.2	36.2
2006	35.9	36.2	36.5	36.9	37.3	38.0	37.6	37.7	37.2	37.0	37.1	37.1	37.0
2007	36.8	36.9	37.4	37.7	38.2	38.9	38.8	38.3	37.8	37.9	37.7	37.7	37.8
2008	37.3	37.6	37.6	38.3	38.8	39.1	39.2	38.9	38.4	38.1	38.1	37.7	38.3
2009	37.3	37.1	37.4	37.4	37.8	38.3	38.0	37.5	36.8	36.9	36.8	36.7	37.3
2010	36.5	36.5	37.1	37.1	37.4	38.1	38.0	37.8	37.5	37.6	37.6	37.3	37.4
2011	37.1	37.2	37.7	37.9	38.1	38.6	39.0	38.9	38.4	38.3	38.3	38.2	38.1
2012	38.0	38.4	38.6	38.7	39.1	39.8	39.8	39.8	39.1	39.4	39.4	39.3	39.1
2013	39.2	39.4	39.8	39.8	40.1	41.2	40.8	40.4	39.8	39.9	39.8	39.8	40.0
Government													
2002	109.1	113.0	113.3	113.4	114.4	108.8	100.9	105.8	114.0	115.8	116.6	116.6	111.8
2003	113.6	115.6	116.2	115.7	116.2	110.2	104.9	109.8	115.3	116.0	115.7	115.7	113.7
2004	114.6	116.2	116.6	115.8	116.3	109.6	101.9	106.2	116.2	117.5	117.5	117.5	113.8
2005	115.7	118.7	118.1	116.6	116.9	108.4	102.1	106.1	116.6	116.1	116.4	116.6	114.0
2006	115.2	118.8	119.2	119.2	120.3	110.3	104.2	108.9	118.9	120.8	121.1	121.6	116.5
2007	117.6	121.1	122.0	121.3	122.5	115.2	107.5	114.8	122.9	123.8	124.6	124.9	119.9
2008	121.0	125.4	126.3	125.4	126.9	119.9	115.8	122.6	126.1	127.3	127.5	127.4	124.3
2009	124.5	127.2	127.5	125.7	126.5	117.0	112.6	120.2	124.4	125.5	125.4	125.6	123.5
2010	124.1	126.1	126.0	126.3	129.1	119.5	112.7	119.3	122.7	124.8	124.9	124.2	123.3
2011	123.2	124.0	124.3	124.3	124.6	114.4	109.5	117.5	121.9	122.8	122.9	123.2	121.1
2012	121.1	123.7	122.8	122.2	123.2	116.2	109.0	121.0	122.5	122.4	122.5	122.2	120.7
2013	118.6	122.5	122.8	122.3	122.8	116.6	109.6	120.2	122.3	122.3	122.4	122.7	120.4

Employment by Industry: Jacksonville, FL, Selected Years, 2002–2013

(Numbers in thousands, not seasonally adjusted)

Industry and year	January	February	March	April	May	June	July	August	September	October	November	December	Annual average
Total Nonfarm													
2002	553.2	555.3	560.8	560.7	562.7	557.0	549.8	558.0	555.9	557.1	560.9	563.7	557.9
2003	553.2	555.9	562.4	561.6	564.2	558.2	553.0	560.7	559.6	562.6	565.4	569.4	560.5
2004	561.6	564.5	570.3	574.5	576.3	573.7	570.7	577.4	576.6	580.5	588.3	595.1	575.8
2005	587.2	592.2	595.3	596.9	599.3	595.7	595.4	605.2	607.4	606.6	613.7	617.6	601.0
2006	609.2	614.9	620.9	618.7	622.8	618.0	615.1	623.3	624.4	626.9	634.2	636.2	622.1
2007	625.5	628.8	634.7	634.0	636.2	631.0	623.5	629.9	628.9	629.7	634.7	634.9	631.0
2008	623.6	626.7	628.0	627.3	627.8	619.1	610.9	613.4	612.7	611.4	612.8	610.2	618.7
2009	592.6	592.3	591.7	588.2	587.6	580.0	574.3	576.6	575.8	579.1	582.9	582.7	583.7
2010	571.1	573.7	577.0	579.0	583.2	576.4	575.1	578.2	580.0	585.5	589.5	590.9	580.0
2011	580.4	584.0	588.6	589.7	590.0	583.0	578.7	583.2	584.9	587.7	591.3	592.8	586.2
2012	584.4	589.0	593.4	595.8	597.9	592.9	588.3	593.6	594.1	598.4	602.7	604.3	594.6
2013	592.2	599.3	603.8	606.1	608.4	604.5	604.1	610.2	611.3	615.1	623.5	623.4	608.5
Total Private													
2002	483.0	484.4	489.9	489.2	491.0	490.5	484.8	486.6	484.7	485.4	488.6	491.0	487.4
2003	481.4	484.1	490.4	489.3	491.2	489.9	486.1	488.8	487.6	489.7	492.1	495.9	488.9
2004	489.0	491.3	496.8	500.8	502.4	504.3	502.7	504.0	502.8	505.6	512.8	518.9	502.6
2005	512.2	516.3	519.2	521.5	523.5	524.7	526.3	530.5	532.3	531.7	538.6	542.4	526.6
2006	534.8	539.7	545.6	544.3	548.6	548.2	546.8	549.7	550.1	551.5	557.8	559.7	548.1
2007	549.9	552.2	557.9	557.0	559.0	558.0	552.8	553.4	552.0	552.3	556.5	556.8	554.8
2008	546.6	548.8	550.0	549.8	550.1	546.1	539.3	537.5	535.7	534.0	534.1	532.1	542.0
2009	516.3	514.9	514.2	510.6	509.7	506.9	502.0	500.7	499.1	501.8	505.4	505.7	507.3
2010	494.1	496.2	499.5	501.1	502.7	502.2	501.5	502.2	503.1	507.8	511.3	513.0	502.9
2011	502.6	505.7	510.3	511.6	512.0	509.6	506.5	507.6	509.0	511.1	514.5	516.1	509.7
2012	509.0	512.5	516.8	520.3	522.5	521.9	517.8	519.9	519.4	522.8	527.0	528.9	519.9
2013	518.1	523.9	528.4	530.7	533.3	534.2	534.6	537.3	537.6	540.5	548.2	547.8	534.6
Goods Producing													
2002	68.8	68.8	69.4	68.7	69.5	70.0	69.4	69.6	69.4	70.1	70.8	70.9	69.6
2003	70.6	71.2	72.0	70.4	71.0	71.8	70.6	70.8	70.8	70.8	71.3	71.9	71.1
2004	71.5	72.5	73.6	74.0	74.5	75.5	76.0	76.2	76.4	76.8	77.6	78.5	75.3
2005	77.3	77.6	78.4	78.8	79.1	80.1	80.6	81.1	81.7	81.1	82.0	82.6	80.0
2006	81.8	83.0	83.9	84.2	85.0	86.0	85.2	85.6	85.4	84.5	84.5	84.3	84.5
2007	82.7	82.6	83.5	82.5	83.6	84.5	83.9	84.0	83.1	81.6	81.5	81.2	82.9
2008	78.8	79.1	78.9	77.4	77.4	77.3	75.9	75.3	75.1	73.5	72.4	71.2	76.0
2009	68.3	67.3	66.4	63.9	62.8	62.6	61.6	61.1	60.5	59.2	58.9	58.6	62.6
2010	56.3	56.1	56.6	56.7	56.7	56.8	57.1	56.7	56.9	56.7	56.5	56.1	56.6
2011	54.2	54.1	54.7	54.9	54.8	54.9	55.4	55.6	55.3	54.9	55.2	54.9	54.9
2012	54.2	54.3	54.7	55.4	55.4	56.0	55.9	56.1	56.3	56.5	56.7	56.5	55.7
2013	56.0	56.7	57.6	57.5	57.7	58.2	58.6	58.6	59.0	59.3	60.6	59.8	58.3
Service-Providing													
2002	484.4	486.5	491.4	492.0	493.2	487.0	480.4	488.4	486.5	487.0	490.1	492.8	488.3
2003	482.6	484.7	490.4	491.2	493.2	486.4	482.4	489.9	488.8	491.8	494.1	497.5	489.4
2004	490.1	492.0	496.7	500.5	501.8	498.2	494.7	501.2	500.2	503.7	510.7	516.6	500.5
2005	509.9	514.6	516.9	518.1	520.2	515.6	514.8	524.1	525.7	525.5	531.7	535.0	521.0
2006	527.4	531.9	537.0	534.5	537.8	532.0	529.9	537.7	539.0	542.4	549.7	551.9	537.6
2007	542.8	546.2	551.2	551.5	552.6	546.5	539.6	545.9	545.8	548.1	553.2	553.7	548.1
2008	544.8	547.6	549.1	549.9	550.4	541.8	535.0	538.1	537.6	537.9	540.4	539.0	542.6
2009	524.3	525.0	525.3	524.3	524.8	517.4	512.7	515.5	515.3	519.9	524.0	524.1	521.1
2010	514.8	517.6	520.4	522.3	526.5	519.6	518.0	521.5	523.1	528.8	533.0	534.8	523.4
2011	526.2	529.9	533.9	534.8	535.2	528.1	523.3	527.6	529.6	532.8	536.1	537.9	531.3
2012	530.2	534.7	538.7	540.4	542.5	536.9	532.4	537.5	537.8	541.9	546.0	547.8	538.9
2013	536.2	542.6	546.2	548.6	550.7	546.3	545.5	551.6	552.3	555.8	562.9	563.6	550.2
Mining and Logging													
2002	0.5	0.5	0.5	0.4	0.5	0.5	0.5	0.5	0.5	0.5	0.5	0.5	0.5
2003	0.5	0.5	0.5	0.5	0.5	0.5	0.5	0.5	0.5	0.5	0.5	0.5	0.5
2004	0.5	0.4	0.4	0.4	0.4	0.4	0.4	0.4	0.4	0.4	0.4	0.4	0.4
2005	0.4	0.4	0.4	0.4	0.4	0.4	0.4	0.4	0.4	0.4	0.4	0.4	0.4
2006	0.4	0.4	0.4	0.4	0.4	0.4	0.4	0.4	0.4	0.4	0.4	0.4	0.4
2007	0.4	0.4	0.4	0.4	0.4	0.4	0.4	0.4	0.4	0.4	0.4	0.4	0.4
2008	0.4	0.4	0.4	0.4	0.4	0.4	0.4	0.4	0.4	0.4	0.4	0.4	0.4
2009	0.4	0.4	0.4	0.4	0.4	0.4	0.4	0.4	0.4	0.3	0.3	0.3	0.4
2010	0.3	0.3	0.3	0.3	0.3	0.4	0.3	0.3	0.3	0.4	0.4	0.4	0.3
2011	0.3	0.3	0.3	0.3	0.3	0.3	0.3	0.3	0.3	0.3	0.3	0.3	0.3
2012	0.3	0.3	0.3	0.3	0.3	0.3	0.3	0.3	0.3	0.4	0.4	0.4	0.3
2013	0.4	0.4	0.4	0.4	0.4	0.4	0.4	0.4	0.4	0.4	0.4	0.4	0.4
Construction													
2002	32.9	32.8	33.5	33.4	34.2	34.6	34.1	34.4	34.4	35.0	35.6	35.8	34.2
2003	35.6	36.0	36.8	36.3	36.6	37.1	36.6	37.0	36.9	36.9	37.4	37.8	36.8
2004	37.9	38.8	39.7	40.0	40.3	41.0	41.6	41.9	42.2	42.5	43.2	43.9	41.1
2005	43.1	43.1	43.8	44.4	44.8	45.6	46.0	46.6	47.1	46.8	47.6	48.1	45.6
2006	47.5	48.7	49.5	50.1	50.7	51.5	50.9	51.4	51.2	50.6	50.7	50.5	50.3
2007	49.0	48.8	49.7	49.4	50.4	51.1	50.5	50.5	49.6	48.3	48.2	47.8	49.4
2008	45.5	45.8	45.7	44.3	44.3	44.3	43.0	42.6	42.4	41.2	40.2	39.1	43.2
2009	36.6	36.3	35.7	33.9	33.3	33.2	32.5	32.0	31.6	30.6	30.3	30.1	33.0
2010	28.3	28.4	29.0	29.2	29.2	29.2	29.4	29.1	29.1	28.6	28.4	27.9	28.8
2011	26.5	26.5	27.1	27.2	27.1	27.2	27.6	27.8	27.7	27.3	27.4	27.1	27.2
2012	26.2	26.3	26.7	27.2	27.1	27.6	27.6	28.0	28.1	28.2	28.4	28.4	27.5
2013	27.7	28.4	29.2	29.2	29.2	29.6	30.1	30.2	30.5	30.9	32.0	31.1	29.8

Employment by Industry: Jacksonville, FL, Selected Years, 2002–2013—*Continued*

(Numbers in thousands, not seasonally adjusted)

Industry and year	January	February	March	April	May	June	July	August	September	October	November	December	Annual average
Manufacturing													
2002	35.4	35.5	35.4	34.9	34.8	34.9	34.8	34.7	34.5	34.6	34.7	34.6	34.9
2003	34.5	34.7	34.7	33.6	33.9	34.2	33.5	33.3	33.4	33.4	33.4	33.6	33.9
2004	33.1	33.3	33.5	33.6	33.8	34.1	34.0	33.9	33.8	33.9	34.0	34.2	33.8
2005	33.8	34.1	34.2	34.0	33.9	34.1	34.2	34.1	34.2	33.9	34.0	34.1	34.1
2006	33.9	33.9	34.0	33.7	33.9	34.1	33.9	33.8	33.8	33.5	33.4	33.4	33.8
2007	33.3	33.4	33.4	32.7	32.8	33.0	33.0	33.1	33.1	32.9	32.9	33.0	33.1
2008	32.9	32.9	32.8	32.7	32.7	32.6	32.5	32.3	32.3	31.9	31.8	31.7	32.4
2009	31.3	30.6	30.3	29.6	29.1	29.0	28.8	28.7	28.5	28.3	28.3	28.2	29.2
2010	27.7	27.4	27.3	27.2	27.2	27.2	27.4	27.3	27.5	27.7	27.7	27.8	27.5
2011	27.4	27.3	27.3	27.4	27.4	27.4	27.5	27.5	27.3	27.3	27.5	27.5	27.4
2012	27.7	27.7	27.7	27.9	28.0	28.1	28.0	27.8	27.9	27.9	27.9	27.7	27.9
2013	27.9	27.9	28.0	27.9	28.1	28.2	28.1	28.0	28.1	28.0	28.2	28.3	28.1
Trade, Transportation, and Utilities													
2002	122.9	122.7	124.1	124.0	124.2	124.0	123.2	124.1	124.1	124.3	126.5	128.9	124.4
2003	124.7	123.9	124.7	124.1	124.2	123.1	123.4	124.4	124.1	125.4	127.8	129.9	125.0
2004	125.5	125.5	126.4	127.5	127.4	126.7	127.0	127.9	127.3	128.9	132.3	134.5	128.1
2005	130.0	130.6	131.5	131.8	132.3	131.8	132.0	132.8	132.9	133.0	135.9	138.0	132.7
2006	133.8	133.6	135.1	135.1	135.8	135.8	135.8	137.1	137.4	138.7	141.2	143.1	136.9
2007	138.0	137.6	139.1	138.9	139.3	138.7	137.9	138.1	138.1	139.1	142.4	143.3	139.2
2008	138.5	138.0	138.3	137.2	137.1	136.0	135.3	135.5	134.2	134.2	135.5	136.0	136.3
2009	130.3	128.9	128.3	126.8	126.8	126.2	125.3	125.0	124.9	125.2	127.1	128.2	126.9
2010	124.3	123.4	123.7	123.7	123.7	123.7	123.1	123.9	123.3	124.5	126.7	128.2	124.4
2011	123.0	123.2	123.9	124.2	123.6	123.7	123.7	123.9	123.4	123.4	125.9	126.7	124.1
2012	124.5	124.5	125.0	124.9	125.3	125.2	124.0	124.8	125.0	125.2	128.0	129.1	125.5
2013	125.4	125.4	126.1	127.2	127.6	127.6	128.2	128.9	128.8	129.4	131.1	132.5	128.2
Wholesale Trade													
2002	25.1	25.3	25.4	25.5	25.6	25.9	25.9	26.1	26.2	26.3	26.6	26.9	25.9
2003	27.1	27.1	27.1	26.8	26.7	26.7	26.7	26.7	26.6	26.6	26.7	26.8	26.8
2004	26.4	26.7	26.8	26.7	26.7	26.9	27.0	26.9	26.7	27.1	27.2	27.2	26.9
2005	27.0	27.3	27.2	27.3	27.5	27.7	27.9	28.0	28.1	28.3	28.4	28.7	27.8
2006	29.0	29.1	29.3	29.4	29.6	29.9	29.8	30.1	30.3	30.6	30.7	30.9	29.9
2007	30.2	30.4	30.6	30.4	30.3	30.4	30.3	30.2	30.0	30.1	29.8	29.7	30.2
2008	29.0	29.0	29.0	28.8	28.7	28.8	28.8	28.7	28.5	28.2	28.0	27.9	28.6
2009	27.7	27.4	27.1	27.0	26.8	26.8	26.6	26.4	26.2	26.2	26.1	26.0	26.7
2010	25.7	25.5	25.4	25.5	25.6	25.7	25.8	25.9	25.7	25.6	25.5	25.5	25.6
2011	24.8	25.0	25.1	24.9	24.9	24.8	24.8	24.8	24.6	24.6	24.6	24.5	24.8
2012	24.5	24.6	24.8	24.7	24.8	24.7	24.9	24.8	24.7	24.7	24.7	24.8	24.7
2013	24.6	24.7	24.8	25.1	25.3	25.4	25.3	25.2	25.2	25.2	25.1	25.2	25.1
Retail Trade													
2002	67.0	66.5	67.4	67.5	68.0	68.2	67.6	68.0	67.9	68.0	69.7	71.2	68.1
2003	68.6	67.9	68.2	67.8	68.2	68.3	68.2	68.4	68.3	68.9	70.8	72.2	68.8
2004	69.4	69.0	69.7	70.5	70.8	70.7	70.9	70.8	70.3	71.5	74.5	75.8	71.2
2005	72.2	72.4	73.3	73.4	73.6	73.8	73.9	73.9	73.7	73.6	75.8	77.0	73.9
2006	72.9	72.8	73.7	73.7	74.0	74.6	74.7	74.9	74.7	75.5	77.7	78.6	74.8
2007	75.5	75.0	76.2	75.7	76.2	76.0	75.7	76.0	75.7	76.2	79.2	80.2	76.5
2008	77.1	76.5	76.8	75.9	76.0	75.5	74.7	74.5	74.0	73.8	75.2	75.3	75.4
2009	70.8	70.0	70.0	69.1	69.4	69.3	68.8	68.7	68.4	68.6	70.4	71.0	69.5
2010	68.8	68.2	68.5	68.5	68.4	68.3	67.9	68.1	67.7	68.6	70.7	71.3	68.8
2011	67.9	67.8	68.3	68.4	68.5	68.8	68.7	68.9	68.7	69.0	71.3	71.8	69.0
2012	69.6	69.5	69.9	69.9	70.3	70.2	69.1	69.5	69.6	69.8	72.2	72.6	70.2
2013	70.1	69.8	70.2	70.6	71.1	71.6	72.3	72.4	72.2	72.7	74.2	75.0	71.9
Transportation and Utilities													
2002	30.8	30.9	31.3	31.0	30.6	29.9	29.7	30.0	30.0	30.0	30.2	30.8	30.4
2003	29.0	28.9	29.4	29.5	29.3	28.1	28.5	29.3	29.2	29.9	30.3	30.9	29.4
2004	29.7	29.8	29.9	30.3	29.9	29.1	29.1	30.2	30.3	30.3	30.6	31.5	30.1
2005	30.8	30.9	31.0	31.1	31.2	30.3	30.2	30.9	31.1	31.1	31.7	32.3	31.1
2006	31.9	31.7	32.1	32.0	32.2	31.3	31.3	32.1	32.4	32.6	32.8	33.6	32.2
2007	32.3	32.2	32.3	32.8	32.8	32.3	31.9	31.9	32.4	32.8	33.4	33.4	32.5
2008	32.4	32.5	32.5	32.5	32.4	31.7	31.8	32.3	31.7	32.2	32.3	32.8	32.3
2009	31.8	31.5	31.2	30.7	30.6	30.1	29.9	29.9	30.3	30.4	30.6	31.2	30.7
2010	29.8	29.7	29.8	29.7	29.7	29.7	29.4	29.9	29.9	30.3	30.5	31.4	30.0
2011	30.3	30.4	30.5	30.9	30.2	30.1	30.2	30.2	30.1	29.8	30.0	30.4	30.3
2012	30.4	30.4	30.3	30.3	30.2	30.3	30.0	30.5	30.7	30.7	31.1	31.7	30.6
2013	30.7	30.9	31.1	31.5	31.2	30.6	30.6	31.3	31.4	31.5	31.8	32.3	31.2
Information													
2002	13.8	13.6	13.7	13.6	13.4	13.2	13.2	13.0	12.9	12.9	12.8	12.8	13.2
2003	12.7	12.8	12.8	12.5	12.8	12.3	12.4	12.3	12.2	12.1	12.1	12.2	12.4
2004	12.0	11.5	11.5	11.3	11.4	11.6	11.5	11.6	11.5	11.7	11.9	12.1	11.6
2005	12.0	12.0	11.9	11.8	12.0	12.0	12.1	12.2	12.0	11.7	11.8	11.4	11.9
2006	11.5	11.5	11.5	11.4	11.3	11.4	11.4	11.1	10.6	10.5	10.4	10.5	11.1
2007	10.1	10.1	10.2	10.2	10.2	10.3	10.2	10.2	10.2	10.1	10.0	10.0	10.2
2008	9.9	9.9	10.0	10.1	10.1	10.2	10.4	10.3	10.4	10.4	10.5	10.5	10.2
2009	10.4	10.4	10.4	10.5	10.5	10.5	10.4	10.4	10.2	10.1	10.2	10.2	10.4
2010	10.2	10.2	10.4	10.4	10.3	10.2	10.2	10.2	10.1	10.0	10.0	9.9	10.2
2011	9.7	9.6	9.6	9.7	9.7	9.6	9.6	9.6	9.5	9.5	9.6	9.5	9.6
2012	9.4	9.3	9.2	9.3	9.3	9.3	9.3	9.1	9.0	9.1	9.1	9.2	9.2
2013	9.1	9.1	9.1	9.0	9.1	9.1	9.2	9.2	9.1	9.1	9.1	9.1	9.1

Employment by Industry: Jacksonville, FL, Selected Years, 2002–2013—*Continued*

(Numbers in thousands, not seasonally adjusted)

Industry and year	January	February	March	April	May	June	July	August	September	October	November	December	Annual average
Financial Activities													
2002	58.6	58.0	57.9	57.9	57.8	57.7	57.6	57.5	57.2	57.3	57.4	57.4	57.7
2003	57.1	56.7	56.9	57.1	57.4	57.6	57.9	58.2	58.2	58.0	58.0	58.4	57.6
2004	57.9	57.8	57.8	58.4	58.5	58.6	58.5	58.7	58.6	58.5	58.7	59.1	58.4
2005	58.8	58.9	59.2	59.1	59.0	59.0	58.9	59.0	58.9	59.5	60.1	60.9	59.3
2006	59.7	60.1	60.3	60.4	60.4	60.2	59.9	59.6	59.4	59.1	59.3	59.6	59.8
2007	58.9	59.1	59.4	59.5	59.8	60.1	60.5	60.8	60.7	60.7	61.1	61.1	60.1
2008	60.7	60.7	60.8	60.7	60.5	60.3	60.0	59.6	59.1	58.6	58.0	57.9	59.7
2009	56.9	56.7	56.5	55.7	55.8	55.7	55.8	55.5	55.0	55.1	55.1	55.2	55.8
2010	54.9	55.0	55.0	54.8	55.1	55.4	55.9	55.9	55.9	56.4	56.9	57.3	55.7
2011	57.0	57.3	57.8	57.8	57.7	58.0	57.9	58.0	58.5	58.4	58.3	59.0	58.0
2012	58.6	59.2	59.5	59.5	59.8	60.0	60.1	60.1	60.2	60.8	61.2	61.4	60.0
2013	60.8	61.1	61.1	61.1	61.2	61.5	61.3	61.2	61.0	60.4	60.7	60.9	61.0
Professional and Business Services													
2002	82.3	83.7	85.0	84.4	84.1	82.7	80.4	80.1	79.7	79.1	78.3	77.8	81.5
2003	77.2	79.3	81.9	82.6	81.8	80.2	78.1	78.1	77.2	77.9	77.2	76.6	79.0
2004	76.4	77.3	79.1	79.7	79.8	80.8	79.2	78.3	77.9	77.5	78.7	79.9	78.7
2005	80.1	81.8	81.3	81.9	82.2	82.9	84.3	85.8	86.7	87.4	88.7	89.3	84.4
2006	88.6	90.4	91.8	90.4	91.7	90.3	90.4	91.1	91.7	93.2	95.5	95.3	91.7
2007	93.8	94.0	94.6	94.2	92.7	91.0	88.8	87.9	87.4	88.2	87.6	86.8	90.6
2008	85.0	86.2	86.6	87.0	87.6	85.8	82.0	81.9	82.7	82.6	82.3	82.1	84.3
2009	79.4	80.1	79.7	79.6	79.5	79.0	77.2	77.3	78.1	80.4	81.4	82.0	79.5
2010	79.2	80.5	81.1	81.0	81.5	81.5	81.2	81.8	83.3	85.6	85.9	85.9	82.4
2011	85.3	87.2	88.0	88.0	88.7	87.5	84.8	85.2	87.3	88.8	89.7	90.0	87.5
2012	89.0	90.1	90.7	92.3	93.1	92.1	89.6	90.4	90.0	91.4	91.7	91.5	91.0
2013	89.0	90.6	92.0	92.6	94.1	94.4	94.1	95.1	95.6	97.4	99.5	99.3	94.5
Education and Health Services													
2002	62.6	62.9	63.3	63.3	63.6	63.7	63.2	63.6	63.7	63.9	64.1	64.3	63.5
2003	63.5	64.0	64.4	64.0	64.4	64.3	64.2	64.6	65.2	66.0	65.9	66.2	64.7
2004	65.8	66.4	66.5	67.4	67.8	67.8	67.5	68.0	68.5	69.3	69.9	70.4	67.9
2005	70.1	70.4	70.6	70.7	71.2	70.8	70.8	71.3	72.3	72.1	72.3	72.7	71.3
2006	72.9	73.5	73.9	73.8	74.0	73.6	73.6	74.5	75.1	76.0	76.4	76.4	74.5
2007	76.2	77.1	77.5	77.4	77.6	77.3	77.0	77.6	78.6	78.9	79.4	79.9	77.9
2008	80.6	81.0	80.9	81.8	81.5	80.9	80.8	80.9	81.5	82.8	83.9	83.8	81.7
2009	82.5	83.2	83.5	83.3	83.4	82.9	82.6	82.9	83.7	85.2	85.9	85.6	83.7
2010	84.5	85.0	85.2	85.4	85.5	84.9	84.6	84.8	85.5	87.5	87.9	88.0	85.7
2011	87.1	87.6	87.7	87.4	87.4	86.4	86.3	86.8	88.1	89.2	89.5	89.8	87.8
2012	87.6	88.4	88.7	88.7	89.0	88.6	88.2	88.9	90.0	90.5	90.8	91.3	89.2
2013	90.0	91.4	91.4	90.7	90.8	90.3	89.6	90.2	90.8	90.7	91.5	91.3	90.7
Leisure and Hospitality													
2002	50.4	51.0	52.3	53.3	54.2	54.7	53.1	53.7	53.1	53.2	53.9	54.1	53.1
2003	51.3	51.7	53.0	53.7	54.5	55.0	54.2	55.2	54.7	54.2	54.5	55.1	53.9
2004	54.2	54.7	56.0	56.7	57.1	57.1	57.0	57.3	57.0	57.6	58.4	61.6	56.8
2005	58.4	59.3	60.5	61.3	61.5	61.6	61.1	62.0	61.4	61.0	61.8	61.6	61.0
2006	60.6	61.3	62.5	62.5	63.6	63.8	63.3	63.6	63.3	62.3	63.1	62.9	62.7
2007	62.6	64.0	65.5	66.7	68.1	68.1	67.0	67.6	67.0	66.7	67.4	67.4	66.5
2008	66.2	66.8	67.4	68.8	69.2	69.1	69.1	68.5	67.8	67.4	67.4	67.0	67.9
2009	65.3	65.1	66.1	67.4	67.6	66.7	66.1	65.4	63.8	63.5	63.6	62.8	65.3
2010	61.8	63.0	64.4	66.0	66.8	66.5	66.4	66.0	65.4	64.2	64.5	64.9	65.0
2011	63.8	64.1	65.8	67.1	68.0	67.7	67.1	67.2	66.0	66.3	66.1	66.3	66.3
2012	65.7	66.6	68.7	69.7	70.1	70.2	70.3	70.1	68.6	69.0	69.3	69.7	69.0
2013	67.8	69.5	70.9	72.2	72.4	72.6	73.1	73.5	72.9	73.8	75.3	74.5	72.4
Other Services													
2002	23.6	23.7	24.2	24.0	24.2	24.5	24.7	25.0	24.6	24.6	24.8	24.8	24.4
2003	24.3	24.5	24.7	24.9	25.1	25.6	25.3	25.2	25.2	25.3	25.3	25.6	25.1
2004	25.7	25.6	25.9	25.8	25.9	26.2	26.0	26.0	25.6	25.3	25.5	25.5	25.7
2005	25.5	25.7	25.8	26.1	26.2	26.5	26.5	26.3	26.4	25.9	26.0	25.9	26.1
2006	25.9	26.3	26.6	26.5	26.8	27.1	27.2	27.1	27.2	27.2	27.4	27.6	26.9
2007	27.6	27.7	28.1	27.6	27.7	28.0	27.5	27.2	26.9	27.0	27.1	27.1	27.5
2008	26.9	27.1	27.1	26.8	26.7	26.5	25.8	25.5	24.9	24.5	24.1	23.6	25.8
2009	23.2	23.2	23.3	23.4	23.3	23.3	23.0	23.1	22.9	23.1	23.2	23.1	23.2
2010	22.9	23.0	23.1	23.1	23.1	23.2	23.0	22.9	22.7	22.9	22.9	22.7	23.0
2011	22.5	22.6	22.8	22.5	22.1	21.8	21.7	21.3	20.9	20.6	20.2	19.9	21.6
2012	20.0	20.1	20.3	20.5	20.5	20.5	20.4	20.4	20.3	20.3	20.2	20.2	20.3
2013	20.0	20.1	20.2	20.4	20.4	20.5	20.5	20.6	20.4	20.4	20.4	20.4	20.4
Government													
2002	70.2	70.9	70.9	71.5	71.7	66.5	65.0	71.4	71.2	71.7	72.3	72.7	70.5
2003	71.8	71.8	72.0	72.3	73.0	68.3	66.9	71.9	72.0	72.9	73.3	73.5	71.6
2004	72.6	73.2	73.5	73.7	73.9	69.4	68.0	73.4	73.8	74.9	75.5	76.2	73.2
2005	75.0	75.9	76.1	75.4	75.8	71.0	69.1	74.7	75.1	74.9	75.1	75.2	74.4
2006	74.4	75.2	75.3	74.4	74.2	69.8	68.3	73.6	74.3	75.4	76.4	76.5	74.0
2007	75.6	76.6	76.8	77.0	77.2	73.0	70.7	76.5	76.9	77.4	78.2	78.1	76.2
2008	77.0	77.9	78.0	77.5	77.7	73.0	71.6	75.9	77.0	77.4	78.7	78.1	76.7
2009	76.3	77.4	77.5	77.6	77.9	73.1	72.3	75.9	76.7	77.3	77.5	77.0	76.4
2010	77.0	77.5	77.5	77.9	80.5	74.2	73.6	76.0	76.9	77.7	78.2	77.9	77.1
2011	77.8	78.3	78.3	78.1	78.0	73.4	72.2	75.6	75.9	76.6	76.8	76.7	76.5
2012	75.4	76.5	76.6	75.5	75.4	71.0	70.5	73.7	74.7	74.7	75.7	75.4	74.7
2013	74.1	75.4	75.4	75.4	75.1	70.3	69.5	72.9	73.7	74.6	75.3	75.6	73.9

Employment by Industry: Kansas City, MO–KS, Selected Years, 2002–2013

(Numbers in thousands, not seasonally adjusted)

Industry and year	January	February	March	April	May	June	July	August	September	October	November	December	Annual average
Total Nonfarm													
2002	958.0	957.0	967.0	975.9	979.4	981.6	946.2	951.6	962.5	962.0	966.8	968.9	964.7
2003	948.2	948.3	953.7	961.6	966.1	971.8	951.2	956.0	966.1	968.7	969.7	970.8	961.0
2004	947.2	945.3	958.2	972.0	975.5	982.3	967.0	966.7	976.9	981.2	982.4	984.1	969.9
2005	957.6	963.5	975.3	985.7	988.8	993.5	975.7	976.9	987.0	989.0	993.1	995.2	981.8
2006	973.7	978.6	988.0	997.8	1,002.7	1,007.7	989.3	993.5	1,005.0	1,004.7	1,010.1	1,014.1	997.1
2007	991.4	994.7	1,010.2	1,016.1	1,022.3	1,026.8	1,017.4	1,020.9	1,023.7	1,022.0	1,027.6	1,024.4	1,016.5
2008	1,004.7	1,007.7	1,017.1	1,028.8	1,028.3	1,031.3	1,019.9	1,018.8	1,021.5	1,022.7	1,017.4	1,012.1	1,019.2
2009	985.2	983.0	985.4	991.7	992.2	993.0	978.5	977.0	978.7	978.1	977.0	974.6	982.9
2010	948.8	951.7	960.6	979.3	986.1	987.0	966.8	967.8	978.6	984.3	984.2	983.7	973.2
2011	957.2	960.1	972.9	983.5	988.6	989.1	978.7	978.2	987.8	992.4	997.1	995.8	981.8
2012	975.2	980.6	991.0	999.7	1,005.4	1,007.7	990.8	998.2	1,000.3	1,006.3	1,008.8	1,005.3	997.4
2013	984.0	987.6	994.3	1,008.4	1,015.1	1,020.0	1,002.2	1,009.1	1,016.5	1,017.2	1,017.5	1,011.2	1,006.9
Total Private													
2002	815.7	813.8	822.4	831.6	834.8	838.5	823.1	826.3	823.2	820.2	824.2	825.1	824.9
2003	805.7	803.3	807.6	814.8	819.3	826.4	819.1	825.8	823.7	824.7	825.5	826.5	818.5
2004	804.9	800.6	812.6	824.9	828.9	836.3	829.9	832.9	832.3	836.4	836.8	838.5	826.3
2005	814.4	817.4	827.6	836.7	841.5	848.1	840.5	844.4	842.6	843.7	846.7	848.8	837.7
2006	829.6	830.1	838.4	848.9	853.3	860.8	854.5	860.3	857.5	856.2	860.6	865.6	851.3
2007	844.1	843.7	857.7	862.1	869.0	874.8	872.5	876.9	873.1	870.3	874.5	873.0	866.0
2008	854.6	854.3	861.9	872.7	871.8	876.1	875.5	873.5	868.2	868.0	862.6	857.4	866.4
2009	832.5	826.2	828.4	833.1	832.9	836.4	833.5	832.6	824.4	823.1	822.1	820.2	828.8
2010	797.3	796.8	804.1	820.9	825.1	829.1	827.8	829.8	826.4	832.0	831.5	831.7	821.0
2011	807.2	807.7	817.9	827.7	833.5	836.0	838.3	839.6	838.1	842.0	846.4	845.1	831.6
2012	827.7	829.4	838.6	846.7	851.8	857.9	853.4	857.1	851.0	855.4	858.1	854.9	848.5
2013	837.3	837.4	843.3	855.2	862.4	870.3	866.2	871.9	866.5	867.2	867.2	861.2	858.8
Goods Producing													
2002	133.0	131.9	133.5	135.2	135.9	137.7	133.6	137.5	135.6	134.6	133.7	133.0	134.6
2003	130.2	130.3	132.2	132.5	134.7	135.7	131.0	136.0	135.4	135.6	134.8	132.7	133.4
2004	129.5	126.9	131.3	134.6	135.3	138.0	134.5	137.7	137.4	137.5	136.9	136.2	134.7
2005	129.3	130.5	134.2	135.9	137.4	139.1	135.4	138.7	137.8	137.7	137.7	136.7	135.9
2006	133.4	133.8	136.7	137.9	138.8	141.8	137.4	140.7	137.7	136.8	138.3	138.2	137.6
2007	133.0	130.4	135.2	135.4	136.7	138.2	136.1	138.2	137.7	134.8	135.9	133.2	135.4
2008	129.2	128.5	131.4	133.0	131.3	133.3	134.4	133.2	132.3	131.6	129.7	126.3	131.2
2009	119.6	117.0	117.9	118.4	117.3	119.0	118.9	117.6	116.0	115.7	114.0	110.9	116.9
2010	106.3	105.9	108.3	111.7	112.0	114.0	113.1	115.2	114.6	114.7	113.6	112.2	111.8
2011	105.7	105.0	108.0	110.3	111.2	112.7	112.7	110.7	112.3	112.0	112.0	111.0	110.3
2012	107.9	107.5	109.7	111.0	111.2	113.3	112.6	113.4	113.1	112.7	112.4	110.0	111.2
2013	108.7	108.3	110.3	112.3	114.5	116.7	114.1	116.3	116.5	117.0	115.7	111.8	113.5
Service-Providing													
2002	825.0	825.1	833.5	840.7	843.5	843.9	812.6	814.1	826.9	827.4	833.1	835.9	830.1
2003	818.0	818.0	821.5	829.1	831.4	836.1	820.2	820.0	830.7	833.1	834.9	838.1	827.6
2004	817.7	818.4	826.9	837.4	840.2	844.3	832.5	829.0	839.5	843.7	845.5	847.9	835.3
2005	828.3	833.0	841.1	849.8	851.4	854.4	840.3	838.2	849.2	851.3	855.4	858.5	845.9
2006	840.3	844.8	851.3	859.9	863.9	865.9	851.9	852.8	867.3	867.9	871.8	875.9	859.5
2007	858.4	864.3	875.0	880.7	885.6	888.6	881.3	882.7	886.0	887.2	891.7	891.2	881.1
2008	875.5	879.2	885.7	895.8	897.0	898.0	885.5	885.6	889.2	891.1	887.7	885.8	888.0
2009	865.6	866.0	867.5	873.3	874.9	874.0	859.6	859.4	862.7	862.4	863.0	863.7	866.0
2010	842.5	845.8	852.3	867.6	874.1	873.0	853.7	852.6	864.0	869.6	870.6	871.5	861.4
2011	851.5	855.1	864.9	873.2	877.4	876.4	866.0	867.5	875.5	880.4	885.1	884.8	871.5
2012	867.3	873.1	881.3	888.7	894.2	894.4	878.2	884.8	887.2	893.6	896.4	895.3	886.2
2013	875.3	879.3	884.0	896.1	900.6	903.3	888.1	892.8	900.0	900.2	901.8	899.4	893.4
Mining, Logging, and Construction													
2002	46.8	46.1	48.1	49.3	50.1	51.9	52.6	52.6	51.4	51.0	50.4	49.9	50.0
2003	47.6	47.5	48.8	50.9	51.6	52.6	52.9	52.9	52.3	52.5	51.5	49.3	50.9
2004	46.3	44.3	48.0	50.7	51.3	52.9	53.8	53.6	53.2	53.4	52.2	51.5	50.9
2005	46.1	47.2	50.3	52.0	53.6	55.1	55.9	55.7	55.1	54.8	54.2	53.0	52.8
2006	51.3	51.8	53.4	54.5	55.1	56.9	56.0	56.0	55.7	54.5	53.9	53.3	54.4
2007	50.3	47.8	51.9	52.6	53.9	55.0	55.6	55.1	54.9	54.1	53.6	51.2	53.0
2008	47.7	46.9	49.4	50.7	52.0	52.6	52.5	52.2	51.2	51.1	49.9	47.1	50.3
2009	42.9	42.6	43.3	43.9	45.1	45.5	45.6	44.1	42.8	42.3	41.4	38.8	43.2
2010	34.0	33.7	36.0	39.1	39.1	40.5	41.1	41.2	40.5	40.7	39.9	38.2	38.7
2011	33.3	32.7	35.5	37.7	38.4	39.3	39.8	39.6	39.3	39.1	38.9	37.9	37.6
2012	35.6	35.2	37.0	38.4	39.8	40.8	40.9	40.9	40.5	40.4	40.0	39.4	39.1
2013	37.0	37.6	38.3	40.1	42.0	43.3	44.2	43.9	43.5	44.3	42.6	39.3	41.3
Manufacturing													
2002	86.2	85.8	85.4	85.9	85.8	85.8	81.0	84.9	84.2	83.6	83.3	83.1	84.6
2003	82.6	82.8	83.4	81.6	83.1	83.1	78.1	83.1	83.1	83.1	83.3	83.4	82.6
2004	83.2	82.6	83.3	83.9	84.0	85.1	80.7	84.1	84.2	84.1	84.7	84.7	83.7
2005	83.2	83.3	83.9	83.9	83.8	84.0	79.5	83.0	82.7	82.9	83.5	83.7	83.1
2006	82.1	82.0	83.3	83.4	83.7	84.9	81.4	84.7	82.0	82.3	84.4	84.9	83.3
2007	82.7	82.6	83.3	82.8	82.8	83.2	80.5	83.1	82.8	80.7	82.3	82.0	82.4
2008	81.5	81.6	82.0	82.3	79.3	80.7	81.9	81.0	81.1	80.5	79.8	79.2	80.9
2009	76.7	74.4	74.6	74.5	72.2	73.5	73.3	73.5	73.2	73.4	72.6	72.1	73.7
2010	72.3	72.2	72.3	72.6	72.9	73.5	72.0	74.0	74.1	74.0	73.7	74.0	73.1
2011	72.4	72.3	72.5	72.6	72.8	73.4	72.9	71.1	73.0	72.9	73.1	73.1	72.7
2012	72.3	72.3	72.7	72.6	71.4	72.5	71.7	72.5	72.6	72.3	72.4	70.6	72.2
2013	71.7	70.7	72.0	72.2	72.5	73.4	69.9	72.4	73.0	72.7	73.1	72.5	72.2

Employment by Industry: Kansas City, MO–KS, Selected Years, 2002–2013—*Continued*

(Numbers in thousands, not seasonally adjusted)

Industry and year	January	February	March	April	May	June	July	August	September	October	November	December	Annual average
Trade, Transportation, and Utilities													
2002	204.4	201.7	203.5	204.2	205.0	203.6	200.4	200.3	201.2	202.6	206.5	207.7	203.4
2003	200.4	198.8	199.1	199.0	199.1	199.9	199.3	201.1	201.9	203.9	207.4	209.2	201.6
2004	200.6	198.5	199.6	201.0	202.4	202.5	200.8	200.6	201.8	204.7	208.5	211.2	202.7
2005	202.5	201.1	202.2	202.5	203.6	203.6	201.5	201.8	202.2	204.3	208.3	210.5	203.7
2006	203.5	201.9	203.1	203.6	204.6	204.6	202.8	203.9	205.1	205.7	209.4	212.2	205.0
2007	204.9	204.0	206.0	206.4	207.3	207.3	207.0	207.6	208.0	208.7	212.9	214.3	207.9
2008	206.2	204.6	204.8	205.9	206.2	205.7	205.4	204.9	204.3	206.8	208.1	208.4	205.9
2009	200.0	197.4	196.8	196.6	196.5	196.6	195.3	195.3	194.3	195.5	198.1	198.2	196.7
2010	191.3	189.7	190.6	193.0	194.5	195.2	194.7	195.2	194.5	196.9	199.9	201.0	194.7
2011	194.2	192.8	194.4	196.5	197.5	197.1	197.3	198.0	197.5	199.0	203.0	204.0	197.6
2012	198.4	196.5	197.6	198.6	200.1	200.6	199.2	199.5	199.2	200.5	204.5	204.9	200.0
2013	198.2	197.0	197.7	199.8	200.8	202.2	201.1	202.2	201.4	202.9	204.6	205.9	201.2
Wholesale Trade													
2002	48.8	48.6	48.7	48.9	48.5	48.6	47.5	47.6	47.2	47.2	47.2	47.3	48.0
2003	47.3	47.5	47.4	47.2	47.1	47.3	47.0	47.0	46.5	46.6	46.5	46.5	47.0
2004	45.4	45.5	46.0	46.3	46.5	46.8	47.1	47.0	46.8	47.5	47.6	47.9	46.7
2005	48.1	48.2	48.5	49.3	49.4	49.6	49.3	49.4	49.2	49.0	49.3	49.4	49.1
2006	48.8	48.8	49.1	48.7	49.1	49.4	49.2	49.5	49.5	49.9	50.0	50.7	49.4
2007	50.2	50.4	51.1	50.7	50.7	51.2	51.3	51.5	51.5	51.8	51.8	51.9	51.2
2008	51.5	51.5	51.3	51.7	51.6	51.6	51.9	51.8	51.4	52.5	52.2	51.9	51.7
2009	51.1	50.6	50.2	49.7	49.1	49.0	48.7	48.2	47.9	48.0	47.9	47.6	49.0
2010	47.2	47.2	47.4	48.7	48.8	49.0	48.9	48.8	48.5	48.8	48.6	48.6	48.4
2011	48.1	48.1	48.3	48.8	49.2	49.2	49.5	49.5	49.4	49.1	49.3	49.5	49.0
2012	49.5	49.5	49.7	49.9	50.1	50.5	50.4	50.4	50.2	50.1	50.2	50.3	50.1
2013	49.7	50.0	49.9	50.2	50.4	50.7	50.7	50.9	50.7	51.1	51.3	51.4	50.6
Retail Trade													
2002	109.1	107.2	108.8	108.7	109.6	110.0	109.0	109.0	109.1	109.5	113.4	115.1	109.9
2003	108.2	106.5	107.0	106.8	107.2	107.9	108.3	109.4	110.0	111.5	115.0	116.6	109.5
2004	110.7	108.4	109.0	109.1	110.0	110.4	109.7	109.2	109.9	110.9	114.6	116.9	110.7
2005	110.2	108.5	109.0	108.8	109.3	109.4	108.9	108.2	107.9	109.5	113.0	114.6	109.8
2006	108.8	107.4	108.2	108.5	109.0	109.2	108.3	108.2	108.3	108.4	111.8	113.2	109.1
2007	107.4	106.5	107.6	108.0	108.7	108.9	108.5	108.2	107.6	108.5	112.2	113.4	108.8
2008	107.5	105.4	106.1	106.4	106.9	107.2	106.9	106.4	105.4	106.4	108.0	108.6	106.8
2009	103.2	101.4	101.9	102.0	102.6	103.2	102.9	102.9	102.2	103.1	105.9	106.2	103.1
2010	100.9	99.6	100.2	101.7	102.8	103.3	103.0	103.0	102.1	103.6	106.5	107.4	102.8
2011	102.3	100.9	102.1	103.5	104.1	104.3	104.3	104.4	103.5	104.8	108.4	108.8	104.3
2012	104.0	102.4	103.3	103.8	105.0	105.0	104.8	104.3	104.1	104.9	108.6	108.9	104.9
2013	103.6	102.2	102.9	104.2	104.8	105.9	105.7	105.7	105.1	106.2	107.1	107.9	105.1
Transportation and Utilities													
2002	46.5	45.9	46.0	46.6	46.9	45.0	43.9	43.7	44.9	45.9	45.9	45.3	45.5
2003	44.9	44.8	44.7	45.0	44.8	44.7	44.0	44.7	45.4	45.8	45.9	46.1	45.1
2004	44.5	44.6	44.6	45.6	45.9	45.3	44.0	44.4	45.1	46.3	46.3	46.4	45.3
2005	44.2	44.4	44.7	44.4	44.9	44.6	43.3	44.2	45.1	45.8	46.0	46.5	44.8
2006	45.9	45.7	45.8	46.4	46.5	46.0	45.3	46.2	47.3	47.4	47.6	48.3	46.5
2007	47.3	47.1	47.3	47.7	47.9	47.2	47.2	47.9	48.9	48.4	48.9	49.0	47.9
2008	47.2	47.7	47.4	47.8	47.7	46.9	46.6	46.7	47.5	47.9	47.9	47.9	47.4
2009	45.7	45.4	44.7	44.9	44.8	44.4	43.7	44.2	44.2	44.4	44.3	44.4	44.6
2010	43.2	42.9	43.0	42.6	42.9	42.9	42.8	43.4	43.9	44.5	44.8	45.0	43.5
2011	43.8	43.8	44.0	44.2	44.2	43.6	43.5	44.1	44.6	45.1	45.3	45.7	44.3
2012	44.9	44.6	44.6	44.9	45.0	45.1	44.0	44.8	44.9	45.5	45.7	45.7	45.0
2013	44.9	44.8	44.9	45.4	45.6	45.6	44.7	45.6	45.6	45.6	46.2	46.6	45.5
Information													
2002	51.0	51.3	51.6	50.8	51.7	52.0	51.3	50.9	50.1	48.6	49.8	50.3	50.8
2003	49.1	48.5	48.3	48.5	48.2	48.5	47.7	47.6	46.9	46.8	46.6	46.7	47.8
2004	46.5	46.1	45.8	45.8	45.7	45.8	45.4	45.3	44.7	43.6	43.8	43.3	45.2
2005	43.2	43.1	43.1	43.0	42.9	43.1	42.8	42.3	42.0	41.1	40.9	40.8	42.4
2006	40.9	40.8	41.1	42.4	42.4	42.8	42.6	42.6	42.6	41.6	41.8	42.2	42.0
2007	42.2	42.1	42.0	42.0	42.3	42.4	42.8	42.6	42.4	42.8	42.9	43.0	42.5
2008	43.0	42.7	42.7	42.0	42.1	42.1	42.0	41.7	41.0	40.5	40.1	39.8	41.6
2009	39.6	39.3	39.1	39.1	38.6	38.3	38.0	37.5	36.7	34.3	33.9	33.9	37.4
2010	32.0	31.6	31.7	32.4	32.3	31.9	31.2	30.9	30.6	30.5	30.3	29.9	31.3
2011	28.8	28.8	28.7	28.9	28.9	29.0	29.0	29.0	29.1	29.0	29.2	29.4	29.0
2012	29.3	29.3	29.3	29.4	29.5	29.7	29.5	29.7	29.4	29.7	29.7	29.9	29.5
2013	29.5	29.6	29.6	29.4	29.5	29.7	30.0	30.0	29.8	30.0	30.0	30.1	29.8
Financial Activities													
2002	70.9	70.7	70.9	71.6	71.7	71.7	71.9	71.3	70.8	70.8	70.9	71.2	71.2
2003	69.8	69.8	69.7	69.9	69.8	70.0	70.0	70.2	69.4	69.1	68.8	68.9	69.6
2004	68.7	68.6	69.2	68.9	68.9	69.9	70.1	69.9	69.6	69.8	69.8	70.3	69.5
2005	70.0	70.1	70.3	70.8	71.0	71.4	71.8	71.6	71.4	71.6	71.7	72.2	71.2
2006	72.0	72.2	72.2	72.5	73.0	73.4	74.1	73.9	73.6	73.1	73.4	73.9	73.1
2007	73.5	73.8	74.5	73.7	73.8	74.4	75.1	74.9	74.3	74.0	74.0	74.2	74.2
2008	73.2	73.5	73.4	73.8	73.8	73.5	73.7	73.3	72.3	71.9	71.3	70.9	72.9
2009	70.3	70.0	70.3	71.0	71.0	71.5	72.0	72.0	70.9	71.0	71.1	70.9	71.0
2010	70.9	71.1	71.2	71.8	72.1	72.1	71.9	71.5	70.9	71.2	71.1	71.2	71.4
2011	70.5	70.7	70.7	71.1	71.7	71.8	71.7	71.7	71.3	72.9	72.9	72.8	71.7
2012	73.2	73.7	74.0	74.1	74.0	74.3	74.5	74.6	73.8	74.0	74.1	73.9	74.0
2013	74.3	74.5	74.1	74.2	74.2	74.8	74.9	74.4	73.8	74.0	74.8	74.4	74.4

Employment by Industry: Kansas City, MO–KS, Selected Years, 2002–2013—*Continued*

(Numbers in thousands, not seasonally adjusted)

Industry and year	January	February	March	April	May	June	July	August	September	October	November	December	Annual average
Professional and Business Services													
2002	125.4	126.8	128.0	128.7	128.0	127.7	123.1	122.8	122.8	122.4	122.7	123.1	125.1
2003	121.0	120.6	120.7	123.2	123.2	125.6	124.5	124.9	124.9	124.7	125.6	127.9	123.9
2004	124.1	124.7	127.6	130.1	129.7	131.5	130.8	131.5	131.9	133.0	133.3	133.7	130.2
2005	131.1	132.9	135.2	137.3	137.0	138.8	138.8	139.6	139.8	139.8	140.8	142.0	137.8
2006	135.9	137.6	139.2	141.1	140.4	141.9	141.6	142.6	143.0	144.8	145.3	146.3	141.6
2007	142.7	143.7	145.7	146.0	147.3	148.6	148.5	149.9	149.8	150.2	151.0	151.2	147.9
2008	147.3	147.9	149.4	151.8	149.4	150.6	150.5	150.2	150.3	148.4	147.8	147.2	149.2
2009	144.1	143.2	142.9	143.2	141.7	141.6	140.8	140.5	139.1	139.2	139.9	141.2	141.5
2010	138.6	138.5	140.0	146.2	145.4	145.6	146.2	145.9	145.3	147.4	147.4	148.5	144.6
2011	145.2	146.3	148.1	150.3	150.2	150.4	151.0	151.9	152.0	152.5	154.0	153.4	150.4
2012	150.3	151.4	153.5	155.9	156.0	157.5	157.3	157.5	157.8	160.6	160.2	159.6	156.5
2013	154.8	155.9	157.4	160.4	160.0	161.9	161.6	163.2	162.0	164.5	164.1	162.5	160.7
Education and Health Services													
2002	103.6	104.2	104.6	105.9	106.3	106.5	105.8	106.2	106.8	107.3	107.7	107.8	106.1
2003	106.6	106.8	106.8	108.1	108.5	107.4	107.7	107.2	108.4	108.7	108.9	108.6	107.8
2004	107.1	107.9	108.1	109.1	109.2	108.7	109.2	108.9	109.9	111.3	111.2	110.8	109.3
2005	109.7	110.5	110.5	111.6	112.0	111.7	110.9	110.9	112.0	113.1	113.3	113.4	111.6
2006	111.8	112.9	112.9	114.2	114.5	114.3	114.3	114.4	116.0	116.6	117.0	117.5	114.7
2007	115.6	116.9	117.6	118.3	118.6	118.5	118.8	119.0	119.7	120.8	121.1	121.0	118.8
2008	120.7	122.3	122.5	124.2	124.2	124.3	124.1	124.0	124.4	126.4	126.7	126.6	124.2
2009	124.6	125.4	125.7	127.0	127.1	126.9	127.9	127.6	128.5	129.9	130.4	130.5	127.6
2010	128.8	129.9	130.0	129.0	129.4	129.2	129.9	129.9	131.0	132.5	132.8	133.3	130.5
2011	131.2	132.7	133.2	132.8	133.0	131.9	132.3	133.5	134.7	136.4	137.0	137.0	133.8
2012	133.9	135.2	135.6	135.6	136.2	135.7	134.5	135.6	135.4	136.9	137.7	138.2	135.9
2013	136.1	136.8	136.2	138.1	139.0	137.8	137.5	138.3	138.2	138.9	138.9	139.3	137.9
Leisure and Hospitality													
2002	85.1	85.0	87.3	91.2	92.3	93.7	92.4	92.9	91.3	90.1	89.0	87.6	89.8
2003	85.0	85.1	87.1	90.0	91.9	94.8	94.2	94.5	93.3	92.6	90.3	89.4	90.7
2004	86.1	85.7	88.5	92.6	95.0	96.7	95.9	96.1	94.4	93.7	90.8	90.5	92.2
2005	86.4	86.7	89.3	93.3	95.4	97.7	96.3	96.6	94.8	93.9	91.9	91.1	92.8
2006	88.7	88.7	91.0	94.8	96.9	98.9	98.6	99.2	96.9	95.2	93.0	92.8	94.6
2007	89.8	90.2	93.8	96.1	98.6	100.4	98.9	99.6	96.7	94.8	92.7	92.2	95.3
2008	90.6	90.3	93.0	97.2	99.8	101.4	100.2	101.2	98.7	97.5	94.1	93.7	96.5
2009	89.8	89.4	91.4	93.2	96.1	97.6	95.9	97.7	95.0	93.3	90.7	90.8	93.4
2010	85.8	86.5	88.8	92.8	95.4	96.9	96.3	96.9	95.7	94.6	92.3	91.5	92.8
2011	87.6	87.6	90.6	93.4	96.6	98.5	99.5	100.2	96.9	95.7	93.9	93.1	94.5
2012	90.9	91.8	94.8	97.9	100.7	102.8	102.1	103.3	99.2	98.0	96.7	95.6	97.8
2013	93.4	93.0	95.7	98.5	101.7	104.2	104.0	104.4	101.9	97.0	96.3	94.4	98.7
Other Services													
2002	42.3	42.2	43.0	44.0	43.9	45.6	44.6	44.4	44.6	43.8	43.9	44.4	43.9
2003	43.6	43.4	43.7	43.6	43.9	44.5	44.7	44.3	43.5	43.3	43.1	43.1	43.7
2004	42.3	42.2	42.5	42.8	42.7	43.2	43.2	42.9	42.6	42.8	42.5	42.5	42.7
2005	42.2	42.5	42.8	42.3	42.2	42.7	43.0	42.9	42.6	42.2	42.1	42.1	42.5
2006	43.4	42.2	42.2	42.4	42.7	43.1	43.1	43.0	42.6	42.4	42.4	42.5	42.7
2007	42.4	42.6	42.9	44.2	44.4	45.0	45.3	45.1	44.5	44.2	44.0	43.9	44.0
2008	44.4	44.5	44.7	44.8	45.0	45.2	45.2	45.0	44.9	44.9	44.8	44.5	44.8
2009	44.5	44.5	44.3	44.6	44.6	44.9	44.7	44.4	43.9	44.2	44.0	43.8	44.4
2010	43.6	43.6	43.5	44.0	44.0	44.2	44.5	44.3	43.8	44.2	44.1	44.1	44.0
2011	44.0	43.8	44.2	44.4	44.4	44.6	44.8	44.6	44.3	44.5	44.4	44.4	44.4
2012	43.8	44.0	44.1	44.2	44.1	44.0	43.7	43.5	43.1	43.0	42.8	42.8	43.6
2013	42.3	42.3	42.3	42.5	42.7	43.0	43.0	43.1	42.9	42.9	42.8	42.8	42.7
Government													
2002	142.3	143.2	144.6	144.3	144.6	143.1	123.1	125.3	139.3	141.8	142.6	143.8	139.8
2003	142.5	145.0	146.1	146.8	146.8	145.4	132.1	130.2	142.4	144.0	144.2	144.3	142.5
2004	142.3	144.7	145.6	147.1	146.6	146.0	137.1	133.8	144.6	144.8	145.6	145.6	143.7
2005	143.2	146.1	147.7	149.0	147.3	145.4	135.2	132.5	144.4	145.3	146.4	146.4	144.1
2006	144.1	148.5	149.6	148.9	149.4	146.9	134.8	133.2	147.5	148.5	149.5	148.5	145.8
2007	147.3	151.0	152.5	154.0	153.3	152.0	144.9	144.0	150.6	151.7	153.1	151.4	150.5
2008	150.1	153.4	155.2	156.1	156.5	155.2	144.4	145.3	153.3	154.7	154.8	154.7	152.8
2009	152.7	156.8	157.0	158.6	159.3	156.6	145.0	144.4	154.3	155.0	154.9	154.4	154.1
2010	151.5	154.9	156.5	158.4	161.0	157.9	139.0	138.0	152.2	152.3	152.7	152.0	152.2
2011	150.0	152.4	155.0	155.8	155.1	153.1	140.4	138.6	149.7	150.4	150.7	150.7	150.2
2012	147.5	151.2	152.4	153.0	153.6	149.8	137.4	141.1	149.3	150.9	150.7	150.4	148.9
2013	146.7	150.2	151.0	153.2	152.7	149.7	136.0	137.2	150.0	150.0	150.3	150.0	148.1

Employment by Industry: Knoxville, TN, Selected Years, 2002–2013

(Numbers in thousands, not seasonally adjusted)

Industry and year	January	February	March	April	May	June	July	August	September	October	November	December	Annual average
Total Nonfarm													
2002	303.5	304.2	307.2	312.0	313.9	315.7	312.8	314.0	315.8	318.8	319.2	321.5	313.2
2003	311.2	311.4	313.7	316.8	318.2	318.9	314.0	316.1	316.8	319.0	320.3	320.8	316.4
2004	315.1	317.9	319.8	321.8	322.8	322.8	323.1	324.3	325.2	325.2	327.6	327.5	322.8
2005	321.7	321.9	324.7	325.4	326.5	327.1	325.0	326.5	329.3	328.3	329.7	330.9	326.4
2006	325.3	326.9	329.9	331.4	332.3	332.0	331.1	334.5	337.6	335.3	336.4	338.2	332.6
2007	331.6	332.5	335.4	336.2	336.7	335.4	334.1	337.6	339.1	337.9	340.0	338.7	336.3
2008	333.5	334.6	335.2	336.8	338.5	336.7	333.1	336.5	338.2	339.1	337.6	335.6	336.3
2009	324.9	323.6	321.8	321.5	321.1	318.8	316.5	317.8	320.2	322.0	324.3	321.6	321.2
2010	314.8	316.2	317.9	322.5	325.1	321.4	322.0	324.4	326.3	326.0	327.4	326.9	322.6
2011	321.1	323.9	325.9	329.1	330.0	327.5	326.9	331.3	333.0	332.5	334.3	332.7	329.0
2012	324.9	326.2	329.3	330.5	331.1	328.5	327.3	331.1	332.6	333.7	335.6	334.6	330.5
2013	326.0	328.4	330.4	331.6	332.0	328.9	328.8	332.9	335.4	335.3	338.4	336.8	332.1
Total Private													
2002	251.4	251.8	254.7	258.0	259.8	262.0	262.0	263.0	263.4	265.2	265.6	267.4	260.4
2003	259.0	258.9	260.9	263.6	265.0	266.3	263.9	265.7	266.1	265.8	267.1	268.0	264.2
2004	262.1	262.9	265.9	269.0	270.6	270.8	272.1	272.9	273.0	271.5	273.8	274.1	269.9
2005	269.3	268.9	271.9	272.6	274.2	275.6	275.0	276.4	277.3	275.4	276.7	277.6	274.2
2006	273.4	274.1	277.3	278.9	280.2	281.8	280.8	283.5	284.5	281.7	282.9	284.2	280.3
2007	279.2	279.3	282.2	283.3	284.5	285.5	284.9	287.3	286.9	285.5	287.5	287.8	284.5
2008	282.8	283.4	284.5	285.7	287.9	288.5	285.4	286.9	286.4	286.2	285.2	284.1	285.6
2009	274.2	272.2	270.6	270.2	270.2	270.2	269.0	270.0	269.9	270.1	271.5	270.4	270.7
2010	264.1	264.4	266.3	270.3	271.5	272.3	273.4	274.6	274.8	274.1	275.6	275.7	271.4
2011	270.9	273.4	275.6	278.4	279.0	279.8	280.4	282.0	282.4	281.9	283.2	282.4	279.1
2012	276.4	277.5	280.1	281.5	282.5	282.9	282.0	284.5	284.2	284.5	286.0	285.4	282.3
2013	278.4	279.8	282.0	282.4	282.9	283.1	283.1	285.8	286.1	285.5	288.0	286.9	283.7
Goods Producing													
2002	54.5	54.4	55.0	55.3	55.7	56.2	56.6	56.6	56.4	57.0	56.6	56.7	55.9
2003	55.7	55.3	55.9	56.0	56.1	55.7	55.1	55.1	55.0	55.1	55.0	54.9	55.4
2004	54.2	54.3	54.8	55.2	55.3	55.1	55.6	55.6	55.6	55.2	55.4	55.1	55.1
2005	55.2	54.7	55.1	54.9	55.0	55.2	55.5	55.7	55.7	55.4	55.3	55.5	55.3
2006	55.6	55.5	56.2	56.6	56.7	57.3	56.8	57.3	57.5	56.4	56.1	55.8	56.5
2007	55.5	55.2	55.8	55.9	56.0	56.3	56.1	56.4	56.6	56.0	55.7	55.4	55.9
2008	53.9	54.0	54.2	54.0	54.5	55.0	54.1	54.2	53.7	53.3	51.9	50.5	53.6
2009	48.6	47.8	47.3	45.9	45.7	45.6	45.3	45.2	45.4	45.7	45.5	44.8	46.1
2010	43.5	43.6	44.2	45.2	45.5	46.1	46.6	46.6	46.8	46.7	46.7	46.6	45.7
2011	45.8	46.3	46.8	46.9	47.1	47.9	48.2	48.5	48.9	49.3	49.1	48.0	47.7
2012	46.5	46.7	46.8	46.7	47.1	47.5	47.5	47.8	47.7	47.8	47.5	46.9	47.2
2013	46.1	46.6	46.7	46.4	46.5	46.6	46.7	47.0	47.0	46.3	46.6	46.4	46.6
Service-Providing													
2002	249.0	249.8	252.2	256.7	258.2	259.5	256.2	257.4	259.4	261.8	262.6	264.8	257.3
2003	255.5	256.1	257.8	260.8	262.1	263.2	258.9	261.0	261.8	263.9	265.3	265.9	261.0
2004	260.9	263.6	265.0	266.6	267.5	267.7	267.5	268.7	269.6	270.0	272.2	272.4	267.6
2005	266.5	267.2	269.6	270.5	271.5	271.9	269.5	270.8	273.6	272.9	274.4	275.4	271.2
2006	269.7	271.4	273.7	274.8	275.6	274.7	274.3	277.2	280.1	278.9	280.3	282.4	276.1
2007	276.1	277.3	279.6	280.3	280.7	279.1	278.0	281.2	282.5	281.9	284.3	283.3	280.4
2008	279.6	280.6	281.0	282.8	284.0	281.7	279.0	282.3	284.5	285.8	285.7	285.1	282.7
2009	276.3	275.8	274.5	275.6	275.4	273.2	271.2	272.6	274.8	276.3	278.8	276.8	275.1
2010	271.3	272.6	273.7	277.3	279.6	275.3	275.4	277.8	279.5	279.3	280.7	280.3	276.9
2011	275.3	277.6	279.1	282.2	282.9	279.6	278.7	282.8	284.1	283.2	285.2	284.7	281.3
2012	278.4	279.5	282.5	283.8	284.0	281.0	279.8	283.3	284.9	285.9	288.1	287.7	283.2
2013	279.9	281.8	283.7	285.2	285.5	282.3	282.1	285.9	288.4	289.0	291.8	290.4	285.5
Mining, Logging, and Construction													
2002	14.0	14.1	14.5	14.8	15.1	15.3	15.6	15.6	15.5	16.0	15.6	15.6	15.1
2003	15.1	14.7	15.4	15.7	16.0	15.9	15.6	15.7	15.8	16.1	16.0	16.2	15.7
2004	15.6	15.6	16.0	16.4	16.6	16.4	16.7	16.8	16.9	16.9	17.0	16.6	16.5
2005	16.6	16.4	16.6	16.5	16.5	16.7	16.8	17.0	17.1	16.9	16.8	16.7	16.7
2006	16.7	16.8	17.5	17.8	18.0	18.6	18.5	18.9	19.3	19.0	18.8	18.4	18.2
2007	18.0	18.0	18.6	18.8	19.0	19.2	19.1	19.4	19.5	19.3	19.1	18.8	18.9
2008	17.6	17.7	18.2	18.4	18.8	19.0	18.8	18.9	18.9	19.0	18.6	17.7	18.5
2009	16.2	16.0	16.1	15.8	16.1	16.4	16.5	16.4	16.5	16.6	16.4	15.8	16.2
2010	14.7	14.8	15.3	15.9	15.9	16.3	16.7	16.7	16.8	16.8	16.6	16.5	16.1
2011	15.2	15.5	15.9	16.0	15.9	16.4	16.7	17.0	17.6	17.8	17.3	16.2	16.5
2012	14.8	14.9	15.1	14.9	15.3	15.6	15.6	15.9	15.9	15.9	15.6	15.3	15.4
2013	14.6	15.1	15.2	15.1	15.3	15.3	15.4	15.7	15.8	15.3	15.2	14.9	15.2
Manufacturing													
2002	40.5	40.3	40.5	40.5	40.6	40.9	41.0	41.0	40.9	41.0	41.0	41.1	40.8
2003	40.6	40.6	40.5	40.3	40.1	39.8	39.5	39.4	39.2	39.0	39.0	38.7	39.7
2004	38.6	38.7	38.8	38.8	38.7	38.7	38.9	38.8	38.7	38.3	38.4	38.5	38.7
2005	38.6	38.3	38.5	38.4	38.5	38.5	38.7	38.7	38.6	38.5	38.5	38.8	38.6
2006	38.9	38.7	38.7	38.8	38.7	38.7	38.3	38.4	38.2	37.4	37.3	37.4	38.3
2007	37.5	37.2	37.2	37.1	37.0	37.1	37.0	37.0	37.1	36.7	36.6	36.6	37.0
2008	36.3	36.3	36.0	35.6	35.7	36.0	35.3	35.3	34.8	34.3	33.3	32.8	35.1
2009	32.4	31.8	31.2	30.1	29.6	29.2	28.8	28.8	28.9	29.1	29.1	29.0	29.8
2010	28.8	28.8	28.9	29.3	29.6	29.8	29.9	29.9	30.0	29.9	30.1	30.1	29.6
2011	30.6	30.8	30.9	30.9	31.2	31.5	31.5	31.5	31.3	31.5	31.8	31.8	31.3
2012	31.7	31.8	31.7	31.8	31.8	31.9	31.9	31.9	31.8	31.9	31.9	31.6	31.8
2013	31.5	31.5	31.5	31.3	31.2	31.3	31.3	31.3	31.2	31.0	31.4	31.5	31.3

Employment by Industry: Knoxville, TN, Selected Years, 2002–2013—*Continued*

(Numbers in thousands, not seasonally adjusted)

Industry and year	January	February	March	April	May	June	July	August	September	October	November	December	Annual average
Trade, Transportation, and Utilities													
2002	64.7	64.5	65.3	65.4	65.2	65.2	65.7	65.9	66.0	66.9	67.7	68.9	66.0
2003	65.4	65.1	65.2	65.4	65.8	66.4	66.0	66.6	66.6	67.1	68.3	69.2	66.4
2004	66.8	66.9	67.7	67.6	68.1	68.0	68.0	68.4	68.5	69.0	70.3	70.9	68.4
2005	69.0	68.7	69.4	68.9	69.4	69.3	69.4	69.8	69.7	69.2	70.5	71.3	69.6
2006	69.5	69.4	70.2	70.2	70.6	70.8	70.6	71.5	72.0	71.5	72.8	74.2	71.1
2007	72.0	71.5	72.3	72.6	73.0	72.8	72.5	73.1	73.1	73.2	74.9	75.2	73.0
2008	73.4	72.7	72.8	72.6	72.3	72.2	71.7	72.0	71.7	72.5	72.9	72.9	72.5
2009	69.3	68.0	67.1	66.7	66.5	66.6	66.1	66.3	66.2	66.6	67.5	68.1	67.1
2010	66.0	65.5	65.5	65.8	66.0	65.9	66.5	66.8	66.6	67.0	68.3	68.6	66.5
2011	66.3	66.2	66.5	67.0	67.2	67.3	67.5	67.5	67.4	67.7	69.2	69.9	67.5
2012	67.7	67.6	68.0	68.2	68.5	68.5	68.8	68.9	68.8	69.6	71.2	71.6	69.0
2013	69.0	68.8	69.2	69.1	69.2	69.2	69.6	69.6	69.4	69.8	71.1	71.3	69.6
Wholesale Trade													
2002	13.8	13.9	14.0	14.0	14.1	14.2	14.6	14.7	14.7	15.0	15.1	15.3	14.5
2003	14.9	14.9	14.9	14.9	14.9	15.1	15.2	15.3	15.3	15.4	15.5	15.6	15.2
2004	15.4	15.5	15.8	15.8	15.9	15.8	16.2	16.2	16.0	16.1	16.2	16.2	15.9
2005	16.0	16.0	16.0	15.8	15.7	15.8	15.8	15.8	15.7	15.5	15.4	15.4	15.7
2006	15.5	15.6	15.7	15.8	15.9	15.9	16.0	16.0	16.1	16.1	16.0	16.2	15.9
2007	16.3	16.2	16.2	16.2	16.4	16.4	16.5	16.7	16.6	16.7	16.7	16.7	16.5
2008	16.6	16.6	16.6	16.8	17.0	17.0	16.9	17.0	17.1	17.2	17.1	17.1	16.9
2009	16.8	16.6	16.3	16.2	16.1	16.0	16.0	15.9	15.9	16.1	16.0	16.0	16.2
2010	16.0	15.9	15.9	15.8	15.7	15.7	15.7	15.6	15.5	15.4	15.4	15.2	15.7
2011	15.2	15.3	15.3	15.6	15.7	15.8	15.8	15.8	15.8	15.7	15.8	15.9	15.6
2012	15.9	16.1	16.1	16.0	16.1	16.1	16.0	16.0	16.1	16.1	16.1	16.0	16.1
2013	16.0	16.0	16.1	16.0	16.0	16.0	16.0	16.0	16.0	16.1	16.2	16.2	16.1
Retail Trade													
2002	40.6	40.3	40.9	40.9	40.8	40.7	40.6	40.6	40.8	41.1	41.9	42.9	41.0
2003	40.5	40.0	40.2	40.4	40.7	41.0	40.7	41.0	41.0	41.2	42.3	43.1	41.0
2004	41.2	41.2	41.6	41.5	41.8	41.8	41.6	41.8	42.0	42.4	43.6	44.0	42.0
2005	42.6	42.3	42.8	42.8	43.2	43.1	42.9	43.1	43.0	42.9	44.2	44.8	43.1
2006	43.2	43.0	43.4	43.5	43.6	43.8	43.7	44.3	44.6	44.3	45.6	46.5	44.1
2007	44.8	44.3	44.9	45.3	45.4	45.2	45.0	45.2	45.3	45.4	47.0	47.3	45.4
2008	45.7	45.0	45.2	44.7	44.2	44.1	43.8	43.8	43.4	44.1	44.5	44.5	44.4
2009	42.1	41.2	40.7	40.7	40.5	40.7	40.3	40.3	40.2	40.4	41.4	41.7	40.9
2010	40.0	39.6	39.6	39.9	40.0	40.0	40.0	40.3	40.1	40.6	41.8	42.0	40.3
2011	40.2	39.9	40.1	40.2	40.2	40.3	40.5	40.4	40.3	40.8	42.1	42.5	40.6
2012	40.7	40.4	40.8	41.1	41.1	41.3	41.7	41.5	41.2	41.8	43.2	43.4	41.5
2013	41.2	40.9	41.1	41.2	41.2	41.2	41.6	41.4	41.1	41.4	42.5	42.6	41.5
Transportation and Utilities													
2002	10.3	10.3	10.4	10.5	10.3	10.3	10.5	10.6	10.5	10.8	10.7	10.7	10.5
2003	10.0	10.2	10.1	10.1	10.2	10.3	10.1	10.3	10.3	10.5	10.5	10.5	10.3
2004	10.2	10.2	10.3	10.3	10.4	10.4	10.2	10.4	10.5	10.5	10.5	10.7	10.4
2005	10.4	10.4	10.6	10.3	10.5	10.4	10.7	10.9	11.0	10.8	10.9	11.1	10.7
2006	10.8	10.8	11.1	10.9	11.1	11.1	10.9	11.2	11.3	11.1	11.2	11.5	11.1
2007	10.9	11.0	11.2	11.1	11.2	11.2	11.0	11.2	11.2	11.1	11.2	11.2	11.1
2008	11.1	11.1	11.0	11.1	11.1	11.1	11.0	11.2	11.2	11.2	11.3	11.3	11.1
2009	10.4	10.2	10.1	9.8	9.9	9.9	9.8	10.1	10.1	10.1	10.1	10.4	10.1
2010	10.0	10.0	10.0	10.1	10.3	10.2	10.8	10.9	11.0	11.0	11.1	11.4	10.6
2011	10.9	11.0	11.1	11.2	11.3	11.2	11.2	11.3	11.3	11.2	11.3	11.5	11.2
2012	11.1	11.1	11.1	11.1	11.3	11.1	11.1	11.4	11.5	11.7	11.9	12.2	11.4
2013	11.8	11.9	12.0	11.9	12.0	12.0	12.0	12.2	12.3	12.3	12.4	12.5	12.1
Information													
2002	5.8	5.8	5.8	5.9	5.9	5.8	5.9	5.9	5.8	6.0	6.0	6.1	5.9
2003	5.9	5.9	5.9	5.9	5.9	6.0	6.0	6.0	6.0	6.0	6.2	6.2	6.0
2004	6.2	6.1	6.2	6.2	6.2	6.1	6.2	6.0	5.9	5.9	5.9	5.8	6.1
2005	5.8	5.8	5.9	5.9	5.9	5.9	6.0	5.9	5.9	5.9	5.9	5.9	5.9
2006	6.0	6.1	6.1	6.1	6.0	6.0	6.0	5.9	5.8	5.8	5.9	5.8	6.0
2007	5.6	5.6	5.6	5.6	5.7	5.7	5.7	5.7	5.6	5.5	5.6	5.6	5.6
2008	5.6	5.6	5.6	5.6	5.7	5.7	5.6	5.5	5.5	5.6	5.6	5.6	5.6
2009	5.6	5.5	5.5	5.5	5.5	5.5	5.5	5.4	5.4	5.4	5.4	5.4	5.5
2010	5.4	5.4	5.4	5.4	5.4	5.5	5.5	5.5	5.4	5.6	5.6	5.6	5.5
2011	5.7	5.7	5.7	5.7	5.6	5.6	5.7	5.6	5.6	5.5	5.5	5.5	5.6
2012	5.5	5.5	5.4	5.5	5.5	5.5	5.6	5.6	5.4	5.6	5.6	5.5	5.5
2013	5.7	5.6	5.6	5.7	5.6	5.7	5.7	5.7	5.5	5.6	5.6	5.6	5.6
Financial Activities													
2002	14.3	14.4	14.4	14.5	14.7	14.9	14.9	14.9	15.1	15.3	15.6	15.8	14.9
2003	15.6	15.7	15.8	15.9	16.1	16.3	16.3	16.5	16.5	16.4	16.4	16.5	16.2
2004	16.4	16.4	16.5	16.6	16.7	16.7	16.8	16.8	16.8	16.8	16.9	17.0	16.7
2005	16.9	16.9	17.0	17.1	17.2	17.4	17.2	17.3	17.2	17.2	17.2	17.3	17.2
2006	17.2	17.2	17.3	17.2	17.3	17.3	17.4	17.6	17.5	17.4	17.5	17.5	17.4
2007	17.3	17.3	17.4	17.4	17.5	17.6	17.6	17.6	17.6	17.6	17.7	17.7	17.5
2008	17.4	17.5	17.6	17.6	17.7	17.9	17.9	18.0	17.9	18.0	18.0	18.0	17.8
2009	17.5	17.6	17.4	17.4	17.4	17.2	17.1	17.1	17.0	16.9	16.9	16.9	17.2
2010	16.9	16.9	16.9	17.1	17.1	17.1	17.0	16.9	16.8	16.8	16.8	16.8	16.9
2011	16.7	16.7	16.7	16.8	16.8	16.9	16.9	17.0	16.9	17.0	17.0	17.1	16.9
2012	17.0	17.1	17.2	17.2	17.3	17.3	17.2	17.2	17.1	17.1	17.1	17.1	17.2
2013	16.9	16.9	17.1	17.1	17.1	17.2	17.3	17.3	17.3	17.3	17.3	17.3	17.2

Employment by Industry: Knoxville, TN, Selected Years, 2002–2013—*Continued*

(Numbers in thousands, not seasonally adjusted)

Industry and year	January	February	March	April	May	June	July	August	September	October	November	December	Annual average
Professional and Business Services													
2002	37.4	37.2	37.9	38.2	38.3	38.5	38.5	38.8	38.8	38.6	37.9	37.8	38.2
2003	37.5	37.6	37.9	39.1	38.9	38.8	38.1	38.8	39.0	38.8	38.4	38.4	38.4
2004	37.3	37.4	38.0	39.2	39.0	39.4	39.4	39.8	39.9	39.4	39.4	39.6	39.0
2005	38.0	38.2	38.8	39.2	39.1	39.1	38.7	39.4	40.0	39.5	39.3	39.3	39.1
2006	38.5	38.8	39.3	39.8	40.0	39.8	39.6	40.3	40.8	40.5	40.5	40.6	39.9
2007	39.7	40.2	40.4	40.8	40.5	40.2	40.2	41.2	41.0	41.0	41.1	41.4	40.6
2008	41.1	41.4	41.3	42.2	42.2	42.0	42.0	42.8	43.4	43.6	43.7	44.0	42.5
2009	42.6	42.2	41.5	41.4	41.2	40.9	41.1	41.9	42.3	42.6	43.2	42.9	42.0
2010	42.3	42.4	42.6	44.3	44.4	43.9	44.8	45.9	46.0	46.4	46.7	46.9	44.7
2011	46.7	47.8	48.3	48.5	48.4	47.6	48.1	48.8	48.9	49.0	49.2	49.0	48.4
2012	47.6	47.9	48.5	48.7	48.8	48.4	47.8	49.2	49.2	48.6	48.8	48.6	48.5
2013	47.7	48.2	48.5	48.6	48.6	48.4	48.5	50.0	50.2	50.0	50.3	49.4	49.0
Education and Health Services													
2002	33.8	34.1	34.2	34.8	35.0	35.5	35.1	35.4	35.7	36.0	36.3	36.3	35.2
2003	35.5	35.6	35.8	36.0	36.2	36.5	36.5	36.6	37.2	37.4	37.6	37.7	36.6
2004	36.7	36.9	37.1	37.3	37.5	37.7	37.9	38.1	38.2	38.2	38.4	38.5	37.7
2005	38.2	38.1	38.5	38.7	39.0	39.3	39.3	39.5	39.7	40.1	40.2	40.3	39.2
2006	39.9	39.8	40.3	40.2	40.4	40.8	40.8	41.0	41.0	41.1	41.1	41.3	40.6
2007	40.9	40.9	41.1	41.3	41.4	41.7	41.9	42.2	42.4	42.6	42.7	42.8	41.8
2008	42.8	43.0	42.9	43.4	43.7	43.8	43.4	43.5	43.4	43.9	44.0	44.2	43.5
2009	43.3	43.4	43.3	44.0	44.3	44.3	44.6	44.7	44.6	44.3	44.2	44.4	44.1
2010	44.0	44.2	44.5	44.7	44.8	44.8	44.7	44.8	45.1	44.9	45.1	45.1	44.7
2011	44.7	45.1	45.3	46.1	46.1	46.2	46.2	46.4	46.6	46.0	45.8	45.7	45.9
2012	45.4	45.5	45.7	45.7	45.9	45.9	45.9	46.2	46.4	46.5	46.4	46.6	46.0
2013	45.3	45.7	45.9	46.0	46.0	45.3	45.2	45.5	45.8	46.2	46.6	46.7	45.9
Leisure and Hospitality													
2002	28.4	28.8	29.3	31.0	31.9	32.6	32.1	32.3	32.2	32.1	32.2	32.3	31.3
2003	29.8	30.0	30.7	31.6	32.2	32.5	31.8	32.2	31.9	31.2	31.4	31.2	31.4
2004	30.7	31.1	31.7	33.0	33.9	33.8	34.3	34.4	34.3	33.4	33.9	33.6	33.2
2005	32.7	33.0	33.6	34.2	34.9	35.5	35.0	35.0	35.3	34.4	34.6	34.2	34.4
2006	33.1	33.6	34.1	35.0	35.3	35.6	35.4	35.8	35.8	35.1	35.0	35.0	34.9
2007	34.1	34.4	35.3	35.6	36.1	36.6	36.4	36.7	36.2	35.2	35.4	35.3	35.6
2008	34.3	34.6	35.4	35.7	36.6	36.9	36.0	36.2	36.1	34.7	34.6	34.4	35.5
2009	32.9	33.3	33.9	34.3	35.1	35.3	34.6	34.7	34.5	33.8	33.8	33.5	34.1
2010	31.9	32.2	32.9	33.8	34.5	35.0	34.6	34.6	34.9	33.7	33.6	33.3	33.8
2011	32.5	33.1	33.7	34.7	35.0	35.2	34.8	35.1	35.3	34.6	34.4	34.2	34.4
2012	33.8	34.2	35.4	36.1	36.0	36.2	35.7	36.2	36.2	36.1	36.3	36.0	35.7
2013	34.8	35.0	35.8	36.3	36.7	37.2	36.7	37.3	37.5	37.0	37.2	36.9	36.5
Other Services													
2002	12.5	12.6	12.8	12.9	13.1	13.3	13.2	13.2	13.4	13.3	13.3	13.5	13.1
2003	13.6	13.7	13.7	13.7	13.8	14.1	14.1	13.9	13.9	13.8	13.8	13.9	13.8
2004	13.8	13.8	13.9	13.9	13.9	14.0	13.9	13.8	13.8	13.6	13.6	13.6	13.8
2005	13.5	13.5	13.6	13.7	13.7	13.7	13.9	13.8	13.8	13.7	13.7	13.8	13.7
2006	13.6	13.7	13.8	13.8	13.9	14.2	14.2	14.1	14.1	13.9	14.0	14.0	13.9
2007	14.1	14.2	14.3	14.1	14.3	14.6	14.5	14.4	14.4	14.4	14.4	14.4	14.3
2008	14.3	14.6	14.7	14.6	15.2	15.0	14.7	14.7	14.7	14.6	14.5	14.5	14.7
2009	14.4	14.4	14.6	15.0	14.5	14.8	14.7	14.7	14.5	14.8	15.0	14.4	14.7
2010	14.1	14.2	14.3	14.0	13.8	14.0	13.7	13.5	13.2	13.0	12.8	12.8	13.6
2011	12.5	12.5	12.6	12.7	12.8	13.1	13.0	13.1	12.8	12.8	13.0	13.0	12.8
2012	12.9	13.0	13.1	13.4	13.4	13.6	13.5	13.4	13.4	13.2	13.1	13.0	13.3
2013	12.9	13.0	13.2	13.2	13.2	13.5	13.4	13.4	13.4	13.3	13.3	13.3	13.3
Government													
2002	52.1	52.4	52.5	54.0	54.1	53.7	50.8	51.0	52.4	53.6	53.6	54.1	52.9
2003	52.2	52.5	52.8	53.2	53.2	52.6	50.1	50.4	50.7	53.2	53.2	52.8	52.2
2004	53.0	55.0	53.9	52.8	52.2	52.0	51.0	51.4	52.2	53.7	53.8	53.4	52.9
2005	52.4	53.0	52.8	52.8	52.3	51.5	50.0	50.1	52.0	52.9	53.0	53.3	52.2
2006	51.9	52.8	52.6	52.5	52.1	50.2	50.3	51.0	53.1	53.6	53.5	54.0	52.3
2007	52.4	53.2	53.2	52.9	52.2	49.9	49.2	50.3	52.2	52.4	52.5	50.9	51.8
2008	50.7	51.2	50.7	51.1	50.6	48.2	47.7	49.6	51.8	52.9	52.4	51.5	50.7
2009	50.7	51.4	51.2	51.3	50.9	48.6	47.5	47.8	50.3	51.9	52.8	51.2	50.5
2010	50.7	51.8	51.6	52.2	53.6	49.1	48.6	49.8	51.5	51.9	51.8	51.2	51.2
2011	50.2	50.5	50.3	50.7	51.0	47.7	46.5	49.3	50.6	50.6	51.1	50.3	49.9
2012	48.5	48.7	49.2	49.0	48.6	45.6	45.3	46.6	48.4	49.2	49.6	49.2	48.2
2013	47.6	48.6	48.4	49.2	49.1	45.8	45.7	47.1	49.3	49.8	50.4	49.9	48.4

Employment by Industry: Las Vegas-Paradise, NV, Selected Years, 2002–2013

(Numbers in thousands, not seasonally adjusted)

Industry and year	January	February	March	April	May	June	July	August	September	October	November	December	Annual average
Total Nonfarm													
2002	709.8	714.2	722.6	727.9	734.2	730.5	726.8	731.6	736.8	743.4	746.1	746.7	730.9
2003	738.2	743.4	749.5	750.0	756.4	754.2	754.0	761.8	770.3	778.8	780.9	785.0	760.2
2004	777.9	781.8	790.7	803.5	808.2	810.4	811.2	815.2	827.4	840.5	841.3	843.9	812.7
2005	832.4	840.6	850.5	867.3	869.9	872.4	870.3	873.4	887.4	892.6	899.2	903.3	871.6
2006	891.4	900.9	910.7	916.0	922.3	923.8	915.7	917.5	925.3	926.7	929.3	927.9	917.3
2007	913.2	923.9	927.9	930.4	936.7	933.3	921.2	921.1	924.6	932.2	935.3	936.3	928.0
2008	919.5	921.4	923.6	926.2	929.6	923.0	910.2	906.7	910.0	903.5	893.5	880.6	912.3
2009	855.7	850.0	842.6	836.1	832.2	824.2	811.1	807.2	815.5	815.6	815.6	816.9	826.9
2010	798.1	798.6	799.5	808.2	811.6	807.6	800.4	799.5	799.7	806.3	807.8	805.4	803.6
2011	797.2	797.3	803.4	810.1	811.2	807.2	804.6	803.5	811.4	817.3	818.3	816.3	808.2
2012	808.6	810.5	815.5	821.9	827.6	826.6	818.8	822.6	830.5	837.7	842.4	838.3	825.1
2013	830.9	832.0	839.4	845.9	850.0	848.8	844.0	850.1	855.2	859.6	866.5	864.3	848.9
Total Private													
2002	635.7	637.1	645.0	650.7	656.5	655.2	655.1	659.7	659.8	662.3	664.3	664.8	653.9
2003	659.9	662.2	667.9	668.5	674.5	675.5	678.9	687.1	689.8	695.9	697.6	701.4	679.9
2004	697.7	699.2	706.6	719.4	723.4	729.4	733.8	738.5	742.8	753.3	753.7	756.2	729.5
2005	748.4	753.5	761.9	778.5	780.8	786.9	788.5	792.6	799.9	801.3	806.9	810.7	784.2
2006	802.8	809.0	818.4	822.5	828.6	833.8	829.8	832.1	833.1	830.2	831.8	830.4	825.2
2007	819.4	826.1	829.6	830.5	836.6	837.3	829.6	831.0	827.5	831.0	833.3	833.9	830.5
2008	820.9	819.1	820.6	822.1	825.6	823.6	814.3	812.1	808.3	797.9	787.8	775.0	810.6
2009	755.1	747.5	740.2	734.3	731.4	727.7	718.0	715.5	717.3	716.5	717.1	718.8	728.3
2010	702.5	700.4	701.1	709.5	710.7	712.3	707.2	708.3	703.9	709.5	710.9	708.6	707.1
2011	702.0	700.5	706.5	713.4	714.9	717.1	715.6	714.4	718.1	722.7	723.7	720.8	714.1
2012	716.0	716.0	719.8	726.3	731.8	735.2	729.5	733.9	736.1	742.3	746.1	741.1	731.2
2013	736.5	736.6	743.2	749.4	753.6	756.3	754.7	759.3	759.7	762.9	769.6	766.8	754.1
Goods Producing													
2002	85.4	85.8	87.5	89.5	91.0	91.1	92.2	93.6	92.9	93.1	92.4	91.8	90.5
2003	90.8	91.3	93.0	94.0	95.6	97.0	98.1	100.0	100.5	102.3	101.8	102.2	97.2
2004	100.5	102.6	104.1	108.4	109.7	111.2	115.1	116.6	118.5	120.8	119.7	120.5	112.4
2005	117.7	120.5	122.3	124.6	124.6	126.0	128.4	129.9	131.9	131.6	131.8	132.9	126.9
2006	130.8	133.6	135.8	137.3	138.5	139.9	138.8	139.3	138.2	135.6	133.7	132.3	136.2
2007	128.1	129.6	131.9	131.0	132.7	132.1	131.5	132.0	129.5	127.9	126.5	125.5	129.9
2008	121.3	121.4	120.9	120.7	121.7	122.0	121.9	120.6	118.0	114.7	109.7	104.8	118.1
2009	99.3	96.8	94.0	90.8	86.5	84.8	82.9	82.2	81.2	79.8	77.2	73.7	85.8
2010	66.8	65.3	64.6	66.8	66.7	66.3	65.2	65.0	63.6	63.0	61.6	60.1	64.6
2011	57.7	57.5	57.2	57.6	57.1	57.2	57.9	58.5	58.0	58.0	57.2	57.0	57.6
2012	54.8	54.7	55.1	55.6	56.6	57.8	58.0	59.5	59.9	60.5	61.0	61.0	57.9
2013	59.3	59.8	60.4	61.2	61.1	61.9	62.2	63.6	63.6	64.1	62.7	62.2	61.8
Service-Providing													
2002	624.4	628.4	635.1	638.4	643.2	639.4	634.6	638.0	643.9	650.3	653.7	654.9	640.4
2003	647.4	652.1	656.5	656.0	660.8	657.2	655.9	661.8	669.8	676.5	679.1	682.8	663.0
2004	677.4	679.2	686.6	695.1	698.5	698.3	696.1	698.6	708.9	719.7	721.6	723.4	700.3
2005	714.7	720.1	728.2	742.7	745.3	746.4	741.9	743.5	755.5	761.0	767.4	770.4	744.8
2006	760.6	767.3	774.9	778.7	783.8	783.9	776.9	778.2	787.1	791.1	795.6	795.6	781.1
2007	785.1	794.3	796.0	799.4	804.0	801.2	789.7	789.1	795.1	804.3	808.8	810.8	798.2
2008	798.2	800.0	802.7	805.5	807.9	801.0	788.3	786.1	792.0	788.8	783.8	775.8	794.2
2009	756.4	753.2	748.6	745.3	745.7	739.4	728.2	725.0	734.3	735.8	738.4	743.2	741.1
2010	731.3	733.3	734.9	741.4	744.9	741.3	735.2	734.5	736.1	743.3	746.2	745.3	739.0
2011	739.5	739.8	746.2	752.5	754.1	750.0	746.7	745.0	753.4	759.3	761.1	759.3	750.6
2012	753.8	755.8	760.4	766.3	771.0	768.8	760.8	763.1	770.6	777.2	781.4	777.3	767.2
2013	771.6	772.2	779.0	784.7	788.9	786.9	781.8	786.5	791.6	795.5	803.8	802.1	787.1
Mining and Logging													
2002	0.4	0.3	0.4	0.3	0.3	0.3	0.3	0.3	0.3	0.3	0.3	0.3	0.3
2003	0.3	0.3	0.3	0.3	0.4	0.4	0.4	0.4	0.4	0.4	0.4	0.4	0.4
2004	0.4	0.4	0.4	0.4	0.4	0.4	0.4	0.4	0.4	0.4	0.4	0.4	0.4
2005	0.4	0.4	0.4	0.4	0.4	0.4	0.4	0.4	0.4	0.4	0.4	0.4	0.4
2006	0.4	0.4	0.4	0.4	0.4	0.5	0.5	0.5	0.5	0.5	0.5	0.5	0.5
2007	0.5	0.5	0.5	0.5	0.5	0.5	0.5	0.5	0.5	0.5	0.4	0.4	0.5
2008	0.4	0.4	0.4	0.4	0.4	0.4	0.4	0.4	0.4	0.3	0.3	0.3	0.4
2009	0.3	0.3	0.3	0.3	0.3	0.3	0.3	0.3	0.3	0.3	0.3	0.3	0.3
2010	0.3	0.3	0.2	0.3	0.3	0.3	0.3	0.3	0.3	0.3	0.3	0.2	0.3
2011	0.2	0.2	0.2	0.2	0.2	0.2	0.2	0.3	0.3	0.3	0.3	0.3	0.2
2012	0.3	0.3	0.3	0.3	0.3	0.3	0.3	0.3	0.3	0.3	0.3	0.3	0.3
2013	0.3	0.3	0.3	0.3	0.3	0.3	0.3	0.3	0.3	0.3	0.3	0.3	0.3
Construction													
2002	64.5	64.9	66.5	68.5	69.8	69.7	70.6	71.9	71.3	71.0	70.3	69.6	69.1
2003	69.1	69.6	71.3	72.2	73.6	74.8	75.7	77.4	77.9	79.4	78.7	79.1	74.9
2004	77.8	79.7	80.9	85.1	86.1	88.3	91.1	92.4	94.3	96.4	95.2	96.1	88.6
2005	93.2	96.0	97.5	99.5	99.4	100.6	102.9	104.3	105.9	105.6	105.7	106.8	101.5
2006	104.6	107.1	108.9	110.0	110.9	112.0	110.8	111.3	110.0	107.7	105.9	104.4	108.6
2007	100.9	102.4	104.5	103.6	105.2	104.4	104.0	104.6	102.3	101.1	99.8	99.0	102.7
2008	95.0	95.2	94.7	94.5	95.4	95.6	95.7	94.6	92.3	89.5	85.2	80.8	92.4
2009	76.2	74.2	71.8	69.0	65.2	63.8	62.0	61.2	60.2	59.1	56.7	53.3	64.4
2010	46.8	45.5	45.0	46.8	46.8	46.4	45.4	45.4	43.9	43.3	41.8	40.5	44.8
2011	38.1	37.9	37.5	37.8	37.4	37.3	38.0	38.2	37.7	37.6	36.9	36.6	37.6
2012	34.8	34.8	35.0	35.3	36.2	37.0	37.3	38.7	39.2	39.8	40.2	40.2	37.4
2013	38.8	39.2	39.7	40.3	40.0	40.7	41.0	42.4	42.4	42.9	41.6	40.9	40.8

Employment by Industry: Las Vegas-Paradise, NV, Selected Years, 2002–2013—*Continued*

(Numbers in thousands, not seasonally adjusted)

Industry and year	January	February	March	April	May	June	July	August	September	October	November	December	Annual average
Manufacturing													
2002	20.5	20.6	20.6	20.7	20.9	21.1	21.3	21.4	21.3	21.8	21.8	21.9	21.2
2003	21.4	21.4	21.4	21.5	21.6	21.8	22.0	22.2	22.2	22.5	22.7	22.7	22.0
2004	22.3	22.5	22.8	22.9	23.2	23.4	23.6	23.8	23.8	24.0	24.1	24.0	23.4
2005	24.1	24.1	24.4	24.7	24.8	25.0	25.1	25.2	25.6	25.6	25.7	25.7	25.0
2006	25.8	26.1	26.5	26.9	27.2	27.4	27.5	27.5	27.7	27.4	27.3	27.4	27.1
2007	26.7	26.7	26.9	26.9	27.0	27.2	27.0	26.9	26.7	26.3	26.3	26.1	26.7
2008	25.9	25.8	25.8	25.8	25.9	26.0	25.8	25.6	25.3	24.9	24.2	23.7	25.4
2009	22.8	22.3	21.9	21.5	21.0	20.7	20.6	20.7	20.7	20.4	20.2	20.1	21.1
2010	19.7	19.5	19.4	19.7	19.6	19.6	19.5	19.3	19.4	19.4	19.5	19.4	19.5
2011	19.4	19.4	19.5	19.6	19.5	19.7	19.7	20.0	20.0	20.1	20.0	20.1	19.8
2012	19.7	19.6	19.8	20.0	20.1	20.5	20.4	20.5	20.4	20.4	20.5	20.5	20.2
2013	20.2	20.3	20.4	20.6	20.8	20.9	20.9	20.9	20.9	20.9	20.8	21.0	20.7
Trade, Transportation, and Utilities													
2002	126.3	125.2	125.9	128.0	128.2	128.5	128.5	128.6	129.3	131.4	133.2	135.3	129.0
2003	129.3	129.1	130.3	129.4	130.0	130.6	130.9	132.7	134.0	136.9	139.8	142.2	132.9
2004	135.2	135.0	136.4	137.1	137.9	139.6	139.8	140.5	141.1	143.7	146.8	149.0	140.2
2005	143.7	143.2	144.0	145.6	146.2	147.3	148.2	149.0	150.6	151.8	155.2	157.2	148.5
2006	152.6	152.1	153.7	153.8	154.8	155.3	155.3	155.9	156.8	158.0	161.4	163.3	156.1
2007	158.4	157.7	158.4	158.8	160.0	160.7	160.0	161.0	161.0	162.1	166.6	168.9	161.1
2008	163.2	161.2	161.6	161.0	160.9	160.9	161.1	161.1	160.3	159.5	160.4	160.0	160.9
2009	152.8	150.0	149.0	147.5	147.4	147.4	146.6	146.5	147.1	147.9	151.1	152.2	148.8
2010	146.5	144.7	144.8	145.1	145.8	146.5	146.7	147.3	146.9	148.4	151.8	152.9	147.3
2011	147.0	145.7	146.0	147.4	147.8	148.3	149.1	149.5	149.8	151.9	156.2	156.6	149.6
2012	152.2	150.3	151.2	151.9	152.8	153.3	153.2	153.4	153.9	154.5	160.1	159.8	153.9
2013	154.5	152.4	151.7	152.2	154.5	155.3	156.0	156.6	157.1	160.0	166.7	166.7	157.0
Wholesale Trade													
2002	19.5	19.7	19.9	20.0	20.0	20.1	19.9	20.0	20.0	20.1	20.1	20.2	20.0
2003	19.7	19.8	19.8	19.7	19.7	19.8	19.9	19.8	19.8	20.0	20.1	20.2	19.9
2004	19.9	20.0	20.1	20.2	20.2	20.4	20.7	20.7	20.8	21.1	21.1	21.2	20.5
2005	21.2	21.4	21.6	21.9	22.0	22.2	22.4	22.5	22.7	22.6	22.7	22.9	22.2
2006	22.8	23.0	23.2	23.4	23.6	23.6	23.7	23.8	24.0	23.9	23.9	24.1	23.6
2007	23.8	23.9	24.0	24.0	24.2	24.3	24.2	24.3	24.3	24.2	24.2	24.2	24.1
2008	24.0	24.0	24.1	23.9	24.0	24.0	24.1	24.1	24.0	23.7	23.4	23.1	23.9
2009	22.5	22.2	21.9	21.6	21.3	21.2	21.1	21.0	20.9	20.9	20.8	20.8	21.4
2010	20.4	20.3	20.4	20.4	20.5	20.5	20.4	20.5	20.4	20.6	20.5	20.5	20.5
2011	20.1	20.1	20.1	20.2	20.2	20.2	20.3	20.2	20.1	20.1	20.1	20.1	20.2
2012	19.9	19.9	20.0	20.0	20.1	20.1	20.2	20.2	20.2	20.2	20.2	20.3	20.1
2013	20.0	20.0	20.1	20.1	20.2	20.3	20.5	20.6	20.6	20.6	20.6	20.7	20.4
Retail Trade													
2002	79.0	77.9	78.3	79.4	79.8	80.2	80.0	79.9	80.4	82.1	85.0	87.3	80.8
2003	81.9	81.3	82.3	81.6	82.3	82.7	83.0	84.6	85.5	87.8	90.4	92.4	84.7
2004	85.9	85.4	86.3	87.2	87.9	89.1	88.7	89.3	89.7	91.3	94.5	96.7	89.3
2005	91.6	90.7	91.1	91.7	91.9	92.6	93.5	93.9	94.9	96.1	99.0	100.5	94.0
2006	96.1	95.4	96.3	96.1	96.6	97.0	96.7	97.1	97.4	98.7	101.6	103.1	97.7
2007	98.7	97.8	98.1	98.5	99.2	99.5	99.4	99.9	99.6	100.2	104.1	106.2	100.1
2008	101.6	99.9	100.0	99.6	99.2	99.4	99.4	99.3	98.8	98.5	99.8	100.0	99.6
2009	94.5	92.2	91.6	90.6	90.8	90.9	90.6	90.7	91.6	92.5	95.5	96.7	92.4
2010	91.6	90.1	90.2	90.6	91.1	91.6	92.0	92.5	92.2	93.5	96.8	97.6	92.5
2011	92.7	91.3	91.5	92.2	92.7	93.0	93.4	94.0	94.2	95.9	100.1	100.5	94.3
2012	96.5	94.8	95.5	96.0	96.4	96.8	96.5	96.7	97.2	98.1	103.6	103.0	97.6
2013	98.0	96.3	96.4	96.7	97.9	98.4	98.9	99.5	99.7	102.3	108.7	108.5	100.1
Transportation and Utilities													
2002	27.8	27.6	27.7	28.6	28.4	28.2	28.6	28.7	28.9	29.2	28.1	27.8	28.3
2003	27.7	28.0	28.2	28.1	28.0	28.1	28.0	28.3	28.7	29.1	29.3	29.6	28.4
2004	29.4	29.6	30.0	29.7	29.8	30.1	30.4	30.5	30.6	31.3	31.2	31.1	30.3
2005	30.9	31.1	31.3	32.0	32.3	32.5	32.3	32.6	33.0	33.1	33.5	33.8	32.4
2006	33.7	33.7	34.2	34.3	34.6	34.7	34.9	35.0	35.4	35.4	35.9	36.1	34.8
2007	35.9	36.0	36.3	36.3	36.6	36.9	36.4	36.8	37.1	37.7	38.3	38.5	36.9
2008	37.6	37.3	37.5	37.5	37.7	37.5	37.6	37.7	37.5	37.3	37.2	36.9	37.4
2009	35.8	35.6	35.5	35.3	35.3	35.3	34.9	34.8	34.6	34.5	34.8	34.7	35.1
2010	34.5	34.3	34.2	34.1	34.2	34.4	34.3	34.3	34.3	34.3	34.5	34.8	34.4
2011	34.2	34.3	34.4	35.0	34.9	35.1	35.4	35.3	35.5	35.9	36.0	36.0	35.2
2012	35.8	35.6	35.7	35.9	36.3	36.4	36.5	36.5	36.5	36.2	36.3	36.5	36.2
2013	36.5	36.1	35.2	35.4	36.4	36.6	36.6	36.5	36.8	37.1	37.4	37.5	36.5
Information													
2002	12.1	11.9	11.6	11.7	11.8	11.4	11.2	11.2	11.2	11.0	11.1	11.0	11.4
2003	10.6	10.4	10.3	10.4	10.6	10.5	10.2	10.0	10.0	10.1	10.2	10.3	10.3
2004	10.2	10.0	10.0	11.1	10.5	10.4	10.4	10.2	10.1	10.5	10.4	10.1	10.3
2005	10.5	10.1	10.1	10.6	11.0	10.4	10.1	10.2	10.2	10.6	10.5	10.3	10.4
2006	10.8	10.8	10.5	10.9	10.9	11.0	11.5	11.5	11.1	11.1	11.0	10.8	11.0
2007	11.3	11.6	11.3	11.4	11.6	11.5	10.9	11.3	10.9	11.4	11.4	11.1	11.3
2008	11.0	11.1	11.1	11.3	11.8	11.2	10.8	10.8	10.7	11.0	10.6	10.2	11.0
2009	9.8	9.9	10.0	9.5	9.5	9.6	9.5	9.6	9.3	9.4	9.4	9.4	9.6
2010	9.0	9.0	8.9	9.3	9.1	9.1	9.4	9.2	9.0	9.1	9.3	9.3	9.1
2011	9.2	9.0	9.1	9.4	9.4	9.4	9.2	9.1	9.4	9.8	9.1	9.6	9.3
2012	9.1	9.2	9.4	9.4	9.5	9.5	9.2	9.5	9.6	10.2	11.3	9.9	9.7
2013	9.1	9.2	9.5	9.6	9.7	10.7	10.0	9.7	9.6	9.8	9.7	9.7	9.7

Employment by Industry: Las Vegas-Paradise, NV, Selected Years, 2002–2013—*Continued*

(Numbers in thousands, not seasonally adjusted)

Industry and year	January	February	March	April	May	June	July	August	September	October	November	December	Annual average
Financial Activities													
2002	40.5	41.0	41.2	41.3	41.3	41.5	41.6	41.5	41.4	41.8	42.3	42.3	41.5
2003	42.1	42.3	42.5	42.8	43.5	43.5	43.9	44.1	44.3	44.4	44.3	44.5	43.5
2004	44.6	44.8	44.9	45.3	45.4	45.8	46.5	46.6	46.7	47.6	47.7	48.4	46.2
2005	47.7	47.6	48.3	48.2	48.4	48.9	48.9	49.1	49.7	49.4	49.6	49.9	48.8
2006	49.0	49.0	49.6	49.6	50.0	50.4	50.5	50.6	50.9	50.6	50.8	51.3	50.2
2007	50.4	50.4	50.7	50.2	50.5	50.6	50.0	49.8	49.7	49.4	48.9	49.0	50.0
2008	48.0	48.1	48.2	48.0	47.9	48.0	47.5	47.1	47.0	46.9	46.4	45.9	47.4
2009	44.1	43.9	43.5	43.1	42.9	42.9	41.7	41.7	41.3	41.4	41.0	40.9	42.4
2010	40.3	39.9	40.0	40.5	40.3	40.1	40.2	39.9	39.8	40.3	40.2	40.3	40.2
2011	39.8	39.6	39.8	40.0	39.9	40.0	39.9	39.7	40.0	40.2	40.2	40.5	40.0
2012	40.2	40.3	40.6	41.4	41.7	41.9	41.8	42.0	42.2	42.8	42.8	42.8	41.7
2013	42.5	42.9	43.6	43.4	43.7	43.6	43.1	43.2	43.2	44.2	44.4	44.0	43.5
Professional and Business Services													
2002	80.0	79.7	81.2	80.5	81.3	80.0	79.7	82.3	82.9	82.4	83.2	81.9	81.3
2003	85.4	85.7	85.4	84.8	85.1	83.5	85.1	87.8	88.0	89.5	88.7	88.3	86.4
2004	93.6	92.2	92.6	94.4	95.1	95.0	95.2	97.0	97.6	101.5	99.3	97.8	95.9
2005	101.5	102.4	103.6	104.9	104.6	105.0	104.4	106.3	107.0	109.7	112.2	112.1	106.1
2006	113.0	114.2	115.3	115.5	116.3	116.6	114.4	115.6	115.2	115.6	116.2	114.0	115.2
2007	116.9	119.5	117.5	117.9	117.9	116.9	113.6	115.3	113.8	116.3	115.3	113.1	116.2
2008	115.9	115.1	115.0	115.0	116.0	113.6	109.8	110.0	110.8	107.9	106.7	103.0	111.6
2009	105.5	103.6	101.4	99.2	99.5	98.4	94.7	95.4	97.6	97.6	99.0	98.5	99.2
2010	100.2	99.1	98.6	99.7	99.6	100.2	98.2	100.4	98.3	100.8	100.6	99.2	99.6
2011	102.7	101.0	101.5	101.8	101.6	101.8	101.1	101.1	102.7	103.9	103.8	102.6	102.1
2012	107.2	106.5	104.9	105.9	106.0	106.6	103.4	106.8	107.8	109.7	108.5	106.8	106.7
2013	111.5	110.1	111.3	112.3	112.6	111.5	108.8	111.2	110.2	111.5	112.9	113.0	111.4
Education and Health Services													
2002	46.0	46.6	47.1	47.4	48.0	47.8	47.8	48.0	48.2	48.8	49.1	49.2	47.8
2003	48.7	49.5	49.7	50.0	50.4	50.3	50.1	50.6	51.2	51.4	52.0	52.2	50.5
2004	51.9	52.6	53.2	53.6	53.5	53.6	54.0	54.3	55.2	55.6	55.7	56.0	54.1
2005	55.8	56.4	57.0	57.7	57.9	58.1	57.6	57.7	58.1	58.0	58.4	59.0	57.6
2006	58.5	59.1	59.8	59.4	59.6	60.2	59.3	59.8	60.7	61.2	61.7	62.1	60.1
2007	61.5	62.4	62.7	62.6	63.2	63.4	63.3	63.5	64.0	64.6	64.9	64.7	63.4
2008	64.6	65.3	65.6	66.3	66.5	66.6	66.2	66.5	67.0	67.2	67.5	67.6	66.4
2009	66.4	66.9	66.9	66.9	67.3	67.5	67.4	67.7	67.7	68.8	68.9	69.0	67.6
2010	68.3	68.6	69.1	69.7	69.8	69.7	69.1	69.3	69.6	70.7	71.1	71.3	69.7
2011	70.8	71.4	71.9	72.5	72.5	72.7	72.3	72.7	73.0	73.7	74.0	74.4	72.7
2012	73.9	74.6	74.6	75.2	75.8	75.4	74.9	76.0	75.9	76.8	76.8	77.2	75.6
2013	76.7	77.8	78.3	78.6	78.8	78.8	78.8	79.4	79.8	80.2	80.8	81.4	79.1
Leisure and Hospitality													
2002	225.6	226.8	230.0	232.0	234.3	234.2	233.7	234.0	233.6	233.6	233.0	233.3	232.0
2003	233.3	234.0	236.5	237.2	239.2	239.6	240.1	241.3	241.2	240.9	240.2	240.9	238.7
2004	240.8	240.5	243.2	247.1	248.4	249.4	249.9	250.4	250.5	250.1	250.8	251.0	247.7
2005	249.2	250.7	253.7	263.9	264.8	267.5	267.2	266.6	268.3	266.2	265.0	264.8	262.3
2006	264.4	266.3	269.4	271.7	273.8	275.3	274.9	274.1	274.7	272.8	271.8	271.5	271.7
2007	268.3	270.4	272.1	273.4	275.1	276.1	274.4	272.1	272.6	273.5	273.8	275.4	273.1
2008	271.1	271.3	272.4	274.1	274.7	275.1	271.1	269.9	268.4	265.0	261.4	258.9	269.5
2009	253.7	253.0	251.9	253.6	254.4	253.2	251.6	248.7	249.4	248.3	247.5	252.1	251.5
2010	248.8	251.1	252.1	255.1	256.0	257.0	254.9	253.6	253.2	253.6	253.2	252.6	253.4
2011	252.1	253.3	257.8	261.4	263.1	264.1	262.4	260.2	261.8	261.9	260.0	256.9	259.6
2012	255.5	257.3	260.6	263.1	265.2	266.2	264.6	262.2	262.2	262.8	261.6	259.9	261.8
2013	259.3	260.6	264.3	267.7	268.5	269.7	271.0	270.9	271.6	268.7	268.3	265.8	267.2
Other Services													
2002	19.8	20.1	20.5	20.3	20.6	20.7	20.4	20.5	20.3	20.2	20.0	20.0	20.3
2003	19.7	19.9	20.2	19.9	20.1	20.5	20.5	20.6	20.6	20.4	20.6	20.8	20.3
2004	20.9	21.5	22.2	22.4	22.9	23.5	22.9	22.9	23.1	23.5	23.3	23.4	22.7
2005	22.3	22.6	22.9	23.0	23.3	23.7	23.7	23.8	24.1	24.0	24.2	24.5	23.5
2006	23.7	23.9	24.3	24.3	24.7	25.1	25.1	25.3	25.5	25.3	25.2	25.1	24.8
2007	24.5	24.5	25.0	25.2	25.6	26.0	25.9	26.0	26.0	25.8	25.9	26.2	25.6
2008	25.8	25.6	25.8	25.7	26.1	26.2	25.9	26.1	26.1	25.7	25.1	24.6	25.7
2009	23.5	23.4	23.5	23.7	23.9	23.9	23.6	23.7	23.7	23.3	23.0	23.0	23.5
2010	22.6	22.7	23.0	23.3	23.4	23.4	23.5	23.6	23.5	23.6	23.1	22.9	23.2
2011	22.7	23.0	23.2	23.3	23.5	23.6	23.7	23.6	23.4	23.3	23.2	23.2	23.3
2012	23.1	23.1	23.4	23.8	24.2	24.5	24.4	24.5	24.6	25.0	24.0	23.7	24.0
2013	23.6	23.8	24.1	24.4	24.7	24.8	24.8	24.7	24.6	24.4	24.1	24.0	24.3
Government													
2002	74.1	77.1	77.6	77.2	77.7	75.3	71.7	71.9	77.0	81.1	81.8	81.9	77.0
2003	78.3	81.2	81.6	81.5	81.9	78.7	75.1	74.7	80.5	82.9	83.3	83.6	80.3
2004	80.2	82.6	84.1	84.1	84.8	81.0	77.4	76.7	84.6	87.2	87.6	87.7	83.2
2005	84.0	87.1	88.6	88.8	89.1	85.5	81.8	80.8	87.5	91.3	92.3	92.6	87.5
2006	88.6	91.9	92.3	93.5	93.7	90.0	85.9	85.4	92.2	96.5	97.5	97.5	92.1
2007	93.8	97.8	98.3	99.9	100.1	96.0	91.6	90.1	97.1	101.2	102.0	102.4	97.5
2008	98.6	102.3	103.0	104.1	104.0	99.4	95.9	94.6	101.7	105.6	105.7	105.6	101.7
2009	100.6	102.5	102.4	101.8	100.8	96.5	93.1	91.7	98.2	99.1	98.5	98.1	98.6
2010	95.6	98.2	98.4	98.7	100.9	95.3	93.2	91.2	95.8	96.8	96.9	96.8	96.5
2011	95.2	96.8	96.9	96.7	96.3	90.1	89.0	89.1	93.3	94.6	94.6	95.5	94.0
2012	92.6	94.5	95.7	95.6	95.8	91.4	89.3	88.7	94.4	95.4	96.3	97.2	93.9
2013	94.4	95.4	96.2	96.5	96.4	92.5	89.3	90.8	95.5	96.7	96.9	97.5	94.8

Employment by Industry: Little Rock-North Little Rock-Conway, AR, Selected Years, 2002–2013

(Numbers in thousands, not seasonally adjusted)

Industry and year	January	February	March	April	May	June	July	August	September	October	November	December	Annual average
Total Nonfarm													
2002	316.5	317.5	319.8	320.1	322.4	322.4	318.6	319.7	322.5	322.3	322.9	324.3	320.8
2003	318.2	319.2	321.2	322.1	323.8	324.0	321.2	324.8	326.2	326.5	326.3	328.3	323.5
2004	322.1	323.4	325.6	326.3	327.7	329.0	327.6	329.8	330.8	330.5	331.8	333.2	328.2
2005	325.4	327.7	330.3	332.8	333.6	334.6	331.3	332.8	335.8	334.8	337.2	338.9	332.9
2006	333.9	336.3	339.9	341.0	341.6	342.8	338.8	340.7	343.6	343.1	343.9	345.6	340.9
2007	339.7	341.2	344.7	345.3	345.7	348.0	343.7	347.0	349.3	348.3	349.7	350.6	346.1
2008	345.4	347.1	348.5	348.6	350.5	349.7	346.1	347.9	349.3	347.4	347.4	346.7	347.9
2009	339.8	340.8	341.4	340.5	339.6	338.8	335.8	335.5	336.1	335.8	337.4	338.0	338.3
2010	331.0	330.8	334.8	336.0	339.0	341.4	337.0	337.1	339.6	340.9	341.5	341.9	337.6
2011	333.9	334.1	337.8	341.2	339.3	338.1	337.0	337.2	339.3	342.2	342.7	342.9	338.8
2012	337.4	339.2	342.2	342.7	344.0	342.9	338.9	341.1	343.2	344.9	346.1	347.2	342.5
2013	340.5	342.8	344.9	346.0	346.4	344.4	342.0	343.4	345.9	347.8	348.2	345.9	344.9
Total Private													
2002	252.9	253.2	255.2	255.6	257.9	259.0	258.2	258.6	258.8	257.9	258.0	259.2	257.0
2003	253.8	254.5	256.4	257.0	259.4	260.1	259.3	262.1	262.0	261.4	260.8	263.2	259.2
2004	257.7	258.3	260.3	261.9	263.4	265.1	265.0	266.3	265.7	265.0	266.0	267.5	263.5
2005	260.7	262.4	264.9	266.5	268.2	269.5	269.1	269.2	270.0	268.6	270.8	272.9	267.7
2006	268.0	269.3	272.7	273.5	274.8	276.4	274.3	275.0	275.7	275.3	276.4	278.2	274.1
2007	272.8	273.5	276.7	276.7	277.9	280.2	279.3	280.0	280.1	278.7	280.0	281.3	278.1
2008	277.3	277.9	279.2	279.1	280.5	280.5	279.6	280.3	279.7	277.3	277.1	276.4	278.7
2009	270.4	270.1	270.6	269.5	269.1	268.7	267.1	267.0	265.8	264.0	265.5	266.1	267.8
2010	259.9	259.2	262.9	264.2	266.4	269.9	268.2	268.3	268.5	269.3	269.7	270.0	266.4
2011	263.4	262.5	266.0	269.1	267.7	267.6	269.3	268.8	268.4	270.7	270.9	271.3	268.0
2012	266.6	267.8	270.7	271.4	273.1	273.0	271.1	272.2	272.6	273.4	274.3	275.3	271.8
2013	269.3	271.0	272.8	274.0	274.9	273.9	273.7	274.4	274.9	276.0	276.2	274.0	273.8
Goods Producing													
2002	44.5	44.3	44.4	44.5	44.9	45.0	45.1	45.2	44.7	44.4	43.7	43.5	44.5
2003	42.8	42.9	43.3	43.4	43.8	44.1	43.8	43.8	43.3	42.7	41.6	42.2	43.1
2004	41.3	41.1	41.5	42.5	43.0	43.6	43.4	43.5	43.3	42.9	42.8	42.6	42.6
2005	42.0	42.1	42.5	42.7	43.0	43.4	43.5	43.7	43.6	43.2	43.2	43.2	43.0
2006	42.9	43.0	43.3	43.5	43.9	44.5	44.1	44.6	44.6	44.2	44.0	44.0	43.9
2007	43.3	43.4	44.3	44.1	44.2	45.0	45.0	45.0	44.7	44.4	44.4	44.4	44.4
2008	43.9	43.5	43.5	43.3	43.9	44.4	44.5	44.6	44.1	43.2	42.6	42.3	43.7
2009	41.4	41.0	40.7	39.8	39.4	39.3	39.4	39.5	39.0	38.0	37.8	37.5	39.4
2010	36.3	35.8	36.2	36.5	37.1	38.3	38.1	37.9	37.7	37.4	37.2	37.1	37.1
2011	35.9	35.6	36.2	36.8	36.6	37.1	37.7	37.4	37.6	37.3	37.2	37.1	36.9
2012	36.8	36.8	37.3	37.0	37.4	37.6	37.4	37.2	37.2	36.9	36.6	36.5	37.1
2013	36.0	35.9	36.1	36.2	36.4	36.5	36.5	36.5	36.3	36.4	35.6	35.5	36.2
Service-Providing													
2002	272.0	273.2	275.4	275.6	277.5	277.4	273.5	274.5	277.8	277.9	279.2	280.8	276.2
2003	275.4	276.3	277.9	278.7	280.0	279.9	277.4	281.0	282.9	283.8	284.7	286.1	280.3
2004	280.8	282.3	284.1	283.8	284.7	285.4	284.2	286.3	287.5	287.6	289.0	290.6	285.5
2005	283.4	285.6	287.8	290.1	290.6	291.2	287.8	289.1	292.2	291.6	294.0	295.7	289.9
2006	291.0	293.3	296.6	297.5	297.7	298.3	294.7	296.1	299.0	298.9	299.9	301.6	297.1
2007	296.4	297.8	300.4	301.2	301.5	303.0	298.7	302.0	304.6	303.9	305.3	306.2	301.8
2008	301.5	303.6	305.0	305.3	306.6	305.3	301.6	303.3	305.2	304.2	304.8	304.4	304.2
2009	298.4	299.8	300.7	300.7	300.2	299.5	296.4	296.0	297.1	297.8	299.6	300.5	298.9
2010	294.7	295.0	298.6	299.5	301.9	303.1	298.9	299.2	301.9	303.5	304.3	304.8	300.5
2011	298.0	298.5	301.6	304.4	302.7	301.0	299.3	299.8	301.7	304.9	305.5	305.8	301.9
2012	300.6	302.4	304.9	305.7	306.6	305.3	301.5	303.9	306.0	308.0	309.5	310.7	305.4
2013	304.5	306.9	308.8	309.8	310.0	307.9	305.5	306.9	309.6	311.4	312.6	310.4	308.7
Mining, Logging, and Construction													
2002	16.3	16.3	16.5	16.7	17.1	17.5	17.7	17.6	17.4	17.3	16.9	16.8	17.0
2003	16.9	16.9	17.3	17.4	17.8	18.1	18.0	18.0	17.7	17.5	17.1	17.0	17.5
2004	16.5	16.3	16.7	17.5	17.8	18.2	18.0	18.0	18.0	17.5	17.3	17.2	17.4
2005	16.7	16.9	17.3	17.5	18.0	18.1	18.1	18.3	18.2	17.7	17.8	17.9	17.7
2006	17.6	17.7	18.1	18.3	18.7	19.1	18.8	19.2	19.3	18.9	18.7	18.8	18.6
2007	18.3	18.4	19.3	19.2	19.4	20.1	20.0	20.1	19.9	19.7	19.6	19.5	19.5
2008	19.1	19.1	19.2	19.1	19.5	19.8	19.9	20.0	19.6	18.8	18.4	18.2	19.2
2009	17.6	17.5	17.5	17.3	17.1	17.2	17.6	17.6	17.3	16.8	16.8	16.6	17.2
2010	15.9	15.6	16.0	16.5	17.0	17.7	17.8	17.7	17.6	17.4	17.2	17.2	17.0
2011	16.2	15.9	16.4	16.9	16.7	17.2	17.6	17.4	17.5	17.3	17.2	17.3	17.0
2012	16.8	16.8	17.1	16.8	17.1	17.3	17.2	17.2	17.2	17.0	16.9	16.8	17.0
2013	16.2	16.2	16.3	16.4	16.8	16.8	16.8	16.8	16.6	16.7	16.0	15.9	16.5
Manufacturing													
2002	28.2	28.0	27.9	27.8	27.8	27.5	27.4	27.6	27.3	27.1	26.8	26.7	27.5
2003	25.9	26.0	26.0	26.0	26.0	26.0	25.8	25.8	25.6	25.2	24.5	25.2	25.7
2004	24.8	24.8	24.8	25.0	25.2	25.4	25.4	25.5	25.3	25.4	25.5	25.4	25.2
2005	25.3	25.2	25.2	25.2	25.0	25.3	25.4	25.4	25.4	25.5	25.4	25.3	25.3
2006	25.3	25.3	25.2	25.2	25.2	25.4	25.3	25.4	25.3	25.3	25.3	25.2	25.3
2007	25.0	25.0	25.0	24.9	24.8	24.9	25.0	24.9	24.8	24.7	24.8	24.9	24.9
2008	24.8	24.4	24.3	24.2	24.4	24.6	24.6	24.6	24.5	24.4	24.2	24.1	24.4
2009	23.8	23.5	23.2	22.5	22.3	22.1	21.8	21.9	21.7	21.2	21.0	20.9	22.2
2010	20.4	20.2	20.2	20.0	20.1	20.6	20.3	20.2	20.1	20.0	20.0	19.9	20.2
2011	19.7	19.7	19.8	19.9	19.9	19.9	20.1	20.0	20.1	20.0	20.0	19.8	19.9
2012	20.0	20.0	20.2	20.2	20.3	20.3	20.2	20.0	20.0	19.9	19.7	19.7	20.0
2013	19.8	19.7	19.8	19.8	19.6	19.7	19.7	19.7	19.7	19.7	19.6	19.6	19.7

Employment by Industry: Little Rock-North Little Rock-Conway, AR, Selected Years, 2002–2013—*Continued*

(Numbers in thousands, not seasonally adjusted)

Industry and year	January	February	March	April	May	June	July	August	September	October	November	December	Annual average
Trade, Transportation, and Utilities													
2002	68.6	68.2	68.7	68.8	69.0	69.0	68.2	68.1	68.2	68.0	69.1	69.9	68.7
2003	67.7	67.3	67.4	67.4	67.6	67.6	67.2	67.7	68.3	69.3	69.7	70.7	68.2
2004	68.0	67.9	68.1	68.0	68.3	68.6	68.7	69.3	69.2	69.3	70.2	71.3	68.9
2005	68.6	68.5	68.7	69.0	69.1	69.0	69.1	69.2	69.8	69.7	71.1	71.9	69.5
2006	69.5	69.3	69.9	70.1	70.5	70.2	69.9	70.3	70.5	70.7	71.8	72.7	70.5
2007	70.1	69.7	70.6	70.0	70.3	70.4	70.2	70.3	70.3	70.0	71.2	72.0	70.4
2008	69.7	69.4	69.7	69.4	69.8	69.7	69.3	69.4	69.2	68.7	69.4	69.4	69.4
2009	66.9	66.4	66.5	65.6	65.2	64.7	63.9	64.1	64.0	63.8	64.9	65.4	65.1
2010	62.8	62.3	63.3	63.6	63.9	64.4	64.2	64.2	64.1	65.6	66.6	67.1	64.3
2011	64.8	64.0	64.7	65.3	64.9	65.0	65.1	65.0	64.8	65.8	67.1	67.5	65.3
2012	65.2	64.9	65.5	66.1	66.3	66.6	66.1	66.3	66.8	67.0	68.4	68.9	66.5
2013	66.6	66.4	66.6	66.6	66.4	66.4	66.8	66.6	66.6	67.0	67.9	67.8	66.8
Wholesale Trade													
2002	16.2	16.2	16.3	16.3	16.3	16.3	16.2	16.2	16.1	16.0	15.9	16.0	16.2
2003	15.9	16.0	15.9	16.0	16.2	16.2	16.3	16.3	16.4	16.5	16.5	16.6	16.2
2004	16.3	16.4	16.5	16.7	16.8	16.9	16.9	16.9	16.9	16.8	16.7	16.9	16.7
2005	16.7	16.8	16.8	16.9	16.9	17.1	17.2	17.2	17.3	17.2	17.3	17.4	17.1
2006	17.3	17.3	17.3	17.5	17.6	17.7	17.6	17.6	17.6	17.4	17.5	17.6	17.5
2007	17.1	17.2	17.3	17.3	17.3	17.4	17.4	17.4	17.3	17.4	17.3	17.4	17.3
2008	17.4	17.5	17.5	17.6	17.7	17.7	17.8	17.9	17.9	17.8	17.7	17.7	17.7
2009	17.6	17.6	17.6	17.5	17.4	17.2	17.0	16.9	16.7	16.7	16.6	16.6	17.1
2010	16.2	16.2	16.4	16.7	16.7	16.8	16.7	16.4	16.2	16.6	16.5	16.4	16.5
2011	15.9	15.9	15.9	16.2	16.0	15.9	16.1	16.0	15.8	16.0	15.9	15.9	16.0
2012	15.5	15.6	15.7	15.9	16.0	16.0	15.7	15.7	15.5	15.5	15.4	15.5	15.7
2013	15.7	15.8	15.8	15.8	15.7	15.7	15.8	15.7	15.7	15.7	15.6	15.7	15.7
Retail Trade													
2002	35.0	34.7	35.1	35.1	35.4	35.5	35.0	34.8	34.9	34.8	36.0	36.7	35.3
2003	34.5	34.1	34.2	34.3	34.4	34.5	34.1	34.5	34.9	35.6	36.2	37.1	34.9
2004	35.0	34.9	35.3	35.3	35.4	35.6	35.5	35.9	35.7	36.0	36.9	37.6	35.8
2005	35.8	35.5	35.6	35.7	35.7	35.7	35.6	35.6	35.8	36.0	37.2	37.8	36.0
2006	35.8	35.5	36.0	35.9	36.0	35.8	35.7	36.1	36.0	36.4	37.5	38.1	36.2
2007	36.5	35.9	36.6	36.1	36.4	36.5	36.4	36.4	36.4	36.3	37.6	38.2	36.6
2008	36.4	36.2	36.5	36.0	36.2	36.4	36.5	36.5	36.2	35.9	36.7	36.9	36.4
2009	35.0	34.7	34.9	34.8	34.9	34.9	34.6	34.8	34.8	34.9	36.1	36.5	35.1
2010	34.7	34.2	34.9	35.0	35.3	35.7	35.5	35.7	35.5	36.6	37.7	38.1	35.7
2011	36.4	35.7	36.2	36.4	36.1	36.1	36.3	36.2	35.8	36.6	37.8	38.0	36.5
2012	36.3	35.9	36.2	36.4	36.4	36.6	36.7	36.7	37.0	37.1	38.4	38.6	36.9
2013	36.4	36.2	36.3	36.4	36.3	36.3	36.8	36.8	36.6	37.0	38.0	37.6	36.7
Transportation and Utilities													
2002	17.4	17.3	17.3	17.4	17.3	17.2	17.0	17.1	17.2	17.2	17.2	17.2	17.2
2003	17.3	17.2	17.3	17.1	17.0	16.9	16.8	16.9	17.0	17.2	17.0	17.0	17.1
2004	16.7	16.6	16.3	16.0	16.1	16.1	16.3	16.5	16.6	16.5	16.6	16.8	16.4
2005	16.1	16.2	16.3	16.4	16.5	16.2	16.3	16.4	16.7	16.5	16.6	16.7	16.4
2006	16.4	16.5	16.6	16.7	16.9	16.7	16.6	16.6	16.9	16.9	16.8	17.0	16.7
2007	16.5	16.6	16.7	16.6	16.6	16.5	16.4	16.5	16.6	16.3	16.3	16.4	16.5
2008	15.9	15.7	15.7	15.8	15.9	15.6	15.0	15.0	15.1	15.0	15.0	14.8	15.4
2009	14.3	14.1	14.0	13.3	12.9	12.6	12.3	12.4	12.5	12.2	12.2	12.3	12.9
2010	11.9	11.9	12.0	11.9	11.9	11.9	12.0	12.1	12.4	12.4	12.4	12.6	12.1
2011	12.5	12.4	12.6	12.7	12.8	13.0	12.7	12.8	13.2	13.2	13.4	13.6	12.9
2012	13.4	13.4	13.6	13.8	13.9	14.0	13.7	13.9	14.3	14.4	14.6	14.8	14.0
2013	14.5	14.4	14.5	14.4	14.4	14.4	14.2	14.1	14.3	14.3	14.3	14.5	14.4
Information													
2002	9.2	9.2	9.1	9.1	9.1	9.2	9.1	9.1	9.1	9.3	9.3	9.3	9.2
2003	9.3	9.3	9.3	9.3	9.4	9.5	9.4	9.5	9.4	9.4	9.5	9.5	9.4
2004	9.6	9.4	9.5	9.5	9.5	9.5	9.5	9.5	9.5	9.4	9.5	9.5	9.5
2005	9.3	9.4	9.3	9.2	9.3	9.4	9.4	9.4	9.3	9.3	9.3	9.4	9.3
2006	9.3	9.3	9.3	9.3	9.3	9.4	9.3	9.3	9.2	9.1	9.2	9.1	9.3
2007	9.4	9.4	9.3	9.4	9.4	9.5	9.4	9.3	9.3	9.3	9.3	9.3	9.4
2008	9.1	9.1	9.1	9.4	9.0	9.1	9.1	9.1	8.9	8.8	8.8	8.8	9.0
2009	8.7	8.6	8.6	8.6	8.6	8.6	8.5	8.4	8.2	8.0	7.9	7.9	8.4
2010	7.7	7.9	7.9	7.9	7.9	8.2	7.8	7.8	7.8	7.8	7.8	7.9	7.9
2011	7.8	7.8	7.8	7.7	7.7	7.7	7.6	7.6	7.5	7.5	7.4	7.4	7.6
2012	7.3	7.3	7.2	7.2	7.3	7.2	7.2	7.3	7.3	7.3	7.3	7.3	7.3
2013	7.3	7.4	7.4	7.2	7.3	7.3	7.3	7.3	7.2	7.2	7.2	7.2	7.3
Financial Activities													
2002	19.1	19.1	19.2	19.1	19.1	19.2	19.3	19.3	19.3	19.2	19.2	19.4	19.2
2003	19.2	19.2	19.2	19.3	19.5	19.7	19.7	19.7	19.7	19.6	19.6	19.9	19.5
2004	19.6	19.7	19.7	19.7	19.7	19.7	19.7	19.7	19.7	19.0	19.0	19.1	19.5
2005	18.8	18.8	18.8	19.5	19.6	19.7	19.8	19.8	19.8	19.7	19.8	20.0	19.5
2006	19.7	19.8	19.8	19.9	20.0	20.0	20.1	20.2	20.1	20.1	20.2	20.3	20.0
2007	20.2	20.2	20.2	20.2	20.2	20.3	20.3	20.2	20.2	20.1	20.0	20.2	20.2
2008	20.1	20.1	20.1	19.8	19.9	19.8	19.9	19.9	19.9	19.8	19.8	19.9	19.9
2009	19.7	19.6	19.6	19.6	19.6	19.7	19.5	19.5	19.4	19.4	19.4	19.5	19.5
2010	19.0	19.0	18.9	18.8	18.8	19.0	19.1	19.1	19.0	19.1	19.2	19.3	19.0
2011	19.1	19.0	19.0	19.0	18.9	19.0	19.3	19.3	19.2	19.5	19.6	19.8	19.2
2012	19.7	19.8	20.0	19.7	19.8	19.8	19.9	19.9	19.7	19.7	19.7	19.9	19.8
2013	19.7	19.8	20.0	20.1	20.2	20.2	20.0	20.1	20.3	20.1	20.1	20.3	20.1

Employment by Industry: Little Rock-North Little Rock-Conway, AR, Selected Years, 2002–2013—*Continued*

(Numbers in thousands, not seasonally adjusted)

Industry and year	January	February	March	April	May	June	July	August	September	October	November	December	Annual average
Professional and Business Services													
2002	37.3	37.2	37.8	37.8	38.3	38.9	39.0	39.4	39.7	39.9	39.3	39.8	38.7
2003	38.9	39.0	39.6	39.2	39.7	39.2	39.5	41.3	41.0	41.1	40.8	41.1	40.0
2004	40.4	40.4	40.9	40.3	40.5	40.5	41.0	41.5	41.2	42.1	42.1	42.4	41.1
2005	40.8	41.2	41.8	41.5	41.4	41.7	41.6	41.6	41.7	41.6	42.1	42.9	41.7
2006	41.7	42.5	43.6	43.1	43.2	43.2	43.1	42.8	43.5	43.1	43.2	43.8	43.1
2007	42.7	43.0	43.2	43.4	43.4	43.6	42.9	43.6	43.8	43.4	43.5	43.7	43.4
2008	43.5	44.1	44.1	43.7	43.7	43.3	42.8	43.0	43.1	42.9	42.8	42.6	43.3
2009	41.4	41.5	41.1	41.4	41.4	41.2	41.0	41.3	41.1	41.4	41.9	42.2	41.4
2010	42.1	42.2	43.2	43.1	43.3	43.9	43.7	43.9	43.9	44.1	44.0	44.0	43.5
2011	42.8	43.1	43.8	44.4	43.7	43.7	44.2	44.1	43.4	43.8	43.0	42.9	43.6
2012	42.1	42.6	43.3	43.7	43.9	44.1	43.7	43.7	43.6	43.7	43.6	43.8	43.5
2013	43.6	44.6	45.0	45.2	45.3	44.6	44.4	44.4	45.4	45.8	45.9	45.4	45.0
Education and Health Services													
2002	38.9	39.3	39.6	39.5	39.8	39.5	39.6	39.7	40.6	40.3	40.5	40.5	39.8
2003	40.0	40.5	40.8	40.9	41.0	41.0	40.8	41.0	41.8	41.8	41.8	41.9	41.1
2004	41.2	41.5	41.6	42.2	42.1	42.1	42.1	42.1	42.8	43.1	43.0	42.9	42.2
2005	42.4	42.9	43.1	43.6	43.6	43.6	43.5	43.5	44.1	44.4	44.4	44.3	43.6
2006	44.2	44.7	45.1	45.0	45.0	45.2	44.9	45.1	45.9	45.7	45.8	46.0	45.2
2007	45.6	46.1	46.5	46.7	46.8	46.9	47.2	47.3	48.0	47.3	47.4	47.3	46.9
2008	47.2	47.7	47.9	48.1	48.0	47.9	47.9	48.1	48.7	48.8	48.7	48.7	48.1
2009	48.5	49.1	49.5	49.4	49.2	49.1	49.0	48.7	49.4	49.4	49.7	50.0	49.3
2010	49.3	49.4	49.8	50.0	49.9	50.1	49.8	49.8	50.7	50.5	50.6	50.4	50.0
2011	49.8	49.8	50.3	50.6	50.3	49.4	49.5	49.8	50.7	51.4	51.5	51.4	50.4
2012	51.3	51.7	51.8	51.8	51.9	50.6	50.4	51.3	52.3	53.1	53.0	52.8	51.8
2013	50.8	51.2	51.1	51.7	51.5	51.0	50.5	51.2	51.9	51.7	51.7	51.1	51.3
Leisure and Hospitality													
2002	23.2	23.8	24.2	24.6	25.3	25.5	25.2	25.1	24.6	24.5	24.5	24.5	24.6
2003	23.7	24.0	24.3	24.9	25.6	25.9	25.8	25.9	25.3	24.3	24.4	24.3	24.9
2004	24.0	24.5	25.2	25.8	26.4	26.8	26.5	26.7	26.1	25.6	25.6	25.9	25.8
2005	25.1	25.7	26.7	26.9	28.0	28.3	27.8	27.7	27.4	26.8	26.9	27.1	27.0
2006	26.6	26.5	27.4	28.2	28.4	29.1	28.1	28.0	27.3	27.9	27.8	27.9	27.8
2007	27.3	27.5	28.3	28.5	29.1	29.5	29.3	29.3	28.8	29.2	29.0	29.1	28.7
2008	28.4	28.5	29.1	29.6	30.2	30.1	29.8	29.9	29.7	29.3	29.3	28.9	29.4
2009	28.2	28.3	29.0	29.6	30.1	30.3	30.1	30.0	29.4	29.1	29.0	28.7	29.3
2010	28.0	28.0	28.9	29.4	30.5	30.7	30.4	30.6	30.3	29.9	29.4	29.3	29.6
2011	28.3	28.3	29.1	30.2	30.5	30.4	30.4	30.4	30.1	30.1	29.9	29.8	29.8
2012	29.1	29.3	30.1	30.8	31.1	31.4	31.0	31.1	30.3	30.3	30.3	30.7	30.5
2013	29.9	30.2	30.9	31.2	32.0	32.1	32.2	32.3	31.6	32.2	32.1	31.0	31.5
Other Services													
2002	12.1	12.1	12.2	12.2	12.4	12.7	12.7	12.7	12.6	12.3	12.4	12.3	12.4
2003	12.2	12.3	12.5	12.6	12.8	13.1	13.1	13.2	13.2	13.2	13.4	13.6	12.9
2004	13.6	13.8	13.8	13.9	13.9	14.3	14.1	14.0	13.9	13.6	13.8	13.8	13.9
2005	13.7	13.8	14.0	14.1	14.2	14.4	14.4	14.3	14.3	13.9	14.0	14.1	14.1
2006	14.1	14.2	14.3	14.4	14.5	14.8	14.8	14.7	14.6	14.5	14.4	14.4	14.5
2007	14.2	14.2	14.3	14.4	14.5	15.0	15.0	15.0	15.0	15.0	15.2	15.3	14.8
2008	15.4	15.5	15.7	15.8	16.0	16.2	16.3	16.3	16.1	15.8	15.7	15.8	15.9
2009	15.6	15.6	15.6	15.5	15.6	15.8	15.7	15.5	15.3	14.9	14.9	14.9	15.4
2010	14.7	14.6	14.7	14.9	15.0	15.3	15.1	15.0	15.0	14.9	14.9	14.9	14.9
2011	14.9	14.9	15.1	15.1	15.1	15.3	15.5	15.2	15.1	15.3	15.2	15.4	15.2
2012	15.1	15.3	15.5	15.1	15.4	15.7	15.4	15.4	15.4	15.4	15.4	15.4	15.4
2013	15.4	15.5	15.7	15.8	15.8	16.0	15.9	15.8	15.8	15.6	15.7	15.7	15.7
Government													
2002	63.6	64.3	64.6	64.5	64.5	63.4	60.4	61.1	63.7	64.4	64.9	65.1	63.7
2003	64.4	64.7	64.8	65.1	64.4	63.9	61.9	62.7	64.2	65.1	65.5	65.1	64.3
2004	64.4	65.1	65.3	64.4	64.3	63.9	62.6	63.5	65.1	65.5	65.8	65.7	64.6
2005	64.7	65.3	65.4	66.3	65.4	65.1	62.2	63.6	65.8	66.2	66.4	66.0	65.2
2006	65.9	67.0	67.2	67.5	66.8	66.4	64.5	65.7	67.9	67.8	67.5	67.4	66.8
2007	66.9	67.7	68.0	68.6	67.8	67.8	64.4	67.0	69.2	69.6	69.7	69.3	68.0
2008	68.1	69.2	69.3	69.5	70.0	69.2	66.5	67.6	69.6	70.1	70.3	70.3	69.1
2009	69.4	70.7	70.8	71.0	70.5	70.1	68.7	68.5	70.3	71.8	71.9	71.9	70.5
2010	71.1	71.6	71.9	71.8	72.6	71.5	68.8	68.8	71.1	71.6	71.8	71.9	71.2
2011	70.5	71.6	71.8	72.1	71.6	70.5	67.7	68.4	70.9	71.5	71.8	71.6	70.8
2012	70.8	71.4	71.5	71.3	70.9	69.9	67.8	68.9	70.6	71.5	71.8	71.9	70.7
2013	71.2	71.8	72.1	72.0	71.5	70.5	68.3	69.0	71.0	71.8	72.0	71.9	71.1

Employment by Industry: Los Angeles-Long Beach-Santa Ana, CA, Selected Years, 2002–2013

(Numbers in thousands, not seasonally adjusted)

Industry and year	January	February	March	April	May	June	July	August	September	October	November	December	Annual average
Total Nonfarm													
2002	5,421.3	5,451.2	5,500.9	5,496.5	5,514.8	5,518.6	5,437.0	5,452.3	5,490.6	5,519.6	5,546.1	5,557.7	5,492.2
2003	5,433.9	5,459.3	5,490.0	5,482.4	5,498.9	5,500.4	5,442.9	5,453.5	5,470.2	5,520.7	5,533.9	5,554.4	5,486.7
2004	5,458.1	5,489.3	5,524.4	5,530.6	5,553.3	5,551.6	5,514.9	5,501.9	5,526.9	5,581.3	5,611.4	5,618.5	5,538.5
2005	5,508.8	5,545.0	5,575.6	5,594.0	5,606.8	5,622.3	5,577.7	5,589.4	5,634.4	5,670.2	5,707.6	5,735.6	5,614.0
2006	5,624.6	5,671.8	5,702.3	5,702.5	5,719.0	5,740.3	5,682.3	5,687.0	5,725.9	5,759.2	5,782.1	5,808.3	5,717.1
2007	5,686.7	5,724.8	5,759.3	5,737.2	5,749.4	5,766.6	5,722.2	5,711.3	5,744.4	5,769.1	5,791.9	5,818.3	5,748.4
2008	5,662.2	5,697.3	5,718.5	5,721.3	5,723.6	5,719.8	5,656.1	5,627.8	5,647.1	5,655.6	5,631.2	5,618.4	5,673.2
2009	5,447.0	5,426.8	5,421.5	5,376.5	5,369.6	5,351.8	5,253.0	5,216.7	5,234.7	5,287.2	5,293.0	5,306.7	5,332.0
2010	5,196.5	5,206.7	5,227.4	5,262.4	5,286.3	5,282.1	5,212.3	5,201.7	5,230.4	5,294.9	5,314.8	5,336.5	5,254.3
2011	5,234.0	5,260.4	5,279.3	5,283.5	5,292.3	5,293.5	5,243.6	5,239.5	5,283.7	5,325.5	5,361.3	5,383.7	5,290.0
2012	5,293.7	5,332.0	5,363.7	5,405.0	5,430.9	5,440.5	5,376.7	5,389.2	5,423.9	5,505.5	5,559.0	5,579.7	5,425.0
2013	5,461.6	5,506.1	5,526.7	5,540.4	5,559.7	5,568.7	5,524.6	5,551.5	5,577.1	5,638.1	5,673.0	5,674.2	5,566.8
Total Private													
2002	4,662.2	4,687.8	4,726.8	4,723.1	4,738.3	4,745.0	4,706.8	4,730.6	4,741.1	4,751.6	4,773.0	4,786.2	4,731.0
2003	4,671.1	4,692.8	4,716.2	4,713.8	4,730.8	4,733.3	4,708.9	4,737.1	4,738.4	4,771.7	4,780.7	4,804.1	4,733.2
2004	4,711.1	4,741.0	4,769.6	4,777.0	4,798.5	4,798.9	4,796.8	4,801.1	4,803.0	4,840.0	4,864.3	4,874.9	4,798.0
2005	4,770.5	4,799.5	4,825.4	4,846.2	4,856.6	4,872.2	4,862.6	4,883.4	4,909.8	4,928.4	4,957.9	4,987.2	4,875.0
2006	4,883.2	4,923.1	4,947.6	4,948.5	4,962.5	4,984.0	4,957.6	4,975.0	4,992.5	5,006.2	5,021.8	5,049.8	4,971.0
2007	4,935.1	4,967.0	4,995.4	4,974.4	4,984.4	5,001.4	4,989.6	4,991.5	5,002.5	5,007.4	5,022.3	5,049.5	4,993.4
2008	4,899.5	4,926.6	4,943.1	4,945.1	4,943.6	4,941.5	4,916.0	4,899.6	4,899.9	4,887.1	4,856.3	4,846.9	4,908.8
2009	4,679.9	4,656.1	4,645.5	4,598.9	4,594.5	4,577.8	4,525.3	4,512.3	4,523.1	4,539.1	4,542.8	4,559.4	4,579.6
2010	4,455.5	4,462.9	4,478.7	4,505.5	4,515.5	4,525.0	4,511.4	4,524.9	4,536.1	4,567.4	4,581.2	4,605.8	4,522.5
2011	4,509.2	4,532.6	4,544.9	4,550.3	4,558.1	4,558.9	4,565.5	4,577.0	4,596.0	4,609.7	4,637.1	4,664.1	4,575.3
2012	4,584.2	4,613.5	4,639.4	4,683.1	4,706.4	4,717.3	4,708.6	4,729.4	4,739.4	4,802.0	4,849.1	4,871.4	4,720.3
2013	4,763.4	4,798.8	4,812.8	4,831.4	4,848.6	4,857.6	4,865.2	4,889.0	4,894.2	4,937.5	4,966.3	4,967.2	4,869.3
Goods Producing													
2002	947.5	952.1	958.5	952.2	954.1	955.1	939.8	943.4	942.9	936.7	933.6	931.0	945.6
2003	912.8	912.0	915.4	909.7	912.1	914.7	903.9	907.4	906.2	902.6	901.8	903.9	908.5
2004	894.3	897.9	904.8	905.5	907.9	913.0	911.4	910.8	911.5	908.9	903.5	901.3	905.9
2005	887.0	895.3	900.2	906.3	910.1	914.5	916.1	918.6	920.4	917.3	916.1	915.4	909.8
2006	904.4	912.5	916.4	915.4	917.7	923.2	918.7	920.5	921.6	914.6	910.9	908.0	915.3
2007	892.2	897.9	902.2	898.3	899.7	906.0	901.8	899.5	895.2	889.5	882.5	878.3	895.3
2008	863.0	864.6	863.9	861.5	860.1	859.2	855.3	852.2	847.0	836.6	823.4	812.2	849.9
2009	787.0	772.9	766.0	753.1	749.1	744.7	730.9	725.3	719.8	715.0	711.2	705.7	740.1
2010	696.7	695.1	697.5	699.5	702.6	705.7	704.9	704.9	701.8	701.9	700.3	697.9	700.7
2011	688.3	690.6	693.4	696.2	699.5	702.0	706.2	707.1	705.5	702.7	702.9	701.1	699.6
2012	696.8	698.7	702.5	705.1	708.7	714.1	716.5	717.2	717.0	716.3	717.8	716.6	710.6
2013	710.4	716.2	717.3	719.1	721.2	726.3	726.5	729.5	727.8	729.1	731.2	726.3	723.4
Service-Providing													
2002	4,473.8	4,499.1	4,542.4	4,544.3	4,560.7	4,563.5	4,497.2	4,508.9	4,547.7	4,582.9	4,612.5	4,626.7	4,546.6
2003	4,521.1	4,547.3	4,574.6	4,572.7	4,586.8	4,585.7	4,539.0	4,546.1	4,564.0	4,618.1	4,632.1	4,650.5	4,578.2
2004	4,563.8	4,591.4	4,619.6	4,625.1	4,645.4	4,638.6	4,603.5	4,591.1	4,615.4	4,672.4	4,707.9	4,717.2	4,632.6
2005	4,621.8	4,649.7	4,675.4	4,687.7	4,696.7	4,707.8	4,661.6	4,670.8	4,714.0	4,752.9	4,791.5	4,820.2	4,704.2
2006	4,720.2	4,759.3	4,785.9	4,787.1	4,801.3	4,817.1	4,763.6	4,766.5	4,804.3	4,844.6	4,871.2	4,900.3	4,801.8
2007	4,794.5	4,826.9	4,857.1	4,838.9	4,849.7	4,860.6	4,820.4	4,811.8	4,849.2	4,879.6	4,909.4	4,940.0	4,853.2
2008	4,799.2	4,832.7	4,854.6	4,859.8	4,863.5	4,860.6	4,800.8	4,775.6	4,800.1	4,819.0	4,807.8	4,806.2	4,823.3
2009	4,660.0	4,653.9	4,655.5	4,623.4	4,620.5	4,607.1	4,522.1	4,491.4	4,514.9	4,572.2	4,581.8	4,601.0	4,592.0
2010	4,499.8	4,511.6	4,529.9	4,562.9	4,583.7	4,576.4	4,507.4	4,496.8	4,528.6	4,593.0	4,614.5	4,638.6	4,553.6
2011	4,545.7	4,569.8	4,585.9	4,587.3	4,592.8	4,591.5	4,537.4	4,532.4	4,578.2	4,622.8	4,658.4	4,682.6	4,590.4
2012	4,596.9	4,633.3	4,661.2	4,699.9	4,722.2	4,726.4	4,660.2	4,672.0	4,706.9	4,789.2	4,841.2	4,863.1	4,714.4
2013	4,751.2	4,789.9	4,809.4	4,821.3	4,838.5	4,842.4	4,798.1	4,822.0	4,849.3	4,909.0	4,941.8	4,947.9	4,843.4
Mining and Logging													
2002	4.4	4.4	4.4	4.1	4.2	4.2	4.2	4.2	4.2	4.2	4.4	4.4	4.3
2003	4.3	4.4	4.4	4.3	4.3	4.3	4.3	4.4	4.2	4.4	4.4	4.4	4.3
2004	4.3	4.3	4.4	4.4	4.3	4.4	4.3	4.3	4.3	4.6	4.6	4.6	4.4
2005	4.5	4.5	4.5	4.3	4.3	4.3	4.4	4.4	4.4	4.3	4.4	4.4	4.4
2006	4.5	4.5	4.5	4.5	4.6	4.7	4.7	4.7	4.7	4.7	4.7	4.7	4.6
2007	4.9	5.0	5.0	4.9	4.9	5.0	5.0	4.9	5.0	5.0	5.1	5.0	5.0
2008	5.0	5.0	5.0	4.9	4.9	5.0	5.0	5.0	5.0	5.1	5.0	5.0	5.0
2009	4.9	4.8	4.8	4.7	4.7	4.7	4.5	4.5	4.4	4.5	4.5	4.3	4.6
2010	4.6	4.7	4.7	4.7	4.7	4.7	4.7	4.6	4.6	4.6	4.5	4.5	4.6
2011	4.5	4.5	4.4	4.5	4.5	4.5	4.5	4.5	4.5	4.7	4.7	4.7	4.5
2012	4.7	4.7	4.7	4.7	4.7	4.7	4.8	4.8	4.8	4.8	4.8	4.8	4.8
2013	5.0	5.0	5.0	5.0	5.0	5.2	5.3	5.2	5.2	5.3	5.3	5.2	5.1
Construction													
2002	208.8	209.5	211.8	209.7	211.7	213.2	212.5	217.9	218.2	217.3	216.6	216.5	213.6
2003	210.3	208.2	211.3	212.3	216.3	219.8	220.0	223.6	223.9	224.1	224.2	225.2	218.3
2004	221.9	222.1	224.7	228.2	230.4	234.1	236.6	239.2	240.5	238.7	236.2	235.3	232.3
2005	226.2	232.9	236.3	241.8	246.4	250.7	254.9	258.5	259.4	259.2	258.8	258.3	248.6
2006	253.9	257.0	259.1	260.0	263.5	267.3	267.9	271.0	272.0	267.9	265.6	264.2	264.1
2007	255.1	257.9	261.6	260.1	261.9	265.8	266.7	266.1	263.8	260.6	255.6	252.7	260.7
2008	242.9	243.3	243.6	241.4	240.6	239.3	237.9	237.9	234.7	230.5	224.9	220.1	236.4
2009	209.1	202.1	201.3	196.0	195.1	193.6	188.3	187.6	184.9	182.7	180.9	176.3	191.5
2010	171.3	169.4	170.9	172.3	173.4	173.9	173.7	174.6	172.7	173.4	173.1	171.2	172.5
2011	167.2	167.8	169.1	171.1	173.3	174.9	177.9	179.6	178.9	177.2	177.4	175.4	174.2
2012	173.8	173.7	175.0	174.8	177.4	181.1	183.5	184.7	185.0	185.1	186.2	185.3	180.5
2013	183.8	186.0	187.6	188.8	190.8	194.2	195.9	198.4	197.0	199.4	202.3	202.2	193.9

Employment by Industry: Los Angeles-Long Beach-Santa Ana, CA, Selected Years, 2002–2013—*Continued*

(Numbers in thousands, not seasonally adjusted)

Industry and year	January	February	March	April	May	June	July	August	September	October	November	December	Annual average
Manufacturing													
2002	734.3	738.2	742.3	738.4	738.2	737.7	723.1	721.3	720.5	715.2	712.6	710.1	727.7
2003	698.2	699.4	699.7	693.1	691.5	690.6	679.6	679.4	678.1	674.1	673.2	674.3	685.9
2004	668.1	671.5	675.7	672.9	673.2	674.5	670.5	667.3	666.7	665.6	662.7	661.4	669.2
2005	656.3	657.9	659.4	660.2	659.4	659.5	656.8	655.7	656.6	653.8	652.9	652.7	656.8
2006	646.0	651.0	652.8	650.9	649.6	651.2	646.1	644.8	644.9	642.0	640.6	639.1	646.6
2007	632.2	635.0	635.6	633.3	632.9	635.2	630.1	628.5	626.4	623.9	621.8	620.6	629.6
2008	615.1	616.3	615.3	615.2	614.6	614.9	612.4	609.3	607.3	601.0	593.5	587.1	608.5
2009	573.0	566.0	559.9	552.4	549.3	546.4	538.1	533.2	530.5	527.8	525.8	525.1	544.0
2010	520.8	521.0	521.9	522.5	524.5	527.1	526.5	525.7	524.5	523.9	522.7	522.2	523.6
2011	516.6	518.3	519.9	520.6	521.7	522.6	523.8	523.0	522.1	520.8	520.8	521.0	520.9
2012	518.3	520.3	522.8	525.6	526.6	528.3	528.2	527.7	527.2	526.4	526.8	526.5	525.4
2013	521.6	525.2	524.7	525.3	525.4	526.9	525.3	525.9	525.6	524.4	523.6	518.9	524.4
Trade, Transportation, and Utilities													
2002	1,033.5	1,027.9	1,030.3	1,032.1	1,036.2	1,042.0	1,037.0	1,040.4	1,044.3	1,045.8	1,063.6	1,084.5	1,043.1
2003	1,037.3	1,031.4	1,031.8	1,027.5	1,029.8	1,033.6	1,027.6	1,028.5	1,033.2	1,048.5	1,054.5	1,070.1	1,037.8
2004	1,028.2	1,024.3	1,029.5	1,032.4	1,037.1	1,043.0	1,039.9	1,041.0	1,042.7	1,053.3	1,074.2	1,086.2	1,044.3
2005	1,052.2	1,045.9	1,045.5	1,046.0	1,049.2	1,054.2	1,057.5	1,060.4	1,064.1	1,073.5	1,093.8	1,114.4	1,063.1
2006	1,072.3	1,067.4	1,071.2	1,068.7	1,071.7	1,077.1	1,077.9	1,082.3	1,086.4	1,093.5	1,115.2	1,132.6	1,084.7
2007	1,092.0	1,083.1	1,081.0	1,080.6	1,082.5	1,086.8	1,092.2	1,091.5	1,092.6	1,100.6	1,122.1	1,141.4	1,095.5
2008	1,093.6	1,085.1	1,080.8	1,077.1	1,076.3	1,076.8	1,073.1	1,067.6	1,063.2	1,064.9	1,068.9	1,074.0	1,075.1
2009	1,027.7	1,010.8	1,002.4	989.3	989.5	985.7	974.1	973.2	976.4	981.5	995.4	1,008.2	992.9
2010	978.0	972.0	970.4	975.9	980.8	982.8	980.9	983.6	981.9	990.5	1,007.8	1,021.6	985.5
2011	988.4	984.9	982.4	986.3	988.9	990.2	992.2	996.1	995.2	999.4	1,022.2	1,035.7	996.8
2012	1,004.6	994.2	995.6	1,002.7	1,007.4	1,011.4	1,010.7	1,013.1	1,014.0	1,019.9	1,050.6	1,060.2	1,015.4
2013	1,024.3	1,018.5	1,014.7	1,019.3	1,023.7	1,027.5	1,028.4	1,031.9	1,030.3	1,039.2	1,068.9	1,074.8	1,033.5
Wholesale Trade													
2002	294.0	295.4	297.4	297.1	297.4	298.4	297.9	298.5	299.1	298.1	298.7	300.0	297.7
2003	295.7	296.3	297.1	295.8	295.8	296.6	294.6	294.4	294.5	293.7	293.0	294.7	295.2
2004	292.2	293.3	295.0	294.9	295.6	297.3	295.8	294.9	294.5	296.9	297.2	297.1	295.4
2005	295.8	296.7	297.8	299.6	300.5	301.3	300.4	300.4	300.6	301.7	301.9	304.5	300.1
2006	301.3	303.5	304.8	305.3	306.3	307.7	308.1	308.1	309.2	309.7	310.0	312.3	307.2
2007	311.0	312.5	313.9	313.4	313.3	313.8	314.0	313.6	314.0	315.3	315.0	316.8	313.9
2008	313.9	314.6	315.0	314.6	313.0	312.8	310.6	308.7	307.9	306.7	303.7	302.4	310.3
2009	295.4	292.9	290.7	287.0	285.6	284.6	279.8	278.4	277.4	278.6	277.6	278.6	283.9
2010	277.0	277.4	278.1	280.1	281.1	281.4	281.0	281.1	280.9	282.8	282.7	283.4	280.6
2011	280.1	281.2	281.1	282.3	282.7	282.4	282.1	282.3	282.7	282.6	282.5	283.9	282.2
2012	281.0	282.1	282.9	287.2	288.7	289.3	288.8	289.9	289.9	291.3	292.5	294.6	288.2
2013	292.0	293.7	294.8	296.4	297.3	298.6	297.5	298.1	297.7	297.8	299.5	300.6	297.0
Retail Trade													
2002	545.3	536.9	540.0	539.1	541.9	546.5	543.5	545.1	548.6	551.4	569.0	587.4	549.6
2003	549.1	542.9	543.0	540.9	543.1	546.3	543.5	545.5	547.9	564.6	571.3	587.2	552.1
2004	548.9	544.2	546.2	548.6	552.3	556.1	554.0	556.1	556.4	561.7	581.9	596.7	558.6
2005	566.7	558.9	558.6	556.1	559.0	563.2	566.8	570.2	573.3	579.7	600.4	617.4	572.5
2006	580.6	572.7	574.5	571.9	573.5	576.6	576.6	580.8	581.9	588.2	608.6	622.7	584.1
2007	587.4	576.9	576.5	573.4	575.5	579.2	583.0	585.1	583.0	589.1	610.6	626.3	587.2
2008	588.6	577.1	575.7	571.4	569.9	570.7	568.1	564.8	563.6	565.1	573.8	579.9	572.4
2009	547.0	535.0	529.4	522.8	524.2	522.8	518.5	519.8	522.7	525.8	540.7	551.1	530.0
2010	526.1	519.2	517.8	520.8	522.1	523.2	523.1	525.2	523.5	528.3	545.9	556.9	527.7
2011	531.8	525.2	524.1	524.9	527.0	528.7	531.1	533.6	533.2	537.1	559.2	569.2	535.4
2012	544.8	533.7	533.2	533.3	536.0	537.9	538.3	540.4	540.5	545.4	574.2	579.1	544.7
2013	548.5	540.6	538.6	540.2	542.9	545.5	546.5	548.6	547.5	555.1	580.5	585.4	551.7
Transportation and Utilities													
2002	194.2	195.6	192.9	195.9	196.9	197.1	195.6	196.8	196.6	196.3	195.9	197.1	195.9
2003	192.5	192.2	191.7	190.8	190.9	190.7	189.5	188.6	190.8	190.2	190.2	188.2	190.5
2004	187.1	186.8	188.3	188.9	189.2	189.6	190.1	190.0	191.8	194.7	195.1	192.4	190.3
2005	189.7	190.3	189.1	190.3	189.7	189.7	190.3	189.8	190.2	192.1	191.5	192.5	190.4
2006	190.4	191.2	191.9	191.5	191.9	192.8	193.2	193.4	195.3	195.6	196.6	197.6	193.5
2007	193.6	193.7	190.6	193.8	193.7	193.8	195.2	192.8	195.6	196.2	196.5	198.3	194.5
2008	191.1	193.4	190.1	191.1	193.4	193.3	194.4	194.1	191.7	193.1	191.4	191.7	192.4
2009	185.3	182.9	182.3	179.5	179.7	178.3	175.8	175.0	176.3	177.1	177.1	178.5	179.0
2010	174.9	175.4	174.5	175.0	177.6	178.2	176.8	177.3	177.5	179.4	179.2	181.3	177.3
2011	176.5	178.5	177.2	179.1	179.2	179.1	179.0	180.2	179.3	179.7	180.5	182.6	179.2
2012	178.8	178.4	179.5	182.2	182.7	184.2	183.6	182.8	183.6	183.2	183.9	186.5	182.5
2013	183.8	184.2	181.3	182.7	183.5	183.4	184.4	185.2	185.1	186.3	188.9	188.8	184.8
Information													
2002	247.2	249.4	257.3	245.3	244.6	245.1	235.2	242.3	235.5	242.6	250.0	234.3	244.1
2003	237.1	241.5	239.6	233.7	237.1	229.3	230.1	241.8	230.9	241.9	246.8	240.9	237.6
2004	246.6	249.6	245.5	244.1	249.4	238.3	241.4	243.1	235.2	249.2	257.1	248.1	245.6
2005	238.6	240.3	245.0	237.9	236.7	236.7	234.5	240.5	240.8	241.0	247.8	244.3	240.3
2006	238.9	245.8	245.1	239.0	239.5	240.9	234.5	235.3	232.2	230.4	230.9	236.8	237.4
2007	234.7	241.2	248.9	237.6	241.1	243.4	240.2	244.2	244.5	233.5	238.0	244.6	241.0
2008	226.6	234.8	243.4	242.6	246.6	248.9	240.1	241.4	245.3	240.5	236.5	237.7	240.4
2009	218.5	221.8	225.4	217.8	216.7	219.3	215.3	216.6	220.9	212.4	215.2	222.6	218.5
2010	211.8	212.4	216.0	210.5	211.4	215.2	215.5	220.4	222.4	216.1	218.7	225.0	216.3
2011	219.0	218.4	219.6	215.5	214.3	214.2	213.7	215.9	214.2	215.4	212.8	216.1	215.8
2012	210.2	210.9	213.0	216.9	213.6	211.2	215.0	217.4	214.0	218.1	222.5	225.7	215.7
2013	216.9	218.7	220.3	219.5	217.8	219.1	220.4	224.6	226.5	229.5	230.9	228.1	222.7

Employment by Industry: Los Angeles-Long Beach-Santa Ana, CA, Selected Years, 2002–2013—*Continued*

(Numbers in thousands, not seasonally adjusted)

Industry and year	January	February	March	April	May	June	July	August	September	October	November	December	Annual average
Financial Activities													
2002	334.2	336.5	337.6	337.8	338.7	340.5	340.7	342.3	342.9	344.3	346.7	349.4	341.0
2003	349.1	351.3	353.7	356.5	358.9	360.9	362.1	364.8	364.7	365.5	365.7	367.8	360.1
2004	367.3	368.7	370.6	370.6	370.4	371.5	372.9	373.2	372.3	374.0	374.9	376.6	371.9
2005	373.0	374.6	376.4	378.1	379.0	379.8	380.7	382.1	382.8	385.0	385.6	388.4	380.5
2006	384.4	385.4	386.4	385.7	386.5	385.5	384.4	384.6	383.9	383.8	383.1	384.9	384.9
2007	380.0	381.1	381.4	377.6	375.3	373.1	371.5	369.4	364.8	363.6	361.0	359.1	371.5
2008	353.8	353.7	352.8	350.7	349.5	348.4	346.9	344.9	341.5	339.4	337.6	337.5	346.4
2009	330.7	328.6	327.8	324.9	322.5	322.1	319.4	317.5	314.8	315.3	314.3	315.4	321.1
2010	310.8	310.9	311.8	311.9	311.9	313.0	313.5	313.5	313.1	314.1	314.2	316.5	312.9
2011	312.7	312.9	313.7	311.5	311.4	312.6	313.2	313.7	312.8	313.8	313.6	315.8	313.1
2012	311.5	312.9	314.5	316.4	317.7	319.4	320.8	321.3	320.8	322.6	323.5	325.6	318.9
2013	322.0	323.1	323.6	324.9	325.7	326.7	326.4	326.0	323.4	324.2	322.4	322.7	324.3
Professional and Business Services													
2002	812.1	815.5	824.2	823.0	823.9	824.3	820.3	826.7	827.7	829.3	828.3	830.6	823.8
2003	806.4	808.9	816.0	812.7	811.7	812.2	808.7	815.7	813.0	813.8	813.8	817.1	812.5
2004	794.8	801.0	808.3	810.0	814.5	818.9	820.8	823.9	821.4	828.9	831.5	834.1	817.3
2005	820.8	827.2	829.6	835.1	834.9	838.7	838.4	845.0	849.0	852.5	855.4	859.0	840.5
2006	846.1	856.3	862.1	865.2	866.4	875.7	875.8	882.6	883.5	889.4	889.0	888.8	873.4
2007	866.5	875.9	881.5	871.5	872.0	878.8	876.4	881.1	882.8	885.4	884.8	887.9	878.7
2008	851.0	859.9	862.2	860.1	855.4	855.0	851.9	850.7	846.2	843.1	831.8	826.1	849.5
2009	795.7	791.1	785.6	772.6	768.4	765.9	755.6	756.5	755.7	766.8	767.2	766.9	770.7
2010	753.1	758.9	760.8	766.9	766.8	771.4	768.6	773.6	771.8	792.1	790.4	790.9	772.1
2011	772.5	780.6	782.6	779.9	780.4	784.7	789.8	792.3	798.3	804.0	806.4	810.7	790.2
2012	792.3	805.9	814.6	820.8	824.9	831.0	829.4	835.0	838.6	848.9	857.0	859.7	829.8
2013	829.7	840.5	844.2	847.5	850.5	852.7	849.7	859.0	859.1	873.0	874.2	876.5	854.7
Education and Health Services													
2002	611.5	622.7	627.8	634.4	635.0	628.2	621.3	623.2	636.7	646.2	649.8	651.9	632.4
2003	638.9	651.5	658.0	664.4	665.1	659.1	653.4	655.4	669.5	679.2	681.6	684.8	663.4
2004	672.4	684.4	689.1	689.9	687.6	678.8	671.2	673.0	686.9	694.8	696.2	698.4	685.2
2005	687.6	698.2	702.0	707.4	707.6	701.6	690.7	694.0	711.7	719.7	722.0	723.8	705.5
2006	710.9	722.8	725.7	727.6	726.3	718.8	707.3	709.6	726.9	736.0	738.1	739.9	724.2
2007	729.1	741.9	746.4	746.7	746.4	737.2	731.3	731.4	750.9	761.0	764.5	766.1	746.1
2008	756.4	768.9	772.3	776.4	775.4	767.4	763.1	764.0	784.2	794.4	799.0	801.5	776.9
2009	786.2	798.9	803.4	805.4	805.4	796.0	788.6	786.8	802.3	813.5	813.5	813.9	801.2
2010	796.1	803.3	806.5	809.7	805.0	793.7	782.6	785.8	803.7	813.0	815.6	817.1	802.7
2011	804.4	816.0	819.1	816.8	813.7	801.5	790.4	792.1	808.3	818.5	823.3	828.1	811.0
2012	822.1	838.0	838.0	844.9	846.2	835.8	822.5	830.0	841.1	882.4	884.5	888.9	847.9
2013	878.1	890.4	893.9	890.8	888.2	877.0	883.8	890.6	901.6	914.5	916.7	917.6	895.3
Leisure and Hospitality													
2002	490.7	495.7	501.5	507.9	513.4	516.5	519.9	520.1	517.7	513.0	508.2	511.2	509.7
2003	499.7	505.0	509.3	516.9	522.7	528.8	531.6	532.2	528.1	527.5	524.7	527.5	521.2
2004	518.4	524.6	529.4	531.9	538.0	541.1	546.6	544.9	540.3	539.0	535.4	538.2	535.7
2005	522.0	526.6	533.5	541.5	544.9	551.2	552.9	551.3	548.0	546.7	544.9	549.3	542.7
2006	536.4	541.3	547.8	554.7	560.5	567.3	567.0	568.1	563.8	564.8	560.8	565.1	558.1
2007	550.4	553.3	560.0	568.0	572.7	579.6	581.7	580.2	575.9	577.4	573.8	576.6	570.8
2008	562.8	566.3	573.2	581.5	585.0	590.6	592.2	588.0	581.1	576.5	569.4	569.3	578.0
2009	550.6	548.8	551.2	554.3	561.0	562.0	562.6	559.3	555.9	554.7	547.4	548.3	554.7
2010	533.3	534.9	539.1	551.7	556.7	561.1	565.3	564.6	561.5	559.0	554.7	558.2	553.4
2011	547.5	551.2	555.6	564.6	569.8	573.2	578.9	579.8	579.6	574.1	574.6	574.4	568.6
2012	566.4	570.8	577.8	590.8	600.5	606.5	606.8	609.1	606.0	604.5	604.6	606.6	595.9
2013	596.0	603.2	609.4	619.6	630.1	636.4	638.4	636.2	633.8	634.0	628.7	629.0	624.6
Other Services													
2002	185.5	188.0	189.6	190.4	192.4	193.3	192.6	192.2	193.4	193.7	192.8	193.3	191.4
2003	189.8	191.2	192.4	192.4	193.4	194.7	191.5	191.3	192.8	192.7	191.8	192.0	192.2
2004	189.1	190.5	192.4	192.6	193.6	194.3	192.6	191.2	192.7	191.9	191.5	192.0	192.0
2005	189.3	191.4	193.2	193.9	194.2	195.5	191.8	191.5	193.0	192.7	192.3	192.6	192.6
2006	189.8	191.6	192.9	192.2	193.9	195.5	192.0	192.0	194.2	193.7	193.8	193.7	192.9
2007	190.2	192.6	194.0	194.1	194.7	196.5	194.5	194.2	195.8	196.4	195.6	195.5	194.5
2008	192.3	193.3	194.5	195.2	195.3	195.2	193.4	190.8	191.4	191.7	189.7	188.6	192.6
2009	183.5	183.2	183.7	181.5	181.9	182.1	178.8	177.1	177.3	179.9	178.6	178.4	180.5
2010	175.7	175.4	176.6	179.4	180.3	181.1	180.1	178.5	179.9	180.7	179.5	178.6	178.8
2011	176.4	178.0	178.5	179.5	180.1	180.5	181.1	180.0	182.1	181.8	181.3	182.2	180.1
2012	180.3	182.1	183.4	185.5	187.4	187.9	186.9	186.3	187.9	189.3	188.6	188.1	186.1
2013	186.0	188.2	189.4	190.7	191.4	191.9	191.6	191.2	191.7	194.0	193.3	192.2	191.0
Government													
2002	759.1	763.4	774.1	773.4	776.5	773.6	730.2	721.7	749.5	768.0	773.1	771.5	761.2
2003	762.8	766.5	773.8	768.6	768.1	767.1	734.0	716.4	731.8	749.0	753.2	750.3	753.5
2004	747.0	748.3	754.8	753.6	754.8	752.7	718.1	700.8	723.9	741.3	747.1	743.6	740.5
2005	738.3	745.5	750.2	747.8	750.2	750.1	715.1	706.0	724.6	741.8	749.7	748.4	739.0
2006	741.4	748.7	754.7	754.0	756.5	756.3	724.7	712.0	733.4	753.0	760.3	758.5	746.1
2007	751.6	757.8	763.9	762.8	765.0	765.2	732.6	719.8	741.9	761.7	769.6	768.8	755.1
2008	762.7	770.7	775.4	776.2	780.0	778.3	740.1	728.2	747.2	768.5	774.9	771.5	764.5
2009	767.1	770.7	776.0	777.6	775.1	774.0	727.7	704.4	711.6	748.1	750.2	747.3	752.5
2010	741.0	743.8	748.7	756.9	770.8	757.1	700.9	676.8	694.3	727.5	733.6	730.7	731.8
2011	724.8	727.8	734.4	733.2	734.2	734.6	678.1	662.5	687.5	715.8	724.2	719.6	714.7
2012	709.5	718.5	724.3	721.9	724.5	723.2	668.1	659.8	684.5	703.5	709.9	708.3	704.7
2013	698.2	707.3	713.9	709.0	711.1	711.1	659.4	662.5	682.9	700.6	706.7	707.0	697.5

Employment by Industry: Louisville/Jefferson County, KY–IN, Selected Years, 2002–2013

(Numbers in thousands, not seasonally adjusted)

Industry and year	January	February	March	April	May	June	July	August	September	October	November	December	Annual average
Total Nonfarm													
2002	586.1	587.1	591.2	596.0	601.4	601.9	594.6	600.6	599.9	600.6	602.5	602.7	597.1
2003	585.5	585.5	590.9	594.2	599.0	601.7	591.3	596.9	598.1	599.3	601.4	603.5	595.6
2004	586.4	587.7	593.2	597.5	599.5	602.9	593.2	603.1	604.2	606.2	609.6	609.3	599.4
2005	591.4	594.4	598.1	604.2	608.2	613.2	601.9	609.7	612.5	613.6	617.2	615.9	606.7
2006	600.9	603.3	611.4	615.7	621.8	625.3	611.1	620.3	622.7	616.5	619.5	626.4	616.2
2007	611.6	611.7	615.0	623.4	631.6	635.8	623.1	626.3	628.8	627.2	633.0	630.7	624.9
2008	615.2	615.6	617.8	623.2	633.0	631.7	619.5	624.4	619.5	618.4	621.5	615.5	621.3
2009	592.0	591.4	593.0	597.4	599.6	599.0	592.6	595.0	595.1	596.0	597.4	595.3	595.3
2010	579.0	573.7	584.5	592.1	599.2	599.4	591.2	594.2	595.8	599.5	603.1	604.8	593.0
2011	584.4	586.4	591.7	597.9	600.0	602.7	593.4	600.4	602.2	603.1	608.1	606.1	598.0
2012	594.2	593.5	601.6	607.5	615.3	617.9	611.5	616.4	618.9	620.9	627.9	628.9	612.9
2013	612.9	613.7	618.8	623.9	628.2	629.2	621.0	630.7	631.6	630.9	634.5	635.2	625.9
Total Private													
2002	510.3	510.1	514.1	518.3	524.1	525.8	523.6	526.5	523.6	523.6	525.4	525.7	520.9
2003	509.9	509.0	513.8	515.6	520.4	523.3	520.1	522.8	521.4	522.1	523.9	526.7	519.1
2004	511.1	510.9	516.0	519.8	522.1	525.7	520.6	528.4	526.7	528.9	531.9	532.4	522.9
2005	514.8	517.0	520.3	526.1	529.7	535.1	527.8	533.6	533.9	534.9	538.2	537.2	529.1
2006	523.1	524.5	532.3	536.2	541.9	546.0	535.6	542.1	541.6	536.5	539.3	546.6	537.1
2007	533.2	532.5	535.4	542.4	550.3	554.8	546.5	547.4	548.2	547.2	552.6	550.2	545.1
2008	535.1	534.5	536.4	541.9	551.3	550.5	542.8	545.6	538.7	537.1	540.0	534.4	540.7
2009	512.0	511.3	512.4	515.8	517.5	517.8	514.7	514.7	512.3	512.4	514.2	513.1	514.0
2010	497.6	492.0	501.1	507.6	512.8	514.9	511.4	513.8	513.8	517.1	520.8	523.3	510.5
2011	503.4	504.7	509.6	515.4	517.3	521.0	515.3	519.6	519.0	519.8	524.4	522.8	516.0
2012	511.4	510.3	517.9	523.7	531.6	535.0	532.7	535.3	535.5	537.1	543.9	545.2	530.0
2013	530.0	529.7	534.2	539.9	543.9	545.8	541.5	548.4	547.3	546.5	549.9	550.9	542.3
Goods Producing													
2002	117.5	117.2	117.5	118.6	118.5	119.6	119.6	120.6	120.4	119.8	119.1	118.8	118.9
2003	114.3	113.7	114.3	114.4	114.8	115.5	115.3	115.8	115.7	116.7	115.7	116.5	115.2
2004	113.9	112.7	113.7	115.6	115.9	116.6	110.6	117.2	117.3	116.8	117.0	116.2	115.3
2005	112.8	112.9	113.7	114.9	115.2	116.9	111.3	116.0	115.5	115.4	115.7	114.5	114.6
2006	112.1	111.8	112.5	113.3	114.3	115.6	109.4	115.2	114.7	109.6	109.3	113.3	112.6
2007	110.2	109.4	107.8	112.1	113.7	115.3	109.5	110.6	113.6	109.2	112.7	109.7	111.2
2008	108.0	108.2	108.5	108.2	111.6	110.5	105.8	108.4	106.1	105.0	107.3	102.7	107.5
2009	97.0	97.1	95.9	96.9	95.9	95.7	94.2	95.1	94.6	94.1	93.4	92.3	95.2
2010	88.9	84.0	88.7	89.5	90.3	91.0	88.6	91.0	91.4	91.2	91.0	90.4	89.7
2011	86.6	86.7	87.6	89.1	89.5	91.2	88.3	91.6	92.0	91.8	92.4	91.4	89.9
2012	90.4	89.3	93.0	94.8	96.4	98.2	98.6	99.1	99.5	99.5	100.0	100.1	96.6
2013	97.9	97.9	98.5	99.7	100.5	101.7	99.0	102.7	102.6	101.0	100.4	98.1	100.0
Service-Providing													
2002	468.6	469.9	473.7	477.4	482.9	482.3	475.0	480.0	479.5	480.8	483.4	483.9	478.1
2003	471.2	471.8	476.6	479.8	484.2	486.2	476.0	481.1	482.4	482.6	485.7	487.0	480.4
2004	472.5	475.0	479.5	481.9	483.6	486.3	482.6	485.9	486.9	489.4	492.6	493.1	484.1
2005	478.6	481.5	484.4	489.3	493.0	496.3	490.6	493.7	497.0	498.2	501.5	501.4	492.1
2006	488.8	491.5	498.9	502.4	507.5	509.7	501.7	505.1	508.0	506.9	510.2	513.1	503.7
2007	501.4	502.3	507.2	511.3	517.9	520.5	513.6	515.7	515.2	518.0	520.3	521.0	513.7
2008	507.2	507.4	509.3	515.0	521.4	521.2	513.7	516.0	513.4	513.4	514.2	512.8	513.8
2009	495.0	494.3	497.1	500.5	503.7	503.3	498.4	499.9	500.5	501.9	504.0	503.0	500.1
2010	490.1	489.7	495.8	502.6	508.9	508.4	502.6	503.2	504.4	508.3	512.1	514.4	503.4
2011	497.8	499.7	504.1	508.8	510.5	511.5	505.1	508.8	510.2	511.3	515.7	514.7	508.2
2012	503.8	504.2	508.6	512.7	518.9	519.7	512.9	517.3	519.4	521.4	527.9	528.8	516.3
2013	515.0	515.8	520.3	524.2	527.7	527.5	522.0	528.0	529.0	529.9	534.1	537.1	525.9
Mining, Logging, and Construction													
2002	30.4	30.7	31.1	31.9	32.6	33.6	33.9	34.2	34.3	33.8	33.6	33.1	32.8
2003	30.8	30.3	31.2	32.1	32.4	32.9	33.4	33.4	33.2	34.2	33.6	33.6	32.6
2004	31.6	31.0	32.1	33.7	34.1	35.0	36.0	35.6	35.7	35.3	35.0	34.4	34.1
2005	31.5	32.1	32.8	34.1	34.7	36.2	37.1	36.2	35.8	35.9	35.5	34.8	34.7
2006	32.5	32.2	32.9	33.4	34.1	34.6	34.7	34.4	34.1	33.6	33.2	33.0	33.6
2007	30.7	30.2	31.8	33.2	34.3	35.2	35.8	35.6	35.5	35.2	35.0	34.3	33.9
2008	32.2	31.9	32.4	34.0	35.2	35.8	35.8	35.8	35.5	35.3	34.6	33.8	34.4
2009	31.3	30.6	30.5	30.9	30.8	31.0	31.2	31.0	30.8	30.8	30.0	28.8	30.6
2010	26.1	25.1	25.8	26.8	26.8	27.3	27.9	27.4	27.0	26.7	26.2	25.3	26.5
2011	23.2	23.1	24.3	25.3	25.6	26.7	27.1	26.9	26.7	26.3	26.2	25.6	25.6
2012	24.0	23.8	24.8	25.5	26.0	26.7	26.7	26.4	26.2	25.8	26.0	25.7	25.6
2013	23.9	23.7	24.5	25.5	26.1	27.0	27.7	27.7	27.6	26.9	25.9	23.8	25.9
Manufacturing													
2002	87.1	86.5	86.4	86.7	85.9	86.0	85.7	86.4	86.1	86.0	85.5	85.7	86.2
2003	83.5	83.4	83.1	82.3	82.4	82.6	81.9	82.4	82.5	82.5	82.1	82.9	82.6
2004	82.3	81.7	81.6	81.9	81.8	81.6	74.6	81.6	81.6	81.5	82.0	81.8	81.2
2005	81.3	80.8	80.9	80.8	80.5	80.7	74.2	79.8	79.7	79.5	80.2	79.7	79.8
2006	79.6	79.6	79.6	79.9	80.2	81.0	74.7	80.8	80.6	76.0	76.1	80.3	79.0
2007	79.5	79.2	76.0	78.9	79.4	80.1	73.7	75.0	78.1	74.0	77.7	75.4	77.3
2008	75.8	76.3	76.1	74.2	76.4	74.7	70.0	72.6	70.6	69.7	72.7	68.9	73.2
2009	65.7	66.5	65.4	66.0	65.1	64.7	63.0	64.1	63.8	63.3	63.4	63.5	64.5
2010	62.8	58.9	62.9	62.7	63.5	63.7	60.7	63.6	64.4	64.5	64.8	65.1	63.1
2011	63.4	63.6	63.3	63.8	63.9	64.5	61.2	64.7	65.3	65.5	66.2	65.8	64.3
2012	66.4	65.5	68.2	69.3	70.4	71.5	71.9	72.7	73.3	73.7	74.0	74.4	70.9
2013	74.0	74.2	74.0	74.2	74.4	74.7	71.3	75.0	75.0	74.1	74.5	74.3	74.1

Employment by Industry: Louisville/Jefferson County, KY–IN, Selected Years, 2002–2013—*Continued*

(Numbers in thousands, not seasonally adjusted)

Industry and year	January	February	March	April	May	June	July	August	September	October	November	December	Annual average
Trade, Transportation, and Utilities													
2002	135.1	133.8	134.6	134.6	135.4	136.0	135.5	135.9	135.1	134.9	137.3	138.4	135.6
2003	131.2	130.3	130.7	130.1	131.0	131.1	130.5	131.4	131.3	132.3	134.3	136.1	131.7
2004	130.5	129.5	130.2	129.6	130.4	131.2	131.3	131.7	131.4	132.6	134.2	135.4	131.5
2005	130.9	130.0	130.9	131.6	132.4	132.8	132.8	133.0	133.5	134.7	137.8	139.4	133.3
2006	133.9	133.0	135.0	135.5	137.1	138.0	136.4	136.9	137.0	137.5	140.6	142.9	137.0
2007	138.1	136.9	137.8	137.9	139.2	140.7	139.3	139.6	139.8	141.5	143.5	145.2	140.0
2008	138.5	136.6	136.4	136.9	138.4	138.1	136.9	137.4	135.4	135.3	137.6	139.8	137.3
2009	131.1	129.3	129.3	128.7	129.4	129.6	128.2	128.0	127.7	128.4	130.8	132.7	129.4
2010	126.2	125.0	126.1	127.7	128.7	129.3	129.5	130.3	130.1	132.1	135.1	138.5	129.9
2011	130.6	130.0	130.9	131.7	131.8	132.5	131.6	131.9	131.3	131.9	135.2	136.7	132.2
2012	130.4	130.1	130.6	130.9	132.2	133.0	132.6	132.6	132.8	133.6	137.3	139.4	133.0
2013	132.9	132.5	133.3	133.5	134.4	135.1	134.6	135.6	136.4	135.9	138.3	141.4	135.3
Wholesale Trade													
2002	29.3	29.3	29.2	29.2	29.3	29.1	29.1	29.6	28.9	29.0	28.9	28.9	29.2
2003	28.5	28.7	28.7	28.5	28.7	28.8	28.7	28.8	29.0	28.9	29.1	29.5	28.8
2004	29.1	29.1	29.2	29.2	29.2	29.3	29.5	29.5	29.3	29.4	29.4	29.5	29.3
2005	29.3	29.4	29.5	29.4	29.5	29.6	29.7	29.6	29.6	29.6	29.7	29.8	29.6
2006	29.9	29.9	30.1	30.0	30.2	30.4	30.1	30.2	30.1	30.2	30.3	30.4	30.2
2007	30.3	30.4	30.5	30.3	30.3	30.4	30.2	30.2	30.3	30.1	30.2	30.3	30.3
2008	29.9	30.0	29.9	30.0	30.1	30.1	30.0	30.0	29.9	29.8	29.6	29.5	29.9
2009	28.7	28.5	28.3	28.3	28.2	28.0	27.9	27.9	28.0	28.0	27.9	27.9	28.1
2010	27.5	27.5	27.7	27.6	27.7	27.8	28.0	28.1	28.0	28.1	28.1	28.0	27.8
2011	27.9	28.0	28.1	28.0	28.1	28.2	28.3	28.4	28.4	28.4	28.4	28.5	28.2
2012	28.1	28.2	28.2	28.3	28.5	28.6	28.7	28.8	28.9	28.9	29.0	28.9	28.6
2013	29.0	29.2	29.2	29.2	29.2	29.3	29.4	29.5	29.6	29.8	29.2	29.7	29.4
Retail Trade													
2002	66.7	65.8	66.7	66.7	67.4	68.2	67.5	67.3	67.1	66.7	69.4	70.7	67.5
2003	65.4	64.4	64.8	64.7	65.5	65.7	65.2	65.6	65.4	65.9	68.0	69.3	65.8
2004	64.9	64.0	64.5	64.2	64.8	65.3	65.2	65.4	65.3	65.7	67.5	68.7	65.5
2005	65.0	63.9	64.4	64.8	65.3	65.5	65.2	65.0	64.9	65.7	67.9	69.2	65.6
2006	65.2	64.3	65.2	65.3	65.7	65.4	64.7	64.3	63.8	64.4	66.7	67.7	65.2
2007	64.7	63.7	64.4	64.3	65.1	65.7	65.6	65.3	65.0	65.2	67.3	67.9	65.4
2008	64.6	63.7	64.2	63.8	64.6	64.6	64.4	64.4	63.3	63.5	65.0	65.6	64.3
2009	61.6	60.4	60.7	60.7	61.3	61.5	61.0	60.7	60.3	61.0	62.7	63.4	61.3
2010	59.9	59.1	59.8	60.0	60.5	60.6	60.6	60.8	60.1	61.3	62.9	63.6	60.8
2011	60.2	59.6	60.2	60.9	61.0	61.0	60.6	60.7	60.0	60.9	62.9	63.6	61.0
2012	60.9	60.3	60.9	61.1	61.8	62.3	62.2	62.0	61.8	62.8	65.6	65.6	62.3
2013	62.2	61.7	62.1	62.5	63.2	63.5	63.2	63.4	63.2	63.0	65.2	65.3	63.2
Transportation and Utilities													
2002	39.1	38.7	38.7	38.7	38.7	38.7	38.9	39.0	39.1	39.2	39.0	38.8	38.9
2003	37.3	37.2	37.2	36.9	36.8	36.6	36.6	37.0	36.9	37.5	37.2	37.3	37.0
2004	36.5	36.4	36.5	36.2	36.4	36.6	36.6	36.8	36.8	37.5	37.3	37.2	36.7
2005	36.6	36.7	37.0	37.4	37.6	37.7	37.9	38.4	39.0	39.4	40.2	40.4	38.2
2006	38.8	38.8	39.7	40.2	41.2	42.2	41.6	42.4	43.1	42.9	43.6	44.8	41.6
2007	43.1	42.8	42.9	43.3	43.8	44.6	43.5	44.1	44.6	46.0	46.1	47.1	44.3
2008	44.0	42.9	42.3	43.1	43.7	43.4	42.5	43.0	42.2	42.0	43.0	44.7	43.1
2009	40.8	40.4	40.3	39.7	39.9	40.1	39.3	39.4	39.4	39.4	40.2	41.4	40.0
2010	38.8	38.4	38.6	40.1	40.5	40.9	40.9	41.4	42.0	42.7	44.1	46.9	41.3
2011	42.5	42.4	42.6	42.8	42.7	43.3	42.7	42.8	42.9	42.6	43.9	44.6	43.0
2012	41.4	41.6	41.5	41.5	41.9	42.1	41.7	41.8	42.1	41.9	42.7	44.9	42.1
2013	41.7	41.6	42.0	41.8	42.0	42.3	42.0	42.7	43.6	43.1	43.9	46.4	42.8
Information													
2002	11.9	11.9	12.0	11.5	11.3	11.4	11.4	11.2	11.2	11.1	11.2	11.3	11.5
2003	11.2	11.2	11.4	10.9	11.0	11.0	11.0	10.8	10.6	10.6	10.5	10.6	10.9
2004	10.4	10.4	10.3	10.2	10.2	10.3	10.3	10.2	10.1	10.0	10.1	10.2	10.2
2005	9.8	9.8	9.8	9.9	10.0	10.1	10.2	10.2	10.1	10.0	10.1	10.2	10.0
2006	9.9	10.0	10.0	10.0	10.1	10.2	10.2	10.2	10.1	10.3	10.3	10.5	10.2
2007	10.5	10.5	10.5	10.5	10.6	10.6	10.7	10.6	10.5	10.4	10.4	10.4	10.5
2008	10.4	10.3	10.4	10.4	10.6	10.9	10.8	10.7	10.5	10.3	10.3	10.2	10.5
2009	10.1	10.0	10.0	9.8	9.9	9.9	9.9	9.9	9.7	9.6	9.7	9.7	9.9
2010	9.4	9.4	9.5	9.5	9.5	9.6	9.5	9.5	9.4	9.3	9.4	9.5	9.5
2011	9.4	9.3	9.3	9.4	9.4	9.3	9.4	9.3	9.3	9.3	9.4	9.5	9.4
2012	9.4	9.3	9.7	9.8	9.8	9.7	9.7	9.7	9.5	9.4	9.5	9.5	9.6
2013	9.6	9.5	9.6	9.5	9.6	9.6	9.7	9.6	9.5	9.4	9.5	9.5	9.6
Financial Activities													
2002	38.0	38.2	38.2	38.4	38.6	38.6	37.8	37.9	38.3	38.1	38.2	38.3	38.2
2003	37.7	37.7	38.0	38.2	38.6	39.1	39.2	39.4	39.5	39.3	39.3	39.5	38.8
2004	39.2	39.2	39.3	39.1	39.0	39.1	39.3	39.2	38.8	38.7	39.0	39.4	39.1
2005	39.1	39.1	39.0	39.2	39.2	39.9	39.7	40.1	40.1	40.3	40.4	40.6	39.7
2006	40.8	41.1	41.4	41.5	41.8	42.2	41.9	42.0	42.2	42.1	42.5	43.1	41.9
2007	43.0	43.0	43.1	43.3	43.3	43.6	43.7	43.6	43.3	43.5	43.5	43.5	43.4
2008	43.2	43.4	43.3	43.3	43.5	43.4	43.5	43.6	43.4	43.2	43.3	43.2	43.4
2009	42.9	42.7	42.6	42.6	42.6	42.6	42.7	42.4	42.1	41.9	41.8	42.0	42.4
2010	41.5	41.3	41.1	40.7	40.8	40.8	40.7	40.5	40.0	40.3	40.5	40.7	40.7
2011	40.4	40.6	40.6	40.1	40.2	40.4	40.4	40.6	40.9	40.8	40.9	41.1	40.6
2012	40.8	40.7	40.9	40.7	41.0	41.5	41.8	41.9	42.0	42.1	42.3	42.7	41.5
2013	42.5	42.5	42.7	42.6	42.8	43.1	43.3	43.4	43.4	43.5	44.3	44.2	43.2

Employment by Industry: Louisville/Jefferson County, KY–IN, Selected Years, 2002–2013—*Continued*

(Numbers in thousands, not seasonally adjusted)

Industry and year	January	February	March	April	May	June	July	August	September	October	November	December	Annual average
Professional and Business Services													
2002	60.4	60.5	61.4	61.8	63.4	63.1	62.5	63.9	63.0	63.5	63.8	63.3	62.6
2003	62.6	62.6	63.6	63.8	64.9	64.5	63.2	64.5	64.7	64.7	65.5	65.4	64.2
2004	61.2	62.0	63.2	63.2	63.8	63.8	64.9	66.4	66.9	68.2	69.3	68.9	65.2
2005	65.3	65.9	66.7	67.7	68.0	68.8	68.2	69.0	70.0	70.8	71.8	71.2	68.6
2006	68.0	68.7	71.6	71.2	71.5	72.3	71.5	72.2	73.1	73.0	73.0	73.2	71.6
2007	70.5	71.2	72.6	72.7	74.4	74.6	73.9	74.2	73.9	75.2	75.8	75.2	73.7
2008	72.1	72.2	72.5	74.0	75.3	76.1	74.9	74.9	74.7	74.8	74.5	72.9	74.1
2009	68.6	69.4	69.4	69.6	69.3	69.3	69.9	70.2	70.3	71.5	72.3	71.5	70.1
2010	69.7	69.9	70.7	72.4	72.8	73.2	73.0	72.7	73.9	73.9	74.6	75.2	72.7
2011	70.9	71.8	72.6	73.1	73.4	73.8	73.5	74.3	74.6	76.1	76.1	76.3	73.9
2012	73.3	72.7	73.3	74.8	75.8	75.8	75.0	76.5	77.3	78.5	79.9	79.8	76.1
2013	75.6	75.1	76.1	77.7	77.7	78.0	77.6	79.8	79.0	80.2	82.0	82.4	78.4
Education and Health Services													
2002	68.3	68.7	68.8	69.6	69.6	69.9	70.6	70.9	71.0	72.1	72.5	72.7	70.4
2003	72.6	72.9	73.4	73.5	73.3	73.3	73.0	73.3	73.8	73.8	73.9	74.2	73.4
2004	74.1	74.3	74.5	74.6	74.5	74.8	75.1	75.0	75.2	76.5	76.6	77.0	75.2
2005	75.5	76.9	76.3	76.4	76.7	76.7	76.7	76.7	76.8	77.0	76.6	76.6	76.6
2006	75.9	76.2	76.5	77.1	76.9	77.0	76.8	76.6	76.8	77.0	76.9	77.4	76.8
2007	76.7	77.1	77.4	77.7	78.3	78.6	79.2	78.8	78.8	79.6	79.4	79.6	78.4
2008	79.2	79.1	79.3	80.3	80.4	80.4	80.3	80.5	80.4	80.9	80.8	80.9	80.2
2009	80.6	80.5	81.0	81.5	81.6	81.8	81.5	82.4	82.7	83.3	83.2	83.4	82.0
2010	82.7	82.8	83.4	83.5	84.0	83.6	83.8	83.9	84.2	84.7	84.9	85.0	83.9
2011	84.3	84.3	84.6	84.0	84.0	84.1	84.2	84.3	84.7	84.5	84.5	83.7	84.3
2012	84.4	84.6	84.7	85.0	85.2	85.4	85.1	85.4	85.7	86.2	86.5	86.7	85.4
2013	85.5	85.7	86.0	86.0	85.6	85.1	85.1	85.1	85.5	85.8	85.2	85.7	85.5
Leisure and Hospitality													
2002	50.7	51.3	52.9	54.8	58.2	57.5	56.9	56.9	55.6	55.0	54.2	53.6	54.8
2003	51.6	51.9	53.4	55.7	57.6	58.9	58.5	58.3	56.9	55.8	55.9	55.3	55.8
2004	53.3	54.0	55.6	58.1	58.8	60.0	59.8	59.4	58.2	57.5	57.3	56.6	57.4
2005	53.2	54.0	55.3	58.2	59.6	61.1	60.6	60.3	59.7	58.4	57.5	56.3	57.9
2006	54.6	55.6	56.9	59.4	61.9	61.9	61.1	60.9	59.9	59.2	59.0	58.2	59.1
2007	56.5	56.7	58.3	60.1	62.4	62.7	62.1	61.9	60.4	60.0	59.5	58.6	59.9
2008	56.4	57.3	58.5	61.1	63.4	62.9	63.0	62.5	61.2	60.2	59.1	57.8	60.3
2009	55.4	56.0	57.8	60.4	62.6	62.4	62.1	60.7	59.5	58.4	57.9	56.4	59.1
2010	54.4	54.8	56.4	59.0	61.2	61.5	60.7	60.4	59.6	60.2	59.9	58.5	58.9
2011	56.0	56.7	58.5	62.5	63.5	63.8	62.0	62.0	60.8	60.1	60.6	58.7	60.4
2012	57.4	58.2	60.1	62.2	65.8	65.6	64.3	64.8	63.6	62.7	63.3	61.7	62.5
2013	60.7	61.1	62.4	65.3	67.6	67.3	66.5	66.5	65.4	65.3	64.8	64.1	64.8
Other Services													
2002	28.4	28.5	28.7	29.0	29.1	29.7	29.3	29.2	29.0	29.1	29.1	29.3	29.0
2003	28.7	28.7	29.0	29.0	29.2	29.9	29.4	29.3	28.9	28.9	28.8	29.1	29.1
2004	28.5	28.8	29.2	29.4	29.5	29.9	29.3	29.3	28.8	28.6	28.4	28.7	29.0
2005	28.2	28.4	28.6	28.2	28.6	28.8	28.3	28.3	28.2	28.3	28.3	28.4	28.4
2006	27.9	28.1	28.4	28.2	28.3	28.8	28.3	28.1	27.8	27.8	27.7	28.0	28.1
2007	27.7	27.7	27.9	28.1	28.4	28.7	28.1	28.1	27.9	27.8	27.8	28.0	28.0
2008	27.3	27.4	27.5	27.7	28.1	28.2	27.6	27.6	27.0	27.4	27.1	26.9	27.5
2009	26.3	26.3	26.4	26.3	26.2	26.5	26.2	26.0	25.7	25.2	25.1	25.1	25.9
2010	24.8	24.8	25.2	25.3	25.5	25.9	25.6	25.5	25.2	25.4	25.4	25.5	25.3
2011	25.2	25.3	25.5	25.5	25.5	25.9	25.9	25.6	25.4	25.3	25.3	25.4	25.5
2012	25.3	25.4	25.6	25.5	25.4	25.8	25.6	25.3	25.1	25.1	25.1	25.3	25.4
2013	25.3	25.4	25.6	25.6	25.7	25.9	25.7	25.7	25.5	25.4	25.4	25.5	25.6
Government													
2002	75.8	77.0	77.1	77.7	77.3	76.1	71.0	74.1	76.3	77.0	77.1	77.0	76.1
2003	75.6	76.5	77.1	78.6	78.6	78.4	71.2	74.1	76.7	77.2	77.5	76.8	76.5
2004	75.3	76.8	77.2	77.7	77.4	77.2	72.6	74.7	77.5	77.3	77.7	76.9	76.5
2005	76.6	77.4	77.8	78.1	78.5	78.1	74.1	76.1	78.6	78.7	79.0	78.7	77.6
2006	77.8	78.8	79.1	79.5	79.9	79.3	75.5	78.2	81.1	80.0	80.2	79.8	79.1
2007	78.4	79.2	79.6	81.0	81.3	81.0	76.6	78.9	80.6	80.0	80.4	80.5	79.8
2008	80.1	81.1	81.4	81.3	81.7	81.2	76.7	78.8	80.8	81.3	81.5	81.1	80.6
2009	80.0	80.1	80.6	81.6	82.1	81.2	77.9	80.3	82.8	83.6	83.2	82.2	81.3
2010	81.4	81.7	83.4	84.5	86.4	84.5	79.8	80.4	82.0	82.4	82.3	81.5	82.5
2011	81.0	81.7	82.1	82.5	82.7	81.7	78.1	80.8	83.2	83.3	83.7	83.3	82.0
2012	82.8	83.2	83.7	83.8	83.7	82.9	78.8	81.1	83.4	83.8	84.0	83.7	82.9
2013	82.9	84.0	84.6	84.0	84.3	83.4	79.5	82.3	84.3	84.4	84.6	84.3	83.6

Employment by Industry: McAllen-Edinburg-Mission, TX, Selected Years, 2002–2013

(Numbers in thousands, not seasonally adjusted)

Industry and year	January	February	March	April	May	June	July	August	September	October	November	December	Annual average
Total Nonfarm													
2002	165.1	166.1	168.1	168.1	168.1	168.0	161.3	165.6	168.4	170.2	172.9	173.7	168.0
2003	172.1	173.8	174.6	174.9	175.6	175.0	170.0	172.7	176.0	178.0	180.9	183.0	175.6
2004	181.4	182.6	184.0	184.9	186.1	184.7	179.3	183.0	185.2	188.0	191.0	192.6	185.2
2005	189.7	191.9	193.3	196.0	195.4	194.8	187.5	192.3	195.1	198.0	199.9	201.8	194.6
2006	200.8	201.7	202.7	202.2	201.6	201.6	192.8	198.2	201.5	205.4	208.4	209.8	202.2
2007	208.1	208.7	209.9	211.8	211.5	210.6	206.3	210.3	211.9	215.8	218.0	219.4	211.9
2008	218.9	219.9	220.3	221.2	220.9	218.4	212.8	215.4	216.3	221.4	222.1	222.9	219.2
2009	218.7	217.9	217.9	219.2	219.3	216.3	211.6	213.8	215.3	219.1	220.5	220.9	217.5
2010	218.6	218.9	220.2	219.7	221.6	219.9	210.5	214.1	217.7	221.3	223.5	225.3	219.3
2011	222.7	223.3	224.9	225.9	226.5	225.2	219.1	222.5	224.2	225.0	228.4	229.4	224.8
2012	226.9	227.8	229.7	229.8	229.8	228.7	221.9	225.1	227.1	230.3	233.7	235.3	228.8
2013	230.7	232.9	234.5	234.8	235.2	234.6	227.1	231.3	233.0	235.4	238.2	238.9	233.9
Total Private													
2002	122.0	122.4	124.0	124.2	124.1	124.5	123.7	125.7	125.6	125.4	127.5	128.4	124.8
2003	127.0	128.5	129.3	129.3	129.8	130.2	130.2	131.4	131.6	132.1	134.1	136.1	130.8
2004	134.9	135.6	136.8	137.6	138.5	138.3	138.0	139.1	138.8	140.3	142.7	144.5	138.8
2005	142.0	143.3	144.6	147.3	146.7	146.7	146.5	147.0	147.5	148.7	150.2	152.1	146.9
2006	150.8	151.0	152.1	152.5	152.0	151.9	151.7	152.4	153.5	154.9	157.4	158.9	153.3
2007	157.9	157.9	158.8	161.2	160.8	160.2	161.3	162.5	161.9	163.9	165.5	166.6	161.5
2008	166.6	167.0	167.1	168.1	167.1	165.9	165.6	166.2	164.4	167.4	167.2	167.8	166.7
2009	164.4	163.1	163.0	164.5	164.2	162.5	163.0	162.9	162.2	164.2	165.0	165.3	163.7
2010	163.6	163.2	164.2	163.3	165.0	164.2	162.2	164.0	165.1	166.3	168.0	170.0	164.9
2011	167.3	167.5	169.2	170.5	170.7	170.5	170.0	171.5	171.4	171.3	173.8	174.9	170.7
2012	172.8	173.2	174.7	175.0	174.9	174.5	173.0	174.6	174.3	175.7	178.4	179.9	175.1
2013	176.1	177.7	178.8	179.5	179.3	179.4	177.4	179.8	179.3	179.8	181.9	182.6	179.3
Goods Producing													
2002	21.0	21.0	21.2	20.6	20.3	20.5	20.4	20.8	20.4	20.1	20.2	20.2	20.6
2003	20.2	20.3	20.3	20.5	20.6	20.4	20.3	20.5	20.5	19.9	20.2	20.3	20.3
2004	19.9	19.9	20.1	19.8	20.0	19.6	19.4	19.4	19.3	19.4	19.4	19.6	19.7
2005	18.8	18.9	19.0	18.8	18.9	19.0	18.6	18.6	18.8	18.9	19.0	19.1	18.9
2006	18.9	19.0	19.2	19.0	18.9	18.9	18.6	18.8	18.9	18.6	19.0	19.2	18.9
2007	19.0	18.9	19.0	19.3	19.3	19.2	18.9	19.5	19.5	19.4	19.4	19.4	19.2
2008	19.3	19.1	19.0	18.7	18.4	18.2	17.6	17.8	17.4	17.9	17.5	17.6	18.2
2009	16.9	16.6	16.3	15.7	15.6	15.4	15.2	15.2	15.0	15.2	15.0	14.9	15.6
2010	15.0	14.7	15.0	14.7	14.8	14.4	14.0	14.3	14.3	14.4	14.5	14.6	14.6
2011	14.6	14.5	14.7	14.4	14.5	14.5	14.6	14.7	14.8	15.0	15.2	15.2	14.7
2012	15.1	15.1	15.3	15.2	15.1	15.2	14.9	15.3	15.2	15.4	15.5	15.7	15.3
2013	15.4	15.6	15.8	15.6	15.6	15.8	15.6	15.9	15.8	15.9	16.0	16.1	15.8
Service-Providing													
2002	144.1	145.1	146.9	147.5	147.8	147.5	140.9	144.8	148.0	150.1	152.7	153.5	147.4
2003	151.9	153.5	154.3	154.4	155.0	154.6	149.7	152.2	155.5	158.1	160.7	162.7	155.2
2004	161.5	162.7	163.9	165.1	166.1	165.1	159.9	163.6	165.9	168.6	171.6	173.0	165.6
2005	170.9	173.0	174.3	177.2	176.5	175.8	168.9	173.7	176.3	179.1	180.9	182.7	175.8
2006	181.9	182.7	183.5	183.2	182.7	182.7	174.2	179.4	182.6	186.8	189.4	190.6	183.3
2007	189.1	189.8	190.9	192.5	192.2	191.4	187.4	190.8	192.4	196.4	198.6	200.0	192.6
2008	199.6	200.8	201.3	202.5	202.5	200.2	195.2	197.6	198.9	203.5	204.6	205.3	201.0
2009	201.8	201.3	201.6	203.5	203.7	200.9	196.4	198.6	200.3	203.9	205.5	206.0	202.0
2010	203.6	204.2	205.2	205.0	206.8	205.5	196.5	199.8	203.4	206.9	209.0	210.7	204.7
2011	208.1	208.8	210.2	211.5	212.0	210.7	204.5	207.8	209.4	210.0	213.2	214.2	210.0
2012	211.8	212.7	214.4	214.6	214.7	213.5	207.0	209.8	211.9	214.9	218.2	219.6	213.6
2013	215.3	217.3	218.7	219.2	219.6	218.8	211.5	215.4	217.2	219.5	222.2	222.8	218.1
Mining, Logging, and Construction													
2002	10.2	10.2	10.4	10.4	10.5	10.8	10.8	11.0	11.0	10.8	10.9	11.0	10.7
2003	10.9	10.9	11.0	11.2	11.3	11.4	11.3	11.4	11.3	11.1	11.1	11.2	11.2
2004	10.8	10.8	11.0	10.9	10.9	10.8	10.8	10.8	10.9	10.7	10.5	10.6	10.8
2005	10.3	10.5	10.5	10.6	10.7	10.9	10.6	10.6	10.7	10.5	10.6	10.6	10.6
2006	10.4	10.6	10.9	10.7	10.8	10.9	11.0	11.1	11.0	10.9	10.9	11.0	10.9
2007	10.9	10.9	11.0	11.1	11.1	11.3	11.4	11.7	11.6	11.3	11.3	11.3	11.2
2008	11.3	11.2	11.1	11.1	10.9	10.8	10.7	10.8	10.6	10.7	10.5	10.5	10.9
2009	10.2	10.0	9.7	9.6	9.4	9.2	9.2	9.0	8.8	8.8	8.7	8.6	9.3
2010	8.6	8.5	8.6	8.5	8.6	8.6	8.4	8.5	8.5	8.4	8.4	8.4	8.5
2011	8.4	8.4	8.6	8.5	8.6	8.6	8.8	8.9	8.9	8.9	8.9	8.9	8.7
2012	8.8	8.9	9.0	9.0	9.0	9.1	9.0	9.2	9.1	9.1	9.1	9.2	9.0
2013	8.8	8.9	9.2	9.2	9.3	9.5	9.5	9.7	9.6	9.6	9.6	9.5	9.4
Manufacturing													
2002	10.8	10.8	10.8	10.2	9.8	9.7	9.6	9.8	9.4	9.3	9.3	9.2	9.9
2003	9.3	9.4	9.3	9.3	9.3	9.0	9.0	9.1	9.2	8.8	9.1	9.1	9.2
2004	9.1	9.1	9.1	8.9	9.1	8.8	8.6	8.6	8.4	8.7	8.9	9.0	8.9
2005	8.5	8.4	8.5	8.2	8.2	8.1	8.0	8.0	8.1	8.4	8.4	8.5	8.3
2006	8.5	8.4	8.3	8.3	8.1	8.0	7.6	7.7	7.9	7.7	8.1	8.2	8.1
2007	8.1	8.0	8.0	8.2	8.2	7.9	7.5	7.8	7.9	8.1	8.1	8.1	8.0
2008	8.0	7.9	7.9	7.6	7.5	7.4	6.9	7.0	6.8	7.2	7.0	7.1	7.4
2009	6.7	6.6	6.6	6.1	6.2	6.2	6.0	6.2	6.2	6.4	6.3	6.3	6.3
2010	6.4	6.2	6.4	6.2	6.2	5.8	5.6	5.8	5.8	6.0	6.1	6.2	6.1
2011	6.2	6.1	6.1	5.9	5.9	5.9	5.8	5.8	5.9	6.1	6.3	6.3	6.0
2012	6.3	6.2	6.3	6.2	6.1	6.1	5.9	6.1	6.1	6.3	6.4	6.5	6.2
2013	6.6	6.7	6.6	6.4	6.3	6.3	6.1	6.2	6.2	6.3	6.4	6.6	6.4

Employment by Industry: McAllen-Edinburg-Mission, TX, Selected Years, 2002–2013—*Continued*

(Numbers in thousands, not seasonally adjusted)

Industry and year	January	February	March	April	May	June	July	August	September	October	November	December	Annual average
Trade, Transportation, and Utilities													
2002	34.5	34.2	34.7	34.8	34.9	34.9	34.7	35.1	35.1	35.0	36.2	37.0	35.1
2003	35.5	35.5	35.8	36.1	36.2	36.3	36.2	36.2	36.2	36.6	37.9	39.2	36.5
2004	38.4	38.3	38.5	39.1	39.1	38.7	38.4	38.7	38.2	38.5	39.7	40.7	38.9
2005	39.4	39.2	39.6	40.8	40.6	40.6	40.7	40.8	40.5	40.8	42.0	42.9	40.7
2006	41.8	41.4	41.9	42.4	42.3	42.1	42.3	42.7	43.2	43.8	45.3	46.0	42.9
2007	44.7	44.3	45.0	45.5	45.2	44.8	45.5	45.8	45.5	46.0	47.3	47.9	45.6
2008	47.0	46.2	46.5	46.7	46.4	46.2	46.3	46.5	45.9	46.5	46.9	47.5	46.6
2009	45.4	44.5	44.6	45.4	45.3	44.9	44.9	45.5	45.1	45.4	46.1	46.7	45.3
2010	44.7	44.1	44.4	44.8	45.2	45.2	44.7	45.3	45.1	45.8	46.9	48.1	45.4
2011	46.1	45.6	46.0	46.7	46.7	46.7	46.6	47.2	46.6	47.0	48.6	49.4	46.9
2012	47.9	47.5	48.0	48.2	48.3	48.5	48.7	49.4	48.7	49.1	51.2	51.7	48.9
2013	49.9	49.6	49.7	50.3	50.2	50.4	49.9	50.2	49.8	49.1	50.6	51.3	50.1
Wholesale Trade													
2002	5.6	5.6	5.8	5.8	5.7	5.7	5.6	5.6	5.6	5.6	5.6	5.8	5.7
2003	5.9	6.0	6.1	6.3	6.3	6.3	6.0	5.9	5.9	5.9	6.0	6.3	6.1
2004	6.2	6.2	6.3	6.8	6.9	6.7	6.5	6.5	6.5	6.4	6.6	6.9	6.5
2005	6.8	6.7	6.7	6.9	6.7	6.7	6.6	6.4	6.5	6.6	6.7	6.8	6.7
2006	6.8	6.9	7.0	7.0	6.9	6.8	6.7	6.6	6.6	6.4	6.4	6.5	6.7
2007	6.3	6.4	6.6	6.9	6.8	6.6	6.7	6.6	6.7	7.0	7.0	7.0	6.7
2008	7.1	6.8	6.9	7.2	7.1	6.9	6.7	6.4	6.3	6.8	6.6	6.7	6.8
2009	6.5	6.4	6.3	6.8	6.6	6.3	6.2	6.2	6.1	6.3	6.2	6.2	6.3
2010	6.1	6.1	6.0	6.2	6.3	6.3	6.1	6.1	6.2	6.3	6.3	6.5	6.2
2011	6.3	6.3	6.5	6.6	6.5	6.4	6.4	6.4	6.4	6.4	6.4	6.5	6.4
2012	6.6	6.6	6.7	6.9	6.9	6.8	6.7	6.8	6.8	7.0	7.0	7.1	6.8
2013	7.1	7.2	7.3	7.6	7.5	7.3	7.2	7.0	7.1	7.1	7.1	7.2	7.2
Retail Trade													
2002	24.3	24.1	24.3	24.4	24.6	24.6	24.5	24.8	24.9	24.8	25.9	26.5	24.8
2003	25.0	24.8	25.0	24.9	25.0	25.0	25.2	25.2	25.3	25.7	26.8	27.8	25.5
2004	27.0	26.9	26.9	27.0	26.9	26.7	26.5	26.8	26.3	26.7	27.7	28.3	27.0
2005	27.1	27.0	27.3	28.2	28.1	28.0	28.1	28.4	28.0	28.4	29.4	30.1	28.2
2006	28.8	28.3	28.5	29.0	28.9	28.6	29.0	29.4	29.9	30.6	32.0	32.5	29.6
2007	31.6	31.0	31.5	31.7	31.4	31.1	31.7	32.1	31.6	32.1	33.5	34.0	31.9
2008	33.0	32.5	32.6	32.4	32.1	32.1	32.5	33.0	32.5	32.9	33.5	33.9	32.8
2009	32.1	31.4	31.5	31.8	31.8	31.6	31.8	32.3	32.1	32.1	32.9	33.4	32.1
2010	31.8	31.2	31.6	31.7	31.8	31.8	31.7	32.2	31.9	32.5	33.6	34.4	32.2
2011	33.0	32.4	32.5	33.0	33.0	33.1	33.0	33.5	33.0	33.3	34.9	35.5	33.4
2012	33.9	33.3	33.6	33.7	33.7	33.9	34.2	34.7	34.3	34.5	36.5	36.8	34.4
2013	35.1	34.7	34.7	34.9	34.9	35.2	34.8	35.2	34.8	34.0	35.3	35.7	34.9
Transportation and Utilities													
2002	4.6	4.5	4.6	4.6	4.6	4.6	4.6	4.7	4.6	4.6	4.7	4.7	4.6
2003	4.6	4.7	4.7	4.9	4.9	5.0	5.0	5.1	5.0	5.0	5.1	5.1	4.9
2004	5.2	5.2	5.3	5.3	5.3	5.3	5.4	5.4	5.4	5.4	5.4	5.5	5.3
2005	5.5	5.5	5.6	5.7	5.8	5.9	6.0	6.0	6.0	5.8	5.9	6.0	5.8
2006	6.2	6.2	6.4	6.4	6.5	6.7	6.6	6.7	6.7	6.8	6.9	7.0	6.6
2007	6.8	6.9	6.9	6.9	7.0	7.1	7.1	7.1	7.2	6.9	6.8	6.9	7.0
2008	6.9	6.9	7.0	7.1	7.2	7.2	7.1	7.1	7.1	6.8	6.8	6.9	7.0
2009	6.8	6.7	6.8	6.8	6.9	7.0	6.9	7.0	6.9	7.0	7.0	7.1	6.9
2010	6.8	6.8	6.8	6.9	7.1	7.1	6.9	7.0	7.0	7.0	7.0	7.2	7.0
2011	6.8	6.9	7.0	7.1	7.2	7.2	7.2	7.3	7.2	7.3	7.3	7.4	7.2
2012	7.4	7.6	7.7	7.6	7.7	7.8	7.8	7.9	7.6	7.6	7.7	7.8	7.7
2013	7.7	7.7	7.7	7.8	7.8	7.9	7.9	8.0	7.9	8.0	8.2	8.4	7.9
Information													
2002	1.1	1.1	1.1	1.0	1.1	1.1	1.0	1.0	1.0	0.9	1.0	1.0	1.0
2003	1.0	1.0	1.0	1.0	1.1	1.3	1.4	1.4	1.4	1.5	1.6	1.7	1.3
2004	1.9	1.8	1.8	1.9	1.9	2.0	2.0	2.0	2.0	2.1	2.1	2.1	2.0
2005	2.0	2.0	2.0	2.1	2.1	2.2	2.2	2.2	2.3	2.3	2.3	2.3	2.2
2006	2.2	2.2	2.3	2.2	2.2	2.2	2.1	2.1	2.1	2.3	2.3	2.2	2.2
2007	2.2	2.2	2.2	2.3	2.3	2.3	2.2	2.2	2.1	2.1	2.2	2.2	2.2
2008	2.2	2.2	2.2	2.2	2.2	2.3	2.3	2.3	2.2	2.2	2.3	2.3	2.2
2009	2.2	2.2	2.2	2.2	2.1	2.1	2.2	2.1	2.1	2.0	2.0	2.0	2.1
2010	2.1	2.0	2.0	2.0	2.0	2.0	1.9	1.9	1.9	1.9	1.9	2.0	2.0
2011	2.1	2.0	2.0	2.1	2.1	2.1	2.1	2.1	2.0	2.0	2.0	2.0	2.1
2012	2.0	2.0	2.0	2.0	2.0	2.0	2.0	1.9	1.9	2.1	2.1	2.1	2.0
2013	2.1	2.1	2.1	2.1	2.1	2.2	2.2	2.2	2.1	2.1	2.1	2.1	2.1
Financial Activities													
2002	6.5	6.5	6.5	6.6	6.7	6.7	6.7	6.7	6.7	6.8	6.9	7.0	6.7
2003	7.0	7.1	7.1	7.1	7.2	7.3	7.3	7.3	7.3	7.4	7.4	7.4	7.2
2004	7.5	7.5	7.6	7.6	7.5	7.7	7.8	7.7	7.7	7.8	7.9	7.9	7.7
2005	7.9	7.9	8.0	8.1	8.0	8.1	8.2	8.2	8.2	8.3	8.3	8.3	8.1
2006	8.3	8.3	8.4	8.2	8.2	8.3	8.4	8.4	8.4	8.6	8.6	8.7	8.4
2007	8.7	8.7	8.7	8.8	8.8	8.8	8.8	8.8	8.8	8.8	8.9	8.8	8.8
2008	8.9	8.9	8.8	8.9	8.8	8.8	8.8	8.7	8.6	8.5	8.5	8.4	8.7
2009	8.3	8.1	8.1	8.0	8.0	7.9	8.0	8.0	7.9	8.0	8.0	8.0	8.0
2010	7.9	7.9	7.9	7.9	8.0	8.0	8.0	8.0	8.1	8.2	8.3	8.4	8.1
2011	8.3	8.3	8.4	8.4	8.4	8.5	8.4	8.5	8.5	8.5	8.5	8.6	8.4
2012	8.7	8.7	8.7	8.6	8.7	8.7	8.7	8.7	8.7	8.8	8.8	8.8	8.7
2013	8.7	8.7	8.7	8.7	8.7	8.7	8.8	8.8	8.9	8.9	8.9	9.0	8.8

Employment by Industry: McAllen-Edinburg-Mission, TX, Selected Years, 2002–2013—*Continued*
(Numbers in thousands, not seasonally adjusted)

Industry and year	January	February	March	April	May	June	July	August	September	October	November	December	Annual average
Professional and Business Services													
2002	11.1	11.1	11.3	11.3	11.0	11.0	10.7	10.9	10.9	11.3	11.4	11.2	11.1
2003	10.9	11.5	11.2	11.1	11.0	11.1	11.0	11.5	11.6	11.7	11.8	12.0	11.4
2004	11.4	11.5	11.4	11.6	11.8	12.0	12.0	12.3	12.1	12.2	12.4	12.5	11.9
2005	12.3	12.8	13.1	13.4	13.2	13.3	13.3	13.5	13.5	13.5	13.6	13.8	13.3
2006	13.8	14.1	14.3	14.0	13.9	14.1	13.8	13.8	13.9	14.0	14.2	14.6	14.0
2007	14.5	14.6	14.8	14.7	14.7	14.7	14.6	14.6	14.7	14.7	14.8	15.0	14.7
2008	15.2	15.4	15.2	14.8	14.7	14.6	14.6	14.6	14.4	14.9	14.9	14.8	14.8
2009	14.6	14.5	14.3	14.4	14.4	14.2	14.1	13.5	13.4	13.5	13.7	13.5	14.0
2010	13.7	13.8	13.7	13.6	13.6	13.8	13.6	13.7	13.7	13.9	14.0	14.2	13.8
2011	14.1	14.3	14.4	15.1	15.0	14.8	14.6	14.7	14.6	14.5	14.6	14.6	14.6
2012	14.9	15.0	14.9	15.3	15.1	14.6	14.6	14.6	14.7	14.8	14.4	14.5	14.8
2013	14.7	15.2	15.4	15.5	15.2	15.1	14.7	15.1	15.0	15.3	15.5	15.5	15.2
Education and Health Services													
2002	28.2	28.4	28.8	29.4	29.7	29.9	30.4	31.0	31.4	31.6	32.1	32.2	30.3
2003	32.4	32.7	33.0	32.9	32.9	32.7	33.1	33.7	34.0	34.3	34.6	34.8	33.4
2004	35.1	35.6	36.0	36.1	36.7	36.8	37.4	37.9	38.7	39.5	40.1	40.5	37.5
2005	40.4	41.0	41.2	41.6	41.7	41.6	41.9	42.3	42.9	43.3	43.5	44.0	42.1
2006	43.6	43.9	43.8	43.9	44.0	44.0	44.0	44.5	44.9	45.0	45.3	45.5	44.4
2007	46.0	46.3	46.3	47.1	47.3	47.1	47.3	47.8	48.2	48.4	48.9	49.0	47.5
2008	49.2	50.1	50.1	50.8	51.0	50.5	50.8	51.0	51.3	52.2	52.5	52.9	51.0
2009	52.4	52.6	52.8	53.7	54.0	53.4	54.0	54.2	54.5	55.5	55.7	55.8	54.1
2010	55.6	55.8	56.0	55.6	56.3	55.9	55.6	56.1	57.1	57.2	57.5	57.7	56.4
2011	57.3	57.6	57.9	58.1	58.4	58.1	58.5	59.1	59.8	59.4	59.8	60.0	58.7
2012	59.3	59.7	59.9	59.7	59.8	59.5	58.5	59.0	59.3	59.6	60.1	60.3	59.6
2013	58.9	59.5	59.6	60.0	60.2	60.0	59.4	60.3	60.6	61.1	61.1	61.2	60.2
Leisure and Hospitality													
2002	15.3	15.7	16.0	15.9	15.9	15.9	15.4	15.8	15.8	15.3	15.3	15.4	15.6
2003	15.5	15.9	16.3	16.1	16.2	16.6	16.5	16.4	16.2	16.3	16.2	16.3	16.2
2004	16.2	16.5	16.8	17.0	16.9	16.9	16.4	16.5	16.3	16.3	16.5	16.6	16.6
2005	16.6	16.9	17.0	17.6	17.3	17.0	16.9	16.7	16.6	16.8	16.7	17.0	16.9
2006	17.6	17.5	17.5	17.9	17.6	17.4	17.4	17.1	16.9	17.4	17.4	17.4	17.4
2007	17.9	17.9	17.7	18.3	18.0	18.0	18.6	18.4	17.8	18.9	18.6	18.7	18.2
2008	19.0	19.2	19.3	19.9	19.7	19.4	19.2	19.3	18.8	19.3	18.8	18.7	19.2
2009	19.0	19.0	19.1	19.3	19.1	18.8	18.9	18.8	18.6	18.9	18.8	18.8	18.9
2010	19.0	19.3	19.5	19.1	19.4	19.2	18.9	19.2	19.3	19.2	19.2	19.4	19.2
2011	19.2	19.5	20.0	20.0	19.9	20.1	19.6	19.6	19.5	19.2	19.4	19.4	19.6
2012	19.2	19.6	20.2	20.2	20.1	20.2	19.8	20.0	20.0	19.9	20.3	20.8	20.0
2013	20.5	21.0	21.5	21.3	21.3	21.2	20.8	21.2	21.2	21.2	21.5	21.3	21.2
Other Services													
2002	4.3	4.4	4.4	4.6	4.5	4.5	4.4	4.4	4.3	4.4	4.4	4.4	4.4
2003	4.5	4.5	4.6	4.5	4.6	4.5	4.4	4.4	4.4	4.4	4.4	4.4	4.5
2004	4.5	4.5	4.6	4.5	4.6	4.6	4.6	4.6	4.5	4.5	4.6	4.6	4.6
2005	4.6	4.6	4.7	4.9	4.9	4.9	4.7	4.7	4.7	4.8	4.8	4.7	4.8
2006	4.6	4.6	4.7	4.9	4.9	4.9	5.1	5.0	5.2	5.2	5.3	5.3	5.0
2007	4.9	5.0	5.1	5.2	5.2	5.3	5.4	5.4	5.3	5.6	5.5	5.6	5.3
2008	5.8	5.9	6.0	6.1	5.9	5.9	6.0	6.0	5.8	5.9	5.8	5.6	5.9
2009	5.6	5.6	5.6	5.8	5.7	5.8	5.7	5.6	5.6	5.7	5.7	5.6	5.7
2010	5.6	5.6	5.7	5.6	5.7	5.7	5.5	5.5	5.6	5.7	5.7	5.6	5.6
2011	5.6	5.7	5.8	5.7	5.7	5.7	5.6	5.6	5.6	5.7	5.7	5.7	5.7
2012	5.7	5.6	5.7	5.8	5.8	5.8	5.8	5.7	5.8	6.0	6.0	6.0	5.8
2013	5.9	6.0	6.0	6.0	6.0	6.0	6.0	6.0	5.9	6.2	6.2	6.1	6.0
Government													
2002	43.1	43.7	44.1	43.9	44.0	43.5	37.6	39.9	42.8	44.8	45.4	45.3	43.2
2003	45.1	45.3	45.3	45.6	45.8	44.8	39.8	41.3	44.4	45.9	46.8	46.9	44.8
2004	46.5	47.0	47.2	47.3	47.6	46.4	41.3	43.9	46.4	47.7	48.3	48.1	46.5
2005	47.7	48.6	48.7	48.7	48.7	48.1	41.0	45.3	47.6	49.3	49.7	49.7	47.8
2006	50.0	50.7	50.6	49.7	49.6	49.7	41.1	45.8	48.0	50.5	51.0	50.9	49.0
2007	50.2	50.8	51.1	50.6	50.7	50.4	45.0	47.8	50.0	51.9	52.5	52.8	50.3
2008	52.3	52.9	53.2	53.1	53.8	52.5	47.2	49.2	51.9	54.0	54.9	55.1	52.5
2009	54.3	54.8	54.9	54.7	55.1	53.8	48.6	50.9	53.1	54.9	55.5	55.6	53.9
2010	55.0	55.7	56.0	56.4	56.6	55.7	48.3	50.1	52.6	55.0	55.5	55.3	54.4
2011	55.4	55.8	55.7	55.4	55.8	54.7	49.1	51.0	52.8	53.7	54.6	54.5	54.0
2012	54.1	54.6	55.0	54.8	54.9	54.2	48.9	50.5	52.8	54.6	55.3	55.4	53.8
2013	54.6	55.2	55.7	55.3	55.9	55.2	49.7	51.5	53.7	55.6	56.3	56.3	54.6

Employment by Industry: Memphis, TN–MS–AR, Selected Years, 2002–2013

(Numbers in thousands, not seasonally adjusted)

Industry and year	January	February	March	April	May	June	July	August	September	October	November	December	Annual average
Total Nonfarm													
2002	603.4	606.9	609.7	613.0	612.6	611.7	610.0	614.2	614.1	618.9	621.5	621.1	613.1
2003	613.0	615.0	618.3	619.6	618.9	614.8	609.0	614.2	616.2	619.9	620.7	620.2	616.7
2004	605.4	610.4	611.5	616.6	614.1	613.3	614.7	620.1	620.9	622.4	624.5	625.3	616.6
2005	610.8	614.7	618.6	625.0	625.6	622.5	626.3	630.9	636.5	632.5	638.0	639.0	626.7
2006	627.8	627.5	632.3	634.2	634.9	633.6	635.5	640.6	643.8	641.2	648.4	649.3	637.4
2007	631.1	632.1	638.1	639.8	641.2	639.8	638.1	643.1	645.3	643.6	648.7	649.2	640.8
2008	632.3	631.3	634.0	636.7	637.6	632.3	631.2	634.2	632.2	630.6	630.9	626.9	632.5
2009	607.9	606.8	605.3	604.2	603.0	600.0	596.2	596.7	596.6	596.7	601.2	598.2	601.1
2010	582.7	584.2	588.7	589.9	595.4	590.0	585.8	589.4	588.2	594.2	596.9	595.7	590.1
2011	582.9	585.0	588.4	594.0	594.5	589.7	590.7	594.9	596.0	599.1	605.3	605.6	593.8
2012	588.8	593.4	597.0	598.4	600.6	598.1	595.8	601.3	603.7	607.5	616.2	616.9	601.5
2013	597.1	602.2	604.5	606.5	607.7	603.2	598.4	602.5	605.1	606.9	613.8	612.7	605.1
Total Private													
2002	516.4	516.9	519.4	522.2	523.9	526.9	527.9	528.3	525.6	527.8	529.3	530.3	524.6
2003	522.1	522.0	524.6	527.0	528.7	530.5	526.2	527.8	527.0	528.9	529.6	529.6	527.0
2004	515.3	516.6	519.7	525.4	525.4	528.4	531.7	532.9	530.5	531.3	533.1	535.0	527.1
2005	521.6	524.2	527.9	534.0	536.4	537.8	542.9	543.9	547.2	542.2	547.4	549.2	537.9
2006	539.3	538.4	542.9	545.2	548.0	550.5	552.7	554.7	554.4	550.2	557.9	558.9	549.4
2007	541.3	541.8	548.1	550.5	553.0	556.3	554.8	556.3	556.0	552.9	557.7	559.0	552.3
2008	542.7	540.3	542.9	545.5	547.3	547.4	546.8	546.3	542.6	540.1	540.5	537.7	543.3
2009	519.7	517.7	516.1	515.2	514.5	515.1	511.6	511.5	508.6	508.1	512.2	510.2	513.4
2010	496.5	496.0	500.2	501.4	505.3	506.2	502.7	504.0	500.5	505.6	508.3	509.0	503.0
2011	495.7	496.3	499.8	505.7	507.3	508.7	510.1	510.5	509.4	511.8	517.6	519.1	507.7
2012	503.2	506.0	509.4	510.8	514.8	517.1	514.6	517.5	516.9	520.6	528.6	530.4	515.8
2013	512.4	514.8	517.3	519.2	522.2	523.1	518.8	520.4	520.9	522.4	528.8	528.7	520.8
Goods Producing													
2002	79.0	78.8	79.5	79.9	80.6	81.5	82.0	81.9	81.8	81.0	80.0	79.6	80.5
2003	77.9	78.2	78.5	79.1	79.6	79.9	79.7	79.5	79.5	79.4	78.8	78.4	79.0
2004	76.7	77.1	78.1	78.9	79.3	80.7	80.9	81.0	80.6	79.2	78.9	77.4	79.1
2005	76.5	77.5	78.5	79.6	80.5	81.4	81.8	80.4	82.6	81.6	81.6	79.2	80.1
2006	79.9	80.4	81.3	81.4	82.0	83.0	82.7	82.6	82.5	80.5	79.9	77.5	81.1
2007	77.5	77.9	79.6	79.4	79.8	80.6	80.0	79.4	78.9	78.4	78.0	77.0	78.9
2008	75.6	75.1	75.9	76.5	77.0	77.2	76.4	76.5	75.9	74.5	73.5	72.3	75.5
2009	70.6	69.2	68.8	68.1	68.1	68.4	67.8	67.8	67.7	66.1	66.6	64.6	67.8
2010	62.5	62.8	63.7	63.9	64.3	64.8	65.0	64.9	64.5	63.6	63.9	63.6	64.0
2011	62.8	62.4	62.7	63.4	64.0	65.0	65.5	65.3	65.0	63.8	64.7	64.2	64.1
2012	63.2	63.3	64.0	64.6	65.2	66.0	66.0	66.3	65.2	64.6	65.3	65.0	64.9
2013	64.3	64.2	64.7	65.1	65.7	66.2	66.0	65.5	65.3	65.2	64.8	64.0	65.1
Service-Providing													
2002	524.4	528.1	530.2	533.1	532.0	530.2	528.0	532.3	532.3	537.9	541.5	541.5	532.6
2003	535.1	536.8	539.8	540.5	539.3	534.9	529.3	534.7	536.7	540.5	541.9	541.8	537.6
2004	528.7	533.3	533.4	537.7	534.8	532.6	533.8	539.1	540.3	543.2	545.6	547.9	537.5
2005	534.3	537.2	540.1	545.4	545.1	541.1	544.5	550.5	553.9	550.9	556.4	559.8	546.6
2006	547.9	547.1	551.0	552.8	552.9	550.6	552.8	558.0	561.3	560.7	568.5	571.8	556.3
2007	553.6	554.2	558.5	560.4	561.4	559.2	558.1	563.7	566.4	565.2	570.7	572.2	562.0
2008	556.7	556.2	558.1	560.2	560.6	555.1	554.8	557.7	556.3	556.1	557.4	554.6	557.0
2009	537.3	537.6	536.5	536.1	534.9	531.6	528.4	528.9	528.9	530.6	534.6	533.6	533.3
2010	520.2	521.4	525.0	526.0	531.1	525.2	520.8	524.5	523.7	530.6	533.0	532.1	526.1
2011	520.1	522.6	525.7	530.6	530.5	524.7	525.2	529.6	531.0	535.3	540.6	541.4	529.8
2012	525.6	530.1	533.0	533.8	535.4	532.1	529.8	535.0	538.5	542.9	550.9	551.9	536.6
2013	532.8	538.0	539.8	541.4	542.0	537.0	532.4	537.0	539.8	541.7	549.0	548.7	540.0
Mining, Logging, and Construction													
2002	24.5	24.1	24.6	25.0	25.7	26.2	26.5	26.3	26.6	25.9	25.6	25.5	25.5
2003	24.3	24.2	24.6	25.2	25.7	25.9	26.0	26.1	26.2	26.0	25.8	25.8	25.5
2004	24.9	25.0	25.7	25.9	26.0	26.8	27.2	27.1	27.0	25.7	25.6	25.1	26.0
2005	23.7	24.1	24.7	25.3	26.0	26.7	26.9	27.2	27.6	26.9	26.8	26.7	26.1
2006	25.8	26.0	26.7	27.1	27.7	28.2	28.3	28.2	28.0	27.0	26.5	26.3	27.2
2007	25.5	25.5	26.0	26.3	26.8	27.3	26.9	27.0	26.8	26.5	26.3	26.2	26.4
2008	24.5	24.5	25.0	25.5	25.7	25.8	25.2	25.1	24.7	23.8	23.4	22.9	24.7
2009	21.7	21.4	21.5	21.5	21.5	22.0	21.7	21.7	21.4	20.5	20.6	20.1	21.3
2010	19.0	18.7	19.2	19.2	19.3	19.7	19.8	19.8	19.6	19.4	19.1	18.9	19.3
2011	18.1	18.2	18.5	19.0	19.4	20.1	20.6	20.7	20.8	20.8	20.7	20.5	19.8
2012	19.5	19.4	20.0	20.4	20.8	21.3	21.3	21.4	21.2	20.7	20.6	20.5	20.6
2013	19.8	19.7	19.9	20.2	20.7	21.1	20.9	20.9	20.8	21.0	20.3	19.2	20.4
Manufacturing													
2002	54.5	54.7	54.9	54.9	54.9	55.3	55.5	55.6	55.2	55.1	54.4	54.1	54.9
2003	53.6	54.0	53.9	53.9	53.9	54.0	53.7	53.4	53.3	53.4	53.0	52.6	53.6
2004	51.8	52.1	52.4	53.0	53.3	53.9	53.7	53.9	53.6	53.5	53.3	52.3	53.1
2005	52.8	53.4	53.8	54.3	54.5	54.7	54.9	53.2	55.0	54.7	54.8	52.5	54.1
2006	54.1	54.4	54.6	54.3	54.3	54.8	54.4	54.4	54.5	53.5	53.4	51.2	54.0
2007	52.0	52.4	53.6	53.1	53.0	53.3	53.1	52.4	52.1	51.9	51.7	50.8	52.5
2008	51.1	50.6	50.9	51.0	51.3	51.4	51.2	51.4	51.2	50.7	50.1	49.4	50.9
2009	48.9	47.8	47.3	46.6	46.6	46.4	46.1	46.1	46.3	45.6	46.0	44.5	46.5
2010	43.5	44.1	44.5	44.7	45.0	45.1	45.2	45.1	44.9	44.2	44.8	44.7	44.7
2011	44.7	44.2	44.2	44.4	44.6	44.9	44.9	44.6	44.2	43.0	44.0	43.7	44.3
2012	43.7	43.9	44.0	44.2	44.4	44.7	44.7	44.9	44.0	43.9	44.7	44.5	44.3
2013	44.5	44.5	44.8	44.9	45.0	45.1	45.1	44.6	44.5	44.2	44.5	44.8	44.7

Employment by Industry: Memphis, TN-MS-AR, Selected Years, 2002–2013—*Continued*

(Numbers in thousands, not seasonally adjusted)

Industry and year	January	February	March	April	May	June	July	August	September	October	November	December	Annual average
Trade, Transportation, and Utilities													
2002	169.1	166.8	167.5	168.0	168.3	168.7	169.7	169.5	169.5	170.7	173.8	175.4	169.8
2003	171.4	170.2	170.8	170.9	170.7	170.8	169.8	170.0	170.3	171.1	173.3	174.1	171.1
2004	167.7	167.4	167.8	168.0	168.0	168.5	170.3	170.0	168.9	170.1	172.7	175.3	169.6
2005	169.8	168.7	169.7	170.0	170.5	170.5	173.5	173.2	173.5	172.9	176.2	178.4	172.2
2006	173.6	172.4	173.0	173.3	174.0	173.7	174.7	175.1	174.9	174.7	178.2	179.9	174.8
2007	173.3	172.5	173.8	174.7	175.5	175.6	175.3	175.3	175.6	174.8	178.0	179.1	175.3
2008	172.8	171.4	171.7	171.7	171.6	171.3	170.8	170.2	169.3	168.3	169.9	170.4	170.8
2009	164.4	163.0	162.3	161.0	161.0	160.5	159.8	159.3	158.6	158.2	159.6	160.7	160.7
2010	157.1	156.3	156.7	157.8	158.0	158.1	158.4	158.3	156.9	158.4	160.8	162.1	158.2
2011	156.7	156.0	156.4	158.0	158.6	158.8	159.5	159.1	159.2	161.1	163.8	164.9	159.3
2012	159.9	159.1	159.8	159.7	160.8	161.2	161.0	161.0	161.4	162.1	165.8	167.2	161.6
2013	161.4	161.1	160.6	161.7	161.7	162.1	162.5	161.8	161.1	162.7	165.5	166.3	162.4
Wholesale Trade													
2002	36.1	36.0	36.1	36.1	36.2	36.4	36.3	36.2	36.2	36.9	37.1	37.3	36.4
2003	37.9	38.1	38.0	37.7	37.5	37.6	36.7	36.6	36.4	36.2	36.4	36.3	37.1
2004	35.8	35.9	36.2	36.5	36.6	36.9	37.3	37.3	37.1	36.8	36.8	36.8	36.7
2005	36.7	36.8	37.1	37.3	37.4	37.5	37.9	38.0	37.7	37.6	37.6	37.7	37.4
2006	37.3	37.4	37.5	37.5	37.7	37.8	37.8	37.9	37.7	37.3	37.5	37.4	37.6
2007	37.0	37.2	37.3	37.5	37.6	37.6	37.5	37.5	37.6	37.3	37.1	37.0	37.4
2008	36.2	36.0	35.9	36.3	36.1	35.8	35.2	35.2	35.0	34.9	34.7	34.3	35.5
2009	33.6	33.6	33.3	33.4	33.3	33.2	32.8	32.7	32.4	32.3	32.2	32.2	32.9
2010	32.0	32.0	32.0	32.8	32.7	32.8	32.7	32.8	32.5	32.6	32.8	32.8	32.5
2011	32.6	32.7	32.6	32.9	33.0	33.0	33.1	33.2	33.1	33.2	33.2	33.1	33.0
2012	33.1	33.3	33.3	33.4	33.7	33.8	33.8	33.8	33.8	33.8	33.9	33.9	33.6
2013	33.4	33.5	33.5	33.8	33.8	34.0	33.9	34.1	34.2	34.5	34.3	34.3	33.9
Retail Trade													
2002	70.4	69.0	69.4	69.6	69.8	70.1	70.4	70.1	70.4	70.4	73.1	74.8	70.6
2003	70.3	69.3	69.8	69.9	69.9	69.8	69.5	69.4	69.9	71.1	73.0	74.3	70.5
2004	69.4	69.3	69.4	69.3	69.4	69.6	70.8	70.3	69.7	70.8	73.0	74.5	70.5
2005	70.5	69.6	69.8	69.8	70.0	70.1	71.5	71.0	71.4	71.4	74.2	75.8	71.3
2006	72.4	71.2	71.8	71.6	71.9	71.8	72.9	72.7	72.6	72.5	75.3	76.3	72.8
2007	72.0	71.0	71.9	72.2	72.5	72.9	72.7	71.8	71.8	71.7	74.8	75.6	72.6
2008	71.6	70.6	71.1	70.5	70.5	70.4	70.5	69.5	68.8	68.4	69.6	69.9	70.1
2009	66.8	65.9	65.6	65.2	65.5	65.7	65.8	65.2	64.8	65.0	66.9	67.7	65.9
2010	64.5	63.9	64.4	64.3	64.5	64.4	64.6	64.0	62.9	63.8	65.7	66.4	64.5
2011	62.4	61.7	61.8	62.5	62.6	62.5	62.7	62.1	61.7	62.5	65.2	65.9	62.8
2012	62.6	61.9	62.5	62.6	63.1	63.2	63.1	62.5	62.2	63.0	65.9	66.2	63.2
2013	63.4	63.0	63.1	63.4	63.7	63.8	64.6	64.3	64.1	65.1	67.7	68.1	64.5
Transportation and Utilities													
2002	62.6	61.8	62.0	62.3	62.3	62.2	63.0	63.2	62.9	63.4	63.6	63.3	62.7
2003	63.2	62.8	63.0	63.3	63.3	63.4	63.6	64.0	64.0	63.8	63.9	63.5	63.5
2004	62.5	62.2	62.2	62.2	62.0	62.0	62.2	62.4	62.1	62.5	62.9	64.0	62.4
2005	62.6	62.3	62.8	62.9	63.1	62.9	64.1	64.2	64.4	63.9	64.4	64.9	63.5
2006	63.9	63.8	63.7	64.2	64.4	64.1	64.0	64.5	64.6	64.9	65.4	66.2	64.5
2007	64.3	64.3	64.6	65.0	65.4	65.1	65.1	66.0	66.2	65.8	66.1	66.5	65.4
2008	65.0	64.8	64.7	64.9	65.0	65.1	65.1	65.5	65.5	65.0	65.6	66.2	65.2
2009	64.0	63.5	63.2	62.4	62.2	61.6	61.2	61.4	61.4	60.9	60.5	60.8	61.9
2010	60.6	60.4	60.3	60.7	60.8	60.9	61.1	61.5	61.5	62.0	62.3	62.9	61.3
2011	61.7	61.6	62.0	62.6	63.0	63.3	63.7	63.8	64.4	65.4	65.4	65.9	63.6
2012	64.2	63.9	64.0	63.7	64.0	64.2	64.1	64.7	65.4	65.3	66.0	67.1	64.7
2013	64.6	64.6	64.0	64.5	64.2	64.3	64.0	63.4	62.8	63.1	63.5	63.9	63.9
Information													
2002	10.2	10.1	10.2	10.1	10.1	10.0	9.6	10.0	9.8	10.0	10.1	10.0	10.0
2003	9.9	9.8	9.8	9.9	9.7	9.6	9.5	9.5	9.2	9.4	9.3	9.4	9.6
2004	9.0	8.9	8.8	8.8	8.6	8.6	8.5	8.6	8.6	8.6	8.6	8.4	8.7
2005	8.2	8.1	8.2	8.2	8.2	8.0	7.8	7.7	7.6	7.7	7.6	7.4	7.9
2006	7.3	7.3	7.3	7.4	7.5	7.5	7.5	7.5	7.8	7.7	7.8	7.9	7.5
2007	7.4	7.4	7.3	7.4	7.4	7.5	7.5	7.4	7.3	7.3	7.4	7.4	7.4
2008	7.4	7.4	7.4	7.4	7.4	7.4	7.2	7.2	7.2	7.3	7.2	7.3	7.3
2009	7.2	7.1	7.0	6.9	6.9	6.8	6.8	6.7	6.7	6.6	6.6	6.6	6.8
2010	6.4	6.3	6.3	6.2	6.3	6.3	6.2	6.2	6.2	6.2	6.2	6.3	6.3
2011	6.2	6.1	6.1	6.1	6.2	6.1	6.1	6.1	6.0	6.0	6.0	6.0	6.1
2012	6.1	6.1	6.1	6.1	6.1	6.0	6.1	6.1	6.0	6.0	6.0	6.0	6.1
2013	5.9	5.9	5.9	5.9	6.0	6.1	6.0	6.0	6.0	6.0	6.0	6.0	6.0
Financial Activities													
2002	32.3	32.4	32.6	32.5	32.6	32.6	32.2	32.3	31.9	32.1	32.3	32.3	32.3
2003	32.5	32.5	32.6	32.7	32.8	32.8	33.0	33.0	32.8	32.8	33.1	33.1	32.8
2004	32.8	32.7	32.6	33.1	33.2	33.2	33.6	33.6	33.4	33.4	33.4	33.5	33.2
2005	32.8	32.7	32.9	32.9	32.9	32.9	32.9	33.0	32.9	32.7	32.8	32.8	32.9
2006	32.7	32.8	32.9	32.7	32.8	33.2	33.1	33.1	33.0	32.5	33.0	33.1	32.9
2007	32.4	32.8	33.0	33.0	33.3	33.6	33.5	33.7	33.5	33.1	33.2	33.2	33.2
2008	32.8	32.7	33.0	33.0	33.0	32.9	32.6	32.5	32.1	32.0	31.9	31.4	32.5
2009	31.2	31.2	31.1	31.1	31.2	31.1	30.8	30.7	30.5	30.2	30.4	30.3	30.8
2010	29.7	29.5	29.4	29.1	29.1	28.9	28.8	28.8	28.5	28.2	28.0	28.0	28.8
2011	27.5	27.3	27.2	27.5	27.5	27.5	27.7	27.7	27.5	27.5	27.5	27.5	27.5
2012	27.3	27.4	27.4	27.3	27.5	27.3	27.5	27.4	27.0	27.3	27.4	27.4	27.4
2013	27.2	27.0	27.0	27.1	27.1	27.3	27.5	27.5	27.5	27.5	27.9	27.7	27.4

Employment by Industry: Memphis, TN–MS–AR, Selected Years, 2002–2013—*Continued*

(Numbers in thousands, not seasonally adjusted)

Industry and year	January	February	March	April	May	June	July	August	September	October	November	December	Annual average
Professional and Business Services													
2002	75.5	77.0	75.8	75.6	74.5	74.9	74.6	74.0	73.6	74.2	74.0	74.2	74.8
2003	72.4	72.3	72.3	73.0	73.6	73.5	71.8	72.9	73.8	74.2	73.8	73.2	73.1
2004	70.2	70.6	70.7	71.9	71.6	72.1	72.9	73.9	73.9	76.1	76.7	77.6	73.2
2005	73.8	75.5	75.2	77.1	77.3	77.2	78.3	80.2	81.3	80.3	81.2	83.8	78.4
2006	79.2	78.9	79.3	79.6	80.0	80.2	81.9	83.5	84.1	83.4	87.2	88.8	82.2
2007	80.4	80.5	81.3	82.0	81.9	81.7	82.7	84.0	85.3	85.4	87.0	87.5	83.3
2008	81.5	81.1	81.0	81.9	81.6	81.5	83.6	84.0	84.1	85.1	85.1	84.0	82.9
2009	77.9	77.8	76.8	75.9	75.0	74.4	73.7	74.7	74.5	76.6	78.0	77.5	76.1
2010	73.9	73.3	74.0	73.2	76.0	75.7	72.8	74.7	75.6	79.7	80.6	80.9	75.9
2011	77.0	78.2	79.2	80.3	80.2	79.8	80.2	81.5	81.6	84.8	86.9	87.6	81.4
2012	80.2	82.0	81.7	81.8	82.9	83.4	81.9	83.3	85.0	87.7	91.3	91.4	84.4
2013	83.5	85.0	86.1	85.0	86.0	85.6	82.3	84.8	86.6	87.4	89.9	90.9	86.1
Education and Health Services													
2002	65.8	66.3	66.9	67.3	67.4	66.8	67.2	67.9	68.9	69.5	69.9	69.9	67.8
2003	69.9	70.5	70.6	70.2	70.4	69.9	69.1	69.9	70.4	71.3	71.0	71.2	70.4
2004	70.0	70.8	71.0	71.6	71.5	71.3	71.3	71.6	72.2	72.7	72.6	72.7	71.6
2005	72.4	73.1	73.3	73.7	73.9	73.4	73.4	74.5	75.1	74.5	75.0	74.7	73.9
2006	75.0	74.7	75.4	75.4	75.2	75.2	75.2	75.6	76.1	76.2	76.1	76.2	75.5
2007	76.1	76.3	77.1	76.9	77.4	77.1	77.0	77.8	78.1	78.3	78.4	79.1	77.5
2008	78.6	78.8	79.3	79.2	79.6	79.2	78.5	78.8	79.2	79.7	79.9	79.8	79.2
2009	78.5	79.3	79.5	80.4	79.8	79.6	79.1	79.4	80.1	81.2	81.8	81.7	80.0
2010	80.1	80.7	81.3	81.2	80.9	80.4	80.3	80.7	80.6	81.3	81.5	81.4	80.9
2011	80.2	80.6	81.1	82.0	81.7	81.2	81.5	82.1	83.1	83.4	83.7	83.7	82.0
2012	83.3	84.2	84.8	83.8	83.8	83.3	83.1	84.6	85.4	85.8	86.4	86.8	84.6
2013	85.6	86.7	86.9	86.7	86.7	85.6	85.2	86.0	87.1	87.3	87.0	86.4	86.4
Leisure and Hospitality													
2002	61.6	62.6	63.9	65.6	67.0	68.7	68.5	68.8	66.3	66.5	65.4	64.9	65.8
2003	64.2	64.5	65.7	66.8	67.6	69.3	68.8	68.4	66.7	66.5	66.1	66.0	66.7
2004	64.9	65.0	66.3	68.8	68.8	69.1	69.4	69.5	68.1	66.6	66.5	65.3	67.3
2005	63.9	64.2	65.5	67.8	68.4	69.4	70.4	70.3	69.6	68.1	68.6	68.6	67.9
2006	67.5	67.7	69.3	71.0	72.1	72.8	72.9	72.7	71.5	71.2	71.7	71.6	71.0
2007	70.5	70.7	71.9	72.8	73.2	75.3	74.3	74.3	73.1	71.5	71.7	71.7	72.6
2008	70.1	69.8	70.5	71.7	72.5	72.8	72.7	72.1	69.9	68.3	68.1	67.5	70.5
2009	65.1	65.2	65.7	66.9	67.4	69.0	68.5	68.0	65.7	64.6	64.7	64.4	66.3
2010	62.4	62.8	64.3	65.2	66.0	67.3	66.9	66.4	64.6	64.3	63.8	63.4	64.8
2011	62.3	62.6	63.9	65.1	65.7	66.6	65.7	64.9	63.3	61.7	61.5	61.6	63.7
2012	59.7	60.4	61.7	63.4	64.2	65.4	64.6	64.6	62.8	63.1	62.4	62.6	62.9
2013	60.8	61.1	62.1	63.7	65.0	65.8	64.9	64.7	63.2	62.3	63.6	63.3	63.4
Other Services													
2002	22.9	22.9	23.0	23.2	23.4	23.7	24.1	23.9	23.8	23.8	23.8	24.0	23.5
2003	23.9	24.0	24.3	24.4	24.3	24.7	24.5	24.6	24.3	24.2	24.2	24.2	24.3
2004	24.0	24.1	24.4	24.3	24.4	24.9	24.8	24.7	24.8	24.6	24.7	24.8	24.5
2005	24.2	24.4	24.6	24.7	24.7	25.0	24.8	24.6	24.6	24.4	24.4	24.3	24.6
2006	24.1	24.2	24.4	24.4	24.4	24.9	24.7	24.6	24.5	24.0	24.0	23.9	24.3
2007	23.7	23.7	24.1	24.3	24.5	24.9	24.5	24.4	24.2	24.1	24.0	24.0	24.2
2008	23.9	24.0	24.1	24.2	24.6	25.1	25.0	25.0	24.9	24.9	24.9	25.0	24.6
2009	24.8	24.9	24.9	24.9	25.1	25.3	25.1	24.9	24.8	24.6	24.5	24.4	24.9
2010	24.4	24.3	24.5	24.8	24.7	24.7	24.3	24.0	23.6	23.9	23.5	23.3	24.2
2011	23.0	23.1	23.2	23.3	23.4	23.7	23.9	23.8	23.7	23.5	23.5	23.6	23.5
2012	23.5	23.5	23.9	24.1	24.3	24.5	24.4	24.2	24.1	24.0	24.0	24.0	24.0
2013	23.7	23.8	24.0	24.0	24.0	24.4	24.4	24.1	24.1	24.0	24.1	24.1	24.1
Government													
2002	87.0	90.0	90.3	90.8	88.7	84.8	82.1	85.9	88.5	91.1	92.2	90.8	88.5
2003	90.9	93.0	93.7	92.6	90.2	84.3	82.8	86.4	89.2	91.0	91.1	90.6	89.7
2004	90.1	93.8	91.8	91.2	88.7	84.9	83.0	87.2	90.4	91.1	91.4	90.3	89.5
2005	89.2	90.5	90.7	91.0	89.2	84.7	83.4	87.0	89.3	90.6	90.6	89.8	88.8
2006	88.5	89.1	89.4	89.0	86.9	83.1	82.8	85.9	89.4	91.0	90.5	90.4	88.0
2007	89.8	90.3	90.0	89.3	88.2	83.5	83.3	86.8	89.3	90.7	91.0	90.2	88.5
2008	89.6	91.0	91.1	91.2	90.3	84.9	84.4	87.9	89.6	90.5	90.4	89.2	89.2
2009	88.2	89.1	89.2	89.0	88.5	84.9	84.6	85.2	88.0	88.6	89.0	88.0	87.7
2010	86.2	88.2	88.5	88.5	90.1	83.8	83.1	85.4	87.7	88.6	88.6	86.7	87.1
2011	87.2	88.7	88.6	88.3	87.2	81.0	80.6	84.4	86.6	87.3	87.7	86.5	86.2
2012	85.6	87.4	87.6	87.6	85.8	81.0	81.2	83.8	86.8	86.9	87.6	86.5	85.7
2013	84.7	87.4	87.2	87.3	85.5	80.1	79.6	82.1	84.2	84.5	85.0	84.0	84.3

Employment by Industry: Miami-Fort Lauderdale-Pompano Beach, FL, Selected Years, 2002–2013

(Numbers in thousands, not seasonally adjusted)

Industry and year	January	February	March	April	May	June	July	August	September	October	November	December	Annual average
Total Nonfarm													
2002	2,188.7	2,198.2	2,217.3	2,201.2	2,206.3	2,197.9	2,152.3	2,161.8	2,193.4	2,201.5	2,225.9	2,249.8	2,199.5
2003	2,203.3	2,219.3	2,231.5	2,213.7	2,210.8	2,196.6	2,151.4	2,158.8	2,189.6	2,207.2	2,217.1	2,244.9	2,203.7
2004	2,217.9	2,237.6	2,254.8	2,259.8	2,260.3	2,251.0	2,219.5	2,229.5	2,245.2	2,280.6	2,311.7	2,340.0	2,259.0
2005	2,295.6	2,319.4	2,330.1	2,345.2	2,347.5	2,320.2	2,306.8	2,346.5	2,362.3	2,357.5	2,376.4	2,409.4	2,343.1
2006	2,365.7	2,389.1	2,409.9	2,396.4	2,406.9	2,383.5	2,352.4	2,391.8	2,401.6	2,405.2	2,436.8	2,462.9	2,400.2
2007	2,415.3	2,433.8	2,449.6	2,428.6	2,436.7	2,408.3	2,366.6	2,406.4	2,414.4	2,410.4	2,441.4	2,463.0	2,422.9
2008	2,406.3	2,420.3	2,426.5	2,397.4	2,391.5	2,347.7	2,300.5	2,325.9	2,321.7	2,315.0	2,327.2	2,335.6	2,359.6
2009	2,265.1	2,259.6	2,254.4	2,232.2	2,223.8	2,186.1	2,152.8	2,175.9	2,178.0	2,190.7	2,213.7	2,226.6	2,213.2
2010	2,180.7	2,192.5	2,200.2	2,199.3	2,207.6	2,172.4	2,150.5	2,178.9	2,181.5	2,203.3	2,229.3	2,247.2	2,195.3
2011	2,211.8	2,224.4	2,230.5	2,243.2	2,237.2	2,202.2	2,186.7	2,217.6	2,231.4	2,249.5	2,278.0	2,297.2	2,234.1
2012	2,261.3	2,274.6	2,287.1	2,288.8	2,290.3	2,259.3	2,237.5	2,267.8	2,279.6	2,306.7	2,338.3	2,350.8	2,286.8
2013	2,313.8	2,333.2	2,344.9	2,346.6	2,350.0	2,321.4	2,302.9	2,336.3	2,346.3	2,364.1	2,392.9	2,414.4	2,347.2
Total Private													
2002	1,880.8	1,889.1	1,905.1	1,890.6	1,893.7	1,893.1	1,868.0	1,875.4	1,882.2	1,889.3	1,911.1	1,933.3	1,892.6
2003	1,889.6	1,903.5	1,913.8	1,897.3	1,892.2	1,886.2	1,861.5	1,867.2	1,875.3	1,890.6	1,900.5	1,928.7	1,892.2
2004	1,902.6	1,920.9	1,937.3	1,941.3	1,941.0	1,938.9	1,927.5	1,935.0	1,927.6	1,959.2	1,990.1	2,018.0	1,945.0
2005	1,975.4	1,998.0	2,007.6	2,020.5	2,022.1	2,023.2	2,013.9	2,025.7	2,038.4	2,031.5	2,051.1	2,083.7	2,024.3
2006	2,041.4	2,063.6	2,082.9	2,071.0	2,081.0	2,085.8	2,058.9	2,069.7	2,075.8	2,078.0	2,106.5	2,133.3	2,079.0
2007	2,088.8	2,105.9	2,119.4	2,098.2	2,105.5	2,106.2	2,068.8	2,078.6	2,082.8	2,080.2	2,108.8	2,129.5	2,097.7
2008	2,075.5	2,087.0	2,093.5	2,065.8	2,058.9	2,044.6	2,001.9	2,000.5	1,994.5	1,988.4	1,998.6	2,005.8	2,034.6
2009	1,937.2	1,933.2	1,927.8	1,905.2	1,898.3	1,888.7	1,858.1	1,859.4	1,859.0	1,869.7	1,891.8	1,904.9	1,894.4
2010	1,862.4	1,873.6	1,881.4	1,879.4	1,878.6	1,876.8	1,861.4	1,868.7	1,870.1	1,889.6	1,915.2	1,933.7	1,882.6
2011	1,899.8	1,910.8	1,918.4	1,931.0	1,927.1	1,918.8	1,906.3	1,914.0	1,924.9	1,939.7	1,969.7	1,988.4	1,929.1
2012	1,956.0	1,968.0	1,981.5	1,983.2	1,985.7	1,980.0	1,960.9	1,969.5	1,977.3	2,001.0	2,032.7	2,045.5	1,986.8
2013	2,010.6	2,027.1	2,038.5	2,040.4	2,043.8	2,041.1	2,025.0	2,037.5	2,042.7	2,056.5	2,084.0	2,105.5	2,046.1
Goods Producing													
2002	236.3	236.3	236.6	234.3	235.1	235.4	231.8	232.9	233.5	233.3	233.6	233.8	234.4
2003	228.3	228.5	228.7	225.5	226.0	226.3	223.9	226.0	227.5	227.6	226.5	228.4	226.9
2004	225.5	227.1	229.7	230.0	231.6	233.4	233.4	235.8	235.5	238.1	240.1	241.8	233.5
2005	238.9	241.0	242.7	244.7	247.1	249.7	250.8	253.1	256.1	256.3	257.6	260.0	249.8
2006	256.1	259.6	262.2	263.6	266.7	269.6	267.3	268.8	270.6	269.1	270.0	270.7	266.2
2007	265.0	266.3	267.4	262.0	263.0	266.0	258.8	259.5	259.4	255.3	254.6	253.8	260.9
2008	244.4	243.3	241.9	234.8	233.4	232.4	225.3	223.9	222.0	217.6	214.1	210.9	228.7
2009	199.1	196.3	193.5	187.4	185.8	184.2	179.5	178.1	177.0	174.7	173.1	172.0	183.4
2010	164.5	165.0	164.9	164.4	165.0	165.7	165.3	165.8	165.6	165.1	164.6	164.3	165.0
2011	160.1	160.7	160.8	161.3	161.4	162.0	161.3	162.2	163.1	163.3	163.8	163.8	162.0
2012	160.9	161.5	162.5	161.5	162.7	164.1	163.1	165.5	166.2	166.6	167.7	167.6	164.2
2013	163.8	165.7	167.0	166.9	169.5	170.9	171.7	174.6	175.3	175.9	176.8	176.9	171.3
Service-Providing													
2002	1,952.4	1,961.9	1,980.7	1,966.9	1,971.2	1,962.5	1,920.5	1,928.9	1,959.9	1,968.2	1,992.3	2,016.0	1,965.1
2003	1,975.0	1,990.8	2,002.8	1,988.2	1,984.8	1,970.3	1,927.5	1,932.8	1,962.1	1,979.6	1,990.6	2,016.5	1,976.8
2004	1,992.4	2,010.5	2,025.1	2,029.8	2,028.7	2,017.6	1,986.1	1,993.7	2,009.7	2,042.5	2,071.6	2,098.2	2,025.5
2005	2,056.7	2,078.4	2,087.4	2,100.5	2,100.4	2,070.5	2,056.0	2,093.4	2,106.2	2,101.2	2,118.8	2,149.4	2,093.2
2006	2,109.6	2,129.5	2,147.7	2,132.8	2,140.2	2,113.9	2,085.1	2,123.0	2,131.0	2,136.1	2,166.8	2,192.2	2,134.0
2007	2,150.3	2,167.5	2,182.2	2,166.6	2,173.7	2,142.3	2,107.8	2,146.9	2,155.0	2,155.1	2,186.8	2,209.2	2,162.0
2008	2,161.9	2,177.0	2,184.6	2,162.6	2,158.1	2,115.3	2,075.2	2,102.0	2,099.7	2,097.4	2,113.1	2,124.7	2,131.0
2009	2,066.0	2,063.3	2,060.9	2,044.8	2,038.0	2,001.9	1,973.3	1,997.8	2,001.0	2,016.0	2,040.6	2,054.6	2,029.9
2010	2,016.2	2,027.5	2,035.3	2,034.9	2,042.6	2,006.7	1,985.2	2,013.1	2,015.9	2,038.2	2,064.7	2,082.9	2,030.3
2011	2,051.7	2,063.7	2,069.7	2,081.9	2,075.8	2,040.2	2,025.4	2,055.4	2,068.3	2,086.2	2,114.2	2,133.4	2,072.2
2012	2,100.4	2,113.1	2,124.6	2,127.3	2,127.6	2,095.2	2,074.4	2,102.3	2,113.4	2,140.1	2,170.6	2,183.2	2,122.7
2013	2,150.0	2,167.5	2,177.9	2,179.7	2,180.5	2,150.5	2,131.2	2,161.7	2,171.0	2,188.2	2,216.1	2,237.5	2,176.0
Mining and Logging													
2003	0.5	0.4	0.4	0.4	0.4	0.4	0.4	0.4	0.4	0.4	0.4	0.4	0.4
2004	0.4	0.4	0.4	0.4	0.5	0.5	0.5	0.5	0.5	0.5	0.5	0.5	0.5
2005	0.5	0.6	0.6	0.6	0.7	0.7	0.7	0.7	0.6	0.6	0.6	0.5	0.6
2006	0.5	0.6	0.6	0.6	0.6	0.7	0.7	0.7	0.7	0.7	0.8	0.8	0.7
2007	0.8	0.8	0.8	0.8	0.8	0.8	0.8	0.8	0.8	0.9	0.9	0.9	0.8
2008	0.7	0.7	0.8	0.8	0.8	0.7	0.6	0.6	0.6	0.6	0.6	0.6	0.7
2009	0.6	0.6	0.5	0.5	0.5	0.5	0.5	0.5	0.5	0.5	0.5	0.5	0.5
2010	0.5	0.5	0.5	0.5	0.5	0.5	0.5	0.5	0.5	0.5	0.5	0.6	0.5
2011	0.6	0.6	0.6	0.7	0.6	0.6	0.6	0.6	0.5	0.6	0.6	0.6	0.6
2012	0.6	0.6	0.6	0.5	0.6	0.6	0.6	0.6	0.6	0.6	0.6	0.6	0.6
2013	0.6	0.6	0.6	0.6	0.6	0.5	0.6	0.6	0.6	0.6	0.6	0.6	0.6
Construction													
2003	119.1	119.6	120.2	119.6	120.9	121.6	122.1	123.5	124.7	125.2	124.7	125.8	122.3
2004	124.2	125.1	126.9	127.4	128.3	130.7	131.9	133.8	134.0	136.4	138.1	139.3	131.3
2005	138.2	139.6	140.7	142.6	144.2	146.3	148.2	149.8	152.3	153.5	154.6	156.1	147.2
2006	153.7	156.7	159.5	161.7	164.4	166.8	165.9	167.0	168.3	168.0	168.4	168.1	164.0
2007	163.6	164.4	165.4	161.4	162.1	164.6	160.1	160.3	160.1	156.3	155.1	154.1	160.6
2008	146.4	145.2	144.5	138.8	137.8	137.2	132.5	131.3	129.6	126.5	123.8	121.5	134.6
2009	112.3	110.5	109.3	105.1	104.3	103.2	100.6	99.2	98.5	96.5	94.7	93.8	102.3
2010	88.0	88.4	88.3	88.2	88.6	88.9	89.3	89.4	89.4	88.6	87.8	87.1	88.5
2011	84.1	84.5	84.7	84.7	84.4	84.7	84.7	85.1	86.1	85.8	86.0	85.8	85.1
2012	83.5	83.6	84.3	84.3	85.1	86.5	86.3	88.1	88.8	88.9	89.5	89.4	86.5
2013	87.4	88.5	89.4	89.6	91.6	92.5	93.6	96.0	96.7	97.6	97.1	97.2	93.1

Employment by Industry: Miami-Fort Lauderdale-Pompano Beach, FL, Selected Years, 2002–2013—*Continued*

(Numbers in thousands, not seasonally adjusted)

Industry and year	January	February	March	April	May	June	July	August	September	October	November	December	Annual average
Manufacturing													
2002	116.4	116.5	116.2	114.5	114.3	113.9	111.8	111.5	111.6	110.4	110.9	111.1	113.3
2003	108.7	108.5	108.1	105.5	104.7	104.3	101.4	102.1	102.4	102.0	101.4	102.2	104.3
2004	100.9	101.6	102.4	102.2	102.8	102.2	101.0	101.5	101.0	101.2	101.5	102.0	101.7
2005	100.2	100.8	101.4	101.5	102.2	102.7	101.9	102.6	103.2	102.2	102.4	103.4	102.0
2006	101.9	102.3	102.1	101.3	101.7	102.1	100.7	101.1	101.6	100.4	100.8	101.8	101.5
2007	100.6	101.1	101.2	99.8	100.1	100.6	97.9	98.4	98.5	98.1	98.6	98.8	99.5
2008	97.3	97.4	96.6	95.2	94.8	94.5	92.2	92.0	91.8	90.5	89.7	88.8	93.4
2009	86.2	85.2	83.7	81.8	81.0	80.5	78.4	78.4	78.0	77.7	77.9	77.7	80.5
2010	76.0	76.1	76.1	75.7	75.9	76.3	75.5	75.9	75.7	76.0	76.3	76.6	76.0
2011	75.4	75.6	75.5	75.9	76.4	76.7	76.0	76.5	76.5	76.9	77.2	77.4	76.3
2012	76.8	77.3	77.6	76.7	77.0	77.0	76.2	76.8	76.8	77.1	77.6	77.6	77.0
2013	75.8	76.6	77.0	76.7	77.3	77.9	77.5	78.0	78.0	77.7	79.1	79.1	77.6
Trade, Transportation, and Utilities													
2002	519.1	515.3	518.6	513.7	514.1	513.6	509.6	512.0	513.4	513.8	522.5	532.0	516.5
2003	513.1	510.7	510.1	508.4	507.5	506.5	504.2	505.6	507.2	510.5	518.9	529.7	511.0
2004	514.0	513.1	514.3	514.5	514.3	513.6	512.5	514.2	511.7	518.0	530.2	540.1	517.5
2005	523.4	523.4	523.9	526.7	528.0	527.4	528.4	530.7	531.6	533.2	539.5	552.2	530.7
2006	538.5	539.1	541.8	540.2	542.3	542.7	538.0	540.2	540.4	543.4	555.1	565.4	543.9
2007	547.6	546.8	549.0	545.7	549.2	549.4	543.5	545.4	545.8	547.4	561.8	570.9	550.2
2008	551.5	550.5	550.5	544.6	544.5	541.6	534.6	534.4	532.8	531.2	537.1	542.6	541.3
2009	519.9	515.8	512.6	505.0	504.3	501.8	495.7	495.8	495.0	499.1	510.4	517.7	506.1
2010	500.4	499.1	500.0	501.1	502.7	502.7	498.9	500.8	500.3	507.3	519.8	528.1	505.1
2011	511.8	511.1	512.1	515.5	515.4	515.5	515.3	517.5	519.5	525.5	538.9	546.7	520.4
2012	532.8	531.7	533.0	533.5	535.3	533.7	530.5	531.1	533.0	538.2	553.4	558.6	537.1
2013	543.9	542.7	543.9	544.4	546.3	547.5	543.3	545.6	546.7	551.0	563.6	575.5	549.5
Wholesale Trade													
2002	132.4	133.1	133.9	132.6	133.1	132.8	132.3	132.9	132.8	133.3	134.1	135.0	133.2
2003	133.8	134.2	134.1	134.1	134.1	134.1	134.3	135.0	135.4	136.2	137.1	139.0	135.1
2004	137.7	138.6	139.6	139.7	140.1	139.8	138.7	138.8	138.4	139.6	140.9	141.5	139.5
2005	140.3	141.3	141.4	142.2	142.8	142.4	141.7	141.9	142.1	142.0	142.1	143.5	142.0
2006	142.3	143.7	144.4	144.3	144.9	145.5	145.0	145.9	146.1	146.5	147.5	149.0	145.4
2007	147.6	149.2	149.8	148.7	149.4	149.2	147.0	147.3	147.5	147.4	148.2	149.3	148.4
2008	146.7	147.6	147.7	146.7	147.1	146.1	144.0	143.8	143.8	143.0	142.8	143.0	145.2
2009	139.5	139.4	138.1	136.7	136.6	135.1	133.2	133.1	132.5	133.2	134.2	135.0	135.6
2010	132.1	132.7	132.8	132.7	133.4	132.7	131.6	131.8	131.7	132.7	133.5	134.5	132.7
2011	132.3	133.3	133.5	134.5	134.1	133.9	133.4	133.8	134.3	135.7	136.7	138.3	134.5
2012	137.0	138.1	139.0	139.4	139.8	139.1	138.3	138.3	138.7	139.5	140.5	141.6	139.1
2013	139.6	140.6	140.9	140.5	141.1	140.7	139.4	139.8	140.2	139.6	138.7	141.5	140.2
Retail Trade													
2002	290.9	286.5	287.5	285.1	284.9	284.7	281.1	282.8	284.3	284.4	291.4	299.0	286.9
2003	283.7	280.9	280.9	279.8	280.1	279.3	278.1	279.1	280.2	282.9	290.4	297.8	282.8
2004	284.2	282.1	282.4	282.5	283.1	282.7	282.3	283.7	281.7	285.6	295.0	302.4	285.6
2005	288.8	287.6	288.0	289.6	290.0	290.7	292.4	295.0	295.4	297.3	302.5	312.2	294.1
2006	300.8	299.8	301.5	300.6	302.7	302.2	299.5	300.0	299.9	302.9	312.7	319.1	303.5
2007	305.1	302.8	303.9	302.0	304.9	304.8	301.7	303.0	303.0	304.1	315.9	321.6	306.1
2008	307.6	305.2	305.1	301.8	301.7	300.8	297.0	296.8	295.8	294.7	300.0	303.8	300.9
2009	288.0	284.6	282.9	278.5	278.7	278.1	274.9	275.3	275.8	278.6	287.7	292.9	281.3
2010	280.1	278.1	278.7	279.9	281.4	282.2	279.9	281.6	281.1	286.4	296.5	302.2	284.0
2011	290.1	287.7	288.2	290.3	290.8	290.9	291.3	293.1	294.4	298.5	309.5	314.0	294.9
2012	303.0	299.9	300.1	300.3	301.7	300.9	298.8	299.5	300.6	303.9	316.8	319.1	303.7
2013	308.7	306.1	306.7	307.4	308.6	309.8	308.2	309.9	310.1	314.8	326.0	333.3	312.5
Transportation and Utilities													
2002	95.8	95.7	97.2	96.0	96.1	96.1	96.2	96.3	96.3	96.1	97.0	98.0	96.4
2003	95.6	95.6	95.1	94.5	93.3	93.1	91.8	91.5	91.6	91.4	91.4	92.9	93.2
2004	92.1	92.4	92.3	92.3	91.1	91.1	91.5	91.7	91.6	92.8	94.3	96.2	92.5
2005	94.3	94.5	94.5	94.9	95.2	94.3	94.3	93.8	94.1	93.9	94.9	96.5	94.6
2006	95.4	95.6	95.9	95.3	94.7	95.0	93.5	94.3	94.4	94.0	94.9	97.3	95.0
2007	94.9	94.8	95.3	95.0	94.9	95.4	94.8	95.1	95.3	95.9	97.7	100.0	95.8
2008	97.2	97.7	97.7	96.1	95.7	94.7	93.6	93.8	93.2	93.5	94.3	95.8	95.3
2009	92.4	91.8	91.6	89.8	89.0	88.6	87.6	87.4	86.7	87.3	88.5	89.8	89.2
2010	88.2	88.3	88.5	88.5	87.9	87.8	87.4	87.4	87.5	88.2	89.8	91.4	88.4
2011	89.4	90.1	90.4	90.7	90.5	90.7	90.6	90.6	90.8	91.3	92.7	94.4	91.0
2012	92.8	93.7	93.9	93.8	93.8	93.7	93.4	93.3	93.7	94.8	96.1	97.9	94.2
2013	95.6	96.0	96.3	96.5	96.6	97.0	95.7	95.9	96.4	96.6	98.9	100.7	96.9
Information													
2002	62.5	62.6	62.8	61.8	61.7	61.9	60.9	60.3	60.0	59.2	59.0	59.1	61.0
2003	57.3	57.0	57.4	56.3	56.4	56.6	56.6	56.6	56.2	56.5	56.6	57.0	56.7
2004	55.4	55.4	55.6	55.6	55.7	55.9	55.8	55.9	55.5	55.9	56.1	56.6	55.8
2005	55.7	56.1	56.2	55.7	55.6	55.7	55.1	54.9	54.8	53.7	54.0	54.1	55.1
2006	53.0	53.4	53.5	52.7	53.1	53.0	52.5	52.3	51.7	51.3	51.3	51.4	52.4
2007	50.7	51.1	51.4	51.2	51.4	51.7	51.3	51.3	50.7	51.0	51.1	51.3	51.2
2008	50.7	50.7	50.7	50.3	50.4	50.3	49.6	49.3	48.9	48.6	48.7	48.4	49.7
2009	47.1	46.9	46.6	45.8	45.7	45.2	44.3	44.2	43.4	43.5	43.5	43.5	45.0
2010	43.1	43.1	43.5	43.4	43.6	43.7	43.6	43.8	43.5	43.9	44.0	44.1	43.6
2011	43.9	43.9	44.0	43.9	43.9	43.9	43.8	44.2	44.2	44.3	44.6	44.7	44.1
2012	44.7	44.7	45.1	45.1	45.1	44.9	45.0	45.1	44.8	45.9	45.9	46.1	45.2
2013	45.4	45.4	46.0	45.8	45.9	46.0	46.1	46.2	46.1	46.5	46.5	46.6	46.0

Employment by Industry: Miami-Fort Lauderdale-Pompano Beach, FL, Selected Years, 2002–2013—*Continued*

(Numbers in thousands, not seasonally adjusted)

Industry and year	January	February	March	April	May	June	July	August	September	October	November	December	Annual average
Financial Activities													
2002	162.1	162.9	163.7	163.1	163.2	163.3	163.6	164.4	164.2	164.6	165.4	165.9	163.9
2003	163.7	164.3	164.6	164.3	164.6	165.0	165.2	165.9	166.1	166.7	166.5	168.2	165.4
2004	166.2	167.3	168.5	170.0	170.4	170.7	172.2	172.1	171.8	174.1	174.2	175.9	171.1
2005	174.3	175.8	176.5	177.8	178.3	179.4	179.8	180.9	181.1	181.3	182.3	184.3	179.3
2006	180.9	183.0	184.2	184.2	184.9	185.6	184.3	185.0	184.2	185.0	185.7	187.7	184.6
2007	183.3	184.3	184.4	183.2	183.0	183.3	182.0	181.7	180.7	179.9	180.9	182.2	182.4
2008	177.5	177.6	177.7	175.2	174.5	173.3	170.7	169.4	167.9	166.6	165.9	166.0	171.9
2009	160.2	159.7	159.1	157.4	157.2	156.8	154.7	154.3	153.2	154.0	154.4	155.2	156.4
2010	151.8	152.3	152.8	152.4	152.6	153.5	153.3	153.3	152.7	154.1	155.1	156.2	153.3
2011	153.4	153.9	154.3	155.6	156.0	155.7	156.2	156.7	157.0	158.3	159.0	160.3	156.4
2012	158.4	159.1	159.7	160.7	161.3	161.6	161.4	161.7	161.1	163.1	163.8	164.9	161.4
2013	162.4	162.7	163.3	163.6	164.1	164.9	165.2	165.5	165.8	166.5	166.8	167.3	164.8
Professional and Business Services													
2002	307.4	309.7	315.1	314.6	316.8	318.7	315.1	314.4	313.8	315.4	319.6	324.3	315.4
2003	314.9	322.1	326.2	321.9	318.1	314.3	308.1	307.5	305.7	312.3	310.6	314.1	314.7
2004	310.7	317.8	323.2	327.6	326.2	325.2	323.8	324.3	323.3	334.6	340.8	347.9	327.1
2005	338.4	346.0	348.7	352.4	352.1	352.6	351.4	353.7	358.5	354.1	359.3	365.5	352.7
2006	353.1	358.7	363.7	361.1	364.4	367.1	362.4	363.9	366.4	365.8	369.7	376.4	364.4
2007	366.6	371.6	373.9	368.7	369.5	369.4	361.9	363.7	363.6	361.8	363.4	365.9	366.7
2008	354.1	358.9	360.8	356.2	353.2	350.9	344.5	344.3	343.3	343.8	343.6	344.3	349.8
2009	327.8	327.8	325.5	321.7	320.0	320.1	316.6	317.9	318.1	321.2	325.2	326.9	322.4
2010	319.6	324.2	325.9	323.8	322.1	323.1	322.8	324.7	325.1	329.3	332.4	336.8	325.8
2011	331.4	336.2	337.7	340.6	338.5	337.3	336.1	336.8	338.7	342.6	346.5	350.0	339.4
2012	341.3	345.8	348.9	350.6	350.4	351.2	349.4	350.7	352.6	361.1	366.0	368.3	353.0
2013	360.9	366.7	368.9	370.5	370.8	370.2	369.4	371.8	371.5	374.3	376.5	378.7	370.9
Education and Health Services													
2002	268.6	271.8	274.5	273.1	274.1	274.5	269.7	272.6	276.8	278.1	279.7	281.7	274.6
2003	278.2	281.5	283.2	282.8	283.6	283.9	279.6	282.0	286.2	288.6	287.8	290.5	284.0
2004	287.3	290.8	291.7	293.3	294.4	293.4	290.0	292.0	293.0	297.4	299.1	300.1	293.5
2005	294.2	298.4	298.9	302.0	302.0	300.3	299.4	302.5	305.1	304.1	304.5	306.4	301.5
2006	300.7	303.7	306.1	306.0	307.9	307.3	304.5	307.9	310.4	311.3	313.3	315.6	307.9
2007	312.0	315.4	316.9	317.2	319.0	318.6	314.5	317.8	321.2	322.1	324.0	326.5	318.8
2008	322.6	326.1	328.0	326.3	328.0	326.6	320.9	324.0	326.1	327.3	329.0	330.0	326.2
2009	325.4	327.2	328.7	329.4	331.5	330.2	326.3	329.0	332.2	335.6	337.0	337.0	330.8
2010	332.6	334.8	335.3	335.5	337.0	335.4	331.6	332.8	335.2	338.2	340.1	340.7	335.8
2011	338.6	341.4	341.7	344.3	343.7	340.6	334.7	336.4	340.6	342.1	343.7	343.8	341.0
2012	339.2	342.3	343.8	343.2	343.1	340.4	334.6	338.6	342.0	343.7	345.3	344.8	341.8
2013	341.9	345.5	346.5	347.1	347.3	345.0	339.5	343.8	346.6	347.9	350.8	352.7	346.2
Leisure and Hospitality													
2002	225.2	229.8	232.5	229.7	228.2	225.2	217.0	218.2	219.3	222.6	227.7	232.0	225.6
2003	230.9	234.8	238.2	233.6	231.3	228.6	221.9	222.1	224.5	226.4	231.6	237.4	230.1
2004	240.1	244.8	248.7	245.9	243.4	240.6	234.7	234.8	230.9	235.9	242.9	248.8	241.0
2005	244.0	249.8	253.3	253.5	251.4	250.8	242.9	243.6	244.5	243.2	247.7	253.8	248.2
2006	251.6	257.3	261.4	256.0	254.3	252.4	244.1	245.6	245.9	246.2	254.6	258.4	252.3
2007	255.8	261.3	265.9	262.6	262.3	259.3	250.0	252.0	253.5	252.9	261.4	265.7	258.6
2008	262.6	267.1	270.3	266.4	263.7	259.1	248.0	247.7	247.1	247.6	254.9	258.2	257.7
2009	254.4	256.3	258.6	255.5	251.4	248.3	240.1	239.5	239.5	240.5	246.4	250.2	248.4
2010	248.9	252.8	256.4	256.0	253.4	250.8	245.4	246.9	247.4	250.5	257.2	261.2	252.2
2011	259.1	261.6	265.2	266.3	264.4	260.9	255.6	256.5	257.5	258.4	266.7	272.0	262.0
2012	271.9	275.2	280.0	279.4	278.6	275.0	268.9	269.3	269.7	273.5	281.0	285.2	275.6
2013	282.9	287.8	291.7	290.4	288.5	285.2	279.4	279.8	280.0	283.1	289.7	293.4	286.0
Other Services													
2002	99.6	100.7	101.3	100.3	100.5	100.5	100.3	100.6	101.2	102.3	103.6	104.5	101.3
2003	103.2	104.6	105.4	104.5	104.7	105.0	102.0	101.5	101.9	102.0	102.0	103.4	103.4
2004	103.4	104.6	105.6	104.4	105.0	106.1	105.1	105.9	105.9	105.2	106.7	106.8	105.4
2005	106.5	107.5	107.4	107.7	107.6	107.3	106.1	106.3	106.7	105.6	106.2	107.4	106.9
2006	107.5	108.8	110.0	107.2	107.4	108.1	105.8	106.0	106.2	105.9	106.8	107.7	107.3
2007	107.8	109.1	110.5	107.6	108.1	108.5	106.8	107.2	107.9	109.8	111.6	113.2	109.0
2008	112.1	112.8	113.6	112.0	111.2	110.4	108.3	107.5	106.4	105.7	105.3	105.4	109.2
2009	103.3	103.2	103.2	103.0	102.4	102.1	100.9	100.6	100.6	101.1	101.8	102.4	102.1
2010	101.5	102.3	102.6	102.8	102.2	101.9	100.5	100.6	100.3	101.2	102.0	102.3	101.7
2011	101.5	102.0	102.6	103.5	103.8	102.9	103.3	103.7	104.3	105.2	106.5	107.1	103.9
2012	106.8	107.7	108.5	109.2	109.2	109.1	108.0	107.5	107.9	108.9	109.6	110.0	108.5
2013	109.4	110.6	111.2	111.7	111.4	111.4	110.4	110.2	110.7	111.3	113.3	114.4	111.3
Government													
2002	307.9	309.1	312.2	310.6	312.6	304.8	284.3	286.4	311.2	312.2	314.8	316.5	306.9
2003	313.7	315.8	317.7	316.4	318.6	310.4	289.9	291.6	314.3	316.6	316.6	316.2	311.5
2004	315.3	316.7	317.5	318.5	319.3	312.1	292.0	294.5	317.6	321.4	321.6	322.0	314.0
2005	320.2	321.4	322.5	324.7	325.4	297.0	292.9	320.8	323.9	326.0	325.3	325.7	318.8
2006	324.3	325.5	327.0	325.4	325.9	297.7	293.5	322.1	325.8	327.2	330.3	329.6	321.2
2007	326.5	327.9	330.2	330.4	331.2	302.1	297.8	327.8	331.6	330.2	332.6	333.5	325.2
2008	330.8	333.3	333.0	331.6	332.6	303.1	298.6	325.4	327.2	326.6	328.6	329.8	325.1
2009	327.9	326.4	326.6	327.0	325.5	297.4	294.7	316.5	319.0	321.0	321.9	321.7	318.8
2010	318.3	318.9	318.8	319.9	329.0	295.6	289.1	310.2	311.4	313.7	314.1	313.5	312.7
2011	312.0	313.6	312.1	312.2	310.1	283.4	280.4	303.6	306.5	309.8	308.3	308.8	305.1
2012	305.3	306.6	305.6	305.6	304.6	279.3	276.6	298.3	302.3	305.7	305.6	305.3	300.1
2013	303.2	306.1	306.4	306.2	306.2	280.3	277.9	298.8	303.6	307.6	308.9	308.9	301.2

Employment by Industry: Milwaukee-Waukesha-West Allis, WI, Selected Years, 2002–2013

(Numbers in thousands, not seasonally adjusted)

Industry and year	January	February	March	April	May	June	July	August	September	October	November	December	Annual average
Total Nonfarm													
2002	829.0	828.2	832.4	839.3	843.8	848.7	840.3	840.5	839.0	844.7	845.0	843.6	839.5
2003	820.0	822.8	824.9	830.9	834.0	839.6	826.8	828.8	828.4	837.1	834.8	837.0	830.4
2004	815.1	817.9	822.8	827.1	833.1	842.0	833.9	836.4	834.8	841.0	841.0	840.5	832.1
2005	822.9	825.2	827.8	839.2	842.1	849.0	843.6	844.8	847.5	847.1	849.0	850.4	840.7
2006	830.0	832.5	836.1	845.8	850.7	859.2	851.7	855.1	858.3	861.4	863.0	863.2	850.6
2007	843.3	843.0	846.0	853.0	861.8	870.8	858.9	861.8	860.1	862.3	863.2	863.5	857.3
2008	843.8	842.9	846.1	853.0	860.1	865.0	854.9	854.7	855.7	856.8	852.8	847.8	852.8
2009	820.7	815.1	810.6	813.4	816.9	819.3	806.3	805.8	810.6	811.5	809.5	808.0	812.3
2010	789.8	789.3	791.9	800.3	808.3	810.1	807.3	809.4	807.8	814.4	816.6	813.9	804.9
2011	795.7	797.6	800.9	808.6	812.9	816.8	814.0	815.4	815.1	815.2	817.8	815.1	810.4
2012	795.8	799.2	805.7	811.3	820.7	823.8	817.4	820.2	821.7	825.9	829.8	827.4	816.6
2013	804.2	811.9	815.6	818.5	826.8	831.5	827.9	831.8	834.1	836.3	836.2	834.3	825.8
Total Private													
2002	734.8	731.1	734.9	742.6	747.8	752.4	753.0	753.2	747.6	746.6	746.5	745.3	744.7
2003	726.6	725.5	728.1	733.7	739.1	744.1	742.2	743.6	740.3	742.0	740.5	742.3	737.3
2004	725.3	723.0	727.5	733.5	739.5	748.5	750.0	751.5	745.0	748.8	747.5	747.6	740.6
2005	731.3	730.4	734.2	745.5	748.7	755.5	758.5	759.4	755.2	754.1	755.5	757.6	748.8
2006	739.8	739.6	742.7	752.1	757.2	765.3	766.2	769.2	766.1	767.8	769.4	770.0	758.8
2007	753.2	751.3	754.0	760.4	768.8	777.2	773.9	776.9	768.6	770.1	771.0	770.5	766.3
2008	752.6	751.6	752.4	759.7	765.8	770.8	769.0	770.1	762.2	761.7	755.9	752.2	760.3
2009	727.5	720.1	715.7	718.1	722.3	725.7	722.7	723.2	719.1	718.5	716.4	714.8	720.3
2010	698.1	697.7	699.9	708.7	714.3	718.8	722.4	725.4	719.8	724.1	724.8	723.8	714.8
2011	706.8	704.8	708.6	717.0	721.9	726.1	726.8	728.8	727.2	728.7	729.3	726.3	721.0
2012	710.0	712.0	716.9	721.2	729.7	734.5	734.1	735.2	734.9	737.3	738.6	738.5	728.6
2013	719.5	723.8	727.5	730.5	739.1	743.6	744.9	746.8	744.4	743.5	743.5	742.8	737.5
Goods Producing													
2002	176.5	174.9	175.4	176.8	178.1	179.8	178.4	179.4	178.0	177.5	176.7	174.6	177.2
2003	169.1	167.9	167.9	169.5	170.7	172.1	171.2	172.8	171.1	170.7	169.9	168.7	170.1
2004	163.7	163.0	163.9	166.1	167.6	170.2	171.1	171.5	170.2	169.5	169.1	168.2	167.8
2005	164.1	163.8	164.4	166.9	168.3	170.7	171.1	170.9	169.4	168.2	167.7	166.7	167.7
2006	164.1	163.0	163.5	166.3	168.1	171.1	170.9	171.8	170.3	170.3	169.7	169.1	168.2
2007	165.8	163.7	164.8	167.2	169.9	172.4	172.0	172.6	170.6	170.3	169.4	167.8	168.9
2008	164.2	163.1	163.6	165.1	167.0	168.6	167.5	167.7	165.0	164.2	162.2	159.1	164.8
2009	153.2	149.4	146.3	145.4	145.0	145.4	143.8	144.0	143.0	142.1	140.5	138.4	144.7
2010	134.9	133.3	133.7	136.4	137.6	140.1	141.8	142.7	141.2	141.4	140.4	138.7	138.5
2011	136.5	135.7	136.8	139.7	141.4	144.5	145.4	145.7	144.2	143.9	143.5	142.0	141.6
2012	139.4	138.9	139.8	142.0	143.2	146.3	147.0	146.5	144.9	144.9	144.3	143.3	143.4
2013	141.2	140.7	141.1	142.3	144.6	147.3	147.6	147.9	146.2	144.9	144.6	142.6	144.3
Service-Providing													
2002	652.5	653.3	657.0	662.5	665.7	668.9	661.9	661.1	661.0	667.2	668.3	669.0	662.4
2003	650.9	654.9	657.0	661.4	663.3	667.5	655.6	656.0	657.3	666.4	664.9	668.3	660.3
2004	651.4	654.9	658.9	661.0	665.5	671.8	662.8	664.9	664.6	671.5	671.9	672.3	664.3
2005	658.8	661.4	663.4	672.3	673.8	678.3	672.5	673.9	678.1	678.9	681.3	683.7	673.0
2006	665.9	669.5	672.6	679.5	682.6	688.1	680.8	683.3	688.0	691.1	693.3	694.1	682.4
2007	677.5	679.3	681.2	685.8	691.9	698.4	686.9	689.2	689.5	692.0	693.8	695.7	688.4
2008	679.6	679.8	682.5	687.9	693.1	696.4	687.4	687.0	690.7	692.6	690.6	688.7	688.0
2009	667.5	665.7	664.3	668.0	671.9	673.9	662.5	661.8	667.6	669.4	669.0	669.6	667.6
2010	654.9	656.0	658.2	663.9	670.7	670.0	665.5	666.7	666.6	673.0	676.2	675.2	666.4
2011	659.2	661.9	664.1	668.9	671.5	672.3	668.6	669.7	670.9	671.3	674.3	673.1	668.8
2012	656.4	660.3	665.9	669.3	677.5	677.5	670.4	673.7	676.8	681.0	685.5	684.1	673.2
2013	663.0	671.2	674.5	676.2	682.2	684.2	680.3	683.9	687.9	691.4	691.6	691.7	681.5
Mining and Logging													
2002	0.4	0.4	0.4	0.4	0.4	0.5	0.5	0.5	0.5	0.4	0.4	0.4	0.4
2003	0.4	0.4	0.4	0.4	0.4	0.5	0.5	0.5	0.5	0.5	0.4	0.5	0.4
2004	0.4	0.4	0.4	0.4	0.5	0.5	0.5	0.5	0.5	0.5	0.5	0.5	0.5
2005	0.4	0.4	0.4	0.5	0.5	0.5	0.5	0.5	0.5	0.5	0.5	0.5	0.5
2006	0.5	0.5	0.5	0.5	0.5	0.5	0.5	0.5	0.5	0.5	0.5	0.5	0.5
2007	0.5	0.4	0.5	0.5	0.5	0.5	0.5	0.5	0.5	0.5	0.5	0.5	0.5
2008	0.4	0.4	0.4	0.4	0.4	0.4	0.4	0.4	0.4	0.4	0.4	0.4	0.4
2009	0.3	0.3	0.3	0.4	0.4	0.4	0.4	0.4	0.4	0.4	0.3	0.3	0.4
2010	0.3	0.3	0.3	0.3	0.3	0.4	0.4	0.4	0.4	0.4	0.4	0.3	0.4
2011	0.3	0.3	0.3	0.3	0.3	0.4	0.4	0.4	0.3	0.4	0.3	0.4	0.3
2012	0.3	0.3	0.3	0.4	0.4	0.4	0.4	0.4	0.4	0.4	0.4	0.3	0.4
2013	0.3	0.3	0.3	0.4	0.4	0.4	0.4	0.4	0.4	0.4	0.3	0.3	0.4
Construction													
2002	29.7	28.9	29.5	32.2	34.0	35.1	35.9	36.1	35.6	35.7	34.9	33.0	33.4
2003	29.9	29.2	29.4	31.5	33.6	34.7	35.7	36.1	35.5	35.4	34.5	33.1	33.2
2004	29.7	29.2	29.9	32.0	33.3	34.7	36.0	36.0	35.4	35.1	34.7	33.5	33.3
2005	30.3	29.9	30.4	32.7	34.4	35.6	36.1	36.0	35.5	35.1	34.8	33.4	33.7
2006	31.2	30.5	31.0	33.5	35.0	36.4	36.7	36.7	36.3	36.1	35.5	34.4	34.4
2007	31.9	30.6	32.3	33.8	36.1	37.5	37.9	37.9	37.1	36.7	36.1	34.0	35.2
2008	31.0	30.2	30.9	32.6	35.0	35.9	36.1	35.9	34.8	35.0	33.6	31.4	33.5
2009	27.6	27.0	26.8	28.4	29.7	30.6	30.8	30.7	29.8	29.3	28.3	26.0	28.8
2010	23.1	22.3	22.6	25.0	25.9	27.1	27.6	28.0	27.2	27.0	25.9	23.9	25.5
2011	21.5	20.8	21.4	23.5	24.9	26.1	26.3	26.4	26.0	25.8	25.2	23.3	24.3
2012	20.6	20.3	20.9	22.8	23.9	25.1	25.4	25.3	24.9	24.9	24.4	23.0	23.5
2013	21.4	21.3	21.7	22.6	25.2	26.3	27.1	27.5	27.0	26.4	25.6	23.4	24.6

Employment by Industry: Milwaukee-Waukesha-West Allis, WI, Selected Years, 2002–2013—*Continued*

(Numbers in thousands, not seasonally adjusted)

Industry and year	January	February	March	April	May	June	July	August	September	October	November	December	Annual average
Manufacturing													
2002	146.4	145.6	145.5	144.2	143.7	144.2	142.0	142.8	141.9	141.4	141.4	141.2	143.4
2003	138.8	138.3	138.1	137.6	136.7	136.9	135.0	136.2	135.1	134.9	135.0	135.1	136.5
2004	133.6	133.4	133.6	133.7	133.8	135.0	134.6	135.0	134.3	133.9	133.9	134.2	134.1
2005	133.4	133.5	133.6	133.7	133.4	134.6	134.5	134.4	133.4	132.6	132.4	132.8	133.5
2006	132.4	132.0	132.0	132.3	132.6	134.2	133.7	134.6	133.5	133.7	133.7	134.2	133.2
2007	133.4	132.7	132.0	132.9	133.3	134.4	133.6	134.2	133.0	133.1	132.8	133.3	133.2
2008	132.8	132.5	132.3	132.1	131.6	132.3	131.0	131.4	129.8	128.8	128.2	127.3	130.8
2009	125.3	122.1	119.2	116.6	114.9	114.4	112.6	112.9	112.8	112.4	111.9	112.1	115.6
2010	111.5	110.7	110.8	111.1	111.3	112.6	113.8	114.3	113.6	114.0	114.2	114.5	112.7
2011	114.7	114.6	115.1	115.9	116.2	118.0	118.7	119.0	117.8	117.8	117.9	118.4	117.0
2012	118.5	118.3	118.6	118.8	118.9	120.8	121.2	120.8	119.6	119.6	119.5	120.0	119.6
2013	119.5	119.1	119.1	119.3	119.0	120.6	120.1	120.0	118.8	118.1	118.7	118.9	119.3
Trade, Transportation, and Utilities													
2002	155.6	152.9	153.7	153.5	154.8	154.6	153.0	152.7	153.4	153.9	157.2	159.1	154.5
2003	152.3	150.4	150.6	151.1	152.3	152.9	149.8	150.7	151.9	153.8	155.6	157.5	152.4
2004	151.4	149.8	150.6	149.7	151.6	153.2	151.3	151.7	152.1	154.1	156.5	157.6	152.5
2005	152.2	150.8	151.3	151.9	153.0	153.6	153.1	153.9	154.2	154.9	157.5	158.9	153.8
2006	153.3	151.5	152.4	152.9	154.2	155.0	153.1	153.6	154.1	155.2	158.2	159.7	154.4
2007	154.2	152.1	152.1	152.0	153.9	154.6	152.7	152.8	152.4	153.2	156.0	156.8	153.6
2008	151.8	149.4	149.5	150.5	151.2	151.8	150.7	150.7	149.8	150.2	150.9	151.4	150.7
2009	145.1	142.6	141.7	140.9	142.6	143.6	140.8	140.6	141.0	143.0	143.5	143.8	142.4
2010	138.5	136.3	136.4	136.6	138.0	138.9	137.5	138.0	138.4	141.5	142.5	143.3	138.8
2011	138.3	136.8	137.3	138.2	138.9	139.3	138.6	139.1	139.9	141.8	143.1	143.5	139.6
2012	139.1	137.4	137.7	136.7	139.2	139.8	138.7	139.3	139.6	140.9	143.7	144.3	139.7
2013	138.7	137.6	137.9	138.1	140.0	140.9	139.7	140.1	139.9	141.3	142.7	143.2	140.0
Wholesale Trade													
2002	41.1	41.0	41.0	40.8	40.9	41.0	41.1	40.9	40.5	40.2	40.2	40.2	40.7
2003	40.0	40.0	40.0	39.9	39.9	40.1	40.1	40.0	39.7	39.5	39.3	39.4	39.8
2004	38.9	38.7	38.9	38.9	38.9	39.3	39.7	39.8	39.5	39.9	40.0	40.1	39.4
2005	39.9	39.9	39.8	40.4	40.5	40.9	41.2	41.0	40.7	40.8	40.9	41.0	40.6
2006	40.4	40.5	40.6	40.8	40.9	41.4	41.6	41.5	41.3	41.4	41.4	41.6	41.1
2007	40.9	41.0	41.0	41.1	41.2	41.8	41.8	41.7	41.3	41.3	41.2	41.2	41.3
2008	40.6	40.6	40.6	40.8	40.8	40.9	41.0	40.9	40.3	39.9	39.9	39.6	40.5
2009	38.9	38.6	38.1	37.6	37.5	37.6	37.2	36.9	36.5	36.5	36.3	36.2	37.3
2010	35.4	35.2	35.1	35.0	35.2	35.5	35.8	35.8	35.4	35.7	35.6	35.6	35.4
2011	35.1	35.1	35.2	35.4	35.5	35.7	36.2	36.2	35.9	36.2	36.1	36.0	35.7
2012	35.6	35.7	35.9	35.9	36.0	36.3	36.3	36.3	35.9	35.9	35.9	36.1	36.0
2013	35.6	35.5	35.5	35.5	35.7	36.0	36.0	36.1	35.6	35.6	35.5	35.2	35.7
Retail Trade													
2002	84.3	81.9	82.5	82.5	83.5	84.2	83.0	83.0	82.5	82.9	86.3	88.2	83.7
2003	82.3	80.3	80.5	80.6	81.7	82.2	81.2	81.8	81.4	83.2	85.3	87.1	82.3
2004	82.5	81.0	81.4	81.1	82.4	83.3	82.4	82.8	82.1	82.9	85.3	86.8	82.8
2005	82.0	80.6	81.1	81.6	82.3	82.8	82.6	83.5	82.7	83.3	85.4	86.6	82.9
2006	82.5	80.6	81.1	81.4	82.4	83.0	82.1	82.7	81.9	82.9	85.9	86.9	82.8
2007	83.3	81.1	81.1	80.5	81.9	82.0	81.7	81.5	80.1	80.8	83.4	84.2	81.8
2008	81.2	78.9	79.1	79.6	80.2	80.7	80.7	80.6	79.2	79.9	81.0	81.7	80.2
2009	77.6	75.6	75.4	75.2	76.4	77.3	76.6	76.6	76.0	77.7	78.5	78.7	76.8
2010	75.4	73.6	73.9	74.3	75.3	75.7	75.3	75.7	75.3	77.5	78.5	79.1	75.8
2011	75.6	74.1	74.5	75.1	75.5	76.1	75.9	76.4	76.0	77.6	78.9	79.5	76.3
2012	76.2	74.4	74.6	74.6	75.7	76.4	76.3	76.8	76.4	77.7	80.3	80.5	76.7
2013	76.6	75.6	75.8	76.2	77.5	78.2	78.1	78.1	77.5	79.0	80.4	81.3	77.9
Transportation and Utilities													
2002	30.2	30.0	30.2	30.2	30.4	29.4	28.9	28.8	30.4	30.8	30.7	30.7	30.1
2003	30.0	30.1	30.1	30.6	30.7	30.6	28.5	28.9	30.8	31.1	31.0	31.0	30.3
2004	30.0	30.1	30.3	29.7	30.3	30.6	29.2	29.1	30.5	31.3	31.2	30.7	30.3
2005	30.3	30.3	30.4	29.9	30.2	29.9	29.3	29.4	30.8	30.8	31.2	31.3	30.3
2006	30.4	30.4	30.7	30.7	30.9	30.6	29.4	29.4	30.9	30.9	30.9	31.2	30.5
2007	30.0	30.0	30.0	30.4	30.8	30.8	29.2	29.6	31.0	31.1	31.4	31.4	30.5
2008	30.0	29.9	29.8	30.1	30.2	30.2	29.0	29.2	30.3	30.4	30.0	30.1	29.9
2009	28.6	28.4	28.2	28.1	28.7	28.7	27.0	27.1	28.5	28.8	28.7	28.9	28.3
2010	27.7	27.5	27.4	27.3	27.5	27.7	26.4	26.5	27.7	28.3	28.4	28.6	27.6
2011	27.6	27.6	27.6	27.7	27.9	27.5	26.5	26.5	28.0	28.0	28.1	28.0	27.6
2012	27.3	27.3	27.2	26.2	27.5	27.1	26.1	26.2	27.3	27.3	27.5	27.7	27.1
2013	26.5	26.5	26.6	26.4	26.8	26.7	25.6	25.9	26.8	26.7	26.8	26.7	26.5
Information													
2002	19.7	19.5	19.6	19.5	19.3	19.3	19.2	19.2	18.9	18.8	18.8	18.8	19.2
2003	18.8	18.6	18.6	18.5	18.3	18.3	18.4	18.4	18.3	18.3	18.3	18.3	18.4
2004	18.5	18.5	18.5	18.6	18.5	18.4	18.6	18.6	18.3	18.2	18.3	18.2	18.4
2005	18.2	18.1	18.1	18.2	18.2	18.3	18.1	18.2	18.1	18.1	18.2	18.3	18.2
2006	18.0	18.1	18.0	17.9	17.9	17.7	17.7	17.7	17.5	17.5	17.5	17.5	17.8
2007	17.5	17.5	17.5	17.5	17.5	17.6	17.5	17.5	17.3	17.4	17.5	17.4	17.5
2008	17.1	17.1	17.0	17.5	17.5	17.7	17.5	17.5	17.3	17.3	17.3	17.3	17.3
2009	16.9	16.9	16.8	16.7	16.5	16.5	16.5	16.4	16.3	16.2	16.2	16.1	16.5
2010	15.6	15.6	15.5	15.5	15.5	15.6	15.9	15.8	15.6	15.2	15.8	15.6	15.6
2011	15.6	15.6	15.4	15.5	15.5	15.5	15.4	15.5	15.4	15.2	15.3	15.1	15.4
2012	15.0	14.9	14.8	14.7	14.7	14.8	14.9	14.9	14.8	14.8	14.8	14.7	14.8
2013	14.6	14.6	14.5	14.6	14.7	14.5	14.6	14.6	14.5	14.5	14.5	14.5	14.6

Employment by Industry: Milwaukee-Waukesha-West Allis, WI, Selected Years, 2002–2013—*Continued*

(Numbers in thousands, not seasonally adjusted)

Industry and year	January	February	March	April	May	June	July	August	September	October	November	December	Annual average
Financial Activities													
2002	57.1	57.1	57.0	57.3	57.4	57.9	58.6	58.6	57.9	57.8	58.1	58.1	57.7
2003	57.8	58.0	58.0	58.1	58.3	58.7	58.7	58.4	57.6	57.5	57.2	57.3	58.0
2004	57.4	57.2	57.4	57.6	57.6	58.1	58.5	58.6	57.5	57.9	57.9	58.1	57.8
2005	57.1	56.8	57.1	57.2	57.2	57.4	57.9	57.7	57.1	56.9	57.1	57.3	57.2
2006	57.0	56.8	56.7	57.3	57.5	57.9	58.4	58.3	58.0	58.0	58.1	58.2	57.7
2007	57.8	57.9	57.6	58.0	58.2	58.7	58.7	58.5	57.7	58.2	58.4	58.6	58.2
2008	58.0	58.2	57.9	58.1	58.5	58.5	59.0	58.9	57.9	58.3	58.2	58.2	58.3
2009	57.7	57.5	57.2	57.6	57.6	57.6	57.8	57.7	56.6	56.8	56.8	56.5	57.3
2010	55.7	55.7	55.9	55.8	55.8	56.0	56.3	56.3	55.8	56.0	56.0	56.3	56.0
2011	55.4	55.4	55.6	55.5	55.5	55.8	56.0	55.8	55.5	55.2	54.9	54.9	55.5
2012	54.5	54.5	54.5	54.4	54.7	55.1	55.1	55.0	54.3	54.4	54.3	54.5	54.6
2013	54.1	54.0	54.0	54.1	54.1	54.5	55.1	54.9	54.2	53.7	53.7	53.5	54.2
Professional and Business Services													
2002	100.1	100.1	101.6	105.3	105.6	105.7	106.3	106.9	106.0	105.6	103.5	102.8	104.1
2003	100.9	101.3	102.5	103.7	103.2	103.6	104.2	104.0	104.5	105.4	104.4	105.4	103.6
2004	102.0	101.6	103.0	104.4	104.0	106.5	107.0	107.6	106.5	106.9	105.9	105.6	105.1
2005	103.5	103.9	104.8	107.9	107.0	108.8	110.6	110.9	111.2	110.8	110.8	111.6	108.5
2006	106.4	107.3	107.9	110.7	110.3	111.9	112.7	113.7	113.9	114.4	114.1	113.6	111.4
2007	110.4	111.0	111.8	113.2	113.8	116.2	115.9	117.7	116.2	115.9	116.1	116.5	114.6
2008	113.1	113.9	112.8	114.3	114.7	116.0	115.9	116.7	116.0	114.6	112.6	111.5	114.3
2009	105.7	103.4	101.9	102.4	102.3	102.8	103.4	103.1	102.4	103.6	103.7	104.3	103.3
2010	100.5	101.7	100.7	104.2	104.8	106.4	108.6	110.1	109.6	110.9	111.9	112.2	106.8
2011	109.1	109.3	110.4	110.6	110.2	112.7	112.5	113.7	113.5	113.0	113.8	112.9	111.8
2012	111.1	111.8	113.3	113.6	114.4	116.6	116.2	117.0	117.9	118.2	118.0	117.5	115.5
2013	114.0	115.7	117.6	116.6	117.7	119.4	120.1	120.8	121.0	119.9	118.3	118.1	118.3
Education and Health Services													
2002	124.4	125.3	125.7	125.9	126.2	125.9	126.0	126.4	126.5	127.9	128.6	128.0	126.4
2003	125.8	128.0	128.1	128.5	128.4	128.0	127.7	127.7	128.1	129.2	129.6	129.4	128.2
2004	129.2	130.0	130.3	130.9	131.2	130.5	130.3	130.5	130.9	132.5	132.8	133.0	131.0
2005	131.1	132.0	132.3	133.2	133.2	132.7	131.7	132.1	133.2	134.8	135.0	135.5	133.1
2006	134.2	135.7	135.6	136.2	136.5	136.1	135.8	136.4	138.2	140.0	140.0	139.9	137.1
2007	137.5	138.9	139.1	139.4	139.8	139.3	138.5	139.4	140.8	141.5	141.9	142.0	139.8
2008	140.0	141.4	141.9	142.3	142.6	141.5	140.6	141.4	142.3	144.6	144.7	145.1	142.4
2009	142.5	143.8	144.2	145.1	145.4	145.0	144.3	144.9	145.9	147.6	147.8	147.8	145.4
2010	146.0	147.6	148.7	148.1	148.0	146.1	145.8	145.4	145.6	147.3	147.6	147.4	147.0
2011	143.9	144.6	145.0	145.9	146.3	143.1	141.8	141.4	145.1	147.1	147.6	147.6	145.0
2012	142.8	146.1	147.6	148.4	148.6	145.4	144.0	144.8	148.7	151.4	151.7	152.0	147.6
2013	147.3	151.2	151.5	152.3	151.3	148.6	147.8	149.0	152.5	154.9	156.0	157.0	151.6
Leisure and Hospitality													
2002	60.4	60.3	60.7	63.0	65.2	67.3	70.0	68.6	65.8	63.8	62.5	62.4	64.2
2003	60.9	60.5	61.3	63.2	67.0	68.8	71.0	70.3	68.0	66.3	64.9	64.8	65.6
2004	62.3	61.9	62.7	64.8	67.7	69.5	71.1	70.9	67.7	67.0	65.3	65.2	66.3
2005	63.8	63.6	64.7	68.4	70.1	71.8	73.9	73.6	70.7	69.2	68.2	68.2	68.9
2006	66.2	66.5	67.8	69.6	71.4	73.7	75.6	75.9	72.5	70.9	70.3	70.2	70.9
2007	68.9	68.9	69.7	70.9	73.8	75.8	76.4	76.5	72.3	71.2	69.5	69.1	71.9
2008	66.7	66.5	67.6	69.3	71.6	73.5	74.6	74.2	71.5	69.6	67.4	67.0	70.0
2009	65.0	65.1	66.0	67.7	70.2	71.4	72.4	72.5	70.0	67.3	65.7	65.4	68.2
2010	63.2	63.3	64.3	67.0	69.8	70.6	71.5	72.2	69.5	67.9	66.9	66.6	67.7
2011	64.8	64.4	65.0	68.1	70.5	71.5	73.2	73.8	70.6	69.3	68.2	67.3	68.9
2012	66.1	66.5	67.3	69.5	72.8	73.7	75.6	75.3	72.7	70.5	69.7	70.0	70.8
2013	68.1	68.5	69.2	70.7	74.7	76.0	77.5	77.0	73.9	71.9	70.6	71.1	72.4
Other Services													
2002	41.0	41.0	41.2	41.3	41.2	41.9	41.5	41.4	41.1	41.3	41.1	41.5	41.3
2003	41.0	40.8	41.1	41.1	40.9	41.7	41.2	41.3	40.8	40.8	40.6	40.9	41.0
2004	40.8	41.0	41.1	41.4	41.3	42.1	42.1	42.1	41.8	42.7	41.7	41.7	41.7
2005	41.3	41.4	41.5	41.8	41.7	42.2	42.1	42.1	41.3	41.2	41.0	41.1	41.6
2006	40.6	40.7	40.8	41.2	41.3	41.9	42.0	41.8	41.6	41.5	41.5	41.8	41.4
2007	41.1	41.3	41.4	42.2	41.9	42.6	42.2	41.9	41.3	42.4	42.2	42.3	41.9
2008	41.7	42.0	42.1	42.6	42.7	43.2	43.2	43.0	42.4	42.9	42.6	42.6	42.6
2009	41.4	41.4	41.6	42.3	42.7	43.4	43.7	44.0	43.9	41.9	42.2	42.5	42.6
2010	43.7	44.2	44.7	45.1	44.8	45.1	45.0	44.9	44.1	43.9	43.7	43.7	44.4
2011	43.2	43.0	43.1	43.5	43.6	43.7	43.9	43.8	43.0	43.2	42.9	43.0	43.3
2012	42.0	41.9	41.9	41.9	42.1	42.8	42.6	42.4	42.0	42.2	42.1	42.2	42.2
2013	41.5	41.5	41.7	41.8	42.0	42.4	42.5	42.5	42.2	42.4	43.1	42.8	42.2
Government													
2002	94.2	97.1	97.5	96.7	96.0	96.3	87.3	87.3	91.4	98.1	98.5	98.3	94.9
2003	93.4	97.3	96.8	97.2	94.9	95.5	84.6	85.2	88.1	95.1	94.3	94.7	93.1
2004	89.8	94.9	95.3	93.6	93.6	93.5	83.9	84.9	89.8	92.2	93.5	92.9	91.5
2005	91.6	94.8	93.6	93.7	93.4	93.5	85.1	85.4	92.3	93.0	93.5	92.8	91.9
2006	90.2	92.9	93.4	93.7	93.5	93.9	85.5	85.9	92.2	93.6	93.6	93.2	91.8
2007	90.1	91.7	92.0	92.6	93.0	93.6	85.0	84.9	91.5	92.2	92.2	93.0	91.0
2008	91.2	91.3	93.7	93.3	94.3	94.2	85.9	84.6	93.5	95.1	96.9	95.6	92.5
2009	93.2	95.0	94.9	95.3	94.6	93.6	83.6	82.6	91.5	93.0	93.1	93.2	92.0
2010	91.7	91.6	92.0	91.6	94.0	91.3	84.9	84.0	88.0	90.3	91.8	90.1	90.1
2011	88.9	92.8	92.3	91.6	91.0	90.7	87.2	86.6	87.9	86.5	88.5	88.8	89.4
2012	85.8	87.2	88.8	90.1	91.0	89.3	83.3	83.0	86.8	86.8	91.2	88.9	88.0
2013	84.7	88.1	88.1	88.0	87.7	87.9	83.0	85.0	89.7	92.8	92.7	91.5	88.3

Employment by Industry: Minneapolis-St. Paul-Bloomington, MN–WI, Selected Years, 2002–2013

(Numbers in thousands, not seasonally adjusted)

Industry and year	January	February	March	April	May	June	July	August	September	October	November	December	Annual average
Total Nonfarm													
2002	1,696.2	1,694.8	1,697.5	1,708.5	1,729.3	1,738.2	1,721.2	1,720.0	1,733.6	1,736.5	1,743.2	1,737.6	1,721.4
2003	1,691.6	1,694.2	1,696.7	1,714.9	1,735.2	1,742.3	1,721.8	1,726.4	1,735.9	1,742.7	1,743.9	1,744.6	1,724.2
2004	1,693.3	1,695.3	1,700.4	1,732.4	1,751.7	1,765.5	1,738.7	1,738.7	1,751.2	1,764.4	1,764.4	1,768.3	1,738.7
2005	1,715.4	1,716.9	1,724.3	1,754.4	1,776.2	1,787.9	1,766.0	1,768.9	1,783.5	1,792.9	1,797.2	1,798.6	1,765.2
2006	1,754.6	1,751.5	1,760.6	1,778.3	1,798.3	1,816.2	1,787.4	1,787.6	1,795.0	1,801.6	1,810.1	1,808.6	1,787.5
2007	1,767.5	1,767.6	1,772.6	1,784.2	1,808.9	1,822.5	1,796.4	1,796.6	1,801.6	1,810.1	1,809.4	1,796.0	1,796.0
2008	1,764.9	1,767.2	1,771.1	1,780.5	1,802.7	1,813.1	1,793.4	1,792.3	1,792.9	1,795.8	1,786.8	1,772.7	1,786.1
2009	1,714.5	1,704.6	1,696.4	1,707.5	1,723.2	1,723.1	1,704.5	1,697.7	1,692.5	1,705.3	1,705.2	1,700.5	1,706.3
2010	1,653.4	1,654.1	1,659.7	1,693.2	1,713.2	1,720.9	1,699.6	1,700.5	1,706.7	1,723.9	1,726.2	1,721.2	1,697.7
2011	1,686.3	1,690.9	1,697.2	1,727.4	1,748.1	1,754.2	1,724.2	1,743.1	1,758.8	1,764.9	1,767.5	1,764.5	1,735.6
2012	1,722.5	1,725.6	1,734.8	1,755.1	1,771.3	1,781.8	1,756.4	1,764.3	1,780.2	1,789.6	1,793.6	1,786.8	1,763.5
2013	1,753.8	1,762.0	1,764.4	1,781.9	1,807.7	1,818.7	1,787.2	1,798.6	1,812.2	1,826.6	1,823.8	1,819.6	1,796.4
Total Private													
2002	1,459.3	1,452.8	1,455.0	1,466.0	1,484.7	1,499.0	1,497.8	1,504.5	1,495.7	1,494.4	1,496.3	1,493.1	1,483.2
2003	1,453.8	1,449.9	1,452.6	1,467.9	1,487.7	1,500.6	1,497.6	1,504.1	1,497.2	1,497.8	1,497.6	1,497.8	1,483.7
2004	1,452.5	1,448.9	1,454.7	1,486.3	1,503.4	1,521.7	1,518.2	1,521.9	1,513.6	1,520.6	1,518.9	1,522.0	1,498.6
2005	1,471.3	1,469.8	1,477.3	1,507.4	1,529.0	1,544.0	1,539.4	1,547.0	1,542.9	1,546.2	1,551.5	1,551.8	1,523.1
2006	1,511.5	1,506.5	1,515.3	1,533.2	1,552.2	1,573.2	1,560.9	1,566.4	1,554.1	1,555.3	1,562.4	1,560.5	1,546.0
2007	1,526.7	1,523.9	1,529.4	1,541.5	1,563.6	1,580.9	1,573.4	1,578.7	1,564.0	1,567.4	1,570.9	1,566.5	1,557.2
2008	1,524.7	1,521.3	1,525.8	1,535.5	1,554.7	1,567.6	1,564.7	1,566.5	1,550.1	1,549.9	1,539.2	1,526.5	1,543.9
2009	1,475.2	1,459.5	1,451.8	1,463.7	1,478.0	1,480.8	1,474.0	1,472.7	1,457.3	1,464.3	1,462.9	1,459.5	1,466.6
2010	1,416.7	1,412.8	1,418.4	1,449.3	1,465.7	1,478.2	1,480.2	1,484.0	1,473.4	1,483.0	1,483.6	1,480.0	1,460.4
2011	1,450.4	1,449.3	1,456.6	1,486.3	1,505.8	1,517.1	1,520.5	1,529.1	1,528.2	1,527.5	1,529.7	1,527.5	1,502.3
2012	1,490.6	1,489.2	1,498.1	1,516.0	1,532.2	1,545.0	1,544.3	1,550.2	1,545.7	1,549.5	1,551.7	1,546.5	1,529.9
2013	1,518.9	1,521.0	1,524.7	1,540.8	1,566.5	1,581.3	1,577.2	1,586.2	1,576.7	1,584.4	1,580.6	1,577.3	1,561.3
Goods Producing													
2002	286.1	283.6	283.7	287.3	293.7	299.3	300.9	303.5	299.4	296.9	293.5	286.8	292.9
2003	277.5	274.2	274.4	279.5	286.5	292.8	292.9	295.1	291.7	289.4	287.1	282.5	285.3
2004	271.8	269.8	271.0	281.1	286.3	293.5	296.0	298.2	295.4	296.0	291.9	288.8	286.7
2005	277.1	275.7	277.3	285.5	293.1	299.8	299.2	301.0	297.8	293.9	292.2	286.5	289.9
2006	277.6	275.0	276.4	283.2	289.4	296.0	294.7	295.8	291.2	289.8	286.4	280.5	286.3
2007	272.0	269.1	269.9	272.7	280.6	286.5	285.7	286.9	281.9	280.8	278.1	272.0	278.0
2008	262.5	259.9	259.6	262.2	270.0	275.2	275.4	275.6	270.7	268.4	261.8	253.1	266.2
2009	240.6	234.1	230.2	231.7	235.5	238.5	238.0	236.8	232.8	231.1	228.2	223.2	233.4
2010	213.9	211.8	212.7	221.1	226.4	231.7	235.0	234.8	232.5	232.6	230.6	226.2	225.8
2011	220.4	219.2	220.6	226.7	233.4	239.2	242.0	243.5	241.2	241.0	238.4	233.8	233.3
2012	226.0	225.1	228.1	234.1	239.2	244.9	247.1	248.1	245.2	244.8	241.9	237.8	238.5
2013	231.9	231.7	233.3	237.1	245.5	251.1	252.9	254.9	252.5	254.7	251.9	244.8	245.2
Service-Providing													
2002	1,410.1	1,411.2	1,413.8	1,421.2	1,435.6	1,438.9	1,420.3	1,416.5	1,434.2	1,439.6	1,449.7	1,450.8	1,428.5
2003	1,414.1	1,420.0	1,422.3	1,435.4	1,448.7	1,449.5	1,428.9	1,431.3	1,444.2	1,453.3	1,456.8	1,462.1	1,438.9
2004	1,421.5	1,425.5	1,429.4	1,451.3	1,465.4	1,472.0	1,442.7	1,440.5	1,455.8	1,468.4	1,472.5	1,479.5	1,452.0
2005	1,438.3	1,441.2	1,447.0	1,468.9	1,483.1	1,488.1	1,466.8	1,467.9	1,485.7	1,499.0	1,505.0	1,512.1	1,475.3
2006	1,477.0	1,476.5	1,484.2	1,495.1	1,508.9	1,520.2	1,492.7	1,491.8	1,503.8	1,511.8	1,523.7	1,528.1	1,501.2
2007	1,495.5	1,498.5	1,502.7	1,511.5	1,528.3	1,536.0	1,510.7	1,509.7	1,519.7	1,529.3	1,536.9	1,537.4	1,518.0
2008	1,502.4	1,507.3	1,511.5	1,518.3	1,532.7	1,537.9	1,518.0	1,516.7	1,522.2	1,527.4	1,525.0	1,519.6	1,519.9
2009	1,473.9	1,470.5	1,466.2	1,475.8	1,487.7	1,484.6	1,466.5	1,460.9	1,459.7	1,474.2	1,477.0	1,477.3	1,472.9
2010	1,439.5	1,442.3	1,447.0	1,472.1	1,486.8	1,489.2	1,464.6	1,465.7	1,474.2	1,491.3	1,495.6	1,495.0	1,471.9
2011	1,465.9	1,471.7	1,476.6	1,500.7	1,514.7	1,515.0	1,482.2	1,499.6	1,517.6	1,523.9	1,529.1	1,530.7	1,502.3
2012	1,496.5	1,500.5	1,506.7	1,521.0	1,532.1	1,536.9	1,509.3	1,516.2	1,535.0	1,544.8	1,551.7	1,549.0	1,525.0
2013	1,521.9	1,530.3	1,531.1	1,544.8	1,562.2	1,567.6	1,534.3	1,543.7	1,559.7	1,571.9	1,571.9	1,574.8	1,551.2
Mining, Logging, and Construction													
2002	72.3	70.9	71.0	75.8	82.6	86.6	89.6	90.7	88.8	87.3	84.6	79.3	81.6
2003	71.5	69.5	69.9	75.2	82.1	87.0	89.3	90.3	88.5	87.6	84.5	79.8	81.3
2004	71.5	70.3	71.9	79.7	85.0	89.0	92.0	92.6	91.1	90.9	88.8	84.3	83.9
2005	74.2	73.3	74.5	81.2	86.6	91.6	93.6	93.7	91.7	89.1	87.4	82.6	85.0
2006	75.0	74.1	74.8	79.7	85.1	89.1	89.4	89.1	87.7	85.3	82.1	77.0	82.4
2007	70.8	68.7	69.9	72.1	78.8	82.7	82.8	83.1	80.7	79.4	76.5	70.8	76.4
2008	64.6	63.2	63.5	65.3	72.0	75.5	76.5	76.5	74.0	71.8	67.0	61.3	69.3
2009	52.6	51.1	50.8	54.0	59.6	61.4	62.0	61.2	59.7	58.2	55.8	51.8	56.5
2010	44.4	43.1	43.8	50.0	53.7	56.8	58.8	59.0	57.8	57.7	55.4	50.7	52.6
2011	46.4	45.7	46.9	51.2	56.2	59.9	61.4	62.5	61.5	60.9	58.2	53.9	55.4
2012	48.1	47.7	49.7	54.9	58.7	62.1	63.8	64.6	63.2	62.6	59.6	55.9	57.6
2013	51.1	51.4	52.6	56.1	63.4	66.9	68.8	70.6	69.6	71.4	68.0	59.9	62.5
Manufacturing													
2002	213.8	212.7	212.7	211.5	211.1	212.7	211.3	212.8	210.6	209.6	208.9	207.5	211.3
2003	206.0	204.7	204.5	204.3	204.4	205.8	203.6	204.8	203.2	201.8	202.6	202.7	204.0
2004	200.3	199.5	199.1	201.4	201.3	204.5	204.0	205.6	204.3	205.1	203.1	204.5	202.7
2005	202.9	202.4	202.8	204.3	206.5	208.2	205.6	207.3	206.1	204.8	204.8	203.9	205.0
2006	202.6	200.9	201.6	203.5	204.3	206.9	205.3	206.7	203.5	204.5	204.3	203.5	204.0
2007	201.2	200.4	200.0	200.6	201.8	203.8	202.9	203.8	201.2	201.4	201.6	201.2	201.7
2008	197.9	196.7	196.1	196.9	198.0	199.7	198.9	199.1	196.7	196.6	194.8	191.8	196.9
2009	188.0	183.0	179.4	177.7	175.9	177.1	176.0	175.6	173.1	172.9	172.4	171.4	176.9
2010	169.5	168.7	168.9	171.1	172.7	174.9	176.2	175.8	174.7	174.9	175.2	175.5	173.2
2011	174.0	173.5	173.7	175.5	177.2	179.3	180.6	181.0	179.7	180.1	180.2	179.9	177.9
2012	177.9	177.4	178.4	179.2	180.5	182.8	183.3	183.5	182.0	182.2	182.3	181.9	181.0
2013	180.8	180.3	180.7	181.0	182.1	184.2	184.1	184.3	182.9	183.3	183.9	184.9	182.7

Employment by Industry: Minneapolis-St. Paul-Bloomington, MN–WI, Selected Years, 2002–2013—*Continued*

(Numbers in thousands, not seasonally adjusted)

Industry and year	January	February	March	April	May	June	July	August	September	October	November	December	Annual average
Trade, Transportation, and Utilities													
2002	339.5	332.6	332.6	333.9	336.7	338.2	334.9	335.0	333.4	336.1	343.3	347.0	336.9
2003	335.4	330.5	330.2	331.2	334.2	335.0	330.9	331.8	331.4	335.3	340.2	343.0	334.1
2004	329.6	326.0	326.0	331.4	335.5	338.7	338.1	338.2	336.3	340.8	347.0	350.6	336.5
2005	335.2	331.4	332.4	337.1	340.5	340.5	338.7	339.1	337.7	342.2	348.7	352.1	339.6
2006	338.7	333.8	334.0	335.7	338.7	341.4	337.4	337.5	336.5	338.8	346.9	349.3	339.1
2007	338.1	334.9	334.1	336.3	340.0	342.5	339.2	339.2	337.8	340.6	346.6	349.5	339.9
2008	336.2	331.0	331.9	331.5	334.5	334.7	331.6	330.9	328.3	329.4	332.5	332.8	332.1
2009	318.3	312.4	310.4	310.0	312.5	313.2	309.5	308.8	306.3	307.8	313.0	314.3	311.4
2010	303.1	299.3	300.0	304.3	307.2	310.1	307.8	307.1	306.2	308.9	314.4	316.9	307.1
2011	305.2	302.1	303.2	308.9	311.8	313.1	313.2	313.4	313.5	314.7	320.6	323.7	312.0
2012	312.4	307.3	308.8	312.6	316.4	317.8	315.6	315.8	314.2	317.3	324.7	325.3	315.7
2013	315.6	311.9	312.1	314.3	319.1	322.3	320.4	322.2	319.7	322.3	325.6	330.5	319.7
Wholesale Trade													
2002	83.8	83.8	83.6	83.6	83.7	84.2	84.4	84.3	83.3	83.6	83.4	83.4	83.8
2003	83.7	83.7	83.7	82.9	83.3	83.9	84.2	84.0	83.2	83.3	83.2	83.3	83.5
2004	82.4	82.4	82.5	84.1	84.5	85.4	86.2	86.0	84.9	84.9	84.8	84.9	84.4
2005	83.8	83.7	83.6	85.9	86.5	86.8	86.4	86.5	85.7	86.3	86.3	86.6	85.7
2006	85.8	85.9	86.4	86.6	87.1	88.1	88.1	88.2	87.2	87.3	87.2	87.3	87.1
2007	86.5	86.6	86.8	87.0	87.7	88.6	88.5	88.4	87.0	86.9	87.1	87.2	87.4
2008	86.3	86.1	86.4	86.1	86.4	87.1	87.2	86.9	85.5	85.3	84.7	84.2	86.0
2009	82.2	81.3	80.4	80.4	80.3	80.6	80.7	80.0	78.2	78.4	78.4	78.2	79.9
2010	76.7	76.4	76.7	77.4	77.9	79.0	79.3	79.0	78.0	78.4	78.3	78.3	78.0
2011	77.9	77.9	78.1	79.1	79.5	80.1	80.7	80.8	79.8	79.7	79.7	79.8	79.4
2012	79.1	78.9	79.3	80.5	81.2	82.1	82.5	82.0	80.9	81.0	81.0	81.1	80.8
2013	80.6	80.6	80.7	81.1	81.8	82.7	82.8	82.6	81.7	82.7	82.9	82.2	81.9
Retail Trade													
2002	187.5	181.7	181.9	182.6	184.9	186.5	185.3	185.6	183.4	185.2	192.7	196.8	186.2
2003	185.8	181.2	181.0	182.8	185.4	186.4	183.2	184.7	183.4	186.0	191.1	194.0	185.4
2004	183.0	179.4	179.2	181.9	185.1	187.4	186.1	186.2	183.7	186.3	192.4	195.9	185.6
2005	184.0	180.1	180.7	184.2	186.4	186.6	185.1	186.1	185.1	188.9	195.2	198.5	186.7
2006	187.2	182.8	182.5	184.3	186.3	188.4	186.0	186.2	183.8	186.1	193.0	195.8	186.9
2007	187.0	183.0	182.9	184.1	186.7	188.6	186.8	186.9	184.6	187.0	192.9	194.7	187.1
2008	184.7	179.6	179.9	180.1	182.3	182.7	181.3	181.1	177.9	179.1	182.8	183.0	181.2
2009	173.7	169.3	167.8	168.1	170.8	172.2	170.2	170.8	167.3	168.7	173.3	174.5	170.6
2010	166.5	163.2	163.5	166.7	168.8	170.7	169.6	170.1	167.3	169.1	173.9	175.7	168.8
2011	166.7	163.6	164.0	168.0	170.1	171.6	171.8	172.6	170.9	172.1	177.7	180.0	170.8
2012	171.4	166.8	167.7	169.9	172.5	174.2	172.8	173.3	171.1	173.7	180.6	180.8	172.9
2013	173.3	169.5	169.6	171.5	174.6	177.6	177.1	178.3	175.3	177.0	180.0	184.6	175.7
Transportation and Utilities													
2002	68.2	67.1	67.1	67.7	68.1	67.5	65.2	65.1	66.7	67.3	67.2	66.8	67.0
2003	65.9	65.6	65.5	65.5	65.5	64.7	63.5	63.1	64.8	66.0	65.9	65.7	65.1
2004	64.2	64.2	64.3	65.4	65.9	65.9	65.8	66.0	67.7	69.6	69.8	69.8	66.6
2005	67.4	67.6	68.1	67.0	67.6	67.1	67.2	66.5	66.9	67.0	67.2	67.0	67.2
2006	65.7	65.1	65.1	64.8	65.3	64.9	63.3	63.1	65.5	65.4	66.7	66.2	65.1
2007	64.6	65.3	64.4	65.2	65.6	65.3	63.9	63.9	66.2	66.7	66.6	67.6	65.4
2008	65.2	65.3	65.6	65.3	65.8	64.9	63.1	62.9	64.9	65.0	65.0	65.6	64.9
2009	62.4	61.8	62.2	61.5	61.4	60.4	58.6	58.0	60.8	60.7	61.3	61.6	60.9
2010	59.9	59.7	59.8	60.2	60.5	60.4	58.9	58.0	60.9	61.4	62.2	62.9	60.4
2011	60.6	60.6	61.1	61.8	62.2	61.4	60.7	60.0	62.8	62.9	63.2	63.9	61.8
2012	61.9	61.6	61.8	62.2	62.7	61.5	60.3	60.5	62.2	62.6	63.1	63.4	62.0
2013	61.7	61.8	61.8	61.7	62.7	62.0	60.5	61.3	62.7	62.6	62.7	63.7	62.1
Information													
2002	48.0	47.8	47.7	48.2	48.2	48.7	48.3	47.4	46.6	46.6	46.7	47.0	47.6
2003	45.6	45.4	45.3	45.9	45.8	45.4	44.9	44.5	43.9	43.7	43.9	44.3	44.9
2004	43.5	43.3	43.5	44.2	44.3	44.1	43.4	42.7	42.2	42.2	42.7	42.9	43.3
2005	42.1	42.1	41.9	43.6	43.6	43.8	43.0	42.5	42.2	42.0	42.2	42.2	42.6
2006	41.7	41.6	41.7	41.3	41.7	41.9	41.7	41.9	41.3	41.3	41.6	41.9	41.6
2007	42.1	42.2	42.4	42.4	42.5	42.7	42.5	42.6	42.2	42.1	42.0	42.3	42.3
2008	41.9	41.7	41.8	41.7	41.7	42.0	42.2	42.1	41.9	41.4	41.5	41.2	41.8
2009	40.7	40.4	40.3	39.9	39.9	40.0	40.2	40.0	39.4	39.1	39.1	39.2	39.9
2010	39.1	38.9	38.9	39.1	38.9	39.1	39.4	39.3	38.9	39.0	38.9	38.9	39.0
2011	39.0	38.9	38.7	39.1	39.1	39.1	39.6	39.8	39.4	39.4	39.4	39.4	39.2
2012	38.4	38.3	38.4	38.8	39.0	39.0	39.1	39.0	38.8	38.9	38.9	39.0	38.8
2013	38.6	38.6	38.6	38.7	38.7	38.7	39.2	39.0	38.5	38.7	38.7	38.9	38.7
Financial Activities													
2002	135.2	135.5	135.5	135.8	136.1	136.7	138.3	138.7	137.9	137.7	138.4	139.0	137.1
2003	136.0	136.6	137.4	139.1	139.8	141.4	142.5	142.8	141.8	140.6	140.5	140.9	140.0
2004	140.3	139.9	139.7	140.5	140.7	141.9	141.9	142.0	140.8	141.1	141.1	141.7	141.0
2005	139.6	139.7	140.0	141.2	141.8	144.0	143.8	144.3	143.3	142.8	143.0	143.7	142.3
2006	142.4	142.5	142.8	142.3	143.0	144.2	143.5	143.2	142.2	142.0	142.2	142.6	142.7
2007	141.7	142.2	142.2	141.3	141.6	142.9	142.7	142.8	141.6	141.5	141.6	142.0	142.0
2008	139.7	140.0	140.1	139.9	139.9	140.7	141.4	140.9	139.5	139.0	138.8	139.3	139.9
2009	137.4	137.1	136.6	136.3	136.7	137.3	137.4	137.0	136.2	136.5	136.4	136.8	136.8
2010	135.0	134.9	134.9	135.3	135.7	137.0	137.4	137.7	137.0	137.8	138.1	138.7	136.6
2011	137.9	137.9	138.1	137.9	138.2	138.8	139.5	139.7	138.8	138.7	138.7	139.0	138.6
2012	139.0	139.3	139.5	139.7	140.2	141.5	141.4	141.3	140.4	140.9	140.9	141.2	140.4
2013	141.0	141.0	141.0	141.1	141.6	143.0	142.7	142.8	141.2	141.9	141.4	141.7	141.7

Employment by Industry: Minneapolis-St. Paul-Bloomington, MN–WI, Selected Years, 2002–2013—*Continued*

(Numbers in thousands, not seasonally adjusted)

Industry and year	January	February	March	April	May	June	July	August	September	October	November	December	Annual average
Professional and Business Services													
2002	241.8	241.0	241.0	242.2	244.2	247.3	247.8	249.2	247.5	248.4	246.7	244.6	245.1
2003	237.2	237.5	237.7	238.8	240.0	242.2	243.1	244.2	244.5	246.2	245.0	245.5	241.8
2004	236.4	237.4	238.7	244.4	245.9	249.2	249.3	249.1	248.0	249.6	248.3	247.3	245.3
2005	238.0	238.4	240.6	247.3	249.4	252.6	251.8	254.0	255.4	259.2	259.2	259.0	250.4
2006	253.2	253.7	255.0	258.3	260.9	265.9	263.4	265.2	263.9	265.4	266.4	266.3	261.5
2007	259.1	259.9	261.5	261.9	263.7	267.9	267.7	270.3	267.0	268.9	269.0	267.7	265.4
2008	260.4	260.9	260.6	262.5	264.2	266.9	268.1	268.2	266.4	267.1	263.9	261.4	264.2
2009	249.1	245.0	242.8	245.4	245.8	246.9	246.4	247.7	244.6	249.4	249.9	250.3	246.9
2010	241.9	242.4	242.0	249.3	251.1	254.0	257.4	258.8	256.0	258.7	259.5	259.1	252.5
2011	253.3	253.6	255.0	261.8	262.9	265.9	270.4	272.8	272.7	274.0	274.5	274.2	265.9
2012	265.6	265.5	266.4	268.8	270.0	272.8	273.9	275.8	274.6	276.7	276.1	275.8	271.8
2013	268.7	271.0	271.0	272.8	274.8	278.4	278.4	279.8	277.9	278.3	275.9	275.8	275.2
Education and Health Services													
2002	194.5	197.8	198.9	199.6	201.1	198.2	198.7	199.3	203.1	206.3	207.9	208.1	201.1
2003	205.7	210.0	210.9	211.4	212.5	210.5	208.8	208.7	210.5	213.5	214.7	214.3	211.0
2004	211.2	213.7	214.7	216.3	217.1	215.8	212.6	212.4	214.6	218.5	219.2	220.4	215.5
2005	216.7	220.5	221.5	222.6	224.0	222.0	221.8	223.0	225.9	228.7	230.3	231.9	224.1
2006	229.7	231.8	233.9	237.2	237.8	237.1	237.0	237.4	238.6	241.7	244.0	245.0	237.6
2007	244.7	246.6	248.1	250.7	252.0	250.4	248.7	249.4	250.1	254.1	256.4	255.8	250.6
2008	253.1	256.0	257.5	260.1	259.6	257.7	256.9	257.0	259.3	264.3	265.3	264.8	259.3
2009	262.1	264.8	265.4	268.2	268.2	263.2	262.3	261.6	263.0	267.6	268.9	269.0	265.4
2010	263.4	266.2	267.9	270.4	271.1	267.5	264.4	266.0	267.9	272.9	274.1	273.4	268.8
2011	272.1	275.1	275.8	279.6	280.2	276.2	272.1	274.0	278.5	281.7	282.9	283.4	277.6
2012	280.3	284.3	284.6	284.2	284.3	279.9	278.4	279.8	285.9	289.6	290.9	290.3	284.4
2013	289.4	293.2	292.8	296.5	297.5	293.1	289.9	291.9	296.2	301.3	303.7	304.5	295.8
Leisure and Hospitality													
2002	141.3	141.5	142.5	145.3	150.8	156.0	153.9	156.1	153.5	148.0	145.1	145.8	148.3
2003	143.1	142.3	142.8	148.2	154.6	158.1	157.1	159.5	156.6	152.6	149.4	150.5	151.2
2004	144.8	144.3	145.9	152.3	157.8	161.9	160.7	162.5	160.5	156.4	153.0	154.1	154.5
2005	148.3	147.7	149.0	153.7	159.1	164.5	164.4	165.9	163.8	160.8	159.4	159.2	158.0
2006	154.2	154.1	156.1	159.3	164.4	169.3	166.4	168.3	164.2	159.8	157.8	157.8	161.0
2007	154.5	154.6	155.5	160.7	167.2	171.4	170.0	170.7	167.7	163.5	160.4	160.1	163.0
2008	155.0	154.7	156.5	159.6	166.8	171.1	170.2	172.3	166.6	162.8	158.3	157.0	162.6
2009	152.0	150.6	151.1	156.2	163.2	164.7	164.0	164.7	160.3	157.2	152.2	151.6	157.3
2010	146.3	145.2	147.1	154.8	160.1	162.4	162.5	163.8	160.0	157.4	152.8	151.8	155.4
2011	148.2	147.9	150.2	156.5	164.2	167.8	166.2	168.1	167.0	161.4	158.7	157.4	159.5
2012	153.3	153.7	156.3	161.4	166.4	170.8	170.9	172.6	170.0	164.6	161.7	160.6	163.5
2013	157.9	157.6	159.5	163.5	171.5	175.8	175.4	176.8	172.7	168.7	164.5	163.0	167.2
Other Services													
2002	72.9	73.0	73.1	73.7	73.9	74.6	75.0	75.3	74.3	74.4	74.7	74.8	74.1
2003	73.3	73.4	73.9	73.8	74.3	75.2	77.4	77.5	76.8	76.5	76.8	76.8	75.5
2004	74.9	74.5	75.2	76.1	75.8	76.6	76.2	76.8	75.8	76.0	75.7	76.2	75.8
2005	74.3	74.3	74.6	76.4	77.5	76.8	76.7	77.2	76.8	76.6	76.5	77.2	76.2
2006	74.0	74.0	75.4	75.9	76.3	77.4	76.8	77.1	76.2	76.5	77.1	77.1	76.2
2007	74.5	74.4	75.7	75.5	76.0	76.6	76.9	76.8	75.7	75.9	76.8	77.1	76.0
2008	75.9	77.1	77.8	78.0	78.0	79.3	78.9	79.5	77.4	77.5	77.1	76.9	77.8
2009	75.0	75.1	75.0	76.0	76.2	77.0	76.2	76.1	74.7	75.6	75.2	75.1	75.6
2010	74.0	74.1	74.9	75.0	75.2	76.4	76.3	76.5	74.9	75.7	75.2	75.0	75.3
2011	74.3	74.6	75.0	75.8	76.0	77.0	77.5	77.8	77.1	76.6	76.5	76.6	76.2
2012	75.6	75.7	76.0	76.4	76.7	78.3	77.9	77.8	76.6	76.7	76.6	76.5	76.7
2013	75.8	76.0	76.4	76.8	77.8	78.9	78.3	78.8	78.0	78.5	78.9	78.1	77.7
Government													
2002	236.9	242.0	242.5	242.5	244.6	239.2	223.4	215.5	237.9	242.1	246.9	244.5	238.2
2003	237.8	244.3	244.1	247.0	247.5	241.7	224.2	222.3	238.7	244.9	246.3	246.8	240.5
2004	240.8	246.4	245.7	246.1	248.3	243.8	220.5	216.8	237.6	243.8	245.5	246.3	240.1
2005	244.1	247.1	247.0	247.0	247.2	243.9	226.6	221.9	240.6	246.7	245.7	246.8	242.1
2006	243.1	245.0	245.3	245.1	246.1	243.0	226.5	221.2	240.9	246.3	247.7	248.1	241.5
2007	240.8	243.7	243.2	242.7	245.3	241.6	223.0	217.9	237.6	242.7	244.1	242.9	238.8
2008	240.2	245.9	245.3	245.0	248.0	245.5	228.7	225.8	242.8	245.9	247.6	246.2	242.2
2009	239.3	245.1	244.6	243.8	245.2	242.3	230.5	225.0	235.2	241.0	242.3	241.0	239.6
2010	236.7	241.3	241.3	243.9	247.5	242.7	219.4	216.5	233.3	240.9	242.6	241.2	237.3
2011	235.9	241.6	240.6	241.1	242.3	237.1	203.7	214.0	230.6	237.4	237.8	237.0	233.3
2012	231.9	236.4	236.7	239.1	239.1	236.8	212.1	214.1	234.5	240.1	241.9	240.3	233.6
2013	234.9	241.0	239.7	241.1	241.2	237.4	210.0	212.4	235.5	242.2	243.2	242.3	235.1

Employment by Industry: Nashville–Davidson-Murfreesboro–Franklin, TN, Selected Years, 2002–2013

(Numbers in thousands, not seasonally adjusted)

Industry and year	January	February	March	April	May	June	July	August	September	October	November	December	Annual average
Total Nonfarm													
2002	674.5	677.8	682.7	685.1	688.1	685.8	688.5	692.9	697.0	698.2	701.6	703.0	689.6
2003	687.4	688.6	691.5	696.9	699.2	695.2	691.8	698.5	701.7	703.4	707.0	710.2	697.6
2004	695.8	701.3	705.5	711.1	711.8	709.5	712.4	719.6	721.6	727.9	732.0	735.5	715.3
2005	713.7	719.2	724.5	732.7	734.1	731.1	733.1	740.6	744.8	746.0	751.3	753.2	735.4
2006	736.9	739.4	746.9	748.8	750.0	750.3	749.6	757.5	760.0	756.1	761.7	764.2	751.8
2007	744.2	747.8	755.6	754.6	758.2	759.4	759.0	769.8	773.6	770.5	778.4	778.6	762.5
2008	756.0	758.9	762.1	762.8	767.4	761.1	753.4	760.6	764.1	760.9	760.2	759.1	760.6
2009	731.4	730.0	728.1	726.2	727.1	717.6	712.4	719.8	724.4	727.8	733.4	733.3	726.0
2010	714.7	717.3	723.7	732.0	738.6	730.6	725.2	732.9	742.4	748.9	752.9	753.2	734.4
2011	732.1	737.3	744.6	752.4	756.0	750.5	751.4	761.0	766.5	771.1	778.1	779.9	756.7
2012	761.4	767.5	777.9	779.6	782.7	779.1	774.6	785.5	791.3	796.9	805.1	806.7	784.0
2013	783.9	792.4	798.5	803.3	807.4	804.3	800.7	812.6	817.6	821.7	828.8	828.7	808.3
Total Private													
2002	582.4	583.9	587.9	591.0	594.6	597.4	602.3	604.9	604.4	604.5	607.8	608.8	597.5
2003	593.5	593.3	595.7	600.4	603.8	606.1	603.1	606.2	606.1	607.6	611.6	613.9	603.4
2004	599.8	601.2	607.0	613.0	615.2	619.9	623.0	626.5	625.8	630.8	634.6	636.9	619.5
2005	617.4	621.0	626.3	634.1	636.5	639.5	641.5	644.8	646.2	647.5	652.7	654.4	638.5
2006	638.7	639.5	646.7	648.7	651.0	657.7	656.2	660.1	659.8	655.8	660.7	662.8	653.1
2007	644.4	646.7	654.4	655.4	660.7	667.4	665.8	670.7	668.9	667.4	673.4	675.2	662.5
2008	653.6	654.7	657.8	659.0	662.5	666.0	658.5	660.7	658.5	654.4	653.0	651.0	657.5
2009	626.6	622.4	621.1	618.7	620.2	622.5	616.4	619.1	618.3	620.0	625.3	625.5	621.3
2010	609.1	610.0	615.9	623.6	628.6	632.1	629.1	631.5	633.4	639.3	643.7	644.5	628.4
2011	626.1	631.3	637.9	645.2	649.0	652.6	653.5	657.4	659.6	664.0	670.8	672.9	651.7
2012	656.1	660.6	670.4	673.0	677.7	683.1	679.4	684.4	686.5	691.3	698.6	700.4	680.1
2013	679.8	686.4	692.2	697.3	703.0	708.7	705.6	711.5	712.7	715.9	722.8	722.5	704.9
Goods Producing													
2002	115.4	114.7	114.5	115.7	116.8	117.5	117.5	118.0	117.6	116.9	116.5	117.1	116.5
2003	114.9	114.7	114.9	115.4	116.4	117.0	116.8	117.0	117.2	117.0	116.6	116.7	116.2
2004	115.0	115.0	115.8	117.6	118.4	119.3	119.5	119.3	119.2	118.7	118.9	119.2	118.0
2005	116.5	117.3	118.2	120.1	120.7	121.7	120.7	121.9	121.8	122.0	122.2	122.5	120.5
2006	121.4	121.3	122.4	123.0	123.0	124.9	124.1	124.8	124.5	123.1	123.4	123.4	123.3
2007	120.7	120.3	121.4	121.0	121.1	122.3	121.3	121.4	121.6	120.4	120.3	119.8	121.0
2008	116.7	116.1	115.7	115.4	115.8	116.1	114.1	113.5	111.4	108.1	106.0	104.3	112.8
2009	99.3	97.8	96.6	94.9	94.0	93.7	93.1	93.1	92.5	91.8	91.6	90.8	94.1
2010	88.0	87.6	88.5	90.4	90.8	92.0	92.0	92.6	92.7	93.1	92.5	92.4	91.1
2011	89.8	90.6	92.2	93.9	94.0	95.1	95.1	95.7	96.0	96.6	96.8	97.0	94.4
2012	94.7	96.0	97.7	97.8	98.4	99.4	99.6	100.6	101.3	100.6	101.0	101.1	99.0
2013	99.4	100.3	101.1	102.6	103.8	105.1	104.2	105.0	105.3	105.6	106.1	107.2	103.8
Service-Providing													
2002	559.1	563.1	568.2	569.4	571.3	568.3	571.0	574.9	579.4	581.3	585.1	585.9	573.1
2003	572.5	573.9	576.6	581.5	582.8	578.2	575.0	581.5	584.5	586.4	590.4	593.5	581.4
2004	580.8	586.3	589.7	593.5	593.4	590.2	592.9	600.3	602.4	609.2	613.1	616.3	597.3
2005	597.2	601.9	606.3	612.6	613.4	609.4	612.4	618.7	623.0	624.0	629.1	630.7	614.9
2006	615.5	618.1	624.5	625.8	627.0	625.4	625.5	632.7	635.5	633.0	638.3	640.8	628.5
2007	623.5	627.5	634.2	633.6	637.1	637.1	637.7	648.4	652.0	650.1	658.1	658.8	641.5
2008	639.3	642.8	646.4	647.4	651.6	645.0	639.3	647.1	652.7	652.8	654.2	654.8	647.8
2009	632.1	632.2	631.5	631.3	633.1	623.9	619.3	626.7	631.9	636.0	641.8	642.5	631.9
2010	626.7	629.7	635.2	641.6	647.8	638.6	633.2	640.3	649.7	655.8	660.4	660.8	643.3
2011	642.3	646.7	652.4	658.5	662.0	655.4	656.3	665.3	670.5	674.5	681.3	682.9	662.3
2012	666.7	671.5	680.2	681.8	684.3	679.7	675.0	684.9	690.0	696.3	704.1	705.6	685.0
2013	684.5	692.1	697.4	700.7	703.6	699.2	696.5	707.6	712.3	716.1	722.7	721.5	704.5
Mining, Logging, and Construction													
2002	31.1	31.0	31.2	31.5	32.5	33.0	33.6	34.1	34.0	33.6	33.8	33.8	32.8
2003	32.7	32.6	33.2	33.9	34.7	35.4	35.7	35.6	35.5	34.9	34.5	34.6	34.4
2004	33.1	32.9	33.4	34.0	34.6	35.4	35.5	35.3	35.1	34.6	34.5	34.5	34.4
2005	32.8	33.1	34.0	35.2	36.1	37.1	37.2	37.5	37.5	37.3	37.2	37.2	36.0
2006	37.0	37.3	38.3	38.7	39.2	40.3	40.1	40.3	40.2	39.6	39.5	39.6	39.2
2007	38.8	39.3	40.8	41.1	41.7	42.9	42.8	43.1	43.1	42.7	42.4	41.9	41.7
2008	40.3	40.1	40.1	40.1	40.5	40.7	40.0	40.0	39.3	38.1	36.9	35.9	39.3
2009	33.5	32.7	32.4	31.7	31.7	31.9	31.9	31.7	31.3	30.9	30.6	30.2	31.7
2010	28.1	27.8	28.7	30.5	30.7	31.7	31.8	32.1	32.0	32.4	31.5	31.1	30.7
2011	28.6	29.2	30.4	31.8	31.9	32.7	32.6	32.9	33.1	32.8	32.5	32.1	31.7
2012	30.8	31.2	32.5	32.0	32.2	32.4	32.2	32.6	32.9	32.0	31.5	31.3	32.0
2013	30.0	30.8	31.5	31.9	32.6	33.3	33.4	33.5	33.5	33.6	33.8	34.6	32.7
Manufacturing													
2002	84.3	83.7	83.3	84.2	84.3	84.5	83.9	83.9	83.6	83.3	82.7	83.3	83.8
2003	82.2	82.1	81.7	81.5	81.7	81.6	81.1	81.4	81.7	82.1	82.1	82.1	81.8
2004	81.9	82.1	82.4	83.6	83.8	83.9	84.0	84.0	84.1	84.1	84.4	84.7	83.6
2005	83.7	84.2	84.2	84.9	84.6	84.6	83.5	84.4	84.3	84.7	85.0	85.3	84.5
2006	84.4	84.0	84.1	84.3	83.8	84.6	84.0	84.5	84.3	83.5	83.9	83.8	84.1
2007	81.9	81.0	80.6	79.9	79.4	79.4	78.5	78.3	78.5	77.7	77.9	77.9	79.3
2008	76.4	76.0	75.6	75.3	75.3	75.4	74.1	73.5	72.1	70.0	69.1	68.4	73.4
2009	65.8	65.1	64.2	63.2	62.3	61.8	61.2	61.4	61.2	60.9	61.0	60.6	62.4
2010	59.9	59.8	59.8	59.9	60.1	60.3	60.2	60.5	60.7	60.7	61.0	61.3	60.4
2011	61.2	61.4	61.8	62.1	62.1	62.4	62.5	62.8	62.9	63.8	64.3	64.9	62.7
2012	63.9	64.8	65.2	65.8	66.2	67.0	67.4	68.0	68.4	68.6	69.5	69.8	67.1
2013	69.4	69.5	69.6	70.7	71.2	71.8	70.8	71.5	71.8	72.0	72.3	72.6	71.1

Employment by Industry: Nashville–Davidson-Murfreesboro–Franklin, TN, Selected Years, 2002–2013—Continued

(Numbers in thousands, not seasonally adjusted)

Industry and year	January	February	March	April	May	June	July	August	September	October	November	December	Annual average
Trade, Transportation, and Utilities													
2002	136.0	134.9	136.2	134.6	135.4	136.1	137.3	137.8	138.4	140.8	143.1	145.5	138.0
2003	139.3	139.0	139.3	139.7	140.0	141.3	140.6	142.0	141.9	143.9	146.5	148.3	141.8
2004	142.5	141.8	142.9	143.0	143.7	144.8	144.9	146.1	146.6	149.2	152.2	153.7	146.0
2005	146.4	146.1	147.3	148.5	149.1	149.1	150.5	150.9	152.1	153.3	156.8	158.5	150.7
2006	151.9	151.4	152.9	152.5	153.0	153.7	152.7	153.6	153.9	153.3	156.4	158.6	153.7
2007	152.6	152.0	153.6	152.8	153.5	153.7	153.4	154.1	154.6	154.9	158.7	160.7	154.6
2008	154.3	153.9	154.8	153.7	153.9	153.9	154.2	154.4	154.4	154.3	156.1	157.5	154.6
2009	150.5	148.2	147.2	145.8	146.3	146.4	146.2	146.9	146.2	147.4	150.0	151.4	147.7
2010	145.4	144.6	145.3	145.9	146.3	147.3	146.9	147.7	147.4	149.6	152.6	154.4	147.8
2011	148.1	148.0	149.2	150.7	151.2	151.5	151.8	152.2	152.7	154.8	158.4	159.8	152.4
2012	154.1	153.2	155.2	155.6	156.5	156.5	156.3	156.9	157.8	159.6	164.5	165.3	157.6
2013	157.4	157.1	157.8	158.6	159.5	160.4	159.8	160.8	161.0	160.6	164.1	166.3	160.3
Wholesale Trade													
2002	34.5	34.2	34.6	34.2	34.3	34.5	34.8	35.0	35.1	35.7	36.3	36.9	35.0
2003	34.8	34.8	34.7	34.7	34.9	34.8	34.5	34.5	34.5	34.2	34.0	33.9	34.5
2004	33.7	33.9	34.1	34.2	34.3	34.6	34.6	35.0	35.1	35.5	35.4	35.5	34.7
2005	35.4	35.7	35.7	36.1	36.3	36.1	36.2	36.3	36.6	36.7	37.0	36.8	36.2
2006	36.4	36.5	36.5	36.4	36.5	36.6	36.5	36.7	36.9	36.3	36.2	36.3	36.5
2007	35.8	36.0	36.3	36.3	36.5	36.7	36.7	36.8	37.2	37.2	37.4	37.4	36.7
2008	37.1	37.3	37.2	37.2	37.6	37.8	38.0	38.2	38.5	38.4	38.4	38.2	37.8
2009	37.2	36.9	36.5	36.3	36.2	36.0	35.8	35.9	35.8	36.0	35.9	35.9	36.2
2010	35.3	35.3	35.4	35.5	35.7	35.6	35.7	35.9	35.8	36.3	36.3	36.5	35.8
2011	36.2	36.4	36.7	36.7	36.9	37.0	37.1	37.2	37.5	37.8	38.0	38.2	37.1
2012	37.7	37.9	38.1	38.2	38.5	38.6	38.7	39.0	39.0	39.2	39.4	39.4	38.6
2013	38.8	39.1	39.4	39.7	39.9	40.1	40.3	40.3	40.5	40.2	40.3	40.5	39.9
Retail Trade													
2002	75.8	75.2	75.9	75.0	75.5	75.9	76.6	76.8	77.2	78.5	79.8	81.1	76.9
2003	78.0	77.5	77.7	78.0	78.0	79.1	78.6	79.8	80.3	82.5	85.1	86.8	80.1
2004	81.9	80.9	81.3	81.2	81.5	82.1	81.9	82.4	82.5	84.3	87.0	88.0	82.9
2005	83.2	82.6	83.6	83.9	84.2	84.1	84.3	84.3	84.9	85.5	88.4	89.7	84.9
2006	84.8	84.3	85.3	85.5	85.8	86.0	85.3	85.8	85.6	85.8	89.1	90.6	86.2
2007	86.4	85.6	86.8	86.1	86.7	86.5	86.1	86.5	86.6	87.3	90.7	92.5	87.3
2008	87.6	87.1	88.1	86.8	86.5	86.2	86.1	86.2	85.8	85.7	87.7	88.6	86.9
2009	83.9	82.5	82.1	81.6	82.1	82.2	82.1	82.5	81.7	82.5	84.7	85.9	82.8
2010	81.9	81.2	81.6	82.3	82.3	83.0	82.5	82.9	82.2	83.3	85.7	86.9	83.0
2011	83.1	83.0	83.6	84.5	84.6	84.9	84.9	85.0	84.9	85.6	88.2	89.3	85.1
2012	85.4	84.3	85.6	85.5	85.7	85.6	85.2	85.0	84.8	85.7	89.0	89.2	85.9
2013	84.6	83.6	83.9	84.3	85.0	85.3	84.9	85.4	85.3	85.4	88.4	89.8	85.5
Transportation and Utilities													
2002	25.7	25.5	25.7	25.4	25.6	25.7	25.9	26.0	26.1	26.6	27.0	27.5	26.1
2003	26.5	26.7	26.9	27.0	27.1	27.4	27.5	27.7	27.1	27.2	27.4	27.6	27.2
2004	26.9	27.0	27.5	27.6	27.9	28.1	28.4	28.7	29.0	29.4	29.8	30.2	28.4
2005	27.8	27.8	28.0	28.5	28.6	28.9	30.0	30.3	30.6	31.1	31.4	32.0	29.6
2006	30.7	30.6	31.1	30.6	30.7	31.1	30.9	31.1	31.4	31.2	31.1	31.7	31.0
2007	30.4	30.4	30.5	30.4	30.3	30.5	30.6	30.8	30.8	30.4	30.6	30.8	30.5
2008	29.6	29.5	29.5	29.7	29.8	29.9	30.1	30.0	30.1	30.2	30.0	30.7	29.9
2009	29.4	28.8	28.6	27.9	28.0	28.2	28.3	28.5	28.7	28.9	29.4	29.6	28.7
2010	28.2	28.1	28.3	28.1	28.3	28.7	28.7	28.9	29.4	30.0	30.6	31.0	29.0
2011	28.8	28.6	28.9	29.5	29.7	29.6	29.8	30.0	30.3	31.4	32.2	32.3	30.1
2012	31.0	31.0	31.5	31.9	32.3	32.3	32.4	32.9	34.0	34.7	36.1	36.7	33.1
2013	34.0	34.4	34.5	34.6	34.6	35.0	34.6	35.1	35.2	35.0	35.4	36.0	34.9
Information													
2002	22.3	22.2	22.4	21.9	21.8	21.5	21.5	21.3	21.0	21.3	21.1	20.9	21.6
2003	20.2	20.1	20.1	19.9	20.0	19.8	19.8	19.8	19.6	19.6	19.8	19.8	19.9
2004	19.5	19.4	19.3	19.3	19.3	19.5	19.5	19.5	19.5	18.8	19.1	19.2	19.4
2005	19.8	19.9	19.8	19.5	19.5	19.7	19.7	19.6	19.6	19.7	19.8	19.8	19.7
2006	19.6	19.6	19.7	19.6	19.7	19.7	19.0	18.9	19.0	19.0	19.1	19.2	19.3
2007	19.0	19.0	19.0	19.2	19.6	19.7	19.9	20.0	20.1	20.3	20.4	20.8	19.8
2008	21.1	21.1	21.2	21.2	21.3	21.3	21.0	21.0	20.9	21.2	21.1	21.2	21.1
2009	20.8	20.7	20.6	20.3	20.2	20.0	19.8	20.0	19.8	19.4	19.5	19.4	20.0
2010	19.4	19.4	19.5	19.4	19.3	19.3	19.3	19.3	19.0	19.0	19.3	19.3	19.3
2011	18.9	18.8	18.8	18.9	19.1	19.2	19.2	19.5	19.2	19.5	19.9	20.0	19.3
2012	19.8	20.0	19.9	20.0	20.8	21.0	19.9	20.1	19.9	20.2	20.1	20.2	20.2
2013	19.9	20.2	20.3	20.2	20.5	21.2	20.4	20.4	20.2	20.2	20.3	20.4	20.4
Financial Activities													
2002	42.7	42.8	42.7	43.1	43.3	43.9	43.8	44.0	43.8	44.1	44.3	44.4	43.6
2003	44.4	44.5	44.7	44.8	44.8	45.1	44.8	44.8	44.6	44.5	44.5	44.7	44.7
2004	44.0	44.0	44.2	44.5	44.4	44.4	44.5	44.6	44.5	44.9	45.1	45.2	44.5
2005	44.4	44.5	44.7	45.1	45.3	45.4	45.5	45.6	45.6	45.4	45.6	45.7	45.2
2006	45.3	45.2	45.5	45.7	45.9	45.9	46.0	45.9	45.7	45.8	45.7	45.9	45.7
2007	45.3	45.6	45.8	46.1	46.6	46.8	46.6	46.6	46.3	46.3	46.2	46.4	46.2
2008	45.9	46.2	46.1	46.1	46.2	46.4	46.3	46.1	45.7	45.3	45.1	45.1	45.9
2009	44.8	44.7	44.5	44.6	44.8	45.1	44.9	45.3	45.1	45.2	45.5	45.8	45.0
2010	45.4	45.5	45.5	46.0	46.3	46.2	46.4	46.7	46.3	46.7	46.9	47.0	46.2
2011	46.2	46.4	46.3	47.1	47.6	47.2	47.5	47.7	47.8	48.0	48.2	48.2	47.4
2012	47.6	48.0	48.0	48.1	48.5	48.8	48.9	49.3	49.3	49.5	49.8	50.2	48.8
2013	49.9	50.2	50.6	50.7	51.1	51.0	51.8	51.6	51.4	51.1	51.0	50.8	50.9

Employment by Industry: Nashville–Davidson-Murfreesboro–Franklin, TN, Selected Years, 2002–2013—*Continued*

(Numbers in thousands, not seasonally adjusted)

Industry and year	January	February	March	April	May	June	July	August	September	October	November	December	Annual average
Professional and Business Services													
2002	84.4	85.7	86.9	87.2	87.5	87.2	88.0	88.7	88.0	86.7	87.4	86.2	87.0
2003	82.4	82.2	82.2	82.8	83.6	84.0	83.0	84.0	84.5	85.4	87.1	87.7	84.1
2004	85.7	86.6	87.7	89.4	89.7	91.0	91.5	93.0	94.0	96.5	96.6	96.5	91.5
2005	92.3	93.4	93.9	95.3	95.2	95.7	96.1	97.8	99.3	99.7	100.5	101.0	96.7
2006	95.4	95.4	96.3	96.6	96.9	99.3	98.7	101.1	102.4	100.8	102.1	102.1	98.9
2007	96.5	97.3	98.9	98.9	100.0	102.6	103.3	104.8	104.2	104.4	106.2	105.8	101.9
2008	99.2	98.9	99.3	100.2	101.1	103.5	98.8	100.5	101.8	102.0	101.9	100.0	100.6
2009	93.4	92.9	92.2	91.2	91.9	93.5	90.2	91.9	92.9	94.5	96.4	95.5	93.0
2010	92.1	92.8	94.2	96.2	100.6	100.4	98.8	99.4	101.4	101.5	103.1	103.2	98.6
2011	99.5	101.7	103.1	104.1	104.9	107.3	107.2	108.7	109.5	110.0	111.4	111.4	106.6
2012	107.4	109.1	112.0	112.0	113.0	115.4	114.4	116.1	117.0	118.6	120.0	119.9	114.6
2013	114.9	116.8	118.2	117.7	118.7	120.6	119.3	122.4	124.0	127.4	129.2	128.6	121.5
Education and Health Services													
2002	87.2	88.0	88.3	89.5	90.0	90.0	92.0	92.0	92.3	92.6	92.8	92.7	90.6
2003	93.0	93.4	93.7	94.9	94.9	94.9	95.5	95.5	95.5	95.6	95.6	95.8	94.9
2004	96.3	96.6	97.2	98.3	97.9	97.9	99.3	99.2	99.0	99.6	99.7	99.8	98.4
2005	98.7	99.4	99.5	101.2	101.7	101.6	102.5	102.5	102.3	102.2	102.3	102.5	101.4
2006	102.2	102.8	103.5	104.1	104.2	104.5	104.8	105.0	105.1	105.2	105.7	105.6	104.4
2007	104.9	105.8	106.2	107.0	107.5	107.8	108.7	109.5	110.2	109.5	109.7	110.0	108.1
2008	108.9	109.7	109.8	111.3	111.5	111.8	112.2	112.9	113.7	113.8	114.2	114.7	112.0
2009	113.6	114.0	114.0	115.1	114.6	114.1	114.5	114.3	115.7	116.0	116.4	116.6	114.9
2010	115.8	116.5	117.0	118.5	117.3	116.9	118.4	118.5	120.4	120.9	121.1	120.9	118.5
2011	119.6	120.9	121.0	121.6	121.1	120.0	120.5	120.7	122.2	122.8	123.4	123.6	121.5
2012	122.8	123.9	124.4	124.6	123.4	123.1	122.7	123.5	125.5	125.8	126.3	126.1	124.3
2013	124.9	126.4	126.9	127.4	127.1	126.5	125.5	126.7	128.2	129.1	129.4	127.8	127.2
Leisure and Hospitality													
2002	65.6	66.3	67.7	69.3	69.5	70.6	71.3	72.4	71.9	70.0	71.0	70.7	69.7
2003	68.1	68.8	70.1	71.9	73.1	73.8	73.0	73.7	73.1	71.8	71.9	71.6	71.7
2004	67.4	68.0	69.5	71.2	72.5	73.5	74.0	74.8	74.2	73.0	72.9	73.3	72.0
2005	70.4	71.3	72.7	74.6	75.4	76.3	76.7	76.8	75.6	75.4	75.4	74.7	74.6
2006	73.2	73.9	75.8	77.1	77.9	78.9	80.4	80.4	78.9	78.2	78.1	78.1	77.6
2007	75.9	76.8	79.0	80.1	81.8	83.8	82.4	83.8	81.6	81.0	81.3	81.2	80.7
2008	77.1	77.9	79.4	80.3	81.6	81.9	80.8	81.4	80.1	78.5	77.8	77.5	79.5
2009	74.4	74.0	75.5	76.8	78.2	79.1	77.5	77.7	76.7	75.9	76.1	76.4	76.5
2010	73.8	74.2	76.3	77.8	78.3	79.6	77.1	77.4	76.1	77.8	77.6	76.5	76.9
2011	73.3	73.8	75.9	77.8	79.7	80.2	80.4	81.4	81.0	81.1	81.3	81.5	79.0
2012	78.6	79.0	81.5	83.1	85.1	86.1	85.1	85.8	83.9	85.1	84.9	85.5	83.6
2013	81.5	83.1	84.8	87.3	89.2	90.3	91.2	91.5	89.8	89.4	89.7	88.6	88.0
Other Services													
2002	28.8	29.3	29.2	29.7	30.3	30.6	30.9	30.7	31.4	32.1	31.6	31.3	30.5
2003	31.2	30.6	30.7	31.0	31.0	30.2	29.6	29.4	29.7	29.8	29.6	29.3	30.2
2004	29.4	29.8	30.4	29.7	29.3	29.5	29.8	30.0	29.5	29.8	30.0	29.3	29.7
2005	28.9	29.1	30.2	29.8	29.6	30.0	29.8	29.7	29.9	29.8	30.1	29.7	29.7
2006	29.7	29.9	30.6	30.1	30.4	30.8	30.5	30.4	30.3	30.4	30.2	29.9	30.3
2007	29.5	29.9	30.5	30.3	30.6	30.7	30.2	30.5	30.3	30.6	30.6	30.5	30.4
2008	30.4	30.9	31.5	30.8	31.1	31.1	31.1	30.9	30.5	31.2	30.8	30.7	30.9
2009	29.8	30.1	30.5	30.0	30.2	30.6	30.2	29.9	29.4	29.8	29.8	29.6	30.0
2010	29.2	29.4	29.6	29.4	29.7	30.4	30.2	30.2	30.1	30.4	30.6	30.8	30.0
2011	30.7	31.1	31.4	31.1	31.4	32.1	31.8	31.5	31.2	31.2	31.4	31.4	31.4
2012	31.1	31.4	31.7	31.8	32.0	32.8	32.5	32.1	31.8	31.9	32.0	32.1	31.9
2013	31.9	32.3	32.5	32.8	33.1	33.6	33.4	33.1	32.8	32.5	33.0	32.8	32.8
Government													
2002	92.1	93.9	94.8	94.1	93.5	88.4	86.2	88.0	92.6	93.7	93.8	94.2	92.1
2003	93.9	95.3	95.8	96.5	95.4	89.1	88.7	92.3	95.6	95.8	95.4	96.3	94.2
2004	96.0	100.1	98.5	98.1	96.6	89.6	89.4	93.1	95.8	97.1	97.4	98.6	95.9
2005	96.3	98.2	98.2	98.6	97.6	91.6	91.6	95.8	98.6	98.5	98.6	98.8	96.9
2006	98.2	99.9	100.2	100.1	99.0	92.6	93.4	97.4	100.2	100.3	101.0	101.4	98.6
2007	99.8	101.1	101.2	99.2	97.5	92.0	93.2	99.1	104.7	103.1	105.0	103.4	99.9
2008	102.4	104.2	104.3	103.8	104.9	95.1	94.9	99.9	105.6	106.5	107.2	108.1	103.1
2009	104.8	107.6	107.0	107.5	106.9	95.1	96.0	100.7	106.1	107.8	108.1	107.8	104.6
2010	105.6	107.3	107.8	108.4	110.0	98.5	96.1	101.4	109.0	109.6	109.2	108.7	106.0
2011	106.0	106.0	106.7	107.2	107.0	97.9	97.9	103.6	106.9	107.1	107.3	107.0	105.1
2012	105.3	106.9	107.5	106.6	105.0	96.0	95.2	101.1	104.8	105.6	106.5	106.3	103.9
2013	104.1	106.0	106.3	106.0	104.4	95.6	95.1	101.1	104.9	105.8	106.0	106.2	103.5

Employment by Industry: New Haven, CT, NECTA, Selected Years, 2002–2013

(Numbers in thousands, not seasonally adjusted)

Industry and year	January	February	March	April	May	June	July	August	September	October	November	December	Annual average
Total Nonfarm													
2002	269.0	270.9	272.6	275.2	277.6	281.3	271.0	270.5	276.0	275.0	277.0	278.1	274.5
2003	267.5	269.0	269.0	270.6	271.6	271.7	265.8	265.1	267.7	271.4	274.6	275.5	270.0
2004	266.6	268.0	269.2	271.5	273.4	273.8	269.8	267.6	271.3	275.5	277.0	278.0	271.8
2005	268.2	270.7	269.3	275.1	275.6	277.6	270.2	268.0	274.5	274.8	277.7	278.8	273.4
2006	270.2	273.7	273.4	276.9	278.8	280.3	272.2	270.5	276.6	278.7	280.5	281.9	276.1
2007	272.3	275.0	273.8	277.8	279.7	281.8	273.8	272.6	278.4	280.9	282.5	283.4	277.7
2008	276.0	278.4	276.9	278.6	280.6	280.4	271.6	270.0	276.1	277.2	279.1	278.4	276.9
2009	268.1	269.1	265.7	266.6	269.0	268.6	260.0	258.5	265.4	266.6	268.2	269.0	266.2
2010	259.1	261.1	259.6	263.8	267.5	267.1	262.2	260.0	265.6	267.4	267.9	267.9	264.1
2011	262.0	263.7	261.8	268.2	269.4	269.7	262.7	261.6	267.6	269.1	270.3	270.6	266.4
2012	265.3	268.5	267.9	272.5	274.6	274.9	267.4	265.5	272.1	273.8	275.4	276.9	271.2
2013	268.2	268.7	269.9	275.8	276.5	277.8	271.5	269.9	275.5	277.8	280.0	280.0	274.3
Total Private													
2002	233.3	234.6	236.4	239.5	241.8	245.1	240.3	239.5	241.9	239.3	240.2	241.3	239.4
2003	231.7	232.9	232.7	234.4	235.5	237.5	234.6	234.3	233.7	236.1	238.2	239.5	235.1
2004	231.8	232.4	233.3	235.8	237.7	239.8	238.3	237.1	237.8	240.3	241.2	242.3	237.3
2005	233.9	235.5	234.2	239.4	240.2	241.8	239.8	238.2	240.8	240.1	242.3	243.3	239.1
2006	234.9	238.2	238.0	241.5	243.1	244.3	241.4	240.1	242.7	243.8	245.1	246.4	241.6
2007	237.3	239.7	238.5	242.6	244.3	245.6	243.2	242.3	244.4	245.7	246.7	247.7	243.2
2008	240.7	242.6	241.4	243.6	244.8	245.1	241.2	240.1	241.8	241.9	243.2	242.7	242.4
2009	232.9	233.8	230.5	231.7	233.3	233.9	230.2	229.4	231.5	232.7	233.5	234.7	232.3
2010	224.7	226.3	225.4	229.5	231.1	231.7	231.6	230.5	231.9	233.7	233.7	233.9	230.3
2011	228.0	229.4	228.4	233.6	235.0	235.4	233.3	232.9	234.8	235.7	236.7	237.0	233.4
2012	232.5	234.4	234.1	238.4	240.8	241.3	238.4	237.6	239.9	241.0	242.0	242.9	238.6
2013	234.7	235.3	236.3	241.1	241.9	242.8	241.3	241.1	242.2	243.9	245.5	245.4	241.0
Goods Producing													
2002	47.5	46.9	47.2	47.4	47.7	48.1	47.7	47.5	47.3	46.8	46.5	46.1	47.2
2003	44.4	44.0	44.0	44.6	45.1	45.7	45.3	45.4	45.1	45.1	45.1	45.0	44.9
2004	43.9	43.5	44.3	45.1	45.7	46.3	46.4	46.4	46.1	45.7	45.6	45.3	45.4
2005	43.9	43.4	43.7	44.2	44.5	45.3	45.3	45.1	44.5	44.2	44.1	43.8	44.3
2006	43.3	43.1	43.3	44.0	44.4	45.0	44.9	44.7	44.1	44.0	43.9	43.7	44.0
2007	42.9	42.5	42.7	43.4	43.6	44.2	43.9	44.1	43.8	43.6	43.7	43.3	43.5
2008	42.6	42.1	42.1	42.3	42.7	42.9	42.8	42.6	42.2	41.8	41.6	40.8	42.2
2009	38.1	37.2	36.9	37.5	37.9	38.2	37.4	37.3	36.8	36.3	36.1	35.9	37.1
2010	34.2	33.8	34.1	34.7	35.4	35.8	35.9	35.9	35.7	35.2	35.1	34.8	35.1
2011	33.9	33.9	34.1	34.7	35.3	35.7	35.6	35.7	35.4	35.3	35.3	35.1	35.0
2012	34.2	34.2	34.2	34.8	35.2	35.6	35.6	35.4	35.3	35.1	34.9	34.8	34.9
2013	33.7	33.5	33.8	34.3	34.8	35.3	35.7	35.7	35.4	35.2	35.1	34.8	34.8
Service-Providing													
2002	221.5	224.0	225.4	227.8	229.9	233.2	223.3	223.0	228.7	228.2	230.5	232.0	227.3
2003	223.1	225.0	225.0	226.0	226.5	226.0	220.5	219.7	222.6	226.3	229.5	230.5	225.1
2004	222.7	224.5	224.9	226.4	227.7	227.5	223.4	221.2	225.2	229.8	231.4	232.7	226.5
2005	224.3	227.3	225.6	230.9	231.1	232.3	224.9	222.9	230.0	230.6	233.6	235.0	229.0
2006	226.9	230.6	230.1	232.9	234.4	235.3	227.3	225.8	232.5	234.7	236.6	238.2	232.1
2007	229.4	232.5	231.1	234.4	236.1	237.6	229.9	228.5	234.6	237.3	238.8	240.1	234.2
2008	233.4	236.3	234.8	236.3	237.9	237.5	228.8	227.4	233.9	235.4	237.5	237.6	234.7
2009	230.0	231.9	228.8	229.1	231.1	230.4	222.6	221.2	228.6	230.3	232.1	233.1	229.1
2010	224.9	227.3	225.5	229.1	232.1	231.3	226.3	224.1	229.9	232.2	232.8	233.1	229.1
2011	228.1	229.8	227.7	233.5	234.1	234.0	227.1	225.9	232.2	233.8	235.0	235.5	231.4
2012	231.1	234.3	233.7	237.7	239.4	239.3	231.8	230.1	236.8	238.7	240.5	242.1	236.3
2013	234.5	235.2	236.1	241.5	241.7	242.5	235.8	234.2	240.1	242.6	244.9	245.2	239.5
Mining, Logging, and Construction													
2002	10.0	10.0	10.4	11.1	11.5	11.7	11.7	11.7	11.5	11.3	11.2	10.6	11.1
2003	9.6	9.4	9.6	10.2	10.8	11.1	11.3	11.4	11.1	11.1	11.0	10.8	10.6
2004	9.9	9.7	10.3	11.3	11.8	12.1	12.3	12.3	12.0	11.7	11.5	11.1	11.3
2005	10.0	9.7	9.9	10.6	11.0	11.4	11.7	11.8	11.4	11.3	11.2	10.9	10.9
2006	10.1	10.1	10.3	11.1	11.5	11.9	12.1	12.1	12.0	11.7	11.6	11.4	11.3
2007	10.7	10.4	10.7	11.3	11.7	12.1	12.3	12.4	12.2	12.1	12.2	11.8	11.7
2008	11.0	10.8	10.9	11.1	11.5	11.6	11.7	11.7	11.4	11.1	11.0	10.5	11.2
2009	9.3	8.9	8.9	9.4	9.8	10.0	9.9	10.0	9.8	9.4	9.3	9.0	9.5
2010	7.7	7.5	7.7	8.4	8.9	9.0	9.2	9.2	9.1	9.0	9.0	8.6	8.6
2011	8.0	8.0	8.1	8.7	9.2	9.4	9.5	9.5	9.3	9.3	9.2	9.0	8.9
2012	8.3	8.3	8.3	8.8	9.1	9.3	9.5	9.5	9.4	9.3	9.2	9.0	9.0
2013	8.1	7.9	8.2	8.8	9.2	9.5	9.8	9.9	9.8	9.7	9.6	9.2	9.1
Manufacturing													
2002	37.5	36.9	36.8	36.3	36.2	36.4	36.0	35.8	35.8	35.5	35.3	35.5	36.2
2003	34.8	34.6	34.4	34.4	34.3	34.6	34.0	34.0	34.0	34.0	34.1	34.2	34.3
2004	34.0	33.8	34.0	33.8	33.9	34.2	34.1	34.1	34.1	34.0	34.1	34.2	34.0
2005	33.9	33.7	33.8	33.6	33.5	33.9	33.6	33.3	33.1	32.9	32.9	32.9	33.4
2006	33.2	33.0	33.0	32.9	32.9	33.1	32.8	32.6	32.1	32.3	32.3	32.3	32.7
2007	32.2	32.1	32.0	32.1	31.9	32.1	31.6	31.7	31.6	31.5	31.5	31.5	31.8
2008	31.6	31.3	31.2	31.2	31.2	31.3	31.1	30.9	30.8	30.7	30.6	30.3	31.0
2009	28.8	28.3	28.0	28.1	28.1	28.2	27.5	27.3	27.0	26.9	26.8	26.9	27.7
2010	26.5	26.3	26.4	26.3	26.5	26.8	26.7	26.7	26.6	26.2	26.1	26.2	26.4
2011	25.9	25.9	26.0	26.0	26.1	26.3	26.1	26.2	26.1	26.0	26.1	26.1	26.1
2012	25.9	25.9	25.9	26.0	26.1	26.3	26.1	25.9	25.9	25.8	25.7	25.8	25.9
2013	25.6	25.6	25.6	25.5	25.6	25.8	25.9	25.8	25.6	25.5	25.5	25.6	25.6

Employment by Industry: New Haven, CT, NECTA, Selected Years, 2002–2013—*Continued*

(Numbers in thousands, not seasonally adjusted)

Industry and year	January	February	March	April	May	June	July	August	September	October	November	December	Annual average
Trade, Transportation, and Utilities													
2002	49.5	48.7	49.0	50.2	50.7	51.4	50.1	49.7	50.5	50.5	51.4	52.3	50.3
2003	49.7	48.8	49.2	48.8	49.4	49.8	48.4	48.4	49.0	50.1	51.0	51.7	49.5
2004	49.8	48.9	49.3	49.2	49.7	50.3	49.7	49.6	50.4	51.2	52.1	52.9	50.3
2005	51.0	50.3	50.2	50.8	51.3	51.6	50.6	50.4	51.1	51.3	52.4	53.1	51.2
2006	51.4	50.4	50.8	51.1	51.7	52.1	50.8	50.5	51.0	51.4	52.5	53.3	51.4
2007	51.6	51.0	51.0	50.9	51.7	52.3	51.1	50.8	51.1	51.5	52.3	52.8	51.5
2008	51.7	50.6	50.6	50.5	50.8	51.2	50.3	49.9	50.2	50.1	50.8	51.2	50.7
2009	49.1	48.3	47.9	47.4	48.3	48.7	47.7	47.6	47.9	48.5	49.4	49.9	48.4
2010	47.7	46.8	46.9	46.7	47.7	48.3	47.7	47.9	47.7	48.2	49.1	49.9	47.9
2011	47.6	47.1	47.1	48.0	48.4	48.7	47.9	48.1	48.1	48.5	49.4	50.2	48.3
2012	48.9	48.1	48.3	48.5	49.5	50.1	49.3	49.2	49.4	50.1	51.4	51.7	49.5
2013	49.9	48.8	49.2	50.1	50.5	51.0	49.9	50.3	50.3	50.6	52.3	52.8	50.5
Wholesale Trade													
2002	11.1	11.0	11.0	11.3	11.4	11.4	11.1	11.1	11.1	11.0	11.0	11.0	11.1
2003	10.8	10.7	10.8	10.8	11.0	11.1	11.1	11.2	11.2	11.5	11.6	11.7	11.1
2004	11.4	11.3	11.4	11.5	11.5	11.6	11.3	11.3	11.4	11.4	11.4	11.5	11.4
2005	11.4	11.3	11.3	11.4	11.4	11.4	11.4	11.4	11.4	11.5	11.6	11.6	11.4
2006	11.5	11.5	11.5	11.6	11.7	11.8	11.7	11.7	11.6	11.5	11.5	11.5	11.6
2007	11.6	11.6	11.5	11.4	11.5	11.6	11.6	11.6	11.6	11.5	11.5	11.6	11.6
2008	11.9	11.8	11.8	11.9	11.9	12.0	12.0	12.0	12.1	12.0	12.1	12.1	12.0
2009	11.9	11.8	11.7	11.5	11.5	11.6	11.5	11.5	11.5	11.4	11.4	11.4	11.6
2010	11.2	11.2	11.2	11.2	11.3	11.4	11.4	11.4	11.4	11.3	11.3	11.3	11.3
2011	11.2	11.2	11.2	11.3	11.3	11.4	11.4	11.4	11.2	11.2	11.2	11.2	11.3
2012	11.1	11.1	11.1	11.2	11.3	11.4	11.3	11.2	11.2	11.2	11.2	11.2	11.2
2013	11.0	10.9	11.0	11.2	11.2	11.3	11.2	11.2	11.1	11.1	11.1	11.2	11.1
Retail Trade													
2002	31.0	30.2	30.6	30.9	31.2	32.0	31.5	31.3	31.4	31.4	32.3	33.2	31.4
2003	31.2	30.4	30.6	30.3	30.6	30.8	30.0	30.0	29.9	30.4	31.2	31.8	30.6
2004	30.4	29.6	29.9	29.7	30.0	30.4	30.6	30.6	30.4	30.8	31.6	32.2	30.5
2005	30.4	29.7	29.5	29.9	30.2	30.5	30.2	30.1	30.1	30.4	31.3	32.0	30.4
2006	30.7	29.8	30.1	30.3	30.8	31.2	30.8	30.7	30.5	31.1	32.2	32.8	30.9
2007	31.2	30.6	30.7	30.7	31.2	31.6	31.0	30.9	30.5	30.8	31.7	32.0	31.1
2008	30.9	29.9	29.9	29.6	29.9	30.1	29.6	29.5	29.1	29.1	29.8	30.2	29.8
2009	28.7	28.0	27.7	27.6	28.2	28.5	28.1	28.1	27.9	28.6	29.5	29.9	28.4
2010	28.2	27.4	27.5	27.3	27.9	28.3	28.2	28.3	27.8	28.3	29.2	29.7	28.2
2011	28.2	27.6	27.6	28.2	28.5	28.6	28.3	28.5	28.3	28.6	29.5	30.2	28.5
2012	29.2	28.4	28.5	28.5	29.2	29.5	29.0	28.9	28.5	29.1	30.4	30.6	29.2
2013	29.1	28.3	28.3	28.8	29.1	29.4	29.0	29.4	29.0	29.2	30.8	31.2	29.3
Transportation and Utilities													
2002	7.4	7.5	7.4	8.0	8.1	8.0	7.5	7.3	8.0	8.1	8.1	8.1	7.8
2003	7.7	7.7	7.8	7.7	7.8	7.9	7.3	7.2	7.9	8.2	8.2	8.2	7.8
2004	8.0	8.0	8.0	8.0	8.2	8.3	7.8	7.7	8.6	9.0	9.1	9.2	8.3
2005	9.2	9.3	9.4	9.5	9.7	9.7	9.0	8.9	9.6	9.4	9.5	9.5	9.4
2006	9.2	9.1	9.2	9.2	9.2	9.1	8.3	8.1	8.9	8.8	8.8	9.0	8.9
2007	8.8	8.8	8.8	8.8	9.0	9.1	8.5	8.3	9.0	9.2	9.1	9.2	8.9
2008	8.9	8.9	8.9	9.0	9.0	9.1	8.7	8.4	9.0	9.0	8.9	8.9	8.9
2009	8.5	8.5	8.5	8.3	8.6	8.6	8.1	8.0	8.5	8.5	8.5	8.6	8.4
2010	8.3	8.2	8.2	8.2	8.5	8.6	8.1	8.2	8.6	8.6	8.6	8.8	8.4
2011	8.2	8.3	8.3	8.5	8.6	8.7	8.2	8.2	8.6	8.7	8.7	8.8	8.5
2012	8.6	8.6	8.7	8.8	9.0	9.2	9.0	9.1	9.7	9.8	9.8	9.9	9.2
2013	9.8	9.6	9.9	10.1	10.2	10.3	9.7	9.7	10.2	10.3	10.4	10.4	10.1
Information													
2002	10.0	10.0	10.0	9.8	9.8	9.8	9.7	9.6	9.6	9.5	9.4	9.5	9.7
2003	9.2	9.2	9.2	9.1	9.1	9.1	9.1	9.1	9.0	8.9	9.0	9.0	9.1
2004	8.7	8.6	8.6	8.6	8.6	8.7	8.7	8.7	8.6	8.7	8.7	8.7	8.7
2005	8.6	8.8	8.5	8.4	8.4	8.5	8.4	8.3	8.3	8.2	8.3	8.2	8.4
2006	8.3	8.3	8.2	8.2	8.2	8.2	8.1	8.1	8.0	8.1	8.1	8.2	8.2
2007	8.1	8.2	8.1	8.2	8.2	8.1	8.1	8.1	8.1	8.1	8.1	8.2	8.1
2008	8.1	8.3	8.0	7.9	7.8	7.8	7.7	7.8	7.6	7.6	7.6	7.5	7.8
2009	7.3	7.3	7.0	6.8	6.7	6.6	6.5	6.4	6.2	6.2	6.1	5.9	6.6
2010	5.7	5.6	5.4	5.3	5.3	5.2	5.1	5.0	4.9	4.9	4.9	4.9	5.2
2011	4.8	4.8	4.8	4.7	4.7	4.7	4.6	4.5	4.5	4.6	4.6	4.6	4.7
2012	4.5	4.5	4.5	4.3	4.3	4.3	4.3	4.3	4.3	4.3	4.3	4.3	4.4
2013	4.3	4.2	4.3	4.2	4.2	4.2	4.2	4.2	4.1	4.1	4.1	4.1	4.2
Financial Activities													
2002	14.0	13.8	13.9	14.1	14.2	14.3	14.6	14.6	14.3	14.2	14.2	14.3	14.2
2003	14.1	14.1	14.1	14.1	14.2	14.4	14.4	14.5	14.4	14.2	14.2	14.3	14.3
2004	14.1	14.1	14.2	14.2	14.2	14.4	14.2	14.1	14.0	14.0	14.0	14.0	14.1
2005	13.8	13.8	13.8	13.9	14.1	14.3	14.3	14.3	14.1	14.0	14.1	14.1	14.1
2006	14.0	14.0	13.9	14.0	14.0	14.1	14.1	14.1	13.9	13.9	14.0	14.0	14.0
2007	13.8	13.8	13.7	13.7	13.8	13.9	13.8	13.7	13.4	13.4	13.3	13.4	13.6
2008	13.3	13.3	13.3	13.0	13.1	13.2	13.1	13.1	12.9	12.7	12.7	12.7	13.0
2009	12.5	12.5	12.5	12.4	12.5	12.6	12.4	12.3	12.1	12.2	12.2	12.3	12.4
2010	12.1	12.1	12.1	12.1	12.2	12.3	12.5	12.5	12.2	12.2	12.2	12.2	12.2
2011	12.3	12.3	12.3	12.2	12.2	12.3	12.3	12.3	12.0	12.0	11.8	12.0	12.2
2012	12.1	12.1	12.1	12.1	12.1	12.3	12.3	12.2	12.1	12.0	12.0	12.1	12.1
2013	12.1	12.0	12.0	12.0	12.1	12.2	12.3	12.3	12.3	12.3	12.4	12.4	12.2

Employment by Industry: New Haven, CT, NECTA, Selected Years, 2002–2013—*Continued*

(Numbers in thousands, not seasonally adjusted)

Industry and year	January	February	March	April	May	June	July	August	September	October	November	December	Annual average
Professional and Business Services													
2002	27.4	27.4	28.0	27.6	27.9	28.9	28.1	28.8	29.0	27.7	27.9	27.9	28.1
2003	26.5	26.7	26.6	26.4	26.6	26.8	26.4	26.6	26.5	26.5	26.8	26.9	26.6
2004	25.2	25.6	25.5	25.7	25.9	26.3	26.0	26.0	25.8	25.1	25.2	25.6	25.7
2005	24.6	24.7	24.8	25.7	25.5	26.5	26.2	26.1	25.9	25.5	25.6	25.9	25.6
2006	25.0	25.6	25.8	26.1	26.4	27.2	25.9	26.1	26.2	26.0	26.2	26.4	26.1
2007	25.4	25.6	25.8	26.0	26.3	26.8	26.4	26.7	26.7	26.6	26.6	27.1	26.3
2008	26.4	26.8	26.6	27.1	27.1	27.5	26.0	26.1	26.1	25.3	25.1	25.3	26.3
2009	24.4	23.9	23.7	23.8	23.8	23.9	23.4	23.9	23.8	24.1	24.4	25.1	24.0
2010	23.9	24.5	24.4	25.0	24.9	25.5	25.6	25.6	25.3	25.4	25.3	25.4	25.1
2011	24.9	25.2	24.9	25.9	25.7	26.3	26.2	26.2	26.1	26.1	26.4	26.6	25.9
2012	26.6	26.6	26.9	27.8	27.8	27.9	27.5	27.5	27.8	27.9	28.0	28.4	27.6
2013	27.8	28.0	28.0	28.3	28.4	28.8	28.7	28.7	28.2	28.0	28.0	27.9	28.2
Education and Health Services													
2002	58.1	60.7	60.3	61.6	61.6	61.5	58.9	58.4	61.8	61.8	62.4	62.6	60.8
2003	60.6	62.6	61.6	62.5	61.5	60.3	59.1	58.7	59.4	61.4	62.4	62.8	61.1
2004	61.5	63.2	62.1	62.8	62.0	60.9	60.2	59.2	61.2	64.7	65.1	64.8	62.3
2005	62.8	65.0	63.5	65.4	64.4	62.3	61.7	60.8	64.8	65.5	66.6	66.8	64.1
2006	62.7	66.7	65.1	66.9	65.9	64.0	63.9	63.1	67.1	68.4	68.9	68.8	66.0
2007	64.9	68.3	66.5	68.7	67.8	66.2	65.8	64.9	68.5	69.9	70.4	70.5	67.7
2008	68.0	70.8	69.4	70.9	70.1	68.4	67.7	67.0	70.1	72.2	73.4	73.0	70.1
2009	71.0	74.0	71.2	72.1	71.3	70.0	69.1	68.6	71.9	73.6	73.8	73.9	71.7
2010	72.0	73.8	72.4	74.6	73.5	71.7	71.6	70.7	73.9	76.0	75.6	74.9	73.4
2011	74.7	75.9	74.5	75.9	75.5	73.5	72.7	72.2	75.4	76.5	76.8	75.7	74.9
2012	74.9	77.4	76.0	77.4	77.6	75.7	74.4	74.0	76.7	78.0	77.8	77.9	76.5
2013	75.4	77.7	76.7	78.5	77.2	75.6	75.1	74.8	77.6	79.7	80.1	79.4	77.3
Leisure and Hospitality													
2002	16.6	16.9	17.6	18.5	19.4	20.5	20.7	20.5	19.1	18.6	18.2	18.2	18.7
2003	17.1	17.5	17.8	18.9	19.5	20.9	21.5	21.3	20.2	19.7	19.3	19.3	19.4
2004	18.4	18.4	19.0	19.8	20.8	22.0	22.1	22.0	21.0	20.3	19.8	20.1	20.3
2005	18.5	18.8	18.9	20.2	21.1	22.1	22.2	22.2	21.3	20.6	20.3	20.3	20.5
2006	19.5	19.5	20.2	20.4	21.5	22.6	22.6	22.4	21.5	20.9	20.4	20.8	21.0
2007	19.7	19.6	20.0	20.8	22.0	22.9	23.0	22.9	21.9	21.6	21.4	21.3	21.4
2008	19.9	20.0	20.5	21.1	22.3	23.0	22.7	22.7	22.0	21.5	21.3	21.3	21.5
2009	19.9	20.0	20.6	21.0	22.2	23.0	23.0	22.7	22.2	21.4	21.1	21.2	21.5
2010	19.0	19.6	19.8	20.8	21.8	22.4	22.7	22.5	21.8	21.5	21.3	21.5	21.2
2011	19.8	20.2	20.7	21.9	22.9	23.6	23.6	23.5	23.0	22.5	22.2	22.4	22.2
2012	21.0	21.2	21.7	22.9	23.8	24.8	24.4	24.3	23.8	23.0	23.0	23.1	23.1
2013	21.2	20.8	21.8	23.1	24.0	24.9	24.7	24.6	23.9	23.6	23.2	23.5	23.3
Other Services													
2002	10.2	10.2	10.4	10.3	10.5	10.6	10.5	10.4	10.3	10.2	10.2	10.4	10.4
2003	10.1	10.0	10.2	10.0	10.1	10.5	10.4	10.3	10.1	10.2	10.4	10.5	10.2
2004	10.2	10.1	10.3	10.4	10.8	10.9	11.0	11.1	10.7	10.6	10.7	10.9	10.6
2005	10.7	10.7	10.8	10.8	10.9	11.2	11.1	11.0	10.8	10.8	10.9	11.1	10.9
2006	10.7	10.6	10.7	10.8	11.0	11.1	11.1	11.1	10.9	11.1	11.1	11.2	11.0
2007	10.9	10.7	10.7	10.9	10.9	11.2	11.1	11.1	10.9	11.0	10.9	11.1	11.0
2008	10.7	10.7	10.9	10.8	10.9	11.1	10.9	10.9	10.7	10.7	10.7	10.9	10.8
2009	10.6	10.6	10.7	10.7	10.6	10.9	10.7	10.6	10.6	10.4	10.4	10.5	10.6
2010	10.1	10.1	10.3	10.3	10.3	10.5	10.5	10.4	10.4	10.3	10.2	10.3	10.3
2011	10.0	10.0	10.0	10.3	10.3	10.6	10.4	10.4	10.3	10.2	10.2	10.4	10.3
2012	10.3	10.3	10.4	10.6	10.5	10.6	10.6	10.7	10.5	10.6	10.6	10.6	10.5
2013	10.3	10.3	10.5	10.6	10.7	10.8	10.7	10.5	10.4	10.4	10.3	10.5	10.5
Government													
2002	35.7	36.3	36.2	35.7	35.8	36.2	30.7	31.0	34.1	35.7	36.8	36.8	35.1
2003	35.8	36.1	36.3	36.2	36.1	34.2	31.2	30.8	34.0	35.3	36.4	36.0	34.9
2004	34.8	35.6	35.9	35.7	35.7	34.0	31.5	30.5	33.5	35.2	35.8	35.7	34.5
2005	34.3	35.2	35.1	35.7	35.4	35.8	30.4	29.8	33.7	34.7	35.4	35.5	34.3
2006	35.3	35.5	35.4	35.4	35.7	36.0	30.8	30.4	33.9	34.9	35.4	35.5	34.5
2007	35.0	35.3	35.3	35.2	35.4	36.2	30.6	30.3	34.0	35.2	35.8	35.7	34.5
2008	35.3	35.8	35.5	35.0	35.8	35.3	30.4	29.9	34.3	35.3	35.9	35.7	34.5
2009	35.2	35.3	35.2	34.9	35.7	34.7	29.8	29.1	33.9	33.9	34.7	34.3	33.9
2010	34.4	34.8	34.2	34.3	36.4	35.4	30.6	29.5	33.7	33.7	34.2	34.0	33.8
2011	34.0	34.3	33.4	34.6	34.4	34.3	29.4	28.7	32.8	33.4	33.6	33.6	33.0
2012	32.8	34.1	33.8	34.1	33.8	33.6	29.0	27.9	32.2	32.8	33.4	34.0	32.6
2013	33.5	33.4	33.6	34.7	34.6	35.0	30.2	28.8	33.3	33.9	34.5	34.6	33.3

Employment by Industry: New Orleans-Metairie-Kenner, LA, Selected Years, 2002–2013

(Numbers in thousands, not seasonally adjusted)

Industry and year	January	February	March	April	May	June	July	August	September	October	November	December	Annual average
Total Nonfarm													
2002	605.7	607.9	611.5	615.5	613.7	616.8	604.0	605.5	610.1	609.1	614.9	615.5	610.9
2003	607.0	610.2	611.6	618.3	617.0	618.4	609.9	607.1	613.0	614.0	619.4	620.5	613.9
2004	611.0	613.2	617.5	623.6	622.7	621.5	613.1	615.1	613.2	617.0	621.3	619.2	617.4
2005	609.7	610.4	616.3	616.2	615.6	619.5	607.8	607.0	476.5	429.1	442.2	454.3	558.7
2006	449.8	459.7	472.5	475.5	481.1	488.2	484.3	488.5	492.8	499.5	506.5	511.1	484.1
2007	507.4	512.1	518.8	511.9	513.2	516.0	510.2	514.8	515.7	526.0	531.0	534.7	517.7
2008	524.7	528.6	532.2	531.3	530.7	530.1	522.9	530.2	523.2	531.5	534.1	536.2	529.6
2009	523.1	525.7	525.7	527.6	528.9	523.9	519.5	523.3	521.3	523.6	525.7	525.7	524.5
2010	516.7	518.7	522.8	525.8	525.5	525.2	517.8	519.3	522.4	525.8	529.4	531.6	523.4
2011	523.6	527.0	529.9	531.6	532.0	527.2	522.9	526.8	529.1	531.8	535.8	537.5	529.6
2012	526.9	529.9	532.2	538.8	540.2	534.5	530.9	533.0	528.9	536.4	541.3	543.6	534.7
2013	539.8	543.7	542.6	544.5	545.0	543.9	538.8	546.7	543.8	550.4	553.7	554.1	545.6
Total Private													
2002	502.8	504.0	507.4	511.6	510.2	511.9	504.7	504.8	507.5	505.9	510.7	511.0	507.7
2003	503.2	505.4	506.4	513.5	512.6	513.2	506.7	506.9	508.5	510.9	515.4	516.6	509.9
2004	507.8	509.2	513.0	516.7	515.8	515.6	509.4	512.4	507.4	512.7	516.3	514.0	512.5
2005	504.5	504.1	509.4	511.1	511.0	514.6	506.4	504.8	374.6	348.8	362.2	374.7	460.5
2006	377.1	386.9	399.0	402.1	407.3	414.8	412.3	415.9	416.9	423.4	429.3	433.1	409.8
2007	431.1	434.7	440.7	439.2	440.1	442.6	438.8	442.4	440.0	447.9	452.2	455.7	442.1
2008	446.8	449.9	453.7	450.6	449.9	450.7	444.4	449.5	441.5	448.9	451.0	453.3	449.2
2009	441.3	443.2	443.8	444.0	445.7	443.2	438.1	440.0	438.2	439.4	441.6	442.3	441.7
2010	434.4	435.9	439.4	442.5	440.7	442.5	437.5	438.4	440.9	443.8	447.1	449.8	441.1
2011	442.8	446.1	449.3	450.7	451.4	448.6	446.1	448.5	449.3	452.4	456.4	458.5	450.0
2012	449.8	452.2	454.7	460.0	461.7	457.2	455.9	456.8	451.7	458.8	463.5	465.9	457.4
2013	463.6	467.1	466.1	467.7	468.4	468.5	465.4	472.1	468.2	474.3	477.6	478.0	469.8
Goods Producing													
2002	80.4	79.9	80.6	80.6	81.1	81.3	80.2	80.7	80.4	80.2	80.1	79.9	80.5
2003	79.4	79.4	79.4	80.5	81.2	81.5	80.3	79.9	79.3	79.4	78.5	78.7	79.8
2004	77.9	77.5	78.2	78.8	78.2	78.4	77.7	77.5	76.9	77.2	76.9	76.9	77.7
2005	75.1	75.8	76.6	76.5	76.9	77.6	77.1	77.2	60.5	65.7	68.8	71.2	73.3
2006	71.5	72.5	73.9	74.5	74.8	76.5	74.8	75.9	75.9	76.6	76.7	76.9	75.0
2007	75.1	75.5	75.8	75.8	76.1	76.8	76.7	77.0	77.1	77.2	77.1	77.4	76.5
2008	77.2	76.7	76.6	77.0	77.4	77.8	78.1	78.4	77.8	78.6	77.8	78.1	77.6
2009	76.3	75.9	75.3	75.3	75.2	75.1	74.0	73.3	72.6	72.9	72.5	71.7	74.2
2010	69.8	69.8	70.1	70.3	70.7	71.4	71.0	70.9	70.6	71.5	70.7	70.7	70.6
2011	69.7	69.9	70.1	70.4	70.4	70.0	70.0	69.9	69.4	69.3	69.2	69.0	69.8
2012	68.2	68.1	68.2	67.9	68.6	69.0	69.4	69.2	69.0	69.2	69.1	68.8	68.7
2013	67.2	67.1	67.5	67.4	67.9	68.8	69.1	69.3	69.2	68.8	69.2	68.2	68.3
Service-Providing													
2002	525.3	528.0	530.9	534.9	532.6	535.5	523.8	524.8	529.7	528.9	534.8	535.6	530.4
2003	527.6	530.8	532.2	537.8	535.8	536.9	529.6	527.2	533.7	534.6	540.9	541.8	534.1
2004	533.1	535.7	539.3	544.8	544.5	543.1	535.4	537.6	536.3	539.8	544.4	542.3	539.7
2005	534.6	534.6	539.7	539.7	538.7	541.9	530.7	529.8	416.0	363.4	373.4	383.1	485.5
2006	378.3	387.2	398.6	401.0	406.3	411.7	409.5	412.6	416.9	422.9	429.8	434.2	409.1
2007	432.3	436.6	443.0	436.1	437.1	439.2	433.5	437.8	438.6	448.8	453.9	457.3	441.2
2008	447.5	451.9	455.6	454.3	453.3	452.3	444.8	451.8	445.4	452.9	456.3	458.1	452.0
2009	446.8	449.8	450.4	452.3	453.7	448.8	445.5	450.0	448.7	450.7	453.2	454.0	450.3
2010	446.9	448.9	452.7	455.5	454.8	453.8	446.8	448.4	451.8	454.3	458.7	460.9	452.8
2011	453.9	457.1	459.8	461.2	461.6	457.2	452.9	456.9	459.7	462.5	466.6	468.5	459.8
2012	458.7	461.8	464.0	470.9	471.6	465.5	461.5	463.8	459.9	467.2	472.2	474.8	466.0
2013	472.6	476.6	475.1	477.1	477.1	475.1	469.7	477.4	474.6	481.6	484.5	485.9	477.3
Mining and Logging													
2005	8.3	8.4	8.6	8.3	8.4	8.6	8.4	8.5	8.1	8.3	8.3	8.4	8.4
2006	7.9	8.0	8.1	8.0	8.0	8.0	8.1	8.4	8.5	8.7	8.5	8.3	8.3
2007	7.8	8.0	8.1	8.3	8.3	8.3	8.4	8.3	8.3	8.6	8.6	8.6	8.3
2008	8.9	8.4	8.4	8.5	8.4	8.4	8.6	8.7	8.8	8.9	8.8	8.7	8.6
2009	8.6	8.5	8.4	8.3	8.2	8.3	7.8	7.8	7.7	7.8	7.7	7.8	8.1
2010	7.5	7.6	7.6	7.6	7.7	7.8	7.7	7.6	7.5	7.6	7.5	7.4	7.6
2011	7.3	7.5	7.5	7.4	7.4	7.5	7.6	7.6	7.5	7.6	7.6	7.6	7.5
2012	7.8	7.7	7.7	7.5	7.6	7.6	7.8	7.7	7.7	7.7	7.6	7.5	7.7
2013	7.4	7.5	7.5	7.5	7.5	7.6	7.8	7.8	7.7	7.7	7.7	7.7	7.6
Construction													
2005	29.2	29.0	29.6	29.8	30.0	30.0	29.8	29.7	21.8	25.8	28.4	29.4	28.5
2006	30.6	31.1	32.2	32.7	32.9	33.7	31.4	32.0	31.8	32.5	32.3	32.3	32.1
2007	31.6	31.6	31.9	31.7	31.9	32.1	32.0	32.4	32.2	32.2	31.9	31.8	31.9
2008	31.8	31.9	31.8	32.4	32.5	32.6	32.9	33.2	33.1	33.5	32.9	33.0	32.6
2009	31.9	31.9	31.7	31.8	32.0	32.0	31.7	31.4	31.0	31.6	31.5	30.7	31.6
2010	29.8	29.9	30.2	29.9	30.1	30.7	30.9	31.0	31.0	32.0	31.7	31.7	30.7
2011	31.0	30.9	31.3	32.3	32.1	31.7	31.5	31.4	31.1	31.0	30.9	30.7	31.3
2012	29.9	30.2	30.5	30.6	30.9	31.3	31.4	31.5	31.6	31.8	31.8	31.5	31.1
2013	30.4	30.4	30.9	30.9	31.1	31.5	31.5	31.7	31.8	32.0	32.0	31.0	31.3

Employment by Industry: New Orleans-Metairie-Kenner, LA, Selected Years, 2002–2013—*Continued*

(Numbers in thousands, not seasonally adjusted)

Industry and year	January	February	March	April	May	June	July	August	September	October	November	December	Annual average
Manufacturing													
2002	41.3	41.2	41.2	41.4	41.5	41.7	41.1	41.3	40.6	40.3	40.4	40.4	41.0
2003	39.5	39.4	39.3	39.1	39.3	39.4	39.3	39.3	39.1	39.3	39.0	39.4	39.3
2004	38.5	38.5	38.4	38.9	38.9	39.2	38.9	39.1	38.8	38.4	38.1	38.4	38.7
2005	37.6	38.4	38.4	38.4	38.5	39.0	38.9	39.0	30.6	31.6	32.1	33.4	36.3
2006	33.0	33.4	33.6	33.8	33.9	34.7	35.0	35.4	35.4	35.4	35.9	36.3	34.7
2007	35.7	35.9	35.8	35.8	35.9	36.4	36.3	36.3	36.6	36.4	36.6	37.0	36.2
2008	36.5	36.4	36.4	36.1	36.5	36.8	36.6	36.5	35.9	36.2	36.1	36.4	36.4
2009	35.8	35.5	35.2	35.2	35.0	34.8	34.5	34.1	33.9	33.5	33.3	33.2	34.5
2010	32.5	32.3	32.3	32.8	32.9	32.9	32.4	32.3	32.1	31.9	31.5	31.6	32.3
2011	31.4	31.5	31.3	30.7	30.9	30.8	30.9	30.9	30.8	30.7	30.7	30.7	30.9
2012	30.5	30.2	30.0	29.8	30.1	30.1	30.2	30.0	29.7	29.7	29.7	29.8	30.0
2013	29.4	29.2	29.1	29.0	29.3	29.7	29.8	29.8	29.7	29.1	29.5	29.5	29.4
Trade, Transportation, and Utilities													
2002	123.1	122.3	123.9	123.9	123.9	125.7	123.5	123.5	123.1	122.6	124.1	126.5	123.8
2003	121.0	120.9	121.3	121.0	120.9	121.4	121.4	121.8	121.1	121.9	124.2	125.6	121.9
2004	121.4	121.3	122.3	123.0	123.3	123.2	122.1	122.4	121.1	122.8	124.2	126.4	122.8
2005	121.5	120.7	121.7	121.3	121.6	122.0	121.1	120.6	88.6	84.1	89.9	94.3	110.6
2006	94.7	96.7	99.3	101.0	102.2	104.0	103.9	104.4	104.2	106.0	107.8	110.1	102.9
2007	107.6	107.2	108.4	107.5	107.7	108.0	107.7	107.8	107.1	109.8	112.3	114.0	108.8
2008	110.0	109.1	109.6	108.6	108.8	108.7	108.2	108.6	106.3	108.3	110.2	111.3	109.0
2009	106.4	105.6	105.5	104.8	104.8	105.1	104.1	104.0	103.6	103.2	104.5	105.2	104.7
2010	102.0	101.4	102.2	102.8	102.8	102.9	103.1	103.1	103.0	104.7	106.5	107.9	103.5
2011	106.1	105.6	105.8	105.9	106.2	105.9	106.0	105.7	105.5	105.9	107.9	108.7	106.3
2012	106.1	105.4	105.7	106.1	106.4	106.2	105.9	105.8	105.2	107.3	110.3	111.2	106.8
2013	109.5	108.4	109.2	108.8	108.9	109.1	109.3	110.2	110.3	111.5	112.8	114.4	110.2
Wholesale Trade													
2002	27.1	27.1	27.3	27.4	27.5	27.6	27.1	27.2	27.0	26.9	26.8	26.8	27.2
2003	27.0	27.1	27.1	26.6	26.6	26.6	26.6	26.6	26.3	26.8	26.7	26.6	26.7
2004	26.3	26.3	26.4	26.4	26.5	26.5	26.3	26.3	26.2	25.8	25.8	25.8	26.2
2005	25.3	25.3	25.4	25.8	25.9	26.0	26.2	26.1	21.8	21.9	22.2	22.5	24.5
2006	21.8	22.2	22.4	22.6	22.8	23.0	23.0	23.1	23.1	23.1	23.2	23.4	22.8
2007	23.6	23.7	24.0	23.8	24.0	24.2	24.6	24.8	24.5	24.9	24.9	25.0	24.3
2008	24.5	24.6	24.7	24.0	24.0	24.0	23.9	23.9	23.7	23.8	23.9	23.9	24.1
2009	23.3	23.3	23.3	23.5	23.5	23.4	22.9	22.8	22.7	22.6	22.6	22.6	23.0
2010	22.0	22.0	22.1	22.1	22.2	22.3	22.2	22.2	22.1	22.3	22.3	22.4	22.2
2011	22.8	22.9	22.9	22.4	22.6	22.6	22.6	22.5	22.5	22.5	22.5	22.5	22.6
2012	22.2	22.2	22.2	22.5	22.5	22.5	22.4	22.4	22.2	22.3	22.3	22.3	22.3
2013	22.9	22.9	23.0	22.9	23.0	23.0	23.1	23.2	23.2	23.4	23.4	23.2	23.1
Retail Trade													
2002	67.5	66.8	68.1	67.4	67.3	68.6	67.0	66.8	66.5	65.7	67.5	69.4	67.4
2003	66.1	65.9	66.5	66.3	66.5	67.0	66.7	67.3	67.0	67.3	69.5	71.0	67.3
2004	67.8	67.4	67.9	68.7	68.7	68.7	67.9	67.6	66.6	68.0	69.5	71.0	68.3
2005	67.6	66.8	67.4	67.5	67.8	68.0	67.2	66.9	44.1	41.0	45.7	48.8	59.9
2006	50.3	51.6	53.2	54.3	55.1	56.2	56.7	56.8	56.8	58.7	60.1	61.3	55.9
2007	59.4	58.9	59.7	59.1	59.4	59.4	59.4	59.0	58.9	60.5	62.8	64.1	60.1
2008	61.4	60.2	60.6	60.1	60.1	60.1	59.8	60.0	58.3	59.5	61.0	62.0	60.3
2009	58.4	58.1	58.0	57.6	57.8	58.1	57.6	57.6	57.3	56.9	58.2	58.7	57.9
2010	56.5	55.9	56.6	56.4	56.3	56.3	56.2	56.0	56.1	57.3	59.2	60.1	56.9
2011	58.1	57.8	58.0	58.3	58.2	58.0	58.1	57.8	57.4	58.2	60.0	60.5	58.4
2012	58.6	57.8	57.9	57.9	58.1	58.0	58.0	57.7	57.3	58.9	61.5	62.0	58.6
2013	59.8	58.8	59.3	59.3	59.5	59.7	59.9	60.3	60.4	60.9	62.3	63.4	60.3
Transportation and Utilities													
2002	28.5	28.4	28.5	29.1	29.1	29.5	29.4	29.5	29.6	30.0	29.8	30.3	29.3
2003	27.9	27.9	27.7	28.1	27.8	27.8	28.1	27.9	27.8	27.8	28.0	28.0	27.9
2004	27.3	27.6	28.0	27.9	28.1	28.0	27.9	28.5	28.3	29.0	28.9	29.6	28.3
2005	28.6	28.6	28.9	28.0	27.9	28.0	27.7	27.6	22.7	21.2	22.0	23.0	26.2
2006	22.6	22.9	23.7	24.1	24.3	24.8	24.2	24.5	24.3	24.2	24.5	25.4	24.1
2007	24.6	24.6	24.7	24.6	24.3	24.4	23.7	24.0	23.7	24.4	24.6	24.9	24.4
2008	24.1	24.3	24.3	24.5	24.7	24.6	24.5	24.7	24.3	25.0	25.3	25.4	24.6
2009	24.7	24.2	24.2	23.7	23.5	23.6	23.6	23.6	23.6	23.7	23.7	23.9	23.8
2010	23.5	23.5	23.5	24.3	24.3	24.3	24.7	24.9	24.8	25.1	25.0	25.4	24.4
2011	25.2	24.9	24.9	25.2	25.4	25.3	25.3	25.4	25.6	25.2	25.4	25.7	25.3
2012	25.3	25.4	25.6	25.7	25.8	25.7	25.5	25.7	25.7	26.1	26.5	26.9	25.8
2013	26.8	26.7	26.9	26.6	26.4	26.4	26.3	26.7	26.7	27.2	27.1	27.8	26.8
Information													
2002	10.0	10.0	10.0	9.6	9.5	9.7	9.6	9.6	9.5	9.3	9.3	9.4	9.6
2003	9.8	9.7	9.9	10.0	10.4	10.7	9.2	9.5	9.4	9.1	9.2	9.2	9.7
2004	9.4	9.8	9.8	10.7	10.4	10.7	9.7	11.2	10.1	11.0	12.7	10.8	10.5
2005	10.8	10.6	10.5	9.5	9.6	9.8	10.1	10.5	9.0	7.3	7.4	7.7	9.4
2006	7.1	7.3	8.8	8.1	8.4	7.5	6.7	6.8	6.9	6.9	7.4	7.5	7.5
2007	7.4	8.2	10.1	9.5	9.2	9.8	8.7	8.3	7.3	7.1	7.4	7.3	8.4
2008	8.0	9.2	11.2	9.8	10.6	11.2	7.2	8.6	8.9	6.9	7.4	7.9	8.9
2009	6.0	6.4	6.6	6.3	6.7	7.1	6.4	6.4	6.4	6.0	6.4	6.1	6.4
2010	6.8	7.3	7.2	6.9	7.5	8.3	6.0	6.3	8.7	6.5	6.9	7.1	7.1
2011	6.9	6.8	8.4	7.6	8.5	8.0	6.8	6.9	7.1	7.4	7.4	8.0	7.5
2012	7.2	7.8	8.0	10.5	11.9	9.2	8.6	8.7	7.8	7.7	8.6	8.9	8.7
2013	9.1	10.1	9.2	9.5	10.1	10.4	8.4	9.0	8.2	8.2	8.6	8.5	9.1

Employment by Industry: New Orleans-Metairie-Kenner, LA, Selected Years, 2002–2013—*Continued*

(Numbers in thousands, not seasonally adjusted)

Industry and year	January	February	March	April	May	June	July	August	September	October	November	December	Annual average
Financial Activities													
2002	33.7	33.9	34.1	34.5	34.6	34.9	34.7	35.2	35.0	35.5	35.6	35.5	34.8
2003	35.1	34.7	34.6	34.4	34.4	34.5	34.6	34.9	34.6	34.6	34.5	34.5	34.6
2004	33.9	33.8	33.8	34.2	34.1	34.2	34.7	34.7	34.3	34.3	34.1	34.2	34.2
2005	33.2	33.2	33.2	32.8	32.7	32.8	32.9	33.0	27.6	26.2	26.1	25.9	30.8
2006	25.7	25.8	26.1	25.7	26.0	26.3	26.4	26.4	26.4	26.6	26.7	26.8	26.2
2007	27.4	27.5	27.3	27.1	27.2	27.4	27.6	27.5	27.3	27.6	27.5	27.5	27.4
2008	27.0	27.2	27.2	26.9	26.9	26.9	26.6	26.4	26.0	26.2	26.1	26.1	26.6
2009	25.7	25.8	25.8	26.2	26.2	26.3	26.2	26.1	26.0	25.9	26.0	26.1	26.0
2010	25.7	25.7	25.8	25.9	26.1	26.1	26.1	26.0	25.8	26.1	26.2	26.2	26.0
2011	26.4	26.4	26.4	26.2	26.3	26.2	26.5	26.5	26.5	26.6	26.7	26.7	26.5
2012	26.4	26.5	26.5	26.5	26.6	26.8	26.7	26.6	26.5	26.8	26.8	26.9	26.6
2013	26.8	26.8	26.9	27.0	27.1	27.2	27.3	27.5	27.4	27.6	27.7	27.7	27.3
Professional and Business Services													
2002	72.8	72.8	73.1	73.4	72.1	72.2	71.5	71.9	71.3	70.4	70.4	70.8	71.9
2003	70.7	71.6	72.3	73.9	72.0	72.5	71.8	71.9	71.6	73.7	74.5	75.1	72.6
2004	72.8	73.4	73.8	75.0	74.6	74.7	71.5	71.7	71.0	73.1	73.7	73.6	73.2
2005	73.2	73.4	74.3	76.9	75.8	75.2	74.1	73.8	54.0	55.6	59.1	61.1	68.9
2006	60.7	62.8	64.4	64.5	65.1	66.3	65.6	66.6	66.2	66.7	67.0	67.4	65.3
2007	67.3	68.4	69.0	68.4	69.0	68.8	66.8	67.9	67.8	69.9	70.1	70.2	68.6
2008	67.1	68.7	69.1	69.5	69.3	68.7	68.3	69.1	67.8	68.8	68.9	69.0	68.7
2009	66.7	67.5	67.3	67.4	67.8	67.3	66.2	66.0	65.9	67.3	67.5	68.1	67.1
2010	65.8	66.6	67.3	69.3	69.2	69.5	69.0	68.6	67.6	68.2	68.4	68.3	68.2
2011	66.9	68.3	68.0	68.5	68.2	67.9	67.1	67.7	67.8	69.4	69.5	69.6	68.2
2012	67.5	68.8	69.2	71.1	70.7	69.0	69.5	68.7	67.7	70.1	70.0	69.7	69.3
2013	69.9	73.2	71.4	71.4	71.0	71.0	71.6	72.2	71.5	73.5	73.2	72.9	71.9
Education and Health Services													
2002	81.6	83.0	82.6	84.7	83.0	81.6	80.0	79.7	85.0	85.5	87.5	85.6	83.3
2003	84.9	85.3	84.4	85.9	85.4	83.6	82.9	82.5	87.3	87.3	89.5	87.9	85.6
2004	87.5	87.2	87.3	87.8	86.9	84.4	85.0	86.0	86.4	86.6	86.5	83.4	86.3
2005	84.1	83.7	84.3	84.5	83.7	85.1	81.7	80.7	66.7	53.4	52.5	53.2	74.5
2006	55.3	55.2	56.6	57.8	58.3	57.9	57.8	58.0	60.1	61.3	63.3	62.5	58.7
2007	64.0	64.7	65.3	65.6	64.4	64.2	64.2	64.1	65.9	67.1	68.9	69.5	69.7	66.1
2008	69.3	70.1	70.6	70.7	68.6	68.5	68.6	70.3	70.4	72.7	73.2	73.3	70.5
2009	73.8	74.6	75.0	75.5	75.8	73.0	73.3	75.1	75.4	77.0	77.3	77.3	75.3
2010	77.2	77.5	78.0	78.8	76.0	75.0	74.9	75.7	76.7	78.0	78.5	78.6	77.1
2011	77.2	78.3	78.8	79.5	79.5	77.0	77.1	78.2	79.9	81.0	81.7	81.2	79.1
2012	79.6	80.6	81.4	81.3	81.3	80.7	80.1	81.7	81.6	82.4	82.6	82.6	81.3
2013	84.1	84.6	84.2	84.6	84.3	82.9	81.3	83.3	83.9	85.2	85.3	85.3	84.1
Leisure and Hospitality													
2002	78.4	79.2	79.9	81.7	82.5	82.9	81.6	80.6	79.7	78.6	79.8	79.1	80.3
2003	78.5	79.8	80.5	83.2	83.5	84.9	83.1	83.0	81.9	81.0	81.1	81.7	81.9
2004	81.3	82.5	83.9	83.7	84.8	86.5	85.1	85.3	84.2	84.3	84.9	85.3	84.3
2005	83.6	83.6	85.5	86.2	87.2	88.6	85.8	85.6	51.7	42.2	44.1	46.3	72.5
2006	47.3	51.2	54.1	54.4	56.1	59.6	60.2	60.7	59.9	61.6	62.7	64.1	57.7
2007	63.5	64.0	65.4	65.1	66.1	67.0	65.9	66.5	64.8	65.5	66.4	67.6	65.7
2008	67.1	67.6	68.1	68.8	68.9	69.4	68.3	69.0	65.4	67.0	66.9	67.2	67.8
2009	66.1	67.0	67.8	67.8	68.4	68.6	67.2	68.2	67.4	66.8	67.0	67.4	67.5
2010	67.4	67.9	69.0	69.6	69.4	70.2	68.6	69.1	69.9	69.7	70.8	71.9	69.5
2011	70.4	71.5	72.5	73.1	73.7	74.0	73.1	74.1	73.7	73.3	74.4	75.7	73.3
2012	75.3	75.5	76.0	76.8	76.4	76.4	75.8	76.3	74.3	75.6	76.4	78.0	76.1
2013	77.3	77.1	77.9	78.9	78.9	78.8	78.0	80.2	77.5	79.1	80.4	80.5	78.7
Other Services													
2002	22.8	22.9	23.2	23.2	23.5	23.6	23.6	23.6	23.5	23.8	23.9	24.2	23.5
2003	23.8	24.0	24.0	24.6	24.8	24.1	23.4	23.4	23.3	23.9	23.9	23.9	23.9
2004	23.6	23.7	23.9	23.5	23.5	23.5	23.6	23.6	23.4	23.4	23.3	23.4	23.5
2005	23.0	23.1	23.3	23.4	23.5	23.5	23.6	23.4	16.5	14.3	14.3	15.0	20.6
2006	14.8	15.4	15.8	16.1	16.4	16.7	16.9	17.1	17.3	17.7	17.7	17.8	16.6
2007	18.8	19.2	19.4	20.2	20.4	20.6	21.3	21.5	21.5	21.9	21.9	22.0	20.7
2008	21.1	21.3	21.3	19.3	19.4	19.5	19.1	19.1	18.9	20.4	20.5	20.4	20.0
2009	20.3	20.4	20.5	20.7	20.8	20.7	20.7	20.9	20.9	20.3	20.4	20.4	20.6
2010	19.7	19.7	19.8	18.9	19.0	19.1	18.8	18.7	18.6	19.1	19.1	19.1	19.1
2011	19.2	19.3	19.3	19.5	19.4	19.6	19.5	19.5	19.4	19.5	19.6	19.6	19.5
2012	19.5	19.5	19.7	19.8	19.8	19.9	19.9	19.8	19.6	19.7	19.7	19.8	19.7
2013	19.7	19.8	19.8	20.1	20.2	20.3	20.4	20.4	20.2	20.4	20.4	20.5	20.2
Government													
2002	102.9	103.9	104.1	103.9	103.5	104.9	99.3	100.7	102.6	103.2	104.2	104.5	103.1
2003	103.8	104.8	105.2	104.8	104.4	105.2	103.2	100.2	104.5	103.1	104.0	103.9	103.9
2004	103.2	104.0	104.5	106.9	106.9	105.9	103.7	102.7	105.8	104.3	105.0	105.2	104.8
2005	105.2	106.3	106.9	105.1	104.6	104.9	101.4	102.2	101.9	80.3	80.0	79.6	98.2
2006	72.7	72.8	73.5	73.4	73.8	73.4	72.0	72.6	75.9	76.1	77.2	78.0	74.3
2007	76.3	77.4	78.1	72.7	73.1	73.4	71.4	72.4	75.7	78.1	78.8	79.0	75.5
2008	77.9	78.7	78.5	80.7	80.8	79.4	78.5	80.7	81.7	82.6	83.1	82.9	80.5
2009	81.8	82.5	81.9	83.6	83.2	80.7	81.4	83.3	83.1	84.2	84.1	83.4	82.8
2010	82.3	82.8	83.4	83.3	84.8	82.7	80.3	80.9	81.5	82.0	82.3	81.8	82.3
2011	80.8	80.9	80.6	80.9	80.6	78.6	76.8	78.3	79.8	79.4	79.4	79.0	79.6
2012	77.1	77.7	77.5	78.8	78.5	77.3	75.0	76.2	77.2	77.6	77.8	77.7	77.4
2013	76.2	76.6	76.5	76.8	76.6	75.4	73.4	74.6	75.6	76.1	76.1	76.1	75.8

Employment by Industry: New York-Northern New Jersey-Long Island, NY–NJ–PA, Selected Years, 2002–2013

(Numbers in thousands, not seasonally adjusted)

Industry and year	January	February	March	April	May	June	July	August	September	October	November	December	Annual average
Total Nonfarm													
2002	8,136.4	8,168.1	8,225.0	8,255.0	8,314.4	8,358.4	8,268.5	8,233.7	8,240.8	8,319.1	8,376.2	8,410.5	8,275.5
2003	8,131.9	8,139.8	8,187.2	8,214.0	8,270.6	8,314.7	8,249.8	8,209.0	8,235.4	8,313.7	8,364.5	8,398.8	8,252.5
2004	8,099.2	8,129.6	8,209.1	8,246.4	8,318.6	8,382.3	8,326.2	8,283.4	8,298.4	8,371.7	8,418.7	8,466.6	8,295.9
2005	8,167.6	8,189.0	8,241.8	8,329.5	8,376.9	8,450.5	8,372.0	8,340.9	8,375.0	8,403.6	8,474.1	8,528.1	8,354.1
2006	8,252.6	8,274.7	8,351.3	8,394.7	8,469.0	8,545.0	8,456.9	8,419.6	8,455.0	8,526.6	8,596.3	8,658.5	8,450.0
2007	8,391.3	8,410.6	8,472.1	8,517.0	8,594.9	8,676.3	8,586.6	8,538.1	8,557.0	8,650.6	8,709.4	8,755.0	8,571.6
2008	8,494.9	8,516.3	8,566.9	8,611.9	8,655.0	8,707.8	8,620.2	8,565.7	8,564.8	8,608.1	8,623.0	8,623.5	8,596.5
2009	8,294.1	8,281.8	8,290.0	8,300.4	8,354.6	8,382.2	8,308.3	8,249.6	8,238.6	8,315.8	8,355.4	8,390.0	8,313.4
2010	8,115.3	8,131.7	8,197.8	8,299.7	8,377.7	8,414.7	8,303.4	8,260.1	8,287.4	8,386.6	8,432.0	8,459.4	8,305.5
2011	8,200.9	8,236.7	8,295.8	8,396.5	8,440.2	8,495.1	8,442.0	8,393.4	8,435.6	8,503.9	8,561.8	8,589.1	8,415.9
2012	8,341.6	8,396.9	8,470.0	8,511.4	8,592.7	8,650.3	8,542.3	8,521.3	8,567.7	8,650.5	8,657.8	8,733.7	8,553.0
2013	8,458.6	8,504.0	8,577.5	8,669.9	8,728.2	8,787.6	8,718.0	8,679.7	8,710.1	8,786.7	8,842.6	8,841.3	8,692.0
Total Private													
2002	6,884.3	6,907.6	6,957.6	6,989.7	7,043.0	7,085.6	7,019.6	7,011.0	7,015.2	7,060.2	7,101.0	7,130.8	7,017.1
2003	6,868.7	6,863.2	6,906.9	6,933.2	6,990.1	7,032.8	6,992.8	6,979.1	7,001.9	7,039.2	7,077.1	7,108.6	6,982.8
2004	6,837.4	6,853.9	6,926.0	6,964.6	7,033.4	7,092.6	7,063.9	7,047.7	7,060.9	7,094.5	7,129.1	7,176.8	7,023.4
2005	6,895.3	6,906.0	6,955.9	7,036.6	7,082.7	7,148.8	7,098.3	7,093.4	7,121.8	7,122.3	7,178.9	7,228.0	7,072.3
2006	6,974.3	6,986.5	7,059.0	7,101.2	7,173.1	7,246.8	7,189.4	7,179.5	7,203.0	7,239.2	7,296.4	7,352.0	7,166.7
2007	7,104.7	7,111.6	7,168.4	7,215.3	7,287.8	7,365.6	7,310.0	7,285.8	7,293.4	7,352.7	7,399.8	7,438.6	7,277.8
2008	7,201.6	7,210.2	7,255.9	7,295.8	7,337.0	7,387.3	7,323.6	7,301.0	7,293.4	7,300.7	7,299.5	7,295.8	7,291.8
2009	6,994.0	6,970.8	6,973.9	6,978.0	7,030.4	7,062.6	6,985.8	6,955.4	6,976.0	7,012.1	7,040.4	7,073.7	7,004.5
2010	6,826.9	6,831.5	6,890.8	6,982.3	7,026.7	7,083.8	7,035.8	7,028.5	7,042.9	7,104.0	7,143.9	7,176.7	7,014.5
2011	6,946.9	6,966.9	7,022.5	7,116.6	7,165.5	7,223.0	7,190.4	7,164.4	7,207.6	7,239.0	7,290.1	7,323.5	7,154.7
2012	7,112.0	7,143.7	7,208.6	7,250.9	7,333.0	7,392.7	7,321.5	7,324.7	7,354.4	7,398.3	7,405.7	7,477.7	7,310.3
2013	7,233.9	7,254.9	7,325.3	7,412.7	7,472.0	7,536.5	7,498.8	7,488.7	7,504.4	7,543.1	7,593.0	7,592.6	7,454.7
Goods Producing													
2002	860.2	862.2	869.3	878.1	886.0	891.1	882.5	888.3	888.0	884.6	878.9	870.4	878.3
2003	827.9	823.9	831.6	841.2	851.6	857.7	850.9	854.1	855.9	851.0	848.3	842.2	844.7
2004	800.1	800.9	815.6	822.7	834.2	846.0	842.3	845.9	847.4	842.4	839.3	835.3	831.0
2005	790.5	787.8	795.6	809.5	818.6	827.7	821.8	828.4	830.8	822.0	824.4	819.2	814.7
2006	787.6	787.3	797.3	809.8	819.6	828.9	821.6	826.6	827.8	824.7	821.8	817.6	814.2
2007	786.2	779.6	788.0	802.2	813.4	823.7	820.1	822.0	820.6	820.8	817.9	810.9	808.8
2008	781.7	778.5	785.8	794.7	799.3	804.0	801.4	802.6	798.0	790.8	779.5	761.5	789.8
2009	711.8	702.8	701.5	702.8	706.5	708.5	703.6	701.1	695.2	692.2	685.7	677.7	699.1
2010	641.8	636.2	645.7	663.2	666.6	672.4	673.2	674.5	671.9	670.6	669.3	659.8	662.1
2011	626.4	625.4	636.1	650.6	659.9	666.7	670.7	674.3	671.8	670.7	670.6	665.1	657.4
2012	639.6	638.6	646.7	655.5	661.7	668.7	669.9	673.0	671.8	673.6	670.9	674.1	662.0
2013	651.4	649.5	658.7	673.5	680.1	685.8	686.3	691.9	690.7	687.5	685.5	670.7	676.0
Service-Providing													
2002	7,276.2	7,305.9	7,355.7	7,376.9	7,428.4	7,467.3	7,386.0	7,345.4	7,352.8	7,434.5	7,497.3	7,540.1	7,397.2
2003	7,304.0	7,315.9	7,355.6	7,372.8	7,419.0	7,457.0	7,398.9	7,354.9	7,379.5	7,462.7	7,516.2	7,556.6	7,407.8
2004	7,299.1	7,328.7	7,393.5	7,423.7	7,484.4	7,536.3	7,483.9	7,437.5	7,451.0	7,529.3	7,579.4	7,631.3	7,464.8
2005	7,377.1	7,401.2	7,446.2	7,520.0	7,558.3	7,622.8	7,550.2	7,512.5	7,544.2	7,581.6	7,649.7	7,708.9	7,539.4
2006	7,465.0	7,487.4	7,554.0	7,584.9	7,649.4	7,716.1	7,635.3	7,593.0	7,627.2	7,701.9	7,774.5	7,840.9	7,635.8
2007	7,605.1	7,631.0	7,684.1	7,714.8	7,781.5	7,852.6	7,766.5	7,716.1	7,736.4	7,829.8	7,891.5	7,944.1	7,762.8
2008	7,713.2	7,737.8	7,781.1	7,817.2	7,855.7	7,903.8	7,818.8	7,763.1	7,766.8	7,817.3	7,843.5	7,862.0	7,806.7
2009	7,582.3	7,579.0	7,588.5	7,597.6	7,648.1	7,673.7	7,604.7	7,548.5	7,543.4	7,623.6	7,669.7	7,712.3	7,614.3
2010	7,473.5	7,495.5	7,552.1	7,636.5	7,711.1	7,742.3	7,630.2	7,585.6	7,615.5	7,716.0	7,762.7	7,799.6	7,643.4
2011	7,574.5	7,611.3	7,659.7	7,745.9	7,780.3	7,828.4	7,771.3	7,719.1	7,763.8	7,833.2	7,891.2	7,924.0	7,758.6
2012	7,702.0	7,758.3	7,823.3	7,855.9	7,931.0	7,981.6	7,872.4	7,848.3	7,895.9	7,976.9	7,986.9	8,059.6	7,891.0
2013	7,807.2	7,854.5	7,918.8	7,996.4	8,048.1	8,101.8	8,031.7	7,987.8	8,019.4	8,099.2	8,157.1	8,170.6	8,016.1
Mining, Logging, and Construction													
2002	309.6	310.0	315.3	326.7	332.3	337.3	340.7	343.7	342.6	342.2	339.8	334.9	331.3
2003	306.5	301.6	308.8	321.6	331.4	336.2	339.1	340.3	340.3	338.3	336.6	331.9	327.7
2004	303.5	301.9	313.3	324.8	333.9	342.0	345.2	347.7	347.6	345.0	343.2	340.1	332.4
2005	309.6	305.5	311.6	328.6	337.2	344.0	345.3	350.4	351.9	344.7	348.1	343.0	335.0
2006	320.4	320.2	329.2	342.8	351.1	358.7	359.7	364.6	365.3	363.3	361.6	359.9	349.7
2007	336.4	330.3	338.5	354.9	365.8	374.6	375.3	378.3	377.2	377.8	376.2	370.5	363.0
2008	346.9	344.6	351.0	362.1	367.9	371.2	374.2	376.1	371.8	368.7	361.2	348.4	362.0
2009	314.9	310.9	313.5	319.4	323.6	325.8	327.5	326.6	321.1	318.1	313.8	306.3	318.5
2010	278.3	272.8	281.1	297.5	300.2	303.8	307.2	309.0	306.3	304.5	303.2	293.8	296.5
2011	268.0	267.0	277.0	291.0	299.6	304.4	311.0	313.3	310.5	309.6	309.1	304.0	297.0
2012	284.4	282.6	288.8	298.5	302.7	307.6	311.7	314.4	311.9	313.5	312.6	315.2	303.7
2013	298.9	296.0	302.9	317.4	322.8	326.6	330.8	334.7	333.1	329.1	326.9	311.6	319.2
Manufacturing													
2002	550.6	552.2	554.0	551.4	553.7	553.8	541.8	544.6	545.4	542.4	539.1	535.5	547.0
2003	521.4	522.3	522.8	519.6	520.2	521.5	511.8	513.8	515.6	512.7	511.7	510.3	517.0
2004	496.6	499.0	502.3	497.9	500.3	504.0	497.1	498.2	499.8	497.4	496.1	495.2	498.7
2005	480.9	482.3	484.0	480.9	481.4	483.7	476.5	478.0	478.9	477.3	476.3	476.2	479.7
2006	467.2	467.1	468.1	467.0	468.5	470.2	461.9	462.0	462.5	461.4	460.2	457.7	464.5
2007	449.8	449.3	449.5	447.3	447.6	449.1	444.8	443.7	443.4	443.0	441.7	440.4	445.8
2008	434.8	433.9	434.8	432.6	431.4	432.8	427.2	426.5	426.2	422.1	418.3	413.1	427.8
2009	396.9	391.9	388.0	383.4	382.9	382.7	376.1	374.5	374.1	374.1	371.9	371.4	380.7
2010	363.5	363.4	364.6	365.7	366.4	368.6	366.0	365.5	365.65	366.1	366.1	366.0	365.6
2011	358.4	358.4	359.1	359.6	360.3	362.3	359.7	361.0	361.3	361.1	361.5	361.1	360.3
2012	355.2	356.0	357.9	357.0	359.0	361.1	358.2	358.6	359.9	360.1	358.3	358.9	358.4
2013	352.5	353.5	355.8	356.1	357.3	359.2	355.5	357.2	357.6	358.4	358.6	359.1	356.7

Employment by Industry: New York-Northern New Jersey-Long Island, NY–NJ–PA, Selected Years, 2002–2013—*Continued*

(Numbers in thousands, not seasonally adjusted)

Industry and year	January	February	March	April	May	June	July	August	September	October	November	December	Annual average
Trade, Transportation, and Utilities													
2002	1,574.0	1,558.0	1,568.4	1,563.6	1,571.7	1,587.5	1,561.9	1,558.1	1,578.3	1,590.9	1,618.9	1,649.6	1,581.7
2003	1,575.2	1,559.6	1,563.9	1,558.0	1,568.7	1,580.4	1,557.8	1,556.1	1,573.8	1,590.2	1,615.1	1,641.3	1,578.3
2004	1,562.3	1,550.4	1,558.9	1,555.8	1,572.8	1,589.2	1,570.8	1,568.4	1,583.4	1,600.8	1,625.9	1,654.4	1,582.8
2005	1,568.2	1,553.5	1,558.3	1,567.7	1,579.3	1,594.0	1,571.3	1,569.4	1,585.6	1,592.3	1,622.8	1,656.9	1,584.9
2006	1,583.2	1,562.0	1,570.6	1,573.1	1,587.3	1,604.2	1,581.5	1,577.1	1,593.5	1,611.6	1,646.7	1,677.9	1,597.4
2007	1,605.7	1,584.6	1,590.4	1,591.6	1,609.5	1,629.3	1,603.0	1,593.1	1,609.5	1,622.1	1,659.2	1,688.2	1,615.5
2008	1,615.8	1,593.9	1,600.3	1,596.4	1,605.7	1,619.2	1,594.2	1,588.8	1,599.5	1,602.5	1,620.1	1,636.6	1,606.1
2009	1,550.0	1,525.4	1,518.9	1,506.9	1,521.0	1,532.7	1,505.2	1,500.7	1,516.9	1,529.1	1,556.6	1,582.0	1,528.8
2010	1,510.4	1,492.8	1,498.6	1,511.2	1,522.3	1,540.6	1,519.9	1,519.3	1,531.7	1,548.6	1,576.3	1,602.2	1,531.2
2011	1,538.0	1,522.1	1,526.0	1,537.3	1,547.0	1,565.1	1,544.3	1,543.9	1,559.3	1,569.7	1,604.7	1,632.0	1,557.5
2012	1,572.0	1,553.8	1,560.8	1,557.2	1,577.4	1,594.8	1,561.4	1,564.7	1,581.0	1,592.4	1,623.7	1,652.1	1,582.6
2013	1,578.5	1,556.8	1,569.6	1,578.3	1,591.1	1,611.5	1,595.7	1,592.5	1,608.5	1,619.4	1,659.7	1,690.5	1,604.3
Wholesale Trade													
2002	434.4	435.0	437.4	432.2	432.5	433.4	429.2	430.2	431.0	432.7	433.4	434.9	433.0
2003	431.8	432.1	433.4	430.9	432.2	433.6	431.9	431.2	431.2	431.7	432.7	434.1	432.2
2004	425.4	426.4	428.9	427.9	429.3	432.2	432.1	431.8	431.5	432.9	433.2	435.1	430.6
2005	424.5	425.6	426.5	427.5	428.8	430.9	428.6	429.5	430.6	430.5	431.6	434.9	429.1
2006	425.3	425.6	427.5	429.4	431.7	434.5	432.9	432.6	432.4	434.4	435.4	438.4	431.7
2007	431.4	431.2	432.2	432.4	434.2	437.7	436.1	435.3	434.6	437.5	437.5	439.4	435.0
2008	432.0	432.0	432.9	431.0	431.6	433.1	430.3	428.8	427.6	425.6	423.0	421.2	429.1
2009	411.8	407.8	405.5	401.6	401.4	401.6	397.4	396.2	395.1	396.6	396.6	397.8	400.8
2010	389.5	388.7	390.2	391.0	392.5	395.4	395.2	394.6	394.4	395.7	396.9	398.5	393.6
2011	392.3	391.7	393.5	394.6	396.0	398.7	398.5	398.6	397.1	397.7	398.0	401.1	396.5
2012	396.8	398.0	399.7	399.4	400.7	403.9	402.2	401.7	400.7	402.1	402.4	404.8	401.0
2013	397.7	398.1	399.4	400.8	402.4	406.3	406.8	406.5	405.9	405.1	405.4	409.1	403.6
Retail Trade													
2002	819.4	802.7	810.2	810.2	816.8	830.6	820.2	820.3	823.8	830.6	859.0	887.9	827.6
2003	825.2	810.3	811.5	813.3	820.6	830.5	821.6	823.0	825.0	837.0	860.6	883.8	830.2
2004	823.2	810.9	815.5	816.1	827.5	839.5	834.6	834.7	835.6	847.2	872.0	897.6	837.9
2005	836.1	820.4	822.1	829.3	836.8	847.0	840.8	840.6	839.1	845.7	872.2	898.0	844.0
2006	843.8	822.7	828.0	829.3	836.7	848.4	843.6	842.0	839.6	854.6	886.1	907.7	848.5
2007	855.8	835.4	838.9	840.9	851.1	864.2	858.1	852.8	850.2	858.5	893.7	915.0	859.6
2008	863.1	841.5	844.9	842.0	848.7	858.7	854.6	852.1	847.8	854.2	873.1	887.1	855.7
2009	825.6	806.5	803.7	798.8	809.8	820.7	814.3	814.3	815.3	824.8	849.3	869.3	821.0
2010	819.3	804.5	808.4	819.2	827.2	840.5	836.6	837.6	833.2	846.8	870.6	889.1	836.1
2011	841.3	827.9	828.7	837.0	843.4	855.9	852.6	853.7	852.6	862.5	892.4	912.4	855.0
2012	868.4	849.2	852.8	854.3	865.8	877.1	869.8	869.9	869.3	879.4	908.2	926.2	874.2
2013	874.3	859.8	864.8	870.6	880.5	895.0	893.5	894.9	892.8	904.0	935.0	955.4	893.4
Transportation and Utilities													
2002	320.2	320.3	320.8	321.2	322.4	323.5	312.5	307.6	323.5	327.6	326.5	326.8	321.1
2003	318.2	317.2	319.0	313.8	315.9	316.3	304.3	301.9	317.6	321.5	321.8	323.4	315.9
2004	313.7	313.1	314.5	311.8	316.0	317.5	304.1	301.9	316.3	320.7	320.7	321.7	314.3
2005	307.6	307.5	309.7	310.9	313.7	316.1	301.9	299.3	315.9	316.1	319.0	324.0	311.8
2006	314.1	313.7	315.1	314.4	318.9	321.3	305.0	302.5	321.5	322.6	325.2	331.8	317.2
2007	318.5	318.0	319.3	318.3	324.2	327.4	308.8	305.0	324.7	326.1	328.0	333.8	321.0
2008	320.7	320.4	322.5	323.4	325.4	327.4	309.3	307.9	324.1	322.7	324.0	328.3	321.3
2009	312.6	311.1	309.7	306.5	309.8	310.4	293.5	290.2	306.5	307.7	310.7	314.9	307.0
2010	301.6	299.6	300.0	301.0	302.6	304.7	288.1	287.1	304.1	306.1	308.8	314.6	301.5
2011	304.4	302.5	303.8	305.7	307.6	310.5	293.2	291.6	309.6	309.5	314.3	318.5	305.9
2012	306.8	306.6	308.3	303.5	310.9	313.8	289.4	293.1	311.0	310.9	313.1	321.1	307.4
2013	306.5	298.9	305.4	306.9	308.2	310.2	295.4	291.1	309.8	310.3	319.3	326.0	307.3
Information													
2002	321.0	324.3	319.8	316.7	322.9	320.5	310.2	312.6	307.4	308.1	312.1	310.3	315.5
2003	296.3	299.3	296.3	293.2	297.8	295.0	292.3	296.2	292.6	294.4	298.4	296.7	295.7
2004	286.4	286.2	288.1	286.7	287.6	287.5	286.6	288.4	288.4	288.3	290.8	290.4	288.0
2005	282.4	284.1	284.9	284.1	286.2	291.0	288.6	289.7	289.7	290.1	292.2	295.1	288.2
2006	287.0	287.7	289.2	286.9	289.1	292.2	290.9	291.9	291.0	288.0	290.0	291.8	289.6
2007	285.1	287.1	287.3	286.3	288.2	290.6	289.4	289.7	288.7	287.3	289.0	290.3	288.3
2008	285.1	287.2	287.4	285.7	287.2	289.9	286.7	287.1	286.5	284.6	284.8	285.5	286.5
2009	278.3	276.5	277.2	278.1	278.0	277.7	276.1	274.9	274.2	273.4	273.7	274.1	276.0
2010	266.8	267.0	268.0	267.9	269.0	271.0	270.8	271.1	271.1	272.9	272.5	276.6	270.4
2011	267.9	268.9	270.7	273.1	273.5	275.2	276.7	260.6	276.4	274.0	275.0	275.9	272.3
2012	272.3	273.8	275.1	275.5	277.3	279.3	276.5	276.1	274.6	276.3	277.1	277.6	276.0
2013	269.4	271.0	272.7	274.5	276.0	278.7	278.0	280.0	277.8	279.0	280.1	279.8	276.4
Financial Activities													
2002	774.9	774.0	773.1	768.8	768.9	776.2	777.5	775.7	767.5	766.8	766.9	770.1	771.7
2003	764.8	762.8	762.4	760.4	762.7	770.0	773.8	772.6	765.7	764.0	765.4	770.2	766.2
2004	759.5	760.4	762.3	763.0	764.4	773.3	780.5	779.5	771.2	774.8	776.0	781.6	770.5
2005	768.0	767.7	770.3	774.4	774.1	784.3	791.0	791.3	784.1	783.2	785.2	790.1	780.3
2006	776.4	778.3	781.3	783.6	786.7	797.6	801.7	802.4	794.4	793.8	795.8	800.7	791.1
2007	788.5	789.9	791.6	791.7	792.5	804.0	807.5	804.8	795.7	797.9	799.4	801.3	797.1
2008	790.6	791.0	791.3	788.0	787.4	794.5	795.7	794.5	780.3	775.7	771.8	771.3	786.0
2009	754.9	749.9	745.8	740.6	738.5	740.4	738.9	735.1	729.6	728.0	726.7	729.1	738.1
2010	718.4	719.4	721.6	722.3	723.5	733.1	735.6	736.4	730.9	730.4	732.5	737.2	728.4
2011	727.1	728.2	729.3	732.1	733.9	744.0	747.2	748.0	739.6	736.9	737.4	739.7	737.0
2012	731.0	733.2	734.2	732.8	733.5	742.4	743.8	742.8	734.0	735.5	735.2	740.6	736.6
2013	727.7	730.0	731.0	733.2	733.4	743.7	747.4	747.3	738.5	740.3	738.8	740.6	737.7

Employment by Industry: New York-Northern New Jersey-Long Island, NY–NJ–PA, Selected Years, 2002–2013—*Continued*

(Numbers in thousands, not seasonally adjusted)

Industry and year	January	February	March	April	May	June	July	August	September	October	November	December	Annual average
Professional and Business Services													
2002	1,213.1	1,217.8	1,228.8	1,240.3	1,242.4	1,250.6	1,242.3	1,244.4	1,239.3	1,245.3	1,248.7	1,249.6	1,238.6
2003	1,195.6	1,192.8	1,205.4	1,214.9	1,218.5	1,230.0	1,227.7	1,231.0	1,231.0	1,235.7	1,239.0	1,243.9	1,222.1
2004	1,194.8	1,199.0	1,215.9	1,229.8	1,235.4	1,247.2	1,243.3	1,244.5	1,240.5	1,243.2	1,248.6	1,255.9	1,233.2
2005	1,206.2	1,207.3	1,216.6	1,240.6	1,242.3	1,259.3	1,255.9	1,259.4	1,258.4	1,256.8	1,264.2	1,269.3	1,244.7
2006	1,219.1	1,227.4	1,244.8	1,256.9	1,266.0	1,286.8	1,284.6	1,289.8	1,284.4	1,289.4	1,299.0	1,307.0	1,271.3
2007	1,260.4	1,265.1	1,281.0	1,295.2	1,304.5	1,325.4	1,328.9	1,332.9	1,322.1	1,334.2	1,339.1	1,342.4	1,310.9
2008	1,298.8	1,304.0	1,313.5	1,327.4	1,329.0	1,343.1	1,343.1	1,340.1	1,328.4	1,322.5	1,317.4	1,311.1	1,323.2
2009	1,253.2	1,246.7	1,245.3	1,247.6	1,247.4	1,257.4	1,249.9	1,245.4	1,240.1	1,244.3	1,248.4	1,251.8	1,248.1
2010	1,211.6	1,217.4	1,229.2	1,251.4	1,255.7	1,273.3	1,271.2	1,273.1	1,267.5	1,278.3	1,283.4	1,286.2	1,258.2
2011	1,251.9	1,257.2	1,269.5	1,292.5	1,296.5	1,315.6	1,319.7	1,321.7	1,319.5	1,323.8	1,332.7	1,332.4	1,302.8
2012	1,289.9	1,298.2	1,313.8	1,329.2	1,339.7	1,358.5	1,354.4	1,363.8	1,361.6	1,370.7	1,378.4	1,386.2	1,345.4
2013	1,334.8	1,340.9	1,354.7	1,372.1	1,380.0	1,398.5	1,401.6	1,405.1	1,397.9	1,404.2	1,402.1	1,400.0	1,382.7
Education and Health Services													
2002	1,278.2	1,299.6	1,311.4	1,315.1	1,320.6	1,306.4	1,292.1	1,283.9	1,306.2	1,335.8	1,346.1	1,348.0	1,312.0
2003	1,320.9	1,333.9	1,345.8	1,345.5	1,347.0	1,333.3	1,316.8	1,304.9	1,330.9	1,358.1	1,366.3	1,367.5	1,339.2
2004	1,334.0	1,351.9	1,365.3	1,363.1	1,368.5	1,352.4	1,335.4	1,324.6	1,345.3	1,377.8	1,385.0	1,390.1	1,357.8
2005	1,353.1	1,373.0	1,382.8	1,389.0	1,388.5	1,371.5	1,353.6	1,344.7	1,375.2	1,402.5	1,412.1	1,417.1	1,380.3
2006	1,383.9	1,402.7	1,414.4	1,417.2	1,420.2	1,404.3	1,379.4	1,370.5	1,403.4	1,435.4	1,445.0	1,453.7	1,410.8
2007	1,418.1	1,437.4	1,448.0	1,444.9	1,446.6	1,430.8	1,405.7	1,395.5	1,428.1	1,463.8	1,469.7	1,477.6	1,438.9
2008	1,445.3	1,466.4	1,475.2	1,477.8	1,477.2	1,462.2	1,430.3	1,424.5	1,456.8	1,488.1	1,498.9	1,506.6	1,467.4
2009	1,473.5	1,494.9	1,501.5	1,503.1	1,504.0	1,489.7	1,457.4	1,451.0	1,482.8	1,519.3	1,529.8	1,538.5	1,495.5
2010	1,504.8	1,524.6	1,536.7	1,540.7	1,538.0	1,516.8	1,486.2	1,479.0	1,511.5	1,547.6	1,559.6	1,561.9	1,525.6
2011	1,528.0	1,551.1	1,561.7	1,567.0	1,565.7	1,538.0	1,509.9	1,502.0	1,542.8	1,569.9	1,579.8	1,587.7	1,550.3
2012	1,553.6	1,581.2	1,595.1	1,595.2	1,602.2	1,574.8	1,542.1	1,534.4	1,580.4	1,606.8	1,602.9	1,618.0	1,582.2
2013	1,585.7	1,612.6	1,625.6	1,636.6	1,635.0	1,605.0	1,578.3	1,568.8	1,608.8	1,644.1	1,662.9	1,662.8	1,618.9
Leisure and Hospitality													
2002	527.6	534.5	547.0	567.1	587.0	607.2	607.9	605.6	588.8	584.4	583.1	585.3	577.1
2003	549.5	551.3	559.4	576.8	597.8	617.6	624.6	617.2	605.2	596.6	594.1	594.5	590.4
2004	560.2	563.1	574.8	592.4	615.5	638.4	646.2	639.3	627.5	611.1	606.3	609.5	607.0
2005	570.6	573.8	586.1	606.3	626.2	649.7	651.1	647.2	634.9	614.1	614.5	614.2	615.7
2006	580.6	583.2	599.7	613.9	640.3	664.2	667.6	661.6	647.3	636.0	635.6	637.5	630.6
2007	600.6	605.5	616.9	637.2	662.3	686.8	689.1	684.5	665.7	660.2	657.4	658.5	652.1
2008	622.8	626.5	638.0	660.3	682.7	703.3	704.6	698.0	679.8	671.2	661.8	658.1	667.3
2009	618.4	619.7	628.1	644.0	675.6	694.2	696.2	690.7	682.9	669.2	661.6	661.7	661.9
2010	623.5	624.7	639.1	670.1	693.2	714.7	719.3	717.0	702.4	695.4	689.8	690.9	681.7
2011	652.6	657.4	670.6	700.5	722.4	747.7	753.4	748.4	732.9	726.9	722.4	721.5	713.1
2012	688.3	698.4	713.3	733.0	764.5	792.1	795.0	793.7	774.6	764.9	741.6	749.8	750.8
2013	715.2	721.4	738.7	765.1	794.5	826.3	827.2	820.1	801.6	785.6	779.8	765.9	778.5
Other Services													
2002	335.3	337.2	339.8	340.0	343.5	346.1	345.2	342.4	339.7	344.3	346.3	347.5	342.3
2003	338.5	339.6	342.1	343.2	346.0	348.8	348.9	347.0	346.8	349.2	350.5	352.3	346.1
2004	340.1	342.0	345.1	351.1	355.0	358.6	358.8	357.1	357.2	356.1	357.2	359.6	353.2
2005	356.3	358.8	361.3	365.0	367.5	371.3	365.0	363.3	363.1	361.3	363.5	366.1	363.5
2006	356.5	357.9	361.7	359.8	363.9	368.6	362.1	359.6	361.2	360.3	362.5	365.8	361.7
2007	360.1	362.4	365.2	366.2	370.8	375.0	366.3	363.3	363.0	366.4	368.1	369.4	366.4
2008	361.5	362.7	364.4	365.5	368.5	371.1	367.6	365.4	364.1	365.3	365.2	365.1	365.5
2009	353.9	354.9	355.6	355.8	359.4	362.0	358.5	356.5	354.3	356.6	357.9	358.8	357.0
2010	349.6	349.4	351.9	355.5	358.4	361.9	359.6	358.1	355.9	360.2	360.5	361.9	356.9
2011	355.0	356.6	358.6	363.5	366.6	370.7	368.5	365.5	365.3	367.1	367.5	369.2	364.5
2012	365.3	366.5	369.6	372.5	376.7	382.1	378.4	376.2	376.4	378.1	375.9	379.3	374.8
2013	371.2	372.7	374.3	379.4	381.9	387.0	384.3	383.0	380.6	383.0	384.1	382.3	380.3
Government													
2002	1,252.1	1,260.5	1,267.4	1,265.3	1,271.4	1,272.8	1,248.9	1,222.7	1,225.6	1,258.9	1,275.2	1,279.7	1,258.4
2003	1,263.2	1,276.6	1,280.3	1,280.8	1,280.5	1,281.9	1,257.0	1,229.9	1,233.5	1,274.5	1,287.4	1,290.2	1,269.7
2004	1,261.8	1,275.7	1,283.1	1,281.8	1,285.2	1,289.7	1,262.3	1,235.7	1,237.5	1,277.2	1,289.6	1,289.8	1,272.5
2005	1,272.3	1,283.0	1,285.9	1,292.9	1,294.2	1,301.7	1,273.7	1,247.5	1,253.2	1,281.3	1,295.2	1,300.1	1,281.8
2006	1,278.3	1,288.2	1,292.3	1,293.5	1,295.9	1,298.2	1,267.5	1,240.1	1,252.0	1,287.4	1,299.9	1,306.5	1,283.3
2007	1,286.6	1,299.0	1,303.7	1,301.7	1,307.1	1,310.7	1,276.6	1,252.3	1,263.6	1,297.9	1,309.6	1,316.4	1,293.8
2008	1,293.3	1,306.1	1,311.0	1,316.1	1,318.0	1,320.5	1,296.6	1,264.7	1,271.4	1,307.4	1,323.5	1,327.7	1,304.7
2009	1,300.1	1,311.0	1,316.1	1,321.5	1,324.2	1,319.6	1,322.5	1,294.2	1,262.6	1,303.7	1,315.0	1,316.3	1,308.9
2010	1,288.4	1,300.2	1,307.0	1,317.4	1,351.0	1,330.9	1,267.6	1,231.6	1,244.5	1,282.6	1,288.1	1,282.7	1,291.0
2011	1,254.0	1,269.8	1,273.3	1,279.9	1,274.7	1,272.1	1,251.6	1,229.0	1,228.0	1,264.9	1,271.7	1,265.6	1,261.2
2012	1,229.6	1,253.2	1,261.4	1,260.5	1,259.7	1,257.6	1,220.8	1,196.6	1,213.3	1,252.2	1,252.1	1,256.0	1,242.8
2013	1,224.7	1,249.1	1,252.2	1,257.2	1,256.2	1,251.1	1,219.2	1,191.0	1,205.7	1,243.6	1,249.6	1,248.7	1,237.4

Employment by Industry: North Port-Bradenton-Sarasota, FL, Selected Years, 2002–2013

(Numbers in thousands, not seasonally adjusted)

Industry and year	January	February	March	April	May	June	July	August	September	October	November	December	Annual average
Total Nonfarm													
2002	238.6	242.0	245.4	246.7	245.4	242.1	239.9	243.5	243.9	245.1	247.3	249.4	244.1
2003	244.9	246.6	248.3	246.5	247.5	247.4	241.7	246.3	247.1	249.4	253.7	257.6	248.1
2004	252.1	254.7	258.0	258.7	260.0	258.1	258.2	261.7	262.2	265.9	269.5	273.7	261.1
2005	268.3	271.7	273.8	273.1	274.1	271.0	269.5	273.0	273.8	274.8	278.1	281.5	273.6
2006	275.8	279.5	283.5	282.0	282.8	280.7	276.3	279.4	279.7	277.8	280.9	282.9	280.1
2007	276.9	278.9	281.1	277.1	276.4	272.5	266.6	270.0	268.6	267.6	270.9	273.6	273.4
2008	268.5	271.0	272.3	266.2	264.8	259.6	254.7	256.9	255.9	253.7	254.1	255.0	261.1
2009	248.3	247.8	248.3	245.5	243.9	239.3	234.7	236.4	235.4	237.8	240.3	241.8	241.6
2010	236.2	238.0	240.0	240.1	241.7	236.5	233.1	235.0	233.6	235.1	238.4	240.5	237.4
2011	236.5	239.6	241.2	243.1	241.1	236.9	235.1	238.4	238.3	239.5	243.9	246.1	240.0
2012	243.2	245.0	248.2	247.7	247.0	242.8	240.0	242.5	243.4	246.8	252.2	253.8	246.1
2013	250.6	254.4	256.1	256.7	257.0	252.7	250.6	253.4	253.8	256.3	259.8	261.2	255.2
Total Private													
2002	213.3	216.3	219.6	221.0	219.5	218.7	216.7	217.9	218.1	219.2	221.1	223.2	218.7
2003	218.7	220.2	221.8	220.1	220.8	223.3	217.8	219.8	220.5	222.7	226.6	230.3	221.9
2004	225.4	227.7	231.0	231.6	232.7	233.5	233.9	234.7	235.4	238.9	242.3	246.3	234.5
2005	241.4	244.6	246.7	245.8	246.7	246.5	245.1	246.0	246.6	247.0	250.1	253.6	246.7
2006	248.0	251.6	255.4	253.6	254.3	255.1	251.0	251.2	251.1	249.2	251.6	253.6	252.1
2007	248.1	249.8	251.9	247.9	247.3	246.4	240.7	241.2	239.7	238.8	241.8	244.5	244.8
2008	239.5	241.8	242.8	236.7	235.3	233.1	228.4	227.7	226.7	224.7	225.3	226.2	232.4
2009	219.7	219.1	219.4	216.2	215.0	213.5	209.1	208.8	207.6	209.8	212.1	213.7	213.7
2010	208.4	210.1	212.0	212.1	212.2	211.0	207.9	208.3	206.5	207.6	210.8	212.9	210.0
2011	209.1	212.0	213.5	215.4	213.9	212.6	211.1	211.3	211.3	212.3	216.5	218.8	213.2
2012	216.0	217.7	220.7	220.4	219.7	218.7	216.0	216.6	216.7	219.6	224.9	226.6	219.5
2013	223.5	227.1	228.7	229.4	229.9	228.6	226.6	227.5	227.2	229.4	232.7	234.2	228.7
Goods Producing													
2002	42.8	43.1	43.0	42.8	43.0	43.0	42.9	43.4	43.1	43.0	43.0	43.2	43.0
2003	42.4	42.9	42.7	42.1	42.3	42.5	42.4	42.5	42.4	42.9	42.8	43.1	42.6
2004	43.3	43.6	44.1	44.4	44.8	45.0	45.5	45.6	45.8	46.4	46.6	47.1	45.2
2005	46.4	47.1	47.4	47.3	48.0	48.2	48.7	49.0	49.6	49.7	50.1	50.6	48.5
2006	50.3	50.9	51.3	51.1	51.6	51.9	51.5	51.5	51.3	50.7	50.2	50.1	51.0
2007	48.6	48.2	48.1	46.7	46.5	46.1	45.0	44.8	43.9	43.0	42.6	42.3	45.5
2008	41.0	40.9	40.4	39.3	39.1	39.0	38.0	37.7	37.4	36.0	35.4	35.2	38.3
2009	32.8	31.9	31.6	30.9	30.8	30.5	29.8	29.6	29.3	29.1	28.9	28.9	30.3
2010	27.8	27.8	27.7	28.0	28.3	28.6	28.6	28.7	28.6	28.4	28.3	28.4	28.3
2011	27.5	27.7	27.9	28.3	28.6	29.0	29.1	29.2	29.4	29.3	29.5	29.6	28.8
2012	29.3	29.4	29.6	29.6	29.9	30.0	29.9	30.2	30.3	30.5	30.8	30.8	30.0
2013	30.4	30.7	30.8	30.8	31.2	31.5	31.6	31.9	32.0	32.2	32.1	32.2	31.5
Service-Providing													
2002	195.8	198.9	202.4	203.9	202.4	199.1	197.0	200.1	200.8	202.1	204.3	206.2	201.1
2003	202.5	203.7	205.6	204.4	205.2	204.9	199.3	203.8	204.7	206.5	210.9	214.5	205.5
2004	208.8	211.1	213.9	214.3	215.2	213.1	212.7	216.1	216.4	219.5	222.9	226.6	215.9
2005	221.9	224.6	226.4	225.8	226.1	222.8	220.8	224.0	224.2	225.1	228.0	230.9	225.1
2006	225.5	228.6	232.2	230.9	231.2	228.8	224.8	227.9	228.4	227.1	230.7	232.8	229.1
2007	228.3	230.7	233.0	230.4	229.9	226.4	221.6	225.2	224.7	224.6	228.3	231.3	227.9
2008	227.5	230.1	231.9	226.9	225.7	220.6	216.7	219.2	218.5	217.7	218.7	219.8	222.8
2009	215.5	215.9	216.7	214.6	213.1	208.8	204.9	206.8	206.1	208.7	211.4	212.9	211.3
2010	208.4	210.2	212.3	212.1	213.4	207.9	204.5	206.3	205.0	206.7	210.1	212.1	209.1
2011	209.0	211.9	213.3	214.8	212.5	207.9	206.0	209.2	208.9	210.2	214.4	216.5	211.2
2012	213.9	215.6	218.6	218.1	217.1	212.8	210.1	212.3	213.1	216.3	221.4	223.0	216.0
2013	220.2	223.7	225.3	225.9	225.8	221.2	219.0	221.5	221.8	224.1	227.7	229.0	223.8
Mining, Logging, and Construction													
2002	22.7	22.9	22.9	22.8	23.1	23.2	23.2	23.5	23.4	23.7	23.8	24.0	23.3
2003	23.5	24.0	24.0	23.7	23.9	24.0	23.9	24.0	24.0	24.4	24.4	24.6	24.0
2004	24.9	25.1	25.5	25.9	26.1	26.2	26.6	26.5	26.7	27.4	27.5	27.8	26.4
2005	27.5	28.1	28.4	28.4	28.9	29.0	29.4	29.6	30.1	30.2	30.6	31.0	29.3
2006	30.9	31.5	31.9	31.8	32.2	32.4	32.2	32.4	32.4	32.0	31.6	31.4	31.9
2007	30.2	30.0	29.9	28.7	28.5	28.1	27.0	26.9	26.1	25.3	24.9	24.6	27.5
2008	23.4	23.3	23.0	22.2	22.0	22.0	21.4	21.3	21.2	20.2	19.7	19.6	21.6
2009	18.0	17.6	17.4	17.0	17.0	16.8	16.5	16.4	16.1	16.0	15.8	15.7	16.7
2010	14.9	14.9	14.9	15.0	15.2	15.5	15.5	15.6	15.5	15.3	15.2	15.1	15.2
2011	14.5	14.6	14.8	14.9	14.9	15.1	15.1	15.1	15.4	15.3	15.4	15.4	15.0
2012	14.9	15.0	15.1	15.2	15.3	15.5	15.5	15.7	15.7	16.0	16.1	16.1	15.5
2013	15.8	16.0	16.1	16.2	16.4	16.7	16.9	17.2	17.2	17.4	17.2	17.2	16.7
Manufacturing													
2002	20.1	20.2	20.1	20.0	19.9	19.8	19.7	19.9	19.7	19.3	19.2	19.2	19.8
2003	18.9	18.9	18.7	18.4	18.4	18.5	18.5	18.5	18.4	18.5	18.4	18.5	18.6
2004	18.4	18.5	18.6	18.5	18.7	18.8	18.9	19.1	19.1	19.0	19.1	19.3	18.8
2005	18.9	19.0	19.0	18.9	19.1	19.2	19.3	19.4	19.5	19.5	19.5	19.6	19.2
2006	19.4	19.4	19.4	19.3	19.4	19.5	19.3	19.1	18.9	18.7	18.6	18.7	19.1
2007	18.4	18.2	18.2	18.0	18.0	18.0	18.0	17.9	17.8	17.7	17.7	17.7	18.0
2008	17.6	17.6	17.4	17.1	17.1	17.0	16.6	16.4	16.2	15.8	15.7	15.6	16.7
2009	14.8	14.3	14.2	13.9	13.8	13.7	13.3	13.2	13.2	13.1	13.1	13.2	13.7
2010	12.9	12.9	12.8	13.0	13.1	13.1	13.1	13.1	13.1	13.1	13.1	13.3	13.1
2011	13.0	13.1	13.1	13.4	13.7	13.9	14.0	14.1	14.0	14.0	14.1	14.2	13.7
2012	14.4	14.4	14.5	14.4	14.6	14.5	14.4	14.5	14.6	14.5	14.7	14.7	14.5
2013	14.6	14.7	14.7	14.6	14.8	14.8	14.7	14.7	14.8	14.8	14.9	15.0	14.8

Employment by Industry: North Port-Bradenton-Sarasota, FL, Selected Years, 2002–2013—*Continued*
(Numbers in thousands, not seasonally adjusted)

Industry and year	January	February	March	April	May	June	July	August	September	October	November	December	Annual average
Trade, Transportation, and Utilities													
2002	49.6	49.3	49.6	49.3	49.0	48.7	48.1	48.3	48.6	48.8	50.1	51.2	49.2
2003	49.3	48.9	49.3	49.2	49.0	48.6	47.9	48.3	48.5	49.1	50.4	52.0	49.2
2004	50.6	50.8	51.0	50.8	50.7	50.5	50.6	50.6	50.6	51.6	53.2	54.1	51.3
2005	52.1	52.5	52.8	52.9	52.8	52.4	51.9	51.8	51.8	51.9	53.0	53.8	52.5
2006	52.0	52.1	52.6	52.7	52.7	52.5	51.4	51.4	51.4	51.4	52.7	53.8	52.2
2007	53.0	52.6	52.9	52.1	52.1	51.7	51.1	50.8	50.5	50.8	52.0	53.4	51.9
2008	51.9	51.7	51.9	50.7	50.4	49.7	48.9	48.6	48.5	48.3	48.8	49.5	49.9
2009	47.5	47.3	46.9	46.2	45.9	45.4	44.6	44.4	44.4	44.7	45.9	46.6	45.8
2010	45.2	45.4	45.6	45.7	45.5	45.2	44.5	44.7	44.5	45.1	46.4	47.4	45.4
2011	46.3	46.2	46.4	46.8	46.4	46.0	45.8	46.0	46.2	46.6	48.4	49.1	46.7
2012	48.1	48.1	48.5	48.6	48.8	48.5	47.9	47.9	48.3	49.1	50.6	51.5	48.8
2013	49.8	50.2	50.1	50.2	50.3	50.3	50.1	50.1	50.1	51.1	52.7	53.9	50.7
Wholesale Trade													
2002	7.1	7.1	7.1	7.2	7.2	7.2	7.2	7.3	7.4	7.5	7.5	7.5	7.3
2003	7.2	7.2	7.4	7.4	7.4	7.3	7.2	7.3	7.4	7.3	7.4	7.5	7.3
2004	7.3	7.4	7.4	7.6	7.6	7.4	7.5	7.5	7.5	7.6	7.9	7.9	7.6
2005	7.8	8.0	8.0	8.2	8.3	8.2	8.1	8.2	8.3	8.3	8.4	8.6	8.2
2006	8.4	8.5	8.6	8.6	8.7	8.8	8.6	8.6	8.7	8.5	8.4	8.6	8.6
2007	8.7	8.7	8.7	8.8	8.9	8.9	8.8	8.8	8.7	8.7	8.7	8.8	8.8
2008	8.5	8.5	8.5	8.4	8.3	8.2	8.1	8.0	8.0	8.0	7.8	7.7	8.2
2009	7.4	7.4	7.3	7.3	7.2	7.3	7.2	7.2	7.2	7.2	7.1	7.2	7.3
2010	7.1	7.1	7.2	7.2	7.2	7.2	7.1	7.1	7.1	7.2	7.2	7.2	7.2
2011	7.3	7.3	7.4	7.3	7.2	7.2	7.2	7.3	7.3	7.2	7.3	7.3	7.3
2012	7.3	7.3	7.4	7.5	7.5	7.5	7.4	7.3	7.4	7.5	7.5	7.5	7.4
2013	7.4	7.5	7.6	7.6	7.6	7.7	7.6	7.6	7.7	7.7	7.7	7.7	7.6
Retail Trade													
2002	38.3	38.0	38.3	37.9	37.6	37.3	36.7	36.9	37.0	37.2	38.4	39.4	37.8
2003	37.9	37.6	37.8	37.6	37.4	37.1	36.4	36.7	36.8	37.5	38.6	39.8	37.6
2004	38.8	38.8	38.9	38.6	38.5	38.5	38.4	38.4	38.4	39.1	40.3	41.2	39.0
2005	39.6	39.8	40.0	39.9	39.7	39.4	39.0	38.8	38.7	38.8	39.5	40.0	39.4
2006	38.8	38.8	39.2	39.2	39.1	38.9	38.1	38.1	37.9	38.1	39.4	39.9	38.8
2007	39.4	39.2	39.4	38.6	38.6	38.2	37.8	37.6	37.4	37.7	38.8	39.8	38.5
2008	39.1	38.9	39.0	38.0	37.8	37.3	36.6	36.4	36.3	36.1	36.7	37.2	37.5
2009	35.9	35.7	35.5	34.7	34.5	34.0	33.4	33.2	33.2	33.5	34.7	35.1	34.5
2010	34.1	34.2	34.3	34.4	34.2	33.9	33.4	33.5	33.3	33.9	35.0	35.7	34.2
2011	34.7	34.7	34.8	35.2	35.0	34.6	34.4	34.5	34.7	35.2	36.8	37.3	35.2
2012	36.4	36.4	36.7	36.9	37.0	36.7	36.3	36.4	36.7	37.3	38.6	39.2	37.1
2013	37.9	38.1	37.9	38.1	38.1	38.1	37.9	37.9	37.8	38.8	40.3	41.3	38.5
Transportation and Utilities													
2002	4.2	4.2	4.2	4.2	4.2	4.2	4.2	4.1	4.2	4.1	4.2	4.3	4.2
2003	4.2	4.1	4.1	4.2	4.2	4.2	4.3	4.3	4.3	4.3	4.4	4.7	4.3
2004	4.5	4.6	4.7	4.6	4.6	4.6	4.7	4.7	4.7	4.9	5.0	5.0	4.7
2005	4.7	4.7	4.8	4.8	4.8	4.8	4.8	4.8	4.8	4.8	5.1	5.2	4.8
2006	4.8	4.8	4.8	4.9	4.9	4.8	4.7	4.7	4.8	4.8	4.9	5.3	4.9
2007	4.9	4.7	4.8	4.7	4.6	4.6	4.5	4.4	4.4	4.4	4.5	4.8	4.6
2008	4.3	4.3	4.4	4.3	4.3	4.2	4.2	4.2	4.2	4.2	4.3	4.6	4.3
2009	4.2	4.2	4.1	4.2	4.2	4.1	4.0	4.0	4.0	4.0	4.1	4.3	4.1
2010	4.0	4.1	4.1	4.1	4.1	4.1	4.0	4.1	4.1	4.0	4.2	4.5	4.1
2011	4.3	4.2	4.2	4.3	4.2	4.2	4.2	4.2	4.2	4.2	4.3	4.5	4.3
2012	4.4	4.4	4.4	4.2	4.3	4.3	4.2	4.2	4.2	4.3	4.5	4.8	4.4
2013	4.5	4.6	4.6	4.5	4.6	4.5	4.6	4.6	4.6	4.6	4.7	4.9	4.6
Information													
2002	4.3	4.3	4.3	4.3	4.3	4.3	4.3	4.2	4.2	4.3	4.3	4.3	4.3
2003	4.3	4.3	4.3	4.2	4.3	4.3	4.3	4.4	4.3	4.2	4.3	4.3	4.3
2004	4.2	4.2	4.2	4.1	4.3	4.3	4.2	4.1	4.1	4.1	4.2	4.2	4.2
2005	4.1	4.2	4.2	4.3	4.3	4.4	4.4	4.4	4.3	4.3	4.4	4.4	4.3
2006	4.2	4.3	4.3	4.3	4.3	4.3	4.4	4.5	4.4	4.6	4.6	4.6	4.4
2007	4.4	4.3	4.3	4.3	4.2	4.2	4.1	4.1	4.1	4.1	4.1	4.0	4.2
2008	4.0	4.0	4.0	3.9	3.9	3.9	3.8	3.8	3.8	3.7	3.6	3.6	3.8
2009	3.6	3.6	3.5	3.5	3.4	3.5	3.4	3.4	3.4	3.4	3.4	3.4	3.5
2010	3.4	3.4	3.3	3.3	3.4	3.4	3.4	3.4	3.4	3.4	3.5	3.5	3.4
2011	3.4	3.5	3.5	3.5	3.4	3.4	3.4	3.4	3.4	3.4	3.4	3.4	3.4
2012	3.5	3.4	3.4	3.4	3.4	3.3	3.3	3.3	3.3	3.3	3.3	3.4	3.4
2013	3.3	3.3	3.4	3.4	3.4	3.4	3.4	3.4	3.3	3.3	3.3	3.3	3.4
Financial Activities													
2002	13.7	13.7	13.7	13.6	13.5	13.7	13.7	13.8	13.7	13.7	13.8	14.0	13.7
2003	13.7	13.6	13.6	13.8	13.8	13.8	14.1	14.1	14.0	14.1	14.1	14.3	13.9
2004	14.1	14.3	14.4	14.5	14.5	14.7	15.0	15.0	15.1	15.4	15.7	15.8	14.9
2005	15.4	15.5	15.4	15.6	15.6	15.7	15.7	15.9	15.9	16.2	16.3	16.5	15.8
2006	16.1	16.2	16.3	16.2	16.2	16.3	16.2	16.1	16.1	16.3	16.3	16.5	16.2
2007	16.0	16.0	16.1	16.4	16.4	16.3	16.2	16.2	16.3	16.5	16.4	16.5	16.3
2008	16.3	16.3	16.2	15.8	15.7	15.7	15.4	15.3	15.2	15.1	15.0	15.0	15.6
2009	14.5	14.4	14.3	14.2	14.2	14.2	14.0	13.9	13.9	13.9	13.9	13.8	14.1
2010	13.6	13.6	13.6	13.7	13.6	13.6	13.7	13.7	13.6	13.7	13.8	13.9	13.7
2011	13.8	13.9	14.0	13.9	14.0	14.0	14.1	14.1	14.0	14.1	14.2	14.3	14.0
2012	14.1	14.1	14.2	14.4	14.4	14.4	14.4	14.4	14.3	14.4	14.4	14.5	14.3
2013	14.3	14.3	14.3	14.6	14.5	14.5	14.5	14.6	14.6	14.6	14.7	14.7	14.5

Employment by Industry: North Port-Bradenton-Sarasota, FL, Selected Years, 2002–2013—*Continued*

(Numbers in thousands, not seasonally adjusted)

Industry and year	January	February	March	April	May	June	July	August	September	October	November	December	Annual average
Professional and Business Services													
2002	22.2	24.5	26.6	29.4	28.5	27.6	27.3	27.1	27.2	27.1	25.7	24.9	26.5
2003	25.2	25.4	25.6	25.9	26.7	30.2	27.1	28.3	29.0	29.6	30.6	31.3	27.9
2004	28.0	29.3	30.1	30.9	31.8	33.1	33.4	34.1	34.7	35.4	35.3	36.7	32.7
2005	35.7	36.8	37.3	37.1	37.8	38.3	38.5	38.7	38.7	38.3	38.4	39.6	37.9
2006	37.5	38.8	40.3	39.0	39.4	40.3	39.3	39.1	39.4	37.5	37.4	37.0	38.8
2007	35.3	36.1	36.7	35.4	35.9	36.5	34.6	35.3	35.1	33.8	34.6	35.2	35.4
2008	33.2	34.4	35.0	33.5	33.8	33.9	33.5	33.7	33.7	32.9	32.9	32.5	33.6
2009	30.8	30.9	31.3	30.4	30.6	31.2	30.2	30.3	30.3	30.6	30.6	30.8	30.7
2010	29.0	29.2	29.6	29.6	31.0	31.1	29.9	30.1	29.2	29.0	29.7	30.1	29.8
2011	28.5	29.8	29.9	31.0	30.9	31.0	30.6	30.6	30.3	30.3	31.0	31.4	30.4
2012	30.4	30.7	31.4	31.3	31.1	31.4	31.0	31.0	31.0	32.1	33.6	33.7	31.6
2013	33.1	33.9	34.5	35.1	35.8	35.7	34.8	35.1	35.2	35.3	36.0	35.5	35.0
Education and Health Services													
2002	35.4	35.5	35.8	35.8	36.0	36.1	36.0	36.5	36.9	37.3	37.8	38.1	36.4
2003	37.4	37.8	38.1	37.8	38.1	38.0	37.4	37.7	38.1	38.3	38.6	38.6	38.0
2004	38.2	38.5	38.7	38.8	39.1	39.0	38.6	38.9	39.2	39.6	39.9	40.1	39.1
2005	39.1	39.4	39.6	39.3	39.5	39.4	39.1	39.3	39.5	39.6	39.9	40.3	39.5
2006	39.5	40.0	40.3	40.2	40.4	40.4	40.0	40.3	40.5	40.3	40.7	41.1	40.3
2007	40.8	41.6	41.5	41.3	41.3	41.3	41.0	41.3	41.6	41.7	42.0	42.2	41.5
2008	42.5	43.0	43.2	42.7	42.7	42.4	41.9	42.1	42.4	42.7	43.1	43.3	42.7
2009	43.3	43.3	43.4	43.2	43.1	42.8	42.3	42.7	42.4	43.3	43.6	43.9	43.1
2010	43.3	43.7	44.0	44.1	43.8	43.5	43.3	43.5	43.5	43.8	44.0	44.2	43.7
2011	44.1	44.5	44.7	44.8	44.7	44.3	44.1	44.3	44.4	44.7	44.9	45.3	44.6
2012	44.7	45.1	45.4	45.2	45.2	44.8	44.3	44.7	45.1	45.4	45.9	45.9	45.1
2013	45.6	46.1	46.1	46.3	46.3	45.6	45.4	45.9	46.0	46.3	46.3	46.5	46.0
Leisure and Hospitality													
2002	31.9	32.4	33.2	32.3	31.7	31.8	31.2	31.4	31.1	31.6	32.9	33.9	32.1
2003	32.9	33.6	34.5	33.8	33.3	32.7	31.6	31.6	31.2	31.5	32.8	33.6	32.8
2004	33.7	34.1	35.0	35.0	34.3	33.6	33.3	33.1	32.7	33.4	34.3	35.1	34.0
2005	35.2	35.7	36.5	36.1	35.5	34.9	33.8	33.9	33.6	33.9	34.9	35.2	34.9
2006	35.0	35.7	36.5	36.4	35.9	35.5	34.7	34.6	34.1	34.5	35.5	36.3	35.4
2007	36.1	37.1	38.2	37.8	37.1	36.2	35.0	34.9	34.3	34.7	35.6	36.2	36.1
2008	36.0	36.7	37.2	36.5	35.5	34.6	33.4	33.2	32.6	33.1	33.9	34.6	34.8
2009	34.9	35.4	36.1	35.6	34.8	33.7	32.9	32.6	32.0	32.9	33.8	34.3	34.1
2010	34.3	35.1	36.1	35.7	34.8	34.0	33.0	32.8	32.4	32.9	33.8	34.0	34.1
2011	34.4	35.2	35.9	35.8	34.7	33.8	33.1	32.9	32.7	33.2	34.4	35.0	34.3
2012	35.4	36.3	37.5	37.1	36.2	35.6	34.7	34.6	33.8	34.3	35.6	36.0	35.6
2013	36.3	37.8	38.6	38.1	37.5	36.8	36.1	35.9	35.3	35.9	36.9	37.4	36.9
Other Services													
2002	13.4	13.5	13.4	13.5	13.5	13.5	13.2	13.2	13.3	13.4	13.5	13.6	13.4
2003	13.5	13.7	13.7	13.3	13.3	13.3	13.2	13.0	12.9	13.0	13.0	13.1	13.2
2004	13.3	12.9	13.5	13.5	13.1	13.2	13.3	13.3	13.3	13.2	13.0	13.1	13.2
2005	13.4	13.4	13.5	13.2	13.2	13.2	13.0	13.0	13.2	13.1	13.1	13.2	13.2
2006	13.4	13.6	13.8	13.7	13.8	13.9	13.5	13.7	13.9	13.9	14.2	14.2	13.8
2007	13.9	13.9	14.1	13.9	13.8	14.1	13.7	13.8	13.9	14.2	14.5	14.7	14.0
2008	14.6	14.8	14.9	14.3	14.2	13.9	13.5	13.3	13.1	12.9	12.6	12.5	13.7
2009	12.3	12.3	12.3	12.2	12.2	12.2	11.9	11.9	11.9	11.9	12.0	12.0	12.1
2010	11.8	11.9	12.1	12.0	11.8	11.6	11.5	11.4	11.3	11.3	11.3	11.4	11.6
2011	11.1	11.2	11.2	11.3	11.2	11.1	10.9	10.8	10.9	10.7	10.7	10.7	11.0
2012	10.5	10.6	10.7	10.8	10.7	10.7	10.5	10.5	10.6	10.5	10.6	10.8	10.6
2013	10.7	10.8	10.9	10.9	10.9	10.8	10.6	10.6	10.7	10.6	10.7	10.7	10.7
Government													
2002	25.3	25.7	25.8	25.7	25.9	23.4	23.2	25.6	25.8	25.9	26.2	26.2	25.4
2003	26.2	26.4	26.5	26.4	26.7	24.1	23.9	26.5	26.6	26.7	27.1	27.3	26.2
2004	26.7	27.0	27.0	27.1	27.3	24.6	24.3	27.0	26.8	27.0	27.2	27.4	26.6
2005	26.9	27.1	27.1	27.3	27.4	24.5	24.4	27.0	27.2	27.8	28.0	27.9	26.9
2006	27.8	27.9	28.1	28.4	28.5	25.6	25.3	28.2	28.6	28.6	29.3	29.3	28.0
2007	28.8	29.1	29.2	29.2	29.1	26.1	25.9	28.8	28.9	28.8	29.1	29.1	28.5
2008	29.0	29.2	29.5	29.5	29.5	26.5	26.3	29.2	29.2	29.0	28.8	28.8	28.7
2009	28.6	28.7	28.9	29.3	28.9	25.8	25.6	27.6	27.8	28.0	28.2	28.1	28.0
2010	27.8	27.9	28.0	28.0	29.5	25.5	25.2	26.7	27.1	27.5	27.6	27.6	27.4
2011	27.4	27.6	27.7	27.7	27.2	24.3	24.0	27.1	27.0	27.2	27.4	27.3	26.8
2012	27.2	27.3	27.5	27.3	27.3	24.1	24.0	25.9	26.7	27.2	27.3	27.2	26.6
2013	27.1	27.3	27.4	27.3	27.1	24.1	24.0	25.9	26.6	26.9	27.1	27.0	26.5

Employment by Industry: Oklahoma City, OK, Selected Years, 2002–2013

(Numbers in thousands, not seasonally adjusted)

Industry and year	January	February	March	April	May	June	July	August	September	October	November	December	Annual average
Total Nonfarm													
2002	535.9	541.5	546.3	548.4	552.4	549.7	539.4	544.4	551.2	549.5	551.6	551.4	546.8
2003	531.6	534.5	535.8	538.0	540.8	534.7	529.4	533.6	541.2	543.4	544.2	545.7	537.7
2004	533.0	537.2	542.7	547.1	549.0	545.3	540.8	545.3	553.8	554.7	556.1	559.1	547.0
2005	541.1	547.8	553.6	559.8	561.3	558.7	553.8	558.0	566.3	566.1	570.7	572.9	559.2
2006	557.8	563.1	568.5	569.4	572.0	571.0	561.1	566.1	573.7	572.6	574.2	576.9	568.9
2007	563.2	568.8	576.1	575.7	578.3	578.3	568.2	574.4	581.1	583.5	588.5	586.8	576.9
2008	573.5	579.7	583.6	585.6	588.3	583.8	576.0	580.9	589.2	589.7	591.6	590.3	584.4
2009	575.5	573.7	575.3	572.2	570.8	566.8	559.3	560.0	565.3	565.2	566.9	566.6	568.1
2010	552.5	555.3	561.8	566.0	569.5	566.6	560.5	564.5	571.3	575.7	578.6	580.6	566.9
2011	564.7	567.7	575.5	582.0	582.2	579.1	574.2	577.8	586.6	587.5	590.8	593.6	580.1
2012	579.5	586.1	591.9	595.4	597.2	595.2	584.3	589.9	596.6	602.5	605.6	606.2	594.2
2013	592.6	599.5	603.9	605.6	609.3	605.8	599.3	604.5	609.6	614.9	621.4	619.8	607.2
Total Private													
2002	423.8	427.4	431.4	433.7	437.5	438.6	437.2	439.4	437.8	434.0	435.8	435.7	434.4
2003	420.9	420.9	422.9	425.3	428.2	425.6	427.8	430.3	429.7	430.4	430.8	432.1	427.1
2004	423.3	424.0	429.1	433.6	435.3	435.0	437.8	438.1	438.6	439.4	440.4	442.8	434.8
2005	428.3	432.7	438.1	443.7	444.8	446.4	448.4	450.4	451.1	449.0	452.9	455.3	445.1
2006	443.4	445.8	450.9	451.7	454.0	457.2	454.7	456.9	457.9	453.5	454.8	457.8	453.2
2007	446.5	449.9	456.5	456.3	458.6	462.1	459.3	462.8	462.9	462.5	466.9	466.1	459.2
2008	457.7	459.9	463.0	465.1	467.2	468.7	467.3	468.0	469.1	467.7	468.6	468.0	465.9
2009	454.9	452.9	453.2	449.8	448.1	448.9	446.3	445.2	444.1	441.0	442.0	441.9	447.4
2010	432.6	432.5	437.8	441.6	443.3	445.7	445.4	447.9	449.0	452.0	454.5	456.1	444.4
2011	445.6	444.9	451.9	458.1	458.2	459.9	459.8	462.6	463.5	462.8	465.6	467.9	458.4
2012	459.4	462.6	467.4	470.4	472.3	475.3	470.8	473.8	473.5	476.2	478.7	480.1	471.7
2013	471.1	473.5	477.3	478.7	481.6	483.3	482.2	485.1	485.2	485.8	491.6	490.2	482.1
Goods Producing													
2002	70.6	71.7	71.9	70.9	72.2	72.4	72.4	72.2	71.5	70.4	70.1	69.9	71.4
2003	68.8	68.6	68.8	69.1	69.4	67.3	70.5	70.7	70.2	70.2	69.7	70.0	69.4
2004	69.3	69.0	69.7	70.8	71.6	70.3	73.1	73.3	73.1	72.9	72.2	73.2	71.5
2005	70.5	72.0	73.2	73.5	73.7	73.1	75.4	75.6	75.5	76.0	76.3	77.3	74.3
2006	76.3	76.7	77.5	77.1	77.5	78.4	77.5	77.9	77.7	77.7	77.3	77.9	77.5
2007	75.4	75.5	76.9	77.1	77.4	78.8	78.6	79.4	79.0	79.2	79.8	79.3	78.0
2008	78.5	79.0	79.6	80.3	81.0	82.1	82.0	82.1	81.6	81.4	80.7	79.7	80.7
2009	77.6	75.9	74.6	72.6	71.8	72.0	71.3	70.6	69.6	68.8	68.7	68.6	71.8
2010	67.6	67.1	68.1	69.1	69.7	70.6	70.9	71.4	71.6	73.1	72.8	73.6	70.5
2011	72.3	72.2	73.4	74.9	75.2	76.3	76.9	77.0	77.1	77.3	77.6	78.6	75.7
2012	77.9	78.5	79.5	80.4	81.0	82.5	81.9	82.3	81.9	82.5	82.5	82.6	81.1
2013	82.1	82.3	82.7	82.9	83.5	84.2	83.7	83.7	83.2	84.5	85.1	83.8	83.5
Service-Providing													
2002	465.3	469.8	474.4	477.5	480.2	477.3	467.0	472.2	479.7	479.1	481.5	481.5	475.5
2003	462.8	465.9	467.0	468.9	471.4	467.4	458.9	462.9	471.0	473.2	474.5	475.7	468.3
2004	463.7	468.2	473.0	476.3	477.4	475.0	467.7	472.0	480.7	481.8	483.9	485.9	475.5
2005	470.6	475.8	480.4	486.3	487.6	485.6	478.4	482.4	490.8	490.1	494.4	495.6	484.8
2006	481.5	486.4	491.0	492.3	494.5	492.6	483.6	488.2	496.0	494.9	496.9	499.0	491.4
2007	487.8	493.3	499.2	498.6	500.9	499.5	489.6	495.0	502.1	504.3	508.7	507.5	498.9
2008	495.0	500.7	504.0	505.3	507.3	501.7	494.0	498.8	507.6	508.3	510.9	510.6	503.7
2009	497.9	497.8	500.7	499.6	499.0	494.8	488.0	489.4	495.7	496.4	498.2	498.0	496.3
2010	484.9	488.2	493.7	496.9	499.8	496.0	489.6	493.1	499.7	502.6	505.8	507.0	496.4
2011	492.4	495.5	502.1	507.1	507.0	502.8	497.3	500.8	509.5	510.2	513.2	515.0	504.4
2012	501.6	507.6	512.4	515.0	516.2	512.7	502.4	507.6	514.7	520.0	523.1	523.6	513.1
2013	510.5	517.2	521.2	522.7	525.8	521.6	515.6	520.8	526.4	530.4	536.3	536.0	523.7
Mining and Logging													
2002	7.4	7.5	7.5	7.3	7.5	7.5	7.6	7.6	7.5	7.4	7.4	7.4	7.5
2003	7.5	7.5	7.5	7.7	7.7	7.8	8.1	8.2	8.2	8.3	8.3	8.4	7.9
2004	8.5	8.5	8.6	8.8	8.9	9.1	9.2	9.2	9.3	9.4	9.5	9.6	9.1
2005	9.7	9.8	10.0	10.1	10.2	10.3	10.6	10.7	10.9	11.0	11.3	11.7	10.5
2006	11.7	12.0	12.2	12.4	12.6	12.8	12.7	13.0	13.1	13.3	13.5	13.8	12.8
2007	13.7	13.7	13.7	13.9	14.0	14.2	14.6	14.9	14.9	15.1	15.3	15.3	14.4
2008	14.9	15.1	15.2	15.6	15.9	16.3	16.4	16.6	16.5	16.8	16.7	16.3	16.0
2009	15.9	15.2	14.5	13.6	13.3	13.2	12.9	12.8	12.6	12.6	12.8	13.1	13.5
2010	13.1	13.2	13.5	13.7	13.9	14.2	14.4	14.6	14.7	15.3	15.1	15.5	14.3
2011	15.6	15.9	16.0	16.4	16.7	17.0	17.3	17.4	17.6	17.8	17.9	18.2	17.0
2012	18.3	18.6	19.0	19.4	19.7	20.3	20.2	20.2	19.9	19.9	19.8	19.7	19.6
2013	20.4	20.2	20.1	20.4	20.5	20.6	19.9	19.9	19.8	19.8	19.9	20.1	20.1
Construction													
2002	21.6	21.4	21.7	21.6	22.1	22.5	22.7	22.6	22.2	22.0	21.8	21.8	22.0
2003	21.5	21.4	21.6	22.0	22.8	23.6	23.6	23.7	23.3	23.2	22.8	22.9	22.7
2004	22.3	22.1	22.7	23.1	23.4	24.0	24.5	24.5	24.3	23.9	23.4	23.9	23.5
2005	23.1	23.2	24.1	24.6	24.9	25.7	26.0	26.1	26.0	26.1	26.2	26.4	25.2
2006	25.8	25.9	26.6	26.2	26.5	27.2	26.7	26.9	26.7	26.3	26.1	26.2	26.4
2007	25.3	25.2	26.2	26.3	26.3	27.3	26.9	27.2	27.0	26.9	27.2	26.8	26.6
2008	26.6	26.9	27.4	27.5	27.9	28.4	28.5	28.3	28.1	27.7	27.4	27.1	27.7
2009	26.1	25.8	26.1	25.7	25.8	26.5	26.4	26.3	25.9	25.1	25.0	24.7	25.8
2010	23.9	23.4	24.1	24.7	25.0	25.5	25.7	25.8	25.7	26.3	26.0	26.2	25.2
2011	25.3	24.7	25.5	26.0	25.9	26.5	26.5	26.2	26.0	25.8	25.8	26.1	25.9
2012	25.4	25.5	25.9	26.3	26.5	27.1	26.7	26.9	26.7	26.9	26.8	26.9	26.5
2013	25.9	26.2	26.6	26.5	26.8	27.3	27.4	27.4	27.3	28.2	28.6	27.6	27.2

Employment by Industry: Oklahoma City, OK, Selected Years, 2002–2013—*Continued*

(Numbers in thousands, not seasonally adjusted)

Industry and year	January	February	March	April	May	June	July	August	September	October	November	December	Annual average
Manufacturing													
2002	41.6	42.8	42.7	42.0	42.6	42.4	42.1	42.0	41.8	41.0	40.9	40.7	41.9
2003	39.8	39.7	39.7	39.4	38.9	35.9	38.8	38.8	38.7	38.7	38.6	38.7	38.8
2004	38.5	38.4	38.4	38.9	39.3	37.2	39.4	39.6	39.5	39.6	39.3	39.7	39.0
2005	37.7	39.0	39.1	38.8	38.6	37.1	38.8	38.8	38.6	38.9	38.8	39.2	38.6
2006	38.8	38.8	38.7	38.5	38.4	38.4	38.1	38.0	37.9	38.1	37.7	37.9	38.3
2007	36.4	36.6	37.0	36.9	37.1	37.3	37.1	37.3	37.1	37.2	37.3	37.2	37.0
2008	37.0	37.0	37.0	37.2	37.2	37.4	37.1	37.2	37.0	36.9	36.6	36.3	37.0
2009	35.6	34.9	34.0	33.3	32.7	32.3	32.0	31.5	31.1	31.1	30.9	30.8	32.5
2010	30.6	30.5	30.5	30.7	30.8	30.9	30.8	31.0	31.2	31.5	31.7	31.9	31.0
2011	31.4	31.6	31.9	32.5	32.6	32.8	33.1	33.4	33.5	33.7	33.9	34.3	32.9
2012	34.2	34.4	34.6	34.7	34.8	35.1	35.0	35.2	35.3	35.7	35.9	36.0	35.1
2013	35.8	35.9	36.0	36.0	36.2	36.3	36.4	36.4	36.1	36.5	36.6	36.1	36.2
Trade, Transportation, and Utilities													
2002	99.0	98.3	99.3	98.7	98.9	98.9	98.7	99.1	98.8	98.0	100.3	101.2	99.1
2003	96.6	95.5	95.9	96.0	96.4	96.4	95.8	96.5	96.5	97.5	99.5	101.0	97.0
2004	96.3	95.7	96.3	96.1	96.3	96.5	96.0	95.8	95.7	96.8	99.3	100.9	96.8
2005	96.4	96.4	97.1	97.8	98.0	98.0	98.6	99.3	99.5	100.0	102.6	104.2	99.0
2006	99.1	99.0	99.5	99.3	99.7	100.1	99.4	100.1	100.4	100.4	102.5	104.0	100.3
2007	100.3	100.3	102.0	100.9	101.3	101.2	100.4	100.7	100.3	100.7	102.9	103.3	101.2
2008	100.4	99.8	100.5	99.8	99.9	100.1	100.5	100.4	100.8	100.9	102.5	102.9	100.7
2009	98.9	97.9	98.2	97.5	97.4	97.6	96.8	96.7	96.3	96.5	97.9	98.4	97.5
2010	94.8	94.4	95.5	95.9	96.4	97.2	97.4	97.6	97.1	98.3	100.3	101.5	97.2
2011	97.9	97.4	98.8	99.2	99.1	99.5	99.5	100.6	100.4	100.7	102.8	103.8	100.0
2012	100.4	100.2	101.0	101.5	102.2	102.6	102.4	102.7	103.0	104.3	106.7	107.8	102.9
2013	103.7	104.0	105.0	105.3	106.1	106.5	106.6	107.4	107.6	107.8	109.4	110.5	106.7
Wholesale Trade													
2002	21.4	21.3	21.4	21.2	21.4	21.5	21.7	21.6	21.6	21.3	21.3	21.3	21.4
2003	21.2	21.1	21.2	21.0	21.0	21.0	20.9	20.9	21.0	21.0	20.9	21.1	21.0
2004	20.8	20.7	20.6	20.6	20.8	21.2	21.2	21.1	21.0	21.2	21.3	21.4	21.0
2005	21.1	21.2	21.3	21.4	21.4	21.6	22.0	22.0	21.9	22.0	22.2	22.4	21.7
2006	22.2	22.4	22.5	22.4	22.6	22.8	22.8	22.9	23.0	23.0	23.0	23.2	22.7
2007	22.8	22.9	23.0	23.0	23.0	23.1	22.9	22.7	22.6	23.0	22.9	23.1	22.9
2008	22.9	22.8	22.9	22.9	22.9	23.1	23.1	22.9	23.0	23.0	22.9	22.9	23.0
2009	22.5	22.4	22.3	22.0	21.8	21.8	21.8	21.7	21.6	21.8	21.6	21.6	21.9
2010	21.5	21.5	21.5	21.7	21.8	22.0	22.2	22.3	22.4	22.7	22.8	22.9	22.1
2011	22.8	22.8	23.1	23.3	23.2	23.5	23.5	23.6	23.7	23.9	23.9	24.0	23.4
2012	24.2	24.4	24.5	24.4	24.7	24.9	25.0	25.2	25.1	25.4	25.6	25.8	24.9
2013	25.9	26.1	26.3	26.2	26.4	26.7	26.6	26.8	26.9	27.0	27.1	27.2	26.6
Retail Trade													
2002	61.4	60.8	61.7	61.2	61.2	61.1	60.5	61.0	60.9	60.6	63.1	64.3	61.5
2003	60.0	59.0	59.2	59.7	60.1	60.2	59.6	60.3	60.3	61.1	63.3	64.7	60.6
2004	60.2	59.8	60.3	60.2	60.2	60.0	59.5	59.4	59.2	59.9	62.3	63.6	60.4
2005	60.0	59.8	60.3	60.7	60.8	60.7	60.6	61.2	61.4	61.9	64.2	65.4	61.4
2006	61.1	60.8	61.1	61.1	61.2	61.4	60.8	61.3	61.3	61.1	63.1	64.2	61.5
2007	61.1	60.9	62.2	61.3	61.7	61.6	61.2	61.7	61.5	61.9	64.3	64.4	62.0
2008	62.5	62.0	62.4	61.5	61.5	61.4	61.4	61.8	61.9	62.2	63.8	64.1	62.3
2009	60.8	60.0	60.2	59.9	60.1	60.2	59.6	59.7	59.6	59.4	61.0	61.4	60.2
2010	58.6	58.2	59.1	59.2	59.7	60.1	60.1	60.2	59.6	60.6	62.3	63.0	60.1
2011	60.1	59.6	60.5	60.8	60.6	60.5	60.7	61.6	61.3	61.3	63.3	63.9	61.2
2012	60.9	60.5	61.2	61.7	61.9	62.0	61.6	61.8	62.2	63.0	65.2	65.9	62.3
2013	62.0	61.7	62.4	63.0	63.5	63.4	63.7	64.3	64.4	64.5	65.9	66.7	63.8
Transportation and Utilities													
2002	16.2	16.2	16.2	16.3	16.3	16.3	16.5	16.5	16.3	16.1	15.9	15.6	16.2
2003	15.4	15.4	15.5	15.3	15.3	15.3	15.2	15.3	15.3	15.2	15.4	15.3	15.3
2004	15.3	15.2	15.4	15.3	15.3	15.3	15.3	15.3	15.3	15.5	15.7	15.9	15.4
2005	15.3	15.4	15.5	15.7	15.8	15.7	16.0	16.1	16.2	16.1	16.2	16.4	15.9
2006	15.8	15.8	15.9	15.8	15.9	15.9	15.9	15.8	15.9	16.1	16.3	16.4	16.0
2007	16.4	16.5	16.8	16.6	16.6	16.6	16.5	16.3	16.3	16.2	15.8	15.7	16.3
2008	15.0	15.0	15.2	15.4	15.5	15.6	15.6	15.6	15.6	15.6	15.7	15.9	15.5
2009	15.6	15.5	15.7	15.6	15.5	15.6	15.4	15.3	15.1	15.3	15.3	15.4	15.4
2010	14.7	14.7	14.9	15.0	14.9	15.1	15.1	15.1	15.1	15.0	15.2	15.6	15.0
2011	15.0	15.0	15.2	15.1	15.3	15.5	15.3	15.4	15.4	15.5	15.6	15.9	15.4
2012	15.3	15.3	15.3	15.4	15.6	15.7	15.7	15.8	15.7	15.7	15.9	16.1	15.6
2013	15.8	16.2	16.3	16.1	16.2	16.4	16.3	16.3	16.3	16.3	16.4	16.6	16.3
Information													
2002	14.3	14.4	14.2	14.1	14.2	14.1	14.0	14.0	13.8	13.7	13.9	13.8	14.0
2003	13.6	13.5	13.5	13.4	13.5	13.4	13.4	13.4	13.4	13.3	13.4	13.5	13.5
2004	13.5	13.4	13.3	13.5	13.7	13.5	13.8	14.0	13.8	13.5	13.8	13.7	13.6
2005	13.6	13.7	13.6	13.7	13.7	13.5	13.6	13.3	13.0	12.9	13.0	13.0	13.4
2006	12.4	12.5	12.6	13.5	13.4	13.3	13.5	13.5	13.4	13.2	13.2	13.6	13.2
2007	13.0	12.6	12.3	12.3	12.2	12.3	12.2	12.2	12.2	12.1	12.2	12.2	12.3
2008	12.2	12.3	12.1	12.3	12.3	12.3	12.4	12.2	12.0	11.9	12.0	11.9	12.2
2009	11.8	11.6	11.6	11.5	11.4	11.3	11.1	10.9	10.6	10.4	10.3	10.2	11.1
2010	10.2	10.1	9.9	9.8	9.7	9.6	9.5	9.3	9.2	9.1	9.2	9.1	9.6
2011	9.2	9.1	8.9	9.0	9.0	9.0	9.0	8.9	8.9	9.0	9.0	9.0	9.0
2012	8.9	8.9	8.8	8.7	8.7	8.6	8.7	8.5	8.3	8.4	8.4	8.3	8.6
2013	8.1	8.1	8.0	8.1	8.1	8.2	8.2	8.2	8.1	8.1	8.1	8.1	8.1

Employment by Industry: Oklahoma City, OK, Selected Years, 2002–2013—*Continued*

(Numbers in thousands, not seasonally adjusted)

Industry and year	January	February	March	April	May	June	July	August	September	October	November	December	Annual average
Financial Activities													
2002	34.8	34.8	34.9	34.9	35.1	35.6	35.6	35.8	35.6	35.5	35.6	35.8	35.3
2003	34.3	34.4	34.5	34.7	34.8	35.0	35.0	35.3	35.2	35.2	35.0	35.1	34.9
2004	34.8	34.9	35.1	35.8	35.7	35.9	35.6	35.5	35.3	35.3	35.2	35.3	35.4
2005	34.1	34.1	34.3	34.3	34.5	34.8	34.9	34.8	34.7	34.2	34.3	35.0	34.5
2006	34.6	34.5	34.6	34.2	34.4	34.4	34.5	34.6	34.5	34.5	34.4	34.4	34.5
2007	34.7	35.1	34.9	34.4	34.5	34.5	34.3	34.3	33.9	33.9	33.9	33.9	34.4
2008	34.2	34.1	34.1	34.2	34.4	34.4	34.5	34.2	34.0	33.9	34.0	34.1	34.2
2009	33.3	33.2	33.3	33.2	33.3	33.4	33.3	33.3	33.1	33.1	33.1	33.3	33.2
2010	32.8	32.8	32.9	32.7	32.9	32.9	32.8	32.7	32.5	32.6	32.6	32.8	32.8
2011	32.0	32.1	32.3	32.4	32.5	32.6	32.7	32.8	32.7	32.9	33.1	33.2	32.6
2012	32.9	33.2	33.3	33.4	33.7	33.9	33.7	33.7	33.6	33.8	33.9	34.2	33.6
2013	33.9	34.1	34.0	34.0	34.1	34.2	34.3	34.3	34.2	34.0	34.3	34.6	34.2
Professional and Business Services													
2002	65.6	67.0	68.1	69.4	69.4	69.5	67.8	68.5	68.5	67.0	66.7	66.8	67.9
2003	63.3	63.5	63.7	64.5	65.2	65.0	65.0	65.5	65.7	65.6	65.3	65.1	64.8
2004	63.1	63.3	64.6	66.5	66.4	66.7	67.6	68.0	67.9	68.0	68.1	68.0	66.5
2005	65.3	66.5	67.5	70.0	69.9	71.2	71.1	72.2	72.2	70.9	71.6	71.0	70.0
2006	69.6	70.1	71.3	71.4	72.1	73.4	73.0	73.6	74.3	72.1	72.5	72.8	72.2
2007	71.3	72.6	73.7	74.0	74.6	75.9	74.6	75.7	76.4	75.6	76.7	76.9	74.8
2008	74.6	75.3	75.5	75.4	75.5	75.6	74.3	74.9	75.4	74.8	74.7	74.7	75.1
2009	71.5	71.7	71.4	70.4	69.2	69.4	69.2	69.1	69.9	69.2	69.0	69.1	69.9
2010	68.0	68.6	69.4	70.0	69.9	70.9	71.8	72.9	73.1	73.9	74.3	74.1	71.4
2011	72.2	72.1	73.0	74.6	74.4	73.9	74.3	75.0	74.5	74.7	74.5	75.1	74.0
2012	73.7	74.7	75.2	75.1	74.5	75.6	74.4	75.4	74.5	75.6	75.4	74.9	74.9
2013	73.9	74.4	75.6	75.4	75.1	75.8	75.6	76.3	75.9	76.0	77.0	75.2	75.5
Education and Health Services													
2002	67.8	68.7	69.2	70.4	71.1	70.9	71.2	72.0	72.1	72.3	73.0	73.0	71.0
2003	71.1	71.9	72.4	72.0	72.0	71.5	71.4	72.1	72.9	72.4	72.7	72.5	72.1
2004	73.4	74.0	74.7	74.5	74.3	73.7	73.2	73.7	74.6	75.1	75.1	75.2	74.3
2005	73.2	73.9	74.5	75.4	75.1	74.9	75.3	76.2	77.2	77.1	77.3	77.7	75.7
2006	75.1	75.9	76.2	76.6	76.8	77.3	76.7	77.2	77.8	77.5	77.3	77.5	76.8
2007	77.1	77.8	78.4	78.8	79.0	79.1	78.7	79.4	80.3	80.9	81.2	81.1	79.3
2008	80.0	80.9	81.0	82.0	82.3	81.7	81.9	82.6	83.1	83.4	83.6	83.6	82.2
2009	83.0	82.9	83.0	82.8	82.8	82.8	82.6	82.8	83.4	82.9	83.0	82.9	82.9
2010	82.0	82.4	82.7	83.3	83.2	83.0	82.2	82.8	83.8	84.3	84.4	84.3	83.2
2011	82.6	82.6	83.5	84.1	84.2	84.3	83.8	84.5	85.5	85.4	86.0	86.0	84.4
2012	84.5	85.2	85.8	86.4	86.6	86.5	85.4	86.5	87.3	87.4	87.7	88.0	86.4
2013	86.9	87.3	87.7	87.6	87.9	87.5	86.6	87.4	88.1	88.7	89.5	89.4	87.9
Leisure and Hospitality													
2002	48.6	49.3	50.4	51.3	52.5	52.9	53.1	53.4	53.1	53.0	52.2	51.1	51.7
2003	49.7	50.0	50.6	52.2	53.3	53.1	53.0	53.3	52.6	52.9	51.9	51.4	52.0
2004	49.9	50.6	52.0	53.0	54.0	54.4	54.8	54.8	55.4	54.7	54.0	53.6	53.4
2005	52.3	53.1	54.8	55.9	56.8	57.6	56.0	55.7	55.7	54.7	54.6	53.9	55.1
2006	53.5	54.2	56.0	56.7	56.9	56.8	56.9	57.0	56.8	55.3	54.9	54.8	55.8
2007	52.1	53.3	55.4	55.5	56.1	56.5	57.0	57.7	57.5	56.9	57.0	56.4	56.0
2008	54.7	55.1	56.6	57.2	57.8	58.3	57.6	57.5	58.1	57.4	57.2	57.3	57.1
2009	55.2	56.1	57.4	58.3	58.7	58.7	58.6	58.7	58.2	57.2	57.0	56.6	57.6
2010	54.7	54.6	56.6	58.0	58.7	58.6	58.2	58.6	59.1	58.0	58.1	57.9	57.6
2011	57.0	57.0	59.5	61.2	60.8	61.3	60.8	61.1	61.6	60.1	59.9	59.6	60.0
2012	58.6	59.3	61.2	62.1	62.8	62.7	61.7	62.4	62.8	62.4	62.3	62.6	61.7
2013	60.9	61.7	62.8	63.9	65.1	65.0	65.2	65.9	66.3	65.0	66.5	67.0	64.6
Other Services													
2002	23.1	23.2	23.4	24.0	24.1	24.3	24.4	24.4	24.4	24.1	24.0	24.1	24.0
2003	23.5	23.5	23.5	23.4	23.6	23.9	23.7	23.5	23.3	23.2	23.2	23.3	23.5
2004	23.0	23.1	23.4	23.4	23.5	23.7	23.5	23.2	23.1	22.8	22.8	22.9	23.2
2005	22.9	23.0	23.1	23.1	23.1	23.3	23.5	23.3	23.3	23.2	23.2	23.2	23.2
2006	22.8	22.9	23.2	22.9	23.2	23.5	23.2	23.0	23.0	22.8	22.7	22.8	23.0
2007	22.6	22.7	22.9	23.3	23.5	23.8	23.5	23.4	23.3	23.2	23.2	23.0	23.2
2008	23.1	23.4	23.6	23.9	24.0	24.2	24.1	24.1	24.1	24.0	23.9	23.8	23.9
2009	23.6	23.6	23.7	23.5	23.5	23.7	23.4	23.1	23.0	22.9	23.0	22.8	23.3
2010	22.5	22.5	22.7	22.8	22.8	22.9	22.6	22.6	22.6	22.7	22.8	22.8	22.7
2011	22.4	22.4	22.5	22.7	23.0	23.0	22.8	22.7	22.8	22.7	22.7	22.6	22.7
2012	22.5	22.6	22.6	22.8	22.8	22.9	22.6	22.3	22.1	21.8	21.8	21.7	22.4
2013	21.6	21.6	21.5	21.5	21.7	21.9	22.0	21.9	21.8	21.7	21.7	21.6	21.7
Government													
2002	112.1	114.1	114.9	114.7	114.9	111.1	102.2	105.0	113.4	115.5	115.8	115.7	112.5
2003	110.7	113.6	112.9	112.7	112.6	109.1	101.6	103.3	111.5	113.0	113.4	113.6	110.7
2004	109.7	113.2	113.6	113.5	113.7	110.3	103.0	107.2	115.2	115.3	115.7	116.3	112.2
2005	112.8	115.1	115.5	116.1	116.5	112.3	105.4	107.6	115.2	117.1	117.8	117.6	114.1
2006	114.4	117.3	117.6	117.7	118.0	113.8	106.4	109.2	115.8	119.1	119.4	119.1	115.7
2007	116.7	118.9	119.6	119.4	119.7	116.2	108.9	111.6	118.2	121.0	121.6	120.7	117.7
2008	115.8	119.8	120.6	120.5	121.1	115.1	108.7	112.9	120.1	122.0	123.0	122.3	118.5
2009	120.6	120.8	122.1	122.4	122.7	117.9	113.0	114.8	121.2	124.2	124.9	124.7	120.8
2010	119.9	122.8	124.0	124.4	126.2	120.9	115.1	116.6	122.3	123.7	124.1	124.5	122.0
2011	119.1	122.8	123.6	123.9	124.0	119.2	114.4	115.2	123.1	124.7	125.2	125.7	121.7
2012	120.1	123.5	124.5	125.0	124.9	119.9	113.5	116.1	123.1	126.3	126.9	126.1	122.5
2013	121.5	126.0	126.6	126.9	127.7	122.5	117.1	119.4	124.4	129.1	129.8	129.6	125.1

Employment by Industry: Omaha-Council Bluffs, NE–IA, Selected Years, 2002–2013

(Numbers in thousands, not seasonally adjusted)

Industry and year	January	February	March	April	May	June	July	August	September	October	November	December	Annual average
Total Nonfarm													
2002	433.7	434.9	436.6	440.9	443.9	446.9	440.9	441.4	440.6	439.7	442.1	441.1	440.2
2003	434.8	434.3	436.1	437.0	441.4	444.0	443.7	444.4	444.4	445.7	446.9	446.0	441.6
2004	436.1	433.7	437.8	440.3	444.9	447.7	443.7	444.5	444.3	444.9	447.9	448.2	442.8
2005	438.3	439.1	442.7	448.1	451.3	454.9	450.8	451.1	452.3	453.8	457.4	457.3	449.8
2006	445.9	448.0	451.7	455.4	460.3	463.8	458.4	458.8	461.5	462.0	465.0	464.5	457.9
2007	452.9	453.7	456.2	461.8	466.8	469.7	464.3	467.0	468.1	470.7	473.4	472.5	464.8
2008	462.5	462.9	465.3	470.2	476.0	475.7	470.5	472.5	472.3	475.5	475.3	472.7	471.0
2009	458.8	457.7	457.9	461.5	464.8	463.9	461.8	461.4	459.5	461.1	462.1	459.0	460.8
2010	448.0	447.4	451.0	458.6	463.3	464.7	461.0	462.0	458.7	464.4	465.0	464.9	459.1
2011	453.2	453.8	455.9	463.9	467.3	467.8	464.8	465.8	464.3	467.6	469.8	469.3	463.6
2012	459.6	459.7	463.5	468.6	473.2	472.4	471.3	471.2	470.2	473.8	476.4	475.4	469.6
2013	465.5	465.9	468.0	472.3	478.8	478.7	477.5	479.1	478.2	481.1	483.1	480.4	475.7
Total Private													
2002	376.7	377.3	379.2	383.5	386.2	389.1	386.1	386.8	384.2	381.7	384.0	383.3	383.2
2003	377.1	376.2	378.4	377.9	382.1	384.6	388.1	390.3	387.9	386.8	388.0	387.6	383.8
2004	377.5	374.9	378.7	381.0	385.2	388.1	386.8	387.7	385.5	384.9	387.9	388.4	383.9
2005	378.7	379.0	382.7	388.0	390.6	394.4	393.4	394.0	392.7	392.7	396.1	396.4	389.9
2006	385.2	387.0	390.7	393.8	398.3	402.1	400.8	401.1	400.7	400.3	403.1	403.2	397.2
2007	391.7	392.1	394.7	399.6	404.2	407.7	407.6	409.3	407.2	408.3	411.0	410.9	403.7
2008	400.8	400.9	403.6	407.2	412.6	413.8	412.4	413.4	410.3	411.4	411.0	409.2	408.9
2009	395.3	393.8	394.1	396.3	398.9	399.7	398.5	398.6	395.4	395.4	396.3	394.5	396.4
2010	383.5	382.6	385.2	392.1	396.0	398.2	398.4	399.0	395.0	398.0	398.6	399.2	393.8
2011	387.8	387.8	390.5	397.1	400.3	402.6	401.7	402.0	399.7	401.1	403.1	403.4	398.1
2012	393.8	393.5	397.8	402.6	406.7	409.3	408.7	408.1	405.9	408.0	410.5	410.4	404.6
2013	400.7	400.5	402.9	406.6	412.4	413.9	414.6	416.0	414.0	415.5	417.2	415.5	410.8
Goods Producing													
2002	55.4	55.2	55.7	57.1	57.6	58.3	58.0	58.0	57.5	57.3	57.3	56.4	57.0
2003	55.9	55.3	55.6	56.7	58.1	59.2	60.7	60.9	60.2	60.1	59.6	58.8	58.4
2004	56.4	55.4	57.1	58.1	59.1	59.7	59.7	59.5	59.0	58.9	58.7	58.3	58.3
2005	56.0	55.6	57.1	58.5	58.7	60.0	60.3	60.1	59.6	59.4	59.2	58.2	58.6
2006	56.4	56.8	57.7	59.2	60.2	61.4	61.6	61.6	61.7	61.1	60.2	59.2	59.8
2007	56.6	55.7	56.2	57.6	58.7	59.8	60.2	60.6	59.9	60.5	60.2	59.1	58.8
2008	57.5	57.3	57.9	59.4	60.6	61.2	60.9	60.9	60.4	60.2	59.4	58.1	59.5
2009	54.9	54.5	54.5	55.8	56.2	56.5	56.5	56.3	55.7	55.0	54.7	53.1	55.3
2010	50.4	49.9	50.4	52.4	52.9	53.3	53.5	53.2	52.6	52.3	52.2	51.3	52.0
2011	49.0	49.0	49.8	51.0	51.6	52.6	52.7	52.4	51.8	52.1	52.1	52.0	51.3
2012	49.9	49.5	50.6	51.7	52.5	53.3	53.6	53.5	53.4	53.6	53.7	53.5	52.4
2013	51.6	52.0	52.4	53.8	55.3	55.7	56.9	56.8	56.6	56.4	56.2	55.4	54.9
Service-Providing													
2002	378.3	379.7	380.9	383.8	386.3	388.6	382.9	383.4	383.1	382.4	384.8	384.7	383.2
2003	378.9	379.0	380.5	380.3	383.3	384.8	383.0	383.5	384.2	385.6	387.3	387.2	383.1
2004	379.7	378.3	380.7	382.2	385.8	388.0	383.8	385.0	385.3	386.0	389.2	389.9	384.5
2005	382.3	383.5	385.6	389.6	392.6	394.9	390.5	391.0	392.7	394.4	398.2	399.1	391.2
2006	389.5	391.2	394.0	396.2	400.1	402.4	396.8	397.2	399.8	400.9	404.8	405.3	398.2
2007	396.3	398.0	400.0	404.2	408.1	409.9	404.1	406.4	408.2	410.2	413.2	413.4	406.0
2008	405.0	405.6	407.4	410.8	415.4	414.5	409.6	411.6	411.9	415.3	415.9	414.6	411.5
2009	403.9	403.2	403.4	405.7	408.6	407.4	405.3	405.1	403.8	406.1	407.4	405.9	405.5
2010	397.6	397.5	400.6	406.2	410.4	411.4	407.5	408.8	406.2	412.1	412.8	413.6	407.1
2011	404.2	404.8	406.1	412.9	415.7	415.2	412.1	413.4	412.5	415.5	417.7	417.3	412.3
2012	409.7	410.2	412.9	416.9	420.7	419.1	417.7	417.7	416.8	420.2	422.7	421.9	417.2
2013	413.9	413.9	415.6	418.5	423.5	423.0	420.6	422.3	421.6	424.7	426.9	425.0	420.8
Mining, Logging, and Construction													
2002	20.9	20.8	21.7	23.3	23.9	24.7	25.1	25.1	24.7	24.7	24.7	23.8	23.6
2003	23.0	22.4	22.8	24.0	25.1	25.9	27.6	27.8	27.1	27.0	26.6	25.8	25.4
2004	23.6	22.8	24.3	25.4	26.2	26.6	26.7	26.5	26.0	25.9	25.8	25.1	25.4
2005	23.1	23.0	24.3	25.5	25.9	27.0	27.2	27.3	26.8	26.7	26.4	25.3	25.7
2006	24.1	24.4	25.2	26.4	27.3	28.3	28.4	28.5	28.7	27.8	26.8	25.8	26.8
2007	23.7	22.7	23.1	24.4	25.3	26.2	26.3	26.6	26.1	26.5	26.2	25.2	25.2
2008	23.6	23.4	24.0	25.5	26.5	27.0	27.0	27.1	26.8	26.5	25.9	25.1	25.7
2009	22.6	22.4	22.8	24.4	24.8	25.2	25.3	25.1	24.5	23.8	23.3	21.8	23.8
2010	19.4	19.0	19.4	21.4	21.7	22.0	22.1	22.0	21.4	21.1	21.0	20.0	20.9
2011	18.2	18.0	18.7	19.7	20.3	21.2	21.3	21.3	21.0	21.0	20.8	20.1	20.1
2012	19.0	18.6	19.5	20.6	21.3	21.8	22.0	22.1	22.0	22.4	22.2	21.9	21.1
2013	20.3	20.4	20.8	22.0	23.1	23.4	24.2	24.2	24.0	24.1	23.8	23.1	22.8
Manufacturing													
2002	34.5	34.4	34.0	33.8	33.7	33.6	32.9	32.9	32.8	32.6	32.6	32.6	33.4
2003	32.9	32.9	32.8	32.7	33.0	33.3	33.1	33.1	33.1	33.1	33.0	33.0	33.0
2004	32.8	32.6	32.8	32.7	32.9	33.1	33.2	33.0	33.0	33.0	32.9	33.2	32.9
2005	32.9	32.6	32.8	33.0	32.8	33.0	33.1	32.8	32.8	32.7	32.8	32.9	32.9
2006	32.3	32.4	32.5	32.8	32.9	33.1	33.2	33.1	33.0	33.3	33.4	33.4	33.0
2007	32.9	33.0	33.1	33.2	33.4	33.6	33.9	34.0	33.8	34.0	34.0	33.9	33.6
2008	33.9	33.9	33.9	33.9	34.1	34.2	33.9	33.8	33.6	33.7	33.5	33.0	33.8
2009	32.3	32.1	31.7	31.4	31.4	31.3	31.2	31.2	31.2	31.2	31.4	31.3	31.5
2010	31.0	30.9	31.0	31.0	31.2	31.3	31.4	31.2	31.1	31.2	31.2	31.3	31.2
2011	30.8	31.0	31.1	31.3	31.3	31.4	31.4	31.1	30.8	31.1	31.3	31.9	31.2
2012	30.9	30.9	31.1	31.1	31.2	31.5	31.6	31.4	31.4	31.2	31.5	31.6	31.3
2013	31.3	31.6	31.6	31.8	32.2	32.3	32.7	32.6	32.6	32.3	32.4	32.3	32.1

Employment by Industry: Omaha-Council Bluffs, NE–IA, Selected Years, 2002–2013—*Continued*

(Numbers in thousands, not seasonally adjusted)

Industry and year	January	February	March	April	May	June	July	August	September	October	November	December	Annual average
Trade, Transportation, and Utilities													
2002	105.6	104.2	103.9	103.6	103.9	103.7	103.0	102.7	102.9	102.3	103.9	104.4	103.7
2003	99.3	98.2	98.9	97.2	97.8	97.9	97.9	97.9	98.0	97.9	99.2	100.1	98.4
2004	96.3	94.9	94.6	95.6	97.0	97.8	97.3	98.5	98.9	98.2	100.7	102.0	97.7
2005	98.1	97.8	98.2	98.1	99.4	99.4	98.8	99.2	99.3	99.8	101.9	102.8	99.4
2006	97.0	96.6	97.4	97.4	98.5	98.7	98.6	98.9	99.1	100.0	102.7	103.7	99.1
2007	98.6	98.1	98.7	99.2	100.0	100.1	99.8	100.3	100.4	100.6	103.2	103.9	100.2
2008	99.4	98.5	99.0	98.7	99.9	99.6	99.0	99.4	98.9	100.1	101.8	102.6	99.7
2009	96.7	95.3	95.1	94.3	95.0	94.5	94.0	94.3	93.9	94.8	96.6	97.1	95.1
2010	92.1	91.3	91.9	93.0	94.1	93.9	93.4	93.5	92.9	94.3	96.4	98.1	93.7
2011	92.6	91.9	92.4	93.1	93.6	93.3	93.0	93.5	93.5	93.9	96.6	97.5	93.7
2012	92.9	91.8	92.4	92.9	94.0	94.0	93.5	93.3	93.4	94.5	97.4	98.6	94.1
2013	93.8	92.5	92.9	92.7	94.3	94.4	94.4	95.2	95.0	96.6	98.9	99.6	95.0
Wholesale Trade													
2002	21.0	21.0	21.1	21.0	21.1	21.2	21.2	21.3	21.2	21.0	21.0	21.0	21.1
2003	20.7	20.7	20.9	20.8	20.6	20.5	20.4	20.3	20.2	19.6	19.7	19.6	20.3
2004	19.2	19.0	19.1	19.1	19.0	19.2	19.2	19.3	19.2	19.2	19.1	19.1	19.1
2005	18.6	18.6	18.8	18.6	18.6	18.6	18.7	18.5	18.3	18.4	18.4	18.4	18.5
2006	18.1	18.2	18.3	18.2	18.3	18.3	18.4	18.2	18.1	18.1	18.1	18.2	18.2
2007	17.7	17.7	17.8	18.0	18.0	18.3	18.3	18.3	18.4	18.4	18.5	18.6	18.2
2008	18.4	18.4	18.5	18.4	18.6	18.6	18.6	18.5	18.4	18.4	18.4	18.3	18.5
2009	18.0	17.9	17.8	17.9	17.9	17.9	18.0	17.9	17.7	17.8	17.9	17.9	17.9
2010	17.5	17.4	17.4	17.6	17.6	17.7	17.6	17.4	17.2	17.3	17.3	17.2	17.4
2011	16.9	16.9	17.0	17.0	17.0	17.1	17.1	17.0	17.1	17.1	17.2	17.1	17.0
2012	16.7	16.7	16.8	16.8	16.9	16.9	16.9	16.8	16.7	16.7	16.8	16.8	16.8
2013	16.6	16.6	16.7	16.8	17.0	17.1	17.1	17.0	16.9	17.1	17.0	16.9	16.9
Retail Trade													
2002	54.4	53.2	53.1	53.4	54.0	54.1	53.8	53.9	54.6	54.6	56.6	57.6	54.4
2003	53.2	52.0	52.3	51.3	51.5	51.4	51.2	51.1	51.2	52.1	53.7	54.6	52.1
2004	51.4	50.2	50.0	50.1	50.8	51.1	50.7	50.6	50.5	51.1	53.1	54.3	51.2
2005	50.8	50.1	50.2	50.6	51.2	51.0	50.8	51.0	50.9	51.8	53.6	54.4	51.4
2006	50.5	49.6	50.1	50.3	50.8	50.9	50.7	50.7	50.7	51.7	54.0	54.8	51.2
2007	50.9	50.2	50.6	51.1	51.9	51.9	51.7	51.7	51.5	52.4	54.5	55.3	52.0
2008	52.1	51.1	51.2	50.9	51.3	51.2	50.8	50.7	50.2	51.0	52.6	53.6	51.4
2009	50.1	49.1	49.0	49.1	49.8	49.8	49.5	49.5	49.2	50.0	51.5	51.6	49.9
2010	48.9	48.3	48.7	49.3	50.1	50.2	49.6	49.6	49.1	50.2	51.8	52.7	49.9
2011	49.3	48.7	49.0	49.6	50.1	49.9	49.7	49.9	49.6	50.3	52.7	53.4	50.2
2012	50.0	49.0	49.4	49.8	50.5	50.5	50.2	50.0	49.9	51.1	53.3	53.8	50.6
2013	50.2	49.4	49.7	49.8	50.6	50.8	50.9	51.1	51.0	52.3	54.6	55.1	51.3
Transportation and Utilities													
2002	30.2	30.0	29.7	29.2	28.8	28.4	28.0	27.5	27.1	26.7	26.3	25.8	28.1
2003	25.4	25.5	25.7	25.1	25.7	26.0	26.3	26.5	26.6	26.2	25.8	25.9	25.9
2004	25.7	25.7	25.5	26.4	27.2	27.5	27.4	28.6	29.2	27.9	28.5	28.6	27.4
2005	28.7	29.1	29.2	28.9	29.6	29.8	29.3	29.7	30.1	29.6	29.9	30.0	29.5
2006	28.4	28.8	29.0	28.9	29.4	29.5	29.5	30.0	30.3	30.2	30.6	30.7	29.6
2007	30.0	30.2	30.3	30.1	30.1	29.9	29.8	30.3	30.5	29.8	30.2	30.0	30.1
2008	28.9	29.0	29.3	29.4	30.0	29.8	29.6	30.2	30.3	30.7	30.8	30.7	29.9
2009	28.6	28.3	28.3	27.3	27.3	26.8	26.5	26.9	27.0	27.0	27.2	27.6	27.4
2010	25.7	25.6	25.8	26.1	26.4	26.0	26.2	26.5	26.6	26.8	27.3	28.2	26.4
2011	26.4	26.3	26.4	26.5	26.5	26.3	26.2	26.6	26.8	26.5	26.7	27.0	26.5
2012	26.2	26.1	26.2	26.3	26.6	26.6	26.4	26.5	26.8	26.7	27.3	28.0	26.6
2013	27.0	26.5	26.5	26.1	26.7	26.5	26.4	27.1	27.1	27.2	27.3	27.6	26.8
Information													
2002	14.4	14.4	14.4	14.3	14.4	14.4	14.4	14.3	14.1	14.0	14.1	14.1	14.3
2003	14.0	14.0	13.9	13.7	13.7	13.8	13.9	13.8	13.7	13.8	13.8	13.9	13.8
2004	13.6	13.6	13.6	13.4	13.5	13.5	13.6	13.5	13.4	13.4	13.4	13.5	13.5
2005	13.3	13.3	13.3	13.2	13.1	13.3	13.3	13.4	13.2	13.3	13.4	13.4	13.3
2006	13.1	13.0	13.0	13.0	13.1	13.1	13.0	12.8	12.7	12.5	12.6	12.6	12.9
2007	12.3	12.4	12.4	12.5	12.6	12.7	12.7	12.7	12.6	12.6	12.6	12.6	12.6
2008	12.3	12.3	12.3	12.4	12.4	12.3	12.3	12.1	12.0	12.0	12.0	11.9	12.2
2009	11.6	11.6	11.6	11.5	11.4	11.5	11.5	11.5	11.4	11.3	11.5	11.5	11.5
2010	11.3	11.3	11.2	11.2	11.3	11.3	11.2	11.2	11.1	11.1	11.1	11.2	11.2
2011	11.2	11.2	11.1	11.1	11.1	11.2	11.4	11.4	11.3	11.3	11.4	11.4	11.3
2012	11.3	11.4	11.4	11.4	11.3	11.3	11.3	11.2	11.2	11.1	11.1	11.1	11.3
2013	11.0	11.0	11.0	11.0	11.1	11.0	11.1	11.1	11.1	11.1	11.1	11.0	11.1
Financial Activities													
2002	35.6	35.9	36.1	36.3	36.8	37.1	37.5	37.6	37.4	37.7	38.0	38.2	37.0
2003	38.2	38.3	38.3	37.3	37.3	37.5	38.2	38.2	38.0	37.8	37.8	38.1	37.9
2004	37.6	37.6	38.0	37.3	37.4	37.6	37.5	37.4	37.1	37.5	37.4	37.5	37.5
2005	37.3	37.3	37.3	37.3	37.5	37.6	37.6	37.8	37.7	37.6	37.7	38.0	37.6
2006	37.8	38.1	38.2	38.3	38.6	39.1	39.2	39.4	39.1	39.1	39.3	39.6	38.8
2007	39.3	39.5	39.7	39.8	40.1	40.3	40.2	40.0	39.9	39.9	39.9	40.1	39.9
2008	40.2	40.5	40.7	40.5	40.8	41.0	40.9	40.7	40.6	40.7	40.6	40.8	40.7
2009	40.1	40.4	40.4	40.0	40.1	40.1	40.0	40.0	39.7	39.8	40.0	40.1	40.1
2010	40.0	40.1	40.3	40.1	40.3	40.5	40.7	40.8	40.5	40.9	40.8	40.9	40.5
2011	40.9	40.9	41.0	41.2	41.4	41.4	41.4	41.3	41.2	41.3	41.5	41.7	41.3
2012	41.3	41.2	41.3	41.5	41.6	41.6	41.8	41.8	41.7	41.8	42.0	42.0	41.6
2013	41.8	41.9	41.9	41.9	42.0	42.2	42.0	42.0	42.0	41.9	41.8	41.9	41.9

Employment by Industry: Omaha-Council Bluffs, NE–IA, Selected Years, 2002–2013—*Continued*

(Numbers in thousands, not seasonally adjusted)

Industry and year	January	February	March	April	May	June	July	August	September	October	November	December	Annual average
Professional and Business Services													
2002	58.0	58.6	59.1	59.6	59.5	60.1	58.1	58.3	57.4	57.7	57.9	57.7	58.5
2003	58.0	58.6	59.2	59.0	59.6	59.5	61.3	62.6	62.6	63.0	62.9	62.9	60.8
2004	61.2	61.0	61.7	60.9	61.1	61.3	60.5	60.9	59.7	60.0	60.3	60.2	60.7
2005	59.4	59.7	60.4	61.5	61.7	62.1	61.7	61.9	62.1	62.6	62.9	63.6	61.6
2006	61.8	62.3	63.1	63.4	63.7	64.6	64.4	64.1	63.9	63.3	63.1	63.2	63.4
2007	62.0	62.7	63.2	63.9	64.3	65.1	65.4	65.3	65.3	65.4	65.9	66.6	64.6
2008	64.8	64.8	65.1	66.1	66.3	66.4	65.8	66.1	65.5	65.5	65.2	64.7	65.5
2009	63.1	62.9	62.5	63.1	63.1	63.4	63.1	63.0	62.1	62.3	62.1	62.3	62.8
2010	61.3	60.9	61.1	62.8	63.2	63.8	64.4	64.8	64.4	65.1	65.0	65.2	63.5
2011	63.3	63.4	63.7	65.3	65.3	66.0	66.8	67.0	67.0	66.6	66.6	66.3	65.6
2012	65.5	65.8	65.7	67.0	67.3	68.5	68.6	68.2	67.8	68.5	68.7	68.3	67.5
2013	67.4	67.4	67.5	68.6	68.8	69.4	69.6	69.5	69.6	69.4	69.9	71.0	69.0
Education and Health Services													
2002	56.2	57.3	57.4	57.9	58.1	58.2	57.3	57.9	58.5	58.3	58.8	58.8	57.9
2003	58.9	59.1	58.9	59.0	58.9	59.1	58.5	59.0	59.2	59.1	60.2	59.9	59.2
2004	59.1	59.3	59.7	60.2	59.9	59.7	59.6	59.6	60.1	60.5	61.2	60.9	60.0
2005	59.5	60.1	60.3	61.3	60.9	61.0	60.9	60.8	61.5	61.8	63.0	62.9	61.2
2006	62.0	62.8	63.1	62.8	63.0	63.0	62.4	62.9	63.9	63.7	65.0	64.4	63.3
2007	63.8	64.7	64.9	65.1	65.4	65.6	65.5	66.3	66.6	67.1	67.6	67.6	65.9
2008	66.9	67.9	68.1	68.4	68.8	68.5	68.6	69.5	69.9	70.1	70.6	70.5	69.0
2009	69.8	70.2	70.1	70.3	70.2	69.7	69.7	69.9	70.5	71.1	71.4	71.2	70.3
2010	70.5	71.1	71.2	71.4	71.6	71.5	71.5	71.8	71.5	72.2	72.2	72.4	71.6
2011	72.0	72.6	72.6	73.2	73.4	73.0	72.3	72.8	73.0	74.1	74.3	74.4	73.1
2012	73.4	73.9	74.6	74.5	74.7	74.3	74.1	74.8	74.9	75.4	75.7	75.5	74.7
2013	74.5	75.1	75.1	75.1	75.3	74.8	74.3	74.9	74.9	75.1	75.6	75.0	75.0
Leisure and Hospitality													
2002	37.2	37.2	38.0	39.6	40.8	42.1	42.4	43.0	41.7	39.7	39.3	39.0	40.0
2003	38.4	38.3	39.0	39.9	41.0	41.8	41.7	42.0	40.5	39.5	38.9	38.4	40.0
2004	37.8	37.6	38.3	39.9	41.5	42.5	42.3	42.3	41.4	40.4	40.2	39.9	40.3
2005	39.2	39.2	40.1	42.1	43.2	44.7	44.4	44.5	43.3	42.1	41.9	41.5	42.2
2006	40.9	41.2	42.0	43.3	44.7	45.6	45.0	44.9	43.9	44.0	43.7	43.9	43.6
2007	42.7	42.6	43.1	44.9	46.5	47.4	47.2	47.6	46.1	45.7	45.0	44.4	45.3
2008	43.2	43.1	43.9	45.1	46.9	48.0	48.1	48.0	46.4	45.8	44.4	43.7	45.6
2009	42.4	42.2	43.2	44.4	45.9	46.8	46.4	46.4	44.9	43.8	42.6	41.7	44.2
2010	40.7	40.8	41.8	43.7	45.0	46.1	45.9	46.0	44.6	44.7	43.5	42.7	43.8
2011	41.5	41.6	42.6	44.8	46.5	47.5	46.6	46.3	44.7	44.6	43.5	43.0	44.4
2012	42.4	42.8	44.5	46.1	47.6	48.4	48.0	47.6	45.9	45.7	44.6	44.1	45.6
2013	43.4	43.5	44.8	46.2	48.2	48.9	48.7	48.9	47.3	47.3	46.0	43.6	46.4
Other Services													
2002	14.3	14.5	14.6	15.1	15.1	15.2	15.4	15.0	14.7	14.7	14.7	14.7	14.8
2003	14.4	14.4	14.6	15.1	15.7	15.8	15.9	15.9	15.7	15.6	15.6	15.5	15.4
2004	15.5	15.5	15.7	15.6	15.7	16.0	16.1	16.0	15.9	16.0	16.0	16.1	15.8
2005	15.9	16.0	16.0	16.0	16.1	16.3	16.4	16.3	16.0	16.1	16.1	16.0	16.1
2006	16.2	16.2	16.2	16.4	16.5	16.6	16.6	16.5	16.4	16.6	16.5	16.6	16.4
2007	16.4	16.4	16.5	16.6	16.6	16.7	16.6	16.5	16.4	16.5	16.6	16.6	16.5
2008	16.5	16.5	16.6	16.6	16.9	16.8	16.8	16.7	16.6	17.0	17.0	16.9	16.7
2009	16.7	16.7	16.7	16.9	17.0	17.2	17.3	17.2	17.2	17.3	17.4	17.5	17.1
2010	17.2	17.2	17.3	17.5	17.6	17.8	17.8	17.7	17.5	17.4	17.4	17.4	17.5
2011	17.3	17.2	17.3	17.4	17.4	17.6	17.5	17.3	17.2	17.2	17.1	17.1	17.3
2012	17.1	17.1	17.3	17.5	17.7	17.9	17.8	17.7	17.6	17.4	17.3	17.3	17.5
2013	17.2	17.1	17.3	17.3	17.4	17.5	17.6	17.6	17.5	17.7	17.7	18.0	17.5
Government													
2002	57.0	57.6	57.4	57.4	57.7	57.8	54.8	54.6	56.4	58.0	58.1	57.8	57.1
2003	57.7	58.1	57.7	59.1	59.3	59.4	55.6	54.1	56.5	58.9	58.9	58.4	57.8
2004	58.6	58.8	59.1	59.3	59.7	59.6	56.9	56.8	58.8	60.0	60.0	59.8	59.0
2005	59.6	60.1	60.0	60.1	60.7	60.5	57.4	57.1	59.6	61.1	61.3	60.9	59.9
2006	60.7	61.0	61.0	61.6	62.0	61.7	57.6	57.7	60.8	61.7	61.9	61.3	60.8
2007	61.2	61.6	61.5	62.2	62.6	62.0	56.7	57.7	60.9	62.4	62.4	61.6	61.1
2008	61.7	62.0	61.7	63.0	63.4	61.9	58.1	59.1	62.0	64.1	64.3	63.5	62.1
2009	63.5	63.9	63.8	65.2	65.9	64.2	63.3	62.8	64.1	65.7	65.8	64.5	64.4
2010	64.5	64.8	65.8	66.5	67.3	66.5	62.6	63.0	63.7	66.4	66.4	65.7	65.3
2011	65.4	66.0	65.4	66.8	67.0	65.2	63.1	63.8	64.6	66.5	66.7	65.9	65.5
2012	65.8	66.2	65.7	66.0	66.5	63.1	62.6	63.1	64.3	65.8	65.9	65.0	65.0
2013	64.8	65.4	65.1	65.7	66.4	64.8	62.9	63.1	64.2	65.6	65.9	64.9	64.9

Employment by Industry: Orlando-Kissimmee-Sanford, FL, Selected Years, 2002–2013

(Numbers in thousands, not seasonally adjusted)

Industry and year	January	February	March	April	May	June	July	August	September	October	November	December	Annual average
Total Nonfarm													
2002	880.4	890.3	897.2	893.8	898.0	890.3	884.7	898.1	900.5	905.3	914.5	922.2	897.9
2003	904.5	909.7	914.3	914.3	915.9	907.1	901.6	916.4	916.8	924.7	931.6	937.5	916.2
2004	931.2	939.2	945.4	954.4	957.8	950.6	949.4	960.9	960.8	973.7	985.6	993.5	958.5
2005	985.0	992.7	1,000.1	1,007.2	1,013.9	1,003.6	1,003.5	1,018.7	1,023.9	1,026.5	1,037.3	1,044.4	1,013.1
2006	1,034.4	1,041.4	1,050.2	1,055.5	1,059.8	1,050.5	1,041.5	1,059.3	1,064.2	1,064.7	1,076.7	1,084.4	1,056.9
2007	1,072.1	1,082.0	1,087.6	1,087.7	1,089.1	1,076.0	1,067.9	1,081.1	1,080.3	1,084.3	1,095.5	1,096.4	1,083.3
2008	1,077.6	1,087.8	1,091.3	1,080.1	1,077.6	1,060.6	1,051.2	1,059.1	1,052.5	1,048.5	1,046.4	1,044.5	1,064.8
2009	1,018.0	1,017.9	1,015.5	1,009.5	1,005.5	988.6	977.7	985.9	984.6	986.6	992.9	993.6	998.0
2010	976.2	982.4	989.9	995.9	1,000.9	989.0	984.3	994.2	989.9	998.1	1,004.3	1,005.7	992.6
2011	989.5	996.1	1,002.5	1,007.5	1,006.9	995.4	993.8	1,004.3	1,009.7	1,012.3	1,022.9	1,025.1	1,005.5
2012	1,011.2	1,021.2	1,031.0	1,030.6	1,031.2	1,021.2	1,018.0	1,029.0	1,031.5	1,043.5	1,056.3	1,057.0	1,031.8
2013	1,037.1	1,051.2	1,058.9	1,059.7	1,063.7	1,057.0	1,053.9	1,068.5	1,068.7	1,080.3	1,087.6	1,093.5	1,065.0
Total Private													
2002	781.0	789.9	796.7	792.7	796.2	799.3	795.6	797.4	798.2	801.5	810.1	817.4	798.0
2003	800.8	805.3	809.8	809.4	810.5	813.0	809.5	813.4	812.4	818.6	824.9	830.6	813.2
2004	825.2	831.9	837.9	847.0	850.2	854.5	855.3	855.5	852.8	863.7	874.7	882.7	852.6
2005	874.9	881.6	888.6	895.7	901.4	903.4	905.4	908.9	911.4	913.3	923.5	930.8	903.2
2006	921.2	926.8	935.7	940.0	944.5	946.1	939.4	944.7	948.1	948.0	959.3	967.8	943.5
2007	955.0	963.4	968.6	968.0	969.7	967.9	962.0	961.9	960.4	965.2	976.3	978.3	966.4
2008	959.9	969.2	971.6	960.3	957.6	952.8	945.6	941.4	933.7	929.7	926.9	925.1	947.8
2009	899.7	898.6	896.1	890.2	887.9	881.9	872.4	870.4	868.3	869.5	875.2	877.0	882.3
2010	859.6	865.6	872.9	878.0	880.2	881.1	877.8	877.5	873.6	880.4	886.6	889.2	876.9
2011	873.2	878.1	884.3	890.1	890.4	889.8	889.1	889.4	893.4	894.7	904.7	907.8	890.4
2012	893.6	901.8	911.1	912.4	914.0	914.7	912.0	911.9	914.3	924.9	936.9	938.5	915.5
2013	919.5	931.8	939.1	939.9	944.8	949.1	946.7	950.3	950.8	961.0	967.8	974.3	947.9
Goods Producing													
2002	106.7	107.2	107.6	106.7	106.9	106.6	106.2	107.1	107.3	108.2	108.5	109.1	107.3
2003	106.9	107.7	108.3	107.8	108.5	109.4	109.1	110.3	111.0	111.8	111.9	113.2	109.7
2004	112.9	114.0	115.4	116.9	117.6	119.1	120.2	120.5	120.4	121.9	123.2	124.3	118.9
2005	124.4	125.5	126.8	128.5	129.6	130.7	131.9	132.4	133.0	132.6	133.5	134.1	130.3
2006	133.0	134.2	136.0	136.3	137.4	138.1	137.1	137.2	136.9	136.4	135.5	135.6	136.1
2007	132.2	131.9	132.4	130.9	130.9	131.1	129.6	129.9	129.4	127.9	127.5	126.0	130.0
2008	121.8	121.8	121.2	118.4	117.7	116.9	115.3	114.2	113.5	110.7	108.3	106.2	115.5
2009	102.8	100.8	99.4	95.4	94.3	93.7	91.3	90.2	88.9	88.0	87.4	86.5	93.2
2010	84.7	85.1	85.7	86.1	86.2	86.9	87.0	86.4	86.0	85.4	84.6	84.3	85.7
2011	83.1	83.2	83.0	83.0	83.0	82.9	83.2	83.4	83.7	83.3	83.4	83.4	83.2
2012	82.6	83.1	83.6	82.3	83.0	83.3	84.1	84.8	85.2	85.9	86.4	85.8	84.2
2013	85.0	86.1	86.9	87.4	88.1	89.0	89.9	90.8	91.2	91.4	92.6	92.9	89.3
Service-Providing													
2002	773.7	783.1	789.6	787.1	791.1	783.7	778.5	791.0	793.2	797.1	806.0	813.1	790.6
2003	797.6	802.0	806.0	806.5	807.4	797.7	792.5	806.1	805.8	812.9	819.7	824.3	806.5
2004	818.3	825.2	830.0	837.5	840.2	831.5	829.2	840.4	840.4	851.8	862.4	869.2	839.7
2005	860.6	867.2	873.3	878.7	884.3	872.9	871.6	886.3	890.9	893.9	903.8	910.3	882.8
2006	901.4	907.2	914.2	919.2	922.4	912.4	904.4	922.1	927.3	928.3	941.2	948.8	920.7
2007	939.9	950.1	955.2	956.8	958.2	944.9	938.3	951.2	950.9	956.4	968.0	970.4	953.4
2008	955.8	966.0	970.1	961.7	959.9	943.7	935.9	944.9	939.0	937.8	938.1	938.3	949.3
2009	915.2	917.1	916.1	914.1	911.2	894.9	886.4	895.7	895.7	898.6	905.5	907.1	904.8
2010	891.5	897.3	904.2	909.8	914.7	902.1	897.3	907.8	903.9	912.7	919.7	921.4	906.9
2011	906.4	912.9	919.5	924.5	923.9	912.5	910.6	920.9	926.0	929.0	939.5	941.7	922.3
2012	928.6	938.1	947.4	948.3	948.2	937.9	933.9	944.2	946.3	957.6	969.9	971.2	947.6
2013	952.1	965.1	972.0	972.3	975.6	968.0	964.0	977.7	977.5	988.9	995.0	1,000.6	975.7
Mining and Logging													
2002	0.4	0.5	0.5	0.5	0.5	0.5	0.5	0.5	0.5	0.5	0.5	0.5	0.5
2003	0.5	0.5	0.5	0.5	0.5	0.5	0.5	0.5	0.5	0.4	0.4	0.4	0.5
2004	0.4	0.4	0.4	0.4	0.4	0.4	0.4	0.4	0.4	0.4	0.3	0.4	0.4
2005	0.3	0.3	0.3	0.4	0.4	0.4	0.3	0.3	0.3	0.3	0.3	0.3	0.3
2006	0.3	0.3	0.3	0.3	0.3	0.3	0.3	0.3	0.3	0.3	0.3	0.4	0.3
2007	0.3	0.4	0.4	0.4	0.4	0.4	0.3	0.3	0.3	0.4	0.4	0.4	0.4
2008	0.4	0.4	0.4	0.4	0.4	0.3	0.3	0.3	0.3	0.3	0.2	0.2	0.3
2009	0.2	0.2	0.2	0.2	0.3	0.3	0.3	0.2	0.2	0.2	0.2	0.2	0.2
2010	0.2	0.2	0.2	0.2	0.2	0.2	0.2	0.2	0.2	0.2	0.2	0.2	0.2
2011	0.2	0.2	0.2	0.2	0.2	0.2	0.2	0.2	0.2	0.2	0.2	0.2	0.2
2012	0.2	0.2	0.2	0.2	0.2	0.2	0.2	0.2	0.2	0.2	0.2	0.2	0.2
2013	0.2	0.2	0.2	0.2	0.2	0.2	0.3	0.3	0.3	0.3	0.3	0.3	0.3
Construction													
2002	59.2	59.5	59.9	59.6	60.0	60.1	60.4	61.4	61.7	62.6	63.1	63.6	60.9
2003	62.0	62.8	63.3	63.6	64.3	65.2	65.3	66.5	67.1	68.1	68.3	69.4	65.5
2004	69.2	70.1	71.2	72.2	72.7	73.9	74.9	75.3	75.2	76.1	77.2	77.9	73.8
2005	78.4	79.4	80.5	81.7	83.0	84.0	85.4	86.2	87.0	86.9	87.9	88.8	84.1
2006	88.1	89.3	90.6	91.1	92.0	92.4	91.7	91.9	91.7	91.1	90.3	90.2	90.9
2007	87.4	86.9	87.2	85.6	85.7	85.8	84.6	85.0	84.6	83.3	82.7	81.2	85.0
2008	77.7	77.7	77.2	74.5	74.0	73.3	72.1	71.5	70.9	68.4	66.5	64.8	72.4
2009	62.3	60.7	59.6	56.3	55.2	54.5	52.7	51.8	50.7	49.9	49.2	48.6	54.3
2010	47.2	47.7	48.0	48.3	47.9	48.5	48.2	47.9	47.5	47.0	46.1	45.6	47.5
2011	44.7	44.7	44.6	44.5	44.6	44.7	45.1	45.3	45.6	45.4	45.4	45.4	45.0
2012	44.4	44.8	45.1	43.9	44.6	44.9	45.8	46.8	47.4	48.0	48.4	47.9	46.0
2013	47.4	48.3	49.1	49.4	50.0	50.7	51.3	52.3	52.4	52.7	53.6	53.5	50.9

Employment by Industry: Orlando-Kissimmee-Sanford, FL, Selected Years, 2002–2013—*Continued*

(Numbers in thousands, not seasonally adjusted)

Industry and year	January	February	March	April	May	June	July	August	September	October	November	December	Annual average
Manufacturing													
2002	47.1	47.2	47.2	46.6	46.4	46.0	45.3	45.2	45.1	45.1	44.9	45.0	45.9
2003	44.4	44.4	44.5	43.7	43.7	43.7	43.3	43.3	43.4	43.3	43.2	43.4	43.7
2004	43.3	43.5	43.8	44.3	44.5	44.8	44.9	44.8	44.8	45.4	45.7	46.0	44.7
2005	45.7	45.8	46.0	46.4	46.2	46.3	46.2	45.9	45.7	45.4	45.3	45.0	45.8
2006	44.6	44.6	45.1	44.9	45.1	45.4	45.1	45.0	44.9	45.0	44.9	45.0	45.0
2007	44.5	44.6	44.8	44.9	44.8	44.9	44.7	44.6	44.5	44.2	44.4	44.4	44.6
2008	43.7	43.7	43.6	43.5	43.3	43.3	42.9	42.4	42.3	42.0	41.6	41.2	42.8
2009	40.3	39.9	39.6	38.9	38.8	38.9	38.3	38.2	38.0	37.9	38.0	37.7	38.7
2010	37.3	37.2	37.5	37.6	38.1	38.2	38.6	38.3	38.3	38.2	38.3	38.5	38.0
2011	38.2	38.3	38.2	38.3	38.2	38.0	37.9	37.9	37.9	37.7	37.8	37.8	38.0
2012	38.0	38.1	38.3	38.2	38.2	38.2	38.1	37.8	37.6	37.7	37.8	37.7	38.0
2013	37.4	37.6	37.6	37.8	37.9	38.1	38.3	38.2	38.5	38.4	38.7	39.1	38.1
Trade, Transportation, and Utilities													
2002	171.9	170.6	171.0	170.6	170.9	170.3	169.2	170.1	170.6	170.9	174.8	178.2	171.6
2003	172.1	171.0	171.2	170.8	170.6	170.5	171.6	172.8	173.6	175.0	178.8	182.4	173.4
2004	176.9	175.7	176.6	179.0	179.9	180.5	181.3	181.8	181.2	184.5	189.4	193.1	181.7
2005	187.7	187.9	189.2	190.8	191.7	191.8	192.8	193.3	193.2	194.4	198.4	201.8	192.8
2006	196.8	196.3	196.7	197.3	198.3	198.1	197.4	198.0	197.8	198.4	203.5	207.1	198.8
2007	200.7	201.2	200.9	201.2	203.1	202.9	202.4	203.5	204.1	205.1	210.1	212.6	204.0
2008	205.7	205.1	204.7	201.9	201.3	200.4	199.0	198.6	197.5	196.3	198.6	199.9	200.8
2009	191.9	190.1	188.4	186.4	185.7	184.6	183.1	183.2	182.6	182.3	186.4	188.0	186.1
2010	182.6	182.9	182.7	183.9	184.6	185.1	185.0	185.8	185.1	187.2	192.7	195.5	186.1
2011	188.8	188.4	188.7	189.3	189.7	189.6	190.5	191.5	191.4	193.5	199.9	202.0	191.9
2012	195.9	194.9	196.1	195.7	196.4	196.3	196.6	196.9	196.5	198.4	205.8	207.5	198.1
2013	200.2	199.6	200.0	200.1	201.2	202.2	203.3	204.2	204.7	205.9	209.6	213.1	203.7
Wholesale Trade													
2002	39.9	39.9	40.0	39.7	39.7	39.4	39.2	39.2	39.3	39.4	39.5	39.4	39.6
2003	39.6	39.6	39.8	39.7	39.8	39.9	40.1	40.2	40.4	40.2	40.4	40.6	40.0
2004	40.8	41.0	41.2	41.9	42.0	42.2	42.3	42.2	42.1	42.3	42.5	42.8	41.9
2005	43.3	43.7	43.7	44.3	44.6	44.8	45.0	45.1	45.3	45.2	45.5	45.9	44.7
2006	45.7	46.1	46.2	46.2	46.8	46.5	46.4	46.0	46.2	46.1	46.1	46.3	46.2
2007	46.6	47.2	47.1	47.1	47.3	47.2	47.2	47.1	47.2	47.6	47.6	47.8	47.3
2008	47.3	48.0	47.5	46.4	46.2	46.0	45.5	45.3	45.0	44.4	44.2	43.9	45.8
2009	42.4	42.5	41.6	41.0	40.7	40.5	39.9	39.7	39.5	39.2	39.0	39.0	40.4
2010	38.4	38.9	38.7	38.7	38.8	38.5	38.1	38.1	38.0	38.2	38.1	38.1	38.4
2011	38.5	38.6	38.6	38.4	38.5	38.4	38.4	38.3	38.3	38.3	38.4	38.6	38.4
2012	38.5	38.5	38.7	38.9	38.8	38.9	39.1	39.3	39.2	39.4	39.6	39.6	39.0
2013	39.2	39.6	39.7	39.9	40.0	40.1	40.0	40.1	40.5	40.5	40.2	40.5	40.0
Retail Trade													
2002	104.9	103.7	104.0	103.4	103.8	103.6	102.7	103.6	104.0	104.5	108.1	110.7	104.8
2003	105.8	105.1	105.2	105.0	105.0	105.2	105.8	106.8	107.5	109.3	112.8	115.5	107.4
2004	110.8	109.2	109.8	111.0	111.7	112.2	113.0	113.3	112.9	115.6	119.9	122.3	113.5
2005	117.5	117.4	118.3	119.0	119.2	119.2	120.0	120.1	119.5	120.7	124.0	126.3	120.1
2006	122.1	121.2	121.3	121.6	121.6	121.6	121.0	121.3	120.6	121.3	126.1	128.4	122.3
2007	122.6	121.8	121.7	121.5	123.0	123.2	122.6	123.3	123.2	123.8	128.4	129.8	123.7
2008	124.5	123.2	123.3	121.6	121.3	121.1	120.6	120.7	120.2	120.0	122.6	123.4	121.9
2009	117.8	116.4	115.8	114.9	114.7	114.3	113.7	114.2	113.8	113.9	118.1	119.1	115.6
2010	114.9	114.3	114.3	115.5	116.0	117.0	117.3	118.1	118.1	117.5	119.4	124.6	126.7	118.0
2011	120.8	120.3	120.2	120.9	121.2	121.2	122.1	123.1	122.9	124.6	130.5	131.7	123.3
2012	126.6	125.5	126.3	125.9	126.7	126.5	126.7	126.9	126.8	128.2	135.1	136.3	128.1
2013	130.4	129.4	129.5	129.4	130.1	131.0	132.4	133.0	132.9	134.0	137.6	140.1	132.5
Transportation and Utilities													
2002	27.1	27.0	27.0	27.5	27.4	27.3	27.3	27.3	27.3	27.0	27.2	28.1	27.3
2003	26.7	26.3	26.2	26.1	25.8	25.4	25.7	25.8	25.7	25.5	25.6	26.3	25.9
2004	25.3	25.5	25.6	26.1	26.2	26.1	26.0	26.3	26.2	26.6	27.0	28.0	26.2
2005	26.9	26.8	27.2	27.5	27.9	27.8	27.8	28.1	28.4	28.5	28.9	29.6	28.0
2006	29.0	29.0	29.2	29.5	29.9	30.0	30.0	30.7	31.0	31.0	31.3	32.4	30.3
2007	31.5	32.2	32.1	32.6	32.8	32.5	32.6	33.1	33.7	33.7	34.1	35.0	33.0
2008	33.9	33.9	33.9	33.9	33.8	33.3	32.9	32.6	32.3	31.9	31.8	32.6	33.1
2009	31.7	31.2	31.0	30.5	30.3	29.8	29.5	29.3	29.3	29.2	29.3	29.9	30.1
2010	29.3	29.7	29.7	29.7	29.8	29.6	29.6	29.6	29.6	29.6	30.0	30.7	29.7
2011	29.5	29.5	29.9	30.0	30.0	30.0	30.0	30.1	30.2	30.6	31.0	31.7	30.2
2012	30.8	30.9	31.1	30.9	30.9	30.9	30.8	30.7	30.5	30.8	31.1	31.6	30.9
2013	30.6	30.6	30.8	30.8	31.1	31.1	30.9	31.1	31.3	31.4	31.8	32.5	31.2
Information													
2002	22.5	22.5	22.4	22.1	22.5	22.4	22.3	22.6	22.3	22.3	22.5	22.6	22.4
2003	22.3	22.8	22.7	22.5	23.1	23.2	22.9	23.3	23.0	23.0	23.4	23.5	23.0
2004	23.1	23.3	23.3	23.5	23.8	23.7	23.9	23.9	23.6	23.7	24.2	24.1	23.7
2005	23.7	24.1	24.0	24.1	25.0	24.8	24.7	24.8	24.8	24.8	25.1	25.3	24.6
2006	25.2	25.4	25.7	25.8	25.9	25.9	25.8	25.6	25.8	25.8	25.9	25.9	25.7
2007	26.1	26.3	26.8	27.1	27.3	27.2	26.9	26.7	26.5	26.5	26.4	26.5	26.7
2008	26.5	26.7	26.7	26.4	26.4	26.4	26.3	26.2	25.5	25.9	25.9	25.8	26.2
2009	25.8	25.9	25.7	25.1	25.1	25.0	24.7	24.4	24.1	23.9	23.9	23.9	24.8
2010	23.9	23.8	23.9	23.8	23.6	23.7	23.7	23.9	23.7	23.7	23.9	23.9	23.8
2011	23.8	23.9	23.9	23.9	24.0	24.0	24.2	24.1	24.1	23.9	24.2	24.1	24.0
2012	23.9	23.9	23.8	23.6	23.5	23.5	23.6	23.5	23.3	23.6	23.5	23.5	23.6
2013	23.2	23.5	23.5	23.6	23.7	23.9	23.9	23.9	23.8	24.0	23.9	23.9	23.7

Employment by Industry: Orlando-Kissimmee-Sanford, FL, Selected Years, 2002–2013—*Continued*

(Numbers in thousands, not seasonally adjusted)

Industry and year	January	February	March	April	May	June	July	August	September	October	November	December	Annual average
Financial Activities													
2002	56.6	56.8	57.3	56.8	57.2	57.6	57.9	58.0	58.2	58.4	58.8	59.4	57.8
2003	59.0	59.4	59.7	59.6	59.7	60.4	60.5	60.9	60.9	61.2	61.4	61.9	60.4
2004	60.4	61.0	61.1	61.7	62.0	62.5	62.9	63.3	62.9	63.6	63.8	64.7	62.5
2005	63.7	64.5	64.9	65.6	66.0	66.4	67.5	67.8	67.9	68.3	68.6	69.2	66.7
2006	68.6	69.1	69.4	69.7	69.9	70.1	69.8	70.2	70.1	70.6	71.1	71.5	70.0
2007	70.3	70.9	71.1	70.6	70.8	71.4	70.9	70.8	70.5	70.5	70.6	70.9	70.8
2008	69.9	70.2	70.3	69.7	70.2	69.8	69.6	69.6	69.0	68.6	68.5	68.6	69.5
2009	67.3	67.1	66.8	66.4	66.2	66.1	65.4	65.3	64.6	64.9	65.2	65.2	65.9
2010	64.1	64.4	64.7	64.6	65.0	65.5	65.5	65.6	65.0	65.7	65.6	65.9	65.1
2011	65.5	65.8	66.1	65.7	65.7	65.5	65.9	65.9	66.1	65.8	66.0	66.2	65.9
2012	65.9	66.3	66.7	66.7	67.0	67.2	67.4	67.4	67.3	68.0	68.4	68.5	67.2
2013	68.0	68.4	68.7	69.0	69.1	69.7	69.7	70.1	70.0	70.7	70.8	71.5	69.6
Professional and Business Services													
2002	141.0	144.1	146.0	143.6	143.7	143.1	143.5	143.1	144.3	146.1	148.2	149.6	144.7
2003	145.1	145.9	146.4	147.4	145.7	144.1	140.5	140.6	139.7	143.7	143.0	140.9	143.6
2004	142.3	144.7	145.7	148.6	148.5	148.6	146.8	147.4	147.3	151.1	152.7	153.5	148.1
2005	154.0	155.4	156.3	158.8	159.7	159.9	159.5	161.0	162.2	163.2	165.4	166.1	160.1
2006	165.4	165.6	168.2	171.1	172.1	172.9	170.2	172.7	175.5	175.1	178.2	180.2	172.3
2007	179.2	181.7	182.3	182.5	182.4	179.3	178.6	178.0	178.3	180.5	182.3	180.8	180.5
2008	178.4	182.5	181.4	179.3	177.9	175.6	174.3	174.2	174.4	175.1	173.1	171.6	176.5
2009	166.7	166.5	165.3	164.0	165.6	163.1	160.3	161.0	163.0	165.0	165.1	164.3	164.2
2010	161.3	161.6	163.0	163.7	163.4	162.2	159.9	160.0	159.7	159.9	159.6	159.0	161.1
2011	157.4	158.8	159.4	161.7	161.8	161.5	160.5	161.4	163.6	164.0	166.1	165.8	161.8
2012	164.7	167.8	169.8	169.7	170.3	168.8	166.1	166.9	168.1	172.0	173.6	173.2	169.3
2013	169.5	173.1	174.3	175.0	176.7	176.9	174.0	175.2	175.7	178.1	178.7	179.6	175.6
Education and Health Services													
2002	86.9	87.8	88.1	88.9	89.3	88.8	88.6	89.9	90.5	90.9	91.3	91.4	89.4
2003	91.5	92.0	92.1	92.7	93.4	93.3	93.1	94.1	94.9	94.8	95.3	95.5	93.6
2004	95.2	96.1	96.5	96.7	97.3	97.1	97.1	97.4	97.7	98.4	99.1	99.3	97.3
2005	99.6	100.1	100.6	100.8	101.7	100.9	101.3	102.8	103.6	104.2	105.0	105.3	102.2
2006	104.8	105.8	106.3	106.4	107.0	106.8	106.3	107.9	108.9	109.3	109.9	110.3	107.5
2007	109.5	110.6	111.0	111.7	112.5	112.3	111.5	112.7	113.7	114.8	115.8	116.1	112.7
2008	115.5	116.3	116.6	116.6	117.2	116.3	115.3	116.0	116.2	116.9	117.0	117.4	116.4
2009	116.0	116.8	117.8	117.7	118.1	117.9	118.0	118.3	118.8	120.2	121.1	121.4	118.5
2010	120.0	120.2	120.7	121.3	121.7	120.8	120.2	120.7	120.3	121.5	122.0	121.1	120.9
2011	121.1	121.9	122.2	123.4	123.6	122.6	122.9	123.6	124.6	124.9	125.6	125.9	123.5
2012	124.3	125.1	125.8	128.4	128.5	127.9	127.6	128.3	129.3	130.5	130.9	131.1	128.1
2013	129.7	130.9	131.4	131.4	131.6	130.5	128.9	131.0	131.2	132.7	133.1	132.4	131.2
Leisure and Hospitality													
2002	156.2	161.3	164.6	164.7	166.0	170.7	168.0	166.4	164.7	164.4	165.5	166.9	165.0
2003	163.9	166.3	169.1	169.0	169.8	172.3	172.2	172.0	169.6	169.5	171.6	173.5	169.9
2004	174.1	176.6	178.4	179.9	180.0	181.3	181.7	180.3	178.4	179.1	180.5	181.8	179.3
2005	180.0	182.1	184.8	184.7	184.7	185.8	184.4	183.4	182.8	182.0	183.6	184.8	183.6
2006	183.0	185.5	188.4	188.5	188.5	188.3	187.0	186.8	185.9	184.7	187.0	188.6	186.9
2007	188.0	191.1	193.9	194.7	193.5	194.8	194.2	193.0	190.8	193.1	197.1	199.3	193.6
2008	196.9	201.2	205.0	203.4	202.5	203.6	202.6	200.3	195.4	194.6	194.6	195.0	199.6
2009	189.1	191.3	192.3	194.7	192.8	191.9	190.4	189.1	187.4	186.4	187.7	189.3	190.2
2010	184.7	189.2	193.6	195.7	196.8	198.0	197.7	196.6	195.5	198.6	199.9	201.4	195.6
2011	195.7	198.2	202.8	205.1	204.9	206.5	205.4	203.7	204.5	204.2	204.8	206.1	203.5
2012	202.2	206.4	210.7	211.2	210.5	212.6	211.7	209.3	209.8	211.3	213.1	213.5	210.2
2013	208.7	214.9	218.8	217.7	218.6	221.0	221.3	219.5	218.6	222.5	223.3	225.0	219.2
Other Services													
2002	39.2	39.6	39.7	39.3	39.7	39.8	39.9	40.2	40.3	40.3	40.5	40.2	39.9
2003	40.0	40.2	40.3	39.6	39.7	39.8	39.6	39.4	39.7	39.6	39.5	39.7	39.8
2004	40.3	40.5	40.9	40.7	41.1	41.7	41.4	40.9	41.3	41.4	41.8	41.9	41.2
2005	41.8	42.0	42.0	42.4	43.0	43.1	43.3	43.4	43.9	43.8	43.9	44.2	43.1
2006	44.4	44.9	45.0	44.9	45.4	45.9	45.8	46.3	47.2	47.7	48.2	48.6	46.2
2007	49.0	49.7	50.2	49.3	49.2	48.9	47.9	47.3	47.1	46.8	46.5	46.1	48.2
2008	45.2	45.4	45.7	44.6	44.4	43.8	43.2	42.3	42.2	41.6	40.9	40.6	43.3
2009	40.1	40.1	40.4	40.5	40.1	39.6	39.2	38.9	38.9	38.8	38.4	38.4	39.5
2010	38.3	38.4	38.6	38.9	38.9	38.9	38.8	38.5	38.3	38.4	38.3	38.1	38.5
2011	37.8	37.9	38.2	38.0	37.7	37.2	36.5	35.8	35.4	35.1	34.7	34.3	36.6
2012	34.1	34.3	34.6	34.8	34.8	35.1	34.9	34.8	34.8	35.2	35.2	35.4	34.8
2013	35.2	35.3	35.5	35.7	35.8	35.9	35.7	35.6	35.6	35.7	35.8	35.9	35.6
Government													
2002	99.4	100.4	100.5	101.1	101.8	91.0	89.1	100.7	102.3	103.8	104.4	104.8	99.9
2003	103.7	104.4	104.5	104.9	105.4	94.1	92.1	103.0	104.4	106.1	106.7	106.9	103.0
2004	106.0	107.3	107.5	107.4	107.6	96.1	94.1	105.4	108.0	110.0	110.9	110.8	105.9
2005	110.1	111.1	111.5	111.5	112.5	100.2	98.1	109.8	112.5	113.2	113.8	113.6	109.8
2006	113.2	114.6	114.5	115.5	115.3	104.4	102.1	114.6	116.1	116.7	117.4	116.6	113.4
2007	117.1	118.6	119.0	119.7	119.4	108.1	105.9	119.2	119.9	119.1	119.2	118.1	116.9
2008	117.7	118.6	119.7	119.8	120.0	107.8	105.6	117.7	118.8	118.8	119.5	119.4	117.0
2009	118.3	119.3	119.4	119.3	117.6	106.7	105.3	115.5	116.3	117.1	117.7	116.6	115.8
2010	116.6	116.8	117.0	117.9	120.7	107.9	106.5	116.7	116.3	117.7	117.7	116.5	115.7
2011	116.3	118.0	118.2	117.4	116.5	105.6	104.7	114.9	116.3	117.6	118.2	117.3	115.1
2012	117.6	119.4	119.9	118.2	117.2	106.5	106.0	117.1	117.2	118.6	119.4	118.5	116.3
2013	117.6	119.4	119.8	119.8	118.9	107.9	107.2	118.2	117.9	119.3	119.8	119.2	117.1

Employment by Industry: Oxnard-Thousand Oaks-Ventura, CA, Selected Years, 2002–2013

(Numbers in thousands, not seasonally adjusted)

Industry and year	January	February	March	April	May	June	July	August	September	October	November	December	Annual average
Total Nonfarm													
2002	278.3	280.2	281.1	280.9	282.4	284.5	281.7	278.9	283.0	283.5	287.5	287.6	282.5
2003	280.4	280.8	283.2	284.3	286.7	288.3	283.9	282.5	285.1	287.5	288.5	288.8	285.0
2004	281.7	284.2	286.8	287.4	287.8	289.5	285.8	284.9	285.8	288.8	290.0	291.7	287.0
2005	286.3	289.0	290.9	292.2	292.8	294.0	290.0	289.8	292.1	293.3	295.6	297.8	292.0
2006	293.3	296.0	297.6	298.6	301.1	302.2	297.7	297.5	299.3	299.3	301.1	302.4	298.8
2007	294.9	296.6	298.5	296.8	299.3	300.8	296.7	296.6	296.9	297.6	299.1	300.3	297.8
2008	292.0	293.9	294.0	294.5	295.3	295.3	290.0	289.2	291.0	291.3	290.5	291.3	292.4
2009	282.6	280.7	279.2	278.9	279.1	278.5	270.6	271.6	272.6	274.1	276.0	276.8	276.7
2010	269.8	270.9	271.3	275.9	278.8	275.9	271.7	272.5	273.5	276.3	278.7	279.7	274.6
2011	273.5	274.4	274.5	276.2	276.7	276.9	273.5	274.3	275.8	278.1	281.3	280.9	276.3
2012	277.0	278.3	279.1	280.0	281.8	282.5	277.4	278.1	279.8	284.6	288.0	289.1	281.3
2013	283.5	285.3	285.7	285.5	287.4	286.8	283.0	284.9	285.9	288.8	291.2	291.5	286.6
Total Private													
2002	232.4	233.7	235.1	235.2	236.8	238.4	237.9	237.2	238.6	238.4	240.8	242.0	237.2
2003	234.9	235.3	237.1	238.5	240.1	242.3	240.9	240.9	241.5	242.7	243.3	245.0	240.2
2004	238.6	240.8	243.1	243.7	244.4	245.7	245.2	245.2	245.0	246.5	247.4	249.0	244.6
2005	244.1	246.3	248.1	249.5	249.7	251.1	249.8	249.9	250.3	251.1	252.7	255.0	249.8
2006	250.8	253.2	254.6	255.6	258.2	259.0	256.8	257.1	256.7	256.8	257.9	259.3	256.3
2007	252.2	253.5	255.2	253.3	255.6	257.0	255.2	255.5	253.9	254.5	255.3	256.5	254.8
2008	248.5	250.0	250.0	250.7	251.2	250.9	248.9	249.0	249.3	248.1	246.8	247.5	249.2
2009	239.4	237.1	235.6	234.7	234.7	234.0	230.6	230.9	231.0	231.3	232.7	233.7	233.8
2010	227.2	227.7	228.0	230.0	231.3	230.9	230.4	230.1	230.2	231.5	233.0	234.2	230.4
2011	228.7	229.1	229.0	230.8	231.5	231.2	232.4	232.4	232.5	233.4	235.7	236.6	231.9
2012	233.1	233.7	234.5	235.5	236.9	237.8	236.9	237.2	237.4	240.8	243.5	244.9	237.7
2013	239.7	240.9	241.1	241.2	242.6	242.2	242.5	243.8	243.4	244.8	246.5	247.3	243.0
Goods Producing													
2002	53.9	54.7	54.7	54.4	54.8	55.2	54.4	54.0	54.2	53.7	54.2	54.0	54.4
2003	52.9	52.7	53.2	53.8	54.4	55.1	55.3	55.2	55.1	54.8	54.7	54.3	54.3
2004	54.0	54.7	55.3	55.8	56.0	56.5	56.7	56.4	56.3	56.4	56.4	56.5	55.9
2005	55.6	56.6	57.3	57.4	57.4	58.1	57.6	57.5	57.5	57.5	57.2	57.5	57.3
2006	57.7	58.8	59.1	59.3	60.2	61.2	61.1	61.2	61.1	60.2	59.8	59.2	59.9
2007	58.0	58.2	58.6	57.9	58.7	59.0	58.3	58.3	57.5	57.3	56.7	56.1	57.9
2008	54.0	54.3	54.2	54.3	54.2	54.3	54.2	53.9	53.8	53.5	52.5	52.0	53.8
2009	50.2	48.9	48.9	48.3	47.7	47.8	46.6	46.3	45.8	45.1	44.6	44.2	47.0
2010	43.6	43.6	43.7	43.7	44.3	44.5	44.6	44.1	44.0	44.1	44.0	43.5	44.0
2011	43.0	43.1	43.1	43.1	43.2	43.2	43.4	43.4	43.3	43.2	43.2	42.8	43.2
2012	42.2	42.3	42.6	42.4	42.7	43.1	43.2	43.3	43.3	43.3	43.2	43.4	42.9
2013	43.2	43.1	43.2	43.0	43.2	43.4	43.6	44.0	43.9	43.8	43.6	43.0	43.4
Service-Providing													
2002	224.4	225.5	226.4	226.5	227.6	229.3	227.3	224.9	228.8	229.8	233.3	233.6	228.1
2003	227.5	228.1	230.0	230.5	232.3	233.2	228.6	227.3	230.0	232.7	233.8	234.5	230.7
2004	227.7	229.5	231.5	231.6	231.8	233.0	229.1	228.5	229.5	232.4	233.6	235.2	231.1
2005	230.7	232.4	233.6	234.8	235.4	235.9	232.4	232.3	234.6	235.8	238.4	240.3	234.7
2006	235.6	237.2	238.5	239.3	240.9	241.0	236.6	236.3	238.2	239.1	241.3	243.2	238.9
2007	236.9	238.4	239.9	238.9	240.6	241.8	238.4	238.3	239.4	240.3	242.4	244.2	240.0
2008	238.0	239.6	239.8	240.2	241.1	241.0	235.8	235.3	237.2	237.8	238.0	239.3	238.6
2009	232.4	231.8	230.3	230.6	231.4	230.7	224.0	225.3	226.8	229.0	231.4	232.6	229.7
2010	226.2	227.3	227.6	232.2	234.5	231.4	227.1	228.4	229.5	232.2	234.7	236.2	230.6
2011	230.5	231.3	231.4	233.1	233.5	233.7	230.1	230.9	232.5	234.9	238.1	238.1	233.2
2012	234.8	236.0	236.5	237.6	239.1	239.4	234.2	234.8	236.5	241.3	244.8	245.7	238.4
2013	240.3	242.2	242.5	242.5	244.2	243.4	239.4	240.9	242.0	245.0	247.6	248.5	243.2
Mining and Logging													
2002	0.6	0.7	0.7	0.7	0.7	0.7	0.7	0.7	0.7	0.7	0.7	0.6	0.7
2003	0.6	0.6	0.6	0.6	0.6	0.6	0.6	0.6	0.6	0.6	0.6	0.6	0.6
2004	0.6	0.6	0.7	0.7	0.7	0.7	0.7	0.7	0.7	0.7	0.7	0.7	0.7
2005	0.7	0.6	0.7	0.7	0.7	0.8	0.8	0.8	0.8	0.9	0.9	0.9	0.8
2006	1.0	1.0	1.0	1.0	1.0	1.0	1.1	1.1	1.1	1.1	1.1	1.1	1.1
2007	1.1	1.1	1.1	1.1	1.1	1.1	1.0	1.0	1.0	1.1	1.1	1.1	1.1
2008	1.0	1.1	1.1	1.1	1.1	1.1	1.2	1.2	1.2	1.3	1.3	1.3	1.2
2009	1.3	1.3	1.3	1.3	1.2	1.3	1.2	1.2	1.2	1.2	1.2	1.2	1.2
2010	1.1	1.1	1.1	1.1	1.2	1.2	1.2	1.2	1.2	1.3	1.3	1.3	1.2
2011	1.2	1.3	1.3	1.2	1.2	1.2	1.2	1.3	1.3	1.3	1.3	1.3	1.3
2012	1.3	1.3	1.3	1.3	1.3	1.3	1.3	1.3	1.2	1.2	1.2	1.2	1.3
2013	1.2	1.2	1.2	1.2	1.2	1.2	1.2	1.2	1.2	1.2	1.2	1.3	1.2
Construction													
2002	15.3	15.8	15.5	15.3	15.4	15.6	15.8	15.8	15.9	16.0	16.0	15.9	15.7
2003	15.3	15.1	15.4	16.0	16.9	17.3	17.6	17.7	17.5	17.1	17.0	16.8	16.6
2004	16.4	16.4	16.5	16.5	16.5	16.9	17.3	17.1	17.2	17.4	17.3	17.5	16.9
2005	16.6	17.4	18.0	18.5	18.7	19.2	19.2	19.4	19.5	19.7	19.5	19.8	18.8
2006	19.8	20.4	20.4	20.4	21.0	21.4	21.2	21.2	21.0	20.2	19.6	19.2	20.5
2007	18.3	18.5	18.7	18.5	19.1	19.7	19.5	19.7	19.1	18.8	18.3	17.9	18.8
2008	16.9	17.1	17.0	17.2	17.1	17.2	17.0	16.7	16.6	16.2	15.7	15.4	16.7
2009	14.2	13.6	13.9	13.7	13.6	13.6	13.2	13.2	12.8	12.4	12.2	11.9	13.2
2010	11.2	11.2	11.3	11.2	11.5	11.5	11.5	11.4	11.2	11.3	11.3	11.1	11.3
2011	11.1	11.0	11.0	11.3	11.3	11.3	11.5	11.5	11.3	11.5	11.5	11.3	11.3
2012	11.2	11.3	11.5	11.4	11.6	11.8	11.8	11.9	12.1	12.1	12.3	12.4	11.8
2013	12.2	12.3	12.2	12.1	12.3	12.4	12.6	12.7	12.7	12.7	12.7	12.1	12.4

Employment by Industry: Oxnard-Thousand Oaks-Ventura, CA, Selected Years, 2002–2013—*Continued*

(Numbers in thousands, not seasonally adjusted)

Industry and year	January	February	March	April	May	June	July	August	September	October	November	December	Annual average
Manufacturing													
2002	38.0	38.2	38.5	38.4	38.7	38.9	37.9	37.5	37.6	37.0	37.5	37.5	38.0
2003	37.0	37.0	37.2	37.2	36.9	37.2	37.1	36.9	37.0	37.1	37.1	36.9	37.1
2004	37.0	37.7	38.1	38.6	38.8	38.9	38.7	38.6	38.4	38.3	38.4	38.3	38.3
2005	38.3	38.6	38.6	38.2	38.0	38.1	37.6	37.3	37.2	36.9	36.8	36.8	37.7
2006	36.9	37.4	37.7	37.9	38.2	38.8	38.8	38.9	39.0	38.9	39.1	38.9	38.4
2007	38.6	38.6	38.8	38.3	38.5	38.2	37.8	37.6	37.4	37.4	37.3	37.1	38.0
2008	36.1	36.1	36.1	36.0	36.0	36.0	36.0	36.0	36.0	36.0	35.5	35.3	35.9
2009	34.7	34.0	33.7	33.3	32.9	32.9	32.2	31.9	31.8	31.5	31.2	31.1	32.6
2010	31.3	31.3	31.3	31.4	31.6	31.8	31.9	31.5	31.6	31.5	31.4	31.1	31.5
2011	30.7	30.8	30.8	30.6	30.7	30.7	30.7	30.6	30.7	30.4	30.4	30.2	30.6
2012	29.7	29.7	29.8	29.7	29.8	30.0	30.1	30.1	30.0	30.0	29.7	29.8	29.9
2013	29.8	29.6	29.8	29.7	29.7	29.8	29.8	30.1	30.0	29.9	29.7	29.6	29.8
Trade, Transportation, and Utilities													
2002	51.9	51.5	51.5	50.6	50.9	51.4	50.8	51.0	51.1	51.7	53.0	54.2	51.6
2003	51.5	51.3	51.3	51.0	51.2	51.3	51.3	51.5	51.8	53.1	53.4	54.9	52.0
2004	52.5	52.6	53.0	52.5	52.8	53.0	52.8	52.8	52.9	53.4	54.7	55.6	53.2
2005	53.7	53.5	53.6	54.0	54.2	54.6	54.5	54.7	55.0	55.3	56.8	58.1	54.8
2006	55.4	55.1	55.2	55.8	56.3	56.5	56.4	56.4	56.1	56.6	58.1	59.1	56.4
2007	56.4	55.8	55.9	55.5	55.8	56.5	56.7	57.1	56.7	56.6	58.3	59.8	56.8
2008	56.5	56.4	56.4	56.1	56.1	56.1	55.7	55.5	55.7	55.6	56.2	57.1	56.1
2009	54.0	52.9	52.0	51.8	51.8	51.7	51.6	51.7	51.8	52.2	53.4	54.8	52.5
2010	52.2	51.8	51.8	53.0	53.0	52.9	52.9	52.7	52.7	53.4	54.9	56.0	53.1
2011	53.4	52.9	52.9	53.7	53.7	53.9	54.1	54.2	53.9	54.4	56.5	57.4	54.3
2012	55.2	54.2	54.0	54.6	55.0	55.1	55.3	55.1	55.1	55.8	58.6	59.4	55.6
2013	56.6	56.3	55.9	56.0	56.6	56.8	56.9	56.9	56.7	57.2	58.9	59.9	57.1
Wholesale Trade													
2002	11.6	11.9	11.8	11.6	11.7	11.7	11.5	11.6	11.5	11.6	11.8	11.8	11.7
2003	11.7	11.8	12.0	12.0	12.0	12.0	11.9	11.9	11.9	11.5	11.6	11.7	11.8
2004	11.6	12.0	12.2	12.1	12.1	12.3	12.5	12.5	12.5	12.4	12.3	12.3	12.2
2005	12.3	12.4	12.4	12.5	12.5	12.6	12.6	12.7	12.7	12.6	12.5	12.6	12.5
2006	12.4	12.6	12.7	12.8	12.9	12.9	12.8	12.6	12.5	12.6	12.4	12.5	12.6
2007	12.6	12.9	13.0	13.1	13.1	13.2	13.1	13.2	13.1	13.0	13.0	13.0	13.0
2008	12.7	12.9	12.8	12.8	12.9	12.9	12.9	12.9	12.9	12.9	12.7	12.8	12.8
2009	12.6	12.4	12.3	12.2	12.1	12.1	11.8	11.8	11.8	11.8	11.7	11.8	12.0
2010	11.8	12.0	12.1	13.0	12.9	12.7	12.5	12.2	12.0	12.1	12.3	12.2	12.3
2011	12.0	12.1	12.3	12.7	12.6	12.6	12.7	12.6	12.6	12.4	12.3	12.3	12.4
2012	12.3	12.3	12.4	12.6	12.6	12.7	12.7	12.7	12.7	12.5	12.5	12.7	12.6
2013	12.5	12.7	12.7	12.8	12.9	12.9	12.9	12.9	12.8	12.7	12.7	12.8	12.8
Retail Trade													
2002	34.4	33.6	33.7	33.3	33.5	33.9	33.6	33.7	34.0	34.4	35.3	36.5	34.2
2003	34.1	33.8	33.7	33.5	33.7	33.8	33.8	34.0	34.2	35.9	36.1	37.5	34.5
2004	35.3	35.0	35.1	34.6	34.9	34.9	34.8	34.8	34.8	35.3	36.6	37.4	35.3
2005	35.7	35.5	35.4	35.6	35.8	36.1	36.2	36.3	36.5	36.9	38.4	39.5	36.5
2006	37.1	36.5	36.5	36.9	37.2	37.3	37.5	37.6	37.4	37.9	39.5	40.3	37.6
2007	37.9	37.0	36.9	36.6	36.7	37.1	37.4	37.7	37.4	37.4	38.9	40.2	37.6
2008	37.5	37.1	37.0	37.0	36.9	37.1	37.0	36.9	37.0	37.1	38.0	38.7	37.3
2009	35.8	35.1	34.4	34.4	34.4	34.3	34.5	34.6	34.6	35.1	36.4	37.5	35.1
2010	35.2	34.6	34.5	34.8	34.9	34.9	35.0	35.1	35.3	36.0	37.3	38.3	35.5
2011	36.1	35.5	35.3	35.6	35.6	35.8	35.8	36.0	35.8	36.5	38.5	39.3	36.3
2012	37.3	36.3	35.9	36.4	36.7	36.7	36.8	36.6	36.6	37.5	40.3	40.7	37.3
2013	38.4	37.8	37.5	37.5	37.9	38.1	38.2	38.2	38.1	38.7	40.3	41.2	38.5
Transportation and Utilities													
2002	5.9	6.0	6.0	5.7	5.7	5.8	5.7	5.7	5.6	5.7	5.9	5.9	5.8
2003	5.7	5.7	5.6	5.5	5.5	5.5	5.6	5.6	5.7	5.7	5.7	5.7	5.6
2004	5.6	5.6	5.7	5.8	5.8	5.8	5.5	5.5	5.6	5.7	5.8	5.9	5.7
2005	5.7	5.6	5.8	5.9	5.9	5.9	5.7	5.7	5.8	5.8	5.9	6.0	5.8
2006	5.9	6.0	6.0	6.1	6.2	6.3	6.1	6.2	6.2	6.1	6.2	6.3	6.1
2007	5.9	5.9	6.0	5.8	6.0	6.2	6.2	6.2	6.2	6.2	6.4	6.6	6.1
2008	6.3	6.4	6.6	6.3	6.3	6.1	5.8	5.7	5.8	5.6	5.5	5.6	6.0
2009	5.6	5.4	5.3	5.2	5.3	5.3	5.3	5.3	5.4	5.3	5.3	5.5	5.4
2010	5.2	5.2	5.2	5.2	5.2	5.3	5.4	5.4	5.4	5.3	5.3	5.5	5.3
2011	5.3	5.3	5.3	5.4	5.5	5.5	5.6	5.6	5.5	5.5	5.7	5.8	5.5
2012	5.6	5.6	5.7	5.6	5.7	5.7	5.8	5.8	5.8	5.8	5.8	6.0	5.7
2013	5.7	5.8	5.7	5.7	5.8	5.8	5.8	5.8	5.8	5.8	5.9	5.9	5.8
Information													
2002	8.3	8.3	8.4	8.3	8.3	8.2	8.0	7.9	7.8	7.8	7.8	7.8	8.1
2003	7.5	7.4	7.4	7.1	7.1	7.1	7.3	7.2	7.1	7.0	7.0	7.0	7.2
2004	6.9	6.7	7.1	7.0	7.0	7.0	6.9	6.8	6.6	6.5	6.4	6.3	6.8
2005	6.1	6.2	6.1	6.2	6.2	6.2	6.1	6.2	6.2	6.1	6.1	6.2	6.2
2006	6.1	6.1	6.1	6.0	6.1	6.0	6.0	5.9	5.8	5.8	5.7	5.8	6.0
2007	5.7	5.9	5.9	5.8	5.9	5.9	5.8	5.8	5.8	5.7	5.8	5.7	5.8
2008	5.7	5.7	5.7	5.7	5.7	5.7	5.6	5.6	5.5	5.5	5.5	5.4	5.6
2009	5.4	5.4	5.3	5.3	5.3	5.3	5.3	5.2	5.2	5.2	5.3	5.3	5.3
2010	5.2	5.2	5.2	5.2	5.2	5.2	5.2	5.2	5.1	4.9	5.0	5.0	5.1
2011	4.9	4.8	4.8	4.8	4.9	4.9	4.9	4.9	4.8	4.8	4.9	5.0	4.9
2012	5.0	5.0	5.1	5.0	5.1	5.2	5.2	5.2	5.1	5.2	5.2	5.3	5.1
2013	5.1	5.1	5.1	5.1	5.1	5.1	5.2	5.2	5.1	5.1	5.1	5.1	5.1

Employment by Industry: Oxnard-Thousand Oaks-Ventura, CA, Selected Years, 2002–2013—*Continued*

(Numbers in thousands, not seasonally adjusted)

Industry and year	January	February	March	April	May	June	July	August	September	October	November	December	Annual average
Financial Activities													
2002	20.9	21.1	21.4	21.8	22.0	22.2	22.5	22.7	22.8	22.9	23.2	23.3	22.2
2003	22.5	22.7	23.1	23.2	23.5	23.8	23.6	23.9	23.7	23.7	23.7	23.7	23.4
2004	23.5	23.8	23.8	24.1	24.2	24.5	24.3	24.3	24.5	24.3	24.4	24.5	24.2
2005	24.1	24.2	24.3	24.1	24.3	24.5	24.4	24.6	24.6	24.7	24.8	25.1	24.5
2006	25.0	24.8	24.9	24.6	24.5	24.4	23.9	23.6	23.3	23.2	22.9	23.3	24.0
2007	22.7	22.7	22.8	22.8	22.9	23.1	23.0	22.8	22.6	22.7	22.1	22.1	22.7
2008	21.5	21.5	21.3	21.4	21.4	21.4	21.1	20.9	20.8	20.7	20.5	20.5	21.1
2009	20.6	20.7	20.6	20.6	20.5	20.4	20.4	20.4	20.5	20.2	20.4	20.5	20.5
2010	20.2	20.3	20.3	20.1	20.1	20.1	20.3	20.4	20.3	20.5	20.6	20.8	20.3
2011	20.6	20.6	20.7	20.7	20.7	20.7	20.7	20.3	20.1	20.0	19.6	19.8	20.4
2012	19.9	19.9	20.0	19.7	19.5	19.5	19.5	19.3	19.2	19.4	19.4	19.4	19.6
2013	19.1	19.1	19.2	18.8	18.8	18.7	18.9	18.9	18.8	18.7	18.6	18.6	18.9
Professional and Business Services													
2002	35.9	36.1	36.3	36.7	36.8	36.9	36.8	36.4	36.7	36.6	36.9	37.0	36.6
2003	35.9	35.9	36.4	36.5	36.7	37.3	37.2	37.1	37.0	37.2	37.4	37.8	36.9
2004	36.4	36.8	37.2	37.1	36.9	37.3	37.2	37.6	37.2	37.9	37.7	38.4	37.3
2005	37.6	38.1	38.3	39.0	38.7	38.7	38.4	38.4	38.0	38.1	38.3	38.4	38.3
2006	38.0	38.8	39.2	39.4	40.0	39.9	39.1	39.6	39.5	39.5	39.4	39.7	39.3
2007	38.8	39.1	39.4	38.5	38.5	38.6	38.0	37.8	37.3	37.2	37.3	37.4	38.2
2008	37.2	37.6	37.6	37.5	37.7	37.8	37.8	38.2	38.4	37.8	37.6	37.8	37.8
2009	36.6	36.1	36.0	35.3	35.1	34.9	34.6	34.5	34.4	34.6	35.0	34.6	35.1
2010	33.5	33.6	33.8	33.5	33.6	33.8	33.6	33.7	33.5	33.7	33.5	33.8	33.6
2011	32.7	32.7	32.7	32.9	32.9	33.0	33.8	33.4	33.2	33.4	33.5	33.7	33.2
2012	33.5	34.0	34.3	34.3	34.4	34.7	34.8	35.0	35.1	35.8	35.9	36.0	34.8
2013	35.5	35.7	36.0	36.0	36.0	35.9	36.5	36.5	36.5	36.8	36.6	36.7	36.2
Education and Health Services													
2002	26.0	26.1	26.4	26.6	26.7	26.6	26.9	26.9	27.6	27.9	27.8	27.8	26.9
2003	27.7	28.0	28.3	28.7	28.8	29.0	27.9	27.9	28.5	28.6	28.7	28.9	28.4
2004	28.0	28.3	28.5	28.6	28.6	28.5	27.9	27.8	28.1	28.7	28.5	28.4	28.3
2005	28.3	28.7	29.0	29.2	29.2	29.3	29.0	28.7	29.3	29.6	29.7	29.8	29.2
2006	29.3	29.8	29.8	30.0	30.1	30.0	29.4	29.4	29.9	30.7	30.8	31.0	30.0
2007	30.5	31.1	31.4	31.2	31.4	31.4	31.0	31.4	31.8	32.6	32.7	32.8	31.6
2008	32.2	33.0	32.8	33.4	33.6	33.1	32.5	33.1	33.8	34.4	34.3	34.6	33.4
2009	33.8	34.4	34.2	34.6	34.7	34.2	32.9	33.5	34.1	34.8	35.0	35.2	34.3
2010	33.9	34.5	34.3	35.2	35.2	34.8	34.0	34.2	34.6	35.2	35.3	35.5	34.7
2011	34.8	35.4	35.1	35.5	35.5	34.8	34.5	35.0	35.9	36.4	36.6	36.7	35.5
2012	36.5	37.2	37.1	37.5	37.6	37.2	36.2	36.7	37.2	38.8	38.7	39.2	37.5
2013	38.4	39.2	39.2	39.2	39.2	38.6	37.6	38.5	38.9	39.5	39.5	40.1	39.0
Leisure and Hospitality													
2002	25.8	26.1	26.5	26.8	27.2	27.6	28.1	28.0	28.0	27.6	27.5	27.5	27.2
2003	26.7	27.0	27.1	27.5	27.7	27.9	27.8	27.8	28.0	27.9	28.1	28.1	27.6
2004	27.1	27.6	27.8	28.1	28.5	28.6	29.0	29.2	29.2	28.9	29.0	29.0	28.5
2005	28.2	28.4	28.8	29.0	29.2	29.3	29.5	29.6	29.4	29.6	29.6	29.7	29.2
2006	29.2	29.6	30.0	30.2	30.6	30.6	30.9	31.0	30.9	30.8	31.1	31.2	30.5
2007	30.6	31.1	31.4	31.7	32.3	32.5	32.5	32.5	32.2	32.0	32.3	32.5	32.0
2008	31.4	31.4	31.8	32.1	32.3	32.3	31.9	31.8	31.3	30.9	30.7	30.6	31.5
2009	29.5	29.4	29.3	29.5	30.2	30.4	30.2	30.1	30.0	29.9	29.7	29.8	29.8
2010	29.5	29.6	29.7	30.1	30.6	30.4	30.7	30.7	30.7	30.5	30.5	30.5	30.3
2011	30.3	30.5	30.6	31.0	31.4	31.6	31.8	32.1	32.0	31.8	31.9	31.8	31.4
2012	31.6	31.7	32.1	32.6	33.0	33.3	33.2	33.2	33.0	33.0	33.2	32.9	32.7
2013	32.4	32.9	33.0	33.5	34.1	34.1	34.1	34.1	33.8	33.9	34.4	34.2	33.7
Other Services													
2002	9.7	9.8	9.9	10.0	10.1	10.3	10.4	10.3	10.4	10.2	10.4	10.4	10.2
2003	10.2	10.3	10.3	10.7	10.7	10.8	10.5	10.3	10.3	10.4	10.3	10.3	10.4
2004	10.2	10.3	10.4	10.5	10.4	10.3	10.4	10.3	10.2	10.4	10.3	10.3	10.3
2005	10.5	10.6	10.7	10.6	10.5	10.4	10.3	10.2	10.3	10.2	10.2	10.2	10.4
2006	10.1	10.2	10.3	10.3	10.4	10.4	10.0	10.0	10.1	10.0	10.1	10.0	10.2
2007	9.5	9.6	9.8	9.9	10.1	10.0	9.9	9.8	10.0	10.4	10.1	10.1	9.9
2008	10.0	10.1	10.2	10.2	10.2	10.2	10.1	10.0	10.0	9.7	9.5	9.5	10.0
2009	9.3	9.3	9.3	9.3	9.4	9.3	9.0	9.2	9.2	9.3	9.3	9.3	9.3
2010	9.1	9.1	9.2	9.2	9.3	9.2	9.1	9.1	9.3	9.2	9.2	9.1	9.2
2011	9.0	9.1	9.1	9.1	9.2	9.1	9.2	9.1	9.3	9.4	9.5	9.4	9.2
2012	9.2	9.4	9.3	9.4	9.6	9.7	9.5	9.4	9.4	9.5	9.3	9.3	9.4
2013	9.4	9.5	9.5	9.6	9.6	9.6	9.7	9.7	9.7	9.8	9.8	9.7	9.6
Government													
2002	45.9	46.5	46.0	45.7	45.6	46.1	43.8	41.7	44.4	45.1	46.7	45.6	45.3
2003	45.5	45.5	46.1	45.8	46.6	46.0	43.0	41.6	43.6	44.8	45.2	43.8	44.8
2004	43.1	43.4	43.7	43.7	43.4	43.8	40.6	39.7	40.8	42.3	42.6	42.7	42.5
2005	42.2	42.7	42.8	42.7	43.1	42.9	40.2	39.9	41.8	42.2	42.9	42.8	42.2
2006	42.5	42.8	43.0	43.0	42.9	43.2	40.9	40.4	42.6	42.5	43.2	43.1	42.5
2007	42.7	43.1	43.3	43.5	43.7	43.8	41.5	41.1	43.0	43.1	43.8	43.8	43.0
2008	43.5	43.9	44.0	43.8	44.1	44.4	41.1	40.2	41.7	43.2	43.7	43.8	43.1
2009	43.2	43.6	43.6	44.2	44.4	44.5	40.0	40.7	41.6	42.8	43.3	43.1	42.9
2010	42.6	43.2	43.3	45.9	47.5	45.0	41.3	42.4	43.3	44.8	45.7	45.5	44.2
2011	44.8	45.3	45.5	45.4	45.2	45.7	41.1	41.9	43.3	44.7	45.6	44.3	44.4
2012	43.9	44.6	44.6	44.5	44.9	44.7	40.5	40.9	42.4	43.8	44.5	44.2	43.6
2013	43.8	44.4	44.6	44.3	44.8	44.6	40.5	41.1	42.5	44.0	44.7	44.2	43.6

Employment by Industry: Philadelphia-Camden-Wilmington, PA–NJ–DE–MD, Selected Years, 2002–2013

(Numbers in thousands, not seasonally adjusted)

Industry and year	January	February	March	April	May	June	July	August	September	October	November	December	Annual average
Total Nonfarm													
2002	2,704.6	2,715.4	2,733.4	2,741.3	2,751.8	2,764.7	2,716.7	2,712.0	2,733.9	2,753.8	2,770.8	2,775.8	2,739.5
2003	2,692.1	2,693.5	2,713.5	2,731.2	2,742.8	2,750.4	2,713.7	2,704.4	2,726.1	2,748.3	2,762.2	2,767.2	2,728.8
2004	2,686.9	2,698.0	2,721.2	2,740.8	2,753.7	2,765.6	2,733.8	2,726.4	2,752.2	2,779.1	2,792.5	2,798.9	2,745.8
2005	2,716.2	2,728.7	2,741.2	2,777.6	2,789.9	2,790.0	2,765.9	2,755.3	2,781.5	2,800.1	2,816.9	2,819.7	2,773.6
2006	2,747.1	2,760.3	2,777.9	2,805.4	2,818.4	2,818.8	2,784.4	2,776.9	2,797.2	2,819.7	2,832.5	2,836.7	2,797.9
2007	2,764.7	2,770.4	2,789.4	2,810.7	2,824.4	2,831.9	2,801.8	2,792.0	2,805.7	2,835.8	2,851.2	2,851.1	2,810.8
2008	2,778.7	2,788.5	2,801.5	2,830.2	2,833.8	2,833.8	2,793.0	2,783.5	2,799.5	2,820.1	2,815.2	2,807.6	2,807.1
2009	2,718.4	2,718.3	2,714.6	2,725.6	2,730.9	2,725.2	2,685.3	2,669.4	2,686.0	2,720.7	2,724.0	2,718.9	2,711.4
2010	2,648.8	2,647.5	2,667.7	2,702.1	2,725.4	2,723.0	2,684.7	2,674.2	2,692.5	2,724.1	2,736.6	2,738.7	2,697.1
2011	2,662.9	2,674.7	2,695.6	2,725.5	2,726.4	2,725.0	2,686.3	2,676.0	2,705.2	2,725.9	2,740.4	2,742.9	2,707.2
2012	2,669.6	2,686.9	2,713.6	2,725.8	2,738.1	2,741.1	2,700.9	2,700.5	2,726.8	2,753.6	2,772.2	2,770.6	2,725.0
2013	2,693.0	2,713.9	2,734.1	2,753.5	2,763.5	2,768.8	2,729.5	2,726.4	2,751.8	2,775.2	2,795.7	2,777.6	2,748.6
Total Private													
2002	2,349.7	2,354.1	2,370.9	2,378.2	2,390.0	2,406.9	2,386.3	2,389.4	2,388.9	2,398.8	2,411.5	2,416.5	2,386.8
2003	2,339.7	2,334.5	2,352.3	2,369.5	2,382.2	2,392.7	2,381.4	2,378.6	2,378.5	2,388.9	2,399.8	2,404.7	2,375.2
2004	2,330.2	2,334.9	2,355.7	2,373.7	2,389.7	2,405.9	2,401.6	2,398.7	2,400.1	2,416.5	2,427.3	2,434.7	2,389.1
2005	2,358.2	2,364.5	2,374.8	2,410.5	2,425.5	2,430.6	2,428.2	2,422.5	2,430.1	2,438.5	2,454.0	2,457.5	2,416.2
2006	2,390.0	2,396.4	2,412.3	2,439.8	2,453.2	2,460.4	2,449.6	2,445.0	2,446.4	2,459.3	2,469.5	2,475.2	2,441.4
2007	2,410.9	2,409.5	2,426.7	2,448.0	2,463.3	2,474.3	2,468.1	2,462.4	2,457.1	2,475.1	2,488.5	2,490.2	2,456.2
2008	2,424.0	2,428.1	2,439.2	2,466.5	2,472.5	2,475.0	2,463.8	2,454.8	2,447.2	2,455.2	2,449.0	2,441.7	2,451.4
2009	2,359.8	2,354.0	2,347.9	2,357.9	2,367.1	2,364.1	2,350.9	2,338.2	2,330.9	2,354.6	2,356.0	2,352.4	2,352.8
2010	2,290.8	2,283.5	2,301.7	2,334.0	2,351.6	2,355.1	2,349.3	2,344.7	2,343.6	2,365.7	2,374.8	2,376.9	2,339.3
2011	2,310.1	2,317.2	2,336.2	2,365.1	2,370.7	2,373.2	2,364.0	2,357.5	2,365.7	2,377.0	2,389.6	2,392.1	2,359.9
2012	2,329.0	2,339.1	2,364.6	2,376.8	2,391.7	2,399.6	2,385.5	2,386.8	2,392.2	2,408.3	2,425.1	2,423.5	2,385.2
2013	2,355.1	2,368.8	2,387.2	2,407.2	2,417.7	2,427.7	2,413.4	2,414.6	2,419.8	2,432.9	2,449.2	2,432.2	2,410.5
Goods Producing													
2002	381.6	380.9	382.3	382.6	385.7	388.0	386.1	387.3	385.1	382.5	380.3	377.3	383.3
2003	362.7	358.1	360.6	364.5	368.4	370.7	369.5	368.8	366.9	365.3	363.5	359.7	364.9
2004	349.9	348.8	353.8	356.5	360.7	364.8	365.8	366.0	364.7	363.3	362.3	359.6	359.7
2005	345.9	344.7	348.2	355.9	360.2	362.4	363.2	364.3	362.8	361.4	364.5	359.3	357.7
2006	351.9	350.6	354.4	359.6	362.8	364.6	362.6	362.6	359.9	358.3	354.5	352.5	357.9
2007	343.2	338.6	342.8	346.9	350.4	354.2	354.4	354.8	352.3	351.9	351.3	347.7	349.0
2008	338.1	337.2	340.0	343.8	344.0	347.4	345.5	344.3	339.5	335.6	332.1	324.7	339.4
2009	309.1	303.2	301.7	301.3	300.8	301.2	299.3	298.0	294.3	294.5	291.1	288.9	298.6
2010	279.7	275.4	279.8	286.5	289.1	291.9	292.6	292.4	290.2	290.8	289.6	286.7	287.1
2011	276.2	275.0	281.0	286.8	287.6	290.1	291.2	291.4	289.5	289.6	288.1	284.6	285.9
2012	276.3	276.0	278.9	280.8	281.6	285.1	285.3	285.8	285.0	284.3	282.2	280.9	281.9
2013	273.7	273.4	277.2	281.0	282.2	285.6	285.7	287.4	285.8	285.8	288.3	283.3	282.5
Service-Providing													
2002	2,323.0	2,334.5	2,351.1	2,358.7	2,366.1	2,376.7	2,330.6	2,324.7	2,348.8	2,371.3	2,390.5	2,398.5	2,356.2
2003	2,329.4	2,335.4	2,352.9	2,366.7	2,374.4	2,379.7	2,344.2	2,335.6	2,359.2	2,383.0	2,398.7	2,407.5	2,363.9
2004	2,337.0	2,349.2	2,367.4	2,384.3	2,393.0	2,400.8	2,368.0	2,360.4	2,387.5	2,415.8	2,430.2	2,439.3	2,386.1
2005	2,370.3	2,384.0	2,393.0	2,421.7	2,429.7	2,427.6	2,402.7	2,391.0	2,418.7	2,438.7	2,452.4	2,460.4	2,415.9
2006	2,395.2	2,409.7	2,423.5	2,445.8	2,455.6	2,454.2	2,421.8	2,414.3	2,437.3	2,461.4	2,478.0	2,484.2	2,440.1
2007	2,421.5	2,431.8	2,446.6	2,463.8	2,474.0	2,477.7	2,447.4	2,437.2	2,453.4	2,483.9	2,499.9	2,503.4	2,461.7
2008	2,440.6	2,451.3	2,461.5	2,486.4	2,489.8	2,486.4	2,447.5	2,439.2	2,460.0	2,484.5	2,483.1	2,482.9	2,467.8
2009	2,409.3	2,415.1	2,412.9	2,424.3	2,430.1	2,424.0	2,386.0	2,371.4	2,391.7	2,426.2	2,432.9	2,430.0	2,412.8
2010	2,369.1	2,372.1	2,387.9	2,415.6	2,436.3	2,431.1	2,392.1	2,381.8	2,402.3	2,433.3	2,447.0	2,452.0	2,410.1
2011	2,386.7	2,399.7	2,414.6	2,438.7	2,438.8	2,434.9	2,395.1	2,384.6	2,415.7	2,436.3	2,452.3	2,458.3	2,421.3
2012	2,393.3	2,410.9	2,434.7	2,445.0	2,456.5	2,456.0	2,415.6	2,414.7	2,441.8	2,469.3	2,490.0	2,489.7	2,443.1
2013	2,419.3	2,440.5	2,456.9	2,472.5	2,481.3	2,483.2	2,443.8	2,439.0	2,466.0	2,489.4	2,507.4	2,494.3	2,466.1
Mining, Logging, and Construction													
2002	114.9	114.8	116.6	118.7	121.5	123.5	124.3	125.3	123.1	123.1	121.7	119.5	120.6
2003	113.0	109.8	112.3	118.9	123.0	124.9	127.3	127.4	126.6	125.3	124.6	121.5	121.1
2004	115.1	113.6	118.5	120.9	124.5	127.3	129.0	129.8	129.9	128.9	127.9	125.2	124.2
2005	116.6	114.7	117.6	125.3	129.1	131.5	133.4	133.4	132.7	133.0	134.3	130.1	127.6
2006	122.8	122.2	126.3	131.6	134.8	136.0	135.8	135.8	134.1	133.1	130.5	128.8	131.0
2007	121.7	117.9	121.7	126.1	128.9	131.3	132.5	133.3	132.4	131.8	129.9	125.9	127.8
2008	120.4	118.6	121.2	126.0	127.2	128.5	128.6	128.2	125.3	123.1	120.1	114.9	123.5
2009	104.6	101.9	103.2	104.3	105.1	106.2	106.8	106.3	103.7	103.7	101.0	98.6	103.8
2010	92.0	89.1	93.5	99.4	101.6	103.1	104.6	104.6	103.1	103.7	102.7	99.3	99.7
2011	90.6	90.0	95.2	100.8	101.5	103.2	104.9	105.2	104.4	104.6	103.3	99.9	100.3
2012	93.4	93.5	96.0	98.2	98.9	101.4	102.2	102.9	103.0	102.6	101.3	99.8	99.4
2013	94.3	94.1	98.1	101.9	102.7	104.7	105.5	106.8	105.8	106.3	107.9	102.6	102.6
Manufacturing													
2002	266.7	266.1	265.7	263.9	264.2	264.5	261.8	262.0	262.0	259.4	258.6	257.8	262.7
2003	249.7	248.3	248.3	245.6	245.4	245.8	242.2	241.4	241.3	240.0	238.9	238.2	243.8
2004	234.8	235.2	235.3	235.6	236.2	237.5	236.8	236.2	234.8	234.4	234.4	234.4	235.5
2005	229.3	230.0	230.6	230.6	231.1	230.9	229.8	230.9	230.1	228.4	230.2	229.2	230.1
2006	229.1	228.4	228.1	228.0	228.0	228.6	226.8	226.8	225.8	225.2	224.0	223.7	226.9
2007	221.5	220.7	221.1	220.8	221.5	222.9	221.9	221.5	219.9	220.1	221.4	221.8	221.3
2008	217.7	218.6	218.8	217.8	216.8	218.9	216.9	216.1	214.2	212.5	212.0	209.8	215.8
2009	204.5	201.3	198.5	197.0	195.7	195.0	192.5	191.7	190.6	190.8	190.1	190.3	194.8
2010	187.7	186.3	186.3	187.1	187.5	188.8	188.0	187.8	187.1	187.1	186.9	187.4	187.3
2011	185.6	185.0	185.8	186.0	186.1	186.9	186.3	186.2	185.1	185.0	184.8	184.7	185.6
2012	182.9	182.5	182.9	182.6	182.7	183.7	183.1	182.9	182.0	181.7	180.9	181.1	182.4
2013	179.4	179.3	179.1	179.1	179.5	180.9	180.2	180.6	180.0	179.5	180.4	180.7	179.9

Employment by Industry: Philadelphia-Camden-Wilmington, PA–NJ–DE–MD, Selected Years, 2002–2013—*Continued*

(Numbers in thousands, not seasonally adjusted)

Industry and year	January	February	March	April	May	June	July	August	September	October	November	December	Annual average
Trade, Transportation, and Utilities													
2002	529.8	521.1	525.3	523.8	527.5	531.3	524.6	526.3	528.6	535.3	545.6	557.0	531.4
2003	528.4	520.6	523.4	525.7	528.7	532.2	525.5	525.5	528.4	534.9	545.0	553.4	531.0
2004	524.9	521.1	522.9	523.2	527.7	531.1	526.4	526.0	527.2	534.0	543.9	552.4	530.1
2005	529.0	523.3	525.0	527.4	531.1	532.1	529.8	528.9	529.8	534.3	544.8	554.6	532.5
2006	531.2	523.3	527.2	527.7	531.0	532.5	527.7	526.3	527.1	533.0	544.4	551.9	531.9
2007	530.8	521.3	523.3	524.2	529.2	532.5	529.3	527.2	527.0	531.5	544.0	551.8	531.0
2008	532.0	522.2	523.9	525.3	528.5	529.1	523.5	521.8	522.4	526.6	530.0	536.0	526.8
2009	509.8	501.5	498.5	496.3	500.6	502.9	495.6	494.3	496.5	502.4	511.7	517.1	502.3
2010	497.4	488.3	491.7	494.8	499.9	502.6	496.3	495.1	496.2	501.6	511.4	520.1	499.6
2011	498.9	493.8	494.8	498.6	500.4	501.7	496.3	495.8	497.9	501.8	513.4	520.9	501.2
2012	500.6	495.5	499.0	498.6	504.3	505.0	500.4	500.4	501.7	507.0	521.1	525.5	504.9
2013	503.9	498.8	500.7	502.4	506.2	509.0	504.6	505.6	507.1	508.1	519.5	526.6	507.7
Wholesale Trade													
2002	129.5	129.1	130.1	130.1	130.4	130.6	129.9	129.9	129.2	130.6	130.5	131.3	130.1
2003	129.1	129.0	129.9	129.8	130.0	130.3	129.5	129.5	129.4	129.4	130.0	130.5	129.7
2004	127.9	128.1	128.9	129.3	129.8	130.3	130.5	130.3	129.6	130.1	129.9	130.2	129.6
2005	129.8	129.1	129.7	129.7	130.1	130.4	130.6	130.5	129.8	129.9	130.1	130.7	130.1
2006	128.6	128.7	129.6	129.9	130.3	131.3	131.3	131.2	130.3	129.9	129.8	130.1	130.1
2007	128.7	128.2	129.0	130.0	130.2	131.4	131.8	131.3	130.4	130.5	131.0	131.4	130.3
2008	130.0	129.8	130.2	130.4	131.0	131.4	131.5	131.0	130.0	130.1	129.1	128.8	130.3
2009	127.2	126.2	125.8	124.9	124.7	124.6	123.5	122.8	121.8	122.0	121.7	121.8	123.9
2010	120.5	119.8	120.2	120.8	121.4	121.7	121.6	121.5	120.9	121.1	121.1	121.3	121.0
2011	120.3	120.4	121.1	121.9	122.1	122.7	123.0	123.0	122.4	122.6	122.6	123.0	122.1
2012	121.0	121.3	122.1	122.2	122.5	123.2	122.8	122.5	121.7	121.9	121.8	122.1	122.1
2013	120.5	120.6	121.2	121.8	122.3	122.9	122.6	122.4	122.4	120.8	121.1	121.9	121.7
Retail Trade													
2002	308.6	300.9	303.5	300.8	303.4	306.9	303.5	305.4	304.7	307.4	318.2	328.6	307.7
2003	304.4	297.0	299.2	300.7	303.6	307.3	304.6	305.7	305.2	310.3	320.2	328.2	307.2
2004	305.1	300.9	301.9	301.7	305.5	308.1	306.6	307.3	305.7	311.7	321.2	328.5	308.7
2005	308.4	303.4	304.0	305.5	308.5	309.0	309.0	308.7	306.6	310.6	319.7	327.5	310.1
2006	309.4	301.1	303.3	303.6	305.1	306.1	304.2	302.8	301.3	307.0	317.7	323.1	307.1
2007	307.5	299.0	299.8	300.2	304.1	305.9	305.1	304.2	302.0	307.3	318.4	324.3	306.5
2008	308.0	298.7	300.0	300.4	302.7	303.9	301.0	300.6	298.8	302.6	307.2	312.0	303.0
2009	291.7	285.0	282.9	281.7	286.0	287.8	285.7	285.6	284.2	289.1	298.0	302.2	288.3
2010	287.0	278.9	282.1	284.0	288.1	290.1	288.3	288.0	285.0	289.8	299.1	305.1	288.8
2011	288.5	283.4	283.4	286.0	287.0	287.8	285.8	286.2	284.3	288.1	298.8	304.1	288.6
2012	289.8	284.0	286.4	287.0	291.0	291.6	290.6	291.3	288.9	292.9	305.9	308.4	292.3
2013	292.0	286.9	287.8	288.9	291.7	294.0	292.8	294.0	291.5	293.3	302.4	306.2	293.5
Transportation and Utilities													
2002	91.7	91.1	91.7	92.9	93.7	93.8	91.2	91.0	94.7	97.3	96.9	97.1	93.6
2003	94.9	94.6	94.3	95.2	95.1	94.6	91.4	90.3	93.8	95.2	94.8	94.7	94.1
2004	91.9	92.1	92.1	92.2	92.4	92.7	89.3	88.4	91.9	92.2	92.8	93.7	91.8
2005	90.8	90.8	91.3	91.8	92.2	92.5	90.3	89.7	93.4	93.8	95.0	96.4	92.3
2006	93.2	93.5	94.3	94.2	95.6	95.1	92.2	92.3	95.5	96.1	96.9	98.7	94.8
2007	94.6	94.1	94.5	94.0	94.9	95.2	92.4	91.7	94.6	93.7	94.6	96.1	94.2
2008	94.0	93.7	93.7	94.5	94.8	93.8	91.0	90.2	93.6	93.9	93.7	95.2	93.5
2009	90.9	90.3	89.8	89.7	89.9	90.5	86.4	85.9	90.5	91.3	92.0	93.1	90.0
2010	89.9	89.6	89.4	90.0	90.4	90.8	86.4	85.6	90.3	90.7	91.2	93.7	89.8
2011	90.1	90.0	90.3	90.7	91.3	91.2	87.5	86.6	91.2	91.1	92.0	93.8	90.5
2012	89.8	90.2	90.5	89.4	90.8	90.2	87.0	86.6	91.1	92.2	93.4	95.0	90.5
2013	91.4	91.3	91.7	91.7	92.2	92.1	89.2	89.2	93.2	94.0	96.0	98.5	92.5
Information													
2002	69.5	69.4	69.9	68.0	68.6	68.5	67.8	67.4	67.0	66.3	66.7	66.4	68.0
2003	65.2	64.9	65.3	64.1	63.6	63.0	62.0	61.1	60.1	58.9	58.6	57.6	62.0
2004	56.7	56.3	56.4	56.4	56.5	56.7	56.8	56.6	55.8	55.7	55.9	56.0	56.3
2005	54.7	54.7	54.9	55.4	55.5	56.1	55.7	55.7	58.6	55.7	56.0	56.3	55.8
2006	55.4	56.1	55.4	55.4	55.7	55.9	55.8	55.9	56.4	56.4	56.3	56.8	56.0
2007	56.4	56.4	56.5	57.1	57.1	57.3	58.1	57.8	58.9	58.2	58.3	58.8	57.7
2008	57.8	57.8	57.6	57.9	57.9	57.6	57.3	57.1	56.5	56.3	56.2	56.1	57.2
2009	55.4	55.1	54.8	54.5	54.3	54.3	54.0	53.6	53.2	53.3	52.7	52.9	54.0
2010	51.8	51.4	51.7	51.9	51.8	52.4	52.1	51.8	51.8	51.0	50.9	51.1	51.6
2011	50.0	50.0	49.7	50.3	50.1	50.5	50.3	47.3	50.4	49.8	50.6	51.6	50.1
2012	48.9	49.6	50.6	48.6	49.4	50.4	48.8	50.9	48.6	48.1	50.6	48.4	49.4
2013	48.0	49.7	49.3	47.6	47.4	47.5	47.5	47.6	47.0	46.9	47.5	47.1	47.8
Financial Activities													
2002	217.9	217.7	218.1	217.9	217.8	219.4	220.1	220.4	218.8	218.7	219.3	220.1	218.9
2003	219.0	219.2	219.7	220.1	220.7	222.2	223.1	222.9	220.5	219.2	219.2	219.5	220.4
2004	218.4	217.7	218.1	218.8	219.5	220.7	221.1	220.4	217.7	217.3	217.8	218.9	218.9
2005	217.9	218.0	218.1	218.4	219.3	221.1	221.9	222.1	220.2	219.8	220.3	221.3	219.9
2006	219.6	219.2	219.2	220.2	220.4	222.0	222.6	222.3	220.5	220.4	220.6	221.1	220.7
2007	219.6	219.6	219.6	219.9	220.0	221.7	222.8	222.1	219.7	220.0	220.0	220.4	220.5
2008	217.8	218.0	218.2	218.1	217.9	218.9	219.4	218.2	215.3	214.1	213.6	212.7	216.9
2009	210.2	209.2	208.4	208.2	208.1	208.3	207.9	206.1	204.0	203.4	202.6	202.1	206.5
2010	200.4	199.8	199.7	199.6	200.3	201.0	201.6	201.4	200.0	200.3	200.5	201.5	200.5
2011	199.6	198.9	198.9	198.9	198.8	199.7	200.6	200.1	199.2	198.7	198.4	199.3	199.3
2012	198.1	198.0	198.5	198.6	199.5	201.1	202.0	202.1	200.8	200.9	201.5	202.4	200.3
2013	201.7	202.5	202.5	202.9	203.2	205.0	205.1	204.8	202.8	204.0	202.7	202.3	203.3

Employment by Industry: Philadelphia-Camden-Wilmington, PA–NJ–DE–MD, Selected Years, 2002–2013—*Continued*

(Numbers in thousands, not seasonally adjusted)

Industry and year	January	February	March	April	May	June	July	August	September	October	November	December	Annual average
Professional and Business Services													
2002	377.4	377.4	382.4	386.3	386.6	389.3	384.7	385.8	383.2	385.4	386.9	387.0	384.4
2003	378.6	377.0	381.3	387.3	388.6	390.4	390.2	391.0	392.6	394.7	396.5	398.3	388.9
2004	388.4	389.5	395.9	398.6	400.8	406.0	405.7	406.0	405.7	410.0	411.0	411.5	402.4
2005	395.7	396.8	399.1	410.7	410.8	413.2	414.7	413.2	413.0	415.3	416.4	417.2	409.7
2006	404.3	407.0	411.8	420.2	421.4	424.6	424.5	425.3	425.2	428.5	430.9	432.2	421.3
2007	417.6	418.3	422.6	430.6	432.6	435.8	434.2	434.7	431.8	435.5	438.5	438.2	430.9
2008	425.4	424.7	428.7	435.4	435.7	437.0	434.4	434.0	430.8	430.9	428.3	425.2	430.9
2009	411.5	408.9	408.3	412.0	410.5	410.2	407.5	406.7	403.1	409.5	409.9	407.3	408.8
2010	396.4	397.3	399.4	408.0	409.8	411.8	411.0	411.3	409.9	414.1	415.5	415.0	408.3
2011	406.5	406.4	410.3	418.8	417.9	420.5	418.2	418.2	419.3	422.0	423.2	422.0	416.9
2012	410.9	412.5	417.9	422.9	424.4	428.0	426.5	427.9	430.1	434.7	436.8	434.3	425.6
2013	421.0	423.6	428.7	435.1	437.5	441.5	437.2	438.4	437.5	442.8	443.2	436.7	435.3
Education and Health Services													
2002	470.2	481.9	482.2	480.0	476.0	474.4	469.5	469.4	478.4	484.9	488.2	485.2	478.4
2003	474.1	483.9	484.7	485.0	480.9	477.0	472.4	470.5	479.2	487.9	490.4	489.0	481.3
2004	476.2	486.7	488.5	490.1	486.7	480.8	479.4	477.4	488.3	497.7	499.9	498.7	487.5
2005	488.6	501.7	498.8	503.4	500.8	490.3	489.7	487.4	500.0	511.3	513.1	510.4	499.6
2006	499.7	512.1	509.6	514.6	512.6	503.5	501.9	499.2	511.1	519.6	521.8	519.3	510.4
2007	511.9	524.0	525.1	525.2	522.1	513.4	513.6	511.2	520.3	533.0	533.3	531.1	522.0
2008	521.4	536.7	534.4	539.7	535.1	525.5	524.5	523.8	534.7	545.8	548.6	548.6	534.9
2009	539.0	551.5	547.6	550.0	546.0	535.9	534.4	530.8	539.9	551.6	554.0	551.4	544.3
2010	542.3	551.6	551.4	553.8	551.8	540.8	540.0	537.3	546.8	560.8	562.0	559.6	549.9
2011	547.2	560.9	561.3	562.0	558.4	547.6	545.9	543.8	556.7	565.1	568.0	567.9	557.1
2012	556.9	569.5	572.0	572.8	568.6	557.4	552.9	550.1	565.9	576.4	577.9	576.0	566.4
2013	564.7	577.5	579.1	578.0	572.2	562.1	558.5	556.4	573.0	580.5	585.7	581.2	572.4
Leisure and Hospitality													
2002	186.5	188.0	192.3	200.3	206.4	212.6	210.9	210.1	206.3	204.9	203.9	202.8	202.1
2003	192.8	191.9	197.2	202.8	210.4	214.8	217.0	217.4	210.8	207.4	205.6	205.7	206.2
2004	196.2	195.0	198.9	207.8	214.6	221.1	221.1	221.0	216.0	214.4	212.3	213.1	211.0
2005	202.4	200.9	205.5	214.2	222.1	228.5	227.4	225.8	221.4	216.8	214.9	214.2	216.2
2006	205.0	205.0	210.5	218.1	224.6	231.5	229.7	229.5	223.6	220.4	218.5	218.9	219.6
2007	210.1	209.7	214.6	221.2	227.9	233.4	231.7	231.1	224.7	222.5	220.4	219.5	222.2
2008	209.8	209.8	214.8	224.8	230.9	236.2	236.3	233.4	226.6	225.1	219.8	218.1	223.8
2009	206.2	206.0	209.6	216.7	226.7	230.3	231.8	229.1	221.7	221.5	215.7	214.3	219.1
2010	205.2	203.0	209.9	220.3	228.6	233.1	235.2	235.0	229.3	227.2	225.0	222.9	222.9
2011	212.8	213.1	220.3	228.9	236.1	240.1	239.7	239.7	232.6	230.0	228.0	225.8	228.9
2012	217.8	218.6	227.6	233.7	242.0	248.9	247.2	247.5	239.2	236.1	234.4	235.0	235.7
2013	222.5	223.4	229.2	239.3	246.9	252.6	252.9	252.4	245.8	243.0	240.3	234.3	240.2
Other Services													
2002	116.8	117.7	118.4	119.3	121.4	123.4	122.6	122.7	121.5	120.8	120.6	120.7	120.5
2003	118.9	118.9	120.1	120.0	120.9	122.4	121.7	121.4	120.0	120.6	121.0	121.5	120.6
2004	119.5	119.8	121.2	122.3	123.2	124.7	125.3	125.3	124.7	124.1	124.2	124.5	123.2
2005	124.0	124.4	125.2	125.1	125.7	126.9	125.8	125.1	124.3	123.9	124.0	124.2	124.9
2006	122.9	123.1	124.2	124.0	124.7	125.8	124.8	123.9	122.6	122.7	122.5	122.5	123.6
2007	121.3	121.6	122.2	122.9	123.8	125.2	124.3	123.2	122.4	122.5	122.7	122.7	122.9
2008	121.7	121.7	121.6	121.5	122.5	123.3	122.9	122.2	121.4	120.8	120.4	120.3	121.7
2009	118.6	118.6	119.0	118.9	120.1	121.0	120.4	119.6	118.2	118.4	118.3	118.4	119.1
2010	117.6	116.7	118.1	119.1	120.3	121.5	120.5	120.4	119.4	119.9	119.9	120.0	119.5
2011	118.9	119.1	119.9	120.8	121.4	123.0	121.8	121.2	120.1	120.0	119.9	120.0	120.5
2012	119.5	119.4	120.1	120.8	121.9	123.7	122.4	122.1	120.9	120.8	120.6	121.0	121.1
2013	119.6	119.9	120.5	120.9	122.1	124.4	121.9	122.0	120.8	121.8	122.0	120.7	121.4
Government													
2002	354.9	361.3	362.5	363.1	361.8	357.8	330.4	322.6	345.0	355.0	359.3	359.3	352.8
2003	352.4	359.0	361.2	361.7	360.6	357.7	332.3	325.8	347.6	359.4	362.4	362.5	353.6
2004	356.7	363.1	365.5	367.1	364.0	359.7	332.2	327.7	352.1	362.6	365.2	364.2	356.7
2005	358.0	364.2	366.4	367.1	364.4	359.4	337.7	332.8	351.4	361.6	362.9	362.2	357.3
2006	357.1	363.9	365.6	365.6	365.2	358.4	334.8	331.9	350.8	360.4	363.0	361.5	356.5
2007	353.8	360.9	362.7	362.7	361.1	357.6	333.7	329.6	348.6	360.7	362.7	360.9	354.6
2008	354.7	360.4	362.3	363.7	361.3	358.8	329.2	328.7	352.3	364.9	366.2	365.9	355.7
2009	358.6	364.3	366.7	367.7	363.8	361.1	334.4	331.2	355.1	366.1	368.0	366.5	358.6
2010	358.0	364.0	366.0	368.1	373.8	367.9	335.4	329.5	348.9	358.4	361.8	361.8	357.8
2011	352.8	357.5	359.4	360.4	355.7	351.8	322.3	318.5	339.5	348.9	350.8	350.8	347.4
2012	340.6	347.8	349.0	349.0	346.4	341.5	315.4	313.7	334.6	345.3	347.1	347.1	339.8
2013	337.9	345.1	346.9	346.3	345.8	341.1	316.1	311.8	332.0	342.3	346.5	345.4	338.1

Employment by Industry: Phoenix-Mesa-Glendale, AZ, Selected Years, 2002–2013

(Numbers in thousands, not seasonally adjusted)

Industry and year	January	February	March	April	May	June	July	August	September	October	November	December	Annual average
Total Nonfarm													
2002	1,568.4	1,583.3	1,594.7	1,607.8	1,603.7	1,591.9	1,564.6	1,588.0	1,599.6	1,610.9	1,634.7	1,633.9	1,598.5
2003	1,589.6	1,608.7	1,617.2	1,623.6	1,625.7	1,607.5	1,585.3	1,612.2	1,624.8	1,645.7	1,659.8	1,671.0	1,622.6
2004	1,629.4	1,651.3	1,665.5	1,680.2	1,682.2	1,667.5	1,657.9	1,678.7	1,698.1	1,728.5	1,744.1	1,760.1	1,687.0
2005	1,718.0	1,746.0	1,761.9	1,786.9	1,789.0	1,772.2	1,765.5	1,791.7	1,820.4	1,829.5	1,852.0	1,864.4	1,791.5
2006	1,833.7	1,866.2	1,883.4	1,887.7	1,895.8	1,876.0	1,859.3	1,884.3	1,905.3	1,912.8	1,927.1	1,934.6	1,888.9
2007	1,887.4	1,913.9	1,926.8	1,920.5	1,924.9	1,904.5	1,887.4	1,916.3	1,927.7	1,937.3	1,948.6	1,949.7	1,920.4
2008	1,903.0	1,915.2	1,911.9	1,902.8	1,896.2	1,857.3	1,824.1	1,854.8	1,859.6	1,854.4	1,851.5	1,839.1	1,872.5
2009	1,778.7	1,773.8	1,767.0	1,753.3	1,741.2	1,696.4	1,672.8	1,685.8	1,697.6	1,705.3	1,718.0	1,717.9	1,725.7
2010	1,678.4	1,691.1	1,701.1	1,705.9	1,710.4	1,666.8	1,648.8	1,671.3	1,683.1	1,707.5	1,724.7	1,729.6	1,693.2
2011	1,696.0	1,710.1	1,720.0	1,729.0	1,725.9	1,682.0	1,667.7	1,704.7	1,726.9	1,740.5	1,760.5	1,764.1	1,719.0
2012	1,734.0	1,748.6	1,761.5	1,762.9	1,760.2	1,730.0	1,710.2	1,752.2	1,772.1	1,789.2	1,813.1	1,820.8	1,762.9
2013	1,782.7	1,801.4	1,810.8	1,815.0	1,812.7	1,779.2	1,763.7	1,802.3	1,818.7	1,833.0	1,854.8	1,862.7	1,811.4
Total Private													
2002	1,361.2	1,368.6	1,379.5	1,390.4	1,391.2	1,391.8	1,375.8	1,384.4	1,382.4	1,388.1	1,405.5	1,410.6	1,385.8
2003	1,377.8	1,386.7	1,395.2	1,401.5	1,404.3	1,401.8	1,393.1	1,403.5	1,406.8	1,421.8	1,435.3	1,445.7	1,406.1
2004	1,415.7	1,427.7	1,441.6	1,455.0	1,457.5	1,461.1	1,460.3	1,466.7	1,471.2	1,497.5	1,512.5	1,527.6	1,466.2
2005	1,496.9	1,514.2	1,531.8	1,555.9	1,559.7	1,563.2	1,564.1	1,574.9	1,588.6	1,595.9	1,616.8	1,629.5	1,566.0
2006	1,610.1	1,632.0	1,649.2	1,653.6	1,659.9	1,665.7	1,653.3	1,663.8	1,669.9	1,673.5	1,687.3	1,697.3	1,659.6
2007	1,656.6	1,673.4	1,684.9	1,678.9	1,682.5	1,685.0	1,671.0	1,680.6	1,681.6	1,689.0	1,697.9	1,699.1	1,681.7
2008	1,653.8	1,661.6	1,658.4	1,649.4	1,644.0	1,632.9	1,611.4	1,615.5	1,608.1	1,600.9	1,596.6	1,585.8	1,626.5
2009	1,533.3	1,522.1	1,516.2	1,502.4	1,494.2	1,479.6	1,463.0	1,462.2	1,455.9	1,460.6	1,472.8	1,475.3	1,486.5
2010	1,440.1	1,446.5	1,457.8	1,461.8	1,459.6	1,452.2	1,441.8	1,448.1	1,447.1	1,468.9	1,484.7	1,492.4	1,458.4
2011	1,462.3	1,471.3	1,481.4	1,489.8	1,487.0	1,478.6	1,474.8	1,485.2	1,492.1	1,502.7	1,521.8	1,529.7	1,489.7
2012	1,502.4	1,510.5	1,523.1	1,524.0	1,526.3	1,523.0	1,513.3	1,528.1	1,534.2	1,549.8	1,572.3	1,580.9	1,532.3
2013	1,547.6	1,561.1	1,571.3	1,574.8	1,575.6	1,571.5	1,565.3	1,578.3	1,580.5	1,592.0	1,613.8	1,624.7	1,579.7
Goods Producing													
2002	265.8	265.5	266.3	266.6	267.1	268.6	268.3	268.7	266.1	263.6	262.5	260.8	265.8
2003	257.3	256.9	257.1	259.6	261.3	263.1	263.1	265.2	265.4	265.5	265.6	266.2	262.2
2004	262.2	264.3	266.6	269.1	271.4	275.0	277.4	279.6	281.1	285.0	286.3	288.6	275.6
2005	283.9	287.3	291.5	297.2	300.1	305.1	306.6	308.5	310.1	310.6	313.5	316.3	302.6
2006	312.8	317.9	321.9	324.1	326.3	329.5	328.3	327.9	325.8	321.6	318.9	317.0	322.7
2007	310.2	311.9	312.4	310.8	311.9	315.1	314.1	314.8	311.1	307.6	301.4	297.1	309.9
2008	288.7	286.5	283.9	281.0	279.8	278.0	274.4	272.7	267.9	261.3	253.3	246.2	272.8
2009	234.9	227.7	223.4	218.8	216.0	214.8	211.3	209.1	206.1	204.0	201.9	199.5	214.0
2010	194.2	194.3	194.8	196.2	196.1	197.2	197.3	196.8	196.1	197.6	197.1	196.7	196.2
2011	193.4	193.3	194.5	196.7	198.3	200.0	202.0	202.4	202.5	202.2	202.3	202.6	199.2
2012	200.8	201.8	204.3	205.3	206.8	210.0	210.8	212.7	212.9	213.3	212.9	212.1	208.6
2013	208.6	210.3	211.8	212.0	213.7	216.6	217.0	217.4	216.3	214.2	214.4	214.2	213.9
Service-Providing													
2002	1,302.6	1,317.8	1,328.4	1,341.2	1,336.6	1,323.3	1,296.3	1,319.3	1,333.5	1,347.3	1,372.2	1,373.1	1,332.6
2003	1,332.3	1,351.8	1,360.1	1,364.0	1,364.4	1,344.4	1,322.2	1,347.0	1,359.4	1,380.2	1,394.2	1,404.8	1,360.4
2004	1,367.2	1,387.0	1,398.9	1,411.1	1,410.8	1,392.5	1,380.5	1,399.1	1,417.0	1,443.5	1,457.8	1,471.5	1,411.4
2005	1,434.1	1,458.7	1,470.4	1,489.7	1,488.9	1,467.1	1,458.9	1,483.2	1,510.3	1,518.9	1,538.5	1,548.1	1,488.9
2006	1,520.9	1,548.3	1,561.5	1,563.6	1,569.5	1,546.5	1,531.0	1,556.4	1,579.5	1,591.2	1,608.2	1,617.6	1,566.2
2007	1,577.2	1,602.0	1,614.4	1,609.7	1,613.0	1,589.4	1,573.3	1,601.5	1,616.6	1,629.7	1,647.2	1,652.6	1,610.6
2008	1,614.3	1,628.7	1,628.0	1,621.8	1,616.4	1,579.3	1,549.7	1,582.1	1,591.7	1,593.1	1,598.2	1,592.9	1,599.7
2009	1,543.8	1,546.1	1,543.6	1,534.5	1,525.2	1,481.6	1,461.5	1,476.7	1,491.5	1,501.3	1,516.1	1,518.4	1,511.7
2010	1,484.2	1,496.8	1,506.3	1,509.7	1,514.3	1,469.6	1,451.5	1,474.5	1,487.0	1,509.9	1,527.6	1,532.9	1,497.0
2011	1,502.6	1,516.8	1,525.5	1,532.3	1,527.6	1,482.0	1,465.7	1,502.3	1,524.4	1,538.3	1,558.2	1,561.5	1,519.8
2012	1,533.2	1,546.8	1,557.2	1,557.6	1,553.4	1,520.0	1,499.4	1,539.5	1,559.2	1,575.9	1,600.2	1,608.7	1,554.3
2013	1,574.1	1,591.1	1,599.0	1,603.0	1,599.0	1,562.6	1,546.7	1,584.9	1,602.4	1,618.8	1,640.4	1,648.5	1,597.5
Mining and Logging													
2002	2.3	2.3	2.3	2.3	2.3	2.3	2.2	2.3	2.1	2.1	2.0	2.0	2.2
2003	2.0	2.0	1.9	2.0	2.0	2.0	2.0	2.0	1.9	1.9	2.0	2.0	2.0
2004	1.9	1.9	1.9	2.0	2.0	2.1	2.1	2.1	2.1	2.2	2.2	2.2	2.1
2005	2.2	2.2	2.2	2.3	2.4	2.4	2.0	1.9	1.9	1.9	2.1	2.4	2.2
2006	2.5	2.4	2.5	2.6	2.6	2.8	2.8	2.9	2.9	2.8	2.9	2.9	2.7
2007	2.9	3.0	3.1	3.0	3.0	3.1	3.4	3.4	3.4	3.5	3.5	3.5	3.2
2008	3.5	3.5	3.6	3.6	3.7	3.9	3.9	4.0	3.9	3.9	3.9	3.8	3.8
2009	3.3	3.3	3.3	3.2	3.0	3.0	2.9	2.9	2.9	3.0	3.0	3.0	3.1
2010	3.0	3.0	3.0	3.0	3.1	3.1	3.0	3.0	3.0	3.0	3.1	3.1	3.0
2011	3.2	3.2	3.2	3.1	3.2	3.3	3.2	3.2	3.2	3.4	3.4	3.5	3.3
2012	3.5	3.5	3.5	3.6	3.6	3.7	3.8	3.9	3.9	3.9	3.9	4.0	3.7
2013	3.9	4.0	4.0	4.0	4.0	4.2	4.2	4.2	4.1	4.1	4.0	4.0	4.1
Construction													
2002	122.2	122.2	123.7	124.6	126.1	127.9	128.2	129.5	128.5	127.4	127.1	126.0	126.1
2003	123.7	124.0	124.6	125.8	127.9	129.7	130.4	132.2	132.9	133.4	133.5	133.8	129.3
2004	130.9	132.4	134.1	136.4	138.3	140.9	143.2	144.9	146.2	149.2	150.2	152.0	141.6
2005	149.0	151.8	155.4	159.7	161.4	165.1	166.8	168.4	170.2	170.7	173.2	174.7	163.9
2006	172.2	176.1	179.5	181.1	183.1	185.6	184.3	184.0	182.6	179.4	177.6	175.5	180.1
2007	169.8	171.0	171.4	170.4	171.3	174.4	172.3	173.1	171.1	167.5	162.2	158.2	169.4
2008	151.5	149.9	148.7	146.0	145.0	143.4	140.5	139.1	135.4	130.1	124.0	118.7	139.4
2009	110.2	105.1	102.8	99.6	98.1	97.7	95.2	93.2	90.7	88.7	86.6	84.2	96.0
2010	81.1	81.3	81.9	82.8	82.3	83.3	83.4	83.1	82.4	83.4	82.7	81.6	82.4
2011	79.2	79.0	80.1	81.7	82.5	84.0	85.5	85.7	86.0	85.2	84.7	84.0	83.1
2012	82.5	83.1	85.0	85.5	86.5	88.7	89.6	91.1	91.5	92.1	91.7	90.5	88.2
2013	88.1	89.3	90.9	91.2	92.6	94.8	95.3	96.1	95.3	93.6	93.8	93.5	92.9

Employment by Industry: Phoenix-Mesa-Glendale, AZ, Selected Years, 2002–2013—*Continued*

(Numbers in thousands, not seasonally adjusted)

Industry and year	January	February	March	April	May	June	July	August	September	October	November	December	Annual average
Manufacturing													
2002	141.3	141.0	140.3	139.7	138.7	138.4	137.9	136.9	135.5	134.1	133.4	132.8	137.5
2003	131.6	130.9	130.6	131.8	131.4	131.4	130.7	131.0	130.6	130.2	130.1	130.4	130.9
2004	129.4	130.0	130.6	130.7	131.1	132.0	132.1	132.6	132.8	133.6	133.9	134.4	131.9
2005	132.7	133.3	133.9	135.2	136.3	137.6	137.8	138.2	138.0	138.0	138.2	139.2	136.5
2006	138.1	139.4	139.9	140.4	140.6	141.1	141.2	141.0	140.3	139.4	138.4	138.6	139.9
2007	137.5	137.9	137.9	137.4	137.6	137.6	138.4	138.3	136.6	136.6	135.7	135.4	137.2
2008	133.7	133.1	131.6	131.4	131.1	130.7	130.0	129.6	128.6	127.3	125.4	123.7	129.7
2009	121.4	119.3	117.3	116.0	114.9	114.1	113.2	113.0	112.5	112.3	112.3	112.3	114.9
2010	110.1	110.0	109.9	110.4	110.7	110.8	110.9	110.7	110.7	110.7	111.2	111.3	112.0	110.7
2011	111.0	111.1	111.2	111.9	112.6	112.7	113.3	113.5	113.3	113.6	114.2	115.1	112.8
2012	114.8	115.2	115.8	116.2	116.7	117.6	117.4	117.7	117.7	117.5	117.3	117.3	116.8
2013	116.6	117.0	116.9	116.8	117.1	117.6	117.5	117.1	116.9	116.5	116.6	116.7	116.9
Trade, Transportation, and Utilities													
2002	321.6	318.8	320.9	322.7	324.0	325.3	322.2	323.2	324.6	326.9	335.0	340.3	325.5
2003	326.5	325.4	325.5	325.2	325.5	324.8	324.4	325.8	325.9	332.2	340.2	345.0	328.9
2004	333.7	333.8	334.8	336.9	337.4	337.5	338.1	339.1	337.4	345.3	354.1	359.3	340.6
2005	352.1	353.3	354.9	357.4	358.0	358.0	361.0	362.0	364.1	366.7	376.3	381.4	362.1
2006	371.4	371.2	374.1	375.2	375.6	375.6	377.2	378.5	378.7	384.2	393.3	399.3	379.5
2007	386.5	385.9	386.9	387.3	388.3	388.4	389.4	390.6	391.9	394.1	403.2	408.3	391.7
2008	391.7	389.9	388.4	386.1	386.2	385.0	378.9	379.6	377.0	377.7	381.9	381.9	383.7
2009	367.0	360.7	359.0	355.5	354.3	351.6	349.2	348.4	347.0	347.4	354.6	357.3	354.3
2010	346.3	345.7	346.0	346.1	346.2	344.0	341.9	341.9	339.6	344.3	352.3	356.5	345.9
2011	345.8	345.7	346.5	348.4	347.9	346.9	346.5	347.2	347.1	351.7	361.3	363.3	349.9
2012	351.7	349.6	350.8	351.0	351.7	350.6	349.7	349.6	350.3	354.6	365.8	368.4	353.7
2013	352.3	351.5	351.0	352.0	353.0	352.9	353.5	354.9	356.0	359.0	370.2	374.9	356.8
Wholesale Trade													
2002	76.9	77.1	77.6	78.0	78.9	79.0	78.8	78.8	78.7	78.9	79.1	79.0	78.4
2003	77.9	78.0	77.8	77.7	78.0	77.8	77.0	77.1	76.9	76.8	77.1	77.5	77.5
2004	77.8	78.1	78.2	78.4	78.6	78.8	79.7	79.8	78.6	80.5	80.7	81.0	79.2
2005	80.4	81.3	81.8	82.5	82.6	82.7	83.3	83.3	83.5	83.9	84.7	85.3	82.9
2006	84.7	85.4	85.7	86.3	86.5	87.0	87.4	87.6	87.9	88.5	88.5	89.1	87.1
2007	88.0	88.5	88.9	89.1	89.3	89.9	90.4	90.4	90.3	90.6	90.7	91.0	89.8
2008	89.5	90.0	89.8	89.6	89.9	89.5	89.0	89.2	89.1	89.3	88.6	88.0	89.3
2009	86.5	85.7	84.9	84.0	83.3	82.6	82.4	82.1	81.4	81.5	81.4	81.2	83.1
2010	79.9	80.3	80.5	80.3	80.3	80.2	80.0	79.8	79.2	79.9	80.3	80.4	80.1
2011	79.6	80.1	80.1	80.5	80.4	80.5	80.4	80.3	80.4	80.6	80.7	80.6	80.4
2012	80.1	80.5	81.0	80.8	80.9	81.3	81.4	81.4	81.4	81.8	81.9	81.9	81.2
2013	80.7	81.3	81.1	81.4	81.4	81.7	81.8	82.2	82.4	82.9	83.2	83.3	82.0
Retail Trade													
2002	187.2	184.3	185.3	186.4	186.5	186.8	184.1	184.8	186.3	187.7	195.5	201.0	188.0
2003	189.0	187.9	188.2	188.2	188.3	188.1	188.7	189.9	190.0	195.7	203.3	207.4	192.1
2004	196.4	196.2	196.6	198.2	198.6	198.5	197.9	198.8	198.7	203.0	211.7	216.8	201.0
2005	210.5	210.5	211.8	213.5	213.3	213.2	215.4	215.7	217.0	219.4	227.2	230.9	216.5
2006	223.2	222.3	224.7	224.6	224.6	224.3	225.0	225.4	224.8	229.8	238.5	242.6	227.5
2007	231.9	230.6	231.3	231.2	231.5	230.9	231.8	232.6	233.7	235.6	244.5	247.8	234.5
2008	235.0	232.3	231.2	229.0	228.9	228.4	223.3	223.6	221.4	222.3	226.6	227.0	227.4
2009	215.4	210.6	209.9	208.4	208.0	206.3	204.5	204.2	203.8	204.7	211.9	214.1	208.5
2010	205.8	204.8	205.1	206.0	205.9	203.9	202.5	202.3	200.5	203.9	211.1	213.6	205.5
2011	205.3	204.5	205.1	206.0	205.5	204.1	204.1	204.7	204.4	207.9	216.7	217.7	207.2
2012	208.2	205.6	206.0	206.9	207.3	206.0	204.7	204.5	205.2	208.9	219.7	221.0	208.7
2013	207.3	205.8	206.1	207.2	207.7	207.4	208.3	209.2	210.0	213.3	222.6	226.0	210.9
Transportation and Utilities													
2002	57.5	57.4	58.0	58.3	58.6	59.5	59.3	59.6	59.6	60.3	60.4	60.3	59.1
2003	59.6	59.5	59.5	59.3	59.2	58.9	58.7	58.8	59.0	59.7	59.8	60.1	59.3
2004	59.5	59.5	60.0	60.3	60.2	60.2	60.5	60.5	60.1	61.8	61.7	61.5	60.5
2005	61.2	61.5	61.3	61.4	62.1	62.1	62.3	63.0	63.6	63.4	64.4	65.2	62.6
2006	63.5	63.5	63.7	64.3	64.5	64.3	64.8	65.5	66.0	65.9	66.3	67.6	65.0
2007	66.6	66.8	66.7	67.0	67.5	67.6	67.2	67.6	67.9	67.9	68.0	69.5	67.5
2008	67.2	67.6	67.4	67.5	67.4	67.1	66.6	66.8	66.5	66.1	66.7	66.9	67.0
2009	65.1	64.4	64.2	63.1	63.0	62.7	62.3	62.1	61.8	61.2	61.3	62.0	62.8
2010	60.6	60.6	60.4	59.8	60.0	59.9	59.4	59.8	59.9	60.5	60.9	62.5	60.4
2011	60.9	61.1	61.3	61.9	62.0	62.3	62.0	62.2	62.3	63.2	63.9	65.0	62.3
2012	63.4	63.5	63.8	63.3	63.5	63.3	63.6	63.7	63.7	63.9	64.2	65.5	63.8
2013	64.3	64.4	63.8	63.4	63.9	63.8	63.4	63.5	63.6	62.8	64.4	65.6	63.9
Information													
2002	40.7	40.5	40.1	40.4	39.9	39.4	39.4	39.1	38.3	37.7	38.3	38.5	39.4
2003	37.5	37.7	38.0	38.1	37.8	37.9	37.2	37.0	36.5	36.5	37.1	36.9	37.4
2004	36.4	36.2	36.6	36.5	35.7	35.5	34.4	33.4	32.6	32.6	32.9	32.5	34.6
2005	32.2	32.9	33.2	34.0	34.1	33.7	33.3	33.0	32.6	32.9	33.5	34.0	33.3
2006	33.1	33.2	33.3	32.8	32.9	32.7	32.1	32.1	31.3	31.1	31.7	32.1	32.4
2007	30.1	31.0	30.9	31.2	31.8	31.8	31.6	31.2	31.0	30.6	31.5	31.1	31.2
2008	30.6	31.6	32.0	31.3	32.3	32.1	30.9	30.6	31.1	30.3	30.7	30.6	31.2
2009	29.7	30.0	29.6	29.6	30.0	29.3	28.9	28.6	28.1	27.6	28.0	27.8	28.9
2010	27.3	27.5	27.8	27.8	27.7	28.1	27.3	27.1	27.0	26.7	27.2	27.7	27.4
2011	27.5	27.5	27.8	28.1	28.2	28.4	28.7	28.7	28.6	29.0	29.7	29.8	28.5
2012	29.8	30.2	30.4	30.7	31.3	31.3	31.4	31.6	31.2	31.3	32.3	32.5	31.2
2013	32.2	32.7	33.1	33.0	33.4	33.2	33.4	33.5	33.0	32.6	33.4	34.0	33.1

Employment by Industry: Phoenix-Mesa-Glendale, AZ, Selected Years, 2002–2013—*Continued*

(Numbers in thousands, not seasonally adjusted)

Industry and year	January	February	March	April	May	June	July	August	September	October	November	December	Annual average
Financial Activities													
2002	130.5	131.7	131.1	132.5	131.6	131.8	131.2	131.4	131.2	132.6	134.3	135.0	132.1
2003	133.2	133.8	135.1	135.0	135.7	136.0	136.4	137.2	136.3	136.1	136.7	137.4	135.7
2004	136.0	136.7	137.5	139.6	139.4	139.7	140.6	141.0	140.8	143.0	143.5	144.6	140.2
2005	143.4	144.8	145.0	147.4	147.6	148.0	149.2	150.3	151.0	152.5	153.0	154.0	148.9
2006	152.7	153.9	154.7	154.5	155.1	155.5	155.5	156.1	156.4	157.0	157.3	158.5	155.6
2007	156.4	157.6	158.1	158.3	158.0	157.5	156.6	155.7	154.9	153.7	153.7	153.9	156.2
2008	150.8	152.0	151.8	151.3	151.1	150.8	149.9	149.4	149.0	149.3	148.4	148.1	150.2
2009	144.7	144.7	144.4	143.7	143.8	143.2	142.4	142.3	141.2	141.0	140.9	141.7	142.8
2010	139.5	140.2	140.9	139.9	139.8	139.8	140.4	140.9	140.5	142.5	143.1	144.1	141.0
2011	142.4	143.2	143.7	144.5	144.3	144.9	145.3	146.1	146.1	146.4	147.2	149.0	145.3
2012	147.5	149.1	149.4	149.1	149.3	149.3	149.5	150.3	150.7	152.6	153.8	154.7	150.4
2013	153.5	156.2	156.2	157.1	157.6	158.1	158.2	158.7	158.7	161.5	164.3	166.6	158.9
Professional and Business Services													
2002	244.1	247.5	252.3	256.2	256.0	256.4	253.2	256.2	254.7	254.2	255.8	255.9	253.5
2003	248.3	252.8	256.2	258.3	259.4	259.3	256.2	258.6	259.8	263.3	264.1	266.6	258.6
2004	257.2	260.4	264.8	270.9	271.5	273.9	275.0	275.8	278.4	284.3	285.3	288.4	273.8
2005	279.9	284.3	288.5	294.4	294.0	296.7	298.0	300.9	304.6	304.3	307.3	308.6	296.8
2006	302.8	310.0	313.1	315.4	317.8	321.4	319.1	322.7	325.7	326.5	327.3	328.7	319.2
2007	317.9	322.3	326.3	324.3	324.6	326.5	324.6	326.8	325.5	328.2	329.1	327.1	325.3
2008	316.7	319.6	316.8	314.8	312.5	309.2	306.4	307.9	305.4	304.4	301.7	298.8	309.5
2009	285.7	283.3	280.5	277.9	274.9	272.5	270.7	268.5	267.9	271.7	274.3	274.5	275.2
2010	265.3	266.4	269.9	272.5	271.5	270.8	268.8	269.6	269.1	275.5	277.1	280.8	271.4
2011	272.4	275.2	276.8	278.5	275.3	274.6	274.8	276.5	277.0	280.3	283.0	287.2	277.6
2012	278.6	279.9	281.8	282.8	283.2	285.3	284.6	287.6	287.6	291.8	297.3	300.6	286.8
2013	295.4	294.6	297.5	299.2	299.6	301.8	299.9	300.7	299.4	302.6	304.8	305.5	300.1
Education and Health Services													
2002	149.7	151.1	152.2	152.1	153.4	153.7	151.2	154.5	155.8	158.5	160.3	161.0	154.5
2003	159.8	161.5	162.2	164.0	164.2	164.1	162.8	165.3	167.1	168.2	169.2	170.0	164.9
2004	169.5	171.3	172.1	174.2	174.6	174.7	173.0	175.4	176.8	179.8	180.7	182.2	175.4
2005	178.2	180.0	182.9	185.9	186.9	185.6	183.7	187.0	188.6	189.8	191.0	191.8	186.0
2006	191.3	194.0	196.1	197.0	197.7	197.2	196.9	200.6	201.9	202.6	203.9	206.1	198.8
2007	202.7	206.1	207.4	206.1	206.6	207.8	205.7	209.5	211.3	214.9	215.4	216.6	209.2
2008	214.0	217.5	218.3	219.6	220.6	219.6	218.7	221.9	223.9	225.1	226.4	228.2	221.2
2009	223.4	225.2	225.9	226.6	227.3	225.8	224.5	228.7	229.9	233.4	235.5	236.8	228.6
2010	234.2	235.3	236.5	236.5	237.4	235.5	234.8	239.5	241.1	245.5	247.0	245.9	239.1
2011	243.0	244.6	245.4	246.3	247.4	242.9	242.3	247.5	250.6	252.3	254.0	254.8	247.6
2012	252.0	254.4	255.0	255.3	255.5	252.0	249.3	255.3	257.6	259.4	261.1	262.4	255.8
2013	257.6	260.4	262.2	262.1	261.1	256.9	255.4	261.5	263.8	267.1	268.8	270.9	262.3
Leisure and Hospitality													
2002	148.9	153.1	155.5	158.0	157.1	153.8	148.9	149.6	149.8	152.7	157.3	157.0	153.5
2003	154.2	157.4	159.3	160.3	159.1	155.1	150.4	151.1	152.3	156.1	158.0	159.1	156.0
2004	157.5	160.8	164.7	164.2	163.9	160.9	157.6	158.1	159.8	162.9	165.1	167.0	161.9
2005	163.5	167.3	170.6	174.0	173.0	169.9	166.2	167.1	170.8	172.1	174.8	175.6	170.4
2006	175.5	179.6	182.6	183.5	182.4	180.3	175.1	176.2	179.4	181.2	184.7	185.1	180.5
2007	182.8	186.9	190.5	189.8	189.1	184.6	177.8	181.0	183.4	187.4	190.2	191.1	186.2
2008	188.0	190.4	192.6	191.5	187.7	184.2	178.6	180.0	180.5	180.5	181.6	180.0	184.6
2009	177.9	179.9	182.9	181.5	179.0	173.5	168.2	169.1	168.6	169.5	171.7	171.9	174.5
2010	169.3	172.4	177.0	179.0	176.6	172.3	167.8	169.2	170.8	173.3	176.8	176.5	173.4
2011	173.9	177.0	181.8	182.4	180.5	175.9	171.3	173.4	176.9	177.9	181.4	180.7	177.8
2012	180.2	183.5	189.0	187.5	185.7	181.3	175.8	179.2	181.7	184.2	186.0	186.9	183.4
2013	185.3	190.9	195.4	195.4	193.0	187.8	184.2	188.3	189.8	191.1	193.4	193.8	190.7
Other Services													
2002	59.9	60.4	61.1	61.9	62.1	62.8	61.4	61.7	61.9	61.9	62.0	62.1	61.6
2003	61.0	61.2	61.8	61.0	61.3	61.5	62.6	63.3	63.5	63.9	64.4	64.5	62.5
2004	63.2	64.2	64.5	63.6	63.6	63.9	64.2	64.3	64.3	64.6	64.6	65.0	64.2
2005	63.7	64.3	65.2	65.6	66.0	66.2	66.1	66.1	66.8	67.0	67.4	67.8	66.0
2006	70.5	72.2	73.4	71.1	72.1	73.5	69.1	69.7	70.7	69.3	70.2	70.5	71.0
2007	70.0	71.7	72.4	71.1	72.2	73.3	71.2	71.0	72.5	72.5	73.4	73.9	72.1
2008	73.3	74.1	74.6	73.8	73.8	74.0	73.6	73.4	73.3	72.3	72.6	72.0	73.4
2009	70.0	70.6	70.5	68.8	68.9	68.9	67.8	67.5	67.1	66.0	65.9	65.8	68.2
2010	64.0	64.7	64.9	63.8	64.3	64.5	63.5	63.1	62.9	63.5	64.1	64.2	64.0
2011	63.9	64.8	64.9	64.9	65.1	65.0	63.9	63.4	63.3	62.9	62.9	62.3	63.9
2012	61.8	62.0	62.4	62.3	62.8	63.2	62.2	61.8	62.2	62.6	63.1	63.3	62.5
2013	62.7	64.5	64.1	64.0	64.2	64.2	63.7	63.3	63.5	63.9	64.5	64.8	64.0
Government													
2002	207.2	214.7	215.2	217.4	212.5	200.1	188.8	203.6	217.2	222.8	229.2	223.3	212.7
2003	211.8	222.0	222.0	222.1	221.4	205.7	192.2	208.7	218.0	223.9	224.5	225.3	216.5
2004	213.7	223.6	223.9	225.2	224.7	206.4	197.6	212.0	226.9	231.0	231.6	232.5	220.8
2005	221.1	231.8	230.1	231.0	229.3	209.0	201.4	216.8	231.8	233.6	235.2	234.9	225.5
2006	223.6	234.2	234.2	234.1	235.9	210.3	206.0	220.5	235.4	239.3	239.8	237.3	229.2
2007	230.8	240.5	241.9	241.6	242.4	219.5	216.4	235.7	246.1	248.3	250.7	250.6	238.7
2008	249.2	253.6	253.5	253.4	252.2	224.4	212.7	239.3	251.5	253.5	254.9	253.3	246.0
2009	245.4	251.7	250.8	250.9	247.0	216.8	209.8	223.6	241.7	244.7	245.2	242.6	239.2
2010	238.3	244.6	243.3	244.1	250.8	214.6	207.0	223.2	236.0	238.6	240.0	237.2	234.8
2011	233.7	238.8	238.6	239.2	238.9	203.4	192.9	219.5	234.8	237.8	238.7	234.4	229.2
2012	231.6	238.1	238.4	238.9	233.9	207.0	196.9	224.1	237.9	239.4	240.8	239.9	230.6
2013	235.1	240.3	239.5	240.2	237.1	207.7	198.4	224.0	238.2	241.0	241.0	238.0	231.7

Employment by Industry: Pittsburgh, PA, Selected Years, 2002–2013

(Numbers in thousands, not seasonally adjusted)

Industry and year	January	February	March	April	May	June	July	August	September	October	November	December	Annual average
Total Nonfarm													
2002	1,123.3	1,125.7	1,134.2	1,142.3	1,153.6	1,158.7	1,141.6	1,139.5	1,146.4	1,148.9	1,149.3	1,141.3	1,142.1
2003	1,117.8	1,113.2	1,121.5	1,134.2	1,141.8	1,147.6	1,130.0	1,128.2	1,137.8	1,145.6	1,146.4	1,143.9	1,134.0
2004	1,110.6	1,110.2	1,122.3	1,133.3	1,143.5	1,151.8	1,134.4	1,127.4	1,137.7	1,143.2	1,145.3	1,143.3	1,133.6
2005	1,110.9	1,110.8	1,118.2	1,134.7	1,142.6	1,147.7	1,133.6	1,129.6	1,138.9	1,141.0	1,144.3	1,141.2	1,132.8
2006	1,110.3	1,115.0	1,124.9	1,135.7	1,145.4	1,151.5	1,136.1	1,130.9	1,144.3	1,149.1	1,151.1	1,150.7	1,137.1
2007	1,120.3	1,119.9	1,132.3	1,142.0	1,156.1	1,164.4	1,147.4	1,145.0	1,151.8	1,157.8	1,159.7	1,156.7	1,146.1
2008	1,125.9	1,128.0	1,135.5	1,150.2	1,161.9	1,165.3	1,151.1	1,147.6	1,154.7	1,160.1	1,157.0	1,149.6	1,148.9
2009	1,112.5	1,111.4	1,114.3	1,123.2	1,131.4	1,132.6	1,115.9	1,111.6	1,119.3	1,124.8	1,126.8	1,124.8	1,120.7
2010	1,090.6	1,088.4	1,102.7	1,122.2	1,134.1	1,142.1	1,130.0	1,127.4	1,135.5	1,143.1	1,144.6	1,143.3	1,125.3
2011	1,116.1	1,118.0	1,128.3	1,142.7	1,152.9	1,160.3	1,144.1	1,140.1	1,153.3	1,160.4	1,162.9	1,159.8	1,144.9
2012	1,130.3	1,137.4	1,151.0	1,160.7	1,168.4	1,170.9	1,154.5	1,150.3	1,160.0	1,169.2	1,170.8	1,165.6	1,157.4
2013	1,133.7	1,140.8	1,148.1	1,158.2	1,167.5	1,169.5	1,156.9	1,153.1	1,162.4	1,169.6	1,171.5	1,162.7	1,157.8
Total Private													
2002	994.9	994.0	1,002.4	1,010.3	1,021.4	1,028.3	1,021.4	1,022.2	1,018.5	1,016.5	1,015.4	1,008.8	1,012.8
2003	987.8	980.5	987.9	1,001.2	1,009.6	1,016.7	1,011.6	1,012.4	1,009.3	1,012.8	1,012.8	1,011.7	1,004.5
2004	981.4	979.0	990.1	1,000.5	1,011.2	1,020.8	1,016.7	1,013.8	1,010.7	1,012.7	1,013.5	1,012.7	1,005.3
2005	983.1	980.8	987.3	1,003.7	1,012.3	1,018.3	1,017.6	1,017.6	1,013.2	1,011.7	1,013.1	1,011.1	1,005.8
2006	983.4	984.9	994.2	1,005.1	1,015.0	1,022.3	1,018.9	1,017.3	1,017.6	1,019.7	1,020.4	1,020.7	1,010.0
2007	993.6	990.4	1,002.0	1,012.2	1,027.5	1,037.1	1,029.8	1,028.8	1,026.4	1,029.4	1,030.2	1,027.6	1,019.6
2008	1,000.5	999.3	1,006.2	1,021.1	1,033.6	1,038.7	1,032.7	1,030.5	1,028.3	1,030.3	1,026.8	1,020.6	1,022.4
2009	987.3	982.6	985.1	992.9	1,002.2	1,004.9	996.5	993.7	992.4	994.7	995.2	993.9	993.5
2010	964.9	958.8	972.1	990.8	1,000.8	1,011.0	1,009.8	1,009.6	1,008.3	1,012.9	1,014.1	1,013.2	997.2
2011	989.5	988.7	998.3	1,013.2	1,025.1	1,034.4	1,028.7	1,026.8	1,031.7	1,035.8	1,037.2	1,034.3	1,020.3
2012	1,010.8	1,013.2	1,026.5	1,036.4	1,044.2	1,049.7	1,041.9	1,038.6	1,040.0	1,046.6	1,047.1	1,042.3	1,036.4
2013	1,015.3	1,018.0	1,025.2	1,035.2	1,044.0	1,050.4	1,046.4	1,043.2	1,043.6	1,048.4	1,049.6	1,040.8	1,038.3
Goods Producing													
2002	172.5	173.1	174.9	178.3	181.1	182.6	181.3	182.7	180.8	180.0	176.7	172.2	178.0
2003	166.5	163.5	166.2	169.6	170.8	172.1	171.6	171.2	169.6	168.9	166.5	162.7	168.3
2004	154.4	153.1	156.8	160.8	164.2	166.8	167.0	165.9	164.6	164.0	162.0	159.0	161.6
2005	151.9	150.8	152.6	158.3	160.7	162.0	163.0	164.0	163.5	162.4	161.1	157.3	159.0
2006	152.1	152.5	155.8	159.5	161.5	163.0	164.2	164.9	164.8	163.7	162.7	160.5	160.4
2007	155.7	153.3	157.5	161.1	164.8	166.8	166.3	166.0	165.4	164.9	163.1	159.2	162.0
2008	154.2	152.6	155.3	160.3	163.6	165.3	165.7	165.8	165.0	164.6	160.7	156.1	160.8
2009	148.2	146.2	146.7	148.2	148.8	149.5	148.1	147.0	146.5	146.9	145.0	141.0	146.8
2010	134.0	131.9	136.5	142.8	145.3	147.2	149.0	148.8	147.8	147.6	146.9	143.3	143.4
2011	137.7	137.7	141.7	145.9	149.2	151.9	153.6	154.0	154.3	154.7	153.3	150.4	148.7
2012	145.5	145.6	148.3	153.1	155.4	157.6	158.0	157.8	157.7	158.5	155.5	151.9	153.7
2013	146.2	146.3	148.7	152.1	154.8	156.6	156.8	156.8	156.1	156.9	155.7	151.1	153.2
Service-Providing													
2002	950.8	952.6	959.3	964.0	972.5	976.1	960.3	956.8	965.6	968.9	972.6	969.1	964.1
2003	951.3	949.7	955.3	964.6	971.0	975.5	958.4	957.0	968.2	976.7	979.9	981.2	965.7
2004	956.2	957.1	965.5	972.5	979.3	985.0	967.4	961.5	973.1	979.2	983.3	984.3	972.0
2005	959.0	960.0	965.6	976.4	981.9	985.7	970.6	965.6	975.4	978.6	983.2	983.9	973.8
2006	958.2	962.5	969.1	976.2	983.9	988.5	971.9	966.0	979.5	985.4	988.4	990.2	976.7
2007	964.6	966.6	974.8	980.9	991.3	997.6	981.1	979.0	986.4	992.9	996.6	997.5	984.1
2008	971.7	975.4	980.2	989.9	998.3	1,000.0	985.4	981.8	989.7	995.5	996.3	993.5	988.1
2009	964.3	965.2	967.6	975.0	982.6	983.1	967.8	964.6	972.8	977.9	981.8	983.8	973.9
2010	956.6	956.5	966.2	979.4	988.8	994.9	981.0	978.6	987.7	995.5	997.7	1,000.0	981.9
2011	978.4	980.3	986.6	996.8	1,003.7	1,008.4	990.5	986.1	999.0	1,005.7	1,009.6	1,009.4	996.2
2012	984.8	991.8	1,002.7	1,007.6	1,013.0	1,013.3	996.5	992.5	1,002.3	1,010.7	1,015.3	1,013.7	1,003.7
2013	987.5	994.5	999.4	1,006.1	1,012.7	1,012.9	1,000.1	996.3	1,006.3	1,012.7	1,015.8	1,011.6	1,004.7
Mining and Logging													
2005	5.1	5.1	4.7	5.1	5.0	5.0	5.0	5.0	5.0	4.9	5.0	5.0	5.0
2006	4.9	4.9	4.9	4.9	4.9	4.9	4.9	4.9	4.8	4.8	4.8	4.8	4.9
2007	4.8	4.7	4.7	4.7	4.8	4.9	5.0	5.0	4.9	4.9	5.0	5.0	4.9
2008	5.0	5.0	5.0	5.1	5.3	5.5	5.5	5.6	5.6	5.7	5.7	5.7	5.4
2009	5.6	5.5	5.3	5.4	5.4	5.5	5.6	5.6	5.7	5.8	5.9	5.9	5.6
2010	5.9	6.0	6.2	6.4	6.5	6.7	6.9	7.1	7.3	7.2	7.3	7.4	6.7
2011	7.5	7.7	7.9	8.2	8.4	8.6	8.9	9.0	9.1	9.2	9.4	9.5	8.6
2012	9.6	9.6	9.7	9.8	9.9	10.0	10.0	10.1	10.1	10.1	10.1	10.1	9.9
2013	10.1	10.2	10.4	10.6	10.7	10.7	10.6	10.6	10.6	10.6	10.4	10.5	10.5
Construction													
2005	46.0	45.3	47.0	52.3	54.8	55.6	57.0	57.9	57.9	57.3	56.0	52.1	53.3
2006	48.1	48.6	51.4	54.7	56.3	57.2	58.4	59.1	59.6	58.5	57.1	54.7	55.3
2007	50.6	48.7	52.5	55.8	59.2	60.5	60.5	60.6	60.8	60.4	58.3	54.4	56.9
2008	50.6	49.2	51.6	56.7	59.4	60.4	61.0	61.4	61.1	60.9	57.8	53.9	57.0
2009	48.7	48.9	50.8	53.1	54.8	55.6	54.9	54.4	54.2	54.0	51.8	47.4	52.4
2010	41.7	40.0	44.0	49.7	51.9	52.6	53.9	53.6	52.7	52.4	51.2	47.5	49.3
2011	42.6	42.3	45.7	49.3	52.2	54.1	55.1	55.6	55.8	56.2	54.5	51.4	51.2
2012	47.1	47.2	49.6	54.1	55.8	57.1	57.4	57.0	57.4	58.3	55.1	51.8	54.0
2013	46.6	46.9	49.0	52.2	54.8	55.9	56.5	56.6	56.4	57.5	56.1	51.8	53.4

Employment by Industry: Pittsburgh, PA, Selected Years, 2002–2013—*Continued*

(Numbers in thousands, not seasonally adjusted)

Industry and year	January	February	March	April	May	June	July	August	September	October	November	December	Annual average
Manufacturing													
2002	116.5	115.9	115.5	115.3	115.5	116.0	114.9	115.0	114.5	114.4	113.7	113.5	115.1
2003	112.4	110.2	110.0	110.4	109.7	109.6	108.3	107.3	106.3	105.5	104.7	104.5	108.2
2004	102.8	102.2	102.5	103.2	103.0	103.9	103.4	103.1	102.7	102.4	102.4	102.3	102.8
2005	100.8	100.4	100.9	100.9	100.9	101.4	101.0	101.1	100.6	100.2	100.1	100.2	100.7
2006	99.1	99.0	99.5	99.9	100.3	100.9	100.9	100.9	100.4	100.4	100.8	101.0	100.3
2007	100.3	99.9	100.3	100.6	100.8	101.4	100.8	100.4	99.7	99.6	99.8	99.8	100.3
2008	98.6	98.4	98.7	98.5	98.9	99.4	99.2	98.8	98.3	98.0	97.2	96.5	98.4
2009	93.9	91.8	90.6	89.7	88.6	88.4	87.6	87.0	86.6	87.1	87.3	87.7	88.9
2010	86.4	85.9	86.3	86.7	86.9	86.9	87.9	88.2	88.1	87.8	88.0	88.4	87.4
2011	87.6	87.7	88.1	88.4	88.6	89.2	89.6	89.4	89.4	89.3	89.4	89.5	88.9
2012	88.8	88.8	89.0	89.2	89.7	90.5	90.6	90.7	90.2	90.1	90.3	90.0	89.8
2013	89.5	89.2	89.3	89.3	89.3	90.0	89.7	89.6	89.1	89.0	89.1	88.6	89.3
Trade, Transportation, and Utilities													
2002	236.6	233.5	234.6	235.2	236.9	237.6	233.9	234.0	234.5	236.3	239.9	241.6	236.2
2003	231.2	227.9	228.2	230.0	231.9	232.7	229.6	230.6	231.7	235.0	238.5	241.4	232.4
2004	231.9	229.5	230.7	231.3	232.6	232.8	229.3	229.2	229.3	231.2	234.6	237.3	231.6
2005	226.6	224.0	224.8	225.9	227.6	227.9	225.5	225.9	225.7	227.8	231.9	235.3	227.4
2006	226.3	223.2	224.4	224.5	226.3	226.2	222.7	223.0	224.5	226.9	230.7	233.9	226.1
2007	225.9	221.5	223.3	223.4	225.9	226.2	222.8	222.1	222.6	224.2	228.8	231.3	224.8
2008	223.6	220.0	220.9	221.1	223.3	223.2	219.4	218.7	220.3	222.6	225.0	227.6	222.1
2009	217.2	213.8	213.0	213.5	215.3	214.5	210.2	210.1	211.3	213.0	217.3	219.4	214.1
2010	211.6	208.0	210.1	211.6	214.0	215.3	212.2	212.5	213.8	217.0	220.8	224.2	214.3
2011	215.3	213.1	213.8	215.6	217.5	217.1	214.4	214.4	216.2	218.1	222.5	225.3	216.9
2012	217.0	214.9	216.7	216.8	218.0	217.2	213.8	212.9	214.5	216.5	221.7	223.3	216.9
2013	214.2	211.6	212.2	212.7	214.8	214.9	212.0	212.7	213.7	214.8	220.1	222.6	214.7
Wholesale Trade													
2002	45.3	45.1	45.2	45.6	46.0	46.3	45.9	45.7	45.4	45.6	45.7	45.4	45.6
2003	45.2	45.1	45.2	45.6	45.8	45.9	46.0	45.9	45.9	46.3	46.4	46.6	45.8
2004	45.8	45.7	45.9	45.8	46.1	46.6	46.7	46.7	46.2	46.3	46.3	46.4	46.2
2005	46.4	46.6	46.7	47.0	47.4	47.7	47.7	47.8	47.6	47.8	48.0	48.1	47.4
2006	48.0	48.0	48.1	48.3	48.7	49.1	49.1	49.2	48.9	49.2	49.1	49.4	48.8
2007	49.1	48.9	49.2	49.1	49.2	49.5	49.5	49.6	49.1	49.0	49.1	49.1	49.2
2008	48.9	48.8	48.9	49.2	49.5	49.7	49.5	49.4	49.0	49.0	48.7	48.6	49.1
2009	47.8	47.4	47.1	46.9	46.9	46.7	46.3	46.1	45.8	45.6	45.5	45.5	46.5
2010	45.3	44.9	45.4	46.0	46.2	46.4	46.7	46.9	46.6	47.1	46.9	47.1	46.3
2011	46.6	46.6	46.9	47.3	47.6	47.3	47.2	47.3	46.9	47.0	46.9	46.9	47.0
2012	46.4	46.6	47.0	47.1	46.8	46.9	46.6	46.3	45.9	45.8	45.7	45.7	46.4
2013	45.0	44.8	45.0	45.2	45.4	45.7	45.5	45.6	45.4	45.4	45.4	45.7	45.3
Retail Trade													
2002	138.1	135.5	136.3	136.7	138.0	139.3	138.4	138.5	137.1	138.0	142.1	144.8	138.6
2003	136.6	133.8	134.3	135.7	137.0	138.2	137.5	138.2	136.9	138.8	142.2	145.1	137.9
2004	137.7	135.6	136.4	136.9	137.8	138.4	137.7	137.4	135.5	136.5	140.3	142.5	137.7
2005	133.9	131.5	132.0	132.8	134.0	134.7	135.0	135.0	132.0	133.8	137.5	140.3	134.4
2006	132.6	129.8	130.6	130.6	131.8	132.4	131.2	131.5	129.8	131.8	135.9	138.3	132.2
2007	131.6	127.7	129.0	129.0	131.2	131.9	131.4	130.9	128.7	130.6	135.3	137.4	131.2
2008	130.9	127.6	128.5	128.0	129.3	129.8	129.2	128.7	127.5	129.0	131.6	133.8	129.5
2009	126.1	123.3	123.2	123.8	125.6	126.2	125.3	125.4	123.7	125.2	129.3	130.8	125.7
2010	124.7	121.8	123.1	123.7	125.6	126.6	126.5	126.6	124.6	126.7	130.4	132.6	126.1
2011	126.0	123.7	124.1	125.2	126.7	127.3	127.5	127.9	126.1	127.5	131.6	133.5	127.3
2012	127.2	124.9	126.0	126.2	127.4	128.1	127.4	127.0	125.3	127.0	132.0	132.8	127.6
2013	125.9	123.7	124.0	124.3	125.9	127.0	126.5	126.8	124.8	125.6	130.1	131.8	126.4
Transportation and Utilities													
2002	53.2	52.9	53.1	52.9	52.9	52.0	49.6	49.8	52.0	52.7	52.1	51.4	52.1
2003	49.4	49.0	48.7	48.7	49.1	48.6	46.1	46.5	48.9	49.9	49.9	49.7	48.7
2004	48.4	48.2	48.4	48.6	48.7	47.8	44.9	45.1	47.6	48.4	48.0	48.4	47.7
2005	46.3	45.9	46.1	46.1	46.2	45.5	42.8	43.1	46.1	46.2	46.4	46.9	45.6
2006	45.7	45.4	45.7	45.6	45.8	44.7	42.4	42.3	45.8	45.9	45.7	46.2	45.1
2007	45.2	44.9	45.1	45.3	45.5	44.8	41.9	41.6	44.8	44.6	44.4	44.8	44.4
2008	43.8	43.6	43.5	43.9	44.5	43.7	40.7	40.6	43.8	44.6	44.7	45.2	43.6
2009	43.3	43.1	42.7	42.8	42.8	41.6	38.6	38.6	41.8	42.2	42.5	43.1	41.9
2010	41.6	41.3	41.6	41.9	42.2	42.3	39.0	39.0	42.6	43.2	43.5	44.5	41.9
2011	42.7	42.8	42.8	43.1	43.2	42.5	39.7	39.2	43.2	43.6	44.0	44.9	42.6
2012	43.4	43.4	43.7	43.5	43.8	42.2	39.8	39.6	43.3	43.7	44.0	44.8	42.9
2013	43.3	43.1	43.2	43.2	43.5	42.2	40.0	40.3	43.5	43.8	44.6	45.1	43.0
Information													
2002	26.7	26.4	26.4	26.1	26.3	26.1	25.9	25.8	25.4	25.2	25.5	25.5	25.9
2003	25.6	25.4	25.6	25.3	25.5	25.5	25.2	25.3	24.9	24.7	24.9	25.1	25.3
2004	24.8	24.5	24.5	24.2	24.3	24.3	24.1	23.8	23.5	23.3	23.2	23.1	24.0
2005	23.2	23.0	23.0	23.0	23.3	23.5	23.3	23.2	22.9	23.0	23.2	23.3	23.2
2006	22.9	22.9	23.0	23.0	23.0	23.1	23.0	22.9	22.6	22.6	22.4	22.7	22.8
2007	22.0	21.9	22.1	21.8	21.9	22.2	21.9	21.8	21.4	21.2	21.2	21.6	21.8
2008	21.3	21.2	21.1	21.3	21.4	21.3	20.8	20.5	20.2	20.1	20.1	20.2	20.8
2009	19.9	19.8	19.8	19.9	19.8	20.0	19.8	19.5	19.3	19.7	19.6	20.3	19.8
2010	18.6	18.5	18.2	18.4	18.4	18.9	18.8	18.5	18.7	18.1	18.2	18.3	18.5
2011	18.2	18.2	18.3	18.5	18.7	18.9	18.8	17.3	18.5	18.6	18.9	18.3	18.4
2012	18.2	18.2	18.5	18.5	19.5	19.0	18.8	18.9	18.7	18.6	18.7	18.5	18.7
2013	18.6	18.2	18.2	18.1	18.3	18.3	18.5	18.4	18.4	18.4	18.6	18.5	18.4

Employment by Industry: Pittsburgh, PA, Selected Years, 2002–2013—*Continued*

(Numbers in thousands, not seasonally adjusted)

Industry and year	January	February	March	April	May	June	July	August	September	October	November	December	Annual average
Financial Activities													
2002	67.7	68.0	68.3	68.0	68.6	69.1	69.1	69.1	68.5	68.2	68.3	68.6	68.5
2003	69.0	68.9	69.2	69.8	70.3	70.7	71.2	71.2	70.6	70.2	70.2	70.3	70.1
2004	70.0	69.7	69.9	69.5	69.8	70.2	70.3	70.0	69.1	69.0	68.9	69.1	69.6
2005	68.7	68.6	68.9	69.0	69.3	69.5	70.1	70.0	69.2	69.1	69.2	69.2	69.2
2006	68.1	68.3	68.4	68.7	69.0	69.6	69.0	68.8	67.9	67.7	67.7	67.9	68.4
2007	67.6	67.8	68.0	67.8	68.2	68.8	68.9	68.8	68.0	67.7	67.8	67.6	68.1
2008	66.8	67.1	67.5	67.7	68.3	69.0	68.9	68.8	67.6	67.4	67.4	67.4	67.8
2009	66.9	66.9	66.8	67.0	67.4	68.1	68.1	68.0	67.4	67.7	67.9	68.1	67.5
2010	67.6	67.4	67.7	68.0	68.4	68.9	69.0	69.0	68.2	68.3	68.3	68.5	68.3
2011	68.6	68.4	68.5	68.8	69.3	70.1	70.4	70.4	69.7	69.9	70.1	70.3	69.5
2012	69.9	70.0	70.3	70.3	70.7	71.7	71.8	71.8	71.0	71.1	71.3	71.3	70.9
2013	70.8	70.9	71.0	71.2	71.4	72.1	72.3	72.4	71.5	71.0	71.5	71.4	71.5
Professional and Business Services													
2002	134.6	134.0	134.6	136.3	137.2	138.5	138.8	139.0	137.1	136.5	136.6	136.6	136.7
2003	131.9	130.6	131.3	134.1	135.0	135.5	135.7	136.9	135.5	136.3	136.7	136.7	134.7
2004	133.7	133.8	135.3	138.4	139.6	141.8	142.5	143.7	143.1	144.7	145.2	145.7	140.6
2005	141.4	141.3	142.5	145.8	145.8	146.8	147.4	147.7	146.1	145.9	145.9	145.5	145.2
2006	141.5	142.5	144.2	146.4	147.4	149.7	151.1	151.2	150.7	151.4	151.6	150.8	148.2
2007	148.2	149.4	151.1	154.2	155.7	159.1	158.7	159.7	158.0	158.3	159.2	159.4	155.9
2008	156.2	156.8	157.2	160.6	161.1	162.8	163.2	163.0	161.0	160.7	160.3	158.6	160.1
2009	154.3	153.7	153.3	153.9	154.7	155.3	154.3	154.3	153.4	153.9	153.8	153.9	154.1
2010	151.0	151.1	152.7	156.6	157.5	159.6	160.6	160.9	159.7	161.1	162.0	161.4	157.9
2011	159.7	160.0	161.1	164.2	165.8	167.0	167.3	167.4	167.4	169.4	169.2	168.1	165.6
2012	167.0	167.6	170.0	172.0	172.9	174.3	173.6	173.0	171.9	174.0	173.8	173.0	171.9
2013	170.6	172.2	173.7	175.5	176.5	177.5	177.8	177.1	175.7	176.2	175.9	174.7	175.3
Education and Health Services													
2002	205.8	208.3	209.8	208.2	206.5	205.6	203.6	202.2	207.2	209.6	209.9	205.9	206.9
2003	211.2	212.9	213.6	212.4	210.1	209.6	207.5	205.2	210.1	214.0	214.7	214.3	211.3
2004	211.7	213.3	214.4	214.7	212.6	212.3	211.4	208.6	213.6	217.0	218.4	218.2	213.9
2005	217.0	218.8	219.3	219.9	217.2	217.1	217.2	215.4	220.1	222.9	224.1	224.6	219.5
2006	221.0	223.6	223.9	223.8	222.0	220.3	219.5	217.9	223.6	226.0	227.3	227.1	223.0
2007	222.6	225.4	226.5	226.4	225.2	224.0	223.3	221.9	226.9	230.7	231.2	230.4	226.2
2008	226.3	229.9	230.1	231.0	229.4	227.4	226.5	225.8	231.1	234.1	235.3	234.0	230.1
2009	231.1	232.7	233.0	234.1	232.8	231.2	230.7	228.4	233.2	235.9	236.9	236.6	233.1
2010	234.2	234.6	235.9	236.4	234.8	234.7	233.7	231.6	236.6	240.0	239.8	239.5	236.0
2011	238.2	240.0	240.6	240.5	238.6	239.1	235.9	234.4	240.3	243.1	244.1	243.2	239.8
2012	240.1	243.5	245.1	244.1	240.7	237.8	235.6	233.0	239.7	243.7	244.5	242.4	240.9
2013	239.6	243.4	243.3	243.1	238.3	236.8	235.0	232.0	239.5	243.4	243.4	241.1	239.9
Leisure and Hospitality													
2002	94.2	93.8	96.3	100.5	106.6	109.8	109.6	110.6	107.2	102.8	100.6	100.3	102.7
2003	95.3	94.3	96.4	101.8	107.5	111.5	111.0	112.3	108.3	104.8	102.5	102.3	104.0
2004	96.2	96.8	99.2	102.6	108.7	112.2	111.4	112.5	108.6	104.7	102.5	101.7	104.8
2005	96.3	96.3	98.0	103.7	110.4	113.4	113.4	114.7	110.9	106.2	103.7	102.7	105.8
2006	97.2	97.9	100.2	104.4	110.7	114.6	113.6	113.5	109.1	107.5	104.2	104.1	106.4
2007	98.7	98.4	100.4	104.2	112.3	116.0	113.8	114.9	111.2	109.5	105.9	105.4	107.5
2008	100.0	99.9	102.0	106.4	113.4	116.1	114.6	114.9	110.7	108.4	105.7	104.2	108.0
2009	98.2	98.1	100.7	104.5	111.1	113.3	112.3	114.0	110.0	106.3	103.6	103.5	106.3
2010	97.6	97.3	100.3	106.2	111.0	114.2	114.1	115.9	112.5	109.7	107.1	106.9	107.7
2011	101.5	100.8	103.4	108.6	114.3	117.8	115.9	116.7	114.0	110.8	107.9	107.4	109.9
2012	102.4	102.5	106.1	109.9	115.0	119.0	117.4	118.9	114.8	112.9	110.5	110.8	111.7
2013	105.2	105.2	107.6	111.8	118.6	122.0	121.6	121.8	117.3	116.6	113.4	109.8	114.2
Other Services													
2002	56.8	56.9	57.5	57.7	58.2	59.0	59.2	58.8	57.8	57.9	57.9	58.1	58.0
2003	57.1	57.0	57.4	58.2	58.5	59.1	59.8	59.7	58.6	58.9	58.8	58.9	58.5
2004	58.7	58.3	59.3	59.0	59.4	60.4	60.7	60.1	58.9	58.8	58.7	58.6	59.2
2005	58.0	58.0	58.2	58.1	58.0	58.1	57.7	56.7	54.8	54.4	54.0	53.2	56.6
2006	54.3	54.0	54.3	54.8	55.1	55.8	55.8	55.1	54.4	53.9	53.8	53.7	54.6
2007	52.9	52.7	53.3	53.3	53.5	54.0	54.1	53.6	52.9	52.9	53.0	52.7	53.2
2008	52.1	51.8	52.1	52.7	53.1	53.6	53.6	53.0	52.4	52.4	52.3	52.5	52.6
2009	51.5	51.4	51.8	51.8	52.3	53.0	53.0	52.4	51.3	51.3	51.1	51.1	51.8
2010	50.3	50.0	50.7	50.8	51.4	52.2	52.4	52.4	51.0	51.1	51.0	51.1	51.2
2011	50.3	50.5	50.9	51.1	51.7	52.5	52.4	52.2	51.3	51.2	51.2	51.3	51.4
2012	50.7	50.9	51.5	51.7	52.0	53.1	52.9	52.3	51.7	51.3	51.1	51.1	51.7
2013	50.1	50.2	50.5	50.7	51.3	52.2	52.4	52.0	51.4	51.1	51.0	51.6	51.2
Government													
2002	128.4	131.7	131.8	132.0	132.2	130.4	120.2	117.3	127.9	132.4	133.9	132.5	129.2
2003	130.0	132.7	133.6	133.0	132.2	130.9	118.4	115.8	128.5	132.8	133.6	132.2	129.5
2004	129.2	131.2	132.2	132.8	132.3	131.0	117.7	113.6	127.0	130.5	131.8	130.6	128.3
2005	127.8	130.0	130.9	131.0	130.3	129.4	116.0	112.0	125.7	129.3	131.2	130.1	127.0
2006	126.9	130.1	130.7	130.6	130.4	129.2	117.2	113.6	126.7	129.4	130.7	130.0	127.1
2007	126.7	129.5	130.3	129.8	128.6	127.3	117.6	116.2	125.4	128.4	129.5	129.1	126.5
2008	125.4	128.7	129.3	129.1	128.3	126.6	118.4	117.1	126.4	129.8	130.2	129.0	126.5
2009	125.2	128.8	129.2	130.3	129.2	127.7	119.4	117.9	126.9	130.1	131.6	130.9	127.3
2010	125.7	129.6	130.6	131.4	133.3	131.1	120.2	117.8	127.2	130.2	130.5	130.1	128.1
2011	126.6	129.3	130.0	129.5	127.8	125.9	115.4	113.3	121.6	124.6	125.7	125.5	124.6
2012	119.5	124.2	124.5	124.3	124.2	121.2	112.6	111.7	120.0	122.6	123.7	123.3	121.0
2013	118.4	122.8	122.9	123.0	123.5	119.1	110.5	109.9	118.8	121.2	121.9	121.9	119.5

Employment by Industry: Portland-Vancouver-Hillsboro, OR–WA, Selected Years, 2002–2013

(Numbers in thousands, not seasonally adjusted)

Industry and year	January	February	March	April	May	June	July	August	September	October	November	December	Annual average
Total Nonfarm													
2002	937.6	941.3	944.0	947.2	950.8	954.0	936.9	937.1	946.9	953.5	954.1	950.5	946.2
2003	928.9	929.7	931.2	933.2	935.9	936.7	929.0	931.7	938.9	946.3	949.2	949.5	936.7
2004	921.7	932.0	939.9	949.6	955.9	961.4	957.1	958.1	966.0	975.7	979.0	980.6	956.4
2005	956.7	965.2	971.3	978.0	983.4	988.3	982.5	986.0	993.3	1,003.1	1,010.3	1,014.7	986.1
2006	988.6	997.7	1,004.4	1,011.4	1,018.9	1,023.8	1,014.6	1,016.1	1,025.1	1,034.4	1,039.9	1,040.2	1,017.9
2007	1,015.6	1,025.1	1,031.8	1,032.2	1,039.4	1,040.8	1,033.0	1,033.9	1,040.6	1,050.7	1,055.4	1,054.4	1,037.7
2008	1,029.5	1,036.2	1,039.8	1,043.3	1,046.3	1,044.1	1,038.0	1,035.3	1,040.7	1,039.5	1,033.6	1,021.5	1,037.3
2009	992.1	988.6	983.5	982.1	982.5	977.4	967.3	963.7	968.0	975.9	976.0	973.4	977.5
2010	953.3	957.5	961.5	969.7	975.9	977.5	967.7	968.2	974.6	989.9	991.9	991.2	973.2
2011	971.3	977.9	981.5	991.6	993.5	994.9	988.4	988.8	994.9	1,005.7	1,010.1	1,010.1	992.4
2012	991.7	998.3	1,002.8	1,009.4	1,015.7	1,017.2	1,009.0	1,011.5	1,015.9	1,027.8	1,031.0	1,029.9	1,013.4
2013	1,007.9	1,017.5	1,021.8	1,031.3	1,037.5	1,039.9	1,032.5	1,037.8	1,043.8	1,051.1	1,055.1	1,055.0	1,035.9
Total Private													
2002	803.1	804.2	806.0	809.1	811.5	814.6	816.3	819.6	817.7	816.6	815.7	813.3	812.3
2003	794.8	794.4	795.5	796.9	798.8	800.8	804.3	808.6	808.7	810.6	812.0	812.8	803.2
2004	787.1	795.2	801.8	811.4	817.2	822.0	827.6	831.2	832.7	836.3	838.9	840.8	820.2
2005	818.4	824.9	830.7	837.7	842.3	846.9	853.6	858.7	861.4	863.8	868.9	874.0	848.4
2006	850.3	857.3	862.9	869.9	875.5	880.8	884.0	888.0	891.5	893.3	896.3	898.0	879.0
2007	874.5	882.2	887.7	887.9	892.9	894.3	898.3	902.3	904.5	905.4	908.4	907.5	895.5
2008	883.8	889.1	891.5	894.7	896.2	894.3	896.9	897.0	897.9	890.0	881.8	870.7	890.3
2009	843.1	837.6	831.7	830.2	829.8	826.3	826.3	825.5	827.7	826.6	825.1	823.5	829.5
2010	804.7	807.5	811.1	820.1	822.5	824.2	828.1	830.9	835.1	841.5	841.5	843.3	825.9
2011	823.0	828.6	832.3	840.7	842.1	846.0	851.3	854.0	857.8	858.9	861.7	863.4	846.7
2012	845.2	850.3	854.8	861.5	866.5	868.8	872.2	876.8	878.7	881.5	883.2	883.6	868.6
2013	862.8	870.2	874.7	883.8	889.1	891.5	898.0	903.9	907.5	905.7	908.0	908.6	892.0
Goods Producing													
2002	176.0	175.7	175.6	175.6	176.0	178.1	180.4	182.5	180.0	177.7	175.0	172.4	177.1
2003	169.5	168.0	167.6	166.8	167.8	169.7	171.7	173.5	172.4	171.4	170.2	169.8	169.9
2004	164.5	166.9	169.1	171.8	174.0	176.9	180.8	182.1	182.1	181.7	179.3	179.1	175.7
2005	176.1	177.0	178.6	179.8	181.4	183.9	187.6	188.9	188.0	188.6	187.0	187.4	183.7
2006	184.0	185.4	186.7	188.1	189.8	193.3	196.0	197.2	196.9	195.3	193.0	192.3	191.5
2007	188.9	190.0	191.1	190.2	192.3	193.2	196.5	197.7	196.5	195.5	193.2	191.2	193.0
2008	186.7	186.9	186.8	186.3	187.2	187.9	189.6	189.1	188.0	183.6	179.6	174.3	185.5
2009	168.7	164.7	161.8	159.5	159.1	159.2	160.2	160.0	159.2	157.6	153.9	152.3	159.7
2010	148.9	148.3	149.1	150.1	151.4	153.0	156.1	156.9	156.9	157.6	155.1	154.4	153.2
2011	151.2	152.6	154.0	155.8	157.2	159.8	162.2	163.5	163.0	162.8	161.5	160.8	158.7
2012	158.2	158.8	159.3	160.5	163.0	164.7	167.4	168.4	167.3	166.7	164.4	162.7	163.5
2013	160.6	161.6	162.5	164.9	166.9	169.0	171.3	172.9	172.7	172.1	170.2	168.4	167.8
Service-Providing													
2002	761.6	765.6	768.4	771.6	774.8	775.9	756.5	754.6	766.9	775.8	779.1	778.1	769.1
2003	759.4	761.7	763.6	766.4	768.1	767.0	757.3	758.2	766.5	774.9	779.0	779.7	766.8
2004	757.2	765.1	770.8	777.8	781.9	784.5	776.3	776.0	783.9	794.0	799.7	801.5	780.7
2005	780.6	788.2	792.7	798.2	802.0	804.4	794.9	797.1	805.3	814.5	823.3	827.3	802.4
2006	804.6	812.3	817.7	823.3	829.1	830.5	818.6	818.9	828.2	839.1	846.9	847.9	826.4
2007	826.7	835.1	840.7	842.0	847.1	847.6	836.5	836.2	844.1	855.2	862.2	863.2	844.7
2008	842.8	849.3	853.0	857.0	859.1	856.2	848.4	846.2	852.7	855.9	854.0	847.2	851.8
2009	823.4	823.9	821.7	822.6	823.4	818.2	807.1	803.7	808.8	818.3	822.1	821.1	817.9
2010	804.4	809.2	812.4	819.6	824.5	824.5	811.6	811.3	817.7	832.3	836.8	836.8	820.1
2011	820.1	825.3	827.5	835.8	836.3	835.1	826.2	825.3	831.9	842.9	848.6	849.3	833.7
2012	833.5	839.5	843.5	848.9	852.7	852.5	841.6	843.1	848.6	861.1	866.6	867.2	849.9
2013	847.3	855.9	859.3	866.4	870.6	870.9	861.2	864.9	871.1	879.0	884.9	886.6	868.2
Mining and Logging													
2002	1.5	1.5	1.5	1.6	1.6	1.7	1.8	1.8	1.8	1.8	1.7	1.6	1.7
2003	1.6	1.6	1.6	1.6	1.6	1.7	1.7	1.7	1.8	1.7	1.7	1.7	1.7
2004	1.5	1.5	1.6	1.6	1.7	1.7	1.8	1.8	1.8	1.8	1.7	1.7	1.7
2005	1.7	1.7	1.7	1.7	1.8	1.8	1.9	1.9	1.8	1.8	1.8	1.7	1.8
2006	1.6	1.6	1.6	1.6	1.7	1.8	1.8	1.8	1.8	1.7	1.6	1.6	1.7
2007	1.5	1.6	1.6	1.6	1.7	1.7	1.7	1.7	1.7	1.7	1.6	1.5	1.6
2008	1.5	1.5	1.5	1.5	1.6	1.6	1.6	1.7	1.6	1.6	1.5	1.4	1.6
2009	1.2	1.2	1.2	1.1	1.2	1.2	1.3	1.3	1.3	1.3	1.2	1.1	1.2
2010	1.0	1.0	1.1	1.0	1.1	1.1	1.1	1.1	1.1	1.1	1.1	1.0	1.1
2011	0.9	1.0	1.0	1.0	1.1	1.1	1.1	1.1	1.1	1.1	1.1	1.0	1.1
2012	0.9	0.9	0.9	0.9	1.0	1.0	1.0	1.0	1.0	1.0	1.0	1.0	1.0
2013	1.0	1.0	1.0	1.0	1.0	1.0	1.1	1.1	1.1	1.1	1.0	1.0	1.0
Construction													
2002	49.3	49.6	49.9	50.1	50.8	51.8	53.6	55.3	54.2	53.5	51.6	49.6	51.6
2003	48.2	47.6	47.6	47.4	48.6	49.6	51.3	53.2	52.8	52.7	51.4	50.7	50.1
2004	47.4	49.0	50.2	51.8	53.3	55.0	56.8	57.8	57.5	57.1	55.8	55.2	53.9
2005	53.3	53.8	55.1	55.8	57.1	58.4	60.8	62.2	62.2	61.8	60.6	60.8	58.5
2006	58.3	59.4	60.1	61.0	62.2	64.3	65.6	66.7	66.6	65.9	64.5	63.7	63.2
2007	61.4	62.2	63.2	63.4	65.4	65.5	67.8	68.9	68.3	67.4	66.0	64.4	65.3
2008	60.9	61.0	61.0	60.9	61.9	62.5	63.2	63.3	62.7	60.4	57.2	54.4	60.8
2009	51.8	50.4	49.4	48.9	49.2	50.0	50.8	50.9	50.3	49.0	46.5	45.4	49.4
2010	42.8	42.4	42.8	43.6	44.3	45.1	47.1	47.7	47.6	47.4	45.2	44.7	45.1
2011	42.3	42.9	43.8	45.0	45.8	47.3	48.7	49.6	49.4	49.1	47.9	47.4	46.6
2012	45.6	45.8	45.9	46.8	48.5	49.0	50.4	51.6	50.7	50.2	48.3	47.1	48.3
2013	45.9	46.5	47.5	49.2	51.0	52.0	54.0	54.9	54.8	54.3	52.7	51.5	51.2

Employment by Industry: Portland-Vancouver-Hillsboro, OR–WA, Selected Years, 2002–2013—*Continued*

(Numbers in thousands, not seasonally adjusted)

Industry and year	January	February	March	April	May	June	July	August	September	October	November	December	Annual average
Manufacturing													
2002	125.2	124.6	124.2	123.9	123.6	124.6	125.0	125.4	124.0	122.4	121.7	121.2	123.8
2003	119.7	118.8	118.4	117.8	117.6	118.4	118.7	118.6	117.8	117.0	117.1	117.4	118.1
2004	115.6	116.4	117.3	118.4	119.0	120.2	122.2	122.5	122.8	122.8	121.8	122.2	120.1
2005	121.1	121.5	121.8	122.3	122.5	123.7	124.9	124.8	124.0	125.0	124.6	124.9	123.4
2006	124.1	124.4	125.0	125.5	125.9	127.2	128.6	128.7	128.5	127.7	126.9	127.0	126.6
2007	126.0	126.2	126.3	125.2	125.2	126.0	127.0	127.1	126.5	126.4	125.6	125.3	126.1
2008	124.3	124.4	124.3	123.9	123.7	123.8	124.8	124.1	123.7	121.6	120.9	118.5	123.2
2009	115.7	113.1	111.2	109.5	108.7	108.0	108.1	107.8	107.6	107.3	106.2	105.8	109.1
2010	105.1	104.9	105.2	105.5	106.0	106.8	107.9	108.1	108.2	109.1	108.8	108.7	107.0
2011	108.0	108.7	109.2	109.8	110.3	111.4	112.4	112.8	112.5	112.6	112.5	112.4	111.1
2012	111.7	112.1	112.5	112.8	113.5	114.7	116.0	115.8	115.6	115.5	115.1	114.6	114.2
2013	113.7	114.1	114.0	114.7	114.9	116.0	116.2	116.9	116.8	116.7	116.5	115.9	115.5
Trade, Transportation, and Utilities													
2002	188.7	187.0	187.2	187.8	188.9	190.0	190.4	189.6	188.9	188.7	191.7	194.0	189.4
2003	186.7	184.8	184.6	184.7	185.8	187.1	187.4	188.0	187.3	189.0	192.5	193.9	187.7
2004	185.7	185.0	185.5	187.1	188.0	189.7	190.6	191.0	190.3	191.9	196.1	198.2	189.9
2005	190.3	189.4	189.9	190.6	191.5	193.2	194.6	195.3	195.5	196.3	200.9	204.1	194.3
2006	195.1	194.1	194.6	195.3	197.0	198.3	199.0	199.5	199.2	199.5	204.2	207.1	198.6
2007	198.7	197.7	198.2	198.2	199.8	201.0	201.7	202.0	202.2	202.4	207.3	209.2	201.5
2008	200.8	199.4	199.1	199.1	199.3	199.2	200.3	200.3	199.7	198.6	199.0	198.9	199.5
2009	190.1	186.9	184.5	183.6	184.4	184.0	183.7	183.5	183.3	183.0	185.2	187.3	185.0
2010	180.4	178.8	179.0	180.2	180.9	181.8	182.8	183.1	183.1	184.5	188.0	190.2	182.7
2011	182.9	181.7	181.7	183.0	184.1	184.9	186.1	185.9	186.1	186.7	190.6	192.2	185.5
2012	185.4	183.9	184.3	185.5	187.5	188.8	188.7	189.2	188.9	190.1	195.0	197.0	188.7
2013	189.4	189.2	189.1	190.4	192.1	192.7	193.8	195.0	195.2	195.6	200.0	202.0	193.7
Wholesale Trade													
2002	51.5	51.4	51.3	51.5	51.6	51.7	52.0	52.1	51.7	51.5	51.6	51.6	51.6
2003	51.6	51.5	51.5	51.5	51.5	51.8	51.9	51.9	51.6	51.3	51.3	51.1	51.5
2004	50.7	51.1	51.1	51.4	51.5	51.8	52.4	52.4	51.8	51.6	51.8	51.9	51.6
2005	51.6	52.1	52.1	52.1	52.3	52.7	53.1	52.9	53.0	52.8	52.9	53.2	52.6
2006	52.3	52.8	52.8	53.3	53.7	53.8	54.0	54.2	53.7	53.8	53.9	53.9	53.5
2007	53.4	53.9	53.9	53.8	54.2	54.2	54.5	54.1	53.7	53.9	53.8	53.8	53.9
2008	53.2	53.5	53.3	53.2	53.6	53.6	54.1	53.8	53.5	53.4	53.1	52.4	53.4
2009	51.4	51.0	50.3	50.3	50.3	49.8	49.8	49.5	48.8	48.5	48.1	48.1	49.7
2010	47.2	47.2	47.2	48.0	48.4	48.4	48.9	48.8	48.5	48.8	49.1	49.0	48.3
2011	48.1	48.5	48.4	49.3	49.8	49.7	50.1	50.1	49.7	50.0	50.0	49.7	49.5
2012	49.3	49.6	49.7	50.7	51.2	51.0	51.4	51.5	51.1	51.3	51.4	51.6	50.8
2013	50.7	51.4	51.2	51.6	52.0	51.9	52.7	52.8	52.7	52.9	53.2	53.2	52.2
Retail Trade													
2002	100.0	98.4	98.6	98.8	99.7	100.6	101.0	100.2	99.9	100.0	103.3	105.5	100.5
2003	98.6	97.3	97.1	97.2	98.1	99.0	99.4	99.7	99.0	100.4	103.9	105.5	99.6
2004	98.4	97.3	97.8	98.9	99.8	101.1	101.6	101.9	101.3	102.3	106.5	108.4	101.3
2005	102.4	100.8	101.1	101.7	102.6	103.7	105.0	105.8	105.4	106.4	110.6	112.7	104.9
2006	105.9	104.1	104.5	105.0	106.1	106.8	107.8	108.1	107.8	107.9	112.4	114.6	107.6
2007	108.1	106.5	106.7	106.9	107.8	108.9	110.1	110.6	110.4	110.3	114.8	116.2	109.8
2008	110.1	108.3	108.2	107.8	107.6	107.8	109.1	109.0	108.4	107.4	109.0	109.4	108.5
2009	102.8	100.8	99.6	99.1	99.8	100.1	100.7	100.8	100.5	100.8	103.4	105.0	101.1
2010	100.1	98.8	99.0	99.0	99.4	100.1	101.2	101.6	101.0	101.9	105.1	106.7	101.2
2011	101.3	100.0	100.0	100.3	100.7	101.6	102.7	102.6	102.2	102.9	106.4	107.8	102.4
2012	102.7	100.9	100.9	101.4	102.6	103.9	104.3	104.5	104.0	104.9	109.2	110.4	104.1
2013	105.1	104.1	104.1	104.7	106.0	106.7	107.9	108.7	108.2	108.9	112.6	113.6	107.6
Transportation and Utilities													
2002	37.2	37.2	37.3	37.5	37.6	37.7	37.4	37.3	37.3	37.2	36.8	36.9	37.3
2003	36.5	36.0	36.0	36.0	36.2	36.3	36.1	36.4	36.7	37.3	37.3	37.3	36.5
2004	36.6	36.6	36.6	36.8	36.7	36.8	36.6	36.7	37.2	38.0	37.8	37.9	37.0
2005	36.3	36.5	36.7	36.8	36.6	36.8	36.5	36.6	37.1	37.1	37.4	38.2	36.9
2006	36.9	37.2	37.3	37.0	37.2	37.7	37.2	37.2	37.7	37.8	38.0	38.6	37.5
2007	37.2	37.3	37.6	37.5	37.8	37.9	37.1	37.3	38.1	38.2	38.7	39.2	37.8
2008	37.5	37.6	37.6	38.1	38.1	37.8	37.1	37.5	37.8	37.8	36.9	37.1	37.6
2009	35.9	35.1	34.6	34.2	34.3	34.1	33.2	33.2	34.0	33.7	33.7	34.2	34.2
2010	33.1	32.8	32.8	33.2	33.1	33.3	32.7	32.7	33.6	33.8	33.8	34.5	33.3
2011	33.5	33.2	33.3	33.4	33.6	33.6	33.3	33.2	34.2	33.8	34.2	34.7	33.7
2012	33.4	33.4	33.7	33.4	33.7	33.9	33.0	33.2	33.8	33.9	34.4	35.0	33.7
2013	33.6	33.7	33.8	34.1	34.1	34.1	33.2	33.5	34.3	33.8	34.2	35.2	34.0
Information													
2002	24.4	24.3	24.1	23.8	23.7	23.7	23.4	23.4	23.2	23.2	23.2	23.1	23.6
2003	22.8	22.5	22.3	22.1	22.3	22.3	22.2	22.1	22.1	22.2	22.4	22.5	22.3
2004	22.3	22.3	22.4	22.2	22.2	22.3	22.4	22.4	22.2	22.1	22.3	22.4	22.3
2005	22.3	22.4	22.4	22.6	22.8	23.0	23.1	23.1	23.1	23.1	23.3	23.5	22.9
2006	23.3	23.4	23.4	23.3	23.4	23.5	24.2	23.9	24.0	24.2	23.8	24.0	23.7
2007	23.9	24.1	24.3	24.3	24.6	24.5	24.6	24.7	24.5	24.6	24.7	24.8	24.5
2008	24.6	24.6	24.6	24.6	24.6	24.5	24.5	24.4	24.2	23.8	23.7	23.5	24.3
2009	23.2	23.1	23.0	22.8	22.7	22.6	22.6	22.5	22.2	22.2	22.3	22.3	22.6
2010	22.0	22.1	22.0	22.1	22.3	22.1	22.1	22.4	22.0	22.1	22.3	22.2	22.1
2011	22.2	22.2	22.1	22.2	22.1	22.0	22.3	22.0	21.8	21.9	22.0	22.0	22.1
2012	21.8	21.8	22.0	22.0	22.0	22.2	22.5	22.4	22.3	22.8	22.9	22.9	22.3
2013	22.6	22.5	22.6	22.5	22.4	22.5	22.7	22.6	22.7	22.9	23.2	23.3	22.7

Employment by Industry: Portland-Vancouver-Hillsboro, OR–WA, Selected Years, 2002–2013—*Continued*

(Numbers in thousands, not seasonally adjusted)

Industry and year	January	February	March	April	May	June	July	August	September	October	November	December	Annual average
Financial Activities													
2002	64.9	65.0	64.8	64.9	65.0	65.3	65.8	66.0	65.8	66.2	66.4	66.8	65.6
2003	66.8	66.9	67.3	67.4	67.1	67.0	66.6	66.7	66.0	65.5	65.0	64.9	66.4
2004	65.0	65.1	65.3	65.8	65.9	66.3	66.5	66.6	66.4	66.4	66.7	66.9	66.1
2005	66.4	66.6	66.7	67.2	67.7	68.2	68.8	69.1	69.1	69.3	69.7	70.0	68.2
2006	69.3	69.5	69.7	70.1	70.3	70.7	71.3	71.5	71.4	71.2	71.3	71.4	70.6
2007	70.7	70.9	71.0	70.8	70.8	70.8	70.9	70.6	69.7	69.5	69.5	69.3	70.4
2008	68.6	68.7	68.4	68.5	68.5	68.1	68.1	67.9	67.2	66.9	66.4	65.9	67.8
2009	65.2	64.7	64.2	64.2	64.1	64.0	63.9	63.7	63.1	63.1	62.8	62.7	63.8
2010	61.9	61.7	61.6	61.9	61.8	62.0	62.2	62.2	61.8	62.0	61.8	62.1	61.9
2011	61.5	61.4	61.2	61.3	61.4	61.7	61.9	61.9	61.6	61.6	61.7	62.0	61.6
2012	61.6	61.7	61.7	62.1	62.0	62.3	62.9	63.1	62.7	62.9	62.8	63.1	62.4
2013	62.4	62.4	62.6	63.1	63.5	63.7	64.3	64.3	64.0	63.2	62.5	63.0	63.3
Professional and Business Services													
2002	124.6	124.8	125.1	125.5	125.2	126.0	126.8	127.4	126.9	126.2	124.5	122.8	125.5
2003	119.3	120.2	120.2	120.8	120.7	121.0	123.0	123.6	124.2	124.1	123.4	123.3	122.0
2004	119.0	120.6	122.1	124.2	125.5	127.3	129.0	129.8	129.0	130.8	130.8	130.5	126.6
2005	126.2	128.0	129.4	131.6	131.8	133.5	135.1	136.3	136.5	136.7	136.8	137.1	133.3
2006	133.2	135.1	136.3	137.9	138.9	140.9	141.2	142.4	142.8	143.4	143.3	141.6	139.8
2007	137.6	139.0	140.6	141.0	140.8	142.0	142.3	143.8	144.0	143.2	142.4	141.7	141.7
2008	139.3	140.9	142.0	143.2	143.1	143.4	144.5	145.3	144.2	142.5	139.7	137.3	142.1
2009	132.9	131.7	131.0	131.2	130.1	130.2	130.7	130.6	129.7	130.5	130.5	130.3	130.8
2010	127.9	129.1	130.6	133.3	132.9	133.8	135.3	136.5	136.5	137.9	137.5	137.5	134.1
2011	134.1	135.4	136.6	138.8	138.6	139.7	142.0	142.7	143.1	143.2	143.3	143.6	140.1
2012	141.4	142.2	143.3	144.6	144.9	146.1	147.4	148.6	148.1	149.2	148.5	148.4	146.1
2013	145.4	146.8	148.5	150.6	151.3	152.6	154.9	156.4	156.0	155.1	154.6	154.3	152.2
Education and Health Services													
2002	109.5	111.7	112.6	113.4	113.0	110.6	108.8	109.1	112.2	115.6	116.4	116.0	112.4
2003	113.8	115.9	116.3	116.7	116.1	113.5	111.6	111.6	114.9	117.6	118.1	118.2	115.4
2004	114.2	117.3	118.1	118.5	117.8	115.0	113.3	113.2	117.8	120.2	120.9	120.8	117.3
2005	118.1	121.3	122.0	122.5	121.9	118.5	117.1	117.7	122.3	124.8	125.6	125.8	121.5
2006	121.8	125.3	126.1	126.7	125.9	122.4	119.8	120.3	124.8	128.5	129.5	129.7	125.1
2007	126.0	129.9	130.8	131.0	130.3	127.1	124.9	125.0	129.9	133.7	134.6	134.2	129.8
2008	130.9	134.8	135.5	136.1	135.2	132.3	130.2	130.2	135.5	138.5	139.2	138.9	134.8
2009	134.8	138.1	138.4	139.3	138.6	135.2	133.3	133.2	139.0	141.7	142.5	141.8	138.0
2010	139.8	142.8	143.5	144.3	143.3	140.0	137.7	137.5	142.8	146.6	147.6	147.6	142.8
2011	144.9	147.7	148.2	148.5	146.8	143.8	141.3	141.5	146.7	149.8	150.6	150.3	146.7
2012	146.7	150.5	151.3	151.8	149.8	146.2	143.4	144.0	149.1	151.6	152.7	152.4	149.1
2013	148.1	152.1	152.3	153.4	151.5	147.8	146.0	146.8	151.9	154.4	154.9	154.8	151.2
Leisure and Hospitality													
2002	81.3	81.7	82.5	84.0	85.6	87.0	87.0	88.0	87.0	85.0	84.4	84.5	84.8
2003	82.3	82.3	83.3	84.5	84.9	86.4	87.9	89.0	87.5	86.6	86.3	86.1	85.6
2004	82.9	83.8	84.6	87.0	88.8	89.3	89.9	91.1	89.7	88.2	88.0	88.5	87.7
2005	85.4	86.1	87.5	89.0	90.6	92.0	92.5	93.5	92.2	90.3	90.8	91.3	90.1
2006	89.3	89.7	91.0	93.1	94.3	95.5	96.4	97.3	96.5	95.2	95.2	95.7	94.1
2007	93.1	94.3	95.3	96.1	97.7	98.8	100.9	101.8	101.0	98.7	98.8	99.3	98.0
2008	96.2	96.9	98.0	99.6	100.8	101.3	102.3	102.5	101.5	98.9	97.5	95.7	99.3
2009	92.6	92.7	93.2	94.2	95.3	95.8	96.7	96.9	96.4	93.9	93.3	92.4	94.5
2010	90.0	90.7	91.2	93.8	95.2	96.2	96.9	97.5	97.1	95.7	94.7	94.7	94.5
2011	91.9	92.9	93.7	96.1	96.8	98.8	99.9	100.7	99.8	97.2	96.4	96.9	96.8
2012	94.5	95.5	96.9	98.6	100.3	101.7	103.1	104.3	103.7	101.4	100.5	100.9	100.1
2013	98.3	99.3	100.7	102.3	104.3	106.3	107.7	108.5	108.0	105.1	105.5	105.4	104.3
Other Services													
2002	33.7	34.0	34.1	34.1	34.1	33.9	33.7	33.6	33.7	34.0	34.1	33.7	33.9
2003	33.6	33.8	33.9	33.9	34.1	33.8	33.9	34.1	34.3	34.2	34.1	34.1	34.0
2004	33.5	34.2	34.7	34.8	35.0	35.2	35.1	35.0	35.2	35.0	34.8	34.4	34.7
2005	33.6	34.1	34.2	34.4	34.6	34.6	34.8	34.8	34.7	34.7	34.8	34.8	34.5
2006	34.3	34.8	35.1	35.4	35.9	36.2	36.1	35.9	35.9	36.0	36.0	36.2	35.7
2007	35.6	36.3	36.4	36.3	36.6	36.9	36.5	36.7	36.9	37.0	37.1	37.1	36.6
2008	36.7	36.9	37.1	37.3	37.5	37.6	37.4	37.3	37.6	37.2	36.7	36.2	37.1
2009	35.6	35.7	35.6	35.4	35.5	35.3	35.2	35.1	34.8	34.6	34.6	34.4	35.2
2010	33.8	34.0	34.1	34.4	34.7	35.3	35.3	35.0	34.8	34.9	35.1	34.5	34.6
2011	34.3	34.7	34.8	35.0	35.1	35.3	35.6	35.8	35.7	35.7	35.6	35.6	35.3
2012	35.6	35.9	36.0	36.4	37.0	36.8	36.8	36.8	36.6	36.8	36.4	36.2	36.4
2013	36.0	36.3	36.4	36.6	37.1	36.9	37.3	37.4	37.0	37.3	37.1	37.4	36.9
Government													
2002	134.5	137.1	138.0	138.1	139.3	139.4	120.6	117.5	129.2	136.9	138.4	137.2	133.9
2003	134.1	135.3	135.7	136.3	137.1	135.9	124.7	123.1	130.2	135.7	136.7	136.7	133.5
2004	134.6	136.8	138.1	138.2	138.7	139.4	129.5	126.9	133.3	139.4	140.1	139.8	136.2
2005	138.3	140.3	140.6	140.3	141.1	141.4	128.9	127.3	131.9	139.3	141.4	140.7	137.6
2006	138.3	140.4	141.5	141.5	143.4	143.0	130.6	128.1	133.6	141.1	143.6	142.2	138.9
2007	141.1	142.9	144.1	144.3	146.5	146.5	134.7	131.6	136.1	145.3	147.0	146.9	142.3
2008	145.7	147.1	148.3	148.6	150.1	149.8	141.1	138.3	142.8	149.5	151.8	150.8	147.0
2009	149.0	151.0	151.8	151.9	152.7	151.1	141.0	138.2	140.3	149.3	150.9	149.9	148.1
2010	148.6	150.0	150.4	149.6	153.4	153.3	139.6	137.3	139.5	148.4	150.4	147.9	147.4
2011	148.3	149.3	149.2	150.9	151.4	148.9	137.1	134.8	137.1	146.8	148.4	146.7	145.7
2012	146.5	148.0	148.0	147.9	149.2	148.4	136.8	134.7	137.2	146.3	147.8	146.3	144.8
2013	145.1	147.3	147.1	147.5	148.4	148.4	134.5	133.9	136.3	145.4	147.1	146.4	144.0

Employment by Industry: Providence-Fall River-Warwick, RI–MA, NECTA, Selected Years, 2002–2013

(Numbers in thousands, not seasonally adjusted)

Industry and year	January	February	March	April	May	June	July	August	September	October	November	December	Annual average
Total Nonfarm													
2002	561.1	562.2	567.4	574.9	580.7	581.6	569.4	574.9	581.8	580.3	582.9	581.6	574.9
2003	565.2	564.0	567.5	576.1	584.1	586.1	573.0	575.7	584.3	586.6	588.7	588.3	578.3
2004	567.0	568.4	572.3	580.9	590.2	591.0	578.1	579.8	588.3	590.5	591.8	590.8	582.4
2005	569.1	570.9	572.5	584.6	589.1	592.0	580.7	582.5	589.8	589.5	591.8	590.1	583.6
2006	566.7	569.4	574.0	586.9	590.7	593.3	580.0	583.2	591.6	593.6	595.2	594.1	584.9
2007	572.0	572.7	575.4	583.5	590.4	592.4	580.5	581.4	585.8	585.3	585.5	584.3	582.4
2008	562.2	563.6	566.0	573.8	579.5	579.3	566.0	566.7	572.6	571.1	568.0	563.9	569.4
2009	538.5	538.4	537.6	542.3	548.5	548.4	536.3	536.3	543.7	545.2	545.2	543.5	542.0
2010	524.8	526.9	530.9	539.2	547.8	547.8	540.8	541.9	547.3	549.8	551.1	548.7	541.4
2011	528.3	531.8	534.1	545.3	551.2	553.2	544.0	543.5	550.6	553.1	553.7	551.0	545.0
2012	533.2	537.4	541.3	548.9	556.2	557.5	547.5	549.8	557.5	558.7	558.4	559.1	550.5
2013	540.2	541.5	545.8	554.7	562.7	566.2	555.3	556.0	564.1	566.2	565.2	560.5	556.5
Total Private													
2002	483.7	484.4	489.1	496.9	502.6	504.2	497.1	503.2	505.0	504.0	505.5	504.7	498.4
2003	488.1	486.8	490.2	499.0	506.5	508.5	503.0	506.3	509.1	510.3	512.2	511.7	502.6
2004	491.3	492.5	495.8	505.2	513.5	514.5	509.6	511.6	513.9	515.2	515.8	515.5	507.9
2005	494.1	495.7	497.5	509.4	513.4	516.5	511.8	514.3	516.6	514.4	516.3	514.7	509.6
2006	492.0	494.2	498.9	512.0	515.5	518.3	510.9	514.5	517.6	518.5	519.1	518.3	510.8
2007	497.1	497.7	500.3	508.5	514.8	517.6	510.7	511.9	512.6	511.1	511.1	509.6	508.6
2008	488.2	489.3	491.5	499.2	504.1	504.9	498.0	499.4	501.0	498.5	494.5	490.7	496.6
2009	466.2	466.0	465.3	469.6	475.5	476.1	470.5	471.0	473.4	473.2	472.8	471.2	470.9
2010	453.2	455.2	458.6	466.9	473.5	475.2	474.4	475.7	477.6	478.3	478.9	476.8	470.4
2011	457.1	460.5	462.3	473.6	479.3	481.6	478.8	478.3	481.3	482.3	482.6	479.8	474.8
2012	462.8	466.6	470.5	477.8	484.4	487.2	482.5	484.7	488.3	487.9	487.1	488.0	480.7
2013	469.5	471.2	474.9	483.8	490.8	495.2	489.9	491.2	494.6	495.2	493.8	489.0	486.6
Goods Producing													
2002	105.3	105.2	106.2	106.9	108.2	108.4	103.3	108.2	108.3	107.4	107.0	105.8	106.7
2003	101.4	100.1	100.6	103.4	105.0	105.7	101.7	105.3	105.9	105.2	105.1	103.7	103.6
2004	98.4	97.6	98.5	101.0	102.6	104.0	101.9	104.2	104.1	103.9	103.6	102.5	101.9
2005	97.3	96.5	96.3	99.4	100.6	102.1	98.7	101.1	100.9	99.7	100.0	98.6	99.3
2006	93.8	93.7	94.3	97.5	98.3	99.7	96.6	99.0	98.5	98.0	96.9	96.2	96.9
2007	92.3	90.9	91.3	92.5	94.1	95.1	92.7	94.9	94.6	93.0	92.1	90.6	92.8
2008	86.3	85.2	85.7	87.5	88.7	89.2	86.7	88.3	87.7	86.1	84.3	82.2	86.5
2009	76.4	74.2	73.1	73.9	74.4	74.7	73.1	73.7	73.3	72.9	72.3	71.2	73.6
2010	67.3	66.8	67.2	69.2	71.0	72.1	71.7	72.9	72.5	72.6	72.4	71.3	70.6
2011	67.6	67.0	67.4	69.8	71.1	72.2	71.7	72.5	72.1	71.9	71.6	70.7	70.5
2012	67.6	67.2	68.0	69.8	70.6	71.8	71.0	72.1	71.7	72.0	71.5	71.3	70.4
2013	67.9	67.1	68.2	70.0	71.5	72.4	71.6	73.0	72.9	73.0	72.5	70.8	70.9
Service-Providing													
2002	455.8	457.0	461.2	468.0	472.5	473.2	466.1	466.7	473.5	472.9	475.9	475.8	468.2
2003	463.8	463.9	466.9	472.7	479.1	480.4	471.3	470.4	478.4	481.4	483.6	484.6	474.7
2004	468.6	470.8	473.8	479.9	487.6	487.0	476.2	475.6	484.2	486.6	488.2	488.3	480.6
2005	471.8	474.4	476.2	485.2	488.5	489.9	482.0	481.4	488.9	489.8	491.8	491.5	484.3
2006	472.9	475.7	479.7	489.4	492.4	493.6	483.4	484.2	493.1	495.6	498.3	497.9	488.0
2007	479.7	481.8	484.1	491.0	496.3	497.3	487.8	486.5	491.2	492.3	493.4	493.7	489.6
2008	475.9	478.4	480.3	486.3	490.8	490.1	479.3	478.4	484.9	485.0	483.7	481.7	482.9
2009	462.1	464.2	464.5	468.4	474.1	473.7	463.2	462.6	470.4	472.3	472.9	472.3	468.4
2010	457.5	460.1	463.7	470.0	476.8	475.7	469.1	469.0	474.8	477.2	478.7	477.4	470.8
2011	460.7	464.8	466.7	475.5	480.1	481.0	472.3	471.0	478.5	481.2	482.1	480.3	474.5
2012	465.6	470.2	473.3	479.1	485.6	485.7	476.5	477.7	485.8	486.7	486.9	487.8	480.1
2013	472.3	474.4	477.6	484.7	491.2	493.8	483.7	483.0	491.2	493.2	492.7	489.7	485.6
Mining and Logging													
2002	0.3	0.3	0.3	0.3	0.3	0.3	0.3	0.3	0.3	0.3	0.3	0.3	0.3
2003	0.2	0.2	0.2	0.3	0.3	0.3	0.3	0.3	0.3	0.3	0.3	0.3	0.3
2004	0.3	0.2	0.2	0.3	0.3	0.3	0.3	0.3	0.3	0.3	0.3	0.3	0.3
2005	0.3	0.2	0.2	0.3	0.3	0.3	0.3	0.3	0.3	0.3	0.3	0.3	0.3
2006	0.2	0.2	0.2	0.3	0.3	0.3	0.3	0.3	0.3	0.3	0.3	0.3	0.3
2007	0.3	0.2	0.2	0.3	0.3	0.3	0.3	0.3	0.3	0.3	0.3	0.3	0.3
2008	0.2	0.2	0.2	0.2	0.3	0.3	0.3	0.3	0.3	0.3	0.3	0.3	0.3
2009	0.2	0.2	0.2	0.2	0.2	0.2	0.2	0.2	0.2	0.2	0.2	0.2	0.2
2010	0.1	0.1	0.1	0.2	0.2	0.2	0.2	0.2	0.2	0.2	0.2	0.2	0.2
2011	0.1	0.1	0.1	0.2	0.2	0.2	0.2	0.2	0.2	0.2	0.2	0.2	0.2
2012	0.1	0.1	0.1	0.2	0.2	0.2	0.2	0.2	0.2	0.2	0.2	0.2	0.2
2013	0.1	0.1	0.1	0.2	0.2	0.2	0.2	0.2	0.2	0.2	0.2	0.2	0.2
Construction													
2002	21.3	21.1	22.0	23.2	24.3	24.8	24.9	25.2	25.1	24.7	24.5	23.7	23.7
2003	21.2	20.3	21.1	23.9	25.8	26.6	27.6	27.9	27.9	27.6	27.3	26.2	25.3
2004	22.6	21.9	22.6	24.9	26.1	27.0	27.7	27.7	27.6	27.7	27.4	26.8	25.8
2005	23.2	22.6	23.0	26.4	27.6	28.8	29.0	29.2	29.0	28.4	28.9	27.7	27.0
2006	24.7	24.2	25.1	28.2	29.1	30.3	30.3	30.6	30.3	29.9	29.3	28.7	28.4
2007	25.9	24.5	25.1	26.6	28.2	29.0	29.5	29.4	28.9	28.3	27.8	26.5	27.5
2008	23.2	22.6	23.1	25.1	26.2	26.9	27.2	27.1	26.8	25.8	24.9	23.3	25.2
2009	20.1	19.5	19.4	20.8	21.7	21.9	22.2	22.1	21.6	21.4	20.8	19.8	20.9
2010	16.9	16.3	16.8	18.9	20.2	20.8	21.5	21.7	21.6	21.1	21.0	20.7	19.6
2011	16.7	16.1	16.5	18.6	19.8	20.6	21.4	21.3	20.9	20.9	20.8	19.9	19.5
2012	17.7	17.1	17.9	19.4	20.1	20.9	21.3	21.3	20.9	21.0	20.6	20.2	19.9
2013	17.5	17.0	17.7	19.3	20.6	21.1	21.9	21.9	21.8	22.0	21.4	19.7	20.2

Employment by Industry: Providence-Fall River-Warwick, RI–MA, NECTA, Selected Years, 2002–2013—Continued

(Numbers in thousands, not seasonally adjusted)

Industry and year	January	February	March	April	May	June	July	August	September	October	November	December	Annual average
Manufacturing													
2002	83.7	83.8	83.9	83.4	83.6	83.3	78.1	82.7	82.9	82.4	82.2	81.8	82.7
2003	80.0	79.6	79.3	79.2	78.9	78.8	73.8	77.1	77.7	77.3	77.5	77.2	78.0
2004	75.5	75.5	75.7	75.8	76.2	76.7	73.9	76.2	76.2	75.9	75.9	75.4	75.7
2005	73.8	73.7	73.1	72.7	72.7	73.0	69.4	71.6	71.6	71.0	70.8	70.6	72.0
2006	68.9	69.3	69.0	69.0	68.9	69.1	66.0	68.1	67.9	67.8	67.3	67.2	68.2
2007	66.1	66.2	66.0	65.6	65.6	65.8	62.9	65.2	65.4	64.4	64.0	63.8	65.1
2008	62.9	62.4	62.4	62.2	62.2	62.0	59.2	60.9	60.6	60.0	59.1	58.6	61.0
2009	56.1	54.5	53.5	52.9	52.5	52.6	50.7	51.4	51.5	51.3	51.3	51.2	52.5
2010	50.3	50.4	50.3	50.1	50.6	51.1	50.0	51.0	51.2	51.4	51.5	51.5	50.8
2011	50.8	50.8	50.8	51.0	51.1	51.4	50.1	51.0	51.0	50.8	50.6	50.6	50.8
2012	49.8	50.0	50.0	50.2	50.3	50.7	49.5	50.6	50.6	50.8	50.7	50.9	50.3
2013	50.3	50.0	50.4	50.5	50.7	51.1	49.5	50.9	50.9	50.8	50.9	50.9	50.6
Trade, Transportation, and Utilities													
2002	101.6	100.0	100.6	101.7	102.7	104.0	102.5	102.7	103.2	103.7	106.2	108.0	103.1
2003	102.2	100.7	100.8	101.6	102.8	103.8	102.2	102.5	103.7	104.8	107.1	108.3	103.4
2004	102.3	101.3	101.5	101.3	103.3	103.6	102.0	101.8	102.6	104.0	105.9	107.1	103.1
2005	101.7	100.8	100.7	102.0	102.6	103.5	102.1	102.5	102.9	103.9	106.0	107.8	103.0
2006	102.0	100.3	100.8	102.2	102.6	103.4	101.5	101.7	102.6	103.6	105.9	107.5	102.8
2007	102.2	100.4	100.7	101.4	102.3	103.3	101.7	101.4	101.9	102.1	104.4	105.8	102.3
2008	100.1	98.5	98.5	98.9	99.8	100.5	99.0	99.1	99.4	99.6	100.3	100.8	99.5
2009	95.2	93.7	93.3	92.6	94.1	94.9	93.2	93.1	94.4	94.9	96.4	97.2	94.4
2010	93.5	92.6	93.0	92.5	93.2	94.4	93.2	93.4	94.3	95.2	96.9	97.7	94.2
2011	93.7	93.0	92.7	94.0	94.9	95.5	94.1	94.3	95.5	96.5	98.5	99.7	95.2
2012	95.5	94.3	94.5	94.9	96.1	97.0	94.9	95.1	96.3	97.0	99.0	99.6	96.2
2013	94.5	93.7	93.6	94.5	95.6	96.4	95.1	95.3	96.3	96.8	97.6	99.4	95.7
Wholesale Trade													
2002	20.3	20.2	20.4	20.5	20.6	20.7	20.4	20.5	20.4	20.4	20.7	20.6	20.5
2003	20.5	20.3	20.4	20.5	20.8	20.9	20.7	20.6	20.5	20.6	20.8	20.6	20.6
2004	20.2	20.2	20.4	20.7	20.7	20.8	20.7	20.7	20.7	20.8	20.9	20.9	20.6
2005	20.5	20.5	20.6	21.0	21.0	21.2	21.1	21.2	21.1	21.1	21.2	21.5	21.0
2006	21.0	21.0	21.1	21.3	21.4	21.5	21.4	21.4	21.4	21.5	21.4	21.4	21.3
2007	21.3	21.1	21.1	21.4	21.4	21.5	21.5	21.4	21.2	21.2	21.3	21.4	21.3
2008	20.8	20.8	20.8	20.9	21.0	21.1	21.0	20.9	20.9	20.9	20.8	20.6	20.9
2009	20.1	19.9	19.9	19.9	19.9	20.0	19.8	19.7	19.9	19.9	19.8	19.8	19.9
2010	19.4	19.4	19.4	19.4	19.7	19.8	19.7	19.8	19.8	19.8	19.9	19.8	19.7
2011	19.5	19.6	19.1	19.3	19.4	19.5	19.6	19.6	19.7	19.7	19.8	20.0	19.6
2012	19.8	19.9	20.0	20.0	20.1	20.3	20.2	20.1	20.1	20.1	20.1	20.0	20.1
2013	19.7	19.7	19.8	19.9	20.0	20.1	20.0	20.1	20.1	20.2	19.9	20.2	20.0
Retail Trade													
2002	68.6	67.3	67.6	68.4	69.0	69.9	69.4	69.4	69.8	70.1	72.4	74.3	69.7
2003	68.9	67.6	67.5	68.1	68.7	69.5	69.0	69.4	69.6	70.7	72.8	74.2	69.7
2004	69.1	68.2	68.2	68.3	69.2	69.6	69.2	69.0	68.6	70.0	71.9	73.1	69.5
2005	68.7	67.8	67.7	68.2	68.6	69.1	68.6	68.8	68.6	69.6	71.6	73.0	69.2
2006	68.4	66.8	67.1	68.0	68.1	68.6	67.9	67.9	67.8	68.7	71.1	72.6	68.6
2007	68.1	66.8	67.0	67.1	67.8	68.4	67.8	67.6	67.2	67.6	69.8	70.8	68.0
2008	66.6	65.1	65.1	65.1	65.6	66.1	65.5	65.5	64.9	65.5	66.5	66.9	65.7
2009	62.8	61.6	61.3	60.7	61.9	62.4	62.1	62.0	61.9	62.6	64.1	64.8	62.4
2010	62.2	61.2	61.6	60.8	61.0	61.8	61.9	62.0	61.6	62.4	64.0	64.7	62.1
2011	61.7	60.9	61.1	61.8	62.4	62.7	62.4	62.8	62.4	63.4	65.3	65.9	62.7
2012	62.7	61.5	61.6	61.9	62.7	63.2	62.6	62.7	62.7	63.4	65.4	65.8	63.0
2013	62.1	61.2	61.0	61.6	62.4	63.0	62.8	62.9	62.7	63.2	64.3	65.4	62.7
Transportation and Utilities													
2002	12.7	12.5	12.6	12.8	13.1	13.4	12.7	12.8	13.0	13.2	13.1	13.1	12.9
2003	12.8	12.8	12.9	13.0	13.3	13.4	12.5	12.5	13.6	13.5	13.5	13.5	13.1
2004	13.0	12.9	12.9	12.3	13.4	13.2	12.1	12.1	13.3	13.2	13.1	13.1	12.9
2005	12.5	12.5	12.4	12.8	13.0	13.2	12.4	12.5	13.2	13.2	13.2	13.3	12.9
2006	12.6	12.5	12.6	12.9	13.1	13.3	12.2	12.4	13.4	13.4	13.4	13.5	12.9
2007	12.8	12.5	12.6	12.9	13.1	13.4	12.4	12.4	13.5	13.3	13.3	13.6	13.0
2008	12.7	12.6	12.6	12.9	13.2	13.3	12.5	12.7	13.6	13.2	13.0	13.3	13.0
2009	12.3	12.2	12.1	12.0	12.3	12.5	11.3	11.4	12.6	12.4	12.5	12.6	12.2
2010	11.9	12.0	12.0	12.3	12.5	12.8	11.6	11.6	12.9	13.0	13.0	13.2	12.4
2011	12.5	12.5	12.5	12.9	13.1	13.3	12.1	11.9	13.4	13.4	13.4	13.8	12.9
2012	13.0	12.9	12.9	13.0	13.3	13.5	12.1	12.3	13.5	13.5	13.5	13.8	13.1
2013	12.7	12.8	12.8	13.0	13.2	13.3	12.3	12.3	13.5	13.4	13.4	13.8	13.0
Information													
2002	11.9	11.9	11.9	11.9	11.9	12.1	12.0	12.0	11.9	11.6	11.9	11.9	11.9
2003	12.0	12.0	11.9	11.9	11.9	12.1	11.9	11.9	11.7	11.9	11.9	11.8	11.9
2004	11.9	11.9	11.9	11.9	11.8	11.8	11.6	11.5	11.4	11.4	11.5	11.5	11.7
2005	11.7	11.7	11.6	11.6	11.5	11.6	11.6	11.6	11.5	11.6	11.8	11.8	11.6
2006	11.9	11.8	11.8	12.2	12.1	12.2	11.6	11.5	11.5	11.4	11.7	11.7	11.8
2007	11.3	11.2	11.2	11.3	11.4	11.5	11.5	11.6	11.5	11.5	11.7	11.7	11.5
2008	11.6	11.9	11.9	11.7	11.8	12.0	11.8	12.2	11.9	11.9	11.7	11.6	11.8
2009	11.6	11.5	11.4	11.6	11.6	11.6	11.2	11.2	11.1	10.9	11.1	11.1	11.3
2010	11.0	11.1	11.2	11.1	11.1	11.2	11.2	11.5	11.6	11.4	11.5	11.5	11.3
2011	11.0	11.0	11.2	11.6	11.8	11.7	11.5	10.6	11.3	11.1	11.2	11.4	11.3
2012	11.1	11.1	11.1	10.9	10.8	10.9	10.7	10.7	10.5	10.5	10.5	10.5	10.8
2013	10.4	10.5	10.3	10.1	10.3	10.3	10.2	10.3	10.1	10.0	10.2	10.0	10.2

Employment by Industry: Providence-Fall River-Warwick, RI–MA, NECTA, Selected Years, 2002–2013—*Continued*

(Numbers in thousands, not seasonally adjusted)

Industry and year	January	February	March	April	May	June	July	August	September	October	November	December	Annual average
Financial Activities													
2002	35.1	35.0	35.0	35.4	35.3	35.9	36.0	36.0	36.0	36.2	36.4	36.6	35.7
2003	36.4	36.4	36.7	36.3	36.6	37.1	37.1	37.1	37.0	37.0	37.1	37.3	36.8
2004	37.0	37.0	37.0	37.1	37.4	37.4	37.3	37.3	37.1	37.3	37.3	37.3	37.2
2005	36.9	37.1	37.1	37.6	37.5	37.8	37.9	37.9	37.7	37.4	37.5	37.8	37.5
2006	37.3	37.3	37.5	37.7	37.9	38.1	38.3	38.7	38.8	38.7	38.9	39.3	38.2
2007	38.4	38.5	38.4	38.5	38.6	38.4	38.1	37.7	37.6	37.2	37.1	37.1	38.0
2008	36.7	36.8	36.6	36.4	36.5	36.4	36.2	36.0	36.1	35.3	35.1	35.1	36.1
2009	34.6	34.5	34.2	33.9	34.0	34.1	33.8	33.5	33.2	33.2	33.4	33.3	33.8
2010	32.9	32.9	33.1	32.9	33.0	33.1	33.2	33.1	33.2	33.4	33.4	33.6	33.2
2011	32.9	33.0	33.0	33.1	33.1	33.6	33.3	33.3	33.3	33.3	33.6	33.5	33.3
2012	33.3	33.5	33.7	33.8	34.1	34.3	34.3	34.3	34.3	34.4	34.4	34.5	34.1
2013	34.2	34.4	34.7	34.8	34.9	35.1	35.1	34.9	34.8	34.9	34.8	34.9	34.8
Professional and Business Services													
2002	55.1	54.6	55.2	56.8	57.1	57.6	56.5	57.0	57.4	57.7	57.2	56.3	56.5
2003	54.6	54.3	54.7	56.6	57.2	58.5	58.3	59.0	58.9	59.4	59.3	59.3	57.5
2004	57.8	57.9	58.4	60.7	61.4	62.2	61.3	62.1	62.5	62.4	62.0	61.5	60.9
2005	59.0	59.0	59.5	62.3	62.2	62.9	62.8	63.5	63.7	62.6	62.5	61.9	61.8
2006	58.8	59.1	59.8	63.0	63.0	64.2	63.1	64.3	65.0	65.0	64.4	63.7	62.8
2007	60.5	60.2	60.6	62.9	63.4	64.5	63.3	63.3	63.0	62.6	62.5	62.2	62.4
2008	59.5	59.0	59.3	61.6	61.4	62.5	61.7	61.9	62.3	61.8	60.8	59.6	61.0
2009	56.9	56.5	56.8	58.1	58.1	58.8	58.1	58.5	58.6	58.5	58.3	57.5	57.9
2010	55.1	55.3	56.2	59.5	59.6	60.4	60.2	60.1	60.2	60.4	60.3	59.2	58.9
2011	56.9	57.3	57.6	59.7	59.9	60.4	60.3	60.7	61.3	61.3	61.2	59.7	59.7
2012	57.6	57.9	59.1	61.3	61.7	62.6	61.9	62.4	62.3	62.1	62.3	62.0	61.1
2013	59.7	60.3	60.6	63.4	64.1	65.5	64.4	64.9	65.1	65.5	65.1	64.4	63.6
Education and Health Services													
2002	99.6	101.9	103.2	103.6	103.6	99.1	98.5	99.6	103.1	104.4	105.4	105.8	102.3
2003	103.5	105.4	106.7	107.0	107.0	102.6	101.3	100.7	104.5	107.1	107.9	108.2	105.2
2004	105.4	107.8	109.0	109.7	109.6	104.9	104.0	103.7	107.5	109.8	110.5	110.9	107.7
2005	107.6	110.2	111.2	111.7	111.4	107.5	106.8	106.5	111.0	113.2	113.8	112.9	110.3
2006	109.1	112.7	114.0	114.6	113.7	109.5	108.0	107.9	111.8	114.8	115.9	115.0	112.3
2007	111.6	115.3	115.9	116.2	116.1	111.8	110.2	110.1	113.9	116.3	117.2	116.5	114.3
2008	113.2	116.6	117.5	117.7	117.0	112.6	111.1	111.1	114.8	117.4	118.0	117.8	115.4
2009	114.1	117.5	118.0	117.9	117.5	113.7	112.5	112.5	116.3	118.7	119.3	119.3	116.4
2010	116.1	118.8	119.7	119.6	119.7	115.0	114.5	114.6	118.5	120.6	121.1	121.4	118.3
2011	117.0	120.4	120.9	121.9	121.9	117.3	116.1	115.5	119.2	122.2	122.3	121.6	119.7
2012	118.1	122.0	122.6	121.6	122.1	117.7	116.2	116.5	122.2	123.6	123.3	124.3	120.9
2013	121.2	123.3	124.0	123.8	123.4	120.3	118.0	117.6	122.9	125.4	126.0	123.3	122.4
Leisure and Hospitality													
2002	49.8	50.4	51.6	55.1	58.1	60.8	61.6	61.3	59.4	57.0	55.5	54.3	56.2
2003	52.0	51.9	52.6	56.2	59.6	61.9	63.3	62.9	61.1	58.6	57.2	56.5	57.8
2004	52.6	53.1	53.4	57.2	60.8	63.7	64.2	63.9	62.2	59.7	58.2	58.0	58.9
2005	53.8	54.3	54.8	58.4	61.0	64.1	64.6	63.9	62.5	59.7	58.3	57.5	59.4
2006	53.6	53.7	54.9	58.5	61.3	64.0	64.5	64.3	63.0	60.3	58.8	58.3	59.6
2007	54.8	55.2	56.0	59.4	62.3	65.6	65.8	65.7	63.8	62.0	59.7	59.1	60.8
2008	55.0	55.5	56.0	59.3	62.6	65.0	64.5	64.1	62.8	60.3	58.4	57.7	60.1
2009	52.3	52.9	53.3	56.2	60.2	62.4	62.3	62.5	61.3	58.6	56.5	56.1	57.9
2010	52.5	52.8	53.3	57.0	60.4	63.3	63.9	63.7	62.0	59.5	57.9	56.8	58.6
2011	53.3	53.9	54.5	58.1	61.0	64.5	64.7	64.4	62.8	60.5	58.5	57.5	59.5
2012	54.6	55.4	56.2	59.6	63.0	66.2	66.4	66.4	64.5	62.2	60.0	59.5	61.2
2013	56.1	56.3	57.6	61.3	64.8	68.3	68.3	68.2	66.3	63.6	61.3	60.4	62.7
Other Services													
2002	25.3	25.4	25.4	25.5	25.7	26.3	26.7	26.4	25.7	26.0	25.9	26.0	25.9
2003	26.0	26.0	26.2	26.0	26.4	26.8	27.2	26.9	26.3	26.3	26.6	26.6	26.4
2004	25.9	25.9	26.1	26.3	26.6	26.9	27.3	27.1	26.5	26.7	26.8	26.7	26.6
2005	26.1	26.1	26.3	26.4	26.6	27.0	27.3	27.3	26.4	26.3	26.4	26.4	26.6
2006	25.5	25.6	25.8	26.3	26.6	27.2	27.3	27.1	26.4	26.7	26.6	26.6	26.5
2007	26.0	26.0	26.2	26.3	26.6	27.4	27.4	27.2	26.3	26.4	26.4	26.6	26.6
2008	25.8	25.8	26.0	26.1	26.3	26.7	27.0	26.7	26.0	26.1	25.9	25.9	26.2
2009	25.1	25.2	25.2	25.4	25.6	25.9	26.3	26.0	25.2	25.5	25.5	25.5	25.5
2010	24.8	24.9	24.9	25.1	25.5	25.7	26.5	26.4	25.3	25.2	25.4	25.3	25.4
2011	24.7	24.9	25.0	25.4	25.6	26.4	27.1	27.0	25.8	25.5	25.7	25.7	25.7
2012	25.0	25.2	25.3	25.9	26.0	26.7	27.1	27.2	26.5	26.1	26.1	26.3	26.1
2013	25.5	25.6	25.9	25.9	26.2	26.9	27.2	27.0	26.2	26.0	26.3	25.8	26.2
Government													
2002	77.4	77.8	78.3	78.0	78.1	77.4	72.3	71.7	76.8	76.3	77.4	76.9	76.5
2003	77.1	77.2	77.3	77.1	77.6	77.6	70.0	69.4	75.2	76.3	76.5	76.6	75.7
2004	75.7	75.9	76.5	75.7	76.7	76.5	68.5	68.2	74.4	75.3	76.0	75.3	74.6
2005	75.0	75.2	75.0	75.2	75.7	75.5	68.9	68.2	73.2	75.1	75.5	75.4	74.0
2006	74.7	75.2	75.1	74.9	75.2	75.0	69.1	68.7	74.0	75.1	76.1	75.8	74.1
2007	74.9	75.0	75.1	75.0	75.6	74.8	69.8	69.5	73.2	74.2	74.4	74.7	73.9
2008	74.0	74.3	74.5	74.6	75.4	74.4	68.0	67.3	71.6	72.6	73.5	73.2	72.8
2009	72.3	72.4	72.3	72.7	73.0	72.3	65.8	65.3	70.3	72.0	72.4	72.3	71.1
2010	71.6	71.7	72.3	72.3	74.3	72.6	66.4	66.2	69.7	71.5	72.2	71.9	71.1
2011	71.2	71.3	71.8	71.7	71.9	71.6	65.2	65.2	69.3	70.8	71.1	71.2	70.2
2012	70.4	70.8	70.8	71.1	71.8	70.3	65.0	65.1	69.2	70.8	71.3	71.1	69.8
2013	70.7	70.3	70.9	70.9	71.9	71.0	65.4	64.8	69.5	71.0	71.4	71.5	69.9

Employment by Industry: Raleigh-Cary, NC, Selected Years, 2002–2013

(Numbers in thousands, not seasonally adjusted)

Industry and year	January	February	March	April	May	June	July	August	September	October	November	December	Annual average
Total Nonfarm													
2002	425.9	427.2	428.3	432.3	435.5	436.3	430.6	433.8	438.7	439.8	441.1	441.8	434.3
2003	429.2	430.2	431.8	436.0	439.3	440.3	433.1	436.6	438.3	442.6	443.6	444.6	437.1
2004	437.0	438.1	441.9	443.4	447.7	449.2	448.4	451.6	454.6	456.9	458.8	461.2	449.1
2005	451.5	453.4	456.9	461.9	465.6	467.0	466.9	472.6	475.3	474.6	479.3	479.8	467.1
2006	472.3	474.2	478.1	485.9	490.3	493.2	490.5	496.8	498.7	502.5	508.0	509.5	491.7
2007	501.5	504.9	509.5	510.7	517.2	520.1	514.4	520.7	520.7	525.1	528.2	528.5	516.8
2008	518.3	520.4	521.6	521.6	525.8	523.6	520.3	524.1	523.9	524.9	522.9	520.1	522.3
2009	503.8	501.9	501.0	501.4	504.0	500.7	496.7	497.9	497.4	498.0	499.8	499.3	500.2
2010	487.7	487.9	492.2	497.6	502.3	502.2	500.7	503.2	502.8	506.8	509.1	508.2	500.1
2011	499.0	502.6	505.6	508.3	509.8	509.2	507.6	511.4	512.2	515.2	517.7	516.8	509.6
2012	512.3	514.7	518.4	522.7	525.9	526.2	524.8	529.9	528.8	531.9	535.4	534.7	525.5
2013	525.5	530.3	533.6	535.3	537.9	537.6	536.4	544.8	547.8	553.0	555.4	556.9	541.2
Total Private													
2002	349.5	349.9	351.8	355.8	358.7	359.8	360.6	362.2	361.1	361.6	362.8	363.9	358.1
2003	351.8	352.3	353.5	357.4	360.3	361.9	358.2	360.8	359.0	360.9	362.6	363.9	358.6
2004	357.1	357.8	361.0	362.4	366.3	368.4	371.0	372.1	370.4	372.5	374.7	377.4	367.6
2005	368.7	369.9	372.9	377.9	381.4	384.1	386.6	387.9	389.2	390.6	393.6	396.4	383.3
2006	387.7	388.7	392.0	398.5	402.3	406.0	406.7	408.7	409.5	412.5	417.4	419.4	404.1
2007	411.7	414.2	418.2	419.1	424.9	429.3	427.0	430.0	428.0	432.1	434.8	435.4	425.4
2008	425.7	427.0	427.7	427.4	431.3	430.8	429.8	431.2	428.4	427.3	426.2	423.8	428.1
2009	410.3	408.2	406.6	405.3	407.9	406.8	406.8	406.7	404.1	403.8	405.6	405.7	406.5
2010	395.6	395.0	398.7	402.6	405.4	407.6	410.3	411.0	408.8	412.3	415.1	414.5	406.4
2011	406.3	409.1	411.8	414.9	416.5	419.1	421.3	422.0	420.6	422.3	425.0	426.1	417.9
2012	421.0	422.2	425.9	430.6	434.4	436.4	438.8	440.1	437.0	439.0	442.4	443.4	434.3
2013	434.0	437.4	440.4	442.6	446.5	449.5	450.7	454.7	454.5	458.7	461.3	463.3	449.5
Goods Producing													
2002	68.2	68.4	68.5	68.8	69.1	68.9	69.0	68.8	68.2	67.9	67.3	66.9	68.3
2003	64.3	64.2	64.3	64.2	65.1	65.4	65.2	65.5	65.0	65.6	65.6	65.6	65.0
2004	63.9	63.9	65.0	65.7	66.3	66.6	67.3	67.0	66.6	67.6	67.4	67.2	66.2
2005	65.7	66.1	66.7	68.0	68.8	69.9	70.4	70.5	70.8	70.7	70.9	70.9	69.1
2006	70.0	70.2	71.4	72.2	73.3	74.3	74.8	75.1	75.0	75.1	75.3	75.5	73.5
2007	74.3	74.5	75.3	75.2	75.8	76.4	76.6	77.2	76.6	76.0	75.8	75.3	75.8
2008	73.6	73.5	73.6	72.6	72.8	72.7	72.6	72.0	71.4	69.9	68.7	67.1	71.7
2009	64.1	63.0	62.4	61.1	60.7	60.7	60.5	60.2	59.6	59.1	58.7	58.6	60.7
2010	56.8	56.5	57.1	57.3	57.9	58.3	59.1	59.2	59.0	59.0	58.9	58.4	58.1
2011	57.4	58.0	58.6	58.6	58.8	59.3	59.8	59.6	59.3	59.0	59.0	59.0	58.9
2012	58.7	59.0	59.5	59.7	60.2	60.8	61.4	61.4	61.2	61.0	61.0	61.0	60.4
2013	59.6	60.0	60.3	60.4	60.8	61.3	61.6	61.7	61.5	61.2	61.7	61.1	60.9
Service-Providing													
2002	357.7	358.8	359.8	363.5	366.4	367.4	361.6	365.0	370.5	371.9	373.8	374.9	365.9
2003	364.9	366.0	367.5	371.8	374.2	374.9	367.9	371.1	373.3	377.0	378.0	379.0	372.1
2004	373.1	374.2	376.9	377.7	381.4	382.6	381.1	384.6	388.0	389.3	391.4	394.0	382.9
2005	385.8	387.3	390.2	393.9	396.8	397.1	396.5	402.1	404.5	403.9	408.4	408.9	398.0
2006	402.3	404.0	406.7	413.7	417.0	418.9	415.7	421.7	423.7	427.4	432.7	434.0	418.2
2007	427.2	430.4	434.2	435.5	441.4	443.7	437.8	443.5	444.1	449.1	452.4	453.2	441.0
2008	444.7	446.9	448.0	449.0	453.0	450.9	447.7	452.1	452.5	455.0	454.2	453.0	450.6
2009	439.7	438.9	438.6	440.3	443.3	440.0	436.2	437.7	437.8	438.9	441.1	440.7	439.4
2010	430.9	431.4	435.1	440.3	444.4	443.9	441.6	444.0	443.8	447.8	450.2	449.8	441.9
2011	441.6	444.6	447.0	449.7	451.0	449.9	447.8	451.8	452.9	456.2	458.7	457.8	450.8
2012	453.6	455.7	458.9	463.0	465.7	465.4	463.4	468.5	467.6	470.9	474.4	473.7	465.1
2013	465.9	470.3	473.3	474.9	477.1	476.3	474.8	483.1	486.3	491.8	493.7	495.8	480.3
Mining, Logging, and Construction													
2002	31.5	32.0	32.2	32.6	33.3	33.1	33.3	33.5	33.0	32.9	32.4	32.0	32.7
2003	30.1	30.1	30.3	30.2	31.0	31.4	31.8	32.1	31.9	32.2	32.1	32.1	31.3
2004	30.8	30.9	31.7	32.5	32.5	33.1	33.2	33.9	33.8	34.0	33.8	33.6	32.9
2005	32.3	32.5	33.0	33.8	34.6	35.3	35.7	35.8	36.0	36.1	36.1	35.9	34.8
2006	35.2	35.4	36.1	37.2	38.0	38.8	39.5	39.7	39.6	39.5	39.6	39.7	38.2
2007	39.2	39.4	40.1	40.3	40.8	41.3	41.5	41.8	41.5	41.1	40.9	40.4	40.7
2008	39.2	39.2	39.3	38.3	38.6	38.5	38.4	38.0	37.6	36.4	35.3	34.2	37.8
2009	31.7	31.1	30.7	29.9	30.0	30.1	30.0	29.8	29.4	28.8	28.5	28.3	29.9
2010	27.0	26.8	27.3	27.7	28.1	28.4	29.0	29.1	28.9	28.9	28.6	28.1	28.2
2011	27.2	27.8	28.2	28.0	28.3	28.8	29.3	29.1	28.9	28.7	28.6	28.6	28.5
2012	28.4	28.6	29.1	29.2	29.6	30.0	30.5	30.5	30.4	30.3	30.2	30.2	29.8
2013	29.0	29.3	29.6	29.6	30.1	30.3	30.3	30.4	30.3	30.0	30.5	30.4	30.0
Manufacturing													
2002	36.7	36.4	36.3	36.2	35.8	35.8	35.7	35.3	35.2	35.0	34.9	34.9	35.7
2003	34.2	34.1	34.0	34.0	34.1	34.0	33.4	33.4	33.1	33.4	33.5	33.5	33.7
2004	33.1	33.0	33.3	33.2	33.2	33.4	33.4	33.2	33.1	33.6	33.6	33.6	33.3
2005	33.4	33.6	33.7	34.2	34.2	34.6	34.7	34.7	34.8	34.6	34.8	35.0	34.4
2006	34.8	34.8	35.3	35.0	35.3	35.5	35.3	35.4	35.4	35.6	35.7	35.8	35.3
2007	35.1	35.1	35.2	34.9	35.0	35.1	35.1	35.4	35.1	34.9	34.9	34.9	35.1
2008	34.4	34.3	34.3	34.3	34.2	34.2	34.2	34.0	33.8	33.5	33.4	32.9	34.0
2009	32.4	31.9	31.7	31.2	30.7	30.6	30.5	30.4	30.2	30.3	30.2	30.3	30.9
2010	29.8	29.7	29.8	29.6	29.8	29.9	30.1	30.1	30.1	30.1	30.3	30.3	30.0
2011	30.2	30.2	30.4	30.6	30.5	30.5	30.5	30.5	30.4	30.3	30.4	30.4	30.4
2012	30.3	30.4	30.4	30.5	30.6	30.8	30.9	30.9	30.8	30.7	30.8	30.8	30.7
2013	30.6	30.7	30.7	30.8	30.7	31.0	31.3	31.3	31.2	31.2	31.2	30.7	31.0

Employment by Industry: Raleigh-Cary, NC, Selected Years, 2002–2013—*Continued*

(Numbers in thousands, not seasonally adjusted)

Industry and year	January	February	March	April	May	June	July	August	September	October	November	December	Annual average
Trade, Transportation, and Utilities													
2002	79.7	79.1	79.6	79.8	80.1	80.1	80.0	80.5	80.7	81.1	82.7	83.7	80.6
2003	79.4	79.0	79.3	80.4	81.1	81.8	79.9	80.8	80.9	82.2	83.6	84.6	81.1
2004	81.2	80.8	80.9	80.8	81.2	81.3	81.4	82.0	82.2	83.0	84.5	85.6	82.1
2005	82.5	81.8	82.3	82.9	83.5	83.6	84.2	84.3	84.3	85.7	87.3	88.9	84.3
2006	85.0	84.2	84.4	85.1	85.5	85.9	87.0	87.9	87.8	89.0	92.0	93.3	87.3
2007	90.0	89.2	90.2	90.2	91.2	91.4	91.3	91.2	91.1	92.1	95.0	96.3	91.6
2008	91.9	91.5	91.9	91.8	91.8	92.0	91.6	91.7	90.9	91.5	92.3	92.8	91.8
2009	88.1	87.1	87.1	86.5	87.0	86.9	87.0	86.8	86.4	87.1	88.7	89.5	87.4
2010	86.0	85.3	85.5	86.0	86.7	86.9	87.2	87.3	86.2	87.6	89.7	91.1	87.1
2011	87.5	87.3	87.8	88.6	88.9	89.2	89.5	89.7	89.6	90.0	92.5	93.5	89.5
2012	91.4	90.6	91.2	90.9	91.8	92.0	92.1	91.9	91.7	92.3	94.7	95.3	92.2
2013	91.5	90.8	91.5	91.3	92.2	92.8	93.0	93.5	93.4	94.8	96.7	97.5	93.3
Wholesale Trade													
2002	20.0	20.0	19.9	19.7	19.9	19.9	20.4	20.4	20.4	20.7	20.6	20.5	20.2
2003	20.1	20.0	20.2	20.1	20.0	20.1	20.0	20.1	20.1	20.2	20.0	20.0	20.1
2004	19.5	19.5	19.7	19.6	19.7	19.8	20.1	20.1	20.1	20.4	20.3	20.4	19.9
2005	19.8	19.8	19.8	19.9	20.1	20.2	20.1	20.3	20.4	20.6	20.5	20.7	20.2
2006	20.4	20.4	20.4	20.5	20.6	20.9	21.1	21.3	21.5	21.4	21.6	21.7	21.0
2007	21.9	22.0	22.2	22.1	22.2	22.2	22.3	22.2	22.2	22.1	22.2	22.2	22.2
2008	22.0	22.2	22.2	22.1	22.2	22.3	22.3	22.4	22.2	22.3	22.0	21.9	22.2
2009	21.4	21.4	21.2	21.0	20.9	20.8	20.7	20.7	20.5	20.5	20.4	20.4	20.8
2010	20.0	20.0	19.9	20.1	20.2	20.2	20.4	20.5	20.3	20.5	20.5	20.5	20.3
2011	20.7	20.7	20.7	21.1	21.3	21.4	21.8	21.9	22.1	21.8	22.1	22.1	21.5
2012	22.5	22.7	22.8	22.7	22.9	22.9	23.3	23.3	23.2	23.0	22.9	22.8	22.9
2013	22.5	22.5	22.5	22.3	22.5	22.7	22.7	22.8	22.7	23.1	23.2	23.2	22.7
Retail Trade													
2002	50.6	50.2	50.7	50.8	50.9	50.9	50.1	50.9	51.2	51.3	53.2	54.3	51.3
2003	50.2	49.9	50.0	51.0	51.8	52.4	50.7	51.3	51.4	52.7	54.4	55.3	51.8
2004	52.6	52.1	52.0	51.8	52.2	52.2	52.2	52.7	53.0	53.5	55.1	56.0	53.0
2005	53.3	52.7	53.0	53.5	53.9	53.8	54.3	54.2	54.2	54.8	56.4	57.8	54.3
2006	54.4	53.6	53.7	54.2	54.5	54.5	55.1	55.7	55.4	56.8	59.3	60.4	55.6
2007	57.1	56.3	57.0	57.0	57.8	58.0	57.9	57.9	57.8	59.1	61.9	62.8	58.4
2008	59.3	58.8	59.1	58.9	58.8	58.9	58.6	58.5	58.0	58.5	59.7	59.9	58.9
2009	56.2	55.4	55.7	55.4	56.1	56.2	56.4	56.3	56.0	56.7	58.3	59.0	56.5
2010	56.2	55.5	55.8	55.9	56.5	56.6	56.7	56.7	56.0	57.1	59.2	60.4	56.9
2011	57.2	57.0	57.4	57.5	57.6	57.7	57.6	57.7	57.3	58.2	60.4	61.1	58.1
2012	58.8	57.9	58.4	58.3	58.9	59.0	58.9	58.7	58.7	59.5	62.0	62.4	59.3
2013	59.2	58.8	59.4	59.5	60.1	60.4	60.6	61.0	60.9	61.7	63.5	64.1	60.8
Transportation and Utilities													
2002	9.1	8.9	9.0	9.3	9.3	9.3	9.5	9.2	9.1	9.1	8.9	8.9	9.1
2003	9.1	9.1	9.1	9.3	9.3	9.3	9.2	9.4	9.4	9.3	9.2	9.3	9.3
2004	9.1	9.2	9.2	9.4	9.3	9.3	9.1	9.2	9.1	9.1	9.1	9.2	9.2
2005	9.4	9.3	9.5	9.5	9.5	9.6	9.8	9.8	9.7	10.3	10.4	10.4	9.8
2006	10.2	10.2	10.3	10.4	10.4	10.5	10.8	10.9	10.9	10.8	11.1	11.2	10.6
2007	11.0	10.9	11.0	11.1	11.2	11.2	11.1	11.1	11.1	10.9	10.9	11.3	11.1
2008	10.6	10.5	10.6	10.8	10.8	10.8	10.7	10.8	10.7	10.7	10.6	11.0	10.7
2009	10.5	10.3	10.2	10.1	10.0	9.9	9.9	9.8	9.9	9.9	10.0	10.1	10.1
2010	9.8	9.8	9.8	10.0	10.0	10.1	10.1	10.1	9.9	10.0	10.0	10.2	10.0
2011	9.6	9.6	9.7	10.0	10.0	10.1	10.1	10.1	10.2	10.0	10.0	10.3	10.0
2012	10.1	10.0	10.0	9.9	10.0	10.1	9.9	9.9	9.8	9.8	9.8	10.1	10.0
2013	9.8	9.5	9.6	9.5	9.6	9.7	9.7	9.7	9.8	10.0	10.0	10.2	9.8
Information													
2002	18.3	18.2	18.4	18.2	18.1	18.2	17.9	17.8	17.7	17.7	17.7	17.7	18.0
2003	17.6	17.7	17.7	17.7	17.8	17.9	17.9	17.8	17.5	17.3	17.3	17.4	17.6
2004	17.5	17.4	17.5	17.1	17.0	17.1	17.0	17.0	16.8	16.5	16.8	16.9	17.1
2005	16.7	16.7	16.9	17.1	17.2	17.3	17.3	17.4	17.2	17.0	17.1	17.2	17.1
2006	17.0	16.9	16.6	16.8	16.8	16.8	16.7	16.6	16.5	16.4	16.4	16.4	16.7
2007	16.3	16.6	16.5	16.4	16.5	16.8	16.9	16.9	16.7	16.9	16.8	16.8	16.7
2008	16.7	16.8	16.7	17.0	17.1	17.2	17.1	17.2	17.1	17.2	17.2	17.3	17.1
2009	17.1	17.0	16.9	17.0	16.8	16.9	16.9	16.8	16.7	16.8	16.8	16.8	16.9
2010	16.5	16.5	16.6	16.6	16.5	16.7	16.8	16.8	16.7	16.7	16.9	16.9	16.7
2011	16.9	17.0	17.0	17.1	17.1	17.4	17.5	17.7	17.5	17.6	17.8	17.8	17.4
2012	17.7	17.7	17.7	17.5	17.5	17.7	17.7	17.7	17.7	17.6	17.6	17.7	17.6
2013	17.7	17.8	17.8	17.8	17.9	18.0	18.1	18.1	17.9	18.0	18.0	18.1	17.9
Financial Activities													
2002	21.9	22.0	21.8	21.6	21.8	22.1	21.7	22.1	22.1	22.1	22.2	22.0	22.0
2003	21.8	21.8	21.9	22.0	22.2	22.3	22.0	22.1	22.2	22.8	22.7	22.8	22.2
2004	23.3	23.5	23.6	23.5	23.3	23.3	23.7	23.6	23.4	23.5	23.6	23.6	23.5
2005	23.4	23.4	23.4	23.4	23.5	23.6	23.8	24.0	24.1	24.4	24.5	24.8	23.9
2006	24.4	24.4	24.6	24.9	25.0	25.2	25.3	25.4	25.4	25.6	25.8	25.9	25.2
2007	25.6	25.7	25.8	26.3	26.6	26.9	27.1	27.3	27.1	27.5	27.4	27.7	26.8
2008	26.8	27.0	27.0	27.1	27.2	27.4	27.4	27.5	27.4	27.5	27.3	27.3	27.2
2009	26.9	26.9	26.7	26.8	26.7	26.8	26.9	26.8	26.4	26.5	26.6	26.8	26.7
2010	26.4	26.4	26.4	26.3	26.4	26.4	26.6	26.6	26.6	26.8	26.7	26.9	26.6
2011	26.4	26.4	26.4	26.3	26.3	26.3	26.3	26.4	26.2	26.2	26.1	26.2	26.3
2012	25.8	26.1	26.2	26.4	26.4	26.5	26.4	26.3	26.2	26.2	26.1	26.2	26.4
2013	26.5	26.4	26.6	26.8	26.9	27.0	27.1	27.2	27.1	27.0	27.0	27.0	26.9

Employment by Industry: Raleigh-Cary, NC, Selected Years, 2002–2013—*Continued*

(Numbers in thousands, not seasonally adjusted)

Industry and year	January	February	March	April	May	June	July	August	September	October	November	December	Annual average
Professional and Business Services													
2002	69.6	69.7	70.0	70.6	71.1	71.5	72.7	73.3	73.1	73.2	73.2	73.9	71.8
2003	71.2	71.3	71.4	72.9	72.5	72.7	71.9	72.2	71.3	71.8	71.8	71.9	71.9
2004	70.7	71.2	71.7	72.5	73.4	74.4	75.6	75.8	75.7	76.4	76.5	77.7	74.3
2005	76.0	76.5	77.0	79.1	78.6	79.1	80.8	81.1	81.5	81.2	81.5	81.8	79.5
2006	80.9	81.2	82.0	83.9	83.9	84.9	85.7	86.1	87.3	88.5	88.8	88.8	85.2
2007	87.3	88.3	89.0	89.4	89.7	91.6	89.2	89.7	89.5	92.2	90.8	90.0	89.7
2008	88.5	88.5	88.6	89.1	89.2	88.9	88.1	89.1	88.1	88.3	87.3	86.0	88.3
2009	84.1	83.3	81.9	81.8	81.8	81.7	81.7	81.8	82.1	82.8	83.5	83.4	82.5
2010	81.8	81.9	82.7	84.3	84.7	85.7	86.2	86.3	86.4	89.2	89.3	89.3	85.7
2011	87.7	88.5	88.4	89.7	90.0	91.0	91.6	91.4	92.1	92.5	92.7	92.9	90.7
2012	92.0	92.1	92.7	95.6	95.9	97.0	98.6	98.9	98.1	98.8	99.6	99.6	96.6
2013	98.4	101.0	101.4	101.7	102.8	103.1	104.1	106.4	106.8	109.0	109.1	109.9	104.5
Education and Health Services													
2002	42.8	43.2	43.4	44.6	44.7	44.6	44.2	44.8	45.4	45.8	46.3	46.1	44.7
2003	45.9	46.5	46.6	46.5	46.7	46.2	46.1	46.6	47.2	47.2	47.4	47.5	46.7
2004	47.2	47.5	48.0	47.7	48.1	47.9	48.0	48.6	49.1	49.5	49.9	49.9	48.5
2005	49.4	49.9	50.2	50.1	50.3	49.9	50.0	50.3	51.4	52.0	52.4	52.3	50.7
2006	51.6	52.2	52.6	53.4	53.9	53.5	53.0	53.3	54.0	54.8	55.6	55.7	53.6
2007	54.9	55.8	56.2	56.6	57.0	56.5	56.1	56.9	57.5	58.5	58.7	58.8	57.0
2008	58.1	58.9	58.9	58.9	59.3	58.4	57.9	58.4	59.1	59.9	60.5	60.2	59.0
2009	59.2	59.8	59.9	60.2	60.8	59.7	59.2	60.0	60.0	60.3	60.4	60.3	60.0
2010	59.6	60.1	60.5	61.3	61.4	60.3	60.3	60.7	60.6	61.0	61.2	60.7	60.6
2011	60.7	61.5	61.6	61.1	61.3	60.6	60.5	60.8	61.0	62.2	62.3	62.1	61.3
2012	62.1	62.8	63.4	63.2	63.8	62.9	62.7	63.3	63.7	64.5	64.7	64.8	63.5
2013	63.5	64.2	64.4	64.5	64.8	63.9	63.9	64.8	65.3	66.5	66.5	66.2	64.9
Leisure and Hospitality													
2002	34.8	35.1	36.0	37.7	38.9	39.5	40.1	40.1	39.4	39.2	38.8	39.1	38.2
2003	37.2	37.3	37.8	38.8	39.2	39.7	39.0	39.7	38.9	38.4	38.5	38.3	38.6
2004	37.2	37.2	38.0	38.6	40.0	40.6	41.2	41.5	40.3	39.6	39.5	40.0	39.5
2005	38.6	39.0	40.0	40.5	42.0	43.0	42.6	42.7	42.8	42.1	42.3	42.8	41.5
2006	41.3	41.8	42.6	44.0	45.4	46.2	45.6	45.9	45.9	45.1	45.2	45.3	44.5
2007	44.7	45.2	45.8	45.5	48.1	49.1	48.8	49.7	49.0	47.5	48.6	48.8	47.6
2008	47.6	48.0	48.5	48.5	50.9	50.9	51.3	51.5	50.8	49.4	49.5	50.1	49.8
2009	48.5	48.6	49.1	49.3	51.4	51.5	51.6	51.5	50.6	49.4	49.4	49.2	50.0
2010	47.4	47.3	48.6	49.7	50.6	51.9	52.7	52.9	52.4	50.9	51.4	50.7	50.5
2011	49.5	50.2	51.5	53.1	53.6	54.3	55.1	55.4	54.2	53.8	53.7	53.9	53.2
2012	52.5	53.0	54.2	55.9	56.9	57.5	57.7	58.1	56.1	55.8	55.9	56.5	55.8
2013	55.1	55.2	56.1	57.7	58.4	60.4	60.1	60.3	59.8	59.3	59.6	60.9	58.6
Other Services													
2002	14.2	14.2	14.1	14.5	14.9	14.9	15.0	14.8	14.5	14.6	14.6	14.5	14.6
2003	14.4	14.5	14.5	14.9	15.7	15.9	16.2	16.1	16.0	15.6	15.7	15.8	15.4
2004	16.1	16.3	16.3	16.5	17.0	17.2	16.8	16.6	16.3	16.4	16.5	16.5	16.5
2005	16.4	16.5	16.4	16.8	17.5	17.7	17.5	17.6	17.1	17.5	17.6	17.7	17.2
2006	17.5	17.8	17.8	18.2	18.5	19.2	18.6	18.4	17.6	18.0	18.3	18.5	18.2
2007	18.6	18.9	19.4	19.5	20.0	20.6	21.0	21.1	20.5	21.4	21.7	21.7	20.4
2008	22.5	22.8	22.5	22.4	23.0	23.3	23.8	23.8	23.6	23.6	23.4	23.0	23.1
2009	22.3	22.5	22.6	22.6	22.7	22.6	23.0	22.8	22.3	21.8	21.5	21.1	22.3
2010	21.1	21.0	21.3	21.1	21.2	21.4	21.4	21.2	20.7	21.2	20.8	20.4	21.1
2011	20.2	20.2	20.5	20.4	20.5	21.0	21.0	21.0	20.7	21.0	20.9	20.7	20.7
2012	20.8	20.9	21.0	21.4	21.9	22.0	22.2	22.5	22.5	22.3	22.3	21.8	21.8
2013	21.7	22.0	22.3	22.4	22.7	23.0	22.8	22.7	22.7	22.9	22.7	22.6	22.5
Government													
2002	76.4	77.3	76.5	76.5	76.8	76.5	70.0	71.6	77.6	78.2	78.3	77.9	76.1
2003	77.4	77.9	78.3	78.6	79.0	78.4	74.9	75.8	79.3	81.7	81.0	80.7	78.6
2004	79.9	80.3	80.9	81.0	81.4	80.8	77.4	79.5	84.2	84.4	84.1	83.8	81.5
2005	82.8	83.5	84.0	84.0	84.2	82.9	80.3	84.7	86.1	84.0	85.7	83.4	83.8
2006	84.6	85.5	86.1	87.4	88.0	87.2	83.8	88.1	89.2	90.0	90.6	90.1	87.6
2007	89.8	90.7	91.3	91.6	92.3	90.8	87.4	90.7	92.7	93.0	93.4	93.1	91.4
2008	92.6	93.4	93.9	94.2	94.5	92.8	90.5	92.9	95.5	97.6	96.7	96.3	94.2
2009	93.5	93.7	94.4	96.1	96.1	93.9	89.9	91.2	93.3	94.2	94.2	93.6	93.7
2010	92.1	92.9	93.5	95.0	96.9	94.6	90.4	92.2	94.0	94.5	94.0	93.7	93.7
2011	92.7	93.5	93.8	93.4	93.3	90.1	86.3	89.4	91.6	92.9	92.7	90.7	91.7
2012	91.3	92.5	92.5	92.1	91.5	89.8	86.0	89.8	91.8	92.9	93.0	91.3	91.2
2013	91.5	92.9	93.2	92.7	91.4	88.1	85.7	90.1	93.3	94.3	94.1	93.6	91.7

Employment by Industry: Richmond, VA, Selected Years, 2002–2013

(Numbers in thousands, not seasonally adjusted)

Industry and year	January	February	March	April	May	June	July	August	September	October	November	December	Annual average
Total Nonfarm													
2002	579.2	582.0	587.4	588.0	592.1	595.4	586.9	587.5	587.1	586.4	588.9	589.9	587.6
2003	576.2	576.1	580.9	589.4	592.9	595.2	587.7	588.0	589.1	593.1	596.6	599.6	588.7
2004	590.5	592.9	599.1	602.5	606.7	610.3	602.6	598.6	606.0	611.5	614.3	615.9	604.2
2005	604.0	606.7	610.7	618.7	621.2	624.7	615.5	612.0	618.6	620.0	623.6	624.0	616.6
2006	613.2	613.7	621.7	623.0	628.5	630.9	627.5	626.0	624.8	632.5	636.6	637.5	626.3
2007	625.3	628.8	631.2	632.1	637.2	643.2	634.1	634.2	634.7	635.9	636.9	638.1	634.3
2008	627.0	628.2	630.8	634.3	634.0	637.8	630.3	629.3	630.5	633.8	632.1	629.6	631.5
2009	614.1	609.2	610.4	610.2	611.1	612.5	600.5	597.3	600.8	604.0	605.4	604.5	606.7
2010	593.3	590.1	596.9	605.4	610.6	612.6	605.1	602.5	603.0	607.0	608.3	608.1	603.6
2011	598.5	600.6	605.2	612.0	612.7	614.4	613.6	610.5	613.5	620.0	623.2	621.6	612.2
2012	609.9	611.6	617.4	622.6	625.4	629.6	623.0	625.9	626.8	631.7	634.6	636.4	624.6
2013	620.5	623.4	627.7	633.0	633.6	636.9	634.0	633.6	634.5	637.2	641.3	638.7	632.9
Total Private													
2002	469.0	470.9	475.9	476.7	480.8	483.7	479.4	479.9	478.9	476.1	477.7	478.6	477.3
2003	464.3	463.0	468.4	475.5	479.9	482.7	479.4	481.4	480.1	482.4	483.7	486.3	477.3
2004	479.0	479.6	484.9	489.0	493.4	497.7	494.4	493.9	494.2	496.4	498.5	500.9	491.8
2005	490.3	491.1	494.6	501.6	505.0	508.9	505.4	504.8	506.4	508.1	510.4	510.7	503.1
2006	499.4	498.9	506.7	508.6	514.0	516.6	517.5	516.5	513.6	518.5	521.3	522.0	512.8
2007	510.0	512.3	515.7	516.7	522.3	529.0	525.0	526.1	526.1	524.9	525.5	527.4	521.8
2008	516.9	517.1	519.7	521.0	521.7	525.1	523.1	522.8	520.3	520.3	517.7	516.9	520.2
2009	500.7	495.4	496.1	495.3	497.1	498.6	493.5	490.3	490.3	490.3	490.5	490.7	494.1
2010	479.7	476.1	482.5	489.6	494.1	496.9	495.3	493.5	492.4	493.9	494.2	494.6	490.2
2011	484.8	486.2	490.5	497.1	499.2	501.5	504.2	502.3	502.1	505.9	508.5	507.4	499.1
2012	496.0	496.5	502.0	508.4	512.3	516.6	515.2	518.1	516.6	519.5	520.8	522.7	512.1
2013	508.0	510.2	514.4	518.7	521.0	524.1	524.7	525.9	523.6	523.8	526.9	524.6	520.5
Goods Producing													
2002	90.1	90.4	91.4	91.7	92.1	92.5	91.6	92.3	92.3	91.8	91.6	91.3	91.6
2003	88.0	87.5	88.7	89.8	90.3	89.7	89.6	89.8	89.3	88.6	88.2	87.9	89.0
2004	86.3	86.1	87.2	87.5	87.7	88.6	89.3	89.1	90.0	89.7	90.2	90.4	88.5
2005	89.3	88.6	88.6	89.3	89.5	90.2	91.1	91.1	90.5	90.0	90.3	90.2	89.9
2006	88.3	88.7	89.4	89.3	89.7	90.5	90.1	90.1	89.3	88.9	88.5	88.5	89.3
2007	87.4	87.1	87.8	88.7	89.5	90.5	90.0	90.2	89.8	89.0	88.3	88.1	88.9
2008	85.5	85.1	84.9	84.8	84.3	84.0	83.6	83.3	82.1	81.7	79.5	78.2	83.1
2009	74.5	71.6	71.4	70.8	70.1	70.3	69.7	69.0	68.8	68.4	68.0	67.5	70.0
2010	65.3	64.2	65.2	66.7	67.1	67.4	68.0	67.3	67.0	67.3	66.9	66.2	66.6
2011	63.8	64.0	64.5	65.0	65.2	65.1	65.6	65.3	65.0	65.6	65.6	65.5	65.0
2012	63.5	63.1	64.0	65.2	65.7	66.2	66.1	66.7	66.4	66.1	66.1	65.9	65.4
2013	64.2	64.9	65.7	66.3	66.6	67.5	67.6	67.5	67.1	66.1	67.4	67.5	66.5
Service-Providing													
2002	489.1	491.6	496.0	496.3	500.0	502.9	495.3	495.2	494.8	494.6	497.3	498.6	496.0
2003	488.2	488.6	492.2	499.6	502.6	505.5	498.1	498.2	499.8	504.5	508.4	511.7	499.8
2004	504.2	506.8	511.9	515.0	519.0	521.7	513.3	509.5	516.0	521.8	524.1	525.5	515.7
2005	514.7	518.1	522.1	529.4	531.7	534.5	524.4	520.9	528.1	530.0	533.3	533.8	526.8
2006	524.9	525.0	532.3	533.7	538.8	540.4	537.4	535.9	535.5	543.6	548.1	549.0	537.1
2007	537.9	541.7	543.4	543.4	547.7	552.7	544.1	544.0	544.9	546.9	548.6	550.0	545.4
2008	541.5	543.1	545.9	549.5	549.7	553.8	546.7	546.0	548.4	552.1	552.6	551.4	548.4
2009	539.6	537.6	539.0	539.4	541.0	542.2	530.8	528.3	532.0	535.6	537.4	537.0	536.7
2010	528.0	525.9	531.7	538.7	543.5	545.2	537.1	535.2	536.4	539.7	541.4	541.9	537.1
2011	534.7	536.6	540.7	547.0	547.5	549.3	548.0	545.2	548.5	554.4	557.6	556.1	547.1
2012	546.4	548.5	553.4	557.4	559.7	563.4	556.9	559.2	560.4	565.6	568.5	570.5	559.2
2013	556.3	558.5	562.0	566.7	567.0	569.4	566.4	566.1	567.4	571.1	573.9	571.2	566.3
Mining, Logging, and Construction													
2002	38.5	38.7	39.9	40.5	41.0	41.0	40.7	41.3	41.3	41.1	40.9	40.6	40.5
2003	38.3	38.0	39.5	40.6	41.4	41.2	41.7	41.9	41.6	41.0	40.5	40.2	40.5
2004	39.2	39.2	40.3	41.2	41.9	42.6	43.3	43.0	43.7	43.8	44.1	44.1	42.2
2005	43.2	42.9	43.3	44.0	44.3	44.9	46.2	46.0	45.4	45.1	45.2	44.9	44.6
2006	43.7	44.2	45.1	45.0	45.7	46.5	46.6	46.5	46.0	46.0	45.8	45.7	45.6
2007	44.8	44.7	45.3	46.3	47.1	47.8	47.7	47.9	47.8	47.0	46.3	45.9	46.6
2008	43.7	43.4	43.6	43.6	43.3	43.3	43.3	43.3	42.3	42.1	40.6	39.7	42.7
2009	37.3	36.2	36.1	36.2	36.1	36.1	35.9	35.5	35.1	35.1	34.7	34.2	35.7
2010	32.4	31.5	32.5	33.9	34.2	34.3	34.9	34.4	34.1	34.5	34.3	33.6	33.7
2011	31.8	31.8	32.3	32.8	33.0	32.9	33.4	33.2	32.9	33.4	33.4	33.3	32.9
2012	32.0	31.6	32.4	33.3	33.7	34.0	34.2	34.6	34.4	34.2	34.2	33.9	33.5
2013	32.5	32.9	33.6	34.2	34.3	35.0	35.1	35.1	34.8	34.0	35.3	35.4	34.4
Manufacturing													
2002	51.6	51.7	51.5	51.2	51.1	51.5	50.9	51.0	51.0	50.7	50.7	50.7	51.1
2003	49.7	49.5	49.2	49.2	48.9	48.5	47.9	47.9	47.7	47.6	47.7	47.7	48.5
2004	47.1	46.9	46.9	46.3	45.8	46.0	46.0	46.1	46.3	45.9	46.1	46.3	46.3
2005	46.1	45.7	45.3	45.3	45.2	45.3	44.9	45.1	45.1	44.9	45.1	45.3	45.3
2006	44.6	44.5	44.3	44.3	44.0	44.0	43.5	43.6	43.3	42.9	42.7	42.8	43.7
2007	42.6	42.4	42.5	42.4	42.4	42.7	42.3	42.3	42.0	42.0	42.0	42.2	42.3
2008	41.8	41.7	41.3	41.2	41.0	40.7	40.3	40.0	39.8	39.6	38.9	38.5	40.4
2009	37.2	35.4	35.3	34.6	34.0	34.2	33.8	33.5	33.7	33.3	33.3	33.3	34.3
2010	32.9	32.7	32.7	32.8	32.9	33.1	33.1	32.9	32.9	32.8	32.6	32.6	32.8
2011	32.0	32.2	32.2	32.2	32.2	32.2	32.2	32.1	32.1	32.2	32.2	32.2	32.2
2012	31.5	31.5	31.6	31.9	32.0	32.2	31.9	32.1	32.0	31.9	31.9	32.0	31.9
2013	31.7	32.0	32.1	32.1	32.3	32.5	32.5	32.4	32.3	32.1	32.1	32.1	32.2

Employment by Industry: Richmond, VA, Selected Years, 2002–2013—*Continued*

(Numbers in thousands, not seasonally adjusted)

Industry and year	January	February	March	April	May	June	July	August	September	October	November	December	Annual average
Trade, Transportation, and Utilities													
2002	111.1	109.9	110.7	110.6	111.3	111.8	111.6	112.2	111.9	112.6	114.4	116.2	112.0
2003	110.8	109.8	109.9	110.8	111.8	112.1	111.7	112.1	111.7	113.7	115.6	117.2	112.3
2004	112.8	111.9	112.4	112.7	113.2	113.5	113.0	112.7	111.9	113.2	114.8	116.1	113.2
2005	111.4	110.5	111.3	111.9	112.4	112.9	113.1	113.5	113.2	113.9	116.5	118.5	113.3
2006	114.5	113.2	114.2	113.9	115.0	115.3	115.1	115.5	114.8	116.6	119.0	121.1	115.7
2007	117.0	116.0	116.8	116.4	117.6	118.4	118.3	118.4	118.5	119.0	121.4	122.8	118.4
2008	117.9	116.4	116.6	116.2	116.7	117.4	117.0	117.0	117.0	117.7	119.2	120.2	117.4
2009	114.5	112.6	111.9	110.9	111.2	111.2	110.3	110.0	109.3	110.6	112.4	113.8	111.6
2010	109.6	107.8	108.6	110.0	111.2	111.7	111.2	111.0	109.9	111.1	113.1	114.7	110.8
2011	110.8	110.1	110.6	111.9	112.4	112.9	113.0	113.1	112.2	113.8	116.2	117.9	112.9
2012	113.3	112.0	113.0	113.5	114.7	114.7	113.7	114.1	114.4	117.5	120.7	124.3	115.5
2013	117.2	115.6	115.5	116.5	117.8	118.2	118.7	119.2	119.1	119.6	121.2	122.4	118.4
Wholesale Trade													
2002	24.3	24.4	24.8	24.7	24.9	25.1	25.3	25.5	25.6	25.6	25.7	25.9	25.2
2003	26.0	26.0	26.1	25.9	26.2	26.2	26.2	26.2	25.9	26.0	26.0	26.1	26.1
2004	25.7	25.8	25.9	26.1	26.2	26.3	26.4	26.2	26.0	26.2	26.1	26.1	26.1
2005	25.8	25.8	25.9	26.2	26.2	26.3	26.5	26.7	26.6	26.6	26.7	26.8	26.3
2006	26.9	27.0	27.1	27.2	27.4	27.6	27.8	27.9	27.8	28.0	28.1	28.1	27.6
2007	28.1	28.3	28.5	28.5	28.6	28.8	28.8	28.8	28.7	28.9	28.7	28.7	28.6
2008	28.5	28.6	28.6	28.6	28.5	28.6	28.7	28.6	28.4	28.3	28.1	27.9	28.5
2009	27.5	27.2	27.0	26.7	26.6	26.4	26.2	26.1	25.8	26.0	25.9	25.9	26.4
2010	25.6	25.5	25.6	26.1	26.3	26.4	26.5	26.5	26.3	26.8	26.8	26.9	26.3
2011	26.9	27.0	27.2	27.2	27.3	27.5	27.7	27.6	27.4	27.3	27.4	27.4	27.3
2012	27.2	27.3	27.6	28.0	28.2	28.4	28.2	28.4	28.3	28.4	28.4	28.4	28.1
2013	28.4	28.5	28.6	28.6	28.8	28.9	29.0	29.0	28.9	28.8	28.2	28.2	28.7
Retail Trade													
2002	66.9	65.8	66.3	65.9	66.4	66.8	66.1	66.4	66.1	66.7	68.3	70.0	66.8
2003	65.1	64.1	64.1	64.8	65.5	65.7	65.2	65.6	65.7	67.2	69.2	70.7	66.1
2004	67.2	66.2	66.6	66.3	66.7	66.9	65.9	65.8	65.4	66.6	68.2	69.2	66.8
2005	65.9	65.0	65.4	65.7	66.2	66.5	66.3	66.5	66.2	66.7	69.0	70.6	66.7
2006	67.3	66.1	66.8	66.6	67.4	67.4	67.0	67.0	66.3	67.7	69.9	71.4	67.6
2007	68.1	67.0	67.4	67.1	68.2	68.6	68.6	68.5	68.6	69.2	71.5	72.4	68.8
2008	68.9	67.4	67.6	67.1	67.6	68.1	67.7	67.8	68.1	69.0	70.5	71.2	68.4
2009	67.0	65.6	65.2	64.8	65.2	65.4	64.7	64.6	64.3	65.4	67.0	68.0	65.6
2010	64.8	63.3	63.8	64.5	65.6	65.9	65.3	65.1	64.2	64.9	66.7	67.7	65.2
2011	64.5	63.7	63.9	64.6	64.8	64.9	64.6	64.8	64.1	65.6	67.8	69.1	65.2
2012	65.6	64.4	64.8	64.9	65.8	65.5	64.8	65.0	65.3	68.3	71.4	74.3	66.7
2013	67.8	66.3	66.1	67.1	68.1	68.3	68.8	69.3	69.2	69.9	72.0	72.9	68.8
Transportation and Utilities													
2002	19.9	19.7	19.6	20.0	20.0	19.9	20.2	20.3	20.2	20.3	20.4	20.3	20.1
2003	19.7	19.7	19.7	20.1	20.1	20.2	20.3	20.3	20.1	20.5	20.4	20.4	20.1
2004	19.9	19.9	19.9	20.3	20.3	20.3	20.7	20.7	20.5	20.4	20.5	20.8	20.4
2005	19.7	19.7	20.0	20.0	20.0	20.1	20.3	20.3	20.4	20.6	20.8	21.1	20.3
2006	20.3	20.1	20.3	20.1	20.2	20.3	20.3	20.6	20.7	20.9	21.0	21.6	20.5
2007	20.8	20.7	20.9	20.8	20.8	21.0	20.9	21.1	21.2	20.9	21.2	21.7	21.0
2008	20.5	20.4	20.4	20.5	20.6	20.7	20.6	20.6	20.5	20.4	20.6	21.1	20.6
2009	20.0	19.8	19.7	19.4	19.4	19.4	19.4	19.4	19.3	19.2	19.2	19.5	19.5
2010	19.2	19.0	19.2	19.4	19.3	19.4	19.4	19.4	19.4	19.4	19.6	20.1	19.4
2011	19.4	19.4	19.5	20.1	20.3	20.5	20.7	20.7	20.7	20.9	21.0	21.4	20.4
2012	20.5	20.3	20.6	20.6	20.7	20.8	20.7	20.7	20.8	20.8	20.9	21.6	20.8
2013	21.0	20.8	20.8	20.8	20.9	21.0	20.9	20.9	21.0	20.9	21.0	21.3	20.9
Information													
2002	12.6	12.6	12.6	12.5	12.6	12.5	12.3	12.4	12.2	11.9	12.2	12.2	12.4
2003	11.7	12.0	12.0	11.9	11.9	12.0	11.9	11.9	11.7	11.5	11.6	11.5	11.8
2004	11.5	11.4	11.5	11.2	11.2	11.2	11.1	11.0	10.9	10.9	11.0	11.0	11.2
2005	11.0	11.0	11.1	11.1	11.1	11.1	11.1	11.1	11.1	11.0	11.1	11.1	11.1
2006	11.0	11.0	11.0	10.8	12.9	10.8	11.8	11.2	11.1	11.1	11.2	11.2	11.3
2007	11.6	11.6	11.5	11.7	11.9	11.6	11.3	11.2	11.0	10.8	10.8	10.6	11.3
2008	10.5	10.5	10.5	10.4	10.3	10.4	10.3	10.2	10.1	10.3	10.4	10.4	10.4
2009	10.5	10.4	10.4	10.4	10.4	10.3	10.2	9.9	9.8	9.7	9.6	9.6	10.1
2010	9.5	9.5	9.4	9.4	9.4	9.5	9.5	9.4	9.5	9.5	9.5	9.4	9.5
2011	9.2	9.2	9.1	8.9	8.9	8.9	9.0	7.6	8.6	9.3	9.3	9.5	9.0
2012	8.1	8.1	8.2	8.0	8.0	8.2	8.1	8.3	7.7	7.7	8.0	8.0	8.0
2013	7.8	8.0	8.0	8.5	7.9	8.0	7.9	8.0	7.8	7.8	7.8	7.8	7.9
Financial Activities													
2002	47.0	47.2	47.3	47.2	47.0	47.1	46.8	46.3	46.4	46.1	45.9	45.7	46.7
2003	45.2	45.4	45.6	46.2	46.5	46.7	47.0	47.2	46.9	46.3	46.5	47.0	46.4
2004	46.6	46.9	46.8	47.1	47.0	47.3	47.1	47.2	46.7	46.5	46.6	46.8	46.9
2005	46.6	46.7	46.8	46.5	46.6	46.7	47.3	47.2	46.7	46.4	46.3	46.5	46.7
2006	46.4	46.5	46.8	46.5	46.7	46.9	47.0	47.0	46.4	46.2	46.0	46.1	46.5
2007	45.7	45.6	45.9	45.9	46.0	46.3	46.2	46.4	45.7	45.3	45.1	45.0	45.8
2008	44.6	44.5	44.5	44.0	43.8	44.0	44.3	44.3	43.7	44.1	44.0	44.1	44.2
2009	43.7	43.4	43.6	43.5	43.0	43.1	43.0	43.1	42.6	42.5	42.5	42.6	43.1
2010	42.2	42.1	42.4	42.5	42.6	43.0	42.7	42.9	42.4	42.7	42.8	43.0	42.6
2011	42.7	42.8	43.1	43.4	43.6	44.0	44.5	44.7	44.5	44.9	45.6	45.9	44.1
2012	45.3	45.5	45.8	46.3	46.6	47.0	47.2	47.4	47.2	47.2	47.4	47.5	46.7
2013	47.0	47.2	47.4	47.4	47.5	47.8	48.2	48.2	47.9	48.2	48.3	48.2	47.8

Employment by Industry: Richmond, VA, Selected Years, 2002–2013—*Continued*

(Numbers in thousands, not seasonally adjusted)

Industry and year	January	February	March	April	May	June	July	August	September	October	November	December	Annual average
Professional and Business Services													
2002	86.5	87.6	88.3	88.6	88.9	89.0	88.3	88.0	87.9	86.4	86.8	86.6	87.7
2003	81.7	81.1	82.3	83.8	84.3	84.9	84.5	84.6	84.3	85.0	85.1	85.7	83.9
2004	84.5	84.6	85.0	86.4	87.4	88.4	88.8	89.4	89.1	90.9	91.1	92.3	88.2
2005	89.7	90.3	90.8	92.3	92.7	93.4	93.8	93.5	93.6	95.2	94.9	95.1	92.9
2006	93.2	93.4	94.3	93.7	94.6	95.4	95.3	95.9	96.4	98.5	98.8	99.3	95.7
2007	97.0	97.7	98.8	98.6	98.3	99.8	99.5	99.7	100.0	100.2	99.8	100.2	99.1
2008	99.4	99.9	100.3	100.1	99.9	100.5	99.7	99.8	99.0	99.1	98.2	97.4	99.4
2009	95.2	94.7	95.0	93.0	92.6	92.1	91.9	91.6	91.4	91.9	92.3	92.3	92.8
2010	90.5	90.5	91.6	92.9	92.8	93.0	94.0	94.3	94.8	95.1	95.1	95.4	93.3
2011	94.7	95.2	96.3	97.2	97.0	96.5	97.2	97.2	98.0	98.3	99.0	97.0	97.0
2012	96.6	97.4	98.1	98.8	99.2	99.9	100.1	100.5	100.9	101.6	100.6	100.3	99.5
2013	97.9	98.8	99.4	98.9	98.6	98.6	98.6	99.3	99.2	99.4	100.0	97.9	98.9
Education and Health Services													
2002	56.2	56.6	56.7	56.8	57.8	58.0	56.0	56.4	58.1	58.6	59.0	59.0	57.4
2003	60.6	60.7	60.8	61.5	61.3	61.0	58.5	60.2	62.4	62.9	63.2	63.6	61.4
2004	64.5	65.0	65.5	65.9	66.7	66.6	63.0	63.2	66.5	67.6	68.3	68.4	65.9
2005	68.1	68.9	68.9	69.5	69.9	69.4	65.7	65.6	70.5	72.1	72.6	71.8	69.4
2006	70.2	69.6	72.1	74.2	72.6	72.3	71.9	71.0	72.2	74.1	74.5	73.3	72.3
2007	72.9	75.3	73.9	72.6	74.0	74.5	72.0	72.5	76.6	78.0	78.9	79.7	75.1
2008	79.4	80.4	80.7	81.9	81.9	81.8	79.6	79.9	82.6	83.6	84.1	84.2	81.7
2009	83.2	83.5	83.4	84.1	85.0	84.8	81.9	81.8	84.7	85.9	86.7	86.5	84.3
2010	85.8	85.7	86.4	86.4	87.1	86.3	83.9	83.6	85.7	86.9	87.2	86.8	86.0
2011	86.2	86.7	86.8	87.6	86.6	86.2	87.1	87.3	88.5	89.6	90.0	88.6	87.6
2012	88.6	89.0	89.3	90.4	89.3	89.3	89.3	90.3	91.8	92.3	92.4	91.5	90.3
2013	91.1	92.0	92.3	93.0	92.3	91.6	91.1	91.8	93.1	92.8	93.6	92.8	92.3
Leisure and Hospitality													
2002	41.1	41.9	44.0	44.4	46.0	47.6	47.7	47.2	45.2	43.9	42.8	42.7	44.5
2003	41.7	41.7	44.1	46.0	47.8	49.6	49.3	48.7	46.7	46.9	45.5	45.2	46.1
2004	44.3	44.5	46.6	48.4	50.2	52.0	52.2	51.4	49.7	48.1	47.0	46.4	48.4
2005	44.8	45.3	47.4	49.3	50.9	52.9	52.9	52.4	50.9	49.4	48.7	47.8	49.4
2006	46.8	47.4	49.6	50.9	52.8	55.4	54.9	54.5	51.8	52.4	51.1	50.9	51.5
2007	48.6	49.1	50.7	51.6	53.8	56.3	56.1	55.7	53.5	52.0	50.6	50.3	52.4
2008	49.0	49.3	51.1	53.1	55.2	57.1	56.7	55.9	53.1	52.0	50.5	50.6	52.8
2009	48.7	48.8	49.9	52.1	54.4	56.2	55.8	54.7	52.9	51.2	49.0	48.8	51.9
2010	47.2	46.6	48.6	51.7	53.9	55.7	55.7	54.8	53.2	51.4	49.7	49.3	51.5
2011	47.8	48.6	50.3	52.9	55.4	57.5	57.5	56.9	55.5	54.5	52.9	53.0	53.6
2012	51.0	51.8	53.7	55.7	58.0	60.3	59.8	59.7	57.4	56.1	54.6	54.7	56.1
2013	52.9	53.6	55.7	57.7	59.6	61.4	61.3	60.6	58.4	58.9	57.5	56.9	57.9
Other Services													
2002	24.4	24.7	24.9	24.9	25.1	25.2	25.1	25.1	24.9	24.8	25.0	24.9	24.9
2003	24.6	24.8	25.0	25.5	26.0	26.7	26.9	26.9	27.1	27.5	28.0	28.2	26.4
2004	28.5	29.2	29.9	29.8	30.0	30.1	29.9	29.9	29.4	29.5	29.5	29.5	29.6
2005	29.4	29.8	29.7	31.7	31.9	32.3	30.4	30.4	29.9	30.1	30.0	29.7	30.4
2006	29.0	29.1	29.3	29.3	29.7	30.0	31.4	31.3	31.6	30.7	32.2	31.6	30.4
2007	29.8	29.9	30.3	31.2	31.2	31.6	31.6	32.0	31.0	30.6	30.6	30.7	30.9
2008	30.6	31.0	31.1	30.5	29.6	29.9	31.9	32.4	32.7	31.8	31.8	31.8	31.3
2009	30.4	30.4	30.5	30.5	30.4	30.6	30.7	30.2	30.8	30.1	30.0	29.6	30.4
2010	29.6	29.7	30.3	30.0	30.0	30.3	30.3	30.2	29.9	29.9	29.9	29.8	30.0
2011	29.6	29.6	29.8	30.2	30.1	30.4	30.3	30.2	29.8	29.9	29.9	30.0	30.0
2012	29.6	29.6	29.9	30.5	30.8	31.0	30.9	31.1	30.8	31.0	31.0	30.5	30.6
2013	29.9	30.1	30.4	30.4	30.7	31.0	31.3	31.3	31.0	31.0	31.1	31.1	30.8
Government													
2002	110.2	111.1	111.5	111.3	111.3	111.7	107.5	107.6	108.2	110.3	111.2	111.3	110.3
2003	111.9	113.1	112.5	113.9	113.0	112.5	108.3	106.6	109.0	110.7	112.9	113.3	111.5
2004	111.5	113.3	114.2	113.5	113.3	112.6	108.2	104.7	111.8	115.1	115.8	115.0	112.4
2005	113.7	115.6	116.1	117.1	116.2	115.8	110.1	107.2	112.2	111.9	113.2	113.3	113.5
2006	113.8	114.8	115.0	114.4	114.5	114.3	110.0	109.5	111.2	114.0	115.3	115.5	113.5
2007	115.3	116.5	115.5	115.4	114.9	114.2	109.1	108.1	108.6	111.0	111.4	110.7	112.6
2008	110.1	111.1	111.1	113.3	112.3	112.7	107.2	106.5	110.2	113.5	114.4	112.7	111.3
2009	113.4	113.8	114.3	114.9	114.0	113.9	107.0	107.0	110.5	113.7	114.9	113.8	112.6
2010	113.6	114.0	114.4	115.8	116.5	115.7	109.8	109.0	111.0	113.1	114.1	113.5	113.4
2011	113.7	114.4	114.7	114.9	113.5	112.9	109.4	108.2	111.4	114.1	114.7	114.2	113.0
2012	113.9	115.1	115.4	114.2	113.1	113.0	107.8	107.8	110.2	112.2	113.8	113.7	112.5
2013	112.5	113.2	113.3	114.3	112.6	112.8	109.3	107.7	110.9	113.4	114.4	114.1	112.4

Employment by Industry: Riverside-San Bernardino-Ontario, CA, Selected Years, 2002–2013

(Numbers in thousands, not seasonally adjusted)

Industry and year	January	February	March	April	May	June	July	August	September	October	November	December	Annual average
Total Nonfarm													
2002	1,042.7	1,050.6	1,056.8	1,068.8	1,077.6	1,082.0	1,062.5	1,067.2	1,077.9	1,083.2	1,097.6	1,103.6	1,072.5
2003	1,084.4	1,087.8	1,097.8	1,101.0	1,107.3	1,112.1	1,100.8	1,099.2	1,113.4	1,128.7	1,138.0	1,145.1	1,109.6
2004	1,134.5	1,140.6	1,151.9	1,164.5	1,171.7	1,174.4	1,165.0	1,165.6	1,180.1	1,197.6	1,211.4	1,219.0	1,173.0
2005	1,198.3	1,209.5	1,221.2	1,233.6	1,234.5	1,235.5	1,223.9	1,227.6	1,244.3	1,254.8	1,268.6	1,278.7	1,235.9
2006	1,260.8	1,269.0	1,279.1	1,283.1	1,287.8	1,292.6	1,277.4	1,274.1	1,282.8	1,286.4	1,295.1	1,297.5	1,282.1
2007	1,277.3	1,282.1	1,289.8	1,287.9	1,294.0	1,293.4	1,279.4	1,274.5	1,278.6	1,284.8	1,293.7	1,296.1	1,286.0
2008	1,263.6	1,262.6	1,263.0	1,261.3	1,256.3	1,252.6	1,228.0	1,225.0	1,223.1	1,227.4	1,228.2	1,223.0	1,242.8
2009	1,193.1	1,183.0	1,182.5	1,176.7	1,173.2	1,167.1	1,140.7	1,139.1	1,135.2	1,148.7	1,157.2	1,157.6	1,162.8
2010	1,135.7	1,136.6	1,143.2	1,151.3	1,154.8	1,151.5	1,124.5	1,131.7	1,132.9	1,146.4	1,160.2	1,162.4	1,144.3
2011	1,137.9	1,142.2	1,146.9	1,150.3	1,149.6	1,144.1	1,127.8	1,135.9	1,141.6	1,153.3	1,168.8	1,168.6	1,147.3
2012	1,158.2	1,160.7	1,165.5	1,175.9	1,179.3	1,178.1	1,158.3	1,168.7	1,173.8	1,199.9	1,217.3	1,214.8	1,179.2
2013	1,202.4	1,208.8	1,214.6	1,222.5	1,225.3	1,223.2	1,205.6	1,219.8	1,228.4	1,242.9	1,258.3	1,265.0	1,226.4
Total Private													
2002	834.7	839.0	845.6	850.0	859.4	863.1	855.5	864.2	868.3	869.3	881.2	887.4	859.8
2003	869.2	872.6	880.5	884.4	892.4	898.0	895.2	899.8	906.5	918.7	925.8	933.8	898.1
2004	922.8	928.7	938.1	949.6	956.7	961.0	959.5	963.7	970.1	983.3	993.5	999.6	960.6
2005	978.3	988.0	998.0	1,009.1	1,010.0	1,015.3	1,013.1	1,017.0	1,026.8	1,032.3	1,044.3	1,053.2	1,015.5
2006	1,039.8	1,047.7	1,055.7	1,057.0	1,060.9	1,065.3	1,061.3	1,062.0	1,064.2	1,061.5	1,068.8	1,071.9	1,059.7
2007	1,052.6	1,056.9	1,062.2	1,059.5	1,064.8	1,064.4	1,062.1	1,061.3	1,059.4	1,056.6	1,063.3	1,064.6	1,060.6
2008	1,032.8	1,031.0	1,029.5	1,026.7	1,021.3	1,018.8	1,006.0	1,002.8	999.4	993.8	992.8	987.0	1,011.8
2009	957.5	947.5	944.8	935.9	932.2	927.7	914.9	910.4	908.6	912.7	919.2	920.1	927.6
2010	898.9	899.2	903.5	909.5	910.1	909.9	903.1	905.7	907.2	913.3	926.5	932.4	909.9
2011	906.6	910.6	913.6	916.9	916.0	913.3	913.8	918.1	921.6	925.4	939.7	941.8	919.8
2012	930.1	932.6	935.9	946.1	949.2	952.0	949.1	953.7	957.1	973.4	988.3	987.8	954.6
2013	975.5	981.6	986.0	994.3	996.0	995.7	995.3	1,003.4	1,007.8	1,015.9	1,029.2	1,036.2	1,001.4
Goods Producing													
2002	199.8	201.4	203.1	204.0	206.0	207.8	208.2	212.4	212.1	212.2	212.5	210.8	207.5
2003	207.6	207.5	210.5	211.2	215.3	217.0	216.8	220.0	220.8	222.7	222.6	223.1	216.3
2004	221.3	223.2	224.2	229.0	231.5	234.4	237.0	238.4	240.2	240.8	239.1	238.2	233.1
2005	230.7	235.3	238.3	242.3	243.2	247.0	248.6	250.7	252.7	253.3	253.1	253.1	245.7
2006	250.4	253.4	254.4	253.7	256.5	259.4	257.1	256.7	255.3	247.7	242.2	240.3	252.3
2007	234.2	234.6	235.8	235.0	236.4	237.8	237.2	236.7	233.1	226.6	222.3	218.5	232.4
2008	208.9	207.2	206.8	205.0	203.8	203.5	200.5	199.4	196.0	190.2	184.9	179.5	198.8
2009	169.8	164.2	163.3	160.3	160.9	159.9	157.1	155.6	153.3	151.7	150.4	147.5	157.8
2010	144.4	143.8	144.9	146.5	147.5	147.8	146.7	147.3	146.3	145.3	145.1	144.2	145.8
2011	140.4	141.9	142.7	144.4	145.3	146.2	147.5	147.8	147.8	146.6	146.2	145.0	145.2
2012	143.8	144.7	145.9	147.1	149.5	152.1	152.8	154.3	154.1	154.5	153.6	153.0	150.5
2013	151.6	153.8	155.2	155.1	155.8	156.8	158.4	159.7	160.1	161.1	161.2	159.2	157.3
Service-Providing													
2002	842.9	849.2	853.7	864.8	871.6	874.2	854.3	854.8	865.8	871.0	885.1	892.8	865.0
2003	876.8	880.3	887.3	889.8	892.0	895.1	884.0	879.2	892.6	906.0	915.4	922.0	893.4
2004	913.2	917.4	927.7	935.5	940.2	940.0	928.0	927.2	939.9	956.8	972.3	980.8	939.9
2005	967.6	974.2	982.9	991.3	991.3	988.5	975.3	976.9	991.6	1,001.5	1,015.5	1,025.6	990.2
2006	1,010.4	1,015.6	1,024.7	1,029.4	1,031.3	1,033.2	1,020.3	1,017.4	1,027.5	1,038.7	1,052.9	1,057.2	1,029.9
2007	1,043.1	1,047.5	1,054.0	1,052.9	1,057.6	1,055.6	1,042.2	1,037.8	1,045.5	1,058.2	1,071.4	1,077.6	1,053.6
2008	1,054.7	1,055.4	1,056.2	1,056.3	1,052.5	1,049.1	1,027.5	1,025.6	1,027.1	1,037.2	1,043.3	1,043.5	1,044.0
2009	1,023.3	1,018.8	1,019.2	1,016.4	1,012.3	1,007.2	983.6	983.5	981.9	997.0	1,006.8	1,010.1	1,005.0
2010	991.3	992.8	998.3	1,004.8	1,007.3	1,003.7	977.8	984.4	986.6	1,001.1	1,015.1	1,018.2	998.5
2011	997.5	1,000.3	1,004.2	1,005.9	1,004.3	997.9	980.3	988.1	993.8	1,006.7	1,022.6	1,023.6	1,002.1
2012	1,014.4	1,016.0	1,019.6	1,028.8	1,029.8	1,026.0	1,005.5	1,014.4	1,019.7	1,045.4	1,063.7	1,061.8	1,028.8
2013	1,050.8	1,055.0	1,059.4	1,067.4	1,069.5	1,066.4	1,047.2	1,060.1	1,068.3	1,081.8	1,097.1	1,105.8	1,069.1
Mining and Logging													
2002	1.1	1.1	1.1	1.2	1.2	1.2	1.3	1.3	1.3	1.2	1.3	1.3	1.2
2003	1.3	1.3	1.3	1.3	1.2	1.2	1.2	1.2	1.2	1.2	1.2	1.2	1.2
2004	1.2	1.2	1.2	1.2	1.2	1.2	1.2	1.2	1.2	1.2	1.3	1.3	1.2
2005	1.3	1.3	1.3	1.3	1.3	1.3	1.4	1.4	1.4	1.4	1.4	1.4	1.4
2006	1.4	1.4	1.4	1.4	1.4	1.4	1.5	1.4	1.4	1.4	1.4	1.4	1.4
2007	1.4	1.3	1.3	1.3	1.3	1.3	1.4	1.4	1.4	1.3	1.3	1.2	1.3
2008	1.3	1.3	1.3	1.2	1.2	1.2	1.2	1.2	1.2	1.1	1.2	1.2	1.2
2009	1.2	1.2	1.2	1.2	1.2	1.2	1.1	1.1	1.1	1.1	1.1	1.0	1.1
2010	1.0	1.0	1.0	1.0	1.0	1.0	1.0	1.0	1.0	1.0	1.0	1.0	1.0
2011	1.0	1.0	1.0	1.0	1.0	1.0	1.0	1.1	1.1	1.1	1.1	1.1	1.0
2012	1.1	1.2	1.2	1.2	1.2	1.2	1.2	1.2	1.2	1.2	1.2	1.2	1.2
2013	1.2	1.2	1.2	1.2	1.2	1.2	1.2	1.2	1.2	1.2	1.2	1.2	1.2
Construction													
2002	84.8	85.7	86.7	87.3	88.7	90.2	91.6	95.1	95.0	95.9	95.8	93.9	90.9
2003	92.7	91.9	94.2	94.6	98.6	99.8	99.7	102.2	102.7	104.0	103.7	103.4	99.0
2004	102.4	103.6	104.0	108.4	110.1	112.2	114.5	115.9	117.4	118.6	117.3	116.6	111.8
2005	109.9	113.8	116.1	120.5	121.7	124.9	125.7	127.6	129.3	130.2	130.2	129.9	123.3
2006	126.7	128.6	128.9	128.3	130.2	132.6	131.6	131.5	130.2	123.9	119.6	117.7	127.5
2007	112.2	112.9	114.2	114.4	115.3	116.6	116.5	116.4	113.6	108.8	105.8	103.2	112.5
2008	95.8	94.8	95.3	94.0	93.6	93.8	92.3	92.0	89.5	85.7	82.5	79.5	90.7
2009	73.6	70.0	70.5	68.9	70.0	69.8	68.4	67.9	66.1	64.6	63.9	61.6	67.9
2010	58.9	58.5	59.8	60.5	61.2	61.3	60.4	60.7	59.7	58.8	58.8	57.7	59.7
2011	55.6	56.9	57.3	58.6	58.9	59.4	60.8	61.0	60.9	60.4	60.0	58.7	59.0
2012	57.9	58.0	58.7	59.3	61.1	63.5	64.4	65.6	65.7	66.1	65.6	65.2	62.6
2013	64.6	66.3	67.1	67.4	67.7	68.6	70.3	71.6	71.9	72.5	72.4	71.5	69.3

Employment by Industry: Riverside-San Bernardino-Ontario, CA, Selected Years, 2002–2013—*Continued*

(Numbers in thousands, not seasonally adjusted)

Industry and year	January	February	March	April	May	June	July	August	September	October	November	December	Annual average
Manufacturing													
2002	113.9	114.6	115.3	115.5	116.1	116.4	115.3	116.0	115.8	115.1	115.4	115.6	115.4
2003	113.6	114.3	115.0	115.3	115.5	116.0	115.9	116.6	116.9	117.5	117.7	118.5	116.1
2004	117.7	118.4	119.0	119.4	120.2	121.0	121.3	121.3	121.6	121.0	120.5	120.3	120.1
2005	119.5	120.2	120.9	120.5	120.2	120.8	121.5	121.7	122.0	121.7	121.5	121.8	121.0
2006	122.3	123.4	124.1	124.0	124.9	125.4	124.0	123.8	123.7	122.4	121.2	121.2	123.4
2007	120.6	120.4	120.3	119.3	119.8	119.9	119.3	118.9	118.1	116.5	115.2	114.1	118.5
2008	111.8	111.1	110.2	109.8	109.0	108.5	107.0	106.2	105.3	103.3	101.3	98.8	106.9
2009	95.0	93.0	91.6	90.2	89.7	88.9	87.6	86.6	86.1	86.0	85.4	84.9	88.8
2010	84.5	84.3	84.1	85.0	85.3	85.5	85.3	85.6	85.6	85.5	85.3	85.5	85.1
2011	83.8	84.0	84.4	84.8	85.4	85.8	85.7	85.7	85.8	85.1	85.1	85.2	85.1
2012	84.8	85.5	86.0	86.6	87.2	87.4	87.2	87.5	87.2	87.2	86.8	86.6	86.7
2013	85.8	86.3	86.9	86.5	86.9	87.0	86.9	86.9	87.0	87.4	87.6	86.5	86.8
Trade, Transportation, and Utilities													
2002	220.0	218.5	220.0	222.2	224.8	226.4	225.9	226.9	228.3	229.1	234.8	238.2	226.3
2003	231.0	229.8	230.7	231.9	233.4	234.7	234.4	235.3	236.7	243.3	245.8	250.2	236.4
2004	243.1	242.1	244.2	247.6	249.9	251.7	253.4	255.6	258.0	266.7	274.1	278.4	255.4
2005	269.5	267.8	269.2	270.8	272.2	273.6	274.6	276.3	279.4	281.2	289.9	296.8	276.8
2006	285.2	283.5	286.1	286.8	288.6	290.6	291.3	291.9	293.0	296.8	305.0	309.4	292.4
2007	299.1	296.7	297.9	297.5	298.9	299.0	300.4	300.7	301.9	303.1	311.7	315.7	301.9
2008	302.1	297.3	296.0	294.8	294.5	293.3	290.1	289.3	288.7	287.1	290.5	291.1	292.9
2009	280.3	275.5	273.0	269.7	270.2	270.1	267.0	266.5	267.9	268.9	274.8	278.6	271.9
2010	268.8	266.6	266.9	267.6	268.7	269.0	267.9	268.0	268.9	271.9	280.7	284.0	270.8
2011	273.5	271.4	271.1	272.1	273.0	272.9	273.5	274.8	275.7	278.1	288.4	290.7	276.3
2012	282.4	278.9	279.5	282.9	284.5	285.2	285.3	287.2	288.7	292.4	305.2	305.9	288.2
2013	294.1	292.5	292.8	293.9	295.6	296.1	296.2	299.2	299.7	302.0	312.8	316.9	299.3
Wholesale Trade													
2002	40.4	40.7	40.9	41.6	41.8	42.2	42.1	42.5	42.7	42.5	42.8	42.9	41.9
2003	42.9	43.3	43.5	44.0	44.1	44.0	43.4	43.4	43.4	43.4	43.0	43.1	43.5
2004	42.9	43.3	43.7	44.2	44.6	45.1	46.2	46.4	46.6	47.6	47.8	48.2	45.6
2005	47.9	48.0	48.5	49.3	49.6	49.9	50.2	50.4	50.8	51.1	51.4	52.1	49.9
2006	52.6	53.1	53.5	54.0	54.0	54.2	54.6	54.6	54.8	54.6	54.8	55.0	54.2
2007	55.3	55.9	56.2	56.3	56.5	56.9	57.1	57.2	57.4	57.5	57.6	57.7	56.8
2008	56.3	56.0	55.6	55.2	55.1	55.0	53.8	53.6	53.1	52.7	51.9	51.2	54.1
2009	50.4	49.8	49.1	48.8	48.7	48.9	48.6	48.4	48.2	48.5	48.5	48.5	48.9
2010	48.3	48.3	48.4	48.7	48.8	48.9	48.8	48.6	48.6	48.8	48.7	48.8	48.6
2011	48.4	48.7	48.8	48.9	49.0	49.0	49.1	49.2	49.2	49.3	49.3	49.3	49.0
2012	49.2	49.4	49.8	51.5	52.0	52.3	52.5	53.1	53.3	53.8	53.8	53.9	52.1
2013	54.4	54.8	55.4	55.6	55.8	55.9	56.1	56.7	56.5	56.5	56.9	56.8	56.0
Retail Trade													
2002	134.3	132.4	133.9	134.8	136.6	137.3	137.1	137.4	138.0	138.6	143.9	146.0	137.5
2003	139.6	138.6	138.9	138.8	139.5	140.4	140.7	141.5	142.0	147.0	150.1	154.2	142.6
2004	147.7	145.8	147.3	148.9	150.5	151.0	151.2	152.6	153.8	158.7	165.8	169.5	153.6
2005	162.3	160.1	160.4	161.0	161.7	162.7	163.4	164.6	166.0	166.9	174.3	179.7	165.3
2006	168.9	166.8	168.1	168.6	169.7	171.0	171.5	171.8	171.7	175.0	182.2	185.1	172.5
2007	176.7	173.2	174.2	173.1	174.1	173.3	173.2	173.5	173.4	174.4	182.4	185.3	175.6
2008	175.2	170.8	170.3	169.2	168.7	168.1	166.7	165.8	165.3	164.7	168.7	169.6	168.6
2009	161.1	157.5	156.0	154.4	154.6	154.1	153.3	153.0	153.5	154.4	160.0	162.7	156.2
2010	154.8	153.0	153.3	153.8	154.1	153.9	153.2	153.1	153.0	155.5	163.0	165.2	155.5
2011	157.3	155.0	154.5	155.5	155.8	155.6	156.3	157.1	157.1	159.0	168.4	170.2	158.5
2012	162.6	158.8	158.4	159.7	160.0	159.3	159.5	159.9	160.0	162.3	173.7	173.2	162.3
2013	163.3	161.1	160.5	161.2	162.4	162.8	162.8	163.6	163.3	165.2	174.1	177.5	164.8
Transportation and Utilities													
2002	45.3	45.4	45.2	45.8	46.4	46.9	46.7	47.0	47.6	48.0	48.1	49.3	46.8
2003	48.5	47.9	48.3	49.1	49.8	50.3	50.3	50.4	51.3	52.9	52.7	52.9	50.4
2004	52.5	53.0	53.2	54.5	54.8	55.6	56.0	56.6	57.6	60.4	60.5	60.7	56.3
2005	59.3	59.7	60.3	60.5	60.9	61.0	61.0	61.3	62.6	63.2	64.2	65.0	61.6
2006	63.7	63.6	64.5	64.2	64.9	65.4	65.2	65.5	66.5	67.2	68.0	69.3	65.7
2007	67.1	67.6	67.5	68.1	68.3	68.8	70.1	70.0	71.1	71.2	71.7	72.7	69.5
2008	70.6	70.5	70.1	70.4	70.7	70.2	69.6	69.9	70.3	69.7	69.9	70.3	70.2
2009	68.8	68.2	67.9	66.5	66.9	67.1	65.1	65.1	66.2	66.0	66.3	67.4	66.8
2010	65.7	65.3	65.2	65.1	65.8	66.2	65.9	66.3	67.3	67.6	69.0	70.0	66.6
2011	67.8	67.7	67.8	67.7	68.2	68.3	68.1	68.5	69.4	69.8	70.7	71.2	68.8
2012	70.6	70.7	71.3	71.7	72.5	73.6	73.3	74.2	75.4	76.3	77.7	78.8	73.8
2013	76.4	76.6	76.9	77.1	77.4	77.4	77.3	78.9	79.9	80.3	81.8	82.6	78.6
Information													
2002	14.5	14.3	14.2	13.9	14.1	14.2	13.9	14.1	13.8	14.0	14.0	14.0	14.1
2003	13.9	13.9	13.8	13.6	13.7	13.8	14.1	14.0	13.9	13.8	14.0	13.9	13.9
2004	13.9	13.7	13.8	13.9	13.9	14.0	14.3	14.0	13.9	14.2	14.4	14.4	14.0
2005	14.3	14.5	14.5	14.6	14.7	14.6	14.5	14.2	14.4	14.4	14.6	14.7	14.5
2006	14.6	14.9	14.9	15.1	15.2	15.4	15.5	15.5	15.5	15.4	15.6	15.7	15.3
2007	15.7	15.6	15.3	15.3	15.5	15.5	15.5	15.4	15.2	15.1	15.3	15.3	15.4
2008	15.3	15.4	15.2	15.1	15.1	14.8	14.7	14.6	14.3	14.2	14.3	14.1	14.8
2009	13.9	13.9	14.0	14.0	14.1	14.3	14.4	14.5	14.4	14.0	14.0	13.9	14.1
2010	14.2	14.2	14.3	14.2	14.2	14.3	14.2	14.0	13.7	13.5	13.5	13.5	14.0
2011	12.8	12.6	12.5	12.3	12.2	12.2	12.2	12.1	11.7	11.5	11.5	11.4	12.1
2012	11.8	11.7	11.7	11.5	11.5	11.6	11.6	11.4	11.3	11.3	11.4	11.5	11.5
2013	11.4	11.3	11.3	11.3	11.4	11.4	11.4	11.3	11.2	11.2	11.3	11.2	11.3

Employment by Industry: Riverside-San Bernardino-Ontario, CA, Selected Years, 2002–2013—*Continued*

(Numbers in thousands, not seasonally adjusted)

Industry and year	January	February	March	April	May	June	July	August	September	October	November	December	Annual average
Financial Activities													
2002	38.7	38.7	38.7	39.4	39.6	39.9	39.3	39.5	39.5	39.6	40.0	40.6	39.5
2003	40.3	40.7	40.9	41.9	42.3	42.9	43.0	43.5	43.8	43.7	44.1	44.4	42.6
2004	44.4	44.5	45.0	45.1	45.4	45.5	46.0	45.9	45.9	46.4	47.0	47.4	45.7
2005	47.6	47.9	48.1	48.5	48.5	48.5	49.0	49.3	49.6	49.9	50.2	50.4	49.0
2006	51.2	51.3	51.6	51.9	52.2	52.1	51.3	51.4	51.3	51.1	51.3	51.2	51.5
2007	51.1	51.3	51.4	50.6	50.3	50.2	49.6	49.4	49.0	48.2	48.2	48.2	49.8
2008	47.0	47.0	46.9	46.7	46.4	46.5	45.7	45.6	45.3	45.3	45.3	45.0	46.1
2009	44.7	44.4	44.1	43.4	42.5	42.2	41.7	41.4	41.1	41.6	41.5	41.6	42.5
2010	41.0	41.1	41.3	41.3	40.9	40.9	40.7	40.6	40.8	41.0	40.9	41.0	41.0
2011	40.1	40.4	40.2	40.2	39.9	39.9	39.6	39.7	39.6	39.8	39.8	39.8	39.9
2012	39.5	39.8	40.1	40.7	40.8	40.8	40.9	40.9	41.0	41.4	41.7	41.9	40.8
2013	41.5	41.7	41.6	41.9	42.0	42.2	42.1	42.0	41.9	42.8	41.9	41.9	42.0
Professional and Business Services													
2002	101.2	102.7	103.7	103.6	105.4	106.5	106.6	109.2	109.9	109.3	111.7	111.8	106.8
2003	109.4	109.6	111.0	111.1	112.6	113.9	117.0	117.8	119.9	120.3	121.1	121.6	115.4
2004	119.5	121.0	123.3	124.8	125.7	127.0	126.5	127.6	127.4	127.8	127.9	127.5	125.5
2005	125.4	128.4	130.3	132.7	131.4	132.7	133.7	135.1	136.4	137.1	137.8	137.0	133.2
2006	138.2	139.5	140.5	141.2	140.6	141.8	143.0	143.2	145.0	145.3	145.9	144.4	142.4
2007	142.4	144.4	145.9	144.3	145.6	145.4	146.2	146.3	146.5	146.8	146.0	144.7	145.4
2008	139.8	140.7	139.5	137.9	136.4	138.7	138.3	138.3	138.2	138.1	137.3	135.2	138.2
2009	130.9	129.5	129.3	127.7	125.1	124.5	122.8	122.3	121.9	123.2	123.1	121.3	125.1
2010	118.5	119.5	120.3	121.6	121.8	123.0	123.4	124.9	125.0	127.2	127.5	128.1	123.4
2011	122.9	125.1	125.6	125.5	124.1	123.3	124.6	127.3	127.9	128.1	128.0	126.6	125.8
2012	124.8	126.6	125.7	128.1	126.8	128.0	127.1	127.4	127.1	129.7	128.3	125.6	127.1
2013	126.5	129.5	128.8	131.7	130.7	131.2	133.0	135.6	136.6	136.0	133.4	137.7	132.6
Education and Health Services													
2002	117.2	118.5	119.2	118.9	120.5	120.6	118.1	119.1	121.5	122.5	123.7	124.6	120.4
2003	122.2	124.4	125.2	126.6	126.8	127.4	125.0	125.2	126.3	127.9	128.4	129.5	126.2
2004	128.3	130.3	131.2	132.3	132.1	132.1	130.2	130.0	130.9	132.6	133.1	133.5	131.4
2005	132.0	133.3	133.8	134.5	134.4	134.4	131.8	131.4	133.1	135.5	135.8	136.0	133.8
2006	134.8	137.0	137.4	137.2	136.9	136.2	134.5	135.0	135.9	137.6	138.2	138.4	136.6
2007	138.2	139.8	140.6	140.6	140.8	140.7	141.4	142.0	142.9	145.6	146.2	146.6	142.1
2008	145.2	148.0	148.6	150.2	149.5	148.5	147.1	147.3	149.0	152.0	152.8	153.4	149.3
2009	151.5	153.8	154.5	155.9	155.4	155.1	154.1	154.5	155.1	156.6	156.7	156.5	155.0
2010	152.5	153.7	153.7	154.3	153.9	152.8	151.6	152.6	153.9	155.2	157.0	157.2	154.0
2011	154.6	156.7	157.1	158.2	157.2	155.8	155.1	155.6	158.3	159.6	160.8	161.5	157.5
2012	162.3	164.2	164.4	165.0	165.0	164.4	162.5	163.4	165.9	175.6	176.2	177.1	167.2
2013	177.5	178.8	179.6	182.4	182.3	181.3	180.1	181.6	183.8	185.3	185.3	185.8	182.0
Leisure and Hospitality													
2002	106.2	107.3	108.7	109.5	110.1	108.8	105.3	104.8	105.0	104.9	106.6	109.5	107.2
2003	107.4	108.8	110.2	109.8	109.6	109.3	107.0	106.3	106.9	108.5	111.3	113.2	109.0
2004	114.1	115.4	117.1	118.2	119.4	117.6	113.4	113.6	115.0	115.8	119.1	121.3	116.7
2005	119.2	120.9	123.4	125.1	125.0	124.3	121.4	120.8	121.2	121.4	123.4	125.4	122.6
2006	125.3	127.2	129.4	130.0	129.4	128.4	127.0	126.6	126.4	126.4	129.5	131.5	128.1
2007	131.7	133.6	134.6	134.6	135.4	133.8	130.7	129.7	129.4	130.2	132.5	134.7	132.6
2008	133.8	134.4	134.9	134.6	133.0	131.3	128.8	127.5	127.5	127.4	128.8	130.2	131.0
2009	129.2	129.1	129.2	127.5	126.5	124.1	120.3	118.7	118.1	119.0	121.0	123.3	123.8
2010	122.4	122.8	124.1	125.2	124.2	122.9	120.2	120.1	120.6	121.1	123.6	126.1	122.8
2011	124.3	124.0	125.8	125.1	125.0	123.6	122.2	121.4	121.3	122.2	125.6	127.4	124.0
2012	126.7	127.5	129.1	130.5	130.5	129.1	128.4	128.4	128.3	128.6	131.9	133.1	129.3
2013	133.2	133.8	135.7	137.1	137.2	135.5	133.2	132.9	133.5	136.5	142.2	143.6	136.2
Other Services													
2002	37.1	37.6	38.0	38.5	38.9	38.9	38.2	38.2	38.2	37.7	37.9	37.9	38.1
2003	37.4	37.9	38.2	38.3	38.7	39.0	37.9	37.7	38.2	38.5	38.5	37.9	38.2
2004	38.2	38.5	39.3	38.7	38.8	38.7	38.7	38.6	38.8	39.0	38.8	38.9	38.8
2005	39.6	39.9	40.4	40.6	40.6	40.2	39.5	39.2	40.0	39.5	39.5	39.8	39.9
2006	40.1	40.9	41.4	41.1	41.5	41.4	41.6	41.7	41.8	41.2	41.1	41.0	41.2
2007	40.2	40.9	40.7	41.6	41.9	42.0	41.1	41.1	41.4	41.0	41.1	40.9	41.2
2008	40.7	41.0	41.6	42.4	42.6	42.2	40.8	40.8	40.4	39.5	38.9	38.5	40.8
2009	37.2	37.1	37.4	37.4	37.5	37.5	37.5	36.9	36.8	37.7	37.7	37.4	37.3
2010	37.1	37.5	38.0	38.8	38.9	39.2	38.4	38.2	38.0	38.1	38.2	38.3	38.2
2011	38.0	38.5	38.6	39.1	39.3	39.4	39.1	39.4	39.3	39.5	39.4	39.4	39.1
2012	38.8	39.2	39.5	40.3	40.6	40.8	40.5	40.7	40.7	39.9	40.0	39.7	40.1
2013	39.7	40.2	41.0	40.9	41.0	41.2	40.9	41.1	41.0	41.0	41.1	39.9	40.8
Government													
2002	208.0	211.6	211.2	218.8	218.2	218.9	207.0	203.0	209.6	213.9	216.4	216.2	212.7
2003	215.2	215.2	217.3	216.6	214.9	214.1	205.6	199.4	206.9	210.0	212.2	211.3	211.6
2004	211.7	211.9	213.8	214.9	215.0	213.4	205.5	201.9	210.0	214.3	217.9	219.4	212.5
2005	220.0	221.5	223.2	224.5	224.5	220.2	210.8	210.6	217.5	222.5	224.3	225.5	220.4
2006	221.0	221.3	223.4	226.1	226.9	227.3	216.1	212.1	218.6	224.9	226.3	225.6	222.5
2007	224.7	225.2	227.6	228.4	229.2	229.0	217.3	213.2	219.2	228.2	230.4	231.5	225.3
2008	230.8	231.6	233.5	234.6	235.0	233.8	222.0	222.2	223.7	233.6	235.4	236.0	231.0
2009	235.6	235.5	237.7	240.8	241.0	239.4	225.8	228.7	226.6	236.0	238.0	237.5	235.2
2010	236.8	237.4	239.7	241.8	244.7	241.6	221.4	226.0	225.7	233.1	233.7	230.0	234.3
2011	231.3	231.6	233.3	233.4	233.6	230.8	214.0	217.8	220.0	227.9	229.1	226.8	227.5
2012	228.1	228.1	229.6	229.8	230.1	226.1	209.2	215.0	216.7	226.5	229.0	227.0	224.6
2013	226.9	227.2	228.6	228.2	229.3	227.5	210.3	216.4	220.6	227.0	229.1	228.8	225.0

Employment by Industry: Rochester, NY, Selected Years, 2002–2013

(Numbers in thousands, not seasonally adjusted)

Industry and year	January	February	March	April	May	June	July	August	September	October	November	December	Annual average
Total Nonfarm													
2002	504.3	505.9	507.4	510.7	516.8	517.3	509.2	509.9	512.1	515.9	517.6	517.8	512.1
2003	500.4	501.8	503.9	504.1	513.4	513.7	506.0	506.5	510.6	514.1	514.1	516.0	508.7
2004	498.4	501.2	503.6	506.5	515.0	516.0	507.7	506.7	511.8	519.3	519.1	519.0	510.4
2005	502.8	506.2	508.4	514.8	519.2	519.5	510.6	510.4	513.8	519.4	521.0	522.3	514.0
2006	502.9	505.2	507.5	511.0	515.2	517.0	506.6	506.6	513.0	518.7	519.6	520.2	512.0
2007	504.6	507.0	508.4	510.2	518.5	520.2	510.2	509.3	514.1	520.6	521.0	521.3	513.8
2008	504.3	508.4	509.1	514.9	521.3	521.7	513.0	512.1	516.9	522.3	519.7	518.4	515.2
2009	499.3	500.2	499.6	499.9	504.7	503.0	498.5	496.6	499.1	506.4	505.8	505.7	501.6
2010	489.9	493.3	495.4	501.5	506.1	506.0	497.8	498.0	502.8	512.0	512.2	510.3	502.1
2011	494.2	498.2	500.2	509.3	511.7	513.2	505.1	505.9	513.0	518.6	519.2	519.6	509.0
2012	500.7	506.3	508.5	510.5	516.9	517.1	507.6	506.3	513.0	520.7	521.2	521.8	512.6
2013	502.0	508.9	510.4	514.6	519.8	518.5	508.2	508.6	515.7	522.9	522.9	521.6	514.5
Total Private													
2002	425.3	423.0	423.8	428.6	434.3	435.4	434.9	435.8	433.8	433.6	434.2	433.2	431.3
2003	419.8	418.3	419.9	421.4	429.8	431.2	431.5	432.4	431.9	432.9	431.9	432.3	427.8
2004	418.4	420.9	422.6	424.2	431.5	433.5	433.2	432.5	433.4	437.2	436.3	434.9	429.9
2005	422.6	423.1	425.0	431.3	435.4	436.6	435.4	435.5	434.7	437.2	437.8	438.2	432.7
2006	423.9	423.8	425.5	429.5	433.7	437.0	434.3	434.4	434.8	438.2	438.2	438.6	432.7
2007	425.7	425.9	427.1	428.7	436.5	438.9	436.8	436.5	435.4	439.2	439.0	438.5	434.0
2008	424.9	426.8	427.2	432.4	438.6	439.7	438.3	438.1	437.2	439.8	436.9	435.3	434.6
2009	419.5	417.9	417.4	417.1	421.8	421.6	421.0	421.0	420.7	423.6	422.6	422.2	420.5
2010	409.0	410.4	412.4	418.4	421.5	422.7	423.4	424.6	424.4	429.3	428.9	426.6	421.0
2011	414.4	415.7	417.7	426.4	429.1	431.4	431.8	432.5	434.4	436.9	436.8	436.6	428.6
2012	421.9	424.5	426.6	429.2	434.9	436.1	435.0	434.3	435.3	440.0	440.2	439.7	433.1
2013	423.9	427.9	429.0	433.5	438.3	438.4	436.1	436.8	438.3	442.4	441.8	439.6	435.5
Goods Producing													
2002	107.5	105.1	104.7	105.4	106.2	106.7	107.4	108.1	105.9	105.4	104.7	102.8	105.8
2003	99.9	98.0	98.0	97.9	99.9	100.9	102.9	103.3	102.1	101.2	100.2	98.9	100.3
2004	96.0	95.0	95.3	96.3	97.8	98.8	100.4	100.0	98.9	99.0	97.9	96.4	97.7
2005	94.1	93.3	93.3	95.1	96.5	97.8	99.2	99.6	98.6	97.9	97.3	95.6	96.5
2006	93.2	92.4	92.2	93.8	95.3	97.2	97.3	97.6	96.3	95.9	95.2	94.0	95.0
2007	91.3	90.2	90.5	91.4	93.1	94.2	94.0	94.1	92.9	92.2	91.4	90.3	92.1
2008	87.9	86.8	86.5	87.4	89.5	90.9	91.9	91.8	90.8	90.0	88.1	86.1	89.0
2009	82.5	80.8	79.7	79.5	80.6	81.1	81.6	82.2	80.7	80.2	78.9	77.3	80.4
2010	74.7	74.0	74.2	75.8	77.1	78.3	79.5	80.0	79.1	79.3	78.8	76.7	77.3
2011	75.2	74.3	74.8	76.3	78.2	80.2	81.1	81.4	80.7	80.3	79.4	78.2	78.3
2012	76.2	75.4	75.6	76.8	78.3	80.2	80.9	80.7	79.6	79.1	78.1	77.5	78.2
2013	75.1	74.2	74.2	75.5	77.2	78.3	79.2	79.8	78.8	78.7	77.6	75.6	77.0
Service-Providing													
2002	396.8	400.8	402.7	405.3	410.6	410.6	401.8	401.8	406.2	410.5	412.9	415.0	406.3
2003	400.5	403.8	405.9	406.2	413.5	412.8	403.1	403.2	408.5	412.9	413.9	417.1	408.5
2004	402.4	406.2	408.3	410.2	417.2	417.2	407.3	406.7	412.9	420.3	421.2	422.6	412.7
2005	408.7	412.9	415.1	419.7	422.7	421.7	411.4	410.8	415.2	421.5	423.7	426.7	417.5
2006	409.7	412.8	415.3	417.2	419.9	419.8	409.3	409.0	416.7	422.8	424.4	426.2	416.9
2007	413.3	416.8	417.9	418.8	425.4	426.0	416.2	415.2	421.2	428.4	429.6	431.0	421.7
2008	416.4	421.6	422.6	427.5	431.8	430.8	421.1	420.3	426.1	432.3	431.6	432.3	426.2
2009	416.8	419.4	419.9	420.4	424.1	421.9	416.9	414.4	418.4	426.2	426.9	428.4	421.1
2010	415.2	419.3	421.2	425.7	429.0	427.7	418.3	418.0	423.7	432.7	433.4	433.6	424.8
2011	419.0	423.9	425.4	433.0	433.5	433.0	424.0	424.5	432.3	438.3	439.8	441.4	430.7
2012	424.5	430.9	432.9	433.7	438.6	436.9	426.7	425.6	433.4	441.6	443.1	444.3	434.4
2013	426.9	434.7	436.2	439.1	442.6	440.2	429.0	428.8	436.9	444.2	445.3	446.0	437.5
Mining and Logging													
2002	0.4	0.4	0.4	0.5	0.6	0.6	0.6	0.6	0.5	0.5	0.5	0.4	0.5
2003	0.4	0.4	0.4	0.5	0.5	0.6	0.6	0.6	0.6	0.6	0.5	0.6	0.5
2004	0.6	0.6	0.6	0.6	0.6	0.6	0.6	0.6	0.6	0.6	0.6	0.6	0.6
2005	0.5	0.5	0.5	0.6	0.6	0.7	0.7	0.7	0.7	0.6	0.6	0.6	0.6
2006	0.5	0.5	0.5	0.6	0.6	0.7	0.7	0.7	0.6	0.6	0.6	0.4	0.6
2007	0.4	0.5	0.5	0.6	0.6	0.6	0.6	0.6	0.6	0.6	0.6	0.6	0.6
2008	0.6	0.5	0.5	0.5	0.6	0.6	0.6	0.6	0.6	0.6	0.6	0.6	0.6
2009	0.5	0.5	0.5	0.5	0.6	0.6	0.6	0.6	0.6	0.6	0.6	0.6	0.6
2010	0.5	0.5	0.5	0.6	0.6	0.6	0.6	0.6	0.6	0.5	0.6	0.5	0.6
2011	0.5	0.5	0.5	0.6	0.6	0.6	0.6	0.6	0.6	0.6	0.6	0.6	0.6
2012	0.4	0.5	0.5	0.5	0.5	0.5	0.5	0.5	0.5	0.6	0.6	0.5	0.5
2013	0.5	0.5	0.5	0.5	0.5	0.6	0.6	0.5	0.5	0.5	0.6	0.6	0.5
Construction													
2002	15.7	15.0	15.1	16.3	17.4	18.3	19.1	19.7	19.1	18.7	18.0	16.7	17.4
2003	14.8	14.3	14.5	15.3	17.0	17.9	19.3	19.6	19.2	18.5	17.8	16.9	17.1
2004	15.2	14.8	15.1	16.5	17.9	18.9	19.9	20.3	19.8	19.6	19.0	17.9	17.9
2005	16.0	15.5	15.4	17.0	18.7	19.2	19.7	20.1	19.6	19.2	18.8	17.5	18.1
2006	16.0	15.3	15.2	16.5	18.0	19.0	19.4	19.6	19.0	18.9	18.3	17.7	17.7
2007	16.2	15.2	15.7	16.9	18.7	19.7	20.0	20.2	19.7	19.6	19.1	18.1	18.3
2008	16.8	16.0	16.1	17.4	19.1	20.0	20.8	21.0	20.6	20.3	19.1	17.9	18.8
2009	15.6	14.9	14.8	15.8	17.4	18.4	19.2	19.5	18.7	18.3	17.5	16.2	17.2
2010	14.5	14.0	14.3	15.9	17.0	18.0	18.8	19.2	18.4	18.3	17.8	16.1	16.9
2011	14.8	14.2	14.6	15.7	17.3	18.6	19.3	19.6	19.2	19.0	18.3	17.2	17.3
2012	15.8	15.3	15.7	16.9	18.1	19.4	20.0	20.1	19.6	19.1	18.4	17.7	18.0
2013	16.1	15.7	15.8	16.8	18.8	19.7	20.2	20.4	19.8	19.5	18.4	16.4	18.1

Employment by Industry: Rochester, NY, Selected Years, 2002–2013—*Continued*

(Numbers in thousands, not seasonally adjusted)

Industry and year	January	February	March	April	May	June	July	August	September	October	November	December	Annual average
Manufacturing													
2002	91.4	89.7	89.2	88.6	88.2	87.8	87.7	87.8	86.3	86.2	86.2	85.7	87.9
2003	84.7	83.3	83.1	82.1	82.4	82.4	83.0	83.1	82.3	82.1	81.9	81.4	82.7
2004	80.2	79.6	79.6	79.2	79.3	79.3	79.9	79.1	78.5	78.8	78.3	77.9	79.1
2005	77.6	77.3	77.4	77.5	77.2	77.9	78.8	78.8	78.3	78.1	77.9	77.5	77.9
2006	76.7	76.6	76.5	76.7	76.7	77.5	77.2	77.3	76.7	76.4	76.3	75.9	76.7
2007	74.7	74.5	74.3	73.9	73.8	73.9	73.4	73.3	72.6	72.0	71.7	71.6	73.3
2008	70.5	70.3	69.9	69.5	69.8	70.3	70.5	70.2	69.6	69.1	68.4	67.6	69.6
2009	66.4	65.4	64.4	63.2	62.6	62.1	61.8	62.1	61.4	61.3	60.8	60.5	62.7
2010	59.7	59.5	59.4	59.3	59.5	59.7	60.1	60.2	60.1	60.5	60.4	60.1	59.9
2011	59.9	59.6	59.7	60.0	60.3	61.0	61.2	61.2	60.9	60.7	60.5	60.4	60.5
2012	60.0	59.6	59.4	59.4	59.7	60.3	60.4	60.1	59.5	59.4	59.1	59.3	59.7
2013	58.5	58.0	57.9	58.2	57.9	58.1	58.4	58.9	58.5	58.7	58.6	58.6	58.4
Trade, Transportation, and Utilities													
2002	86.2	84.0	83.8	84.0	85.5	86.5	85.4	85.7	84.6	84.8	86.2	87.2	85.3
2003	84.5	82.5	82.6	82.4	84.1	85.0	83.6	84.0	83.8	84.3	85.4	86.4	84.1
2004	82.9	81.8	81.9	81.5	84.2	85.3	84.7	84.6	84.7	85.5	86.6	87.9	84.3
2005	84.3	82.7	82.8	83.4	84.5	85.9	85.1	85.5	84.3	85.1	86.3	88.1	84.8
2006	84.3	82.0	82.2	82.2	83.5	85.2	84.1	84.6	83.8	84.9	86.3	87.5	84.2
2007	84.4	82.2	82.6	82.2	85.1	86.3	85.5	85.1	84.4	85.5	87.0	87.9	84.9
2008	84.9	82.9	82.8	83.4	84.8	85.5	84.4	84.2	83.3	84.3	84.6	85.3	84.2
2009	81.3	79.4	79.2	78.8	80.6	81.5	80.9	80.8	79.7	80.7	81.5	82.6	80.6
2010	79.6	78.4	78.8	79.6	80.9	82.1	81.1	81.4	80.6	82.1	82.7	83.6	80.9
2011	80.5	79.3	79.3	80.4	81.2	82.4	81.4	81.6	80.8	82.2	83.2	84.6	81.4
2012	81.1	79.3	79.7	79.8	81.9	83.1	82.2	82.1	81.4	82.7	84.0	84.6	81.8
2013	81.1	79.6	79.7	80.2	81.5	82.6	81.5	81.3	80.9	81.5	83.0	83.7	81.4
Wholesale Trade													
2002	17.9	17.8	17.6	17.9	18.1	18.2	18.2	18.1	17.7	17.4	17.4	17.4	17.8
2003	17.2	17.0	17.1	17.1	17.3	17.5	17.6	17.5	17.2	17.0	17.0	17.0	17.2
2004	17.0	17.1	17.1	17.2	17.4	17.7	17.6	17.6	17.2	17.4	17.3	17.4	17.3
2005	17.3	17.3	17.3	17.3	17.4	17.6	17.7	17.7	17.3	17.0	17.3	17.2	17.4
2006	17.3	17.2	17.2	17.2	17.3	17.7	17.8	18.1	17.6	17.4	17.4	17.5	17.5
2007	17.4	17.4	17.4	17.4	17.6	17.9	18.1	18.0	17.7	17.8	17.7	17.7	17.7
2008	17.3	17.2	17.1	17.4	17.6	17.7	17.8	17.7	17.5	17.8	17.6	17.5	17.5
2009	17.1	16.9	16.8	16.6	16.8	16.8	16.8	16.7	16.5	16.5	16.3	16.5	16.7
2010	16.0	16.0	16.1	16.2	16.3	16.5	16.5	16.5	16.4	16.5	16.4	16.5	16.3
2011	16.1	16.1	16.2	16.4	16.5	16.7	16.7	16.6	16.5	16.9	16.8	16.8	16.5
2012	16.4	16.4	16.5	16.9	17.1	17.2	17.2	17.1	16.9	17.2	17.2	17.3	17.0
2013	17.1	17.0	17.0	17.1	17.2	17.4	17.4	17.4	17.4	17.3	17.4	17.5	17.3
Retail Trade													
2002	58.9	56.8	56.9	56.8	58.0	58.8	58.4	58.8	57.6	57.9	59.4	60.4	58.2
2003	57.8	56.2	56.2	55.9	57.4	58.2	57.4	57.8	57.2	57.7	58.8	59.7	57.5
2004	56.4	55.2	55.3	54.4	56.7	57.4	57.3	57.3	57.3	57.8	59.0	60.2	57.0
2005	57.0	55.4	55.4	55.9	56.8	57.9	57.6	57.9	56.5	57.4	58.3	60.0	57.2
2006	56.6	54.4	54.6	54.5	55.6	56.7	56.1	56.3	55.5	56.8	58.2	59.2	56.2
2007	56.6	54.5	54.9	54.6	57.0	57.9	57.4	57.1	56.1	57.0	58.5	59.3	56.7
2008	57.1	55.2	55.2	55.4	56.4	57.0	56.4	56.4	55.5	56.2	56.7	57.3	56.2
2009	54.4	52.7	52.8	52.5	53.9	54.7	54.3	54.3	53.3	54.1	55.2	55.8	54.0
2010	53.8	52.7	53.0	53.6	54.7	55.6	55.2	55.5	54.3	55.6	56.3	57.0	54.8
2011	54.8	53.6	53.5	54.2	54.8	55.7	55.3	55.6	54.3	55.3	56.5	57.6	55.1
2012	55.1	53.3	53.6	53.4	55.0	55.9	55.7	55.7	54.6	55.6	56.9	57.1	55.2
2013	54.4	53.0	53.1	53.5	54.5	55.3	54.9	54.8	53.6	54.3	55.6	56.0	54.4
Transportation and Utilities													
2002	9.4	9.4	9.3	9.3	9.4	9.5	8.8	8.8	9.3	9.5	9.4	9.4	9.3
2003	9.5	9.3	9.3	9.4	9.4	9.3	8.6	8.7	9.4	9.6	9.6	9.7	9.3
2004	9.5	9.5	9.5	9.9	10.1	10.2	9.8	9.7	10.2	10.3	10.3	10.3	9.9
2005	10.0	10.0	10.1	10.2	10.3	10.4	9.8	9.9	10.5	10.7	10.7	10.9	10.3
2006	10.4	10.4	10.4	10.5	10.6	10.8	10.2	10.2	10.7	10.7	10.7	10.8	10.5
2007	10.4	10.3	10.3	10.2	10.5	10.5	10.0	10.0	10.6	10.7	10.8	10.9	10.4
2008	10.5	10.5	10.5	10.6	10.8	10.8	10.2	10.1	10.3	10.3	10.3	10.5	10.5
2009	9.8	9.8	9.6	9.7	9.9	10.0	9.8	9.8	9.9	10.1	10.0	10.3	9.9
2010	9.8	9.7	9.7	9.8	9.9	10.0	9.4	9.4	9.9	10.0	10.0	10.1	9.8
2011	9.6	9.6	9.6	9.8	9.9	10.0	9.4	9.4	10.0	10.0	9.9	10.2	9.8
2012	9.6	9.6	9.6	9.5	9.8	10.0	9.3	9.3	9.9	9.9	9.9	10.2	9.7
2013	9.6	9.6	9.6	9.6	9.8	9.9	9.2	9.1	9.9	9.9	10.0	10.2	9.7
Information													
2002	13.5	13.1	13.3	13.0	13.1	12.9	12.7	12.6	12.5	12.4	12.4	12.5	12.8
2003	12.3	12.3	12.2	12.2	12.5	12.4	12.3	12.3	12.2	12.3	12.3	12.3	12.3
2004	12.4	12.3	12.3	12.2	12.2	12.2	12.1	12.0	12.0	12.0	12.0	11.9	12.1
2005	11.8	11.6	11.6	11.6	11.7	11.7	11.6	11.6	11.6	11.8	11.7	11.8	11.7
2006	11.7	11.6	11.5	11.1	11.1	11.1	10.9	10.7	10.5	10.6	10.6	10.5	11.0
2007	10.6	10.5	10.5	10.6	10.7	10.7	10.7	10.7	10.6	10.6	10.6	10.7	10.6
2008	10.5	10.5	10.5	10.4	10.4	10.4	10.4	10.4	10.2	10.3	10.4	10.4	10.4
2009	10.2	10.0	10.0	10.2	10.1	10.0	10.0	9.9	9.7	9.7	9.8	9.7	9.9
2010	9.5	9.4	9.4	9.4	9.4	9.5	9.5	9.5	9.3	9.3	9.3	9.2	9.4
2011	9.2	9.2	9.1	9.1	9.1	9.1	9.1	9.2	9.0	9.0	9.0	9.0	9.1
2012	8.5	8.5	8.5	8.5	8.8	8.8	9.0	9.0	8.9	8.9	9.1	9.0	8.8
2013	8.9	8.7	8.7	8.7	8.6	8.7	8.7	8.7	8.4	8.4	8.5	8.4	8.6

Employment by Industry: Rochester, NY, Selected Years, 2002–2013—*Continued*

(Numbers in thousands, not seasonally adjusted)

Industry and year	January	February	March	April	May	June	July	August	September	October	November	December	Annual average
Financial Activities													
2002	20.7	20.7	20.6	20.6	20.9	21.3	21.7	21.8	21.1	21.2	21.2	21.2	21.1
2003	21.0	20.9	20.9	21.1	21.7	22.0	22.3	22.3	21.8	21.9	21.9	22.2	21.7
2004	21.5	21.5	21.6	21.7	21.8	22.1	22.6	22.7	22.2	21.9	21.9	22.1	22.0
2005	21.7	21.5	21.6	21.5	21.8	22.0	22.2	22.2	21.7	21.7	21.9	22.0	21.8
2006	21.7	21.5	21.5	21.5	21.7	22.1	22.5	22.5	21.6	21.8	21.6	21.6	21.8
2007	21.6	21.5	21.5	21.5	21.5	22.0	22.3	22.3	21.4	21.4	21.4	21.5	21.7
2008	21.0	21.0	21.0	21.1	21.5	21.9	22.1	22.1	21.4	21.3	21.2	21.2	21.4
2009	20.4	20.2	20.1	20.2	20.7	21.1	21.2	21.3	20.9	20.6	20.5	20.6	20.7
2010	20.2	20.0	20.2	20.2	20.4	21.0	21.0	20.9	20.1	20.2	20.1	20.2	20.4
2011	20.1	20.1	20.2	20.5	20.7	21.4	21.7	21.7	21.1	21.1	21.0	21.2	20.9
2012	21.2	21.2	21.0	21.1	21.3	22.0	22.0	22.1	21.3	21.4	21.3	21.5	21.5
2013	21.0	21.0	20.9	21.1	21.3	21.8	22.0	22.0	21.3	21.3	21.5	21.6	21.4
Professional and Business Services													
2002	55.2	55.2	55.3	57.2	58.0	59.0	58.8	58.7	58.7	58.3	58.6	58.3	57.6
2003	55.9	55.9	56.2	57.4	58.2	59.0	58.2	58.5	58.2	58.8	58.3	58.5	57.8
2004	55.6	56.3	56.4	57.1	57.7	59.3	58.7	58.7	58.8	59.8	59.5	58.9	58.1
2005	57.2	57.4	58.1	60.2	60.5	61.1	61.6	61.1	60.8	61.2	61.5	61.7	60.2
2006	59.2	58.6	59.4	60.7	60.5	61.9	61.6	61.4	62.2	62.4	61.8	62.3	61.0
2007	60.8	61.2	61.2	61.2	61.9	63.1	62.6	62.8	61.9	62.8	62.3	62.3	62.0
2008	61.1	61.5	61.7	63.3	63.5	64.7	64.4	65.0	63.9	64.3	63.7	63.2	63.4
2009	61.1	60.6	60.5	59.7	59.6	60.6	60.3	60.3	60.0	60.8	60.8	60.7	60.4
2010	58.8	59.1	59.4	60.1	60.1	61.5	62.3	62.8	61.9	63.1	63.0	62.2	61.2
2011	60.3	60.2	61.0	63.4	63.3	64.9	65.6	65.8	66.1	65.3	65.7	65.5	63.9
2012	64.2	64.4	64.6	65.7	66.0	67.2	66.7	66.4	65.6	66.3	66.6	65.9	65.8
2013	64.6	64.6	64.7	65.7	66.2	67.5	67.5	67.5	66.9	67.2	66.0	64.8	66.1
Education and Health Services													
2002	89.8	92.1	92.8	92.7	92.1	89.4	88.8	88.8	93.2	94.9	95.3	95.5	92.1
2003	92.4	95.0	95.4	95.1	94.3	91.7	90.9	90.9	95.0	96.8	97.1	97.3	94.3
2004	95.8	99.4	100.0	98.9	98.2	94.6	93.0	92.8	97.5	100.4	100.8	100.2	97.6
2005	98.0	100.9	101.3	101.4	99.8	95.8	94.1	93.9	98.9	101.6	102.3	102.1	99.2
2006	99.4	102.7	102.8	102.9	102.0	98.0	95.8	95.8	101.2	104.0	104.7	104.5	101.2
2007	101.2	104.3	104.5	104.7	103.2	99.2	98.1	98.4	104.0	106.9	107.3	107.2	103.3
2008	103.3	107.3	107.6	108.0	106.5	102.6	101.2	100.9	107.1	109.6	110.3	110.5	106.2
2009	107.2	110.5	110.8	110.5	108.4	104.1	103.0	102.8	108.4	111.5	112.1	112.3	108.5
2010	108.9	112.5	112.7	113.3	111.0	106.5	105.3	105.2	111.6	114.4	114.9	115.1	111.0
2011	110.6	113.9	114.0	115.5	113.0	108.1	107.0	106.8	113.3	116.0	116.4	116.4	112.6
2012	110.9	115.7	116.2	115.9	113.6	108.3	107.4	107.3	114.6	117.7	118.3	118.6	113.7
2013	112.7	118.5	118.9	118.9	116.7	110.9	109.0	109.5	116.6	119.5	120.2	121.0	116.0
Leisure and Hospitality													
2002	34.8	35.1	35.6	37.6	40.3	41.3	41.7	41.5	39.4	38.1	37.2	37.1	38.3
2003	35.4	35.3	36.0	36.6	40.2	41.3	42.3	42.2	40.1	38.8	37.8	37.7	38.6
2004	35.7	35.9	36.3	37.5	40.4	42.0	42.7	42.8	40.6	39.6	38.7	38.5	39.2
2005	36.6	36.7	37.1	38.6	41.1	42.8	42.4	42.6	40.0	38.9	37.8	37.8	39.4
2006	35.5	36.0	36.8	38.2	40.4	42.5	43.0	43.0	40.5	39.7	38.9	38.8	39.4
2007	36.6	36.8	37.1	37.9	41.5	43.9	44.3	43.8	41.2	40.4	39.6	39.1	40.2
2008	36.9	37.5	37.8	39.2	42.6	43.9	44.0	44.0	41.2	40.5	39.1	39.1	40.5
2009	37.3	36.9	37.5	38.7	42.1	43.5	44.1	44.0	41.9	40.6	39.3	39.2	40.4
2010	37.8	37.7	38.4	40.4	43.0	44.1	44.7	44.8	42.3	41.1	40.2	39.6	41.2
2011	38.7	38.9	39.2	40.8	43.2	44.9	45.4	45.5	43.1	42.6	41.6	40.9	42.1
2012	39.1	39.4	40.1	40.5	43.8	45.2	46.0	46.0	43.6	43.3	42.2	41.9	42.6
2013	40.0	40.7	41.3	42.6	45.6	47.1	47.2	47.0	44.8	45.0	44.1	43.5	44.1
Other Services													
2002	17.6	17.7	17.7	18.1	18.2	18.3	18.4	18.6	18.4	18.5	18.6	18.6	18.2
2003	18.4	18.4	18.6	18.7	18.9	18.9	19.0	18.9	18.7	18.8	18.9	19.0	18.8
2004	18.5	18.7	18.8	19.0	19.2	19.2	19.0	18.9	18.7	19.0	18.9	19.0	18.9
2005	18.9	19.0	19.2	19.5	19.5	19.5	19.2	19.0	18.8	19.0	19.0	19.1	19.1
2006	18.9	19.0	19.1	19.1	19.2	19.0	19.1	18.8	18.7	18.9	19.1	19.4	19.0
2007	19.2	19.2	19.2	19.2	19.5	19.5	19.3	19.3	19.0	19.4	19.4	19.5	19.3
2008	19.3	19.3	19.3	19.6	19.8	19.8	19.9	19.7	19.3	19.5	19.5	19.5	19.5
2009	19.5	19.5	19.6	19.5	19.7	19.7	19.9	19.7	19.4	19.5	19.7	19.8	19.6
2010	19.5	19.3	19.3	19.6	19.6	19.7	20.0	20.0	19.5	19.8	19.9	20.0	19.7
2011	19.8	19.8	20.1	20.4	20.4	20.4	20.5	20.5	20.3	20.4	20.5	20.8	20.3
2012	20.7	20.6	20.9	20.9	21.2	21.3	20.8	20.7	20.3	20.6	20.6	20.7	20.8
2013	20.5	20.6	20.6	20.8	21.2	21.5	21.0	21.0	20.6	20.8	20.9	21.0	20.9
Government													
2002	79.0	82.9	83.6	82.1	82.5	81.9	74.3	74.1	78.3	82.3	83.4	84.6	80.8
2003	80.6	83.5	84.0	82.7	83.6	82.5	74.5	74.1	78.7	81.2	82.2	83.7	80.9
2004	80.0	80.3	81.0	82.3	83.5	82.5	74.5	74.2	78.4	82.1	82.8	84.1	80.5
2005	80.2	83.1	83.4	83.5	83.8	82.9	75.2	74.9	79.1	82.2	83.2	84.1	81.3
2006	79.0	81.4	82.0	81.5	81.5	80.0	72.3	72.2	78.2	80.5	81.4	81.6	79.3
2007	78.9	81.1	81.3	81.5	82.0	81.3	73.4	72.8	78.7	81.4	82.0	82.8	79.8
2008	79.4	81.6	81.9	82.5	82.7	82.0	74.7	74.0	79.7	82.5	82.8	83.1	80.6
2009	79.8	82.3	82.2	82.8	82.9	81.4	77.5	75.6	78.4	82.8	83.2	83.5	81.0
2010	80.9	82.9	83.0	83.1	84.6	83.3	74.4	73.4	78.4	82.7	83.3	83.7	81.1
2011	79.8	82.5	82.5	82.9	82.6	81.8	73.3	73.4	78.6	81.7	82.4	83.0	80.4
2012	78.8	81.8	81.9	81.3	82.0	81.0	72.6	72.0	77.7	80.7	81.0	82.1	79.4
2013	78.1	81.0	81.4	81.1	81.5	80.1	72.1	71.8	77.4	80.5	81.1	82.0	79.0

Employment by Industry: Sacramento–Arden-Arcade–Roseville, CA, Selected Years, 2002–2013

(Numbers in thousands, not seasonally adjusted)

Industry and year	January	February	March	April	May	June	July	August	September	October	November	December	Annual average
Total Nonfarm													
2002	821.3	823.8	834.4	833.8	840.6	844.7	839.0	841.5	843.6	845.9	849.7	850.7	839.1
2003	839.1	841.0	846.2	851.5	857.1	863.6	856.9	858.6	860.2	857.8	865.8	867.0	855.4
2004	853.8	856.0	860.8	866.9	870.0	876.6	871.9	870.0	875.5	876.9	879.7	882.4	870.0
2005	873.0	876.5	881.9	886.2	890.6	895.0	894.4	895.0	899.9	901.5	906.9	910.9	892.7
2006	900.4	904.1	905.8	902.7	912.5	920.4	913.4	914.3	916.7	914.3	917.1	918.8	911.7
2007	905.7	909.0	916.0	913.8	920.3	924.5	918.8	919.5	919.3	916.1	919.3	919.9	916.9
2008	899.6	903.2	904.9	903.5	906.4	907.3	899.0	894.4	891.9	888.4	886.9	885.1	897.6
2009	866.0	860.9	859.2	856.9	857.8	855.8	838.5	833.7	832.0	839.5	840.4	838.4	848.3
2010	821.0	820.6	824.1	828.0	833.6	834.9	822.3	819.9	821.2	826.9	827.7	825.2	825.5
2011	814.0	816.7	818.3	822.0	823.7	825.1	816.3	821.0	824.7	829.1	833.2	831.3	823.0
2012	820.4	826.0	829.2	839.8	845.0	852.8	838.2	842.0	841.5	852.3	858.4	855.7	841.8
2013	850.7	856.3	860.0	860.5	864.7	869.5	859.0	864.0	865.7	870.1	875.6	876.9	864.4
Total Private													
2002	599.3	600.0	605.2	604.5	610.0	615.0	615.4	617.1	617.5	618.3	621.7	623.2	612.3
2003	614.1	614.1	618.5	623.5	626.9	634.7	632.6	636.0	635.6	634.4	638.0	642.6	629.3
2004	631.3	632.9	637.8	643.3	645.6	651.7	654.3	654.8	656.2	655.5	657.0	661.3	648.5
2005	651.2	653.7	657.9	661.1	664.4	668.9	673.4	675.3	675.9	676.1	680.6	684.8	668.6
2006	675.3	676.8	677.2	673.7	682.8	689.6	687.8	691.2	689.5	684.6	685.4	686.1	683.3
2007	674.3	676.1	680.0	677.7	682.7	685.7	687.5	688.7	685.3	679.7	681.8	682.2	681.8
2008	662.6	664.3	664.1	663.5	664.4	665.4	662.9	662.1	657.4	650.9	648.0	646.2	659.3
2009	627.3	620.5	617.0	614.3	615.0	615.1	613.0	611.5	606.1	604.9	605.4	605.2	612.9
2010	590.1	588.6	590.5	591.6	593.5	597.8	599.6	600.6	597.1	596.9	596.9	599.2	595.2
2011	586.7	587.6	588.0	591.1	594.2	596.8	602.2	606.0	605.5	603.9	608.0	610.3	598.4
2012	598.7	602.1	603.0	613.3	618.4	625.1	625.8	629.1	625.5	630.1	635.3	636.9	620.3
2013	630.0	633.8	635.3	636.3	639.5	643.8	645.0	649.0	647.3	645.6	649.3	654.5	642.5
Goods Producing													
2002	99.0	99.0	100.3	101.7	104.1	105.3	105.8	107.7	107.6	107.9	106.3	104.5	104.1
2003	100.8	101.8	103.7	105.3	107.7	111.0	110.8	113.5	113.9	113.5	111.5	109.9	108.6
2004	107.5	107.8	110.6	111.8	113.6	116.5	117.5	119.0	118.7	117.3	114.8	113.8	114.1
2005	110.8	112.0	113.7	114.5	116.1	118.0	119.8	121.7	122.0	121.0	119.1	117.4	117.2
2006	113.0	113.1	111.3	109.3	114.4	117.2	116.8	119.0	119.0	115.1	112.2	109.6	114.2
2007	107.2	107.4	108.5	108.1	110.7	112.0	111.1	112.3	110.5	107.2	104.6	101.6	108.4
2008	95.0	94.9	95.2	95.3	96.9	98.3	98.7	99.4	97.9	95.1	91.4	88.8	95.6
2009	83.2	79.8	79.1	78.3	79.2	79.9	79.0	79.0	77.8	77.1	75.3	72.9	78.4
2010	69.7	68.6	69.5	70.3	71.4	73.1	73.9	74.8	73.8	73.0	71.4	69.7	71.6
2011	67.1	67.0	66.6	68.2	69.5	70.8	72.6	74.1	74.5	74.0	72.3	70.4	70.6
2012	68.2	68.1	67.3	69.1	71.7	73.8	75.5	77.0	76.8	76.0	74.7	73.7	72.7
2013	72.4	73.4	74.2	75.5	77.1	78.9	79.7	81.6	81.0	76.7	77.0	77.1	77.1
Service-Providing													
2002	722.3	724.8	734.1	732.1	736.5	739.4	733.2	733.8	736.0	738.0	743.4	746.2	735.0
2003	738.3	739.2	742.5	746.2	749.4	752.6	746.1	745.1	746.3	744.3	754.3	757.1	746.8
2004	746.3	748.2	750.2	755.1	756.4	760.1	754.4	751.0	756.8	759.6	764.9	768.6	756.0
2005	762.2	764.5	768.2	771.7	774.5	777.0	774.6	773.3	777.9	780.5	787.8	793.5	775.5
2006	787.4	791.0	794.5	793.4	798.1	803.2	796.6	795.3	797.7	799.2	804.9	809.2	797.5
2007	798.5	801.6	807.5	805.7	809.6	812.5	807.7	807.2	808.8	808.9	814.7	818.3	808.4
2008	804.6	808.3	809.7	808.2	809.5	809.0	800.3	795.0	794.0	793.3	795.5	796.3	802.0
2009	782.8	781.1	780.1	778.6	778.6	775.9	759.5	754.7	754.2	762.4	765.1	765.5	769.9
2010	751.3	752.0	754.6	757.7	762.2	761.8	748.4	745.1	747.4	753.9	756.3	755.5	753.9
2011	746.9	749.7	751.7	753.8	754.2	754.3	743.7	746.9	750.2	755.1	760.9	760.9	752.4
2012	752.2	757.9	761.9	770.7	773.3	779.0	762.7	765.0	764.7	776.3	783.7	782.0	769.1
2013	778.3	782.9	785.8	785.0	787.6	790.6	779.3	782.4	784.7	793.4	798.6	799.8	787.4
Mining and Logging													
2002	0.7	0.7	0.8	0.8	0.8	0.8	0.8	0.8	0.8	0.8	0.8	0.8	0.8
2003	0.6	0.6	0.6	0.6	0.6	0.7	0.7	0.7	0.7	0.7	0.7	0.7	0.7
2004	0.6	0.6	0.7	0.7	0.7	0.7	0.8	0.8	0.8	0.8	0.7	0.7	0.7
2005	0.7	0.7	0.7	0.7	0.7	0.7	0.8	0.8	0.7	0.7	0.7	0.7	0.7
2006	0.7	0.7	0.7	0.6	0.6	0.8	0.7	0.8	0.8	0.7	0.7	0.7	0.7
2007	0.6	0.6	0.6	0.6	0.7	0.7	0.7	0.7	0.7	0.7	0.7	0.7	0.7
2008	0.6	0.6	0.6	0.7	0.7	0.7	0.7	0.7	0.7	0.7	0.6	0.6	0.7
2009	0.4	0.4	0.4	0.4	0.4	0.4	0.5	0.5	0.5	0.5	0.5	0.4	0.4
2010	0.3	0.3	0.4	0.4	0.4	0.5	0.5	0.5	0.5	0.5	0.5	0.5	0.4
2011	0.4	0.4	0.4	0.4	0.4	0.4	0.5	0.5	0.5	0.5	0.5	0.5	0.5
2012	0.4	0.4	0.4	0.3	0.4	0.4	0.4	0.4	0.4	0.5	0.5	0.4	0.4
2013	0.4	0.3	0.4	0.4	0.4	0.5	0.5	0.5	0.5	0.5	0.5	0.5	0.5
Construction													
2002	55.8	56.5	57.6	58.8	61.0	62.3	63.1	64.9	64.9	64.6	64.1	62.3	61.3
2003	60.1	60.9	62.7	64.2	66.1	68.2	68.3	70.0	70.2	70.4	69.2	67.5	66.5
2004	65.3	65.8	68.5	69.6	70.9	73.2	73.5	74.2	73.5	73.2	71.3	70.3	70.8
2005	67.8	68.9	70.4	71.8	73.1	74.8	76.0	76.5	76.6	76.5	75.2	73.2	73.4
2006	69.5	69.6	67.9	66.1	71.1	73.3	73.4	74.6	74.3	71.4	69.7	67.1	70.7
2007	65.7	65.7	67.0	66.8	69.0	70.0	69.6	69.8	68.2	66.1	63.9	61.1	66.9
2008	55.2	55.3	55.5	55.7	57.2	58.5	59.2	59.0	57.6	56.2	53.6	51.2	56.2
2009	47.0	44.2	43.9	43.5	44.4	45.0	44.3	43.9	42.7	42.3	41.5	39.4	43.5
2010	37.1	36.1	36.8	37.6	38.6	40.0	40.5	40.5	39.5	39.2	38.2	36.4	38.4
2011	34.4	34.2	33.6	35.1	36.2	37.2	39.2	39.6	39.6	39.2	38.5	36.4	36.9
2012	34.7	34.6	33.9	35.4	37.7	39.4	40.7	41.4	41.2	41.3	40.5	39.7	38.4
2013	38.7	39.6	40.5	41.5	42.9	44.1	45.2	46.3	46.0	43.1	43.1	43.6	42.9

Employment by Industry: Sacramento–Arden-Arcade–Roseville, CA, Selected Years, 2002–2013—*Continued*

(Numbers in thousands, not seasonally adjusted)

Industry and year	January	February	March	April	May	June	July	August	September	October	November	December	Annual average
Manufacturing													
2002	42.5	41.8	41.9	42.1	42.3	42.2	41.9	42.0	41.9	42.5	41.4	41.4	42.0
2003	40.1	40.3	40.4	40.5	41.0	42.1	41.8	42.8	43.0	42.4	41.6	41.7	41.5
2004	41.6	41.4	41.4	41.5	42.0	42.6	43.2	44.1	44.4	43.3	42.8	42.8	42.6
2005	42.3	42.4	42.6	42.0	42.3	42.5	43.0	44.4	44.7	43.8	43.2	43.5	43.1
2006	42.8	42.8	42.7	42.6	42.7	43.1	42.7	43.6	43.9	43.0	41.8	41.8	42.8
2007	40.9	41.1	40.9	40.7	41.0	41.3	40.8	41.8	41.6	40.3	40.0	39.8	40.9
2008	39.2	39.0	39.1	38.9	39.0	39.1	38.8	39.7	39.6	38.2	37.2	37.0	38.7
2009	35.8	35.2	34.8	34.4	34.4	34.5	34.2	34.6	34.6	34.3	33.3	33.1	34.4
2010	32.3	32.2	32.3	32.3	32.4	32.6	32.9	33.8	33.8	33.3	32.7	32.8	32.8
2011	32.3	32.4	32.6	32.7	32.9	33.2	32.9	34.0	34.4	34.3	33.3	33.5	33.2
2012	33.1	33.1	33.0	33.4	33.6	34.0	34.4	35.2	35.2	34.2	33.7	33.6	33.9
2013	33.3	33.5	33.3	33.6	33.8	34.3	34.0	34.8	34.5	33.1	33.4	33.0	33.7
Trade, Transportation, and Utilities													
2002	138.5	137.4	138.5	138.6	139.0	140.2	140.3	140.5	140.7	141.8	145.0	146.8	140.6
2003	141.6	139.6	139.6	140.2	140.8	142.3	142.9	143.5	143.3	144.5	148.4	150.9	143.1
2004	144.1	143.1	143.0	143.9	144.8	145.9	145.8	145.7	145.8	147.5	151.0	152.3	146.1
2005	147.0	145.9	146.2	146.2	146.7	147.2	148.4	148.7	149.1	150.1	154.1	157.5	148.9
2006	151.2	149.9	150.8	150.4	151.8	153.1	154.3	155.1	154.4	154.6	157.8	159.9	153.6
2007	153.9	152.2	152.0	151.2	151.7	152.2	152.8	152.7	152.2	152.3	156.3	158.2	153.1
2008	150.5	148.5	148.2	147.3	147.0	147.1	146.4	145.7	144.3	143.7	145.2	145.8	146.6
2009	138.1	135.4	134.0	133.5	134.6	134.7	133.8	133.2	133.4	133.6	136.9	137.7	134.9
2010	132.3	130.3	130.3	130.7	131.4	131.5	131.8	132.5	132.1	133.4	136.1	138.0	132.5
2011	132.5	131.0	130.9	131.2	132.0	132.7	133.2	134.0	134.0	135.6	139.8	141.7	134.1
2012	135.8	134.0	134.5	136.7	137.6	138.6	138.6	139.4	139.5	140.3	144.9	146.2	138.8
2013	140.3	139.1	139.1	139.6	140.4	141.0	141.7	141.9	141.8	143.0	147.6	149.4	142.1
Wholesale Trade													
2002	25.3	25.5	25.7	25.5	25.6	25.5	25.5	25.6	25.5	25.7	25.8	25.7	25.6
2003	25.9	26.0	26.0	26.2	26.2	26.3	26.3	26.4	26.4	26.4	26.5	26.6	26.3
2004	26.3	26.4	26.4	26.3	26.4	26.6	26.7	26.8	26.7	26.6	26.5	26.6	26.5
2005	26.4	26.5	26.5	26.7	26.7	26.7	26.9	27.0	27.1	27.4	27.5	27.6	26.9
2006	27.7	28.0	28.3	28.1	28.5	28.7	28.8	28.8	28.6	28.7	28.6	28.4	28.4
2007	28.4	28.2	28.5	28.1	28.0	28.1	27.8	27.7	27.5	27.4	27.3	27.5	27.9
2008	27.0	27.0	26.8	26.8	26.9	26.8	26.6	26.3	26.2	26.0	25.7	25.4	26.5
2009	25.0	24.7	24.4	24.3	24.6	24.6	24.1	23.7	23.5	23.5	23.5	23.0	24.1
2010	23.0	22.8	22.6	22.9	22.9	22.7	22.6	22.7	22.6	22.8	22.8	22.8	22.8
2011	22.8	22.7	22.7	23.3	23.5	23.7	23.6	23.7	23.8	24.2	24.5	24.7	23.6
2012	24.5	24.7	25.1	25.5	25.5	25.5	25.2	25.2	25.0	25.1	25.1	25.1	25.1
2013	24.9	24.8	24.9	25.0	25.1	25.2	25.2	25.0	25.1	25.1	24.4	25.0	25.0
Retail Trade													
2002	91.3	89.9	90.7	90.6	90.8	92.0	92.1	92.3	92.8	93.8	96.9	99.0	92.7
2003	94.2	92.2	92.2	92.5	92.9	94.1	94.6	94.8	94.6	95.7	99.5	101.9	94.9
2004	95.2	94.3	94.3	95.1	95.9	96.6	96.4	96.0	95.9	97.3	101.1	102.3	96.7
2005	97.3	96.3	96.4	96.5	96.8	97.2	98.3	98.3	98.5	99.3	103.1	105.8	98.7
2006	100.1	98.7	99.1	98.9	99.7	100.3	100.9	101.0	100.3	100.6	103.7	105.2	100.7
2007	100.4	98.9	98.4	98.2	98.6	98.7	99.5	99.3	98.9	99.3	103.3	104.4	99.8
2008	98.4	96.3	96.1	95.5	95.2	95.2	94.5	94.1	92.9	92.8	94.8	95.4	95.1
2009	89.3	87.0	86.1	85.9	86.9	87.0	86.9	86.5	86.8	87.3	90.4	91.6	87.6
2010	87.1	85.6	85.7	86.3	86.9	87.1	87.6	88.1	88.0	89.0	91.7	93.2	88.0
2011	89.0	87.6	87.3	87.1	87.5	87.9	88.5	89.0	89.0	90.1	93.9	95.3	89.4
2012	90.7	88.7	88.8	89.7	90.3	90.9	91.1	91.8	91.9	92.6	97.0	97.8	91.8
2013	92.8	91.7	91.6	92.0	92.5	92.8	93.4	93.6	93.3	94.3	98.9	99.7	93.9
Transportation and Utilities													
2002	21.9	22.0	22.1	22.5	22.6	22.7	22.7	22.6	22.4	22.3	22.3	22.1	22.4
2003	21.5	21.4	21.4	21.5	21.7	21.9	22.0	22.3	22.3	22.4	22.4	22.4	21.9
2004	22.6	22.4	22.3	22.5	22.5	22.7	22.7	22.9	23.2	23.6	23.4	23.4	22.9
2005	23.3	23.1	23.3	23.0	23.2	23.3	23.2	23.4	23.5	23.4	23.5	24.1	23.4
2006	23.4	23.2	23.4	23.4	23.6	24.1	24.6	25.3	25.5	25.3	25.5	26.3	24.5
2007	25.1	25.1	25.1	24.9	25.1	25.4	25.5	25.7	25.8	25.6	25.7	26.3	25.4
2008	25.1	25.2	25.3	25.0	24.9	25.1	25.3	25.3	25.2	24.9	24.7	25.0	25.1
2009	23.8	23.7	23.5	23.3	23.1	23.1	22.8	23.0	23.1	22.8	23.0	23.1	23.2
2010	22.2	21.9	22.0	21.5	21.6	21.7	21.6	21.7	21.5	21.6	21.6	22.0	21.7
2011	20.7	20.7	20.9	20.8	21.0	21.1	21.1	21.3	21.2	21.3	21.4	21.7	21.1
2012	20.6	20.6	20.6	21.5	21.8	22.2	22.3	22.4	22.6	22.6	22.8	23.3	21.9
2013	22.6	22.6	22.6	22.6	22.8	23.0	23.1	23.3	23.4	23.6	24.3	24.7	23.2
Information													
2002	24.1	23.8	23.7	23.5	23.7	23.6	23.3	22.7	22.4	22.3	21.9	21.6	23.1
2003	21.8	22.0	21.7	22.2	22.6	22.8	21.7	21.6	21.3	21.4	21.5	21.6	21.9
2004	21.3	21.5	21.3	21.1	21.1	21.1	21.0	20.8	20.5	20.4	20.5	20.6	20.9
2005	20.5	20.6	20.2	20.3	20.1	19.9	19.8	19.8	19.5	19.2	19.4	19.5	19.9
2006	19.6	19.8	19.7	19.9	19.9	19.8	20.4	20.3	20.1	20.0	20.1	20.4	20.0
2007	20.4	20.7	20.4	20.1	20.3	20.0	20.0	20.0	19.8	19.7	19.7	19.7	20.1
2008	19.5	19.7	19.5	19.4	19.4	19.4	19.3	19.3	19.1	18.6	18.8	18.8	19.2
2009	18.9	18.8	18.6	18.1	18.3	18.2	18.4	18.3	18.1	18.0	18.0	18.3	18.3
2010	17.8	17.7	17.4	17.3	17.2	17.6	17.1	16.9	16.7	16.7	17.0	17.0	17.2
2011	16.8	16.8	16.8	16.7	16.6	16.5	16.4	16.2	15.9	15.9	15.7	15.6	16.3
2012	15.5	15.6	15.6	15.7	15.7	15.8	15.7	15.5	15.3	15.3	15.5	15.5	15.6
2013	15.3	15.3	15.0	15.2	15.2	15.2	15.1	15.0	14.7	14.7	14.8	14.8	15.0

Employment by Industry: Sacramento–Arden-Arcade–Roseville, CA, Selected Years, 2002–2013—*Continued*

(Numbers in thousands, not seasonally adjusted)

Industry and year	January	February	March	April	May	June	July	August	September	October	November	December	Annual average
Financial Activities													
2002	52.9	53.2	53.3	53.9	53.8	54.1	54.9	55.4	56.2	57.1	57.6	58.1	55.0
2003	57.6	58.2	58.3	59.2	59.4	59.5	59.6	59.9	59.5	59.1	59.0	59.3	59.1
2004	58.4	58.8	58.8	59.5	59.7	59.9	60.5	60.8	60.8	61.2	61.2	61.7	60.1
2005	61.6	61.9	62.3	62.6	63.1	63.1	63.5	63.7	63.8	63.9	64.1	64.4	63.2
2006	64.9	65.0	65.0	64.8	64.7	64.9	64.5	64.3	64.1	63.2	63.4	63.2	64.3
2007	62.7	62.9	62.5	62.5	62.3	62.1	61.9	61.4	60.7	60.2	59.6	59.6	61.5
2008	58.6	58.6	58.2	58.0	57.7	57.5	57.4	56.9	56.5	55.8	55.6	55.4	57.2
2009	55.5	55.3	55.1	53.9	53.4	53.1	52.7	52.4	51.3	51.0	50.6	50.6	52.9
2010	49.8	49.5	49.5	49.0	48.6	48.7	48.2	48.0	47.8	47.5	46.5	46.4	48.3
2011	46.3	46.0	46.2	46.4	46.7	46.7	47.0	47.3	47.0	46.7	46.5	46.7	46.6
2012	46.9	47.1	47.2	47.5	47.8	48.2	48.6	48.7	48.4	48.8	48.7	49.1	48.1
2013	48.9	49.1	49.1	49.4	49.5	49.7	50.2	50.2	49.6	50.1	49.1	49.3	49.5
Professional and Business Services													
2002	98.3	99.4	101.7	100.5	100.4	102.1	102.6	102.5	103.0	100.5	100.7	100.8	101.0
2003	99.5	100.0	100.2	100.3	100.3	101.2	100.5	100.9	101.4	100.2	101.5	101.5	100.6
2004	100.1	100.8	101.6	103.2	103.0	103.6	104.0	104.2	104.0	104.4	104.0	104.4	103.1
2005	103.6	105.0	106.3	107.7	107.9	109.7	109.7	109.7	109.7	110.5	111.3	112.0	108.6
2006	111.0	112.0	112.3	111.7	112.4	113.5	112.9	113.3	112.7	113.1	113.0	112.6	112.5
2007	108.6	110.0	110.8	111.4	111.3	112.3	113.3	113.7	113.2	113.5	113.4	113.9	112.1
2008	110.0	111.2	110.9	111.3	110.8	110.2	110.0	109.9	109.4	109.9	108.8	108.3	110.1
2009	103.8	103.1	102.2	101.2	100.0	100.0	101.2	101.2	99.7	100.7	100.2	100.1	101.1
2010	98.9	100.4	100.9	101.5	101.5	102.8	103.7	103.7	103.1	103.9	103.1	102.6	102.2
2011	100.3	102.1	101.3	102.5	102.7	103.1	105.2	106.4	106.0	106.7	106.8	107.0	104.2
2012	103.8	106.1	105.6	109.7	111.2	112.8	113.7	114.5	112.1	114.0	113.7	112.8	110.8
2013	111.9	113.5	112.7	112.4	112.8	113.7	113.5	115.2	115.8	116.9	115.8	117.1	114.3
Education and Health Services													
2002	85.0	84.2	84.6	83.7	85.8	84.6	84.2	83.7	84.8	86.1	87.4	86.6	85.1
2003	88.6	87.5	88.9	90.5	91.0	91.0	91.1	89.9	91.6	92.0	92.7	92.9	90.6
2004	93.9	93.9	94.2	95.2	95.8	95.5	95.9	94.4	97.7	97.5	97.7	98.2	95.8
2005	98.8	98.4	98.8	99.7	100.4	99.9	100.0	99.4	101.0	101.9	102.5	102.3	100.3
2006	103.9	103.4	104.1	104.2	105.4	105.5	104.5	104.1	105.5	107.1	106.7	106.7	105.1
2007	108.2	108.5	110.1	110.0	111.2	110.3	110.5	110.3	112.0	112.3	114.1	113.7	110.9
2008	113.5	114.8	114.7	115.4	115.8	114.8	113.8	114.4	115.4	115.8	117.0	116.6	115.2
2009	116.3	116.7	116.7	117.0	117.7	116.4	115.1	115.3	115.8	117.3	117.3	117.0	116.6
2010	114.5	114.3	114.5	115.4	116.1	115.0	113.8	114.0	114.6	115.6	116.3	116.2	115.0
2011	115.8	115.9	116.4	117.1	117.6	116.4	115.7	116.2	117.2	117.5	118.6	118.6	116.9
2012	119.7	120.5	121.2	121.2	121.7	120.9	118.2	118.4	119.8	124.0	125.2	124.8	121.3
2013	126.0	127.0	127.7	126.7	127.7	126.2	125.5	126.2	127.6	129.8	131.0	130.6	127.7
Leisure and Hospitality													
2002	73.9	74.8	75.3	74.9	74.5	76.6	76.0	76.6	74.8	74.2	74.5	76.4	75.2
2003	76.9	77.4	78.5	77.5	76.5	78.1	77.7	78.4	76.6	75.9	75.7	78.7	77.3
2004	78.3	79.1	80.1	80.1	78.8	80.6	80.8	81.2	79.8	78.4	79.3	81.7	79.9
2005	80.6	81.3	81.4	81.0	81.1	82.3	83.7	83.9	82.4	81.4	82.2	84.0	82.1
2006	83.8	85.2	85.5	85.2	85.5	86.9	86.5	87.0	85.2	83.2	83.9	85.6	85.3
2007	85.5	86.2	87.2	85.8	86.1	87.6	88.6	88.8	87.4	85.1	85.0	86.2	86.6
2008	87.0	87.7	88.4	87.1	86.7	88.1	87.1	86.3	84.6	82.2	81.8	83.3	85.9
2009	82.6	82.4	82.5	82.9	82.4	83.6	83.7	83.3	81.3	78.7	78.8	81.0	81.9
2010	79.5	80.2	80.6	79.3	78.9	80.6	82.4	82.1	80.4	78.5	78.6	81.7	80.2
2011	80.4	81.2	82.2	80.9	80.9	82.3	83.6	83.4	82.4	79.7	80.6	82.5	81.7
2012	80.9	82.7	83.2	84.8	83.7	85.7	86.9	86.9	85.1	83.3	84.2	86.5	84.5
2013	87.0	87.9	88.7	88.7	87.8	89.9	90.2	89.7	87.7	86.0	84.8	87.4	88.0
Other Services													
2002	27.6	28.2	27.8	27.7	28.7	28.5	28.3	28.0	28.0	28.4	28.3	28.4	28.2
2003	27.3	27.6	27.6	28.3	28.6	28.8	28.3	28.3	28.0	27.8	27.7	27.8	28.0
2004	27.7	27.9	28.2	28.5	28.8	28.6	28.8	28.7	28.9	28.8	28.5	28.6	28.5
2005	28.3	28.6	29.0	29.1	29.0	28.8	28.5	28.4	28.4	28.1	27.9	27.7	28.5
2006	27.9	28.4	28.5	28.2	28.7	28.7	27.9	28.1	28.5	28.3	28.3	28.1	28.3
2007	27.8	28.2	28.5	28.6	29.1	29.2	29.3	29.5	29.5	29.4	29.1	29.3	29.0
2008	28.5	28.9	29.0	29.7	30.1	30.0	30.2	30.2	30.2	29.8	29.4	29.2	29.6
2009	28.9	29.0	28.8	29.4	29.4	29.2	29.1	28.8	28.7	28.5	28.3	27.9	28.8
2010	27.6	27.6	27.8	28.1	28.4	28.5	28.7	28.6	28.6	28.3	27.9	27.6	28.1
2011	27.5	27.6	27.6	28.1	28.2	28.3	28.5	28.4	28.5	27.8	27.7	27.8	28.0
2012	27.9	28.0	28.4	28.6	29.0	29.3	28.6	28.7	28.5	28.4	28.4	28.3	28.5
2013	28.2	28.5	28.8	28.8	29.0	29.2	29.1	29.2	29.1	28.4	29.2	28.8	28.9
Government													
2002	222.0	223.8	229.2	229.3	230.6	229.7	223.6	224.4	226.1	227.6	228.0	227.5	226.8
2003	225.0	226.9	227.7	228.0	230.2	228.9	224.3	222.6	224.6	223.4	227.8	224.4	226.2
2004	222.5	223.1	223.0	223.6	224.4	224.9	217.6	215.2	219.3	221.4	222.7	221.1	221.6
2005	221.8	222.8	224.0	225.1	226.2	226.1	221.0	219.7	224.0	225.4	226.3	226.1	224.0
2006	225.1	227.3	228.6	229.0	229.7	230.8	225.6	223.1	227.2	229.7	231.7	232.7	228.4
2007	231.4	232.9	236.0	236.1	237.6	238.8	231.3	230.8	234.0	236.4	237.5	237.7	235.0
2008	237.0	238.9	240.8	240.0	242.0	241.9	236.1	232.3	234.5	237.5	238.9	238.9	238.2
2009	238.7	240.4	242.2	242.6	242.8	240.7	225.5	222.2	225.9	234.6	235.0	233.2	235.3
2010	230.9	232.0	233.6	236.4	240.1	237.1	222.7	219.3	224.1	230.0	230.8	226.0	230.3
2011	227.3	229.1	230.3	230.9	229.5	228.3	214.1	215.0	219.2	225.2	225.2	221.0	224.6
2012	221.7	223.9	226.2	226.5	226.6	227.7	212.4	212.9	216.0	222.2	223.1	218.8	221.5
2013	220.7	222.5	224.7	224.2	225.2	225.7	214.0	215.0	218.4	224.5	226.3	222.4	222.0

Employment by Industry: Salt Lake City, UT, Selected Years, 2002–2013

(Numbers in thousands, not seasonally adjusted)

Industry and year	January	February	March	April	May	June	July	August	September	October	November	December	Annual average
Total Nonfarm													
2002	567.5	572.3	564.2	562.7	560.1	561.9	557.2	558.7	560.6	560.8	565.0	568.0	563.3
2003	553.8	553.5	553.4	553.5	553.4	554.9	552.2	555.5	556.4	558.2	562.0	567.8	556.2
2004	554.2	556.1	558.7	560.9	560.0	564.4	563.3	565.9	567.6	570.3	575.9	583.1	565.0
2005	572.1	574.9	576.4	581.5	580.8	585.2	586.5	591.3	594.3	595.2	601.5	608.9	587.4
2006	597.5	601.4	605.6	608.2	608.4	614.8	612.3	617.9	620.2	620.6	628.5	636.2	614.3
2007	625.8	628.6	632.4	633.9	634.1	639.5	635.2	639.9	639.7	641.0	646.9	653.0	637.5
2008	640.0	641.3	642.5	643.1	640.1	642.7	638.6	642.5	641.6	639.2	637.7	640.6	640.8
2009	620.7	617.1	615.1	611.1	607.2	607.1	601.1	603.1	604.8	606.1	608.1	613.9	609.6
2010	601.0	600.2	604.0	606.1	605.1	607.2	604.9	606.7	609.3	613.5	617.0	622.5	608.1
2011	610.8	612.6	614.9	617.8	614.1	617.8	616.7	621.1	624.0	624.6	629.7	636.4	620.0
2012	627.2	629.7	632.8	640.5	641.4	645.5	637.6	642.8	646.2	650.4	658.8	662.9	643.0
2013	652.0	655.9	658.9	661.4	658.7	661.7	658.4	662.0	663.9	667.0	671.0	675.5	662.2
Total Private													
2002	479.5	485.8	475.7	474.0	472.0	473.2	471.8	474.6	472.0	472.1	475.9	478.7	475.4
2003	464.9	464.2	464.4	464.0	464.6	466.1	467.0	470.9	467.9	469.3	473.2	478.9	468.0
2004	465.4	467.1	469.7	470.8	470.6	474.8	476.8	479.1	477.5	480.0	485.6	492.3	475.8
2005	481.6	484.1	485.9	490.4	490.2	494.5	498.4	502.9	503.1	503.7	509.7	516.8	496.8
2006	506.1	509.4	513.7	516.1	516.8	522.5	523.1	528.6	528.1	528.1	535.9	543.2	522.6
2007	533.6	536.2	540.0	541.0	541.4	546.1	545.7	549.8	546.7	547.4	553.0	558.8	545.0
2008	546.1	547.1	547.9	548.4	545.3	547.3	547.2	550.0	545.4	542.7	540.9	543.7	546.0
2009	524.8	520.8	518.8	514.1	510.4	510.3	508.6	509.7	507.9	508.6	510.8	516.4	513.4
2010	504.2	503.4	507.1	508.6	505.9	508.9	510.6	512.0	510.6	514.0	517.7	524.1	510.6
2011	513.0	514.7	516.9	519.1	515.1	518.6	521.7	525.5	525.2	526.0	530.5	536.9	521.9
2012	527.8	529.9	533.0	539.3	540.7	544.6	541.6	546.8	545.9	548.8	557.5	562.4	543.2
2013	551.9	555.3	558.4	559.2	556.1	559.1	560.2	564.1	560.9	562.7	566.8	572.0	560.6
Goods-Producing													
2002	86.8	84.8	85.1	85.6	86.8	87.9	88.0	88.3	87.9	87.4	86.6	85.4	86.7
2003	82.3	81.9	82.0	83.1	84.9	85.5	85.8	86.4	86.1	86.3	85.6	84.8	84.6
2004	81.8	81.8	83.0	84.9	86.9	88.0	89.1	89.5	89.4	89.1	88.5	88.5	86.7
2005	86.2	86.5	87.1	89.6	91.2	93.0	94.3	95.4	95.5	94.7	94.9	94.7	91.9
2006	92.8	93.9	95.4	97.0	99.7	102.0	102.4	103.7	104.2	104.3	104.4	103.9	100.3
2007	101.5	101.8	103.4	104.7	106.7	108.9	108.9	110.0	108.8	107.8	106.9	105.4	106.2
2008	102.1	101.0	101.7	102.2	103.0	104.1	104.4	104.6	103.4	102.1	99.4	97.3	102.1
2009	91.0	88.7	88.3	87.2	88.6	89.0	89.6	89.6	89.2	89.0	88.0	86.8	88.8
2010	83.9	83.2	83.6	85.1	86.3	87.0	87.8	88.7	88.8	88.8	87.9	86.9	86.5
2011	84.6	84.3	84.9	85.9	87.0	88.5	90.5	91.4	90.9	90.7	90.3	89.3	88.2
2012	87.2	87.7	88.3	89.8	91.9	92.8	92.7	93.4	93.0	92.7	92.2	91.6	91.1
2013	89.1	89.0	89.7	91.1	91.8	92.3	92.2	93.0	92.3	93.9	93.7	91.8	91.7
Service-Providing													
2002	480.7	487.5	479.1	477.1	473.3	474.0	469.2	470.4	472.7	473.4	478.4	482.6	476.5
2003	471.5	471.6	471.4	470.4	468.5	469.4	466.4	469.1	470.3	471.9	476.4	483.0	471.7
2004	472.4	474.3	475.7	476.0	473.1	476.4	474.2	476.4	478.2	481.2	487.4	494.6	478.3
2005	485.9	488.4	489.3	491.9	489.6	492.2	492.2	495.9	498.8	500.5	506.6	514.2	495.5
2006	504.7	507.5	510.2	511.2	508.7	512.8	509.9	514.2	516.0	516.3	524.1	532.3	514.0
2007	524.3	526.8	529.0	529.2	527.4	530.6	526.3	529.9	530.9	533.2	540.0	547.6	531.3
2008	537.9	540.3	540.8	540.9	537.1	538.6	534.2	537.9	538.2	537.1	538.3	543.3	538.7
2009	529.7	528.4	526.8	523.9	518.6	518.1	511.5	513.5	515.6	517.1	520.1	527.1	520.9
2010	517.1	517.0	520.4	521.0	518.8	520.2	517.1	518.0	520.5	524.7	529.1	535.6	521.6
2011	526.2	528.3	530.0	531.9	527.1	529.3	526.2	529.7	533.1	533.9	539.4	547.1	531.9
2012	540.0	542.0	544.5	550.7	549.5	552.7	544.9	549.4	553.2	557.7	566.6	571.3	551.9
2013	562.9	566.9	569.2	570.3	566.9	569.4	566.2	569.0	571.6	573.1	577.3	583.7	570.5
Mining, Logging, and Construction													
2002	33.7	32.1	32.5	33.4	34.5	35.7	36.1	36.3	36.1	35.8	35.1	34.1	34.6
2003	31.8	31.5	31.7	32.6	34.0	34.5	34.9	35.4	35.1	35.1	34.3	33.4	33.7
2004	31.0	31.1	32.0	33.5	34.8	35.7	36.6	37.0	37.0	36.7	36.0	35.9	34.8
2005	34.0	34.1	35.1	37.0	38.1	39.2	40.4	41.2	41.3	41.0	41.0	40.6	38.6
2006	39.0	39.7	41.0	42.4	44.5	46.2	46.6	47.5	47.9	47.9	47.6	47.1	44.8
2007	45.2	45.2	46.4	47.5	49.2	50.7	50.7	51.4	50.5	49.5	48.4	46.9	48.5
2008	43.6	42.6	43.3	44.2	45.1	46.1	46.4	46.9	46.0	44.9	42.9	41.3	44.4
2009	36.5	35.4	35.4	34.9	36.3	36.6	37.1	37.3	37.1	36.8	36.0	34.5	36.2
2010	32.2	31.6	32.0	32.9	34.2	34.6	35.1	35.7	36.0	36.4	35.5	34.4	34.2
2011	32.1	31.7	32.3	33.1	33.9	35.0	36.4	37.1	36.6	36.6	36.0	34.9	34.6
2012	33.1	33.6	33.9	35.2	36.9	37.4	37.2	37.8	37.5	37.2	36.8	36.1	36.1
2013	34.1	34.0	34.7	35.9	36.6	37.0	37.0	37.8	37.4	38.2	37.9	36.3	36.4
Manufacturing													
2002	53.1	52.7	52.6	52.2	52.3	52.2	51.9	52.0	51.8	51.6	51.5	51.3	52.1
2003	50.5	50.4	50.3	50.5	50.9	51.0	50.9	51.0	51.0	51.2	51.3	51.4	50.9
2004	50.8	50.7	51.0	51.4	52.1	52.3	52.5	52.5	52.4	52.4	52.5	52.6	51.9
2005	52.2	52.4	52.0	52.6	53.1	53.8	53.9	54.2	54.2	53.7	53.9	54.1	53.3
2006	53.8	54.2	54.4	54.6	55.2	55.8	55.8	56.2	56.3	56.4	56.8	56.8	55.5
2007	56.3	56.6	57.0	57.2	57.5	58.2	58.2	58.6	58.3	58.3	58.5	58.5	57.8
2008	58.5	58.4	58.4	58.0	57.9	58.0	58.0	57.7	57.4	57.2	56.5	56.0	57.7
2009	54.5	53.3	52.9	52.3	52.3	52.4	52.5	52.3	52.1	52.2	52.0	52.3	52.6
2010	51.7	51.6	51.6	52.2	52.1	52.4	52.7	53.0	52.8	52.4	52.4	52.5	52.3
2011	52.5	52.6	52.6	52.8	53.1	53.5	54.1	54.3	54.3	54.1	54.3	54.4	53.6
2012	54.1	54.1	54.4	54.6	55.0	55.4	55.5	55.6	55.5	55.5	55.4	55.5	55.1
2013	55.0	55.0	55.0	55.2	55.2	55.3	55.2	55.2	54.9	55.7	55.8	55.5	55.3

Employment by Industry: Salt Lake City, UT, Selected Years, 2002–2013—*Continued*

(Numbers in thousands, not seasonally adjusted)

Industry and year	January	February	March	April	May	June	July	August	September	October	November	December	Annual average
Trade, Transportation, and Utilities													
2002	120.9	120.1	118.6	119.0	119.5	119.6	119.7	119.9	119.3	120.4	122.6	123.7	120.3
2003	116.9	115.8	115.8	115.4	116.0	116.1	116.4	117.2	116.5	117.4	119.8	121.6	117.1
2004	117.0	116.2	116.3	116.5	117.0	118.1	118.4	118.6	118.2	119.4	122.1	123.8	118.5
2005	119.8	119.5	119.9	120.7	121.2	121.4	122.4	123.3	123.0	124.2	126.6	128.5	122.5
2006	124.2	123.9	124.3	124.2	124.7	125.9	126.1	127.5	127.5	127.7	131.2	133.9	126.8
2007	129.9	129.4	130.2	129.9	130.6	131.2	131.6	132.5	132.3	132.9	136.0	138.1	132.1
2008	133.2	132.2	132.2	132.5	132.6	133.3	132.8	133.3	132.4	132.5	133.7	134.4	132.9
2009	128.3	126.5	125.6	124.1	124.0	123.6	122.8	122.9	122.8	122.9	125.1	126.4	124.6
2010	121.7	121.0	121.2	121.1	121.6	121.9	122.1	122.9	122.3	123.4	125.8	127.2	122.7
2011	122.7	122.4	122.9	123.8	123.7	124.4	124.8	125.6	125.4	125.8	128.9	130.4	125.1
2012	127.1	126.7	127.7	128.6	129.3	130.2	129.7	130.3	130.7	131.5	135.0	135.7	130.2
2013	132.0	131.6	131.6	131.3	132.2	132.8	133.5	134.1	133.4	134.4	137.0	138.6	133.5
Wholesale Trade													
2002	28.2	28.2	28.1	28.3	28.6	28.5	28.6	28.7	28.6	28.6	28.6	28.5	28.5
2003	27.1	27.0	27.1	27.2	27.4	27.3	27.3	27.4	27.3	27.2	27.2	27.3	27.2
2004	27.0	27.1	27.3	27.5	27.7	28.0	27.9	27.9	27.9	28.1	28.3	28.3	27.8
2005	28.1	28.2	28.4	28.5	28.7	28.6	28.7	28.7	28.6	28.7	28.8	28.8	28.6
2006	28.5	28.8	28.9	29.0	29.3	29.6	29.6	29.7	29.7	29.8	29.9	30.3	29.4
2007	30.0	30.1	30.2	30.2	30.5	30.7	30.8	31.0	30.9	30.9	31.0	31.2	30.6
2008	30.9	30.9	30.9	31.3	31.4	31.5	31.4	31.5	31.3	31.1	31.0	31.0	31.2
2009	30.2	30.1	29.8	29.5	29.4	29.3	29.2	29.1	29.0	28.9	28.8	28.9	29.4
2010	28.4	28.3	28.5	28.6	29.0	28.9	29.1	29.2	29.0	29.2	29.3	29.6	28.9
2011	29.4	29.7	29.9	30.1	30.2	30.4	30.5	30.7	30.7	30.6	30.8	30.9	30.3
2012	30.7	30.9	31.1	31.1	31.2	31.2	31.0	31.1	30.9	30.8	30.8	30.8	31.0
2013	31.0	31.0	30.9	31.0	31.2	31.2	31.3	31.4	31.2	30.9	31.5	31.6	31.2
Retail Trade													
2002	64.3	63.3	62.8	62.9	63.3	63.5	63.3	63.5	63.2	63.7	66.0	67.3	63.9
2003	62.9	62.1	62.1	62.0	62.2	62.4	62.5	63.0	62.6	63.5	65.9	67.4	63.2
2004	63.2	62.4	62.3	62.6	62.9	63.4	63.9	64.1	63.8	64.7	66.9	68.3	64.0
2005	64.5	63.5	63.5	63.7	64.0	64.3	65.1	66.0	65.7	66.6	68.6	70.1	65.5
2006	66.4	65.8	66.1	66.0	66.2	66.9	67.1	67.9	67.8	68.0	71.0	72.4	67.6
2007	69.3	68.6	69.2	69.0	69.3	69.5	69.8	70.3	69.9	70.2	72.9	74.3	70.2
2008	71.1	70.1	70.2	70.2	70.3	71.0	70.6	71.0	70.4	70.7	72.1	72.8	70.9
2009	68.1	66.8	66.6	65.9	66.2	66.3	65.5	66.0	66.1	66.4	68.7	69.6	66.9
2010	66.0	65.3	65.3	65.1	65.3	65.4	65.4	65.8	65.3	65.9	67.9	68.5	65.9
2011	64.8	64.2	64.4	64.9	64.9	65.1	65.4	65.9	65.7	66.5	69.0	69.8	65.9
2012	67.0	66.3	66.9	67.4	67.9	68.5	68.9	69.1	69.4	70.2	73.3	73.5	69.0
2013	69.9	69.5	69.6	70.2	70.8	71.3	71.5	72.0	71.6	72.8	74.0	74.9	71.5
Transportation and Utilities													
2002	28.4	28.6	27.7	27.8	27.6	27.6	27.8	27.7	27.5	28.1	28.0	27.9	27.9
2003	26.9	26.7	26.6	26.2	26.4	26.4	26.6	26.8	26.6	26.7	26.7	26.9	26.6
2004	26.8	26.7	26.7	26.4	26.4	26.7	26.6	26.6	26.5	26.6	26.9	27.2	26.7
2005	27.2	27.8	28.0	28.5	28.5	28.5	28.6	28.6	28.7	28.9	29.2	29.6	28.5
2006	29.3	29.3	29.3	29.2	29.2	29.4	29.4	29.9	30.0	29.9	30.3	31.2	29.7
2007	30.6	30.7	30.8	30.7	30.8	31.0	31.0	31.2	31.5	31.8	32.1	32.6	31.2
2008	31.2	31.2	31.1	31.0	30.9	30.8	30.8	30.8	30.7	30.7	30.6	30.6	30.9
2009	30.0	29.6	29.2	28.7	28.4	28.0	28.1	27.8	27.7	27.6	27.6	27.9	28.4
2010	27.3	27.4	27.4	27.4	27.3	27.6	27.6	27.9	28.0	28.3	28.6	29.1	27.8
2011	28.5	28.5	28.6	28.8	28.6	28.9	28.9	29.0	29.0	28.7	29.1	29.7	28.9
2012	29.4	29.5	29.7	30.1	30.2	30.5	29.8	30.1	30.4	30.5	30.9	31.4	30.2
2013	31.1	31.1	31.1	30.1	30.2	30.3	30.7	30.7	30.6	30.7	31.5	32.1	30.9
Information													
2002	20.0	19.9	19.2	18.9	19.2	19.0	19.0	18.6	18.5	18.6	18.7	18.5	19.0
2003	17.9	17.7	17.6	17.4	18.0	18.1	17.9	18.2	18.0	18.3	18.1	18.4	18.0
2004	17.4	17.9	17.9	17.9	17.9	18.1	17.5	17.5	17.6	17.8	18.3	18.1	17.8
2005	17.9	18.3	18.7	18.2	18.2	18.1	18.6	19.0	18.8	18.4	18.7	18.6	18.5
2006	18.2	18.3	18.3	18.6	19.3	19.4	18.6	18.8	18.7	18.5	18.8	18.7	18.7
2007	18.7	18.6	18.8	17.6	17.8	17.6	17.5	17.7	17.3	17.2	17.3	17.4	17.8
2008	17.0	17.6	17.7	18.0	18.3	18.2	17.9	18.0	17.8	17.5	17.7	17.7	17.8
2009	17.3	17.4	17.2	16.9	17.0	17.2	16.9	16.8	16.6	16.7	16.8	16.9	17.0
2010	16.3	16.4	16.8	16.9	16.8	16.8	16.8	16.5	16.6	16.6	17.2	17.2	16.7
2011	16.3	16.5	16.6	16.3	16.4	16.4	16.4	16.5	16.4	16.3	16.8	16.8	16.5
2012	16.2	16.4	16.4	18.7	19.3	19.3	17.9	18.1	17.8	18.1	18.9	18.8	18.0
2013	19.5	19.6	19.6	18.2	18.3	18.3	18.3	18.5	18.1	18.6	18.0	18.6	18.6
Financial Activities													
2002	46.1	46.0	45.5	45.3	45.5	45.6	45.1	45.3	44.9	45.3	45.1	45.6	45.4
2003	45.7	46.1	45.6	45.9	45.9	45.4	45.5	45.6	45.1	44.9	44.8	45.2	45.5
2004	44.5	44.7	44.7	44.8	44.6	44.4	44.6	44.5	44.5	44.7	45.2	45.8	44.8
2005	45.1	45.5	44.9	45.9	45.7	46.0	46.5	46.6	46.7	46.9	47.3	48.1	46.3
2006	47.6	48.2	48.3	48.5	48.5	48.8	49.2	49.4	49.3	50.0	50.4	51.1	49.1
2007	51.0	51.7	51.8	51.9	52.0	52.1	52.1	52.0	51.7	52.1	52.2	52.6	51.9
2008	51.5	52.0	51.8	51.8	51.5	51.3	51.4	51.4	50.9	50.8	50.5	51.1	51.3
2009	50.4	50.6	50.4	49.8	49.4	49.3	48.6	48.7	48.4	48.2	48.2	48.7	49.2
2010	47.6	47.1	47.2	46.8	46.6	46.6	46.8	47.0	47.1	47.4	47.7	48.0	47.2
2011	47.3	47.5	47.6	47.6	47.3	47.6	47.7	47.9	47.7	47.7	47.9	48.3	47.7
2012	47.7	47.8	47.9	48.0	47.8	48.2	48.4	49.1	48.8	49.0	49.4	50.2	48.5
2013	49.3	49.7	49.7	50.0	49.9	50.8	51.3	51.7	51.3	51.5	52.0	52.4	50.8

Employment by Industry: Salt Lake City, UT, Selected Years, 2002–2013—*Continued*

(Numbers in thousands, not seasonally adjusted)

Industry and year	January	February	March	April	May	June	July	August	September	October	November	December	Annual average
Professional and Business Services													
2002	82.8	85.7	82.6	82.8	83.4	83.3	82.9	84.1	83.5	82.9	83.3	82.6	83.3
2003	79.9	79.9	80.7	81.7	82.5	82.7	83.2	84.1	83.3	83.8	84.0	84.7	82.5
2004	81.8	82.5	83.1	83.9	84.5	85.3	85.7	86.7	85.8	87.5	87.7	88.7	85.3
2005	86.0	86.4	87.0	89.3	90.2	91.3	91.9	93.2	93.5	94.2	95.0	95.6	91.1
2006	92.8	93.6	94.8	96.4	97.2	97.9	98.6	99.0	98.7	98.2	99.2	99.3	97.1
2007	96.5	97.3	97.8	100.0	101.4	102.0	101.6	102.3	101.7	103.3	104.0	103.9	101.0
2008	100.5	100.8	100.8	101.3	101.9	101.7	101.9	102.6	101.8	100.9	99.6	99.1	101.1
2009	94.9	94.5	93.7	93.6	93.6	93.5	93.4	93.4	93.1	93.9	93.7	94.1	93.8
2010	91.4	92.0	93.8	94.6	95.7	96.7	97.3	96.7	95.9	97.0	97.5	98.2	95.6
2011	95.9	96.7	97.4	98.5	99.0	99.3	100.1	101.0	101.3	103.0	103.4	103.4	99.9
2012	100.7	101.6	102.4	102.7	103.8	104.8	104.9	106.3	106.4	108.4	109.3	108.8	105.0
2013	104.7	106.4	107.6	110.3	109.7	110.2	110.9	112.0	112.1	110.7	110.4	110.0	109.6
Education and Health Services													
2002	48.0	48.5	48.4	48.8	48.8	48.8	48.4	49.2	50.1	50.3	50.5	50.9	49.2
2003	50.4	50.7	51.0	50.7	50.8	50.9	50.7	51.1	51.7	52.1	52.3	52.5	51.2
2004	51.7	52.3	52.7	52.7	52.8	52.9	52.6	52.8	53.5	53.9	54.3	54.4	53.1
2005	53.9	54.5	54.5	55.0	55.0	55.1	54.5	54.7	55.5	55.8	56.3	56.4	55.1
2006	55.4	55.9	56.3	56.2	56.5	56.7	55.8	56.8	57.4	58.1	58.4	58.3	56.8
2007	57.8	58.4	58.8	59.2	59.3	59.2	58.8	59.9	60.8	61.1	61.6	61.8	59.7
2008	61.4	62.4	62.5	62.5	62.5	62.3	62.0	62.6	63.5	64.6	65.4	65.5	63.1
2009	64.5	64.8	65.3	65.3	65.2	64.8	64.0	64.7	65.9	67.1	67.5	67.8	65.6
2010	67.1	67.4	67.6	67.8	67.4	67.2	66.5	66.6	68.0	69.0	69.1	69.0	67.7
2011	68.4	69.0	68.9	69.3	68.7	68.1	66.8	67.3	68.9	69.5	69.7	69.4	68.7
2012	69.1	69.5	69.5	72.1	72.0	71.6	69.7	70.5	71.6	72.6	73.3	73.4	71.2
2013	73.7	74.4	74.7	74.2	74.1	73.4	71.8	72.7	73.3	74.2	75.0	75.1	73.9
Leisure and Hospitality													
2002	56.6	61.5	57.7	55.0	50.1	50.3	49.7	50.2	49.2	48.8	50.4	53.6	52.8
2003	53.8	54.1	53.7	51.7	48.5	49.3	49.2	49.9	49.2	48.6	50.6	53.7	51.0
2004	53.5	53.9	54.0	51.9	48.7	49.7	50.0	50.6	50.1	49.5	51.3	54.7	51.5
2005	54.5	55.1	55.3	53.1	50.2	51.0	51.0	51.6	51.2	51.0	52.4	56.2	52.7
2006	56.7	57.1	57.5	56.3	51.8	52.4	52.9	53.9	52.9	52.3	54.5	58.7	54.8
2007	59.2	59.9	59.9	58.4	54.0	55.3	55.1	55.2	54.4	53.5	55.5	60.0	56.7
2008	61.1	61.6	61.6	60.5	55.8	56.6	56.6	56.8	55.6	55.0	55.4	59.3	58.0
2009	59.5	59.4	59.3	58.2	53.5	53.7	53.9	54.2	53.1	52.1	53.0	57.0	55.6
2010	57.6	57.7	58.0	57.7	52.8	54.0	54.2	54.5	53.4	53.2	54.0	59.1	55.5
2011	59.5	59.8	60.1	59.1	54.1	55.2	56.0	56.3	55.5	54.1	54.7	60.4	57.1
2012	61.0	61.2	61.6	60.2	57.2	58.2	58.3	59.0	57.9	56.8	59.7	64.1	59.6
2013	63.9	64.5	65.1	63.4	59.2	61.0	61.4	61.3	60.2	59.0	60.7	65.2	62.1
Other Services													
2002	18.3	19.3	18.6	18.6	18.7	18.7	19.0	19.0	18.6	18.4	18.7	18.4	18.7
2003	18.0	18.0	18.0	18.1	18.0	18.1	18.3	18.4	18.0	17.9	18.0	18.0	18.1
2004	17.7	17.8	18.0	18.2	18.3	18.3	18.9	18.9	18.4	18.1	18.2	18.3	18.3
2005	18.2	18.3	18.5	18.6	18.5	18.6	19.2	19.1	18.9	18.5	18.5	18.7	18.6
2006	18.4	18.5	18.8	18.9	19.1	19.4	19.5	19.5	19.4	19.0	19.0	19.3	19.1
2007	19.0	19.1	19.3	19.3	19.6	19.8	20.1	20.2	19.7	19.5	19.5	19.6	19.6
2008	19.3	19.5	19.6	19.6	19.7	19.8	20.2	20.7	20.0	19.3	19.2	19.3	19.7
2009	18.9	18.9	19.0	19.0	19.1	19.2	19.4	19.4	18.8	18.7	18.5	18.7	19.0
2010	18.6	18.6	18.9	18.6	18.7	18.7	19.1	19.1	18.5	18.6	18.5	18.5	18.7
2011	18.3	18.5	18.5	18.6	18.9	19.1	19.4	19.5	19.1	18.9	18.8	18.9	18.9
2012	18.8	19.0	19.2	19.2	19.4	19.5	20.0	20.1	19.7	19.7	19.7	19.8	19.5
2013	19.7	20.1	20.4	20.7	20.9	20.3	20.8	20.8	20.2	20.4	20.0	20.3	20.4
Government													
2002	88.0	86.5	88.5	88.7	88.1	88.7	85.4	84.1	88.6	88.7	89.1	89.3	87.8
2003	88.9	89.3	89.0	89.5	88.8	88.8	85.2	84.6	88.5	88.9	88.8	88.9	88.3
2004	88.8	89.0	89.0	90.1	89.4	89.6	86.5	86.8	90.1	90.3	90.3	90.8	89.2
2005	90.5	90.8	90.5	91.1	90.6	90.7	88.1	88.4	91.2	91.5	91.8	92.1	90.6
2006	91.4	92.0	91.9	92.1	91.6	92.3	89.2	89.3	92.1	92.5	92.6	93.0	91.7
2007	92.2	92.4	92.4	92.9	92.7	93.4	89.5	90.1	93.0	93.6	93.9	94.2	92.5
2008	93.9	94.2	94.6	94.7	94.8	95.4	91.4	92.5	96.2	96.5	96.8	96.9	94.8
2009	95.9	96.3	96.3	97.0	96.8	96.8	92.5	93.4	96.9	97.5	97.3	97.5	96.2
2010	96.8	96.8	96.9	97.5	99.2	98.3	94.3	94.7	98.7	99.5	99.3	98.4	97.5
2011	97.8	97.9	98.0	98.7	99.0	99.2	95.0	95.6	98.8	98.6	99.2	99.5	98.1
2012	99.4	99.8	99.8	101.2	100.7	100.9	96.0	96.0	100.3	101.6	101.3	100.5	99.8
2013	100.1	100.6	100.5	102.2	102.6	102.6	98.2	97.9	103.0	104.3	104.2	103.5	101.6

Employment by Industry: San Antonio–New Braunfels, TX, Selected Years, 2002–2013

(Numbers in thousands, not seasonally adjusted)

Industry and year	January	February	March	April	May	June	July	August	September	October	November	December	Annual average
Total Nonfarm													
2002	737.2	745.0	751.6	755.2	760.8	759.5	750.6	756.1	760.0	756.5	758.0	758.2	754.1
2003	739.0	745.3	751.3	752.1	755.0	755.2	747.1	751.0	751.9	754.2	756.9	757.4	751.4
2004	742.0	749.8	756.5	759.8	763.3	765.4	759.5	764.0	764.1	763.8	765.7	766.2	760.0
2005	756.7	765.9	771.9	778.3	783.1	785.5	780.7	784.9	789.9	791.2	796.0	799.3	782.0
2006	787.0	795.1	803.8	809.7	814.5	817.6	809.8	814.2	818.8	819.9	823.3	825.9	811.6
2007	809.3	820.2	826.5	829.7	837.2	840.2	833.9	836.8	840.3	840.8	848.0	852.1	834.6
2008	836.2	846.0	850.9	855.8	860.0	861.1	852.2	853.6	853.5	854.7	856.8	855.5	853.0
2009	833.0	837.5	838.8	839.7	841.2	842.9	832.1	831.6	832.3	835.7	840.5	842.0	837.3
2010	826.6	834.6	841.3	845.1	851.9	851.9	840.6	841.9	842.2	848.9	851.6	853.8	844.2
2011	839.6	846.8	854.8	859.9	863.1	864.9	859.9	861.6	864.4	865.2	869.1	871.6	860.1
2012	857.6	865.8	872.7	877.0	882.4	887.2	879.6	885.8	887.5	891.0	896.6	899.9	881.9
2013	883.6	894.4	900.0	903.8	907.6	913.4	906.4	908.0	910.3	914.2	915.8	918.5	906.3
Total Private													
2002	597.0	601.7	607.9	611.9	616.6	620.2	617.6	621.2	618.4	612.3	613.2	613.6	612.6
2003	596.6	600.5	606.6	606.8	609.5	614.1	611.3	613.8	610.7	611.1	612.4	613.4	608.9
2004	600.8	605.3	612.3	615.4	618.4	624.6	623.6	625.5	621.0	619.7	621.3	621.9	617.5
2005	614.2	620.6	626.7	632.7	637.5	642.5	643.6	646.1	646.2	645.3	649.1	652.4	638.1
2006	641.6	647.3	656.2	660.3	665.4	670.8	670.4	673.6	672.5	670.5	673.0	675.9	664.8
2007	660.6	669.1	675.0	678.5	685.8	691.5	690.4	692.8	689.8	689.8	694.9	698.0	684.7
2008	683.2	690.5	695.0	700.3	704.3	706.2	704.1	704.8	700.8	697.4	698.2	697.3	698.5
2009	675.9	677.8	678.9	678.4	680.9	683.7	679.8	679.6	674.8	674.5	678.1	680.1	678.5
2010	667.4	672.3	678.2	681.5	685.8	688.8	686.6	686.2	681.6	684.8	686.8	689.6	682.5
2011	678.0	682.6	691.2	696.7	699.9	703.1	705.0	707.4	705.5	704.1	707.6	710.0	699.3
2012	698.1	704.2	711.2	715.5	721.5	728.7	727.3	731.7	727.9	729.6	734.4	737.7	722.3
2013	723.4	731.7	737.5	741.2	745.4	752.3	750.2	752.2	749.5	751.1	752.4	755.5	745.2
Goods-Producing													
2002	95.6	95.4	96.3	96.1	96.4	97.3	96.5	96.0	94.7	93.2	92.9	92.9	95.3
2003	91.0	91.5	91.4	91.8	92.1	92.5	91.9	91.8	91.4	91.1	90.6	90.6	91.5
2004	88.8	89.0	89.4	90.0	90.1	91.0	91.7	91.4	91.4	91.8	91.8	91.8	90.7
2005	90.6	91.2	92.4	93.8	94.0	94.7	95.1	94.9	95.6	95.4	95.7	96.7	94.2
2006	96.0	97.4	98.8	98.2	99.0	100.4	100.1	100.2	100.7	99.9	100.1	100.3	99.3
2007	98.8	100.2	100.6	100.7	101.9	103.6	103.2	103.6	103.3	104.0	104.0	104.6	102.4
2008	103.2	104.0	104.4	104.6	105.1	105.7	104.4	104.5	103.5	102.8	101.9	100.5	103.7
2009	97.6	96.5	95.9	95.3	94.9	94.7	94.3	93.8	92.8	92.0	91.6	91.6	94.3
2010	90.7	90.2	90.4	91.0	91.2	91.1	91.5	91.0	90.1	90.4	90.0	90.0	90.6
2011	88.5	88.7	89.5	90.1	90.3	91.1	91.4	91.2	90.9	90.5	90.3	89.8	90.2
2012	89.5	89.8	90.2	90.8	91.2	92.4	92.8	93.2	92.7	93.0	93.3	93.3	91.9
2013	92.4	92.7	93.5	94.5	94.9	96.0	96.5	96.7	96.4	95.8	94.0	94.8	94.9
Service-Providing													
2002	641.6	649.6	655.3	659.1	664.4	662.2	654.1	660.1	665.3	663.3	665.1	665.3	658.8
2003	648.0	653.8	659.9	660.3	662.9	662.7	655.2	659.2	660.5	663.1	666.3	666.8	659.9
2004	653.2	660.8	667.1	669.8	673.2	674.4	667.8	672.6	672.7	672.0	673.9	674.4	669.3
2005	666.1	674.7	679.5	684.5	689.1	690.8	685.6	690.0	694.3	695.8	700.3	702.6	687.8
2006	691.0	697.7	705.0	711.5	715.5	717.2	709.7	714.0	718.1	720.0	723.2	725.6	712.4
2007	710.5	720.0	725.9	729.0	735.3	736.6	730.7	733.2	737.0	736.8	744.0	747.5	732.2
2008	733.0	742.0	746.5	751.2	754.9	755.4	747.8	749.1	750.0	751.9	754.9	755.0	749.3
2009	735.4	741.0	742.9	744.4	746.3	748.2	737.8	737.8	739.5	743.7	748.9	750.4	743.0
2010	735.9	744.4	750.9	754.1	760.7	760.8	749.1	750.9	752.1	758.5	761.6	763.8	753.6
2011	751.1	758.1	765.3	769.8	772.8	773.8	768.5	770.4	773.5	774.7	778.8	781.8	769.9
2012	768.1	776.0	782.5	786.2	791.2	794.8	786.8	792.6	794.8	798.0	803.3	806.6	790.1
2013	791.2	801.7	806.5	809.3	812.7	817.4	809.9	811.3	813.9	818.4	821.8	823.7	811.5
Mining and Logging													
2002	3.1	3.0	3.1	2.8	2.8	2.7	3.2	3.2	3.1	3.1	3.2	3.1	3.0
2003	2.5	2.7	2.7	2.8	2.7	2.8	2.8	2.8	2.9	2.9	2.9	3.0	2.8
2004	2.9	2.9	2.9	2.8	2.8	2.8	2.7	2.7	2.5	2.4	2.4	2.3	2.7
2005	2.3	2.4	2.4	2.4	2.4	2.5	2.6	2.6	2.6	2.8	2.8	2.8	2.6
2006	2.9	3.0	3.0	3.0	3.1	3.0	3.0	3.1	3.1	3.0	3.1	3.1	3.0
2007	3.0	3.1	3.1	3.1	3.2	3.2	3.2	3.3	3.3	3.4	3.4	3.5	3.2
2008	3.4	3.4	3.4	3.5	3.6	3.7	3.6	3.6	3.5	3.5	3.4	3.3	3.5
2009	3.3	3.2	3.2	3.1	3.0	3.0	3.0	3.0	3.0	2.9	3.0	3.0	3.1
2010	2.9	3.0	2.9	2.9	3.0	3.0	3.0	3.0	2.9	2.9	2.9	2.9	2.9
2011	2.8	2.9	2.9	2.9	3.0	3.1	3.2	3.2	3.3	3.4	3.4	3.4	3.1
2012	3.4	3.5	3.7	3.9	3.9	4.1	4.4	4.4	4.5	4.6	4.7	4.8	4.2
2013	4.9	5.0	5.1	5.4	5.5	5.6	6.1	6.1	6.1	6.1	6.0	6.1	5.7
Construction													
2002	42.2	42.5	43.0	43.4	43.9	44.6	43.7	43.9	43.0	42.0	41.6	41.4	42.9
2003	41.3	41.1	41.3	41.5	42.1	42.5	42.4	42.6	42.0	41.9	41.6	41.6	41.8
2004	40.6	40.5	40.8	41.1	41.5	42.4	42.8	43.1	43.1	43.4	43.6	43.8	42.2
2005	43.0	43.3	44.4	45.6	45.9	46.4	46.3	46.3	46.7	46.1	46.1	46.5	45.6
2006	45.9	46.7	47.6	47.4	47.7	48.7	48.3	48.3	48.2	47.6	47.5	47.4	47.6
2007	46.6	47.8	48.7	48.6	49.5	50.8	50.7	51.1	50.9	51.4	51.5	52.1	50.0
2008	51.6	52.7	53.2	53.6	54.0	54.5	53.9	54.2	53.7	53.3	52.6	51.6	53.2
2009	49.6	49.0	48.7	48.5	48.4	48.6	48.3	48.0	47.1	46.1	45.5	45.1	47.7
2010	44.6	43.9	44.3	44.5	44.3	43.8	44.1	43.5	42.6	42.5	41.9	41.8	43.5
2011	40.4	40.5	41.4	41.7	41.7	42.0	42.1	41.9	41.4	40.9	40.6	40.0	41.2
2012	39.9	40.0	40.2	40.1	40.6	41.4	41.6	42.1	41.6	41.7	41.7	41.6	41.0
2013	41.1	41.4	42.3	42.9	43.2	44.1	44.3	44.5	44.2	43.5	41.9	42.3	43.0

Employment by Industry: San Antonio–New Braunfels, TX, Selected Years, 2002–2013—*Continued*

(Numbers in thousands, not seasonally adjusted)

Industry and year	January	February	March	April	May	June	July	August	September	October	November	December	Annual average
Manufacturing													
2002	50.3	49.9	50.2	49.9	49.7	50.0	49.6	48.9	48.6	48.1	48.1	48.4	49.3
2003	47.2	47.7	47.4	47.5	47.3	47.2	46.7	46.4	46.5	46.3	46.1	46.0	46.9
2004	45.3	45.6	45.7	46.1	45.8	45.8	46.2	45.6	45.8	46.0	45.8	45.7	45.8
2005	45.3	45.5	45.6	45.8	45.7	45.8	46.2	46.0	46.3	46.5	46.8	47.4	46.1
2006	47.2	47.7	48.2	47.8	48.2	48.7	48.8	48.8	49.4	49.3	49.5	49.8	48.6
2007	49.2	49.3	48.8	49.0	49.2	49.6	49.3	49.2	49.1	49.2	49.1	49.0	49.2
2008	48.2	47.9	47.8	47.5	47.5	47.5	46.9	46.7	46.3	46.0	45.9	45.6	47.0
2009	44.7	44.3	44.0	43.7	43.5	43.1	43.0	42.8	42.7	43.0	43.1	43.5	43.5
2010	43.2	43.3	43.2	43.6	43.9	44.3	44.4	44.5	44.6	45.0	45.2	45.3	44.2
2011	45.3	45.3	45.2	45.5	45.6	46.0	46.1	46.1	46.2	46.2	46.3	46.4	45.9
2012	46.2	46.3	46.3	46.8	46.7	46.9	46.8	46.7	46.6	46.7	46.9	46.9	46.7
2013	46.4	46.3	46.1	46.2	46.2	46.3	46.1	46.1	46.1	46.2	46.1	46.4	46.2
Trade, Transportation, and Utilities													
2002	136.7	135.3	136.4	137.2	137.8	137.9	137.7	138.3	138.5	137.8	140.2	141.2	137.9
2003	134.0	133.2	134.3	133.6	133.5	133.9	134.0	134.4	134.7	136.7	138.3	139.9	135.0
2004	134.4	133.9	135.0	135.6	135.8	135.9	136.2	137.5	136.9	137.4	139.6	141.2	136.6
2005	136.5	136.1	137.1	137.8	138.3	138.8	139.7	140.5	140.0	140.8	143.9	145.5	139.6
2006	141.0	140.4	142.0	142.0	142.5	142.8	143.1	144.5	144.7	146.8	150.7	152.7	144.4
2007	147.7	146.5	147.5	147.5	148.1	148.3	149.5	150.4	149.6	150.2	153.8	155.6	149.6
2008	149.9	149.4	150.2	149.5	149.4	149.6	150.3	151.5	150.0	150.4	152.1	152.6	150.4
2009	146.1	144.6	143.7	143.4	143.3	143.6	143.1	144.1	143.2	143.3	145.4	146.4	144.2
2010	141.3	140.4	140.9	141.4	141.5	141.9	141.7	142.9	141.9	143.2	145.4	147.3	142.5
2011	143.0	141.8	142.7	143.7	143.7	144.3	144.8	146.0	145.4	146.9	149.8	151.5	145.3
2012	147.0	146.1	146.5	147.4	147.9	148.8	148.9	149.9	149.8	151.5	155.6	156.5	149.7
2013	151.7	151.4	151.4	151.5	152.0	152.7	153.3	154.8	154.5	155.1	158.9	161.0	154.0
Wholesale Trade													
2002	27.0	26.9	27.1	27.1	27.2	27.4	27.4	27.4	27.3	27.2	27.3	27.3	27.2
2003	26.6	26.7	26.9	26.9	27.0	27.2	27.4	27.3	27.4	27.5	27.3	27.2	27.1
2004	27.0	27.0	27.0	27.1	27.1	27.1	27.2	27.1	26.8	26.7	26.3	26.2	26.9
2005	26.3	26.4	26.5	26.7	26.9	27.1	27.2	27.3	27.3	27.1	27.4	27.5	27.0
2006	27.5	27.6	27.7	27.8	28.0	28.4	28.4	28.5	28.6	28.7	29.1	29.1	28.3
2007	28.9	29.0	29.2	29.4	29.5	29.6	29.6	29.7	29.6	29.7	29.7	29.8	29.5
2008	29.3	29.4	29.4	29.4	29.4	29.5	29.5	29.7	29.5	29.4	29.3	29.1	29.4
2009	28.8	28.7	28.5	28.5	28.5	28.5	28.0	28.0	27.9	28.1	28.1	28.0	28.3
2010	27.9	27.9	27.3	28.1	28.1	28.3	28.2	28.3	28.3	28.6	28.5	28.5	28.2
2011	28.1	28.2	28.5	28.7	28.7	29.0	29.1	29.1	29.0	29.3	29.4	29.3	28.9
2012	29.4	29.4	29.6	29.8	29.9	30.1	30.2	30.3	30.1	30.3	30.2	30.2	30.0
2013	30.6	30.8	30.5	29.7	29.8	30.0	30.0	30.1	30.1	30.5	30.6	30.5	30.3
Retail Trade													
2002	90.9	89.5	90.0	90.7	90.9	90.6	90.5	90.9	91.4	90.7	92.8	93.9	91.1
2003	87.6	86.7	87.4	87.2	86.9	86.9	86.8	87.3	87.3	89.0	90.8	92.3	88.0
2004	87.4	86.7	87.6	88.2	88.2	88.3	88.6	90.0	89.7	90.4	92.9	94.4	89.4
2005	90.0	89.4	90.2	90.6	90.6	90.7	91.3	91.8	91.1	92.2	94.6	95.9	91.5
2006	92.0	91.2	92.4	92.3	92.5	92.3	92.7	93.9	93.9	95.9	99.2	100.8	94.1
2007	93.8	93.0	93.8	93.5	93.7	93.8	93.7	94.8	93.7	94.7	96.9	98.5	94.5
2008	94.7	93.4	93.9	94.5	94.5	94.6	94.9	95.9	95.1	96.4	99.0	100.3	95.6
2009	96.5	95.5	95.5	96.0	96.3	96.7	96.7	97.3	97.4	98.9	102.8	103.2	97.7
2010	98.4	98.1	98.3	99.1	99.5	99.8	100.6	101.8	101.6	101.7	105.1	106.7	100.9
2011	94.7	93.4	93.9	94.5	94.5	94.6	94.9	95.9	95.1	96.4	99.0	100.3	95.6
2012	96.5	95.5	95.5	96.0	96.3	96.7	96.7	97.3	97.4	98.9	102.8	103.2	97.7
2013	98.4	98.1	98.3	99.1	99.5	99.8	100.6	101.8	101.6	101.7	105.1	106.7	100.9
Transportation and Utilities													
2002	18.8	18.9	19.3	19.4	19.7	19.9	19.8	20.0	19.8	19.9	20.1	20.0	19.6
2003	19.8	19.8	20.0	19.5	19.6	19.8	19.8	19.8	20.0	20.2	20.2	20.4	19.9
2004	20.0	20.2	20.4	20.3	20.5	20.5	20.4	20.4	20.4	20.3	20.4	20.6	20.4
2005	20.2	20.3	20.4	20.5	20.8	21.0	21.2	21.4	21.6	21.5	21.9	22.1	21.1
2006	21.5	21.6	21.9	21.9	22.0	22.1	22.0	22.1	22.2	22.2	22.4	22.8	22.1
2007	22.2	22.4	22.6	22.7	22.6	22.7	22.6	22.7	22.6	22.4	22.4	22.5	22.5
2008	21.8	21.8	21.9	21.8	21.9	21.8	22.0	21.9	21.8	21.7	21.7	21.8	21.8
2009	21.1	20.8	20.8	20.3	20.3	20.2	20.0	20.0	19.9	19.9	20.0	20.0	20.3
2010	19.6	19.5	19.8	19.8	19.7	19.8	19.8	19.8	19.9	19.9	20.0	20.3	19.8
2011	20.2	20.2	20.3	20.5	20.5	20.7	20.8	21.0	21.3	21.2	21.4	21.9	20.8
2012	21.1	21.2	21.4	21.6	21.7	22.0	22.0	22.3	22.3	22.3	22.6	23.1	22.0
2013	22.7	22.5	22.6	22.7	22.7	22.9	22.7	22.9	22.8	22.9	23.2	23.8	22.9
Information													
2002	24.5	24.4	24.1	23.9	23.9	23.8	22.9	22.9	22.5	22.7	22.8	22.4	23.4
2003	22.2	22.0	22.2	22.2	22.3	22.4	22.6	22.5	22.4	22.4	22.7	22.5	22.4
2004	22.0	21.8	21.8	22.2	22.2	22.0	21.9	21.7	21.3	21.4	21.3	21.0	21.7
2005	20.6	20.7	20.5	20.2	20.4	20.8	20.7	20.8	20.7	20.8	21.1	21.1	20.7
2006	20.7	20.5	20.6	20.6	21.0	21.3	21.2	21.3	21.1	21.4	21.7	21.9	21.1
2007	21.7	21.9	21.7	21.6	21.8	21.8	21.8	21.6	21.4	21.4	21.5	21.5	21.6
2008	21.5	21.6	21.7	21.5	21.7	21.5	21.1	21.0	20.7	20.8	20.8	20.6	21.2
2009	20.5	20.5	20.6	20.2	19.9	19.5	19.1	18.9	18.5	18.4	18.4	18.3	19.4
2010	18.2	18.2	18.6	19.1	18.9	18.6	18.4	18.2	18.0	17.8	18.1	18.1	18.4
2011	18.3	18.4	18.7	19.0	19.0	18.6	19.4	19.2	19.0	19.0	19.2	19.4	18.9
2012	19.4	19.4	19.8	20.0	20.0	20.0	20.0	20.1	20.0	19.9	20.2	20.2	19.9
2013	20.1	20.3	20.5	21.1	21.1	21.1	21.2	21.0	20.7	20.8	20.9	21.0	20.8

Employment by Industry: San Antonio–New Braunfels, TX, Selected Years, 2002–2013—*Continued*

(Numbers in thousands, not seasonally adjusted)

Industry and year	January	February	March	April	May	June	July	August	September	October	November	December	Annual average
Financial Activities													
2002	58.7	58.8	59.1	59.4	59.9	60.1	60.1	60.4	60.3	60.6	60.8	61.2	60.0
2003	60.2	60.4	60.7	60.5	60.5	61.0	60.9	61.1·	60.7	60.6	60.7	61.1	60.7
2004	60.6	60.7	60.8	61.5	61.6	62.0	62.3	62.3	62.2	61.5	61.7	61.8	61.6
2005	61.2	61.4	61.3	61.5	61.8	62.3	63.3	63.4	63.3	63.4	63.4	63.7	62.5
2006	63.0	63.1	63.2	63.6	63.9	64.2	64.4	64.3	64.4	64.5	64.6	64.9	64.0
2007	64.3	64.9	64.7	65.4	65.9	65.8	65.8	65.6	65.3	65.5	65.6	65.8	65.4
2008	65.1	65.4	65.2	67.0	67.3	67.1	67.5	66.9	66.6	66.3	65.9	66.5	66.4
2009	64.8	65.0	64.4	64.5	64.8	65.3	65.7	65.7	65.6	65.8	65.8	66.1	65.3
2010	65.7	66.3	66.4	66.3	67.0	67.6	67.5	67.4	66.9	67.8	68.2	68.6	67.1
2011	68.0	68.8	69.1	69.3	69.6	70.0	70.6	70.2	70.0	70.2	70.2	70.6	69.7
2012	70.6	71.0	71.2	71.3	71.7	72.2	72.9	73.0	73.1	73.7	74.1	74.7	72.5
2013	74.3	75.1	75.5	75.6	75.7	76.4	76.8	76.7	76.5	76.3	76.0	76.5	76.0
Professional and Business Services													
2002	83.3	84.6	85.2	86.7	87.1	88.0	88.7	90.1	90.1	89.0	88.1	87.8	87.4
2003	84.6	85.6	87.0	86.8	87.7	88.2	87.7	89.0	88.1	88.6	89.0	88.4	87.6
2004	87.0	87.6	88.7	88.9	89.2	90.5	89.5	90.4	89.5	89.4	89.3	89.4	89.1
2005	92.2	93.7	94.1	96.7	97.4	97.9	96.7	97.8	99.4	99.9	100.0	101.1	97.2
2006	98.9	100.3	101.9	103.7	104.5	104.9	105.1	105.8	105.7	103.9	103.4	104.1	103.5
2007	101.5	102.7	103.4	104.8	105.7	106.3	105.6	106.3	106.4	107.0	107.6	107.5	105.4
2008	106.8	108.3	108.5	109.3	108.9	108.7	106.5	106.6	107.0	105.6	105.4	104.7	107.2
2009	101.3	100.8	100.9	99.9	99.5	100.3	98.2	99.2	98.6	100.0	101.5	102.7	100.2
2010	101.6	102.3	102.7	101.8	101.2	101.7	100.3	100.5	100.2	101.3	101.2	101.2	101.3
2011	100.8	101.8	102.9	103.1	102.4	102.7	102.4	103.7	104.7	104.0	104.1	105.0	103.1
2012	103.1	104.4	105.3	105.7	106.1	106.8	107.0	109.1	109.2	109.0	109.6	110.9	107.2
2013	108.1	109.7	110.3	110.1	109.6	110.7	110.3	110.9	111.8	111.9	112.7	111.5	110.6
Education and Health Services													
2002	94.5	96.1	96.4	96.7	97.0	95.8	95.0	96.7	98.6	98.9	99.4	99.5	97.1
2003	97.9	99.0	99.2	99.5	99.4	99.1	97.9	99.5	101.1	101.6	101.9	101.8	99.8
2004	101.4	102.1	102.9	102.7	102.5	103.1	101.9	103.2	103.7	105.2	105.5	105.6	103.3
2005	103.8	105.6	106.1	105.5	105.6	105.3	105.4	106.7	108.7	109.1	109.7	110.2	106.8
2006	108.5	109.7	110.4	109.5	109.9	109.5	108.5	110.3	112.2	112.1	112.2	112.2	110.4
2007	110.1	112.5	113.2	112.8	113.6	113.5	112.9	114.0	115.3	115.9	116.7	117.1	114.0
2008	114.1	116.2	116.2	117.0	118.0	116.9	116.7	117.8	120.1	121.3	121.8	122.6	118.2
2009	119.7	121.5	121.9	122.5	123.4	122.8	123.0	123.2	124.7	126.0	126.5	126.8	123.5
2010	125.2	127.1	127.8	128.3	128.8	129.0	128.5	128.8	129.8	131.0	131.3	131.6	128.9
2011	129.9	130.9	131.6	132.8	133.1	132.4	132.4	133.9	135.7	135.7	136.2	136.7	133.4
2012	134.4	136.0	136.7	136.4	137.3	137.4	135.0	136.6	136.8	137.3	137.9	138.3	136.7
2013	135.5	137.1	137.9	138.4	138.9	138.8	135.8	137.4	138.3	140.9	140.2	140.3	138.3
Leisure and Hospitality													
2002	76.2	79.2	82.3	83.5	85.8	88.1	88.0	88.0	84.9	81.7	80.1	80.0	83.2
2003	78.5	80.5	83.1	84.0	85.6	88.1	88.0	87.2	84.3	82.6	81.3	81.4	83.7
2004	79.2	82.5	85.8	86.8	89.2	91.9	92.5	91.4	88.6	86.2	85.0	84.2	86.9
2005	82.8	85.4	88.4	90.0	92.8	95.1	95.1	94.5	91.0	89.0	88.3	87.2	90.0
2006	86.8	88.9	92.0	94.6	96.2	98.9	99.3	98.5	94.9	93.4	91.5	91.3	93.9
2007	89.0	92.4	95.7	97.3	100.0	102.7	102.3	101.8	98.7	96.1	95.4	95.7	97.3
2008	92.7	95.3	98.1	100.4	102.7	105.2	106.0	105.0	101.7	99.5	99.4	99.1	100.4
2009	95.5	98.2	100.8	101.8	103.9	106.0	105.2	103.6	100.7	98.4	97.7	97.3	100.8
2010	94.1	96.9	100.3	102.2	105.5	107.1	107.1	105.8	103.1	101.8	101.1	101.0	102.2
2011	98.6	101.0	105.4	107.0	110.0	112.1	112.0	111.2	107.9	106.2	105.8	105.4	106.9
2012	102.3	105.5	109.1	111.4	114.7	117.8	117.5	116.7	113.1	112.1	110.3	110.6	111.8
2013	108.2	111.8	114.6	116.2	119.0	122.2	121.8	120.4	117.1	116.2	115.4	116.3	116.6
Other Services													
2002	27.5	27.9	28.1	28.4	28.7	29.2	28.7	28.8	28.8	28.4	28.9	28.6	28.5
2003	28.2	28.3	28.7	28.4	28.4	28.9	28.3	28.3	28.0	27.5	27.9	27.7	28.2
2004	27.4	27.7	27.9	27.7	27.8	28.2	27.6	27.6	27.5	26.8	27.1	26.9	27.5
2005	26.5	26.5	26.8	27.2	27.2	27.6	27.6	27.5	27.5	26.9	27.0	26.9	27.1
2006	26.7	27.0	27.3	28.1	28.4	28.8	28.7	28.7	28.8	28.5	28.8	28.5	28.2
2007	27.5	28.0	28.2	28.4	28.8	29.5	29.3	29.5	29.8	29.7	30.3	30.2	29.1
2008	29.9	30.3	30.7	31.0	31.2	31.5	31.6	31.5	31.2	30.7	30.9	30.7	30.9
2009	30.4	30.7	30.7	30.8	31.2	31.5	31.2	31.1	30.7	30.6	31.2	30.9	30.9
2010	30.6	30.9	31.1	31.4	31.7	31.8	31.6	31.6	31.6	31.5	31.5	31.8	31.4
2011	30.9	31.2	31.3	31.7	31.8	31.9	32.0	32.0	31.9	31.6	32.0	31.6	31.7
2012	31.8	32.0	32.4	32.5	32.6	33.3	33.2	33.1	33.2	33.1	33.4	33.2	32.8
2013	33.1	33.6	33.8	33.8	34.2	34.4	34.5	34.3	34.2	34.1	34.3	34.1	34.0
Government													
2002	140.2	143.3	143.7	143.3	144.2	139.3	133.0	134.9	141.6	144.2	144.8	144.6	141.4
2003	142.4	144.8	144.7	145.3	145.5	141.1	135.8	137.2	141.2	143.1	144.5	144.0	142.5
2004	141.2	144.5	144.2	144.4	144.9	140.8	135.9	138.5	143.1	144.1	144.4	144.3	142.5
2005	142.5	145.3	145.2	145.6	145.6	143.0	137.1	138.8	143.7	145.9	146.9	146.9	143.9
2006	145.4	147.8	147.6	149.4	149.1	146.8	139.4	140.6	146.3	149.4	150.3	150.0	146.8
2007	148.7	151.1	151.5	151.2	151.4	148.7	143.5	144.0	150.5	151.0	154.1	154.1	149.9
2008	153.0	155.5	155.9	155.5	155.7	155.7	154.9	148.1	148.8	152.7	157.3	158.6	158.2	154.5
2009	157.1	159.7	159.9	161.3	160.3	159.2	152.3	152.0	157.5	161.2	162.4	161.9	158.7
2010	159.2	162.3	163.1	163.6	166.1	163.1	154.0	155.7	160.6	164.1	164.8	164.2	161.7
2011	161.6	164.2	163.6	163.2	163.2	161.8	154.9	154.2	158.9	161.1	161.5	161.6	160.8
2012	159.5	161.6	161.5	161.5	160.9	158.5	152.3	154.1	159.6	161.4	162.2	162.2	159.6
2013	160.2	162.7	162.5	162.6	162.2	161.1	156.2	155.8	160.8	163.1	163.4	163.0	161.1

Employment by Industry: San Diego–Carlsbad–San Marcos, CA, Selected Years, 2002–2013

(Numbers in thousands, not seasonally adjusted)

Industry and year	January	February	March	April	May	June	July	August	September	October	November	December	Annual average
Total Nonfarm													
2002	1,211.4	1,222.2	1,229.0	1,235.5	1,242.3	1,249.1	1,225.8	1,230.7	1,230.9	1,242.9	1,251.1	1,257.5	1,235.7
2003	1,227.5	1,233.0	1,238.4	1,243.6	1,248.2	1,254.0	1,241.6	1,247.9	1,248.1	1,257.5	1,260.1	1,268.1	1,247.3
2004	1,241.8	1,248.7	1,256.6	1,264.0	1,268.3	1,275.4	1,267.1	1,269.0	1,272.0	1,280.1	1,285.7	1,294.1	1,268.6
2005	1,265.1	1,273.3	1,280.2	1,289.7	1,294.5	1,300.0	1,288.6	1,291.8	1,296.8	1,296.6	1,305.8	1,313.6	1,291.3
2006	1,287.5	1,297.0	1,303.7	1,304.9	1,313.4	1,322.2	1,307.6	1,311.8	1,316.4	1,317.1	1,327.2	1,330.0	1,311.6
2007	1,299.4	1,307.9	1,315.6	1,313.8	1,322.4	1,330.9	1,321.6	1,322.3	1,321.6	1,320.7	1,327.3	1,333.4	1,319.7
2008	1,302.7	1,311.2	1,316.1	1,315.7	1,319.9	1,324.0	1,312.3	1,311.9	1,307.9	1,306.9	1,306.1	1,302.7	1,311.5
2009	1,265.6	1,261.4	1,259.1	1,251.1	1,252.7	1,252.1	1,228.8	1,229.2	1,224.5	1,235.1	1,240.9	1,242.7	1,245.3
2010	1,213.3	1,216.9	1,221.8	1,235.4	1,246.4	1,247.8	1,236.3	1,239.5	1,237.6	1,242.9	1,247.9	1,251.9	1,236.5
2011	1,229.4	1,237.1	1,240.5	1,243.1	1,246.0	1,249.6	1,239.5	1,242.8	1,246.8	1,251.9	1,261.7	1,263.9	1,246.0
2012	1,240.8	1,249.5	1,256.1	1,274.1	1,283.4	1,291.1	1,275.8	1,281.7	1,281.6	1,297.0	1,308.1	1,311.4	1,279.2
2013	1,286.9	1,294.6	1,302.6	1,308.8	1,313.4	1,318.8	1,307.3	1,313.0	1,312.2	1,323.9	1,330.6	1,331.6	1,312.0
Total Private													
2002	991.5	999.4	1,005.3	1,012.4	1,019.5	1,025.9	1,015.1	1,020.3	1,018.0	1,021.5	1,028.3	1,035.0	1,016.0
2003	1,006.6	1,011.5	1,016.2	1,021.9	1,027.2	1,033.0	1,032.6	1,039.6	1,036.4	1,040.6	1,043.4	1,051.6	1,030.1
2004	1,028.7	1,032.9	1,039.9	1,045.4	1,050.9	1,057.6	1,061.2	1,064.5	1,061.0	1,063.2	1,068.5	1,077.3	1,054.2
2005	1,050.1	1,056.5	1,062.6	1,071.7	1,075.8	1,080.9	1,080.7	1,086.5	1,085.3	1,080.6	1,087.9	1,096.1	1,076.2
2006	1,071.3	1,078.2	1,084.0	1,085.0	1,093.4	1,101.0	1,097.0	1,103.6	1,101.9	1,096.9	1,104.3	1,106.9	1,093.6
2007	1,077.9	1,084.2	1,090.6	1,088.7	1,097.4	1,105.2	1,106.7	1,110.1	1,103.5	1,096.3	1,101.4	1,106.3	1,097.4
2008	1,078.5	1,083.7	1,087.4	1,087.9	1,091.1	1,093.9	1,095.6	1,096.6	1,087.8	1,080.1	1,078.1	1,075.3	1,086.3
2009	1,039.4	1,034.5	1,030.6	1,021.3	1,023.3	1,022.1	1,014.3	1,017.0	1,008.4	1,008.8	1,013.3	1,016.2	1,020.8
2010	988.8	991.3	994.4	1,000.6	1,005.7	1,009.8	1,010.7	1,015.7	1,010.1	1,011.0	1,014.6	1,019.7	1,006.0
2011	999.3	1,004.2	1,006.7	1,009.3	1,013.3	1,016.0	1,019.8	1,025.6	1,023.6	1,022.3	1,030.6	1,034.1	1,017.1
2012	1,014.1	1,020.1	1,025.2	1,043.3	1,052.1	1,059.0	1,057.7	1,062.7	1,058.6	1,067.6	1,076.0	1,080.2	1,051.4
2013	1,059.3	1,064.6	1,070.2	1,076.9	1,081.1	1,084.8	1,086.8	1,092.1	1,086.3	1,092.3	1,096.9	1,098.6	1,082.5
Goods-Producing													
2002	188.2	188.5	189.5	189.5	191.1	191.8	189.3	189.9	188.9	188.0	187.7	186.9	189.1
2003	182.1	180.5	182.9	183.0	185.0	186.9	188.0	189.6	188.5	188.0	186.9	188.3	185.8
2004	185.9	187.0	189.0	190.1	191.6	193.2	195.1	195.8	195.7	195.6	195.0	195.0	192.4
2005	189.0	191.7	193.6	195.0	196.8	197.9	198.8	198.9	198.0	196.2	195.8	196.6	195.7
2006	194.2	196.1	197.4	196.6	198.8	200.3	198.4	198.8	198.1	196.0	195.6	194.6	197.1
2007	189.8	190.4	191.4	189.9	191.6	193.1	192.2	191.6	189.5	187.0	185.9	185.3	189.8
2008	181.0	181.0	181.3	180.3	180.9	181.6	181.2	180.6	179.0	177.0	174.5	172.1	179.2
2009	167.4	164.5	163.2	159.4	158.2	157.3	154.7	154.1	151.9	150.8	150.2	149.8	156.8
2010	148.3	147.3	147.9	149.6	150.0	149.6	149.3	149.9	148.6	147.6	147.9	147.9	148.7
2011	146.8	147.4	147.5	147.8	148.5	149.4	149.3	150.3	149.8	149.6	149.2	149.1	148.7
2012	147.0	147.2	148.2	150.1	151.4	152.8	153.3	153.9	153.5	153.5	154.5	154.2	151.6
2013	152.8	153.7	154.1	155.1	155.0	156.1	156.8	157.6	157.0	158.0	158.3	159.1	156.1
Service-Providing													
2002	1,023.2	1,033.7	1,039.5	1,046.0	1,051.2	1,057.3	1,036.5	1,040.8	1,042.0	1,054.9	1,063.4	1,070.6	1,046.6
2003	1,045.4	1,052.5	1,055.5	1,060.6	1,063.2	1,067.1	1,053.6	1,058.3	1,059.6	1,069.5	1,073.2	1,079.8	1,061.5
2004	1,055.9	1,061.7	1,067.6	1,073.9	1,076.7	1,082.2	1,072.0	1,073.2	1,076.3	1,084.5	1,090.7	1,099.1	1,076.2
2005	1,076.1	1,081.6	1,086.6	1,094.7	1,097.7	1,102.1	1,089.8	1,092.9	1,098.8	1,100.4	1,110.0	1,117.0	1,095.6
2006	1,093.3	1,100.9	1,106.3	1,108.3	1,114.6	1,121.9	1,109.2	1,113.0	1,118.3	1,121.1	1,131.6	1,135.4	1,114.5
2007	1,109.6	1,117.5	1,124.2	1,123.9	1,130.8	1,137.8	1,129.4	1,130.7	1,132.1	1,133.7	1,141.4	1,148.1	1,129.9
2008	1,121.7	1,130.2	1,134.8	1,135.4	1,139.0	1,142.4	1,131.1	1,131.3	1,128.9	1,129.9	1,131.6	1,130.6	1,132.2
2009	1,098.2	1,096.9	1,095.9	1,091.7	1,094.5	1,094.8	1,074.1	1,075.1	1,072.6	1,084.3	1,090.7	1,092.9	1,088.5
2010	1,065.0	1,069.6	1,073.9	1,085.8	1,096.4	1,098.2	1,087.0	1,089.6	1,089.0	1,095.3	1,100.0	1,104.0	1,087.8
2011	1,082.6	1,089.7	1,093.0	1,095.3	1,097.5	1,100.2	1,090.2	1,092.5	1,097.0	1,102.3	1,112.5	1,114.8	1,097.3
2012	1,093.8	1,102.3	1,107.9	1,124.0	1,132.0	1,138.3	1,122.5	1,127.8	1,128.1	1,143.5	1,153.6	1,157.2	1,127.6
2013	1,134.1	1,140.9	1,148.5	1,153.7	1,158.4	1,162.7	1,150.5	1,155.4	1,155.2	1,165.9	1,172.3	1,172.5	1,155.8
Mining and Logging													
2002	0.3	0.3	0.3	0.3	0.3	0.3	0.3	0.3	0.3	0.3	0.3	0.3	0.3
2003	0.3	0.3	0.3	0.3	0.3	0.3	0.3	0.4	0.4	0.4	0.4	0.4	0.3
2004	0.4	0.4	0.4	0.4	0.4	0.4	0.4	0.4	0.4	0.4	0.4	0.4	0.4
2005	0.4	0.4	0.4	0.4	0.4	0.4	0.4	0.4	0.4	0.4	0.4	0.4	0.4
2006	0.5	0.4	0.4	0.4	0.5	0.5	0.5	0.5	0.5	0.5	0.5	0.5	0.5
2007	0.4	0.4	0.4	0.4	0.4	0.4	0.4	0.4	0.4	0.4	0.4	0.4	0.4
2008	0.4	0.4	0.4	0.4	0.4	0.4	0.4	0.4	0.4	0.4	0.4	0.4	0.4
2009	0.4	0.4	0.4	0.4	0.4	0.4	0.4	0.4	0.4	0.3	0.3	0.3	0.4
2010	0.4	0.4	0.4	0.4	0.4	0.4	0.4	0.4	0.4	0.4	0.4	0.4	0.4
2011	0.4	0.4	0.4	0.4	0.5	0.4	0.4	0.5	0.5	0.4	0.4	0.4	0.4
2012	0.4	0.4	0.4	0.4	0.4	0.4	0.4	0.4	0.4	0.4	0.4	0.4	0.4
2013	0.4	0.4	0.4	0.4	0.4	0.4	0.4	0.4	0.4	0.4	0.4	0.4	0.4
Construction													
2002	73.6	73.3	74.0	75.3	76.9	77.7	77.0	78.2	77.6	77.9	77.8	78.0	76.4
2003	75.9	74.5	76.2	76.5	78.9	80.7	82.8	84.3	83.5	83.4	82.3	83.2	80.2
2004	82.5	83.4	84.8	85.8	86.8	88.0	89.5	90.4	90.9	90.7	90.0	89.8	87.7
2005	84.1	86.6	88.5	89.9	91.5	92.7	93.4	93.7	93.5	91.9	91.6	92.4	90.8
2006	90.5	91.8	92.5	92.1	94.1	95.1	93.4	94.2	93.7	92.2	91.6	90.7	92.7
2007	86.8	87.6	88.3	87.9	89.5	90.9	89.1	88.8	87.0	83.9	82.4	81.3	87.0
2008	78.0	78.0	77.9	77.0	77.5	77.9	77.7	76.9	75.7	73.8	72.0	70.2	76.1
2009	66.0	64.2	64.0	62.1	62.1	61.7	60.5	60.4	58.7	58.3	58.0	57.5	61.1
2010	55.7	54.8	55.0	55.7	56.2	56.1	56.1	56.3	55.3	54.4	54.5	54.1	55.4
2011	53.6	54.2	54.2	54.6	55.0	55.4	55.8	56.6	55.9	56.0	55.6	55.1	55.2
2012	54.1	54.1	55.0	56.0	57.0	58.0	57.6	58.1	57.8	58.1	58.8	58.3	56.9
2013	57.9	58.5	58.8	59.9	60.1	61.4	61.8	62.5	61.9	63.3	63.6	64.1	61.2

Employment by Industry: San Diego–Carlsbad–San Marcos, CA, Selected Years, 2002–2013—*Continued*

(Numbers in thousands, not seasonally adjusted)

Industry and year	January	February	March	April	May	June	July	August	September	October	November	December	Annual average
Manufacturing													
2002	114.3	114.9	115.2	113.9	113.9	113.8	112.0	111.4	111.0	109.8	109.6	108.6	112.4
2003	105.9	105.7	106.4	106.2	105.8	105.9	104.9	104.9	104.6	104.2	104.2	104.7	105.3
2004	103.0	103.2	103.8	103.9	104.4	104.8	105.2	105.0	104.4	104.5	104.6	104.8	104.3
2005	104.5	104.7	104.7	104.7	104.9	104.8	105.0	104.8	104.1	103.9	103.8	103.8	104.5
2006	103.2	103.9	104.5	104.1	104.2	104.7	104.5	104.1	103.9	103.3	103.5	103.4	103.9
2007	102.6	102.4	102.7	101.6	101.7	101.8	102.7	102.4	102.1	102.7	103.1	103.6	102.5
2008	102.6	102.6	103.0	102.9	103.0	103.3	103.1	103.3	102.9	102.8	102.1	101.5	102.8
2009	101.0	99.9	98.8	96.9	95.7	95.2	93.8	93.3	92.8	92.2	91.9	92.0	95.3
2010	92.2	92.1	92.5	93.5	93.4	93.1	92.8	93.2	92.9	92.8	93.0	93.4	92.9
2011	92.8	92.8	92.9	92.8	93.0	93.6	93.1	93.2	93.4	93.2	93.2	93.6	93.1
2012	92.5	92.7	92.8	93.7	94.0	94.4	95.3	95.4	95.3	95.0	95.3	95.5	94.3
2013	94.5	94.8	94.9	94.8	94.5	94.3	94.6	94.7	94.7	94.3	94.3	94.6	94.6
Trade, Transportation, and Utilities													
2002	206.0	204.8	205.7	206.6	207.6	209.2	207.1	207.5	207.3	207.8	212.6	217.6	208.3
2003	205.7	204.7	205.0	205.3	206.5	207.2	208.2	209.4	209.9	215.6	217.1	221.7	209.7
2004	211.5	210.8	210.6	211.9	213.4	214.6	213.8	214.3	213.9	217.9	223.5	227.2	215.3
2005	217.6	216.1	215.6	215.4	216.5	216.7	217.7	218.8	220.0	220.3	226.2	231.3	219.4
2006	220.7	219.3	218.9	218.3	219.5	220.0	220.1	221.3	221.4	222.4	229.4	232.8	222.0
2007	222.3	220.4	219.9	218.9	220.3	220.8	221.9	223.1	221.6	221.0	226.8	230.5	222.3
2008	219.5	216.9	215.9	215.9	214.9	215.0	216.3	215.3	214.3	213.4	215.8	217.1	215.9
2009	204.1	200.9	199.0	197.3	198.4	198.1	196.8	196.9	196.5	197.8	202.6	205.2	199.5
2010	194.8	193.3	192.6	193.9	195.0	195.9	196.8	197.6	196.9	198.5	204.2	207.6	197.3
2011	198.2	196.1	195.8	197.0	197.8	198.4	200.1	201.1	201.4	202.4	209.0	212.0	200.8
2012	204.3	201.9	201.6	204.0	205.7	206.5	206.7	207.2	207.3	209.3	218.3	220.1	207.7
2013	210.3	208.4	208.3	208.9	210.3	210.8	211.1	212.1	211.0	213.6	220.4	222.0	212.3
Wholesale Trade													
2002	40.4	40.8	40.9	41.4	41.6	41.8	41.4	41.6	41.4	41.5	41.6	41.6	41.3
2003	40.9	41.2	41.4	41.5	41.8	41.9	41.6	41.7	41.6	41.6	41.9	41.9	41.6
2004	41.2	41.7	41.4	42.1	42.2	42.1	41.8	41.9	41.4	42.2	42.4	42.6	41.9
2005	42.3	42.8	42.7	43.3	43.6	43.7	43.8	43.9	44.2	44.2	44.5	44.5	43.6
2006	44.3	44.9	44.8	45.0	45.4	45.3	45.1	45.2	45.1	45.0	45.2	45.3	45.1
2007	44.7	45.2	45.3	45.2	45.7	45.7	46.0	45.9	45.7	45.4	45.6	45.5	45.5
2008	44.8	45.2	45.0	45.5	44.9	44.7	45.3	45.2	44.8	44.6	44.3	44.2	44.9
2009	42.1	42.0	41.4	41.0	41.0	40.4	39.9	39.8	39.5	39.9	39.9	39.8	40.6
2010	38.7	38.9	38.7	39.4	39.7	39.9	40.2	40.4	40.4	41.2	41.6	41.9	40.1
2011	40.6	40.9	40.9	41.2	41.3	41.2	41.3	41.5	41.4	41.7	41.9	41.9	41.3
2012	41.6	42.2	42.1	43.0	43.5	43.3	43.6	43.8	43.6	44.1	44.4	44.2	43.3
2013	43.9	44.4	44.2	44.2	44.7	44.4	44.1	44.2	44.1	43.9	44.4	44.5	44.3
Retail Trade													
2002	136.6	134.7	135.4	135.5	136.3	137.5	136.2	137.1	138.1	138.7	143.6	148.8	138.2
2003	138.6	137.3	137.0	136.9	137.6	138.0	139.0	139.9	140.4	145.8	147.2	151.7	140.8
2004	142.5	141.1	141.1	141.7	142.9	144.0	143.6	144.1	144.1	146.5	152.0	155.6	144.9
2005	146.8	144.8	144.4	143.9	144.5	144.8	145.5	146.6	147.4	148.1	153.6	158.1	147.4
2006	148.2	146.2	145.8	145.0	145.7	146.0	146.2	147.3	147.3	148.6	155.1	157.7	148.3
2007	149.5	146.9	146.6	145.8	146.4	146.4	146.7	147.9	146.6	146.7	151.9	155.2	148.1
2008	145.7	142.3	141.7	141.5	141.0	141.3	141.9	141.1	140.5	140.2	143.0	144.2	142.0
2009	134.1	131.6	130.3	129.1	130.2	130.1	129.6	129.8	129.8	130.9	135.9	138.2	131.6
2010	129.9	128.3	127.8	128.2	128.7	129.3	129.8	130.4	129.8	130.9	136.1	138.7	130.7
2011	131.5	129.5	129.1	130.1	130.7	131.3	132.7	133.3	133.6	134.7	141.0	143.3	133.4
2012	136.4	133.3	132.9	134.1	135.0	135.5	135.5	135.8	136.1	137.8	146.2	147.4	137.2
2013	139.2	136.9	136.9	137.5	138.4	139.3	139.8	140.8	140.3	142.8	148.5	149.7	140.8
Transportation and Utilities													
2002	29.0	29.3	29.4	29.7	29.7	29.9	29.5	28.8	27.8	27.6	27.4	27.2	28.8
2003	26.2	26.2	26.6	26.9	27.1	27.3	27.6	27.8	27.9	28.2	28.0	28.1	27.3
2004	27.8	28.0	28.1	28.1	28.3	28.5	28.4	28.3	28.4	29.2	29.1	29.0	28.4
2005	28.5	28.5	28.5	28.2	28.4	28.2	28.4	28.3	28.4	28.0	28.1	28.7	28.4
2006	28.2	28.2	28.3	28.3	28.4	28.7	28.8	28.8	29.0	28.8	29.1	29.8	28.7
2007	28.1	28.3	28.0	27.9	28.2	28.7	29.2	29.3	29.3	28.9	29.3	29.8	28.8
2008	29.0	29.4	29.2	28.9	29.0	29.0	29.1	29.0	29.0	28.6	28.5	28.7	29.0
2009	27.9	27.3	27.3	27.2	27.2	27.6	27.3	27.3	27.2	27.0	26.8	27.2	27.3
2010	26.2	26.1	26.1	26.3	26.6	26.7	26.8	26.8	26.7	26.4	26.5	27.0	26.5
2011	26.1	25.7	25.8	25.7	25.8	25.9	26.1	26.3	26.4	26.0	26.1	26.8	26.1
2012	26.3	26.4	26.6	26.9	27.2	27.7	27.6	27.6	27.6	27.4	27.7	28.5	27.3
2013	27.2	27.1	27.2	27.2	27.2	27.1	27.2	27.1	26.6	26.9	27.5	27.8	27.2
Information													
2002	34.7	34.7	34.9	34.8	34.8	34.5	33.7	33.4	33.0	35.0	35.0	34.7	34.4
2003	34.3	34.6	33.9	33.5	33.3	33.3	33.4	33.2	33.0	32.9	32.9	32.6	33.4
2004	32.6	32.6	32.4	32.1	32.2	32.5	32.6	32.5	32.3	32.6	32.7	32.9	32.5
2005	32.8	32.9	32.7	32.7	32.8	32.7	32.7	32.5	32.2	32.1	32.3	32.3	32.6
2006	31.9	31.8	31.5	31.2	31.3	31.6	32.1	32.0	31.4	31.8	31.7	31.9	31.7
2007	31.5	31.6	31.4	31.3	31.1	31.1	31.2	31.2	30.9	31.1	31.3	31.5	31.3
2008	31.3	31.4	31.2	31.0	31.3	31.6	31.9	31.9	31.4	31.2	31.3	31.3	31.4
2009	30.5	30.3	29.9	29.2	28.8	28.5	28.2	27.6	26.8	26.5	26.2	26.0	28.2
2010	25.7	25.4	25.3	25.2	25.2	25.3	25.1	25.1	24.7	24.6	24.6	24.6	25.1
2011	24.4	24.3	24.2	24.1	24.1	24.0	24.2	24.2	24.2	24.1	24.1	24.2	24.2
2012	24.4	24.3	24.3	24.6	24.6	24.7	24.6	24.5	24.3	24.4	24.5	24.6	24.5
2013	24.3	24.1	24.1	24.1	24.3	24.2	24.0	24.1	23.9	24.0	24.2	24.2	24.1

Employment by Industry: San Diego–Carlsbad–San Marcos, CA, Selected Years, 2002–2013—*Continued*

(Numbers in thousands, not seasonally adjusted)

Industry and year	January	February	March	April	May	June	July	August	September	October	November	December	Annual average
Financial Activities													
2002	72.2	73.1	73.5	74.0	74.6	75.1	75.0	75.7	75.7	76.3	77.3	77.9	75.0
2003	77.5	78.2	78.6	79.5	80.3	80.7	80.7	81.0	80.7	80.5	80.6	80.6	79.9
2004	80.6	80.9	81.4	81.7	81.8	81.8	82.4	82.4	82.2	82.6	82.5	83.0	81.9
2005	81.7	82.1	82.3	82.8	82.9	83.2	83.6	83.8	83.5	84.1	84.2	84.4	83.2
2006	83.9	84.4	84.4	84.2	84.7	84.5	83.5	83.6	83.2	82.8	82.6	82.6	83.7
2007	80.9	81.9	81.9	81.2	81.5	81.6	80.7	80.2	79.3	78.6	77.9	77.8	80.3
2008	76.3	76.7	76.6	76.6	76.3	75.9	75.4	75.0	74.1	73.7	73.2	72.9	75.2
2009	71.6	72.0	71.7	70.4	70.3	70.1	69.5	69.0	68.1	68.4	68.2	68.0	69.8
2010	67.0	67.2	67.2	67.0	66.8	67.0	67.3	67.0	66.8	67.7	67.5	67.7	67.2
2011	66.9	67.2	66.9	67.0	67.0	67.3	67.9	67.7	67.8	68.2	68.2	68.7	67.6
2012	68.2	68.4	68.8	69.6	69.8	70.2	71.0	70.8	70.3	70.9	71.2	71.5	70.1
2013	70.8	71.1	71.3	71.3	71.5	71.6	71.9	71.8	71.1	71.3	71.8	71.7	71.4
Professional and Business Services													
2002	201.0	204.0	205.2	204.1	204.1	205.4	204.0	205.8	205.3	206.3	207.3	208.2	205.1
2003	202.8	205.1	205.2	204.9	203.6	204.2	203.3	204.4	203.8	205.4	206.7	207.4	204.7
2004	204.3	205.6	207.3	207.3	206.6	208.0	210.0	209.7	209.7	210.4	211.0	213.3	208.6
2005	210.4	212.4	213.4	216.3	215.3	216.9	215.1	216.0	216.5	216.4	216.9	217.6	215.3
2006	214.3	216.9	218.1	218.3	219.0	220.9	219.9	221.5	221.9	220.0	220.2	219.9	219.2
2007	218.0	220.4	221.4	221.7	222.0	224.0	224.7	225.7	225.1	225.1	224.9	225.0	223.2
2008	222.0	224.4	225.2	225.1	224.0	223.6	222.4	223.6	221.9	220.0	217.8	217.0	222.3
2009	211.7	210.5	208.0	206.3	205.5	204.9	205.4	205.6	203.4	205.6	206.7	207.9	206.8
2010	201.9	203.7	203.2	205.3	205.9	207.6	209.2	211.2	210.7	211.4	210.5	211.8	207.7
2011	208.0	209.5	210.0	209.2	208.1	208.4	209.8	211.6	210.1	210.5	211.2	211.9	209.9
2012	207.5	210.7	211.4	216.4	216.9	218.4	217.0	218.4	216.9	220.1	219.5	221.3	216.2
2013	218.8	221.1	221.6	221.1	221.9	222.3	223.7	224.4	224.0	226.1	224.2	222.5	222.6
Education and Health Services													
2002	122.3	124.8	124.9	125.3	125.8	125.0	122.4	122.3	123.8	126.0	126.7	127.0	124.7
2003	125.9	126.8	127.8	130.0	130.5	130.2	127.5	128.1	129.2	129.8	130.7	131.6	129.0
2004	129.1	129.2	130.8	131.0	130.8	130.3	127.2	127.7	128.7	130.8	131.2	132.0	129.9
2005	130.1	130.5	131.4	132.8	132.6	131.9	129.4	129.7	132.0	132.4	134.1	134.3	131.8
2006	132.4	133.3	134.7	135.0	135.2	134.9	133.3	133.6	135.8	136.9	138.0	138.1	135.1
2007	136.0	137.5	139.4	139.5	140.6	139.7	138.6	140.0	141.9	143.0	143.9	145.3	140.5
2008	144.4	146.7	147.6	148.0	149.0	148.6	148.3	149.7	151.1	154.3	155.9	156.9	150.0
2009	155.2	156.8	158.4	157.5	158.3	157.8	154.5	156.3	158.0	160.5	162.0	163.1	158.2
2010	158.3	159.9	160.7	159.9	160.3	159.4	156.8	157.3	159.0	160.5	161.1	161.6	159.6
2011	161.0	162.9	163.5	162.6	163.1	162.2	160.2	160.6	162.7	163.5	165.4	165.5	162.8
2012	164.2	166.0	167.1	169.7	171.1	170.1	167.7	168.4	170.2	176.5	176.8	177.4	170.4
2013	177.1	178.2	180.2	180.9	179.9	177.8	175.2	177.0	178.7	181.1	181.4	183.7	179.3
Leisure and Hospitality													
2002	123.8	125.6	127.1	132.0	134.9	137.3	137.5	140.3	138.3	136.3	135.8	136.6	133.8
2003	132.9	135.9	136.8	138.7	140.5	142.2	144.4	146.7	144.0	142.0	142.1	142.6	140.7
2004	138.3	140.0	141.3	144.3	147.0	149.0	151.1	153.2	149.5	145.2	144.4	145.3	145.7
2005	141.0	142.5	144.9	147.7	149.7	152.2	154.2	157.5	154.4	150.5	149.7	150.7	149.6
2006	147.0	148.7	151.3	153.0	155.9	159.4	161.7	164.8	161.3	158.3	158.0	158.1	156.5
2007	152.1	154.2	157.0	158.5	161.9	165.7	168.5	169.7	166.5	162.5	162.4	162.4	161.8
2008	156.6	158.7	161.1	162.9	166.1	168.2	171.0	171.4	167.7	162.4	161.5	159.9	164.0
2009	152.6	152.5	153.1	154.2	156.5	157.9	158.6	160.4	157.5	152.8	151.1	149.9	154.8
2010	147.3	148.4	150.8	154.3	156.4	158.4	159.7	161.2	157.6	154.4	152.9	152.7	154.5
2011	148.3	150.0	152.0	153.8	156.2	158.0	160.2	162.2	159.4	155.8	155.7	155.3	155.6
2012	151.3	153.3	155.1	159.6	162.7	165.9	167.9	170.3	166.7	163.1	162.2	162.2	161.7
2013	157.6	159.8	162.4	166.9	169.1	172.1	174.1	175.1	171.0	168.5	166.7	166.1	167.5
Other Services													
2002	43.3	43.9	44.5	46.1	46.6	47.6	46.1	45.4	45.7	45.8	45.9	46.1	45.6
2003	45.4	45.7	46.0	47.0	47.5	48.3	47.1	47.2	47.3	46.4	46.4	46.8	46.8
2004	46.4	46.8	47.1	47.0	47.5	48.2	49.0	48.9	49.0	48.1	48.2	48.6	47.9
2005	47.5	48.3	48.7	49.0	49.2	49.4	49.2	49.3	48.7	48.6	48.7	48.9	48.8
2006	46.9	47.7	47.7	48.4	49.0	49.4	48.0	48.0	48.8	48.7	48.8	48.9	48.4
2007	47.3	47.8	48.2	47.7	48.4	49.2	48.9	48.6	48.7	48.0	48.3	48.5	48.3
2008	47.4	47.9	48.5	48.1	48.6	49.4	49.1	49.1	48.3	48.1	48.1	48.1	48.4
2009	46.3	47.0	47.3	47.0	47.3	47.5	46.6	47.1	46.2	46.4	46.3	46.3	46.8
2010	45.5	46.1	46.7	45.4	46.1	46.6	46.5	46.4	45.8	46.3	45.9	45.8	46.1
2011	45.7	46.8	46.8	47.8	48.5	48.3	48.1	47.9	48.2	48.2	47.8	47.4	47.6
2012	47.2	48.3	48.7	49.3	49.9	50.4	49.5	49.2	49.4	49.8	49.0	48.9	49.1
2013	47.6	48.2	48.2	48.6	49.1	49.9	50.0	50.0	49.6	49.7	49.9	49.3	49.2
Government													
2002	219.9	222.8	223.7	223.1	222.8	223.2	210.7	210.4	212.9	221.4	222.8	222.5	219.7
2003	220.9	221.5	222.2	221.7	221.0	221.0	209.0	208.3	211.7	216.9	216.7	216.5	217.3
2004	213.1	215.8	216.7	218.6	217.4	217.8	205.9	204.5	211.0	216.9	217.2	216.8	214.3
2005	215.0	216.8	217.6	218.0	218.7	219.1	207.9	205.3	211.5	216.0	217.9	217.5	215.1
2006	216.2	218.8	219.7	219.9	220.0	221.2	210.6	208.2	214.5	220.2	222.9	223.1	217.9
2007	221.5	223.7	225.0	225.1	225.0	225.7	214.9	212.2	218.1	224.4	225.9	227.1	222.4
2008	224.2	227.5	228.7	227.8	228.8	230.1	216.7	215.3	220.1	226.8	228.0	227.4	225.1
2009	226.2	226.9	228.5	229.8	229.4	230.0	214.5	212.2	216.1	226.3	227.6	226.5	224.5
2010	224.5	225.6	227.4	234.8	240.7	238.0	225.6	223.8	227.5	231.9	233.3	232.2	230.4
2011	230.1	232.9	233.8	233.8	232.7	233.6	219.7	217.2	223.2	229.6	231.1	229.8	229.0
2012	226.7	229.4	230.9	230.8	231.3	232.1	218.1	219.0	223.0	229.4	232.1	231.2	227.8
2013	227.6	230.0	232.4	231.9	232.3	234.0	220.5	220.9	225.9	231.6	233.7	233.0	229.5

Employment by Industry: San Francisco–Oakland–Fremont, CA, Selected Years, 2002–2013

(Numbers in thousands, not seasonally adjusted)

Industry and year	January	February	March	April	May	June	July	August	September	October	November	December	Annual average
Total Nonfarm													
2002	2,027.4	2,034.8	2,047.9	2,041.9	2,049.7	2,053.7	2,029.3	2,032.3	2,036.6	2,041.5	2,050.7	2,052.0	2,041.5
2003	1,995.7	2,003.6	2,006.8	1,999.3	2,001.7	2,005.8	1,979.6	1,981.1	1,985.5	1,988.3	1,994.2	2,002.0	1,995.3
2004	1,956.3	1,966.6	1,977.2	1,980.8	1,989.0	1,995.6	1,980.9	1,976.7	1,983.3	1,996.0	2,004.8	2,015.7	1,985.2
2005	1,968.2	1,981.3	1,988.9	1,995.8	2,000.3	2,008.5	1,996.2	1,996.5	2,009.5	2,015.7	2,028.3	2,036.2	2,002.1
2006	1,994.4	2,010.7	2,019.3	2,020.1	2,037.6	2,048.0	2,031.3	2,035.3	2,045.5	2,053.8	2,064.6	2,067.8	2,035.7
2007	2,023.3	2,039.5	2,050.8	2,044.5	2,060.6	2,069.1	2,060.0	2,062.6	2,068.6	2,074.8	2,088.0	2,094.1	2,061.3
2008	2,044.4	2,057.6	2,060.6	2,064.0	2,068.9	2,073.6	2,063.5	2,057.3	2,055.6	2,057.2	2,050.1	2,045.8	2,058.2
2009	1,985.8	1,976.1	1,968.2	1,961.3	1,957.7	1,954.3	1,928.9	1,911.6	1,917.5	1,935.7	1,937.3	1,935.6	1,947.5
2010	1,892.7	1,895.2	1,902.5	1,917.0	1,928.0	1,930.4	1,910.8	1,904.9	1,920.9	1,933.7	1,936.7	1,941.0	1,917.8
2011	1,908.3	1,916.7	1,921.4	1,939.9	1,947.8	1,950.3	1,948.4	1,952.1	1,962.7	1,975.3	1,983.7	1,988.8	1,949.6
2012	1,958.1	1,971.4	1,981.5	2,005.7	2,021.5	2,032.5	2,026.0	2,032.6	2,037.9	2,064.5	2,078.7	2,086.6	2,024.8
2013	2,048.4	2,065.9	2,078.1	2,093.8	2,104.4	2,104.2	2,101.4	2,112.3	2,114.6	2,132.5	2,142.3	2,149.2	2,103.9
Total Private													
2002	1,713.7	1,717.8	1,726.7	1,719.4	1,726.8	1,733.2	1,724.9	1,728.7	1,722.8	1,719.6	1,727.4	1,730.3	1,724.3
2003	1,677.8	1,683.1	1,684.9	1,678.9	1,681.6	1,687.5	1,676.5	1,680.8	1,677.8	1,675.8	1,681.2	1,690.3	1,681.4
2004	1,646.6	1,654.1	1,662.6	1,666.2	1,674.3	1,681.6	1,679.1	1,680.1	1,679.7	1,684.4	1,690.9	1,703.2	1,675.2
2005	1,657.8	1,667.3	1,673.7	1,679.3	1,683.0	1,692.3	1,691.0	1,695.7	1,699.2	1,700.0	1,710.2	1,720.5	1,689.2
2006	1,680.1	1,693.0	1,699.3	1,700.7	1,717.5	1,729.5	1,722.1	1,728.4	1,730.6	1,732.1	1,739.9	1,746.7	1,718.3
2007	1,704.3	1,716.1	1,725.6	1,719.4	1,732.9	1,742.6	1,745.9	1,749.4	1,746.9	1,758.0	1,768.6	1,775.4	1,740.4
2008	1,729.5	1,739.9	1,741.6	1,744.4	1,750.0	1,752.8	1,753.1	1,750.6	1,744.2	1,741.8	1,733.2	1,730.8	1,742.7
2009	1,672.8	1,660.7	1,651.4	1,643.2	1,641.6	1,637.9	1,628.5	1,623.5	1,617.8	1,629.6	1,631.2	1,633.5	1,639.3
2010	1,592.8	1,593.2	1,599.0	1,608.0	1,612.7	1,619.7	1,624.5	1,622.2	1,622.1	1,631.5	1,631.4	1,637.4	1,616.2
2011	1,607.3	1,613.0	1,615.4	1,633.2	1,640.9	1,645.1	1,658.0	1,661.8	1,669.7	1,675.6	1,682.9	1,690.1	1,649.4
2012	1,661.9	1,672.3	1,679.7	1,703.7	1,719.2	1,731.4	1,735.3	1,743.8	1,745.5	1,767.7	1,777.2	1,786.6	1,727.0
2013	1,752.7	1,768.1	1,776.4	1,791.5	1,802.1	1,806.5	1,814.1	1,824.1	1,820.3	1,831.7	1,839.2	1,847.4	1,806.2
Goods-Producing													
2002	261.0	262.2	263.5	264.5	265.8	269.3	267.9	270.4	268.5	267.0	263.7	260.9	265.4
2003	252.9	252.5	252.6	251.4	251.5	253.1	253.4	255.7	255.7	256.4	255.4	254.0	253.7
2004	248.2	248.6	250.1	251.8	253.5	256.1	257.8	259.0	258.5	257.0	254.4	252.9	254.0
2005	244.8	246.6	248.4	248.9	249.4	252.8	255.0	256.3	256.4	256.0	255.5	253.8	252.0
2006	248.0	250.2	250.3	248.3	254.5	258.5	259.0	261.8	261.1	259.6	257.9	254.6	255.3
2007	249.1	249.6	252.1	251.5	253.4	256.2	257.0	258.8	257.4	256.9	256.2	254.3	254.4
2008	246.8	247.7	246.5	245.2	245.7	246.6	246.9	246.0	243.9	240.7	235.1	231.2	243.5
2009	221.9	214.9	213.0	208.4	207.8	207.9	206.6	206.4	204.9	204.9	204.3	201.4	208.6
2010	195.7	194.2	195.9	191.9	194.1	195.7	197.9	198.3	196.6	197.0	195.7	194.3	195.6
2011	192.0	191.9	190.0	192.4	194.4	196.2	201.3	202.3	201.3	201.1	199.9	198.9	196.8
2012	195.5	195.7	195.4	196.9	201.2	204.4	207.7	208.0	208.7	208.8	207.9	206.9	203.1
2013	203.2	205.2	205.9	206.9	209.0	211.3	213.3	215.9	215.6	216.2	216.1	214.7	211.1
Service-Providing													
2002	1,766.4	1,772.6	1,784.4	1,777.4	1,783.9	1,784.4	1,761.4	1,761.9	1,768.1	1,774.5	1,787.0	1,791.1	1,776.1
2003	1,742.8	1,751.1	1,754.2	1,747.9	1,750.2	1,752.7	1,726.2	1,725.4	1,729.8	1,731.9	1,738.8	1,748.0	1,741.6
2004	1,708.1	1,718.0	1,727.1	1,729.0	1,735.5	1,739.5	1,723.1	1,717.7	1,724.8	1,739.0	1,750.4	1,762.8	1,731.3
2005	1,723.4	1,734.7	1,740.5	1,746.9	1,750.9	1,755.7	1,741.2	1,740.2	1,753.1	1,759.7	1,772.8	1,782.4	1,750.1
2006	1,746.4	1,760.5	1,769.0	1,771.8	1,783.1	1,789.5	1,772.3	1,773.5	1,784.4	1,794.2	1,806.7	1,813.2	1,780.4
2007	1,774.2	1,789.9	1,798.7	1,793.0	1,807.2	1,812.9	1,803.0	1,803.8	1,811.2	1,817.9	1,831.8	1,839.8	1,807.0
2008	1,797.6	1,809.9	1,814.1	1,818.8	1,823.2	1,827.0	1,816.6	1,811.3	1,811.7	1,816.5	1,815.0	1,814.6	1,814.7
2009	1,763.9	1,761.2	1,755.2	1,752.5	1,749.9	1,746.4	1,722.3	1,705.2	1,712.6	1,730.8	1,733.0	1,734.2	1,738.9
2010	1,697.0	1,701.0	1,706.6	1,725.1	1,733.9	1,734.7	1,712.9	1,706.6	1,724.3	1,736.7	1,741.0	1,746.7	1,722.2
2011	1,716.3	1,724.8	1,731.4	1,747.5	1,753.4	1,754.1	1,747.1	1,749.8	1,761.4	1,774.2	1,783.8	1,789.9	1,752.8
2012	1,762.6	1,775.7	1,786.1	1,808.8	1,820.3	1,828.1	1,818.3	1,824.6	1,829.2	1,855.7	1,870.8	1,879.7	1,821.7
2013	1,845.2	1,860.7	1,872.2	1,886.9	1,895.4	1,892.9	1,888.1	1,896.4	1,899.0	1,916.3	1,926.2	1,934.5	1,892.8
Mining and Logging													
2002	1.5	1.5	1.5	1.5	1.5	1.4	1.3	1.3	1.2	1.2	1.2	1.2	1.4
2003	1.0	1.0	1.0	1.0	1.0	1.0	1.0	1.0	1.0	1.4	1.4	1.4	1.1
2004	1.4	1.4	1.4	1.4	1.4	1.4	1.4	1.4	1.4	1.3	1.4	1.4	1.4
2005	1.3	1.4	1.3	1.3	1.3	1.3	1.4	1.3	1.3	1.3	1.3	1.3	1.3
2006	1.3	1.3	1.3	1.3	1.4	1.4	1.4	1.5	1.5	1.5	1.5	1.5	1.4
2007	1.4	1.5	1.4	1.5	1.5	1.5	1.4	1.5	1.4	1.4	1.4	1.4	1.4
2008	1.4	1.4	1.4	1.4	1.4	1.4	1.4	1.4	1.4	1.4	1.4	1.4	1.4
2009	1.4	1.4	1.4	1.4	1.4	1.4	1.4	1.4	1.4	1.4	1.4	1.4	1.4
2010	1.4	1.4	1.4	1.4	1.4	1.5	1.5	1.6	1.5	1.4	1.4	1.4	1.4
2011	1.4	1.4	1.4	1.4	1.4	1.4	1.3	1.3	1.3	1.3	1.2	1.2	1.3
2012	1.3	1.3	1.3	1.3	1.3	1.3	1.3	1.4	1.3	1.3	1.3	1.3	1.3
2013	1.3	1.3	1.3	1.3	1.3	1.3	1.3	1.3	1.3	1.3	1.2	1.2	1.3
Construction													
2002	106.7	107.9	108.9	110.2	111.3	114.2	114.0	116.6	115.6	114.9	112.8	110.9	112.0
2003	107.9	108.1	108.6	108.1	108.6	110.5	111.5	113.7	113.6	113.8	112.6	110.8	110.7
2004	106.2	106.1	107.2	109.5	111.1	113.3	115.0	116.3	116.8	116.0	113.4	112.2	111.9
2005	106.3	108.0	110.1	111.4	112.4	115.3	117.3	118.5	118.5	118.5	117.6	115.8	114.1
2006	110.1	112.0	111.0	109.7	115.5	118.4	120.0	122.3	122.1	121.2	118.8	116.2	116.4
2007	112.3	112.3	114.7	114.8	116.5	118.8	120.5	121.7	120.3	119.3	117.7	115.9	117.1
2008	110.3	110.8	109.8	109.5	110.2	110.9	111.6	111.3	109.9	108.9	104.7	102.0	109.2
2009	95.5	90.7	90.3	88.4	88.5	88.9	88.6	88.5	87.1	86.7	86.3	83.5	88.6
2010	78.3	76.6	78.0	78.3	79.7	80.7	82.3	82.5	81.1	81.7	79.9	78.5	79.8
2011	76.3	76.1	74.1	76.3	78.1	79.7	84.0	85.3	85.7	85.7	84.7	83.9	80.8
2012	81.3	81.5	80.8	81.7	85.5	88.2	91.0	91.5	92.1	92.7	92.2	91.2	87.5
2013	88.7	90.4	90.5	91.3	92.8	94.5	96.1	97.6	96.9	96.9	96.9	95.5	94.0

Employment by Industry: San Francisco–Oakland–Fremont, CA, Selected Years, 2002–2013—*Continued*

(Numbers in thousands, not seasonally adjusted)

Industry and year	January	February	March	April	May	June	July	August	September	October	November	December	Annual average
Manufacturing													
2002	152.8	152.8	153.1	152.8	153.0	153.7	152.6	152.5	151.7	150.9	149.7	148.8	152.0
2003	144.0	143.4	143.0	142.3	141.9	141.6	140.9	141.0	141.1	141.2	141.4	141.8	142.0
2004	140.6	141.1	141.5	140.9	141.0	141.4	141.4	141.3	140.3	139.7	139.6	139.3	140.7
2005	137.2	137.2	137.0	136.2	135.7	136.2	136.3	136.5	136.6	136.2	136.6	136.7	136.5
2006	136.6	136.9	138.0	137.3	137.6	138.7	137.6	138.0	137.5	136.9	137.6	136.9	137.5
2007	135.4	135.8	136.0	135.2	135.4	135.9	135.1	135.6	135.7	136.2	137.1	137.0	135.9
2008	135.1	135.5	135.3	134.3	134.1	134.3	133.9	133.3	132.6	130.4	129.0	127.8	133.0
2009	125.0	122.8	121.3	119.0	117.9	117.6	116.6	116.5	116.4	116.8	116.6	116.5	118.6
2010	116.0	116.2	116.5	112.2	113.0	113.5	114.1	114.2	114.0	113.9	114.4	114.4	114.4
2011	114.3	114.4	114.5	114.7	114.9	115.1	116.0	115.7	114.3	114.1	114.0	113.8	114.7
2012	112.9	112.9	113.3	113.9	114.4	114.9	115.4	115.1	115.3	114.8	114.4	114.4	114.3
2013	113.2	113.5	114.1	114.3	114.9	115.5	115.9	117.0	117.4	118.0	118.0	118.0	115.8
Trade, Transportation, and Utilities													
2002	382.8	379.7	380.2	375.9	377.4	379.3	378.6	377.5	378.3	379.7	386.7	391.3	380.6
2003	374.4	370.1	368.7	363.3	363.8	364.6	362.2	361.4	360.6	361.6	368.5	374.4	366.1
2004	356.5	353.9	354.3	355.0	357.3	358.8	357.4	356.9	356.4	360.9	368.8	375.9	359.3
2005	359.8	356.0	355.1	355.2	355.9	357.8	357.2	357.9	358.6	357.6	365.0	372.7	359.1
2006	359.6	356.1	356.4	354.9	357.0	359.4	358.4	359.0	359.3	360.5	368.2	374.6	360.3
2007	363.0	359.6	359.4	356.3	357.9	359.4	359.8	360.5	360.1	361.2	369.9	375.9	361.9
2008	361.5	357.2	356.4	353.0	353.6	353.8	353.0	351.8	348.9	348.2	351.4	353.4	353.5
2009	340.0	334.7	331.1	328.0	327.6	326.5	323.5	323.2	322.7	324.2	330.7	335.4	329.0
2010	321.8	318.1	317.2	317.8	318.5	319.8	318.6	318.9	318.2	320.2	326.4	332.0	320.6
2011	319.3	316.9	316.3	318.8	320.0	320.7	322.4	323.5	322.9	324.8	333.3	338.2	323.1
2012	327.9	323.6	323.9	327.2	329.5	331.1	332.4	334.0	333.3	336.6	347.3	352.3	333.3
2013	340.7	338.0	337.5	338.5	340.8	342.6	344.0	345.6	345.0	348.5	356.1	361.5	344.9
Wholesale Trade													
2002	83.1	83.5	83.7	82.1	82.4	82.4	82.0	81.9	81.7	81.3	81.2	81.3	82.2
2003	79.5	79.5	79.5	78.9	78.7	78.4	77.6	77.4	77.0	76.9	76.6	76.8	78.1
2004	74.3	74.4	74.8	75.7	75.7	76.2	76.0	75.8	76.0	76.1	76.4	76.6	75.7
2005	74.6	74.3	74.2	74.9	74.7	75.2	74.7	74.6	74.5	74.4	74.5	74.7	74.6
2006	74.1	74.5	74.9	75.2	75.6	76.0	75.4	75.6	75.8	76.1	76.1	76.6	75.5
2007	75.7	76.1	76.6	75.5	76.0	76.2	75.6	75.6	75.4	75.7	75.5	75.6	75.8
2008	75.1	75.3	75.3	75.1	75.2	74.9	74.5	74.1	73.9	73.6	73.0	72.6	74.4
2009	70.6	70.2	69.4	69.0	68.7	68.3	67.7	67.3	66.6	66.9	66.7	66.5	68.2
2010	65.4	65.4	65.2	65.8	65.9	66.1	65.9	65.8	65.6	66.2	66.0	65.8	65.8
2011	65.1	65.3	65.4	66.0	66.4	66.5	67.0	67.2	67.3	67.6	67.9	68.1	66.7
2012	67.3	67.4	67.7	68.8	69.5	69.7	70.4	70.6	70.3	70.7	71.0	71.3	69.6
2013	71.0	71.0	71.0	71.6	72.0	72.5	73.2	73.3	73.3	73.8	72.8	73.4	72.4
Retail Trade													
2002	209.4	205.9	206.7	205.6	206.5	207.8	207.7	207.0	208.2	209.5	217.0	221.4	209.4
2003	208.8	205.1	204.0	201.3	201.9	202.9	202.6	202.6	202.5	203.5	211.3	216.5	205.3
2004	202.5	200.0	199.9	199.8	201.5	202.2	202.2	202.5	201.6	204.0	211.4	218.0	203.8
2005	206.4	202.7	202.0	201.9	202.3	203.4	203.6	204.9	205.2	205.6	212.5	219.2	205.8
2006	208.2	203.8	203.6	202.5	203.5	204.8	205.5	206.1	205.2	206.5	214.0	218.7	206.9
2007	210.0	205.9	205.7	203.5	204.4	205.3	206.7	207.1	206.5	207.2	215.8	220.8	208.2
2008	209.6	204.9	204.2	202.6	202.2	203.1	203.1	202.3	200.0	199.8	203.5	205.4	203.4
2009	196.9	192.3	190.1	187.9	187.5	187.0	185.5	185.8	185.9	186.9	193.6	198.0	189.8
2010	188.0	184.3	183.8	184.4	185.2	185.7	185.5	186.1	185.1	186.6	192.7	197.0	187.0
2011	187.1	184.6	184.0	185.0	185.6	186.0	187.1	187.8	187.1	188.7	196.3	199.6	188.2
2012	191.8	187.6	187.2	188.7	190.1	190.8	191.9	192.8	192.3	194.5	204.0	207.4	193.3
2013	197.6	194.9	194.6	194.4	195.8	197.2	197.5	198.7	197.9	200.2	208.2	211.2	199.0
Transportation and Utilities													
2002	90.3	90.3	89.8	88.2	88.5	89.1	88.9	88.6	88.4	88.9	88.5	88.6	89.0
2003	86.1	85.5	85.2	83.1	83.2	83.3	82.0	81.4	81.1	81.2	80.6	81.1	82.8
2004	79.7	79.5	79.6	79.5	80.1	80.4	79.2	78.6	78.8	80.8	81.0	81.3	79.9
2005	78.8	79.0	78.9	78.4	78.9	79.2	78.9	78.4	78.9	77.6	78.0	78.8	78.7
2006	77.3	77.8	77.9	77.2	77.9	78.6	77.5	77.3	78.3	77.9	78.1	79.3	77.9
2007	77.3	77.6	77.1	77.3	77.5	77.9	77.5	77.8	78.2	78.3	78.6	79.5	77.9
2008	76.8	77.0	76.9	75.3	76.2	75.8	75.4	75.4	75.0	74.8	74.9	75.4	75.7
2009	72.5	72.2	71.6	71.1	71.4	71.2	70.3	70.1	70.2	70.4	70.4	70.9	71.0
2010	68.4	68.4	68.2	67.6	67.4	68.0	67.2	67.0	67.5	67.4	67.7	69.2	67.8
2011	67.1	67.0	66.9	67.8	68.0	68.2	68.3	68.5	68.5	68.5	69.1	70.5	68.2
2012	68.8	68.6	69.0	69.7	69.9	70.6	70.1	70.6	70.7	71.4	72.3	73.6	70.4
2013	72.1	72.1	71.9	72.5	73.0	72.9	73.3	73.6	73.8	74.5	75.1	76.9	73.5
Information													
2002	88.3	87.5	87.4	85.9	86.8	86.9	85.8	85.7	85.1	83.7	84.2	84.0	85.9
2003	81.7	82.1	80.6	79.5	79.5	79.2	78.4	78.0	77.2	76.4	76.9	76.6	78.8
2004	75.5	75.7	75.7	75.3	75.3	75.3	75.3	74.7	74.0	73.5	73.5	73.5	74.8
2005	73.1	73.5	72.5	71.8	71.7	71.7	71.3	71.3	70.6	70.1	70.2	69.9	71.5
2006	69.4	69.6	69.3	68.7	68.8	68.9	68.7	69.1	68.7	68.9	69.3	69.5	69.1
2007	68.2	68.4	68.4	68.3	68.7	68.7	69.0	69.0	68.5	68.2	68.1	68.1	68.5
2008	67.9	68.3	68.0	68.5	68.7	68.7	69.7	69.5	68.8	68.6	68.4	68.2	68.6
2009	67.3	66.6	66.3	64.9	64.7	64.7	65.0	64.5	63.8	63.8	63.7	63.7	64.9
2010	63.0	62.6	62.6	62.3	62.4	62.9	63.0	62.7	62.2	62.3	62.7	63.0	62.6
2011	63.2	63.6	64.1	64.4	64.9	65.7	66.5	66.9	66.8	67.3	67.8	68.1	65.8
2012	68.6	69.1	69.2	70.1	70.6	71.6	72.0	72.2	72.0	72.1	72.9	73.3	71.1
2013	71.5	72.1	71.9	72.6	73.0	73.9	74.2	74.2	73.4	73.6	73.8	73.9	73.2

Employment by Industry: San Francisco–Oakland–Fremont, CA, Selected Years, 2002–2013—*Continued*

(Numbers in thousands, not seasonally adjusted)

Industry and year	January	February	March	April	May	June	July	August	September	October	November	December	Annual average
Financial Activities													
2002	153.3	153.3	153.6	153.8	153.8	154.7	154.5	155.5	154.5	155.1	155.6	156.4	154.5
2003	154.2	155.0	155.5	154.7	155.0	154.9	153.1	152.9	152.2	151.0	150.6	151.1	153.4
2004	150.1	150.1	150.2	149.3	149.8	150.5	150.4	150.5	149.8	150.4	150.6	151.4	150.3
2005	151.0	151.4	151.8	151.8	152.4	153.4	153.0	152.8	152.5	151.9	151.9	152.5	152.2
2006	150.9	151.4	151.7	151.7	152.2	152.1	150.6	150.6	150.2	149.5	148.8	148.3	150.7
2007	146.2	146.8	146.9	145.8	146.2	146.0	145.4	145.2	144.0	142.2	142.3	141.6	144.9
2008	139.1	139.0	138.8	138.0	137.9	138.2	137.2	137.0	135.7	135.3	134.2	134.1	137.0
2009	129.4	128.8	128.0	126.4	125.7	125.2	123.5	122.7	121.7	122.5	121.8	121.8	124.8
2010	121.7	122.1	122.0	121.9	122.3	122.2	122.6	122.5	122.3	121.9	121.5	122.2	122.1
2011	120.1	120.4	120.3	120.2	120.3	120.9	121.6	121.7	121.9	121.3	121.4	122.0	121.0
2012	121.2	122.0	122.3	122.8	123.4	124.2	124.3	124.5	123.9	124.5	124.3	125.1	123.5
2013	124.7	125.3	125.4	125.9	126.1	126.5	126.6	126.8	126.3	126.0	125.8	125.9	125.9
Professional and Business Services													
2002	341.9	342.3	343.8	340.1	338.3	338.5	334.6	334.7	331.9	329.7	331.9	332.1	336.7
2003	322.3	323.7	324.6	322.9	320.8	322.1	320.6	321.7	320.2	319.9	320.8	323.4	321.9
2004	318.4	320.8	323.3	323.9	324.0	326.5	325.2	326.1	325.1	328.3	330.3	333.2	325.4
2005	328.3	331.6	333.7	334.4	333.5	335.9	337.1	339.0	339.3	341.1	344.0	347.1	337.1
2006	340.8	344.8	347.4	347.8	349.3	353.2	352.6	354.6	354.8	356.0	357.5	359.9	351.6
2007	350.9	354.5	356.6	355.2	357.8	361.3	364.4	366.6	365.6	376.3	377.5	378.6	363.8
2008	372.4	374.7	375.6	375.5	374.5	376.6	377.8	378.6	376.6	376.7	373.4	372.0	375.4
2009	361.4	358.6	355.9	352.4	349.0	349.7	349.0	348.2	345.4	350.8	350.6	350.2	351.8
2010	343.2	345.1	347.1	349.6	348.9	352.5	356.1	356.1	355.7	357.7	357.6	357.9	352.3
2011	356.4	358.6	360.3	364.6	365.5	368.4	373.6	375.7	378.0	380.0	381.6	382.8	370.5
2012	379.9	382.6	385.7	392.8	394.6	399.5	400.9	404.0	404.0	409.0	409.4	410.1	397.7
2013	404.2	407.0	409.4	413.8	413.5	416.3	419.7	423.2	420.4	424.1	424.8	426.7	416.9
Education and Health Services													
2002	227.9	231.8	234.0	230.0	230.8	227.7	228.1	227.6	229.3	231.5	233.3	233.4	230.5
2003	230.3	235.7	237.3	240.7	241.6	240.2	238.5	238.1	240.2	241.1	242.6	243.3	239.1
2004	239.4	243.8	244.5	244.7	244.2	242.6	239.8	239.8	242.5	245.1	246.3	246.8	243.3
2005	240.5	246.0	246.6	246.4	246.8	244.2	242.7	242.7	245.7	248.1	249.3	249.9	245.7
2006	245.4	250.5	251.8	253.8	254.6	252.7	249.7	249.7	253.3	255.7	257.1	258.2	252.7
2007	252.7	259.4	261.5	259.7	260.7	260.1	256.8	255.7	259.1	262.9	264.9	265.7	259.9
2008	261.1	268.0	269.7	273.4	275.0	271.4	271.1	271.1	275.6	279.7	281.2	282.6	273.3
2009	276.8	281.0	281.8	283.4	283.5	280.2	277.2	275.3	278.6	282.0	282.5	283.3	280.5
2010	278.7	281.2	283.0	283.8	284.1	280.4	278.8	276.2	281.1	284.3	284.1	284.6	281.7
2011	279.8	282.8	283.4	284.5	284.0	278.9	276.6	275.4	281.5	284.5	285.2	286.2	281.9
2012	282.6	289.7	290.9	293.4	294.0	291.0	288.4	288.3	292.0	304.3	305.6	307.7	294.0
2013	305.6	313.3	315.6	316.8	317.6	312.8	312.3	312.7	315.1	317.7	318.7	320.9	314.9
Leisure and Hospitality													
2002	183.1	184.7	187.5	192.4	196.7	199.1	197.6	199.9	197.8	196.3	195.2	195.3	193.8
2003	187.0	187.9	189.4	190.5	193.3	196.9	195.2	197.9	196.6	195.0	192.4	193.2	192.9
2004	186.2	188.2	190.6	192.1	195.8	197.4	198.9	199.6	199.7	196.3	194.6	196.5	194.7
2005	189.3	190.6	193.1	197.7	200.1	202.6	201.8	203.6	204.0	202.7	202.2	202.0	199.1
2006	195.1	198.6	200.0	202.6	207.1	210.0	209.0	209.9	209.5	208.5	207.9	208.0	205.5
2007	202.0	204.4	206.6	208.5	213.2	215.7	217.8	218.1	216.9	214.8	214.2	215.3	212.3
2008	207.1	210.3	211.5	215.1	218.4	221.1	220.9	220.9	219.4	216.7	214.3	214.2	215.8
2009	203.2	203.5	202.8	206.0	210.0	210.6	210.9	210.8	209.1	208.7	205.3	205.6	207.2
2010	197.9	198.7	199.7	208.0	209.1	212.3	213.6	214.4	213.4	214.3	210.4	210.4	208.5
2011	204.3	206.3	208.2	213.8	217.4	219.5	220.4	221.2	222.1	220.8	218.0	218.4	215.9
2012	212.4	214.9	216.9	224.2	228.2	231.3	231.9	235.2	233.7	234.2	231.6	232.6	227.3
2013	226.1	229.3	232.2	237.2	242.1	242.8	243.8	245.4	244.6	245.3	243.7	244.0	239.7
Other Services													
2002	75.4	76.3	76.7	76.8	77.2	77.7	77.8	77.4	77.4	76.6	76.8	76.9	76.9
2003	75.0	76.1	76.2	75.9	76.1	76.5	75.1	75.1	75.1	74.4	74.0	74.3	75.3
2004	72.3	73.0	73.9	74.1	74.4	74.4	74.3	73.5	73.7	72.9	72.4	73.0	73.5
2005	71.0	71.6	72.5	73.1	73.2	73.9	72.9	72.1	72.1	72.5	72.1	72.6	72.5
2006	70.9	71.8	72.4	72.9	74.0	74.7	74.1	73.7	73.7	73.4	73.2	73.6	73.2
2007	72.2	73.4	74.1	74.1	75.0	75.2	75.7	75.5	75.3	75.5	75.5	75.9	74.8
2008	73.6	74.7	75.1	75.7	76.2	76.4	76.5	75.7	75.3	75.9	75.2	75.1	75.5
2009	72.8	72.6	72.5	73.3	73.3	73.1	72.8	72.4	71.6	72.7	72.3	72.1	72.6
2010	70.8	71.2	71.5	72.7	73.3	73.9	73.9	73.1	72.6	73.8	73.0	73.0	72.7
2011	72.2	72.5	72.8	74.5	74.4	74.8	75.6	75.1	75.2	75.8	75.7	75.5	74.5
2012	73.8	74.7	75.4	76.3	77.7	78.3	77.7	77.6	77.9	78.2	78.2	78.6	77.0
2013	76.7	77.9	78.5	79.8	80.0	80.3	80.2	80.3	79.9	80.3	80.2	79.8	79.5
Government													
2002	313.7	317.0	321.2	322.5	322.9	320.5	304.4	303.6	313.8	321.9	323.3	321.7	317.2
2003	317.9	320.5	321.9	320.4	320.1	318.3	303.1	300.3	307.7	312.5	313.0	311.7	314.0
2004	309.7	312.5	314.6	314.6	314.7	314.0	301.8	296.6	303.6	311.6	313.9	312.5	310.0
2005	310.4	314.0	315.2	316.5	317.3	316.2	305.2	300.8	310.3	315.7	318.1	315.7	313.0
2006	314.3	317.7	320.0	319.4	320.1	318.5	309.2	306.9	314.9	321.7	324.7	321.1	317.4
2007	319.0	323.4	325.2	325.1	327.7	326.5	314.1	313.2	321.7	316.8	319.4	318.7	320.9
2008	314.9	317.7	319.0	319.6	318.9	320.8	310.4	306.7	311.4	315.4	316.9	315.0	315.6
2009	313.0	315.4	316.8	318.1	316.1	316.4	300.4	288.1	299.7	306.1	306.1	302.1	308.2
2010	299.9	302.0	303.5	309.0	315.3	310.7	286.3	282.7	298.8	302.2	305.3	303.6	301.6
2011	301.0	303.7	306.0	306.7	306.9	305.2	290.4	290.3	293.0	299.7	300.8	298.7	300.2
2012	296.2	299.1	301.8	302.0	302.3	301.1	290.7	288.8	292.4	296.8	301.5	300.0	297.7
2013	295.7	297.8	301.7	302.3	302.3	297.7	287.3	288.2	294.3	300.8	303.1	301.8	297.8

Employment by Industry: San Jose–Sunnyvale–Santa Clara, CA, Selected Years, 2002–2013

(Numbers in thousands, not seasonally adjusted)

Industry and year	January	February	March	April	May	June	July	August	September	October	November	December	Annual average
Total Nonfarm													
2002	934.8	935.7	941.0	931.3	929.9	928.4	917.4	911.2	903.4	902.9	899.6	896.6	919.4
2003	876.6	875.5	876.9	878.7	879.0	880.4	870.5	868.1	866.8	869.4	870.4	873.3	873.8
2004	854.3	859.0	864.5	864.3	869.5	874.3	866.8	866.5	865.2	873.0	875.6	878.5	867.6
2005	862.3	865.5	869.2	869.9	873.5	879.3	876.7	878.4	878.0	884.3	887.6	894.0	876.6
2006	879.2	887.0	890.3	890.3	897.4	903.2	900.2	902.4	902.6	904.5	908.0	913.8	898.2
2007	899.5	905.8	911.9	909.0	916.5	924.6	923.8	922.5	921.5	927.5	931.3	932.9	918.9
2008	919.9	923.6	927.5	925.4	929.0	931.8	926.0	930.0	928.4	924.0	920.0	916.2	925.2
2009	890.3	882.4	878.2	872.1	872.5	872.6	849.5	852.9	855.5	862.6	865.5	865.4	868.3
2010	849.9	851.6	856.0	862.9	870.0	871.5	860.0	860.8	865.0	876.3	880.5	882.3	865.6
2011	868.4	873.8	877.1	881.1	884.3	890.3	880.3	883.6	889.8	898.5	901.3	904.4	886.1
2012	892.3	898.7	904.9	913.6	919.4	927.8	916.8	922.1	925.9	939.5	944.8	947.5	921.1
2013	933.2	941.5	945.7	953.1	959.5	964.5	957.8	967.9	970.6	976.8	983.3	987.6	961.8
Total Private													
2002	833.6	833.5	837.6	826.7	825.2	824.0	816.1	812.6	803.7	799.7	796.0	793.5	816.9
2003	774.4	774.5	775.2	776.9	777.6	779.6	773.6	773.5	771.5	770.8	771.9	776.3	774.7
2004	758.4	762.2	766.6	766.4	771.4	776.7	772.0	773.6	771.7	776.8	778.2	782.5	771.4
2005	766.8	769.3	772.3	772.9	776.1	782.3	782.4	784.7	784.2	788.1	791.0	797.8	780.7
2006	783.5	790.5	793.6	793.0	799.6	805.8	805.1	808.7	808.3	806.8	810.4	816.3	801.8
2007	801.8	808.8	813.6	810.9	818.2	826.8	828.7	828.6	826.6	829.2	832.7	834.6	821.7
2008	820.9	825.4	828.4	827.0	830.0	833.2	832.0	835.5	830.4	825.3	821.7	818.4	827.4
2009	792.9	785.6	780.6	772.6	772.3	772.3	764.4	764.1	759.5	764.1	766.2	767.3	771.8
2010	753.9	755.4	758.4	763.5	769.1	774.9	775.0	777.3	775.1	780.9	783.5	786.2	771.1
2011	773.8	778.5	781.4	784.6	787.5	794.1	799.0	801.2	798.9	804.7	806.9	810.0	793.4
2012	800.6	805.8	810.9	819.4	825.2	832.9	835.7	839.0	835.7	846.0	850.7	854.2	829.7
2013	840.6	847.5	852.6	858.9	863.7	871.0	879.2	884.0	879.3	882.9	887.7	891.9	869.9
Goods-Producing													
2002	256.0	252.4	253.3	248.9	248.5	248.2	246.3	244.5	240.3	236.4	231.5	228.0	244.5
2003	223.0	220.6	220.0	218.1	216.5	216.9	216.2	215.7	214.6	212.1	210.7	210.6	216.3
2004	208.5	206.6	207.6	207.9	209.0	211.1	211.9	212.7	211.8	210.8	209.4	208.9	209.5
2005	205.5	205.2	205.2	207.5	207.6	209.9	211.6	212.0	211.2	210.9	209.4	209.9	208.8
2006	207.7	208.5	208.3	207.3	209.7	210.7	212.6	213.4	212.5	210.8	208.7	208.8	209.9
2007	207.1	208.7	209.5	209.5	211.3	215.1	217.7	218.3	217.5	216.0	214.1	212.8	213.1
2008	210.7	210.9	210.6	210.4	212.2	213.3	214.9	215.2	213.3	210.5	207.0	205.1	211.2
2009	198.5	194.8	192.6	190.0	188.5	188.0	187.0	186.9	185.9	184.0	183.3	182.1	188.5
2010	180.5	180.0	180.9	180.8	181.9	184.5	186.0	187.4	186.9	186.6	185.2	185.1	183.8
2011	183.0	183.4	184.2	185.2	186.1	188.5	190.6	191.6	190.0	188.2	186.9	186.8	187.0
2012	186.0	186.3	186.7	188.2	190.3	193.6	194.1	195.0	193.5	192.1	191.4	191.1	190.7
2013	188.2	188.5	189.3	190.1	190.9	193.9	196.7	197.9	197.0	196.7	197.5	198.8	193.8
Service-Providing													
2002	678.8	683.3	687.7	682.4	681.4	680.2	671.1	666.7	663.1	666.5	668.1	668.6	674.8
2003	653.6	654.9	656.9	660.6	662.5	663.5	654.3	652.4	652.2	657.3	659.7	662.7	657.6
2004	648.5	652.4	656.9	656.4	660.5	663.2	654.9	653.8	653.4	662.2	666.2	669.6	658.2
2005	656.8	660.3	664.0	662.4	665.9	669.4	665.1	666.4	666.8	673.4	678.2	684.1	667.7
2006	671.5	678.5	682.0	683.0	687.7	692.5	687.6	689.0	690.1	693.7	699.3	705.0	688.3
2007	692.4	697.1	702.4	699.5	705.2	709.5	706.1	704.2	704.0	711.5	717.2	720.1	705.8
2008	709.2	712.7	716.9	715.0	716.8	718.5	711.1	714.8	715.1	713.5	713.0	711.1	714.0
2009	691.8	687.6	685.6	682.1	684.0	684.6	662.5	666.0	669.6	678.6	682.2	683.3	679.8
2010	669.4	671.6	675.1	682.1	688.1	687.0	674.0	673.4	678.1	689.7	695.3	697.2	681.8
2011	685.4	690.4	692.9	695.9	698.2	701.8	689.7	692.0	699.8	710.3	714.4	717.6	699.0
2012	706.3	712.4	718.2	725.4	729.1	734.2	722.7	727.1	732.4	747.4	753.4	756.4	730.4
2013	745.0	753.0	756.4	763.0	768.6	770.6	761.1	770.0	773.6	780.1	785.8	788.8	768.0
Mining and Logging													
2002	0.3	0.3	0.3	0.2	0.2	0.2	0.2	0.2	0.2	0.2	0.2	0.2	0.2
2003	0.2	0.2	0.2	0.2	0.2	0.2	0.2	0.2	0.2	0.2	0.2	0.1	0.2
2004	0.1	0.1	0.1	0.1	0.1	0.2	0.1	0.2	0.2	0.2	0.1	0.1	0.1
2005	0.1	0.1	0.1	0.2	0.2	0.2	0.2	0.2	0.2	0.3	0.3	0.2	0.2
2006	0.3	0.3	0.2	0.2	0.2	0.3	0.3	0.3	0.3	0.3	0.3	0.3	0.3
2007	0.3	0.3	0.3	0.3	0.3	0.3	0.3	0.3	0.3	0.3	0.3	0.3	0.3
2008	0.3	0.3	0.3	0.3	0.3	0.3	0.3	0.3	0.3	0.3	0.3	0.3	0.3
2009	0.3	0.2	0.2	0.2	0.2	0.2	0.2	0.2	0.3	0.2	0.2	0.2	0.2
2010	0.2	0.2	0.2	0.2	0.2	0.2	0.2	0.2	0.2	0.2	0.2	0.2	0.2
2011	0.2	0.2	0.2	0.2	0.2	0.2	0.2	0.2	0.2	0.2	0.2	0.2	0.2
2012	0.2	0.2	0.2	0.2	0.2	0.2	0.2	0.3	0.3	0.3	0.3	0.2	0.2
2013	0.2	0.2	0.2	0.2	0.2	0.2	0.3	0.3	0.3	0.3	0.3	0.3	0.3
Construction													
2002	43.7	43.3	44.1	43.6	44.4	45.3	45.6	46.7	45.6	44.5	43.8	42.2	44.4
2003	40.0	39.9	40.2	40.1	40.4	41.2	41.9	43.3	43.5	43.2	42.7	42.3	41.6
2004	40.3	40.8	41.2	41.7	42.4	43.7	44.2	44.6	44.5	44.8	44.2	43.9	43.0
2005	41.6	41.7	42.3	43.0	43.6	45.0	45.7	46.4	46.7	46.3	46.0	45.9	44.5
2006	44.9	45.4	45.1	44.3	46.2	47.4	47.9	48.7	48.9	48.2	47.6	46.9	46.8
2007	45.0	45.5	46.3	46.0	47.0	47.9	48.6	49.2	49.2	48.3	47.3	46.6	47.2
2008	44.3	44.6	44.2	44.0	44.6	45.1	45.5	45.9	45.1	43.7	41.9	40.9	44.2
2009	37.8	36.2	35.9	34.9	34.2	34.2	33.8	33.8	33.4	33.2	33.1	32.3	34.4
2010	31.2	30.8	31.2	31.8	32.1	32.9	33.4	33.2	33.1	32.8	32.0	31.7	32.2
2011	29.8	29.7	30.2	30.2	30.5	31.2	32.8	33.1	33.4	32.9	32.8	32.6	31.6
2012	31.9	32.1	32.4	33.2	34.7	35.6	35.7	35.9	35.6	35.9	35.9	36.0	34.6
2013	34.9	35.3	35.6	35.9	36.4	37.4	38.8	39.3	38.8	39.2	39.2	39.2	37.5

Employment by Industry: San Jose–Sunnyvale–Santa Clara, CA, Selected Years, 2002–2013—*Continued*

(Numbers in thousands, not seasonally adjusted)

Industry and year	January	February	March	April	May	June	July	August	September	October	November	December	Annual average
Manufacturing													
2002	212.0	208.8	208.9	205.1	203.9	202.7	200.5	197.6	194.5	191.7	187.5	185.6	199.9
2003	182.8	180.5	179.6	177.8	175.9	175.5	174.1	172.2	170.9	168.7	167.8	168.2	174.5
2004	165.4	165.7	166.3	166.1	166.5	167.2	167.6	167.9	167.1	165.8	165.1	164.9	166.3
2005	163.8	163.4	162.8	164.3	163.8	164.7	165.7	165.4	164.3	164.3	163.1	163.8	164.1
2006	162.5	162.8	163.0	162.8	163.3	163.0	164.4	164.4	163.3	162.3	160.8	161.6	162.9
2007	161.8	162.9	162.9	163.2	164.0	166.9	168.8	168.8	168.0	167.4	166.5	165.9	165.6
2008	166.1	166.0	166.1	166.1	167.3	167.9	169.1	169.0	167.9	166.5	164.8	163.9	166.7
2009	160.4	158.4	156.5	154.9	154.1	153.6	153.0	152.9	152.2	150.6	150.0	149.6	153.9
2010	149.1	149.0	149.5	148.8	149.6	151.4	152.4	154.0	153.6	153.6	153.0	153.2	151.4
2011	153.0	153.5	153.8	154.8	155.4	157.1	157.6	158.3	156.4	155.1	153.9	154.0	155.2
2012	153.9	154.0	154.1	154.8	155.4	157.8	158.2	158.8	157.6	155.9	155.2	154.9	155.9
2013	153.1	153.0	153.5	154.0	154.3	156.3	157.6	158.3	157.9	157.2	158.0	159.3	156.0
Trade, Transportation, and Utilities													
2002	139.8	138.3	138.8	137.0	137.0	136.8	136.4	136.0	135.8	135.5	137.6	139.5	137.4
2003	133.1	131.2	130.9	131.0	131.0	131.3	130.8	131.1	130.8	131.7	134.3	136.6	132.0
2004	130.7	129.6	129.2	128.8	129.8	130.1	129.8	130.1	129.9	131.4	134.2	136.6	130.9
2005	131.3	130.2	130.3	130.2	130.7	131.2	132.1	132.8	133.5	134.2	137.1	140.0	132.8
2006	135.3	133.8	133.8	133.7	134.4	135.2	136.4	137.6	138.1	138.6	142.6	145.1	137.1
2007	139.3	137.6	137.8	137.2	137.8	138.8	140.0	139.9	139.6	140.0	143.3	145.3	139.7
2008	140.2	138.7	138.9	137.1	137.2	136.9	137.3	137.5	136.3	136.0	137.4	138.1	137.6
2009	130.7	128.5	126.9	125.2	125.9	125.4	124.4	124.3	124.1	124.7	127.8	129.2	126.4
2010	124.6	123.4	123.0	123.6	124.5	125.1	125.6	126.2	125.7	126.2	129.8	131.2	125.7
2011	125.7	124.5	124.1	125.3	125.7	126.6	127.4	128.0	128.0	129.4	133.1	135.1	127.7
2012	129.6	127.9	127.9	129.2	130.0	130.9	132.1	132.3	131.8	133.2	138.3	139.8	131.9
2013	133.8	132.9	132.5	132.7	133.1	134.3	135.9	136.2	135.5	137.2	141.1	142.3	135.6
Wholesale Trade													
2002	38.6	38.1	38.2	37.2	37.0	36.5	35.9	35.5	34.9	34.6	34.0	33.6	36.2
2003	33.6	33.6	33.8	34.1	34.2	34.2	34.3	34.5	34.3	34.3	34.2	34.3	34.1
2004	34.0	33.9	33.9	34.3	34.4	34.6	34.5	34.6	34.5	34.9	34.9	34.5	34.5
2005	34.8	35.1	35.1	35.2	35.5	35.8	36.1	36.3	36.5	36.5	36.4	36.7	35.8
2006	37.0	37.3	37.4	37.8	37.9	38.2	38.7	38.8	39.0	39.0	39.1	39.3	38.3
2007	38.9	39.3	39.3	39.0	39.2	39.8	40.0	40.0	40.1	40.4	40.5	40.8	39.8
2008	40.5	40.4	40.9	40.2	40.3	40.1	39.6	39.4	39.3	39.2	38.8	38.4	39.8
2009	37.1	36.7	36.3	36.1	35.9	35.7	35.1	35.0	34.7	35.0	34.9	34.9	35.6
2010	34.5	34.6	34.6	34.7	34.9	35.0	35.3	35.2	35.3	35.0	34.8	34.8	34.9
2011	34.5	34.4	34.2	33.9	33.8	33.7	33.8	33.7	33.5	33.6	33.5	33.7	33.9
2012	33.9	34.2	33.9	34.3	34.5	34.6	35.2	35.3	35.1	35.9	35.8	35.8	34.9
2013	35.8	36.0	36.0	36.0	36.0	36.2	37.1	37.1	37.0	36.9	36.9	36.9	36.5
Retail Trade													
2002	86.5	85.4	85.8	84.8	84.6	84.9	85.1	85.2	85.6	85.5	88.3	90.6	86.0
2003	84.9	83.2	82.8	82.3	82.4	82.6	82.3	82.4	82.5	83.3	86.1	88.4	83.6
2004	82.9	81.9	81.5	81.1	81.9	81.9	82.0	82.3	82.0	83.0	85.8	88.2	82.9
2005	83.4	82.0	82.1	81.9	82.1	82.3	82.9	83.5	83.9	84.8	87.8	90.3	83.9
2006	85.8	83.9	83.8	83.4	83.7	84.0	84.8	85.6	85.8	86.5	90.1	92.3	85.8
2007	87.5	85.3	85.4	84.8	85.1	85.2	86.2	86.1	85.6	85.9	89.1	90.6	86.4
2008	86.5	84.9	84.6	83.6	83.3	83.1	84.3	84.6	83.5	83.4	85.2	86.0	84.4
2009	80.9	79.3	78.5	77.2	77.8	77.7	77.5	77.5	77.5	77.8	81.1	82.3	78.8
2010	78.3	77.1	76.7	77.2	77.6	78.0	78.2	78.8	78.1	79.1	82.9	84.0	78.8
2011	79.4	78.2	78.0	79.5	79.8	80.7	81.4	82.2	82.3	83.7	87.4	88.8	81.8
2012	83.4	81.4	81.7	82.5	82.9	83.4	83.8	83.8	83.3	83.9	89.0	90.1	84.1
2013	84.6	83.2	82.9	83.0	83.4	84.2	84.6	84.9	84.2	86.0	89.8	90.9	85.1
Transportation and Utilities													
2002	14.7	14.8	14.8	15.0	15.4	15.4	15.4	15.3	15.3	15.4	15.3	15.3	15.2
2003	14.6	14.4	14.3	14.6	14.4	14.5	14.2	14.2	14.0	14.1	14.0	13.9	14.3
2004	13.8	13.8	13.8	13.4	13.5	13.6	13.3	13.2	13.4	13.5	13.5	13.5	13.5
2005	13.1	13.1	13.1	13.1	13.1	13.1	13.1	13.0	13.1	12.9	12.9	13.0	13.1
2006	12.5	12.6	12.6	12.5	12.8	13.0	12.9	13.2	13.3	13.1	13.4	13.5	13.0
2007	12.9	13.0	13.1	13.4	13.5	13.8	13.8	13.8	13.9	13.7	13.7	13.9	13.5
2008	13.2	13.4	13.4	13.3	13.6	13.7	13.4	13.5	13.5	13.4	13.4	13.7	13.5
2009	12.7	12.5	12.1	11.9	12.2	12.0	11.8	11.8	11.9	11.9	11.8	12.0	12.1
2010	11.8	11.7	11.7	11.7	12.0	12.1	12.1	12.2	12.3	12.1	12.1	12.4	12.0
2011	11.8	11.9	11.9	11.9	12.1	12.2	12.2	12.1	12.2	12.1	12.2	12.6	12.1
2012	12.3	12.3	12.3	12.4	12.6	12.9	13.1	13.2	13.4	13.4	13.5	13.9	12.9
2013	13.4	13.7	13.6	13.7	13.7	13.9	14.2	14.2	14.3	14.3	14.4	14.5	14.0
Information													
2002	37.9	37.8	37.6	36.6	35.8	35.2	34.5	34.2	33.8	33.4	33.6	33.1	35.3
2003	32.7	33.0	32.6	32.2	32.1	32.2	32.2	32.1	32.0	32.3	32.5	32.7	32.4
2004	32.7	33.0	33.2	33.0	33.1	33.4	33.5	33.4	33.6	34.1	34.5	34.8	33.5
2005	34.6	34.9	35.2	34.8	35.2	35.8	36.3	36.6	36.5	37.1	37.8	38.2	36.1
2006	38.0	38.2	38.3	38.2	38.4	38.6	38.8	38.9	38.5	38.1	38.3	38.6	38.4
2007	38.8	39.4	39.7	39.2	40.0	40.9	41.4	41.7	41.5	41.7	42.3	42.6	40.8
2008	42.5	42.5	42.3	42.8	43.4	43.8	45.0	44.9	44.3	44.0	44.3	44.0	43.7
2009	44.7	43.6	43.3	42.8	43.0	43.4	44.5	44.3	44.0	44.0	44.3	44.4	43.9
2010	44.1	44.4	44.1	44.8	45.4	46.6	47.6	47.8	47.5	47.9	48.5	48.6	46.4
2011	49.2	49.7	49.7	50.0	50.4	51.9	52.7	52.7	52.1	52.1	52.2	52.5	51.3
2012	52.1	52.6	52.8	53.3	53.5	54.5	55.5	55.2	54.9	55.0	55.2	55.6	54.2
2013	56.3	56.6	57.0	57.0	57.1	58.9	60.3	60.2	59.5	59.8	60.6	60.7	58.7

Employment by Industry: San Jose–Sunnyvale–Santa Clara, CA, Selected Years, 2002–2013—*Continued*

(Numbers in thousands, not seasonally adjusted)

Industry and year	January	February	March	April	May	June	July	August	September	October	November	December	Annual average
Financial Activities													
2002	35.4	35.6	35.6	35.1	35.5	35.4	35.4	35.6	35.2	35.2	35.1	35.1	35.4
2003	34.7	34.7	34.9	34.9	35.0	34.9	35.1	35.2	35.0	34.8	34.7	34.9	34.9
2004	34.5	34.6	34.8	34.9	35.2	35.2	35.3	35.3	35.3	35.8	35.7	35.9	35.2
2005	35.7	35.6	35.8	35.7	35.8	36.0	36.1	36.4	36.2	36.5	36.5	36.8	36.1
2006	36.5	36.6	36.8	36.9	37.3	37.0	37.1	37.0	36.9	36.9	36.9	36.9	36.9
2007	37.0	37.1	37.1	37.0	37.2	37.0	37.1	36.9	36.8	36.6	36.2	36.3	36.9
2008	35.3	35.5	35.1	34.9	34.8	34.5	34.3	34.0	33.8	33.4	32.7	32.8	34.3
2009	32.2	31.9	31.9	31.8	31.7	31.4	31.3	31.2	30.9	31.2	31.2	31.3	31.5
2010	30.8	30.9	31.5	30.2	30.6	30.8	30.9	31.1	30.9	31.4	31.7	31.7	31.0
2011	31.6	31.8	31.7	31.9	31.9	32.3	32.5	32.5	32.5	32.9	33.1	33.3	32.3
2012	32.8	32.7	33.0	33.0	33.1	33.5	33.6	33.4	33.4	33.7	33.8	33.7	33.3
2013	32.7	33.0	33.3	33.5	33.9	33.9	34.0	34.1	33.8	33.7	33.4	33.2	33.5
Professional and Business Services													
2002	180.5	180.8	180.9	177.6	175.7	175.5	174.1	173.1	171.2	171.0	170.1	169.8	175.0
2003	166.4	166.7	166.9	168.1	168.5	169.2	166.2	167.9	168.4	166.9	167.0	168.3	167.5
2004	164.8	165.8	166.0	165.3	165.1	166.6	163.8	165.0	164.8	166.2	166.5	167.6	165.6
2005	164.3	165.9	166.7	165.0	165.1	165.9	164.4	165.3	165.8	166.2	166.5	168.4	165.8
2006	166.2	168.6	169.3	169.5	169.7	171.5	172.5	173.8	174.7	174.2	175.0	177.7	171.9
2007	176.1	177.6	177.7	177.1	177.5	178.1	178.6	178.2	178.1	178.8	179.7	180.3	178.2
2008	177.2	178.3	179.5	179.6	178.7	180.0	179.9	180.4	179.6	177.9	176.9	175.7	178.6
2009	168.2	166.4	164.9	161.1	159.7	160.1	158.9	158.6	157.9	158.5	159.0	159.4	161.1
2010	156.7	157.8	158.6	160.0	160.5	162.0	162.8	163.4	162.7	164.0	164.2	164.9	161.5
2011	163.1	164.3	165.3	165.6	165.1	166.7	169.4	169.9	169.0	169.5	169.3	169.8	167.3
2012	168.9	170.9	172.7	175.7	176.1	178.5	181.5	182.9	181.9	183.7	184.6	186.6	178.7
2013	184.5	186.8	188.1	188.3	188.7	191.3	194.3	196.6	195.1	193.1	193.2	194.3	191.2
Education and Health Services													
2002	91.4	94.2	95.3	95.4	95.4	95.0	91.9	92.1	91.9	94.4	95.6	95.7	94.0
2003	94.2	96.3	97.1	98.1	98.7	98.2	96.7	95.5	95.4	98.2	99.2	99.7	97.3
2004	98.7	99.8	101.0	100.5	101.6	101.8	99.3	99.2	99.3	102.2	103.2	103.4	100.8
2005	102.5	103.1	103.3	102.8	103.0	103.3	102.0	102.1	102.1	105.4	106.8	107.1	103.6
2006	105.3	107.9	108.6	107.9	108.6	109.1	106.0	105.7	106.0	108.3	109.4	109.2	107.7
2007	107.0	109.8	111.1	109.4	111.2	112.1	110.2	109.8	110.0	113.7	115.2	115.2	111.2
2008	116.0	118.7	119.2	118.8	118.5	118.2	114.8	118.2	118.1	119.7	121.2	121.2	118.6
2009	120.3	121.8	121.9	121.8	122.5	122.0	118.4	118.8	117.8	122.7	122.9	123.2	121.2
2010	121.2	122.3	122.4	124.5	125.1	124.7	121.9	121.6	121.2	124.7	125.4	125.9	123.4
2011	124.8	126.6	126.8	125.7	126.1	125.3	122.0	122.3	122.8	127.8	129.5	129.7	125.8
2012	130.0	133.2	133.4	133.5	134.0	132.9	129.2	130.4	130.2	138.4	139.5	139.7	133.7
2013	139.0	141.1	141.8	144.1	144.9	143.4	143.3	144.5	144.1	148.5	149.3	149.9	144.5
Leisure and Hospitality													
2002	66.3	67.7	69.2	69.4	70.6	71.2	70.8	70.5	69.3	68.1	66.5	66.5	68.8
2003	65.5	66.9	67.7	68.8	70.1	71.1	70.9	70.9	70.2	69.5	68.1	68.2	69.0
2004	66.9	68.0	69.9	70.8	72.2	73.1	73.2	72.9	72.0	71.3	69.7	70.2	70.9
2005	68.4	69.5	70.9	72.1	73.7	74.8	75.2	75.3	74.5	73.5	72.7	73.1	72.8
2006	70.5	72.4	73.8	74.7	76.2	77.9	76.9	77.4	76.6	75.4	74.9	75.3	75.2
2007	72.6	74.0	75.9	76.7	78.0	79.2	78.6	78.7	77.7	76.9	76.5	76.7	76.8
2008	74.3	75.6	77.3	77.9	79.3	80.6	80.5	80.2	79.5	78.3	76.9	76.3	78.1
2009	73.8	74.0	74.4	75.1	76.1	77.1	75.9	76.2	74.8	74.7	73.1	73.2	74.9
2010	71.5	71.7	72.7	75.5	76.9	76.7	76.4	76.1	76.3	75.9	74.4	74.7	74.9
2011	72.4	73.9	75.3	76.4	77.5	78.1	79.5	79.7	79.9	80.1	78.0	78.1	77.4
2012	77.1	78.0	80.1	81.7	83.2	83.8	84.6	84.9	85.3	85.0	83.1	83.1	82.5
2013	81.4	83.6	85.5	87.8	89.3	89.6	89.2	89.2	89.0	88.2	87.1	87.4	87.3
Other Services													
2002	26.3	26.7	26.9	26.7	26.7	26.7	26.7	26.6	26.2	25.7	26.0	25.8	26.4
2003	24.8	25.1	25.1	25.7	25.7	25.7	25.5	25.1	25.1	25.3	25.4	25.3	25.3
2004	24.3	24.8	24.9	25.2	25.4	25.4	25.2	25.0	25.0	25.0	25.0	25.1	25.0
2005	24.5	24.9	24.9	24.8	25.0	25.4	24.7	24.2	24.4	24.3	24.2	24.3	24.6
2006	24.0	24.5	24.7	24.8	25.3	25.8	24.8	24.9	25.0	24.5	24.6	24.7	24.8
2007	23.9	24.6	24.8	24.8	25.2	25.6	25.1	25.1	25.4	25.5	25.4	25.4	25.1
2008	24.7	25.2	25.5	25.5	25.9	25.9	25.3	25.1	25.5	25.5	25.3	25.2	25.4
2009	24.5	24.6	24.7	24.8	24.9	24.9	24.0	23.8	24.2	24.3	24.6	24.5	24.5
2010	24.5	24.9	25.2	24.1	24.2	24.5	23.8	23.7	23.9	24.2	24.3	24.1	24.3
2011	24.0	24.3	24.3	24.5	24.7	24.7	24.9	24.5	24.6	24.7	24.8	24.7	24.6
2012	24.1	24.2	24.3	24.8	25.0	25.2	25.1	24.9	24.7	24.9	24.8	24.6	24.7
2013	24.7	25.0	25.1	25.4	25.8	25.7	25.5	25.3	25.3	25.7	25.5	25.3	25.4
Government													
2002	101.2	102.2	103.4	104.6	104.7	104.4	101.3	98.6	99.7	103.2	103.6	103.1	102.5
2003	102.2	101.0	101.7	101.8	101.4	100.8	96.9	94.6	95.3	98.6	98.5	97.0	99.2
2004	95.9	96.8	97.9	97.9	98.1	97.6	94.8	92.9	93.5	96.2	97.4	96.0	96.3
2005	95.5	96.2	96.9	97.0	97.4	97.0	94.3	93.7	93.8	96.2	96.6	96.2	95.9
2006	95.7	96.5	96.7	97.3	97.8	97.4	95.1	93.7	94.3	97.7	97.6	97.5	96.4
2007	97.7	97.0	98.3	98.1	98.3	97.8	95.1	93.9	94.9	98.3	98.6	98.3	97.2
2008	99.0	98.2	99.1	98.4	99.0	98.6	94.0	94.5	98.0	98.7	98.3	97.8	97.8
2009	97.4	96.8	97.6	99.5	100.2	100.3	85.1	88.8	96.0	98.5	99.3	98.1	96.5
2010	96.0	96.2	97.6	99.4	100.9	96.6	85.0	83.5	89.9	95.4	97.0	96.1	94.5
2011	94.6	95.3	95.7	96.5	96.8	96.2	81.3	82.4	90.9	93.8	94.4	94.3	92.7
2012	91.7	92.9	94.0	94.2	94.2	94.9	81.1	83.1	90.2	93.5	94.1	94.3	91.4
2013	92.6	94.0	93.1	94.2	95.8	93.5	78.6	83.9	91.3	93.9	95.6	95.7	91.9

Employment by Industry: Seattle–Tacoma–Bellevue, WA, Selected Years, 2002–2013

(Numbers in thousands, not seasonally adjusted)

Industry and year	January	February	March	April	May	June	July	August	September	October	November	December	Annual average
Total Nonfarm													
2002	1,590.3	1,590.6	1,593.2	1,594.4	1,606.1	1,614.2	1,604.4	1,603.6	1,609.2	1,606.7	1,616.4	1,610.0	1,603.3
2003	1,575.8	1,580.2	1,581.4	1,583.5	1,596.3	1,601.2	1,592.7	1,592.3	1,601.1	1,602.5	1,610.0	1,611.3	1,594.0
2004	1,570.9	1,580.6	1,590.9	1,598.1	1,608.7	1,620.1	1,612.7	1,609.9	1,621.6	1,628.1	1,639.6	1,640.4	1,610.1
2005	1,605.6	1,612.9	1,624.5	1,635.1	1,649.6	1,660.7	1,658.8	1,659.6	1,661.6	1,675.5	1,690.2	1,695.2	1,652.4
2006	1,660.3	1,671.5	1,680.1	1,687.3	1,703.8	1,719.6	1,706.9	1,711.0	1,726.4	1,724.7	1,737.5	1,740.0	1,705.8
2007	1,707.4	1,727.4	1,735.1	1,740.4	1,757.1	1,772.2	1,764.9	1,766.7	1,770.4	1,776.1	1,790.6	1,790.8	1,758.3
2008	1,756.8	1,769.2	1,769.9	1,775.2	1,785.4	1,793.7	1,788.0	1,787.6	1,786.5	1,757.4	1,774.8	1,759.6	1,775.3
2009	1,716.6	1,710.3	1,700.4	1,691.5	1,695.3	1,696.3	1,682.7	1,668.3	1,677.0	1,674.6	1,673.0	1,669.6	1,688.0
2010	1,636.6	1,639.2	1,646.3	1,657.8	1,670.8	1,677.9	1,675.0	1,664.3	1,675.3	1,683.9	1,688.6	1,688.0	1,667.0
2011	1,657.0	1,664.9	1,670.1	1,684.9	1,694.3	1,704.5	1,706.7	1,699.7	1,708.1	1,713.2	1,721.1	1,720.9	1,695.5
2012	1,690.6	1,699.2	1,710.1	1,719.8	1,736.5	1,749.2	1,745.3	1,741.9	1,750.2	1,759.1	1,769.4	1,767.7	1,736.6
2013	1,741.6	1,751.4	1,758.2	1,768.5	1,784.5	1,794.2	1,796.1	1,796.3	1,801.7	1,802.9	1,807.8	1,811.7	1,784.6
Total Private													
2002	1,343.4	1,340.3	1,342.8	1,343.9	1,354.8	1,362.4	1,363.4	1,370.0	1,364.6	1,357.1	1,360.0	1,358.4	1,355.1
2003	1,325.3	1,326.3	1,328.0	1,330.4	1,338.9	1,346.4	1,350.8	1,355.9	1,355.2	1,351.8	1,353.8	1,356.3	1,343.3
2004	1,320.7	1,326.7	1,336.7	1,344.4	1,354.1	1,363.9	1,368.5	1,373.4	1,372.9	1,376.0	1,380.7	1,385.6	1,358.6
2005	1,353.8	1,359.1	1,369.5	1,380.4	1,394.0	1,404.2	1,414.0	1,422.6	1,412.5	1,422.5	1,431.1	1,440.7	1,400.4
2006	1,407.3	1,414.7	1,423.1	1,431.4	1,446.7	1,462.0	1,462.1	1,473.5	1,477.2	1,470.8	1,477.7	1,485.2	1,452.6
2007	1,454.3	1,470.4	1,478.0	1,483.6	1,499.2	1,513.2	1,515.2	1,523.2	1,522.5	1,519.2	1,527.7	1,531.9	1,503.2
2008	1,498.9	1,506.1	1,508.6	1,513.6	1,522.2	1,529.1	1,531.8	1,536.5	1,530.5	1,492.7	1,503.5	1,493.8	1,513.9
2009	1,451.1	1,443.6	1,433.3	1,421.3	1,425.1	1,429.2	1,424.1	1,420.8	1,419.0	1,408.9	1,405.5	1,406.3	1,424.0
2010	1,371.9	1,373.0	1,380.0	1,389.4	1,396.6	1,407.3	1,414.7	1,415.9	1,417.5	1,419.2	1,421.5	1,426.3	1,402.8
2011	1,394.1	1,400.5	1,405.8	1,420.4	1,428.6	1,441.6	1,450.6	1,454.8	1,457.7	1,451.4	1,458.1	1,462.0	1,435.5
2012	1,430.2	1,437.7	1,447.0	1,456.2	1,472.3	1,487.5	1,489.5	1,497.5	1,497.5	1,496.3	1,504.6	1,507.6	1,477.0
2013	1,479.9	1,487.7	1,494.3	1,504.0	1,519.3	1,531.1	1,541.2	1,549.9	1,547.7	1,539.6	1,542.8	1,550.0	1,524.0
Goods-Producing													
2002	282.2	279.9	279.0	277.8	280.2	281.2	280.9	282.5	278.9	275.9	272.0	268.1	278.2
2003	260.9	259.8	259.3	259.3	261.5	262.9	264.4	266.1	264.8	262.9	260.3	258.3	261.7
2004	252.9	254.1	256.4	257.5	259.8	261.8	266.0	267.4	266.6	268.1	266.9	266.3	262.0
2005	261.4	263.7	267.6	270.3	273.5	277.3	282.7	285.3	271.6	281.1	285.5	286.3	275.9
2006	283.1	286.9	288.5	290.5	294.3	299.0	301.5	303.9	305.3	304.5	303.1	302.4	296.9
2007	299.3	304.6	305.7	307.4	311.9	317.4	319.8	322.3	322.0	320.0	318.9	316.0	313.8
2008	310.9	312.8	311.8	311.0	312.8	314.0	315.7	316.7	313.4	285.4	301.3	294.5	308.4
2009	283.7	280.8	274.1	269.7	268.4	268.1	267.2	266.0	263.9	259.8	255.5	251.8	267.4
2010	247.5	246.5	246.2	247.2	248.2	250.7	254.5	255.5	255.1	254.1	251.2	249.1	250.5
2011	244.8	245.9	246.9	249.3	251.6	255.6	260.1	262.0	263.5	262.0	260.4	259.9	255.2
2012	255.6	256.8	258.6	260.5	263.8	268.9	272.0	275.2	275.6	274.9	273.9	272.5	267.4
2013	269.8	271.4	272.8	273.6	275.9	279.6	282.7	285.2	284.6	279.8	276.3	274.2	277.2
Service-Providing													
2002	1,308.1	1,310.7	1,314.2	1,316.6	1,325.9	1,333.0	1,323.5	1,321.1	1,330.3	1,330.8	1,344.4	1,341.9	1,325.0
2003	1,314.9	1,320.4	1,322.1	1,324.2	1,334.8	1,338.3	1,328.3	1,326.2	1,336.3	1,339.6	1,349.7	1,353.0	1,332.3
2004	1,318.0	1,326.5	1,334.5	1,340.6	1,348.9	1,358.3	1,346.7	1,342.5	1,355.0	1,360.0	1,372.7	1,374.1	1,348.2
2005	1,344.2	1,349.2	1,356.9	1,364.8	1,376.1	1,383.4	1,376.1	1,374.3	1,390.0	1,389.4	1,404.7	1,408.9	1,376.5
2006	1,377.2	1,384.6	1,391.6	1,396.8	1,409.5	1,420.6	1,405.4	1,407.1	1,421.1	1,420.2	1,434.4	1,437.6	1,408.8
2007	1,408.1	1,422.8	1,429.4	1,433.0	1,445.2	1,454.8	1,445.1	1,444.4	1,448.4	1,456.1	1,471.7	1,474.8	1,444.5
2008	1,445.9	1,456.4	1,458.1	1,464.2	1,472.6	1,479.7	1,472.3	1,470.9	1,473.1	1,472.0	1,473.5	1,465.1	1,467.0
2009	1,432.9	1,429.5	1,426.3	1,421.8	1,426.9	1,428.2	1,415.5	1,402.3	1,413.1	1,414.8	1,417.5	1,417.8	1,420.6
2010	1,389.1	1,392.7	1,400.1	1,410.6	1,422.6	1,427.2	1,420.5	1,408.8	1,420.2	1,429.8	1,437.4	1,438.9	1,416.5
2011	1,412.2	1,419.0	1,423.2	1,435.6	1,442.7	1,448.9	1,446.6	1,437.7	1,444.6	1,451.2	1,460.7	1,461.0	1,440.3
2012	1,435.0	1,442.4	1,451.5	1,459.3	1,472.7	1,480.3	1,473.3	1,466.7	1,474.6	1,484.2	1,495.5	1,495.2	1,469.2
2013	1,471.8	1,480.0	1,485.4	1,494.9	1,508.6	1,514.6	1,513.4	1,511.1	1,517.1	1,523.1	1,531.5	1,537.5	1,507.4
Mining and Logging													
2002	2.1	2.2	2.3	2.2	2.2	2.2	2.2	2.2	2.2	2.2	2.1	2.1	2.2
2003	2.0	2.0	2.1	1.9	1.8	1.8	1.7	1.8	1.7	1.8	1.7	1.7	1.8
2004	1.6	1.6	1.6	1.6	1.7	1.7	1.6	1.6	1.6	1.6	1.6	1.6	1.6
2005	1.5	1.5	1.5	1.5	1.5	1.5	1.5	1.5	1.5	1.5	1.5	1.5	1.5
2006	1.4	1.5	1.5	1.5	1.5	1.5	1.5	1.5	1.5	1.5	1.5	1.5	1.5
2007	1.4	1.5	1.4	1.6	1.6	1.6	1.7	1.6	1.5	1.6	1.5	1.5	1.5
2008	1.3	1.4	1.4	1.4	1.4	1.4	1.4	1.4	1.4	1.4	1.3	1.3	1.4
2009	1.3	1.3	1.2	1.1	1.1	1.1	1.1	1.1	1.1	1.1	1.1	1.0	1.1
2010	1.0	1.1	1.0	1.0	1.1	1.1	1.1	1.1	1.1	1.1	1.0	1.0	1.1
2011	1.0	1.0	1.0	1.0	1.0	1.0	1.0	1.0	1.0	1.1	1.1	1.1	1.0
2012	1.0	1.0	1.0	1.0	1.0	1.0	1.0	1.1	1.0	1.1	1.0	1.0	1.0
2013	1.0	1.0	1.0	1.0	1.0	1.1	1.1	1.1	1.1	1.1	1.1	1.1	1.1
Construction													
2002	88.4	88.9	88.9	89.1	91.4	92.8	94.6	97.5	96.5	94.5	92.2	89.6	92.0
2003	86.2	86.4	86.6	88.3	90.9	92.8	94.9	97.0	96.6	95.7	94.0	92.4	91.8
2004	88.8	90.3	91.9	92.7	94.6	96.2	99.2	100.4	99.4	99.9	98.6	97.3	95.8
2005	93.1	94.9	97.1	98.9	101.1	103.2	106.5	108.7	109.9	108.9	107.9	107.9	103.2
2006	104.3	106.8	108.8	110.6	113.4	116.4	117.9	120.1	120.5	119.8	117.6	116.5	114.4
2007	114.4	117.5	119.7	121.6	124.9	128.2	128.8	131.1	130.3	128.3	126.4	124.5	124.6
2008	120.0	120.2	120.7	120.7	121.7	122.5	123.7	124.1	122.2	119.0	113.3	108.4	119.7
2009	101.2	98.8	97.0	94.8	94.8	94.9	94.7	94.0	93.1	90.6	87.0	84.3	93.8
2010	80.4	79.6	79.8	80.6	81.9	82.9	85.6	86.6	85.9	85.1	81.8	79.7	82.5
2011	75.5	75.3	75.5	76.6	78.2	80.1	82.1	83.2	83.4	82.1	79.9	79.0	79.2
2012	75.0	76.1	76.8	78.4	80.6	83.2	85.1	87.2	87.4	87.3	85.9	85.1	82.3
2013	82.4	83.8	84.5	85.7	87.8	89.7	92.6	94.9	94.5	90.8	88.2	86.4	88.4

Employment by Industry: Seattle–Tacoma–Bellevue, WA, Selected Years, 2002–2013—*Continued*

(Numbers in thousands, not seasonally adjusted)

Industry and year	January	February	March	April	May	June	July	August	September	October	November	December	Annual average
Manufacturing													
2002	191.7	188.8	187.8	186.5	186.6	186.2	184.1	182.8	180.2	179.2	177.7	176.4	184.0
2003	172.7	171.4	170.6	169.1	168.8	168.3	167.8	167.3	166.5	165.4	164.6	164.2	168.1
2004	162.5	162.2	162.9	163.2	163.5	163.9	165.2	165.4	165.6	166.6	166.7	167.4	164.6
2005	166.8	167.3	169.0	169.9	170.9	172.6	174.7	175.1	160.2	175.7	176.1	176.9	171.3
2006	177.4	178.6	178.2	178.4	179.4	181.1	182.1	182.3	183.3	183.2	184.0	184.4	181.0
2007	183.5	185.6	184.6	184.2	185.4	187.6	189.3	189.6	190.2	190.1	191.0	190.0	187.6
2008	189.6	191.2	189.7	188.9	189.7	190.1	190.6	191.2	189.8	165.0	186.7	184.8	187.3
2009	181.2	180.7	175.9	173.8	172.5	172.1	171.4	170.9	169.7	168.1	167.4	166.5	172.5
2010	166.1	165.8	165.4	165.6	165.2	166.7	167.8	167.8	168.1	167.9	168.4	168.4	166.9
2011	168.3	169.6	170.4	171.7	172.4	174.5	177.0	177.8	179.1	178.8	179.4	179.8	174.9
2012	179.6	179.7	180.8	181.1	182.2	184.7	185.9	186.9	187.2	186.5	187.0	186.4	184.0
2013	186.4	186.6	187.3	186.9	187.1	188.8	189.0	189.2	189.0	187.9	187.0	186.7	187.7
Trade, Transportation, and Utilities													
2002	308.9	304.5	304.0	303.7	306.0	308.4	309.5	309.5	308.6	308.6	313.1	316.7	308.5
2003	304.4	301.3	300.8	300.3	302.0	304.0	306.5	306.1	305.2	305.8	311.2	316.1	305.3
2004	301.3	300.1	301.3	303.5	305.6	308.0	308.6	310.1	309.2	310.8	316.0	320.4	307.9
2005	307.0	305.6	306.6	307.2	310.4	312.3	313.6	315.3	315.0	315.7	322.0	327.7	313.2
2006	313.8	311.4	312.5	312.5	315.6	318.9	318.9	320.6	319.8	319.2	326.1	331.3	318.4
2007	319.5	319.0	319.5	320.1	322.9	325.3	326.8	327.4	325.8	326.7	334.3	338.2	325.5
2008	326.5	324.4	324.2	323.7	324.6	326.0	327.4	328.5	325.3	323.9	325.4	327.6	325.6
2009	312.9	307.5	304.8	301.8	303.4	303.8	304.3	303.9	303.4	301.6	304.9	308.4	305.1
2010	297.1	295.2	295.5	297.0	298.8	301.2	302.4	303.1	302.0	304.1	308.9	314.1	301.6
2011	301.7	300.5	301.4	302.7	305.1	308.0	310.5	311.5	310.2	310.3	316.2	319.8	308.2
2012	308.6	306.6	308.0	308.8	313.0	317.1	319.5	320.2	319.1	320.0	326.9	329.3	316.4
2013	319.3	317.3	317.8	318.9	323.4	326.1	329.3	331.1	329.8	331.3	337.4	342.0	327.0
Wholesale Trade													
2002	77.6	77.6	77.7	77.2	77.5	77.6	77.2	77.3	76.8	75.9	75.8	75.8	77.0
2003	75.7	75.8	76.0	75.8	75.9	75.9	76.4	76.3	76.0	75.9	75.9	76.1	76.0
2004	75.7	76.1	76.7	77.1	77.2	77.2	77.7	77.5	77.4	77.2	77.0	77.3	77.0
2005	76.6	76.9	77.4	77.6	78.0	78.4	78.9	79.3	79.4	79.4	79.6	80.2	78.5
2006	80.2	80.4	80.9	80.7	81.3	81.8	82.1	82.2	82.2	81.8	82.1	82.2	81.5
2007	81.6	82.0	82.3	82.4	83.0	83.5	83.7	83.8	83.5	83.6	84.0	84.4	83.2
2008	83.5	83.9	84.0	84.0	84.4	84.6	84.4	84.6	84.1	83.5	83.0	82.6	83.9
2009	81.8	80.8	80.2	79.4	79.1	79.0	78.9	78.3	78.0	77.5	77.2	77.2	79.0
2010	76.1	76.4	76.5	76.8	76.9	76.9	77.0	77.0	76.7	76.8	77.0	77.0	76.8
2011	76.4	76.7	76.9	77.3	77.6	77.8	78.1	78.0	77.8	77.6	77.5	77.8	77.5
2012	77.2	77.3	77.7	78.1	78.4	78.8	79.3	79.7	79.3	79.0	79.2	79.5	78.6
2013	78.9	79.5	79.8	79.9	80.2	80.7	81.2	81.4	81.4	82.3	82.4	81.9	80.8
Retail Trade													
2002	171.4	167.0	167.1	167.2	168.5	170.1	170.7	170.6	170.3	170.9	176.0	179.7	170.8
2003	168.7	166.1	165.7	165.4	166.6	168.1	169.5	169.3	168.7	169.6	175.2	179.3	169.4
2004	167.2	165.7	166.0	166.7	168.5	169.8	169.6	171.3	170.0	171.2	176.8	180.6	170.3
2005	170.3	168.0	168.3	169.1	171.3	172.3	173.4	174.8	173.9	175.1	180.8	184.8	173.5
2006	172.9	170.3	170.6	170.5	172.3	174.3	174.2	175.6	174.5	175.2	181.8	185.5	174.8
2007	176.2	175.1	175.0	174.9	176.7	177.8	179.3	179.6	178.5	179.4	186.7	189.3	179.0
2008	180.8	177.9	177.8	177.3	177.2	178.1	179.5	180.6	178.5	178.7	181.1	183.0	179.2
2009	170.6	167.7	166.1	164.0	165.6	166.3	166.8	167.2	166.9	166.5	170.5	173.1	167.6
2010	165.0	163.0	163.1	164.2	165.5	167.1	167.6	168.3	167.5	169.6	174.3	177.8	167.8
2011	168.3	166.6	166.5	167.0	168.9	171.0	172.2	173.3	172.0	173.4	178.9	181.3	171.6
2012	172.7	170.4	171.0	171.3	174.1	176.9	178.7	178.9	178.5	180.3	186.6	188.1	177.3
2013	180.4	178.2	178.3	179.1	182.4	184.4	186.7	188.0	186.6	187.1	193.7	197.8	185.2
Transportation and Utilities													
2002	59.9	59.9	59.2	59.3	60.0	60.7	61.6	61.6	61.5	61.8	61.3	61.2	60.7
2003	60.0	59.4	59.1	59.1	59.5	60.0	60.6	60.5	60.5	60.3	60.1	60.7	60.0
2004	58.4	58.3	58.6	59.7	59.9	61.0	61.3	61.3	61.8	62.4	62.2	62.5	60.6
2005	60.1	60.7	60.9	60.5	61.1	61.6	61.3	61.2	61.7	61.2	61.6	62.7	61.2
2006	60.7	60.7	61.0	61.2	62.0	62.8	62.6	62.8	63.1	62.2	62.2	63.6	62.1
2007	61.7	61.9	62.2	62.8	63.2	64.0	63.8	64.0	63.8	63.7	63.6	64.5	63.3
2008	62.2	62.6	62.4	62.4	63.0	63.3	63.5	63.3	62.7	61.7	61.3	62.0	62.5
2009	60.5	59.0	58.5	58.4	58.7	58.5	58.6	58.4	58.5	57.6	57.2	58.1	58.5
2010	56.0	55.8	55.9	56.0	56.4	57.2	57.8	57.8	57.8	57.7	57.6	59.3	57.1
2011	57.0	57.2	58.0	58.4	58.6	59.2	60.2	60.2	60.4	59.3	59.8	60.7	59.1
2012	58.7	58.9	59.3	59.4	60.5	61.4	61.5	61.6	61.3	60.7	61.1	61.7	60.5
2013	60.0	59.6	59.7	59.9	60.8	61.0	61.4	61.7	61.8	61.9	61.3	62.3	61.0
Information													
2002	76.6	76.4	76.0	75.6	75.7	76.0	76.2	76.2	75.5	75.5	75.8	75.6	75.9
2003	74.6	74.5	74.0	73.6	74.1	74.3	74.7	75.4	75.0	75.1	75.4	75.8	74.7
2004	74.9	74.9	75.2	75.1	75.6	76.0	76.3	76.5	75.8	76.2	76.6	76.9	75.8
2005	76.2	76.8	76.6	76.8	77.1	77.3	78.1	78.8	78.1	77.6	78.4	78.9	77.6
2006	77.9	78.1	78.7	79.2	79.8	82.1	82.5	83.3	83.4	82.8	83.6	84.0	81.3
2007	83.3	84.3	83.9	84.3	85.1	85.9	86.1	86.4	86.0	85.1	86.2	86.4	85.3
2008	85.9	87.0	87.2	87.5	88.0	89.1	90.4	91.2	90.2	89.6	90.6	90.7	89.0
2009	88.9	89.4	89.1	87.8	88.4	88.6	88.9	88.4	87.6	87.0	87.3	87.1	88.2
2010	86.6	86.9	86.8	86.5	87.0	88.1	88.3	88.8	88.7	87.9	88.3	88.6	87.7
2011	87.2	88.0	87.7	87.8	88.0	89.1	90.1	90.4	89.6	88.9	89.2	88.9	88.7
2012	88.8	89.3	89.0	88.8	89.6	90.7	90.7	91.0	89.7	89.1	89.6	89.5	89.7
2013	89.0	89.8	89.3	89.7	90.3	91.1	92.4	93.0	92.1	91.3	91.5	90.7	90.9

Employment by Industry: Seattle–Tacoma–Bellevue, WA, Selected Years, 2002–2013—*Continued*

(Numbers in thousands, not seasonally adjusted)

Industry and year	January	February	March	April	May	June	July	August	September	October	November	December	Annual average
Financial Activities													
2002	101.3	101.9	102.3	102.3	102.7	102.8	103.1	103.7	103.6	103.6	104.3	104.6	103.0
2003	104.1	104.6	104.8	105.2	106.0	106.3	107.2	107.7	107.2	107.0	106.8	106.5	106.1
2004	105.2	105.2	106.0	105.2	105.4	105.8	106.1	106.2	105.7	105.6	105.5	106.4	105.7
2005	104.3	104.7	104.8	105.1	105.7	106.2	107.7	108.4	108.1	108.3	108.5	108.9	106.7
2006	107.6	108.0	107.8	107.9	108.1	108.3	108.6	108.5	107.8	107.5	107.3	107.6	107.9
2007	106.4	106.7	107.2	107.3	107.3	107.6	107.9	107.9	106.7	106.8	107.2	107.1	107.2
2008	106.0	106.0	105.8	105.4	106.0	105.8	105.3	105.3	104.3	102.9	102.6	102.0	104.8
2009	100.0	99.9	98.7	98.1	97.9	97.8	96.9	96.1	95.5	94.4	93.8	93.6	96.9
2010	91.9	91.7	91.7	91.8	91.8	92.0	92.8	92.3	92.2	92.2	92.1	92.4	92.1
2011	91.4	91.6	91.7	92.1	92.0	92.2	92.6	92.5	92.3	91.9	92.2	92.2	92.1
2012	91.1	91.4	91.7	91.9	92.7	93.3	94.2	94.1	94.0	94.3	94.8	95.2	93.2
2013	95.0	95.5	96.1	96.3	96.9	97.2	98.0	98.1	97.5	97.1	97.6	97.3	96.9
Professional and Business Services													
2002	193.3	194.5	195.1	196.3	197.3	198.4	199.8	202.4	201.7	200.9	201.7	199.0	198.4
2003	192.8	194.1	194.3	195.1	195.1	195.8	197.1	199.2	199.0	199.5	199.1	198.1	196.6
2004	193.7	196.6	198.3	200.7	201.5	203.3	205.7	207.2	207.1	209.0	209.5	208.3	203.4
2005	203.6	206.2	207.4	210.1	212.0	213.8	216.8	218.9	220.6	220.4	221.3	221.2	214.4
2006	215.2	217.4	219.6	222.6	225.2	228.3	229.9	232.7	233.3	233.6	234.5	234.6	227.2
2007	228.0	232.3	234.7	235.2	237.1	239.7	240.6	242.6	243.0	242.4	243.2	244.1	238.6
2008	237.5	239.5	240.5	243.2	244.4	244.9	245.7	245.5	244.9	242.8	238.3	234.5	241.8
2009	228.3	226.3	224.4	221.4	220.0	221.1	219.9	219.5	219.7	218.8	218.4	219.2	221.4
2010	212.1	213.2	216.1	218.6	219.2	220.8	223.8	223.0	223.9	225.1	225.1	225.8	220.6
2011	220.3	222.5	223.9	228.0	227.9	229.3	232.5	233.1	233.9	234.3	234.7	234.6	229.6
2012	228.9	231.3	232.6	236.4	238.6	240.8	239.8	242.6	242.7	244.1	244.8	244.6	238.9
2013	240.2	242.3	242.8	245.2	246.9	249.0	250.0	252.6	252.6	252.7	252.1	252.9	248.3
Education and Health Services													
2002	188.3	190.2	191.0	190.6	191.4	189.9	186.5	186.7	189.0	192.4	194.2	193.9	190.3
2003	192.2	194.4	195.7	196.3	196.3	194.9	191.6	191.1	193.2	196.0	197.0	196.2	194.6
2004	193.3	194.8	195.4	195.6	196.2	194.7	190.6	190.8	193.6	196.8	197.9	197.0	194.7
2005	195.7	197.2	198.5	199.6	200.4	198.1	194.2	194.7	198.5	200.8	201.8	201.0	198.4
2006	199.4	201.4	202.5	202.7	203.7	201.3	196.4	197.3	200.9	203.9	204.7	204.3	201.5
2007	203.1	205.6	207.2	207.5	208.9	206.2	202.4	203.0	206.5	211.6	212.9	212.5	207.3
2008	210.1	213.1	213.3	214.3	215.6	214.4	211.3	211.9	215.2	220.1	220.8	220.8	215.1
2009	220.5	222.8	223.8	223.8	225.3	224.2	220.4	220.5	224.1	229.7	230.6	230.7	224.7
2010	228.0	230.0	231.1	231.6	232.4	230.9	227.2	226.8	230.6	235.8	237.3	236.0	231.5
2011	235.0	237.5	238.2	238.6	238.6	237.4	234.2	233.6	236.8	240.0	242.0	240.9	237.7
2012	238.2	240.9	242.5	241.8	242.8	240.9	236.2	235.9	238.8	242.4	244.0	244.0	240.7
2013	240.1	244.0	244.8	245.3	245.6	243.1	241.4	241.3	244.9	248.8	250.9	252.3	245.2
Leisure and Hospitality													
2002	135.0	134.9	137.0	138.6	142.0	145.3	146.4	147.7	146.9	140.7	139.3	140.6	141.2
2003	137.1	138.0	139.3	140.9	143.6	147.3	148.3	149.5	150.4	145.8	144.1	145.1	144.1
2004	140.3	141.4	144.0	146.3	148.9	152.5	153.0	153.0	153.3	148.5	147.3	149.1	148.1
2005	145.1	144.0	146.5	149.9	153.1	156.7	158.2	158.5	158.5	152.1	152.1	154.7	152.5
2006	149.3	150.0	151.6	154.0	157.5	160.8	161.3	164.0	163.7	157.5	156.5	158.7	157.1
2007	153.7	155.9	157.3	159.5	163.0	167.4	168.0	169.6	169.1	163.7	161.9	164.3	162.8
2008	159.3	160.0	161.9	164.3	165.9	169.6	170.2	171.5	171.6	163.6	160.1	159.9	164.8
2009	153.3	153.3	154.4	154.9	157.8	161.3	162.0	162.1	161.5	154.8	152.6	152.9	156.7
2010	147.4	148.0	150.8	154.5	156.4	159.9	161.2	161.8	161.5	156.1	154.5	156.4	155.7
2011	150.7	151.2	152.4	157.5	160.3	164.0	163.9	165.2	165.6	158.7	158.1	160.1	159.0
2012	154.4	156.1	158.7	161.8	165.2	168.4	169.0	170.7	170.2	164.5	163.5	165.6	164.0
2013	161.2	161.6	164.5	168.3	172.9	177.0	178.4	179.7	178.3	170.9	169.6	172.2	171.2
Other Services													
2002	57.8	58.0	58.4	59.0	59.5	60.4	61.0	61.3	60.4	59.5	59.6	59.9	59.6
2003	59.2	59.6	59.8	59.7	60.3	60.9	61.0	60.8	60.4	59.7	59.9	60.2	60.1
2004	59.1	59.6	60.1	60.5	61.1	61.8	62.2	62.2	61.6	61.0	61.0	61.2	61.0
2005	60.5	60.9	61.5	61.4	61.8	62.5	62.7	62.7	62.1	61.5	61.5	62.0	61.8
2006	61.0	61.5	61.9	62.0	62.5	63.3	63.0	63.2	63.0	61.8	61.9	62.3	62.3
2007	61.0	62.0	62.5	62.3	63.0	63.7	63.6	64.0	63.4	62.9	63.1	63.3	62.9
2008	62.7	63.3	63.9	64.2	64.9	65.3	65.8	65.9	65.6	64.4	64.4	63.8	64.5
2009	63.5	63.6	64.0	63.8	63.9	64.3	64.5	64.3	63.3	62.8	62.4	62.6	63.6
2010	61.3	61.5	61.8	62.2	62.8	63.7	64.5	64.6	63.5	63.9	64.1	63.9	63.2
2011	63.0	63.3	63.6	64.4	65.1	66.0	66.7	66.5	65.8	65.3	65.3	65.6	65.1
2012	64.6	65.3	65.9	66.2	66.6	67.4	68.1	67.8	67.4	67.0	67.1	66.9	66.7
2013	65.3	65.8	66.2	66.7	67.4	68.0	69.0	68.9	67.9	67.7	67.4	68.4	67.4
Government													
2002	246.9	250.3	250.4	250.5	251.3	251.8	241.0	233.6	244.6	249.6	256.4	251.6	248.2
2003	250.5	253.9	253.4	253.1	257.4	254.8	241.9	236.4	245.9	250.7	256.2	255.0	250.8
2004	250.2	253.9	254.2	253.7	254.6	256.2	244.2	236.5	248.7	252.1	258.9	254.8	251.5
2005	251.8	253.8	255.0	254.7	255.6	256.5	244.8	237.0	249.1	253.0	259.1	254.5	252.1
2006	253.0	256.8	257.0	255.9	257.1	257.6	244.8	237.5	249.2	253.9	259.8	254.8	253.1
2007	253.1	257.0	257.1	256.8	257.9	259.0	249.7	243.5	247.9	256.9	262.9	258.9	255.1
2008	257.9	263.1	261.3	261.6	263.2	264.6	256.2	251.1	256.0	264.7	271.3	265.8	261.4
2009	265.5	266.7	267.1	270.2	270.2	267.1	258.6	247.5	258.0	265.7	267.5	263.3	264.0
2010	264.7	266.2	266.3	268.4	274.2	270.6	260.3	248.4	257.8	264.7	267.1	261.7	264.2
2011	262.9	264.4	264.3	264.5	265.7	262.9	256.1	244.9	250.4	261.8	263.0	258.9	260.0
2012	260.4	261.5	263.1	263.6	264.2	261.7	255.8	244.4	252.7	262.8	264.8	260.1	259.6
2013	261.7	263.7	263.9	264.5	265.2	263.1	254.9	246.4	254.0	263.3	265.0	261.7	260.6

Employment by Industry: St. Louis, MO–IL, Selected Years, 2002–2013

(Numbers in thousands, not seasonally adjusted)

Industry and year	January	February	March	April	May	June	July	August	September	October	November	December	Annual average
Total Nonfarm													
2002	1,309.2	1,312.0	1,321.0	1,333.4	1,341.2	1,351.2	1,324.9	1,330.0	1,340.6	1,340.5	1,342.3	1,345.4	1,332.6
2003	1,309.6	1,308.9	1,317.5	1,326.4	1,333.2	1,337.9	1,315.2	1,318.1	1,326.1	1,331.1	1,327.8	1,329.7	1,323.5
2004	1,296.2	1,294.7	1,310.2	1,323.8	1,331.1	1,335.9	1,313.7	1,320.4	1,332.0	1,338.5	1,339.3	1,341.5	1,323.1
2005	1,307.8	1,313.6	1,325.6	1,345.0	1,349.1	1,353.4	1,330.2	1,341.1	1,351.1	1,349.5	1,352.1	1,354.6	1,339.4
2006	1,323.0	1,327.9	1,339.3	1,355.0	1,362.0	1,369.6	1,346.6	1,349.4	1,364.3	1,366.0	1,365.9	1,371.0	1,353.3
2007	1,332.0	1,335.4	1,352.4	1,364.6	1,377.8	1,378.5	1,349.5	1,357.8	1,370.6	1,373.0	1,376.8	1,378.3	1,362.2
2008	1,344.9	1,350.9	1,354.5	1,366.2	1,379.2	1,382.4	1,348.9	1,357.1	1,364.3	1,358.6	1,350.7	1,344.4	1,358.5
2009	1,303.8	1,302.8	1,304.9	1,313.5	1,318.2	1,314.9	1,285.9	1,291.7	1,297.7	1,296.7	1,294.4	1,295.5	1,301.7
2010	1,267.2	1,272.5	1,284.1	1,297.3	1,306.0	1,302.6	1,279.3	1,291.7	1,297.6	1,305.1	1,304.4	1,301.8	1,292.5
2011	1,278.0	1,280.8	1,293.7	1,315.4	1,320.8	1,316.5	1,297.3	1,305.6	1,313.7	1,314.7	1,313.3	1,314.2	1,305.3
2012	1,281.8	1,287.1	1,299.5	1,312.2	1,320.3	1,316.8	1,292.3	1,301.6	1,309.4	1,316.3	1,316.7	1,319.0	1,306.1
2013	1,287.3	1,294.5	1,301.3	1,320.4	1,330.4	1,326.0	1,306.1	1,315.7	1,322.9	1,326.2	1,325.9	1,325.9	1,315.2
Total Private													
2002	1,139.0	1,140.5	1,149.0	1,161.4	1,167.4	1,180.9	1,176.9	1,178.8	1,171.6	1,168.7	1,169.3	1,172.6	1,164.7
2003	1,140.6	1,138.3	1,146.4	1,154.3	1,159.9	1,167.5	1,165.9	1,167.0	1,158.5	1,161.3	1,157.1	1,159.3	1,156.3
2004	1,128.2	1,125.3	1,140.3	1,153.3	1,159.4	1,168.6	1,165.1	1,168.4	1,163.8	1,168.6	1,168.4	1,170.6	1,156.7
2005	1,140.6	1,143.3	1,155.4	1,173.0	1,176.2	1,184.5	1,179.4	1,184.9	1,181.6	1,179.0	1,180.1	1,183.1	1,171.8
2006	1,155.1	1,157.1	1,168.2	1,182.7	1,188.6	1,202.1	1,195.6	1,194.6	1,193.8	1,193.7	1,192.5	1,197.5	1,185.1
2007	1,162.4	1,162.7	1,179.6	1,191.4	1,203.4	1,210.1	1,203.0	1,204.4	1,199.5	1,198.9	1,201.5	1,203.3	1,193.4
2008	1,173.9	1,175.5	1,180.0	1,191.3	1,202.3	1,211.8	1,199.3	1,200.1	1,190.4	1,181.8	1,173.8	1,168.0	1,187.4
2009	1,130.7	1,127.3	1,128.6	1,133.4	1,138.0	1,139.7	1,134.1	1,131.9	1,121.7	1,119.5	1,117.7	1,118.7	1,128.4
2010	1,094.9	1,097.4	1,108.7	1,119.9	1,124.4	1,132.2	1,131.7	1,133.0	1,126.6	1,132.2	1,131.2	1,129.4	1,121.8
2011	1,108.7	1,109.8	1,122.0	1,142.6	1,147.1	1,151.7	1,152.9	1,152.7	1,144.2	1,144.6	1,143.2	1,143.8	1,138.6
2012	1,116.1	1,118.5	1,130.1	1,141.6	1,149.0	1,154.0	1,150.4	1,151.1	1,143.2	1,149.0	1,149.4	1,151.5	1,142.0
2013	1,124.1	1,128.2	1,134.4	1,152.4	1,161.8	1,165.9	1,167.4	1,168.5	1,160.1	1,162.1	1,161.3	1,161.0	1,153.9
Goods-Producing													
2002	231.9	232.5	234.5	235.6	236.0	239.6	240.4	239.4	238.1	235.7	234.7	234.3	236.1
2003	226.4	224.4	227.3	228.5	230.3	233.1	231.3	233.6	230.5	229.9	228.2	226.9	229.2
2004	220.4	218.7	223.8	226.0	227.5	230.6	225.4	231.2	230.3	228.4	227.2	226.4	226.3
2005	219.4	219.8	223.2	225.9	227.5	229.5	224.5	229.7	229.1	228.4	227.4	225.9	225.9
2006	220.1	220.2	222.7	224.4	225.0	229.3	228.4	225.8	227.3	225.4	224.1	222.7	224.6
2007	214.2	214.0	219.4	220.9	224.0	225.3	222.4	223.8	223.0	222.1	220.9	218.7	220.7
2008	209.3	210.0	209.0	211.7	215.1	219.1	214.3	214.3	213.5	209.9	204.8	200.3	210.9
2009	187.8	186.3	185.6	182.3	181.5	181.4	182.0	179.2	177.2	175.7	172.6	170.1	180.1
2010	163.6	162.7	166.3	168.8	169.4	173.2	173.3	173.2	172.8	173.7	172.5	170.7	170.0
2011	167.9	168.1	171.9	175.4	176.7	179.1	180.0	179.1	176.9	174.5	172.1	171.0	174.4
2012	164.8	164.6	167.2	169.5	171.5	173.7	174.1	174.1	172.3	172.0	170.3	169.9	170.3
2013	164.9	165.6	166.4	169.7	172.6	176.2	176.7	176.6	175.5	174.8	174.2	169.7	171.9
Service-Providing													
2002	1,077.3	1,079.5	1,086.5	1,097.8	1,105.2	1,111.6	1,084.5	1,090.6	1,102.5	1,104.8	1,107.6	1,111.1	1,096.6
2003	1,083.2	1,084.5	1,090.2	1,097.9	1,102.9	1,104.8	1,083.9	1,084.5	1,095.6	1,101.2	1,099.6	1,102.8	1,094.3
2004	1,075.8	1,076.0	1,086.4	1,097.8	1,103.6	1,105.3	1,088.3	1,089.2	1,101.7	1,110.1	1,112.1	1,115.1	1,096.8
2005	1,088.4	1,093.8	1,102.4	1,119.1	1,121.6	1,123.9	1,105.7	1,111.4	1,122.0	1,121.1	1,124.7	1,128.7	1,113.6
2006	1,102.9	1,107.7	1,116.6	1,130.6	1,137.0	1,140.3	1,118.2	1,123.6	1,137.0	1,140.6	1,141.8	1,148.3	1,128.7
2007	1,117.8	1,121.4	1,133.0	1,143.7	1,153.8	1,153.2	1,127.1	1,134.0	1,147.6	1,150.9	1,155.9	1,159.6	1,141.5
2008	1,135.6	1,140.9	1,145.5	1,154.5	1,164.1	1,163.3	1,134.6	1,142.8	1,150.8	1,148.7	1,145.9	1,144.1	1,147.6
2009	1,116.0	1,116.5	1,119.3	1,131.2	1,136.7	1,133.5	1,103.9	1,112.5	1,120.5	1,121.0	1,121.8	1,125.4	1,121.5
2010	1,103.6	1,109.8	1,117.8	1,128.5	1,136.6	1,129.4	1,106.0	1,118.5	1,124.8	1,131.4	1,131.9	1,131.1	1,122.5
2011	1,110.1	1,112.7	1,121.8	1,140.0	1,144.1	1,137.4	1,117.3	1,126.5	1,136.8	1,140.2	1,141.2	1,143.2	1,130.9
2012	1,117.0	1,122.5	1,132.3	1,142.7	1,148.8	1,143.1	1,118.2	1,127.5	1,137.1	1,144.3	1,146.4	1,149.1	1,135.8
2013	1,122.4	1,128.9	1,134.9	1,150.7	1,157.8	1,149.8	1,129.4	1,139.1	1,147.4	1,151.4	1,151.7	1,156.2	1,143.3
Mining, Logging, and Construction													
2002	73.8	73.5	75.3	77.1	78.0	81.0	82.8	82.3	81.2	80.1	78.8	77.9	78.5
2003	72.8	71.1	73.5	76.4	78.2	80.6	82.9	82.9	81.8	81.7	80.3	78.8	78.4
2004	74.0	72.2	77.0	79.8	81.1	83.1	84.8	84.3	83.6	82.1	81.1	80.0	80.3
2005	74.3	74.8	78.1	80.5	82.2	83.7	85.2	85.2	84.6	83.8	82.8	81.1	81.4
2006	78.2	78.0	79.8	82.4	83.0	86.0	86.1	86.0	85.1	83.8	82.5	80.8	82.6
2007	77.4	74.4	79.9	81.4	84.3	87.2	86.7	86.6	84.7	84.1	83.0	80.4	82.5
2008	76.2	74.1	76.5	78.4	80.4	82.5	82.7	82.6	81.1	78.4	75.4	72.0	78.4
2009	64.3	63.3	64.9	65.1	65.9	67.1	68.1	67.1	66.1	64.9	62.5	60.3	65.0
2010	55.2	54.2	57.5	59.7	59.9	62.7	62.9	62.7	62.3	62.3	60.9	58.8	59.9
2011	56.9	56.9	60.2	63.4	64.4	65.7	65.9	65.2	63.1	60.9	59.0	57.4	61.6
2012	52.2	51.8	53.9	56.1	57.7	59.2	60.0	60.4	59.9	59.3	57.9	57.3	57.1
2013	52.6	52.7	53.9	56.8	59.4	62.1	63.4	62.6	61.8	61.1	60.6	56.6	58.6
Manufacturing													
2002	158.1	159.0	159.2	158.5	158.0	158.6	157.6	157.1	156.9	155.6	155.9	156.4	157.6
2003	153.6	153.3	153.8	152.1	152.1	152.5	148.4	150.7	148.7	148.2	147.9	148.1	150.8
2004	146.4	146.5	146.8	146.2	146.4	147.5	140.6	146.9	146.7	146.3	146.1	146.4	146.1
2005	145.1	145.0	145.1	145.4	145.3	145.8	139.3	144.5	144.5	144.6	144.6	144.8	144.5
2006	141.9	142.2	142.9	142.0	142.0	143.3	142.3	139.8	142.2	141.6	141.6	141.9	142.0
2007	136.8	139.6	139.5	139.5	139.7	138.1	135.7	137.2	138.3	138.0	137.9	138.3	138.2
2008	133.1	135.9	132.5	133.3	134.7	136.6	131.6	131.7	132.4	131.5	129.4	128.3	132.6
2009	123.5	123.0	120.7	117.2	115.6	114.3	113.9	112.1	111.1	110.8	110.1	109.8	115.2
2010	108.4	108.5	108.8	109.1	109.5	110.5	110.4	110.5	110.5	111.4	111.6	111.9	110.1
2011	111.0	111.2	111.7	112.0	112.3	113.4	114.1	113.9	113.8	113.6	113.1	113.6	112.8
2012	112.6	112.8	113.3	113.4	113.8	114.5	114.1	113.7	112.4	112.7	112.4	112.6	113.2
2013	112.3	112.9	112.5	112.9	113.2	114.1	113.3	114.0	113.7	113.7	113.6	113.1	113.3

Employment by Industry: St. Louis, MO–IL, Selected Years, 2002–2013—*Continued*

(Numbers in thousands, not seasonally adjusted)

Industry and year	January	February	March	April	May	June	July	August	September	October	November	December	Annual average
Trade, Transportation, and Utilities													
2002	256.1	252.2	253.4	254.4	256.1	258.9	256.9	257.5	258.7	258.5	263.5	267.1	257.8
2003	258.8	254.8	255.3	256.0	256.5	256.0	255.7	255.0	254.3	259.1	261.3	264.0	257.2
2004	251.7	248.2	249.8	250.7	252.7	253.3	253.6	252.1	252.1	254.8	259.9	263.2	253.5
2005	253.5	250.4	251.9	253.5	254.5	254.8	254.9	255.4	254.0	254.8	259.7	262.9	255.0
2006	252.9	249.8	251.2	252.4	254.1	255.5	254.3	255.0	254.9	256.6	261.3	265.1	255.3
2007	256.1	253.0	256.1	257.3	259.6	260.3	258.8	258.1	258.4	259.4	265.5	268.2	259.2
2008	260.2	256.7	257.8	258.1	259.6	260.7	258.4	258.8	257.4	256.9	259.5	260.8	258.7
2009	250.5	247.1	246.5	246.6	247.3	246.9	244.3	245.3	244.7	244.1	247.7	249.2	246.7
2010	240.8	238.4	240.0	240.7	242.2	242.4	241.2	242.5	241.2	242.1	245.8	248.5	242.2
2011	241.6	239.9	241.1	244.0	245.0	245.0	244.2	244.9	243.9	244.2	249.0	251.2	244.5
2012	242.9	240.7	242.2	244.2	245.8	245.7	244.8	246.0	245.6	247.6	252.9	254.8	246.1
2013	244.6	241.9	242.3	244.2	246.0	246.3	245.9	247.5	246.7	247.3	251.2	254.2	246.5
Wholesale Trade													
2002	56.6	56.5	56.7	56.7	56.9	57.2	56.8	56.8	56.5	56.2	56.0	55.9	56.6
2003	57.1	56.9	56.9	57.5	57.5	57.7	58.5	58.5	57.8	57.9	57.8	57.9	57.7
2004	58.2	58.2	58.6	58.6	58.7	59.1	60.4	59.7	59.5	58.9	58.9	59.1	59.0
2005	59.8	59.2	59.4	59.8	59.8	60.2	60.6	60.8	60.0	59.7	59.8	60.1	59.9
2006	59.5	59.4	59.7	60.5	60.8	61.5	61.6	61.7	61.5	61.5	61.5	62.0	60.9
2007	61.4	61.6	62.0	61.8	62.2	62.7	63.0	62.9	62.7	62.8	62.9	63.1	62.4
2008	62.8	62.8	62.9	63.2	63.4	63.8	63.7	63.7	63.3	62.7	62.2	62.1	63.1
2009	60.9	60.6	60.3	60.0	59.7	59.9	59.7	59.5	59.0	59.4	59.1	59.4	59.8
2010	58.7	58.6	59.0	60.8	60.8	60.7	60.4	60.0	59.7	59.7	59.5	59.7	59.8
2011	59.3	59.3	59.5	59.7	59.8	60.2	60.6	60.4	60.1	60.1	60.2	60.2	60.0
2012	59.9	59.9	60.2	60.8	61.1	61.5	61.3	61.6	61.1	61.2	61.2	61.4	60.9
2013	60.1	60.1	60.2	60.2	60.7	61.1	61.3	61.4	61.2	61.9	61.7	61.8	61.0
Retail Trade													
2002	146.1	142.8	143.5	143.9	145.0	146.8	146.0	146.4	147.1	146.6	152.0	156.3	146.9
2003	147.3	143.8	144.9	145.1	146.0	146.5	146.0	146.5	146.0	150.6	154.1	156.8	147.8
2004	145.4	141.9	142.7	143.7	145.2	146.2	145.8	144.6	144.0	147.1	152.1	154.6	146.1
2005	145.9	143.4	144.2	145.2	146.1	146.6	147.1	147.1	145.4	146.9	151.4	153.5	146.9
2006	145.4	142.4	143.4	144.2	145.2	146.2	145.6	145.5	144.7	146.7	151.4	153.9	146.2
2007	146.3	143.3	145.5	146.7	148.0	148.9	147.5	146.4	146.0	146.9	152.6	154.5	147.7
2008	148.0	144.6	145.4	145.5	146.5	147.5	145.8	145.5	143.9	144.2	147.1	148.3	146.0
2009	140.3	137.7	137.6	138.5	139.3	140.0	138.6	138.8	138.1	138.2	142.1	143.0	139.4
2010	136.5	134.4	135.5	136.1	137.4	138.7	138.1	138.1	136.6	137.5	141.2	143.3	137.8
2011	137.8	136.0	136.8	138.9	139.5	140.2	139.9	139.6	138.3	138.7	143.2	144.7	139.5
2012	138.4	136.1	137.2	138.1	138.9	139.5	139.1	138.4	138.0	139.9	144.9	145.7	139.5
2013	138.9	136.4	136.5	138	139.1	140.2	139.8	139.9	138.9	139.4	142.4	144.1	139.5
Transportation and Utilities													
2002	53.4	52.9	53.2	53.8	54.2	54.9	54.1	54.3	55.1	55.7	55.5	54.9	54.3
2003	54.4	54.1	53.5	53.4	53.0	51.8	51.2	50.0	50.5	50.6	49.4	49.3	51.8
2004	48.1	48.1	48.5	48.4	48.8	48.0	47.4	47.8	48.6	48.8	48.9	49.5	48.4
2005	47.8	47.8	48.3	48.5	48.6	48.0	47.2	47.5	48.6	48.2	48.5	49.3	48.2
2006	48.0	48.0	48.1	47.7	48.1	47.8	47.1	47.8	48.7	48.4	48.4	49.2	48.1
2007	48.4	48.1	48.6	48.8	49.4	48.7	48.3	48.8	49.7	49.7	50.0	50.6	49.1
2008	49.4	49.3	49.5	49.4	49.7	49.4	48.9	49.6	50.2	50.0	50.2	50.4	49.7
2009	49.3	48.8	48.6	48.1	48.3	47.0	46.0	47.0	47.6	46.5	46.5	46.8	47.5
2010	45.6	45.4	45.5	43.8	44.0	43.0	42.7	44.4	44.9	44.9	45.1	45.5	44.6
2011	44.5	44.6	44.8	45.4	45.7	44.6	43.7	44.9	45.5	45.4	45.6	46.3	45.1
2012	44.6	44.7	44.8	45.3	45.8	44.7	44.4	46.0	46.5	46.5	46.8	47.7	45.7
2013	45.6	45.4	45.6	46.0	46.2	45.0	44.8	46.2	46.6	46.0	47.1	48.3	46.1
Information													
2002	30.8	30.7	30.5	30.4	30.6	30.5	29.8	29.9	29.4	29.3	29.3	29.4	30.1
2003	30.8	31.1	31.0	29.3	29.0	29.2	29.1	28.9	28.5	28.3	28.3	28.5	29.3
2004	29.5	29.5	29.5	29.5	29.5	29.6	29.5	28.8	28.8	29.4	29.4	29.3	29.4
2005	29.1	29.1	29.1	29.4	29.4	29.7	30.0	29.9	29.9	30.1	30.1	30.3	29.7
2006	30.1	29.9	29.9	29.9	30.0	30.2	30.4	30.3	30.1	30.5	30.5	30.7	30.2
2007	29.8	29.7	29.8	30.1	30.4	30.6	30.4	30.4	30.3	30.7	30.9	30.9	30.3
2008	30.4	30.2	30.3	30.8	31.2	31.3	31.2	31.0	30.8	30.9	31.0	31.1	30.9
2009	30.8	30.7	30.6	30.3	30.3	30.5	30.5	30.5	30.2	29.9	29.9	30.2	30.4
2010	29.9	29.7	29.6	31.7	31.3	31.8	31.5	31.5	31.2	30.9	30.8	31.0	30.9
2011	30.5	30.3	30.2	31.0	31.2	31.4	31.7	31.6	31.4	31.0	30.9	30.9	31.0
2012	30.7	30.6	30.4	30.1	30.3	30.2	30.3	30.1	29.7	29.4	29.3	29.3	30.0
2013	29.2	29.3	29.3	29.6	29.9	29.9	29.8	29.7	29.5	29.7	29.7	29.8	29.6
Financial Activities													
2002	76.6	76.7	77.2	77.4	77.9	78.5	78.7	79.0	78.4	78.8	79.2	80.0	78.2
2003	77.8	77.7	78.1	78.5	78.9	79.7	79.7	80.1	79.0	78.9	78.5	78.6	78.8
2004	76.7	76.5	76.7	76.9	77.2	78.0	78.9	78.7	77.9	78.3	78.1	78.5	77.7
2005	76.5	76.9	77.0	78.1	78.0	78.7	79.3	79.2	78.9	78.4	78.2	78.5	78.1
2006	77.5	77.7	77.9	78.6	79.2	79.7	79.6	79.7	79.2	79.0	79.1	79.3	78.9
2007	78.7	78.8	79.0	79.2	80.0	80.5	80.7	80.5	79.8	79.9	79.5	79.8	79.7
2008	80.2	80.4	80.5	80.0	80.1	80.2	79.7	80.0	79.2	78.5	78.3	78.2	79.6
2009	78.3	78.5	78.6	79.1	79.2	79.5	79.5	79.3	78.7	79.0	78.6	78.6	78.9
2010	78.5	78.5	78.6	79.9	80.1	80.6	81.4	81.4	80.9	81.8	81.7	81.7	80.4
2011	80.8	80.7	80.8	82.2	82.4	82.3	83.2	83.4	82.9	83.4	83.6	83.6	82.4
2012	83.1	83.4	84.0	84.5	84.8	85.2	85.4	85.6	85.2	86.1	86.4	86.3	85.0
2013	84.2	84.5	84.7	85.2	86.0	86.6	86.5	86.5	85.9	86.4	86.5	87.5	85.9

Employment by Industry: St. Louis, MO–IL, Selected Years, 2002–2013—*Continued*

(Numbers in thousands, not seasonally adjusted)

Industry and year	January	February	March	April	May	June	July	August	September	October	November	December	Annual average
Professional and Business Services													
2002	177.7	178.6	179.6	180.1	179.2	180.3	179.1	179.8	178.3	178.4	178.7	178.6	179.0
2003	176.1	177.1	178.2	178.4	177.4	178.9	178.9	180.0	178.8	179.9	178.2	178.4	178.4
2004	174.7	175.0	178.7	180.1	179.2	181.5	180.8	181.8	181.0	181.6	181.5	182.0	179.8
2005	180.7	181.8	184.5	188.8	187.4	189.3	188.1	188.9	188.9	188.4	188.6	188.9	187.0
2006	185.7	186.6	189.3	192.4	192.1	195.3	193.5	194.7	194.8	195.7	194.5	196.0	192.6
2007	189.1	189.7	192.3	194.8	194.9	195.7	195.0	195.7	195.3	195.3	194.9	195.2	194.0
2008	193.7	195.2	196.8	200.3	199.1	200.4	198.7	198.7	195.9	194.1	191.5	189.6	196.2
2009	183.9	183.7	182.4	184.5	183.4	183.5	182.5	182.4	181.0	181.1	181.3	181.7	182.6
2010	179.1	181.0	182.6	188.0	187.3	188.2	189.2	189.4	188.3	190.1	189.8	189.0	186.8
2011	187.1	187.9	190.0	194.3	192.7	192.9	192.6	192.1	191.4	191.7	191.5	190.9	191.3
2012	186.4	187.1	189.2	193.3	192.8	193.9	191.6	191.5	190.7	192.4	192.9	193.1	191.2
2013	189.5	191.2	194.1	197.5	197.8	198.4	199.7	200.6	199.5	200.6	199.2	201.0	197.4
Education and Health Services													
2002	186.4	188.8	189.1	190.8	192.0	192.1	192.0	192.9	194.1	193.7	194.6	195.1	191.8
2003	190.4	191.8	192.4	191.7	191.3	190.9	191.4	191.3	192.7	193.2	193.3	194.2	192.1
2004	190.5	193.0	193.7	194.2	194.0	193.4	193.7	193.4	195.3	197.2	197.6	197.4	194.5
2005	195.3	197.9	198.2	198.8	198.1	197.6	197.4	197.0	199.8	200.9	201.6	202.2	198.7
2006	199.5	202.5	203.7	203.7	203.4	203.2	201.8	201.7	204.6	206.8	207.4	207.8	203.8
2007	204.1	206.8	207.9	208.8	208.9	208.3	208.1	207.9	210.5	212.1	213.1	213.6	209.2
2008	208.6	211.8	211.6	212.3	212.2	211.4	211.2	211.5	214.0	215.5	216.2	216.6	212.7
2009	213.3	215.6	215.8	215.3	215.8	214.7	214.3	214.8	217.1	218.7	220.4	222.5	216.5
2010	220.6	223.5	223.9	225.0	224.9	223.9	222.4	222.5	225.5	229.2	229.9	229.5	225.1
2011	227.6	230.2	230.6	232.0	231.6	229.9	230.0	230.0	233.1	235.4	236.9	237.0	232.0
2012	234.6	237.6	238.0	234.3	233.2	231.1	230.9	230.7	233.8	235.9	235.9	236.4	234.4
2013	233.4	237.2	236.3	238.2	236.2	232.5	233.2	233.0	234.8	235.0	236.2	235.2	235.1
Leisure and Hospitality													
2002	122.0	122.2	125.1	132.5	135.6	140.4	140.0	140.4	135.4	135.2	130.2	129.0	132.3
2003	123.1	123.4	125.6	132.9	137.0	139.7	140.9	139.6	137.0	134.2	131.8	130.9	133.0
2004	128.1	127.3	130.2	137.7	141.3	143.9	144.4	144.1	140.4	140.3	136.4	135.2	137.4
2005	129.1	129.9	133.5	140.6	143.6	146.5	147.3	147.1	144.1	140.6	137.4	137.0	139.7
2006	132.7	133.7	136.4	143.6	147.1	150.4	149.4	149.2	145.0	142.1	138.1	138.2	142.2
2007	133.7	133.8	137.7	142.7	147.7	151.2	149.8	150.2	145.1	142.0	139.2	139.6	142.7
2008	134.7	134.4	136.8	140.6	146.9	150.3	147.7	147.9	142.3	138.4	135.4	134.7	140.8
2009	130.5	129.9	133.3	139.3	144.3	147.2	145.5	145.3	138.4	135.9	132.2	131.3	137.8
2010	127.9	129.1	132.6	139.9	143.2	145.8	146.5	146.4	141.3	138.7	135.0	133.2	138.3
2011	128.3	127.8	131.9	137.2	140.9	143.8	143.8	144.5	137.9	138.0	133.0	132.8	136.7
2012	128.1	128.9	133.1	139.7	144.1	147.3	146.5	146.6	140.1	139.8	136.0	136.0	138.9
2013	132.4	132.5	135.2	142.2	147.1	149.2	149.3	148.3	143.0	142.5	138.4	137.9	141.5
Other Services													
2002	57.5	58.8	59.6	60.2	60.0	60.6	60.0	59.9	59.2	59.1	59.1	59.1	59.4
2003	57.2	58.0	58.5	59.0	59.5	60.0	58.9	58.5	57.7	57.8	57.5	57.8	58.4
2004	56.6	57.1	57.9	58.2	58.0	58.3	58.8	58.3	58.0	58.6	58.3	58.6	58.1
2005	57.0	57.5	58.0	57.9	57.7	58.4	57.9	57.7	56.9	57.4	57.1	57.4	57.6
2006	56.6	56.7	57.1	57.7	57.7	58.5	58.2	58.2	57.9	57.6	57.5	57.7	57.6
2007	56.7	56.9	57.4	57.6	57.9	58.2	57.8	57.8	57.1	57.4	57.5	57.3	57.5
2008	56.8	56.8	57.2	57.5	58.1	58.4	58.1	57.9	57.3	57.6	57.1	56.7	57.5
2009	55.6	55.5	55.8	56.0	56.2	56.0	55.5	55.1	54.4	55.1	55.0	55.1	55.4
2010	54.5	54.5	55.1	45.9	46.0	46.3	46.2	46.1	45.4	45.7	45.7	45.8	48.1
2011	44.9	44.9	45.5	46.5	46.6	47.3	47.4	47.1	46.7	46.4	46.2	46.4	46.3
2012	45.5	45.6	46.0	46.0	46.5	46.9	46.8	46.5	45.8	45.8	45.7	45.7	46.1
2013	45.9	46.0	46.1	45.8	46.2	46.8	46.3	46.3	45.2	45.8	45.9	45.7	46.0
Government													
2002	170.2	171.5	172.0	172.0	173.8	170.3	148.0	151.2	169.0	171.8	173.0	172.8	168.0
2003	169.0	170.6	171.1	172.1	173.3	170.4	149.3	151.1	167.6	169.8	170.7	170.4	167.1
2004	168.0	169.4	169.9	170.5	171.7	167.3	148.6	152.0	168.2	169.9	170.9	170.9	166.4
2005	167.2	170.3	170.2	172.0	172.9	168.9	150.8	156.2	169.5	170.5	172.0	171.5	167.7
2006	167.9	170.8	171.1	172.3	173.4	167.5	151.0	154.8	170.5	172.3	173.4	173.5	168.2
2007	169.6	172.7	172.8	173.2	174.4	168.4	146.5	153.4	171.1	174.1	175.3	175.0	168.9
2008	171.0	175.4	174.5	174.9	176.9	170.6	149.6	157.0	173.9	176.8	176.9	176.4	171.2
2009	173.1	175.5	176.3	180.1	180.2	175.2	151.8	159.8	176.0	177.2	176.7	176.8	173.2
2010	172.3	175.1	175.4	177.4	181.6	170.4	147.6	158.7	171.0	172.9	173.2	172.4	170.7
2011	169.3	171.0	171.7	172.8	173.7	164.8	144.4	152.9	169.5	170.1	170.1	170.4	166.7
2012	165.7	168.6	169.4	170.6	171.3	162.8	141.9	150.5	166.2	167.3	167.3	167.5	164.1
2013	163.2	166.3	166.9	168.0	168.6	160.1	138.7	147.2	162.8	164.1	164.6	164.9	161.3

Employment by Industry: Tampa–St. Petersburg–Clearwater, FL, Selected Years, 2002–2013

(Numbers in thousands, not seasonally adjusted)

Industry and year	January	February	March	April	May	June	July	August	September	October	November	December	Annual average
Total Nonfarm													
2002	1,118.5	1,130.9	1,138.0	1,136.0	1,136.9	1,120.4	1,109.7	1,122.6	1,123.5	1,126.2	1,139.0	1,145.1	1,128.9
2003	1,118.7	1,127.5	1,137.6	1,133.9	1,133.1	1,119.9	1,110.7	1,123.8	1,126.9	1,133.6	1,138.1	1,146.4	1,129.2
2004	1,137.8	1,151.2	1,163.1	1,171.6	1,173.2	1,163.3	1,155.8	1,167.7	1,168.9	1,181.2	1,192.9	1,201.7	1,169.0
2005	1,185.7	1,199.8	1,206.2	1,211.4	1,213.6	1,200.0	1,194.7	1,207.2	1,212.2	1,211.3	1,220.8	1,228.5	1,207.6
2006	1,212.2	1,221.9	1,237.9	1,236.2	1,238.7	1,228.0	1,216.6	1,233.6	1,236.5	1,233.5	1,241.2	1,249.8	1,232.2
2007	1,228.5	1,236.9	1,248.6	1,243.0	1,239.8	1,230.5	1,212.7	1,225.3	1,222.1	1,219.9	1,227.8	1,232.3	1,230.6
2008	1,207.0	1,214.9	1,219.6	1,206.3	1,201.2	1,185.3	1,168.1	1,178.5	1,173.4	1,168.1	1,167.4	1,169.2	1,188.3
2009	1,139.3	1,139.7	1,140.2	1,132.8	1,125.2	1,109.3	1,095.6	1,105.0	1,102.9	1,104.2	1,106.9	1,109.7	1,117.6
2010	1,089.8	1,098.8	1,107.4	1,106.9	1,113.1	1,100.2	1,093.1	1,103.7	1,102.1	1,113.9	1,118.8	1,123.9	1,106.0
2011	1,106.7	1,115.2	1,123.2	1,127.3	1,123.2	1,110.6	1,107.6	1,121.3	1,128.4	1,132.4	1,139.8	1,145.2	1,123.4
2012	1,132.2	1,140.7	1,148.3	1,153.0	1,152.0	1,139.9	1,132.3	1,146.7	1,147.0	1,155.2	1,165.8	1,172.0	1,148.8
2013	1,155.0	1,165.5	1,173.8	1,178.3	1,179.9	1,167.6	1,164.4	1,178.6	1,179.5	1,184.0	1,196.2	1,198.5	1,176.8
Total Private													
2002	971.5	982.1	988.9	986.9	988.8	983.9	974.5	976.3	975.5	976.6	988.4	993.4	982.2
2003	971.4	978.2	988.5	985.9	984.7	983.4	975.2	977.8	979.5	984.8	989.2	998.0	983.1
2004	991.6	1,002.0	1,014.3	1,022.6	1,023.8	1,025.8	1,019.0	1,020.4	1,020.2	1,030.9	1,042.0	1,050.8	1,022.0
2005	1,037.2	1,048.7	1,055.9	1,061.9	1,063.7	1,061.9	1,057.4	1,059.4	1,062.4	1,060.2	1,069.3	1,077.8	1,059.7
2006	1,062.6	1,071.5	1,087.6	1,085.4	1,088.4	1,089.5	1,079.2	1,084.4	1,084.4	1,079.7	1,087.7	1,096.9	1,083.1
2007	1,076.2	1,083.5	1,094.5	1,089.2	1,087.6	1,088.2	1,071.4	1,074.1	1,068.0	1,064.5	1,072.4	1,077.3	1,078.9
2008	1,053.6	1,059.1	1,064.1	1,051.5	1,048.0	1,042.6	1,026.7	1,026.0	1,017.7	1,011.7	1,010.4	1,011.2	1,035.2
2009	983.7	981.6	982.7	974.3	969.6	963.8	950.9	950.6	947.7	947.7	950.8	954.1	963.1
2010	935.3	941.4	950.4	950.6	951.8	952.3	946.5	949.8	946.4	957.5	962.2	968.8	951.1
2011	951.8	957.8	966.1	971.0	968.7	966.3	965.0	969.6	973.3	977.0	984.7	990.1	970.1
2012	977.5	985.5	993.5	997.3	997.3	995.8	989.5	995.8	994.2	1,002.0	1,011.6	1,018.2	996.5
2013	1,000.7	1,010.0	1,018.4	1,022.8	1,026.3	1,024.5	1,022.5	1,027.7	1,026.8	1,030.5	1,041.9	1,044.9	1,024.8
Goods-Producing													
2002	149.2	149.1	149.2	149.0	149.4	150.3	150.0	151.3	151.8	151.8	152.0	151.6	150.4
2003	147.9	148.8	148.7	148.2	148.9	149.5	148.2	149.1	149.0	148.8	148.7	149.9	148.8
2004	149.6	150.9	152.9	155.3	155.7	156.7	157.1	157.8	158.6	160.9	161.0	161.8	156.5
2005	160.1	161.6	162.7	163.7	164.9	166.1	167.8	168.5	169.4	169.7	171.0	171.5	166.4
2006	170.2	171.4	173.2	173.4	174.4	175.4	173.6	174.4	173.8	172.4	171.4	171.2	172.9
2007	168.9	169.1	169.8	166.2	166.2	166.3	162.8	162.0	161.1	158.4	157.1	156.7	163.7
2008	153.3	154.0	153.8	151.3	151.0	151.0	148.4	147.2	145.4	142.3	139.8	137.4	147.9
2009	131.1	129.3	127.6	125.3	123.9	123.2	120.6	119.8	118.4	116.8	115.2	114.0	122.1
2010	110.6	110.6	110.8	110.5	111.6	111.7	112.0	111.9	111.0	110.9	110.4	110.3	111.0
2011	108.4	109.0	110.2	111.1	111.7	112.0	112.5	112.4	113.1	112.7	112.3	112.5	111.5
2012	110.7	111.7	112.5	112.8	113.6	114.6	114.2	114.9	114.2	114.6	114.9	115.0	113.6
2013	112.7	113.4	114.5	116.0	116.6	117.3	117.4	118.1	118.1	120.3	120.9	120.3	117.1
Service-Providing													
2002	969.3	981.8	988.8	987.0	987.5	970.1	959.7	971.3	971.7	974.4	987.0	993.5	978.5
2003	970.8	978.7	988.9	985.7	984.2	970.4	962.5	974.7	977.9	984.8	989.4	996.5	980.4
2004	988.2	1,000.3	1,010.2	1,016.3	1,017.5	1,006.6	998.7	1,009.9	1,010.3	1,020.3	1,031.9	1,039.9	1,012.5
2005	1,025.6	1,038.2	1,043.5	1,047.7	1,048.7	1,033.9	1,026.9	1,038.7	1,042.8	1,041.6	1,049.8	1,057.0	1,041.2
2006	1,042.0	1,050.5	1,064.7	1,062.8	1,064.3	1,052.6	1,043.0	1,059.2	1,062.7	1,061.1	1,069.8	1,078.6	1,059.3
2007	1,059.6	1,067.8	1,078.8	1,076.8	1,073.6	1,064.2	1,049.9	1,063.3	1,061.0	1,061.5	1,070.7	1,075.6	1,066.9
2008	1,053.7	1,060.9	1,065.8	1,055.0	1,050.2	1,034.3	1,019.7	1,031.3	1,028.0	1,025.8	1,027.6	1,031.8	1,040.3
2009	1,008.2	1,010.4	1,012.6	1,007.5	1,001.3	986.1	975.0	985.2	984.5	987.4	991.7	995.7	995.5
2010	979.2	988.2	996.6	996.4	1,001.5	988.5	981.1	991.8	991.1	1,003.0	1,008.4	1,013.6	995.0
2011	998.3	1,006.2	1,013.0	1,016.2	1,011.5	998.6	995.1	1,008.9	1,015.3	1,019.7	1,027.5	1,032.7	1,011.9
2012	1,021.5	1,029.0	1,035.8	1,040.2	1,038.4	1,025.3	1,018.1	1,031.8	1,032.8	1,040.6	1,050.9	1,057.0	1,035.1
2013	1,042.3	1,052.1	1,059.3	1,062.3	1,063.3	1,050.3	1,047.0	1,060.5	1,061.4	1,063.7	1,075.3	1,078.2	1,059.6
Mining and Logging													
2002	0.5	0.5	0.5	0.5	0.5	0.5	0.5	0.5	0.5	0.5	0.5	0.5	0.5
2003	0.5	0.5	0.5	0.5	0.5	0.5	0.5	0.5	0.5	0.5	0.6	0.6	0.5
2004	0.6	0.6	0.6	0.6	0.6	0.6	0.6	0.6	0.6	0.6	0.6	0.6	0.6
2005	0.6	0.6	0.6	0.6	0.7	0.7	0.7	0.7	0.8	0.8	0.8	0.8	0.7
2006	0.9	0.9	0.9	0.9	0.9	0.8	0.7	0.6	0.6	0.6	0.6	0.7	0.8
2007	0.6	0.6	0.6	0.7	0.7	0.7	0.7	0.7	0.7	0.7	0.7	0.7	0.7
2008	0.7	0.6	0.7	0.7	0.7	0.7	0.6	0.6	0.6	0.5	0.5	0.5	0.6
2009	0.5	0.5	0.5	0.5	0.5	0.5	0.5	0.5	0.5	0.5	0.5	0.5	0.5
2010	0.5	0.5	0.5	0.5	0.5	0.5	0.5	0.5	0.5	0.5	0.5	0.5	0.5
2011	0.5	0.5	0.5	0.5	0.5	0.5	0.5	0.5	0.5	0.5	0.5	0.5	0.5
2012	0.5	0.5	0.5	0.5	0.5	0.5	0.5	0.5	0.5	0.5	0.5	0.5	0.5
2013	0.5	0.5	0.5	0.5	0.5	0.5	0.5	0.5	0.5	0.5	0.5	0.5	0.5
Construction													
2002	67.5	67.9	67.9	68.1	68.9	69.2	69.3	70.4	71.0	71.5	71.9	71.7	69.6
2003	69.6	70.6	70.8	70.9	71.9	72.6	72.0	72.9	72.8	73.0	73.0	74.1	72.0
2004	73.7	74.8	76.3	77.7	78.1	78.6	79.4	79.8	80.7	82.8	82.9	83.6	79.0
2005	83.1	84.4	85.4	86.0	87.0	87.8	89.4	89.7	90.2	90.5	91.7	92.2	88.1
2006	91.0	92.1	93.3	94.0	94.7	95.3	94.5	95.0	94.6	93.7	92.9	92.7	93.7
2007	91.3	91.3	92.2	88.9	88.8	89.0	86.3	85.6	84.9	83.1	82.4	82.2	87.2
2008	79.2	80.0	79.8	78.0	77.8	77.9	75.8	75.1	74.1	72.1	70.5	69.1	75.8
2009	64.4	63.2	62.3	61.2	60.4	60.2	59.2	58.8	58.2	57.0	55.9	55.2	59.7
2010	52.4	52.4	52.6	52.2	52.7	52.7	53.0	52.7	52.2	52.4	51.6	51.4	52.4
2011	50.1	50.5	51.3	52.0	52.5	52.5	52.8	52.6	53.3	53.2	52.8	52.9	52.2
2012	51.3	52.0	52.6	52.8	53.5	54.4	54.0	54.5	54.5	54.7	55.0	55.1	53.7
2013	53.4	54.0	54.8	55.5	56.2	56.7	56.9	57.5	57.6	59.4	59.3	58.1	56.6

Employment by Industry: Tampa–St. Petersburg–Clearwater, FL, Selected Years, 2002–2013—*Continued*

(Numbers in thousands, not seasonally adjusted)

Industry and year	January	February	March	April	May	June	July	August	September	October	November	December	Annual average
Manufacturing													
2002	81.2	80.7	80.8	80.4	80.0	80.6	80.2	80.4	80.3	79.8	79.6	79.4	80.3
2003	77.8	77.7	77.4	76.8	76.5	76.4	75.7	75.7	75.7	75.3	75.1	75.2	76.3
2004	75.3	75.5	76.0	77.0	77.0	77.5	77.1	77.4	77.3	77.5	77.5	77.6	76.9
2005	76.4	76.6	76.7	77.1	77.2	77.6	77.7	78.0	78.4	78.4	78.5	78.5	77.6
2006	78.3	78.4	79.0	78.5	78.8	79.3	78.4	78.8	78.6	78.1	77.9	77.8	78.5
2007	77.0	77.2	77.0	76.6	76.7	76.6	75.8	75.7	75.5	74.6	74.0	73.8	75.9
2008	73.4	73.4	73.3	72.6	72.5	72.4	72.0	71.5	70.7	69.7	68.8	67.8	71.5
2009	66.2	65.6	64.8	63.6	63.0	62.5	60.9	60.5	59.7	59.3	58.8	58.3	61.9
2010	57.7	57.7	57.7	57.8	58.4	58.5	58.5	58.7	58.3	58.0	58.3	58.4	58.2
2011	57.8	58.0	58.4	58.6	58.7	59.0	59.2	59.3	59.3	59.0	59.0	59.1	58.8
2012	58.9	59.2	59.4	59.5	59.6	59.7	59.7	59.9	59.2	59.4	59.4	59.4	59.4
2013	58.8	58.9	59.2	60.0	59.9	60.1	60.0	60.1	60.0	60.4	61.1	61.7	60.0
Trade, Transportation, and Utilities													
2002	232.0	230.3	230.4	229.0	229.2	226.9	224.9	226.4	224.8	226.0	228.8	232.5	228.4
2003	222.0	220.7	220.7	220.2	221.1	220.2	219.4	219.7	220.8	223.5	226.3	229.8	222.0
2004	225.3	224.9	225.3	225.3	226.1	226.0	224.7	224.5	224.4	227.7	233.1	236.9	227.0
2005	231.0	231.1	232.1	233.9	234.6	234.0	232.9	233.0	232.9	234.3	238.9	243.4	234.3
2006	236.9	236.3	238.3	236.1	236.5	235.6	234.0	234.3	234.1	234.3	239.2	243.3	236.6
2007	235.6	234.4	235.6	234.4	235.1	234.6	232.2	232.9	232.9	232.8	238.8	241.3	235.1
2008	233.5	232.6	232.6	229.3	229.1	227.2	224.4	223.9	222.2	222.1	224.6	226.5	227.3
2009	217.2	214.6	213.2	210.8	210.7	209.0	206.7	206.7	206.3	207.2	210.9	213.4	210.6
2010	206.6	206.5	207.3	207.6	208.7	208.7	207.5	208.1	207.9	210.5	214.7	218.7	209.4
2011	210.9	210.3	211.3	211.9	212.1	211.2	211.6	212.6	212.9	214.1	219.4	222.6	213.4
2012	217.7	217.3	216.8	217.4	218.3	217.2	216.7	217.4	217.4	218.9	225.0	227.5	219.0
2013	220.8	220.7	220.4	220.0	221.0	220.9	220.9	221.7	221.6	223.3	228.6	233.2	222.8
Wholesale Trade													
2002	54.1	54.1	54.1	53.6	53.9	53.4	52.9	52.9	52.7	52.6	52.6	52.7	53.3
2003	51.0	51.1	50.8	51.0	51.0	50.6	50.1	50.0	50.0	49.8	49.8	50.0	50.4
2004	50.4	50.9	50.7	50.6	50.8	51.1	50.7	50.8	50.8	51.0	51.5	51.8	50.9
2005	52.1	52.1	52.6	52.9	53.3	53.1	52.6	52.6	52.6	52.8	52.9	53.6	52.8
2006	53.3	53.5	53.8	53.8	54.2	54.0	53.7	54.0	54.0	54.1	54.6	55.0	54.0
2007	54.4	54.5	54.6	54.3	54.6	54.5	53.8	54.0	53.8	54.0	54.6	54.8	54.3
2008	54.3	54.3	54.2	53.8	54.0	53.4	52.5	52.2	51.8	51.5	51.4	51.2	52.9
2009	50.0	49.4	49.1	48.4	48.3	47.5	46.7	46.6	46.4	46.6	46.5	46.7	47.7
2010	45.7	45.8	46.2	46.1	46.5	46.2	45.6	45.6	45.5	45.9	45.8	46.3	45.9
2011	45.5	45.5	45.7	45.8	46.1	45.8	46.1	46.3	46.6	46.8	47.2	47.8	46.3
2012	48.2	48.5	48.3	48.4	48.7	48.4	47.9	48.2	48.3	48.4	49.1	49.0	48.5
2013	48.9	49.0	49.1	48.8	49.0	48.7	48.5	48.8	48.7	48.6	50.2	50.4	49.1
Retail													
2002	144.9	143.2	143.7	142.6	142.7	141.0	139.6	141.1	140.3	141.6	144.7	148.1	142.8
2003	140.5	139.2	139.4	138.7	139.4	139.1	138.4	138.7	139.5	142.2	145.0	147.5	140.6
2004	143.2	142.2	142.7	142.7	143.1	142.8	142.1	141.8	142.0	144.8	149.6	152.8	144.2
2005	147.1	147.0	147.4	148.8	149.3	149.2	148.9	149.1	149.1	150.4	154.7	157.6	149.9
2006	152.4	151.6	153.2	151.2	151.2	150.7	149.6	149.7	149.8	150.5	154.8	157.4	151.8
2007	151.9	150.9	151.8	151.1	151.7	151.2	149.5	149.9	150.2	150.0	155.2	156.7	151.7
2008	151.0	150.0	150.1	147.3	146.9	145.8	144.5	144.5	143.3	143.4	146.0	147.1	146.7
2009	140.3	138.7	137.9	136.4	136.5	135.8	134.5	134.8	134.7	135.8	139.5	140.8	137.1
2010	136.1	135.9	136.4	136.6	137.1	137.6	136.9	137.5	137.4	139.3	143.4	145.8	138.3
2011	140.0	139.5	140.1	140.7	140.4	139.8	139.7	140.5	140.4	141.4	146.0	147.5	141.3
2012	143.2	142.4	142.1	142.5	143.0	142.2	142.2	142.9	142.7	144.1	149.2	150.9	144.0
2013	145.1	144.6	144.2	143.9	144.7	144.8	145.3	145.8	145.9	147.6	151.0	154.6	146.5
Transportation and Utilities													
2002	33.0	33.0	32.6	32.8	32.6	32.5	32.4	32.4	31.8	31.8	31.5	31.7	32.3
2003	30.5	30.4	30.5	30.5	30.7	30.5	30.9	31.0	31.3	31.5	31.5	32.3	31.0
2004	31.7	31.8	31.9	32.0	32.2	32.1	31.9	31.9	31.6	31.9	32.0	32.3	31.9
2005	31.8	32.0	32.1	32.2	32.0	31.7	31.4	31.3	31.2	31.1	31.3	32.2	31.7
2006	31.2	31.2	31.3	31.1	31.1	30.9	30.7	30.6	30.3	29.7	29.8	30.9	30.7
2007	29.3	29.0	29.2	29.0	28.8	28.9	28.9	29.0	28.9	28.8	29.0	29.8	29.1
2008	28.2	28.3	28.3	28.2	28.2	28.0	27.4	27.2	27.1	27.2	27.2	28.2	27.8
2009	26.9	26.5	26.2	26.0	25.9	25.7	25.5	25.3	25.2	24.8	24.9	25.9	25.7
2010	24.8	24.8	24.7	24.9	25.1	24.9	25.0	25.0	25.0	25.3	25.5	26.6	25.1
2011	25.4	25.3	25.5	25.4	25.6	25.6	25.8	25.8	25.9	25.9	26.2	27.3	25.8
2012	26.3	26.4	26.4	26.5	26.6	26.6	26.6	26.3	26.4	26.4	26.7	27.6	26.6
2013	26.8	27.1	27.1	27.3	27.3	27.4	27.1	27.1	27.0	27.1	27.4	28.2	27.2
Information													
2002	35.9	35.5	35.7	35.3	35.2	34.8	34.6	34.5	34.6	34.4	34.9	34.8	35.0
2003	34.3	34.1	34.2	34.5	34.4	34.0	33.9	33.6	33.5	32.9	32.9	32.8	33.8
2004	32.6	32.3	32.9	32.0	32.1	32.2	31.6	31.8	31.8	31.8	31.9	32.0	32.1
2005	31.6	31.6	31.8	31.5	31.6	31.6	31.8	32.0	32.4	32.2	32.3	32.2	31.9
2006	32.1	32.2	32.0	31.8	31.9	32.0	31.8	31.7	31.6	31.5	31.6	31.7	31.8
2007	31.6	31.8	31.9	32.1	32.2	32.4	31.9	31.9	31.7	31.4	31.4	31.3	31.8
2008	30.9	31.1	31.0	31.0	30.9	30.7	30.3	30.0	29.5	29.6	29.3	29.0	30.3
2009	28.7	28.6	28.5	28.1	27.8	27.7	27.6	27.3	26.9	26.5	26.5	26.5	27.6
2010	26.0	26.0	26.0	25.8	25.8	25.7	25.7	25.6	25.5	25.5	25.6	25.6	25.7
2011	25.8	25.9	25.7	25.6	25.7	25.8	26.0	25.9	25.9	26.0	26.1	26.2	25.9
2012	25.8	25.7	25.7	25.7	25.6	25.8	25.7	25.6	25.6	25.9	25.9	25.9	25.7
2013	26.1	26.1	26.2	26.3	26.4	26.6	26.4	26.3	26.2	26.1	26.1	26.1	26.2

Employment by Industry: Tampa–St. Petersburg–Clearwater, FL, Selected Years, 2002–2013—*Continued*

(Numbers in thousands, not seasonally adjusted)

Industry and year	January	February	March	April	May	June	July	August	September	October	November	December	Annual average
Financial Activities													
2002	92.8	93.8	93.8	93.4	93.5	93.9	94.2	94.4	94.0	94.3	94.9	95.4	94.0
2003	94.4	95.1	95.2	95.4	95.7	95.9	95.8	96.1	95.5	95.3	95.1	95.6	95.4
2004	95.2	95.7	96.1	97.3	97.4	97.1	96.9	97.0	96.8	97.7	98.1	98.6	97.0
2005	98.2	98.9	98.9	100.1	100.5	101.3	101.6	101.0	101.5	102.3	102.8	104.2	100.9
2006	103.2	104.0	104.6	104.8	105.0	104.9	104.1	104.1	103.7	103.8	103.6	104.3	104.2
2007	103.2	104.2	104.3	104.4	104.2	104.0	103.7	102.8	102.4	102.1	102.0	101.8	103.3
2008	100.5	100.5	100.2	99.3	99.1	98.6	98.3	98.0	97.4	97.2	97.0	96.9	98.6
2009	96.0	95.3	95.0	94.4	94.2	93.7	93.0	92.6	91.8	91.1	90.7	90.8	93.2
2010	89.3	89.2	89.4	89.1	89.1	89.2	89.0	89.5	89.0	89.6	89.7	90.5	89.4
2011	89.7	89.9	90.3	90.5	90.4	90.9	91.2	92.1	93.0	93.5	93.4	94.2	91.6
2012	93.3	93.8	94.4	94.5	94.8	95.5	95.5	96.0	96.1	96.9	97.6	98.1	95.5
2013	97.6	98.4	99.0	98.8	99.2	99.6	99.9	100.2	99.8	100.8	100.7	101.1	99.6
Professional and Business Services													
2002	154.8	161.6	162.8	162.9	163.1	160.7	158.3	154.6	154.3	153.5	159.6	158.9	158.8
2003	156.7	160.8	166.9	165.5	162.4	162.1	159.6	159.6	160.0	164.7	165.4	167.1	162.6
2004	167.2	171.5	175.4	181.2	180.4	182.5	180.8	180.6	179.0	182.2	184.9	187.9	179.5
2005	184.2	189.3	190.2	192.0	191.2	189.7	188.7	190.1	191.9	187.9	189.6	190.4	189.6
2006	188.5	191.1	197.5	198.0	198.7	199.9	199.1	201.4	200.8	197.5	198.9	200.6	197.7
2007	196.9	198.2	201.1	201.3	199.1	200.9	196.9	198.2	193.7	192.4	192.8	193.3	197.1
2008	188.0	189.1	190.6	185.9	184.0	184.4	181.9	182.1	179.7	177.0	176.2	177.2	183.0
2009	172.6	172.8	173.0	171.2	169.4	170.1	168.0	168.4	168.2	167.6	168.6	169.6	170.0
2010	167.0	169.8	172.2	172.1	172.1	174.2	173.8	175.9	174.5	178.8	179.2	180.6	174.2
2011	177.6	179.8	180.6	182.1	180.7	181.5	182.4	183.8	183.7	184.2	186.2	188.0	182.6
2012	185.8	188.4	190.3	190.9	190.3	190.0	189.8	191.6	190.2	192.9	194.7	196.3	190.9
2013	192.1	195.6	196.9	198.4	200.2	199.6	200.4	201.6	201.4	200.2	204.9	202.9	199.5
Education and Health Services													
2002	142.3	143.4	144.9	145.3	146.1	145.8	144.6	145.9	146.8	147.8	149.2	149.8	146.0
2003	146.6	147.9	149.2	150.0	150.6	150.2	149.6	151.5	152.7	152.2	153.0	153.6	150.6
2004	152.1	153.4	154.2	155.2	155.9	155.4	154.3	155.2	155.8	156.3	157.3	157.7	155.2
2005	155.9	156.8	157.4	158.5	158.1	157.5	156.5	157.4	157.6	158.3	158.8	159.6	157.7
2006	158.0	159.5	160.7	161.0	161.3	160.9	159.2	160.4	162.1	163.2	164.7	166.1	161.4
2007	164.2	166.0	167.9	168.2	168.4	168.2	166.1	168.2	169.2	171.0	172.6	173.4	168.6
2008	171.6	172.9	174.0	173.6	173.9	172.1	170.4	171.7	172.3	173.5	174.9	175.6	173.0
2009	172.1	172.9	174.3	174.2	174.6	173.4	172.2	173.0	174.3	176.5	177.8	178.6	174.5
2010	176.4	177.3	179.3	178.5	178.1	177.2	175.8	176.1	176.8	179.5	180.4	180.6	178.0
2011	179.0	180.1	181.1	182.5	181.6	179.7	178.6	179.8	181.0	182.0	182.9	182.8	180.9
2012	180.7	182.0	182.9	183.5	183.1	182.0	179.2	181.1	182.1	183.1	183.7	184.2	182.3
2013	182.2	183.6	185.0	185.7	185.5	183.6	182.0	184.1	185.0	186.8	188.6	189.0	185.1
Leisure and Hospitality													
2002	117.7	121.1	124.5	124.8	124.8	123.5	120.1	121.3	121.3	120.1	120.1	121.2	121.7
2003	120.5	121.9	124.9	124.2	123.8	123.4	121.2	121.2	120.9	120.7	121.0	122.0	122.1
2004	122.0	125.2	128.6	128.0	127.4	126.3	124.6	124.8	124.8	125.0	125.9	126.3	125.7
2005	126.4	129.1	132.3	132.0	132.5	131.4	129.0	129.0	128.5	128.1	128.7	129.5	129.7
2006	128.2	130.9	134.7	134.0	133.6	133.4	130.6	131.6	131.6	130.3	131.5	132.5	131.9
2007	129.4	132.6	136.0	136.1	135.2	133.9	131.1	131.4	130.4	129.1	129.8	130.9	132.2
2008	128.0	130.6	133.7	133.5	132.0	130.5	126.1	126.4	125.2	124.8	123.8	124.1	128.2
2009	122.2	124.4	127.2	126.8	125.4	123.3	120.1	120.1	119.3	119.3	118.6	118.8	122.1
2010	117.8	120.0	123.3	124.8	124.1	123.1	120.7	121.0	120.3	120.6	120.5	120.7	121.4
2011	119.1	121.2	124.8	125.2	124.5	123.7	121.5	122.1	123.0	123.8	123.8	123.2	123.0
2012	123.1	125.9	129.8	131.3	130.4	129.5	127.5	128.3	127.5	128.5	128.4	129.7	128.3
2013	128.1	130.8	134.7	135.4	135.1	134.4	133.3	133.4	132.5	131.0	130.1	130.3	132.4
Other Services													
2002	46.8	47.3	47.6	47.2	47.5	48.0	47.8	47.9	47.9	48.7	48.9	49.2	47.9
2003	49.0	48.9	48.7	47.9	47.9	48.1	47.5	47.0	47.1	46.7	46.8	47.2	47.7
2004	47.6	48.1	48.9	48.3	48.8	49.6	49.0	48.7	49.0	49.3	49.8	49.6	48.9
2005	49.8	50.3	50.5	50.2	50.3	50.3	49.1	48.4	48.2	47.4	47.2	47.0	49.1
2006	45.5	46.1	46.6	46.3	47.0	47.7	46.8	46.5	46.7	46.7	46.8	47.2	46.7
2007	46.4	47.2	47.9	46.5	47.2	47.9	46.7	46.7	46.6	47.3	47.9	48.6	47.2
2008	47.8	48.3	48.5	47.6	48.0	48.1	46.9	46.7	46.0	45.2	44.8	44.5	46.9
2009	43.8	43.7	43.9	43.5	43.6	43.4	42.7	42.7	42.5	42.7	42.5	42.4	43.1
2010	41.6	42.0	42.1	42.2	42.3	42.5	42.0	41.7	41.4	42.1	41.7	41.8	42.0
2011	41.3	41.6	42.1	42.1	42.0	41.5	41.2	40.9	40.7	40.7	40.6	40.6	41.3
2012	40.4	40.7	41.1	41.2	41.2	41.2	40.9	40.9	41.1	41.2	41.4	41.5	41.1
2013	41.1	41.4	41.7	42.2	42.3	42.5	42.2	42.3	42.2	42.0	42.0	42.0	42.0
Government													
2002	147.0	148.8	149.1	149.1	148.1	136.5	135.2	146.3	148.0	149.6	150.6	151.7	146.7
2003	147.3	149.3	149.1	148.0	148.4	136.5	135.5	146.0	147.4	148.8	148.9	148.4	146.1
2004	146.2	149.2	148.8	149.0	149.4	137.5	136.8	147.3	148.7	150.3	150.9	150.9	147.1
2005	148.5	151.1	150.3	149.5	149.9	138.1	137.3	147.8	149.8	151.1	151.5	150.7	148.0
2006	149.6	150.4	150.3	150.8	150.3	138.5	137.4	149.2	152.1	153.8	153.5	152.9	149.1
2007	152.3	153.4	154.1	153.8	152.2	142.3	141.3	151.2	154.1	155.4	155.4	155.0	151.7
2008	153.4	155.8	155.2	154.8	153.2	142.7	141.4	152.5	155.7	156.4	157.0	158.0	153.0
2009	155.6	158.1	157.5	158.5	155.6	145.5	145.4	154.4	155.2	156.5	156.1	155.6	154.4
2010	154.5	157.4	157.0	156.3	161.3	147.9	146.6	153.9	155.7	156.4	156.6	155.1	154.9
2011	154.9	157.4	157.1	156.3	154.5	144.3	142.6	151.7	155.1	155.4	155.1	155.1	153.3
2012	154.7	155.2	154.8	155.7	154.7	144.1	142.8	150.9	152.8	153.2	154.2	153.8	152.2
2013	154.3	155.5	155.4	155.5	153.6	143.1	141.9	150.9	152.7	153.5	154.3	153.6	152.0

Employment by Industry: Tucson, AZ, Selected Years, 2002–2013

(Numbers in thousands, not seasonally adjusted)

Industry and year	January	February	March	April	May	June	July	August	September	October	November	December	Annual average
Total Nonfarm													
2002	341.0	344.3	345.2	346.9	346.1	338.5	329.1	335.8	341.8	345.6	349.2	349.9	342.8
2003	340.5	343.6	345.7	345.7	346.0	338.4	333.2	340.2	346.8	350.5	353.1	356.6	345.0
2004	349.8	353.8	354.5	358.7	358.5	351.5	345.2	351.6	357.6	363.4	367.2	369.0	356.7
2005	355.8	361.7	363.7	368.0	367.9	360.5	358.0	364.0	370.1	370.7	374.1	378.0	366.0
2006	370.6	377.5	378.2	379.3	379.1	372.6	368.5	375.0	380.6	385.0	387.2	390.8	378.7
2007	379.5	386.4	387.6	386.1	386.1	377.8	374.7	378.1	385.2	387.2	390.1	390.4	384.1
2008	377.8	383.8	383.7	384.1	383.0	374.8	373.9	378.2	380.9	380.1	380.0	379.3	380.0
2009	368.1	368.3	365.8	364.2	361.9	352.3	349.9	354.4	357.9	358.0	359.9	360.9	360.1
2010	351.2	355.3	354.7	356.8	357.3	345.1	341.4	347.5	350.4	353.1	356.2	358.0	352.3
2011	350.3	354.2	355.0	356.1	355.8	344.2	339.4	350.7	355.2	358.0	361.8	361.4	353.5
2012	356.2	360.2	361.8	361.8	361.2	351.3	343.4	354.5	359.8	362.2	366.0	367.1	358.8
2013	359.3	363.3	364.6	365.5	364.5	351.1	348.7	355.3	362.4	364.6	366.8	367.9	361.2
Total Private													
2002	266.3	267.4	268.3	268.7	268.7	267.1	264.3	266.3	266.9	268.2	270.8	271.7	267.9
2003	264.8	265.5	267.2	267.5	267.7	267.7	266.5	269.5	270.8	272.4	275.2	277.6	269.4
2004	273.3	274.9	275.6	279.6	279.5	277.9	278.7	280.5	279.7	283.5	286.7	288.2	279.8
2005	279.6	282.2	283.8	288.3	288.3	287.6	287.6	290.6	292.5	292.4	295.2	299.3	289.0
2006	294.9	299.1	300.0	300.7	301.2	301.3	300.0	302.6	304.9	305.8	307.6	310.9	302.4
2007	302.7	306.3	307.8	306.5	307.4	306.3	303.8	304.7	304.6	306.5	308.8	309.3	306.2
2008	301.1	302.4	303.0	302.4	301.2	300.0	298.9	300.2	299.7	298.1	297.4	297.1	300.1
2009	288.5	286.7	284.8	282.4	281.0	279.1	277.3	278.3	277.8	277.3	279.0	280.3	281.0
2010	273.1	274.6	275.3	276.0	275.0	273.5	271.1	272.1	271.1	273.6	275.3	277.8	274.0
2011	273.3	274.4	275.6	276.5	276.7	275.7	273.5	275.8	276.4	278.2	281.5	283.1	276.7
2012	278.7	280.2	281.9	281.7	281.2	280.0	276.8	279.3	279.8	281.8	285.3	286.7	281.1
2013	281.4	282.9	284.3	284.9	284.6	282.2	280.9	282.9	283.5	284.5	286.4	287.8	283.9
Goods-Producing													
2002	55.1	54.5	54.6	54.4	54.7	55.0	54.9	55.1	54.7	54.2	54.0	53.9	54.6
2003	53.0	52.3	52.7	52.2	52.6	53.0	52.9	53.1	52.5	53.1	52.9	53.2	52.8
2004	52.9	52.8	52.9	53.2	53.4	53.6	54.2	54.0	54.1	54.4	54.4	54.8	53.7
2005	53.1	53.8	54.2	54.8	55.1	55.8	55.8	56.4	56.5	56.0	56.3	56.9	55.4
2006	56.3	57.3	57.0	57.5	57.8	58.5	58.8	58.6	58.4	58.1	56.6	56.3	57.6
2007	54.9	56.4	56.0	55.5	55.9	56.5	56.4	56.5	55.9	55.2	54.9	54.3	55.7
2008	53.6	53.3	53.2	52.5	52.4	52.8	52.6	52.4	51.6	50.4	49.3	48.3	51.9
2009	46.2	45.1	44.3	43.7	43.6	43.8	43.4	43.0	42.5	42.0	41.7	41.7	43.4
2010	40.6	40.7	40.7	40.9	41.0	41.2	41.1	41.1	40.7	40.7	40.4	40.5	40.8
2011	39.9	39.8	40.0	39.7	40.0	40.2	40.1	40.0	39.8	39.7	39.4	39.4	39.8
2012	39.0	38.9	39.2	39.3	39.5	40.1	40.2	40.4	40.2	40.3	40.6	40.9	39.9
2013	40.2	40.2	40.5	40.7	40.8	41.4	41.6	41.4	40.8	40.8	40.9	40.8	40.8
Service-Providing													
2002	285.9	289.8	290.6	292.5	291.4	283.5	274.2	280.7	287.1	291.4	295.2	296.0	288.2
2003	287.5	291.3	293.0	293.5	293.4	285.4	280.3	287.1	294.3	297.4	300.2	303.4	292.2
2004	296.9	301.0	301.6	305.5	305.1	297.9	291.0	297.6	303.5	309.0	312.8	314.2	303.0
2005	302.7	307.9	309.5	313.2	312.8	304.7	302.2	307.6	313.6	314.7	317.8	321.1	310.7
2006	314.3	320.2	321.2	321.8	321.3	314.1	309.7	316.4	322.2	326.9	330.6	334.5	321.1
2007	324.6	330.0	331.6	330.6	330.2	321.3	318.3	321.6	329.3	332.0	335.2	336.1	328.4
2008	324.2	330.5	330.5	331.6	330.6	322.0	321.3	325.8	329.3	329.7	330.7	331.0	328.1
2009	321.9	323.2	321.5	320.5	318.3	308.5	306.5	311.4	315.4	316.0	318.2	319.2	316.7
2010	310.6	314.6	314.0	315.9	316.3	303.9	300.3	306.4	309.7	312.4	315.8	317.5	311.5
2011	310.4	314.4	315.0	316.4	315.8	304.0	299.3	310.7	315.4	318.3	322.4	322.0	313.7
2012	317.2	321.3	322.6	322.5	321.7	311.2	303.2	314.1	319.6	321.9	325.4	326.2	318.9
2013	319.1	323.1	324.1	324.8	323.7	309.7	307.1	313.9	321.6	323.8	325.9	327.1	320.3
Mining and Logging													
2002	1.7	1.6	1.6	1.6	1.6	1.6	1.4	1.4	1.5	1.4	1.4	1.4	1.5
2003	1.3	1.1	1.2	1.1	1.2	1.2	1.2	1.2	1.2	1.2	1.2	1.2	1.2
2004	1.2	1.2	1.2	1.3	1.3	1.3	1.3	1.3	1.4	1.4	1.4	1.4	1.3
2005	1.4	1.4	1.5	1.5	1.5	1.5	1.2	1.2	1.2	1.2	1.4	1.5	1.4
2006	1.4	1.5	1.5	1.5	1.5	1.6	1.6	1.6	1.6	1.6	1.7	1.7	1.6
2007	1.7	1.7	1.7	1.7	1.8	1.8	1.8	1.8	1.8	1.8	1.8	1.9	1.8
2008	1.9	1.9	1.9	1.9	1.9	2.0	2.0	2.0	2.0	1.9	1.9	1.9	1.9
2009	1.8	1.8	1.7	1.7	1.7	1.7	1.7	1.7	1.7	1.7	1.7	1.8	1.7
2010	1.7	1.8	1.8	1.8	1.8	1.8	1.8	1.9	1.8	1.9	1.9	1.9	1.8
2011	1.9	1.9	1.9	1.9	1.9	1.9	1.9	1.9	1.9	2.0	2.0	2.0	1.9
2012	2.0	2.0	2.0	2.1	2.1	2.1	2.1	2.2	2.1	2.2	2.2	2.2	2.1
2013	2.2	2.2	2.2	2.3	2.3	2.3	2.3	2.3	2.2	2.3	2.3	2.3	2.3
Construction													
2002	21.9	21.8	22.0	21.8	22.2	22.6	22.9	23.3	23.0	23.0	23.0	23.0	22.5
2003	22.5	22.3	22.4	22.5	22.8	23.2	23.1	23.2	22.8	23.4	23.3	23.4	22.9
2004	23.3	23.3	23.3	23.6	23.8	23.9	24.3	24.2	24.2	24.6	24.6	24.9	24.0
2005	23.7	24.2	24.6	25.3	25.5	26.0	26.2	26.5	26.8	26.4	26.6	26.8	25.7
2006	26.3	26.7	26.9	27.5	27.9	28.4	28.7	28.7	28.7	28.7	28.5	28.3	27.9
2007	27.1	26.9	26.9	26.5	26.8	27.1	26.9	26.9	26.3	25.8	25.4	24.8	26.5
2008	24.0	23.8	23.8	23.3	23.2	23.3	23.3	23.2	22.6	21.8	20.8	20.0	22.8
2009	18.7	17.8	17.3	16.7	16.7	16.8	16.5	16.3	16.0	15.7	15.5	15.4	16.6
2010	14.6	14.5	14.6	14.9	15.0	15.3	15.2	15.3	15.1	15.3	15.0	15.0	15.0
2011	14.6	14.6	14.8	14.5	14.6	14.8	14.7	14.6	14.4	14.3	14.1	14.0	14.5
2012	13.7	13.5	13.8	13.8	14.0	14.5	14.6	14.7	14.7	14.8	15.0	15.3	14.4
2013	14.9	14.8	15.2	15.3	15.4	15.8	15.8	15.6	15.3	15.3	15.4	15.3	15.3

Employment by Industry: Tucson, AZ, Selected Years, 2002–2013—*Continued*

(Numbers in thousands, not seasonally adjusted)

Industry and year	January	February	March	April	May	June	July	August	September	October	November	December	Annual average
Manufacturing													
2002	31.5	31.1	31.0	31.0	30.9	30.8	30.6	30.4	30.2	29.8	29.6	29.5	30.5
2003	29.2	28.9	29.1	28.6	28.6	28.6	28.6	28.7	28.5	28.5	28.4	28.6	28.7
2004	28.4	28.3	28.4	28.3	28.3	28.4	28.6	28.5	28.5	28.4	28.4	28.5	28.4
2005	28.0	28.2	28.1	28.0	28.1	28.3	28.4	28.7	28.5	28.4	28.3	28.6	28.3
2006	28.6	29.1	28.6	28.5	28.4	28.5	28.5	28.3	28.1	27.8	26.4	26.3	28.1
2007	26.1	27.8	27.4	27.3	27.3	27.6	27.7	27.8	27.8	27.6	27.7	27.6	27.5
2008	27.7	27.6	27.5	27.3	27.3	27.5	27.3	27.2	27.0	26.7	26.6	26.4	27.2
2009	25.7	25.5	25.3	25.3	25.2	25.3	25.2	25.0	24.8	24.6	24.5	24.5	25.1
2010	24.3	24.4	24.3	24.2	24.2	24.1	24.1	23.9	23.8	23.5	23.5	23.6	24.0
2011	23.4	23.3	23.3	23.3	23.5	23.5	23.5	23.5	23.5	23.4	23.3	23.4	23.4
2012	23.3	23.4	23.4	23.4	23.4	23.5	23.5	23.5	23.5	23.4	23.3	23.4	23.4
2013	23.1	23.2	23.1	23.1	23.1	23.3	23.5	23.5	23.3	23.2	23.2	23.2	23.2
Trade, Transportation, and Utilities													
2002	54.1	53.8	53.8	54.0	54.4	54.2	53.5	53.6	53.5	54.4	55.9	57.0	54.4
2003	54.0	54.0	54.4	54.1	54.1	54.2	54.0	54.9	54.9	55.7	57.6	58.8	55.1
2004	56.2	56.1	56.4	57.1	57.8	57.9	57.9	58.0	57.7	58.5	60.3	61.0	57.9
2005	58.0	58.0	58.2	58.3	58.3	58.3	58.8	59.4	59.8	60.8	62.6	64.1	59.6
2006	61.1	61.0	61.2	61.3	61.3	61.7	61.5	61.9	62.7	63.1	63.8	65.5	62.7
2007	63.9	63.3	64.0	63.8	64.1	63.8	63.7	64.0	64.0	64.5	66.1	66.7	64.3
2008	63.6	62.9	63.0	62.2	62.4	62.4	62.2	62.7	62.3	62.5	63.0	63.2	62.7
2009	60.6	59.3	58.6	58.0	57.8	57.4	57.4	57.7	57.4	57.2	58.3	59.2	58.2
2010	57.0	56.7	56.6	56.7	56.7	56.6	56.5	56.7	56.1	56.4	58.1	58.7	56.9
2011	57.2	56.8	56.9	57.1	57.2	57.4	57.0	57.9	57.3	57.8	59.9	60.3	57.7
2012	58.0	57.3	57.3	57.3	57.1	57.1	56.6	57.4	57.4	57.7	59.7	60.5	57.8
2013	58.4	57.6	57.9	57.9	58.2	58.1	58.2	59.0	58.8	59.2	61.0	61.6	58.8
Wholesale Trade													
2002	7.5	7.4	7.4	7.2	7.3	7.3	7.2	7.3	7.3	7.4	7.4	7.4	7.3
2003	7.2	7.3	7.3	7.3	7.4	7.4	7.4	7.5	7.5	7.5	7.6	7.6	7.4
2004	7.5	7.5	7.6	8.1	8.4	8.4	8.3	8.2	8.2	8.0	8.1	8.2	8.0
2005	8.0	8.1	8.2	8.3	8.4	8.5	8.6	8.7	8.9	9.0	9.0	9.2	8.6
2006	9.0	9.1	9.2	9.2	9.3	9.4	9.5	9.7	9.8	9.7	9.8	9.9	9.5
2007	9.6	9.6	9.8	9.7	9.8	9.9	9.8	9.9	9.9	9.9	9.9	9.9	9.8
2008	9.7	9.7	9.8	9.7	9.7	9.7	9.7	9.7	9.7	9.6	9.5	9.4	9.7
2009	9.1	8.9	8.6	8.5	8.5	8.4	8.5	8.5	8.4	8.4	8.4	8.4	8.6
2010	8.1	8.1	8.0	8.1	8.1	8.0	8.1	7.9	7.8	7.8	7.8	7.8	8.0
2011	7.7	7.8	7.8	7.8	7.8	7.8	7.8	7.8	7.9	7.9	7.9	7.9	7.8
2012	7.6	7.7	7.7	7.8	7.8	7.8	7.8	7.9	7.9	7.8	7.9	8.0	7.8
2013	7.8	7.7	7.8	7.7	7.8	7.8	7.6	7.6	7.7	7.7	7.8	7.8	7.7
Retail Trade													
2002	39.1	38.8	38.8	39.1	39.4	39.2	38.6	38.6	38.7	39.2	40.7	41.8	39.3
2003	39.0	38.9	39.3	39.0	38.9	39.0	38.8	39.2	39.3	40.0	41.8	42.9	39.7
2004	40.6	40.5	40.7	40.8	41.1	41.2	41.3	41.4	41.1	41.7	43.4	43.9	41.5
2005	41.2	41.0	41.0	41.1	41.0	40.8	41.3	41.8	42.0	42.8	44.6	45.8	42.0
2006	43.1	42.9	43.0	43.0	43.2	42.9	43.1	43.7	43.9	44.7	46.2	47.3	43.9
2007	45.1	44.6	45.0	44.9	44.9	44.6	44.6	44.7	44.7	45.3	46.8	47.1	45.2
2008	44.6	43.9	44.0	43.4	43.6	43.6	43.4	43.7	43.3	43.6	44.2	44.2	43.8
2009	42.2	41.1	40.8	40.6	40.5	40.2	40.2	40.4	40.2	40.0	41.1	41.7	40.8
2010	40.0	39.7	39.5	39.6	39.6	39.5	39.2	39.6	39.1	39.4	41.0	41.3	39.8
2011	39.9	39.3	39.4	39.6	39.6	39.7	39.4	40.2	39.4	40.0	41.9	42.1	40.0
2012	40.6	39.7	39.7	39.6	39.5	39.5	39.1	39.8	39.8	40.4	42.3	42.7	40.2
2013	41.2	40.5	40.8	41.0	41.1	41.0	41.1	41.8	41.5	41.9	43.5	44.0	41.6
Transportation and Utilities													
2002	7.5	7.6	7.6	7.7	7.7	7.7	7.7	7.7	7.5	7.8	7.8	7.8	7.7
2003	7.8	7.8	7.8	7.8	7.8	7.8	7.8	8.2	8.1	8.2	8.2	8.3	8.0
2004	8.1	8.1	8.1	8.2	8.3	8.3	8.3	8.4	8.4	8.8	8.8	8.9	8.4
2005	8.8	8.9	9	8.9	8.9	9	8.9	8.9	8.9	9	9	9.1	8.9
2006	9.0	9.0	9.0	9.1	9.2	9.2	9.3	9.3	9.4	9.4	9.5	9.8	9.3
2007	9.2	9.1	9.2	9.2	9.4	9.3	9.3	9.4	9.4	9.3	9.4	9.7	9.3
2008	9.3	9.3	9.2	9.1	9.1	9.1	9.1	9.3	9.3	9.3	9.3	9.6	9.3
2009	9.3	9.3	9.2	8.9	8.8	8.8	8.7	8.8	8.8	8.8	8.8	9.1	8.9
2010	8.9	8.9	9.1	9.0	9.0	9.1	9.2	9.2	9.2	9.2	9.3	9.6	9.1
2011	9.6	9.7	9.7	9.7	9.8	9.9	9.8	9.9	10.0	9.9	10.1	10.3	9.9
2012	9.8	9.9	9.9	9.9	9.8	9.8	9.7	9.7	9.7	9.5	9.5	9.8	9.8
2013	9.4	9.4	9.3	9.2	9.3	9.3	9.5	9.6	9.6	9.6	9.7	9.8	9.5
Information													
2002	7.9	8.0	8.0	7.9	8.0	7.8	7.8	7.9	7.8	7.8	7.9	7.8	7.9
2003	7.6	7.7	7.5	7.5	7.6	7.5	7.5	7.6	7.3	7.4	7.7	7.7	7.6
2004	7.5	7.7	7.5	7.5	7.6	7.5	7.6	7.8	7.3	7.4	7.7	7.6	7.6
2005	7.3	7.2	7.2	7.2	7.2	7.2	7.2	7.2	7.2	7.2	7.2	7.3	7.2
2006	7.5	7.5	7.4	6.9	6.9	6.9	6.7	6.5	6.5	6.3	6.2	6.0	6.8
2007	6.3	6.2	6.2	6.1	6.1	5.8	5.7	5.7	5.7	5.8	5.8	5.7	5.9
2008	5.7	5.5	5.4	5.3	5.3	5.2	5.2	5.1	5.1	5.0	5.1	5.2	5.3
2009	5.1	5.1	4.9	4.9	4.8	4.6	4.6	4.5	4.5	4.4	4.4	4.5	4.7
2010	4.5	4.5	4.5	4.4	4.4	4.4	4.3	4.3	4.2	4.2	4.2	4.2	4.3
2011	4.2	4.3	4.1	4.1	4.2	4.2	4.2	4.3	4.2	4.2	4.3	4.3	4.2
2012	4.2	4.4	4.3	4.3	4.4	4.2	4.2	4.3	4.1	4.1	4.2	4.2	4.2
2013	4.2	4.4	4.2	4.3	4.6	4.3	4.3	4.4	4.2	4.2	4.2	4.3	4.3

Employment by Industry: Tucson, AZ, Selected Years, 2002–2013—*Continued*

(Numbers in thousands, not seasonally adjusted)

Industry and year	January	February	March	April	May	June	July	August	September	October	November	December	Annual average
Financial Activities													
2002	13.9	14.0	14.1	14.1	14.3	14.2	14.1	14.2	14.3	14.6	14.6	14.7	14.3
2003	14.7	14.8	15.0	14.8	15.0	15.0	15.3	15.5	16.0	16.1	15.9	16.0	15.3
2004	15.9	16.0	15.9	16.0	15.9	15.6	15.8	15.7	15.5	15.5	15.5	15.6	15.7
2005	15.3	15.5	15.5	15.8	16.0	16.2	16.3	16.7	16.8	16.8	16.9	17.2	16.3
2006	16.4	16.6	16.7	17.0	17.1	17.2	17.3	17.5	17.7	18.0	18.1	18.4	17.3
2007	18.1	18.2	18.3	18.4	18.5	18.5	18.5	17.4	17.0	17.0	17.0	17.3	17.9
2008	16.5	16.6	16.7	16.9	16.8	17	17	17	16.9	16.5	16.5	16.8	16.8
2009	16.5	16.6	16.6	16.8	16.9	16.9	17.4	17.4	17.2	17.3	17.3	17.5	17.0
2010	17.4	17.5	17.2	17.0	17.2	17.2	17.1	17.1	16.9	17.0	17.0	17.2	17.2
2011	16.9	16.9	16.9	16.8	16.7	16.8	16.8	16.7	16.7	16.7	16.7	16.9	16.8
2012	16.7	16.8	16.6	16.5	16.6	16.7	16.7	16.8	16.8	17.0	17.0	17.2	16.8
2013	16.9	17.0	17.0	16.9	17.0	17.1	17.0	16.9	17.0	17.1	17.2	17.4	17.0
Professional and Business Services													
2002	40.4	41.0	41.3	41.5	40.9	41.1	41.2	41.9	42.0	42.0	42.4	42.2	41.5
2003	40.6	40.6	40.7	41.0	40.8	41.5	41.2	41.6	42.1	41.7	41.5	41.5	41.2
2004	41.2	41.7	41.8	43.4	42.7	42.8	43.5	43.9	43.8	45.3	45.3	45.4	43.4
2005	44.1	44.5	44.5	45.8	45.5	45.5	46.3	47.0	47.0	46.5	46.6	47.6	45.9
2006	47.3	48.4	48.5	48.6	48.6	49.1	49.5	50.0	50.9	50.9	52.0	53.1	49.7
2007	51.5	52.1	52.3	52.1	52.0	52.5	52.0	52.9	53.0	53.6	53.9	53.6	52.6
2008	51.8	52.0	52.3	52.3	51.4	51.2	51.7	51.9	51.6	50.6	50.0	50.2	51.4
2009	49.0	48.3	48.0	47.2	46.5	46.5	46.4	46.4	46.3	46.4	46.8	47.0	47.1
2010	45.8	46.1	46.4	46.2	45.2	45.2	45.1	45.0	44.8	45.9	45.8	46.8	45.7
2011	45.6	45.9	46.3	46.3	46.0	46.1	45.9	46.1	47.1	47.9	48.3	49.0	46.7
2012	47.7	48.2	48.9	48.6	48.2	48.3	47.9	47.9	48.1	48.9	49.2	49.2	48.4
2013	49.0	49.4	49.8	50.1	49.7	48.7	48.3	48.3	48.9	49.5	49.0	49.8	49.2
Education and Health Services													
2002	42.9	43.4	43.4	43.4	43.7	43.4	42.7	43.5	43.9	44.0	44.3	44.3	43.6
2003	44.3	44.9	45.0	45.4	45.5	45.3	45.3	46.1	46.5	46.1	46.6	46.8	45.7
2004	46.7	46.7	46.9	47.1	47.5	47.2	47.2	48.2	48.5	48.9	49.1	49.2	47.8
2005	49.1	49.5	49.7	50.2	50.5	49.8	49.9	50.8	51.4	51.6	51.7	52.2	50.5
2006	51.6	52.1	52.5	52.0	52.3	52.0	51.7	52.6	53.0	53.3	53.6	54.2	52.6
2007	53.5	54.0	54.3	54.0	54.7	54.1	54.0	54.6	54.9	55.9	55.9	56.2	54.7
2008	55.0	55.6	56.0	57.0	57.1	56.6	56.7	57.6	58.1	58.4	58.8	58.8	57.1
2009	58.4	58.7	58.7	58.4	58.5	58.0	57.8	58.4	58.7	58.8	58.9	59.1	58.5
2010	58.0	58.2	58.4	58.5	58.6	58.0	57.4	58.1	58.3	58.7	58.7	59.1	58.3
2011	58.6	59.1	59.0	59.8	59.9	59.4	59.2	60.0	60.4	60.4	60.8	61.1	59.8
2012	61.0	61.2	61.4	61.2	61.1	60.6	59.7	60.4	60.7	61.1	61.3	61.6	60.9
2013	60.5	61.0	61.2	61.2	61.1	60.5	60.6	61.5	61.6	62.2	61.9	61.6	61.2
Leisure and Hospitality													
2002	37.8	38.4	38.8	38.7	37.9	36.7	35.5	35.6	36.2	36.8	37.3	37.4	37.3
2003	36.4	36.9	37.5	37.9	37.5	36.6	35.7	36.1	36.9	37.5	38.2	38.9	37.2
2004	38.6	39.4	39.7	40.5	39.8	38.6	37.7	38.3	38.4	38.8	39.7	40.0	39.1
2005	38.7	39.6	40.2	41.6	41.1	40.4	39.0	38.9	39.6	39.1	39.4	39.6	39.8
2006	39.7	40.9	41.2	41.9	41.1	40.2	39.3	39.9	40.8	40.5	40.7	40.9	40.6
2007	39.8	41.1	41.5	41.5	41.0	39.9	38.6	38.7	39.3	39.6	40.3	40.7	40.2
2008	40.3	41.7	41.6	41.3	41.0	39.9	38.8	39.0	39.7	40.4	40.4	40.6	40.4
2009	39.1	39.9	39.9	39.9	39.5	38.5	37.0	37.6	38.1	38.1	38.5	38.2	38.7
2010	37.4	38.4	38.9	39.5	39.1	38.0	36.8	37.1	37.4	38.0	38.4	38.6	38.1
2011	38.4	39.0	39.7	40.1	40.1	39.0	37.8	38.4	38.7	39.1	39.6	39.6	39.1
2012	39.7	40.8	41.4	41.8	41.4	40.0	38.6	39.3	39.8	39.9	40.4	40.4	40.3
2013	39.8	40.7	41.0	41.0	40.4	39.3	38.2	38.8	39.7	38.9	39.5	39.7	39.8
Other Services													
2002	14.2	14.3	14.3	14.7	14.8	14.7	14.6	14.5	14.5	14.4	14.4	14.4	14.5
2003	14.2	14.3	14.4	14.6	14.6	14.6	14.6	14.6	14.6	14.8	14.8	14.7	14.6
2004	14.3	14.5	14.5	14.8	14.8	14.7	14.8	14.6	14.4	14.7	14.7	14.6	14.6
2005	14.0	14.1	14.3	14.6	14.6	14.4	14.3	14.2	14.2	14.4	14.5	14.4	14.3
2006	15.0	15.3	15.5	15.5	15.7	15.9	14.8	14.8	14.5	14.9	14.9	15.0	15.2
2007	14.7	15.0	15.2	15.1	15.1	15.2	14.9	14.9	14.8	14.9	14.9	14.8	15.0
2008	14.6	14.8	14.8	14.9	14.9	14.9	14.7	14.5	14.4	14.3	14.3	14.0	14.6
2009	13.6	13.7	13.8	13.5	13.4	13.4	13.3	13.3	13.1	13.1	13.1	13.1	13.4
2010	12.4	12.5	12.6	12.8	12.8	12.9	12.8	12.7	12.7	12.7	12.7	12.7	12.7
2011	12.5	12.6	12.7	12.6	12.6	12.6	12.5	12.4	12.2	12.4	12.5	12.5	12.5
2012	12.4	12.6	12.8	12.7	12.9	13.0	12.9	12.8	12.7	12.8	12.9	12.7	12.8
2013	12.4	12.6	12.7	12.8	12.8	12.8	12.7	12.6	12.5	12.6	12.7	12.6	12.7
Government													
2002	74.7	76.9	76.9	78.2	77.4	71.4	64.8	69.5	74.9	77.4	78.4	78.2	74.9
2003	75.7	78.1	78.5	78.2	78.3	70.7	66.7	70.7	76.0	78.1	77.9	79.0	75.7
2004	76.5	78.9	78.9	79.1	79.0	73.6	66.5	71.1	77.9	79.9	80.5	80.8	76.9
2005	76.2	79.5	79.9	79.7	79.6	72.9	70.4	73.4	77.6	78.3	78.9	78.7	77.1
2006	75.7	78.4	78.2	78.6	77.9	71.3	68.5	72.4	75.7	79.2	79.6	79.9	76.3
2007	76.8	80.1	79.8	79.6	78.7	71.5	70.9	73.4	80.6	80.7	81.3	81.1	77.9
2008	76.7	81.4	80.7	81.7	81.8	74.8	75.0	78.0	81.2	82.0	82.6	82.2	79.8
2009	79.6	81.6	81.0	81.8	80.9	73.2	72.6	76.1	80.1	80.7	80.9	80.6	79.1
2010	78.1	80.7	79.4	80.8	82.3	71.6	70.3	75.4	79.3	79.5	80.9	80.2	78.2
2011	77.0	79.8	79.4	79.6	79.1	68.5	65.9	74.9	78.8	79.8	80.3	78.3	76.8
2012	77.5	80.0	79.9	80.1	80.0	71.3	66.6	75.2	80.0	80.4	80.7	80.4	77.7
2013	77.9	80.4	80.3	80.6	79.9	68.9	67.8	72.4	78.9	80.1	80.4	80.1	77.3

Employment by Industry: Tulsa, OK, Selected Years, 2002–2013

(Numbers in thousands, not seasonally adjusted)

Industry and year	January	February	March	April	May	June	July	August	September	October	November	December	Annual average
Total Nonfarm													
2002	410.6	410.5	412.3	414.7	417.1	413.3	406.5	408.5	407.7	406.0	406.7	407.3	410.1
2003	398.8	398.3	398.7	400.1	401.5	398.1	394.8	396.1	396.6	398.0	398.9	400.2	398.3
2004	394.7	396.7	399.5	399.7	400.1	400.9	399.1	400.6	402.1	403.4	403.6	405.5	400.5
2005	401.8	404.5	407.8	410.8	414.1	415.8	412.6	415.7	418.7	418.9	421.7	424.0	413.9
2006	418.2	420.4	425.0	424.4	429.2	430.4	423.2	426.1	428.8	430.3	431.7	433.9	426.8
2007	424.2	428.2	433.8	434.4	437.5	437.7	433.2	435.0	436.5	439.9	441.2	439.3	435.1
2008	435.1	438.6	441.5	441.5	444.5	442.1	438.1	439.7	442.2	441.9	441.5	441.0	440.6
2009	428.1	427.1	427.3	424.3	424.4	421.5	413.5	413.8	414.8	417.2	417.9	416.7	420.6
2010	406.5	408.0	411.2	414.9	417.7	416.3	410.1	409.2	411.9	417.2	418.8	419.4	413.4
2011	407.6	405.1	411.6	414.5	415.8	415.6	414.2	414.1	417.9	421.7	422.6	423.7	415.4
2012	414.0	417.7	420.4	424.2	426.8	426.5	421.4	422.3	425.6	431.0	434.0	434.5	424.9
2013	422.6	425.1	428.0	429.9	432.2	432.4	428.9	430.2	432.2	435.7	439.3	438.7	431.3
Total Private													
2002	360.4	359.4	360.9	363.0	364.5	362.8	358.9	360.2	357.8	354.5	355.3	355.7	359.5
2003	348.7	347.5	347.9	349.5	350.4	348.6	347.5	348.7	346.7	347.4	348.4	349.4	348.4
2004	345.0	345.9	348.5	348.7	349.0	350.7	350.0	350.9	350.0	350.6	351.6	353.1	349.5
2005	349.3	351.1	354.2	357.1	359.6	361.8	363.0	364.7	365.2	363.5	366.4	368.5	360.4
2006	363.4	364.8	369.0	369.3	373.3	376.3	374.0	376.2	375.0	374.7	376.5	378.8	372.6
2007	370.7	373.3	378.4	378.9	381.6	384.7	384.0	385.3	382.2	383.8	385.3	383.7	381.0
2008	380.8	382.9	385.6	385.1	387.5	388.3	387.6	388.5	385.7	383.2	382.9	382.4	385.0
2009	372.3	369.8	369.4	365.7	365.3	366.5	363.0	361.1	357.0	357.0	357.6	356.8	363.5
2010	349.5	349.9	352.3	355.4	356.6	358.3	358.8	358.3	356.0	358.6	360.0	360.7	356.2
2011	351.5	348.3	354.4	357.3	358.9	360.7	362.5	362.4	362.8	363.9	364.7	365.7	359.4
2012	358.5	360.6	362.7	366.8	369.1	371.7	370.7	371.3	369.7	372.9	375.6	376.2	368.8
2013	366.4	367.3	369.9	372.1	374.2	376.5	376.2	377.5	375.6	376.3	380.0	379.3	374.3
Goods-Producing													
2002	78.4	77.3	77.1	76.7	76.8	76.6	75.4	75.3	73.9	73.0	72.6	72.7	75.5
2003	71.7	71.0	71.1	71.3	71.4	71.8	72.2	72.1	71.6	70.8	70.5	70.8	71.4
2004	69.4	69.4	69.8	69.8	70.2	70.9	71.4	70.8	70.3	70.0	69.7	69.9	70.1
2005	68.9	69.0	69.9	70.6	71.2	72.0	72.7	73.1	73.3	73.2	73.7	75.0	71.9
2006	74.5	75.0	76.2	75.0	76.3	77.5	77.7	78.4	78.2	78.3	78.7	79.0	77.1
2007	77.8	77.8	79.1	78.6	79.4	80.6	81.4	81.9	81.0	81.8	82.1	81.8	80.3
2008	81.9	82.2	82.9	82.8	83.8	84.2	84.5	84.5	84.0	82.9	82.6	82.9	83.3
2009	81.0	79.1	77.8	75.7	74.4	74.6	73.0	72.2	71.1	70.2	69.6	69.3	74.0
2010	68.0	68.1	68.5	68.9	69.4	70.5	71.2	70.9	70.7	71.6	72.0	72.6	70.2
2011	70.7	70.0	71.7	72.5	72.8	73.7	74.1	73.9	74.3	75.0	75.3	75.5	73.3
2012	74.4	74.8	75.4	76.3	77.1	77.6	77.8	78.1	78.1	80.1	80.6	80.4	77.6
2013	78.1	78.2	78.7	79.0	79.0	79.8	80.1	80.5	79.8	80.7	81.5	81.0	79.7
Service-Providing													
2002	332.2	333.2	335.2	338.0	340.3	336.7	331.1	333.2	333.8	333.0	334.1	334.6	334.6
2003	327.1	327.3	327.6	328.8	330.1	326.3	322.6	324.0	325.0	327.2	328.4	329.4	327.0
2004	325.3	327.3	329.7	329.9	329.9	330.0	327.7	329.8	331.8	333.4	333.9	335.6	330.4
2005	332.9	335.5	337.9	340.2	342.9	343.8	339.9	342.6	345.4	345.7	348.0	349.0	342.0
2006	343.7	345.4	348.8	349.4	352.9	352.9	345.5	347.7	350.6	352.0	353.0	354.9	349.7
2007	346.4	350.4	354.7	355.8	358.1	357.1	351.8	353.1	355.5	358.1	359.1	357.5	354.8
2008	353.2	356.4	358.6	358.7	360.7	357.9	353.6	355.2	358.2	359.0	358.9	358.1	357.4
2009	347.1	348.0	349.5	348.6	350.0	346.9	340.5	341.6	343.7	347.0	348.3	347.4	346.6
2010	338.5	339.9	342.7	346.0	348.3	345.8	338.9	338.3	341.2	345.6	346.8	346.8	343.2
2011	336.9	335.1	339.9	342.0	343.0	341.9	340.1	340.2	343.6	346.7	347.3	348.2	342.1
2012	339.6	342.9	345.0	347.9	349.7	348.9	343.6	344.2	347.5	350.9	353.4	354.1	347.3
2013	344.5	346.9	349.3	350.9	353.2	352.6	348.8	349.7	352.4	355.0	357.8	357.7	351.6
Mining and Logging													
2002	4.3	4.4	4.4	4.3	4.3	4.5	4.2	4.2	4.1	4.0	3.9	3.9	4.2
2003	4.0	3.9	3.9	3.8	3.8	3.8	3.9	3.9	4.0	4.0	4.0	4.0	3.9
2004	4.4	4.4	4.3	4.3	4.3	4.4	4.5	4.4	4.4	4.4	4.3	4.4	4.4
2005	4.8	4.8	4.8	4.9	5.0	5.1	5.3	5.3	5.4	5.3	5.4	5.5	5.1
2006	5.6	5.7	5.8	6.2	6.1	6.2	6.3	6.3	6.3	6.2	6.3	6.3	6.1
2007	6.4	6.4	6.5	6.4	6.5	6.7	6.9	6.9	6.8	7.0	7.0	7.1	6.7
2008	7.0	7.1	7.1	7.0	7.1	7.4	7.5	7.5	7.4	7.2	7.1	7.1	7.2
2009	7.3	7.1	6.9	6.8	6.7	6.8	6.8	6.9	6.8	6.6	6.6	6.6	6.8
2010	6.7	6.6	6.6	6.7	6.8	7.0	7.1	7.1	7.1	7.2	7.3	7.3	7.0
2011	7.2	7.2	7.3	7.3	7.4	7.5	7.6	7.7	7.7	7.8	7.9	7.9	7.5
2012	7.4	7.4	7.5	7.4	7.5	7.5	7.7	7.7	7.7	8.0	8.0	7.8	7.6
2013	7.4	7.4	7.4	7.5	7.4	7.4	7.7	7.7	7.7	7.6	7.7	7.7	7.6
Construction													
2002	20.8	20.7	20.6	20.3	20.6	20.7	20.8	21.1	20.4	20.2	19.9	20.0	20.5
2003	19.4	19.1	19.4	20.1	20.4	20.6	20.9	20.8	20.4	19.7	19.4	19.5	20.0
2004	18.6	18.5	18.8	18.9	19.2	19.6	20.3	20.1	19.9	19.6	19.3	19.2	19.3
2005	18.4	18.4	18.9	19.3	19.7	20.1	20.7	20.8	20.8	20.6	20.5	20.9	19.9
2006	20.7	20.7	21.2	21.1	21.3	21.9	21.8	21.9	21.9	22.1	22.0	22.1	21.6
2007	20.6	20.6	21.5	21.3	21.5	22.2	22.2	22.5	22.1	22.4	22.5	22.1	21.8
2008	22.1	22.2	22.7	22.9	23.2	23.3	23.6	23.5	23.3	23.0	22.8	22.7	22.9
2009	21.7	21.5	21.5	21.0	20.7	21.0	20.8	20.5	20.1	19.9	19.5	19.4	20.6
2010	18.6	18.8	19.1	19.2	19.4	19.8	20.1	19.9	19.9	20.3	20.3	20.5	19.7
2011	19.0	18.4	19.4	19.7	19.7	19.9	19.7	19.5	19.6	19.8	19.6	19.5	19.5
2012	19.0	19.0	19.2	19.6	19.9	20.0	20.1	20.2	20.3	21.4	22.1	21.7	20.2
2013	20.0	20.1	20.7	21.1	21.3	21.9	21.8	22.3	21.9	22.9	22.7	21.8	21.5

Employment by Industry: Tulsa, OK, Selected Years, 2002–2013—*Continued*

(Numbers in thousands, not seasonally adjusted)

Industry and year	January	February	March	April	May	June	July	August	September	October	November	December	Annual average
Manufacturing													
2002	53.3	52.2	52.1	52.1	51.9	51.4	50.4	50.0	49.4	48.8	48.8	48.8	50.8
2003	48.3	48.0	47.8	47.4	47.2	47.4	47.4	47.4	47.2	47.1	47.1	47.3	47.5
2004	46.4	46.5	46.7	46.6	46.7	46.9	46.6	46.3	46.0	46.0	46.1	46.3	46.4
2005	45.7	45.8	46.2	46.4	46.5	46.8	46.7	47.0	47.1	47.3	47.8	48.6	46.8
2006	48.2	48.6	49.2	47.7	48.9	49.4	49.6	50.2	50.0	50.0	50.4	50.6	49.4
2007	50.8	50.8	51.1	50.9	51.4	51.7	52.3	52.5	52.1	52.4	52.6	52.6	51.8
2008	52.8	52.9	53.1	52.9	53.5	53.5	53.4	53.5	53.3	52.7	52.7	53.1	53.1
2009	52.0	50.5	49.4	47.9	47.0	46.8	45.4	44.8	44.2	43.7	43.5	43.3	46.5
2010	42.7	42.7	42.8	43.0	43.2	43.7	44.0	43.9	43.7	44.1	44.4	44.8	43.6
2011	44.5	44.4	45.0	45.5	45.7	46.3	46.8	46.7	47.0	47.4	47.8	48.1	46.3
2012	48.0	48.4	48.7	49.3	49.7	50.1	50.0	50.2	50.1	50.7	50.5	50.9	49.7
2013	50.7	50.7	50.6	50.4	50.3	50.5	50.6	50.5	50.2	50.2	51.1	51.5	50.6
Trade, Transportation, and Utilities													
2002	85.0	84.1	84.9	86.1	86.3	85.8	85.1	85.1	85.0	84.4	85.9	86.7	85.4
2003	83.7	82.7	82.7	83.0	82.9	82.1	81.7	81.9	81.3	82.0	83.5	84.6	82.7
2004	80.9	79.8	80.8	80.8	81.2	81.2	79.8	79.7	79.2	79.6	80.8	81.5	80.4
2005	79.9	79.3	79.4	79.7	80.1	80.2	80.8	81.3	81.4	81.7	83.2	84.2	80.9
2006	81.3	80.8	81.7	83.2	84.0	83.9	83.4	83.5	83.6	83.8	85.5	86.7	83.5
2007	83.8	83.9	85.2	84.7	85.0	85.3	84.9	84.3	84.2	85.1	86.7	86.7	85.0
2008	83.6	83.9	84.8	85.3	85.6	85.6	86.2	86.4	85.8	85.7	86.9	87.3	85.6
2009	83.6	82.8	83.1	83.6	84.0	83.9	83.0	82.8	82.2	82.6	83.8	84.3	83.3
2010	80.5	79.9	80.3	80.4	80.9	81.0	81.1	80.9	80.0	80.5	82.1	82.7	80.9
2011	79.7	78.7	79.8	80.7	81.0	81.2	81.4	81.5	81.5	81.9	83.7	84.4	81.3
2012	81.7	81.3	81.8	82.1	82.5	83.1	82.5	82.2	81.9	82.9	84.9	85.3	82.7
2013	81.1	80.7	81.2	81.8	82.3	82.7	82.7	83.0	82.9	83.2	85.5	86.8	82.8
Wholesale Trade													
2002	17.6	17.4	17.6	17.7	17.7	17.7	17.7	17.8	17.7	17.4	17.5	17.5	17.6
2003	17.0	16.8	16.9	16.9	16.8	16.8	16.9	16.8	16.8	16.8	16.7	16.8	16.8
2004	16.3	16.0	16.0	16.0	16.2	16.3	16.3	16.3	16.4	16.3	16.4	16.6	16.3
2005	16.7	16.7	16.8	16.9	17.0	17.2	17.5	17.5	17.5	17.5	17.6	17.7	17.2
2006	17.4	17.3	17.4	17.7	17.8	17.9	17.7	17.7	17.7	17.7	17.7	17.7	17.6
2007	17.8	18.0	18.2	18.3	18.2	18.3	18.2	18.0	17.9	18.0	18.0	17.9	18.1
2008	17.7	17.7	17.7	17.5	17.4	17.4	17.5	17.4	17.3	17.1	17.1	17.0	17.4
2009	16.6	16.5	16.4	16.3	16.2	16.0	15.8	15.6	15.4	15.4	15.2	15.2	15.9
2010	15.1	15.1	15.1	15.1	15.2	15.3	15.3	15.3	15.3	15.2	15.3	15.3	15.2
2011	15.0	15.0	15.1	15.1	15.1	15.1	15.4	15.3	15.3	15.2	15.2	15.2	15.2
2012	15.0	15.1	15.2	15.3	15.4	15.5	15.3	15.4	15.5	15.6	15.5	15.5	15.4
2013	15.3	15.3	15.3	15.5	15.6	15.6	15.7	15.8	15.8	15.8	15.8	15.8	15.6
Retail Trade													
2002	46.8	46.2	46.6	46.9	47.1	46.6	45.7	45.7	45.5	45.5	46.9	47.6	46.4
2003	45.2	44.5	44.5	44.9	45.0	44.7	44.4	44.6	44.3	44.9	46.5	47.4	45.1
2004	44.7	43.8	44.7	44.8	44.9	44.7	43.4	43.2	42.7	43.5	44.7	45.2	44.2
2005	43.2	42.6	42.6	42.8	43.0	42.8	43.2	43.5	43.8	44.2	44.5	46.3	43.6
2006	43.4	43.4	43.9	44.4	44.9	44.6	44.4	44.2	44.2	44.6	46.1	47.0	44.6
2007	44.1	43.8	44.9	44.7	45.0	45.1	44.5	44.4	44.3	44.9	46.4	46.5	44.9
2008	43.9	44.2	45.1	45.7	45.9	45.8	46.0	46.2	45.6	45.5	46.6	46.9	45.6
2009	44.8	44.3	44.8	44.9	45.5	45.6	45.1	45.2	45.0	45.3	46.7	47.0	45.4
2010	44.8	44.1	44.5	44.9	45.2	45.3	45.3	45.2	44.4	45.0	46.5	46.8	45.2
2011	44.7	43.7	44.5	45.2	45.4	45.3	45.1	45.3	45.3	45.7	47.4	47.7	45.4
2012	45.5	44.8	45.3	45.5	45.8	46.2	45.9	45.6	45.4	46.3	48.4	48.7	46.1
2013	45.5	45.1	45.6	45.9	46.4	46.8	46.5	46.7	46.6	46.9	49.2	50.4	46.8
Transportation and Utilities													
2002	20.6	20.5	20.7	21.5	21.5	21.5	21.7	21.6	21.8	21.5	21.5	21.6	21.3
2003	21.5	21.4	21.3	21.2	21.1	20.6	20.4	20.5	20.2	20.3	20.3	20.4	20.8
2004	19.9	20.0	20.1	20.0	20.1	20.2	20.1	20.2	20.1	19.8	19.7	19.7	20.0
2005	20.0	20.0	20.0	20.0	20.1	20.2	20.1	20.3	20.1	20.0	20.1	20.2	20.1
2006	20.5	20.1	20.4	21.1	21.3	21.4	21.3	21.6	21.7	21.5	21.7	22.0	21.2
2007	21.9	22.1	22.1	21.7	21.8	21.9	22.2	21.9	22.0	22.2	22.3	22.3	22.0
2008	22.0	22.0	22.0	22.1	22.3	22.4	22.7	22.8	22.9	23.1	23.2	23.4	22.6
2009	22.2	22.0	21.9	22.4	22.3	22.3	22.1	22.0	21.8	21.9	21.9	22.1	22.1
2010	20.6	20.7	20.7	20.4	20.5	20.4	20.5	20.4	20.3	20.3	20.3	20.6	20.5
2011	20.0	20.0	20.2	20.4	20.5	20.8	20.9	20.9	20.9	21.0	21.1	21.5	20.7
2012	21.2	21.4	21.3	21.3	21.3	21.4	21.3	21.2	21.0	21.0	21.0	21.1	21.2
2013	20.3	20.3	20.3	20.4	20.3	20.3	20.5	20.5	20.5	20.5	20.5	20.6	20.4
Information													
2002	15.7	15.8	15.4	14.6	14.4	14.2	14.0	13.9	13.8	13.7	13.6	13.2	14.4
2003	12.9	12.8	12.5	12.6	12.6	12.4	12.0	11.7	11.6	11.8	11.8	12.0	12.2
2004	12.0	12.0	11.9	11.5	11.3	11.2	11.1	10.8	10.5	10.5	10.5	10.5	11.2
2005	10.8	10.7	10.5	10.6	10.6	10.7	10.7	10.7	10.8	10.8	11.0	11.0	10.7
2006	10.5	10.3	10.3	10.0	10.1	10.1	10.0	10.0	9.7	9.8	9.8	10.2	10.1
2007	9.9	10.1	10.0	9.9	10.0	9.9	10.0	9.9	9.9	10.0	10.0	10.0	10.0
2008	9.8	9.9	9.8	10.0	10.0	10.0	10.0	9.8	9.7	9.6	9.7	9.7	9.8
2009	9.4	9.4	9.2	9.1	9.0	8.9	8.9	8.8	8.5	8.5	8.5	8.5	8.9
2010	8.4	8.3	8.3	8.7	8.7	8.5	8.7	8.5	8.4	8.3	8.3	8.4	8.5
2011	8.3	8.2	8.2	8.1	8.2	8.2	8.3	8.3	8.2	8.2	8.1	8.2	8.2
2012	8.1	8.0	8.0	7.9	7.9	7.9	8.0	7.9	7.9	7.9	7.9	7.9	7.9
2013	7.8	7.8	7.8	7.8	7.9	7.9	8.0	7.8	7.7	7.7	7.7	7.7	7.8

Employment by Industry: Tulsa, OK, Selected Years, 2002–2013—*Continued*

(Numbers in thousands, not seasonally adjusted)

Industry and year	January	February	March	April	May	June	July	August	September	October	November	December	Annual average
Financial Activities													
2002	25.0	24.9	24.8	24.9	24.9	25.0	25.0	24.9	24.7	24.5	24.5	24.5	24.8
2003	24.4	24.4	24.4	24.6	24.7	24.7	24.6	24.5	24.4	24.4	24.3	24.2	24.5
2004	24.7	24.8	24.9	24.7	24.7	24.8	24.6	24.7	24.5	24.5	24.6	24.6	24.7
2005	25.1	25.2	25.2	24.9	24.9	25.1	25.2	25.2	25.0	24.9	25.1	25.1	25.1
2006	25.3	25.4	25.5	25.3	25.4	25.7	25.3	25.4	25.3	25.4	25.5	25.7	25.4
2007	24.9	25.1	25.3	25.0	25.0	25.1	25.2	25.1	24.9	25.0	24.8	24.8	25.0
2008	24.6	24.6	24.6	24.6	24.6	24.6	24.9	24.8	24.5	24.5	24.4	24.5	24.6
2009	24.0	23.9	23.9	24.0	24.1	24.0	24.2	23.9	23.6	23.5	23.5	23.4	23.8
2010	23.2	23.2	23.2	23.3	23.3	23.2	23.2	23.2	23.0	23.0	22.9	23.0	23.1
2011	22.7	22.6	22.6	22.6	22.5	22.6	22.6	22.6	22.5	22.6	22.6	22.7	22.6
2012	22.4	22.5	22.4	22.2	22.3	22.4	22.5	22.5	22.4	22.6	22.6	22.7	22.5
2013	22.6	22.6	22.6	22.7	22.8	22.8	23.0	23.0	22.8	22.9	22.9	23.0	22.8
Professional and Business Services													
2002	51.5	51.8	52.0	52.6	53.4	52.8	51.6	51.8	51.2	50.7	50.2	50.1	51.6
2003	48.6	48.8	48.7	48.8	49.0	48.6	48.7	49.5	49.5	50.2	50.3	50.0	49.2
2004	50.6	51.8	51.5	52.2	51.8	52.4	53.4	54.1	54.9	56.1	56.2	56.6	53.5
2005	56.2	57.7	58.3	59.3	59.8	59.8	59.9	60.3	61.2	60.5	61.1	61.0	59.6
2006	59.8	60.7	61.1	61.1	61.7	61.8	61.2	62.1	61.9	61.4	61.4	60.5	61.2
2007	60.2	61.0	61.7	62.1	62.8	62.7	62.4	63.6	62.8	63.1	63.0	62.5	62.3
2008	63.3	64.0	64.4	64.2	64.1	63.9	63.3	63.8	63.5	62.7	62.0	60.6	63.3
2009	57.2	57.0	56.4	55.1	55.0	55.1	54.4	54.4	53.7	54.5	54.7	54.6	55.2
2010	53.6	54.0	54.4	55.3	55.1	55.3	55.2	55.1	54.9	55.7	55.1	54.6	54.9
2011	53.0	52.8	53.7	53.7	53.8	53.9	54.6	54.8	55.4	55.6	55.1	55.1	54.3
2012	53.3	54.6	54.8	55.9	56.1	56.8	56.9	57.4	57.0	57.3	57.4	56.9	56.2
2013	55.7	56.0	56.8	57.1	57.5	58.1	58.6	58.9	58.6	58.7	58.6	58.4	57.8
Education and Health Services													
2002	56.3	56.7	56.9	56.8	56.5	55.8	56.5	57.6	58.4	57.9	58.8	58.8	57.3
2003	58.5	58.6	58.5	58.8	58.6	57.7	57.5	57.9	58.2	58.0	58.1	57.8	58.2
2004	57.9	58.2	58.5	58.6	58.3	57.8	57.9	58.5	59.2	58.9	58.9	59.1	58.5
2005	58.5	58.9	59.3	59.6	59.8	59.8	59.7	60.0	60.2	60.2	60.4	60.5	59.7
2006	60.1	60.5	60.7	60.8	61.2	61.8	61.3	61.6	62.3	62.5	62.6	62.9	61.5
2007	61.9	62.5	63.0	63.4	63.6	64.2	63.7	63.9	64.0	64.0	63.9	63.6	63.5
2008	63.8	64.2	64.4	63.4	63.7	63.6	62.8	63.0	63.2	63.1	63.2	63.2	63.5
2009	63.4	63.7	64.0	63.3	63.6	64.2	64.2	64.2	63.9	64.8	64.8	64.7	64.1
2010	64.6	64.8	65.0	65.2	65.2	65.2	65.3	65.7	65.6	66.4	66.6	66.7	65.5
2011	66.0	65.4	66.1	66.3	66.7	66.6	66.8	66.8	66.7	67.0	66.6	66.6	66.5
2012	66.1	66.1	65.9	66.6	66.8	66.8	66.5	66.9	67.1	67.4	67.6	68.0	66.8
2013	67.6	68.0	68.1	67.9	67.9	67.7	66.7	67.1	67.4	67.3	67.0	66.6	67.4
Leisure and Hospitality													
2002	32.8	33.1	33.9	34.7	35.6	35.6	34.4	35.0	34.3	34.1	33.5	33.5	34.2
2003	32.4	32.6	33.2	33.9	34.5	34.4	34.0	34.4	33.5	33.5	33.3	33.2	33.6
2004	32.7	33.1	34.0	34.2	34.6	35.1	34.8	35.3	34.6	34.2	34.1	34.0	34.2
2005	33.1	33.4	34.5	35.5	36.2	36.9	37.6	36.8	36.1	35.2	34.9	34.6	35.3
2006	34.8	35.0	36.2	36.5	37.2	37.6	37.4	37.6	36.5	36.2	35.6	36.3	36.4
2007	35.0	35.6	36.6	36.9	37.4	37.8	37.6	37.7	36.8	36.4	36.4	36.0	36.7
2008	35.5	35.8	36.4	36.8	37.6	38.0	37.4	37.9	37.0	36.7	36.3	36.4	36.8
2009	36.1	36.4	37.4	37.6	38.0	38.3	37.7	37.4	36.8	35.8	35.6	35.0	36.8
2010	34.3	34.7	35.6	36.7	37.1	37.3	37.1	37.2	36.7	36.4	36.3	36.1	36.3
2011	34.8	34.3	35.8	36.9	37.3	37.6	37.8	37.9	37.6	37.0	36.6	36.5	36.7
2012	36.0	36.7	37.7	38.6	39.1	39.6	39.1	39.1	38.4	37.8	37.7	38.1	38.2
2013	36.9	37.3	38.1	39.1	40.0	40.2	39.9	40.1	39.5	38.9	40.0	39.0	39.1
Other Services													
2002	15.7	15.7	15.9	16.6	16.6	17.0	16.9	16.6	16.5	16.2	16.2	16.2	16.3
2003	16.5	16.6	16.8	16.5	16.7	16.9	16.8	16.7	16.6	16.7	16.6	16.8	16.7
2004	16.8	16.8	17.1	16.9	16.9	17.3	17.0	17.0	16.8	16.8	16.8	16.9	16.9
2005	16.8	16.9	17.1	16.9	17.0	17.3	17.6	17.3	17.2	17.0	17.0	17.1	17.1
2006	17.1	17.1	17.3	17.4	17.4	17.9	17.7	17.6	17.5	17.3	17.4	17.5	17.4
2007	17.2	17.3	17.5	18.3	18.4	19.1	18.8	18.9	18.6	18.4	18.4	18.3	18.3
2008	18.3	18.3	18.3	18.0	18.1	18.4	18.5	18.3	18.0	18.0	17.8	17.8	18.2
2009	17.6	17.5	17.6	17.1	17.2	17.5	17.6	17.4	17.2	17.1	17.1	17.0	17.3
2010	16.9	16.9	17.0	16.9	16.9	17.3	17.0	16.8	16.7	16.7	16.7	16.6	16.9
2011	16.3	16.3	16.5	16.5	16.6	16.9	16.9	16.6	16.6	16.6	16.7	16.7	16.6
2012	16.5	16.6	16.7	17.2	17.3	17.5	17.4	17.2	16.9	16.9	16.9	16.9	17.0
2013	16.6	16.7	16.6	16.7	16.8	17.3	17.2	17.1	16.9	16.9	16.8	16.8	16.9
Government													
2002	50.2	51.1	51.4	51.7	52.6	50.5	47.6	48.3	49.9	51.5	51.4	51.6	50.7
2003	50.1	50.8	50.8	50.6	51.1	49.5	47.3	47.4	49.9	50.6	50.5	50.8	50.0
2004	49.7	50.8	51.0	51.0	51.1	50.2	49.1	49.7	52.1	52.8	52.0	52.4	51.0
2005	52.5	53.4	53.6	53.7	54.5	54.0	49.6	51.0	53.5	55.4	55.3	55.5	53.5
2006	54.8	55.6	56.0	55.1	55.9	54.1	49.2	49.9	53.8	55.6	55.2	55.1	54.2
2007	53.5	54.9	55.4	55.5	55.9	53.0	49.2	49.7	54.3	56.1	55.9	55.6	54.1
2008	54.3	55.7	55.9	56.4	57.0	53.8	50.5	51.2	56.5	58.7	58.6	58.6	55.6
2009	55.8	57.3	57.9	58.6	59.1	55.0	50.5	52.7	57.8	60.2	60.3	59.9	57.1
2010	57.0	58.1	58.9	59.5	61.1	58.0	51.3	50.9	55.9	58.6	58.8	58.7	57.2
2011	56.1	56.8	57.2	57.2	56.9	54.9	51.7	51.7	55.1	57.8	57.9	58.0	55.9
2012	55.5	57.1	57.7	57.4	57.7	54.8	50.7	51.0	55.9	58.1	58.4	58.3	56.1
2013	56.2	57.8	58.1	57.8	58.0	55.9	52.7	52.7	56.6	59.4	59.3	59.4	57.0

Employment by Industry: Urban Honolulu, HI, Selected Years, 2002–2013

(Numbers in thousands, not seasonally adjusted)

Industry and year	January	February	March	April	May	June	July	August	September	October	November	December	Annual average
Total Nonfarm													
2002	401.8	408.4	411.0	405.0	414.7	419.5	408.0	409.0	413.0	416.5	421.3	426.2	412.9
2003	414.2	418.8	421.0	416.6	421.2	420.8	414.1	414.6	417.2	420.9	426.4	429.8	419.6
2004	419.0	423.2	425.9	426.3	429.8	430.3	424.7	425.9	429.3	435.2	442.5	444.1	429.7
2005	429.9	437.3	440.0	440.4	443.5	444.3	437.6	441.0	444.2	446.2	451.1	456.3	442.7
2006	440.0	449.6	452.7	448.9	453.5	454.9	445.5	448.7	453.9	451.8	460.1	461.4	451.8
2007	447.2	454.2	457.2	449.9	457.3	458.9	448.3	449.7	456.2	458.0	462.3	465.8	455.4
2008	450.9	456.6	459.0	451.6	455.5	455.5	445.7	447.2	449.4	450.1	455.7	454.3	452.8
2009	440.4	443.5	444.6	439.3	440.4	439.0	429.1	427.6	432.0	435.2	436.4	439.7	437.3
2010	427.9	432.9	434.8	434.1	437.0	433.2	428.8	425.0	433.2	438.0	442.9	445.4	434.4
2011	429.2	439.3	442.0	439.1	439.8	437.7	433.4	430.8	440.2	443.4	448.8	451.9	439.6
2012	430.7	444.7	446.8	447.5	450.3	448.3	441.2	446.1	449.3	453.4	461.3	461.2	448.4
2013	440.6	455.4	457.4	453.7	458.4	455.4	450.5	448.1	455.6	460.0	466.7	466.8	455.7
Total Private													
2002	310.7	313.1	314.5	314.6	317.4	319.8	319.9	320.3	322.2	321.6	324.8	328.2	318.9
2003	319.5	321.5	323.2	322.1	323.5	324.1	324.3	325.5	326.7	325.5	329.4	332.4	324.8
2004	324.7	326.6	327.9	329.0	331.1	333.5	334.5	335.4	336.4	339.2	343.4	346.0	334.0
2005	337.8	340.5	342.4	343.6	345.4	347.6	348.0	349.8	351.7	350.7	354.1	358.3	347.5
2006	348.8	352.5	354.7	351.8	354.6	357.5	355.7	357.6	358.7	354.6	358.7	361.7	355.6
2007	352.6	355.4	357.7	355.4	357.7	360.9	358.2	359.8	360.6	360.2	362.9	365.5	358.9
2008	355.4	357.4	358.6	356.1	356.2	356.2	353.6	353.4	352.4	349.8	351.3	352.5	354.4
2009	342.1	343.2	342.8	337.9	337.7	338.3	335.7	335.5	336.3	336.7	336.9	339.6	338.6
2010	332.1	333.9	334.5	333.4	334.6	334.3	334.7	335.1	337.2	338.9	340.4	344.5	336.1
2011	335.2	338.8	341.0	338.4	338.4	338.7	339.8	341.3	343.9	344.2	347.9	350.5	341.5
2012	341.7	343.8	345.2	345.9	348.1	348.8	348.9	351.4	352.1	353.6	357.8	359.5	349.7
2013	351.5	354.2	355.9	355.3	356.3	357.2	358.3	358.4	358.6	360.3	364.0	365.0	357.9
Goods-Producing													
2002	28.7	28.6	29.1	28.9	29.2	30.0	30.1	30.3	30.0	29.9	30.1	30.2	29.6
2003	29.6	29.7	30.2	30.3	30.7	30.9	31.2	31.4	31.4	31.7	31.8	31.7	30.9
2004	31.2	31.3	30.7	31.7	32.3	32.9	33.1	33.2	33.4	33.4	33.4	33.7	32.5
2005	33.1	33.5	34.0	34.4	34.8	35.2	35.4	35.9	36.3	36.1	36.2	36.5	35.1
2006	35.5	35.7	35.7	35.5	36.2	36.7	36.9	37.3	37.7	37.3	37.8	38.1	36.7
2007	37.0	37.3	37.4	37.4	37.9	38.6	38.7	39.0	39.2	39.0	39.3	39.3	38.3
2008	38.4	38.6	38.7	38.2	38.0	37.8	38.0	37.9	37.7	36.9	36.9	36.5	37.8
2009	34.8	34.5	34.3	33.6	33.6	33.6	33.5	33.2	33.0	32.7	32.3	32.5	33.5
2010	32.0	31.8	31.8	31.7	31.7	31.5	31.8	31.7	31.9	32.4	32.4	32.6	31.9
2011	31.5	31.9	32.1	32.2	32.2	32.8	33.1	33.3	33.6	33.3	33.1	33.1	32.7
2012	32.4	32.3	32.3	32.2	32.2	32.6	32.8	33.0	33.4	33.5	33.7	33.5	32.8
2013	32.9	33.2	33.5	33.5	34.0	33.8	34.0	34.2	34.1	34.1	34.3	34.8	33.9
Service-Providing													
2002	373.1	379.8	381.9	376.1	385.5	389.5	377.9	378.7	383.0	386.6	391.2	396.0	383.3
2003	384.6	389.1	390.8	386.3	390.5	389.9	382.9	383.2	385.8	389.2	394.6	398.1	388.8
2004	387.8	391.9	395.2	394.6	397.5	397.4	391.6	392.7	395.9	401.8	409.1	410.4	397.2
2005	396.8	403.8	406.0	406.0	408.7	409.1	402.2	405.1	407.9	410.1	414.9	419.8	407.5
2006	404.5	413.9	417.0	413.4	417.3	418.2	408.6	411.4	416.2	414.5	422.3	423.3	415.1
2007	410.2	416.9	419.8	412.5	419.4	420.3	409.6	410.7	417.0	419.0	423.0	426.5	417.1
2008	412.5	418.0	420.3	413.4	419.3	417.7	407.7	409.3	411.7	413.2	418.8	417.8	415.0
2009	405.6	409.0	410.3	405.7	406.8	405.4	395.6	394.4	399.0	402.5	404.1	407.2	403.8
2010	395.9	401.1	403.0	402.4	405.3	401.7	397.0	393.3	401.3	405.6	410.5	412.8	402.5
2011	397.7	407.4	409.9	406.9	407.6	404.9	400.3	397.5	406.6	410.1	415.7	418.8	407.0
2012	398.3	412.4	414.5	415.3	418.1	415.7	408.4	413.1	415.9	419.9	427.6	427.7	415.6
2013	407.7	422.2	423.9	420.2	424.4	421.6	416.5	413.9	421.5	425.9	432.4	432.0	421.9
Mining, Logging, and Construction													
2002	16.5	16.5	16.9	17.1	17.4	18.1	18.4	18.7	18.5	18.5	18.7	18.7	17.8
2003	18.3	18.4	18.8	19.0	19.3	19.4	19.7	19.8	19.8	19.9	19.9	19.7	19.3
2004	19.3	19.4	19.4	18.9	20.3	20.7	21.1	21.2	21.4	21.5	21.5	21.8	20.6
2005	21.4	21.6	22.1	22.6	23.0	23.4	23.7	24.0	24.4	24.3	24.4	24.6	23.3
2006	23.9	24.0	24.0	23.9	24.5	24.8	25.0	25.3	25.7	25.5	25.8	26.1	24.9
2007	25.2	25.4	25.6	25.7	26.1	26.7	26.9	27.1	27.3	27.3	27.4	27.3	26.5
2008	26.6	26.8	26.8	26.4	26.1	26.0	26.2	26.1	26.0	25.5	25.4	25.0	26.1
2009	23.7	23.4	23.2	22.7	22.7	22.7	22.8	22.4	22.2	22.0	21.6	21.7	22.6
2010	21.4	21.3	21.3	21.3	21.3	21.2	21.5	21.3	21.4	21.9	21.8	21.9	21.5
2011	20.9	21.2	21.3	21.5	21.5	22.1	22.4	22.5	22.7	22.4	22.1	22.2	21.9
2012	21.6	21.5	21.6	21.6	21.7	22.0	22.2	22.3	22.6	22.7	22.8	22.6	22.1
2013	22.2	22.4	22.7	22.8	23.2	23.0	23.2	23.4	23.1	23.0	23.1	23.3	23.0
Manufacturing													
2002	12.2	12.1	12.2	11.8	11.8	11.9	11.7	11.6	11.5	11.4	11.4	11.5	11.8
2003	11.3	11.3	11.4	11.3	11.4	11.5	11.5	11.6	11.6	11.8	11.9	12.0	11.6
2004	11.9	11.9	11.8	12.0	12.0	12.2	12.0	12.0	12.0	11.9	11.9	11.9	12.0
2005	11.7	11.9	11.9	11.8	11.8	11.8	11.7	11.9	11.9	11.8	11.8	11.9	11.8
2006	11.6	11.7	11.7	11.6	11.7	11.9	11.9	12.0	12.0	11.8	12.0	12.0	11.8
2007	11.8	11.9	11.8	11.7	11.8	11.9	11.8	11.9	11.9	11.7	11.9	12.0	11.8
2008	11.8	11.8	11.9	11.8	11.9	11.8	11.8	11.8	11.7	11.4	11.5	11.5	11.7
2009	11.1	11.1	11.1	10.9	10.9	10.9	10.7	10.8	10.8	10.7	10.7	10.8	10.9
2010	10.6	10.5	10.5	10.4	10.4	10.3	10.3	10.4	10.5	10.5	10.6	10.7	10.5
2011	10.6	10.7	10.8	10.7	10.7	10.7	10.7	10.8	10.9	10.9	11.0	10.9	10.8
2012	10.8	10.8	10.7	10.6	10.5	10.6	10.6	10.7	10.8	10.8	10.9	10.9	10.7
2013	10.7	10.8	10.8	10.7	10.8	10.8	10.8	10.8	11.0	11.1	11.2	11.5	10.9

Employment by Industry: Urban Honolulu, HI, Selected Years, 2002–2013—*Continued*

(Numbers in thousands, not seasonally adjusted)

Industry and year	January	February	March	April	May	June	July	August	September	October	November	December	Annual average
Trade, Transportation, and Utilities													
2002	75.9	75.3	75.1	75.3	75.8	76.3	76.6	76.8	76.7	76.9	78.2	79.6	76.5
2003	76.6	76.3	76.1	75.7	75.6	76.0	76.3	76.5	76.5	76.6	78.1	79.6	76.7
2004	77.2	76.7	76.9	77.7	78.2	79.0	79.2	79.6	80.0	81.5	83.3	84.3	79.5
2005	81.8	81.7	81.9	82.3	83.1	83.9	84.6	85.1	85.4	85.3	86.7	88.1	84.2
2006	85.3	85.0	85.7	85.2	85.5	86.4	86.0	86.7	86.7	85.7	87.7	88.9	86.2
2007	86.3	85.3	85.8	85.0	85.3	85.5	85.5	85.6	85.4	85.9	88.0	89.7	86.1
2008	86.2	84.9	84.9	83.7	83.7	83.4	82.7	82.9	82.4	81.7	82.6	83.2	83.5
2009	80.6	80.0	79.4	78.3	78.3	78.5	78.2	78.1	78.3	78.4	79.7	80.9	79.1
2010	78.3	77.6	77.4	77.7	77.3	77.9	78.3	78.5	78.2	78.7	80.3	81.6	78.5
2011	79.2	78.7	78.7	78.3	78.4	78.6	78.9	79.1	79.4	80.2	82.0	83.0	79.5
2012	80.9	80.4	80.6	80.4	81.1	81.5	81.8	81.9	82.2	82.7	85.2	86.1	82.1
2013	82.8	82.6	82.9	82.5	82.6	83.1	83.0	83.2	82.9	83.8	86.0	87.0	83.5
Wholesale Trade													
2002	13.3	13.3	13.3	13.3	13.5	13.5	13.5	13.5	13.6	13.6	13.7	13.8	13.5
2003	13.5	13.6	13.6	13.7	13.7	13.7	13.7	13.7	13.7	13.7	13.6	13.7	13.7
2004	13.6	13.6	13.7	13.7	13.8	13.9	13.9	13.9	13.8	13.8	13.9	14.0	13.8
2005	13.8	13.9	14.0	14.0	14.1	14.1	14.2	14.3	14.4	14.4	14.4	14.5	14.2
2006	14.2	14.2	14.2	14.3	14.3	14.5	14.4	14.6	14.5	14.6	14.7	14.9	14.5
2007	14.6	14.6	14.7	14.7	14.8	14.9	14.9	15.0	15.0	15.0	15.1	15.3	14.9
2008	15.0	15.0	15.1	15.1	15.1	15.1	15.1	15.1	15.1	15.0	15.0	15.0	15.1
2009	14.7	14.6	14.5	14.4	14.4	14.3	14.3	14.3	14.3	14.2	14.2	14.3	14.4
2010	14.1	14.1	14.1	14.2	14.2	14.2	14.3	14.3	14.3	14.3	14.3	14.4	14.2
2011	14.1	14.0	14.0	14.0	14.1	14.1	14.1	14.2	14.2	14.2	14.2	14.3	14.1
2012	14.1	14.1	14.1	14.0	14.1	14.2	14.2	14.3	14.3	14.3	14.3	14.4	14.2
2013	14.2	14.2	14.3	14.2	14.2	14.2	14.2	14.2	14.2	14.2	14.5	14.4	14.3
Retail Trade													
2002	43.7	43.0	42.7	42.7	42.9	43.2	43.6	43.6	43.5	43.6	44.6	46.0	43.6
2003	43.4	42.9	42.7	42.4	42.5	43.0	43.3	43.4	43.3	43.6	44.9	46.4	43.5
2004	44.2	43.7	43.7	43.5	43.8	44.3	44.5	44.9	45.1	46.1	47.6	48.8	45.0
2005	46.3	45.9	45.9	45.7	45.8	46.1	46.7	46.9	46.9	47.3	48.6	49.9	46.8
2006	47.5	47.1	47.2	46.6	46.5	46.9	46.6	46.7	46.5	46.5	48.2	49.0	47.1
2007	47.0	46.3	46.5	45.9	46.0	46.2	46.1	46.1	46.0	46.3	48.2	49.3	46.7
2008	46.7	46.3	46.9	46.1	46.0	46.3	46.4	46.5	46.3	45.9	46.8	47.5	46.5
2009	45.7	45.2	44.8	44.1	44.0	44.3	44.2	44.1	44.5	44.8	46.0	46.9	44.9
2010	44.8	44.2	44.1	44.1	43.8	44.2	44.5	44.6	44.5	44.8	46.3	47.3	44.8
2011	45.5	45.0	45.0	44.8	44.8	44.8	45.1	45.2	45.5	46.1	47.8	48.6	45.7
2012	46.8	46.4	46.4	46.3	46.8	46.9	47.0	46.9	47.1	47.4	49.8	50.4	47.4
2013	47.8	47.4	47.5	47.2	47.2	47.4	47.4	47.5	47.2	47.9	49.8	50.7	47.9
Transportation and Utilities													
2002	18.9	19.0	19.1	19.3	19.4	19.6	19.5	19.7	19.6	19.7	19.9	19.8	19.5
2003	19.7	19.8	19.8	19.6	19.4	19.3	19.3	19.4	19.5	19.4	19.5	19.5	19.5
2004	19.4	19.4	19.5	20.5	20.6	20.8	20.8	20.9	21.1	21.5	21.7	21.5	20.6
2005	21.7	21.9	22.0	22.6	23.2	23.7	23.7	23.9	24.1	23.6	23.7	23.7	23.2
2006	23.6	23.7	24.3	24.3	24.7	25.0	25.0	25.4	25.7	24.6	24.8	25.0	24.7
2007	24.7	24.4	24.6	24.4	24.5	24.4	24.5	24.5	24.4	24.6	24.7	25.1	24.6
2008	24.5	23.6	22.9	22.5	22.6	22.0	21.2	21.3	21.0	20.8	20.8	20.7	22.0
2009	20.2	20.2	20.1	19.8	19.9	19.9	19.7	19.7	19.5	19.4	19.5	19.7	19.8
2010	19.4	19.3	19.2	19.4	19.3	19.5	19.5	19.6	19.5	19.6	19.7	19.9	19.5
2011	19.6	19.7	19.7	19.5	19.5	19.7	19.7	19.7	19.7	19.9	20.0	20.1	19.7
2012	20.0	19.9	20.1	20.1	20.2	20.4	20.6	20.7	20.8	21.0	21.1	21.3	20.5
2013	20.8	21.0	21.1	21.1	21.2	21.5	21.4	21.5	21.5	21.7	21.7	21.9	21.4
Information													
2002	9.8	9.7	9.7	9.5	9.5	9.3	9.1	9.2	9.9	9.1	9.1	9.7	9.5
2003	8.9	9.0	9.0	8.8	9.4	9.2	8.3	8.2	8.2	8.1	8.3	8.2	8.6
2004	8.4	8.4	8.7	8.5	9.0	8.8	9.2	9.2	9.2	9.3	9.8	9.7	9.0
2005	8.6	8.8	8.6	8.9	9.0	8.7	8.7	9.1	9.1	9.1	9.3	9.8	9.0
2006	9.0	9.3	9.2	8.4	9.2	8.9	8.5	8.7	9.2	8.4	8.8	9.0	8.9
2007	8.4	8.9	8.9	8.6	9.3	9.2	8.5	9.0	8.6	8.4	8.5	8.6	8.7
2008	7.8	8.3	8.6	8.7	9.0	9.4	8.0	7.8	7.8	7.6	8.1	8.3	8.3
2009	7.4	7.9	7.7	7.7	7.3	7.4	7.0	7.2	7.3	7.6	7.3	7.3	7.4
2010	7.3	8.1	8.3	7.7	8.9	8.3	7.0	7.5	9.4	8.3	7.9	8.8	8.1
2011	6.9	7.9	8.7	6.6	6.5	6.3	6.8	6.8	6.7	6.8	7.1	7.2	7.0
2012	6.8	7.0	7.1	7.0	7.0	6.3	6.7	6.9	6.9	7.2	7.7	7.5	7.0
2013	6.9	7.0	7.1	7.0	6.6	6.5	8.2	6.9	7.3	7.0	7.3	7.2	7.1
Financial Activities													
2002	21.1	21.3	21.4	21.3	21.5	21.5	21.6	21.5	21.5	21.6	21.7	21.8	21.5
2003	21.3	21.5	21.6	21.5	21.7	21.9	22.0	22.1	22.1	22.1	22.1	22.2	21.8
2004	22.0	22.0	22.1	22.1	22.2	22.2	22.2	22.1	22.0	22.3	22.3	22.4	22.2
2005	22.1	22.3	22.3	22.2	22.4	22.5	22.5	22.6	22.7	22.6	22.8	22.9	22.5
2006	22.5	22.7	22.9	22.8	22.9	23.2	23.0	23.0	22.8	22.9	22.9	23.0	22.9
2007	22.8	22.7	23.0	22.8	22.9	23.1	23.1	23.0	22.9	23.1	23.0	23.1	23.0
2008	22.6	22.7	22.9	22.9	22.9	22.8	22.7	22.7	22.5	22.3	22.3	22.3	22.6
2009	21.7	21.6	21.5	21.4	21.5	21.4	21.3	21.1	21.1	21.1	21.0	21.0	21.3
2010	20.6	20.7	20.7	20.6	20.6	20.5	20.7	20.6	20.6	20.6	20.5	20.7	20.6
2011	20.3	20.3	20.3	20.3	20.3	20.2	20.4	20.3	20.2	20.3	20.5	20.4	20.3
2012	20.0	20.1	20.1	20.1	20.2	20.4	20.4	20.4	20.4	20.4	20.5	20.4	20.3
2013	20.1	20.2	20.4	20.3	20.4	20.5	20.5	20.3	20.4	20.6	20.7	20.6	20.4

Employment by Industry: Urban Honolulu, HI, Selected Years, 2002–2013—*Continued*

(Numbers in thousands, not seasonally adjusted)

Industry and year	January	February	March	April	May	June	July	August	September	October	November	December	Annual average
Professional and Business Services													
2002	52.4	53.5	53.7	54.0	54.5	55.3	55.7	56.3	56.4	56.4	56.5	58.1	55.2
2003	56.6	56.5	56.8	56.5	56.4	56.8	56.9	57.6	57.9	56.5	57.4	58.0	57.0
2004	56.6	57.2	57.5	57.1	56.3	56.9	57.2	57.6	57.2	57.7	58.3	59.1	57.4
2005	58.0	58.5	59.0	59.2	58.7	59.4	59.9	60.4	60.3	60.9	61.7	62.5	59.9
2006	61.0	62.5	62.8	62.0	61.7	62.5	62.2	62.3	61.6	60.2	60.4	61.1	61.7
2007	59.3	59.8	60.2	59.4	59.4	60.9	60.5	60.8	61.1	61.3	61.2	61.8	60.5
2008	60.2	60.6	60.8	60.6	60.1	60.2	60.4	60.6	60.2	60.1	60.0	60.9	60.4
2009	59.3	59.3	59.4	57.9	57.5	57.6	57.1	57.0	57.0	57.8	57.4	58.1	58.0
2010	57.0	57.3	57.4	57.5	57.5	57.6	58.1	58.0	58.1	58.6	58.7	59.3	57.9
2011	59.0	60.0	60.5	60.4	60.0	60.2	60.0	60.8	61.1	60.9	61.4	62.6	60.6
2012	60.6	61.0	61.5	62.1	62.5	62.7	62.2	62.9	62.5	63.0	63.5	63.8	62.4
2013	62.9	63.6	63.9	63.7	63.4	63.6	64.0	64.3	64.1	65.1	64.8	64.5	64.0
Education and Health Services													
2002	48.6	49.7	49.8	50.0	50.4	50.2	50.1	49.6	50.6	50.9	52.0	51.2	50.3
2003	50.3	51.6	51.9	51.9	52.1	51.7	51.9	51.7	52.6	52.7	53.4	53.6	52.1
2004	52.0	52.8	53.2	53.2	53.9	53.7	53.3	53.1	54.0	54.3	55.1	55.4	53.7
2005	54.4	55.1	55.5	55.3	55.7	55.5	54.9	54.6	55.5	55.3	55.7	56.1	55.3
2006	54.4	55.2	55.7	55.7	56.3	56.6	55.8	55.9	56.7	56.7	57.2	57.6	56.2
2007	56.3	57.3	57.6	57.6	57.8	58.2	57.2	57.0	57.8	57.8	58.1	58.1	57.6
2008	56.9	57.9	58.2	58.0	58.3	58.5	58.0	57.8	58.3	58.5	59.0	59.3	58.2
2009	58.0	58.7	59.0	58.4	58.5	58.6	57.8	57.7	58.3	58.5	58.7	59.2	58.5
2010	58.1	58.8	59.0	58.7	59.1	58.7	58.6	58.3	58.3	59.5	59.7	60.1	58.9
2011	58.1	59.5	59.6	59.5	59.8	59.1	59.2	58.9	60.0	60.1	60.8	61.0	59.6
2012	59.0	60.1	60.1	60.4	60.8	60.4	60.0	60.8	61.2	61.3	61.6	62.2	60.7
2013	60.7	61.7	62.0	62.1	62.2	62.1	61.4	61.8	62.2	62.7	63.2	62.3	62.0
Leisure and Hospitality													
2002	55.7	56.4	56.9	56.8	57.6	58.3	57.8	57.8	58.1	57.9	58.1	58.5	57.5
2003	57.5	57.9	58.5	58.1	58.3	58.3	58.5	58.8	58.8	58.6	59.0	59.8	58.5
2004	58.6	59.3	59.6	59.7	60.0	60.7	61.2	61.5	61.7	61.4	61.9	62.1	60.6
2005	60.8	61.5	61.9	61.8	61.9	62.7	62.4	62.4	62.6	61.7	61.8	62.3	62.0
2006	61.2	62.0	62.4	62.0	62.4	62.8	63.0	63.2	63.5	62.9	63.2	63.4	62.7
2007	62.5	63.7	64.2	64.2	64.6	64.9	64.2	64.8	64.8	63.8	63.9	64.0	64.1
2008	62.8	63.4	63.3	62.8	62.9	63.1	63.0	62.9	62.5	61.7	61.4	61.1	62.6
2009	60.2	60.8	61.1	60.4	60.8	61.1	60.7	60.9	60.9	60.2	60.1	60.2	60.6
2010	58.9	59.4	59.6	59.5	59.5	59.9	60.2	60.4	60.7	60.7	60.9	61.4	60.1
2011	60.5	60.6	61.2	61.1	61.1	61.4	61.3	61.9	62.4	62.1	62.5	62.6	61.6
2012	62.0	62.6	63.1	63.3	63.7	64.4	64.6	64.9	64.9	64.9	65.0	65.5	64.1
2013	64.6	65.2	65.4	65.4	66.4	66.8	66.5	66.9	66.7	66.2	66.4	67.1	66.1
Other Services													
2002	18.5	18.6	18.8	18.8	18.9	18.9	18.9	18.8	19.0	18.9	19.1	19.1	18.9
2003	18.7	19.0	19.1	19.3	19.3	19.3	19.2	19.2	19.2	19.2	19.3	19.3	19.2
2004	18.7	18.9	19.2	19.0	19.2	19.3	19.1	19.1	18.9	19.3	19.3	19.3	19.1
2005	19.0	19.1	19.2	19.5	19.8	19.7	19.6	19.7	19.8	19.7	19.9	20.1	19.6
2006	19.9	20.1	20.3	20.2	20.4	20.4	20.3	20.5	20.5	20.5	20.7	20.6	20.4
2007	20.0	20.4	20.6	20.4	20.5	20.5	20.5	20.6	20.8	20.9	20.9	20.9	20.6
2008	20.5	21.0	21.2	21.2	21.3	21.0	20.8	20.8	21.0	21.0	21.0	20.9	21.0
2009	20.1	20.4	20.4	20.2	20.2	20.1	20.1	20.3	20.4	20.4	20.4	20.4	20.3
2010	19.9	20.2	20.3	20.0	20.0	19.9	20.0	20.1	20.0	20.1	20.0	20.0	20.0
2011	19.7	19.9	19.9	20.0	20.1	20.1	20.1	20.2	20.5	20.5	20.5	20.6	20.2
2012	20.0	20.3	20.4	20.4	20.6	20.5	20.4	20.6	20.6	20.6	20.6	20.5	20.5
2013	20.6	20.7	20.7	20.8	20.7	20.8	20.7	20.8	20.9	20.8	21.3	21.5	20.9
Government													
2002	91.1	95.3	96.5	90.4	97.3	99.7	88.1	88.7	90.8	94.9	96.5	98.0	93.9
2003	94.7	97.3	97.8	94.5	97.7	96.7	89.8	89.1	90.5	95.4	97.0	97.4	94.8
2004	94.3	96.6	98.0	97.3	98.7	96.8	90.2	90.5	92.9	96.0	99.1	98.1	95.7
2005	92.1	96.8	97.6	96.8	98.1	96.7	89.6	91.2	92.5	95.5	97.0	98.0	95.2
2006	91.2	97.1	98.0	97.1	98.9	97.4	89.8	91.1	95.2	97.2	101.4	99.7	96.2
2007	94.6	98.8	99.5	94.5	99.6	98.0	90.1	89.9	95.6	97.8	99.4	100.3	96.5
2008	95.5	99.2	100.4	95.5	101.1	99.3	92.1	93.8	97.0	100.3	104.4	101.8	98.4
2009	98.3	100.3	101.8	101.4	102.7	100.7	93.4	92.1	95.7	98.5	99.5	100.1	98.7
2010	95.8	99.0	100.3	100.7	102.4	98.9	94.1	89.9	96.0	99.1	102.5	100.9	98.3
2011	94.0	100.5	101.0	100.7	101.4	99.0	93.6	89.5	96.3	99.2	100.9	101.4	98.1
2012	89.0	100.9	101.6	101.6	102.2	99.5	92.3	94.7	97.2	99.8	103.5	101.7	98.7
2013	89.1	101.2	101.5	98.4	102.1	98.2	92.2	89.7	97.0	99.7	102.7	101.8	97.8

Employment by Industry: Virginia Beach–Norfolk–Newport News, VA–NC, Selected Years, 2002–2013

(Numbers in thousands, not seasonally adjusted)

Industry and year	January	February	March	April	May	June	July	August	September	October	November	December	Annual average
Total Nonfarm													
2002	714.8	719.6	726.2	731.3	738.3	747.6	735.4	739.2	737.1	739.9	743.1	744.8	734.8
2003	722.8	724.8	731.5	732.3	739.3	746.7	742.3	744.8	740.8	742.7	747.8	747.9	738.6
2004	730.4	731.3	739.3	747.1	752.5	760.7	757.7	760.4	756.7	755.4	759.1	760.8	751.0
2005	739.3	742.4	750.3	760.4	765.9	775.4	771.1	774.6	772.1	761.6	765.8	766.1	762.1
2006	748.9	751.1	760.3	767.2	772.4	781.9	775.1	776.2	769.2	769.9	774.4	776.0	768.6
2007	759.3	760.5	768.8	774.1	779.8	787.7	789.5	788.1	783.1	774.0	777.9	776.4	776.6
2008	754.6	757.9	764.2	768.0	774.8	782.3	778.3	778.2	769.9	764.0	761.4	758.0	767.6
2009	737.6	736.1	739.4	743.2	748.2	752.8	744.7	745.0	739.9	740.5	739.9	738.7	742.2
2010	720.2	719.5	726.9	737.4	743.0	747.9	744.3	744.2	739.1	740.1	739.2	738.0	736.7
2011	719.8	721.7	729.8	739.7	743.2	750.1	748.3	747.8	744.6	741.6	742.1	742.1	739.2
2012	727.0	730.3	736.7	743.5	746.4	752.5	749.6	750.9	746.6	751.9	753.8	753.6	745.2
2013	738.0	740.5	746.4	752.1	755.9	762.4	760.4	762.3	755.6	750.7	754.2	753.7	752.7
Total Private													
2002	567.2	570.5	576.0	581.3	587.3	596.1	590.1	593.7	588.1	588.9	591.8	593.8	585.4
2003	573.5	574.5	580.5	583.3	589.7	596.1	595.2	598.3	591.7	593.9	597.2	597.3	589.3
2004	580.6	580.2	587.5	595.5	600.3	607.7	609.9	611.5	605.9	603.7	605.6	607.8	599.7
2005	589.7	591.4	598.8	608.0	613.0	621.3	621.8	624.9	620.8	610.4	612.9	614.2	610.6
2006	598.3	599.4	608.0	613.1	618.2	626.8	623.9	625.4	618.2	616.1	618.9	620.9	615.6
2007	605.6	605.4	613.2	618.9	624.6	631.7	636.7	635.4	628.6	618.8	620.4	619.8	621.6
2008	599.8	600.9	606.7	611.7	618.0	624.1	624.0	623.8	613.9	606.1	601.3	599.3	610.8
2009	579.9	577.7	580.3	583.9	589.3	593.1	592.1	590.7	583.8	581.0	578.7	579.0	584.1
2010	561.6	560.1	566.9	576.9	580.3	586.0	589.1	588.7	580.9	580.6	579.5	578.6	577.4
2011	561.7	562.7	570.0	579.8	583.6	590.1	592.1	591.1	585.4	585.4	580.8	579.8	579.7
2012	567.3	569.5	576.5	583.3	586.5	592.3	594.2	595.4	589.2	592.3	592.8	593.4	586.1
2013	580.5	581.5	587.4	593.1	597.5	604.3	606.3	607.8	599.3	592.8	595.3	595.5	595.1
Goods-Producing													
2002	104.0	104.1	104.4	104.0	104.6	105.2	103.8	105.5	104.8	105.0	105.0	105.2	104.6
2003	103.9	104.4	105.5	105.0	106.3	107.1	104.6	107.3	106.2	108.5	110.0	108.9	106.5
2004	106.2	105.2	106.4	107.6	108.5	109.7	108.6	110.0	109.7	110.3	110.3	110.0	108.5
2005	108.3	108.3	109.0	110.4	110.6	111.4	110.0	112.0	111.2	109.2	109.0	109.2	109.9
2006	107.2	107.2	108.6	109.0	109.5	110.3	107.9	109.8	107.2	106.7	106.7	108.1	108.2
2007	105.9	104.8	105.7	106.8	107.0	107.6	107.5	107.5	107.0	105.2	105.1	104.5	106.2
2008	102.2	101.9	101.9	102.1	102.5	103.0	102.9	102.8	101.5	100.5	99.7	98.4	101.6
2009	94.2	93.1	92.8	92.2	92.0	92.0	92.0	91.8	91.2	91.0	90.3	90.4	91.9
2010	87.8	87.5	88.3	89.2	89.6	89.2	89.4	89.3	89.0	88.6	88.4	87.7	88.7
2011	85.6	85.5	86.4	86.5	87.1	87.6	88.2	88.2	87.8	86.8	86.7	86.7	86.9
2012	86.4	86.7	87.1	86.8	86.4	86.5	89.5	89.3	89.6	89.3	89.3	89.3	88.0
2013	87.8	88.2	88.5	88.6	89.0	89.6	90.3	90.3	90.1	87.3	87.7	87.9	88.8
Service-Providing													
2002	610.8	615.5	621.8	627.3	633.7	642.4	631.6	633.7	632.3	634.9	638.1	639.6	630.1
2003	618.9	620.4	626.0	627.3	633.0	639.6	637.7	637.5	634.6	634.2	637.8	639.0	632.2
2004	624.2	626.1	632.9	639.5	644.0	651.0	649.1	650.4	647.0	645.1	648.8	650.8	642.4
2005	631.0	634.1	641.3	650.0	655.3	664.0	661.1	662.6	660.9	652.4	656.8	656.9	652.2
2006	641.7	643.9	651.7	658.2	662.9	671.6	667.2	666.4	662.0	663.2	667.7	667.9	660.4
2007	653.4	655.7	663.1	667.3	672.8	680.1	682.0	680.6	676.1	668.8	672.8	671.9	670.4
2008	652.4	656.0	662.3	665.9	672.3	679.3	675.4	675.4	668.4	663.5	661.7	659.6	666.0
2009	643.4	643.0	646.6	651.0	656.2	660.8	652.7	653.2	648.7	649.5	649.6	648.3	650.3
2010	632.4	632.0	638.6	648.2	653.4	658.7	654.9	654.9	650.1	651.5	650.8	650.3	648.0
2011	634.2	636.2	643.4	653.2	656.1	662.5	660.1	659.6	656.8	654.8	655.4	655.4	652.3
2012	640.6	643.6	649.6	656.7	660.0	666.0	660.1	661.6	657.0	662.6	664.5	664.3	657.2
2013	650.2	652.3	657.9	663.5	666.9	672.8	670.1	672.0	665.5	663.4	666.5	665.8	663.9
Mining, Logging, and Construction													
2002	43.6	44.0	44.6	44.3	44.8	45.3	45.7	45.5	44.6	44.7	44.4	44.5	44.7
2003	43.9	44.5	45.2	45.6	47.0	47.5	48.1	48.1	47.1	49.3	50.2	49.5	47.2
2004	46.9	46.3	47.2	48.3	48.9	49.8	50.4	49.9	49.3	49.6	49.2	49.3	48.8
2005	48.1	48.1	48.7	50.0	50.3	50.8	51.5	51.4	51.2	49.7	49.8	50.1	50.0
2006	48.6	48.6	49.8	50.4	50.6	51.1	50.6	50.3	49.8	49.3	49.3	49.3	49.8
2007	48.0	47.9	48.6	48.7	48.8	49.2	49.7	49.7	49.2	47.8	47.5	46.9	48.5
2008	45.5	45.4	45.6	45.8	46.1	46.4	46.4	46.3	45.2	44.6	43.8	42.6	45.3
2009	39.9	39.2	39.0	38.7	38.5	38.5	38.6	38.4	37.9	37.6	37.0	37.1	38.4
2010	35.8	35.5	36.2	37.1	37.5	37.5	37.8	37.7	37.4	37.0	36.9	36.3	36.9
2011	34.8	34.9	35.1	35.6	35.6	35.8	35.7	35.6	35.1	34.7	34.5	34.5	35.2
2012	33.4	33.5	33.8	34.3	34.8	35.4	35.5	35.3	34.7	34.9	34.6	34.5	34.6
2013	33.9	34.1	34.4	34.4	34.8	35.3	35.5	35.5	35.3	33.2	33.4	33.6	34.5
Manufacturing													
2002	60.4	60.1	59.8	59.7	59.8	59.9	58.1	60.0	60.2	60.3	60.6	60.7	60.0
2003	60.0	59.9	60.3	59.4	59.3	59.6	56.5	59.2	59.1	59.2	59.8	59.4	59.3
2004	59.3	58.9	59.2	59.3	59.6	59.9	58.2	60.1	60.4	60.7	61.1	60.7	59.8
2005	60.2	60.2	60.3	60.4	60.3	60.6	58.5	60.6	60.0	59.5	59.2	59.1	59.9
2006	58.6	58.6	58.8	58.6	58.9	59.2	57.3	59.5	57.4	57.4	57.4	58.8	58.4
2007	57.9	56.9	57.1	58.1	58.2	58.4	57.8	57.8	57.8	57.4	57.6	57.6	57.7
2008	56.7	56.5	56.3	56.3	56.4	56.6	56.5	56.5	56.3	55.9	55.9	55.8	56.3
2009	54.3	53.9	53.8	53.5	53.5	53.5	53.4	53.4	53.3	53.4	53.3	53.3	53.6
2010	52.0	52.0	52.1	52.1	52.1	51.7	51.6	51.6	51.6	51.6	51.5	51.4	51.8
2011	50.8	50.6	51.3	50.9	51.5	51.8	52.5	52.6	52.7	52.1	52.2	52.2	51.8
2012	53.0	53.2	53.3	52.5	51.6	51.1	54.0	54.0	54.9	54.4	54.7	54.8	53.5
2013	53.9	54.1	54.1	54.2	54.2	54.3	54.8	54.8	54.8	54.1	54.3	54.3	54.3

Employment by Industry: Virginia Beach–Norfolk–Newport News, VA–NC, Selected Years, 2002–2013—*Continued*

(Numbers in thousands, not seasonally adjusted)

Industry and year	January	February	March	April	May	June	July	August	September	October	November	December	Annual average
Trade, Transportation, and Utilities													
2002	138.1	136.4	135.3	136.6	138.3	140.2	138.7	139.2	138.9	141.3	145.1	147.3	139.6
2003	138.1	135.9	135.5	133.0	133.6	134.1	134.3	135.2	134.9	137.3	141.8	144.5	136.5
2004	136.8	135.8	135.4	136.8	138.1	139.2	139.6	140.1	139.5	141.2	144.7	146.1	139.4
2005	138.0	136.6	137.6	139.4	140.2	141.0	142.1	142.3	142.2	142.4	146.3	146.9	141.3
2006	139.9	138.3	139.7	140.4	141.6	142.6	142.4	141.9	140.8	143.2	147.9	148.4	142.3
2007	142.3	140.5	141.3	140.8	142.2	143.4	145.4	144.7	143.0	143.2	147.7	147.9	143.5
2008	140.0	138.0	138.3	138.2	138.9	139.9	139.6	139.4	138.0	136.5	139.1	139.8	138.8
2009	130.8	128.2	127.9	128.4	129.9	130.3	130.0	129.6	128.3	128.9	131.4	132.6	129.7
2010	126.8	125.2	126.3	127.6	129.1	129.5	129.6	129.7	128.1	129.6	131.9	133.4	128.9
2011	127.2	126.2	126.7	128.0	128.5	129.3	128.8	128.9	127.7	128.1	131.0	132.3	128.6
2012	126.5	125.3	126.2	127.0	128.3	128.9	128.4	127.8	126.6	128.6	131.6	132.5	128.1
2013	126.7	125.5	126.0	126.7	127.9	129.0	129.7	130.1	129.0	130.5	133.3	134.3	129.1
Wholesale Trade													
2002	25.2	25.2	25.2	25.5	25.6	25.7	25.3	25.3	25.2	25.3	25.5	25.5	25.4
2003	25.1	24.8	24.5	24.6	24.3	23.9	23.5	22.9	22.8	23.1	23.1	23.2	23.8
2004	22.8	22.9	23.0	23.1	23.2	23.4	23.6	23.6	23.4	23.5	23.6	23.7	23.3
2005	23.5	23.6	23.6	23.9	24.0	24.1	24.1	24.2	24.1	24.0	24.1	24.3	24.0
2006	23.9	23.9	24.0	24.1	24.1	24.2	24.3	24.1	24.1	24.1	24.2	24.2	24.1
2007	24.1	24.2	24.3	24.2	24.3	24.3	24.4	24.2	24.1	23.7	23.7	23.7	24.1
2008	23.5	23.4	23.4	23.5	23.5	23.5	23.4	23.4	23.1	22.9	22.7	22.6	23.2
2009	22.3	22.1	22.1	22.0	22.0	21.9	21.9	21.9	21.6	21.5	21.6	21.5	21.9
2010	20.9	20.7	20.8	21.0	21.1	21.1	21.1	21.2	21.1	21.1	21.1	21.1	21.0
2011	20.7	20.6	20.7	20.7	20.8	20.8	20.7	20.6	20.4	20.3	20.3	20.4	20.6
2012	20.2	20.2	20.2	20.2	20.2	20.2	20.3	20.2	20.0	20.2	20.2	20.1	20.2
2013	19.7	19.7	19.7	19.8	19.8	19.8	19.9	20.0	20.0	19.9	19.9	19.9	19.8
Retail Trade													
2002	87.7	85.8	84.7	85.7	86.9	88.1	87.1	87.8	87.7	89.5	93.0	95.0	88.3
2003	87.9	86.3	85.8	83.7	84.7	85.4	85.3	86.6	86.5	87.8	92.2	94.7	87.2
2004	88.7	87.5	86.9	88.1	89.2	89.9	90.1	90.4	90.2	91.3	94.7	95.8	90.2
2005	88.7	87.2	87.4	89.1	89.8	90.4	91.5	91.7	91.9	92.1	95.4	95.9	90.9
2006	90.6	88.9	89.9	90.5	91.5	92.2	92.1	91.7	90.7	92.8	97.1	97.8	92.2
2007	93.0	91.1	91.6	91.2	92.3	93.1	94.6	94.5	93.1	93.5	97.8	98.1	93.7
2008	92.0	90.0	90.4	89.6	90.2	90.8	90.6	90.4	89.5	88.3	90.8	91.5	90.3
2009	84.7	82.7	82.5	82.9	84.3	84.8	84.3	84.2	83.2	83.6	85.6	86.8	84.1
2010	82.7	81.5	82.4	83.3	84.3	84.6	84.3	84.4	82.8	83.7	85.9	87.3	83.9
2011	82.5	81.8	82.2	83.3	84.1	84.8	84.5	84.6	83.4	83.9	86.6	87.8	84.1
2012	83.2	81.8	82.7	83.3	84.2	84.6	84.2	83.8	82.8	84.2	87.4	88.2	84.2
2013	83.7	82.8	83.4	83.8	84.7	85.5	85.8	86.1	85.1	86.7	89.5	90.5	85.6
Transportation and Utilities													
2002	25.2	25.4	25.4	25.4	25.8	26.4	26.3	26.1	26.0	26.5	26.6	26.8	26.0
2003	25.1	24.8	25.2	24.7	24.6	24.8	25.5	25.7	25.6	26.4	26.5	26.6	25.5
2004	25.3	25.4	25.5	25.6	25.7	25.9	25.9	26.1	25.9	26.4	26.4	26.6	25.9
2005	25.8	25.8	26.6	26.4	26.4	26.5	26.5	26.4	26.2	26.3	26.8	26.7	26.4
2006	25.4	25.5	25.8	25.8	26.0	26.2	26.0	26.1	26.0	26.3	26.6	26.4	26.0
2007	25.2	25.2	25.4	25.4	25.6	26.0	26.4	26.0	25.8	26.0	26.2	26.1	25.8
2008	24.5	24.6	24.5	25.1	25.2	25.6	25.6	25.6	25.4	25.3	25.6	25.7	25.2
2009	23.8	23.4	23.3	23.5	23.6	23.6	23.8	23.5	23.5	23.8	24.2	24.3	23.7
2010	23.2	23.0	23.1	23.3	23.7	23.8	24.2	24.1	24.2	24.8	24.9	25.0	23.9
2011	24.0	23.8	23.8	24.0	23.6	23.7	23.6	23.7	23.9	23.9	24.1	24.1	23.9
2012	23.1	23.3	23.3	23.5	23.9	24.1	23.9	23.8	23.8	24.2	24.0	24.2	23.8
2013	23.3	23.0	22.9	23.1	23.4	23.7	24.0	24.0	23.9	23.9	23.9	23.9	23.6
Information													
2002	16.4	16.4	16.4	16.4	16.6	16.6	16.4	16.5	16.3	16.3	16.6	16.7	16.5
2003	16.1	16.1	16.1	16.1	16.0	16.3	16.3	15.9	15.9	15.8	15.9	15.9	16.0
2004	15.8	15.8	15.8	15.5	15.6	15.7	15.7	15.6	15.4	15.1	15.1	15.0	15.5
2005	15.0	14.8	14.7	14.9	15.0	15.1	15.3	15.4	15.3	15.2	15.3	15.5	15.1
2006	15.5	15.5	15.5	15.4	15.5	15.6	15.6	15.5	15.3	15.2	15.3	15.4	15.4
2007	15.5	15.6	15.6	15.6	15.7	15.8	15.6	15.6	15.4	15.2	15.2	15.3	15.5
2008	15.3	15.2	15.1	15.0	15.2	15.2	15.0	14.9	14.5	14.2	14.0	13.9	14.8
2009	13.7	13.7	13.6	13.5	13.6	13.5	13.3	13.2	12.9	12.9	12.8	12.8	13.3
2010	12.6	12.4	12.5	12.3	12.4	12.4	12.2	12.2	12.0	11.8	11.8	11.7	12.2
2011	11.6	11.5	11.6	11.6	11.7	11.8	11.9	10.9	11.6	11.4	11.4	11.6	11.6
2012	11.6	11.6	11.7	11.7	11.8	11.8	11.5	11.7	11.3	11.4	11.6	11.6	11.6
2013	11.5	11.6	11.6	11.4	11.6	11.6	11.6	11.6	11.3	11.4	11.3	11.2	11.5
Financial Activities													
2002	35.5	35.8	36.0	36.3	36.8	37.9	37.0	37.3	36.6	37.1	37.2	37.4	36.7
2003	36.2	36.5	36.7	36.9	37.5	38.2	38.7	38.7	38.3	37.6	37.5	37.8	37.6
2004	38.3	38.4	38.7	39.4	39.7	40.4	41.1	41.0	40.2	39.5	39.5	39.6	39.7
2005	38.4	38.6	38.7	39.9	40.2	41.4	41.5	41.4	40.7	39.3	39.3	39.8	39.9
2006	39.1	39.3	39.5	40.2	40.6	41.7	41.9	41.9	41.2	40.9	40.9	41.1	40.7
2007	40.9	41.1	41.3	41.6	41.8	42.3	42.5	42.5	41.8	41.1	40.8	40.8	41.5
2008	40.3	40.5	40.5	40.3	40.3	41.0	41.3	41.0	40.2	39.3	38.8	38.7	40.2
2009	38.2	38.1	37.9	37.9	37.9	38.3	38.1	38.0	37.1	36.3	36.0	36.0	37.5
2010	36.0	35.9	35.9	36.2	36.1	37.1	37.4	37.4	36.7	36.2	36.1	36.1	36.4
2011	36.0	36.1	36.1	36.9	37.0	37.5	37.9	37.7	37.0	36.6	36.5	36.8	36.8
2012	36.4	36.7	36.8	37.2	37.1	37.9	38.3	38.2	37.7	37.7	37.6	37.7	37.4
2013	37.1	37.1	37.2	37.6	37.8	38.5	38.5	38.3	37.8	37.3	37.1	36.5	37.6

Employment by Industry: Virginia Beach–Norfolk–Newport News, VA–NC, Selected Years, 2002–2013—Continued

(Numbers in thousands, not seasonally adjusted)

Industry and year	January	February	March	April	May	June	July	August	September	October	November	December	Annual average
Professional and Business Services													
2002	101.6	103.9	105.8	105.6	104.6	105.9	104.2	105.9	104.9	104.5	104.8	104.6	104.7
2003	101.8	102.4	104.3	106.2	104.2	105.0	104.6	105.0	104.6	105.9	105.0	103.2	104.4
2004	98.4	98.0	99.3	100.2	99.6	100.8	101.2	101.7	101.1	100.4	101.2	101.6	100.3
2005	99.2	100.2	101.3	101.4	101.7	102.6	102.3	102.6	102.8	101.0	101.2	101.3	101.5
2006	99.7	100.4	101.5	101.6	102.4	102.6	102.0	102.2	102.5	102.7	102.8	103.0	102.0
2007	100.0	100.4	101.7	102.1	102.5	103.0	103.4	104.1	104.3	103.5	104.5	104.9	102.9
2008	101.8	102.6	103.7	105.1	105.3	106.5	106.2	107.1	106.5	105.4	104.2	104.0	104.9
2009	100.7	100.4	100.5	100.2	99.2	99.5	98.9	99.2	99.0	99.0	100.1	99.7	99.7
2010	96.9	96.3	96.5	97.9	96.7	97.7	99.2	99.4	98.9	99.5	100.0	99.1	98.2
2011	96.7	96.8	97.4	99.1	98.8	98.9	99.7	100.5	100.9	99.7	99.4	99.1	98.9
2012	97.7	98.3	98.9	99.8	99.5	99.7	99.6	100.4	100.1	101.9	102.2	101.9	100.0
2013	101.3	101.9	102.3	103.1	102.7	103.4	103.2	103.8	102.2	100.9	102.9	102.7	102.5
Education and Health Services													
2002	75.8	76.7	77.5	77.0	77.7	77.9	76.8	76.9	78.4	79.3	79.8	80.1	77.8
2003	77.5	77.9	78.4	79.0	78.4	78.4	78.7	79.2	80.3	80.1	80.7	80.8	79.1
2004	82.2	82.7	83.5	83.4	82.3	81.3	81.8	82.3	83.7	84.4	84.7	85.3	83.1
2005	84.7	85.0	85.3	85.4	84.7	84.8	84.5	85.6	87.7	87.6	88.0	88.5	86.0
2006	87.1	87.8	88.2	88.0	87.3	87.4	87.1	87.5	89.8	90.1	90.3	90.9	88.5
2007	89.7	90.1	90.7	91.0	90.1	89.9	90.3	90.9	92.5	92.6	92.8	93.4	91.2
2008	90.7	91.5	92.0	92.3	91.4	91.3	91.4	92.1	93.0	94.0	93.9	94.3	92.3
2009	94.0	94.2	94.5	94.3	93.3	92.9	93.2	93.7	95.2	95.8	95.7	96.0	94.4
2010	94.2	94.6	95.5	95.8	94.7	94.0	94.5	94.9	95.5	97.3	97.5	97.7	95.5
2011	97.1	97.9	98.5	99.2	98.2	97.9	98.2	98.5	100.0	100.3	100.6	99.3	98.8
2012	99.7	100.5	100.8	101.3	100.0	100.1	99.5	100.5	102.1	103.8	104.2	103.4	101.3
2013	103.9	104.6	104.8	105.1	103.8	103.7	103.1	104.5	105.6	105.9	107.0	107.2	104.9
Leisure and Hospitality													
2002	67.7	68.8	71.7	76.6	79.8	83.2	84.0	83.4	79.1	76.2	74.3	73.5	76.5
2003	69.6	70.2	72.5	74.8	79.9	83.0	84.2	83.6	78.6	75.9	72.9	72.4	76.5
2004	69.3	70.6	74.3	78.6	82.4	86.2	87.5	86.4	81.9	78.6	76.0	76.0	79.0
2005	72.1	73.6	77.7	81.7	85.4	89.7	90.8	90.2	85.3	80.5	78.6	77.8	82.0
2006	75.8	76.7	80.4	84.6	87.2	92.3	92.9	92.4	87.2	83.4	81.0	79.8	84.5
2007	77.2	78.5	82.3	85.2	88.7	93.5	95.9	94.7	89.7	84.4	81.0	80.2	85.9
2008	78.1	79.6	83.4	86.4	90.9	94.2	94.7	93.7	87.9	84.1	79.4	78.1	85.9
2009	74.3	75.9	78.8	83.0	88.8	91.8	91.9	90.7	86.0	82.9	78.4	77.5	83.3
2010	74.0	74.9	78.2	83.7	87.2	91.6	92.0	91.1	86.4	83.2	79.6	79.2	83.4
2011	74.0	75.0	79.1	83.7	87.3	91.8	92.0	91.0	85.3	82.9	79.4	79.3	83.4
2012	75.0	76.1	80.3	83.7	87.5	91.2	91.4	91.4	86.3	83.6	80.4	81.2	84.0
2013	76.8	77.0	81.2	84.5	88.4	91.9	93.4	92.9	87.5	83.6	80.3	80.1	84.8
Other Services													
2002	28.1	28.4	28.9	28.8	28.9	29.2	29.2	29.0	29.1	29.2	29.0	29.0	28.9
2003	30.3	31.1	31.5	32.4	33.8	34.0	33.8	33.4	32.9	32.8	33.4	33.8	32.8
2004	33.6	33.7	34.1	34.0	34.1	34.4	34.4	34.4	34.4	34.2	34.1	34.2	34.1
2005	34.0	34.3	34.5	34.9	35.2	35.3	35.3	35.4	35.6	35.2	35.2	35.2	35.0
2006	34.0	34.2	34.6	33.9	34.1	34.3	34.1	34.2	34.2	33.9	34.0	34.2	34.1
2007	34.1	34.4	34.6	35.8	36.6	36.2	36.1	35.4	34.9	33.6	33.3	32.8	34.8
2008	31.4	31.6	31.8	32.3	33.5	33.0	32.9	32.8	32.3	32.1	32.2	32.1	32.3
2009	34.0	34.1	34.3	34.4	34.6	34.8	34.7	34.5	34.1	34.2	34.0	34.0	34.3
2010	33.3	33.3	33.7	34.2	34.5	34.5	34.8	34.7	34.3	34.4	34.2	33.7	34.1
2011	33.5	33.7	34.2	34.8	35.0	35.3	35.4	35.4	35.1	35.0	34.8	34.7	34.7
2012	34.0	34.3	34.7	35.8	35.9	36.2	36.0	36.1	35.5	36.0	35.9	35.8	35.5
2013	35.4	35.6	35.8	36.1	36.3	36.6	36.5	36.3	35.8	35.9	35.7	35.6	36.0
Government													
2002	147.6	149.1	150.2	150.0	151.0	151.5	145.3	145.5	149.0	151.0	151.3	151.0	149.4
2003	149.3	150.3	151.0	149.0	149.6	150.6	147.1	146.5	149.1	148.8	150.6	150.6	149.4
2004	149.8	151.1	151.8	151.6	152.2	153.0	147.8	148.9	150.8	151.7	153.5	153.0	151.3
2005	149.6	151.0	151.5	152.4	152.9	154.1	149.3	149.7	151.3	151.2	152.9	151.9	151.5
2006	150.6	151.7	152.3	154.1	154.2	155.1	151.2	150.8	151.0	153.8	155.5	155.1	153.0
2007	153.7	155.1	155.6	155.2	155.2	156.0	152.8	152.7	154.5	155.2	157.5	156.6	155.0
2008	154.8	157.0	157.5	156.3	156.8	158.2	154.3	154.4	156.0	157.9	160.1	158.7	156.8
2009	157.7	158.4	159.1	159.3	158.9	159.7	152.6	154.3	156.1	159.5	161.2	159.7	158.0
2010	158.6	159.4	160.0	160.5	162.7	161.9	155.2	155.5	158.2	159.5	159.7	159.4	159.2
2011	158.1	159.0	159.8	159.9	159.6	160.0	156.2	156.7	159.2	160.8	162.3	162.3	159.5
2012	159.7	160.8	160.2	160.2	159.9	160.2	155.4	155.5	157.4	159.6	161.0	160.2	159.2
2013	157.5	159.0	159.0	159.0	158.4	158.1	154.1	154.5	156.3	157.9	158.9	158.2	157.6

Employment by Industry: Washington–Arlington–Alexandria, DC–VA–MD–WV, Selected Years, 2002–2013

(Numbers in thousands, not seasonally adjusted)

Industry and year	January	February	March	April	May	June	July	August	September	October	November	December	Annual average
Total Nonfarm													
2002	2,139.2	2,144.4	2,160.0	2,166.6	2,180.7	2,198.2	2,179.0	2,176.4	2,182.3	2,189.0	2,197.6	2,204.9	2,176.5
2003	2,176.6	2,178.8	2,197.4	2,218.4	2,233.7	2,249.7	2,248.1	2,240.4	2,251.2	2,253.5	2,262.6	2,273.1	2,232.0
2004	2,229.4	2,242.5	2,269.7	2,278.5	2,296.9	2,313.4	2,306.2	2,305.8	2,313.1	2,329.6	2,340.3	2,346.6	2,297.7
2005	2,293.0	2,304.7	2,319.8	2,337.1	2,351.3	2,364.0	2,364.9	2,360.3	2,364.8	2,364.9	2,382.6	2,390.9	2,349.9
2006	2,344.9	2,354.9	2,375.6	2,381.5	2,396.0	2,414.6	2,402.5	2,396.9	2,397.6	2,405.5	2,413.9	2,425.2	2,392.4
2007	2,374.9	2,383.1	2,401.3	2,405.9	2,419.4	2,431.8	2,423.7	2,414.7	2,412.8	2,430.2	2,439.7	2,448.6	2,415.5
2008	2,392.3	2,401.7	2,417.1	2,430.7	2,445.6	2,452.3	2,450.8	2,441.8	2,432.3	2,435.6	2,437.3	2,436.7	2,431.2
2009	2,382.1	2,381.4	2,387.6	2,387.1	2,399.8	2,407.9	2,409.0	2,392.5	2,377.7	2,397.7	2,408.9	2,409.7	2,395.1
2010	2,355.3	2,338.7	2,375.1	2,405.6	2,425.7	2,435.5	2,435.7	2,405.6	2,407.8	2,428.0	2,438.3	2,441.6	2,407.7
2011	2,394.9	2,403.7	2,421.4	2,443.8	2,442.5	2,457.6	2,467.9	2,447.7	2,459.4	2,463.1	2,473.8	2,475.9	2,446.0
2012	2,426.3	2,438.9	2,460.2	2,473.7	2,484.4	2,495.7	2,488.2	2,477.9	2,488.5	2,508.3	2,520.3	2,517.0	2,481.6
2013	2,468.1	2,481.2	2,492.9	2,507.7	2,515.6	2,517.3	2,513.8	2,500.0	2,507.4	2,519.2	2,533.0	2,530.2	2,507.2
Total Private													
2002	1,640.8	1,645.6	1,658.3	1,667.4	1,677.9	1,692.8	1,687.3	1,686.8	1,677.7	1,680.4	1,689.0	1,693.3	1,674.8
2003	1,661.0	1,658.7	1,675.1	1,695.1	1,708.1	1,722.7	1,724.6	1,723.9	1,724.1	1,728.9	1,737.4	1,747.2	1,708.9
2004	1,706.9	1,715.9	1,739.1	1,750.6	1,765.7	1,784.6	1,784.9	1,786.0	1,784.7	1,791.7	1,798.6	1,805.6	1,767.9
2005	1,761.1	1,771.0	1,784.0	1,800.5	1,811.5	1,825.5	1,828.3	1,826.2	1,827.6	1,821.4	1,834.1	1,843.1	1,811.2
2006	1,804.8	1,811.0	1,828.5	1,834.9	1,846.5	1,867.9	1,858.2	1,856.3	1,853.2	1,854.0	1,861.5	1,871.0	1,845.7
2007	1,834.2	1,836.7	1,852.6	1,856.9	1,867.2	1,882.6	1,875.8	1,870.5	1,865.0	1,872.3	1,879.0	1,885.9	1,864.9
2008	1,840.7	1,843.1	1,854.8	1,872.5	1,884.3	1,891.4	1,888.7	1,882.4	1,875.4	1,869.9	1,868.1	1,865.8	1,869.8
2009	1,818.5	1,810.8	1,813.4	1,815.4	1,825.8	1,834.1	1,826.9	1,820.3	1,808.6	1,819.7	1,826.3	1,827.7	1,820.6
2010	1,781.1	1,761.8	1,792.5	1,821.8	1,832.2	1,844.4	1,837.3	1,834.7	1,826.0	1,837.6	1,844.6	1,850.3	1,822.0
2011	1,815.8	1,818.1	1,832.2	1,856.9	1,854.8	1,870.9	1,883.3	1,879.5	1,875.8	1,877.3	1,887.4	1,889.4	1,861.8
2012	1,850.9	1,857.0	1,873.8	1,889.1	1,899.6	1,912.0	1,911.7	1,915.7	1,907.8	1,919.5	1,930.4	1,927.7	1,899.6
2013	1,890.2	1,896.2	1,906.1	1,921.6	1,928.1	1,933.2	1,938.8	1,940.4	1,929.3	1,936.3	1,948.9	1,945.7	1,926.2
Goods-Producing													
2002	168.0	169.1	170.7	171.7	173.5	175.4	175.2	176.1	174.8	174.0	173.0	170.8	172.7
2003	166.6	166.2	168.2	171.2	173.8	175.7	178.1	178.8	178.3	177.9	177.2	176.1	174.0
2004	172.2	172.3	175.8	178.4	180.9	182.8	185.6	186.1	185.6	185.7	185.5	184.9	181.3
2005	179.8	180.1	181.9	186.5	188.9	192.3	194.1	195.1	194.8	192.4	193.0	192.2	189.3
2006	187.3	187.7	190.6	191.9	193.6	196.6	196.8	196.3	194.2	190.6	188.9	188.4	191.9
2007	182.9	180.6	183.4	184.2	185.7	188.3	187.8	187.8	185.8	183.6	181.9	179.8	184.3
2008	174.9	174.1	174.9	175.2	175.5	176.6	176.5	176.5	175.0	172.6	169.4	166.2	174.0
2009	157.4	154.8	153.8	154.0	154.1	154.3	154.1	153.5	151.8	149.4	147.9	146.4	152.6
2010	139.7	133.5	139.9	144.5	145.7	146.6	148.2	148.3	147.0	145.9	145.1	143.4	144.0
2011	138.1	137.8	139.6	143.1	144.0	146.0	149.0	148.8	146.8	145.4	145.0	144.5	144.0
2012	139.9	139.9	142.2	143.9	145.1	147.7	148.9	148.3	147.1	147.4	146.4	145.3	145.2
2013	140.9	140.9	142.2	144.4	146.3	148.1	149.0	149.7	147.9	145.1	146.2	143.9	145.4
Service-Providing													
2002	1,971.2	1,975.3	1,989.3	1,994.9	2,007.2	2,022.8	2,003.8	2,000.3	2,007.5	2,015.0	2,024.6	2,034.1	2,003.8
2003	2,010.0	2,012.6	2,029.2	2,047.2	2,059.9	2,074.0	2,070.0	2,061.6	2,072.9	2,075.6	2,085.4	2,097.0	2,058.0
2004	2,057.2	2,070.2	2,093.9	2,100.1	2,116.0	2,130.6	2,120.6	2,119.7	2,127.5	2,143.9	2,154.8	2,161.7	2,116.4
2005	2,113.2	2,124.6	2,137.9	2,150.6	2,162.4	2,171.7	2,170.8	2,165.2	2,170.0	2,172.5	2,189.6	2,198.7	2,160.6
2006	2,157.6	2,167.2	2,185.0	2,189.6	2,202.4	2,218.0	2,205.7	2,200.6	2,203.4	2,214.9	2,225.0	2,236.8	2,200.5
2007	2,192.0	2,202.5	2,217.9	2,221.7	2,233.7	2,243.5	2,235.9	2,226.9	2,227.0	2,246.6	2,257.8	2,268.8	2,231.2
2008	2,217.4	2,227.6	2,242.2	2,255.5	2,270.1	2,275.7	2,274.3	2,265.3	2,257.3	2,263.0	2,267.9	2,270.5	2,257.2
2009	2,224.7	2,226.6	2,233.8	2,233.1	2,245.7	2,253.6	2,254.9	2,239.0	2,225.9	2,248.3	2,261.0	2,263.3	2,242.5
2010	2,215.6	2,205.2	2,235.2	2,261.1	2,280.0	2,288.9	2,287.5	2,257.3	2,260.8	2,282.1	2,293.2	2,298.2	2,263.8
2011	2,256.8	2,265.9	2,281.8	2,300.7	2,298.5	2,311.6	2,318.9	2,298.9	2,312.6	2,317.7	2,328.8	2,331.4	2,302.0
2012	2,286.4	2,299.0	2,318.0	2,329.8	2,339.3	2,348.0	2,339.3	2,329.6	2,341.4	2,360.9	2,373.9	2,371.7	2,336.4
2013	2,327.2	2,340.3	2,350.7	2,363.3	2,369.3	2,369.2	2,364.8	2,350.3	2,359.5	2,374.1	2,386.8	2,386.3	2,361.8
Mining, Logging, and Construction													
2002	119.4	120.4	121.8	123.0	125.0	127.0	127.1	128.2	126.9	126.9	126.3	124.4	124.7
2003	120.7	120.1	122.8	126.5	129.3	131.1	133.5	134.5	134.0	134.0	133.3	132.3	129.3
2004	128.7	128.9	132.1	134.5	137.0	138.6	140.9	141.5	141.0	141.5	141.3	140.7	137.2
2005	136.2	136.4	138.0	142.3	144.5	147.6	149.4	150.3	150.1	148.5	148.8	148.0	145.0
2006	144.2	144.6	147.3	148.3	150.1	152.7	152.4	152.2	150.4	147.7	146.2	145.6	148.5
2007	141.0	138.6	141.5	142.4	143.8	145.9	145.4	145.6	143.8	141.9	140.3	138.2	142.4
2008	133.8	133.0	133.9	134.3	134.5	135.4	135.3	135.2	133.9	131.8	129.0	125.9	133.0
2009	118.8	116.8	116.0	116.3	116.4	116.9	117.2	116.7	115.4	113.0	111.6	110.1	115.4
2010	104.5	98.7	104.9	109.3	110.4	111.3	113.2	113.4	112.3	110.9	110.2	108.6	109.0
2011	103.8	103.6	105.2	108.7	109.7	111.6	114.7	114.8	113.0	111.6	111.2	110.7	109.9
2012	106.4	106.9	108.9	110.8	111.9	114.3	115.4	114.9	114.0	114.4	113.4	112.8	112.0
2013	108.7	108.8	110.1	112.1	113.9	115.6	116.6	117.4	116.0	114.0	115.4	113.8	113.5
Manufacturing													
2002	48.6	48.7	48.9	48.7	48.5	48.4	48.1	47.9	47.9	47.1	46.7	46.4	48.0
2003	45.9	46.1	45.4	44.7	44.5	44.6	44.6	44.3	44.3	43.9	43.9	43.8	44.7
2004	43.5	43.4	43.7	43.9	43.9	44.2	44.7	44.6	44.6	44.2	44.2	44.2	44.1
2005	43.6	43.7	43.9	44.2	44.4	44.7	44.7	44.8	44.7	43.9	44.2	44.2	44.3
2006	43.1	43.1	43.3	43.6	43.5	43.9	44.4	44.1	43.8	42.9	42.7	42.8	43.4
2007	41.9	42.0	41.9	41.8	41.9	42.4	42.4	42.2	42.0	41.7	41.6	41.6	42.0
2008	41.1	41.1	41.0	40.9	41.0	41.2	41.2	41.3	41.1	40.8	40.4	40.3	41.0
2009	38.6	38.0	37.8	37.7	37.7	37.4	36.9	36.8	36.4	36.4	36.3	36.3	37.2
2010	35.2	34.8	35.0	35.2	35.3	35.3	35.0	34.9	34.7	35.0	34.9	34.8	35.0
2011	34.3	34.2	34.4	34.4	34.3	34.4	34.3	34.0	33.8	33.8	33.8	33.8	34.1
2012	33.5	33.0	33.3	33.1	33.2	33.4	33.5	33.4	33.1	33.0	33.0	32.5	33.2
2013	32.2	32.1	32.1	32.3	32.4	32.5	32.4	32.3	31.9	31.1	30.8	30.1	31.9

Employment by Industry: Washington–Arlington–Alexandria, DC–VA–MD–WV, Selected Years, 2002–2013—Continued

(Numbers in thousands, not seasonally adjusted)

Industry and year	January	February	March	April	May	June	July	August	September	October	November	December	Annual average
Trade, Transportation, and Utilities													
2002	301.5	297.5	298.4	299.0	301.3	304.4	303.0	302.8	302.7	304.8	310.9	317.1	303.6
2003	302.1	298.7	300.6	303.3	305.9	309.5	308.8	309.7	309.7	312.6	319.9	326.4	308.9
2004	310.4	308.0	310.7	309.6	313.2	318.6	315.7	316.0	314.8	321.0	327.7	334.0	316.6
2005	318.8	316.3	317.8	317.9	320.1	322.3	322.3	321.8	319.6	321.7	328.7	337.2	322.0
2006	320.9	314.0	315.8	314.6	318.4	321.5	319.7	319.7	318.8	320.8	328.3	335.0	320.6
2007	320.6	315.1	316.7	317.2	320.1	322.9	322.1	320.7	319.1	320.6	328.8	335.5	321.6
2008	319.6	314.3	314.7	315.2	317.1	319.5	318.2	316.9	314.6	314.1	318.8	323.1	317.2
2009	306.2	300.4	299.8	298.1	300.9	302.4	300.3	299.8	299.2	300.9	307.9	312.7	302.4
2010	298.5	290.8	295.6	298.5	301.5	304.6	302.9	303.6	301.3	305.9	313.2	319.5	303.0
2011	304.6	301.0	302.1	304.7	305.7	307.9	308.1	308.2	306.2	309.0	316.6	322.1	308.0
2012	308.3	304.7	306.3	305.9	309.0	311.0	309.9	310.0	308.7	311.2	320.5	324.9	310.9
2013	309.9	305.7	306.9	308.7	310.8	313.0	312.3	312.4	311.0	315.6	323.9	328.1	313.2
Wholesale Trade													
2002	51.4	51.3	51.4	51.3	51.4	51.5	51.5	51.4	51.0	51.5	51.8	52.1	51.5
2003	52.5	52.5	52.8	52.8	53.0	53.1	52.3	52.2	51.8	52.7	53.0	53.3	52.7
2004	53.3	53.5	53.9	52.9	52.9	53.4	53.5	53.4	53.4	54.5	54.9	55.0	53.7
2005	55.0	55.3	55.5	56.0	56.0	55.8	56.3	56.3	55.7	54.9	55.0	55.2	55.6
2006	53.9	54.0	54.4	54.3	54.7	54.9	54.7	54.7	54.4	54.6	54.7	54.9	54.5
2007	54.8	54.8	55.0	55.0	55.2	55.5	55.0	55.1	54.8	55.0	55.1	55.2	55.0
2008	54.6	54.9	54.8	54.8	54.9	55.1	54.8	54.6	54.1	53.8	53.3	53.0	54.4
2009	52.5	52.2	51.9	51.5	51.4	51.3	50.8	50.7	50.2	50.0	49.9	50.0	51.0
2010	49.2	48.9	49.1	48.9	49.1	49.3	49.2	49.2	48.8	49.3	49.0	49.2	49.1
2011	48.9	49.0	49.1	49.1	49.0	49.0	49.2	49.3	48.8	48.7	48.6	48.6	48.9
2012	48.3	48.6	48.8	48.1	48.7	49.0	49.2	49.5	49.3	49.4	49.5	49.5	49.0
2013	49.5	49.6	49.7	49.8	49.8	49.9	49.8	49.7	49.5	49.6	49.3	49.8	49.7
Retail Trade													
2002	191.9	188.2	189.2	189.6	191.5	193.7	191.9	191.7	192.7	193.5	199.0	205.3	193.2
2003	190.2	187.1	188.4	190.4	192.3	195.5	194.7	196.0	196.8	198.9	205.9	211.7	195.7
2004	198.5	195.9	197.6	198.0	200.9	204.8	202.4	202.4	200.9	205.6	211.7	217.6	203.0
2005	204.4	201.3	202.4	202.6	204.5	206.5	206.5	206.1	204.9	206.8	213.1	219.8	206.6
2006	208.6	203.5	204.5	203.7	206.5	208.7	207.9	208.1	207.1	209.4	216.4	220.6	208.8
2007	209.9	204.3	205.5	206.2	208.5	210.2	210.1	208.6	207.4	209.1	216.7	221.0	209.8
2008	209.2	203.6	204.3	204.7	206.1	207.7	206.9	205.6	204.2	204.3	208.6	211.5	206.4
2009	198.3	193.8	193.4	192.5	194.7	195.9	194.9	194.8	194.5	196.8	203.2	206.5	196.6
2010	196.0	189.1	193.1	195.7	197.9	199.9	198.9	199.5	197.6	201.9	208.2	212.2	199.2
2011	200.8	197.6	198.2	200.8	201.7	203.3	202.7	202.8	202.0	204.8	211.9	215.7	203.5
2012	205.0	201.1	202.7	202.2	204.1	205.3	204.5	204.2	203.5	205.7	214.3	216.3	205.7
2013	205.1	202.2	202.8	204.4	206.0	207.7	207.9	208.1	207.1	211.7	218.0	221.2	208.5
Transportation and Utilities													
2002	58.2	58.0	57.8	58.1	58.4	59.2	59.6	59.7	59.0	59.8	60.1	59.7	59.0
2003	59.4	59.1	59.4	60.1	60.6	60.9	61.8	61.5	61.1	61.0	61.0	61.4	60.6
2004	58.6	58.6	59.2	58.7	59.4	60.4	59.8	60.2	60.5	60.9	61.1	61.4	59.9
2005	59.4	59.7	59.9	59.3	59.6	60.0	59.5	59.4	59.0	60.0	60.6	62.2	59.9
2006	58.4	56.5	56.9	56.6	57.2	57.9	57.1	56.9	57.3	56.8	57.2	59.5	57.4
2007	55.9	56.0	56.2	56.0	56.4	57.2	57.0	57.0	56.9	56.5	57.0	59.3	56.8
2008	55.8	55.8	55.6	55.7	56.1	56.7	56.5	56.7	56.3	56.0	56.9	58.6	56.4
2009	55.4	54.4	54.5	54.1	54.8	55.2	54.6	54.3	54.5	54.1	54.8	56.2	54.7
2010	53.3	52.8	53.4	53.9	54.5	55.4	54.8	54.9	54.9	54.7	56.0	58.1	54.7
2011	54.9	54.4	54.8	54.8	55.0	55.6	56.2	56.1	55.4	55.5	56.1	57.8	55.6
2012	55.0	55.0	54.8	55.6	56.2	56.7	56.2	56.3	55.9	56.1	56.7	59.1	56.1
2013	55.3	53.9	54.4	54.5	55.0	55.4	54.6	54.6	54.4	54.3	56.6	57.1	55.0
Information													
2002	101.4	100.8	100.6	98.9	98.7	98.4	96.0	95.3	93.8	92.5	92.8	92.3	96.8
2003	92.3	92.6	92.5	91.6	92.2	92.5	92.5	92.5	91.8	91.1	91.7	91.9	92.1
2004	91.6	91.2	91.9	90.2	89.9	89.7	90.4	89.5	87.8	85.1	84.8	84.3	88.9
2005	83.1	83.6	83.4	82.7	82.6	83.0	82.8	82.1	81.5	81.2	81.3	81.4	82.4
2006	80.4	80.7	81.4	80.4	80.5	80.5	80.2	79.5	79	78	77.9	77.7	79.7
2007	78.3	78.2	78.0	77.0	77.2	77.7	77.9	77.4	76.8	76.6	76.7	76.7	77.4
2008	75.6	76.0	75.9	75.5	75.4	75.4	75.0	74.6	73.8	72.5	72.4	71.7	74.5
2009	70.0	69.9	68.9	68.1	67.8	68.0	67.2	66.5	65.6	65.4	65.3	65.2	67.3
2010	64.4	64.0	64.0	63.7	63.5	64.3	64.8	64.9	65.4	65.7	65.7	66.7	64.8
2011	64.7	65.1	65.4	66.6	64.7	66.6	66.3	62.4	65.2	62.1	63.4	64.8	64.8
2012	61.2	62.5	63.3	61.9	62.5	63.7	62.8	64.0	62.1	62.1	63.6	62.1	62.7
2013	61.7	63.2	63.0	61.8	62.2	62.3	62.5	63.5	61.6	61.5	61.2	61.6	62.2
Financial Activities													
2002	108.9	109.5	109.8	109.2	109.4	110.4	110.1	110.4	109.5	110.1	110.6	111.3	109.9
2003	111.1	111.1	111.3	112.9	113.3	114.3	115.2	114.6	113.3	112.5	111.8	112.0	112.8
2004	111.2	111.3	112.0	114.3	115.1	115.9	114.8	114.8	114.4	115.0	114.9	115.6	114.1
2005	114.1	114.5	114.4	115.8	116.4	116.8	117.2	117.0	116.5	115.8	115.7	116.4	115.9
2006	115.2	115.7	116.4	115.7	116.5	117.6	117.6	117.0	116.4	115.7	115.4	116.3	116.3
2007	115.4	115.8	116.0	115.0	115.3	116.1	115.9	114.6	113.6	112.7	112.2	112.2	114.6
2008	110.8	110.7	110.7	111.2	111.3	111.9	111.9	111.2	110.4	109.6	109.3	109.0	110.7
2009	106.9	106.2	105.8	105.4	105.6	106.5	106.2	106.0	106.0	105.2	105.8	105.7	106.0
2010	104.5	104.1	104.9	104.9	105.4	106.5	106.5	106.0	104.8	106.1	106.3	106.3	105.5
2011	105.2	105.1	105.5	106.7	106.9	107.4	108.0	108.0	107.7	107.8	107.7	108.0	107.0
2012	106.9	107.3	107.7	108.4	108.6	109.7	109.9	109.7	109.3	109.9	110.1	110.4	109.0
2013	109.7	110.0	110.5	110.8	110.9	112.1	112.3	112.2	111.5	112.2	112.6	112.7	111.5

Employment by Industry: Washington–Arlington–Alexandria, DC–VA–MD–WV, Selected Years, 2002–2013—*Continued*

(Numbers in thousands, not seasonally adjusted)

Industry and year	January	February	March	April	May	June	July	August	September	October	November	December	Annual average
Professional and Business Services													
2002	441.9	444.5	447.7	449.3	449.5	453.2	451.1	449.2	446.1	448.7	449.8	450.9	448.5
2003	455.3	455.7	459.5	470.4	473.0	477.5	479.4	480.0	478.6	482.1	484.4	487.9	473.7
2004	478.8	483.6	490.7	494.6	498.0	505.1	509.7	511.0	509.8	512.0	511.6	515.3	501.7
2005	506.1	511.0	515.2	520.1	521.2	527.1	532.1	532.1	532.4	530.1	531.2	532.2	524.2
2006	523.6	529.1	533.4	537.0	538.7	547.4	546.6	546.3	543.7	543.5	544.0	545.0	539.9
2007	538.9	543.4	547.4	550.1	551.7	557.6	555.4	555.5	549.9	555.7	555.9	556.7	551.5
2008	548.4	551.6	554.5	559.6	560.0	563.9	564.2	562.8	558.8	559.6	558.4	556.7	558.2
2009	550.4	550.2	550.6	549.8	549.7	553.8	554.9	552.8	546.5	553.9	554.7	554.2	551.8
2010	544.8	545.1	550.2	559.1	559.7	564.2	560.9	559.3	554.2	560.2	560.5	561.4	556.6
2011	557.1	559.3	562.8	566.3	565.6	569.6	575.9	576.1	571.3	575.2	575.6	574.0	569.1
2012	567.7	570.8	574.8	581.9	582.1	586.9	588.9	590.3	583.1	588.8	589.8	586.5	582.6
2013	579.0	582.8	583.8	586.5	584.6	587.0	587.9	589.3	580.6	579.0	580.4	580.0	583.4
Education and Health Services													
2002	227.4	229.3	230.3	231.1	231.9	230.8	230.6	231.6	233.7	236.5	238.2	237.8	232.4
2003	228.3	230.4	232.9	231.6	229.1	226.1	223.1	221.9	230.0	231.6	232.8	232.5	229.2
2004	230.8	236.0	238.2	238.4	236.3	233.1	228.0	227.5	236.6	240.6	241.9	240.7	235.7
2005	238.4	242.9	243.5	243.4	241.7	237.2	233.6	233.2	242.9	245.8	249.6	249.2	241.8
2006	244.3	249.4	250.9	251.3	248.4	244.7	239.8	239.7	249.2	254.7	258.2	258.6	249.1
2007	255.1	260.2	262.2	261.1	258.2	254.0	249.8	248.9	259.2	265.6	266.8	267.2	259.0
2008	260.9	264.0	265.2	267.4	268.5	263.9	261.7	262.0	270.1	273.0	274.6	275.4	267.2
2009	272.4	274.7	275.6	277.8	277.8	272.4	269.2	268.2	274.0	281.6	283.5	283.7	275.9
2010	279.8	278.6	282.3	286.4	286.5	279.9	277.7	277.7	284.6	286.2	288.1	287.3	282.9
2011	289.1	290.9	292.1	295.1	289.2	286.4	288.5	287.7	297.3	299.1	300.3	297.7	292.8
2012	297.0	298.9	300.1	302.3	299.9	293.0	291.1	293.8	305.0	309.6	310.7	309.3	300.9
2013	307.1	310.4	311.6	313.9	310.8	301.2	305.1	305.4	315.3	321.5	321.9	320.3	312.0
Leisure and Hospitality													
2002	164.9	167.2	172.2	179.0	184.2	189.7	190.0	189.6	186.3	182.9	182.8	181.5	180.9
2003	175.2	173.6	178.0	183.9	189.9	195.1	195.1	194.7	191.4	189.4	187.7	187.5	186.8
2004	180.1	181.0	186.1	190.7	197.0	202.7	203.0	203.8	199.4	197.0	196.2	195.5	194.4
2005	187.9	189.1	193.2	198.8	204.8	210.2	209.3	208.4	204.3	199.7	199.3	198.5	200.3
2006	191.3	192.2	196.8	200.0	205.6	213.0	210.8	211.1	206.3	202.8	201.1	201.3	202.7
2007	195.2	194.7	199.4	204.1	209.6	215.2	216.2	216.1	211.7	208.1	206.6	206.7	207.0
2008	200.7	201.8	207.0	215.2	221.6	224.6	225.0	223.3	218.5	214.4	210.9	209.0	214.3
2009	201.9	201.3	205.3	209.9	216.9	222.0	220.9	219.5	214.1	211.9	210.2	207.5	211.8
2010	199.9	197.2	205.3	213.1	217.4	224.5	223.1	222.6	217.8	215.9	213.9	213.4	213.7
2011	206.3	207.5	212.9	220.7	224.5	231.5	230.9	232.7	226.9	224.1	223.2	221.9	221.9
2012	215.1	217.4	223.1	229.0	235.9	242.1	240.6	241.2	235.0	232.9	231.2	230.0	231.1
2013	224.8	226.0	230.7	237.0	243.4	249.2	249.5	248.4	242.5	242.2	243.1	239.6	239.7
Other Services													
2002	126.8	127.7	128.6	129.2	129.4	130.5	131.3	131.8	130.8	130.9	130.9	131.6	130.0
2003	130.1	130.4	132.1	130.2	130.9	132.0	132.4	131.7	131.0	131.7	131.9	132.9	131.4
2004	131.8	132.5	133.7	134.4	135.3	136.7	137.7	137.3	136.3	135.3	136.0	135.3	135.2
2005	132.9	133.5	134.6	135.3	135.8	136.6	136.9	136.5	135.6	134.7	135.3	136.0	135.3
2006	141.8	142.2	143.2	144.0	144.8	146.6	147.2	146.7	145.6	147.9	147.7	148.7	145.5
2007	147.8	148.7	149.5	148.2	149.4	150.8	150.7	149.5	148.9	149.4	150.1	151.1	149.5
2008	149.8	150.6	151.9	153.2	154.9	155.6	156.2	155.1	154.2	154.1	154.3	154.7	153.7
2009	153.3	153.3	153.6	152.3	153.0	154.7	154.1	154.0	152.2	150.8	151.1	151.9	152.9
2010	149.5	148.5	150.3	151.6	152.5	153.8	153.2	152.3	150.9	151.7	151.8	152.3	151.5
2011	150.7	151.4	151.8	153.7	154.2	155.5	156.6	155.6	154.4	154.6	155.6	156.4	154.2
2012	154.8	155.5	156.3	155.8	156.5	157.9	159.6	158.4	157.5	157.6	158.1	159.2	157.3
2013	157.1	157.2	157.4	158.5	159.1	160.3	160.2	159.5	158.9	159.2	159.6	159.5	158.9
Government													
2002	498.4	498.8	501.7	499.2	502.8	505.4	491.7	489.6	504.6	508.6	508.6	511.6	501.8
2003	515.6	520.1	522.3	523.3	525.6	527.0	523.5	516.5	527.1	524.6	525.2	525.9	523.1
2004	522.5	526.6	530.6	527.9	531.2	528.8	521.3	519.8	528.4	537.9	541.7	541.0	529.8
2005	531.9	533.7	535.8	536.6	539.8	538.5	536.6	534.1	537.2	543.5	548.5	547.8	538.7
2006	540.1	543.9	547.1	546.6	549.5	546.7	544.3	540.6	544.4	551.5	552.4	554.2	546.8
2007	540.7	546.4	548.7	549.0	552.2	549.2	547.9	544.2	547.8	557.9	560.7	562.7	550.6
2008	551.6	558.6	562.3	558.2	561.3	560.9	562.1	559.4	556.9	565.7	569.2	570.9	561.4
2009	563.6	570.6	574.2	571.7	574.0	573.8	582.1	572.2	569.1	578.0	582.6	582.0	574.5
2010	574.2	576.9	582.6	583.8	593.5	591.1	598.4	570.9	581.8	590.4	593.7	591.3	585.7
2011	579.1	585.6	589.2	586.9	587.7	586.7	584.6	568.2	583.6	585.8	586.4	586.5	584.2
2012	575.4	581.9	586.4	584.6	584.8	583.7	576.5	562.2	580.7	588.8	589.9	589.3	582.0
2013	577.9	585.0	586.8	586.1	587.5	584.1	575.0	559.6	578.1	582.9	584.1	584.5	581.0

Employment by Industry: Worcester, MA–CT, NECTA, Selected Years, 2002–2013

(Numbers in thousands, not seasonally adjusted)

Industry and year	January	February	March	April	May	June	July	August	September	October	November	December	Annual average
Total Nonfarm													
2002	240.8	240.6	241.3	244.6	246.6	246.5	241.3	241.1	245.8	246.5	247.2	247.8	244.2
2003	241.5	240.3	241.2	243.0	245.0	245.2	241.7	240.5	245.4	247.2	247.0	247.3	243.8
2004	239.9	240.2	241.8	244.9	246.6	247.8	243.1	243.3	246.6	247.2	247.7	248.3	244.8
2005	240.8	241.6	242.0	245.2	247.2	247.8	243.4	242.5	246.8	247.5	248.8	249.2	245.2
2006	243.7	243.2	244.8	247.9	249.5	250.7	246.6	247.1	250.3	252.2	252.0	252.4	248.4
2007	245.5	246.2	247.1	248.9	251.8	253.4	246.7	246.9	250.1	252.9	253.9	253.0	249.7
2008	246.5	247.5	247.9	249.2	250.6	250.8	245.7	245.5	249.2	250.4	248.8	247.4	248.3
2009	240.8	240.3	239.5	241.0	241.8	240.8	236.6	236.5	239.6	242.3	241.9	243.0	240.3
2010	236.8	237.0	237.4	240.4	243.0	243.2	239.2	239.0	241.5	244.4	244.7	246.1	241.1
2011	240.2	240.9	241.9	244.4	245.4	244.8	243.1	241.6	246.0	248.2	248.2	248.5	244.4
2012	242.3	242.1	244.2	245.0	246.1	248.0	244.2	244.1	247.2	249.0	249.6	248.8	245.9
2013	243.5	244.3	246.1	248.7	250.5	251.0	245.7	246.8	248.5	250.4	250.9	250.2	248.1
Total Private													
2002	204.8	204.2	205.0	208.1	209.7	210.0	207.8	208.3	209.9	210.4	210.7	211.3	208.4
2003	205.8	204.3	205.0	207.0	208.8	209.0	208.1	207.5	209.4	211.5	211.5	211.2	208.3
2004	204.8	204.7	205.9	208.8	210.5	212.1	209.8	210.3	210.6	210.8	211.0	211.4	209.2
2005	204.7	204.9	205.6	208.9	210.6	211.4	210.3	210.3	211.2	210.7	211.9	212.3	209.4
2006	207.1	206.6	208.0	210.8	212.1	213.9	213.1	213.6	213.7	214.8	214.2	214.7	211.9
2007	208.5	208.8	209.7	211.3	213.6	215.6	212.6	213.2	213.1	215.2	215.9	214.9	212.7
2008	209.3	209.8	210.1	211.4	212.6	213.6	211.4	211.8	212.3	212.6	211.0	209.8	211.3
2009	203.5	202.4	201.5	202.8	203.6	203.2	202.0	202.0	202.4	204.0	203.6	203.8	202.9
2010	199.0	198.9	199.2	202.1	203.9	204.9	204.7	204.6	204.3	206.6	206.5	207.7	203.5
2011	202.9	203.1	203.9	206.4	207.0	207.3	208.5	207.6	208.9	210.4	210.4	210.6	207.3
2012	205.2	204.4	206.1	207.4	208.3	210.4	210.0	209.9	210.0	211.3	211.6	210.7	208.8
2013	206.7	206.1	207.8	210.2	211.9	213.6	211.7	212.3	212.1	213.2	213.5	212.8	211.0
Goods-Producing													
2002	43.2	42.6	42.6	43.1	43.4	43.6	42.7	43.1	43.0	42.7	42.5	42.3	42.9
2003	41.3	40.3	40.1	40.6	40.9	41.2	40.9	40.9	40.9	41.0	40.8	40.4	40.8
2004	39.1	38.5	38.8	39.9	40.4	40.8	40.7	41.2	41.0	40.7	40.7	40.5	40.2
2005	38.7	38.2	38.2	39.2	39.8	40.2	40.0	40.0	39.9	39.7	39.8	39.8	39.5
2006	38.9	38.5	38.4	39.3	39.8	40.4	40.4	40.6	40.2	40.0	39.7	39.6	39.7
2007	38.2	37.6	37.7	38.1	38.7	39.5	39.4	39.4	39.3	39.5	39.5	39.1	38.8
2008	37.9	37.3	37.3	37.6	38.0	38.6	38.3	38.1	38.1	38.0	37.5	36.7	37.8
2009	34.8	33.8	33.2	33.3	33.5	33.8	33.7	33.6	33.6	33.6	33.4	33.1	33.6
2010	32.0	31.4	31.5	32.3	32.7	33.2	33.2	33.1	33.0	33.1	33.1	33.1	32.6
2011	31.8	31.5	31.4	32.3	33.1	33.7	34.4	34.3	34.2	34.3	34.2	34.1	33.3
2012	32.2	31.7	31.8	32.3	32.3	32.9	32.9	32.7	32.7	32.6	32.4	31.8	32.4
2013	30.9	30.8	30.8	31.3	31.8	32.5	32.6	32.7	32.3	32.5	32.3	32.1	31.9
Service-Providing													
2002	197.6	198.0	198.7	201.5	203.2	202.9	198.6	198.0	202.8	203.8	204.7	205.5	201.3
2003	200.2	200.0	201.1	202.4	204.1	204.0	200.8	199.6	204.5	206.2	206.2	206.9	203.0
2004	200.8	201.7	203.0	205.0	206.2	207.0	202.4	202.1	205.6	206.5	207.0	207.8	204.6
2005	202.1	203.4	203.8	206.0	207.4	207.6	203.4	202.5	206.9	207.8	209.0	209.4	205.8
2006	204.8	204.7	206.4	208.6	209.7	210.3	206.2	206.5	210.1	212.2	212.3	212.8	208.7
2007	207.3	208.6	209.4	210.8	213.1	213.9	207.3	207.5	210.8	213.4	214.4	213.9	210.9
2008	208.6	210.2	210.6	211.6	212.6	212.2	207.4	207.4	211.1	212.4	211.3	210.7	210.5
2009	206.0	206.5	206.3	207.7	208.3	207.0	202.9	202.9	206.0	208.7	208.5	209.9	206.7
2010	204.8	205.6	205.9	208.1	210.3	210.0	206.0	205.9	208.5	211.3	211.6	213.0	208.4
2011	208.4	209.4	210.5	212.1	212.3	211.1	208.7	207.3	211.8	213.9	214.0	214.4	211.2
2012	210.1	210.4	212.4	212.7	213.8	215.1	211.3	211.4	214.5	216.4	217.2	217.0	213.5
2013	212.6	213.5	215.3	217.4	218.7	218.5	213.1	214.1	216.2	217.9	218.6	218.1	216.2
Mining, Logging, and Construction													
2002	9.0	8.7	8.8	9.5	9.9	10.1	10.2	10.3	10.1	10.0	10.0	9.7	9.7
2003	8.8	8.2	8.3	9.2	9.9	10.1	10.5	10.7	10.6	10.7	10.6	10.2	9.8
2004	9.1	8.8	9.1	10.0	10.5	10.8	11.2	11.3	11.1	10.9	10.8	10.4	10.3
2005	9.2	8.8	8.9	9.9	10.5	10.8	11.2	11.2	11.1	10.8	10.9	10.6	10.3
2006	9.8	9.5	9.6	10.4	10.8	11.1	11.4	11.5	11.2	11.0	10.6	10.2	10.6
2007	9.1	8.6	8.7	9.2	9.9	10.3	10.5	10.5	10.5	10.3	10.2	9.7	9.8
2008	8.7	8.4	8.5	9.0	9.5	9.9	9.9	9.9	9.8	9.6	9.3	8.7	9.3
2009	7.6	7.2	7.1	7.6	7.9	8.2	8.4	8.5	8.4	8.3	8.1	7.8	7.9
2010	6.9	6.5	6.6	7.3	7.7	8.0	8.2	8.1	8.0	8.1	8.0	7.8	7.6
2011	6.9	6.6	6.6	7.4	7.9	8.3	8.8	8.8	8.8	8.8	8.7	8.4	8.0
2012	7.6	7.2	7.4	8.0	8.1	8.4	8.7	8.7	8.6	8.4	8.3	8.1	8.1
2013	7.4	7.3	7.3	7.8	8.3	8.8	9.0	9.0	8.8	8.9	8.7	8.4	8.3
Manufacturing													
2002	34.2	33.9	33.8	33.6	33.5	33.5	32.5	32.8	32.9	32.7	32.5	32.6	33.2
2003	32.5	32.1	31.8	31.4	31.0	31.1	30.4	30.2	30.3	30.3	30.2	30.2	31.0
2004	30.0	29.7	29.7	29.9	29.9	30.0	29.5	29.9	29.9	29.8	29.9	30.1	29.9
2005	29.5	29.4	29.3	29.3	29.3	29.4	28.8	28.8	28.8	28.9	28.9	29.2	29.1
2006	29.1	29.0	28.8	28.9	29.0	29.3	29.0	29.1	29.0	29.0	29.1	29.4	29.1
2007	29.1	29.0	29.0	28.9	28.8	29.2	28.9	28.9	28.8	29.2	29.3	29.4	29.0
2008	29.2	28.9	28.8	28.6	28.5	28.7	28.4	28.2	28.3	28.4	28.2	28.0	28.5
2009	27.2	26.6	26.1	25.7	25.6	25.6	25.3	25.1	25.2	25.3	25.3	25.3	25.7
2010	25.1	24.9	24.9	25.0	25.0	25.2	25.0	25.0	25.0	25.0	25.1	25.3	25.0
2011	24.9	24.9	24.8	24.9	25.2	25.4	25.6	25.5	25.4	25.5	25.5	25.7	25.3
2012	24.6	24.5	24.4	24.3	24.2	24.5	24.2	24.0	24.1	24.2	24.1	23.7	24.2
2013	23.5	23.5	23.5	23.5	23.5	23.7	23.6	23.7	23.5	23.6	23.6	23.7	23.6

Employment by Industry: Worcester, MA–CT, NECTA, Selected Years, 2002–2013—*Continued*

(Numbers in thousands, not seasonally adjusted)

Industry and year	January	February	March	April	May	June	July	August	September	October	November	December	Annual average
Trade, Transportation, and Utilities													
2002	45.2	44.5	44.9	45.2	45.2	45.6	44.6	44.3	45.0	45.6	46.2	46.8	45.3
2003	45.1	44.2	44.6	45.0	45.3	45.7	45.2	45.2	45.8	46.1	46.6	46.8	45.5
2004	45.0	44.5	44.7	45.0	45.2	45.7	44.5	44.5	44.8	45.5	46.2	46.6	45.2
2005	45.4	44.7	44.8	45.1	45.5	45.6	44.9	45.1	45.3	45.5	46.3	46.7	45.4
2006	45.3	44.6	45.0	45.2	45.3	45.6	45.3	45.7	46.2	46.5	47.0	47.4	45.8
2007	46.1	45.5	45.9	45.9	46.4	46.9	46.0	45.8	46.1	47.0	47.8	48.1	46.5
2008	46.8	45.8	46.1	46.1	46.3	46.4	45.6	45.7	46.0	46.4	46.6	46.7	46.2
2009	44.6	43.7	43.6	43.5	43.7	44.1	43.0	42.9	43.3	43.8	44.4	44.8	43.8
2010	43.6	43.2	43.6	44.4	45.0	45.5	44.7	44.8	44.8	45.4	46.1	46.9	44.8
2011	45.0	44.5	44.7	44.9	45.1	45.1	44.6	44.6	45.2	46.1	46.9	47.5	45.4
2012	45.8	45.1	45.4	45.7	46.2	46.6	46.0	46.1	46.4	47.0	47.7	47.7	46.3
2013	46.1	45.5	45.7	46.4	47.2	47.7	46.7	46.6	46.8	47.6	48.4	48.4	46.9
Wholesale Trade													
2002	9.7	9.6	9.6	9.8	9.7	9.9	9.8	9.8	9.8	10.0	10.0	10.0	9.8
2003	10.0	9.9	10.0	10.0	10.0	10.0	10.1	10.0	9.9	9.8	9.8	9.7	9.9
2004	9.5	9.5	9.6	9.7	9.7	9.8	9.5	9.5	9.5	9.4	9.5	9.4	9.5
2005	9.4	9.3	9.4	9.6	9.6	9.7	9.6	9.8	9.7	9.8	9.9	9.9	9.6
2006	9.7	9.8	9.9	9.9	9.9	9.9	10.0	10.1	10.1	10.1	10.1	10.1	10.0
2007	9.9	9.9	10.0	10.0	10.1	10.1	10.1	10.1	10.0	10.4	10.5	10.4	10.1
2008	10.4	10.4	10.6	10.7	10.8	10.8	10.8	10.9	10.8	11.0	10.9	10.9	10.8
2009	10.3	10.2	10.2	10.2	10.1	10.0	10.0	10.0	9.9	10.0	9.9	9.8	10.1
2010	9.8	9.7	9.7	9.7	9.7	9.7	9.5	9.4	9.3	9.5	9.4	9.3	9.6
2011	9.1	9.0	9.0	9.2	9.2	9.2	9.2	9.1	9.1	9.2	9.2	9.2	9.1
2012	9.3	9.2	9.3	9.4	9.5	9.6	9.6	9.6	9.6	9.8	9.8	9.6	9.5
2013	9.5	9.5	9.6	9.5	9.6	9.7	9.7	9.6	9.6	9.8	9.8	9.7	9.6
Retail Trade													
2002	27.9	27.4	27.8	27.7	27.8	28.0	27.8	27.6	27.7	27.9	28.5	29.0	27.9
2003	27.6	27.0	27.2	27.5	27.8	28.2	28.0	28.2	28.4	28.6	29.2	29.5	28.1
2004	28.3	27.8	27.9	28.0	28.2	28.5	28.1	28.2	28.1	28.6	29.3	29.8	28.4
2005	28.8	28.2	28.1	28.2	28.5	28.5	28.2	28.3	28.0	28.1	28.7	28.9	28.4
2006	28.1	27.4	27.6	27.7	27.7	27.9	27.9	28.2	28.1	28.3	28.8	29.1	28.1
2007	28.2	27.6	27.9	27.9	28.2	28.6	28.2	28.0	27.8	28.4	29.0	29.2	28.3
2008	28.1	27.2	27.3	27.2	27.3	27.5	27.4	27.5	27.2	27.4	27.7	27.8	27.5
2009	26.6	25.9	25.8	25.8	25.9	26.4	25.8	25.7	25.6	25.9	26.4	26.9	26.1
2010	26.0	25.6	26.0	26.5	26.8	27.1	26.9	27.0	26.5	26.9	27.5	28.0	26.7
2011	27.0	26.5	26.6	26.8	26.9	27.0	26.9	27.0	27.1	27.8	28.4	28.8	27.2
2012	27.6	27.0	27.1	27.2	27.5	27.8	27.7	27.7	27.6	27.9	28.5	28.5	27.7
2013	27.5	26.9	27.0	27.5	28.1	28.4	28.0	28.1	27.8	28.3	29.0	28.9	28.0
Transportation and Utilities													
2002	7.6	7.5	7.5	7.7	7.7	7.7	7.0	6.9	7.5	7.7	7.7	7.8	7.5
2003	7.5	7.3	7.4	7.5	7.5	7.5	7.1	7.0	7.5	7.7	7.6	7.6	7.4
2004	7.2	7.2	7.2	7.3	7.3	7.4	6.9	6.8	7.3	7.5	7.4	7.4	7.2
2005	7.2	7.2	7.3	7.3	7.4	7.4	7.1	7.0	7.6	7.6	7.7	7.9	7.4
2006	7.5	7.4	7.5	7.6	7.7	7.8	7.4	7.4	8.0	8.1	8.1	8.2	7.7
2007	8.0	8.0	8.0	8.0	8.1	8.2	7.7	7.7	8.3	8.2	8.3	8.5	8.1
2008	8.3	8.2	8.2	8.2	8.2	8.1	7.4	7.3	8.0	8.0	8.0	8.0	8.0
2009	7.7	7.6	7.6	7.5	7.7	7.7	7.2	7.2	7.8	7.9	8.1	8.1	7.7
2010	7.8	7.9	7.9	8.2	8.5	8.7	8.3	8.4	9.0	9.0	9.2	9.6	8.5
2011	8.9	9.0	9.1	8.9	9.0	8.9	8.5	8.5	9.0	9.1	9.3	9.5	9.0
2012	8.9	8.9	9.0	9.1	9.2	9.2	8.7	8.8	9.2	9.3	9.4	9.6	9.1
2013	9.1	9.1	9.1	9.4	9.5	9.6	9.0	8.9	9.4	9.5	9.6	9.8	9.3
Information													
2002	4.5	4.4	4.4	4.3	4.4	4.4	4.4	4.3	4.2	4.2	4.2	4.2	4.3
2003	4.1	4.1	4.0	4.0	4.0	4.0	4.0	3.9	3.8	3.9	3.9	3.9	4.0
2004	3.9	3.9	3.9	3.9	4.0	4.2	4.2	4.1	3.9	3.9	3.9	3.9	4.0
2005	3.9	3.9	3.9	3.7	3.7	3.6	3.6	3.6	3.6	3.6	3.6	3.6	3.7
2006	3.6	3.6	3.6	3.6	3.6	3.7	3.7	3.7	3.7	3.7	3.7	3.7	3.7
2007	3.9	3.9	3.9	3.9	4.0	4.0	4.0	4.0	3.9	4.0	4.0	3.9	4.0
2008	4.0	4.0	4.0	4.1	4.1	4.1	4.0	4.0	3.9	3.6	3.6	3.6	3.9
2009	3.5	3.5	3.4	3.4	3.4	3.5	3.4	3.4	3.4	3.4	3.4	3.4	3.4
2010	3.4	3.5	3.5	3.6	3.6	3.6	3.6	3.6	3.5	3.5	3.5	3.5	3.5
2011	3.5	3.5	3.5	3.5	3.5	3.5	3.6	3.3	3.5	3.6	3.5	3.5	3.5
2012	3.5	3.5	3.5	3.5	3.6	3.6	3.6	3.7	3.6	3.5	3.6	3.6	3.6
2013	3.6	3.5	3.6	3.6	3.6	3.7	3.7	3.7	3.6	3.6	3.6	3.6	3.6
Financial Activities													
2002	14.0	14.0	14.0	14.2	14.2	14.2	14.2	14.3	14.1	14.3	14.3	14.3	14.2
2003	13.9	13.9	14.0	14.1	14.1	14.2	14.3	14.3	14.2	14.2	14.2	14.2	14.1
2004	14.2	14.1	14.1	14.1	14.2	14.2	14.3	14.3	14.1	14.0	13.9	14.0	14.1
2005	13.8	13.8	13.9	14.0	14.0	14.2	14.3	14.3	14.2	14.1	14.2	14.3	14.1
2006	14.2	14.2	14.2	14.3	14.3	14.4	14.3	14.2	14.0	14.1	14.0	14.0	14.2
2007	13.9	13.8	13.8	13.8	13.7	13.7	13.7	13.7	13.5	13.6	13.6	13.6	13.7
2008	13.4	13.5	13.4	13.5	13.5	13.6	13.7	13.6	13.5	13.4	13.5	13.4	13.5
2009	13.5	13.4	13.4	13.4	13.4	13.5	13.5	13.5	13.4	13.3	13.3	13.3	13.4
2010	13.3	13.3	13.3	13.2	13.2	13.3	13.4	13.3	13.2	13.5	13.4	13.5	13.3
2011	13.3	13.3	13.3	13.3	13.3	13.3	13.5	13.5	13.5	13.6	13.6	13.6	13.4
2012	13.6	13.5	13.5	13.6	13.6	13.6	13.7	13.7	13.5	13.6	13.6	13.6	13.6
2013	13.5	13.5	13.5	13.5	13.5	13.7	13.7	13.7	13.5	13.5	13.5	13.5	13.6

Employment by Industry: Worcester, MA–CT, NECTA, Selected Years, 2002–2013—*Continued*

(Numbers in thousands, not seasonally adjusted)

Industry and year	January	February	March	April	May	June	July	August	September	October	November	December	Annual average
Professional and Business Services													
2002	26.6	26.6	26.7	27.2	27.3	27.2	28.1	28.1	28.4	27.3	27.6	27.1	27.4
2003	26.6	26.5	26.6	27.1	27.3	27.4	27.6	27.6	27.7	27.9	28.0	28.3	27.4
2004	27.3	27.6	27.8	28.6	28.8	29.2	29.3	29.5	29.5	29.2	29.3	29.4	28.8
2005	27.7	27.9	28.2	29.1	29.5	29.7	29.6	29.7	30.0	29.8	30.1	30.0	29.3
2006	28.7	28.5	29.0	29.4	29.9	30.2	30.5	30.6	30.1	30.2	29.8	29.7	29.7
2007	28.1	28.1	28.1	28.9	29.3	29.7	28.9	28.8	28.5	28.4	28.6	28.6	28.7
2008	27.1	27.1	27.0	27.4	27.6	27.9	27.6	27.9	27.8	27.4	27.2	27.1	27.4
2009	26.2	25.7	25.5	25.5	25.5	25.1	25.0	25.2	24.9	25.3	25.2	25.0	25.3
2010	24.4	24.1	24.3	24.8	25.0	25.4	25.6	25.6	25.4	25.5	25.3	25.8	25.1
2011	26.2	26.1	26.0	27.1	26.6	26.8	26.9	26.6	26.6	26.4	26.3	25.8	26.5
2012	25.0	24.6	25.1	25.5	25.2	25.7	25.5	25.7	25.3	25.5	25.5	25.2	25.3
2013	24.6	24.6	24.9	25.3	25.5	25.6	25.3	25.5	25.2	25.2	25.0	25.5	25.2
Education and Health Services													
2002	43.9	44.8	45.0	46.0	46.1	45.4	44.5	44.4	45.9	46.7	46.7	47.0	45.5
2003	46.1	46.9	47.1	47.4	46.8	46.0	44.7	44.4	46.5	47.4	47.5	47.1	46.5
2004	46.2	47.0	47.2	47.1	46.6	46.2	45.2	45.1	46.4	47.0	47.1	47.0	46.5
2005	46.1	47.3	47.3	47.5	47.2	46.8	46.3	46.3	47.5	48.0	48.3	48.0	47.2
2006	47.2	48.3	48.5	48.8	48.4	47.6	47.1	47.0	48.4	49.7	49.7	49.7	48.4
2007	48.5	50.0	50.1	50.3	50.1	49.4	48.8	49.3	50.9	51.9	52.0	51.7	50.3
2008	50.5	52.4	52.5	52.4	51.7	51.2	50.8	51.0	52.5	53.6	53.6	53.5	52.1
2009	52.8	54.1	54.1	54.5	53.8	52.7	53.0	53.4	54.5	55.3	55.6	55.7	54.1
2010	54.6	56.0	55.9	55.6	55.2	54.2	54.3	54.4	55.9	56.8	57.1	57.0	55.6
2011	55.8	56.9	57.3	56.7	56.3	55.2	55.7	55.7	57.0	57.7	57.9	58.0	56.7
2012	57.3	58.3	58.9	58.6	58.3	57.8	57.9	57.7	59.1	59.9	60.2	60.2	58.7
2013	59.6	60.2	60.9	60.9	60.4	59.6	59.1	59.4	60.8	61.3	61.7	60.8	60.4
Leisure and Hospitality													
2002	18.6	18.5	18.6	19.4	20.3	20.7	20.6	20.9	20.8	21.0	20.6	20.9	20.1
2003	20.0	19.7	19.9	20.1	21.6	21.5	22.0	21.9	22.0	22.1	21.5	21.5	21.1
2004	20.2	20.1	20.4	21.3	22.3	22.7	22.2	22.2	22.0	21.6	21.0	21.1	21.4
2005	20.2	20.1	20.3	21.2	21.9	22.2	22.1	21.9	21.5	20.9	20.5	20.7	21.1
2006	20.1	19.9	20.2	21.1	21.7	22.7	22.4	22.4	22.0	21.7	21.3	21.5	21.4
2007	20.8	20.9	21.2	21.4	22.3	23.0	22.3	22.7	21.8	21.8	21.3	20.9	21.7
2008	20.7	20.8	20.8	21.5	22.5	22.9	22.3	22.6	22.0	21.7	20.6	20.5	21.6
2009	19.9	19.9	20.0	20.8	21.9	21.9	21.7	21.5	21.2	21.2	20.3	20.5	20.9
2010	19.9	19.6	19.3	20.3	21.3	21.6	21.5	21.6	20.8	21.1	20.3	20.3	20.6
2011	19.8	19.8	20.0	20.9	21.4	21.9	21.8	21.8	21.4	21.3	20.6	20.8	21.0
2012	20.5	20.4	20.7	20.9	21.7	22.6	22.5	22.5	22.0	21.6	20.9	20.9	21.4
2013	20.7	20.5	20.8	21.5	22.2	22.9	22.4	22.6	22.2	21.8	21.3	21.2	21.7
Other Services													
2002	8.8	8.8	8.8	8.7	8.8	8.9	8.7	8.9	8.5	8.6	8.6	8.7	8.7
2003	8.7	8.7	8.7	8.7	8.8	9.0	9.4	9.3	8.8	8.9	9.0	9.0	8.9
2004	8.9	9.0	9.0	8.9	9.0	9.1	9.4	9.4	8.9	8.9	8.9	8.9	9.0
2005	8.9	9.0	9.0	9.1	9.0	9.1	9.5	9.4	9.2	9.1	9.1	9.2	9.1
2006	9.1	9.0	9.1	9.1	9.1	9.3	9.4	9.4	9.1	8.9	9.0	9.1	9.1
2007	9.0	9.0	9.0	9.0	9.1	9.1	9.4	9.5	9.1	9.0	9.1	9.0	9.1
2008	8.9	8.9	9.0	8.8	8.9	8.9	9.1	8.9	8.5	8.5	8.4	8.3	8.8
2009	8.2	8.3	8.3	8.4	8.4	8.6	8.7	8.6	8.2	8.1	8.0	8.0	8.3
2010	7.8	7.8	7.8	7.9	7.9	8.1	8.4	8.2	7.7	7.7	7.7	7.6	7.9
2011	7.5	7.5	7.7	7.7	7.7	7.8	8.0	7.8	7.5	7.4	7.4	7.3	7.6
2012	7.3	7.3	7.2	7.3	7.4	7.6	7.9	7.8	7.4	7.6	7.7	7.7	7.5
2013	7.7	7.5	7.6	7.7	7.7	7.9	8.2	8.1	7.7	7.7	7.7	7.7	7.8
Government													
2002	36.0	36.4	36.3	36.5	36.9	36.5	33.5	32.8	35.9	36.1	36.5	36.5	35.8
2003	35.7	36.0	36.2	36.0	36.2	36.2	33.6	33.0	36.0	35.7	35.5	36.1	35.5
2004	35.1	35.5	35.9	36.1	36.1	35.7	33.3	33.0	36.0	36.4	36.7	36.9	35.6
2005	36.1	36.7	36.4	36.3	36.6	36.4	33.1	32.2	35.6	36.8	36.9	36.9	35.8
2006	36.6	36.6	36.8	37.1	37.4	36.8	33.5	33.5	36.6	37.4	37.8	37.7	36.5
2007	37.0	37.4	37.4	37.6	38.2	37.8	34.1	33.7	37.0	37.7	38.0	38.1	37.0
2008	37.2	37.7	37.8	37.8	38.0	37.2	34.3	33.7	36.9	37.8	37.8	37.6	37.0
2009	37.3	37.9	38.0	38.2	38.2	37.6	34.6	34.5	37.2	38.3	38.3	39.2	37.4
2010	37.8	38.1	38.2	38.3	39.1	38.3	34.5	34.4	37.2	37.8	38.2	38.4	37.5
2011	37.3	37.8	38.0	38.0	38.4	37.5	34.6	34.0	37.1	37.8	37.8	37.9	37.2
2012	37.1	37.7	38.1	37.6	37.8	37.6	34.2	34.2	37.2	37.7	38.0	38.1	37.1
2013	36.8	38.2	38.3	38.5	38.6	37.4	34.0	34.5	36.4	37.2	37.4	37.4	37.1

APPENDIX

SEVENTY-FIVE LARGEST METROPOLITAN STATISTICAL AREAS (MSAs) AND COMPONENTS
(As defined December 2010)

Albany–Schenectady–Troy, NY
Albany County, NY
Rensselaer County, NY
Saratoga County, NY
Schenectady County, NY
Schoharie County, NY

Albuquerque, NM
Bernalillo County, NM
Sandoval County, NM
Torrance County, NM
Valencia County, NM

Allentown–Bethlehem–Easton, PA–NJ
Warren County, NJ
Carbon County, PA
Lehigh County, PA
Northampton County, PA

Atlanta–Sandy Springs–Roswell, GA
Barrow County, GA
Bartow County, GA
Butts County, GA
Carroll County, GA
Cherokee County, GA
Clayton County, GA
Cobb County, GA
Coweta County, GA
Dawson County, GA
DeKalb County, GA
Douglas County, GA
Fayette County, GA
Forsyth County, GA
Fulton County, GA
Gwinnett County, GA
Haralson County, GA
Heard County, GA
Henry County, GA
Jasper County, GA
Lamar County, GA
Meriwether County, GA
Morgan County, GA
Newton County, GA
Paulding County, GA
Pickens County, GA
Pike County, GA
Rockdale County, GA
Spalding County, GA
Walton County, GA

Austin–Round Rock, TX
Bastrop County, TX
Caldwell County, TX
Hays County, TX
Travis County, TX
Williamson County, TX

Bakersfield–Delano, CA
Kern County, CA

Baltimore–Columbia–Towson, MD
Anne Arundel County, MD
Baltimore County, MD
Carroll County, MD
Harford County, MD
Howard County, MD
Queen Anne's County, MD
Baltimore city, MD

Baton Rouge, LA
Ascension Parish, LA
East Baton Rouge Parish, LA
East Feliciana Parish, LA
Iberville Parish, LA
Livingston Parish, LA
Pointe Coupee Parish, LA
St. Helena Parish, LA
West Baton Rouge Parish, LA
West Feliciana Parish, LA

Birmingham–Hoover, AL
Bibb County, AL
Blount County, AL
Chilton County, AL
Jefferson County, AL
St. Clair County, AL
Shelby County, AL
Walker County, AL

Boston–Cambridge–Newton, MA–NH
Boston, MA Metropolitan Division
       Norfolk County, MA
       Plymouth County, MA
       Suffolk County, MA
Cambridge–Newton–Framingham, MA Metropolitan Division
       Essex County, MA
       Middlesex County, MA
Rockingham County–Strafford County, NH Metropolitan Division
       Rockingham County, NH
       Strafford County, NH

Bridgeport–Stamford–Norwalk, CT, NECTA
Fairfield County, CT

Buffalo–Cheektowaga–Niagara Falls, NY
Erie County, NY
Niagara County, NY

Charlotte–Concord–Gastonia, NC–SC
Cabarrus County, NC
Gaston County, NC

Charlotte–Concord–Gastonia, NC–SC—*Continued*
Iredell County, NC
Lincoln County, NC
Mecklenburg County, NC
Rowan County, NC
Union County, NC
Chester County, SC
Lancaster County, SC
York County, SC

Chicago–Naperville–Elgin, IL–IN–WI
Chicago–Naperville–Arlington Heights, IL Metropolitan
Division
        Cook County, IL
        DuPage County, IL
        Grundy County, IL
        Kendall County, IL
        McHenry County, IL
        Will County, IL
Elgin, IL Metropolitan Division
        DeKalb County, IL
        Kane County, IL
Gary, IN Metropolitan Division
        Jasper County, IN
        Lake County, IN
        Newton County, IN
        Porter County, IN
Lake County–Kenosha County, IL–WI Metropolitan
Division
        Lake County, IL
        Kenosha County, WI

Cincinnati–Middletown, OH–KY–IN
Dearborn County, IN
Franklin County, IN
Ohio County, IN
Union County, IN
Boone County, KY
Bracken County, KY
Campbell County, KY
Gallatin County, KY
Grant County, KY
Kenton County, KY
Pendleton County, KY
Brown County, OH
Butler County, OH
Clermont County, OH
Hamilton County, OH
Warren County, OH

Cleveland–Elyria–Mentor, OH
Cuyahoga County, OH
Geauga County, OH
Lake County, OH
Lorain County, OH
Medina County, OH

Columbia, SC
Calhoun County, SC
Fairfield County, SC
Kershaw County, SC
Lexington County, SC
Richland County, SC
Saluda County, SC

Columbus, OH
Delaware County, OH
Fairfield County, OH
Franklin County, OH
Hocking County, OH
Licking County, OH
Madison County, OH
Morrow County, OH
Perry County, OH
Pickaway County, OH
Union County, OH

Dallas–Fort Worth–Arlington, TX
Dallas–Plano–Irving, TX, Metropolitan Division
        Collin County, TX
        Dallas County, TX
        Delta County, TX
        Denton County, TX
        Ellis County, TX
        Hunt County, TX
        Kaufman County, TX
        Rockwall County, TX
Fort Worth–Arlington, TX, Metropolitan Division
        Johnson County, TX
        Parker County, TX
        Tarrant County, TX
        Wise County, TX

Dayton, OH
Greene County, OH
Miami County, OH
Montgomery County, OH

Denver–Aurora–Lakewood, CO
Adams County, CO
Arapahoe County, CO
Broomfield County, CO
Clear Creek County, CO
Denver County, CO
Douglas County, CO
Elbert County, CO
Gilpin County, CO
Jefferson County, CO
Park County, CO

Detroit–Warren–Livonia, MI
Detroit–Livonia–Dearborn, MI, Metropolitan Division
        Wayne County, MI
Warren–Troy–Farmington Hills, MI, Metropolitan
Division
        Lapeer County, MI
        Livingston County, MI
        Macomb County, MI
        Oakland County, MI
        St. Clair County, MI

El Paso, TX
El Paso County, TX
Hudspeth County, TX

Fresno, CA
Fresno County, CA

Grand Rapids–Wyoming, MI
Barry County, MI
Kent County, MI
Montcalm County, MI
Ottawa County, MI

Greensboro–High Point, NC
Guilford County, NC
Randolph County, NC
Rockingham County, NC

Greenville–Anderson–Mauldin, SC
Anderson County, SC
Greenville County, SC
Laurens County, SC
Pickens County, SC

Hartford–West Hartford–East Hartford, CT, NECTA
Hartford County, CT
Middlesex County, CT
Tolland County, CT

Houston–The Woodlands–Sugar Land, TX
Austin County, TX
Brazoria County, TX
Chambers County, TX
Fort Bend County, TX
Galveston County, TX
Harris County, TX
Liberty County, TX
Montgomery County, TX
Waller County, TX

Indianapolis–Carmel–Anderson, IN
Boone County, IN
Brown County, IN
Hamilton County, IN
Hancock County, IN
Hendricks County, IN
Johnson County, IN
Madison County, IN
Marion County, IN
Morgan County, IN
Putnam County, IN
Shelby County, IN

Jacksonville, FL
Baker County, FL
Clay County, FL
Duval County, FL
Nassau County, FL
St. Johns County, FL

Kansas City, MO–KS
Johnson County, KS
Leavenworth County, KS
Linn County, KS
Miami County, KS
Wyandotte County, KS
Bates County, MO
Caldwell County, MO
Cass County, MO
Clay County, MO

Clinton County, MO
Jackson County, MO
Lafayette County, MO
Platte County, MO
Ray County, MO

Knoxville, TN
Anderson County, TN
Blount County, TN
Campbell County, TN
Grainger County, TN
Knox County, TN
Loudon County, TN
Morgan County, TN
Roane County, TN
Union County, TN

Las Vegas–Henderson–Paradise, NV
Clark County, NV

Little Rock–North Little Rock–Conway, AR
Faulkner County, AR
Grant County, AR
Lonoke County, AR
Perry County, AR
Pulaski County, AR
Saline County, AR

Los Angeles–Long Beach–Anaheim, CA
Anaheim–Santa Ana–Irvine, CA, Metropolitan Division
    Orange County, CA
Los Angeles–Long Beach–Glendale, CA, Metropolitan Division
    Los Angeles County, CA

Louisville/Jefferson County, KY–IN
Clark County, IN
Floyd County, IN
Harrison County, IN
Scott County, IN
Washington County, IN
Bullitt County, KY
Henry County, KY
Jefferson County, KY
Oldham County, KY
Shelby County, KY
Spencer County, KY
Trimble County, KY

McAllen–Edinburg–Mission, TX
Hidalgo County, TX

Memphis, TN–MS–AR
Crittenden County, AR
Benton County, MS
DeSoto County, MS
Marshall County, MS
Tate County, MS
Tunica County, MS
Fayette County, TN
Shelby County, TN
Tipton County, TN

Miami–Fort Lauderdale–Pompano Beach, FL
Fort Lauderdale–Pompano Beach–Deerfield Beach, FL,
Metropolitan Division
        Broward County, FL
Miami–Miami Beach–Kendall, FL, Metropolitan
Division
        Miami–Dade County, FL
West Palm Beach–Boca Raton–Delray Beach, FL,
Metropolitan Division
        Palm Beach County, FL

Milwaukee–Waukesha–West Allis, WI
Milwaukee County, WI
Ozaukee County, WI
Washington County, WI
Waukesha County, WI

Minneapolis–St. Paul–Bloomington, MN–WI
Anoka County, MN
Carver County, MN
Chisago County, MN
Dakota County, MN
Hennepin County, MN
Isanti County, MN
Le Sueur County, MN
Mille Lacs County, MN
Ramsey County, MN
Scott County, MN
Sherburne County, MN
Sibley County, MN
Washington County, MN
Wright County, MN
Pierce County, WI
St. Croix County, WI

Nashville–Davidson-Murfreesboro–Franklin, TN
Cannon County, TN
Cheatham County, TN
Davidson County, TN
Dickson County, TN
Hickman County, TN
Macon County, TN
Maury County, TN
Robertson County, TN
Rutherford County, TN
Smith County, TN
Sumner County, TN
Trousdale County, TN
Williamson County, TN
Wilson County, TN

New Haven–Milford, CT, NECTA
New Haven County, CT

New Orleans–Metairie, LA
Jefferson Parish, LA
Orleans Parish, LA
Plaquemines Parish, LA
St. Bernard Parish, LA
St. Charles Parish, LA

St. James Parish, LA
St. John the Baptist Parish, LA
St. Tammany Parish, LA

New York–Newark New Jersey, NY–NJ–PA
Dutchess County–Putnam County, NY Metropolitan
Division
        Dutchess County, NY
        Putnam County, NY
Nassau County–Suffolk County, NY Metropolitan
Division
        Nassau County, NY
        Suffolk County, NY
Newark, NJ–PA Metropolitan Division
        Essex County, NJ
        Hunterdon County, NJ
        Morris County, NJ
        Somerset County, NJ
        Sussex County, NJ
        Union County, NJ
        Pike County, PA
New York–Jersey City–White Plains, NY–NJ
Metropolitan Division
        Bergen County, NJ
        Hudson County, NJ
        Middlesex County, NJ
        Monmouth County, NJ
        Ocean County, NJ
        Passaic County, NJ
        Bronx County, NY
        Kings County, NY
        New York County, NY
        Orange County, NY
        Queens County, NY
        Richmond County, NY
        Rockland County, NY
        Westchester County, NY

North Port–Bradenton–Sarasota, FL
Manatee County, FL
Sarasota County, FL

Oklahoma City, OK
Canadian County, OK
Cleveland County, OK
Grady County, OK
Lincoln County, OK
Logan County, OK
McClain County, OK
Oklahoma County, OK

Omaha–Council Bluffs, NE–IA
Harrison County, IA
Mills County, IA
Pottawattamie County, IA
Cass County, NE
Douglas County, NE
Sarpy County, NE
Saunders County, NE
Washington County, NE

Orlando–Kissimmee–Sanford, FL
Lake County, FL
Orange County, FL
Osceola County, FL
Seminole County, FL

Oxnard–Thousand Oaks–Ventura, CA
Ventura County, CA

Philadelphia–Camden–Wilmington, PA–NJ–DE–MD
Camden, NJ, Metropolitan Division
       Burlington County, NJ
       Camden County, NJ
       Gloucester County, NJ
Montgomery County–Bucks County–Chester County, PA
Metropolitan Division
       Bucks County, PA
       Chester County, PA
       Montgomery County, PA
Philadelphia, PA, Metropolitan Division
       Delaware County, PA
       Philadelphia County, PA
Wilmington, DE–MD–NJ, Metropolitan Division
       New Castle County, DE
       Cecil County, MD
       Salem County, NJ

Phoenix–Mesa–Scottsdale, AZ
Maricopa County, AZ
Pinal County, AZ

Pittsburgh, PA
Allegheny County, PA
Armstrong County, PA
Beaver County, PA
Butler County, PA
Fayette County, PA
Washington County, PA
Westmoreland County, PA

Portland–Vancouver–Hillsboro, OR–WA
Clackamas County, OR
Columbia County, OR
Multnomah County, OR
Washington County, OR
Yamhill County, OR
Clark County, WA
Skamania County, WA

Providence–Warwick, RI–MA, NECTA
Bristol County, MA
Bristol County, RI
Kent County, RI
Newport County, RI
Providence County, RI
Washington County, RI

Raleigh–Cary, NC
Franklin County, NC
Johnston County, NC
Wake County, NC

Richmond, VA
Amelia County, VA
Caroline County, VA
Charles City County, VA
Chesterfield County, VA
Dinwiddie County, VA
Goochland County, VA
Hanover County, VA
Henrico County, VA
King William County, VA
New Kent County, VA
Powhatan County, VA
Prince George County, VA
Sussex County, VA
Colonial Heights city, VA
Hopewell city, VA
Petersburg city, VA
Richmond city, VA

Riverside–San Bernardino–Ontario, CA
Riverside County, CA
San Bernardino County, CA

Rochester, NY
Livingston County, NY
Monroe County, NY
Ontario County, NY
Orleans County, NY
Wayne County, NY
Yates County, NY

Sacramento–Arden-Arcade–Roseville, CA
El Dorado County, CA
Placer County, CA
Sacramento County, CA
Yolo County, CA

Salt Lake City, UT
Salt Lake County, UT
Tooele County, UT

San Angelo, TX
Irion County, TX
Tom Green County, TX

San Antonio–New Braunfels, TX
Atascosa County, TX
Bandera County, TX
Bexar County, TX
Comal County, TX
Guadalupe County, TX
Kendall County, TX
Medina County, TX
Wilson County, TX

San Diego–Carlsbad, CA
San Diego County, CA

San Francisco–Oakland–Hayward, CA
Oakland–Hayward–Berkeley, CA Metropolitan Division
       Alameda County, CA
       Contra Costa County, CA

San Francisco–Oakland–Hayward, CA—*Continued*
San Francisco–Redwood City–South San Francisco, CA
Metropolitan Division
       San Francisco County, CA
       San Mateo County, CA
San Rafael, CA Metropolitan Division
       Marin County, CA

San Jose–Sunnyvale–Santa Clara, CA
San Benito County, CA
Santa Clara County, CA

Tampa–St. Petersburg–Clearwater, FL
Hernando County, FL
Hillsborough County, FL
Pasco County, FL
Pinellas County, FL

Tucson, AZ
Pima County, AZ

Tulsa, OK
Creek County, OK
Okmulgee County, OK
Osage County, OK
Pawnee County, OK
Rogers County, OK
Tulsa County, OK
Wagoner County, OK

Virginia Beach–Norfolk–Newport News, VA–NC
Currituck County, NC
Gates County, NC
Gloucester County, VA
Isle of Wight County, VA
James City County, VA
Mathews County, VA
York County, VA
Chesapeake city, VA
Hampton city, VA
Newport News city, VA

Norfolk city, VA
Poquoson city, VA
Portsmouth city, VA
Suffolk city, VA
Virginia Beach city, VA
Williamsburg city, VA

Washington–Arlington–Alexandria, DC–VA–MD–WV
Silver Spring–Frederick–Rockville, MD Metropolitan
Division
       Frederick County, MD
       Montgomery County, MD
Washington–Arlington–Alexandria, DC–VA–MD–WV
Metropolitan Division
       District of Columbia, DC
       Calvert County, MD
       Charles County, MD
       Prince George's County, MD
       Arlington County, VA
       Clarke County, VA
       Culpeper County, VA
       Fairfax County, VA
       Fauquier County, VA
       Loudoun County, VA
       Prince William County, VA
       Rappahannock County, VA
       Spotsylvania County, VA
       Stafford County, VA
       Warren County, VA
       Alexandria city, VA
       Fairfax city, VA
       Falls Church city, VA
       Fredericksburg city, VA
       Manassas city, VA
       Manassas Park city, VA
       Jefferson County, WV

Worcester, MA–CT
Windham County, CT
Worcester County, MA

Note. Delineations as established in OMB Bulletin Number 13-01, Metropolitan Statistical Areas, Metropolitan Divisions, Micropolitan Statistical Areas, Combined Statistical Areas, New England City and Town Areas, and Combined New England City and Town Areas, February 28, 2013